# BIRDS OF OREGON

## Sponsors

National Fish and Wildlife Foundation
U.S. Fish and Wildlife Service
Leupold and Stevens, Inc.
Izaak Walton League of America, Portland Chapter
U.S. Geological Survey, Forest and Rangeland Ecosystem Science Center
Mazamas
Oregon Department of Fish and Wildlife, Wildlife Diversity Program
The Weyerhaeuser Company Foundation
Oregon Field Ornithologists
Backyard Bird Shops
U.S. Bureau of Land Management
Merlin S. and Elsie K. Eltzroth
Dr. and Mrs. Richard E. Markley
Society for Northwestern Vertebrate Biology
U.S. Forest Service
Audubon Society of Portland
Central Oregon Audubon Society
Anne and Charles Jacobs
Oregon Wildlife Heritage Foundation
Portland General Electric
The Wildlife Society, Oregon Chapter

We also recognize four major sponsors who elected to remain anonymous

# BIRDS OF OREGON

## A GENERAL REFERENCE

**David B. Marshall**
**Matthew G. Hunter**
**Alan L. Contreras**

*Editors*

Harry B. Nehls

*Senior Contributor*

M. Ralph Browning

*Taxonomic Editor*

Jonathan P. Brooks

*Cartographer*

Rachel White Scheuering

*Editorial Assistant*

Incorporating contributions from 100 authors
*and*
data from the Oregon Breeding Bird Atlas Project

*Illustrations by*
Elva Hamerstrom Paulson

**OREGON STATE UNIVERSITY PRESS**
**Corvallis, Oregon**

## Recommended Citations

Book:
Marshall, D.B., M.G. Hunter, and A.L. Contreras, Eds. 2003, 2006. Birds of Oregon: A General Reference. Oregon State University Press, Corvallis, OR. 768 Pp.

A Chapter or Species Account:
Cite by author or authors as listed at end of chapter or account. Fictitious example:
Byrd, C.E. Full-winged Gull. Pp. 40-45 in Birds of Oregon: A General Reference. D.B. Marshall, M.G. Hunter, and A.L. Contreras, Eds. Oregon State University Press, Corvallis, OR.

```
REF 598 BIRDS
BIRDS OF OREGON
A GENERAL REFERENCE
```

The paper in this book meets the guidelines for permanence and durability of the Committee on Production Guidelines for Book Longevity of the Council on Library Resources and the minimum requirements of the American National Standard for Permanence of Paper for Printed Library Materials Z39.48-1984.

The Library of Congress has cataloged the hardcover edition as follows:
Birds of Oregon : a general reference / David B. Marshall, Matthew G. Hunter, Alan L. Contreras, editors.
    p. cm.
Includes bibliographical references (p.  ).
 ISBN 0-87071-497-X (alk. paper)
 1. Birds—Oregon. I. Marshall, David B. II. Hunter, Matthew G., 1963-
III. Contreras, Alan, 1956-
  QL684.O6 B56 2003
  598'.07'234795--dc21

                    2002154684

ISBNs for this edition: 0-87071-182-2, 978-0-87071-182-4

Oregon State University Press
500 Kerr Administration
Corvallis OR 97331
541-737-3166 • fax 541-737-3170
http://oregonstate.edu/dept/press

# Dedications

*To Stanley G. Jewett, William L. Finley, and Ira N. Gabrielson whose guidance and support during my youth expanded my interest in birds and other wildlife and caused me to enter the wildlife conservation and management field professionally.*—David B. Marshall

*To Martha Sawyer, my first birding buddy, and to my wife Lisa, daughter Katy, and son Daniel, who enjoy with me a curiosity of things created.*—Matt Hunter

*For Sayre Greenfield, who asked me, when we were children, if I wanted to go look at birds. To the 35 years of our friendship and mutual enjoyment of birds that have followed, I dedicate my work on this book.*—Alan Contreras

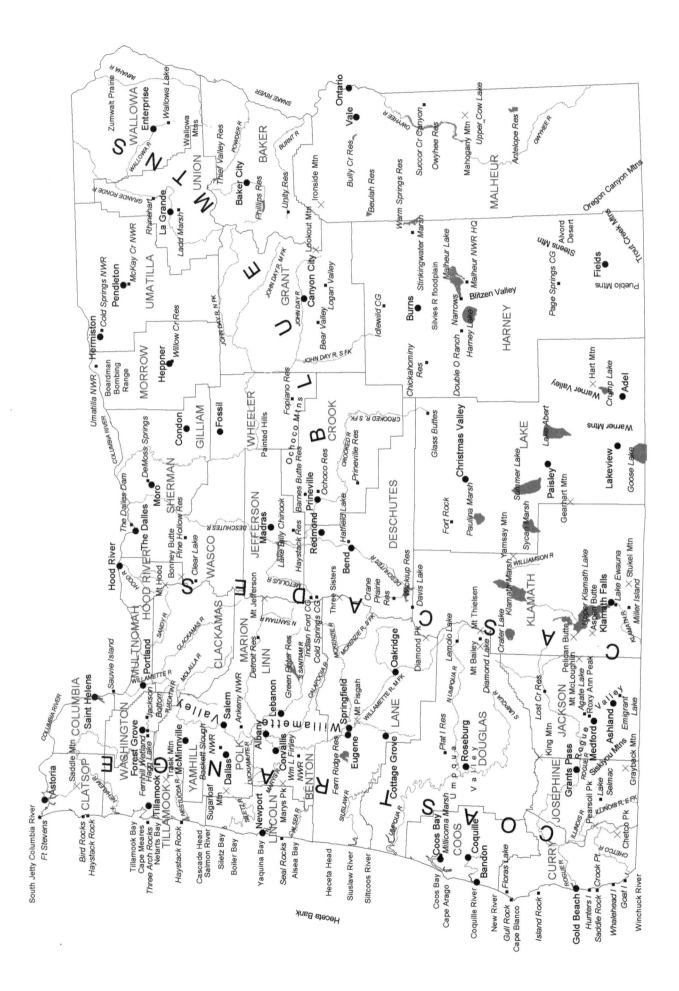

# Contents

# Preface

About 65 years ago, two distinguished government wildlife biologists, Ira N. Gabrielson and Stanley G. Jewett, began writing the first Birds of Oregon. It was published in 1940 by what was then Oregon State College (now Oregon State University). Gabrielson and Jewett's book was a landmark for the day, and is widely cited in this volume. Like this work, it is not an identification book; rather it emphasizes distribution, habitat, and population status. It represents not only 35 years of field work conducted by these two early biologists in conjunction with their duties as animal control agents of the U.S. Biological Survey, but also the writings, research, and collecting of others, including but not limited to Meriwether Lewis, William Clark, John Kirk Townsend, Charles Bendire, Alfred Webster Anthony, O.B. Johnson, Arthur Roy Woodcock, Alfred C. Shelton, Alex Walker, George Willett, and William L. Finley.

Gabrielson and Jewett worked at a time when field guides were nonexistent and good optics were primitive and financially out of reach of the average person. The state's transportation infrastructure was also primitive, and parts of the state were accessible to automobiles only during part of the year, or not at all. Extensive offshore birding as we know it today was not within reach of these two men.

This was also a time when collecting both birds and eggs was in vogue as a hobby and scientific endeavor. The basic tool for an ornithologist was a .410 gauge shotgun loaded with dust shot. Specimens were prepared as study skins and eggs blown so they could be preserved. Only with specimens could a new finding or unusual record be confirmed. Museum specimens left few identification doubts when sightings were difficult and impossible to confirm with photographs or follow-up observations. At the beginning of the 20th century, birding as we know it today was nonexistent. The inability of amateur birders to conduct satisfactory surveys can be illustrated by the fact that Portland's first Christmas Bird Count, conducted in 1915, listed only 16 species recorded by three people. Not until 1933 did the count exceed 30 species. This contrasts with 100+ species recorded by about 75 people today.

Since Gabrielson and Jewett's time, birding has become a popular and fashionable hobby. Just before and immediately after World War II, universities began training significant numbers of wildlife biologists and ornithologists who gradually became a force in resource agencies and universities. The information contained in this volume includes contributions from (1) research financed by resource agencies and conducted in part by graduate students, (2) resource agency biologists, and (3) observations made by an army of advanced birders. Examples of the latter include the recent completion of the Oregon Breeding Bird Atlas project headed by Paul Adamus of Oregon State University, the Breeding Bird Survey sponsored by the Biological Resources Division of the U.S. Geological Survey, and the quarterly journal of Oregon Field Ornithologists, Oregon Birds, now in its 26th year.

While professionals have worked mainly on habitat and life history requirements, amateurs have concentrated on distribution. However, there has been much overlap, and both have contributed, through various means, information on population numbers and trends.

During the early years of my professional career spent as a field biologist in various states, I came to appreciate the value of state bird books as references and realized the need to update the original Birds of Oregon, but full-time employment precluded my participation. Fortunately, Birds of Oregon: Status and Distribution (Gilligan et al. 1994) filled an important void. It is frequently cited in this volume, but the reader will find Birds of Oregon: A General Reference differs in terms of delineating habitat requirements, population numbers, historical changes, and by citing information sources in the species accounts. Other recent contributions to Oregon ornithology include Northwest Birds in Winter (Contreras 1997b); the Atlas of Oregon Wildlife (Csuti et al. 1997; 2nd edition 2001), which features distribution maps based on habitat types for birds and mammals that reproduce in the state; and the Oregon Breeding Bird Atlas available on compact disk.

Some history on how this book emerged appears appropriate. Since boyhood, I had realized that the time would come to update Gabrielson and Jewett's book and that I could even become involved. Gabrielson and Jewett were both mentors of mine. In 1997, I learned that Oregon State University Press was interested in publishing a new state bird book. I submitted to them a proposal which included sample species accounts and a book outline that I felt would represent the needs of a wide group, including wildlife biologists, other natural-resource professionals, conservationists, birders, and hunters. Two very capable individuals, Matthew G. Hunter and Alan L. Contreras, volunteered to help as co-editors. Each brought special talents to the project. Hunter was experienced as an offshore and inland birder, had worked on several avian research projects in Oregon, and had academic experience and needed computer skills. Contreras' perspective was that of one of the state's premium birders with a wide knowledge of published literature on Oregon birds. We began enlisting experts on various species as potential authors; very few declined the invitation to write accounts, and others whom we had not thought of volunteered. An impressive list of professional wildlife biologists and ornithologists, along with some advanced amateur ornithologists, emerged.

Soon after the first draft species accounts had been written, it became clear to the editors that neither they nor the authors were qualified to adequately address the taxonomic status of subspecies. We began consulting with M. Ralph Browning, an Oregonian who had recently retired from his position as an avian taxonomist with the U.S. National Museum. Browning subsequently consented to become Taxonomic Editor. Harry B. Nehls, longtime secretary for the Oregon Bird Records Committee of the Oregon Field Ornithologists, also became a major contributor. Nehls' background on bird rarities of the state made him an important reviewer and author of vagrant or rare species accounts.

Another need was for illustrations. Hunter introduced me to Elva Hamerstrom Paulson, whose superb artistic talents were obviously a fit. Her background as the daughter of two famous ornithologists undoubtedly contributed to this. Finally, Jonathan P. Brooks, a cartographer with Oregon State University, consented to prepare maps based on Oregon Breeding Bird Atlas data.

Our main objectives for this book were to (1) document the status and distribution of the state's birds as known at the beginning of the 21st century; (2) set forth what is known of their habitat requirements in terms of food, cover, and space; and (3) stimulate research and continued investigations by showing what is not known. One of my hopes is that the book will dampen some of the rhetoric and misunderstandings that have emerged from resource extractors on one side and environmentalists on the other regarding the needs of controversial species. And by describing habitat requirements, we also show that habitat destruction for one group of species invariably creates habitat for another group; yet maintaining habitat diversity is necessary to sustain all of the state's birds.

More than anything else, we hope this book will constitute a contribution to the conservation and enjoyment of birds found throughout Oregon.

*David B. Marshall*

## Preface to Paperback Edition

Since publication of the first printing in 2003, Co-editor Matthew G. Hunter has maintained a website which invites readers to submit corrections to the first printing. For this printing, the editors incorporated corrections found in the website which involved substantial or factual errors, including misspellings of names of individuals. Other errors of a typographical nature were not corrected, but can be found on the website. No attempt was made to incorporate new information that has emerged since the original printing except for the listing of new species to the state, as well as taxonomic and name changes, which are found on page 22. In total, the additions to the state list and changes in taxonomy have increased the Oregon state bird list to 500 in this book (499 by AOU, ABA, and OBRC count, because Brant species are lumped by these organizations).

*Editors*
*March 2006*

# Acknowledgments

Hundreds of people were involved in some way in the production of this book. Many of these we know, and attempt to list here, but others we are sure helped without our full knowledge.

Early on, and at various junctures along the way, we recruited specific help from key people without whom there would not be a Birds of Oregon: A General Reference. At the very beginning of the project we asked Elva Hamerstrom Paulson to do the drawings. These have brought life and beauty to many pages of the book. Similarly, the Oregon Breeding Bird Atlas project, headed by Paul Adamus, contributed data to prepare maps that accompany many species accounts. It became evident early in the process that more help was needed with particular issues. Several people began as consultants and became integral parts of the staff necessary to complete the book. This included Harry B. Nehls whose knowledge of Oregon bird records, particularly rare species, was unmatched. Avian taxonomist M. Ralph Browning guided us through the confusing and controversial mass of subspecies in the state. Jonathan Brooks, also a birder, volunteered to prepare the maps used in this book with the support of the Oregon Forest Research Laboratory and the Oregon State University Forest Resources Department. The "life-saver" at the end was Rachel White Scheuering, whose editorial skills in organizing over 4,000 references and nearly 300 personal citations, correcting the citation of these in the text, and assisting with a myriad of other editing tasks helped us meet our final deadlines with the publisher.

Approximately 80 volunteer authors and 20 co-authors made this book so comprehensive. Biographies of each are contained at the end of the book. Over 95% of the people we asked to write species accounts accepted; others we did not think of volunteered to help. We asked authors to estimate the time they spent researching and writing a full species account (excluding accidentals). The average was over 30 hr per species, which at a rate of $25 per hr was valued at $262,500. Obviously this does not include many thousands of hours devoted to the project by editors, consultants and others.

Contributors of another type were the hundreds of scientists and birders who participated indirectly through published and unpublished material, including research project reports, Christmas Bird Counts, Breeding Bird Surveys, the Oregon Breeding Bird Atlas, and government agency and non-government organization reports. Examples include the U.S. Fish and Wildlife Service, which made available unpublished waterfowl and seabird inventories from their files or actually took authors into the field. Marty Drut, Jim Hainline, Meg Laws, Bob Trost, and Jim Voelzer of the Portland office, Roy Lowe and David Pitkin of the Newport office, and Jock Beall of the Willamette Valley refuges were among these. Many from the Oregon Department of Fish and Wildlife helpfully provided field knowledge and material from files, including Ron Anglin, Bradley Bales, Charles Bruce, Tom Collom, Martin Nugent, Marty St. Louis, John Thiebes, Daniel VanDyke, Walt VanDyke, and Simon Wray. Others from various organizations included Robert Marheine of PGE, David Heye with the U.S. Coast Guard, Jan Hodder with Oregon Institute of Marine Biology, Sandy Bryce with the U.S. Environmental Protection Agency, Jeff Comstock with Indus Corporation, and Jimmy Kagan of the Oregon Natural Heritage Advisory Council. Others who provided information in the form of knowledge, notes, unpublished reports or papers in preparation include Range Bayer, Kelly Bettinger, Joseph Buchanan, Greg Concannon, Mike Evanson, Bill Haight, Jeremy Hatch, Tom Mickel, Marjorie Moore, Gary Page, Mark Stern, Oriane Taft, Chip Weseloh, Nils Warnock, and Herb Wisner, and numerous people recognized in the Sources section under personal communications.

Museum personnel provided a wealth of information on existing specimens that is rarely included in state bird books. Richard C. Banks of the National Museum of Natural History and Chair of the American Ornithologists' Union Committee on Classification and Nomenclature, provided much appreciated and invaluable assistance on certain specimens, data, and publications. Others who assisted by providing access to specimens or data were Ned K. Johnson of the Museum of Vertebrate Zoology in Berkeley, California, Pamela Endzweig of the University of Oregon Museum of Natural History, Gary Shugart of the Slater Museum of Natural History at University of Puget Sound, and Phil Unitt of the San Diego Natural History Museum. We thank others from staffs of the following additional museums for access to collections (locations excluded where obvious): American Museum of Natural History, New York; British Museum of Natural History, Tring; California Academy of Science, San Francisco; Cleveland Museum of Natural History; Crater Lake National Park; Carnegie Museum of Natural History, Pittsburgh; Delaware Natural History Museum, Greenville; Denver Natural History Museum; Douglas Co. Museum; Museum of Comparative Zoology, Harvard University; Oregon State University,

Corvallis; and Southern Oregon University, Ashland. Additionally, we thank the staffs of other collections that helped in reaching distributional and taxonomic conclusions reflected in this book: Canadian Museum of Nature; Field Museum of Natural History, Chicago; Peabody Museum of Natural History, Yale University; Royal British Columbia Museum, Victoria; University of Michigan; University of Washington; and University of Utah. Other museums were acknowledged in various species accounts in Chapter 3.

Experts who reviewed one or more accounts for authors prior to submission included M. Ralph Browning, Douglas Bell, Kathy Merrifield, Alan Reid, Peter Sanzenbacher, Oriane Taft, and Liv Wennerberg. Others who assisted by assembling references by species, or compiling records and other data included Vjera Arnold, Barbara Combs, and Larry McQueen. Some of the leading birders of the state, as well as others, read all or portions of the first drafts. They added missing material and made editorial comments. In this group were Norm Barrett, M. Ralph Browning, Char Corkran, Mike and Merry Lynn Denny, David Fix, Steve Heinl, Dave Irons, Donna Lusthoff, Tom McAllister, Harry B. Nehls, Tim Rodenkirk, and Paul T. Sullivan. The appendices list scientific names for plants and various animal groups. Taxonomic specialists who assisted with this were Scott Sundberg of the Oregon State University Department of Botany and Plant Pathology, and Hal Weeks who did fishes. Noah Strycker assisted with editing the appendices. Clarice Watson diligently and thoroughly checked order and spelling of all common and scientific bird names and avian taxonomic groups. Special thanks to the staff of Rogue Community College for providing space for our marathon taxonomic work session.

A book of this nature is expensive to produce because of its size and limited sales (mostly one state). Through donations to Oregon State University Foundation, we were able to keep production costs down and thereby make the book available to more users. There were also editorial and miscellaneous costs. The latter were handled through a fund established by the Audubon Society of Portland. We thank David Eshbaugh, Executive Director, Bill Clemons, Finance Director, and Candice Guth, former Finance Director, for administering this fund. Major donors to both organizations are listed as sponsors on an adjoining page. Other donors included: The Weyerhauser Wildlife Fund, Don and Lynn Herring, Mary Brodie, Claire Puchy, Mary and William Telfer, and the Oregon Division of the Izaak Walton League of America. Numerous people became fundraisers. Among them were authors of this book and individuals from government and non-government organizations who understood this project and saw its value to the missions of their organizations. Mary Anne Sohlstrom, President of Oregon Field Ornithologists, Jeanne Norton, President of the Portland Chapter of the Izaak Walton League of America, and Krystyna Wolniakowski of the National Fish and Wildlife Foundation are examples.

We thank Jeffrey B. Grass, former director of OSU Press, and his staff for encouragement, patience with deadlines we did not meet, and firmness in coming up with a final manuscript deadline, and Jo Alexander for much helpful editing advice along the way.

No one deserves more credit than family members. This book took just over four and a half years to write or about double our first estimate. In Marshall's case this constituted nearly a full time job, but it was his wife, Georgia, of just over three years, who deserves the credit for being so patient and supportive during this period. Co-editor Hunter put in nearly as much time. We are indebted to his wife, Lisa, and growing family for their support. M. Ralph Browning's wife, Linda Ray, also provided her support, as well as the family of Rachel White Scheuering. We must also credit Elva Hamerstrom Paulson's husband, Dale, who took many of the bird photographs that Elva used for models.

Many thanks to all.

—David B. Marshall, Matthew G. Hunter, Alan L. Contreras

# About This Book

The reader is urged to read this section before proceeding, as it will lead to a better understanding of how to use this book.

## Style

The writing style used in this book is sometimes tight and cryptic to provide maximum utilization of space. Abbreviations are extensively used. Definitions of species abundance and frequency are given below.

The text is extensively referenced, using peer-reviewed journals, other published literature, unpublished reports, field notes, and personal communications, in order to assemble as much available information as possible on each species within a limited space. These references add credibility to the book's content and allow researchers to follow up on subjects of interest in more detail and to assess for themselves the reliability of information presented. In cases of unpublished observations made by authors or editors, observer initials are shown in italics (see below). The sources have been combined in a common list.

Only those geographical features judged to be unfamiliar to most readers are identified by county.

## Abbreviations

### Units of Measure:
Used when preceded by a number:
- ac = acre(s)
- cm = centimeter(s)
- fm = fathom
- ft = feet or foot
- g = gram(s)
- ha = hectare(s)
- hr = hour(s)
- in = inch(es)
- km = kilometer(s)
- m = meter(s)
- mm = millimeter(s)
- mi = mile(s) (statute for land; nautical for at-sea.)
- min = minute(s)
- mo = month(s)
- oz = ounce(s)
- sec = second(s)
- wk = week(s)
- yr = year(s)

### Geographic Areas:
To show sections of a state or other location:
- c. = central
- e. = east or eastern
- ec. = east-central
- n. = north or northern
- nc. = north-central
- ne. = northeast or northeastern
- nw. = northwest or northwestern
- s. = south or southern
- sc. = south-central
- se. = southeast or southeastern
- sw. = southwest or southwestern
- w. = west or western
- wc. = west-central

Sections of continental land masses or oceans:
- M. America = Middle America
- N. America = North America
- N. Pacific = North Pacific Ocean
- S. America = South America
- S. Pacific = South Pacific Ocean

### Other Geographic Entities
- CG = Campground
- Co. = County
- Cr. = Creek
- Ft. = Fort
- HQ = Headquarters
- I(s). = Island(s)
- L. = Lake
- Mt. = Mount
- Mtn(s). = Mountain or Mountains
- N. Antelope R. = National Antelope Refuge
- NF = National Forest
- NP = National Park
- NRA = National Recreation Area
- NWR = National Wildlife Refuge
- Pt. = Point
- R. = River
- RD = Ranger District
- Res. = Reservoir
- RS = Ranger Station
- SP = State Park
- U.S. = United States
- W.A. = Wildlife Area
- WMA = Wildlife Management Area

## Museums

AMNH = American Museum of Natural History, New York

BM(NH) = British Museum (Natural History)

CAS = California Academy of Science, San Francisco

CMNH = Cleveland Museum of Natural History, Ohio

CLNP = Crater Lake National Park, Oregon

CM = Carnegie Museum of Natural History, Pittsburgh, Pennsylvania

DEL = Delaware Natural History Museum, Greenville

DEN = Denver Natural History Museum, Colorado

DCM = Douglas County Museum, Oregon

LACM = Los Angeles County Museum, California

MCZ = Museum of Comparative Zoology, Harvard University, Massachusetts

MVZ = Museum of Vertebrate Zoology, University of California, Berkeley

PSU = Portland State University, Portland, Oregon

OSU = Oregon State University, Corvallis

UO = University of Oregon, Eugene

SMNH = Slater Museum of Natural History, University of Puget Sound, Tacoma, Washington

SDNHM = San Diego Natural History Museum, California

SOU = formerly SOC and SOSC, now Southern Oregon University, Ashland

UCLA = University of California, Los Angeles

USNM = National Museum of Natural History, Smithsonian Institution, Washington, D.C.

## Editors and Authors

Editor comments or observations are shown by initials. DBM = David B. Marshall, MGH = Matthew G. Hunter, ALC = Alan L. Contreras, MRB = M. Ralph Browning. In addition, observations by authors of individual accounts are shown by their respective initials in italics.

## Other Abbreviations

AOU = American Ornithologists' Union

BBL = Bird Banding Laboratory

BBS = Breeding Bird Survey

BLM = U. S. Department of Interior, Bureau of Land Management

BRD = Biological Resources Division of the U.S. Geological Survey

CBC(s) = Christmas Bird Count or Counts

dbh = diameter at breast height (in reference to trees)

ENSO = El Nino/Southern Oscillation

EPA = Environmental Protection Agency

NAS = National Audubon Society

NPS = National Parrk Service

OBBA = Oregon Breeding Bird Atlas

OBRC = Oregon Bird Records Committee

ODF = Oregon Department of Forestry

ODFW = Oregon Department of Fish and Wildlife

OFO = Oregon Field Ornithologists

ONHP = Oregon Natural Heritage Program

p.c. = personal communication

ppm = parts per million

PRBO = Point Reyes Bird Observatory

SD = standard deviation

USACE = U.S. Army Corps of Engineers

USDI = U.S. Department of Interior

USFS = U.S. Department of Agriculture, Forest Service

USFWS = U.S. Department of Interior, Fish and Wildlife Service

## Definitions of Bird Abundance and Frequency

Observers commonly use the words "abundant," "common," "rare," etc. to describe the status of a given species; but such terms can carry different meanings, depending upon the observer, size of the bird, detectability, and other factors. The editors instructed authors to use definitions described by Arbib (1957); with minor modifications, the most frequently used definitions are as follows:

### Non-breeding Occurrences

Abundant: Occurring in such numbers that a competent observer might see or hear more than 500 individuals in a single day.

Very common: 101-500 in a single day.

Common: 26-100 in a single day.

Fairly common: 6-25 in a single day.

Uncommon: 1-5 in a single day and no more than 25 per season.

Rare: 1-5 in a single day, but no more than 5 per season.

Very rare: No more than 1 per day or 1 per season.

### Frequency Standards

Regular: Recorded every year.

Irregular: Recorded less than once every year, but no less than once in 5 years on the average.

Casual: Recorded less than once in 10 years, but no less than once in 20 years on the average.

Additional details can be found in Arbib (1957).

**Breeding Abundance Scale for Territorial Species**

| Term | Breeding Density | |
|---|---|---|
| | Flicker Size or Smaller | Larger than Flicker |
| Abundant | 1 pair per 1-5 ac (.4-2.2 ha) | 1 pair per 1-25 ac (.40-10 ha) |
| Very Common | 1 pair per 6-25 ac 2.3-10 ha) | 1 pair per 26-125 ac (11-50 ha) |
| Common | 1 pair per 26-125 ac (11-50 ha) | 1 pair per 126-640 ac (51 ha-236 ha) |
| Uncommon | 1 pair per 1-5 mi² (2.6 -14 km²) | 1 pair per 6-25 mi² (16-65 km²) |
| Rare | 1 pair per 6-25 mi² (15-65 km²) | 1 pair per 26-125 mi² (66-324 km²) |

## The Organization of This Book

### Chapter 1:
### Summary of Changes to Oregon's Avifauna Since 1935

This chapter summarizes the need for this book. It describes the state of knowledge in 1935 (when data was cut off for the last general reference to Oregon's birds) and changes that have occurred in species distribution, and abundance since that date. The numbers of species known to occur in the state in 1935 are compared with those known to occur today.

### Chapter 2: Avian Environments of Oregon's Ecoregions

This chapter provides brief descriptions of the state's ecoregions in terms of habitats and bird communities, including historical changes.

### Chapter 3: Species Accounts

Species accounts comprise the main body of this book. Included are those species listed in the current Oregon checklist maintained by the OBRC of OFO, which is periodically published in Oregon Birds. This includes all native Oregon extant species and established self-sustaining introduced species that meet the committee's standards.

Sequence and Nomenclature: Species nomenclature and sequence follow the 7th edition of the AOU Check-list of North American Birds and the 42nd and 43rd checklist supplements (AOU 1998, 2000, Banks et al. 2002) unless otherwise stated in the species accounts.

Treatment of Subspecies: Despite numerous uncertainties and discrepancies, the editors chose to cover subspecies, in part because the accounts address conservation needs and problems and subspecies often have different conservation problems. For example, the Willamette Valley supports remnant populations of subspecies of the Vesper Sparrow and Horned Lark, both of which were formerly abundant, but are now rare. In addition subspecies can constitute populations, usually from a geographic area, as so

clearly shown in the Canada Goose account. As noted by Joe Marshall in The Birds of Arizona (Phillips et al. 1964), subspecies are "permanently marked by nature" and are therefore ideal for studies of migration and distribution. However, in most instances, Birds of Oregon: A General Reference does not identify vagrants and other wanderers to the subspecies level unless they are represented by specimens from Oregon that were identified by a taxonomist.

The last AOU list of North American subspecies appeared in the Check-list of North American Birds, 5th edition (AOU 1957). Most bird books produced in recent times have ignored subspecies, including the 6th and 7th editions of the AOU check-lists. This deficiency is noted in the Preface of the 7th edition with the words, "As in the sixth edition, for reasons of expediency, the Committee reluctantly excluded the treatment of subspecies in the current volume. Their omission should not be interpreted as a devaluation of that taxonomic rank. To the contrary, the Committee strongly and unanimously continues to endorse the biological reality and practical utility of subspecies."

Since 1957, new subspecies that have not been independently evaluated with the benefit of specimens have been proposed for recognition in the literature. This situation was addressed by Browning (1990), who evaluated new subspecies that had been proposed since publication of the 5th edition of the AOU checklist. We follow Browning (1990) and use the 5th edition as a starting point; however, we do not necessarily recognize all subspecies the 5th edition listed, and likewise we do recognize some other subspecific names not listed in the 1957 edition. Reasons for these departures are provided in the individual species accounts. Sources for taxonomic evaluations also include various works, principally those of Phillips (1991) and various papers by Browning. In all instances subspecies recognized in Oregon are based on specimens except where otherwise stated. The majority of identifications of those specimens, whether reported in the literature or deposited in museums, were verified by Browning. Our conclusions do not always agree with those reached in the species accounts in The Birds of North America edited by Poole and Gill (1992 - ongoing).

Taxonomists now recognize subspecies only by scientific names. English names for subspecies, as used in the original Birds of Oregon, came from the AOU in the 4th check-list (AOU 1931), and almost without exception are obsolete. However, exceptions are made herein for a few obvious subspecies that can be identified in the field, whose names are well established or are used for special purposes, as for example in endangered, threatened, or critical species listings or for other wildlife management or regulatory purposes. Examples of widely used common names for subspecies include the Harlan's Hawk subspecies within the Red-tailed Hawk group; the split of the Yellow-rumped Warbler into Audubon's and Myrtle Warblers; the two Northern Flickers known as Yellow-shafted Flicker and Red-shafted Flicker; the Dark-eyed Junco which in Oregon can usually be split out between Oregon Juncos, Slate-colored Juncos, and Gray-headed Juncos. Subspecies names used for regulatory or management purposes include the Columbian Sharp-tailed Grouse, Northern Spotted Owl, and various subspecies of the Canada Goose and Sandhill Crane.

Account Content: Account lengths vary according to the Oregon status and amount of appropriate information available. In general there are three categories of accounts: (1) species that regularly breed in Oregon, (2) species that regularly winter in or migrate through Oregon but do not breed here, and (3) species that occur as accidentals or vagrants.

Regularly Occurring Species: About 360 species regularly occur or are established in Oregon as breeders, migrants, or winter visitors. Those that breed in the state are often covered in more detail than those that occur only as migrants or winter visitors. For example, nesting habitat and breeding behavior for the non-breeders are not covered because breeding activities occur outside the state. Identical subheadings are used for all regularly occurring species.

In each account, the introductory section briefly describes the subject species and anything that is particularly unusual, unique, or interesting is mentioned.

The General Distribution section briefly describes the North American (and where applicable the worldwide) range of the species. The intent here is to place Oregon in the context of the range of the species as a whole. We refer those who want North American or worldwide range in detail to the 7th AOU Check-list of North American Birds (AOU 1998). Authors excerpted their general distribution information from this check-list unless otherwise noted. Species without subspecies are noted here as monotypic; if subspecies have been accepted, the approximate number in either N. America or the world is designated here.

The Oregon Distribution section centers on the Oregon range of each species, and distributions are provided in as much detail as possible, along with a statement on relative abundance or rarity and seasons in which the species is present. It has not always been possible or practical to cover every case in which a species has strayed outside its normal range. Oregon ranges are separated by subspecies where they exist, but oftentimes the exact ranges of subspecies are unknown for lack of museum specimens.

Maps of Oregon breeding distributions during 1995-1999 are shown for 205 species. These are based on OBBA data (Adamus et al. 2001, which show OBBA results for 275 species), with only a few updates. Hexagon shades indicate the level of breeding confirmation during the atlas period based on criteria described in Adamus et al. (2001). Because these maps are based on actual observations, they differ in some respects from some of the ranges shown in Csuti et al. (1997), which are based largely on habitat. Extralimital occurrences are not shown on the maps.

We encourage the reader to carefully interpret the meaning of "possible" and "probable" levels of breeding confirmation. For easily observed species such as waterfowl, these may represent occurrences of non-breeding individuals or they may indicate the presence of pioneering individuals. For secretive or difficult to observe species such as owls, these may represent actual breeding populations that are very difficult to verify.

The Habitat and Diet section describes habitats used based on Oregon data to the extent available, including required habitat components, e.g., snags and presence of certain plant species as applied to seasonal or year-round needs including reproduction. Home range sizes are provided here if known. Types of foods consumed are described.

The Seasonal Activity and Behavior section covers such topics as seasonal changes in abundance and activities, the life-history activities that take place in Oregon, and arrival and departure times of migrants.

The Detection section gives tips on how, where, and when each species can be observed and the likelihood of sightings.

The Population Status and Conservation section provides information on population levels, densities, and trends as well as historical changes, particularly since the 1930s. Habitat changes and how they have affected a species in terms of the past, present, and future are mentioned here. Any threats to the well-being of the species (and subspecies where appropriate) in Oregon are mentioned. The future outlook for the species and subspecies and conservation problems are also covered here.

Accidentals, Vagrants, and Other Wanderers: So-called rare species that are infrequently reported or occur casually or rarely, of which there are 135, are covered with only brief accounts without subheadings. These species are represented by as few as one or as many as 35 OBRC accepted records (though there may be additional unsubmitted reports), and the OBRC is seeking additional records for most of them. Most can now be considered regular but rare migrants. It can be assumed that only a small fraction of actual occurrences in the state among this group is seen and reported, and more species will be added to this list over time. However, in terms of the requirements of these species as whole, Oregon is not believed important; nor is enough information available on them to adequately describe their habitat needs or distribution within the state. For these reasons, and because of limited space, this book does not concentrate on birds of this group. However, they represent a challenge to those birders who enjoy seeking out rarities.

## Chapter 4: Supplemental Species Accounts

This is an annotated list that includes extirpated species; those for which we have records of their having been unsuccessfully introduced to the state; introduced species whose establishment is in question in terms of being self-sustaining over time; and commonly reported escapees from captivity. This list also identifies those birds which have been reported in other publications, but which have not been accepted by the OBRC.

## Glossary

The glossary includes terms, usually of a technical nature, that are used in the text and may not be familiar to some readers.

## Appendices

Appendix A, List of Common and Scientific Names of Plants and Animals. Chapters 2 and 3 mention, by common names only, numerous plants and animals. Rather than list the scientific names in the text for these taxa, which would be highly repetitive for some,

like Douglas-fir, this appendix provides a combined listing. It also includes some birds that do not occur in Oregon but are mentioned in the text. (Scientific names of Oregon's birds are listed with the species accounts.)

Appendix B, Changes in Scientific Bird Names Since Publication of Gabrielson and Jewett (1940). This appendix provides a comparison of scientific names used in the 1940 publication named above with those used in this book.

Appendix C, Oregon Breeding Bird Atlas, Christmas Bird Counts, and Breeding Bird Surveys. Considerable information in the species accounts, including nesting data, breeding distribution, and population trends are based on these surveys, which are described in this appendix.

## Sources

Although it is customary to list references following each species account, this book departs from that procedure to avoid duplication and save space. This combined list has two parts: 1) published and unpublished literature, and 2) names and associations of those individuals and organizations that have contributed information to authors in the form of personal communications.

The large number of references in the Sources Cited presented complications for citing these sources in the species accounts. Particular difficulties arose when multiple publications had authors with the same last name (but different first name) and the same year of publication; and cases where more than one publication had the same senior author and same year, but different junior authors. In these cases, we followed the Council of Science Editors guidelines and inserted initials or added junior authors' names in the text citation to eliminate ambiguity.

The cut-off for receipt of information contained in this book was 31 Dec 2001, with a few exceptions.

# Chapter 1
## A Summary of Changes to Oregon's Avifauna Since 1935

The first complete bird book on Oregon (Gabrielson and Jewett's *Birds of Oregon*), while published in 1940, was essentially completed by 1935. Much has been learned about individual species since its publication, and many changes have since occurred in the status of the state's avifauna. Throughout this book, we have attempted to place the state's avifauna in historical perspective since 1935.

First, some statistics. Using current nomenclature, Gabrielson and Jewett (1940) listed 338 species as having acceptable records of occurrence in the state. In this book, we recognize all but four of them in Chapter 3, which comprises species accounts for birds on the official list maintained by the Oregon Bird Records Committee (OBRC). Of the remaining four, we relegated three to Chapter 4, the supplementary species accounts, because they had not been accepted by the OBRC or otherwise for insufficient evidence. Also moved to Chapter 4 was the California Condor, which has not been known to occur in Oregon for nearly 100 yr. Since Gabrielson and Jewett's time, another 150 species have been added to the official list of state birds maintained by the OBRC, making a total of 486 recognized herein in Chapter 3. While most of the added 150 species comprise vagrants found at various times by increasing numbers of competent birders, other species have expanded their range into Oregon and adjoining states either as migrants, breeders, or some combination of both.

Again using current nomenclature, Gilligan et al. (1994) accounted for 476 species. In this book we excluded two of them and placed four in the supplemental species accounts in Chapter 4. Since publication of Gilligan et al. (1994), 14 more species were added to the state list and are covered in Chapter 3.

Now let us consider some specific examples of changes, which are of course covered in more detail in Chapter 3. Perhaps the most spectacular immigration has been that of the Cattle Egret, which came to the Americas from Africa and to Oregon from the E. Coast of N. America (Telfair 1994). Other species that expanded their breeding range westward into Oregon include the Barred Owl and Grasshopper Sparrow. From the northeast came the Franklin's Gull, Least Flycatcher, and Northern Waterthrush, and from California the White-tailed Kite, Red-shouldered Hawk, Anna's Hummingbird, Black Phoebe, and Blue-gray Gnatcatcher, all of which have been found nesting in Oregon or show strong evidence of doing so. While it is possible Gabrielson and Jewett overlooked one or more of these species, they are widely recognized as having expanded their range within the past 50 yr (Johnson 1994). Most are also sufficiently conspicuous

that it is doubtful they were overlooked. Currently breeding species that may have been present as breeders in the 1930s, but overlooked, include the Horned Grebe, Red-necked Grebe, and Black Swift. There are still others, e.g. the Virginia's Warbler, which we suspect breed in Oregon, but for which actual nesting has not been confirmed.

Among the most obvious changes since the 1930s and 1940s have been the occupation of rural, suburban, and urban areas of nw. Oregon by the Western Scrub-Jay and House Finch, and the inundation of Oregon by the European Starling, which began in the 1950s. Also significant is the statewide expansion through agricultural and urban areas of the Brown-headed Cowbird both in terms of range and population numbers; it was described by Gabrielson and Jewett as being confined almost entirely to e. Oregon as a "not common resident." In addition, the world's largest known Caspian Tern colony now exists near the mouth of the Columbia R. on human-made islands, whereas none nested there historically. During the latter half of the last century, White-faced Ibis, Sandhill Cranes, and Black-necked Stilts began nesting in far greater numbers, and expanded their Oregon range over that previously known. The Acorn Woodpecker's range has slowly extended northward in w. Oregon nearly to the north edge of the Willamette Valley, and the Wrentit expanded its range inland from the coast to the Willamette Valley and in some locales eastward.

Other changes have taken place among migrant and wintering populations, mostly with species already present in the state, but which now occur in expanded numbers or where not previously found. The Great Egret, a longtime summer resident and breeder in se. and sc. Oregon, now winters in Oregon (west of the Cascades) and nests at Coos Bay. During the summer months, numbers of Brown Pelicans which wander north along the Oregon coast and into the Columbia R. estuary now number in the thousands rather than in the hundreds. Small numbers of Elegant Terns, not known from Oregon until 1983, have subsequently migrated most years from California up the Oregon coast. Ross's Geese, considered very rare in N. America in the 1950s, are now commonplace. Gabrielson and Jewett did not detect a number of rare but regular migrants including the Tufted Duck, Tennessee

Warbler, Black-throated Blue Warbler, Palm Warbler, Blackpoll Warbler, Black-and-white Warbler, Ovenbird, and Clay-colored Sparrow. This may have been due to inadequate coverage.

Perhaps the most dramatic change is the hundreds of thousands of Canada Geese that now winter in the state, mainly in the Willamette Valley and secondarily in the Columbia Basin east of the Cascades. Canada Geese wintered in small numbers in Oregon before the 1940s. Much to the consternation of farmers, the geese are attracted to the Willamette Valley by the grass seed industry that developed after World War II. Due to transplant efforts by goose enthusiasts and the state, Canada Geese now nest statewide instead of just east of the Cascades as in the 1940s. Willamette Valley grass fields, as reported in this book, also support unusually large concentrations of wintering Killdeer and Dunlin. The fields recently began serving Tundra Swans that formerly relied on native wetland plants now overrun by reed canarygrass. The Trumpeter Swan, formerly a wintering bird in small numbers, was successfully introduced as a breeding species in the 1960s.

Increases in Bald Eagle and Osprey populations over the past 50 yr following declines are well documented in their respective accounts in Chapter 3. The Peregrine Falcon has been re-established, at least in part through artificial means, after its reported (although questioned) extirpation in Oregon following widespread use of the insecticide DDT.

Gabrielson and Jewett and their small number of cooperators did not have the opportunity that we have today to detect birds. Gabrielson once told me that he and Jewett did not have funds for offshore pelagic trips, and that the few they did take occurred through interest of some fishing-boat captains. Even so, it appears they were unable to go offshore a sufficient distance to detect such seabirds as the Laysan Albatross and Long-tailed Jaeger. Other regular seabird migrants that they did not detect include the Flesh-footed Shearwater and South Polar Skua.

On the negative side, Oregon has lost two formerly common breeding species, the Yellow-billed Cuckoo and Sharp-tailed Grouse (a re-introduction of the latter is too recent for the outcome to be known). Oregon's Upland Sandpiper population, probably the largest west of the Rocky Mountains, is close to extirpation. The changing status of other species is often documented by the Breeding Bird Survey (BBS), but in many cases the declines occurred prior to initiation of the BBS in Oregon in 1969. For this we have only anecdotal information, including Gabrielson and Jewett (1940) and the memory of a few like myself from the 1930s. But when vast areas of former habitat known to support certain species in substantial numbers is now composed of housing and industrial developments, or when former high-quality wetlands are gone, the results are obvious. Overall trends for many species remain

unknown, but declines, some serious, are apparent in others. Examples include the Black Brant, Canvasback, Swainson's Hawk, Ruffed Grouse, Blue Grouse, Mountain Quail, Snowy Plover, Black Tern, Marbled Murrelet, Burrowing Owl, Common Nighthawk, Rufous Hummingbird, Lewis's Woodpecker, Olive-sided Flycatcher, Willow Flycatcher, Purple Martin, Western Bluebird, Swainson's Thrush, Yellow Warbler, Yellow-breasted Chat, and Purple Finch; and in the Willamette Valley the Horned Lark, Vesper Sparrow, Western Meadowlark, and Lazuli Bunting.

The picture for introduced game birds is mixed. While the Ring-necked Pheasant has undergone a major decline, and the Northern Bobwhite has virtually disappeared after having done well in the first half of the 20th century, the outlook for two recently introduced game birds, the Chukar and Wild Turkey, looks bright, at least for now.

Reasons for the numerous changes run from the obvious to completely unknown (Johnson and Jehl 1994). Human-caused habitat changes are the most obvious. Examples include replacement of natural grasslands and prairie with agriculture; changes in agricultural practices; riparian losses from livestock grazing; silvicultural practices including fire control, logging, and plantings; urbanization; introductions of non-native species (e.g. carp, European Starling, reed canary grass, cheat grass, and Himalayan blackberry); conversion of free-running rivers into impoundments by dams; loss in sagebrush steppe diversity and area from agriculture, grazing, fire control, and severe fires caused by fire control and introduced plants; and a decline in wetland diversity and acreage. Other human factors include bird feeding, human disturbance, establishment of wildlife refuges, and nest parasitism by the Brown-headed Cowbird. The latter is believed to have occurred because cowbirds are attracted to agricultural areas and livestock. Many of these changes are discussed in more detail in Chapter 2. They range from highly negative to positive depending upon the species and activity.

Johnson (1994) described range expansions by species that did not previously nest in the state as "natural range expansions." In other cases the birds themselves have habituated to human intrusions. Examples of the latter include the recent exploitation of food sources in urban areas of Portland and other Willamette Valley cities by substantial numbers of species not previously thought of as "city birds." This includes the Double-crested Cormorant, Great Blue Heron, Canada Goose, Bald Eagle, Peregrine Falcon, Mourning Dove, Band-tailed Pigeon, and American Crow. The latter three species commonly use bird feeders whereas they did not, at least in Oregon, in the 1930s. Even the Pileated Woodpecker, often considered a wilderness species in the northwest, now appears in sections of metropolitan Portland having large trees.

This book therefore delineates the status of the state's avifauna at the beginning of the 21st century. Climate change, more natural range changes, changes in the composition of marine food chains, and continued habitat changes caused by human activities will continue to create changes in avian communities. Changes should not be looked at in terms of Oregon alone since many of the state's migratory birds winter in w. Mexico, and in some cases even as far away as Argentina. Others breed as far north as Arctic Alaska and Canada. Some of the seabirds that occur off or along the Oregon coast move between Arctic and Antarctic waters.

Another type of change has to do with bird nomenclature. As the science of taxonomy progresses, changes in bird names are inevitable. Some species will be split, some will be combined, and new subspecies will be named. With DNA analysis and other new techniques, this change could be accelerated, as illustrated by the recent splits that created the Greater Sage-Grouse and Gunnison Sage-Grouse from the former Sage Grouse and the Juniper Titmouse and Oak Titmouse from the former Plain Titmouse.

This book also describes in brief terms what has been learned about individual species since the late 1930s. Today, inventories of waterfowl, colonial nesting birds at nest sites, and many raptors are routine. The BBS provides an index to population changes since its initiation for common species that lend themselves to roadside inventories. Unfortunately, this survey was not initiated until 24 yr after World War II, by which time some gross changes in bird populations had already taken place in the state. The Oregon Breeding Bird Atlas project was recently completed. It documented the breeding status of most species that nest in the state in a systematic basis using several hundred volunteers. An increasing number of Christmas Bird Counts, now numbering approximately 40, held throughout the state provide an index to wintering populations and have documented many changes.

On an individual species basis, extensive habitat requirement studies, population inventories, and life history studies have been conducted on some of Oregon's species of concern, including some that are listed as threatened under state and federal endangered species legislation. The reader who looks at accounts for the Harlequin Duck, Osprey, Bald Eagle, Northern Goshawk, Greater Sage-Grouse, Yellow Rail, Sandhill Crane, Snowy Plover, Long-billed Curlew, Marbled Murrelet, Flammulated Owl, Burrowing Owl, Spotted Owl, Vaux's Swift, White-headed Woodpecker, Black-backed Woodpecker, Pileated Woodpecker, and Olive-sided Flycatcher will see results of some of this work. Although the quantity of accumulated data on many of these species is impressive, it also shows we are only beginning to learn the basics of most species. Perhaps the most striking illustration of knowledge gained since the 1930s is the fact that it was not known at that time that the Marbled Murrelet, a seabird, flies inland to nest in trees.

*David B. Marshall*

## Chapter 2
# Avian Habitats in Oregon Ecoregions

Oregon is one of the most diverse states in the union. All four of the world's major biotic terrestrial community types or biomes—arctic alpine or tundra, desert, grassland, and forest—occur in Oregon. In addition the region is bordered by the Pacific Ocean along over 300 mi (480 km) of coastline. Approximately 45% of the state's 61,778,976 ac (25,001,951 ha) or 96,529 mi² (247,107 km²) consists of forest or woodland (predominantly conifer), 34% shrub-steppe and grassland, 7% mosaic or mixed tree-shrub structure, 10% agriculture, 1% alpine rock, lava, dunes, and other lightly vegetated types, 1% urban, and 1% open water and wetland (Oregon Natural Heritage Advisory Council [hereafter ONHAC] 2002).

The human population stood at 3,421,399 in 2000, an increase of 17% from 1990 (Loy et al. 2001). Approximately 70% of these people resided in the Willamette Valley, and three-fourths of those lived in 94 incorporated cities. The human population runs from fewer than three people/mi² (0.01/ha) in seven e. Oregon counties to 1,424/mi² (5.49/ha) in Multnomah and Washington counties (Portland metro area) (Defenders of Wildlife 1998). West to east, climate varies from the mild and wet coastal region to relatively mild valleys, to mountains that rise to over 11,000 ft (3,300 m) and have heavy snowfall and glaciers, to arid plateaus, and finally to expanses of high desert.

Approximately 44% of Oregon is privately owned, 25% is administered by each of the USFS and BLM, 3% is state owned and another 3% is owned by other entities including the USFWS, NPS, and tribes (Loy et al. 2001).

This varied climate and the resulting diverse vegetation provide for a varied avifauna including many subspecies. At press time, 486 species of birds had been recorded as occurring in a wild state in Oregon, well over half the total number of birds reported in the contiguous 48 states, and a total matched or exceeded in the U.S. only by Florida, New Mexico, Arizona, Texas, and California (Maybank 2000). Species that have a large part of their range in Oregon include

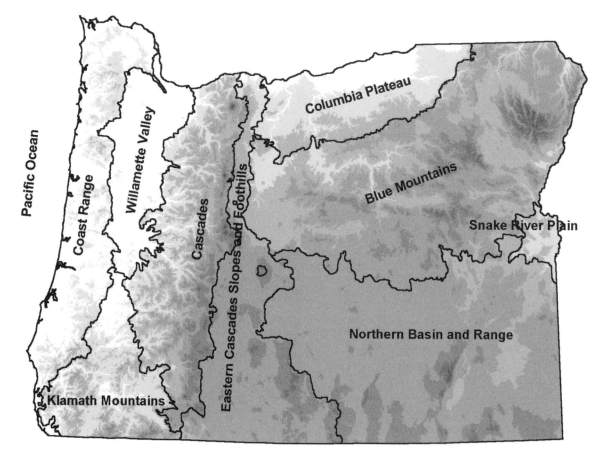

Wrentit, Hermit Warbler, and Marbled Murrelet. The Wallowa subspecies of the Gray-crowned Rosy-Finch (*Leucosticte tephrocotis wallowa*) and the sw. Oregon subspecies of the Wrentit (*Chamaea fasciata margra*) are the only endemic breeding avian taxa in Oregon. Bird species found nearly statewide include Canada Goose, Mallard, Great Blue Heron, Red-tailed Hawk, Mourning Dove, Violet-green Swallow, Killdeer, Northern Flicker, American Kestrel, Great Horned Owl, American Robin, Brewer's and Red-winged Blackbirds, and Dark-eyed Junco.

Several publications have delineated physiographic provinces or ecoregions in Oregon and adjoining states (e.g., Franklin and Dyrness 1973, Bailey 1976, 1978, ONHAC 1988). These have typically been based on previous works on geology and physiography (Fenneman 1931, Baldwin 1964, Orr et al. 1992). In our discussion of avian habitats in Oregon's ecoregions we are using the most current concept accepted by state and federal agencies and described in the *Atlas of Oregon* (Loy et al. 2001), and a new edition of the *Oregon Natural Heritage Plan* (ONHAC 2002). These publications combined the former High Lava Plains ecoregion into the Blue Mountains ecoregion and the former Owyhee Uplands ecoregion into the Northern Basin and Range ecoregion. We occasionally refer to other designations when they are helpful in discussing avian habitats. Also, we describe as an ecoregion the Pacific Ocean from the coastline to the 200-mi (322-km) territorial limit, since it provides habitat for a number of Oregon's birds.

This chapter is not extensively referenced. We relied heavily on the Oregon Biodiversity Project (Defenders of Wildlife 1998), Johnson and O'Neil (2001), Loy et al. (2001) and the draft Oregon Natural Heritage Plan (ONHAC 2002). Much of the information in the above publications is duplicative, and we saw little point in repeating them as references. Information on birds was taken from species accounts in Chapter 3 of this book. We also relied upon our own knowledge acquired through a long history of travel in Oregon.

The following discussions are intended to provide readers a broad view of the state in terms of: (1) ecological conditions and processes that affect birds, (2) the most common and unique aspects of each ecoregion, and (3) the important avian habitats and sites in each ecoregion.

## Pacific Ocean Ecoregion

The factors having the most influence on species composition, numbers, and condition of birds present off Oregon's coast are food supply and weather conditions. Whereas landbirds prefer certain structural characteristics in their habitats, such as bare ground, grass, shrubs, or a tree canopy, marine birds, so far as we know, do not require a particular physical structure

of the surface water. In contrast, the structure of their habitat is open ocean. What they look for is food. Some birds, such as the Black-footed Albatross, leave their chicks for weeks at a time and fly between the Hawaiian Is. and offshore Oregon to forage on squid and other marine prey. What guides them here we do not know, but they find food here. Similarly, large numbers of Sooty Shearwaters sometimes congregate near shore (e.g., the mouth of the Columbia R.) in "great screaming, struggling, fighting masses" (Gabrielson and Jewett 1940) to forage on huge schools of anchovies, which concentrate there to breed.

Locally, pelagic birds (e.g., shearwaters, jaegers, fulmars) are sometimes held near shore by offshore fog banks, or offshore by near-shore fog banks, or are driven near shore or even inland by strong west winds. On a larger scale, it appears that, during fall, weather systems to the north of Oregon (e.g., fronts in the Gulf of Alaska) may push large numbers of northern birds to migrate south along the coast (P. Pickering p.c.).

Oceanic processes influencing the distribution and abundance of food for marine birds are many, interrelated, and difficult to understand. They may include temperature, salinity, depth to bottom, currents, upwelling, and life histories of aquatic organisms. At a large scale, within the N. Pacific, temperature, salinity, and depth to sea floor work together to form broad distinctions in the oceanic ecosystem. Mean sea surface temperatures over the shelf are 46-50° F (8-10° C) in winter and 52-59° F (11-15° C) in summer, generally colder closer to shore, but large variations occur along the coast and among years (Landry et al. 1989).

Locally off the Oregon coast, upwelling—an annual offshore movement of surface water and onshore movement of deep water—is probably the most important process. Deeper water brought to the surface near shore brings with it abundant nutrients and an associated food chain. Upwelling is produced by winds generally from the north and can occur at any time of year, but on average predominates May through Aug and often Sep (Landry et al. 1989). This process is present along the west coasts of many continents, and is generally referred to as an "eastern boundary current."

Along the Oregon coast, the seafloor extends out in a shallow slope (continental shelf) 15-30 mi (24-48 km) offshore. The shelf reaches a depth of approximately 100-200 fm (182-364 m) before it drops more steeply to 1,000-2,000 fm (1,828-3,658 m), 50-75 mi (80-120 km) off the coast (nautical charts). Several significant seafloor features occur off the Oregon Coast, the most prominent of which are Astoria Canyon, Heceta Bank, and Coquille Bank.

A relatively small-scale feature that influences local ocean conditions and the food base for seabirds is the freshwater input of coastal rivers. Freshwater from rivers is less dense than salt water and floats over the top of the

*Offshore fishing scene in the Pacific Ocean Ecoregion*

salt water as it diffuses into the sea. This mixing of salt and fresh water creates a unique mix of forage species off the mouths of larger rivers. Most rivers in Oregon, however, are too small to have noticeable effects. The freshwater plumes of rivers follow the prevailing winds and currents on the ocean. The Columbia R. freshwater plume is pressed north along the Washington coast in winter and southwest to offshore Oregon in summer (Landry et al. 1989).

Over a longer time interval, larger-scale oceanic processes such as El Niño and La Niña can have a pronounced effect on the temperature and salinity of shelf waters, the frequency and fruitfulness of upwelling, and the marine faunal community.

In addition to the natural processes already described, human activity on the ocean has had an effect on local distribution of some birds for at least the latter half of the 20th century. Through the mid-1980s, huge factory ships (primarily foreign) worked off the coast of Oregon, processing massive quantities of fish, and discarding many tons of waste. These ships attracted swarms of thousands of Sooty Shearwaters, Northern Fulmars, and gulls; hundreds of Black-footed Albatross; and dozens of jaegers and other species (see Tom Crabtree's photo in Carlson 1988). In 1983, the U.S. established an Exclusive Economic Zone, extending 200 mi (320 km) offshore in order to protect declining fish stocks. Enforcement of regulations within this zone greatly reduced all foreign fishing vessels near Oregon's shores. Numbers of domestic ships have not increased substantially and their time at sea is so brief that they have not been encountered on many recent pelagic birding trips. However, the domestic trawler and shrimp fisheries remain active off the coast and attract up to a thousand or so total birds. Wahl and Tweit (2000a) reported that the distribution of Black-footed Albatross off the coast of Washington 1977-98 was affected by the location and activity of commercial fishing, from which the albatross, fulmars, and other species scavenged.

Along the w. coast of N. America, primary production and seabird biomass are highest over the continental shelf, moderate over the slope, and lowest in deep (>1094 fm [>2000 m]) offshore waters (Tyler et al. 1993). Bird density at sea is highest during spring and fall migration, and higher during summer than winter (Tyler et al. 1993). However, it should be noted that species composition changes rapidly with distance from shore as well. Some species are more numerous near shore, while others are rare near shore and present only farther from shore. These associations with distance from shore are thought to reflect locations of upwellings (typically over the continental shelf and near shore). Nearshore we find loons, grebes, pelicans, cormorants, scoters, alcids, and gulls. At the inner shelf are shearwaters and the Parasitic Jaeger, while at the shelf break Black-footed Albatross and Long-tailed Jaeger are present. In deep water we find Fork-tailed and Leach's Storm-Petrels, Laysan Albatross, Long-tailed Jaeger, and Horned Puffins.

One of the most amazing features of Oregon's oceanic avifauna is the broad geographic origin of the species that occur here. Northern Fulmars and Black-legged Kittiwakes are most likely from breeding colonies on coasts and islands of Alaska; three species of jaegers from the arctic tundra; Fork-tailed Storm-Petrels, Rhinoceros Auklets, and Cassin's Auklets from along the w. coast of N. America; Black-footed and Laysan Albatrosses from the Hawaiian Is.; Pink-footed Shearwaters from the w. coast of S. America; Sooty Shearwaters primarily from the southern tip of S. America and perhaps islands near New Zealand; Buller's Shearwaters from New Zealand; Short-tailed Shearwaters from Australia; and South Polar Skuas from the Antarctic! Many of these species can be seen in a single day in late summer or early fall in Oregon waters.

Looking ahead, it is difficult to predict what we might see. We are rapidly learning about global ocean cycles (e.g., El Niño and La Niña as Pacific Ocean examples) and how these conditions, in combination with national fisheries, alter the aquatic food base and thus seabird populations. It is conceivable that Short-tailed Albatross may be observed annually off the coast of Oregon in a decade or two if the breeding population in Japan continues to expand as it has been doing (Morgan 2001). Primary threats to offshore birds are fisheries, floating oil, and toxic chemicals (Tyler et al. 1993).

## Coast Range Ecoregion

From the shores of the Pacific Ocean to the edge of the Willamette and Umpqua valleys and south to the California line, this ecoregion straddles a variety of rich habitats. The Coast Range proper makes up most of the ecoregion, but from the Coquille R. south the ecoregion comprises only a strip between the sea and the Klamath Mtns. The Coast Range is mostly forested with a mix of forest successional stages ranging from clearcuts to mature stands, but there is little true old-growth because of logging and past wild fires. This province has the highest number of bird species of any of the state's ecoregions, largely due to the interface of the forested mountains with the sea. Here colonial seabirds nest on erosion-resistant headlands and offshore islands locally called sea stacks. There are rocky coves, stretches of sand dunes, and over 12 true estuaries that are visited by thousands of waterbirds and shorebirds. Extending back from the estuaries are river valleys that have been turned into pastures for dairy cattle, the main agricultural pursuit in the province. Overall, the coastline presents a beautiful mix of rocky headlands and coves, beaches, sand dunes, and shallow estuaries. The coastline from Cape Arago south is particularly rocky, while great expanses of sand dunes are present between Cape Arago and Heceta Head and from Seaside to the Columbia R.

By western standards, the Coast Range is low; the highest point in the range, which is Marys Peak, Benton Co., rises to only 4,097 ft (1,249 m) (Loy et al. 1976). The general crest line is 1,476 ft (450 m). The range comprises a series of ridges divided by numerous creeks and rivers resulting from heavy precipitation, which ranges from 60 to 80 in (152-203 cm) annually along the immediate coast and up to 200 in (508 cm) at some of the higher locations (Loy et al. 2001). The Coast Range and Klamath Mtns. are the first in Oregon to take their share of precipitation from moist air masses coming in from the Pacific Ocean. While most precipitation occurs in the form of rain, it is not uncommon for snow to frustrate motorists crossing Coast Range passes in winter, and the highest peaks are typically snow covered through the winter months. This accounts for Gray-crowned Rosy-Finches frequenting Marys Peak in winter. Coastal temperatures are mild with the smallest annual range in Oregon, typically 60-70° F (15-21° C) in summer and 40-50° F (4-10° C) in winter, with southern and inland locations becoming warmer in summer (Taylor and Hannan 1999). High winds of sufficient intensity to preclude tree growth on some headlands and mountaintops buffet the coast in winter. The winds are accompanied by heavy rain.

Approximately 61% of the ecoregion is privately owned, 28% is in federal and 11% state ownership, with the remainder owned by miscellaneous entities, e.g., tribal, county, and city. Major federal owners are USFS at 13% and BLM at 13%. State lands include numerous parks and the Tillamook and Clatsop forests. A minor owner in terms of acreage but of major importance to wildlife is the USFWS, which has jurisdiction over the Three Arch Rocks NWR, Oregon Is. NWR, and some recently acquired estuaries and tidelands. The former two refuges support the largest seabird colonies in the U.S. outside Alaska.

Exact figures are not available for the resident human population; a rough calculation based on year 2000 county data from Loy et al. (2001) indicates this ecoregion has approximately 206,000 residents. This is swelled by large numbers of weekenders and summer

*Three Arch Rocks NWR and Cape Meares, at the juncture of the Pacific Ocean and Coast Range Ecoregions*

*Estuary at the interface of the Pacific Ocean and Coast Range Ecoregions*

vacationers who seek out the beaches and camping, fishing, birding, whale-watching, and sightseeing opportunities. Numerous vacation homes dot the area. For the most part humans concentrate along beaches, lower riverine corridors, and estuaries where private land exists. The largest town is Coos Bay which, combined with adjoining North Bend, has a population of 24,918 (Loy et al. 2001).

Vegetation of the province has been variously described by Franklin and Dyrness (1973), Johnson and O'Neil (2001), and ONHAC (2002). Forest vegetation begins along the coastal strip, often with narrow bands of young lodgepole (shore) pine which invade recently stabilized sandy soils. Developed soils near the coastal fog zone support a Sitka spruce/western hemlock/western redcedar maritime forest, found only in this ecoregion. Douglas-fir/western hemlock/western redcedar forest otherwise dominates this and the Cascades Ecoregion, but red alder can be prominent and in pure stands, especially where soil conditions are moist and disturbances have taken place. Bigleaf maple is also prominent. At the southern end of the province, coast redwood, Pacific madrone, Port-Orford cedar, and tanoak occur. Overall, most of the private land in the Coast Range presents a patchwork ranging from recent clearcuts to even-aged Douglas-fir in blocks, each block representing a different stage of forest succession up to pole-sized trees, at which time harvest again takes place. Unlike clearcuts in the shrub stage, and mature and old-growth stands, young artificially planted Douglas-fir forests have relatively low species richness, and are harvested before they are sufficiently mature to support most cavity-nesting species. Forests on public lands tend to be older, are likely to be of mixed age classes, and are more variable

in terms of species composition. True old-growth is largely confined to public lands. Overall, Coast Range forests show the effects of logging that began early in the 20th century followed by successive waves of wildfires that reached a peak in the 1930s. Shrub cover below the forest canopy varies from almost impenetrable stands of salal, to vine maple, to sword ferns.

Clearcut logging, as practiced in the Coast Range in the latter half of the 20th century, did not replicate natural disturbances caused by fire and wind, nor did it replicate the type of "high-grade" logging that occurred before the use of chain saws when economics dictated a policy of removing only the largest Douglas-firs, Sitka spruce, and western redcedars. Many trees at the time considered of no value blew down or were knocked down in the process. From a human perspective, the result was an unsightly mess, but this provided ideal habitat for species like the Mountain Quail and Olive-sided Flycatcher. Natural fires left standing snags used by a variety of wildlife, including cavity-nesters. This is especially true of those snags in the large diameter classes, which eventually fell and provided cover.

Looking at typical birds of the ecoregion beginning from the edge of the sea and going west, at least 16 species of sea and shorebirds nest along the coast. This includes Common Murres and Leach's Storm-Petrels, which nest on offshore rocks in the hundreds of thousands, all three species of cormorants found in the state, Glaucous-winged and Western Gulls, Rhinoceros and Cassin's Auklets, Pigeon Guillemots, Tufted Puffins, and Black Oystercatchers. Massive nesting failures sometimes occur in the murre colonies due to food shortages related to El Niño effects. In the

Columbia R. estuary is the largest Caspian Tern colony known to exist in the world. Coastal Snowy Plovers, which nested in the many dune areas, are now listed under the Endangered Species Act because of invasion of European dune grass and human activities.

Shorebirds are mainly spring and fall migrants. Approximately 30 occur in the state, some of which appear in the thousands, e.g., Sanderlings, Least Sandpipers, Dunlins, and Long-billed Dowitchers.

Avifauna that use estuaries for migration or wintering include loons, grebes, Brown Pelicans, various ducks including dabbling (e.g., Northern Pintails, American Wigeon) and diving (e.g., scoters, Buffleheads, and mergansers) ducks, Canada Geese, and Black Brant. The portion of the Columbia R. within the ecoregion holds up to 3,000 Tundra Swans in winter and is a migration corridor for the Dusky Canada Goose.

Prominent raptors include the Bald Eagle and Peregrine Falcon. Some landbirds such as the Band-tailed Pigeon and Wilson's Warbler reach highest densities in Oregon in the Coast Range. This and the Klamath Mtns. ecoregion are strongholds for the Wrentit. The most abundant breeding birds in conifer and mixed conifer-deciduous forests of the Coast Range include: Winter Wren, Chestnut-backed Chickadee, Golden-crowned Kinglet, Hermit Warbler, Wilson's Warbler, Western Flycatcher, Brown Creeper, Hammond's Flycatcher, Swainson's Thrush, Varied Thrush, Red-breasted Nuthatch, Steller's Jay, Dark-eyed Junco, Western Tanager, Hutton's Vireo, and Hairy Woodpecker. In early seral growth dominated by shrubs, grasses, and forbs, the following birds are typically most abundant: Rufous Hummingbird, White-crowned Sparrow, Swainson's Thrush, Song Sparrow, Spotted Towhee, American Goldfinch, Willow Flycatcher, Orange-crowned Warbler, MacGillivray's Warbler, Wilson's Warbler, Dark-eyed Junco, Bewick's Wren, American Robin, Black-headed Grosbeak, and Wrentit. Addition of suitable snags brings House Wren into the list.

Declining species include the Mountain Quail. Of special interest is the Semidi Is. population of the Aleutian Canada Goose that winters near Pacific City.

Problems include estuary health, human disturbances on beaches and in and along estuaries, loss of shorebird habitat, and declining diversity in forest habitats.

## Willamette Valley Ecoregion

This is Oregon's smallest major ecoregion, covering 3,395,806 ac (1,374,264 ha) or 5% of the state. Approximately 94% of it is private land, with only small inclusions of federal, state, county, and city lands. This is the center of agriculture and commerce in the state and, as mentioned earlier, houses 70% of the human population.

The Willamette Valley's climate is mild with winter temperatures only occasionally going below freezing and summer temperatures seldom climbing above 100° F (38° C). However, it has a high percentage of cloudy days and annual precipitation is in the 40-in (102-cm) range, most of which falls in the winter, with less in the spring and fall. Summer months are dry with little rainfall occurring some years in Jul, Aug, and Sep. The valley is particularly attractive to wintering waterfowl because grasses grow through the winter and waters rarely freeze over.

The upper end of the valley floor lies at approximately 600 ft (180 m) elevation and the lower end where the

*Sauvie Island, at the north end of the Willamette Valley Ecoregion*

*Agricultural scene in the Willamette Valley Ecoregion*

Willamette R. enters the Columbia is subject to tidal action. Much of the valley is slightly hilly with buttes and small hills protruding above the valley floor.

Fifty-eight percent of the Willamette Valley is classed as agricultural land. Bottomlands are typically used for grass-seed crops, small grains, tree and shrub nurseries, and small inclusions of livestock pasture, while sloping foothills are often given to Christmas tree farms and vineyards. Over half of Oregon's urban area occurs in this ecoregion. The flanks of the valley are composed of Douglas-fir/western hemlock/western redcedar forest that merges with the Coast Range and Cascades ecoregions. Small scattered patches of Oregon white oak forest are present on hillsides, especially in the central and southern portions of the valley. For lack of fire, they have been gradually inundated by Douglas-fir. Major wetlands occur along the Columbia R., but are otherwise scattered. Small inclusions of other habitats in this ecoregion are hawthorn/willow shrubland and black cottonwood-Oregon ash-willow forest.

This and Columbia Plateau are the most heavily altered of Oregon's ecoregions (Habeck 1962, Towle 1974). At the time of Euro-American settlement, the valley was dominated by prairie, including wet and dry types, Oregon white oak savannahs, riparian forests of black cottonwood and lowland white fir along major streams, numerous wetlands, and even some ponderosa pine stands. Agriculture began changing that in the 1840s, and the valley has undergone continuous alteration since, with changes in agricultural practices, wetland drainage, and urbanization. Since the early 1940s, small diversified farms with their vegetated fence rows and pastures have been replaced by large monocultures that are largely devoid of fence rows. Few birds find useful habitat in nurseries. Wetlands, where not drained, have been invaded by reed canary grass, which replaced native sedges, bulrushes, wapato, and other native aquatic plants. Another prominent introduced plant is Himalayan blackberry, which proliferates in uncared-for places. The numerous changes that have taken place in bird populations in Oregon (discussed in Chapter 1) are no doubt in part due to environmental changes such as these.

Lewis's Woodpeckers and Yellow-billed Cuckoos were formerly among the ecoregion's breeding birds. Still present but in much reduced numbers are the "Streaked" Horned Lark (*Eremophila alpestris strigata*), Western Meadowlark, Common Nighthawk, "Oregon" Vesper Sparrow (*Pooecetes gramineus affinis*), Yellow Warbler, Canvasback, Lazuli Bunting, Yellow-breasted Chat, and Western Bluebird.

Nonetheless, distinctive bird communities remain in the valley's forests, woodlands, open fields, wetlands, river-bottoms, wetlands, and parks. Distinctive birds frequent replacement habitats. Among these are rye-grass fields where increasing numbers of Canada Geese winter (see the discussion in Chapter 1 and the Canada Goose account in Chapter 3). Also common in this habitat are other waterfowl such as various ducks and several thousand Tundra Swans. Increasing numbers of Sandhill Cranes winter and migrate through the valley. Numerous species are adapting to urban areas, as discussed in Chapter 1, and parks in the major cities such as the Portland metro area have some good bird habitats. Typical species in or over urban yards are: Band-tailed Pigeon, Mourning Dove, Anna's Hummingbird, Vaux's Swift, Downy Woodpecker, Northern Flicker, Steller's Jay, Western Scrub-Jay, American Crow, Violet-Green Swallow, Black-capped Chickadee, Bushtit, Bewick's Wren, American Robin, Varied Thrush, European Starling, Yellow-rumped Warbler, Spotted Towhee, Fox Sparrow, Song Sparrow, Golden-crowned Sparrow, Dark-eyed Junco, Black-headed Grosbeak, House Finch, American Goldfinch, and Evening Grosbeak. Many of these are seasonal.

For waterfowl and other birds, the Willamette Valley has some outstanding protected and managed wintering areas, which are frequently mentioned in Chapter 3. From north to south, they include Sauvie I. and the Sauvie I. W.A. north of Portland, Baskett

Slough NWR near Rickreall in Polk Co., Ankeny NWR south of Salem, William L. Finley NWR south of Corvallis, and Fern Ridge Res. west of Eugene in Lane Co.

## Klamath Mountains Ecoregion

This is perhaps the most variable ecoregion in the state in terms of topography, vegetation, land uses, and climate. It covers 3,864,245 ac (1,563,839 ha) or about 6% of Oregon's area. It is approximately evenly divided among federal and private lands, with the federal lands being nearly equally shared by USFS and BLM. This ecoregion extends from the c. Umpqua Valley southwest to include the Klamath Mtns., south to the Rogue Valley and Siskiyou Mtns., and southeast to the sw. Cascades. The Klamath Mtns., often poorly defined in maps and literature, adjoin the Coast Range south of the Coquille R. drainage and extend south into California. East of this range and south of Grants Pass lie the famous Siskiyou Mtns., which are a part of this ecoregion. Overall, the ecoregion presents a pattern of "steep, dissected mountains and canyons to gentle foothills and flat valley bottoms" (ONHAC 2002). Elevations run from 100 ft (30 m) to over 7,500 ft (2,300 m). High elevations near the coast receive over 100 in (254 cm) of precipitation, whereas the driest parts of the Rogue Valley receive 20 in (50 cm). Maximum temperatures in the same valley reached 105° F (40° C) during the 1950-80 period but average high is around 90° F (32° C). Minimum temperatures during the same period reached a low of 15° F (-9° C).

The Umpqua Valley is an agricultural area with diversified crops and livestock grazing. The valley of the Rogue R. and its tributaries, particularly Bear Cr., form the other major agricultural area in the ecoregion. Most of the human population of the ecoregion lives in these valleys along the I-5 corridor and to a limited extent in the Illinois Valley to the southwest. About 10% of Oregon's population resides in the ecoregion. They rely mainly on agriculture, forestry products, and tourism.

The Klamath Mtns. are noted among botanists for their diversified plant life, caused in part by numerous soil types and varied climatic conditions. About half of the state's 4,000 plant species, including 30 different conifers, occur here (ONHAC 2002). Over 60% of the ecoregion is in conifer or mixed conifer/deciduous forest and 18% is in agriculture. Oregon white oak/grassland types occur, especially in the foothills of the Umpqua Valley. Other vegetation types include regenerating young forests with grasses, saplings, and shrubs. Specific forest types include Douglas-fir/white fir/tanoak/Pacific madrone forests, Douglas-fir dominant mixed conifer forests, and Douglas-fir/western hemlock/western redcedar types. Although totaling less than 10% of this ecoregion, the following vegetation types are largely restricted to this ecoregion: Jeffrey pine forest and woodland, serpentine conifer woodland, Siskiyou Mtns. serpentine shrubland, manzanita dominant shrubland, Siskiyou Mtns. mixed deciduous forest, and Oregon white oak forest.

Although there are extensive areas of wilderness, these forests differ from pre-European times because of logging and fire suppression. Originally there was a

*Mixed evergreen and dry shrubby hillside in the Klamath Mountains Ecoregion*

*Oak savannah among the Umpqua Valley foothills, Klamath Mountains Ecoregion*

relatively frequent fire interval (e.g., 16-64 yr) in the Siskiyous, but they were generally fire-free from 1921 (Agee 1991) until recent years. Transformation of shrub habitats from ceanothus and others to Himalayan blackberry has already taken place, especially in the Umpqua Basin.

A unique set of birds occurs here, including the California Towhee, Black Phoebe, Oak Titmouse, and Blue-gray Gnatcatcher, all of which have the bulk of their Oregon range in this ecoregion. Other interesting species that are prevalent include the Common Poorwill, Acorn Woodpecker, Flammulated Owl, and Lark Sparrow. This is the only regular wintering area for Lewis's Woodpeckers in w. Oregon. No major wetlands occur here, but otherwise avian species composition resembles the Willamette Valley and Cascades ecoregions.

## Cascades Ecoregion

This was formerly known as the Western Cascades and High Cascades Physiographic Provinces (Franklin and Dyrness 1973) and later the Western Slopes and Crest Oregon Cascades Ecoregion (ONHAC 1988); these names are much more descriptive than Cascades since this ecoregion does not include the entire Cascade Range, but comprises the western slopes plus a strip that spills over the crest east of the Cascade summit.

This ecoregion consists of 7,142,099 ac (2,890,368 ha), covering 12% of Oregon's area. The Cascade Range extends north and south from British Columbia to n. California. In Oregon it is broken only by the Columbia R. Six major river drainages exit west from the Cascades, including the Clackamas, Molalla, Santiam, McKenzie, Willamette, Umpqua, and Rogue rivers. The latter two flow independently to the Pacific Ocean on the s. Oregon coast, while the others flow into the Willamette, which finds its way to the ocean via the Columbia R.

A series of glaciated peaks extends along the crest of the Cascade Range, the highest of which is Mt. Hood at 11,239 ft (3,425 m). Others mentioned in the species accounts in Chapter 3 include Mt. Jefferson and the North, Middle, and South Sister peaks (known as the Three Sisters). Also perched along the crest of the Cascades is Crater L. NP. Passes through the Cascades typically sit at 4,000-5,000 ft (1,219-1,524 m). Precipitation ranges from a low of approximately 30 in (76 cm) in southern, low-elevation portions of the ecoregion to a high of 100 in (254 cm) in northern, high elevations. Annual precipitation is dominated by snow above about 3,000 ft (914 m), and reaches as high as 500 in (1,270 cm) annually on the highest peaks (Loy et al. 2001).

The resident human population is confined to small towns in foothill valleys and small settlements based on the tourist industry (formerly logging), and for the most part it is concentrated along lower riverine corridors where private land exists. The largest town is Oakridge with a 1997 population of 3,148. The population swells during the summer and again in the winter, as this is a popular area for camping, hiking, backpacking, fishing, hunting, and winter sports. Hundreds of vacation homes are also present.

Ownership is dominated by USFS (65%) and private (23%), with smaller acreages of BLM (7%), NPS (3%), tribal lands (2%), and others.

This ecoregion is dominated by conifer forest: 44% of it is western hemlock/Douglas-fir forest, predominantly located on the western slope of the Cascades; 14% is mountain hemlock/true fir forests (Pacific silver fir in the north and Shasta red fir in the south), predominantly located above 3,500 ft (1,067 m) where snow cover is more persistent. Some large inclusions of lodgepole pine forest are present in the c. and s. Cascades (especially), and mixed conifer forests, including subalpine fir, grand fir, Pacific silver fir, noble fir, lodgepole pine, western white pine, mountain hemlock, and Engelmann spruce, occur along the

Cascades crest. Conifer forests of the ecoregion present a patchwork of successional stages due to fire, mostly in the past, and timber harvesting. Deciduous woods are present, primarily in riverine corridors and damp lower-elevation slopes. Dominant deciduous trees are black cottonwood, red alder, willows, and bigleaf maple, with smaller trees including Sitka alder, vine maple, and bitter cherry. Two evergreen broadleaf trees, golden chinkapin and Pacific madrone, are scattered throughout the western slopes of the ecoregion, with greatest abundance in the south. A variety of fire sizes and intensities have been documented in the w. Cascades (Agee 1993).

Earliest human uses within this ecoregion include subsistence hunting and gathering, especially huckleberry picking by native Americans. In the 1800s, huge flocks of sheep were herded to high mountain meadows from e. Oregon ranches. One or more of the sheep ranchers set fires in the fall to destroy conifers in favor of shrubs. Sheep grazing was gradually phased out as trees replaced shrubs. Beginning in the 1930s a huge effort to suppress forest fires began. The effects of fire suppression in this ecoregion have not been addressed. Timber harvest in this ecoregion began in the late 1800s, but remained very slow-paced until the 1950s. By the 1970s, over 20,000 ac (8,094 ha) per year were being harvested in this ecoregion. Lawsuits and eventually the Northwest Forest Plan (USDA/ USDI 1994) slowed the harvest and placed more emphasis on thinning and partial-cutting practices

*Old-growth forest in the Cascades Ecoregion*

instead of clearcutting. If harvest is curtailed and fire continues to be suppressed in this ecoregion, many open-area, shrub-nesting birds will likely be reduced in population as young conifer plantations grow and canopies close. At smaller scales, insects, pathogens, floods, and landslides have shaped, and will continue to shape, avian habitats.

Distinct bird habitats here include the low- and high-elevation forests and their seral stages including shrubs. In addition there are rivers, lakes, alpine tundra, meadows, and wetlands, some of which are human-made by creation of reservoirs.

Species common in most forested habitats include Hermit Warbler, Winter Wren, Chestnut-backed Chickadee, Hammond's Flycatcher, Pacific-slope Flycatcher, Red-breasted Nuthatch, Varied Thrush, Gray Jay, and Steller's Jay. Species more abundant in older forests include Vaux's Swift, Pileated Woodpecker, Red Crossbill, Hairy Woodpecker, and Red-breasted Nuthatch. Most of the state's Spotted Owls reside in this ecoregion. Black-throated Gray Warblers flank the western foothills and make their way up river valleys and adjacent slopes, sometimes with Hutton's Vireos. American Dippers and Common Mergansers frequent streams. Cascade streams are the only place in Oregon where Harlequin Ducks breed consistently. Barrow's Goldeneyes also breed almost exclusively in this ecoregion at high-elevation lakes where at some sites they are joined by Buffleheads. This ecoregion boasts the only known breeding sites in the state for the Black Swift. In mid- to high-elevation shrub-lands are Fox Sparrows and Green-tailed Towhees (mostly east-side but west-side in south). Also in shrublands and open forests are Townsend's Solitaires and Dusky Flycatchers; and in wet meadows, Lincoln's Sparrows. Fish introduced to many high lakes and reservoirs attract Double-crested Cormorants, Common Mergansers, California and Ring-billed Gulls, and in some cases Eared and Western Grebes. Alpine areas support Gray-crowned Rosy-Finches, American Pipits, and Clark's Nutcrackers. The majority of Oregon's Peregrine Falcon nests are located in this ecoregion, particularly in the south, likely because of a combination of relatively abundant nest ledges and avian prey. Many species have subspecies boundaries running along the Cascade summit.

The status of several species remains unclear in this ecoregion. Common Poor-wills have been observed in western foothill clearcuts, but no widespread survey effort adequately detecting or monitoring this species has occurred. The Boreal Owl has been detected, but it is unclear whether it breeds or is only a migrant and winter visitant. Flammulated Owls have been detected in the southern portion of the ecoregion, but their status has not been assessed. A population of subalpine-nesting Brewer's Sparrow has been discovered north of Mt. Jefferson and deserves further investigation.

## Eastern Cascades Slopes and Foothills Ecoregion

Aside from the crest and its immediate slopes, this ecoregion comprises the eastern slopes of the Cascades and mountain ranges and intervening valleys of sc. Oregon. In the north it starts with a narrow band that extends southward from the Columbia R. at Hood River, across the Warm Springs Indian Reservation and southward. From Bend it extends not only south but also southeast to Newberry Crater, Winter Ridge, the Warner Mtns. east of Lakeview, and finally to the California border. The absence of formal names for the numerous mountain ranges and intervening valleys of this portion of the ecoregion–including parts of the Deschutes, Fremont, and Winema NFs—was a handicap to designating bird ranges in this book. Also included are Klamath and Goose L. basins. Elevations run from approximately 750 ft (229 m) on the Columbia R. to the 8,456 ft (2,577 m) Crane Mtn. in the Warner Mtns. This ecoregion covers 7,012,961 ac (2,838,145 ha) or about 11% of the state. The northern portion of the region is drained by the Deschutes R., a tributary to the Columbia R. Rivers and streams in the southern portion of the ecoregion drain into the Klamath R. except for those in the southeast corner, which drain into various inland basins. Since the Coast Range and western slopes of the Cascades catch much of the westward flow of moisture from the Pacific, this is a relatively dry region with annual precipitation of 14-26 in (35-66 cm). Temperatures vary with elevation, but waters generally freeze over in winter.

This ecoregion supports about 120,000 people or about 6% of Oregon's population as estimated from county populations shown in Loy et al. (2001). The economy is based largely on agriculture, forest products, and tourism. The largest city, Bend, population 52,000, borders this ecoregion. It is a popular retirement area and tourist center for outdoor recreational activities centered in the adjoining Cascade Range. Other important cities include Hood River, Klamath Falls, and Lakeview. Land ownership breaks down as approximately 57% USFS, 32% private, 5% tribal, 3% BLM, 1% state, and 1% other.

This is one of the most diverse ecoregions in terms of vegetation. Approximately 7% is in agriculture starting with pear and apple orchards of the Hood R. valley. Elsewhere wheat, barley, alfalfa hay, onions, and potatoes are important crops. The crops are artificially irrigated, as are developed pastures.

Considering natural vegetation types, one source (ONHAC 2002) classifies 22% of the area as ponderosa-lodgepole pine on pumice (largely restricted to this ecoregion), 20% ponderosa pine forest and woodland, 7% Douglas-fir dominant mixed conifer forest, 6% ponderosa pine dominant mixed conifer forest (largely restricted to this ecoregion), 6% sagebrush steppe, 5% western juniper woodland, 5% grass-shrub-sapling or regenerating young forest, 4% lodgepole pine forest and woodland (largely restricted to this ecoregion), 3% ponderosa pine-western juniper woodland (predominantly in this ecoregion). Of ornithological interest are the ponderosa pine/white oak forest and woodland east of Mt. Hood. Aquatic habitat includes wet meadows, marshes, and lakes, including Upper Klamath L., the largest in the state.

Human impacts have included livestock grazing over most of the ecoregion at various times, timber harvest, fire suppression, clearing for agriculture, water diversions, and drainage for agriculture. Current problems include competition for water among agricultural, wildlife, and fisheries needs. Ponderosa pine forests, which dominate forest lands, are in poor condition from fire suppression, removal of mature and old-growth pines, and grazing. This has changed the landscape from park-like stands of sparsely spaced mainly mature and old-growth trees to crowded stands of small pines and shrubs, and this change has a marked effect on birds like the White-headed Woodpecker.

*Klamath Marsh NWR in the Eastern Cascades Slopes and Foothills Ecoregion*

Yellow Rails are currently known in the state only from this ecoregion and the only permanent nesting group of Red-necked Grebes in the state is on Upper Klamath L. The Klamath Basin is known for supporting the largest concentrations of migrating waterfowl in the U.S. as well as hundreds of wintering Bald Eagles. White-headed Woodpeckers and all three western nuthatches are in the pine forests. Lewis's Woodpeckers nest in the oak woodlands east of Mt. Hood. The southeast portion of this ecoregion hosts a large number of hybrid Red-naped and Red-breasted Sapsuckers, particularly in the Fremont NF of s. Lake Co. (OBBA).

As can be surmised from the above, the Klamath Basin complex of national wildlife refuges, including Klamath Marsh NWR, Upper Klamath NWR, Lower Klamath NWR (on the Oregon-California border), and Tule L. NWR (in California) are "must sees" for birders at proper seasons. These refuges are frequently mentioned in the species accounts in Chapter 3. Sycan Marsh, a preserve operated by The Nature Conservancy in Lake and Klamath counties is another important site. It supports the second largest concentration of nesting Sandhill Cranes in the state. For forest birds, the reader will find that Indian Ford and Cold Springs campgrounds in Deschutes NF, Deschutes Co., and Cabin L. CG, also Deschutes NF, but in nw. Lake Co., are commonly mentioned along with Davis L. in n. Klamath Co. for both aquatic and terrestrial species.

## Blue Mountains Ecoregion

The new designation for the state's ecoregions has combined the former High Lava Plains Ecoregion (which adjoined the East Cascades Ecoregion on the west) into the Blue Mountains Ecoregion, which means that this ecoregion now covers 25% of Oregon or 15,425,783 ac (6,242,729 ha). This is a generally mountainous region with numerous intervening valleys and canyons. Elevations run from approximately 2,500 ft (762 m) in the irrigated cropland area near Madras, Jefferson Co., to peaks in the Strawberry (Grant Co.) and Elkhorn (Baker Co.) ranges and Wallowa Mtns. (Wallowa Co.) that are over 9,000 ft (2,700 m) in elevation, the highest being Eagle Cap in the Wallowas. The most prominent ranges are the Ochoco, Blue, and Wallowa mountains, but the name Blue Mtns. is vague and variable. It can include the numerous ranges extending from Washington to the Harney Basin in Harney Co. There are numerous broad river valleys supporting cattle ranches that irrigate alluvial areas for hay production. Examples include valleys and floodplains associated with Deschutes, Crooked, John Day, Powder, Wallowa, Silvies, and Grande Ronde rivers. Major cities are also located in these valleys, including Madras, Redmond, Baker City, John Day, La Grande, and Enterprise. Over half of the eastern border of the ecoregion is bordered by Hells Canyon of the Snake R.

Because most of this ecoregion lies above 3,000 ft (914 m) and is beyond the rain-shadows of the Coast and Cascade ranges, this is generally an arid area with temperature extremes. Annual precipitation runs from 9 in (23 cm) at Redmond to 80 in (200 cm) in high sections of the Wallowa Mtns. Much of this comes in the form of snow, especially at high elevations. Temperatures below 0° F (-18° C) in winter and above 100° F (38° C) in summer are not uncommon.

Sixty-one percent of the ecoregion is federally owned with 53% of the federal land being USFS and 8% BLM. Private lands make up nearly 38% and state and tribal lands make up most of the remainder. This is a sparsely populated region that supports fewer than 100,000 people. While covering 25% of the state's area, it has <3% of the people. The economy is based on cattle ranching, farming, timber, and tourism. In the vicinity of Madras, farmland is devoted to growing alfalfa hay, onions, potatoes, garlic, grass seed, and other crops. Tourism, based in part on spectacular scenery, includes camping, fishing, hunting, and wilderness trips, especially in the Wallowa Mtns.

Natural vegetation of this ecoregion is difficult to describe because it is varied, complex, and changing. The former High Lava Plains to the west were originally

*Ponderosa pine forest in the Eastern Cascades Slopes and Foothills Ecoregion and Blue Mountains Ecoregion*

*High-elevation meadow, parkland, and fir forests of the Blue Mountains Ecoregion*

dominated by big sagebrush steppe, western juniper woodlands, and native grasslands. Today much of this has been converted to agriculture and pastures. Because of fire suppression, the western juniper woodlands have expanded in area at the expense of native grasslands. The newly established juniper areas lack some of the species richness of the original old-growth juniper woodlands (Reinkensmeyer 2001). In the forests that dominate the ecoregion, ponderosa pine was once the main tree. However, former open pine stands are changing to mixed ponderosa pine-Douglas-fir forests. Grand fir is also a major tree, and at high elevations Engelmann spruce and subalpine fir are common.

Valley bottomlands, now largely irrigated for pasture, were formerly wetlands and included bottomland hardwood trees such as black cottonwood and willow. Some of this habitat still exists along major streams. The 123,000-ac (49,800-ha) Zumwalt Prairie north of the Wallowa Valley is a major grassland. Mountain meadows exist in many areas although they have been modified for livestock grazing. A limited amount of treeless tundra-type habitat is present on high peaks like Eagle Cap. Rivers, lakes, and reservoirs occur at many locales. Some are important to aquatic birds.

Problems from a wildlife perspective include loss of native grasslands due to livestock grazing, western

*Western juniper/ sagebrush of the Blue Mountains Ecoregion*

ELVA H PAULSON

juniper expansion, and invasion of introduced plants, particularly cheatgrass. Other concerns are old-growth forest losses, the almost complete loss of ponderosa pine forests in their original state, and loss of riparian vegetation due to livestock grazing.

Forest and grassland birds star in this ecoregion, and include species not found elsewhere in the state. There are few special sites to name for these species, and most tend to be found in the Wallowa Mtns. and adjoining lowlands. Nearly all the forest birds named for the Eastern Cascade Slopes and Foothills Ecoregion are also found here. Additionally, birds like the Red-eyed Vireo, Veery, Gray Catbird, and American Redstart occur in lowlands, especially along river corridors. The Pine Grosbeak breeds in high-elevation forests of the Wallowas. Bohemian Waxwings, Common Redpolls, and Pine Grosbeaks are irregular winter visitors along with flocks of Gray-crowned Rosy-Finches in agricultural areas. Endemic as a breeder to the Wallowa Mtns. is the Wallowa subspecies of the Gray-crowned Rosy-Finch. Bear and Logan valleys in Grant Co. are hold-outs for a remnant breeding population of the Upland Sandpiper. Zumwalt Prairie is the transplant site for the Sharp-tailed Grouse, and supports sizeable nesting populations of Ferruginous and Swainson's Hawks. Other species to look for in conifer forests of the ecoregion are Flammulated and Great Gray Owls. Many of Oregon's Boreal Owl records come from this ecoregion, but it is not known if they nest here. The most likely area to find Pinyon Jays in Oregon is in the western juniper woodlands in the western portion of the ecoregion.

## Columbia Plateau Ecoregion

This relatively small ecoregion borders the Columbia R. in the north-central section of the state. Portions of it are rolling hills and other parts are relatively flat. In general this ecoregion slopes towards the Columbia R. It covers 4,253,759 ac (1,721,473 ha) or 7% of Oregon's area. Land ownership is approximately 90% private, 7% federal (BLM and Dept. of Defense), and 3% state. About 100,000 people reside here, totaling just over 3% of the state's population. Two of its counties, Sherman and Gilliam, had just under 2,000 people each in 2000 according to Loy et al. (2001).

Most of the population resides in Umatilla Co., where the city of Pendleton is located. Elevations in the ecoregion range from <500 ft (150 m) along the Columbia R. to 4,000 ft (1,200 m) on isolated buttes and along the edges of the Blue Mtns. Precipitation is 8-12 in (20-30 cm).

Along with the Willamette Valley, this is the most human-modified of any of the state's ecoregions. Agriculture takes up 41% of the land area, much of which is dominated by dryland wheat, but there are also extensive acreages of irrigated crops and pastures. Livestock grazing occurs over most non-irrigated sites. Originally this ecoregion was dominated by native grassland types. Rocky terrain and canyons preclude cultivation in some areas, as seen in the scablands, which support bluebunch wheatgrass and Idaho fescue. Sandy shrub-steppe occurs near the Columbia R., and is limited in area. It includes bitterbrush, needle-and-thread grass, sagebrush, and western juniper. Above 1,000 ft (300 m) the former Palouse grasslands have been largely converted to agriculture. Big sagebrush is an important component of some grassland types. An extension of the oak woodland east of Mt. Hood that was mentioned in a previous ecoregion description occurs on the western edge of this ecoregion. Riparian habitat has changed due to dam construction and water diversions. Introduced Russian- olive trees are found along reservoirs. Their impact is not all negative, as they are extensively used by birds for cover and food. Cheatgrass and introduced weed invasions have further altered the region. The Columbia R. is of course no longer a free-flowing stream. Three dams, The Dalles, John Day, and McNary, have backed-up water creating reservoirs along the Columbia R. bordering this ecoregion.

This ecoregion does not have any bird specialties confined to it, but the Grasshopper Sparrow occurs in a few remnant grasslands in much greater numbers here than in any other ecoregion. Other birds of interest here include the Burrowing Owl and Long-billed Curlew. Anthropogenic changes here have had mixed effects on birds. Conversion of the Columbia R. into pools where none previously existed, combined with adjoining croplands, have made this an important migration and wintering area, particularly for Canada Geese and other waterfowl. Wetlands created by

*Natural grassland in the Columbia Plateau Ecoregion*

*Upper Columbia River in the Columbia Plateau Ecoregion*

irrigation in combination with grasslands make this a major nesting area for Long-billed Curlews. Waterfowl like Greater Scaups, which were not known to occur here before dam construction, accept still-water areas along river edges. Islands in the river support nesting colonies of colonial birds. Irrigated areas are used by many species of wetland-oriented birds. Aquatic habitat that resulted from dam construction also made possible several national wildlife refuges, the largest of which is the Umatilla NWR.

## Northern Basin and Range Ecoregion

This 15,252,161- ac (6,172,464-ha) ecoregion occupies the southeastern corner of the state. It comes to 25% of the state's total or about the same as the Blue Mtns. Ecoregion. In coming up with these numbers, we took the liberty of incorporating the Snake R. Plain Ecoregion into this discussion. It comprises the agricultural areas near Ontario, Vale, and Nyssa, Malheur Co. Also incorporated herein is a segment of the Central Basin and Range Ecoregion, which occurs in Nevada except for a segment in the Alvord Basin east of Steens Mtn. The Northern Basin and Range Ecoregion includes the former Basin and Range and Owyhee Uplands Ecoregions.

From an ornithological viewpoint, this is one of the most exciting ecoregions in the state, in large part because of Malheur NWR and Steens Mtn. This is the heart of the so-called high desert region where there are extensive expanses of sagebrush steppe, great inland marshes and lakes without outlets to the sea, mountain ranges running in the 8,000-9,000 ft (2,400-2,740 m) elevation ranges, the rugged canyons of Snake R. tributaries like the famous Owyhee R. and Succor Cr., and large ranches separated by many miles.

The western two-thirds of the ecoregion is dominated by basin and range topography with north-south fault-block mountain ranges separated by basins or valleys that are in the 4,100 ft (1,250 m) elevation range. Precipitation from the mountains either soaks into the ground or runs into the basins where it evaporates. Basins range from open-water alkaline lakes to marshes to extensive alkali flats that rarely hold water. West to

*Steens Mountain, in the Northern Basin and Range Ecoregion*

*Malheur NWR, in the Northern Basin and Range Ecoregion*

east, prominent ranges and basins include Summer L., Chewaucan Marshes (fed mainly by mountains of Fremont NF to the west), L. Abert, Abert Rim, Warner Valley or Basin, Hart Mtn., Catlow Valley, Steens Mtn., and Alvord Basin. Major portions of Steens Mtn. also drain northwest via the Blitzen R. to feed Malheur and Harney lakes and east into the Alvord Basin. Most of these areas are prominently mentioned in the species accounts along with the Pueblo, Trout Cr., and Oregon Canyon mountains along the southern border of the ecoregion. The eastern third of the ecoregion, formerly referred to as the Owyhee Uplands, is lower than the mountain ranges but is a high plateau that drains mainly northward into the Owyhee and Snake rivers. Mahogany Mtn. is a prominent landmark here at 6,522 ft (1,987 m). The Snake R. plain stands at about 2,100 ft (640 m) elevation.

This is an arid region with low areas in the 9- to 12-in (25- to 30-cm) precipitation zone and both daily and annual temperature extremes. Steens Mtn. holds patches of snow through the summer and snow accumulates through the winter on all major ranges.

Precipitation on Steens Mtn. is approximately 60 in (152 cm), but is subject to annual changes that have a profound effect on the condition of wetlands like Malheur L.

The human population of this ecoregion is estimated at 44,000 based on county figures, but about 70% of this is in the eastern one-third of the ecoregion, mainly on the Snake R. plain where the city of Ontario is located. The western two-thirds of the ecoregion has about 15,000 residents, many of whom reside in Burns and Hines. The economy is based mainly on ranching, farming, and tourism. The richest farming area is on the Snake R. plain, but elsewhere, unpredictable summer frosts preclude growing most crops except alfalfa for hay. Cattle ranches typically occur along and at the terminus of streams where water diversions enable hay to be irrigated and grown for winter livestock feed. For the spring and summer, many of the ranches have allotments on BLM lands and in national forests to the north. A major area devoted to growing of wild hay is referred to in this book as the Lower Silvies R. floodplain south and east of Burns. The flooded wild

*Owyhee Region of the Northern Basin and Range Ecoregion*

hay meadows are a major stopping point for waterfowl migrating north in the spring, and are the main basis for the John Scharff Migratory Bird Festival held in early Apr in Burns.

Since most of this ecoregion was unsuitable for homesteading and is not forested, about 71% is under the jurisdiction of BLM. Private lands, mainly arable land suitable for farming or irrigation, make up 22%. National wildlife refuges (Hart Mtn. and Malheur) cover about 3%, as does state land.

Over half of this ecoregion is covered with various species and varieties of sagebrush. Salt desert scrub types composed of shadscale, greasewood, spiny hopsage, and other shrubs dominate poorly drained sites in many areas. There are also areas of western juniper-sagebrush steppe and extensive stands of curl-leaf mountain mahogany, particularly on Mahogany Mtn. and on Mahogany Ridge in the Trout Cr. Mtns. Stands of snowberry and snowbrush also occur in higher parts of the Trout Cr. Mtns. Riparian vegetation, mainly willows, border streams. Wet areas above 5,000 ft (1,500 m) in many of the mountains have extensive aspen stands, which are important bird habitats. An isolated stand of ponderosa pine located on Hart Mtn. is often referred to in this book. The highest reaches of Steens Mtn. are dominated by grasses and low-growing alpine plants. Not to be forgotten are extensive areas with little or no vegetation including lava fields and dry lakebeds like the Alvord Desert.

In addition to the Silvies R. floodplain, some important wetlands include the Malheur NWR, Summer L. W.A., the Warner Lakes wetlands in Warner Basin, and L. Abert. Important wetland plants in these areas include pondweeds, hardstem bulrush, giant burreed, alkali bulrush, spikerushes, and sedges, though these sites vary in terms of vegetation. L. Abert has little vegetation but is important to birds because of aquatic invertebrates.

Ecological problems in this ecoregion that affect birds include the continuous erosion of the quality and quantity of sagebrush steppe. Fire suppression, grazing, and introduced cheatgrass and forb invasions have all taken a toll. Plantings of the introduced crested wheatgrass have also reduced sagebrush steppe. Water is critical in this region, and is undependable.

The number of species worthy of special mention from this ecoregion is large. Foremost are wetland associates. Malheur L. has the greatest concentration of colonial nesting waterbirds in the state, including grebes, herons, egrets, ibis, Franklin's Gulls, and Black and Forster's Terns. It also supports the largest number of Sandhill Cranes found nesting in Oregon. Many of these same species nest in other wetlands like Summer L., e.g., Avocets are particularly prominent there. Summer L. is also turning out to be a major stopover place for Tule White-fronted Geese, and like the Lower Silvies R. valley, is known for spectacular migratory concentrations of Snow Geese: Summer L. in the fall

*Succor Creek Canyon in the Northern Basin and Range Ecoregion*

and the Silvies in the spring. Foraging with Snow Geese in the Silvies R. valley are Ross's Geese. This is also an important area for Long-billed Curlews. Thousands of Eared Grebes visit L. Abert to feed on its brine shrimp. White Pelican colony locations vary according to water conditions, but periodically occur at Malheur NWR and in Warner Valley. Snowy Plovers nest at L. Abert and along Summer and Harney lakes.

Terrestrial species of note are sagebrush inhabitants, including the Gray Flycatcher, Sage Thrasher, and Brewer's and Sage Sparrows. In the mountains are Green-tailed Towhees in shrub stands and nesting Mountain Bluebirds in aspens. Along the rim of Steens Mtn. can be found Oregon's only summering Black Rosy-Finches. Oregon's first known breeding "Gray-headed Juncos" (*Junco hyemalis caniceps*), a distinctive subspecies of the Dark-eyed Junco, were recently found in canyons of the Oregon Canyon and Trout Cr. mountains. The Greater Sage-Grouse reaches greatest abundance in Oregon in this ecoregion. White-throated Swifts are sure-finds in canyons of the eastern portion of the ecoregion.

*Matthew G. Hunter and David B. Marshall*

## Addendum to Paperback Edition

Since the first printing in May 2003, the following species have been accepted or are anticipated to be accepted by the OBRC as having occurred in the state. Changes in taxonomy are described and common and scientific name changes are also listed.

### Juan Fernandez Petrel *Pterodroma externa*
One observed 51 mi (82 km) west of Brookings 7 June 2002 (Nehls 2005).

### Cook's Petrel *Pterodroma cookii*
Two photographed 92 mi (148 km) west of Cape Sebastian, Curry Co., 20 Oct 2005 (Nehls p.c.).

### Manx Shearwater *Puffinus puffinus*
Single birds at Boiler Bay, Lincoln Co., 12 Sep 2000 (Nehls 2003) and Tierra Del Mar, Tillamook Co., 7 Sep 2002 (Nehls 2004).

### Cackling Goose *Branta hutchinsii*
Now considered a separate species from the Canada Goose (Banks et al. 2003), and incorporating the following subspecies that occur in Oregon: *B. h. minima* (commonly referred to simply as Cackling Goose), Aleutian Cackling Goose (*B. h. leucopareia*), and Taverner's (*B. h. taverneri*) Cackling Goose.

### Falcated Duck *Anas falcate*
One adult male photographed at Kirk Pond, Lane Co. 14 Feb 2004 and one photographed at Coburg, Lane Co., 16 Jan 2005 (Nehls 2004, 2005). Re-appeared nearby area 5 Feb 2006 (R. & B. Robb p.c.).

### Crested Caracara *Caracara plancus*
Observed 5 mi (8 km) east of Gold Beach 10 Feb 1990, one photographed south of Bandon, Coos Co., 25 Apr 2005, and one photographed near Corvallis, Benton Co., March 2006 (Nehls 2003, Nehls p.c., Contreras p.c.).

### White-rumped Sandpiper *Calidris fuscicollis*
One adult photographed at New River, Coos Co., 28 Jun 2003 (Nehls p.c.).

### Iceland Gull *Larus glaucoides*
One at Moolack Beach, Lincoln Co., 24 Feb 1991 and one photographed at Salem 25 Feb 1996 (Nehls 2004).

### Yellow-throated Vireo *Vireo flavifrons*
One at Malheur NWR HQ 9 Jun 2000 (Nehls 2003).

### Sedge Wren *Cistothorus platensis*
One territorial bird photographed N. Spit of Coos Bay, Coos Co., 30 May 2003 (Nehls 2004).

### White Wagtail *Motacilla alba*
The Black-backed Wagtail discussed on page 498 is no longer considered to be a distinct species from the White Wagtail. Consequently, Black-backed Wagtails should be referred to as White Wagtails (Banks et al. 2005).

### Red-throated Pipit *Anthus cervinus*
One photographed Wickiup Res., Deschutes Co. 6 Oct 2003 (Nehls 2004) and 2 adults photographed Cape Blanco 29 Apr 2004 (Nehls 2005).

### Sprague's Pipit *Anthus spragueii*
One photographed near Langlois, Coos Co., 1 Oct 2005 (Nehls p.c.).

### Smith's Longspur *Calcarius pictus*
One photographed N. Portland 17 Oct 2003 (Nehls 2004).

In addition to these changes, a few common and scientific names have changed. These are:

Rock Dove changed to Rock Pigeon. Band-tailed Pigeon genus changed to *Patagioenas*. Western Screech-Owl genus changed to *Megascops*. Snowy Owl scientific name changed to *Bubo scandiacus*. Three-toed Woodpecker changed to American Three-toed Woodpecker, and specific scientific name changed to *dorsalis*. Black-capped Chickadee specific scientific name changed to *aurocapillus*. Ovenbird specific scientific name changed to *aurocapilla*.

## Sources

Banks, R.C., C. Cicero, J.L. Dunn, A.W. Kratter, P.C. Rasmussen, J.V. Remsen Jr., J.D. Rising and D.F. Stotz. 2003. Forty-fifth supplement to the American Ornithologists' Union check-list of North American birds. Auk 121:985-995.

Banks, R.C., C. Cicero, J.L. Dunn, A.W. Kratter, P.C. Rasmussen, J.V. Remsen Jr., J.D. Rising and D.F. Stotz. 2005. Forty-sixth supplement to the American Ornithologists' Union check-list of North American birds. Auk 122:1026-1031.

Nehls, H. 2003. The records of the Oregon bird records committee, 2002-2003. Oregon Birds 29:101-103.

Nehls, H. 2004. The records of the Oregon bird records committee, 2003-2004. Oregon Birds 30:73-77.

Nehls, H. 2005. The records of the Oregon bird records committee, 2004-2005. Oregon Birds 31:2-4.

# Chapter 3

# Species Accounts

This chapter, comprising most of the book, provides information for all native species known for the state except the California Condor, which is extirpated, as well as a few self-sustaining introduced species. Basically the collection of species included in this chapter follows the list of species approved by the Oregon Bird Records Committee (OBRC) of the Oregon Field Ornithologists.

## Order GAVIIFORMES

### *Family Gaviidae*

**Red-throated Loon** *Gavia stellata*
A small loon holding its slender head erect and narrow upswept bill upward is most always a Red-throated. The sloped forecrown, domed hindcrown, and slim neck further define this smaller of the two "smiling" loons. In winter it is wispy and pale, its unpatterned neck blending dorsal gray and ventral white. The "stars" that earned its specific epithet are small white spots evenly strewn over its gray back during winter. Unlike other loons, in basic plumage the adult's eye is broadly surrounded by white. In alternate plumage, the adult's head is dark blue-gray, throat deep dull red, and back plain brown. A quick flyer, it can be identified by rapid deep wing-beats, humpbacked body with head and neck extending below the body, and wings appearing far to the rear due to the usual invisibility of the small feet. Often feeding near the surf, it may be spotted by beachcombing humans. It can take flight from a small water area, and can also, if pressed, take flight from land. Known in Europe as the Red-throated Diver. The greatest life span recorded for this species is 23 yr.

**General Distribution:** In N. America, breeds from n. Alaska across n. Canada and Greenland, south along the Pacific coast to s. Vancouver I.; also in similar latitudes along the Atlantic coast and across n. coastal Europe and Asia (Gabrielson and Lincoln 1959, Palmer 1962, Campbell et al. 1990a). Postbreeding dispersal extends from c. Alaska south along the Rocky Mtn. crest to nw. Wyoming (Palmer 1962). Winters along the Pacific coast from the Alaska Peninsula and Aleutians to n. Baja California and n. Sea of Cortez, along the Atlantic coast from Nova Scotia to the w. coast of Florida, and in similar latitudes and coasts in Eurasia (Palmer 1962, Campbell et al. 1990a, Stallcup 1994). Monotypic (Storer 1978).

**Oregon Distribution:** Abundant nearshore transient and uncommon to locally common in winter, mostly within 0.5 mi (0.8 km) of shore, along the coast, and in the lower Columbia R. estuary from fall through

spring. It is progressively less frequent farther from the coast up the Columbia R. at least to Portland, and on lakes and large rivers away from the coast (Gilligan et al. 1994, Contreras 1997b, D. Irons p.c.). Very rare in e. Oregon, with a few wintering (Johnson J 1989b, 1991b, Contreras 1997b). Immatures remain on the ocean throughout the year, but are rare in summer at most Oregon wintering areas (Gilligan et al. 1994).

**Habitat and Diet:** Winters primarily on coastal salt water, including bays, estuaries, harbors, and open ocean (Palmer 1962, Cogswell 1977, Campbell et al. 1990a). More common on shallow waters and closer to shore than other loon species (Palmer 1962, Johnsgard 1987, Campbell et al. 1990a).

Almost exclusively piscivorous in both breeding and wintering areas (Johnsgard 1987). Saltwater fishes consumed frequently in the ne. Pacific and Bering Sea, include herring, smelt, cod, sculpins, surfperches, sand lance, gobies, and, less frequently, capelin, tomcod, killifish, gunnels, and prickleback (Ainley and Sanger 1979, Johnsgard 1987, Campbell et al. 1990a). In the same area, freshwater fishes consumed include whitefish, grayling, and trout; estuarine fishes included sticklebacks and char (dolly varden and bull trout) (Ainley and Sanger 1979, Johnsgard 1987). One stomach examined in Oregon in 1921 contained two Pacific staghorn sculpin (Gabrielson and Jewett 1940). Also consumes crustaceans, aquatic insects, newts, frogs, squid and other mollusks, insects, crustaceans, mosses, and seaweeds (Johnsgard 1987).

**Seasonal Activity and Behavior:** Adult bills begin to turn dark in late Mar, and alternate plumage is first noted in early Apr, often in northward-flying birds only (*KM*). Transition to basic plumage begins in early Oct and continues through mid-Dec (*KM*).

During 2000, seawatches from Boiler Bay showed northward flight during Mar-Jun that peaked in Apr (P. Pickering unpubl. data). Numbers seen flying or on water from promontory censuses taken at the s. jetty of the Columbia R. in 1997-2000 peaked at less than 20/ hr in late Mar (M. Patterson unpubl. data). Numbers from 45-min censuses conducted up to 1.1 mi (1.8 km) offshore at three locations in Lincoln Co. during 1991-

98 peaked at 10-40 from mid-Jan to late Apr (*KM*). Present in lower Yaquina Bay from Jan through mid-May. Peak at 14-23 per census in Jan-Mar (Merrifield 1998). May be common in Columbia R. downstream from Portland during Feb-Mar smelt runs (Gilligan et al. 1994). A few remain as rare nonbreeding summer coastal visitors (Gilligan et al. 1994).

Southbound, off Boiler Bay Sep 1999-Dec 2000, adults flew by from late Aug through Oct, peaking in early Sep; a second wave of mixed ages peaked from late Oct through mid-Nov, but extended through mid-Dec; about 500-1,000/hr were observed during peaks (P. Pickering unpubl. data). Off the Columbia R. s. jetty 1997-2000, promontory census numbers increased in late Aug to mid-Nov and peaked at about 80/hr (M. Patterson unpubl. data). Numbers from censuses conducted 1991-98 to 1.1 mi (1.8 km) offshore at three locations in Lincoln Co. peaked at 10-60 from Sep through early Nov (*KM*). Rare in Nov at large bodies of water east of the Cascade crest, such as Wickiup Res., Deschutes Co., and below John Day Dam (P. T. Sullivan p.c.). Up to 200 observed annually in coastal CBCs; occurs sporadically with decreasing frequency upstream to Hood River in Columbia R. CBCs.

**Detection:** Easily located along the coast in flight and on open water, especially during migration. Tends to be the lowest flyer among the loons, often just over the surf (D. Irons p.c.).

**Population Status and Conservation:** Numerous, though numbers may be decreasing in some areas; not globally threatened (Cogswell 1977, Carboneras 1992b). Oregon CBC numbers 1959-88 suggest no population changes (Contreras 1997b). Over 33,000 were recorded during spring migration off California in 1979 (Carboneras 1992b). Estimated 1975-83 populations off California north of Point Conception were 3,800-16,000 in Apr and about a third less in fall; numbers dropped to about 2,000-3,000 in winter (Briggs et al. 1987). Similar estimates are not available for Oregon, but up to 1,000/hr pass Boiler Bay during peak migration (P. Pickering unpubl. data).

Highly vulnerable to oil spills, especially where large concentrations may form at rich winter fishing grounds (Palmer 1962, Carboneras 1992b). Some were illegally shot on wintering range (Palmer 1962), and some drown in fishing nets (Johnsgard 1987, Carboneras 1992b).—*Kathy Merrifield*

## Arctic Loon *Gavia arctica*

The Arctic Loon is primarily a Eurasian bird breeding across Europe and Asia to w. Alaska. It winters mainly south to the Mediterranean, Black and Caspian Seas, China, and Japan. It is casual in winter in Alaska and southward along the Pacific coast to California. A basic-plumaged individual, well seen and photographed, at Yaquina Bay, Lincoln Co., 16 May to 7 Jun 1998 is the only accepted Oregon record (Lillie 1998). Distinguishing this species from the Pacific Loon is very difficult, even in the hand. Probable hybrids have been reported (Storer 1978). Arctic and Pacific Loons, considered conspecific by AOU (1957), are separate species (AOU 1983). The Arctic Loon is monotypic.—*Harry B. Nehls*

## Pacific Loon *Gavia pacifica*

The flight of Pacific Loons by the thousands along the coast each spring and fall is one of Oregon's most dramatic bird migrations. Stunning plumage often clothes these fast-flying travelers. The crown and nape of breeding adults is frosty gray to white. Black-checked white scapulars against the black backs, fine black and white vertical stripes bordering the purple-iridescent black throats, and white underparts complete this study in contrast. The dark gray upperparts and white underparts of basic plumage are crisply divided, and a black line separates the dark hindneck from the white foreneck. The dark of the upper head extends below the eye, as if a hat were pulled over the face. Plumage of summer immatures resembles that of winter adults except that crowns and napes are light gray to white. The straight bill, distinguishing Pacific from Red-throated and Yellow-billed, is less robust than that of Common Loons; Pacific's head is larger and its neck thicker than those of the Red-throated. In flight, Pacific's wing-beats are faster than those of Common, the feet appear larger, the forecrown is rounder, and the hindcrown more sloped than those of Red-throated. In Eurasia, called Pacific Diver.

**General Distribution:** Breeds in e. Siberia and in N. America from the Arctic coast of Alaska and n. Canada east to Baffin I. and Hudson Bay southward to latitude 59° 23' N; winters south to Japan and along Pacific coast of N. America from se. Alaska through Baja California and the Sea of Cortez (Palmer 1962, Campbell et al. 1990a). Monotypic (AOU 1957). See Arctic Loon.

**Oregon Distribution:** This is the most abundant loon off the Oregon coast (though not in estuaries), especially in Apr and May and possibly in Oct (Briggs et al. 1992, Stallcup 1994); abundance varies widely by year and location (Contreras 1997b). Usually 5-20 but sometimes over 100 present on coastal CBCs. Occasionally inland in fall throughout state (*Oregon Birds* field notes, F. Conley p.c., P. T. Sullivan p.c., *MGH*). D. Irons (p.c.) reports they are regular in small numbers in Cascade lakes, including Big L., Linn Co.; Suttle L., Jefferson Co.; and Odell L., Klamath Co. Up to two are occasionally present on interior w. Oregon CBCs; other localities with multiple records include Timothy L., Clackamas Co.; and Henry Hagg L., Washington Co. On Columbia R. CBCs, usually 10 or fewer but up to 110 are found nearly every year at the Columbia estuary; they are observed with diminishing frequency upstream. Localities with multiple records along the Columbia R. include Sauvie I., Portland, Deschutes R. mouth, and John Day Dam; e. Oregon localities include Malheur NWR and the following reservoirs: Ana, Lake Co.; Haystack, Jefferson Co.; Pine Hollow, Wasco Co.; Wickiup, Deschutes Co.; Phillips, Baker Co.; Wallowa L., Wallowa Co. (F. Conley p.c.); and Antelope, Malheur Co.

**Habitat and Diet:** The Pacific Loon occurs most often on coastal salt water but sometimes on freshwater lakes, reservoirs, and rivers; prefers deeper water than other loons (Palmer 1962, Campbell et al. 1990a). Most common in lower estuaries and open ocean (Johnsgard 1987, Stallcup 1994, Contreras 1997b); least common loon in Yaquina Bay (Merrifield 1998). Most off California are within 6.2 mi (10 km) from land (Briggs et al. 1987).

Almost exclusively piscivorous; it usually eats only one or two kinds of food at a time, preferring small schooling fish (Johnsgard 1987). Frequent diet components in the ne. Pacific and Bering Sea include squid and saltwater fishes including herring, cod, sand smelt, stickleback, and sand lance, and less frequently the saltwater fishes sculpin, surfperch, gobies, butterfish, and prickleback, snakeblenny (or eelblenny); freshwater fishes include trout, grayling, carp, dace, and perch, and the estuarine char as well as salamanders, frogs, mollusks, insects, crustaceans, leeches, and rarely plants (Palmer 1962, Ainley and Sanger 1979, Johnsgard 1987).

Prey is captured with up to 57 dives/hr averaging less than 1 min usually to 20 ft (6.1 m) but as deep as 150 ft (46 m) (Palmer 1962, Johnsgard 1987). Diving Pacific Loons participate in feeding flocks composed of shearwaters, pelicans, cormorants, gulls, and alcids; also attracted to feeding flocks initiated by other diving birds (Pearse 1950, *KM*).

**Seasonal Activity and Behavior:** Alternate plumage is complete in Apr (*KM*). Migration timing varies between years (Russell and Lehman 1994). Up to 5,000/hr may pass a given point (Lillie 1996, P. Pickering unpubl. data). Spring migration off Oregon appears more compressed than fall (P. Pickering unpubl. data). Northward migration off Lincoln Co. begins from early to mid-Mar and extends as late as early Jun (Merrifield 1997, Pickering unpubl. data.). Numbers from censuses conducted 1991-98 (approximately 45-min count of all birds sitting on the water) up to 1.1 mi (1.8 km) offshore at three locations in Lincoln

Co. peaked at 15-170 in Mar through May (*KM*). In 1997-2000 promontory censuses off the s. jetty of the Columbia R. up to 350/hr indicate a spring peak in late Apr (M. Patterson unpubl. data). Nonbreeders form oversummering flocks on ocean (Gilligan et al. 1994).

Fall transitional plumage extends through late Oct (Hagenstein 1936, *KM*). Oct to mid-Nov southbound censuses conducted to 1.1 mi (1.8 km) offshore at three locations in Lincoln Co. during 1991-98 (approximately 45-min count of all birds sitting on the water) peaked at 25-80 (*KM*). Promontory censuses off the Columbia R. s. jetty had totals of up to 385/hr and indicated a fall peak in mid-Oct (M. Patterson unpubl. data). Southward migration off Lincoln Co. begins in late Aug, peaks from late Oct through mid-Nov, and continues through early Dec; highest numbers have followed weather fronts in the Gulf of Alaska (P. Pickering unpubl. data). In early Nov 2000, 8,000/hr flew south off Lincoln Co. (W. Hoffman p.c., P. Pickering p.c.). Inland records pick up in Oct and Nov and extend through winter (*Oregon Birds* field notes, F. Conley p.c., P. T. Sullivan p.c., *MGH*). Uncommon along the coast through most of winter, but may form rafts in late winter and spring (Gilligan et al. 1994, Contreras 1997b).

**Detection:** Migration distance from the coast and thus detectability may vary among years (Fix 1985a). Migrating birds fly steadily in small groups or in long, loose flocks, usually within 50 ft (81 m) of the water (Cogswell 1977). Most easily found by scanning open ocean, especially from headlands and jetties, nearshore sky, and lower bays.

**Population Status and Conservation:** The world population is probably in the millions, but numbers are decreasing throughout the southern portion of its range (Johnsgard 1987, Carboneras 1992b). Off California, over one million were recorded during spring migration in 1979 (Carboneras 1992b). Approximately 10,000-15,000 winter along the California coast (Briggs et al. 1987); no numbers for Oregon. Oregon CBCs indicate a 1.9 % annual increase (Contreras 1997b).

Some drown in fishing nets (Johnsgard 1987, Carboneras 1992b) and some were illegally shot during winter (Palmer 1962), but no known reports of either from Oregon. Vulnerable to oil pollution on migration and wintering areas (Palmer 1962, Johnsgard 1987), especially near rich winter fishing waters where many concentrate (Carboneras 1992b).—*Kathy Merrifield*

## Common Loon *Gavia immer*

Great Northern Diver, as it is known in Eurasia, aptly describes the Common Loon. This largest of the commonly encountered loons breeds predominantly north of the Canadian border. It is perfectly built for underwater prey pursuit. "Loon" may be derived from Old Norse or Swedish words alluding to its wild laughing territorial call or perhaps to its ungainliness on land, the price it pays for being a great diver. Large and blocky-headed, with a straight, robust bill, the Common Loon is separated from the Yellow-billed by its straight bill and winter face pattern and from smaller loons by its more angular head and often-retracted robust neck. Black head, white "necklace," incomplete black-and-white neckband, and white-checked black back define breeding adult. Dark gray upperparts of winter adults shade to white underparts. Take-off is impossible from land and labored on water, but flight is swift, direct, and steady. Flying Common Loons appear large in front due to blocky heads, thick necks, and large bills; their big black feet are obvious behind the tail.

**General Distribution:** Breeds from Aleutian Is. and Bering Sea coasts east throughout boreal lake country to s. Baffin I. and south to Great Lakes, Newfoundland, Iceland, Greenland, and occasionally Scotland (Harrison 1985). Formerly bred, now perhaps casually, south to about 41º N Lat including ne. California (Bent 1919, Palmer 1962). In w. N. America this species winters mostly along marine coasts but occasionally on fresh water from Aleutian Is. to n. Baja California and the Sea of Cortez. In e. N. America winters from Newfoundland to Florida and the Gulf states, and in Europe from Scandinavia to n. Spain, mostly off sw. Britain (Harrison 1985, Campbell et al. 1990a, Stallcup 1994). Monotypic (Storer 1978, 1988).

**Oregon Distribution:** Common to abundant transient along coast; uncommon to locally common on large freshwater bodies; less frequent east of the Cascades. Numbers and frequency decrease progressively upstream in Columbia R. CBCs; occasional on the Columbia R. throughout the year from the coast through Portland to McNary Dam, Umatilla Co. (M. Denny p.c.). Flight during migration extends to 20-25 mi (32-40 km) from land along the coast and over a broad front inland (Palmer 1962, Campbell et al. 1990a, P. Pickering unpubl. data). Common Loons are the most widespread loon in winter, occurring on both salt and fresh water and regularly on the Columbia R. to e. Oregon; this is the only loon regular on inland fresh water (Stallcup 1994, Contreras 1997b). In summer, most immatures remain on coastal salt water (Palmer 1962), as corroborated by basic plumage of the few summering in Oregon estuaries (*KM*). There

are scattered summer records (Gilligan et al. 1994, Adamus et al. 2001), with one positive breeding record in Oregon; others are suspected as described below.

**Habitat and Diet:** In winter and during migration, Common Loons utilize coastal bays, coves, harbors, estuaries, inland lakes, reservoirs, or rivers that have sufficient food and open water to take flight (Palmer 1962, Campbell et al. 1990a). May raft at night, especially in estuaries. All identified in 1989-90 surveys off Oregon were within 3 mi (5 km) of shore, most within 0.3 mi (0.5 km) (Briggs et al. 1987, 1992). Most numerous and widely dispersed loon in Yaquina Bay 1993-94 (Merrifield 1998). Many fall stopover sites appear to be traditional large lakes along migratory routes (Johnsgard 1987).

Information to define breeding habitat in Oregon is insufficient, but Cascade lakes are the most likely breeding habitat. Elsewhere breed on freshwater lakes, sloughs, marshes, lagoons, and rivers (Campbell et al. 1990a). Need abundant supply of small fish in water clear enough to allow efficient foraging. Islands influence nest location, but artificial islands do not affect lake selection (McIntyre 1975). In Minnesota, require lakes larger than 10 ac (4 ha) to form territory, 25 ac (10.1 ha) to raise one chick, and 50 ac (20.2 ha) to raise two (McIntyre 1975). Breeding negatively correlated with recreational use in some studies, but unrelated in others (McIntyre 1975, Robertson and Flood 1980, Johnsgard 1987).

Diet is usually about 80% fishes (Palmer 1962). Saltwater fishes consumed include capelin, codfishes, eelpout, flounder, gobies, herring, killifish, pipefish, rockfish, sand dabs, sand lance, sardines, sculpins, shiner perch, smelt, steelhead, sticklebacks, surf fish, and surfperch, mostly of little economic value (Palmer 1962, Cogswell 1977, Ainley and Sanger 1979). Several freshwater fishes are also consumed, presumably during breeding (Palmer 1962, Ainley and Sanger 1979, Carboneras 1992b). Up to 20% of diet may be crustaceans, including shrimps, crabs, and amphipods (Palmer 1962, Carboneras 1992b). Other foods include various annelids, fish eggs, sea stars, amphibians, insects, and mollusks including clams, snails, and squid (Palmer 1962, Johnsgard 1987, Paulson 1988, Ford and Gieg 1995). Crayfish are important in inland areas of Oregon (C. Corkran p.c.)

**Seasonal Activity and Behavior:** Development of alternate plumage begins in early Mar with dark areas on the face or around the bill; some birds have nearly completed pre-alternate molt by mid-Mar while others are just beginning (*KM*). Spring migration off Oregon and Washington peaks in Apr and May (Briggs et al. 1992). In promontory censuses off the Columbia R. s. jetty 1997-2000, numbers were generally quite small,

*Common Loon*

peaking at 6-7/hr from early May through mid-Jul, with maximum in mid-May (M. Patterson unpubl. data). Inland, spring flocks sometimes exceeding 400 (e.g., Summers 1993c) peak in mid-Apr at Wickiup Res., Deschutes Co. (numerous reports in *Oregon Birds*), while smaller numbers may be found on many sizeable inland lakes and reservoirs (P. T. Sullivan p.c., *MGH*), including lakes and reservoirs in the Bull Run watershed of Mt. Hood NF (C. Corkran p.c.) and Odell L., Klamath Co. (D. Irons p.c.)

Courtship behavior or competitive male displays observed in mid-Apr in Yaquina Bay (Merrifield 2001a), Tillamook Bay, and Bull Run Res. (C. Corkran p.c.). No nesting dates for Oregon, but most newly completed first clutches along the southern extreme of breeding range are from mid-May to late Jun (Palmer 1962, Harrison 1985, Campbell et al. 1990a). Dates for most broods observed in British Columbia ranged from mid-Jun to mid-Jul. Oregon's only breeding record was an observation of an adult with a young riding on its back in late Jun or early Jul 1991 on Lower Eddeeleo L., in the Waldo L. Wilderness Area, Lane Co. (C. Heath p.c.).

During surveys between 1 Jun and 6 Aug 1988, C. Corkran (p.c.) saw Common Loons at 10 of 89 lakes visited. While most were coastal, an adult and immature were in the Bull Run watershed northwest of Mt. Hood and two adults were on Waldo L., e. Lane Co., 21 and 22 Jul 1988. Jun and Jul records also come from Diamond L. (J. Bohler p.c.). Two adults with two well-developed juvenile or immature birds on Waldo L. on 7 Aug 1948 (T. McAllister p.c.) may have been breeding birds, but could also have been nonbreeders or early fall migrants. An immature 8 Aug 1985 on Lookout Point Res., Lane Co. (*MGH*), and two adults with one fully grown juvenile on Diamond L., e. Douglas Co.,

23 Aug 1988 (Heinl and Fix 1989, Fix 1990a), were judged early fall migrants (*MGH*).

Development of basic plumage begins in mid-Aug with white areas on the lower face or around the bill and is about half complete by mid-Oct. By mid-Nov only dark smudges remain on the face (*KM*). Fall numbers are usually highest in Oct or Nov. Three to 30/hr fly south along the coast from about Sep through early Dec, peaking in mid-Nov (Briggs et al. 1992, P. Pickering unpubl. data). On 17 Nov 1999, 150/hr flew south (P. Pickering unpubl. data). In promontory censuses from the Columbia R. s. jetty conducted 1997-2000, numbers peaked at 6-8/hr from mid-Sep to late Oct; an analysis indicated a maximum in mid- to late Oct (M. Patterson unpubl. data). From three locations in Lincoln Co. 1991-98, censuses out to 1.1 mi (1.8 km) offshore numbers (approximately 45-min counts of birds on the water) peaked at 4-15 from early Aug through late Nov (*KM*). Inland, the same pattern is again indicated by Wickiup Res. records: fall flocks of up to 250 peak in mid-Oct to early Nov, while smaller numbers and individuals may be found on many sizeable inland lakes and reservoirs (P. T. Sullivan p.c., *MGH*).

Winters along the outer coast (P. Pickering unpubl. data, *KM*). Numbers from censuses to 1.1 mi (1.8 km) offshore at three locations in Lincoln Co. 1991-98 peaked at 5-15 (approximately 45-min count of birds on the water) from Jan through Mar (*KM*). Winter averages of 15-40 in Yaquina Bay were highest in Feb (Merrifield 1998). Ten to 200 recorded yearly in coastal CBCs. Up to eight have been present during some years in CBCs encompassing large water bodies.

Activity budgets not recorded in Oregon. Off Rhode Island in winter, 23-38% of time is spent feeding (Ford and Gieg 1995). In winter, dives averaged 52 sec off se. Alaska (Stewart 1967) and 40 sec off Virginia to depths of 6-15 ft (1.8-4.6 m) (McIntyre 1978). Dives to 200 ft (61 m) have been reported (Palmer 1962).

**Detection:** Rarely heard in Oregon. Most easily found by scanning sky and ocean along the shore, bays, estuaries, the Columbia and other large rivers, and large inland lakes and reservoirs. Often scattered among other loon species (P. Pickering unpubl. data). Easily the highest flier of the loons over the ocean (D. Irons p.c.).

**Population Status and Conservation:** Other than the summer sightings mentioned previously, there are scattered sightings that may or may not indicate breeding activity in Oregon. Two presumed Common Loon eggs were collected from a nest on a floating log at Loon L., Douglas Co., in 1852 (McArthur 1992); current location of the eggs is unknown. A pair summered at Devils L., Lincoln Co., 1931-34 (Gabrielson and Jewett 1940). One to two have been at Bull Run L. and Upper Res., Mt. Hood NF, since at least the late 1970s; pairs in 1984-86 exhibited courtship and nesting behavior but apparently did not nest, perhaps due to fluctuating water levels (C. Corkran p.c.). Two in alternate plumage were at Timothy L., Clackamas Co. summer 1991 (Johnson 1992a), and one in alternate plumage was at Detroit L., Linn Co. 27 Jun 1997 (Johnson 1997a). Positive signs of breeding in Oregon remain elusive. In 1988, C. Corkran (p.c.) searched 87 lakes within the state that have reported loons in the past, but did not find evidence of actual reproduction. On 5-7 Aug 2002, she checked out Diamond L. and seven lakes in the Waldo L. area including the Eddeeleo complex, but did not find loons. In Washington, there were 16 confirmed and 23 possible breeding localities as far south as King Co. in the late 1980s (Smith et al. 1997); about eight more confirmed statewide 1987-1996 (T. R. Wahl p.c.).

Not globally threatened: world population comprises a few hundred thousand birds; numbers decreased during 1900s in southern range (Carboneras 1992b). Johnsgard (1987) estimated a breeding population of 15,000 south of Canada. Off California 1975-83, 6,000-11,000 were offshore, and many more on estuarine waters were not counted (Briggs et al. 1987). Entanglement in fish nets and oiling cause most winter mortality (Palmer 1962, Johnsgard 1987, Carboneras 1992b). Major oil disasters of the last few decades have severely affected several populations; some may take decades to recover (Carboneras 1992b).

Declining food supplies may alter feeding habits. More time is devoted to feeding when food populations decline. Further fish population declines in New England may result in loon population decline (Ford and Gieg 1995). Many fish and invertebrate populations declined during the pronounced 1983 El Niño (McGowan et al. 1998), and populations of some smelt and rockfishes are declining off British Columbia (Gillespie and Westrheim 1997); such declines could conceivably affect Oregon Common Loon populations.

This species is easily disturbed by humans, especially in breeding habitat (Palmer 1962, Smith et al. 1997). In extreme southern breeding range, numbers have been greatly reduced or locally extirpated through shooting and from disturbance from vacationers, airplanes, and motorboats (Palmer 1962, Robertson and Flood 1980, Carboneras 1992b). Mercury poisoning in Common Loons occurs in ne. N. America (Frank et al. 1983, Barr 1986).—*Kathy Merrifield*

## Yellow-billed Loon *Gavia adamsii*

This large loon breeds in the Arctic tundra from nw. Russia across Siberia and Alaska through Canada to Hudson Bay. It winters in N. America along the coast of s. Alaska and British Columbia, and regularly in small numbers south to Baja California. There are records of transient birds on large inland bodies of water. Difficulties in separating this species from the widespread Common Loon can lead to mis-identification. Following recognition that this species ranged in the U.S. south of Alaska, observers began publishing sightings (Remsen and Binford 1975). First Oregon record at the s. jetty of the Columbia R. 8 Mar 1969 (Crowell and Nehls 1969b).

The majority of Oregon records are of transient birds found between early Nov and early Jun. Wintering individuals were at Yaquina Bay, Lincoln Co., from 14 Jan to 14 Feb 1980 (OBRC); at Netarts Bay, Tillamook Co., 1 Mar to 5 Apr 1980 (Watson 1989), and at Garibaldi, Tillamook Co., 14 Dec 1991 to 19 Jan 1992 (Johnson 1992b). Individuals are occasionally found from early Jul to late Sep that appear to be nonbreeding, mostly subadult, summer transients. An adult in alternate plumage was photographed at Coos Bay, Coos Co., 15 Jul 1972 (Crowell and Nehls 1972d). An injured subadult bird was at Yaquina Bay from 20 Jul to 15 Aug 1985, when it was found dead (Heinl 1986b). Inland records include: individuals at Fern Ridge Res., Lane Co., 31 Dec 1989 (OBRC); Timothy L., Clackamas Co., 16 May 1988 (Mattocks 1988b); Boyle Res., Klamath Co., 29 Apr 1993 (OBRC); Wallowa L. 12-13 Feb 2000 (Korpi 2000); and again 17 Dec 2000 to 20 Jan 2001 (Spencer 2001b). Most Oregon records are verified by detailed descriptions and some by identifiable photographs in OBRC files (Watson 1989). An adult in basic plumage was found dead on Clatsop Beach, Clatsop Co., 8 Apr 1977 (spec. no. 942 PSU). Monotypic (AOU 1957).—*Harry B. Nehls*

# Order PODICIPEDIFORMES
## *Family Podicipedidae*

## Pied-billed Grebe *Podilymbus podiceps*

Also known as "dabchick" or "helldiver," this wary bird sinks like a submarine when disturbed, rather than diving, and re-emerges with only its head above water. This is a brownish grebe with a black vertical bar in the middle of the rather stubby, whitish bill, and jet-black throat patch on both sexes in alternate plumage (Wetmore 1924). It has a surprisingly loud "yelping" call within a marsh. Young have striking stripes on head.

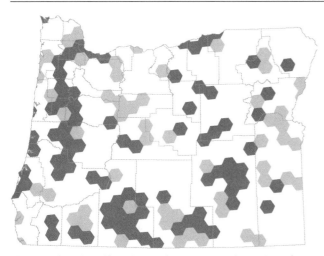

**General Distribution:** Across N. America from Canada south through U.S., Mexico, M. and S. America, to southern parts of Argentina. Oregon birds belong to *P. p. podiceps*, the subspecies breeding in N. America (AOU 1957).

**Oregon Distribution:** The Pied-billed Grebe is a common breeder in Klamath, Lake, and Harney counties (Gabrielson and Jewett 1940, Gilligan et al. 1994), and in Malheur Co. (Contreras and Kindschy 1996). Rare to uncommon breeder along coast and uncommon to common breeder in the Willamette Valley. Uncommon breeder in Josephine Co. (OBBA, D.Vroman p.c.) and Douglas Co. (Sawyer and Hunter 1988, Hunter et al. 1998). Rare to uncommon breeder in nc. and ne. Oregon. In ne. Oregon, it is an uncommon spring and fall migrant and summer resident, and occasional winter resident at lower elevations (Evanich 1992a). The majority winter along the coast, and in the Willamette and Rogue valleys. Also winter on the Columbia R. from John Day Dam upstream into Washington (M. Denny p.c.).

**Habitat and Diet:** At Malheur NWR, the Pied-billed Grebe nests on lakes, ponds, channels, and sloughs with emergent vegetation (Littlefield 1990a); nests at Double O Unit of the refuge were located in Baltic rush and built of Baltic rush or spikerush stems and algae (Foster 1985). On Malheur L. nests on floating mass of hardstem bulrush from the previous year (*DBM*). In Jackson Co. found on shallow ponds and reservoirs (Browning 1975a). In Klamath Co. most nests found in or near edges of dense cattails and bulrush; forage in open water in all seasons (*KS*). This species also nests on small stock ponds in Malheur, Harney, and Baker counties (M. Denny p.c.).

In winter along coast it prefers freshwater lakes, ponds, slow-moving rivers, and backwaters (Gabrielson and Jewett 1940, Bayer and Krabbe 1984, Contreras 1997b). In winter east of the Cascades this species occurs around warm freshwater springs and moving open water such as on Blitzen R., Malheur NWR

(Littlefield 1990a, Evanich 1992e, Contreras 1997b), and Ana R. and Summer L., Lake Co. (Anderson DA 1990d), or slow-moving water of L. Ewauna and Link R. at Klamath Falls (Coopey 1938, Korpi 1997, *KS*).

Comprehensive Oregon diet data are not available; probably consumes many species of fish and invertebrates. Consumed bluegill perch Dec-Feb in Jackson and Josephine counties (D. Vroman and C. Brumitt p.c.). Possible fish consumed in Sep at Cook Slough, Clatsop Co., include yellow perch, largemouth bass, peamouth chub, American shad, sculpins, and carp (L. Cain p.c.). Food item percentages from birds taken in e. U.S. included: 20% fish, 17% crustaceans, 4% dragonfly nymphs, 21% bugs, 33% beetles, with a greater proportion of aquatic insects, mainly dragonfly and damselfly larvae, taken during summer (Wetmore 1924). Fish are eaten in small quantities May-Aug, and crustaceans taken mostly Dec-Feb (Wetmore 1924). Fish included catfish, bullheads, suckers, chubs, sunfish, perch, sculpins, and carp. Amphibians included frogs, toads, and salamanders. Insects included dragonfly and damselfly nymphs, grasshoppers, bugs, beetles, fly larvae, wasps, bees, and ants (Wetmore 1924). Young are fed dragonfly nymphs (Deusing 1939). Like other grebes, it consumes feathers, which retains bones and chitin in stomach where bones dissolve, then cast pellet of feathers and chitin (Wetmore 1920, Storer 1961).

**Seasonal Activity and Behavior:** The Pied-billed Grebe is most abundant east of the Cascades early Mar to Apr. At Malheur NWR, average arrival 11 Mar (Ivey, Herziger, and Scheuering 1998). Solitary nester (Gabrielson and Jewett 1940, Faaborg 1976, Littlefield 1990a) and fierce defender of territory (Wetmore 1924). Like other grebes, this species has elaborate courtship displays involving numerous ceremonies including stretching upright on water while beating wings and treading water, various postures, head shaking, diving, and swimming side by side (Kilham 1954, Storer and Muller 1999). At Malheur NWR, nesting begins in late Apr and early May, peaks in late May to early Jun (Littlefield 1990a); nests initiated mid-May (Foster 1985). In Iowa, nests were constructed in 3-7 days (Glover 1953). Limited clutch-size data from Oregon include: two eggs, Fern Ridge Res., Lane Co. (Gullion 1951); seven eggs, William L. Finley NWR, Benton Co. (Evenden et al. 1950); elsewhere in N. America, 1-8 (Storer and Muller 1999). Eggs dull bluish white. Nests often left covered with rotting vegetation (Storer and Muller 1999), including nests found on Malheur L. (*DBM*) and at William L. Finley NWR (Evenden et al. 1950). This practice maintains proper temperatures—coolness from the water below during warm air temperatures and heat from putrefaction of vegetation. Nests with eggs or young observed 24 May to 14 Jul (n=4); recently hatched young away from nests observed

5 Jun to 17 Aug, with most late Jun and Jul (n=25) (OBBA). Newly hatched young swim and dive soon after leaving egg (Gabrielson and Jewett 1940). After nesting and feather molt, birds appear more often in open (Wetmore 1924). At Malheur NWR, flightless young have been seen through Aug, begin leaving in mid-Aug, peak migration in Sep, and most are gone by Oct (Littlefield and Cornely 1984, Littlefield 1990a). On the coast early fall arrival is 30 Jul, Lincoln Co. (Johnson J 1994a); coastal numbers subsequently build up in the fall. At Upper Klamath L. numbers peak Oct and drop sharply by Nov (Coopey 1938, *KS*).

**Detection:** Spring vocalizations, *cowp-cowp-cowp-cowp*, heard from great distances, allow detection within dense emergent vegetation. Sinks when approached, re-emerging a short distance away with only head above waterline. Seldom seen in flight; migrates by night (Storer and Muller 1999). Wariness and elusiveness may contribute to underestimation of numbers.

**Population Status, and Conservation:** BBS shows stable population 1968-87 in Oregon (Sharp 1990). CBC data in Oregon show slight upward trend (Contreras 1997b). Average CBC numbers 1979-98 along coast 8-43; in the Willamette Valley 13-44; in the Rogue Valley 14-23; east of the Cascades 2-38. High CBC counts west of the Cascades 258 at Lincoln City in 1985 (Contreras 1995), and east of the Cascades 159 at Klamath Falls in 1997 (*KS*). Other reported high numbers include 415 in late Dec at Devils L., Lincoln Co. (Heinl 1985).—*Kevin Spencer*

## Horned Grebe *Podiceps auritus*

In alternate plumage this striking bird's lower neck, chest, and sides are bright chestnut. Three groups of yellow plumes adorn the sides of the head. Head and throat are black. In basic plumage, they are mainly gray and white with black crowns. Young are almost black above with grayish white stripes and spots on head.

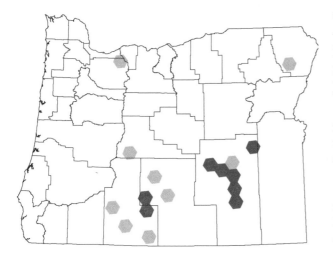

**General Distribution:** Holarctic. In N. America breeds from Alaska and n. Yukon south to e. Oregon and Idaho and east across s. Canada to New Brunswick and south as far as S. Dakota, c. Nebraska, and c. Wisconsin. N. American wintering range includes Pacific coast from Aleutian Is. south to n. Baja California and Atlantic coast from Nova Scotia to Florida and w. to Texas. Limited inland wintering in mild waters. Contrary to AOU (1957), this species is monotypic (Cramp and Simmons 1977).

**Oregon Distribution:** Rare breeder east of the Cascades. Malheur NWR has averaged 4-5 pairs per summer since 1958 (Marshall 1959, Littlefield 1979, 1990a, Anderson 1987d); nests are not found there each year (Evanich 1993). Horned Grebes nested at Downey L., Wallowa Co., where in 1979, eight pairs were on nests with eggs (Evanich 1992a, M. A. Stern p.c.). There are individual nest records from Sycan Marsh, Lake Co. (Stern, Del Carlo, et al. 1987) and near Riley, Harney Co. (Sullivan PT 1995a). Present late Jun at Upper Klamath L. (*KS*) where up to 10 birds have been observed (Gilligan et al. 1994).

Rare along coast in summer. Uncommon spring and fall transient on lakes, reservoirs, and large rivers west of the Cascades, and uncommon to common east of the Cascades. In winter, common along coast in estuaries and near-shore ocean (Gabrielson and Jewett 1940, Contreras 1997b); uncommon in the Willamette and Umpqua valleys, and rare east of the Cascades. CBC numbers on coast usually 20-50, with high of 325 at Coos Bay in 1996; inland along Columbia R. average is 29 at Hood River; Willamette Valley average is 3-4; east of the Cascades average is three in Wallowa Co.; very scarce elsewhere. In winter inland presence dependent on open ice-free water, usually near springs or moving water (*KS*).

**Habitat and Diet:** At Malheur NWR the Horned Grebe favors semi-permanent ponds for nesting such as Buena Vista, Wright's, Warbler, and Knox (Littlefield 1990a); one nest in Double O Unit was built of rush stems and algae in a stand of Baltic rush (Foster 1985). At Sycan Marsh this species nested in sedge at edge of open water, with depth less than 3 ft (1 m), and at Downey L., Wallowa Co., nested in same area with Eared Grebes (M. A. Stern p.c.). In Montana, one nest was a platform of coarse fresh green grasses floating in 1 ft (30 cm) of water (DuBois 1919). In sw. Manitoba nests in water >8 in (20 cm) with average depth of 16 in (40 cm); anchored to previous season's vegetation or to new emergent vegetation (Ferguson and Sealy 1983).

Diet in summer consists of fish, crayfish, and aquatic insects including: caddisflies, damselflies, mayfly larvae, leeches, beetles, flies, gnats, true water bugs, water striders, water boatmen, backswimmers, and sand fleas

(Wetmore 1924, Storer 1969). In winter, Pacific coast diet is predominately crayfish, shrimp, prawns, and fish including sculpin, stickleback, anchovy, carp, silversides, and eel (Wetmore 1924). Consumes own feathers like other grebes (Gabrielson and Jewett 1940).

**Seasonal Activity and Behavior:** Numbers increase in early spring along coast, with a high of 100 at Boiler Bay on 9 Apr (Lillie 1995). Most have departed w. Oregon by early May (Irons 1984b). Transients are fairly common during Apr in high Cascade and e. Oregon lakes and reservoirs; two were very late 26 May 1988 at Diamond L., e. Douglas Co. (Fix 1990a). At Malheur NWR, earliest arrival is 8 Apr (Summers 1985a, Littlefield 1990a), mean 20 Apr (Ivey, Herziger, and Scheuering 1998). In Deschutes, Crook, and Jefferson counties, earliest arrival is 3 Mar; mean 2 Apr (C. Miller unpubl. data).

Courtship display on breeding grounds involves attraction posturing, ritualized preening, offerings of vegetation, and "rushing displays" where the pair races atop the water (Storer 1969). Territorial attachment shown by both sexes (Ferguson 1981). In N. Dakota, aggressively defended against other Horned Grebes; nests separated by at least 140 ft (56 m) of open water (Faaborg 1976). Earliest eggs at Malheur NWR 7 Jun (Foster 1985); earliest young 10 Jul (Littlefield 1990a). In sw. Manitoba renesting after failure peaks mid- to late Jun; eggs hatch after 23 days; chicks are brooded constantly first 3 days on adult's back; capture own food at 12 days, and most are fledged by 45-50 days (Ferguson and Sealy 1983). Eggs per nest 3-7; white, stained by nest material to a dirty brown (Reed 1965). At Malheur NWR individuals migrate from area soon after young fledge, usually Aug-Sep (Littlefield 1990a). During Oct-Nov, 45-65 typically observed at Wickiup Res., Deschutes Co., and John Day Dam (Anderson 1987b, 1988b, 1991a, Evanich 1992b, Summers 1994a, Sullivan PT 1995b), and 10-20 at Pelican Marina, Upper Klamath L. (S. Summers unpubl. data, *KS*). A high count of 100 at Antelope Res., Malheur Co., 25 Oct 1995 (Contreras and Kindschy 1996). Earliest fall arrival at Diamond L. 9 Oct, maximum 20 on 16 Oct 1989, latest fall departure 21 Nov (Fix 1990a). They reach coast by late Aug to early Sep (Contreras 1979a, Fix 1987a). Most depart e. Oregon by early Dec (*KS*).

**Detection:** Conspicuous on open water in all seasons, although can be missed in rough water due to small size. Gives variety of trills and high squeaks when advertising on breeding ground; quiet away from breeding areas (Storer 1969).

**Population Status and Conservation:** A nest with eggs, 24 Jun 1958, Blitzen Valley, Malheur NWR, was the first Oregon nesting record (Marshall 1959). Breeding in Harney and Lake counties is at southwestern edge of breeding range (Littlefield 1990a). Declining water levels during breeding season may strand shallow-water nests (Ferguson and Sealy 1983). Rough water from high winds may cause nest damage or failure (Dubois 1919, Littlefield 1990a). Late fall departure coincident with severe storm can result in mass grounding and high mortality (Eaton 1983).—*Kevin Spencer*

## Red-necked Grebe *Podiceps grisegena*

This medium-sized shy grebe has bright white cheeks that contrast sharply against a dark crown and rust-red neck during the breeding season. Its bill is long and straight, yellowish at its base and dark at the tip, but proportionately more stout than bills of Western or Clark's Grebes. Red-necked Grebes have large, distinctive white secondaries that contrast with dark upper wings and back in flight. In basic plumage, grayish cheeks are noticeable against a dark gray hind neck and crown, and a slightly paler whitish upper breast. First-year birds in winter are distinguished by pale brown eye vs. dark in adults (Palmer 1962). This is the least common grebe in Oregon in all seasons.

**General Distribution:** Breeds from British Isles east to Siberia, and in N. America from c. Alaska south and southeast through the Yukon to e. Oregon and Idaho east to Manitoba; formerly bred south to n. Utah in the west and in s. New England in the east. Winters on Atlantic and Pacific coasts (Palmer 1962). The subspecies *P. g. hólböllii* occurs in N. America (AOU 1957).

**Oregon Distribution:** Five to 20 birds at Rocky Pt., Upper Klamath L. NWR (Kebbe 1958b, Watkins 1988) form the only consistent breeding population in Oregon. Summer inland records away from Upper Klamath L. include three records at Howard Prairie Res., Jackson Co., including one pair with two young, 23 Jun 1965 (Baldridge and Crowell 1965), two adults with three young, 22 Jun 1969 (Browning 1975a), and one pair, 4 Jul 1976 (Crowell and Nehls 1976d). Numerous pairs seen at Klamath Marsh (H. Nehls p.c.), including a nesting pair Jun 1964 (Marshall 1969). Other inland records include one, 20-29 Jun 1980, at Malheur NWR (Littlefield et al. 1985, Littlefield 1990a); one adult and two young, 25-26 Jul 1993, at Benson Pond (Crabtree 1994a) constituting the only breeding record at Malheur NWR; one pair on nest, Jul 1988, at Indian L., Umatilla Co. (Rogers 1988c); one pair and one young 6 Jun 1998 at Big Lava L., Deschutes Co. (Spencer 1998); one summered on Fish L., Jackson Co. 1989 (Fix and Heinl 1990); and one was collected at Diamond L. 5 Aug 1931 (Gabrielson and Jewett 1940). The Red-necked Grebe reaches its greatest numbers during winter along the coast. Coastal CBC averages 1979-98 are: Tillamook 14; Coos Bay 14; Florence 5; Yaquina Bay 12; and Port Orford 7; with a high of 91 at Lincoln City 1986 CBC (Drennan 1986). Rarely occurs on Willamette Valley CBCs; usually one if present. Extremely rare in winter away from the coast. During peak fall and spring migration can be locally uncommon on larger waterways in the Willamette Valley. Rare in Wallowa Co. (Evanich 1992a) south to s. Malheur Co. (Contreras and Kindschy 1996) and in the Klamath Basin away from Upper Klamath. L. (Summers 1993a).

**Habitat and Diet:** Breeding habitat consists of extensive clear, deep-water marshy lakes and ponds in timbered regions (Bent 1946, Johnsgard 1987, Watkins 1988). The area at Upper Klamath L. where Red-necked Grebes breed is dominated by emergent vegetation that grows in clear cool water of varying depths, protected from harsh weather and winds (Watkins 1988). Pondweed and waterweed are common aquatic plants found here. They harbor large numbers of aquatic insects important in the first weeks for newly hatched young. Adult diet is composed of small fish, aquatic and terrestrial insects and their larvae, tadpoles, salamanders, crustaceans, mollusks, and aquatic worms. Content of 46 stomachs taken in British Columbia and n. U.S., by number of items, was 3% vegetation, 55% fish, 22% insects, and 20% crustaceans, including sculpin, stickleback, common shrimp, crawfish, caddisfly, and adult dragonfly (Wetmore 1924). Fish are increasingly important after the first week of life and make up 50-75% of adult diet (Palmer 1962). Young at Upper Klamath L. are fed insects and some vegetation, and adults feed on fathead minnows, blue chub, and yellow perch (Watkins 1988). Two stomachs examined from Multnomah and Tillamook counties contained balls of grebe feathers, water striders, scarabid beetles, water beetles, and a bee or wasp (Gabrielson and Jewett 1940). Feathers aid in retention of bones and insect chitin in the stomach, allowing strong stomach acids to dissolve bones, while chitin and feathers are later cast by pellet (Storer 1961). In winter, they are seen most often in lower parts of estuaries and protected waters such as the lee side of islands and sheltered coves of the open coast, but are also seen on the open ocean where in some years form rafts of scores of birds at some locations (Drennan 1986, Contreras 1997b).

**Seasonal Activity and Behavior:** Arrive in breeding areas by mid-Apr. Courtship displays consist of swimming around each other, stopping with breasts close, then treading water, rising nearly upright, uttering *teck-teck-teck*, and then settling down (Palmer 1962, W. Watkins p.c.). After diving, pairs emerge together, sometimes with vegetation in their bills, and then slowly sink. Swimming simultaneously or "dueting," they mirror each others' motions while their crowns are erect, then race along the water's surface with feet and wings thrashing (Palmer 1962, W. Watkins p.c.). Nest building begins within emergent vegetation in early May on an anchored floating nest of cattails, sedges, and rushes (Palmer 1962, Watkins 1988). Female lays 3-6 eggs of a dingy white color (Reed 1965). Kebbe (1958b) reported three nests at Rocky Pt., Upper Klamath L. on 30 May with three, three, and four eggs, two sets of which were considered fresh. They were 0.25 mi (0.4 km) apart. Hatching occurs the last week of Jun or first week of Jul. Young ride on parents' backs, staying close to nest sites the first week after hatching. By second week at Pelican Bay, Upper Klamath L., young swim and dive with adults, are fed aquatic insects and some plants, and move further from nesting area, using a wider range of the marsh (Watkins 1988). By early Sep most depart breeding areas and numbers increase coastally Aug to Nov, with a fall high of 36 at Netarts Bay, 21 Oct 1986 (Fix 1987a). Migration to inland breeding areas occurs Mar to early May while coastal numbers decrease.

**Detection:** Stockier build helps distinguish the Red-necked Grebe from other grebes. Silent during winter. A summer visit to Rocky Pt., Upper Klamath L., provides the best opportunity for observing breeding behavior, full alternate plumage, as well as the striped-faced young. Easily detected on open water during nonbreeding season.

**Population Status and Conservation:** First knowledge of breeding in Oregon was summer of 1945 at Rocky Pt., Upper Klamath L.; four adults present 7 Sep 1948; observations of adults with young regular by 1952 (Kebbe 1958b). Thirteen adults raised six young in summer of 1988 there (Watkins 1988). Twenty-eight adults with 10 young in eight broods observed there 11 Jul 1989 (Marshall et al. 1996). Rarely encountered prior to 1940 during summer months in e. Oregon (Gabrielson and Jewett 1940). Gabrielson and Jewett visited the marsh at Upper Klamath L. on a number of occasions and did not encounter this species. It is not known if the breeding population became established after 1940 or if it was not discovered until then. Breeding status in Oregon is precarious considering low numbers at only one consistent localized breeding location on Upper Klamath L. It could be affected by deteriorating water quality due to agricultural run-off, drought, and pollution (Marshall et al. 1996). Susceptible to low reproduction from pesticides and PCBs, and human water-recreation disturbances (Bent 1946, DeSmet 1987, Watkins 1988). Long take-off on water required; encroaching ice may prohibit a late fall departure (Wetmore 1924).—*Kevin Spencer*

## Eared Grebe *Podiceps nigricollis*

This salt-loving bird is possibly the most abundant grebe in the world (Johnsgard 1987, Jehl 2001). It was once in great demand for millinery purposes, but has prospered since plumage-taking laws were passed and enforced starting in Oregon in 1903 (Gabrielson and Jewett 1940). In alternate plumage, crown, neck, back, and throat are black, flanks chestnut, and underparts bright white. A golden orange, loose, fan-shaped tuft extends from rear of eyes to back of head. Irises scarlet. In basic plumage, breast is silky white, back dark gray, neck light gray, with small patches of white behind eyes and on throat. Sexes indistinguishable in the field.

**General Distribution:** Breeds widely in w. N. America from sw. Canada south through w. U.S. to n. Texas, Arizona, and California, except for w. Washington and Oregon, and nw. California. Winters Pacific coast from Washington south to s. Mexico; majority to Salton Sea and Gulf of California (Jehl and Yochem 1986). Worldwide, north of Bogota, in Andes, S. America, across Europe and Africa. One subspecies, *P. n. californicus,* occurs in N. America (AOU 1957).

**Oregon Distribution:** The Eared Grebe has been reported breeding in nearly every e. Oregon county, but principal breeding areas are in Klamath, Lake, and Harney counties. A common breeder on Malheur NWR at Boca L. (C. Herziger p.c.), Knox Pond (Hill et al. 1997), Diamond Swamp (Evanich 1992d), and Malheur L.; in Klamath Co. at Tingley and Spring lakes (*KS*), Gerber Res. (Sullivan 1997c), and Davis L. (Anderson 1991b, Sullivan 1996b); in Malheur Co. at Copeland and Bully Cr. Res. (Spencer 1999), Upper Cow L. (M. St. Louis p.c.); in Crook Co. at Rabbit Valley Res. (C. Gates p.c.), Difficulty Res. (Spencer 2000a), and Rockhouse, Blevens, and Chevally reservoirs (Spencer 1998). Local elsewhere east of the Cascades including Wallowa and Union counties (Evanich 1992a); Lake Co., Summer L. W.A. (M. St. Louis p.c.); and Grant Co. at Olive L., (Sullivan

1999b). It has bred at Boardman and La Grande sewage ponds where invertebrates are abundant (Anderson 1991b, Boe 1992, Evanich 1992b) and at Juniper Butte Ranch, Wheeler Co., and in Morrow Co. (D. Lusthoff p.c.). Not known to summer or breed near coast. In Aug and Sep, it is abundant at L. Abert (Boula 1986), uncommon in the Cascades at Diamond L. (Fix 1990a) and Wickiup Res.; rare to uncommon in the Willamette and Rogue valleys, and rare on coast. In winter, very uncommon on coastal bays; CBCs average 2-3; high of 23 at Coos Bay. Rare to very uncommon in winter in the Willamette and Rogue valleys; CBCs average about one each. Very rare in winter most years in e. Oregon, where CBCs average 1-3 birds at Bend and Summer L.; also L. Abert (Contreras 1997b), Klamath Falls with a high of 129 in 1996, and Malheur NWR with a high of 25 in 1960. Greater numbers winter east of the Cascades with mild temperatures: 3,620 on 9 Dec at L. Abert (C. Miller p.c.). Several hundred wintered 1995-2000 at Gutierrez Ranch, Crook Co. (C. Gates p.c.).

**Habitat and Diet:** Nests near shore on small freshwater lakes and reservoirs where open water is intermixed with emergents such as hardstem bulrush and cattails (M. St. Louis p.c., *KS*). At Dutchy L. and Gold Dike, Summer L. W.A., attaches nest to watermilfoil and pondweed (M. St. Louis p.c.). Nest substrate in hardstem bulrush on Boca L. and Knox Pond; in goosefoot at Malheur L. in 1993 (Hill et al. 1997). Terrestrial plants such as goosefoot can become flooded and utilized as nest substrate (G. Ivey p.c.). Nests at Malheur NWR constructed of fresh spikerush stems and algae (Foster 1985). Nests in water 1-4 ft (0.3-1.2 m) deep, cup shaped with rim slightly above the water (McAllister 1958). Mean nest spacing at Malheur NWR about 3-10 ft (0.7-3.3 m) apart (Hill et al. 1997).

During fall migration at L. Abert and Mono L., California, this species feeds on seasonally superabundant invertebrates including brine shrimp, brine flies, long-legged flies, other flies, an amphipod, water fleas, and beetles (Mahoney and Jehl 1985b, Boula 1986). Elsewhere, it is largely insectivorous, consuming beetles, flies, ants, wasps, centipedes, spiders, moth and butterfly pupae, leech eggs, caddisfly, damselfly, dragonfly larvae, with a few fish, including sculpin (Wetmore 1924). Obtains water from prey, shrimp being 80% water (Mahoney and Jehl 1985b). Consumes own feathers (Wetmore 1920). When in alkaline waters, utilizes glands capable of removing large amounts of salts to prevent salt loading; large tongue may also exclude alkaline water when feeding (Mahoney and Jehl 1985b). This species uses coastal saltwater estuaries in winter, rarely ocean (Contreras 1997b), fresh water in summer, fresh and alkaline water in fall, and sewage treatment ponds in all seasons.

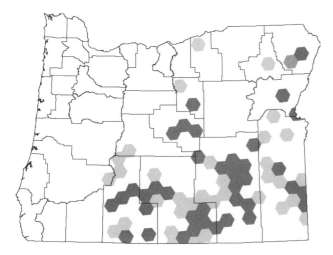

**Seasonal Activity and Behavior:** Numbers decrease on coast in Feb. Mean spring migrant arrival 30 Mar at Malheur NWR (Ivey, Herziger, and Scheuering 1998); mid-Mar in Klamath Co. (*KS*). On coast, Coos Co., latest departure date is 23 May (Contreras 1998). Courtship includes elaborate postures and movements including advertising, preening, and head shaking (McAllister 1958). Nests in dense colonial groups were initiated late Jun to early Jul, Malheur NWR; highly synchronized within colony (Hill et al. 1997). Nests mid-Jul to late Aug at Summer L. W.A., Lake Co. (M. St. Louis p.c.); on nests mid-Aug at Tingley and Spring L., Klamath Co. (*KS*). Fresh egg dates 12 May to 4 Jul (Gabrielson and Jewett 1940). Aggression, nesting infanticide, and brood parasitism increased with nest density at Malheur and Boca lakes and Knox Pond, Malheur NWR (Hill et al. 1997). Migrates mid-Aug in e. Oregon (Sullivan 1998a); peaks at Malheur NWR Sep to early Oct; latest departure 23 Nov (Littlefield and Cornely 1984). Large numbers of migrants in spring and fall stop and feed at L. Abert (Boula 1986, Summers 1994a, Sullivan 1996a, 1998a, 1999a); 30,000 estimated in Apr 1994 (Tweit and Summers 1994); 15,500 on 21 Sep 1996 (C. Miller p.c.). Jehl (1988) stated postbreeders arrive at L. Abert in Aug, peak in Sep, and depart in Oct. At L. Abert in late summer, they molt flight feathers, double body weight with fat deposits, and allow pectoral muscles to atrophy to less than that needed for flight. Then 2-3 wk before departure date, they use one-third of fat reserves to rebuild flight muscles (Jehl 1997). The Eared Grebe utilizes solar energy by spreading wings, a sunbathing posture, to expose black base to back feathers and very dark pigmentation of skin (Storer et al. 1976). It is a weak flyer requiring a long take-off on water (Johnsgard 1987), so timing of fall departure precedes freezing of open waters.

**Detection:** Easily observed when present on open water. Colonies and nests are conspicuous. Sometimes confused with Horned Grebe.

**Population Status and Conservation:** The population of *P. n. californicus*, estimated at 3.7 million, is almost 12 times all other N. American grebes combined; numbers attributed to superabundance of prey in fishless, hypersaline lakes; likely increased in post-Pleistocene era climates (Jehl 2001).

Nest counts include: 800 in 1984 at Malheur L. (G. Ivey p.c.), 700 in 1997 at Boca L., Malheur NWR (C. Herziger p.c.); 74 in 1994 at Knox Pond, Malheur NWR (Hill et al. 1997); 250 in 2000 at Rabbit Valley Res., Crook Co. (C. Gates p.c.); and 22 pairs in 1998 at Copeland Res., Malheur Co. (Spencer 1999); 50 pairs at Difficulty Res., Malheur Co. (Spencer 2000a); and 112 in 2000 at Tingley and Spring lakes, Klamath Co. (*KS*).

Colony nesting locations are subject to annual changes in water conditions; may change nesting location year to year (Boe 1992). This has been very evident at Malheur NWR and vicinity where responds to newly flooded areas following dry years or drawdowns (Ivey, Cornely, Paullin, and Thompson unpubl. ms., *DBM*). Unused lakes and ponds may be used in other years, so retention is important in total potential nesting pool (Boe 1992).

Negatively impacted by fishing, boating, and other human disturbances (Boe 1992). Nesting failure can be caused by rising water levels (Evanich 1993), waves from high winds (Hill et al. 1997, M. St. Louis p.c.), and water receding before eggs hatch or young fledge (Littlefield 1990a). Increased nest predation by American Coot associated with increased nest distances (Hill et al. 1997). L. Abert is a critically important fall staging location. Nocturnal migration in large groups has resulted in significant mortality during severe storms or collisions with other Eared Grebes (Jehl 1996).—*Kevin Spencer*

## Western Grebe *Aechmophorus occidentalis*

The species known earlier as Western Grebe by Gabrielson and Jewett (1940) and AOU (1957) included pale morphs (Clark's Grebe) and dark morphs (Western Grebe), now recognized as separate species (AOU 1985). These, the largest of Oregon's grebes, have a long white neck, black cap, bright red iris, long straight bill, dark back, bright white breast, and they appear tailless. While excellent divers, they are unable to walk on land because their body weight is forward of their legs. Differences in appearance between Western and Clark's Grebes are subtle. In the Western Grebe, the black cap typically extends down to the eye whereas white facial plumage extends slightly above the eye on Clark's Grebe, but this is not always diagnostic in winter (Sibley 2000). Clark's Grebe also has a slightly shorter, brighter yellow-orange bill and flanks are mottled in black and white (Evanich 1982e, Ratti et al. 1983).

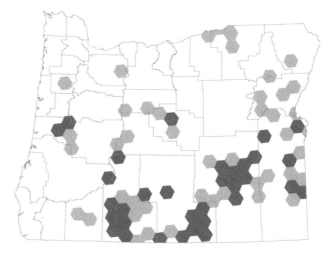

The portion of the courtship display in which a pair rushes in tandem atop the water is perhaps the most spectacular display exhibited by any Oregon bird.

**General Distribution:** Breeds on large lakes, reservoirs, and waterways from s. British Columbia to sw. Ontario south through w. U.S. to w. Texas, c. Arizona, and s. California (Storer and Neuchterlein 1992); found year-round in c. California, Baja, and on Mexican Plateau. Winters along Pacific coast from se. Alaska to Baja, Mexico. Two subspecies; *A. o. occidentalis* occurs in Oregon (Dickerman 1986, Storer and Neuchterlein 1992).

**Oregon Distribution:** Common breeder in e. Oregon, especially at large lakes and marshes having open water in Klamath, Harney, Goose L., and Warner basins (Gabrielson and Jewett 1940, Stern 1988, Littlefield 1990a, Hill et al. 1995, *KS*). Also breeds at numerous smaller water bodies among which are Spring and Tingley lakes, Klamath Co. (*KS*); Chickahominy Res., Harney Co.; Dog L. (C. Miller p.c.), Cottonwood and Drews Res. (F. Isaacs p.c.), and Summer L. W.A. (M. St. Louis p.c.), Lake Co.; Ochoco Res., Crook Co. (Anderson 1989b); Antelope, Beulah, Bully Cr., Chevally and Cow lakes, Malheur Co., and Unity Res. (Contreras and Kindschy 1996, Sullivan 1997c, Spencer 1999). West of the Cascades it first bred at Fern Ridge Res., Lane Co., in the 1990s (Johnson J 1993a, 1997a, Lillie 1997); it is now a regular breeder there.

During spring and fall, concentrations on Cascade Mtn. lakes include but are not limited to Davis L., Klamath Co.; Wickiup Res., Deschutes Co. (Anderson 1991a); and Suttle L., Jefferson Co. (Korpi 2000). As many as 2,000 *Aechmophorus* grebes were observed on Davis L. in May 1990 (Anderson DA 1990b) and 2

Aug 1992 (*DBM*). Other spring and fall concentrations include Upper Klamath L. (*KS*), Hood River (Anderson DA 1990b), Columbia Gorge (Fix 1991), and John Day Dam (Sullivan 1997a).

In winter, most common in coastal bays, on the ocean near shore, and in the Columbia R. estuary. Small numbers winter in the Willamette Valley and even fewer east of the Cascades. CBC averages per circle on the coast run into the hundreds; <100 per circle in the Willamette, Umpqua and Rogue R. valleys; average 41 1999-2001 Hood River CBC, and <10 at selected e. Oregon circles. Flocks often winter behind John Day Dam (D. Irons p.c.).

**Habitat and Diet:** The Western Grebe breeds in marshes having open water and on lakes and reservoirs supporting emergent vegetation along shorelines. Typical emergent vegetation in Oregon breeding areas includes hardstem bulrush, broad-leaf cattail, and giant burreed (*DBM*). Nesting sites on floating mats of vegetation are constructed of available aquatic vegetation and are held in place through contact with bottom or submerged vegetation. Muskrat houses are used as nest support at Harney L. (G. Ivey p.c.). At Malheur NWR and Summer L. W.A., nest materials can be sago pondweed, watermilfoil, widgeon grass, hardstem bulrush, alkali bulrush, alkali saltgrass, or other plants (M. St. Louis p.c., *DBM*). Open water expanses are used for rearing young (*DBM*). Migration and wintering habitat includes those habitats mentioned above plus lakes, large rivers, estuaries, and open ocean.

It is difficult to distinguish foods taken from breeding vs. migration and wintering areas, but fish comprise much of the diet. No formal food habits studies known for Oregon, but sculpin are known to be consumed by adults and young during summer and fall at Upper Klamath L. (*KS*) and carp, tui chub, and brown bullhead at Malheur NWR (G. Ivey p.c.). Tui chub and possibly roach are the only fish available at Summer L. W.A. (M. St. Louis p.c.). At Clear L., c. California, Lawrence (1950) found that fishes comprised 81% by volume of all foods consumed by 27 Western and/or Clark's grebes collected Jun-Sep. Main fish taken was bluegill perch at 71% of total volume. Other foods taken included a large selection of arthropods. During breeding season in se. British Columbia, Forbes and Sealy (1990) found Western Grebes consumed yellow perch and pumpkinseed. At Netarts Bay, Wetmore (1924) reported numerous smelt taken. Other reported foods, not necessarily from Oregon, include sala-manders, crustaceans, polychaete

*Western Grebe*

ELVA HAMERSTROM PAUlson

worms, and a variety of other aquatic forms (Storer and Neuchterlein 1992).

Foraging strategies differ between Western and Clark's Grebes. Feerer (1977) wrote that Western Grebes (referred to as "dark form" Western Grebes in the paper) captured significantly larger fish than Clark's Grebes (referred to as "light form" grebes), and exhibited niche partitioning of food resources in spring. Clark's Grebes reach greater depths than Western Grebes if dive times are interpreted as indicative of deeper dives (Neuchterlein and Buitron 1989). At L. Ewauna near Klamath Falls and on Upper Klamath L., Western Grebes used a level dive in shallow water near shore compared to Clark's Grebes, which used deeper water and a "springing dive" (Neuchterlein 1981) whereby the entire body emerges from the water with breast and tarsus clearly visible upon diving (Lawrence 1950). According to Neuchterlein and Buitron (1989), differences in diving strategies results in ecological separation of the two species.

Like other grebes, Western Grebes line stomach with feathers and hold bones for digestion. Indigestible chitin and feathers are eventually cast as pellets (Wetmore 1920, Ryser 1985).

**Seasonal Activity and Behavior:** Earliest arrival is 10 Mar in Klamath Co. (Summers 1985b); average arrival is 20 Mar at Malheur NWR (Ivey, Herziger, and Scheuering 1998). Courtship displays begin late Mar to early Apr in Klamath Co. (*KS*). Displays include a variety of spectacular actions including a display known as rushing wherein pairs run atop the water in tandem by furiously churning their feet and flapping their wings, pointing bills at one another while shaking their heads, and rising out of the water with vegetation displayed to mates (Neuchterlein and Storer 1982, 1989, Storer and Neuchterlein 1992). At Malheur NWR, nesting begins mid-May and extends well into Aug; flightless young can be seen into mid-Sep (Littlefield 1990a). Timing similar in Klamath Co. (*KS*). Nests both solitarily and colonially with one colony reported reaching 850 nests on 1 ac (0.4 ha) at Harney L., Malheur NWR in 1983 (Littlefield 1990a).

Young ride on backs of adults 2-4 wk, and adults even dive with young on their backs. Young dependent on parents 6-7 wk (Storer and Neuchterlein 1992). Older immatures follow adults, beg for food, and wait at water's surface for adults to return to surface with food. Nocturnal migrant. Begin departure from breeding areas in Aug; peaking Sep-Oct. Most depart from Malheur NWR by Nov (Littlefield and Cornely 1984).

**Detection:** Easily spotted on large water bodies. Seen in rafts just past the breakers on the coast. Give double note *kreek-kreek* as opposed to long single note *kreeeek* of Clark's Grebe. Separation of Western and Clark's Grebes, which can be challenging, especially in winter, is summarized by Ratti (1981). Moore Park and Pelican Marina near Klamath Falls are good observation sites for both species in spring and summer.

**Population Status and Conservation:** Estimated to be >120,000 in N. America (Jehl 2001). From the early 1890s until about 1906, Western and Clark's Grebes were slaughtered for their skins which were used in the millinery trade (Bent 1919, Storer and Neuchterlein 1992). Their tough skins called "fur" were scraped like hides, and resembled mammal fur. During this period of exploitation a large colony survived at Lower Klamath NWR (Finley 1907c).

Surveys at Malheur NWR have not separated Western from Clark's Grebes because aerial techniques were used (G. Ivey p.c.). Malheur NWR population numbers of these two species fluctuate widely due to ever-changing water conditions which in turn affect forage availability and nest substrates (Littlefield 1979, Ivey, Cornely, Paullin, and Thompson unpubl. ms., *DBM*). Availability of forage fish here, mainly carp, depends in part upon effects of carp control operations, which are periodically carried out during low water years. During such times, carp are restricted largely to adults, which are too large for grebes to handle. Following carp control operations and/or with increasing water conditions, young age classes of carp suitable for the grebes again appear, causing a population rebound. When forage is inadequate in Malheur L., nesting is confined mainly to the Blitzen Valley. When Harney L. had exceptionally high water levels in 1993 and was heavily populated with small tui chubs and dense stands of widgeon grass for nesting substrate, grebes of the genus *Aechmophorus* (Western and Clark's) nested there as well as on Malheur L. (Ivey, Cornely, Paullin, and Thompson unpubl. ms.). During 1980-98, populations of these birds at Malheur NWR averaged 2.5 times higher during wet than dry years. They did not breed at all during high-water years of 1989 and 1990 at Malheur L., when high water inundated aquatic vegetation (Anderson DA 1990c, 1991b). In 1984, peaks of 1,055 and 1,309 nests of Western and Clark's Grebes combined were recorded at Harney L. and Malheur L. respectively. These peak numbers were caused by flooding, which provided millions of young fish as prey (G. Ivey p.c.).

At Upper Klamath L. a boat trip from Howard Bay to Shoalwater Bay on 14 Jun 2002 tallied approximately 1,150 Western Grebes and 340 Clark's Grebes. If these numbers are representative of the entire lake, which is a reasonable assumption, the total population there would approximate 5,000 Western Grebes and 1,500 Clark's Grebes (*KS*).

Wave action destroyed Western Grebe colonies at Malheur NWR in the late 1950s (*DBM*). In Utah, this along with both flooding and drops in water levels have been reported to destroy nests as well (Lindvall and Low 1982). Nationwide, this species is subject to mortality from numerous causes, including botulism (G. Ivey p.c.), pesticides, oil spills, capture in gill nets and fishing gear (Storer and Neuchterlein 1992).—*Kevin Spencer*

### Clark's Grebe *Aechmophorus clarkii*

Clark's Grebe, first described in 1858, was not recognized (e.g., AOU 1957) until the two morphs of what was earlier known as the Western Grebe (e.g., Gabrielson and Jewett 1940) were recognized as separate species (AOU 1985). Clark's Grebe is very similar in plumage, habitat, and behavior to the Western Grebe (see that species for further description). Exceptions are noted in both accounts.

**General Distribution:** Breeds from sc. British Columbia east across s. Canada as far as sw. Manitoba and south to e. Washington, N. and S. Dakota south to sw. U.S., but distribution is spotty along northern edges of the range. Winters sparingly from s. British Columbia south along the Pacific coast and more commonly from c. California south to s. Baja California. Resident at some lakes that do not freeze, e.g., Clear L. (c. California), and in Mexico. Two subspecies; *A. c. transitionalis* is the U.S. subspecies (Dickerman 1986, Storer and Neuchterlein 1992).

**Oregon Distribution:** Breeding range in Oregon overlaps that of Western Grebe, but Clark's is not as common. Upper Klamath L. and Goose L. in Oregon's Lake Co. and California's Modoc Co. support the largest known concentrations of this species within its range (Ratti 1979, 1981). All *Aechmophorus* grebes seen 13 Jul 1985 at Goose L. SP were Clark's Grebes; 100 Western and 115 Clark's Grebes were at Pelican Marina in Klamath Falls Jul 1985 (Summers 1985a). About 23% of *Aechmophorus* grebes counted on Upper Klamath L. in Jun 2002 were Clark's (see Western Grebe account). On 24 Aug 1985 along Hwy 205 in Harney Co., 40% of low 100s were Clark's Grebes, and 85% of grebes on Harney L. were Clark's Grebes (Hunter 1985). Proportions of Clark's vs. Western Grebes is different in some areas in different years. Clark's Grebe has been present during summer on Fern Ridge Res., Lane Co., in recent years where breeding took place in 1998-99 (*ALC*). It is unclear what proportion of *Aechmophorus* grebes that spend spring and fall in high Cascade lakes are Clark's. In winter, this species occurs in w. Oregon, mostly along the coast in very low numbers. Very small numbers are regular in winter in the Coos Bay area (T. Rodenkirk p.c.). Because the taxonomic split is relatively new, the winter range of each species is not clear.

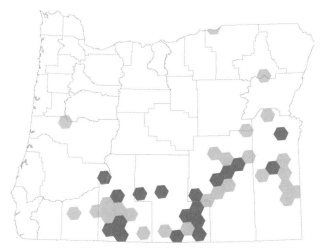

**Habitat and Diet:** Habitat is like that described for Western Grebe, but Clark's Grebe is more adapted to foraging in deeper water, farther from shore, and on smaller fish (Neuchterlein 1981, Ratti 1985, Neuchterlein and Buitron 1989). See Western Grebe for additional details.

**Seasonal Activity and Behavior:** Earliest arrival in the Klamath Basin is 10 Mar 1985 (Summers 1985b); average arrival at Malheur NWR is 4 May (Ivey, Herziger, and Scheuering 1998). No data on departure dates from breeding areas, but assumed to be similar to Western Grebe; see that species for additional details.

**Detection:** See Western Grebe.

**Population Status and Conservation:** N. American population estimated to be 10-20,000 (Jehl 2001). Littlefield (1990a) reported an increase in Clark's Grebe at Malheur L. during years of increasing lake size (1980s), which may be related to the preference of Clark's Grebe for relatively small fish, since Malheur L. has greater numbers of large fish while shrinking and greater numbers of small fish while expanding (G. Ivey p.c., *DBM*). Population threats similar to Western Grebe; see that species for more details.—*Kevin Spencer*

## Order PROCELLARIIFORMES
### Family Diomedeidae

### Shy Albatross *Thalassarche cauta*

The Shy Albatross, also known as the White-capped Albatross, breeds on islands near s. Australia and New Zealand and ranges widely at sea in the S. Pacific and Indian Oceans. There are seven records from the e. N. Pacific. Single individuals were photographed over the north end of Heceta Bank, 25 mi (40.2 km) west of Yachats, Lincoln Co., Oregon, 5 Oct 1996 (Hunter and Bailey 1997, *MGH*), and 7 Oct 2001 (OBRC). Of three subspecies, all ne. Pacific birds are of the widespread subspecies *T. c. cauta* according to Cole (2000).—*Harry B. Nehls*

## Laysan Albatross *Phoebastria immutabilis*

Popularly called "Gooneybird" for its elaborate mating antics and clumsy takeoffs and landings at breeding islands, this is a large, spectacular seabird. Though small for an albatross, it glides on wind currents just above the ocean waves on long narrow wings which span approximately 6.5 ft (2 m). The dark gray wings, back, and tail contrast with a white body and upper tail coverts. Singles or small groups are reported occasionally on offshore Oregon birding trips, primarily in winter.

**General Distribution:** Ranges widely through the N. Pacific from Japan to Baja California and north to the Gulf of Alaska and Bering Sea. Breeding confined mainly to the Hawaiian Archipelago from Kure Atoll in NW. Hawaiian Is. east to Kauai (Whittow 1993b); eggs laid Nov-Dec (Harrison 1983). Small numbers breed south of Japan on the Bonin Is., and new colonies have recently become established on islands off the coast of Baja California and the w. coast of Mexico. Monotypic (AOU 1957).

**Oregon Distribution:** Uncommon winter visitor and rare at other seasons far offshore. In 30 at-sea observations where distance was recorded, sightings ranged from 12 to 529 mi (21-936 km) offshore; median 30 mi (53 km) (*GG*). Four sightings from shore. Ten records of dead or dying birds washed up on beaches.

**Habitat and Diet:** Pelagic. Primarily found seaward of the continental shelf near areas of strong upwelling and along boundaries between different water masses (McDermond and Morgan 1993). Prefer water saltier than 0.32%; thus more common far offshore away from freshwater runoff (McDermond and Morgan 1993). Away from breeding islands generally avoid water warmer than 52°F (13°C) (Stallcup 1990).

No dietary studies from Oregon, but in reference to the range as a whole, McDermond and Morgan (1993) and Whittow (1993b) reported diet consists principally of squids. Other foods include crustaceans, fishes, and carrion (Whittow 1993b). This species will feed at chum and waste from ships (P. T. Sullivan p.c.).

**Seasonal Activity and Behavior:** The Laysan Albatross appears off the W. Coast mainly in fall and winter, and at other seasons is more confined to c. and w. Pacific (McDermond and Morgan 1993). Oregon records exist for every month with most for Dec-Mar and Aug-

Oct; the latter is the season of the majority of historical oceanic birding trips (*GG*). Record number of birds seen was 15 in Jan 1963 (Sanger 1972), 43 on 13-14 Dec 1998 (Tice 1999b), and 94 on 13 Dec 1999 (Tice 2000c), all from cruise or research vessels.

This species spends less time afloat than the Black-footed Albatross (Whittow 1993b), thus most often seen flying over the ocean in a sweeping glide-like pattern. Wind is necessary for flight. May sail up to 11 min without flapping (Sanger 1970). Forage mainly at night while sitting on the water. It will take discards from ships, but not to the extent of Black-footed Albatross; not readily chummed. Sometimes follows large ships or fishing vessels.

**Detection:** For most of the year seeing this species on an offshore trip appears to be a matter of luck. Likelihood of seeing one increases with distance offshore. Rough seas often prevent exploring Oregon's offshore waters in winter, but deep water close to shore off Coos Bay, Dec-Mar, may provide a good chance for single-day quests. In recent years, 1-7 birds found on most trips to Perpetua Bank, 32 mi (50 km) offshore from Yachats, Lincoln Co., from late Oct into May.

**Population Status and Conservation:** World population estimated at 2.5 million; most breeding on Laysan I., Hawaii (Harrison 1990). Recent w. Mexican breeding population is only about 100 pairs (McDermond and Morgan 1993), thus probably not responsible for the vast majority of Oregon records.

First sight record in Oregon was in Mar or Apr 1949 (McHugh 1950); first specimen (USNM) was a dead beached bird on 30 Jan 1953 (McAllister 1954), and a second beached bird, erroneously reported to be the first Oregon specimen, on 13 Jul 1960 (Fredrich 1961); about 75 records of at least 220 birds through 1999 (*GG*). Detected annually since 1976. Much of our understanding of the Oregon status results from Sanger's (1965, 1970, 1972) research from 1960-66. Sanger (1970) recorded a mean daily abundance of three birds and an occurrence rate of 75% in Jan and Nov 1965 on transects from 25 to 375 mi (44-664 km) off Oregon and Washington.

There are no known conservation problems in Oregon. There has been a major population recovery since the decimation by plume hunters on breeding colonies up to the early 20th century. Threats on breeding colonies include introduction of exotic plants and predators such as Polynesian rats. Drift nets incidentally killed an estimated 17,548 Laysan Albatrosses in 1990, but this has been partially curtailed (McDermond and Morgan 1993). Mortality from long-line tuna and swordfish fisheries in the c. Pacific is of current concern (Kalmer et al. 1996, Skillman 1997). Annual losses from these fisheries exceeded 1,000 Laysan Albatrosses in both 1994 and

1995. Plastic ingestion is high and also of concern (McDermond and Morgan 1993).—*Greg Gillson and David B. Marshall*

## Black-footed Albatross *Phoebastria nigripes*

"My distinct impression of the Black-footed Albatross is that of a big, cleanly, well-mannered bird of friendly, even playful disposition, with an abundant and perhaps excusable curiosity as to our presence and our activities within the realm of open ocean over which he presides" (Miller 1940). Long-winged, to 7 ft (2.1 m), and dark sooty-brown; adults have white rump and feathering, which juveniles lack, around base of a large bill. Every sighting of these gentle giants gliding up to the boat evokes delight.

**General Distribution:** N. Pacific. Breed on islands of c. and w. Pacific, from NW. Hawaiian Is. to Japanese island of Torishima; eggs laid Nov-Dec. Disperse north to Bering Sea, east to the W. Coast of N. America. Immatures are wide-ranging, not returning to breeding colonies until three or four yr of age (Harrison 1983). Monotypic (AOU 1957).

**Oregon Distribution:** Regular visitant spring through fall offshore; irregular in winter. Greatest abundance occurs at shelf break and upper slope in water depth over 100 fm (180 m) (Miller 1940). Local concentrations occur around fishing vessels. Locations with higher than average numbers off Oregon are Astoria Canyon off the Columbia R., off Cape Blanco, and around the margins of Heceta and Stonewall banks off the c. coast (Briggs et al. 1992). As in Washington (Wahl 1975), it is rare within 15 mi (27 km) of shore or in less than 75 fm (135 m) of water. Occurs in low numbers off the continental shelf. However, 53 birds observed at stationary ship 465 mi (823 km) west of Cape Blanco, Oregon, in Jul and Aug 1944 seems unusually high (Yocom 1947).

**Habitat and Diet:** Pelagic. Off Oregon and Washington they do not appear to select water of any particular temperature or temperature gradient (Briggs et al. 1992). Glean squid, fish, and fish eggs from surface; also eat galley scraps, especially fatty or greasy foods, pastries, but not raw vegetables; described as "feathered pig" (Miller 1940). Scavenge fish and shrimp scraps around fishing vessels (Briggs et al. 1992). Albatrosses following the offal of a processing ship prefer entrails and organs over heads, fins, and skin (P. T. Sullivan p.c.).

**Seasonal Activity and Behavior:** Arrive in good numbers off the Oregon coast in Apr, which may correspond to the arrival of failed and nonbreeding birds from nesting colonies (Whittow 1993a). However, at least some radio-tagged adults nesting at French Frigate Shoals, Hawaii, seek food for older nestlings on the W. Coast of N. America in Apr and May during month-long forays (David Anderson p.c.). Unlike the population in California which peaks May-Jul, numbers off Oregon and Washington remain "remarkably consistent" Apr-Sep (Wahl 1975, Briggs et al. 1992). The highest numbers on Oregon pelagic trips were 274 on 7 Oct 2001, 400 on 25 Aug 2000 (both Contreras 2002b), and 456 on 7 Oct 2000 (Korpi 2001a). Numbers drop significantly by late Oct. Few, usually all-dark juveniles occur offshore in winter.

Black-footed Albatrosses have a curious nature; are attracted to any flotsam, including ocean sunfish. They quickly "appear out of nowhere" to find chum when none were seen in the distance (Stallcup 1990, *GG*). On a chartered pelagic trip, where no albatrosses had yet been seen, seven appeared to inspect a hat blown overboard which was retrieved within 3 min (*GG*). Respond aggressively to chum. A group of 180 birds on 4 Apr 1998, 47 mi (83 km) off Depoe Bay, crowded right up to the boat, whistling and bleating as they churned the water to froth, furiously paddling their huge webbed feet, in an attempt to out-eat their companions (*GG*). They have an acute sense of smell (Whittow 1993a). Yocom (1947) observed that albatrosses off Oregon were attracted to ships and boats of all sizes, following up to 60 mi (106 km). They soar 26-35 mph (42-57 km/hr), but only 10-45 sec without flapping. Unlike larger relatives, they can fly on calm days, running up to 100 ft (30 m) on surface of water to become airborne. Usually, however, they congregate in rafts and "peacefully loiter away most of an afternoon" on calm days. When landing, set wings and lower webbed feet, skiing 4-8 ft (1.2-2.4 m) on water's surface before coming to a stop. On water float high with neck extended in alert-looking posture. Feed by tip-up method, similar to puddle ducks; rarely submerge. Active predawn feeder. Protect food with spread wings and scream with wide-open bill.

**Detection:** Regular on pelagic trips Apr-Oct at least 20 mi (35 km) offshore. Low numbers usually detected, except near active fishing vessels, or if chummed with fish scraps, beef fat, bread, or popcorn. More difficult to find on foggy days when albatrosses cannot see other birds feeding around boat. On 16 one-day pelagic trips Jul-Oct 1994-98, recorded on 100% of trips; average number of birds 30; maximum 110 (*GG*). Occasionally seen from shore (D. Fix, D. Irons p.c.).

**Population Status and Conservation:** Possibly declining (McDermond and Morgan 1993); 61,339 breeding pairs worldwide with a total population of about 240,000 (B. Flint p.c.). Oregon/Washington average density was 0.26-0.39 birds/mi² (0.10-0.15 birds/km²) at 100-400 fm (180-720 m) on summer aerial surveys in 1989-90 (Briggs et al. 1992).

There are few hazards in Oregon. Commercial fishing techniques off Japan, Alaska, and Hawaii cause mortalities. Up to 4,500 Black-footed Albatrosses drowned in high-seas drift nets each year prior to a 1993 ban (Alexander et al. 1997). Hawaiian longline fishery incidentally killed an average of 1,640 Black-footed Albatrosses per year 1994-96 (Dalzell 1997), but new techniques are being developed to reduce mortalities (e.g., Melvin et al. 2001). Other threats include ingestion of plastics, PCB pollution in Hawaiian Leeward Is., volcanic or flood disturbance to breeding areas, and avian pox (Alexander et al. 1997).—*Greg Gillson*

### Short-tailed Albatross *Phoebastria albatrus*

Formerly, this large white-bodied albatross was a common nesting bird on many islands in the w. Pacific. When not breeding it wandered over much of the N. Pacific, regularly along the W. Coast of N. America. Exploited for its feathers, it was near extinction at the beginning of the 20th century. It now breeds on Torishima and other nearby islands south of Japan. Although still quite rare it has slowly increased in numbers in recent years, and sightings away from the nesting colonies have increased (Hasegawa and DeGange 1982). There are three accepted Oregon records: an immature photographed at Perpetua Bank, 32 mi (51.4 km) west of Yachats, Lincoln Co., 11 Dec 1961 (Wyatt 1963); an immature observed 20 mi (32.2 km) southwest of the mouth of the Columbia R. 19 Jun 1978 (OBRC); and another immature observed 9 Nov 1996 about 51 mi (82 km) west of Arch Cape, Clatsop Co. (OBRC). There are unsubstantiated sight records 20 mi (32.2 km) west of Depoe Bay, Lincoln Co., 19 Sep 1989 (Fix and Heinl 1990), 21 mi (33.8 km) off Curry Co., 13 Dec 1999 (Tice 2000c), and at Perpetua Bank 21 Oct 2000 (Korpi 2001a). An immature was photographed at Perpetua Bank 24 Mar 2001 (Lillie 2001). Monotypic (AOU 1957). — *Harry B. Nehls*

## Family Procellariidae

### Northern Fulmar *Fulmarus glacialis*

One of Oregon's characteristic offshore seabirds, these stocky gull-like birds with steep foreheads come in a broad range of color morphs from quite white to slaty, with buffy, bluish-gray, mottled, and brown intermediates. The round head and pecking motion of birds feeding on the water is reminiscent of the shape and behavior of pigeons. The heavy hooked bills are divided into colorful plates of green, yellow, and orange, with a large tubed nostril atop. The Icelandic name, fulmar, means "foul gull," a reference to their musky odor.

**General Distribution:** N. Pacific and Atlantic. Breed on islands and coasts in Bering Sea, N. Pacific, Arctic, and N. Atlantic. Nonbreeders range south to Japan, Baja California, France, and New England. Of three subspecies, only *F. g. rogersii* occurs in Oregon (AOU 1957).

**Oregon Distribution:** Irregularly common to abundant winter visitor, especially beyond 5 mi (8.9 km) from shore. Highest concentrations are along the shelf break; but widely dispersed from inshore to deep waters beyond the continental shelf (Briggs et al. 1992). One inland record: 9 Feb 1983 at Steamboat, Douglas Co. (Gilligan et al. 1994, Tice 1997).

**Habitat and Diet:** Pelagic. Ainley (1976) reported that fulmars off California prefer cold water of high salinity. Briggs et al. (1992) found no consistent selection of any particular temperature, bottom topography, or depth for fulmars off Oregon and Washington. However, they are usually seen in water deeper than 40 fm (72 m) (Wahl 1975).

Primary foods are squid, fish, and invertebrates which are scavenged on the surface, alive or as carrion. Eight species of squids were identified as prey items in a group of fulmars washed up on the beaches of Washington in 1986-87 (Hill and Fiscus 1988). Fish discards from nets of fishing trawlers and draggers are a significant source of food in some areas (Lockley 1974). Fulmars following the offal of a processing ship prefer entrails and organs over heads, fins, and skin (P. T. Sullivan p.c.).

**Seasonal Activity and Behavior:** Variably common Jul-Mar; typically rare Apr-Jun (Gilligan et al. 1994) when most of the population is near breeding colonies in Alaska. As in Washington, however (Wahl 1975), this can be quite variable; some of the highest densities have been in mid-summer (Briggs et al. 1992). Peak numbers in Oct. Highest numbers on Oregon pelagic trips were 1,275 on 24 Oct 1992 (Gilligan 1993a) and 3,610 on 7 Oct 2000 (*GG*).

Usually solitary (Stallcup 1990), contrary to Harrison (1983), but chum readily and large flocks attracted to by-catch from fishing vessels (Wahl 1975). Briggs et al. (1992) note that "curiously, although several sightings of large numbers of fulmars (to several hundreds of birds) were made from near factory fishing vessels during summer flights, only a very small portion of the total number of fulmar sightings pertained to vessels." They swim up close to boat when feeding on chum (Stallcup 1990). Defend food successfully from larger gulls by threatening with wide-open bill and issuing a clucking or quacking *guk-guk-guk* (*GG*). Rarely noted to dive for food (Wahl 1984).

*Northern Fulmar*

**Detection:** Flight is similar to that of shearwaters with shallow stiff-winged flapping and glides low along the water. The Northern Fulmar differs from Sooty Shearwaters by having slower and more sustained flapping and longer glides, higher off the water and with more frequent high wheeling and banking. Presence of active fishing vessels increases chances of detection dramatically. Often they are the first seabirds to respond to chum such as buttered popcorn or fish scraps. On 16 one-day pelagic trips Jul-Oct 1994-98, recorded on 94% of trips; average number of birds 133; maximum 772 (*GG*). May be driven inshore by strong westerly winds (Gilligan et al. 1994), and seen from low headlands such as at Cape Arago, Coos Co.; Boiler Bay, Lincoln Co.; Ecola SP, Clatsop Co.; and the s. jetty of the Columbia R.

**Population Status and Conservation:** Abundant. Atlantic population increased greatly in the 20th century, probably in response to fishery waste (Lockley 1974). Alaskan population numbers about 2 million birds. Oregon winter average 0.16-0.52 birds/mi$^2$ (0.06-0.20 birds/km$^2$), locally 15.5-31.1 birds/mi$^2$ (6-12 birds/km$^2$) on surveys in 1989-90; rare to irregularly common in summer with local peaks to 28.5 birds/mi$^2$ (11 birds/km$^2$) in Jun 1990 (Briggs et al. 1992). The majority of birds (8:1) (Stallcup 1990) are medium or dark colored, not light, evidently originating from the breeding colonies on the Aleutian Is. and s. Alaska (Hatch 1993). Variable in abundance, periodically invading in large numbers in cold-water winters and remaining the following summer (Ainley 1976).

A low rate of plastic ingestion is documented in Oregon (Bayer and Olsen 1988). Hundreds occasionally die in severe storms and wash up onto beaches (Gabrielson and Jewett 1940). Annual adult mortality of 2-3%, one of lowest of all birds. Introduced foxes on Alaskan breeding islands have reduced or eliminated some breeding populations. Small numbers are harvested by native Alaskans. They are at risk from oil spills; an extensive spill around the Semidi Is. could affect 1/3 of Alaskan breeding population (Shallenberger 1984).—*Greg Gillson*

**Murphy's Petrel** *Pterodroma ultima*
This obscurely marked species breeds on islands in the sc. Pacific. Following nesting the birds move northward through the e. Pacific to the Gulf of Alaska, then south along the west side of the Pacific back to their breeding islands. Many nonbreeding birds remain in the N. Pacific throughout the year (Bartle et al. 1993). Recent sightings off California indicate that they are regular transients off the N. American Pacific coast from Mar through Jun (Bailey et al. 1989).

Difficulties in identifying dark-plumaged petrels make sight records, and even some photographs, difficult to confirm. Both Murphy's Petrel and the very similar Solander's Petrel have been observed off Washington and California (Bailey et al. 1989), in numbers of up to 100 a day at times, and a Great-winged Petrel has recently been reported off California (D. Shearwater p.c.). On 20 May 1981, four dark petrels were observed 55-70 mi (88-112 km) offshore between the mouth of the Columbia R. and Heceta Head, Lane Co. (Bailey et al. 1989). On 3 May 1997, 14 were observed approximately 127 mi (204 km) off the s. Oregon coast; on 12 May 1997, two were 161 mi (259 km) off the s. Oregon coast (Lillie 1997); and on 19 Sep 1999, one was 65 mi (104.5 km) off Clatsop Beach, Clatsop Co. (Gilligan 2000).

There are three Oregon specimens of Murphy's Petrel; one dead on the beach near Lost Cr., Lincoln Co., 15 Jun 1981 (spec. no. 571368 USNM); one moribund on Horsfall Beach, Coos Co., 6 Mar 1987 (spec. no. 103774 LACM, Bailey et al. 1989); and one, 2 mi (3.2 km) south of Cape Blanco, Curry Co., 27 Mar 1988 (specimen also LACM, Bailey et al. 1989). Monotypic (Harrison 1983).—*Harry B. Nehls*

**Mottled Petrel** *Pterodroma inexpectata*
The Mottled Petrel breeds Oct-Apr on New Zealand and nearby islands, and ranges throughout much of the Pacific Ocean, mostly far from land. It is a common May to Oct visitant in the n. and e. N. Pacific, with nonbreeding birds occurring during the winter months (Ainley and Manolis 1979).

A long-dead Mottled Petrel was found on the beach north of Alsea Bay, Lincoln Co., 25 Jul 1959 for the first w. N. American record south of Alaska (spec. no. 142570 MVZ, Wallace 1961). Two were found dead 18-19 Mar 1972 on the beach south of Yaquina Beach, Lincoln Co. (OBRC, skulls 555219 and 555218 USNM); one was found dead and photographed at Driftwood SP, Lincoln Co., 15 Dec 1986 (OBRC); a leucistic bird was chased and attacked by dogs in downtown Cannon Beach, Clatsop Co., 13 Jan 1988 (Johnson 1988a, Watson 1989); the wings of one dead on Clatsop Beach, Clatsop Co., were photographed 15 Nov 1989 (Fix and Heinl 1990); the wings of one dead on Bayocean Beach, Tillamook Co., were photographed 14 Apr 1993 (OBRC); one was found dead on Oceanside Beach, Tillamook Co., 1 Dec 1995 (spec. to Tillamook County Museum, Johnson 1996b).

One was observed 105 mi (169 km) west of Tillamook Co., 16 Feb 1971 (Ainley and Manolis 1979). Nine were observed 60 mi (97 km) west of Waldport, Lincoln Co., 31 Mar 1981. On 19 Apr 1985, 62 Mottled Petrels were recorded off the s. Washington and n. Oregon coast, of which 28 were about 97 mi (156 km) west of the Oregon coast (Mattocks 1985b). One was observed off Boiler Bay Viewpoint, Lincoln Co., 10 Dec 1987 (OBRC), and three were 45 mi (72 km) west of Tillamook and Lincoln counties 11 Dec 1990 (OBRC); one was 14 mi (25.9 km) w. of Cape Blanco 12 Dec 1999 (Tice 2000c); and 12 were 20-215 mi (38-409 km) off the Oregon coast 20 Oct to 2 Nov 2001 (Sullivan 2002). Monotypic (AOU 1957).—*Harry B. Nehls*

## Streaked Shearwater *Calonectris leucomelas*
This is a bird of the w. Pacific, breeding on islands about Japan, Korea, and China and dispersing over nearby seas. Individuals occasionally occur in the fall at Monterey Bay, California. There is one accepted sight record from Oregon, a bird observed from a research vessel over Heceta Bank, 35.3 mi (57 km) west of Lane Co. 13 Sep 1996 (Force et al. 1999). One was reported 50 mi (80.6 km) west of Cape Lookout, Tillamook Co., 17 Sep 2000 (Korpi 2001a). Monotypic (Harrison 1983).—*Harry B. Nehls*

## Pink-footed Shearwater *Puffinus creatopus*
The world population of this species, which probably does not exceed 25,000 pairs, is quite low for a seabird. Nevertheless, these are the common light-bellied shearwaters off Oregon in summer. They are larger, bulkier, and fly more deliberately than the usually much more abundant Sooty Shearwaters with which they associate. They are uniform gray-brown above; the underparts are white; the vent and underwings variably smudged with dusky. The pinkish bill is dark-tipped and the feet are pink. Considered by Palmer (1962) to be a light morph of Flesh-footed Shearwater, with which it shares behavior, flight-style, and soft-part coloration.

**General Distribution:** Restricted to the e. Pacific. Breed on three islands off Chile: Robinson Crusoe (Más á Tierra) and Santa Clara in the Juan Fernandez Is., and Isla Mocha; eggs laid Dec-Jan (Harrison 1983). Range north to Oregon and Washington, rarely to se. Alaska (Ainley 1976). Monotypic (AOU 1957).

**Oregon Distribution:** Common summer visitor and very common fall transient offshore on shallow shelf waters. Usually seen seaward of 40 fm (72 m) depth (Wahl 1975), approximately 5-10 mi (8.9-17.7 km) off Oregon's shores. Infrequently seen from shore.

**Habitat and Diet:** Pelagic. Off California largest numbers occur over the shelf where sea temperatures are warmest (Ainley 1976). However, off Oregon and Washington density seems independent of environmental variables. Instead, density is highest where Sooty Shearwaters are also dense, "where one species occurred, so also did the other" (Briggs et al. 1992). This association with Sooty Shearwaters is long recognized (Bent 1922, Peterson 1961). Food consists of small fish and crustaceans picked from surface or pursued by shallow dives (Bent 1922).

**Seasonal Activity and Behavior:** Arrive in low numbers in Feb-Mar; gradually build in numbers becoming common Jul-Oct; depart in Nov. Absent Dec-Jan, or very rare in warm-water winters (Gilligan et al. 1994). Highest number on an Oregon pelagic trip was about 1,000 on 24 Sep 1998 (*GG*), and 3,450 on 2 Sep 2000 (Korpi 2001a), both off Newport, corresponding to Sep peak in Washington (Wahl 1975).

Often seen in flocks resting in bunched rafts on the water. Congregate to feed on fish (Bent 1922). Otherwise, individuals tend only loosely to associate with each other and flocks of Sooty Shearwaters. Large numbers attracted to fishing boats (Wahl 1975). Characteristic flight is "languid and unhurried" (Harrison 1983). Fly higher off the water on average than Sooty Shearwaters, with slower deeper wing strokes ("lumbering," Stallcup 1990), and much gliding and wheeling.

**Detection:** Easily found in small numbers at all seasons except winter 10-20 mi (18-35 km) offshore. More common from mid-Aug to mid-Oct when 50 to several hundred may be encountered on a typical pelagic trip (Gilligan et al. 1994). On 16 one-day pelagic trips Jul-Oct 1994-98 recorded on 100% of trips; average number of birds 119 (*GG*). They do not always feed on chum, but attracted to the periphery of feeding flocks of fulmars and albatrosses which are attracted to chum. In bright sunlight, especially at dawn, underparts can appear immaculately white, and upperparts can look two-toned. At such times they may be momentarily mistaken for Buller's Shearwaters.

**Population Status and Conservation:** A "few thousand" pairs breed on Robinson Crusoe I. and up to 3,000 pairs on Santa Clara I. (Collar et al. 1994). Guicking (1999) recently studied the birds on Isla Mocha, and made the first population estimate for this island—roughly 13,000-17,000 breeding pairs. Rare off Peru in warm-water El Niño years when local anchovy population crashes; then more abundant than usual in California (Ainley 1976). Average Oregon/ Washington density 0.03-0.23 birds/mi² (0.01-0.09 birds/km²) Apr-Nov on surveys conducted in 1989-90, with local densities 2.6-7.8 birds/mi² (1-3 birds/km²) Apr-Jun and 15.5-36.3 birds/mi² (6-14 birds/km²) Jul-Sep (Briggs et al. 1992).

Listed as "vulnerable" by BirdLife International as population is small and restricted. Known threats on the breeding islands include predation by feral cats and coatimundis, and soil erosion by goats and rabbits (Collar et al. 1994). From 3,000 to 5,000 chicks are harvested for food each year on Isla Mocha (Guicking 1999). There are no reports of significant fishery-related mortality (Everett and Pitman 1993).—*Greg Gillson*

## Flesh-footed Shearwater *Puffinus carneipes*

These are always exciting birds to find, as they are one of the rarest of the seabirds to occur annually in Oregon. Single birds are sometimes found in flocks of other shearwaters. They are very similar to Sooty Shearwaters but they are larger with pink or pale whitish feet and dark-tipped pale bills. In addition, their plumage is a deep chocolate-brown, lacking the grayness of the upperpart coloration of Sooty Shearwaters; and the underwing does not show the Sooty's white coverts.

**General Distribution:** Western and ne. Pacific and Indian Oceans to Arabian Sea, breeding on islands off w. Australia and New Zealand; eggs laid Nov-Dec (Harrison 1983). New Zealand breeders disperse northward off Asia then east to Gulf of Alaska and the W. Coast of N. America; Australian breeders disperse into Indian Ocean (Lockley 1974). Probably monotypic (Palmer 1962).

**Oregon Distribution:** Rare late fall transient offshore at the western edge and slopes of the continental shelf. Rare or irregular at other times of yr. For 29 birds observed at sea where distance was recorded, sightings ranged from 5-60 mi (8.9-106 km) from land; median 29 mi (51.3 km). Four sightings from shore (Gillson 2000).

**Habitat and Diet:** Pelagic. Found in waters 52-61° F (11-16° C) (Ainley 1976). Feed on fish and squid. Especially attracted to shrimp trawlers off Washington (Wahl 1975).

**Seasonal Activity and Behavior:** Most records fall between 27 Aug-31 Oct; otherwise one or two records each in Feb, Mar, Apr, May, Jul, and Dec (Gillson 2000, Lillie 2001, *GG*). Record high number in Oregon in a single day is six birds 7 Oct 2001 on Perpetua Bank (Contreras 2002b). In Washington this species is present May-Oct with peak Sep-Oct (Wahl 1975). Likewise in California it is uncommon May-early Nov (Ainley 1976); very rare other times of year (Stallcup 1990).

Flesh-footed Shearwaters compete vigorously for discards from fishing vessels (Wahl 1975). Sometimes feed by skimming surface, treading water, ending in belly flop (Harrison 1983). Dive for food (Palmer 1962, Harrison 1983). Usually seen singly among flocks of other shearwaters. Characteristic flight resembles that of Pink-footed Shearwaters (Harrison 1983). They fly higher off the water on average than Sooty Shearwaters, with slower, deeper, wing strokes, and much gliding, wheeling, and circling.

**Detection:** Difficult due to scarcity, narrow migration window, occurrence well offshore, and similarity to abundant Sooty Shearwaters. On 16 one-day pelagic trips Jul-Oct 1994-98 recorded on 25% of trips (67% of trips from 12 Sep-18 Oct); average number of birds 0.8; maximum four (*GG*). About 70% of detections in Washington were around fishing boats (T. R. Wahl p.c.). Thus, the best chance to find these birds would be to seek out shrimp trawlers in Sep as they pull in nets. Identification is often difficult because of sea conditions. From above or behind appear similar to Pink-footed Shearwaters; from underneath look like Sooty Shearwaters. Surprisingly, though, the most difficult separation in flight can be with some dark-morph Northern Fulmars, which also have dark chocolate-brown plumage, pink feet, pale bills, and leisurely wheeling flight style (Harrison 1983, *GG*).

**Population Status and Conservation:** World population about 300,000 breeding pairs (Everett and Pitman 1993). First recorded in Oregon on 12 Sep 1965 inside the Columbia R. mouth in a large flock of Sooty Shearwaters (H. Nehls p.c.). Second record on 13 Jul 1973 about 20 mi (35 km) off Newport (Crowell and Nehls 1973c); about 31 records of 43 birds through 1999 (Gillson 2000). Detected annually since 1978, except 1989 and 1999. Absent in California during years of cold-water anomalies (Ainley 1976). Wahl also noted yearly fluctuations in abundance in Washington (Wahl 1975).

Because it is a deep diver, it is frequently entangled in nets and vulnerable to fishery mortality. Some destruction of breeding habitat on Lord Howe I. Nevertheless, no existing substantial threats to population (Everett and Pitman 1993).—*Greg Gillson*

## Wedge-tailed Shearwater *Puffinus pacificus*

This species is by far the most abundant and widespread breeding shearwater in the tropical Pacific and Indian Ocean (Marchant and Higgins 1990). It breeds northward to Baja California through the c. and w. Pacific to Japan. Both dark and light color morphs occur with many intermediate individuals reported. It does not regularly occur in the N. Pacific. In recent years there have been several California records of individuals in Monterey Bay, and one at Salton Sea. A dark morph bird was found dead on the beach at Newport, Lincoln Co., 26 Mar 1999 (Leal 1999). A live bird was observed in flight 25 mi (46.3 km) west of Depoe Bay 2 Oct 1999 (Hunter 2000). Monotypic (Harrison 1983).—*Harry B. Nehls*

## Buller's Shearwater *Puffinus bulleri*

Few seabirds have been labeled "stunning" (Harrison 1983); but with their graceful flight, boldly patterned upperparts, and brilliant white underparts, these birds truly are one of the most beautiful in Oregon waters. They have a black cap, wings angled forward, long body and tail, and a unique dark 'M' pattern against light gray back and wings. Often seen in small groups mixed among other more abundant shearwaters, they sometimes form pure flocks all flying in gracefully synchronized flight. While regular in late fall, they are still uncommon enough to excite observers when encountered at sea.

**General Distribution:** Pacific. Breed only on Poor Knights Is. in n. New Zealand; eggs laid Nov-Dec (Harrison 1983). Range east to Chile, north to Japan, and Gulf of Alaska. "Movements and routes little known" (Harrison 1983). Few found south of Baja California in fall; apparently fly directly to New Zealand from c. California (Ainley 1976). Monotypic (AOU 1957).

**Oregon Distribution:** Common to very common regular late fall transient offshore on shelf and slope waters. Most are found over 5 mi (8.9 km) from shore (Gilligan et al. 1994). Rarely seen from shore.

**Habitat and Diet:** Pelagic. Prefer the boundary between warm and cold water (Ainley 1976); near or seaward of the shelf break on warmer sides of sea surface temperature fronts, in waters 58-61° F (14.5-16° C) (Briggs et al. 1992). They eat squid, crustaceans, and small fish picked from the surface, probably primarily at night when plankton rise (Wahl 1986).

**Seasonal Activity and Behavior:** Single early birds sometimes arrive in late Jul; variably common Aug-Nov, peak late Sep-mid-Oct; rare to Dec; matching relative abundance and timing in California (Stallcup 1990) and Washington (Wahl 1975). Highest numbers on Oregon pelagic trips were 442 off Depoe Bay on 18 Oct 1997 and 290 off Newport on 5 Oct 1996 (Gilligan 1997). Harrison (1983) reports 1,000 per day off Oregon, though the basis of this report is unknown. On 16 one-day pelagic trips Jul-Oct 1994-98 recorded on 56% of trips (100% of trips from 27 Aug-18 Oct); average number of birds 76; maximum 442 (*GG*).

Usually occur in small mixed flocks of shearwaters (Harrison 1983), but occasionally large monotypic flocks. Not attracted to discards from fishing boats (Wahl 1975). Feeding method is primarily like surface-feeding ducks, swinging bill from side to side as they swim forward. Also feed by contact dipping: feeding in flight while suspended in breeze with outstretched wings, sometimes pushing off water with feet, and then plunging head into water to grab food. Occasionally fly low and flop into water submersing head to grab fish. Only rarely dive for food (Wahl 1986).

**Detection:** Distinctive plumage allows easy detection. In bright sun, Pink-footed Shearwaters sometimes mistaken for this species. Characteristic flight is more buoyant and higher off the water on average than Sooty Shearwaters, with slow deep wing strokes. Sometimes glide long distances without wing strokes. In normal flight they wheel up sharply, then gracefully glide down on bowed wings angled forward. Sometimes engage in an amazing synchronized flight when flocking (Wahl 1975, Stallcup 1990, *GG*).

**Population Status and Conservation:** Reduced to 100 pairs by 1938 on Aorangi I.—a major nesting colony among the Poor Knights Is.—from trampling of the island by pigs. The pigs were removed, and the population on that island rapidly expanded to 200,000 pairs. Current total population is about 2.5 million birds (Everett and Pitman 1993). Noticeable fluctuations in numbers reaching our shores from year to year. Numbers seem greatest in years preceding an El Niño event: "Buller's Shearwaters occurring in high numbers off California seem to foretell a period of warm water to follow" (Ainley 1976).

Listed as "near threatened" by BirdLife International as breeding population restricted (Collar et al. 1994). Less vulnerable to fishery mortality than other shearwaters because they usually don't dive (Everett and Pitman 1993). —*Greg Gillson*

## Sooty Shearwater *Puffinus griseus*

This seabird, the most abundant in Oregon, has recently suffered severe declines or significant population shifts in the e. N. Pacific. Similar in shape to thin, long-winged gulls, Sooty Shearwaters are dark sooty gray with limited amounts of white on the underwing coverts. They glide on wind currents along wave troughs on stiff wings. Gregarious, they form huge loose flocks in migration, often passing for hours within sight of land-based observers.

**General Distribution:** Wide-ranging in the Pacific and Atlantic. Breed on islands off s. S. America and in the Australasian region, primarily off New Zealand; eggs laid Nov-Dec (Harrison 1983). Most S. American breeders depart north into the Pacific, reaching California, where this is the commonest shearwater Jul-Nov when flocks of several million often seen from shore. Many continue north to Alaska. Return migration begins in Aug. Band returns indicate some of e. Pacific population originates from New Zealand (Ainley 1976), suggesting a clockwise migration in the N. Pacific (Everett and Pitman 1993). Monotypic (AOU 1957).

**Oregon Distribution:** Abundant summer visitor and transient offshore on the inner shelf. Most numerous 3-6 mi (5-10 km) off shore (Wahl 1975, Briggs et al. 1992). They can be found in small numbers in deeper waters off the continental shelf. Frequently viewed from shore, especially from elevated viewpoints, sometimes in huge numbers. Also occur regularly within the mouth of the Columbia R., rarely upriver to Hammond where 5,000 were seen on 16 Sep 1990 (Fix 1991).

**Habitat and Diet:** Pelagic. From Jul-Sep prefer warmer waters, 50-57° F (10-14° C), over flat seafloor of n. Oregon (Briggs et al. 1992); but in California generally prefer cool water over the rugged seafloor of n. California rather than the flatter seafloor and very warm waters of s. California (Ainley 1976).

Food of the Sooty Shearwater includes fish, squid, and crustaceans picked from the water's surface. They eat anchovies in Willapa Bay and Grays Harbor, Washington (Wahl 1975). Particularly fond of squid; stomachs of birds off Oregon contained many eye lenses and mandibles of squids (Gabrielson and Jewett 1940). Most aggressive feeder following offal from processing ships. They will dive under hull of ship for choice food items (P. T. Sullivan p.c.).

**Seasonal Activity and Behavior:** Begin arriving in Oregon in Mar, peak in Jul; southward migration begins Aug, abundant to Oct, most are gone by mid-Dec; rare in winter. Tens to hundreds of thousands of birds may be seen migrating past coastal points Jul-Sep

(Gilligan et al. 1994); over 750,000 off Clatsop Co. on Aug 25-26, 1979 (Contreras 1979a).

Gregarious, forming huge loose flocks (Harrison 1983). Response to offal from fishing boats is inconsistent, perhaps due to abundance or lack of natural food. Wahl (1975) and Stallcup (1990) assert these birds are usually not attracted to shrimp or bottom trawlers and usually ignore chum. However, Bent (1922) and Wahl (1986) report that they are "readily attracted" to discards and chum to fish livers or any greasy offal. They show significant avoidance of flocks with California and Western Gulls, and Fork-tailed Storm-Petrels (Briggs et al. 1992). Usually silent, except when squabbling over food; then low, guttural *wok-wok-wok* (Bent 1922). "Often follow great schools of anchovies close inshore, congregating in great screaming, struggling, fighting masses as the fishes come close to the surface" (Gabrielson and Jewett 1940). Characteristic flight: 2-8 quick, stiff, wing-beats to rise a few feet above waves; followed by a banked glide of 3-5 seconds; wingtips occasionally shear the water. They show more wheeling and gliding in high winds. While flying may dive into the water for food from about 3 ft (1 m) height. Propel themselves rapidly under water with wings. Submersed birds may burst right out of the water into full flight, rather than running on surface to take wing (*GG*).

**Detection:** Regular from shore Jul-Oct, especially during strong onshore winds, as they migrate just beyond the breakers. Also noted inshore when calm and foggy over the ocean. Most abundant on the n. Oregon coast; can be seen especially from the s. jetty of the Columbia R. Migrate close to shore, thus huge numbers not usually encountered by pelagic trips 20-30 mi (35-53 km) from shore. One of the most abundant birds offshore Apr-Oct. On 16 one-day pelagic trips Jul-Oct 1994-98 recorded on 100% of trips; average number of birds 143; maximum 672 (*GG*).

**Population Status and Conservation:** Worldwide population is about 20 million birds. About 1 million were estimated moving south from Tillamook 21 Aug 1978 (Hunn and Mattocks 1979a). Similar numbers were reported previous years (H. Nehls p.c.). Off Oregon and Washington Apr-Sep average 0.16-6.5 birds/mi² (0.06-2.50 birds/km²), with local densities >5,180 birds/mi² (>2000 birds/km²) (Briggs et al. 1992). There has been a 90% decline in numbers in California Current since 1987 (Veit et al. 1996). Recent studies (Spear and Ainley 1999) suggest a "progressive increase in number of shearwaters" migrating to the c. N. Pacific from the Peru Current, "consistent with a concurrent sharp decline of these birds in the California Current" due to a long-term increase in sea-surface temperature of the California Current. The high seas squid drift-net fleet took up to 400,000 Sooty Shearwaters annually as incidental bycatch prior to 1993 ban on this fishery (Everett and Pitman 1993). In Oregon, one newspaper report (*The Oregonian* 1971) described a catch of about 2,000 Sooty Shearwaters in nets of a single boat in the lower Columbia R., and mentioned that other boats had similar experiences. Substantial mortality of migrants, especially first-year birds, off e. Australia when food abnormally scarce (Shallenberger 1984).—*Greg Gillson*

## Short-tailed Shearwater *Puffinus tenuirostris*

These very abundant seabirds are uncommon off Oregon in winter. Their arrival coincides with some of the Pacific Northwest's stormiest weather. Complicating detection difficulties is their identification; they look very much like the abundant Sooty Shearwaters—all dark, but slightly smaller with shorter bills and tails. Studied on their Tasmanian breeding grounds continuously for over 45 yr; once they leave for the open ocean little is known about them. Popularly known as "muttonbirds," they have been harvested as food for centuries on their southern seas breeding islands. Even today, up to 300,000 chicks are harvested in Tasmania each year (Davies 1997).

**General Distribution:** Breed when at least 5 yr old on islands of S. Australia, Victoria, New South Wales, and Tasmania; eggs laid in 3-wk period in late Nov (Ainley 1976). The largest of about 280 breeding colonies is on Babel I., which is riddled with 3 million nest burrows. Migrate north past Japan, to n. coast of Alaska (to Point Barrow); then majority return south through the c. Pacific to their breeding islands. Some nonbreeders in Nov-Dec migrate along the W. Coast of N. America, to Baja California, then return to the sw. Pacific. Monotypic (AOU 1957).

**Oregon Distribution:** Uncommon to fairly common late fall and winter transient; irregular spring transient offshore. Occasionally seen from shore in early winter, sometimes in large flocks.

**Habitat and Diet:** Pelagic. Poorly known off Oregon. Over entire range, they eat fish, crustaceans, and squid taken from surface or by diving and pursuing underwater (Bent 1922).

**Seasonal Activity and Behavior:** Small numbers noted offshore beginning in Sep; variably common Nov-Jan; remaining in some years until May; very rare or absent in summer. May be the most numerous (often the only) shearwater offshore from late Nov-Feb. Actual status difficult to ascertain because of similarity to abundant Sooty Shearwaters. Migratory flocks often noted from shore Nov-early Dec (Gilligan et al. 1994). Highest

numbers are seen from shore: 500 from Boiler Bay on 15 Nov 2000, 300 from Boiler Bay on 12 Dec 2000 (P. Pickering p.c.), and 100 from Bandon on 8 Jan 1989, a rather late date for such numbers (Johnson 1989b).

Over most of its range the species is highly gregarious; it usually occurs in dense flocks (Harrison 1983). Most sightings are from pelagic trips; however, singles or small groups (generally less than 20) are seen from shore (*GG*). More frequently attracted to chum than Sooty Shearwater (Stallcup 1990). Their characteristic flight is composed of rapid swift-like wing strokes ("snappy" [Stallcup 1990]), faster and more continuous than Sooty Shearwater with less gliding and more darting changes in direction.

**Detection:** Generally difficult to identify at sea. Very similar in behavior and plumage to Sooty Shearwater. Few are seen on early spring or fall pelagic trips; seas are generally unfavorable to get offshore during peak abundance in late fall and early winter. Distant views from headlands of dark shearwaters gliding through the wave troughs often go unidentified as to species. On 16 one-day pelagic trips Jul-Oct 1994-98 recorded on only 12.5% of trips (33% of trips Sep-Oct); average number of birds 2.7; maximum 40 (*GG*).

**Population Status and Conservation:** Current population estimate 23 million birds (Everett and Pitman 1993). Early in the 20th century one flock in the Bass Strait, between Australia and Tasmania, was estimated at over 150 million birds (Bent 1922). Change in seasonal status since last century; in California formerly common all year, now uncommon winter visitor, mid-Sep through Apr (Stallcup 1990), peak mid-Nov (Ainley 1976). More common in California when water abnormally cold in fall and winter (Ainley 1976).

Only known threat off Oregon is normal migratory hazard of exhaustion and starvation; sometimes wash up dead on beaches following winter storms. During times of poor food conditions off e. Australia, migration mortality can be high, especially of first-year birds (Shallenberger 1984). Whole breeding colonies have been destroyed by introduction of pigs, cattle, and sheep to breeding islands. Feral cats eat chicks. The N. Pacific drift-net fishery incidentally drowned "hundreds of thousands" of these birds annually until a 1993 ban (Everett and Pitman 1993). Harvest of chicks is closely monitored as 200,000 commercially, and 100,000 recreationally, are killed annually in Tasmania for food (Davies 1997); this down from 700,000 in 1993 (Everett and Pitman 1993). Plastic ingestion is a possible contributor to deaths. Nevertheless, the population seems stable (Everett and Pitman 1993).—*Greg Gillson*

## Black-vented Shearwater *Puffinus opisthomelas*

The Black-vented Shearwater breeds from Jan to Jun on islands off the Pacific coast of Baja California. Following nesting it disperses along the Pacific coast from Mexico north to c. California and casually north to Vancouver I., British Columbia.

Several species of small black-and-white shearwaters occur in the N. Pacific and the identity of many sight records remains in question. The Black-vented Shearwater is the expected species off the N. American Pacific coast. However, the Manx Shearwater has been verified from Washington and California (Howell et al. 1994). There are many sight records of unidentified small black-and-white shearwaters from Oregon, most seen between late Aug and early Nov (OBRC), some of which may have been Manx Shearwaters. While most have been at or just off the beaches, some have been found up to 16 mi (26 km) offshore. One was west of Newport, Lincoln Co., 28 Mar 1982 (Mattocks and Hunn 1982b). One observed 22 Nov 1992 flying over the surf at Bandon, Coos Co., has been accepted by the OBRC as a Black-vented Shearwater. Monotypic (Harrison 1983).—*Harry B. Nehls*

## Family Hydrobatidae

## Wilson's Storm-Petrel *Oceanites oceanicus*

This species breeds on islands in the S. Pacific, Atlantic, and Indian Oceans. After nesting it ranges throughout the Atlantic and Indian Oceans and the S. Pacific. It is casual northward in the e. Pacific Ocean. There are numerous fall records for California, mainly Monterey Bay, from mid-Jul to early Nov. It is much less regular in spring (Small 1994). There are two sight records for Oregon. One was among a concentration of shearwaters and storm-petrels off the s. jetty of the Columbia R., Clatsop Co., 31 May 1976. A lone bird was observed from a research vessel about 80 mi (129 km) west of Nestucca Bay, Tillamook Co., 24 Jul 1996. Both reports have been accepted by the OBRC. The subspecies of birds that have occurred in Oregon is unknown.—*Harry B. Nehls*

## Fork-tailed Storm-Petrel *Oceanodroma furcata*

In Oregon, Fork-tailed Storm-Petrels breed in numbers that are only a tiny fraction of those of Leach's Storm-Petrels. Other than records of presence at nesting colonies and reports of offshore sightings, little is known of the biology of this species in Oregon. This is the larger of two storm-petrels breeding in Oregon; it is gray in color and sexually monomorphic. These birds leave and return to breeding colonies only at night, when they are best detected by their distinct raspy call (Simons 1981). At sea distinguished by quick, buoyant flight with short glides interspersed with wing fluttering to maintain position at food source.

**General Distribution:** Confined to the N. Pacific with nesting colonies from the Kuril Is. south to n. California. At sea from the Bering Sea south through the N. Pacific along the W. Coast of N. America to c. California and west to Japan and the Volcano Is. Two subspecies; *O. f. plumbea* breeds in Oregon (AOU 1957).

**Oregon Distribution:** Fewer than 20 nests have been found in Oregon, all located in the same habitat as colonies of Leach's Storm-Petrels (Browning and English 1972, Pitman et al. 1985, USFWS unpubl. data) with nests recorded at Three Arch Rocks and Haystack Rock, Tillamook Co.; Island Rock, Hunters I., N. Crook Pt. Rock, Saddle Rock, Whalehead I., and Goat I., Curry Co. During breeding season the Fork-tailed Storm-Petrel does not forage as far offshore as Leach's Storm-Petrel (Vermeer and Devito 1988). It can be seen over the outer shelf, at the margins of offshore banks such as the Heceta-Stonewall complex, and along the margins of the Columbia plume (Briggs et al. 1992). Tyler et al. (1993) detected highest numbers in Jun and Jul over the upper continental slope where they were most common in waters on the warmer seaward side of the shelf break fronts.

At sea are present all year but found primarily on the continental slope in waters 600-6,200 ft (200-2,000 m) deep during the breeding season, and greater than 6,200 ft (2,000 m) in Nov and Jan (Briggs et al. 1992). Attracted to fishing vessels and frequently follow ships (Sanger 1970). Occasionally observed from land singly or in small flocks of 20 or more (Gilligan et al. 1994, Contreras 1998). Unusually large numbers nearshore on occasion; in late Aug/early Sep 1983, recorded from shore on the s. and c. coast (Evanich and Fix 1983, Bayer 1985b); 100 seen in Yaquina Bay on 8 Feb 1984 (Heinl 1985). In 1985 countless sightings were made from land Mar-May from s. British Columbia to Monterey, California (Fix 1985a). In Oregon, 200 seen at the mouth of the Rogue R. in May 1995 (Lillie 1995), and a pelagic trip in late Apr 1985 recorded about 500 just outside the jetties of Tillamook Bay (Evanich 1986b). A partially eaten adult bird found on the trail above Elk Cr. Falls, Siskiyou NF, on 31 Jul 1999, possibly dropped by a Great Horned Owl, is the only known inland record (M. Graybill p.c.).

**Habitat and Diet:** Marine. In Oregon, nests in burrows dug in the soil of areas vegetated with grasses and herbaceous vegetation. In California also uses rocky crevices for nest sites (Harris 1974), and in British Columbia nests beneath roots of spruce trees and under fallen logs (Vermeer et al. 1988).

They feed from the surface. There are no dietary studies in Oregon. Diets elsewhere vary with season and location. On the Queen Charlotte Is., amphipods, euphausiids, copepods, and fish were fed to chicks (Vermeer and Devito 1988). Birds collected Jul-Oct in Alaska fed on scyphomedusae and their associated hyperiid amphipods, squid, crustaceans, and larval fish (Harrison N 1984).

**Seasonal Activity and Behavior:** No published studies of breeding chronology in Oregon. The overall nesting season is approximately 6 mo in length and they nest 4-8 wk earlier than Leach's Storm-Petrels. At the beginning of the breeding season they arrive on the colony earlier in the evening than Leach's Storm-Petrels with peak arrivals around midnight (Vermeer et al. 1988). At the Farallon Is. they leave the colony earlier than Leach's Storm-Petrels. Peak of egg laying is Apr in California (Harris 1974) and late May in Alaska (Boersma et al. 1980); both sexes incubate single white egg. Neglect of egg during incubation appears to be more common in this species than in Leach's Storm-Petrel, which lengthens the incubation period. Boersma and Wheelwright (1979) recorded the mean duration of egg neglect in Alaska to be 1.7 days with a mean cumulative number of 11 days. Eggs that hatched were most commonly neglected for 1 or 2 days at a time, but some experienced up to 7 consecutive days of neglect. Such neglect results in a mean incubation period of 50 days, although the mean for the number of days that the egg was actually attended was 38.6 days. Eggs need 34-35 days of warmth to hatch (Boersma and Silva 2001). Incubation periods, however, can be as long as 68 days and as short as 37 (Boersma and Wheelwright 1979). Incubation shifts by the male and female average 2-3 days and as long as 5 days and they spend an average of 32 min (standard deviation 38 min) together during incubation change-overs, range 5-235 min (n=43) (Simons 1981).

In British Columbia most hatched late May and early Jun, although some not until mid-Aug (Vermeer et al. 1988). Chicks are brooded for 1-8 days after hatching (Simons 1981). Both parents feed the chick by regurgitation, returning to the colony at night. Frequency of visits varied from 2/night to once every 4 days. In British Columbia mean fledging period 62 days (standard deviation 2.4 days), range 58-68 days after hatching (n=20) (Vermeer et al. 1988). Chicks attain peak body mass several weeks before fledging (Boersma and Silva 2001), and there is a distinct prefledging mass loss, but they still fledge at 120% of average adult weight (Simons 1981). In British Columbia chicks fledged before Leach's Storm-Petrels, leaving the colony from late Jul to early Sep (Vermeer et al. 1988). At a colony in n. California a few present at the colony throughout winter (Harris 1974). It is unknown if this occurs in colonies farther north.

Fork-tailed Storm-Petrels have two distinct calls: a common raspy 3- to 5-note call made by both sexes and a single-note call, often repeated many times, which is made by males when on the ground or in the burrow (Simons 1981). It is unknown if they call at sea.

**Detection:** Rarely seen near colonies, as they are nocturnal. Even offshore the likelihood of detection can be low as they are small birds and easily missed in the waves and swells unless close to a boat. Binoculars and calm sea conditions aid detection. Birding trips conducted offshore in Lane, Lincoln, and Tillamook counties during Apr-Oct 1994-98 detected no birds closer than 11 mi (18 km) from shore (G. Gillson p.c.). At a distance can be confused with phalaropes.

**Population Status and Conservation:** Censusing is difficult; the total population size is estimated at 5-10 million (Boersma and Groom 1993). Estimated Oregon breeding population estimates only a few hundred according to 1979 and 1988 surveys (Pitman et al. 1985, USFWS files).

Threats to the colony include predation and trampling of burrows by introduced mammals, which fortunately are not currently present on colonies in Oregon. River otter and avian predation occurs on some colonies (Quinlan 1983); seven eaten individuals were found at Haystack Rock, Tillamook Co. (Pitman et al. 1985). Storm-petrels spend considerable time away from Oregon waters and can be influenced by activities throughout the Pacific. As they feed at the surface, they are vulnerable to oil slicks; petroleum hydrocarbons have been found in the crops of Fork-tailed Storm-Petrels (Holmes 1984). Storm-petrel eggs were the only seabird in which DDT and toxaphene were detected in samples taken from Oregon (Henny et al. 1982). A single Fork-tailed Storm-Petrel egg collected at Haystack Rock in 1979 contained the highest concentration of organochlorines and PCBs in 10 species of seabirds measured (Henny et al. 1982).—*Jan Hodder*

## Leach's Storm-Petrel *Oceanodroma leucorhoa*

The smallest and most pelagic of Oregon's breeding seabirds flies the farthest offshore of any of Oregon's breeding seabirds to feed. It spends the nonbreeding season in the subtropical and equatorial Pacific. It is the second most abundant breeding seabird in Oregon, and is rarely seen from land or close to shore. It comes to its breeding islands, where it nests in burrows, only under the cover of darkness. Sexes are monomorphic; the plumage is black and Oregon populations have a distinct white rump. Leach's Storm-Petrels are long-lived birds characterized by long-term pair bonds and may breed yearly for up to 30 yr (Mauck et al. 1995).

**General Distribution:** Occur in both the N. Pacific and N. Atlantic. Breeding colonies in the N. Pacific range from Japan, across the Aleutian chain south to

c. Baja California. Ranges at sea from breeding areas south to the Hawaiian, Revillagigedo, and Galapagos Is., and in the w. Pacific to Indonesia and New Guinea. Two N. American subspecies; nominate *leucorhoa* in Oregon (includes *beali* as a synonym, Browning and Cross 1999).

**Oregon Distribution:** Nests on about 15 soil-covered offshore islands within the Oregon Is. NWR. Seven islands in Curry Co. account for the bulk of the population, with Goat I. and the islands off Crook Pt. accounting for 68% of the breeding population in 1979 (Pitman et al. 1985) and 66% in 1988 (USFWS unpubl. data). They feed during the day in warmer waters of the continental shelf edge and slope, so they fly 50+ mi (80+ km) offshore each day and are normally seen only by observers at this distance (Johnson 1992a), although small numbers are occasionally seen closer in (Johnson 1990a).

Major wintering areas are warm subtropical waters west of the California current (Boersma et al. 1980) and waters of the equatorial Pacific (Crossin 1974, Ainley 1980) and thus few are seen in Oregon's waters during the nonbreeding season. During Nov and Jan none were seen offshore during aerial surveys (Briggs et al. 1992) and numbers were low in Mar and Sep. In late Mar, Pitman (1981) recorded 250, 60 mi (96 km) off Waldport during 1 hr of observation. During all months in which they were sighted they were more common in waters > 6,200 ft (2,000 m) deep but during the breeding season birds foraged closer to shore in waters < 6,200 ft (2,000 m) deep. In May, population densities reached 640/mi² (250/km²) over the continental shelf (Briggs et al. 1992). They follow ships. Occasionally forced close to shore by gales and on a few occasions blown inland where they have been observed in w. Oregon valleys and waterways (Tice 1997). This most often happens in the autumn, but has occurred in spring (Heinl 1988a, Gilligan 1994, Browning and Cross 1999).

**Habitat and Diet:** Marine. Nests on islands on the s. coast are often located where cover of grass of the genus *Phalaris* is present (Browning and English 1972). Must have sufficient soil cover for digging a burrow (Browning and English 1972). On islands where soil cover is poor, are known to nest in rock crevices (Ainley et al. 1975), but not in Oregon. Non-nesting periods are spent on the open ocean. Tend to concentrate at fronts, eddies, and internal waves where upwelling brings food close to the surface (Haney 1986).

Leach's Storm-Petrels acquire individual prey items at the surface by capturing them while hovering above or sitting on the water. They eat a variety of plankton and nekton that varies seasonally and geographically (Huntington et al. 1996). Food of adults nesting in Oregon is unknown. Provision chicks by regurgitating previously swallowed food, some of which has been converted to lipid-rich oil. As the chick grows, the quantity of oil decreases and amount of solid food increases (Vermeer et al. 1988). Food destined for the chick can be collected from adults returning from sea captured in mist nets. Analysis of these remains from Goat I. collected in 1973 by W. Pearcy (p.c.) showed they were feeding chicks a variety of prey including the by-the-wind sailor (a jellyfish-like hydrozoan *Velella velella*), euphausiids (primarily *Euphausia pacifica*), oplophorid shrimps (*Hymenodora* sp.), calanoid copepods, hyperid amphipods, fish, and squid. A similar species list was obtained from samples collected at Saddle Rock, Curry Co., in 1987 and 1988. A more detailed analysis of fish remains from these samples found the following species: California headlight fish, hake, lampfish, and lanternfish (W. Walker p.c.).

**Seasonal Activity and Behavior:** There are few published studies of the biology of Leach's Storm-Petrels breeding in Oregon. In n. California absent from colonies from late Oct until early Feb (Huntington et al. 1996). By mid-Feb birds return and males begin digging burrows. Fidelity to nesting colony is high, as is reuse of previous year's burrow, particularly for pairs successful in raising a chick in previous years (Huntington et al. 1996). Peak of burrow digging and courtship is Mar-May. From late Mar to early Jun, pairs regularly found in burrows before eggs are laid. Large numbers of immatures visit the Farallon Is. off San Francisco Bay in the first 3 wk of Jun.

A single white egg is laid, often on bits of vegetation brought in by adults. Laying is relatively synchronous. In California it begins in mid-May, peaks in late May to early Jun, and is completed by early Jul. The mean incubation period at the Farallon Is. is 43 days, and ranges 42-48 days (Ainley, Henderson, and Strong 1990). Both sexes incubate with bouts averaging 3 days but can be as long as 7 days (Mauck et al. 1995). The first young hatched in late Jun, and peaked in mid- to late Jul (Ainley, Henderson, and Strong 1990). The blue-gray down-covered nestling is brooded for about 5 days and then left unattended in the burrow, the adults returning at night to deliver food (Mauck et al. 1995). On the Farallon Is. fledging began in mid-Aug, peaked in late Aug to Sep, and the last young fledged in late Oct. Limited data from Saddle Rock, Curry Co., indicate the timing in Oregon is similar. In British Columbia the average nestling period is 63 days, range 59-70 days (n=30) (Vermeer et al. 1988). Chicks typically attain 1.5 times adult mass but lose much of this weight in the nest and fledge at adult weight (Ainley et al. 1975). Adults typically arrive 30-60 min after complete darkness, and leave 50-90 min before sunrise (Harris 1974, Ainley, Henderson, and Strong 1990). Peak of arrival is just after midnight. The presence of bright moonlight reduces the number of birds that return to the colony before incubation, but after that time has little or no effect in n. California (Harris 1974), but did reduce the numbers on the Farallon Is. (Ainley, Henderson, and Strong. 1990). Individuals begin to breed when 4-5 yr of age (Ainley, Henderson, and Strong 1990).

Three distinct vocalizations are known from adult Leach's Storm-Petrels. As individuals fly about the colony at night they utter a loud chatter call which can be used to determine sex, although this is difficult to discern (Taoka et al. 1989).

**Detection:** Although this is an abundant breeding seabird in Oregon, it is rarely seen because it flies well offshore under the cover of darkness. During breeding season can be seen from land at a lumber mill north of Brookings, Curry Co., where on foggy nights birds are attracted to lights, which results in a number of collision mortalities (Dillingham 1992).

**Population Status and Conservation:** Worldwide population estimate is >8 million nesting pairs with an unknown large population of nonbreeders (Huntington et al. 1996). Numbers of breeders are difficult to estimate as burrow densities differ in different habitats ranging 1-9 active burrows per 10.7 ft² (1 m²) in Oregon (Pitman et al. 1985, USFWS unpubl. data). Many areas on colonies cannot be censused due to steepness of slopes or the likelihood of crushing burrows. So far as can be determined, Browning and English (1972) conducted the first nesting population surveys in Oregon. Their population estimate for Curry Co., where most of these birds nest in Oregon, was 1,011,000 breeding birds in 1966-67. This exceeds the first statewide estimate in 1979, which was 354,412 breeding birds (Pitman et al. 1985). For 1988, USFWS (unpubl. data) shows 435,000 breeders. The largest colony is on Goat I., Curry Co., with 535,800 breeding birds estimated in 1966-67, 116,000 in 1979, and 102,060 in 1988 (Browning and English 1972, Pitman et al. 1985, USFWS unpubl. data). Other large colonies, all in Curry Co., are N. Crook Pt., estimated in 1966-67 at 101,500 birds, in 1979 at 72,500 birds, and in 1988 at 99,090 breeders; Saddle Rock with 49,900 in 1966-67, 53,000 in 1979, and 87,520 in 1988; Hunters I. with 208,100 in 1966-67, 45,000 in 1979, and 19,740 in 1988; and islands off Whalehead Cr. with 118,300 in 1966-67, 40,000 in 1979, and 81,284 in 1988 (Browning and English 1972, Pitman et al. 1985, USFWS unpubl. data). Far fewer birds nest on the n. coast where there are only three colonies of note: the two Haystack Rocks in Tillamook and Clatsop counties, and the Three Arch Rocks NWR complex, also Tillamook Co.

Changes in soil cover on islands can influence numbers nesting; for example Finley (1902) noted that there were "a great many" Leach's Storm-Petrels and "a whole acre of nesting holes" (Finley 1905) on Shag Rock in the Three Arch complex. The 1979 seabird survey noted that there was little suitable habitat on this rock for nesting storm-petrels, and in 1988 Roy Lowe climbed onto Shag Rock and found there were few nesting petrels (USFWS unpubl. data).

Storm-petrels are inconspicuous at colony sites and at sea major declines can occur without notice (Huntington et al. 1996). A major cause of natural mortality for both adults and chicks at colonies is avian and mammalian predation. Such predation may modify the timing of breeding events in this species (Ainley, Henderson, and Strong 1990). Western Gull and river otter predation (*JH*) have been recorded from Saddle Rock, Curry Co., and Saw-whet Owl, Bald Eagle, and Common Raven predation noted in Alaska and British Columbia (Quinlan 1983, Vermeer et al. 1988). River otter predation eliminated colonies in British Columbia (Vermeer et al. 1988).

As a result of their feeding mode, storm-petrels pick up non-food items from the ocean surface. A study of nesting Leach's Storm-Petrels in Japan found that 6-19% of stomachs pumped contained plastic particles (Watanuki 1985). Also vulnerable to contamination by surface oil slicks. Petroleum hydrocarbons have been found in crops (Holmes 1984). Experimental work has shown that there is decreased survival and growth in chicks attended by one or two oil-dosed nesting adults (Trivelpiece et al. 1984, Butler et al. 1988), and that metabolic rate is elevated in adults that are fed small quantities of oil (Butler et al. 1986).—*Jan Hodder*

**Black Storm-Petrel** *Oceanodroma melania*
This large dark storm-petrel breeds on islands off s. California and Baja California and ranges at sea from c. California to Peru. Large numbers regularly occur at Monterey Bay, California, and casually northward to n. California (Harris 1991). A flock of 10 was photographed at Seaside, Clatsop Co., Oregon, 8 Sep 1983 (OBRC). Monotypic (AOU 1957).—*Harry B. Nehls*

# Order PELECANIFORMES
*Family Sulidae*

**Blue-footed Booby** *Sula nebouxii*
This tropical species breeds in n. S. America and Mexico and is a rare and irregular post-breeding visitor to s. California (Small 1994). There is one record for Washington (AOU 1998). A subadult (subspecies

unknown) was photographed at Yaquina Head, Lincoln Co., 7-9 Sep 2002.—*Harry B. Nehls*

## Brown Booby *Sula leucogaster*

This widespread tropical species breeds in America on the coasts of n. S. America, about the Gulf of Mexico, the Caribbean, and on both coasts of Mexico. It is casual northward along the Atlantic coast and elsewhere in s. U.S. It has been recorded in California and Washington. The single Oregon record was a juvenile observed 3 Oct 1998 by many on an offshore birding trip 15 mi (10 km) west-southwest of Depoe Bay, Lincoln Co. (OBRC). The subspecific identity of this bird is unknown.—*Harry B. Nehls*

## Family Pelecanidae

## American White Pelican

*Pelecanus erythrorhynchos*

Large and primarily white, the American White Pelican has the longest wingspan of any bird in Oregon, reaching 8.0-9.5 ft (2.5-3.0 m). It also has an enormous orange bill, and flies with neck withdrawn. During the breeding season the top of the bird's head becomes dusted with black and a horn grows on the upper mandible; this projection serves as a target for aggressive encounters to avoid injury to the essential bill pouch, but is shed after eggs are laid (Knopf 1975). Makes unusually long flights for feeding and migration, and at great distances soaring flocks (appearing to be a single object) have been reported as UFOs. American White Pelicans can be mistaken for Snow Geese, which are much smaller with a stubby pink bill and fly with neck extended. Fossils from the Pleistocene appearing similar to this species have been found at Fossil L., Lake Co. (Miller 1911).

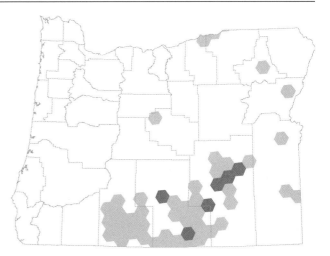

**General Distribution:** Breeds primarily inland N. America, from British Columbia east to Ontario, and in scattered locations as far south as n. California and Colorado (Evans and Knopf 1993). Winter range extends from c. California south to Nicaragua, the Gulf coast, and to Yucatan Peninsula (Evans and Knopf 1993). Monotypic (AOU 1957).

**Oregon Distribution:** Regularly occurs only east of the Cascades (Evanich 1990). Breeds at a few interior sites with differing regularity, including Malheur, Lower Klamath, and Upper Klamath NWRs; Summer L. W.A.; Warner Basin; and on islands in the Columbia R. east of Arlington (Paullin et al. 1988, Evanich 1990, Nehls 2001, OBBA, M. St. Louis unpubl. data). Locally common to abundant Mar-Oct in Klamath, Lake, and Harney counties (Summers 1993a, Gilligan et al. 1994). Other eastern locations in spring and summer (nonbreeding sites) include near Prineville, Crook Co.; Hermiston, Umatilla Co.; La Grande, Union Co.; Richland, Baker Co.; and Vale and Jordan Valley, Malheur Co. (OBBA). Postbreeding, this species may occur anywhere in e. Oregon (Evanich 1990), particularly at Malheur L. and reservoirs east of the Cascades (Marshall et al. 1996). Small numbers

*American White Pelican*

occur occasionally in w. Oregon, most regular at Fern Ridge Res., Lane Co.; other locations include Sauvie I. (Johnson 1997a, Lillie 2000, Tice 2000a); Portland (exceptionally, 102 in summer 2001) (Nehls 2001); Tillamook Bay (Lillie 1995, 1998), Baskett Slough NWR (Tice 2000a); Warrenton sewage ponds, Clatsop Co. (Lillie 1999); and Agate L., Dead Indian Plateau, and Howard Prairie Res., Jackson Co. (Gilligan 1997, Lillie 1998, Korpi 2001a). Rare across state in winter (Gilligan et al. 1994); CBC records primarily from southeast, accidental at Malheur NWR (Littlefield 1990a), Sauvie I. (Korpi 2001c), and Milwaukie (Tice 1999b). Interestingly, two were at Fern Ridge Res. winters of 1997-2000 (Tice 2000c, Korpi 2001c).

**Habitat and Diet:** Breeds on isolated lakes and freshwater marshes. Historically nested at Malheur NWR on islands, switched to floating bulrush mats in early 1900s, then flooded haystacks 1938-40 (Thompson et al. 1979). Recently nested mostly on barren islands with some greasewood, saltgrass, Great Basin wild rye, and trace amounts of forbs (Paullin et al. 1988). Nests in similar habitat at Pelican L. in Warner Basin: islands sparsely vegetated with greasewood and saltgrass (Stern 1988). Feeds in shallow water in marshes and canals near water-control structures (e.g., diversion dams, lift gates, pipes, etc.) where fish concentrate (Puchy and Marshall 1993). Unlike the Brown Pelican, which dives for food, this species feeds cooperatively in shallow water by encircling fish or driving them to the shallows with bill dipping and wing beating, then scooping up prey in bills (Evans and Knopf 1993).

At Malheur L., fed on suckers in 1875 (Bendire 1876), on cyprinids (chub) in 1918 (Willett 1919). By 1952 carp was the dominant fish in Malheur L. Currently, chub are still present, but suckers are not likely because of carp infestation, carp now regular and important food item (*GLI*). At Malheur NWR, size and distribution of carp population determine presence of pelicans; numbers of birds decrease when carp are too big and significantly more nests occurred during years when lake levels decline, which concentrates fish (Ivey, Cornely, Paullin, and Thompson unpubl. ms.). These birds feed primarily on chub in the Klamath and Goose L. basins, and white crappie in Warner Basin (Smith et al. 1984). To rear one young to fledging takes an estimated 182 lbs (68.1 kg) of fish (Evans and Knopf 1993).

**Seasonal Activity and Behavior:** First arrives in Klamath Basin in early Mar (Gilligan et al. 1994). Average arrival date at Malheur NWR is 24 Mar with first nearly a month earlier (Ivey, Herziger, and Scheuering 1998); average at Warner Basin is 2 Apr (Stern 1988). Low nesting site tenacity; adapts to take advantage of changing food sources due to fluctuating

water levels and other factors (Evans and Knopf 1993). Nesting season begins Apr or May, and during this time, birds are highly sensitive to disturbance; human visits result in reduced nesting success or desertion, leaving eggs and young exposed to predators and weather (Marshall et al. 1996). The parent not incubating may make regular trips up to about 60 mi (100 km) and be gone for 2-3 days early in incubation period (McMahon and Evans 1992). Local examples include Warner Basin birds flying to Malheur L. to feed on carp (Puchy and Marshall 1993). After 3 wk young gather in groups called "pods," which spread out during day to be fed by parents and huddle to save energy in cold weather (Evans and Knopf 1993). Most young fledge by Aug (Smith et al. 1984).

Migrating pelicans make interesting travels. Color-marked birds from Lower Klamath NWR, Clear L. NWR in California, and Pyramid L. in Nevada have been noted at Malheur L. (Thompson et al. 1979). In addition, a bird marked with a satellite transmitter in the summer of 1997 in Nevada stayed there for 2.5 mo, then flew to Burns, Oregon; to sw. Idaho; then Bear R. NWR, Utah (late Aug); and on to Wyoming (late Sep); Salton Sea, California (late Oct); and Mexico (early Nov) (Yates 1999). This bird was timed flying with a tailwind at 70 mph (113 kph). Another bird from the Nevada project was next located at Malheur NWR; se. Idaho (mid-Sep); Great Salt L., Utah; Salton Sea; and Mexico (early Dec) (Yates 1999). Several color-banded birds seen west of the Cascades have come from the Stum L. colony in British Columbia; it is unknown what proportion of w. Oregon birds come from this or other sources (H. Nehls p.c.).

**Detection:** Easily located from great distances due to large size and white plumage.

**Population Status and Conservation:** In U.S., American White Pelicans were historically shot because they were blamed for decline of commercial fish stocks, even though prefers fish of low economic value (Evans and Knopf 1993). Also threatened from changing water levels and disturbance until early 1970s (Evans and Knopf 1993); number of colonies west of Rocky Mtns. declined from 24 to eight by 1984 (Paullin et al. 1988). Population now appears stable, with some recolonization of previous sites, although disturbance and habitat degradation from flooding and drought still a threat (Evans and Knopf 1993).

In Oregon, they nested at Malheur L. in late 1800s and were described by Bendire as "common" (Thompson et al. 1979). However, by 1932 there were no colonies in the state due to drought and draining. Next nesting occurred in 1934 and only at Upper Klamath L. (Gabrielson and Jewett 1940). In the 1940s, regularly recorded at Fern Ridge Res. in summer with numbers up to 100, but nesting not confirmed (Gullion 1951). About 40 remained there through the summer of 2001 (*ALC*). Malheur L. colony was used sporadically due to nest inundations from storms, receding lake levels, and predators, eventually abandoned in 1960 (Paullin et al. 1988), but several thousand birds continued to summer (Littlefield 1990a). Nesting resumed in 1985 after 25-yr absence, with seven pairs occupying new islands pioneered by other species (Great Blue Herons, Great Egrets, Snowy Egrets, Black-crowned Night-Herons, California and Ring-billed Gulls, and Caspian Terns) (Paullin et al. 1988). Nest numbers peaked at Malheur L. in 1988 with 2,045 pairs (Ivey, Cornely, Paullin, and Thompson unpubl. ms.). Estimated 200 pairs each at Upper Klamath L. (Gilligan et al. 1994) and Warner Basin (Stern 1988); nested at Summer L. W.A. for the first time in 1999 (eight pairs) (M. St. Louis unpubl. data).

Threats are many. Deaths at Malheur NWR have resulted from botulism and hitting powerlines, and in 1990 over 500 birds died primarily at Malheur NWR and the nearby Silvies R. floodplain, but necropsies could not determine cause (*GLI*). Starvation may have been possible, or perhaps Newcastle's Disease, diagnosed in other regions (*GLI*). Fluctuating water levels also a concern. For instance, chicks were stranded in 1992 at Pelican L. (Warner Basin) when the lake dried up (Puchy and Marshall 1993), and 325 nests at Malheur NWR were destroyed due to high water in 1998 (Ivey, Cornely, Paullin, and Thompson unpubl ms.). Disturbance can lead to colony abandonment; over 800 nests were abandoned at Malheur L. in 1988 after human trespassers visited one colony in canoes (Ivey, Cornely, Paullin, and Thompson unpubl. ms.). Size of nesting islands in Upper Klamath L. and Warner Basin is limited and erosion of islands has been a problem (Marshall et al. 1996). Listed as Sensitive Species in Oregon by ODFW (ODFW 1997) because of wetland loss, drought, and disturbance (Puchy and Marshall 1993).—*Caroline Herziger and Gary L. Ivey*

## Brown Pelican *Pelecanus occidentalis*

Commonly found along beaches and about estuaries, this large, ponderous bird is a conspicuous member of the summer coastal community, easily recognized by its large size, massive bill, and brownish plumage. Highly gregarious, it often forms large flocks; regularly observed foraging over the ocean just offshore. This species often joins mixed flocks of birds attracted to schools of small fish.

**General Distribution:** A coastal marine species that rarely occurs inland or far offshore. Nests on islands along Atlantic and Pacific coasts of N. and S. America from Maryland and s. California to Chile and Brazil.

Disperses after breeding to British Columbia and Nova Scotia, occasionally inland. Of seven subspecies only *P. o. californicus*, commonly referred to as the California Brown Pelican, occurs along the Pacific coast of N. America (AOU 1957, Shields 2002).

**Oregon Distribution:** Common spring, summer, and fall visitor along the coast. Formerly considered occasional in winter (Tweit 1988, Tice 1998a), but now occurs in small numbers in winter about Charleston and Coos Bay (Contreras 1998). Starting in the late 1990s, large numbers began concentrating inside the Columbia R. mouth in and around East Sand I. (D. Jaques p.c., D. Pitkin p.c.). The possibility of breeding on East Sand I. became evident in 2001 (Wright et al. 2002, D. Roby p.c.). This possibility was based in part on the following: early spring arrival (9 Apr), large numbers present from Jun to late Nov, presence of a breeding colony of cormorants that act as an attractant, abundance of anchovy as prey, breeding behavior including courtship displays and copulation, and finally nest building. This situation was repeated in 2002 (D. Roby p.c.). A possible colony here was unexpected considering the nearest breeding colonies are otherwise on California Channel Is.

Extralimital records follow: On 1 Dec 1985 a storm-driven immature was 13 mi (21 km) up Elk R., Curry Co. (Heinl 1986c). There are several records from the Willamette Valley north of Salem, including four on 14 Dec 1977 (Hunn and Mattocks 1978); three or more during Dec 1987 (Johnson 1988a); one on 21 Jul 1991 (Johnson 1992a); one on 24 Nov 1997 (Gilligan 1998); two on 3 Dec 1998 (Tice 1999b); a flock of 12 on 16 Aug 1996 (Gilligan 1997); a moribund bird in full alternate plumage in Milwaukie 4 Feb 2001 (Korpi 2001c); and an immature at a farm pond near McMinnville, Yamhill Co., 30 Oct 2001 (Contreras 2002b). On 13 Oct 1997, one was at McNary Dam 13 Oct 1997; it or another was near mouth of Deschutes R. on 19 Oct 1997 (Sullivan 1998a). None of these inland records appear to be storm related.

An immature found dead near Coos Bay, Coos Co., 19 Dec 1982, that was banded 3 May 1982 on w. Anacapa I., California (Mattocks and Hunn 1983a) is one of numerous Brown Pelican bands recovered in Oregon from birds banded at Anacapa I. and Gulf of California (D. Anderson p.c.).

**Habitat and Diet:** Brown Pelicans occur near shore and in large bays and river mouths; feed on fish taken from the surface by diving from up to 50 ft (15 m) overhead. Occasionally feed on invertebrates (Shields 2002) and offal around ports (Dan Anderson p.c.). Roost on sandy shores and offshore rocks. Wintering birds visit estuaries and offshore rocks (*HBN*), but also travel upstream from the Columbia R. mouth where D. Jaques and C. Strong (p.c.) observed 2,600 in Nov

2001. Gulls, especially Heermann's, often rob the pelican as it surfaces and prepares to swallow prey (Bent 1921, Jewett et al. 1953). The northern anchovy is now the primary food source for pelicans in the California Current System (Anderson and Gress 1982, Tyler et al. 1993). Brown Pelicans are opportunistic feeders, however, and will take what is available (Anderson and Anderson 1976). One Nov bird taken at Netarts, Tillamook Co., contained two surfperch (Gabrielson and Jewett 1940). Pacific herring and Pacific sand lance were the main species taken off Vancouver I., British Columbia, during the fall of 1997 (Burger et al. 1998).

**Seasonal Activity and Behavior:** Nonbreeding adult and subadult birds begin to reach Oregon during Apr in most years (Lillie 1998, HBN). Postbreeding adults arrive during May and Jun (Gilligan 1992b); juveniles during Jul and Aug (Anderson and Anderson 1976). Peak numbers occur during Aug and Sep. During late Aug 1982, 2,000 were on Tillamook Bay, Tillamook Co. (Evanich 1982a); 1,000 were there 24 Aug 1988 (Heinl and Fix 1989); and 1,800 were on the Curry Co. coast 13 Aug 1987 (Mattocks 1988a). Of these gatherings 60-75% were juveniles or subadult birds. However, the locations of these birds vary from year to year.

The main southward movement takes place during Nov most years, but during stormy, unsettled falls many leave during Oct. In mild falls with good food supplies, many linger through Dec. In some years many attempt to overwinter, especially along the s. Oregon coast (Evanich 1983b, Tice 1998a). High mortality can occur during Nov and Dec storms (Tweit 1988).

**Detection:** Conspicuous and easily recognized on water, beaches, and in flight; however, easily overlooked when sitting on offshore rocks and even more so in piles of driftwood.

**Population Status and Conservation:** This species was officially listed as endangered by the federal government in 1970 (35 *Federal Register* 16047), making it one of the first birds to be so listed. Reasons for the listing included widespread reproductive failures caused by eggshell thinning from DDT and other pollutants, as described in the recovery plan for the species (Anonymous 1983). Starting in the early 1970s, the situation began improving (Anderson et al. 1975, Anderson and Gress 1983). The total California Brown Pelican population estimate currently stands at 50,000-51,000 breeding pairs (Shields 2002).

Numbers of Brown Pelicans that move north up the Pacific coast vary. Variations have been attributed not only to the total population and reproductive success, but other factors working in combination, including oceanographic conditions in the California Current

(Tyler et al. 1993) and prey availability (Anderson and Anderson 1976, Jaques 1994). Increasing seasonal occurrence of Brown Pelicans north of California first became evident in 1972 coincident with the beginning of a warm water regime in the California Current System (Crowell and Nehls 1972a, Anderson and Anderson 1976, Jaques et al. 1992, Burger et al. 1998), and numbers have increased dramatically in recent years (Jaques et al. 1992, Wahl and Tweit 2000a).

Combined Oregon-Washington mid-Sep numbers increased from 4,194 in 1987 to 10,119 in 1991 (Jaques 1994). An aerial survey conducted 21 Sep 2001 from Cape Sebastian, Curry Co., northward through Oregon resulted in a count of 1,014 pelicans on rocks and coastal waters plus 5,081 at E. Sand I. inside the Columbia R. mouth (USFWS unpubl. data, D. Pitkin p.c.). Total Oregon bird numbers came to 6,095. A similar survey run the following day from the Washington-Oregon line north to Pt. Grenville, Grays Harbor Co., Washington, yielded 2,650 additional pelicans for a total of nearly 9,000 in the two states. Some sections were missed because obscured by fog. Pelicans at E. Sand I. had to be counted from aerial photos because most were visually undetectable in piles of drift logs (D. Pitkin p.c.).—*Harry B. Nehls*

## Family Phalacrocoracidae

**Brandt's Cormorant** *Phalacrocorax penicillatus*
Brandt's Cormorants nest colonially on offshore islands and mainland cliffs and are the most common of the cormorants on the Oregon coast in summer. In the breeding season males are easily distinguished by their intense blue gular pouches, displayed with a skyward pointing of the bill. They also have wispy white plumes along the side of their head and on their back, which show well against the solid black of the rest of their plumage. In bright light they have a green iridescence. During all seasons they can be distinguished from the two other Oregon cormorant species by buff-colored feathers that outline the gular region. Monotypic (AOU 1957).

**General Distribution:** Endemic to shores bounded by the California Current. Resident but exhibit short movements along the Pacific coast from Alaska to the Gulf Is. of Baja California. Monotypic (AOU 1957).

**Oregon Distribution:** Present all year. This cormorant nests along the entire Oregon coast where rocky islands or mainland cliffs are available for nesting. They recently colonized E. Sand I. near the mouth of the Columbia R. where 30-40 pairs nest on wood piling dikes associated with the rocky jetty (D. Craig p.c.). While they do not appear to have distinct migrations, movements are evident in summer when flocks are seen flying north low over the ocean beyond the surf line, and flying south in the fall (Fix 1987a, Anderson 1991b). Fewer are present in winter than summer (Scott 1973, H. Nehls p.c.). Confined mostly to waters within 14 mi (20 km) of the coast (Briggs et al. 1992).

**Habitat and Diet:** Marine and estuarine. In almost all situations, they nest on flat or sloped surfaces of rocky islands and headlands. The nest is built of seaweed and terrestrial vegetation taken near the nesting site. Cormorants are foot-propelled divers; during spring and summer Brandt's feed on a variety of fish from rocky areas and from mid-water levels. Scott (1973) recorded anchovies and smelts, rockfish, flatfish, and sculpins from adults collected off Newport. The diet at the Farallon Is. off San Francisco Bay is dominated by mid-water schooling rockfish and in British Columbia by Pacific herring (Wallace and Wallace 1998). Fall and winter diet is unknown from Oregon. Winter samples from 11 birds from Monterey Bay, California, found Pacific sand dabs, English sole, plain midshipman, and rockfish dominant (Talent 1984), and in British Columbia Pacific herring and shiner surf perch (Wallace and Wallace 1998). Prey fed to chicks is difficult to characterize as adults feed by regurgitation, passing small amounts of food into young chick's mouths, and as chicks age they insert their heads into parent's mouth and throat.

**Seasonal Activity and Behavior:** No detailed studies of breeding Brandt's Cormorant have been conducted in Oregon, so much of the following information is taken from known-age birds at the largest colony in the world at the Farallon Is. Timing for Oregon birds is likely to be a little later. Dates of arrival on the colony for males vary with age. The oldest males (9+ yr) arrive in mid- to late Mar, with peak of arrival for previous breeders from mid-Apr to early May. Inexperienced males do not arrive until later (Boekelheide and Ainley 1989). Females do not show such an age-related pattern with the exception of young females, which arrive last, in late May and Jun. Females breed at an earlier age (modal age 2 yr) than males (modal age 4 yr) but do not live as long (Boekelheide and Ainley 1989).

Brandt's Cormorants have an extensive behavioral repertoire, which is well summarized in Johnsgard (1993). The conspicuous advertisement display of males consists of the bird squatting on its nest with its breast almost touching the substrate, its tail cocked and spread, and the neck drawn back so the nape almost touches the back. In this position, blue gular pouch is maximally displayed and the white plumes are conspicuous. The male then rhythmically waves its wings causing the primaries to oscillate rapidly. The presence of females close to the nest causes an increase in this activity (Johnsgard 1993). Behavior associated with copulation involves even more displays, some of which include collection and deposition of nest material.

Five to 30 days after arrival (mean 13.6 days) the female begins to lay. Pale bluish-white eggs are laid at night or in early morning; normal clutch size is 3-4, but can range 1-6, with younger birds laying smaller clutches. Interval between each egg is 2.6 days. Older birds lay second clutches if first clutch is lost (Boekelheide and Ainley 1989). Nests with eggs observed from late Apr to mid-Jun (n=37) (OBBA), first eggs observed at Yaquina Head late May (Scott 1973). Eggs incubated for 30 days; chicks hatch naked 1 day apart and are dependent on parents for food and shelter. Hatching begins in early Jun (USFWS unpubl. data). Parents continue to brood chicks 5-10 days after hatching. Chicks exhibit crèching behavior; small chicks (10–25 days old) from adjacent nests huddle closely, particularly at night. As chicks age, they form larger crèches culminating in groups of fledglings involving chicks older than 25 days (Carter and Hobson 1988).

Fledging success variable and influenced by warm ocean water events (Ainley et al. 1995). On the Farallon Is. 1976-82 the number of chicks fledged per nest ranged 0.46-2.56 (Boekelheide et al. 1990c). During the 1982-83 ENSO birds at Bandon, Curry Co., had abandoned nesting by mid-Jul (Graybill and Hodder 1985), and only 0.56 chicks were fledged per nest at the colony north of Sea Lion Caves, Lane Co. (Hodder and Graybill 1985). Scott (1973) records 1.56 chicks fledged per nest in 1973 at Yaquina Head, Lincoln Co. On the Farallon Is. the "average" Brandt's Cormorant bred for 2-3 seasons and fledged 2-4 chicks over a lifetime. Prior breeding experience had little influence on reproductive success, and birds commonly skipped a breeding year (Boekelheide and Ainley 1989). Mate fidelity between seasons is low (Boekelheide and Ainley 1989).

Brandt's Cormorants continue to feed chicks after they leave the nest, sometimes into late Sep and Oct (Boekelheide et al. 1990c). At the end of breeding season some movement into estuaries occurs (Scott 1973). Fall and winter movements of Oregon birds are unclear, although there is a northerly movement (Contreras 1998) with a resulting increase in numbers in Puget Sound and British Columbia (e.g., Mattocks and Hunn 1980a, Fix 1987a). Of 161 nestlings banded at Three Arch Rocks NWR in 1939 and 1940, five were recovered, all within 1 yr of fledging. Two were found off Vancouver I., one in Puget Sound, one in n. Oregon and one in Santa Cruz, California (Bayer and Ferris 1987). Juveniles and some adults from the Farallon Is. move north at least as far as the Oregon coast at the end of the breeding season (Boekelheide et al. 1990c). Maximum life span is 18 yr (Wallace and Wallace 1998).

**Detection:** Brandt's Cormorants can readily be seen on breeding colonies from Apr to Aug. The easiest sites for viewing are Yaquina Head, Lincoln Co., Heceta Head, and Sea Lion Caves, Lane Co., and offshore rocks at Bandon, Coos Co. During the rest of the year they can be seen in estuaries and close to shore in the open ocean.

**Population Status and Conservation:** World population size unknown. Boekelheide et al. (1990c) listed 75,639 breeding pairs in N. America for 1965-79 but this includes only 79 pairs from Oregon. In 1979, 16,188 breeding birds were counted in Oregon (Pitman et al. 1985), and in 1988, 22,816 were recorded nesting (USFWS unpubl. data). In 1979 the largest colony was on the mainland at Sea Lion Caves, where 4,502 birds were counted. The second-largest colony was Bird Rocks, Clatsop Co., with 1,450 birds; a further 21 sites had more than 100 pairs (Pitman et al. 1985). In 1988 the largest breeding colonies were Bird Rocks with 3,100 breeders and the mainland colony at Heceta Head, Lane Co., with 1,840 birds (USFWS unpubl. data). Care must be taken in interpreting changes in numbers at specific sites as Brandt's Cormorant colonies vary from year to year in size and location (Boekelheide et al. 1990c). For example, in 1979 no birds bred at the mainland Heceta Head colony (Pitman et al. 1985), whereas in 1988 the mainland Sea Lion Caves colony had only 628 breeding birds (USFWS unpubl. data).

It appears the population is increasing in Oregon. Anecdotal evidence suggests that prior to the 1960s birds were shot in Oregon to reduce perceived competition with humans. This likely served to lower population numbers.

Disturbance on nesting colonies is the most serious threat to Brandt's Cormorants, which readily desert nests during incubation. Since 1994, Bald Eagles have caused abandonment of nests along the n. Oregon coast (R. Lowe p.c.). Seven eggs collected in Oregon in 1979 had low PCB and DDE concentrations (Henny et al. 1982). In Sept 1991 large numbers of Brandt's Cormorants in Monterey Bay, California, exhibited symptoms of domoic acid poisoning, and some birds died from the toxin produced by the diatom *Pseudonitzschia australis* (Fritz et al. 1992).—*Jan Hodder*

## Double-crested Cormorant

*Phalacrocorax auritus*
Adaptable and opportunistic, this species is the most abundant and widespread of the three cormorant species found in Oregon, occurring inland and on the coast (Brand 1982, Harrison 1983). Adults have deep, coppery feathers, bordered in black, that glisten with a green iridescence and offset a rich orange throat atop a

long curved neck. The bird earns its name from plumes, ranging from white to black, that crown either side of the head during the breeding season (Gabrielson and Jewett 1940, Brand 1982, Harrison 1983, Hatch and Weseloh 1999).

**General Distribution:** Common breeder along the coasts of N. America, from the Aleutian Is. and Newfoundland, south to nw. Mexico and the Gulf coast. Inland, from Great Lakes west through the prairies of Canada and nc. U.S., with smaller numbers in mid-Atlantic and se. U.S. states. Some Pacific coast populations are resident, but considerable migration is evident among others, with dispersal south to se. California, Sinaloa and Nayarit, Mexico, and a portion northward in British Columbia. Four N. American subspecies, *albociliatus* occurs on the W. Coast south of s. British Columbia (AOU 1957), but the subspecies east of the Cascades needs to be determined (*MRB*).

**Oregon Distribution:** Common breeder in spring and summer at bays and estuaries, and on islands and cliffs along the coast and lower Columbia R. (Carter, Sowls, et al. 1995, R. Lowe p.c.). Smaller breeding populations are present along the upper Columbia and Snake rivers, and other large rivers, shallow lakes, marshes, and reservoirs in the s. Cascades and se. Oregon. Breeding sites for multiple years include Siuslaw and Umpqua river estuaries, Crane Prairie Res., Deschutes Co., Upper Klamath NWR, Malheur NWR, Pelican L. (Warner Valley), and Summer L. W.A. Migrant and wintering birds are uncommon to sometimes abundant along the coast, on larger rivers, lakes, and reservoirs in w. Oregon, particularly in the Portland area, the lower Columbia R., and c. and s. Cascades. A few winter east of the Cascades on unfrozen water bodies (Gabrielson and Jewett 1940, Thompson et al. 1979, Ryser 1985, Gilligan et al. 1994, Contreras 1997b, Hatch and Weseloh 1999), but generally considered absent in winter from se. Oregon (Brand 1982, Stern 1988, Littlefield 1990a, Gilligan et al. 1994, Contreras and Kindschy 1996, Marheine et al.

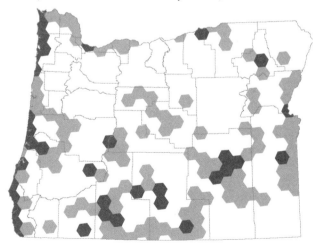

unpubl. data, OBBA, ONHP 1999). However, M. Denny (p.c.) reports small numbers winter along the Snake R. from Farewell Bend southward, Malheur Co. Occasional spring and summer transient in ne. Oregon (Evanich 1992a).

**Habitat and Diet:** The Double-crested Cormorant breeds in colonies. Prefers isolated sites on or adjacent to water, but rarely seen far from land (Hatch and Weseloh 1999, ONHP 1999). On the coast, nests are perched on pilings, channel markers, rocks, and cliff ledges; in conifers at river mouths; and on bare ground, sand, and mats of emergent vegetation on islets, dredged material, and offshore rocks (*SEM*). Freshwater rookeries are found on floating bog marshes (J. Hainline p.c.), nestled among scattered greasewood shrubs and desert saltgrass on lake islands, and in hardstem bulrush stands (Thompson et al. 1979, Ryser 1985, Stern 1988, Malheur NWR files, *DBM*). Before the 1983 floods at Malheur L., nesting took place in hardstem bulrush stands. By 1983 all nesting cormorants had moved to tree sites (G. Ivey p.c.). As tree-nesting options diminished, they later moved to island colonies, nesting with pelicans, gulls, and terns. Nests are assembled from sticks, twigs, grasses, weeds, and tules, topped by a profuse layer of guano (Gabrielson and Jewett 1940, Siegel-Causey and Hunt 1986). New nest may be built, or a used one refurbished by adding a tier of fresh material (Ryser 1985).

Throughout the year, roost on rocks, pilings, and other protruding structures. D. Lusthoff (p.c.) has observed 150-200 roosting in winter on power line towers at The Dalles Dam, Wasco Co.

Seldom forage in the ocean (D. Fix p.c.). These cormorants feed opportunistically on aggregated or readily caught fish (Brand 1982, Roby et al. 1998, Hatch and Weseloh 1999). Foraging flocks may form lines and circles to herd and condense prey aggregations (Nelson 1979). During daylight, dive from surface in pursuit of prey, using totipalmate feet to propel underwater for a peak recorded

*Double-crested Cormorant*

duration of 70 sec (Lewis 1929, Mendall 1936, Palmer 1962, Ryser 1985, Johnsgard 1993, King et al. 1995). Known to dive as deep as 72 ft (22 m), but most forage in water <33 ft (10 m) deep (Palmer 1962, Knopf and Kennedy 1981).

**Seasonal Activity and Behavior:** Birds arrive as early as Feb at Malheur (Malheur NWR files) and Upper Klamath breeding grounds (Gilligan et al. 1994); nesting generally commences in Apr (Gabrielson and Jewett 1940, OBBA, Roby et al. 1998). First breed at 2-3 yr, laying 2-8, usually 3-5 pale-blue eggs (Palmer 1962, Brand 1982, Siegel-Causey and Hunt 1986, Roby et al. 1998). Frequently nest alongside White Pelicans and Great Blue Herons in s. Oregon (*SEM*). Both sexes participate in nest building, incubation, and feeding of young (Ryser 1985); egg dates are Apr-Jul (Palmer 1962, Harrison 1983, Roby et al. 1998). Renesting is common following loss of clutch or brood to disturbance (ONHP 1999).

Young are altricial, fledge at 6-8 wk, and are fully independent at 9-10 wk (Reilly 1968, Johnsgard 1993, Hatch and Weseloh 1999). There is some migration, beginning in Aug (Bent 1922, Reilly 1968, Bayer and Lowe 1995), to the Columbia R. (east to Tri-cities area), n. Willamette R., freshwater sites west of the Cascades, and marine locations extending from British Columbia to the Gulf of California. Departures peak mid-Sep to mid-Nov; birds concentrated in winter areas by Dec (Bent 1922, Reilly 1968, Bayer and Lowe 1995).

**Detection:** Easily observed at many breeding colonies, though some require a boat or plane to census. Birds nesting in trees can be identified by dead or decaying limbs and underbrush caused by accumulations of guano. On the water, this species often resembles a periscope with only its long neck and up-tilted head visible above the surface (*SEM*). Migrant flocks often seen along coast Sep-Nov (Bayer and Lowe 1995).

**Population Status and Conservation:** The Double-crested Cormorant has flourished over the past two decades after being almost decimated throughout its N. American range (Hatch 1995, Krohn et al. 1995). Recent population expansion can be attributed, in part, to its efficiency in adapting to anthropogenic environments, such as dams, dredged material, hatcheries, and aquaculture facilities (Nettleship and Duffy 1995). In addition, reductions in pollutants, persecution, and disturbance have resulted in dramatic increases in Double-crested Cormorants since the mid-1970s (Carter, Sowls, et al. 1995, Roby et al. 1998). About 6,249 pairs nested in coastal Oregon in 1991-92 compared to 989 in 1979 (Carter, Sowls, et al. 1995). East Sand I. in the Columbia R. estuary supports the largest colony on the Pacific coast of

N. America peaking at 7,242 breeding pairs in 1999 (Collis et al. 1999). A complete census of marine populations has not been conducted since 1992, but current observations indicate that total coastal numbers have risen slightly (KC). Interior populations fluctuate with water levels, inclement weather, and disturbance. Malheur NWR averaged 60 breeding pairs/yr in the 1970s, 629 in the 1980s, and 307 during 1990-98 (Thompson et al. 1979, Malheur NWR files, G. Ivey p.c.). Upper Klamath NWR averaged 675 pairs in the late 1980s, decreasing slightly to 535 in the 1990s (no estimates available for 1995, 1996, or 1998) (Klamath Basin NWR unpubl. data, J. Hainline p.c.). Summer L. supported 35-60 pairs/yr in the early 1990s, and 16-36 1998-2000 (Summer L. W.A. files). Crane Prairie had 53 pairs in 1998 and 61 in 1999 (C. Heath p.c.).

As its numbers increased, so did concern for its impact on commercial and recreational fisheries. Studies conducted in Oregon concluded that avian predation can have an effect on survival of juvenile salmonids and, potentially, the recovery of listed salmonid stocks, but ocean conditions, habitat modifications, harvest, and hatchery stock release practices are also contributing factors (Brand 1982, Bayer 1989b, Schaeffer 1992, Independent Multidisciplinary Science Team 1998, Roby et al. 1998).

Killing cormorants has been illegal under federal law since 1972 (Oregon State Game Commission 1971). In 1988, ODFW granted commercial boats permits to harass cormorants at Nehalem and Tillamook bays to reduce predation on hatchery-released salmon and steelhead smolts (Bayer 1989b). In 1995, the Oregon Legislature legalized the harassment of cormorants in Tillamook Co. estuaries (ORS 498.247, Carter, Sowls, et al. 1995).—*Shelley Espeland Matthews, David P. Craig, Ken Collis, and Daniel D. Roby*

## Pelagic Cormorant *Phalacrocorax pelagicus*

Seemingly misnamed, Pelagic Cormorants are rarely seen far from land. During the breeding season the distinct white flank patches contrast markedly with their black plumage. In bright light the slender neck has a purple iridescent sheen, and the back shines green accenting white filoplumes. They nest on cliff ledges.

**General Distribution:** Breeds from the s. Chukchi Sea south through the Bering Sea to the Aleutian Is., and along the Pacific coast to n. Baja California, and from Wrangel I. east along the Arctic coast of Siberia to the Bering Strait and south to n. Japan. Winters from the Aleutian Is. south to c. Baja California and from Kamchatka south to China. Two subspecies; *P. p. resplendens* occurs in Oregon (AOU 1957).

**Oregon Distribution:** Common year round along the entire coast; not found away from salt water. Breeds where rocky cliffs with ledges are present; does not breed along the sandy coast from Coos Bay to Florence. The colony at Cape Foulweather, Lincoln Co., is one of the largest on the Pacific coast with up to 925 breeding birds (R. Lowe p.c.), but most breeding colonies tend to be much smaller. This species is seen in estuaries during all months; no distinct migrations. Not found inland away from salt water.

**Habitat and Diet:** Nearshore marine and estuarine. They nest in loose colonies on ledges on vertical cliffs on rocky islands and headlands. In British Columbia and Washington they have habituated to nesting on human-made structures such as lighthouses, docks, pilings, and bridges (Hobson and Wilson 1985), but such nesting is rare in Oregon and occurs only on the Yaquina and Alsea Bay bridges. Nest is constructed of terrestrial vegetation and algae cemented to the cliff ledge with excrement; both sexes contribute (Hobson 1997). Some are built inside caves. In British Columbia some colony sites not used each year (Carter et al. 1984). Roost on islands, cliffs, logs, pilings, and sandbars (Hobson 1997). Occasionally range several miles up large estuaries.

Foot-propelled divers, they have been caught in fishing nets set at 100 ft (35 m) (Johnsgard 1993). Average dive time at Barkley Sound, British Columbia, was 35 sec (Hobson and Sealy 1985). Diet is particularly difficult to determine as birds capture and often swallow prey underwater. Likewise it is difficult to determine chick diet as chicks feed by placing their heads into the adult's mouth and throat to eat regurgitated food. Little information is available for Oregon populations. Stomach contents of 12 adults from Newport were empty or contained cottids (Scott 1973). Contents of six stomachs from Washington contained flounder, sculpin, herring, and smelt (Jewett et al. 1953). In California, nesting birds feed on non-schooling fish and decapod crustaceans in rocky reef or sand/mud areas within a few miles of nest site (Ainley et al. 1981). No data on nonbreeding season diet for any area, and no information on chick diet in Oregon. In British Columbia, gunnels, sandlance, clingfish, sculpins, pricklebacks, and shrimp were fed to chicks (Robertson 1974). When food is abundant, participate in multispecies feeding flocks initiated by gull activity (Scott 1973, Chilton and Sealy 1987). Adults and fledging-age chicks regurgitate a pellet of indigestible materials almost daily, usually just before dawn. The presence of nematodes in the pellet suggests regurgitation may function as a parasite control (Ainley et al. 1981).

**Seasonal Activity and Behavior:** Detailed studies of breeding biology throughout its range are rare as only in a few locations can data be easily collected. One such location is a colony approximately 1 mi (1.6 km) south of Sunset Bay, Coos Co. (named the OIMB colony), where University of Oregon students have been monitoring an average of 34 nests for the past 26 yr. Breeding success at this colony and others on the Pacific coast is variable (Hodder and Graybill 1985, Boekelheide et al. 1990a).

Breeding begins when birds are 2-3 yr of age (Johnsgard 1993). At the OIMB colony birds start to establish nest sites in late Mar, and nesting material is present by late Apr. At five other sites, nest building was noted from late Mar to early May (OBBA). Breeding displays involve head, neck, and wing movements (Johnsgard 1993, Hobson 1997). Timing of nest building completion is variable and ranges from May to the end of Jun, but birds continue to add to the nest until fledging. Copulation occurs on nest site (Hobson 1997).

Laying is asynchronous and timing varies considerably between years, influenced by prey availability (Ainley 1990). On the Farallon Is. clutch initiation ranged from 2 wk to 3 mo, although more than 50% of eggs are laid within a 2-wk period (Boekelheide et al. 1990a). First eggs were observed at the OIMB colony in mid-May and Yaquina Head during the last week of May (Scott 1973), although at some other sites they have been seen as early as mid-Apr (OBBA). Eggs are laid at an average interval of 2 days, although the laying interval is longer for eggs laid later (Boekelheide et al. 1990a). On the Farallon Is., mean clutch size was 3.4, mode 4, and range 1-5 (Boekelheide et al. 1990a).

Eggs are incubated between the top of the feet and the breast feathers (Robertson 1974). Incubation begins with the first egg and averages 31 days; range 27–37 days (Johnsgard 1993). Both sexes incubate and 3.3-5.4 nest exchanges occur during the day; females incubate at night (Hobson 1997). When relieved from the nest, adult always bathes at sea and often bathes immediately after foraging bouts (Hobson 1997). Hatching at the OIMB colony begins in mid-Jun but has been seen in early Jun at other sites (OBBA), chicks hatch naked and rely on parental protection for warmth and defense. During the second week of nestling period parental protection is relaxed and chicks begin to exercise their wings. In situations where a number of nests are present on a ledge, 2- to 3-wk-old chicks from different nests will group together in a crèche while adults are absent. By the third week they can swim or dive if chased into the water and may make short trips beyond the nest if conditions allow (Hobson 1997). Parents forage close to the nest site. At the OIMB colony adults feed the young several times during the day with a peak of feedings in early morning.

Fledging success in the 26-yr period was quite variable at the OIMB colony; averaged 1.88 chicks/nest and ranged 0-3.11 chicks/nest. Years in which breeding success was lower than normal at this site were associated with positive sea surface temperature anomalies. Chicks depart the nest when 40-50 days old (Boekelheide et al. 1990a) and often remain at a communal roosting area where they are fed by the parents sometimes as late as early Oct (Hobson 1997).

Breeding season can continue through Aug. Postbreeding local dispersal occurs and there is some movement into estuaries (Scott 1973); there is little evidence of any seasonal migration. Limited returns from banded birds along the Pacific coast indicate they do not disperse far from their natal site (Hobson 1997). Some birds return to breed on the same colony, but others change colonies between years (Carter et al. 1984). Oldest known bird was from British Columbia at 17 yr, 10 mo of age (Clapp et al. 1982).

**Detection:** During breeding season, nests are visible along the entire rocky coastline where suitable small ledges are available. Once chicks are present the nests are visible from afar by streaks of white guano on the rock below nest site. Sites at which breeding birds can be easily seen are Coquille Point Rocks and Bandon, Curry Co., Yaquina Head, and Haystack Rock at Cannon Beach, Clatsop Co. Easily seen foraging in estuaries and nearshore.

**Population Status and Conservation:** The world population is undocumented because the size of the Asian population is unknown. The estimated N. American population is 130,000 adults (Johnsgard 1993), the majority of which are in Alaska. In Oregon 6,496 breeding birds were estimated in 1979 with over half in the southern third of Oregon (Pitman et al. 1985), and in 1988, 11,000 breeding birds were counted (USFWS unpubl. data).

Pelagic Cormorants are sensitive to human disturbance. They flush from the nest, leaving their eggs vulnerable to predation by American Crows, Common Ravens, and gulls and will often abandon nesting attempts or shift locations. In 1979, four Pelagic Cormorant eggs had the lowest organochlorine levels of the three species of cormorant in Oregon (Henny et al. 1982). Nest sites can be flooded by storm waves and in Alaska heavy rains caused chick mortality and nest destruction (Hatch and Hatch 1990).—*Jan Hodder*

## Family Fregatidae

### Magnificent Frigatebird *Fregata magnificens*

This species breeds from Florida and the Gulf of Mexico, and from Baja California southward through most of coastal S. America. It ranges north to N. Carolina and n. California, and sporadically to New

England and s. coastal Alaska. It is casual elsewhere in the U.S. First Oregon record was a bird found dead at Tillamook Light, Clatsop Co., 18 Feb 1935 (Gabrielson and Jewett 1940, specimen No. 9530 SDNHM and its skeleton is No. 322266 at USNM). One was at Gold Beach, Curry Co., 24 Jul 1979 (OBRC). An immature was at Florence, Lane Co., and Yaquina Bay, Lincoln Co., 29 Jul 1983 (OBRC); a juvenile was photographed at Charleston, Coos Co., 7-11 Mar 1987 (Heinl 1987a, Watson 1989); an adult male was at Yaquina Bay 18 Aug 1987 (Heinl 1988a); and a juvenile was at Cape Arago, Coos Co., 1 Feb. 1992 (OBRC). An immature at Portland, Multnomah Co., 4 Jun 1987 was possibly ship assisted (OBRC). Monotypic (Bourne 1957).—*Harry B. Nehls*

# Order CICONIIFORMES
## *Family Ardeidae*

**American Bittern** *Botaurus lentiginosus*
Skulking through wetlands, the American Bittern is rarely seen, for it has an extremely slow and stealthy walk, and when a threat approaches it freezes and mimics marshland plants with upright posture and beak pointed skyward. These behaviors combined with its cryptic plumage effectively camouflage the bird. However, it is occasionally seen in flight, and its low, gurgling song, described by Gibbs et al. (1992a) as *pump-er-lunk* or *dunk-a-doo* can be heard over long distances. Pleistocene fossils of what appears to be the same species have been found at Fossil L., Lake Co. (Gibbs et al. 1992a).

**General Distribution:** Nests primarily south of 55°N latitude from Canada south to California, Nevada, Utah, New Mexico, Colorado, Nebraska, Missouri, Kentucky, and Virginia (Gibbs et al. 1992a). Winters mainly on southern coastal plain areas where temperatures remain

above freezing, concentrated in the west at Salton Sea and San Joaquin Valley of California (Gibbs et al. 1992a). Monotypic (AOU 1957).

**Oregon Distribution:** Uncommon to fairly common breeder east of the Cascades, including Warner Basin, Malheur NWR, Summer L., Klamath Basin (Summers 1993a), Sycan Marsh (Lake Co.), and the Blue Mtns. (OBBA). Rare migrant in Malheur Co. (Contreras and Kindschy 1996); also noted at mountain lakes east of the Cascades; Goose L., Lake Co.; near Fossil, Wheeler Co.; and near Pendleton, Umatilla Co. (OBBA). In w. Oregon, uncommon along the coast, Sauvie I., and the Willamette Valley (Contreras 1998, OBBA); also noted in spring in ne. Jackson Co. (OBBA). Wintering birds found throughout the state except for Blue Mtns. (Puchy and Marshall 1993); rare to uncommon on coast (Brown et al. 1996, Contreras 1998), and very rare east of the Cascades (Gilligan et al. 1994), including Malheur NWR (Littlefield 1990a). Casual in all seasons in Umpqua Valley (Hunter et al. 1998).

**Habitat and Diet:** Entire life cycle depends on wetlands, with abundance positively correlated with wetland size (Gibbs et al. 1992a). The American Bittern nests in freshwater marshes with emergent vegetation; at Malheur NWR in Baltic rush, bulrush, burreed, cattail, common reed, creeping wildrye, and Nevada bluegrass (Foster 1985, *GLI*). Water depths for nests are shallow, may dry up underneath (Foster 1985). Occur, but not necessarily nesting, in extensive reed canarygrass at Fern Ridge Res., Lane Co. (*MGH*) and in the marsh on Cedar Canyon Rd. west of Banks, Washington Co. (*DBM*). Molting birds may move to isolated areas such as islands (Dechant et al. 1999). No detailed diet information available from Oregon, but nationally documented feeding on insects, fish, crustaceans, frogs, snakes, and small mammals (Gibbs et al. 1992a).

**Seasonal Activity and Behavior:** Average arrival date at Malheur NWR is 4 Apr, but noted as early as

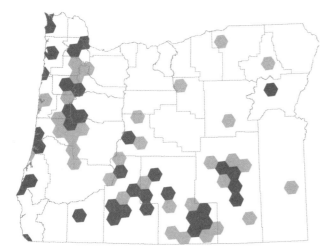

*American Bittern*

22 Feb (Ivey, Herziger, and Scheuering 1998). Well-known low-frequency song is produced by contortions that inflate the esophagus, which is used for territorial signal and to attract a mate (Gibbs et al. 1992a). Male displays white plumes rising from scapulars and extending down back during courtship (Brewster *in* Bent 1926). Solitary nester, with initiation dates varying from early May to late Jun at Malheur NWR (Foster 1985, Littlefield 1990a). Young leave the nest when only a few days old (Jewett 1919); fledglings observed 5 Jun to 29 Aug (n=3) (OBBA). Migration starts in Jul, peaks in late Sep at Malheur NWR (Littlefield 1990a). Feeds alone, standing motionless and waiting, or moving almost imperceptibly until final dart (Gibbs et al. 1992a).

**Detection:** Best located by song in spring or watching for flying birds, especially near dusk. Sometimes confused with immature Black-crowned Night-Heron. The marsh near Cedar Canyon Rd., Washington Co., is a favorite place to observe this species (D. Lusthoff p.c.).

**Population Status and Conservation:** Threats on a national scale include loss of wetlands (over half in the contiguous U.S. have been lost), eutrophication, silt-ation, chemicals, and human disturbance (Gibbs et al. 1992a). National management concerns include protecting wetlands and adjacent uplands (Dechant et al. 1999). First reported in Oregon by Newberry in 1857, believed to be common by Gabrielson and Jewett (1940). Stern (1988) described status as uncommon in Warner Basin, uncommon at Malheur NWR as well (*GLI*). Numbers declining in this region, and therefore American Bitterns are listed as Nongame Species of Management Concern by USFWS (1995a).—*Caroline Herziger and Gary L. Ivey*

## Least Bittern *Ixobrychus exilis*

Inconspicuous and a master of stealth, the Least Bittern inhabits densely vegetated deep-water marshes, making observations rare and difficult; its call is often the only way to detect this secretive species. The smallest of herons, its long neck and legs make it appear larger. Crown, back, and tail of male vivid greenish black; purple-chestnut on female. Neck, flanks, and underparts brown and white; wings buff.

**General Distribution:** Breeds locally in w. N. America in s. Oregon, interior and s. coastal California, s. Arizona, and Baja California; in c. and e. N. America from s. Manitoba, N. Dakota, east to ne. U.S.; and south to Gulf and Atlantic states to s. Florida, Rio Grande Valley, Mexico, and S. America to e. Brazil and n. Argentina. Winters in areas south of prolonged winter frosts, including Atlantic coastal plain, Gulf states, lower Colorado R., and Baja California into Mexico and S. America. Five subspecies; *I. e. exilis* occurs in N. America (Dickerman 1973).

**Oregon Distribution:** Rare spring and summer resident in larger freshwater marshes of e. Oregon. Field notes in *Oregon Birds* and *American Birds* 1971-97 report five records for Upper Klamath L., at Odessa, Rocky Point, and Malone Spring, and two for Klamath Marsh NWR, 10 for Malheur NWR. Also, 5-6 at Crump and Hart lakes, 1993-98, Lake Co. (W. DeVaurs p.c.). Very rare spring through fall in the Rogue Valley (Boggs and Boggs 1961, Crowell and Nehls 1973a), and Willamette Valley at Fern Ridge Res., Lane Co. (Crowell and Nehls 1968c), Buena Vista near Ankeny NWR (Crowell and Nehls 1975d), and Baskett Slough NWR (Crowell and Nehls 1970c). Only recent breeding evidence in Oregon: pair 13 Jun 1975, Malheur L.; one adult and two immatures 30 Jun 1981, Malheur L. (Littlefield 1990a).

**Habitat and Diet:** At Upper Klamath NWR, Malheur NWR, and Klamath Marsh NWR, this species occurs in islands or edges of dense marsh vegetation of hardstem bulrush and cattail (F. Isaacs p.c., *DBM, KS*). At Crump and Hart L., Lake Co., it occurs in islands of cattails surrounded by deeper water, or at edges of marsh along shore with deeper water on at least one side of emergent vegetation (W. DeVaurs p.c.). Only one nest has been reported from Oregon, early 1900s, at Malheur L., in tall vegetation near open water (Willett 1919).

In e. California, 87.5% of 24 broods found in islands of dense emergent surrounded by open water 6 ft (2 m) in depth (Kirk 1995). In s. Florida, Iowa, and Maine, nests in stands of cattail, bulrush, and other coarse dense semiaquatic vegetation, sometimes sedge bogs, with nearly equal parts vegetation and open water (Weller 1961, Palmer 1962, Gibbs et al. 1992b). Nest is an elevated platform of aquatic vegetation and sticks built by male with overhead canopy in cattail and bulrush; average < 30 ft (10 m) from open water (Weller 1961, Gibbs et al. 1992b). In s. Florida, nests < 30 ft apart in highly productive areas or concentrated due to drought (Kushlan 1973).

In Iowa feeds on small fishes, snakes, frogs, tadpoles, salamanders, leeches, slugs, crayfish, insects, and occasionally shrews and mice (Weller 1961, Gibbs et al. 1992b). Of 93 stomachs in Florida, 40% contained small fish, 21% dragonflies, 12% other aquatic insects, and 10% crustaceans (Weller 1961). Highly insectivorous at peak nesting in Jun (Gibbs et al. 1992b).

**Seasonal Activity and Behavior:** Arrives in Oregon by late Apr and May (Rogers 1977, Evanich 1992c, Summers 1994b). Male and female equally help to rear young (Weller 1961, Gibbs et al. 1992b). Average

4.5 eggs per nest in Iowa (Weller 1961); 3.3 nestlings per nest in e. California (Kirk 1995). In Iowa and e. California young are capable of leaving nest for brief periods by age 7 days, abandons nest by 17 days; attains flight by 25 days (Weller 1961, Kirk 1995). Young observed flying mid-Jul at Malheur L. (Willett 1919). In Iowa builds foraging platforms; uses during late-incubation and brooding (Weller 1961). Repeated use of nest locations in e. California suggests nest-site fidelity (Kirk 1995). In se. Michigan forages by stalking along edges of open water side of emergent vegetation, grasping plants with long toes and claws, standing in place, walking slowly, swaying neck, and "wing flicking" (Sutton 1936). Burrow through dense vegetation, fly weakly away, or stand motionless and erect when encountered (Gibbs et al. 1992b). Latest dates in Oregon in Sep (Scott 1971, Kingery 1972a, Crowell and Nehls 1973a, Summers 1993b, Sullivan 1997a).

**Detection:** Detected by calls in appropriate habitat, especially from canoe or kayak (Gibbs and Melvin 1993, Kirk 1995). Low descending calls heard from Odessa Cr. channel, Upper Klamath L., in canoe, 100 yds downstream, 22 May 1983, 2000-2100 hr (F. Isaacs p.c.); similar calls tape-recorded at Malheur NWR (Watson 1983). Variety of calls in e. California and Iowa include dove-like cooing in spring, *gack-gack* call from nest, *tut-tut-tut* alarm call, an *ank-ank* call when flushed; weak peeps from just hatched to raspy cheeps and shrieks from young 7-40 days after hatch (Weller 1961, Gibbs et al. 1992b, Kirk 1995). In Maine and New York did not respond to tape broadcasts early May, response peaked mid-May to late Jun; declined early Jul and most vocal 0800-1000 hr. (Swift et al. 1988, Gibbs and Melvin 1993). Gabrielson and Jewett (1940) suspected numbers in Oregon to be much greater because of their stealthy nature. Elusive; not detected despite numerous day and night canoe trips at Malone Spring, Rocky Point, and Odessa, at Upper Klamath NWR, 1994-2000 (*KS*), or at Malheur L., 1955-60, where air boat travel through marsh failed to flush any (*DBM*). Potentially mistaken for Green Heron or rail; some immature Green Heron mistaken for Least Bittern.

**Population Status and Conservation:** Thorough censuses are lacking, and modern status is not well known in Oregon. Fluctuating water levels at Malheur L. alter habitat year to year. During deeper-water years at Malheur NWR, it may be forced out of preferred habitat into peripheral habitat (Littlefield 1990a). Willett (1919), without details, reported only nest ever found in Oregon and the bittern as a common breeder at Malheur L. Present-day conditions different than early 1900s. Introduction of carp to Malheur L. in 1930s (*DBM*) undoubtedly impacted invertebrate and amphibian populations, but effects on Least Bittern are unknown. Reported to be adversely affected by marsh drainage, pollution, insecticide spraying, and other human activities (Palmer 1962).—*Kevin Spencer*

## Great Blue Heron *Ardea herodias*

This is one of the most widespread and familiar waterbirds in Oregon. Also known as "shidepoke" or "blue crane." It is the largest heron in N. America, standing approximately 4 ft (1.2 m) tall (Palmer 1962, Butler 1992). It is slate gray with a white crown, cheeks, and throat, rusty thighs and a uniformly yellow bill. Adults develop long gray-white plumes on chest, neck, and back during breeding. Juveniles have similar plumage but may be distinguished by absence of breeding plumes, a dark crown, and dark upper bill (Hancock and Kushlan 1984). Great Blue Herons frequent many habitats from shallow areas of marshes, lakes, streams, and oceans, where they feed on fish, amphibians, and aquatic invertebrates; to pastures and dry fields where they hunt for rodents, primarily during the winter (Palmer 1962, Hancock and Elliot 1978). Herons are highly adaptable and may be found hunting in urban settings such as ponds of city parks.

**General Distribution:** Resident populations from Maine to Florida and across to the W. Coast with the exception of high elevation mountains. Also found along the W. Coast of British Columbia and s. coast of Alaska, in Florida Keys, in coastal Mexico and in the Caribbean. Migrant populations generally breed in southern half of Canada from Manitoba to Quebec and south through the Great Plains states and nw. Minnesota, as well as the Caribbean, Greater Antilles, and Galapagos Is. Wintering populations in M. America and n. S. America, Haiti, Dominican Republic, and Cuba (Hancock and Kushlan 1984, Butler 1992). Six N. American subspecies: *treganzai*, *hyperonca*, and *fannini* occur in Oregon; *treganzai* and *hyperonca* were provisional synonyms of *A. h. herodias* by Browning

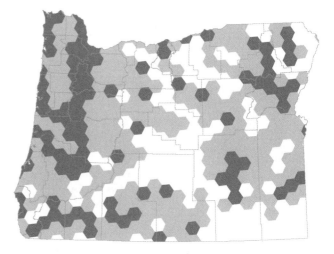

and Cross (1999), who remarked that additional study is needed.

**Oregon Distribution:** The Great Blue Heron is a fairly common to common resident and breeder along estuaries, streams, marshes, and lakes throughout the state. However, ice in winter often precludes presence or causes reduction in numbers in e. Oregon and at high-elevation lakes. Most common year-round in the Coast Range, Willamette Valley, and along the Columbia R. Also present at Cascade lakes and reservoirs spring through fall. *A. h. hyperonca* is the breeding subspecies in w. Oregon, *A. h. treganzai* breeds in e. Oregon (Gabrielson and Jewett 1940, AOU 1957). The subspecies which nests in the Cascades is unknown. *A. h. fannini*, which nests in Washington, has been taken in Tillamook Co. in Jan as per specimen in CMNH. Although nesting birds in the Portland area were identified as *fannini* by Griffee and Rapraeger (1937), specimens from the region are intergrades between *fannini* and *hyperonca*, but closer to the latter (Gabrielson and Jewett 1940).

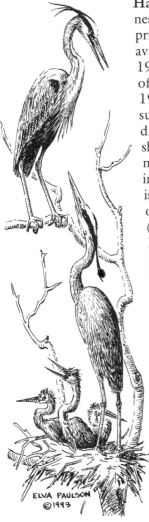

ELVA PAULSON
©1993

**Habitat and Diet:** Suitable nest locations are determined primarily by proximity and availability of food (Gibbs 1991, Butler 1992), level of disturbance (Vos et al. 1985), and suitability of substrate. Nests on many different substrates (e.g. shrubs, trees, river channel markers). Numbers of nests in coastal Oregon colonies is positively related to area of nearby foraging habitat (Werschkul et al. 1977, Bayer and McMahon 1981). Nest-site fidelity is weak, but fidelity to choice of tree within a colony is strong (Butler 1992). Nest trees include black cottonwood, Sitka spruce, red alder, western hemlock, canyon live oak, Oregon white oak, ponderosa pine, bigleaf maple, and Douglas-fir (Henny and Bethers 1971, Werschkul et al. 1977, English 1978, Ellingson 1988, Thomas 1997). Average height and dbh of nest trees were 79 ft (24 m) and 4.5 ft (1.36 m), but ranged 43-120 ft (13.2-36.6 m) and 1.5-6.0 ft (0.45-1.83 m), respectively (Henny and Bethers 1971, Werschkul et al. 1977, English 1978). Nest in the top third of the nest tree; height in black cottonwoods was 69-110 ft (21.0-33.5 m) (Henny and Bethers 1971). Occasionally nest in hardstem bulrush (Cornely et al. 1993), black greasewood (G. Ivey p.c.), sagebrush, Pacific willow, and on channel markers along the Columbia R. (Henny and Kurtz 1978). Birds observed using channel markers thought to have nested in nearby cottonwoods eliminated in 1968 when the John Day Dam was completed (Henny and Kurtz 1978). During the 1983-87 flood at Malheur L., most nesting switched from emergent vegetation to trees (Ivey, Cornely, Paullin, and Thompson unpubl. ms.).

Colonies are periodically abandoned, and birds relocate in nearby areas. Julin (1986) suggested that herons contribute to the decline of nest tree health by defecating on leaves or needles, causing abnormal tissue loss and blocking photosynthesis.

Great Blue Herons forage in salt- and freshwater environments, including shallow waters and shores of lakes, ponds, marshes, streams, estuaries, bays, and occasionally oceans (Palmer 1962, Hancock and Elliot 1978, Hancock and Kushlan 1984). Also in wet meadows, pastures, and dry fields (Palmer 1962, Hancock and Elliot 1978, Bayer 1981, Butler 1992). In coastal Oregon, forage in water <1.3 ft (40 cm) deep; peak of feeding activity occurs 3 hr before and after low tide (Bayer 1978). Along the Columbia R. and in the Willamette Valley, forage in quiet waters up to 2.0 ft (60 cm) deep. Little information available on preferred water depths east of the Cascades.

Diet varies locally. Feeds primarily on fish but also on amphibians, aquatic invertebrates, reptiles, mammals, and birds (Palmer 1962, Henny and Bethers 1971, English 1978, Hancock and Kushlan 1984, Bayer 1985a, Wolf and Jones 1989, Butler 1992, Thomas 1997, Thomas and Anthony 1999). In Yaquina Bay, prey included bay pipefish, staghorn sculpin, shiner perch, saddleback gunnel, snake prickleback, and starry flounder (Bayer 1985a). Along the Columbia and Willamette rivers, prey included American shad, brown bullhead, carp, cutthroat trout, largescale sucker, northern squawfish, Pacific lamprey, peamouth chub, warmouth, white crappie, bullfrog, and crayfish (Henny and Bethers 1971, English 1978, Thomas 1997, Thomas and Anthony 1999). Little information available on preferred prey sizes in Oregon; researchers in other areas report mean prey length 3.1 in (8 cm) (Hom 1983) and range 2.0-12 in (5-30 cm) (Butler 1992).

Two reported cases of death by asphyxiation due to ingesting prey items that were too large. Both cases involved Pacific lamprey that were 1.9 ft (57.6 cm) and 2.0 ft (61.9 cm) long and 1.6 in (4 cm) wide; both occurred in California (Wolf and Jones 1989).

**Seasonal Activity and Behavior:** The following information on life history is a compilation of data from Palmer (1962), Henny and Bethers (1971), Werschkul et al. (1977), English (1978), Hancock and Elliot (1978), Hancock and Kushlan (1984), Butler (1992), and Thomas (1997). Highly asynchronous nesters. They gather at colonies during Feb (late Jan to mid-Mar); larger colonies have earlier arrival dates. Males choose nest sites and court females. Upon arrival, initiate courtship as early as Jan; pair formation and nest building in mid-Feb. Displays may continue through early Apr for late arrivals. Unusual periods of low temperatures, high winds, and/or rain may delay courtship displays and nesting attempts. Eggs laid from late Feb through Apr, with most eggs laid in Mar. Both sexes incubate and feed young. Clutch size is usually 2-6 eggs. Incubation takes 28 days and eggs hatch from early Apr through the end of May. At least one adult is present at nest almost continuously until 3-4 wk after eggs hatch. During the first 1-2 wk after hatch, adults spend most time brooding. Three wk past hatch, adults stand within 13 ft (4 m) of nest. Nest attendance decreases by week 4 and by week 7 adults return to nests only to feed chicks. Young fledge from early Jun through mid-Aug, typically at 7-8 wk of age. Early chicks leave nest at approximately 81 days (64-91 days) while chicks from later nest attempts leave nest at an average of 67 days. Young birds return to nests to be fed for 1-3 wk after fledging. Few data available for Oregon on dispersal of fledglings. Hatch-year birds frequently seen in Cascade lakes and reservoirs Jul-Oct. Subadults begin breeding at approximately 2 yr. Based on band-recovery data, Henny (1972) suggests that few subadults return to their natal colony.

Daily activity is influenced by tides in coastal and Columbia R. colonies, with peak feeding around low tide (Bayer and McMahon 1981). D. Irons (p.c.) observed adults taking food at night at Crystal Springs, Portland, in the late 1970s and early 1980s. They presumably came from the Ross I. colony.

**Detection:** When hunting, they are easily detected in wetlands, estuaries, bays, rivers, and streams. Colonies in conifers difficult to detect due to dense foliage. Large colonies in deciduous trees easily detected during early spring prior to leaf-out.

**Population Status and Conservation:** Overall population and range in Oregon may be static, but nesting and foraging habitat has been reduced due to urban development and tree harvesting. A statewide survey conducted in 1972 by Nehls (1972) revealed about 2,000 active nests at 70 sites. A 1988 survey found a slight decrease in the number of active nests along the Willamette R. compared to a 1977 survey. However, 54% more colonies were identified, suggesting that fragmentation of older colonies was

occurring (Ellingson 1988). In 1991 Clint Smith (Oregon Dept. Forestry, unpubl. report) confirmed presence of 133 rookeries in the state with an additional 61 unconfirmed.

Willett (1919) reported a record 600 pairs at Malheur NWR in 1918. A new record was set during the flood years of 1983-87, when 688 nests were found. With a subsequent drought, they have shown a significant declining trend of –28.85/yr (Ivey, Cornely, Paullin, and Thompson unpubl. ms.). This correlated with Malheur L. elevations and surface area, which is likely related to shoreline feeding area.

Habitat loss is the most significant threat to current populations (English 1978, Ellingson 1988, Butler 1992). Species is extremely sensitive to disturbance during the early portion of the breeding cycle (courtship, pair formation, and egg laying). Colonies of any size should be avoided from Jan through Mar as disturbance during this period may result in colony abandonment.—*Carmen Thomas*

### Great Egret *Ardea alba*

Formerly called American Egret (Gabrielson and Jewett 1940), the Great Egret is much larger than Snowy or Cattle Egrets, and has a unique combination of yellow bill, black legs, and a cape of feathers draping beyond the tail in the breeding season. This attractive plumage nearly led to the extirpation of this species at Malheur NWR due to excessive market hunting. Malheur and Lower Klamath NWRs were set aside primarily to promote the protection and recovery of this species. Its former genus name *Casmerodius* means "adorned ornament"; nicknames include "angel bird" (Terres 1980).

**General Distribution:** Breeds on every continent except Antarctica. In N. America, found primarily in sc. Canada; Atlantic coastal states south to Gulf coast and Mexico; on the Pacific coast to San Francisco Bay and the Central Valley of California and Mexico; also in scattered inland locations. Winters along Atlantic

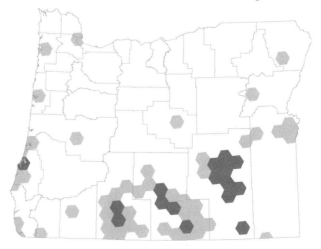

and Gulf coast states, and from s. Washington south through coastal and interior Mexico. Four subspecies, *A. a. egretta* occurs in Oregon (AOU 1957).

**Oregon Distribution:** As a breeder, most abundant east of the Cascades, primarily in Goose L., Harney, Warner, Summer L., and Upper Klamath L. basins, Silvies R. floodplain near Burns, and Chewaucan marshes and Garrett's Wetlands, Lake Co. (Stern 1988, Gilligan et al. 1994, Marshall et al. 1996, OBBA, M. St. Louis unpubl. data). Present year-round in the Klamath Basin, but more common Apr-Nov (Summers 1993a). Fairly common to abundant on the s. coast except during summer months when uncommon to fairly common (Brown et al. 1996, Contreras 1998). In summer, it is rare west of the Cascades, but is a regular local breeder around Coos Bay, Coos Co. (Rainboth 1990, Contreras 1998). In fall, occurs statewide, especially in the sc. and se. Willamette Valley and coast (Marshall et al. 1996). In winter, rare east of the Cascades and accidental at Malheur NWR (Littlefield 1990a), but locally common on coast and in the Willamette Valley (Gilligan et al. 1994); uncommon to fairly common in Umpqua Valley (Hunter et al. 1998). Presence in w. Oregon is a relatively recent phenomenon.

**Habitat and Diet:** Nests in riparian, marsh, and tree habitats (Puchy and Marshall 1993); at Malheur NWR in hardstem bulrush (Cornely et al. 1993), willows (Littlefield 1990a), poplars, and rarely on islands in greasewood with American White Pelicans (Ivey, Cornely, Paullin, and Thompson unpubl. ms.). In Coos Co. nests in trees with Great Blue Herons (Rainboth 1990, Marshall et al. 1996, Contreras 1998), in Warner Basin on islands sparsely vegetated with greasewood and saltgrass, also in cattails with American White Pelicans, Black-crowned Night-Herons, Double-crested Cormorants, and Great Blue Herons (Stern 1988). Nest numbers were significantly higher at Malheur NWR in wet years (Ivey, Cornely, Paullin, and Thompson. unpubl. ms.).

The Great Egret feeds in lakes, marshes, meadows, pastures, ponds, sloughs, streams, and urban areas (Puchy and Marshall 1993, Brown et al. 1996), in fall near Malheur L. in drying ponds and sloughs north of lake (Littlefield 1990a). No diet information available specifically for Oregon, but feeding on small fishes, frogs, lizards, snakes, mice, moles, crustaceans, snails, and insects documented elsewhere (Bent 1926); even observed consuming a sandpiper on the E. Coast (Repenning 1977).

**Seasonal Activity and Behavior:** Average arrival date at Malheur NWR is 26 Mar (Ivey, Herziger, and Scheuering 1998), 12 Apr at Hart Mt. N. Antelope R./Warner Valley (Stern 1988), the earliest of the egrets at both sites. Nests colonially from late Apr to Jun at Malheur NWR (Littlefield 1990a); in Coos Bay, nestlings were observed during the first week of Jul in 1988, and in and near nests 11 Jun 1989 (Rainboth 1990). Most young fledge by the end of Jul at Malheur NWR and then depart with adults, with peak numbers in Sep and early Oct; few remain by Nov (Littlefield 1990a). Early dispersants to interior sw. Oregon arrive in c. Douglas Co. in late Jul and are uncommon to fairly common by late Oct through mid-Jan, after which they decline in numbers and are casual by May (Hunter et al. 1998). Timing is generally similar farther north (*MGH*) with 50 or more present at Fern Ridge Res., Lane Co., in late summer and fall (D. Irons p.c.). Band returns from Malheur NWR nestlings indicated that migration and wintering areas are near Chandler, Arizona; Fallon, Nevada; Lissie, Texas; and Baja California, Jalisco, and Sonora in Mexico (Thompson et al. 1979).

**Detection:** Easily observed because of large size, white coloration, and habit of foraging in open areas.

**Population Status and Conservation:** The first colony was found at Malheur L. in 1875 by Bendire; also known to nest historically at Upper Klamath L. (Gabrielson and Jewett 1940). Described as "moderately common" breeder by Bendire (Thompson et al. 1979). Early reports attracted plume hunters to Malheur L.; colonies there were nearly destroyed in 1890s, but creation of Malheur NWR in 1908 helped protect them (Cornely et al. 1993). That year only two Great Egrets were noted in the entire Harney Basin, and nesting did not resume until 1912, population numbers varying with water conditions (Thompson et al. 1979). It is now a common breeder, particularly in Harney Basin. Number of nesting pairs increased greatly in the early 1980s when Malheur L. flooded, creating new habitat by increasing lake size and isolating trees; pairs numbered 605 compared to 1966-81 average of 235 (Ivey and Littlefield 1986). Peak number of nests 755 in 1983; most recently 331 were recorded in 1998, but 1980-98 data indicate a significant declining trend (Ivey, Cornely, Paullin, and Thompson unpubl. ms.). Considered common at Warner Basin, with over 140 nests in 1987 (Stern 1988), peak of 116 at Summer L. W.A. in 1994 (M. St. Louis unpubl. data). Eggs at Malheur L. had relatively high DDE contamination and eggshell thinning in 1980, with less nest success for those with higher amounts of contaminants (Cornely et al. 1993).

The Great Egret is a recent invader to w. Oregon. Up to 1940 Gabrielson and Jewett (1940) reported one bird in 1933 at Swan I. in downtown Portland for the only w. Oregon record. In 1958, one was found there on nearby Sauvie I. (Schultz 1959), and by the 1960s they had become regular at Sauvie I., Fern Ridge Res., and finally elsewhere in w. Oregon (H. Nehls p.c.).—*Caroline Herziger* and *Gary L. Ivey*

## Snowy Egret *Egretta thula*

Formerly called Brewster's Egret (Gabrielson and Jewett 1940), the Snowy Egret is intermediate in size between Great and Cattle Egrets, and much more common in Oregon than the latter. Adults have black bill and legs and bright yellow feet; immatures show yellow on the back of their legs. In the breeding season, plumes are present on head and breast, and curve upwards on the back. Bent (1926) described the species as "one of nature's daintiest and most exquisite creatures, ... the most charming of all our marsh birds." However, the beautiful appearance of the bird led to a demand for its plumage and subsequently a drastic population decline. Historically, it was hunted much more heavily than the Great Egret for fashionable hat plumes since it was more numerous and widespread, less shy, and the more delicate feathers were in greater demand (Bent 1926).

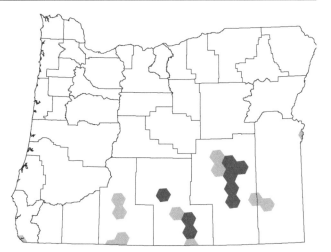

**General Distribution:** Found only in W. Hemisphere. Nesting distribution varies due to fluctuations of habitat, but includes the Great Basin, California, Gulf coast states north through Texas, Oklahoma, Kansas, and Arkansas; along Atlantic coast to Maine; locally in many western interior states; and extending south mainly along coasts through Mexico to Argentina and Chile (Parsons and Master 2000). Winters primarily from Gulf coast south, but also as far north as the Oregon coast (Evanich 1990). Two subspecies (AOU 1957); the western subspecies, *E. t. brewsteri*, occurs in Oregon (Palmer 1962, e.g. specimen [USNM] from Burns, Harney Co., 13 Aug 1957).

**Oregon Distribution:** Breeds regularly but in varying numbers primarily in e. Oregon, at Malheur NWR, Silvies R. floodplain near Burns, Summer and Upper Klamath lakes, and Warner Basin (Stern 1988, Evanich 1990, Marshall et al. 1996, OBBA, M. St. Louis unpubl. data). Uncommon to fairly common spring through fall in the Klamath Basin (Summers 1993a), occasional to uncommon in ne. Malheur Co. (Contreras and Kindschy 1996, Spencer 1999), rare in the Rogue Valley (Gilligan et al. 1994). On s. coast it is rarely found in summer, but occurs, primarily at Coos Bay in winter (Brown et al. 1996, Contreras 1998). Accidental in winter at Malheur NWR (Littlefield 1990a).

**Habitat and Diet:** Nests in riparian, marsh, and tree habitats (Puchy and Marshall 1993); at Malheur NWR in hardstem bulrush (Cornely et al. 1993) and shrub willows (Ivey, Cornely, Paullin, and Thompson unpubl. ms.); at Summer L. W.A. in hardstem bulrush (Marshall et al. 1996); at Warner Basin on islands sparsely vegetated with greasewood and saltgrass, and in cattails (Stern 1988). Of interest is nest vegetation at non-Oregon locations: blackberry, blueberry, cactus, grape, and holly (Parsons and Master 2000). At Malheur NWR, nest numbers were significantly higher in wet years, and correlated with Malheur L. elevations and surface area; lake elevation was a better predictor of nests (Ivey, Cornely, Paullin, and Thompson unpubl. ms.). The Snowy Egret forages in lakes, meadows, marshes, ponds, streams, and urban habitats (Puchy and Marshall 1993), in pastures on the coast (Brown et al. 1996). No food information available for Oregon, but like other herons it is an opportunistic feeder on earthworms, aquatic and terrestrial insects, crustaceans, snails, fish, frogs, snakes, and lizards (Parsons and Master 2000).

**Seasonal Activity and Behavior:** Average arrival date at Malheur NWR is 18 Apr with earliest record over a month earlier (Ivey, Herziger, and Scheuering 1998), at Hart Mt. N. Antelope R./Warner Valley average date is 2 May (Stern 1988). Usually nests yearly in mixed colonies with other egrets at Malheur L. and Silvies R. floodplain (*GLI*), with earliest record of 16 May, and season extending into Jun (Littlefield 1990). Nested later than Great Egrets in Warner Basin (Stern 1988). Young fledge in Jul and Aug at Malheur NWR; most birds have left by Oct (Littlefield 1990a).

A very active and visual feeder, it uses the greatest variety of foraging techniques of any heron to frighten prey into view (Parsons and Master 2000). This range of techniques is not correlated to different kinds of prey, as only a few food items make up a majority of their diet; rather, Snowy Egrets adapt to different environmental and social foraging conditions (Parsons and Master 2000). Behaviors include "tongue flicking" in areas where prey is widely dispersed with high water levels (Master 1991), "foot dragging" (dragging feet in water while in flight) when water levels are lower and fish less available (Kushlan 1972), and "hovering-stirring" (hovering near water while feet stir water or vegetation) (Kushlan 1972). Such techniques use a lot of energy, so they spend more time feeding than other herons (Parsons and Master 2000). Foraging birds serve as "local enhancement" species, attracting others to food aggregations, and benefiting themselves as well; feeding with other waders improves foraging success, and efficiency increases when with non-wader species (Parsons and Master 2000). Birds have been noted in other states stopping feeding to walk or fly to shore to defecate, then returning to feeding in water; it has been theorized that this is to reduce the chance of parasitic infection (Recher and Recher 1972).

**Detection:** Easily spotted because of white plumage, but can disappear in high vegetation.

**Population Status and Conservation:** Nationally, plumes for women's hats sold for $32/oz in 1886, twice the price of gold at the time (Parsons and Master 2000). Peak numbers were killed in 1903, but by 1913, the McLean Bill to forbid transportation of plumage finally passed, and the 1916 Migratory Bird Act protected migratory birds and their eggs (Parsons and Master 2000). Unfortunately, collecting continued longer in M. and S. America to meet European demand but recovery followed, with range expansion farther north on both coasts than before heavy hunting (Parsons and Master 2000). However, this species is currently declining in the northeast, midwest, and California due to wetland loss and competition with other species (particularly Black-crowned Night-Heron and Cattle Egret), and contaminants (Parsons and Master 2000).

In Oregon, it historically bred in the Harney Basin in late 1800s. Bendire considered species "moderately common" in 1877 along Silvies R., then the only known breeding site in the state (Gabrielson and Jewett 1940). Numbers were greatly reduced by hunters; by late 1800s no Snowy Egrets were noted (Thompson et al. 1979). Malheur NWR was established in 1908, but nesting did not resume in the Harney Basin (Malheur L.) until 1941 (three nests); population stabilized in 1950s, then fluctuated with water conditions (Thompson et al. 1979). When Malheur L. flooded in the early 1980s, numbers increased to 167 pairs, up 94% from a long-term average of 86 for 1966-81 (Ivey and Littlefield 1986). Eggshell thinning and pesticide residues were recorded in eggs at Malheur L. in 1981 (Cornely et al. 1993). Peak pair numbers occurred in 1985 (227), but have been much lower in recent years with none in 1997 and five in 1998. Data from 1980-98 indicate a significant declining trend (Ivey, Cornely, Paullin, and Thompson unpubl. ms.). This parallels a declining trend reported by Parsons and Master (2000) for many regions across N. America. Considered uncommon at Warner Basin with 10 nests in 1987 (Stern 1988); first nested at Summer L. W.A. in 1990, with peak of 15 in 1991 (M. St. Louis unpubl. data). Not recorded regularly west of the Cascades until the late 1970s (Gilligan et al. 1994). Currently

listed as Sensitive Species by ODFW (1997) because of limited distribution, wetland loss, and natural causes (Puchy and Marshall 1993).—*Caroline Herziger* and *Gary L. Ivey*

## Little Blue Heron *Egretta caerulea*
This small dark heron breeds from c. S. America northward to s. California, across the southern states, and north along the E. Coast of the U.S. Immature Little Blue Heron is white and very similar to immature Snowy Egret, making identification difficult at this age. Prior to the southward migration, a postbreeding dispersal brings many birds north of their regular range, but this does not fit Oregon records. It is sporadic and very rare in the Pacific Northwest (Rodgers and Smith 1995). An adult was photographed at Buena Vista, Marion Co., 16-18 May 1985 (Watson 1989); an adult was at Milwaukie, Clackamas Co., 18 Jun 1987 (OBRC); and a white immature was photographed at Brownsmead, Clatsop Co., 20 Jan to 11 Mar 1990 (Fix 1990c). Monotypic (Peters 1979 *contra* AOU 1957).—*Harry B. Nehls*

## Tricolored Heron *Egretta tricolor*
This small dark heron with white underparts breeds along the Atlantic coast and from the s. U.S. into S. America. Postbreeding dispersals bring it rarely, but regularly, to s. California during the fall and winter. It is casual farther north and in the Pacific Northwest. One individual, identified as *E. t. ruficollis*, was collected at Malheur NWR on 31 Oct 1945 (Scharff 1944). Others have not been identified to the subspecies level, including an adult in alternate plumage photographed at Finley NWR, Benton Co., 12-31 May 1976 (Watson 1989), and an adult in basic plumage photographed at Ona Beach SP, Lincoln Co., 11-13 Nov 1993 (Gillson 1994, Sherrell 1994b).—*Harry B. Nehls*

## Cattle Egret *Bubulcus ibis*
Cattle Egrets are the smallest of Oregon's three egret species, with short, stout neck and legs, and white body with orange-buff plumes on the head and nape in spring and early summer. They are named for their association with livestock, including cattle, horses, and other large mammals, consuming insects on their backs or stirred up by their hooves. Their range has expanded remarkably. Birds apparently spread to the Americas on their own from other continents using prevailing winds, and have been seen flying in extreme situations: from ships in the middle of the Atlantic and at 11,500 ft (3,500 m) (Telfair 1994).

**General Distribution:** Worldwide range primarily in temperate and tropical zones. Breeds in N. America from s. Canada south through U.S. to M. America and W. Indies (Telfair 1994). Winters mainly south of 32°N latitude where temperatures rarely fall below 39°F (4°C), including such locations as the Salton Sea, California, and the Gulf coast (Telfair 1994). The subspecies in Oregon probably belongs to *B. i. ibis* (AOU 1998) or less likely to *B. i. coromadra*, known as a visitor to Alaska (Gibson and Kessell 1992).

**Oregon Distribution:** Casual transient in spring in the Klamath Basin (Summers 1993a), rare at Malheur NWR (Littlefield 1990a). The least widespread of the state's egrets during the breeding season; rare breeder in Great Basin with only a few pairs occasionally nesting at Malheur NWR and elsewhere in the Harney Basin (Thompson and Paullin 1985, OBBA). In fall, it is uncommon east of the Cascades (Evanich 1992f) including Malheur NWR (Littlefield 1990a) and upper Columbia Basin near Milton-Freewater, Umatilla Co. (Sullivan 1998a). Also seen near Mitchell, Wheeler Co., in Oct 1993 (D. Lusthoff p.c.). Uncommon to rare on coast, very rare in western interior valleys fall through spring (Gilligan et al. 1994). Records from all coastal counties, most in Dec (Evanich 1992f), especially at Coos, Nehalem, Tillamook, and Winchester Bays and Coquille R. Valley (Evanich 1990).

**Habitat and Diet:** Recorded nesting in the Harney Basin in hardstem bulrush over approximately 24 in (60 cm) of water with Black-crowned Night-Herons, Eared Grebes, Franklin's Gulls, Great Blue Herons, Great Egrets, Snowy Egrets, and White-faced Ibis (Thompson and Paullin 1985). Also has nested in willows (Thompson and Paullin 1985). The Cattle Egret may compete for nest sites with other egrets or herons although arrives later, likely does not compete for food since different food and foraging methods (Burger 1978). Wintering birds on s. coast found in pastures, golf courses, and grassy areas, sometimes with livestock (Brown et al. 1996, Contreras 1998).

This species feeds in marshes, lowland meadows, and irrigated hay meadows (Puchy and Marshall 1993), also regionally in parks, dumps, fields being plowed (Telfair 1994), even with agricultural workers (Menon 1981). No analysis of foods of Oregon birds, but diet varies with habitat and prey availability nationally, includes grasshoppers, crickets, spiders, frogs, moths, flies on carrion, with many earthworms in fall, frogs important for chicks (Telfair 1994). Observed feeding on night crawlers near Milton-Freewater, Umatilla Co. 15 Nov 1997 (M. Denny p.c.). One adult with three chicks eats more than 55% of its body weight per day to feed itself and its young (Telfair 1994).

**Seasonal Activity and Behavior:** Average arrival date at Malheur NWR is 6 May, more than 2 wk later than Snowy Egrets, and 6 wk after Great Egrets (Ivey, Herziger, and Scheuering 1998). Gregarious, both nesting and feeding in groups of mixed species (Telfair 1994); however, in one study of nesting egrets and herons in the east, this species was twice as aggressive as any other, conflicts were more vigorous, and it won more interactions with other species (Burger 1978). It is the only species of heron able to breed in its first year (Kohlar *in* Terres 1980). Nesting occurred in Jun and Jul at Malheur NWR (Littlefield 1990a); chicks do not fledge until 1 mo old (Telfair 1994), usually in Jul at Malheur NWR (*GLI*). Birds from the Pacific states travel south to s. California and wc. Mexico to winter; route may have been initially established while traveling with other egrets (Telfair 1994). Last birds to migrate are young of that year, most will not return to natal area to breed (Telfair 1994). Latest departure date from Malheur NWR is 10 Oct (Littlefield 1990a), birds present on coast Oct-Apr, most records from 15 Nov to 10 Jan (Evanich 1992f).

**Detection:** Easily spotted during nonbreeding season, often with livestock. Difficult to locate the few breeding pairs in the state when present due to remoteness of nesting marshes.

**Population Status and Conservation:** Native to Portugal, Spain, India, Japan, Australia, and Africa, but now spread throughout most of the world. Rapid broadening of the species' range can be attributed to gregariousness, feeding and breeding adaptability, and especially the conversion of landscapes to livestock pastures (Telfair 1994). It was first noted in U.S. in Florida in 1941, no records in w. U.S. until 1960. Breeding now confirmed in all but six of the contiguous states (Telfair 1994). First record in Oregon at Sauvie I. in 1965, noted yearly since 1972 (Evanich 1992f), first nesting confirmed in 1982 near Lawen, Harney Co. (Thompson and Paullin 1985). A record number of six pairs were found nesting in Harney Basin in 1986, but none 1987-98. However, a few birds have been observed in the area almost annually, and it is likely nests were missed during surveys (Ivey, Cornely, Paullin, and Thompson unpubl. ms.). Species could be listed as sensitive if confirmed as a permanent breeder (ODFW 1997).—*Caroline Herziger and Gary L. Ivey*

## Green Heron *Butorides virescens*

Though less conspicuous than Great Blue Herons, Green Herons are well-established residents of w. Oregon. Distinguished by small size, glossy greenish-black cap and back, yellow legs, blackish-green wings, gray underparts, and dark red neck. One of

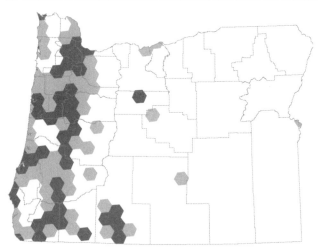

the few tool-using birds, Green Herons are experts at making and using baits and lures, such as bread crusts, mayflies, earthworms, sticks, and feathers, to catch fish (Davis and Kushlan 1994). The sixth edition of the AOU check-list (AOU 1983) considered the Green Heron conspecific with *B. striatus*, and gave it the name "Green-backed Heron," although *striatus* is more commonly referred to as the "Striated Heron." However, the current AOU check-list (1998) reverted to the original conclusion, which separated these two taxa, thus restoring the name "Green Heron."

**General Distribution:** Year-round resident along coastlines of extreme s. U.S. and California. Breeds throughout the U.S. except for drier areas of the interior west. Along the Pacific coast, breeds near marine or freshwater habitat from British Columbia south through Baja California, including western portions of Washington, Oregon, and California (Davis and Kushlan 1994). Three subspecies in N. America: *B. v. anthonyi* occurs in Oregon (*MRB*).

**Oregon Distribution:** Uncommon but regular migrant and summer resident throughout w. and sc. Oregon (Jobanek 1988). Detection of nests is difficult and breeding status uncertain in some areas due to secretive habits. Observations are reported regularly on the s. coast (Broadbooks 1946a, Bayer 1995a), in the southwest interior (Browning 1975a, Hunter et al. 1998, Browning and Cross 1999, Janes et al. 2001), in wc. (Graf 1946, Merrifield 1996b, Contreras 2002b), and in sc. (K. Spencer p.c.) Oregon. Accidental in the Cascades (Fix 1990a) and elsewhere in e. Oregon (McAllister and Marshall 1945, Littlefield 1990a, Contreras and Kindschy 1996). Rare in winter with most in sw. Oregon (Contreras 1997b, Contreras 1998, Hunter et al. 1998).

**Habitat and Diet:** Little is known of nesting habitat in Oregon. The Green Heron has been observed nesting in platforms of loosely fitting branches and sticks in willow trees up to 20 ft (7 m) above water

(K. Spencer p.c.). It has used Oregon ash and bigleaf maple for nesting in Eugene, sometimes 0.25 mi (0.4 km) from water (*ALC*). In habitat studies outside Oregon, found to prefer swampy thickets, riparian zones along creeks and streams, ditches, canals, ponds, lake edges, mudflats, parks, and harbors, avoiding open flats frequented by longer-legged herons (Davis and Kushlan 1994).

Little documentation of diet in Oregon. Elsewhere, diet consists mostly of small fish, supplemented with frogs, invertebrates of all kinds such as crayfish and aquatic insects, and occasionally terrestrial species, such as mice, snakes, and snails (Davis and Kushlan 1994).

**Seasonal Activity and Behavior:** Little is known of life history in Oregon. Noticeable influx of migrants in Oregon in mid-Apr. In w. Oregon, breeding and nest building start mid-Apr with observations of nest building, nest and eggs, birds entering or leaving a probable nest site, and nestlings 28 Apr to 25 Jun (n=21), and recently fledged young 5 Jun to 18 Aug (n=17) (OBBA). In Klamath Co., nesting behavior reported 13 May to 23 Jun (n=3) (K. Spencer p.c.).

**Detection:** Despite notoriously secretive habits, Green Herons can be found by repeatedly visiting appropriate habitat, especially riparian and swampy areas (*NKS*). In flight, they appear crow-sized, with conspicuously trailing orange legs and slow wing-beats (Forshaw et al. 1994). Their call, a *skow* or *skeow*, can be heard when in flight, sounding like a scolding squawk and often accompanied by a stream of white defecation. This habit is responsible for folk names such as "fly-up-the-creek," "shite-polk," and "chalk-line" (Davis and Kushlan 1984).

**Population Status and Conservation:** Increasing in the state since the 1920s (Jobanek 1988). Jewett established the first definite breeding record for Oregon in 1945 in Portland (Jewett 1945a). Gabrielson and Jewett (1940) called the bird "a decided rarity," citing observations of only one or two birds in Multnomah, Klamath, Josephine, and Linn counties. CBC data indicate small winter populations for Oregon; BBS trends show stable populations in w. Oregon over the past 30 yr with some range expansion in nw. Oregon (Sauer et al. 1999). Because of a higher intake of fish and fewer invertebrates compared to other herons, Green Herons tend to exhibit higher levels of pesticide residue contamination, which has been associated with eggshell thinning (Niethammer et al. 1984).—*Noah K. Strycker*

## Black-crowned Night-Heron
*Nycticorax nycticorax*

Although quite common in the U.S., the Black-crowned Night-Heron's nocturnal and crepuscular feeding habits can make it difficult to locate. Its habitat consists of marshes, lakes, rivers, and other wetlands, where it feeds mostly on fish. It is a thick-billed, medium-sized, stocky heron with relatively short neck and legs. Adults have a black back and cap which contrast with the pale gray or whitish underparts. Immatures have brown backs with large pale spots and heavily streaked underparts. A distinctive choking *squawk* call is often heard at dusk.

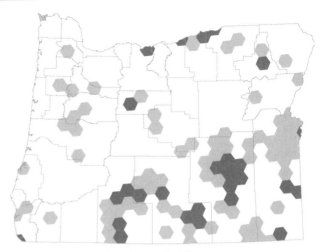

**General Distribution:** A cosmopolitan species that breeds on every continent except Australia and Antarctica (Davis 1993). In N. America breeds locally from Washington in the west through Quebec and New Brunswick in the east, south through coastal Mexico, locally in M. America, the Caribbean, and Hawaii (Palmer 1962, Hancock and Kushlan 1984, Davis 1993). Generally, coastal areas contain the largest breeding concentrations.

Individuals that breed in N. America winter from n. Oregon, s. Nevada, n. Utah, c. New Mexico, s. Texas, the lower Ohio Valley, Gulf coast, and s. New England south throughout Mexico and M. America. Suitable wetland habitat appears to control its breeding and wintering range (Palmer 1962). Four subspecies; *N. n. hoactli* occurs in Oregon (Davis 1993).

*Black-crowned Night-Heron*

**Oregon Distribution:** Fairly common summer resident east of the Cascades where it breeds locally at large wetlands. This species has nested on Malheur L., Malheur NWR, since at least 1918 (Thompson et al. 1979, Cornely et al. 1993) and continues to breed there (Ivey, Cornely, Paullin, and Thompson unpubl. ms.). In the 1980s several other colonies were documented, including Silver L., Lake Co., and Harney L., Island Ranch, Vogler Marsh, Squarewell, Knox Pond, Boca L., along the Silvies R. at Graves Ranch, and Mud L., Harney Co. (Ivey, Cornely, Paullin, and Thomspon unpubl. ms.). Not all these colonies have been active in recent years. Night-herons are known to shift colony locations in response to changing water conditions. During this same period, night-herons also bred at Summer L. W.A., Lake Co., and continued to nest there through 1994 (M. St. Louis p.c.). A colony has occurred in Malheur Co. near Vale since the mid-1980s (Contreras and Kindschy 1996). Colonies also have been found in Malheur Co. near Westfall, in the Batch L. complex, and Crow I. on the Snake R. north of Nyssa (Keister 1991, Contreras and Kindschy 1996). Other documented colonies include Three Mile I. on the Columbia R., Morrow Co.; Ladd Marsh W.A., Union Co. (Henny et al. 1984, Blus et al. 1997); and Catherine Cr., Union Co. (*SLF*). Although frequently observed during summers at Klamath Marsh NWR and upper Klamath NWR, Klamath Co., nesting colonies have not been documented (J. Hainline p.c.). Other small colonies may exist in e. Oregon where suitable habitat exists.

Observed more widely when postbreeding adults and young disperse, and may be locally abundant during fall in e. Oregon favored locations such as Malheur NWR (Gilligan et al. 1994). Gilligan et al. (1994) reported that about 100 birds usually winter in the Klamath Basin, Klamath Co., primarily along the Link R. in Klamath Falls. During some winters they remain at Malheur NWR, Summer L., and Umatilla NWR (Gilligan 1994). Fourteen night-herons were observed at the wildlife area west of

McNary Dam, Umatilla Co., on 23 Feb 2001 and one at Umatilla NWR, Morrow Co., the same day (*SLF*). There are also mid-Aug observations in the Cascades at Davis L., Deschutes Co. (L. McQueen p.c.).

Occasionally observed during early summer in w. Oregon (Dillingham 1994, Brown et al. 1996, Contreras 1998, Hunter et al. 1998, Adamus et al. 2001, Janes et al. 2001), and may nest, but nesting has not been documented since the early 1900s (Gabrielson and Jewett 1940, Gilligan et al. 1994). In late summer through early spring, night-herons are rare to uncommon in w. Oregon. Local roosts or regular sightings are known from lower Rogue and Chetco rivers, Coos Bay, near Tillamook, Medford, Grants Pass, Myrtle Point, Roseburg, and Portland (Gilligan et al. 1994, Hunter et al. 1998, Janes et al. 2001, *Oregon Birds* field notes).

**Habitat and Diet:** Black-crowned Night-Herons usually breed in colonies with other species of colonial nesting waterbirds. They use a broad spectrum of habitat types for nesting from the ground up to 160 ft (48.8 m) in trees (Palmer 1962). Breeding colonies are typically found on islands, in marshes, or over water. Colony sites probably chosen to avoid predators such as raccoons. A variety of substrates are used for nesting. Most nesting colonies in Oregon are in emergent vegetation composed of cattails or hardstem bulrush. However, in the 1980s they were documented nesting in flooded willows and greasewood near the shores of Malheur L., and in flooded greasewood in Harney L., Malheur NWR (Ivey, Cornely, Paullin, and Thompson unpubl. ms.). Colonies also located on a greasewood island in Mud L. and in flooded shrub-willows at Boca L. in the s. Blitzen Valley, Malheur NWR, and at Graves Ranch in the Silvies R. floodplain southeast of Burns (Ivey, Cornely, Paullin, and Thompson unpubl. ms.). Blus et al. (1997) indicated that night-herons nested in mulberry except for one nest in big sagebrush on Three Mile I., Morrow Co. Nests at Catherine Cr., Union Co., colony are on lower branches of large black cottonwoods or in small trees (*SLF*).

Palmer (1962) indicated that the foraging habitats used by the Black-crowned Night-Heron over its extensive range are "so varied as to be difficult to describe." Throughout their range they use a wide variety of wetland habitats including swamps, streams, rivers, margins of pools, ponds, lakes, lagoons, tidal mudflats, salt marshes, human-made ditches, canals, reservoirs, and wet agricultural fields (Davis 1993). Usage of wetlands can vary dramatically because of fluctuating water levels. Also known to forage in dry grasslands (Hancock and Kushlan 1984). Roost in trees.

They feed opportunistically on a variety of items. Main foods include freshwater and marine fish, leeches, earthworms, aquatic and terrestrial insects including moths, prawns and crayfish, mussels, squid, amphibians, lizards, snakes, rodents, birds, eggs, carrion, plant material, garbage/refuse at landfills (Bent 1926, Kushlan 1978, Davis 1993). Normally solitary foragers and defend feeding territories (Davis 1993).

**Seasonal Activity and Behavior:** Although Gross (1923) indicated that Black-crowned Night-Herons arrive at breeding grounds in Oregon in mid-Apr, many individuals arrive in late Mar (Gilligan 1994). Usually nest colonially with males choosing nest sites and advertising for females. Davis (1986) indicated that pair formation and nest building are essentially contiguous events, especially when old nests are used. Copulation usually occurs on the first or second day after pair formation and the first egg is laid an average of 3.3 days after the first copulation (Allen and Mangels 1940). Both parents incubate eggs starting with the first egg. Eggs laid at 2-day intervals until clutch (3-5 eggs) is complete. In 1991, at Three Mile I., Morrow Co., the approximate peak of egg laying was 1-6 May with a secondary peak 15-20 May (Blus et al. 1997). In this colony most young had already fledged by 23 Jul. At Ladd Marsh W.A., Union Co., 4 of 12 nests contained chicks by 18 May, in 1979 (ODFW unpubl. data). The other nests still contained eggs. Hatching occurs in 23-26 days (Hancock and Kushlan 1984). After 2 wk young capable of leaving the nest and typically fledge when 6-7 wk old (Davis 1993). Typically have one brood per season but will renest if first nest fails (Nickell 1966, Henny 1972). Most individuals nest at 2-3 yr old, but yearlings sometimes breed (Custer and Davis 1982).

Beginning in Jul and Aug, postbreeders and young are observed more often away from colonies as they begin dispersal. Numbers build at Malheur NWR in Sep and most are gone by early Nov, while birds are present year-round in the Klamath Basin (Gilligan et al. 1994). In c. Douglas Co., birds are usually found at roosts mid-Jul through mid-Apr (Hunter et al. 1998).

Migration routes and wintering areas of Oregon birds are not well documented. Night-herons banded in Idaho and Nevada colonies wintered in Mexico (Henny, Blus, and Hulse 1985, Henny and Blus 1986), and breeders from e. Oregon may do the same. It is unknown if birds wintering in the Klamath Basin are from Oregon breeding colonies or elsewhere.

**Detection:** Crepuscular and nocturnal feeding habits make this species difficult to locate, especially outside the breeding season. Typically heard before observed, often while the bird is flying to and from the roost (Hancock and Kushlan 1984). Especially vocal from colonies during the breeding season. Juveniles can be confused with American Bittern but lack dark neck streaks and dark flight feathers.

**Population Status and Conservation:** Although aerial surveys are useful for locating active colonies, they often grossly underestimate true numbers of nesting individuals (Erwin 1980, Portnoy 1980). Counts of active nests can also be difficult to obtain during ground surveys because of necessary precautions to prevent human impacts (Tremblay and Ellison 1979). Thus, population status and trends are difficult to assess. Overall, Oregon historical and recent population data are lacking except from Malheur NWR and elsewhere in the Harney Basin. The largest Oregon nesting population exists on Malheur L. In 1918 this area contained a total of 500 active nests in several sub-colonies (Thompson et al. 1979). Apparently, numbers of active nests declined dramatically during the drought years of the 1930s and early 1980s at Malheur L. (Henny et al. 1984). From 1965 to 1980, the population fluctuated between 250 and 1,000 pairs (Thompson et al. 1979, Henny et al. 1984). At Malheur NWR and Harney Basin during 1980-98 estimates of active nests ranged 29-1,031, indicating a significant declining trend (Ivey, Cornely, Paullin, and Thompson unpubl. ms.). The colony at Summer L. W.A. contained 80 active nests in 1980 (Henny et al. 1984). From 30 to 325 nesting pairs existed there 1988-95 but no active nests were found 1996-2000 (M. St. Louis p.c.). Thompson and Tabor (1981) reported 26 and 31 nests at Three Mile I., Morrow Co., in 1977 and 1978, respectively. Henny et al. (1984) counted 31 nests on the island in 1979 and 32 nests in 1980. At least 54 active nests were located there in 1991 (Blus et al. 1997). In 1979, 12 active nests were found in the Ladd Marsh W.A. colony (Henny et al. 1984). Night-herons have not nested at Ladd Marsh in recent years. It is believed that night-herons that formerly nested there now nest in a colony with Great Blue Herons along Catherine Cr., Union Co. (*SLF*). According to Contreras and Kindschy (1996) several dozen pairs breed in dense marshes in the Batch L. complex near Cow Lakes, Malheur Co. It also breeds along the Snake R. on Crow I., Malheur Co., north of Nyssa (Keister 1991).

Gabrielson and Jewett (1940) mention a colony with 200 nests near Portland, citing Finley (1906), but this was an error. A careful read of Finley (1906) reveals that the colony of 200 near Portland consisted exclusively of Great Blue Herons; a colony near San Francisco, abundantly described in the article, contained many Black-crowned Night-Herons. Nevertheless, during the spring of 1951, H. Nehls (p.c.) found four pairs of night-herons nesting in the Ross I. Great Blue Heron colony in Portland. It is possible that a few pairs still nest there or at the large colony on Bachelor I. in Ridgefield NWR, sw Washington (H. Nehls p.c.). Small colonies may exist in w. Oregon and should be looked for.

Habitat destruction, particularly drainage of wetlands for development and agriculture, development along coastal marshes, and increased human disturbance and usage of islands continues to be a problem for this species (Davis 1993). At Malheur NWR, nest numbers were correlated with annual precipitation (Ivey, Cornely, Paullin, and Thompson. unpubl. ms.). Because Black-crowned Night-Herons are high on the food chain they accumulate pesticides and other contaminants. Populations may have declined in the late 1960s and 1970s because of exposure to DDT (Ohlendorf et al. 1979, Custer et al. 1983, Henny et al. 1984, Findholt and Trost 1985, Blus et al. 1997). Henny et al. (1984) discovered that night-herons breeding (mostly on refuges) in Oregon and Idaho were less contaminated with DDE than those in Nevada. Interestingly, the birds did not share the same wintering area (Henny and Blus 1986). The Nevada birds (Ruby L. NWR) wintered in DDE-contaminated sites in the sw. U.S., with some in n. Mexico. The less-contaminated Oregon night-herons used a leap-frog migration and primarily wintered farther south in coastal Mexico. Management of night-herons has not been a major focus since most populations are stabilized or increasing (Davis 1993). In Oregon, most large colonies are on national wildlife refuges or state wildlife areas and thus are protected from human development. In contrast, most roosts in w. Oregon are on private land (*MGH*).—*Scott L. Findholt*

## Family Threskiornithidae

### Subfamily Threskiornithinae

**White Ibis** *Eudocimus albus*
Adults of this medium-sized heron-like bird with a downcurved bill are white with black wing-tips and pinkish face, bill, and legs; immatures are brownish. Resident in coastal salt marshes from s. U.S. into S. America; casual elsewhere in N. America. An adult photographed at Newport, Lincoln Co., 15-16 Nov 2000 (OBRC, Korpi 2001a) is the only Oregon record. Monotypic (AOU 1957).—*Harry B. Nehls*

**White-faced Ibis** *Plegadis chihi*
During market hunting days of the late 19th and early 20th centuries, ibises were shot en masse and peddled as "black curlew." Sporting the form of a curlew, this medium-sized marsh wader is almost always found in flocks, flying in formation and quacking like ducks. Their long, down-curved bill complements their long neck and legs. Although their feathers appear black, a closer look will reveal an iridescence of bronze, purple, maroon, and green. They are named for their "white face," which appears in alternate plumage as a narrow border of white

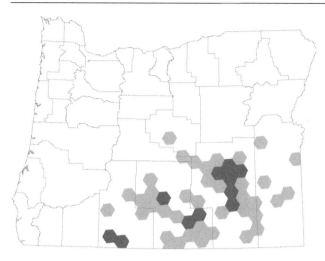

feathers along the edge of their reddish-purple facial skin, delineating a mask around the red eye.

**General Distribution:** Breeds locally in dispersed wetland basins from s. Alberta, c. and w. Montana, N. and S. Dakota, w. Wyoming, se. Idaho, n. and w. Utah, w. and ne. Nevada, se. Oregon, California, Colorado, Kansas, Louisiana, Texas, Mexico, and s. S. America. Winters primarily in coastal and southern regions of Mexico, and also along the Gulf coast and in c. and s. California (Ryder and Manry 1994). This is *P. guarauna* of Gabrielson and Jewett (1940) and *P. mexicana* of Oberholser (1974; Banks and Browning [1995] recommended the continued use of *chihi*). Monotypic (AOU 1957).

**Oregon Distribution:** Breeding restricted to Malheur L. for most of the 20th century, but the species experienced an exponential population increase and range expansion beginning in the 1980s (Ivey, Stern, and Carey 1988). By the late 1990s, colonies were documented at several wetland sites in Harney and Lake counties, including Blitzen Valley, Double-O, and Malheur L. on Malheur NWR, and Silver L. in Harney Co.; Chewaucan Marsh, Garrett Marsh (near Goose L.), Paulina Marsh, Silver L., Summer L. W.A., Sycan Marsh, and Warner Basin (Anderson L., Crump L., and Greaser Res.) in Lake Co. (Earnst et al. 1998); and Swan L. and Wood R. Wetlands in Klamath Co. (Ivey, Cornely, Paullin, and Thompson unpubl. ms.). Additionally, a new colony site appeared at Lower Klamath NWR, just south of the Oregon border. During this range expansion, there were increased observations of migrant ibis away from breeding areas. East of the Cascades, generally common from May through Sep near breeding areas (Harney, Lake, Klamath counties). Other spring and fall birds noted at Crook, Grant, Malheur, and Wallowa counties. (Anderson DA 1990c, Evanich 1992b, Summers 1993c, Gilligan et al. 1994, M. St. Louis p.c.). West of the Cascades its presence has recently become apparent

on the coast and occasionally in the Willamette Valley in spring (Gilligan et al. 1994). In winter, occasional to rare on the coast and at Sauvie I. and Malheur NWR (Evanich 1982d, Mattocks and Hunn 1982a, Irons 1984a, Littlefield 1990a, Gilligan et al. 1994, Contreras 1998).

**Habitat and Diet:** Usually breeds in mixed colonies in areas isolated from disturbance and predators with other colonial-nesting waterbirds. Nest sites are over water in emergent vegetation, including hardstem bulrush, cattail, broad-fruited burreed, and Baltic rush. It feeds in seasonal wetlands along shallow lake shores and in irrigated agricultural fields (particularly alfalfa and hay). Opportunistic in feeding, this species often focuses on receding wetlands where prey is concentrated. Known foods in Oregon include earthworms, aquatic insects, leeches, and carp minnows. Studies elsewhere have documented crustaceans, frogs, crayfish, and small bivalves (Ryder and Manry 1994).

**Seasonal Activity and Behavior:** Average arrival at Malheur NWR is 28 Apr; earliest 7 Apr (Ivey, Herziger, and Scheuering 1998). Exhibits nomadic behavior, regularly shifting nesting colonies between years in response to changing wetland conditions. Begins nest building in late May and is occupied with incubation and rearing of young through Jul. During this time, it constantly makes flights to and from colonies and feeding areas to feed mate and young. Post-fledging, ibises wander widely during Aug and Sep; most depart the state by mid-Oct; occasional as late as early Nov. Winter records include Malheur NWR in Jan and Feb 1964 (Littlefield 1990a), Tillamook in Dec 1979 (Mattocks and Hunn 1980b), and Sauvie I. in Dec 1981 and Oct 1983 (Evanich 1982d, Irons 1984a).

**Detection:** Located most easily by scanning seasonal wetlands and hay fields near breeding colonies. Most dependable places are Blitzen Valley of Malheur NWR and Silvies R. floodplain south of Burns. Listen for soft quacking calls and look for low-flying flocks of dark birds.

**Population Status and Conservation:** Jobanek (1987) reviewed historical records of White-faced Ibis in Oregon, and reported the earliest specimen was collected by Henry W. Henshaw from Warner L. in 1877. He listed additional early records, including a sighting from Lower Klamath L. in 1914 and Crump L. in 1922, and noted that A. G. Prill collected three ibises at Adel in the Warner Valley in 1931. William L. Finley found the species nesting at Malheur L. in 1908 where he and Herman T. Bohlman discovered a colony of 500 (Finley 1908b). In 1912, L. A. Lewis recorded 200 adults and several nests on Malheur NWR (Ryder 1967), and Willett (1919) observed 100 pairs with young there in 1918. Ryder (1967) reported that the only colony in Oregon was at Malheur L.

After recovering from market hunting, the species faced another threat in the 1960s and 1970s, when most populations decreased because of pesticide contamination and loss of habitat (Ryder 1967, Capen and Leiker 1979, King et al. 1980). Nevertheless, breeding pairs at Malheur L. increased from 10 in 1963 to 190 in 1979 (Thompson et al. 1979). Even though DDT was banned in the U.S. in the early 1970s, eggshell thinning and DDE contamination in White-faced Ibis eggs was still noted in the early 1980s on Malheur L. (Cornely et al. 1993). Beginning in the mid-1980s, the species began increasing and expanding its breeding range in Oregon and other regions of the w. U.S. (Ivey, Stern, and Carey 1988, Earnst et al. 1998). Earnst et al. (1998) cataloged over 8,000 breeding pairs in Oregon during the late 1990s. In 1998, 10,250 pairs were counted at Malheur NWR and an additional 275 pairs at Chewaucan and Paulina marshes (Ivey et al. 2003). These latter sites are private ranches managed for livestock grazing where the management of cattle and water may not be conducive to continued use by ibises.

Nomadic species pose special management and conservation challenges because of the large area they occupy and their unique population dynamics. White-faced Ibis movements exemplify the ecological connectivity among wetlands in se. Oregon and other western states, and indicate that wetland management decisions should be made in a regional context. Maintaining a mosaic of wetlands at a scale that ensures independence from water fluctuations would benefit White-faced Ibis population stability. In order to accomplish this, maintenance of colony sites on private lands through acquisition, easement, or cooperative agreements in order to maintain emergent marsh habitats and water conditions suitable for ibis would be needed.

White-faced Ibises are exposed to pesticide applications because they feed in agricultural fields, and especially because many winter in Mexico where few restrictions on chemical uses are enforced. This makes ibis a good candidate for monitoring as an indicator of environmental health.—*Gary L. Ivey*

## Family Cathartidae

**Turkey Vulture** *Cathartes aura*
This, perhaps the most visible bird in Oregon, is a fine example of the paradox of avian commonness and concomitant human ignorance of a bird. Few nests have been observed, and few details on nests have been published for the state. The Turkey Vulture, known locally as "buzzard," is a common sight spring through fall throughout the state, except in the highest

mountains and featureless desert expanses in summer where they are uncommon. Debate raged for nearly 140 yr whether this species could locate its usual foul meals by smell or whether it depended on visual cues (Stager 1964). Some even postulated an "occult sense" (Beck 1920), or that the sound of carrion-eating rodents or insects attracted vultures (Taber 1928, Darlington 1930). While it is now clear that Turkey Vultures have a sense of smell (Stager 1964, Bang and Cobb 1968), the question of its power is still being debated (Smith and Paselk 1986). Turkey Vultures are large-winged soaring birds with overall dark plumage except for a silvery sheen on the undersides of the flight feathers. Adults have small, featherless, red heads, while juveniles have gray heads.

**General Distribution:** Breeds throughout the conterminous U.S. and s. Canada south through M. and S. America to the Straits of Magellan; also in the Greater Antilles. Winters from n. California and Maryland south along the coast and inland to s. Arizona, Texas, and much of se. U.S., south through the breeding range in M. America, the Greater Antilles, and S. America. Three N. American subspecies; *meridionalis* in Oregon; *teter* and *meridionalis* are synonyms (Wetmore 1964, Browning 2002).

**Oregon Distribution:** The Turkey Vulture is a common to abundant transient throughout the state and an uncommon to common summer resident except in high mountains. It is most common at lower elevations (Fix 1990a) and in large valleys (Gullion 1951).

**Habitat and Diet:** Nests have been reported in caves, old stumps, hollow logs, and similar places (Gabrielson and Jewett 1940). Turkey Vultures have been reported to nest in rimrock areas near Malheur NWR where pairs are frequently seen (Jewett 1936, Littlefield 1990a); one nest was found in Mud Cr. Canyon in 1978 (Littlefield 1990a). Nests were reported from Diamond Craters, Malheur NWR, in summer 1979 (Rogers TH 1979). Concentrations of sloppy whitewash at several small pothole caves in tall cliffs in the Cascades of e. Douglas Co. were attributed to vultures, and a flightless juvenile was found at the base of nearby similar cliffs (Fix 1990a). Numerous nests have been reported from abandoned buildings elsewhere in U.S., but not in the vicinity of human activity—thus it is not surprising that no vulture nests were recorded in the Portland area (Griffee and Rapraeger 1937). No detailed descriptions of nests published for Oregon until recently when Rochelle (2001) described a nest in an old cedar stump in an active clearcut in Linn Co. The birds successfully hatched two young, which were believed to have successfully fledged. Unpublished brief descriptions of nests include one found in a large hollow elevated log in a white oak stand on Bald Hill, just north of Corvallis, in 1998 (D. Vesely p.c.); one under an upturned tree in an ash swale along Beaver Cr. near Lebanon, Linn Co., in 2000 (*fide* P. and J. Harding); and one in a "tunnel" more than 10 ft (3 m) long through bracken fern and Himalayan blackberry at the wooded edge of a field in se. Polk Co. (J. Geier p.c.). Most nests appear to be either highly inaccessible, such as in cliff faces, or hidden in or under large structures in wooded environments.

Turkey Vultures primarily forage over open country, where visual cues may assist in locating food. However, they are occasionally observed on the ground, presumably foraging or searching for food, in oak stands in the Willamette Valley (Anderson SH 1970), and in young (40- to 55-yr-old) Douglas-fir stands in the Coast Range (Hagar et al. 1996) and w. Cascades (*MGH*). They are regularly found foraging in more open forests of sw. and e. Oregon (*MGH*).

Turkey Vultures roost primarily on large, tall, open structures such as dead or partly dead trees or tall towers. They typically have an associated pre- and post-roost site. Probably the most important characteristic of a morning post-roost site is exposure to sunshine (Davis D 1979).

They are predominantly carrion eaters, but contrary to popular belief (e.g. Anonymous 1973), do on a rare occasion take live, typically helpless prey (Mueller and Berger 1967, Glading and Glading 1970, Jackson et al. 1978, Titus and Mosher 1980, Smith 1982). Occasional nest predation on Ring-necked Pheasant in the Willamette Valley was attributed to vultures (Eklund 1942).

**Seasonal Activity and Behavior:** At Malheur NWR, the earliest arrival is 18 Feb 1976, with average arrival

*Turkey Vulture*

16 Mar; peak of spring migration is 5-25 Apr, with most migrants gone by 5 May (Littlefield 1990a). In the s. Willamette Valley, the first individuals are noted during Feb in most years; many arrive in Mar, with peak migration in mid-Apr (Gullion 1951). Timing of pair formation or nest-site selection is probably in Apr; a "pair" was reported 3 Apr 1949 west of Salem (Flahout 1949). Birds have been reported on nests as early as 30 Apr 1998 at Bald Hill, Corvallis (OBBA, D. Vesely p.c.).

Eggs are laid May-Jul. A nest in Harney Co. 12 May contained two fresh eggs; other egg dates are from 2 May to 10 Jun in Klamath and Jackson counties. (Gabrielson and Jewett 1940); 29 May, Baker Co., 14 Jun, Klamath Co. (OBBA); 30 Apr (D. Vesely p.c.) and 29 May (P. and J. Harding p.c.) in the Willamette Valley. Downy young were on Spencer Butte, near Eugene, Jul 1942 (Gullion 1951). Birds on nests (status unknown) observed 30 Apr to 26 Jul (n=10), with young in nests beginning 1 Jun (n=4) (OBBA). Young vultures just learning to fly 29 Jul near Bend (Roger 1955). Fledglings observed 20 May to 26 Aug (n=3) (OBBA).

A famous roost at P Ranch, Malheur NWR (Littlefield 1990a), consisting of a tall tower and adjacent large cottonwoods, is used during spring, summer, and fall. Vultures usually arrive 1.5 hr before sunset in late spring, and 2.5 hr before sunset in early and mid-summer, earlier during inclement weather (Davis D 1979). Typical departure time was 3-4 hr after sunrise; earlier when a breeze was present and later when there was no breeze. Marked vultures used the roost only 58-79% of the evenings observed (n=28), and number of vultures ranged 68-151, suggesting that they may switch roosts or roost near a food source some nights. Pre-roost structures adjacent to roosts may function to allow unobstructed sunning, preening, and stretching activities, as well as intense interactions among vultures (Davis D 1979).

Over 200 vultures have been counted on the P Ranch tower during migration. Most birds appeared to be subadults or nonbreeders during summer; a few dark-headed young birds appeared in fall migration (Littlefield 1990a). Forty-three of 200 vultures soaring over Malheur NWR, 9 Sep 1971, were judged to be young of the year (Kingery 1972a). At Bonney Butte, near Mt. Hood, vultures are observed from the beginning of the monitoring season (late Aug); bulk of passage is in the second half of Sep; median passage date was 22 Sep for the Sep-Oct monitoring period 1994-98; latest observation was 10 Oct; numbers ranged 41-93 birds/100 hr of observation time, averaged 64 birds/100 hr during Sep-Oct 1994-99 (Vekasy and Smith 2000). In the s. Willamette Valley, fall migration is most noticeable mid-Sep to early Oct, when a peak of 280 birds was reported (Gullion 1951). At Malheur NWR, fall migration begins in Aug, peaks 1-15 Sep; most have left by Oct; latest is 20 Oct 1965. Large numbers are consistently reported in the Rogue Valley in fall; e.g., "Approximately 100 Turkey Vultures were seen over the Rogue R. Valley in s. Oregon" on 20 Sep, and "funnels of 30, 50, and 80 birds" were seen there ahead of a storm on 26 Sep (Crowell and Nehls 1973a). Fall migrants peak in late Sep and early Oct in s. California at the southern terminus of the Sierra Nevada (Rowe and Gallion 1996).

The first 20th-century winter record was 28 Dec 1952 on the Eugene CBC (Robbins 1953). In winter 1978-79, an immature attempted to winter at Roseburg but died during a Jan freeze, despite supplemental feeding by a farmer (Mattocks 1979). By the next year Mattocks and Hunn (1980b) proclaimed "That a few Turkey Vultures are found here [Pacific coast west of the Cascades] in winter is now normal." One near Cove, Union Co., 8 Feb 1981 (Rogers TH 1981b) was one of few e. Oregon winter records, or perhaps a very early migrant. One spent the 1975-76 winter near Frenchglen Spring (Littlefield 1990a).

**Detection:** Gullion (1951) detected the vulture on 147 of 222 days during their season of occurrence in the s. Willamette Valley. Turkey Vultures are rarely observed flying before 10:00 during spring and early summer (*MGH*) so typical point counts and BBS routes which span 05:00-10:00 are not adequate to assess the presence or abundance of this species. In Oregon, identification problems are limited primarily to occasional confusion with the Golden Eagle, but young Turkey Vultures, which have dark heads, are occasionally reported as Black Vultures (*MGH*).

**Population Status and Conservation:** Remains of Turkey Vultures were found in an Indian midden near The Dalles, estimated to be several thousand years old (Miller 1957), indicating the species' long historical presence. Generally this is a very adaptable bird due to its diverse nest-site selection and foraging habits. Most likely threats include a reduction in food supplies over a large region and chemical contaminants (Pattee and Wilbur 1989). One raven-control study in Oregon was conscientious enough to cease poisoning ravens when vultures were first noted in spring (Larsen and Dietrich 1970). Some eggshell thinning has been shown from California, Texas, and Florida, but not of magnitudes typically associated with declines in productivity (Wilbur 1978).

Summer censuses of the P Ranch roost, including the tower and nearby cottonwoods, revealed an average of 46.6 (range 35-54) birds in 1981 and 54.0 (range 33-74) birds in 1982, down from a single count of 92 in 1976 (Taylor 1986b), and an average of 90 (peak of 110) birds over approximately the same period in 1973 (Davis D 1979). Hypotheses that might explain this decline include an overall decrease in vulture numbers in the region, or a change in distribution and establishment of new roost sites, perhaps due to the reduction in cattle population and associated carrion availability (Taylor 1986b).—*Matthew G. Hunter*

# Order ANSERIFORMES
## *Family Anatidae*

### Subfamily Dendrocygninae

**Fulvous Whistling-Duck** *Dendrocygna bicolor*
This tropical duck breeds from S. America into the s. U.S. It formerly bred in the Central Valley of California and in s. California but is now reduced to occasional visitants. It regularly wanders, often in large flocks, to areas outside of its normal range. Numbers have decreased in recent years, as have reports of wandering birds (Bellrose 1976). A flock of 11 remained at a pothole lake in the North Spit of Coos Bay 14-24 Feb 1970 (Anonymous 1970, Watson 1989). One of these birds was collected and is now a mounted specimen at the Audubon Society in Portland. One was reported without details from Haystack Res., Jefferson Co., 24 May 1965 (Rogers 1965). Monotypic (Hellmayr and Conover 1948, Monroe 1968).—*Harry B. Nehls*

### Subfamily Anserinae

**Greater White-fronted Goose** *Anser albifrons*
While not as abundant or conspicuous as the more familiar Canada and Snow Geese, Greater White-fronted Geese represent one of the first signs of fall. Laugh-like calls from small skeins of these birds are heard high overhead in Aug-Sep through the n. Willamette Valley and across the Cascades to sc. Oregon and ne. California. The prefix "Greater" was applied to this species when a split into two species within the white-fronted goose complex was recognized by the AOU (1983). (The Lesser White-fronted Goose is found in Eurasia only.) The Greater White-fronted Goose is gray-brown in body color and has orange feet. Adults have the namesake white forehead, pinkish-orange bill, and black speckled/barred breast and belly, the latter responsible for the common nickname, "speckle-belly." Young birds lack white forehead and black belly markings through their first fall. Considered among the most delectable of geese, this bird is a favorite among waterfowl hunters across N. America, although, on

average fewer than 1,500 are harvested annually in Oregon (Drut and Trost 2000).

**General Distribution:** Nearly circumpolar in the N. Hemisphere. In N. America, breeds in the Arctic and sub-Arctic from Alaska east to Hudson Bay and winters in California, Texas, and Mexico. Two populations are recognized: the larger mid-continent population of the Central and Mississippi Flyways and the Pacific Flyway population. The entire Pacific Flyway population originates in Alaska and winters in California's Central Valley and in w. Mexico (Ely and Takekawa 1996). Three subpopulations comprise the Pacific Flyway population. Two are composed of *A. a. frontalis* and one consists of *A. a. elgasi* (popularly called Tule Goose). Each subpopulation differs in morphology, timing of migration, and location of primary breeding and wintering grounds (Orthmeyer et al. 1995, Ely and Takekawa 1996).

The most common and widespread N. American Greater White-fronted Goose subspecies is *A. a. frontalis*, often referred to as the "Pacific White-fronted Goose" by waterfowl biologists. Taxonomy of the remaining birds is complex. Pacific and Central Flyways each support a population of subspecies that are noticeably larger and darker than *frontalis* and have separate breeding areas. One originates in Alaska's Cook Inlet and the other at Old Crow Flats in nw. Yukon (Timm et al. 1982). The first described of the large dark birds was taken in Texas and given the subspecific name *gambelli*. Large dark "white-fronts" called Tule Geese wintering in the Sacramento Valley were erroneously assumed to be this subspecies (Swarth and Bryant 1917). However, Delacour and Ripley (1975) described the Tule Goose as a separate subspecies using specimens from California, and gave it the name *elgasi*. This terminology was accepted by Browning (1990) and R. Banks (p.c.). However, Bellrose (1976), Timm et al. (1982), Ely and Dzubin (1994), and waterfowl biologists in general have continued to refer to the Tule Goose as *gambelli*. We accept the name *elgasi*, and also recognize the widespread English name, Tule Goose. It may deserve full species rank (Krogman 1979, AOU 1998).

Despite much effort and speculation, the breeding grounds of the Tule Goose were not located until 1980 (Timm et al. 1982). Through radio and plastic color-collaring on both breeding and wintering areas, it was found to breed at Susitna Flats and Redoubt Bay in Alaska's Cook Inlet Lowlands (Timm et al. 1982, Orthmeyer et al. 1995). It winters in the Sacramento Valley and Suisun Marsh of California (Bauer 1979, Timm and Dau 1979, Wege 1984) and migrates through Oregon spring and fall (Timm et al. 1982).

**Oregon Distribution:** Greater White-fronted Geese unidentified by subspecies, but mostly *frontalis*, are fairly common in flight statewide during spring and fall migrations. Foraging birds concentrate in the major basins east of the Cascades, especially Klamath. Lesser numbers stop along the lower Columbia R. and coast. Probably least frequent in migration along the s. Oregon coast (Brown et al. 1996, Sawyer and Hunter 1988), particularly in spring (Contreras 1998). Low densities winter with Canada Geese in the Willamette Valley and Klamath Basin.

Tule Geese stop in the fall at Summer L. W.A. and Malheur NWR (Timm et al. 1982, Pacific Flyway Council 1991b). Spring stopover locations include Summer L., the Lower Chewaucan drainage, S. Deep Cr. of Warner Valley (all Lake Co.) (M. St. Louis p.c.) and irrigated hay meadows in the Lower Silvies R. floodplain south of Burns (*DBM*). H. Nehls (p.c.) observed two, one of which was collared, at John Day Dam 27 Oct 1995. Status of the Tule Goose in w. Oregon not clear. Derek Minear, a goose collar reader, read the numbers on a collared Tule Goose south of Dayton, Yamhill Co., on 12 Dec 1998 (*DAB*); it had been banded as an adult female 1 Jul 1997 in the Kahiltna R. Valley north-northwest of Anchorage (C. Ely p.c.). A neck-collared bird from Cook Inlet was observed at Sauvie I. (Timm et al. 1982). On 2 Oct 1997, *DBM* observed two large dark-necked individuals at Sauvie I. They took flight, leaving a flock of more typical "white-fronts" (see detection section). A flock of 10 that included one neck-collared bird was observed at Sauvie I. 30 Sep 1994 (H. Nehls p.c.). A group of six spent most of Feb 1998 at Baskett Slough NWR (*HBN*). They are also regularly seen in Clatsop Co. (M. Patterson p.c.).

There are no museum specimens of a Tule Goose from Oregon. Their presence in Oregon is confirmed by birds neck-collared at Cook Inlet and in the Sacramento Valley and seen at Summer L. W.A., Malheur NWR, the Klamath Basin, and elsewhere as named above. At Summer L. sizeable numbers have been identified at the hunter check station through morphological characteristics (M. St. Louis p.c.). Rocket-netting and tagging with satellite transmitters of Tule Geese took place there in fall 2001 with expectations of tracing migration routes with greater accuracy.

**Habitat and Diet:** These geese utilize both aquatic and terrestrial habitats. In Oregon they take advantage of agricultural crops, feeding on waste barley, corn, and potatoes; but also graze on a variety of grasses (Ely 1992). Feeding sites often located near suitable roost sites, typically large bodies of water or ice. Tule Geese prefer marshes and feed more in wetland habitats and less in agricultural fields than *frontalis* (Bauer 1979).

**Seasonal Activity and Behavior:** Except during the nesting season, Greater White-fronted Geese are gregarious and social birds; family bonds are maintained for years (Ely 1993). They are the first geese to migrate south; begin arriving in Summer L. and Klamath basins in late Aug. Earliest arrivals: 21 Aug Malheur NWR (Littlefield 1990a), 22 Aug flying south over e. Douglas Co. (Fix 1985f), and 22 Aug flying south over E. E. Wilson W.A. (*DAB*). First arrivals are probably from the Bristol Bay Lowland subpopulation of *frontalis*, which stages during late Aug and Sep in the Klamath Basin and winters in Mexico (Ely and Takekawa 1996). Remainder of the *frontalis* population begins arriving in late Sep. In the Klamath Basin numbers peak in late Oct and early Nov. Although most *frontalis* winter south of Oregon, small numbers winter in w. Oregon, the Klamath Basin, and sometimes Malheur NWR. Tule Geese also begin arriving in late Aug in Oregon (Pacific Flyway Council 1991b). In recent years, a peak of 1,500-2,000 Tule Geese at Summer L. has been reached in mid-Sep. (M. St. Louis p.c.). In Mar and Apr, Tule Geese can again be observed at Oregon sites.

Spring migrants, not identified as subspecies, are most common at Malheur NWR 15-25 Mar (Littlefield 1990a). Up to 4,000 known to stage at Conley L., Union Co., Feb-Apr (Evanich 1985). Fix (1988b) documented a large movement over e. Douglas Co. on 26 and 27 Apr., and reports this is an annual event within a narrow corridor (D. Fix p.c.). Large movements were also noted over E. E. Wilson W.A. 1992-2001 with peaks for each year usually 24-27 Apr (*DAB*).

**Detection:** In flight, flocks are most frequently detected by unique laughing *kah-ah-luck* vocalizations. Experienced observers with spotting scopes can separate *frontalis* from Tule Geese under ideal field conditions, especially if both are within good viewing distance for comparison. Tule Geese are noticeably larger with proportionately larger bills and darker necks and heads. They tend to be in small groups, fly lower with a slower wing beat than the more common *frontalis*, and segregate from *frontalis* (Bauer 1979, *DBM*).

**Population Status and Conservation:** With more than 1 million Greater White-fronted Geese in N. America, the most recent 3-yr average for *frontalis* in the Pacific Flyway was 332,912 birds (Drut and Trost 2000); the population of the Tule Goose is probably stable at an average of 7,500 birds (Pacific Flyway Council 1991b). *A. a. frontalis* reached a population low near 100,000 in 1984, with over-harvest on breeding grounds by subsistence hunters and on wintering grounds by sport hunters likely a contributing factor (Timm and Dau 1979). The population has grown at an average annual rate exceeding 7% for the past 10 yr (Drut and Trost 2000). The management objective for *frontalis* is a 3-yr average population of 300,000 based on coordinated fall surveys (Pacific Flyway Council 1987). Annual production and winter surveys closely monitor population trends.

The management objective for the Tule Goose is a 3-yr average of 10,000 based on peak fall and winter surveys (Pacific Flyway Council 1991b). Conservation measures designed to protect this less numerous subspecies have been adopted and annual surveys monitor the population. Their Cook Inlet breeding area is major gas and oil producing area (Timm et al. 1982).—*David A. Budeau*

## Emperor Goose *Chen canagica*

The Emperor is a medium-sized, stocky goose with a white head and metallic blue-gray body reminiscent of a blue-morph Snow Goose. Dark throat and undertail coverts as well as yellow feet distinguish it from the latter. Juveniles are brown with a gray-black head and neck that becomes white with black flecking in late fall. Vocalizations include in-flight call *kla-ha, kla-ha, kla-ha*, and an alarm call a deep ringing *u-lugh, u-lugh, u-lugh* (Peterson et al. 1994).

**General Distribution:** Breeds on the west coast of Alaska from Kotzebue Sound south to Kuskowim Bay, St. Lawrence, and Nunivak Is. and the Siberian coast of the Bering Sea. Most of the population breeds on Alaska's Yukon R. Delta. Winters in the Aleutian Is., Alaska Peninsula, Kodiak I., and on the Kamchatka Peninsula in Siberia. A few Emperors winter along the Gulf of Alaska and Cook Inlet; stragglers can occasionally be found from British Columbia to California. Monotypic (AOU 1957).

**Oregon Distribution:** Wilbur and Yocom (1971) described the Emperor as a rare but regular visitor in Oregon during migration and in winter. Most commonly found on the coast; sightings have been reported from Tillamook (*DBM*), Siletz Bay (Irons 1984a), Yaquina Bay (Scott and Haislip 1969, Bayer and Krabbe 1984, Fix 1985f), Yachats (Irons 1984b), Winchester Bay (Sawyer and Hunter 1988), Coos Co. (Contreras 1998, T. Rodenkirk p.c.) and Gold Beach (Rowe 1943). In interior w. Oregon, Emperors have been found near Eugene (Gabrielson and Jewett 1940), in Westmoreland Park in Portland (Irons 1984b), at Sauvie I. (Roberson 1980), on the lower Sandy R. just east of Portland (*RKM*), and at Baskett Slough NWR winter of 1977-78 (D. Irons p.c.). East of the Cascades, one sighting has been reported at Malheur NWR; one on the lower Silvies R. floodplain near Burns; several in the Klamath Basin (Roberson 1980, Littlefield 1990a) and at Hart Mtn. (Wilbur and Yocom 1971).

Most sightings are of single birds, but Rowe (1943) reported a flock of 17 at Gold Beach, Curry Co., in Apr 1943, and T. Rodenkirk (p.c.) reported a group of four in Coos Co, Jan 2001.

**Habitat and Diet:** Data on habitat and diet in Oregon are lacking. Elsewhere the birds use the intertidal zone almost exclusively as their winter habitat and feed on benthic invertebrates (Peterson et al. 1994).

**Seasonal Activity and Behavior:** Emperors have been observed as early as 15 Oct at Nehalem (H. Nehls p.c.) and 16 Oct at Siletz Bay (Irons 1984b). Most birds move on, but some linger through the winter and longer. Single birds have spent the winter including those cited above at Yachats and Westmoreland Park in Portland. A wintering bird stayed in the Nehalem area into Jun (H. Nehls p.c.). At Coos Bay a bird cited above stayed through 10 Apr and another stayed into late summer (Contreras 1998). An Emperor first observed in Dec 1996 in Gresham is assumed to be the same bird that subsequently appeared along the Sandy R. and remained there into 1999 (H. Nehls p.c.); it associated with domestic mallards at both locations. Association with domestic waterfowl also occurred at Westmoreland Park, near Tillamook (*DBM*) and Veneta, Lane Co. (Evanich 1982d). Under such situations they become quite unwary.

**Detection:** Easily observed when in grassy or mudflat surroundings, but sometimes quite camouflaged when perched on jetties or intertidal rocks. Juveniles with their dull brown plumage are more difficult to spot than adults. Check geese with white heads and dark bodies carefully to distinguish Emperors from blue morph Snow or Ross's geese.

**Population Status and Conservation:** Gabrielson and Jewett (1940) reported observations from Lane, Lincoln, Multnomah, Tillamook counties. Since then the Emperor Goose population in Alaska declined markedly from 139,000 in 1964 to 42,000 in 1986. Although poorly understood, the cause of the decline may be related to coastal pollution and/or native subsistence hunting. Populations recovered somewhat since the 1986 low, but are still below pre-1986 levels (Peterson et al. 1994). Sightings in Oregon, perhaps due to increasing numbers of birders in the field, have not shown a commensurate decrease.—*R. Kahler Martinson*

## Snow Goose *Chen caerulescens*
The skies near favored stopover locations are filled twice annually with the sights and sounds of these geese as they migrate between Arctic breeding grounds and wintering areas farther south. Snow geese share very similar all-white plumage and black wing tips with the less common Ross's Goose. These are our only wild white geese. Immatures show considerable amount of sooty gray on the head, neck, and wing coverts that fades as birds molt those feathers and attain nearly all-white plumage. The blue form or morph, identified by its white head and upper neck, slate gray body and pearly-gray wing coverts, is rare in Oregon. Owing to their gregarious nature, flocks of thousands are not uncommon and are an awesome migratory bird spectacle. Where concentrations occur during the hunting season, the species can be an important game bird.

**General Distribution:** Breeds across the N. American Arctic and sub-Arctic regions and into the Far East and Siberian arctic regions of Russia. During migration and in winter, found across the Canadian provinces and northern tier of states south into the Mexican highlands of Chihuahua and Sinaloa provinces. Major wintering populations are found in sw. British Columbia and nw. Washington, n. and c. California, New Mexico, Texas panhandle, the Mississippi Gulf states, and Arkansas (Bellrose 1976). The one N. American subspecies, *C. c. caerulescens*, is commonly referred to as the "lesser snow goose" by waterfowl managers.

**Oregon Distribution:** Predominately a spring and fall migrant, it is especially abundant in the large wetland and agricultural complexes such as Malheur NWR and the Silvies R. floodplain in Harney Co., Lower Klamath NWR, and Klamath W.A. in the Klamath Basin, and Summer L. W.A., Goose L. and other Lake Co. locales. Population estimates in these areas range from 50,000 to 100,000 individuals (ODFW files, Summer L. W.A. files). Smaller numbers (e.g., 1-50, rarely a few thousand) are uncommon in spring or fall elsewhere in e. Oregon (Evanich 1992a, Contreras and Kindschy 1996), and rare to uncommon from the w. Cascades to the coast (Fix 1990a, Contreras 1998, Herlyn 1998, Hunter et al. 1998).

Wintering Snow Geese in Oregon are found primarily along the lower Columbia R. between the mouth of the Willamette R. and Astoria where a few hundred to several thousand can sometimes be found (ODFW files, Summer L. W.A. files). The Sauvie I. W.A. hosts a population numbering from a few hundred to several thousand annually. Small flocks numbering 250-300 birds can sometimes be found in the Columbia Basin near the confluence of the Umatilla R. with the Columbia R. near Umatilla NWR (M. Kirsch p.c.). Elsewhere in w. Oregon, individuals or small flocks are casual to rare in winter (Contreras 1998, Herlyn 1998, Hunter et al. 1998); those in the Willamette Valley usually present among flocks of Canada Geese (Herlyn 1998). Occasionally winter in the Klamath Basin (Summers 1993a), especially when weather conditions are mild (J. Hainline p.c.).

Very unusual was a nesting record at Malheur L. in 1960 (Marshall 1962), which could have involved pairing by crippled adults.

**Habitat and Diet:** Freshwater and brackish-water emergent marshes seem to be the preferred habitat of Snow Geese during migration in se. and sc. Oregon (*MStL*). During winter, coastal and freshwater marshes are utilized along the lower Columbia R. In spring, heavy use is also made of shallow flooded fields and grassy flats where emerging shoots of various grass species are utilized. Farmed and native hay meadows and other cultivated fields are used extensively in many locales (*MStL*). Underground stems of emergent rushes and grasses seem to be the preferred food at inland marsh sites, especially during fall migration (Martin et al. 1951). Having a well-suited bill, Snow Geese grub pond bottoms and remove roots and tubers, especially from alkali bulrush and American three-square bulrush. Salt grass and Lemmon's alkali grass are used to a lesser degree (*MStL*). In the Klamath Basin predominately, Snow Geese often become field feeders on waste small grains found in agricultural fields. Occasional use is also made of alfalfa fields, where young shoots and rhizomes are dug up and consumed (T. Collom p.c.). Use alfalfa fields in spring in and around Umatilla NWR, Morrow Co. (M. Denny p.c.).

**Seasonal Activity and Behavior:** In e. Oregon, arrive in late Sep, becoming abundant in Oct (Summers 1993b, *MStL*). In w. Oregon, have been seen as early as Sep (Hunter et al. 1998, Patterson 1998b), but most are observed beginning late Oct and Nov (Fix 1990a, Herlyn 1998, Patterson 1998b).

Large concentrations develop in locations providing ample food resources and security. Typically, birds loaf or roost on large water bodies and fly en masse to and from feeding areas. At major fall stopover sites in e. Oregon, Snow Geese remain until weather, usually snow accumulation and freeze-up of open water areas, precludes foraging on wetland plants. At Summer L. W.A. most depart in late Nov or early Dec (ODFW files, Summer L. W.A. files); timing is similar in the Klamath Basin (Summers 1993a). Timing of winter use is variable along the Columbia R. corridor as birds wander, utilizing wetland areas from the mouth upstream to Umatilla NWR, Morrow Co.

Spring migration and arrival are very dependent on weather conditions, but usually begin in early to mid-Feb (ODFW files, Summer L. W.A. files, Summers 1993c). By early to mid-Mar, migration is in full swing and large numbers can be found in all major stopover areas of e. Oregon (*MStL*); smaller numbers may be found in lesser-used areas (Contreras and Kindschy 1996).

Population monitoring (neck collar observation and radio telemetry) has documented birds moving from one basin to another, north to south (e.g., Klamath Basin to Summer L. W.A. to Harney Basin) with stopovers suspected to be dictated largely by weather conditions and the thawing of ice- or snow-covered habitat (ODFW files, Summer L. W.A. files). Departure from Oregon usually complete by early to mid-Apr (Summers 1993a, *MStL*) although many observers have reported small groups or individuals lingering into late spring or early summer.

**Detection:** Due to their gregarious nature, Snow Geese are easily detected by their distinctive plumage, wavy and undulating skeins in flight, and shrill and constant calls.

**Population Status and Conservation:** Two major subpopulations, the Wrangel I., Russia subpopulation (WIP), and Western Canadian Arctic subpopulation (WCAP) pass through Oregon during annual migration. A small breeding colony on the North Slope in Alaska (500 birds) is considered a satellite colony of the WCAP subpopulation (Kerbes et al. 1999). WCAP birds are the most numerous due to their explosive population growth, suspected to be a result of extensive use of agricultural fields in staging areas and throughout wintering areas in California and elsewhere in the Pacific and Central Flyways (Kerbes et al. 1999). Population monitoring has documented a strong showing by WCAP birds throughout Oregon during spring migration and occasionally during the fall (ODFW files, Summer L. W.A. files). In fall 2000, the Pacific Flyway portion of this subpopulation was estimated at 656,800 birds (USFWS 2001a). WIP birds show the strongest fidelity to an Oregon migration, spending 4-5 mo passing through and utilizing wetlands located primarily in e. Oregon (Kerbes et al. 1999). Alaska birds are the least numerous and generally co-mingle with WIP birds (*MStL*).

In earlier times of abundance, 30-40 yr ago, over 500,000 birds were found on Summer L. W.A. in Lake Co. (ODFW files, Summer L. W.A. files). In recent years, that number has rarely exceeded 100,000 birds. This radical reduction in numbers can be attributed to a shift in migrational patterns, a severe decline in some breeding populations, and adverse weather patterns (Kerbes et al. 1999).

Wintering populations found along the lower Columbia R. are predominately WIP birds (ODFW files, Summer L. W.A. files) probably associated with wintering snow geese found in coastal Washington and British Columbia.

Conservation measures primarily include maintaining and managing the large wetland complexes required to support thousands of these birds in Harney, Summer L., Warner, and Klamath basins. Wetland enhancement and restoration through state and federal programs and in partnership with non-governmental organizations (e.g., Ducks Unlimited, The Nature Conservancy, and others) continues to broaden and improve the habitat base supporting this species.

Management plans containing habitat-enhancement and protection goals, population monitoring and special studies developed through the Pacific Flyway Council guide conservation efforts for both subpopulations (Pacific Flyway Council 1992a, 1992b).—*Martin J. St. Louis*

## Ross's Goose *Chen rossii*

This small white goose is similar in plumage to the Snow Goose in all ages—white body and black primaries of adult and subadult birds, gray plumage in juveniles. In mixed flocks, the Ross's smaller size, shorter neck, head and bill profile, and more rapid wing-beat may be apparent. In hand or at close range, the small size and stubby bill lacking the grinning patch separate the Ross's from the Snow Goose. Vocalizations are higher pitched, but similar to those of the Snow Goose: when disturbed, *kork* or *kouk*, in flight, *keek keek keek* (Ryder and Alisauskas 1995). A rare blue morph similar to that of the Snow Goose has been observed in the Burns area (Littlefield 1990a) and the Klamath Basin (Summers 1993a). The species is not an important game bird in Oregon with very few taken incidentally by hunters seeking other species.

**General Distribution:** Breeds in the c. Canadian Arctic lowlands of the Queen Maud Gulf, Mackenzie District, Northwest Territories. Small numbers have been found breeding on the w. and s. coasts of Hudson Bay, on Southhampton and Baffin Is., and in the w. Arctic. Winters in the interior valleys of California with increasing numbers in New Mexico, Texas, Oklahoma, Missouri, Arkansas, Louisiana, and the north-central highlands of Chihuahua and Durango, Mexico. Monotypic (AOU 1957).

**Oregon Distribution:** Common spring and fall migrant through Klamath and Harney basins (Marshall 1959, Wilbur and Yocom 1971, Littlefield 1990a, Summers 1993a) with records also from Warner Valley, Summer L. (Wilbur and Yocom 1971) and ne. Oregon (Jewett 1946c, Evanich 1985). Rare or occasional visitor to Malheur Co. (Contreras and Kindschy 1996). Irregular in the Willamette Valley (Heinl 1986a, Lillie 1994, 1998, Gilligan 1998), Umpqua Valley (Hunter et al. 1998), and coast (Heinl 1986c, T. Rodenkirk p.c.). A few occasionally remain in the Klamath Basin through winter.

**Habitat and Diet:** During migration and on wintering grounds the Ross' Goose uses lakes and shallow marshes for roosting, and agricultural crops and irrigated hay meadows for feeding. On migration in the Burns area, feeds in pastures and cut hay fields (Littlefield 1990a). In the San Joaquin Valley of California, it uses green-grass fields with Cackling Canada Geese while Snow Geese feed in waste grain fields (*DBM*). Ross's Geese also observed foraging with Cackling Canada Geese in grass fields in the Willamette Valley (D. Irons p.c.), but also take grasses, sedges, and waste grain (*RKM, DBM*).

**Seasonal Activity and Behavior:** Flocks arrive at Malheur NWR 27 Oct-16 Nov, peak 3-12 Nov, and move on south soon thereafter (Littlefield 1990a). During spring migration, Ross's Geese move into the Klamath Basin in late Feb and Mar (Gilligan et al. 1994). At Malheur NWR their earliest arrival date is 2 Feb with the greatest abundance 1-15 Apr; most have departed by May (Littlefield 1990a).

**Detection:** Found by scanning flocks of geese for small white birds and carefully studying flocks of white geese to find the smaller Ross's Goose. There is a high probability of observing this species during late Mar and Apr at Miller I. in the Klamath Basin, Summer L., and Harney Basin, particularly in meadows south and east of Burns; and in Nov in the Klamath Basin.

**Population Status and Conservation:** Ross's Geese were thought to be rare at the turn of the century and sport hunting was closed in 1931 when numbers were estimated at 5,000-6,000 (Alisauskas and Ryder 1995). Gabrielson and Jewett (1940) reported only two specimens and concluded its main migration was to the east of Oregon. Numbers were thought to have remained dangerously low through the 1950s and Canada delayed hunting for white geese in the 1960s and 1970s to protect them. Subsequently numbers recorded on surveys have increased significantly: 188,000 in 1989 on the breeding grounds (Alisauskas and Ryder 1995), and Canadian biologists now believe the population may be as high as 1 million (USFWS undated). In the Burns area, Littlefield (1990a) concluded that Ross's Geese are increasing as Snow Geese are decreasing. Some of the apparent recovery of the species can be attributed to improved survey techniques, but counts in recent years have documented a steady expansion in both population and range (Bellrose 1980, Ryder and Alisauskas 1995). Abundance during spring migration is illustrated by a flock of 25,000, including three blue morphs, observed on the Silvies R. floodplain south of Burns 22 Apr 2001 (Sullivan 2001b).—*R. Kahler Martinson*

## Canada Goose *Branta canadensis*

Canada Geese, with their distinctive black neck and head and white cheek patches, need little description because they are one of Oregon's most familiar and conspicuous birds. However, they represent a very complex pattern in terms of subspecies and populations which include both residents and long-distance migrants. They are one of the state's most important game birds; are known as ferocious defenders of their nest and family; and show lifelong faithfulness to their mates. Their "V" flight pattern and honking call thrill many people and have made them an icon of wildness. Canada Geese are loved by many, but because wintering concentrations sometimes cause damage to agricultural crops, and resident birds foul some park and golf course lawns, they can be despised. More is known about this species than perhaps any other Oregon bird.

The life-history traits of Canada Geese promote formation of numerous subspecies that often comprise discrete populations. Traits such as lifetime pair bonds, young remaining with their parents for nearly a full year, natal philopatry, and pair formation on breeding areas, result in stable populations composed of interwoven extended families.

Although some authors recognize only eight subspecies (Schorger 1976, Owen 1980), most, including Delacour (1954), Johnsgard (1975b), Bellrose (1980), and this account recognize 11 subspecies. No official vernacular names are currently recognized by the AOU for subspecies and the unofficial common names regularly used by waterfowl managers for Canada Goose subspecies are used herein. Some subspecies show much variation among sub-populations. Pierson et al. (2000) detected differences in the genome of some sub-populations, but did not propose dividing them into distinct subspecies. The 11 subspecies range in size from the 2.5-lb (1.1-kg) Cackling Canada Goose (*B. c. minima*) to the 15-lb (6.8-kg) Giant Canada Goose (*B. c. maxima*), and in color from the rich chocolate brown of the Dusky Canada Goose (*B. c. occidentalis*) to the silvery-breasted Western Canada Goose (*B. c. moffitti*). (Note the nomenclatural anomaly: Dusky Canada Goose is *occidentalis*, which means "western," while Western Canada Goose is *moffitti*, after the naturalist James Moffitt.) The Western subspecies has also been referred to as the Great Basin Canada Goose. Seven and perhaps eight of the 11 subspecies occur in Oregon, six as winter migrants (*leucopareia, occidentalis, fulva, minima, taverneri,* and *parvipes*), and one or two as permanent residents (*moffitti* and *maxima*).

As a further complication, numerous poorly documented and undocumented releases of Canada Geese have been made in the western states from privately owned captive flocks (former decoy flocks) (Hanson 1965), in some cases representing several subspecies and probably hybrids. Some of these mixed-origin birds became semi-wild "park" geese, which, when they became a nuisance, were "managed" by transplanting them to other locales. Many resident populations in w. Oregon originated through transplant operations. Consequently, the taxonomic identity of many local breeding populations is problematic. Western Canada Geese, however, comprise by far the largest component of the mixed gene pool, and all resident populations are classed as Western Canada Geese herein, though some show characteristics of other ancestors, e.g. Giant and Dusky Canada Geese, and probably Atlantic and Vancouver Canada Geese.

Separation of Canada Goose subspecies can be difficult, especially in the field. They can be grouped into three size categories. The largest is the Giant Canada Goose, imported to Knappa, Clatsop Co. (McAllister 1981, Gilligan et al. 1994), but has undoubtedly since mixed with other subspecies. The other large Canada Geese that occur in Oregon include the silvery-breasted Western Canada Goose and the dark-breasted but slightly smaller Dusky and Vancouver (*B. c. fulva*) Canada Geese. Medium-sized Canada Geese include the light-breasted Lesser (*B. c. parvipes*) and the slightly smaller and tannish-gray-breasted Taverner's (*B. c. taverneri*) Canada Geese; these two often are confused in local field guides. The Aleutian Canada Goose (*B. c. leucopareia*) is generally classed as a small Canada Goose, although it is only slightly smaller than Taverner's Canada Goose, which it also resembles in breast color. One distinguishing character of the Aleutian Canada Goose is a high, abrupt forehead that results from enlargement of the supraorbital salt gland in response to consumption of salt water by this coastal bird. Another distinguishing character is a broad white band that extends completely around the base of the neck between the black neck and gray breast, though a few adults and many juveniles lack the complete neck ring. Weighing little more than a Mallard, the very dark-breasted Cackling Canada Goose is the smallest. It often has a white neck ring, but it rarely extends around the back of the neck as in the Aleutian Canada Goose.

**General Distribution:** The species as a whole occurs throughout most of N. America from about 70º N latitude to extreme n. Mexico (Bellrose 1980). Introduced and established in w. Europe and New Zealand. Among natural populations, the smallest subspecies breed farthest north and originally wintered farthest south, but agriculture and reservoir construction have disrupted the winter pattern. Dark-colored subspecies breed in coastal areas of w. N. America while light-colored subspecies originate in the interior. Only Oregon subspecies are covered below.

Western Canada Goose (*B. c. moffitti*) breeds from s. British Columbia and Alberta, south to Utah, Nevada, and n. California. Winters in southern portion of this range, and south into Arizona and s. California (Bellrose 1980).

Aleutian Canada Goose (*B. c. leucopareia*) breeds in the Aleutian and Semidi Is., Alaska. Those from the Aleutian Is. winter mainly in the Central Valley of California, while those from the Semidi Is. winter on the Oregon coast (Springer and Lowe 1998).

Dusky Canada Goose (*B. c. occidentalis*) breeds in the Copper R. Delta, Alaska, and Middleton Is. in the Gulf of Alaska, although the mostly resident Canada Geese from Prince William Sound may represent a sub-population. Winter almost exclusively in sw. Washington and nw. Oregon (Jarvis and Bromley 1998).

Vancouver Canada Goose (*B. c. fulva*) breeds in the rainforest of se. Alaska, where most also winter (Bellrose 1980), but small numbers migrate as far south as Oregon (Ratti and Timm 1979).

Cackling Canada Goose (*B. c. minima*) breeds in narrow coastal band on the Yukon-Kuskokwim Delta in w. Alaska (Bellrose 1980, USFWS 1986a). Formerly wintered in the Central Valley of California, and staged during fall and spring in the Klamath Basin, but now winter mostly in nw. Oregon and sw. Washington.

Taverner's Canada Goose (*B. c. taverneri*) breeds broadly across tundra regions of Alaska and w. Canada, but specific distribution is poorly known. Winters at scattered locations throughout much of the intermountain west.

Lesser Canada Goose (*B. c. parvipes*): breeding distribution poorly known, but apparently breeds broadly across Alaska and nw. Canada; most reports from forested river valleys. Winters broadly across w. U.S., apparently including the short-grass plains of Colorado and Texas.

Giant Canada Goose (*B. c. maxima*) breeds in the northern two-thirds of the prairies and winters in the southern two-thirds (Hanson 1965). Once thought extinct. Kept extensively in captive flocks. Has been re-introduced throughout its former range, and introduced elsewhere in N. America, including Oregon.

**Oregon Distribution:** As a whole the species is widely distributed throughout Oregon, with the exception of mountainous and desert areas lacking reservoirs, lakes, or large rivers. Concentrations of wintering and breeding Canada Geese occur wherever agriculture and other human developments provide green forage or small grains and water bodies provide sanctuary. Major breeding areas include the Klamath Basin, Malheur NWR, and elsewhere in Harney Basin, Summer L. W.A., Warner Valley, and most major river systems, e.g. Columbia, Snake, and Willamette. Major wintering areas include the Willamette Valley-lower Columbia R., the upper Columbia R. Basin, and Klamath Basin.

Western Canada Goose. Common permanent resident throughout most of the state, augmented in winter by birds from British Columbia and Alberta (Ball et al. 1981, USFWS 1989). Wherever geese occur in Oregon, this subspecies is present. Although originally restricted to areas east of the Cascades, especially during breeding season, escapees from captive breeding flocks and enthusiasm for transplanting geese have resulted in broad distribution across the state. Releases from captive flocks of mixed origins undoubtedly introduced genes from other subspecies. Most recent expansions include the Willamette Valley and lower Columbia R. in the 1970s and 1980s, and coastal bays in the 1990s.

Aleutian Canada Goose. Migrate mainly along the coast where occasional transients are seen. Sporadically observed in fall and winter at Sauvie I. and elsewhere in the Willamette Valley, and at New R. near Langlois and Bandon on the s. coast during fall (Oct-Nov) and spring (Feb-Apr) migration (Springer and Lowe 1998). A small population (~120 birds) of Aleutian Canada Geese that originates on the Semidi Is. winters near Pacific City, Tillamook Co. They forage in a pasture along the lower Nestucca R. east of Pacific City and roost on Haystack Rock offshore from Pacific City as well as in the ocean at Haystack Rock (Springer and Lowe 1998, D. Pitkin p.c.). These birds are easily traced by red-and-white neck collars placed on birds captured in the Semidi Is. This is an unusual population in terms of roosting on the ocean.

Dusky Canada Goose. Winters almost exclusively in the Willamette Valley and to a lesser degree along the lower Columbia R. (Chapman et al. 1969, USFWS 1997a, Cornely et al. 1998). Small numbers also winter on the Oregon coast, especially on Nestucca NWR (confirmed by red collars placed in the Copper R. in Alaska) and on Goat I. NWR, near Brookings; the latter possibly remnants of a flock that formerly wintered at Lake Earl, Crescent City, California (P. Springer p.c., R. Lowe p.c., *RLJ*). Browning (1973a) reported Canada Geese during spring, mostly on Goat and Hunters islands, and Saddle and Crook Pt. rocks, Oregon Is. NWR. Perhaps the same population Gabrielson and Jewett (1940) reported for the s. Oregon coast, which could have been either Dusky or Vancouver Canada Geese or others.

Vancouver Canada Goose. Sight records and recoveries of banded birds (Hanson 1962, Ratti and Timm 1979) indicate a few probably migrate to nw. Oregon on a regular basis. Similarity to Dusky Canada Geese makes sight and even specimen records suspect; equally important, many birds likely go undetected. A few hundred assumed to winter in Oregon (Jarvis and Bromley 1998).

Cackling Canada Goose. Common winter resident in the Willamette Valley and lower Columbia R. (Drut and Trost 1999). Transient during migration on the coast, Klamath Basin, other e. Oregon basins.

Taverner's Canada Goose. Concentrations winter in the Willamette Valley and along the lower Columbia R.

(Jarvis and Cornely 1988, Jarvis and Bromley 1998) and in the upper Columbia R. Basin. A smattering can also be found along the coast including Nestucca Bay NWR (D. Pitkin p.c.), and at most areas in e. Oregon harboring spring and fall or wintering concentrations of Canada Geese, e.g. Klamath Basin, Malheur L., Summer L., Goose L., Warner Valley, and Snake R. near Ontario.

Lesser Canada Goose. Concentrations occur in the Willamette Valley and along the lower Columbia R. (Jarvis and Cornely 1988, Jarvis and Bromley 1998) and in the upper Columbia R. Basin. Those that winter in the Willamette Valley and along the lower Columbia R. breed in upper Cook Inlet near Anchorage, and until recently were all silvery-breasted birds. In the 1990s dark-breasted lesser-sized geese began breeding in the expanding suburban area of Anchorage (T. Rothe p.c.). At least some of these latter birds migrate to Oregon, where most concentrate around Baskett Slough NWR along with silvery-breasted Lesser Canada Geese. As with Taverner's Canada Geese, a few Lesser Canada Geese can be also found on the coast and at most areas in e. Oregon harboring spring and fall or wintering concentrations of Canada Geese. A specimen from Silver L., Lake Co., is at USNM.

Giant Canada Goose. A pair purchased from a Minnesota game-bird breeder by Robert Ziak was introduced near Knappa, Clatsop Co., in 1938; increased to about 300 birds by 1981 (McAllister 1981, Gilligan et al. 1994). Interbreeding with the expanding Western Canada Goose population on the lower Columbia, and with Dusky Canada Geese from a former semi-captive flock at Willapa NWR, now makes racial identity of these birds problematic. While individuals may occasionally show "Giant" characteristics, the subspecies is probably extirpated in Oregon.

**Habitat and Diet:** For protection from mammalian predators, Canada Geese nest on small islands or various elevated structures, e.g. muskrat houses, artificial structures, cliffs, and abandoned raptor and heron nests. Broods need water bodies large enough to allow them to escape by swimming while their parents harass pursuing predators. Lastly, succulent green forage is needed in or adjacent to brood-rearing wetlands. These three elements have been provided intentionally by wildlife managers, but also unintentionally as a result of agricultural and rural/suburban development (*RLJ*).

Wintering habitat consists of sanctuary in an agricultural environment that provides food and is provided by lakes, reservoirs, and large rivers, often associated with wildlife refuges (*RLJ*). Canada Geese are grazers showing a strong preference for succulent tips of young grasses and grass-like plants (Schorger 1976, Baldasarre and Bolen 1994). Selective both in which plants and which plant parts they consume. During winter, often forage on waste grain, although

show a preference for green forage when available. This preference has created conflicts with farmers, park managers, and golf course operators (*RLJ*).

**Seasonal Activity and Behavior:** Although Canada Geese form permanent year-round pair bonds, they re-pair quickly when a mate is lost. Nesting begins in Mar in most areas of Oregon; a few may start as early as Feb or as late as Apr. Secure nest sites are at a premium and the territory around them is vigorously defended against other pairs. Throughout the laying and incubation period (30-35+ days), the male stands guard, ready to repel both intruding geese and predators. Females take infrequent breaks during the ~28-day incubation period and consequently have almost no remaining fat reserves when goslings hatch. Broods present Mar-Aug; most young flying by Jul. During latter part of the gosling stage, parents molt flight feathers and are flightless for 3+ wk; they regain flight at same time the goslings are first able to fly at about 8 wk of age. While breeders are incubating, most Oregon nonbreeders, which includes all yearlings, many 2-yr-olds, and failed breeders, migrate to n. Alberta and British Columbia, s. Yukon, and Northwest Territories, where they molt (Furniss et al. 1979, Ball et al. 1981). They return in early fall to natal areas to rejoin breeders, which have regained flight, and new recruits which are flying for the first time.

In fall, the earliest migrant Dusky Canada Geese arrive in late Sep, but the first large influx of migrants, including all subspecies, usually comes in early Nov. Most migrants arrive by Dec, but in the Oregon portion of the upper Columbia R. Basin, peak numbers may not occur until Jan. During winter, they typically make two daily foraging flights from nocturnal roost areas. The first occurs about sunrise and is usually a mass departure to feeding areas. They filter back to roost areas throughout mid-morning. Disperse for afternoon feeding flights throughout mid- to late afternoon; often return to roost sites at dusk or shortly after. Nocturnal feeding is apparently uncommon. During periods of heavy overcast, may remain in fields during most of the diurnal period. During periods of intense cold, minimize energy expenditures by making single foraging forays during midday (*RLJ*).

Because of migration and nesting demands, they begin accumulating fat reserves prior to departure from wintering grounds. Increased foraging activity begins up to 1 mo or more before departure, with increased activity levels becoming very noticeable 2-3 wk before. All migratory birds undergo period of "migratory restlessness," easily observed in Canada Geese: feeding intensity increases, they become more vocal and more "flighty" in the couple of weeks before departure (*RLJ*).

Spring departure of wintering birds is timed for arrival on breeding grounds at the beginning of spring ice break-up. Breeders leave first in mass migration on very predictable schedule. Nonbreeders leave later, on dispersed schedule. For example, Cackling Canada Geese leave Oregon in late Apr and stop at several staging areas in Alaska before arriving on the Yukon-Kuskokwim Delta at the beginning of May. Nonbreeders may not leave wintering grounds until early to mid-May. Dusky Canada Geese arrive on the Copper R. Delta in mid-Apr, but do not stop along the way. Hence, breeders typically depart Oregon 10-15 Apr and arrive on the Copper R. Delta a couple days later (Bromley and Jarvis 1993).

D. Pitkin (p.c.) says the Semidi Is. Aleutian Canada Geese depart Semidi Is. late Sep and arrive at Pacific City in mid-Oct. It is unknown where they make stopovers.

**Detection:** Canada Geese are so widespread and obvious both vocally and visually that there is little need for comment. Concentrations can be spectacular. Sauvie I., Willamette Valley NWRs, upper Columbia R. Basin, and Klamath Basin provide ideal opportunities to observe large concentrations during winter. Nesting and brooding geese are more secretive, but are widespread and can be observed with patience.

**Population Status and Conservation:** Major changes have occurred in the distribution and numbers in Oregon since Gabrielson and Jewett's (1940) time. Resident breeders have increased in numbers and in distribution. Rural and suburban development, along with increases in golf courses and parks, have produced an abundance of semi-wild "park" geese. Because of proximity to humans, these populations are difficult to control, and in many places have become annoyances to local residents and landowners. Numbers of winter migrants have also increased. Some of the increase comes from a northern shift in wintering distribution of geese that previously wintered in California; this shift is at least partly attributed to agriculture and river impoundments. Long-term warming trends across the Arctic likely contributed to increases of migrant Canada Geese.

Discussions are divided into four areas: (1) Willamette Valley/lower Columbia R.; (2) upper Columbia R. Basin (including Columbia R. Gorge); (3) Klamath Basin; and (4) other rivers and basins.

Willamette Valley/lower Columbia R. This area, which stretches from Astoria to Portland to Eugene, has the most complex wintering aggregation of geese in N. America, and the most controversial management scheme (Jarvis and Cornely 1988, Jarvis and Bromley 1998). All seven (eight if Giant Canada Goose is included) of Oregon's subspecies winter in this area, five in substantial numbers. This is a dynamic wintering flock. Early in the 20th century few geese apparently wintered in this area; the first specimen of a Dusky Canada Goose

observed by Stanley G. Jewett was shot by a hunter near Salem in 1927 (Jewett 1932) (Jewett also reported a mounted specimen shot near Eugene, which he had not seen, as a valid Dusky Canada Goose). By the 1940s, about 1,500 geese were wintering in the Fern Ridge area east of Eugene; about two-thirds were Dusky Canada Geese and one-third light-breasted (Taverner's and/or Lesser?) Canada Geese (Gullion 1951). In the late 1940s, from 4,000 to 7,000 were wintering south of Corvallis at McFadden Marsh, now part of the William L. Finley NWR (Evenden et al. 1950). By the middle of the 20th century, about 10,000 geese were present, nearly all Dusky Canada Geese (Jarvis and Cornely 1988, Jarvis and Bromley 1998). Dusky Canada Geese increased through the 1960s and mid-1970s to about 30,000 as refuges were created and hunting regulations tailored to the geese were implemented. Dusky Canada Geese comprised 95% of geese in the Willamette Valley/lower Columbia R. in 1971. Taverner's Canada Geese, a few of which apparently always were present, began increasing in the early 1970s, leveling off at about 50,000 by the end of the decade (Simpson and Jarvis 1979). Cackling Canada Geese declined from 400,000-500,000 at mid-century to 25,000 by 1984. Under protective harvest regulations, including agreements with native hunters, the population has since expanded and shifted its wintering grounds to the Willamette Valley/Lower Columbia R. area. Wintering numbers currently stand at about 250,000 and continue to expand (Drut and Trost 1999).

Cackling Canada Geese, which previously migrated over this area to winter in California's Central Valley, first remained in substantial numbers in 1985. Wintering component of this subspecies expanded rapidly under protective hunting regulations. Western Canada Geese expanded distribution and numbers within this area during the 1980s and 1990s from population growth and transplants. Thus, from about 10,000 Dusky Canada Geese at mid-century, the wintering flock has grown to more than 300,000 geese, mostly Cackling, Taverner's and Western Canada Geese.

Upper Columbia R. Basin. Canada Geese have been a major beneficiary of the damming of the Columbia R. (Hanson and Eberhardt 1971, Ball et al. 1981). Pools behind dams provide sanctuary for roosting, and the resulting irrigated agricultural developments provide food. One flock, wintering upstream from The Dalles into e. Washington along the Columbia R., numbers about 150,000 birds. Between The Dalles and Arlington, they feed in dryland wheat fields, primarily on the Oregon side of the river. This portion of the flock is mostly Western Canada Geese, with a small mixture of Taverner's and Lesser Canada Geese. From about Arlington upstream, they feed in irrigated cropland on both sides of the river. This portion of the winter flock comprises mostly Taverner's and Lesser

Canada Geese, with perhaps 25% Western Canada Geese. Breeding-ground origins of these Taverner's and Lesser Canada Geese are unknown. There is, however, much subtle color variation within both of these subspecies here, which may indicate multiple breeding grounds for both. The Oregon portion of the wintering flock varies annually depending upon weather and food availability. Western Canada Geese wintering in this area breed throughout the upper Columbia R. Basin in Oregon, Washington, Idaho, and British Columbia.

**Klamath Basin.** The Klamath Basin, which straddles the Oregon-California border, now winters about 10,000-15,000 Canada Geese, nearly all Western Canada Geese (D. Mauser p.c.). A few Taverner's and Lesser Canada Geese pass through during migration. Most of the Western Canada Geese wintering here are local breeders, augmented by birds that breed in surrounding areas at higher elevation, and by migrants from British Columbia. Formerly the entire population of Cackling Canada Geese stopped in the Klamath Basin during fall and spring (O'Neill 1979).

**Other Rivers and Basins.** Other rivers and basins in Oregon support wintering concentrations. Most are composed of Western Canada Geese, originating from local and nearby areas. Occasionally a few Taverner's and Lesser Canada Geese are present, mostly during fall and spring migration. These rivers and basins hold from a few hundred to a few thousand geese each. All have two things in common: (1) water bodies that retain some open water during winter; and (2) food—green forage or waste grain—that does not become snow covered for extended periods.

Annual Oregon Canada Goose hunter harvest is about 50,000 (Trost RE 1999). The breeding population of Western Canada Geese in Oregon averaged about 55,000 during 1994-99, excluding a few breeding areas that were not inventoried (ODFW files).

Although the Dusky Canada Goose population currently numbers about 15,000 (Drut and Trost 1999), the status of this subspecies remains precarious because of low productivity, which is likely to continue into the foreseeable future. Habitat changes on the Copper R. Delta breeding grounds, resulting from a seismic uplift in 1964, have adversely impacted productivity (Cornely, Campbell, and Jarvis 1985). Very severe limitations on harvest have been imposed to minimize mortality of adults, and seem to have succeeded in stabilizing the population for now. These regulations require training of hunters and are highly controversial, but have allowed recreational hunting to provide some relief from goose depredations to farmers' crops.

The Aleutian Canada Goose was close to extinction as recently as the 1970s, when its population was estimated at 790 individuals (Woolington et al.

1979, USFWS 1982). Eradication of introduced fox populations from key islands in the Aleutian chain followed by reintroductions helped restore populations (*DBM*). Current numbers are about 30,000 (Drut and Trost 1999). The subspecies was downgraded from endangered to threatened in 1990 (USFWS 1990) and proposed for de-listing in 1999 (Degange 1999). The small discrete group that breeds on the Semidi Is., Alaska and winters on the Oregon coast numbered approximately 130 birds as of spring of 2002, and has experienced reproductive failures in recent years (D. Pitkin p.c.). Its small population size warrants continuation in threatened status.

The Cackling Canada Goose now numbers about 250,000, up from a low of about 25,000 in 1985 (Drut and Trost 1999). Numbers for other wintering Canada Goose subspecies constitute rough estimates because there are no accurate censuses by subspecies. Taverner's Canada Geese in the Willamette Valley/lower Columbia R. number about 50,000 (Jarvis and Cornely 1988, Jarvis and Bromley 1998) with perhaps another 50,000 in the upper Columbia R. Basin. Lesser Canada Geese numbers stand at 3,000-5,000 and ~50,000 for the same two areas, respectively.—*Robert L. Jarvis*

## **Brant** *Branta bernicla*

See Black Brant, which follows, for the basis of considering this and the Black Brant as separate species. This common pale-bellied brant of the Atlantic coast is accidental in Oregon, but occasionally appears on the coast and at Sauvie I. These birds belong to the subspecies *B. b. hrota*, which nests in arctic areas of e. N. America (Browning 2002). Most Oregon reports of Brant are coastal (Batterson 1968, Crowell and Nehls 1974b, Hoffman and Elliott 1974, Gilligan et al. 1994), but two were on Sauvie I. in Oct and Nov 1984 (Hunn and Mattocks 1985, *DBM*). A brant observed at Yaquina Bay, Lincoln Co., during summer and fall of 1973 and another recovered at Coos Bay were characterized by Hoffman and Elliot (1974) as pale bellied, with nearly complete white neck markings; the identity of these birds cannot be confirmed (*MRB*).—*Harry B. Nehls*

## **Black Brant** *Branta orientalis*

With four wing-beats each second pushing them to 62 mph (100 kph), brant, including this species, are the fastest and strongest geese in flight and among the swiftest of all large birds. Ancient observers were not aware of the brant's northern breeding areas and believed that they originated from barnacles or wood-boring sea worms. Tough enough to live for 20 yr and resilient enough to ride out storms on the open ocean, they may not be sufficiently tough and resilient to survive degradation of their habitat.

Until publication of the sixth edition of the AOU check-list (AOU 1983), the Brant (*B. bernicla*) of the Atlantic coast and Black Brant of the Pacific coast, then referred to as *B. nigricans*, were recognized as two separate species. The sixth edition listed the two former species as conspecific under the species name Brant (*B. bernicla*). We follow Browning (2002), which again recognizes the Black Brant as a full species but under the name *B. orientalis*. Black Brant comprise the vast majority of brant occurring in Oregon. These small geese have smoky black backs and bellies, and dissected white collars and white around the tails provide striking contrast. There are a few Oregon records of the light-bellied Brant of the Atlantic coast (*B. bernicla hrota*). In Europe, the English name for Brant is "Brent Goose," and the names "Light-bellied Brent Goose" or "Pale-bellied Brent Goose" refer to Brant, while "Dark-bellied Brent Goose" refers to Black Brant.

The Black Brant was a popular game bird among a few dedicated Oregon hunters (Einarsen 1965), but numbers taken in recent years are minimal.

**General Distribution:** Breeds in arctic w. N. America and e. Asia. Winters along the N. American Pacific coast and nearby islands from Alaska to the wc. Mexican coast and s. Baja California, and in the w. Pacific from Kamchatka to s. China (Leopold and Smith 1953, Smith and Jensen 1970, Dau and Hogan 1985, AOU 1998). Several thousand may winter in Izembek Bay, Alaska, especially during mild winters (Bellrose 1976). The largest breeding area is on the outer Yukon Kuskokwim Delta (Bellrose 1976). Other breeding areas include the N. Slope and Kotzebue Sound, Alaska, and Liverpool Bay and Banks I. Peninsula, Canada (Bellrose 1976). A few breeding locations overlap that of Brant (Bellrose 1976).

**Oregon Distribution:** From the 1960s until 1993, about 800 Black Brant wintered in Netarts, 300-400 in Yaquina, and 100 or fewer in Tillamook Bay (Batterson 1968, Bayer 1996d). Statewide wintering numbers have averaged 640 during 1994-98, a 50% reduction

from previous years (D. Pitkin p.c.). Coos Bay, a former wintering area, is no longer regularly occupied by sizeable numbers due to eelgrass reduction, human activity, or both (Batterson 1968, Contreras 1997b), but flocks of up to 2,100 occur along the Coos Co. coast during northward migration in Mar and Apr (Contreras 1998, T. Rodenkirk p.c.). On 4 Apr 1998, a flock of 16 was observed flying north offshore about 90 mi (145 km) west of Depoe Bay (G. Gillson p.c., *MGH*). In some years, from 20 to 106 Brant have been observed during the Florence, Coos Bay, Coquille Valley, Port Orford, and Gold Beach CBCs (Bayer 1996a). Individuals or small flocks regularly summer in coastal estuaries (Gilligan et al. 1994, Bayer 1995a).

Black Brant are rare inland, usually occurring as individuals among flocks of Cackling Canada Geese (Gilligan et al. 1994, Contreras 1997b). West of the Cascades, they are most often observed in the Willamette Valley and at Sauvie I. (Contreras 1997b, Tice 1997). Localities with multiple records east of the Cascades are Warner Valley (Einarsen 1965) and Summer L. (Wilbur and Yocum 1971), both in Lake Co. A total of nine were observed in Deschutes, Klamath, Sherman, Umatilla, and Harney counties in Oct, Dec, Mar, May, and Jun (Tice 1997).

**Habitat and Diet:** Black Brant usually winter in large shallow bays with eelgrass beds (Batterson 1968, Smith and Jensen 1970, Cogswell 1977), but have also been observed along the open coast (Bayer 1996a). In Coos and Yaquina bays, they are most abundant in embayments and mouths (Bayer 1983a, Bayer 1996a, Wetzel 1996, Contreras 1998, Merrifield 1998). Occasionally observed in upland fields (Leopold and Smith 1953, Einarsen 1965, Batterson 1968, Bayer 1996a) often when eelgrass is depleted by disease (Smith and Jensen 1970). Black Brant may roost on the open ocean at night or when disturbed (Batterson 1968, Henry 1980, Bayer 1996a, Wetzel 1996), and they are comfortable on stormy seas (Einarsen 1965).

Black Brant have perhaps the most specialized and least adaptable food and feeding requirements among N. American waterfowl (Cottam et al. 1944, Einarsen 1965). They tip, swim, and stalk in shallow water, steal from other birds, or glean shore drift to procure eelgrass and sea lettuce (Cottam et al. 1944, Einarsen 1965, Baldwin and Lovvorn 1994, Bayer 1996a, Wetzel 1996). Black Brant wintering from Alaska to California consume other foods to a lesser extent, perhaps when eelgrass and sea

*Black Brant*

lettuce cannot be reached (Cottam et al. 1944). Surfgrass along the open coast (Bayer 1996a), glasswort and other salt marsh plants, and upland grasses may be eaten (Cottam et al. 1944, Bayer 1996a). Diatoms, bryozoans, gastropods, shrimp, and insects are also ingested, probably incidentally (Einarsen 1965).

**Seasonal Activity and Behavior:** Following pre-basic molt, Black Brant leave breeding areas in late Aug or early Sep, and virtually all spend 6-9 wk at and near Izembek Lagoon, Alaska, accumulating energy reserves (Bellrose 1976, Dau and Hogan 1985). Departing together in late Oct or early Nov, most migrate directly to Baja California (Cottam et al. 1944, Einarsen 1965, Bellrose 1976) in as little as 56 hr (R. Lowe p.c.) Land-based records of southward flight are unusual (i.e., Bayer 1997). Arrivals in Oregon bays, probably of immatures, may begin as early as mid-Aug (Einarsen 1965, Batterson 1968, Contreras 1998). Larger numbers of all ages arrive in late Oct or early Nov (Bayer 1996a, Bellrose 1976).

In Tillamook, Netarts, and Yaquina bays, numbers build to a winter plateau, fluctuate during late winter, and reach higher spring peaks probably due to supplementation by northward migrants (Cottam et al. 1944, Einarsen 1965, Batterson 1968, Bellrose 1976, Bayer 1983a, Bayer 1996a, Wetzel 1996). Those wintering at Yaquina Bay have shown strong winter site fidelity (D. Pitkin p.c.).

Gradual northward movement along the Pacific coast begins soon after some birds arrive in Baja California in winter (Bellrose 1976, Dau and Hogan 1985). Peak populations develop in eelgrass and sea lettuce habitats during late winter and early spring (Einarsen 1965, Bellrose 1976). The onset of northward movement in Oregon is often not clearly delineated and may vary from year to year, starting as early as Jan but usually from mid-Apr through mid-Jun to as late as mid-Jul (Bayer 1996a, 1996d, Batterson 1968, Contreras 1998). Northward flight along the coast is commonly observed in Mar and Apr (Browning 1973a, Hunn and Mattocks 1981b, Faxon 1990). Black Brant arrive at Izembek Lagoon, Alaska, in late Apr and early May and reach maximum numbers on the Yukon Delta breeding grounds by the last week in May and in arctic and w. Canada by mid-Jun (Cottam et al. 1944, Dau and Hogan 1985).

A few Black Brant summer in Oregon (Einarsen 1965, Batterson 1968, Bayer 1995a, 1996a, Contreras 1998). Have reportedly bred in Coos and Humboldt bays, California (Cottam et al. 1944, Einarsen 1965), but Harris (1991) suggests these may have been molting adults mistaken for young. Because their rapid digestion necessitates prolonged feeding, and because extreme low tides are more frequent during early evening or after dark, their daylight search for food is continual (Einarsen 1965). Feeding is usually most intense during low tides (Wetzel 1996). Black Brant will snatch plant material from the bills of coots and diving ducks during high tides (Cottam et al. 1944, Einarsen 1965, Wetzel 1996).

**Detection:** Easily seen feeding on open mudflats or along rocky shores. During migration in late winter and spring, they may often be observed along open coasts and flying northward over the ocean.

**Population Status and Conservation:** Natural climatic events combined with human and animal predation have caused dramatic Black Brant population fluctuations (Smith and Jensen 1970, Dau and Hogan 1985). Populations were about 140,000-170,000 along the entire Pacific coast 1951-79 (Leopold and Smith 1953, Smith and Jensen 1970, Bellrose 1976, Dau and Hogan 1985), 109,300 in 1981-83, 133,430 in 1984, and 144,800 in 1985 (Dau and Hogan 1985). The 1981 Black Brant Management Plan, recommended by the Pacific Flyway Council, calls for closing all sport hunting of Black Brant if the 3-yr running average drops below 120,000 (Dau and Hogan 1985).

Average numbers of Black Brant wintering in Oregon have declined from 3,628 in 1936-60 to 1,041 in 1981-90, and yearly totals have declined from 1,399 in 1990 to 546 in 1998 (Pacific Flyway Council 1991a). The 1994-98 5-yr statewide average is the lowest on record (D. Pitkin p.c.) Populations along the s. British Columbia coast have dropped drastically since the 1950s to about 100-200 (Bellrose 1976, Contreras 1997b). Winter averages in California declined from 58,000 from 1930-42 to 43,800 in 1952 (Bellrose 1976) to 751 in 1981-90 (Pacific Flyway Council 1991a). Pollution, disturbance, and elimination of eelgrass have rendered some California bays unsuitable winter habitat (Smith and Jensen 1970, Cogswell 1977, Dau and Hogan 1985). Numbers wintering in Mexico have increased since 1969 (Dau and Hogan 1985). From 1960 through 1990, numbers have averaged 98,656 to 112,582 in Baja California (Smith and Jensen 1970, Pacific Flyway Council 1991a) and up to 35,100 have wintered on the Mexican mainland coast beginning in 1959 (Smith and Jensen 1970).

As early as 1965, Einarsen warned that changes in the supply of eelgrass and sea lettuce might bring Black Brant to extinction. In spite of protection, eelgrass beds are threatened (Dau and Hogan 1985). Brant use of estuaries is positively correlated with eelgrass presence, and decline in Black Brant use is associated with eelgrass decline, strongly suggesting that brant use of bays is limited by eelgrass availability (Wilson and Atkinson 1995, Wetzel 1996). A shortage of eelgrass during the critical spring staging period may lead to low reproductive success (Wilson and Atkinson 1995).

Eelgrass is the host for eelgrass blight slime mold, which nearly eradicated eelgrass on the Atlantic coast and had a marked but lesser effect along the Pacific coast in the early 1940s (Einarsen 1965, Smith and Jensen 1970, Hawksworth et al. 1983). The southward wintering shift may be related to eelgrass decline (Leopold and Smith 1953, Wilson and Atkinson 1995).

Hunting, chasing, and general shoreline activities disturb Black Brant and force them out of estuaries (Einarsen 1965, Batterson 1968, Smith and Jensen 1970, Dau and Hogan 1985, Bayer 1996a, Wetzel 1996). Human activities affect the extent of Black Brant use of eelgrass areas within Yaquina Bay (Wetzel 1996). Pollution, dredging and other development, and boat and airplane traffic have disturbed staging Black Brant at Izembek Bay, Alaska, and diminished the usefulness of San Diego, Mission, San Francisco, and Humboldt bays in California to Black Brant, even though adequate eelgrass was present in some (Leopold and Smith 1953, Cogswell 1977, Henry and Springer 1981, Dau and Hogan 1985). Disturbed Black Brant may fly to the ocean or to sanctuaries within bays that are safe from humans and other predators (Batterson 1968, Bayer 1996a, Wetzel 1996). Black Brant decline could negatively impact estuarine nutrient cycling due to increased eelgrass and sea lettuce decomposition time without brant digestion (Baldwin and Lovvorn 1994).—*Kathy Merrifield*

## Trumpeter Swan *Cygnus buccinator*

The majestic Trumpeter Swan is the largest of our native waterfowl and one of the heaviest flying birds in the world, with males sometimes exceeding 30 lbs (13.6 kg). Historically hunted to the brink of extinction, it was recognized as an endangered species long before there was an Endangered Species Act, and its recovery is a conservation success story. The adult's snow-white plumage with contrasting black bill and feet and 8-ft (2.4-m) wingspan define this magnificent bird. Their neck is as long as their body and is used to reach food at the marsh bottom. Juvenal garb is a subdued mouse-gray. Identification is difficult, as this species is very similar in appearance to Tundra Swans, but trumpeters normally lack the yellow lores found on most tundras, have a longer neck, and a larger, more wedge-shaped head and bill. Also, the black mask of the trumpeter engulfs the eye, whereas the tundra's eye appears distinct. Deep-toned trumpet voice is the best confirmation of the species, in contrast to the high pitched *purr-rr* of the Tundra Swan.

**General Distribution:** Rocky Mountain population trumpeters breed in Canada in the Yukon and Northwest Territories south to Montana, Idaho, and Wyoming, with 90% wintering in the three latter states (Pacific Flyway Council 1998b). Restoration flocks in e.

Washington, Oregon, and Nevada are considered part of this population, and are generally nonmigratory. The Pacific coast population breeds primarily in Alaska and n. British Columbia, and winters from Alaska south through British Columbia to coastal and w. Oregon (Pacific Flyway Council 1998a). Interior population range is in scattered locations from Wyoming e. to Ontario, with most wintering locally. Monotypic (AOU 1957).

**Oregon Distribution:** In spring, the Trumpeter Swan is a locally uncommon breeder east of the Cascades, most notably at Malheur NWR (Ivey et al. 2000). Pinioned birds have been released on the Deschutes R. in Bend (Carey and Liedblad 2000). Most Malheur NWR birds remain for the winter, although some have traveled elsewhere in the eastern portion of the state including Summer L. W.A., and to California and Nevada (Ivey 1990). West of the Cascades, wintering birds are most consistently noted in w. Polk Co. and Sauvie I., also along n. coast, lower Columbia R., Forest Grove, and Trojan Nuclear Power Plant (Paullin 1987b, Evanich 1990, Pacific Flyway Council 1998a, Gilligan et al. 1994). Identification problems preclude a better determination of status in w. Oregon; source of Oregon's wintering trumpeters needs to be determined.

**Habitat and Diet:** Nesting birds need semipermanent marshes and an abundance of submergent vegetation on which to feed (Rule et al. 1990). At Malheur NWR, this species usually nests in ponds greater than 20 ac (8 ha) with bulrush and occasionally cattail or burreed; may nest on top of muskrat houses (Rule et al. 1990). Nests are constructed by the female ("pen") from materials brought by the male ("cob"), range 6-12 ft (2-4 m) across (Bellrose 1976). Molting birds seek large marshes with good food and emergent cover to escape predators (Rule et al. 1990). Feed in estuaries, lakes, marshes, and ponds (Puchy and Marshall 1993). In winter at Malheur NWR, freezing limits food so birds occur in ice-free areas maintained by springs or moving water (Rule et al. 1990). Summer L. W.A. retains more ice-free water, has an abundance of aquatic vegetation, and provides better winter habitat (Ivey and Carey 1991). Coastal wintering birds roost in estuaries and fresh water, and forage in croplands, pastures, and estuaries (Mitchell 1994).

Feeds in shallow water by putting head and neck below surface, but tips up in deeper water, and may dig holes on bottom with feet to dislodge roots (Banko 1960). Sago pondweed is most important plant food at Malheur NWR; milfoil and other plants used when pondweed not available (Rule et al. 1990). Also feeds on tubers of emergents, especially in spring where a burn has occurred the previous fall or winter (Rule et al. 1990). Young, known as cygnets, eat aquatic beetles and crustaceans for a month, then shift to vegetation like adults (Banko 1960). Primary food along the lower Columbia R. is wapato (Palmer 1976, H. Nehls p.c.). Adults in Montana eat nearly 20 lbs (9 kg, wet weight) of aquatic vegetation a day (Bellrose 1976).

**Seasonal Activity and Behavior:** Pairs at Malheur NWR establish territories in late Apr, begin nesting in early May (Rule et al. 1990); disturbance at this time will cause abandonment (Mitchell 1994). Males are very aggressive in territorial defense; one even attacked a plane in Alaska (Hansen et al. 1971). Cygnets hatch in Jun, adults molt in Jul and Aug and are flightless for 30-40 days (Rule et al. 1990). By early Sep cygnets are usually fledged (Rule et al. 1990), but may not be independent from parents until following spring (Mitchell 1994). Wintering pairs defend feeding areas (Mitchell 1994, *GLI*). Migrant trumpeters usually arrive on the coast in Dec, but sometimes as early as late Oct, leave Feb-Mar (Gilligan et al. 1994).

**Detection:** Easy to see because of color and large size, but difficult to distinguish from other swans without careful study of subtle features. Characteristic call is helpful in identification.

**Population Status and Conservation:** Trumpeter Swans were once found coast-to-coast before hunting pressure decreased both range and numbers dramatically. With expansion of the fur trade and European settlement, they were collected for skins and feathers, and nearly became extinct south of the U.S.-Canadian border with only 66 left in Wyoming by the 1930s, but increased after protection from hunting, habitat preservation, and restoration programs (Mitchell 1994). Trumpeters require a long time to reach breeding age, have only one brood per year, and experience high winter mortality, so population growth is slow (Mitchell 1994). In 1968, they were declared no longer endangered, but are considered a Nongame Species of Management Concern by USFWS (1995a).

Whether or not Trumpeter Swans historically nested in Oregon is unclear. Although Banko (1960) found no evidence of breeding, birds may have been eliminated by European settlers or Native Americans. Fossil remains found at Fossil L. indicate a long presence (Ivey and Carey 1991), and presence in winter was noted historically. Lewis and Clark noted the species at the mouth of the Columbia R. in 1806, Townsend considered them abundant at this location in 1836, and Johnson regarded Trumpeter Swans more common than Tundra Swans in the Willamette Valley in 1880 (Jobanek and Marshall 1992). A single bird seen in 1929 at Davis L. presumed to be a Trumpeter Swan was the last noted until introduction program began in 1939, which moved birds from Red Rock

Lakes NWR, Montana, to Malheur NWR (Cornely, McLaury, et al. 1985). First nesting occurred in 1958, with the flock slowly growing to a peak of 77 in the early 1980s (Ivey 1990), but a shortage of winter food due to flooding and the invasion of carp, compounded by sedentary behavior, resulted in increased mortality, thereby limiting the population (Ivey et al. 2000). By 1989, a harsh winter dropped the total to 18 birds and only two nesting pairs (Ivey and Carey 1991). Because of this declining trend, a proposal was developed in 1990 to enhance conditions in Oregon by increasing the breeding population and expanding their breeding and wintering range (Ivey and Carey 1991). Implementation began in 1991 with summering sites only in Harney Co.; by 1999 had expanded to Lake, Klamath, Crook, Grant, and Baker counties (Ivey et al. 2000). Two pinioned pairs successfully hatched young in 2002 in Bend (C. Carey p.c.). For 79 known fatalities in Oregon 1958-99, 33% were due to powerlines, 27% from predation, 20% from shooting, 9% from emaciation, 8% from lead poisoning, 2% from fence collisions, and 1% from disease (Ivey et al. 2000).—*Gary L. Ivey and Caroline Herziger*

## Tundra Swan *Cygnus columbianus*

Of several swans found in Oregon, the Tundra Swan, formerly called Whistling Swan, is by far the most common during the nonbreeding season. First described from specimens taken by Meriwether Lewis at the mouth of the Columbia R., resulting in the appropriate Latin name *columbianus* (Cutright 1969). Most readily distinguished from the similar-appearing Trumpeter Swan by voice, although subtle differences in physical appearance and behavior can separate the two with difficulty.

The name "Tundra Swan" resulted from a decision by the AOU (1983) to consider conspecific the former Bewick's Swan (*C. bewickii*) of Eurasia and the former Whistling Swan (*C. columbianus*) of N. America, and use the name Tundra Swan for both. This decision occurred with acknowledgment of the lack of a complete published investigation of the taxonomy of the genus *Cygnus* (see AOU 1998).

**General Distribution:** Breeds across N. American and Russian northern tundra regions from nw. Alaska south to Alaska Peninsula and east across Arctic coast to Baffin I., and south around Hudson Bay, Quebec. Also nw. Russia east along Arctic coast almost to Finland. Winters in N. America on Pacific coast from s. British Columbia to s. California, inland to interior valleys and Intermountain West east to Montana and Wyoming and south rarely to Mexico; locally in the e. Great Lakes region; and along the Atlantic coast and Piedmont from New Jersey to S. Carolina. In Eurasia south to British Isles, n. Europe, the Caspian Sea,

Japan, Korea, and the coast of China. Migrates widely through interior N. America. Two subspecies; both have occurred in Oregon.

**Oregon Distribution:** *C. c. columbianus* is a fairly common transient throughout the state but most abundant at large bodies of water and wetland complexes east of the Cascades including Malheur NWR and the surrounding Harney Basin, Summer L. W.A., and the Klamath Basin. Key migratory sites west of the Cascades include Sauvie I. and the lower Columbia R.

During winter it occurs locally in large numbers west of the Cascades. Several thousand, and rarely up to about 10,000, annually winter in the Willamette Valley and 500-1,000 are usually found along the lower Columbia R. (USFWS undated). The Rogue Valley is used to a lesser extent. Along the coast this species is frequently encountered in larger bays and estuaries. The Siuslaw and Umpqua river estuaries have both been noted as significant wintering areas (Bayer and Lowe 1988, Gilligan et al. 1994). East of the Cascades many birds move on to wintering areas in California. However as many as 1,500 and 5,000 birds regularly winter at Summer L. W.A. and the Klamath Basin respectively, and smaller numbers remain at other scattered locations (USFWS undated). In milder winters as many as 10,000 or more may remain at these sites (USFWS undated).

*C. c. bewickii* is reported as accidental. Gilligan et al. (1994) reported fewer than 10 records of this subspecies, most from the Klamath Basin with additional records from Sauvie I. and Nehalem, Tillamook Co. Ongoing reports include one at Malheur NWR on 21 Dec 1997, four in a close group at Lower Klamath NWR on 31 Jan 1998 (Korpi 1998), and one on Antone Reservoir, Wheeler Co., on 10 Mar 2002 (H. Nehls p.c.). No records have been accepted by OBRC, which generally does not review subspecies (H. Nehls p.c.); no specimens taken.

**Habitat and Diet:** The Tundra Swan utilizes shallow lakes, ponds and marshes, sloughs, rivers, estuaries, and agricultural fields in Oregon. Mostly herbivorous, feeding primarily on the seeds, stems, roots, and tubers of submerged and emergent aquatic plants, particularly sago pondweed (Limpert and Earnst 1994). Also eats grasses, sedges, and thin-shelled mollusks. No food habits studies have been conducted in Oregon but concentrated use in areas known to support certain food plants is evident. This includes sago pondweed at Malheur NWR and Warner Valley and wapato at Sauvie I. (*DBM*). With loss of natural foods (e.g., wapato) through invasion of reed canarygrass, livestock use, and wetland loss, Tundra Swans wintering in the Willamette Valley have in recent years taken to foraging in rye-grass fields (*DBM*). Introduction of carp has also had a major impact on swan food plants, especially sago pondweed. Widely fluctuating numbers of swans using Malheur L. relate to habitat conditions affected by carp abundance and water levels (*EJS, DBM*).

**Seasonal Activity and Behavior:** Arrives early to mid-Oct east of the Cascades (Littlefield 1990a, Summers 1993a) and in early Nov on the west side (Browning 1975a, Bayer 1977, Gilligan et al. 1994). Numbers peak in mid-Nov and transients move south through Dec. At Malheur NWR, birds may winter in limited numbers if sago pondweed is abundant on Malheur L. and open water present. Spring migration numbers in the Klamath Basin peak in mid-Feb. Mean spring arrival date for non-wintering birds at Malheur NWR is 11 Feb (Ivey, Herziger, and Scheuering 1998) and numbers usually peak at several thousand, up to 22,000, in mid-Mar (Littlefield 1990a). At Sauvie I. the spring peak is late Feb (Gilligan et al. 1994). Lone birds occasionally summer in Oregon and sometimes associate with Trumpeter Swans (*EJS*).

Gene Kridler initiated a marking study at Malheur NWR during fall migration in 1961 and found migratory corridors were southwest through n. California and the Klamath and Pit river valleys to primary wintering areas in the Central Valley, similar to the pattern of Greater Sandhill Cranes (Paullin and Kridler 1988). During spring migration, swans returned to Malheur NWR mostly through the Klamath Basin, and then continued to the northeast and were observed primarily in n. Idaho, w. Montana, and c. Alberta, a pattern comparable to Snow and Ross's Geese. Additional observations came from c. British Columbia and e. Idaho. A secondary spring migratory route through the Willamette Valley and north along the coast was noted. Sightings from the lower Columbia R., Willamette Valley, and c. Oregon coast were of collared swans marked at Izembek NWR near Cold Bay, Alaska, in a separate study (Lowe 1988).

Each year's offspring remain with their parents throughout their first fall and winter and return to the breeding grounds with them. Territoriality not observed during nonbreeding season and birds travel, forage, and roost in flocks. Pair bond maintained year-round (Limpert and Earnst 1994).

Vocalizations include 1- 3-syllable variations of *ou, oh,* and *oo.* Flight calls common before dusk when migratory and winter flocks come together for the night (Limpert and Earnst 1994).

**Detection:** This swan is reliably found at key sites and easily detected where it occurs due to size, color, and tendency to congregate. Often heard from great distances before they are visually located because of distinctive voice. Care must be taken to distinguish from Trumpeter Swan.

**Population Status and Conservation:** The N. American population reportedly doubled during the last half of the 20th century (Limpert and Earnst 1994). The 1990s saw a steady significant increase in numbers in the Pacific Flyway and the number of swans recorded on Midwinter Waterfowl Surveys averaged 84,600 birds over the 10-yr period 1992-2001 compared to the long-term average of 55,300 during 1949-2000 (Pacific Flyway Council 2001). In Oregon the average wintering population 1992-2001 was just over 9,000 swans (Pacific Flyway Council 2001).

Hunting of western wintering populations has the most direct impact on the species, although there is no legal hunting of swans in Oregon. Mortality from lead poisoning on migratory stopover and wintering sites from ingestion of lead shot or fishing sinkers is a habitual problem more common to the eastern seaboard, but has never appeared to have large-scale effects despite localized large die-offs (Limpert and Earnst 1994). No reports of such die-offs are known from Oregon. Die-offs numbering over 1,000 birds caused by avian cholera have been reported from California (Limpert and Earnst 1994).—*Eric J. Scheuering*

## Whooper Swan *Cygnus cygnus*

A small number of this common Eurasian species regularly winter on the outer Aleutian Is. Casual on the Alaskan mainland. Since the fall of 1991 individuals have been found wintering in the Klamath Basin or among swan flocks elsewhere in n. California (Bailey and Singer 1996). Up to five reported from the Lower Klamath NWR during the winter of 1997-98 (Korpi 1998). During the fall of 1991 up to three Whooper Swans observed at Summer L. W.A., Lake Co. Single individuals were there 9 Mar 1992, 24 Nov 1993, and 10 Nov to 3 Dec 1994 (St. Louis 1995). An adult with three possible hybrid young were there 1-6 Nov 2000 (Sullivan 2001a). One was photographed near Airlie, Polk Co., 27 Nov to 1 Dec 1997 (Tice 1998a). Monotypic (AOU 1957).—*Harry B. Nehls*

### Subfamily Anatinae

## Wood Duck *Aix sponsa*

The drake Wood Duck is the most colorful of N. American ducks, having iridescent greens, blues, and purple on head, crest, speculum, and wing coverts; a white chin, cheek stripes, and belly; black and white edging on yellow flanks; and even a bill of red, white, and black. The brown hen also has a crest, distinctive white eye-ring, white belly and purplish-blue iridescence on wing coverts and speculum. Both sexes have a prominent tail that can be a field mark in flight. As their name implies, associated with timbered wetlands, nesting in cavities and sometimes even feeding in trees. Hens utter a fairly wide range of

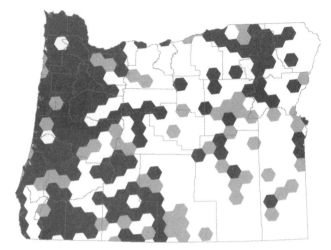

un-duck like sounds, but most common is a loud *wee-e-e-k, wee-e-e-k*. The call of the drake is a low nasal *swheeet, swheet*. Although the Wood Duck constitutes only 2-3% of the duck harvest in Oregon and is a minor game bird in the west, they make up a significant part of the hunting kill in e. U.S.

**General Distribution:** Breeds from s. British Columbia across s. Canada to the Maritime Provinces south to Florida, Cuba, and the Gulf coast in the east and c. New Mexico, c. Arizona, and c. California in the west. Winters throughout the breeding range and n. Mexico in the west; in the east, in the southern parts of the breeding range north to e. Colorado, s. Kansas, s. Minnesota, the Ohio R. valley, and New England, and in Cuba and the Bahamas. Monotypic (AOU 1957).

**Oregon Distribution:** Regular breeder in the Willamette Valley (Evenden et al. 1950, Gullion 1951, OBBA), along slow reaches and backwaters of Cascade and Coast Range rivers, lakes, and ponds, and along the Columbia R. and coastal counties (Adamus et al. 2001). The Wood Duck breeds locally in e. Oregon at McNary Dam and along the Umatilla R., Umatilla Co.; La Grande, Union Co.; Enterprise, Wallowa Co.; Phillips Res. and Haines, Baker Co.; and Ontario, Nyssa, and other sites in Malheur Co. (OBBA, Contreras and Kindschy 1996). Other areas include Warner Valley (Kebbe 1956b), the upper Deschutes area (Roest 1957), the Silvies R. north of Burns (Littlefield 1990a), and the Klamath Basin (Klamath Basin NWR files).

During spring and fall migration the species is locally uncommon in ne. Oregon (Evanich 1992a), locally common in Malheur Co. (Contreras and Kindschy 1996), occasional at Malheur NWR (Littlefield, 1990a), uncommon to fairly common in the Klamath Basin (Summers 1993a). Fairly common migrant in the Willamette Valley (*RKM*) and c. Douglas Co. (Hunter et al. 1998). Common at the Columbia R. estuary and coast (Sawyer and Hunter 1988, Brown et al. 1996, Contreras 1998, Patterson 1998b).

This species winters locally in Malheur Co. (Contreras and Kindschy 1996), Bend (Summers 1985b), Malheur NWR (Littlefield 1990a), and a significant concentration of hundreds is typically present in the pool below McNary Dam and on the McNary NWR (M. Denny p.c.), but most wintering birds are found in w. Oregon (USFWS undated). Sauvie I. and the Portland area are important fall and winter areas (Irons and Heinl 1984, Heinl 1985), with some birds present throughout the Willamette Valley (Gullion 1951, *RKM*). Rare to very uncommon in c. Douglas Co. (Hunter et al. 1998), but common to fairly common on the Douglas Co. coast (Sawyer and Hunter 1988). Found irregularly in major coastal bays (Bayer and Krabbe 1984), but more commonly in sloughs and flooded farmlands in the lower valleys of coastal rivers (Contreras 1998).

*Wood Duck*

ELVA HAMERSTROM Paulson

**Habitat and Diet:** Breeding habitat is wooded swamps, wooded riparian zones of rivers, streams, marshes, sloughs, and lakes. They require cavities in trees for nesting and have been known to use vacated nests of other species such as the Pileated Woodpecker (Grinnell GB 1901, Bull 1986). Nest boxes, placed where birds will find them, are readily accepted in lieu of tree cavities. Migration and winter habitat is similar to that used during the breeding season. Wood Ducks feed on acorns, seeds of trees, shrubs, and aquatic plants, berries, and grapes. Although most feeding is done in flooded areas, sometimes forage above ground level in search of berries and grapes, and also forage on acorns and waste grain (Bellrose 1980). In Oregon they have been observed feeding on hazelnuts in orchards (J. Sayre p.c., W. Mathewson p.c.), and on Russian olive berries on McNary NWR (M. Denny p.c.).

**Seasonal Activity and Behavior:** Migrants begin moving north from their wintering areas by Mar. Irons (1984b) reported migrant flocks along the Oregon coast after mid-Mar. In most of their breeding range, they start nesting as early as Feb and most have nested by the end of Apr. However, H. Nehls (p.c.) has observed downy young as late as the end of Jun at Fernhill Wetlands, Washington Co. Average clutch size is 12 and incubation appears to be longer than most ducks' with a wide range of 28-37 days (Bellrose 1980). Young tend to disperse from rearing areas and some move north before fall migration begins (Bellrose 1980). Wood Ducks are seldom seen in large flocks, with singles, pairs, and small groups the rule. However, when coming in to roost at dusk birds are more apt to bunch and as they arrive in a short span of time this sometimes appears to constitute one large flock (*RKM*).

**Detection:** Wood Ducks are often difficult to locate due to their preferred habitat of wooded sloughs, streams, and flooded timber, but distinctive call often gives them away from some distance.

**Population Status and Conservation:** Gabrielson and Jewett (1940) noted that, although the species had become rare along the Columbia R. by 1912, it had recovered and was exceedingly common—so numerous in fact, that hunters complained about them eating wheat bait intended for other species. Those authors noted that Sauvie I. and Carlton L., Yamhill Co., held the major concentrations of Wood Ducks in the state. Carlton L. has since been drained, but early fall concentrations still occur on Sauvie I. (*RKM*). In recent years, Wood Ducks seem to be holding their own if not increasing in Oregon (Heinl 1985, USFWS undated). Elsewhere in N. America, after what was perceived as near-extinction in the early 1900s, the species gradually recovered and expanded its range northwestward into Minnesota, the Dakotas, and s. Canada and now makes up an important part of the hunting kill in the Mississippi and Atlantic Flyways. Habitat recovery, widespread use of nest boxes, and reduction of kill, in that order, are likely responsible for the population increase and range expansion.—*R. Kahler Martinson*

## Gadwall *Anas strepera*

The drake Gadwall is a large mostly gray dabbling duck, known appropriately as "grayduck" in some regions. Adult drakes have a black bill, buff head, gray body, and black upper and lower tail coverts. Hens are nondescript brown ducks with a spotted, yellowish-orange bill with black edges. Unique among dabbling ducks in having a partly white speculum which can be observed in flight. Common vocalizations include the deep, reed-like sounds of the male, and the female's quacking, similar to, but more nasal and higher pitched than, the Mallard hen's. Hens also make a *tickety-tickety-tickety* chatter like the Mallard (Leschack et al. 1997). The species is an important game species in e. Oregon and good table fare.

**General Distribution:** Breeds from s. Alaska, s. Yukon, south and east to c. Saskatchewan east through sw. Quebec to the Maritimes south to s. California, east to sc. Texas, Kansas, n. Iowa, to n. Pennsylvania and N. Carolina on the Atlantic coast. Core breeding habitat is in the prairie pothole region. Winters from s. Alaska, s. British Columbia, Idaho to s. S. Dakota, the s. Great Lakes, and s. New England south to n. Baja California, Oaxaca, Yucatan, the Gulf coast, Florida, the Bahamas, and W. Indies. Largest wintering concentrations are in the coastal marshes of Louisiana. Oregon birds belong to *A. s. strepera*; the subspecies *couesi* of the Pacific Is. is extinct (AOU 1998).

**Oregon Distribution:** Abundant breeder locally in e. Oregon, uncommon breeder in w. Oregon. Common to abundant spring and fall migrant in e. Oregon, common migrant in w. Oregon. Breeds locally in ne. Oregon (Evanich 1992a) and Malheur Co. (Contreras and Kindschy 1996). Abundant breeder at Malheur NWR (Cornely 1982, Littlefield 1990a), Summer L. W.A. (W.A. files), and in the Klamath Basin (Klamath Basin NWR files). Nesting is rare in w. Oregon, but Heinl (1986c) reported two males courting a female at the s. jetty of the Columbia R. in May and Patterson (1998b) described it as uncommon, but

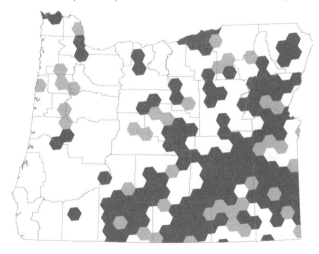

regular summer resident in the Columbia R. estuary. Nesting has been confirmed in Clatsop (OBBA) and Washington counties (Johnson J 1991a, H. Nehls p.c.).

Common spring and fall migrant in ne. Oregon (Evanich 1992a), Malheur Co. (Contreras and Kindschy 1996), and the Klamath Basin (Summers 1993a). Abundant in spring and fall at Malheur NWR (Littlefield 1990a). In the Willamette Valley, rated a common fall migrant by Gullion (1951) and occasional in fall and spring by Evenden et al. (1950). Rare to very uncommon in c. Douglas Co. (Hunter et al. 1998) and the Douglas Co. coast (Sawyer and Hunter 1988). Migrants, especially in the fall (Heinl 1986a), are more common in the Columbia R. estuary and some areas on the coast (Brown et al. 1996, Contreras 1998, Patterson 1998b).

As a winter visitant, Gadwalls are occasional in ne. Oregon (Evanich 1992a), uncommon but widespread during open winters in Malheur Co. (Contreras and Kindschy 1996), uncommon at Malheur NWR (Littlefield 1990a), and uncommon to fairly common in the Klamath Basin (Summers 1993a). Winter in the Willamette Valley in small numbers, though rather inconsistently (Evenden et al. 1950, Irons 1984b). In recent winters, 200-400 have wintered around Eugene (D. Irons p.c.). Wintering birds are common on the coast (Bayer and Krabbe 1984, Heinl 1985, Brown et al. 1996, Contreras 1998) and in the Columbia R. estuary (Patterson 1998b). Winter survey counts show small numbers of Gadwalls statewide, with most in sc. and w. Oregon (USFWS undated).

**Habitat and Diet:** Littlefield (1990a) describes their spring and summer habitat at Malheur NWR as flooded meadows, canals, and ponds and fall habitat as the larger lakes. At the refuge, nested in dry sites, in dense vegetation, often in greasewood stands. Will select islands for nesting sites and prefer more open brood ponds that other dabbling ducks (Leschack et al. 1997). Migration and wintering habitats include permanent wetlands such as lakes, reservoirs, large permanent marshes, and coastal estuaries as well as seasonally flooded pastures and marshes in the Willamette Valley (D. Irons p.c.). Data from Oregon are not available but studies elsewhere suggest that foods are aquatic plants and seeds, with invertebrates becoming more important during the breeding season (Leschack et al. 1997).

**Seasonal Activity and Behavior:** At Malheur NWR, Gadwalls arrive, mostly in pairs, in Apr with peak numbers in early May (Littlefield 1990a). Studies in the midcontinental prairies show that the species nests later than most dabbling ducks, significantly later than Mallards and Northern Pintails, peaking in late May and early Jun (Bellrose 1980). The breeding home range of Gadwalls, unlike most other ducks, may overlap, especially where nesting is concentrated, and the male defends a "moving" territory around the female (Duebbert 1966). At Malheur NWR, nesting takes place mid-May through late Jun. Clutches average 9.1 eggs, hatching peaks in Jul, and flightless young are seen until early Sep. Males begin arriving at the refuge to molt in mid-Jul and, with American Wigeon and American Coot, congregate in deeper parts of Malheur L. Gadwalls begin leaving the refuge in late Aug and early Sep after molt is completed (Littlefield 1990a). At Malheur NWR numbers again increase in late Sep as migrants arrive and peak in mid- to late Oct. Most Gadwalls depart the refuge by mid-Nov. The few birds remaining for the winter, usually not more than 100, are found at Double O Ranch and s. Blitzen Valley (Littlefield 1990a). On the Oregon coast, migrants have stayed as late as 2 May before moving to their breeding areas (Contreras 1998). In Coos Co., the earliest fall arrival date for Gadwalls was 1 Oct (Contreras 1998). Usually observed in singles, pairs, and small groups; rarely in large flocks (Grinnell GB 1901, Evenden et al. 1950).

**Detection:** Gadwalls are sometimes overlooked at a distance because of their drab plumage. The black stern on the drake and the white speculum in flight help distinguish.

**Population Status and Conservation:** Gabrielson and Jewett (1940) found the species to be a common breeder in the "great tule marshes" of e. Oregon and occurring in winter in w. Oregon based on specimens brought to them by hunters for identification. McAllister and Marshall (1945) found the species breeding in the Fremont NF in sc. Oregon. At Malheur NWR, numbers of breeding birds have declined since the 1940s and 1950s (Cornely 1982) due to unfavorable water levels and encroachment of emergent vegetation around ponds and lakes (R. Erickson p.c., *DBM*). Statewide winter surveys suggest that the small numbers of birds wintering here have increased in recent years (USFWS undated). Continental Gadwall population increased during the droughts of the 1950s and 1960s when most other prairie ducks suffered severe population declines. After relative stability in the 1970s and 1980s, numbers again increased to record highs in the 1990s (USFWS undated). Late nesting and preference for dense cover may have sheltered Gadwalls from the effects of agriculture that have been detrimental to earlier-nesting species such as Northern Pintails and Mallards.—*R. Kahler Martinson*

## Eurasian Wigeon *Anas penelope*

This foreign visitor is regularly found in Oregon among wintering flocks of American Wigeon. Drakes are easily distinguished from American Wigeon drakes by reddish brown head, gray flank, and lack of green eye stripe. Hens are similar to American Wigeon hens and difficult to distinguish. Eurasian X American Wigeon hybrids may exhibit a weak eye stripe, buff head, and gray flank (Merrifield 1993). Call of the male is a shrill, whistling, *whe'e-you*; the female's voice a low purr or a croak (Kortright 1943).

**General Distribution:** Breeds from Iceland and British Isles, across n. Europe and Asia to the Bering Sea. Winters across Eurasia to Japan, n. and c. Africa, Arabia, s. Asia, the Malay Peninsula, Taiwan and the Philippines. Regular visitor to both U.S. coasts and occasional in the N. American interior. Monotypic (AOU 1957).

**Oregon Distribution:** Rare to uncommon visitant east of the Cascades. Recorded in ne. Oregon at Ladd Marsh and Pete's Pond (Evanich 1992a), and in Malheur Co. at Farewell Bend and Antelope Res. (Contreras and Kindschy 1996). Annual in small numbers along the Columbia R. in Umatilla and Morrow counties (M. Denny p.c.). Eurasian Wigeon have been observed near Burns, the Double O Ranch, and Frenchglen, Harney Co., and in Bend (Summers 1985a, 1985b, 1986a). At Malheur NWR, first recorded in the 1940s by Erickson (1948), but numerous sightings since, with five observed at one time on 2 Apr 1966 (Littlefield 1990a). They have been found in Lake Co. at Silver L. (Summers 1985a), Summer L., L. Abert, and Thompson Res. (Summers 1985a, C. Miller p.c.). Rare to very uncommon in the Klamath Basin (Summers 1993a). Uncommon, but regular in recent years among American Wigeon flocks in western interior valleys from Portland south to Albany (J. Fleischer p.c.), Corvallis (Evanich 1983b), Eugene (Contreras 2002a), c. Douglas Co. (Hunter et al. 1998), Grants Pass (D. Vroman p.c.) and Medford (Evanich 1983b). Small numbers regularly found among large wintering flocks of American Wigeon from the Portland area (Irons 1984b) to the Columbia R. estuary (Patterson 1998b), and on the coast (Bayer and Krabbe 1984, Sawyer and Hunter 1988, Brown et al. 1996), occurring on 14 of 25 Coos Bay CBCs with a high of nine birds (Contreras 1998).

**Habitat and Diet:** In Oregon identical to the American Wigeon.

**Seasonal Activity and Behavior:** Most observations in Oregon are made Dec to May. Eurasian Wigeon have been observed in fall as early as 16 Sep at Summer L. (C. Miller p.c.). In w. Oregon, Contreras (1998) noted the earliest fall arrival at Coos Bay was 1 Oct. In Linn Co. the earliest fall arrival was 15 Oct (Gillson 1998). Spring departure dates were 7 Apr in Linn Co. (Gillson

1998) and 2 May at Coos Bay (Contreras 1998). One 24 Jun at Malheur NWR was unusually late (Littlefield 1990a). The species' close relationship with American Wigeon results in relatively frequent hybridization with that species (Heinl 1985, Merrifield 1993, *RKM*).

**Detection:** Look for Eurasian Wigeon in large flocks of American Wigeon. The red head of the drakes stands out, but the hens will elude you. Because hybrids are possible, a careful look at atypical drakes is worthwhile. In the Portland area, Eurasians are regularly found at Westmoreland Park and Commonwealth L.

**Population Status and Conservation:** Records from the first half of the 20th century (Gabrielson and Jewett 1940) were few and largely reported by hunters. As numbers of knowledgeable observers with spotting scopes increased, reports throughout Oregon increased. In recent years, small but increasing numbers of Eurasian Wigeon have been found in almost all the areas that harbor wintering American Wigeon. Heinl (1985) suggested that the gradual increase in numbers reported probably reflects observer awareness rather than a real increase in numbers of birds. More recently, D. Vroman (p.c.) leaves open the possibility that, although the increasing observations of the species may be due to careful searching through American Wigeon flocks, there may also be more birds to be found. A. L. Contreras (p.c.) points out that because the hard-to-identify hens are under-reported, absolute numbers of Eurasian Wigeon visiting Oregon are much larger than reported.—*R. Kahler Martinson*

## American Wigeon *Anas americana*

Wigeon drakes are beautifully marked with white pate, green eye stripe, purplish breast and flanks, white belly and wing covert patch, and iridescent black/green speculum. The white pate is the basis for their once being called baldpates. The grayish hen shows white on the wing covert patch. Medium-sized flocks are common in fall and winter, and like geese, will be found grazing pastures, park lawns, and golf courses. Drakes give a three-note whistle and get progressively noisier as spring approaches and courting flights begin. Sometimes associates with diving ducks, a habit which made them a pest to early market hunters when their early flush would alert the diver flock to impending danger. This is an important Oregon game bird ranking as second in the duck harvest (USFWS undated). It is a good table bird, but coastal birds can be strong flavored when on a diet of animal foods (Gabrielson and Jewett 1940, Bayer 1980).

**General Distribution:** Breeds from c. Alaska, c. Yukon to ne. Manitoba, n. Ontario and the Maritimes south to ne. California, n. Nevada, and n. Utah east to

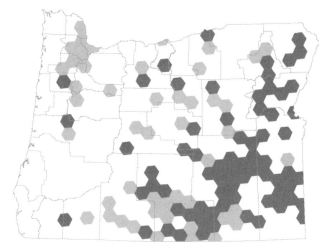

Nebraska, Wisconsin, New York, and the Atlantic coast. Although most breed in the prairie pothole region of sw. Canada and the Dakotas, American Wigeon, like Northern Pintail, breed in substantial numbers in the far north of Canada and Alaska. Winters from s. Alaska, s. British Columbia, Idaho, and Colorado across c. U.S. to the s. Great Lakes and Atlantic coast north to Nova Scotia and south throughout s. U.S., M. America, W. Indies, and n. S. America. Largest numbers are found wintering in the Central Valley of California and the Louisiana Gulf coast (Bellrose 1980). Monotypic (AOU 1957).

**Oregon Distribution:** Rare to locally common breeder in e. Oregon, rare in summer in w. Oregon. Common to abundant migrant and wintering bird statewide. In ne. Oregon, an uncommon summer resident, but nests locally at Ladd Marsh W.A. (Evanich 1992a). A common breeder at Batch L. and Bogus L. in Malheur Co. and locally elsewhere in the county when water conditions are favorable, including Cow Lakes, Beulah Res., and Bully Cr. Res. (Contreras and Kindschy 1996). Cornely (1982) recorded annual production of several hundred wigeon 1942-80 on Malheur NWR; and Littlefield (1990a) reported 200-400 pairs nesting there. Regular but rare breeder at Summer L. (Summer L. W.A. files) and occasional and rare breeder in the Klamath Basin (Klamath Basin NWR files). Gilligan et al. (1994) described the bird as a rare breeder in w. Oregon, although we do not know of specific breeding records. Rare summer resident in the Columbia R. estuary (Patterson 1998b) and very rare in the Willamette Valley and coast. A common spring and fall migrant in ne. Oregon (Evanich 1992a) and Malheur Co., abundant at Malheur NWR (Littlefield 1990a), in the Klamath Basin (Summers 1993a), in the Willamette Valley (Evenden et al. 1950, Gullion 1951), c. Douglas Co. (Hunter et al. 1998), the lower Columbia R. and on the coast (Sawyer and Hunter 1988, Brown et al. 1996, Contreras 1998, Patterson 1998b). Winter waterfowl surveys have found the birds statewide, but with several times the numbers in nw. Oregon than elsewhere (USFWS undated). Wintering wigeon are occasionally reported in ne. Oregon (Evanich 1992a), and uncommonly in Malheur Co. (Contreras and Kindschy 1996), but M. Denny (p.c.) reports 300-400 winter at Hat Rock SP, Umatilla Co. A few hundred spend the winter at Malheur NWR (Littlefield 1990a), and they are uncommon to fairly common in the Klamath Basin in winter (Summers 1993a). Common winter visitants in the Willamette Valley (Evenden et al. 1950, Gullion 1951) and c. Douglas Co. (Hunter et al. 1998), abundant in the Columbia estuary (Patterson 1998b) and on the coastal bays (Gabrielson and Jewett 1940, Bayer and Krabbe 1984, Sawyer and Hunter 1988, Brown et al. 1996, Contreras 1998).

**Habitat and Diet:** Throughout their range American Wigeon breed in small seasonal and semi-permanent wetlands in prairie, parkland, and river delta areas (Bellrose 1980). At Malheur NWR, nesting wigeon favor sites in dense willows along streams and small ponds (Littlefield 1990a). Migrants and wintering birds use the coastal bays, lakes, reservoirs, the Willamette R., Columbia R., and nearby pastures. They eat plant foods, but unlike most other dabblers prefer leaves and stems rather than seeds. At Malheur L., unlike other dabbling ducks, prefer hardstem bulrush stands in the middle of the lake (Littlefield 1990a), where they associate with swans, diving ducks, or coots, stealing food which would normally be out of their reach (*DBM*). Regularly leave the water to feed on grasses and clover on pastures, park lawns, and golf courses (*RKM*). Animal matter, as for most other ducks, frequently makes up part of their diet. Bayer (1980) found wigeon feeding on herring eggs in the Yaquina estuary.

**Seasonal Activity and Behavior:** Migrating American Wigeon leave the state in early Apr (Irons 1984b), arriving in their core breeding grounds in the prairie pothole region in Apr, later than Mallards and Northern Pintails. On the coast, the latest departure from Coos Bay was 2 May (Contreras 1998). Nest in May, later than Mallards and Northern Pintails, but earlier than Gadwalls and Blue-winged Teal. Clutch size 7-9 and incubation 23 days. Young fledge in 45-48 days (Bellrose 1980). At Malheur NWR, Littlefield (1990a) found nesting in progress by late May with young showing up from mid-Jun through Jul. Although adult males arrive at Malheur NWR in late Jul to molt (Littlefield 1990a), first fall migrants arrive in Aug (Gabrielson and Jewett 1940, Contreras 1998) with good-sized flocks along the coast in Sep (Irons 1984a) and Oct (Gabrielson and Jewett 1940). Statewide, wigeon numbers peak in Nov and Dec (Hitchcock et al. 1993). From Malheur NWR, most wigeon migrate

southwest to California with only a few going south through w. Nevada (Littlefield 1990a).

**Detection:** During migration and winter, wigeon are easy to locate because of their open-area feeding habits. The whistle calls of drakes can be heard and identified at long distances. Distinguishing hens from Eurasian Wigeon hens as well as Eurasian x American hybrids can be quite difficult to impossible in the field.

**Population Status and Conservation:** Gabrielson and Jewett (1940) reported the species breeding at Malheur L. and Cold Springs NWR, Umatilla Co., and as an abundant migrant and wintering bird on the coast and in the valleys of coastal streams. Winter surveys in Oregon suggest that numbers were lower in the 1980s than in either 1965-79 or the 1990s. Oregon harvest data show that the species has remained the second most abundant duck in the bag since 1961 (USFWS undated). In the early and mid-1950s, prior to the establishment of standardized waterfowl surveys, American Wigeon, as well as Northern Pintails, were likely at record numbers in Oregon and the w. U.S. as reflected by the severe crop depredations by these species in the Central and Imperial valleys of California. Since then, the continental American Wigeon population has fluctuated markedly with lows in the 1960s and 1980s, higher numbers in the 1950s and 1970s, and has been increasing since 1990.—*R. Kahler Martinson*

## American Black Duck *Anas rubripes*

Common and widespread throughout e. N. America. Postbreeding dispersal takes many individuals well away from their normal range with some reaching Alaska and the Pacific Northwest. Private introductions and releases for hunting purposes have complicated determination of the origin of most of these out-of-range records. There are many published and unpublished W. Coast reports, including many shot by hunters and birds captured at banding operations (Roberson 1980). Noted as an Oregon bird as early as 1887 (Lincoln 1932). An adult male was banded at Malheur NWR, Harney Co., 14 Nov 1930 (Lincoln 1932). Another was seen there 5 May 1977 (Littlefield 1990a). One was observed on Sauvie I., Multnomah Co., 26 Dec 1971, where at least four had been identified in hunters' bags up to that time (Crowell and Nehls 1972b). One was at Eugene, Lane Co., 25 Dec 1984 (Mattocks 1985a). One was collected at Summer L. W.A. 12 Nov 1950 (specimen at OSU), and one was banded near Ontario, Malheur Co., 5 Mar 1951 (Jewett 1954c). An adult male remaining at Hood River from 4 Jan 1998 to mid-Dec 2000 has been accepted by the OBRC. Monotypic (AOU 1957).—*Harry B. Nehls*

## Mallard *Anas platyrhynchos*

When mention is made of ducks, many people first think of the Mallard. Its ability to tolerate human disturbance and adapt to urban as well as rural habitats make it the N. Hemisphere's most abundant and widespread waterfowl. Known as fine table fare, the Mallard is a highly sought game bird and the most harvested waterfowl species in N. America.

Females are mottled-brown, with a dark brown stripe through the eye, orange bill with black splotching, and yellowish-orange to dark-orange legs. Males have a green head with chestnut-brown chest separated by a white neck ring, yellow to yellowish-green bill, and dark-orange legs. Sides are gray with a brownish back, black rump, and black upper and under-tail coverts. Immatures resemble adult females until males acquire nuptial plumage usually by mid-Nov. Males enter the eclipse molt in Jun and resemble hens until mid-Sep. Wings of both sexes have a violet-blue speculum bordered in front and behind by a pronounced white stripe.

**General Distribution:** Breed in much of N. America, and across Europe and Asia south as far as the Mediterranean region and Japan. Winters as far south as n. Africa and India. Introduced to Hawaii, New Zealand, and Australia. In N. America breeds from n. Alaska and n. Yukon southeast across Canada to s. Maine and south through the Aleutian Is. to s. California, and east to Texas and across n. and c. U.S. to Virginia with local breeding on the Gulf coast and Florida. Highest breeding density is in the prairie pothole region of sc. Canada and nc. U.S. (Crissey 1969). The N. American wintering range extends from the s. Alaska coast, including the Aleutian Is., across s. Canada south to c. Mexico, the Gulf coast, s. Florida, and Cuba. Largest wintering concentrations occur in the Mississippi Flyway where over 3 million winter annually (Bellrose 1976). The Pacific Flyway winters approximately 1.7 million (Trost 2000).

It is one of the latest fall migrants, migrating only as far as necessary to find open water and obtain food. Migration occurs along numerous corridors, with highest concentration found along Mississippi R. from n. Illinois to e. Arkansas and Mississippi (Bellrose 1976). In w. U.S. the most important corridor extends from s. Alberta to the Columbia Basin of Oregon and Washington, where as many as 750,000 may winter. Another important corridor exists from s. Alberta through the Snake R. region of Idaho and Oregon, continuing south to the Klamath Basin of sc. Oregon and n. California (Baldassarre and Bolen 1994).

Extensive interbreeding in sw. U.S. with the Mexican Duck (formerly *A. diazi*) has resulted in grouping *diazi* under *A. platyrhynchos* (AOU 1998). Two subspecies; *A. p. platyrhynchos* occurs in Oregon

(Browning 1978).

**Oregon Distribution:** Common transient and summer and winter resident throughout the state. Large numbers breed in the marshes of se. and sc. Oregon. Nesting is known in every county. Largest concentrations winter in the Klamath and Columbia basins, where over 250,000 birds have been noted (Bellrose 1976). Other significant wintering areas include the Willamette Valley and lower Columbia R. region from Portland to Astoria (Bellrose 1976). Free-ranging domestic birds and Mallard-Pekin duck hybrids are also common in municipal parks.

**Habitat and Diet:** Temporary and seasonal wetlands serve as major habitats prior to the nesting season (Dwyer et al. 1979, Baldassarre and Bolen 1994). In the Willamette Valley, Rickerson (2002) documented extensive use of seasonal and semi-permanent wetlands by breeding females. Breeding home range sizes differ greatly depending upon habitat and population density (Bellrose 1980) and have been reported from 500 ac (203 ha) to over 1,700 ac (700 ha) (Dzubin 1955, Titman 1973, Gilmer et al. 1975, Dwyer et al. 1979, Rickerson 2002). Nest site selection is highly variable and ranges from over-water human-made structures to grassland and shrub habitat located up to 1 mi (1.6 km) or more from water. In the Willamette Valley, agricultural cropland, black hawthorn riparian, and Oregon ash riparian zones were the three most highly utilized nesting cover types (Rickerson 2002).

Nesting adults and ducklings feed in shallow temporary to semi-permanent wetlands with abundant emergent cover, e.g., sedge, cattail, bulrush (Talent et al. 1982). In summer when temporary and seasonal wetlands dry up, Mallards move to permanent ponds and lakes where aquatic insects dominate the invertebrate fauna (Swanson et al. 1974, Swanson and Meyer 1977). Postbreeding (molting) males are

*Mallard*

ELVA HAMERSTROM Paulson

commonly found on large shallow marshes with extensive emergent and submergent vegetation that provides abundant cover and food and minimal disturbance (Hochbaum 1944, Oring 1964, Salomonsen 1968).

Main foods taken include grain (corn, barley, and wheat), moist-soil and aquatic plant seeds, and aquatic invertebrates. Invertebrates (Diptera, Gastropoda, and Oligochaeta) are particularly important to females during pre-laying and laying periods and ducklings during the first 6 wk after hatch (Swanson and Nelson 1970, Krapu 1974, Swanson et al. 1974, Swanson and Meyer 1977).

**Seasonal Activity and Behavior:** In w. Oregon, pairs begin establishing territories by early Feb with first nesting attempts occurring late-Feb, and nesting continuing through early Jun (Rickerson 2002). In e. Oregon, egg laying begins in late-Mar, with incubation beginning late-Apr and peaking in May (Littlefield 1990a). Females lay one egg/day until clutch of 9-11 eggs is complete (on average) and incubate approximately 26 days. Ducklings are highly mobile and follow the female up to 1 mi (1.6 km) or more to water within 24 hr of hatch. Fledging (first flight) occurs 52-60 days after hatch (Gollop and Marshall 1954).

Mallards forage singly or with mate in nesting season and in flocks during nonbreeding season. Forage while walking in dry fields or in shallow water. Dabble for food items at water surface and tip up in shallow wetlands. Occasionally dive to reach bottom vegetation or aquatic seeds.

**Detection:** One of the most vocal of all ducks; exhibits a variety of quacks especially noticeable during fall and winter when birds are concentrated. Easily located by scanning most water bodies including municipal parks, coastal estuaries, and wetlands throughout the state.

**Population Status and Conservation:** From 1996 to 1999, the average Mallard breeding population in Oregon was 112,800 birds (ODFW unpubl. data). Seasonal marshes of sc. and se. Oregon contain the largest breeding numbers with approximately 61,400 birds or 18.5 birds/mi² (7.2 birds/km²). Other large breeding segments include the Willamette Valley (20,240 birds or 7.4 birds/mi² [2.9 birds/km²]), lower Columbia R. region from Sauvie I. to Youngs Bay at Astoria (5,592 birds or 25 birds/mi² [9.8 birds/km²]), and forested wetlands of sc. Oregon (4,400 birds or 6.6 birds/mi² [2.6 birds/km²]). Remainder of the breeding population is distributed throughout the lakes and rivers of the state in low to moderate densities.

In 1999, the Mallard breeding population within the traditional survey area of sc. Canada and nc. U.S. was 10.8 million birds, up 12% from 1998 and 46% above long-term average (1955-98) (Trost 1999). Rapid changes in Mallard populations result from rapidly changing water abundance in the prairie pothole region (Posphala et al. 1974).

There are no conservation threats to this species; however, hybridization between the Mallard and other duck species has created problems for waterfowl managers when it occurs with a species of concern such as the American Black Duck and Pacific Gray Duck (Braithwaite and Miller 1975, Johnsgard and DiSilvestro 1976).—*Eric V. Rickerson*

## Blue-winged Teal *Anas discors*

The Blue-winged Teal is one of Oregon's least common ducks. It is a small, warm-weather duck usually found in Oregon only from late spring until the weather cools in early fall. Except for adult drakes in alternate plumage, blue-wings are difficult to distinguish from Cinnamon Teal. For that reason its status in Oregon is less clear than that of other ducks. Adult blue-wing drakes have a gray head with white crescent between the eye and bill. Hens and young of both species are nondescript small brown ducks, but show the prominent blue wing-covert patch in flight. In flight drakes utter a *peep* call and the hen's quack is softer and weaker than that of the Green-winged Teal. Blue-wings are not an important game species in Oregon and only a few are taken annually because their early autumn migration usually precedes the hunting season and they rarely winter.

**General Distribution:** Breeds from ec. Alaska, s. Yukon south and east to c. Manitoba and east to the Maritimes south to ne. California, c. Nevada east to Texas, Tennessee, and N. Carolina. The core breeding area is the prairie pothole region of sw. Canada and the Dakotas. Winters from n. California, s. Arizona, to the Gulf coast and N. Carolina south throughout M. America, the W. Indies, and c. S. America. Although some blue-wings regularly winter in S. Carolina, Georgia, and Florida, the only large wintering concentration in the U.S. is in the Louisiana coastal

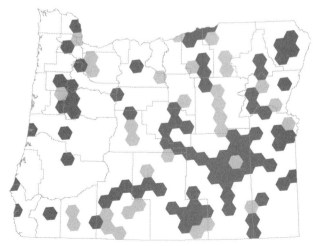

marshes. Most winter south of the U.S. in Colombia, Venezuela, M. America, Mexico, and the W. Indies. Monotypic (Delacour 1964).

**Oregon Distribution:** Uncommon summer resident in ne. Oregon (Evanich 1992a). Regular on McKay Cr. NWR, Umatilla Co., with 20-30 birds in May-Jun (M. Denny p.c.). Breeds locally in Malheur Co. (Contreras and Kindschy 1996) and is a regular but uncommon breeder at Malheur NWR (Wheeler 1965, Littlefield 1990a). Regular but rare breeder at Summer L. (Summer L. W.A. files) and in the Klamath Basin (Klamath Basin NWR files). Nesting has also been confirmed in Wallowa, Union, Morrow, Wasco, Klamath, and Lake counties (OBBA). Breeding in the Willamette Valley has been verified (OBBA), but is rare (McAllister 1949, Wheeler 1965, Irons 1984b). Although no breeding was reported, Hunter et al. (1988) listed it as casual during summer in c. Douglas Co., and S. Pinnock (p.c.) reported up to eight at Jackson Bottoms, Washington Co., during May and Jun 2000. On the coast, blue-wings have been observed occasionally throughout the summer suggesting possible breeding in Coos Co. (Contreras 1998) and in Clatsop Co. (M. Patterson p.c.).

These birds are common spring and fall migrants in ne. Oregon (Evanich 1992a) and Malheur Co. (Contreras and Kindschy 1996). Littlefield (1990a) found the species to be an uncommon spring migrant at Malheur NWR. In w. Oregon, Gullion (1951), undoubtedly using a different abundance rating, called it a common spring and fall migrant in the s. Willamette Valley while Evenden et al. (1950) described it as sporadic at McFadden's Swamp (now McFadden's Marsh, William L. Finley NWR). Hunter et al.(1998) noted the species as a casual spring and early fall migrant in c. Douglas Co. Blue-wings are rare and irregular migrants on the coast (Brown et al. 1996, Contreras 1998, Patterson 1998b).

In winter, irregularly reported with records from Malheur NWR (Littlefield 1990a), a record from ne. Oregon (Evanich 1992a), and several from w. Oregon (Bayer and Krabbe 1984, Heinl 1985, Heinl 1986c).

**Habitat and Diet:** At Malheur NWR, it selects the moist zones between marshes and uplands for nesting (Littlefield 1990a). W. Oregon nesting sites have been near shallow marshes (Wheeler 1965), including McFadden's Marsh (McAllister 1949) and sewage ponds (Irons 1984b). Feeds on plant and animal matter. This species differs from the Green-winged Teal, with which they are seen feeding in early fall, in that they eat the vegetative parts of the plants whereas the green-wings eat the seeds (Bellrose 1980).

**Seasonal Activity and Behavior:** Earliest arrival for Blue-winged Teal at Malheur NWR is 27 Feb with the average 11 Apr; most birds arrive paired with no discernable peak in spring migration (Littlefield 1990a). Average arrival in Crook, Deschutes, and Jefferson counties is 28 Apr with earliest recorded 13 Apr (C. Miller unpubl. data). In w. Oregon, spring arrival has been as early as 16 Mar (Fix 1985a, Heinl 1986c). In 1984, Irons (1984b) reported its arrival throughout the region during the last week in Apr. In the Corvallis area, A. McGie (p.c.) observed 21 Apr as the earliest and 7 May as the average arrival date over 18 yr. In Coos Co. the earliest arrival date was 14 Mar and latest 11 Jun (Contreras 1998). Studies elsewhere suggest that clutch size is 8-11; incubation 23-27 days (Bellrose 1980), but no data are available for Oregon. At Malheur NWR, young were evident in Jun and Jul; most were fledged by early Sep and left shortly thereafter (Littlefield 1990a). Because of the identification problem with Cinnamon Teal, Littlefield (1990a) was not able to identify an autumn peak in numbers or departure date, but speculated that, like the Cinnamon Teal, numbers peaked in the last half of Aug and most had migrated by mid-Oct.

**Detection:** Females and juveniles are very difficult to distinguish from Cinnamon Teal. Although not great, the likelihood of detecting this species is best where they occur as breeding pairs in e. Oregon marshes.

**Population Status and Conservation:** Although they found blue-wings in summer in both e. and w. Oregon, Gabrielson and Jewett (1940) reported only a single nesting record, a nest with eggs found in Warner Valley. Erickson (1948) reported that the species nested at Malheur NWR in the 1940s. Hebard (1949) found a pair in Jul at Hart L. in Warner Valley. Fluctuations in populations in Oregon may be related to habitat conditions elsewhere. Littlefield (1990a) noted that numbers of breeders at Malheur NWR usually increase when drought persists in the prairie pothole region. Although the continental Blue-winged Teal population shows some of the effects of drought in the prairie pothole region, it has exhibited a stable long-term trend with an upswing in the 1990s (USFWS undated). The late nesting habit of the species, with nest initiation after some ponds have dried and agriculture is underway, may have mitigated the effects that the drought had on more early-nesting ducks in the prairie pothole region.—*R. Kahler Martinson*

## Cinnamon Teal *Anas cyanoptera*

The bright rusty plumage of the male Cinnamon Teal, a bird of w. N. America, is a visual delight. In flight, both males and females show powder blue in the wings as they fly fast and low, timed at nearly 60 mph (97 kph). They weigh only about 1 lb (0.4 kg) (Terres 1980). Cinnamon Teal are one of the least studied

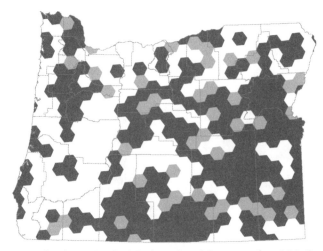

waterfowl species in N. America (Gammonley 1996). Fossil evidence shows they have been in Oregon since the Pleistocene (Miller 1911).

**General Distribution:** The only duck other than Ruddy that breeds in both N. and S. America (Terres 1980). Only one of five Cinnamon Teal subspecies occurs in U.S. and Canada (Gammonley 1996). *A. c. septentrionalium* nests in British Columbia, Alberta, and Saskatchewan, in the U.S. west of the Great Plains primarily in the Great Basin and western intermountain regions, also south through c. Mexico (Gammonley 1996). Winters from coastal nw. and s. Sacramento Valley areas of California to Arizona, New Mexico, south to Guatemala (Gammonley 1996).

**Oregon Distribution:** Common to fairly common breeder throughout state except rare or absent in w. Oregon and high Cascades. Most common east of the Cascades with greatest numbers at Malheur NWR, Summer L. W.A., and Klamath Basin. Local breeder along coast and western interior valleys (Evanich 1990, Puchy and Marshall 1993, Summers 1993a, Gilligan et al. 1994, Hunter et al. 1998). It is uncommon to rare fall through spring on s. coast, Sauvie I., Forest Grove, and Fern Ridge Res., and in e. Oregon at Malheur NWR (Evanich 1990, Littlefield 1990a, Brown et al. 1996, Contreras 1998).

**Habitat and Diet:** Nests in marshes, irrigated meadows, and grass and forb habitats (Puchy and Marshall 1993). At Malheur NWR, the Cinnamon Teal nests near water primarily in meadows, secondarily in uplands, preferring grassy nest sites (Rule et al. 1990) often in creeping wild rye and saltgrass (*GLI*), occasionally over water (Paullin 1981, Foster 1985). Nests more in partially mowed fields than other duck species (Ivey 1979, Paullin 1981), and requires lower vegetation height and density than other ducks except Northern Shoveler (Paullin 1981). Nest initiation is earlier and success higher in burned fields (Ivey et al. 1987). At Bear and Silvies valleys in the Blue Mtns., it

nests more abundantly in herbaceous xeric shrub and continuous mesic shrub habitats (Sanders and Edge 1998). Broods are often found in wet meadows at Malheur NWR (Rule et al. 1990), but in Washington they feed over dense floating mats of submerged vegetation at moderate water depths, similar to Gadwalls (Monda and Ratti 1988). Males molt in wetlands near breeding areas or in large marshes with abundant emergent vegetation (Gammonley 1996). Migrant and wintering birds use lakes, flooded fields, and sewage ponds (Gilligan et al. 1994).

This species feeds in estuaries, marshes, meadows, and urban habitats (Puchy and Marshall 1993), often on midges and midge larvae (*GLI*). No other diet information available for Oregon, but in N. American range as a whole feed in shallow water on seeds of bulrush and saltgrass, leaves of bulrush and pondweed, also mollusks and insects (Bellrose 1976). Social feeding occurs throughout the year with birds dabbling at water stirred up by those in front (Gammonley 1996).

**Seasonal Activity and Behavior:** Usually migrates nocturnally (Gammonley 1996). Most arrive in spring already paired at Malheur NWR (Littlefield 1990a); average arrival 28 Feb (Ivey, Herziger, and Scheuering 1998); average arrival date at Hart Mt. N. Antelope R./Warner Valley 4 Apr (Stern 1988). This is one of the earliest nesting duck species at Malheur NWR, starting in Apr (Ivey 1979, Paullin 1981, Foster 1985) running to late Jun (Rule et al. 1990). Peak numbers at Warner Basin were mid-Apr and May (Stern 1988). Pairs select nest site by first flying over area together, then female travels on foot (Bellrose 1976). Defends only a very small territory and so has greater pair densities than other dabblers (Rule et al. 1990). Males guard females until late into incubation period, then leave to form small flocks with other males to molt, and begin fall migration in summer, earlier than most other ducks (Gammonley 1996). Eggs hatch early May to late Jul (Rule et al. 1990). Females have been described as the best mothers of any duck species, keeping their broods near cover, and diverting attention while young hide from danger (Spencer *in* Bellrose 1976). Ducklings feed themselves on their first day, but do not fledge until about 50 days, with males developing red eyes at 8 wk (Gammonley 1996). At Malheur NWR, young fledge by early Sep. Most winter on Mexico's w. coast (Littlefield 1990a). Some birds winter in Oregon, most commonly along the coast and in interior western valleys (Evanich 1990, Brown et al. 1996, Contreras 1998).

**Detection:** Male Cinnamon Teal in alternate plumage can be easily identified even without binoculars due to distinctive plumage and because they are often found in water sources adjoining roads. However, females, young, and molting males are difficult to distinguish from other teal species; males can be identified by their red eyes.

**Population Status and Conservation:** Overall in N. America, this is one of the least abundant dabbling ducks, not harvested as much as others because of limited range and early migration (Gammonley 1996). Availability and quality of wetlands and surrounding uplands may be limiting factor on population; predation limits recruitment and competition with Blue-winged Teal may limit range expansion (Gammonley 1996). Threats include wetland loss, upland vegetation degradation from grazing, and selenium poisoning from agricultural drainage in California (Gammonley 1996).

In Oregon, Willett (1919) described this species as "abundant" on and near Malheur L. in 1918. Gabrielson and Jewett (1940) reported them so common that, "In May, June, and early July every roadside pond and water-filled ditch in e. Oregon is likely to display some of these very beautiful ducks." Currently, it is the most common breeding duck at Malheur NWR (Ivey 1979, Paullin 1981, Rule et al. 1990), also at Warner Basin (Stern 1988). Oregon population estimates from 1994-99 ranged from 34,669 to 52,629 individuals with about 85% on the east side of the Cascades (B. Bales p.c.). Botulism kills birds in late summer and fall in the Great Basin (Gammonley 1996), including Malheur NWR (Malheur NWR files). Limiting factors for birds at Malheur NWR are predation, nesting cover, and carp that limit aquatic foods (Rule et al. 1990). BBS data 1986-91 show significant population decline in state (Gammonley 1996).—*Caroline Herziger and Gary L. Ivey*

## Northern Shoveler *Anas clypeata*

The Northern Shoveler's specialized bill earned it the nickname "Spoonbill" or "Spoonie" among waterfowl hunters. The drake is strikingly handsome with a dark head, white breast, reddish belly, blue wing coverts and an iridescent green speculum. Brown hens also have blue wing patch similar to that of the Cinnamon Teal and Blue-winged Teal. Vocalizations include a *paaay . . . took-took . . . took-took* by drakes in the fall and early winter and weak quacks by the hen (Dubowy 1996). Bill and feeding behavior lead to a largely undeserved reputation among hunters as a poor table bird. Gabrielson and Jewett (1940) attributed poor table quality to the birds being in poor condition while in Oregon. The species ranks about sixth, after the Gadwall, in the hunting harvest of ducks in Oregon.

**General Distribution:** Breeds from n. Alaska, n. Yukon southeast to n. Manitoba and n. Ontario south to s. California, s. Arizona, east to Oklahoma, n. Missouri, c. Ohio, New York, and Delaware. Greatest

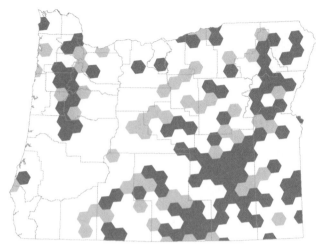

density and numbers of breeding shovelers occur in the prairie pothole region of the Great Plains. Winters from coastal and s. British Columbia to w. Montana, Colorado, and c. Texas, the Gulf coast and Maryland south through M. America, Bermuda, the W. Indies, to n. S. America. Largest numbers are in Mexico, California, and Louisiana. Monotypic (AOU 1957).

**Oregon Distribution:** Locally common in summer in e. Oregon, uncommon in w. Oregon. Common spring and fall migrant statewide, rare to locally abundant winterer in e. Oregon, uncommon to common in winter in w. Oregon. The Northern Shoveler breeds locally in Malheur Co. (Contreras and Kindschy 1996) and on the Umatilla NWR complex in Morrow and Umatilla counties (M. Denny p.c.). Often found at sewage ponds in e. Oregon (M. Denny p.c.). Common in summer at Malheur NWR with 500-700 pairs nesting there (Littlefield 1990a) and average annual production sometimes exceeding 1,000 young (Cornely 1982). Regular and common breeder at Summer L. (Summer L. W.A. files) and in the Klamath Basin (Klamath Basin NWR files). Breeding west of the Cascades has become widespread and regular, especially around sewage ponds (H. Nehls p.c.). There are breeding records from the n. Oregon coast (Hunn and Mattocks 1977, Tweit and Heinl 1989), Portland (Harrington-Tweit et al. 1978), and the Willamette Valley (OBBA), as well as one record from Coos Co. (Contreras 1998).

It is a common spring and fall migrant in ne. Oregon (Evanich 1992a), Malheur Co. (Contreras and Kindschy 1996), the Klamath Basin (Summers 1993a), and abundant at Malheur NWR (Marshall 1959, Littlefield 1990a). Fairly common migrant in the Willamette Valley (Evenden et al. 1950, Gullion 1951) and on the s. coast (Brown et al. 1996). Uncommon to fairly common in c. Douglas Co. (Hunter et al. 1998). Common migrant in Coos Co. (Contreras 1998) and the Columbia R. estuary (Patterson 1998b).

In winter, rare in ne. Oregon (Evanich 1992a) and

Malheur Co. (Contreras and Kindschy 1996). It is an occasional winterer at Malheur NWR (Evanich 1983b, Littlefield 1990a), but when conditions are favorable, large numbers may linger into Dec (Marshall 1959). In some years, large numbers remain in the Klamath Basin (USFWS undated). Uncommon winterer in the Willamette Valley (Evenden et al. 1950, Irons and Heinl 1984). Sometimes especially common at sewage ponds and in c. Douglas Co. (Hunter et al. 1998). Uncommon on the s. coast (Brown et al. 1996) and Douglas Co. coast (Sawyer and Hunter 1988). Common to abundant in Coos Bay (Contreras 1998), common in the Columbia R. estuary (Patterson 1998b) and other large coastal bays (Bayer and Krabbe 1984).

**Habitat and Diet:** Breeding habitat consists of open, shallow wetlands, including sewage ponds. Migration and wintering habitat includes a wide range of habitats such as fresh and salt marshes, sewage and wastewater lagoons, and shallow lakes (Dubowy 1996). Uses specialized bill to strain small swimming crustaceans from the water surface. When Harney L. has high invertebrate populations, Northern Shovelers can be the most abundant duck in the region, with numbers that approached 250,000 in the late 1950s (Littlefield 1990a, *DBM*); also occurs in large concentrations some years on L. Abert (*DBM*). Occasionally will feed with head under water or tip up. Although animal life is the principal food, some plant seeds are consumed. Unlike most other dabbling ducks, does not feed on land (Dubowy 1996).

**Seasonal Activity and Behavior:** Spring migration is later than Northern Pintails and Mallards. In e. Oregon, Gabrielson and Jewett (1940) found shovelers arriving as early as 22 Mar, but it was well into Apr before most were there. At Malheur NWR, Littlefield (1990a) reported the first birds arriving in late Feb or early Mar with the peak mid- to late Apr; most migrants were gone by mid-May. In Coos Co. the latest spring arrival was 16 May (Contreras 1998). Nesting at Malheur NWR occurred from late Mar to late Jun, clutch size averaged 9.3, and young were observed Jun through Jul (Littlefield 1990a). Males are the most territorial of dabbling ducks and may be seen defending territories until hatching time (Littlefield 1990a, Dubowy 1996). Fall migrants begin arriving at Malheur NWR mid- to late Aug and peak in early Sep (Littlefield 1990a). On the coast in Coos Co. the earliest arrival was 4 Aug (Contreras 1998). Many local breeders depart in Sep (Gabrielson and Jewett 1940), but some may still be present in mid-Nov (Littlefield 1990a), and occasionally until Dec (Gabrielson and Jewett 1940, Marshall 1959). In fall and winter, usually seen in small flocks as well as pairs and singles, but have been found in large autumn concentrations (see habitat

and diet). Hunters find the species unpredictable, sometimes coming into decoys with abandon, and other times quite indifferent to even the most enticing decoy sets.

**Detection:** With birds on the water, the large bill angled downward aids identification of this species at long distances. The feeding habit of skimming the surface of the water can also aid in detection.

**Population Status and Conservation:** Gabrielson and Jewett (1940) described the Northern Shoveler as an abundant summer resident of e. Oregon marshes, fairly common during winter in the Portland area, and occurring on the Columbia R. and larger coastal bays. Recent trends in Oregon winter survey counts are variable, with highest numbers in years when winter conditions in the east and south-central regions of the state are favorable (USFWS undated). The continental population of the Northern Shoveler has increased to record highs in the 1990s from lows in the late 1950s and early 1960s (USFWS undated). Although habitat degradation in the prairie pothole region has undoubtedly reduced productivity, the bird's nesting habits have made it less affected by agricultural practices than early nesters such as the Mallard and Northern Pintail.—*R. Kahler Martinson*

### Northern Pintail *Anas acuta*

The pintail is a large, long-necked duck of open spaces. The long-tailed, full-plumaged drake is striking with a chestnut head, gray back and flanks, bright white breast and front of neck, and iridescent green-bronze speculum. The brown hen is nondescript, but shares the long neck and graceful shape of the drake. Common vocalizations are the two-note flute-like whistle of the drake and harsh *gaak*, either single or in a series, of the hen (Austin and Miller 1995). In fall and winter, pintails travel in medium to large flocks. In Oregon, flocks seem to fly exceptional distances in daily foraging and can be seen traveling many miles

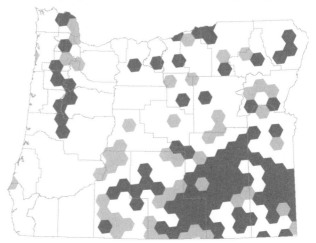

from their Sauvie I. roost along the Willamette R. and Columbia R. throughout the morning hours. Pintails are an important game bird in Oregon. Although ranking fourth numerically in the duck harvest, it rates at the top with the Mallard in terms of hunter preference.

**General Distribution:** Breeds from n. Alaska across the Canadian arctic as far north as Banks I. to c. Labrador south to s. California, n. Arizona, to nw. Missouri, New York, and Massachusetts. The prairie pothole region, when ponds are full, is the core breeding range for the Northern Pintail, which concentrate there in great abundance. Winters from the s. Alaska coast, s. interior British Columbia, c. Washington, s. Idaho, Montana, to c. Missouri, the s. Great Lakes, and along the Atlantic coast from Massachusetts, south throughout the s. U.S., M. America, Bermuda, and the W. Indies to n. Colombia, n. Venezuela, and the Guianas. Highest winter concentrations are in the central valleys of California and coastal marshes of Louisiana and Texas. Insular Old World birds are a separate species (*contra* AOU 1983, see Stahl et al. 1984, Livezey 1991), while New World and mainland Old World birds remain *A. acuta*. Thus the species is monotypic.

**Oregon Distribution:** Uncommon to common breeder and abundant migrant east of the Cascades; it is a rare breeder, but an abundant migrant and winter visitant west of the Cascades. Nests locally in counties adjacent to Idaho (Evanich 1992a, Contreras and Kindschy 1996) and at Malheur NWR (Littlefield 1990a). Common breeder in the Klamath Basin (Klamath Basin NWR files) and regular but rare breeder at Summer L. (Summer L. W.A. files). In w. Oregon, M. Patterson (p.c.) reported a hen with ducklings near Karlson I. in the Columbia R. estuary and a female with eight young was reported from the Nehalem sewage ponds 23 Jul 1990 (Johnson J 1991a). Probably breeds locally elsewhere in w. Oregon (Contreras 1998, OBBA).

Common spring and fall migrants in ne. Oregon (Evanich 1992a) and Malheur Co. (Contreras and Kindschy 1996). Littlefield (1990a) found them the most abundant migrant duck in Harney-Malheur Basin with numbers approaching 250,000 in some springs. Common to abundant spring and fall migrant in the Klamath Basin (Summers 1993a) and the Willamette Valley (Evenden et al. 1950, Gullion 1951). Rare to very uncommon migrant in c. Douglas Co. (Hunter et al. 1998). Common migrant in the Columbia R. estuary (Patterson 1998b) and along the Oregon coast (Sawyer

and Hunter 1988, Brown et al. 1996, USFWS undated).

Uncommon winter visitant in Malheur Co. (Contreras and Kindschy 1996) and at Malheur NWR (Littlefield 1990a); common in winter in ne. Oregon (Evanich 1992a), the Klamath Basin (Summers 1993a), and the Willamette Valley (Evenden et al. 1950, Gullion 1951). Rare to very uncommon in c. Douglas Co. (Hunter et al. 1998). Common migrant and winter visitor in Lower Columbia R. from Sauvie I. to Astoria (Patterson 1998b, USFWS undated) and in coastal bays and estuaries (Bayer and Krabbe 1984, Sawyer and Hunter 1988, Brown et al. 1996, Contreras 1998). A majority of the Oregon wintering population usually found on Sturgeon L. on Sauvie I., with next largest concentrations in the Klamath Basin and Columbia R. below Portland (J. Voelzer p.c.).

**Habitat and Diet:** Although Northern Pintails can be found in a variety of habitats, throughout their breeding range they prefer open country, nesting in grasslands and treeless tundra. At Malheur NWR, they nest in short, open vegetation (Littlefield 1990a). Migration and wintering habitat includes open, shallow wetlands, flooded agricultural fields, and coastal estuaries. Spring migrants at Malheur NWR are attracted to newly flooded meadows and, in the fall, use shallow portions of large lakes. Pintails are largely vegetarian, feeding on marsh plant seeds and waste grain and rice (latter in California). Invertebrates are important during breeding and rearing and have been found in the diets of wintering birds from Sauvie I. and Netarts Bay (Gabrielson and Jewett 1940).

**Seasonal Activity and Behavior:** Pairing takes place in fall and winter. They migrate north from wintering grounds in Feb and Mar. First migrants arrive in e. Oregon at ice breakup (Gabrielson and Jewett 1940). At Malheur NWR, it is one of the earliest spring migrants, arriving in mid-Feb; numbers peak in mid-Mar. With Mallards, pintails are the earliest nesting

*Northern Pintail*

ducks and all but the local breeders have left by early May (Littlefield 1990a). On the coast, Contreras (1998) noted 2 May as the latest departure from Coos Co. Littlefield (1990a) reported nesting in progress by mid-Apr and peaking in May at Malheur NWR. Highly promiscuous, and pursuit flights of several unmated drakes after a paired hen are common through spring (Bellrose 1980). At Malheur NWR, clutches averaged 7.5 eggs and hatched in 23 days (Littlefield 1990a). Adult males from northern breeding areas arrived at Malheur NWR in Jun to molt (Littlefield 1990a). Young may be on the wing in Jul, but with renesting, flightless young may be present in late Jul and Aug (Littlefield 1990a). Migrants begin arriving in Oregon as early as Jul (Heinl 1986b). Coincidental with the arrival of northern migrants, dispersing young show up in high mountain lakes in early Aug, and by mid-Aug Northern Pintails have become common throughout the state (Gabrielson and Jewett 1940). Fall migration peaks 25 Aug-10 Sep at Malheur NWR (Littlefield 1990a). Earliest fall arrival at Coos Bay was 8 Aug (Contreras 1998) and substantial numbers have arrived on the Oregon coast by early Sep (Irons 1983). Migration extends through Nov with numbers peaking in mid-Nov. Wintering pintails move from coastal estuaries to the Willamette Valley to Sauvie I. in response to food availability affected by water level changes and freezing. Up to 4,000 were on Fern Ridge Res., Lane Co., in late Dec 2001, but departed in Jan 2002 (D. Irons p.c.). Large flocks also travel considerable distances within and between those regions in daily foraging in winter. Attracted to shallow water on agricultural fields and respond overnight when flooding creates such habitat (*RKM*).

**Detection:** The pintail's distinctive slender shape and loud call, as drakes become progressively noisier through the winter, make the species recognizable from some distance.

**Population Status and Conservation:** Gabrielson and Jewett (1940) reported the species as an abundant breeder in the alkaline marshes of e. Oregon and one of the most abundant ducks found in the state during migration and winter. At Malheur NWR, pintail production was high in 1942-50, but declined several-fold during 1951-80 (Cornely 1982). Widespread heavy growth of emergent vegetation in the area after the 1940s was the likely reason for the decline (*DBM*). There is also a suggestion of the inverse relation between production at Malheur NWR and that in the prairie pothole region that Littlefield (1990a) cited for the Blue-winged Teal. Winter counts of Northern Pintail in Oregon are highly variable, but suggest that fewer birds wintered here 1980-95 than in the 1970s. Counts for 1996-98 were similar to those of the 1970s (USFWS undated). Continental populations

of Northern Pintails flourished during the 1950s when the prairie pothole region was wet, grain farming in s. Canada was just beginning to expand, and favorable spring weather combined to provide optimum nesting conditions for such early-nesting species. Numbers declined drastically when droughts dried up prairie habitat in the late 1950s and early 1960s, rebounded somewhat in the 1970s, but subsequently decreased to record lows in the 1990s (USFWS undated). Increasing agricultural pressure in the prairie pothole region is likely responsible for the recent decline (Miller and Duncan 1999).—*R. Kahler Martinson*

### Garganey *Anas querquedula*

Small numbers of this widespread Eurasian duck occur as spring and fall transients to the Aleutian Is. and irregularly to the N. American continent (Spear et al. 1988). In other than full adult male plumage it is quite difficult to separate Garganey from other duck species. There are two Oregon records; a male photographed in full eclipse plumage at the Nehalem sewage ponds, Tillamook Co., 17-19 Sep 1988 (Johnson and Lethaby 1991), and an adult male in alternate plumage at the Bay City sewage ponds, Tillamook Co., 9-13 May 1992 (photo *Oregon Birds* 18:[4] cover). Monotypic (Madge and Burn 1988).—*Harry B. Nehls*

### Baikal Teal *Anas formosa*

This colorful Asian duck occurs casually in N. America from Alaska southward along the Pacific coast to s. California. There is a single Oregon record, an adult male shot by a hunter 2 mi (3.2 km) east of Finley NWR, Benton Co., 12 Jan 1974. Mounted specimen is now at OSU (Nehls 1992b). Monotypic (AOU 1957).—*Harry B. Nehls*

### Common Teal *Anas crecca*

This abundant duck of Eurasia, often called Eurasian Teal in N. America and Teal in Europe, was formerly considered conspecific with the Green-winged Teal of N. America (Browning 2002). In addition to Eurasia, the Common Teal breeds in the Aleutian Is. Only the adult male can be separated in the field from the Green-winged Teal. Common Teal are found in flocks of Green-winged Teal along the Pacific and Atlantic coasts south to Florida and California and occasionally inland (AOU 1998). In Oregon it is a rare but regular winter resident from mid-Nov to Mid-Apr with an average of 2-5 reported each year. Several Oregon specimen records including an adult male taken on Sauvie I. 20 Jan 1954 (spec. No. 9901 OSU) (Jewett 1954a), and an adult male taken during Mar 1964 at Malheur NWR (spec. HSU 898 Humboldt State University) (Jarvis 1966). Many reports of *A. crecca* X

*A. carolinensis* hybrids (Korpi 2002, *HBN*). Monotypic (Browning 2002).—*Harry B. Nehls*

### Green-winged Teal *Anas carolinensis*

Formerly *A. crecca carolinensis*, but see Sangster et al. (2001) and Browning (2002). The Green-winged Teal is the smallest N. American dabbling duck. Green-wings are common migrants along all the flyways. After the Mallard, it is the second most abundant duck in the bag of hunters in the U.S. and third most abundant in Oregon (USFWS undated). In alternate plumage, green-wing drakes have a cinnamon-colored head with green eye-stripe, gray back, flanks, and wing with a iridescent green speculum. Hens are brown with a green speculum. Vocalizations include a piping whistle by the drake, and 4-7 descending quacks by the hen (Johnson K 1995). Green-wings appear to have a fast wing-beat and frequently travel in medium-sized flocks in erratic flight at low altitudes, moving quickly in and out of range of the observer or hunter. When alarmed, will flare almost straight up before regrouping and continuing on their way.

**General Distribution:** Breeds from w. Alaska, including the e. Aleutians, east across boreal Canada to Newfoundland and south to w. Washington, c. Oregon, and n. Nevada east to s. Minnesota, s. Ontario, and Massachusetts. Winters from s. Alaska, s. British Columbia, c. Montana, S. Dakota, the Great Lakes, New England, and the Maritimes south to Baja California, Oaxaca, the Gulf coast, s. Florida, Bermuda, and the Bahamas. Largest wintering concentrations occur in the coastal marshes of Louisiana and the interior valleys of California. Monotypic (Gibson and Kessel 1997).

**Oregon Distribution:** Mainly a migrant and winter visitor. Uncommon summer resident and breeder in ne. Oregon (Evanich 1992a), Malheur Co. (Contreras and Kindschy 1996), Malheur NWR (Cornely 1982, Littlefield 1990a), Lake and Klamath counties (OBBA). M. Denny (p.c.) found them breeding in wet meadows along the Middle Fork John Day R. drainage. Rare summer resident and very rare breeder west of the Cascades (Gilligan et al. 1994, Contreras 1998, OBBA). Uncommon spring and fall migrant in ne. Oregon (Evanich 1992a). Common spring and fall migrant in Malheur Co. (Contreras and Kindschy 1996), Malheur NWR (Littlefield 1990a), the Klamath Basin (Summers 1993a), c. Douglas Co. (Hunter et al. 1988), the Willamette Valley (Evenden et al. 1950, Gullion 1951), the Columbia R. estuary (Patterson 1998b), the Douglas Co. coast (Sawyer and Hunter 1988), Coos Co. (Contreras 1998), and the south coast (Brown et al. 1996). Uncommon winterer in ne. Oregon (Evanich 1992a), Malheur Co. (Contreras and

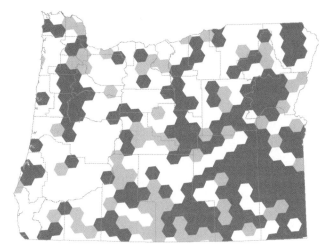

Kindschy 1996), Malheur NWR (Littlefield 1990a), and the Klamath Basin (Summers 1993a). It is a common wintering bird in the Willamette Valley (Evenden et al. 1950, Gullion 1951, USFWS undated), c. Douglas Co. (Hunter et al. 1998), Columbia R. estuary (Patterson 1998b), and coastal bays and estuaries (Bayer and Krabbe 1984, Sawyer and Hunter 1988, Brown et al. 1996, Contreras 1998, USFWS undated).

**Habitat and Diet:** Little is known of this species' preferred breeding habitat in Oregon, but in Malheur, Grant, and Union counties it nests in meadows in dense grass cover (M. Denny p.c.). Elsewhere it breeds in deciduous parklands, boreal forest, large river deltas and mixed prairies (Johnson K 1995). During migration and winter, uses shallow inland and coastal wetlands, mudflats, and flooded agricultural fields. At Malheur NWR commonly uses shallow ponds in remote areas (Littlefield 1990a). Feeds on seeds of grasses and sedges; invertebrates are important during breeding and rearing (Johnson K 1995).

**Seasonal Activity and Behavior:** Pairing begins in fall. Birds begin moving north from their wintering areas in Feb. Arrive at Malheur NWR mid-Feb and numbers peak in mid-Mar (Littlefield 1990a), but have arrived as late as mid-Apr in other Oregon areas (Irons 1984b). Contreras (1998) noted the latest spring departure from Coos Co. was 30 May. Gabrielson and Jewett (1940) noted that most green-wings had departed the state by mid-Apr. Of four nests examined by C. Foster at the Double O Unit of Malheur NWR, nest initiation was 1 May-7 Jun with clutches averaging 10 eggs (Littlefield 1990a). Incubation is about 20-23 days (Johnson K 1995). At Malheur NWR, the small number of breeders are joined in Jul by the males from northern breeding areas arriving to molt (Littlefield 1990a). In Coos Co., fall arrivals have been as early as 17 Jul (Contreras 1998), but the main fall migration on the coast begins in Aug with substantial numbers in Oregon coastal bays and estuaries in Sep (Irons

1984a). Numbers peak at Malheur NWR 1-15 Oct and most have departed by mid-Dec. In w. Oregon, large numbers of green-wings remain through the winter (USFWS undated).

**Detection:** Because of their small size and habit of resting on or near shore or on mud flats, these birds may be overlooked. In flight, their erratic maneuvers may cause them to be mistaken for shorebirds. In late winter and spring, the piping whistle of the male can be heard at a distance and helps in identification.

**Population Status and Conservation:** Although Gabrielson and Jewett (1940) cited reports of nesting in the 1800s in Harney Valley, Warner Valley, and Washington Co., they did not find it breeding during their years in Oregon. More recently the bird has been reported to be a breeder in e. Oregon (Cornely 1982, Littlefield 1990a, M. Denny p.c.) and a rare breeder in the western part of the state (OBBA). Gabrielson and Jewett (1940) reported that it appeared in abundance in late Sep and early Oct in Oregon. Those authors found it wintering in Oregon wherever there was open water and stated it was one of the most common ducks on the Columbia R. near Portland. Winter survey counts in Oregon are highly variable, but suggest that the population trend is upward. Continental green-wing populations generally have shown an upward trend from lows in the early 1960s to high population levels in the 1990s (USFWS undated). One reason for the success of the species is its widespread breeding range, much of which has not been impacted by human development nor subject to the periodic droughts of the prairies of Canada and north-central states.—*R. Kahler Martinson*

## Canvasback *Aythya valisineria*

A prized game bird and magnificent diver, the Canvasback was the "gold standard" of the wildfowl markets in the late 19th century. It figured prominently in the Portland market, both in numbers and in value (T. McAllister p.c.), and brought higher prices than Mallards and Northern Pintails in the Klamath Basin (Mathewson 1997); however, the renowned table quality could suffer when their diet turned to animal foods (Gabrielson and Jewett 1940). Areas where they concentrated on migration routes and wintering grounds were among the first acquired by hunting clubs. A sought-after game bird in Oregon, but currently accounts for only a trace of the duck harvest (USFWS undated). Canvasbacks are large; adults in good condition are as heavy as Mallards and second in size only to the White-winged Scoter among common Oregon ducks. Drakes have a reddish head and neck; black breast, lower back, and tail coverts; nearly white back, flank, and belly, and dark gray tail. The hen is

grayish brown with a darker brown head, neck, breast, and tail coverts. Not a vocal species; calls include *ick ick coo* notes by the male during courtship and a quack by the female (Bent 1925).

**General Distribution:** Breeds from c. Alaska south to ne. California and east to c. Canada and nc. U.S. Winters along Pacific coast from c. Aleutians and s. coastal Alaska to Baja California, and from interior Washington east to Montana, Nebraska, Iowa, the Great Lakes, and from New England, on the Atlantic coast, to Florida, the Gulf coast, and the n. and c. Mexican highlands. Monotypic (AOU 1957).

**Oregon Distribution:** Occasional summer resident in ne. Oregon nesting locally only at Ladd Marsh, Union Co. Uncommon breeder at Batch L. and Bogus L. in Malheur Co. (Contreras and Kindschy 1996). Uncommon summer resident and breeder at Malheur NWR (Erickson 1948, Cornely 1982, Littlefield 1990a). Regular but rare breeder at Summer L. (Summer L. W.A. files) and common breeder in the Klamath Basin (Klamath Basin NWR files). Breeding has been verified in Lake Co. (OBBA). Occasional summer resident west of the Cascades with no known nesting records.

Uncommon spring and fall migrant in ne. Oregon (Evanich 1992a) and Malheur Co. (Contreras and Kindschy 1996); occasional in winter in those areas. Regular in winter and spring on the Umatilla NWR complex in Morrow and Umatilla counties (M. Denny p.c.). Common at Malheur NWR in spring and fall; occasional in winter (Littlefield 1990a). Common spring and fall migrant in the Klamath Basin and, depending on conditions, several thousand may winter there (USFWS undated). Uncommon in fall, winter, and spring in the Willamette Valley (Evenden et al. 1950, Gullion 1951). Locally common in w. Washington Co. in late winter (C. Polityka p.c.). Rare to very uncommon in c. Douglas Co. (Hunter et al. 1998). Common fall and spring migrant and winter visitant on the Columbia R. (USFWS undated)

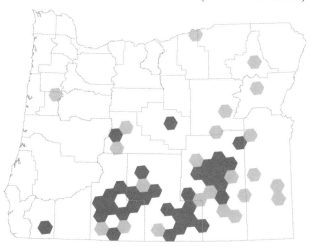

and Columbia R. estuary (Patterson 1998b). It was formerly a common migrant in coastal bays and estuaries (Bayer and Krabbe 1984, Sawyer and Hunter 1988, Brown et al. 1996, Contreras 1998), but has recently become a less common transient and winter visitant and is consistent only in Youngs Bay, Clatsop Co.,Yaquina Bay, Lincoln Co., and Siltcoos L., Lane Co. (W. Mathewson p.c.).

**Habitat and Diet:** In its northern breeding habitat the Canvasback is primarily a small-pothole nester in parklands and subarctic deltas, but in Oregon and the remainder of the Great Basin, it can be found nesting in large marsh habitat similar to that preferred by Redheads. Nest sites are in emergent vegetation, over water. At Malheur NWR, they prefer hardstem bulrush (Erickson 1948, Littlefield 1990a), but will use burreed and cattail (Littlefield 1990a). In migration and winter, found on large marshes, lakes, reservoirs, rivers, estuaries, and bays. Gabrielson and Jewett (1940) reported diets similar to those of other ducks in the Klamath Falls area: chiefly the seeds and tubers of pondweed, along with a variety of other plants. Fall transient Canvasbacks linger on Malheur L. when sago pondweed is abundant; when it is not, they move through in a short time (Littlefield 1990a). In fall and winter, Canvasbacks are present at grain terminals on the Snake R. and mid-Columbia R. (P. T. Sullivan p.c.). In early spring at Malheur NWR have been observed associating with swans, which keep the water open and uproot submerged plants that the Canvasbacks eat (Littlefield 1990a). Not as vegetarian as the Ring-necked Duck or Redhead; when plant foods are lacking, readily substitutes an animal diet. On the Oregon coast, remains of mollusks and crabs have been found in stomachs (Gabrielson and Jewett 1940), and Canvasbacks have been observed to consume herring eggs (Bayer 1980).

**Seasonal Activity and Behavior:** At Malheur NWR, it arrives in late Feb, numbers peak in mid-Apr, and most migrants are gone by early May (Littlefield 1990a). On the coast, Gabrielson and Jewett (1940) found the species lingering as late as 5 May. More recently, has lingered as late as 30 Jun at Coos Bay (Contreras 1998). At Malheur NWR, the first flocks in spring were mostly males, but 68% were paired during the peak of migration during 1942, 1946, and 1947 (Erickson 1948). The earliest nesters of the *Aythya*, nesting began as early as 22 Mar and hens were found on the nest as late as 5 Aug at Malheur NWR; clutches averaged 9.9 eggs with many nests containing more eggs from parasitism by Redheads; incubation was 25 days (Erickson 1948). Young fledge in 56-58 days (Bellrose 1980). At Malheur NWR, juveniles made short flights after their 10th wk and left the ponds by the first half of Aug (Erickson 1948). Gabrielson and Jewett

(1940) noted that the "vanguard" of Canvasbacks from northern breeding areas arrived in Oregon in Sep, but the species did not become common until Nov in Oregon. At Malheur NWR, fall migrants began arriving in mid-Sep, peaking in mid- to late Oct with most gone by mid-Dec (Littlefield 1990a). Earliest arrival at Coos Bay was 30 Sep (Contreras 1998). Numbers in coastal estuaries and lakes increase through Nov and remain through the winter.

**Detection:** The white backs of adult males are visible from a great distance, and separate Canvasbacks from scaup when head color is not discernable. The gray females, which blend with gray water and shoreline, are less easily detectable. Females with broods are apt to head for open water when alarmed so are more easily spotted than the puddle duck species. At Malheur NWR, look on Malheur, Boca, and Derrick lakes and Wright and Knox ponds. In w. Oregon the coastal bays such as Yaquina, Alsea, and Coos are the place to look for Canvasbacks.

**Population Status and Conservation:** In the late 1800s, Canvasbacks were abundant in the Portland area, on lakes along the lower Columbia R. and in the Willamette Valley, as well as in the large eastern marshes, coastal estuaries, and lakes along the coast. By the turn of the 20th century, once abundant transient and wintering flocks had abandoned the Willamette Valley and the lower Columbia R. floodplain after carp introductions had destroyed the wapato marshes (T. McAllister p.c.). In their time, Gabrielson and Jewett (1940) noted that the species was decreasing in Oregon and did not find a nest until 1936 when they reported a few pairs nesting at Malheur L. In N. America, migration stopovers and wintering locations have changed dramatically in response to availability of preferred foods. Once known for their preference for wild celery and other aquatics, Canvasbacks deserted traditional areas in the upper Midwest when these foods disappeared and began using areas such as the Mississippi R., where animal foods predominated in their diet. Continent-wide, the prairie droughts of the 1930s and again in the late 1950s and 1960s led to hunting closures and bag-limit restrictions, usually coupled with restrictions on Redheads. Concern continued during the 1970s and 1980s due to uncertain results from nesting studies, changes in distribution on migration and wintering grounds, and the vulnerability of the birds. Aerial breeding-ground survey data collected in recent years show no long-term trend and may actually suggest an increase in the continental population. However, winter surveys in Oregon indicate that fewer birds are wintering here in the 1990s than in the previous 25 yr (USFWS undated). Agricultural draining and filling of prairie and parkland ponds, and degradation of wintering habitat by fill and pollution continue to be the greatest threats to the species' survival. At Malheur NWR, carp affect Canvasback use of the area by preventing the growth of sago pondweed (Ivey, Cornely, and Ehlers 1998, *DBM*).—*R. Kahler Martinson*

## Redhead *Aythya americana*

Although not as imposing as the Canvasback, the Redhead is a large, handsome, fast-flying diver. The drake has a red head, black breast and tail coverts, and steel gray back, flanks, and tail. Hens are a medium brown. During courtship, the drake utters a very un-duck-like *meow*. Known for nest parasitism, laying eggs in the nests of other birds, usually other diving ducks, but Redhead eggs have been found in the nests of a variety of species. A highly desirable game bird in other flyways, but only locally important in e. Oregon where it is usually taken incidental to other species. As a table bird, the Redhead closely approaches the Canvasback (Grinnell GB 1901) and since it is less likely to take animal food, seldom has the fishy flavor the Canvasback sometimes acquires (Kortright 1943).

**General Distribution:** Breeds locally in interior sc. and se. Alaska, and from c. and ne. British Columbia, sw. Mackenzie, n. Saskatchewan, c. Manitoba, and Minnesota south to s. California, New Mexico, Texas, Kansas, and n. Iowa. Most abundant in prairie pothole region; abundant locally in the large marshes of the Great Basin. Winters from coastal and s. British Columbia, Washington, n. Idaho, w. Montana, Kansas, the middle Mississippi and Ohio valleys, the Great Lakes, and from New England south throughout the s. U.S. and most of Mexico to Guatemala, the W. Indies, Bermuda, and the Bahamas. The largest wintering concentration is in the Laguna Madre of Texas and Mexico. Monotypic (AOU 1957).

**Oregon Distribution:** An uncommon summer resident in ne. Oregon (Evanich 1992a), but commonly breeds at Batch L. and Bogus L. and locally

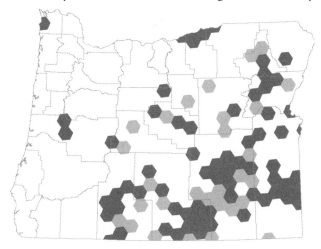

elsewhere in Malheur Co. (Contreras and Kindschy 1996). During 1942-80, Redheads were the second- or third-most-prolific breeding duck at Malheur NWR (Cornely 1982). Later, Littlefield (1990a) reported it the third-most abundant breeder among ducks there, with 2,000-3,000 pairs commonly nesting. It is an abundant breeder at Summer L. (Summer L. W.A. files) and in the Klamath Basin (Klamath Basin NWR files). McAllister and Marshall (1945) found Redheads nesting at Dog L. in the Fremont NF. Nesting has been confirmed in Klamath, Morrow, Lake, and Deschutes counties (OBBA). Nesting has not been documented in w. Oregon, where summer observations are generally rare; several pairs summered at Fern Ridge Res., Lane Co., in 2000 and 2001 (*ALC*).

Common spring and fall migrant in ne. Oregon (Evanich 1992a) and an uncommon migrant in Malheur Co. (Contreras and Kindschy 1996). It is a common wintering species on the Columbia R. and the Umatilla NWR complex in Umatilla and Morrow counties (M. Denny p.c.). Abundant in spring and fall at Malheur NWR (Littlefield 1990a) and in the Klamath Basin (Gabrielson and Jewett 1940). Very uncommon during spring and fall in w. Oregon (Irons 1984b, Hunter et al. 1998). Uncommon spring and fall migrant in the Columbia R. estuary (Patterson 1998b), Coos Co. (Contreras 1998), and on the south coast (Brown et al. 1996). Winter surveys have found small and annually variable numbers throughout the state (USFWS undated). Gabrielson and Jewett (1940) reported only three winter records in e. Oregon. It has since been found to be an occasional winter visitant in ne. Oregon (Evanich 1992a), in Malheur Co. (Contreras and Kindschy 1996), and at Malheur NWR (Littlefield 1990a). Uncommon to fairly common in winter in the Klamath Basin (Summers 1993a). In w. Oregon, a very few winter inland (Irons 1984, Fix 1985f, Heinl 1985, 1986c, Hunter et al. 1998). Uncommon in the Columbia R. estuary (Patterson 1998b) and on coastal bays (Evanich 1984a, Irons and Heinl 1984). Regular in small numbers in Yaquina Bay (H. Nehls p.c.). Although concentrations of as many as 200 birds have been found from time to time on Coos Bay (Bayer and Krabbe 1984, Irons and Heinl 1984, Contreras 1998), in recent years has been uncommon to rare in Coos Co. (T. Rodenkirk p.c.).

**Habitat and Diet:** Nests in potholes, sloughs, and ponds, but commonly selects large marshes and pioneers these habitats when they become available. The Redhead is primarily an over-water nester like the Canvasback, but sometimes nests on land, usually close to water. At Malheur NWR, Littlefield (1990a) reported nesting in spikerush, Baltic rush, burreed, and cattail, but most used hardstem bulrush like the Canvasback. During migration and winter uses large marshes, lakes, reservoirs, estuaries, inlets, and protected ocean bays. In fall and winter, found at grain terminals on Snake R. and mid-Columbia R. (P. T. Sullivan p.c.). Food is predominantly vegetable, less animal food than the Canvasback.

**Seasonal Activity and Behavior:** Gabrielson and Jewett (1940) reported that spring migrants arrived in Oregon as early as 11 Mar. A late coastal date, probably a nonbreeder, was 30 Jun in Coos Co. (Contreras 1998). At Malheur NWR, Redheads usually began arriving in late Feb with numbers building until nesting began in May (Littlefield 1990a). Hens commonly parasitize nests of other Redheads as well as those of other species (Erickson 1948, Littlefield 1990a). Because of parasitism, Littlefield (1990a) believed that the average of 9.3 eggs/clutch at Malheur NWR may be high, representing the eggs of more than one hen. Nesting at the refuge peaks in late May and newly hatched young observed from mid-Jun to mid-Jul (Littlefield 1990a). Redheads are poor parents and hens often abandon broods, although survival of the young can be satisfactory because they frequent the deeper, more permanent habitat that tends to have few predators (Littlefield 1990a). Young have fledged and adult males began to congregate for the molt in Jul (Littlefield 1990a). Fall migration began in Aug and most birds had left the refuge by late Oct. Unlike most duck species, which migrate southwestward from the refuge, most Redheads head southeast (Littlefield 1990a), probably to their wintering grounds on the Laguna Madre in s. Texas and nw. Mexico. Fall migrants may arrive relatively late on the coast, as Contreras (1998) noted the earliest arrivals in Coos Co. on 6 Nov.

**Detection:** Early in spring, the *meow*, and on the breeding marshes, the distinctive *err*, are aids to detection. In e. Oregon during winter, look for Redheads on the Columbia R. at Starvation Cr. SP, between Hood River and The Dalles, and at Upper Klamath L. On the coast, a few wintering Redheads are usually found on Yaquina Bay (H. Nehls p.c.). Malheur L. during summer and fall is a particularly good location.

**Population Status and Conservation:** Gabrielson and Jewett (1940) noted that Redheads, once a common breeding duck in the state, bred in much reduced numbers in "the freshwater ponds and lakes of the southern half of the state east of the Cascades." Gabrielson and Jewett (1940) and Kortright (1943) expressed grave concern about the decline of Redheads in their time due to the drought of the 1930s, agriculture, and other development within the species' breeding range. In recent years, the continental population has fluctuated with lows in the early 1960s and late 1980s, higher populations in

between, and an increase in the late 1990s when record highs were recorded on breeding ground surveys (USFWS undated). Restrictive hunting regulations, including closed seasons (usually linked with those for Canvasbacks), were implemented for Redheads during the 1930s and subsequently over most of the past 40 yr. Continued destruction of breeding habitat and, to a lesser degree, wintering habitat has been the most serious permanent threat to the species throughout its range in recent times (*RKM*). At Malheur NWR, the single most important breeding area in Oregon, productivity is affected by carp abundance and water levels (Ivey, Cornely, and Ehlers 1998, *DBM*).—*R. Kahler Martinson*

## Ring-necked Duck *Aythya collaris*

The Ring-necked Duck, which would have been better named "Ring-billed Duck" and is called "Blackjack" in the se. U.S., frequents different habitats than the scaups with which it is often confused. The black back, white crescent on the side just in front of the wing, and white-ringed bill separate the drake ring-neck from the scaups. The brownish neck ring of the male in alternate plumage is not prominent. Hen is a small dark brown duck with a buff face. Drakes in courtship give a head-throw accompanied by a *wow* note (Hohman and Eberhardt 1998) while hens utter a growling *purr* similar to, but softer than, that of the scaups (Mendall 1958). Although the species is most common in the Mississippi Flyway and southern one-third of the Atlantic Flyway in the U.S., they regularly occur in Oregon. Predilection for small waters makes it available to hunters, but the scarcity of this good table bird limits it to less than 2% of the annual Oregon duck harvest.

**General Distribution:** Breeds from ec. and se. Alaska, and ne. British Columbia, s. Yukon, across n. Canada to Newfoundland to the Maritimes south to coastal British Columbia, nw. Washington, c. Oregon, n. California, c. Nevada east to n. Nebraska, n. Iowa, Wisconsin,

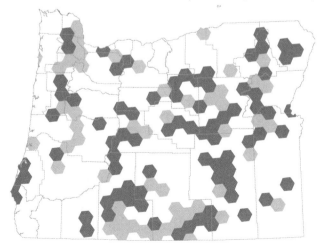

Michigan, n. Ohio, New York to Maine. Most breed in the boreal forests of the District of Mackenzie and the northern portions of Alberta, Saskatchewan, Manitoba, and Ontario. Winters on the Pacific coast from se. Alaska, in the interior from Washington, Idaho, w. Montana, Colorado, Oklahoma, the lower Mississippi and Ohio valleys, the s. Great Lakes region, and New England south through the s. U.S., M. America, and the W. Indies to Panama and Grenada. Largest numbers winter in Florida and Louisiana. Monotypic (AOU 1957).

**Oregon Distribution:** A locally uncommon breeder in Oregon. Ring-necks are uncommon summer residents in ne. Oregon (Evanich 1992a) and occasional breeders at lakes with emergent vegetation in Malheur Co. (Contreras and Kindschy 1996). There are breeding records from Little Morgan L., Union Co. (Watson 1979a); Penland L., Morrow Co. (M. Denny p.c.); Olive L., Grant Co. (M. Denny p.c.); Malheur NWR (Marshall and Deubbert 1965, Cornely et al. 1980, Littlefield 1990a); Warner Pond on Hart Mtn. NWR (Summers 1986a); and Upper Klamath L. (Marshall and Deubbert 1965). A rare breeder at Summer L. (Summer L. W.A. files), a common breeder in the Klamath Basin (Klamath Basin NWR files), and in the forested wetlands of the s. Fremont NF (M. St. Louis p.c.). Several nests were found each year at Sycan Marsh (Stern, Del Carlo, et al. 1987). Indication of breeding has been reported also from Hood River, Deschutes, Morrow, Grant, and Lake counties (OBBA). Groups of 5-7 nonbreeding males are frequently noted during summer on stock ponds and large lakes in e. Oregon (M. Denny p.c.). Breeding in w. Oregon has been reported at Trillium L., Clackamas Co., in the Cascades (Marshall and Deubbert 1965), and at Jackson Bottoms wetlands, Hillsboro (S. Pinnock p.c.). Breeding has been confirmed in Polk, Lane, Clackamas, and Coos counties, and is possible elsewhere (Adamus et al. 2001).

Ring-necks are uncommon spring and fall migrants in ne. Oregon (Evanich 1992a), in Malheur Co. (Contreras and Kindschy 1996), and at Malheur NWR (Littlefield 1990a), and are common to abundant in the Klamath Basin (Summers 1993a). Gullion (1951) noted that the birds were uncommon migrants in the Willamette Valley, although recently they have been described as widespread in small numbers in that area (*MGH*). Common in c. Douglas Co. (Hunter et al. 1998). Common spring and fall in the Columbia R. estuary (Patterson 1998b) and on the

coast (Irons 1984b, Sawyer and Hunter 1988, Brown et al. 1996, Contreras 1998).

Winter surveys have found several thousand ring-necks in Oregon, most in the western part of the state (USFWS undated). Wintering birds are occasional in ne. Oregon (Evanich 1992a), in Malheur Co. (Contreras and Kindschy 1996), at Malheur NWR (Evanich 1984a, Littlefield 1990a) and uncommon in the Klamath Basin (Summers 1993a). Regular in winter on the Umatilla NWR complex in weed-edged ponds (M. Denny p.c.). They occur in small numbers on small ponds, lakes, and sewage ponds throughout the Willamette Valley (Evanich 1984a, Irons and Heinl 1984, *MGH*). Common to abundant in c. Douglas Co. (Hunter et al. 1998) and w. Washington Co. (*RKM*). A common winter visitant in the Columbia R. estuary (Patterson 1998b) and on the coast (Sawyer and Hunter 1988, Brown et al. 1996, Contreras 1998) and coastal freshwater such as Siltcoos L. (W. Mathewson p.c.).

**Habitat and Diet:** At Malheur NWR, Littlefield (1990a) usually found the species on the larger lakes and ponds, but they occasionally used canals, ditches, and the smaller ponds during migration. Elsewhere this species nests in shallow but stable freshwater wetlands with abundant submerged and emergent vegetation; nests are in emergent or floating vegetation or on islands, but close to water (Bellrose 1980, Hohman and Eberhardt 1998). In w. Oregon, small lakes, ponds, sewage ponds, sloughs, and river eddies and backwaters are commonly used by migrating and wintering Ring-necks (D. Fix p.c., *MGH*). When water levels rise, they can be found in flooded riparian areas along the lower Columbia R. (*RKM*). Diet is more vegetarian than other *Aythya* especially during fall and winter.

**Seasonal Activity and Behavior:** In Oregon, Irons (1984b) reported 700 in the Coquille Valley 24 Mar and throughout the region from mid-Mar to mid-May that he thought to be migrants. In Coos Co., the latest spring migrant left the area 21 May (Contreras 1998). The species arrives at Malheur NWR in mid-Feb, numbers peak mid-Mar, and the latest

*Ring-necked Duck*

ELVA PAULSON

arrival was 24 May Littlefield (1990a). Pairing occurs during spring migration in Mar and Apr. Few nesting data are available for Oregon. A nest with eggs was photographed at Davis L., Klamath Co., on 27 Jun 1985 (N. Barrett p.c.). Elsewhere nesting may occur from Apr through Jul depending on latitude; clutches are about nine eggs and hatch in 26 days after start of incubation (Hohman and Eberhardt 1998). Fall migration may be protracted, but appears to be earlier than that of the scaups in Oregon (*RKM*). The earliest autumn migrant at Malheur NWR was 24 Aug, but ring-necks usually did not show up until late Sep, with greater numbers in Oct, peaking in Nov, and most gone by early Dec (Littlefield 1990a). The earliest fall arrival in Coos Co. was 30 Oct (Contreras 1998). Wintering birds in Oregon are usually in pairs and small groups although occasional larger flocks and aggregations have been observed (Evanich 1984a, Irons and Heinl 1984, Littlefield 1990a).

**Detection:** Ring-necks are relatively difficult to find in Oregon during the breeding season not only because of their scarcity, but because of their affinity for areas of emergent vegetation. However, they are consistent at Trillium L. near Government Camp, Clackamas Co. In migration and winter they are more abundant and much more easily spotted on the open water they inhabit in those seasons.

**Population Status and Conservation:** Ring-necked Duck status appears to have changed over the past 100 yr in Oregon. Although Gabrielson and Jewett (1940) mentioned that James Merrill reported nesting at Ft. Klamath, Klamath Co., in the 1880s, they reported no further evidence of nesting in the state. Subsequently, a report of nesting without details came from the same area in 1954, as reported by Deubbert and Marshall (1965). These authors found nesting Ring-necked Ducks at Trillium L. west of Mt. Hood in 1963 and at Malheur NWR in 1964. This was followed by numerous subsequent sightings throughout the state as reported herein. Likewise, numbers of migrant and wintering Ring-necked Ducks appear to have increased in historical times. Jewett (Gabrielson and Jewett 1940) believed that the species became more common in his time, and *DBM* believes he has witnessed a further increase since the 1940s. Winter survey counts suggest that numbers of wintering birds have increased since 1965 and especially in the last 10 yr (USFWS undated). Interestingly, the first specimen of a Ring-necked Duck taken from the Americas was one collected by the Lewis and Clark expedition at Deer I., Columbia Co. (Gabrielson and Jewett 1940). Ring-necks sustain a fairly high rate of hunting harvest, but much of their breeding range has been impacted neither by human development nor by the droughts that have devastated prairie duck habitat (*RKM*).

The continental population is thought to be stable or increasing and the bird has expanded its range west to Yukon (Hohman and Eberhardt 1998), which may be responsible for the increase in the Oregon wintering population.—*R. Kahler Martinson*

## Tufted Duck *Aythya fuligula*
This Eurasian diving duck regularly occurs in the Aleutian Is. and with increasing regularity in N. America, especially along the W. Coast. Now reported annually in Oregon. The first Oregon record was of a male photographed at Portland, Multnomah Co., 14 Feb to 26 Mar 1960 (Olson 1961, Watson 1989). All subsequent Oregon records have fallen between mid-Oct and early May, with most during Jan and Feb. All were from the coastal lowlands or the Willamette Valley, except for one on a small pond at Kerby, Josephine Co., 12 Mar 1989 (photo cover *Oregon Birds* 15[4]); a male at Cascade Locks, Hood River Co., 17 Apr 1995 (Lillie 1995); a female at Antelope Res., Malheur Co., 28 Oct 1995 (Contreras and Kindschy 1996); a female at Rufus, Sherman Co., 31 Oct and 13 Dec 1997 (Korpi 1998, Sullivan 1998a); and one at Hatfield L., Deschutes Co., 6 May 2000 (Sullivan 2000b), and 23 Mar to 8 Apr 2001 (Sullivan 2001b). Closely related to the scaups and often associated with them. Many records of Tufted Duck X scaup hybrids. One such hybrid was at the Monmouth sewage ponds, Polk Co., during the winters of 1987, 1988, and 1989 (OBRC, Tweit and Johnson 1990). Monotypic (AOU 1957).—*Harry B. Nehls*

## Greater Scaup *Aythya marila*
Called "Broadbills" on Long I. Sound and other northeast wintering areas, Greater Scaup are almost the size of Redheads. In hand, they are easily distinguishable from Lesser Scaup by size and by the white wing stripe extending beyond the secondaries into the primaries. In the field the two species are sometimes difficult to separate. Drakes are "black on both ends and white in the middle"—black head, neck, breast, tail coverts and tail, gray back, white flanks. Hens are dark brown with a white mask around the base of the bill. The common vocalizations are the discordant *scaup* and purring *pbbbbrr* of the female (Kortright 1943). Greater Scaups form large flocks, sometimes mingling with Lesser Scaups in fall and winter. Only fair as a table bird and can be strong flavored when feeding on certain animal foods. Makes up only a small part of the duck harvest in Oregon, but has become more popular as a game bird in recent years.

**General Distribution:** Breeds from w. Alaska east across n. Yukon, n. Mackenzie, s. Keewatin to Hudson Bay, James Bay, and n. Quebec casually or irregularly south to se. Alaska, s. Mackenzie, c. Manitoba, to the Maritimes. Most of the breeding population is in Alaska. Winters from the Aleutians, se. Alaska, coastal and s. British Columbia, c. Washington, w. Montana, the Great Lakes, and Newfoundland on the Atlantic coast south to n. Baja California, and se. California, the Gulf coast, Florida, and Bermuda. The largest concentration of wintering birds is between s. New England and Chesapeake Bay. Two subspecies; *A. m. nearctica* in N. America and Oregon (Browning 2002).

**Oregon Distribution:** Except for regular occurrence in the Columbia R. estuary (Patterson 1998b) and Coos Bay (T. Rodenkirk p.c.), there are few summer records (Evanich 1992a). An exception was in 1999 when hundreds summered on the Oregon coast (Harrington-Tweit et al. 1999). Not known to breed in Oregon.

Abundant migrant and winter visitor in the Columbia R. estuary (Patterson 1998b, *RKM*) and common to abundant on coastal bays and lower river segments (Bayer and Krabbe 1984, Irons 1984b, Sawyer and Hunter 1988, Brown et al. 1996, Contreras 1998). Rare to uncommon migrant and winterer in inland areas west of the Cascades (Heinl 1986c, Hunter et al. 1998), but locally common on reservoirs near Eugene (*MGH*), and on Lost Cr. Res., Jackson Co. (N. Barrett p.c.). Annual winter survey counts on the Columbia R. show scaup species regularly occurring in all counties from Clatsop Co. upstream to Umatilla Co. (USFWS undated), and, although the two species are not differentiated in these counts, field observations indicate that Greater Scaup are locally common east of Portland and outnumber Lesser Scaup 2-3:1 east of the John Day Dam (Irons 1984b, Heinl 1986c, Gilligan et al. 1994, H. Nehls p.c., M. Denny p.c.). It winters by the thousands on the Columbia R. in Umatilla Co. (M. Denny p.c.). Occasional to rare migrant and winter visitant in Union and Wallowa counties (Evanich 1992a), Malheur Co. (Contreras and Kindschy 1996), at Malheur NWR (Kridler and Marshall 1962, Littlefield 1990a), and in the Klamath Basin (Summers 1993a).

**Habitat and Diet:** The Greater Scaup uses large lakes, reservoirs, rivers, estuaries, and bays on migration. More apt than Lesser Scaup to frequent salt- or brackish-water habitats. Most winter on coastal bays, estuaries, and the Columbia R., where substantial numbers are found well inland. They feed on both animal and plant life, but small clams are the most common item in most areas (Bellrose 1980) including the Columbia R. estuary (*RKM*). Bayer (1980) found them feeding on herring eggs at Yaquina Bay.

**Seasonal Activity and Behavior:** Less is known about the Greater Scaup than the Lesser Scaup. Migration timing is likely similar to that of the Lesser Scaup, but Bellrose (1980) speculates that the species may migrate earlier in the spring and later in the fall. In Oregon, large numbers pass along the coast with Lesser Scaup from late Mar through early May (Irons 1984b). Pairing probably occurs during late winter and spring migration and it is likely that some birds do not breed in their first year (Bellrose 1980). A late bird, likely a nonbreeder, was noted 18 Jun in Coos Co. (Contreras 1998). Fall migration begins in Sep, but most move to major wintering grounds in Oct and Nov. Contreras (1998) reported the first Greater Scaup arriving in Coos Co. 28 Sep. Fall migrants sometimes aggregate into huge flocks and make long, nonstop flights to wintering areas (Bellrose 1980). In Oregon, flocks form large rafts, often with Lesser Scaup, on the broad waters of the Columbia R. and coastal bays. They also disperse rather randomly among larger, highly mixed-species assemblages on most bays (D. Fix p.c.). In daily activities, small groups break off the rafts to fly to feeding areas.

**Detection:** Readily spotted on open-water habitats. Care is needed to distinguish from Lesser Scaup.

**Population Status and Conservation:** Although they had several reports of birds taken in both coastal and inland areas, Gabrielson and Jewett (1940) felt that definite information on the species was meager and confusion with Lesser Scaup complicated its status. They speculated that it was regular only on the coast and a straggler inland except that it possibly occurred regularly in small numbers on the Columbia R. and should be found on the Snake R. Since their time, the impoundments on the Columbia R. have attracted significant numbers of scaups from Portland to Umatilla. Although there has been a decline in continental scaup populations (Austin et al. 1998), Oregon winter survey counts, which combine the two species, suggest an increase in wintering populations in recent years (USFWS undated). Since Pacific Flyway winter counts of scaups have not increased (USFWS undated), the increase in Oregon may be related to attractive habitat conditions such as maturing of the Columbia R. impoundments that have attracted the birds since the time of Gabrielson and Jewett (1940).—*R. Kahler Martinson*

**Lesser Scaup** *Aythya affinis*
Known as "Bluebill" to most hunters, this species is one of the most abundant and widespread of N. American ducks. The Lesser Scaup is similar to the Greater Scaup in appearance and habits, but is smaller and lacks the white on the primaries. In the field, however, the black-

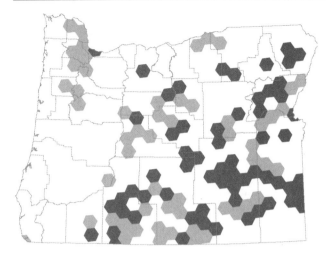

and-white drakes and brown hens are very similar to Greater Scaups. The common vocalization is the *purr* call of the female; drakes are usually silent, but utter a low single-note whistle in courtship (Austin et al. 1998). In general, the Lesser Scaup is more apt to be found in interior and/or freshwater habitats while the Greater Scaup is more a coastal bird, but many exceptions occur (see Greater Scaup). Both scaup make up only a small portion of the Oregon duck harvest. On the best of feed, Lesser Scaup are mediocre table fare, and while on some coastal diets Gabrielson and Jewett (1940) described them as inedible.

**General Distribution:** Breeds from c. Alaska, c. Yukon, southeast to n. Manitoba and n. Ontario south through interior British Columbia, to n. Wyoming, ne. S. Dakota and c. Minnesota. Also to e. Washington, Oregon, and California. Most breed in the boreal forests and parklands from interior Alaska to Ontario; greatest densities in the Yukon Flats and large river deltas of nw. Canada. Winters from s. Alaska and coastal and s. British Columbia, east to Montana, Kansas, the s. Great Lakes region, and New England south throughout the s. U.S., and farther south than other *Aythya* species into M. America, the W. Indies, and n. S. America. Largest wintering concentrations are in Florida and Louisiana. Monotypic (AOU 1957).

**Oregon Distribution:** Uncommon breeder at Malheur NWR (Cornely 1982, Littlefield 1990a). Nests regularly at Batch L. and Bogus L. and locally elsewhere in Malheur Co. (Contreras and Kindschy 1996). Occasional summerer and very local nester in ne. Oregon (Evanich 1992a). Rare breeder at Summer L (Summer L. W.A. files) and rare to common breeder in the Klamath Basin (Klamath Basin NWR files). Nesting has also been noted in Grant Co. (OBBA). This species occurs regularly during Jun and Jul on Davis L., Hosmer L., and Wickiup Res. in the c. Cascades, although evidence of nesting is lacking (L. McQueen p.c.).

Uncommon migrant in Union and Wallowa counties (Evanich 1992a), but common in Umatilla Co. on the Columbia R. (M. Denny p.c.). Common in Malheur Co. (Contreras and Kindschy 1996) and at Malheur NWR (Littlefield 1990a) although migration peaks rarely exceed 5,000 (Littlefield 1990a). Common to abundant migrant in the Klamath Basin (Summers 1993a). Uncommon to fairly common migrant in c. Douglas Co. (Hunter et al. 1998) and large numbers gather at Diamond L. in Nov: 1,100+ there most of Nov 1987 (Heinl 1988a). Common migrant during spring and fall on the Columbia R. west of Portland, on the coast and lakes and rivers near the coast (Gabrielson and Jewett 1940, Irons 1984, Heinl 1986c, Sawyer and Hunter 1988, Brown et al. 1996, Contreras 1998), and in the Columbia R. estuary (Patterson 1998b).

The Lesser Scaup is a rare winter visitant in Union and Wallowa counties (Evanich 1992a) and occasional in Malheur Co. (Contreras and Kindschy 1996). It winters by the thousands on the Snake and Columbia rivers, east of the John Day Dam (M. Denny p.c.). At Malheur NWR, uncommon in winter, occurring in 23 CBCs, but with all but two counts less than 100 (Littlefield 1990a). Common to abundant winterer in the Klamath Basin (Summers 1993a), and a regular, if somewhat uncommon, visitor in the Willamette Valley (Evenden et al. 1950, Gullion 1951, Irons 1984a). Uncommon to fairly common in c. Douglas Co. (Hunter et al. 1998). Winter survey counts show scaups (the two species combined) in counties along the Columbia R. (USFWS undated) and observations from the ground verify the presence of Lesser Scaup in these areas (Gilligan et al. 1994). Common winterer in the Columbia R. estuary (Patterson 1998b) and along the coast (Bayer and Krabbe 1984, Sawyer and Hunter 1988, Brown et al. 1996, Contreras 1998), especially on lower river segments (P. T. Sullivan p.c.).

**Habitat and Diet:** Breeding habitat is seasonal and semi-permanent shallow wetlands and lakes. Lesser Scaup are not over-water nesters, usually nesting out of water and are the only *Aythya* species that nest in uplands. At Malheur NWR, select nest sites in meadows, dry uplands, or islands (Littlefield 1990a). On migration they use large wetlands, lakes, reservoirs, rivers, and estuaries. Wintering habitat is broad water; fresh, brackish, and salt water, although saltwater areas are used less by this species than by Greater Scaup (Austin et al. 1998). In the Columbia R. estuary, Lesser Scaup mingle with greaters, but may be most common in the nearshore and inter-island channels, while greaters predominate in the more open expanses toward mid-channel (*RKM*). In large coastal freshwater bodies such as Siltcoos L., lessers are the predominant scaup species with greaters rare in these habitats (W. Mathewson p.c.). Common winter habitats include sloughs, backwaters of rivers, quarry borrow pits, log ponds, and sewage ponds (D. Fix p.c.). Food tends to be primarily animal—mollusks, crustaceans, and aquatic insects—although vegetation is eaten (Austin et al. 1998). Large rafts are often near wheat terminals on the Columbia R. east of The Dalles Dam (M. Denny p.c.). In the Klamath Basin, just south of the Oregon border, Gammonley and Heitmeyer (1990) found that invertebrates were the primary spring food of Lesser Scaup, making up 66-77% of the volume (59-72% dry weight). At Yaquina estuary, Bayer (1980) reported that the species fed on herring eggs, as did several other species of ducks.

**Seasonal Activity and Behavior:** Lesser Scaup are late spring migrants; some birds linger south of their breeding grounds until mid-May or later. At Malheur NWR, spring migrants arrive mid- to late Feb, peak in mid-Apr, and most are gone by mid-May (Littlefield 1990a). A late bird, likely a nonbreeder, was present 18 Jun in Coos Co. (Contreras 1998). Pairing is later than for most other ducks and takes place on spring migration. Not all birds breed in their first spring and trios—two drakes with one hen—are commonly observed on the northern breeding grounds (*RKM*). Oregon nesting information is confined to Malheur NWR where nesting begins in late May and young are present in late Jun and Jul (Littlefield 1990a). Elsewhere clutches are 8-10 eggs, the incubation period is 21-27 days, and young fledge in 47-61 days (Austin et al. 1998). Lesser Scaup are the latest of the *Aythya* and of all ducks to migrate in the fall, often among the last ducks holding out until freeze up. At Malheur NWR, fall migrants begin arriving in late Aug, peak in mid- to late Oct, and most are gone by early Dec, but may remain through Dec in mild years (Littlefield 1990a). Earliest arrivals in Coos Co. were 14 Oct (Contreras 1998). Tend to migrate in large flocks of hundreds or even thousands (Bellrose 1980). In the Columbia estuary wintering flocks aggregate in large rafts with small bunches periodically leaving for their feeding areas (*RKM*).

**Detection:** Readily detected in their open-water habitats. Care should be taken to distinguish from Greater Scaup.

**Population Status and Conservation:** Gabrielson and Jewett (1940) noted that stragglers remained in the summer, especially in Harney and Klamath counties, but believed they were nonbreeders. They reported the species a common migrant and winterer on the Columbia R. west of Portland, on coastal bays and lakes near the coast, and that it could be found in e. Oregon wherever open water occurred on any considerable body of water. Aerial surveys on breeding and wintering grounds (Lesser and Greater Scaup combined) suggest a

downward trend in recent years (Austin et al. 1998). In Oregon, however, winter surveys suggest an increasing trend in wintering populations of scaups (USFWS undated). The cause of the continental decline has not been identified, but wintering ground deficiencies seem most likely since much of their breeding range has not been seriously impacted by human development. The apparent increase in wintering in Oregon may be the result of attractive habitat, such as maturing of the impoundments on the Columbia R., since there is no indication of increases in other Pacific coast states (USFWS undated).—*R. Kahler Martinson*

## Steller's Eider *Polysticta stelleri*
This sea duck breeds from the Arctic coast of c. Russia east locally to nw. Canada, and winters south along the sw. Alaskan coast and casually to s. California. There is one Oregon record, an adult male photographed at the n. jetty of Coos Bay 10-18 Feb 1992 (Griffith 1992). Monotypic (AOU 1957).—*Harry B. Nehls*

## King Eider *Somateria spectabilis*
The King Eider is a large Arctic sea duck with a circumpolar breeding range. It winters south to the Aleutian Is., n. New England, and occasionally to s. California and Florida. There are 13 Oregon records between early Oct and late Apr. All have been females or subadult males found on the ocean from rocky headlands, jetties, or in lower bays. The first was a female at Tillamook Bay 10-20 Mar 1976 (OBRC). Oregon's only specimen is a female found dead on the beach at Cape Arago, Coos Co., 18 Nov 1980 (spec. no. A-0114 Oregon Institute of Marine Biology, Charleston). Monotypic (AOU 1957).—*Harry B. Nehls*

## Harlequin Duck *Histrionicus histrionicus*
This small, boldly-patterned duck can be found in Oregon throughout the year, either around rocky headlands on the coast or inland on mountain streams. No other breeding duck in Oregon feeds almost exclusively on benthic invertebrates, often swimming underwater and upstream against swift current in search of prey. Though the males are striking in appearance, these and the drab brown females can be difficult to see when at rest on a mid-stream rock or dodging behind rocks as they evade observers.

**General Distribution:** Breed in mountainous areas in n. and e. Asia, east through Alaska and the Yukon, and south to Wyoming, Idaho, and Oregon; formerly in Colorado and n. California. In e. N. America, breed from Labrador to the Gaspe Peninsula and possibly Newfoundland, with concentrations in Iceland and

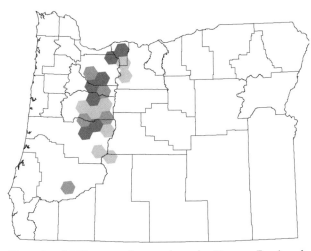

Greenland. Winter as far south as the Korean Peninsula and n. Japan, in w. N. America from the Aleutians south to c. California, and on the Atlantic coast south to New England. Monotypic (AOU 1957, Johnsgard 1975b).

**Oregon Distribution:** Broods have been observed or nests located on tributaries in the following river basins of the w. Cascades: Clackamas, McKenzie, Middle Fork of the Willamette, Molalla, N. Santiam, Sandy, and S. Santiam. Pairs have been observed on at least two tributaries of the Umpqua R. without direct evidence of nesting. Breeding has been confirmed in the Hood R. basin. Records from the east slope of the Cascades are limited to the White R. on the eastern flank of Mt. Hood, and single reports from the Metolius R., Jefferson Co., and the Klamath R., Klamath Co. (*SGD*). In the Coast Range, birds have been observed on the Trask, Wilson, and Nestucca rivers, Tillamook Co., and from Lobster Cr. in the Alsea R. basin, Lincoln Co. Eggs were collected from a Wilson R. nest in 1940 by Alex Walker (Bayer 1994b), and breeding was confirmed on the Nestucca R. in 1994 (Johnson J 1995a). In ne. Oregon, broods were found on the Imnaha, Lostine, and Wallowa rivers draining the Wallowa Mtns. prior to 1935, and birds have been reported on the W. Fork Wallowa R. Individual birds were found on the Grand Ronde R., Union Co. (Gabrielson and Jewett 1940), and adults and pairs have been reported there through 1992 (Evanich 1992c).

They are found at the Oregon coast throughout the year (nonbreeders through spring and summer, usually in small numbers). Larger concentrations of wintering birds are usually seen in Lane, Lincoln, and Coos counties (Bayer 1994b). Wintering birds on the Oregon coast are of unknown origin, though at least three birds banded on breeding streams in Montana and one from Washington have been seen in Oregon (Genter et al. 1998, Schirato and Hardin 1998, D. Pitkin p.c.). Of approximately 250 harlequins of all ages banded on breeding streams in Oregon, only two

drakes—banded as adults in Apr at Quartzville Cr., Linn Co.—have been relocated (by radio telemetry) on the Oregon coast, both in early Jun of 1994 (Dowlan 1996a). At least four birds banded as breeders on the Nestucca R., Tillamook Co., have been sighted or recaptured in successive years as molting birds near Protection I., Washington. At Protection I., the birds from Nestucca R. were in the company of other harlequins from three states and three provinces (Schirato and Hardin 1998, G. Schirato p.c.). Two drakes banded during molt drives at Protection I. have been observed on the Table Rock Fork of the Molalla R., Clackamas Co., in 1995, 1996, and 1999 (*SGD*). They are essentially unobserved in migration, so one 17 Aug 1978 in Malheur Co. (perhaps a postbreeding bird from the Rocky Mtn. population) is of note (Contreras and Kindschy 1996).

**Habitat and Diet:** In the w. Cascades, breeding pairs are observed on low to moderate gradient (1-7%) third- to fifth-order streams in the western hemlock zone, typically with simple (vs. constricted or braided) channels and abundant in-stream rocks which serve as "loaf sites." Most observations occur in reaches containing bedrock, boulder, and cobble substrates, usually where riffle and glide channel units are present, followed in order of frequency by rapids, pools, and chutes (Bruner 1997). Pools, chutes, and backwaters occasionally are used (Thompson et al. 1993, Bruner 1997). Sandy substrates and constricted or braided channel types are infrequently used (Bruner 1997, *SGD*). The Nestucca R. breeding site in Tillamook Co., the only recent breeding location in the Coast Range, is generally of lower gradient, with a sandier substrate and fewer loaf sites (*SGD*). Breeding stream characteristics in the Blue Mtns. region have not been documented.

Nesting in Oregon occurred along first- through fifth-order streams (Bruner 1997) in a variety of seral stages and forest stand characteristics, ranging from relatively undisturbed and stable (90-300 yr old) at upslope sites to frequent disturbance in riparian stands (5-45 yr old) in stream channel sites. The nest is a scooped depression lined with down. Of 20 nests in Bruner's (1997) study, 35% were placed on exposed shelves of logs or rootwads and on the ground in floodplains within 3.3 ft (1 m) of the ground, and 65% were on natural ledges on slopes or cliffs. Nests on the ground in riparian zones were less successful than upslope sites on cliffs or steep slopes. Vertical cover within 3 ft (1 m) of the nest was present at 95% of the western Cascades sites, though nests situated on slopes were generally accompanied by small level clearings, presumably to accommodate airborne approach. Horizontal distance to water ranged 1-82.5 ft (0.3-25 m) for all nests. Five nests were located on islands. Surrounding cover up to 3.3 ft (1 m) high appears to be important for concealing the incubating hen. Nest predation occurred at five nests in Bruner's study, and hens were killed by an unknown predator at two of these. At least 29 nests have been found in Oregon (Dowlan 1996a). Nesting density was as high as eight nests per 16 km (10 mi) on Quartzville Cr., Linn Co. (Bruner 1997).

Diurnal feeder (Johnsgard 1975b, Palmer 1975). Observations of hens with broods and fecal analysis from 33 harlequins on Quartzville Cr., Linn Co., indicate it forages heavily on the limnephelid caddisfly *Dicosmeocus gilvipes*, especially from late Jun on, when broods are present (Wright et al. 2000). Some mayflies and stoneflies were also consumed, though 12 of the samples contained 100% *D. gilvipes*. One female was observed eating fish, a behavior apparently not recorded previously. K. K. Wright's (1997) study indicated a correlation between timing of brood hatching and the later instars of *D. gilvipes*, though this relationship apparently did not extend to a correlation between higher numbers of birds where caddisflies were also most abundant in the stream system. Presence of harlequins at particular sites was positively associated with bedrock substrate, which may allow for increased visibility of prey and a reduction in invertebrate refuges.

Molting and wintering harlequins may be found at rocky headlands, offshore rocks, and jetties and occasionally around sandy beaches (*SGD*) at the coast. In Washington, harlequins generally concentrate over shallow (<33 ft [10m]) water inside the surf line, usually over eelgrass (*Zostera* spp.) and kelp communities (Hirsch 1980). Food on winter range typically consists of intertidal and subtidal invertebrates, especially crabs, amphipods, and gastropods, and occasional small fish and fish roe (Robertson and Goudie 1999). Rough water is not a deterrent to harlequin presence.

**Seasonal Activity and Behavior:** Migration is apparently direct to and from breeding grounds (Robertson and Goudie 1999). A few very early records on breeding streams include a pair on Lost Cr. in the McKenzie R. drainage Jan 1992 and an unspecified number on the McKenzie R. in late Feb 1991 (Latta 1992). Males and females typically arrive on breeding streams beginning the first week of Mar (Dowlan 1996a). Pairs are seen on breeding streams in greatest numbers between the second week of Apr and the end of May, though a few pairs can be found through Jun (Dowlan 1996a).

The following nesting data are from Bruner (1997). Initiation dates in the w. Cascades ranged 20 Apr-8 Jun. Forty-three percent of paired (all marked) females nested (n=42); nest success was 74% overall. Nest-site fidelity was high for adult females, and at least nine nests (45%) contained buried egg membranes indicating use in previous years. Clutch size 3-7. Hatch dates ranged 24 May-25 Jun. Eggs incubated approximately 28 days, consistent with other N. American populations. Of 44 females observed, 15.9% produced broods. Females may remain still as the nest is approached (Palmer 1975, *SGD*). Jewett (1931) recounted the experience of a small boy who actually lifted a hen from a nest along the Zigzag R., Clackamas Co.

Marked drakes left the breeding streams by the first week in Jun 1994 and 1995 (Bruner 1997), usually shortly after hens began to incubate. Non-nesting males and females may form "clubs" at popular loafing sites prior to migration from breeding to molting areas, a behavior noted in populations elsewhere (Robertson and Goudie 1999). At Quartzville Cr., five or more males have been observed together in this fashion, though no female groups of that size have been seen (*SGD*).

Birds of the year are present on breeding streams as early as the first week of Jun and as late as Aug. Duckling survival from hatching to fledging for 13 broods was 60%, with the highest mortality in the first 2 wk (Bruner 1997). Brood rearing has been observed to occur in close proximity to areas occupied by pairs, or in other areas generally downstream (*SGD*), possibly determined by stream morphology (Wright et al. 2000). Broods may temporarily join together during feeding or resting (*SGD*). Average date of departure has not been documented, though birds of unknown age have been seen on breeding streams as late as the first week in Sep (*SGD*). Two female brood-mates banded on Quartzville Cr., Linn Co., in 1995 returned as nonbreeders in 1997, then successfully nested in 1998 (R. Jarvis p.c.). Males are not known to return to natal streams (*SGD*).

Drakes migrate first to molting areas. Large rafts form in Puget Sound and in the Strait of Juan de Fuca (Schirato 1993), Strait of Georgia, and Hecate Strait (Savard 1988, Breault and Savard 1991, Wright and Clarkson 1998). Sixty or more males

*Harlequin Duck*

ELVA PAULSON

are present on Smith I., Island Co., Washington, after 15 Jun annually (M. Denny p.c.). Prebasic molt begins soon after arrival at sheltered sites. Small numbers of molting drakes may be seen along the Oregon coast. Pair bonds are reestablished at wintering areas (Gowans et al. 1997) beginning in Oct, after females complete molt. Pairs banded and monitored at White Rock, British Columbia, reunited on the wintering grounds 79% of the time (Smith et al. 1998).

On the Oregon coast, numbers increase in Oct and diminish by Jun, with only rare nonbreeders present through summer. Peak numbers at Yaquina Bay and Seal Rocks, Lincoln Co., occur in Mar (Bayer 1994b). Latta (1992) estimated the entire wintering population on the Oregon coast at 200 individuals.

**Detection:** In general, this is an unwary species. Harlequins are most detectable at breeding streams in spring when pairs are present, and least detectable in Jun and Jul when hens are on the nest (*SGD*). Jarvis and Bruner (1997) determined an approximate 30% probability of detecting harlequins present on a stream during a single dedicated survey. In a similar investigation in Washington, Schirato and Perfito (1998) determined that, assuming a female is present, six surveys on a given stream reach would be necessary for a 90% chance of detecting harlequins. Numbers from annual BLM spring counts on Quartzville Cr., Linn Co., and the Molalla R., Clackamas Co., conducted since 1993, vary considerably from year to year, and broods have been found in Jul in survey areas in which no pairs were detected by single-visit spring survey efforts (*SGD*). Intensive surveys in 1993 found breeding populations of multiple pairs on streams from which no previous sightings were reported (Thompson et al. 1993).

Detection is fairly reliable at regular coastal sites, though birds move between wintering areas. Harlequins are usually observed within the surfline adjacent to or on exposed rocks, and are generally somewhat more approachable than other sea ducks (Robertson and Goudie 1999, *SGD*).

**Population Status and Conservation:** Harlequin Ducks are not monitored by BBS efforts, and monitoring of a few breeding streams began only in the early 1990s. Latta (1992) cited an estimate of 100 breeding pairs for Oregon from Bellrose (1976), but Marshall (1992a) speculated that <50 pairs actually bred in the state. Historic population numbers are unknown. Thompson et al. (1993) reported observations of up to 47 pairs for the w. Cascades based on single year's spring surveys, though some of these are multiple observations of the same pair on different dates (*SGD*). Broods were observed on eight other streams where spring surveys had not been conducted. CBC data are of limited use due to the small number of coastal counts, the vagaries of

observer effort, the small number of birds present, and the likelihood that birds may move in and out of CBC circles. Among three counts with regular occurrence since 1980 (Tillamook, Yaquina Bay, Port Orford) no trend is obvious. In Puget Sound and the Strait of Juan de Fuca, Washington, well-monitored molting and wintering populations are on an increasing trend (Schirato and Hardin 1998).

Very high breeding-site fidelity and dependence on forested, montane riparian canyons in the w. Cascades makes the species vulnerable to both natural and human disturbances (Bruner 1997). Wright et al. (2000) postulates that severe flood events which reduce or set back benthic invertebrate populations, e.g., the Feb 1996 floods on Quartzville Cr., may reduce nesting frequency and brood success in harlequins. Thompson et al. (1993) found human activity as close as 10-30 ft (3-9 m) at 48% of sites where Harlequin Ducks were observed, usually in the form of road traffic, fishing or hiking. Reports vary on the species' tolerance of human activity, though the highest known density in the state is along a section of Quartzville Cr. which is heavily used for recreation (Bruner 1997), including suction-dredge mining (*SGD*). Direct effects of timber harvesting, mining, road building or other activities have not been documented.

The relatively small, widely scattered Oregon coastal population is subject to most if not all of the disturbance factors relevant to seabirds in general, especially those which might impact intertidal zones (*SGD*). The effects of the *Exxon Valdez* oil spill on the numbers of breeding and wintering harlequins in Prince William Sound, Alaska, are inconclusive (Robertson and Goudie 1999), though continued exposure to oil may still be occurring. Hunting pressure on wintering harlequins in Oregon and the w. U.S. in general is thought to be low to moderate, though reliable estimates of harvest cannot be obtained from hunter surveys and questionnaires (Robertson and Goudie 1999).—*Stephen G. Dowlan*

**Surf Scoter** *Melanitta perspicillata*
In contrast to the other scoters, the Surf Scoter is exclusively N. American. Although the least numerous scoter on the continent, it is the most common scoter along the Pacific coast south of Alaska and winters by the thousands off Oregon. Adult males' plumage, black except for white patches on the forehead and nape, yields attention to the bill, a swollen white, red-orange, yellow, and black wedge feathered squarely along its base. This highly visible standard advertises males' presence for up to a mile. Dark-billed adult females and subadults are dark brown above and paler brown below, with two indistinct light patches on the cheeks and sometimes one on the nape. A flattened head profile and heavier bill distinguish this species from

other scoters; feathering over the bill extends farther down the culmen than in black but not as far forward as in white-winged.

**General Distribution:** Breeds in boreal forest freshwater regions (Bellrose 1980) from nw. Alaska to Hudson Bay and wc. Quebec, south to ne. British Columbia and east to Labrador (Campbell et al. 1990a, Savard et al. 1998). Along the Pacific coast, winters principally from the e. Aleutian Is. and se. Alaska south to c. Baja California and in n. Gulf of California to c. Sonora, Mexico; less numerous along the Atlantic coast, wintering from Newfoundland south to the Gulf coast (Savard et al. 1998). A few winter on interior waters (Cottam 1939). Monotypic (AOU 1957).

**Oregon Distribution:** Abundant on salt water along the coast from fall through spring and uncommon during summer. Uncommon on fresh water near the coast, but does not breed in Oregon. Inland, several are recorded from west of the Cascades and a few from e. Oregon most years, usually in fall on large lakes and reservoirs (Gilligan et al. 1994, Contreras 1997b).

**Habitat and Diet:** Preferring water less than 33 ft (10 m) deep, most Surf Scoters winter within 0.6 mi (1 km) of land (Savard et al. 1998). On the ocean, they usually congregate just outside the breaker line and often dive through breaking waves. In bays and estuaries, most occur in lower reaches or where herring eggs are available (Bayer 1980, Varoujean 1985, Merrifield 1998). Often congregate over substrates of gravel and sand and are the only scoters to dive regularly over solid rock (Brown and Fredrickson 1997, Savard et al. 1998). Synchronous diving and surfacing may help maintain cohesion during foraging, facilitate location of patches of sessile prey, and reduce vulnerability to predation (Savard et al. 1998). The spawning of Pacific herring in estuaries in late winter and spring coincides with the northward movement of scoters and may attract thousands of Surf Scoters (Bayer 1980, Campbell et al. 1990a).

Most dives last 19-32 sec (Cottam 1939, Carboneras 1992a). Diet averaged from all wintering regions consists of 61% bivalves (mussels; bent-nose, razor, and littleneck clams), 9% gastropods (periwinkles, basket whelks, and olive shells), 10% crustaceans (barnacles, mole and true crabs, and amphipods), 3% fishes, and <1% chitons (Cottam 1939), mostly inhabitants of the lower mid-littoral zone (Kotzloff 1993). Mussels are probably torn from rocks with bills, and all mollusks are swallowed shell and all (Savard et al. 1998). Fewer heavier-shelled mollusks are consumed than by White-winged and Black Scoters (Cottam 1939, Brown and Fredrickson 1997, Savard et al. 1998). Plants (pondweed, eelgrass, wigeongrass, horned pondweed) eaten more on summer than winter range (Cottam 1939).

Herring eggs may be important as a source of nutrition for fat deposition prior to or during spring migration (Bayer 1980), and scoters appear to adjust winter and spring concentrations to take advantage of spawning Pacific herring on Washington waters, where at spawns surfs outnumbered white-wingeds by about 10:1 (Wahl et al. 1981).

**Seasonal Activity and Behavior:** Fall migration is more diffuse than spring passage due to separation of sex and age classes among molting, staging, and breeding areas; many migrate overland at night (Savard et al. 1998). Most leave the nc. Alaska Peninsula by early Sep but are reported in northern prairie provinces until early Nov (Savard et al. 1998). Males leave Beaufort Sea coastal molting areas from late Aug to early Sep (Savard et al. 1998).

Arrival in northwest coastal wintering areas begins in late Aug, and numbers peak in Nov (Campbell et al. 1990a, Contreras 1998, Merrifield 1998). Total scoter numbers on the Oregon and Washington continental shelf increase markedly in Sep and peak in Nov; highest concentrations are off c. Oregon and n. Washington (Briggs et al. 1992). In 1991-98 censuses (approximately 45-min count of all birds sitting on the water) to 1.1 mi (1.8 km) offshore from three Lincoln Co. coastal points, Surf Scoter total numbers peaked at 300-1,100 in Sep and Oct (*KM*). Large southbound flocks are routinely seen from shore points during Oct.

Wintering Surf Scoters forage in flocks of a few to several hundred to thousands (Savard et al. 1998). In Jan-Mar, total scoter numbers on outer continental shelf diminished south of Tillamook, and less than 5/mi² (2/km²) were south of Newport (Briggs et al. 1992). Pairs form on both wintering and staging grounds; interactions include threats, rushes, and aerial pursuits (Palmer 1975, Savard et al. 1998). Courtship displays have been observed in Oregon, mostly in Mar (Johnsgard 1965, *KM*).

Females begin northward migration in late Mar, but most coastal movement is from mid-Apr to mid-May; some fly overland at night (Campbell et al. 1990a, Gilligan et al. 1994, Savard et al. 1998). Staging is difficult to document due to gathering at herring spawns (Savard et al. 1998). Arrival on interior lakes begins in late Mar, but most occurs from late Apr through May (Campbell et al. 1990a, Savard et al. 1998). Off Oregon, 1,000s/hr may pass a given point for short periods during peak migration, but sustained rates are in 100s/hour (Gilligan et al. 1994). In 1991-98 censuses (approximately 45-min count of all birds sitting on the water) to 1.1 mi (1.8 km) offshore from three Lincoln Co. coastal points, numbers peaked at 350-850 during Feb-Apr (*KM*). Most have left Oregon by early May (Contreras 1998, Merrifield 1998).

Many immatures remain in coastal wintering areas during summer (Campbell et al. 1990a, Contreras 1998). In 1991-98 censuses (see above for details), the surf was the only scoter present during midsummer; numbers were lowest in Jun and Jul (*KM*). In 1989 and 1990 aerial censuses, overall scoter populations dwindled on the Oregon and Washington outer continental shelf in Jun and Jul, but higher concentrations remained in Washington (Briggs et al. 1992).

In mid-Aug to early Sep, western population males migrate to the British Columbia and Alaska coasts and to the Bering Sea to molt in thousand-strong groups; unsuccessful and then successful breeding females follow a month later (Bellrose 1980, Campbell et al. 1990a, Carboneras 1992a, Savard et al. 1998).

**Detection:** Most easily found by scanning the nearshore ocean and large bays, estuaries, and inland lakes and reservoirs. Also seen in flight over nearshore ocean during migration from coastal promontories.

**Population Status and Conservation:** This least numerous of the scoters, inhabiting only N. America, far outnumbers other scoters in Oregon waters. Not globally threatened and fairly common, surfs are probably in decline, possibly related to hunting in other regions, breeding habitat loss, or oil pollution (Carboneras 1992a, Savard et al. 1998). An estimated 765,000 winter south of Alaska (Bellrose 1980), and 536,000 breed in nw. N. America (Savard et al. 1998). Numbers in Oregon marine waters reach into the thousands in winter; total scoters off Oregon number about 30,000 (Briggs et al. 1992).—*Kathy Merrifield*

## White-winged Scoter *Melanitta fusca*

Perhaps because of its southerly breeding range, the White-winged Scoter is the most studied of the scoters and suffers most from breeding-habitat disturbance. The white secondaries of all plumages form a conspicuous square wing patch during flight but are often hidden during rest. Other than the secondaries, males' plumage is entirely black except for a small white teardrop around each eye. Females and immatures are dark brown above and pale below with diffuse white patches in front of and behind the eyes. A black knob graces the males' swollen, white-ridged, orange bills, while females' and immatures' bills are dark; the feathering of all extends almost to the nostril. Sexual maturity is achieved at 2-3 yr; the oldest recorded banded bird was 12 yr old.

**General Distribution:** Occurs in Eurasia and N. America. Largely extirpated from former breeding areas in the n. U.S., white-wingeds still breed from interior Alaska to Manitoba, rarely to nc. N. Dakota, and sparingly in portions of e. Canada (Bellrose 1980, Brown and Fredrickson 1997). Winter along Atlantic coast from the Gulf of St. Lawrence to the Gulf coast, along Pacific coast from Alaska to Baja California, most commonly from British Columbia to Oregon, and rarely inland (Cottam 1939, Carboneras 1992a, Brown and Fredrickson 1997). The subspecies *M. f. deglandi* occurs in N. America; this is *M. deglandi deglandi* of Gabrielson and Jewett (1940) and AOU (1957) but *deglandi* and *M. fusca* are conspecific (Delacour and Mayr 1945), and *dixoni* and *M. f. deglandi* are synonyms (Delacour 1959).

**Oregon Distribution:** Abundant along the coast from fall through spring, White-winged Scoters are uncommon during summer on the ocean and inshore marine waters. Especially during migration peaks, congregate farther seaward than surfs. Inland, casual to rare during most years on large water bodies on both sides of the Cascades (Gilligan et al. 1994, Contreras 1997b). Waters with multiple records include Summer, Malheur, Upper Klamath, Hatfield, and Suttle lakes, McKay, Wickiup, Crane Prairie, Ana, and Haystack reservoirs; Willamette and Columbia rivers; and Sheridan and Monmouth sewage ponds.

**Habitat and Diet:** Most winter in marine waters, including large bays, estuaries, and open coastline over shellfish beds in hard sand or gravel; on the ocean, they congregate beyond breaking waves and within about 1 mi (1.6 km) of shore (Palmer 1975, Brown and Fredrickson 1997). Preferred waters are shallow but on average deeper than those chosen by Surf Scoters (Campbell et al. 1990a). Densities are higher in lower sections of estuaries than in upper sections (Varoujean 1985, Merrifield 1998). Feeding dives are to depths of up to 40 ft (12 m), but usually are less than 15 ft (4.5 m), and average about 60 sec, with surface intervals averaging 12 sec (Cottam 1939, Palmer 1975). White-wingeds tear mussels loose by grasping them with their bills and paddling their feet vigorously in a vertical head-down position (Palmer 1975). Small food is swallowed underwater and larger food at the surface (Palmer 1975).

In marine waters, 94% of food is animal and is mostly mollusks, including their shells, particularly bivalves (Cottam 1939). Where all scoters occur together, white-wingeds usually select larger prey in deeper water farther from shore (Brown and Fredrickson 1997). Mollusks, including native littleneck, bent-nose, soft-shelled, and surf clams; native oysters, mussels, scallops, basket whelks, slipper shells, and chitons compose 63% of the diet (Cottam 1939). Crustaceans, including rock, mud, and other crabs; amphipods, and barnacles compose 13%, fishes, 2%, and various small invertebrates including echinoderms, 1% of the diet (Cottam 1939). On the

Pacific coast, native littleneck clams were the single most important food item, followed by native oysters, mussels, and bent-nose and razor clams (Cottam 1939, Bellrose 1980). Native littlenecks are most abundant in protected sandy or gravelly mud; native oysters often live on undersides of rocks, usually in quieter waters; California mussels are most abundant from 0.0-4.0 ft (0.0-1.2 m), often in surge channels or on vertical surfaces; and razor and bent-nose clams inhabit mud or sand (Kotzloff 1993). Because large mollusks themselves serve as effective grinding material, only small quantities of gravel may be consumed (Cottam 1939). White-wingeds consume fewer herring eggs than Surf Scoters; eelgrass may be ingested coincidentally (Bayer 1980, Wahl et al. 1981). Plant foods, composing 6% of the diet, are usually consumed during breeding (Cottam 1939, Martin et al. 1951)

**Seasonal Activity and Behavior:** In Lincoln Co. marine waters, they first arrive as early as 4 Jul, and larger numbers in late Jul to early Sep (Merrifield 1998, *KM*). Most southward migration begins in about Sep and extends through early Nov (Palmer 1975, Bellrose 1980, Campbell et al. 1990a). In 1991-98 censuses (approximately 45-min count of all birds sitting on the water) to 1.1 mi (1.8 km) offshore from three Lincoln Co. coastal points, numbers peaked at 100-1,200 during Oct-Dec (*KM*). In Oregon, more likely to be on inland waters both east and west of the Cascades in fall, usually Oct and Nov, than in spring. Courtship activities become common in late winter (Palmer 1975, Campbell et al. 1990a, *KM*).

A northward coastal shift begins in Mar (Palmer 1975), and migration, often overland at night, extends through May (Palmer 1975, Campbell et al. 1990a). In 1991-98 censuses (see details above), daily peaks were 60-150 in Feb and Mar (*KM*). Most leave the coast by mid-May (Contreras 1998, Merrifield 1998). Most first-summer birds move to more northern marine waters (Palmer 1975, Brown and Fredrickson 1997). First nonbreeders, then males followed by some females migrate to northern coastal waters to molt (Palmer 1975, Bellrose 1980, Campbell et al. 1990a). Nonbreeders less common off Oregon than are Surf Scoters, but small numbers may remain through the summer (Contreras 1998, *KM*)

**Detection:** Most easily found by scanning the nearshore ocean and large bays, estuaries, and inland lakes and reservoirs. Also seen in flight over nearshore ocean during migration from coastal promontories. White wing-patches can be seen from great distances.

**Population Status and Conservation:** About 675,000 White-winged Scoters breed in N. America (Bellrose 1980, Brown and Fredrickson 1997). Carboneras (1992a) estimated a winter population of

1 million in N. America, 250,000 in the Palearctic, and unknown numbers in Asia. Declining due to reduction in prairie breeding habitat (Cottam 1939, Brown and Fredrickson 1997); highly vulnerable to oil spills, susceptible to being trapped in fishing nets, and may further concentrate toxins accumulated in mussels (Carboneras 1992a, Brown and Fredrickson 1997). This second most common scoter in Oregon comprises about 30% of wintering scoters; numbers vary more than those of Surf Scoter (Gilligan et al. 1994, Contreras 1997b).—*Kathy Merrifield*

## Black Scoter *Melanitta nigra*

Adult male scoters of all species are black, but Black Scoters are the blackest; their shiny black plumage bears no white. The swollen bright orange-yellow knob on the otherwise black bill has invited common names including "yellowbill" and "butternose," but the bill is smaller than that of other scoters. Males are distingushed in flight by the flashing silver-gray of underwing flight feathers against black wing linings and by the all-black body. Females' uniform sooty upperparts and dark head cap are clearly delineated from paler cheeks; their bills are usually dark. Immatures resemble females, but most males acquire some black feathering the first fall. Sexual maturity is achieved in 2-3 yr; the oldest banded bird was 16 yr old. The least common and most local scoter in the Pacific Northwest.

**General Distribution:** Occurs Eurasia and N. America. The western of two distinct N. American populations breeds mainly in w. Alaska; the eastern population breeds mainly in n. Quebec (Campbell et al. 1990a, Bordage and Savard 1995). In N. America, winter abundance decreases from north to south in the Bering-Pacific area from the Pribilof and Aleutian Is. to s. California and is greatest off Alaska to n. Washington (Cottam 1939, Campbell et al. 1990a, Bordage and Savard 1995). Alaskan breeders winter along the Pacific coast; Quebec breeders winter on the Atlantic (Cottam 1939, Bellrose 1980, Campbell et al. 1990a). One subspecies in Oregon, *M. n. americana* of N. America (AOU 1957).

**Oregon Distribution:** Uncommon to locally common along the coast fall through spring, usually on the ocean; abundance is highest in n. Lincoln, Tillamook, and s. Clatsop counties (Contreras 1997b). Up to several hundred may aggregate in traditional areas along the coastline, often in sheltered waters around headlands and away from easy human visibility. Only occasionally noted in lower estuaries. These factors may contribute to blacks being Oregon's least frequently noted scoter (Fix 1991). The least likely scoter to oversummer along the Oregon coast (Contreras 1998, *KM*).

Inland, have been recorded from Salem, Monmouth sewage ponds, Sauvie I., Cascade Locks, Summer L., Lake Co., Haystack Res., Jefferson Co., and Willow Cr. Res., Morrow Co. (Kebbe 1956a, Heinl 1985, Summers 1985a, Anderson DA 1990a, Anderson 1991a, Gilligan et al. 1994).

**Habitat and Diet:** Migrants and winterers frequent a variety of coastal waters including exposed coastlines, estuaries, bays, harbors, and inlets less than 36 ft (11 m) deep (Campbell et al. 1990a, Bordage and Savard 1995). Black Scoters appear to prefer gravel and cobble substrates in British Columbia but sandy substrates in Washington (Bordage and Savard 1995); gravelly substrates, especially gravelly clay, also preferred by native littleneck clams, an important prey species (Ricketts et al. 1968). They may (Campbell et al. 1990a) or may not (Bordage and Savard 1995) concentrate over large blue mussel beds.

Feed almost exclusively by diving (Carboneras 1992a) to 40 ft (12 m) but usually less than 21 ft (7 m) (Cottam 1939). Where the three scoters occur together, blacks consume fewer bivalves and more crustaceans than surfs and smaller prey in shallower water than white-wingeds (Cottam 1939, Brown and Fredrickson 1997). Average diet is 65% bivalves including native littleneck clams, mussels, razor clams, and bent-nose clams (Cottam 1939, Bellrose 1980). Native littlenecks alone provide 17-36% of the diet along the Washington coast in Jan and Feb (Bellrose 1980). Crustaceans, including barnacles, amphipods, and isopods, are next in importance, followed by gastropods (periwinkles and limpets), fishes including herring eggs, echinoderms, and chitons. Some foods may be eaten in larger quantities when available. Black Scoters congregate at Pacific herring spawns less regularly than other scoters (Bordage and Savard 1995). Insects, freshwater gastropods, and plants including muskgrass and wigeongrass are consumed more during breeding than wintering (Martin et al. 1951). Eelgrass and kelp are consumed in winter, perhaps with herring eggs (Martin et al. 1951, Bellrose 1980).

**Seasonal Activity and Behavior:** In 1991-98 censuses (approximately 45-min count of all birds sitting on the water) to 1.1 mi (1.8 km) offshore from three Lincoln Co. coastal points, a few arrived in mid-Aug; numbers peaked at 150-650 in Oct-Dec (*KM*); also arrives off Coos Co. in Aug (Contreras 1998). First nonbreeders, then males, and then females migrate southward in early Sep-Dec; movement off British Columbia peaks in late Oct (Campbell et al. 1990a, KM). Most inland records are Oct-Dec.

In winter, they feed mostly in homogeneous groups and often form larger roosting flocks (Bordage and Savard 1995). In 1991-98 censuses (see details above), numbers peaked at 120-400 in Feb (*KM*). Winter pair formation, including courting flights, inciting by females, and ritualized displays by males (Palmer 1975), has been observed in Oregon (*KM*). Although blacks are the most vocal of scoters (Bordage and Savard 1995), calls are usually inaudible amid ocean noise.

A northward coastal shift begins in Mar; breeders depart on high-altitude, probably nonstop flights to breeding areas through the first half of May (Palmer 1975, Bellrose 1980, Campbell et al. 1990a). A few remain off Oregon through May (Gilligan et al. 1994, Contreras 1998). Arrival off the Yukon Delta begins in mid-May, and courtship continues through the month (Bellrose 1980). In late Jun to mid-Jul, males and some females and yearlings undergo a migration to offshore molting sites mostly north of Oregon (Bellrose 1980, Bordage and Savard 1995). Small numbers, probably yearlings, summer along the nw. coast (Campbell et al. 1990a).

**Detection:** Most easily found by scanning the nearshore ocean, large bays, and estuaries. Also seen in flight over nearshore ocean during migration from coastal promontories.

**Population Status and Conservation:** Bordage and Savard (1995) estimated 51,000 breeding pairs in Alaska and 25,800 in Quebec. Carboneras (1992a) estimated 500,000 in both Quebec and Alaska before breeding. No more than 5,000 winter along the Pacific coast south of Anchorage (Bellrose 1980); specific numbers for Oregon are not available. Widespread and common over most of their range, blacks are probably declining, but not rapidly (Carboneras 1992a, Goudie et al. 1994). Reductions in populations may be due to a decrease in breeding habitat, to oil pollution, or to unknown factors related to food or predation in breeding areas (Carboneras 1992a). Highly vulnerable to oil spills (Bordage and Savard 1995). Die-offs at Cape Yakataga, Alaska, may have been due to elevated cadmium levels in mussels (Goudie et al. 1994).—*Kathy Merrifield*

## Long-tailed Duck *Clangula hyemalis*
This restless diver of cold oceans and bays, formerly called Old Squaw in N. America, is one of the prize waterfowl to see on a coastal winter day. Although the loud, musical call of males is seldom heard in Oregon, we can still be cheered on a chilly day by this energetic visitor from the north. Winter males' bodies are mostly white except for black breast and central back; the wings are dark, scapulars long and gray, and the dark central tail feathers elongate. Winter females are darker

above with a light head; scapulars and tail feathers are short and dark. Dark areas mark females' heads and males' necks. Because of age and sex differences and individual variations during the pre-breeding molt, confusing patterns occur in spring (Bellrose 1976). Basic plumage transforms to alternate plumage with a spring head and body molt. Whether this summer plumage is an eclipse is controversial (Kortright 1943, Johnsgard 1965, Carboneras 1992a).

**General Distribution:** Long-tailed Ducks nest in the circumpolar high arctic, in N. America south to the Aleutians, sw. Hudson Bay, and Labrador (Bellrose 1976). They winter on the Great Lakes and along N. Hemisphere seacoasts, to Florida in the Atlantic, and from the limit of ice in the Bering Sea to s. California, Korea, and Japan in the Pacific; small numbers winter across the n. and c. U.S. and similar latitudes in Eurasia (Bellrose 1976, Cogswell 1977, AOU 1998). Monotypic (AOU 1957).

**Oregon Distribution:** Long-tailed Ducks are rare to uncommon winter visitors along the coast (Rogers D 1982, Sawyer and Hunter 1988, Contreras 1998) and rare inland on the Columbia R. and on lakes throughout the state (Summers 1982a, Gilligan et al. 1994, Contreras 1997b). Typically occur singly or in pairs (Gilligan et al. 1994, Contreras 1998), but groups of up to 13 (exceptionally) have been observed along the coast (Carlson 1978, Fix 1984b, 1990b, Johnson J 1990b, 1994b, Contreras 1997b, 1998, T. Rodenkirk p.c.).

E. Oregon waters with multiple records include Summer L. (Anderson 1989e, Evanich 1991b, Sullivan 1996a), Wallowa L. (Summers 1986a, Crabtree 1996b), Harney L. (Anderson 1987b), Malheur L. and nearby Sod House Spring (Marshall 1959, Scott 1959, 1965, Littlefield 1990a, Sullivan PT 1995b), Haystack Res. (Anderson 1988c, Evanich 1992b), Sunriver sewage pond (Summers 1985b), and the Columbia R., particularly at John Day Dam (Anderson 1989b, Crabtree 1995b, Sullivan PT 1995b, 1996b). Inland w. Oregon waters with multiple records include the Monmouth sewage ponds (Fix 1984b), the Willamette R. at Salem (Heinl 1986a), and Toketee Res. (Heinl 1986a, 1987c, Gilligan 1997, Johnson 1997b).

**Habitat and Diet:** Long-tailed Ducks favor sheltered waters, and deep, calm coves or lower estuaries, but also occur on the open ocean; they are rare on inland lakes (Rogers D 1982, Summers 1982a, Contreras 1997b). No diet information is available from the Pacific Northwest. Crustaceans, especially isopods, amphipods, and crabs and mollusks averaging 0.5 in (11.3 mm) long, including mussels, periwinkles, basket whelks, bent-nose clams, and cockles, comprise the highest percentage of the diet by collective volume in

ducks examined from 13 eastern and western states and eight Canadian provinces, including 66 birds (34% of total) from Alaska and British Columbia (Cottam 1939), off Newfoundland (Goudie and Ankney 1986), and the Baltic Sea (Stempniewicz 1995). Fish and fish eggs, polychaetes, sea anemones, aquatic insects, and plant material are also consumed in small amounts (Cottam 1939, McGilvrey 1967, Bellrose 1976, Goudie and Ankney 1986, Stempniewicz 1995). The targeted amphipods, isopods, and periwinkles live on rocks, pilings, and the leaves of bay and ocean seagrasses; bent-nose clams and cockles occur in sand or mud, whelks are subtidal rock-dwellers, and mussels adhere to rocks and pilings (Kotzloff 1993). Gravel, sought for internal food crushing, comprises more of the stomach volume than in ducks such as scoters, which consume a higher proportion of harder foods and therefore need less gravel (Cottam 1939).

**Detection:** This duck may remain isolated or join flocks of scoters on the ocean or in bays. Long-tailed Ducks with extensive white plumage are easily detected due to contrast, but those in darker or less contrasting plumage are more difficult to see. May be missed in quick scans due to long dive times.

**Seasonal Activity and Behavior:** Following nesting in the high arctic, flocks begin to form on the ocean in Jun; flightless adults have been observed in Jul and Aug, and flight feathers are regained in Sept (Bellrose 1976). Oct and Nov southward movement in British Columbia (Campbell et al. 1990a) coincides with a Nov observation peak in Oregon. Usually observed in Oregon from Oct through Apr, most frequently in Nov inland both west and east of the Cascades, and in Mar along the coast (Marshall 1959, Rogers D 1982, Sawyer and Hunter 1988, Littlefield 1990a, Bayer 1996b, Johnson 1996b, Contreras 1998). The earliest fall record for e. Oregon is from Harney L. on 28 Sep 1986 (Anderson 1987b). The earliest fall inland w. Oregon record is from Big L., Linn Co., on 24 Oct 1987 (Gilligan et al. 1994). The record high CBC total was 20 in Port Orford in 1988 (Contreras 1991). The latest e. Oregon record is from Summer L. on 24 Apr 1996 (Sullivan 1996b), and the latest w. Oregon inland record is from Toketee Res. 29 Jan through 1 Mar 1987 (Fix 1990a). Scattered coastal observations have occurred from Sep through May (Sawyer and Hunter 1988, Johnson J 1991b, Bayer 1995a, Johnson J 1995b, 1996b, 1998a). A report of Long-tailed Ducks flying north off Cape Blanco on 12 May 1979 (Rogers D 1979a) was retracted by the author; they are thought to have been Pacific Loons (D. Rogers p.c.). The complex courtship ritual (Johnsgard 1965) has not been reported in Oregon.

Long-tailed Ducks routinely dive to 74 ft (22.5 m) but often deeper—in one instance to 240 ft (73 m)

(Cottam 1939, Cogswell 1977). Dives of 15-36 ft (4.6-11.0 m) averaged 59.3 sec, and interdive pauses averaged 28.2 sec (Dow 1964). In n. Europe, Long-tailed Ducks are day-active, and feeding intensity is highest during the coldest months (Nilsson 1970).

**Population Status and Conservation:** The world Long-tailed Duck population may exceed 10 million (Carboneras 1992a), and Bellrose (1976) estimated an early summer N. American population of 3-4 million. As of 1995, however, Henny et al. (1995) reported a decline in Alaska breeding populations. Long-tailed Ducks risk mass exposure to oil pollution, because they gather in large rafts in the Bering Sea and off se. Alaska following nesting and during winter (Carboneras 1992a). Many drown when entangled in fishing nets (Carboneras 1992a).

In recent years, totals of 5-23 Long-tailed Ducks have been reported annually along the Oregon coast, and these small numbers do not appear to be declining. Long-tailed Ducks were observed 12 of 25 yr on the Coos Bay CBC, averaging one bird, with a maximum of three. They were observed 14 of 34 yr on the Tillamook Bay CBC, where the maximum was five. During the Columbia Estuary CBC, single birds were seen three out of 17 yr.

At the time of Gabrielson and Jewett's (1940) writing in the late 1930s, the species was not known to occur away from the coast. Its presence could have been overlooked before that time, but most inland records are from human-constructed impoundments, including most of the Columbia R., which flowed swiftly before it was dammed in the early 1930s (*DBM*). Thus, the recent appearance of Long-tailed Ducks inland may have been human-influenced. There are currently no conservation concerns for Long-tailed Ducks in Oregon.—*Kathy Merrifield*

**Bufflehead** *Bucephala albeola*
Originally called "buffalo-head" because its puffy head seemed large in comparison to its pint-size body,

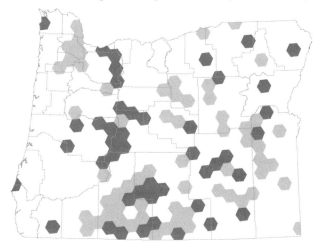

this species has also been referred to colloquially as "butterball" for its buoyancy and plumpness. The Bufflehead is N. America's smallest diving duck, giving it the advantage of being able to nest in abandoned holes of Northern Flickers, a plentiful resource off-limits to larger cavity-nesting ducks. It is a swift flyer and takes wing from the water more easily and neatly than other diving ducks. Widely distributed throughout the state in winter, males attract attention with their striking white body, black back, and iridescent black head with a large notch of white; females and juveniles are dark charcoal-gray with a conspicuous white patch behind and below the eye.

**General Distribution:** Breeds from c. Alaska south through British Columbia to n. Washington, and west through s. and wc. Canada to wc. Quebec. Isolated breeding populations in Oregon, California, Montana, Wyoming, and nc. U.S. Winters along the Pacific coast from Alaska to n. Baja California, on Atlantic coast from Newfoundland to n. Florida and Bermuda; and locally throughout the interior from Washington, the Great Lakes, and the Ohio and Mississippi river valleys south to interior Mexico and Gulf coast. Monotypic (AOU 1957).

**Oregon Distribution:** Local, uncommon breeder in c. and s. Cascades. In Aug 1946 a pair with four young was observed at Red Butte L., Linn Co., for the first recorded evidence of nesting in Oregon (Evenden 1947). Other known nesting sites include Fish L., Linn Co.; Hosmer L., Crane Prairie Res., Twin Lakes, Wickiup Res., Davis L., and along the Little Deschutes R., all Deschutes Co.; Diamond L. sewage ponds, Douglas Co.; and Dayton Hyde's Res., Klamath Co. (Griffee 1961a, Stern, Wise, and Theodore 1987, Fix 1990a, Marshall 1996). Broods have also been seen at small lakes near the crest of the Cascades in e. Lane and w. Deschutes counties (C. Corkran unpubl. data). Perhaps the easternmost confirmed breeders were several broods 4 Jul 2001 on Hatfield L. east of Bend, Deschutes Co. (J. Meredith p.c.).

Rare in summer away from breeding locations in the Cascades. One female was seen at North Spit effluent pond, Coos Co., in Jul 1998 (Tice 1999a). A few nonbreeders have summered in Multnomah, Clatsop, Lincoln, and Tillamook counties (Gilligan et al. 1994). The OBBA shows breeding in Warner Valley, Lake Co., and probable breeding elsewhere in e. Oregon. These reports need further investigation, especially in areas like Warner Valley that lack nesting cavities. Marshall (1959) reported the species summering at Boca L., Malheur NWR, in 1957, and there have been several additional records since, most of which are probably subadults (Littlefield 1990a). There are several Jun reports from se. Oregon (e.g., Spencer 1998), but none have been reported to nest. A male discovered in a grove of flooded cottonwoods at upper Bully Cr. Res., Malheur Co., in mid-Jun 1995 could possibly indicate breeding (Contreras and Kindschy 1996). A more suggestive observation was made of a pair at Peterson Cr. Res., east end of Big Summit Prairie, Crook Co., 17 May 2001: the female was observed to fly into a cavity in a ponderosa pine adjacent to the reservoir (J. Geier p.c.).

Common migrant throughout the state in both spring and fall. It winters throughout Oregon. It is possibly the most ubiquitous diving duck in w. Oregon during late fall through early spring, with two or three present at many small impoundments. At larger water bodies, it can be abundant, especially at coastal locations. Concentrations in the thousands build up at Coos Bay in particular (Gilligan et al. 1994, Contreras 1997b). Winters regularly on Toketee L. in the s. Cascades, and may do so on other lakes in the region that do not completely freeze (Fix 1990a). It is also quite common in the Klamath Basin (Gilligan et al. 1994). Uncommon to locally common elsewhere east of the Cascades in winter where open water permits (Littlefield 1990a, Evanich 1992a, Gilligan et al. 1994, Contreras and Kindschy 1996, Contreras 1997b).

**Habitat and Diet:** Typically nests at high-elevation forested lakes in c. Cascades, using cavities or artificial nest boxes in trees close to water (Gilligan et al. 1994, Marshall 1996). Use of former Northern Flicker cavities has been documented: a nest with eight eggs was found in an old flicker cavity in a cottonwood snag near Fish L., Linn Co., in 1959, and a similar nest was discovered near Wickiup Res., Deschutes Co., in 1961 (Griffee 1961a). Another cavity nest was found in a lodgepole pine snag on the edge of a dense stand of trees bordering Davis L. in 1986 (Stern, Wise, and Theodore 1987). No studies have been done in Oregon on water body characteristics needed for nesting.

In migration and winter, Buffleheads use sheltered freshwater lakes, freshwater ponds, sewage ponds, slow-moving rivers, estuaries, bays, and backwaters (Gauthier 1993, Gilligan et al. 1994, AOU 1998). They are almost never seen on the open ocean (Contreras 1997b), preferring to feed in shallow water over tidal mudflats in large bays (Gilligan et al. 1994). At Malheur NWR, they use larger ponds and lakes (Littlefield 1990a). Found on the larger, deeper bodies of water in ne. Oregon and Malheur Co. (Evanich 1992a, Contreras and Kindschy 1996).

Buffleheads studied during spring in the California portion of the Klamath Basin primarily ate animal matter, especially midge larvae. Other common food items included water boatmen, physid snails, and seeds of smartweed, alkali bulrush, and sago pondweed (Gammonley and Heitmeyer 1990). Known to eat herring eggs seasonally on the Oregon coast (Bayer 1980) and noted by Kortright (1943) to consume "the maggoty flesh of rotting salmon" in Pacific coastal rivers. Nothing is known of the breeding-season diet in Oregon.

**Seasonal Activity and Behavior:** Peak of spring migration is mid-Mar through late Apr, with a few migrants lingering into May (Gilligan et al. 1994). Migrants arrive at Malheur NWR in late Feb and move through the refuge in small flocks, peaking in early to mid-Apr and disappearing by late May (Littlefield 1990a). In late May 1997, three or four pairs were noted at Beulah Res., Malheur Co. (Sullivan 1997b). Pairs have been seen displaying on lakes and reservoirs in the c. Cascades on 18 May 1997 (Sullivan 1997b); courtship has also been observed 15 Jun (OBBA). A female was flushed from a nest cavity on 6 Jun 1986 at Davis L., Klamath Co., and nesting was completed by 29 Jun (Stern, Wise, and Theodore 1987). On 4 Jul 1989 a brood of six very young ducklings was observed at the Diamond L. sewage ponds, e. Douglas Co., and a brood of four young was there 25 Jun 1990 (Fix 1990a). Generally, fledged young have been observed throughout Jun and early Jul (n=12), but have been seen as late as 17 Aug (OBBA).

*Bufflehead*

Fall migrants begin arriving in Oregon in late Sep, generally peaking in late Oct or early Nov (Gilligan et al. 1994). Peak migration into the Klamath Basin is a little later, in late Nov and early Dec (Gammonley and Heitmeyer 1990). Mainly migrate in small flocks, but occasionally seen in larger concentrations: in early Nov of 1988 and 1989 numbers reached 1,000 at Diamond L., e. Douglas Co., (Fix 1990a), and 320 were seen at Cow Lakes, Malheur Co., 21 Nov 1995 (Sullivan 1996a). A flock of 156 birds was noted at Farewell Bend, Malheur Co., on 22 Jan 2000 (Korpi 2000), a very large number for the Snake R. (M. Denny p.c.).

**Detection:** Easily noted in suitable habitat in migration and winter, especially males, whose striking contrast of black and white make them stand out. Wariness makes them more difficult to locate in summer.

**Population Status and Conservation:** Gabrielson and Jewett (1940) found this species to be "one of the most abundant and widely distributed winter ducks" in Oregon, but noted decreases in numbers by 1930 consistent with severe reductions everywhere due to overshooting. As protective measures like the Migratory Birds Treaty Act Convention took effect, populations showed steady increases across the continent (Gauthier 1993). In recent decades, hunting pressure has decreased in the Pacific Flyway (Gauthier 1993), but other factors may have an impact on population status in Oregon, such as human disturbance from high recreation use at Cascade lakes and a shortage of suitable natural nesting cavities due to forestry practices (Marshall 1996). The Oregon breeding population is considered sensitive by ODFW because of small size and limited nesting habitat.— *Rachel White Scheuering*

## Common Goldeneye *Bucephala clangula*
The drake Common Goldeneye is a strikingly handsome black-and-white diver about the size of a Greater Scaup. Goldeneyes are strong, fast flyers nicknamed "Whistlers" for the sound of their primaries as they zoom past on a still day. Drakes have a black head with a white spot below and in front of the eye, white neck, breast and flanks, and a black back and tail. Hens have a brown head, light neck, breast and belly, brown back and flanks. Fairly silent. Usually alone or in small groups, goldeneyes tend to remain apart from other ducks. This habit is reflected in their avoidance of hunters' decoys and has led to the use of a few goldeneye decoys by those seeking to bag them. Not a good table bird; Gabrielson and Jewett (1940) reported that their flesh was frequently "strong and unpalatable." They make up only a trace of the duck harvest in Oregon.

**General Distribution:** Breeds in low densities over a wide range from Kotzebue Sound in w. Alaska, n. Yukon to n. Manitoba, n. Ontario, n. Quebec, c. Labrador and Newfoundland south to c. Alaska, s. British Columbia, to c. Montana, nw. Wyoming, n. N. Dakota, n. Minnesota, n. Michigan, s. Ontario, New York, Vermont, and Maine. Winters from the Aleutians and se. Alaska to s. British Columbia and across the n. U.S., the Great Lakes, and s. Canada to Newfoundland south to Baja California, Sonora, the Gulf coast and Florida. Widespread, but nowhere abundant in winter. Two subspecies; *B. c. americana* in most of N. America and Oregon (Browning 2002).

**Oregon Distribution:** Although there have been reports of breeding in Oregon, none have been substantiated (*MGH*). An extremely rare summer visitor in ne. Oregon (Evanich 1992a) and casual to rare in summer in the Klamath Basin (Summers 1993a). Two males were observed on Dowell Res., Malheur Co., on 24 Jun 1998 (Spencer 1999). Littlefield (1990a) reported only one summer record at Malheur NWR.

This species is a common spring and fall migrant in ne. Oregon (Evanich 1992a), common to locally abundant in Malheur Co. and on the Snake R. between Oregon and Idaho (Contreras and Kindschy 1996), common at Malheur NWR (Littlefield 1990a) and in the Klamath Basin (Summers 1993a). Irregular in c. Douglas Co. (Hunter et al. 1998). They are uncommon migrants in the Columbia R. estuary (Patterson 1998b) and on the coast (Brown et al. 1996, Contreras 1998).

Gabrielson and Jewett (1940) reported the species common in winter on the Snake R., the entire course of the Columbia R., and the Klamath R., and expected it to winter in all other lakes and streams of the state wherever there was open water. Winter surveys find small numbers of goldeneyes (species unidentified) in most areas of the state, with highest numbers in Baker, Klamath, and coastal counties (USFWS undated). A common winter visitant in ne. Oregon (Evanich 1992a) and at Malheur NWR (Littlefield 1990a), common to abundant in Malheur Co. and on the Snake R. (Contreras and Kindschy 1996) and in the Klamath Basin (Summers 1993a). When open water permits, goldeneyes occur on Cascade lakes, Black Butte Ranch ponds, and Paulina L. (*DBM*). Common in winter on Lost Cr. Res. and on the upper Rogue R., Jackson Co. (N. Barrett p.c.). An uncommon winter visitant in the Willamette Valley (Evenden et al. 1950, Gullion 1951). Uncommon but regular winter visitant in the Columbia R. estuary (Patterson 1998b), the Nehalem R. valley (*RKM*), and on the coast (Bayer and Krabbe 1984, Brown et al. 1996, Contreras 1998).

**Habitat and Diet:** Nesting should be looked for in cavities in trees near high-elevation lakes. Common Goldeneyes frequent a variety of habitats on migration and during the winter including lakes, reservoirs, rivers, ponds, estuaries, coastal bays, and flooded fields. Noted for their diet of animal foods and Bayer (1980) found the species eating herring eggs at Yaquina Bay. Elsewhere it has been known to eat some plant life, supplementing a mainly animal diet (Bellrose 1980). Hundreds gather at Biggs, Boardman, and McNary at granaries and barges in winter on the Columbia R. (M. Denny p.c.).

**Seasonal Activity and Behavior:** Wintering Common Goldeneyes may be heard vocalizing as they engage in courtship displays by early Feb (Fix 1990a). An amazing 5,000 birds were along the Snake R. from Farewell Bend to Annex during the winter of 1994-95 (Crabtree 1995b), and a congregation of 2,300 was at Farewell Bend, Malheur Co., on 22 Jan 2000 (Korpi 2000). They migrate early, following the spring breakup and are the first ducks to appear at Malheur NWR (Littlefield 1990a). Migrants at Malheur NWR peak in Mar and early Apr (Littlefield 1990a), and leave e. Douglas Co. (Fix 1990a), Jackson Co. (N. Barrett p.c.), and Coos Co. (Contreras 1998) by late Apr; a few stragglers may persist until mid-May (Irons 1984b, Littlefield 1990a). Nests in Apr and May depending on latitude (Bellrose 1980).

In fall, young usually reach wintering grounds before the adults, which seem to move south just ahead of freeze up. The earliest Malheur NWR observation was 23 Sep, but the bird is usually not seen until late Oct or Nov, with peak numbers in early Dec (Littlefield 1990a). On the coast, an early report was 7 Oct at "D" Lake (Heinl 1986a). Fix (1985f) listed the species at Boiler Bay and Salem in mid-Oct, but noted that they moved south "in force" in early Nov. Earliest fall arrival in Coos Co. was 11 Nov (Contreras 1998). This species is among the latest waterfowl to leave high lakes before freeze up, typically in Nov or Dec, and may stay all winter if open water is available (Fix 1990a). During migration and winter usually found in small flocks, singles, and pairs and rarely mingles with other species. However, on the Columbia R. from The Dalles Dam to Umatilla Co., forms large winter flocks and freely mingles with other divers (M. Denny p.c.).

**Detection:** Males, with their contrasting black-and-white plumage, are easy to spot on open water, but females and juveniles often blend into a dark water surface. Females and juveniles of the two Goldeneye species are difficult to distinguish. Sod House Spring at Malheur NWR, Upper Klamath L., the Snake R., the Deschutes R. at the town of Warm Springs, Enterprise, Wallowa L., and coastal bays, as well as most of the Columbia R., are likely places to find Common

Goldeneyes. The calls of the male sound remarkably like the flight note of the Common Nighthawk (Fix 1990a).

**Population Status and Conservation:** Gabrielson and Jewett (1940) reported the bird very common in winter on the Snake R., and regularly and commonly on the entire length of the Columbia R. in the state as well as on the Deschutes R. and Klamath R. Although numbers are small, never reaching 3,000, winter survey counts in Oregon since 1965 show a wide distribution of the birds throughout the state and an upward trend for wintering populations (USFWS undated). Because of their low density throughout a wide range, aerial surveys are not dependable for assessing continental breeding populations. —*R. Kahler Martinson*

## Barrow's Goldeneye *Bucephala islandica*

Medium-sized diving ducks, Barrow's Goldeneyes are the expected of the two goldeneye species in Oregon in summer, but typically less numerous in winter. Drakes show graceful patterns of black and white, purple-glossed head, white crescent-shaped patch between eye and bill, steep forehead, and short bill. Females and juveniles have a chocolate-brown head, slate-gray back, wings and tail; adult females have a golden bill. The only waterfowl species known to defend winter territories different from breeding territories (Eadie et al. 2000). Vocalizations are relatively quiet and rarely heard, but the musical whistling sound made with its whirring wings (similar to Common Goldeneye) is heard often, giving rise to the colloquial name "Whistler."

**General Distribution:** Two distinct and widely separated ranges. The larger range includes the wild montane regions of nw. N. America, with >90% of the world population breeding west of the Rocky Mtns. from c. Alaska to n. California. Smaller numbers can be found in Montana, Wyoming, and e. Canada, with a breeding population recently found in the forested

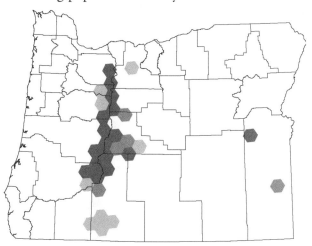

regions of se. Quebec. Breeding also occurs in Iceland. Winter distribution in w. N. America concentrates on the Pacific coast from Alaska to n. Washington; smaller numbers winter inland on lakes and rivers south to n. California and as far east as Yellowstone NP. Eastern population winters in Quebec and in very small numbers along ne. U.S. coast (AOU 1998, Eadie et al. 2000). Monotypic (AOU 1957).

**Oregon Distribution:** Uncommon from the Cascades eastward in both breeding season and winter, but it may concentrate in winter at certain favored spots. Breeds in small numbers at numerous alpine and subalpine lakes in the n. and c. Cascades. Barrow's Goldeneye is the most common nesting duck at Diamond L. in the s. Cascades (Fix 1990a), and can be seen every summer at Lost L. on Santiam Pass. Ducklings of this species have also been seen at Fish L. and Big L., Linn Co., Sparks L., Deschutes Co. (A. Reid p.c.), Waldo L. in e. Lane Co. (D. Irons p.c.), and at other small lakes in Lane, Douglas, Deschutes, Linn, Jefferson, Marion, and Clackamas counties (C. Corkran unpubl. data).

Although not mentioned as occurring in summer in ne. Oregon by Evanich (1992a), this species may be extremely rare at that season in the n. Blue and Wallowa mountains. Broods and adults have been seen at Langdon L. near Tollgate, e. Umatilla Co., and in the Wallowas at Duck L. and nearby vernal ponds in s. Wallowa Co. (R. Anderson p.c.). Also regularly nests on Bogus L. in sc. Malheur Co. when water levels permit, and probably breeds on nearby Batch L. complex as well (Contreras and Kindschy 1996).

Winters mainly on e. and w. Cascade lakes and streams and scattered areas in c. and e. Oregon. Known to congregate at Hatfield L. and Wickiup Res., Deschutes Co. (Rogers 1980b); Toketee L., Douglas Co. (Fix 1990a); Lost Cr. Res., Jackson Co. (N. Barrett p.c.); and at Brownlee Dam, Baker Co., where 200 were reported wintering in 1980 (Contreras and Kindschy 1996). One hundred or more birds have been noted on the Columbia R. at Biggs during several visits in late Jan (M. Denny p.c.). Other wintering locations include various open bodies of water in the northeast part of the state (e.g., Wallowa L.), in the Klamath Basin, along the Columbia R. near The Dalles, and at Malheur NWR (Heinl 1986c, Littlefield 1990a, Gilligan et al. 1994). Barrow's Goldeneye is a very rare winter visitant and transient west of the Cascades inland and along the n. coast and casual to rare on the coast south of Lincoln Co. (T. Rodenkirk p.c.).

**Habitat and Diet:** Breeds mainly at cold inland waters such as alpine and subalpine lakes, reservoirs, and rivers. Females often use nest cavities in dead or dying trees (Eadie et al. 2000), though this has not been proven in Oregon. However, females have been observed entering holes in snags at Lost L. during

nesting season and have been documented using nest boxes there (A. Reid p.c.). Breeds mostly in forested country in Oregon, mostly on high-elevation lakes in the Cascades. Regularly nests at Diamond L., a natural subalpine lake at an elevation of 5,182 ft (1,580 m). Also nests on the nearby Diamond L. sewage ponds, consisting of four treatment ponds adjacent to an isolated mixed-vegetation marsh (Fix 1990a). At Bogus L., two seasonal playa lakes bordered by marsh in Oregon's high desert, nests in dense stands of cattail and hardstem bulrush, breaking from its norm of cavity nesting (R. R. Kindschy p.c.).

In winter, Barrow's Goldeneyes occur in a wide variety of habitats in Oregon. Favored wintering sites range widely, from the 10,000-ac (4,049-ha) Wickiup Res. to the less than 30-ac (12-ha) Carmen Res., Lane Co., and from the Columbia R. to the ice-free reaches of the Blitzen R. near Page Springs (Littlefield 1990a). A group of 500 were attending grain elevators on the Columbia R. at Biggs on 23 Jan 1999 (Korpi 1999). Coastal birds typically appear in the lower portions of estuaries; they tend to be more partial to shoreline waters than Common Goldeneyes. Occurrences inland in w. Oregon have been at borrow pits, larger log ponds, river backwaters, and reservoirs (D. Fix p.c.).

While food habit data for Barrow's Goldeneye are unavailable for Oregon, studies conducted in British Columbia, Alaska, and sc. Washington indicate that adults and juveniles feed predominantly on aquatic invertebrates, and also take some buds and tubers of wild celery and some pondweed seeds. Diet was shown to shift markedly with season and habitat; on breeding grounds, diets were more restricted to aquatic insects. In winter, mollusks make up a major proportion of the diet, and salmon eggs and fingerlings also are taken where available (Fitzner and Gray 1994, Eadie et al. 2000).

**Seasonal Activity and Behavior:** The Barrow's Goldeneye has not been closely studied in Oregon. Elsewhere it is known to be a medium-distance migrant between wintering and breeding areas, with an additional early-summer migration for males from breeding to molting areas (Eadie et al. 2000). Wintering birds at Toketee L., e. Douglas Co., where they do not appear to breed, depart by mid-Apr (Fix 1990a). At Malheur NWR, where they also do not breed, they have been noted as late as 28 Apr (Littlefield 1990a). A maximum number for spring was 185 recorded at the Diamond L. sewage ponds, e. Douglas Co., on 29 Apr 1990 (Fix 1990a). Family groups may be encountered anywhere along the Diamond L. shore from Jun to Sep; a boat survey of the entire shoreline 30 Jul 1989 revealed nine broods, with ages ranging from 1 wk old to nearly adult-sized. Average number of ducklings per brood was six, range of 2-14. Nine broods totaling 53 young were located on Lost L.

on 16 Jul 1998 (Tice 1999a). A lone female seen at Lost L. with a group of 35 ducklings appeared to be exhibiting crèching behavior, and was later relieved by a second female (A. Reid p.c.). Barrow's Goldeneye was the most common duck during Jun and Jul at the Diamond L. sewage ponds, e. Douglas Co., during the last half of the 1980s (Fix 1990a).

As early as late Oct, birds begin showing up at Malheur NWR, with abundance peaking Dec through Feb (Littlefield 1990a). They also arrive at Toketee L., e. Douglas Co., beginning in Oct, with flocks peaking over the winter at 50-75 birds (Fix 1990a).

**Detection:** Males are conspicuous and can be readily picked out from groups of Common Goldeneyes. Much more care must be taken to distinguish females and juveniles of the two species.

**Population Status and Conservation:** The Barrow's Goldeneye has a restricted distribution and a relatively small population worldwide (estimated at less than 200,000), but populations seem stable throughout most of their range (Eadie et al. 2000). No serious declines have been reported for Oregon, but because of its restricted distribution, this species should be monitored. Potential threats in the state might include recreational development on breeding lakes or loss of nesting habitat due to forestry practices which eliminate tree cavities.—*Rachel White Scheuering*

## Smew *Mergellus albellus*

This small, striking Eurasian merganser ranges rarely but regularly to the Aleutian Is. and casually in winter along W. Coast of N. America. Reports from elsewhere in N. America, and perhaps some of the W. Coast records, may be of escaped captive waterfowl. There are at least two Oregon records. An adult male was photographed and seen by many from 26 Jan to 1 Apr 1991 on both sides of the Columbia R. around Stevenson, Washington, and Cascade Locks, Hood River Co., Oregon (Evanich 1991a, 1991b). It, or another adult male, was in the same area 2 Jan-16 Feb 1992, when it evidenced serious injuries, which were thought probably mortal (Evanich 1992e). An adult male was photographed at Malheur NWR HQ, 26-28 Feb 2001 (OBRC). Monotypic (AOU 1957).—*Harry B. Nehls*

## Hooded Merganser *Lophodytes cucullatus*

In quiet backwaters and wooded wetlands, these stunning ducks can occasionally be seen skulking near the shoreline as they search for fish. The male with a striking black head and extensible white crest, white breast, black back, and chestnut sides is truly a sight to behold. Females and immatures are quite plain by

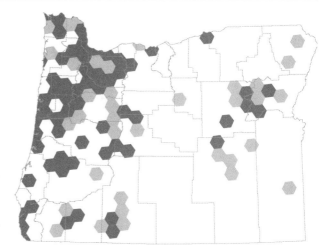

comparison: dull grayish-brown except for a reddish-brown crest. Juvs lack the white greater coverts and tertials that females possess while first year males show varying amounts of white in their crest (Madge and Burn 1988). These elegant ducks do not reach reproductive maturity until their second year after hatching (Morse et al. 1969).

**General Distribution:** Breed in wooded wetlands from se. Alaska east to w. Alberta and south to sw. Oregon, c. Idaho and w. Montana (casually south to California and New Mexico). Also breeds from c. Saskatchewan east to s. Nova Scotia and south to n. Georgia and n. Louisiana, primarily from the Appalachians westward. Winters along the Pacific coast from s. Alaska south to s. Baja California and on the Atlantic coast from New England to Florida and along the Gulf coast to Texas. Away from the moderating effects of the coast, winters locally in s. Canada and the continental U.S. south (rarely) to n. Mexico. Oregon birds tentatively belong to *M. s. serrator*, the N. American subspecies (AOU 1957); *M. s. schioleri* of Greenland may not be distinct (see Palmer 1975, Cramp 1977).

**Oregon Distribution:** Hooded Mergansers are surprisingly secretive and local during the breeding season. The breeding range in Oregon is not entirely clear, but they breed locally throughout the Willamette Valley west to the coast and south to Coos Co. (Kitchin 1934, Griffee 1936, Evenden et al. 1950, Gullion 1951, Kebbe 1954, Morse et al. 1969, OBBA). Additionally, ducklings have been found at Bull Run Res., Trillium L., and Timothy L., e. Clackamas Co., as well as other small lakes in the n. and c. Cascades (C. Corkran p.c.). In e. Oregon has been recorded breeding about 60 mi (108 km) north of Malheur NWR (Littlefield 1990a), and two females with 10 ducklings were observed on Unity Res., Baker Co., on 13 Jul 1999 (Spencer 2000a). Probable breeding has also been recorded in Wasco, Morrow, Grant, Deschutes, Jefferson, and Klamath counties, and in sw.

Oregon in Josephine and Jackson counties (OBBA). Casual from Apr to early Oct in the Umpqua Valley (Hunter et al. 1998); but a brood was observed near Umpqua during a BBS (D. Fix p.c.). During migration, it is widespread though uncommon across Oregon, usually in sheltered areas of lakes and ponds and much less commonly on estuaries (Contreras 1998, Hunter et al. 1998). Winters throughout Oregon on open water, though most common in w. Oregon (Root 1988, Contreras 1997b, Hunter et al. 1998).

**Habitat and Diet:** Found on woodland ponds, lakes, and other wooded wetlands (Evenden et al. 1950). Nest in cavities near undisturbed bodies of water (Morse et al. 1969). Scant data on preferred forest type exist for Oregon; the only published detailed nest description is of one in an aspen snag in a ponderosa pine forest (Griffee 1954). In Washington, nests have been reported from a variety of forest types below 3,000 ft (900 m) (Griffee 1954, Beall 1990, Smith et al. 1997). They readily nest in nest boxes designed for Wood Ducks (Kitchin 1934, Griffee 1936, Kebbe 1954, Morse et al. 1969, Beall 1990). In Oregon and elsewhere in N. America, they are most frequently reported nesting within 15 ft (5 m) of the ground (Kitchin 1934, Griffee 1936, Kebbe 1954, Morse et al. 1969, Baicich and Harrison 1997).

No data are available on food preferences in Oregon, although it is widely believed that the diet consists of invertebrates and small fish (Gabrielson and Jewett 1940, Littlefield 1990a). Diet studies from Michigan support this belief as small fish (including yellow perch, sunfish, bass, catfish, sculpin, darters), crayfish, aquatic insects, other crustaceans, and amphibians were frequently found in stomachs examined (Salyer and Lagler 1940, Stewart 1962).

Hooded Mergansers are visual feeders, typically feeding in water <5 ft (1.5 m) deep (Dugger et al. 1994). They have the ability to radically adjust the refractive properties of their lenses (Sivak et al. 1985). This, combined with the high transparency of their nicitans, is thought to provide them with excellent underwater vision (Sivak and Glover 1986). They pursue prey underwater by propelling with their feet; saw-edged bills allow firm grip on food (Brooks 1945).

**Seasonal Activity and Behavior:** Data on pair-bond formation in Oregon are lacking, but in sw. British Columbia they begin pairing in mid-Nov, much earlier than either Red-breasted or Common Mergansers

(Coupe and Cooke 1999). Migrants in Oregon begin arriving in Feb and peak in Mar, adding to the winter population (Littlefield 1990a, Contreras 1997b). Nest initiation begins in late Feb and eggs are typically laid in Mar. A bimodal distribution of egg laying occurs with more experienced females laying during the first week of Mar and first-time nesters laying during the last week of Mar. An average of 9-11 white, nearly spherical eggs are laid (9.4 eggs on average for first-time nesters, 10.4 eggs for more experienced nesters) at a rate of one egg per 2 days. When 87% (on average) of the eggs have been laid, female will begin depositing down in her nest. Incubation in Oregon lasts an average of 32.6 days, range 29-37 days. Nests with eggs have been observed as late as 17 May (OBBA). Males disappear when incubation begins, presumably relocating to nearby areas (Morse et al. 1969).

Ducklings are precocial and typically remain in the nest for 24 hr after hatching (McGilvrey 1966, Morse et al. 1969). A nest with young was observed 19 May northwest of Portland (OBBA). Broods are typically observed during May and Jun (Evenden et al. 1950, Morse et al. 1969), but young are discernable through Aug (OBBA). Young birds are able to fly after approximately 71 days (McGilvrey 1966). Adults go through a molt starting in Jun or early Jul that lasts until Oct. Because the flight feathers are molted simultaneously, it is estimated that Hooded Mergansers are flightless for about 1 mo during this molt (Palmer 1975).

They apparently move north after the end of the breeding season (Bellrose 1980). Arrive on wintering grounds in early Oct and numbers usually peak by late Nov (Littlefield 1990a, Fix 1991). During this month they become most apparent on w. Cascade reservoirs (*MGH*). Although it may be difficult to locate a single individual during the breeding season (particularly in Apr), they frequently gather in small flocks during the nonbreeding season (Gullion 1951, Littlefield 1990a, Fix 1991). Males and females apparently reunite at this time (Coupe and Cooke 1999).

**Detection:** Easily overlooked in their wooded wetland habitat, even in places where they may be fairly common. Plumage of both male and female blends in surprisingly well with the dappled sunlight that

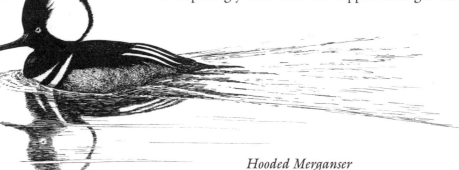

*Hooded Merganser*

falls on the surface at the water's edge. Additionally, their unobtrusive nature may lead to underreporting. However, if one patiently scouts around the edges of wooded ponds, lakes, and streams, it is fairly easy to find these birds outside of the breeding season. Nests (excluding nest boxes), however, remain surprisingly difficult to locate.

**Population Status and Conservation:** The status of this handsome duck in N. America is not well known. Bellrose (1980) estimated the nationwide population at 76,000, a value that seems low as between 83,100 and 99,100 were killed annually 1970-85 (USDI 1988). A more reasonable population estimate may be that proposed by Dugger et al. (1994) of 270,000-385,000 birds. It is estimated that Oregon contains 1,000 breeding birds (Bellrose 1980). Approximately 11% of the population winters in the Pacific states (Dugger et al. 1994). In Oregon, CBC data indicate that there has been a slight increase of 1.5% per year (Contreras 1997b).—*Chris Butler*

## Common Merganser *Mergus merganser*

From coastal bays to the high Cascades, in all corners of Oregon and far beyond, Common Mergansers ply the rivers and peer into still waters in their efficient pursuit of fish. A white form on the distant water may be the sides and breast of an adult male, whose deep green head and dark back are less visible far away. The pearl-gray bodies and white breasts of females, subadults, and eclipse males are starkly delineated from their full-crested chestnut heads. Long, slender, saw-toothed bills are held horizontally during surface swimming and grip squirming prey after an underwater chase. Among the gray-plumaged birds, red bills and feet indicate adult females, while yellow bills and feet indicate immatures of either sex (Anderson and Timken 1971). Though streamlined, Common Mergansers rank among the longest and heaviest of ducks (Erskine 1966, Bellrose 1976). Like their close relatives the goldeneyes and scoters, they do not reproduce until the second year

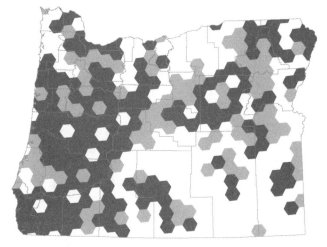

after hatching, retaining their chestnut-headed gray plumage until breeding (Erskine 1966).

**General Distribution:** Three subspecies occur throughout the closed boreal and montane forest zones of Eurasia and N. America (Bellrose 1976, Cogswell 1977). *M. m. americanus* breeds in subarctic and cold temperate zones across N. America south to s. Canada and ne. U.S., through the Rockies to n. Mexico, and in the western mountains to c. California (Bellrose 1976, Cogswell 1977, AOU 1998). It winters along the Atlantic coast from Newfoundland to Florida, inland from the Great Lakes to the Gulf of Mexico, and along the Pacific coast from the Aleutian Is. into Mexico (Bellrose 1976, Cogswell 1977).

**Oregon Distribution:** Breeds commonly in mountainous areas but is nearly absent as a breeder in the Columbia Basin and the Great Basin, where open water is scarce. Although they avoid lower estuaries during most months (Bayer and Lowe 1988, Contreras 1998), large estuarine flocks may form following breeding (Vermeer et al. 1994, Bayer 1996c, Merrifield 1998). A common migrant and winter resident where open water remains (Gullion 1951, Roberts 1970, Eley and Eley 1972, Littlefield 1990a, Contreras 1997b).

**Habitat and Diet:** Common Mergansers appear to prefer large bodies of water but will forage in any water deep enough to provide adequate fish for food (Anderson et al. 1974, Cogswell 1977, Littlefield 1990a, Kerekes et al. 1994, Contreras 1997b). They may congregate and nest near profitable feeding areas such as spawning channels and hatcheries, where densities of juvenile salmon can be many times greater than those found in nature (Wood 1987). From spring through early fall, four individuals/6 mi (10 km) were observed on larger streams in the Coast Range, with significantly fewer on smaller streams (Loegering and Anthony 1999).

Hollow trees with entrances 50 ft (15 m) above the ground near available prey are preferred nest sites, but loose boulders, brush, streambank hollows, rocky ledges, nest boxes, and even buildings may be used (Bent 1923, Bellrose 1976, Campbell et al. 1990a, Cunningham 1991). Two Oregon nests have been described (Griffee 1958): 10 eggs were observed in a hole in a cliff above the Umpqua R. on 26 May 1895, and a female sat on 11 eggs along the Wilson R. below the Tillamook Burn, 12 Apr 1958.

Common Mergansers eat freshwater and marine fishes including carp, suckers, perch, bullhead catfish, sculpins, sticklebacks, gizzard shad, freshwater drum, white bass, creek chub, river lamprey, brook trout, Coho salmon, and steelhead (Latta and Sharkey 1966, Timken and Anderson 1969, Bellrose 1976, Sjoberg 1985, Wood 1985, Wood and Hand 1985, Littlefield

1990a). Shrimp, clams, nematodes, mayfly larvae, fly larvae and adults, shore crabs, sowbugs, centipedes, beetle larvae, moss, and Sitka spruce and hemlock needles are also consumed (Fritsch and Buss 1958, Littlefield 1990a). They prefer fish less than 8 in (20.5 cm) long (Latta and Sharkey 1966, Cogswell 1977). Freshwater foragers in some studies fed mostly on salmonids, but sculpins and blennies comprised the majority of the diet of those feeding in tidal waters (Wood 1987). In warm-water areas, food consists mostly of nongame fishes usually shorter than 7.25 in (18.6 cm) (Alcorn 1953, Bellrose 1976). In small streams, almost any kind of fish was consumed, whereas in larger bodies of water, fish in large schools were consumed more often than other fish (Timken and Anderson 1969). Often feed in areas below dams in which fish killed or injured by hydropower turbines accumulate (Anderson et al. 1974).

**Seasonal Activity and Behavior:** Migrants arrive in Oregon beginning in Feb, adding to the wintering population. Pairs and small flocks form prior to the May departure of migrants to breeding areas in Oregon or to the north (Foreman 1979, Watson 1979c, Littlefield 1990a, Sullivan 1996b). Pairs are often observed on rivers in the Cascades during Mar and Apr (D. Fix p.c.), where they likely will begin nesting. In Apr or May, resident females take about 15 days to lay 9-12 eggs, which hatch in 30-35 days (Bent 1923, Griffee 1958, Bellrose 1976, Cunningham 1991).

Adult and yearling males leave breeding areas early in incubation and have been observed moving to estuaries or large lakes for wing molt (Erskine 1966, Bellrose 1976, Cunningham 1991), but in Oregon, estuarine abundance has been low through mid-summer (Foreman 1979, Merrifield 1998). Yearling birds, not known to reproduce, flock throughout the breeding season (Erskine 1966, Bellrose 1976).

Within 2 days after hatching, ducklings jump from their cavities in response to females' calls (Bellrose 1976). Broods have been observed May-Aug (Foreman 1979, Littlefield 1990a, Bayer 1994a). Upstream broods gradually move downstream (gone from middle portion of John Day R. by mid-summer [P. T. Sullivan p.c.]), often joining other broods by the time they reach estuaries and can fly, which occurs after 65-70 days (Erskine 1966, Bellrose 1976). These aggregations form when many young spontaneously cluster behind the most stimulating adult (Batt et al. 1992). Females undergo wing molt during about 4 wk from mid-Aug through early Oct (Bellrose 1976).

Fall migrants provide the highest concentrations of the year, peaking Oct through late Nov; many leave by mid-Dec (Littlefield 1990a, Sullivan 1997a, Merrifield 1998). Estuarine flocks in late summer and fall are composed mostly of basic-plumaged birds characterized by synchronous swimming and diving

(Merrifield 1998). Synchronous diving has also been observed in late Oct on Trillium L. near Mt. Hood, Clackamas Co. (*DBM*). They disperse from their native stream systems in Nov (Bellrose 1976). Males and females reunite in winter (Campbell et al. 1990a).

In studies from e. Canada and Sweden, Common Mergansers foraged by sight during the day (Erskine 1966, Nilsson 1970, Sjoberg 1985). Random searching and probing techniques as well as direct pursuit were employed (Sjoberg 1985). Began feeding late in the morning and ended well before sunset or followed a morning and evening pattern during spring (Nilsson 1970, Sjoberg 1985). Daily activity correlated with prey behavior (Sjoberg 1985). Number of prey items pursued per unit time was much lower than that of Red-breasted Mergansers (probably due to latter species' smaller prey size) and is higher during colder months (Nilsson 1970). Common Mergansers usually move continuously while foraging, repeatedly submerging their heads and at times accelerating suddenly (Wood and Hand 1985). No evidence of cooperative foraging has been found, but concurrent foraging may facilitate success (Wood and Hand 1985).

**Detection:** Common Merganser nests are difficult to locate, and few have been described. They are easily observed on open water bodies. Care must be taken to distinguish eclipse males, females, and subadults from similarly plumaged Red-breasted Mergansers (Kaufman 1990).

**Population Status and Conservation:** Of the estimated 878,000 breeding in N. America, 1,200 breed in Oregon (Bellrose 1976). Of the 165,000 wintering in N. America, 24,000 winter in the Pacific Flyway (Bellrose 1976); no numbers are available for Oregon. Birds tend to concentrate in winter; west of the Cascades, >100 have been observed in 13 separate CBC locations. Oregon's highest CBC total was 928 in Eugene in 1976 (Contreras 1991); hundreds may gather there on Fern Ridge Res. (Contreras 1997b). East of the Cascades, high winter counts, usually of several hundred, have occurred on Malheur and Harney lakes, Wickiup and Thompson reservoirs, and behind John Day Dam (Anderson 1987c, Littlefield 1990a, Evanich 1991b, 1992b, 1992e, Sullivan 1996a, 1996b); >100 observed during five CBCs. CBC data indicate an increase in Oregon 1959-88 (Contreras 1997b), perhaps due to an increase in reservoirs (*ALC*).

Long regarded as a menace to sport fish populations, they are indeed efficient predators of juvenile salmonids (Wood 1987). However, fish available for sport harvest are larger if there is a regular cropping of the smaller sizes, and Common Mergansers prefer fish under 8 in (20.5 cm) long (Latta and Sharkey 1966, Cogswell 1977). Average daily food requirement is approximately 14 oz (400 g) (Atkinson and Hewitt

1978, Wood and Hand 1985). Because energy gain is constrained by digestion time rather than hunting performance, daily consumption of 1.5-oz (43-g) salmonid smolts will not exceed 9.3-11.6 smolts during a 12-hr day (Wood and Hand 1985). Common Mergansers had an insignificant effect upon salmon in the Unikwik Inlet area of se. Alaska (Fritsch and Buss 1958).—*Kathy Merrifield*

## Red-breasted Merganser *Mergus serrator*

Swimming and diving with grace and energy, Red-breasted Mergansers arrive in fall but save their complex, contorting courtship display for early spring. A ragged-crested dark green head and reddish-brown breast mark the male, along with a dark back and gray sides. Females share the ragged crest; their rufous heads and gray bodies may make separation from Common Merganser females difficult. Their bills, however, are noticeably slimmer.

**General Distribution:** Breed throughout the southern tundra and lakes of the boreal forest from n. Alaska to Labrador and south to nw. British Columbia, c. Alberta, Minnesota, the Great Lakes, and Maine and in comparable latitudes in Greenland, Iceland, and Europe (Bellrose 1976, Cogswell 1977, Campbell et al. 1990a). Winter along the Pacific coast from the Aleutian Is. to s. Baja California, on the Atlantic coast from Newfoundland to the s. U.S., and uncommonly on the Great Lakes or inland (Munro and Clemens 1939, Cogswell 1977, Campbell et al. 1990a, AOU 1998). Eurasian birds winter from the Baltic and North seas to the n. Mediterranean, Black, Caspian, and Aral seas and from the Kamchatka Peninsula south through coastal Japan, Korea, and China (Bellrose 1976). Oregon birds are tentatively considered to belong to nominate *serrator*, the Palearctic population; however, *schioleri* may not be distinct (see Palmer 1975, Cramp 1977), thus the species may be monotypic.

**Oregon Distribution:** Red-breasted Mergansers are common from fall through spring, mostly in coastal bays and estuaries but occasionally on the open ocean. There are, however, more than 120 inland records including 48 from along the Columbia R., where some probably winter, as well as about 35 west and 41 east of the Cascades away from the Columbia, usually in larger bodies of water (Tice 1997, 1998b). Inland w. Oregon localities with multiple records include Sauvie I., the Portland and Salem areas, Fern Ridge Res., Forest Grove sewage ponds, and Diamond L. (Anonymous 1978b, Gordon 1980, Irons and Heinl 1984, Heinl 1986c, 1987c, Johnson J 1991b, 1992b, Gilligan 1995, Johnson 1996b, Tice 1998b) and the Hood River, Portland, and Sauvie I. CBCs. E. Oregon localities with multiple records include Upper Klamath L., Malheur NWR, Wickiup Res., Pine Hollow Res.

(Wasco Co.), and Summer L. (Jewett 1954d, Evanich 1983a, Heinl 1987c, Anderson 1988b, 1988d, Littlefield 1990a, Anderson 1991a, Johnson J 1991b, Evanich 1992e, Summers 1994b, Gilligan 1997, Sullivan 1997a) and the Klamath Falls CBC.

**Habitat and Diet:** Red-breasted Mergansers winter more frequently on salt than on fresh water (Bellrose 1976), although some probably winter along the Columbia R. (Tice 1997). Most are observed in lower estuaries and close inshore on the ocean (Bayer and Lowe 1988, Contreras 1998, Merrifield 1998), and few travel upstream above tidal influence (Munro and Clemens 1939).

No diet information is available from Oregon. In British Columbia, birds were often observed pursuing herring, especially during the Feb and Mar herring spawn (Munro and Clemens 1939, Bellrose 1976). Wintering birds also ate eulachon, sticklebacks, sculpins, blennies, rock fishes, salmonids, and crustaceans including shrimp and crabs (Munro and Clemens 1939). Observations in Mexico and Florida suggest that cooperative pursuit may increase hunting success (Des Lauriers and Brattstrom 1965, Emlen and Ambrose 1970).

**Seasonal Activity and Behavior:** Migration data from the Oregon coast are not available. Southward migration along the British Columbia coast from late Aug to early Dec peaks from mid-Sep to early Nov (Munro and Clemens 1939, Campbell et al. 1990a). A few have been reported along the Oregon coast as early as Aug, but most arrive in Oct or Nov (Contreras 1979b, 1998, Thornburgh 1981, Bayer 1983a, 1995a, Merrifield 1996a, 1998). A few have also been reported inland by late Aug, but they are most commonly seen from Nov through Jan (Tice 1997). Most Willamette Valley records are in Nov and Dec (Tice 1998b). Courtship displays may be observed in coastal bays in late Feb and early Mar (Merrifield 1996a).

Northward migration along the British Columbia coast from mid-Mar to early May peaks in Apr; interior Oregon and British Columbia sightings follow the same pattern (Campbell et al. 1990a, Tice 1997). Arrival in far northern breeding areas is from mid- to late May (Bellrose 1976).

Red-breasted Mergansers observed in Oregon during the summer are nonbreeders (Bayer 1995b, Merrifield 1998). Not known to breed before their second year, and males do not acquire full alternate plumage until their second fall (Bellrose 1976). Individuals in partial male alternate plumage have been observed in summer along the Oregon coast (Bayer 1998a).

Feeding habit studies have not been undertaken in Oregon. In a Swedish study, Red-breasted Mergansers were day-active (Nilsson 1970). In British Columbia studies, hunted by sight with heads submerged and usually dived for food (Munro and Clemens 1939,

Dow 1964). Feeding dives averaged 42-48 sec separated by a 24-sec pause (Dow 1964).

**Detection:** Located most easily by meticulously scanning open water. Care should be taken to separate Red-breasted from Common Merganser females and immatures, particularly in late summer and early fall.

**Population Status and Conservation:** Bellrose (1976) estimated a N. American population of 237,000 Red-breasted Mergansers. Although Bellrose estimated that only 250 of 6,000 Pacific coast wintering birds were in Oregon, Gilligan et al. (1994) indicated that up to 300 may be present on some individual bays. Oregon CBC data indicate a 3% decrease 1959-88 (Contreras 1997b). Counts from 1982-83 through 1997-98 ranged 33-297 at Tillamook Bay, 8-45 at Florence, 4-103 in the Columbia Estuary, and 19-75 in Yaquina Bay. The 25-yr median for the Coos Bay CBC is 46, and the highest count 121 (Contreras 1998). Although Red-breasted Mergansers are not threatened globally and apparently are stable, water pollution and human alterations of breeding habitat such as dam construction and forest destruction could harm them (Carboneras 1992a).—*Kathy Merrifield*

### Ruddy Duck *Oxyura jamaicensis*

Small in size and displaying a showy, almost comical alternate plumage, the male Ruddy Duck is an unforgettable sight. Bent (1925) described it as a "little gem of bird life," saying: "He knows he is handsome as he glides smoothly along . . . his saucy springtail held erect or even pointed forward till it nearly meets his upturned head; he seems to strut like a miniature turkey gobbler." Breeding males are unmistakable with their rich chestnut back, black crown, white cheek, sky-blue bill, and proportionately long stiff tail. Female plumage is drab in comparison, being dusky dark brown with a dark facial stripe across the mostly white cheek, quite similar to the male's basic plumage. However unimpressive the tiny female's coloration,

she makes up for it with the outlandish size of the eggs she lays, which are substantially larger than a Mallard's, a duck three times her size. Also known for their peculiar courtship display in which the male draws his head down and slaps his bill against his breast repeatedly in increasing tempo, creating a bubbling in the water and a hollow tapping sound (Palmer 1975). A consummate diver, this bird rises off the water only after an industrious pattering along the surface, and is nearly helpless on land.

**General Distribution:** Extensive breeding range through w. and c. N. America, from c. and ne. British Columbia west to c. and se. Manitoba, south to s. California, and west to w. and s. Texas. Casual breeder in ec. Alaska. Sporadic or former breeder from c. Ontario, s. Quebec, and Nova Scotia south in scattered locations in e. U.S., Mexico, Guatemala, El Salvador, and the Bahamas. Winters from n. Washington, sw. Idaho, Colorado, Kansas, the Great Lakes, and Massachusetts south throughout s. U.S. and Mexico to Honduras, and throughout the Bahamas. Two to three subspecies worldwide; *O. j. jamaicensis* in N. America (AOU 1957).

**Oregon Distribution:** Locally common east of the Cascades in summer, particularly in freshwater marsh complexes in sc. and se. Oregon (Gilligan et al. 1994). Common to abundant year-round in the Klamath Basin (Summers 1993a). Most important breeding areas are wetland basins in Klamath, Lake, and Harney counties, though small numbers breed at scattered locations throughout the state (Gilligan et al. 1994). Average statewide breeding population 1994-99 was 44,000 (B. Bales p.c.). Uncommon summer resident in ne. Oregon; nests sporadically and very locally at Downey L., Wallowa Co., and possibly elsewhere (Evanich 1992a). Recently fledged young have been reported in the s. Willamette Valley (Gordon 1984b). Adults were reported lingering into May at the Forest Grove sewage ponds (now Fernhill Wetlands), Washington Co. (Irons 1984b), and since then downy chicks have been documented there (G. Gillson p.c.). Several pairs were known to nest at Delta Park in n. Portland (Gilligan et al. 1994). There is a nesting record from 1990 at the Diamond L. sewage ponds, e. Douglas Co., in the s. Cascades (Fix 1990a).

Ruddy Ducks move into western interior valleys and coastal estuaries to winter, with many migrants using Upper Klamath L. and Malheur NWR en route (Littlefield 1990a, Gilligan et al. 1994). Uncommon, irregular fall migrant on Diamond L., though 140 congregated there in Nov 1987 (Fix 1990a). Common along the coast in winter, particularly at major estuaries. They are known to concentrate at Devils L., Lincoln Co. Gabrielson and Jewett (1940) found Ruddy Duck to be the most abundant species there in winter; more recently a count of 730 was recorded in late Dec 1984 (Heinl 1985). Locally common along the Columbia R. (Contreras 1997b), and an uncommon but regular winter visitor in the Willamette Valley, with groups of 1-30 birds in scattered locations where suitable water occurs (Gabrielson and Jewett 1940, Gullion 1951). Other commonly used wintering grounds include areas of open water in Jackson Co. (Browning 1975a) and the Klamath Basin (Contreras 1997b).

**Habitat and Diet:** Ruddy Ducks occur in lakes, marshes, deep sloughs, and ponds that allow enough open space for long running take-off. For nesting, in e. Oregon, they often use dense stands of hard-stem bulrush or cattail, which are matted down to form a simple platform (*RWS, EJS*). Historically, clutches were also found on Malheur L. in the sides and on top of muskrat houses (Willett 1919). Favored nesting localities at Malheur NWR include Malheur L., Boca and Derrick lakes, and Knox, Buena Vista, Warbler, and Wright's ponds (Littlefield 1990a). Wintering habitats additionally include estuaries, borrow pits, and other such water bodies devoid of nesting habitat.

Food habits of Ruddy Ducks in Oregon have not been closely studied. Gabrielson and Jewett (1940) noted that while on the coast the birds regularly consume mollusks and "other aquatic life." Elsewhere known to rely on midge larvae or pupae in the summer, with other important food sources being seeds and vegetative parts of pondweed, bulrushes, and wigeongrass (Johnsgard and Carbonell 1996).

**Seasonal Activity and Behavior:** Spring migration west of the Cascades from Feb through early Apr, though individuals may remain along the coast into early May (Gilligan et al. 1994). First appear at Malheur NWR in late Feb, with numbers peaking in late Apr or early May (Littlefield 1990a). Concentrations of up to 15,000-18,000 individuals, primarily males, have been noted at The Narrows, Harney Co., in late Apr each year since 1997 (D. Evered and L. Messick p.c.). Nesting at Malheur NWR begins in mid-May and continues through Jun (Littlefield 1990a). In addition

*Ruddy Duck*

to distinctive courtship displays, Ruddy Ducks are also noted for brood parasitism, laying eggs in the nests of other ducks, often Redheads or Canvasbacks (Joyner 1982, *EJS, RWS*). Males often accompany hens with young broods in Jun, but by late Jul both males and females have deserted the young, which then fledge in Aug or Sep (Littlefield 1990a). Adults undergo a postbreeding molt from Aug to Oct, producing a dull brown plumage concomitant with a change in the male's bill color. Males resemble females at this point, except for their solid white cheek patch, and retain this plumage until Apr (Palmer 1975).

Fall migration begins in Sep and continues into Dec when numbers peak at coastal locations (Gilligan et al. 1994). In early Oct 1995, 300 were seen at Phillips Res., Baker Co., and in late Nov of that year there were 190 at L. Abert, Lake Co. (Sullivan 1996a). There were 200 birds at the Lakeview sewage ponds from mid-Sep through mid-Oct 1997 (Sullivan 1998a). Most birds have left Malheur NWR by late Oct, but may linger into Nov if sufficient submergent vegetation and open water are available; an estimated 50,000 remained on the refuge on 8 Nov 1959 (Littlefield 1990a).

**Detection:** Males in alternate plumage are conspicuous and hard to mistake. However, much suitable habitat (deep open water and marsh) is not easily accessible to humans and therefore many individuals are likely to go undetected during the breeding season. During winter, the Ruddy Duck is among the most commonly seen diving ducks on still or slow-moving waters of any size.

**Population Status and Conservation:** Breeding population in N. America estimated at about 380,000 birds (Johnsgard and Carbonell 1996). Described as delicious table birds and easily decoyed, Ruddy Ducks historically have been popular with hunters (Kortright 1943). Bent (1925) remarked that it would not take long for a gunner to bag the legal limit of 35 a day. Gabrielson and Jewett (1940) reported an "alarming" decrease in numbers breeding in the inland lake country of s. Oregon since 1930, though they still found it fairly common along the coast. Palmer (1975) described great declines in the N. American population in the early part of the 20th century due to unrestricted hunting, and speculated that with continuing loss of breeding habitat, the population would probably never be more than a small fraction of its former numbers.

Hunter harvest of Ruddy Ducks in N. America has declined sharply over the last few decades, indicating either long-term population declines or the species' decreasing popularity with hunters (Johnsgard and Carbonell 1996). Declines have not been documented in Oregon recently, but clearly this species warrants close observation.—*Rachel White Scheuering and Eric J. Scheuering*

# Order FALCONIFORMES
*Family Accipitridae*

## Subfamily Pandioninae

### Osprey *Pandion haliaetus*

This large bird of prey is dark above, white below, and has a visible dark spot at the wrist of the wing when flying. The head is black and white. Juveniles have buffy-tipped dark feathers above. In flight, the wings have a noticeable angle or "crook." This highly migratory fish-eating species is frequently found nesting along larger rivers, lakes, and reservoirs. A large bulky nest at the very top of a live, broken top, or dead tree and more recently on utility poles, channel markers, pilings, and cell phone towers near fishable waters is good evidence of Ospreys.

**General Distribution:** Cosmopolitan, in temperate and tropical areas of all continents. In N. America breed from c. Alaska and northern portions of Canadian provinces south to s. Baja California, coastal Sinaloa, Mexico, and the southern tip of Florida (Henny and Anderson 1979, Henny 1983). In the U.S., four general regions of Osprey concentrations were noted: forested Pacific Northwest (Oregon, Washington, n. California, n. Idaho, w. Montana, nw. Wyoming), Great Lakes (Minnesota, Wisconsin, Michigan), N. Atlantic coast (Maine to and including Chesapeake Bay), and S. Atlantic and Gulf coast (Carolinas to and including all of Florida). Although nesting Ospreys were concentrated in the above locations, only 17 states, located primarily in the mid-portion of the continent, were without nesting pairs during the early 1980s. There are four subspecies worldwide, with *P. h. carolinensis* in N. America (Prevost 1983).

**Oregon Distribution:** Breeds statewide except in arid treeless regions of se. Oregon and Columbia Basin grasslands. Found commonly nesting along larger rivers including the Columbia, Willamette, Rogue, Umpqua, and Deschutes. Other haunts include natural lakes and reservoirs in the Cascades, along the coast, and elsewhere. Nesting pairs east of the Cascades forested zone are limited to some along the Columbia R. east to Umatilla, and localized nesting in the Blue and Wallowa mountains, including the Snake R. In winter, very rare on the s. coast and in w. Oregon interior valleys. Casual elsewhere.

**Habitat and Diet:** This species historically nested only in forested regions of Oregon because of requirement for large live tree (often broken top) or dead tree (snag) for nest sites. Nests in Oregon are usually located within 2 mi (3.2 km) of water with an accessible fish population. By the mid-1970s, Ospreys along the

Willamette R. began nesting on utility poles, allowing them to breed in locations previously limited by lack of nest sites because of land clearing for agriculture. Similarly, the recent use of channel markers for nest sites on the Columbia R. permitted the species to utilize sites where suitable nesting trees were no longer available, and to extend the present breeding range eastward beyond the forested Columbia R. Gorge (*CJH*). They have also been noted to use artificial nest platforms placed for Canada Geese at Fern Ridge Res. (N. Barrett p.c.), and to have traditional nest sites (previously built by Osprey) usurped by early-nesting Canada Geese along the Willamette and Umpqua rivers (*CJH, MGH*).

Ospreys dive feet first into the water for fish, but can only reach about 18 in (45 cm) under the surface. Therefore, fish are always caught near the surface, and favored hunting areas are often over shallow water, when available. Clear water is critical to fishing success. Feed almost exclusively on live fish, but dead ones are taken occasionally (Nesbitt 1974). Fish in the 4- to 12-in (11- to 30-cm) size class constituted the bulk of the diet (89%) in Idaho (Van Daele and Van Daele 1982). The list of non-fish species taken by Ospreys is long (Wiley and Lohrer 1973) and includes mammals, birds, amphibians, and reptiles, but represents a minute percentage of the overall diet. Lind (1976) calculated that adult Ospreys required 286 kcal/day and assumed fish contained 1 kcal/gm (0.035 oz) of body weight. Nordbakke (1980) suggested daily food requirements were slightly higher (300-400 gm; 10.5-14 oz) and concluded that an Osprey pair raising two young consumed about 375 lbs (170 kg) of fish during a breeding season. The nesting season in Finland was shorter, but yielded comparable findings (Häkkinen 1977) if adjusted to the time period spent on the Oregon breeding grounds. The 234 pairs nesting along the Willamette R. and lower Santiam R. between Portland and Eugene (Henny and Kaiser, unpubl. data) probably ate about 88,000 lbs (40,000 kg) of fish during the 2001 nesting season. A few nonbreeders (perhaps 5% of the population) were also present, consuming additional fish. The vast majority of fish taken were largescale suckers (82.8% on a biomass basis), followed by northern pikeminnow (7.3%), common carp (6.4%), largemouth and/or smallmouth bass (1.5%), and brown bullhead (1.0%) with no other species above 1.0% (Henny et al. 2003).

**Seasonal Activity and Behavior:** Some Ospreys that breed in Oregon begin returning from the wintering grounds in late Feb and early Mar, but the large influx generally starts near the first day of spring (20 Mar) and continues over the next several weeks. Older experienced breeders generally arrive first, younger breeders a few weeks later (Poole 1985). Established pairs nearly always return to their old nest sites. Both members of a pair nesting along the Columbia R. near St. Helens in 1996 received satellite transmitters to evaluate timing of migration and wintering localities (Martell et al. 1998). The female departed the nesting area between 23 Aug and 2 Sep; the male left later (between 16 and 26 Sep). Both birds wintered in Sinaloa on the w. coast of Mexico (at Mazatlan and about 200 mi [320 km] to the north). They had not seen each other for about 7 mo, and met at the nest site the following spring (between 28 Mar and 7 Apr) to continue their long-term relationship.

Aerial displays by males are first seen on warm spring days, followed shortly by nest building and/or repairs. Extrapolations from the development of a single egg collected from 16 clutches in the Willamette Valley in 1993 and 1998 indicate that eggs are laid between 23 Apr and 8 May (mean 30 Apr). Ospreys usually lay three eggs (range 1-4) with a mean of 2.92 for 39 nests studied on the Columbia and Willamette rivers 1993-99 (Henny and Kaiser unpubl. data). Unlike many birds of prey, males share the incubation of eggs (about 25%) (Garber and Koplin 1972). Eggs hatch in about 38 days, and after hatch the female remains in almost constant attendance brooding the young for the first 30 days, while the male provides all the fish for female and young (Poole 1989). The male spends non-hunting time perched nearby. Young make first flights at 50-55 days (Poole 1989) which, for the Willamette Valley, is in late Jul and early Aug; they return to the nest site for food for several weeks. Based upon satellite telemetry information for 15 adults from Oregon, departure dates (not calculated if more than 10-day gap between last signal on breeding grounds and first in migration) for the wintering grounds occurred between 28 Aug and 24 Sep (Martell et al. 2001). Most wintered near the coast of s. Mexico (13), with others in El Salvador (1) and Honduras (1). At Bonney Butte, near Mt. Hood, median passage date (during Sep-Oct monitoring period) averaged 17 Sep for 1994-98, with only occasional birds after early Oct. Numbers (Sep-Oct) have been rather low: 10/100 hr of observation time in 1994, and consistently 17-21/100 hr from 1995 to 1999, constituting only about 2% of total raptor numbers (Vekasy and Smith 2000).

**Detection:** This is perhaps the most visible nesting bird of prey in Oregon. Quite tolerant of human activities if not molested. Nests are bulky and conspicuous. Many nests in the Willamette Valley are on utility poles in the middle of farmers' fields. Double cross-arm poles chosen are often at wells and irrigation pumps. Most Oregon residents in Osprey country recognize the species and relate its arrival to the coming of spring. Males' screaming call during the sky-dance display in spring can be heard from great distances, while the bird is high in the sky and barely visible to the naked eye. Its limited nesting distribution, near large rivers, lakes, and reservoirs, coupled with extreme visibility of the nests renders the species easily visible during aerial surveys. Thus, the Osprey has been monitored by wildlife biologists in this manner over much of its range to evaluate changes in populations over time (e.g., Henny et al. 1974, 1978, Henny and Anderson 1979). From a population perspective, the Osprey is one of the best understood birds of prey in the U.S.

**Population Status and Conservation:** Gabrielson and Jewett (1940) reported Ospreys as formerly common along the Columbia and Willamette rivers, the Klamath Basin, and about the larger Cascade lakes, but "now must be considered one of the rarer Oregon hawks." They mentioned specifically the "sadly diminished" numbers in the Klamath Basin, and that a few scattered pairs were found along the coast, the Rogue, Umpqua, Deschutes, John Day, and Columbia rivers. Why Gabrielson and Jewett singled out the Klamath Basin was not fully understood until an unpublished manuscript written by Vernon Bailey was found in the Smithsonian Archives (Henny 1988). Bailey reported 500 Osprey nests located near the foothills along the northeast corner of Tule L. in 1899, about 4 mi (6.4 km) from Malin, Oregon. Henny (1988) estimated from Bailey's report that perhaps 250-300 pairs nested at the site that year. Within 10 yr, Tule L. was drained by the Bureau of Reclamation's Klamath Project and now the former lake bed is farmed. The number nesting at the 1899 colony about equaled the 308 pairs recorded for all of Oregon in 1976 (Henny, Collins, and Deibert 1978). Thus, Ospreys declined in Oregon by 1940, and habitat alteration (drainage and cutting of potential nest trees) was at least part of the problem.

Ospreys declined rapidly during the 1950s and 1960s in many parts of the U.S. following the widespread use of DDT, which resulted in thin-shelled eggs and reduced productivity (Henny 1977b). By the early 1980s (Henny 1983) only an estimated 8,000 pairs were nesting in the U.S. After the nationwide ban of DDT in 1972, evidence of decreasing DDT/DDE residues in eggs—followed by improved productivity and increasing populations—became apparent. By 1994, the U.S. population had nearly doubled to about 14,200 pairs (Houghton and Ryman 1997). The Oregon population increased from 308 pairs in 1976 to 675-700 pairs in 1994. The Willamette and lower Santiam rivers (Portland to Eugene) had only 13 pairs in 1976, but numbers increased to 78 pairs by 1993 (Henny and Kaiser 1996), 151 pairs in 1998, 177 pairs in 1999, 202 pairs in 2000, and 234 pairs in 2001 (Henny and Kaiser unpubl. data). The Columbia R., supporting few pairs in 1976 (Henny et al. 1978), had more than 100 pairs (between the Pacific Ocean and Umatilla) in 1997 (Henny unpubl. data). The entire length of the Rogue R. had 33 pairs in 1976 (Henny, Collins, and Deibert 1978) and the lower one-third had 42 pairs in 1996 (Blithe and Dillingham 1997). The population increase during the past two decades returned Ospreys to their former prominence at most locations in Oregon specifically mentioned by Gabrielson and Jewett (1940), with the notable exception of the drained Tule L. However, additional habitat was created by reservoirs constructed over the last 50 yr, which Ospreys have pioneered. The shortage of natural nest sites was compensated with human-made structures. Ospreys adapted much later in the west to human-made structures, while they were regularly reported to do so by 1900-20 in the e. U.S. (Bent 1937). This delayed use, or delayed adaptation, is probably related to the shorter time period that human structures have been present in the west.

Wintering numbers of Ospreys in Oregon have increased; probably in relation to the general population increase. Prior to 1970 there were only two records on CBCs. Ospreys (typically individuals) were detected in 60% of years during CBCs in the 1970s and 1980s, and every year since 1987, with an average of 2.5 birds per year for the state during 1990-2000 (NAS 2002). The import of the few wintering Ospreys is unknown.—*Charles J. Henny*

### Subfamily Accipitrinae

## White-tailed Kite *Elanus leucurus*
As the winter day turns to dusk, White-tailed Kites drop into their roosts and Short-eared Owls rise to take their place on the local hunting grounds. White-tailed Kites in Oregon often roost communally in winter, but they disperse in early spring and are more difficult to find during the breeding season. By day, they are conspicuous as they hover over rural fields searching for prey, in part because of their pale appearance. The tail is entirely white, as are the head and the underparts. Dark crescents on the underwing can be seen when a bird is flying or hovering. Above, they are light gray with black shoulder patches. Young-of-the-year are easily distinguished by a rusty band across the breast,

rusty markings on the head, and a thin gray band near the end of the tail.

**General Distribution:** Resident from sw. Washington to Baja California on the W. Coast, and in Arizona, Kansas, s. Oklahoma, and Gulf coast states. Also resident in parts of Mexico and M. America, south through Brazil and Bolivia to Chile and Argentina. Casual or accidental as far east as Massachusetts and as far north as British Columbia and N. Dakota. Two subspecies; *E. l. majusculus* in N. America (Dunk 1995).

**Oregon Distribution:** Rare to very rare breeder, probably permanent resident, in the Willamette, Umpqua, Rogue, Illinois, and Applegate valleys, and along the coast (OBBA, CBC). The highest concentration of known nest locations is in the Medford, Jackson Co., area. Nests have also been found in Clatsop, Tillamook, Polk, Benton, Lane, Douglas, and Curry counties. Other nesting evidence (but no nests) has been found in Coos and Josephine counties. An immature was in the Portland, Multnomah Co., area in Jul 1986 (Heinl 1987b), but whether it fledged in the vicinity is unknown. The extent of the visitant population west of the Cascades at any season is unknown, but kites are uncommon to locally common fall through winter. They are irregular visitants east of the Cascades in all seasons, primarily south of the Wallowa and Ochoco mountains.

**Habitat and Diet:** White-tailed Kites nest in trees in and around fields and agricultural areas. The first nest found in Oregon was in Benton Co. in the top of a 16-ft (5-m) tall hawthorn (Henny and Annear 1978). A Douglas Co. nest was in a fork in the top of an old oak (K. Wilson p.c.). One Tillamook Co. nest was 75 ft (23 m) up in a Sitka spruce, about 10-12 ft (3-3.7 m) from a damaged top (F. Schrock p.c.); another was in a 35-ft (11-m) spruce about 6 ft (2 m) from the top (Henry 1983). A Jackson Co. nest was low enough in an oak tree to be obscured from view by Himalayan

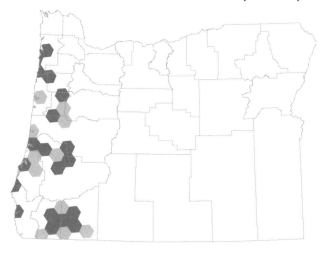

blackberry bushes (M. Brazelton p.c.). A nest about 0.5 mi (0.8 km) south of Fern Ridge W.A., Lane Co., was about a quarter of the way down a 75-ft (23-m) tall Douglas-fir, and placed about 1-2 ft (0.3-0.6 m) from the trunk on a branch (W. Morrow p.c.).

Consistent with the description of a Tillamook Co. nest located by Floyd Schrock (p.c.), Bent (1937) and Dunk (1995) describe the nest as consisting of sticks for the outer part, the inner part lined with softer plant material. One Oregon nest was lined with gray-tailed vole hair (Henny and Annear 1978). Birds nesting in an established territory may not reuse the previous year's nest (F. Schrock p.c.).

During the nonbreeding season in w. Oregon, kites are typically found in uncultivated open lowlands, prairie, and coastal estuauries. They appear in coastal dunes during this period as well. Winter roost sites in Oregon include a dense second-growth spruce-hemlock stand (Henry 1983); an ash swale at William L. Finley NWR, Benton Co. (J. Fisher p.c.); the transition area between wetlands and uplands, where reed canarygrass gives way to remnant prairie dotted with small ash and hawthorn trees at Fern Ridge Res., Lane Co. (D. Fix, S. Heinl, W. Morrow p.c.s); a dead fruit tree in an old orchard (M. Moore p.c.); and the mouth of the Wilson R., Tillamook Co., where habitat consists of canarygrass, cattails, small willows, red elderberry, and scattered Sitka spruce (Irons and Heinl 1984, J. Gilligan p.c.). In California, a roost was located on power lines (Scott 1994). Easily scared away from a roost by human disturbance (Dunk 1995). May be absent from an established roost site during times when it would normally be used (Watson 1981a).

Studies of pellets in California and Chile showed that over 95% of the diet consisted of mice, voles, and other small mammals (Dunk 1995). Other dietary items reported include birds, snakes, lizards, frogs, and insects (Bent 1937). No information is available on seasonal variation in diet or on diets of Oregon individuals. Near Tillamook, the highest hunting success was observed in unmown fields with tall grass. Preferred perching sites before and after hunts are bare trees, snags, and shrubs less than 50 ft (15 m) tall in open fields (Henry 1983).

**Seasonal Activity and Behavior:** In Oregon, the earliest courtship reported was 27 Feb (OBBA). Copulation was witnessed 23 Mar 2002 near a known nesting area along the Little Nestucca R., Tillamook Co. (F. Schrock p.c.). Nest building is infrequently observed, but occurs into Aug (Henny and Annear 1978). Nests with eggs were found from 14 Mar (OBBA) through 4 Aug (F. Schrock p.c.). Based on the fledging date, egg laying in one nest was estimated to have occurred 17-23 Apr in Tillamook Co. in 1983 (Henry 1983). Clutches range 3-6 eggs (Bent 1937). A nest at the Nestucca NWR, Tillamook Co., contained

"five brownish blotchy eggs about the size of very small chicken eggs" (F. Schrock p.c.). Incubation begins after the first or second egg has been laid, and lasts about 30-32 days (Dunk 1995). Chicks fledge after about 35-40 days (Thiollay 1994). The earliest report of fledged young came from Douglas Co. on 17 May (OBBA). This report came from the same hexagon as the earliest reported courtship that year. At the first nest discovered in Oregon, young were being fed 11 Apr (Henny and Annear 1978) and would have fledged before 17 May had they survived that long. Most reports of birds in juvenal plumage range from early Jul to early Sep. Kites may nest a second time in one season (Dunk 1995); although this has not been reported in Oregon, a wide range of egg dates is consistent with this possibility. A 28 Oct 2000 report of juveniles in fresh plumage accompanied by an adult at the Little Nestucca R., Tillamook Co., was suggestive of a second nesting (F. Schrock p.c.). No information is available on the timing of departures from breeding areas.

In-flight prey exchanges were observed during nesting season (Bent 1937). Adults were seen exchanging object during courtship in Curry Co. 26 Apr 1998 (Wander 1998), and 18 Jun 1998 in Tillamook Co. (F. Schrock p.c.). A prey exchange from an adult to an immature was observed 19 Sep 1998 in Yamhill Co. (F. Schrock p.c.). One was seen mounting an aerial attack on a Red-tailed Hawk in Josephine Co. 26 Jun 2000 (D. Vroman p.c.).

Origins of wintering birds are uncertain. Kites are present in some breeding areas all year, but it is not known whether the same individuals are there year-round, or whether birds that remain on breeding territory use communal roosts. The largest winter roost was at Fern Ridge Res., Lane Co., with 20 individuals in 1979 (Mattocks 1979). In winter 1992-93, a White-tailed Kite shared a roost with Northern Harriers in Polk Co. (Johnson J 1993b). Roosts at Fern Ridge Res. (Mickel and Mickel 2000) and the Rain River Preserve, mouth of Wilson R., Tillamook Co. (Gilligan 1990), have been shared with Northern Harriers and Short-eared Owls (D. Fix p.c., D. Irons p.c.). Birds arrive at roosts as early as 6 Sep (Gilligan 1999) and leave as late as May (Heinl 1987a), but some may leave before the end of Feb (Irons and Heinl 1984) or even Dec (Heinl 1985). The largest midday congregation was of 28 kites on 8 Oct 2001 at Cabell Marsh, William L. Finley NWR, Benton Co. (P. Vanderheul p.c.). It is not known whether individuals that leave a roost early move to breeding areas or to other roost sites. Nothing is known about where birds from particular winter roosts go to breed.

East of the Cascades, about one-third of visitants have appeared in Aug; the remainder occurred in other months. Some fall/winter visitants have lingered as long as a month (Littlefield 1977/78, Anderson DA 1990a, Korpi 1998).

**Detection:** White-tailed Kites are easy to spot when hovering over a field, but easy to miss when they are perching on low trees or bushes. White-tailed Kites in Oregon are notable for their infrequent use of human-made perches (D. Fix p.c.). They are more difficult to find during the breeding season than at other times. Male Northern Harriers are occasionally misidentified as this species, particularly at a distance.

**Population Status and Conservation:** The White-tailed Kite is a recent pioneer to Oregon. In the 1930s, they neared extirpation in a much-reduced range in California (Bent 1937). The first published first-hand report of White-tailed Kite in Oregon was of one seen near Scappoose, Columbia Co., 23 Feb 1933 (Jewett 1933). This article also reported an earlier sighting from about 1923-25 at Blue L., Multnomah Co. Two immatures were noted about 25 mi (40 km) west of Bend 4 Aug 1947 (Laval 1947); one individual at Reedsport 13 May 1958 (Schultz 1958); 1 at William L. Finley NWR 13 Feb 1967 (Henny and Annear 1978); and two "almost certain" sightings near Dufur 15 Mar and 23 Apr 1967 (Rogers 1967b). The first Oregon CBC record was at Ruggs-Hardman on 20 Dec 1968, followed by a Eugene bird seen 25 Dec 1968 through 18 Jan 1969 (Crowell and Nehls 1969b) and recorded on the Eugene CBC on 29 Dec 1968. California population increases led to range expansion into Oregon in the 1970s (Henny and Annear 1978). They have been seen in the state every year since 1972. The first Medford CBC record was in 1973. There were no CBC records in 1974, but numbers increased rapidly afterward. CBCs on which at least 10 individuals have been counted since 1990 include Coos Bay, Coquille Valley, Eugene, and Medford. The highest count was of 26 birds in Eugene in 1993.

Since nesting was first detected in 1976 (Henny and Annear 1978), nesting evidence was reported in each year in Oregon except for 1979 and 1980. Apparent population fluctuations during the period of increase may be partly due to fluctuations in vole populations, but also to variability in observer effort and reporting. In response to a 1980 report that numbers were declining, David Fix and Tom Lund searched appropriate habitat and estimated that wintering kite numbers were about 40% higher than previous estimates (Mattocks and Hunn 1980b). Oregon reports have increased in number over the years to more than 80 in winter 1998 (Tweit, Gilligan, and Mlodinow 1999). In Washington, first sighted in 1975 (Harrington-Tweit 1980), and first breeding evidence found in 1988 (Anderson and Batchelder 1990). California populations may now be declining, however (Dunk 1995). Considered by ODFW to be a recent immigrant that could become a sensitive species (Marshall et al. 1996).—*Barbara Combs*

## Bald Eagle *Haliaeetus leucocephalus*

The Bald Eagle is one of eight species of sea-eagle (genus *Haliaeetus*) worldwide (Brown 1977), and the only sea-eagle found throughout N. America (Stalmaster 1987). It is one of the most studied N. American birds (Buehler 2000). Large size, wingspan of 6.6-8.0 ft (200-243 cm) (Stalmaster 1987), and the contrast of white head and tail, and yellow eyes, beak, and legs, to dark brown body and wings make the adult Bald Eagle one of our most distinctive raptors. Six age-related plumages have been recognized; adult plumage is acquired at 4.5 or 5.5 yr of age (McCollough 1989). Sexes have similar plumages, but females are larger than males (Stalmaster 1987), and sex of individuals in breeding pairs can usually be determined by size when they perch close together. The mottled plumage of juveniles and subadults is less distinctive, and results in confusion with Golden Eagles. The word "bald" is derived from a word for "shining white," and refers to head color rather than bare skin (Choate 1985). The scientific name means "white-headed sea-eagle" (Choate 1985). Its large size, striking adult plumage, superb hunting and flying skills, loyalty to its nest site, and position at the top of the food chain make it a popular symbol. The species is important spiritually to indigenous cultures and was chosen as the official emblem of the American colonies in 1782, and as the emblem of the U.S. in 1787 (Herrick 1934). Images of the adult Bald Eagle often are used as school mascots, and to promote government programs, private organizations, and commercial products. The longevity record for a wild eagle is 28 yr (Schempf 1997); two lived 47 yr in captivity (Stalmaster 1987).

**General Distribution:** Resident of N. America. Found throughout Alaska, Canada, the contiguous U.S. (AOU 1998), as far south as Baja California Sur, Mexico (Henny, Anderson, and Knoder 1978), and as far west as the Aleutian Is., Alaska (Anthony et al. 1999). Although two subspecies were described, and distinguished by size—*H. l. alascanus*, the larger northern subspecies and *leucocephalus*, the smaller

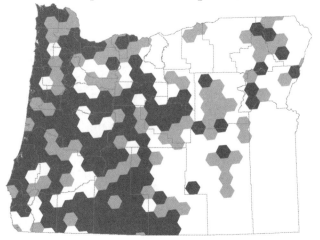

southern subspecies—the geographical line dividing them (e.g., the Oregon/California border) crosses a gradual north-south cline that led Amadon (1983) to doubt recognizing subspecies. Genetic variation in western populations also shows a gradual north-south cline rather than significant genetic differences and does not support recognizing subspecies (Morizot et al. 1985). Monotypic (*MRB*).

Resident year-round where food is available, otherwise migrates or wanders to find food. When not breeding, may congregate where food is abundant, even away from water (Stalmaster 1987). Migrants passing through Glacier NP generally followed north-south flyways similar to those of waterfowl (McClelland et al. 1994). In contrast, juveniles from Yellowstone NP area traveled west into Oregon and Washington (Harmata and Oakleaf 1992), and juveniles and subadults from California traveled north to Oregon, Washington, and British Columbia in late summer and fall (D. K. Garcelon p.c., R. E. Jackman p.c.).

**Oregon Distribution:** Breed in 32 of 36 Oregon counties; not reported nesting in Sherman, Gilliam, Morrow, and Malheur counties (Isaacs and Anthony 2001). It is a fairly common breeder at Upper Klamath L., along the Columbia R. below Portland, and at Crane Prairie and Wickiup reservoirs, Deschutes Co. An uncommon to very rare breeder elsewhere, except deserts of Malheur Co., where breeding has not been reported. Found throughout the state during the nonbreeding season. Variation locally in number of eagles and timing of peak abundance is due to weather and food supply. Very common in winter and early spring in the Klamath (Keister et al. 1987) and Harney (Isaacs and Anthony 1987) basins, Columbia R. estuary (Garrett et al. 1988), and L. Billy Chinook (Concannon 1998); common in winter and early spring at Hells Canyon, Oxbow, and Brownlee reservoirs, and along the Wallowa and Grande Ronde rivers (Isaacs et al. 1992), the Crooked R. Valley above Prineville Res. (Isaacs et al. 1993), the south end of the Willamette Valley (Isaacs unpubl. data), the John Day R. above Service Cr. (Isaacs et al. 1996), the Columbia R. in the Umatilla NWR area (Isaacs unpubl. data), Goose L. Valley (Isaacs unpubl. data), Summer L. and Chewaucan R. downstream of Paisley (R. L. Madigan p.c.), and at Sauvie I. (Isaacs unpubl. data); common in fall at Wickiup Res. (Isaacs unpubl. data, G. J. Niehuser p.c.) and Odell L. (Crescent RD 1998).

An understanding of population structure, abundance, and distribution is complicated by multiple age classes, breeding status, nesting chronology, origin and movements of individuals, local and regional distribution and abundance of prey, local and regional weather, and season. For example, native and non-native juveniles (<1 yr old), subadults (1-4 yr old), nonbreeding adults, and breeding adults can all occur in the same area (e.g., Klamath Basin) in winter and early spring.

**Habitat and Diet:** Usually associated with large bodies of water, but it can occur in any habitat with available prey. Primarily nests in forested areas near the ocean, along rivers, and at estuaries, lakes, and reservoirs (Isaacs and Anthony 2001). Consequently, shoreline is an important component of nesting habitat; 84% of Oregon nests were within 1 mi (1.6 km) of water (Anthony and Isaacs 1989); a nest in the Ft. Rock Valley was the most distant from water at 18 mi (29 km) from the nearest shoreline (Isaacs and Anthony unpubl. data). The highest-elevation nest known west of the Cascade crest is at Waldo L., 5,500 ft (1,676 m), and east of the crest at East L., 6,520 ft (1,987 m) (Isaacs and Anthony unpubl. data). All nests observed in Oregon have been in trees, primarily Sitka spruce and Douglas-fir west of the Cascades and ponderosa pine, Douglas-fir, and sugar pine in e. Oregon (Anthony and Isaacs 1989). Use of black cottonwood for nesting has increased recently as Columbia and Willamette river populations have increased. Bald Eagles also nest in white fir, red fir, grand fir, incense-cedar, Oregon white oak, quaking aspen, and willow (Isaacs and Anthony unpubl. data). Of 870 nests, 98.9% were built in live trees, but often use the same nest after the tree dies. Nesting success is similar in dead and live trees. Ninety-four percent of nests persisted from one year to the next (Isaacs and Anthony unpubl. data). Nest trees are usually large and prominent (Anthony et al. 1982); they average 42.0 in (106.8 cm) dbh in Douglas-fir/mixed conifer, 43.0 in (109.1 cm) in ponderosa pine, and 67.2 in (170.7 cm) in Douglas-fir/western hemlock and spruce/hemlock forest types (Anthony and Isaacs 1989). Large old trees have large limbs and open structure required for eagle access and nest support, and provide a view of the surrounding territory. Some use has been made of artificial platforms placed in trees modified for Osprey (Witt 1996, Isaacs and Anthony unpubl. data, R. Opp p.c.). Cliff nesting is thus far unknown, but possible, especially in sparsely forested areas of se. Oregon.

Breeding-season home range (95% harmonic mean) (Dixon and Chapman 1980) averaged 8.38 mi$^2$ (21.7 km$^2$) on the Columbia R. estuary (Garrett et al. 1993), 1.75 mi$^2$ (4.52 km$^2$) at Devils L., Lincoln Co., and 2.71 mi$^2$ (7.02 km$^2$) at Siletz Bay (Anthony et al. 1990). Home ranges for the same pairs were similar when not breeding (Anthony et al. 1990, Garrett et al. 1993). Home ranges for resident adults in sc. Oregon averaged 2.55 mi$^2$ (6.60 km$^2$); range 1.25-5.34 mi$^2$ (3.25-13.84 km$^2$) (minimum convex polygon) (Frenzel 1983). Winter home range for winter adult visitant in the Klamath Basin was 658 mi$^2$ (1,705 km$^2$) (minimum convex polygon) (McClelland et al. 1994).

Freedom from human disturbance is important for successful hunting (McGarigal et al. 1991), feeding of young (Steidl and Anthony 2000), and nesting (Anthony and Isaacs 1989). Nests at locations with high human activity, e.g., Ross I. in Portland, suggest tolerance in some situations.

Research on winter habitat has focused on communal roosts because of high eagle use, e.g., there are regularly 300-400 at Bear Valley in the Klamath Basin (Keister et al. 1987, R. R. Opp p.c.). Communal roosts have been reported along the Columbia R. (Anderson et al. 1985, Watson and Anthony 1986), in the Willamette Valley (DellaSala et al. 1989), and throughout e. Oregon (Opp 1980a, Isaacs and Anthony 1987, Keister et al. 1987, Isaacs et al. 1992, 1993, 1996). Roosts are located in Douglas-fir/western hemlock, Douglas-fir/mixed conifer, ponderosa pine, and Blue Mtn./mixed conifer forest types. Eagles have also been found roosting in black cottonwood in riparian areas and deciduous trees planted as windbreaks. Roost trees are deciduous or coniferous (Isaacs et al. 1996), large with an open limb structure (Isaacs et al. 1993); average dbh of roost trees was 27.4 in (69.6 cm) in the Klamath Basin (Keister and Anthony 1983), 34.0 in (86.3 cm) in the Harney Basin (Isaacs and Anthony 1987), and 37.8 in (96.0 cm) along the Crooked R. (Isaacs et al. 1993).

Bald Eagles consume a variety of prey that varies by location and season. Prey are taken alive (57% at Columbia R. estuary, 77% at Upper Klamath L., 59% at Wickiup Res.), scavenged (24% at Columbia R. estuary, 16% at Upper Klamath L., 13% at Wickiup Res.), and pirated (19% at Columbia R. estuary, 7% at Upper Klamath L., 28% at Wickiup Res.) (Frenzel 1985, Watson et al. 1991). Fish were the most frequent prey among 84 species identified (16 fish, 46 birds, 20 mammals, two invertebrates) at nest sites in sc. Oregon, and a tendency was observed for some individuals or pairs to specialize in certain species (Frenzel 1985). Waterfowl (68% of castings collected at night roosts) and montane voles (31%) were the most important prey for eagles wintering in the Klamath Basin. At these locations 94% of the remains below perches were waterfowl, 91% of the waterfowl were scavenged, and montane voles were captured at flooded agricultural fields (Frenzel and Anthony 1989). On the Columbia R. estuary, prey consisted of 90% fish, 7% birds, and 3% mammals annually; the proportion of birds was 16% higher and fish 16% lower during the nonbreeding season (Watson et al. 1991). At Devils L., 87.8% of prey consisted of fish and 9.8% birds when breeding; 28.6% were fish and 57.1% birds when not breeding (Anthony et al. 1990). At L. Billy Chinook, kokanee salmon comprised 73% of items delivered to nests in 1996, and 60% in 1997 (Clowers 1997b). Seabird remains were observed in nests along the coast during aerial surveys (R. Lowe p.c.). Domestic sheep remains

(93.3%), waterfowl (4.4%), and small rodents (2.2%) were found in 45 castings collected from roosts in the Willamette Valley. Eagles eating sheep fed exclusively on carrion and afterbirth; no attempts to prey on live domestic sheep were observed (DellaSala et al. 1989, Marr et al. 1995). Wintering and migrant eagles in e. Oregon fed on large mammal carrion, especially road-killed mule deer, domestic cattle that died of natural causes, and stillborn calves, as well as cow afterbirth, waterfowl, ground squirrels, other medium-sized and small rodents, and fish. Proportions varied by month and location. In general, outside the Klamath Basin where waterfowl were important throughout the winter, carrion was the most important until ground squirrels emerged or migrant waterfowl arrived (Isaacs and Anthony 1987, Isaacs et al. 1992, 1993, 1996). Food habits are unknown for nesting eagles over much of the state.

**Seasonal Activity and Behavior:** Bald Eagles are most abundant in Oregon in late winter and early spring, because resident breeders (engaged in early nesting activities), winter residents, and spring transients are all present. Nest building and repair occur any time of year, but most often observed from Feb to Jun (Isaacs and Anthony unpubl. data). These eagles are territorial when breeding but gregarious when not (Stalmaster 1987). They exhibit strong nest-site and mate fidelity (Jenkins and Jackman 1993), but "divorce" has been documented (Frenzel 1985, Garrett et al. 1993). Cooperative nesting by three adults was reported

*Bald Eagle*

ELVA HAMERSTROM Paulson

(Garcelon et al. 1995). Both sexes build nest, incubate eggs, and brood and feed young (Stalmaster 1987). Egg laying occurs mid-Feb to late Apr; hatching late Mar to late May; and fledging late Jun to mid-Aug (Isaacs and Anthony unpubl. data). Banded juveniles from Oregon have traveled as far as British Columbia, Canada, and Sonora, Mexico (Anthony unpubl. data). Reviews of published literature (Harmata et al. 1999, Jenkins et al. 1999) suggested that survival varies by location and age; hatch-year survival was usually >60%, and survivorship increased with age to adulthood. However, recent work by Harmata et al. (1999) showed survival lowest among 3- and 4-yr-old birds.

Resident breeders remained at or near nest sites year-round (Frenzel 1985, Frenzel 1988, Garrett et al. 1993), or left breeding areas during late summer and fall (Garrett et al. 1993, Isaacs and Anthony unpubl. data); e.g., eagles that nested in w. Washington traveled to British Columbia (Watson and Pierce 1998). Migrant adults were mostly gone by late Apr (Isaacs and Anthony 1987, Keister et al. 1987, Garrett et al. 1988, Isaacs et al. 1992, 1993, 1996). Eagles probably are least abundant late May and early Jun when migrants are gone and young not fledged, or Aug-Oct if some natives leave Oregon after breeding. Migrant eagles are highly mobile. Eagles radioed at Glacier NP averaged 59 mi/day (95 km/day); one traveled nearly 311 mi (500 km) in 1 day (McClelland et al. 1994). Color-marked or radio-tagged individuals from Washington (Watson and Pierce 1998), Montana, Idaho, Wyoming (Harmata and Oakleaf 1992), Arizona (D. Hwang p.c.), and n. (Jenkins et al. 1999) and s. California (D. K. Garcelon p.c.) have visited Oregon. An adult radio-tagged at Glacier NP, Montana, wintered in the Klamath Basin, then traveled to Northwest Territories, Canada, in spring (McClelland et al. 1994).

Resident breeders spent >90% of the time perched (Popp and Isaacs 1989, Anthony et al. 1990, Watson et al. 1991). Breeders roost at nest sites (Watson and Anthony 1986, Clowers 1996, 1997a). Hunting was concentrated during early morning and low tide at Columbia R. estuary (Watson et al. 1991), and during morning and evening at Siletz Bay (Anthony et al. 1990). Clowers (1997b) reported that the proportion of daily total prey items delivered to nests increased throughout the day at L. Billy Chinook (0400-0800, 18%; 0800-1200, 21%; 1200-1600, 25%; 1600-2000, 36%).

Migrants or wanderers roosted singly or in groups (Isaacs et al. 1996) in suitable trees adjacent to hunting areas. Large congregations (>100) have been reported in fall (Crescent RD 1998), winter, and spring (Isaacs and Anthony 1987, Keister et al. 1987, Garrett et al. 1988, Isaacs et al. 1992, Concannon 1998). It roosts communally where abundant prey attracts many eagles; largest count 500+ at Bear Valley in the Klamath Basin (R. R. Opp p.c.). Klamath Basin, Oregon and California, has one of the largest concentrations of Bald Eagles in the lower 48 states (Opp 1980a, Keister et al. 1987). Most fly from the roost to hunting areas at dawn, then return to the roost throughout the afternoon, with a peak around sunset. Wintering birds flew 13 mi (21 km) from hunting area to roost along the Crooked R. (Isaacs et al. 1993); they may fly 20+ mi (32+ km) in the Harney Basin or other sparsely forested areas of e. Oregon (*FBI*).

Habitat use and movements of native juveniles, subadults, and nonbreeding adults unknown.

**Detection:** Bald Eagles are best detected by searching suitable habitat by eye, binoculars, or spotting scope. Adults easier to see than subadults because their heads are highly visible, and they perch at prominent locations, often in trees, but will use rock outcrops, utility poles, fence posts, pilings, logs, stumps, root wads, boulders, cut banks, low hills, or flat ground. During the nesting season, they are best located by searching shorelines of rivers, lakes, and reservoirs by boat. Wintering birds best located by boating as above, or by driving along rivers, in wildlife areas, and through agricultural areas where waterfowl congregate, livestock are kept, or ground squirrels are abundant.

Good areas to find birds during nesting are generally also good year-round: Columbia R. estuary, Sauvie I., Odell L., Upper Klamath L., Crane Prairie and Wickiup reservoirs, and L. Billy Chinook. Areas good in winter or early spring are Ankeny, Baskett Slough, and Finley NWRs, Crooked R. above Prineville Res., Klamath Basin near the California border and Klamath W.A., Ft. Rock Valley, Summer L. W.A., Harney Basin, Wallowa Valley, and Snake R. reservoirs (Hells Canyon, Oxbow, and Brownlee). A birder visiting any of those areas should see one or more eagles/day. Dawn flyout from the Bear Valley roost in the Klamath Basin provides an excellent opportunity to observe numerous eagles Jan-Mar; best viewed from Bear Valley Rd., west of Hwy 97, southwest of Worden. Often seen in winter along highways in e. Oregon perched near road-killed animals. Nests are typically found by searching shoreline trees for large stick nests, or by watching adults during the breeding season. Communal roosts are best located by watching late afternoon or evening flights from hunting areas to roosts.

**Population Status and Conservation:** By 1940, the Bald Eagle had "become rather an uncommon bird" except along the coast and Columbia R., and in Klamath Co. (Gabrielson and Jewett 1940). Habitat loss (cutting of nest trees) and direct persecution (shooting, trapping, poisoning) probably caused a gradual decline prior to 1940. Between 1945 and 1974 over 4.5 million ac (1.8 million ha) of NF in Oregon were sprayed with DDT (Henny and Nelson 1981).

Undocumented quantities were also applied on private forests and agricultural crops, and for mosquito control around municipalities. Consequently, the deleterious effects of DDT on reproduction (Stalmaster 1987) joined habitat loss and direct persecution as causes of decline through the early 1970s when the population may have reached its historical low. By then, nesting pairs were extirpated from ne. Oregon (Isaacs and Anthony 2001), where applications of DDT on NF land were common and widespread (Henny and Nelson 1981).

Surveys of local nesting populations began in 1970 on the Deschutes NF (Shull 1978) and 1971 on Weyerhaeuser Company land in the Klamath Basin (Anderson RJ 1985). The USFWS coordinated statewide nesting surveys during 1972-77 (USFWS undated). A study of the Oregon nesting population by the Oregon Cooperative Fish and Wildlife Research Unit at Oregon State University began in 1978 (Isaacs et al. 1983) and has continued to the present (Isaacs and Anthony 2001). Distribution of nesting eagles in 1978 was similar to that described by Gabrielson and Jewett (1940): concentrated on the coast, lower Columbia R., and at Upper Klamath L.; in addition, a concentration of sites was present on the Deschutes NF (Isaacs et al. 1983). Since then, the minimum nesting population increased from 56 to 393 pairs, nearly doubling each decade (Isaacs and Anthony 2001). The Oregon distribution is now nearly continuous, with five densely populated areas, and several sites are occupied in ne. Oregon (Isaacs and Anthony 2001). Thirty-five percent of nest trees are on land owned by private companies and individuals, and 47% are on USFS and BLM land (Isaacs and Anthony 2001). The nesting population is expected to increase for several more years.

Annual surveys (1971-2001) showed that 93% of known breeding sites were occupied, 61% of occupied sites were successful, an average of 0.95 young were produced per breeding pair, and 1.55 young were produced per successful pair (Isaacs and Anthony 2001). Probable causes of 89 nesting failures in sc. Oregon and along the lower Columbia R. 1980-87 were: pesticides (32%), effects related to nearest neighbor (11%), infertile eggs (7%), nestling mortality (3%), human disturbance (2%), change in member of pair (1%), and unknown (21%) (Anthony et al. 1994). Survival rates and causes of mortality need study.

Less is known about migrant and winter populations. Midwinter Bald Eagle Surveys (MBES) conducted in early Jan 1979-83 (Opp 1979, 1980b, ODFW unpubl. data) and 1988-2001 indicate that the Jan population is stable or increasing (1988-92 average 593, 1997-2001 average 692) (Isaacs unpubl. data). The MBES does not take place when eagles are most abundant; local populations have 2-3 times more eagles in Feb and early Mar (Isaacs and Anthony 1987, Keister et al. 1987, Garrett et al. 1988, Isaacs et al. 1992, 1993, 1996), indicating a minimum population during peak abundance of 1,400-2,100.

Declared threatened in Oregon, Washington, Michigan, Minnesota, Wisconsin, and Florida, and endangered in other 43 contiguous states in 1978 under federal Endangered Species Act (ESA) because of a declining number of nesting pairs and reproductive problems caused by environmental contaminants (USDI 1978). The recovery plan for Pacific states was completed in 1986 (USFWS 1986b). The Bald Eagle was listed as threatened under the Oregon ESA in 1987 (Marshall et al. 1996). Listing resulted in protection of eagle habitat and restrictions on human activities near nest and roost sites. Site-specific planning was recommended for nest and roost protection (USFWS 1986b). Forest management in nesting (Arnett et al. 2001) and roosting (DellaSala et al. 1998) habitat proved useful when declining forest health or fire danger threatened nest and roost trees. Habitat protection and management, the ban on use of DDT (Grier 1982), and reduced direct persecution due to education (e.g., annual Klamath Basin Bald Eagle Conference and Eagle Watch at L. Billy Chinook) were followed by a recent population increase. Improved nesting success and a population increase led to a 1999 proposal to delist federally (USDI 1999). Oregon also may propose to delist the species.

The upward population trend could reverse if the species is delisted without maintaining habitat-protection measures implemented under the ESA (e.g., USFS and BLM special habitat management for Bald Eagles, Oregon Forest Practices Rules protecting Bald Eagle sites on nonfederal forest land, and local zoning laws that protect wildlife habitat). Habitat degradation and a population decline could go undetected if monitoring of nesting and wintering populations is not continued. Contaminants have been implicated in reduced productivity of nesting pairs on the Columbia R. downstream of Portland (Anthony et al. 1993, Buck 1999) and warrant continued monitoring.—*Frank B. Isaacs and Robert G. Anthony*

## Northern Harrier *Circus cyaneus*

Formerly known as the Marsh Hawk, the Northern Harrier is a slender, medium-sized hawk commonly encountered in large expanses of open country. Characterized by a noticeably long tail, bold white rump patch, and owl-like face. Its main hunting technique is through use of a distinctive buoyant, gliding flight low over the ground that relies heavily on visual as well as auditory cues to detect prey (MacWhirter and Bildstein 1996). A sexually dimorphic species; the larger females have rich brown upperparts while adult males are mostly light to medium gray, sometimes appearing almost ghostly silvery-white, earning them

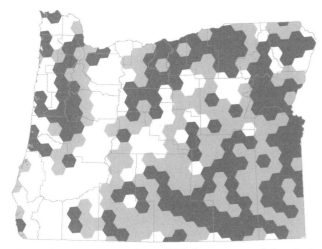

the nickname "gray ghost." Males are noted for their high-spirited and acrobatic courtship displays, in particular a series of dives and barrel rolls in multiple loops that serve as a means of advertising territory occupancy.

**General Distribution:** Breeds across N. America and Eurasia. Breeds from n. Alaska and Canada south to n. Baja California, Mexico, and east to s. New Mexico, c. Texas, s. Kansas, s. Illinois, se. Virginia, and formerly Florida. Absent from some areas in ne. U.S. Winters predominantly from s. Canada throughout most of the contiguous U.S. and M. America. Two subspecies; *C. c. hudsonius* occurs across N. America (MacWhirter and Bildstein 1996, AOU 1998).

**Oregon Distribution:** Common during summer and migration in open habitats east of the Cascades, with numbers decreasing in most areas during winter. An exception is in the lowlands of Umatilla and Morrow counties, where the harrier is common in winter due to an influx of wintering birds (M. Denny p.c.). The harrier also remains common year-round in the Klamath Basin (Summers 1993a) and is the second most commonly encountered wintering raptor at Malheur NWR (Littlefield 1990a). West of the Cascades, they occur in the interior valleys and along coastal lowlands as locally uncommon summer residents and common transients and winterers. Along the coast they are most common in winter. They are common postbreeding wanderers over rangelands and casual transients above timberline and over forested habitats statewide.

**Habitat and Diet:** Northern Harriers are birds of open country. During the breeding season, may be found in a variety of open habitats including wetland complexes with wet meadows and freshwater or brackish marshes, grasslands, sagebrush steppe, and agricultural fields. Nest on the ground mostly within patches of tall dense vegetation. On Malheur NWR most documented nests have been in ungrazed dense emergent vegetation, particularly hardstem bulrush

and broad-fruited burreed, as well as in weedy fields and among shrubs (Littlefield 1990a, *EJS*). Littlefield and Thompson (1987) reported that, during a 5-yr study at Malheur NWR, Northern Harriers were more frequently found in habitat that was not, nor had been, grazed by cattle. They presumed that there were significantly greater numbers of voles in idle fields. No formal studies of habitat preferences have been conducted west of the Cascades. In the nonbreeding season, most frequently encountered in large open areas including marshes, dry meadowlands, and cultivated fields. It has occasionally been observed hunting over bare ground (*MGH*). Roosts communally in nonbreeding season in dense, tall grass often at traditional sites, such as at the southern section of Oak I. on Sauvie I., Multnomah Co., at the mouth of the Wilson R., Tillamook Co., and marshes near Coyote Cr. at Fern Ridge Res., Lane Co.

No thorough examinations of diet have been completed in the state. They principally eat small and medium-sized mammals, especially voles and mice, and infrequently black-tailed jackrabbits. Of 36 whole prey found at a nest at Malheur NWR where the female had been killed and the male continued to provide food to the nestlings, most prey were montane and long-tailed voles in addition to a few ground squirrels (Thompson and Cornely 1982). At Malheur NWR, montane voles are the most important prey source in winter (Littlefield and Thompson 1987). Occasionally consume birds, including ducks, American Coots, Sandhill Crane chicks (Ivey and Scheuering 1997), and snakes.

**Seasonal Activity and Behavior:** Partial and long-distance migrant. In late Feb numbers begin to increase across e. Oregon as abundance declines in coastal areas. Peak of migration at Malheur NWR occurs between mid-Mar and mid-Apr. Most transients have left the refuge by early May and nesting is in progress by late Apr continuing through Jun (Littlefield 1990a).

Annual breeding numbers and productivity are influenced by prey availability (MacWhirter and Bildstein 1996). Males perform a sky-dancing display to advertise territory that includes about 25 and as many as 74 deep U-shaped undulations, mostly coming within 65 ft (20 m) of ground (MacWhirter and Bildstein 1996, *EJS*). Males are generally monogamous but will occasionally mate with with two or more females if more abundant prey is available (Littlefield 1990a, MacWhirter and Bildstein 1996). No other raptor species is known to exhibit this degree or regularity of polygamy (Simmons et al. 1986). The nest is built mainly by female, although both sexes collect materials. Harriers are single-brooded and nests usually contain 4-6 eggs. Females incubate and brood young while males provide most of food for mate and nestlings for about 60 days from pre-laying

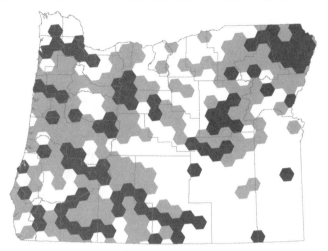

to early nestling stage. In the breeding season, hunting activity is generally distributed throughout the day, but there may be temporal peaks and midday heat may be avoided (MacWhirter and Bildstein 1996).

Recently fledged juveniles appear in Jul at Malheur NWR. Throughout the state, dispersal begins in late Jul and continues into Sep. Fall migration at Malheur NWR peaks from mid-Sep to mid-Oct and numbers begin to increase along the coast in Sep. Most near the coast are immatures or females. A marked harrier observed near the coast in Lincoln Co. in Oct 1999 was a female from the Puget Sound area that had been banded when it had five nestlings in Jun of that year (Bayer 1999b).

Most migrants have left by Dec and the number of wintering birds depends on winter severity and prey populations. Numbers at winter roosts range 8-20 and these aggregations occasionally include other species such as Short-eared Owl, White-tailed Kite, and Merlin (Gilligan 1990, Lethaby 1990). In se. Washington in winter, hunting flights most often occur in the afternoon (MacWhirter and Bildstein 1996).

**Detection:** Foraging birds are readily detected throughout the year due to their distinctive, low-level flight. Occasional high-flying harriers seem out of place to many observers and are sometimes mistaken for falcons or accipiters. Even perched birds are often misidentified as other species. Local congregations can be detected at evening roosts.

**Population Status and Conservation:** Numbers across the U.S. declined in the 20th century, mostly due to loss of habitat through extensive draining of wetlands, conversion of undisturbed native grasslands to monotypic farming, and reforestation of farmlands (MacWhirter and Bildstein 1996). Although no studies have been conducted, the harrier likely has suffered declines due to habitat loss associated with conversion of native wetlands and prairies to monocultural agricultural practices, particularly in the Willamette Valley and Columbia Basin. Continued destruction of habitat, including freshwater and estuarine wetlands, poses the greatest threat to the future of this species.—
*Eric J. Scheuering*

### Sharp-shinned Hawk *Accipiter striatus*

The Sharp-shinned Hawk is N. America's smallest and most migratory accipiter (Bildstein and Meyer 2000). As a hunter of songbirds (and sometimes young chickens) it historically endured harsh reproach, and was often depicted as a blood-thirsty villain, even by some ornithologists (Bent 1937). Gabrielson and Jewett (1940) felt that "because of its comparative abundance [it] is undoubtedly the most destructive hawk in the state." Across the U.S. many thousands were shot

in the first half of the 20th century. But prevailing attitudes have changed, and today a glimpse of this slender, secretive hawk darting through the treetops is more likely to elicit admiration than malice.

Adult plumage, nearly identical to the slightly larger Cooper's Hawk, consists of slate gray back and wings, breast and sides barred with rufous and white, and a black and gray banded tail. The eyes of adults are a striking crimson. The most sexually dimorphic of all N. American raptors; males average about 57% the body mass of females (Bildstein and Meyer 2000).

**General Distribution:** Breeds from wc. Alaska across c. Canada to Newfoundland, and locally south to c. California, c. Arizona, nc. Texas, and northern portions of Gulf states; also in ne. U.S. from Minnesota to Maine, south through Appalachians to w. Virginia, w. N. Carolina, and w. S. Carolina (Bildstein and Meyer 2000); also to M. America; and S. America. Winters from s. Alaska and Nova Scotia south through U.S. and M. America to c. Panama and Bermuda; also in breeding ranges in tropical America. Number of subspecies is complex and unsettled according to Bildstein and Meyer (2000); two have been recorded in Oregon.

**Oregon Distribution:** All but two Oregon specimen records from all seasons refer to the subspecies *velox*, which breeds in much of Canada and the U.S. The subspecies *perobscurus*, which breeds from s. coastal Alaska to the Olympic Peninsula, Washington, is known in Oregon from two specimens, one from Portland in Nov and a specimen from Tillamook in Nov (Brodkorb 1940).

The Sharp-shinned Hawk is an uncommon breeder throughout Oregon in forested areas from sea level to timberline (Gilligan et al. 1994). In a study by Reynolds et al. (1982) 1969-74, nests were found in Coast Range, Siskiyou, Cascades, Bly (Klamath Co.), Warner, Steens, Ochoco, Blue, and Wallowa mountains. Mean distance between nests of conspecifics was 2.5 mi (4.1 km), with nest density of approximately one nest per

6,793 ac (2,750 ha) in the Bly study area (Reynolds and Wight 1978). It is least common in the breeding season in se. Oregon, where most forests are widely disjunct and separated by arid brushland (Contreras and Kindschy 1996, OBBA).

Uncommon transient and winter visitor across the state in wooded areas or semi-open country (Gilligan et al. 1994). During fall migration, many birds move through the state to wintering grounds farther south (Gilligan et al. 1994). Migrating birds often pass along higher ridges of the Cascades in fall (Fix 1990a). Uncommon in both spring and fall in e. Douglas Co. (Fix 1990a). Also uncommon at Malheur NWR in spring and fall, and occasional in winter (Littlefield 1990a). May move downslope in winter (Evanich 1992a, Contreras 1997b). CBCs in Oregon 1959-88 averaged 0.32 birds per 100 party hours (Sauer et al. 1996).

**Habitat and Diet:** Throughout most of the state the Sharp-shinned Hawk coexists with two other accipiters, the Cooper's Hawk and the Northern Goshawk, both of which are competitors and even potential predators (Bildstein and Meyer 2000). Studies of these closely related species in Oregon have described patterns of resource partitioning: each species tends to utilize different prey sizes, different forest stand structures for nesting, and different foraging zones within the canopy (Reynolds et al. 1982, Reynolds and Meslow 1984).

Breed in forest types with a wide variety of tree species, though most are dominated by conifers (Reynolds et al. 1982, Gilligan et al. 1994). Nests have been located at elevations from 393 ft (120 m) in the Coast Range to 6,593 ft (2,010 m) on Bly Mtn. (Reynolds et al. 1982). Vegetative characteristics consistently found at nest sites include high tree density and dense canopy cover, which generally produce cool, shady conditions (Reynolds 1983). Mean tree density at nest sites was 478 trees/ac (1,180 trees/ha) for all sites in Oregon, with a range of 257 trees/ac (636 trees/ha) in nw. Oregon's old-growth forest to 1,057 trees/ac (2,610 trees/ha) in e. Oregon (Reynolds et al. 1982). No nests found in large expanses of open conifer forests, probably due to lack of suitable dense cover (Reynolds and Meslow 1984). Nesting habitat differs structurally in terms of forest stand age from that used by Cooper's Hawk and Northern Goshawk in Oregon, with Sharp-shinned Hawk preferring the youngest forests, usually 25-50-yr-old, even-aged stands (Reynolds et al. 1982).

In w. Oregon, typical nesting habitat is often composed of young Douglas-fir in pure stands or sometimes mixed with western hemlock, red alder, or bigleaf maple (Reynolds and Wight 1978). Canopies often sufficiently closed to restrict ground vegetation to sword fern, bracken fern, and mosses (Reynolds et al. 1982). In e. Oregon all nest sites found by Reynolds et al. (1982) were in even-aged stands of either white fir, Douglas-fir, ponderosa pine, or aspen, with ground vegetation limited to annual grasses and creeping barberry (Reynolds et al. 1982). Open western juniper forests were not included in the study, though it is known to nest in juniper stands occasionally (Gilligan et al. 1994).

The immediate nest site, including nest tree, roosts, prey plucking perches, and outlying area used by nesting pair during breeding period (excluding foraging areas), typically measures approximately 10 ac (4 ha) (Reynolds et al. 1982). Nest trees studied by Reynolds et al. (1982) in nw. Oregon were all within 298 ft (91 m) of water (average distance was 148 ft [45 m]), whereas in e. Oregon average distance of nest to water was 590 ft (180 m). Nests usually placed against trunk or in crotch of split trunk in a dense part of lower canopy, at a mean nest height of 39 ft (12 m) in second-growth forest to 79 ft (24 m) in mature sites (Reynolds et al. 1982). Mean dbh of nest trees was 16 in (41 cm) in nw. Oregon and 9 in (23 cm) for the rest of the state (Reynolds et al. 1982).

In winter this hawk is routinely encountered in urban areas, perhaps due in part to availability of bird feeders, which concentrate small birds in suitable foraging and roosting habitats (Gilligan et al. 1994, Contreras 1997b). Less likely than Cooper's Hawk to appear in uninhabited open country in winter, probably because of reduced prey availability (Contreras 1997b). Browning (1975a) noted increased numbers in winter in chaparral-oak associations of sw. Oregon, especially along streams.

Diet in Oregon composed almost entirely of birds (<5% mammals), the majority small passerines such as sparrows, finches, chickadees, nuthatches, and warblers (Reynolds and Meslow 1984). In a study by Reynolds and Meslow (1984), mean prey size of birds in n. Coast Range (0.45 oz [12.8 g]) was significantly less than mean prey size of birds elsewhere in the state (0.99 oz [28.4 g]). At Malheur NWR, prey has included California Quail, Mourning Dove, Varied Thrush, American Robin, Red-eyed Vireo, and House Sparrow (Littlefield 1990a). Observed pursuing Clark's Nutcrackers and Dark-eyed Juncos, and feeding on grasshoppers (Farner 1952). Two juveniles were observed pursuing a Pileated Woodpecker, larger than usual prey for this species, and were apparently adopting a cooperative hunting strategy (Smith 1983). Mammal species consumed include Douglas squirrel, northern flying squirrel, jumping mouse, and microtine voles (Reynolds and Meslow 1984). Adept at capturing birds at bird feeders (Bildstein and Meyer 2000). Plucks prey before eating, often at an established plucking perch near nest site (Reynolds et al. 1982).

**Seasonal Activity and Behavior:** Numbers begin increasing at Malheur NWR in late Feb, with peak spring migration occurring by mid-Apr (Littlefield 1990a). Arrive on nest sites in late Apr-early May (Reynolds 1983, Reynolds and Meslow 1984). Most breeding-season activity, including copulation and prey handling, takes place upslope from nest tree (Reynolds 1983). It is the latest of Oregon's three accipiters to nest, in concurrence with the generalization that larger species tend to start earlier to complete longer breeding cycles (Henny et al. 1985). Completion of clutch generally ranges from 14 May to 21 Jun (Reynolds and Wight 1978, Henny, Olson, and Fleming 1985). Incubation lasts 30-32 days, nestling stage is 21-24 days, and young remain in vicinity after fledging and continue to be fed by adults for 30-40 days (Reynolds and Wight 1978, Reynolds and Meslow 1984).

Southward migration begins in mid-Aug and peaks mid-Sep to mid-Oct (Gilligan et al. 1994, Smith 2001). Median passage date during fall migration counts conducted 1994-99 at Bonney Butte, near Mt. Hood, was 5 Oct (Smith 2001); average number passing was 1,058 (38% of total raptor numbers and 70% of accipiter numbers) (Smith 2001). Migration behavior along ridgelines well-described by Fix (1990a): "Like other raptors *en passant* across the w. Cascades, they do not assemble in kettles, but move through individually, achieving lift by ringing up on prevailing winds moving upslope, gaining altitude above a transverse ridgeline, going into a tuck, and repeating the process upon reaching the next prominent ridge."

**Detection:** Secretive. Can be detected by call in the breeding season. Several sources speculate that this species is more common in Oregon than records indicate (Gabrielson and Jewett 1940, Farner 1952, Marshall 1987, Fix 1990a). Rarely seen during breeding season, and considered to be one of the most difficult birds to census in N. America (Bildstein and Meyer 2000). Often the best clues to its presence are a mound of bird feathers and bones on the ground, or a sudden scattering of small birds from an area. Best seen during migration when it is more likely to be encountered in open habitats.

**Population Status and Conservation:** Across its range, insufficient census data make any generalizations about current population trends difficult (Bildstein and Meyer 2000). Historical declines documented in ne. U.S. during mid-1900s were attributed to widespread use of DDT (Snyder et al. 1973), and this was a concern in Oregon as well. Extremely high DDE residues (highest of the three *accipiter* species) were found in both plasma and eggs of Sharp-shinned Hawks following a single DDT spray project in ne. Oregon in 1974 (Henny and Meeker 1981).

This species' dependence on dense, continuous forest for breeding certainly influences its abundance and distribution (Bildstein and Meyer 2000). Its nesting-habitat requirements for vegetative structure are very specific; therefore forest management practices that alter certain conifer stands can pose a threat (Reynolds 1983). Adequate stand densities should be maintained in nesting areas, with uncut buffers of 9.8 ac (4 ha) left around active nests, including portions upslope from the nest for use as roosts and plucking perches (Reynolds 1983).—*Rachel White Scheuering and Gary McAtee*

## Cooper's Hawk *Accipiter cooperii*

Cooper's Hawks are smallish "bird hawks" (slightly smaller than American Crows) with rounded wings, a long rounded tail, and long yellow legs. This is the mid-sized accipiter nesting in Oregon and is larger than the Sharp-shinned Hawk, but smaller than the Northern Goshawk. The usual mode of flight consists of several rapid wing-beats alternating with brief periods of sailing. Juveniles are dark above with underparts streaked vertically. Adults tend to have a bluish cast to their gray upperparts and have brownish-orange and white underparts. The long tail is barred dark and light with a narrow whitish band at the tip. The Cooper's Hawk is restricted to N. America, and birds from the northern portion of its range are migratory, although some remain behind in winter—even in Canada (Palmer 1988).

Historically, this species was called the "blue darter" or "chicken hawk" and was much maligned for its prowess at killing birds. In fact, Gabrielson and Jewett (1940) called it one of the few species in the state that was almost consistently destructive, living to a large extent on poultry, game, and insectivorous birds. Typical ammunition advertisements as recently as the late 1940s (e.g., *True—The Man's Magazine*, May 1948) promoted shooting them: "Nothing can be said in his favor. That's why you should ask your dealer for the lightning-fast 22 ... Hollow Point. Its

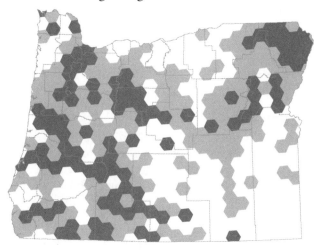

*Cooper's Hawk*

bullet, zipping through space at 1400 feet per second as it leaves your gun muzzle, will drop him—sure!" Unfortunately, all hawks suffered retribution, and "chicken hawk" was loosely applied to accipiters and buteos alike. Neither state nor federal laws protected birds of prey until the National Audubon Society pushed for a Model Hawk Law through its state affiliates in the 1950s. The Oregon Audubon Society (now Audubon Society of Portland) drafted HB 628 based on the national model in 1959 and saw it passed in the Oregon Legislature. All hawks and owls were given protection with the proviso that the owner or occupant of the land could kill a hawk or owl that was destroying poultry. Without that exception, the bill never would have passed in that era. Subsequently, by an Amendment to the Federal Migratory Bird Treaty Act with Mexico in 1972, hawks and owls and several other families of birds became fully protected.

**General Distribution:** Nest in N. America from s. Canada to n. Mexico; winter from n. U.S. to n. M. America (Palmer 1988). Most winter within the U.S., but are also widespread in Mexico. Monotypic (AOU 1957).

**Oregon Distribution:** An uncommon breeder in forests and woods throughout state except in arid treeless areas of se. Oregon. Littlefield (1990a) reports

regular nesting on Steens Mtn., and one summer record for Malheur NWR. Pairs were located along Denio Cr. and Van Horn Cr. in the Pueblo Mtns., Harney Co., in Jun 1997 (Spencer 1998). Reynolds et al. (1982) reported Cooper's Hawks nesting from an elevation of 50 ft (15 m) in the Willamette Valley to 5,775 ft (1,760 m) in the Bly Mtns, Klamath Co. Reynolds and Wight (1978) reported one pair/4,589 ac (1,857 ha) and one pair/5,436 ac (2,200 ha) in e. and w. Oregon study areas, respectively. An uncommon transient and winter visitor statewide (Gilligan et al. 1994, CBC).

**Habitat and Diet:** This hawk can be found in coniferous, mixed, and deciduous forests, as well as riparian, juniper, and oak woodlands. Habitat was studied at 70 Cooper's Hawk nest sites from the Cascades, Coast Range, Siskiyou, Steens, Wallowa, Blue, Ochoco, Bly, and Warner mountains in Oregon (Reynolds et al. 1982, Moore and Henny 1983). The vegetative profile around nests (n=39) was trees 30-60 and 50-70 yr old in nw. and e. Oregon, respectively, with a tree density of 265/ac (655/ha) and 469/ac (1,159/ha) (Reynolds et al. 1982). Moore and Henny (1983) found a slightly higher tree density (n=31) of 730/ac (1,804/ha) in the Blue and Wallowa mountains. Each coexisting accipiter used habitats with different structural characteristics associated with forest stand age. Nest sites were characterized as dense young stands for Sharp-shinned Hawks, more widely spaced older trees for Cooper's Hawks, and mature stands with varying densities of overstory trees for Northern Goshawks (Reynolds et al. 1982). Goshawks tend to build nests below the crown in more exposed positions, while Cooper's and Sharp-shinned Hawks build up in the canopy (Moore and Henny 1983). Of 37 female breeding Cooper's Hawks in ne. Oregon that were aged, eight (22%) were 1 yr old with their nests associated with younger successional stages than adult female nest sites (Moore and Henny 1984). Reynolds et al. (1982) reported Cooper's Hawks commonly nesting in deformed trees infected with dwarf-mistletoe, and Moore and Henny (1983) reported 20 of 31 nests (64.5%) on a mistletoe nesting substrate. Adult females also utilized mistletoe for nest structures more than 1-yr-old females (Moore and Henny 1984).

Diet in nw. Oregon consisted of 74% birds (average size 79.2 g [2.80 oz]) and 25% mammals (average size 296.4 g [10.45 oz]) and in e. Oregon 47% birds (average size 123.7 g [4.36 oz]) and 53% mammals (average size 147.5 g [5.2 oz]) (Reynolds and Meslow 1984). Combining both areas, 23.2% of the prey was either young mammals or nestling and fledgling birds. Cooper's Hawks preyed upon 39 known species of birds and nine species of mammals in nw. Oregon, with the American Robin, Steller's Jay,

Dark-eyed Junco, and Spotted Towhee most frequent. Townsend's chipmunk, brush rabbit, Douglas' squirrel, and woodrats (not identified to species) were most numerous mammals. In e. Oregon, preyed upon 20 known species of birds and six species of mammals with the Steller's Jay, Dark-eyed Junco, American Robin, and Northern Flicker most frequent. Mammals frequently taken included chipmunks (not identified to species) and golden-mantled ground squirrels. Reynolds and Meslow (1984) assigned all bird and mammal species to one of four height zones (ground-shrub, shrub-canopy, canopy, and aerial) and concluded that Cooper's Hawks foraged in the ground-shrub and shrub-canopy zones.

**Seasonal Activity and Behavior:** Reynolds and Wight (1978) reported the earliest pair of Cooper's Hawks at its nest site on 28 Mar (w. Oregon), while most pairs throughout Oregon were observed at or about their nest sites by mid-Apr, with the earliest completed clutch 1 May (w. Oregon) and latest 30 May (e. Oregon). In ne. Oregon completed their clutches nearly 1 mo after Northern Goshawks (mean date 22 May, range 12-31 May, n=35 nests) (Henny, Olson, and Fleming 1985). Timing similar to the 19 May mean (n=8) for se. Oregon, but later than the 11 May mean (n=12) for w. Oregon (Reynolds and Wight 1978). In general, 1-yr-old females completed clutches in ne. Oregon about 5 days later than adult females (mean 26 May vs. 21 May) (Henny, Olson, and Fleming 1985). Females in juvenal plumage accounted for 22% (8 of 37) of the nesting females that were aged in ne. Oregon (Moore and Henny 1984), but only 6% (2 of 34) of those observed by Reynolds and Wight (1978). The incubation period was 30-32 days and the nestling period 27-30 days, with young dependent upon adults for many weeks (up to 53 days) after fledging (Reynolds and Wight 1978).

Although generally recognized as permanent residents in Oregon by Gabrielson and Jewett (1940), the breeding population in the Blue and Wallowa mountains of ne. Oregon is highly migratory (Henny 1990). In fact, a Cooper's Hawk from this population banded as a nestling provided one of the southernmost species records (Zihuatanejo, Guerrero, Mexico). Two others were reported on 22 Sep and 20 Oct in w. Mexico (Sonora and Sinaloa), but perhaps were still migrating. Thus, Cooper's Hawks from ne. Oregon apparently winter in w. Mexico, perhaps from Sonora to Guerrero. Migratory status of birds breeding in w. Oregon is unknown. Birds presumably breeding north of Oregon are counted during fall migration at Bonney Butte, near Mt. Hood. Median passage date (during Sep-Oct monitoring period) averaged 25 Sep for 1994-98 (20 Sep for juveniles, 30 Sep for adults), with a gradual decline to almost no birds in late Oct. Numbers (Sep-Oct) have ranged 72-150/100 hr of observation time during 1994-99, and constituted about 13% of total raptor numbers. A hatch-year female banded at Bonney Butte 20 Sep 1998 was captured and released at San Simeon, California, on 24 Sep 1999, a distance of approximately 545 mi (875 km) (Vekasy and Smith 2000).

**Detection:** This species is quite shy and secretive, and seeing a Cooper's Hawk is largely a matter of accident. Much effort is required to locate nests, especially in coniferous forests. The degree of defensiveness at the nest site depends upon the stage in the nesting cycle, with the protective instinct increasing with progression to the fledging period (Palmer 1988). Cooper's Hawks are sometimes detected by their call in woodlands. Juveniles are often difficult to distinguish from Sharp-shinned Hawk.

**Population Status and Conservation:** Around 1900, Cooper's Hawks were considered a common nesting raptor in the U.S., but a widespread decline occurred soon afterward, especially in the e. U.S. (Palmer 1988). Shooting may have been responsible for the early declines; even Gabrielson and Jewett (1940) refer to the species as a bird-killing hawk. This perspective probably resulted in many being shot. Henny and Wight (1972) reported that 15.7% of nestling Cooper's Hawks banded (primarily ne. U.S.) from 1929-40 were shot during their first year of life (as reported to Bird Banding Laboratory). Shooting decreased during war years (1941-45) to 8.3%, and after the war (1946-57) to 6.8%. Actual losses were undoubtedly higher, since some bands from shot birds were not noticed and others not reported.

About the time shooting pressure abated, DDT came on the market (in 1946) as a pesticide, although its eggshell-thinning properties and adverse effects on productivity of birds were not recognized for more than two decades (Ratcliffe 1967). Clutch size showed no change over time (mean 4.18 eggs), but the number of young banded per successful nest (mostly ne. U.S.) decreased (1929-40, 3.52 young; 1941-45, 3.54; 1946-48, 3.08; 1949-67, 2.67) (Henny and Wight 1972). This decline in production rates may have been underestimated as information on complete nest failures was not available and could not be included. Four Cooper's Hawk eggs collected in Oregon in 1969-71 averaged 1.73 ppm DDE (geometric mean 1.47 ppm) (Snyder et al. 1973). Although the peak use of DDT occurred in the mid- to late 1960s, it was banned nationwide in 1972 by the EPA. The USFS received special approval for emergency use of DDT in 1974 to control Douglas-fir tussock moths on 426,159 ac (172,460 ha) of forest in Oregon, Washington, and Idaho (Henny 1977a). Following the single application at 0.75 lbs/ac (0.84 kg/ha), DDT/DDE residues increased in the blood of raptors living in the spray area

(Henny 1977a), and Cooper's Hawks laid eggs in spray areas (almost all from Oregon) in 1975-79 with 4.91 ppm DDE (geometric mean, range 1.89-95.5, n=12), while eggs > 2 mi (3.2 km) from the spray areas had 1.63 ppm (range 0.42-11.33, n=20) (Henny unpubl. data). The Cooper's Hawk nest in the spray area with the highest DDE egg residues (95.5 ppm) contained several broken eggs; thin-shelled eggs were common in spray areas in contrast to eggs collected away from spray areas.

More recently, White (1994) summarized the status of Cooper's Hawks in w. N. America as undetermined; migration data suggested recent increases. Number of young banded per successful nest (again mostly in the ne. U.S.) increased from 2.67 (1949-67) to 3.36 (1968-74) (Braun et al. 1977), nearly back to pre-DDT era rates of 3.52-3.54. Frequent use of dwarf-mistletoe as a nesting substrate for Cooper's Hawks and its use by other wildlife species prompted Parks et al. (1999) to suggest that some areas where dwarf-mistletoe is frequent and severe may be best used to manage wildlife species that use the large brooms formed in severely infected trees.—*Charles J. Henny*

### Northern Goshawk *Accipiter gentilis*

Of the three U.S. and Canadian forest hawks known as accipiters, this is by far the most impressive because of its size and aggressiveness. Like others of the genus, it is morphologically adapted to maneuvering through forest landscapes and usually uses an ambush approach to capturing prey; although if prey tries to escape, it quickly pursues. From Turkey to Japan, goshawks are favored over falcons for falconry (Beebe 1974, Palmer 1988), and a limited number of permits are issued in Oregon for taking goshawks for falconry purposes (C. Bruce p.c.).

This and the other two accipiters, the pigeon-sized Sharp-shinned Hawk and crow-sized Cooper's Hawk, have short, broad, round-tipped wings and long tails. The Northern Goshawk (hereafter referred to as goshawk) approximates the size of the Common

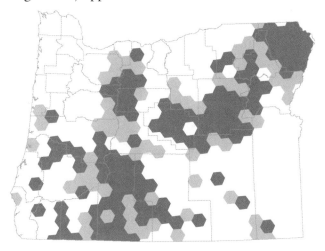

Raven (Johnsgard 1990). Adult plumage color is generally silver-gray on the upperparts and barred pale grayish-white on the underparts. Immatures are generally brown with strong striping on the underparts. An eye-stripe, if present, helps identify a goshawk. When perched, the short wings of the goshawk do not reach the midpoint of the tail. Tails of both adults and immatures have dark bands.

Because of its somewhat specialized habitat requirements, reclusiveness, and large home-range size, seeing a goshawk can be an unexpected and exciting event; but near a nest they become conspicuous and have a reputation for attacking human investigators with their talons (Bendire 1892, Bent 1937, Speiser and Bosakowski 1991). Likewise they attack avian territorial intruders as large as Great Horned Owls and Red-tailed Hawks (Squires and Reynolds 1997).

**General Distribution:** Holarctic, nesting in forested areas of Eurasia and N. America as far south as the Mexican highlands. Also occurs in treeless areas during migration and winter. In Eurasia winter as far south as n. Africa, India, and Burma; and in N. America as far south as N. Mexico, Texas, the Gulf states and Florida. Both resident and migrant populations, depending upon locale and year. Invasions occur, but have not been recorded in Oregon.

Old and New World forms are sufficiently different to be considered separate species (AOU 1998). Of two N. American subspecies, *A. g. atricapillus* is a resident in Oregon; *A. g. laingi*, breeding as far south as Vancouver I., British Columbia, is known from a female (USNM) from Glendale, Douglas Co., 18 Jun 1897, and is probably a postbreeding wanderer (*MRB*).

**Oregon Distribution:** Uncommon to fairly common permanent resident in suitable habitat between 1,900 ft (480 m) and 6,100 ft (1,860 m) elevation in forested portions of the Cascade, Blue, and Klamath mountains (Reynolds and Wight 1978, Reynolds et al. 1982, Marshall 1992b). Highest densities are found east of the Cascade crest. Goshawks were found nesting in the Coast Range in 1995 when one nest each was found in the Yachats R., Lincoln Co., and Siuslaw R., n. Lane Co., drainages (Thrailkill and Andrews 1996). OBBA listed two nestings in the Coast Range of Douglas Co. Breed locally on Steens Mtn., Hart Mtn., and in the Oregon Canyon Mtns. (Gabrielson and Jewett 1940, Green 1978, Reynolds et al. 1982, Denny 2000a, T. McAllister p.c.). Considering its presence on Steens Mtn., Oregon Canyon Mtns., and similar ranges in n. Nevada, goshawks are to be looked for in the Trout Cr. Mtns.

Uncommon to rare transient and winter resident; can appear anywhere in the state in forested and unforested habitats. Some individuals represent out-of-state breeders. Fall raptor counts conducted 1994-99 at Bonney Butte south of Mt. Hood yielded a mean of 29 goshawks annually compared to 319 Cooper's Hawks and 938 Sharp-shinned Hawks (Vekasy and Smith 2000). Contreras (1997b) reported only 0.09 goshawks per 100 party hr on Oregon CBCs. However, Littlefield (1990a) described them as "occasional" in autumn, winter, and spring in sagebrush habitat in the vicinity of Malheur NWR. Several goshawks banded in ne. Oregon wintered within 100 mi (161 km) of their nesting sites (C. J. Henny p.c.), which suggests that goshawks that breed in Oregon may remain in the region year round.

**Habitat and Diet:** Reproductive home range has three components: foraging area, nest area, and post-fledging family area (Graham et al. 1994). Foraging areas are typically 4,900-5,900 ac (2,000-2,400 ha), comprising a forest mosaic including large trees, snags, and down logs interspersed with openings. These areas must support a wide range of suitable prey, especially species that are ground dwellers or occur near the forest floor. Heavy shrub layers are believed to inhibit goshawk foraging (Reynolds and Meslow 1984, Speiser and Bosakowski 1987, Crocker-Bedford 1990), the probable cause of their rarity in the Coast Range (DeStefano and McCloskey 1997).

Goshawks often use alternate nests in different years. Nests are typically built in one of the largest trees within 20-39 acre (8-12 ha) dense patches of large old trees. Forest canopy at nest sites can be single-layered or multi-layered. Woodbridge et al. (1988) summarized common nest-site characteristics for the western states as follows: "Mature stands—high basal area of large trees. High canopy closure. Open understory. Moderate slopes—sites on benches, toe of slope or level ground. Often close to perennial water."

Three separate studies (Reynolds et al. 1982, Moore and Henny 1983, Bull and Hohmann 1994) totaling 120 Oregon nests show nesting in a wide range of conifer species and forest types including Douglas-fir, true firs, lodgepole and ponderosa pines, western larch, and quaking aspen. Only two of the studied nests were west of the Cascades.

Oregon nests studied by Reynolds et al. (1982) were below the upper canopy and placed on large, horizontal limbs either against the trunk or up to 13 ft (4 m) from the trunk. Nests were built of sticks. Bull and Hohmann (1994) reported 12 Wallowa Co. nests averaged 37 in (94 cm) X 26 in (66 cm) across and 14 in (36 cm) high. Heavy limbs are necessary for support. Mean dbh of 61 e. Oregon nest trees studied by Reynolds et al. (1982) was 32 in (82 cm); average dbh of 12 Wallowa Co. nests was 25 in (65 cm) (Bull and Hohmann 1994).

Habitat of breeding goshawks that nest in aspen stands in desert ranges dominated by sagebrush-steppe in the Northern Basin and Range ecoregion of se. Oregon has not been well studied. Younk and Bechard (1994) reported that in n. Nevada nests are in closed canopy aspen stands with little understory.

Post-fledging family areas that surround nest sites are typically a 300- to 600-ac (120- to 240-ha) mosaic of large mid-aged trees and snags with large down logs and small openings, with an herbaceous understory (Graham et al. 1994).

Their diet has been studied in many areas; varies by region and season. Comprises a variety of birds and mammals ranging from passerines to grouse and hares (Marshall 1992b). Analysis of prey remains at plucking sites near and at nests has shown that birds slightly exceed mammals. Reynolds and Meslow (1984) identified prey remains at 59 Fremont NF nests. They found Steller's Jays, American Robins, Northern Flickers, Mountain Quail, Mourning Doves, Blue Grouse, and Gray Jays dominated the bird catch; snowshoe hares, golden-mantled ground squirrels, chipmunks of several species, northern flying squirrels, Douglas' squirrels, unidentified hares, and western gray squirrels the mammal catch. Bull and Hohmann (1994) reported on remains at plucking sites in Wallowa Co. American Robins, Northern Flickers, Western Meadowlarks, Western Tanagers, Clark's Nutcrackers, Gray Jays, Hairy Woodpeckers, Ruffed Grouse, and Dark-eyed Juncos were taken in that order of frequency, while snowshoe hares, ground squirrels (mainly Columbian), red squirrels, and yellow pine chipmunks dominated the mammal catch.

In n. Nevada areas similar to desert ranges of se. Oregon, diet was primarily composed of Belding's ground squirrels until time of that species' aestivation, after which birds such as Northern Flickers and American Robins were taken (Younk and Bechard 1994). In the same area, Herron et al. (1985) mentioned capture of golden-mantled ground squirrels and cottontail rabbits.

No information is available on goshawk food habits in Oregon outside breeding areas.

**Seasonal Activity and Behavior:** Nest building begins Mar or Apr. In ne. and sc. Oregon, clutches complete 10 Apr-2 Jun (Reynolds and Wight 1978, Henny, Olson, and Fleming 1985, Bull and Hohmann 1994). Average clutch size 3.1; incubation 30-32 days. Egg attendance and feeding of young conducted mainly by female (Squires and Reynolds 1997). Food brought to nest by male. Young in nest 42-47 days, then move to nearby perches. Fledglings are dependent upon parents for food into early Sep (Reynolds and Wight 1978), and remain in post-fledging family areas (Reynolds et al. 1991). Nest sites and post-fledging areas defended.

At the Bonney Butte HawkWatch site, 80% of fall passage occurred 11 Sep-17 Oct (Vekasy and Smith 2000). No information is available on young dispersal in Oregon, and little is known about wintering biology.

**Detection:** Goshawk sightings outside breeding areas reflect an element of chance, but males regularly soar over breeding territories (Squires and Reynolds 1997). This species is also seen during fall migration over mountains, e.g. Bonney Butte in Mt. Hood NF. The use of recorded vocalizations in likely nesting habitat is very effective for detection during the nesting season (Kennedy and Stahlecker 1993). Nest searches are also used.

**Population Status and Conservation:** Population numbers unknown. DeStefano et al. (1994) reported on density of active nesting territories as ranging from 0.105/1,000 ac (405 ha) to 0.356/1,000 ac with an average of 0.283/1,000 ac in the Fremont, Malheur, and Wallowa-Whitman NFs.

Reliance, although not exclusively, on mature and old-growth timber, especially for nesting, makes this a species of concern. Desimone (1997) found that re-occupancy of nest sites in the Fremont NF was clearly related to the amount of mid-aged and late structural forest stages having >50% canopy closure. Conservation must consider not only nest sites, but also post-fledging family areas and foraging areas (Graham et al. 1994). Fire exclusion that has allowed a buildup of heavy shrub layers, together with timber harvest, has likely made former foraging and nesting areas unusable, but no population declines have been documented. Management recommendations used by BLM and USFS in varying degrees were developed mainly for habitats in the sw. U.S. (Reynolds et al. 1991).

The need to list this species under the Endangered Species Act has been debated (Kennedy 1997, Smallwood 1998). In 1998, USFWS denied a petition for listing in western states, but as of this writing the issue may end up in the courts (C. Bruce p.c.).—*David B. Marshall*

## Red-shouldered Hawk *Buteo lineatus*

Only recently documented as a breeding species in Oregon, the Red-shouldered Hawk has been the subject of growing attention and curiosity. Whereas populations in the ne. U.S. appear to have declined with loss of contiguous woodland in the past two centuries, Oregon's population has recently been increasing both in range and number (Crocoll 1994, Contreras 1997b, Gilligan 1999). A medium-sized hawk, it has bold black-and-white flight feathers and rusty shoulder patches. Seen in flight from underneath, especially when lit from above by the sun, its wings show a translucent "window" near the tips. It relies on perches for hunting, and is closely affiliated with wooded wetlands and riparian bottomlands.

**General Distribution:** Breeds from wc. and sw. Oregon (Adamus et al. 2001) south, west of the

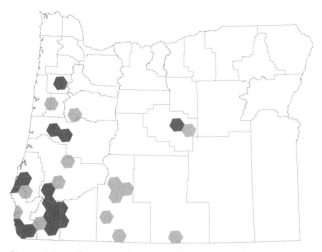

Sierra Nevada, to c. Baja California; also breeds from c. Minnesota through ne. U.S. to sw. Quebec south into Texas, along the Gulf coast, and into Florida. Winters sporadically through the breeding range, though not in the northernmost portions of its range in e. N. America. Five subspecies; *B. l. elegans* occurs in Oregon, according to Crocoll (1994).

**Oregon Distribution:** Locally uncommon breeder in sw. Oregon and s. Willamette Valley. Breeding locations include coastal Curry and Coos counties, Rogue Valley, sw. Douglas Co., c. Lane Co., and just east of Dallas, Polk Co. (OBBA). Occasionally seen in summer at Miller I., Odessa CG, and along Upper Klamath L., all Klamath Co., where nesting status unknown (Spencer 2001a, K. Spencer p.c.).

Locally uncommon to common in breeding locations in winter, as well as along the c. coast (Contreras 1997b, Hunter et al. 1998, Tice 1999b, Korpi 2001b). It is especially common in Coquille Valley: CBCs there have counted highest numbers in state, e.g., 19 in 1995, 24 in 1996, and 26 in 1999 (Contreras 1997b, Tice 1999b). Rare in winter in the n. Willamette Valley and along the n. coast (Tice 2000c, Korpi 2001b). East of the Cascades, most observations are in fall and winter. Very uncommon winter visitor in the Klamath Basin: most often near Upper Klamath L. and along the Klamath R. at L. Ewauna, Miller I., or Link R., but has also been seen along Lost R. (Korpi 1997, 1999, 2000, K. Spencer p.c.). It is also seen almost annually in fall on or near Malheur NWR since mid-1990s, and occasionally in sc. Deschutes Co. (Gilligan et al. 1994, Sullivan 1998a, 1999a, 2001a). An average of one bird/100 hr observation was seen in fall at Bonney Butte, south of Mt. Hood, during 1994-2000 (Smith 2001).

**Habitat and Diet:** In the breeding season this hawk is found in moist woodlands with at least a few deciduous trees (Henny and Cornely 1985). It prefers riparian bottoms, especially those near shallow wetlands or open meadows (Gilligan et al. 1994). On the s. coast uses lightly wooded coastal meadowlands (Evanich 1990). Its method of hunting from perches links it to wooded areas (Crocoll 1994); in California use of non-woodland habitat occurred only where there were substitute perch structures such as utility lines or fenceposts (Bloom et al. 1993). Across its range, appears to adapt habitat usage to what is available (Bloom et al. 1993, Crocoll 1994). In some cases habitat selection may be influenced by competition with the more xeric-adapted Red-tailed Hawk (Evanich 1990, Crocoll 1994, Moorman and Chapman 1996).

A nest found by Bendire (1892) along Archies Cr., Harney Co., was in a tall juniper. Near Brookings, Curry Co., one nest was approximately 80 ft (24 m) up in a Sitka spruce, and another 50 ft (15 m) up in a red alder. Both were constructed of sticks and were well concealed in forks of branches within the upper canopy (C. Dillingham p.c.).

In winter may use more open lands such as found in the Rogue and Willamette valleys (Gilligan et al. 1994), depending on perches available for hunting. In the Klamath Basin usually seen near water (K. Spencer p.c.). At Fern Ridge Res., Lane Co., tends to inhabit wet alder-oak woodlots in winter (Evanich 1990). Also associated with ash trees (*ALC*).

Diet undocumented for Oregon. Elsewhere found to take a variety of prey, including small mammals, snakes, lizards, amphibians, and small birds (Crocoll 1994). Crayfish known to be an especially important prey item in some areas (Crocoll 1994).

**Seasonal Activity and Behavior:** Timing of pair formation and breeding in Oregon is still poorly understood. Elsewhere in range, circling over breeding territory functions as courtship and possibly also territorial display (Crocoll 1994). This behavior has been documented in Oregon from 24 Jan to 4 Jun: however, the peak of territory establishment is likely Mar-Apr (Henny and Cornely 1985, Tice 1999a, 2000b). Copulating pair seen 12 Feb (Korpi 2001b). Nest building observed 9 Jun, nests with young 1 and 26 Jun, and fledglings 24 Jun and 3 Aug (Adamus et al. 2001). Populations in Oregon are largely non-migratory (Crocoll 1994). Postbreeding dispersal into Klamath Basin and other wintering areas generally occurs late Aug-Mar (Gilligan et al. 1994, K. Spencer p.c.). Seen at or near Malheur NWR regularly in Sep (Gilligan et al. 1994).

**Detection:** Often perches inconspicuously in wooded habitats (Evanich 1990), and therefore may be under-represented in forest habitat censuses (Crocoll 1994). Breeding birds are likely to be heard before seen (Crocoll 1994).

**Population Status and Conservation:** The first published observations in Oregon include a vague record from the Willamette Valley (Johnson 1880), and two nest records from Archie's Cr., Harney Co. (Bendire 1892). With the absence of any corroborating reports for nearly a century, these observations were viewed with growing skepticism over the years (Gabrielson and Jewett 1940). However, Browning (1973b) measured the eggs collected by Bendire and verified his identification. During the early 1970s additional sightings started trickling in, mainly from Curry Co. and the Fern Ridge Res. area (Rogers D 1979b, Henny and Cornely 1985). Records for the s. coast and s. Willamette Valley became more regular in the 1980s, and range expansion outside of these areas became increasingly evident; e.g. first observed in winter in the Klamath Basin during this period (Henny and Cornely 1985, K. Spencer p.c.). Now record numbers are being seen in strongholds of sw. Oregon, especially in winter (Johnson 1997b, Korpi 2001b). Also seen more and more often in nw. Oregon in fall and winter (Gilligan 1998, Tice 2000c): in winter 1997-98 they were reported in 14 of the 19 counties of w. Oregon (Tice 1998a). Meanwhile, reports continue to accumulate for sc. and se. Oregon, especially in the Klamath Basin (Sullivan 1998a, 1999a).

Outside Oregon, population declines have been attributed to fragmentation of contiguous forest and subsequent displacement by the more aggressive Red-tailed Hawk, which favors more open space (Bednarz and Dinsmore 1982, Moorman and Chapman 1996). Interactions between Red-shouldered Hawks and other hawks have not been studied in Oregon. An agonistic interaction was observed at Malheur NWR: a Red-shouldered Hawk attempting to roost was harassed and chased off by eight Red-tailed Hawks (Littlefield 1990a).—*Rachel White Scheuering and Gary McAtee*

## Broad-winged Hawk *Buteo platypterus*

This small, stout hawk breeds throughout the e. U.S., across s. Canada to c. Alberta. It winters primarily in M. and S. America. The main migratory routes are east of the Rocky Mtns., but it is rare but regular through the w. U.S. (Goodrich et al. 1996). Migrant broad-wings have been reported almost yearly from the Bonney Butte HawkWatch site, Hood River Co., since its inception in 1994. On 29 Sep 1999 a kettle of 65 passed over the station (Vekasy and Smith 2000). While kettles of this species are routine east of the Rockies, such occurrences are virtually unknown on the W. Coast. In addition, there have been 14 published sightings in Oregon since the species was first reported in the state in 1983. Of these, nine have been from Harney Co. The five spring records range from mid-May to early Jun; the seven fall records from mid-Sep to early Oct. Early birds were seen in the Coast Range of Washington Co., 6 Aug 1983 (OBRC) and near Madras, Jefferson Co., 17 Aug 1999 (OBRC). A subadult at Malheur NWR, Harney Co., 29 May 1983 was photographed (Watson 1989). Oregon observers are just beginning to grasp the status and movements of this species in the state. The subspecies represented by these records is unknown.—*Harry B. Nehls*

## Swainson's Hawk *Buteo swainsoni*

A century ago Swainson's Hawks were the most abundant buteo in much of Oregon east of the Cascades (Gabrielson and Jewett 1940). They could be regularly seen lazily soaring over fields and grasslands searching for small rodents and large insects, and in late summer large flocks assembled in areas of high prey concentrations in preparation for the fall migration. By the late 1960s, Marshall (1969) considered them to be rare and still declining. Swainson's Hawks are medium-sized buteos, smaller than Red-tailed and Ferruginous Hawks. Plumage beneath varies along a continuum from very pale to nearly black below. Lighter-plumaged birds have a distinct chest band. They have relatively long, pointed wings that contribute to superior flying skills. In flight the wings are held in a dihedral. The dark flight feathers contrast with the paler wing lining in all but the darkest birds.

**General Distribution:** Breeds in grasslands from w. Canada south through the U.S. from the prairie states west and on into Mexico. A few breed in Alaska and the Yukon and N. Territories. Winter in s. S. America, largely Argentina, though a small number have wintered in s. Florida and the Sacramento Valley of California in recent years (Stevenson and Anderson 1994, Herzog 1996). Monotypic (AOU 1957).

**Oregon Distribution:** Breeds in the bunchgrass prairies east of the Cascades with highest concentrations in the foothills of the Blue and Wallowa mountains, with densities reaching 13.7-42.2 pairs/100 mi² (5.3-16.3 pairs/100 km²) (Cottrell 1981, Janes 1985b). Local and uncommon in the southeast quarter of the

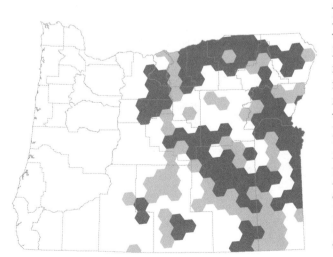

state, most often in the vicinity of irrigated hayfields. Rare in the Klamath Basin though common just across the California border. There are a few records from west of the Cascades during migration (Gullion 1951, Browning 1975a) and one winter record at Fern Ridge Res., 1968-69 (L. McQueen p.c.).

**Habitat and Diet:** Prefer open country. These hawks have little need for numerous trees or utility poles since they forage extensively while in flight and may include only the nest tree in their home range (Janes 1985b). Due to preference for habitat with rich and stable prey populations, they are most common in fertile bunchgrass prairie and irrigated farmland, especially alfalfa fields supporting abundant ground squirrels and pocket gophers (Janes 1985b). However, not all farmland supports high prey densities; Cottrell (1981) found they avoided cultivated land on Zumwalt Prairie, Wallowa Co.

With few exceptions, Swainson's Hawks nest in trees. The tree required for nesting may be quite small, and some nests are placed less than 6 ft (2 m) off the ground (Green and Morrison 1983). Build a relatively small nest (Green and Morrison 1983), often made of tumbleweeds. Single instances of Oregon birds constructing nests on a utility pole and in a large sagebrush have been observed (*SWJ*). Prior to European settlement, probably nested most often in willows that lined the streams in bunchgrass country (Bendire 1877), moving out over the grasslands to forage. This can still be observed in the Heppner area, though such habitat is much reduced in Oregon today.

Adults prey most often on small mammals, typically ground squirrels, pocket gophers, and voles early in the season. After the young fledge in late summer and on the wintering area, feed extensively upon insects such as grasshoppers (Jaramillo 1993).

**Seasonal Activity and Behavior:** Mean arrival is 5 Apr at Malheur NWR (Littlefield 1990a), and 5-10 Apr in Wasco Co. Peak movement occurs during 10-25 Apr. Swainson's Hawks arrive in Oregon at a time when most other buteos are incubating. Thus, much habitat has already been occupied, especially those areas richest in prey. Males often displace resident buteos from portions of their territories, which often involves numerous aerial encounters. They usually are successful within 24 hr of arrival (Janes 1984b, 1985b, 1994a). Defend a relatively small territory for a buteo (0.42-1.00 mi² [1.09-2.59 km²]) (Janes 1984b, 1985b). Incubation of 2-3 eggs, rarely 4, commences about 15 May with the female performing most of the incubation duties (*SWJ*). Young hatch in mid-Jun and fledge about 1 Aug. Fledge an average of 1.27-1.84 young/pair (Cottrell 1981, Janes unpubl. data). Migratory flocks of nonbreeding birds begin assembling in late Jun and grow in number until departure for S. America (Johnson et al. 1987). Fall migration begins in Aug with peak movement 20 Aug-10 Sep. Flocks of 20-30 are regular in the Horse Heaven Hills (Oregon Hills) of n. Umatilla Co. through 20 Sep (M. Denny p.c.).

Swainson's Hawks spend more time flying than Red-tailed Hawks, and males stay aloft nearly twice as much as females during the breeding season (Janes 1984b). Besides territorial defense and seeking prey, another possible reason that males fly extensively is to detect predators. For example, a Golden Eagle was once observed to attempt the capture of an incubating female from its nest (*SWJ*).

**Detection:** Swainson's Hawks can easily be overlooked if one simply searches utility poles and treetops for perched birds; one must look up for flying birds. Nests can be located by examining tops of junipers and other short trees for dried tumbleweeds. Agricultural lands around La Grande and in n. Malheur Co. offer some of the best opportunities for viewing. Though relatively few in number, they can usually be found in Christmas Valley, at Summer L., and in pastures at the north end of the Alvord Desert.

**Population Status and Conservation:** The Swainson's Hawk was formerly the most common buteo east of the Cascades (Gabrielson and Jewett 1940). In the early part of the 20th century Gabrielson and Jewett (1940) still considered them common although they had noted declines. Further losses were registered in the late 1950s (Littlefield et al. 1984). Have declined precipitously elsewhere west of the Rocky Mtns., particularly in California, where they occur at 5% of former abundance (Bloom 1980). Populations on the Great Plains have not suffered as greatly.

A number of factors appear to have contributed to their troubles on their breeding grounds and in S. America where they winter. They are vulnerable because of high concentrations in their wintering area in Argentina. Pesticide kills exceeding 1,000 birds have been noted (Goldstein et al. 1996). Now aware of the problem, farmers are reportedly working to reduce the threat to these birds. However, this does not explain the declines earlier in the 20th century, nor why populations in the intermountain region experienced the worst declines. Loss of bunchgrass prairie to agriculture—and subsequent loss of prey base and riparian woods for nesting—is probably an important factor. Another factor is grazing and the associated reduction in the incidence of fire. Western junipers spread widely during the 20th century without fire to confine them to less productive rimrock country (Burkhardt and

Tisdale 1976). Active fire suppression and grazing in more productive grasslands, which reduces fuel loads, have led to reduced seedling mortality. Red-tailed Hawks have followed this spread of perches, apparently to the detriment of Swainson's Hawks (Janes 1987). Unlike many other raptors, reproductive performance of Swainson's Hawk was not seriously affected by pesticide residues (e.g. DDE) during the 20th century (Henny and Kaiser 1977).—*Stewart W. Janes*

### Red-tailed Hawk *Buteo jamaicensis*

One of the most familiar sights along the roads of Oregon is a Red-tailed Hawk soaring high in the sky over a field, or perched on a utility pole, waiting patiently for prey. Found throughout the state in every habitat and at every elevation, though they are scarce in more densely forested areas. Red-tailed Hawks are large-bodied raptors with relatively broad wings. The back is mottled brown, and the tail of mature birds is orangish red with a thin, dark subterminal band. Some adults retain dark barring in the tail feathers normally present in immatures. Perched birds can be identified from behind even when the tail is concealed by the white mottling on the scapulars forming a faint 'V.' Most individuals can be assigned unambiguously to one of two color morphs, light or dark. Both are similar from the back, but underneath the light-morph birds are largely white or off-white with a belly band of varying extent and darkness. The lower surface of the wing is also light with a diagnostic dark patagial mark. Dark-morph birds are dark brown to nearly black on

*Red-tailed Hawk*

the belly, and the wing linings are dark in contrast to the light primaries and secondaries. Dark-morph birds are more abundant east of the Cascades. First-year birds lack the reddish tail and instead have a brownish tail with narrow dark bands. The breast tends to be whiter, and the belly band tends to be both darker and more mottled in appearance than in adult birds.

**General Distribution:** Found throughout N. America except for the Arctic. Breed from treeline south to Panama and islands of the Caribbean. In winter, retreat from the coldest areas, ranging from s. Canada and the n. U.S. south as far as Panama. Fifteen subspecies are currently recognized; three have been recorded in Oregon.

**Oregon Distribution:** *B. j. calurus* is a common permanent resident throughout the state, though local in colder areas at high elevations and east of the Cascades in winter. Attains highest breeding densities along the northern foothills of the Blue and Wallowa mountains where grasslands and forests meet, and in the Klamath Basin. In Wasco, Wheeler, Morrow, and Wallowa counties, breeding densities of 13-61 pairs/100 mi² (5.1-23.7 pairs/100 km²) have been observed (Cottrell 1981, Janes 1985b). A common migrant and locally abundant winter resident. *B. j. alascensis* (female OSU, Scio, Nov 1928, reported as *harlani* by Prill [1937] but reidentified by MRB) and presumed sightings (Lavers 1975) of *harlani*, a dark subspecies, are very rare winter visitors from Alaska.

**Habitat and Diet:** Red-tails are largely perch hunters. Although often observed soaring in thermals, this is seldom used as a vantage point from which to spot prey (Ballam 1984). Consequently any habitat that provides suitable perches (trees, utility poles, outcrops, etc.) and is open enough to permit the detection of ground-dwelling prey typically supports Red-tailed Hawks. Preston (1980) observed that dark- and light-morph birds select different perches apparently according to the degree of concealment they offer from prey. Light-morph birds tend to perch higher, where they are silhouetted against the sky, dark-morph birds lower, where they are more likely to be silhouetted against vegetation.

Frequent woodlands, agricultural land, clearcuts, grasslands, sagebrush plains, alpine environments, and urban areas. In winter when the energetic demands of rearing young are less, they expand their range into areas with fewer perches than during the breeding season (Janes unpubl. ms.[c]). Pairs inhabiting environments that provide greater opportunities for perch foraging rear more young (Janes 1984b). Immatures tend to occupy even more open real estate than adults (Janes and Bloom unpubl. ms.). Immatures have longer wings and tails, enhancing flight performance in these open environments like those of the open country buteos: Swainson's, Ferruginous, and Rough-legged Hawks (Janes and Bloom unpubl. ms.).

Red-tails construct nests in a variety of situations including trees, utility poles, and cliffs and place their nest higher than other buteos (Cottrell 1981).

They consume a wide variety of prey including small to medium-sized rodents such as ground squirrels, cottontails, voles, and pocket gophers, as well as snakes (Janes 1979, 1984a, Cottrell 1981, Lein 1982, Littlefield 1990a). Occasionally eat prey as varied as porcupines and Great Horned Owls (*SWJ*).

**Seasonal Activity and Behavior:** Resident pairs begin defending territories in Jan on Sauvie I. while migrants east of the Cascades establish territories immediately upon their return about 20 Mar. The peak of the spring movement of returning breeding birds and transients occurs in Mar. They defend their territory against other buteos and Golden Eagles (Cottrell 1981, Janes 1984a, 1985b, 1994a), and defend a greater vertical space than either Ferruginous or Swainson's Hawks (Janes unpubl. ms. [b]). Mean territory size for populations of Red-tailed Hawks east of the Cascades ranged 0.8-1.6 mi² (2.2-4.27 km²) (Janes 1975, 1985b) while on Sauvie I. individual territories varied 0.1-1.4 mi² (0.31-3.73 km²) (Lein 1982).

Nests may be used repeatedly in succeeding years, and birds show a high degree of fidelity to territories (Janes 1984a). Sites as scattered as Harney, Multnomah, Jackson, Wasco, and Wallowa counties all report mean dates for the initiation of incubation between the last week of Mar and the first week of Apr (Janes 1979, 1985a, Cottrell 1981, Lein 1982, Littlefield 1990a). Males take a greater role in defending the territory (Janes unpubl. ms.[c]) while females are more active in defense of the nest (Anderson DE 1990). Males remain aloft more than females during the breeding season, even allowing for incubation duties. Both males and females share incubation duties, but the male's contribution is relatively minor.

Clutch size varies 1-4 with a mean of 2.1-2.7, and the mean number of young fledged/pair is 1.3-1.4 (Cottrell 1981, Janes 1985b). Young tend to fledge in mid-Jun about 6 wk following hatching. The fall influx of northerly populations into the state occurs from late Aug to mid-Nov with the peak passage of adults in the last week of Sep and the first 2 wk of Oct (Smith 2000, 2001). Immatures tend to move a week earlier than the adults. Among many populations in Oregon (Harney, Multnomah, Jackson counties), redtails are largely resident (Lein 1982, Littlefield 1990a, *SWJ*), remaining on their territories year round. However, other populations tend to be migratory. In Wasco and Wheeler counties only about 10% of the pairs remain on breeding territories (*SWJ*).

**Detection:** Perched birds are easily located by scanning likely perches. Nests may be easy or difficult to find depending on the foliage density near the nest. Cliff nests may be located by searching for streaks of droppings. Loud cries and rapid circling over an observer often indicate a nearby nest. Winter concentrations at Sauvie I., the southern half of the Willamette Valley, and the Klamath Basin provide some of the best opportunities for viewing. Urban wintering birds are harassed heavily by crows and perched birds can often be detected by the escort and calling of crows.

**Population Status and Conservation:** Red-tailed Hawk populations have apparently increased with Euro-American settlement (Janes 1987). The clearing of forests for agriculture and the introduction of trees and utility poles in areas previously lacking elevated foraging perches have increased available habitat. Reduction in the incidence of fire east of the Cascades has contributed to the spread of junipers (Burkhardt and Tisdale 1976), further benefiting this species by providing perches and nest structures where none or few previously existed. Red-tailed Hawks are reportedly nesting among the vast acres of hybrid poplars being planted in Morrow and Umatilla counties (M. Denny p.c.).

While the status of many other raptors in the state is of concern, Red-tailed Hawk populations seem secure. Most human activities have worked to the advantage of this species by creating more habitat and increasing prey populations, chiefly meadow mice, ground squirrels, and pocket gophers. They often nest close to human dwellings and in suburban areas affording seemingly little opportunity for foraging. In 2000 a pair nested in the Portland Park Blocks (*DBM*).—*Stewart W. Janes*

## Ferruginous Hawk *Buteo regalis*

This largest of Oregon's hawks inhabits the most open country of the state's buteos, and watches over its home range on long, motionless wings for extended periods in search of prey. Ferruginous Hawks are sensitive to human disturbance and tend to reside in remote areas. They occur in two color morphs, but dark-morph birds are rare in Oregon. Light-morph birds are white below with few markings except for the ruddy-colored leg feathers. The back and wing coverts are rust colored, and the tips of the primaries and end of the tail tend toward dark, smoky gray. From above in flight, white at the base of the primaries and tail coupled with the ferruginous mantle are diagnostic. Dark-morph birds are the same above but with uniform dark brown body and wing linings below. Immatures are similar in appearance to adults but have a rusty wash on the chest. In profile Ferruginous Hawks are heavier chested than other buteos; this is particularly noticeable in flight.

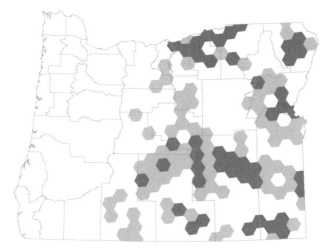

**General Distribution:** Breeds in semiarid western plains from s. Alberta, Saskatchewan, and Manitoba south to Arizona, New Mexico, and Kansas. Winters in reduced abundance over much of their breeding range south to Baja California, n. Mexico, and Texas. Monotypic (AOU 1957).

**Oregon Distribution:** Uncommon to rare resident in open landscapes east of the Cascades. Most common in n. Malheur Co. and along the foothills of the Blue Mtns. from Zumwalt Prairie (Wallowa Co.) west to the Columbia R. floodplain of Gilliam Co. Isolated breeding attempts have been recorded in Wasco Co. (*SWJ*). Although locally common in the Ft. Rock basin and Christmas Valley, they are less common in c. and sc. Oregon to rare in the Klamath Basin. Densities range 7.5-26.9 pairs/100 mi² (2.9-10.4 pairs/100 km²) (Lardy 1980, Cottrell 1981, Janes 1985a). Few remain in their Oregon breeding range during winter. The species is casual in winter in w. Oregon but has been seen annually in recent years. In the Rogue Valley it is a regular but rare winter visitor (Janes et al. 2001).

**Habitat and Diet:** This species is at home in the sagebrush plains of the high desert as well as in the bunchgrass prairies along the northern foothills of the Blue Mtns., wherever their principal prey— ground squirrels, rabbits, and hares—are common. In Washington, they prey largely upon northern pocket gophers as well as lesser numbers of other mammals, birds, and reptiles (Richardson et al. 2001). Surprisingly, they also feed on a number of insects, mostly Mormon crickets.

Ferruginous Hawks tend to live in areas of lower topographic relief than other buteos, though they can be found in the steep hill country near Heppner (Janes 1985a, 1985b). They forage over treeless grasslands and sagebrush plains. In comparison with sympatric Red-tailed and Swainson's Hawks, they occupy habitat with the lowest tree densities and areas of relatively shallow soils (Cottrell 1981, Janes 1985a, 1985b). Less common in cultivated areas than other buteos. Their home range may include only a single small tree—the nest tree—where the junipers give way to sagebrush or in a cottonwood along a small stream in the bunchgrass prairie. Some home ranges lack trees.

Nests are commonly placed on short cliffs or on the ground on small promontories or rises that can be approached on foot. Where riparian gallery forests were available in a 150-mi² (384-km²) study area in c. Morrow Co., most pairs nested in willows or cottonwoods along creeks (Janes 1985b). In comparison with the Swainson's Hawk, Ferruginous Hawks build a bulkier nest placed lower in junipers (10 vs. 15 ft [2.9 vs. 4.7 m]) (Green and Morrison 1983). However, Cottrell (1981) found Ferruginous Hawks placed their nests higher than Swainson's Hawks in a variety of trees on the Zumwalt Prairie (33 vs. 23 ft [10 vs. 7 m]). Sturdiness of the substrate appears to be the deciding factor. Avoid shaded nest sites (Howard and Hilliard 1980, Woffinden and Murphy 1983).

**Seasonal Activity and Behavior:** Typically arrive on their breeding territories in late Mar. Where they co-occur with other buteos, Ferruginous Hawks tend to occupy less productive sites, which is reflected in their relatively large home ranges (1.3-3.1 mi² [3.4-8.1 km²]) (Janes 1985b). They produce larger clutches than other buteos (up to eight eggs) (Smith and Murphy 1978, Smith et al. 1981), averaging 3.9 eggs in Malheur Co. (Lardy 1980), and fledge an average of 1.6-3.2 young/nest (Lardy 1980, Cottrell 1981). In areas where rabbits and hares are the dominant prey, reproductive success varies considerably, corresponding to annual changes in prey abundance (Smith et al. 1981). Incubation begins about 1 Apr and young fledge in mid-Jun. Fall migration occurs from Sep through mid-Nov.

Like most buteos, they sometimes perch on exposed perches where they search for prey. However, in spring and summer, they more often hunt while in flight. They interact with Red-tailed and Swainson's Hawks, but usually give way to these more aggressive relatives in territorial disputes (Cottrell 1981, Janes 1985a).

**Detection:** During the breeding season, Ferruginous Hawks fly extensively. Because most are bright white underneath, perched birds can often be located at great distances. The best opportunity to see this bird is late in the summer when the fledged young and adults are often seen perched on utility poles. Though it can be observed in many locations east of the Cascades, highest concentrations and best opportunities for viewing are in n. Malheur Co.; Harney Co. east of Burns and s. to Crane; the Fort Rock basin and Christmas Valley, Lake Co.; and Zumwalt Prairie, Wallowa Co. (*SWJ*).

Also, frequently noted between Pilot Rock and Nye Junction, Umatilla Co. (M. Denny p.c.).

**Population Status and Conservation:** Populations have declined on Malheur NWR since the 1940s with none breeding on the refuge in the 1980s (Littlefield 1990a). However, no declines have been noted for the state as a whole (Bechard and Schmutz 1995).

Much of the higher-quality habitat for this species has been converted into agricultural land in the past century, particularly along the floodplain of the Columbia R. Susceptible to further conversion of rangeland to agriculture particularly if it results in the loss of ground squirrels, cottontails, and jackrabbits (Bechard and Schmutz 1995). The loss of riparian gallery forests along streams due to grazing and other management practices in the bunchgrass prairies has undoubtedly reduced nesting opportunities (*SWJ*). More than most other raptors, Ferruginous Hawks are sensitive to human disturbance and will readily abandon nests especially during the period of egg laying and incubation (Olendorff and Stoddard 1974, White and Thurow 1985). This is exacerbated by the tendency to nest in very short trees and even on the ground where the nest can be easily approached. Increased use of public lands for recreational purposes could cause further reductions. Stream and rangeland rehabilitation and discouraging human activities near nesting areas would benefit this species. Wind turbines have been erected or are proposed in areas with nesting Ferruginous Hawks in Umatilla Co. and other places (M. Denny p.c.). The effect of these structures should be investigated.—*Stewart W. Janes*

## Rough-legged Hawk *Buteo lagopus*

Characteristic of open country and cold weather, the Rough-legged Hawk can be found soaring over exposed terrain or perched on utility poles across much of the state in winter. The rough appearance of its legs comes from the feathers covering their length, an adaptation that provides extra warmth in frigid weather. In flight, dark wrist patches and belly help identify this large buteo, though like other hawks it is subject to much variation in plumage. From a distance it frequently appears to have a frosty upper half. Often hovers over fields while hunting, a behavior that is rare among most other buteos.

**General Distribution:** Breeds from nw. Alaska across n. Yukon and the Arctic islands to n. Labrador, south through n. Mackenzie, n. Manitoba, and extreme n. Ontario to Newfoundland; also in arctic Eurasia from Scandinavia to n. Siberia. Winters from s. Canada south to s. California, through sw. U.S. to n. Texas, and northeast to Virginia; in Eurasia from British Isles, s. Scandinavia, and c. Russia south to s. Europe, s. Russia, and Japan. Two subspecies; *B. l. sanctijohannis* occurs in Oregon (AOU 1957).

**Oregon Distribution:** Uncommon to common in winter in open country throughout the state (Gilligan et al. 1994). Numbers vary markedly from year to year (Gilligan et al. 1994), perhaps in relation to fluctuations in prey abundance (Littlefield et al. 1992). Most common in open areas east of the Cascades, where it can be abundant in some years (Contreras 1997b). It is especially common at Malheur NWR, where CBCs have several times recorded the highest number of this species in N. America (Littlefield 1990a). Some show obvious site fidelity to wintering grounds; many individuals have returned year after year to Malheur NWR, some for at least 7 yr (Littlefield 1990a).

Generally uncommon west of the Cascades in interior valleys, though can be locally common in some years (Gilligan et al. 1994, Contreras 1997b). Least common on the coast and in sw. Oregon: in years of lower numbers may be absent from these areas altogether (Contreras 1997b).

In migration this hawk regularly passes south along Cascade crest (Fix 1990a, Smith 2001). An average of five birds/100 hr of observation time passed Bonney Butte, south of Mt. Hood, during 1994-2000 (Smith 2001). Considered a casual fall migrant on Diamond L. RD (Fix 1990a), and uncommon fall migrant at Sycan Marsh, Lake Co. (Stern, Del Carlo, et al. 1987). It is sometimes seen at higher elevations during migration, e.g., at approximately 8,000 ft (2,439 m) on Steens Mtn. (*ALC*).

**Habitat and Diet:** Winter habitat includes open fields, grasslands, pastures, open woodland, agricultural land, and sagebrush flats at low to moderate elevations (Gabrielson and Jewett 1940, Contreras and Kindschy 1996). They reach high densities in drainage basins and valleys with seasonally flooded wetlands and native meadows (Littlefield et al. 1992). Densities of wintering birds in Colorado are negatively correlated with amount of urban development (Berry et al. 1998). A study of effects of land use practices on Rough-legged Hawks wintering at Malheur NWR revealed their strong preference for land ungrazed by cattle, used disproportionately more than grazed or hayed lands, likely because ungrazed land at Malheur NWR has a much higher density of voles (Littlefield et al. 1992).

Diet consists mainly of rodents, montane voles particularly important in some areas (Littlefield et al. 1992). Known to congregate in areas with jackrabbits (Gabrielson and Jewett 1940). Black-tailed jackrabbit carrion makes up a significant portion of prey consumed by a population in Idaho, which often hunts from power lines paralleling roads (Watson 1986). Rarely takes birds (McAtee 1935), but has been observed attacking California Quail in heavy snow cover (Contreras and Kindschy 1996).

**Seasonal Activity and Behavior:** Usually begin arriving mid-Oct, with peak numbers in late Nov and early Dec (Littlefield 1990a). Some migrants pass through on their way farther south (Gilligan et al. 1994). Most start leaving the state late Mar to early Apr, but timing appears affected by weather (Littlefield 1990a). Peak numbers most often occur around mid-Apr (Littlefield 1990a). Exceptionally late birds have been recorded in May (Fix 1985a, Gilligan et al. 1994, Sullivan 1998b). There is some evidence that pair bonding may occur on wintering areas, as the birds often travel and arrive on breeding grounds already paired (Bent 1937). Aberrant records exist for summer, including an immature seen in late Jun and Jul 1998 (Spencer 1999), and a bird in late Aug 1985 (Summers 1986a).

**Detection:** This large bird is generally conspicuous in open winter landscapes and its hovering is often quite obvious.

**Population Status and Conservation:** Since abundance of this species varies greatly from year to year, short-term population trends are difficult to detect (Contreras 1997b), though data from Oregon CBCs for 1959-88 show an overall increase (Sauer et al. 1996). Some changes in distribution have occurred in the state. Gabrielson and Jewett (1940) and Jewett (1946a) considered it a rare straggler in w. Oregon where it is now considered uncommon to locally common (Gilligan et al. 1994).

Throughout its range, it appears to be strongly influenced by local prey population cycles (Baker and Brooks 1981, Littlefield et al. 1992). Therefore, abundance may be affected by land use practices that increase or decrease prey populations. Urbanization may present a limiting factor in some areas (Berry et al. 1998).—*Rachel White Scheuering and Gary McAtee*

## Golden Eagle *Aquila chrysaetos*

The largest soaring raptor inhabiting open country and mountainous terrain in e. Oregon. A powerful and skillful hunter, worshipped by Native Americans for its spiritual powers and persecuted by early 20th-century livestock owners, the Golden Eagle has become the raptorial icon of the American West. A very large, dark raptor, the nape golden in all plumages. Sexes similar in appearance, females slightly larger. Wing span measures up to 90 in (230 cm) in females and 83 in (210 cm) in males. Differentiated from smaller dark-morph raptors by larger size and massive bill. Adults may be difficult to distinguish from immature Bald Eagles at a distance. Juvenile birds show white patches at the base of the

primaries and a white tail with a broad dark terminal band. Gold-colored feathers on the head and back of neck, and fully feathered tarsus, are diagnostic.

**General Distribution:** Holarctic; occurs throughout Eurasia south to n. Africa; in N. America, is locally distributed from Alaska across Canada, rare in the northeast, south to c. Mexico. In the U.S., breeds from Alaska south and west of the east slope of the Rocky Mtns. Northern populations are migratory, southern populations resident. Number of subspecies worldwide not certain, *A. c. canadensis* occurs in N. America (Palmer 1988).

**Oregon Distribution:** Common to uncommon year round resident in all counties east of the Cascade Range. Highest densities of nesting birds are found in the Northern Basin and Range ecoregion in Lake, Harney, and Malheur counties. Nest records exist for Clackamas, Coos, Curry, Douglas, Jackson, Josephine, and Linn counties of w. Oregon (Issacs and Opp 1991, Gilligan et al. 1994). Irregularly observed in winter in nw. Oregon and along the coast (CBC). Uncommon fall migrant along Cascades summit (Smith 2001, *MGH*).

**Habitat and Diet:** The Golden Eagle inhabits shrub-steppe, grassland, juniper, and open ponderosa pine, and mixed conifer/deciduous habitats. It forages in a variety of habitat types and successional stages, preferring areas with an open shrub component that provides food and cover for prey. Suitable nesting and foraging habitat can be found in mountains, canyons, and rolling hills. Of 506 occupied nests in 1982, 35% were in mature trees and 65% on ledges along rims and cliffs (Isaacs and Opp 1991). Nests are massive, often 3-10 ft (1-3 m) tall and 3 ft (1 m) wide weighing many hundreds of pounds. Nest trees are typically large live ponderosa pine with sturdy open branching and a trunk dbh > 30 in (75 cm). Nests persist for many years and are often rebuilt in same location if destroyed.

It occasionally builds nests on electric transmission towers (*CGC*).

Golden Eagles have large breeding territories ranging 10-40 mi$^2$ (26-100 km$^2$) that may encompass several habitat types (Newton 1979, Collopy and Edwards 1989). Home ranges are larger during the nonbreeding season although the degree of increase is highly individualistic (Marzluff et al. 1993). Availability of suitable nest sites and abundance of prey influence nesting density and productivity. Nest territories may contain several alternate nests in close proximity. One territory along L. Billy Chinook, Jefferson Co., has eleven alternate nests (*CGC*).

Throughout most of the Great Basin, black-tailed jackrabbits are the main prey item and numerous studies have correlated eagle production with jackrabbit abundance (Olendorff 1976, Kochert 1980, Thompson et al. 1982). In c. Oregon, where jackrabbit populations have been depressed since the mid-1980s, a study of diet and prey selection conducted in 1999-2000 showed a great variety of prey species. Remains of the following prey items were found in the nests or observed delivered to young: mountain cottontail, California and Belding's ground squirrels, marmots, woodrats, other small mammals, Kokanee salmon, and a variety of birds including pheasants, waterfowl, and rock doves (*CGC*). Golden Eagles will occasionally kill newborn deer and pronghorn fawns, and mountain sheep and domestic lambs (Palmer 1988). They will eat fresh carrion and are skilled at pirating prey from other raptors (*CGC*).

**Seasonal Activity and Behavior:** Courtship displays begin as early as mid-Feb at low-elevation sites. Egg laying occurs from late Feb to mid-Apr. A clutch of two eggs is typically laid, rarely one or three, and incubated primarily by the female for 35-45 days. Incubation starts with the first egg laid. Young birds fledge in 65-84 days, between late Jun and early Aug. The adult male delivers more prey items to the nest but the female usually feeds young. Post-fledging period, when the young have left the nest but are still dependent on the adults for food and developing hunting skills, is about 11 wk (Collopy 1984, *CGC*).

They show a wide range of tolerance to disturbance at their nest sites. A pair of eagles at Smith Rock SP has become accustomed to rock climbers and thousands of annual visitors and nests successfully most years. Other eagle pairs may move away or abandon nests if disturbed. (*CGC*).

Most adult pairs in Oregon are resident year round and exhibit strong fidelity to nest territories. Young disperse in early fall and a study in sw. Idaho found 78% remain within 60 mi (100 km) of the natal region during Oct-Mar (Steenoff et al. 1984). Some family groups stay together until the start of the next breeding season.

There is a small migratory movement of northern birds through the state in fall. Raptor counts at Bonney Butte, Mt. Hood NF, Wasco Co., during Sep and Oct 1994-99, averaged 30.8 (+/- 6.6) Golden Eagles per 100 viewing hr (Smith 2001).

**Detection:** Often observed perched on power poles, large trees, or other high spots in preferred habitats. Soars on afternoon thermals. Three flight displays have been described: high circling, undulating, and tumbling flights function in maintaining pair bonds and territorial defense. Generally silent, occasionally gives weak calls during courtship, territorial defense, or to communicate with young. Young give a clearly audible food-begging call (Palmer 1988). Large nests may be easily observed on cliff faces and trees. Good places to observe eagles are in the canyon and rim country along the major river drainages in c. and e. Oregon.

**Population Status and Conservation:** In 1982 it was estimated that 1,000-1,500 pairs of Golden Eagles nested in Oregon (Isaacs and Opp 1991). In Harney Co., quarterly road surveys conducted 1985-93 showed medium abundance with a mean of 4.67 (+/-2.28) observations per 100 mi (160 km) of survey route (Keister and Ivey 1994). At the Pelton-Round Butte area in Jefferson Co. the 6-yr mean of 13.5 occupied territories averaged 79% successful with an average of 1.4 young produced per successful territory (Concannon 1998). In se. Oregon, breeding data from 1940 and 1966-80 showed 51% nest success with an average 1.7 young fledged per successful nest (Thompson et al. 1982). Golden Eagles counted during the mid-winter Bald Eagle survey in Oregon for 1992-2001 have varied from 79 to 128 and averaged 97 (Isaacs 2001).

The population trend in Oregon is unknown. Regionally, the population of resident Golden Eagles in the northern portions of the Great Basin, particularly Idaho and N. Utah, have shown indications of a decline (M. Kochert p.c.). The reasons are complex and may be related to a decline in jackrabbit abundance due to habitat alteration caused by the introduction of exotic range plants, devastating wildfires, and excessive livestock grazing. Some nest territories in c. Oregon have been lost to urban sprawl, residential developments, and disturbing recreational activities such as off-highway vehicles (*CGC*).

Provisions of the Bald Eagle Protection Act were extended to the Golden Eagle in 1962 because of concerns with declining numbers and the similarity in appearance of immatures. A special federal permit is required to have possession of any part of any eagle. Native Americans can obtain eagle feathers for ceremonial purposes from the USFWS.

Monitoring activities include protection of nest sites, occasional surveys for nest site occupancy and productivity, fall migration counts at Bonney Butte near Mt. Hood, and counts during the mid-winter Bald Eagle survey. Nest sites are protected by state and federal laws. In 1982, 75% of Oregon nests were on public lands and 25% on private lands (Isaacs and Opp 1991). Deschutes, Jefferson, Crook, and Wasco counties have adopted ordinances under Goal 5 of Oregon's land use laws that regulate the siting and construction of new roads and dwellings within a 0.25-mi (0.4-km) buffer zone around Golden Eagle nest sites. There are no state land use provisions for protecting eagle foraging habitats.—*Chris G. Carey*

## Family Falconidae

### Subfamily Falconinae

### American Kestrel *Falco sparverius*
Formerly known in American literature as the Sparrow Hawk, this is the smallest (dove-sized) and most familiar and abundant member of the family Falconidae in N. America, and one of the easiest raptors to observe. It has two considerably different plumages: adult male and adult female, and juvenile males differ somewhat from adult males until post-juvenal molt in fall (Wheeler and Clark 1995). Adult males have rufous backs and tails with blue-gray upper wing coverts. The tail has a wide black subterminal band. Juvenile males are similar to adult males but have heavily streaked breasts. Females are slightly larger than males and have reddish-brown backs and upper wing coverts that are barred with dark brown. These birds soar with their long and pointed wings flat, and regularly hover over open and partly open country with scattered trees, including cultivated lands and occasionally suburban areas. Nesting in boxes is frequent and widespread and was recorded at least as early as 1909 (Palmer 1988).

**General Distribution:** Breed in N. America from the Arctic treeline south to s. Baja California, the highlands of M. America, the Gulf coast and s. Florida; in the Bahamas and the Antilles, and the lowland pine forest of e. Honduras and ne. Nicaragua; breeds throughout most of S. America, but absent from heavily forested regions such as Amazon Basin, south to Tierra del Fuego. Three subspecies recognized in N. America, although others are reported throughout S. America (Palmer 1988); *F. s. sparverius* occurs in Oregon (AOU 1957).

**Oregon Distribution:** The kestrel breeds statewide in open terrain from sea level to the alpine zone in the mountains. Open habitat is limited in forested landscapes of the w. Cascades and Coast Range, and nesting cavities are sometimes limited in vast open spaces. It winters throughout the breeding range except at high elevations where deep snow restricts foraging opportunities. It is less common in winter in e. Oregon. In contrast, numbers increase with the incursion of wintering birds at low elevations in w. Oregon. At all seasons it is least common, even rare, on the outer coast.

**Habitat and Diet:** In summer, this is a bird of roadsides, prairies, and grasslands, grassy forest openings, or sagebrush and desert lands (Beebe 1976). Perches on snags, posts, and utility wires, making short flights out over open areas hunting for prey. It likes to face into the wind and hover while searching the ground for small prey. Since available nest cavities (often old excavations made by Northern Flickers or other woodpeckers) are a prerequisite for nesting, a lack of old trees with cavities can limit nesting distribution. They have also nested in holes in fenceposts and cutbanks, cavities in cliffs or rimrock, and sometimes in openings under the eaves of residences and other buildings (e.g., see Littlefield [1990a] for Malheur NWR). They take well to nest boxes.

Kestrels are almost exclusively insectivorous except when insect food is difficult to obtain (Fisher 1893). Much literature discusses kestrels eating grasshoppers and crickets almost exclusively when they are abundant. It is an opportunistic predator; in cold weather, when insects are dead or dormant, must obtain other kinds of food including voles, mice, shrews, other small mammals, and various species of birds (Fisher 1893, May 1935). Thus, dramatic seasonal shifts occur in types of prey eaten in Oregon.

**Seasonal Activity and Behavior:** Most nesting kestrels from more northern latitudes are migratory (Henny 1972), but the percentage migrating decreases in a clinal manner at nesting localities progressively farther south. An estimated 89.5% of American Kestrels nesting in e. Oregon, e. Washington, and Idaho (excluding the Snake R. plain) are migratory, moving primarily to w. Mexico for winter (Henny and Brady 1994). Banding data imply that the remaining kestrels nesting in the region (10.5%) are permanent residents. Henny and Brady (1994) found 2.8% of a nc. Oregon population (Umatilla and Morrow counties) on nesting territories in Jan 1981 (permanent residents). A higher percentage appears to be permanent residents in valleys with agriculture along the Snake R. plain than in the remainder of Idaho, e. Oregon, and e. Washington. Limited evidence indicates that permanent resident kestrels in nc. Oregon nest earlier than migrants (Henny and Brady 1994).

West of the Cascades in Oregon, a permanent resident population is present, but some individuals migrate south to winter in Mexico and perhaps California (Henny and Brady 1994). Precise estimates of permanent residents in the w. Oregon breeding

population cannot be made at this time, although it is likely much higher than for e. Oregon. Most kestrels nesting in California are permanent residents (Bloom 1985).

In spring, migrant kestrels arrive at Malheur NWR in late Mar and reach a peak 1-25 Apr, with most being transients (Littlefield 1990a). When kestrels arrive on breeding grounds, initial reproductive behavior is characterized by flight display (Beebe 1976). Displays are typical for falcons, and primarily an activity of the male, taking the form of steep ascents and plunges above the flying or perched female. The male is extremely noisy at this time (Beebe 1976). Clutch completion dates for 220 kestrels nests in nc. Oregon 1979-81 (excluded first year boxes established) ranged 20 Mar (a permanent resident) to early Jun with 3 (1.4%) in Mar, 102 (46.4%) in Apr, 111 (50.5%) in May, and 4 (1.8%) in Jun (Henny and Brady 1994). Clutch size in 1981 generally decreased from Mar (5.50 eggs) to Apr (5.29 eggs) to May (5.04 eggs). The male usually brings all food to the female from the time preceding egg production through incubation, and shares with incubation (Beebe 1976).

In general, kestrels produce one brood per year, but occasionally two broods have been produced at more southern latitudes. Steenhof and Peterson (1997) reported the first double brooding by kestrels nesting above latitude 40° N near Boise, Idaho (43°N, 116°W) in 1996. The female that raised two broods (fledged 10 young) was known to spend at least part of one winter near her nesting territory. Steenhof and Peterson (1997) estimated a minimum of 120 days to raise two broods successfully. They probably require at least 5 days for laying eggs, 27 days to incubate, and 30 days for brood rearing (Porter and Wiemeyer 1972). In sw. Idaho, begin laying eggs as early as mid-Mar, and young have fledged as late as early to mid-Aug, a window of about 150 days.

At Bend, local kestrels drift south in Sep with movements depending on local food and weather, but are gone by mid-month (Roest 1957a). At Bonney Butte, on the southeast flanks of Mt. Hood, few kestrels were counted annually; 95% of the passage occurred 31 Aug to 20 Oct (HawkWatch International, files for 1994-99). Peak counts at Malheur NWR occur 20 Aug to 15 Sept (Littlefield 1990a).

**Detection:** American Kestrels are easily seen because of their habit of hunting and perching in the open.

**Population Status and Conservation:** Gabrielson and Jewett (1940) reported the species very common. Of all N. American raptors, has been the least persecuted and it has become unsuspicious and tame (Beebe 1976). Nest boxes have been used successfully to concentrate kestrels for research, especially for contaminant studies. In 1978, 217 nest boxes were generally placed in riparian zones that meandered through the wheat-growing regions of Umatilla and Morrow counties in nc. Oregon. This was an area where few kestrels were seen during the breeding season in earlier years, presumably because the region lacked nest cavities. The first year 86 pairs (40% occupancy rate) nested in the boxes (Henny et al. 1983), and the occupancy rate increased in later years. Similarly, nest boxes were placed near openings in the forested Blue and Wallowa mountains of ne. Oregon, but the occupancy rate was much lower (Henny 1977a). Thus, many kestrels look for nest cavities as they migrate through e. Oregon in spring, presumably en route toward natal areas in Washington, British Columbia, and farther north.

Henny (1972) provided some evidence that the number of young banded per successful nest declined in the ne. U.S. during the 1960s, compared to 1925-45 and 1946-59, and Anderson and Hickey (1972) reported 12-14% eggshell thinning (a problem related to DDT) in New York and Indiana 1952-63. However, other species including the bird-eating Peregrine Falcon showed much more serious eggshell thinning during the same time period. Kestrels were studied during the last major DDT spray project (to control Douglas-fir tussock moths) in the U.S. in 1974 (426,000 ac [172,350 ha] sprayed once at 0.75 lbs/ac [0.85 kg/ha]) which included the Blue and Wallowa mountains of Oregon (Henny 1977a). One year after the spraying, DDT and its metabolites were five times higher in kestrel eggs from the spray area than those collected more than 10 mi (16 km) from the spray area (reference area). In 1975, eggshells were 10.4% thinner in the spray area than in the reference area and 11.5% thinner than during the pre-DDT era. The accipiters (Northern Goshawk, Cooper's Hawk, and Sharp-Shinned Hawk) in the spray area accumulated much higher concentrations of DDT and its metabolites (Henny 1977a). The kestrel was also studied in Oregon 1974-79 to evaluate heptachlor used as a wheat seed treatment for wireworm control in Umatilla and Morrow counties. Heptachlor reduced productivity of kestrels and caused some adult mortality (Henny et al. 1983). Following the restrictions in 1979, heptachlor epoxide residues in kestrel eggs in 1980 and 1981 decreased and productivity improved. White (1994) reported kestrels stable/increasing in w. N. America with the increases regional or local, while Fuller et al. (1995) reported the species stable throughout the U.S. based upon the BBS.—*Charles J. Henny*

## Merlin *Falco columbarius*

With short pointed wings and long narrow tails, these small falcons are well built for fast pursuit and mid-air attacks. Sexes differ in color and size, with adult males 24-30% smaller by weight than females (Sodhi et al. 1993). Males range from blackish gray to pale blue-gray on the back with a reddish wash along sides of breast and a banded tail; females have brownish backs. Formerly called "pigeon hawk" in recognition of *columbarius*, the Latin binomial (Gruson 1972).

**General Distribution:** Circumboreal; breeds in Alaska, most of Canada, parts of nw. and ne. U.S., Britain, Scandinavia, Finland, Iceland, Siberia, and nc. Russia (Sodhi et al. 1993). N. American populations winter in sw. Alaska, coastal w. Canada, w. and s. U.S., south into Panama, the W. Indies, M. America, n. S. America. Ten subspecies worldwide; two of the three subspecies that occur in N. America can regularly be found in Oregon; a third has been reported.

**Oregon Distribution:** *F. c. suckleyi*, "Black Pigeon Hawk" or "Black Merlin," was considered by Gabrielson and Jewett (1940) a "rare winter resident of coast. Only of casual occurrence inland." Based on sightings, Gilligan et al. (1994) listed it as "an uncommon winter visitant and transient in lowland areas along the coast and in inland w. Oregon." *F. c. columbarius* (*bendirei* of Gabrielson and Jewett [1940] and *columbarius* are synonyms [Brown and Amadon 1968, Temple 1972]), sometimes called "Taiga Merlin," was first reported as nesting in Oregon in 1857 near Klamath L. (Gabrielson and Jewett 1940). Those authors described *F. c. columbarius* as a "very rare breeding bird and uncommon migrant and winter resident in e. Oregon. Very rare straggler west of Cascades." Based on sightings, Gilligan et al. (1994) described *columbarius* as occurring throughout Oregon, most frequently east of the Cascades listed as "uncommon to rare as a transient, and generally rare at lower elevations in winter."

Buchanan et al. (1988) reported *F. c. columbarius* and *F. c. suckleyi* during their study of wintering Merlins in w. Washington estuaries (outer coast and Puget Sound). T. Gleason (p.c.) reported that of nesting or territorial pairs he observed on the Olympic Peninsula, which in theory should be *F. c. suckleyi*, several comprised one dark and one light bird and three comprised two dark birds. Observers at the Dutchman Peak Hawk Watch site in sw. Oregon tentatively identified the subspecies of 13 migrating Merlins as follows: nine *F. c. columbarius*, two *F. c. suckleyi*, and two *F. c. richardsonii* "prairie Merlin" (Smith 2000). Another unusual report of *F. c. richardsonii* comes from near the town of Merlin in Josephine Co., 28 Jan 2001 (D. Vroman p.c.). A specimen (USNM) forming the basis for Gabrielson and Jewett (1940) listing *richardsonii* on their hypothetical list was reidentified as *columbarius* by S. A. Temple (Browning 1974); sightings of *richardsonii* probably are the nominate subspecies (S. A. Temple p.c., *MRB*). Positive identification of *F. c. richardsonii* in Oregon requires specimens.

There are no confirmed breeding records for Oregon from recent decades, but regular reports of Merlins in summer (Jun-Jul) from the 1970s, 1980s, and 1990s, including at least 33 sighting reports during the 1995-99 OBBA effort (Gilligan et al. 1994, OBBA, D. Fenske p.c.). Breeding-season reports come from throughout most of w. and e. Oregon, with the exception of sc. and se. Oregon. Particular areas of concentrations of summer reports over the past few decades include the central high Cascades and Douglas Co. Several observations in e. Oregon strongly indicate breeding. On 19 and 21 Jun and 24 Jul 2001, Mike and MerryLynn Denny (p.c.) observed a Merlin apparently hunting at the southern body of Twin Lakes, near the Wallowa/Baker Co. border, then later in the day on 24 Jul approximately 3 mi (2 km) east and 1 mi (0.8 km) south (along Buck Crossing Trail in Baker Co.) they saw a pair of adult Merlins, one of which was carrying a stick and being followed by the other. Lastly, on 10–11 Jul 1998, a bird was reported to be on territory near Potamus Point, Morrow Co. (Spencer 1999). In w. Oregon, the strongest recent evidence of possible breeding is a pair of Merlins seen Jun 1997 and later a family group of five seen Jul-Oct at a decadent cottonwood grove along the Middle Fork Willamette R. near Pleasant Hill, Lane Co.; this grove was damaged by wind during the winter of 1997-98 and only single birds were subsequently seen near the grove during the breeding season 1998-2000; they were not seen in 2001 (D. Allen p.c.).

Merlins are more common in Oregon in migration and winter; though still uncommon at best. Unusually high counts for inland areas were reported from three CBCs: three birds Jan 1988 on the Hood River CBC; six birds Dec 1997 on the Sauvie I. CBC in Multnomah Co.; four birds Dec 1997 on the Dallas CBC in Polk Co. (Anderson 1988c, Tice 1998a). It was considered a strong showing for the area when at least four individuals spent the winter in Klamath and Lake counties (two in each) in 1978 (Summers 1978). Coastal CBCs often tally as many as six or seven individuals, with Coquille Valley CBC averaging 3.8, Coos Bay CBC 3.0, Tillamook CBC 2.4 (CBC data).

**Habitat and Diet:** In winter, can be found throughout the state in open or semi-open habitats, but most regular near major estuaries, lakes, reservoirs, and occasionally in cities where food supplies are reliable (Contreras 1997b).

For nesting, Merlins use old crow, raven, hawk, or magpie nests, tree cavities, or cliff ledges. In w. Washington, they seem to prefer "waterfront property" and nest near lakes, rivers, and along Puget Sound, perhaps because these areas provide breaks in otherwise continuous forest and/or because prey species are more abundant (T. Gleason p.c.). In Washington, up to 13 nests and an additional five territorial pairs of *F. c. suckleyi* were found in the 1980s and 1990s in Skagit, Snohomish, Clallam, Grays Harbor, San Juan, and Jefferson counties (Smith et al. 1997, T. Gleason p.c.). Of nine nests monitored in the late 1990s, all were in old corvid nests and eight were in Douglas-fir or western hemlock trees with diameters ranging from 24 in (61 cm) to 13 ft (4 m) (T. Gleason p.c.).

They hunt a variety of small to medium-sized birds, usually specializing in one or two locally abundant species; also will feed to a lesser extent on large flying insects, such as dragonflies, and small mammals and reptiles (Sodhi et al. 1993). Dunlins are an important food item in winter in Washington; of 111 hunting flights observed at estuarine sites Nov-Mar 1979-85 and 51 hunting flights observed over beach habitat Nov-Feb 1983-90 and Nov-Mar 1993-94, all were directed at Dunlin flocks (Buchanan 1996, Buchanan 1988b, Buchanan et al. 1988). *F. c. suckleyi* were reported on several occasions hunting House Sparrows and harassing pigeons in the cities of Portland and Seattle, and successfully capturing pigeons in Eugene (Gabrielson and Jewett 1940, Jewett et al. 1953, D. Irons p.c.).

**Seasonal Activity and Behavior:** *F. c. suckleyi* is considered mostly sedentary, *F. c. columbarius* mostly migratory.

Spring migrants noted 17 Mar to 3 Apr in the w. Cascades of e. Douglas Co. (Fix 1990a). Spring migrants are typically gone by the end of Apr, but reports of birds through mid-May do occur (Heinl 1986c, 1987a, Gilligan et al. 1994). In Oregon, reports of a pair of Merlins, a territorial bird, and a bird carrying food were noted Jun-Jul during the OBBA effort. Rangewide, eggs typically in May and young in Jun (Sodhi et al. 1993).

Fall migrants begin appearing in early Sep, rarely late Aug (Gilligan et al. 1994). Early arrivals in w. Oregon include 20 Aug 1989 at Newport, 23 Aug 1987 at Roxy Ann Butte, Jackson Co., and 30 Aug 1987 in Ashland (Heinl 1988a, Fix and Heinl 1990). Sixty-five migrating Merlins were tallied in 2000 at the Bonney Butte HawkWatch site southeast of Mt. Hood (Smith 2001). Birds were first observed 7 Sep and last observed 24 Oct with the bulk of passage between 20 Sept and 22 Oct. Mean annual count of Merlins 1994-2000 at Bonney Butte is 66 (range 36-104). At Dutchman Peak HawkWatch site near Medford 29 and 53 birds were tallied in 1997 and 1998 respectively (Smith 2000). In 1998 at this site, Merlins were first observed 22 Sep and last observed 2 Nov, with bulk of passage between 30 Sep and 29 Oct.

**Detection:** Very difficult to locate nests. Tom Gleason (p.c.) spent 5 yr and many hours of patient searching and watching to find just eight nests in w.

Washington. More abundant in winter and tend to be easier to see as they occupy more habitats than are used for breeding. Can be confused by sight with Peregrine Falcon, American Kestrel, Cooper's Hawk, or Sharp-shinned Hawk, and even pigeons, especially at a distance. Usually silent except around immediate vicinity of nest.

**Population Status and Conservation:** Oregon is at the edge of the species' breeding range, therefore the number of breeding pairs in the state, if any at present, has always been small and variable. No Merlin nests have been confirmed in Oregon since the late 1800s (Gabrielson and Jewett 1940, Gilligan et al. 1994), though at least five possible nests have been observed in recent decades: a cavity in a large snag along the Smith R. near Reedsport in the early 1960s; an adult carrying a small bird entered a tree cavity in a snag near Keno, Klamath Co., in 1970; a tree cavity near Cottage Grove in 1972; a tree cavity west of Roseburg in 1988 or 1989; and a stick nest on the upper Metolius plus perhaps a second in a tree cavity in the same area (no date; D. Fenske p.c.). BBS trends 1966-2000 throughout the U.S. and Canada, in the w. BBS region, and in the British Columbia, California, Oregon, and Washington region are all increasing (BBS). Thus, Merlins could be confirmed breeders in Oregon in the near future.

Analysis of CBC data for the Northwest region (British Columbia, Washington, Oregon) shows short-term (1961-84) and long-term (1946-85) increasing population trends (Buchanan 1988a).

As with the Peregrine Falcon, DDT use was associated with eggshell thinning in the Merlin, and studies in the 1960s in the Great Plains and Canada documented a 30% decline in Merlin reproductive success when compared to pre-1950 data (Sodhi et al. 1993). Though most Merlin populations are currently thought to be reproducing well, a study of eggs collected 1980-88 in the Canadian prairie provinces showed that 35.7% of the eggs still contained levels of DDE likely to negatively affect reproductive success (Noble and Elliot 1990). No Merlin eggs have been tested in Oregon or Washington, but eggshells from some Peregrine Falcon nests in the region still contain levels of DDE that warrant concern (J. Pagel p.c.). Organochlorine contaminants, including high levels of DDE, were found in shorebirds in w. Washington during winter and spring sampling 1975-81 (Schick et al. 1987). Dunlins, an important Merlin food item, were among those tested.

Of the nine nests monitored by Tom Gleason in w. Washington in the 1990s, adults at two nests were shot and an additional two nest trees were cut down by landowners. All nine nests were on private land and many were near homes in low-density waterfront neighborhoods with mature conifer trees.—*Kelly A. Bettinger*

## Gyrfalcon *Falco rusticolus*

This large powerful falcon is a circumpolar breeder. In N. America it breeds in the high Canadian Arctic and Alaska. Most breeding birds are permanent residents where possible (Palmer 1988), but many disperse southward in winter through Canada and into the n. U.S. Oregon is at the southern edge of its normal winter range. The majority of Gyrfalcons seen in Oregon are immatures or adults of the "gray" type, but there are several reports of "white" birds. The Gyrfalcon is a regular winter visitant to Oregon, usually with fewer than five reports per year. Reported sightings have been increasing in recent years, probably owing to better coverage rather than an increase in birds. Have been reported from Oregon from late Sep to late Apr, usually as single individuals. Two were photographed together at Wickiup Res., Deschutes Co., 5 Dec 1987 (Miller and Crabtree 1989). Photographs were taken of an adult near Joseph during the winter of 1994-95 (Schmidt 1995), of a brown immature at Finley NWR during the winter of 1994-95 (*Oregon Birds* 21[3]: cover and p. 99), and in Wallowa Co. on 20 Jan 2002 (*Oregon Birds* 28[2]:58). The majority of sightings come from coastal and Willamette Valley lowlands near waterfowl concentrations. Individuals have been seen chasing and feeding on geese, ducks, and gulls. "Gyrs" forage by flying low over the ground flushing prey, then often giving spectacular tail chases. If a bird refuses to flush the hunt is usually unsuccessful. East of the Cascades, occurs around open meadowlands and prairies, as well as about waterfowl concentrations. No information available on prey species in these areas. There is often interaction among this species and other birds of prey, but it is seldom seriously aggressive. Although Gabrielson and Jewett (1940) and AOU (1957) recognized *F. r. obsoletus*, the species is monotypic (Vaurie 1961).—*Harry B. Nehls*

## Peregrine Falcon *Falco peregrinus*

"The most efficient flying machine, the best-designed bird, the fiercest and fastest bird—all these superlatives have been claimed for the Peregrine," noted Roger Tory Peterson (1988). Peregrine Falcons are among the most charismatic and noted of the world's birds. They are described as the fastest animal on the planet, and have been recorded reaching speeds in excess of 240 mi/hr (380 km/hr) in dives after prey. They are one of Oregon's boldest raptors, and have been observed usurping active Golden Eagle nest sites, stealing fish from Ospreys and ground squirrels from Red-tailed Hawks, as well as regularly driving away adult Bald Eagles who stray into their territories (*JEP*). Has, for perhaps 4,000 yr, been used by falconers because of its skill in capturing game birds in tandem hunts with humans.

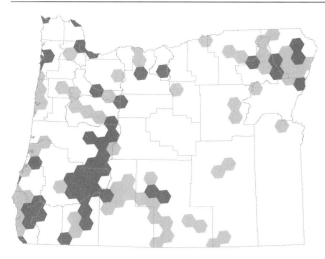

Peregrines are medium-sized raptors, and share characteristics with all falcons: bill conspicuously toothed and notched, presence of a nasal cone, and pointed wings for swift flight. The male (tiercel) is about one-third smaller than the female; the male is about the size of an American Crow, while the female is nearly as large as a Common Raven. Their plumage allows them to be extremely cryptic when perched in trees or on cliffs. In the Pacific Northwest, there are four gradations of breast plumage in adults, ranging from bright white to deep, rich, reddish-chocolate/black (*JEP*). Upper wing coverts, back, and tail feathers in adults can range from black to a dark gray. Juvenal plumage is darker than the adults' in overall appearance, with a chestnut-colored, vertically striated breast and a distinct brownish tinge in all plumages. In level flight, peregrines have a short, choppy wing-beat; however they regularly use thermals and updrafts at cliffs to gain altitude when hunting, playing (juveniles), and when nest site protection is critical. Their pointy, swept-back wing silhouette is an often-used field characteristic.

Because of organochlorine contaminants, peregrines were extirpated throughout much of their range. Following the banning of DDT in the U.S. in 1972 (with a single exception made in the Blue Mtns. of Oregon, Washington, and Idaho in 1974 [Henny 1977a]) and subsequent protective actions at nest sites by state and federal agencies, populations have increased throughout Oregon and N. America.

The most widespread peregrine subspecies in N. America, *F. p. anatum*, was referred to as the "Duck Hawk" prior to publication of the 1957 AOU checklist. *P. p. pealei* was referred to as "Peale's Falcon" (AOU 1931).

**General Distribution:** Breed on every continent except Antarctica. They use or pass through all terrestrial ecosystems and nearby waters. In N. America, breed from the Arctic coast south to s. Baja California, the coast of Sonora, s. Arizona, New Mexico, and Texas and the highlands of Mexico. Formerly extirpated east of the Mississippi R. in the U.S., but reintroduced to much of their historic range in s. Canada and the U.S. Worldwide 19 subspecies recognized by White and Boyce (1988), of which three occur in N. America and Oregon. While the AOU no longer recognizes English names for subspecies, the three subspecies are sometimes referred to by English names. The migratory, light-colored Arctic Peregrine Falcon (*F. p. tundrius*) breeds north of the tree line. At the edge of its range, it intergrades clinally with the slightly larger American Peregrine Falcon (*F. p. anatum*), which has a very large breeding range extending from the northern tree line south into Mexico with the exception of the perimeter of the Gulf of Alaska from the Aleutian Is. south into Washington. The latter area is occupied by the largely resident coastal Peale's Peregrine Falcon (*F. p. pealei*) (Jewett et al. 1953, AOU 1957).

**Oregon Distribution:** In Oregon, peregrines occur as resident and migratory populations. *F. p. anatum* is a regular breeder and uncommon migrant. They nest on cliffs >75 ft (23 m) in height, and within 1 mi (1.6 km) of some form of water (*JEP*). Nesting occurs in xeric areas of e. Oregon, marine habitats of w. Oregon, montane habitats that extend to over 6,000 ft (1,800

*Peregrine Falcon*

m) elevation, small riparian corridors statewide, and more recently in urban habitats of the lower Willamette and Columbia rivers.

Evidence of *anatum* migration through Oregon includes two nestlings banded on the Yukon R. and Charley R. (a Yukon R. tributary) in Alaska, which were subsequently found on 20 Nov and 1 Apr in San Jose and Long Beach, California, respectively (Anderson et al. 1988).

Historically, *pealei* was first noted through collected specimens to be an uncommon but regular migrant and winter resident along the Oregon coast (Gabrielson and Jewett 1940). Although no banded *pealei* have been reported in Oregon, three banded as nestlings along the n. coast of British Columbia were recovered in coastal California at Point Reyes, Santa Cruz, and San Diego (Anderson et al. 1988). Those recoveries and numerous reports by *JEP* and birders (as frequently reported in *Oregon Birds*) suggest that *pealei* may continue to move through Oregon. A breeding individual was recently observed on Oregon's n. coast that exhibited characteristics of *pealei* (*JEP*). Jewett et al. (1953) list *pealei* as nesting the entire length of the Washington coast. Hayes and Buchanan (2002) indicate that both *anatum* and *pealei* are represented by peregrines nesting on the Washington coast. Thus, the possibility exists that *pealei* has nested in Oregon, but a bird in hand would be required for confirmation.

Evidence of *F. p. tundrius* movements through Oregon include a nestling banded along the Colville R., Alaska, that was recovered in the Willamette Valley near Monmouth 21 Oct 1986; another, banded on the Colville R., was found dead on San Miguel I., California (Anderson et al. 1988). In recent years, birds showing characteristics of *tundrius* have been regularly reported in the fall and spring in the Klamath Basin (*JEP*). Nevertheless, it is difficult to determine the frequency at which *tundrius* moves through Oregon because *anatum* and *tundrius* are difficult to separate in the field. The recent recognition of *tundrius* as being distinct from *anatum* (White 1968) explains the absence of early Oregon records.

**Habitat and Diet:** The Peregrine Falcon has adapted to a wide range of prey and nesting locations. As suggested by Beebe (1976), the common threads of habitat of the peregrine are so variable that even the most carefully recorded accounts can be contradictory. By making 750 entrees to 150 nest cliffs that contained 180 nest ledges in the Pacific Northwest (n. California, Oregon, and Washington) during 1983-2001, *JEP* was able to characterize nesting sites in the area. In Oregon, currently nest on cliffs ranging in height from a 75 ft (23 m) escarpment at a reclaimed quarry to monolithic 1,500-ft (457-m) high cliffs, as well as on structural features of bridges. Average occupied cliff size in the Cascade Mtns. is 229 ft (70 m), and in the Siskiyou

Mtns. of Oregon and n. California 135 ft (41 m).

Cliff nests are on ledges and potholes with and without protective overhangs. Stick nests originally constructed by Common Ravens, Golden Eagles and Red-tailed Hawks were recorded at five Oregon locations. At some nest sites, a clear preference was shown for the same nest ledge in successive years, whereas at other locations resident pairs have selected different nest ledges each year. Smallest nest ledge was 6 in (15 cm) deep by 12 in (30 cm) wide; the largest was 22 ft (6.7 m) wide and 9 ft (2.7 m) deep. Ledges are usually located within 40-80% of total cliff height.

From 1983 to 1998, 92 prey species have been identified at Pacific Northwest nest sites (*JEP*). Rock Doves (domestic racing and feral pigeons), starlings, and gulls are major prey items at many Oregon sites. Avian prey ranged in size from hummingbirds to Western Gulls; adult Aleutian Canada geese have also been killed and eaten in at least two instances in coastal areas (Stabins 1995, D. Pitkin p.c.). Doves/pigeons, sandpipers, and starlings are strongly represented. Examples from other families show the wide range of birds consumed during the nesting season: Green Heron, Cooper's Hawk, Northern Goshawk, American Kestrel, Pigeon Guillemot, Marbled Murrelet, Northern Pygmy-Owl, Spotted Owl, Black Swift, Hairy Woodpecker, Clark's Nutcracker, Common Raven, Hermit Thrush, Cedar Waxwing, and Western Tanager (Henny and Nelson 1981, D. Pitkin and J. Schmitt p.c.s, *JEP*). Mammal prey included at least two species of bats, California ground squirrel, gray squirrel, chipmunks, and mountain beaver (J. Schmitt p.c., *JEP*). From other groups were one species of lizard, two species of fish (derived through kleptoparasitism from Osprey) and at least four species of insects (*JEP*).

Adults and subadults flying or sallying through mayfly hatches to catch individual insects in their talons have been documented (*JEP*). D. Davis (p.c.) observed juvenile peregrines flushing grasshoppers, which they took with their feet over a meadow. Not all prey is caught on the wing; D. Pitkin (p.c.) has twice observed peregrines scavenging beached seabird remains during winter.

Hundreds of racing pigeon bands found deep in the detritus of active nest scrapes, including one from 1937 (Willamette NF) and another from 1942 (Klamath NF), suggest that many currently active sites were used historically (*JEP*). The 1937 pigeon was used by a forest fire lookout within several miles of the nest to send messages to the district office (K. Byford p.c.).

**Seasonal Activity and Behavior:** Adults remain in the vicinity of nest sites throughout the year at Pacific Northwest locales below approximately 4,000 ft (1,200 m) elevation (*JEP*). Flight displays associated with courtship include spectacular chases and aerobatics

(Beebe 1976). At lower-elevation Pacific Northwest sites, clutches are usually complete by mid-Mar to mid-Apr, but may vary at any single site up to 6 wk annually (*JEP*). Usual clutch size is 2-4 eggs laid at about 2-day intervals; incubation is shared, but done mainly by the female (Palmer 1988). In Oregon, eggs are incubated for 31-33 days, during which time the male usually brings food to the female. Normal departure from the nest (first flight) is at 37-54 days (Sherrod 1979, Palmer 1988). Fledging occurs late May through mid-Aug, but this is dependent on chronology dictated usually by site elevation and weather patterns (*JEP*). Upper-elevation nest sites show high levels of asynchronous hatching within clutches. Due to the high variability, clutches at these sites may not be completed until mid- to late May, and fledging can extend to mid-Aug (*JEP*).

**Detection:** Not commonly observed during breeding season because numbers are low and most cliff habitats are remote and difficult to access. Regularly seen during winter on the lower Columbia R., along the Oregon coast, and at anytime of year in urban Portland. Cape Meares, Tillamook Co., has a well-known eyrie that can be readily seen.

**Population Status and Conservation:** The history of Oregon breeding populations prior to their decline and near loss in the mid-1900s unfortunately is little known. In the late 1800s, were reported breeding at Malheur L. (Bendire 1877) and resident at Ft. Klamath (Merrill 1888). Anthony (in Woodcock 1902) stated that a few were seen along the river below Portland. Bretherton (in Woodcock 1902) also referred to the species as a common breeding resident at Cape Foulweather near Newport. In the early 1900s, Gabrielson and Jewett (1940) considered them relatively rare in Oregon, and reported knowing only one nesting pair since 1920 (in Lake Co.). However, several active nest sites were known in the 1930s and early 1940s (*DBM*). Nelson (1969) reported that R. M. Bond knew of 13 pairs historically nesting along the Columbia R., primarily in the Gorge. Bond (1946) believed that the actual number of breeding pairs in the western contiguous U.S. was more than twice the numbers known.

Unprecedented declines throughout much of the N. Hemisphere became apparent at the Madison Peregrine Falcon Conference in 1965 (Hickey 1969). Ratcliffe (1967) showed a significant decrease in eggshell weight of peregrines in Britain beginning in 1947 or 1948 and reported breakage of eggs. Hickey and Anderson (1968) demonstrated the same finding in N. America. Then the relationship between eggshell thickness and DDE (a metabolite of DDT) in eggs was established for peregrines in Alaska (Cade et al. 1971, Peakall et al. 1975).

The population decline in Oregon appears to have paralleled the decline at other N. American locations. Although comprehensive surveys were not conducted, there were few known occupied peregrine eyries in Oregon after the 1950s (Henny and Nelson 1981). In 1978 and 1979, Henny and Nelson (1981) searched Oregon for occupied sites and reported a site on the Crater L. caldera where a geodetic survey team had found an active nest. In reconstructing historic information, they conservatively reported 42 nesting sites with 18 in coastal and w. Oregon, 19 in the Cascade Mtns. and e. Oregon, and five along the Columbia R. within both Oregon and Washington. D. Fenske (p.c.) interviewed oologists and falconers between 1966 and 1985 to reconstruct historic nesting information and concluded there were at least 90 confirmed historic nest sites in Oregon. Many have yet to be reoccupied.

Following the 1972 ban on DDT and later bans on several other persistent insecticides, numbers increased in Oregon. Walton et al. (1988) reported two pairs breeding in se. Oregon and four other pairs in the state in 1986. By 1994, Enderson et al. (1995) tallied 37 pairs from various sources. In 1999, from 80 known sites surveyed, 54 active pairs were reported to have fledged 72 young, but 18 of the 54 pairs failed in their nesting attempts (data from *JEP* on file at ODFW, Portland). While a population increase is unquestionable, the increase in the number of known nests was in large part due to refined nest-survey techniques (Pagel 1992), which broadened the type of cliffs to be searched and standardized the ground techniques, and great increases in survey efforts by many agencies and individuals. Approximately 20% of 96 Oregon nest sites identified as having been used at least once 1975-2001 were at historic locations identified by D. Fenske (*JEP*). Eggshells collected from wild nests throughout Oregon during 1986-98 and measured by Sam Sumida at the Western Foundation for Vertebrate Zoology still showed significant thinning (eggshells collected since 1998 have not been measured).

Beginning in the mid-1970s, state and federal agencies and private organizations conducted programs to locate, monitor, study, and assist peregrines in Oregon and elsewhere in N. America. The first direct nest-site intervention was the 1981 replacement of three wild-layed eggs that failed to hatch with two captive-reared chicks at Crater L. by Lee Aulman of the Santa Cruz Predatory Bird Research Group. During 1981-90, 96 captive-reared peregrine chicks were released by hacking or other nest manipulations in Oregon (Haight 1992). Similar programs occurred in adjacent states during this period. During 1991-95 (the last year of release), another 83 captive-reared chicks were released in Oregon (Peregrine Fund files). Some from private breeders may not have been pure

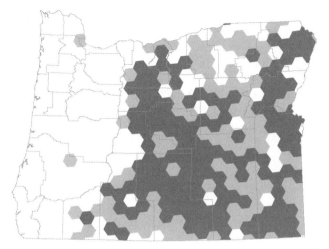

*anatum* stock. To date however, only one bird at Cape Meares and another on the Fremont NF were positively identified to originate from a hack site, as indicated by a USFWS color band (*JEP*). Oregon wild productivity 1975-2000 was just over 500 birds, with the most productive nests at scattered sites throughout the n. Cascades, and an artificial site on the Lower Columbia R. (*JEP*).

Both *anatum* and *tundrius* were listed under the Endangered Species Conservation Act of 1969, and subsequently transferred to the protection of the Endangered Species Act of 1973. *F. p. pealei* was later protected by the Act's similarity-of-appearance clause [16 U.S.C. 1533:4(e)]. *F. p. tundrius* was federally delisted in 1994, and *anatum* was federally delisted in 1999 despite concerns (*Federal Register* 64:46541-46558, Pagel et al. 1996, Cade et al. 1997, Pagel et al. 1997, 1998, Doremus and Pagel 2001). At this time, the peregrine is still state listed as endangered in Oregon but is subject to reclassification (M. Nugent p.c.).

The peregrine population's resurgence throughout the Pacific Northwest and the world has been nothing less than remarkable. Work to increase the population included countless hours of collaborative effort by birders, conservationists, falconers, rock climbers, as well as federal and state employees. In Oregon, work by state, federal, and private entities to enhance nest sites, protect habitat around known sites, and exhaustive work to monitor the birds has resulted in a better ecological understanding of its current status. However, sustained and continued vigilance is required, and further research is needed.—*Charles J. Henny and Joel E. Pagel*

## Prairie Falcon *Falco mexicanus*

One of the most impressive sights in the unforested regions east of the Cascades is a Prairie Falcon strafing a Belding's ground squirrel colony repeatedly at full speed in hopes of catching one emerging from its burrow at just the wrong moment. Prairie Falcons are most common in rimrock country, where they nest, but may travel great distances in search of prey. Large falcons, sandy brown above and off-white with variable amounts of streaking below. The face has a vertical stripe below the eye, as do many falcons. In flight, the long, pointed wings and long tail identify it as a falcon, and the dark axillars at the base of the underwing identify it as a Prairie Falcon. The shallow, flat wing-beats also help distinguish it from the Peregrine Falcon. The female (1.8 lbs [801 g]) is noticeably larger than the male (1.1 lbs [496 g]) (Snyder and Wiley 1976).

**General Distribution:** Breeds from c. British Columbia east to N. Dakota; south to Baja California and Texas. Winters over much of its breeding range south into Mexico. Band returns suggest a general movement southeast towards the s. Great Plains in fall (Enderson 1964). Monotypic (AOU 1957).

**Oregon Distribution:** Breeds throughout the open country east of the Cascades wherever cliffs and outcrops provide opportunities for nesting (*SWJ*). Breeding densities of 3.9-8.0 pairs/100 mi² (1.5-3.1 pairs/100 km²) are typical in the rimrock country of Wasco and Wheeler counties (Janes 1975). Lardy (1980) found higher average densities in Malheur Co. (9.8-14.0/100 mi² [3.8-5.4 pairs/100 km²], and in the area of greatest density, he recorded 168 pairs/100 mi² [65 pairs/100 km²]). In the Blue Mtns., a few long-standing pairs nest above 5,400 ft (1,650 m) on exposed andesite cliffs surrounded by dense mixed-conifer forest, but within easy foraging flight of lithosol openings and natural meadows (M. Denny p.c.). West of the Cascades, breeding has been documented at two locations in Jackson Co. (J. Harper p.c.).

May be found throughout their breeding range in winter though in reduced numbers. Rare fall and winter visitors to open areas of interior w. Oregon (Gilligan et al. 1994). For at least two decades, they have wintered almost annually in nc. Lane Co. and sc. Linn Co., sw. of Brownsville (D. Irons p.c.). Interestingly, long-time falcon watchers in the Willamette Valley report only females there (D. Fenske p.c., D. Fix p.c.). In Jackson Co., more regular and are considered uncommon in winter (Browning 1975a, *SWJ*). Casual on the coast (Dillingham et al. 1994, Gilligan et al. 1994, Contreras 1998).

**Habitat and Diet:** A combination of rimrock or other outcrops and adjacent open country provides ideal breeding habitat. Cliffs need not be large: Denton (1976) found 59% of nests on cliffs less than 100 ft (30 m) in height, some as low as 15 ft (5 m). They have even been known to nest below ground level among cracks and entrances to caves in recent lava flows (Haak and Denton 1979), but almost always nest on cliffs, usually in recesses and potholes. They do not build a nest of their own but use natural depressions and old nests of other birds, most often those of the Common Raven. The principal requirement is that the nest site be sheltered from above (Bent 1938, Webster 1976); this appears to reflect a need for shade (Webster 1976) and possibly protection from predators. They defend only the area in the immediate vicinity of the nest (0.25 mi [0.4 km] radius) (Haak 1982a), but have a huge home range for a raptor of moderate size. Home ranges for three radio-tagged males ranged 13-150 mi² (34-389 km²) with a mean of 88 mi² (228 km²) (Haak 1982a). Grasslands are the preferred habitat although they also occur in less-productive areas dominated by sagebrush. They may be especially common around irrigated hayfields where ground squirrels are abundant. The principal requirement for foraging appears to be low and sparse vegetation that accommodates their foraging style. Prey most often consists of small mammals, usually ground squirrels (Denton 1976, Haak 1982b). Also prey upon birds, especially in winter, including Western Meadowlarks, Horned Larks, and Northern Flickers (Steenhof 1998).

**Seasonal Activity and Behavior:** Prairie Falcons appear at their nesting sites in Oregon by late Mar. Mean date for initiation of incubation is approximately 16-24 Apr, for hatching about 20 May, and for fledging 24-26 Jun (Denton 1976, Haak 1982b). The female incubates at night and during 82% of the day (Steenhof 1998). Denton (1976) and Haak (1982b) observed mean clutch sizes of 3.3 and 4.0 and mean number of young fledged/active nest of between 2.3 and 2.5. Ten nesting attempts over a 4-yr period in se. Wasco Co. produced an average of 3.7 young/pair (Janes 1975). Begin departing from the breeding area as soon as prey becomes difficult to find; this usually coincides with the onset of aestivation of ground squirrels in Jul. At this time, Prairie Falcon numbers increase at higher elevations as they follow spring up into the mountains. Even frequent meadows above timberline in the Cascades in late summer.

Their favored mode of hunting is a low course where the bird drops low from a perch and flies directly at its intended victim from just above the vegetation (mean attack distance of 1,390 ft [424 m]) (Haak 1982a). Radio-tagged birds in the Klamath Basin traveled an average of 4.5 mi (7.2 km) from nests to forage (Haak 1982a). Haak observed that one out of every three attempts resulted in a capture. Occasionally Red-tailed Hawks displace Prairie Falcons from kills (Haak 1982a). Great Horned Owls sometimes prey upon Prairie Falcons (McFadden and Marzluff 1996, *SWJ*).

**Detection:** Because of low density and wide-ranging habits, Prairie Falcons can be difficult to locate. Utility poles located near irrigated hayfields may provide the best opportunity. Nests can often be located by scanning cliffs for whitewash streaks (droppings) below recesses. Birds can be encountered almost anywhere east of the Cascades. The Fort Rock Basin, Christmas Valley, and the Klamath Basin offer some of the more dependable viewing opportunities.

**Population Status and Conservation:** Fortunately Prairie Falcons tend to feed lower on the food chain than their relative, the Peregrine Falcon. Ground squirrels and other herbivorous rodents do not carry concentrations of pesticides as high as those found in the avian prey of Peregrine Falcons. Consequently, Prairie Falcons did not experience the reproductive failure that impacted the peregrine 1950-70 as a result of the accumulation of DDT and its metabolites in its tissues. Still, as predators, they tend to be more sensitive than other animals to chemicals in the environment. Populations, including those in Oregon, appear to be stable (White 1994).—*Stewart W. Janes*

# Order GALLIFORMES
## *Family Phasianidae*

### Subfamily Phasianinae

**Chukar** *Alectoris chukar*
Standing atop rocky spires and cackling frequently, Chukars entertain campers and boaters along many remote byways in e. Oregon, especially during spring and summer. These same cackles become taunting laughter in the fall as they echo from canyons during the hunting season and dare hunters to test their boots, endurance, and dogs against the steep and rocky terrain Chukars call home. Coloration is gray with 8-13 prominent black and white flank bars per side, dark eyestripes, and a white throat encircled by a black necklace. Red legs, eyelids, and beak starkly contrast with the nondescript plumage. They are ground-loving birds that quickly run uphill or burst from cover with

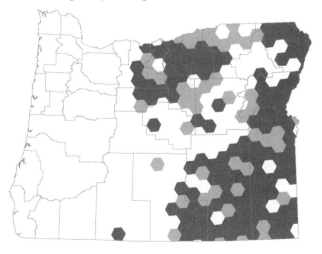

rapid wing-beats and a characteristic *whitoo* call if alarmed. Introduced (1930-70) by managers wishing to increase hunting opportunities in arid w. N. America, the Chukar is a very successful exotic species that occupies habitats where few other gamebirds exist. It is the most-harvested upland bird in Oregon and Nevada with over 20 million birds taken in N. America since 1950 (Christensen 1996).

**General Distribution:** Native in Eurasia from se. Europe to Manchuria, n. China and w. Himalayas; introduced widely and established from s. British Columbia to California, Idaho, Montana, Wyoming, Colorado, New Mexico (Christensen 1996) and Hawaii (AOU 1998). Numerous subspecies. Long (1981) reported that at least some of those released in e. Oregon are known to have been *A. c. chukar*. Birds in adjoining Nevada were identified by Christensen (1970) as *A. c. chukar*, who remarked that other subspecies may have been introduced. Specimens are needed to confirm subspecies identifications.

**Oregon Distribution:** Common permanent resident of e. Oregon. Populations are distributed in steppe habitats along the breaks of the Columbia, John Day, Snake, Owyhee, Deschutes, Malheur, Burnt, and Grande Ronde rivers, and lesser watercourses or reservoirs. Found throughout other suitable areas including Steens, Hart, and Trout Cr. mountains, Abert Rim and Succor Cr. Canyon.

**Habitat and Diet:** Suitable habitat is variegated topography with a mix of annual grass, bunchgrass, rock, and shrub cover types in close proximity to each other and with permanent water sources nearby. Dominant shrubs in these areas include sagebrush, bitterbrush, rabbitbrush, and others with similar structure. Major grasses are the native bluebunch wheatgrass, Idaho fescue, Sandberg's bluegrass, and the exotic cheatgrass. Other habitats may include scattered western juniper or saltbrush components. Details of habitat use have not been well investigated, but recent radiotelemetry projects suggest selection of rocky areas for escape cover and loafing as well as a preference for southeast slopes for nesting and foraging (Lindbloom 1998, Walter 2000). Nests primarily under rocks and in bunchgrasses (Lindbloom 1998, Walter 2000). Broods used shrub cover types more than adults and steep slopes less than adults in Oregon (Walter 2000). Summer distribution is closely linked to water availability (*HW*). Mean spring-summer 90% minimum convex polygon home range of adults in Succor Cr. SP was 44-62 ac (18-25 ha) (Walter 2000). During winter Chukars use snow-free slopes or lower-elevation valleys.

The success of Chukar introductions has probably been aided by their opportunistic foraging habits. A total of 72 diet items, including seeds, leaves, forbs, arthropods, and grit were found in an Oregon sample of 140 crops (Walter 2000). New-growth leaf-blades and mature seeds of cheatgrass are a major food during all seasons (Galbreath and Moreland 1953, Weaver and Haskell 1967, Christensen 1970, Knight et al. 1979). Cheatgrass, subterranean bulbils of prairie starflower, sagebrush galls, and fiddleneck are important in Oregon (Walter 2000). Insects are seasonally important to adults, but diet of chicks may consist largely of insects (Harper et al. 1958). Much temporal and spatial variation in habitat use and diet likely is attributable to climate and phenological responses of plants (*HW*). Additional investigations are required to determine productivity and density in various habitats to identify potential threats to suitable habitat and beneficial management options.

**Seasonal Activity and Behavior:** Coveys break up in spring and spacing occurs. Site fidelity by males has been observed, but whether this is territoriality or mate guarding is unclear (*HW*). Pairing starts early to mid-Mar and nesting begins early to mid-Apr. (*HW*). Mean clutch size 13 in Oregon (Walter 2000). Incubation lasts approximately 24 days (*HW*). Nest success averaged 50% in e. Oregon during 1997-98 (Walter 2000). The Chukar is an avid renester if the nest is destroyed, regardless of the stage of incubation. Hatching occurs late May to Aug. Precocial chicks are capable of flight at 10-15 days. The female tends the brood for the first 4-8 wk, after which mixed coveys occur. Cold, wet weather may delay or adversely affect nesting or brood survival. Mean spring-summer daily movement was 925 ft (282 m) (Walter 2000). Mixed coveys occur in late summer through fall. Larger coveys (10-50) occur in winter.

**Detection:** Chukars can be observed year-round, but are most visible during summer and fall when populations are high. Broods and coveys are often encountered near stock ponds, reservoirs, and along rivers and roads in summer. Nesting and pair spacing decrease observability in spring. Cackles of the rally call can be heard at a distance during spring through fall, frequently in the morning.

**Population Status and Conservation:** Large numbers of Chukars were first released in Oregon in 1952 on the John Day R. (Masson 1954). Over 100,000 birds were subsequently released in many parts of the state 1955-70. Breeding was documented in 1968 (Christensen 1970). Chukars quickly expanded their range and increased in number and are now widespread permanent residents of e. Oregon, although their annual distribution and density fluctuate. No known disease threats to this species. Habitat loss is not a factor because most range is on public lands, but invasive weeds such as yellow starthistle may be detrimental (Lindbloom 1998), as well as replacement of shrub and bunchgrass cover types with large homogeneous expanses of annuals including cheatgrass or medusahead. The timing of temperature and precipitation is probably the most influential factor on survival and reproduction because of its effects on thermal requirements and food availability. Hunting harvests fluctuate, but the risk of overhunting is negligible considering terrain and the species' wide range. Ingested shot pellets were found in approximately 5% of gizzards in Succor Cr. SP, and further investigations in heavily hunted areas are needed (Walter 2000). Further research is required on factors affecting nesting, brood survival, seasonal movements, behavior, and ecosystem interactions.— *Hanspeter Walter*

## Gray Partridge *Perdix perdix*

The Gray Partridge was released in N. America as early as 1790 (Lever 1987) from its native range in Europe and Asia, but it was not until the 1900s that this stocky gamebird became well established in many states and some Canadian provinces. Also called the Hungarian Partridge, and this name is often shortened to "Hun" by hunters. Adults are tawny cinnamon on the head with a prominent buffy brown crown and ear patches. Upperparts are grayish to brownish with dark mottling on the wing region and conspicuous white shaft streaks on the scapulars. The breast is finely vermiculated gray and the abdomen has a prominent chestnut brown horseshoe marking, much more pronounced in males. During spring, males emit the "rusty gate" or *kee-uk* call, especially during early morning and evening. They are often encountered in coveys of 10-20 birds, frequent open areas such as grasslands, meadows, and agricultural fields, and shun forested habitats.

**General Distribution:** Breeds across most of Europe from Ireland and the British Isles to s. Scandinavia south to n. Spain and east from Italy to nw. Iran. Breeding

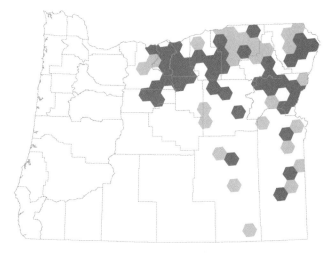

range extends farther east to Mongolia, China, and north to Russia. In N. America, widely established in s. Canada and n. U.S. Small isolated populations occur in New York, Ontario, Quebec, Vermont, Prince Edward I., and Nova Scotia (Johnsgard 1975a, Lever 1987, Carroll 1993). Eight subspecies have been described, at least two of which, *lucida* and *perdix*, were probably introduced to N. America based on source localities (Lever 1987), but current composition of specific N. American populations is unknown.

**Oregon Distribution:** Introduced in the 1900s to w. and e. Oregon; all populations west of the Cascades have failed. The Gray Partridge currently thrives mainly in the valleys of the ne. and Columbia Basin counties (Evanich 1986a). A few still occur in the Malheur-Harney lakes basin; two birds were observed south of Malheur NWR headquarters in 1986 and two near Boca L. in 1987 (Littlefield 1990a). A few are present in c. Malheur Co. around Rome, along the Owyhee R. near Adrian, and north to Vale through Keeney Pass (M. Denny p.c.). Occasionally sighted elsewhere, e.g., nc. Grant Co. (Sullivan 2000a); Haystack Res., Jefferson Co.; and w. Oregon locations, probably from incidental introductions by dog trainers or bird fanciers (*MGH*).

**Habitat and Diet:** Found primarily in and along the margins of cultivated fields, especially wheat, grasslands, meadows, and pastures. They are occasionally found in sagebrush or grasslands several miles from agricultural areas (Evanich 1986a, Gilligan et al. 1994). There are no descriptions of nests in Oregon. Elsewhere, nests consist of a shallow depression on the ground lined with dead herbaceous vegetation and often located in thick grass, alfalfa field, or under a bush (Johnsgard 1975a).

There is no information on diet in Oregon but 20 crops obtained from Okanogan Co., Washington, during a 1-yr period (Sep-Jul) revealed that 14 food items were present but only six amounted to more than 1% of a season's total food volume. Gray Partridges exhibit heavy reliance on grass seeds and leaves (more than 90%). Winter diet (Dec-Feb) comprised primarily (65%) leaves of cheatgrass and fall wheat; seeds of wheat and cheatgrass were also eaten. Other plant species consumed included common Russian thistle (seeds) and fescue grass (leaves) (Knight et al. 1979). Although animal matter was not detected in crops, insects are an important source of protein for chicks elsewhere and this is likely the case in Oregon (*KI*). Succulent leaves of alfalfa, clover, dandelion, and other forbs probably supplement the diet.

**Seasonal Activity and Behavior:** Resident throughout the year. Relatively sedentary, coveys seldom travel more than a quarter of a mile. During spring, coveys break apart and previously paired birds will often remate (Johnsgard 1975a). The rusty-gate call is the unmated male's principal advertisement call. Pair formation is a protracted event and birds often change mates before finally selecting one for the breeding season that starts in late May (Johnsgard 1975a). Clutch size ranges 6-20 eggs with 10 the norm. Incubation lasts 24-25 days; while the female is incubating, male often remains close by. Both parents tend to the precocial chicks (Johnsgard 1975a). In Oregon, parents with chicks observed 15 Jun to 31 Aug (n=4) (OBBA). During fall, coveys form that consist of the breeding pair and their surviving young and additional unsuccessful nesters (Johnsgard 1975a). Two or more family groups may join together to form a social unit that lasts through fall and winter.

**Detection:** Elusive and seldom observed during summer (Evanich 1992a). They are probably best observed during winter months when present in coveys, or late summer/early fall when large broods occasionally cross gravel roads while moving from one agricultural field to another (*KI*). Can be detected by rusty-gate call uttered primarily from late winter to spring, most often in mornings and evenings, just prior to sunrise and after sunset (Carroll 1993).

**Population Status and Conservation:** In 1900, 97 birds were released in Marion Co., west of Salem in the Willamette Valley. In 1913, 218 and in 1914, 1,522 were released in 23 counties, especially Baker, Deschutes, Gilliam, Grant, Jefferson, Klamath, Umatilla, Union, Wallowa, and Wasco. Between 1925 and 1932, 401 additional birds were released, and by 1934, this species was well established over much of the eastern part of the state but only locally elsewhere. A further 1,255 were released in the Willamette Valley 1956-57, and 691 during 1969-76 (Gabrielson and Jewett 1940, Evanich 1986a, Lever 1987). About 1,500 birds were introduced to Jackson Co. 1960-62 and were periodically sighted shortly after release, especially east of Ashland near Pompadour Bluffs. The last sighting at this locale occurred in 1964 (Browning 1975a).

Oregon population numbers are unknown. No conservation problems have been identified in Oregon although highly mechanized agricultural practices may impact populations. They are not globally threatened and estimated to number several million birds; however, numbers have declined markedly in many parts of its native and introduced ranges as a direct result of the intensification of agricultural practices (del Hoyo et al. 1994).—*Kamal Islam*

## Ring-necked Pheasant *Phasianus colchicus*

Oregon hosted the first successful introduction of the Ring-necked Pheasant in N. America. This exotic game bird, released for sport hunting from China, is now widely introduced and distributed throughout N. America. A medium to large bird, both sexes have a long, barred, and pointed tail. Adult males are unmistakable with an iridescent blue-green head, white collar, scarlet facial skin, and rich coppery chestnut underparts. Females are buff overall with prominent chestnut and black mottling, particularly on the upperparts. During spring, males parade in open areas with tail cocked, periodically emitting a harsh *ko-or ok* call, often accompanied by rapid wing-beats. Even the sound of a door slamming or a train whistling can cause several males to crow. Males usually seen in company of a harem of several females. Although more likely to run than fly, will explode into the air if startled producing a distinctive sound from rapid wing-beats. Inhabits open areas such as grasslands, agricultural fields, and brushy areas, and avoids forested habitats.

**General Distribution:** Distributed extensively across Europe and Asia. Introduced widely in the British Isles, continental Europe, W. Indies, S. America, Australia, and New Zealand. Also introduced to the N. American continent (Canada, U.S., and n. Mexico). In the U.S., established populations occur in most states including Hawaii; exceptions are Alaska and the southeastern states (Long 1981, Johnsgard 1986b, Lever 1987, Giudice and Ratti 2001). Of 30 subspecies (AOU 1957), at least three, "Chinese Pheasant," *P. c. torquatus*, "Mongolian Pheasant," *P. c. mongolicus*, and "Sichuan Pheasant," *P. c. strauchi*—and plus many birds with apparently mixed parentage—have been introduced to Oregon (Evanich 1986a, E. V. Rickerson p.c.).

**Oregon Distribution:** Generally rare and local along the coast; most regular along the s. Oregon coast, but still encountered on < 25% of field trips (Brown et al. 1996). Most abundant in the agricultural regions of

e. Oregon (Evanich 1986a, Gilligan et al. 1994), and suburban sprawl (D. Fix p.c.). Numbers have greatly declined in the Willamette Valley in recent decades due primarily to changes in agricultural practices (Evanich 1986a, Haensly et al. 1987, Gilligan et al. 1994). Its stronghold continues to be the agricultural areas of n. Malheur Co., the "wheat belt" counties along the Columbia R. in c. Oregon, and the foothill regions of the Blue Mtns. (Evanich 1986a).

**Habitat and Diet:** The pheasant is associated primarily with agricultural areas such as wheat fields, which provide cover in the form of tall vegetation. In the Willamette Valley, also occurs in orchards, large urban parks, and suburbs. It avoids deserts, high mountains, and dense forests (Browning 1975a, Gilligan et al. 1994). Nests consist of a shallow scrape sometimes lined with dry vegetation (Gabrielson and Jewett 1940). Pen-reared hen pheasants released in the Willamette Valley nested in strip habitats consisting of fencerows, along roadsides and ditch banks, and in non-strip habitats composed of agricultural fields and woodland-grassland areas (Haensly et al. 1987).

Little information is available on diet in Oregon. According to one study, green herbaceous vegetation formed the bulk of the winter diet in the Willamette Valley (Einarsen 1945). Nineteen pheasant crops collected from Sep to Jul from Okanogan Co., Washington, yielded 45 different food items. Fruits and berries comprised 76% and 30% of the fall (Sep-Nov) and winter (Dec-Feb) diets, respectively. Knight et al. (1979) suggested that the high proportion of fruits and berries in the fall diet was reflective of both selective feeding habits and association with agricultural croplands and berry patches. Seeds (33.4%) and leaves (32.3%) were particularly important items in the winter diet but were relatively unimportant (seeds 3.4%, leaves 1.6%) in the fall diet. Animal matter, primarily grasshoppers, comprised 8.5% of the fall diet (Knight et al. 1979). Food items singled out as particularly important included hawthorn berries, rose hips, alfalfa leaves, milkvetch seeds, tumbleweed seeds, apples, and grasshoppers.

**Seasonal Activity and Behavior:** Resident throughout the year with movement generally restricted to a few square miles. However, one pair was reported to have traveled 50 mi (81 km) in 2 mo from the point of release (Bent 1932). During spring, males become extremely aggressive and defend territories, which are several acres in size. Through constant crowing and wing-whirring displays, commencing as early as Feb, dominant males attract and mate with several females during the breeding season (Littlefield 1990a). Eggs are laid in Apr and May and clutch size ranges from 6-16; however, 10-12 eggs generally laid (Gabrielson and Jewett 1940, Littlefield 1990a). The female

alone incubates the eggs, which hatch in 23-28 days (Johnsgard 1975a, 1986b). Precocial young are brooded by the female with no male involvement; chicks are capable of flight within 2 wk of hatching (Johnsgard 1986b). Usually one brood is raised per year; however, females renest if their clutch is lost. Recently hatched chicks were observed 3 Jun to 13 Jul (n=10) (OBBA), but as late as 1 Sep (n=1) (OBBA), suggesting renesting efforts (Littlefield 1990a). During fall, become gregarious when up to 40 birds may concentrate around an abundant food source. These flocks remain together through winter; however, flocks of pheasants usually remain sexually segregated Dec to Feb (Johnsgard 1975a, Littlefield 1990a).

**Detection:** Males are more likely to be encountered than females, especially during spring (*KI*); this may be a reflection of biased sex ratio in favor of males or conspicuous visual and aural detections of males. During spring, brightly colored males are often encountered in open areas; even when hidden under cover, males are easily detected by their crowing call.

**Population Status and Conservation:** The first attempt to establish Ring-necked Pheasants in N. America occurred in 1880 when a shipment of 70 birds was sent to Oregon by Judge Owen Nickerson Denny, then U.S. Consul General posted at Shanghai, China. The birds reached Port Townsend, Washington, safely but perished before reaching Portland, Oregon (Gabrielson and Jewett 1940, Lever 1987). Undaunted by this initial failure, Judge Denny shipped an additional 30 birds to Oregon in 1881, of which 26 survived and were liberated on Peterson Butte, Linn Co. (Bent 1932). In 1882, 48 birds were released at the same locality (Evanich 1986a). All these initial introductions consisted of the Chinese subspecies (*P. c. torquatus*). By 1893, the first shooting season for Ring-necked Pheasants opened in the Willamette Valley and more than 30,000 birds were harvested. The following year, harvest rates increased to between 250,000 and 500,000 (Evanich 1986a, Lever 1987). Gene Simpson of Corvallis, Benton Co., started rearing pheasants commercially in the early 1900s and this operation was later leased to the Oregon Game Commission (now ODFW), which continued to raise and release pheasants throughout Oregon (Lever 1987). In 1924, a shipment of the Mongolian subspecies (*P. c. mongolicus*) from China was added to the breeding stock (Gabrielson and Jewett 1940). Ring-necked Pheasants were first introduced to the Malheur-Harney lakes basin in 1913 with additional releases in 1939 and 1940 (Littlefield 1990a) and in ne. Oregon during the 1920s and 1930s (Evanich 1992a). Since these early introductions, have been successfully introduced in most counties. The latest introduction constituted 18,689 "Sichuan" subspecies

(*P. c. strauchi*) from China to the Willamette Valley (E. V. Rickerson p.c.). Oregon population numbers are unknown. They are not threatened globally; the total world population numbers over 50 million (Johnsgard 1986b, del Hoyo et al. 1994).—*Kamal Islam*

## Subfamily Tetraoninae

### Ruffed Grouse *Bonasa umbellus*

Ruffed Grouse are named for a series of black iridescent feathers on the sides of the neck called the ruff, which is erected by males to form an umbel-shaped ring around the neck during courtship displays. This forest-dwelling species, favored by upland game-bird hunters, also is well known for the drumming of the males during courtship displays in the spring. Both sexes are mottled in rich brown, black, and white. Two color morphs occur, with some intermediates. Gray birds have tails barred with alternating bands of black and gray, whereas red birds have tails banded with black and rust. Most in w. Oregon are red, those in e. Oregon are gray; however, both morphs occur in mixed broods on both sides of the state.

**General Distribution:** Resident of forested regions of c. Alaska and Yukon, s. Northwest Territories, and most of s. Canadian Provinces. In w. U.S., occupies coastal and Cascade mountains of w. Washington, Oregon, and nw. California, and the Rocky Mtns. of e. Washington and Oregon, n. Idaho, w. Montana and Wyoming, and ne. Utah. Small populations in ne. Nevada and w. N. Dakota and S. Dakota. In e. U.S., resident of New England and Great Lakes states including Minnesota, Wisconsin, and Michigan, where dense populations may occur in conjunction with aspen habitats. Extends south through Appalachian Mtns. in e. Ohio, Kentucky and Tennessee, W. Virginia, w. Virginia, N. Carolina, and S. Carolina, and n. Georgia. Three of 11 subspecies occur in Oregon (Johnsgard 1983b).

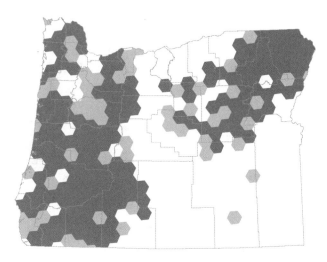

**Oregon Distribution:** Common resident throughout most forested regions of the state (Durbin 1979). *B. u. affinis* occupies most forests at low to moderate elevations east of the Cascade crest (Browning 2002), primarily the east slope of the Cascades (e.g., specimens from Ft. Klamath [USNM] and Upper Klamath L. [SDMNH]) and Blue Mtns., but also forested extensions to lowlands. It is not present in riparian or aspen stands of se. Oregon desert regions, except for a single report along the Blitzen R. at 6,000 ft (1,828 m) on Steens Mtn. 15 May 1997 (Sullivan 1997b). *B. u. sabini* occurs in forested areas of the c. and s. Coast Range, Willamette Valley, Klamath Mtns., and w. Cascades (Browning 2002). *B. u. castanea* occurs in the nw. Coast Range (Aldrich 1963, Browning 2002). The species has been seen all the way to the dune line in coastal forests, e.g., at Fort Stevens SP (M. Patterson p.c.), and on the north spit of the Umpqua R. (*MGH*).

**Habitat and Diet:** Closely associated with dense deciduous or deciduous/evergreen forest, represented primarily by alder-dominated stands in w. Oregon and stands containing alders, quaking aspens, hawthorns, and other small trees and shrubs in e. Oregon (Durbin 1979). Dense conditions favored by the species are characteristic of riparian zones and young, regenerating forest stands. Natural disturbances and timber-management activities that result in small forest clearings favor the species (Johnsgard 1983b). In the relatively dry habitat of the Blue and Wallowa mountains, Ruffed Grouse frequently congregate along stream corridors and drainages that afford dense vegetation and a diversity of berries, catkins, and other food sources. They may be less concentrated in w. Oregon, where sufficient habitat is more widespread (Durbin 1979).

Spring habitat of males is usually centered on a log, or occasionally a group of logs or other elevated surfaces, used as platforms for drumming. These "drumming logs" are frequently located in mid-successional deciduous stands, often with conifer and dense understory components (Johnsgard 1983b). Nests are usually in mid-aged deciduous or mixed deciduous-conifer habitat, and often at the base of a tree or stump or under a log, shrub, or brushpile (Johnsgard 1983b). Nests are shallow depressions lined with feathers.

Like other galliformes, Ruffed Grouse are omnivorous; diet varies tremendously, but in spring consists primarily of leaves, buds, and flowers of grasses and forbs. Microarthropods increase in the diet during summer, and berries and other fruits such as salal, hawthorn, and blackberry become common in diet as they ripen (Durbin 1979). As in some other grouse, diets become relatively specialized during winter, mainly including buds and seeds of deciduous trees.

Throughout most of their range, buds and catkins of aspen are major winter foods; in areas of Oregon where aspen does not predominate or occur, feed on alder, willow, birch, dogwood, hawthorn, and others. Ferns and some other ground-level evergreen plants are also utilized during winter (Durbin 1979).

Although much of their winter diet is derived from deciduous trees, Ruffed Grouse use conifers for roosting. Where snow depth permits and winter temperatures are extreme, may fly into snowdrifts and roost overnight under the surface for thermal cover and possibly protection from predators (Bump et al. 1947), although this activity has not been documented in Oregon.

**Seasonal Activity and Behavior:** Although males exhibit territorial behavior throughout the year, territoriality increases in early Mar, peaks in late Mar or Apr, and declines in May (Johnsgard 1983b). During this time, the male selects a log, which is used for visual strutting displays and drumming. A single drumming log often is used throughout the life of a Ruffed Grouse, and many have been used by numerous successive generations. The drumming display, a series of wing-beats beginning at 1-sec intervals and progressing to a continuous crescendo, usually lasts 8-11 sec and occurs every 3-5 min during crepuscular hours throughout peak of breeding season, although they can occur every few sec or only sporadically (Bump et al. 1947). Drumming is also occasionally heard in fall. Visual displays may include upright strutting, a "bowing" movement, and a rush sequence (Hjorth 1970). Sullivan (1992b) described an observation of a display in the Wallowa Mtns. as "rattlesnake" behavior due to the rattle-like sound of the tail following the rush sequence.

Polygamous. After copulation, the female seeks a nest site. Eggs are laid at a rate of two per 3 days; average clutch size 11. Incubation begins after the last egg is laid and usually lasts 23 or 24 days. May renest if the first nest is destroyed; the number of eggs in the second nest averages seven or eight (Bump et al. 1947). Chicks are precocial, hatch in early or mid-Jun, and gain flight in approximately 2 wk. During summer, Ruffed Grouse, and particularly broods, frequent habitat with dense invertebrate populations, such as logging roads or other disturbed locations with herbaceous growth.

They do not migrate; however, some populations exhibit seasonal variation in mobility (Johnsgard 1983b). Chambers and Sharp (1958) noted most moved <0.25 mi (0.40 km) prior to fall dispersal, whereas over half of young dispersed >1 mi (1.60 km) after broods broke up. Hale and Dorney (1963) noted a juvenile grouse in Wisconsin that was shot 12 mi (19.3 km) from the site at which it was banded 31 days earlier. Long and erratic flights of immature

Ruffed Grouse—termed "crazy flight" and apparently unrelated to dispersal—are thought to be a function of fright and inexperience. Movements of both juvenile and adult grouse decline in winter, and by spring they are sedentary (Johnsgard 1983b).

**Detection:** Despite the dense habitat favored by the species, individuals and broods frequently are observed along logging roads throughout spring, summer, and fall. Adult birds typically are wary; however, hens frequently defend broods aggressively. Males may defend territories with impunity, but become warier as hunting season progresses. Ruffed Grouse are more frequently heard than seen; the drumming of males in spring, and occasionally in the fall, may be heard at great distances, but, as with the hooting of the Blue Grouse, the source of the sound is particularly difficult to pinpoint.

**Population Status and Conservation:** Although density is highly variable among areas and years, the population status in Oregon appears favorable. Range remains consistent with that noted by Gabrielson and Jewett (1940). Population density data are unavailable, but data from ODFW hunter surveys indicated harvest 1979-96 ranged from an estimated 23,983 in 1985 to 74,290 in 1992. Intensive hunter harvest data in Wallowa Co. suggest relatively stable populations. The *Oregon Sportsman* magazine reported that approximately 425 Ruffed Grouse were harvested there in 1926, and 396 in 1986 (V. L. Coggins p.c.). Populations in some states exhibit 10-yr cycles of alternating abundance and relative scarcity (Johnsgard 1983b); insufficient data exist on cyclic fluctuations in Oregon.

Timber harvest creates a mosaic of young timber stands favorable for the species. Additionally, alder is an abundant food resource in w. Oregon. In the relatively dry Blue and Wallowa mountains, streamside buffer zones facilitate dense stands of hawthorn and other food-producing shrubs ideal for the species. The outlook for Ruffed Grouse in Oregon is positive.—*Eric Pelren*

## Greater Sage-Grouse
*Centrocercus urophasianus*
Greater Sage-Grouse, also called sage hens or sage chickens, are best known for their elaborate courtship displays, which occur on traditional strutting grounds, known as leks, where males gather each spring. At all seasons both sexes are readily identified by large size and chicken-like build. Adults are mottled dark gray, black and buff, with black bellies and pointed tails (Johnsgard 1983b). Males have whiter breast feathers than females and a dark v-shaped pattern on the neck lined by a narrow white band. At 4-6 pounds (1.8-

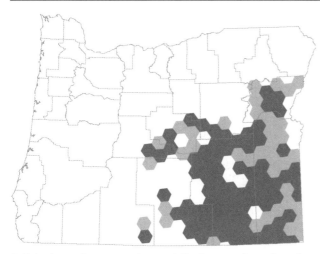

Washington. There are no geographic or other barriers separating the subspecies. Genetic differences between samples representing the two recognized (AOU 1957) subspecies (Benedict et al. unpubl. ms.) suggests further work is required.

**Oregon Distribution:** Formerly widespread in sagebrush-dominated areas east of the Cascades (Aldrich 1963). Aldrich (1946) listed specimens from Fremont, Blitzen Valley, Huntington, Juntura, and Mt. Harney. By the 1940s sage-grouse range had contracted by about 50%, with populations lost in the Columbia Plateau and Blue Mountains ecoregions of Oregon. Currently the northernmost Oregon population is in the Baker Valley. Most common in the southeastern desert regions (Northern Basin and Range); generally limited to sagebrush habitats (Crawford and Lutz 1985).

**Habitat and Diet:** Sage-grouse are sagebrush obligates, relying on the plant for food and cover throughout the year. Leks are generally located in openings in sagebrush. Windswept ridges, small meadows or drainages, and bare openings are often used. New leks have formed on small burned areas (*JB*).

The nest is a shallow depression lined with grass or sagebrush leaves, usually under a sagebrush. Big sagebrush cover types are used for nesting more than low sagebrush. Successful nests have greater cover of grasses >7 in (18 cm) tall immediately surrounding the nest (Gregg et al. 1994, Hanf et al. 1994, DeLong et al. 1995). Most unsuccessful nests are lost to predators. Common Ravens and coyotes are the most common, but badgers and ground squirrels also take nests (DeLong 1993).

Broods use big and low sagebrush habitat types for cover and food. In se. Oregon, broods used sites with higher forb availability than what occurred randomly in the landscape (Drut et al. 1994a). A study area south of Burns had lower forb availability and larger brood home ranges than Hart Mtn. N. Antelope R. and long-term sage-grouse productivity was higher at Hart Mtn. (Drut et al. 1994a). Broodless hens flock together, remain separate from broods, and use a wider variety of cover types than broods.

2.7 kg), males are substantially larger than females, which are usually 2-3.5 pounds (1-1.8 kg). Males have specializations used in display. Their tail feathers are long and pointed with white spots on the undertail coverts. They have yellow combs over each eye and a chest sac with two bare, yellow patches of skin, which are inflated during display. The display lasts only a few seconds and is a combination of color, movement, and sound. Males attend leks for several hours each morning and display repeatedly.

The name was recently changed from Sage Grouse when the Gunnison Sage-Grouse of sw. Colorado and se. Utah was separated (AOU 2000, Young et al. 2000).

**General Distribution:** Currently resident across large portions of se. Oregon, s. Idaho, Nevada, Montana, and Wyoming. Scattered populations in Colorado and Utah. Two isolated populations in c. Washington, and populations in e. California, se. Alberta, sw. Saskatchewan, sw. N. Dakota, and nw. S. Dakota (Johnsgard 1983b). Historical range included sc. British Columbia, n. Arizona, and New Mexico, extreme nw. Nebraska and a small population in the Oklahoma panhandle. Range has contracted within all states and provinces currently occupied.

AOU (1957) recognized two subspecies. Ranges, as described by Aldrich (1963), place both in Oregon with *C. u. phaios* in extreme se. Oregon and *C. u. urophasianus* over the rest of Oregon north into

*Greater Sage-Grouse*

Sage-grouse are the only galliform in the world in which the gizzard is not muscular, so they are limited to soft foods. Sagebrush is a principal food throughout much of the year, but forbs and insects are critical to successful reproduction in spring and summer. Grasses are rarely eaten. Hens take forbs as soon as they are available in Mar and Apr. Forbs important in Oregon include desert parsley, hawksbeard, long-leaf phlox, mountain-dandelion, clover, milkvetches, Oregon sunshine, western yarrow and paintbrush (Barnett and Crawford 1994, Hanf et al. 1994). Insects are critical food for chicks in the first weeks of life. In a captive feeding trial, chicks fed only plant material the first 10 days of life died or had stunted growth (Johnson and Boyce 1990). In se. Oregon, chicks ate a wide variety of forbs and insects, but a few items made up the bulk of the diet. Important chick foods included milky-juiced composites (Cichorieae), milkvetch, microsteris, beetles, ants, and sagebrush (Drut et al. 1994b). Several family groups were observed foraging on grasshoppers in cheatgrass and crested wheatgrass areas of Malheur Co. (M. Denny p.c.). By late fall, sagebrush is the only item in the diet and remains so until spring (Wallestad 1975).

They congregate in mixed-sex flocks in winter where sagebrush is available above the snow or on windswept ridges. Near Prineville, mountain big sagebrush and low sagebrush cover types used most frequently, but silver sagebrush and grassland types used also (Hanf et al. 1994).

**Seasonal Activity and Behavior:** Males begin attending leks in late Feb; strut primarily in the mornings, beginning before dawn, but occasionally in the evening and throughout moonlit nights as well. Hens attend leks later, peaking in late Mar on Hart Mountain. Peak lek attendance by males is in mid-Apr. The sole function of the lek is courtship display and copulation. Hens select a mating center, rather than an individual male, and these centers are traditional. Males that occupy these centers are called master cocks, and perform the majority of copulations (Johnsgard 1983b, Ryser 1985). Strutting of the master cock looks no different to humans from that of other males. Males with territories next to the master cock mate only occasionally.

After mating, males have no further role in reproduction; they leave leks by mid-May and gather in flocks, but stay separate from broodless hens and broods until late summer. Hens disperse to surrounding uplands to nest after mating. Six to nine eggs are typically laid and incubated for 28 days. At a laying rate of two eggs every 3 days, it takes 10-13 days for a female to lay a clutch. Hens that lose their first nest may return to a lek, breed again, and renest. Renesting attempts are not common: renesting rates at Hart Mtn averaged 22% over a 12-yr period (M.

Byrne p.c.) and were even lower during the Prineville study (Hanf et al. 1994).

Nest success is highly variable. At Hart Mtn, nest success averaged 31% (range 20-60%) (M. Byrne p.c.). Data from Prineville were similar (Hanf et al. 1994). Nest success in Oregon seems to be lower than that reported throughout the entire Greater Sage-Grouse range (Schroeder et al. 1999).

Most clutches hatch late May to mid-Jun. Downy chicks are precocial and leave the nest within 24 hr of hatching. They feed themselves, but are brooded by the hen for warmth. Fly in 10-14 days. Hens with broods remain separate from other hens and seek out forb-rich areas within sagebrush communities. Brood movements are highly variable. Some broods spend the entire summer in a small area while others move large distances. In an extreme case on Hart Mtn., a hen moved her brood over 20 mi (32 km) the first week, then spent the rest of the summer in a small area (M. Gregg p.c.). Chicks remain with the hen for 10-12 wk. Successful nesters raise only one brood and hens do not renest after brood loss.

As forbs desiccate in the uplands, sage-grouse move to places where forbs are still available such as wet meadows, lakebeds, or irrigated fields. Timing of these movements depends on weather, which influences forb availability. Meadows and lakebeds play a larger role in Oregon than for populations in eastern portions of their range (Montana, Wyoming, Colorado), where forbs are available in the uplands longer.

During winter, sage-grouse concentrate in large flocks where sagebrush is available, not buried by snow.

**Detection:** Most easily seen in spring on leks and in late summer and fall when congregated at meadows, lakebeds, and waterholes. Early morning and late evening are the best times to look. Leks represent the best viewing opportunities but can be difficult to access; repeated human disturbance at leks can cause decreased attendance and eventual abandonment of the lek.

During other times sage-grouse are widely dispersed throughout sagebrush habitats. Their camouflage and tendency to crouch and freeze when danger approaches makes them easy to miss. Most often seen while observers are walking or driving and the birds flush.

**Population Status and Conservation:** Marked declines are being reported for Greater Sage-Grouse populations throughout their range (Braun 1998). Concern about declines has prompted petitioning of the USFWS to list the species under the Endangered Species Act. In Oregon, numbers of males counted at leks declined approximately 60% from the late 1950s to the early 1980s (Crawford and Lutz 1985). Populations typically show marked variation within the span of a decade, making short-term analysis of trends difficult and potentially misleading. For example, at

Hart Mtn. N. Antelope R., males on five leks near headquarters varied from 239 in 1990, to 42 in 1996, to 168 in 2001 (Hart Mtn. NAR files).

This bird may be a good indicator species for shrub-steppe habitat since they require large expanses of sagebrush with healthy, native understories. The best habitat has a diversity of cover types and seral stages, including riparian or other moist habitats.

Sage-grouse are affected by anything that affects sagebrush-dominated habitat. Impacts occur chiefly through loss, fragmentation, or degradation of habitat. Habitat loss, primarily through conversion for agriculture, has been implicated as a major factor in population declines throughout portions of their range (Miller and Eddleman 2000). Habitat loss and fragmentation also occur via sagebrush-control projects, large wildfires, and urbanization.

Juniper expansion threatens sage-grouse habitat. In many remaining sagebrush communities, the proportion of trees, shrubs, grasses, and forbs has changed (Miller and Eddleman 2000). In some areas, woody plants have increased while herbaceous plants have decreased. In these areas, sagebrush remained available for food and cover, but the important herbaceous layer was reduced or lost. Reduced productivity due to loss of important foods and nesting cover may be the consequence in such areas. In other areas, weedy species and fire frequency have increased, and native plants, including sagebrush, have been greatly reduced. The result is a loss of sage-grouse habitat unless sagebrush can be restored. Miller and Eddleman (2000) implicated livestock grazing, introduction of exotic plants, change in fire regimes, and herbicides as causes of such changes in these sagebrush communities.—*Jenny Barnett*

## Spruce Grouse *Falcipennis canadensis*

This northern grouse reaches Oregon only in the forests of the Wallowa Mtns. in ne. Oregon. Gabrielson and Jewett (1940) considered it "Oregon's rarest and most local species of upland game bird." Dusky and slightly smaller than Ruffed Grouse. Sexes are different in coloration; males have a black breast with white spotting on the sides, white spots at the base of a black tail, and a red comb above the eye. Females are heavily barred with dark brown and white and have a dark tail. Both sexes lack the neck ruffs and crown feather crests of Ruffed Grouse, the species with which they are most often confused. They have been protected from hunting in Oregon for many years because of their lack of wariness and limited distribution in the state.

**General Distribution:** Resident of boreal conifer forest from Alaska east to Quebec and Labrador south into Washington, Idaho, Wyoming, Montana, ne. Oregon, the n. Great Lakes and n. New England

states. Successfully introduced to Newfoundland and Anticosti I. in the mid-1980s (Boag and Schroeder 1992). Five subspecies, *F. c. franklinii* in Oregon (AOU 1957).

**Oregon Distribution:** Typically uncommon in conifer forest above 5,000 ft (1,500 m) in the Wallowa Mtns. of Baker, Union, and Wallowa counties. They may still inhabit the Hat Point area on the rim of Hells Canyon (*VLC*). Most are found within the Wallowa-Whitman NF, with the majority in or near the Eagle Cap Wilderness. No specimens or documentation from other sections of Oregon are known. Early reports indicate they may have been present in the n. Cascades (Gabrielson and Jewett 1940). Spruce Grouse are occasionally reported from the Blue Mtns. outside the Wallowas, but no reports have been confirmed.

**Habitat and Diet:** Closely associated with conifer-dominated forests, Spruce Grouse appear to prefer dense, relatively young stands (Boag and Schroeder 1992). They are most frequently seen in summer in Engelmann spruce, lodgepole pine, and subalpine fir forests. During the winter, they prefer the needles of lodgepole but will utilize spruce needles if pine is not available (Boag and Schroeder 1992). During the snow-free time of the year, feed chiefly on the ground, clipping off the growing tips of shrubs and forbs as well as eating small insects. They nest on the ground, generally with overhead cover at the base of a conifer (Boag and Schroeder 1992). Juvenile diets are mostly animal matter in the first months of life (Pendergast and Boag 1970).

**Seasonal Activity and Behavior:** Very little is known about Spruce Grouse in Oregon. Elsewhere, it is known that males are territorial and perform display flights in the spring. Loud wing claps are produced only by *F. c. franklinii* (McDonald 1968) and can be heard at up to 500 ft (150 m) (Schroeder and Boag 1987). Egg laying begins about 17 days after the ground becomes 50% snow-free (Keppie and Towers 1990). Clutch size

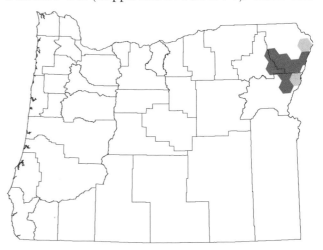

averaged 4.8 for 40 nests and renesting occurred with a reduced number of eggs if the first clutch was lost (Keppie 1982). In the Wallowas, broods are normally seen in Aug. On an annual 10-mi (16-km) vehicle survey route near Hat Point during Aug 1960-2000, a total of six broods were observed (all on the plateau); broods consisted of 2-6 chicks (average 3.8) (*VLC*). Spruce Grouse in sw. Alberta were recorded to move up to 7 mi (11 km) from breeding ranges to wintering areas (Schroeder 1985). Movements of Oregon birds are unreported.

**Detection:** August is the best month to find the birds by slowly walking trails or driving roads in early morning. Trails into the Eagle Cap Wilderness that offer good viewing opportunities are McCully Cr., Big Sheep Cr. to Bonny Lakes, and Salt Cr. Summit to Wing Ridge. Can occasionally be seen along the Wallowa Mtn. Loop road between Salt Cr. Summit and the Lick Cr. CG during the summer. Access is difficult in winter and birds are seldom seen at this time of year.

**Population Status and Conservation:** Spruce Grouse appear to have declined in ne. Oregon over the past 50 yr. In Sep 1950, 17 were seen in the Hat Point (Snake R. Divide) area during a 3-day period by an ODFW biologist (Laughlin 1950); none have been seen by ODFW personnel in this area since 1983. Brood count routes established in the area in 1960 have also shown a decline with 34 total birds counted 1960-83 and *none* seen 1984-2000. This declining trend was also apparent in forest-grouse wing collections started in 1980. While Spruce Grouse are protected, some incidental harvest occurs. During 1985-98, wings from 106 Spruce Grouse were deposited at collection stations in Wallowa, Baker, and Union counties with 80% taken in Wallowa Co. Wing deposits were highest in 1988 with 27. The most taken in 1 yr in the 1990s was 10 (Crawford and Swanson 1999). While illegal hunting could be a factor in the apparent decline, most hunting occurs on or near roads while the majority of habitat is roadless. Road closures would help protect birds in areas outside designated wilderness.

Habitat loss from wildfires and logging are suspected to have caused some of the decline in the e. Wallowa Mtns. and Hells Canyon rim. As these areas regenerate, habitat should become more favorable. In contrast, in the w. Wallowa Mtns., lack of fire has resulted in more old-growth forest that appears to be less-suitable Spruce Grouse habitat (*VLC*). Status needs to be determined before it is lost, especially isolated populations such as those on the Hat Point plateau and in unconfirmed areas such as the n. Blue Mtns. outside the Wallowas. A limited study to determine distribution, habitat use, and population status was begun by ODFW and OSU in 2001.—*Victor L. Coggins*

## "Blue Grouse" complex *Dendragapus obscurus*

This popular upland game bird is the largest of Oregon's three forest grouse. It is well known for the distinctive hooting call emitted by courting males in the spring. This call is accompanied by an extravagant courtship display involving exposure of blood-engorged, featherless shoulder spots and eyecombs, which are yellow among coastal populations and reddish to orange in interior populations. Gabrielson and Jewett (1940), following AOU (1931), listed coastal and interior populations as two species: Richardson's (*D. obscurus*) and Sooty Grouse (*D. fuliginosus*), respectively. Blue Grouse was split into Sooty Grouse (*D. fuliginosus*) (w Oregon) and Dusky Grouse (*D. obscurus*) (Blue Mtns), 47th Supp. to AOU Check-List, R. Banks et al., *Auk* 123:926-36 (July 2006). Males are predominantly dull gray; females are mottled brown. Leucism (white pigmentation) was observed in 0.1% of 1,018 Oregon birds collected 1974-85 (Crawford 1987). Some individuals allow close approach by humans, which has earned the species the pseudonym "fool hen."

**General Distribution:** Local short-distance migrant throughout the coniferous forests of the N. American Cordillera (Zwickel 1992). Resident of the southeastern corner of the Northwest Territories, s. Yukon, British Columbia, w. Alberta, and the islands of Alaska's southeastern panhandle. The range extends south through the Coast Range, Cascades, and Olympic Mtns. in Washington, the contiguous mountains of w. and ne. Oregon, and the Sierra Nevada in n. and s. California and w. Nevada; also in the mountains of Idaho, Montana, Wyoming, Utah, and Colorado, with fragmented populations in Arizona and New Mexico. Three of eight subspecies occur in Oregon (Aldrich 1963, Browning 2002).

**Oregon Distribution:** *D. o. fuliginosus* is a fairly common resident in coniferous forests from the Cascade crest to the coast, with broad areas of absence

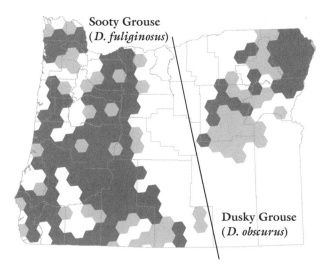

Sooty Grouse
(*D. fuliginosus*)

Dusky Grouse
(*D. obscurus*)

around low-elevation urban and unforested valley areas. *D. o. sierrae* is limited primarily to the east slope of the Cascades, but intergrades with *D. o. fuliginosus* on the west slope of the Cascades in ne. Jackson Co. and near the Cascade crest in Crater L. NP (Browning and Cross 1999) and probably to the north. *D. o. pallidus* occupies coniferous forests of the Blue and Wallowa mountains (Johnsgard 1983b).

**Habitat and Diet:** Blue Grouse use a wide variety of habitats in spring and summer, including forests and forest edges, and may occur 1.2 mi (2 km) or more from forest within open grassland or shrubland (Zwickel 1992). They also use regenerating clearcuts and riparian habitats with dense deciduous cover. Females construct shallow ground nests lined with leaves and feathers. Nesting habitat ranges from nearly bare ground with no overhead cover to dense vegetation beneath full forest canopies (Zwickel 1992, Pelren and Crawford 1999). Pelren and Crawford (1999) observed the greatest nesting success among nests beneath logs. Females with young broods often use open sites, mesic sites, and lush vegetation, perhaps in response to invertebrate abundance in these areas (reviewed in Zwickel 1992). Individuals throughout the state spend a great deal of time in trees during spring and summer; however, individuals in ne. Oregon were predominantly on the ground during summer (Popper et al. 1996).

Winter range includes conifer forests from sea level to subalpine elevations, where this species occurs principally in association with forests dominated by Douglas-fir and true firs (Beer 1943), and, in e. Oregon, ponderosa pines (Pelren 1996). It is also associated with forests dominated by spruce, lodgepole pine, limber pine, western hemlock, and mountain hemlock (Zwickel 1992). Commonly uses subalpine fir and witches brooms in dwarf-mistletoe-infested Douglas-firs for thermal protection while roosting in winter (Pelren 1996). Individuals may remain in the same tree continuously for several weeks. Both sexes and age groups in ne. Oregon selected open park-like stands of mature ponderosa pine and Douglas-fir rather than more heavily forested stands (Pelren 1996). Like some other galliformes, Blue Grouse occasionally roost beneath the surface of snow in winter; this aids in thermoregulation and/or predator-avoidance, and likely occurs in Oregon where snow depths are adequate. Observations on the ground increased throughout winter in ne. Oregon from 8% of Dec radiolocations to 57% of Mar radiolocations (Pelren 1996).

Arthropods compose virtually 100% of the diet of the precocial chicks, but the young birds also begin to eat vegetation in late summer and fall. As fall approaches, diets increasingly include conifer seeds, western larch needles (in e. Oregon), and berries of deciduous shrubs. Mike Denny (p.c.) reports that huckleberries are a common food source Jul-Sep in the Blue Mtns. Crawford et al. (1986b) found early fall diets of Blue Grouse in ne. Oregon were composed of over 50 plant and animal species, but primarily contained short-horned grasshoppers, prickly lettuce, yellow salsify, wild buckwheat, and snowberry. Conifer needles, stems, and buds represent the majority of the diet during winter (Pelren 1996). In e. Oregon, these are primarily needles from Douglas-fir and needles and buds from ponderosa pine (Pelren 1996). In studies elsewhere, winter diets included needles of true firs, lodgepole and limber pine, and western and mountain hemlock (Beer 1943, Zwickel 1992).

**Seasonal Activity and Behavior:** Pelren (1996) observed a Blue Grouse hooting in the Wallowa Mtns. on 16 Feb 1992, somewhat earlier than typical. Male breeding behavior usually increases in Mar and peaks in Apr. Male courtship display is characterized by the exposure of cervical apteria, or shoulder spots, on the sides of the neck and superorbital apteria, or eyecombs, above the eyes. The feathers which normally cover the shoulder spots are drawn back and create a white border; the apteria themselves are engorged with blood and are reddish in interior populations and yellow in coastal populations. This visual display is accompanied by a series of low-pitched hoots. In coastal populations, males typically emit six hoots in succession, often from trees; the call may be audible up to 1 mi (1.6 km). Interior males frequently hoot from the ground; their call usually consists of five notes and is significantly quieter than that of coastal males, seldom audible beyond 100-200 yds (91-183 m) (Zwickel 1992).

Polygamous. After copulation, females move to isolated locations to nest. Egg laying occurs at the approximate rate of one egg every 1.5 days (Zwickel 1992); the average number of eggs per clutch was 7.7 in ne. Oregon, which represented the largest mean clutch sizes for any Blue Grouse populations for which such data exist (Pelren and Crawford 1999). Incubation begins after the last egg is laid and takes approximately 26 days (Zwickel 1992). Hatch dates in ne. Oregon ranged from 1 May to 8 Jul (Crawford et al. 1986a); mean hatch date was 31 May (Pelren and Crawford 1999). Chicks are precocial and gain rudimentary flight capability in approximately 2 wk. No similar data are available from w. Oregon.

Travel toward winter range begins in early summer; females with broods have limited mobility and delay travel until mid- or late summer. Birds in w. Oregon use trees heavily during this time, but birds in e. Oregon usually stay on the ground during nocturnal roosting (Popper et al. 1996).

Broods exhibit mixing and combining during late summer and early fall; during this time groups of over three dozen birds occasionally are observed in ne. Oregon. Mean number of grouse per group was three in Dec and two from Jan through Mar in ne. Oregon; percent of occasions in which radio-equipped birds were observed in groups with at least one other bird increased from 42% in Dec to 66% in Mar (Pelren 1996).

The distance between winter and spring range varies from none to several kilometers. An adult female in the Wallowa Mtns. moved 7.5 mi (12 km) between winter and spring range (Pelren 1996). Elevational movements between winter and spring range have been documented in numerous studies (Zwickel 1992), and likely occur in response to spatially separated spring and winter habitats in some areas.

**Detection:** Blue Grouse are extremely difficult to locate in trees. Males can be located in spring by their hooting, although many people are frustrated by an inability to localize the low-pitched call. Females may be located with broods in early summer; a chick distress call may be used to lure brood hens within close distances. Territorial males also may allow close approach; Tice (1995) documented the capture of one such individual by hand in the c. Coast Range. Lundsten (1995) observed numerous Blue Grouse by sight and sound near Marys Peak, Benton Co., from Mar through Oct. Along the breaks of Hells Canyon and its tributaries, frequently observed individually and in groups ranging 2-30 or more. In the Cascades and Coast Range, frequently located along secondary roads and around the edges of harvested timber stands (*EP*). During Jul-Oct, sometimes use bald or grassy ridgelines (D. Fix p.c.).

**Population Status and Conservation:** Densities of adult male Blue Grouse in e. Oregon and other interior populations have ranged 5-50/mi$^2$ (2-19/km$^2$) (Zwickel 1992). Densities in w. Oregon are difficult to estimate due in part to the dense vegetation they occupy and the frequent use of trees. Estimated densities of adult males in British Columbia ranged 10-264/mi$^2$ (4-102/km$^2$) (Zwickel 1992), but populations in w. Oregon are presumed to be much lower.

ODFW has been involved in telemetry studies and other research since the 1980s to better understand Blue Grouse populations and habitat needs. Harvest data indicated that, from the late 1970s to the mid-1990s, the approximate number of hunters declined from 10,000 to 5,000 in e. Oregon and from 20,000 to 8,000 in w. Oregon, with a concomitant decline in harvest from approximately 25,000 to under 15,000 in e. Oregon, and from 25,000 to under 20,000 in w. Oregon.

The early succession forest habitat used for breeding and brood rearing is created by active timber harvest; however, timber harvest may also reduce mature Douglas-fir and other coniferous habitat used in winter. In e. Oregon, prescribed burning and other methods that maintain mature park-like stands would likely benefit the species (Pelren 1996).—*Eric Pelren*

## Sharp-tailed Grouse *Tympanuchus phasianellus*

Sharp-tails, commonly called "prairie chickens" by early Oregon residents, were abundant in the grasslands and foothills of Oregon east of the Cascade Mtns. prior to the late 1800s (Anonymous 1915, Gabrielson and Jewett 1940, Olson 1976). They were considered extirpated from the state by the 1970s, but recent reintroduction programs give a glimmer of hope that sharp-tails may once again hold their own in ne. Oregon. The subspecies in Oregon, Columbian Sharp-tailed Grouse (*T. p. columbianus*) is the palest and grayest of six. Adult sharp-tails are about the size of Ruffed Grouse. The feathers of the lower back are mottled in shades of black and buff while the underside feathers are white or white surrounded with brown. The two middle tail feathers extend beyond the other tail feathers several inches and appear pointed, thus the name. Sexes have similar plumage. Sharp-tails are well adapted to northern climates, with feathers extending to the first joint of the toes, aiding heat retention. Snowshoe-like scales along the toes, present only in winter, allow the birds to walk more easily on the snow. The males congregate on leks or dancing grounds in the spring and perform elaborate social displays.

**General Distribution:** Resident from c. Alaska east to c. Quebec, south to Colorado and Utah, and west to Washington and Oregon (Johnsgard 1973). The Columbian Sharp-tailed Grouse was found historically in Oregon. Historic range included British Columbia and all western states except Arizona. Range has been substantially reduced and sharp-tails have been extirpated from about 90% of the area they formerly inhabited (Miller and Graul 1980). Six subspecies; *T. p. columbianus* in Oregon (AOU 1957).

**Oregon Distribution:** Formerly, sharp-tails were found in the grassland and sagebrush steppe of e. Oregon with records from all counties east of the Cascades (Anonymous 1915, Bent 1932, Gabrielson and Jewett 1940). The last generally accepted sighting was at Little Lookout Mtn., Baker Co., in 1967 (Woodruff 1982). A small breeding population has been established 4 mi (6 km) north of Enterprise in the Parsnip Cr. drainage of Wallowa Co. since 1994. Sharp-tails have also been reported near Findley Buttes on the Zumwalt Prairie and on Tick Hill north of Wallowa, but these sightings have not been confirmed. In the 1990s, several unconfirmed sightings were reported in Baker Co. near Little Lookout Mtn. (G. Keister p.c.).

It is possible birds could be reoccupying historic range from small populations in w. Idaho that are within 20 mi (32 km) of Baker Co.

**Habitat and Diet:** Sharp-tailed Grouse are found in grassland or grass-shrub habitats and utilize deciduous shrubs and trees for wintering (Hart et al. 1950, Rogers 1969, Johnsgard 1973). Adults feed extensively on forbs during the spring and summer. Chicks depend on insects, especially during the first seven weeks (Hillman and Jackson 1973). In Wallowa Co., sharp-tails utilize Conservation Reserve Program (CRP) fields planted to grasses and forbs for lek sites and native prairie for early spring feeding, nesting, and early summer brood rearing. CRP fields remain green through late summer and early fall and receive heavy use by sharp-tails at this time. During 1991-98, 13 nests were in an area 4 mi (6 km) north of Enterprise; 11 were in native bunchgrass habitats and two in CRP fields. During winter when snow depths prohibit ground feeding, sharp-tails have been observed feeding on buds of quaking aspen, common chokecherry, black hawthorn, and willow (*VLC*). Grassland is a very important habitat component. In Idaho, where the birds are still hunted, the harvest went from about 1,500 in 1983 to more than 8,000 in 1993 following large-scale conversions of cropland to CRP grassland (T. Hemker p.c.).

**Seasonal Activity and Behavior:** Males utilize leks from early Mar through early Jun. In Wallowa Co., courtship activity appears to peak in late Apr. Display activity begins before dawn and continues for several hours. Evening activity also occurs. Nesting occurs in May and Jun. The mean completed clutch size was 11 eggs. Renesting has been documented on several occasions. Broods of young have normally been seen in Aug. During the winter, birds moved as far as 4 mi (6 km) to deciduous shrub patches following heavy snowfall (*VLC*).

**Detection:** Sharp-tails in Oregon have very limited distribution and are currently found only on private land. Winter provides some viewing opportunity, especially following heavy snowfall. Sharp-tails can sometimes be seen north of Enterprise along Leap Lane, Dunham Rd., and Highway 3 by carefully searching deciduous shrubs and trees for feeding birds. This is best accomplished from public roads using proper optics and looking for birds in the upper half of shrubs and small trees. Occasionally, sharp-tails can be seen on the ground near the base of shrubs. Permission should be secured before entering private lands. Limited viewing opportunity is available at lek sites in Apr and May but landowners need to be contacted in advance. Additional information on sharp-tails is available at the Wallowa District office of ODFW.

**Population Status and Conservation:** They were abundant during the late 1800s, but declined rapidly and were considered extirpated by the 1970s. Sharp-tailed Grouse restoration began with an attempted introduction of Plains Sharp-tailed Grouse (*T. p. jamesi*) in Jefferson and Wasco counties in 1963, but was unsuccessful (Olson 1976). From 1991 to 1993, 86 Columbian sharp-tails were reintroduced 18 mi (29 km) east of Enterprise on Clear L. Ridge. In 1993, it became apparent that this site was unsuitable and an area 4 mi (6 km) north of Enterprise was selected after several radioed Clear L. Ridge birds moved there. Between 1993 and 1997, 98 Columbian sharp-tails were obtained from Idaho and released at this location. Birds were translocated within 48 hr of capture and released at night near established leks. Most remained in the lek area and did not disperse great distances as many Clear L. birds did. Also predation on transplants was much lower at the Enterprise site. The population in spring 1998 was estimated at 50-75 birds on the Wallowa Co. restoration site. Twenty-six birds were counted on three leks during Apr 1998. Nine males and three females were trapped on the primary lek 1997-99; of these, nine were locally hatched birds. Sharp-tails appear to be slowly increasing but are at such low numbers that their status is still uncertain. The birds are on the west side of the Zumwalt prairie with many square miles of unoccupied habitat available. Future surveys are planned in habitats adjacent to existing sharp-tail use areas as well as Baker Co. sites where birds were last documented.

An ODFW Columbian sharp-tail restoration plan to establish a second population west of the Blue Mtns. is in progress. The primary management emphasis is the continued reintroduction to suitable former habitats. Sources of birds for translocation are limited. Idaho Fish and Game has generously supplied birds for Oregon from the Curlew and Pocatello valleys near Malad. Restoration of grassland and riparian areas has restored some large blocks of habitat, especially where CRP seedings have replaced extensive areas of grain. Hopefully, this species can be restored to historic range in Oregon where suitable habitat exists.—*Victor L. Coggins*

## Subfamily Meleagridinae

### Wild Turkey *Meleagris gallopavo*

The Wild Turkey is the largest game bird in N. America with mature males (gobblers) weighing >20 lb (9 kg) and standing 40 in (102 cm) tall. These large terrestrial birds are generally dark brown to black in appearance, but iridescent color in feathers ranging from gold and copper to green and black gives an intriguing, metallic appearance, particularly in full sunlight. Males and approximately 10% of females (Keegan and Crawford unpubl. data) sport a unique beard of keratinous filaments (Pelham and Dickson 1992) that protrudes from the junction of the breast and neck. Beards grow continuously but rarely exceed 10 in (25 cm) in length because the ends wear off from friction with the ground. Females are smaller and duller in appearance. The head of both sexes is sparsely feathered.

Turkeys have an important place in N. American history, providing an important food source for native Americans and European settlers. The s. Mexican subspecies *M. g. gallopavo*, now probably extinct in the wild, was domesticated before Spanish explorers arrived, and turkeys remain the only American species under significant domestication (Williams 1984). Nearly extirpated early in the 20th century by market and subsistence harvest and forest clearing; restoration of this important game bird is a major success story of modern wildlife management. Has been reestablished throughout its original range in the U.S. and widely introduced outside the historic range. Wild Turkeys are hunted in every state except Alaska.

**General Distribution:** Endemic to N. America, historic distribution included the e. and mid-western U.S., stretching from s. Maine west to S. Dakota and southwest to Arizona, and south through most of Mexico. Currently, populations are found in all lower 48 states, Hawaii, n. Mexico, and five Canadian provinces (Wunz 1992). Two of six subspecies occur in Oregon, and a third subspecies exists primarily in a feral state. Subspecific identifications in this account derive primarily from knowledge of source localities.

**Oregon Distribution:** Densities are highest in forests and interspersed open habitats at low to mid-elevation in the Klamath, Ochoco, Blue, and Wallowa mountains, w. Cascades, Umpqua Valley, Willamette Valley, and ne. Cascades. Local in the Coast Range, e. Columbia Basin, High Lava Plains, and se. Cascades. Rio Grande Wild Turkeys (*M. g. intermedia*) occur in all areas listed above. A population of Merriam's Wild Turkeys (*M. g. merriami*) existed in the ne. Cascades, but releases of Rio Grande Turkeys in that area in the late

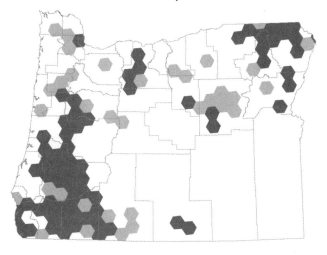

1990s will likely result in an area of intergradation. A predominantly feral population of Eastern Wild Turkeys (*M. g. silvestris*) persists in the Coburg Hills, Lane and Linn Cos. (W. Castillo p.c.). Turkeys are occasionally found at high elevations (>5,000 ft [1500 m]) in sw. and e. Oregon mountains (M. Denny p.c., *TK*).

**Habitat and Diet:** Turkeys are often considered generalists in both habitat use and diet. Nevertheless, specific habitat characteristics are seasonally important or necessary for specific life-history phases. Because turkeys roost above the ground at night, distribution is limited to forested habitats. However, they will roost on human-made objects where trees are rare or absent. Locally common in forested habitats including mixed conifer, oak woodlands and savannas, and ponderosa pine. Meadows and grassland edges within and adjacent to these forested habitats are important foraging areas.

Wild Turkeys are ground nesters. Keegan (1996) reported that Rio Grande Turkeys nested in low shrub patches <65 ft (20 m) in diameter and nest sites were heavily screened by vegetation (>75% horizontal screening 0-24 in [60 cm] above ground). Merriam's Turkeys in nc. Oregon frequently nested in slash left from precommercial thinning (Lutz and Crawford 1987a). Broods used relatively open stands dominated by bare ground, with moderate vegetative cover (44-52%) (Keegan and Crawford 1997). Average roost trees in sw. Oregon were >105 yr old, 20 in (50 cm) dbh, and 108 ft (33 m) tall (n=565) (Keegan 1996). Douglas-fir and ponderosa pine accounted for >90% of roost trees (Lutz and Crawford 1987b, Keegan 1996). Some roost sites are used repeatedly within seasons (particularly winter) and among years. In Douglas Co., average 95% minimum convex polygon annual home range size was 9,815 ac (3,972 ha, n=43) (Keegan and Crawford 2000).

Best described as opportunistic omnivores, turkeys consume a wide variety of green vegetation, seeds, and soft and hard mast (Hurst 1992). Animal matter is occasionally taken, but typically comprises a small percentage of annual diets. Consumption of insects and snails by females increases during nesting (Beasom and Pattee 1978). Poults (young turkeys <4 wk old) consume large amounts of insects during the first few weeks of life, but quickly switch to a diet consisting chiefly of vegetative matter (Hurst 1992). Therefore, adequate insect density in early and mid-summer is important to annual productivity.

**Seasonal Activity and Behavior:** Wild Turkeys are gregarious birds, usually found in flocks of several to as many as several hundred. Although permanent residents, turkeys often move seasonally to winter at lower elevations (often in association with agricultural land), and move to higher elevations to nest and raise broods. Male breeding displays (Mar-May) are impressive: they gobble loudly and strut in front of females with feathers erect, wings dragging on the ground, and tail feathers fanned out. In sw. Oregon, mean adult nest initiation occurred during the second week in Apr; corresponding mean hatch dates were the third week in May (Keegan and Crawford 1999). Yearling females nested later than adults. Clutch size averages 11. Precocious poults leave nests within 12-24 hr of hatching. As poults grow older, brood flocks tend to congregate and slowly move toward wintering areas.

Wild Turkeys are credited with 28 distinct vocalizations (Williams 1984). The most well-known call is the gobble of the male, heard primarily in early morning (beginning while birds are still on the roost) and evening. Males gobble in response to calls of females and other gobbles, but will also respond to loud noises (e.g., thunder, coyote howl, slamming car door).

**Detection:** Several methods are valuable for determining presence of Wild Turkeys, but reliable census techniques are lacking. During spring breeding period, most easily detected by gobbling call of males. However, gobble counts may not provide reliable population estimates because of wide variation in gobbling frequency (Kurzejeski and Vangilder 1992). Direct counts of flocks from mid-summer through winter when birds may be conspicuous in meadows and pastures can provide an index to population status. Track counts in snow can contribute data regarding presence and relative abundance. Turkeys are vocal during early morning and evening through much of the year; under appropriate conditions, flocks can be located by listening for calls from high points.

**Population Status and Conservation:** Wild Turkeys are not native to Oregon. Early attempts to introduce game-farm-reared Eastern Turkeys failed (except for a feral population in the Coburg Hills). Wild Merriam's Wild Turkeys were captured from sites within the exclusive native range and released at four locations in e. Oregon during the early 1960s (Durbin 1975, ODFW undated files [b]). Only one of these releases, in Hood R. and Wasco counties, resulted in a viable population, primarily in the foothills east of Mt. Hood. Birds of the Rio Grande subspecies (acquired from the state of California) were first released in Rogue R. Valley in 1975 (Durbin 1975). Subsequent sources for wild-trapped Rio Grande Wild Turkeys were within the exclusive native range of that subspecies in western Texas and Kansas (ODFW undated files [b]). Since then, turkey populations have substantially increased, chiefly because of a continued translocation program with the Rio Grande subspecies and natural expansion.

Populations in Oregon will likely continue to grow and expand into suitable unoccupied habitat, both as a result of natural movements and continued translocation programs. However, periodic severe winter weather in parts of e. Oregon may limit their eventual range. Harvest of males during spring seasons increased from 563 in 1988 to >2,500 in 1999 (ODFW 1999b) and 3,699 in 2002 (ODFW 2002).—*Tom Keegan*

## Family Odontophoridae

**Mountain Quail** *Oreortyx pictus*
This is the largest native quail in N. America and one of the least understood. Males and females have identical plumage characterized by distinctive white flank barring and prominent vertical head plumes. The first documented description was in Lewis and Clark's journals when hunters from their outbound expedition to the Pacific collected two birds near Rooster Rock, 14 mi (23 km) east of Portland along the Columbia R. (Burroughs 1961). In 1826, David Douglas collected two pairs near Elkton in sw. Oregon and provided the first taxonomic description (Douglas 1829).

**General Distribution:** Mountain Quail have the most northerly distribution of any quail in w. N. America, ranging north to Washington and south to Baja, Mexico (Johnsgard 1973), and occur as high as 3,500 m (11,482 ft). In the Intermountain Region, can be found in w. Nevada, w. Idaho, and along many tributaries of the Snake R. Five subspecies are recognized by the AOU (1957); *pictus* breeds west of the Cascades and *palmeri*, a paler subspecies, breeds east of the Cascades (Browning 1977, 2002). As with almost all so-called upland game species, introductions and transplantations have obscured present morphologies and ranges (*MRB*).

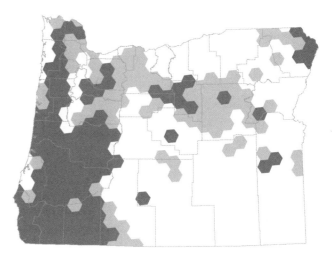

**Oregon Distribution:** In e. Oregon, range appears reduced from historical accounts (Gabrielson and Jewett 1940). In Wallowa Co., they are located primarily along eastern tributaries of the Imnaha R. and the Snake R. (*MP*), but generally considered occasional in Union and Wallowa counties (Evanich 1992a). They have been observed along many of the tributaries of the John Day R. in Wheeler and Grant counties, and some tributaries of the Deschutes and Crooked rivers in Wasco, Jefferson, Deschutes, and Crook counties (OBBA, *MP*). Also in the Mosier Cr. drainage, Wasco Co. (C. Corkran p.c.). Rare in extreme nw. Malheur and n. Harney counties (OBBA); rare along L. Owyhee, Succor Cr., and Bully Cr., and on Mahogany Mtn. in c. Malheur Co. (Contreras and Kindschy 1996); rare on west slope of Steens Mtn. in s. Harney Co. (C. Littlefield p.c.), and Trout Cr. Mtns. in s. Malheur Co. (Contreras and Kindschy 1996). Rare along the east slope of the Cascades, but more widespread in sw. Klamath Co.; rare and local in Lake Co. (OBBA). In w. Oregon, found in most forested mountainous areas generally above 1,640 ft (500 m) (OBBA, *MP*), but may move to valley bottoms in winter (Fix 1990a, *MP*), and are occasionally at backyard bird feeders (*MP*). Low numbers are found in nw. Oregon. Casual along the outer coast, where it is usually found along the beachgrass-forest ecotone (*ALC*).

**Habitat and Diet:** Observed in a variety of habitat types across its range but generally found in shrub-dominated communities (Gutiérrez and Delehanty 1999). In w. Oregon, associated with early successional vegetation composed of a diverse array of shrubs, often associated with early seral conifer plantations. In fall and spring, Mountain Quail are often observed foraging along logging roads and open, shrubby mountain slopes and ridge tops. In the semi-arid, eastern portion of Oregon range, are associated with riparian areas; usually along the ecotone of riparian core vegetation and more grassy, open uplands (Contreras and Kindschy 1996, *MP*). Nest sites vary with open-shrub-dominated communities often selected for nest sites in w. Oregon and grass or shrub patches near riparian areas in e. Oregon.

They are primarily seed eaters, but consume a variety of greenery, berries, and insects if available (Gutiérrez and Delehanty 1999). In fall in the western portion of their range, they forage on many different plant species, especially legumes. No data exist on diets in e. Oregon, but in w. Idaho, Ormiston (1966) reported hawthorn, clover, and grass seeds consumed extensively in early fall while chickweed and microsteris were the most important food items during spring. In se. Washington, Yocum and Harris (1953) found that sumac, vicia, elderberry, clover, hackberry, and chickweed were important food sources. In w. Oregon, fall diets consisted primarily of vetch, clover, Scot's-broom, black medic, peavine, and blackberry (Pope 1999).

**Seasonal Activity and Behavior:** Because of their secretive habits and occurrence in remote areas with rugged terrain, many life-history characteristics have not been studied. Mostly monogamous. Males display little territoriality. Beginning in early Mar, winter coveys start to break apart and pair bonds begin to form. By the end of Mar most birds are paired with mates and either remain in winter ranges to nest or migrate to new breeding sites in higher-elevation habitats. May move 15-19 mi (25-30 km) to breeding ranges. High reproductive output in response to high annual adult mortality, low chick survival, high nest-loss rates, and fluctuating resource conditions. Females may lay eggs in two simultaneous clutches (Heekin et al. 1994, Pope 1999). Males will incubate one clutch and females the other. Consequently, during May, females may deposit as many as 26 eggs in two separate nests. Clutch size averages 11 eggs (Gutiérrez and Delehanty 1999, Pope 1999). Have unusually long incubation periods of 26 days (Pope 1999). Peak of hatch is the first week in Jul (Pope 1999), but broods frequently observed mid-Jun through Jul, and rarely as early as May (OBBA, Fix 1990a). Males and females generally brood their chicks separately until the chicks are capable of short flights. May remain in nesting area or immediately move their broods 1-3 mi (2-4 km). Fall coveys average 8-15 birds. In early Dec, Mountain Quail that had migrated to breeding ranges in spring return to winter range habitats (*MP*). In e. Douglas Co., wintering birds present at Toketee RS Oct-Mar (Fix 1990a).

**Detection:** In late summer and fall, when covey sizes are large, they are often observed foraging along logging roads and brushy clearcuts in w. Oregon. Several hours after sunrise or several hours before sunset are the best times to observe Mountain Quail. They frequently respond to simulated yelp calls during Apr, May, and occasionally through fall. They are generally difficult to locate during winter but pairs frequent roadsides during Apr and May.

**Population Status and Conservation:** Earlier in the 20th century Mountain Quail were present in almost every county of e. Oregon (Gabrielson and Jewett 1940), c. and sw. Idaho, and w. and se. Washington. Distributions have contracted in the Pacific Northwest with the species rare or absent in se. Oregon, present in low numbers in ne. Oregon, and rare in most parts of se. Washington and w. Idaho. They are rare if not extirpated in many historic ranges in Nevada, se. Washington, and w. Idaho. Populations have persisted but appear to be declining in ne. Oregon (ODFW 1999a). Appear to be stable and abundant in sw. Oregon. May have declined in nw. Oregon (*DBM*).

They are hunted in w. Oregon during Sep-Jan with a 10-bird/day limit, but seasons closed for most of e. Oregon with the exception of Wallowa Co. with a 2-bird/day limit (*MP*).—*Mike Pope*

### California Quail *Callipepla californica*

California Quail are the most widely distributed upland game birds in Oregon. Most easily recognized by the comma-shaped, black plume, or "topknot," which bends forward and is larger on the male. In the adult male, the top of the head, back of the neck, and flanks are olive-brown; the flanks and sides are streaked with white. The face is black, bordered by a white stripe, except for a small tan to brown forehead; the remaining upperparts are brownish gray with black and white vermiculations on the neck. The upper breast, sides, back, and tail are bluish gray; the belly is tan with a black scale pattern except for a central chestnut patch. Adult female is similar but with duller tones and brownish overall although the nape is clearly patterned, head is entirely brownish gray and belly is "scaly" without the chestnut patch.

**General Distribution:** Best described by Leopold (1977), the native range included all of Baja California and California (except for Colorado and e. Mojave deserts and high elevations), a small portion of w. Nevada and sw. Oregon. Widely introduced elsewhere from s. British Columbia through the Pacific states to Baja, including Idaho, Nevada, and Utah (Calkins et al. 1999). Six subspecies in N. America; two subspecies, *brunnescens* and *californica*, occur in Oregon (AOU 1957, Browning 2002). A seventh, *orecta*, recognized by Johnsgard (1973) as found in Oregon, is a synonym with *californica* following Miller (1941, AOU 1957).

**Oregon Distribution:** In the 1800s, *C. c. brunnescens* was resident along humid coastal areas from Coos Co. south, and *C. c. californica* in the relatively dry valleys of s. Oregon, primarily the Rogue and Klamath watersheds (Browning 2002). Mixing of populations through transplant activities, began as early as 1870 by hunters (Gabrielson and Jewett 1940) and 1912 by the Oregon State Game Commission (now ODFW) (Finley 1914), has likely obscured subspecies differences and ranges. It has been a resident statewide since the early 1900s (Gabrielson and Jewett 1940), except for most forests of the n. Coast Range and w. Cascades; it is generally absent along the coast north of Coos Bay (Gilligan et al. 1994). Also absent from high-elevation areas of the e. Cascade range and e. Oregon mountains. They have recently expanded up many drainages in the western face of the Blue Mtns. to elevations of 3,500 ft (1,066 m) in summer (M. Denny p.c.). They extend into the Cascades and Coast Range via lowland river valleys primarily where there are dispersed farms and residences. Common resident in rural and even some suburban areas (*KB*), particularly in e. Oregon where many coveys gather at feeding stations during winter (M. Denny p.c., D. Irons p.c.).

**Habitat and Diet:** Highly adaptable as evidenced by its wide distribution. California Quail are relatively sedentary birds that rely on edge components of a variety of habitats including agricultural lands, brushy streamcourses, forested areas, and even sagebrush environments. Require patches of dense trees or tall shrubs for roosting, escape, and loafing cover as well as adjacent, more open areas for foraging, brood rearing, and travel lanes. Nesting occurs on the ground in a simple nest, typically in the vicinity of open grassland areas (Kilbride et al. 1992). They are common visitors to backyard feeders in rural and some suburban locations. Generally forage in open-ground areas such as roadsides, openings adjacent to cover, and sparse grass areas.

They consume a wide variety of foods: primarily green plant material during the late winter, spring, and summer, and seeds during fall and early winter. Major plants that contribute the bulk of the diet throughout the year (green material and seeds) include legumes, composites (especially the milky-juiced, dandelion forbs), grains, grasses, and other forbs (primarily annuals) (Crawford 1993). Invertebrates constituted less than 1% of the diet by weight in w. Oregon but were consumed year-round (Blakely et al. 1988). Insects were common in the diet during spring and summer (>75% birds examined); ants were the most frequently consumed insect (Blakely et al. 1988). Diet studies throughout Oregon have shown adapt-ability to agricultural crops, weedy species, and even Russian-olive fruits (Crawford 1993).

**Seasonal Activity and Behavior:** Beginning in late Feb, pairs begin to form while males give a single-note advertisement

*California Quail*

call. Nesting begins as early as Apr (Anthony 1970, Leopold 1977). These primarily monogamous quail have one of the largest clutch sizes (often 15-20 eggs) of any N. American game bird. Eggs hatch from May through Sep with a peak in Jul (Crawford 1993). High reproductive rate is necessary to offset equally high annual mortality. Home range during breeding season in w. Oregon averaged 35-50 ac (14-20 ha) (Kilbride et al. 1992). Family group broods stick together and often join others to form large coveys beginning in Sep and continuing through fall and winter. Coveys are generally associated with specific cover patches of rather dense, tall shrubs or trees adjacent to food sources. Daily covey movements of more than 1 mi (1.6 km) are exceptional.

**Detection:** Springtime advertisement calls by the males and the trademark *chi-ca-go* or *cu-CA-cow* call throughout the year. Coveys are most commonly located by calling birds or by observing a male sentinel atop a post or shrub poised to quickly warn of dangers. Alerted quail give a *pit-pit* call at high rates. Small bowl-like depressions on the ground in dry dirt used for dusting are often found next to covey use areas.

**Population Status and Conservation:** In Oregon, California Quail are one of the most heavily hunted game birds with an average of 70,000 birds taken annually (ODFW 1999a). Readily respond to management activities that address the most limiting and essential habitat components within the range of a covey of birds. Techniques include planting trees/shrubs, artificial roosts, planting food plots, and mechanically opening areas of dense cover for food, travel, and foraging access. Improvement of natural water sources and distribution of artificial watering devices (guzzlers) are also important and common management tools (*KB*).—*Kevin Blakely*

## Northern Bobwhite *Colinus virginianus*

Widely distributed throughout the eastern and midwestern U.S. and into Mexico, the Northern Bobwhite is one of the most familiar—and economically one of the most important—game birds in N. America. As a result, has been studied intensively by scientists, and has been used as a model to test the physiological and behavioral effects of pesticides on wildlife. Adult males have a white line above and through the eye and a white throat bordered by black. The head is slightly crested. Underparts are buffy with reddish on sides and narrowly barred with black throughout. Upperparts are reddish brown and black. Adult females are similar except that the white on the face is replaced by buff. During spring, males give the familiar *bob-bobwhite* call throughout the day.

**General Distribution:** Resident from S. Dakota, s. Minnesota, s. Ontario (Canada), and Maine south to Florida, Gulf coast, and Texas. Distribution extends farther south from e. Mexico to extreme sw. Guatemala and several Caribbean Is. (Johnsgard 1975a, Lever 1987, Brennan 1999). Has been introduced to Europe (British Isles, France, Germany), Australasia, New Zealand, and the West Indies (Lever 1987). In the U.S., introduced populations occur in Washington, Oregon, and possibly Idaho (Brennan 1999). Of 22 recognized subspecies, *C. v. virginianus* and *taylori* were introduced to Oregon (AOU 1957). However, the only specimens of the species are *taylori* (Aldrich 1946, Browning 2002). Populations surviving in e. Oregon were presumed by Long (1981), Evanich (1986a), and Lever (1987) without the benefit of specimens to belong to *taylori*.

**Oregon Distribution:** Although single birds are still reported in the Willamette Valley (OBBA), these are undoubtedly released or escaped individuals. This species continues to be a favorite exhibit at state and county fairs and is used by bird-dog trainers throughout the valley. By the early 1990s, only two breeding populations were believed to persist in e. Oregon. One remained in the irrigated farmlands of n. Umatilla Co. near Hermiston and Milton-Freewater. A second population was located in extreme ne. Malheur Co. in the farmlands surrounding Ontario (Evanich 1986a). However, record snowfall in 1993 is believed to have eliminated the population in n. Umatilla Co. (Gilligan et al. 1994). A small population has been present in the Nestucca Bay//Neskowin area since at least the 1990s (R. Lowe p.c.).

**Habitat and Diet:** There is little information on habitat in Oregon; Northern Bobwhites are generally associated with agricultural areas. Elsewhere, they frequent a wide variety of early successional vegetation ranging from grasslands and agricultural fields to open park-like pine and mixed pine-hardwood forests (Brennan 1999). Both sexes participate in building a nest, a shallow depression in the ground lined with grass or other leafy material. Nests are frequently arched over the top with woven grass, effectively concealing the eggs (Gabrielson and Jewett 1940, Johnsgard 1975a, Brennan 1999).

There is no information on diet in Oregon. Elsewhere in their natural range, bobwhites feed mainly on seeds of legumes, cultivated grains (corn, soybean, wheat), weedy herbs, and leaves of succulent plants. Young depend heavily on insects during their first 6-8 wk. Females consume four times as many arthropods as males prior to egg laying (Johnsgard 1975a, Brennan 1999).

**Seasonal Activity and Behavior:** Resident throughout the year with little movement within home range except for unmated males. During spring, coveys disband and previously paired birds may renew their pair bond. Unmated males seek females by uttering their familiar *bobwhite* call throughout the day (Johnsgard 1975a, Brennan 1999). Clutch size varies from 7 to 28 eggs with an average of 12-14 eggs/clutch. Females begin incubation after the last egg is laid and males are known to incubate clutches, especially if the female is killed. Incubation lasts 22-24 days. In general, one brood is reared per breeding season but two and three have been documented (Gabrielson and Jewett 1940, Johnsgard 1975a, Brennan 1999). Both sexes brood precocial young for the first 2 wk of life. During fall, bobwhites form coveys consisting of related and unrelated adults and their broods, ranging in size from 12-17 birds. They have a peculiar habit of roosting together on the ground in a tight circle with each member facing outward. At the approach of danger, explode into the air and fly off in different directions. Reunite by constantly uttering contact calls. Coveys form a social unit through winter and into early spring (Johnsgard 1975a, Brennan 1999).

**Detection:** Except for the single small population in Ontario, Malheur Co., unlikely to be encountered except by driving along farmlands during spring and listening for the familiar *bobwhite* call. Peak calling hours are early morning (05:00-06:00), midday (14:00-15:00), and evening (18:00-19:00) (Brennan 1999).

**Population Status and Conservation:** In 1882, six birds from Indiana were released in the Willamette Valley by Solomon Wright of Tangent, Linn Co. (Gabrielson and Jewett 1940). After this early introduction, numerous releases were undertaken by the Oregon Game Commission (now ODFW) and private individuals from 1899 to 1929 throughout Oregon. These early introductions did well particularly in the following areas: the Willamette Valley, n. Morrow and Umatilla counties, along the Columbia and Umatilla rivers, in Wallowa Co., and in the Ontario region of Malheur Co. Numbers peaked between 1930 and 1950 before rapidly decreasing. By the 1960s small populations persisted in the Willamette Valley (e.g., nw. Beaverton farm area) and some areas of e. Oregon, but by 1975 breeding populations in the Willamette Valley had completely disappeared (Gabrielson and Jewett 1940, Evanich 1986a). This species was still being reported in "fair" numbers from e. Clackamas Co. as late as 1983 (Evanich and Fix 1983). Oregon population numbers are unknown but are probably very small and decreasing. Northern Bobwhite are not threatened globally, but recent changes in agriculture (heavy use of pesticides and

removal of hedgerows between fields) and forestry practices (high-density pine plantations) have negative effects on populations in some parts of their natural range. In addition, suppression of fire necessary to set back plant succession, together with fragmentation of habitat, have resulted in further deterioration of suitable habitat (del Hoyo et al. 1994, Brennan 1999).—*Kamal Islam*

# Order GRUIFORMES
## *Family Rallidae*

**Yellow Rail** *Coturnicops noveboracensis*
A small, secretive rail that is seen and heard far less than any other rail in Oregon. Males vocalize during the breeding season with a five-note call *tic-tic, tic-tic-tic* repeated incessantly during hours of dark, 2200-0400, and call infrequently during the day. Call sounds much like two small rocks being tapped together. Yellow Rails are quite small and have a white patch on the trailing edge of the inner wing (secondaries), more extensive than that on juvenile Soras. Males in the breeding season have a distinct yellow bill and are slightly larger, but otherwise sexes are alike. Chicks are downy black and have a pink bill.

**General Distribution:** Breeds locally in wet meadows in Canada, including Alberta, Saskatchewan, Manitoba, Quebec, Ontario, New Brunswick, and possibly Nova Scotia; in n. U.S. in a tier of states from N. Dakota east to Maine, possibly including Montana, and formerly Ohio; reported from Jackson NWR, Wyoming, in 1998 (B. R. Casler p.c.); and in Mexico (Taylor 1998). Primary winter range is coastal marshes in se. U.S., S. Carolina to Texas. *C. n. noveboracensis* is the subspecies in N. America north of Mexico (AOU 1957).

In the west, a small breeding population was historically reported from sc. Oregon and e. California,

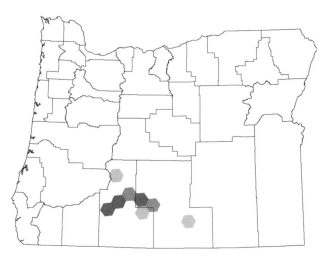

with nest records in California from Bridgeport and Long Valley, Mono Co., in 1922, 1930, 1947, and 1950 (Grinnell and Miller 1944, McCaskie et al. 1988). Two sightings during Jul of 1980 and 1985 from Tuolumne and Mono counties, California (Gaines 1988), and more recently from the extreme northeast corner of Modoc Co., California in late May 2002 (G. Keller p.c.). Winter records along California coast from 1970s in Riverside, Monterey, and Marin counties (McCaskie et al. 1988). More recently, Harris (1996) reported three, possibly four, sightings in Humboldt Co. during winter 1978-91, and one from Mendocino Co. in 1995. Observations also from Tomales Bay, Marin Co., in Dec of 1986, 1987, and 2000 (J. Evens p.c.). In Nov 1998 and 1999, two dead rails found near San Diego and Santa Barbara, and one dead rail found in Del Norte Co. in Oct 1999. From Washington, three records during migration: Skagit R. mouth Nov 1935 (Jewett et al. 1953), Herman Slough, Adams Co., in Apr 1969 (Furrer 1974), and spring 1982 from Columbia NWR, Adams Co. (Rogers TH 1982c).

**Oregon Distribution:** The first Oregon record was female specimen taken 1 Feb 1900 near Scio, Linn Co. (Prill 1937). Subsequently, S. E. Carter and J. E. Patterson found at least two and possibly four nests at Aspen L., Klamath Co., in late May and early Jun of 1926 and 1930, and yet another nest at Shoalwater Bay on Upper Klamath L. on 26 May 1926 (Griffee 1944, Contreras 1993). No Yellow Rails were reported thereafter in Oregon, and as of 1983, the bird was thought to have been extirpated from both Oregon and California (AOU 1983). In 1982, however, Loren Hughes reported two calling Yellow Rails 19-20 Jun near Fort Klamath Historic Monument. The report set off a flurry of sightings in the Fort Klamath and adjoining Wood R. Valley area, with reports from a half-dozen or so sites (Gordon 1984a). From 1988 to 1992, an intensive inventory located calling rails at 27 sites concentrated in Wood R. Valley and at Klamath Marsh NWR; rails were also heard at Sycan Marsh, Lake Co. (Stern et al. 1993). In May 1989, a set of recently predated eggs was found by G. Rosenberg and M. A. Stern near Jack Spring, the first documented breeding record in the w. U.S. in nearly 40 yr (Stern et al. 1993). From 1995 to 1998, 34 nests were found in the Wood R. Valley, the largest sampling of nests ever found in the U.S. (Popper and Stern 2000, *KJP*). In 1991, Yellow Rails were heard calling at Camas Prairie, 8 mi (13 km) east of Lakeview, on 3 Jun, and have since been reported irregularly at Big Marsh, in n. Klamath Co. More recently, they were reported from the Sprague R. Valley at several sites between Copperfield Draw and Beatty in Jul 2002 (S. Lundsten p.c.). There have also been rumors of Yellow Rails at Malheur NWR near Page Springs, but no confirmed sightings.

Other sightings in Oregon include 22 Sep 1988 near Dayton, Yamhill Co. (G. Dorsey p.c.), in a wet meadow near Tillamook in Sep 1989 (A. Pampush p.c.), one found dead in the road near Prineville in the 1970s (J. Pesek p.c.), a sighting in the backwaters of Carty Res., Morrow Co., in the 1980s (J. Ruppe p.c.), a small flock observed at Delta Park, Multnomah Co., in May 1985 (H. Nehls p.c.), and a reported sighting from the wetlands north of Hart L. in the late 1990s (W. DeVaurs p.c.). These sightings are probably associated with migration, but from where and to where remains a matter of interest.

**Habitat and Diet:** Calling male Yellow Rails are found in shallowly flooded sedge meadows at 4,100-5,000 ft (1,250-1,524 m) elevation. Water depth at 660 male calling sites averaged 2.9 +/- 1.4 in (7.3 +/- 3.6 cm [1 standard deviation]) (Lundsten and Popper 2002). Thirty-four nests found 1995-98; 29 were completely or nearly completely covered with a canopy of senescent vegetation, and the other five had domes of live vegetation. Within 11.7-ft$^2$ (1-m$^2$) plots surrounding the nest sites, senescent and live vegetation each accounted for 49% of the cover, with bare ground 2% (Popper and Stern 2000). Short beaked sedge comprised 26% of the live cover; additional species included beaked sedge, inflated sedge, spike rush, Baltic rush, Sierra rush, narrow spiked reedgrass, and tufted hairgrass. Areas with habitat similar to that described often are not occupied.

Based on 23 radio-tagged males, home ranges averaged 47.7 ac (19.3 ha), with range of 11.4-111.7 ac (4.6-45.2 ha). Males moved their territories in response to changing water levels during the breeding season, selecting habitats with water depths of approximately 2.4-2.8 in. (6-7 cm) (Popper and Stern 1996).

The summer diet of Yellow Rails in Quebec included invertebrates (68%) and seeds of sedges and rushes (32%), with beetles and spiders the most common invertebrates (Robert et al. 1997). In Michigan and Minnesota, fed primarily on freshwater snails (Walkinshaw 1939, Savaloja 1981).

**Seasonal Activity and Behavior:** First heard calling in late Apr, with peak calling 1 May to 9 Jun along the west side of the Wood R. Valley 1995-2001 (Lundsten and Popper 2002). Most rails are quiet by late Jul, although many may still be in residence; heard calling as late as early Sep. At Fourmile Cr. sites, incubation was initiated 20 May-21 Jul, hatching occurred 8 Jun-9 Aug, and fledging 13 Jul-13 Sep. Most banded males remain on territory during breeding season; however in 2000 and 2001, three moved 2.6-6.7 mi (4.2-10.7 km) within the Wood R. Valley in Jun and Jul, and one traveled 35 mi (57 km) from Klamath Marsh NWR to Sycan Marsh (Popper and Lundsten 2001, Lundsten and Popper 2002).

During 1995-2000, 242 rails were banded in the Fourmile Cr./Mares Egg Spring area in Klamath Co.; 27 were recaptured the following year at mean distance of 500 yd (547 m) from original location. Overall, only 11% of rails recaptured in subsequent year, and only two rails captured in three successive years (Lundsten and Popper 2002). The low rate of return of male Yellow Rails in successive years is surprising considering the relative constancy of a few discrete breeding areas, but may be indicative of low survivorship and a relatively short life span.

**Detection:** Rarely observed, these rails are detected by their characteristic nocturnal call. High detection (call only) likely in May and Jun at habitual breeding locations; likelihood of visual sighting is low. Radiotelemetry and banding studies have shown that the number of males present may exceed the number calling by as much as 30% (Popper and Stern 1996). The secretive nature of this species leads one to speculate that its distribution may be more wide ranging than currently known, especially in the west, particularly for migrant and wintering populations.

**Population Status and Conservation:** The Oregon population is geographically restricted to a small portion of the state and apparently disjunct from the main population that occurs east of the Rocky Mtns. Currently, they breed on both private and publicly managed lands, though a majority of the rails and the more-optimal habitats occur on public lands at Klamath Marsh NWR, and on BLM and USFS Winema NF lands in the Fourmile Cr. and Jack Spring area. Recent estimates indicate approximately 235-285 pairs breeding in Oregon (Lundsten and Popper 2002).

The most persistent threat to Yellow Rails is the loss of wetland habitat through various types of development. Specifically, diking, ditching, and draining of wetlands is not only a direct and obvious threat, but the subtle ditching and deepening of creeks, ditches, and irrigation canals often lowers the water table in the adjoining wetlands, effectively making the site too dry for rails. Three specific examples of this during the 1980s in the Wood R. Valley led to abandonment of the sites by rails in subsequent years. Fortunately, Yellow Rails may also colonize restored wetlands, as evidenced by their recent discovery and continued presence at the BLM's Wood R. wetland restoration project.

Management practices at wetland nesting sites may also threaten this species. Nesting Yellow Rails use senescent vegetation from the previous year to conceal their nests; intensive livestock grazing that removes more than 50% of the cover may render potential nesting areas unsuitable in the following year. Also, flood irrigation practices may deliver a pulse of water to nesting meadows in Jun or Jul, inundating active

Yellow Rail nests. Loss of wintering habitat along the coast of California may also threaten Yellow Rails from Oregon, though further study is needed to confirm the location of wintering areas and identify migration routes for this population that breeds in Oregon.—*Mark A. Stern and Kenneth J. Popper*

### Virginia Rail *Rallus limicola*

With its long, decurved bill, the black and cinnamon Virginia Rail probes the mud for much of its food. Its narrow body is specially designed for slipping through a densely vegetated marsh, so it rarely has to move away from cover. Known for its staccato *kidik, kidik* call, this rail also contributes grunts, clicks, churs, squeaks, *skeeuws*, and quack-like noises to the marsh chorus.

**General Distribution:** Breeds all across Canada south through the U.S. and portions of Mexico, probably to Guatemala; moves away from colder areas during winter. Resident in sw. Colombia and Peru in S. America. *R. l. limicola* is the subspecies in N. America (Taylor 1998).

**Oregon Distribution:** This is a rare to locally abundant breeder. In w. Oregon, breeds in freshwater and brackish marshes. In e. Oregon, large marshes in Klamath, Lake, and Harney counties host numerous breeders each year, as do smaller wetland patches. It is also found in small marshes scattered in the midst of wooded areas (*BC*), and occasionally in high-elevation marshes (Gilligan et al. 1994). It is a regular spring and fall transient throughout the state. Largest numbers winter in marshy areas on and near the coast, but may be found wintering in any marshy habitat that remains usable (Contreras 1997b). It is absent from cold, inhospitable areas in winter such as Sycan Marsh, Lake Co. (Stern, Del Carlo, et al. 1987), but regularly present at the Wallowa Fish Hatchery pond at Enterprise, Wallowa Co. (Evanich 1982d, 1991b, Korpi 2000).

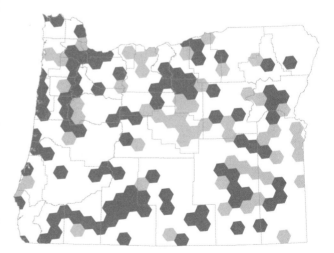

**Habitat and Diet:** The most preferred habitat is wetland, about half covered by vegetation, the remainder consisting of open water, mudflats, and matted vegetation; this type of wetland is the most productive for the macroinvertebrate food source (Conway 1995). At Sycan Marsh, Lake Co., breeds in wet meadows, including sedge, rush, and tufted hairgrass types (Stern, Del Carlo, et al. 1987). Prefers emergent stands, primarily hardstem bulrush, at Malheur NWR, Harney Co. One nest, considered unusual, found in creeping wild rye on dry land near Double O Ranch, Malheur NWR (Littlefield 1990a). In Union and Wallowa counties, the Virginia Rail mainly uses low-elevation cattail and tule marshes (Evanich 1992a), and cattail and bulrush marshes in Malheur Co. (Contreras and Kindschy 1996). In Washington, it is not present in most high-elevation wet meadows where Soras are present (Smith et al. 1997). Also uses coastal saltwater marshes (Thornburgh 1991). Nest is well concealed on a tussock, mat of vegetation, or driftwood, or at the base of a clump of cattails; woven of coarse marsh vegetation and may include a canopy and an entrance runway (Ripley 1977, Conway 1995, Taylor 1996, Taylor 1998). Thick clumps of sedge were the most common nest location at McFaddens Marsh in the 1940s (now a part of William L. Finley NWR, Benton Co.) (Evenden et al. 1950), but habitat is drastically changed there now (*DBM*). Male builds 1-5 brood nests in close proximity to one another (Taylor 1996).

May be found using wet fields and roadside ditches during migration in the Willamette Valley (Herlyn 1998). Rarely found in dry habitats. Singles were found in a logged-over burn just east of La Pine, Deschutes Co., 23 Jun 2001 (T. Rodenkirk p.c.), and in a dry grassy field at E. E. Wilson W.A., Benton Co., in Nov 1990 (Herlyn 1998). In spring migration, it has been found in the bottomlands of the John Day R., Grant Co, where flood irrigation is used in the hay fields (Sullivan 1990). They are also regular at the Fields oasis in migration (D. Irons p.c.). On the coast in winter, it uses vegetated wet areas such as grassy swales, sumps, ditches, holes, and willow thickets with standing water but without marsh vegetation, as well as typical marshes (Contreras 1992, 1998).

This rail eats worms, insects and their larvae, caterpillars, spiders, slugs, snails, small aquatic invertebrates, small fish, amphipods, crustaceans, frogs, and small snakes, as well as aquatic plants and seeds. In winter, diet includes a larger proportion of seeds (Conway 1995). No information on Oregon diet, but preferred food plants in an Iowa study included duckweed, sedge, and smartweed (Horak 1970), all of which are represented in Oregon marshes. It has wing claw that enables it to climb through marsh vegetation (Taylor 1998). With long claws on its feet, it can walk on floating vegetation while foraging (Conway 1995).

Feeds primarily by probing in mud on shore, in shallow water, or under floating vegetation (Taylor 1998). Relies more on animal material than Sora, which may partly explain why the two species successfully share nesting territories (Horak 1970).

**Seasonal Activity and Behavior:** Average spring arrival in Corvallis, Benton Co., is 26 Mar, although some may arrive much earlier (Gillson 1998). E. Oregon migrants begin to arrive in Mar; average arrival date at Malheur NWR is 20 Apr (Ivey, Herziger, and Scheuering 1998). Peak migration at Malheur NWR is the last week of Apr to the first week of May (Littlefield 1990a). Nesting begins by mid-May at Malheur NWR (Littlefield 1990a). Average nest has 8.5 eggs, range 4-13 (Taylor 1996). A nest found at Malheur NWR had 10 eggs (Littlefield 1990a). Incubation begins at least 1 day before final egg is laid; lasts 18-20 days. All eggs usually hatch within 48 hr of each other (Conway 1995). Downy young found as early as 22 Apr at McFaddens Marsh (Evenden et al. 1950) and 9 May in e. Oregon (OBBA), and are found into Aug statewide (Littlefield 1990a, OBBA). Peak hatching time is the last week in May at Sauvie I., Columbia/Multnomah Cos, in 1968 (Crowell and Nehls 1968b). Downy chicks are black and lack orange bristles on chin that Sora chicks have (Kaufmann 1987). Young can run, drink, and swim by end of first day (Conway 1995). Parents may carry chicks in bill (Taylor 1998). Young can feed on their own within 3-7 days, although fed by adults for up to 3 wk (Taylor 1998). Thermoregulation and development of wing limbs and flight feathers take longer (Kaufmann 1987). Brooded for 3-4 wk. Young can fly within 4 wk (Taylor 1998). Postjuvenal molt begins when chicks are 12-14 wk. May double brood, especially in the s. U.S. (Taylor 1998). They are not known to double brood in Oregon, but breeding season is long enough to allow it.

Generally, the Virginia Rail will winter coastally and inland where temperature does not go below 20° F (7° C) (Root 1988). Many coastal and some inland CBCs have tallied over 20 individuals; highest was 86 at Port Orford in 1998. Nearly all CBCs in the state have had at least one record of Virginia Rail.

**Detection:** Easier to hear than see. Best viewing times are during early morning hours or near dusk, when it is away from cover, but may be seen at other times of day by those with the patience to spend a lot of time watching edges and open spots in marsh vegetation. It will respond to tapes and other noises such as clapping, tapping two stones together, or imitations of its call or that of Sora. It is more vocal from about Apr to Jul, especially within 1 hr or so of dawn or dusk; after Jul, vocalization less frequent, so detection more difficult (Conway 1995).

**Population Status and Conservation:** Not globally threatened (Taylor 1996). The Virginia Rail is as common as or more common than Sora all along the Oregon coast, with the possible exception of Beaver Cr. marsh, Lincoln Co. (Faxon 1995), and in most of the rest of the state, except for Sycan Marsh, Lake Co. (Stern, Del Carlo, et al. 1987), Malheur NWR (Littlefield 1990a), and ne. Oregon (Evanich 1992a). From BBS data, a statistically significant population increase occurred in the combined area of British Columbia, California, Oregon, and Washington 1966-99; data for Oregon alone showed an increase that was not statistically significant.

It may collide with towers, utility wires, and wire fences while migrating at low altitudes at night (Taylor 1996). Subject to predation by other birds, such as Great Egret, Sandhill Crane, and raptors. Minks, coyotes, and feral house cats prey on both adults and young (Conway 1995).

Habitat loss has probably reduced some populations over the long term, since over 1 million acres (given as 456,119 ha) of wetland and riparian habitat have been lost in the Willamette Valley since Euro-American settlement (Titus et al. 1996). Oregon as a whole has lost about 38% of its original freshwater wetlands, including 75% of the original wetlands in the Klamath Basin (Oregon Progress Board 2000). While Guard (1995) states that marsh birds use reed canarygrass for food, shelter, and nesting, more research is needed to determine the impacts of the spread of this aggressive, monoculture-forming plant on populations of species such as Sora and Virginia Rail (*DBM*). New wetlands being established in Willamette Valley wildlife refuges and efforts to rejuvenate wildlife habitats elsewhere should assist in the maintenance and expansion of Virginia Rail populations (*BC, DBM*). Actions that keep 30-60% of wetland in open water or mudflat, while improving emergent vegetation in the remainder, will benefit Virginia Rail the most (Conway 1995).—
*Barbara Combs*

## Sora *Porzana carolina*

The Sora's call is difficult to translate into human syllables: *koo-wa, ker-wee, ka-e, kooEE, surrrr-eeeee,* and *soar-UH* are several of many attempts. The notes are clear and steady, with the second syllable higher-pitched than the first. Smaller than a robin, this shy skulker is difficult to see, even though it is present during the nesting season in marshes throughout the state. The Sora is mostly brown with a black face and a stout yellow bill. Its chicks are small black balls of fluff with a bit of orange feathering under their chins.

**General Distribution:** Breeds across N. America from se. Alaska through Canada south into s. New Mexico in the west, through c. Oklahoma and Illinois,

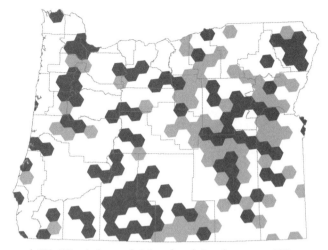

and W. Virginia and Maryland in the east. Winters from Oregon south through California and across the western states to New Mexico and Texas, east to Maryland. Monotypic (AOU 1957).

**Oregon Distribution:** Rare to locally abundant breeder in freshwater marshes throughout Oregon, including a few locations at fairly high elevations (e.g., 7,300 ft [2,224 m] at Lily L., Steens Mtn., Harney Co.) (Lundsten 1993). The Sora is known to breed on the coast at the Astoria mitigation bank, Clatsop Co. (Patterson 1998b), and the saltmarsh at Bandon (Thornburgh 1991, Brown et al. 1996). A representative sample of breeding sites in interior w. Oregon includes Ankeny NWR, Marion Co. (Tice 1999b), McFadden's Marsh (now part of William L. Finley NWR) (Evenden et al. 1950), Fern Ridge Res., Lane Co. (Rodgers 1993, ODFW undated checklist [a]), and possibly Jackson Co. (Browning 1975a, Janes et al. 2001). In Linn Co., it has bred at a farm in the lowlands (Gillson 1998), as well as in the vicinity of Clear L. in the w. Cascades (OBBA). Breeds in the Sunriver area, Deschutes Co. (Sunriver Nature Center undated). The most extensive breeding areas are large marshes of Klamath, Lake, and Harney counties, including Sycan Marsh (Stern, Del Carlo, et al. 1987), the Klamath Falls area (Summers 1993a), the Warner Valley (USFWS 1994b), and Malheur NWR (Littlefield 1990a, OBBA). It is not as common at Summer L. W.A. (ODFW undated checklist [c]). In Malheur Co., Preble (1915) found breeding birds in meadows by Succor Cr. and in the marsh at Cow Lakes. Regular spring and fall transient throughout the state in suitable habitat.

The Sora chiefly winters where Jan temperatures stay above 30º F (-1º C) (Root 1988), but winter records exist for all months in both e. and w. Oregon. Winters annually in the Rogue Valley, Jackson Co. (Contreras 1997b, Janes et al. 2001) and on the coast (Contreras 1992, 1998, Tweit 1989), often at Millicoma Marsh (Rodenkirk 2000), but not limited to these locations. It is regular on Coquille Valley and Medford CBCs; the high count for the state was nine in Medford in 1993. As many as five wintered at Port Orford in 1985-86 (Heinl 1986c). More likely to overwinter in e. Oregon when weather is mild and open water is present. It is not detected every winter in the Klamath Basin (Summers 1982a). No location in e. Oregon stands out as preferred by the wintering birds that are irregularly found there. Sites where they are found are typically marshy and not frozen over. Single individuals have been found on John Day, Fort Klamath, and Klamath Falls CBCs, and there is one count-week record for Malheur NWR.

**Habitat and Diet:** In the breeding season, Soras use wet meadows, including sedge, rush, and hair grass types, but also wet areas with emergent vegetation, particularly cattails and tules (Stern, Del Carlo, et al. 1987, Littlefield 1990a, Kristensen et al. 1991) and coastal saltmarsh habitat (Thornburgh 1991). The two most preferred breeding vegetative habitat types are edges of freshwater marshes, and lake/pond shoreline and islands (OBBA). At McFadden's Marsh in Benton Co., Evenden et al. (1950) found nests in dense clumps of sedge (but habitat there is very different now) (*DBM*). In migration and in winter, it uses wet fields and some upland habitat, as well as fresh- and saltwater marshes (Melvin and Gibbs 1996). They have been observed in irrigated hayfields in the bottomlands along the John Day R., Grant Co., during spring migration (Sullivan 1990).

The Sora eats invertebrates, seeds, plant leaves, and stems. No dietary information is available specific to Oregon, but food plant types listed by Taylor (1998) that are represented in Oregon include smartweed, loosestrife, sticktight, rush, sedge, flatsedge, bulrush, spike-rush, witchgrass, cockspur, leersia, foxtail, duckweed, and pondweed. Invertebrate prey includes mollusks, crustaceans, and insects. Soras consume more invertebrates in spring than in other seasons (Melvin and Gibbs 1996). They feed by pecking, and may use their feet or bill to move vegetation aside (Melvin and Gibbs 1996). They rely more on plant material than the Virginia Rail, which may partly explain why the two species successfully share nesting territories (Horak 1970).

**Seasonal Activity and Behavior:** Spring arrival begins with a trickle of individuals in Mar. Generally present at coastal sites by early Apr (Contreras 1992); average arrival in Corvallis, Benton Co., area is 7 Apr (Gillson 1998). An arrival date of 7 Feb for flocks in the Klamath Falls area (Watson 1980b) has been questioned as possibly representing overwintering birds (Contreras 1992). Common in Mar in the Klamath Basin (Summers 1982a). Average arrival date at Malheur NWR is 20 Apr (Ivey, Herziger, and Scheuering 1998); peak spring migration at Malheur NWR is 5-15 May (Littlefield 1990a).

At Malheur NWR, nesting begins in early May and peaks in the last half of the month (Littlefield 1990a). Clutches generally consist of 10-12 eggs (Bent 1926); an average of 10.6 eggs were found in eight clutches at the Double O Ranch, Malheur NWR (Littlefield 1990a). Nests have been found in late Apr and early May in Benton Co. (Evenden et al. 1950). Young have been found in e. Oregon from 20 May to 27 Jul (OBBA), with some into Aug (Littlefield 1990a).

At Malheur NWR, fall migration begins in late Aug and peaks in the first half of Sep; most birds are gone by mid-Oct (Littlefield 1990a). Migration timing in w. Oregon is similar (Herlyn 1998). Winters annually in w. Oregon on the coast and inland (Contreras 1992, Brown et al. 1996, Contreras 1998, Rodenkirk 2000).

**Detection:** Rarely seen. Soras usually stay hidden in vegetation. As a result, confirmed breeding records are less numerous than might be expected based on actual abundance. Dawn and dusk are probably the best times to see a Sora at the edge of a marsh's vegetative cover. Soras are frequently heard; they vocalize more often than the Virginia Rail. Their distinctive two-note call and descending series of single notes are easily recognizable. They also make a nonmusical *keck* sound. Readily respond to taped or imitated calls, particularly during the breeding season, including those of its own species and the Virginia Rail. In Colorado, responses tapered off by late Jun (Glahn 1974).

**Population Status and Conservation:** The Sora has the largest range of any rail in N. America and is the most numerous rail species (Melvin and Gibbs 1996). Most Oregon checklists consider Sora to be as common as or less common than Virginia Rail, but checklists for Sycan Marsh, Lake Co. (Stern, Del Carlo, et al. 1987), Malheur NWR, and ne. Oregon (Evanich 1992a) list Sora as more common. Possibly excepting Beaver Cr. marsh, Lincoln Co. (Faxon 1995), is less common than Virginia Rail all along the Oregon coast. Oregon BBS data for 1966-99 indicate growth in population (but not statistically significant).

Accidental mortality occurs by ingestion of lead shot and capture in traps meant for fur-bearing mammals (Melvin and Gibbs 1996). A juvenile found hit by a car and threatened by a cat in a Newport, Lincoln Co., parking lot (Fix 1991) epitomized other threats to the species. Soras often fly low and may become victims of collisions with fencing material such as barbed wire (Knight and Skriletz 1980). They are preyed upon by other marsh birds and several species of raptors and small mammals (Melvin and Gibbs 1996).

See the Virginia Rail account for a summary of wetland loss in Oregon. Wetland loss is the greatest problem for the survival of rail species (Eddleman et al. 1988). Most suitable types of vegetation need more study. Guard (1995) stated that marsh birds used reed canarygrass for food, shelter, and nesting, but more research is needed to determine the impacts of the spread of this aggressive, monoculture-forming plant on populations of species such as Sora and Virginia Rail (*DBM*). New wetlands being established in Willamette Valley wildlife refuges and efforts to establish and rejuvenate wildlife habitats elsewhere should assist in the maintenance and expansion of Sora populations (*BC, DBM*), particularly if emergent vegetation is emphasized (Melvin and Gibbs 1996). Soras have accepted the Astoria mitigation bank as a breeding area (Patterson 1998b).—*Barbara Combs*

## Common Moorhen *Gallinula chloropus*

This coot-like bird with a bright red bill and shield breeds throughout much of the e. and s. U.S. and from the Sacramento Valley, California, southward through M. and S. America. All but one of the nine Oregon records are in May, and all but one are of single individuals. There are five records from Malheur NWR: 20 May 1972 (Kingery 1972b); 22-24 May 1981 (Rogers 1981, photos OBRC); 12-16 May 1982 (Rogers TH 1982b, Watson 1989); and during May 1984 (Littlefield 1990a). A displaying pair was at Malheur NWR from 17 May to 17 Jul 2001 but no nest or young were observed (Spencer 2001a, *HBN*). One was photographed at Garrison L. in Port Orford, Curry Co., 1 May 1976 (OBRC). One was at the Denman W.A., Jackson Co., 30 May 1982 (Hunn and Mattocks 1982b). A male was collected along Winema Cr., Tillamook Co., 13 Feb 1983 (spec. no. S-8202 CM). One was at Elk R., Curry Co., 16-17 May 2001 (OBRC). The subspecies of birds occurring in Oregon is unknown.—*Harry B. Nehls*

## American Coot *Fulica americana*

Often mistaken for a duck, the American Coot is actually a member of the rail family. It is a smallish, slate-gray water bird with a white bill. At home swimming in ponds and marshes, it seems to propel itself through the water by rhythmically extending its neck. During the nesting season it can be seen enthroned on a sizable nesting platform built from marsh vegetation. It has the largest Oregon breeding population of any waterfowl. Rafts of thousands of coots stage for migration in spring and fall on lakes throughout Oregon.

**General Distribution:** Breeds across Canada southward across the U.S. to Cuba, Jamaica, and Grand Cayman. Winters from British Columbia through the Pacific Northwest and California; across the U.S. from n. Arizona to W. Virginia, south to Panama. Casual in northern areas from the Aleutians to Churchill to Greenland. *F. a. americana* is the subspecies in N. America (AOU 1957).

**Oregon Distribution:** Found throughout most of Oregon in all seasons where open water is available. Some birds are permanent residents (Gullion 1951, Summers 1982a). Very rare local breeder in coastal Lincoln, Lane, Douglas, and Coos counties (Sawyer and Hunter 1988, Contreras 1998, OBBA). Locally very common to rare breeder inland west of the Cascades. Breeds regularly at Sauvie I. (Crowell and Nehls 1968b, OBBA); in Washington Co. (Woodcock 1902, Evanich 1981b, G. Gillson p.c.); William L. Finley NWR, Benton Co. (Woodcock 1902, Herlyn 1998, OBBA); Fern Ridge Res., Lane Co. (Gullion 1951, OBBA); and the marshes north of Medford, Jackson Co. (Browning 1975a, OBBA). It is not known to breed in Hood River Co. (Anderson 1987a). Abundant breeder at large e. Oregon marshes (Stern, Del Carlo, et al. 1987, Littlefield 1990a). Regular spring and fall transient and winter visitant statewide where water remains open.

**Habitat and Diet:** The American Coot breeds in freshwater wetlands with a mix of open water and emergent vegetation (Taylor 1998, *BC*). It uses ponds, cattle-watering reservoirs, marshes, and lakes, often at wildlife refuges such as Malheur NWR and William L. Finley NWR, Benton Co. (Green 1978, Stern, Del Carlo, et al. 1987, Littlefield 1990a, OBBA, *BC*) and nearby wet meadows (Willett 1919). Dominant aquatic plants in major Oregon nesting areas, e.g., Malheur NWR, Summer L. W.A., and Klamath Basin NWR, include hardstem bulrush, broad-leaved cattail, broad-fruited burreed, Baltic rush, western watermilfoil, and pondweeds (*DBM*). The nest is a large platform made of nearby vegetation. In Harney Co., nests seen both in open water and adjacent to emergent vegetation (*BC*). Outside of breeding season, habitat use expands to include sluggish water along the Columbia R.; reservoirs, lakes, and ponds that may lack breeding habitat; coastal marshes and estuaries; grassy fields and cultivated lands; and park lawns and golf courses (Bent

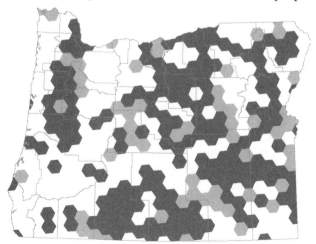

1926, Ehrlich et al. 1988, Taylor 1998, D. Kirkpatrick p.c., *BC, DBM*).

Omnivorous, at times even cannibalistic (Paullin 1987a, Taylor 1998). In a se. Washington study, most frequently consumed plants were pondweeds, water milfoil, and filamentous algae. Invertebrates comprised 21% of the diet in juveniles, and 11% of the diet in adults (Fitzner et al. 1980). May prey on eggs and young of other birds, such as Yellow-headed Blackbird (Hurd 1992, Taylor 1998). Known as "mud hen," it has chicken-like feeding habits when on land (Bent 1926). Especially in winter and during migration, may forage with American Wigeon on lawns such as those at Westmoreland Park in Portland (*BC, DBM*), or in grassy fields such as those adjacent to the Kirtland Road sewage ponds near Medford, Jackson Co. (D. Kirkpatrick p.c.). It is able to feed in deeper water than dabbling ducks, so better able to forage in fall and winter when there is less surface vegetation on the water. American Wigeon are frequently seen associating with American Coots to feed on vegetation that coots break free from weed beds on the bottom (Graves 1996, *MGH*); Wigeon and Gadwall may even steal food from coots in that situation (Ryan 1981, Graves 1996, Taylor 1998). Coots, in turn, may take advantage of food items floating to the surface as a result of feeding behaviors of ducks such as the Canvasback (Anderson 1974) and may steal food from them (Taylor 1998).

**Seasonal Activity and Behavior:** At Malheur NWR, spring arrivals begin in mid-Feb; peak numbers occur in mid-Apr; transients leave by mid-May. Breeding begins late Apr and peaks in mid-May (Littlefield 1990a). It can lay up to 56 eggs in one breeding season. Littlefield (1990a) calls coots a "predator buffer" since the availability of so many coot eggs means that other species experience less predation. Average clutch size (viewed as a minimum because lost/destroyed eggs not included) in e. Washington 6.7, range 6-10 (Fitzner et al. 1980); average 9-10 in other Washington studies (Hill 1986, 1988b). Renested readily in w. Manitoba when first clutch lost or destroyed (Arnold 1993). Incubation 21-27 days (Taylor 1998). At Malheur NWR, incubation starts after first egg is laid. One egg hatches per day. Female tends precocial chicks while male incubates remaining eggs (Littlefield 1990a). Downy young, which may be found in Oregon from late Apr (Kristensen et al. 1991) into late Aug (Littlefield 1979), are largely black with reddish bristles on forehead, lores, and chin. Bare reddish skin on crown (Taylor 1998).

Throughout the state beginning in Sep, the coot gathers on larger lakes for autumn migration. Up to 500,000 have been at Malheur NWR in fall (Littlefield 1990a), though 20,000 to 40,000 is typical. Begins to depart from Malheur NWR in Sep, with most departing 20 Sep-10 Oct (Littlefield 1990a), but fall

numbers have peaked there in early Oct (Anderson 1987b). Large flocks may remain at some lakes into Nov, e.g., 5,000 at Thompson Res., Lake Co., 2 Nov 1997 (Sullivan 1998a); 12,000 in the Davis L./ Wickiup Res. area bordering Deschutes and Klamath counties 2 Nov 1978 (Rogers TH 1979a); more than 2,000 at Haystack Res., Jefferson Co., 4 Nov 1984 (Rogers 1985a); 10,000 at Diamond L., Douglas Co., 11 Nov 1988 (Heinl and Fix 1989); 20,000 at Mann L., Harney Co., 14 Nov 1987 (Anderson 1988b); 250 at Painted Hills Res., Wheeler Co., 16 Nov 1996 (Sullivan 1997a); and 1,600 at L. Selmac Co. Park, Josephine Co., 18 Nov. 2000 (Korpi 2001a). Portions of these flocks may remain into Dec (Winter 1976), or all winter if water remains open. Arrive in Hood River Co. in mid-Sep (Anderson 1987b); full wintering contingent is usually present mid-Oct to late Mar (Anderson 1987e). More numerous on coast in winter than at other times of year. Coastal populations begin to increase to winter levels in Sep (Rogers D 1982, Brown et al. 1996, Contreras 1998, Patterson 1998b). In winter, hundreds to thousands are often found in coastal areas where little or no breeding occurs. State CBC record high is 5,568 in Lincoln City in 1985. They are largely gone from Lincoln Co. by first week of May, but may remain later in some years (Bayer 1995a).

**Detection:** Usually easy to detect because it is common and uses open water, but can hide in vegetation and is elusive in late summer. Very vocal. Calls of females (e.g., *poonk, punk-unk*) generally described as nasal compared to those of male (e.g., *puhlk, puhk-ut*) (Taylor 1998).

**Population Status and Conservation:** From 1955 through 1997, the number in the Pacific Flyway increased from about 600,000 to nearly 5 million. Oregon breeding population estimated at 194,419 in 1999. Harvest was 5,279 birds by 704 hunters in 1998 (ODFW 2000). The American Coot is adaptable and able to take advantage of newly created wetlands (Taylor 1998). Improvements in permanent and semi-permanent wetlands at Ankeny and Baskett Slough NWRs have provided year-round benefits to American Coots, including an increase in the nesting population, particularly at Baskett Slough (J. Beall p.c.). Hunting opportunities for this species are predicted to grow (ODFW 2000).

Some factors limit the population, but none are currently a serious threat. Nest failures can result from water level changes and predation (Ohlendorf et al. 1989). In 1989, predation at the XL Spring pond, Lake Co., resulted in only one chick fledging (Kristensen et al. 1991). At times it is caught in traps meant for furbearers (Eddleman et al. 1988). Observers in Oregon have witnessed predation by Bald Eagles

(Bayer 1987, D. DeWitt p.c., *BC*) and gulls (F. Chancey p.c.). Eggs and live birds eaten by Common Ravens at Malheur NWR (Stiehl and Trautwein 1991). Grass carp introduction at Devils L., Lincoln Co., has reduced winter numbers there (Bayer 1999c). Many birds have died due to outbreaks of avian cholera (Paullin 1987a) and botulism (Littlefield 1979) at Malheur NWR. Vacuolar myelinopathy (Coot and Eagle Brain Lesion Syndrome, or CEBLS) has affected American Coots in Arkansas, Georgia, N. Carolina, S. Carolina, and Wisconsin (Clinbeard 1999, USGS 1999) but not yet known in Oregon.—*Barbara Combs*

## Family Gruidae

### Subfamily Gruinae

### Sandhill Crane *Grus canadensis*

Oregon's tallest bird. In many cultures cranes are associated with longevity, fidelity, peace, beauty, wisdom, and nobility, and have inspired cultural rituals in Japan, China, Africa, and Australia (Grooms 1992). This large majestic crane has a guttural gurgling or bugling call, and is easily noticed in flight by its profile, with long neck and head extending straight ahead and long legs trailing behind. The Sandhill Crane is distinguished by its red crown and white cheek patches, contrasting with a light gray body. Fledged young resemble adults, but have a feathered forehead, a lighter tawny plumage, and lack the red crown and white cheek patches during their first fall. Fledged young have a squeaky *cheap* call often heard in flight during fall and winter. Adults look alike, though males are larger than females. Subspecies differ in size: Lesser Sandhill Cranes (*G. c. canadensis*) are 10-20% smaller than Greater Sandhill Cranes (*G. c. tabida*), but difficult for inexperienced observers to distinguish. A third subspecies, Canadian Sandhill Crane (*G. c. rowani*), is intermediate in size, and is observed in Oregon during migration. The dancing behavior of cranes is usually associated with disturbance and agitation, and not courtship ritual as so often reported. Cranes are a major attraction at Malheur NWR.

**General Distribution:** Breeds primarily in Alaska, Canada, south through Washington and Oregon to ne. California, and east through Idaho, Colorado, Wyoming, Montana, Minnesota, Wisconsin, and Michigan (Johnsgard 1983a). Nonmigratory populations occur in Florida, Georgia, Mississippi, and Cuba. Migratory flocks winter primarily in Oregon, Washington, California, Arizona, New Mexico, Texas, Florida, and n. Mexico. Six subspecies (Johnsgard 1983a, Browning 1990); three occur in Oregon.

**Oregon Distribution:** Most of the references to subspecies (whether scientific or English names) in Oregon are based on sightings only. The Greater Sandhill Crane breeds throughout se., sc., ne., and c. Oregon in large emergent marsh-meadow wetlands, as well as scattered smaller meadows among the Blue Mtns. A few pairs also nest in high montane meadows in the w. Cascades. The largest breeding concentrations occur at Malheur NWR, Sycan Marsh, the Silvies R. floodplain (near Burns), Chewaucan Marshes, Warner Valley, and Klamath Marsh NWR (Littlefield et al. 1994, Ivey and Herziger 2000). Marked birds breeding in Oregon winter in the Central Valley of California (Pogson and Lindstedt 1991).

The Lesser Sandhill Crane is reported to be a common spring and fall migrant in the Malheur-Harney Basin (Littlefield and Thompson 1982). Large flocks of Lesser Sandhill Cranes stage on the Silvies R. floodplain in Mar and Apr (C. D. Littlefield unpubl. data). Jewett (1954f) collected a specimen at Sauvies I. in Oct.

In fall, the Sandhill Cranes that stage on Sauvie I. and Ridgefield NWR in Washington are frequently heard as they migrate south over the Willamette Valley. An increasing winter population of cranes on Sauvie I. was thought to consist of Lesser Sandhill Cranes (H. Nehls p.c., *MAS*). A recent radio-tagging study documented extensive use of Sauvie I. by Canadian sandhills during late Nov and Mar. Greater sandhills may also be present there (Pogson and Lindstedt 1991). These subspecies are difficult to identify in the field and additional in-hand measurements and/or radio-tagging studies are needed to better document the subspecies composition at different seasons (Ivey, Hoffman, and Herziger unpubl. ms.).

**Habitat and Diet:** Sandhill Cranes generally build large floating nests in 0.5-3.0 ft (0.19-1.09 m) of water, and forage in nearby wet meadows or grain fields, if available. At Malheur NWR, of 800 nests, 348 were in broad-fruited burreed, 325 in hardstem

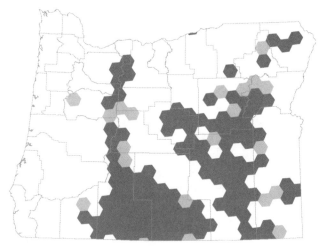

bulrush, 68 in meadow, and 59 in broad-leaved cattail (Littlefield 1995b). At Sycan Marsh, nests located in deeper water bulrush areas survived to hatching with greater frequency than shallower nest sites in sedge wetland and grass meadow habitats (Stern, Pampush, and Del Carlo 1987), as access to nests by and visibility to coyotes was reduced in bulrush sites.

No dietary study of Sandhill Cranes has been done in Oregon, but they are omnivores, feeding on a variety of plant parts, invertebrates, amphibians, reptiles, small mammals, eggs, and young birds; waste grain and other seeds are the dominant foods in autumn and winter (*CDL*).

**Seasonal Activity and Behavior:** Greater Sandhill Cranes migrate northward from the Central Valley of California, arriving in Oregon in late Feb or early Mar. Cranes typically retain the same mate and nest territory in successive years; arriving cranes may loaf at foraging sites, or go directly to their nesting territory. Cranes are long lived, with band records from Malheur NWR of adult cranes living in excess of 34 yr. Nest initiation begins as early as late Mar, but more typically extends from early Apr through Jun, with young fledged between mid-Jul and mid-Sep (Stern, Pampush, and Del Carlo 1987). Greater sandhills migrate asynchronously. Those in Harney Co. and points north, including approximately 3,000 Greater Sandhill Cranes that nest in British Columbia, formerly staged at Malheur NWR in Sep and Oct; peak number was 3,400 recorded in 1979 (Littlefield 1986). More recently, these birds have moved on earlier, probably because of improved conditions in California and changes in management practices at Malheur NWR (DBM). Sandhills nesting at Sycan Marsh are known to migrate south through Langell Valley in Klamath Co., Oregon (Stern et al. 1986), and it is presumed that those nesting at the Klamath Marsh NWR and other sites in Klamath Co. also migrate through Langell Valley. Most Greaters leave Oregon by early Nov. Greaters from Malheur NWR typically winter at the Sacramento R. Delta, whereas those from Sycan Marsh usually winter in the n. Central Valley near Gray Lodge W.A. in the Butte Sinks Basin. In Dec, however, some cranes from Gray Lodge may migrate south to the Delta area; the total wintering population is estimated at 6,600-8,500 Greater sandhills, including up to 893 Canadian sandhills (Pogson and Lindstedt 1991, CDL).

Lesser Sandhill Cranes wintering in the Central Valley of California arrive on the shallowly flooded Silvies R. floodplain in Mar, with typical peak numbers reaching 6,000 in early Apr (Littlefield and Thompson 1982). Smaller groups of spring migrants are also found throughout wetland sites in Lake and Klamath counties. Most Lessers depart Oregon by the third week in Apr, though some may linger into May. Band information suggests that at least some Lessers that migrate through e. Oregon breed on low-lying wetlands on the north shore of Bristol Bay in sw. Alaska (Pogson 1987) and around Cook Inlet in sc. Alaska (B. Bortner p.c.). Fall migration in e. Oregon is less noticeable because most wetlands are dry and most Lessers bypass traditional spring staging areas. Migrant flocks of Lessers are regularly observed in fall and spring as they pass through the interior valleys of w. Oregon. In Douglas Co., regular reports of cranes in both spring and fall from Tiller and Glide; also a flock of 98 cranes overflew Toketee RS on 16 Oct 1984, and flocks of 3, 4, and 13 cranes were reported there in mid-Nov 1987 (Fix 1990a). In w. Oregon, fall migrant Sandhill Cranes arrive on Sauvie I. the first week of Sep, though they have been reported from late Aug in some years (MAS). Fall counts of cranes (predominantly Lesser, but including some Canadian and perhaps Greater Sanhill Cranes) flying into evening roosts on Sauvie I. and the adjacent Ridgefield NWR, Washington 1991-2000 averaged 3,353 (1,218-4,273) (E. Anderson unpubl. data, MAS); counts on Sauvie I., where they roost at different sites on Sturgeon L., averaged 2,319 (887-3,281). The proportion of Canadian and Greater Sandhill Cranes migrating through Sauvie I. and Ridgefield is uncertain, though Pogson and Lindstedt (1991) reported 893 intermediate cranes (aka

*Sandhill Cranes*

Canadians) on Sauvie I. in spring 1982. High water levels, such as those caused by the flood of Feb 1996, may inundate roost sites on Sauvie I. and force cranes to use sites at Ridgefield NWR. Wintering cranes on Sauvie I. increased from approximately 100 in the 1980s to a high count of 600 in Dec 1997 (H. Nehls p.c.).

**Detection:** Large size and prominent call make this species highly detectable in accessible breeding areas, especially in early spring when vegetation has yet to grow. Pairs more reclusive when brooding young. Spring flocks of migrant Lesser Sandhill Cranes are predictably viewed on Silvies R. floodplain south of Burns, and migrants are easily detected on Sauvie I. in fall and spring, less so in winter. Migrant flocks in flight detected by frequent call as they circle upwards to catch thermals prior to or during departure.

**Population Status and Conservation:** Greater Sandhill Cranes nesting in Oregon, ne. California, Washington, and in British Columbia constitute what is called the Central Valley Population. Gabrielson and Jewett (1940) reported cranes from Harney, Lake, and Klamath counties, but numbers were much lower than found now. Also, they did not report cranes wintering on Sauvie I., or breeding in the Cascades, suggesting that crane populations in Oregon have increased since the early 1900s.

In 1999-2000, the estimated breeding population in Oregon, California, and Washington was 3,270 cranes (Ivey and Herziger 2000, 2001). A majority of nesting pairs (1,151) occurred in Oregon, perhaps as many 465 pairs in California, and 19 pairs in Washington (Engler and Brady 2000); an estimated 3,000 cranes also are presumed to summer in British Columbia. Overall trend data indicate that breeding Greater Sandhill Cranes increased in Oregon, Washington, and California between 1986-88 and 1999-2000 survey periods. Breeding pair numbers increased 22% in Oregon and 68% in California (Ivey and Herziger 2000, 2001).

Between the early 1970s and 1986 the number of breeding pairs of cranes at 19 sites in Baker, Deschutes, Grant, Harney, Lake, Malheur, and Union counties wase stable, except for a dramatic 23% decline from 236 to 181 pairs at Malheur NWR, Oregon's largest breeding concentration (Littlefield et al. 1994). Population declines at Malheur NWR were attributed to poor productivity in the late 1970s and 1980s, partly because 1080 (a poison used to kill coyotes) was banned in 1972. Coyotes, Common Ravens, and raccoons were identified as the principal cause of egg loss; coyotes were also implicated in chick mortalities (Littlefield and Lindstedt 1992, Littlefield 1995a). Subsequent management efforts to control predators at Malheur NWR resulted in a tremendous

upswing in productivity and an associated increase in the population, from 168 pairs in 1989 to 251 pairs in 1996. At Sycan Marsh, Oregon's second largest concentration of breeding cranes, predation of eggs and flightless young by coyotes was the primary cause of poor productivity 1981-84 (Stern et al. 1986, Stern, Pampush, and Del Carlo 1987); surveys in Apr 2000 at Sycan found an estimated 113-135 pairs, approximately the same number as the 126 pairs recorded in 1983 (*MAS*).

Ongoing threats include conversion of wetlands and pasture to farmland in breeding areas, predation of eggs and flightless young by coyotes, ravens, and other predators, and loss of habitat on wintering grounds in California (*MAS, CDL, GLI*).—*Mark A. Stern, C. D. Littlefield, and Gary L. Ivey*

# Order CHARADRIIFORMES
## *Family Charadriidae*

### Subfamily Charadriinae

**Black-bellied Plover** *Pluvialis squatarola*
Western Oregon observers enjoy these large, elegant plovers almost year-round, and as a consequence they are one of the most familiar larger shorebirds. This, the Gray Plover of Eurasia, is indeed gray for most of its time in Oregon, but the black belly is a trademark visible at great distances in late spring and on some birds during summer and fall. The black axillars, white rump, and distinctive plaintive whistle make them easy to identify.

**General Distribution:** Breeds from nc. Russia eastward to c. Canada; winters in the temperate Old World and from British Columbia and s. New England southward, mainly along coasts, to S. America. Monotypic.

**Oregon Distribution:** Fairly common to common transient on the coast (Bayer 1988b, Sawyer and Hunter 1988, Contreras 1998, Patterson 1998b); rare to locally uncommon transient in western interior valleys (Gullion 1951, Herlyn 1998, Gillson 1999). Considered very rare in Jackson Co. by Browning (1975a) but the subsequent creation of sewage ponds there has attracted many birds and resulted in this species becoming occasional in Apr and early May (C. Brumitt p.c.).

East of the Cascades, the Black-bellied Plover is an uncommon transient in the Klamath Basin (Summers 1993a) and at Malheur NWR (Littlefield 1990a). Rare to absent along the Columbia R. east to the Umatilla NWR complex (USDI 1968, 1973, Anderson 1987d,

M. Denny p.c.), in c. Oregon (C. Miller unpubl. data), ne. Oregon (Evanich 1992a), and Malheur Co. (Contreras 1996a).

In winter it is a common resident on the coast, rare to locally uncommon in western interior valleys (mainly c. and s. Willamette Valley), and absent east of the Cascades.

**Habitat and Diet:** Almost all migrants and winterers visiting Oregon inhabit mudflats and open wet dirt fields. A few can be found on sand beaches and even occasionally on rocks, but the great majority are found feeding and resting on open mud. Birds wintering in the Willamette Valley often use wet fields of short grass. This preference for wide-open mudflats may explain in part why this species is reasonably regular at Malheur NWR and in the Klamath Basin, especially in fall, while nearly absent elsewhere east of the Cascades.

Paulson (1993) indicated that polychaete worms and small bivalves are important prey items for coastal Black-bellied Plovers, but they also forage on other invertebrates on the surface of the mud. No food studies have been conducted in Oregon.

**Seasonal Activity and Behavior:** Movements of adults vs. immatures are not well known. Southbound adults begin arriving in Oregon in early Jul (a few sometimes appear in late Jun), with a peak in Aug probably comprising adults, while immatures begin arriving in late Aug and probably comprise the bulk of the early Sep peak. Another peak occurs in Oct, probably birds that have molted prior to leaving the breeding grounds (Paulson 1993). Peak fall counts include 600 in upper Coos Bay 21 Oct 2001 (T. Rodenkirk p.c.), 330 at the n. spit of Coos Bay, Coos Co., 17 Nov 1997 and 300 at Bandon, Coos Co., 25 Aug 1996 (Contreras 1998). Eastside peak counts are much lower, with unusually high counts of 25 at Cold Springs NWR, Umatilla Co., in fall 1982 (Rogers 1983a) and 21 at Malheur NWR on 7 Nov 1987 (Littlefield 1990a).

Most winter birds concentrate at larger estuaries, though many can be found on wet pastureland near the coast. Peak CBC counts include 607 at Coos Bay in 1982 and 467 at Tillamook Bay in 1979. CBC counts in the Willamette Valley are usually very low, with scattered single birds typically present. Small concentrations of 20-30 are sometimes found around Fern Ridge Res, Lane Co.; a remarkable 132 were in short-grass fields near there in winter 1999-2000 (*MGH*).

Spring movements are obscured by the presence of a sizable wintering population on the coast, but there is obvious movement from mid-Apr through mid-May. Most birds are gone by late May (Paulson 1993). The 100 birds at Merrill, Klamath Co., on 3 May 1981 (Rogers TH 1981c) is a remarkable count, perhaps the largest flock ever reported east of the Cascades. The few birds found in early Jun on the coast are probably nonbreeders that summer locally.

**Detection:** This is one of Oregon's obvious and easily found shorebirds, feeding on open mudflats and calling attention to itself with its loud but mellow whistle and active feeding.

**Population Status and Conservation:** No systematic surveys have been done in Oregon comparing the number of birds present over time. CBC numbers suggest that wintering populations are relatively stable, with CBC data and anecdotal evidence suggesting that more birds are wintering in the Willamette Valley than was previously known. Gullion (1951) did not mention records after late Dec in Lane Co.; the species has been regular there in winter for some years. It is possible that the advent of extensive grass-seed farming in the c. and s. Willamette Valley has provided more usable winter habitat for this species.—*Alan L. Contreras*

## American Golden-Plover *Pluvialis dominica*

These elegant shorebirds are found as often in dry or damp upland areas as on mudflats or beaches. The plain brown immature birds of autumn become spangled with black and gold as breeding approaches.

**General Distribution:** Breed from n. Alaska eastward across n. Canada to n. Ontario and Baffin I. Winter in S. America. Migrant continent-wide, mostly east of the Rocky Mtns. The two N. American golden-plovers (American [*dominica*] and Pacific [*fulva*]) were distinguishable as subspecies for more than two centuries (AOU 1957, Connors 1983) and have been recognized as separate species since 1993 (Connors et al. 1993). Monotypic.

**Oregon Distribution:** Occasional to uncommon migrant in w. Oregon (mainly coastal) and locally rare, irregular migrant in e. Oregon, with most reports at Malheur NWR (Littlefield 1990a), in the Klamath Basin (Summers 1993a), and in Umatilla Co. (miscellaneous notes in *Oregon Birds* and *American Birds*). The true status of American vs. Pacific Golden-Plover in Oregon is still unclear because many published sight records cannot be distinguished to species, as indeed some birds in the field cannot. See Evanich (1989) and Paulson (1993) for further information.

**Habitat and Diet:** These plovers use mudflats and a variety of drier habitats such as short-grass fields, gravel pans, freshly tilled fields, and sometimes beaches. Diet information is unavailable for Oregon.

**Seasonal Activity and Behavior:** Because of the uncertainty of many sight records, the golden-plover accounts rely somewhat more than usual on specimen data; these provide a solid outline of status, but many details have yet to be determined. Certain high counts of golden-plovers of unknown species are included in this account, while the Pacific account includes all winter reports of golden-plovers.

This is mainly a southbound migrant in Oregon, with birds of known identity occurring primarily in Sep and early Oct. Specimens have been collected 7 Sep 1912 near Netarts (Bayer 1989a: SDNHM No. 20735), 7 Sep 1959 at Malheur L. (USNM No. 466754), two on 12 Sep 1926 at the California state line in Curry Co. (Bayer 1989a: SDNHM Nos. 20736 and 20738), 6 Oct 1918 near Mercer, Lane Co. (Bayer 1989a: OSUFW No. 10190), and 4 Nov 1935 (a late date) at The Narrows, Malheur NWR (SDNHM No. 20737).

Fall sight records are numerous, mainly from late Aug through Oct, but include some reports of adults in Jul, as well as birds as late as 4 Nov 1987 near Malheur NWR HQ (Littlefield 1990a; field notes) and 4 Nov 1997 at Coos Bay (Contreras 1998). Rare in the Willamette Valley, with one Sep record from Benton Co. and a few records not clearly identified to species from Linn Co. (Herlyn 1998, Gillson 1999), as well as scattered reports from the n. valley and Sauvie I. (*Oregon Birds* field notes).

Single birds and flocks of fewer than 10 are the norm; peak fall counts of golden-plovers (of uncertain identity) include 30 on 26 Sep 1987 at Tillamook (Paulson 1993), 15 at Pony Slough, Coos Bay, 10 Sep 1940 (Contreras 1998), and 15 (careful comparison suggested the presence of eight American and seven Pacific) at the north spit settling ponds, Coos Bay, 16 Sep 1999 (T. Rodenkirk p.c.). The latter flock built and dissipated over a period of nearly a month, with the first plover seen 9 Sep and the last 2 Oct, though it is not certain that the same birds were involved. Peak counts of 8-9 birds of uncertain identity at the s. jetty of the Columbia R. have all come in the first three weeks of Sep (M. Patterson p.c.). Winter reports of golden-plovers are few and are discussed under Pacific Golden-Plover, to which they probably pertain.

Far fewer birds thought to be of this species pass through Oregon in spring. The small number of sight records are mostly from May or the last few days of Apr (Littlefield 1990a, *Oregon Birds* and *American Birds* field notes), with a few outliers, e.g., 18 Apr 1987 near Adel, Lake Co. (Stern 1988). West of the Cascades, the peak count of golden-plovers of uncertain species is 11 near Tillamook in the last week of Apr 1984 (Irons 1984b).

**Detection:** Fairly easy within a limited habitat and migration window. Observers who spend time in flat, drier habitats on the outer coast in Sep are likely to come across them. Care must be taken to distinguish the relatively dull juveniles from bright juvenile Black-bellied Plovers as well as from the more golden juvenile Pacific Golden-Plover. Distinctions between American and Pacific are subtle; see standard field guides and Paulson (1993) for details.

**Population Status and Conservation:** A very small portion of the population passes through Oregon and uses human-generated as well as natural habitats. Conservation practices in Oregon are unlikely to affect this species.—*Alan L. Contreras*

## Pacific Golden-Plover *Pluvialis fulva*

These delicate and truly golden plovers that pass through Oregon in fall are always a delight to find on an open beach or grassy coastal plain. Juveniles are relatively easy to identify because of the golden-yellow suffusion of the face, neck, and coverts; adults that have already lost their breeding plumage are more difficult to distinguish from American Golden-Plovers. Formerly conspecific with American Golden Plover; historical reports not distinguishing the species are generally discussed under the account for American Golden-Plover.

**General Distribution:** Breeds from nw. Siberia eastward to the Bering Sea coast of Alaska. Winters mainly from ne. Africa westward across s. Asia and China, also to Wallacea and the s. Pacific islands to Hawaii. Rare in winter along the w. coast of N. America from British Columbia south to California. Migrates in small numbers along the Pacific coast of N. America. Monotypic.

**Oregon Distribution:** Rare to uncommon migrant; most birds occur in fall on the outer coast. Very rare to rare in winter on the coast and in the Willamette Valley.

**Habitat and Diet:** Most often reported in drier settings such as open short-grass fields, beaches, gravel pans, and the drier parts of mudflats. Feeds mainly in the open. No dietary information is available from Oregon.

**Seasonal Activity and Behavior:** Mainly a fall migrant, but spring reports have increased in recent years. This may reflect the presence of more birds, more observers, increased observer experience with methods of distinguishing this species from American Golden-Plover, or wishful thinking on the part of observers. The species is confirmed for Oregon by a juvenile female collected 28 Sep 1940 at Bayocean, Tillamook Co. (PSM No. 00014). Sight records of southbound birds in w. Oregon range from 12 Jul to 24 Nov (Nehls 1994), with reports of most birds in Sep. A remarkably early two molting adults at the n. spit of Coos Bay 25 Jun 2000 were apparently southbound birds. Peak fall counts thought to be of this species include seven at the s. jetty of the Columbia R. on 7 Sep 1992 (M. Patterson p.c.), seven at the n. spit settling ponds, Coos Bay on 16 Sep 1999 (T. Rodenkirk p.c.), five on 28 Sep 1996 on the n. spit of the Coquille R. (Contreras 1998), and five at Coos Spit on 23 Oct 2001 (Contreras 2002b).

There are no specimens or photo-documented records east of the Cascades, but one at Wickiup Res., Deschutes Co., 10 Oct 1998 was thought to be of this species (Sullivan 1999a), as were singles at the Boardman sewage ponds, Morrow Co., from 28 Sep to 5 Oct 1990 (Anderson 1991a) and at Cold Springs NWR, Umatilla Co., on 21 Sep 1992 (Summers 1993b).

A few winter reports of golden-plovers are probably of this species, based on its pattern of wintering in very small numbers on the Pacific coast (Paulson 1993). Coastal reports thought to be Pacifics include one on 18 Dec 1976 at Tillamook Bay (D. Fix p.c., CBC), one on 4 Jan 1997 at Bandon (Johnson 1997b), a remarkable eight reported on a golf course on the 16 Dec 1979 Coos Bay CBC, one seen 18 and 23 Jan 1980 near Coquille, Coos Co., conceivably part of the golf course flock, as the locations are within 10 air miles (16 km) (Mattocks and Hunn 1980b, Watson 1980c), two on 30 Dec 1981 at Pony Slough, Coos Co. (Evanich 1982d), and one at Coos Bay on 11 Dec 1982 (Evanich 1983b). Inland winter reports include one in alternate plumage near the Forest Grove sewage ponds 10-11 Jan 1987 (Heinl 1987c), one (species not certain) on 21 Jan 1994 near Tangent, Linn Co. (Gillson 1999), and one on 21 Dec 1995 near Corvallis (Johnson 1996b).

Although data are still limited, it is likely that this species (though rare to uncommon) is more regular on the coast in spring than is the American. Migrants have been reported from 17 Apr to 25 May, with most records in May (*Oregon Birds* field notes). A report from 12 Jun 1998 at New R., Coos Co. (Tice 1999a), is hard to classify, although given the rather late southbound movement of this species (rarely reported before Aug), this was probably a late northward migrant or a nonbreeder. Spring reports usually involve one or at most two birds, but nine were at Cape Blanco, Curry Co., on 27 Apr 1999 (Lillie 1999). There are very few inland reports in spring. A bird was reported at Ankeny NWR on 25 May 1999 (Lillie 1999), and singles were at Finley NWR on 19 May 1990 and (photographed) at the Kirtland Rd. sewage ponds, Jackson Co., 11-12 May 1990 (Fix 1990c).

**Detection:** Moderately difficult owing to its coloration, sparse numbers, limited preferred habitat, and tendency to feed in drier upland areas where it is less easy to see than, for example, a Black-bellied Plover on an open mudflat. It sometimes requires intense scanning of otherwise birdless expanses to be rewarded with one or two birds. Care is required to distinguish it from the American Golden-Plover.

**Population Status and Conservation:** Oregon represents a tiny sliver of this species' migratory range. The species is fairly adaptable to human-created habitats such as tilled fields, and also uses open beaches and occasionally mudflats. No conservation measures in Oregon are apparent for this species.—*Alan L. Contreras*

### Mongolian Plover *Charadrius mongolus*
This colorful shorebird breeds across n. Asia and sparingly in Alaska. It winters in Asia. There are a few fall N. American records away from Alaska, primarily along the Pacific coast. There are three Oregon records, each of which involved a bird that remained for several days; an adult in basic plumage photographed at Tillamook Bay 11-17 Sep 1977 (Anonymous 1977b, Roberson 1980, Watson 1989); an adult in prebasic molt photographed at the s. jetty of the Columbia R. 16-21 Oct 1979 (Mattocks and Hunn 1980a, Nehls 1980); and an alternate-plumaged adult photographed at Bandon Marsh NWR 11 Jul to 14 Aug 1986 (Heinl 1987b).—*Harry B. Nehls*

### Snowy Plover *Charadrius alexandrinus*
This small shorebird moves along the sand by foot rather than flight. It has a distinct black cap behind a white forehead, a dark line through the eye, and an incomplete black breast band. Males have darker and more distinct breeding plumage than females; both sexes lose coloration during late summer. Snowy Plovers breeding along the Oregon, Washington, and

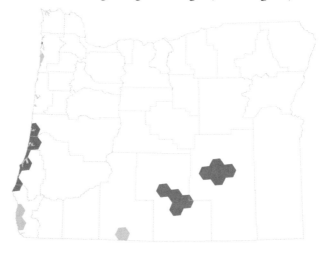

California coast are listed as Threatened under the ESA (Federal Register 1993). It is the only shorebird that regularly breeds on Oregon's beaches.

**General Distribution:** Worldwide distribution (breeds on five continents) except Australia and Antarctica. In N. America, breeds from coast of s. Washington south to s. Baja California. Inland, also at scattered locales extending through the western tier of states (except Idaho) east to s. Saskatchewan and south through Kansas, Texas, and c. Mexico. Also along the Gulf coast of Texas and Florida south along the east coast of Mexico and east in parts of the Caribbean region. N. American birds winter mainly in coastal areas from Washington south to M. America along both the Pacific and Gulf coasts. One N. American subspecies, *C. a. nivosus*; *tenuirostris* of the Gulf coast and *nivosus* are synonyms (Blake 1977).

**Oregon Distribution:** East of the Cascades, the Snowy Plover is a summer resident breeding on alkaline flats and salt pans found in and around Harney L., Stinking L., Alvord Desert, L. Abert, Alkali L., Summer L., and other smaller sites in Harney and Lake counties. It is reported intermittently from White L., Klamath Co. (Summers 1982b, Sullivan 1996b). These summer residents winter along California coast and Baja, and rarely if at all in Oregon (Page, Stern, and Paton 1995). On the Oregon coast this species is found year-round between Heceta Head and Cape Blanco, breeding at Sutton/Baker Beach, Siltcoos R. mouth, the Dunes NRA Overlook, Tahkenitch Spit south to Threemile Cr., Tenmile R. mouth, s. end of the Coos Bay North Spit, on the Bandon beaches, on New R. Spit, at overwashes along the south end of New R., and the beaches west of Floras L. Nesting at Bayocean Spit, Tillamook Co., was last documented in 1995, although lingering pairs in late Apr 1998 indicated the potential for nest activity. Nesting was documented at Necanicum R. mouth, Clatsop Co., in 2000. Incidental reports have come from several other places along the coast during the breeding season, e.g., Pistol R., Euchre Cr., and Sixes R. mouths in Curry Co., and one from Sand L., Tillamook Co., in May 1995. This plover was formerly a more widespread breeder on the Oregon coast, but now is gone from many n. coast sites.

In winter, they are known from coastal breeding sites, with concentrations typically found at Bandon, Siltcoos, and Sutton beaches. A few wintering birds have also been found at Bayocean Spit through 2000.

**Habitat and Diet:** East of the Cascades, Snowy Plovers are found on alkaline playas that may be sparsely vegetated with alkali saltgrass, typically in association with springs, seeps, or lake edges. At L. Abert they nest in a vast saltgrass playa at the north end of the lake; following hatching, adults take broods about 2 mi (3.2 km) and congregate along the north lake shore where they feed on abundant concentrations of brine flies (Stern, Kristensen, and Morawski 1990). On the Oregon coast, they nest on open sand areas along the upper beach below the foredune, on unvegetated spits at mouths of small estuaries, and in sandy overwash areas between large hummocks vegetated by beachgrass that typically occur at sites where the foredune has not yet developed. At the Coos Bay North Spit, they also nest on old dredge spoils that lie adjacent to the beach. Nesting substrate varies from white, crusty alkaline soils at interior sites to soft sand, pebbly gravel, or dredged materials from the bays at coastal sites. Nests are a small depression in the sand or alkali, often occurring near a small object such as a dried-up piece of kelp, a small piece of driftwood, or a cowpie, or near or within a sparse clump of beachgrass or saltgrass. Plovers at coastal sites will sometimes line a nest with small pebbles or shell fragments. Food items at coastal sites include shore flies, rove beetles, and other small insects commonly associated with seaweed and other tidal debris found in the high tide wrackline (Stern, McIver, and Rosenberg 1990).

**Seasonal Activity and Behavior:** Inland, plovers return to breeding sites in Apr, and nesting begins late Apr, with peak nest initiation from mid-May to mid-Jun (Stern, Kristensen, and Morawski 1990). On the coast, wintering plovers disperse to breeding sites in Mar; pair bonds form immediately and nesting occurs from early Apr, occasionally late Mar, through Jul, with peak nesting activity mid-May through mid-Jul. Late season broods may not fledge until mid-Sep on coast (Castelein et al. 2001).

*Snowy Plover*

Though nesting pairs are occasionally found in isolation, most are semi-colonial and found in proximity to each other. A typical clutch has three eggs, and incubation takes approximately 28 days, with fledging another 28-30 days after hatching (Page, Warriner, et al. 1995). The male and female share incubation duties, females during the day, and males at night. If the nest fails, the pair may renest several times within a breeding season. The male usually raises the brood of 1-3 chicks alone as the female deserts her mate and brood and re-mates. Males will also re-mate after their young fledge or the brood fails. Female may help male with the last brood of the summer. Plovers may have 2-3 successful nests and broods per season, though this occurs more frequently at coastal sites where nesting season is longer (Page, Warriner, et al. 1995). In some years, relatively few individuals may account for a majority of the young hatched and raised through fledging (*MAS*).

Broods at coastal sites have traveled along the linear beach as far as 6 mi (9.6 km) from their nest; the mean maximum distance traveled for 56 broods in 1999 and 2000 was 3681 ft (1122 m), ranging 210-18,350 ft (64-5593 m) (Castelein et al. 2001).

Wintering flocks of 2-25 plovers are often found together in tightly spaced groups. On the beach, they escape the strong coastal winds by standing or sitting behind small pieces of driftwood or other debris, or by hunkering down in depressions in the sand. Pair bonds are not maintained through winter, but individuals often reunite with mate from previous year during breeding season (*MAS, DJL, KAC*).

On the Oregon coast, 30-50% of young fledged return the following year, and most breed as first-year adults. Other surviving young disperse to other breeding sites, including Leadbetter Point in Washington, and Humboldt and Monterey Bays in California. Oldest adult recorded is 15-yr old male in California (Page, Warriner, et al. 1995); 11-yr old male on the Oregon coast (originally banded as an adult on 26 Jun 1990 at New R., Coos Co., and observed in Jun 2001 in same general area), but typical life expectancy much less. In Utah, estimated mean life span was 2.7 yr (Paton 1994).

**Detection:** Small and camouflaged within its habitat, can be difficult to find in the breeding season. Wintering birds are less wary, and may be approached. When flushed from the nest, incubating females have a characteristic head bob and sentinel-like behavior. If disturbed or threatened, both males and females with broods or near nest at time of hatching will press body to ground, extend wings and tail, and do a 'tail drag' much like the Killdeer's feigned broken-wing act in attempt to draw attention away from nest or brood.

**Population Status and Conservation:** Listed as Threatened by State of Oregon in 1975, and the coastal population in Oregon, California, and Washington listed as Federal Threatened by USFWS in 1993. Inland breeding populations fluctuate in abundance and distribution depending on lake levels at nesting sites. In 1980, Herman et al. (1988) surveyed all sites in se. Oregon and portions of w. Nevada, and tallied 1047 breeding plovers in Oregon, with peak counts of 400 and 345 at Harney L. and L. Abert, respectively. In the early 1980s, when abundant snowfall led to record high lake levels throughout se. Oregon, nesting sites at Harney L. and other sites were inundated; overall numbers in e. Oregon then dwindled. Annual surveys of known breeding sites in e. Oregon 1982-94 reported totals that ranged from 198 in 1981 to peak of 850 in 1987, with numbers ranging 521-735 during 1992-94 (ODFW unpubl. data). Largest numbers consistently found at L. Abert and Summer L.; population at Harney L. recovered but never attained levels noted in 1980.

Survey information about plovers on the Oregon coast prior to 1978 is sparse. Annual single-day efforts to survey breeding plovers along the Oregon coast 1978-2001 found peak count of 139 adults in 1981; numbers dropped to lows of 35 and 30 in 1991 and 1992, respectively (USFWS 2001b). Plover numbers rose through mid-1990s to 86 in 1996, but have since dropped slightly to 81 in 2001 (Castelein et al. 2001). Beginning in 1993, additional population information was gathered from intensive observation of color-marked plovers through the breeding season. The number of plovers observed during the breeding season showed a similar trend, with estimates of 72 plovers in 1993, a peak of 141 in 1997, and 111-113 in 2001 (Castelein et al. 2001).

Main threats to plovers on coast are loss of habitat due to encroachment by European beachgrass, predation of eggs by American Crows, Common Ravens, red fox, and striped skunks. Predation of young prior to fledging by red fox may also threaten plovers. Beginning in 1991, there has been an intensive effort to minimize impacts of predation through placement of fenced exclosures at nest sites. Based on 763 nests monitored during 1990-2001, nest success of nests with exclosures was 66.8 ± 10.8% compared to 17.3 ± 19.2% for nests without exclosures (Castelein et al. 2001).

Avian predators, mostly American Crows, occasionally enter exclosures through the top; this may represent one or two individuals who learned how to enter the exclosures. Experimental use of a battery-powered hot wire around the top perimeter has reduced likelihood of avian predators entering the exclosures, though it is labor intensive to install. To alleviate the stress of unusually high predation rates, state and federal management agencies are now evaluating implementation of a predator-control program at coastal sites (*MAS, DJL, KAC*).

Adults incubating nests within exclosures may themselves be subject to predation, either from red fox as noted in California and suspected at New R., Coos Co., and from migrating falcons; these predators apparently key in on the exclosures. In 2000, an estimated 6-12 adult plovers were lost to an avian predator at exclosed nests in early May, a time when Merlins are known to migrate through the area. In response to these events, placement of exclosures is now delayed until mid-May when Merlins have presumably migrated further north (*MAS, DJL, KAC*).

Beginning in 1994, the Coos Bay District BLM and Dunes NRA initiated habitat-restoration efforts to remove beachgrass. On the Coos Bay North Spit, BLM, the Army Corp of Engineers and ODFW expanded the nesting area around the dredge spoil from 23 ac (9 ha) to 185 ac (75 ha). Here, annual tilling of the area during winter prior to nesting season has kept beachgrass from recolonizing the site. Placement of shell hash (e.g., broken-up oyster shells) attracts plovers. At New R., BLM has also recreated open overwash areas by bulldozing breaches in the foredune, which in turn allow overwash during winter storm surges. The Dunes NRA has used several methods of controlling beachgrass, including plowing and tilling, as well as using herbicides. At both the Dunes and BLM sites, plovers have re-colonized new or enhanced nesting areas. Beachgrass is persistent and expands rapidly, and routine maintenance is required to keep restored sites free of this invasive non-native species (*MAS, DJL, KAC*).

Recreation and unintended human disturbance have led to both direct and indirect loss of eggs and young plovers. Closure of beaches to vehicles and people has occurred at key sites. In some instances, human activities may unknowingly force a plover to leave a nest, and the nest may then be buried by blowing sand. In other instances, nests have been lost to direct human activity, including being stepped on (*MAS, DJL, KAC*).

Coastal plovers may also be at risk from oil spills. In Feb 1999, the freighter *New Carissa* ran aground on the Oregon coast, spilling an estimated 20,000-140,000 gallons of fuel oil into the ocean. Within the following 2 mo, approximately 62% (n=73) of individually color-banded plovers observed on the Oregon coast were sighted with some oiling (Stern et al. 2000). Relatively few were severely oiled, and overall population and productivity levels in 1999 were essentially the same as or higher than the immediately preceding years. Nonetheless, the possibility of a major oil spill remains an ongoing threat to Snowy Plovers on the Oregon coast.

The Draft Recovery Plan for the coastal population of threatened Snowy Plovers released by the USFWS in 2001 calls for 200 breeding plovers on the Oregon coast (USFWS 2001b). Attaining this goal will require a coordinated and concerted effort among state and federal agencies to restore and maintain habitat, to further reduce the impacts of predation on nest loss and brood failure, and to ensure that human disturbance does not impact breeding plovers.—*Mark A. Stern, Dave J. Lauten, and Kathy A. Castelein*

## Wilson's Plover *Charadrius wilsonia*

This thick-billed plover breeds along the Pacific and Atlantic coasts from c. S. America northward through Mexico, about the Gulf of Mexico, and to New Jersey. It is casual elsewhere in N. America. There are several records for coastal California. The only Oregon record was from Bullards Beach SP, Coos Co., where a bird remained from 9 Sep to mid-Oct 1998. There are numerous photographs in the files of the OBRC.—*Harry B. Nehls*

## Semipalmated Plover *Charadrius semipalmatus*

These small, chunky plovers are uncommon to locally abundant migrants statewide, where they are among the most visible and easily identified small shorebirds. The only single-banded plover that occurs in Oregon, 'Semis' can be remarkably easy to see when they are moving about on mud flats, and remarkably hard to detect when only their unmoving brown backs are visible against the mud.

**General Distribution:** Breeds from w. Alaska to ne. Canada, rarely south to Washington and Oregon. Winters from s. British Columbia and mid-Atlantic region south to S. America, mainly along coasts. Migrant continent-wide. Monotypic.

**Oregon Distribution:** Uncommon to locally abundant migrant, with most birds at coastal estuaries and some concentrations in spring at larger lakes of se. Oregon; rare in fall in the Cascades (Fix 1990b, D. Lusthoff p.c., C. Miller p.c.). In winter, uncommon at larger estuaries, especially on the south coast; rare in western interior valleys; essentially absent east of the Cascades.

Rare local breeder. Single pairs bred at Stinking L. in 1987 and Harney L. in 1989; a pair was present at Harney L. in 1988 but no evidence of breeding was found (Ivey, Fothergill, and Yates-Mills 1988, Ivey and Baars 1990). Single pairs bred at the n. spit of Coos Bay in 1993, 1994 (possibly two pairs, Hallett et al. 1995), and 2000 (D. Lauten and K. Castelein p.c.). As many as 20 were present at Coos Spit in summer 2000 (some giving display flights) and other nests were suspected (D. Lauten p.c., K. Castelein p.c.).

**Habitat and Diet:** Breeding birds at Malheur NWR used alkali flats with patches of dried algae adjacent to an area of open greasewood (Ivey, Fothergill, and Yates-Mills 1988). Coastal breeders were in sandy dredge spoil with shell fragments in a low dune habitat (Hallett et al. 1995). In both locations the same habitat was also being used by breeding Snowy Plovers.

Migrants and winter birds are usually found on open mudflats, where they form loose running groups, pausing and picking food from the mud surface. Some use open beaches.

No detailed dietary information is available from Oregon. Polychaete worms may be the primary food on beaches (Paulson 1993). Has been observed eating worms in Umatilla Co. (M. Denny p.c.)

**Seasonal Activity and Behavior:** These are among the most obvious migrant shorebirds in Oregon, with large flocks often present on the coast. Southbound adults appear in Oregon by early Jul, with peak numbers including 600 at Tillamook Bay 24 Jul 1985, 400 there on 6 Aug 1986 (Paulson 1993), and 400 at Bandon, Coos Co., on 20 Jul 1997 (Contreras 1998). Juveniles begin arriving in mid-Aug, with peak numbers such as 400 at Coos Bay 31 Aug 1996 dropping slowly throughout the fall. Significant flocks are often present through Oct, e.g., 225 at Bandon 5-6 Oct 1996 (Contreras 1998). In the western interior valleys, numbers are much lower, with peak flocks of 16 in Linn Co. (Gillson 1999), eight in Benton Co. (Herlyn 1999), and 22 in Lane Co. (Gullion 1951).

The species is annual on the coast in winter, but numbers vary from year to year. The Coos Bay CBC has found the species on 22 of 25 counts, with a high of 224 and a median of 20. The only winter record east of the Cascades is of seven at Malheur NWR 16 Dec 1989 (Nehls 1994). Rare in the western interior valleys in winter.

Peak of spring passage is mid-Apr to mid-May. Coastal peak counts include an amazing 700 at Coos Spit on 10 May 2001 (Lillie 2001), 109 at Pony Slough, Coos Co., on the early date of 31 Mar 1979 (Contreras 1998) and 400 at New R., Coos Co., in late Apr 1984 (Paulson 1993). Numbers are usually much lower east of the Cascades, but large concentrations sometimes occur, e.g., 1029 at Summer L. 1 May 1987 and 200 at L. Abert in early May 1989 (Nehls 1994). Peak of passage at Malheur NWR is the first half of May (Littlefield 1990a). Generally absent from late May through early Jul, with rare summering and breeding birds.

**Detection:** Easy to find, observe, and identify. Many birds in flight are first detected by call. Somewhat skittish and less tolerant of sudden movements than most shorebirds. Often approaches a careful observer, but always remains alert and loose flocks can suddenly rise and fly to the far side of an estuary with no obvious provocation.

**Population Status and Conservation:** Populations using Oregon show no sign of decline in the past 25 yr based on migration counts and CBC data. However, that information is limited. Because the species is essentially limited to open mudflats on the coast, loss to development or vegetative incursions would limit utility for this species. East of the Cascades most habitat is already protected in refuges and wildlife management areas.—*Alan L. Contreras*

### Piping Plover *Charadrius melodus*

This small pale plover breeds around the Great Lakes and along the n. Atlantic coast of N. America. It winters along the s. Atlantic coast and in the Caribbean. It is much reduced in numbers and is now endangered. W. coast records are few. There is one sight record for Oregon, a bird on Neahkahnie Beach, Tillamook Co., 6-8 Sep 1986 (Mattocks and Harrington-Tweit 1987a).—*Harry B. Nehls*

### Killdeer *Charadrius vociferus*

With a widespread distribution and affinity for open habitats, the Killdeer is one of the most common and recognized birds throughout much of N. America. Killdeer are large for a plover and easily distinguished from other N. American plovers by their characteristic two black or brownish-black breast bands. Initially, downy young have a single band but soon resemble adults in appearance. Killdeer are well known for their loud and persistent call of "kill-dee, kill-dee," heard at all times of day or night on both the breeding and wintering grounds. Killdeer often nest close to human activities. Adults perform an elaborate and exaggerated broken-wing display to lure humans and potential predators away from their nests.

**General Distribution:** Restricted to the New World. Vagrant to Europe, Hawaiian Is., and far e. Russia (Jackson and Jackson 2000). Breeds throughout N. America from the southern extent of arctic Alaska and Canada southward to the Gulf states and parts of Mexico. Information on population structure and residency patterns is limited, although known to exhibit partial migration with both residents and migrants. Generally, northern breeders are migratory and the proportion of resident birds increases farther south (Schardien 1981, Heck 1985). Small numbers winter as far north as s. Alaska, although most birds are found from s. British Columbia, across middle latitudes of the continental U.S., and farther south into regions of M. America and n. S. America. Migrants also winter in the W. Indies and Caribbean. Three recognized subspecies; *C. v. vociferus* in N. America (AOU 1957).

**Oregon Distribution:** Common spring and summer resident throughout the state with breeding records from every county, although absent or rare at higher elevations (Gabrielson and Jewett 1940, Fix 1990a, Gilligan et al. 1994, Nehls 1994). During winter, Killdeer are uncommon to rare in e. Oregon, but common to abundant west of the Cascades. In particular, large numbers are found in the agricultural landscape of the Willamette Valley. Winter flocks as large as 1,000 birds are not uncommon in the c. and s. Willamette Valley. Partial surveys there in the winter of 1998 and 1999 tallied as many as 8,162. A majority of wintering birds are migrants, but some individuals are year-round residents (Sanzenbacher and Haig 2002a). Small groups and solitary birds winter on the coast along beaches and in coastal fields. Coastal numbers increase during periods of inclement weather at more northerly or inland areas (Gilligan et al. 1994).

**Habitat and Diet:** Killdeer occur in a diversity of wetland and upland habitats from coastline to alpine zones. Natural habitats include mudflats, sandbars, and grassland, as well as various human-modified habitats such as cultivated fields, athletic fields, airports, golf courses, and even gravel parking lots. Further, Killdeer exhibit a particular affinity for nesting on gravel substrates including road shoulders, railroad tracks, and rooftops (Jackson and Jackson 2000, *PMS*). General characteristics of habitat are open areas with short and/or sparse vegetation or bare ground. They often occur near fresh water, particularly during the breeding season when water is important for foraging, belly-soaking, and brood rearing. The nest is a small scrape situated on bare ground or in short vegetation (Jackson and Jackson 2000, Mabee and Estelle 2000). Nests are often lined with small pebbles or bits of vegetation (*PMS*). In the w. Great Basin (Honey L., California), breeding home ranges averaged 15 ac (6.0 ha) and movements were influenced by the distance of nests from water (Plissner, Oring, and Haig 2000). Winter habitats are similar to those used during the

breeding season. In w. Oregon, winter rains saturate and flood agricultural fields providing prime habitat for Killdeer. Winter home ranges of birds in the Willamette Valley averaged 1,675 ac (670 ha) (Sanzenbacher and Haig 2002a).

Killdeer are opportunistic foragers that exhibit a flexible diet of terrestrial invertebrates and to a lesser extent aquatic invertebrates and seeds. In analyses of stomach content across the species' range, > 98% was animal matter. Significant prey items included earthworms, beetles, and grasshoppers (Jackson and Jackson 2000). Information on Killdeer diet in Oregon is lacking, but winter observations of individuals in agricultural fields of the Willamette Valley suggest earthworms are a significant prey item (*PMS*), and Kamm (1973) found sod webworms in the digestive tracts of Willamette Valley Killdeer.

**Seasonal Activity and Behavior:** Killdeer are socially monogamous breeders that often maintain pair bonds between years and exhibit a high degree of breeding site fidelity (Powers 1997, Jackson and Jackson 2000). However, the degree of pair retention and fidelity varies with prior reproductive success and other factors (Powers 1997). They have nested at the same nest site at E.E. Wilson W.A., Benton Co., since 1994, and one adult marked in 1999 returned the following 2 yr (D. A. Budeau p.c.). Clutch size is typically four eggs, although renesting attempts often include only three eggs (Jackson and Jackson 2000, L. Oring p.c.). Killdeer initiate breeding activities earlier than most Oregon birds. In the Willamette Valley, eggs are found as early as mid-Mar, with peak laying dates from late Mar to Apr, and late-season nests found into Jul (*PMS*, OBBA). Present in high Cascades of e. Douglas Co. beginning in Apr (Fix 1990a). Breeding dates are later east of the Cascades. Mean nest-initiation date at Summer L. W.A., Lake Co., was 17 May (n=32) and 25 May (n=31) in 1996 and 1997 respectively, with earliest nests found in mid-Apr (*SMH*). Incubation period ranges 23-29 days and precocial, nidifugous young are capable of flight at 20-31 days (Jackson and Jackson 2000). Both sexes participate in parental activities, although studies have found that males tend to adopt a greater role, particularly during later phases of incubation and brood rearing (Brunton 1988, Warnock and Oring 1996). Birds may renest multiple times following loss of clutch to predation or disturbance (Powers 1997, Jackson and Jackson 2000, D. A. Budeau p.c.,). There are no reported data on annual reproductive success in Oregon. They retreat from the higher Cascades of e. Douglas Co. before Oct (Fix 1990a).

*Young Killdeer*

**Detection:** Due to their vigilant and vocal nature, Killdeer are generally visible at all times of year. Give alarm call when approached and, if pressed, tend to walk or run, as opposed to taking flight (*PMS*). During breeding activities, adults are quick to respond to disturbance near nest sites with agitated calling and broken-wing displays. However, incubating birds are highly cryptic and in some cases remain silent on nests (*PMS*). Stationary birds are difficult to detect in vegetated habitats (e.g., agricultural fields). Thus, diligently scanning Willamette Valley agricultural fields in winter often results in finding large flocks that would otherwise go unnoticed (*PMS*). Downy young with single breast bands are sometimes confused with Semipalmated Plover.

**Population Status and Conservation:** The rangewide population estimate for the species is 1,000,000 individuals, although the precision of this estimate is poor and warrants further efforts (Morrison et al. 2000). Widespread hunting in the 1800s and early 1900s led to a continent-wide reduction in numbers. However, it is likely that large-scale conversion of native habitats, particularly forested areas, to agriculture and other open habitats has led to an increase in Killdeer populations in many regions. Regardless, large-scale avian surveys (BBS and CBC) indicate significant long-term negative population trends, particularly in Canada and the w. U.S. (Page and Gill 1994, Sanzenbacher and Haig 2001). In Oregon, there are few data on historical or current numbers, but there was a significant decline in numbers on BBS routes 1966-2000 (Sauer et al. 2001).

Potential threats to Killdeer in Oregon include enhanced levels of disturbance and predation in altered habitats. For example, road graders destroy many nests along shoulders of rural roads (*PMS*). Off-road vehicles and cattle destroy eggs and chicks, especially in e. Oregon where Killdeer often nest near stock tanks. Studies from other regions have also documented potential harmful effects of toxins on Killdeer in agricultural habitats (Fair et al. 1994, Warnock and Schwarzbach 1995).—*Peter M. Sanzenbacher and Susan M. Haig*

## Mountain Plover *Charadrius montanus*
The Mountain Plover breeds on the high plateaus of the Rocky Mtns. from Montana to Colorado. It winters in s. Texas, Mexico, and s. California. A small number winter in the Central Valley of California. It is casual elsewhere in the West, but there are eight Oregon records. Two appeared within a large flock of Killdeer near the Corvallis Airport, Benton Co.; one was collected and the other remained from 2 Jan to 10 Mar 1967 (Crowell and Nehls 1967c). A remarkably unwary bird was photographed on Bayocean Beach,

Tillamook Co., 19-26 Nov 1977 (Fix 1977b). Another was photographed at Siletz Bay, Lincoln Co., 3-21 Feb 1983 (Mattocks and Hunn 1983a), and one was on Tahkenitch Beach, Douglas Co., 23 Jan 1988 (OBRC). Two were on the beach at Bandon SP, Coos Co., 6 Dec 1989 (Tweit and Johnson 1990). One was at Ankeny NWR, Marion Co., 4 Dec 1995, and it or another was photographed near Corvallis 19-21 Dec 1995 (Johnson 1996b), one near Floras L., Curry Co., 7 Nov 1999 (Gilligan 2000), and one at Dunes Overlook, Douglas Co., 16 Nov 1999 to 8 Jan 2000 (Gilligan 2000, OBRC). Monotypic.—*Harry B. Nehls*

## Eurasian Dotterel *Charadrius morinellus*
The dotterel is a breeding bird of the alpine tundra across Eurasia and locally into Alaska. It winters from s. Europe to Iran, and casually to Japan. It is casual in fall along the w. coast of N. America. One was photographed near the s. jetty of the Siuslaw R., Lane Co., 24-26 Sep 2000 (Contreras et al. 2001, OBRC) for the only Oregon record.—*Harry B. Nehls*

## Family Haematopodidae

## Black Oystercatcher *Haematopus bachmani*
Easily recognized with its black plumage, long, straight, laterally compressed, orange-red bill with a yellow tip, orange-red eye ring, yellow iris, and pale pink legs. Black Oystercatchers are restricted to rocky coastal shorelines where they feed in the intertidal zone.

**General Distribution:** Resident from w. Aleutians south along the Pacific coast to c. Baja California. Monotypic.

**Oregon Distribution:** Uncommon to fairly common resident on rocky shores and sand/gravel beaches along entire coast. Along sandy central coast, present only as occasional dispersing or wandering individual, typically on jetties.

**Habitat and Diet:** No detailed habitat studies have been done in Oregon. Territory chosen for breeding usually contains a nest site above the high-water mark and an adequate intertidal foraging area. Rock flakes, pebbles, and shell fragments are tossed into the nest area using the bill. The nest bowl is made by pressing the chest into the nest material or into the sediment. Most feeding takes place during low tides and food sources are dependent upon tidal height, surf conditions, and location. A wide array of intertidal invertebrates are commonly eaten (Hartwick 1976). Diet of chicks has been determined from refuse left in the vicinity of the nest or chick roosting site. Particularly notable are mollusks including mussels, limpets, and chitons. They also forage within the interstices of the mussel beds taking crabs, particularly *Oedignathus inermis* and the lined shore crab, and whelks, barnacles, sipunculids, nemertines, and polychaetes. At Cape Arago their foraging influences the distribution of limpets, which in turn affects algal distribution (Frank 1982). Foraging on bivalves occurs in more gravel/sand areas (Andres and Falxa 1995). Black Oystercatchers feeding in California safely ingest doses of paralytic shellfish toxins that are lethal to most other vertebrates (Andres and Falxa 1995).

**Seasonal Activities and Behavior:** Few studies exist on the breeding biology of this species in Oregon. Reproductive success measured in Alaska, British Columbia, and Washington appears to be quite variable among sites and years (Andres and Falxa 1995). Although both sexes participate in nest building, the male does the bulk of the work. Pairs nesting in California used the same nest site for a 5-yr period (Andres and Falxa 1995). Sometimes multiple nests are made and the female chooses in which one to lay (Webster 1941). During breeding season, adults are territorial and defend a section of intertidal habitat where foraging takes place (Hartwick 1976).

Throughout its range, egg laying takes place in May and early Jun. A nest with eggs was recorded from Goat I., Curry Co., on 23 May 1965 (Browning 1973a), and eggs were observed in late May at two other sites (OBBA) and as late as 15 Jun at Barview, Tillamook Co. (D. Fix p.c.). Females lay 1-3 eggs: rarely four or five. The modal clutch size in Alaska was three, and the mean clutch size varied from 2.07 to 2.69 (Andres and Falxa 1995). Average incubation is 26-28 days, range 26-32 days (Andres and Falxa 1995); both sexes incubate and exchanges are frequent during the day, especially during low-tide foraging periods. Hatching success 34-70%. Eggs flooded at high tides have hatched in some instances. Shells of hatched eggs are never found in the nest bowl (Andres and Falxa 1995).

Chicks are brooded, most commonly by the female parent, continuously for 1-2 days, and then intermittently until 13-20 days old. When not brooding, one parent stands and guards the chicks while the other forages. The chick can walk and swim competently 3 days after hatching, and after 5 days begins to pick at food items (Webster 1941). Most provisioning of the young at the nest is done by the male (Purdy and Miller 1988). As early as 7 days after hatching the chick will begin to accompany parents to the nearby feeding areas. Here the female will deliver a greater portion of the food (Andres and Falxa 1995).

Chicks are capable of flight at 38-40 days but remain with their parents in the territory. Acquisition of foraging skills by the chick is slow; 50-day-old chicks still receive more than 50% of their nutritional biomass from their parents (Groves 1984). Parents have been observed to feed chicks that were more than 120 days old (Williams 1927). Offspring are ejected from the territory during Jan to Mar of the following year when courtship intensifies (Helbing 1977). Birds take up to 3 yr to develop a complete repertoire of foraging skills (Andres and Falxa 1995). In nonbreeding season they will form groups of up to 30 (rarely, 45) (Gilligan et al. 1994, Contreras 1998, *ALC*) and use traditional feeding and roosting areas. Individuals will move into bays during rough weather on the outer coast (Andres and Falxa 1995). During storms, large numbers will roost together on a rock that is protected from wave action. One such example is the 49 birds seen roosting on the landward side of a rock at N. Cove, Cape Arago in Dec 1994 (*JH*). Females are heavier than males and have longer narrower bills (Helbing 1977). The few records of the life span of Black Oystercatchers indicate they live 9 to 16 yr (Purdy and Miller 1988, Andres and Falxa 1995).

**Detection:** Despite the small numbers in Oregon, Black Oystercatchers can be easily seen all year on rocky shores. During the breeding season individuals or pairs are often detected by sound. If they sense the presence of humans, birds give an alarm call, a brief, sharp note given singly or in multiples probably associated with higher levels of alarm (Andres and Falxa 1995). Chicks freeze, hide, or run short distances for cover in response to these calls. Foraging activities in the intertidal zone can sometimes be detected by the presence of upside-down limpet shells with chipped edges and their contents eaten (Frank 1982).

**Population Status and Conservation:** The total world population is estimated at 11,000 (Andres and Falxa 1995) with an estimated 350 in Oregon (Pitman et al. 1985, USFWS undated). This species is very vulnerable to oil spills that come ashore; ironically, cleanup activities can disrupt breeding and feeding areas. The presence of hydrocarbons in mussel beds can provide a chronic source of exposure to this species (Andres 1994). Four of five eggs collected in Oregon for contaminant analysis in 1979 contained no detectable organochlorine residues (Henny et al. 1982). Numerous mammalian and avian predators on the eggs and chicks have been recorded (Andres and Falxa 1995), while adults are relatively immune to predation. Human disturbance can result in nest failure if eggs or chicks become unattended and open to predation.—*Jan Hodder*

## Family Recurvirostridae

**Black-necked Stilt** *Himantopus mexicanus*
This fragile-looking bird with bold black-and-white plumage and exaggerated, long reddish legs is often associated with American Avocets at shallow inland ponds and lakes. Very noisy and aggressive in protection of its nest and young, using a variety of distraction displays, including an impressive broken-leg act to lure away interlopers.

**General Distribution:** Local summer resident from Washington, Montana, and Colorado, and along e. coast from Pennsylvania, south through S. America to Chile and Argentina. Casually occurs and occasionally breeds elsewhere in N. America. Winters from California, Florida, and the Gulf coast south through S. America. Of three subspecies *H. m. mexicanus* occurs in Oregon (Robinson et al. 1999).

**Oregon Distribution:** Locally uncommon to fairly common summer resident of Klamath, Lake, Harney, and Malheur counties. Largest Oregon breeding colony is at Summer L. (Rogers 1980a, Paulson 1993). Since 1980 have become regular spring and fall migrants through e. Oregon and irregular spring and casual fall migrants through w. Oregon. Since 1985 nesting colonies have been established in Umatilla, Morrow, and Union counties (Summers 1985a, Anderson DA 1989d, 1990b). Nested in the Willamette Valley at Baskett Slough NWR during 2000 (P. Thompson p.c.) and 2001 (Korpi 2001b); at least two pairs bred at Fern Ridge Res., Lane Co., in 2002, raising three young (J. Sullivan p.c., D. DeWitt p.c.).

**Habitat and Diet:** Nests colonially, often with Avocets, at vegetated edges of alkaline and, preferably, freshwater ponds and lakes (Wetmore 1925, Robinson et al. 1999). Nests usually well scattered, but more concentrated on islands when available (Paulson 1993, Robinson et al. 1999). Forages in water up to 5 in (130

mm) deep and about muddy edges (Robinson et al. 1999). Uses similar habitat in migration (*HBN*).

Nest usually a depression on the ground lined with weed stalks, twigs, and grasses. If water rises during incubation, parents will add to the nest, keeping the eggs above the water. Nest may be raised up to 8 in (203 mm) above the ground (Dawson 1923, Bent 1927, Gabrielson and Jewett 1940).

Opportunistic forager of insects, aquatic bugs, and beetles (Bent 1927). Brine shrimp and brine flies major food item in alkaline situations (Hamilton 1975, Paulson 1993,), crawfish, water-boatmen, beetles, flies, and small fishes in fresh water (Wetmore 1925).

**Seasonal Activities and Behavior:** Spring movements taken in small flocks and occasionally individually. Numbers involved highly variable, influenced primarily by habitat availability at traditional sites (Littlefield 1990a, Paulson 1993, Nehls 1994). Main movement during Apr and May with peak during mid-Apr (Nehls 1994, Sullivan 2001b). Earliest at Klamath NWR 19 Mar 1979 (Watson 1979c), and at Malheur NWR 20 Mar 1984 (Ivey, Herziger, and Scheuering 1998).

Monogamous. One brood per season. Usual clutch size 3-4 eggs. Both parents incubate and care for young. Incubation period 25-26 days; precocial young become independent in 28-32 days after hatching (Baicich and Harrison 1997). There is little information on Oregon nesting. Nesting at Malheur NWR early May, earliest 3 May, with most eggs hatching late Jun (Littlefield 1990a). Nest and eggs have been observed mid-May to late Jun (n=18), and flightless young mid-Jun to late Jul (n=9, OBBA). Two early chicks were noted near Boardman 16 May 1990 (Anderson DA 1990b).

There is some wandering away from nesting sites prior to departure, but not as conspicuously as in spring. There are two fall records west of the Cascades, one near Woodburn 17 Aug 1979 and three near Roseburg 16 Sep 1979 (Hunn and Mattocks 1980). They seldom move to staging areas prior to migration, but occasionally form impressive concentrations; e.g., 1,338 at Malheur NWR late Aug 1991 (Evanich 1992b), 2,436 there 18 Aug 1994 (G. L. Ivey p.c.), and 563 at Summer L. 3 Aug 1987 (Rogers 1987b). The peak of fall movement occurs during Aug with much lower numbers through Sep; latest at Malheur NWR 26 Oct (Paulson 1993) and at Lower Klamath NWR 27 Oct 1999 (Sullivan 2000a).

**Detection:** Easily located in its specialized shallow water habitat where it is loud and conspicuous. Most common at se. Oregon alkaline lakes and playas.

**Population Status and Conservation:** Breeding habitat is susceptible to naturally occurring drought and floods causing periodic abandonment. Severe

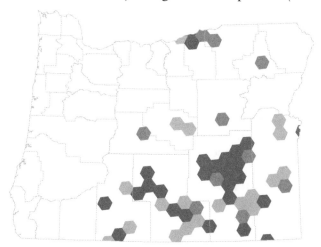

drought and subsequent flooding in the Great Basin during the 1970s and 1980s forced stilts to temporarily abandon traditional nesting sites in search of more suitable sites elsewhere (Littlefield 1979, 1990a, Alberico 1993, Paulson 1993, Nehls 1994). Breeding in the Willamette Valley from 2000 through 2002 is probably due in part to improved wetland habitat at wildlife areas.

Mobile, with nomadic tendencies, this species is able to find currently suitable sites and maintain a stable population. Such fluctuation in the number of birds at nesting colonies requires assessment of migrants and wintering birds to obtain population estimates. Page and Gill (1994) estimate at least 25,000 winter in N. America west of the Rocky Mtns. Peak number of migrants through se. Oregon were estimated at approximately 2,000 (ODFW *in* Robinson et al. 1999).

Studies during 1980-83 found organochlorine pesticides in Black-necked Stilt eggs at Malheur NWR and at other Great Basin colonies, but it did not cause eggshell thinning or affect reproduction (Henny, Blus, and Hulse 1985). Selenium from irrigation runoff is a serious problem and has reduced egg viability in many areas, but apparently not in Oregon (Robinson et al. 1999). Habitat loss remains the primary conservation concern in Oregon. Natural instability of Black-necked Stilt nesting habitat should be considered in all wetland management decisions to ensure that suitable alternate sites will always be available (*HBN*).—*Harry B. Nehls*

### American Avocet *Recurvirostra americana*

A conspicuous wader of shallow wetland habitats with a striking appearance and graceful movements. These long-legged shorebirds have contrasting black and white upperparts and during the breeding season, the head and neck turn from gray or white to a deep rust color. One of their most notable traits is a long, slender, upturned bill for which the genus, *Recurvirostra*, is named. The bill is well-adapted for capturing aquatic and terrestrial invertebrates as foraging birds sweep their bill through the water column or pick prey off the surface of land and water. Males and females are similar in appearance except that the degree of bill curve is greater in females.

**General Distribution:** Restricted to N. America. Exhibit a disjunct breeding distribution associated with the occurrence of appropriate wetland habitats. Breeding birds are found along the Pacific coast from San Francisco Bay, California, south to n. Baja, Mexico, at inland sites extending from se. British Columbia to sw. Ontario and south to interior regions of Mexico, and on the Gulf coast of Texas and Mexico (del Hoyo et al. 1996, Robinson et al. 1997). Small breeding populations are known on the Atlantic coast as far

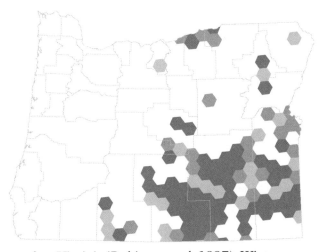

north as Virginia (Robinson et al. 1997). Winter range overlaps much of the breeding range, particularly at coastal and southern sites. Also winters in parts of M. America as far south as Guatemala (Hamilton 1975). Monotypic.

**Oregon Distribution:** A common breeder east of the Cascades at wetlands of sc. and se. Oregon. Distribution and number of breeding birds vary annually depending on regional and local water levels and habitat availability. Regardless, most breeders occur in the w. Great Basin counties of Klamath, Lake, Harney, and Malheur (Gilligan et al. 1994). Sites with consistently high numbers of breeding birds include the Harney Basin, L. Abert, and Summer L. (Nehls 1994). In addition, Goose L. is an important site that straddles the border of Oregon and California. Intensive searches at Summer L. W.A. in 1995 resulted in 232 nests found (*SMH*). Smaller numbers also occur in adjacent areas and northeastern parts of the state where habitat is appropriate.

In late summer and early fall, birds are common and locally abundant at various staging sites with greatest numbers found at L. Abert, Summer L., Goose L., and Malheur L. For example, peak 1997 fall counts at Summer L. (26 Aug) and L. Abert (13 Aug) were 15,460 and 15,345 birds respectively (Warnock et al. 1998). In w. Oregon, sightings in the Willamette Valley are rare with records of migrants for wetland refuges such as William L. Finley NWR (Merrifield 1996b) and the Fernhill Wetlands (Nehls 1998). On the coast, spring and fall migrants are uncommon with annual reports from Tillamook and Coos Bay (Nehls 1994, H. Nehls p.c.). Wintering birds are rare to occasional in the state with single birds found in the Coos Bay area 18 Oct 1998-28 Feb 1999 and 16 Dec 2001 through at least 3 Mar 2002 (T. Rodenkirk p.c.).

**Habitat and Diet:** American Avocets frequent a range of shallow wetland habitats throughout the annual cycle. Generally, birds occur in open areas with little emergent vegetation and water depths of 0-8 in (0-12 cm) (Boettcher et al. 1995, Robinson et al. 1997). Preferred breeding habitats in Oregon are alkaline lakes, marshes, and freshwater sites. In particular, access to freshwater inflows or other sources of fresh water are critical for chick survival because their salt glands are not fully developed, resulting in a low tolerance of saline environments (Rubega and Robinson 1997). Nest sites are along shorelines and in adjacent upland areas with sparse or no vegetation (Robinson et al. 1997). When available, birds will also nest on islands that provide protection from mammalian predators (*PMS*). From studies at L. Abert and Summer L. W.A., 95% of nests (n=204) were within 164 ft (50 m) of water and greater than half were less than 33 ft (10 m) from water (*SMH*). Nests are shallow scrapes that are either bare or lined with small pebbles and bits of vegetation (Hamilton 1975, *PMS*). Prior to migration, postbreeding birds occupy habitats similar to the breeding period but also use wet meadows and flooded agricultural fields. On migration routes and wintering grounds outside of Oregon, birds occupy a greater diversity of habitats including coastal estuaries and artificial habitats such as evaporation ponds and rice fields (Evans and Harris 1994, Robinson et al. 1997).

American Avocets are generalist tactile and visual foragers that feed on a range of aquatic and terrestrial invertebrates throughout the annual cycle. In stomach analyses of birds from different regions, seeds and vegetable matter were also found to be a substantial portion of diets (Wetmore 1925, Baldassarre and Fischer 1984). At L. Abert, various life stages of brine fly accounted for a majority of prey biomass consumed by postbreeding birds followed by long-legged flies (Boula 1986). Of interest, brine shrimp are abundant at L. Abert but accounted for < 2% of biomass consumed (Boula 1986).

**Seasonal Activity and Behavior:** American Avocets are socially monogamous breeders that form pair bonds at wintering sites and on migration (Sordahl 1984, Robinson and Oring 1997). However, some birds have been observed copulating with multiple individuals within a breeding season (Gibson 1971, *PMS*). Birds arrive at Summer L. W.A. and other sites in the w. Great Basin from late Mar through Apr (Gibson 1971, Nehls 1994). Displays at breeding sites include an astounding dance performed immediately after copulation in which the male and female cross bills and then rapidly walk forward together (Hamilton 1975, *PMS*). Nests both solitarily and semi-colonially and lays a clutch of four eggs from late Apr to May (Gibson 1971, *SMH*). Nests with as many as eight eggs have been found and

are considered a result of "dumping" by other females (Gibson 1971, *SMH*). Anti-predator behavior near colonies includes mobbing and distraction displays (Gibson 1971, Robinson et al. 1997). Incubation period ranges between 22 and 28 days (Robinson et al. 1997). Young are downy and nidifugous at hatch (Gibson 1971). Both sexes participate in parental care activities including incubation and brood rearing (Hamilton 1975, Robinson et al. 1997).

Postbreeding birds in Oregon and throughout the w. Great Basin visit multiple wetland sites, often travel hundreds of miles between sites, and may remain at sites for months prior to fall migration (Plissner, Haig, and Oring 2000). Studies indicate a northerly movement direction of many postbreeding birds to these sites, with peak numbers occurring in late Aug and early Sep (Nehls 1994, Plissner et al. 1999). Birds depart for wintering grounds in Sep and Oct, although there are records of flocks lingering into Nov (Bent 1927, Paulson 1993, Nehls 1994). Winter surveys and reports of marked birds suggest that many American Avocets breeding in Oregon winter along the coast of California (e.g., San Francisco Bay) and Baja, Mexico (Engilis et al. 1998, Page et al. 1999).

**Detection:** American Avocets are conspicuous birds throughout the annual cycle due to their size, gregarious nature, and affinity for open, unvegetated habitats. In Oregon, huge flocks are easily observed at isolated postbreeding sites in the w. Great Basin and adjacent areas.

**Population Status and Conservation:** North American breeding population estimate is 450,000 individuals (Morrison et al. 2000). Overall, the w. Great Basin is a region of critical importance for breeding and

*American Avocet*

postbreeding American Avocets and other shorebirds. Based on survey results and guidelines of the Western Hemisphere Shorebird Reserve Network, Summer L. and L. Abert qualify as sites of international importance and Goose L. qualifies as a site of regional importance to American Avocets (Warnock et al. 1998). Potentially the greatest threats to breeding and migrating birds in Oregon stem from local and regional variation in water levels due to drought and water-management practices for agriculture and grazing (Alberico 1993, Robinson et al. 1997, Reed et al. 1997). Low water levels can result in increased salinity levels, decreased availability of fresh water, and greater accessibility of island nesting sites to predators. But rising water levels at L. Abert from snow melt and other events can flood large numbers of nests and result in breeding failure (*SMH*). Other threats include trampling of nests by cattle (*PMS*) and effects of selenium and other contaminants (Williams et al. 1989). The potential for these different factors to affect large segments of the population is enhanced at sites where large numbers of birds congregate.—*Peter M. Sanzenbacher and Susan M. Haig*

## Family Scolopacidae

### Subfamily Scolopacinae

### Greater Yellowlegs *Tringa melanoleuca*
This tall, pale wader is often first detected by its ringing calls as a small flock maneuvers to land in shallow water along an estuary or lakeshore. The long, often slightly upturned bill and very long yellow legs make this one of the easier shorebirds to identify despite its subdued, speckled gray and white plumage.

**General Distribution:** Breeds from w. Alaska across n. and c. Canada to the Maritime Provinces and Quebec. Winters from British Columbia and s. New England south coastally and in mild climates in the interior to S. America. Migrates continent-wide. Monotypic (AOU 1957).

**Oregon Distribution:** Uncommon to locally common migrant on shorelines and open wet areas statewide. Winters on the coast and locally inland. A single pair bred at Downey L., a wooded swamp at 4,850 ft (1,478 m) elevation, 10 mi (16 km) northeast of Joseph, Wallowa Co., each summer 1983-86 (Paulson 1993). This is the only known breeding locale south of Canada. Young were fledged in 1984, 1985, and probably 1983 and 1986 (F. Conley p.c.). Breeding has apparently not occurred there since 1986; the swamp is dry in some years.

**Habitat and Diet:** In addition to using shallow water in estuaries and along lake margins, these birds can often be found in flooded pastureland, especially in winter, when they seem to prefer this habitat to the more typical estuarine areas (*ALC*). Studies outside Oregon have shown that this species eats small fish as well as crustaceans, snails, and small worms (Paulson 1993, Kaufman 1996).

**Seasonal Activity and Behavior:** Significant southbound movements begin early, with small flocks of adults usually appearing during the last few days of Jun, increasing in Jul (Gullion 1951, Littlefield 1990a, Paulson 1993, Contreras 1998). Widespread after early Jul, with peak of juvenile passage in Sep (Littlefield 1990a, Paulson 1993). Counts from fall movements are rarely published in local and regional studies, but recent reports include high counts of 93 at Thompson Res., Lake Co., 12 Oct 1995 (Sullivan 1996a), 68 at Malheur NWR 20 Sep-8 Oct 1998 (Sullivan 1999a) and 40 at The Narrows, Malheur NWR on 20-24 Sep 1997 (Sullivan 1998a). Most birds are gone from e. Oregon by early Nov, but some linger in mild years.

They winter along the entire coast, but most (sometimes scores) are at Coos Bay (CBC) and only smaller flocks are scattered northward along the coast in most years. Peak counts at Coos Bay can be impressive, e.g., 137 at Pony Slough alone on 4 Jan 1997 (Johnson 1997b). Small numbers winter locally in the Willamette Valley (Gullion 1951, Herlyn 1998, Gillson 1999, CBC) where peak CBC counts are usually under 20 even in favored areas. They winter more rarely in the Umpqua and Rogue valleys (Browning 1975a, Hunter et al. 1998). A few can also be found in the Klamath Basin (Summers 1993a) and Umatilla Co. (CBC) in winter, with scattered records elsewhere (especially along the Columbia R.) in mild years when open water with unfrozen edges is available for foraging.

Spring movements in w. Oregon are somewhat obscured by the presence of a significant wintering population on the south coast, but a noticeable movement occurs in late Mar and especially Apr, with some birds present through early May and stragglers rarely to early Jun. Small flocks are the norm, but occasional large gatherings occur. Peak counts west of the Cascades during spring passage in recent years include 200 at Cedar Canyon marsh, Washington Co., 30 Mar 1997 (Lillie 1997), 150 at Tillamook on 20 Apr 1992 (Gilligan 1992b), 100 near Lebanon, Linn Co., and 92 at the Kirtland Rd. sewage ponds, Jackson Co., both on 9 Apr 1994 (Lillie 1994). In some years extraordinary spring movements occur, e.g., the 500 found along New R., Curry Co., 27 Apr 1984 (Irons 1984b). Spring movement is more apparent east of the Cascades owing to the absence of wintering birds in most locations. Average arrival at Malheur is 17 Mar

(Ivey, Herziger, and Scheuering 1998) and peak of passage is in the first half of Apr (Littlefield 1990a). A similar pattern holds true in the Klamath Basin (Summers 1993a). Peak counts include 100 in the Klamath Basin on 21-22 Mar 1997 (Sullivan 1997b) and 61 at Klamath Marsh NWR on 12 Apr 1993 (Summers 1993c).

**Detection:** These are among the easiest Oregon shorebirds to locate and observe, owing to their size, sounds, and preference for open shorelines. Typically approachable, but the best views are often obtained by remaining stationary along a shoreline while birds stalk the shallows toward the observer.

**Population Status and Conservation:** Migratory movements in Oregon have not been studied over a long enough period to allow any meaningful statement about the populations that move through Oregon. Winter numbers have remained stable or perhaps have increased, though this may be an artifact of more CBCs being conducted on the coast.—*Alan L. Contreras*

## Lesser Yellowlegs *Tringa flavipes*

This small, remarkably delicate long-legged wader can be found in migration across most of Oregon. It is speckled gray and white with some variation by season, and is typically noticed mincing about in shallow pools and in the water adjacent to mudflats.

**General Distribution:** Breeds from nw. Alaska south and east across most of Canada to extreme w. Quebec. Winters mainly from M. America southward, with small numbers along the warmer southern fringe of N. America, rarely north (coastally) to British Columbia and New York. The bulk of migration is east of the Rocky Mtns. but a recent study showed a major staging through e. Idaho, with up to 800 birds found in a day and many daily counts above 100 birds (Taylor et al. 1992). Monotypic (AOU 1957).

**Oregon Distribution:** Uncommon to common migrant, most birds in fall. In the eastern one-third of Oregon, it usually outnumbers Greater Yellowlegs in fall. A survey of sites at Summer L. and Malheur NWR in Aug 1993 found 130 Lesser and 33 Greater Yellowlegs (Summers 1994a). Numbers drop significantly farther west, where Greater is usually far more common west of the Cascades. However, some years bring remarkably large flights to w. Oregon. On the outer coast this is one of the less common regular migrant shorebirds, with numbers usually much lower than those of Greater Yellowlegs.

**Habitat and Diet:** This is a wader of shallow pools. It is often found in the water near mudflats or on seasonally flooded fields, as well as in small isolated ponds. It occurs even in isolated patches of habitat in montane regions, e.g., five at Big L., Linn Co., 1 Aug 1968 (Gillson 1999) and several fall records at the Diamond L. sewage ponds, Douglas Co. (Fix 1990a).

Dietary information is not available from Oregon.

**Seasonal Activity and Behavior:** Southbound movements of adults begin fairly early, e.g., 22 Jun 1940 at Malheur NWR (Littlefield 1990a), 25 Jun 1985 (Heinl 1986b) and 24 Jun 1993 at Ankeny NWR (Johnson J 1994b), and 29 Jun 1989 at the Diamond L. sewage ponds (Fix 1990a). The bulk of movement begins in early Jul and continues through Sep, with a peak in Aug at Malheur NWR involving chiefly juveniles (Littlefield 1990a). Sometimes lingers on the coast through the fall (Paulson 1993, Summers 1993a, Nehls 1994, Patterson 1998b, field notes) and, rarely, into winter.

Unlike those of the Greater Yellowlegs, fall movements have a narrow peak in late Aug-early Sep and then drop off sharply. Peak fall numbers in w. Oregon include 123 at Sauvie I. in early Sep 1989 (Nehls 1994), 96 at Nehalem 23 Aug 1980 (Hunn and Mattocks 1981a) and 85 at Tillamook Bay on 18 Aug 1985 (Paulson 1993), while more typical peaks include 35 at Sauvie I. 7 Sep 1996 and 13 at Astoria 12 Oct 1996 (Gilligan 1997). Typical high counts east of the Cascades are 20-30 in late Aug and early Sep at favored sites (*Oregon Birds* field notes). Peak fall numbers east of the Cascades include 70 near Hermiston 28 Aug 1992 (Summers 1993b), 40 (compared to 3 Greaters at the same location) near Malheur NWR HQ on 17-18 Sep 1999 (*ALC*) and 38 at Summer L. 15 Aug 1986 (Paulson 1993).

Winter status is poorly known but there are some well-documented records, mostly from the outer coast and interior sw. Oregon. At least two winter records have photographic documentation, one near Fern Ridge Res., Lane Co., that remained with Greater Yellowlegs during the winter of 1995-96 and one at Summer L. 26 Dec 1996 (Contreras 1997b). Another wintered near Fern Ridge Res. in 1994-95 and yet another was seen near there by multiple observers in early Jan 1999 (J. Johnson, D. Bailey et al.). A good written description was provided for a bird seen on the Tillamook Bay CBC in 1992. There are widely accepted multiple-observer sight records for Coos Bay in Dec 1976 (CBC; *ALC*), 12 Jan 1992 (Johnson J 1992b) and one that wintered in 2000-01 (H. Herlyn p.c., CBC, *ALC*). One for which details are unavailable was reported 7 Dec 1984 along the Malheur R. near Riverside (Rogers 1985b). Paulson (1993) notes that a few have wintered in the Klamath Basin. However, there are many reports, especially on CBCs, for which documentation is lacking.

Spring movements involve far fewer birds than are seen in fall. Migration begins with small numbers in late Mar (Nehls 1994, Contreras 1998, Herlyn 1998, Gillson 1999), including birds in e. Oregon. Peak counts are low; highs include 30 at New R. 22 Apr 1998 (Lillie 1998), 25 at the Forest Grove sewage ponds, Washington Co., 22 Apr 1991 (Gilligan 1991) and at the Kirtland Rd. sewage ponds, Jackson Co., 17 Apr 1994 (Summers 1994b), and 24 at Seaside 25 Apr 1999 (Lillie 1999). Numbers east of the Cascades are even lower, with 18 at McKay Cr. NWR 6 May 1995 the highest in the past 10 yr (Sullivan PT 1995a).

**Detection:** While quieter than the Greater Yellowlegs, it is easily observed at close range in many situations; especially obvious in fall at major e. Oregon staging areas such as Malheur NWR, where dozens may be compared to Greater Yellowlegs at preferred wetlands. Even more than Greater, this yellowlegs tends to remain in the same feeding area for several days in fall, allowing easy location and repeated studies.

**Population Status and Conservation:** Lack of long-term sampling of migrants precludes any definitive statement about the condition of the population that passes through Oregon. Numbers are moderate even in peak years, but this seems to have been the case for decades. Winter reports are increasing, which may represent an actual tendency to winter farther north or may simply represent better coverage and reporting.

This species uses mainly shallow water habitats, including temporarily wet areas, and seems fairly adaptable to such situations as wet agricultural lands. Estuaries are important migration stops, and any filling of such areas would be detrimental.—*Alan L. Contreras*

## Spotted Redshank *Tringa erythropus*
This vociferous Eurasian shorebird appears as an occasional migrant in the Aleutian Is. and as a casual visitant elsewhere in N. America. There is one Oregon record, a bird photographed at the s. jetty of the Columbia R. 21 Feb to 15 Mar 1981 (Mattocks and Hunn 1981, Watson 1989).—*Harry B. Nehls*

## Solitary Sandpiper *Tringa solitaria*
The enigmatic Solitary Sandpiper may be one of the least understood of Oregon's regularly occurring shorebirds. As its name implies, the species is most often found singly, and it rarely occurs in groups of more than two individuals. The Solitary Sandpiper frequents habitats not often utilized by other migrant shorebirds, such as smaller and often partly wooded patches of water, and high-altitude bogs and wet meadows. It often tips repeatedly forward; when

alighting, it holds its wings high over the body before folding them closed. Normally a boreal forest breeder, the Solitary Sandpiper has been all but confirmed as breeding in Oregon, with two records of territorial birds in the c. Oregon Cascades.

**General Distribution:** Breeds to northern tree line in boreal forests of n. N. America from w. interior Alaska to c. Labrador coast, south to sc. Ontario and se. Quebec (Paulson 1993, Moskoff 1995); breeding also suspected in Cariboo Parklands, Okanagan Valley, and Manning L. in s. British Columbia (Paulson 1993). Winters se. Texas and much of M. and S. America (Moskoff 1995a). Two subspecies; only *T. s. cinnamomea* documented in Oregon (Conover 1944), but both probably occur (see below).

**Oregon Distribution:** Uncommon to rare migrant in fresh water or brackish habitats throughout Oregon; rarest along outer coast and in alkali habitats. Spring adults more common in western interior valleys; fall juveniles are more common than adults in all regions and more common east of the Cascades (Paulson 1993); occasional in extreme e. Oregon (Evanich 1992a, Contreras 1996a).

Only a handful of the many Oregon records expressly identify the subspecies. All records for the state prior to 1940 were attributed to *T. s. cinnamomea* (Gabrielson and Jewett 1940), while most modern records do not include a subspecific designation. *T. s. solitaria* has been positively identified from interior Washington, Idaho, and s. California (Brooks 1923, Paulson 1993).

**Habitat and Diet:** Prefers fresh water, even at coast; rarely found on saltwater marshes and mud flats. In migration, frequents muddy ponds and sewage lagoons as well as livestock wallows (Paulson 1993, Moskoff 1995a). Sometimes found in migration at high elevation lakes; at least three records over 6,000 ft (1,800 m) elevation: Munson Meadow in Crater L. NP, 6,397 ft (1,950 m) (Farner 1952); Summit Ridge near Lookout Mtn., Wallowa Co., 6,722 ft (2,050 m) (Summers 1985a), and Little Three Cr. L., Deschutes Co., 6,797 ft (2,070 m) (SS).

Two Oregon locations where nesting may have occurred were high-elevation bogs and wet meadows surrounded by mixed coniferous forest (Sawyer 1981, Lundsten 1996). While other N. American sandpipers can be observed perching in trees on their nesting grounds, the Solitary Sandpiper is the only arboreal nesting species (Johnsgard 1986a). In its traditional breeding range, the species often utilizes abandoned nests of Rusty Blackbirds, which also prefer wet, open habitats; other species whose nests are used include robins, waxwings, kingbirds, and jays (Moskoff 1995a).

Across N. America, diet consists mainly of insects as well as some arachnids, amphibians, annelids, small fishes, and gastropods; in winter (outside Oregon) consumes various terrestrial and aquatic invertebrates. Has been observed extracting freshwater snails from their shells (Moskoff 1995a), but one study showed the crops of breeding birds to contain small snails, swallowed whole (Swarth 1935). Whether on the breeding grounds or in migration, often feeds at pond edges or in shallow puddles by vibrating forward foot to stir up insects on the bottom (McGillivray and Semenchuk 1998). Other feeding behavior includes surface picking or vigorous probing for invertebrates (Paulson 1993).

**Seasonal Activity and Behavior:** Earliest spring record west of the Cascades from Coos Co., 24 Mar 1987 (Contreras 1998); documentation is scant for this extremely early sighting; early spring record east of the Cascades of two birds in Hines, Harney Co., 4 Apr 1997 (*SS*). Most spring sightings last week of Apr through first week of May. Late spring record for w. Oregon from Seaside, 20 May 2000 (Lillie 2000); late spring e. Oregon record from Fields, 30 May, unspecified year (Gilligan 1994). The spring high count is eight from Banks, Washington Co., last week of Apr 1984 (Irons 1984b).

Two locations in the Oregon Cascades have hosted probable nesting of Solitary Sandpiper: Gold L. bog in the Willamette NF, Lane Co. (Sawyer 1981), and Olallie Meadows in the Mt. Hood NF, Marion Co. (Lundsten 1996). Two territorial individuals were first observed at Gold L. bog on 28 Jun 1981; four individuals were later observed at the same location on 25 Jul 1981, although it could not be confirmed that any of the four were fledglings (Sawyer 1981). Territorial adults were observed in the same region almost annually until 1987 (Paulson 1993). At Olallie Meadows, the first evidence of probable breeding was documented on 1 Jul 1995, yet through 12 Jul 1995 only one territorial individual was ever observed at once (Lundsten 1996). At both locations, individual birds were observed perching in trees, a habit commonly attributed to breeding birds but not to migrants (Paulson 1993). Possible breeding individuals have also occurred at Downey L., e. Wallowa Co., just outside Wallowa-Whitman NF (Paulson 1993).

An early fall record was 2 Jul 1990 at Seaside, Clatsop Co.; the main movement begins late Jul (Nehls 1994). Fall adults arrive before juveniles, but juveniles are more common and remain through late Sep. A late fall record west of the Cascades at the n. spit Coos Bay was 22 Oct 1997 (Contreras 1998); a late fall e. Oregon record from an unspecified location was 20 Sep 1985 (Summers 1986a). A fall high count was six at Malheur NWR, Harney Co., 17 Aug 1977 (Nehls 1994).

**Detection:** This species is nearly always observed singly; occasionally among small flocks of other shorebirds, especially yellowlegs. It is occasionally confused with the Spotted Sandpiper, with which it may occur at higher elevations, and the Lesser Yellowlegs. Its call is distinctive.

**Population Status and Conservation:** Merrill (1888) first reported Solitary Sandpiper in Oregon in May and Aug 1887 at Fort Klamath. In Oregon, this species is not present during BBS or CBC efforts, and no other monitoring currently in place effectively samples this species. In the species' normal breeding range, little is known of its population trends (Moskoff 1995a).—*Stephen Shunk*

## Willet *Catoptrophorus semipalmatus*

At first look, the Willet is a rather drab and nondescript medium-sized shorebird found in wetland habitats and nearby uplands. However, further observation reveals subtle patterning in its relatively uniform grayish plumage and birds in flight expose a distinct, bold white wing bar that contrasts with a black border. Sexes are similar in appearance at all times of year. Willets are present on breeding grounds in Oregon for a short period of time during spring and summer, but displaying birds are conspicuous and emit a loud and persistent "pill-will-willet" call. These vigilant and vocal individuals often hover overhead and alight on fence posts or the tops of bushes near nesting territories.

**General Distribution:** The species is restricted to the New World. There are two recognized subspecies based primarily on disjunct breeding distributions, as well as differences in ecology, morphology, and vocalizations (Bent 1927, Lowther et al. 2001). Studies indicate that individuals recognize and discriminate between calls of the different subspecies (Douglas 1998). Western Willets (*C. s. inornatus*) breed at isolated and dispersed sites of the Great Basin, n. Great Plains, and Prairie regions. A majority of the population winters along the

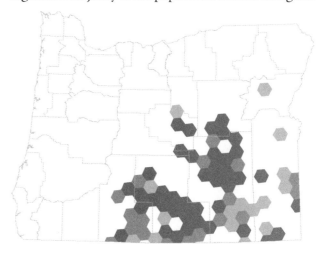

Pacific coast from Humboldt Bay, California south as far as Chile. Large numbers of w. Great Basin Willets concentrate in the San Francisco Bay area during winter (Haig et al. 2002), whereas Prairie Canada breeders apparently winter farther south (Lowther et al. 2001). In addition, some Western Willets are also known to winter along the Atlantic and Gulf coasts (Lowther et al. 2001). Eastern Willets (*C. s. semipalmatus*) breed along the Atlantic and Gulf coasts from New Brunswick and Nova Scotia south to northern areas of Mexico (Howe 1982, Lowther et al. 2001). They winter along the Atlantic coast from Virginia south, including the Caribbean and in some cases areas as far south as Brazil (Lowther et al. 2001).

**Oregon Distribution:** Willets are a common spring and summer resident east of the Cascades in Klamath, Lake, Harney, Malheur, and Grant counties (Gilligan et al. 1994, Nehls 1994). Also confirmed in Crook Co. (OBBA). Occurrence and abundance of breeding birds vary with availability of sites with upland nesting habitats adjacent to water. In late summer, postbreeding birds are common to uncommon at wetland staging areas adjacent to breeding sites. There are no winter records of Willets east of the Cascades (Nehls 1994).

Willets are very rare spring and fall migrants in the Willamette Valley and other inland areas west of the Cascades (Browning 1975a, Gilligan et al. 1994, Nehls 1994, Hunter et al. 1998). In coastal areas, birds are rare during spring and fall (Gilligan et al. 1994, Nehls 1994). Also rare in winter on the coast, but small groups are reported regularly in Yaquina Bay and Coos Bay, and occasionally in Bandon (Paulson 1993, Gilligan et al. 1994, Nehls 1994). Small numbers (1-8 birds) have wintered at Coos Bay in recent years (T. Rodenkirk p.c., *ALC*).

**Habitat and Diet:** Willets are a wetland-associated species throughout the annual cycle and the western subspecies exhibits seasonal differences in habitat use between coastal wintering areas and inland breeding sites. Oregon breeding birds

nest in upland habitats including short grassland, sagebrush, and saltbrush flats (Nehls 1994, Haig et al. 2002). Nest sites are generally adjacent to alkaline lakes, freshwater wetlands, wet meadows, or other sources of water used for foraging and brood-rearing activities (Reed et al. 1997, Haig et al. 2002). However, distances of nest sites from water are variable and in some cases Willets in western states have been found nesting as far as 1.7 mi (2.7 km) from any water (Lowther et al. 2001). Nests are shallow scrapes, lined with small pebbles and fine grasses, situated on bare ground or short vegetation, or at the base of shrubs (e.g., sagebrush; Lowther et al. 2001, *PMS*). Haig et al. (2002) found that home range size of breeding birds at the Goose L. airport averaged 413 ac (167 ha; standard deviation ± 358 ac, n=18 birds). Adults generally remained within 3 mi (4.8 km) of nests and during incubation breaks birds were found at an average distance of 2,262 ft (689 m) from nests (SD ± 1,128 ft, n=28 birds). Wintering birds occur in various coastal habitats including tidal mudflats, marshes, sandy beaches, and rocky shores (Lowther et al. 2001).

Knowledge of Willet diet is lacking for all regions and most information is descriptive in nature. Based on their bill morphology, visual and tactile foraging strategies, and the range of habitats they occupy, Willets are likely generalists that feed on a diversity of aquatic and terrestrial invertebrates (Lowther et al. 2001, *PMS*). Major prey items identified from the breeding sites in e. Oregon include aquatic beetles and to a lesser extent spiders and fish (Mendenhall 1970). Diet at coastal wintering sites includes numerous crab species, sandworms, nereid worms, clams, and amphipods (Lowther et al. 2001).

*Willet*

**Seasonal Activity and Behavior:** Willets appear synchronously at most Oregon breeding sites in mid-Apr (Gabrielson and Jewett 1940, Gilligan et al. 1994), with an early date from Malheur NWR (Harney Co.) of 21 Mar (Littlefield 1990a). Depending on the site, birds exhibit both semi-colonial (e.g., Goose L. airport, Lake Co.) and solitary (e.g., Summer L. W.A., Lake Co., L. Abert; Haig et al. 2002, *PMS*) nesting behavior. For example, at the Goose L. airport, 28 nests were found within a 161-ac (65-ha) area (Haig et al. 2002) and at another w. Great Basin site, Oring and Reed (1997) cite as many as 50 pairs breeding around 250 ac (100 ha) of ponds near Honey L., California. Mean nest initiation dates over consecutive years at the Goose L. airport and Summer L. W.A. were in mid-May (Haig et al. 2002). Willets are socially monogamous and lay a clutch of four eggs (Lowther et al. 2001).

Following breeding activities, some Willets congregate at pre-migratory wetland staging sites. High counts at three w. Great Basin breeding areas in 1997 were 466 birds at Goose L. (1 Jul), 125 birds at Summer L. and Summer L. W.A. (24 Jun), and 73 birds at L. Abert (9 Jul) (Warnock et al. 1998, *SMH*). Regardless, Willets are present at w. Great Basin breeding areas for a relatively short period and depart for coastal wintering sites in Jun and early Jul. In 1998 and 1999, departure dates of radio-marked adults from Goose L. were variable and averaged the last week of Jun (Haig et al. 2002). Adults with failed nests departed approximately a week prior to other birds. Following departure, results of searches along the Pacific coast as far south as Mexico found that 80% (32/40) of birds re-located were within 30.5 mi (49 km) of the San Francisco Bay area. In addition, birds from the w. Great Basin showed fidelity to local wintering areas with some adults (n=6) found at the same wintering site in multiple years (Haig et al. 2002). In contrast, winter resights of Willets from Alberta breeding sites were found farther south in Mexico and Costa Rica (Lowther et al. 2001).

**Detection:** Willets are easy to detect and observe at breeding sites in e. Oregon, particularly during prebreeding activites in Mar and Apr. Breeding pairs are territorial and displaying individuals in flight and on high perches emit loud and continuous calls. In contrast, incubating birds are extremely secretive and nests highly cryptic. Birds often sit tightly on nests until intruders are within a few feet or less (*PMS*). Although birds depart Oregon shortly after breeding activities, postbreeding birds can be found in flocks at lakes and other wetland sites. In particular, areas of Malheur NWR, Summer L. W.A., and Goose L. provide excellent viewing opportunities.

**Population Status and Conservation:** Morrison et al. (2000) estimated the rangewide Willet population at 250,000 birds and Western Willets may represent as many as 160,000 birds (Lowther et al. 2001). Historically, populations on the east coast were greatly reduced as a result of hunting and egg collecting (Bent 1927). Information on Willets in the west is less extensive, although the dramatic loss and degradation of native grasslands (Knopf 1994) has undoubtedly affected populations. Potential threats to birds in Oregon include the effects of agriculture and invasive plant species on breeding habitat (Lowther et al. 2001), grazing activities (Powers and Glimp 1997), and variation in water levels at wetlands due to drought and water-management practices for agriculture and grazing (Reed et al. 1997). Oregon breeding birds also face threats of habitat loss and degradation at coastal wintering sites. For example, a large proportion of Oregon birds winter in San Francisco Bay where the extent of tidal mudflat and other shorebird habitats has been greatly reduced over the past two centuries (Lowther et al. 2001, Haig et al. 2002). Also, the effects of introduced invertebrates and plants on shorebirds in coastal estuaries are not well understood.—*Peter M. Sanzenbacher and Susan M. Haig*

## Wandering Tattler *Heteroscelus incanus*

The presence of this medium-sized shorebird often is announced by its high-pitched ringing call as it forages along rocky coastlines amid crashing waves. Adults in winter plumage have uniform gunmetal gray upperparts which extend to the sides, breast, and upper belly. The chin, abdomen, and undertail coverts are dull white, and the head has a prominent white supercilium. The dark bill is straight and slender, the legs are dull yellow. Spring migrants have heavily barred gray and white underparts. Unlike most shorebirds, this species is a loner and is rarely encountered in flocks. Loose aggregations may sometimes be found together, e.g., strung out along jetties in migration.

**General Distribution:** Breeds from ne. Siberia across the Bering Strait to mountains of w., c., and s. coastal Alaska, Yukon, and nw. British Columbia (Richards 1988). Winters primarily on islands in the c. and s. Pacific to Australia and New Zealand. Some winter from c. California (rare) south to Ecuador (Johnsgard 1981). Monotypic (AOU 1957).

**Oregon Distribution:** Coastal. Fairly common migrant during spring and fall along the entire Oregon coast (Evanich 1990, Gilligan et al. 1994). Rare to casual in winter (Gilligan et al. 1994, Nehls 1994). Vagrant inland with eight reports; two from Klamath Co., three from Lake Co., and one each from Grant, Jackson and Malheur counties (Tice 1997, Sullivan 1998a, Spencer 2000a).

**Habitat and Diet:** Frequents rocky headlands, offshore rocks, and jetties. Also visits rocky and gravelly flats in estuaries (Gabrielson and Jewett 1940, Nehls 1994). No food habit studies undertaken in Oregon but likely feeds on abundant mollusks, marine invertebrates, and arthropods which are exposed during low tide.

**Seasonal Activity and Behavior:** Fall movement along the Oregon coast extends from early Jul through Oct with peak numbers noted from late Jul to mid-Aug (Nehls 1994). The latest departure date is 22 Nov (Gabrielson and Jewett 1940, Nehls 1994), though there are a few winter reports. Observed on 25-75% of field trips along the s. Oregon coast from mid-Jul through 3rd week in Sep (Brown et al. 1996). Six of eight inland sightings were made during fall migration (Tice 1997).

Rare and irregular in winter along the Oregon coast with sightings reported from mid-Dec through mid-Mar (Nehls 1994); a high count of 13 reported on the Coos Bay CBC is considered erroneous and probably referable to Willets.

Spring migration occurs from mid-Apr to early Jun with peak numbers moving through the state during early May (Nehls 1994). Detected on 25-75% of field trips along the s. Oregon coast from the second week in Mar through mid-May (Brown et al. 1996). The two inland records during spring occurred on 7 May (Summers 1993c) and 22 Jun (Spencer 2000a), the latter conceivably a southbound migrant.

Like the Spotted Sandpiper, it bobs and teeters while foraging over exposed rocks or beaches at low tide (Gabrielson and Jewett 1940, Johnsgard 1981). Usually observed singly or rarely in small groups. Said to form communal roosts (Hayman et al. 1986) but this has not been observed in Oregon. Allows close approach; when alarmed either crouches or remains perfectly still and blends well with the rocky background (Johnsgard 1981, Hayman et al. 1986). When flushed, emits a series of 6-10 *u-li-li-li-li-li* plaintive, whistled notes, all at the same pitch (Hayman et al. 1986).

**Detection:** Difficult to locate usually because of dull coloration, but calls audible over the sound of crashing waves (Hayman et al. 1986, Paulson 1993).

**Population Status and Conservation:** Oregon population numbers unknown. Generally found as singles although aggregations may range from two to 55 birds, the latter tally being birds using the entire s. jetty of the Columbia on 8 May 1977 (Nehls 1994, D. Fix p.c.). No conservation problems have been identified for this species in Oregon or in other parts of its range. However, oil spills potentially pose a threat during fall and spring migrations, and on wintering grounds.—*Kamal Islam*

## Spotted Sandpiper *Actitis macularia*

This unusual shorebird breeds along rivers, streams, and lakes in a variety of habitat types throughout the state, from sea level to near timberline. Conspicuous by its distinctive teetering behavior, boldly spotted underparts, and noisy alarm calls, it is usually the only breeding shorebird present in its preferred habitat. The appearance of a sandpiper along a tiny tributary in the upper reaches of a heavily forested watershed can be startling to one unfamiliar with the species' ubiquitous nature. In its gray-brown winter and juvenal plumage, it is much less conspicuous, though the white stripe on the primary and secondary wing feathers and the distinct flutter-and-glide behavior quickly identify a bird in flight.

**General Distribution:** Breed throughout N. America north to the subarctic tree line. Winters in small numbers on the Pacific coast and interior valleys close to the coast from extreme s. British Columbia south along the Pacific slope, east across the southern edge of the U.S. to coastal N. Carolina. Winter concentrations occur along major river systems and lakes within this area, and in the Florida Everglades (Root 1988). Monotypic (Browning 1990).

**Oregon Distribution:** The Spotted Sandpiper is a widespread transient and breeder throughout the state; referred to as "unusually ubiquitous" by Paulson (1993). Gabrielson and Jewett (1940) noted that the species was found "in nearly every county in Oregon," and further stated that the species "is one of the most frequently mentioned water birds in all the published literature on Oregon avifauna." Though it is frequently referred to in site reports, numbers are seldom mentioned. Most birds depart the state by Oct, though a few remain west of the Cascades. Winter occurrence in Oregon is seldom reported apart from a few on CBCs.

**Habitat and Diet:** No field studies of this species have been conducted in Oregon. Spotted Sandpipers may be found near water within a wide spectrum of habitat types, from streams coursing through heavy conifer forest to ponds and lakes in open arid country. In general, the species breeds along the margins of streams, rivers, ponds, lakes, and marshes wherever flat shoreline is available for foraging and herbaceous vegetation is present for nest concealment (Paulson 1993). Breeding habitat suitability may undergo rather frequent change as a result of natural plant succession, hydraulic scouring, predation, or human activity, which may cause local disappearance or present new opportunities for colonization (Oring et al. 1997). Streams in the w. Cascades often lack substantial floodplains, and many undergo large-scale hydraulic disturbance almost annually (*SGD*).

In migration and postbreeding dispersal, the species may be found around almost any inland body of water, as well as coastal estuaries, headlands, and jetties, and rarely on open beaches (Jewett 1929, Oring et al. 1997). In winter, it is most likely to be found around the margins of fresh or salt water which include some exposed rocky substrate, woody debris, or occasionally formed concrete, as in urban parks or sewage ponds. Often uses log booms, the edges of boat basins, and other sheltered sites.

Gabrielson and Jewett (1940) indicated that breeding records were "exceedingly numerous" and described nests as "on the ground, lined with dry grass and weeds, usually in a tuft of grass or a small bush." Still, physical descriptions of nests are infrequent in ornithological literature for Oregon. One nest on Quartzville Cr., Linn Co., was concealed in the center of an elevated tuft of grass on an open gravel bar, and was located by the relative intensity of the distraction display (*SGD*).

Primarily a visual forager, the Spotted Sandpiper picks invertebrates from rocky substrate in shallow water or dry banks and bars sometimes well away from water (*SGD*). A wide variety of terrestrial and aquatic prey is consumed, including flying insects which might be caught in the air, various insect larvae, grasshoppers, crickets, grubs, worms, beetles, young fish, and small crustaceans (Tyler 1929).

**Seasonal Activity and Behavior:** Northbound migrants begin to appear in early Apr; average arrival dates are 16-30 Apr for w. Oregon (G. Gillson p.c.), early May in the Cascades of e. Douglas Co. (Fix 1990a), 28 Apr for c. Oregon (C. Miller p.c.), and 2 May for Malheur NWR (Littlefield 1990a). Though a small number may occasionally be seen together in the same area, the species does not migrate in flocks. Egg dates range 2 May-22 Jul for the entire state (Gabrielson and Jewett 1940), with most recent observations mid-Jun to early Jul (n=15; OBBA). Clutch size ranges 3-5, typically four (Gabrielson and Jewett 1940, Alcorn 1978). Family groups are noted beginning the last half of Jun in the Cascades of e. Douglas Co. (Fix 1990a), and e. Lane Co. (*MGH*), with most fledglings observed during Jul (24 of 38 reports; OBBA). A canoe trip taken Jul through fall on the Willamette R. or any of its tributaries may produce numerous encounters with family groups on gravel bars and banks (*SGD*). Specific egg and brood dates are not well-reported for higher elevations, though Farner (1952) recorded an observation of a nest for Crater L. NP which hatched between 18 and 22 Jul, and related an observation of young with parents on 2 Jul. Jewett (1929) recorded a nest with eggs 11 Jul 1924 at 5,000 ft (1,524 m) elevation in the Blue Mtns., Umatilla Co. One pair and nest was found at Gold L. bog 8 Jul 1988 (P.T. Sullivan p.c.).

In Minnesota studies, females usually arrived first to establish territories, a behavior not previously reported in any other sandpiper species. Usual sex roles are reversed, with females more aggressive and active in courtship. Brooding and parental care primarily by the male (Oring et al. 1997). It is not known if any of the northwest breeding population is polyandrous, as is true of populations elsewhere in N. America (Paulson 1993). When flushed or pursued near a nest, males engage in a Killdeer-like distraction display, usually running clumsily away as if struggling with an injury, calling frequently and remaining just ahead of a pursuer. They may fly only a short distance and run, or not fly at all, and they are just as likely to move away from the water's edge as towards it (Oring et al. 1997). Some occasionally perch in vegetation in a songbird-like fashion (*SGD*).

Fall migration is not well known but peaks at Malheur NWR during Aug (Littlefield 1990a) and in w. Oregon most birds are gone after Sep (Gabrielson and Jewett 1940). Observations in fall 2001 (V. Arnold p.c.) suggest that local breeders near Eugene leave by late Sep while the small number of local winter birds do not arrive until late Nov (Contreras 2002b).

CBC records 1985-2000 indicate that the species is regularly detected in small numbers in count circles with increasing frequency from north to south (high of 17 in Grants Pass in 1996), though no obvious pattern is evident from coastal areas to western interior valleys. Extremely rare in CBC circles east of the Cascades, with irregular scattered detections of single birds over many years.

**Detection:** In Oregon breeding habitat, this is usually the only sandpiper present, and it normally makes little or no effort to conceal its presence. Loud, repeated high-pitched whistles are given in flight, and the breeding song, a high rather sweet *pit-a-weet, pit-a-weet*, is not likely to be confused with any other bird. May be easily detected when silent by a constant "teetering" motion, during which it repeatedly pumps the rear end of the body up and down, the purpose of which is unknown (Oring et al. 1997). This behavior may increase in frequency when the bird is agitated. When they fly very low over the water, stiff fluttering wing beats make them unlikely to be confused with any other N. American sandpiper.

**Population Status and Conservation:** Breeding populations around N. America are apparently stable (Oring et al. 1997). BBS data for the state of Oregon as a whole are not sufficient for a statistically significant trend to be identified. Among data sets for regions within Oregon, the trend from the Cascades indicates a 4.2% annual increase 1966-98 (p=0.02), with non-significant declines for the Columbia Plateau and Basin and Range provinces, and for n. Pacific rainforests as a whole. Oregon CBC trend data are insufficient for a statistically valid trend to be observed. Only six counts have reported 10 or more individuals since 1984 (Sauer et al. 1999), though detections for w. Oregon interior and coastal counts appear to be generally increasing (Contreras 1997b), perhaps due to an increase in observer skill and more thorough coverage of suitable habitat within CBC circles.

This species has a very broad distribution within the state and non-specialized habitat requirements. Though population dynamics for western Spotted Sandpipers have not been studied, yearly variation in breeding density in Oring's Minnesota study area was caused primarily by fluctuations in egg predation the previous year, which led to emigration by males and reduced immigration of females, as well as reduced recruitment of yearlings. Alterations to breeding habitat caused by natural disturbance to floodplain and riparian areas during the breeding season may destroy nests, though these events may also create new territories for subsequent breeding cycles.—*Stephen G. Dowlan*

## Upland Sandpiper *Bartramia longicauda*

One of Oregon's rarest breeders, this distinctive "shorebird" is known for its courtship display flight and loud curlew-like call. It often perches in pine trees or on fenceposts adjacent to nesting areas. A small plover-like head and short, straight bill seem out of proportion to its body, which is reminiscent of a small curlew. The only species in this genus.

**General Distribution:** Breeds in prairie-grassland habitats from Alaska south through Canada into plains states; core areas in U.S. are N. Dakota and adjacent states but populations are declining. In the west, a small relict and disjunct population in Oregon and Idaho persists, though it is more common in Oregon. Winters in pampas of c. S. America. Monotypic (AOU 1957).

**Oregon Distribution:** The Upland Sandpiper is a rare breeder in large montane meadows within forests of e. Oregon. Breeding was documented in Bear Valley, Grant Co., in 1977 by H. Nehls and M. Koninendyke, and at both Bear and nearby Logan valleys in the 1980s by S. Herman, J. Scoville and others (Herman et al. 1985, Herman and Scoville 1988). It also bred at Sycan Marsh, Lake Co., in 1981 (Stern and Rosenberg 1985), and more recently one or two pairs were defending young at Logan Valley in 1993 (Akenson 1993). One or two birds reported from Sycan Marsh have been reported in some years since 1981 (*MAS*), including one observed 18 Jun 1998 (K. Popper p.c.) but no additional breeding has been confirmed there.

Breeding may have occurred elsewhere in e. Oregon. In 1987, one was observed 21 Jun along the west edge of Big Summit Prairie, Crook Co., two pairs were found 12 May at Bridge Cr. W.A., and one pair and a trio were observed 6 May on Campbell Flats on Starkey Forest and Range Experiment Station (FRES), Union Co. In Umatilla Co., a pair were at Pine Cr., three pairs at Albee, and an individual at French Ranch in the n. Ukiah Basin (Herman and Scoville 1988). A pair had been reported previously from Campbell Flats in mid-summer 1973 and 1984 (E. Bull p.c.). In 1991, a pair was reported from Cable Cr., e. Ukiah Basin and in 1992 and 1993 pairs were reported from several sites in the Marley Cr. area on Starkey FRES (Akenson 1993).

Upland Sandpipers are almost never observed away from the breeding grounds in Oregon. Transient records from and adjacent to Malheur NWR are on 31 May 1964 (Marshall 1969), 2 May 1987, and 12 Aug 1987 (Littlefield 1990a). There are two records from the Boardman Bombing Range, Morrow Co., in 1995 and 1996 (Green and Livezey 1999). One was at Papersack Canyon, Gilliam Co., on 30 May 1994 (D. Lusthoff p.c.).

There are four records from w. Oregon, 23-28 Jul 1987 at Hatfield Marine Science Center, Lincoln Co. (Gilligan et al. 1994), 22 May 1999 at Cape Blanco, Curry Co. (Lillie 1999), 16 Sep 2000 at McKenzie Ranch near New L., Coos Co. (Korpi 2001a, not at Wahl Ranch as published), and 20 Jun 2001 at Coos Spit (Korpi 2001b).

**Habitat and Diet:** In Oregon, this sandpiper is found in montane meadows ranging 1,000-30,000 ac (400-12,000 ha) at 3,400-5,060 ft (1,036-1,542 m) elevation, generally surrounded by lodgepole and sometimes ponderosa pine forests. Meadows include native and non-native grasses and forbs, often with a small intermittent creek nearby; they may have a component of sagebrush within or along the margin. Presence of forbs such as cinquefoil may be a critical component of nesting habitat (Herman and Scoville 1988). At Bear Valley, nests found in 1984 and 1987 were in or near an ecotone (Herman and Scoville 1988).

In the Midwest, birds foraged in vegetation less than 2.5 in (10 cm) tall (Dorio and Grewe 1979), and nested in taller vegetation (6-12 in [16-31 cm]) that provided cover and concealment (Kirsh and Higgins 1976). Nest success was highest in ungrazed and recently burned grasslands (Kirsh and Higgins 1976), though some evidence suggests that late-season grazing may not affect nest densities and success (Bowen and Kruse 1993). In Nebraska, 50% occupancy of suitable habitats was attained at sites of 165 ac (55 ha) and 100% occupancy attained at sites 350 ac (140 ha) and larger; sites with smaller perimeter-area ratios were more likely to be occupied (Helzer and Jelinski 1999). Insects are primary food, but no detailed information is available from Oregon.

**Seasonal Activity and Behavior:** At Bear and Logan valleys, birds returned in the first week of May; courtship flights were most common in the third week of May but were apparent through Jun and early Jul; egg laying occurred 18 May-14 Jun, and incubation occurred as late as 10-12 Jul. Fledging was observed 15 Jul-12 Aug (Herman et al. 1985). No departure information is available.

**Detection:** Display flights in courtship can be quite apparent, but otherwise birds are very secretive and difficult to detect during incubation and brood rearing. This species is easily missed even when present.

**Population Status and Conservation:** It was first reported breeding in Oregon from the Ft. Klamath area in 1887 (Merrill 1888). Other early reports were from Harney Valley by Bendire (Merrill 1888), Big Summit Prairie, Crook Co., on 9 Aug 1919 (Jewett 1930), near Ukiah in Umatilla Co. on 16 May 1931, and in Bear and Logan valleys, on 23-24 May 1931 (Jewett 1931b). The next report was 26 Jun 1968, a single bird by T. R. Wahl from Silvies, Grant Co.

Continental range has decreased in the last two centuries due to hunting in the late 1800s and conversion of prairie habitat to intensive farming and grazing (White 1983). Populations east of the Rocky Mtns. are stable and perhaps increasing in n. prairie states, expanding in Quebec, and numbers are higher than previously thought in Alaska (Robbins et al. 1986), but are probably decreasing in ne U.S. due to loss of habitat to agricultural practices (Bollinger 1991).

In the nw. U.S., the small population in e. Washington is now thought to be extirpated owing to habitat loss, and numbers in Idaho are few and irregular from year to year. In Oregon, 75-79 adult Upland Sandpipers were found in 1984; number of pairs declined from 24 to 18 in Bear Valley, and from 12 to 8 in Logan Valley by 1987 (Herman and Scoville 1988). In 1991, numbers at Bear Valley were the same, but numbers decreased at Logan Valley from 16 to 10 birds (Scoville 1991), with only three reported at Logan Valley in 1993 (Akenson 1993). Likewise, five sites in Umatilla and Union counties had 18 individuals in 1987 compared to only seven in 1991 (Akenson 1991, Scoville 1991).

Reasons for decline are uncertain, but may include habitat loss caused by encroachment of pine into meadows and use of herbicides to control and eliminate the forb component of the nesting meadows. Overgrazing of meadows, especially in spring and early summer during incubation and brood rearing, can have a direct impact, and any resultant downcutting of streams in riparian areas that might lead to a lowering of the water table can lead to drying of adjacent meadows. The relationship of breeding birds in Oregon and Idaho to the core population east of the Rocky Mtns. is unknown, but continued low numbers in the Northwest threaten the viability of this subpopulation. Habitat loss and management practices on wintering grounds may also threaten Oregon and Idaho birds, but no information is available.

No monitoring program for this species is in place. Its continued existence in the Northwest, including Oregon, is obviously precarious. Without immediate research to fully define its habitat requirements and other possible causes for its decline followed by implementation of remedial measures, the species will likely become the third known breeding bird in Oregon to be extirpated after the Yellow-billed Cuckoo and Sharp-tailed Grouse.—*Mark A. Stern*

## Whimbrel *Numenius phaeopus*

This large brown shorebird is the most wide-ranging of the curlew species. It is distinctive, having contrasting light-brown and dark-brown head stripes and a long decurved bill that it uses to probe for food on coastal mud flats and beaches.

**General Distribution:** Breeds in n. Eurasia and N. America, winters on all continents from temperate to southern latitudes, except Antarctica. Disjunct breeding populations in N. America: Alaska and the western and southern shores of Hudson Bay in Canada (Skeel and Mallory 1996). The N. American population winters in coastal areas of the s. U.S. as well as in Mexico, M. and S. America. *N. p. hudsonicus* is the regularly occurring subspecies in N. America (AOU 1957).

**Oregon Distribution:** Common spring and fall migrant in coastal areas although also found rarely in small numbers inland as well (Gilligan 1994). All reports in Oregon have been of the N. American subspecies, *N. p. hudsonicus,* with the exception of two sight records that are consistent with typical individuals of the e. Eurasian subspecies *N. p. variegatus.* One of these white-backed birds was observed along Clatsop Beach 25 Sep 1985 and photographed several days later (Heinl 1986a, Evanich 1987); the other was observed at Yaquina Bay 31 May 1995 (Lillie 1995).

The Whimbrel is a rare spring migrant in the Willamette Valley with generally about one record annually, typically in late Apr or early May. It is a rare spring migrant in e. Oregon with most records occurring in May at favored migratory shorebird stopovers such as Klamath Basin NWRs, Malheur NWR, Summer L., and Hatfield L. It is a casual fall migrant inland.

**Habitat and Diet:** Most commonly found on coastal estuarine mud flats and on sandy ocean beaches. Occasionally found on the coast on rocky beaches and in pastures. Inland records have been from fields and from mud flats around lakes or ponds (Gilligan et al. 1994).

Primary diet consists of marine invertebrates including crabs and other crustaceans, marine worms, mollusks, and fish. On breeding grounds eats berries, insects, and occasionally flowers (Skeel and Mallory 1996). No published data on its diet in Oregon are available, but marine invertebrates are likely the predominant food source.

**Seasonal Activity and Behavior:** The earliest coastal spring record is 14 Mar in Newport (Bent 1922) but northward migrants generally first appear in early Apr (Gilligan et al. 1994). The earliest inland record is of two birds 7 Apr 1996 near Canby, Clackamas Co. (Lillie 1996). Peak numbers of spring migrants occur in late Apr and early May. The largest flocks reported in spring consisted of 2150 birds west of Langlois, Curry Co., 11 May 2002 (T. J. Wahl p.c.), and over 1,000 at Elk R. Meadows, Curry Co., on 18 May 1999 (Lillie 1999), but flocks rarely contain over 300 birds. Inland sightings have generally been of individual birds, but flocks of up to 15 have been reported (Gilligan et al. 1994) and one flock of 24 was near Malheur NWR HQ on 20 May 1989 (Anderson 1989c). Few migrants are seen after mid-May. A few nonbreeding birds usually summer at favored estuaries such as Yaquina Bay (Bayer 1984, Gilligan et al. 1994, R. Bayer p.c.) and Necanicum Estuary as well as on open beaches in Clatsop Co. (M. Patterson p.c.).

Adult fall migrants generally begin arriving in early Jul with the peak of fall migration occurring in Aug (Gilligan et al. 1994). Juveniles do not arrive before late Aug and reach peak numbers in Sep (Paulson 1993). The largest fall migrant flock reported was of 240 birds at Florence 24 Aug 1997 (Gilligan 1998); the largest inland flock in fall was 15 at Fern Ridge Res., Lane Co., on 2 Aug 2001 (Contreras 2002b). Southbound migrants may be seen as late as Nov.

Winters in small numbers on the s. Oregon coast, primarily at Bandon and Coos Bay (Contreras 1998) and also sometimes at Yaquina Bay (Gilligan et al. 1994). The largest winter flock consisted of at least nine and possibly as many as 14 birds at Yaquina Bay 29 Dec 1979 (R. Bayer p.c.); it is not known whether these birds remained all winter. The northernmost winter record in Oregon is of an individual at the Columbia R. Estuary (CBC 1982), but it has wintered previously as far north as s. Vancouver I. (Paulson 1993).

The Whimbrel walks or runs as it pecks and probes for food. On the breeding grounds, males make an aerial display ascending as high as 985 ft (300 m) and flying in circles as large as 1,312 ft (400 m) in diameter. Not highly social, particularly during the breeding season, but may form larger flocks during migration (Skeel and Mallory 1996).

**Detection:** In favored coastal habitats the Whimbrel is generally easily detected when present since it favors exposed mud flats and open beaches. Its loud piercing call can be heard from great distances.

**Population Status and Conservation:** The world population is estimated to be approximately 800,000 birds, of which 57,000 breed in N. America (Morrison et al. 2001). Market hunters caused significant declines in total population in the late 19th century, but total numbers seem to be increasing since then (Kaufman 1996). No conservation problems have been identified in Oregon other than the continued incremental decrease in estuarine mudflats.—*Tim Janzen*

### Bristle-thighed Curlew *Numenius tahitiensis*
The Bristle-thighed Curlew breeds in Alaska and winters in Hawaii and other S. Pacific islands. It flies directly over the ocean to the wintering islands. There are very few records away from this migration route. Two were with Whimbrels near Bandon Marsh NWR 16 Sep 1981 (OBRC). During the unique weather-related landfall made by this species from n. California to Washington in 1998, one was observed at Floras L., Curry Co., 6 May and 19 May 1998; two were at Yaquina Bay 13-19 May 1998; three were at the s. jetty of the Columbia R. 9-21 May 1998; and one was at Pony Slough, Coos Bay, 13 May 1998 (OBRC). Photographs of four of these birds are in Patterson (1998a) and Lillie (1998). One observed flying past the Boiler Bay Viewpoint, Lincoln Co., 29 Sep 2000 is being evaluated by the OBRC. Monotypic (AOU 1957).—*Harry B. Nehls*

### Long-billed Curlew *Numenius americanus*
The Long-billed Curlew is the largest N. American shorebird. Its most striking morphological characteristic, the long decurved bill, is an adaptation for foraging on earthworms or burrow-dwelling organisms like shrimp and crab. The bill was also the inspiration

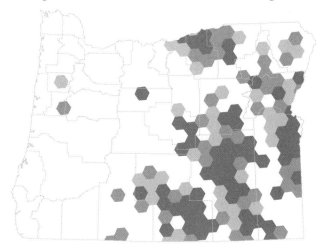

for its generic name (*Numenius* is derived from the Greek word *noumenios*, meaning new moon) and the vernacular name, Sicklebill (Dugger and Dugger 2002). The name "curlew" comes from the species' most common call, which is given equally by either sex throughout the year. Body plumage is a rich buff with a tinge of cinnamon or pink. Sexes have similar plumage, but females are larger with a longer bill. It can be distinguished from other curlews in flight by its bright cinnamon underwings. When observed on the ground, the Long-billed Curlew's head lacks the strongly streaked pattern of other curlews or Whimbrel.

**General Distribution:** Breeds in short-grass and mixed-grass habitats of the w. Great Plains, Great Basin, and intermountain valleys of U.S. and Canada (Dugger and Dugger 2002). Within its breeding range, distribution is patchy. During winter, this curlew occurs on the Gulf coast from sw. Louisiana to Yucatan Peninsula. On the Pacific coast, it is common from San Francisco Bay south to Colima, Mexico (including Baja Peninsula), occasionally to Costa Rica (Dugger and Dugger 2002). Inland, winter concentrations occur in California's Central Valley (Shuford et al. 1998); in Mexico, it is locally common below 7,500 ft (2,500 m) south to Guatemala. Two subspecies have been described, *N. a. parvus* and *N. a. americanus*; according to Oberholser (1918) *parvus* breeds in Oregon. However, the distribution of putative subspecies is uncertain. Subspecies delineation was based on measurements of 23 birds occurring at the extreme northern and southern end of breeding distribution (Bishop 1910). Recent analysis of 250 specimens from throughout the breeding range indicated that the size difference described by Bishop may also be explained as clinal variation in body size with latitude; body size increases from north to south (Dugger and Forsythe unpubl. data).

**Oregon Distribution:** The Long-billed Curlew is a locally common breeder in open grassland areas east of the Cascades in Klamath, Lake, Harney, Crook, Umatilla, Morrow, Union, Malheur, and Baker counties (Gilligan et al. 1994, Contreras and Kindschy 1996, *DBM*). This species is not known to nest in Wallowa Co. in recent years (Evanich 1992a). It is most abundant in the Columbia R. basin followed by the Harney/ Malheur L. area (Pampush 1980, Littlefield 1990a); small numbers of breeders likely occur in most short-grass habitats at L. Abert and other alkaline lakes in sc. and se. Oregon (Kristensen et al. 1991, M. St. Louis p.c.). During migration, this species occurs in the same habitats as during the breeding season;

rare in the Willamette Valley, more commonly observed in spring than fall (Gilligan et al. 1994); also found in small numbers in estuaries along the coast (Contreras 1997b). Have been observed during all months on the coast. It is not present in winter along the coast in all years, but became more regular during the 1990s south from Coos Bay, where a state CBC record of nine birds was recorded in 1995 (Contreras 1998).

**Habitat and Diet:** Nests primarily in short-grass or mixed-prairie habitat with flat to rolling topography; will nest in agricultural fields including short dry cereal grain fields, wheat stubble, and fallow fields (Pampush 1981). In the Columbia R. basin, the Long-billed Curlew generally avoids habitats with trees, high density of shrubs (e.g., sagebrush), and tall, dense grass (Pampush and Anthony 1993). This species has nested at highest densities in cheatgrass-dominated grasslands (23.3 nests/mi2 [9.0/km$^2$]), followed by bunchgrass (9.1 nests/mi$^2$ [3.5/km$^2$]), dense forb (8.5 nests/mi$^2$ [3.3/km$^2$]), open low shrub (6.5 nests/mi$^2$ [2.5/km$^2$]), and bitterbrush (3.4 nests/mi$^2$ [1.3/km$^2$]) habitats (Pampush and Anthony 1993). Saltgrass meadows are used in sc. Oregon (Littlefield 1990a). Activities like fire and grazing that maintain short, open landscapes are generally beneficial. Nest is a shallow depression in ground, generally located in a relatively dry, exposed site. Taller, denser grass is used during brood-rearing when shade and camouflage from predators is presumably more important for chicks, but may also reflect a decline in availability of shorter habitats with season. During migration, curlews more readily use agricultural habitats. Along the coast, use tidal estuaries, wet pastures, and sandy beaches; but unlike Willet and Marbled Godwit, use of sandy beaches is relatively uncommon (Stenzel et al. 1976,

*Long-billed Curlew*

EPaulson

Colwell and Sundeen 2000). Roost in high-elevation salt marsh, low dunes, coastal airports, and pastures during high tide (Page et al. 1979, *ALC*).

Data on diet in Oregon are lacking; elsewhere on breeding grounds Long-billed Curlews appear to be opportunistic foragers, supplementing a diet dominated by invertebrates like grasshoppers and beetles with bird eggs and small vertebrates including nestlings (Sadler and Maher 1976, Redmond and Jenni 1985). On estuaries in California, its diet is more specialized than other shorebirds including Willet and Marbled Godwit (Stenzel et al. 1976, Boland 1988). Curlews feed primarily by probing for large burrow dwellers like mud crab, ghost shrimp, and mud shrimp; but significant numbers of bivalves and marine worms may be taken (Stenzel et al. 1976, Boland 1988, Leeman et al. 2001). Earthworms are important food in wet coastal pastures (Leeman 2000).

**Seasonal Activity and Behavior:** Long-billed Curlews do not breed until 2-4 yr old. Birds arrive, typically in small groups of 3-10, on breeding areas beginning mid-Mar (Pampush 1981). Extremely territorial, the male establishes a territory immediately after arrival and defends it from pre-laying through hatching (Pampush 1981). Pair formation on breeding grounds is highlighted by a conspicuous aerial display. Aerial displays by unpaired males are observed through Jun (12-14 wk after arrival) (Pampush 1981). In w. Idaho and e. Washington, territory size ranged 13-31 ac (6-14 ha). Nest construction usually begins within 1 wk of pairing. The male initiates most nest building with scraping behavior related to courtship (Jenni et al. 1981). Earliest egg laying reported is late Mar; lays 2-5 eggs, four most common. Both male and female incubate and defend nest from predators, but the female often leaves brood care to the male shortly after chicks hatch. Mean hatch date is mid-May, ranging 1 May to 4 Jun (Pampush and Anthony 1993). Broods frequently leave territories after hatch; chicks fledge at 38-45 days. Renesting has not been documented.

Some females depart breeding grounds by mid-Jun (Gilligan et al. 1994); a few birds arrive on the coast beginning in late Jun. Although not documented for Oregon, individuals may establish and defend feeding territories on coastal mudflats during summer and fall (Colwell 2000). Most adults remain on breeding areas till late Jul; juveniles are noted into mid-Aug (Gilligan et al. 1994). Near Malheur NWR, fall migration peaks 5-25 Aug, most are gone by mid-Sep, and the latest record is 5 Oct (Littlefield 1990a); elsewhere east of the Cascades birds have been reported as late as Nov. During migration, flocks of 10-50 are common, sometimes 100 are seen, but up to 500 have been reported in nc. Oregon (Pampush 1981).

**Detection:** Large size and long, decurved bill make this species easy to detect and identify when feeding on open mudflats in coastal estuaries. On breeding grounds, the male's display flight is conspicuous early in season, but birds can be difficult to locate during incubation and chick rearing. More commonly, birds locate the human during this period, flying long distances from the nest to perform aggression or distraction displays.

**Population Status and Conservation:** There is no reliable recent information on breeding population size in Oregon. In 1980, estimates included 2,500 breeding pairs in mid-Columbia Basin, and 750 pairs in the closed basins of sc. and se. Oregon. (Pampush 1980). However, significant habitat changes have occurred since 1980; Evanich (1992a) noted the species was "seriously declining in ne. Oregon" and development of agriculture in the Columbia Basin has drastically altered habitats. BBS data (1979-2000) suggest the species is stable or possibly increasing along surveyed routes in Oregon. Conflicting reports may reflect scarcity of data or differing trends by region within the state. Breeding habitat loss, primarily conversion of grassland to agriculture, is a major threat throughout species' range. However, in areas where cheatgrass has supplanted sage-dominated communities in Oregon, breeding habitat may be improving. Work is needed to understand population size and trend in Oregon.—*Bruce Dugger and Katie Dugger*

### Hudsonian Godwit *Limosa haemastica*

This long-distance migrant breeds in nc. Canada and in Alaska and winters in s. S. America. In fall, most migrate to the Atlantic coast then south over the ocean. In spring it migrates north through the interior of N. America. It is casual in migration along the w. coast. There are 12 fall records for Oregon from early Aug through Oct (Egger 1980, OBRC). A group of 16 flew in from the open ocean and dropped onto Tillamook Bay, Tillamook Co., 17 Aug 1980 (Watson 1989). This is the only flock recorded for the state. One was at the s. jetty of the Columbia R., Clatsop Co., 31 May 1983 (OBRC), one was at Ankeny NWR, Marion Co., 10-11 May 1994 (Lillie 1995), and one was at Miller I. W.A., Klamath Co., 30 May 2000 (Sullivan 2000b).—*Harry B. Nehls*

### Bar-tailed Godwit *Limosa lapponica*

This godwit breeds across n. Eurasia to w. Alaska. In winter it is found in s. Eurasia, Africa, and the s. Pacific islands. It is casual along the Atlantic coast of N. America and is rare but regular along the Pacific coast, predominantly in fall. Oregon spring records range from late Apr to early Jun. A group of four at

Bandon Marsh NWR, Coos Co., 14 May 1988 is the largest reported Oregon flock (OBRC); oddly all four birds were in basic plumage (D. Fix p.c.). Oregon fall records range from late Jun to mid-Oct. One was at Coos Bay 3 Nov to 7 Dec 2001 (Contreras 2002b, T. Rodenkirk p.c.). There are photographs of many of these birds in the files of the OBRC (Watson 1989). No specimens from Oregon; a female *baueri* was taken from Arcata, California, 17 Jul 1968 (Gerstenberg and Harris 1970).—*Harry B. Nehls*

## Marbled Godwit *Limosa fedoa*

A large, long-legged wader distinguished from similar species in flight by flashing rufous underwings and dark brown primaries. Overall appearance is cinnamon-brown. Sports a long, slightly upturned, bicolored bill, black at tip and pink on the basal half. Nonbreeding adults and juveniles in fall similar to adults in breeding plumage but lack brown breast streaks and bars on the sides. Feet extend beyond tail tip in flight. This is a long-lived species: adults banded at Humboldt Bay, California, were observed foraging there nearly 26 yr later (Colwell et al. 1995). The oldest recorded individual was >29 yr (Gratto-Trevor 2000).

**General Distribution:** Marbled Godwits breed in three widely separated populations. The largest is the prairie-breeding population on the n. Great Plains of the U.S. and Canada. The other two are small, little-known tundra-breeding populations of 1000-3000 birds (Gratto-Trevor 2000). One breeds along sw. James Bay, Canada, and the other breeds at Ugashik Bay on the north side of the Alaska Peninsula (Gibson and Kessel 1989). These breeding populations belong to two subspecies. The n. Great Plains and James Bay populations belong to *L. f. fedoa* and winter from c. California to n. Chile. Inland records of Marbled Godwits in Oregon probably represent this subspecies (Paulson 1993). The Alaska population, *L. f. beringiae*, may migrate on a direct transoceanic flight in spring and fall (Gibson and Kessel 1989), although large flocks at Yakutat Forelands, Alaska, suggest this subspecies is more of a coastal migrant (Andres and Browne 1998). *L. f. beringiae* winters locally from Vancouver I., British Columbia, to San Francisco Bay, California (Gibson and Kessel 1989, Paulson 1993). Specimens of *fedoa* have been collected in Oregon, but *beringiae* has not (*MRB*).

**Oregon Distribution:** Regular spring and fall migrant on the Oregon coast; irregular in winter, mainly from Coos Bay southward. Rare and irregular spring and fall migrant in the Willamette Valley. Occasional spring migrant in the Rogue Valley, but absent in fall. Irregular spring and fall migrant in e. Oregon. Absent in summer and winter in inland valleys; casual in e. Oregon in winter.

**Habitat and Diet:** Migrants and wintering birds in Oregon prefer coastal mudflats, sandy ocean beaches, wet margins of large reservoirs or brackish lakes, and sewage ponds. May forage on coastal golf courses in spring (Paulson 1993) and sometimes almost exclusively on plant tubers during migration (Gratto-Trevor 2000).

Food habit studies have not been conducted in Oregon. Studies at Elkhorn Slough, California (Ramer et al. 1991), showed that polychaete worms and small clams such as gem and bent-nosed were among the highest-ranking prey items in fall or winter. In spring, clams (primarily species of macoma and littlenecks) and green shore crabs were most often eaten. These prey items are also found in Oregon estuaries.

**Seasonal Activity and Behavior:** Spring migration commences in early Apr and extends through early Jun on the coast. In e. Oregon, average arrival at Malheur NWR is 27 Apr (Ivey, Herziger, and Scheuering 1998); latest record is 7 Jun 1956 at the Double O Unit, Malheur NWR (Marshall 1959). Flocks generally consist of fewer than 50 birds on the coast. The largest flock recorded was 250 at Bandon Marsh, Coos Co., 27 Apr 1988 (Mattocks 1988b). Counts in the Willamette Valley consist of single birds in Apr and May. In the Rogue Valley, a record 145 were seen at Ashland, Jackson Co., 26 Apr 1981 (Watson 1981b), although only three published records exist for the Rogue Valley. Most spring records in e. Oregon consist of 1-10 birds at any one locality. The largest flock was 73 at the Joseph sewage ponds, Wallowa Co., 15 May 1982 (Evanich 1982b); 59 were at Antelope Res., Malheur Co. on 21 Apr 2000 (M. Denny p.c.).

Juveniles migrate south several weeks later than most adults (Gratto-Trevor 2000). The first southbound migrants appear in mid-Jun. Two peaks occur on the coast, the first from late Aug to early Sep, and the second in late Sep. Most flocks are on the coast and contain 5-30 birds, but 200 were at Bandon Marsh 22 Sep 1978 (Nehls 1994). After mid-Nov, a few stragglers are seen until late Dec and thereafter become scarce until spring migration resumes. The latest record in e. Oregon is five at Summer L., Lake Co., 13 Oct 1990 (Anderson 1991a).

Winter records are mostly confined to the Coos and Coquille R. estuaries, Coos Co., although there are scattered reports from Tillamook, Siletz, and Yaquina bays in Tillamook and Lincoln counties. Largest number is 45 recorded on the Tillamook Bay CBC 14 Dec 1974 (Thackaberry 1975, Contreras 1995). Between mid-Oct and Apr, only wandering strays are recorded east of the Coast Range. One bird was at Malheur NWR, 28 Feb 1991, possibly representing a very early spring migrant (Tweit and Johnson 1991a).

**Detection:** Foraging behavior is diagnostic at a distance (Paulson 1993). Marbled Godwits probe deeply into the mud with their long bills, often submerging their heads below the water surface. They tend to remain in flocks as they deliberately peck or probe for food, and often accompany Whimbrels, Willets and Long-billed Curlews at roosting sites and in flight. Their call is a two-syllabled *kerreck* (Paulson 1993) or a series of *reck* calls in rapid succession (Wishart and Sealy 1980). Interestingly, Dodd and Colwell (1996, 1998) reported that Marbled Godwits may sometimes forage at night in Humboldt Bay, California, primarily in fall during a visible moon. This suggests that comprehensive foraging studies of this species would need to consider possible nocturnal activities.

**Population Status and Conservation:** Braly (1938) stated that Marbled Godwits were seldom recorded in migration in Oregon. Gabrielson and Jewett (1940) indicated they were a "very rare transient" in Oregon. Numbers of Marbled Godwits in Oregon are obviously much larger than were perceived by these authors or have grown. As early as the mid-1950s, Marshall (1959) reported several sightings of up to 50 migrants during spring and fall at Malheur NWR. Change in status since the 1940s may be the result of increased numbers of birds coupled with increased coverage of proper habitat by more birders in recent years.

Breeding areas in Alaska remain unaltered and are not under proximate pressure for development (Gratto-Trevor 2000), but some concern has been expressed about proposed oil and gas activity in the area (Mehall-Niswander 1997). Wetland drainage and alteration of native mixed short-grass prairies by agricultural practices in the n. Great Plains has a deleterious effect on breeding and post-breeding Marbled Godwits (Ryan et al. 1984, Page and Gill 1994). No immediate conservation problems were identified for Marbled Godwits in Oregon other than protection of a mosaic of freshwater marshes, estuarine tidelands, and short-grass upland sites required for foraging and loafing.—*Alan McGie*

## Ruddy Turnstone *Arenaria interpres*

The noisy and frenetic Ruddy Turnstone is a stocky, plover-like bird whose breeding plumage is a clown-like pattern of black, rust, and white. Young and winter birds are generally duller, but the white throat and collared breast help distinguish it from the Black Turnstone. Its call is a chatter, lower in pitch than that of Black Turnstone (Hoffmann 1927, Paulson 1993), and may be uttered nearly continuously while feeding (Paulson 1993). Ruddy Turnstones have been found foraging in the company of many other shorebird species, including Black Turnstone (Browning 1973a, Johnson 1988c, Contreras 1998); Surfbird, Sanderling, Dunlin, Red Knot, and Pectoral Sandpiper (Paulson 1993); Whimbrel (B. Godfrey p.c.); and Least and Western Sandpiper (Anderson and Bellin 1988, Anderson DA 1990a).

**General Distribution:** Circumpolar breeder along n. coasts of the Arctic Ocean and on nearby islands, at times along coasts slightly to the south. Migrates primarily along the coasts, but some pass through c. Canada and the U.S. interior. Number of w. U.S. migrants lower than in the east. Winters along Pacific coast from sw. British Columbia to Tierra del Fuego; from Hawaii to w. Pacific Is., Australia, and New Zealand; along European coasts from s. Scandinavia through the Mediterranean; and along Asian coasts from se. China through Indonesia and India to s. African coast. Along Atlantic coast, winters from n. Massachusetts south to Caribbean Is. and Tierra del Fuego, and from s. Europe to s. Africa. Two subspecies, both of which occur in Oregon (AOU 1957).

**Oregon Distribution:** *A. i. interpres* is the most common subspecies in Oregon (Browning 1974 *contra* Gabrielson and Jewett 1940), with example specimens (SMNH) from Lincoln and Coos counties, in May and Sep, respectively. *A. i. morinella* is thought to occur less commonly along the Pacific coast (Paulson 1993), and there is at least one specimen (OSU) from Mercer, Oregon (*MRB*).

The species is an uncommon to common spring and fall transient along the coast; a few birds remain to winter there each year. Largest flocks (175 or more) seen during spring and fall migration at Bandon (Watson 1981b, Gilligan 1992b). Irregular spring and occasional fall transient inland west of the Cascades. There is a spring record from Marion Co. (Lillie 1998) and single fall records from Washington (Heinl 1988a) and Linn (P. T. Sullivan p.c.) counties. There are both spring and fall sightings in Jackson Co. (Heinl 1986a, Anderson 1988a, Heinl 1989a, Gilligan 1991, Lillie 1996, Janes et al. 2001). It is an irregular spring and fall transient in e. Oregon, particularly at Malheur NWR (Littlefield 1990a); in Lake Co. (Tice 1997), including Summer L. W.A. (Anderson 1988b, Evanich 1991a, Sullivan 1998a, Sullivan 1999a); and at sites along the Columbia R. (Summers 1986b, Anderson DA 1990a, 1990b, Evanich 1992b).

**Habitat and Diet:** Found on rocky shores, jetties, open ocean beaches, mud flats (especially those littered with stones or rocks), salicornia marshes (Paulson 1993), grass flats such as the area around the North Bend airport (Contreras 1977), and flooded fields (Johnson 1988c). No information is available on diet specific to Oregon, but this turnstone is an opportunistic feeder. Its diet generally includes crustaceans, marine worms, mollusks, sea anemones, sea stars, sea urchins, bird eggs (especially those of gulls and terns), insects, spiders, small fish, carrion, human food garbage, and waste from fisheries (Nettleship 2000). Feeds by moving beach stones or debris with beak, then pecking at or chasing prey item. May use head and body to move obstacles.

**Seasonal Activity and Behavior:** This species is usually found singly or in small flocks. Larger flocks are occasional in fall and spring. Earliest fall arrivals are generally the second week of Jul, although one arrival was reported as 30 Jun 1997 (Johnson J 1998a). A flock of 200 individuals was reported at Bandon, Coos Co., on 19 Jul 1981 (Watson 1981b). Juveniles' arrival dates are scattered throughout the fall migratory period, beginning in late Aug. In some years there are fewer juvenile than adult migrants (Contreras 1998). Numbers decrease during Sep and birds are scarce by Oct, rare through winter (Gilligan et al. 1994, Contreras 1998). Fall records inland west of the Cascades include 11-13 Aug 2002 at Villa Wetlands near Brownsville, Linn Co. (P. T. Sullivan p.c.); 12 Sep 1985 at Kirtland Road sewage ponds near Medford, Jackson Co. (Anderson 1988a); and 14-15 Sep 1987 at Forest Grove sewage ponds, Washington Co. (Heinl 1988a). East of the Cascades, there are numerous fall records from 3 Aug (Anderson 1988b) to 30 Sep (Sullivan 1998a).

Spring migrants usually arrive late Apr (Lillie 1999). A flock of 85 birds was seen migrating north along the Lincoln Co. coast 10 May 1995 (Lillie 1995). Flocks of 175 birds at Bandon, Coos Co., and 86 birds north of the Rogue R. mouth, Curry Co., were sighted 11 May 1992 (Gilligan 1992b). Absent by end of May; Oregon records are almost nonexistent in Jun and early Jul. Juveniles reportedly spend first summer on wintering grounds (Paulson 1993) Inland west of the Cascades, two seen 13 May 1998 at Mohoff Pond, Ankeny NWR, Marion Co. (Lillie 1998). Jackson Co. spring records from 24 Apr to 13 May at Kirtland Road sewage ponds near Medford (Heinl 1986c, Anderson 1988a, Heinl 1989a, Gilligan 1991, Lillie 1996, Janes et al. 2001). Spring records in c. and e. Oregon from 8 May (Evanich 1991a) to 4 Jun (Anderson and Bellin 1988).

**Detection:** Easy to spot on debris-free sandy beaches, but rock configurations can make this species difficult to detect on jetties and natural rock masses along the coast. Constant and often frenzied motion while feeding aids in detection.

**Population Status and Conservation:** N. American population stable at about 267,000 (Morrison et al. 2000, Nettleship 2000). Migrant groups in Oregon usually small. Oregon coastal CBCs generally report fewer than 10 individuals; sometimes missed entirely.

State CBC record high is 31 individuals at Coos Bay 17 Dec 1995. Human activities threaten food availability and accessibility at migratory stopover points and in wintering habitats, but effect on population has not been determined (Nettleship 2000).—*Barbara Combs*

## Black Turnstone *Arenaria melanocephala*

Along coastal shores and islands, the chatter and flight calls of Black Turnstones invite an observer to look more closely at the rocky substrates to find these birds busily picking about in their search for food. While belly and undertail coverts are white, black, or dark gray, upperparts blend well with the color of coastal rocks. When a group takes flight, bold white and black markings on upperparts and wings are revealed, and the observer soon realizes that there were more birds in the flock than had initially been detected.

**General Distribution:** Breeds along the w. and s. Alaska coast, but may occur anywhere along the Pacific coast south to n. Baja California in summer. Winters from s. Alaska coast to s. Baja California and c. Sonora. Scattered inland records in coastal provinces and states in w. N. America. Monotypic.

**Oregon Distribution:** The Black Turnstone is a common transient and winter visitant on the coast; rare in early summer. The only e. Oregon record is of two individuals at Ochoco Res., Crook Co., 8 Sep 1985 (Summers 1986a). There are nine inland records of single individuals west of the Cascades: 28 Aug 1994 at Sauvie I., Columbia Co. (Gilligan 1995); 12 Nov 1913 at Wapato L., Washington Co. (Nehls 1994); 19 Dec 1974 at Coburg, Lane Co. (Nehls 1994); 25 Apr 1999 at Fernhill Wetlands, Washington Co. (Lillie 1999); three records from late Apr to early May (1984, 1987, 1994) at Kirtland Road sewage ponds near Medford, Jackson Co. (Anderson 1988a, Janes et al. 2001); one in alternate plumage 13 May 1986 at Ankeny NWR, Marion Co. (Anderson and Bellin 1990), and one in alternate plumage 24 Jul 2002 at Lost Cr. Res., Jackson Co. (N. Barrett p.c.).

**Habitat and Diet:** Primarily uses rocky shores, jetties, and offshore islands, but may also be found on shorebird flats and sandy beaches (Nehls 1994). Has been observed foraging in pasturelands near Siletz Bay, Lincoln Co. (*BC*), in Curry Co. in flooded fields near Cape Blanco (Johnson 1988c), and with Mew Gulls in fields near Floras L., Curry Co. (N. Wander p.c.), as well as in grass flats at Yachats, Lincoln Co. (J. Simmons p.c.), and around the North Bend, Coos Co., airport during migration and in winter (Contreras 1977). Known to feed on log booms, woody and shell debris, boat ramps and mudflats (Contreras 1998).

Roosts in loose flocks on elevated rocks near feeding areas (Paulson 1993), as well as roofs of buildings, pilings, and log booms (Bayer 1999b, *ALC*).

The nonbreeding diet is believed to consist mainly of crustaceans such as acorn barnacles and mollusks such as limpets. The turnstone either hammers the shell with its beak or inserts its bill into the gap in the shell to open it (Paulson 1993). Despite its name, this turnstone is more often seen moving vegetation with its beak or pecking around shore debris than turning over stones or other items while foraging (Nehls 1994). In Oregon, it is regularly seen picking through piles of oyster shells at an oyster plant at Bay City, Tillamook Co. The largest flock there was 100 on 14 Mar 1998 (Lillie 1998). Similar behavior has been observed at Garibaldi, Tillamook Co. (N. Barrett p.c., W. Hoffman p.c.); upper Yaquina Bay, Lincoln Co., about 7 mi (11 km) east of Newport (R. Bayer p.c., E. Horvath p.c., D. Knutsen p.c.); and Bandon, Coos Co. (*ALC*). R. Bayer (p.c.) has observed them going through clumps of algae in the Newport area, Lincoln Co., turning them over while foraging. P. Pickering (p.c.) saw about a dozen Black Turnstones feeding on white rice scattered at "D" R. Wayside, Lincoln Co. At a ground feeder in Depoe Bay, Lincoln Co., one "gobbled" millet (Denny 1992). Black Turnstones eat herring eggs while at Prince William Sound in May (Handel and Gill 2001).

**Seasonal Activity and Behavior:** Early migrants arrive in early Jul; migration continues through mid-Dec (Woodcock 1902, Nehls 1994, Bayer 1995a, Johnson 1996a). Adults arrive first; juveniles begin to arrive 6-17 Aug (Handel and Gill 2001). Wintering birds scatter along the coast in small flocks. Never missed on Tillamook Bay, Lincoln City, Yaquina Bay, Florence, Coos Bay, Coquille Valley, Port Orford, and Gold Beach CBCs; missed on about one-third of Columbia Estuary CBCs (CBC Data). The 1980 Port Orford CBC holds the record high for Oregon of 327 individuals (Contreras 1991). About 400-500 individuals is the usual total found on all Oregon coastal CBCs combined (but over 700 found in both 1999 and 2000). Begin to depart in mid-Feb

(Nehls 1994). Generally gone by mid-May, rare late May to early Jul.

The most frequent flock size is 25-30. Reports of flocks of 300 or more include 350 on 16 Oct 1980 at Tillamook Bay (Nehls 1994), 300 on 9 Jan 1994 (R. Robb p.c.), 300 on 16 Feb 1997 (T. Mickel p.c.), both at Florence, 400 on 19 Feb 1980 at Seal Rock (Nehls 1994), and 300 on 6 Apr 1996 at Bandon (R. Robb p.c.). Associates with other species such as Surfbirds and Ruddy Turnstones when using same habitat (Woodcock 1902, Browning 1973a, Paulson 1993).

**Detection:** Difficult to detect when hidden by irregularities of the rocky seacoast. Often first detected due to high-pitched pipping sound. Obvious in flight.

**Population Status and Conservation:** The U.S. breeding population is estimated at 80,000 (Morrison et al. 2000). An estimate published in 1992 was 61,000-99,000; the population trend at that time was unknown (Handel and Gill 1992). Predictions for the future are mixed. An apparent population decline was suggested in a prioritization system developed for the U.S. Shorebird Conservation Plan (Manomet 2000). Paulson (1993) suggested that there appeared to be a decline in numbers based on 1974-98 CBC data. Including Oregon CBC data through the 2001 season, no such trend is apparent (*BC*). Oil spills may be a significant threat to both breeding and migratory areas (Manomet 2000).—*Barbara Combs*

*Black Turnstone*

## Surfbird *Aphriza virgata*

This stocky, medium-sized shorebird is a denizen of Oregon's rocky shoreline, foraging as close to the crashing waves as possible, hence its name. Birds wintering in Oregon have the upperparts, head, neck, and breast slate gray with a whitish eye-ring. Indistinct supercilium and chin are white, whereas the belly and abdomen are white with dark brown streakings. Legs are short and yellow, while the plover-like bill, well adapted for plucking off young barnacles, mussels, and snails, is brown with an orange base.

**General Distribution:** Breeds in c. Alaska and Yukon with some nonbreeding individuals summering as far south as Panama. Very rarely encountered away from the coast during migration; it is a rare spring migrant in Texas and a vagrant to Pennsylvania (Richards 1988). Winters along the Pacific coasts of N., M., and S. America from se. Alaska to the Straits of Magellan (Johnsgard 1981). Monotypic (AOU 1957).

**Oregon Distribution:** Strictly coastal with no inland records (Nehls 1994). Fairly common migrant along the coast during fall and spring with large numbers resident during the winter months (Gabrielson and Jewett 1940, Evanich 1990, Gilligan et al. 1994).

**Habitat and Diet:** Uses the rocky intertidal zone which includes jetties, offshore rocks and rocky shorelines, sea stacks, and tidal pools (Gabrielson and Jewett 1940, Evanich 1990, Nehls 1994, Merrifield 1998). Occasionally found on sandy beaches interspersed with groups of rocks, and on mudflats near the mouth of the Coquille R. (Gilligan et al. 1994). Sometimes uses freshwater outfalls for bathing (D. Fix p.c.).

Marsh (1983, 1986) analyzed 19 stomachs of specimens collected along the Oregon coast from Jan 1979 to Mar 1981, supplemented with 102 fecal samples. Principal prey items included mussels, barnacles, and gastropods. Mussels of the genus *Mytilus* were present in >95% of fecal samples analyzed; on average, 30% of prey items/stomach consisted of this genus. Of 104 mussels consumed by Surfbirds, size ranged from 0.1-0.4 inches (2-10 mm) indicating that only small mussels are consumed in Oregon despite higher frequency and abundance of larger potential prey. Although limpets are abundant in rocky intertidal habitats, Surfbirds did not consume this food item. Marsh (1983) suggested that its short, stout bill adapted for tugging may prevent exploitation of this low-profile prey, unless a limpet is loosely attached to an algal mat allowing for easy extraction.

**Seasonal Activity and Behavior:** Fall movement begins in early Jul (earliest arrival date reported is 23 Jun [Johnson J 1994a]) with peak number noted during the latter two weeks in Jul (an estimated 500 present at Seal Rock SP on 15 Jul); adults arrive first followed by juveniles (Johnson 1990a, Nehls 1994). During winter, large flocks (up to 100 individuals) often assemble along the rocky coastline with a high of 375 reported along the Columbia R. estuary during a CBC (Contreras 1991) and 350 recorded 19 Feb at Seal Rock SP (Nehls 1994). The highest 10-yr average for a CBC (1983-92) in Oregon (Tillamook) is 104.8 (range 3-215) (Senner and McCaffery 1997). Spring migration appears as a gradual reduction in numbers (from early Mar through Apr) with no noticeable peak departure period (Nehls 1994). Latest departure date recorded is 28 May (Lillie 1998).

Primarily silent, except for an occasional plaintive whistle *kee-wee-ah*, as it forages for intertidal invertebrates on rocks at and above the splash zone (Hayman et al. 1986). It uses its entire body, not just bill motion, to remove mussels and barnacles by tugging and pulling; on the Oregon coast, 63% of *Balanus glandula* barnacles were obtained by tugging, 33% by pecking, and 4% by hammering (Marsh 1983, Senner and McCaffery 1997). Rapid pecking motion, consisting of a series of hard jabs at substrate, is often associated with high densities of small snails (Marsh 1983). Occasionally a pushing tactic, similar to that of Black Turnstone, is used to obtain prey from algal substrates (Marsh 1983). Prey items usually are swallowed whole with the shell later regurgitated (Paulson 1993).

Highly gregarious, often forming mixed-species foraging flocks with Rock Sandpipers and Black Turnstones. Often aggressive toward conspecifics and other species when foraging or bathing in close proximity to one another (Paulson 1993, D. Fix p.c.). Roosts communally in either conspecific or mixed-species flocks on dry rocks above the splash zone (Paulson 1993).

**Detection:** No information on detection rates throughout Oregon, but found on >75% of all field trips along the s. Oregon coast from mid-Jul through Apr, and observed on 25-75% of all trips from first week of May to mid-May and from end of first week in Jul to mid-Jul (Brown et al. 1996). Seal Rock SP has the largest assemblage of Surfbirds, Black Turnstones, and Rock Sandpipers anywhere along the Oregon coast (Nehls 1994).

**Population Status and Conservation:** Oregon population numbers unknown. Usually occurs in flocks which vary in size from 4-5 to 100-300. Large numbers are often present during winter (Nehls 1994). No conservation problems identified; however, entire Pacific coast migration and wintering habitats are along oil tanker routes and thus vulnerable to oil spills. In addition, human encroachment on its feeding and roosting habitat along the Pacific coast may result in increased disturbance (Senner and McCaffery 1997).—*Kamal Islam*

## Great Knot *Calidris tenuirostris*

This Asian species breeds in Siberia and winters southward to the S. Pacific islands. It is casual in spring to Alaska. There have been one verified and several unverified sightings along the Pacific coast south to Oregon. One was observed at Newport, Lincoln Co., 28 Sep 1978 (Paulson 1993), and a juvenile was seen by many and photographed at Bandon Marsh and the lower Coquille R., Coos Co., 1-17 Sep 1990 (Lethaby and Gilligan 1991, 1992).Monotypic (AOU 1957).—*Harry B. Nehls*

## Red Knot *Calidris canutus*

These stocky shorebirds stand out among their fellow migrants in spring, resplendent with rich rufous breasts shading into white on the lower belly. In contrast, migrants in fall, which are primarily juveniles, are bland pale gray at most distances and blend in with fellow shorebirds; though at close examination juveniles have a beautiful scalloped pattern on their back and wing coverts. Red Knots have short, black bills tapering to a fairly fine tip; short legs give them a low-slung appearance. They are highly gregarious and tend to form tight foraging and roosting flocks.

**General Distribution:** Breed locally in tundra of Canada, Siberia, and Alaska, and on Canadian islands from Victoria to Ellesmere. Individuals may annually commute as far as New Zealand, Australia, S. Africa, and Tierra del Fuego (Harrington 1983). Migrates along the Pacific Coast of N. America (Tomkovich 1992) and probably winters in M. America, as well as the w. coast of Florida and Texas coast (Piersma and Davidson 1992). Many nonbreeding individuals remain in southern wintering grounds all year (Hayman et al. 1986), especially on the Atlantic and Gulf coasts of the U.S. (AOU 1998).

Conover (1943) recognized two subspecies. AOU (1957) recognized *C. c. rufa* as the subspecies that migrates in Oregon. Tomkovich (1990) proposed the name *C. c. roselaari* for a subspecies from Wrangel I. and Alaska (Tomkovich 1992). Paulson (1993) indicated that Pacific coast birds are probably from a population that breeds on Wrangel I., Siberia, and are distinct from any named subspecies. More recently, five subspecies have been recognized with three found in the w. Hemisphere (Engelmoer and Roselaar 1998, Harrington 2001), each with widely divergent migration strategies (Piersma and Davidson 1992). Oregon specimens from Malheur NWR, May 1970 (USNM), and one near Corvallis, May 1959 (OSU,

Porter 1960), are darker and larger than *rufa*, and identified tentatively as *roselaari* (*MRB*).

**Oregon Distribution:** In contrast to California and Washington, most Red Knots bypass Oregon (Nehls 1994). Primarily found on the coast where they are regular transients in spring and fall. Casual in summer and occasional in winter along the Oregon coast. Casual in spring and fall in the Willamette Valley. Occasional in the Rogue Valley in spring, but casual in fall. It is a rare transient in spring and fall in e. Oregon.

**Habitat and Diet:** Knots forage on open estuarine tide flats; less commonly on margins of sandy ocean beaches. Inland, found on margins of sewage ponds and at large brackish lakes such as Malheur L. and Summer L. Rarely found on the margins of large freshwater lakes or reservoirs.

Feed by probing mud or sand. No food habit studies are available from Oregon. Almost entirely dependent on bivalve mollusks that are swallowed whole, based on studies of fall migrants in Europe (Zwarts and Blomert 1992) and spring migrants in Argentina (Gonzalez et al. 1996). Eggs of horseshoe crabs provide an important alternate diet for northward migrants at Delaware Bay, bordering Delaware and New Jersey (Harrington 2001). They have heavy muscular gizzards that are adapted to crush hard-shelled mollusks (Piersma et al. 1993). Food studies in England (Goss-Custard et al. 1977) showed that the most important prey were baltic clams. These clams are found near the surface of most Oregon estuaries (Hancock et al. 1979) and may be an important food source for Red Knots in Oregon.

Knots have a remarkable ability to quickly gain a substantial amount of body fat. Individuals may double their weight in a few weeks before undergoing an extended migration where the fat is quickly burned up (Harrington 1983). This may explain why they often congregate at a few favorable staging sites such as Grays Harbor, Washington, and Delaware Bay where food supplies are seasonally abundant and easily accessible.

**Seasonal Activity and Behavior:** Red Knots are rapid transients through Oregon in spring. They arrive on the coast and inland valleys in mid-Apr (earliest date 7 Apr at Yaquina Bay) and depart by the end of May (Nehls 1994). In e. Oregon, they have been seen as late as 6 Jun at Stinking L. and Harney L., Malheur NWR (Littlefield 1990a). The largest flock recorded was 143 at Tillamook Bay 10 May 1976 (Nehls 1994). Reported more frequently from the Rogue Valley than Willamette Valley. Observed numbers range 1-11 individuals in inland valleys in spring. Generally, only 1-3 individuals seen in e. Oregon in spring, although 12 appeared at Summer L. 11-13 May 1991 (Evanich 1991a). Knots rarely summer on the Oregon coast.

Three reports of solitary birds were between 9 Jun and 12 Jul (Nehls 1994). There are no inland summering records in Oregon.

Fall migration is underway by the third week of Jul, peaks the last week of Aug and first week of Sep when juveniles arrive, and thereafter dwindles into mid-Nov. There is only one fall record from the Willamette Valley, a single individual at St. Paul sewage pond, Marion Co., 13 Sep 1991 (Gilligan 1992a). There are eight records in e. Oregon (all single birds); dates recorded for five range from 24 Aug to 26 Sep. A few scattered individuals winter on the Oregon coast. The maximum winter number is 22 on the Coos Bay CBC in 1976, which remained all winter (Contreras 1995). Single birds are more typical in winter. There are no records from inland valleys or e. Oregon in winter.

**Detection:** Easily detected in spring when in bright nuptial plumage. Much harder to distinguish at other seasons in drab basic plumage when they often blend in with the more abundant Dunlins and dowitchers of similar size. Forms larger flocks in spring than in fall. Rarely heard in Oregon; typically quiet when foraging or when flushed. Flight call is a soft, melodious *cur-ret* (Paulson 1993).

**Population Status and Conservation:** Gabrielson and Jewett (1940) listed the Red Knot as a rare straggler on the Oregon coast, but expanded coverage by many observers since that time suggests that was not the case. An injured Red Knot was collected at McFaddens Marsh (Benton Co.) on 6 May 1959 and seven more were seen in the area, representing the first known record east of the Coast Range in Oregon (Porter 1960).

No conservation problems have been identified in Oregon. Harrington (1983) indicated that tidal power generation schemes, pollution, uncontrolled recreational use of beaches, and habitat loss in major staging areas in N. and S. America threaten the population. The rapid spread of exotic and invasive Smooth Cordgrass on intertidal mudflats of Willapa Bay, Washington, poses a significant threat to foraging shorebirds (Buchanan and Evenson 1997). Global warming may have especially strong impacts in polar and temperate latitudes where Red Knots breed and winter, respectively (Davidson and Piersma 1992, Harrington 2001).—*Alan McGie*

## Sanderling *Calidris alba*

These small gray-and-white sandpipers are commonly seen on beaches from early fall through late spring running in and out along the surf's edge. Buffier, spangled juveniles can be seen in late summer but the stunning rufous breeding plumage is less often seen and can be startling and confusing. The larger size, larger bill, and different habits of the Sanderling help distinguish it in all plumages from other small calidrids.

**General Distribution:** Circumpolar local tundra breeder at high latitudes. Migrates nearly worldwide, mostly coastal. Winters on coasts nearly worldwide except ne. continental Asia. Monotypic (AOU 1957).

**Oregon Distribution:** Common to locally abundant on open sand beaches from fall through spring. Rare to locally uncommon migrant inland statewide; most often reported along the Columbia R. and at e. Oregon lakes. Rare migrant in ne. Oregon (Evanich 1992a) and Malheur Co. (Contreras and Kindschy 1996); occasional with infrequent larger movements at Malheur NWR (Littlefield 1990a); rare in c. Oregon (C. Miller p.c.) and in the Klamath Basin (Summers 1993a); very rare throughout interior sw. Oregon (Hunter et al. 1998); rare but regular migrant in the Willamette Valley (Heinl and Hunter 1985, Herlyn 1998, Gillson 1999).

**Habitat and Diet:** Most Oregon birds use the wave-washed part of flat ocean beaches (not dunes), with a few coastal birds found on mudflats and even mixed into flocks of Black Turnstones and Surfbirds using rocky habitats. Diet of coastal birds is not well known, but a Washington study found young razor clams to be a principal prey item (Paulson 1993). Paulson also notes that Sanderlings farther south on the Pacific coast eat "a variety of small invertebrates, particularly amphipod crustaceans" and that some carrion is used.

Inland birds are usually found on wet edges of alkali playas or on muddy lakeshores, with a few along muddy shores of the largest rivers. Diet of inland birds is essentially unknown but probably includes sand flies and other invertebrates found in wet muddy areas.

**Seasonal Activity and Behavior:** Present in Oregon except in late Jun. First southbound migrants appear in early Jul; birds are common to abundant on coast from Jul onward (Contreras 1998, Patterson 1998b). Fall migrants tend to be in small flocks (100-200 birds) but build through the season until flocks of 1,000 or more are found on beaches by Nov. As a consequence this abundant species can be somewhat local in winter, with large clusters separated by miles of empty beach.

Away from the outer coast this species moves in very small numbers from Jul through Oct, rarely Nov. The species is regular in small numbers at Malheur NWR, with records from 11 Jul to 2 Oct and peak of passage in Aug (Littlefield 1990a). The largest number reported from e. Oregon is 124 found on the playas of Harney L. 12 Sep 1990 (Anderson 1991a).

Winter populations move somewhat along the outer beaches, with a noticeable tendency to concentrate by late Feb as birds begin staging to move north. Beaches from Coos Bay to Florence and in Clatsop Co. are principal spring staging areas (Nehls 1994). Peak of passage on the coast is late Apr through mid-May, with extended buildups in some areas (especially near the Columbia R.) and fewer birds in other locations by mid-May. The earliest spring date at Malheur NWR is 24 Apr, with a late date of 8 Jun (Littlefield 1990a).

**Detection:** It is difficult to imagine a more obvious and approachable bird, as these playa-feeders are truly shorebirds when in Oregon, visible and fairly approachable on open beaches much of the year. Juveniles are occasionally mistaken for Semipalmated Sandpipers and adults in alternate plumage are occasionally mistaken for Red-necked Stints by inexperienced or rarity-seeking observers.

**Population Status and Conservation:** Migration numbers are difficult to gauge over time. Winter numbers within long-standing CBC areas vary widely from year to year, but whether this is due to actual population change or local movements is not known. The 25-yr median at Coos Bay is 501, but the low count was 91 and the high was 5,238 (in back-to-back years). Numbers at Tillamook Bay CBC have ranged from 31 to 3,118. At the Columbia Estuary CBC, which contains part of one of the species' main wintering grounds, the high count was 5,853, the low was seven, and the median was 287.

A flock of 80,000 on Clatsop Beach 23 Jul to 6 Aug 1983 is the largest single assemblage reported in Oregon (Nehls 1994). Other peak counts include 20,000 on 21 May 1977 on Sunset Beach, Clatsop Co. (Crowell and Nehls 1977c), 1200/mi near the s. jetty of the Columbia R. 15 May 1978, and an estimated 30,000 in 3 mi (4.8 km) of beach near the s. jetty of the Columbia R. 25 May 1978 (Mattocks and Hunn 1978b). Note that these three peak counts come from essentially the same beaches.

It is not clear whether Sanderlings migrating through and wintering in Oregon are significantly affected by any current habitat changes or management practices. They are, of course, highly sensitive to any adverse conditions, such as oil spills, affecting the outer sand beaches. Likewise, constant human disturbance or harassment (e.g., by dogs or off-road vehicles) will render feeding difficult.—*Alan L. Contreras*

## Semipalmated Sandpiper *Calidris pusilla*

This tiny sandpiper is the rarest of the regularly occurring "peeps" in Oregon. Its scarceness in the state, however, belies its abundance in e. N. America, where it is the most abundant transient shorebird. Only a handful of individuals are reported in Oregon each year, mostly during fall migration and usually in mixed flocks with Least and Western Sandpipers. Like

the Western Sandpiper, the Semipalmated has black legs, but its bill is generally shorter, straighter, and more blunt. Well-known as a transoceanic migrant, the Semipalmated Sandpiper may be one of the fastest flying of the long-distance shorebirds. An individual banded in Massachusetts was found 4 days later, 2,800 mi (4,500 km) south, in Guyana, an average of nearly 30 mph (48 kph) for 96 hr without touching land (Knight-Ridder 1997).

**General Distribution:** Breeds from coastal w. Alaska east to shores of Hudson Bay and n. Labrador; also Chukchi Peninsula, ne. Siberia. Winters mainly in S. America, rare in s. Florida (Gratto-Trevor 1992). Spring migration is primarily continental, with all but eastern nesters crossing N. America through plains states (Paulson 1993). Fall migration mainly along e. coast of N. America where up to 1 million individuals, 95% of the western hemisphere population, stage in the Bay of Fundy each Aug (Weidensaul 1999). Monotypic (AOU 1957).

**Oregon Distribution:** Rare irregular spring transient throughout Oregon, very uncommon coastal and rare inland fall transient (Gilligan et al. 1994, Nehls 1994).

**Habitat and Diet:** Usually found inside coastal bays along intertidal sand or mud flats, and occasionally on exposed ocean beaches (Paulson 1993); also found at the borders of grassy marsh and tidal flats, such as Bayocean Spit near Tillamook. Inland birds frequent muddy edges of shallow freshwater lakeshores and sewage lagoons. Occasionally seen at small irrigation ponds e. of the Cascades (*SS*).

No dietary data are available specific to Oregon. Elsewhere, diet consists mainly of small arthropods, mollusks, and annelids, occasionally insects and spiders; during migration in particular also known to consume small shrimp and algae (Gratto-Trevor 1992). Feeding behavior includes both surface pecking and probing, depending on seasonal prey sources available. Birds observed at sewage lagoons and pond edges during migration mostly peck at surface (Gratto-Trevor 1992).

**Seasonal Activity and Behavior:** Most spring sightings in Oregon are late Apr through late May; the earliest spring record west of the Cascades is from Medford, 14 Apr 1964; early spring record east of the Cascades is from Hatfield L. near Bend, 3 May 1987 (Paulson 1993). Most individuals arriving in Oregon likely breed in Alaska (Paulson 1993). Males arrive on breeding grounds a few days earlier than females and therefore may precede females in Oregon by several days in spring. There are no records between 21 May and 29 Jun (Nehls 1994).

Adults return in early Jul; earliest coastal fall date Tillamook 29 Jun 1986; earliest interior fall date from Hatfield L., 7 Jul 1984. The peak of adult movement (which involves very few birds) is in mid-Jul, with some reported through early Aug. Nonbreeding adults usually arrive first, followed by breeding females; males remain with the brood on the northern breeding grounds and follow the females by about 5 days (Gratto-Trevor 1992). Juveniles arrive in late Jul and peak mid-Aug to mid-Sep (again, very few birds are involved); the latest coastal fall date is from Manzanita, 25 Sep 1987; the latest interior fall date is from Malheur NWR, 25 Sep 1983. The juvenile high count is an extraordinary 15 at Tillamook 18 Aug 1985 (Paulson 1993, Nehls 1994). There are no verified Oregon records from 25 Sep to 2 Apr.

**Detection:** Most commonly associated with Western Sandpipers (Paulson 1993). Individual variation among bills and plumages of Western Sandpipers and Eurasian stints makes separation of juvenile Semipalmated difficult, and basic-plumaged birds nearly impossible. The call, if learned, is very helpful for field identification.

**Population Status and Conservation:** Townsend listed the Semipalmated Sandpiper as occurring in "the territory of Oregon" in 1839, but a century later this could not be verified (Gabrielson and Jewett 1940). The next documented sighting occurred at Hoover's Lakes near Medford on 14 Apr 1964; however, since no individual had been collected to date, the species remained hypothetical in Oregon (Browning 1975a). A sighting 13 yr later from the same region generated the first verified Oregon record: one photographed on 19 and 21 Aug 1977 at Agate Res. in Jackson Co. (OBRC). The bird remained an OBRC review species until 1984.

No detectable trends in Oregon. Surveys of wintering birds in S. America generated estimates of 2 million individuals in 1989; no significant population declines noted in 12 yr of International Shorebird Surveys; current populations may be threatened by loss of wetlands used during migration (Gratto-Trevor 1992). Staging areas of significant importance to the species have been identified by the International Shorebird Reserve Network, but none currently exists in Oregon (Gratto-Trevor 1992).—*Stephen Shunk*

## Western Sandpiper *Calidris mauri*

At certain estuaries and interior alkali lakes, flocks of many thousands of these migrants can be observed swirling around over shallow water, landing to frantically feed, before resuming migration. Falcons often attack Westerns, and their acrobatic, tightly coordinated escape flights are breathtaking to observe. In winter, these small sandpipers (length 6-7 in [14-17 cm]) are gray above with white underparts. In breeding plumage they have a rich rufous-chestnut back, cheeks, and cap, dark-centered scapulars with rufous-chestnut edges, grayish throats streaked with dark chevrons through the flank, and whitish underparts. Longer-billed females generally are larger than males but are otherwise similar in appearance.

**General Distribution:** The Western Sandpiper is the most numerous shorebird along the Pacific Flyway (Page and Gill 1994). They breed principally in the subarctic zone of w. Alaska, on parts of the Alaska Peninsula north to the Yukon-Kuskokwim Delta, with smaller numbers in n. Alaska and ne. Russia (Gill et al. 1981, Bishop and Warnock 1998). They winter primarily along the coast from California to C. and S. America as far south as Peru, as well as along the s. Atlantic coast, and the Gulf of Mexico (Wilson 1994). Monotypic (AOU 1957).

**Oregon Distribution:** Along the coast of Oregon, the Western Sandpiper is the most abundant shorebird in estuaries and along beaches during migration. Generally, larger flocks are seen in fall than in spring. The largest concentrations of migrant birds are usually found at Tillamook Bay, Bandon Marsh, and the Columbia R. estuary (Nehls 1994, Point Reyes Bird Observatory [PRBO] unpubl. data). During winter along the coast, Westerns are occasional to uncommon, with most birds found around Coos Bay,

*Western Sandpiper*

Tillamook Bay, and the Columbia R. estuary (Paulson 1993, Contreras 1997b, PRBO unpubl. data). Within inland valleys west of the Cascades, Western Sandpipers are common migrants in spring and fall. Highest concentrations in the Willamette Valley are usually found at Ankeny, Baskett Slough, and Finley NWRs, especially in the spring (T. Mickel unpubl. data). Their occurrence at western interior sites during the winter is rare, although a few birds are found most winters at Fern Ridge Res. near Eugene (Contreras 1997b). Small numbers of birds are seen in and along the w. Cascades during spring and fall migration (Browning 1975a, Fix and Sawyer 1991). East of the Cascades, Western Sandpipers do not winter, but are common spring and fall migrants at lower elevations, uncommon in summer (Evanich 1992a, Nehls 1994). In wetlands at higher elevations, such as Sycan Marsh, Lake Co., small numbers have been observed, but not on a regular basis (Stern, Del Carlo, et al. 1987). Notable concentrations of many thousands of birds occur in e. Oregon at Harney L., Malheur NWR, and at L. Abert (Littlefield 1990a, Kristensen et al. 1991, Oring and Reed 1997), although numbers vary greatly among years depending on lake levels (Warnock et al. 1998).

**Habitat and Diet:** On the coast, the largest concentrations of feeding Western Sandpipers occur at estuaries with large expanses of mudflats. In California, these birds have been shown to prefer mudflats for foraging, and unlike Dunlin, rarely feed in agricultural fields (Long 1993, Warnock and Takekawa 1995). Birds will roost on a variety of different substrates when tides are high including beaches (where they will also feed), rock jetties, and other structures above the high tide line (*NW*). At interior sites, they occur at permanent and seasonal wetlands. In the Cascades, migrating birds are occasionally seen along shorelines of reservoirs, lakes, ponds, and wet meadows (Stern, Del Carlo, et al. 1987, Fix and Sawyer 1991). In e. Oregon, some of the largest concentrations of birds are found in the shallow water or on the exposed mudflats of alkali lakes such as L. Abert. Managed wetlands, flooded playas, and other bodies of water are also used.

Little is known about the diet of Western Sandpipers in Oregon. At coastal sites, they commonly feed on invertebrates including but not limited to crustaceans, worms, and small clams (Wilson 1994). In coastal w. Washington, small crustaceans, chiefly amphipods, seem to be especially important prey items (Couch 1966, Wilson 1994). At interior sites in Oregon, Western Sandpipers probably feed on insects, especially flies (Wilson 1994). At alkali lakes such as L. Abert they probably feed on brine flies, as this is the most abundant invertebrate prey consumed by other shorebird species there (Boula 1986), and brine flies are a known prey

item of Western Sandpipers in other areas (Anderson W 1970).

**Seasonal Activity and Behavior:** Records for Western Sandpipers on the coast mainly occur from Mar through May, and late Jun to early Oct (Nehls 1994). Spring migration of Western Sandpipers is more compressed than fall migration (Nehls 1994, Warnock et al. 1998), and individuals pass through the region quickly. An estimated 15,000 "peeps" (mostly Westerns) were counted at L. Abert on 4 May 1989, dropping to 5,000 by 9 May and 1 by 11 May (Kristensen et al. 1991). Spring migrants spend an average of 2.6 days at Honey L., in ne. California, 3.3 days at Humboldt Bay in nw. California, and 2.3 days at Grays Harbor in w. Washington (Warnock and Bishop 1998). In spring 2002, of 60 Western Sandpipers radiomarked at Bahia Santa Marina, Sinaloa, Mexico, in early Apr, six were detected in Oregon within 3 wks of being marked (Warnock et al. 2002). The length of stay of these birds in Oregon was 1 day or less at Bandon Marsh (three birds), Coos Bay (two), Yaquina Bay (one), and Siletz Bay (one) (Warnock et al. 2002).

Small numbers of birds are present along the coast during fall and winter months from Oct through Feb. Five-year CBC averages of Western Sandpipers 1974-88 have ranged between 676 and 771 birds at Coos Bay, 65-244 birds at Tillamook Bay, and 56-119 birds at Yaquina Bay (Paulson 1993). In San Francisco Bay, Western Sandpipers have been shown to exhibit strong local winter site fidelity (Warnock and Takekawa 1996), but the strength of winter site fidelity in Oregon is unknown.

Main spring migration west of the Cascades is from mid-Apr to early May (Nehls 1994), with a peak generally in last few days of Apr and first few of May (*NW*). East of the Cascades, the first arrival and peaks of Westerns are approximately a week later. In c. Oregon, the earliest arrival date was 16 Apr with an average first detection of 22 Apr (n=15 yrs, C. Miller unpubl. data). At Malheur NWR, the earliest arrival for Western Sandpiper was 2 Apr 1966 while the latest first detection was 5 May 1973 with an average first detection date of 21 Apr (Ivey, Herziger, and Scheuering 1998). During the "fall" migration, the first southbound adults appear in the last week of Jun. Along the coast, peak of adult movement is late Jul and early Aug, followed by a higher peak of juveniles in late Aug; east of the Cascades, the pattern is similar but high counts have been recorded late into Sep, such as 23,000 birds at Malheur NWR in late Sep 1979 (Nehls 1994). As on the coast, southbound adults are found inland as early as late Jun. 2,500 Western Sandpipers counted at Summer L. on 12 Jul 1997 (Spencer 1998).

Recent banding and radiotelemetry projects on Western Sandpipers have revealed that many of those migrating through the Pacific Northwest breed in w. Alaska from the Yukon-Kuskokwim Delta up to the Seward Peninsula (Butler et al. 1996, Bishop and Warnock 1998). Seven wintering birds banded in Panama and one in Mexico, and five summering birds banded on the Seward Peninsula in Alaska were observed in Oregon during migration (Butler et al. 1996). Most sightings in Oregon were from the coast but one was seen at Sauvie I. and one at Salem (Butler et al. 1996).

**Detection:** Because of their habit of feeding in large compact flocks on open mudflats and in shallow water, Western Sandpipers are easy to detect when present. In winter, these birds are often confused with the Dunlin, Least Sandpiper, and Sanderling (Contreras 1997b). It is easy to confuse Western Sandpipers, especially short-billed, juvenile males, with similar sized and colored, although rarer, Semipalmated Sandpipers (Paulson 1993). The Western Sandpiper's monosyllabic *dzheet* flight call is higher pitched than the short, sometimes doubled *chert* call of the Semipalmated Sandpiper (Paulson 1993).

**Population Status and Conservation:** The world population of Western Sandpipers is estimated between 2.8 and 4.3 million birds (Morrison et al. 2000). In Oregon, shorebird surveys coordinated by the PRBO 1990-95 at the larger coastal estuaries revealed that highest mean spring and fall concentrations were in Clatsop Co. with mean (+/- SD) spring numbers of 2,695 birds +/- 6,620 (n=11 surveys), and mean fall numbers of 3,326 birds +/- 4,441 (n=14 surveys). Other high counts during spring and fall migration periods include 100,000 at Tillamook Bay, 23,000 at L. Abert, and 22,325 at the lower Columbia R. estuary (Littlefield 1990a, PRBO unpubl. data).

Highest winter concentrations of Western Sandpipers were in Coos Co. with mean (+/- SD) numbers of 768 birds +/- 1,010 (n=8 surveys); most in Coos Bay (PRBO unpubl. data, see also Contreras 1997). During winter (Dec) from 1991 to 1994, the mean number of Western Sandpipers counted along the coast of Oregon was 3,715 birds +/- 2,689 (range 719 -2, 6,728 birds) (PRBO unpubl. data); this probably represents the range of mean winter population size of Western Sandpipers in Oregon, since few birds are found away from the coast in the winter. The highest number ever recorded in Oregon on a CBC (up to 1995) was 2,437 birds seen at Coos Bay in 1991 (Contreras 1995).

These birds were once hunted in Oregon; dozens at a time were killed when hunters shot into densely packed flocks of birds roosting on the beaches (Gabrielson and Jewett 1940). While they are no longer hunted, hundreds have been illegally killed by people driving through roost flocks on beaches in the Pacific Northwest (Buchanan 1999). Continued degradation of coastal habitat in Oregon will likely negatively affect numbers of Western Sandpipers. The spread of non-native cord grass in coastal estuaries as seen at Willapa Bay in Washington could also negatively affect Western Sandpiper numbers as has been described in Britain for Dunlin (Goss-Custard and Moser 1988). In e. Oregon, water-diversion programs that affect the large alkaline lakes could have important implications for migrating birds (see Jehl 1994). Likewise, factors affecting brine fly production at alkaline lakes such as L. Abert will also affect Western Sandpiper migration through this part of the state as brine flies are probably the major food item of Western Sandpipers at these lakes (Boula 1987). The spread of purple loosestrife has reduced habitat at Cold Springs NWR in Umatilla Co. (M. Denny p.c.).—*Nils Warnock*

## Red-necked Stint *Calidris ruficollis*

This small colorful shorebird breeds across n. Siberia to w. Alaska. It winters southward to the S. Pacific islands. It occurs casually in migration along the Pacific coast, and more rarely elsewhere in N. America. Adults in alternate plumage are unmistakable (though observers sometimes mis-report alternate-plumage Sanderlings) but this species is difficult to separate from Little Stints and Semipalmated Sandpipers in basic or juvenal plumages. Only adults have been identified along the w. coast. Four different adults were photographed in the shorebird congregation on Bayocean Spit at Tillamook Bay, Tillamook Co., during the fall of 1982. The first was 20 Jun (Harrington-Tweit et al. 1982); another on 3 Jul (Nehls 1989a); a third 19-22 Aug (OBRC), and a 4th 21-26 Aug (Watson 1989). There are accepted sight records of an adult at Bandon Marsh 25 Jun 1984 (OBRC), and at the s. jetty of the Columbia R., Clatsop Co., 19 Jul 1997 (Johnson J 1998a). One at the North Spit of Coos Bay 15 Jul 1999 (Tice 2000b), and two at the mouth of Siltcoos R. 3 Sep 2001 (Contreras 2002b) are being evaluated by the OBRC. Monotypic (AOU 1957).—*Harry B. Nehls*

## Little Stint *Calidris minuta*

The Little Stint breeds in n. Europe and Asia and winters in Africa and the Middle East. It occurs casually in N. America, with most records from Alaska. Adults in alternate plumage are unmistakable, but it is difficult to separate from Rufous-necked Stints and Semipalmated Sandpipers in basic or juvenal plumages. Three birds in juvenal plumage have been photographed in Oregon: on the Bayocean Spit of Tillamook Bay, Tillamook Co., 7 Sep 1985 (Johnson 1987); Bandon Marsh, Coos Co., 12 Sep 1986 (Fix 1987a); and s. jetty of the Columbia R., Clatsop Co., 10-11 Aug 1995 (Gilligan 1996). An adult showing considerable alternate plumage was videotaped at Coos Spit on 13 Jul 2002 (K. Castelein,

D. Lauten, T. Rodenkirk) just as this book was going to the publisher; the record has not been considered by the OBRC but acceptance is likely. Monotypic (Johnsgard 1981).—*Harry B. Nehls*

## Long-toed Stint *Calidris subminuta*

This small shorebird breeds in Siberia and winters southward to the S. Pacific islands. It is a rare migrant to Alaska, and is casual along the w. coast of N. America. It is almost indistinguishable from the more common Least Sandpiper. A juvenile was photographed and its voice recorded at the s. jetty of the Columbia R., Clatsop Co., 2-6 Sep 1981 (Hunn and Mattocks 1982a, Gilligan et al. 1987). A sight record of an adult at the s. jetty of the Columbia R. 17 Jul 1983 has been accepted by the OBRC. Monotypic (AOU 1957)—*Harry B. Nehls*

## Least Sandpiper *Calidris minutilla*

This is the world's smallest "peep" and can usually be picked out by its brownish coloration, dull yellowish legs, and hunched, creeping foraging style. Least can be found in small flocks in Oregon almost year-round; juveniles and spring adults are somewhat brighter.

**General Distribution:** Breeds from Alaska east across n. Canada to Newfoundland. Winters in small numbers from British Columbia s. more commonly on the coast (with a few birds inland) to California, across the southern tier of states and to n. S. America. Monotypic (AOU 1957).

**Oregon Distribution:** Uncommon to locally abundant statewide in migration, with most birds along the coast and at larger lakes and marshes inland. Found in appropriate habitat statewide. Locally common on the coast in winter; smaller numbers winter in the western interior valleys, where small flocks can be found at larger lakes, locally in flooded fields and sometimes even at marginal sites such as sewage ponds. A few birds sometimes winter east of the Cascades where appropriate habitat remains open.

**Habitat and Diet:** Feeds on open mud with Western Sandpipers but often feeds where some grass, salicornia, or other cover is present, avoiding walking in the water as Western often do. Will use flat wet stony areas within estuaries, e.g., on a falling tide, but does not usually use steeper rocky habitats. Except for roosting, generally does not use beaches and very dry "upland" grassy or open soil sites (*ALC*). Sometimes uses wet pastures and moist tilled fields, especially in winter.

No dietary studies are available from Oregon. Studies in Washington and in e. Canada show that small amphipods, gastropods, and terrestrial invertebrates (especially flies) are principal prey items. It is an opportunistic feeder, using the commonest prey available (Cooper 1994).

**Seasonal Activity and Behavior:** A few southbound adults appear in the last week of Jun, with most adult movement in Jul (*ALC*). Peak counts during southbound movements of adults include 1,500 at Tillamook Bay 2 Jul 1988 (Paulson 1993). Juvenile movement is extended and peak numbers can be found from mid-Aug through Nov, though late Aug and early Sep are typical peak times (Nehls 1994). Peak of southbound passage at Malheur NWR is 25 Jul to 25 Aug (Littlefield 1990a). An estimated 9,000 were at Tillamook and Netarts Bay (peak of juvenile passage) 25-26 Aug 1979 (Paulson 1993), 4,000 at Tillamook 18 Aug 1985 (Paulson 1993), 1,000 at Bandon 26 Aug 1989 (Fix and Heinl 1990), and 3,000 there on 2 Sep 1990 (Fix 1991). The latter part of fall movement sometimes offers large flocks (e.g., 1,000 at Coos Bay 12 Nov 1961, Boggs and Boggs 1962), some of which winter.

Least are locally common in winter along the coast, with hundreds of birds typically present at Coos Bay and smaller clusters elsewhere. The 25-yr median count at the Coos Bay CBC is 358; the all-time high is 3,268. Small numbers winter in the Willamette Valley (very few in the Umpqua and Rogue valleys) and it is rare in winter east of the Cascades (Littlefield 1990a, Gilligan et al. 1994).

Spring movement is more compressed, with most birds moving from early Apr through early May (Nehls 1994). Peak of passage at Malheur NWR is 20 Apr to 5 May (Littlefield 1990a). Spring peaks at some inland locations are very high, e.g., 23,150 at Summer L. 1 May 1987 and 6,000 at L. Abert 1 May 1971 (Nehls 1994). Numbers at coastal sites are lower but still substantial, e.g., 3,500 at Tillamook Bay 30 Apr 1991 (Nehls 1994), 1,200 at Yaquina Bay 17 Mar 1968 (Paulson 1993), 3,000 at s. jetty of the Columbia R. 24 Apr 1968 (Crowell and Nehls 1968b), and 3,000 at New R. 27 Apr 1984 (Paulson 1993).

**Detection:** Its tendency to feed in drier and even grassy areas, its presence almost year-round in temperate Oregon and its tolerance for close approach make this the easiest "peep" to find, observe, and learn. Although birds tend to disappear into mudholes and behind dank tufts of grass, there are usually so many of them that a reasonably patient observer can't help but obtain good looks.

**Population Status and Conservation:** Numbers reported in Oregon seem fairly consistent over the past 30 yr, with peaks in the multiple thousands in the 1960s and still reaching such levels today, though coverage of habitat is more complete now than in the

1960s. Most of these birds use areas that already enjoy some protection, e.g., Summer L. and coastal estuaries. As long as adequate natural estuarine habitat remains available, the species is likely to remain common in Oregon.—*Alan L. Contreras*

## Baird's Sandpiper *Calidris bairdii*

These large "peeps" are seen in Oregon mainly in late summer and fall, when their size, scalloped buffy plumage, and long profile help them stand out in flocks of other small sandpipers.

**General Distribution:** Breeds from Greenland across the Canadian tundra to Alaska and extreme ne. Siberia. Migrates throughout N. America, with most birds e. of the Rockies. Winters in S. America. Monotypic (AOU 1957).

**Oregon Distribution:** Uncommon migrant statewide, with most birds southbound juveniles. Can occur in suitable habitat anywhere in Oregon, but numbers are usually very low and sizable flocks almost nonexistent. Most often reported from the high Cascades eastward and on the coast; less common in the western interior valleys, perhaps owing to paucity of habitat. Rare in Linn (Gillson 1999) and Benton (Herlyn 1998) counties, and is at best uncommon even at Fern Ridge Res., Lane Co. Rare in the Umpqua and Rogue valleys (Browning 1975a, Hunter et al. 1998) and the s. Cascades (Fix 1990a).

**Habitat and Diet:** This is usually a drier-habitat calidrid. Although it will feed with other "peeps" on mudflats, it is more often observed on drier sand, higher dry mud margins of lakes and marshes, and even beaches and gravelly areas (Paulson 1993, *ALC*). It is well known as a fall migrant at high elevations, where it uses alpine lake margins and even snowfields as foraging areas (Evanich 1992a, Paulson 1993, A. Prigge p.c.).

No dietary studies are available from Oregon.

**Seasonal Activity and Behavior:** Annual numbers are quite variable. Southbound movements of adults begin by early Jul, although most years bring few birds. Peak of passage of juveniles is from mid-Aug to early Sep (Contreras 1998, Patterson 1998b). Most birds have gone by late Sep, but stragglers have been reported at Malheur NWR as late as 14 Oct (Littlefield 1990a), at Fern Ridge Res. 20 Nov. 1994 (Gilligan 1994), and on the coast as late as 20 Nov 1995 at Coos Bay (Contreras 1998) and 28 Nov 1976 at Yaquina Bay (Paulson 1993). Peak fall numbers are unimpressive compared to other shorebirds, e.g., 35 at Bend 14 Aug 1985 (Rogers 1986), 30 at Sauvie I. 13 Aug 1977 (Mattocks and Hunn 1978a), 30 at Borax L. (Harney

Co.) 25 Aug 1985 (Summers 1986a), 14 at Coos Bay 25 Aug 1980 (Contreras 1998), 14 at La Grande 17 Jul 1982 (Evanich 1982c). The highest counts known from Oregon are a remarkable 120 at Nehalem Bay in Aug, probably 1975 (T. Lund, *fide* D. Fix p.c.) and an equally amazing 95 at Malheur NWR 22 Aug 1991 (Evanich 1992b).

The species does not winter in N. America; there are no valid winter records from Oregon.

Spring numbers are even lower, sometimes absent, and those few that are seen are often east of the Cascades. The peak of this very limited passage at Malheur NWR is 20-30 Apr, with the earliest report 8 Apr and the latest 8 May (Littlefield 1990a). The latest record for w. Oregon is 6 Jun 1983 at Yaquina Bay (Nehls 1994).

**Detection:** Fairly easy to distinguish when present, but numbers are so low that some diligence is required to find them. Careful attention to drier and high-elevation shorebird habitat in season should produce this species. Dry call distinctive, but can be confused with that of Pectoral Sandpiper.

**Population Status and Conservation:** Oregon hosts a very small portion of the population. As long as beaches, mudflats, and other littoral habitats are available and not damaged by pollutants, these sandpipers will not be significantly affected.—*Alan L. Contreras*

## Pectoral Sandpiper *Calidris melanotos*

These brownish, heavily streaked, medium-sized shorebirds are often seen peering over grass in the more overgrown parts of mudflats, especially in fall. There is considerable variation in brightness and size even among same-age birds, but the two-tone bills, sharply offset breast streaking, and dull yellowish legs help distinguish this species from others.

**General Distribution:** Breeds from ne. Siberia across Alaska to nc. Canada, winters mainly in S. America. Migrates throughout N. America. Monotypic (AOU 1957).

**Oregon Distribution:** Found statewide in migration; largest numbers in fall, sometimes all but absent in spring. Common on the outer coast but also in wet coastal pastures. More local inland but large flocks can be found in preferred habitat (Littlefield 1990a, Evanich 1992a, Nehls 1994, Contreras 1998, Hunter et al. 1998, Patterson 1998b).

**Habitat and Diet:** Pectorals are shorebirds of wet grassy areas along mudflats, salicornia, wet pastures, and similar areas where there is some cover and some mud in wet situations (*ALC*). On the outer coast they are often found in wet dairy pastures or freshly turned fields. Gabrielson and Jewett (1940) note a record of two birds eating insects off the snow at 9,600 ft (2,926 m) in the Wallowa Mtns.

Diet information is not available for Oregon. Given the species' proclivity for feeding in grassier areas, it may have different dietary preferences than do mudflat feeders.

**Seasonal Activity and Behavior:** Fall numbers vary considerably from year to year, with some years bringing a trickle and other years a flood (Nehls 1994). Very few adult birds move through Oregon; the few that occur pass through from early Jul through Aug. Peak of juvenile passage is later than for many other shorebirds, with numbers not building until Sep and sometimes remaining quite high through Oct, e.g., 20 near Astoria 30 Oct 1996 (Gilligan 1997). Peak fall numbers include 500 around Tillamook and Nehalem 19 Sep 1982 (Hunn and Mattocks 1983), 350 at Stinking L., Harney Co., Sep 1975, and 250 there in Sep 1976 (Littlefield 1990a). Flocks of fewer than 100 are more usual at principal e. Oregon and coastal sites, and groups of 10 or fewer are the norm in the western interior valleys (Herlyn 1998, Gillson 1999), though Sauvie I. sometimes supports larger numbers, e.g., 50 there 24 Sep 1989 (Heinl and Fix 1989). In fall, 2001, over 100 were at Fern Ridge Res., Lane Co. (D. Irons p.c.).

A few birds linger, such as the one on 7 Nov 1987 at Malheur NWR (Littlefield 1990a) and a remarkable 150 on 11 Nov 1989 at Willow Cr. W.A., Morrow Co. (Anderson DA 1990a). There is one sight record of two birds on the Portland CBC in Dec 1959 (Contreras 1997b, CBC), and there are photos of birds in Dec and reputable sight records as late as early Jan as far north as British Columbia, suggesting that birds could occasionally pass through Oregon even into early winter. However, most winter reports are probably referable to Least Sandpipers. Any records after Nov should be documented.

Spring movements are much smaller, and in some years essentially invisible. Movement can begin early, e.g., 9 Apr 1964 (Boggs and Boggs 1964) and is usually over by mid-May, though there are some late spring records, e.g., 2 Jun 1989 at Warrenton, Clatsop Co., and 5 Jun 1989 at Florence, Lane Co. (Johnson 1990a). A bird 20 Jun 1970 at the s. jetty of the Columbia R. may have been either a late spring or early fall migrant (Crowell and Nehls 1970c).

**Detection:** Fairly easy, though in some years numbers are very low. Tends to feed in heavier vegetation than most shorebirds, thus a flock of Pectorals can appear as a curiously serpentine movement in the grass with only an occasional head emerging to delight the attentive observer. Sometimes remain still in grass for extended periods, making observation difficult. As is true of most shorebirds, patience is usually rewarded; even Pectorals don't stay in the grass forever. Call distinctive, though rather similar to Baird's Sandpiper.

**Population Status and Conservation:** Oregon receives relatively few birds out of the continental population and numbers vary considerably from year to year, so an assessment of their actual status is difficult. However, the elimination of marsh edges and wet grassy habitat would clearly have a negative effect on the species' ability to move through Oregon.—*Alan L. Contreras*

## Sharp-tailed Sandpiper *Calidris acuminata*

This is a portly, brightly colored shorebird, typically found in coastal salt marshes, mud flats, and sandy margins of freshwater ponds. Migrant juveniles rather than adults appear in Oregon (Gilligan et al. 1994). They have a flattish, dark rufous-colored crown with fine black streaking. The crown gives the appearance of a jaunty "cap" sitting forward on the head and abruptly ending at the rear. The breast is a rich orange-buff (unique among calidrid waders) shading into the white lower breast and belly. The well-defined creamy-white supercilium broadens behind the eye and is visible at a considerable distance. This is one of the most distinctive field marks on juveniles. Juveniles molt into first-winter plumage after passing through the Northwest (Paulson 1993).

**General Distribution:** Breeds in the ne. Siberian tundra in a small strip well north of the Arctic Circle, entirely within the breeding range of Pectoral Sandpipers (Mlodinow 2001). Migrates by both continental and oceanic routes (Paulson 1993). Most adults fly south across e. Russia but, later in the season, most juveniles take an alternate route to the Pacific coast before migrating south (Mlodinow 2001). In N. America, it appears mostly as a fall migrant or stray. Good numbers may be seen in some years in Alaska and it is regularly seen in British Columbia and Washington; irregular in very small numbers farther south on the Pacific coast and rarely elsewhere (Kaufman 1987). W. coast fall migrants probably travel over the Pacific Ocean on a long flight to tropical Pacific islands or perhaps Australia and New Zealand. They apparently do not return by this route as few adults are seen anywhere in N. America (Paulson 1993). Winters primarily in New Zealand and Australia where it is a common, widespread wader (Hayman et al. 1986). Monotypic (AOU 1957).

**Oregon Distribution:** Irregular transient in fall on the Oregon coast, and only 1 spring record. Occasional in the Willamette Valley and in e. Oregon. In coastal Oregon, 1-12 birds (but usually <6) have been reported each year since 1980. The peak number at a single site was six at Bandon (Coquille R. estuary) between 22 Sep and 28 Oct 1990 (Tweit and Fix 1991). One to four birds occasionally seen in the Willamette Valley; most reported from Sauvie I. Five records in e. Oregon consist of single individuals at widely scattered localities from 1987 through 1995 (Hatfield L., Deschutes Co.; Wamic, Wasco Co.; Malheur L., Harney Co.; near Lower Klamath NWR, Klamath Co.; and Bully Cr. Res., Malheur Co.).

**Habitat and Diet:** No habitat or foraging studies have been conducted in Oregon, but they are often observed in association with Pectoral Sandpipers. Usually found foraging in salt marshes and mud flats in coastal estuaries or nearby sandy margins of freshwater ponds and at sewage ponds; rarely in freshwater marshes or plowed fields. Inland, usually on exposed mud with sparse vegetation.

**Seasonal Activity and Behavior:** The earliest fall record is 2 Sep 1989 at Nehalem sewage ponds and the latest is 12 Nov 1991 at the same locality (Gilligan et al. 1994, Nehls 1994). Reports in Aug likely refer to other species. Most migrate though Oregon in the last few days of Sep, tapering off through mid-Oct (Contreras 1988b). This pattern seems consistent for the coast, inland w. Oregon, and e. Oregon. The single spring record was 24 May 2000 at New R., Coos Co. (Lillie 2000, incorrectly reported as 24 Mar 2000 in Lauten and Castelein 2000) and provided only the second regional spring record for Oregon and Washington (Mlodinow et al. 2000a).

During migration, Sharp-tailed's calls resemble the liquid notes of Barn Swallows, consisting of a soft *plee* or *pleep* or double *tuwit* (Britton 1980, Paulson 1993). Paired notes are given in flight (Webb and Conry 1979). These calls are rarely heard in Oregon. May exhibit aggressive behavior toward approaching Pectoral Sandpipers (Paulson 1993) or neighboring Sharp-tailed Sandpipers (Webb and Conry 1979).

**Detection:** Often observed with Pectoral Sandpipers. Usually picked out by brighter, warmer tones, especially on the cap, face, and breast, but beware of bright juvenile Pectoral Sandpipers. Eye-ring often more noticeable than on Pectoral Sandpiper. Sharp-tailed Sandpipers are rather slow moving while feeding, spending long periods deliberately picking at the substrate in a small area (Kaufman 1987). May crouch, snipe-like, to avoid detection (Hayman et al. 1986).

Most consistently found at the s. jetty of the Columbia R., Clatsop Co. Inland, most sightings occur on Sauvie I., Multnomah and Columbia counties (Nehls 1994). Finding this species is largely a matter of luck and seasonal timing. The beautifully marked juveniles remain distinctive during their stay in Oregon.

**Population Status and Conservation:** One seen at Tillamook Bay 16 Oct 1965 (Baldridge and Crowell 1966) is the first published record of Sharp-tailed Sandpiper in Oregon. The earliest record accepted by OBRC is a juvenile seen at Bayocean Spit, Tillamook Bay, 23 Oct 1977 (Watson 1989). The OBRC accepted 13 records consisting of 17 birds prior to removing Sharp-tailed Sandpiper from the review list in 1983 (Contreras 1988b). Sightings in Oregon have increased since the 1960s, but are probably a reflection of more birder coverage of shorebird habitat. Tends to occur in larger numbers in years when juvenile Pectoral Sandpipers also appear in larger numbers (Gilligan et al. 1994).

Roberson (1980) lists a record of 2-3 birds at s. jetty of the Columbia R. 13 Aug-20 Sep 1978 as accepted by OBRC, but according to H. Nehls (p.c.) the committee did not accept the record. Instead they were determined to be brightly colored Pectoral Sandpipers (H. Nehls p.c.). A report of a bird by Hunn and Mattocks (1979a) on 13-28 Aug 1978 may refer to the same record (Contreras 1988b). One published record (Hoffman 1972) was determined to be a Buff-breasted Sandpiper on the basis of photographs (Watson 1987).

No immediate conservation problems were identified for this species beyond the need to preserve estuarine and freshwater staging areas for shorebirds.—*Alan McGie*

## Rock Sandpiper *Calidris ptilocnemis*

The W. Coast equivalent of the Purple Sandpiper, this medium-sized, stocky sandpiper is rarely observed away from the rocky coastline as it forages close to the zone of salt spray. During winter, the upperparts, head, and upper breast are dark brownish-gray. Lower breast and flanks are dull white streaked with dusky gray. Chin is whitish and the supercilium is grayish-white. The bill is all dark except for a yellow or orange base with a slight droop to the tip. Its short legs are greenish-yellow. These birds often stretch their wings when disturbed exposing the extensive white wing stripe. Loosely associates with flocks of Surfbirds and Black Turnstones.

**General Distribution:** Breeds on the n. coast of Siberia on the Chukotski Peninsula from Providence Bay to Kolyucha Bay, the Commander, Kuril, and Sakhalin Is., many of the islands in the Bering Sea including the Pribilofs, Shumagin and the Aleutians, and from wc. Alaska south to the w. Alaska Peninsula

(Johnsgard 1981, Godfrey 1986, Richards 1988). Southern breeding populations on the N. American Pacific coast are year-round residents (Campbell et al. 1997). Winters to Japan along the w. Pacific; e. Pacific populations winter from Alaska south through British Columbia, Washington, Oregon, and n. California (Johnsgard 1981, Richards 1988, Paulson 1993, Campbell et al. 1997). Vagrant south to Los Angeles, California, and nw. Baja California, Mexico (Godfrey 1986, Hayman et al. 1986). Extremely rare inland with a report from Atlin, nw. British Columbia (Hayman et al. 1986). Of four subspecies described, only *C. p. tschuktschorum* occurs in Oregon (Hayman et al. 1986; specimens, including those available to Gabrielson and Jewett [1940] are of this subspecies [*MRB*]); *couesi*, listed for Oregon by Gabrielson and Jewett (1940), is not known outside its breeding range (AOU 1957).

**Oregon Distribution:** Strictly coastal with no inland records. Uncommon to rare migrant and winter visitor along the entire rocky coastline although greater numbers recorded for the northern counties (Gilligan et al. 1994, Nehls 1994).

**Habitat and Diet:** Found on jetties, rocky headlands, offshore rocks, rocky estuaries, and tide pools; rarely on estuarine mudflats (Evanich 1990, Gilligan et al. 1994, Nehls 1994). No information on diet in Oregon but probably feeds on the abundant mussel and barnacle beds and other intertidal invertebrates along the rocky shoreline.

**Seasonal Activity and Behavior:** Primarily a late fall migrant with the major influx into Oregon occurring during the last week in Oct and into early Nov (Nehls 1994). The earliest arrival date reported is 21 Aug (Gilligan et al. 1994). Generally, single digits are recorded during the winter months; however, a high count of 31 reported on a Tillamook CBC (Contreras 1991). Spring migration involves few birds and is rather protracted with no discernable peak; most birds depart by the third week of Apr. Latest departure date recorded is 14 May (Gilligan et al. 1994).

Generally silent during migration and on wintering grounds. Often found singly or in small groups with foraging Black Turnstones and Surfbirds. Cryptic plumage makes it difficult to observe as it forages slowly over mussel and barnacle beds in typical sandpiper fashion. Roosts on rocks with Black Turnstones and Surfbirds near feeding grounds, just above the spray zone (Paulson 1993).

**Detection:** No information on detection rates throughout Oregon, but found on <25% of field trips to the s. Oregon coast conducted from third week in Aug to Dec and from Jan to the first week in May (Brown et al. 1996). Seal Rock SP is a particularly reliable site to observe this species during Dec and Jan.

**Population Status and Conservation:** Oregon population numbers unknown. Usually seen as singles although small flocks (2-8) occasionally noted; rarely up to 18 individuals observed in a single flock (Nehls 1994).

No conservation problems have been identified for this species in Oregon. However, entire migration and wintering range occurs along oil tanker routes making it vulnerable to oil spills. Paulson (1993) noted a regional decrease in wintering populations in the Pacific Northwest based on CBC data. Indeed, 5-yr averages of the number of birds noted at three CBC coastal locations in Oregon all indicate a decrease in abundance. Buchanan (1999a) postulated that the 1982-83 El Niño/Southern Oscillation (ENSO) event may have been responsible for the decline in numbers. He reanalyzed the CBC data for the above three localities in Oregon into the following two periods: before (1968-69 to 1981-82) and after (1983-84 to 1996-97) the 1982-83 ENSO event. Mean number of birds detected on CBCs declined significantly for all three localities as follows: Coos Bay, from 5.13 (n=8) to 1.55 (n=11, p<0.05); Tillamook Bay, from 12.21 (n=14) to 3.57 (n=14, p<0.001); Yaquina Bay, from 7.33 (n=9) to 0.93 (n=14, p<0.005). Buchanan (1999a) provided no cogent explanation as to how an ENSO event might affect abundance of Rock Sandpipers and cautioned that the above relationship was correlative rather than causal.—*Kamal Islam*

## Dulin *Calidris alpina*

Formerly known as the Red-backed Sandpiper, the Dunlin undergoes one of the most dramatic changes in appearance of all shorebirds when it molts from winter to breeding plumage. In winter, these medium-sized sandpipers (length 6.3-8.7 in [16-22 cm]) are brownish gray above with white underparts, but in breeding plumage they have a striking rufous-brown back and cap and a black belly. Females are larger than males but otherwise similar in appearance. Juveniles are difficult to distinguish from adults in the field since they replace most juvenal feathers near the breeding grounds. Dunlin molt flight feathers while still on or near their breeding grounds, and as a consequence are the last of the sandpipers to arrive in Oregon in the fall except for the very small wintering population of Rock Sandpipers.

**General Distribution:** There are up to 11 recognized subspecies of this Holarctic breeder, including three found in N. America, breeding from sw. Alaska north and east to James Bay, Canada (Browning 1977b, 1991, Greenwood 1986, Nechaev and Tomkovich 1988). The majority of N. American Dunlin winter in coastal areas of the U.S. and n. Mexico. The subspecies that winters along the west coast of N. America, *C.*

*Dunlin*

*a. pacifica* (called by Gabrielson and Jewett [1940] *Pelidna alpina sakhalina*), breeds mainly on coastal, grassy meadows in w. Alaska. While a few birds may winter as far north as the Alaska Peninsula, the majority of birds winter from s. British Columbia south to Baja California and w. mainland Mexico (Howell and Webb 1995, Warnock and Gill 1996). In California, large numbers winter in the Central Valley, especially in wet years (Warnock et al. 1995).

Marking studies have revealed that fall-staging Dunlin on the Yukon-Kuskokwim Delta in Alaska tend to winter in the Pacific Northwest, while fall-staging Dunlin on the Alaska peninsula winter in California (Warnock and Gill 1996). Recent analyses of mtDNA control-region sequences of Dunlin suggest occasional movements of birds between e. Siberia and the Pacific Northwest (Wenink and Baker 1996, Wennerberg 2001).

**Oregon Distribution:** Abundant transient and winter visitant in estuaries and occasionally on beaches along the coast of Oregon, but significant numbers (some flocks >15,000 birds) winter in the Willamette Valley, especially the southern part (Johnson J 1993b, 1994b, Sanzenbacher and Haig 2002b). Small numbers show up during migration and winter in the Rogue and Umpqua valleys (Gilligan et al. 1994). In e. Oregon, smaller numbers (up to a few thousand) of Dunlin are seen at a variety of wetlands during migration, mainly in spring, especially around Klamath Basin and southeastern alkaline lakes such as Summer L. and L. Abert (Nehls 1994, Sullivan 1997b). Dunlin are rare spring and fall migrants at lower elevations in ne. Oregon (Evanich 1992a).

**Habitat and Diet:** On the coast, largest concentrations of feeding Dunlin occur at estuaries with large expanses of mudflats (on low tides). Birds will roost on a variety of different substrates when tides are high including beaches (where they will occasionally feed), rock jetties, pastures, log rafts, and other structures above the high tide line (Brennan et al. 1985, *NW*). Within the Willamette Valley, birds are found roosting in flooded rice fields, sewage ponds, and managed impoundments (Sanzenbacher and Haig 2002b). Feeding birds are often seen in flooded parts of bare to newly planted fields (especially grass fields), and can occur in large numbers at permanent and seasonal wetlands. In the Cascades, occasionally seen along shorelines of reservoirs, lakes, ponds, wet meadows, and other bodies of water during migration (Fix and Sawyer 1991). In e. Oregon, some of the largest concentrations are found in the shallow water or on the exposed mudflats of alkali lakes such as L. Abert. Managed wetlands, flooded playas, and other bodies of water are also used.

Little is known about the diet of Dunlin in Oregon. At coastal sites, Dunlin commonly feed on invertebrates including but not limited to arthropods (especially orders Tanaidacea and Amphipoda), annelids, and small clams (Warnock and Gill 1996). In w. Washington, amphipods seem to be an especially important prey item (Buchanan et al. 1985, Brennan et al. 1990). At interior sites in Oregon, Dunlin probably feed on insects, especially flies, and earthworms as these are common prey items at other interior sites (Warnock and Gill 1996). These are common prey items collected in agricultural wetlands used by Dunlin in the Willamette Valley (Taft and Haig unpubl. data).

**Seasonal Activity and Behavior:** Records for Dunlin on the coast mainly occur from mid-Sep to early May. Birds are largely absent in Jun, Jul, and most of Aug, although there are occasional records in these months. Birds seen Dec-Feb most likely winter in Oregon. In the Willamette Valley, high concentrations (10,000 +) of Dunlin are reported Jan-Mar (Johnson J 1993b, 1994b, Lillie 1995), with major movements in Mar (Nehls 1994). Appearance of birds in winter in the Willamette Valley is thought to coincide with seasonal rains (Strauch 1967), as seen in California where some Dunlin move from the coast into the Central Valley to feed in flooded agricultural fields and seasonal wetlands (Warnock et al. 1995). Studies of radio-marked birds indicate that Dunlin observed in the Willamette Valley during winter months range over large areas (mean home range 101 +/- 18 mi$^2$ [258 +/- 45 km$^2$]) and are winter residents. The mean departure date of 17 radio-marked birds in spring 2000 was 22 Mar +/- 1.8 days (Sanzenbacher and Haig 2002b). Main migration west of the Cascades is from mid-Apr to mid-May (Nehls 1994).

In spring, at Malheur NWR, the earliest arrival for Dunlin was 28 Mar 1985 while the latest first detection was 15 May (1966 and 1971) with an average first detection date of 27 Apr (Ivey, Herziger, and Scheuering 1998). Mid-Apr to mid-May appears to be the main spring migration period for Dunlin in this region. Timing of fall passage of Dunlin east of the Cascades is not well understood, although it is rare to see birds Jul to mid-Sep, and uncommon to see them late Sep into Nov with a few records in Dec (Gilligan et al. 1994). In the w. Great Basin region of Nevada, peak fall numbers of Dunlin occurred in early Oct (Hainline 1974). Dunlin generally do not winter east of the Cascades.

**Detection:** Hundreds of foraging and resting Dunlin may be nearly invisible in wet, plowed fields in winter. Detecting birds in this habitat requires careful searching, often with a scope. They are most easily detected when at edges of water or when in flight in large, tight, well-coordinated flocks. Their *treer* or *krree* call is distinctive, but in appearance they are easily confused with the smaller Western Sandpiper. During the winter, some of the most reliable places to see Dunlin include Coos Co., especially Bandon Marsh and the Coos Bay area (PRBO unpubl. data). Large flocks of Dunlin also can be found in the Willamette Valley. Areas around Eugene, including Fern Ridge Res., the Eugene Airport, and Halsey have produced large (10,000+) flocks of Dunlin (Johnson J 1993b, 1994b, 1995b, 1996b, Lillie 1995, 1996, Contreras 1997b). Listed as a common winter resident (seen on 21% of surveys of suitable habitat) in the s. Willamette Valley in the 1930s and 1940s (Gullion 1951). In spring, highest concentrations of Dunlin are found in Clatsop Co., especially around the lower Columbia R. estuary (PRBO unpubl. data). Areas along the Columbia R. are also important as demonstrated by 10,000 birds at Brownsmead, Clatsop Co. on 30 Apr 1995 (Lillie 1995). National and state wildlife refuges including Sauvie I.-Ridgefield, Finley, Ankeny, and Baskett Slough have been good areas for Dunlin. East of the Cascades, the large lakes in Klamath, Harney, and Lake counties are good places to detect Dunlin (Gilligan et al. 1994).

**Population Status and Conservation:** The world population of *C. a. pacifica* is estimated at 450,000-600,000 (Page and Gill 1994). During winter (Dec), between 1991 and 1994, the mean number of Dunlin counted along the coast of Oregon was 7,334 birds (SD +/- 2,868; low year was 1991 with 3,860 birds and high year was 1992 with 10,166 birds) (PRBO unpubl.

data). In the Willamette Valley, surveys of Dunlin by ODFW 1994-97 revealed a Jan average of 17,461 birds (SD +/- 5,162; low year was 1995 with 10,346 birds and high year was 1996 with 22,714 birds) (T. Mickel unpubl. data), but note high count of over 30,000 roosting birds in winter 2002 (P. Sanzenbacher unpubl. data). If one assumes that 7,334 is a minimum number of Dunlin found along the coast and that 17,461 Dunlin is the minimum average winter population of Dunlin in the Willamette Valley, then in an average winter the minimum Oregon population of Dunlin probably lies around 25,000 birds, depending on whether birds found in the Willamette Valley are the same birds using the coast. The highest number of Dunlin ever found on a CBC in Oregon was 20,483 birds at Columbia R. estuary in 1980 (Contreras 1995).

Interestingly, the presence of Dunlins wintering in the Willamette Valley by the thousands, if not tens of thousands, appears to be a recent phenomenon (*DBM*). Neither Gabrielson and Jewett (1940) nor Gullion (1951) mention numbers of this magnitude. The first reference to such is in Gilligan et al. (1994).

Shorebird surveys coordinated by PRBO 1990-95 at most of the major coastal estuaries and beaches in Oregon revealed that highest winter numbers of Dunlin were in Coos Co. with a mean number of 1,477 birds (SD +/- 2,473; n=8 surveys); most at Bandon Marsh and the Coos Bay area (PRBO unpubl. data). In spring, highest Dunlin counts occurred in Clatsop Co. with a mean of 1,879 birds (SD +/- 4,869; n=11 surveys) (PRBO unpubl. data). High spring counts can occur at the lower Columbia R. estuary (Nehls 1994, PRBO unpubl. data), such as 20,000 birds at the s. jetty on 5 May 1996 (Lillie 1996). Occasionally, concentrations of birds are noted east of the Cascades including an estimated 1,000 at Klamath Basin 21-22 Mar 1997 (Sullivan 1997b), 1,680 at Summer L. on 21 Apr 1987 (Nehls 1994), and 3,000 at L. Abert on 28 Apr 1994 (Summers 1994b).

Current status of the population is unknown, although it has been suggested that winter numbers in the Northwest have declined in some areas (Paulson 1993). CBCs in Oregon show a +1.7 % annual change from 1959 to 1988 with 165 birds being seen per 100 party-hours (Contreras 1997b). Continued degradation of coastal habitat in Oregon will likely negatively impact numbers of Dunlin. The spread of non-native cordgrass in coastal estuaries as seen at Willapa Bay in Washington could also negatively impact Dunlin numbers as has been described in Britain (Goss-Custard and Moser 1988).—*Nils Warnock*

## Curlew Sandpiper *Calidris ferruginea*

This colorful shorebird breeds across n. Siberia and casually into n. Alaska. It winters in Africa, the Middle East, and south to the S. Pacific islands. It is a casual migrant throughout N. America. Oregon records are of an adult at Yaquina Bay, Lincoln Co., 21 Jul 1976 (OBRC); an adult at Seven Devils Wayside, Coos Co., 16 Aug 1976 (OBRC); a juvenile at the s. jetty of the Columbia R., Clatsop Co., 16 Sep 1982 (OBRC); an adult photographed at Bandon Marsh, Coos Co., 25-30 Jul 1985 (Watson 1989); an adult photographed at Tillamook Bay, Tillamook Co., 17 Aug 1985 (OBRC); a juvenile photographed at Tillamook Bay 20-25 Aug 1985 (Heinl 1986a, Watson 1989); a juvenile at the s. jetty of the Columbia R. 23 Sep 1986 (OBRC); at Bandon 25 Sep to 2 Oct 2000 (OBRC); and at the n. jetty of the Siuslaw R. 18 Sep 2000 (OBRC). One was photographed on the n. spit of Coos Bay 1 Oct 2001; the same bird was probably at the mouth of the Siltcoos R. the previous day (Contreras 2002b). Monotypic (AOU 1957).—*Harry B. Nehls*

## Stilt Sandpiper *Calidris himantopus*

This slender sandpiper is a rare but nearly annual visitor to Oregon. Although easily overlooked, its drooped bill, light eyeline, long neck, long greenish legs, and unstriped wings in flight help set this medium-sized shorebird apart from similar species.

**General Distribution:** Breeds from n. Alaska eastward to Hudson Bay. Winters primarily in the southern half of S. America, although a few remain in southern climes of N. America. Migration is primarily through the Great Plains and to a lesser extent along the e. coast. Southward migration brings a few wanderers, usually juveniles, to the Pacific Northwest each year. Monotypic (Jehl 1973).

**Oregon Distribution:** Rare fall and occasional spring transient, most frequently found in estuarine habitat along the coast. Also found along shorelines of the Great Basin region of sc. and se. Oregon. However, it has occurred in appropriate habitat throughout the state (Nehls 1994, *CRM*).

**Habitat and Diet:** Preferred habitat during migration is shallow freshwater, usually avoiding mudflats and beaches. In coastal areas utilizes estuarine wetlands, shallow lagoons, and ponds. Inland habitat includes natural lakes, managed wetlands, reservoirs, and sewage ponds (Paulson 1993, Klima and Jehl 1998). Feeds on invertebrates such as midge, beetle, and mosquito larvae (Alexander et al. 1996, Klima and Jehl 1998).

**Seasonal Activity and Behavior:** Migrates in long nonstop flights for hundreds or thousands of miles (Klima and Jehl 1998). In Oregon, spring sightings are truly exceptional, with only four records, each east of the Cascades: one in "early May" 1962 at the Klamath Marsh (Scott 1962, Fix 1979); one on 8 May 1991 at

Malheur NWR (Evanich 1991a); three on 12-15 May 1995 at Summer L. W.A. (Sullivan PT 1995b) and one on 22 Apr 1998 at Malheur NWR (Sullivan 1998b).

First migrants heading south from their breeding grounds are adults, which pass through Oregon from early Jul through mid-Aug (Paulson 1993, *CRM*). Adult records are quite unusual, averaging only about one sighting every 3 yr and account for only about 7% of all occurrences (*CRM*). However, in Jul of 1988 four or more adults were recorded (Johnson 1989a). The earliest southbound record was 2 Jul 1993 at the s. jetty of the Columbia R. (Johnson J 1994a). Latest record of an adult was 8 Sep 1993 at L. Abert (Summers 1994a).

Juvenile birds migrating southward to wintering grounds make up the bulk of occurrences in Oregon. Found primarily 19 Aug-24 Sep, peaking the last week of Aug. There are only six records after 1 Oct. Latest fall records were both in 1989, one on the very late date of 25 Nov at Ochoco Res. in c. Oregon (Anderson DA 1990a), the next latest record a month earlier, one on 22 Oct at Bandon, Coos Co. (Fix 1990b). Some years bring significant influxes, such as 1982 when a total of 15 were found in six locations, 1986 when 12 were found in nine locations, and most significantly in 1989 when 34 were found in 11 locations. Tend to be found singly or in pairs, but occasionally found in small flocks. The largest concentration in a single area was a flock of 13 seen in flight at Hines, Harney Co., on 23 Aug 2000 (D. Evered p.c.) followed by 12 juveniles observed on Sauvie I., 30 Aug 1989 (Fix 1990b, N. Lethaby p.c.). Feeding behavior can be a "sewing machine" method similar to that of dowitchers; also use a more deliberate slower probing.

**Detection:** Generally difficult to detect because of intermediate size and tendency to mix with large shorebird flocks of similar appearance, especially dowitchers. Flight call, a single soft *tyur*, inconspicuous and rarely given during migration (Paulson 1993, Klima and Jehl 1998). Bill shape is usually best initial clue to distinguish from other species. Often found associated with dowitcher flocks.

**Population Status and Conservation:** Unrecorded in Oregon until 1962 when one was found in early May at the Klamath Marsh (Scott 1962, Fix 1979). Gabrielson and Jewett (1940) make no mention of the species. Since 1974, however, there have been one or more reports of this species nearly every year with about 80 records to date. Since 1974 only 2 yr (1978 and 1992) have passed without at least one record. The reason there were no records prior to 1962 is unclear, but improved coverage, better field guides, and improved identification skills by field ornithologists have no doubt contributed to the number of records since then.

No major threats are identified in Oregon, although loss of wetland habitat would undoubtedly be detrimental. Status as a rare migrant in the state minimizes the potential detrimental impact to the population as a whole.—*Craig R. Miller*

## Buff-breasted Sandpiper *Tryngites subruficollis*

Resembles a plover with a high-stepping, pigeon-like gait. One of the few Oregon shorebirds that frequents dry, sparsely vegetated coastal grasslands. Fall migrants in Oregon consist of juveniles (Gilligan et al. 1994). Has scaly, buffy-brown upperparts, yellow legs, a small head, and a short black bill. Beady black eyes stand out on a plain, pale face. Bobs head while moving. Gleaming white underwings are displayed in a graceful flight pattern. Unique among N. American shorebirds in having a lek mating system (Myers 1979, Lanctot and Laredo 1994).

**General Distribution:** Nests in dry tundra in n. Alaska and upper reaches of Canada. Outside the Americas, the western population breeds on Wrangel I. and in w. Chukotka, Russia (Lanctot and Laredo 1994). Winter in the southern part of S. America (Paraguay, Uruguay, and n. Argentina) where they occupy heavily grazed grasslands and savannah in shrub-steppe habitats and freshwater wetlands (Love 1990a, 1990b, Lanctot and Laredo 1994). Spring migrants primarily move through the c. U.S. east of the Rocky Mtns. (Hayman et al. 1986). Secondary fall migration is along the Atlantic coast. Migration of juveniles is more widespread than adults (Campbell and Gregory 1976). Juveniles are more prevalent on the Atlantic coast with far fewer along the Pacific coast (Paulson 1993). Very few records away from the outer coast (Paulson 1993). Vagrant in continental Europe, Africa, Japan, c. Pacific islands, and Australia (Hayman et al. 1986). Monotypic (AOU 1957).

**Oregon Distribution:** This is a rare but regular fall migrant on the Oregon coast where it has been recorded in every coastal county. Sporadic fall migrant on Sauvie I. Casual in the Rogue Valley. Two fall records east of the Cascades, one near Prineville, Crook Co., from 24 Sep to 5 Oct 1990 (Anderson 1991a, Nehls 1994) and one at the Redmond sewage ponds, Deschutes Co., 24-25 Aug 2001 (Sullivan 2002). There is only a single spring record, one seen 12 Apr 1981 in alternate plumage at Wilson R. Meadows, Tillamook Co. (Watson 1981c). There are no winter records.

Generally 1-6 birds can be found at favored sites along the Oregon coast. Counts at Sauvie I. range 1-3 birds. Peak number at a single site was 14 in the deflation plain near the s. jetty of the Siuslaw R., Lane

Co., 11 Sep 1985, one of the largest flocks ever found on the west coast (Heinl 1986a).

**Habitat and Diet:** Usually forages on sparsely vegetated deflation plains, lawns, golf courses, grassy airport margins, and plowed fields, and on shores of inland reservoirs, lakes, and sewage ponds. Sometimes found on open beaches (Contreras 1998). Rarely ventures out onto mudflats to join other shorebirds.

There are no food habit studies in Oregon. Insects and surface invertebrates such as various crustaceans picked off the surface near shore are food sources (Paulson 1993), also spiders and a few seeds from aquatic vegetation (Ehrlich et al. 1988).

**Seasonal Activity and Behavior:** Fall migration through Oregon extends from mid-Aug to mid-Oct. Early dates are 13 Aug 2001 at Tenmile Cr. Estuary, Coos Co. (Contreras 2002b, erroneously placed in Douglas Co.), and 15 Aug 1985 at the s. jetty of the Columbia R., Clatsop Co.; migration peaks from the last week of Aug to mid-Sep (Nehls 1994); latest record 17 Oct 1988 at Clatsop Beach, Clatsop Co. Inland migrants in Oregon appear within the same time frame as coastal ones.

**Detection:** Mostly silent. Soft flight calls are an instantly forgettable, low, gruff *chu* (Vinicombe 1983), scarcely audible at moderate distances (Paulson 1993). Therefore, they are almost exclusively detected visually. Foraging actions are erratic, with quick directional changes or "run and stop" actions reminiscent of plovers (Paulson 1993). Most consistently found at the s. jetty of the Columbia R., meadows around Tillamook Bay, and the Siuslaw deflation plain in early fall. Inland, most sightings are from Sauvie I.

**Population Status and Conservation:** The first Oregon record was apparently one seen at the s. jetty of the Columbia R. in Sep 1960, but not submitted for publication because no additional verification was obtained (Baldridge and Crowell 1966). The first published record was one at Tillamook Bay on 11 Sep 1965 (Baldridge and Crowell 1966). The first record verified by OBRC is one seen at Yaquina Bay, Lincoln Co., 1 and 3 Sep 1968 (Watson 1989). The OBRC accepted 15 records consisting of 18 birds before removing Buff-breasted Sandpiper from the review list in Apr 1985. The regular reports of this species since publication of Gabrielson and Jewett (1940), who did not record the species in Oregon, may be the result of increased coverage of proper habitats by observers rather than increased numbers of the birds.

Buff-breasted Sandpipers currently face loss of upland winter habitat by agricultural conversions of S. American grasslands (Ehrlich et al. 1988). Vulnerable to pesticides/herbicides in agricultural fields, lawns, and golf courses during migration and on wintering grounds (Lanctot and Laredo 1994). In Oregon, favorable Buff-breasted Sandpiper habitat may be lost by the rampant growth of exotic European beachgrass planted to stabilize sand dunes and by extensive plant succession in coastal deflation plains.—*Alan McGie*

## Ruff *Philomachus pugnax*

The male Ruff is a relatively large, distinctive, Eurasian shorebird that in breeding plumage sports head tufts and neck plumes from which it gained its name. However, most Ruffs seen in Oregon are juveniles that appear as lanky, buff-colored, pot-bellied, short-billed sandpipers showing white on both sides of the rump in flight. Females are about 20% smaller than males and are referred to as reeves.

**General Distribution:** Breeds in arctic, subarctic, and temperate n. Eurasia and winters mostly in s. Europe, and s. Asia south to s. Africa. In N. America, occurs largely as a coastal migrant in Alaska, along the east coast south to the Lesser Antilles, and to a more limited extent along the west coast. Very rare breeder in Alaska. Monotypic (AOU 1957).

**Oregon Distribution:** Rare fall transient and very rare spring transient, usually on the coast. Casual in winter on the coast. Some records are from inland in w. Oregon, particularly from Sauvie I. near Portland. There are four records from e. Oregon.

**Habitat and Diet:** In Oregon usually found on mudflats of coastal estuaries or in adjoining wet meadows (H. Nehls p.c.). No published data regarding Oregon diet, but studies elsewhere indicate species takes mostly aquatic insects, especially beetles, flies, crustaceans, mollusks, and some worms as well as freshwater algae, weed seeds, and grain (Terres 1995). In migration seeds may be more important than during the breeding season (Kaufman 1996).

**Seasonal Activity and Behavior:** Peak period of occurrence in Oregon is late Aug–early Sep. Earliest fall record for a juvenile is 11 Aug and latest is 11 Oct (Gilligan et al. 1994). Adults reported between 25 Jul and 11 Oct (Gilligan et al. 1994). Five spring records, all of single birds, include three from e. Oregon and two from the coast as follows: near Klamath Falls 3-9 Apr 2001, White L., Klamath Co. 30 Apr 2000, Summer L. 12-14 Apr 1991, Coos Bay 18 Apr 1997, and Tillamook Co. 2 Jun 1984 (Harrington-Tweit and Mattocks 1984, Evanich 1991a, Lillie 1997, Sullivan 2000b, D. Haupt p.c., J. Meredith p.c.). Although it is known to winter in California, the only winter record for Oregon was an individual in the Coquille Valley, Coos Co., 18 Jan 1980 (Watson 1980c).

Ruffs are unwary and approachable. They forage while wading or walking by picking up items from the ground or by probing in the mud or water (*TJ*).

**Detection:** Generally easy to detect when present since it occurs on mudflats or in low vegetation. Sometimes confused with other large shorebirds such as Lesser Yellowlegs, Pectoral Sandpiper, or Buff-breasted Sandpiper (especially reeves).

**Population Status and Conservation:** World population is at least 1 million based on congregations found in W. Africa (Rossair and Cottridge 1995). Wetland losses have caused population declines in parts of Europe (Kaufman 1996). Not found breeding in N. America until 1976, when nest found on Alaska's arctic coastal plain (Gibson 1977). Current size and status of Alaskan breeding population somewhat uncertain, but at least several dozen pairs have been breeding there recently (Morrison et al. 2001).

The first accepted Oregon record was of an individual seen at the s. jetty of the Columbia R. 8 Sep 1979 (Mattocks and Hunn 1980a). Approximately 60 subsequent records from Oregon; currently reported at rate of about five annually. While most are of single birds, up to four have been seen together (Gilligan et al. 1994).—*Tim Janzen*

## Short-billed Dowitcher *Limnodromus griseus*

These chunky medium-small shorebirds are quite colorful in oranges and browns during most of their time in Oregon, when they are found mainly along the coast and locally in muddy areas inland. Their feeding motion has been likened to a sewing machine as flocks move slowly through shallow water and wet mud, probing with long straight bills. Identification of winter birds is difficult because of similarity to Long-billed Dowitcher and is best made by voice.

**General Distribution:** Breeds in disjunct locations across subarctic Canada and in s. Alaska. Winters from s. coastal U.S. to n. S. America. Migrates across most of N. America except in the Rocky Mtn. region, where rare. Three subspecies, of which two have been documented in Oregon based on specimen records (Nehls 1989a).

**Oregon Distribution:** Common to locally abundant coastal migrant, less common and more local in western interior valleys, rare but regular east of the Cascades. Records east of the Cascades are widespread but numbers reported are very low, often consisting of one or two birds in large flocks of Long-billed Dowitchers. Although Littlefield (1990a) lists only one probable record for Malheur NWR, the species is now known to be a rare migrant there in spring and fall (C. Miller p.c., *ALC*). Has been recorded as far east as Malheur Co. (Contreras and Kindschy 1996) and ne. Oregon (Evanich 1992a). Except in winter, when usually absent, this is the commonest dowitcher on the outer coast.

Most Oregon specimens are referable to the Alaskan breeding form *L. g. caurinus*. Pitelka (1950) listed specimens of *caurinus* from Clatsop and Lincoln counties. At least one specimen from Oregon (OSU No. 3084) and a few from e. Washington and Idaho have been identified as *L. g. hendersonii*, which breeds in c. Canada and migrates for the most part through the center of the continent. However, many Idaho specimens identified as *hendersonii* by Burleigh (1972) and Weber (1985) were reidentified as *caurinus* by Paulson (1993). It seems likely that at least the eastern part of Oregon receives occasional migrants to and from the c. Canadian breeding grounds (Nehls 1989b, Paulson 1993), possibly representing *hendersonii* or *caurinus*. Further specimens are needed to understand these movements.

**Habitat and Diet:** Short-billed Dowitchers are primarily birds of wet mud or shallow water with underlying mud. Occasionally seen in marginal areas such as flooded pastures, but less likely than Long-billed to use such upland locations (*ALC*). Most are found on tidal mudflats and adjacent shallow water, where large assemblages sometimes form. No detailed habitat studies have been conducted in Oregon. No dietary information is available from Oregon.

**Seasonal Activity and Behavior:** Spring movements begin in late Mar and the peak of passage is in late Apr (Nehls 1989b, Paulson 1993). Stragglers appear through May. Numbers seen in spring migration are not high compared to the thousands seen in Washington, with most flocks comprising fewer than 100 birds. Peak numbers are 200 on 28 Apr 1989 and 400 on 26 Apr 1990, both at Bandon (Contreras 1998); 200 at New R., Coos Co., on 27 Apr 1984; 200 at Yaquina Bay 19 Apr 1977; and 200 at Tillamook Bay on 9 May 1984 (Paulson 1993). East of the Cascades single birds or very small numbers are the norm.

Southbound movements begin with the arrival of the first adults in the last days of Jun. Peak of passage for adults is mid-Jul, with numbers similar to those found in spring migration. Immatures begin arriving in early Aug and peak in late Aug and early Sep, with stragglers through early Oct (Nehls 1989b, Paulson 1993). Numbers are somewhat higher, with flocks of several hundred not uncommon, and a record high of 2,000 on 18 Aug 1990 at Bandon, Coos Co. (Fix 1991). There are reliable reports of calling birds found as late as early Nov (Gilligan 1999) and a few CBC reports of calling birds, but there are no winter records confirmed by specimen or voice recording.

**Detection:** Best observed on the outer coast during southbound migration, where the immature plumage is easiest to distinguish from Long-billed. Not shy but sometimes difficult to approach simply because they often feed inconveniently far away across mudflats. Best studied at locations where shorebirds gather at higher tides.

**Population Status and Conservation:** Oregon is not a major staging area for this species in most years, with only small portions of the population using Oregon sites. However, within the state this species has a relatively specialized habitat: most birds use open estuarine mudflats. Thus significant damage to such habitat or loss of habitat to invading vegetation would reduce the utility of Oregon habitat to the portion of the population that passes through the state.—*Alan L. Contreras*

## Long-billed Dowitcher
*Limnodromus scolopaceus*
This medium-sized shorebird is the most common dowitcher in e. Oregon and inland locations, where it sometimes gathers in large flocks feeding in shallow water. Although breeding-plumage adults are reddish below and heavily patterned above, most birds seen in Oregon are duller postbreeding adults or browner immatures During winter, when shorebirds are hard to find, a small flock of softly chattering dowitchers, even in plain gray basic plumage, often brightens a day in w. Oregon.

**General Distribution:** Breeds from ne. Siberia across n. and w. Alaska, n. Yukon and nw. Mackenzie. Migrates mainly across w. N. America, winters on coast from sw. coastal British Columbia to n. M. America, also along the U.S. western Gulf of Mexico coast, locally inland. Pitelka (1950) listed several specimens from Oregon. Monotypic (AOU 1957).

**Oregon Distribution:** Common to locally abundant migrant statewide. This is by far the most common dowitcher (sometimes the most common shorebird at a given site) found in migration east of the Cascades. It is also the dowitcher most likely to be found at most inland locations in the state and the only dowitcher that regularly winters.

In migration can be found at almost any shallow-water site in the state, from Malheur L. to small potholes in the western interior valleys and the mudflats of the outer coast. Winter distribution is more limited, with most birds on the coast but small numbers in the western interior valleys. Rare in winter from the Cascades eastward.

**Habitat and Diet:** Somewhat more eclectic in its habitat tastes than the Short-billed Dowitcher, being more willing to use freshwater habitats far from the coast. During rainy periods, can be found as often on flooded pastureland (even on the coast) as on mudflats.

Although food studies are not available from Oregon, studies from the c. coast of California show that these long-billed probers tend to eat polychaete worms (*Capitella* spp.), tube-dwelling amphipods (mostly *Corophium* spp.), Cumacea, bivalves, and various other foods (Stenzel et al. 1983, Takekawa and Warnock 2000). Consistent use of pastureland, especially in winter, suggests that earthworms and other terrestrial invertebrates may form a significant portion of the diet at certain seasons.

**Seasonal Activity and Behavior:** Movement patterns are similar to those of other nonbreeding shorebirds that visit Oregon, but fall movements extend later in the season. Adults appear in early Jul (mostly east of the Cascades until mid-Jul), with a peak of passage in late Jul and very early Aug. Juveniles begin arriving in numbers in Aug, with a buildup in late Aug and a lower extended peak throughout Sep, with some movement still underway in early Oct (Nehls 1994). High counts of adults in southbound movements include 800 at Sauvie I. 30 Jul 1989, and 5,262 at Summer L. 3 Aug 1987 (Nehls 1994).

Numbers of immatures peak at Malheur NWR in late Aug. High counts there sometimes reach spectacular numbers, e.g., over 30,000 birds sometimes present on the refuge (Littlefield 1990a). Peak counts include 4,000 in one extended flock near Malheur NWR HQ for much of early Sep 1999 (M. Denny p.c., *ALC*), 17,200 at Malheur NWR 31 Aug 1973 (Paulson 1993), and 20,000 at Malheur L. 12 Oct 1991 (Nehls 1994). Peak counts west of the Cascades are much lower, with 2,000 at Sauvie I., 13 Oct 1988, the highest reported at one site (Nehls 1994) and normal numbers in the dozens to hundreds at a given site. Because this species molts before winter begins, it is not known whether most Oregon winterers are adults or hatch-year birds (Paulson 1993).

Most are gone from Oregon east of the Cascades by Dec, with only rare stragglers reported during winter. Latest record at Malheur is 26 Nov 1971 (Littlefield 1990a). Absence from e. Oregon may be related to feeding strategy: shorebirds such as Killdeer, Least Sandpiper, and Greater Yellowlegs that occasionally winter in small numbers east of the Cascades are surface pickers, while dowitchers are deep probers and are as a consequence more likely affected by ground freezing.

A few birds can be found most winters in the western interior valleys. Small flocks remain along the coast all winter, but total numbers and locations of large flocks vary from year to year. The 25-yr median at Coos Bay CBC is 36, with a high of 532 and 2 yrs in which the species was unreported.

Northbound movements are smaller and blend somewhat with wintering flocks on the coast, but significant movements are underway by Mar and a noticeable peak occurs in late Apr. Largest spring flocks reported are 550 at Tillamook Bay on 25 Apr 1981 and 779 at Summer L. 1 May 1987 (Nehls 1994).

**Detection:** Dowitchers are easy to see statewide at many seasons, but some care must be exercised in identifying them. They may often be approached closely, though they also spook easily and move about a feeding area unexpectedly.

**Population Status and Conservation:** There is not enough information available (especially for spring movements) to make a definitive statement about populations that pass through Oregon, but the continued presence of large flocks in appropriate habitat suggests that no serious diminution is occurring. Because this species requires inundated habitats, reduction in wetlands or increase in invasive plants in mudflat situations would reduce habitat available to migrants.

Winter birds in the western interior valleys and along the coast are found more often in flooded pastureland, grass-seed fields, and other temporary habitat than on mudflats, thus certain agricultural practices that result in short-grass habitat subject to seasonal flooding (coastal dairying, valley grass-seed farming) probably benefit the species.—*Alan L. Contreras*

# Wilson's Snipe *Gallinago delicata*

Cryptically colored, usually solitary and somewhat secretive, the snipe are often flushed before being seen, sometimes exploding from practically underfoot and rocketing off in a corkscrew flight. This plump-bodied, long-billed bird of open marshland is primarily crepuscular, peaking in feeding activity at dusk and

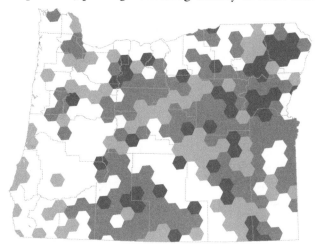

dawn, and often sleeping during the day. In breeding season they become more flamboyant, appearing atop fence posts and displaying their unique winnowing flights from high in the air, their outer tail feathers vibrating with an eerie whistling sound. Nevertheless, confirmation of nesting is a difficult task. N. American hunters often call this species "jack snipe," a name no doubt brought from Europe because of its similarity to the Jack Snipe there.

**General Distribution:** Breeds throughout Alaska, east across n. Canada to n. Newfoundland, south to c. California (generally east of the Cascades), and east to s. Colorado, also in northern portions of Midwestern and New England states. Winters from se. Alaska, s. British Columbia, east into Idaho, throughout the c. U.S., Pennsylvania and s. New England south through M. America and the W. Indies to n. S. America. North American birds, formerly Common Snipe (*G. gallinago*), with *delicata* as a subspecies (e.g., AOU 1957), are now recognized (Banks et al. 2002) as a separate species, *G. delicata*. Monotypic.

**Oregon Distribution:** Uncommon and local west of the Cascades in summer (Gilligan et al. 1994). Probable westside breeding locations include areas in n. and s. Willamette Valley, where they are uncommon and local; also n. Clatsop Co. and n. Jackson Co. (OBBA). Twelve were at Baskett Slough NWR 22 Jul 1998 (Tice 1999a). Observation of courtship flight at Fern Ridge Res. 12 Jun 1947 (Gullion 1951) may have indicated breeding there; breeding has recently been confirmed in nw. Linn Co. (OBBA). Two marshes on Saddle Bag Mtn. in the Coast Range are the only locations where they appear to nest in Lincoln Co. (Bayer et al. 1994).

Uncommon and local in the Cascades in the breeding season (Gilligan et al. 1994). At Summit Meadow (between Government Camp and Trillium L.) appear after snow melt and perform winnowing flights (*DBM*). Also found displaying at Little Crater L. meadows, Salmon R. meadows and Big Meadows on the Warm Springs Indian Reservation (D. Lusthoff p.c., C. Corkran p.c.). Breed at Sycan Marsh, Lake Co., where common in spring, abundant in summer, and uncommon in fall (Stern, Del Carlo, et al. 1987). Winnowing displays observed at the marsh south of Diamond L. probably indicate breeding attempts (Fix 1990a).

Common summer resident east of the Cascades (Gilligan et al. 1994). Gabrielson and Jewett (1940) recorded it as an especially common breeder in Ft. Klamath area. Many breeding records confirmed in the Blue and Wallowa mountains region, and also breeds throughout freshwater wetland complexes of sc. and se. Oregon (OBBA, Gilligan et al. 1994). One of the most common nesting shorebirds at Malheur NWR

(Littlefield 1990a); also common summer resident in extreme e. Oregon (Contreras and Kindschy 1996).

Uncommon to common in winter at lower elevations along the coast and in inland valleys (Gilligan et al. 1994), and can be locally abundant where birds gather to feed in coastal pastures and other wetlands (Contreras 1997b). Very large winter concentrations have been recorded in these areas, giving Oregon the highest CBC numbers of this species on the continent in 1980 and 1983, though these concentrations vary widely from year to year (Paulson 1993). Uncommon to fairly common winter resident throughout interior w. Oregon valleys (Browning 1975a, Heinl and Hunter 1985, Herlyn 1998, Hunter et al. 1998). Uncommon east of the Cascades in winter, and in especially severe cold may not be present at all (Contreras 1997b). Can be found at Malheur NWR in winter where open water remains; accounted for on almost all CBCs (Littlefield 1990a). Also occasional winter resident in extreme e. Oregon (Contreras and Kindschy 1996). Can be found almost anywhere statewide during spring and fall (Gilligan et al. 1994).

**Habitat and Diet:** Nest is a slight depression on ground, lined with grass (Gabrielson and Jewett 1940). Breeding habitat in Oregon generally restricted to wet meadows, marshes of sedge or grass, cattail marsh edges, or riparian bogs (Gilligan et al. 1994, Mueller 1999). Favored locations are swampy areas including expanses of open water interspersed with clumps of shrubs, small trees, and stands of marsh vegetation (e.g., hardhack, red willow, Oregon ash, slough sedge,

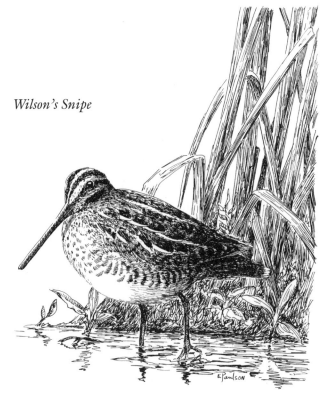

*Wilson's Snipe*

creeping spike-rush, smartweed, and other common marsh plants) (Evenden et al. 1950). In extreme e. Oregon found in wet fields, boggy areas, and grassy lake margins at low to moderate elevations (Contreras and Kindschy 1996). Outside of Oregon, breeding habitat described as areas with soft soil rich in food organisms near surface, with surrounding vegetation in open clumps allowing for good visibility (Mueller 1999). Tend to avoid marshes with tall and/or dense vegetation such as cattails (Mueller 1999).

In winter, drawn to wet or damp fields and marshes and edges of flooded pastures, and single birds may be found in ditches, near small ponds or other small patches of boggy habitat (Contreras 1997b). One bird was seen in winter in a small spring-fed meadow on slopes of Mt. McLoughlin, Jackson Co., at 5,000 ft (1,524 m) elevation (Gabrielson and Jewett 1940). Prefers freshwater habitats, but will use brackish areas (Gilligan et al. 1994).

Besides a few reports of birds feeding on earthworms (Gabrielson and Jewett 1940, Littlefield 1990a), diet not described in much detail for Oregon. Elsewhere reported to consume larval insects, worms, snails, some adult insects, and rarely some small vertebrates (Mueller 1999). Plant materials also appear to be taken, but probably do not contribute much nutrition (Mueller 1999). Feed by probing in mud, and though not often seen in flocks, large numbers may occur loosely associated in prime feeding areas.

**Seasonal Activity and Behavior:** Birds breeding in wetland complexes of sc. and se. Oregon typically begin arriving in Mar (Gilligan et al. 1994). Spring influx at Malheur NWR occurs 20-30 Mar, with pairs on territory by Apr (Littlefield 1990a). Winnowing can be heard Mar-Jul (Littlefield 1990a).

Nest-building observed in the Blue Mtns. on 30 May (OBBA). At Malheur NWR nesting begins in early May and continues into Jul (Littlefield 1990a). Nests with eggs have been found throughout Jun and into early Jul (n=5; OBBA). Fledged young have been seen from late May to early Aug (n=4; OBBA). By mid-Jul presumed fall migrants sometimes observed away from breeding areas (Gilligan et al. 1994). Numbers at Malheur NWR begin declining in Sep, with migrants still seen through Oct (Littlefield 1990a).

In w. Oregon, fall arrivals appear in Aug-Sep and depart Mar-Apr (Herlyn 1998, Hunter et al. 1998)

**Detection:** Camouflaged plumage and stealthy foraging habits can make this bird difficult to detect, especially in nonbreeding seasons. Crepuscular habits and association with marshy, muddy habitat further reduce chances of observation. During spring migration and breeding season birds are more conspicuous, especially given their winnowing displays and habit of perching on posts.

**Population Status and Conservation:** While generally common, relatively little is known about this species. Bent (1927) reported this bird as "formerly exceedingly abundant" in N. America, but states that numbers had been greatly depleted. Recent rangewide population estimates are sketchy, and trends difficult to quantify based on inadequate BBS data (Mueller 1999). Nonetheless, a rangewide decrease has been documented for 1980-95 (Mueller 1999), which correlates with noted significant decline of this species in Oregon over the past two decades (Gilligan et al. 1994). Once listed as common permanent resident of s. Willamette Valley (Gullion 1951), but is not so common in summer anymore (*MGH*). The invasion of valley wetlands by tall, thick stands of reed canarygrass has undoubtedly impacted snipe habitat (*DBM*). For example, reed canarygrass has completely altered plant composition at McFadden Marsh (now part of Finley NWR), where snipe were formerly common.

The Wilson's Snipe is classified as a game species, hunted concurrently with duck seasons, though its current season length of 107 days will likely be maintained even as duck seasons are reduced in the future (B. Bales p.c.). It is estimated that there are 1,100 snipe hunters in Oregon who harvest approximately 3,500 birds annually.—*Rachel White Scheuering*

## Subfamily Phalaropodinae

### Wilson's Phalarope *Phalaropus tricolor*

This is the largest and the most terrestrial of the three species of phalaropes. It shares with its congeners a mating system only rarely seen among birds: females are larger and more brightly colored than males, and they compete for mates, which solely perform incubating and brood-rearing duties. It is similar in shape to other phalaropes, but larger size, longer bill and neck, lack of bar on the wing, and white rump distinguish it from congeners in all plumages. In adaptation to more terrestrial life than other phalaropes, its toes are fringed, not lobed.

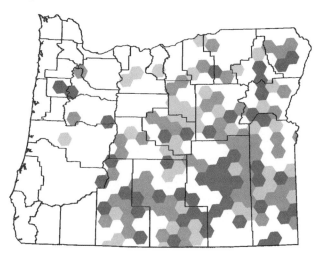

**General Distribution:** Strictly New World, vagrant elsewhere. Breeds mainly in w. N. America, extending east to Manitoba, Nebraska, and Oklahoma, and continuing in a narrow band from Wisconsin to sw. Quebec. Also breeds locally in many scattered locations outside this range from c. and sc. Alaska east to Nova Scotia, and in the south from s. California to Texas. Winters at highly saline lakes in w. and s. S. America. Smaller numbers winter along the coast and inland from Peru and Uruguay to Tierra del Fuego (Jehl 1988). Monotypic (AOU 1957).

**Oregon Distribution:** Common transient and breeder east of the Cascades. Largest numbers breed on the great marshes of se. Oregon (Malheur, Harney, Lake, and Klamath counties). In the Cascades, breeds to at least 5,100 ft (1,700 m), mainly in Deschutes, Douglas (rare), and Klamath counties (Fix 1990a, Gilligan et al. 1994). Local breeder in wet valleys east of the Cascades (e.g., Wallowa Co., Evanich 1992a; valleys in the Blue Mtns., Umatilla Co.).

Historically a rare visitor west of the Cascades, but increasing, with several recent breeding records. In sw. Oregon, bred at Hoovers L., Jackson Co., until 1969 (Browning 1975a), and near Howard Prairie Res. (Janes et al. 2001). In 1990s through 2002, bred in small numbers at Baskett Slough NWR, Polk Co. (Dowlan 1996b), in Ankeny NWR (Tice 1999a, 2000b, Contreras 2002b), and probably in other locations of Linn Co. (Tice 2000a), and at Fern Ridge Res., Lane Co. (Contreras 2002a). Occasionally seen during migration on coastal estuaries and salt marshes (e.g., several spring observations at Coos Bay) (Contreras 1998). Abundant in Basin and Range ecoregion during the fall. There are no documented winter records from the state (Contreras 1997b).

**Habitat and Diet:** Nests are placed in bulrushes or dense grass in wet meadows, croplands, and grazed or idle pastures in vicinity of lakes and ponds, on islands, marshes, sloughs, even at roadside ditches. Utilizes seasonal, semi-permanent and permanent wetlands.

No specific studies regarding diet conducted in Oregon. In other places known to feed on flies, true bugs, and beetles, also on crustaceans and seeds of aquatic plants (Colwell and Jehl 1994). Feeds on the edges of shallow, grassy ponds, swimming in shallow water or walking along the shores; may also feed in deep water and on dry land, less frequently along beaches. On land, gleans insects, their eggs, and crustaceans from the vegetation or mud surface, may hop to catch flying insects, also catches flying insects while swimming (Burger and Howe 1975). When feeding in the water, may take food from the surface or immerse head and neck in water. Often spins, like other phalaropes, to bring otherwise immobile food items close to the surface. Frequency of spinning depends on food availability, and is rarely seen when food abundant (Colwell and Jehl 1994). Also follows other feeding birds (e.g., American Avocets, Northern Shovelers) to feed on items brought by them to the surface (Williams 1953, Siegfried and Batt 1972, Pinkowski 1981a). Rarely scythes in the manner of avocets (Jehl 1988). When competition for food is high, may defend small feeding territories (Howe 1975b).

During migration and on wintering grounds forages on hypersaline lakes, where it feeds on brine shrimp and brine flies. Foraging behavior and diet vary with age, sex, and season (Jehl 1988). Able to feed in hypersaline environments over prolonged periods without attaining elevated levels of sodium concentration (Mahoney and Jehl 1985a).

**Seasonal Activity and Behavior:** Arrives in e. Oregon during late Apr and the first week of May (earliest 2 Apr at Malheur NWR) (Littlefield 1990a), with females greatly outnumbering males in the earliest flocks. Spring movements in recent years in w. Oregon have been similar, with an average arrival in Benton Co. of 10 May (earliest 20 Apr) and most arrival records in the mid-valley and Washington Co. from the middle third of May (Herlyn 1998, Gillson 1999, D. Lusthoff p.c.). The earliest Willamette Valley report is 9 Apr in 1964 (Herlyn 1998). Arrival patterns in the Rogue Valley (where few birds occur) are similar (Browning 1974, Janes et al. 2001).

Neither sex establishes territories; instead females compete among themselves for access to males. Competition among males is sporadic and may occur when the local sex ratio is male-biased (Colwell and Oring 1988). This part of courtship may or may not take place in the direct vicinity of the nesting places (Hohn 1967, Howe 1975b).

When a bond is established, a pair seeks a nesting place. After the general area is chosen, a pair makes several nest scrapes during a highly ritualized sequence of behavior (Hohn 1967). Either sex may prepare a scrape. One or 2 days before onset of laying, a male pulls vegetation from several of the earlier prepared scrapes, which may be located 20-90 ft (7-30 m) apart (Howe 1975a). The decision on which will be used is probably made by the female just before laying. The first egg is usually deposited in the bare scrape, which is lined later by the male. Some males accompany females to the nest, and guard them from a short distance when the egg is being laid. Successive eggs are laid 26 hr apart. Only male incubates; continuous incubation starts after the third egg, intermittent incubation starts earlier, especially during hot days (Howe 1975a). Incubation period averages 23 days (range 18-27 days) (Colwell and Oring 1988). In Oregon, adults on nest observed 31 May to 12 Jul (n=6) (OBBA).

The role of females after completion of the clutch differs among years and locations: some desert immediately, others stay for various periods until hatching and assist their mates in mobbing intruders (Merrill 1888, Johns 1969, Howe 1975a, Murray 1983, Colwell and Oring 1988). The last females are seen close to broods 1 or 2 days after hatching. Some females are possibly prompted to leave by their mates (Howe 1975a). Occasionally females acquire another mate and complete a second clutch with him (four such instances observed over 6 yr) (Colwell and Oring 1988). A female may start courting a new mate within a few hours of completion of her first clutch (Howe 1975a).

Chicks leave the nest within a few hours after hatching (Johns 1969). When several broods occur in close proximity, males may join together in deterring predators. Females, which otherwise pay no attention to the broods, may also join such a ruckus (Johns 1969).

They depart nesting grounds as soon as breeding is completed, gathering in great numbers at several hypersaline lakes in the nw. U.S. (mainly Mono L., California; Great Salt L., Utah; Abert L., Oregon) where they undergo partial molt and acquire fat needed for further migration (Jehl 1987b). After staging for 3-4 wk, adults proceed to S. America over the Pacific, whereas juveniles move more slowly over the w. U.S. Northbound migration follows a different, mainly overland route.

Peak numbers at staging sites occur late Jul and early Aug. L. Abert (Lake Co.) is the major staging area in Oregon and one of the largest in N. America, holding concentrations of up to 70,000 in late Jul (Jehl 1988). Boca and Stinking lakes (Malheur NWR) at times stage 5,000 and 15,000, respectively, and Summer L. (Lake Co.) may support more than 10,000 phalaropes (Littlefield 1990a). Present in Oregon until Sep (latest 22 Sep) (Gabrielson and Jewett 1940).

**Detection:** Easily located when feeding due to active habits. Nesting birds often engage in distraction behavior when an observer nears the nest (Dowlan 1996b). Premigratory concentrations easily seen in Jun and Jul on Great Basin lakes.

**Population Status and Conservation:** Fall population of migrants in 1980s estimated at 1.5 million, based on counts from major staging areas throughout the U.S., but variable (Jehl 1988, 1999). The species may be vulnerable to habitat changes, because virtually whole adult population stages during fall migration in a small number of places.—*Joanna Klima and Joseph R. Jehl, Jr.*

# Red-necked Phalarope *Phalaropus lobatus*

The thick, dense feathering on its underparts allows this dainty shorebird to float high on the water. Its lobed toes give it considerable maneuverability while swimming (Terres 1980). It is equally at home on the roughest seas and the smallest farm pond. A highly sociable bird and extremely trusting. Smaller size and slender bill separate this species from the Wilson's and Red Phalaropes.

**General Distribution:** Almost completely circumpolar, breeding on the subarctic tundra. Winters chiefly on the open ocean in the s. Hemisphere and regularly in small numbers to c. California. N. American populations regularly migrate over the Pacific and Atlantic oceans and through w. N. America, with major staging areas at L. Abert, Oregon; Mono L., California; and Great Salt L., Utah. Lesser numbers migrate through the prairie and eastern states. Monotypic (AOU 1957).

**Oregon Distribution:** Common to abundant migrant along the coast and over the ocean within 31 mi (50 km) of shore. Coastal and w. Oregon sightings fluctuate markedly from year to year, apparently depending on conditions offshore (Wahl 1975, Campbell et al. 1990a, Wahl et. al 1993, Paulson 1993). There is a secondary flyway through c. Oregon that brings large numbers to L. Abert, Lake Co., and to other alkaline lakes (Sullivan PT 1995b, 1998a). Over most of the state small groups of up to 10-12 birds are regularly seen (Gabrielson and Jewett 1940, Paulson 1993). Hundreds often gather on sewage ponds (Kingery 1972a, Fix 1990b, Paulson 1993). Small numbers occasionally remain to summer east of the Cascades (Littlefield 1990a, Spencer 1999).

**Habitat and Diet:** Offshore it concentrates along tide rips and over upwellings. In shallow waters it stirs the bottom with its feet or spins rapidly to expose the tiny organisms that it picks up with its needlelike bill. An opportunistic forager of small animal life; insects, especially flies, and copepod crustaceans are its main source of food (Johnsgard 1981). Its diet while at sea is almost entirely copepods (Briggs et. al 1982). Brown and Harris (1988) found mostly carpenter ants, larvae of cancer crabs, and beetles in 103 individuals checked at Trinidad, Humboldt Co., California 6 May 1969. The primary food source at inland alkaline lakes are brine flies and brine shrimp (Kristensen et al. 1991).

**Seasonal Activity and Behavior:** Early fall migrants begin arriving in late Jun at interior alkaline lakes staging areas (Shuford et al. 1989, Kristensen et al. 1991). They increase through Jul to a peak in Aug and early Sep; most are gone by late Sep with stragglers into

Oct (Sullivan PT 1995b, 1996a, 1998a). Peak number at L. Abert was 43,450 on 27 Aug 1995 (Sullivan 1996a). Up to 5,500 were on the Lakeview sewage ponds, Lake Co., 24 Aug 1972 (Kingery 1972a). A late bird was at Hatfield L., Deschutes Co., 17 Nov 1984 (Summers 1985b).

Fall movements west of the Cascades are inconspicuous and involve mostly small flocks. Early birds begin passing offshore in early Jul, with the main movement occurring from late Jul through Sep, with stragglers to early Nov (Gabrielson and Jewett 1940, Crowell and Nehls 1970a, 1975d, Johnson J 1998a).

Unlike in fall, spring movements are often highly conspicuous along the coast and much less so inland. Main movements east of the Cascades occur during May. Early birds arrive during Apr, and the last leave by mid-Jun (Littlefield 1990a, Nehls 1994). Main coastal movements occur from late Apr to early Jun, with peak numbers during the first week of May. Early birds arrive during Mar, with one at Yaquina Bay 11 Mar 1989 (Heinl 1989b). Peak movements are often spectacular and may continue for several days. Large numbers often occur in the Willamette Valley during these movements. Unusually heavy migrations were noted 8 May 1965 (Hesse and Hesse 1965), and 8-9 May 1976 (Crowell and Nehls 1976c) with many thousands of birds involved.

**Detection:** Almost always at or in the water, even when associated with other species of shorebirds. A swimming shorebird is most likely a phalarope. Offshore, Red-necked are often difficult to separate from Red Phalaropes (Paulson 1993), and at inland alkaline lakes they join Wilson's Phalaropes to make extremely large flocks. Individuals can be picked out by their much smaller size, but estimating the number of each species present is problematic.

**Population Status and Conservation:** The most abundant and most widespread of the phalaropes. It breeds in remote tundra areas and winters at sea where human interference is minimal. Strong storms and high winds often push large numbers shoreward and into the interior, but unlike the Red Phalarope there is little apparent loss of life.—*Harry B. Nehls*

### Red Phalarope *Phalaropus fulicarius*

"Flying low over the water in small flocks or riding the ocean swells like puffs of down … a more incongruous picture can hardly be imagined than these dainty mites riding the waves during rough weather, apparently entirely indifferent to the tumult of the waters" (Gabrielson and Jewett 1940). Pelagic shorebirds, they come to shore only to breed. Adapted to life on the sea, they have glands that allow them to expel salt from the seawater they drink, and lobed, coot-like toes

to swim. Brick red in their breeding plumage, they are mostly gray and white in winter; thus their British name, Grey Phalarope. Even their breeding biology is unusual: females are more brightly colored than males, and after laying eggs the female leaves and males assume all the nest duties and raise the young.

**General Distribution:** Breed mainly above the Arctic Circle in N. America, Europe, and Asia. Migrate through Atlantic and Pacific and along coastlines. Winter at sea primarily in s. Hemisphere in Pacific and Atlantic. Monotypic (AOU 1957).

**Oregon Distribution:** Uncommon to common spring and fall transient, primarily offshore; small numbers regular onshore; irregularly rare to common in winter. Generally found on waters 5.6-373 fm (10-666 m) deep, average 128 fm (228 m) deep on the upper slope (Briggs et al. 1992). This agrees with Wahl (1975), who stated that these birds prefer waters farther offshore in fall. Blown inshore, and occasionally inland nearly annually west of the Cascades, especially during Nov storms. Recorded east of the Cascades 19 times; half the records are from May-Jun and are not storm-related, indicating a small number of birds migrate overland in spring (Tice 1997).

**Habitat and Diet:** Primarily pelagic; on coastal ponds or inland sewage ponds after fall storms; very rare on large inland lakes during spring migration. On the ocean prefer the cooler edge of waters having high surface gradients such as in or near recent upwellings. "Often occurred at visible surface features [such as] natural slicks and color boundaries" (Briggs et al. 1992). At sea diet changes from insects to larval fishes, crustaceans, and small jellyfish (Johnsgard 1981).

**Seasonal Activity and Behavior:** Migrate offshore from late Apr to early Jun (earliest 14 Apr) and mid-Jul-Dec. Paulson (1993) notes migration peaks for the Pacific Northwest in mid-May, Aug-Sep (adults), and late Oct to early Nov (juveniles); agreeing with Wahl's (1975) migration timing for Washington. Gilligan et al. (1994) provide slightly different timing, with spring migration in Oregon extending from mid-Apr to late Jun; odd records in every week of Jun and Jul; fall adult migration beginning in late Jul; juveniles arriving in late Aug with peak numbers from late Sep to mid-Dec. In general, prefer deeper waters and migrate 1 mo later during spring and fall than Red-necked Phalaropes (Briggs et al. 1992). High count 15,000 at Cape Arago 25 Nov 1990 (Fix 1991). May occasionally winter offshore Jan-Mar; thousands blown to shore in Oregon and Washington after a storm 18 Jan 1986 (Paulson 1993).

Gregarious, they fly in loose flocks or lines rather than the bunched flocking behavior and generally larger flock size of Red-necked Phalaropes (Paulson 1993). Persistent swimmers; Reds often turn in tight circles while foraging (Johnsgard 1981). Spinning draws up tiny invertebrates that are picked from the surface or just under the water (Paulson 1993). Fully two-thirds of phalaropes spin to the right. They also zigzag with head bobbing action, upend, and sometimes dive (Lockley 1974). Buoyant, they float cork-like on the ocean swells. Sometimes feed in association with whales (Mayfield 1984). Call note is a musical, metallic *pit* (Paulson 1993).

**Detection:** Hit and miss during migration from boats at sea. On 16 1-day pelagic trips Jul-Oct 1994-98 recorded on 31% of trips; average number of birds 24; maximum 300 (*GG*). During or immediately after late fall storms with strong west or southwest winds check estuaries, tidal or rain puddles behind jetties and foredunes, and sewage ponds. Small numbers may be found along the coast even during apparently normal weather conditions (Gilligan et al. 1994). Fall juveniles and nonbreeding adults may be confused with Red-necked Phalaropes at sea (Gilligan and Schmidt 1980); thus, many phalaropes at sea go unidentified as to species (Briggs et al. 1992).

**Population Status and Conservation:** No population estimates have been made, but one of the most common breeding shorebirds in the high Arctic (Johnsgard 1981).

Severe late fall and early winter storms, with winds of 70-100 mph (113-161 km/h) sometimes cause thousands of phalaropes to be blown inland to the Willamette Valley and even the Cascades (Fix 1990a). Many birds die, but others are found on any odd body of water for several days following such a storm (Mayfield 1984, Paulson 1993).—*Greg Gillson*

## Family Laridae

### Subfamily Stercorariinae

**South Polar Skua** *Stercorarius maccormicki*
Fierce and powerful, with a commanding presence, a skua comes in low, targets a shearwater, forces it to disgorge, then streaks away with a meal. Skuas are the size of Western Gulls, dark with a pale nape and large white patches on the bases of the primaries on both the upper and lower surfaces. Polymorphic, there is a continuous cline in body color which may be grouped into light, intermediate, or blackish types.

**General Distribution:** Breed in Antarctica, primarily in three locations along the Pacific, Atlantic, and Indian oceans; eggs laid Nov-Dec (Harrison 1983). Range widely in nonbreeding season through all southern

oceans. Also migrate to Greenland and nw. Atlantic, and appear to migrate clockwise around the Pacific north as far as Alaska (Olsen and Larsson 1997). *Catharacta*, formerly used with this species (AOU 1998), and *Stercorarius* are synonyms (AOU 2000). Monotypic (Furness 1987).

**Oregon Distribution:** Rare to uncommon fall transient offshore, primarily over the continental slope. In 48 at-sea observations where distance was recorded, sightings ranged from 10 to 65 mi (18-115 km) offshore; median 38 mi (67.3 km) (*GG*). This is farther offshore than most chartered boat trips reach. Six sightings from shore, mostly in Sep.

**Habitat and Diet:** Pelagic. Furness (1987) showed that skuas in the Pacific follow the movements of a surface fish, Pacific saury, north in spring in the w. Pacific, south in fall in the e. Pacific, in water with a preferred temperature of 59-64° F (15-17.8° C) (McCrae 1994), which is a typical fall temperature 20 mi (35 km) or more from Oregon's shores. Olsen and Larsson (1997) report that these skuas feed mainly on fish by shallow plunge-dives. Plunge-diving is apparently unknown in the ne. Pacific (J. Danzenbaker p.c., T. R. Wahl p.c., *GG*). Rather, they attack shearwaters, forcing them to regurgitate food (*GG*).

**Seasonal Activity and Behavior:** Skuas arrive in late Jun (earliest 1 Jun), present in low numbers from late Jul-Aug, peak from 8 Sep-9 Oct (latest 18 Oct), three records from Dec (one beached alive), one from Apr. This pattern matches records in California and Washington (Wahl 1975, Stallcup 1990, Olsen and Larsson 1997). Record numbers in any 1 day: eight on 5 Oct 1996 (Gilligan 1997), seven on 30 Sep 1978 (Hunn and Mattocks 1979a), four on 29 Sep 1979 (Watson 1981c), and four on 12 Sep 1998 (*GG*), all off the c. coast.

Solitary. Flight low and direct with heavy flapping and little gliding; gull-like. Steal food from other seabirds; aggressive, bordering on predatory: "May grab a shearwater's head, wing, or tail and shake and kick the bird until it vomits. We have seen skuas land on a sitting shearwater's back and push it under water again and again" (Stallcup 1990). A prolonged attack of this sort was directed against a Pink-footed Shearwater about 18 mi (32 km) off Garibaldi on 21 Sep 1996 (*GG*). Pink-footed Shearwaters seem to be a preferred target in n. California as well (J. Danzenbaker p.c.), perhaps because they are large and slow. More often, though, skuas are seen flying steadily by, seemingly in a hurry to be elsewhere.

**Detection:** Chances of detection are best around flocks of shearwaters feeding behind fishing boats (Wahl 1975). On 16 1-day pelagic trips Jul-Oct 1994-98 recorded on 38% of trips (60% of trips from 20 Aug-18 Oct); average number of birds 1.1; maximum 8 (*GG*). Sometimes dark phase Pomarine Jaegers are misidentified as skuas. Also, immature dark morph Parasitic Jaegers can show large white wing patches and may cause confusion. Onshore reports of skuas should be well documented to eliminate the possibility of misidentified jaegers.

**Population Status and Conservation:** 5,000-10,000 pairs breed around Antarctica (Olsen and Larsson 1997). First detected in Oregon on 27 Jun 1972 about 65 mi (115 km) off Yaquina Head (Crowell and Nehls 1972d); about 79 records of 125 birds through 1998 (*GG*). Detected every year since 1974 (except 1983). While 80-87% of adult birds in Antarctica are pale or intermediate colored (Olsen and Larsson 1997), the majority of birds seen off the w. coast are dark (Stallcup 1990). These may be immatures as some have assumed, but more observations are needed to clarify this. Skua taxonomy is in flux, and identification and migration routes are still being determined. The possibility certainly exists that some of these dark birds might be something other than South Polar Skuas (Hunter and Gillson 1997). Interestingly, a wash-up on a Coos Co. beach on 9 Jul 1980 had been banded 22 Feb 1980 in Antarctica on the Indian Ocean, rather than on the Pacific (Contreras 1998). In California lower numbers are seen during fall in warm-water years (Ainley 1976).

Even though skuas are top predators, there is no direct evidence of serious effects from pollutants. Some young are preyed upon by Subantarctic Skua, a subspecies of Brown Skua (Olsen and Larsson 1997).—*Greg Gillson*

## Pomarine Jaeger *Stercorarius pomarinus*

These, the most numerous jaegers off Oregon, are slightly smaller than Herring Gulls. Gull-like and graceful, these piratical birds steal food from smaller seabirds. Polymorphic, they come in a bewildering array of light and dark individuals, confounded by age and sexual differences. The adult light morph bird has a black cap, yellow cheeks and collar, and white underparts with a wide dark band across the chest. Wings are wide and pointed, with a large white flash on the bases of the underwing primaries. Breeding adults have a pair of elongated central tail feathers which are twisted with rounded ends, projecting 6-7 in (15.2-17.8 cm) past the rest of the tail. Juveniles are barred and take 4 yr to attain adult plumage. Immatures maintain barring on underwing coverts until adulthood. Juveniles and winter adults lack the long central tail feathers, but immatures may have intermediate-length central tail feathers.

**General Distribution:** Breed on coastal Arctic tundra; nearly circumpolar except for lemming-free areas of Greenland and Murman Peninsula in n. Russia. Winter widely at sea along coasts, most near or north of the equator: California to Chile, se. U.S. and Caribbean, Great Britain south including all of African coast, Red Sea, Persian Gulf, coasts of se. Asia, around Australia and New Zealand, and Hawaii (Olsen and Larsson 1997). Monotypic (AOU 1957).

**Oregon Distribution:** Uncommon spring and fairly common fall transient offshore 2-50 mi (3.5-89 km), following shearwaters (Stallcup 1990). Sightings centered near the continental shelf edge (Briggs et al. 1992). More than 90% are seen >5.6 mi (>10 km) from shore (Wahl 1975). Occasionally observed from shore in fall. Five inland records: two on 10 Nov 1975 at Fern Ridge Res. (Crowell and Nehls 1976a); one adult dark-morph photographed at Summer L., Lake Co., during a fall in the 1980s (*MGH*); one each on 2 Sep 1985 (Gilligan 1994) and 28 Sep 1997 (Sullivan 1998a) at McNary Dam; and one found alive that later died 28-30 Jun 1999 at Halfway, Baker Co. (Hammar 2000). Rare winter visitor.

**Habitat and Diet:** Pelagic. No particular ocean conditions off Oregon are preferred, rather they occur at feeding concentrations of other seabirds. They feed nearly exclusively (97%) on lemmings on Arctic breeding grounds; otherwise scavenge fish or kleptoparasitize birds, kill weakened seabirds. Red-necked Phalaropes may be main food in winter off S. America (Olsen and Larsson 1997).

**Seasonal Activity and Behavior:** Spring migration begins in Mar, uncommon to May; rare Jun; return migration begins in Jul, peak Aug-Sep, common through Oct; rare Nov-Feb. An astounding 750 were observed on a full-day cruise 50 miles off the Oregon coast 17 Sep 2000 (J. Gilligan p.c.). Other high numbers include 50-200 daily 25-27 Jul 1989 (T. Thompson unpubl. data), 80-100 on 29 Jul 1975 (Crowell and Nehls 1975d), and 31 on 30 Sep 1978 (Hunn and Mattocks 1979a). An amazingly high number so late in the season was 15 seen from Cape Arago after a storm on 25 Nov 1990 (Fix 1991).

Usually solitary; attracted to feeding flocks of shearwaters and other seabirds. Often parasitize Sabine's Gulls (Briggs et al. 1992). Flight steady and gull-like with little gliding except in high winds (Olsen and Larsson 1997). Fly high while searching for food and during migration (Stallcup 1990). Piratical attacks against seabirds are direct and aggressive, often directed at the bird rather than the food they carry. May kill birds up to the size of kittiwakes. May utter sharp calls when attending trawlers (Olsen and Larsson 1997); vocalizations are unreported from Oregon.

**Detection:** This is the most frequently encountered jaeger at sea beyond 10 mi (18 km) from shore. Attracted to flocks of seabirds behind fishing vessels. The most reliable way to find these birds is to attract large numbers of gulls and seabirds to the boat with chum, then wait for the jaegers to appear. On 16 1-day pelagic trips Jul-Oct 1994-98, they were recorded on 75% of trips; average number of birds 5.9; maximum 22 (*GG*). Easily confused with Parasitic Jaeger. Identification of many immature birds can be difficult at sea. Many jaegers go unidentified as to species because of distant, poor, or brief views. Larger dark-morph birds with missing tail streamers may be mistaken for South Polar Skuas.

**Population Status and Conservation:** Total breeding population unknown. Breeding density directly correlated to density of lemmings (Olsen and Larsson 1997). Because of widespread and remote breeding and wintering sites, no jaegers are threatened with conservation problems (Maher 1984).—*Greg Gillson*

## Parasitic Jaeger *Stercorarius parasiticus*

The "sea falcons" are strong, fast fliers with a flash of white on the bases of the underwing primaries. They follow migrating Arctic Terns from which they pirate food in swift aerobatic attacks. Polymorphic; northern breeding populations are 90% dark morph, southern populations (including s. Alaska) 50% dark morph (Olsen and Larsson 1997). The size of Mew Gulls, adult light-morph birds are brown above with yellow cheeks and dark caps, have white underparts, and have a narrow pale breast band, if any. Dark-morph birds can be completely sooty colored. Adults have a pair of elongated, sharply pointed tail feathers, extending 2-3 in (51-76 mm) beyond the rest of the tail. Immatures are strongly barred below and on the underwing, and take several years to attain adult plumage.

**General Distribution:** Circumpolar; breed in the Arctic and along shores of the Baltic Sea (Olsen and Larsson 1997). Winter at sea along both coasts of s. S. America, w. and s.coasts of Africa, Persian Gulf, s. and e. coasts of Australia, New Zealand. Rare in winter north to California (Olsen and Larsson 1997). Monotypic (AOU 1957).

**Oregon Distribution:** Uncommon fall and rare spring transient offshore. Most within 14 mi (25 km) of coast (Briggs et al. 1992). In California most 1-2 mi (1.8-3.5 km) offshore (Stallcup 1990). Rare fall migrant inland—at least 22 records (some of multiple birds), 10 at lakes of Harney Co. and four at Fern Ridge Res., Lane Co. (Tice 1997).

**Habitat and Diet:** Breeding habitat tundra where food consists primarily of birds, but will eat all available invertebrates, berries, rodents, and fish. Pelagic during migration and in winter, most near shore. Obtain fish primarily by kleptoparasitism of terns and small gulls (Olsen and Larsson 1997). Occasionally may make a pass at shorebirds over bays and beaches, then return directly to sea.

**Seasonal Activity and Behavior:** Rare spring migrant Mar-Jun. Fall migration begins in Jul, peaks in Sep when common, corresponding to migration of Arctic Terns. Rare Nov-Dec, absent Jan-Feb. A few reported on CBCs in late Dec, but similar Pomarine Jaeger more likely then. High number on Oregon pelagic trip was 40 on 20 Sep 1980 (Hunn and Mattocks 1981a). Regularly viewed from shore in fall, however largest number, 10 from Bandon on 1 Jun 1980, were apparently very late spring migrants (Watson 1980b). Inland fall migrants range from 5 Jul-18 Oct (Tice 1997).

Flight low and unlabored; falcon-like wing-beats alternate with shearwater-like glides. Chase terns and small gulls for up to several minutes until they disgorge food. Start with low flight, culminate in a sudden rising assault, with spectacular abrupt turns and dives (Olsen and Larsson 1997). Normally silent away from breeding grounds. Less prone to following trawlers than other jaegers (Olsen and Larsson 1997). Fix (1983) noted three jaegers in fall at the s. jetty of the Columbia R. soar up in a thermal over the dunes to about 1,500 ft high (464 m) and disappear inland.

**Detection:** This is the most frequently seen jaeger from shore (Stallcup 1990) and sometimes enters estuaries. Best chance for detection is in Sep, within 3 mi (5.3 km) of shore. Also, watch for them to come in from sea and pass over beaches where shorebirds have gathered. Frequently seen from the s. jetty of the Columbia R. On 16 1-day pelagic trips Jul-Oct 1994-98 recorded on 56% of trips; average number of birds 0.8; maximum three (*GG*). Easily confused with both Long-tailed and Pomarine Jaegers.

**Population Status and Conservation:** Several hundred thousand pairs breed circumpolar. Combined Alaska and Canada subpopulation is estimated at 200,000 (Olsen and Larsson 1997). No conservation problems have been identified on breeding or wintering grounds (Maher 1984).—*Greg Gillson*

## Long-tailed Jaeger *Stercorarius longicaudus*

Graceful and buoyant fliers, adults are light gray-brown above with black caps, have dark flight feathers contrasting with grayer mantles and light underparts. Breeding adults have central pair of tail feathers extremely long and pointed, extending up to 8 in (20.3 cm) past the rest of the tail. Immatures lack the long central tail feathers, are barred on the underparts and underwings, and take several years to attain adult plumage. Not usually as aggressive as other jaegers; rely as much on food they pick from the ocean's surface as they do from food they steal from other small seabirds.

**General Distribution:** Breed in Arctic. Circumpolar. Migrate south across Atlantic and Pacific; occasionally in Mediterranean Sea; occasionally inland in N. America. Winter in Atlantic from 40° N to 50° S, in Pacific from 10° S to 50° S off S. America. Northward spring migration farther offshore than in fall. Once split into two subspecies, *S. l. pallescens* with pale belly most prevalent type seen off Oregon. Complete overlap of measurements; now considered monotypic with a cline from dark- to light-bellied birds (AOU 1957, Harrison 1983, Olsen and Larsson 1997).

**Oregon Distribution:** Rare to fairly common fall transient and rare spring (seven records) transient far offshore—the most pelagic of jaegers (Olsen and Larsson 1997). Found at an average water depth of 162 fm (289 m) in Aug 1989 (Briggs et al. 1992). In 68 at-sea observations where distance was recorded, sightings ranged from 12 to 140 mi (21-248 km) offshore; median 36.5 mi (64.6 km) (*GG*). Sixteen sightings from shore. Ten records of inland fall migrants, with most records east of the Cascades (Tice 1997). One specimen from 25 mi (40 km) south-southwest of Burns, Harney Co., 14 Aug 1976 (Grayson and Maser 1978).

**Habitat and Diet:** Pelagic. Well offshore over warm water. Outside breeding season feed primarily on fish by kleptoparisitism or scavenging from surface (Olsen and Larsson 1997). In breeding areas primarily eat rodents; also insects, passerines, and berries.

**Seasonal Activity and Behavior:** Spring migration dates range 19 Apr-27 May with main movement in mid-May. Fall migration dates extend 7 Jul-6 Nov with peak numbers occurring during a 4-wk period centered in late Aug. As in California, absent Dec-Mar (Stallcup 1990). Astonishing were 925 observed on a full-day cruise 50 miles off the Oregon coast 17 Sep 2000 (J. Gilligan p.c.). Other high numbers include 62 on 20 Aug 1987 about 37 mi (65 km) off Lincoln Co. (Sullivan 1988), 62 on 12 May 1997 about 140 mi (248 km) off s. Oregon (Lillie 1997), and 125 on 25 Aug 2001 about 32 mi (56 km) off Newport (Contreras 2002b). Inland fall records range 21 Jul-19 Sep but most records occur 14 Aug-6 Sep, corresponding to peak abundance offshore (Tice 1997).

Parasitize Arctic Terns and Sabine's Gulls (Stallcup 1990) with brief attacks; also hover and pick food from surface (Olsen and Larsson 1997). Flight high, graceful, tern-like (Stallcup 1990); buoyant, body moves up and down in time with wing-beats; often shearwater-like flight without flapping (Olsen and Larsson 1997). In-flight shrug-preen (also common to other jaegers): "[rises] to about 50 feet [(15 m)] above the water, stops flapping, and shudders its body from front to back, shuffling each feather … back to its proper position" (Stallcup 1990). Sometimes migrate in large, well-ordered flocks (Olsen and Larsson 1997).

**Detection:** Best chance of detection mid-late Aug or early Sep at least 25 mi (44 km) from shore. Usually detected when Arctic Terns and/or Sabine's Gulls are in high numbers. Sabine's Gulls are only moderately interested in chum and terns not at all, but chumming may sometimes bring jaegers in to look over a concentration of feeding birds. On 16 1-day pelagic trips Jul-Oct 1994-98 recorded on 44% of trips (71% of trips 10 Aug-12 Sep); average number of birds 1.8; maximum 13 (*GG*). Separating some immature Long-tailed and Parasitic jaegers can be difficult.

**Population Status and Conservation:** There are tens of thousands of breeding pairs in Alaska (Olsen and Larsson 1997). The first two Oregon records washed ashore in Sep 1940 in Lincoln Co. (Jewett 1942); at least 122 records of 987 birds through 1998 (*GG*). Detected nearly every year since 1972 (but apparently not 1973, 1979, or 1993). No conservation problems due to widespread breeding and wintering range in areas remote from human disturbance (Maher 1984).—*Greg Gillson*

## Subfamily Larinae

### Laughing Gull *Larus atricilla*

This mostly coastal gull breeds along the Atlantic coast, the Caribbean and n. S. America, and from Mexico south on the Pacific coast. Postbreeding dispersals bring many to Salton Sea, s. coastal California, and casually to the n. California coast from mid-Apr to Nov (Small 1994). There are two accepted Oregon records: an alternate-plumaged bird photographed 24 Apr 1983 at the Lower Klamath NWR, Klamath Co. (OBRC), and a basic-plumaged adult photographed at Bay City, Tillamook Co., that remained for much of Oct 1998 (OBRC). A report of a subadult near the mouth of the Columbia R. 31 Jul 1999 was submitted to the OBRC. Monotypic (AOU 1957)—*Harry B. Nehls*

## Franklin's Gull *Larus pipixcan*

The nasal meow of the Franklin's Gull can be heard as it soars above wetlands and meadows, and colonies of this species are reported to be the loudest of all the gulls. In breeding plumage, the black hood contrasts sharply with white breast and bright red bill. This species depends much more on insects and other invertebrates than do other gulls, and is therefore considered economically beneficial and favored by farmers. The size of the salt gland varies to adapt to its habitat; enlarged upon arrival on breeding grounds, its size decreases, then grows for migration to coastal wintering sites (Burger and Gochfeld 1994).

**General Distribution:** Nests in interior N. America, primarily in Alberta, Saskatchewan, Manitoba, and northern states directly below these provinces, and locally as far south as Utah and Nevada (Burger and Gochfeld 1994); Oregon is on the western edge of its range (Littlefield and Thompson 1981). Winters on w. coast of S. America, primarily from Peru to Chile, also s. California, sc. U.S., M. America, Galapagos Is., and other S. America locations (Burger and Gochfeld 1994). Monotypic (AOU 1957).

**Oregon Distribution:** Recorded in the southeast portion of the state in spring and summer, especially Harney Basin, rare west of the Cascades (Evanich 1990, Gilligan et al. 1994, OBBA). Nests locally in most years only at Malheur NWR (breeding specimens, Jewett 1949) and Hart Mtn. N. Antelope R. (Burger and Gochfeld 1994), abundantly at the former and in small numbers at the latter. Rare in Klamath Basin May-Aug

*Franklin's Gull*

(Summers 1993a). In fall, may be found throughout e. Oregon; rare but regular on coast and in interior valleys where also rare in winter and spring (Evanich 1990, Gilligan et al. 1994, Marshall et al. 1996).

**Habitat and Diet:** Only gull to nest exclusively in marshes (Burger 1973). Requires large area with emergents and deep water to prevent drying and predator access (Burger and Gochfeld 1994). At Malheur NWR, nests in bulrush but avoids areas of dense vegetation (Littlefield and Thompson 1981), also uses burreed (*GLI*). Nests are nearest to water's surface of seven colonial species (Cornely et al. 1993). Has nested with White-faced Ibises, Snowy Egrets, and Black-crowned Night-Herons at Malheur NWR, with Great Egrets at Hart Mtn. N. Antelope R., and with Forster's Terns at California portion of Lower Klamath NWR (Burger and Gochfeld 1994). The number of nests at Malheur NWR averages significantly higher during wet years and correlates strongly with the level of Malheur L. (Ivey, Cornely, Paullin, and Thompson unpubl. ms.).

Feeds in marshes, irrigated hay meadows, and grass and forb habitats (Puchy and Marshall 1993). Most food is insects caught in flight (Littlefield 1990a), but also eats earthworms, grubs, mice, and fish (Burger and Gochfeld 1994). Birds nesting at Malheur NWR feed in nearby meadows primarily on invertebrates, and in uplands and plowed fields on grasshoppers (Littlefield and Thompson 1981). Birds found in w. Oregon are typically on beaches or lakeshores with other gulls (D. Fix p.c., S. Heinl p.c.).

**Seasonal Activity and Behavior:** Average arrival date at Malheur NWR is 13 Apr, with earliest record nearly a month earlier (Ivey, Herziger, and Scheuering 1998). Colonial nester, beginning early Jun (Littlefield and Thompson 1981). Competition with American Coots may be a problem, as in other states they intensely fight for nest sites, often causing Franklin's Gulls to abandon nests when coots persistently attack (Burger 1973). Nests sink as vegetation decays, so material is constantly added by adults and even older chicks (Burger and Gochfeld 1994). Vegetation frequently gathered by adults stealing from other nests, which may cause eggs or young chicks in those nests to roll out. Chicks remain on nest in undisturbed colonies; where disturbance causes young to leave a nest, adults will coax or grab them and drag them back to it (Burger and Gochfeld 1994). Young fledge in Jul and early Aug at Malheur NWR, with most departed by Sep (Littlefield 1990a). Because only small numbers of Franklin's Gulls winter in s. California, it is likely that most Oregon birds travel to the primary wintering grounds in S. America. The only other gull to migrate south of the equator is Sabine's (Burger and Gochfeld 1994).

**Detection:** These birds may best be located by listening for their calls above Malheur L. in spring, or watching for birds flying over nearby meadows feeding on the wing. After the breeding season, they may be found in a more dispersed area in e. Oregon, sometimes following plows or hay swathers.

**Population Status and Conservation:** Historically, threatened by habitat loss nationwide due to large-scale drainage projects and major droughts, but has regained numbers in recent years with creation of large wetlands (Burger and Gochfeld 1994). However, colony sites continue to shift depending on drought or fluctuating water levels. Birds will abandon nesting sites if disturbed (Burger and Gochfeld 1994). BBS data not appropriate for this species since it nests in remote marshes with few routes nearby, and birds counted on this survey are failed breeders away from colonies, not breeding populations (Burger and Gochfeld 1994).

Franklin's Gulls were unknown in the Great Basin in the 19th century (Burger and Gochfeld 1994). They were first recorded in Oregon in 1943 at Malheur NWR, with first documented nesting in 1947 (Jewett 1949, see also Littlefield and Thompson 1981); not at California portion of Lower Klamath NWR until 1990 (Burger and Gochfeld 1994). Unlike other colonial species at Malheur L., flooding conditions decreased pair numbers (Ivey and Littlefield 1986), possibly linked to carp population. During years with plentiful carp, the number of nesting birds diminishes as little food is available—these fish muddy the water, reduce water quality, and therefore reduce aquatic invertebrates (Littlefield and Thompson 1981). Peak numbers recorded at Malheur L. in 1997 with 4,500 nests; in 1998 there were 1,850, but all failed due to flooding. Malheur NWR data indicate a significant increasing trend (Ivey, Cornely, Paullin, and Thompson unpubl. ms.). Other threats include pesticides (Cornely et al. 1993). Listed as a Sensitive Species by ODFW (1997) because of limited distribution and threat of drought (Puchy and Marshall 1993).—*Caroline Herziger and Gary L. Ivey*

## Little Gull *Larus minutus*

This small gull with dark underwings breeds across n. Eurasia and sparingly in e. Canada. It winters south of its breeding range and is a rare migrant and winter visitant along the w. coast of N. America; Oregon has 7-8 records. One was at Tillamook Bay, Tillamook Co., 4 Nov 1975 (OBRC); one was photographed at Yaquina Bay, Lincoln Co., 20 Aug to early Oct 1979 (Roberson 1980, Watson 1989); one photographed at Tillamook Bay 10 Oct 1981 (OBRC); one photographed at Yaquina Bay 13-25 Oct 1981 (OBRC); it or another was there 15 Dec 1981 (OBRC). A juvenile was at John Day Dam on the Columbia R., Sherman Co.,

21-28 Nov 1989 (Anderson DA 1990a). An adult was photographed at Summer L., Lake Co., 7-27 Sep 1998 (OBRC, Sullivan 1999a); one was there 18-27 Sep 1999 (Sullivan 2000a), and one was there 30 Apr 2000 (Sullivan 2000b). A subadult was on the n. spit of Coos Bay, Coos Co., 7 Jul 1999 (Tice 2000a), and one was at the s. jetty of the Columbia R. 23 Sep 2000 (Korpi 2001a). Monotypic (AOU 1957).—*Harry B. Nehls*

## Black-headed Gull *Larus ridibundus*

The Black-headed Gull breeds across n. Eurasia and occasionally in e. Canada. It winters south of its breeding range and is a rare migrant and winter visitant along the w. coast of N. America. An adult was near Warrenton, Clatsop Co., 20 Dec 1981 (OBRC) and an immature was photographed at the Bay City sewage ponds, Tillamook Co., 3-19 Dec 1992 (OBRC). An adult was near Grass Valley, Sherman Co., 19 Oct 1996 (Sullivan 1997a). The subspecies occurring in Oregon is unknown.—*Harry B. Nehls*

## Bonaparte's Gull *Larus philadelphia*

Graceful and tern-like in many of its actions, this striking little gull displays flashing white outer primaries that contrast with a gray back. The black head turns white in winter showing a dark ear patch. A small black bill separates this species from other gulls with similar plumage. Unlike other gulls, it regularly nests in trees, placing the scanty stick nest in the open on the outer branches.

**General Distribution:** Breeds in taiga regions of Alaska, across Canada to s. James Bay and south to c. British Columbia, Wisconsin, and Quebec. Winters from British Columbia, the Great Lakes, and Massachusetts south to Mexico and the Caribbean. Abundant in winter in n. Puget Sound and s. coastal British Columbia; rare to uncommon elsewhere in the Northwest. Monotypic (AOU 1957).

**Oregon Distribution:** Abundant spring and fall transient along the coast, primarily over the ocean just offshore. Fairly common and widespread transient elsewhere in Oregon, usually in flocks of less than 100 (Summers 1986a, Fix 1991). Larger flocks of up to 1,000 have occurred at Fern Ridge Res., Lane Co., during extreme storm conditions (Crowell and Nehls 1976b); in the Klamath Basin (Rogers TH 1979a, Summers 1986a); and occasionally about coastal estuaries (Crowell and Nehls 1976a, Contreras 1998). The number of individuals occurring away from the coast varies considerably each year, probably owing in significant part to weather patterns, and their movements are often unpredictable. Rare but regular in summer (Littlefield 1990a, Sullivan 1997c). Irregular in winter along the coast (small numbers present in most years), and rare in the Willamette Valley (Contreras 1998, CBC).

**Habitat and Diet:** Flocks are most often observed flying swallow-like over the ocean or over inland waters gleaning flying insects and daintily picking food from the surface of the water (Gabrielson and Lincoln 1959). Primary food is insects, with crustaceans and other aquatic animals regularly taken (Bent 1921, Gabrielson and Jewett 1940, Jewett et al. 1953).

Often observed picking food from the surface of coastal tidal flats, at inland shore edges, and occasionally on wet meadows or farm fields. Small numbers regularly gather over outflows of Columbia R. dams during Nov and early Dec, picking food from the surface of the disturbed waters (Summers 1993b, Sullivan 1996a, 1998a). Most at Malheur NWR occur on or near Stinking and Harney lakes, where crustaceans probably constitute a large percentage of the food items consumed (Littlefield 1990a). Inexplicably, apparently does not occur in numbers at food-rich L. Abert, Lake Co. (Kristensen et al. 1991, *HBN*).

Four birds collected in May at Tillamook Bay, contained the small isopod *Exosphaeroma oregonensis*; a Nov bird on Netarts Bay, Tillamook Co., contained bits of fish and an aquatic beetle (Gabrielson and Jewett 1940). It is a serious predator on downstream migrant hatchery-released salmon fry in British Columbia (Mace 1983), but this is apparently not a problem in Oregon.

**Seasonal Activity and Behavior:** The spring migration is rapid and often spectacular. Early birds arrive during the later half of Mar with the main movement occurring during Apr and continuing to mid-May; the numbers drop rapidly to straggling flocks which continue to mid-Jun (Gabrielson and Jewett 1940, Littlefield 1990a, Lillie 1998). Weather often pushes the offshore movement shoreward. Thousands were along the Curry Co. coast 23 Apr 1966 (Crowell and Nehls 1966b); an estimated 100 birds/hr were passing the s. jetty of the Columbia R. 27 Apr 1974 (Crowell and Nehls 1974b); on 8 May 1976 an estimated 200 birds/ hr were passing along the Tillamook Co. coast (Crowell and Nehls 1976c). Inland records during the spring are plentiful but seldom involve large numbers.

A few nonbreeding individuals and small groups, almost all subadults, remain to summer and might be found anywhere in the state (Littlefield 1990a, Crowell and Nehls 1966b, Sullivan 1997c). Up to 100 are often found at selected coastal spots (Crowell and Nehls 1976d, Contreras 1998). About 270 remained about the mouth of the Columbia R. during the summer of 1978 (Harrington-Tweit et al. 1978).

Early birds from the north begin to arrive in Jul with a general movement by early Aug, which includes brown juveniles (Gabrielson and Jewett 1940, Jewett et al. 1953, Crowell and Nehls 1974c, *HBN*). Peak numbers occur from late Oct through Nov with most gone by mid-Dec (Crowell and Nehls 1976a, Summers 1993b, Tyler et al. 1993). Six at the Umatilla R. mouth, Umatilla Co., 23 Dec 1999 (Korpi 2000) are the latest migrants reported.

**Detection:** Conspicuous and easily identified; most often observed in flight. They seldom flock with other gulls but remain in separate groups nearby.

**Population Status and Conservation:** World population estimated at 85,000-175,000 pairs (Enticott and Tipling 1997). They nest in remote and often inaccessible areas. No conservation problems known at this time in Oregon or elsewhere.—*Harry B. Nehls*

## Heermann's Gull *Larus heermanni*

Heermann's Gulls, the warm-water gulls of summer and fall, accompany Brown Pelicans as they fly north each summer. Seeming to reverse the southward fall movement characteristic of many gulls, they disperse northward to the Pacific Northwest coast following spring breeding in southern waters. The species was named for Adolphus Heermann, a doctor and U.S. Army officer who collected it on the Pacific Railway Survey. It is the only N. American gull species that as an adult is uniformly gray below. Black-tipped red bills, white heads, black tails terminally banded with white, and white-tipped black flight feathers define breeding adults. Younger birds are sooty brown. In flight, all ages of this dark gull may suggest a jaeger at first glance because of their size, strong wing-beats, dark color and occasional pale area in the primaries. Also, their habit of coursing low and fast through the wave-troughs and occasionally pursuing other gulls tends to deceive observers.

**General Distribution:** Breed mainly on Isla Raza in the Gulf of California; smaller numbers breed on other islands in the Gulf of California and locally off Baja California (Cogswell 1977). They also bred once on Alcatraz I., San Francisco Bay, California (Harrison 1985). Although a few spread southward (Cogswell 1977), most postbreeding birds move north in mid-summer, some as far as Vancouver I., British Columbia (Cogswell 1977, Drury 1984), rarely to s.e Alaska. Several juveniles observed 26 Aug to 30 Sep 1992 at the Columbia R. s. jetty were banded during the 1992 breeding season at Isla Raza (H. Nehls p.c.). In fall, they move south again, until by late Nov few are found north of Pt. Conception, California (Drury

1984). Heermann's Gulls winter along the Pacific coast typically from c. California to Guatemala (Cogswell 1977). Monotypic (AOU 1957).

**Oregon Distribution:** Heermann's Gulls are locally common on outer seacoasts, beaches, bays, and estuaries. They are strongly associated with outer coasts and adjacent ocean waters (Cogswell 1977), mostly within a few miles of shore (Drury 1984, Briggs et al. 1987, 1992). A few wander inland during the fall southward retreat. Twelve inland records are from west of the Cascades, including one record of six at Ford's Pond west of Sutherlin on 14 Nov 1981 (Evanich 1982d, *MGH*) and five on separate dates at the Monmouth sewage ponds (Tice 1997). Three of the five records east of the Cascades have been along the Columbia R.; the other two were 18 Oct 1998 at Klamath Falls, Klamath Co., and 16 Oct 1990 at Thompson Res., Lake Co. (Denny 1995).

**Habitat and Diet:** Heermann's Gulls have been observed to select open beaches rather than sheltered river mouths (Merrifield 1994) and lower rather than upper estuaries (Merrifield 1998). In the Siuslaw R. estuary, they chose mudflats rather than rocks as a daytime roosting site (Bayer and Lowe 1988). Although most feed along the shore or in the ocean, some feed on tideflats (Cogswell 1977, Contreras 1998, Drury 1984). They prey on small fish, shrimp, amphipods, and mollusks and will eat dead animals of almost any kind (Cogswell 1977). Often steal food from Brown Pelicans. May take fish directly from the pelicans' bills immediately after a dive (Cogswell 1977, Contreras 1998, Drury 1984, Tershy et al. 1990) or claim food that pelicans have located, discarded, or disturbed (Contreras 1998). In a study in the Gulf of California, Heermann's Gulls attempted food-stealing after 13% of pelican dives (Tershy et al. 1990).

**Seasonal Activity and Behavior:** Arrive at breeding colonies in Mar; egg dates primarily Apr and May (Harrison 1985). They move north to the s. Oregon coast in late spring (Contreras 1998), becoming locally common by mid-summer. Flocks of hundreds are sometimes observed roosting or in flight, but a few score is the usual limit of local concentrations (*ALC*). Earliest observations vary from 18 Apr to 11 Jul (Contreras 1996a, Evanich 1982c) but are usually in the last half of Jun (Bayer 1995a), usually coincident with influxes of Brown Pelicans (Contreras 1997b, 1998). In recent years, Heermann's Gulls have been observed earlier with increasing frequency (Gilligan et al. 1994). Northward movement usually peaks in the second half of Jul (Gilligan et al. 1994, Merrifield 1994).

Southward movement begins in Sep (Gilligan et al. 1994), peaks in Sep and Oct (Contreras 1998, Merrifield 1998), and has been observed over coastal waters in Nov (Boggs and Boggs 1963a, Heinl 1986a). Most leave by mid-Nov (Contreras 1997b). Latest observations vary from 30 Nov through late Dec (Bayer 1995a, Carlson 1980, Evanich 1983b, Heinl and Fix 1989, Johnson J 1994b, Tice 1998a), merging with the few noted mostly along the southern coast during CBCs and later in winter (Carlson and Gordon 1981, Combs 1981, Contreras 1998). In 1972, however, large numbers remained into mid-Dec, and 119 were counted during the Tillamook Bay CBC (Contreras 1991, 1997b). In Jan 1998 a small incursion moved into coastal Oregon, remaining through Mar, with a peak count in Coos Co. of 16 birds (T. Rodenkirk p.c.).

**Detection:** May be spotted among similar-sized gulls by their darker plumage and lack of wing pattern. Often found on the water near Brown Pelicans feeding off jetties or the open coast.

**Population Status and Conservation:** About 600,000 Heermann's Gulls breeding on Isla Raza in the Gulf of California comprise over 90% of the world's population (Harrison 1985, Velarde 1992). Limitation of most breeding pairs to one large colony may render them vulnerable to breeding disturbances. However, proportions of hatch-year birds among postbreeding visitors to Oregon and Washington have been high (Tweit and Johnson 1996b), indicating recent breeding success.

In contrast to their comparative rarity in the early 1930s, when Gabrielson and Jewett (1940) wrote their account, Heermann's Gulls have been common in recent decades. Totals along the Oregon coast counted during Aug Breeding Bird and Coast Birding Weekend surveys vary from minima of 34 in 1977 and 168 in 1981 to a maximum of 918 in 1979 (Contreras 1979a, Rogers D 1981). Higher transient populations during some years are indicated by the "thousands" at coastal resting areas during the summer of 1984 (Irons 1984b), 1,000 at the Columbia R. s. jetty in fall 1986 (Fix 1987a), 700 off Coos Bay on 24 Jul 1969 (Contreras 1998), 500/hr flying northward past Newport on 28 Jul 1979, and 1,200 on Sunset Beach, Clatsop Co., in Oct 1980 (Gilligan et al. 1994).

In Oregon, Heermann's Gull numbers appear to be positively correlated with El Niño/Southern Oscillation (ENSO) patterns. The species was more common and widespread than usual in 1983 and 1993, both strong ENSO years (Hunn and Mattocks 1984, Tweit and Gilligan 1993), and the many that were reported along the coast in winter 1997-98 were coincident with another marked ENSO.—*Kathy Merrifield*

## Mew Gull *Larus canus*

This small, gentle-looking gull, called Common Gull in Eurasia, is one of the most abundant wintering gulls along the Pacific coast. It is often found foraging in mixed flocks with Ring-billed and, to a lesser extent, with California Gulls. Its small size, plover-like head and bill, and habit of bobbing its head while walking, make it fairly easy to identify. In flight the black wingtips show a larger white spot than do those of other small gulls.

**General Distribution:** Breeds across n. Europe and Siberia to Kamchatka, through Alaska and across Canada to Hudson Bay, and south to c. Saskatchewan and through w. British Columbia to the U.S. border (Campbell et al. 1990a). N. American birds winter along the Pacific coast to Baja California, and rarely elsewhere in N. America.

There are four distinct subspecies of *L. canus* with *L. c. brachyrhynchus* the N. American breeding form. The European *L. c. canus* occasionally occurs along the Atlantic coast of N. America and the large, dark Siberian race, *L. c. kamtschatschensis*, occurs on the outer Aleutians.

**Oregon Distribution:** This is an abundant migrant and winter visitor along the coast, the lower Columbia R. and in the Willamette Valley (Baldridge and Crowell 1966, Hunn and Mattocks 1979b, Mattocks and Hunn 1980b, Gillson 1989); rare along the Columbia R. east of the Cascades and in the Klamath Basin (Summers 1982a, Anderson DA 1987b, 1990a, Sullivan PT 1995b); very rare elsewhere (Anderson DA 1987b, Tweit and Gilligan 1991, Evanich 1992a, Summers 1993c, 1994a, Sullivan PT 1995b). Occasional in summer (Gilligan et al. 1994).

**Habitat and Diet:** Although an opportunistic feeder like other gulls, and sometimes found at landfills, fish runs, and other places where gulls congregate, its small size and delicacy are no match for larger, more aggressive gulls. Most often found actively foraging with similar-sized gulls on coastal farm fields and short-grass meadows and lawns when such habitat is moist (Fix 1988c). Along the outer coast regularly found along the tideline on extensive low tide estuarine mud flats and occasionally on sandy beaches, typically near creek mouths (Tangren 1982, D. Irons p.c., *HBN*). Often feeds along jetties and in tide rips at the mouth of estuaries (*ALC*). In most situations tends to roost and feed on wetter ground than do some other gulls (D. Irons p.c.). Consumes more insects and small crustaceans than do larger species of gulls. Two birds collected 16 Sep 1927 at Diamond L., Douglas Co. were filled with ants, and one taken 14 Jan 1921 at Netarts, Tillamook Co., contained insects, mostly beetles (Gabrielson and Jewett 1940). An active participant at the annual smelt (eulachon) runs in the Lower Columbia R. and tributaries, and at late winter Pacific herring runs at coastal estuaries.

**Seasonal Activity and Behavior:** The first southbound migrants arrive in late Jul (rare), usually adults in heavy molt; occasionally juveniles. Their numbers build slowly through Aug (very few) and Sep to a conspicuous movement along the coast starting in mid-Oct (Baldridge and Crowell 1965, Crowell and Nehls 1971a, Fix 1987a). A very heavy movement the last week of Nov brings wintering numbers to the Willamette Valley (Irons 1984a, J. Gatchet p.c.). Flocks of 10,000 or more along the north coast are not uncommon into early winter; over 20,000 were in the fields about Tillamook Bay 28 Dec 1980 (Mattocks and Hunn 1981). Later they scatter, but remain abundant along the coast throughout the winter (Mattocks and Hunn 1980b). On 4 Mar 1989 over 2,000 attended the Pacific herring run into Yaquina Bay (Pat Muller p.c., Linda Weiland p.c.). Flocks of up to 3,000-4,000 are occasionally seen in the Willamette Valley, but the birds seldom concentrate (Irons 1984a, Fix 1988c, J. Gatchet p.c.). On 26 Feb 1981 an estimated 50,000 Mew Gulls were along 50 mi (80 km) of the Columbia R. from Astoria to the mouth of the Cowlitz R. at Longview, Washington (Mattocks and Hunn 1981).

Gradually leave wintering areas from late Mar (bulk of movement) through Apr (Irons 1984b, Lillie 1998), with lingering birds noted to mid-May (Irons 1984b). Sharp declines in the Willamette Valley population often coincide with lower Columbia R. smelt run. A flock of 20 was at Ochoco Res. 22 Mar 1986 (D. Lusthoff p.c.).

**Detection:** Easy to observe in winter along the coast at major estuaries. Less common in the Willamette Valley but a careful search of gull flocks in midwinter and early spring may reveal some. They may be more regular inland than the published records indicate and should be looked for in flocks of Ring-billed Gulls.

**Population Status and Conservation:** There are indications that in recent years the Mew Gull has increased and has established new breeding colonies, especially in s. British Columbia (Campbell et al. 1990a). Sightings in e. Washington and Oregon, and other western states have increased (Tweit, Tice, and Mlodinow 1999). Willamette Valley numbers are higher now than they were in the 1970s, perhaps owing to changes in agricultural practices (D. Fix p.c.).—*Harry B. Nehls*

## Ring-billed Gull *Larus delawarensis*

A small gull, somewhat larger and bulkier than Mew Gull with a shorter bill and narrower, more pointed wings than California Gull. It also has a paler mantle than either of the aforementioned species. Frequently seen in urban locations such as school fields, parking lots, and fast-food locations as well in more customary gull habitat.

**General Distribution:** Endemic to N. America. Breeds from c. British Columbia east to Newfoundland and south to ne. California (Honey Lake), ne. Utah, n. Illinois and c. New York. Winters along the Pacific coast from s. British Columbia to s. Mexico and along the Atlantic coast from the Gulf of St. Lawrence to Florida. Wintering birds occur locally in the interior from s. British Columbia to the Great Lakes region and south to c. Mexico. Nonbreeding individuals may be found throughout the wintering range during summer. Monotypic (AOU 1957).

**Oregon Distribution:** The Ring-billed Gull is a local breeder east of the Cascades and a fairly common wintering gull throughout Oregon. It is one of four gull species to breed in the interior of Oregon. Conover (1983) reported breeding at Baker City sewage ponds in Baker Co.; Pelican L., (in Warner Valley) and Summer L. in Lake Co.; and at Upper Klamath L. in Klamath Co. Five hundred pairs bred at Crump L. in the Warner Valley in 1987, while Summer L. contained 1,331 pairs of Ring-billed/California Gulls in 2000 (Stern 1988, M. St. Louis unpubl. data). During 1977, bred in the Columbia R. on Miller Rocks, Sherman Co., (960 pairs) and at Threemile Canyon I., Morrow Co. (4,380 pairs); similar numbers were present through the early 1990s (Gilligan et al. 1994). According to Littlefield (1990a), 200 pairs bred just southeast of Burns, Harney Co. On Malheur L., peak numbers were 1,050 nests in 1989, although in most years fewer than 300 pairs nested (G. L. Ivey p.c.). Nonbreeding birds are uncommon in summer in w. Oregon, the Cascade lakes (D. Irons p.c.), and along the coast, but are

fairly common in e. Oregon at lakes and large rivers (Aldrich 1940, Gullion 1951, Farner 1952, Contreras and Kindschy 1996, Contreras 1998).

Widespread and common during spring and fall. During the winter, common in the Willamette Valley, along the coast, in the Klamath Basin and along the Columbia R. (Contreras 1997b). Casual from early Jul through late Apr in the Umpqua Valley; during Aug it is rare to very uncommon (Hunter et al. 1998). Formerly very rare during the winter in e. Oregon away from the Columbia R. but numbers have slowly increased during the 20th century. Now local and uncommon in winter, with small numbers regularly recorded at Summer L., Baker City, and north of Burns (Sooter 1941b, Littlefield 1990a, CBCs 1986-2000). Also winters locally along the Snake R. (Contreras 1997b).

**Habitat and Diet:** Oregon nesting colonies are typically situated on islands covered with sand and gravel, and often include some tall grass and low shrubs (Broadbooks 1961, Hayward 1993). Greatest reproductive success occurs when nests are located in tall grass (Hayward 1993). Forage in a wide variety of habitats including lakes, estuaries, beaches, pastures, garbage dumps, and parking lots (Aldrich 1940, Gullion 1951, Farner 1952, Wahl 1977, Contreras and Kindschy 1996, Contreras 1998).

Unlike California Gulls, consistently build a small nest, a small cup on the ground made of twigs, grasses, lichens, and moss (Vermeer 1970), usually near water (Broadbooks 1961, Conover 1984, Littlefield 1990a, Hayward 1993). Information on their preferred nesting substrate in Oregon is skimpy, but in Washington will nest in tall grass (ashy wildrye), shorter herbs and grass (cheatgrass, fiddle neck, and flixweed tansy), and bare ground (Hayward 1993). Fledging rates in Washington are highest when they nest in tall rye grass (Hayward 1993).

Will eat nearly anything that can be swallowed without a struggle. Some of the more common items include insects, fish, small mammals, earthworms, crustaceans, grain, and garbage (Gabrielson and Jewett 1940, Aldrich 1940). Earthworms form an important component of the diet immediately before the breeding season when fields are being plowed in Manitoba (Wellham 1987). Kleptoparasitism has also been observed in other parts of the country (Clapp, Morgan-Jacobs, and Banks 1983, Elston and Southern 1983) but has not yet been reported from Oregon.

**Seasonal Activity and Behavior:** First appear at nesting sites in Oregon during the last week of Feb (Broadbooks 1961, Littlefield 1990a), with an average arrival date of 22 Feb (Ivey, Herziger, and Scheuering 1998). Pair formation typically occurs as birds begin arriving on territory (Moynihan 1958). Nesting colonies are usually shared with California

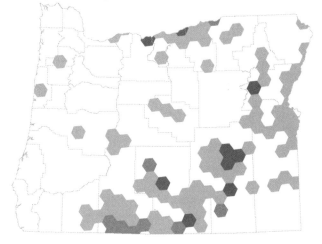

Gulls. Egg laying in Oregon and Washington begins during the last week of Apr and continues through the second week of Jun (Broadbooks 1961, Conover 1984, Littlefield 1990a, Hayward 1993). Typically 2-3 eggs in a clutch in Washington, although clutch sizes may range 1-6 eggs (Conover 1984, Hayward 1993). Clutches of greater than four occur when two females deposit eggs in the same nest. When males are scarce, females may pair with other females to raise young (Conover 1984). Typically attempt nesting during their third year (Vermeer 1970). Monogamous; both sexes incubate the eggs, which usually hatch after 24-29 days in Washington (Hayward 1993). Parents take turns feeding young, which typically leave the nest on their second day, but remain near the nest (Vermeer 1970). In Alberta, adult birds may travel as far as 19 mi (31 km) from the nest site in search of food although usually travel far less (Vermeer 1970). Five wk after hatching, young birds are capable of flying and typically leave the nesting grounds 5-10 days later (Vermeer 1970). Adults follow shortly thereafter, so by mid-Jul or Aug, populations in nonbreeding areas begin increasing (Vermeer 1970).

In e. Oregon, most common during Aug and begin arriving along the coast during this month (Littlefield 1990a, Contreras 1998). Large flocks numbering in the thousands are frequently reported from several e. Oregon lakes including L. Ewauna, Klamath Co., and L. Abert (c. 20,000 birds in 1996), Lake Co., during fall migration (Sullivan 1996a, 1997a). However, the largest flocks appear to occur in Malheur NWR during Aug when as many as 25,000 have been seen at Stinking L. (Littlefield 1990a). Numbers west of the Cascades peak during Oct-Dec (Contreras 1998). Thereafter numbers decline although there is another peak during Mar (Contreras 1998). Most have left the coast by May, although a few remain through the summer (Contreras 1998).

Many gulls that move to the coast after breeding do so along the Columbia R. (Gilligan et al. 1994). However, flocks of Ring-billed and California Gulls are frequently seen in the Cascades during late summer and fall, indicating that birds may migrate across a wider region than previously thought, although they are rare in the Diamond L. district in Douglas Co. (Fix 1990a, Sullivan 1997a).

**Detection:** Easily located when present, although nesting colonies often remote. Hatch-year birds sometimes confused with hatch-year Mew Gull. Large flocks may occur during migration and winter in their usual habitats.

**Population Status and Conservation:** Although Ring-billed Gulls are now very numerous (with an estimated world population of 3 to 4 million), such was not always the case. Heavily persecuted during the late

19th century and the population declined precipitously (Ryder 1993). By the 1920s, were only known to nest in 12 colonies in the w. U.S. and it was estimated that the population was less than 5,000 (Conover 1983). The only two colonies known to exist in Oregon during the 1930s were at Malheur L. and in the Klamath Basin (Gabrielson and Jewett 1940).

During the following decades, this gull gradually increased its population in the Northwest. Discovered nesting for the first time on islands in the Columbia R. in 1956 (Broadbooks 1961). By 1980, known to nest in 57 colonies in the w. U.S. with at least four in Oregon and 11 in Washington (Conover 1983). Began nesting near the coast in w. Washington by 1976 (Smith et al. 1997).

The reason for this continued increase is unclear. A reduction in human disturbance (particularly persecution of the nesting sites) may have helped colonies increase. Additionally, the establishment of reservoirs and the increase in the number of garbage dumps may have played a role (Conover 1983). The trend from CBCs indicates that this species continues to increase in numbers in the Pacific Northwest and further expansion seems likely (Contreras 1997b).—*Chris Butler*

## California Gull *Larus californicus*

Although gulls are often associated with seashores, California Gulls are inland breeders, with nesting colonies located near water amid vast expanses of desert or plains. Perhaps the most famous gull in the world, the California Gull reportedly saved the Mormon settlers from famine by devouring the grasshoppers that plagued their crops in 1848. A statue commemorating this event can be seen in Salt Lake City's Temple Square. These gulls are slightly larger than Ring-billed Gulls with longer bills, longer wings, and a darker mantle.

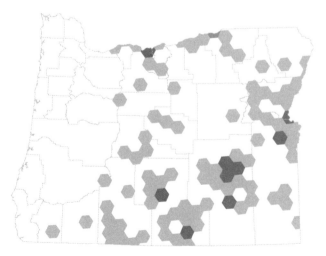

**General Distribution:** Breeds from s. British Columbia south to n. California, east to ne. S. Dakota and c. Colorado and north to Great Slave L. in the Northwest Territories. Winters from sw. British Columbia to e. Idaho; south to s. Baja California and locally to c. Mexico (Jehl 1987a). Nonbreeding individuals may be found in the winter range during the breeding season. Two subspecies are recognized (Jehl 1987a, Browning 1990); only *L. c. californicus* specimens available from Oregon (e.g., USNM [*MRB*]), but *albertaensis*, said to migrate along the coast from British Columbia to Baja California (Jehl 1987a), has been photographed in very small numbers (*MGH*).

**Oregon Distribution:** Colonies of *L. c. californicus* are in a constant state of flux in terms of location and numbers due to variable water conditions. During the early 1990s populations were at 500 pairs in Harney Co., 2,000 pairs in Lake (Pelican L., Warner Valley, and Summer L.) and Klamath counties (Upper Klamath L.), a small population in Baker (Baker City sewage pond) and approximately 5,000 pairs along the Columbia R. (Conover 1983, Gilligan et al. 1994). At Malheur L., numbers of nests are highly variable and peaked at 1,500 in 1997, but averaged 630 nests 1990-98 (G. L. Ivey p.c.). Warner Valley contained 301 pairs in 1987 while Summer L. contained 1,331 pairs of Ring-billed/California Gulls in 2000 (Stern 1988, M. St. Louis unpubl. data). The colony at Threemile Canyon I. in Morrow Co. (active during the early 1990s) was not reported by the OBBA. Nonbreeding birds are widely scattered throughout e. Oregon and are uncommon along the coast (Aldrich 1940, Gullion 1951, Farner 1952, Contreras 1998).

California Gulls are widespread during migration; they may be encountered up to 70 mi (113 km) offshore (Wahl 1977, Gilligan et al 1994). They are casual from late Jun through early May in the Umpqua Valley, except during Aug when rare to very

uncommon (Hunter et al. 1998). During winter, locally common in the Willamette Valley, along the coast, in the Klamath Basin and along the Columbia R. to Hood River (Contreras 1997b). Rare elsewhere in e. Oregon during the winter with the exception of a small population near Baker City. Both *californicus* and presumed *albertaensis* winter, but *californicus* is by far the most common (*MGH*).

**Habitat and Diet:** Oregon colonies are typically situated on relatively bare islands, although some vegetation may be present (e.g., greasewood, other shrubs, saltgrass, and other grass), and are relatively inaccessible to predators (Vermeer 1970, Conover 1984, Stern 1988, Winkler and Shuford 1988, Littlefield 1990a, Hayward 1993, Winkler 1996, *DBM*). Although it has been stated by Hayward (1993) that California Gulls nest almost exclusively on rocky hummocks within sparsely vegetated areas, this does not appear to be the case in Oregon as birds will also nest on sandy beaches and bulrush mats (Finley 1907a, Gabrielson and Jewett 1940, Marshall and Giles 1953). They frequently build a small nest for their eggs, although the amount of material in the nest varies greatly from a cup of dried grass and other vegetation to nearly bare ground (Gabrielson and Jewett 1940).

California Gulls disperse widely during the nonbreeding season and can be found at lakes, ponds, large rivers, and flooded fields, as well as garbage dumps, the coastline, and over the ocean (Aldrich 1940, Gullion 1951, Farner 1952, Wahl 1977, Contreras 1996a, Contreras 1998).

Diet includes insects, fish, small mammals, eggs, crustaceans, and garbage (Aldrich 1940, Gabrielson and Jewett 1940, Wahl 1977, Jehl and Mahoney 1983). Interestingly, have been observed landing in cherry trees and eating ripe cherries (Cottam 1935, Tweit and Johnson 1992). Even more astonishingly, one was once observed catching a Barn Swallow in flight, then alighting in the water and eating it (Laymon 1983).

**Seasonal Activity and Behavior:** They first appear back on their colonies during the second week of Mar (Littlefield 1990a). Pair-bond formation timing is unknown. Nesting colonies frequently shared with Ring-billed Gulls. Egg laying begins during the last week of Apr and continues through Jun and occasionally into Jul (Gabrielson and Jewett 1940, Conover 1984, Littlefield 1990a, Hayward 1993). Typically 2-3 eggs in a clutch, although clutch sizes may range 1-5 eggs (Conover 1984, Hayward 1993). Clutches of greater than four eggs occur when two

*California Gull*

ELVA PAULSON

females deposit eggs in the same nest. When males are scarce, females may pair with other females to raise the young (Conover and Hunt 1984). Birds typically attempt nesting during their third year (Vermeer 1970). Monogamous, and both sexes incubate the eggs (Vermeer 1970, Conover 1984, Hayward 1993). Data from Oregon are lacking, but in Utah eggs typically hatch after 21-26 days (Behle and Goates 1957). Parents take turns feeding the young, which are able to leave the nest on their second day, but will remain near the nest (Vermeer 1970). Five wk after hatching, young birds are capable of flying; typically leave the nesting sites 5-10 days later (Vermeer 1970, Winkler 1996). Adults follow shortly thereafter, so by mid-Jul populations in nonbreeding areas begin increasing (Vermeer 1970).

After the young fledge, California Gulls gradually make their way west or northwest toward the coast (Pugesek et al. 1999). Banded birds recovered in Malheur Co. came from areas predominantly to the east, including Idaho, Utah, Wyoming, and Colorado (Contreras and Kindschy 1996). Birds banded as fledglings in Utah were found later in Oregon at mostly coastal locations, but also at Portland and Malheur L. (Woodbury et al. 1946, Behle and Woodbury 1952). Many gulls follow the Columbia R. to the coast after breeding (Gilligan et al. 1994), but many also travel via other routes, e.g., large flocks of Ring-billed and California Gulls are frequently seen in the Cascades during late summer and fall (Sullivan 1997a).

Birds begin arriving during Jun and Jul in the Cascades of e. Douglas Co. (Fix 1990a), and in mid-Jul on the coast (*ALC, MGH*). These birds are typically subadult birds that presumably did not breed, but these flocks also include postbreeders and many hatch-year birds. Numbers peak in e. Oregon during Aug when up to 8,000 individuals have been reported from L. Abert. Large movements occur in the lower Columbia in Aug-Sep, and on the outer coast they tend to peak in Oct when flocks of thousands are frequently encountered; most movement is very close to shore (Fix 1990a, Tweit and Gilligan 1992, Merrifield 1994, Sullivan 1996a). From Nov onwards, numbers typically dwindle as California Gulls begin a leisurely migration towards s. California and n. Mexico, although many remain throughout the winter in Oregon (Gilligan et al. 1994, Pugesek et al. 1999). Highest CBC count involved 5,901 birds recorded on the Salem CBC in 1981 at Minto Brown I. dump (which is now closed) (Contreras 1991). As winter thaws, they begin migrating en masse to inland breeding colonies (Woodbury and Knight 1951, Pugesek et al. 1999).

**Detection:** California Gulls are easily located when present. Nesting colonies often in remote locations but gulls are frequently seen in surrounding areas. Birds can sometimes be attracted by tossing french fries or pieces of bread.

**Population Status and Conservation:** Although now very numerous (with an estimated world population of 500,000 to 1 million individuals), such was not always the case (Winkler 1996). By the 1920s, only known to nest in 15 colonies in the w. U.S. and it was estimated that their population was approximately 100,000 (Conover 1983). The only three colonies known to exist in Oregon during the 1930s were at Malheur L., Summer L., and in the Klamath Basin (Gabrielson and Jewett 1940).

During the following decades, populations gradually increased in the Northwest. By 1980, California Gulls were known to nest in 80 colonies in the w. U.S. with at least four colonies in Oregon and nine in Washington (Conover 1983). Nonbreeding abundance across the state increased proportionally during this time. Until the 1940s, for example, they were considered a "winter straggler" to the s. Willamette Valley (Gullion 1951), but are now common. Eugene, for example, has recorded an average of 166 California Gulls during 15 CBCs 1986-2000.

The reason for this continued increase since the 1940s is unclear. The creation of reservoirs, increase in the number of garbage dumps, protection of breeding sites, and increase in irrigated farmland may all have played a role (Conover 1983, DBM, Winkler 1996). CBC trends indicates that this species continues to increase in numbers in the Pacific Northwest and continued expansion seems likely (Contreras 1997b).—*Chris Butler*

## Herring Gull *Larus argentatus*

Identification of the large pink-footed gulls (Herring, Thayer's, Glaucous-winged, Western, and Glaucous) along the W. Coast is difficult. Their plumages are similar and they are often found mixed together in the same flock. To make matters worse, those with overlapping ranges hybridize frequently, producing many intermediate-plumaged birds (Williamson and Peyton 1963, Spear 1987). A number of these hybrids winter along the w. coast (Grant 1986). Also, northern populations of Western Gull have paler mantles than do southern birds, a fact only recently made visible in field guides. Many historical CBC counts of Herring vs. Western Gull clearly misstate their relative abundance. Finally, the uncertain taxonomic status of Iceland Gull (which has been reported in Oregon) adds a layer of complication to the situation. Thus both the historical status and present identification of these gulls remain somewhat problematic.

Jewett (Gabrielson and Jewett 1940, Jewett et al. 1953), who recognized *thayeri* as a subspecies of *argentatus*, reported very few records of Herring Gulls in Oregon and Washington and noted that there was considerable confusion among the early ornithologists on proper taxonomic classification. That situation continues today. Herring Gulls are large and pink-legged, and have very pale mantles contrasting with black primary tips, fairly flat heads, usually a yellow eye, and a fairly heavy bill.

**General Distribution:** Circumboreal breeder of the n. Hemisphere, ranging across Siberia and Russia to the coastlines of Europe and around the Mediterranean. In N. America breeds from S. Carolina to Labrador, across Canada to Alaska, and south to sc. British Columbia. Migrates to winter along coastlines and large rivers and lakes south to China, Japan, n. Africa, Mexico, and the Caribbean.

The taxonomic relationship of many of the large gull species is complex (Grant 1986). There are probably at least four subspecies, with *L.a. smithsonianus* the only subspecies that regularly breeds in N. America. The dark-backed Asian race, *L. a. vegae*, occurs regularly to w. Alaska and occasionally south to British Columbia (only one specimen). Bayer (1989a) records a female *vegae* collected by Alex Walker at Netarts, Tillamook Co., 19 Feb 1930 as being spec. no. 18515 in the CMNH. There have been several other reports of *vegae* wintering in Oregon (OBRC).

**Oregon Distribution:** Common migrant and winter visitor offshore (Sanger 1970, 1973). Common fall migrant and very common spring migrant along the coast; fairly common, but in variable numbers, along the coast during the winter (Fix 1984a, Gillson 1989, Contreras 1996a). Moderate numbers winter in the Willamette Valley, concentrating with other gulls at landfills and other food sources. Flocks of 500 or more have been noted (rarely) in the Portland metropolitan area (Gilligan et al. 1994), but numbers seldom exceed 100 elsewhere in the Willamette Valley (Fix 1988c, Gillson 1989) and in most years only a few are present in flocks of other gulls. Most common near Portland and Eugene, least regular in the central valley now that Salem's Minto Brown I. dump (which accounted for record gull counts in the 1970s) is closed (*ALC*, D. Irons p.c.).

Fairly common in winter east of the Cascades near Klamath Falls (Summers 1982a, Rogers 1985b), and along the Columbia R. (Sullivan PT 1995b). Scattered individuals occur elsewhere where open water and food are available (Littlefield 1990a, Evanich 1991b, Contreras and Kindschy 1996). The majority of Herring Gulls wintering in Oregon are adults (Force and Mattocks 1986, Fix 1988c). Summering individuals are occasionally reported (Rogers 1985c, Contreras and Kindschy 1996, Sullivan 1997c, 1998a).

**Habitat and Diet:** An opportunistic scavenger that regularly concentrates about landfills, food processing plants, and other sources of refuse. Many are observed foraging along the more productive rivers and estuaries. During early morning and in inclement weather large numbers gather on farm fields, meadows, and lawns capturing worms, grubs, and insects. Large numbers attend the smelt runs up the Columbia R. and tributaries in the spring (Hunn and Mattocks 1979b, Force and Mattocks 1986). Small fishes, crustaceans, and invertebrates, along with dead fish, birds, and other carrion are the primary foods taken (Pierotti and Good 1994). Sanger (1973) found the pelagic barnacle and other barnacle species the main food for gulls far offshore.

**Seasonal Activity and Behavior:** Early birds begin arriving in early Aug and become common by Oct. The coastal movement is mostly offshore and is usually inconspicuous. However, on 28 Oct 1980, 1,500 were among a migrant gull concentration on Clatsop Beach, Clatsop Co. (Hunn and Mattocks 1982a). Sanger (1970,1973) found Herring Gulls common between the coast and 600 mi (960 km) offshore in winter, and noted that a dispersal away from land in fall and a return to land in spring is indicated. J. M. Scott (p.c.) found that 95% of all gulls offshore, out of sight of land, from Garibaldi, Tillamook Co., to Newport, Lincoln Co., 5-6 Mar 1983, were Herring Gulls. On 27 Dec 1998, 597 were at Yaquina Bay (Merrifield 2001b); about 1,000 were at Siletz Bay during the winter of 2000-01 (Korpi 2001c). Severe winter storms often bring large flocks briefly to estuaries and spits.

The main northward movement in spring occurs in Apr and May. Wintering numbers in the Willamette Valley decline during Mar and Apr with no apparent migratory movement. Spring movements along the coast are often very conspicuous with large numbers flying low over the beaches and offshore. On 3 May 1980 they were passing Cape Meares, Tillamook Co., at a rate of 80 birds/hr (J. Gilligan and O. Schmidt p.c.). Fifty birds/hr were passing along Clatsop Beach 2 May 1984 (Fix 1984a). Large numbers of subadult birds regularly trail the movement of adult birds (Lillie 1998, D. Fix p.c.).

A hatch-year Glaucous-winged/Herring Gull hybrid was banded 20 Jul 1983 at Skilak L. on the Kenai Peninsula, Alaska. It was resighted 15 Jan 1984 on Sauvie I., Multnomah Co., and again during the winters of 1988-90 with other hybrid gulls at Laurelhurst Park in mid-town Portland. (K. Bollinger p.c., *HBN*).

**Detection:** Most winter gull concentrations along the coast and in the Willamette Valley contain Herring Gulls, but they are usually far outnumbered by Glaucous-winged Gulls and their hybrids. In the Portland area Thayer's Gull is sometimes more common than Herring Gull. The similarity in plumages makes detection difficult.

**Population Status and Conservation:** Population increases in Europe and e. N. America have led to range expansions and local population control measures (Cramp and Simmons 1983). Western N. American populations appear to be little changed from historical levels. The Herring Gull is one of the most abundant gulls in the world and needs no additional protection.—*Harry B. Nehls*

## Thayer's Gull *Larus thayeri*

This mid-sized, pink-legged gull has caused much of the confusion in w. coast gull classification and identification. See the general discussion of pink-footed gulls in the Herring Gull account. Its plumage characteristics are similar to Herring, Iceland, and some Glaucous-winged hybrids, and great care is needed for correct identification. For many years the Thayer's Gull was considered a subspecies of the Herring Gull but it was not until it was elevated to a full species in 1973 that any serious attempt was made to gather data on its identification and distribution. It differs from the Herring Gull in having a much smaller bill, a darker eye, less black in the wing-tips and, often, a more rounded head.

**General Distribution:** Breeds on cliff faces in the Canadian Arctic from Banks and Victoria I. to Ellsmere and Baffin I., and nw. Greenland. Winters primarily along the Pacific coast, less commonly around the Great Lakes, and irregularly elsewhere in N. America. Largest wintering numbers occur along the coast of n. Washington and s. British Columbia. Some nonbreeding individuals summer in the winter range.

The Thayer's Gull was given full species status by the AOU (1973). Interbreeding between *L. thayeri* and *L. kumlieni* (Kumlien's gull, see below for specific status), in some colonies (Gaston and Decker 1985, Gaston et al. 1985, Snell 1989) was questioned by Banks and Browning (1999). Salomonsen (1950) thought *thayeri* and *kumlieni* and *glaucoides* (Iceland Gull) were conspecific and Godfrey (1986) concluded that "Thayer's Gull [is] a dark western subspecies of the Iceland Gull." However, the relationships between these taxa are not yet fully understood (Banks and Browning 1999). Howell and Elliott (2001) believed that *thayeri* and *glaucoides* are best considered separate species. Because of a lack of taxonomic evidence Browning (2002) recommended that *thayeri*, *kumlieni*, and *glaucoides* be recognized as separate species until demonstrated otherwise.

**Oregon Distribution:** Common migrant and fairly common winter visitor along the coast; uncommon on the south coast. The largest wintering numbers are found in the Portland metropolitan area where flocks of several hundred are not uncommon. Lesser numbers winter elsewhere in the Willamette Valley, usually about landfills (Fix 1988c, Gillson 1989). Rare along the Columbia R. east of the Cascades (Sullivan PT 1995b); and in the Klamath Basin (Summers 1982a, 1993a). Very rare elsewhere (Summers 1985b, Evanich 1991b, Contreras and Kindschy 1996, Sullivan 1998a). The majority of Thayer's Gulls wintering in Oregon are adults (Force and Mattocks 1986, Fix 1988c).

**Habitat and Diet:** Opportunistic feeders with a diet similar to that of the Herring Gull, they regularly concentrate about landfills, food-processing plants, and over fish runs. However, spend more time than Herring Gulls foraging over farm fields, golf courses, and city parks in search of worms, grubs, and insects, and less time along rivers and estuaries (*HBN*). Large numbers attend the smelt runs up the Columbia R. and its tributaries in spring (Hunn and Mattocks 1979b, Force and Mattocks 1986).

**Seasonal Activity and Behavior:** Early fall migrants arrive along the coast during late Aug; earliest were two at the Nehalem sewage ponds, Tillamook Co., 22 Aug 1983 (Irons 1984a). Numbers remain very low until the main movement arrives in mid-Oct, and it is mid-Nov before wintering numbers arrive in the Willamette Valley. No obvious migratory movement usually noted, but on 28 Oct 1980, 800 were among a migrant gull concentration on Clatsop Beach, Clatsop Co. (Hunn and Mattocks 1981a). The coastal population becomes less conspicuous by Dec with most coastal CBCs recording fewer than 10 individuals (Gillson 1989).

Wintering numbers in the Willamette Valley begin to decline by late Feb and most are gone by mid-Mar; small groups, mostly subadults, remain to mid-Apr (Fix 1984a). This decline often corresponds with the movement of smelt into the lower Columbia R. There is an increase in numbers along the coast during Mar each year, but there is no noticeable migration. Most are gone by late Mar, but small numbers remain into May. Twenty were at Hammond, Clatsop Co., 10 May 1987 (Mattocks and Harrington-Tweit 1987b).

**Detection:** As with other gull species it is conspicuous when present. However, identification is a challenge and the major drawback in the detection of this species. Pale individuals are sometimes mistaken for Kumlien's/Iceland Gull.

**Population Status and Conservation:** Breeds in the Arctic away from most human contact. Recent closings of landfills, sanitizing food-processing plants, and reduced fish runs appear to have affected winter distribution, but not overall population levels (*HBN*). At the present time there appear to be no conservation problems concerning the Thayer's Gull.—*Harry B. Nehls*

### Slaty-backed Gull *Larus schistisagus*

This large, dark-backed gull breeds along the Siberian coast from the Bering Sea to Japan and winters primarily in Asia. Alaskan sightings have increased and breeding was recently confirmed near Cape Romanzof (McCaffery et al. 1997). Reports of migrants or wintering individuals have increased elsewhere in N. America. Several adult and subadult Slaty-backed Gulls were photographed among a large gull concentration at a food-processing plant on Sauvie I., Multnomah Co., 29 Dec 1992 to 20 Mar 1993 (Finnegan 1993, Lehman 1993, Nehls 1993b, Gustafson and Peterjohn 1994). An adult was photographed at the same plant 7 Jan to early Feb 1995 (Johnson J 1995b). Two adults were photographed on Sauvie I., and a subadult was photographed there and at Westmoreland Park in Portland, Multnomah Co., during the winter of 1997-98 (Tice 1998a).—*Harry B. Nehls*

### Western Gull *Larus occidentalis*

The Western Gull has one of the smallest populations of any N. American gull but is the most abundant gull on the Oregon coast, and one of only two species to breed there. Upon reaching adult plumage at 4 yr of age it is distinguished by its large size, slate-gray mantle, black wingtips with white spots at the tip, and pink legs. Eye color varies from tan-yellow to brown—browner in the north, probably because of interbreeding with Glaucous-winged Gull. See the general discussion of pink-footed gulls in the Herring Gull account. Males are slightly larger than females. Juveniles are quite dark with some pale scalloping. When begging for food from adults they appear hunch-backed.

**General Distribution:** Endemic to the region of the California current. Breeds along the Pacific coast from sw. British Columbia to wc. Baja California and Guadalupe I. Winters from s. coastal British Columbia south to s. Baja California, casually to interior Oregon and Washington and s. California, and to the coast of Sonora, Mexico. There are two subspecies. The northern subspecies *L. o. occidentalis* breeds from Washington to c. California and is larger with slightly paler upperparts and darker eyes than the southern subspecies *L. o. wymani*. During the non-breeding season *wymani* is casual north to Washington (AOU 1957) and reported to disperse to Oregon (Coulter 1975). Western Gulls and Glaucous-winged Gulls interbreed where their ranges overlap from Coos Bay to the Strait of Juan de Fuca, Washington, and produce fertile hybrids (Scott JM 1971, Hoffman et al. 1978, Bell 1997).

**Oregon Distribution:** Present all year and breeds along the entire coast. At all times of the year abundance at sea highest from Reedsport south; numbers at sea north of Reedsport are highest in summer. Seldom more than 35 mi (50 km) seaward off the shelf break; most birds occur on the inner and mid-shelf regions (Briggs et al. 1992). Nonbreeders occur year-round north of the breeding range, although their distribution shifts towards the south during winter (Spear et al. 1986). Birds banded in Oregon have been found north and south of the state (Gilligan et al. 1994). Westerns will follow rivers inland for a few miles during salmon runs (Small 1994). Small numbers of immatures and adults are found in fall and winter along the Columbia R. and as far inland as the John Day Dam and the Portland and Eugene areas. Rare inland records include sightings in Umatilla and Klamath counties and Summer L., Lake Co. (Gilligan et al. 1994). Becoming more regular along the Columbia in se. Washington (M. Denny p.c.).

**Habitat and Diet:** Breeds primarily on offshore islands, but will use mainland cliffs, abandoned piers and pilings, channel markers, and bridges. Diet is diverse and depends upon location during the breeding season (Pierotti and Annett 1995). Includes intertidal and pelagic fish and invertebrates, eggs, chicks, and adults of other seabirds, and eggs and chicks of conspecifics. Also scavenge. More females forage offshore than males (Spear 1988). Hard shell prey such as bivalves and gastropods are sometimes dropped in flight onto a hard surface to smash them open (Bent 1921). There is an age-related increase in foraging site fidelity (Spear 1988) and some adults exhibit foraging specializations (Spear et al. 1986, Spear 1993).

Immature birds congregate in areas such as the intertidal, harbors, docks, and refuse dumps, where food is reliably obtained. Some adults, principally males (2:1 ratio at Santa Clara R. dump, Ventura, California [Pierotti and Annett 1995]) are found at dumps during the nonbreeding season (Spear 1988), especially when other foods are unavailable (Pierotti and Annett 1995), but most feed offshore (Briggs et al. 1987). Gull numbers foraging at dumps peaked in Jan and Feb, and gull densities at dumps were higher in Oregon than in California (Spear 1988). In recent decades many open landfills closed, and the number of gulls feeding at the replacement refuse-transfer sites is much lower. Western Gulls act as an initiator of mixed species feeding flocks (Chilton and Sealy 1987).

**Seasonal Activity and Behavior:** Western Gulls have a complex behavior repertoire, often linked with vocalizations that are well described by Pierotti and Annett (1995). No systematic study of the entire breeding season has been conducted, however, it is well studied elsewhere (Penniman et al. 1990) and much of the following information is from California. In Oregon, return to colonies mid-Feb. On the Farallon Is., California, males recruit to the breeding population at a mean of 5 yr, range 3-9 yr, and females at a mean of 6 yr, range 4-10 yr (Spear et al. 1995), although age of first breeding varies at different colonies depending on breeding density (Coulson and White 1956, Coulson et al. 1982).

Males are responsible for territory acquisition, after which both sexes defend the territory from intruders. Both sexes build the nest with vegetation in areas of bare rock or low vegetation that are protected from the prevailing wind (Pierotti and Annett 1995). One brood/yr but can lay a replacement clutch. Clutches of 2-3 eggs initiated late May to early Jul (Pierotti and Annett 1995); the mean length of the laying period on the Farallon Is. was 40 days (range 25-46 days). Penniman et al. (1990) suggested the onset of egg laying is governed more by changes in day length than by local environmental factors. On the Farallon Is. an average of 73% of all nests had 3 eggs; clutches were smallest in warm-water years (Penniman et al. 1990). Eggs laid in morning at approximately 2-day intervals. Male feeds female during this period.

Incubation begins with first egg and lasts 25-30 days (Penniman et al. 1990, Pierotti and Annett 1995). Both sexes participate; daytime shifts are 2-4 hr each, and females incubate at night. Chicks hatch covered with gray down marked with black spots and can move about the nest in 2-3 days. Chicks brooded until 7-10 days. Chick adoption is common (5-10%) on some colonies (Pierotti and Annett 1995) but is low on others (Hunt and Hunt 1975, Carter and Spear 1986). Bayer (1983b) reports that three chicks, 20+ days or older, which fell from nests on pilings were fed and guarded by adults until they could fly. Chicks fledge 6-7 wk after hatching (Spear et al. 1986); late Jul in Oregon (*JH*), and are fed on the nesting territory after fledging (Pierotti and Annett 1995). Fledging success varies with ocean conditions (Penniman et al. 1990) but a diverse diet buffers them more than other seabirds breeding in Oregon. A high percentage of fish in the chick's diet, however, is positively correlated with fledging success, and a high percentage of food scavenged from dumps is negatively correlated with fledging success (Penniman et al. 1990). Chicks leave the colony by early Sep. After fledging, young remain with parent(s) for 1-2 mo on parents' preferred foraging areas, and some chicks associate with parents for up to 6 mo (Spear et al. 1986). One distinctly marked Western Gull at Yaquina Bay provided extended parental care in two different years (Spear et al. 1986).

After the breeding season the majority of fledglings from the Farallon Is. move north, and then move south for their first winter, and north in the following spring. This pattern is repeated as individuals age, but the distance moved away from the breeding colony decreases (Spear 1988, Penniman et al. 1990). Males moved shorter distances from the breeding colony than females (Spear 1988). During its prebreeding years an individual finds an area to which it returns year after year during the postbreeding period (Spear 1988). On the Farallon Is., survival in the first year (following fledging) was 55%, after which it was about 85% (Spear et al. 1987). Roosts in large groups, often mixed species in areas such as beaches and parking lots where predators can be seen at a distance. At night usually fly to offshore locations such as islands.

**Detection:** A very visible and easily identifiable gull, though judgment of the extent of hybridization with Glaucous-winged Gulls is often difficult. Color of the mantle and the primary tips are the best determining factors of hybrids (Bell 1996), which are usually separable by paler wing tips and back, but hybrids and especially back-crosses can be very similar to "pure" Western Gulls. Western Gulls that breed in Washington and Oregon have lighter backs than those that breed farther south (Bell 1996). Hybrid adults are thought to have more head markings in winter.

**Population Status and Conservation:** Limited in distribution, *L. o. occidentalis* has a total population of 40,000, with more than 50% nesting on South East Farallon I. (Carter et al. 1992). The southern subspecies *L. o. wymani* numbers about 15,000 birds (Pierotti and Annett 1995). Gabrielson and Jewett's (1940) summary that Western Gulls breed on nearly every suitable rock in Oregon is unchanged and they are common along rocky coastlines. The 1979 census of Oregon colonies recorded 10,000 breeding at 147 colonies (Pitman et al. 1985), and Briggs et al. (1992) noted 16,400 breeders at 238 sites. Major colonies are the two Haystack Rocks, Clatsop and Tillamook counties; Three Arch Rocks, Tillamook Co.; Table Rock, Coos Co.; and Island Rock, Hunters I., and Goat I., Curry Co. Numbers of pure Western Gulls in the northern part of the state are difficult to count due to the presence of hybrids. At Yaquina Head 32% were hybrids (n=34) and at Gregory Point, south of Coos Bay, 2% were hybrids (n=46) (Bell 1997). The hybrid zone has expanded moderately since that described by Hoffman et al. (1978) as the relative proportions of hybrids at the northern and southern ends of the zones have increased (Bell 1997) and both Western and Glaucous-winged Gulls have expanded their breeding ranges (Bell 1996). The mid-point of the hybrid zone is still centered on Gray's Harbor, Washington, and has not shifted since the mixed colonies were first reported by (Dawson 1908). Bell (1997) suggested that inter-annual variations in relative fitness, resulting from a response to environmental conditions, may shift between the various morphotypes and that this is responsible for maintaining the hybrid zone. Hybrids are most fit in some years whereas pure types are most fit in others. This fluctuation in fitness prevents complete swamping of the parental type and complete elimination of the hybrids. Good et al. (2000) determined that the increase in reproductive success measured in pure hybrid or mixed pairs in Washington resulted from hybrids having nesting and feeding behavior that combines adaptive traits of both parental species.

Major threats are human disturbance on the breeding colony, oil spills, and pollutants. In California in the 1950s to 1970s the sex ratio on colonies in the Channel Is. was weighted 3:2 to females, and female-female pairs were common (Hunt and Hunt 1975, Pierotti 1981). Although the sex ratio was also skewed significantly towards higher numbers of females on the Farallon Is. in the 1980s (Spear et al. 1987), no female-female pairs have been recorded there. In s. California, the skewed sex ratio was attributed to DDT residues causing the feminization of male embryos (Fry et al. 1987), but on the Farallon Is. it was attributed to lower survival rates of males during the first year (Spear et al. 1987). Although both sexes fledge at similar sizes, the males must grow more following fledging to obtain adult size. This growth occurs during the fall and winter of the first year when mortality is the highest during the life cycle of these gulls.—*Jan Hodder*

### Glaucous-winged Gull *Larus glaucescens*

This is one of the two most common large gulls in Oregon. An uncommon breeder, the Glaucous-winged Gull hybridizes with Western Gulls in Oregon and Washington, and farther north hybridizes with Slaty-backed, Herring, and Glaucous Gulls (Bell 1996). See the general discussion of pink-footed gulls in the Herring Gull account. Pure adult Glaucous-winged Gulls have pale gray mantles, flesh colored legs, and dark grayish-brown iris, but because of hybridization plumage can be quite variable.

**General Distribution:** Breeds from the s. Bering Sea through s. Alaska along the Pacific coast to nw. Oregon. It is a rare breeder along the Columbia R. in se. Washington (M. Denny p.c.). Winters in N. America from the s. Bering Sea to Baja California, including the Gulf of California, and in Asia from Bering Is. to Japan. Casual or accidental in Hawaiian Is., interior w. N. America and the Revillagigedo Is. Monotypic.

**Oregon Distribution:** Glaucous-wings were first noticed breeding in Oregon in 1969 (Scott JM 1971).

Hoffman et al. (1978) recorded breeding as far south as Parrot Rock, Lane Co., in 1975. Breeds mainly along the n. coast and at the mouth of the Columbia R.; accurate numbers are difficult to determine because of hybridization. Bell (1997) suggested that Glaucous-winged Gulls will not be able to penetrate the hybrid zone to any great extent as they are not adapted to the upwelling zone of the California current, and that the Oregon coast, with the exception of a few bays, does not provide suitable breeding habitat for them. The largest breeding colony in Oregon is at East Sand I. in the Columbia R. Small numbers breed inland in Ring-billed and California Gull colonies at Memaloose I. in the Columbia R. near The Dalles, and Miller Rock, upstream from the mouth of the Deschutes R. (DuWors et al. 1984). They breed occasionally farther east along the Columbia R. as habitat permits (H. Nehls p.c.). A Western/Glaucous-winged Gull pair nested at Willamette Falls in 1993 and 1994 (Johnson J 1994a, 1995a).

These gulls are abundant fall through spring at the coast, up coastal rivers, and in flooded areas (Contreras 1998). CBCs show numbers of Glaucous-winged Gull and Western/Glaucous-winged Gull hybrids in the hundreds in the Portland and Sauvie I. counts, with smaller numbers upriver as far as Salem and Hood River. They are present in winter in the Willamette Valley, rare but regular in e. Oregon along the Columbia R. (H. Nehls p.c.) and occasional in interior sw. Oregon (Hunter et al. 1998). Never as abundant offshore as Western Gulls, they occur over the continental shelf fall through spring (Briggs et al. 1992). They have been recorded over 600 mi (1080 km) offshore (Sanger 1970).

**Habitat and Diet:** Glaucous-wings prefer bays, estuaries, beaches, mud flats, dumps, dredge spoil islands, and inland waterways and are found in the same habitat year-round (Verbeek 1993). They nest on the

*Glaucous-winged Gull*

ground on rock or in vegetated areas (Verbeek 1993) and on roofs of waterfront buildings (Eddy 1982). The nest consists of loosely stacked terrestrial vegetation, algae, and occasional refuse.

They eat a wide variety of fish, marine invertebrates, garbage, and carrion. Diet varies with location (Vermeer 1982, Verbeek 1993); for example, predation pressure by Glaucous-winged Gulls on Caspian Tern eggs and chicks in the Columbia R. in 2000 was intense at Rice I. but rare at East Sand I. (Lowe 2000). They drop shelled items such as clams on hard substrates to break them open. If they ingest shellfish affected by paralytic poisoning the birds can detect it and regurgitate before any harm is done (Kvitek 1991). Will feed in mixed flocks with other seabirds, and exploit food trapped at the surface by subsurface predators such as sea lions (Baltz and Morejohn 1977) and diving birds. Young are fed mostly fish, with some intertidal invertebrates and garbage (Verbeek 1993).

**Seasonal Activity and Behavior:** Very little is published about the small number of birds that nest in Oregon. The following account is from work in British Columbia by Vermeer (1963) and Verbeek (1986) unless noted otherwise. Timing of movements and breeding is likely a bit earlier in Oregon. The first birds arrive at colonies in early Feb; most have arrived by late Apr. Age at first breeding averages 5.4 yr, (range 4-7 yr) (Reid 1988). Eggs are laid mid-May to mid-Jun (mean clutch size 2.8, range 1-4, n=896). Both sexes incubate; the incubation period is 26.9 days (SE=0.08, n=128). The median date of hatching is the end of Jun. Eggshells are removed and carried away from nest (Verbeek 1993). Chicks remain in or near the nest 2 days after hatching, then start to move around the territory, seeking shade to avoid overheating. Chicks recognize their parents' mew call over considerable distances but parents do not recognize their own chicks (Galusha and Carter 1987). First flight is at 43.8 days (range 37-53, n=67) and young leave the colony on average at 57 days. Associations after fledging are poorly known (Verbeek 1993). Banded birds in British Columbia mostly disperse southward along the coast, with first-year birds dispersing farther than all other age classes (Verbeek 1993).

**Detection:** At all ages, precise identification of Glaucous-winged Gulls is difficult because of hybridization with Western Gulls. Birds with worn plumage look pale, even white, and can be confused with Glaucous Gulls (Pickering 2000); these birds are often so worn that feather shafts are visible.

**Population Status and Conservation:** Total nesting population is estimated at 200,000 pairs (Vermeer and Irons 1991) with 18,500 pairs in Washington (Speich and Wahl 1989). Population has increased in the last few decades (Verbeek 1993). Exact numbers breeding in Oregon are unavailable because of difficulty with identification. In 1997, 9,957 gulls in the Glaucous-winged/Western Gull species complex nested on three dredge spoil islands created in the mid-1980s in the Columbia R. (Collis et al. 1999). The largest breeding colony is at East Sand I. in the Columbia R. where Gilligan et al. (1994) reported 720 gulls breeding in 1975; between 5,500 and 7,000 gulls nested there 1996-98 (Collis et al. 1999). At this site 33% of breeding gulls were hybrids (n=156) (Bell 1997).

Outside of Oregon, river otters and Bald Eagles take adults and chicks. Threats to the population include introduced mammals (Verbeek 1993) and flooding of nesting habitat in dam-controlled rivers (DuWors et al. 1984). Susceptible to oil, as it is a surface feeder.—*Jan Hodder*

## Glaucous Gull *Larus hyperboreus*

This large arctic gull visits the Northwest in winter, where its pale bulk often stands out in gull flocks. Finding one is a highlight of winter birding. Even at a distance the size and frosty tones of this bird can be spotted in a flock. Most Oregon birds are in the whitish first- or second-year plumage showing a pinkish bill with sharply delineated black tip, but third-year birds and adults occur now and then, mainly on the north coast and at Sauvie I. See the general discussion of pink-footed gulls in the Herring Gull account.

**General Distribution:** Breeding range circumpolar, arctic and subarctic; winters south to mid-latitudes of the N. Hemisphere. In N. America breeds from w. Alaska to Greenland, including n. Quebec and n. Hudson's Bay. Winters regularly south to Oregon, the Great Lakes, and Virginia, with most southerly reports coastal. Two N. American subspecies, *L. h. leuceretes* of e. Canada and n. Europe and the smaller, slightly darker *L. h. barrovianus*, the Alaska breeding subspecies (Banks 1986). Specimens of *barrovianus* have been collected in Oregon (Johnston 1955, Bayer 1989a) and no specimens of any other subspecies have been reported from the w. coast of North America (Banks 1986).

**Oregon Distribution:** Rare but regular along the coast and the Columbia R.; local and rare in the Willamette Valley. It can be uncommon midwinter at Sauvie I. Very rare elsewhere; unrecorded in the Umpqua (Hunter et al. 1998) and Rogue (Browning 1975a) valleys. Present every winter in coastal Oregon and up the Columbia R. to Portland, but numbers vary. In winter 1992-93 "several dozen" were thought to be in the huge gull flocks at Sauvie I. (Gilligan et al. 1994) but that is an atypical high count, with 3-5 birds more normal at that location (*ALC*).

Most coastal CBCs record the species with some regularity, usually only one or two birds, but less frequent farther south. The Columbia Estuary CBC has reported it on nine of 19 counts, with a high of three. At Tillamook Bay the species has been found on 17 of 34 counts, also with a high of three. Coos Bay has reported it on only six of 29 counts, nearly always single birds, although the species is annual in Coos Co. (CBC, Contreras 1998). Differences in discovery of this species on CBCs may relate to the fact that gulls concentrate in some count areas, allowing easy sifting for uncommon species, while in other areas gulls are spread thinly (and distantly) over most of the circle.

Rare east of the Cascades, with fewer than 10 records along the Columbia R. and two from Klamath Falls (C. Corder p.c., C. Miller p.c., K. Spencer p.c., CBC).

Offshore status is little known but it is likely very rare. Sanger (1970) noted a probable immature photographed "925 km [498 mi] off Oregon" in Jan 1965. Of 11 offshore trips Nov-Apr 1995-2000, none reported Glaucous Gull (G. Gillson unpubl. data).

Some observers note that coastal birds are sometimes smaller and smaller-billed than birds seen at Sauvie I. and other interior sites (J. Gilligan p.c., *ALC*). This possibility has not been systematically studied owing to the limited number of specimens.

**Habitat and Diet:** Has the usual eclectic feeding habits of large gulls, and is equally at home at dumps, beaches, and riverfronts. Rare in the open areas of the Willamette Valley. Dietary information in Oregon is not available.

**Seasonal Activity and Behavior:** Arrives rather late in autumn and leaves fairly early in spring, with most birds first reported in late Oct or Nov and few reliable reports after Apr (Dillingham 1994, Bayer 1995a, Contreras 1998, Patterson 1998b). Tend to stay in one general area for the winter once they arrive, but move with other gulls, flocks of which often fly long distances between feeding and resting areas. Not averse to feeding in flooded pastures with smaller gulls when that is a good food source (*ALC*). Likewise willing to spend time at landfills with large gulls.

Harder to find by early spring and seems to have an early departure date, though actual late dates are hard to come by. One collected 28 Apr 1915 in coastal Lane Co. is the latest spring report confirmed by specimen (Gabrielson and Jewett 1940, Bayer 1989a). A bird was photographed at Tillamook Bay on 20 Jun 1982 (Gilligan et al. 1994), an astoundingly late date for what may have been an injured or nonbreeding bird. At least three were at Lincoln City in Jun 1999 (Pickering 2000).

**Detection:** Easy to detect when present in gull flocks owing to their size (though *barrovianus* is smaller

than *leuceretes*), two-tone bill on first- and second-year birds and frosty primaries. From spring to mid-summer beware of pale, worn first-year Glaucous-winged Gulls, which are often whiter than real Glaucous Gulls, most of which when viewed at close range show very fine light brown scalloping on much of their plumage through their second winter (Pickering 2000). Presumed hybrids with Glaucous-winged Gulls create additional identification problems (H. Nehls p.c.).

**Population Status and Conservation:** Small numbers have occurred in Oregon as far back as the early 20th century (Gabrielson and Jewett 1940), and numbers wintering in the past 20 yr (CBC) seem relatively constant. As long as coastal and estuarine habitat remains available this species is likely to continue to occur in Oregon. Closure of landfills and similar sources of food would probably reduce inland occurrence.—*Alan L. Contreras*

## Sabine's Gull *Xema sabini*

The striking tri-colored upperwing pattern on this graceful little gull is diagnostic in all plumages—a bold white triangle bordered by black outer primaries and gray back and inner wing. It is a highly pelagic species that is most often observed well offshore during the spring and fall migration. This is the only gull to have a complete molt (flight and body feathers) in spring and a partial molt (primarily body feathers) in fall; other gulls have the opposite sequence.

**General Distribution:** Circumpolar, breeding on arctic tundra. Primarily pelagic when not breeding. Migrates over the ocean to winter at sea in the tropical Pacific and Atlantic oceans. Rare migrant through the interior of N. America. One N. American subspecies (Vaurie 1965), *X. s. sabini*.

**Oregon Distribution:** Common to abundant spring and fall transient over continental shelf well offshore. Irregular but fairly common in fall and uncommon in spring along the coast; casual inland west of the Cascades. Rare but regular fall migrant east of the Cascades. Casual in summer and winter.

**Habitat and Diet:** Most often observed flying in steady migration over the ocean. Seldom observed foraging offshore and is only mildly attracted to fish operations and chum, often hanging back 0.25 mi (0.4 km) (G. Gillson p.c., P.T. Sullivan p.c.). When ashore, found about coastal estuaries and inland lakes and impoundments; avoids rivers and streams (Day et al. 2001). Often observed picking food from the surface of the water, from tidal flats, and along inland mud flats and shore edges.

An opportunistic feeder on small fish, aquatic worms, insects and larvae, and small crustaceans (Bent 1921). Two in Tillamook Co. were full of insects: weevils, carabid beetles, ants, and a few other insects (Gabrielson and Jewett 1940). Two at Stinking L. in Malheur NWR, Harney Co., 17 Sep 1975 were observed feeding on invertebrates (Littlefield 1990a).

**Seasonal Activity and Behavior:** Pelagic migrations are taken individually or in medium-sized flocks of up to 60 birds (Gabrielson and Jewett 1940, Cogswell 1977, *HBN*). Larger flocks are occasionally reported (Campbell et al. 1990a), e.g., 200 over the north end of Heceta Bank, 25 mi (40.2km) west of Yachats 25 Aug 2001 (Contreras 2002b). Pomarine Jaegers regularly shadow the flocks, kleptoparasitizing the birds (Briggs et al. 1992).

The fall movement occurs from mid-Jul to late Nov with the peak from late Aug to mid-Sep (G. Gillson p.c.). Gabrielson and Jewett (1940) observed a major movement 30 Aug 1929, 6 to 9 mi (3.7 to 5.6 km) offshore, "All day long there was a constant flight of Sabine's Gulls headed southward, either single individuals or small companies. Many hundreds passed us during the day." A very large number gathered 19-27 Sep 1920 on and about Netarts Bay (Gabrielson and Jewett 1940). Unusually large numbers were along the coast with several in the Willamette Valley during the fall of 1997 (Gilligan 1998).

Rare but regular fall migrant east of the Cascades between early Sep and mid-Nov with up to five reports yearly, some involving 2-3 individuals (LaFave 1965, Littlefield 1990a, Sullivan 1996a, 1997a). Two spring and two fall records in the Rogue Valley (Janes et al. 2001).

Little is known of the pelagic status of the species during the winter and early spring because offshore sea conditions preclude regular boat trips. An immature was off Cape Arago, Coos Co., 17 Dec 1978 (Mattocks 1979); an adult was off the s. jetty of the Columbia R. 15 Dec 1979 (Mattocks and Hunn 1980a); one was off Cape Arago 20 Dec 1981 and five were there 5 Dec 1987 (Contreras 1998); and one was off Curry Co., 7 Jan 2001 (T. J. Wahl p.c.). A bird in breeding plumage at Yaquina Bay 22 Feb 1992 (Johnson J 1992b) may have been an early spring migrant.

Early spring migrants arrive by mid-Mar increasing to the main movement during May. The latest were two off Boiler Bay, Lincoln Co., 2 Jun 1992 (Johnson J 1993a) and one at the s. jetty of the Columbia R. 6 Jun 1999 (T. Thornton p.c.). One off Coos Co., 21 Jun 1982 (Contreras 1998) and one at Brownlee Res., Baker Co., 19 Jun 1999 (Spencer 2000a) may have been late spring migrants or nonbreeding summering individuals.

There are few spring inland records. Individuals were at the Hines sewage ponds, Harney Co., 19 May 1971 (D. Baccus p.c.); in Jackson Co. in May 1993 (Janes et al. 2001), at the Kirtland Road sewage ponds, Jackson Co., 14 May 1976; at Fern Ridge Res. 19-20 May 1996 (Lillie 1996); and at Baskett Slough NWR 18 May 1999 (R. Gerig p.c.).

**Detection:** Conspicuous and easily identified but pelagic habits and scarcity inland makes it unlikely to be encountered unless an offshore boat trip is taken during the migratory period. At a distance, might be mistaken for terns or Bonaparte's Gulls because of buoyant flight with wing strokes mostly above the horizontal (G. Gillson p.c.). Subadult Black-legged Kittiwakes are often misidentified as this species because of the pale rear wing triangle bordered in front by a dark wedge on outer primaries and gray and black upperwing.

**Population Status and Conservation:** Total population unknown, probably under 100,000 pairs (Enticott and Tipling 1997). Nesting and wintering grounds are well away from human influences. No conservation problems are known in Oregon or elsewhere.—*Harry B. Nehls*

## Black-legged Kittiwake *Rissa tridactyla*

These small agile gulls are predominantly pelagic, but can often be seen from shore and even idling around lower estuaries. Because they are usually offshore and have such distinctive plumage it is always a delight to come across these delicate long-winged birds onshore, whether as gray-mantled adults with frosty primaries and solid black wingtips or in the wing-striped immature plumage.

**General Distribution:** Circumpolar arctic and subarctic breeder, wintering from the Arctic Ocean south mainly over the open sea and along coasts to Baja California; rare inland. Two subspecies; *R. t. pollicaris* in Oregon (AOU 1957).

**Oregon Distribution:** Uncommon to common migrant and winter resident along the outer coast and offshore. Peak numbers are seen from boats and along the outer coast during migration. Winter numbers offshore generally unrelated to seafloor depth, slope or water temperature; densities in 1990 recorded at 3-33 birds/mi$^2$ (1-13 birds/km$^2$) from shore to 100 mi (160 km) offshore (Briggs et al. 1992).

Rare in interior w. Oregon, mainly at large bodies of water after storms. Examples include late fall at Fern Ridge Res., Lane Co. (Heinl and Hunter 1988), rare at Sauvie I. (Klein 1977), two records in fall and one in late winter in Benton Co. (Herlyn 1998). Unrecorded from interior sw. Oregon.

Very rare east of the western interior valleys. One was at John Day Dam 24 Nov to 5 Dec 1995 (Tweit and Johnson 1996a). One was in Heppner, Morrow Co., on 12 Nov 1967 (Rogers 1968a). There were no records from Malheur NWR (Littlefield 1990a) until a single injured bird appeared near Frenchglen in late May 2001 (S. Wright p.c.). Unreported from the Oregon side of the Klamath Basin (Summers 1993a) or in c. Oregon (C. Miller p.c.), Malheur Co. (Contreras and Kindschy 1996), or Union and Wallowa counties (Evanich 1992a).

**Habitat and Diet:** Found primarily on salt water. Does not usually forage in dumps and pastures as most gulls do; rather, it stays over open ocean, along beaches and in lower estuaries, sometimes resting on the water or on jetties, sand spits and similar bare areas. They are often attracted to feeding swarms of loons, pelicans, tubenoses and other seabirds, darting in and out for scraps. On occasion hundreds of birds stream past coastal headlands when winds force migrating swarms eastward (*ALC*, P. Pickering p.c.). No dietary information is available from Oregon. Feeds on surface by dipping, picking, and plunging (Ashmole 1971), primarily on fish (Hatch et al. 1993).

**Seasonal Activity and Behavior:** First reports in fall are usually in early Sep near shore. Kittiwakes are often present in the mouth of the Columbia R. well before they are seen along the remainder of the Oregon coast (*MGH*). Weekly surveys in 1997 at the s. jetty of the Columbia R., found 12 on 7 Sep, and they were recorded on six of seven surveys from that date through 8 Nov, when 167 were seen (M. Patterson p.c.). On 10 offshore trips 1995-2001 in Sep, no kittiwakes were found (G. Gillson p.c.), suggesting that the early fall movement may be largely coastal. Regular seawatches at Boiler Bay overlook, Lincoln Co., 1996-98 found kittiwakes in passage from mid-Sep through early Dec, and sometimes in winter. Peak fall counts there are usually quite low, e.g., 25 on 17 Oct 1996 (*ALC*). At Cape Arago, Coos Co., 300 were seen during storm conditions on 30 Nov 1990 (Contreras 1998).

Regular offshore in winter, uncommon but regular onshore. Typical high hourly counts at Boiler Bay include 60 on 1 Dec 1996 and 30 on 25 Jan 1998 (*ALC*). CBC data show the species found on 21 of 28 counts at Coos Bay, with a high of 62 and a median of three. At Tillamook Bay it has been found 32 yr out of 34, with a high of 27 birds. Large numbers can sometimes be found onshore in early winter, e.g., 85 on the Coquille Valley CBC 31 Dec 2000, 165 at Yaquina Bay CBC in 1986 (Contreras 1997b) and an astonishing 623 on 30 Dec 2000 at Port Orford (CBC).

In some years many dead kittiwakes are found washed up on beaches in winter or early spring.

Harrington-Tweit (1979) suggests that these washups die mainly because of lack of food, perhaps owing to brief periods of warm-water incursion. Considerable numbers must winter offshore or move north by late winter; witness the 200 at the s. jetty of the Columbia R. on 24 Feb 1977 (Crowell and Nehls 1977b). Early spring numbers can be quite high, such as the 157 seen on a pelagic trip off Newport 20 Mar 1999, 350 off Newport 11 Mar 1995, and 312 off Depoe Bay 28 Feb 1998 (G. Gillson p.c.). A record 9,000 were carefully estimated from Boiler Bay wayside during a 3.75-hr seawatch on 16 Mar 2002 (P. Pickering p.c.). Movements in Apr and early May are often composed mainly of first-winter birds (P. Pickering p.c.).

Generally absent in summer. Weekly surveys at the s. jetty of the Columbia R. did not find the species 18 Jun through 29 Aug 1997, but a few summer stragglers are sometimes found, with some years having extraordinary concentrations of birds, e.g., the "flocks up to 500" blown inshore by unusual winds at the Columbia R. mouth 7-21 May 1965 (Hesse and Hesse 1965) and 1,000 there on 20 Jun 1965 (Baldridge and Crowell 1965).

**Detection:** Fairly easy to see at a distance by using a scope from coastal headlands. Sometimes quite approachable on jetties or at beach roosts where gulls gather.

**Population Status and Conservation:** No studies have been conducted in Oregon. Based on limited CBC data, there has been no major change in numbers wintering along the Oregon coast in the past 25 yr. Habitat use in Oregon is mainly limited to the ocean, with occasional visits to open beaches, jetties and estuaries where human impact is not likely to have a significant effect.—*Alan L. Contreras*

## Red-legged Kittiwake *Rissa brevirostris*

This pelagic gull breeds on the Pribilof and Aleutian Is. and winters over the nearby ocean. It occurs casually southward to n. Oregon. There are five specimen records of this species from Oregon beaches: DeLake, Lincoln Co., 28 Jan 1933 (Gabrielson and Jewett 1940, spec. no. 589514 USNM); Waldport, Lincoln Co., 25 Mar 1951 (Munro 1953, spec. no. 81827 Royal Ontario Museum, Toronto); Nehalem, Tillamook Co., 12 Mar 1955 (Walker 1955, spec. no. 81826 Royal Ontario Museum, Toronto); Cannon Beach, Clatsop Co., 30 Dec 1981 (spec. no. 39589 Burke Museum, University of Washington). One was found dead on Clatsop Beach, Clatsop Co., 24 Jan 1982 (OBRC); and another at the n. spit Coos Bay 5 Mar 1999 (Ford et al. 2001). On 7 Aug 1983 an adult landed on a fishing boat 15 mi (24 km) west of Tillamook Head, Clatsop Co., and was photographed (Watson 1989). On 16

Jan 1989 an oiled and weakened bird was found on Rockaway Beach, Tillamook Co., and was taken to a rehabilitation center where it later died (OBRC). Monotypic (AOU 1957).—*Harry B. Nehls*

## Ross's Gull *Rhodostethia rosea*

This Arctic gull breeds in n. Siberia and n. Canada and winters over the Arctic oceans. It is casual southward in N. America but reports are increasing. From 18 Feb to 2 Mar 1987 a rather unwary basic-plumaged adult was photographed at Yaquina Bay, Lincoln Co. (Nehls 1987c, Watson 1988). A bright adult was at McNary Dam on the Columbia R., Umatilla Co., 27 Nov to 1 Dec 1994 (Sullivan T 1995, Sullivan, PT 1995b).—*Harry B. Nehls*

### Subfamily Sterninae

## Caspian Tern *Sterna caspia*

The largest species of tern in the world, the Caspian Tern is easily recognizable by its black cap, pale gray upperparts, scarlet bill, and gull-like size. Although scarce or declining throughout much of its range, most populations in N. America have recently grown, including the Pacific coast/Western states population. Oregon currently hosts the largest known Caspian Tern nesting colony in the world (on East Sand I. in the Columbia R. estuary), but the future of this colony is uncertain. The species has recently gained notoriety in the Pacific Northwest as a predator on young salmon and its management has become highly controversial.

**General Distribution:** Breeds at scattered sites in N. America, Eurasia, Africa, Australia, and New Zealand (Cramp 1985, Cuthbert and Wires 1999). Widespread but disjunct breeding distribution in N. America: Atlantic coast from Newfoundland to N. Carolina; Gulf coast from Florida to Texas; Great Lakes region; c. Canada; Pacific coast from Alaska to Baja California; Great Basin region. Wintering range in N. America mostly coastal: N. Carolina to Florida, Gulf coast, Caribbean islands (rarely), and south to Honduras. On the Pacific coast, it winters along the coast of s. California, Mexico, M. America, and extreme n. S. America. Monotypic (AOU 1945); includes *imperator*, a subspecies in Gabrielson and Jewett (1940).

**Oregon Distribution:** Breeding colonies in recent years have been on islands in the Columbia R. estuary in extreme nw. Oregon; on the mid-Columbia R. east of the Cascades in nc. Oregon; Malheur and Harney lakes in se. Oregon; Summer L. and lakes in the Warner Valley in sc. Oregon. Most colony sites have a history of intermittent use. It is a locally common summer resident during breeding season within foraging distance of nesting colonies (30-40 mi [50-65 km]); rare elsewhere. Later in the breeding season, failed breeders wander widely and occur farther from active colonies (Anderson SK in prep.). It is fairly common in bays and estuaries along the coast during spring and fall migration. Smaller numbers are found on inland waters during migration, including mid-Columbia, Willamette, and Snake rivers, large lakes in the western interior valleys, and lakes and reservoirs east of the Cascades and in sc. Oregon. Occasional along the coast and inland in late fall and early spring (Gilligan et al. 1994).

**Habitat and Diet:** Found in a variety of marine, brackish, and freshwater habitats, usually on or near large water bodies, where forage fishes 4-10 in (10-25 cm) in length are readily available at surface. Most numerous along the coast, especially in bays and estuaries; rarely beyond sight of land. Breeds in colonies, often in association with other colonial waterbirds, especially gulls. For nesting prefers unvegetated sites on islands that are isolated, free of mammalian predators, and in large bodies of water. On coast, nests on sandy

*Caspian Tern*

islands, including dredge spoil sites. The nest is usually a shallow scrape in sand or gravel with little or no nest material; frequently adjacent to driftwood or other debris. Occasionally nests amidst vegetation or on mats of floating vegetation (e.g., at Malheur L., Upper Klamath Basin) (Finley 1907a, KC).

Caspian Terns are almost entirely piscivorous and forage opportunistically on fish at or near the surface. Normally forages alone or, if prey aggregated, in loose foraging flocks, often with other piscivorous birds (e.g., Double-crested Cormorants). Dives from heights up to 100 ft (30 m) into water to capture prey (Cuthbert and Wires 1999). Diet on Rice I. in Columbia R. estuary was mostly juvenile salmonids (73-90% of prey items), including coho salmon, chinook salmon, and steelhead (Collis et al. 2001, Collis et al. 2002, Roby et al. 2002). Diet on Threemile Canyon I. in mid-Columbia R. was also mostly salmonids (81% of prey items), with smaller amounts of bass, yellow perch, and suckers (Collis et al. 2002, Antolos in prep.). Diet on East Sand I. in Columbia R. estuary mostly non-salmonids: anchovy, herring, sardines, surfperch, sand lance, sculpins, smelt, and flatfish (Roby et al. 2002). East Sand I. and Rice I. are only 13 mi (21 km) apart; diet largely reflects local forage fish availability. Only limited diet data are available from Malheur L. or sc. Oregon, but food is assumed to consist mostly of small carp, minnows, suckers, centrarchids, and perch. During 1994-95, they fed chiefly on tui chub (G. L. Ivey p.c.).

**Seasonal Activity and Behavior:** Reaches Oregon in early Mar; 3 Mar 2002 at Brookings the earliest recent arrival (D. Munson p.c.). Arrival of breeding adults at colonies begins in late Mar/early Apr; continues to mid-May. Courtship displays, courtship meal exchange, and copulation commence soon after arrival at a colony, indicating some pairing prior to arrival. Age at first reproduction is 3-4 yr (Cuthbert and Wires 1999); maximum longevity is 25 yr based on a banded adult recovered on Rice I. (Suryan et al. unpubl. ms.). Frequently nests alongside California and Ring-billed Gulls in interior Oregon; nests near Glaucous-winged/Western Gulls in Columbia R. estuary (Roby et al. 2002). Egg laying commences during the third or fourth week in Apr; earliest egg dates are 18 Apr in Columbia R. estuary and 22 Apr at Threemile Canyon I. (Columbia Bird Research [CBR] unpubl. data, Antolos in prep.). Laying peak is variable, but usually early May. If nesting habitat available and/or if earlier nesting attempts fail, egg laying (presumably by renesters) can occur in Jun and (rarely) early Jul (CBR unpubl. data). Clutch size 1-3 eggs; supernormal clutches of 4-6 eggs uncommon and may reflect female-female pairs (Thompson and Tabor 1981, Cuthbert and Wires 1999). Average clutch size 2.0 eggs at Rice I. in Columbia R. estuary

(Roby et al. 1998) and 2.1 eggs at Threemile Canyon I. (Antolos in prep.).

Incubation period 26-27 days (Penland 1981, DDR). Earliest hatching date 15 May in Columbia R. estuary (CBR unpubl. data). Hatching peak variable, but usually about 1 Jun. Young semi-precocial, down-covered at hatch, semi-nidifugous, able to leave nest scrape within 2 days of hatching (Cuthbert and Wires 1999). Eggs and hatchlings are especially vulnerable to gull predation; older chicks may succumb to starvation, abandonment, and aggression from adults. Young tend to form creches when predators (e.g., Bald Eagles) flush adults from colony, leaving chicks vulnerable. Nesting success varied from 0.06 to 0.55 young raised per pair at Rice I. during 1997-2000, and from 0.57 to 1.40 young raised per pair at East Sand I. during 1999-2001 (Roby et al. 1998, Roby et al. 2002).

Young-of-year first fly late in Jun at 6-7 wk post-hatch; most young fledge and leave natal colony by late Jul when 7-8 wk post-hatch (CBR unpubl. data, Antolos in prep.). Renesting is common following loss of clutch to predators or disturbance (Cuthbert 1988); thus some fledging occurs through Aug and (rarely) into Sep for renesting pairs (CBR unpubl. data). Breeding adults may depart colonies in Jun if nesting attempt fails, or from mid-Jul through Aug if accompanied by fledglings.

Extended post-fledging parental care; parents may continue to feed young several months after fledging (Cuthbert and Wires 1999). Thus adults feeding young can be seen hundreds of miles from the nearest active colony. Adults and fledglings disperse widely across the Pacific Northwest, coastal British Columbia, California, and Alaska before southward migration to wintering grounds (CBR unpubl. data). Most birds drift south along Oregon coast during late Jul to mid-Sep; sightings trail off in late Sep and Oct; few records of stragglers in early Nov (Gilligan et al. 1994).

**Detection:** Readily observed during breeding season in the Columbia R. estuary; along The Dalles, John Day, and McNary dam impoundments on mid-Columbia R.; at Malheur NWR, Summer L., and Warner Valley lakes in sc. Oregon (DDR, KC). Readily observed during spring and fall migration in bays and estuaries along the coast of Oregon; frequently rests on sandy spits with gulls. Caspian Terns are often detected first by their characteristic harsh, raucous calls, given in flight and audible for considerable distances day and night. These calls have become a characteristic sound at most Oregon estuaries in late summer when adults accompanied by squealing juveniles can be found all along the coast.

**Population Status and Conservation:** Five breeding populations in N. America: (1) Pacific coast/Western states, (2) Central Canada, (3) Great Lakes, (4) Atlantic coast, (5) Gulf coast (Wires and Cuthbert 2000). Pairs breeding in Oregon belong to Pacific coast/Western states population (Wires and Cuthbert 2000). Band recoveries indicate widespread movement of individuals among colonies along Pacific coast (Gill and Mewaldt 1983, Suryan et al. unpubl. ms.). Pacific coast/Western states population increased from about 4,500 pairs in 1960 to about 15,000 pairs in 2000 (Gill and Mewaldt 1983, Suryan et al. unpubl. ms.).

Recent trends in Oregon reflect general trends in Pacific coast/western States. In 1940, fewer than 1,000 pairs nested throughout Oregon and colonies were restricted to Malheur L. and a few shallow lakes in sc. Oregon. These small, declining colonies were of conservation concern (Gabrielson and Jewett 1940, Bent 1921). During the latter half of the 20th century, breeding habitat/distribution shifted dramatically from inland lakes and reservoirs in se. and sc. Oregon to the lower Columbia R. in nw. Oregon. The statewide breeding population currently approaches 10,000 pairs. Factors responsible for increase include creation of nesting habitat on dredge spoil islands and other anthropogenic sites; changes in availability of forage fishes, especially hatchery production of salmonid smolts; displacement from former breeding colonies, especially along the Washington coast (*DDR*, CBR unpubl. data).

Nesting in Oregon has occurred at only a few sites in recent years. Most nesting now occurs in the Columbia R. estuary, the only coastal colonies in Oregon (Collis et al. 1999, Roby et al. 2002). The first record of a breeding colony along the Oregon coast was in 1984 on East Sand I.; nesting by up to 1,000 pairs continued there through 1986. First recorded nesting on Rice I. in Columbia R. estuary in 1986 (A. Clark p.c.); by 1998 the Rice I. colony had increased to 8,700 breeding pairs. Nesting on Miller Sands Spit occurred in 1998; no young were raised.

In 1977 a colony of about 200 pairs was discovered on Threemile Canyon I. on the Oregon side of the John Day pool in the mid-Columbia R. near Boardman (Thompson and Tabor 1981). This colony was adjacent to a large California and Ring-billed Gull colony and consisted of 200-400 pairs during 1997-99 (Collis et al. 2002, CBR unpubl. data). The colony was abandoned in 2000 due to mink activity and not reoccupied in 2001 or 2002 (Antolos in prep.).

There is a long but sporadic history of nesting at Malheur NWR/Harney L. in se. Oregon (Willett 1919). Colony sizes and locations have been variable; breeding ceased in 1961 due to drought; resumed in 1983 (Littlefield 1990a) and continued until drought in early 1990s; 600 pairs returned in 1994 following flood (Suryan et al. unpubl. ms.); 200-300 pairs nested on two separate islands at the north end of the lake in 2000 (*KC*); less than 100 pairs at only one site in 2001, a drought year (R. Roy p.c., M. Laws p.c.).

A few small colonies are still present in sc. Oregon, but nesting is sporadic due to fluctuating water levels (*KC*, M. Laws p.c., M. St. Louis p.c.). Has nested on islands in several lakes in the Warner Valley, including Pelican, Crump, and Bluejoint lakes (Stern 1988). In 2000, about 150 pairs nested on Crump L. and no nesting colonies were found elsewhere in the Warner Valley (*KC*). Summer L. in recent years has supported less than 50 nesting pairs (M. St. Louis p.c.). Formerly as many as 500 pairs nested on Upper Klamath L. (Finley 1907a), but no recent breeding records in the Upper Klamath Basin.

Small numbers previously reported nesting on islands on the Oregon side of Snake R. near Ontario and Nyssa in e. Oregon, but no confirmed nesting records in recent years (Contreras and Kindschy 1996).

Beginning in 1999, federal, state, and tribal resource management agencies attempted relocating the Rice I. colony (river mile 21) to East Sand I. (river mile 5) to reduce predation on juvenile salmonids in Columbia R. estuary (USACE 2001). By 2001, all nesting in Columbia R. estuary had shifted to East Sand I., where the proportion of salmonids in diet was less than half that on Rice I., and where nesting success was more than twice as high (Roby et al. 2002). At 8,900 pairs in 2001, the East Sand I. colony is currently home to about two-thirds of the Pacific coast/Western states population, one-quarter of the N. American metapopulation, and one-tenth of the worldwide population (Roby et al. 2002).

The unprecedented breeding aggregation in the Columbia R. estuary has an uncertain future. Large breeding aggregations are vulnerable to oil spills, severe storms, disease outbreaks, and disruption by predators. But prospects for restoring or creating suitable nesting habitat elsewhere are not good, and nearby colony sites appear to be at capacity. Additionally, there is no long-term assurance that habitat on East Sand I. will be maintained for terns or that terns would be allowed to recolonize Rice I. if East Sand I. habitat is lost. Caspian Terns are in need of a region-wide management plan; assurance of sufficient suitable nesting habitat through ongoing management efforts is essential if current population size is to be maintained.—*Daniel D. Roby, Ken Collis, Donald E. Lyons, David P. Craig, and Michelle Antolos*

## Elegant Tern *Sterna elegans*

A slender, orange bill, pearl gray upperparts, and fringed black crest adjoining a white face and neck indeed render this graceful hunter from the south elegant. Adults' foreheads turn white in postbreeding plumage, their usual state in Oregon. Elegant Terns were observed in Oregon for the first time in 1983, a strong El Niño/Southern Oscillation (ENSO) year.

Mostly adults with a few immatures have been observed in that and subsequent years. Elegant Terns are our graceful harbingers of ocean warming.

**General Distribution:** These terns formerly nested at about a dozen island and coastal mainland sites in Baja California and in the Gulf of California, Mexico (Schaffner 1986). The five known breeding colonies are in the Gulf of California and in San Diego Bay and Bolsa Chica Ecological Reserve, California (Schaffner 1986, Collins et al. 1991). The establishment of the San Diego colony, a 319-mi (500-km) extension of the known breeding range, followed the ENSO event of 1957-58 and was coincident with an increase in anchovy abundance in waters off s. California (Schaffner 1986). Abundance has increased dramatically since the 1970s, as illustrated by the new California breeding colonies and northward extensions of postbreeding dispersals (Harrison CS 1984, Collins et al. 1991, Contreras 1998). They commonly disperse to the s. and c. California coast, particularly from Jul to Oct, occurring with diminishing northward frequency in n. California and along the Oregon, Washington, and British Columbia coasts (Cogswell 1977, Collins et al. 1991, AOU 1998). They winter along the Pacific coast of Ecuador, Peru, and Chile and occasionally in s. California (Cogswell 1977, Collins et al. 1991). Monotypic (AOU 1957).

**Oregon Distribution:** Elegant Terns have been recorded 10 of 15 yr in the period 1983-97. Virtually all records are coastal or within 0.5 mi (0.8 km) of shore (Briggs et al. 1987). None reported inland. Peak counts include 319 at the Necanicum R. mouth in Aug 1984, 200 at the Rogue R. mouth in Sep 1984, 200 in lower Coos Bay in Jul 1992, and 215 at the Rogue R. mouth in Sep 1992 (Hunn and Mattocks 1984, Watson 1984, Contreras 1998). Localities with multiple records include the Chetco and Rogue R. mouths, Coos Bay, Siuslaw R. estuary, Alsea Bay, Yaquina Bay, Tillamook Bay, Nehalem Bay, the mouth of the Necanicum R. and the s. jetty of the Columbia R.

**Habitat and Diet:** These terns frequent quiet waters or lagoons when diving for fish, but also dive in calm ocean waters. Roost with flocks of gulls and other terns on coastal spits, estuarine sandbars, and on mudflats close to bay mouths (Harrison CS 1984, *KM*). Northern anchovies are the principal food of adults throughout their range (Schaffner 1984, Schaffner 1986, Hay et al. 1992, Love 1996). Diets at nesting colonies are also composed of other fish averaging 1.6 to 6.4 in (4.0 to 16.4 cm) long, including topsmelt and surfperch, both of which inhabit Oregon waters, and longjaw mudsucker, other anchovies, and grunion, all of which inhabit California but not Oregon waters (Schaffner 1986, Love 1996)

**Seasonal Activity and Behavior:** Postbreeding birds disperse north and enter Oregon beginning in late Jun; the earliest record is 10 Jun 1997 (Johnson J 1998a). Anchovies, which are abundant off the Oregon coast, peak in Aug (Wiens and Scott 1975, Hay et al. 1992, Love 1996), coinciding with Elegant Terns' seasonal appearance. Most records have been of adults (Hunn and Mattocks 1984, Tweit and Fix 1991). They are typically observed plunge-diving for prey, circling above bay mouths, or flying over the open ocean near shore (*KM*). Numbers usually diminish rapidly along the Oregon coast after late Aug (Hunn and Mattocks 1984, Tweit and Fix 1991, Contreras 1998); the latest record is 13 Nov 1983 (Contreras 1998).

**Detection:** Typically located by scanning birds in flight over estuaries, river mouths, and surf, or by searching through roosting flocks of gulls and/or terns. Call can alert observers to its presence.

**Population Status and Conservation:** The first Oregon Elegant Tern was sighted 4 Aug 1983 in Coos Bay. By late Aug, many had been reported along the length of the coast, and several had reached Washington and British Columbia (Hunn and Mattocks 1984). During the 1983 ENSO, the range of many entire fish and invertebrate populations shifted north along the Pacific coast (McGowan et al. 1998), coinciding with the first Elegant Tern influx in Oregon.

Common occurrence of Elegant Terns is relatively recent even in California, where large flocks have been regularly sighted only since 1950 (Harrison CS 1984). Limitation of breeding to so few colonies renders them vulnerable to breeding disturbances (Kaufman 1996). Heavy dependence on a single food species makes their status as a breeding species in California highly precarious and sensitive to environmental variability and its associated effect on northern anchovy abundance and availability (Schaffner 1984). At Isla Raza, breeding Elegant Terns suffer from predation by introduced rats and mice as well as commercial egg collectors (Harrison CS 1984). Although the Mexican government has declared Isla Raza a sanctuary, trespassing by egg collectors, poachers, and well-meaning tourists continues to disturb the terns (Harrison CS 1984). No known threats in Oregon.—*Kathy Merrifield*

## Common Tern *Sterna hirundo*

A traveling or foraging flock of this graceful species never fails to bring pleasure to the observer. This is the small tern most often seen along the coast flying along the beaches or hovering and diving over a school of fish just offshore. Breeding-plumage adults have sharp black caps, reddish bills, and forked tails, and are pale grayish above and white to pale gray below. Immatures have reduced black caps, less reddish bills, less fork in the tail, and more patterning on the upperwings.

**General Distribution:** Breeds widely in Europe, Asia, and in N. America from Alberta and Montana east to Newfoundland and New York, and along the Atlantic coast to N. Carolina. Some breed about the Gulf of Mexico. Winters along the coasts of Africa, and from s. California and S. Carolina south to s. S. America. Four subspecies; *S. h. hirundo* occurs in N. America (AOU 1957).

**Oregon Distribution:** Common to abundant spring and fall transient over the ocean, usually within 15 mi (24 km), irregularly along the coast and in the estuaries. Casual w. Oregon away from the coast. Rare spring and uncommon fall transient east of the Cascades, casual in summer.

**Habitat and Diet:** Found along the coast and offshore; always near water when inland. Nearshore and inland flocks are often observed resting in compact flocks on nearby shores or on floating objects, or flying about over the water in search of small fish. When fish are spotted the flock gathers over the school, hovering overhead, then diving headfirst into the water, birds often going completely under. They seldom swim or forage on the water. Food is almost entirely small fish not over 3-4 in (7.6-10.2 cm) long, primarily sand lance and anchovies; occasionally crustaceans and insects (Bent 1921, Ainley and Sanger 1979, Safina and Burger 1988).

**Seasonal Activity and Behavior:** Gregarious. Regularly observed in medium-sized flocks, seldom exceeding 60 individuals, migrating offshore, although nearshore movements often involve large numbers. Most migrate in a rather brief peak period. In migration the flight is fast and direct with the birds widely spaced. Numbers of jaegers, especially the Parasitic Jaeger, regularly accompany the tern flocks and heavily parasitize the birds (*HBN*).

Little is known of the pelagic status of the species during the winter and early spring because of rough seagoing conditions; there are no coastal records from late Oct to late Mar. An early bird was at Ecola SP, Clatsop Co., 29 Mar 1998 (Lillie 1998). The spring offshore movement is primarily from mid-Apr to mid-May with smaller numbers to mid-Jun. A flock of 25 at the s. jetty of the Columbia R., Clatsop Co., 12-17 Jun 1976 (Crowell and Nehls 1976d) was the latest. Individuals or small flocks are regularly reported in spring but coastal movements are often quite spectacular and often include Arctic Terns. Many small flocks, totaling 500-700 birds/hr, passed the mouth of the Columbia R. 2-4 May 1974 (Crowell and Nehls 1974b, *HBN*); 150 birds/hr were passing the mouth

of Tillamook Bay, 8 May 1976 (Crowell and Nehls 1976c). Spring records east of the Cascades are during the same time period as the coastal movement with each involving 1-2 individuals. Two at the Kirtland Road sewage ponds, Jackson Co., 11 May 1994 (Lillie 1994) is the only w. Oregon spring record away from the coast.

Three remained about the mouth of the Columbia R. throughout the summer of 1978 (Harrington-Tweit et al. 1978). Three were at the s. jetty of the Columbia R. 9 Jul 1992 (Johnson J 1993a). Singles were at Cold Springs NWR, Umatilla Co., 25 Jul 1992 (Evanich 1993); at Harbor, Curry Co., 13 Jul; at Florence, Lane Co., 19 Jul 1994 (Johnson J 1995a); and at Hart Mtn., Lake Co., 12 Jul 1997 (Spencer 1998).

The fall movement occurs from mid-Aug to late Oct with a peak period in late Aug and early Sep. Six on Sauvie I. 5 Aug 1996 (Gilligan 1997) were early. The latest was one at The Dalles, Wasco Co., 8 Nov 1997 (Sullivan 1998a). Fall flocks seldom exceed 150 individuals. The largest inland flocks were 23 at John Day Dam, Sherman Co., 29 Aug to 11 Sep 1994 (Sullivan PT 1995b) and 23 at L. Abert, Lake Co., 2 Sep 1997 (Sullivan 1998a).

**Detection:** Easily identified as one of the medium-sized terns, but separation from Forster's and, especially, Arctic Terns requires close examination and care. A combination of features specific to the appropriate age class (e.g., immature vs. adult) is recommended.

**Population Status and Conservation:** Worldwide population is estimated at 250,000 to 500,000 pairs (Enticott and Tipling 1997). Returned from near extirpation over much of its range during the 19th and early 20th centuries and is now close to its former abundance in N. America, but still much reduced in Europe (Bent 1921, Cramp 1985). No conservation concerns known in Oregon.—*Harry B. Nehls*

## Arctic Tern *Sterna paradisaea*

This graceful tern, with its aerodynamic body and streamlined wings, is infrequently seen from land in Oregon. It is most often encountered at sea as it makes one of the most incredible journeys in the animal kingdom, migrating from the Arctic to the Antarctic and back again each year, a journey of nearly 22,000 mi (35,400 km). A medium-sized bird with a reddish bill, it has a black cap and nape, and a white throat and cheek shading to a light gray body. It closely resembles the Common Tern, and many individuals have to be passed off as "commic" terns. However, when seen well a combination of features separate both immature and adult birds.

**General Distribution:** Holarctic, breeding in Greenland and Iceland, across n. Europe to n. Siberia (del Hoyo et al. 1996). In N. America breeds from n. Alaska east through the Yukon and the Northwest Territories to New Brunswick and south locally along the coast to n. British Columbia and Massachusetts. During 1977-95, a disjunct population bred at Everett, Washington (Manuwal et al. 1979, Smith et al. 1997). Winters in waters around Antarctica in the Atlantic, Pacific, and Indian oceans. Monotypic (AOU 1957).

**Oregon Distribution:** It is an uncommon offshore transient in Oregon waters and an occasional migrant along the coast (Anderson 1989c, Lillie 1995). The bulk of the population is thought to migrate 10-40 mi (19-74 km) from land (Stallcup 1990). Rarely reported inland but may turn up nearly anywhere.

**Habitat and Diet:** No specific habitat requirements are known for Oregon. When seen from shore, however, they are usually seen at jetties, in bays, or at river mouths. Often found mixed in with flocks of Common Terns (Fix 1991). Oregon diet unknown. On breeding grounds in the Northwest Territories of Canada observed to prey upon various small fish, insects, amphipods, shrimp, and other crustaceans (Drury 1960, Abraham and Ankney 1984). Feed by hovering above the water and then plunging beakfirst in pursuit of prey (Drury 1960).

**Seasonal Activity and Behavior:** During spring, Arctic Terns may appear as early as mid-Apr, but are most regular during May, with some birds passing through until mid-Jun (Gilligan et al. 1994, Contreras 1998). Accidental in Oregon during summer (Tice 1997). Fall migration is more extended, and occurs from mid-Aug through mid-Oct with the bulk of reports in mid-Sep. It has been recorded as early as mid-Jul and as late as 25 Nov (Gilligan et al. 1994, Tweit and Gilligan 1997, Gilligan 1999). Occasionally, flocks of as many as 50 are reported and once an exceptionally large flock of 250 was seen on a fall pelagic trip (Gilligan 1999). Most inland records refer to only one or two birds. Given the difficulty of field identification of this species and the relative difficulty of field identification in general in the early 1900s, some historical inland reports are questionable (without reference to a specimen), e.g., a flock of a dozen at Sauvie I. in 1939 (Jewett 1940a), and a flock of 40 over Government I., Multnomah Co., Aug 1902, (Jewett and Gabrielson 1929). Unrecorded during winter; a Portland CBC record is considered erroneous.

**Detection:** Most frequently encountered offshore, where it is difficult to observe this small, swift bird from a moving platform. Greater study is often obtained during rare observations from land. It is difficult to separate from Common Tern. Many reports are unaged, and thus questionable. Arctic Terns have been reported most often (other than pelagic records) at the s. jetty of the Columbia R., Yaquina Bay, Tillamook Bay, Depoe Bay, Coos Bay, and the mouth of the Umpqua R.

**Population Status and Conservation:** Estimated at 500,000 breeding pairs worldwide. The Alaskan coastal population is estimated at 12,500 pairs but the inland population may be much greater (del Hoyo et al. 1996). Substantial declines have occurred in the ne. Atlantic and this is attributed to the decline in sandeel stocks (Suddaby and Ratcliffe 1997, Wanless et al. 1998). No information on trends in Oregon.—*Chris Butler*

## Forster's Tern *Sterna forsteri*

Terns are generally associated with marine environments and salt marshes, but in nw. N. America, the Forster's Tern inhabits freshwater areas in the Great Basin and occurs along major rivers. During the breeding season this graceful bird is e. Oregon's resident small white tern. Typical of terns, the Forster's employs the dramatic hunting method of plunge-diving into shallow waters to capture small fish, the bird sometimes submerging completely.

**General Distribution:** Breeds locally from San Francisco Bay area, s. California south to Baja California Norte, northeast to ec. Alberta and wc. Saskatchewan, Columbia Basin, Klamath Basin, Great Basin, n. Great Plains, Great Lakes, mid-Atlantic coast, ne. Florida, Gulf coast from Florida panhandle to n. Tamaulipas. Winters San Francisco Bay area south to El Salvador, Atlantic coast from Delaware s. to Florida, Gulf coast from s. Florida to Yucatan Peninsula, and c. Mexico (Sauer et al. 1997, Howell and Webb 1995). Some winter on Humboldt Bay, California (D. Fix p.c.). Monotypic (AOU 1957).

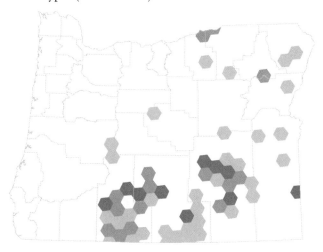

**Oregon Distribution:** This is an uncommon but highly visible colonial breeder east of the Cascades. It is fairly common at Malheur NWR where breeding sites have included Malheur L., Boca L., Derrick L., and Wright's and Warner's Ponds (Littlefield 1990a) and in sc. Oregon at Sycan Marsh (Stern, Del Carlo, et al. 1987). Known to have bred some years at Upper Klamath L., Klamath Marsh NWR, Summer L., Silver L., and Warner Valley lakes. Recent presence at these sites suggests continued breeding (Stern 1988, W. DeVaurs p.c., J. Hainline p.c., M. St. Louis p.c.). Seventeen colonies totalling about 400 pairs were found along the Columbia R. 1977-78 (Thompson and Tabor 1981); one of these colonies, at Rufus Bar below John Day Dam, was in Oregon. Small groups and nonbreeding individuals are occasionally seen during summer away from breeding colonies. Transients are common and widespread east of the Cascades during spring as far east as the Malheur R. and Owyhee R. watersheds (Contreras and Kindschy 1996). Small numbers are reported in some springs at larger lakes in w. Oregon, esp. Fern Ridge Res. (*ALC*, D. Irons p.c.). They are rare in w. Oregon in the Willamette and Rogue valleys, along the Columbia R. and along the coast during fall migration (Gilligan et al. 1994). A single bird seen after storms at Bandon 13 Dec 1995 is the only winter record for Oregon (Contreras 1997b).

**Habitat and Diet:** In Great Basin, including e. Oregon, they nest in emergent vegetation at edges of large lakes or in marshes, but habitat has not been studied in detail. In the n. Great Plains, select nest sites in a variety of wetland types, often on top of muskrat houses or on mats of floating vegetation (Bent 1921, Bergman et al. 1970, McNicholl 1982), a habit also observed at Malheur L. (Littlefield 1990a). Island-nesting birds in the Columbia R. laid eggs on sand-cobble substrate (Thompson and Tabor 1981). Over 70% of these nests successfully fledged at least one chick compared to a much lower 16.5% for marsh-nesting birds in a Manitoba study (McNicholl 1971, Hall 1989). Studies in Wisconsin marshes (Mossman 1989) suggest habitat requirements include nesting substrate,

sites protected from wind and wave action, vegetation of appropriate density to shelter chicks that have left the nest, sites sufficiently protected from humans and predators, and extensive uncontaminated foraging areas nearby. Also in Wisconsin, Forster's Terns utilizing floating artificial nest platforms outproduced those using natural substrates. Although they tend to be located in the same sites repeatedly, nest sites in Wisconsin are transitory and change locations with habitat conditions (Mossman 1989). This appears to be the case in Great Basin populations of Oregon as well, where water levels and availability of prey fish of appropriate size are highly variable and are important in determining nesting sites from year to year (*DBM*).

Prey is captured by plunge-diving, typically in wide expanses of open, shallow water. Fish make up a very high percentage of diet (Gabrielson and Jewett 1940). In a Virginia study, Reed (1985) found about 80% of prey fish to be 2-2.75 in (5-7 cm) in length. Also known to take insects from air and water surface, and occasionally eats frogs and small crustaceans (Kaufman 1996).

**Seasonal Activity and Behavior:** Arrives mid- to late Apr (Gabrielson and Jewett 1940); migration peaks early May (Gilligan et al. 1994). Nesting at Malheur NWR begins early Jun (Littlefield 1990a). During courtship a pair may engage in aerial maneuvers together (Hoffmann 1927), or the male may offer the female a fish (*SCS*). Eggs laid late May to early Jun (Gabrielson and Jewett 1940). Observed on nest in Klamath Basin 8 Jun, fledged 11 Jul in Harney Basin, and carrying food to young 16 and 26 Jul in Klamath Basin (OBBA). Hall (1988, 1989) found that for Columbia R. colonies clutch size averaged 2.9, incubation lasted about 24 days, and young move from the nest after about 2 days, led by walking or flying parents to dispersal areas with vegetative cover. The semiprecocial chick apparently establishes an early bond with parent and can recognize the parent's unique call before leaving the nest. Young were able to fly 4-5 wk after hatching (Hall 1988). Fall migration begins in Jul, and peaks late Aug to early Sep (Gilligan et al. 1994). Littlefield (1990a) reports 20 Oct as a late interior record.

*Forster's Tern*

**Detection:** Easily detected in flight vs. on nest among thick marsh vegetation. High-pitched *churrr* call may alert observers to bird's presence. Inaccessibility and concealed nature of nests can make it difficult to confirm breeding in this species.

**Population Status and Conservation:** Before conservation laws were established early in the 20th century, populations of Forster's Terns were severely threatened by hunters, as the bird's beautiful plumage was highly sought by the fashion industry to adorn womens' hats and attire (Ryser 1985). At Malheur NWR, nest counts peaked at 320 in 1993 and are higher in high-water years (Ivey, Cornely, Paullin, and Thompson unpubl. ms.). Sharp (1990) reported Forster's Tern recently showing "highly significant declines" in Oregon, speculating not only habitat loss in Oregon as the cause, but also contamination of Latin American wintering grounds by agricultural chemicals. More recent data from BBS routes (Sauer et al. 1997) are difficult to interpret. There seems to be a slightly increasing population trend over the western region, though data strictly from Oregon indicate a decreasing trend, at significant levels for some time intervals. Small sample sizes, changing water and food conditions from year to year, and a dearth of local studies make status of Forster's Tern in Oregon uncertain.—*Stuart C. Sparkman*

## Least Tern *Sterna antillarum*

This very small tern breeds along both coasts from Maine and c. California south into S. America. There are scattered colonies along rivers in the interior of N. America. It winters from Mexico southward. It occurs casually elsewhere in N. America. Two adult males were collected at the s. jetty of the Columbia R., Clatsop Co., on 21 May 1964 and are now in the Tillamook Co. Mus. in Tillamook (Walker 1972). One was photographed at the same location 31 May 1976 (Roberson 1980). Four adults were observed on the south sandspit of the Siuslaw R., Lane Co., 19 Aug 1973 (OBRC). One was photographed near the same location 8 Jun 1997 (Johnson J 1998a). An adult was observed at Harris Beach SP, Curry Co., 9 Jul 1998 (OBRC), a subadult was photographed at Yaquina Bay, Lincoln Co., 26 Jul to 10 Aug 1998 (OBRC); and an adult was photographed at the Fernhill Wetlands in Forest Grove 6-10 Mar 1999 (OBRC). Oregon birds belong to nominate *antillarum*, the northern subspecies. Because of similarities of named northern populations (Burleigh and Lowery 1942), *browni* from the w. coast, *athalassos* from the Mississippi Valley, and *antillarum* are synonyms (Massey 1976, Thompson et al. 1992).—*Harry B. Nehls*

## Black Tern *Chlidonias niger*

This is Oregon's smallest breeding tern, with black head and body and gray wings during the breeding season. Sexes are alike, although males are generally larger than females; almost always so within mated pairs (Stern and Jarvis 1991). Adults in late summer molt and juveniles have much white on the head and underparts. Black Terns are delicate, graceful fliers, reminiscent of a nighthawk or swallow.

**General Distribution:** Locally common and concentrated during breeding season in productive freshwater wetlands throughout northern half of temperate N. America; areas of highest abundance are Minnesota., S. and N. Dakota and prairie provinces of Alberta, Saskatchewan, and Manitoba (Dunn and Argo 1995), but range extends from California to Maine and from sw. Northwest Territories to Colorado, Nebraska, and Indiana. Winter range is poorly documented, but known to be along the w. coast of M. America and coastal portions of n. S. America. Two subspecies; *C. n. niger* in the Old World and *C. n. surinamensis* in the Americas and Oregon.

**Oregon Distribution:** Breeds in marsh wetland complexes of se., sc., and c. Oregon, including Malheur NWR, Catlow Valley, Chewaucan Marshes, Warner Valley, Sycan Marsh, Klamath Marsh NWR, Upper Klamath Lake NWR and numerous smaller wetlands throughout Harney, Lake, Klamath and Deschutes counties (e.g., Camas Prairie, north end Goose L., Davis L., Aspen L., Round L., around Upper Klamath L., and Big Marsh). Three records from Malheur Co. at Batch Lakes (2 Jun 1977, 15 Jun 1982), and Bully Cr. Res. (16 Jun 1995), but not known to breed there (Contreras and Kindschy 1996). Infrequent spring and summer sightings from Union and Wallowa counties, but again not suspected to breed there (Evanich 1992a).

In w. Oregon, a very small breeding population is found at a few sites in the Willamette Valley, though not reported in all years from all locations. Two small

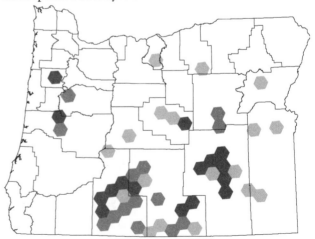

colonies with an estimated 12 nests were reported from Fern Ridge Res., Lane Co., in 1992 (Papish 1993), where the species has bred annually in subsequent years (*ALC*, D. Irons p.c.). Black Terns were also reported in May and Jun from small marshes in Linn Co. south and southeast of Corvallis since at least 1995 (P. Adamus p.c.), and regular summer sightings of a few in 1999-2000 from Baskett Slough NWR, Polk Co. Black Terns are not expected to be numerous in w. Oregon except at Fern Ridge Res.; most sightings elsewhere report fewer than 10 individuals, and often only two or three.

One record of a Black Tern banded at Sycan Marsh in summer 1982 recovered in Guatemala Feb 1983; but otherwise specific migration and wintering areas for Oregon birds unknown. Rare migrant outside breeding range in spring and later summer/early fall (Sawyer and Hunter 1988, Gilligan et al. 1994, Contreras 1998).

**Habitat and Diet:** Black Terns are loosely colonial, with colony size ranging from a couple of nests to large clusters that may number 50 or more. Breeding Black Terns are usually found in emergent marshes and flooded meadows, typically associated with hardstem bulrush. Of 305 nests found at Sycan Marsh in 1982, 170 were in sedge-rush habitats with 4-8 in (11-20 cm) water, 126 in hardstem bulrush in 24 in (60 cm) water, and 11 in tufted hairgrass/rush habitats with 2-6 in (4-15 cm) of standing water. Sedge and rush habitats are characterized by inflated sedge, Nebraska sedge, Sierra rush and Baltic rush (Stern 1982). At Malheur NWR, most nesting occurs in broadfruited bur-reed (G. L. Ivey p.c.). At Sycan Marsh, nest success in 1982 was similar among habitats types, ranging 71-77%.

The nest is a small flat floating platform, sometimes attached to marsh vegetation, with a small bowl made of residual vegetation, occasionally augmented with current year's growth. Flightless young may move to a nearby feeding platform after hatching (*MAS*).

They feed on the wing, flying low over open water, along lake edges, ponds, marshes, sloughs, and irrigation ditches that may be 0.5 mi (0.8 km) or more from a colony. Primarily insectivorous, often taking caddisflies and other aquatic insects, including nymphs and larvae (Gabrielson and Jewett 1940), but will also take small fish and tree frogs (*MAS*). In courtship, male will bring prey items back to female, who waits on nearby perch such as a fence post in or near open water.

**Seasonal Activity and Behavior:** This is a widespread transient east of the Cascades during Apr and May; very rare west of the Cascades (Gilligan et al. 1994). It typically arrives on breeding grounds in e. Oregon in the first wk of May. Nest initiation begins at the end of May and continues through mid-Jun; renesting from

pairs with failed nests at Sycan Marsh occurred slightly later (*MAS*). Young hatch 3 wk after nest initiation and fledge approximately 3 wk later, with most young fledged by mid-Jul. Nesting is synchronized within colonies. Most adults and fledged young leave breeding areas by 1 Aug. Gabrielson and Jewett (1940) reported extreme dates of 10 Apr in Klamath Co. and 11 Oct in Harney Co. In w. Oregon, breeding season may be extended as evidenced by record of black downy chick on nest at Fern Ridge Res., Lane Co. on 27 Jul 1992 (Papish 1993). Gullion (1951) reported extreme dates of 10 May 1948 and 8 Aug 1949 in w. Oregon. Peak autumn migration at Malheur NWR is 10-20 Aug (Littlefield 1990a). Occasional in w. Oregon and along the coast through Dec (Gilligan et al. 1994).

Stern (1987) banded 778 adult terns at Sycan Marsh in 1982-84, with a 15% return rate in successive years. When adjusted for annual survival, it is estimated that 40% of the surviving adult population returned in successive years. The location of other surviving adults is unknown. Mate fidelity is high if both birds return to the same breeding area; at Sycan Marsh, five pairs remained intact in consecutive years, while 18 found new mates as the mate from the previous year was not present (Stern 1987).

**Detection:** Flying birds are easily spotted in the vicinity of a colony, but colony location is not readily visible unless terns are alarmed, in which case the entire colony may rise off nests and mob an intruder. Nests are rarely if ever found in association with other colonial species. Best viewing opportunities are at Malheur NWR, Upper Klamath L. and Klamath Marsh NWRs. Birds can often be viewed closely at colonies at Fern Ridge Res., Lane Co.

**Population Status and Conservation:** BBS data indicate that Black Terns throughout N. America declined 3.1% annually 1966-96, though most of the decline was in Canada. Primary cause of this decline is deterioration and loss of breeding habitat (Dunn and Argo 1995). Populations have apparently leveled out or risen slightly in the 1990s (Shuford 1997). No information is available on trends in Oregon. Most breeding concentrations in e. Oregon are in association with large, publicly managed refuges and wetland areas in e. Oregon, and these habitats are generally secure and not subject to human disturbance (*MAS*). Some marshes may have diminished habitat quality due to closing in of emergent marsh, and decreasing areas of open water.

Small recurrent breeding populations have been found in the Willamette Valley since the late 1940s, though they are not present or at least not reported in every year except at Fern Ridge Res. since 1992. Suspected nesting by Black Terns at Fern Ridge Res. was first reported in 1948-49 by Gullion (1951), who also characterized the species as a common visitor to the s. Willamette Valley. There were subsequent reports of suspected nesting at Fern Ridge Res. in 1969 (Papish 1993). In Benton Co., six nests were found near Corvallis in 1963 (Boggs and Boggs 1963d), and summering Black Terns were reported again in that vicinity in 1979 and 1981. Two were seen at Tanasbrook Pond, Washington Co., on 1 Jun 1977 (J. Buchanan p.c.). Summer sightings have also been reported from Baskett Slough NWR, Marion Co., and Ankeny NWR, Polk Co., in the 1970s, with four immatures sighted at Ankeny NWR on 13 Jun 1972 (Papish 1993). In s. Oregon, Black Terns formerly nested at Hoover's Lakes and the Game Ponds (now Denman WMA) in Jackson Co., north of Medford (Browning 1975a), but none have been reported since then.—*Mark A. Stern*

## Family Alcidae

### Common Murre *Uria aalge*
The most common seabirds breeding in Oregon, Common Murres are easily recognized by their distinct black and white breeding plumage and their upright stance at colonies. They nest on rocky islands and cliffs in colonies of tens or hundreds of thousands of birds packed together almost shoulder to shoulder. Wing-beats are rapid and like all alcids they can fly underwater. They are often seen over the ocean in long lines of 10-40 or more birds.

**General Distribution:** Breeds in the N. Pacific and N. Atlantic. They are found in the Pacific from w. Alaska south through Norton Sound and the Bering Sea and from the Aleutian Is. to c. California. They are also found from Kamchatka south to Korea and Japan. Murres winter offshore in areas near their breeding grounds and south to s. California. Two subspecies in the Pacific Ocean; *U. a. californica* occurs in Oregon (AOU 1957, Browning 2002).

**Oregon Distribution:** Major nesting concentrations in Oregon are on the s. and n. coasts reflecting the availability of suitable nesting habitat. Thirty-three colonies north of Cascade Head represent 53% of the total breeding population. The largest colony complex in Oregon is Three Arch Rocks NWR, where 131,481 birds were counted in 1988. Thirty-one colonies south of Bandon represent 41% of the total breeding population. Three of these locations—an unnamed rock off Whalehead Cr., Gull Rock, both Curry Co., and Cat and Kittens Rocks at Coquille Point, Bandon—each have over 20,000 nesting birds (USFWS unpubl. data). Murres are the most abundant bird over the continental shelf during all months (Briggs et al. 1992) although winter densities are lower than in summer months

(Tyler et al. 1993). They are commonly present in large estuaries in late summer and fall.

**Habitat and Diet:** Marine. Breeding occurs on the tops and ledges of unvegetated rocky offshore islands and cliff faces of headlands. No nest is constructed; a single egg is laid on the bare ground. Common Murres are wing-propelled divers capable of relatively deep long dives; they have been found entangled in gill nets at depths of 600 ft (180 m) (Piatt and Nettleship 1985). The average adult dive time during chick feeding at sea off Newport was 104 sec with dives as long as 154 sec (Scott 1990). Similar results were found off Coos Bay (Hansell 1983) where average dive times for chick feeding adults were 91.5 sec and maximum dive time was 200 sec. Periods of constant diving can last as long as 118 min (Scott 1990) and are interspersed with periods of resting and preening. On rare occasions they can be found up to a mile or two up large coastal rivers (M. Denny p.c., *MGH*).

The most important prey during the breeding season are mid-water fish (vs. surface-living or bottom fish). A collection of 635 murres 1979-82 off Coos Bay, Newport, and the Columbia R. revealed that 29 species of fish, crustaceans, and mollusks were represented in their diet (Matthews 1983). Sand lance, juvenile rockfish, pacific tomcod, whitebait smelt, northern anchovy, speckled sanddab, Pacific herring, market squid, crab megalops, and euphausiids were the most common prey items, but the importance and proportions of these varied with year and location of the sample (Matthews 1983). Scott (1990) collected 18 adult and seven juvenile murres off Newport 1970-1972 and found anchovies, rockfish, and other scorpionfishes predominated in the diet. Chicks are fed single fish ranging <1-5 in (2-15 cm) in length (Parrish et al. 1998). Murres catch slower fish by the tail and faster ones by the head; both are swallowed at the surface (Swennen and Duiven 1977). Little information is available on diet in winter; crustaceans dominated in samples from Alaska, and herring in samples from British Columbia (Vermeer et al. 1987).

**Seasonal Activity and Behavior:** Murres do not breed until 4 or 5 yr of age and probably do not visit the breeding colony until age 2 or 3 (Birkhead and Hudson 1977). There are no published studies that detail the breeding chronology of Common Murres in Oregon. On the Farallon Is., California, they return to the breeding colony in late Oct and visit the nest sites in an irregular pattern during the winter months (Boekelheide et al. 1990b). From mid-Jan to mid-Mar murres are present on about 33% of the days at one colony and only 15% of the days at another more recently formed colony (Sydeman 1993). Murres have been reported on Three Arch Rock NWR in mid-Dec (Bayer 1988a); at Coquille Point, Bandon, in Jan (Roy

Lowe p.c.); in the water at Yaquina Head in late Dec and early Jan but not on the colony until mid-Feb (Bayer and Herzing 1985, Bayer 1988a); and on Cape Meares in mid-Feb (Heinl 1985).

Timing of egg laying on the Farallon Is. is variable, with the mean laying date range from 9 May to 9 Jun, although within years egg laying is closely synchronized, with more than 50% of the single egg clutches laid within a 10-day period (Boekelheide et al. 1990b). Scott (1973) reported first egg dates at Yaquina Head as 5-29 May and Browning and English (1972) mentioned that 10% of breeders on Goat I., Curry Co., had eggs on 14 May 1966. The egg is approximately 11% of the adult weight (Gaston and Jones 1998). Experiments have shown that murres are capable of discriminating between their own and others' eggs (Gaston et al. 1993). At the Farallons, ground color is thought to vary from year to year in response to changes in diet (Boekelheide et al. 1990b).

Length of the breeding season, measured by the presence of eggs or chicks, is about 100 days (Gaston and Jones 1998). Both males and females incubate for an average of 32 days (range 26-39) (Boekelheide et al. 1990b), although females spend more time incubating and brooding than males (Sydeman 1993). The chick is fed a single fish 3-5 times daily for an average of 22-25 days (Gaston and Jones 1998). Both parents feed the chick, carrying the fish to the colony in their bills (Birkhead 1977), although males feed more often than females (Sydeman 1993).

Murre chicks leave the nest site at 20-25% of their adult weight (Birkhead 1977). Unable to fly, they leave the colony at dusk (Gaston and Jones 1998) and go to sea accompanied by the male parent (Scott 1973, Boekelheide et al. 1990b). Chick/adult pairs are first seen at sea on the central coast during late Jun or early Jul (Scott 1973, Bayer 1983a, Williams 1992). Females continue to visit the colony for 13-18 days after the chicks leave (Wanless and Harris 1986). The colony at Yaquina Head is abandoned by early Aug (Bayer 1988a). Hatch-year murres off Oregon reach 90-95% of their adult weight 45-60 days after departing the colony (Varoujean et al. 1979). It is not clear when the young become independent from the male, although Williams (1992) reports fully grown chicks unaccompanied by adults in early Oct. While caring for the chicks at sea the male undergoes postbreeding molt and is flightless for 4-6 wk (Gaston and Jones 1998).

There is some evidence of a general movement of adults north after the breeding season (Bayer et al. 1991, Johnson J 1994a). Small numbers occur in s. Oregon during the non-breeding season but most occur farther north (Manuwal and Carter 2001). Some murres from Oregon colonies are thought to winter on marine inland waters of Washington (Wahl et al. 1989), and the large number observed in the fall off

sw. Vancouver I. are thought to be from Oregon as numbers nesting in British Columbia are low (Vermeer et al. 1989). First-year murres may disperse much farther than older ones, as hatch-year birds do not return to the colony in the subsequent year (Birkhead and Hudson 1977). At Cape Lookout and Three Arch Rocks, 2,820 murres were banded 1930-40; 98 band returns from both chicks and after-hatch-year birds confirm these general movements (Bayer and Ferris 1987).

Most adult calls are guttural and a variation on a deep growling *aargh*. The chick makes a higher-pitched *WEE-wee-wee* call on leaving the colony and at sea with the parent (Gaston and Jones 1998). The latter call is contagious: nearby chicks may begin to call together.

**Detection:** Easily seen on the colonies during breeding season. Good locations are Pillar Rock at Cape Meares, Cascade Head, Yaquina Head, and Coquille Pt. Rocks, Bandon. During the breeding season murres are common inshore close to the colonies and in larger estuaries, although birds can be seen throughout shelf waters (Briggs et al. 1992). Chicks normally swim within 6 ft (2 m) of and behind the adult, calling frequently. Chicks rarely occur more than 15 mi (24 km) offshore (Scott 1990). Easily seen on the water because of large size and contrasting dark and light plumage. Murre chicks are sometimes mistaken for Marbled or Xantus's Murrelets.

**Population Status and Conservation:** The population of murres breeding in Oregon represents 66% of birds breeding south of Alaska (Carter et al. 2001). They are difficult to census, as the number on the colony at any one time depends on a host of variables including ocean productivity, nesting chronology, time of day, weather conditions, disturbance by avian predators, and tidal state (Birkhead 1978, Slater 1980, Rodway 1990). The first count of the total number of murres nesting in Oregon was in 1964 when 408,700 murres were visually estimated during an aerial survey, 300,000 of which were at Three Arch Rocks NWR (Carter et al. 2001). Similar surveys 1966-74 counted an average of 122,673 murres breeding in Oregon (Carter et al. 2001). USFWS surveys in 1975 and 1976 counted 162,350 and 202,960, respectively. A 1979 survey of Oregon colonies used aerial photography and 261,227 birds were counted at 63 colony sites (Varoujean et al. 1979). This figure is probably low as 28 of the colonies were photographed in mid-Jul, by which date a large percentage of the breeding birds would have left the colony. The most comprehensive survey was in 1988, and found 66 colonies and 426,278 birds. Using a correction factor of **x1.67** to account for birds away from the rock at the time of photography, the total population of breeding birds in Oregon in 1988 was estimated at 711,900 (Carter et al. 2001).

Breeding success is variable and is associated with ocean productivity (Sydeman 1993). Large segments of the population will not breed if conditions are unfavorable (Boekelheide et al. 1990b) and they may fail to initiate nesting or may abandon the colony before eggs hatch (Johnson J 1994a). During strong ENSO years, when ocean productivity is low, murre breeding success is correspondingly low (Hodder and Graybill 1985, Bayer 1986a). This can be a statewide phenomenon as in 1983, or can only affect parts of the state. For example, in 1998 no hatchlings were observed at sea in s. Oregon, indicating complete nesting failure, whereas 36 hatchlings/mi² (14 hatchlings/km²) were observed in n. Oregon (Strong 1999). During the 1982/83 ENSO dead adult murres were reported during the breeding season (Evanich and Fix 1983, Hodder and Graybill 1985) with over 4.8 adults/mi (3 adults/km) found on a 7.4 mi (12 km) stretch of beach in Lincoln Co. in Jul 1983 (Graybill and Hodder 1985). In some years large die-offs of chicks occur Jul-Sep after fledging (Bayer et al. 1991). Large die-offs of chicks once they have left the colony can in some instances be associated with high breeding success as was reported in 1967 and 1969 (Nehls 1988a). In 1986, a large die-off of fledglings was attributed to lung disease (Fix 1987a). Such die-offs can be statewide or can be restricted to only parts of the coast.

Common Murres are vulnerable to disturbance by humans or avian predators. On Tatoosh I., Washington, egg predation by Glaucous-winged Gulls and Northwestern Crows, facilitated by the presence of Bald Eagles flushing incubating murres from the colony, caused a decline in reproductive success of murres nesting on the island top (Parrish and Paine 1996). Similar observations of flushing by Bald Eagles have been made at Three Arch Rocks NWR, Bird Rock, Haystack Rock at Cannon Beach, and Yaquina Head (Lowe and Pitkin 1996). During the winter on the Farallons small numbers are taken by Peregrine Falcons (Sydeman 1993).

Chronic oiling and net entanglement have been factors in murre mortality (Burger and Fry 1993, DeGange et al. 1993) and have the potential to affect populations in Oregon. From 1978 to 1990, however, a sample of 791 after-hatch-year and 5,458 hatch-year murres found dead on beaches of the central coast found none shot and very few oiled or tangled in fishing gear (Bayer et al. 1991). Analysis of eight murre eggs for organochlorine residues in 1979 found low levels (Henny et al. 1982).—*Jan Hodder*

## Thick-billed Murre *Uria lomvia*

The Thick-billed Murre is an abundant breeding species of the N. Pacific and N. Atlantic oceans and winters in nearby waters. Small numbers wander southward over both oceans. There have been several reports of this species along the Oregon coast, but difficulties in distinguishing it from the much more common Common Murre bring sight records into question. There are three specimen records for Oregon: one collected out of Depoe Bay, Lincoln Co., 14 Jan 1933 (spec. no. 9258 Yale Peabody Museum, New Haven); one found dead on Sutton Beach, Lane Co., 30 Jan 1933 (Scott and Nehls 1974, Watson 1989); and one found dead at the s. jetty of the Columbia R., Clatsop Co., 15 Sep 1972 (Scott and Nehls 1974). These specimens were of the western race *U. l. arra* (identification of the specimens was verified at USNM). One live oiled bird on Nye Beach in Newport 25 Aug 2001 was rehabilitated and released 6 Oct 2001 (photo in Contreras 2002b).—*Harry B. Nehls*

## Pigeon Guillemot *Cepphus columba*

During the breeding season Pigeon Guillemots are easily seen flying low over the water along rocky coastlines or in estuaries. They have striking red feet, legs, and mouth linings and their large white wing patches contrast markedly with the rest of their black plumage. When standing on land they have a distinctive upright posture and often emit a high-pitched squeal. In the nonbreeding season they move offshore and look entirely different when their black plumage becomes mottled with white.

**General Distribution:** Breeds from n. Alaska to s. California and from e. Siberia to Kamchatka. Largest breeding colonies are at the Farallon Is., California, and in the Chukot Peninsula, nw. Pacific. Nonbreeding individuals occur in summer in Baja California. Winter densities are highest in s. Alaska and Washington, with relatively few birds elsewhere (Ewins et al. 1993). Two subspecies: *C. c. columba* occurs in Oregon (AOU 1957, Browning 2002).

**Oregon Distribution:** Occurs during the breeding season all along the coast wherever offshore islands or rocky cliffs are present. Most breed in small colonies of < 40 birds. Off Oregon and Washington groups of birds are regularly seen flying north along the continental shelf in late Aug to early Sep (Ewins 1993). Occasionally seen in winter as solitary individuals close to shore or in estuaries; they prefer sheltered inshore waters rather than exposed coastlines (Ewins 1993)

**Habitat and Diet:** Marine and estuarine. Nest sites are crevices in cliffs or boulders, burrows in soil, or under tree roots on cliffs. Have adapted to human-made structures such as docks, bridges, navigational aides, and beach debris (Ewins 1993). One of the largest such colonies is at Sitka Dock in Coos Bay, although deterioration of the abandoned pier is reducing the number of nesting sites. They breed in smaller numbers in piers on the c. Oregon coast at Winchester Bay and Florence where no natural nesting habitat exists.

They fly underwater to capture prey, using feet as rudders. Guillemots dive for 10-144 sec to a maximum depth of 140 ft (45 m) (Ewins 1993). During the breeding season feed inshore, close to the colony in waters less than 100 ft (30 m) deep. Bring fish one at a time to chicks, so food is easily observed. Prey fed to chicks is varied but benthic fish comprise a high portion of the diet (Follet and Ainley 1976, Vermeer et al. 1987). At the Sitka Dock colony in Coos Bay, gunnels, pricklebacks, sand lance, sculpins, surf perch, and flat fish are common items brought to the chicks. Adult diet is more difficult to determine and for Oregon is unknown. In Alaska diet varied by season with fish and shrimp important in winter and capelin, codfishes, and Pacific sandfish in summer (Vermeer et al. 1987).

**Seasonal Activity and Behavior:** Considerable behavioral repertoire is associated with breeding, well summarized by Ewins (1993). Adults return to Oregon breeding sites in early to late Mar, and experienced males occupy nest sites up to 2 wk before females (Nelson 1987). Courtship displays take place on land and in water and involve lengthy bouts of billing and vocalizations. Occasionally large numbers can be seen on the water during courtship; for example 298 were seen at Yaquina Head on 22 Mar 1992 (Gilligan 1992b) and 300 on 27 Mar 1994 (Lillie 1994). Monogamous, but extra-pair copulations occur (Ewins 1993). Copulation occurs on land and is preceded by intense billing between the pair (Ewins 1993). Females are absent from the colony just prior to laying and presumably are at sea feeding (Nelson 1987).

Colony attendance usually peaks during the morning and evening (Ewins 1993). No nest is constructed; eggs are laid in a scrape or a depression in the floor of the cavity. Tend to nest in the same site in successive years (Nelson 1991). Breeding biology of this species was studied during 1982-85 and 1989 at Sitka Dock in Coos Bay (Hodder and Graybill 1985, McLaren 1991). One- or two-egg clutches were laid from mid-May to early Jun. Individual females had characteristic laying dates and eggs were laid 1-5 days apart (Ewins 1993). At Sitka Dock, during 1983-85 and 1989, 14-45% of the clutches consisted of 1 egg, and mean clutch size ranged 1.57-1.86 (Hodder and Graybill 1985, McLaren 1991). Incubation period ranged 29-32 days (Ainley, Boekelheide, Morrell, and Strong 1990b). They will successfully incubate an egg laid by another bird, suggesting that they do not recognize their own eggs (McLaren 1991). Sexes alternate incubation shifts; the intervals are irregular ranging from 40 min to 17 hr (Ewins 1993).

The first chicks hatch in late Jun to early Jul and are covered with black down. The first egg usually hatches 1-2 days before the second. Limited information indicates siblicide may occur (Rasmussen 1988). Brooded continuously until at least 3 days old, and then at intervals until 5-7 days old (Ewins 1993). Hatching success at Sitka Dock was 30-64% for one-egg clutches and 57-82% for two-egg clutches (McLaren 1991). Both parents feed the chick whole fish during daylight hours.

Young depart the nest without parents at 90% of adult weight 35-39 days after hatching (Ewins 1993). Mean fledging success at Sitka Dock in 1982 was 0.74 chicks/nest (n=110 nests) and in 1983, 0.72 chicks/nest (n=89 nests). In 1983, 1.3 chicks/nest were fledged from 11 nests at Seal Rocks (Hodder and Graybill 1985). Guillemots have been observed lingering in the vicinity of breeding areas into Nov and Dec (Fix 1991) although most often have moved away by early Sep (Heinl 1985). Postbreeding movements are unclear; recoveries of 12 birds banded in Oregon were all within 112 mi (180 km) of their natal/breeding colonies (Ewins 1993). In contrast, birds banded on the Farallon Is. migrated as far north as the sheltered coasts of Washington and British Columbia after breeding (Ainley, Boekelheide, Morrell, and Strong 1990b). Many Oregon birds may also follow this pattern as the number of birds in the sheltered waters of Washington and British Columbia increases in the winter (Campbell et al. 1990a, Wahl and Tweit 2000b).

Birds first bred on the Farallon Is. at 3 yr old, but more commonly at 4 or 5 yr (Nelson 1991). Annual survival of breeders ranged 76-89% on the Farallon Is. and average life span once breeding was 4.5 yr (Nelson 1991). The oldest recorded bird is 14 yr (Ewins 1993). During the breeding season breeding and nonbreeding birds partake in communal "water-games" or a "water-dance" (Drent 1965) where they chase each other in flight or under and on the surface of the water, flashing their white wing patches.

Highly vocal at colonies, having a variety of distinct calls which have been well studied on the Farallon Is. (Nelson 1984, 1985). Repeated bill-dipping is seen when birds are sitting on the water, commonly when birds are alarmed by a potential predator or disturbance; at the colony this is usually accompanied by a scream alarm call (Ewins 1993).

**Detection:** Easily spotted at breeding colonies or on the water during breeding season because of contrasting plumage, bright red bare parts, and frequent calls. Good locations for viewing are Coquille Pt. Rocks, Bandon, lower Coos Bay, Sea Lion Caves, the Seal Rock area, lower Yaquina Bay, Yaquina Head, the small rocks at the mouth of Tillamook Bay, and Haystack Rock, Tillamook Co.

**Population Status and Conservation:** Pigeon Guillemots are difficult to count as they show marked diurnal, tidal, and seasonal variations in colony attendance. Nelson (1991) gives a world population estimate of 235,170 birds. In 1979, 2,734 individuals were counted nesting in Oregon (Pitman et al. 1985), and in 1988, 4,855 breeding birds were counted (USFWS unpubl. data).Vulnerability to oil is high due to coastal habits, and this species was strongly impacted by the *Exxon Valdez* spill (Piatt et al. 1990). In California inshore gill nets have caused significant local mortality (King 1984). Concentrations of DDE and PCBs were low in five eggs collected from Oregon in 1979 (Henny et al. 1982).—*Jan Hodder*

### Long-billed Murrelet *Brachyramphus perdix*
Long-billed Murrelets breed in Russia on the Kamchatka Peninsula, the Kuril Is., Sakhalin I., and along the w. coasts of the Sea of Okhotsk and the Sea of Japan (Konyukhov and Kitaysky 1995, Nelson SK 1997). They may also breed on e. Hokkaido I., Japan (Brazil 1991), although no nests have been located there (Nelson et al. 1997, 2002). During migration in late summer and fall, individuals are found in N. America, perhaps carried east on the jet stream or during storms as birds move south from northern breeding areas. At least 44 definite N. American records between early Jul and late Dec extend from the Pacific eastward to the Atlantic, and from Alaska south to Florida (Jehl and Jehl 1981, Sealy et al. 1982, 1991, Sibley 1993a, Konyukov and Kitaysky 1995, Di Labio 1996, Mlodinow 1997, Gilligan 1999, American Birding Association 1999, 2000, C. S. Strong p.c.).

Long-billed and Marbled Murrelets were for a short time (c. 1934-1997) recognized as conspecifics, but recent molecular genetic evidence (Zink et al. 1995, Friesen et al. 1996a, b) verified that these two forms merited recognition at the species level (AOU 1997). Several publications have described the identification of these species (Sibley 1993a, Konyukhov and Kitaysky 1995, DiLabio 1996, Mlodinow 1997, Lethaby 2000), and several recent field guides illustrate their differences (e.g., NGS 1999, Sibley 2000). Consequently, the frequency of Long-billed Murrelet sightings has increased in N. America.

This species has been sighted in the nearshore waters along the Pacific Coast of N. America in late summer and early fall almost every year since 1994. Most of these sightings have occurred during intensive surveys for Marbled Murrelets. In Oregon, individual Long-billed Murrelets have been observed at Boiler Bay, Lincoln Co., 6 Nov 1998; 2.5 mi (4 km) south of the Yaquina R., Lincoln Co., 30 Jul 1998; 3.7 mi (6 km) north of Yachats (near Big Cr.), Lincoln Co., 30 Jul 1998; at Lily Cr., north of Heceta Beach, Lane Co., 30 Jul 1998; at Arago Reef, Coos Co., 13 Aug 1994;

0.6 mi (1 km) north of Coos Bay, Coos Co., 15 Jul 1996; 1.2 mi (2 km) north of Bandon, Coos Co., 14 Aug 1996; 0.3 mi (0.5 km) north of the Winchuck R., Curry Co., 30 Aug 1996; and just south of the Winchuck R. (Stateline Rocks), Curry Co., 22 Jul 1998 (Gilligan 1999, C. Strong p.c.). Many of these individuals have been photographed or verified based on detailed descriptions (e.g., Mlodinow 1997). May also be vagrant on inland lakes; a probable sighting of this species occurred in early Aug 1997 on Leaburg Res., Lane Co. (S. Madsen p.c.).—*S. Kim Nelson*

### Marbled Murrelet *Brachyramphus marmoratus*
These small, fast-flying seabirds are unique among alcids in N. America in their use of coastal coniferous forests, primarily old-growth trees, as nesting habitat. Their solitary nests are usually concealed within the forest canopy, and breeding birds are cryptic and primarily crepuscular at nest sites (Nelson and Hamer 1995b, Nelson and Peck 1995). Because of their secretive behavior and elusive nests, Marbled Murrelets were considered the "enigma of the Pacific" (Guiguet 1956) and were one of the last ornithological mysteries in N. America (Arbib 1970), as the first nest was not discovered until 1974.

Adults are sexually monomorphic in plumage, but alternate and basic plumages are distinct. Breeding adults can be recognized by their sooty-brown to brownish-black upperparts, with rusty margins on the back feathers, and reddish scapulars (Ridgway 1919, Carter and Stein 1995). In winter, adults are blackish brown above and white below. Juvenal plumage is similar to adult basic plumage, but white underparts are speckled with blackish brown spots. Within about 2 mo of fledging, juveniles are generally indistinguishable from adults.

**General Distribution:** Year-round resident of nearshore waters along the west coast of N. America, except in portions of Alaska and British Columbia where they are not present in winter. Generally found

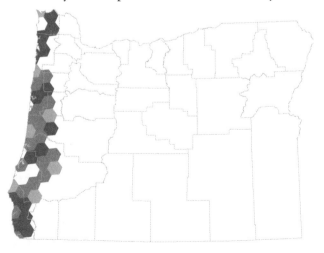

within 3 mi (5 km) of shore south of Alaska, and within 31 mi (50 km) off Alaska. In winter found as far as 22 and 186 mi (35 and 299 km) offshore in California and Alaska, respectively. Nests in forested or rocky areas on islands and the mainland near the coast from the Aleutian Is. in Alaska south along the coasts of sc. and se. Alaska, British Columbia, Washington, and Oregon to c. California (Santa Cruz Co.). A small proportion of the Alaska population from Prince William Sound west (about 3%) (Piatt and Naslund 1995) and a few individuals in British Columbia (F. Cooke p.c.) nest on rocky shorelines or talus slopes near the coast. The remainder of the population nests in trees, or on tree roots on cliffs, in forests within 55 mi (89 km) of the coast, although a grounded juvenile was found 63 mi (101 km) inland in British Columbia (Rodway et al. 1992, Nelson SK 1997). In the winter found as far south as n. Baja (Carter and Erickson 1992, Erickson et al. 1995).

**Oregon Distribution:** Breeds on forested slopes of the Coast Range. Distribution at inland nesting sites is fragmented, as birds occur only in areas where suitable habitat (see below) remains. Furthest inland nest recorded was 31 mi (50 km) from the coast in Douglas Co., near the small community of Umpqua (Witt 1998). Sighted as far inland as 36 mi (58 km) in the Coast Range; also three unverified reports from the Cascades east of Salem between 60 and 80 mi (96 and 129 km) inland (Nelson SK 1997). Inland distribution is constricted south of the upper S. Fk. Coquille drainage in s. Coos Co., following the western hemlock/tanoak vegetation type inland (Dillingham et al. 1995) only up to about 16 mi (26 km) in c. and s. Curry Co. (Alegria et al. 2002).

Visits inland breeding sites at all times of year, except during the prebasic molt in early fall. Present year-round on nearshore waters. Uncommon to rare along entire coast, but densities greatest off the central coast between Cascade Head and Cape Arago (Strong et al. 1995). Generally found within a few miles of shore during the breeding season and up to 6 mi (10 km) in winter.

**Habitat and Diet:** Nest primarily in old-growth trees in old-growth and mature coniferous forests (Hamer and Nelson 1995a). Also found nesting in younger trees (65-200 yr in age) in second-growth Sitka spruce/western hemlock forests in nw. Oregon (Tillamook and Clatsop counties) (Nelson and Wilson 2001). Suitable nest trees within these stands generally occur in small patches, and were either in residual (left behind during management

or natural perturbations) or second-growth western hemlock trees that were heavily infected with dwarf mistletoe. Dwarf mistletoe creates large deformations or platforms suitable for murrelet nesting. Overall, nests in Oregon have been in large (57.0 in [144.8 cm] dbh), tall (185.0 ft [56.4 m]) conifer trees of a variety of species (n = 64) (Nelson SK 1997, *SKN*). Nests are generally in the middle one-third of live crowns (height 117.5 ft [35.8 m]) on large (10.0 in [25.3 cm] diameter), moss-covered limbs. Murrelets do not build a nest, but simply lay their single egg on moss or duff on a tree limb. The availability of platforms (>4 in [10 cm] diameter and >30 ft [9 m] high) is the most important habitat component. In addition, moss abundance and the availability of cover at nest sites are key characteristics of nest sites. Nests located next to the tree bole and with high overhead cover generally have the lowest predation rates (although habitat fragmentation and proximity to humans may also affect predation levels) (Nelson and Hamer 1995a).

Forage in shallow water (generally < 200 ft [60 m]) in nearshore and protected coastal waters. Dive to at least 160 ft (49 m) (Thoresen 1989, Sealy 1975, Jodice and Collopy 1999). Forage in small groups (generally 2) or individually, except in the northern portion of their range where they can be found in large, mixed-species feeding flocks (Chilton and Sealy 1987). Hatch-year birds usually forage very close to shore and in *Nereocystis* kelp beds, but not with adults and generally alone (Kuletz and Piatt 1999). Opportunistic in diet (Burkett 1995), feeding primarily on a variety of small schooling fish, including Pacific sand lance, northern anchovy, Pacific herring, surf smelt, and Pacific sardine. During the spring (and sometimes other seasons) also feed on euphausiids. Currently not known to use

*Marbled Murrelet*

freshwater lakes in Oregon, but feed on a variety of salmon species in freshwater lakes in Washington and British Columbia (Carter and Sealy 1986).

**Seasonal Activity and Behavior:** Courtship is initiated at sea in winter and early spring, when some adults are still in winter plumage. Egg-laying begins in Apr and extends until Jul (Hamer and Nelson 1995b). Murrelets lay a single egg that is incubated for 28-30 days. Both adults participate in incubation, exchanging duties at the nest every 24 hr at dawn, usually within 30 min of sunrise (Nelson SK 1997). Chicks are semi-precocial on hatching and remain in the nest for 27-40 days. Chicks are brooded for only 1-2 days and then left alone on the nest. Adults return to feed the chick up to eight times daily; most feedings at dawn and dusk although adults visit nest during any hour of the day. Juvenal plumage develops under down (both feather types grow from same sheath), providing camouflage on nest until the chick preens off its down 8-48 hr before fledging. Young fledge at dusk between mid-Jun and late Sep and fly directly to sea. No evidence of parental care during fledging and after departure. Marbled Murrelets have an asynchronous breeding season compared with other alcids, possibly related to renesting after failure or individual differences in physiological preparedness (Nelson and Peck 1995).

Although these seabirds nest solitarily, they often nest in stands with other pairs of murrelets. Therefore at dawn and dusk, groups of murrelets often seen flying and circling above or within the forest canopy while calling loudly. Marbled Murrelets have a variety of vocalizations but the most common is described as the "keer" call (Nelson SK 1997). This activity at inland sites occurs year round, but is most pronounced during the breeding season, and is more common at dawn than dusk. In spring and summer they fly inland for nesting and prospecting, and in winter most likely for maintaining pair bonds and nest sites (Naslund 1993, Nelson SK 1997). The peak of this flight and vocalization activity is most pronounced in Jul, when non-breeders are suspected to join breeding birds in the forest, perhaps to select nest sites and mates (O'Donnell et al. 1995). Activity is lowest from Feb to Mar and mid-Aug to Oct during prealternate and prebasic molts. Groups of murrelets return to the same forest stands year after year (Nelson SK 1997). Nest trees occasionally reused; in Oregon 4 of 19 active nest trees (through 1998) reused in successive years, although not always the same platform.

Marbled Murrelets are considered non-migratory, although they are found farther offshore in winter compared with breeding season. Some birds may also move into Washington or California during the fall and winter to take advantage of prey concentrations, but more study is needed on seasonal movements (Nelson SK 1997).

**Detection:** Difficult to detect, even in good habitat. At sea, they can be found just beyond the breakers near other inshore feeders such as scoters. Usually occur in small groups (2-5) or individually; rarely found in large numbers or mixed feeding flocks. Popular locations for at-sea viewing during the breeding season include Boiler Bay and Yaquina Head in Lincoln Co., the Cape Perpetua area in Lincoln and Lane counties, and off the Winchuck and Chetco rivers in Curry Co. At breeding sites, murrelets can be seen or heard calling at dawn while flying inland to nests. Vocalizations are unique and quite recognizable in the forest to anyone with knowledge of their calls. Difficult to detect visually, as they are secretive at nest sites, fly up to 98 mi/hr (158 km/hr), and nest high in conifer trees (Nelson and Hamer 1995b, Nelson and Peck 1995, Burger 1997). The best places to find murrelets at inland sites during the breeding season are the coastal Oregon state parks that have suitable nesting habitat.

**Population Status and Conservation:** Thought to be declining throughout their range. Primary threat is habitat loss from logging and development (USFWS 1992). Also susceptible to oil spills, over-fishing, pollution, predation, and entrapment in gill nets (Carter and Kuletz 1995, Carter et al. 1995, Fry 1995, Nelson and Hamer 1995a). Federally listed as Threatened in Washington, Oregon, and California (USFWS 1992); State listed as Threatened (Oregon Administrative Rule 635-100-125, 1995).

Exact status and rate of decline unknown, however murrelets once described as abundant or common throughout nearshore areas off Oregon (Gabrielson and Jewett 1940). Currently considered rare or uncommon along entire Oregon Coast (Nelson et al. 1992). Estimates of the Oregon population range from 6,600-20,000 individuals (Strong et al. 1995, Varoujean and Williams 1995). Suitable inland habitat rare in Clatsop, Tillamook, n. Lincoln, Douglas, and Coos counties. In existing suitable habitat, fragmentation and proximity to humans may affect predation rates at nests. Sixty-six percent of murrelet nests have failed and most (57%) have failed from predation (Nelson and Hamer 1995a, Nelson SK 1997, SKN). Corvids are the most common predators, although some chicks have been killed by accipiters and owls. There is some evidence from artificial nest studies that small mammals may also be nest predators (J. Marzluff p.c.).

Habitat management or conservation plans (HCPs) have been developed for federal, state and private lands (e.g., U.S. Departments of Agriculture and Interior 1993, ODF 1995, USFWS 1996, 1997b). The Northwest Forest Plan (U.S. Departments of Agriculture and Interior 1993) established a series of late-successional reserves for murrelets and other species that rely on older forests. However, habitat in large portions of these reserves will not be suitable for 50 to100 yr. The future of the Marbled Murrelet in the Pacific Northwest and California is tenuous during this 50- to 100-yr time period. Suitable murrelet habitat continues to be harvested through HCPs, land exchanges, and mis-classification of sites during dawn surveys (Ralph et al. 1994, Evans et al. 2000) in proposed timber sales, and populations are thought to be declining at a rate of 4-7% per year (Beissinger 1995). The Marbled Murrelet Recovery Plan (USFWS 1997b) calls for stabilizing the population by increasing population productivity, improving the distribution and amount of suitable habitat, and minimizing threats to survivorship (e.g., minimizing habitat loss). Additional research on their biology (e.g., determining aspect of their demography and the habitat conditions that provide for successful nesting) and monitoring of populations and their habitat are needed.—*S. Kim Nelson*

## Xantus's Murrelet *Synthliboramphus hypoleucus*

The Xantus's Murrelet is a warm-water species that breeds on islands off s. California and Baja California. After nesting it disperses northward along the California coast and casually to British Columbia. One collected 28 Jul 1970, 115 mi (185 km) west of Cape Falcon (Scott et al. 1971, OSU), and 1 found dead on the n. spit of Coos Bay 26 Jun 1998 (OBRC, OSU) were both *S. h. scrippsi*, as are most Oregon sightings (*HBN*). Xantus's Murrelet records in Oregon have occurred between late Jun and late Nov. All live birds were well offshore, except for single individuals just off the Boiler Bay Wayside, Lincoln Co., 7-8 Nov 1987 (Heinl 1988a) and off Bray's Point, Lane Co., 23 Jul 1991 (Johnson J 1992a). Photographs were taken of a bird 65 mi west of Newport, Lincoln Co., 19 Nov 1969 (Scott, Butler, et al. 1971, Roberson 1980, Watson 1989) and of 1 out of Garibaldi, Tillamook Co., 14 Sep 1985 (Heinl 1986a). One was at the s. jetty of the Columbia R. 14 Jun 2001 (Korpi 2001b). An astonishing 42, including both *scrippsi* and *hypoleucus*, were observed offshore between 10 Aug and 20 Oct 2001 by multiple observers (Contreras 2002b). During Jun 1973 a bird of the subspecies *S. h. hypoleucus* was photographed 65-165 mi (104-264 km) west of Newport. The exact location and date have been lost (Roberson 1980, Watson 1989).—*Harry B. Nehls*

## Ancient Murrelet *Synthliboramphus antiquus*

In winter plumage, the crisp black head, white neck patch, and gray back are striking, and when combined with a pale bill this species is readily distinguished from small alcids in Oregon. Wing-propelled divers, they are nonbreeding visitors to Oregon's offshore waters. They are the only seabirds whose young are reared entirely at sea.

**General Distribution:** Breeds from s. Alaska to the Queen Charlotte Is., British Columbia, casually to nw. Washington; and in e. Asia from the Commander Is. to Korea. Winters at sea from the Aleutian Is. to c. California, and in Asia from the Commander Is. south to Taiwan. The e. Pacific wintering range is between 40 and 50° N (Gaston and Jones 1998). This is the most commonly reported alcid in inland N. America; records are often associated with storms (Verbeek 1966). Monotypic (AOU 1957).

**Oregon Distribution:** Uncommon to common fall migrant and winter visitant in shelf waters near shore; rare to uncommon in spring; absent to rare in summer. Vagrant inland, particularly in fall. Two observations in summer 1993 of an adult with a young chick at Yaquina Head and one record in summer 1997 of an adult/small chick pair south of Newport may be evidence of breeding on the c. Oregon coast (C. Strong p.c.). However, as young Ancient Murrelets are at sea with parents within 2 days of hatching and begin to disperse at that time (Gaston 1992), it is conceivable that these sightings could represent extreme instances of rapid southward dispersal rather than Oregon nesting (D. Fix p.c.).

**Habitat and Diet:** Marine. Found mainly on continental slope and shelf waters (Gaston and Jones 1998) but will occur closer to shore in areas where tidal currents create concentrations of prey, such as euphausiids (Gaston, Carter, and Sealy 1993). Compared to most seabirds, there is little information on diet because they do not bring food to chicks in the colony. During the breeding season they eat euphausiids, decapod larvae, and a variety of small fish (Gaston 1992, Gaston and Jones 1998). The only study of winter diet is from waters off Vancouver I. where birds were exclusively eating *Euphausia pacifica*, the euphausiid (Gaston, Carter, and Sealy 1993).

**Seasonal Activity and Behavior:** After breeding there is a general dispersal southward (Gaston and Jones 1998), and birds typically arrive in Oregon in Sep (Fix 1985f). Most sightings are in the late fall and winter (Fix 1991) with flocks of 10-20 normal. Larger concentrations of hundreds are less frequent (Johnson 1996b, Contreras 1998). Inland reports are irregular and very rare, mostly Sep-Nov (Tice 1997), but one was in Medford in Mar (Browning 1971). During offshore surveys in 1989 and 1990 small numbers (1-4) seen in Jan, Mar, Apr, Jun, and Sep off Washington and Oregon (Briggs et al. 1992). Summer sightings are occasional from land (Watson 1981b, Johnson J 1993a, 1994a); in Jun and Jul 1997 they were seen at numerous locations along the Oregon coast (Johnson J 1998a). Most leave by Mar or early Apr (Contreras 1998).

**Detection:** Birds may be viewed from boats at sea or from coastal promontories. Regular fall and winter sightings are made from the overlook at Boiler Bay, Lincoln Co. (Fix 1987a, Heinl 1988a, Johnson 1996b).

**Population Status and Conservation:** No population estimates are available from Oregon. Estimates are poor except in British Columbia where 500,000 birds breed in the Queen Charlotte Is. (Gaston and Jones 1998). The world population is probably between 1 and 2 million, and throughout its range numbers are diminished as a result of the deliberate or accidental introduction of non-native mammals (Gaston and Jones 1998). Sensitive to disturbance during incubation, will desert burrow (Gaston 1994). Taken by Peregrine Falcons; one such predation event was witnessed at Cape Arago in Jan 1999 (JH).—*Jan Hodder*

## Cassin's Auklet *Ptychoramphus aleuticus*

Despite being one of the most widely distributed Pacific alcids, probably fewer than 1,000 Cassin's Auklets nest at about 8 sites on the Oregon coast. They are burrow nesters, laying a single egg, but are the only known N. Hemisphere seabird that on rare occasions can raise two broods during a single season. They are steel gray above with a white belly, and a white eyebrow that flashes when the bird blinks. There is a pale spot at the base of the lower mandible. Feet and legs are bright blue.

**General Distribution:** Breeds locally on coastal islands from s. Alaska west to Buldir I. in the Aleutians, south to s. Baja California. Seventy-six percent of Cassin's Auklets breed in British Columbia. Winters along the Pacific coast from s. British Columbia to s. Baja California. Two subspecies; *P. a. aleuticus* occurs in Oregon (AOU 1957).

**Oregon Distribution:** Although few Cassin's Auklets nest in Oregon, nesting sites are found along the entire coast where offshore rocks provide appropriate habitat. Unknown as a breeder in s. Oregon in 1958 (Thoresen 1964), 50 individuals were found nesting in Curry Co. on Goat I., the most seaward rock off Whalehead Cr., in 1966 (Browning and English 1968), and in 1967 on Hunter I., Curry Co. (Browning and English 1972). In 1967, nesting birds were also found on Conical Rock (near Heceta Head, Lane Co.) and Haystack Rock (Tillamook Co.); because suitable habitat was present nesting was suspected at Haystack Rock (Clatsop Co.), Parrot Rock (Lane Co.), and Whalehead I. (Curry Co.) (Browning and English 1972). In 1979, nests were again found on Goat I. as well as Island Rock,

both Curry Co. (Pitman et al. 1985). Nesting was again noted at Hunter I. in 1992 (R. Lowe p.c.), and remains suspected but unverified at Three Arch Rocks in Tillamook Co. and Haystack Rock of Clatsop Co. (Pitman et al. 1985).

During the nonbreeding season this is the most abundant alcid seen at sea in Oregon. They are present offshore all year (Briggs et al. 1992); except in the breeding season, most of the birds at sea are from out-of-state breeding colonies. Numbers present during the summer are influenced by the timing and success of the breeding season at colonies in Washington and British Columbia. During summer and fall large numbers have been seen moving south offshore (Graybill 1980) and from land (Fix 1991). They are widespread at sea, occurring within a few miles of the coast out to at least the continental slope (Briggs et al. 1992). They can occasionally be seen on the water from land (Fix 1985f, Contreras 1998). Concentrations occur over the outer shelf and upper continental slope, particularly in winter. The British Columbia population appears to move south in the winter. The Farallon Is. population is apparently sedentary (Ainley, Boekelheide, Morrell, and Strong 1990a). There are three inland records, all from the Columbia R. (Tice 1997), which suggests the possibility that they were brought in by ships (Gilligan 1994).

**Habitat and Diet:** Marine. Nest on soil-covered islands. Colonial cavity nesters, they dig burrows using bills and feet, but also use natural crevices and caves. Nesting takes place on steep cliffs, sloped and level areas. No nest material is used (Thoresen 1964). Adults and chicks eat the same prey (Ainley et al. 1996), which are captured underwater. Diet varies with location and time of year. Average depth of dives is 60 ft (28 m) (Burger and Powell 1990). There is no information on diet in Oregon. On the Farallon Is. adults and chicks feed on euphausiids, amphipods, larval crabs, squid, and juvenile fish (Manuwal 1974c, Ainley et al. 1996). In British Columbia calanoid copepods and euphausiids were the primary prey during the breeding season with lesser amounts of caridean shrimp and larval fish (Vermeer et al. 1985). In the fall they fed exclusively on hyperiid amphipods that occur in association with salps (Vermeer et al. 1989). Chicks are fed at night with food stored in the adult's gular pouch, from which it is regurgitated.

**Seasonal Activity and Behavior:** There are no published accounts of the breeding biology in Oregon. Both sexes excavate the nest site, although the male takes a more active role than the female (Ainley, Boekelheide, Morrell, and Strong1990a). The nest site is used repeatedly by the same pair (Manuwal 1974a). On the Farallon Is., Cassin's

Auklets usurp the nesting cavities of the smaller storm-petrels, and in turn may be evicted by Tufted Puffins or Pigeon Guillemots (Ainley, Boekelheide, Morrell, and Strong1990a). Cassin's Auklets are nocturnal on the breeding colony and most birds begin breeding at 2-3 yr of age.

On the Farallon Is. courtship occurs Jan to Apr. Peak of laying tends to be during Apr in California, and mid-Apr to late May in British Columbia (Vermeer et al. 1985), although it can occur over a wide time period ranging from mid-Mar to early Jul. At the Farallon Is., egg laying is correlated with a decline in sea surface temperature indicating that coastal upwelling of cooler, nutrient-rich water has occurred (Ainley et al. 1996). Cassin's Auklets are capable of laying two eggs in a season; at least 10% of eggs lost on the Farallon Is. are replaced (Ainley, Boekelheide, Morrell, and Strong 1990a). In 9 of 14 yr from 1970 to 1983, when food supplies were adequate, an average of 12% of the population on the Farallon Is. produced a second brood during the nesting season. This is the only population known to do this but fledging success is very low for this second brood (<0.1 chicks/pair).

Both sexes incubate the egg, alternating duties every 24 hr. Over 60% of second clutches are incubated with a re-feathered brood patch (Manuwal 1974b). Incubation period averages 39 days and ranges 37-57 days (Ainley, Boekelheide, Morrell, and Strong 1990a). Chicks hatch covered with down, stay in the burrow for about 30 days, and then leave periodically after dusk to exercise wings and take first flights. Fledge at 41-50 days with no parental assistance. Food availability has a major influence on breeding productivity. On the Farallon Is. and in British Columbia, productivity is strongly positively correlated with the upwelling index (Vermeer 1981, Ainley, Boekelheide, Morrell, and Strong 1990a).

**Detection:** Unlikely to be seen at breeding sites due to the small numbers in Oregon and nocturnal habits. As a result of the low numbers breeding in the state it is likely that some sites are not used in all years, for example Browning and English (1968) found 9 burrows on Parrot (not Conical) Rock, Heceta Head. A thorough search in 1979 and 1988 revealed no nesting (Pitman et al. 1985, USFWS unpubl. data). They can be difficult to see at sea because of small size, but are sometimes seen from pelagic birding trips.

**Population Status and Conservation:** The worldwide population estimate is 3.57 million breeding individuals (Manuwal and Thoresen 1993). The Oregon breeding population is estimated at fewer than 500 representing less than 0.01% of the worldwide breeding population. Southeast Farallon I. is the largest colony to the south, with 105,000 breeding individuals (Manuwal and Thoresen 1993),

but from 1971 to 1989 this population declined by 50% (Ainley et al. 1994) coincident with the general decline of zooplankton in the California Current (Ainley et al. 1996). Triangle I., British Columbia, is the largest breeding colony in the world with 370,000 breeding pairs (Gaston and Jones 1998). Gulls eat adults and chicks; on the Farallon Is. Western Gulls take 7-8% of nestlings; fledglings are vulnerable as they take practice flights before leaving the island, particularly on moonlit nights (Manuwal 1974c). Sensitive to introduced predators and human activities that cause burrow collapse.—*Jan Hodder*

## Parakeet Auklet *Aethia psittacula*

The Parakeet Auklet is an abundant nesting species in Alaska, including the Aleutian Is. Following nesting the adults and young scatter widely over the open ocean, drifting southward far offshore. Monotypic. Most records along the w. coast and from Hawaii are of dead birds washed onto beaches. Gabrielson and Jewett (1940) include a number of records of birds washed up on Oregon beaches. Eight of these specimens are in the SDNHM (spec. nos. 21869-21876). There are 10 more recent Oregon specimen records from early Dec to late Apr: Bayocean Beach, Tillamook Co. 3 Dec 1977 (Roberson 1980, Watson 1989); Wandamere Beach, Lincoln Co., 18 Apr 1982 (OBRC); Clatsop Beach, Clatsop Co., 12 Dec 1994 (OBRC), and Beverly Beach, Lincoln Co., 24 Feb 1996 (Lillie 1996). In addition seven were found dead on the beaches following the Feb 1999 *New Carissa* oil spill (Ford et al. 2001).

Two live birds were observed on the water off Cape Meares (not Cape Lookout, G. Gillson p.c.), Tillamook Co., 13 Aug 1977 (Mattocks and Hunn 1978a). Four live birds were observed 20 mi (32 km) west of Garibaldi, Tillamook Co., 7 Sep 1986 (OBRC). Individuals were reported 50 mi (81 km) west of Seaside, Clatsop Co., and 50 mi (81 km) west of Curry Co., 17 Sep 2000 (Korpi 2001a). Monotypic (AOU 1957)—*Harry B. Nehls*

## Rhinoceros Auklet *Cerorhinca monocerata*

One of the rarer breeding alcids in Oregon. Adults are easily recognized during the breeding season by the vertical "horn" at the base of the upper mandible. Birds in breeding plumage have brownish gray backs, a gray-brown chest, and a dirty white belly. Two distinct cream-colored plumes are present on the head, one above and one below the eye. The bill is orange. In nonbreeding plumage the horn is greatly reduced, the plumes absent or reduced, and the bill duller.

**General Distribution:** Breeds from Alaska to s. California, and from s. Sakhalin south to Korea and

Japan. Winters from s. British Columbia south to Baja California, and in Asia in the southern part of the breeding range. Monotypic.

**Oregon Distribution:** Nest in small numbers (<1,000) in Oregon with Goat I. and Hunter I. having the largest concentrations of breeding birds. Offshore in winter months, detected as far out as the seaward side of the continental slope (Briggs et al. 1992). At sea, mainly found in continental shelf waters, and along the shelf break (Gaston and Jones 1998). Occasionally found in lower estuaries, primarily during summer and fall.

**Habitat and Diet:** Marine. Nest on offshore islands in burrows dug in soil in a variety of habitats including under shrubs, tree stumps, and logs and in areas covered with herbaceous vegetation. Burrows can be up to 20 ft (6 m) in length, although on the Farallon Is. they use only natural cavities in rocks due to the shallow soils (Ainley, Morrell, and Boekelheide 1990). For foraging, prefer waters greater than 50 ft (15 m) deep and can dive to 200 ft (60 m); average dive depth is 100 ft (30 m) (Burger et al. 1993).

There is no information on diet in Oregon. Adults feeding in flocks off Washington, British Columbia, and Alaska take schooling sand lance, capelin, or herring (Gaston and Jones 1998). Throughout their range sand lance, northern anchovy, herring, and greenlings are the most common fish fed to chicks; of secondary importance are rockfish, smelt, capelin, and salmon (Gaston and Jones 1998). One to 19 fish are delivered at one time, averaging 5/load (Burger et al. 1993) with the largest bill load weighing 2 oz (55 g) (Bertram et al. 1991). There is no information on winter diet. May use bubbles, emitted from the mouth, to concentrate schooling fish close to the sea surface to facilitate feeding (Sharpe 1995).

**Seasonal Activity and Behavior:** Less is known about the behavior of Rhinoceros Auklets than almost any other alcid, and there is little information on Oregon's birds. They raft offshore of the colony before sunset, then fly over the colony in a group after the sun sets before entering the burrow (Gaston and Jones 1998). Closely related to puffins, they have efficient terrestrial locomotion, often dropping to the ground and then walking up to 60 ft (20 m) to their burrows (Vermeer 1979). In most cases they leave the colony before sunrise. Both partners dig new burrows and excavate old ones (Ainley, Morrell, and Boekelheide 1990). Burrows on Goat I. were occupied by the end of Mar (Browning and English 1968). Median laying dates on the Farallon Is. vary from mid-Apr to mid-May, being later in warm-water years. In Washington, a peak of laying was recorded during May (Gaston and Dechesne 1996). The single off-white egg is incubated for an average of 45 days, range 39-52 days

(Wilson and Manuwal 1986). Incubation shifts are normally 24 hr but can be as long as 4 days (Gaston and Dechesne 1996). In Washington hatching is from mid-Jun to mid-Jul (Wilson and Manuwal 1986). Chicks are brooded for the first 4 days after hatching (range 0-9 days) (Wilson and Manuwal 1986), and are then fed nightly by both parents. On Protection I., Washington, adults fed the chicks twice per night (Richardson 1961). The mean nestling period is 50 days but the growth rate of nestlings is the slowest of the alcids and chicks leave the nest at 50-80% of adult weight (Bertram et al. 1991).

Usually nocturnal at the colony (Richardson 1961) but at sites throughout their range, including Goat I. and Sea Lion Caves, they bring food to chicks during the day (Scott et al. 1974, Thoresen 1980). Ainley, Morrell, and Boekelheide (1990) suggest they are principally nocturnal at most sites to avoid interference with Tufted Puffins. Western Gulls did not interfere with Rhinoceros Auklets bringing food to their burrows at Sea Lion Caves or the Farallon Is. (Scott et al. 1974). In the nonbreeding season they move offshore, but for a brief period in late summer and early fall they are often found close to shore and in the mouths of estuaries. There are occasional records of birds close to shore after the breeding season in large numbers, for example during Sep 1991, 1,500 were off Barview, 410 off Yaquina Head, and 200 off the Siuslaw R. (Fix 1991). Birds from British Columbia probably winter off the Oregon and California coasts (Kaiser et al. 1984). This may account for the extraordinary migratory movement seen 12 and 13 Mar 2002 off Boiler Bay, when 2,500 and 6,500, respectively, were seen (P. Pickering p.c.). Movements are usually all but invisible. Banded birds found dead on the beach near Newport were from Triangle I., British Columbia (R. Lowe p.c.).

**Detection:** During the breeding season can be seen during the day offshore and occasionally in estuaries. The best viewing location is Sea Lion Caves, Lane Co., where they are diurnal; almost everywhere else in Oregon they return to the colony only at night. At sea large size makes them visible at greater distances than the similarly colored Cassin's Auklet.

**Population Status and Conservation:** Population estimates for this species are unreliable because of the difficulty of establishing whether burrows are occupied. World population is estimated at 1.5 million breeding birds with 461,000 breeding in N. America. Of these, fewer than 2,000 breed in California and 61,000 in Washington (Gaston and Jones 1998). The first records of breeding in Oregon were in 1966 when an adult was discovered in a burrow and four dead birds were found on Goat I., Curry Co. (Browning and English 1968). A year later adults were seen during the breeding season at Sea Lion Caves (Crowell and Nehls 1969d). Goat I. was confirmed as a breeding site by Scott et al. (1974), who unearthed chicks from burrows in 1973. Since the 1960s, the number of Rhinoceros Auklets has increased along the ne. Pacific coast (Gaston and Dechesne 1996), but the number breeding in Oregon is not large, probably because little suitable nesting habitat is available. An estimated 400 breeders were present in 1979 although many of the colonies on which birds were suspected of breeding were not visited (Pitman et al. 1985). The 1988 survey of Oregon's breeding seabirds estimated 1,000 breeding birds (USFWS unpubl. data).

Predation on colonies in Oregon is high. Twenty-five dead Rhinoceros Auklets were found on Goat I. and 25 on Hunter I., Curry Co., in 1979 (Pitman et al. 1985), and a smaller number (<10) on Hunter I. in 1988 (USFWS unpubl. data). All of the heads were missing and the skins neatly pulled inside out with all the muscle and viscera stripped away, suggesting an avian predator, possibly Great Horned Owl (Pitman et al. 1985). On Protection I., Washington, regurgitated pellets from a single family of Great Horned Owls (two adults, three juveniles) found 93% of 129 pellets contained the remains of Rhinoceros Auklets (Hayward et al. 1993). Also at that site, Glaucous-winged Gulls are known to take chicks (M. Denny p.c.). Denny once observed an adult taken from the water's surface from below by an orca. Bald Eagles and Peregrine Falcons are also predators (Gaston and Dechesne 1996). Older chicks emerge from the burrows at night to exercise, sometimes wandering around (Gaston and Dechesne 1996) thus making them vulnerable to predation. Human activities that affect Rhinoceros Auklets include investigator disturbance on the colony, the introduction of non-native mammals to breeding islands, net entanglement, and oil pollution (Gaston and Dechesne 1996).—*Jan Hodder*

## Horned Puffin *Fratercula corniculata*

Horned Puffins have an unmistakable black and white plumage and a large, distinct, yellow and orange bill during the breeding season. They winter offshore in the n. Pacific and nest mainly in Alaska and Russia. Rare in Oregon, they are most commonly encountered dead on the beach in winter or spring, or sighted more than 50 mi (80km) offshore in spring.

**General Distribution:** Breeds on islands and along coasts of the Chukchi and Bering seas and along the Alaska and British Columbia coast. Nonbreeding birds occur in summer south to s. California. Winters from the Bering Sea to the nw. Hawaiian Is., off the N. American coast to s. California and from ne. Siberia to Japan. Monotypic (AOU 1957).

**Oregon Distribution:** Rare to sometimes abundant visitor to the offshore waters of the ne. Pacific (Pitman and Graybill 1985). Specimens are listed by Hoffman et al. (1975). Occasionally found dead on beaches, most commonly in winter (Stallcup 1990), and occasionally in large numbers (Gilligan et al. 1994). During winter they are rarely seen over the continental shelf and normally return northward to the breeding grounds in spring from offshore waters. In some years, however, they move over the shelf during this migration and this may account for the preponderance of spring sightings (Pitman and Graybill 1985, Contreras 1998). Since about 1970, Horned Puffins have regularly been seen off the Oregon coast in small numbers during the summer months. These sightings probably reflect the development of recreational seabird watching and more detailed seabird inventories rather than a change in distribution (Pitman and Graybill 1985). Individual birds, or possibly pairs, occasionally stay in Oregon for the breeding season and are seen attending colonies with Tufted Puffins (Pitman and Graybill 1985), but there are no records of breeding in Oregon. Individuals were seen in seabird colonies during the breeding season at Yaquina Head in 1973 (Hoffman et al. 1975) and 1974; Island Rock, south of Port Orford, in 1979; Hunter I., Curry Co., in 1984 (Pitman and Graybill 1985) and 1987 (Roy Lowe p.c.); at Cape Lookout, Tillamook Co., in 1968 (Hoffman et al. 1975), 1976, 1977 (Anonymous 1977b), and 1981 (Watson 1981b); and at Goat I., Curry Co., in 1998 (Roy Lowe p.c.).

**Habitat and Diet:** Marine. No nests yet recorded in Oregon, but elsewhere, nest located in rock crevices or under boulders, occasionally dig burrows. Diet is poorly known for adults throughout their range and there are no data from Oregon. Winter diet is unknown. In summer includes fish, squid, polychaete worms, and crustaceans. More complete information is available for chicks, who are fed almost entirely fish (Gaston and Jones 1998).

**Seasonal Activity and Behavior:** Offshore in all monthss, but precise timing of offshore activities unknown.

**Detection:** Unmistakable in the Pacific basin due to puffin bill shape and contrasting black and white plumage.

**Population Status and Conservation:** Population off Oregon not known. Total population is estimated at 1.2 million breeders with the majority (62%) breeding on the Alaska peninsula (Gaston and Jones 1998). Breeds in low numbers in s. British Columbia (Campbell et al. 1979). Threats to populations include by-catch in net fisheries, introduced mammals in colonies, and the ingestion of plastic while feeding. Wehle (1982) examined 85 adults and eight subadults from Gulf of Alaska and found 7% of adult and 48% of subadult stomachs contained plastic.—*Jan Hodder*

## Tufted Puffin *Fratercula cirrhata*

The Tufted Puffin is the most recognized seabird in Oregon. It is common to abundant at breeding rocks but rare to uncommon elsewhere owing to its pelagic feeding habits. It is easily identified in the breeding season by the colorful laterally compressed bill, a distinct white face with long cream colored facial plumes, black body, and red feet. In winter it moves offshore and loses most of its colorful plumage and bill plates.

**General Distribution:** Breeds from the Diomede Is. south along the Alaskan coast to s. California; in e. Asia from the Kolyuchin Is. to n. Japan. Winters offshore from s. Alaska and Kamchatka south through the breeding range to c. California and Japan. Monotypic (AOU 1957).

**Oregon Distribution:** It nests along the entire Oregon coast where soil-covered islands are present. It also nests on headlands such as Cape Meares, Cape Lookout, Cape Foulweather, and Yaquina Head. Major nesting concentration is in the north of the state, with two-thirds of nesting birds at Three Arch Rocks. No nesting habitat is available from Coos Bay to north of Florence. During the nonbreeding season, puffins disperse offshore, where they forage as individuals often far past the continental slope (Briggs et al. 1992). There are records of their presence offshore in all months of the nonbreeding season although numbers appear low in Nov and Dec (Tyler et al. 1993, G. Gillson p.c.). Some portion of the Oregon population may move south as numbers in California increase in the winter (Briggs et al. 1992), but the origin of California birds is unclear. Jan and Mar sightings were seaward of the continental slope off n. and c. Oregon (Briggs et al. 1992), although Pitman (1981) sighted 20 birds 60 mi (96km) off Waldport in Mar. Rarely seen from land in winter.

**Habitat and Diet:** Marine. Puffins nest on islands and headlands with steep grassy slopes and deep soil for burrowing; less often use natural rock crevices. Nesting burrows are up to 6 ft (2 m) long and are used repeatedly. Nest site location is influenced by the bird's ability to take off and land; steep slopes or cliff edges are favored, and rarely are nests constructed in areas with shrubs (Vermeer 1979). Diet of adults is not known in Oregon. Squid, fish, and small amounts of crustaceans and polychaetes were found in samples from Alaska taken during the breeding season (Wehle 1982,

Vermeer et al. 1987). Chick diet is easier to determine as adults bring whole fish to the nest. The chick diet at Goat I., Curry Co., varied by year: in 1981 chicks were fed northern anchovy, Pacific herring, and sand lance; in 1982, when sample sizes were larger, rockfish, Pacific sanddab, rex sole, and squid were included in the diet (Boone 1985). The location of the colony no doubt affects the diet of chicks. At the Farallones chicks are primarily delivered rockfish (Ainley, Morrell, and Boekelheide 1990), whereas in British Columbia they receive a more diverse diet of sand lance, bluethroat argentine, Pacific saury, and small amounts of rockfish and squid (Vermeer 1979). No information is available on the diet during the nonbreeding season.

**Seasonal Activity and Behavior:** They have been recorded as early as 7 Mar at Bandon (Contreras 1998). At the beginning of the breeding season they aggregate offshore from the colony, engaging in intensive courtship with frequent copulations (Gaston and Jones 1998). The only study of Tufted Puffins

*Tufted Puffin*

nesting in Oregon was conducted on Goat I., Curry Co., where 40 artificial nest boxes were monitored for two breeding seasons (Boone 1985). At this site puffins returned to their nesting sites in early Apr. A single white egg, representing 12% of the female's body weight (Ainley, Morrell, and Boekelheide 1990), was laid in early May to mid-Jun; peak of laying was mid-May (Boone 1985). Both sexes incubated. On Goat I., incubation was 42 days (SD 4.8 days) and eggs hatched in early Jul (Boone 1985). If the first egg was lost, a second was laid in some instances (Boone 1985).

Adults bring back several whole fish at a time to the chick. At Goat I. the number of food deliveries per nest per day ranged 0-12, with a mean of 4.7, and the average weight of fish was 71.3g/day (Boone 1985). On the Farallon Is. Adults usually bring one, sometimes two, loads per day (Ainley, Morrell, and Boekelheide 1990), whereas on Triangle I., British Columbia, chicks received an average of 3.5 feeds/day (Gaston and Jones 1998). At Goat I., two peak periods of chick feeding were seen: one shortly after dawn, and the other from 1800 hr until dark (Boone 1985).

Chicks fledge at night, unaided by their parents, at 64-68% of adult weight. Nestling period varies 40-59 days (Gaston and Jones 1998). On Goat I., time to fledging was 57.6 days (SD. 7.5 days) in 1981 and 50.6 days (SD 6.6 days) in 1982, although only 8 chicks fledged in each year (Boone 1985). Adults leave the colonies in late Aug to early Sep (Fix 1987, Fix 1991, Contreras 1998).

**Detection:** During incubation one of the pair will often stand outside the burrow during the day or sometimes sit on the water adjacent to the colony. After chicks hatch, adults are more commonly seen in the evening after delivering their last load of fish (Ainley, Morrell, and Boekelheide 1990). Best seen from shore at Parrot Rock off Heceta Head and Haystack Rock, Cannon Beach. Elephant Rock, part of the Coquille Rock complex at Bandon was formerly an excellent site for viewing but in 2002 non-native red foxes eliminated nesting of most seabirds at this colony. Immatures are sometimes confused with Rhinoceros Auklets.

**Population Status and Conservation:** Like all burrow nesters, puffins are difficult to census accurately and no estimate for the world population has been published. The bulk of the population is in Alaska. There are fewer than 70,000 birds south of Alaska, with one colony in British Columbia accounting for 50,000 (Gaston and Jones 1998). They continue to nest at all the sites listed by Gabrielson and Jewett (1940). In 1979, 6,560 nesting birds were estimated in Oregon with 64% (4,200) at Three Arch Rocks (Pitman et al. 1985). In 1988 a total of 5,031 breeding birds were counted of which 3,040 were at Three Arch Rocks (USFWS unpubl. data). Four other colonies (Goat

I. and Island Rock, Curry Co., and Haystack Rocks, Tillamook and Clatsop counties.) each have over 300 nesting birds but the majority of the rest of the nesting colonies have fewer than 100. The Elephant Rock colony is in decline as weathering has caused soil erosion in recent years.

Threats to the population include oil spills, net entanglement, and disturbance at the colonies. Mammalian and avian predators take birds on the colonies and avian predated Tufted Puffins have been found on Goat I. and Hunter I. (USFWS unpubl. data), and at Gregory Point. Ingestion of plastic particles has been studied in Alaska, where 18.5% of stomachs contained plastic (n= 135 birds) (Wehle 1982).—*Jan Hodder*

# Order COLUMBIFORMES
## *Family Columbidae*

### Rock Dove (Feral Pigeon) *Columba livia*

This pigeon of city streets, barns and bridges originated from the Rock Dove native to the Old World. Oregon representatives of this species, as well as those in most other parts of the world, originated from escaped birds. This species was probably the first to have been domesticated for food, some 5000-10,000 yr ago, most likely in the e. Mediterranean (Sossinka 1982), and it is mentioned in early Egyptian literature as a domestic bird (Johnston and Janiga 1995). However, confusion between *C. livia* and *C. oenas* (Stock Dove) existed in the early literature (see Banks and Browning 1995).

The varied plumage colors shown by feral pigeons were created through domestic breeding. Most common are birds having dark green and purple iridescent head and neck plumage, gray backs, black wing bars and tail, and orange feet. Some possess various combinations of brown and white plumage, or are nearly all white, as are the domestic doves that are commonly released for ceremonies or that serve as symbols of peace.

The homing abilities of this species and the ease with which it can be raised in captivity have made it a subject of numerous research papers on bird navigation and orientation (Johnston and Janiga 1995), and a number of hobbyists in Oregon and elsewhere release domestic pigeons >100 mi (160 km) from their lofts and time their arrival home. Occasionally some of these birds, which are banded, go astray or become exhausted. They are picked up by well-meaning citizens, but in reality they are considered losers by pigeon owners. Racing pigeons, crossing the Cascades or other wild landscapes, are regularly taken by Peregrine Falcons, as shown by leg bands found in falcon eyries (J. Pagel p.c.). Between 16 and 25 bands have been found at

some falcon nests with others scattered below the nest.

**General Distribution:** In a wild form, probably occurred from the Faeroes across n. Europe to Russia, the Middle East, India and south to n. Africa, but this not entirely certain because of early unrecorded escapes or releases of domestic pigeons (Johnston 1992). Extirpated as a wild bird from much of this range, including Europe, except for Portugal. Feral forms found throughout most of the world. N. American birds are a combination of several subspecies (AOU 1957).

**Oregon Distribution:** Common to abundant statewide in cities, towns, and agricultural areas (OBBA, *DBM*). Distribution is more scattered in steppe habitats east of the Cascades according to available habitat. Pigeons are not found in forested areas, but occur in some small towns and villages in otherwise forested landscapes on west slopes of the Cascades (*MGH, DBM*).

**Habitat and Diet:** Found in and about human-created structures, e.g., masonry buildings, parking structures, barns, abandoned houses, bridges, water towers, and freeway overpasses that possess cornices, ledges, and cave-like cavities used for nesting and shelter. Such structures replicate natural cliff habitats. Nesting material comprises small amounts of feathers, droppings, grasses, twigs, and other plant material (Johnston and Janiga 1995).

Pigeons forage in city streets and parks on food refuse, public handouts, and weed seeds, and on grain spilled at shipping facilities and along transportation corridors. In agricultural areas they forage in livestock feedlots and fields, particularly where spilled or waste grain is present. Numerous populations have also become established in a habitat type used by the original Rock Dove, specifically in basalt cliffs and rimrock containing cavities, particularly along major rivers and canyons in e. Oregon. These sites are typically near foraging sites, e.g., grain fields or

transportation corridors where spilled grain is present (*RRK, DBM*).

Between 1958 and 1963, Kindschy (1964) studied a population of >1000 doves breeding in Succor Cr. Canyon, Malheur Co., some 10 mi (16 km) from their primary foraging site in Homedale, Idaho. This distance appears to be the outer limit in terms of distance between nesting and foraging sites (Contreras and Kindschy 1996). Kindschy's study included the only food habit studies found for Oregon. Contents of 20 crops taken at different times of year comprised 95.5% domestic grains, of which 35% was corn and 60.5% wheat and similar grains as a percentage of total volume. Seeds from wild plants common to the canyon area comprised 3.5% of the total volume. Wild grasses and forbs amounted to only 1%.

Johnston (1992) summarized what is known about foods taken in various parts of the U.S. It duplicates what might be expected for Oregon. He lists the same grains shown above plus oats and numerous weed seeds, e.g., knotweed as well as the seeds of American elm. The latter two are taken about the park blocks of Portland (*DBM*). Bread, peanuts, popcorn, and other human snacks are readily taken from city streets and parks.

**Seasonal Activity and Behavior:** Nest in colonies and singly (Johnston and Janiga 1995). Monogamous, but readily re-mate after loss of a partner. In some parts of the world, pigeons are known to breed at 6 mo of age. They can breed during any month of the year over most of their range and may produce more than one brood per year (Johnston 1992, Johnston and Janiga 1995). At Newport, Lincoln Co., they have been observed copulating as early as 15 Jan (*MGH*). The only Oregon study was at Succor Cr. Canyon, where mating activity commenced in Feb and Mar (Kindschy 1964). Reproductive activities are assumed to have continued through the summer (*RRK*). Incubation there took 12-15 days. Hatching was completed by mid-Apr, when egg shells were dropped to the canyon floor or to the base of cliffs. Individuals occupied specific ledges and aggressively defended sites against others. Eggs are white in color; clutch size normally two, but sometimes one or three. Young are hatched naked except for scattered bits of filamentous down, and are first fed "pigeon milk," a fluid secreted from the adults' crop. Later this is supplemented with partially digested seeds of waste grain from the parents' crop. Both sexes participate in nest building, incubation, and young care.

In the Kindschy (1964) study, flocks of 10 or more left cliff ledges at intervals during the daylight hours. They would soon return to ledges or depart for Homedale to forage on agricultural lands or in livestock feed lots. Here they joined local feral pigeons. This foraging pattern occurred year-round.

Feral pigeon flocks range in size from several birds to >50. They typically fly from feeding sites or perches, fly for a minute or two, and alight again, often in the same place (*RRK*).

**Detection:** The flocking pattern, conspicuousness, flapping sound made by the wings, low-pitched cooing, and large size all make this an easily recognized and well-known bird.

**Population Status and Conservation:** The first known importation of domestic Rock Doves to N. America was to Nova Scotia in 1606 followed by one to Virginia in 1622. Numerous importations followed (Schorger 1952). It is not clear when these birds first escaped from captivity in N. America, or what the relative roles of subsequent releases and range expansions were in their spread across N. America. Considering that domestic Rock Doves were first raised for food and then for carrying messages and for racing as a hobby, wild populations are assumed to have been augmented by domestic birds on an ongoing basis throughout their worldwide range.

A review of sources available to the writers did not reveal when domestic or feral Rock Doves were imported and escaped in or immigrated to Oregon. A search of historical information on early Northwest agriculture might provide such information. Outside cities and towns, Gabrielson and Jewett (1940) report their presence only along the Umatilla R. As related above, they are now widespread along river canyons throughout e. Oregon. BBS and CBC data are inconclusive with regard to recent population trends, and birders generally ignore their presence, as did early writers like Lord (1902). No conservation concerns.

Like the House Sparrow and European Starling, this is an unprotected species in Oregon for good reasons. They can be highly destructive in terms of defacing buildings with excrement, and as a result are subject to control programs in many cities (Johnston 1992). Architects consider pigeons in some structure designs, and wire and metal devices to prevent their using office buildings and parking structures are often installed at considerable expense. On a positive side, they provide the only opportunity for some inner-city residents to observe and feed birds. Unlike House Sparrows and European Starlings, they utilize only human-made habitats with the exception of cliffs. Any major adverse impacts on native birds is not discernible, and in cities like Portland they constitute the main food source for Peregrine Falcons.—*Robert R. Kindschy and David B. Marshall*

## Band-tailed Pigeon *Columba fasciata*
About the size of the domestic pigeon, this swift-flying species is popular among sport hunters, offering a pursuit unlike any other game bird. An arboreal bird, it is often observed perched alone on top of a tall tree or in flocks when flying about feeding areas and mineral sites. It is one of only two extant native species of pigeon or dove in n. temperate N. America. They appear bluish-gray overall, but a closer inspection reveals brilliant colors including black wing tips, straw yellow legs and feet, straw yellow bill tipped in black, purplish-brown head and breast, coral red eye-ring, a white crescent atop an iridescent bronze green nape, and a long square-ended tail with a distinct pale gray band bordered above by a narrower black band. The white crescent is absent on juveniles.

**General Distribution:** Occurs from w. N. America through M. America into mid-S. America. Eight subspecies are recognized; however, only two occur north of Mexico, including the interior *C. f. fasciata* and the coastal *C. f. monilis*. Interior birds breed from n. Colorado and ec. Utah south through Arizona, New Mexico, extreme w. Texas into the Sierra Madre Occidental of Mexico; and winter from n. Mexico south to at least Michoacan (Braun et al. 1975, AOU 1957). Coastal birds breed from w. British Columbia south into w. Washington, w. Oregon, California, and extreme w. Nevada, primarily west of the Cascade and Sierra Nevada ranges, and into Baja California. They winter from c. California into n. Baja California (AOU 1957). Some in Mexico and s. California and those wintering north of s. California may represent non-migratory populations. Subspecies are geographically separated, but based on banding recoveries some interchange occurs (Schroeder and Braun 1993). Only *monilis* recorded breeding in Oregon (AOU 1957); nominate *fasciata* occurs rarely. Birds occasionally seen in se. Oregon (more reports in recent years, mainly from Harney Co.) are of unknown subspecies.

**Oregon Distribution:** This is a common summer resident in forested areas west of the Cascade crest. It typically nests in forested mountain areas (<4,000 ft [1,220 m] in the w. Cascades) but frequents valleys

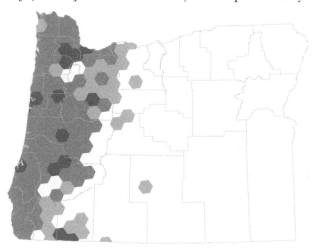

to exploit mineral sites and feed (especially at bird feeders and silage stockpiles). Most abundant in the Coast Range with abundance increasing from east to west, most likely in response to the distribution of food (Sanders 1999). Rare east of the Cascade crest, occurring as a vagrant in riparian habitat and at desert oases from late Mar to Oct (Gabrielson and Jewett 1940). Occur east of the Cascades at Mosier along the Columbia R. and occasionally elsewhere in Wasco Co. (D. Lusthoff p.c.). In winter, uncommon and highly local resident, mainly in Portland and in sw. Oregon.

**Habitat and Diet:** Inhabits coniferous forests. Habitat components identified as important for reproducing Band-tailed Pigeons include: (1) closed-canopy forest for nest sites, (2) open-canopy forests for foraging, and (3) mineral sites. Highly mobile; breeding home range averages 27,482 ac (11,121 ha), ranges 774–446,739 ac (314–180,800 ha); may travel 32.1 miles (51.6 km) from nest locations to food or mineral (Leonard 1998). In the c. Coast Range, equally abundant up to 23 mi (37 km) from the nearest known mineral site (Sanders 1999).

Band-tails nest primarily in Douglas-fir, occasionally in hardwoods and shrubs, within closed-canopy conifer or mixed hardwood and conifer forest stands (Leonard 1998). Nests are loosely constructed twig platforms. Placement is highly variable, ranging 6-120 ft (1.8–36.3 m, averaging 34 ft [10.3 m]) above ground, near the bole and in dense foliage (Leonard 1998).

Diet includes buds, flowers, and fruits of deciduous trees and shrubs, especially oak, madrone, elderberry, cherry, cascara, huckleberry, and blackberry, but varies seasonally and by location (Braun 1994). Elderberry and cascara shrubs are naturally prevalent in early to intermediate forest successional stages, and occur in open areas. Cultivated crops, silage stockpiles, and bird feeders are readily exploited, but natural foods are preferred. Corn is the most preferred grain, but field peas and wheat are also readily consumed and barley and oats are used to a lesser extent (Braun 1994). Berries of red elderberry are consumed late Jun-Aug, cascara from Aug-Sep, and blue elderberry Sep-Oct, consistent with the fruiting phenology of these shrubs (Jarvis and Passmore 1992).

In w. Oregon, 65 known mineral sites are currently used: 33 springs, 22 estuaries, five dry sites, three wastewater sites, and two livestock salting areas (Sanders and Jarvis 2000). Use of these sites is thought to be related to a mineral-poor diet (March and Sadleir 1972, Jarvis and Passmore 1992, Sanders 1999), in combination with inefficient retention of sodium associated with dietary potassium loading (Sanders 1999). Use of mineral sites appears dependent upon salt content and the availability of ample nearby perching sites (Sanders and Jarvis 2000).

**Seasonal Activity and Behavior:** Pigeons begin arriving in Mar, with initiation and timing of reproductive activity generally dependent upon food supply (March and Sadleir 1970, 1972, Gutiérrez et al. 1975, Jarvis and Passmore 1992): generally May-Sep, peaks late Jul. In some years birds begin arriving earlier, e.g., multiple arrivals were reported throughout w. Oregon on 17-18 Feb 2002 (D. Irons p.c.). Successive nest attempts take place at 45- to 50-day intervals. Life history traits consistent with other pigeons or doves: single egg clutches, sequential nest attempts averaging two successful nests per year with three possible, and both adults incubate clutches and feed young regurgitated crop milk (Jarvis and Passmore 1992, Leonard 1998). Males attend nests from mid-morning until mid-afternoon and females from mid-afternoon until the following morning.

Use of mineral sites occurs Jun-Sep with a peak in Aug (Jarvis and Passmore 1992). Band-tails use one or multiple adjacent sites within a year and in subsequent years. Both males and females are thought to use mineral sites once per week while nesting (Jarvis and Passmore 1992). The daily use of mineral sites is daylight to noon, with two times of arrival: early morning (dawn-1000 hr) and late morning (1000-1200 hr). Males predominate in early morning and females in late morning, coinciding with nest attendance schedules. Band-tailed Pigeons remain at mineral sites 1-2 hr, where they loaf and preen while perched in trees adjacent to the mineral source (Jarvis and Passmore 1992).

*Band-tailed Pigeon*

The Band-tailed Pigeon's coo call, usually given by adult males, is low frequency (200-600 Hz) and consists of a faint *oo* followed by a series of five *whoo-oo* sounds (Keppie 1970, Sanders 1999). They call on arrival in Oregon and continue through mid-Aug, but most frequent calling is mid-Jun to early Aug and especially during Jul (Sisson 1968, Keppie et al. 1970). Cooing is typically from a prominent perch near the nest site between about sunrise and 4 hr after sunrise, and to a much lesser extent between 3.5 and 1.5 hr before sunset (Sisson 1968, Keppie et al. 1970). Morning calling commences at about 12 min before sunrise and peaks at or just after sunrise.

Most birds leave in Oct. Those that remain form nomadic aggregations throughout winter.

**Detection:** The likelihood of observing this species in seemingly good nesting habitat can be low. However, in a Coast Range study 1996-98, mid-Jun to late Jul, the probability of hearing at least one Band-tailed Pigeon during a 60-min period beginning 10 min before sunrise at a random forest location was 0.83 (Sanders 1999). The Band-tailed Pigeon's coo call may be audible for at least 0.7 mi (1.1 km), depending on forest conditions (Sanders 1999). This species may be observed in large, conspicuous aggregations at mineral sites or feeding in open forested areas; they can be especially visible near the coast in Sep.

**Population Status and Conservation:** Population size of *C. monilis* is unknown because of difficulty in locating and observing individuals. However, indices of abundance are available. BBSs in the coastal area of British Columbia, Washington, Oregon, and California indicated a long-term (1966-2000) population trend of -2.8% annually (p<0.002, 90% CI=-4.2 to -1.4), while the short-term (1991-2000) trend is inconclusive (trend=-1.5%, p=0.662, 90% CI=-7.2 to 4.2). Visual counts at mineral sites in Oregon indicated a decreasing trend from 1951 to the late 1980s and a slight increasing trend from the late 1980s to 2000 (p<0.001) (*TAS*).

Downward population trends are possibly due to disease and historically liberal hunting regulations. Federal regulations have permitted hunting since 1932 following a 20-yr moratorium (Neff 1947). Between 1957 and 1992, total harvest in the three coastal states ranged from a peak of 724,000 birds in 1972 to a low of 70,000 in 1988 (Pacific Flyway Council 1994). The long-term harvest decreased by 20,000 birds annually from 550,000 in 1968 to 70,000 in 1988 (Braun 1994). From 1957 to 1987, Washington, Oregon, and California respectively accounted for 22%, 23%, and 55% of the total harvest, and in Oregon an average of 12,300 hunters (range 5,900–20,300) harvested an average of 86,000 birds per year (range 45,000–122,000) (Jarvis and Passmore 1992). Since 1987, state agencies in Washington, Oregon, and California have responded with increasingly restrictive hunting regulations. There has been no open hunting season in Washington since 1991 and British Columbia since 1994 due to concern for this species' status. Baja California had no open season except 1981-86.—*Todd A. Sanders and Robert L. Jarvis*

### Eurasian Collared-Dove *Streptopelia decaocto*

During the 1600s this Indian species began to expand its range until today it occurs in all of Europe and most of Asia. After introductions in the Bahamas in 1974 and Guadeloupe in 1976 it soon expanded throughout the Caribbean and reached Florida by 1980. It is now expanding into other parts of N. America, reaching New Mexico, Colorado, and Montana by 1997; Oregon in 1998 (Romagosa and McEneaney 1999); and Washington in 2000 (Mlodinow et al. 2000b). It is expected to eventually colonize most of N. America. S. California populations are from releases beginning in 1994 and are not part of the expansion from the east (Romagosa and McEneaney 1999).

Individuals were observed at Fields, Harney Co., 19 Jun 1999 (Spencer 2000a); in Oregon City, Clackamas Co., 23 Dec 1999 (Tice 2000b); near Astoria, Clatsop Co., 3 Apr 2000 (Lillie 2000); and in Joseph, Wallowa Co., much of the winter of 2001-02 (*ALC*).

The Eurasian Collared-Dove is quite similar to the Ringed Turtle-Dove (*S. 'risoria'*) but is somewhat larger with grayer underparts and darker primaries. It is a bird of agricultural areas and readily visits bird-feeding stations in urban and rural neighborhoods.—*Harry B. Nehls*

### White-winged Dove *Zenaida asiatica*

This medium-sized dove breeds from the s. U.S. south through S. America. Many northern birds migrate south to winter in C. and S. America. It has a propensity to wander northward in the fall and has been recorded casually throughout the U.S. Single birds were observed at the s. jetty of the Columbia R., Clatsop Co., 28 Aug 1976 (OBRC); photographed at the Hatfield Marine Science Center on Yaquina Bay, Lincoln Co., 28-30 Oct 1979 (OBRC); observed at Tillamook Bay, Tillamook Co., 20 Dec 1986 (OBRC); photographed at Brookings, Curry Co., 5-11 Oct 1995; seen at Malheur NWR HQ, Harney Co., 12 May 1998 (OBRC); and photographed on the n. jetty of the Rogue R., Curry Co., 6 Sep 2000 (OBRC). The 1995 bird at Brookings was later found dead after striking a window (Gilligan 1996). Subspecies unknown.—*Harry B. Nehls*

## Mourning Dove *Zenaida macroura*

The mournful, drawn-out *coo, coo, coo* vocalization of a male Mourning Dove advertising for a mate is a familiar sound to suburbanites and country-dwellers alike. This is a streamlined medium-sized dove with a small head and long tail. Its plumage is generally grayish-brown above and buffy below with black spots on the wing coverts. The tail is dark gray with a white border.

**General Distribution:** It occurs from s. Canada south to Panama, Costa Rica, and Caribbean Is. Occurs year-round except in prairie provinces of Canada and north plains states (Mirarchi and Baskett 1994) where absent in winter because of southward migration to Mexico and M. America. Much reduced in winter north of a line from about c. California east to Virginia because of fall exodus (Aldrich 1993). Five subspecies, two of which occur in the U.S.; *Z. m. marginella* occurs across the western half of N. America (Aldrich and Duvall 1958).

**Oregon Distribution:** This species is abundant in spring, summer, and early fall statewide in open landscapes, except along the coast and in the higher elevations of the w. Cascades where it is uncommon to rare (OBBA, ODFW undated files[c]). It is absent from alpine areas and densely forested sites, especially at the highest elevations. Fairly common to uncommon in valleys in winter. Reported from over 80% of CBC circles (n=35) in both e. and w. Oregon for the 1998-99 and 1999-2000 count years, with numbers exceeding 100 on nine counts. Most Oregon Mourning Doves pass through California and Nevada to winter in the Imperial Valley of California, sc. Arizona, and nc. Mexico (Tomlinson 1993). It is not clear whether those that winter in Oregon are migrants from farther north, are permanent residents, or both. Year-round behavioral patterns of a pair found in a residential area of Lake Oswego indicate that at least some remain year-round (*DBM*), as discovered through banding with an urban population in Berkeley, California (Tomlinson 1993).

**Habitat and Diet:** Doves have adapted to a wide variety of habitats ranging from open forests and clearcuts to deserts, as well as urban and agricultural areas. In Oregon, abundant in grass, shrub, juniper steppe, and agricultural areas (*DBM*). Less so in open ponderosa pine forests and suburban and urban areas, but have adapted increasingly to the latter. Tend to frequent edges where trees are present. In the Willamette Valley, they are often seen along roadsides and fencerows supporting small trees and shrubs and also perch on utility and fence wires. In some areas, doves associate with grain-processing and shipping facilities (*RRK*). These doves feed on the ground.

The Mourning Dove is a nest-site generalist that nests in trees where available, but otherwise on the ground under shrubs, or even on structural components of buildings (Sayre and Silvy 1993).

A nearby source of drinking water is required; they typically visit stock-watering ponds in e. Oregon. Doves feed on cereal grains and a great variety of other seeds, too numerous to name other than to provide examples. While no food habit data are available for Oregon, general observations and work in other western states show that seeds of grasses and some trees, e.g., willows and cottonwoods, and numerous herbaceous plants are important (Lewis 1993, Mirarchi and Baskett 1994). Examples of herbaceous plant seeds occurring in Oregon that were found in dove stomachs from adjoining states include goosefoots, saltbushes, sunflowers and other composites, smartweeds, and mustards. Annual sunflower is a popular food in e. Oregon (*RRK*). Doves occur about bird feeders where they take seeds, particularly millet, spilled on the ground. Animal matter, comprising insects and snails, comprises less than 1% of the diet (Lewis 1993).

**Seasonal Activity and Behavior:** Migrants return late Mar-early Apr in e. Oregon (Gabrielson and Jewett 1940, Littlefield 1990a), but it is difficult to discern migration in many areas because of presence of birds year-round (*DBM*). Males select nesting sites (Sayre and Silvy 1993) and females are attracted by the male's cooing. Pairs are monogamous, at least seasonally. There is a high degree of fidelity to previous nesting sites (Tomlinson 1993). Nests are flimsy, loosely assembled bits of twigs and grass (Sayre and Silvy 1993) normally containing two, but sometimes three, white eggs. Incubation lasts approximately 2 wk, and both sexes participate. Young remain in the nest 10-15 days. They are initially fed a fatty substance produced in the crop of adults. Young fend for themselves several days after fledging (Sayre and Silvy 1993).

One complete nesting cycle lasts only 32 days (+/- 5 days). Nesting cycles sometimes overlap because females lay new clutches even while young from the previous brood require care. This strategy allows multiple broods annually. Littlefield (1990a) reported up to three broods annually at Malheur NWR. In the Rogue Valley as many as four clutches have been laid in a season (N. Barrett p.c.). There can be up to five or six broods in southern parts of N. America (Sayre and Silvy 1993). Gullion (1951) reported a 26 Apr-27 Aug breeding period for the Willamette Valley from nest building to fledging, and Gabrielson and Jewett (1940) reported fresh eggs between 20 Apr and 3 Sep for the state as a whole. OBBA data showed nests with eggs as early as 21 Mar (Rogue Valley) and as late as Jul 17, but timing of the OBBA project did not coincide with the entire nesting season.

Aside from wintering Mourning Doves, the typical seasonal pattern, according to Tomlinson (1993), is for immatures that are independent of their parents to gather in wandering flocks of up to about 50 beginning in Jul. They are subsequently joined by adults. Southward migration begins as early as late Jul at Malheur NWR with a peak 25 Aug to 10 Sep (Littlefield 1990a), but Gabrielson and Jewett (1940) reported substantial numbers remaining into early Oct in e. Oregon. Doves generally travel less than 100 mi (160 km) per day (Tomlinson 1993).

**Detection:** Readily seen and heard in good habitat. Cooing can be heard by humans up to 0.25 mi (0.40 km) or more (*RRK*). Flight is swift and direct without gliding. A whistling sound made by the wings is diagnostic.

**Population Status and Conservation:** Although not as popular a game bird in Oregon as in some states, the ~50 million Mourning Doves taken annually by over 2.7 million dove hunters in N. America exceeded the take of all other game birds combined in the 1970s and 1980s (Baskett and Sayre 1993, Sadler 1993). This level of harvest is possible in part because of the bird's high reproductive rate, its coast-to-coast distribution, and the degree to which it has adapted to human-altered landscapes. As a backyard bird, it ranked second behind the Dark-eyed Junco among the most-frequently reported feeder birds in the U.S. and Canada in 1997-98 (Barker and Tessaglia-Hymes 1999).

Continental populations are monitored by roadside call-counts initiated in the early 1950s by federal and state wildlife agencies (Dolton 1993), and the BBS initiated in the 1960s. For Oregon, call counts showed adjusted mean numbers of doves per route dropped from 12 in 1966 to <4 in 2000, a statistically significant annual decline of 3%/yr (USFWS files). Similarly, the BBS shows a significant overall decline averaging 3%/yr for Oregon 1966-98, although a slight increase is indicated between 1993 and 1998 (Sauer et al. 1999). Declines are also evident in other western states.

With forest clearing and agriculture, Mourning Doves are undoubtedly more numerous than prior to Euro-American settlement (Reeves and McCabe 1993). We assume that this statement also applies to Oregon. However, since World War II, ongoing land-management practices in Oregon could easily account for the population decline shown above. For example, Reeves et al. (1993) mention sagebrush loss to cultivation or conversion to plantings of introduced grasses, pointing out that Mourning Doves nest under sagebrush in areas void of trees. They also list changes in agricultural practices in orchards of the Rogue Valley, e.g., turbine sprayers that are capable of destroying nests, and conversion to dwarf tree varieties. Extensive changes in the Willamette Valley, including

urbanization, conversion of cereal grain and grass seed production to nurseries, intensive farming practices that have reduced shrub and tree cover along field borders and weed patches, have adversely affected or eliminated dove habitat (*DBM*).

Although Mourning Doves have a very short average life span (most < 1 yr), their high reproductive rate overall offsets this. Accidents (largely vehicle collisions), predators, disease, weather, and miscellaneous causes are believed to take 4-5 times as many doves annually as hunting in the U.S. (Sadler 1993). A tabulation of 577 USFWS banding recoveries resulting from predation showed 70% of the reported kills having been caused by domestic cats and nearly 14% by domestic dogs (Sadler 1993).

The number of Oregon dove hunters hit a high of 24,000 in 1981 and dropped to 10,100 by 1987, the last year for which data are available (Reeves et al. 1993). Their annual take averaged 11.2 birds per hunter during 1983-87.—*Robert R. Kindschy and David B. Marshall*

# Order CUCULIFORMES
## *Family Cuculidae*

### Subfamily Coccyzinae

**Yellow-billed Cuckoo** *Coccyzus americanus*
The Yellow-billed Cuckoo virtually disappeared as an Oregon breeder long before there was an Endangered Species Act. The only other known extirpated breeder in Oregon is the Sharp-tailed Grouse. The Yellow-billed Cuckoo, one of two New World cuckoos found in N. America, is a slender, long-tailed bird about 12 in (30 cm) long, with a yellow bill and mostly grayish-brown upperparts, and is generally white below. The primaries have a rufous cast and the underside of the tail is black with white spots. It is popularly referred to as the rain crow because of its alleged trait of calling before it rains. J. K. Townsend (*in* Jobanek and Marshall 1992) noted in 1832 that this traditional belief, which he heard in e. N. America, also existed among the Indians of the Lower Columbia R. region. Although not to the extent of the Common Cuckoo of Europe, this species is known to lay eggs in the nests of other species. It is remarkable in that only 17 days are required from egg laying to fledging, and only 2 hr elapse between hatching and the nestlings becoming fully feathered (Hughes 1999).

**General Distribution:** Breeds over most of the U.S. and n. Mexico, but extirpated over much of its western range. Winters in S. America as far south as n. Argentina. Two subspecies, *C. a. americana* and *C.*

*a. occidentalis* (formerly known as California Cuckoo), were recognized starting in 1887 (AOU 1957); but the split was determined invalid by Banks (1988). This conclusion was questioned by Franzreb and Laymon (1993) and Pruett et al. (2001). However, the most recent investigation of this issue commissioned by USFWS concluded the species is monotypic (Fleischer 2001).

**Oregon Distribution:** Currently a rare, irregular visitor east of the Cascades; very rare and sporadic west of the Cascades. There is no known breeding population in the state. Single individuals have been reported almost every year from riparian areas east of the Cascades. There have been about 40 reports from e. Oregon in the 1970s-90s (B. Combs p.c.). Eleven of these were from Malheur NWR and 10 from Fields (Harney Co). Other locales included Pueblo Mtns. (also Harney Co.), Cow Cr. and Owyhee R. near Adrian (both Malheur Co.), Logan Valley (Grant Co.), Haystack Res. (Jefferson Co.), Imnaha (Wallowa Co.), Umatilla, Bend, Hart Mtn., Upper Klamath L., and L. Abert. Many of these reports were accepted by the OBRC, and some involved photographs and birds found dead. During the same period, only four w. Oregon reports were published; two were from Sauvie I. and one each from Sams Valley (Jackson Co.) and West Linn (Clackamas Co.). Over half of all reports were for Jun; but the months of Jul and Aug were also represented. Obviously the locales reflect areas frequented by birders. There is some evidence that cuckoos bred in Oregon within the last 30 yr. Reports of a nesting in La Grande in 1980 remain unconfirmed (Marshall et al. 1996). One found dead and photographed after hitting a window in Bend 500 yds (457 m) from the Deschutes R. (Anderson 1991a, photo in *Oregon Birds* 17: 94) had a brood patch, according to files of the OBRC (specimen with ODFW, Bend).

**Habitat and Diet:** Habitat where Townsend (Jobanek and Marshall 1992) and later Gabrielson and Jewett (1940) found this species was composed of large expanses of riparian forest, particularly black cottonwood, Oregon ash, and willow. Nearly all of this habitat has been converted to agriculture or industry. E. Oregon habitat where most recent reports have originated is riparian, dominated by willows. Eastern Oregon probably lacks habitat blocks of sufficient size and quality to support breeding populations, based on data from California (*DBM*).

Specific historical habitat data are lacking from Oregon. The closest breeding populations are in the Sacramento Valley, California. California habitats overall have been described by Gaines (1974), Gaines and Laymon (1984), Laymon and Halterman (1987), and Halterman et al. (2001). A synopsis of their work shows that trees are dominated by willows with a cottonwood overstory and that birds are found within 328 ft (100 m) of water. Habitat patches are usually in strips adjoining rivers, sloughs, and marshes with high humidity. Minimum width and length of habitat strips is 328 ft (100 m) and 984 ft (300 m) respectively. However, the width and/or length must exceed this amount to reach the required minimum habitat patch size of 62 ac (25 ha). Other descriptors include canopy height 16-82 ft (5-25 m) and canopy cover 30-90%. High foliage density including dense low-level foliage in nesting territories is also needed. Contrary to the above, Laymon and Halterman (1987) reported minimum habitat area for a pair of cuckoos was 37 ac (15 ha). Habitat patches need to be adjoining or in close proximity, but maximum allowable distance between patches was not provided. In the Sacramento Valley, cuckoos sometimes forage in adjoining orchards if tent caterpillars are present.

Nests are frail flimsy affairs of sticks and dried leaves usually placed in willows or shrubs (Bent 1940, Hughes 1999).

Throughout the range of the species, Hughes (1999) listed caterpillars, grasshoppers, katydids, and crickets as comprising nearly 80% of the diet. Food in the Sacramento Valley was determined to be mainly caterpillars (Gaines and Laymon 1984). Green (1978) reported one feeding on fall webworms at Little Alvord Cr., Harney Co. on 20 Jun 1976.

**Seasonal Activity and Behavior:** There is little information from Oregon. Extreme dates for observations cited by Gabrielson and Jewett (1940) are 19 May-5 Sep. This is a late arrival to Oregon in spring, with most reports in Jun. They nest late Jun to early Aug in California. Usually 2-3 eggs, incubation 9 days, fledge 7-9 days (Hughes 1999).

**Detection:** This is a secretive bird that tends to perch unnoticed in the shadows, but can be detected by guttural *ka-ka-ka-ka-ka-kow-kow-kowlp-kowlp-kowlp-kowlp* sounds (Hughes 1999). They also give repetitive cooing notes. A cuckoo's presence can be easily missed, a fact which may in part explain the scarcity of records.

**Population Status and Conservation:** The Yellow-billed Cuckoo has undergone a precipitous decline throughout its range (BBS), particularly in the western states (Hughes 1999). J. K. Townsend, in reference to the Columbia R. at Sauvie I. and nearby Ft. Vancouver during the 1830s, described this species as being "abundant in summer" (Jobanek and Marshall 1992). Ornithologists at the end of the 1890s and early 1900s cited by Gabrielson and Jewett (1940) describe the bird as being "rare" in the Willamette Valley; but otherwise Gabrielson and Jewett describe the species as "not a common bird anywhere in Oregon." However, they also said the species "was most abundant in the willow bottoms of the Columbia and Willamette Rivers, and was erratic or more common some seasons than others." They further stated, "We observed at least a dozen birds on Jun 8, 1923, and obtained many other records and specimens during each of the three seasons. Since then our records have been rather sporadic." They cited only three records from e. Oregon, all between 1876 and 1910. The 1876 record was by Bendire (1877), who described a nest along the Snake R. The 1923 birds represent the last indication of this bird's presence in the lower Columbia R./Willamette Valley region in any numbers.

In more recent times, most cuckoo reports have come from e. Oregon. Quaintance (1944) reported a bird in La Grande on 28 Nov 1943 (an unusually late date). It was not until 1970 that cuckoos were again found in Oregon, this time at Malheur NWR (Littlefield and McLaury 1973). This represented the beginning of periodic reports from e. Oregon. The usual pattern is single birds, but during the summer of 1975, four were "observed for a period of time at Pike Creek," Harney Co. (Green 1978); and beginning 8 Aug 1980, two remained through the month in La Grande (Rogers TH 1981c). Between 12 and 28 Aug 1988, Littlefield (1988) conducted a survey using recorded calls in an attempt to locate cuckoos at likely areas in e. Oregon, but found none. He recognized, as have numerous other writers, including Hughes (1999), that cuckoo population numbers reflect tent caterpillar and other large-sized insect outbreaks. There is no other known explanation for the periodic cuckoo presence in e. Oregon.

Elsewhere in the western states, the species has undergone a precipitous decline with extirpation (at least as a breeding species) having taken place in British Columbia, Washington, and possibly Nevada (Hughes 1999). The species nested at least until 1990 in Idaho, but otherwise the situation in that state is similar to Oregon's in that periodic sightings occur, mainly along the Snake R. (Taylor 2000). An extensive survey of California populations showed 61-67 pairs and 61-68 unmated individuals in 2000 (Halterman et al. 2001). As is true elsewhere in the west, this situation is attributed to loss of riparian forests, especially considering the large territory size required for a nesting pair. The rareness of the species in other western states adds to the mystery of where Oregon birds could be coming from.

The potential adverse impact of DDT on western populations needs investigation. Eggshell fragments from three California nests averaged 19% thinning over pre-DDT shells (Laymon and Halterman 1987). Wintering grounds could be the source of the DDT.

The population decline of the species has led to petitions to the USFWS to list the western population of the species under the Endangered Species Act, but this was initially denied based on the conclusion that the western subspecies was not a valid entity. The fact that western birds differ from eastern populations behaviorally and ecologically and constitute a significant part of the bird's range was eventually accepted by USFWS. On 25 Jul 2001, USFWS announced that listing the western population as a distinct population segment was warranted but precluded (Fed. Reg. 66 (143: 38611). This action places it in the low-priority candidate category for listing (D. Harvey p.c.).

Actions to restore the Yellow-billed Cuckoo as a breeding species in Oregon have been discussed but there are no current plans to attempt this (*DBM*). Laymon and Halterman (1987) specifically mentioned the Willamette Valley as a possibility. Whether sufficient habitat is available or could be restored to provide a stable population requires further study. Other considerations include minimum population size required, the effect of Himalayan blackberry understories that now exist in many areas, the effect of flood control on understory shrub communities, and presence of adequate caterpillar populations in the face of insect-control operations.—*David B. Marshall*

# Order STRIGIFORMES
## *Family Tytonidae*

### Barn Owl *Tyto alba*
One of the most startling sounds in the black of night is the loud, harsh call of the Barn Owl as it flies over field or marsh in search of small rodents. By day this bird is well known to rural residents who have a barn or shed, so familiar that this bird is known by many names: heart-faced owl, monkey-faced owl, and ghost owl. Because of its spotting, it is sometimes even mistakenly identified as the Spotted Owl and its white color sometimes results in it being confused with the Snowy Owl. Barn Owls are not closely related to other owls and are placed in their own family, Tytonidae.

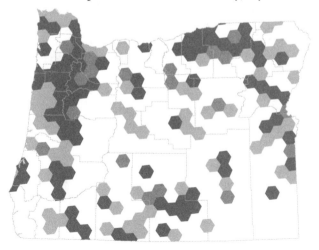

They are white to tan beneath with fine spotting ranging from almost none to fairly extensive. The face has a well-defined facial disc that acts as a parabolic dish collecting the faint sounds of its prey, allowing it to hunt successfully in total darkness. The back is mottled tan and gray with light spotting. Male and female Barn Owls are similar in appearance though the female is somewhat larger (1.25 lb vs. 1.05 lb [570 g vs. 470 g]) (Marti 1992).

**General Distribution:** Cosmopolitan. It occurs on every continent except Antarctica. In N. America it breeds south of a line extending from British Columbia east to New England. Resident over much of its breeding range, though some retreat from northern areas in winter. Thirty-five subspecies have been described. The N. American subspecies is *T. a. pratincola* (Bunn et al. 1982; Browning 2002).

**Oregon Distribution:** A fairly common permanent resident in open country west of the Cascades. East of the Cascades it is more local in its distribution, being most common in agricultural areas. It is absent from much of the open country, most notably in the southeast corner of the state. It is an occasional resident of Malheur NWR, but experiences high winter mortality in some years (Littlefield 1990a). Less common over much of its range in winter.

**Habitat and Diet:** Does not construct a nest, but uses recesses in cliffs, hollow trees, barns, bridges, and even Wood Duck nesting boxes. Suitable roosting and nesting sites appear to be one of the more crucial habitat features for this species. While they often roost in trees, they prefer the greater protection afforded by barns and cliffs. Barn Owls forage in a variety of open habitat including farmland, marshland, and even open fields in developed areas. They frequently can be heard flying over residential areas in Willamette Valley towns (D. Irons p.c., *MGH*).

While many owls wait patiently on a perch for prey to reveal itself, Barn Owls are largely aerial foragers coursing over field and meadow. Long, narrow wings facilitate this effort. In the Klamath Basin, Rudolph (1978) found that they tended to avoid areas with perches. Areas without perches are less likely to harbor the perch-hunting Great Horned Owl, which regularly preys upon Barn Owls.

Unlike Great Horned Owls, which feed upon a wide variety of prey, Barn Owls have a relatively narrow diet consisting largely of mammals 0.5-3 oz (15-80 g). Wherever they occur and at all seasons, field mice (voles) comprise 55-91% of the prey items (Maser and Brodie 1966, Maser and Hammer 1972, Maser et al. 1980, Taylor 1984b, Bull and Akenson 1985). Deer mice regularly make up another 6-32% of the diet, and the balance of the diet usually includes shrews, moles,

kangaroo rats, other mice, pocket gophers, cottontails, and small birds. In some locations they eat more birds; pellets found near the Eugene airport, Lane Co., have included bones of European Starling, Red-winged Blackbird and Wilson's Snipe (S. Heinl p.c.)

Adult pocket gophers and cottontails exceed the normal range of prey size for this owl, and owls preferentially capture young (Janes and Barss 1985) explaining, at least in part, the abundance of gophers in the spring diet (Bull and Akenson 1985). Whether they assess prey size before attempting capture or whether larger gophers are better able to avoid capture is unknown. Lizards, insects, scorpions, and even crayfish appear in the diet, but rarely (Marti 1992). They consume an average of 4 oz (110 g) of food/day in summer (Marti 1974) and 5 oz/day (150 g/day) in winter (Evans and Emlen 1947). They regurgitate 1-2 pellets/day (Marti 1973).

**Seasonal Activity and Behavior:** While Barn Owls breed most frequently in the spring, they are known to breed at any time of the year when field mice (voles) are abundant. In California two peaks of breeding occur, one in May and the second in Oct (Verner and Boss 1980). A single breeding effort appears to be normal for many Oregon birds with young of bandable age most often found in late Apr. Jim Harper (p.c.) has only observed one winter breeding attempt among Barn Owls of the Rogue Valley. However, Scott Findholt (p.c.) has some evidence that Barn Owls in the Grand Ronde Valley may rear two or even three broods a year. Mean clutch size for N. American birds from 4.9 in Texas (Otteni et al. 1972) to 7.0 in Utah (Marti 1992). Barn Owls in the Rogue Valley lay as many as 10 eggs in a clutch (Jim Harper p.c.). The female alone incubates the eggs for 31 days and young fledge about 64 days after hatching (Smith et al. 1974). Unlike many birds, females do not wait until the clutch is complete before initiating incubation. Consequently the young hatch at different times. During years of plentiful prey, all may survive. If prey is scarce, younger individuals may starve. The mean number of young banded per nest in the Grand Ronde Valley 1998-2000 was 4.91-5.77 (range=1-9, n=65 nests) (S. Findholt p.c.). Most Barn Owls are resident, and evidence for migration in any population is weak. However, juveniles often disperse great distances. One bird banded in New Jersey was recovered 1,180 mi (1,900 km) away (Soucy 1980).

**Detection:** Because it is nocturnal, this species can be difficult to observe even when common. Often a harsh cry given while foraging is the only evidence that they frequent an area. Check structures where a pair may roost; roosting birds may be observed by day in shadowed recesses at known roost sites such as the one on the Oregon State University campus, or Fort Rock or other cliffs in agricultural areas. Inspecting dense vegetation in otherwise open areas may uncover roosting birds, especially in e. Oregon in winter, where it sometimes forages in daylight during deep snow conditions (M. Denny p.c.). Nighttime drives in agricultural areas such as Sauvie I. or the Tillamook area may also offer opportunities to observe this bird.

**Population Status and Conservation:** The classic red barn is a fading institution. Modern structures in agricultural areas often do not provide opportunities for roosting and nesting. Some observers suspect that populations have declined in recent years for this reason. Wood Duck nest boxes are used by some, and in recent years some people have constructed and erected nest boxes designed specifically for use by this bird, with reasonable success.—*Stewart W. Janes*

## Family Strigidae

### Flammulated Owl *Otus flammeolus*

This diminutive owl is one of the smallest in N. America, with a body mass of about 1.9 oz (55 g). Once thought to be rare over its range, but investigations in the last three decades have revealed higher densities than previously assumed and have documented many aspects of its life history. This owl has dark eyes, brown plumage with darker and reddish variegations, and small ear tufts. The Flammulated Owl is unique among owls in the Pacific Northwest in that it preys almost exclusively on insects and is a neotropical migrant. Additionally, the pitch of its rather ventriloquial hoot is among the lowest of all N. American owls.

**General Distribution:** Breeds in open forest in all of the eleven contiguous western states, s. British Columbia, and high elevation areas in n. Mexico (McCallum 1994b, AOU 1998). The winter range of this species includes c. and s. Mexico, Guatemala, and perhaps El Salvador (McCallum 1994b). Specific

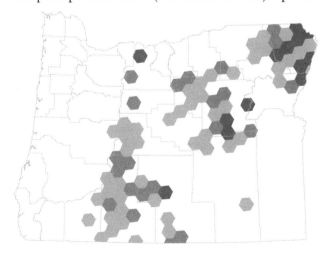

migration routes are not known. Opinions vary as to the systematics of this species. McCallum (1994b) considers this species monotypic because the purported differences do not merit subspecific status, but several subspecies are recognized (Browning 2002). The subspecies *idahoensis*, recognized by Marshall (1978) and Browning (1990) occurs in Oregon (Browning 2002).

**Oregon Distribution:** Breeds on the eastern slope of the Cascades, in the Blue and Wallowa mountains, and in small numbers in the mountains of sw. Oregon. West of the Cascade crest, it has been reported in extreme se. and s. Douglas Co. (Fix 1987b), throughout Jackson Co. (G. Rible p.c., S. Small p.c.), and west to nc. Josephine Co. (S. Small p.c.). It likely migrates throughout its range; also known from Great Basin sites including Hart Mtn. (Mewaldt 1980) and Malheur NWR (Littlefield 1990a). The capture of 16 owls between 29 May and 25 Jun 1977 at Hart Mtn. indicates the species may be a regular and uncommon migrant in the Great Basin (Mewaldt 1980). Records in Jun led Mewaldt (1980) to speculate that this owl spent the summer, and perhaps nested, in the "Blue Sky" pine stand on Hart Mtn. (he was unable to find a nest and was absent from the site after Jun).

**Habitat and Diet:** Found in drier forests with limited understory at mid-elevations; four nests in ne. Oregon were between 3,880 and 4,600 ft elevation (1,183-1,402 m) (Bull and Anderson 1978). Elevational limits vary throughout its range as a function of habitat distribution, prey availability, and thermoregulatory limitations (McCallum 1994c). Tend to nest on upper portions of gently sloping south- and east-facing slopes or on ridges (Bull et al. 1990). During migration, similar habitats are probably used (Balda et al. 1975), but the species also has been found in aspen groves and in patches of ornamental tree plantings within the Great Basin (Littlefield 1990a).

Most closely associated with ponderosa pine forest, but also nests in mixed coniferous stands dominated by ponderosa pine, but including Douglas-fir, grand fir and/or western larch, and in sw. Oregon including Shasta red fir, mountain hemlock, and lodgepole pine. Forest stands used for nesting tend to have moderate to high levels of canopy closure (mean=67%, range=31-94%, n=4 [Bull and Anderson 1978]; 55%, n=33 [Bull et al. 1990]) with rather open understory or an open area adjacent. These areas also contain very dense patches of saplings or shrubs which are used as roost sites (Goggans 1985).

The Flammulated Owl is a cavity nester. In ne. Oregon 62% of 37 nest cavities were excavated by Pileated Woodpeckers, and 32% by Northern Flickers (Bull and Anderson 1978, Bull et al. 1990,). Most nest cavities are in snags, but some (9% [Bull et al.

1990]) are found in live trees. Ponderosa pine was most commonly used (70%) in ne. Oregon, followed by western larch (27% [Bull et al. 1990]). Snags and trees used for nesting averaged 22 and 28 in (56 and 72 cm) dbh in two Oregon studies (Goggans 1985, Bull et al. 1990).

In ne. Oregon, diet was dominated by crickets (Goggans 1985). Moths and beetles were important in other parts of the species' range (McCallum 1994b), and may be important in other areas of Oregon. Scarcity of substantiated records of mammalian prey (Cannings 1994) indicates that they rarely use this prey source.

**Seasonal Activity and Behavior:** Arrives in Oregon primarily during May (Gilligan et al. 1994). Records from Malheur NWR span 30 Apr-7 Jun (Littlefield 1990a); 26 of 36 (72%) spring records at Hart Mtn. were from the period 21 May to 10 Jun (Mewaldt 1980). The earliest record from the Pacific Northwest is 10 Apr 1990 in e. Washington (Buchanan in prep.); records prior to late Apr at this latitude are considered rare (McCallum 1994b). Males begin calling soon after their arrival on the breeding grounds. Unpaired males may vocalize for much of the breeding season (Reynolds and Linkhart 1987). Nest occupancy in Oregon occurs early in Jun (12 Jun [Goggans 1985]). The average clutch size is generally 2-4, and in Oregon was 2.7 (n=6 nests) (Goggans 1985). Incubation was documented 8 Jun-3 Jul in ne. Oregon (Bull and Anderson 1978). Nestlings were present in ne. Oregon 30 Jun-2 Aug, and fledging occurred at 13 nests 19 Jul-16 Aug (Bull and Anderson 1978, Goggans 1985). A fledgling was found near Ashland in early Aug 1985 (Heinl 1986a). The fledging rate at nine Oregon nests averaged 2.66 young/nest (Goggans 1985). Autumn migration probably begins in Aug, and appears to peak in Sep or Oct (Balda et al. 1975, Gilligan et al. 1994). Small numbers may linger through mid-Nov, but records beyond late Oct are rare. The late record from Oregon is 13 Nov 1991 in Harney Co. (Gilligan et al. 1994); one was found dead just across the border in Walla Walla, Washington, on 17 Nov 1979 (Buchanan in prep.), and one was found freshly dead in British Columbia on 15 Nov 1988 (Cannings 1994).

In ne. Oregon, densities are reported at 46 pairs/100 ac (40.5 ha) (Goggans (1985), 0.10 and 0.16/100 ac based on nests, and 0.18 to 0.47/100 ac based on calling sites (Bull et al. 1990). Average home range size at the onset of incubation in ne. Oregon was 39 ac (15.9 ha); this decreased to 19.5 ac (7.9 ha) during the nestling stage and 8.9 ac (3.6 ha) during fledging (Goggans 1985).

**Detection:** Most readily located by its primary call, which occurs at a surprisingly low pitch, and is well known for its ventriloquial qualities (McCallum

1994b). Calling rates in May are apparently higher during the first two hours after sunset (Bull et al. 1990). In Colorado, once eggs have hatched, calling occurs later at night (McCallum 1994b).

**Population Status and Conservation:** Although more common than formerly recognized, there is concern about its population status because of preference for a diminished habitat, older ponderosa pine forest. These forests are being harvested for timber production and in many areas have experienced structural and compositional changes due to the effects of fire suppression (Agee 1993) and salvage logging (D. Fix p.c.), which likely render them less suitable for this owl. Disruption of successional dynamics resulting from fire suppression may reduce recruitment rates of appropriate snags needed for nesting (McCallum 1994a). In addition, use of chemicals or other substances to control forest insect populations may affect the species (McCallum 1994b, 1994a). Very little is known about the population size or status of this species. No systematic study has been made of sw. Oregon populations; their status is poorly known.— *Joseph B. Buchanan*

## Western Screech-Owl *Otus kennicottii*

Almost strictly nocturnal, the Western Screech-Owl hunts discreetly at night and roosts during the day in dense woodlands, its perfectly streaked plumage allowing it to pass as tree bark. These habits make it difficult to see, and it is more common than many are aware. A small owl with yellow eyes and feathered ear tufts, it is superficially almost identical to the Eastern Screech-Owl, with which it was long considered conspecific. It exhibits geographic variation in plumage color and pattern: both gray morphs and brown morphs occur in the Pacific Northwest. Sexes are alike. As is true of many owl species, much of the biology of the Western Screech-Owl remains ambiguous.

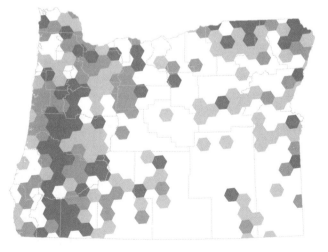

**General Distribution:** Resident from the se. coast of Alaska, coastal and sc. British Columbia, and w. Montana south through Baja California, se. Colorado, sc. Texas, and into the Mexican highlands. Ten subspecies of what is now *O. kennicotti* recognized by AOU (1957); the subspecies, *kennicottii* (with *brewsteri* as a synonym) and *bendirei* (with *macfarlanei* as a synonym) (Marshall 1967, Browning 2001) occur in Oregon.

**Oregon Distribution:** Fairly common year-round resident in lower-elevation woodlands throughout the state (Gilligan et al. 1994). Usually found below 3,000 ft (915 m) in w. Oregon, but has occurred at least to 4,100 ft (1,250 m) in the w. Cascades (Fix 1990a), and Farner (1952) lists one record for Crater L. NP at the southern entrance to the park, elevation 4,400 ft (1,341 m). In w. Oregon, common in lowlands; fairly common in Siskiyou Mtns., along the coast, in the Coast Range, and in low to mid-elevations of w. Cascades (Gullion 1951, Browning 1975a, OBBA, Gilligan et al. 1994). East of the Cascades, it is uncommon at low to moderate elevations (Evanich 1992a, Contreras and Kindschy 1996, OBBA).

*O. k. kennicottii* breeds west of the Cascade summit; e.g., specimens from Clatsop, Tillamook, and Multnomah counties (Marshall 1967), and winter specimens from Rogue Valley (SOU). *O. k. bendirei* breeds in sw. Oregon, with specimens from Grants Pass (CM), Ashland (SOU), Prospect (SOU), and east of

*Western Screech-Owl*

ELVA H PAULSON

the Cascades, with specimens from Steens Mtn. (Jewett 1941). Cannings and Angell's (2001) recognition of *macfarlanei* as distinct from *O. k. kennicottii* and intergradation between them requires qualification (*MRB*).

**Habitat and Diet:** Prefers forest edges and riparian woodland habitats—especially those with older deciduous trees—adjacent to open pastures or fields (Contreras 1997a). Common in woodlots, orchards, and farms (Gillson 1999). Nests in suburbs and city parks if large trees are present (Gilligan et al. 1994). On the coast, many are found where rolling pastures edged with riparian thickets of alder, blackberry, and weeds are interspersed with low forested hills supporting older second-growth Sitka spruce, western hemlock, Douglas-fir, red alder, and bigleaf maple, with an understory of salmonberry, salal, and similar shrubs (Fix 1987c). In sw. Oregon they are most common in chaparral-oak in the valley foothills, where grassy hills surround island groves of Oregon white oak and California black oak mixed with wedgeleaf ceanothus and white manzanita (Browning 1975a). They are sometimes also found in mixed coniferous-deciduous forest (Browning 1975a).

In e. Oregon, these owls can be found in riparian areas with sufficiently large trees, deciduous or mixed woodlands, canyons or rimrock areas, or near human structures (Contreras and Kindschy 1996). They generally avoid wide-open country and purely coniferous forests (Contreras and Kindschy 1996, Contreras 1997a), but are sometimes found in small habitat patches in e. Oregon. Stands of large juniper are known to support populations (Gilligan et al. 1994).

Birds in Idaho chose diurnal roost sites based on density of cover, preferring conifers in spring before leafout, but after leafout 45% of roosts were in deciduous trees (Hayward and Garton 1984). In Oregon, sometimes found roosting in old woodpecker cavities, abandoned farmhouses, or in nest boxes intended for Wood Ducks or Northern Flickers (Contreras and Kindschy 1996, *DBM*). Known to use cliffs or buildings when tree roosts are unavailable (Contreras and Kindschy 1996). Nests in tree cavities, typically old woodpecker holes (Gabrielson and Jewett 1940). Readily occupy nest boxes (Gillson 1999), and occasionally nest on cliffs or banks (Marti and Marks 1989). Reported using an old Black-billed Magpie nest in an area where tree cavities were scarce in sw. Idaho (Marks 1983).

Throughout their range, the diet shows enormous seasonal and regional variation (Cannings and Angell 2001). Known prey includes crayfish, Pacific treefrogs, voles, mice, Song Sparrows, tidepool sculpins, spiders, beetles, and centipedes (Gabrielson and Jewett 1940, Earhart and Johnson 1970, Brown et al. 1986,

Cannings and Angell 2001). Annually observed catching big brown bats exiting an attic roost in Albany, Linn Co., and feeding them to juveniles (Gillson 1999, Tice 1999a, Fleischer 2002). This hunting effort appears to coincide with fledging of juveniles, and has occurred at least since 1998 (Fleischer 2002).

**Seasonal Activity and Behavior:** Breeding phenology is poorly understood. There are few nesting data for Oregon. Throughout range, courtship commences in Jan and Feb (Cannings and Angell 2001) and includes distinctive "bouncing ball" song and presentation of food by male to female (McQueen 1972, Cannings and Angell 2001). OBBA data indicate majority of fledglings seen Jun-Jul, but observations ranged from 27 Apr to 31 Aug (n=22). There is no evidence of migration in this species, though there may be some movement downslope into lowlands or residential areas in winter (Evanich 1992a).

**Detection:** Highly nocturnal. Best detected in the breeding season when vocal; best heard at dusk. Responds to imitations, occasionally during the day (*MGH*). Sometimes betrayed by mobbing jays or songbirds (Fix 1990a, Cannings and Angell 2001).

**Population Status and Conservation:** Status in Oregon uncertain. At one time they were thought to be uncommon on the coast, but a phenomenal count of 48 Western Screech-Owls on the 1986 Florence CBC pointed out limitations in understanding of habitat and distribution of this species, and reinforced the significance of concentrated owling efforts (Fix 1987c). An overall upward trend in Pacific Northwest CBC numbers in the past 30 yr almost certainly reflects improvements in observer effort as opposed to increasing populations (Contreras 1997b).

Considered adaptable and known to utilize certain suburban habitats with adequate trees (Contreras 1997b, Cannings and Angell 2001). Nevertheless, it is undoubtedly affected by loss or degradation of riparian habitat (Marti and Marks 1989), though no specific habitat study has been done on this species in Oregon. Some evidence from Oregon and elsewhere points to a risk of chemical contamination in this species, e.g., from organochlorine pesticides (known to cause eggshell thinning) (Henny, Blus, and Kaiser 1984) and anticoagulant rodenticides (Merson et al. 1984). Additionally, the Barred Owl, a predator of this species, has expanded its range into the Pacific Northwest, and anecdotal evidence hints at potentially serious negative impacts to populations in the region due to this new predation pressure (Cannings and Angell 2001).—*Rachel White Scheuering and Gary McAtee*

## Great Horned Owl *Bubo virginianus*

The Great Horned Owl is the most commonly encountered owl in Oregon. It is a large, stocky, powerful owl with large yellow eyes and distinctive feather tufts or "ears" above the eyes. Plumage color varies from dark brown in w. Oregon to pale grayish brown in se. Oregon. The throat is white. The other owls in Oregon that have feather tufts above the eyes (Western Screech, Long-eared, Flammulated, and Short-eared Owls) are all much smaller than the Great Horned Owl. Because of its large size, powerful feet, and aggressive behavior, the Great Horned Owl has a well-deserved reputation as the "tiger" of the air (Bent 1938). In most areas where it occurs it is at or near the top of the avian food chain.

**General Distribution:** Resident in forested regions of Alaska, Canada, Labrador, and Newfoundland, south throughout most of the Americas (except W. Indies and most of Amazonia), to Tierra del Fuego (Bent 1938, AOU 1998). Number of subspecies vary (AOU 1957, Johnsgard 1988, König et al. 1999); three occur in Oregon (Browning 2002).

**Oregon Distribution:** A fairly common permanent resident throughout the state, but generally absent in areas above timberline. *B. v. saturatus* occurs from the Cascades westward, *B. v. subarcticus* occurs in se. Oregon (CM, USNM), and *B. v. lagophonus* occurs in ne. Oregon (USNM, AMNH) (Browning 2002). The name *subarcticus* replaces *wapacuthu* of AOU (1957)(Browning and Banks 1990), and *occidentalis* as used by Gabrielson and Jewett (1940) and *subarcticus* are synonyms (Dickerman 1991).

**Habitat and Diet:** This highly adaptable owl occurs in a broad array of habitats, including virtually all forest types in Oregon, agricultural areas, urban areas, and the high deserts of se. Oregon. Relative abundance in different habitats is poorly understood. Although it has been suggested that Great Horned Owls are less common in areas dominated by extensive areas of old forest (Johnson DH 1993), evidence supporting this hypothesis is weak.

Most nests are in platforms or cavities in trees, or on ledges on cliffs, but will nest in many other locations, including on the ground (Kebbe 1958a). These owls frequently use stick nests built by hawks, eagles, ravens, or crows. They will also use artificial nest platforms constructed for geese or Ospreys.

An aggressive, opportunistic, nocturnal predator. The diet is influenced by whatever kinds of prey are most available, but in most areas the diet is dominated by rabbits, hares, mice, and voles. They capture a large variety of other prey, including squirrels, woodrats, mountain beavers, gophers, muskrats, weasels, skunks, hawks, falcons, other owls, waterfowl, grouse, pheasants, turkeys, quail, shorebirds, woodpeckers, songbirds, insects, snakes, and fish (Bent 1938, Austing et al. 1966, Maser and Brodie 1966, Brodie and Maser 1967, Maser et al. 1970, Rusch et al. 1972, Frounfelker 1977, Rudolph 1978, Knight and Jackman 1984, Duncan and Lane 1988). Occasionally kills domestic animals if the opportunity presents, including house cats, small dogs, chickens, geese, and even swans (Racey 1926, Bent 1938). The Great Horned Owl is the major predator of Spotted Owls in Oregon and Washington (Forsman et al. 1984, *EDF*), and has been reported to kill adult Red-tailed Hawks and Red-shouldered Hawks (Bent 1938).

**Seasonal Activity and Behavior:** Permanent resident. Can be heard calling at almost any time of year, but pairs tend to be most vocal in Jan and Feb, just before females lay eggs, which is typically late Feb or Mar (Bent 1938). Observed on nest as early as 31 Jan (OBBA), presumed incubating predominantly in Mar-Apr (n=41); young observed in nest 15 Mar-27 Jul, predominantly Apr-May (n=46); fledglings observed 7 Apr-12 Aug, predominantly May-Jun (n=46) (OBBA). Juveniles disperse in Sep, and most do not acquire territories until they are 2-3 yr old (Rhoner 1997). Adults are also quite vocal in Oct and Nov, after the young disperse. Although Great Horned Owls occasionally disperse long distances, the majority of banded juveniles are recovered within 15 mi (25 km) of their natal sites (Adamcik and Keith 1978). Of 30 radio-marked juveniles studied by Rhoner (1997), 16 settled within 31 mi (50 km) of their natal sites.

Flight is characterized by rapid, powerful wing-beats, alternating with periods of gliding. Normally reclusive, but can be very aggressive around nests if the young are threatened. The most commonly heard calls consist of a series of deep, mellow hoots. When hooting, Great Horned Owls assume a unique wren-like posture in which the body is tipped forward, the tail is raised vertically over the back, and the white throat patch is prominently displayed. The begging call of juveniles is a loud raspy screech that can be heard at any time of day (D. Fix p.c.).

**Detection:** Often heard calling at night. Responds to imitations of its calls by hooting, and will often approach the suspected intruder. Not normally active during the day, but can sometimes be found by searching trees near suspected nest sites, or by inspecting stick nests or cliff ledges with binoculars. Almost always present at Malheur NWR HQ and at Benson Pond on the refuge; also at other isolated groves of large trees in e. Oregon. Pellets, whitewash, molted feathers, and prey remains under roosts are also good clues. A good method for locating incubating females in deciduous forests is to check old hawk nests with binoculars during early spring, before leaves obscure the nests. Nests in coniferous forests are difficult to locate.

**Population Status and Conservation:** Common and widespread. No quantitative information on population trends.—*Eric D. Forsman*

## Snowy Owl *Nyctea scandiaca*

The Snowy Owl is the largest N. American owl. Its white plumage makes it is uniquely adapted for life in the arctic and sub-arctic. Adult males are nearly pure white, females have black spots and some barring. Young birds can be strongly barred. Every few years, for reasons which are still not fully understood, Snowy Owls move south of their normal winter range into Oregon. During these irruptive events, they can be found on coastal dunes, open high desert, agricultural areas, airport margins, and occasionally atop buildings in populated areas.

*Great Horned Owl*

ELVA PAULSON ©1993

**General Distribution:** Holarctic, breeding in open arctic tundra. Most move south in winter. In N. America, these movements are usually to the open Great Plains of c. Canada and the n. U.S. Irruptive events have pushed some as far south as c. California and Texas (Weir and Lein 1989). Monotypic (AOU 1957).

**Oregon Distribution:** Irregular in small numbers to Oregon; generally associated with large-scale irruptive events. The first well-recorded irruption was in 1897 (Gabrielson and Jewett 1940). A larger irruption occurred in the winter of 1916-17, during which many specimens were taken. CBC data document irruptions in 1947, 1955, 1966, 1973, 1984, and 1996 (Shipman 1998). Of these, the irruption of 1973 was the largest recent movement in Oregon and included multiple birds in the Willamette Valley to Eugene and along the coast to Yaquina Bay. Eleven were counted on the Tillamook Bay CBC. In the irruption of 1996-97, as many as eight were in the dunes near the s. jetty of the Columbia R. In 1984 one bird reached the Rogue Valley by late Nov (N. Barrett p.c.). They occur occasionally in non-irruption years, most often on coastal dunes of the n. coast or in high deserts and agricultural areas of c. and ne. Oregon.

**Habitat and Diet:** In winter, they occur in open prairies, fields, or shorelines, spending most of the day sitting on low perches with unrestricted views. Winter diet probably reflects availability of prey items (Weir and Lein 1989). Well-studied individuals during the 1996-97 irruption were seen chasing Black-bellied Plover and Sanderlings near Sequim, Washington. Owl pellets found near perches contained rodent bones (Victor 1997). A bird at Sauvie I. in 1973-74 fed mainly on Mew Gulls (H. Nehls p.c.), while those at Iona I., British Columbia, during a peak invasion year were found to be catching many Horned Grebes (Campbell et al. 1990b).

**Seasonal Activity and Behavior:** In Oregon, Snowy Owls begin to appear from late Nov to Dec. Numbers peak in mid-Jan. They were well tracked in Oregon and Washington during the irruption of 1996-97. Numbers at several sites fluctuated markedly from week to week suggesting that some owls were not attached to a particular territory (Victor 1997). Snowy Owls seen in Oregon during the irruption of 1996-97 remained into mid-Mar (*MP*).

**Detection:** Highly visible when present in areas without snow; can be difficult to locate in snowy landscapes. In peak irruptive years, several individuals may be seen in a relatively small area.

**Population Status and Conservation:** Occurrence in Oregon is irregular and irruptive, the reasons for which are controversial. Shelford (1945) made a case, which has persisted in the literature, that ties periodic irruptions with crashes in lemming populations in the Arctic. However, Snowy Owls that appear in the n. Great Plains were found in generally good condition. Accidents, mainly collisions with human-made objects, were the main mortality cause there (Kerlinger and Lein 1988). Food habits information summarized in Parmelee (1992) also show that Snowy Owls utilize a wide source of food, including seabirds, in addition to lemmings.

CBC data analysis does not support the common idea of cyclical irruptions (Kerlinger et al. 1985). Numbers fluctuate significantly from winter to winter and from region to region. Found to be regular winter migrants in the Great Plains, and time series analysis does not support the contention that irruptions in the east and west are regular and periodic. Kerlinger suggests that irruptive events are more probably associated with large-scale weather events.

Snowy Owls are not considered to be under any kind of threat in their breeding grounds. In the past, many were shot during irruptive movements into the south, but this practice is now illegal (Weir and Lein 1989).—*Mike Patterson*

### Northern Hawk-Owl *Surnia ulula*

The Northern Hawk-Owl is a resident of n. Canada and Alaska. In winter many move south to s. Canada and a few casually farther south into the n. U.S. One was observed on Sauvie I., Multnomah Co., 4 Nov to 22 Dec 1973 (OBRC); another was photographed near Palmer Junction, Union Co., 15-20 Jan 1983 (Evanich 1983b, Watson 1989). Subspecies unknown.—*Harry B. Nehls*

### Northern Pygmy-Owl *Glaucidium gnoma*

This tiny owl has a reputation as an aggressive predator on everything from mice and voles to birds and mammals over twice its size (Bent 1938, Balgooyen 1969). Coloration is highly variable with brown and gray morphs. In Oregon, color varies from dark brown in coastal mountains to gray in e. Oregon, with an intermediate pale grayish-brown form in the Cascade Mtns. (Gabrielson and Jewett 1940). About the length of a White-crowned Sparrow, it has striking yellow eyes, dark vertical streaks on the breast and abdomen, and dark "eyespots" on the back of the head. Flight is slightly undulating with rapid wing beats. Imitations of its calls will usually provoke energetic mobbing responses in local songbirds. It is primarily diurnal and can often be approached quite closely when it is hunting or responding to an apparent territorial challenge.

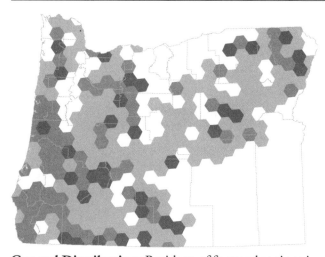

**General Distribution:** Resident of forested regions in w. N. America from se. Alaska, British Columbia, and wc. Alberta to the Southwest, w. Texas, and possibly nw. Mexico. Found from the W. Coast inland to the east slope of the Rocky Mtns. Taxonomy of the Northern Pygmy-Owl is controversial (Heidrich et al. 1995, AOU 1998). The 1998 AOU check-list recognized, as did AOU (1957), the northern birds as *G. gnoma*, with three "groups" within the species; König et al. (1999), without providing evidence, elevated the three groups to species. Of five N. American subspecies listed by AOU (1957) and the subsequently recognized *pinicola* (Marshall *in* Phillips et al. 1964), three apparently occur in Oregon (Gabrielson and Jewett 1940, Pyle 1997). The number of specimens examined by Gabrielson and Jewett (1940) and collected since then is insufficient for a thorough evaluation of the subspecific taxonomy (*MRB*).

**Oregon Distribution:** Based on a statewide survey 1996-97, Sater (1999) concluded that the Northern Pygmy-Owl was fairly common throughout forested areas of Oregon, including the Coast Range, Klamath Mtns., Cascade Mtns., and Blue Mtns. It is rare or absent in the isolated mountains of se. Oregon (Steens Mtn., Pueblo Mtns.) and in the deciduous forests of the Willamette, Umpqua and Rogue valleys (Sater 1999). Considered a resident, but little is known about seasonal movements. During winter, sometimes observed in areas not used for breeding, including suburban backyards, deciduous riparian areas, and western juniper shrubland, but rarely far from forests.

Based on specimens (localities in parenthesis) from numerous museums, *MRB* concluded that during breeding, *grinnelli* occurs in northwest counties (Cedar Mills, Washington Co.); *californicum* breeds in the remainder of the state (Eugene, Lane Co.; Philomath, Benton Co.; Paulina L. and Tumalo Cr., Deschutes Co.; Ft. Klamath, Bly, Spencer, Crater L. NP, Klamath Co.; Arkansas Flat, Lake Co.; Roseburg, Douglas Co.; Prospect, Jackson Co); except for ne.

Oregon where *pinicola* breeds (Enterprise, Wallowa Co.; N. Fork Malheur R., Grant Co.). A male and a female specimen from Toledo, Lincoln Co., 27 Jul 1936, matched *californicum* and *grinnelli* respectively, and demonstrate the difficulty in identifying subspecies from west of the Cascades. Subspecies ranges in the w. Willamette Valley are problematic, with intergrades between *grinnelli* and *californicum* from Scio, Linn Co., in Nov; Spencer Butte near Eugene, 27 Feb.; and Toledo in Jul. There are nonbreeding specimens of *grinnelli* from Tillamook, Lincoln, Douglas, Linn, and Jackson counties; *californicum* from Lane, Harney, Klamath, and Josephine counties; and *pinicola* from Wallowa Co.

**Habitat and Diet:** Occurs in a variety of forests and woodlands. Most common in large tracts of contiguous forest, but also occurs in forests fragmented by timber harvest or other types of disturbance. Detection rates on statewide surveys 1996-97 increased with the diameter of the dominant overstory trees (Sater 1999). Detection rates were highest in tall, mature conifer forests, and lowest in isolated riparian areas, small woodlots, and early seral forest. Relatively uncommon or absent from open western juniper woodland, except in some places in the Blue Mtns. ecoregion, where juniper stands are dense and dominated by relatively large trees. Hunting tactics (see below) may lead to preference for forest with a structurally complex overstory and an open understory. Dense cover is probably important because Northern Pygmy-Owls are preyed upon by other birds such as the Spotted Owl and Northern Saw-whet Owl (Bent 1938, Forsman et al. 1984, Grove 1985).

Nests primarily in cavities excavated by woodpeckers, including Hairy and Acorn Woodpeckers, Northern Flickers and sapsuckers (Bendire 1883, Braly 1930, Bent 1938, Bull et al. 1986, Bull et al. 1987, Reynolds et al. 1988, Marshall 1992a). May also use natural cavities (Johnsgard 1988). Bull et al. (1987) reported two nests in ne. Oregon, one in a flicker cavity and the other in a cavity that had apparently been excavated by a Williamson's Sapsucker. Nests found in e. Oregon were in conifers or quaking aspen, but nests in California have been found in oaks and sycamores as well (Bent 1938). Eight nests located on the Olympic Peninsula in w. Washington were all in cavities excavated by woodpeckers (Giese 1999). Virtually nothing is known about nest characteristics in w. Oregon.

Diet includes small mammals, birds, reptiles, and insects. Diet composition varies by region, year, and season, apparently because of variation in prey availability (Marshall 1957, Earhart and Johnson 1970, Holt and Leroux 1996). Diet of one pair in ne. Oregon contained approximately equal numbers of mammals, birds, and insects (Bull et al. 1987). Prey captured by eight pairs on the Olympic Peninsula, Washington, contained 51% mammals, 35% birds and 14% insects (Giese 1999). Typically a perch-and-wait forager. On the Olympic Peninsula, they were observed dropping from perches onto prey and sometimes sprinted after prey on the ground. Also observed to systematically remove nestlings from nests of small passerines (*ARG*). Caching observed on ground (Holt and Norton 1986) and on tree limbs (*ARG*). Use of cavities for caching has been reported for the closely related Eurasian Pygmy-Owl (Mikkola 1983), but this behavior has not been reported in N. America.

**Seasonal Activity and Behavior:** Generally resident, though apparent movements to lower altitudes during winter have been reported in Montana (D. Holt p.c.), Colorado (Aiken and Warren 1914), and Nevada (Ryser 1985). Bent (1938) believed altitudinal movements of Pygmy-Owls were sporadic and influenced by weather. Oregon populations probably exhibit both altitudinal migration and year-round residency depending on latitude, elevation, and regional climate. One example of this is the birds that appear in Nov in the Mill Cr. drainage in e. Umatilla Co. each year, disappearing, presumably upslope, in Mar (M. Denny p.c.).

Territorial and monogamous (Holt and Norton 1986). In Oregon, territorial calling begins in Mar, and egg laying probably begins in Apr or early May. Clutch size 3-7, usually four. In Oregon, Braly (1930) reported six eggs in a nest on 21 May, and Bendire (1883) reported four nestlings in early Jun. Hatching is nearly synchronous and juveniles leave the nest in Jun or early Jul. On the Olympic Peninsula, Washington, juveniles left the nest from 18 Jun to 17 Jul (*ARG*).

The territorial call is a single whistled *toot* given steadily and repeatedly at 2- to 4-sec intervals, sometimes for over an hour. A soft trill about 3 sec long is also frequently heard, often followed by one or more *toots*. The trill call is sometimes given when the owl is agitated (P.T. Sullivan p.c.), and when it flies from one perch to another (*MGH*). Territorial vocalizations may be heard year-round, but are most common in early spring and again in autumn (Bent 1938).

Primarily diurnal, with peak activity in morning and evening. May be less responsive to acoustic lure surveys during midday (Sater 1999). Radio-marked owls in w. Washington were not observed to move during darkness, indicating that they were generally inactive at night (*ARG*).

**Detection:** Most easily detected by imitating vocalizations and listening for a response. In flight may not be recognized as an owl because of its small size and rapid flight. It often calls from the tops of conifers where it can be easily sighted. The call is sometimes ventriloquial, especially when the owl is directly overhead. Detection rates on acoustic lure

surveys in Oregon during the breeding season in 1996-97 averaged 0.91 owls per survey hour (range 0-4.8) (Sater 1999). Gray Jays often imitate pygmy-owl calls, which can make it difficult to determine what species is calling.

**Population Status and Conservation:** Overall range in Oregon apparently unchanged since description by Gabrielson and Jewett (1940). No information on population trends. Simplification of forest structure and a decrease in large trees and snags may be detrimental, but no information is available on reproductive success or survival rates in different habitats.—*Dawn M. Sater, Alan R. Giese and Eric D. Forsman*

## Burrowing Owl *Athene cunicularia*

This small owl is unusual in that it nests in earthen burrows in open shrub-steppe regions and grasslands. This habit is even more curious in Oregon since most burrows used for nesting were previously excavated by badgers, a major predator of Burrowing Owl eggs and young (Green 1983, Green and Anthony 1989). These long-legged, short-tailed owls are generally brownish buff with spots across the back and barring across the front. Males are usually lighter-colored than females, possibly because they spend more time exposed to the elements. Males also average 5% larger than females, a situation rare among owls (Earhart and Johnson 1970).

**General Distribution:** These owls range from s. Canada south through w. U.S. and all of Mexico, C. America, and S. America, exclusive of the Amazon Basin, with isolated populations in Florida and the Bahamas/Caribbean (Johnsgard 1988). There are five subspecies; the w. N. American subspecies (*A. c. hypugaea*) inhabits the open grasslands and shrub-steppe of the intermountain West and Great Plains. Generally migratory in the n. Great Basin and Great Plains and resident in the se. U.S. (Johnsgard 1988).

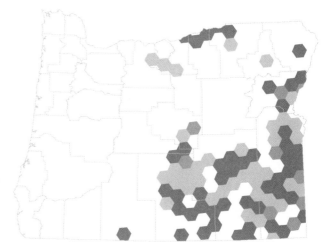

*Burrowing Owl*

ELVA PAULSON
© 1991

**Oregon Distribution:** A spring and summer visitant in open grassland and shrub-steppe habitats in all ecoregions of e. Oregon (except higher mountains). Probably most common in the Columbia Basin and in se. Oregon. Formerly bred in the Rogue and Umpqua valleys (Gabrielson and Jewett 1940, Hunter et al. 1998). Rare annual visitor to the Willamette Valley and s. coast, especially during winter (Jewett 1944b, *Oregon Birds* field notes). Failed introduction attempts were made at William L. Finley NWR near Corvallis (*GAG*) and the Denman W.A. near Medford (T. Farrell p.c.) in the 1980s.

**Habitat and Diet:** Open grasslands and shrub-steppe including rangelands, pastures, golf courses, and airports. In e. Oregon, Burrowing Owls are largely dependent on badgers for providing nesting burrows, although Oregon owls will also occasionally use yellow-bellied marmot, coyote, and Columbia ground squirrel burrows (Dobyns 1928, M. Denny p.c., *GAG*), as

well as artificial structures and burrows (Henny and Blus 1981, *GAG*). Rogue Valley populations were probably dependent on California ground squirrels. Green and Anthony (1989) found that Burrowing Owls in nc. Oregon selected for nesting inactive badger burrows surrounded by low vegetation stature (<6 in [15 cm]) and a high proportion (40-70%) of bare ground. Where average vegetation height was >2 in (5 cm) (but <6 in [15 cm]), owls selected nest sites with nearby elevated perches. Low vegetation structure and elevated perches extended the owls' horizontal vision, probably important in early detection of predators (Green and Anthony 1997). In the Columbia Basin, abundant bare ground or, conversely, sparse vegetative cover, provides habitat for large invertebrate prey (Rickard and Haverfield 1965, Rogers and Fitzner 1980, Gano and Rickard 1982) and small mammals (Rogers and Hedlund 1980, Gano and Rickard 1982), and improves detectability of prey by owls. Rich (1986) found Idaho Burrowing Owls to also select habitats with substantial bare ground. Green and Anthony (1989) found Columbia Basin Burrowing Owls to prefer habitats with annual short grass, or sparse shrubs (sagebrush and bitterbrush) with suitable perches over taller bunchgrass and rabbitbrush habitats which did not provide adequate elevated perches.

In w. Oregon, wintering individuals are typically located in roadside ditches or other locations where culverts are present. The culverts are presumably used for roosting. Little is known about the habitat use or foraging habits of these rare wintering birds. Pellets of a bird wintering under a low bridge about 8 mi (13 km) north of Eugene contained remains of a Barn Swallow and deer mouse (Gullion 1948b).

During spring and summer, they feed predominantly on small mammals and large ground-dwelling arthropods. While small mammals contribute only about 10-15% of the diet in Oregon in terms of individuals captured, they generally contribute over 90% of the biomass due to their large size (Maser, Hammer, and Anderson 1971, Brown et al. 1986, Green et al. 1993). Sagebrush voles, Great Basin pocket mice, and deer mice were the dominant vertebrate prey for Burrowing Owls in c. Oregon (Maser, Hammer, and Anderson 1971), while in se. Oregon, Ord's kangaroo rats, northern pocket gophers, and sagebrush voles were numerically most important (Brown et al. 1986). Similarly, pocket mice, deer mice, and pocket gophers were the dominant small mammal prey in nc. Oregon (Green et al. 1993). In all three studies, the northern pocket gopher, due to its larger body size, contributed greatly to the biomass.

Major arthropod prey includes grasshoppers, crickets, darkling beetles, carrion beetles, scarab beetles, and scorpions (Maser, Hammer, and Anderson 1971, Brown et al. 1986, Green et al. 1993). In particular, Jerusalem crickets, grasshoppers (Acrididae), and burying beetles were common in the diets from all three studies. In addition, scarab beetles were a major contributor to both c. Oregon (Maser, Hammer, and Anderson 1971) and se. Oregon (Brown et al. 1986) diets. The coulee cricket and darkling beetle were important in nc. Oregon (Green et al. 1993).

**Seasonal Activity and Behavior:** Paired adults return as early as Mar to the same burrow they previously inhabited if it is still available (Martin 1973). Nesting territories are vigorously defended from other Burrowing Owls (Thomsen 1971). Egg laying occurs from early Apr to late May (Gabrielson and Jewett 1940), although (reclutching?) incubation has been observed as late as Jul (*GAG*). Incubation period 27-30 days (Henny and Blus 1981) with incubation commencing with the first egg laid (Thomsen 1971), although Henny and Blus (1981) believed incubation to not occur until late in the egg laying stage. Green (unpubl. data), however, observed numerous broods of both similar and widely varied ages supporting both contentions. The number of eggs laid ranges from 6-12 (Henny and Blus 1981, Johnsgard 1988), which may offset a high (up to 70%) first-year mortality rate (Thomsen 1971). Female highly secretive during the incubation and brooding period (Thomsen 1971, Green 1983, Johnsgard 1988), probably to draw less attention to nest occupants. Males rarely enter the nest burrow (Martin 1973, Green 1983).

Adults commonly line their burrows with shredded cow or horse dung, which may serve to camouflage the owls' scent from predators (Martin 1973). Green and Anthony (1989) found nest losses to mammalian predators to be significantly higher in unlined than in lined nests. Green and Anthony (1989) also found higher incidences of nest desertion when adjacent pairs nested closer than 360 ft (110 m), suggesting intraspecific competition pressures.

Nestlings first become visible at the burrow entrance at about 3 wk of age (late May-Jun), and become independent of adults and the nest burrow at about 7-8 wk of age (Green 1983). In the Columbia Basin, adults and juveniles begin leaving the nesting territory between Jul and Sep, and are generally gone from the region before Oct (Green 1983).

Burrowing Owls are observed as early as late Oct in w. Oregon, but more typically appear in Nov or Dec, and are often seen into late Feb or Mar.

**Detection:** Likelihood of detecting nesting pairs early in the nesting season is high due to visible adults, low grass stature, and exaggerated green growth around previously used burrows due to nitrogen loading (scats, prey remains, etc.). During egg laying and brooding, both male and female become more secretive (Thomsen 1971, Green 1983, Johnsgard 1988). They become highly visible again when nestlings begin to fledge.

**Population Status and Conservation:** In general, there has been no detectable trend in Columbia Basin Burrowing Owl populations since 1968 (Saab and Rich 1997), although these populations are at serious risk from habitat loss due to continued agricultural development pressures. However, in recent years, populations in n. Umatilla Co. have declined by at least 10 active nest sites, probably owing to habitat loss, reductions in burrowing mammals, and shooting (M. Denny p.c.). Populations in se. Oregon appear stable (G. Keister p.c.), while populations in c. Oregon, especially near Bend, appear to have experienced significant declines due to incidental shooting and habitat loss from housing and small ranchette developments (C. Carey p.c.). Nesting opportunities in c. Oregon may also have been lost via destruction of badgers. Incidental take of badgers during a coyote-trapping program may have dramatically reduced burrow availability at one location in the Columbia Basin (*GAG*). Livestock grazing appears to benefit these owls by reducing vegetation cover and increasing prey availability, although livestock trampling of nest burrows can occur where soils are friable (*GAG*).

Management for Burrowing Owl populations often has involved providing artificial nesting structures in suitable habitat (Collins and Landry 1977, Olenick 1987, 1990, Trulio 1995). Artificial burrows have been used to gain insight on below-ground nesting ecology (Collins and Landry 1977, Henny and Blus 1981, Olenick 1987, 1990), supplement existing owl populations (Collins and Landry 1977), and passively relocate owls from areas scheduled for disturbance (Trulio 1995). Trulio (1997) has argued that passive relocation, providing artificial nesting burrows near existing nests and allowing owls to relocate on their own, achieves higher successes than active relocation or reintroduction. In an attempt to stem declining populations in Saskatchewan, Wellicome et al. (1997) provided predator-proof artificial burrows and supplemental feeding with inconclusive results.

Using information based on their previous studies (Green and Anthony 1989, Green et al. 1993), and recognizing four important aspects of nesting ecology (predator avoidance, intraspecific competition, brood protection, and prey selection), Green and Anthony (1997) provided six recommendations for managing Burrowing Owls in the Columbia Basin. These are: (1) Provide elevated perches near potential burrows (natural or artificial) in grassland areas where the average height is 2-6 in (5-15 cm); (2) Provide fresh cattle dung near nesting areas if not already available; (3) Place artificial nest boxes no closer than 360 ft (110 m) to avoid territorial competition; (4) Use artificial boxes that are large (>14 in [36 cm] to a side) or expandable (one earthen wall); (5) Select areas for owl propagation with 40-70% bare ground and average shrub cover of <15%; and (6) Explore use of prescribed burning as a tool for enhancing owl habitat.—*Gregory A. Green*

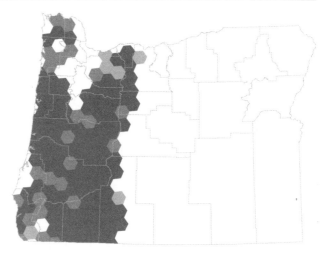

## Spotted Owl *Strix occidentalis*

Because of its association with old forests, this inconspicuous, dark brown owl has become one of the most controversial birds in the Pacific Northwest. The dark eyes and creamy white mottling on the breast and abdomen are distinctive, as is the lack of fear of humans. Both adults and young will typically allow humans to approach within a few feet, and it is not unusual for curious juveniles to follow hikers through the woods. The only other owl with which it might be confused is the Barred Owl, which is slightly larger, much more wary around humans, and which has dark vertical streaks on the lower abdomen rather than brown and white mottling. Because of its central role in the debate over management of old-growth forests, the Spotted Owl has become one of the best known and most intensively studied owls in the world (e.g., see Forsman et al. 1984, 1996, Thomas et al. 1990, Verner et al. 1992, Gutiérrez et al. 1995, USDI 1995, Franklin 1997, Marcot and Thomas 1997, Thrailkill et al. 1997, Franklin et al. 1999, Noon and Franklin 2002).

**General Distribution:** Resident in forested mountains of the w. coast from sw. British Columbia—at least as far north as Carpenter L., 130 mi north of the international border (I. Blackburn p.c.)—to San Francisco; in the Sierra Nevada and coastal mountains of s. California; and in a series of disjunct populations in the mountains of the sw. U.S. and Mexico (Gutiérrez et al. 1995). Recent studies (Haig et al. 2001) support recognition of three subspecies (AOU 1957), but also suggest that mixing has occurred between the Northern Spotted Owl (*S. o. caurina*), which occurs in Oregon, and the California (*S. o. occidentalis*) subspecies.

**Oregon Distribution:** Permanent resident in forested regions of w. Oregon, from the coastal mountains to the eastern foothills of the Cascade Range (Forsman et al. 1987). A few pairs also occur in the Saddle Mtn. area immediately e. of Klamath L. Absent from lowland interior valleys of w. Oregon and from high-elevation subalpine forests, except for occasional stragglers. It occurred to 5,600 ft. (1,867 m) in e. Douglas Co. in the late 1980s (D. Fix p.c.).

**Habitat and Diet:** Occurs in all coniferous forest types that occur at low to mid-elevations in w. Oregon. On the east slope of the Cascades occurs primarily in mixed conifer associations of Douglas-fir, grand fir, ponderosa pine, and incense cedar, but also occurs in the Shasta red fir and Pacific silver fir zones. Most abundant in old-growth and mature forests, where resident pairs are typically spaced about 1-2 mi (1.6-3.2 km) apart (Forsman et al. 1984, Thomas et al. 1990). Less common in younger forests, where it is often associated with residual patches of old trees that survived previous wildfires or logging (Forsman et al. 1977, 1984, Gutiérrez et al. 1995). Radiotelemetry studies have shown a consistent selection of old forests for foraging and roosting (Forsman et al. 1984, Thomas et al. 1990, Carey et al. 1992), but Spotted Owls make extensive use of young forest in areas where old forests are uncommon (Forsman et al. 1984, Diller and Thome 1999, Thome et al. 1999, Irwin et al. 2000).

Nests in cavities or platforms in trees or snags (Forsman et al. 1984, Forsman and Giese 1997, Hershey et al. 1998). Although Spotted Owls in the sw. U.S. often nest on cliff ledges, there are only three confirmed cases of cliff nesting in Oregon (M. Brown p.c., A. Ellingson p.c., J. Mowdy p.c.). Cavity nests are usually in the top of a broken tree or in a large hole in the side of a tree trunk. Platform nests include old stick nests built by other birds or mammals, or accumulations of debris on tree limbs. Use of platform nests is most common on the east slope of the Cascades and in s. Oregon. Most cavity nests are in live trees that have dead tops and rotten boles, but 3-27% of cavity nests are in dead trees (Forsman et al. 1984, Forsman and Giese 1997, Hershey et al. 1998). Nest trees in s. Oregon and on the east slope of the Cascades are often heavily infected with dwarf mistletoe, which causes the limbs to grow in dense, deformed clumps. Average nest height in Oregon was 99 ft (30 m) for cavity nests and 72 ft (22 m) for platform nests (Forsman et al. 1984). Although most nests are high in large trees, some have been found as low as 10 ft (3 m) above ground, and platform nests have been found in trees as small as 11 in (28 cm) in diameter (S. G. Sovern p.c.).

Annual home ranges of radio-marked adults in w. Oregon are typically 3,000-4,500 ac (1,215-1,822 ha) (Forsman et al. 1984, Carey et al. 1992). Home ranges are too large to defend consistently and typically overlap by 3-25% (Forsman et al. 1984).

Diet includes about 90% forest mammals and is dominated by flying squirrels in nw. Oregon and woodrats in sw. Oregon (Forsman et al. 1984). Also takes small birds, insects, and an occasional snake or frog (Verner et al. 1992, Forsman et al. 2001, Hamer et al. 2001). Hunts primarily by sitting quietly and ambushing prey from above.

**Seasonal Activity and Behavior:** Normally resident on the same territory throughout the year, but home range areas are largest during winter when some individuals wander extensively (Forsman et al. 1984). During winter, the male and female on each territory are generally found roosting and foraging separately, and rarely vocalize. Most vocal during spring and early summer (Mar-Jun). Spotted Owls are irregular nesters. On average about 62% of the resident pairs nest each year (range 16-89%) (Forsman et al. 1984). Females lay 1-3 eggs (usually 2) in late Mar or Apr. Incubation is 30 +/-2 days. Juveniles leave the nest at 34-36 days of age in late May or Jun. Males feed the female and young but do not assist with incubation or brooding. Juveniles disperse Sep-Oct and typically do not acquire territories until they are 1-4 yr old. Median straight-line distances from the natal site to the location where juveniles eventually settled were 9 mi (14.6 km) for males and 15 mi (24.5 km) for females (range 1-69 mi [0.6-111 km], n=376 males, 328 females) (Forsman et al. 2002).

**Detection:** Easily located by imitating vocalizations and listening for responses. This method has been used by biologists to locate and band thousands of Spotted Owls in Oregon, California, Washington, and British Columbia in 1980-98. Although primarily nocturnal, Spotted Owls will respond during the day, and can be visually located by homing in on them as they call from day roosts. Good areas to look include almost any old coniferous forest habitats in w. Oregon or on the east slope of the Cascades.

**Population Status and Conservation:** The Northern Spotted Owl was federally listed as "Threatened" in 1991, primarily because of habitat loss from logging. An analysis of banding data collected in 1985-93 suggested that the population was declining and that adult survival rates were declining as well (Burnham et al. 1996). A more recent analysis of a much larger data set that covered the period 1985-98 suggested that, while there was still evidence of a population decline, there was no evidence of a decline in survival rates or reproductive rates (Franklin et al. 1999). Estimates of

population trend are hotly contested, because numerous biases can affect survival estimates from banding studies (Bart 1995, Burnham et al. 1996, Franklin et al. 1999). Regardless of the rate of population change, the known population of resident pairs is still quite large, and extensive areas of suitable habitat remain, especially in the Olympic Peninsula, Cascades, sw. Oregon, and n. California. The Northwest Forest Plan, which was adopted in 1994 (USDA/USDI 1994), included an extensive network of reserves on federal lands that are managed to develop and maintain habitat for the Spotted Owl and other species of plants and animals associated with old forests.

The recent invasion of the Pacific Northwest by the Barred Owl probably represents a serious threat to the Spotted Owl (Hamer et al. 1994, Herter and Hicks 2000, Kelly 2001). There is evidence that Barred Owls have displaced Spotted Owls in some areas, and the two species occasionally hybridize. Hybrids have been observed to back-cross with both Spotted Owls and Barred Owls (Hamer et al. 1994, *EDF*).—*Eric D. Forsman*

### Barred Owl *Strix varia*

The Barred Owl was first reported in Oregon in the early 1970s and it has since spread to forested areas throughout most of the state; in some areas it has become fairly common. Sometimes confused with the closely related Spotted Owl, and some authors consider these two owls a superspecies (AOU 1998). A large, grayish-brown owl, slightly larger than the Spotted Owl, with dark eyes and no ear tufts. It is 17-24 in (43-61 cm) long and has a wingspan of 40-50 in (102-127 cm; Terres 1996). It is easily distinguished from the Spotted Owl by the pronounced horizontal barring across the throat and upper breast, vertical brown streaks on the lower breast and abdomen.

**General Distribution:** Resident se. Alaska, southern half of Canada, e. U.S., nw. Montana, n. Idaho, Washington, Oregon and n. California. Three N.

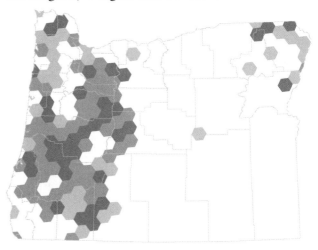

American subspecies north of Mexico (AOU 1957); the subspecies in Oregon is unknown.

**Oregon Distribution:** Rapidly expanding. First detected in 1974; detected at over 706 locations by 1998 (Taylor and Forsman 1976, Kelly 2001). A permanent resident in forests of the Cascades, Coast Range, Blue, Wallowa, Strawberry and Klamath mountains, recently reached w. Curry Co. (T. Rodenkirk p.c.). Rare or absent in non-forested regions of the Willamette, Umpqua and Rogue valleys, and high desert region of se. Oregon. Elevational limits of sightings range 250-7,000 ft (76-2121 m) (Johnson DH 1991).

**Habitat and Diet:** It occurs in a wide variety of conifer and mixed conifer-deciduous forests (Herter and Hicks 2000, Kelly 2001). In British Columbia it is often associated with mixed hardwoods and conifers in riparian zones, but also occurs in upland coniferous forest (Dunbar et al. 1991). Radio-marked Barred Owls in n. Washington generally used old-growth, mature and young forests in proportion to availability, suggesting that they did not prefer any particular forest age class for foraging (Hamer et al. 1989).

In the e. U.S., associated with dense forests, isolated woodlots, or large, contiguous tracts of mature or old-growth forest; primarily nests in tree cavities (Godfrey 1986, Allen 1987, Laidig and Dobkin 1995, Haney 1997). Occasionally uses stick nests built by squirrels, hawks or crows (Johnsgard 1979, Terres 1996). One Union Co. nest was on an abandoned raven platform (M. Denny p.c.). Has been used as an indicator species for forest management and is considered threatened in some states (Haney 1997).

Little diet information from Oregon. Pellets collected at a nest site near Pilot Rock, Umatilla Co. showed a preponderance of chipmunks and microtines (M. Denny p.c.). Elsewhere, diet is diverse, including shrews, voles, mice, chipmunks, squirrels, hares, opossums, weasels, skunks, birds, snails, crayfish, fish, frogs, snakes, salamanders, lizards, insects and spiders (Bent 1938, Hamer et al. 1991, Terres 1996, *EDF*). In n. Washington, three species of mammals (snowshoe hare, northern flying squirrel and Douglas squirrel) comprised 67.5% of the biomass in Barred Owl diets (Hamer et al. 2001)

**Seasonal Activity and Behavior:** No information from Oregon. Primarily nocturnal, but sometimes hunts during the day when skies are overcast, or at dawn and dusk (Terres 1996). Hamer (1988) reported that average annual home range size in n. Washington was 1,591 ac (644 ha) for individual owls and 2,236 ac (905 ha) for pairs. Home ranges were largest during winter. Courtship typically begins with vocalizations near nest sites in late Feb or Mar. In n. Washington,

Hamer (1988) found that eggs appear to be laid by the end of Mar and that juveniles fledged by the first week of Jun. Bent (1938) reported that juveniles left the nest when they were about 42 days old. Clutch size usually 2-3, rarely four, incubation lasts 28-33 days and is primarily carried out by the female (Bent 1938, Johnsgard 1979, Terres 1996). Not much known about dispersal, but a female hybrid between a Barred Owl and Spotted Owl in Washington moved 182 mi (292 km) from her natal site in the Cascades to her territory near the northeast tip of the Olympic Peninsula (Forsman et al. 2002).

Vocalizations include a variety of hoots, cackles, shrieks, and wails. The most commonly heard call is a nine-syllable series of loud hoots, usually described phonetically as 'who-cooks-for-you, who-cooks-for-you-all.' Another common vocalization is a series of six to nine regularly spaced and evenly accentuated ascending hoots that ends with a descending 'hoo-aw.' A single loud, prolonged 'whooooooo-aww' with a tremulous, nasal quality is also common. When excited, pairs often engage in a raucous duet of "cackles hoots caws and gurgles" (Bent 1938, McGarigal and Fraser 1985).

**Detection:** Easily located by imitating vocalizations and listening for a response. Tend to be most vocal just before the egg laying period (Johnsgard 1979). Hamer (1988) reported a decline in responsiveness to imitated calls after Jun. Although Barred Owls are most active between dusk and dawn, they will respond during the day. Unlike the closely related Northern Spotted Owl, Barred Owls are somewhat wary of humans, and tend to be more difficult to approach (*EDF*).

**Population Status and Conservation:** Historic range was limited to the e. U.S. and e. Canada (Bent 1938), but rapidly expanded westward across Canada and into the Pacific Northwest during the 1900s. First reported in British Columbia in 1943 (Grant 1966). There was also an unconfirmed report from nw. Montana in 1927 (Weydemeyer 1927). The range expansion continued during the next 50 yr, with Barred Owls gradually spreading west into se. Alaska and s. into w. Montana, n. Idaho, Washington, Oregon, and n. California (Rogers 1966, Campbell 1973, Shea 1974, Taylor and Forsman 1976, Boxall and Stepney 1982, Sharp 1989, Dunbar et al. 1991, Groves et al. 1997, Dark et al. 1998, Wright and Hayward 1998). As a result of its recent range expansion, the range of the Barred Owl now overlaps most of the range of the Northern Spotted Owl. Currently, the southernmost limit of the range is Sonoma and Yuba counties, California (Dark et al.1998). There is speculation that changes in climate and/or forest cover were factors in the Barred Owl's range expansion across Canada.

(Johnson DH 1993, Wright and Hayward 1998, Dark et al. 1998). Although some have suggested that the range expansion of the Barred Owl was facilitated by timber harvest practices (Hamer 1988, Root and Weckstein 1994, Dark et al. 1998, König et al. 1999), it is equally possible that forest management practices had nothing to do with the range expansion (Johnson DH 1993, Kelly 2001).

The first Oregon record was a pair observed in the Wenaha R. drainage of the Blue Mtns. of ne. Oregon in Jun 1974 (Taylor and Forsman 1976). Two sightings were reported in the Oregon Cascades range near Mt. Hood in Clackamas and Wasco counties in 1979 (Harrington-Tweit et al. 1979). In 1981 an adult was detected in the s. Cascade Range in the Mountain Lakes Wilderness, Winema NF, Klamath Co., and a male was detected on the west side of the c. Cascade Range, Cottage Grove RD, Umpqua NF, Lane Co. (OBRC 1998). Numbers are still increasing in Oregon and elsewhere in the Pacific Northwest, which has led to speculation that the Barred Owl may represent a significant threat to the Spotted Owl (Taylor and Forsman 1976, Dunbar et al. 1991, Hamer et al. 1994, Dark et al. 1998). Barred Owls appear to dominate Spotted Owls in most interactions, and will aggressively chase Spotted Owls away. May sometimes kill Spotted Owls (Leskiw and Gutiérrez 1998).

At least 50 hybrid owls have been observed at 31 different territories in Washington and Oregon, and seven hybrids have been found in California (Kelly 2001, Dark et al. 1998). First generation (F1) hybrids can be identified in the field based on unique plumage characteristics (Hamer et al. 1994), but offspring produced by back-crosses between F1 hybrids and Spotted Owls or Barred Owls may be difficult to differentiate from Barred Owls or Spotted Owls. F1 hybrids have been observed to back-cross with both Barred and Spotted Owls (Hamer et al. 1994, Kelly 2001).—*Elizabeth G. Kelly and Eric D. Forsman*

### Great Gray Owl *Strix nebulosa*

It was once thought that Great Gray Owls bred only north of the Canadian border (Bent 1938). The scattered sightings and specimens collected in Oregon extending as far back as early 1800s were considered winter visitors and vagrants. Gradually, it was realized that this bird, though not common, enjoys a wide distribution in the state breeding in the Blue, Cascade, and Siskiyou mountains. In length it is Oregon's largest owl, though it weighs less than Great Horned and Snowy Owls. It is sooty gray to brownish above and lacks ear tufts. The prominent facial disc, outlined in black, contains a series of fine concentric rings that surround piercing yellow eyes. Despite its large size, both feet and bill are small. Sexes are similar.

**General Distribution:** Occurs in boreal forests throughout the N. Hemisphere. In N. America breed from Alaska to c. Canada and south in the Rocky Mtns. to n. Wyoming and in the Pacific states to the c. Sierra Nevada of California (Yosemite NP). In years of prey scarcity, may visit the northern tier of states east of the Rockies. Two subspecies, *S. n. nebulosa* in N. America (AOU 1957).

**Oregon Distribution:** Uncommon to rare inhabitant of forests adjacent to openings above 3,000 ft (900 m) in the Cascade, Blue, and Wallowa mountains. Most observations in the Cascades are from east of the crest, though they have been discovered breeding west of the crest in the Willamette NF (Goggans and Platt 1992). Recently, a population has been discovered in the Siskiyou Mtns. (Fetz et al. unpubl. ms.). Unlike birds elsewhere in Oregon, most of the Siskiyou Mtn. birds occur at lower elevations (1,400-3,000 ft [440-900 m]).

**Habitat and Diet:** Great Grays inhabit mature to old-growth coniferous forests adjacent to openings in the forest, usually meadows. Sixty of 63 owl observations were within 0.2 mi (0.3 km) of openings 15-250 ac (6-100 ha) in size in the s. Cascades (Bryan and Forsman 1987). Roost and nest within the forest and forage in the adjacent openings that support abundant small rodents (Bull, Henjum, and Rohweder 1988b). Preferred foraging habitat for males includes open canopy forests (11-59% canopy cover) with an abundant herbaceous layer (Bull, Henjum, and Rohweder 1988b). Mean perch height of foraging birds was 18 ft (5.5 m) (Bull, Henjum, and Rohweder 1988b). In the Blue Mtns. they are most often found breeding in mixed Douglas-fir/grand fir and western larch/lodgepole pine forests (Bull, Henjum, and Rohweder 1988b). In the c. and s. Cascades, they occur most often among old lodgepole pine or lodgepole mixed with ponderosa pine, and in the Siskiyous, they occur in areas of high topographic relief where north-facing slopes below 3,000 ft (900 m) support late-successional Douglas-fir in close

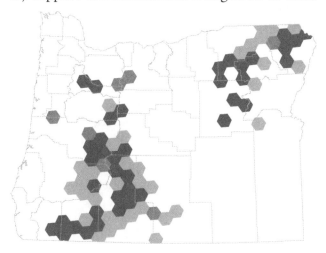

proximity to south-facing slopes with meadows, Oregon white oak woodlands, and chaparral. Great Gray Owls sometimes use clearcuts and partial cuts for foraging (Bull and Henjum 1990, Goggans and Platt 1992). Birds in the s. Cascades and Siskiyou Mtns. are associated with natural openings (Bryan and Forsman 1987, Fetz et al. unpubl. ms.), though N. Barrett (p.c.) has also found them using old shelterwoods and clearcuts. Shrubs and/or young trees usually regrow in clearcuts before a layer of herbaceous vegetation can develop to support sufficient prey populations. In winter, Great Gray Owls tended to occupy areas with <16 in (40 cm) of accumulated snow (Bull, Henjum, and Rohweder 1988a).

Nest sites are another critical habitat feature for this owl. They build no nests of their own, thus depend upon pre-existing nesting sites. These include natural depressions in the tops of large-diameter trees that have broken off, mistletoe clumps, and stick nests built by other animals, often those of Northern Goshawks and Red-tailed Hawks (Bryan and Forsman 1987, Bull, Henjum, and Rohweder 1988b). Stick nests of Western Gray Squirrels appear to be the most frequent choice in the Siskiyous (Fetz et al. unpubl. ms.). They accept artificial nesting platforms provided for their use (Bull, Henjum, and Rohweder 1988b). Since young typically leave the nest before they can fly, leaning trees are an important feature near nesting sites as they allow young to clamber up to safe perches.

Oregon Great Gray Owls prey most often upon voles (45-55% of all individuals) and pocket gophers (10-61%) (Bull, Henjum, and Rohweder 1989a, Goggans and Platt 1992, Fetz et al. unpubl. ms.). In the Siskiyous they also feed extensively upon moles (30%) (Fetz et al. unpubl. ms.). Additional prey include other mice, squirrels, chipmunks, and birds, especially in winter when preferred prey may be difficult to obtain.

**Seasonal Activity and Behavior:** Although some disperse during winters of prey scarcity, they are largely resident. Calling occurs most frequently from late Feb through Apr. They annually produce one clutch of 3-5 eggs beginning in Mar (Bull and Duncan 1993). The incubation period is about 30 days, and an average of 2.3 young (Bull, Henjum, and Rohweder 1989b) leave the nest at about 3-4 wk of age between mid-May and mid-Jun. Juveniles move to thicker cover and climb to an elevated perch. Can fly 1-2 wk after leaving the nest and may be fed by the male for as long as 3 mo (Bull, Henjum, and Rohweder 1989b). Dispersal of juveniles within their first year averaged 11.5 mi (18.5 km) (Bull, Henjum, and Rohweder 1988a). Occupy home ranges encompassing an average of 26 mi² (67.3 km²; range 1.5-120 mi² [4-312 km²]) (Bull, Henjum, and Rohweder 1988a, b). No difference was observed among home range size of males and females.

Great Gray Owls show a high degree of fidelity to both nesting and wintering areas (Bull, Henjum, and Rohweder 1988b), but less to a specific nest site. Seven of 18 nesting sites were used from one year to the next in the Blue Mtns. (Bull, Henjum, and Rohweder 1988b) while none of 10 nests were occupied in succeeding years in the Siskiyous (Fetz et al. unpubl. ms.). Average distance between alternate nests in the Blue Mtns. was 0.8 mi (1.3 km, Bull, Henjum, and Rohweder 1988b). Mates tend to go separate ways when not breeding.

**Detection:** Detection of Great Gray Owls is a challenge. They are largely nocturnal, vocalizations are soft, and they call most often at a time of year when snow makes access into much of their range difficult. Calls most frequently in the first three hours after sunset (Bull and Henjum 1990). Many mistake the call of the Blue Grouse for that of the Great Gray Owl. For years the refuse pit at Fort Klamath presented an opportunity to observe a roosting bird. Today, the forest edges near Howard Prairie in Jackson Co., Spring Cr. west of La Grande, and the La Pine area at dusk offer the best chances to observe this bird.

**Population Status and Conservation:** They are elusive and thus difficult to study, and little is known of numbers or changes in populations. Minimum densities recorded at two small sites (<4 mi² [<10 km²]) in the

*Great Gray Owl*

Blue Mtns. were 2.9-6.6 pairs/mi² (0.74-1.72/km²) (Bull, Henjum, and Rohweder 1988a). Creation of clearcut openings in closed canopy forests may present limited benefit to this species. However, nesting and roosting requirements involve old-growth. Bryan and Forsman (1987) suggest that populations may have declined in recent years due to habitat loss resulting from harvest of old-growth timber as well as urban sprawl in Deschutes Co. More work is needed before the status of this bird can be determined. Oregon lists the Great Gray Owl as a sensitive species.—*Stewart W. Janes*

## Long-eared Owl *Asio otus*
This medium-sized owl is easily recognized by its conspicuous "ear" tufts, yellow eyes set in a round facial disk, size, and mottled plumage of black, brown, gray, buff, and white. Legs and toes are densely feathered. Females are larger and darker in coloration than males (Marks et al. 1994). Wings are long and rounded with a wing loading ratio of 4.61, adapting this species for hunting on the wing (Marti 1974). Strictly nocturnal; secretive during nesting. Perhaps the least understood owl in w. Oregon.

**General Distribution:** Breeds from n. Yukon, s. and e. British Columbia, across c. Canada to Maritime Provinces; south to nw. Baja California, s. Arizona, s. New Mexico; east to Pennsylvania, New York, and n. New England. Also down Appalachian Mtns. to Virginia. Winters in N. America from s. Canada to n. Baja California, Mexico, s. Texas, Gulf coast, Georgia, and casually to Florida (Marks et al. 1994, AOU 1998). New World *A. wilsonianus*, as listed by Gabrielson and Jewett (1940), and Old World *A. otus* are conspecific (Peters 1940; AOU 1944). The AOU (1957) included Oregon in the range of *A. o. tuftsi*, but specimens from Oregon cannot be identified with *tuftsi* or with *wilsonianus* (a darker eastern subspecies) and may represent another subspecies (Browning and Cross 1999).

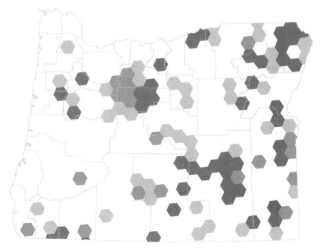

**Oregon Distribution:** A fairly common breeder in open country east of the Cascades in wooded riparian areas and junipers. A common breeder on Boardman Bombing Range, Morrow Co. (Green and Livezey 1999), and widespread in Malheur Co. (Contreras and Kindschy 1996). Uncommon in conifer forests in ne. Oregon below about 5,500 ft (1,650 m), and in pine forests at low to moderate elevations on the east slope of the Cascades (Gilligan et al. 1994). A rare breeder in foothills of the Willamette Valley, where fewer than five nesting records have been reported (Maser and Gordon 1965, Gilligan et al. 1994). Its status is particularly unclear in the w. Cascades and Coast Range where there are no confirmed nesting records except at Hagg L., Washington Co., where a pair has been present since 1990 (D. Lusthoff p.c.). There were two calling birds in mid-Apr 1989 in e. Lane Co., one visual observation in late Apr 1989 in e. Linn Co. (D. Johnson p.c.), and one visual observation 28 Jul 1985 at Mt. Thielsen, e. Douglas Co. (Fix 1990a). There are a few coastal records from Coos, Curry, and Tillamook counties (Gilligan et al. 1994).

May winter throughout the breeding range, but sites at higher elevations are probably vacated in winter (*EB*). Birds breeding in more northerly locations may winter in the state (Gilligan et al. 1994). In e. Oregon, groups of 10 or more birds may roost together in thickets during winter (Gilligan et al. 1994), but there are no winter records for ne. Oregon (Evanich 1992a). Uncommon in winter in the Willamette and Rogue valleys (Gilligan et al. 1994), where regular wintering groups have been found at Finley NWR (E. Forsman p.c.) and E. E. Wilson WMA (*MGH*). Two winter (Dec) and one possible migration record (Mar), for the Umpqua Valley (Hunter et al. 1998). Very little is known about migration routes, or which populations might be more migratory vs. sedentary.

**Habitat and Diet:** Typically nests and roosts in dense vegetation (either deciduous or coniferous stands) adjacent to grasslands, shrublands, or open forests (Marks et al. 1994). Also may inhabit parks, orchards, riparian woodlands, junipers, and dense tangled thickets. Birds in n. Jackson Co. are associated with dense post-fire chinquapin stands (N. Barrett p.c.). Hunts primarily in open areas or in open forested stands.

Nests on existing platforms, which are usually stick nests constructed by other species or broom structures. In ne. Oregon, nests in coniferous forests were in brooms formed by dwarf mistletoe in Douglas-fir trees or on stick platforms built by accipiters (Bull, Wright, and Henjum 1989). On the Boardman Bombing Range, 28 of 30 nests were in old Black-billed Magpie nests, one was in an old Swainson's Hawk nest, and one was in an old Ferruginous Hawk nest (Holmes and Geupel 1998). Maser and Gordon (1965) located a nest in Benton Co. on a stick nest in a Douglas-fir. In se. and sw. Idaho, abandoned nests used by this owl were often built by American Crows or Black-billed Magpies (Craig and Trost 1979, Marks and Yensen 1980). Marks and Yensen (1980) also found one nest in a natural cavity in a limestone cliff in sw. Idaho. An occupied nest along Becker Cr., Malheur Co. was in a particularly large big sagebrush (M. Denny p.c.). In desert areas, the height of the nests above the ground was crucial to nest success; nests low to the ground had more predation than those higher in the trees (Marks and Yensen 1980).

Roosts in dense vegetation for concealment and thermal cover in summer and winter. Conifer stands used commonly for roosting in winter in e. U.S. (Randle and Austing 1952); deciduous thickets used in arid areas in w. U.S. (Marks et al. 1994). Fifty-seven percent of 37 breeding season roosts in ne. Oregon were in dwarf-mistletoe brooms in Douglas-fir (Bull, Wright, and Henjum 1989).

Numerous studies on diet of this owl report a predominance of small mammals, particularly voles, deer mice, and kangaroo rats (Maser and Brodie 1966, Marti 1974, 1976, Sonnenberg and Powers 1976, Marks and Yensen 1980), though the majority of these studies occurred in open habitats. Mean weight of prey was 1.3 oz (37 g), with a daily requirement of about 2.1 oz (60 g) per day (Marti 1976). A predominance (56% by frequency) of pocket gophers made up the diet in a population nesting in coniferous forests in ne. Oregon; 78% of the pocket gophers were juveniles (Bull, Wright, and Henjum 1989). Pocket mice, deer mice, kangaroo rats, and harvest mice comprised the majority of the diet on the Boardman Bombing Range (G. Green, p.c.). Pocket gophers made up the majority of the diet in se. Idaho (Craig and Trost 1979).

**Seasonal Activity and Behavior:** Spring migration thought to be primarily in Mar (Gilligan et al. 1994), but little is known about the timing or migratory habits of these birds. Winter roosts in the Columbia Basin begin breaking up during the last week in Feb (M. Denny p.c.). Male advertising song is given Feb-May in Idaho and Montana, peaking in Feb and Mar. In ne. Oregon, males actively singing in the vicinity of a nest in Mar and Apr (*EB*). Timing of pair bond formation is not known. Pairs are defensive in the immediate vicinity of the nest. First clutches are usually laid mid-Mar to mid-May in Idaho, and nests initiated later at higher elevations (Marks 1986). Clutch initiation ranged from 27 Feb to 16 May on the Boardman Bombing Range (Holmes and Geupel 1998). In ne. Oregon, females observed on eggs between 15 Apr and 26 May (Bull, Wright, and Henjum 1989). A bird was observed in a cavity in incubating position, likely on nest, 11 Jun 1997 in sw. Klamath Co. (OBBA, F. Isaacs p.c.). Normally one clutch each year, although

may lay second clutch if first lost during incubation (Marks et al. 1994). Clutch size averaged 5.5 (n=15) in sw. Idaho (Marks and Yensen 1980), 3.0 in 1975 and 5.3 in 1976 in se. Idaho (Craig and Trost 1979), and ranged 3-5 at 5 nests in ne. Oregon (Bull, Wright, and Henjum 1989). Incubation by female only for 26-28 days, beginning with laying of first egg (Marks et al. 1994). During this time, male provides female with food. Female broods young for at least 2 wk after hatching; female may assist with hunting prey for young after this time. Nests with young observed from late Apr to mid-Jun (n=4) (OBBA). Young leave the nest and perch on nearby branches at about 21 days, although they are unable to fly until about 35 days old. Recently fledged birds observed mid-May to late Jun (n=3) (OBBA).

Nest success was 70% in ne. Oregon with 3.0 young per nest (Bull, Wright, and Henjum 1989). On the Boardman Bombing Range, 78% of the nests were successful with 3.8 young fledged per successful nest and 2.9 young per nesting attempt (Holmes and Geupel 1998). Nest success was 77% in se. Idaho with 4.1 young per nest (Craig and Trost 1979). In Idaho, 52% of 122 females raised >1 young to fledging (Marks 1986); most nestling deaths probably due to starvation and predation. In Idaho, raccoons commonly destroyed nests near water (Marks 1986). In California, nestlings killed by Cooper's, Red-tailed, and Red-shouldered Hawks (Bloom 1994). In ne. Oregon, accipiters killed adults and fledglings; the leg of an adult was found in a Great Horned Owl nest (Bull, Wright, and Henjum 1989). Several pairs of wings were found in an area frequented by Great Horned Owls near Umapine, Umatilla Co. (M. Denny p.c.). Predation at nests on the Boardman Bombing Range was attributed to coyotes and Common Ravens (Holmes and Geupel 1998), and the leg of a juvenile Long-eared Owl was found under an active Ferruginous Hawk nest (G. Green p.c.).

May roost communally in summer and winter (Randle and Austing 1952, Craig et al. 1985); the same roosts may be used all year (Marks et al. 1994), but the individuals may differ with time of year. Fall migration is thought to primarily be in Oct (Gilligan et al. 1994), but virtually nothing is known about the distances that Oregon birds move, the routes they use, or which populations are relatively migratory vs. sedentary.

Marks et al. (1994) described vocalizations in some detail, as follows. A complex array of vocalizations is used during breeding season, although they are mostly silent the rest of the year. The male advertising call is series of 10 to >200 notes evenly spaced about 2-4 sec apart; typically about 30 notes per bout; often ascending at end. The most common call of the female is a soft nasal *shoo-oogh* which is higher pitched than the male's call and does not end as abruptly; repeated at intervals of 2-8 sec. Numerous alarm calls are given by both sexes; call is often a high-pitched barking *ooack ooack ooack*. Human disturbance can elicit a cat-like growl or scream at nests with fledglings.

**Detection:** Responds readily to playback calls near nest at night during the breeding season. Diurnal search for pellets and whitewash in the vicinity of vocalizations often reveals nest or roost. Can be found roosting in riparian habitat in arid or open areas where roosting sites are scarce, particularly in fall and winter.

**Population Status and Conservation:** Little known about long-term trends. Nomadic behavior and fluctuating numbers make it difficult to determine population status. Nest densities 0.18 pairs/mi² (0.07 pairs/km²) in se. Idaho (Craig and Trost 1979) and 11.7 pairs/mi² (4.5 pairs/km²) in sw. Idaho (Marks 1986).

Elimination of riparian woodlands in arid areas, of dense stands of coniferous forest with dwarf-mistletoe brooms, and of open habitats would be detrimental to these species. The conservation of these habitat features for nesting, roosting, and foraging would enhance populations. Retaining nesting habitat of the American Crow and Black-billed Magpie will provide nest structures for Long-eared Owls. Artificial platforms can provide nest structures for this species (Garner 1982).—*Evelyn Bull*

### Short-eared Owl *Asio flammeus*

The Short-eared Owl is one of our most conspicuous owls owing to its use of open country and crepuscular habits. Often seen hunting low over the ground across marshes, fields, and other open areas on its buoyant, long wings, flying slowly and irregularly like a giant moth. This owl also differs from most other owls as it seldom vocalizes and is more often seen than heard. It was named for its inconspicuous "ear" tufts arising from the center of the forehead, though field observers rarely see these tufts. Distinguishing characteristics

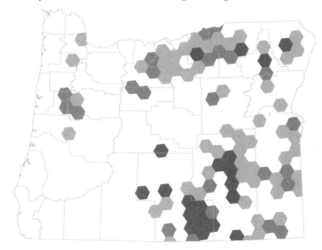

include a pale buff facial disk and a broad tawny patch at the base of the primaries that causes a conspicuous flash in flight above. Black wrist marks are visible below, as are coarse dark brown streaks on the chest with the rest of the underparts finely streaked dark brown on a buff background.

**General Distribution:** This is one of the most widely distributed owls. It breeds from n. Alaska east across Canada and south to the c. U.S., but is now mostly absent from the ne. U.S. It also breeds in S. American grasslands from Colombia and Venezuela south to Tierra del Fuego. In Eurasia it occurs from Iceland and the British Isles across n. Europe and Russia south to s. Europe and c. Asia. In N. America and M. America it winters from s. Canada to s. Mexico and in the Old World south to n. Africa, Asia Minor, Sri Lanka, China and Japan, and casually to many Atlantic and Pacific islands. Disjunct populations exist in Hawaii, the Galapagos, and the Caribbean (AOU 1998, Holt and Leasure 1993). *A. f. flammeus* occurs across N. America (AOU 1957).

**Oregon Distribution:** Locally common to rare in open country throughout the state. Considerable variation in its distribution from year to year is likely due to fluctuations in prey base (Holt and Leasure 1993, Gilligan et al. 1994). East of the Cascades it is locally common in the breeding season, particularly in the large wetland complexes (Adamus et al. 2001). It may have largely disappeared as a breeder from Klamath, Deschutes, and Crook counties (Adamus et al. 2001) where it was historically considered common (Gabrielson and Jewett 1940). It is very uncommon locally west of the Cascades. It is uncommon year-round in the Willamette Valley, becoming more rare in the northern portion, but breeding status is currently unknown and it may possibly be extirpated as a nesting species there (Adamus et al. 2001, P. T. Sullivan p.c.).

Uncommon in winter. In ne. Oregon it is most common in the Grande Ronde Valley and s. Union Co. (Evanich 1992a). Some remain in winter along the Columbia R. lowlands. Gabrielson and Jewett (1940) reported winter concentrations from the Grande Ronde Valley, Malheur R. Valley, and Klamath Basin though status may have changed since then. Numbers increase in western interior valleys and along the coast in winter. An uncommon to rare visitor to Rogue Valley (Browning 1975a, S. Janes p.c.) and occasional to rare along the coast (Bayer 1988b, Brown et al. 1996) with usually at least one found in most years on coastal CBCs. Widespread in migration. Several reports of birds at sea including an individual 70 mi (113 km) west of Newport, Lincoln Co., on 22 Sep 1984 (Fix 1985f, Gilligan et al. 1994).

**Habitat and Diet:** Found in open country, marshes, grasslands, shrub-steppe, and weedy fields. Nests on the ground, often in a sheltered, shallow hollow, sparsely lined with dry vegetation and down, usually beneath a shrub or next to dense bunchgrass to conceal incubating female (Holt and Leasure 1993). At Malheur NWR, uplands surrounded by wet meadows and marshes are their preferred nesting habitat, usually on dry sites; nests are also found among mosaics of wet meadow and marsh habitats (*EJS*).

During a 3-yr study by Maser et al. (1970) on the Crooked R. National Grassland, Jefferson Co., pellets were examined and the most important prey item during the breeding season was found to be the northern pocket gopher (41.5%), followed by the Great Basin pocket mouse (18.9%). Pocket mice were most important in winter months (32.4%), followed closely by deer mice (26.9%). Montane voles were not particularly abundant in the study area and appeared to only be taken incidentally. Kangaroo rats and harvest mice were also only taken incidentally, predominantly during winter. Although numerous in the area, sagebrush voles were rarely taken. Minor components of the diet included rabbits, snakes, birds, and insects. No ground squirrels or shrews were found in pellets although the latter were found in considerable numbers in the area.

Three hundred pellets were collected from a communal roost of unknown size 1.5 mi. (2.4 km) sw. of Bonanza, Klamath Co., on 22 Mar 1970; 295 contained remains of montane voles while five contained signs of deer mice and two contained harvest mice. Authors speculated that these owls may have found a concentration of montane voles and stopped to take advantage of the food supply (Maser et al. 1971). Microtine voles have been shown to be an important prey item throughout the species' range (Holt and Leasure 1993).

**Seasonal Activity and Behavior:** Periodically irruptive during breeding and nonbreeding seasons. Spring migration occurs in Mar and Apr. At Malheur NWR nests containing eggs have been found as early as 14 Mar and most pairs are ready to nest by Apr and May (Littlefield 1990a). A loosely colonial breeder (Holt and Leasure 1993).

This otherwise quiet owl has a spectacular courtship flight including aerial acrobatic displays accompanied by "song" and a wing-clapping sound made by the two wings or carpal bones striking each other (Holt and Leasure 1993, *EJS*). The typical call heard is a high raspy barking sound, most common in the breeding season.

Courses low over the ground while hunting, much like Northern Harrier, often quartering on slightly dihedral wings, and is able to quickly adjust flight and change direction to capture prey (Holt and Leasure

1993, *EJS*). They often start hunting before dusk in late afternoon and earlier on cloudy days, continuing into full darkness (Maser et al. 1970).

Young leave the nest at 12-17 days but do not fly until about 10 days later (Holt and Leasure 1993). Gullion (1948d) found a juvenile away from its nest with fully formed primaries but incapable of flight at Fern Ridge Res., Lane Co., on 14 Jun 1947. Dispersing juveniles can be found in Aug as fall migration begins. At Malheur NWR autumn migration peaks in late Oct and into Nov (Littlefield 1990a). An individual recovered near Nyssa on 27 Nov 1938 had been banded 21 Jun of the same year in N. Dakota (Contreras and Kindschy 1996).

Location of winter populations is quite variable and apparently related to prey abundance. Short-ears tend to concentrate at favored locations, particularly in winter. They roost on the ground or on low, open perches, sometimes in trees and dense vegetation in winter, often communally, sometimes interspecifically with Long-eared Owls, Barn Owls, Northern Harriers, and White-tailed Kites (Gilligan 1990, Holt and Leasure 1993, *EJS, ALC*). In the late 1970s on the southern part of Sauvie I., Multnomah Co., a winter roost was known to include up to approximately 27 Short-eared Owls; an analogous situation occurred during the winter of 2001 when as many as 10 owls were flushed from a dense weedy area near the Medford airport (S. Janes p.c.). Communal winter roosts may turn into local nesting territories if the food base is abundant (Holt and Leasure 1993).

**Detection:** Only occasionally seen despite wide distribution except in irruptive years when many individuals may be found in close proximity to one another. Most easily detected at dusk during foraging flights or courtship displays. Males give primary song during courtship flight and are most vocal around the nest (Holt and Leasure 1993). Small aggregations can be found at evening roosts in wetland or riparian habitats, particularly in fall and winter. May be confused in flight with the similar Long-eared Owl.

**Population Status and Conservation:** It is difficult to assess the status for such a highly irruptive and wide-ranging species. It has become one of the rarer breeding species in the Willamette Valley and may no longer nest there at all owing to widespread habitat loss through conversion of native prairies and wetlands to expansive homogenous patches of agricultural crops. Nomadism and nesting habits make species highly susceptible to habitat loss, though efforts to conserve habitat to benefit waterfowl have likely benefited this species in some areas (Holt and Leasure 1993). Contreras (1997b) noted regionwide decline in numbers shown by CBC trend data and others have noted declines in wintering numbers in w. Oregon (J. Gilligan p.c.).—*Eric J. Scheuering*

## Boreal Owl *Aegolius funereus*

This small, brown, earless owl with a black-framed, square face was long thought to be restricted to the boreal forests of Canada and Alaska, with occasional dispersal of individuals southward into the U.S. During the early 1980s it was found breeding in the Rocky Mtns. of Idaho and Colorado (Hayward and Garton 1983, Palmer and Ryder 1984). Subsequently it was found breeding throughout the Rockies from New Mexico into Canada, in e. Washington, and found but not confirmed breeding in Oregon. It is a difficult species to study as it is strictly nocturnal and lives in areas often covered by deep snows and with few passable roads. Known as Tengmalm's Owl in Eurasia.

**General Distribution:** A permanent resident in boreal and subalpine forests of Eurasia and N. America. It is somewhat nomadic in winter with periodic invasions to the south of the breeding range. One regular N. American subspecies (AOU 1957), *A. f. richardsoni.*

**Oregon Distribution:** Presumed to be a permanent resident but breeding unconfirmed. First reported 21 Mar 1902 when an apparent transient individual was collected at Fort Klamath, Klamath Co. (Gabrielson and Jewett 1940). It was not reported again until the fall of 1987 when 17 individuals were found in Baker, Umatilla, Union, and Wallowa counties (Whelton 1989). It has since been regularly observed about the Wenaha-Tucannon Wilderness in ne. Umatilla and nw. Wallowa counties (Anderson 1989c, Sullivan 2001a); near Todd L. and the south slopes of South Sister Mtn., Deschutes Co. (Tweit and Gilligan 1991, Sullivan PT 1995b, Sullivan 2001a); above Waldo L., Lane Co. (Tweit and Fix 1990a); and on Mt. Pisgah, Wheeler Co. (Tweit and Gilligan 1993, Summers 1994a). USFS surveys found birds in the Willamette, Deschutes, and Umatilla NFs in 1993 (Verner 1994). Most detections were of birds attracted to recorded songs and calls played during Sep and Oct.

**Habitat and Diet:** In Oregon, it occurs in subalpine forests interspersed with openings and meadows, usually above 5,000 ft (1,524 m) in elevation (Teale 1988). Nothing known of nesting habitat in Oregon, but several descriptions are available of habitat in fall. D. Herr (OBRC) describes the habitat where observations have been made at 5,682 ft (1,731.9 m) in nw. Wallowa Co. as pole to small sawtimber-sized subalpine fir and Engelmann spruce, with ground vegetation including big huckleberry and grouse huckleberry. Rocky meadows (without cattle) are located throughout the area. At a nearby 5,600-ft (1,707-m) ridge near Bone Springs CG, T. Winters (OBRC) found Boreal Owls in a comparatively open 10- to 20-yr-old forest with species composition of 40%

subalpine fir, 25% lodgepole pine, and 25% Engelmann spruce. Mike Denny (p.c.) found them in the Umatilla NF in mixed western larch, subalpine fir and lodgepole pine. He notes that subalpine fir is currently suffering high mortality in the n. Blue Mtn. region, which may have consequences for Boreal Owls. Near Todd L., C. Miller (OBRC) found several birds at the edge of meadows in old-growth mountain hemlock forests.

No information on Oregon nests. Generally nests in cavities or unused woodpecker holes, using no nesting material except what is present in the cavity. They will use nest boxes (Hayward and Hayward 1993). In c. Idaho, cavity dimensions average 12.4 in (310 mm) deep and 7.6 in (190 mm) horizontal diameter. Cavity entrances measured 4 in (102 mm) high and 3.8 in (95 mm) wide. Nest cavities average 41.6 ft (12.7 m) above ground, and 51% of tree height (Hayward 1989).

No information on Oregon diet. Elsewhere their primary prey is the red-backed vole, along with other rodents and small to medium-sized birds (Hayward and Hayward 1993). In Idaho, red-backed vole comprises 26-45% of annual diet; years in which few red-backed voles are available are poor breeding years (Hayward 1989).

**Seasonal Activity and Behavior:** Little Oregon information is available. In Idaho, males give the primary song on territory as early as 20 Jan, reaching greatest intensity by late Mar; song becomes uncommon by late Apr and stops when females begin incubation (Hayward and Hayward 1993). Territorial defense is confined to the nest site, seems to include less than 328 ft (100 m) radius and does not encompass the entire home range or foraging area (Mikkola 1983). Primary songs were heard from 2-3 birds at 5,700 ft (1,737 m) near Mt. Bachelor, Deschutes Co., 22 Apr 1991 (Tweit and Gilligan 1991).

Monogamous. They produce one brood per season, from a mean clutch size in Idaho of 3.25 eggs. The female incubates; the male brings food but does not guard the nest. Idaho laying dates are 12 Apr to 24 May, with an average incubation period of 26-32 days; young fledge 28-36 days after hatching (Hayward and Hayward 1993). Fledglings achieve independence after 3-6 wk outside nest cavity (März 1968).

Males resume territorial defense Aug-Nov (Kampfer-Lauenstein 1991). One responded to recorded songs at Waldo L. 31 Jul 1994 (Johnson J 1995a); three responded there through 4 Nov 1989 (Tweit and Fix 1990a). Responds in fall to recorded songs with *skiew* calls (Palmer and Rawinski 1986). This should not be considered evidence of a breeding site (Hayward and Hayward 1993). No information is available on Oregon birds during the winter months.

**Detection:** Similarity of size and calls to Saw-whet Owl can cause confusion and some mis-identification. Boreal Owls are usually found in remote high-elevation forests where travel is difficult and conditions uncomfortable, especially at night. Responds well to recorded calls played in spring and fall but mostly silent and unresponsive during the nesting season.

**Population Status and Conservation:** No information is available on the Oregon population. Surveys in Idaho show extreme yearly variation that corresponds with rodent abundance. Reliable indication of long-term trends is unavailable because of difficulty in surveying and censusing (Hayward and Hayward 1993).

Mature and older forests provide quality nesting, foraging, and summer roosting habitat. Timber harvest often reduces primary prey population and removes nest cavities. "Because forest succession is slow in spruce-fir forests, management must acknowledge that clearcut sites will remain unsuitable for roosting or foraging up to a century and new nest trees will not develop for nearly two centuries" (Hayward and Hayward 1993).—*Harry B. Nehls*

## Northern Saw-whet Owl *Aegolius acadicus*

The Northern Saw-whet Owl is one of the most common forest owls in Oregon, but like most other owls it is more often heard than seen. It is a small owl, approximately 8 in (20 cm) long, with a large head, large yellow eyes, and no ear tufts. The facial disk is reddish brown with small white streaks radiating outward from the eyes and a prominent white V above the eyes and beak. The back and wings are brown with white spots. The breast is white with rust-colored vertical streaking. Juveniles have a distinctive chocolate brown plumage, with a tan or buff-colored chest. They molt out of this plumage before fall dispersal.

Confusion exists about how the Saw-whet got its name. One frequently repeated story is that it was named Saw-whet because one of its calls

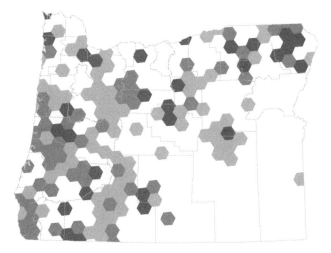

supposedly sounded like a saw being whetted. Another explanation, which we believe is more likely, is that the name Saw-whet was derived from the French word *chouette*, which means "small owl" (de la Torre 1990). Although the Saw-whet has at least nine different vocalizations (Cannings 1993), none of them resemble the sound of a saw being whetted. The most frequently heard vocalization is a monotonous series of whistle-like toots, given at half-second intervals, which can continue for hours.

**General Distribution:** It is a resident of forested areas across N. America from c. and se. Alaska to s. California in the west through much of the montane region west of the Rocky Mtns. In the east, this species is restricted to the southern half of Canada and the ne. U.S. around the Great Lakes and in New England. There are small disjunct populations at high elevations elsewhere (AOU 1998). In the fall and winter a varying number of individuals move south of the breeding range from New Jersey south to n. Florida, across the Midwest into Texas and into the deserts of Arizona and California (AOU 1998, Brinker et al. 1997). Of two subspecies, only *A. a. acadicus* occurs in Oregon (Pyle 1997).

**Oregon Distribution:** Breeds in low to mid-elevation coniferous and mixed deciduous/coniferous forests statewide. Found at higher elevations to tree line in lower numbers (Cannings 1993, *MGH*). Relatively uncommon in dry oak forests, juniper woodlands, and chaparral (Gilligan 1994). In the Coast Range, this is the most common forest owl detected during nocturnal surveys for Spotted Owls in Apr-May (*DKB*). Occasionally found during the nonbreeding season in isolated woodlots and riparian thickets in the Willamette Valley (*DKB*) and high desert regions of e. Oregon (Littlefield 1990a).

**Habitat and Diet:** Usually found in coniferous forests during the breeding season, but may breed occasionally in riparian forests (Kebbe 1959, Marks and Doremus 1988). No published information on the age, composition, or structure of stands used for foraging in Oregon, but the fact that Saw-whets occur in many different forest types and age-classes suggests that they utilize a broad range of forest conditions. Based on locations of calling owls in Idaho, Hayward and Garton (1984) reported that Saw-whets "favored non-deciduous forest stands with a well-developed mid-canopy layer and shrubs in the 1-2 meter range." Hayward and Garton (1984) also reported that breeding season home ranges of three radio-tagged Northern Saw-whet Owls in Idaho were bisected by streams and riparian vegetation. In British Columbia, home ranges of two males that were radio-tracked during the breeding season were 355 ac (142 ha) and 398 ac (159 ha) (Cannings 1987). A Saw-whet that was radio-tracked for 20 days during winter in Minnesota had a range of 285 ac (114 ha) (Forbes and Warner 1974).

Nests primarily in flicker or other woodpecker cavities in trees or snags (Bent 1961, Cannings 1993), but will also use nest boxes (Kebbe 1959, Cannings 1987, Marks and Doremus 1988, Marks et al. 1989). Feeds mainly on mice and voles, but also takes a variety of other small mammals, birds, and insects (Cannings 1987, 1993, Marks and Doremus 1988, Holt and Leroux 1996). Grove (1985) reported a Northern Pygmy-Owl in a saw-whet pellet in Washington. In ne. Oregon, Boula (1982) reported a diet of over 75% deer mice. In w. Oregon, Forsman and Maser (1970) reported a diet of deer mice and voles, including red tree voles. A Portland-area nest contained downy Wood Duck chicks in addition to mice (H. Nehls p.c.). The saw-whet is in turn preyed upon by larger owls (Forsman et al. 1984).

**Seasonal Activity and Behavior:** Territorial during the breeding season. Males advertise territories primarily by calling at night, but may also call during the day. Normally monogamous, but polygyny has been reported in a study where nest boxes were in close proximity in Idaho (Marks et al. 1989).

Nesting begins in Apr and May when males begin calling to defend territories and attract females. Clutch size is 4-7 along the w. coast (Murray 1976) and 5-7 in s. British Columbia (Cannings 1987). Females incubate eggs for 27-29 days (Cannings 1987). Males feed females and young during incubation and brooding period. Juveniles leave the nest after about 29-36 days (Cannings 1987). Flight-capable juveniles are observed in late Jun in the Coast Range (*DKB*). Broods remain together and are fed by adults until they disperse. The precise timing of juvenile dispersal is not known, but is presumed to be about 8 wk after the young leave the nest (Cannings 1993).

Although a southward migration has been well documented on the e. coast during fall and winter (Brinker et al. 1997), similar behavior has not been documented in the Pacific Northwest. However, recent counts of hundreds of these owls at the Boise Ridge, Idaho banding station suggest that a significant fall movement takes place in the w. Rocky Mtns. From 5 Aug to 26 Oct 1999, 848 Saw-whets were captured there, which seems remarkably high for local dispersal (Trochlell 2000). Barrett and Ratti trapped 96 Saw-whets in mist nets at a single location near Florence in Oct-Nov of 1996-98. We do not know if this represents directional migration or random dispersal of young owls. Gilligan (1994) suggested that Saw-whet owls migrate "vertically" in Oregon because they are detected during winter in low-elevation riparian thickets outside the breeding range, but the actual origin of these lowland owls is unknown.

Based on the fact that Saw-whets were rarely found at the same site for more than 1 yr, Marks (1997) suggested that they might be nomadic in some parts of their range, settling in areas of high prey availability encountered during winter. However, Cannings (1993) reported recapturing 5 of 36 adults at the same or an adjacent site in different years. He suggested that site fidelity was underestimated because not all adults were captured and not all nests were found in all years.

**Detection:** The nocturnal nature of this species makes it difficult to see, but auditory detection is easily achieved by going into the forest and listening in the spring. The incessant repetitive singing of males is a common night-time sound during the months of Apr and May, and into Jun at higher elevations. Mimicking the calls or replaying tape-recorded calls can yield detections at virtually any time of year. Finding Saw-whets during the day is a challenge because they typically roost in dense foliage or woodpecker cavities. One technique that often works is to home in on flocks of small forest birds while they are mobbing a roosting owl. Tapping on snags during the breeding season will sometimes cause a female to stick her head out of the cavity.

**Population Status and Conservation:** Common and widespread, but population trends unknown. Detections have declined on BBSs, while winter observations from CBCs seem to be increasing in the w. U.S. (Stokes and Stokes 1996). Not listed as sensitive or threatened by federal or state agencies. Forest management practices and clearing for agriculture and development are probably affecting its numbers. Research is needed to determine habitat requirements, population status, and dispersal behavior.—*Douglas K. Barrett, Laura L. Ratti, and Eric D. Forsman*

# Order CAPRIMULGIFORMES
*Family Caprimulgidae*

## Subfamily Chordeilinae

**Common Nighthawk** *Chordeiles minor*
A nearctic migrant with one of the longest migration distances of any N. American bird, and one of the last migrants to arrive in Oregon. Long, slender wings are marked by a white patch on the "hand," visible in flight from great distances. When perched on the ground, the cryptic brown, gray, and black mottling makes the bird almost invisible, but this camouflage is of limited use when silhouetted on tree limbs or fence posts. Males have a white throat and a white bar on the undertail, while females have a tawny throat, lack the

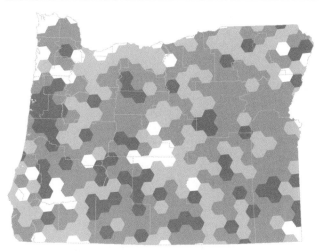

white bar on the undertail, and often have a reduced white wing patch. The erratic, buoyant, bat-like flight of this "bullbat" is frequently observed during warm summer evenings, especially in e. Oregon. Another signature flight behavior is a steep dive ending with an abrupt swoop upward that creates a "booming" sound from the change in angle of the wing feathers. The location of this activity often indicates the presence of its mate. Often seen in large flocks during migration (especially fall) and at prime foraging sites during the breeding season.

**General Distribution:** Breeds from c. Canada south to s. California, s. Nevada, s. Arizona, Texas, n. Mexico, the Gulf coast, and s. Florida, and locally through M. America to Belize, Honduras, and Costa Rica (Poulin et al. 1996). Winters throughout much of S. America to n. Argentina, although distribution remains poorly known. Eight subspecies in N. America (Selander 1954, Browning 1990); two in Oregon.

**Oregon Distribution:** Breeds and migrates at all elevations throughout the state. Fairly common to locally common within and e. of the Cascades; rare to locally uncommon w. of the Cascades. Two breeding subspecies; *C. m. minor* in w. Oregon (Selander 1954) south to Josephine Co. (Browning 2002) and *C. m. hesperis* in the remainder of the state). Intergrades between *minor* and *hesperis* have been found in Deschutes and Crook counties (Browning 2002). More work is required to define ranges.

**Habitat and Diet:** Nesting habitat is characterized by open landscapes with little ground cover. Most abundant in sagebrush and rocky scablands and rimrock habitats of e. Oregon. Also nests in dry creekbeds, burned areas, coastal dunes, forest clearings, unused gravel roads, abandoned parking areas and equipment yards, power substations, Christmas tree farms (Altman 1999b), and at least until recently, gravelly roofs of buildings in towns (Gilligan et al. 1994). Historically nested on "gravely islands in the Willamette River"

(Johnson 1880), and may still nest on gravel bars or sparsely vegetated/bare ground on islands in the larger rivers of w. Oregon such as the Columbia and Willamette (Noyes 1981, Altman 1999b). Nests on the ground with little or no vegetation, usually in gravel, dirt, or plant debris.

Foraging can occur in many places with open, unobstructed aerial foraging space such as farmland, urban areas, and forest burns. Often associated with riparian or open water habitats that provide abundant insect hatches. A recent survey in the Willamette Valley indicated that most foraging birds occurred in association with larger bodies of water (e.g., the Willamette R.) and open upland areas dominated by grass fields and Christmas tree farms (Altman 1999b). It also forages over forested habitats and the expansive high desert country of e. Oregon. Mostly opportunistic in foraging; dependent on insect hatches and availability of flying insects. Forages communally where insect hatches are occurring and may forage long distances from nest sites, including coming down from mountains into valleys. Daytime roosts are usually on the limbs of trees or on logs or fences, where it perches along, not across the perch. Also roosts on the ground in habitats similar to nesting habitat.

Diet is almost exclusively insectivorous, although some vegetable matter reported (Rust 1947). No data are available, but they are suspected to get most prey biomass from medium and large flying insects, of which there are often less than more common, small insects.

**Seasonal Activity and Behavior:** Typically arrives in the last week of May in e. Oregon and first week of Jun in w. Oregon. In e. Oregon, average arrival near Bend is 29 May (n=15) (C. Miller unpubl. data), and 24 May at Malheur NWR with little variation between the earliest (20 May) and latest (28 May) dates (Littlefield 1990a). In w. Oregon, the average arrival date is 31 May in Lincoln Co. (Bayer 1995a), 5 Jun (n=26) in Yamhill Co. (Bayer 1986b), and 4 Jun near Corvallis (n=10) (A. McGie p.c.). Reported early arrival dates include 4 May in Oakridge (Mattocks 1985b), 9 May in the s. Willamette Valley (Gullion 1951), 10 May in Philomath (Mattocks 1985b), and 12 May at Eugene (Lillie 1996). Extremely early arrival dates of 17 Apr (Gilligan et al. 1994) and 28 Apr at Malheur NWR (Ivey, Herziger, and Scheuering 1998) may be vagrant occurrences of Lesser Nighthawk, a species which arrives much earlier than Common Nighthawk in n. California (Gilligan et al. 1994). Any nighthawk seen in Oregon before mid-May should be identified with care.

No nest is built. There are usually two eggs per clutch and the species raises only one brood (Poulin et al. 1996). Nests with eggs are reported from 15 Jun to 29 Jul (n=17) (OBBA). Young fledge mid-Jul through early Aug. Territory size is variable and some pairs will nest relatively close (e.g., <250 ft [75m]) (Poulin et al. 1996).

Some fall migration may begin in Jul (Gullion 1951, Gilligan et al. 1994). Migration flights occur both during day and night, but most often in early evening, and often in large flocks (Poulin et al. 1996). Peak migration is 15-31 Aug at Malheur NWR (Littlefield 1990a), and early Sep in the s. Willamette Valley (Gullion 1951). Large flocks include 100+ birds in 30 min at Malheur NWR on 25 Aug 1984 (Littlefield 1990a), 144 and 300 birds, 11 and 18 Aug respectively at Summer L. WMA (Sullivan 1996a, 1999a) and as many as 300 birds in early Sep in the s. Willamette Valley (Gullion 1951), numbers not seen in the valley today. Occasional birds are reported annually throughout the state in the last 10 days of Sep. Late autumn records include 3 Oct at Malheur NWR (Littlefield 1990a), 5 Oct in Portland (Mattocks and Hunn 1980a), 9 Oct in the s. Willamette Valley (Gullion 1951), and 17 Oct south of Salem (Nehls 1986). There are no winter records (Gilligan et al. 1994).

Nighthawks forage in flight, primarily in late afternoon and early evening, and to a lesser extent early morning. Occasionally seen foraging at midday, most often under low light conditions or during prolonged periods of cool weather (Brigham 1994).

**Detection:** Highly detectable in flight due to large size, characteristic flight, and call. Imitations of calls by European Starlings can be indistinguishable by field observers, thus the source of a call should be determined for early or late-season detections. Roosting and incubating adults have low detectability due to "freezing" behavior and camouflaged plumage. Roosting or incubating birds can be confused with Common Poorwill.

**Population Status and Conservation:** Anecdotal reports indicate a drastic reduction in numbers in the Willamette Valley during the latter half of the 20th century (*DBM*). Reported as common to abundant from the late 1800s through the mid-1900s (Johnson 1880, Anthony 1886, Anthony 1902, Gabrielson and Jewett 1940, Gullion 1951). Currently uncommon to rare and local in the Willamette Valley. As a breeding species, most abundant in e. Oregon and least abundant along the coast. In a Willamette Valley survey 1996-97, the highest numbers were reported from the Sublimity/Waldo Hills area east of Salem and from lowlands in the historic floodplain along the Willamette R. from south of Dayton to south of Corvallis. A survey of foraging birds in the Willamette Valley recorded 49-74 birds per evening on 2 days in 1996 and 2 days in 1997, based on the efforts of 118 people in 1996 and 79 people in 1997 (Altman 1999b). Nesting on gravel roofs in Willamette Valley towns apparently occurred through the 1970s (*ALC*), but regular urban sightings during the nesting season have diminished precipitously in the last 20 yr; it is unlikely that nighthawks nest at all in these places today.

Slightly declining but non-significant BBS trends in Oregon: long-term (1966-98) trends -1.1%/yr, short-term trends (1980-98) -0.6%/yr (Sauer et al. 1999). Within different BBS physiographic regions in Oregon, the only significant declining trend is from w. Oregon (-6.8%/yr). These data include the Puget lowlands of Washington. Trends from the Cascades and e. Oregon (includes Oregon and Washington) mirror the state trend; slight declines but non-significant.

Although they have adapted to human-created environments (e.g., gravel-coated urban rooftops and clearcuts), several factors may render birds using these areas non-sustainable populations. Speculation on the loss of nesting nighthawks on urban rooftops has focused on a reduction in the number of buildings with gravel-coated roofs; the increased urban presence of American Crow and its potential impact as a nest predator; and increased urban insecticide spraying (e.g., for mosquitoes), which has reduced the prey base.

*Common Nighthawk*

In clearcuts and other sites within managed forests, ground-disturbing activities and human presence during the breeding season may affect nesting success, and insecticide spraying on private forest lands may negatively affect the prey base of aerial insectivores.

Of great conservation importance is the presence of areas with high availability of aerial insects. These productive areas are often wet habitats such as riparian/wetland areas, recent burns, or shrublands. Another conservation issue is mortality from automobiles while feeding low over highways. Flood control may have limited annual or semi-annual creation of sandy or gravelly nesting habitats (on gravel bars and floodplains) for this species (*MGH*).—*Bob Altman*

## Subfamily Caprimulginae

### Common Poorwill *Phalaenoptilus nuttallii*

The seldom-seen Common Poorwill was aptly described by Gabrielson and Jewett (1940) when they wrote, "Few Oregonians are acquainted with this bird by sight, and those who are, know it as a pair of shining eyes that gleam from the roadway in the lights of a car or as a ghostly shape that flits for an instant across the beam of those same headlights." Others know this nocturnal species by its call on summer evenings or as a blur fluttering quickly up from secondary roads. Cryptic mottled brownish-gray plumage helps it blend in with dry, barren ground and to conceal it from predators. Common Poorwills are smaller and shorter-tailed than other nightjars; when observed in the air their flight resembles a moth or bat, noiseless and low over the ground.

Bouts of extended torpor in winter have led to the conclusion that this is the only bird species that "hibernates" but this is probably not true hibernation. It regularly enters a state of deep torpor as a response to stresses of cold or hunger. Body temperatures as low as 5° C have been recorded in torpid birds, the lowest for any bird species, with oxygen consumption reduced

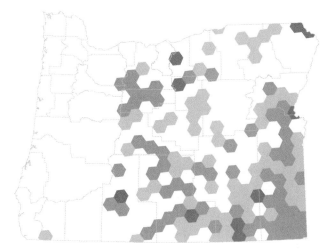

by over 90% (Csada and Brigham 1992). It is also well known for its ability to tolerate high temperatures.

**General Distribution:** Breeds from s. interior British Columbia, Montana, se. Saskatchewan, c. N. Dakota, sw. S. Dakota and south through e. Washington, Oregon, and California to s. Baja California and c. Mexico, and east to e. Kansas and c. Texas. Winters in southern parts of breeding range in California and Arizona and south to limits of the breeding range (Csada and Brigham 1992, AOU 1998). Five subspecies in N. America; two in Oregon.

**Oregon Distribution:** Uncommon to locally common east of the Cascades; locally uncommon in Jackson Co., uncommon to rare farther west in Josephine Co. (Browning 1975a, Marshall 1987, Littlefield 1990a, Evanich 1992a, Summers 1993a, Contreras and Kindschy 1996, Adamus et al. 2001, R. Cooper p.c., D. Vroman p.c.). Common along the Snake, Wenaha, and lower Grande Ronde rivers (Evanich 1992a) and in ranges of se. Oregon (Marshall 1987, Contreras and Kindschy 1996). Uncommon to fairly common in Klamath Basin along Hamaker Mtn. Road, Klamath R. canyon, and Kimball SP, as well as Miller I. W.A. (Summers 1993a). Uncommon summer resident in chaparral-oak in Rogue R. Valley, particularly Roxy Ann Peak (Browning 1975a) where it has bred successfully (Swisher 1978, 1982), and on open, lower-elevation serpentine sites in Josephine Co. (R. Cooper p.c., D. Vroman p.c.).

Numerous records from spring through fall in the w. Cascades from Douglas Co. north to Linn Co., on isolated buttes of the s. Willamette Valley, and south of Hood River (Horn and Marshall 1975, Fix 1985c, Heinl 1986b, Johnson J 1992a, Gilligan et al. 1994, Contreras 2002a, *MGH*) but breeding status unknown. Spring migrants have reached Portland as well as other n. Willamette Valley sites (Gilligan et al. 1994). Several records from spring and fall for Coos and Curry counties (Heinl 1985, Gilligan et al. 1994, Brown et al. 1996).

There are two breeding subspecies in the state; *P. n. californicus* in Jackson and Josephine counties and *P. n. nuttallii* east of the Cascades (Gabrielson and Jewett 1940, Jewett 1948b, AOU 1957, *MRB*). There are specimens (CM) of migrant *californicus* from s. Lake Co. Specimens from Crater L. NP include a late Jul specimen of *californicus* and an early Sep specimen of *nuttalli* (Farner 1952). A young female specimen identified as *nuttallii* from Tillamook Co. (Walker 1934) needs verification. Nonbreeding specimens of *nuttallii* are reported from w. Washington (Edson 1942) and considered casual there and in w. Oregon (AOU 1957). Subspecies of summering birds in the w. Cascades and Willamette Valley are unknown.

**Habitat and Diet:** Breeds in dry, brushy country of shrub-steppe and native grasslands with rimrock outcroppings, and western juniper or ponderosa pine woodlands (Gabrielson and Jewett 1940, Marshall 1987, Evanich 1992a). Terrain may often be rocky or gravelly (Csada and Brigham 1992). Also found in scattered oak and chaparral in sw. Oregon and in forest clearings on the west slope of the Cascades (Browning 1975a, Horn and Marshall 1975, Fix 1985c). One observed on the Umpqua NF was along an overgrown skid road within an old clearcut partly filled in with clumps of small coniferous trees and patches of snowbrush, and containing many narrow skid trails (Fix 1985c).

No data exist on diet in Oregon. Across their range poorwills feed primarily on night-flying large insects such as moths and beetles in addition to flies, grasshoppers, and flying ants (Csada and Brigham 1992). Young are fed regurgitated insects (Csada and Brigham 1992).

**Seasonal Activity and Behavior:** The migratory period is not well known. Some spring migrants arrive in late Apr (Gilligan et al. 1994, Contreras 2002a). Records on 14 Mar 1964 at Malheur NWR (Littlefield 1990a) and 30 Mar 1992 at the Hermiston airport, Umatilla Co. (Gilligan et al. 1994) are the earliest known. The average arrival date at Malheur NWR is 14 May (Ivey, Herziger, and Scheuering 1998) although actual arrival may be many days earlier due to low detectability of this species. The breeding period extends from early Jun through early Jul (Adamus et al. 2001). It nests on bare ground in a slight depression or scrape, often beneath a shrub such as sagebrush or greasewood (Gabrielson and Jewett 1940, Denny 1996). On 10 Jun 1997, two poorwills were observed near dark on a gravel road southeast of Pine Mtn., Deschutes Co. Facing one another approximately 10 in (25cm) apart, the male did a head-bob similar to that observed in waterfowl. With each pump of the head it flashed its white throat (P.T. Sullivan p.c.).

Nests have been found in Oregon from 10 Jun through 4 Jul and all have contained two eggs or young (Gabrielson and Jewett 1940, Marshall 1987, Denny 1996, Adamus et al. 2001). Browning (1975a) noted an adult feeding young on 20 Jul 1971 at Roxy Ann Peak. Both parents incubate and brood young (Csada and Brigham 1992). Performs distraction behavior when disturbed from its nest (Denny 1996).

Singing is noted through the end of Jul (Adamus et al. 2001). At Malheur NWR numbers decline in early Sep with the latest noted on 3 Oct 1977 (Littlefield 1990a). Elsewhere, small concentrations have been noted in mid-Sep. There are many records from late Oct through late Nov from throughout the state (Walker 1934, Jewett 1948b, Heinl 1985, Littlefield 1990a, Evanich 1992a, Contreras 2002a). Late records

have included active birds, birds in torpid condition, and dead birds, all indicating possible attempts at local overwintering.

Forages at dusk, dawn, and periods of night with moonlight (Csada and Brigham 1992). Generally forages by flying up from ground or low perch to capture prey and often returning to same perch though occasionally forages in longer, extended flights (Csada and Brigham 1992).

**Detection:** Poorwills are widely overlooked due to their crepuscular and nocturnal habits. They do not fly during daytime and remain motionless at a roost site. They are most often detected by their distinctive song, *poor-will-up*, which sounds like a simple, soft *poor will* whistle from a distance. The third phrase is heard at close range. Calling is most frequent during twilight, when they are easily heard but often difficult to locate. Reflecting red eyes can be seen in headlights along dirt roads that run through suitable habitat. They usually will not flush until an observer is only a few feet away (Horn and Marshall 1975, *EJS*).

**Population Status and Conservation:** Widespread and not considered threatened. Studies have found it to be more abundant in many areas of its range than previously thought (Csada and Brigham 1992). Although assessing trends in a nocturnal species is complex, BBS long-term trends indicate population increases (Csada and Brigham 1992). Clearings in forests created by clearcut logging practices or fires may increase nesting and roosting habitat.—*Eric J. Scheuering*

# Order APODIFORMES
*Family Apodidae*

## Subfamily Cypseloidinae

**Black Swift** *Cypseloides niger*
Insects swept up in a rising air mass are favorite prey of this species nicknamed the "cloud swift." It could as well be nicknamed the "waterfall swift" because it prefers to nest near or even behind the curtain of a waterfall. Its status in Oregon is enigmatic. It has been seen during the breeding season at Salt Cr. Falls for many years and is believed to nest there, but no one has seen a nest or a young bird. Breeding season sightings from throughout the state suggest that there may be additional nesting areas. This dark swift glides for long distances, often very high in the sky, with its wings held somewhat downward. It is larger and darker than the more common Vaux's Swift, and has a slightly forked tail.

**General Distribution:** In N. America, they breed mostly in mountains from the Stikine R. in Alaska east through sw. Alberta. south to s. California, and across the west through Colorado, se. Arizona, and n. New Mexico. They also breed from Chihuahua and Durango south through Mexico into parts of M. America and the Caribbean islands. They migrate south through the w. U.S. and Mexico through M. America, presumably to winter in S. America. Wintering grounds are unknown, but probably south of s. Colombia (Stiles and Negret 1994). There are three subspecies, *C. n. borealis* in N. America (AOU 1957).

**Oregon Distribution:** Rare to uncommon spring and fall transient and summer visitant (suspected breeder) throughout state. The first probable nest site was located in 1982 at Salt Cr. Falls, e. Lane Co. (Evanich 1982c); 6-8 birds were seen flying behind the falls in 1984 (Gordon 1984b), and up to 15 individuals have been observed at this location (P.T. Sullivan p.c.). In 1998, a new site was located at a waterfall in e. Lane Co., about 3 mi (5 km) west-northwest of Diamond Peak and 7 mi (11 km) southwest of the Salt Cr. Falls site, ironically in the Swift Cr. basin (McAtee 2001). The species is strongly suspected to breed in other locations along the coast, in the Cascades, the Columbia R. gorge, and other canyons and mountain ranges in e. Oregon. Breeding season (Jun to mid-Aug) records away from e. Lane Co. include: two singles in Lincoln Co. (Crowell and Nehls 1973a, Bayer 1995a); single and multiple individuals in Jun in Coos and Curry counties (K. Castelein p.c., D. Lauten p.c., T. Rodenkirk p.c., P. T. Sullivan p.c.); eight at Albany (Gillson 1998); several in the Columbia Gorge from the Portland area to Multnomah Falls and Mosier (Egger 1977b, Evanich and Fix 1983, Anderson 1989d, Anderson DA 1990c, Johnson J 1991a, Tice 2000a, Wieland 2000); 1 at Pamelia L., e. Linn Co. (Johnson 1990a); several birds at Madras, Jefferson Co. (Watson 1981b); several at Crooked R. Canyon, Deschutes Co. (Spencer 2000a) and along the Crooked R. near Paulina, Crook Co. (OBBA); several Wallowa Co. sightings north of Enterprise (Evanich and Fix 1983), at Hat Point (Sullivan 1997c), and in Hells Canyon (OBBA), and six in Kiger Gorge on Steens Mtn., Harney Co. (Anderson 1988b).

**Habitat and Diet:** The two waterfalls with swifts in e. Lane Co. are 286 ft (87 m) and about 40 ft (12 m) tall, at 4,000 ft (1,219 m) and 4,800 ft (1,463 m) elevation respectively, in a setting of true fir/mountain hemlock forest. Rather than elevation or surrounding vegetation type, critical factors for nest locations in other states appear to be (1) temperature moderation due to dripping water and little or no direct solar exposure, and (2) high humidity to help attach nest to substrate (Marín 1997). In the Washington Cascades they breed on steep cliffs and behind waterfalls, and on the coast on rocky shorelines (Smith et al. 1997). The summary by Marín (1997) includes several locations in the w. U.S., where they nest near waterfalls, dripping water, or in damp caves both coastally and inland. Nests cited by Bent (1940) were 6-90 ft (2-27 m) above water. In a cave in s. California, nest height above ground was 1.6-20 ft (0.5-6 m). They usually nest out of direct sunlight on a protected rock ledge or knob, or in a crevice. Nest shape is a full or half cup, or an inverted cone made mostly of moss, but may include seaweed or fern tips. It may have a pine needle lining. Inside diameter averages about 3.5 in (9.0 cm). Outside diameter is highly variable. The nest may also be a hollowed-out spot in the mud with no material added (Marín 1997).

Black Swifts feed on the wing above both forested and open areas. An indiscriminate feeder, mostly catching insects but also spiders. Stomach contents of birds collected near Seattle included flies, beetles, termites, flying ants, plant lice, leafhoppers, treehoppers, wasps, moths, and spiders, but no plant matter (Bent 1940). May forage at some distance from the nest site (Smith et al. 1997).

**Seasonal Activity and Behavior:** The earliest spring report is of two birds over Corvallis, Benton Co., on 31 Mar (Crowell and Nehls 1975b); the date suggests an erroneous identification. First arrivals are usually about 10-16 May. They are most often seen as singles or in flocks of fewer than 15 birds, at times in association with a larger number of Vaux's Swifts (both spring and fall). The largest flocks consisted of 80 birds at Thurston, Lane Co., 5 May 1949 (Gullion 1951) and 50 at Elk R. bottoms, Curry Co., 13 May 1998 (Lillie 1998). Wayne Weber (p.c.) indicates that most birds have arrived on nesting grounds in British Columbia by 31 May. The status of early Jun sightings in Oregon away from known breeding areas is probably indeterminable.

At the site near Diamond Peak in e. Lane Co., McAtee (2001) observed a pair carrying nest material behind the falls on 16 Jun 1998, and a possible nest exchange, with an inbound bird carrying food; both observations were made 11:30-12:30 (G. McAtee p.c.). Nests are reused by the same pair each year. Copulation occurs while in flight (Rathbun 1925). A nest data card cited by Marín (1997) indicated that one nest was built in 4 days. A single dull white egg is laid 10-14 days after the nest is complete. In s. California, peak egg laying was in mid-Jun (Marín 1999). Incubation is accomplished over about 24 days by both adults, with incubation shifts often longer than 4 hr. Young hatch naked, but are covered with down-like semiplumes in about 2 wk. Nestling period is about 48 days, until young reach at least 113% of normal adult weight. Adults feed young infrequently, often at dusk (Marín

1997). In s. California, peak fledging was mid- to late Aug (Marín 1999). A young bird nearly ready to fledge was observed 22 Aug in Yosemite NP (Michael 1927). Normally fledge before 08:00. Once fledging occurs, adults and young do not return to the nest site that year. Single brooded; not known to renest if egg destroyed (Marín 1997). Fewer birds are detected in fall migration, which occurs from late Aug through Sep. Hundreds swarmed in the Brookings area, Curry Co., 14 Sep 1968 (Crowell and Nehls 1969b). Usually absent after about 20 Sep; latest sighting is 11 Oct in Eugene, Lane Co. (Gilligan 1998).

**Detection:** Difficult. They often feed high in the sky making them difficult or impossible to detect with the naked eye and even with binoculars (Rathbun 1925). Many possible nesting locations are difficult to observe, and adults are not present at sites most of the day when observers are likely to be present. Colonies are small, thus few birds are at any one location. They leave the nest site well before dawn, and though they may linger in the area, they normally depart before there is enough light to see them clearly (Bent 1940). One approach is to locate a potential nest site, then stake out a location where it can be intently observed, particularly at dusk when adults might be returning to nest. Usually silent, but occasionally detected by its high-pitched twitter during migration and breeding season.

**Population Status and Conservation:** Status uncertain; may be threatened or endangered, but more information is needed (The Nature Conservancy 1998). Was on the first list of Oregon's Sensitive Species in 1992, and remains there, with an assumed breeding population, in the category "peripherally or naturally rare" (Marshall et al. 1996). For the entire western region of California, Oregon, Washington, Idaho, and Nevada, there was a 1968-87 estimated population increase of 12.2% (but not statistically significant) (Sharp 1990).

Breeding season records throughout Oregon indicate a need to search for additional nesting sites. Many possible locations exist, such as coastal rocky headlands and shores, waterfalls, damp canyons in numerous locations in the state, and high-elevation cliffs with moisture from snowmelt. A likely pair of locations is Marion Falls (on Marion Cr.) and Gatch Falls (near Lake Ann), both about 100 ft (30.5 m) tall, and less than 6 mi (10 km) southwest of Pamelia L., e. Linn Co. The falls are about 16 mi (26 km) from the Breitenbush area, where Black Swifts were seen during the entire summer of 1987 (Tweit and Mattocks 1987b). These falls are not accessible by vehicle, and have not been closely monitored by birders.—*Barbara Combs*

## Subfamily Chaeturinae

### Vaux's Swift *Chaetura vauxi*

This small swift is best known for its quick flight and dazzling aerial agility, perching only when nesting or roosting. It is aerodynamically designed for fast speeds with long, pointed wings, short, stout legs, and a compact body. Plumage is a plain grayish brown, with a slight green iridescence visible at times. Plumage of sexes is similar. Vaux's Swifts are unusual in that they nest and roost in the hollows of large-diameter trees, but also in towns and cities where chimneys take the place of trees. At a time when there were no towns or cities in Oregon, J. K. Townsend (Jobanek and Marshall 1992), in reference to this bird, wrote, "...but in this savage country he has to accommodate himself with the trunk of some hollow tree in which to rear his brood instead of the more congenial dwelling which he always selects in civilized countries." At the time Townsend assumed he was observing the Chimney Swift of e. N. America rather than its similar western counterpart. Today biologists are concerned instead about a shortage of hollow trees.

**General Distribution:** Breeding range in w. N. America from se. Alaska, nw. and s. British Columbia, n. Idaho, and w. Montana south to c. California; in sw. Tamaulipas and se. San Luis Potosí; on the Yucatan Peninsula; in w. Mexico, south to Panama; and coastal mountains of n. Venezuela. Winter range is from c. Mexico south throughout the breeding range in M. America and Venezuela; casual in winter in c. California; possibly in s. Louisiana and Florida. Of two subspecies, the northern subspecies *C. v. vauxi* occurs in Oregon (AOU 1957).

**Oregon Distribution:** A transient and summer resident nesting in older forests and brick chimneys statewide except in se. Oregon, where it occurs only during migration. Fairly common throughout forested regions of the state and in urban areas having brick chimneys. Rare in extensive, treeless areas such as

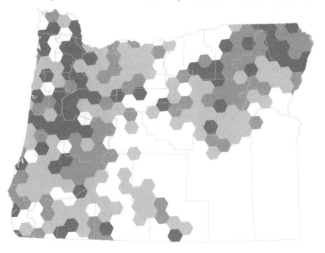

the desert regions of e. Oregon. Concentrations of more than 10,000 swifts may be seen at roosts during migration.

**Habitat and Diet:** Occurs in late seral stages of coniferous and deciduous forests and in urban areas. More common in old-growth forests than in younger stands (Manuwal and Huff 1987, Gilbert and Allwine 1991, Huff and Raley 1991, Bull and Hohmann 1992). Large-diameter hollow trees (live or dead) and brick chimneys are used for nest and roost sites (Griffee 1961b, Bull and Collins 1993b). The majority of known roost sites are in chimneys, although several roosts in hollow trees have been located in ne. Oregon (Bull and Blumton 1997). Most reported swift nests are also in chimneys. Their presence in chimneys has raised concerns over nestling noise, the welfare of nestlings that fall from nests into fireplaces, and the harmful effects of using chimneys for heating while birds are present. Swift use of chimneys should not be construed

*Vaux's Swift*

as a preference because swifts using chimneys are very visible and in close proximity to people, whereas swifts using hollow trees are difficult to detect and in remote areas without many observers.

Twenty-one nests in ne. Oregon were located in live or dead grand fir that contained hollow interiors as a result of heartwood decay (Bull and Cooper 1991). Nest trees averaged 27 in (68 cm) dbh and 83 ft (25 m) tall. Nests were constructed on the inside wall of the hollow chamber and were made of small sticks cemented in place with sticky saliva. Average diameter and depth of the inside hollow chamber was 11 in (28 cm) and 19 ft (5.7 m) respectively. Swifts entered nest trees either through broken-off tops or holes in trunks excavated by Pileated Woodpeckers.

During breeding season this swift forages exclusively in the air. In ne. Oregon radio-tagged swifts spent 60% of their time foraging over forests, 30% over water, and 10% over grasslands; ponds and streams were used more than expected based on availability (Bull and Beckwith 1993). Radio-tagged swifts foraged up to 3.4 mi (5.4 km) from the nest. Adults returned to the nest with a food bolus in their mouth to feed nestlings.

Diet during the breeding season in ne. Oregon includes flies, hover flies, ants, bees, planthoppers, aphids, spindlebugs, lanternflies, bark beetles, moths, mayflies, true bugs, and spiders. Based on 223 food boluses containing 24,141 arthropods, diet was 43% Homoptera, 27% Diptera, 18% Ephermerida, 7% Hymenoptera, 2% Coleoptera, and <1% Lepidoptera, Arachnida, Hemiptera, Psocoptera, and unknowns (Bull and Beckwith 1993). Diet did not differ among five study areas or by time of day. A pair of swifts feeds an average of 5,344 arthropods to their nestlings each day, and an average of 154,976 arthropods during the nestling growth period (Bull and Beckwith 1993). Cold, wet weather during migration and breeding reduces insect availability, probably causing birds to starve.

Swifts drink from ponds or streams by flying low over the water and dipping their beak. They make numerous passes over the water.

**Seasonal Activity and Behavior:** Most arrive in Oregon in late Apr and early May and depart from mid-Aug to late Oct (Gullion 1951, Bull and Collins 1993a, Van Brocklin 2000). They congregate at communal roost sites and migrate in large flocks. Dates during which swifts were observed using roosts during the spring migration were recorded as 28 Apr-19 May 1996 in McMinnville, 13 Apr-21 May 1996 in Eugene, 29 Apr-31 May 1995 in Roseburg, and 26 Apr-11 May 1996 in La Grande (ELB). Dates for the fall migration in 1995 were 25 Aug-20 Oct in Portland, 28 Aug-2 Oct in McMinnville, 18 Aug-10 Oct in Eugene, 11 Aug-15 Oct in Roseburg, and 17 Aug-11 Sep in La Grande (*ELB*).

Birds pair shortly after arriving on breeding grounds in May. Usually occur in groups and may nest in close proximity, although usually not in the same tree; not territorial. Nest building was observed in ne. Oregon 3-23 Jun (Bull and Collins 1993a), and in May in w. Oregon (Thompson 1977). In ne. Oregon, incubating birds were observed from 18 Jun to 25 Jul; nestlings from 2 Jul to 4 Sep; fledging dates 26 Jul to 4 Sep (Bull and Collins 1993a). Egg laying was completed by 12-14 Jun in w. Oregon (Griffee 1961b). Eggs: 5-7 typical; incubation 18-19 days; normally one brood/ season (Bull and Collins 1993b). Both sexes share in nest building, incubation, and feeding of young. There is strong breeding-site fidelity, with the same birds using the same nest tree for consecutive years (Bull and Collins 1993b).

A high-pitched, rapid chipping and buzzy twitter is given in flight and is more pronounced when in groups, in courtship, and after young fledge. Nestlings give a series of rasping notes in rapid succession. A nonvocal sound, called "booming," is made by an adult in the nest cavity by fluttering its wings while in midair; this behavior is thought to be a defense against predators (Griffee 1961b, Thompson 1977).

**Detection:** Most easily observed during spring and fall migrations at roosts in brick chimneys in towns. Birds can be observed entering the roosts in the hour before dark. Known roosts in Oregon with large congregations of birds using brick chimneys occur in Corvallis (First Presbyterian Church, 9th and Monroe), Eugene (17th and Columbia; Agate Hall, 17th and Agate), La Grande (4th and Adams), McMinnville (church chimney at 8th and Cowls), Pendleton (318 S. Main), Portland (Chapman School at N.W. 26th and Raleigh), Roseburg (Umpqua Valley Art Center Pottery Shed off Harvard Ave.), and Union (Union High School). Swifts are difficult to detect over forest unless they are calling, but are more easily observed over water, meadows, and in towns.

**Population Status and Conservation:** While Oregon BBS data show a statistically significant statewide increase of 3.7%/yr during 1966-1999 (Sauer et al. 2001), Sharp (1992) calculated an 8.9%/yr decrease during the 1980s using only routes on National Forests. Population trends in Oregon deserve more regional analysis.

In 2000, ODFW facilitated a volunteer fall survey that provided estimates of swift numbers entering chimneys to roost in the Willamette Valley. This survey resulted in an estimate of approximately 55,000 birds 10-22 Sep. The largest count (20,000 birds) was at Chapman School in Portland and the second largest (16,500 birds) came from Agate Hall in Eugene (Van Brocklin 2000).

The harvest of late seral stages of coniferous forests in Oregon has probably reduced the number of nest and roost sites available to swifts in forested areas. In 1990, Bull (1991) observed about 100 swifts using a roost in a hollow tree all summer in ne. Oregon and suspected they were not nesting because nest sites were not available. In ne. Oregon, conversion of stands dominated by grand fir to an earlier seral stage dominated by ponderosa pine would probably further decrease the number of nest and roost sites because all nests and roosts located in this area were in grand fir trees (Bull 1991, Bull and Cooper 1991). Large-diameter grand fir trees typically contain extensive heartwood decay which creates hollow chambers suitable for nesting; this same phenomenon rarely occurs in ponderosa pine.

Public support for swifts can be illustrated by the case of the chimney at Chapman School in Portland. For several years, the school's heating plant remained closed until the swifts left in the fall, forcing the children to dress accordingly. Finally, Dave Eshbaugh, Executive Director of the Audubon Society of Portland, spearheaded a program to raise funds to rebuild the heating system and allow the chimney to remain unused for heating purposes. Funds came from citizens, metro, Portland Public Schools, and several foundations. The University of Oregon decided not to demolish the unused chimney on Agate Hall largely because of public support for the swifts.

Much is yet to be determined regarding habitat use, survival, and population status of the Vaux's Swift, especially outside ne. Oregon. Additional research is warranted in various parts of the state in natural and constructed habitats.—*Evelyn L. Bull*

## Subfamily Apodinae

### White-throated Swift *Aeronautes saxatalis*
High overhead at the top of the rimrock in Oregon's desert country, the White-throated Swift swoops, soars, and darts about erratically, hunting and catching insects. At great speed, it disappears into a crevice on a cliff without appearing to slow down. Its long, strong claws enable it to crawl deep inside these crevices to roosting and nesting areas, which often cannot be seen from the entrance. The White-throated Swift is a large, dark swift with white flank patches and a white streak extending down from its throat, narrowing as it reaches the belly. Its rapid flight has earned it the reputation as possibly the fastest flying bird in existence.

**General Distribution:** Breeds from s. British Columbia eastward to s. S. Dakota, and south through Baja California and w. Texas. Also breeds in the interior of Mexico and south to Guatemala, El Salvador, and Honduras. Winters from c. California south to the southern end of its breeding range, and east across c.

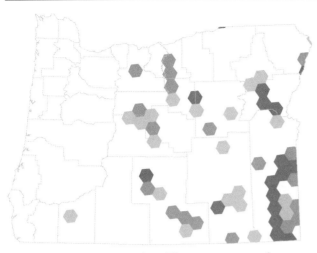

Arizona and s. New Mexico. There are scattered reports as far east as Michigan and the Dominican Republic. Two subspecies; *A. s. saxatalis* in U.S. (Behle 1973).

**Oregon Distribution:** Based on numerous reports in *Oregon Birds* and *American Birds*. This species is a locally common to abundant breeder, primarily on e. Oregon cliffs. Occasional spring and sporadic fall migrant in w. Oregon along the coast, in the Willamette Valley, and on the w. slope of the Cascades. Well-known c. and e. Oregon breeding locations today include Fort Rock, Lake Co.; Smith Rock SP, Deschutes Co.; Peter Skene Ogden Scenic Wayside, on the border of Deschutes and Jefferson counties; Clarno, Wheeler Co.; Picture Gorge, Goose Rock, and John Day Fossil Beds, Grant Co.; Steens Mtn. Rim, Harney Co.; Catlow Rim, Harney Co.; Succor Cr. canyon, Malheur Co.; many sites along the Owyhee R.; the Burnt R. Canyon, Baker Co.; and Hells Canyon along the Snake R., Wallowa Co. A small colony at Lower Table Rock, Jackson Co. was first detected 28 Apr 1990 and later from 1992 through 1994 (M. Moore p.c.). Its current status is unknown. Few birders visit the site due to the miles of difficult terrain that must be traversed to reach the cliff and explore the area (S. Janes p.c.). A 7 May 1996 record from nearby White City, Jackson Co., indicates its possible continued presence, however (M. Moore p.c.). Gilligan et al. (1994) suggest that breeding may also occur near Davis L., Deschutes/Klamath Co.; at Crater L., Klamath Co.; and in the Kalmiopsis Wilderness, Curry Co. A report of one bird at Elgin Rim (Anderson 1989c), suggestive of Wallowa Co., should have been reported as being from Egli Rim, near Summer L., Lake Co. (F. Zeillemaker p.c.).

**Habitat and Diet:** Dry cliffs or rimrock with openings such as crevices, holes, or cracks used for nesting and roosting are essential, whatever the surrounding vegetative habitat may be (Bent 1940). Surrounding habitat in Oregon includes sagebrush steppe and western juniper woodlands, as well as alpine rock and snowfields at Steens Mtn. (OBBA, *BC*). Heights of

nests range from about 10 ft (3 m) to over 200 ft (61 m) (Hanna 1917, Bent 1940, Campbell et al. 1990b, Ryan and Collins 2000). Observed using rock crevices for nest sites in Oregon (Hoffman 1982). Near Tygh Valley, Wasco Co., they were seen entering unused Cliff Swallow nests for 3 yr (D. Lusthoff p.c.). Traditional nest site use has been suggested in Nevada (Dobkin et al. 1986) and is consistent with Oregon observations. For example, T. H. Rogers (1979b) noted that a colony of White-throated Swifts had been at Picture Gorge, Grant Co., for many years. This colony was still active in 2000 (J. Rodecap p.c.). Outside Oregon, has nested in buildings and sea cliffs (Ryan and Collins 2000). No information on Oregon nests; elsewhere nest is cup-shaped and made of grasses, mosses, seed down, and many feathers, held together and attached to the substrate by saliva (Hanna 1909, Pough 1957, Chantler and Driessens 1995).

No dietary information specific for Oregon. Generally, consists of flying insects caught on the wing (Terres 1980). Not known to consume vegetable matter. Often feeds where insects have been swept into an updraft. May also be found foraging over habitat such as grassland and agricultural areas; may follow farm machinery to harvest displaced insects (Alden and Mills 1976). Known to feed at some distance from the nesting area (Ryan and Collins 2000). May drink and/or bathe while skimming over open ponds or other quiet water, especially in the early morning (Ryan and Collins 2000, *MGH*).

**Seasonal Activity and Behavior:** Earliest arrival date is 17 Mar (Summers 1994b, C. Corder p.c.). Regular at nesting cliffs by Apr. Sometimes seen in migration and at breeding colonies with Violet-green Swallows and Cliff Swallows. Oregon colonies of 50 or more birds have been reported (Summers 1994a, Spencer 1998). Seen in courtship falls and copulating in flight on nesting grounds east of Silver L., Lake Co., on 15 Jun 1970 (Reynolds and Forsman 1971). In courtship fall, pair comes together frontally and tumbles and gyrates downward for several seconds, dropping as much as 500 ft (152 m), and separates before reaching the ground (Bent 1940). They also copulate in nesting crevices (Bent 1940). Nest building may take a mo or more (Hanna 1909). Clutch size 3-6 eggs (Ryan and Collins 2000). Little is known about the timing of egg laying, incubation, nestling period, and fledging. Eggs are found in nests from Mar through Jul (as early as Mar in Arizona and California; as late as Jul in Colorado and British Columbia) (Ryan and Collins 2000). A clutch reported from s. California contained one egg May 16 and was complete at four eggs by May 24 (Hanna 1909). The incubation period was 20-29 days for a sample of nine nests in British Columbia. Adults accumulate food in mouth and glue it together with saliva to form a bolus to feed young. In British

Columbia, young fledged after 40-46 days. Not known to double brood (Ryan and Collins 2000). Moves away from breeding areas in late summer. May form flocks to migrate; a flock of over 120 individuals was near the summit of Steens Mtn. 30-31 Aug 2000 (T. Bray p.c.). Gone from the state by mid- to late Sep. Of fall reports from east of the Cascades, 2 Oct 1989 (at Summer L., Lake Co.) is the latest. An 11 Oct 1997 report at Toketee, Douglas Co., is the latest for the state (Anderson DA 1990a). No winter records. In wintering grounds in California, individuals have been found dormant in rock crevices (Terres 1980), seemingly engaged in a sort of hibernation.

**Detection:** Patience is required when observers are standing at the bottom of high cliffs looking upward, because birds may be out of view over the land above and beyond the cliff. Frequent vocalizations aid in detection, especially when the high-pitched descending *hee hee hee* echoes through a canyon. While it sometimes takes several minutes or more of observation before one is seen, this species is hard to miss during the breeding season at cliffs where they are known to nest.

**Population Status and Conservation:** Found by early observers only in Malheur Co. (Gabrielson and Jewett 1940). Preble (1915) provided the first documented sighting in Oregon, west of McDermitt, Malheur Co., on 4 Jun 1915. He later saw single birds near Disaster Peak and at the summit of Mahogany Mtn., four southwest of Watson, and a breeding colony at the northern base of the Mahogany Mtns. First noted at Fort Rock, Lake Co., in the late 1960s (J. Anderson p.c.). Reynolds and Forsman (1971) found 20-25 at Table Rock, Lake Co., on 15 Jun 1970. The birds were probably nesting, as copulation was observed. It was well established in the Steens Mtn. area (Harney Co.) by 1976 (Green 1978). Consistent with Oregon observations, its range appears to be expanding. It is now found in appropriate habitat throughout c. and e. Oregon. Pesticide use probably affects availability of insects for food (Ryan and Collins 2000).—*Barbara Combs*

## Family Trochilidae

### Subfamily Trochilinae

**Broad-billed Hummingbird** *Cynanthus latirostris*
This Mexican species breeds northward to Texas and Arizona, and winters primarily in Mexico. It is casual in winter to the s. U.S., and is accidental farther north in the Midwest. Most California records are from coastal lowlands from mid-Sep to mid-Nov, with some wintering individuals (Small 1994). A subadult male was photographed at John Day, Grant Co., 12-14 Sep

1998 (OBRC). A male was photographed at Gearhart, Clatsop Co., 6-14 Oct 2001 (Contreras 2002b). Subspecies unknown.—*Harry B. Nehls*

## Black-chinned Hummingbird
*Archilochus alexandri*
The Black-chinned Hummingbird has a widespread breeding distribution in w. N. America, occurring most abundantly in riparian habitats of the sw. U.S. Farther north, populations become more scattered. Noteworthy as a generalist, it appears in a wide variety of habitats, including lush river bottoms, urban settings and desert canyons (Baltosser and Russell 2000). Below the male's velvety black gorget is an iridescent purple band that can also look black in poor light. At rest, the wingtips are relatively broad and curved, unlike any other N. American hummingbird.

**General Distribution:** Breeds from sw. British Columbia south to Baja California and east through Nevada to New Mexico and Texas. Winters in Mexico. Monotypic (AOU 1957).

**Oregon Distribution:** A rare to locally common summer resident east of the Cascades (Gilligan et al. 1994). Least common in Klamath and Lake counties (OBBA). Fairly common in foothills near the Blue and Wallowa mountains in summer, also in areas of Wasco Co., and in the Snake and Owyhee valleys (Gilligan et al. 1994, Sullivan 1998a, Spencer 1999). Nesting confirmed at Vale, Malheur Co. (OBBA); and it has probably nested in other areas of extreme e. Oregon such as Ontario, and near Adrian, both Malheur Co., and near Huntington, Baker Co. (Contreras and Kindschy 1996). Recorded as a breeding species along Little Sheep Cr. near Imnaha, Wallowa Co. (Evanich 1990). Migrates through se. and sc. Oregon (Gilligan et al. 1994); occasional in spring at Malheur NWR (regular at Page Springs), and accidental in fall (Littlefield 1990a).

West of the Cascades there is little documented

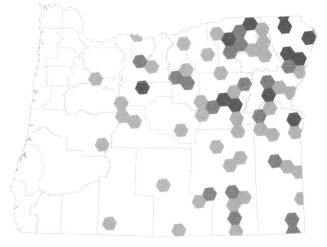

evidence of nesting. One pair was reported to breed at Roseburg 1996-97 (OBBA), but photos of the bird showed an immature male Anna's Hummingbird (*MGH*, D. Tracy p.c.). Six individuals (adult females and immatures) on Saddle Mtn., Clatsop Co., 3 Jul 1985 (Heinl 1986b), may indicate an extralimital breeding there. There are a few records from the Willamette Valley (Marshall 1989a, Gilligan et al. 1994, Lillie 1997), including at least eight Lane Co. records (Contreras 2002a), all from Eugene eastward into the Cascades (*ALC*). Rare spring migrants have been recorded along the coast in Coos, Lincoln, Tillamook, and Clatsop counties, usually at feeders (Hunn and Mattocks 1981b, Gilligan et al. 1994). It is also occasionally reported from the Rogue Valley in spring and summer (Gilligan et al. 1994, Lillie 2000). There are no reliable winter records.

**Habitat and Diet:** Summer habitat in e. Oregon includes canyons, juniper woodlands, and desert riparian zones (Contreras and Kindschy 1996). In the foothills of the Blue and Wallowa Mtns, found along stream bottoms and gulches (Evanich 1990). Also inhabits oak and scrub areas, open woodlands, and towns (Gilligan et al. 1994). Breeding habitat along Little Sheep Cr. in ne. Oregon consists of dry canyonlands with thick riparian growth; and includes the nearby town of Imnaha, with ornamental plantings and gardens (Evanich 1990). These observations are consistent with studies from other parts of its range where nests are typically found in riparian corridors of willow and cottonwood in arid regions, often in canyons (Baltosser and Russell 2000). Adult males may select drier habitats nearby (Baltosser and Russell 2000). Migrants in se. and sc. Oregon use desert oases and towns (Gilligan et al. 1994).

Nest is "a beautiful cup," made of plant down, and usually within a few feet of the ground (Gabrielson and Jewett 1940). Nests from other parts of its range composed of cottonwood or willow down and held together with spider webs and insect cocoon fibers (Baltosser and Russell 2000). In its southern breeding range it is known to use a wide variety of riparian trees and shrubs, orchard trees, or introduced shrubs and vines in urban areas as substrates (Brown 1992).

Diet studies have not been conducted in Oregon. Elsewhere it has been observed using a wide variety of nectar plants. Some of the most important groups include penstemon, larkspur, paintbrush, and sage (Baltosser and Russell 2000), all of which occur in Oregon.

**Seasonal Activity and Behavior:** They begin arriving in mid- to late Apr with peak migration mid- to late May (Gilligan et al. 1994). There are at least four late Mar reports, all from west of the Cascades: two at Coos Bay, one at Shady Cove, Jackson Co., and one at Eugene (Browning 1975a, Gilligan et al. 1994, B. Gleason p.c.). Males wander and migrate early, arriving on breeding grounds before females (Gilligan et al. 1994). In the breeding season, males perform repeated shallow U-shaped dives, which are presumed to be an essential element of courtship, though they may also play a role in aggressive interactions (Baltosser and Russell 2000).

Breeding phenology is not well documented in Oregon. Fledged young have been reported mid-Jun to late Jul (n=5) (OBBA). Most males leave by early Aug, and females and immatures leave by late Aug (Gilligan et al. 1994). At least three females were at Malheur NWR HQ 6-7 Sep 2002 (*ALC*). Latest detection was a male 30 Sep 1998 at a feeder in Reedsport, Douglas Co. (Gilligan 1999).

**Detection:** Males distinctive if seen in good light, but sometimes confused with first-year male Anna's Hummingbirds. Can be detected by their unique calls.

**Population Status and Conservation:** Gabrielson and Jewett's (1940) inclusion of this species on Oregon's bird list was based on only two specimens. They attributed the low frequency of detection to a lack of permanent observers in e. Oregon, and presumed it to be a fairly regular migrant and local breeder there. The first record for Malheur NWR was in 1970 and by the 1980s it had become a regular spring migrant (Littlefield 1990a). Though reasons for this increase are not understood, data for the Pacific Northwest suggests it has become more common and widespread in the region (Baltosser and Russell 2000), and in Oregon specifically (Browning 1975a). The introduction of food supplies, in the form of exotic plants and hummingbird feeders, has significantly affected this and other hummingbird species rangewide, primarily by increasing population levels and vagrant occurrences in urban settings (Baltosser and Russell 2000).—*Mike Patterson and Rachel White Scheuering*

## Anna's Hummingbird *Calypte anna*

Anna's Hummingbird, the largest hummingbird common to our region, is a recent addition to the avifauna of the Pacific Northwest. It is the only hummingbird regularly found in Oregon in winter, during which time it is exposed to short daylengths, limited sources of food, and periods of intense cold. It has successfully withstood ambient temperatures in Portland as low as 12° F (-11°C) (Taylor and Kamp 1985). It is more vocal than most other hummingbirds, with males uttering a dry, scratchy buzz of a song that can be heard throughout the year.

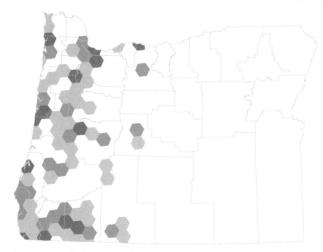

**General Distribution:** A year-round resident of the Pacific coast from s. British Columbia to n. Baja California. Partial postbreeding dispersal occurs casually north to s. coastal Alaska, east to w. Montana and c. New Mexico, and south into nc. Mexico. Rare and irregular migrant through the w. and se. U.S. Monotypic (AOU 1957).

**Oregon Distribution:** A rare to locally uncommon summer resident west of the Cascades in interior valleys and along the coast; also along the Columbia R. east to The Dalles (Gilligan et al. 1994). Occurs and probably breeds into the w. Cascades at some urban developments such as Oakridge (MGH). In winter, uncommon to fairly common in w. Oregon at lower elevations, especially where feeders are present (Contreras 1997b). Casual winter visitor in s. Cascades at Toketee Ranger Station, elevation 2,550 ft (777 m) (Fix 1990a).

In e. Oregon, locally uncommon in spring and summer in several locations along the eastern flank of the Cascades, with most reports from the Klamath Basin and c. Oregon (Deschutes, Crook, and Jefferson counties.) (Gilligan et al. 1994). Breeding suspected in and around Bend, where it is the most common hummingbird species in summer (Crabtree 1983). Has been found as far east as Ukiah, Umatilla Co. (Evanich 1993). Though generally absent east of the Cascades in winter, birds have overwintered in Bend (Gilligan et al. 1994, Korpi 1998).

**Habitat and Diet:** Preferred breeding habitat includes urban areas and parks, especially if they include flowering exotic plants (Gilligan et al. 1994, Russell 1996). Almost never seen away from urban habitats except in shrubland communities of c. and sw. Oregon (MGH). It is regular in summer in chaparral-oak areas of the lower Rogue R. and Bear Cr. valleys (Browning 1975a). Also use brushy riparian creek bottoms in the lowland valleys of c. Douglas Co. (Evanich 1990, Hunter et al. 1998). Known breeding habitats in California also include coastal scrub (Russell 1996).

Winter habitats are almost exclusively near human habitations with steady food resources and available dense cover for nighttime roosts (MP). In especially cold weather birds may ameliorate exposure by roosting near external sources of heat such as chimneys or lights (Taylor and Kamp 1985).

A nest in an ornamental pine tree in downtown Medford had an exterior of lichens bound with spider webs (Paczolt 1987). It was on a branch 10 ft (3 m) up from the ground and secured to the top of a pine cone, with the "nest and cone blending so well as to make the nest invisible" (Paczolt 1987).

Diet unstudied in Oregon. It is known to utilize many plants, for example penstemon, manzanita, and columbine (Russell 1996), all of which occur in Oregon. Cultivated fuchsias, azaleas, and other winter-blooming ornamentals attract them as well (DBM, MP). Also use sap wells left by sapsuckers, when available, for sap and trapped insects (Russell 1996). Insects are captured by hawking or gleaning from plants or spider webs. A bird near Brookings in late Mar was observed feeding among willow catkins and salmonberry (Browning and English 1967a). Observed at Toketee Ranger Station, near Roseburg, during winter, gleaning among mountain whitethorn bushes and beneath eaves of a residence (Fix 1990a). Hummingbird feeders, flowers in actively managed winter gardens, and arthropods provide primary winter diet (MP). May enter torpor while roosting if available energy reserves fall below nominal levels (Russell 1996).

**Seasonal Activity and Behavior:** Arrives in c. Oregon in late Apr or early May (Gilligan et al. 1994), but breeding activities begin earlier in w. Oregon. Rangewide, adult males defend territories with spectacular dive displays, climbing to a height of about 100 ft (30 m) and plummeting in a vertical dive, ending with a loud rattling squeak (Russell 1996). Timing of these displays in Oregon is not well known.

At a nest in Medford, egg laying estimated to begin 27 Jan, based on mid-Feb hatch date for two young (Paczolt 1987). In Newberg a nest was found in Feb 1992 (D. Powers p.c.). A nest located in Portland in 1981 had two young on 30 Mar that fledged on 18 Apr (Hunn and Mattocks 1981b). OBBA records show eggs in nest on 5 Apr and young or fledglings mid-Mar through early Jul (n=5).

Postbreeding movements are difficult to assess. They usually depart c. Oregon by mid-Oct, and numbers in w. Oregon begin increasing during Sep and Oct (Gilligan et al. 1994). Wintering populations appear to be greater than breeding populations, suggesting some northward migration from California (MP).

**Detection:** The only hummingbird species regularly found in winter. Often first detected by diagnostic vocalizations including a complex squeaky song and numerous chittery call notes.

**Population Status and Conservation:** Oregon's first record was 17 Dec 1944, at North Bend, Coos Co. (Contreras 1999b) and first specimen (SOU) 20 Mar 1966, at Brookings, Curry Co. (Browning and English 1967a). By the 1960s it had become established, and range expansion occurred rapidly thereafter (Zimmerman 1973). BBS shows breeding populations in Oregon steadily increasing ever since mid-1980s (Sauer et al. 2001). Human activities have undoubtedly had an impact on the population status of this species, e.g., feeders have probably raised population levels in urban areas. Also, this species is probably more dependent on introduced garden flowers than other hummingbird species (*MP*). Nevertheless, none of these possible associations have been studied.—*Mike Patterson and Rachel White Scheuering*

## Costa's Hummingbird *Calypte costae*

This attractive hummingbird primarily inhabits Sonoran and Mojave desert and s. Great Basin scrub, and coastal scrub. The adult male Costa's crown and gorget reflect iridescent purple and blue, with the gorget extending past the wing shoulder. The female has green upperparts, an unmarked throat (may have a small purple patch), and white underparts. Costa's Hummingbirds tend to pump their tails up and down while feeding, as do Black-chins. The male's display is a series of loop dives with an accompanying whistle.

**General Distribution:** Breeds from c. California (including Channel Is.), s. Nevada and sw. Utah, s. Arizona to s. Baja California and adjacent islands, Sonora, and sw. New Mexico. Winters from s. California and s. Arizona, south to Baja California and nw. coastal Mexico. They have been documented in small numbers north to sw. British Columbia, Oregon, c. Nevada, and east to c. and s. Texas, accidental s. coastal Alaska; there is a sight report for s. Alberta. Monotypic (AOU 1957, Baltosser and Scott 1996).

**Oregon Distribution:** Known from sight records only. Very rare spring and summer visitant to c. and sw. Oregon and coastal locations (Summers and Miller 1993, Gilligan et al. 1994, Patterson 1998b). Records exist during spring and breeding months in Clatsop, Clackamas, Lane, Jackson, and Deschutes counties, and during postbreeding in Lincoln, coastal Lane, Clackamas, Mutnomah, Douglas, and Jackson counties (Baltosser 1989). A nesting attempt occurred near Harbor, Curry Co. (Johnson J. 1992a) but this female appeared to be paired with a male Allen's Hummingbird (Gilligan et al. 1994). Males are sometimes present for the entire year in the Rogue Valley (*DPV*). A male visited a feeder in Grants Pass during most months (except about late Jun to mid-Sep) 1996-99 (*DPV*). A male visited a Central Point feeder continuously for 2 yr (1997-98) until the feeder was removed (A. Buckmaster p.c.). Costa's is a very rare fall and winter visitor to coastal and Portland area locations (Contreras 1997b, Contreras 1998, Tice 1998a). A male visited a Bend area feeder from 1984 to 1988 during spring/summer seasons (T. Crabtree p.c.). There were 24 Oregon sight records 1972-92 (Gilligan et al. 1994), and 27 reported (some possible repeats) in *Oregon Birds* during 1993-2000: one on the central coast, 10 in the Rogue Valley, one in the Umpqua Valley, four in the Portland area, eight in Bend, and three in the Klamath Falls area.

**Habitat and Diet:** Little is known about Oregon habitat preferences, as present knowledge is limited to urban, residential and other human habitation. Such areas may in fact be preferred by Costa's, as is true of Anna's Hummingbird. In the Rogue Valley, males have been observed in canopy-free riparian habitat along Bear Cr. and semi- open 10- to 15-ft (3- to 4.6-m) tall white oaks at the edge of Agate L. in winter, some distance from feeders (*DPV*). Food sources include: flower nectar and small insects and spiders obtained by fly-catching, hawking and gleaning. Feeders appear to be an important nectar substitute for birds in Oregon. They likely forage for small insects in riparian habitat in the Rogue Valley (*DPV*).

**Seasonal Activity and Behavior:** Arrival dates in the Bend area are 30 Mar to 20 May (n=5) (T. Crabtree p.c.); in the Roseburg-Sutherlin area 4 Apr 1990, 27 Apr 1989 (R. Maertz p.c.). A displaying male was seen late Apr 1989 in the n. Umpqua Valley (R. Maertz p.c.). The only known Oregon nesting attempt, a female on eggs in mid-Jun 1991, failed when the nest was destroyed by a passing vehicle (Johnson J 1992a). Departure dates not well documented; one individual was seen 11 Nov 1977 in the Roseburg area (R. Maertz p.c.). Oregon sight reports include all months of year.

**Detection:** Many birds may go undetected because of similarity with other hummingbird species, especially females. Most observations are feeder-related males detected by sight.

**Population Status and Conservation:** Breeding range appears to be expanding north in coastal and c. California (Small 1994). Since Oregon's first record in 1972, sight reports have steadily increased (Gilligan et al. 1994, Contreras 1997b). Increased reports may be due to improved identification efforts at feeders.— *Dennis P. Vroman*

## Calliope Hummingbird *Stellula calliope*

This tiny jewel is the smallest breeding bird in N. America and the smallest long-distance avian migrant in the world (Calder and Calder 1994). The average weight of males is approximately 0.09 oz (2.6 g), about half that of an Anna's Hummingbird (Calder and Calder 1994), and little more than the weight of a penny. Breeds predominately in mountain habitats, and despite its diminutive size successfully withstands the chilly summer nights at high elevations. The iridescent burgundy-red gorget of the adult male is separated into distinct rays that fan across its throat, unlike any other N. American hummingbird. The female closely resembles female Rufous and Allen's Hummingbirds, but is smaller with a shorter bill, and a shorter tail with less rust at its base (Kaufman 1990).

**General Distribution:** Breeds in mountains from c. British Columbia to c. California, Nevada, and Utah, and east to Wyoming. Winters in Mexico. Johnsgard (1997) recognized two subspecies, a northern subspecies and another he erroneously believed to be endemic to Mexico, but the latter was based on a migrant (*MRB*); the species does not breed there (AOU 1998). We follow AOU (1957) and others in considering the species to be monotypic.

**Oregon Distribution:** A common summer resident of the Blue and Wallowa mountains and other high ranges east of the Cascade summit, including Steens and Hart mountains (Gabrielson and Jewett 1940, Gilligan et al. 1994). "Almost a guaranteed species" in the Blue Mtn. foothills along the Grande Ronde R. near La Grande (Evanich 1990). Spring and fall migrants are rare to locally uncommon at lower elevations elsewhere east of the Cascades (Littlefield 1990a, Gilligan et al. 1994). Based on accumulating records from the Alvord Basin, Littlefield (1990a) speculated that this valley might be an important migration corridor to and from mountains in e. Oregon.

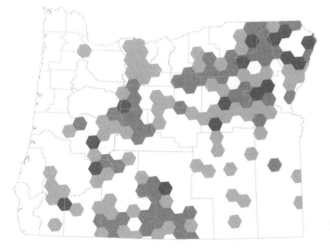

In the w. Cascades, scattered records exist from Mt. Hood to Crater L. NP (Farner 1952, Eltzroth 1984), but repeat observations are rare and nesting has not been documented. At Thorn Prairie, Douglas Co., this species is a regular summer resident (Fix 1990a). Generally very uncommon to rare north of there, at moderate to high elevations (*MGH*).

West of the Cascades, it is locally uncommon in the Siskiyou Mtns. and the Rogue Valley (Browning 1975a, Gilligan et al. 1994). Spring migrants are rare in the Willamette Valley and along the coast, though reports appear to be increasing (Lillie 1997, 1998). It has been a rare but regular spring migrant in the foothills of central Lane Co. since at least the mid-1970s (*ALC*). Multiple females and/or juveniles have been seen almost annually in Jun-Jul on Saddle Mtn., Clatsop Co., since 1995; its status there is unknown (*MP*). A single bird was reported at Eugene during the winter of 1980-81 but without details or documentation (Gilligan et al. 1994).

**Habitat and Diet:** Calliopes frequent open mountain meadows (Gabrielson and Jewett 1940). They are also found in open forests, meadow edges, and riparian areas. They breed mainly at middle elevations, but also occasionally down to lower forest margins and as high as timberline (Gilligan et al. 1994). They are regular in ceanothus in the Rogue Valley (Gilligan et al. 1994). Calliopes can be found in various habitats in the Diamond L. area: clearcuts with an understory including snowbrush, currant, and greenleaf manzanita; montane riparian mostly above 3.500 ft (1.067 m) with willows, Sitka alder, red-osier dogwood, shrubs, and nearby meadows; at human habitations; and at timberline, mostly above 7,000 ft (2,134 m; Fix 1990a). In the Wallowa Mtns. they are associated with areas such as Moss Springs, elevation 6,000 ft (1,829 m), characterized by rocky terrain; streams with lush understory; dense coniferous forests of high-elevation tree species such as white fir, larch, lodgepole pine, and Engelmann spruce; and open grassy meadows with abundant wildflowers (Evanich 1990). They are often detected along the Grande Ronde R. in boggy willow thickets, with nearby groves of cottonwood and alder interspersed with ponderosa pines (Evanich 1990). Territorial males there are typically seen perched on the highest available willow branch (Evanich 1990).

Nests at Fort Cr. near Fort Klamath were described as averaging 1.25 in (3.2 cm) across and 1.25 in (3.2 cm) deep on the outside; with the inner cup 0.75 in (1.9 cm) wide by 0.5 in (1.3 cm) deep, constructed of bits of bark and cone and lined with willow down (Bendire 1895). These nests were typically placed on or adjacent to dry cones on small dead limbs of lodgepole pine, 8-15 ft (2.4-4.5 m) off the ground. The majority were "ingeniously saddled on two small cones, [with their] outward appearance resembling a cone very closely," and positioned beneath larger branches for protection (Bendire 1895).

Diet not studied in Oregon. Observed elsewhere to take nectar from various flowers, typically tubular ones such as squaw currant, paintbrushes, monkeyflowers, penstemons, and scarlet gilia (Calder and Calder 1994), all of which can be found in Oregon. They have been seen feeding on flowering madrone at Skinner's Butte, Lane Co. (Fix 1985d). Birds arriving in British Columbia before flowers bloom consume small insects (Armstrong 1987).

**Seasonal Activity and Behavior:** Most arrive mid-Apr to early May (Gilligan et al. 1994). The earliest detection is 22 Mar 1998 at Lebanon, Linn Co. (Lillie 1998). Based on rangewide migratory patterns, males are assumed to arrive first. By the end of May, birds have traveled to montane breeding territories (*MP*). Breeding phenology is not well described for Oregon. Males on territory perform dive displays, a series of U-shaped plunges from a height of 33-98 ft (10-30 m), that function variably as courtship displays and agonistic behavior (Calder and Calder 1994). As many as 15-20 males have been observed displaying at Thorn Prairie, Douglas Co., and displays there have been reported mid- to late May (Irons 1984b, Sawyer 1985, Fix 1990a). Most adult males have left Oregon by early Jul, and most females and immatures leave late Aug-early Sep (Gilligan et al. 1994). A few records exist for late Sep.

**Detection:** Males aggressively defend territories in the breeding season; dive displays are conspicuous. Males are also noticeable atop "lookout" perches on breeding territory. Adopt a low profile in migration and are likely to be overlooked among more pugnacious hummingbirds (Calder and Calder 1994).

**Population Status and Conservation:** Nesting in Oregon was first documented in the Wood R. Valley near Fort Klamath (Bendire 1895). Current status is not clearly understood. BBS data indicate a significant decline in Oregon's population, averaging -10.9 %/yr (Sauer et al. 2001), suggesting the need for increased monitoring.

At the same time, this species appears to be increasing its range west of the Cascades. Gabrielson and Jewett (1940) reported it only in e. Oregon, except for a small handful of records from the Siskiyou Mtns., and one from Douglas Co. It is now considered fairly common in the Siskiyous (Gilligan et al. 1994), and a regular summer resident in areas of Douglas Co., e.g., at Thorn Prairie (Fix 1990a). In 1984 no records existed for the coast (Eltzroth 1984), but by 1994 there were several spring records for Coos, Lincoln, and Clatsop counties (Gilligan et al. 1994), with more added almost every year (Lillie 1997, 1998, 2000). In addition, until recently it was considered a rare transient in the Willamette Valley. But in the mid-1970s they began to appear in the Eugene area (Eltzroth 1984), and now occur there annually in small numbers (Lillie 1997). From 2 Apr to 13 May 2000 there were 13 reports in the Willamette Valley (Lillie 2000).

However, these increases may actually reflect growing numbers of observers and improved road access to mountain habitats, rather than a growing population of birds (*MGH*). It has been noted elsewhere that forest openings caused by clearcutting may allow for increased growth of favored nectar flowers (Calder and Calder 1994). The long-term effects of deforestation are unknown, as are specific impacts of clearcutting in Oregon. As with all hummingbird species, populations are undoubtedly affected by supplemental food sources provided by feeders.— *Rachel White Scheuering and Mike Patterson*

## Broad-tailed Hummingbird
*Selasphorus platycercus*

Perhaps the most enigmatic hummingbird found regularly in Oregon, the Broad-tailed Hummingbird has so far eluded documentation of its breeding in the state, likely due to identification uncertainties and the remoteness of its preferred habitat. Primarily a Rocky Mtn. species, its hard-to-define breeding range seems to reach its limit at Oregon's eastern edges, where reports of this beautiful and rare species arise each summer. The relatively large adult male has a rose-red gorget and green plumage with no dorsal rufous coloration. Females and immatures are nearly indistinguishable in the field from those of the more common Rufous Hummingbird.

**General Distribution:** Breeds in the c. Rocky Mtns. from Idaho, Wyoming, and Colorado west to Nevada and south to Arizona and New Mexico. Also a rare breeder in e. Guatemala. Winters in Mexico and in the breeding range in Guatemala. Two subspecies; *S. p. platycercus* occurs in Oregon (AOU 1957).

**Oregon Distribution:** Poorly understood. A very uncommon summer resident and migrant in e. Oregon (Gilligan et al. 1994). The Blue and Wallowa mountains of ne. Oregon harbor local populations, and this species has been found there during the breeding season (Evanich 1981a). A few records hint at birds on breeding territories: an adult male at Spring Cr. near La Grande on 3 Jul 1981 appeared to have been displaying, and similar sightings have been reported from the Eagle Cap Wilderness Area, Wallowa Co. (Evanich 1981a). In se. Oregon they are reported fairly often from Steens Mtn. (Gabrielson and Jewett 1940, Contreras and Kindschy 1996) and Mahogany

Mtn. (Gilligan and Smith 1980, Spencer 1999); and encountered on Hart Mtn. during breeding season (Evanich 1981a). The OBBA found summering birds of both sexes in s. Malheur Co. Probably breeds locally in many of these areas, but nesting remains unconfirmed (Contreras and Kindschy 1996). Some of the records from se. Oregon such as those from Fields, Andrews, and Adel probably involve migrants, as these places are below the usual breeding elevations (Evanich 1981a).

Generally absent west of the Cascades, with a few notable exceptions. For several years in the late 1960s and early 1970s a displaying male came to a feeder at Shady Cove, Jackson Co. (Browning 1975a, Evanich 1981a). More recently, a male came to a feeder near Jacksonville 22 Jul 1998 (Tice 1999a). A male seen in Salem 1 May 2001 is the first known record for the Willamette Valley (Lillie 2001). No winter records.

**Habitat and Diet:** Found in Oregon's mountains, especially in canyons with riparian vegetation and in subalpine meadows (Contreras and Kindschy 1996). Known breeding habitats elsewhere are at high elevations, mostly in dense streamside thickets (including willow, alder, or dogwood) amid coniferous forests with aspen, Douglas-fir, and ponderosa pine (Calder and Calder 1992).

Nests have not been described in Oregon. They are known to construct nests of plant fibers bound with spider webs, and to camouflage exterior with lichens, bits of bark, and moss (Calder and Calder 1992). The nest is usually within 1-5 ft (0.3-1.5 m) of ground, and often shielded by an overhanging branch (Calder and Calder 1992).

Diet is unstudied in Oregon, but known nectar plants from other parts of the range include red tubular flowers such as paintbrushes, scarlet gilia, and penstemon (Calder and Calder 1992), which occur in Oregon as well. Earlier in spring they may also feed at pussywillows, currants, or black twinberry (Calder and Calder 1992). Also take small insects in the air or by gleaning. Birds may enter torpor at night in response to inadequate energy intake (Calder and Calder 1992).

**Seasonal Activity and Behavior:** Probably arrive in mid-Apr; arrival data are scarce. The earliest reliable observation is 12 Apr 1997 at Mosier, Wasco Co. (Sullivan 1997b). They have been observed setting up temporary territories at feeders in residential areas in ne. Oregon for a few weeks during May before disappearing, presumably into higher elevations to breed (Evanich 1981a). Courtship display of males is a series of high climbs and dives near a perched female. Males also defend territory by issuing a vocal challenge (a raspy chitter) and/or chasing intruders (Calder and Calder 1992).

Based on rangewide studies, breeding season is known to correlate with the brief flowering season of high-elevation meadows (Calder and Calder 1992), e.g., breeding in Colorado occurs late May to late Jul (Johnsgard 1997). Males do not participate in nesting and depart before females and juveniles (Calder and Calder 1992). The latest detection is 4 Sep 1994 on Steens Mtn. (Sullivan PT 1995b).

**Detection:** The most distinctive characteristic of males is a unique metallic trilling sound produced by wing tips in flight. In forested areas this bird can be difficult to detect unless the male's trilling is heard. Females and juveniles lack this trill, and as with all *Selasphorus* can be very difficult to identify.

**Population Status and Conservation:** Difficult to assess. In 1980 this species was removed from the OBRC review list, and it was no longer considered a rare bird in the state (Irons and Watson 1984). However, the lack of field observers in some of the remote areas of e. Oregon continues to confound attempts to define this species' status and distribution in Oregon. Breeding populations over its range appear to be stable (Sauer et al. 2001), but focused study is needed in Oregon.—*Rachel White Scheuering and Mike Patterson*

### Rufous Hummingbird *Selasphorus rufus*

The Rufous Hummingbird is the most common and widespread of Oregon hummingbirds. This rusty-red and fearless nectar feeder is a popular yard bird, inspiring even the most modest of nature lovers to set up a feeder of sugar water and become a bird watcher. Rufous Hummingbird may also be the most wide ranging hummingbird in N. America. It has occurred in every state and most Canadian provinces. Increased awareness of hummingbird field marks by feeder watchers, and capture efforts by avocational banders, are largely responsible for increasing our understanding of distribution patterns of the species (Heidcamp 1997).

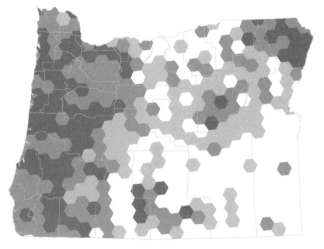

**General Distribution:** Breeds from s. Alaska south to just north of the California line, and east to Idaho and Montana. Occurs throughout the w. U.S. in postbreeding dispersal. Most winter in c. Mexico, but a few regularly winter along the Gulf Coast; casual elsewhere in the U.S. during migration and winter. Monotypic (AOU 1957).

**Oregon Distribution:** Common transient and breeder throughout most of w. Oregon, especially in forested regions. It is uncommon on the east slope of the Cascades, uncommon at higher elevations of the Blue Mtns., and uncommon to fairly common in the Wallowa Mtns. (Evanich 1992a, Gilligan et al. 1994, OBBA). Summering birds are rare in arid se. Oregon (Littlefield 1990, Gilligan et al. 1994, OBBA) where they are usually found in areas with trees, deciduous shrubs, flowers, and water (Gilligan et al. 1994, *MGH*). Breeding has not been confirmed in Harney and Malheur counties (Contreras and Kindschy 1996), the Columbia Plateau, or c. Oregon (OBBA). Most winter records of *Selasphorus* hummingbirds in w. Oregon have been assumed to be this species, but no thorough documentation of these individuals has been obtained.

**Habitat and Diet:** Found in a wide variety of habitats, though it shows a breeding preference for wooded areas with a fairly high canopy and well-developed understory. Nests are usually built between near ground level and 16 ft (5 m) in understory foliage or low branches of evergreen trees (Johnsgard 1997). The nest is typically constructed from fine plant material, animal fur, and spider webs. The outside is camouflaged with bits of lichen, moss, and bark (Baicich and Harrison 1997). Nests are regularly reused from year to year though it is not clear that they are reused by the same individual (Calder 1993).

Many sources tie spring arrival to early blooming plants such as flowering currant, salmonberry, and pacific madrone (Johnsgard 1997). While these are undoubtedly important nectar sources, neither currant nor salmonberry regularly bloom until mid-Mar (Haskin 1934), though the latter has been found in bloom by late Jan on the Oregon coast in some years (M. Denny p.c.). Birds are probably dependent on insects gleaned from willow catkins and beneath leaves in the first few weeks after arrival and are also more likely to take advantage of hummingbird feeders (Calder 1993).

A state of torpor can be induced when air temperatures drop below 50°F (10°C), reducing energy requirements to about 7% of active body temperature. Entry into torpor is regulated by energy reserves and is more likely to occur during periods when food resources are low. Arousal to a higher metabolic rate is triggered by daylight (Calder 1993).

Dispersal to higher elevations and into c. and e. Oregon may be more closely tied to the availability of nectar-producing plants (Calder 1993). Preference is shown for tubular flowers, including paintbrushes, columbine, and penstemons, which are more likely to contain nectar. Grant and Grant (1967) were able to demonstrate a significant benefit to scarlet gilia from cross pollination by Rufous Hummingbirds.

**Seasonal Activity and Behavior:** In most years, they begin to arrive in w. Oregon in mid-Feb. First detections are invariably along the s. Oregon coast; the earliest arrival date is 19 Jan 1998 at Coos Bay, Coos Co. (Thomas 1999). The average arrival date for Curry Co. is 2 Feb; Lincoln Co. 15 Feb; and 3 Mar for Clatsop Co. (composite of data from *Oregon Birds* field notes, *MP*). Western interior valley arrival dates fall behind coastal dates by about 1 wk. Peak migratory movements occur from late Mar through the first wk of Apr (*MP*). There are very few first detection reports e. of the Cascades, but arrival is probably discretionary and weather dependent, ranging from late Mar through Apr (Littlefield 1990a, Calder 1993). Arrival in the Blue Mtns. is typically during the first week of Apr (M. Denny p.c.).

*Rufous Hummingbird*

Males arrive about 2 wk before females, presumably to set up territories. Males select a prominent perch from which to watch a territory and vigorously defend it. Territory size is determined by availability of food resources. Males are polygynous and do not participate in nesting (Calder 1993).

Males move away from breeding territories as early as Jun. Some females and immature birds begin dispersal in Jul but a female has been found feeding young in the nest as late as 28 Jul 2001 near Zigzag, Clackamas Co. (B. Altman p.c.). Postbreeding dispersal has confused the issue of breeding ranges somewhat and many high Cascades, Wallowa, and se. Oregon montane records may be of dispersed birds rather than breeders. Males will use displays generally associated with breeding purely in defense of feeding territories (Calder 1993). Most leave the state by late Aug, though a few are encountered into Sep (composite of *Oregon Birds* field notes).

There are scattered winter records of *Selasphorus* hummingbirds from CBCs, most in the Willamette Valley (Shipman 1998). All recent winter records are associated with hummingbird feeders.

**Detection:** Separation from Allen's Hummingbird should be done with care. Adult males with mostly rufous backs may be safely identified, but some males may have significant amounts of green in the back (Patterson 1990, McKenzie and Robbins 1999). It is generally believed that green-backed males are second-year birds, but ageing of this species needs more investigation (Pyle 1997).

Most field guides published before the late 1990s describe the Rufous display as oval (e.g., Johnsgard 1997). This is incorrect. The display is more properly described as a series of J-shaped high dives (e.g., Sibley 2000) with a loud "zubbing" sound at the bottom of each arc. The upward return from each dive also approximates a J-shape, but is a less strictly held pattern (Hunn 1983, Calder 1993, *MP*).

Rufous females and immature birds have wider rectrices than Allen's, but this is extremely difficult to see in the field (Stiles 1972, Heidcamp 1997). Female and immature *Selasphorus* hummingbirds cannot be safely sorted except by range or in-hand measurements.

**Population Status and Conservation:** They were first recorded by Lewis and Clark at the mouth of the Columbia R. in 1806 and were well studied by Kobbe there in 1900 (Gabrielson and Jewett 1940, Johnsgard 1997). A downward trend in population for Oregon is indicated by BBS data (Sauer et al. 1997). Reasons for this are unclear and deserve further study. Artificial feeders provide supplemental food in times of low availability of natural resources, but may also increase potential for predation, disease, and window collision (Calder 1993).—*Mike Patterson*

## Allen's Hummingbird *Selasphorus sasin*

Allen's Hummingbird is a common breeder in the coastal fog belt from California into s. Oregon. It is closely related to the more wide-ranging Rufous Hummingbird. As is often the case with sibling species, the subtle differences in plumage, behavior, and vocalization are more apparent to the species involved than they are to a human observer. Adult males have a red gorget and a bright, reddish-brown body with an iridescent bronze-green back. Females and immatures are identifiable only in the hand, and even adult males can present a special challenge.

**General Distribution:** Breeds along the coasts of California and s. Oregon. Winters mostly in c. Mexico, and casually along Gulf coast to Alabama. Two subspecies; *S. s. sasin* occurs in Oregon (AOU 1957).

**Oregon Distribution:** This is a fairly common spring and summer resident along the s. Oregon coast as far north as Bandon (Gilligan et al. 1994) and is uncommon up the Coquille Valley to Powers; breeding has been verified only in Curry Co. (OBBA). It is very uncommon at Coos Bay and rare at Reedsport, Douglas Co. (Gilligan at al. 1994). In s. Curry Co., Rufous Hummingbird is thought to be limited to higher-elevation inland areas while Allen's breeds on the outer coast (D. Munson p.c.).

It occurs as a very rare vagrant in other parts of w. Oregon, but physical similarities to Rufous Hummingbird make reports difficult to evaluate. A specimen obtained in 1983 from Philomath, Benton Co., was confirmed as an Allen's (Patterson 1987). A pair of *Selasphorus* hummingbirds that was netted, measured, and photographed 10 Mar 1988 at Astoria, Clatsop Co., was identified with near certainty as this species—but that far north of their expected range they were most likely accidentals (Patterson 1988, Patterson 1990, Gilligan et al. 1994). This is a very rare summer visitant in the Rogue Valley (Gilligan et al. 1994).

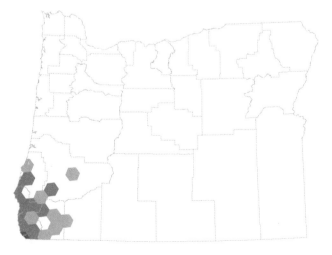

Individuals reported by OBBA in Josephine Co. may have been transients rather than breeders (*MP*). There are no confirmed winter records but see the Rufous Hummingbird account for identification issues.

**Habitat and Diet:** Very little information for Oregon. Rangewide, known to breed only in the narrow, moist coastal fog zone (Mitchell 2000). Males select territories in open areas of coastal scrub, showing a preference for willow, blackberry, and poison oak (Mitchell 2000, *MP*). Females choose nesting sites in wooded areas away from male territories, often in dense vegetation with at least some cover (Johnsgard 1997, Mitchell 2000). Favored nest substrates in California include dense riparian tangles such as blackberry vines or fern thickets (Mitchell 2000). Nests are usually placed fairly low and constructed from plant down and spider webs, camouflaged with lichen, bark, and conifer needles (Baicich and Harrison 1997). No nests have been described for Oregon.

Very little is known about specific feeding preferences in Oregon. Nectar sources identified in California include ceanothus, Pacific madrone, monkey-flowers, and mint—all of which occur in Oregon as well (Johnsgard 1997). Birds in Santa Cruz, California, have been seen hawking insects and possibly picking ants off the ground (Johnsgard 1997). They are regularly reported at hummingbird feeders in Curry Co.

**Seasonal Activity and Behavior:** Spring migrants arrive early, beginning in late Feb. Males arrive first, followed by females, and by late Mar most have returned (Gilligan et al. 1994). Displaying males produce a series of pendulum arcs ending in a final J-shaped high dive (Johnsgard 1997).

The nesting period in Oregon is unknown, but probably Mar through May (*MP*). Males mist-netted in mid-Jun at higher elevations in e. Curry Co. and Josephine Co. suggest a postbreeding dispersal upslope into the Siskiyous (D. Vroman p.c.). Fall migration begins early, peaking in Jul, and few are recorded after early Aug, though this may be a result of identification uncertainties with females and immatures (Gilligan et al. 1994). Reports of *Selasphorus* hummingbirds on the s. coast into Sep could include this species.

**Detection:** Males in flight produce a metallic buzz with wingtips. Also command attention during breeding season with agonistic and/or courtship dive displays, and when chasing intruders off their territories. Males on territory often perch conspicuously on exposed branches (Mitchell 2000).

**Population Status and Conservation:** Survey-wide, BBS data show declining numbers, though no statistically significant trends (Sauer et al. 2001). In general, analysis of BBS data for this and other hummingbird species is limited by low detectability. Confusion with Rufous Hummingbird also makes the Oregon status of this species unclear. Male and female *Selasphorus* hummingbirds captured and measured in Clatsop Co. (Patterson 1988, Patterson 1990) were likely this species, although they appeared to be intermediate based on the keys from Stiles (1972). McKenzie and Robbins (1999) suggest that birds with intermediate characters are possibly Rufous x Allen's hybrids, though they were unable to show an increase in frequency of intermediate characters in the zone of sympatry. There are no proven records of hybridization between the two species. Hybrids have been found between Allen's and Anna's hummingbirds, which show similar habitat preferences and a significant overlap in range (Johnsgard 1997). A focused study in the extremely narrow zone of Rufous/Allen's sympatry (i.e., n. Curry Co. and extreme s. Coos Co. near the outer coast) would help in sorting out status and ecology of this superspecies in our region.—*Mike Patterson and Rachel White Scheuering*

# Order CORACIIFORMES
## *Family Alcedinidae*

### Subfamily Cerylinae

**Belted Kingfisher** *Ceryle alcyon*
This majestically crested bird is often heard before being seen due to its conspicuous harsh rattling call. It is slate-blue with white underparts and pectoral band. Unusual sexual dimorphism is shown by the presence of a single blue-gray breast-band on the male bird, while the more colorful female also exhibits a rufous lower breast-band and rufous flanks often concealed by closed wings.

**General Distribution:** Found across N. America except the Arctic, from Canada south to n. S. America. Subspecies are weakly defined (Todd 1963) and Phillips (1962) considered the species monotypic. Two subspecies are recognized provisionally; *C. a. caurina* in Oregon (*MRB*).

**Oregon Distribution:** This is a common permanent resident throughout most of the state, except in n. Lake and e. Deschutes counties, where open water is generally absent (OBBA, Gilligan et al. 1994). It is local in s. Harney and Malheur counties, in agricultural areas along the Columbia R., and at high elevations where habitat is limited (OBBA).

During winter, kingfishers will withdraw from areas where ice is present on feeding sites (Fix 1991, Evanich 1992a, Contreras and Kindschy 1996). It is known to

*Belted Kingfisher*

attempt to winter up to 2,400 ft (800 m) in e. Douglas Co. (Fix 1990a). It remains throughout e. Oregon where open water permits (CBC); in Klamath Co. it uses open water found along geothermal water routes in towns (K. Spencer p.c.).

**Habitat and Diet:** Kingfishers are most frequently associated with lake and pond shorelines and islands, as well as coastal dunes with ponds and widely scattered shrubs and trees, w. Oregon riparian woodland, streamside, wetland shrublands, and the edges of freshwater marshes (OBBA). In a c. Coast Range study, kingfishers were more abundant in larger (6th-order) than in smaller (4th-order) streams, and used pool channel units more often than riffle channel units relative to their availability. In the same study, kingfishers were associated with the presence of streambank trees (presumably for perches) and unconstrained reaches, which often have greater abundance of small fish (Loegering and Anthony 1999).

Nests in earthen banks generally near water, but will also use ditches, road cuts, landfills, and sand or gravel pits (Hamas 1994), as well as headwall failures (Loegering and Anthony 1999). Both the male and female will excavate the nesting burrow, with the female working half as much as the male. Active nests are at least 31 in (80 cm) long (Hamas 1994). It often breeds near or alongside N. Rough-winged Swallows (M. Patterson p.c., S. Shunk p.c.).

Kingfishers hunt from a vantage point above water such as an overhead branch, telephone wires along a shore line, or pilings of piers. Diet consists primarily of fish but will take other prey such as mollusks, crustaceans, insects, amphibians, reptiles, young birds, small mammals, and in the winter even berries (Hamas 1994). In Clatsop Co., have caught three-spined stickleback and coho salmon smolts (M. Patterson p.c.). Indigestible parts of prey are regurgitated as pellets (Hamas 1994).

**Seasonal Activity and Behavior:** Somewhat difficult to determine onset of breeding. Adults entering probable nest sites were reported 30 Apr to 15 Jul (n=16); carrying of food into nest sites and nests with young reported 8 Jun to 30 Jul (n=16); and fledged young observed 24 May to 3 Aug (n=9) (OBBA). Fall movements are poorly known. Over 200 were along the Deschutes R. between Warm Springs and Sherar's Bridge, approximately 3.6 birds/mi (2.25 birds/km), 22-25 Sep 1987 (Anderson 1988b). A Lincoln Co. survey Nov 1993 to Jan 1994 found 13 males and seven females, which could indicate an unequal sex ratio in winter (R. Bayer p.c.).

**Detection:** Easy to locate by harsh rattle call, or scan shoreline for likely perches. Breeding locations easily confirmed by burrows chiseled out of cut banks (OBBA).

**Population Status and Conservation:** On four streams in the c. Oregon Coast Range in 1992, average densities of kingfishers ranged 5.3-7.2 individuals/6.25 mi (10 km) of stream (Loegering and Anthony 1999). Can be very common in good habitat: 38 pairs were found during a survey of the lower Luckiamute R., Polk Co., on 27 Jul 1974 (Crowell and Nehls 1974c). Oregon BBS data show a significant decline of 2.5%/yr during 1966-2000, but a non-significant increase 1966-79 and a non-significant decrease 1980-2000 (Sauer et al. 2001). Oregon CBC data show a non-significant 1%/yr increase 1959-88 (Sauer et al. 1996). Reasons for the trends are unknown.—*Luke Bloch*

# Order PICIFORMES
*Family Picidae*

## Subfamily Picinae

### Lewis's Woodpecker *Melanerpes lewis*
The Lewis's Woodpecker was named for Meriwether Lewis, who first described the species in 1805. This medium-sized, vaguely crow-like woodpecker relies on flycatching during the spring and summer and stored mast in the fall and winter. It is easily distinguished from other western woodpeckers by its flycatching behavior and its distinctive plumage. Adults have

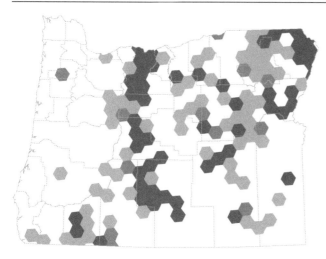

iridescent greenish-black backs, silvery gray collars and breasts, and red facial patches and bellies. This is one of several species that have experienced drastic declines in breeding range in the state.

**General Distribution:** Breeds from s. British Columbia, sw. Alberta, Montana, and parts of S. Dakota and Nebraska south to c. California and portions of Colorado, Arizona, and New Mexico. Winters in milder portions of this range from n. Oregon south to n. Mexico and w. Texas. Monotypic (AOU 1957).

**Oregon Distribution:** Formerly widespread (Gabrielson and Jewett 1940). It is currently common year-round only in the white oak-ponderosa pine belt east of Mt. Hood. Also, it breeds in low numbers in open habitat along e. Oregon river and stream valleys such as the John Day, Grande Ronde, lower Deschutes, Wallowa, Imnaha, Burnt (Baker Co.), and Klamath rivers, and Squaw (Jefferson and Deschutes counties), Murderers (Grant Co.), and Pike creeks (Harney Co.) (Thomas 1979, K. Spencer p.c., *CG, DBM*, BBS, OBBA). In w. Oregon, this was a fairly common summer resident in Jackson Co. as recently as 1975 (Browning 1975a), and is listed as breeding by Janes et al. (2001), but with few recent breeding records. Winters in oak savannah east of Mt. Hood, in the upper Rogue R. valley and along Bear Cr. in the Medford area (Browning 1975a, CBC); uncommon and very local in the Willamette Valley, especially in recent years (*ALC*), occasional in Josephine Co. (D. Vroman p.c.); casual in Umpqua Valley (Hunter et al. 1998). Winter populations depend on the availability of acorns and fluctuate with the amount and location of the acorn crop. A regular transient in small numbers west of the Cascades, uncommon east of the Cascades, and most common in open habitats (e.g., burns) in and near Cascade forests. Very rare on the coast.

**Habitat and Diet:** Associated with open woodland habitat near water. Primarily breeds in Oregon white oak, ponderosa pine, and riparian cottonwood communities. Winters in oak savannah.

Important components of breeding habitat include an open woodland canopy and large-diameter dead or dying trees. They seldom excavate their own nest cavities; most often reusing existing nest holes excavated by other woodpeckers such as Northern Flicker and Hairy Woodpecker (Bock 1970). For that reason nest trees are typically in an advanced state of decay. On the eastern edge of Mt. Hood NF, they nest in Oregon white oak-ponderosa pine savannah. Of 53 nests found in 1989, 43% were in Oregon white oak, 42% in ponderosa pine, 9% in Douglas fir, and 6% in cottonwood. The majority of oak nests were in living and declining trees. Nests in ponderosa pine were typically in snags in various decay stages, often with less than 50% of the bark remaining. The mean dbh of nest trees was 26 in (66 cm) with a range of 12.5-43 in (31.8-109 cm); the mean height of nest trees was 41 ft (12.5 m) with a range of 10-100 ft (3-30 m) (Galen 1989). In the Blue Mtns, nesting occurs along streams. Of 49 nests, 72% were in cottonwood, 12 % in ponderosa pine, 10% in juniper, 4% in willow, and 2% in fir (Thomas 1979). A nest was found in aspen at Mahogany Mtn., Malheur Co. (M. Denny p.c.).

Lewis's Woodpecker is an opportunistic feeder; foraging efforts focus on locally and temporarily abundant insect populations during spring and summer, and on ripe fruits and acorns during fall and winter (Bock 1970, Galen 1989). It catches insects by flycatching and gleaning; insects commonly included in diet are carpenter ants, bees, wasps, mayflies, beetles, and grasshoppers (Bock 1970, Tobalske 1997). Nest sites are often associated with streams, wet meadows, or dense shrub cover where insects are abundant. Often flies to higher elevations (e.g., Cascades) for fruits such as elderberry, currant, cherry, serviceberry, and poison oak. Acorns are harvested and shelled, mast is broken into pieces and stored in cracks in snags and power poles and crevices in bark of oak and pine to eat during the winter and early spring. Storage sites for mast are an essential component of winter habitat; they are often conspicuous by the accumulation of shells at a tree or snag base (Bock 1970, Galen 1989).

**Seasonal Activity and Behavior:** In a detailed study east of Mt. Hood, courtship began in Apr and continued through May with loud vocalizations and flight displays; eggs were incubated 13-16 days during May and early Jun; nestlings were present late May through mid-Jul; birds fledged in Jul and left the nest area seeking additional forage in early Aug; winter residents returned to oak habitat and began storing acorns in late Sep (Galen 1989). At Malheur NWR, where transient, average spring arrival is 26 Apr, peak of passage is 1-12 May; fall peak is 10-25 Sep (Littlefield 1990a). Migrants form flocks in Sep; up to 30-50 individuals were in a flock observed in Klamath Falls area in mid-Sep (K. Spencer p.c.). A regular movement of these woodpeckers occurs along Cascade ridges in fall; transients were observed in the Cascades of e. Douglas Co. 16 Aug- 2 Nov, most during Oct (Fix 1990a, D. Fix p.c.).

Birds defend the area in the immediate vicinity of their nest cavity during the breeding season and protect mast storage sites during fall and winter. Drumming and vocalizations are generally limited to the breeding season. Drumming is of low intensity and sounds like a faint creaky door. Vocalizations are loud and attract attention. Breeding males give a short, loud *churr* call 3-8 times in quick succession to attract a mate and defend the nest tree. Both sexes give chatter calls and alarm notes.

**Detection:** Easily detected during early breeding season when quite vocal and during the summer when flycatching behavior is conspicuous. Easy places to find this species are in the White R. W.A., oaks east of Mosier, Wasco Co., Klamath R. Canyon, Malheur NWR HQ in Sep, foothills around Medford in winter, and along numerous streams in e. Oregon.

**Population Status and Conservation:** It is declining throughout its range, possibly due to loss of suitable habitat, prospects for nest and food storage trees, competition for nest holes, and effects of pesticides (Tobalske 1997). Formerly, "abundant" in Oregon (Gabrielson and Jewett 1940), including the Willamette Valley, but substantially depleted in numbers since the 1960s and there have been no nesting records in the Willamette Valley since 1977 (Gilligan et al. 1994). Drastic decline in Oregon since the mid-1960s speculated to be from destruction of lowland oak habitat and competition with European Starling (Gilligan et al. 1994).—*Christie Galen*

## Acorn Woodpecker *Melanerpes formicivorus*

"Its noisy calls break the midday silence of the hottest summer day," wrote Gabrielson and Jewett (1940). Spirited vocalizations make this handsome clown-faced woodpecker one of the more conspicuous residents of much of Oregon's oak woodland. Its red crown and the striking white eye on this black-and-white woodpecker render it unmistakable. Unique among Oregon woodpeckers with its habits of communal living and acorn storage. Oregon was the northern limit of its range until 1989, when a small colony was found in Washington. Formerly known as the California Woodpecker.

**General Distribution:** Resident (mostly west of the Cascades and Sierra Nevada) from sc. Washington, nw. Oregon south to s. California; from s. Utah and n. New Mexico, w. and c. Texas, ne. Mexico with scattered populations south to M. and n. S. America. (Koenig et al. 1995, AOU 1998). Of seven subspecies, only *M. f. bairdi* is found in Oregon (Short 1982).

**Oregon Distribution:** Fairly common in the Rogue Valley and adjacent hills (Browning 1975a, Gilligan et al. 1994). Locally common in the Klamath R. Canyon in sw. Klamath Co., uncommon in the Klamath Mtns. north to n. Curry Co. (Gilligan et al. 1994, Adamus et al. 2001), and the Umpqua R. Valley (Hunter et al. 1998). Likely extirpated in Coos Co. where it existed from at least the late 1920s until the 1990s (Neff 1928, Contreras 1998, T. Rodenkirk p.c.). Locally common in the s. Willamette Valley, becoming uncommon and local just south and west of Portland (Gilligan et al. 1994, *DBM*). Probably extirpated at The Dalles where it was found intermittently from 1960 through 1991 (Verner 1965b, Evanich 1991b). Colony sites change intermittently (Marshall et al. 1996) and individuals may be noted away from colonies at any time of year (H. Nehls p.c.). There are only about a dozen extralimital records (Neff 1928, Crowell and Nehls 1969b, Anderson 1989c, Bayer 1995d, Bayer 1998b); near Upper Klamath L. is the only repeat location with at least three sightings (Bendire 1895, Gordon 1979, Summers 1993a, Spencer 2001a). One extralimital specimen from Crater L. NP, 14 Aug 1961 (Crater Lake spec. no. 1450, *MRB*).

**Habitat and Diet:** Typically restricted to oaks, mixed conifer/oak, and tanoak, but uses adjacent stands (Doerge 1978, Jobanek 1994c, Dillingham and Vroman 1997, Johnson EM unpubl. ms.). In the Rogue Valley found in Oregon white oak savanna, ponderosa pine/Oregon white oak forests, riparian cottonwood habitat near oaks and cities where oaks exist (Browning 1975a, S. Janes p.c., D. Vroman p.c.). Noted often in tanoak in the Klamath Mtns., and to a lesser degree in "pockets of black oak, white oak and canyon live oak … on various meadows and oak savannas" (Dillingham and Vroman 1997, D.

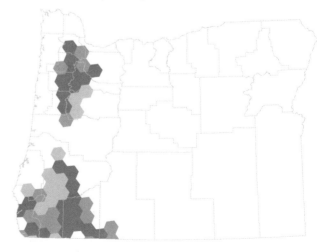

Vroman p.c.). Repeatedly observed in tanoak adjacent to clearcuts with scattered residual Douglas-fir trees, a habitat structurally similar to pine-oak savannas (Dillingham and Vroman 1997). Noted at the juncture of serpentine and non-serpentine soils: open habitat and Jeffrey pine snags are provided in the serpentine soils, and forage in the form of oaks is provided in both habitat types (D. Vroman p.c.).

Oak habitat in Oregon north of c. Lane Co. is limited to one species, Oregon white oak (Peck 1961). Oak groves in the Willamette Valley, in which understory vegetation has been removed, provide the open area under a high canopy preferred by this species (Marshall et al. 1996). In Benton Co., 95% of 20 colony sites were mowed or grazed (Johnson EM unpubl. ms.). Doerge (1978) located 32 colony sites in the mid-Willamette Valley with oaks estimated at 80-120 yr of age; 69% had less than moderate understory, 56% were in residential or work areas and

*Acorn Woodpecker*

41% provided shade or pasture for livestock. Eight Benton Co. oak stands with Acorn Woodpeckers had trees significantly larger in diameter, significantly more dead limbs, and a mean density significantly less than a separate group of eight Benton Co. oak stands without Acorn Woodpeckers. The same eight occupied stands had a mean density of 107.45 trees/ac (265.51 trees/ha), a mean of 167.1 trees per home range, a mean tree dbh of 19.2 in (48.7 cm), and a mean number of dead limbs per tree of 2.07 (Doerge 1978). Surveys of some oak woodlands in the Willamette Valley (Anderson SH 1970, Hagar and Stern 2001) detected few or no Acorn Woodpeckers in less open oak groves with more understory.

Nests have been noted in Oregon white oak, Douglas-fir, black cottonwood, utility poles, and a nest box; California black oak is probably also used (Bendire 1895, Harrington-Tweit et al. 1981, Dillingham and Vroman 1997, N. Barrett p.c., E. Johnson p.c., D. Vroman p.c.). In nw. California, nests in Pacific madrone were noted in mixed Douglas-fir/tanoak/madrone forest (Raphael 1995). Precise nest parameter data are lacking for Oregon. In the Rogue Valley, Bendire (1895) noted "several" nests 15-25 ft (5-8 m) in height. J. Lundsten (p.c.) observed the height of a nest in the Willamette Valley as "about 45 ft" (14 m), and Gabrielson and Jewett (1940) described nests as "generally well up from the ground." D. Vroman (p.c.) noted an apparent bias for excavating utility pole cavities near the top. Competes aggressively for nest cavities with European Starling (Gilligan et al. 1994) and perhaps competes for oak habitat with Lewis' Woodpecker (Doerge 1978).

Granary trees are used by colonies for storing acorns in holes drilled just large enough for each acorn stored (Neff 1928). Typically trees used are dead or have dead branches, and occasionally are live trees with softer wood or thick bark, such as Douglas-fir and ponderosa pine (Dillingham and Vroman 1997, N. Barrett p.c., S. Janes p.c., J. Kemper, p.c., J. Lundsten p.c., D. Vroman p.c.). Other trees observed are Oregon white oak, sugar pine, Jeffrey pine, lodgepole pine, black cottonwood, bigleaf maple and giant sequoia (Bendire 1895, Dillingham and Vroman 1997, Johnson EM unpubl. ms., S. Janes p.c., J. Lundsten p.c., D. Vroman p.c.). Utility poles, fence posts, and wooden buildings, inhabited and not, are also used (Bendire 1895, Gabrielson and Jewett 1940, Johnson EM unpubl. ms., N. Barrett p.c., D. Vroman p.c.).

In Benton Co., granary trees generally were larger in diameter, had shorter brush cover nearby, and were among higher basal area patches than non-granary trees (Johnson EM unpubl. ms.); each of 20 colonies had large numbers of small granaries, mostly in dead oak limbs (E. Johnson p.c.). Of 8 colonies in Benton Co., Doerge (1978) found a mean of 75.2 granaries, and a mean of 3,561.5 storage holes per colony. Numerous small granaries in oak groves have been noted in the Rogue Valley, but use of large ponderosa pine occurs there and in the Umpqua Valley (*MGH*, N. Barrett p.c., S. Janes p.c., J. Kemper p.c.). Granary trees may also be used for nesting and roosting (Johnson EM unpubl. ms.).

Diet per contents of 72 stomachs collected year-round from the Rogue R. Valley averaged 38% plant material, 50% "mineral matter or grit," and 12% insects. Acorns accounted for 30%, manzanita seeds 4%, fruit (all from Dec) < 1%, and miscellaneous plant matter 4%. Ants averaged 5% (including 22% in Jun and as high as 70% in "a few" stomachs), all beetles 4%, and other insects 3%. The grit averaged 80% white quartz (Neff 1928). Acorns are taken from Oregon white oak, black oak (typically within Oregon white oak or pine/oak habitat), canyon live oak, tanoak, and probably Brewer's oak and Huckleberry oak (Doerge 1978, Dillingham and Vroman 1997, Johnson EM unpubl. ms., N. Barrett p.c., S. Janes p.c., D. Vroman p.c.). Caching of filberts has been noted (L. McQueen p.c.).

Flycatching from high on a tree or pole is a common method used to catch insects throughout the year (Doerge 1978, Johnson EM unpubl. ms.); Walker (1952) observed flycatching and catching insects on the ground, caching on a fence post, and taking all to a presumed nest. Sap wells are a source of food (Koenig et al. 1995); J. Lundsten (p.c.) noted a bird using about six non-linear holes on an Oregon white oak. Observed at feeders with suet, sunflower seeds, and other commercial seed (Watson 1979, J. Harding p.c., A. McGie p.c., *MGH*), and at hummingbird feeders (R. Ketchum p.c.); N. Barrett (p.c.) noted they "hang by one foot, rip the bee guards off and drink from it." Besides granary trees, acorn storage has been noted in nest boxes (S. Janes p.c.), moss on tree limbs, and knotholes (E. Johnson p.c.). At a colony site where dead branches were removed, J. Lundsten (p.c.) noted acorns wedged into bark crevices. Granaries and sap wells are generally fiercely defended against intruders such as Western Scrub-Jays and squirrels (Neff 1928, MacRoberts 1970, Nicpon 1995, E.M. Johnson p.c.).

**Seasonal Activity and Behavior:** In wc. California, Acorn Woodpeckers live in social groups or colonies composed of breeding birds and nonbreeding helpers. The colony defends its territory, which includes granaries and a communal nest (Koenig and Mumme 1987). While data on breeding practices are lacking in Oregon, they are colonial: in eight Benton Co. colonies, the average group size was 4.25 birds with a range of 2-8 birds, and the average home range was 1.7 ac (0.69 ha) (Doerge 1978); E.M. Johnson (p.c.) noted a maximum of 8 birds at 20 Benton Co. sites.

MacRoberts (1970) provides timing of dietary habits in wc. California: sapsucking and flycatching begin in spring and continue into summer. Nest

excavation has been noted 28 Mar and in Apr (Gullion 1951, E.M. Johnson p.c.). In wc. California, 50% of nest holes were reused from year to year (Koenig et al. 1995). Both sexes excavate and incubate. Four to six eggs are laid and young are still in the nest from early May to early Sep (n=27); most records (n=23) fall between early May and early Jul (Bendire 1895, Neff 1928, Gabrielson and Jewett 1940, Walker 1952, Baldridge and Crowell 1965, Adamus et al. 2001, T. Janzen p.c., J. Lundsten p.c., C. Paynter p.c., P. T. Sullivan p.c.). As in wc. California, mid-summer records may be second broods or renesting, and Aug and Sep nesting may be "fall nests" related to good acorn crops (Koenig and Mumme 1987). Fledglings have been noted from early Aug to mid-Sep (n=3) (Mattocks and Hunn 1980a, *MGH*, J. Lundsten p.c.). Green acorns replace sapsucking as a major food source in Aug and Sep, storage of ripened acorns begins in mid-Sep, and stored acorns are the primary winter food (MacRoberts 1970, D. Vroman p.c.). Nest cavities are typically used for winter roosting (Johnson EM unpubl. ms.); D. Vroman (p.c.) observed enlarging of the entrance hole and roosting in a nest box.

**Detection:** Often detected by distinctive *waka* calls (usually repeated several times) used primarily to greet each other, or any of several other less common vocalizations or drumming (MacRoberts and MacRoberts 1976). Granary trees are often conspicuous.

**Population Status and Conservation:** Expanded its range into nw. Oregon during the 20th century. Recorded in the Umpqua Valley in 1855, but didn't reach Eugene until 1920 (Baird et al. 1858, Jobanek 1994c). Birds and signs of past presence noted in Corvallis in 1950; a dead bird was found near Salem in 1952 (Walker 1952, Jewett 1954b). First reported in McMinnville in 1968, Tigard in 1975, and Banks, Washington Co., in 1976 (Crowell and Nehls 1969a, 1975c, 1976b). In Wasco Co., noted at The Dalles 1960-67, at Tygh Valley in 1978, and at The Dalles again in 1991 (Verner 1965b, Rogers TH 1978b, Evanich 1991a, 1991b, W. Hoffman p.c.). Sporadically recorded 10 mi (16 km) west in Lyle, Washington, from 1979 to 1995 and regularly since (*American Birds* field notes 1979-1998, W. Cady p.c.). Present in Coos Co. since at least the late 1920s, it was last observed in the early 1990s (Neff 1928, Contreras 1998). Closed-canopy oak forests in the Willamette Valley were developed over the last 150 yr as a result of suppression of periodic ground fires, which formerly maintained open oak savannas (Thilenius 1964). Thus, Doerge (1978) hypothesized that the range extension of the Acorn Woodpecker may have occurred as a result of settlement by immigrants and the practice of fire suppression, since the resulting closed-canopy oak forests were favorable to the species.

Jobanek (1994c) suggested that w. Oregon offers poor habitat due to the lack of diversity of oak species resulting in some years of low food supply. Oregon white oak produces acorns on a roughly 2-yr cycle, leaving northern groups vulnerable, which may cause the extreme variation in numbers that occurs (Harrington-Tweit et al. 1979). BBS data show a non-significant 0.9%/yr increase 1966-2000 for Oregon (Sauer et al. 2001). Oregon CBC data 1959-88 show a non-significant decrease of 0.9%/yr (Sauer et al. 1996). Populations may be stable now, but Marshall et al. (1996) warn of an imminent threat because large oak trees, upon which the species depends, are not being replaced and are declining due to clearing of land, use as firewood, urbanization, and invasion by Douglas-fir that is assisted by fire suppression.—*Jamie Simmons*

## Williamson's Sapsucker *Sphyrapicus thyroideus*

Male and female Williamson's Sapsuckers look so different that until 1873 ornithologists thought they represented two distinct species (Bent 1939). The mostly black male has a bright yellow belly and red chin. The female is pale brown with barred back and wings and dull yellow belly. This is a highly adaptable species using a variety of coniferous forest types within its range. In Oregon it is most often found in ponderosa pine forests during the breeding season. It is usually quiet and retiring and often overlooked. Its loud code-like drumming is more distinctive than any of its various call notes.

**General Distribution:** A summer resident on the east slopes of the Cascades east to the Rocky Mtns. from s. British Columbia south into Mexico and Baja California. Winters from n. California, Arizona, Texas, and New Mexico south through Mexico, casually farther north. Monotypic (Browning and Cross 1999, *contra* AOU 1957).

**Oregon Distribution:** A common to uncommon summer resident of forests in the Blue Mtns., and on the east slope of the Cascades, east to Warner Mtns. in the south. A few breed west of the Cascade summit (Fix and Sawyer 1991, Johnson 1996a), where they are locally common in the high Cascades of e. Jackson Co. (N. Barrett p.c.), and may breed in the Siskiyou Mtns., s. Jackson Co. (Gabrielson and Jewett 1940, Browning 1974, Small 1994). Postbreeding dispersants and transients are found to the high Cascades and lower elevations of e. Oregon; casual in winter (Littlefield 1990a, Evanich 1992a, Summers 1993a). A casual vagrant to w. Oregon below the high Cascades (Crowell and Nehls 1972b, Tweit and Heinl 1989, Brown et el. 1996).

**Habitat and Diet:** Breeds in mid- to high-elevation mature or old-growth conifer forests with fairly open canopy cover (Thomas, Anderson, et al. 1979, Sanderson et al. 1980). At Crater L. NP, Klamath Co., Farner (1952) found "the principal requirement is simply a forest with large dead trees suitable for nest cavities. Ponderosa pine, shasta [red] fir, mountain hemlock, and aspen all seem adequate." In Oregon there seems to be a strong preference for ponderosa pine over other tree species (Gabrielson and Jewett 1940, Thomas, Anderson, et al. 1979, Bull et al. 1980). Snags are a critical component of breeding habitat (Thomas, Anderson, et al. 1979, Conway and Martin 1993). All nests that N. Barrett (p.c.) observed in e. Jackson Co., were in thinned stands or selective cuts.

It is a weak excavator, selecting soft and decayed wood for nesting sites regardless of tree species (Bull et al. 1980). Nests are placed in snags or in injured or diseased live trees with heart rot. Although the nest tree may be as small as 12 in (30.7 cm) dbh, preference is for larger trees. On Starkey Experimental Forest in the Blue Mtns., 86 nest trees averaged 27 in (69 cm) dbh (Bull et al. 1986). Nest trees often contain several nest cavities, as pairs regularly return to the same tree, building a new nest most years (Dobbs et al. 1997, *HBN*). A nesting cavity in a partly dead pine near Fort Klamath was 8 in (20.5 cm) deep and about 5 in (12.8 cm) wide at the bottom, with an entrance hole 1.5 in (3.8 cm) in diameter (Bendire 1895).

The main diet consists of conifer tree sap, phloem fibers, cambium, and insects. Sap wells are drilled mainly in ponderosa pine and Douglas-fir (Bull et al. 1986). They take insects attracted to sap and gleaned from the bark of trunk and limbs. They also scale bark in search of insects and to reach phloem and cambium. In ne. Oregon 75% of foraging observations were at sap wells, 25% pecking on trees (Bull et al. 1986). Carpenter ants and wood ants constitute the majority of insects consumed (Short 1982). Beetles, flies, and aphids are also taken (Dobbs et al. 1997).

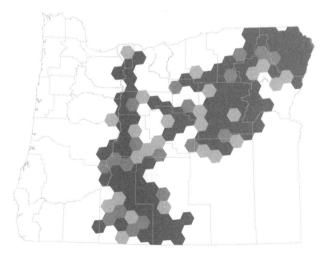

**Seasonal Activity and Behavior:** Spring migration occurs Mar to early May (Phillips et al. 1964, Short 1982). Early birds arrive in Oregon during Mar, but most arrive during Apr. Males arrive up to 2 wk earlier than females. On arrival males are extremely active and vociferous, displaying and chasing each other through the forest (Gabrielson and Jewett 1940, *HBN*). Territories are established prior to the arrival of females. The birds then become quiet and unobtrusive through the rest of their stay.

Monogamous. Produces one brood per season, with a clutch of 4-6 eggs incubated by both sexes for 12-14 days (Dobbs et al. 1997). Egg sets were taken near Fort Klamath, Klamath Co., 2-12 May (Gabrielson and Jewett 1940). Incubation was observed mid-May to mid-Jun in ne. Oregon (Bull et al. 1986). Young fledge 31-32 days after hatching (Martin and Li 1992). Fledging dates for 19 nests in ne. Oregon were 19 Jun–20 Jul (Bull et al. 1986).

Families usually disperse immediately after young fledge (Dobbs et al 1997). Southward movements are not conspicuous with birds remaining scattered. Most leave late Aug to mid-Oct, with lingerers noted through Nov (Anderson 1987b, Gilligan et al. 1994).

**Detection:** Although quiet and unassuming this species is not secretive. The young in the nest are vociferous and the adults solicitous. After postbreeding dispersals detection is low, even in proper habitat.

**Population Status and Conservation:** This species is highly adaptable and able to withstand considerable disturbance. Most studies show a fairly stable population, but forestry practices that remove snags cause concern. In the Pacific Northwest, 150 snags of at least 12 in (30.5 cm) dbh per 100 ac (40 ha) are estimated necessary to support "maximum population" (Thomas, Anderson, et al. 1979). Thomas, Anderson, et al. (1979) estimated territory size in ne. Oregon at 10 ac (4 ha), but others have estimated territories up to 22 ac (9 ha) in other parts of the breeding range (Dobbs et al. 1997). Population density is thought to be affected by uneven distribution of snags in Oregon forests (Thomas, Anderson, et al. 1979, Bull et al. 1980). Conservation of existing snags and providing for additional or replacement snags is highly recommended (Thomas, Anderson, et al. 1979, Bull et al. 1980, Scott et al. 1980).—*Harry B. Nehls*

### Yellow-bellied Sapsucker *Sphyrapicus varius*

This eastern sapsucker breeds east of the Rocky Mtns. from ec. Alaska (rare), across Canada, and south to n. Georgia. It winters from the se. U.S. through C. America. It is casual to rare elsewhere in N. America. It is closely related to the Red-breasted and Red-naped Sapsuckers and hybridizes limitedly with them. There

are 19 Oregon sight records, 15 between early Oct and late Feb. In addition to birds in the typical fall-winter ocurrence pattern, an adult male and an immature female were at Scoggins Valley Park, Washington Co., 9 Jul 1976 (OBRC); an adult female was photographed near Gilchrist, Klamath Co., 5 Jul 1983 (OBRC) and an adult male was observed at La Grande, Union Co., 11 Jul 1980 (OBRC).—*Harry B. Nehls*

### Red-naped Sapsucker *Sphyrapicus nuchalis*

Lines of neatly drilled holes in even the smallest stand of aspen east of the Cascade summit are likely the work of the Red-naped Sapsucker. The black breast patch and red forehead of this black-and-white woodpecker distinguish it from other common Oregon woodpeckers. Sexes are similar and not always separable in the field. Formerly classified as conspecific with Yellow-bellied Sapsucker and Red-breasted Sapsucker; hybrids with the latter occur in Oregon. Considered a double keystone species as its nest cavities are used by secondary cavity-nesters and its sap wells provide food for a variety of other animals, from insects to other birds to squirrels (Daily et al. 1993).

**General Distribution:** Breeds in the Rocky Mountain region from sw. Canada, w. and c. Montana, and sw. S. Dakota south, east of the Cascades and Sierra Nevada, to ec. California, s. Nevada, c. Arizona, s. New Mexico, and extreme w. Texas, and east to sw. S. Dakota. Winters from s. California (casually in Oregon), s. Nevada, s. Utah, and c. New Mexico south to s. Baja California, and nw. and nc. Mexico. Monotypic.

**Oregon Distribution:** A common summer resident throughout forested mountains east of the crest of the Cascades. A spring and fall migrant through the same mountains and lower elevations, preferring areas with trees. Rare in winter along the east slope of the Cascades and very rare elsewhere east of the Cascades. Casual in all seasons west of the Cascades summit; about 60% of 52 records (in *Oregon Birds* and *American Birds* field notes 1974-2000) were during spring migration (Eltzroth MS 1987b, Nehls 1987a, Gilligan et al. 1994, Contreras 1997b). Winter and westside observations should be made with care since the very similar Yellow-bellied Sapsucker is casual in Oregon. Hybridizes with Red-breasted Sapsucker mostly along the east slope of the Cascades and in sc. Oregon (Howell 1952, Browning 1977c, Johnson and Johnson 1985, Trombino 1998, Adamus et al. 2001). In the Paisley and Lakeview RDs of the Fremont NF in sc. Oregon, Trombino (1998) found the proportion of hybrids to be lower than expected at 32.5%.

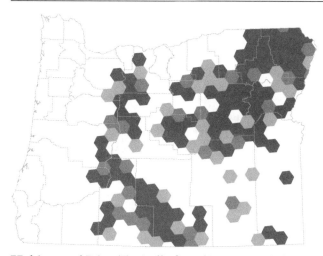

**Habitat and Diet:** Typically found in riparian habitats, especially aspens, as well as cottonwoods, alders, and pine forests, and less frequently in mixed conifer forests (Gabrielson and Jewett 1940, Jackman 1974, Pedersen et al. 1975, Bull 1980, Mannan 1982, Littlefield 1990a, Evanich 1992a, Dobkin et al. 1995, Contreras and Kindschy 1996, Trombino 1998). Bendire (1888) found them breeding "sparingly" at about 5,000 ft (1,525 m) elevation in sc. Oregon—records Gabrielson and Jewett (1940) overlooked (Browning 1973b)—and found nests more abundant between 6,000 and 7,000 ft (1,825-2,125 m) in the Blue Mtns. Bull (1980) found only eight nests (of a total of 306 nests of various woodpecker species) between 3,500 and 5,000 ft (1,070-1,525 m) in the Blue Mtns. in ne. Oregon. Numerous nests were found in two areas of sc. Oregon, at elevations of 5,200-6,600 ft (1,600-2,010 m) and 5,650-7,550 ft (1,725-2,300 m) (Dobkin et al. 1995, Trombino 1998). On Hart Mtn., Dobkin et al. (1995) noted foraging occurring "largely or entirely" in the riparian forest. Bendire (1888) noted foraging in winter in low-elevation riparian willow thickets far from "timber of any size."

Aspen nest trees often have heartwood decay likely caused by fungi (Kilham 1971a); 72% of live aspen with woodpecker-excavated cavities at Hart Mtn. had visible fungi (Dobkin et al. 1995). On the east slope of the Cascades in Washington, Stegen (2001) noted that the newest cavities tended to be the highest cavities in the trees, and in Colorado Daily (1993) noted that, due to the typical start of heartwood decay at the roots and base, Red-naped Sapsuckers generally make first nests low on aspens, then situate them increasingly higher in succeeding years.

Of 25 nests (four pairs had one Red-breasted Sapsucker x Red-naped Sapsucker hybrid per pair) in riparian and snowpocket aspen woodlands on Hart Mtn., 92-100% were in aspens. Dead trees (8%) and live trees (92%) were used in proportion to availability. Mean dbh, tree height, cavity height, and entrance diameter were 10.8 in (27.4 cm), 47.9 ft (14.6 m), 13.8 ft (4.2 m), and 1.7 in (4.3 cm), respectively. Less

than 4% of all aspens were >33 ft (10 m) in height and >9 in (24 cm) in dbh, yet were preferred as nest trees. No nests were located along the riparian woodland edge nor were any oriented in that direction (Dobkin et al. 1995). In the Paisley and Lakeview RDs of the Fremont NF in sc. Oregon, of 17 nests in aspens believed to be >90 yr old, mean dbh, tree height and cavity height were 15.2 in (38.6 cm), 53.1 ft (16.2 m), and 19.7 ft (6.0 m), respectively (Trombino 1998). In ne. Oregon, Bull (1986) noted nests in trees similar to those of Williamson's Sapsucker, weak excavators that use recently dead trees with much decay and bark and branches intact. In the Blue Mtns. of ne. Oregon, of eight nests, seven (88%) were within 330 ft (100 m) of open water. Nests were in western larch, lodgepole pine, Douglas-fir, grand fir, and ponderosa pine; two were in live trees. Trees retained 70-100% of original bark and were likely dead less than 10 yr. Mean dbh, tree height and cavity height were 20 in (52 cm), 66 ft (20 m), and 30 ft (9 m), respectively (Bull 1980). Bendire (1888) examined a nest cavity in an aspen "about 8 in deep and 4 in. wide at bottom." The eggs lay "embedded in a layer of fine chips." Also breeds in cottonwoods (Contreras and Kindschy 1996); 5 of 20 nests on the east slope of the Cascades in Washington were in cottonwood and two were in willows (Stegen 2001).

In mixed coniferous forests of ne. Oregon, densities per 100 ac (40 ha) were 0-0.5 in managed forests and from less than 0.1 to 0.5 in old growth (Mannan 1982). In mixed coniferous and aspen forests (six sites ranging from 1 to 98% aspen) at 9,000 ft (2,750 m) on the west slope of the Rocky Mtns. in Colorado, densities ranged 0-3 birds per 100 ac (40 ha) (Scott and Crouch 1988).

Sapsucker diet in general includes sap, cambium, and soft parts beneath the bark. Neat rows of holes are drilled in the bark or the bark may be removed in strips to collect the oozing sap and insects attracted to it (Gabrielson and Jewett 1940, Howell 1952, Ehrlich and Daily 1988). A variety of trees are used; some noted in Oregon are aspen, willow, elm, apple, and ornamental pine (K. Spencer p.c., D. Tracy p.c., *JS*). Westside vagrants have been observed using Oregon ash, big-leaf maple, black cottonwood, Douglas-fir, English holly, and ornamental elm (J. Fairchild p.c., J. Harding p.c., D. Vroman p.c., *MGH*). Juniper, "various pines," and "firs" are other trees included in a long list used by this species within its range (McAtee 1911). Other general Red-naped Sapsucker food items include "small beetles, spiders, grasshoppers, ants, and such larvae as are to be found under the loose bark of trees" and "wild berries of different kinds" (Bendire 1895). Birds foraging on aspen snags with peeling bark on Steens Mtn. may have been seeking larvae (D. Tracy p.c.). Stoneflies and crane flies were eaten at sap wells in the Rocky Mtns. in wc. Colorado (Ehrlich and Daily 1988).

**Seasonal Activity and Behavior:** In spring, arrives at Malheur NWR as soon as early Feb and peaks late Apr to early May (Littlefield 1990a, Ivey, Herziger, and Scheuering 1998). On the central east slope of the Cascades, some arrive as early as late Feb, with an average first arrival of mid-Apr (Miller 1998). May be dependent on conifer sap for food until deciduous trees bud and insects are available, as in Montana (Tobalske 1992). A comprehensive account detailing observations of Red-naped and Red-breasted Sapsuckers in ne. California and British Columbia was written by Howell (1952). Courtship and territorial displays may involve drumming and posturing. Territories range from about 1.6 to >14.6 ac (0.7 to >5.9 ha). Both sexes begin excavating a nest cavity before copulation. Three to seven eggs are laid, typically four or five, and both parents incubate (Bendire 1895, Gabrielson and Jewett 1940, Howell 1952). Incubation occurs and young are still in the nest cavity from mid-May to late Jul (n=59) (Bendire 1877 *in* Gabrielson and Jewett 1940, Bendire 1888, Gabrielson and Jewett 1940, Anderson 1988e, Anderson 1989d, Spencer 2000b, Adamus et al. 2001, T. Janzen p.c., *JS*). Interspecific helping behavior at nests, rare in sapsuckers, was observed as a female Red-naped Sapsucker, a female hybrid, and a (presumed) male Red-breasted Sapsucker fed young in sc. Oregon (Trombino 2000). Fledglings are typically observed early to late Jul (n=8) (Adamus et al. 2001, T. Janzen p.c., M. LaFaive p.c.). Trombino (1998) found that adult survivorship is reduced in hybrids, while nestling success is not. Fall migration at Malheur NWR occurs mid-Aug to mid-Oct, with most sightings from mid- to late Sep (Littlefield 1990a). A few individuals winter at low elevations in the southwest part of their range (Contreras 1997b).

**Detection:** Frequent, characteristic drumming and five distinctive calls may be heard, mostly during the breeding season (Howell 1952). Generally quiet and secretive outside breeding (Farrand 1983b).

**Population Status and Conservation:** BBS data for Oregon showed a non-significant 0.5%/yr increase 1966-2000 (Sauer et al. 2001). Thomas, Anderson, et al. (1979), probably having included some Yellow-bellied Sapsucker data (vs. Red-naped Sapsucker only), estimated that 150 snags per 100 ac (40 ha) of at least 10 in (25 cm) dbh were necessary to support the "maximum population" in forests of the Blue Mtns. Long-term widespread degradation of aspen and other riparian forests through intensive livestock grazing and fire suppression is a threat considering Red-naped Sapsucker's dependence on large aspen trees and snags for nesting in many areas. A lack of tree regeneration may lead to inevitable loss of large trees, which could result in significant declines in cavity-nesting species (Dobkin et al. 1995). Maintaining undisturbed aspen

groves and mixed ponderosa pine and aspen forests, as well as the adjacent foraging zones, would be beneficial (Jackman 1974, Trombino 1998).—*Jamie Simmons*

### Red-breasted Sapsucker *Sphyrapicus ruber*

The only sapsucker regularly found in w. Oregon, the Red-breasted Sapsucker, with its raspberry-red head and breast, is unmistakable among Oregon's avifauna. Earlier in the 20th century it was considered a pest among nut and fruit growers, because it damaged orchards by deforming and girdling trees (Neff 1928, Gabrielson and Jewett 1940).

The taxonomic status of this species has been treated variously (e.g., Grinnell J 1901, Howell 1952, Short 1969, Browning 1977c). It was long regarded as a full species until it was designated a subspecies of the Yellow-bellied Sapsucker by the AOU (1931). It was later re-evaluated and restored to full species status (AOU 1983). Crosses between sapsuckers are infrequent, and hybrids may have less success in obtaining a mate (Johnson and Johnson 1985).

**General Distribution:** Breeds in forested areas from the Alaska panhandle into interior British Columbia, southward primarily west of the Cascades into nw. California. It is also found in the Sierra Nevada range of California east into w. Nevada, and in the high mountains of s. California. Winter range includes most of the breeding range west of the Cascade-Sierra Nevada ranges (withdraws from much of its Alaska and British Columbia breeding range), and extends south into Baja California. Two subspecies; both occur in Oregon.

**Oregon Distribution:** *S. r. ruber* is a fairly common breeder in the northern part of the state from the coast to the Cascades and south to the s. Cascades (Browning 1977c). Breeds locally on the eastern slope, particularly in c. Oregon (Browning 1977c). In sw. Oregon, *S. r. ruber* intergrades with *S. r. daggetti*, which gradually replaces it to the south, probably near s. Douglas Co.

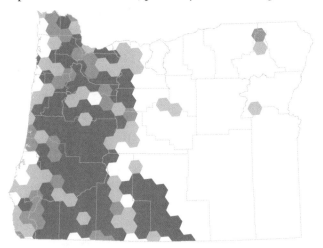

(*MRB*). *S. r. daggetti* is found from s. Douglas and Josephine counties east to the Warner Mtns. (Howell 1952). Southern coastal birds were considered intergrades by Devillers (1970) but more specimens are required to verify ranges in sw. Oregon.

Both subspecies are known to hybridize with Red-naped Sapsuckers in localized zones of overlap east of the Cascades summit: near Sisters (*S. r. ruber* X *S. nuchalis*; Howell 1952, Browning 1977c), Ft. Klamath and Warner Valley (*S. r. daggetti* X *S. nuchalis*; Browning 1977c), and especially in the Warner Mtns. (Howell 1952, Short 1969, Johnson and Johnson 1985, OBBA). A specimen (MCZ) from Ft. Klamath reported as a possible hybrid between *S. ruber* and *S. varius* by Dickinson (1953) is a hybrid between *S. ruber* and *S. nuchalis* (*MRB*)

Recently a vagrant visitant to the Ochoco, Wallowa, and Blue mountains (Evanich 1992a, Gilligan et al. 1994, OBBA) and an irregular transient in the Harney Basin (Littlefield 1990a). Winters in the Coast Range and lowlands of w. Oregon, with small numbers found in river valleys of the w. Cascades (*MGH*), the Klamath Basin, and sc. Oregon (Contreras 1997b).

**Habitat and Diet:** It is found in moist coniferous coastal forest and mixed deciduous-coniferous forest west of the Cascade crest, and in aspen-ponderosa pine forests east of the Cascades (Howell 1952). It uses a wider range of wooded habitat in winter and migration. Studies in the Oregon Cascades, Coast Range, and s. Washington Cascades showed increasing abundance with stand age and a close association with old-growth forest (Mannan et al. 1980, Nelson 1988, Carey et al. 1991, Gilbert and Allwine 1991, Huff and Raley 1991, Lundquist and Mariani 1991). In the c. Coast Range, detections were most numerous in riparian areas during the breeding season (Mannan 1977), and a preference was shown for nest sites in snag patches with dense midstory and understory cover and sites in close proximity to water (Nelson 1988). In the Umpqua NF, nest sites were strongly associated with stand edges (Brett 1997). Rarely nests in clearcuts (Schreiber 1987).

Nest cavities are typically in large snags or live trees with decayed interiors (Bent 1939, Howell 1952). Hard snags were preferred in the Coast Range (Nelson 1988) and the Umpqua NF (Brett 1997). In the Coast Range, nine of 18 nests were in dead branches of live bigleaf maple trees (Chambers et al. 1997). It generally has no preference for species of tree, using those common to the area, including aspen, cottonwoods, alders, Douglas-fir, grand fir, bigleaf maple, white fir, and western hemlock (Bendire 1888, Bent 1939, Nelson 1988, Brett 1997). In the Coast Range, mean dbh of nine snags with nests was 40 in (101 cm) with a range of 22-85 in (56-216 cm) in one study (Mannan et al. 1980) and mean dbh was 44 in (113

cm) for 30 nest trees with a range of 15-98 in (37-250 cm) in another study (Nelson 1988). In the Umpqua NF, mean dbh of 68 nest trees was 31.6 in (80.5 cm) (Brett 1997). Mean nest cavity heights in two Coast Range studies were 56.4 ft (17.2 m) (range 20.0-73.1 ft [6.1-22.3 m]; n=9) (Mannan et al. 1980) and 87.2 ft (26.6 m) (range 26-171 ft [8-52 m]; n=30) (Nelson 1988). Mean nest height in the Umpqua NF was 66.9 ft (20.4 m; n=68) (Brett 1997). Mean heights of nest trees were 110.5 ft (33.7 m) (range 43-184 ft [13-56 m]) in the Coast Range (Nelson 1988) and 90.2 ft (27.5 m) in the sw. Cascades (Brett 1997).

Sapsuckers drill holes in the bark of trees to access sap. Sap wells are visited frequently to consume sap as well as insects and other arthropods attracted to it, and are vigorously defended from other bird species (Bent 1939, Howell 1952). One or two trees within 5-100 yards (5-91 m) of the nest are worked constantly for insects, which are the primary food for young (Howell 1952). Sixty-four stomachs, taken from every month of the year in Oregon (primarily from the Willamette Valley, with a few from s. Oregon) contained 53% animal and 40% vegetable food. Ants made up 32% of annual diet (but 80% in Jul). The remaining animal matter consisted of beetles, caddis flies, aphids, crane flies, and unidentified insects. Cambium or inner bark made up 31%, primarily consumed Oct-Apr. Fruit made up 4% of diet, with bark and other vegetable matter comprising 5% (Neff 1928). Over 67 species of trees including fruit, nut, and ornamental trees have been reported used. Neff (1928) reported that deciduous trees were frequently used from early spring to late autumn, while drilling was more confined to conifers from late Nov through Feb (broadleaf evergreens were not addressed). In the Coast Range, Carey et al. (1991) observed foraging primarily on the trunks of Douglas-fir, bigleaf maple, and western hemlock in good condition. Forty-seven percent of foraging observations were recorded in the mid-canopy, with 23% in lower and 19% in upper canopy (n=99). Foraging trees were primarily 8-39 in (20-100 cm) dbh.

**Seasonal Activity and Behavior:** Possibly arrives on territory earlier than Red-naped Sapsucker, which may limit hybridization (Howell 1952, 1953, Johnson and Johnson 1985). In the Klamath Basin, the bulk of migrants arrive in mid-Mar (Summers 1993a).

Howell (1952) provides a detailed life history based on observations of Red-breasted and Red-naped Sapsuckers in California and British Columbia. Both adults take part in all nesting activities. Nest excavation lasts 6-14 days. Several cavities may be started before a final site is selected (Howell 1952). Nest construction and egg laying begin late Apr to early May (OBBA). As soon as the nest is completed incubation begins (Howell 1952). Incubation is generally mid-May to late Jun (n=7) (OBBA). Hatching occurs in about 14 days (Howell 1952). Young are in nest from late May through Jul (n=28) (OBBA), and fledge after about 24 days, leaving the nest over a period of 2 days or more (Howell 1952). Fledglings observed primarily mid-Jun through late Jul (n=12) (OBBA).

Departure and/or downslope movement of birds in fall from the Cascades may depend on weather conditions (Contreras 1997b). Dates of movement are unclear, as the species winters throughout much of its Oregon breeding range. It is also unknown whether birds that leave higher elevations in Oregon move to local valleys or migrate southward. Extent of migration is unclear, but altitudinal migration of both subspecies occurs (Gabrielson and Jewett 1940, Howell 1952, Devillers 1970). It is not clear whether winter influxes into w. Oregon are from the Cascades or from more northerly populations. Specimens of *S. r. ruber* have been collected in s. California and Arizona in winter, suggesting that at least some migration occurs out of the Northwest, but it is not clear whether these are Oregon birds or "leapfrogging" birds from Alaska or British Columbia (Phillips et al. 1964, Devillers 1970).

**Detection:** Its irregular drumming may be heard for a considerable distance, occuring most often in early morning, particularly early in the breeding season; it may respond to imitations (Howell 1952). Easiest to detect during the nesting season when adults and young are more vocal as large nestlings and fledglings beg for food. Fresh sapsucker holes provide evidence of recent activity, and old scars on trees can be seen for many years.

**Population Status and Conservation:** Dependence on large snags and association with old-growth forest are the chief causes of concern for the future. Since average-sized nesting snags take about 100 yr to replace, loss of mature and old trees through short-rotation logging may be detrimental to Red-breasted Sapsucker populations (Carey et al. 1991, Huff and Raley 1991).—*Karen Viste-Sparkman*

**Nuttall's Woodpecker** *Picoides nuttallii*
This small woodpecker is a resident of oak woodlands and riparian streamsides from Baja California to the north end of the Central Valley of California. There were several reports prior to 1900 of Nuttall's Woodpeckers in Oregon. One was reportedly collected in the Umpqua Valley, Douglas Co., during Aug 1855 (Short 1965b, spec. no. 4471 USNM). The exact location where this bird was taken has been questioned in Short (1965b), but the Umpqua Valley location was accepted in Browning and Cross (1994). A male and a female collected near Ashland, Jackson Co., 3 Feb and

4 Feb 1881 are now in the BM (Short 1965b). One was found dead near Trail, Jackson Co., in fall 1991 (Browning and Cross 1994, spec. no. 1697 SOU). Monotypic (AOU 1957).—*Harry B. Nehls*

**Downy Woodpecker** *Picoides pubescens*
This active and often unwary woodpecker, the smallest in N. America, is generally the most often seen black-and-white woodpecker in human-settled areas. Its facial pattern, clear pale back, and light spotting on the wings are distinctive, but similar to its larger cousin, the Hairy Woodpecker. The pale parts of Downy Woodpecker plumage grade from pure white in e. Oregon to brownish-gray in coastal Oregon. Males have a red patch on the nape. Juveniles of both sexes have red on the crown only.

**General Distribution:** A permanent resident from w. and c. Alaska across Canada to Newfoundland; south to s. California, c. Arizona, s. New Mexico, c. Texas, the Gulf coast, and s. Florida (Browning 1995b, AOU 1998). Three of 7-8 subspecies occur in Oregon (AOU 1957, Browning 1997).

**Oregon Distribution:** Found mostly at low to moderate elevations in deciduous and mixed deciduous-coniferous forests, and less often in coniferous forests (Gilligan et al. 1994). Most abundant in riparian areas and red alder (Adamus et al. 2001). In the w. Cascades, it occurs in deciduous river corridors and in some large patches of deciduous habitat (*MGH*). *P. p. leucurus* occurs in e. Oregon (specimens from Union and Umatilla counties [Burleigh 1961]), *P. p. turati* along the east slope of the Cascades and through sw. Oregon (Klamath, Jackson, and Josephine counties), and *P. p. gairdnerii* elsewhere in w. Oregon (Browning 1997).

**Habitat and Diet:** In e. Oregon, most often found in deciduous stands, especially riparian, composed of alder, cottonwood, willow, and aspen (Gabrielson and

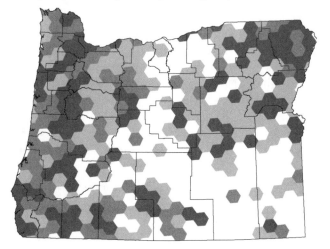

Jewett 1940, Bull 1986, Littlefield 1990a, Trombino 1998, *JS*). It is less common in mixed conifers, such as in the Blue Mtns. and in ponderosa pine (Gabrielson and Jewett 1940, Pedersen et al. 1975, Gashwiler 1977). Nests in aspen groves and meadows east of the Cascades (Littlefield 1990a, Trombino 1998). It has nested in willow and apple in e. Washington (Jewett et al. 1953). In the Willamette Valley and the Coast Range, inhabits riparian deciduous and oak-dominated woodlands, and is rarely found in closed-canopy conifer forests (Anderson SH 1970, McGarigal 1993, Hagar and Stern 2001). Along the Willamette and Columbia rivers it has nested in "old willow stubs and branches" and Oregon ash (Gabrielson and Jewett 1940, *JS*). Nested in madrone and tanoak in nw. California (Raphael 1995). It may be found at farms, orchards, parks, or other developed areas (Neff 1928, Evanich 1992a). It visits areas of burned trees; five were noted at the Awbry Hall burn near Bend in Jan 1991 (Evanich 1991b).

All but one of several nest reports from Oregon were in dead trees (Neff 1928, Nelson 1988, *JS*). However, Jewett et al. (1953) noted a few nests in live (including partly dead) trees in Washington. A preference is shown for decayed wood for nesting, though sound wood is also utilized (Brown 1985, Bull 1986). Nest data for Oregon are limited; in the Coast Range, one nest was found in an old-growth evergreen snag with light to moderate decay, with dbh of 15.4 in (39 cm), tree height of 26.2 ft (8.0 m), tree diameter at nest height of 11.0 in (28.0 cm), and cavity height of 26.2 ft. (8.0 m) (Nelson 1988). Neff (1928) noted that nests were at a height of 3-30 ft (1-9 m) and Gabrielson and Jewett (1940) said that they were "usually ... 10 to 12 ft" (3-4 m). A nw. Washington nest was found in red alder with a dbh of 8 in (20 cm), nest height of 6 ft (2 m), and tree diameter at nest height of 7 in (18 cm) (Zarnowitz and Manuwal 1985).

Densities per 100 ac (40 ha) were found to be 11-22 in white oak stands in the Willamette Valley (Anderson 1972), 0.1 in early-growth vegetation on clearcuts in the Coast Range (Morrison and Meslow 1983a), and 3.6 and 0.9 pairs on ungrazed and grazed willow and aspen riparian habitat, respectively, during the breeding season in ne. Nevada (Medin and Clary 1991). Maximum densities of 0.3 and 0.8 in summer and fall, respectively, were found in young-growth Douglas-fir in nw. California (Marcot 1985).

Diet according to the contents of 68 stomachs, "most of them from the Willamette Valley," averaged 39.50% scale insects (Coccids), 21.61% beetles (Coleoptera), 12.82% other insects and spiders, 8.14% miscellaneous insect fragments, 17.47% miscellaneous vegetable matter (bark, wood fiber, cambium, etc.), and 0.46% fruit (elderberry and madrona) (Neff 1928). Birds in n. and c. California yielded an average of 39.9% beetles (Coleoptera), 32.4% ants (Hymenoptera), 18.1% scale

and other Homoptera, 7.2% other invertebrates, and 2.4% plant material (Otvos and Stark 1985). They have been observed feeding on aphids and scale on large cottonwoods close to the Willamette R. during summer, with as many as 10 birds in a single tree. During late winter feed on scale and weevils in the blossoms and catkins of the same cottonwoods. Weevils are taken from common mullein, and oak galls are torn open for wasp larvae. It is the most effective woodpecker predator of the codling moth, an orchard pest (Neff 1928). It has taken "small white grubs," possibly larvae of a cynipidae wasp, from galls on thimbleberry stalks in the Coast Range (D. Faxon p.c., B. Newhouse p.c.). Morrison and Meslow (1983a) noted foraging in clearcuts in the Coast Range by individuals nesting in adjacent mature stands.

Downy Woodpeckers are a common visitor to suet at feeders and an individual even drank from a hummingbird feeder in Seattle, Washington (D. Paulson p.c., *JS*). In the foothills of the Sierra Nevada in c. California, Dennis (1999) noted foraging on 30 living trees and six dead trees. Hammering was used as the "attack maneuver" in 35 instances and pecking in one, and foraging occurred on all parts of the tree. In ne. Washington in a burned mixed-conifer forest, 80% of foraging was on branches and 80% on ponderosa pine (Kreisel and Stein 1999). In winter it frequently forages with flocks of smaller birds (Jackman 1974, *JS*). Of 20 Downy Woodpeckers observed in winter in riparian habitat in sw. Washington, 18 were in 14 mixed flocks with mostly Black-capped and Chestnut-backed Chickadees, and Golden-crowned and Ruby-crowned Kinglets. Foraging time was nearly equally split between pecking and gleaning (LaGory et al. 1984).

**Seasonal Activity and Behavior:** Subsequent to courtship and drumming activity, excavation of a fresh nest cavity takes place approximately 26 Apr to 22 May (n=2; w. Oregon). Eggs are laid and young are still in the nest cavity from late Apr to late Jul (n=50). Eggs may number three to seven; four or five is most common. Fledglings are typically observed from mid-Jun to late Jul (n=13) (Bendire 1895, Neff 1928, Griffee and Rapraeger 1937, Gabrielson and Jewett 1940, Brown 1985, Adamus et al. 2001, *JS*). Both home range and territory size in w. Oregon are 5-8 ac (2-3 ha) (Brown 1985); territory size is 5-9 ac (2-3.6 ha)/pair in the Blue Mtns. (Thomas, Anderson, et al. 1979). In fall/winter some local movements occur as a few individuals move to lower elevations and/or populated areas, such as Malheur NWR or Bend (Roest 1957b, Littlefield 1990a, Contreras 1997b). Excavation of a winter roost cavity was noted in the Willamette Valley (J. Weikel p.c.) and repeated use of a nest box for roosting has been observed in Roseburg (A. Parker p.c.).

**Detection:** Often detected by sound, either tapping, drumming, or call, a short *pik* or a whinny or rattle call. Calls may be infrequent and require patience to locate tapping or detect movement on trees or in flight from one tree to another. It may be confused with the larger, longer-billed Hairy Woodpecker.

**Population Status and Conservation:** According to Morrison and Morrison (1983), Downy Woodpeckers are experiencing a general decline in numbers in the Pacific Northwest. CBCs in s. Oregon, Portland, and Spokane, Washington, showed significant decreases in numbers of Downy Woodpecker observations per party mile from 1952-53 to 1981-82, while CBCs in w. Oregon outside Portland showed significant increases. Oregon CBC data from 1959 to 1988 show no significant trends with an increase of 0.3%/yr. (Sauer et al. 1996). BBS data show no significant change with a 0.4%/yr decline 1966-2000 for Oregon (Sauer et al. 2001), but Sharp (1996) shows a moderately significant decline of 3.5%/yr in Oregon per BBS data for 1968-94. Thomas, Anderson, et al. (1979) estimated that 300 snags per 100 ac (40 ha) of at least 6 in (15 cm) dbh were necessary to support the "maximum population" in relevant forests of the Blue Mtns. while Neitro et al. (1985) calculated that 16.0 snags per 100 ac (40 ha) of at least 11 in (28 cm) dbh were needed in areas of forest in w. Oregon Douglas-fir habitat. Raphael (1995) computed that five madrone of dbh >12 in (30 cm) per 100 ac (40 ha) might be needed in Douglas-fir forests of nw California. Degradation and elimination of habitat, such as replacement of oak or alder habitat with coniferous habitats and grazing in e. Oregon riparian habitats, seem to pose the greatest risks for this species (Jackman 1974, Medin and Clary 1991, Hagar and Stern 2001).—*Jamie Simmons*

## Hairy Woodpecker *Picoides villosus*

This medium-sized woodpecker may be found in virtually any forested area in Oregon. Its facial pattern, clear light back, and light spotting on the wings are distinctive and resemble its smaller cousin, the Downy Woodpecker. The pale parts of Hairy Woodpecker plumage are white in far e. Oregon and grade to gray-brown in coastal Oregon. Males have a red patch on the nape. Juveniles of both sexes have orange or red (rarely yellow) on the crown only.

**General Distribution:** Permanent resident of coniferous and deciduous forests from c. and e. Alaska, across Canada to Newfoundland; south to n. Baja California, ec. California, and Arizona, through most highlands of M. America to w. Panama, to the Gulf coast, s. Florida and the Bahamas. Northern populations are partially migratory southward in winter. Three of 12 subspecies found in N. America occur in Oregon.

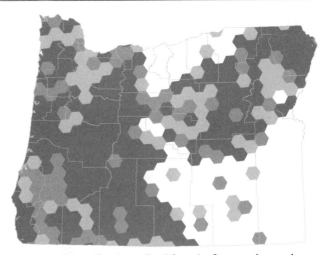

**Oregon Distribution:** Resident in forests throughout Oregon with the exception of juniper. Common throughout most of range, but uncommon to fairly common along the coast and in western interior valleys. Most common in burns or in areas with trees that are dead from or infested with mountain pine beetles (Bull 1983). *P. v. monticola* breeds in ne. Oregon (Blue and Wallowa mountains); *P. v. orius* breeds on the east slope of the Cascades south from the Columbia R. to Diamond L., and east through Klamath Co., s. Lake Co., and in parts of Rogue Valley of Jackson and Josephine counties; *P. v. harrisi* breeds from the Oregon coast east to the summit of the Cascades south to parts of Jackson and Josephine counties, and in Coos and Curry counties. Intergrades exist between *monticola* and *orius* from Warm Springs (USNM), and between *orius* and *harrisi* from Mt. Hood, w. Klamath Co., and localities in Rogue Valley (Browning 2002).

**Habitat and Diet:** Found primarily in mixed-conifer and ponderosa pine forests, as well as adjacent deciduous stands, especially during the breeding season (Meslow and Wight 1975, Mannan et al. 1980, Bull et al. 1986, Nelson 1988, Carey et al. 1991, Gilbert and Allwine 1991, Hagar et al. 1996, Trombino 1998, Weikel and Hayes 1999, Hagar and Stern 2001). In some areas occurrence has been noted across all ages of trees or thinned stands during the breeding season while a preference for old-growth or unthinned stands has been found in winter (Anthony et al. 1996, Hagar et al. 1996). A preference for nesting in coniferous trees older than 100 yr has been observed in areas where they occur (Mannan et al. 1980, Nelson 1988, Ralph et al. 1991) and Gilbert and Allwine (1991) noted a significant association with older stands in spring in the Cascades. Where only young trees occur, they prefer thinned stands, consistent with a general selection for open stands (Hagar et al. 1996). Readily move into burns; an estimated 100 were found at the Pringle Falls burn in the Cascades in Jan 1999 (D. Hale p.c., J. Meredith p.c.).

Nesting in dead trees with light to moderate decay is preferred (Mannan et al. 1980; Bull et al. 1986, Brett 1997, Weikel unpubl. data). Nests are typically freshly excavated (Gabrielson and Jewett 1940). Of 59 nests in the Blue Mtns. in forests ranging from young to old-growth, 68% were in ponderosa pine, 17% in lodgepole pine, 10% in western larch, and 5% in Douglas-fir; 93% were in dead trees. The mean dbh, tree height, and cavity height were 17 in (42 cm), 49 ft (15 m) and 26 ft (8 m), respectively (Bull et al. 1986). In the Paisley and Lakeview RDs of the Fremont NF in sc. Oregon, 10 nests in aspens had a mean dbh, tree height, and cavity height of 14.4 in (36.7 cm), 56.8 ft (17.3 m), and 17.7 ft (5.4 m), respectively. Nest trees averaged 24.1% live growth (Trombino 1998). In the s. Oregon Cascades in a mixed-conifer-dominated forest, of 32 nest trees, the mean dbh, tree height, and cavity height were 31.7 in (80.4 cm), 91.9 ft (28.0 m), and 61 ft (18.6 m), respectively; 81% had broken tops (Brett 1997). At Crater L. NP nesting has occurred in cottonwood, lodgepole pine, and Shasta (red) fir (Farner 1952). Neff (1928) noted that *harrisi* commonly nest in "dead cottonwoods, alders, willows, etc." In the Coast Range, of 23 nests in stands of mostly unmanaged trees ranging in age from 40 to >200 yr, 74% were in Douglas-fir, 13% in grand fir, and 13% in bigleaf maple. The mean dbh, tree height, and cavity height were 28.4 in (72.2 cm), 98.8 ft (30.1 m), and 71.2 ft (21.7 m), respectively; 78% were dead trees (Nelson 1988). Also in the Coast Range with stands ranging from 10 to >200 yr old, seven nests were found only in stands 110 yr or more in age, in snags with a mean dbh and cavity height of 36.2 in (92 cm) and 59.7 ft (18.2 m), respectively (Mannan et al. 1980). In 35- to 45-yr-old Douglas-fir forests in the Coast Range, of 16 nests, all in snags, 38% were in red alder, 12% in Douglas-fir, 6% each in western hemlock and noble fir, and 38% in unidentified residual snags. The mean dbh and tree height were 21.5 in (54.5 cm) and 28.2 ft (8.6 m), respectively (Weikel unpubl. data). Nine nest snags in clearcuts in the Coast Range had a mean dbh, snag height, and cavity height of 23 in (58 cm), 21.0 ft (6.4 m), and 22.3 ft (6.8 m), respectively (Schreiber 1987).

Densities per 100 ac (40 ha) were 1-3 birds in the Wallowa Mtns. (Mannan 1982); 2.0-8.9 in ponderosa pine and 0.5-2.9 in Douglas-fir/western hemlock forests on the east and west slopes of the Cascades, respectively (Bate 1995); 0.50 birds in summer and 1.80-5.40 birds in winter in riparian areas of the w. Cascades (Anthony et al. 1996); 0-12 birds in stands of mostly Oregon white oak in the Willamette Valley (Anderson SH 1970); and 0.3-72 birds in the Coast Range (Mannan et al. 1980, Morrison and Meslow 1983a, Nelson 1988, Carey et al. 1991). Mannan et al. (1980), Mannan (1982), Nelson (1988), Carey et al. (1991), and Anthony et al. (1996) noted that

density increased with age of trees; Nelson (1988) found significant differences in 1 of 2 yr.

Contents of 57 stomachs of birds from the Willamette Valley and Rogue R. and Klamath areas were 62% beetles (Coleoptera), 5% ants, 15% other insects and spiders, 11% miscellaneous plant matter, and 2% each elderberry, corn, and mast (mostly acorns); a few seeds were also noted (Neff 1928). Beetle larvae and carpenter ants were noted as diet in the Coast Range (Weikel and Hayes 1999). Regular visitors to suet feeders (*DBM*), they have been observed drinking from hummingbird feeders at two locations in c. Oregon (L. Kunzman p.c., L. Wentworth p.c.). A preference was shown for foraging on mature and old-growth coniferous trees in the Blue Mtns. (Bull et al. 1986) and in two studies in the Coast Range (Mannan 1977, Carey et al. 1991), with most activity occurring on unhealthy live trees and trees dead about 1-3 yr. Weikel and Hayes (1999) noted a selection for foraging on deciduous over coniferous trees during the breeding season in the Coast Range. Live trees were foraged on 55% and 64% of the time in forests of mixed-age trees in the Blue Mtns. and the Coast Range, respectively (Bull et al. 1986, Carey et al. 1991). Morrison and Meslow (1983a) noted foraging in clearcuts in the Coast Range by individuals nesting in adjacent mature stands. Douglas-fir comprised 71% of the trees foraged on in a mixed-age forest in the Coast Range (Carey et al. 1991) and ponderosa pine and lodgepole pine made up 84% in the Blue Mtns., though a preference was shown for western larch where it occurred (Bull et al. 1986). In the Willamette Valley, Neff (1928) noted foraging on dead willows, cottonwood, and alder. In the Coast Range in a 35- to 45-yr-old Douglas-fir forest, during 85 observations, Weikel and Hayes (1999) noted foraging on snags (46%), logs (31%), hardwoods (13%), and conifers (10%). Bull et al. (1986) found that Hairy and Black-backed Woodpeckers both feed in the same habitat with the same strategies; this could lead to competition when resources are limited.

**Seasonal Activity and Behavior:** Few consistent seasonal movements are known. Some wandering occurs outside the breeding season (*JS*). At Malheur NWR spring migration begins in Mar or Apr and ends by late May (Littlefield 1990a). Following spring courtship and drumming activity, cavity excavation takes place mid-Apr to mid-Jun (n=24). Eggs are laid and young are still in the nest cavity early May to mid-Jul (n=112) (Bendire 1895, Bull 1980, Adamus et al. 2001, Weikel unpubl. data). Eggs may number three to six; four to five is most common (Griffee and Rapraeger 1937, Gabrielson and Jewett 1940). Fledglings are typically observed mid-Jun to late Jul (n=53) (Gullion 1951, Bull 1980, Adamus et al. 2001, Weikel unpubl. data). Bull et al. (1986) found that of seven species of woodpeckers, Hairy Woodpecker young fledged earliest and Black-backed Woodpecker young fledged latest, providing an advantageous temporal separation of resource utilization. Territory size in the Blue Mtns. was 6-9 ac (2-4 ha) (Thomas, Anderson, et al. 1979) and averaged 7 ac (3 ha) in w. Oregon where home range was 22-37 ac (9-15 ha) (Brown 1985). Fall migration at Malheur NWR begins in early Oct, peaks in late Oct, and ends by mid-Nov; small numbers winter (Littlefield 1990a). Regular movement into residential areas has been noted in winter, especially when conditions are severe (Neff 1928, Evanich 1992a, Contreras and Kindschy 1996).

**Detection:** Not adequately sampled on point counts due to infrequent drumming and calling, and short duration of surveys, otherwise easy to detect (*MGH*), including when tapping (*DBM*). Worn birds with reduced spotting, and immature birds with orange or yellow on crown may be mistaken for Three-toed Woodpecker. Sometimes reported as Downy Woodpecker by inexperienced observers conducting forest bird surveys (*MGH*).

**Population Status and Conservation:** Portland area CBCs showed significant decreases in number of Hairy Woodpeckers observed per party mile from 1952-53 to 1981-82, likely due to habitat loss caused by urbanization. CBCs in s. and w. Oregon did not show significant correlations while all areas of Washington did (Morrison and Morrison 1983). Oregon CBC data 1959-88 show no significant trends with a decrease of 0.9%/yr (Sauer et al. 1996). BBS data show a non-significant 0.5%/yr decline 1966-2000 for Oregon (Sauer et al. 2001), but Sharp (1996) reported a significant decline of 5.5%/yr on non-NF lands in Oregon per BBS data for 1968-94. Thomas, Anderson, et al. (1979) estimated that 180 snags per 100 ac (40 ha) of at least 10 in (25 cm) dbh were necessary to support the "maximum population" in relevant forests of the Blue Mtns. and Neitro et al. (1985) calculated that 132 and 192 snags per 100 ac (40 ha) were needed in areas of shrub/open sapling-pole and forest, respectively, in w. Oregon Douglas-fir habitat. The "loss of old growth would negatively affect cavity-using bird populations," with severe effects for woodpeckers (Carey et al. 1991). These "habitat generalists" can have their needs met with management for snag habitat islands and shelterwoods within managed forests or in clearcuts (Nelson 1988). Both appropriate nesting and foraging habitat need to be provided, including patches of hardwoods and old-growth living conifers, snags, and logs (Weikel and Hayes 1999).—*Jamie Simmons*

## White-headed Woodpecker
*Picoides albolarvatus*

This medium-sized woodpecker is one of the most striking and unique animals found in Oregon's ponderosa pine forests because of its contrasting plumage. It is the only woodpecker that relies heavily on the seeds of ponderosa pine for food and is the only one with a mostly white head and fully black body. Males are distinguished by a red patch on the nape. The black of juveniles is dull instead of glossy, and the nape patch tends to be orange (Winkler et al. 1995, Garrett et al. 1996) or rose-colored (R. W. Frenzel p.c.). In flight, white wing-patches and a dark back and rump separate this from other woodpeckers.

**General Distribution:** Resident of montane coniferous forests from s. interior British Columbia south through c. Washington, n. Idaho, e. and sw. Oregon, n. and c. California, and the western edge of c. Nevada to the mountains of s. California. Occasionally found in lowlands outside the breeding season. *P. a. gravirostris* occurs in s. California and *P. a. albolarvatus* occurs in the remainder of the species' range (AOU 1957).

**Oregon Distribution:** An uncommon permanent resident in forests of the Ochoco, Blue, and Wallowa Mtns. and the east side of the Cascades, but suitable habitat is restricted. Local west of the Cascade crest in upper reaches of the Umpqua R. basin, in the Siskiyou Mtns., and in the north part of the east slope of the Cascades (Marshall 1997). Fewer than 10 records exist outside this range, including coastal sites and Malheur NWR (Rogers J 1978, Littlefield 1990a, Tweit and Johnson 1990).

**Habitat and Diet:** It occurs mainly in open ponderosa pine or mixed-conifer forests dominated by ponderosa pine (Bull et al. 1986, Dixon 1995a, 1995b, Frenzel 2000). Exceptions include: (1) wandering or vagrant birds that can occur almost anywhere, (2) occasional foraging bouts from stands dominated by ponderosa

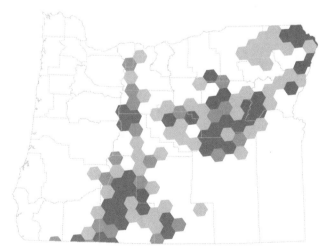

pine to lodgepole pine, Engelmann spruce, and other species; and (3) a small population in true firs in the Siskiyou Mtns. southwest of Ashland that extends south into California (Marshall 1997). The latter population has not been studied and could show variations from findings in ponderosa pine habitat that are cited below. Dixon (1995a, 1995b) found White-headed Woodpecker population density increased with increasing volumes of old-growth ponderosa pine and a positive association with large-diameter ponderosa pines in both contiguous and fragmented sites. However, it is not present at many sites that provide seemingly good habitat.

In addition to uncut old-growth, they commonly use areas which have undergone various silvicultural treatments if large-diameter ponderosa pines and other old-growth components remain (Dixon 1995a, 1995b, Frenzel 2000). Nest sites are not representative of overall habitat needs, and tend to be in the open. Average canopy closure at 66 nests sites studied by Frenzel (2000) from the Deschutes and Winema NFs was only 12%. Of the 66 sites, 86.4% had undergone various silvicultural treatments, including 25 nests in partial cuts, nine in clearcuts (in stumps or snags), 11

*White-headed Woodpecker*

in shelterwoods or seed tree cuts, seven in overstory removals, two in commercial thins, and three in pre-commercial thins.

They usually excavate nest cavities in snags, but other commonly recorded substrates found in Oregon, Idaho, and California include stumps, leaning logs, and dead tops of live trees (Milne and Hejl 1989, Frederick and Moore 1991, Dixon 1995a, 1995b). Mean dbh of nest snags or trees was 25.6 in (65 cm) for 43 nests in the Deschutes NF and 31.5 in (80 cm) for 16 nests in the Winema NF (Dixon 1995a, b). Similarly, the 203 nest trees and snags subsequently studied by Frenzel (2000) over 4 yr had a mean dbh of 26.2 in (66.5 cm). Among western woodpeckers, requirements for nest tree diameter are exceeded only by the Pileated Woodpecker (*DBM*). Mean canopy closure for 205 nests was 10.3% (Frenzel 2000). Nests can be close to the ground. Mean cavity height of 16 Winema NF nests, where tall snags are scarce, was only 4.6 ft (1.4 m; range 1.2 - 9.8 ft [0.37 - 3.0 m]) (Dixon 1995a). They use separate cavities for roosting (Dixon 1995a, b).

In the Deschutes NF, the Jul-Dec median minimum convex polygon annual home range size for contiguous and fragmented habitats was 257 ac (104 ha) (range 165-403 ac or 67-163 ha, n=7) and 793 ac (321 ha) (range 141-1099 ac or 57-445 ha, n=3) respectively (Dixon 1995b).

Diet varies locally and seasonally; it includes seeds, invertebrates, and sap. Ponderosa pine seeds are the most important vegetable food item in Oregon (Bull et al. 1986, Dixon 1995b), but sugar pine is utilized locally (Dixon 1995a). Information specific to Oregon regarding the invertebrate part of the diet is absent other than Dixon's (1995b) observations of birds taking spruce budworm, larvae, ants, and cicadas. From a rangewide perspective, ants, beetles, and scale insects constitute the bulk of the insect diet (Garrett et al. 1996). More observations in Oregon may show similar results.

Dixon (1995a, 1995b) made over 5,000 observations of radio-tagged White-headed Woodpeckers in the Winema and Deschutes NFs. Seventy percent of 3,473 Jul-Dec observations in the Deschutes NF involved foraging, which broke out as 35% gleaning, 31% cone-feeding, 24% pecking, 7% sapsucking, and 3% other, including excavating, scaling, flycatching, and ground foraging. In the Winema NF more time was spent gleaning and pecking and only 5% at cone-feeding. Unlike other woodpeckers, spend little time excavating or scaling bark for food. In the Deschutes NF, 42% of foraging took place in branches, 23% on the upper trunk, 22% on the mid-trunk, and 13% on the lower trunk of ponderosa pines having a mean dbh of 27 in (68 cm). Bull et al. (1986) reported foraging as occurring mainly on the lower trunks of ponderosa pines in ne. Oregon.

**Seasonal Activity and Behavior:** No consistent seasonal movements are known, but limited movements or wandering outside breeding areas and seasons occur as noted in the distribution sections above. Dixon (1995a, b) found 30 radio-tagged breeding adults occupying the same home range from Jul into Dec. She detected foraging bouts involving adults with young up to 5 mi (8 km) from a breeding territory to feed on spruce budworms, and up to 8 mi (13 km) for sugar pine seeds.

The following life history information, taken from Garrett et al. (1996), incorporates information that is applicable to the species in Oregon based on the work of Dixon. Pairs occupy the same territory in succeeding year. They defend the area around the nest site during the breeding season, but the defended area is small compared to home range. Excavation of nest cavities often involves false starts; begins around 1 May and takes 3-4 wk. They commonly excavate a new cavity each year. Frenzel (2000) found 16.6% of 175 nests were in re-used cavities with additional nests excavated from old starts or old entrances.

Garrett et al. (1996) reported nests with eggs 30 May - 25 Jun, but Frenzel (2000) reported a clutch as early as 15 May. Clutch size is usually 4 to 5 (Garrett et al. 1996). A mean clutch size of 4.1 (n=41) was found by Frenzel (2000). Young fledge at approximately 26 days old, typically from mid-Jun to mid-Jul (Frenzel 2000). Parents remain with young into Aug. Both adults share in cavity construction, incubation, and feeding of young.

Both sexes use a *pee-dink* call and a rattle similar to the more common Hairy Woodpecker. Also drum on hollow logs or snags. Vocalizations and drumming occur year-round, but are more frequent during breeding season (Garrett et al. 1996).

The 30% of the time budget on the Deschutes NF not devoted to foraging included 10% flying, 6% resting, 5% preening, 2% calling, 2% interacting or displaying, and 5% other activities including feeding young, climbing, and drumming (Dixon 1995b). They frequently drink water at springs, guzzlers, and streams.

**Detection:** Even in seemingly good habitat, the likelihood of detecting this species can be low. However, in specific areas a concerted effort will result in finding the bird, especially during the breeding season, when it is most active. Popular locales for observing it in Deschutes Co. include the Camp Sherman and Black Butte Ranch areas and Cold Springs and Indian Ford CGs.; and in Klamath Co. from the road that runs along the west side of Upper Klamath L. It is also often seen at Cabin L. Guard Station north of Ft. Rock in Deschutes Co. and at Idlewild CG north of Burns in Harney Co. It is most frequently detected when flying or by its rattly call.

**Population Status and Conservation:** The overall range in Oregon appears not to have changed from the historical pattern based on Gabrielson and Jewett (1940), but seems to have become more patchy because of habitat deterioration. No population data are available, but densities in the Deschutes and Winema NFs, based on line transects conducted 15 Apr-24 May 1991, ranged 0-2.53 birds per 100 ac (40 ha) (Dixon 1995b). Densities per 100 ac found in 1997 on five study areas each in the Deschutes and Winema NFs by Frenzel and Popper (1998) were 0.03-1.54 and 0-1.23 respectively.

Most habitat available to this species has been subjected to silvicultural treatments. Amounts of old-growth ponderosa pine remaining in Oregon and Washington are probably less than 10% of what existed prior to Euro-American settlement (Henjum et al. 1994). Much of this exists in stands that are too small to support populations of old-growth associates. This has occurred through a combination of fire suppression that precludes natural thinning and results in replacement of pines with firs; livestock grazing that restricted grasses needed to carry ground fires; and timber harvest that has concentrated on large-diameter ponderosa pines (Agee 1993, Oliver et al. 1994, Brown 2000, Covington 2000). Habitat deterioration in terms of both quality and quantity provided the impetus for studies of this species, and is reflected by research monies devoted to it by ODFW and the USFS, including Dixon's (1995, 1995a) research and follow-up studies by the ONHP (Frenzel 2000).

While the above research clearly shows a positive relationship between this species and large-diameter ponderosa pines, Frenzel (2000) acquired additional information which led to the conclusion that population recruitment for this woodpecker was insufficient to offset mortality in his 11 study areas in the Deschutes and Winema NFs. For the period 1997-2000, he found nesting success was only 35.6% (95% CI: 28.6-44.2; n=154) at nest sites in silvicultural treatments as opposed to 62.0% (95% CI: 47.9-80.1; n=46) for nests in uncut stands. Uncut sites had big tree (>21 in [53 cm] dbh) density >12 trees/ac (0.4 ha). Weighted adult mean survivorship was calculated at only 0.561 for 1997 to 2000, based on a sample of 46 marked birds.

Shrub growth on the forest floor and increased understories, which has resulted from fire suppression, may be factors affecting levels of mammalian nest predation and vulnerability of adults to avian predation (Frenzel 2000). Some sites subjected to partial and shelterwood cuts may more closely replicate the original open park-like ponderosa pine stands than some existing uncut stands with heavy shrub understories. White-headed Woodpeckers are possibly drawn to relatively open sites to avoid predation (Frenzel 2000).

A population decline in this species can be assumed to be ongoing in the above two NFs, which contain some of the best remaining habitat for this bird in Oregon. Determining if, when, and where the population might level off will require continued monitoring and studies, but the long-term stability of this bird in Oregon (and Washington) appears to rest with reversing the declining health of ponderosa pine forests (*DBM*).—*David B. Marshall*

## Three-toed Woodpecker *Picoides tridactylus*

At first glance, Oregon seems to offer this compact, finely marked woodpecker a bonanza of trees and forest types to choose from, yet actual sightings are cause for celebration. The white-barred back and black-and-white face might cause the casual hiker to mistake it for the common Hairy Woodpecker, or the barred flanks, reduced spotting on the wings, and male's yellow crown might suggest the Black-backed Woodpecker. The reason for this bird's rarity may lie in its very narrow diet or nesting requirements, which offer the diligent observer much opportunity for discovery.

**General Distribution:** Holarctic: Scandinavia, n. Europe and Asia; disjunct populations in c. and s. Europe, Tibet, China, and Japan. Broadly distributed through n. N. America from Alaska to Newfoundland. In the Rocky Mtns. south to n. Arizona and New Mexico, but in the Cascades only to s. Oregon, and absent from the Sierra Nevada. The range of this species overlaps the range of spruce trees almost perfectly (Bock and Bock 1974). Three N. American subspecies, *P. t. fasciatus* in Oregon (AOU 1957).

**Oregon Distribution:** Rare and local, particularly near and w. of the Cascade summit, often near high-elevation lakes or beetle outbreaks (*MGH*). Reports come sparingly from both slopes of the Cascades including Crater L. and the upper Rogue R. drainage (Farner 1952), Olallie Lake (*DBM*), the Bear Springs RD area of Wasco Co. (D. Lusthoff p.c.) and the Blue

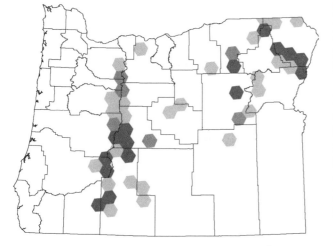

Mtns. including the Wallowas (Bull et al. 1986, Evanich 1992a, Leonard 2001). Southernmost records are from Mt. McLoughlin (Gabrielson and Jewett 1940). There is one record from Hart Mt. (Lake Co.) and two from west of the Cascades (Roxy Anne Peak and Mt. Ashland, Jackson Co.) (Gilligan et al. 1994).

**Habitat and Diet:** Inhabits lodgepole pine, Blue Mtn. mixed conifer, true fir/mountain hemlock, and Douglas-fir/mixed conifer habitat types. Forest type may not be as important as the presence of bark beetles (Baldwin 1968, Bock and Bock 1974). In Oregon, they tend to use higher-elevation forests than Black-backed Woodpecker (but the two species overlap). Goggans et al. (1989) found 20 nests in the Deschutes NF at 4,500–5,600 ft (1,360–1,700 m), but none at a nearby 4,350-ft (1,320 m) elevation study area. In a mountain pine beetle outbreak in the Blue Mtns., 69% of observations were in grand fir forest types, but these forests always contained lodgepole pines, the host tree of this bark beetle species (Bull et al. 1986). Three-toed Woodpeckers fed exclusively on lodgepole pine (mean dbh 9.4 in [24 cm]); most fed-upon trees had been dead less than 3 yr (Bull et al. 1986). More abundant in burned than adjacent unburned forests of ne. Washington; 85% of foraging was on trees >9 in (23 cm) dbh even though these trees made up <40% of the forest (Kreisel and Stein 1999). Nests are often fairly low; nest trees are often smaller in diameter than those used by other cavity nesters (Hejl et al. 2000). Habitat requirements may include trees with heartrot for nesting and high densities of bark or wood-boring beetles (Goggans et al. 1989).

Eats larvae of bark beetles (Scolytidae) and wood-boring beetles (Cerambycidae and Buprestidae) (Leonard 2001). Suggested to be a bark beetle specialist (Murphy and Lehnhausen 1998). Bark beetle larvae rarely exceed 0.2 in (5 mm) length, whereas wood-borer larvae can exceed 2 in (5 cm), so food value differs between these 2 types of prey. In an Alaska burn, Murphy and Lehnhausen (1998) found that 18 Three-toed Woodpecker stomachs contained an average of 43 ± 10 scolytid larvae and 20 ± 10 cerambycid larvae. They noted that the cerambycid larvae were early instars (i.e., small). However, in Idaho burned forests Three-toed Woodpeckers often fed nestlings large wood-borer larvae and pupae (0.4–0.8 in [10–20 mm] length) (*HDP*).

Often forages by flaking bark (Goggans et al. 1989, Villard 1994) or making shallow holes (*HDP*), exposing insects at the bark-wood interface. The beak is markedly shorter than Black-backed Woodpecker's (Bock and Bock 1974). Three-toed Woodpeckers investigate deeper foraging holes made by larger woodpeckers (*HDP*). In areas of sympatry with Black-backed Woodpecker, this species forages higher on the trunk and on limbs of trees (Villard 1994). In the Old

World, this species is known for feeding on sap, but this behavior is much rarer in N. America (Villard 1994).

**Seasonal Activity and Behavior:** Begins breeding in late May to late Jun (n=2), territorial defense observed 23 May; courtship/copulation observed 18 Jun; nest with young observed 19 Jul, and fledged young found 9 Jul to 9 Aug (n=6) (OBBA). An adult male with a fledgling was seen in the Cache Cr. burn on Forest Road 590 near Sisters on 21 Jul 2001 (S. Shunk p.c.). This species may breed relatively late in the season owing to its tendency to occupy high-elevation forests (Goggans et al. 1989). One was observed feeding recently fledged young as late as 4 Aug 1984 in extreme nw Klamath Co. (D. Fix p.c.).

The call is a high-pitched, descending rattle. During aggression, gives a more urgent, constant-pitch rattle while wing-fluttering and clinging to the bark with tail held free from trunk (Leonard 2001, *HDP*). Drum accelerates at end, very similar to Black-backed Woodpecker but often with a shorter constant-tempo introduction (Leonard 2001, *HDP*).

**Detection:** Less conspicuous than Black-backed Woodpecker because of less-frequent vocalizations (Goggans et al. 1989). Nevertheless, fairly readily detected early in the breeding season from drumming, or late in the breeding season from the nearly constant begging calls of nestlings. Responds to playback of drumming during Apr–May (Goggans et al. 1989).

**Population Status and Conservation:** Status in Oregon is not well known. Oregon is the southern limit of this species' range on the w. coast, although curiously it occurs as far south as Arizona along the Rocky Mtns. Although the overlap of the species' global range with spruce trees suggests an explanation (spruce trees are absent from the Sierra Nevada but present in the Rockies) (Bock and Bock 1974), it is not as simple a solution as would at first seem. Three-toed Woodpeckers are often found in forest types that do not include spruce, especially in Oregon, where they occupy lodgepole pine forests at least as frequently (Bull et al. 1986, Goggans et al. 1989). More research is needed to determine why Three-toed Woodpeckers are rare in this state, and to identify important habitat components.

The Three-toed Woodpecker has been linked with infestations of the spruce beetle and other bark beetles, and it is also recorded from burned forests. Bark-beetle outbreaks appear to provide important habitat in Oregon (Bull et al. 1986, Goggans et al. 1989), as they do in much of this species' range (Baldwin 1968, Fayt 1999). In other parts of the West, Three-toed Woodpeckers take advantage of insect outbreaks and plentiful nest sites following forest fires (Hutto 1995a, Murphy and Lehnhausen 1998, Hejl et al. 2000), but the importance of burned forests in Oregon has not yet been documented. This species appears to thrive in areas traditionally evaluated as diseased and undesirable, making it a difficult species to protect without altering our perception of healthy forests.—*Hugh D. Powell*

## Black-backed Woodpecker *Picoides arcticus*

You may walk many miles through Oregon forests in search of this woodpecker before you find one. On the other hand, if your trail leads into the open expanses of a recent forest fire or the twiggy closets of a bark-beetle outbreak, you are much more likely to glimpse this charcoal bird. Your ears may draw you to it via an accelerating drum ringing from a prominent snag, or its snarling call. Once you've found it, look for the yellow crown (males), barred flanks, dark face, and unmarked black back. This last trait distinguishes this species from all other medium-sized area woodpeckers except the gaudy Williamson's Sapsucker and the distinctive White-headed Woodpecker. Field guides often overlook two subtle fieldmarks: the near absence of a postocular stripe and the much-reduced wing spotting compared with Hairy Woodpeckers.

**General Distribution:** Broadly distributed across Canada and north into c. Alaska. In U.S., they are largely confined to northernmost tier of states. Isolated population in S. Dakota Black Hills. Occurs south in Rocky Mtns. to n. Wyoming; in the Cascade Range through Washington and Oregon; in Sierra Nevada to c. California. In e. U.S., irruptive south of normal range. Monotypic (AOU 1957).

**Oregon Distribution:** A rare to locally common resident near the summit and on nearby plateaus and ridges on the west side of the Cascades (Fix 1990a, *MGH*); more widespread on the east slope (Gilligan et al. 1994). Uncommon in the Blue Mtns., where it is less common than the Three-toed Woodpecker (the reverse of the rest of Oregon) (Evanich 1992a, OBBA).

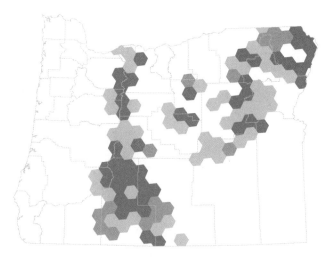

In nw. Oregon, there have been several sightings from the Clackamas R. drainage (R. W. Scharpf unpubl. data, *MGH*). The westernmost extent of its range is in the Siskiyou Mtns. (Marshall et al. 1996, Contreras 1998). The reported center of abundance is the lodgepole pine forest east of the Cascade crest between Bend and Klamath Falls (Gabrielson and Jewett 1940, Gilligan et al. 1994). Merrill (1888, cited in Farner 1952) reported this species abundant in mountains around Ft. Klamath. Inhabits the Warner Mtns. of California, so it may occur in this range in adjacent sc. Oregon (Dixon and Saab 2000).

**Habitat and Diet:** It has been recorded in most types of conifer forest including ponderosa pine, lodgepole pine, Douglas-fir/mixed conifer, Blue Mtn. mixed conifer, and to a lesser extent true fir/mountain hemlock, but odds of finding this species in any forest type increase dramatically if the forest contains a high proportion of dead trees (Bent 1939, Bock and Bock 1974, Fix 1990a, Gilligan 1994). Across its range, it is best known from and apparently most abundant in recently burned forests (Apfelbaum and Haney 1981, Hutto 1995a, Dixon and Saab 2000), but in Oregon, bark-beetle-killed forests are frequently occupied, including lodgepole pine forests of e. Cascades (n=35 nests over 2 yrs) (Goggans et al. 1989) and pine and mixed-conifer forests of the Blue Mtns. (n=9 nests) (Bull et al. 1986). Home range size in a bark beetle outbreak ranged 173–810 ac (81–368 ha, min. convex polygon; n=3 radio-marked birds) (Goggans et al. 1989). Observations of high density of this species in burned forests suggest that home range can vary greatly according to food availability (Murphy and Lehnhausen 1998, Dixon and Saab 2000). Salvage-logged burned forests contain fewer nests than unlogged burns (Hejl et al. 2000). Nest is often low in a tree; both living and dead trees are used, but may require heartrot for excavation of nest cavities (17 of 17 nest trees had heartrot [Goggans et al. 1989]). Nest trees are often smaller in diameter than those used by other cavity nesters (Raphael and White 1984, Hejl et al. 2000). Gilligan (1994) reported elevational range in Oregon as 4,000–7,800 ft (1,200–2,400 m), but some Clackamas R. sightings may have been lower (*MGH*).

Primarily eats larvae of wood-boring beetles (families Cerambycidae and Buprestidae). Beal (1911) reported 75% of stomach contents consisted of wood-borers (this figure is the root of almost all published diet descriptions prior to 1998). In burned spruce forests of Alaska, this species ate almost exclusively Cerambycidae larvae (n=18 stomachs) (Murphy and Lehnhausen 1998). In burned forests of Montana and Idaho, nestlings were fed 59–74% wood-borer larvae > 0.4 in (10 mm) long (Powell 2000). Observations of this species inhabiting bark-beetle outbreaks indicate bark beetles (family Scolytidae) are also eaten (Bull

et al. 1986, Goggans et al. 1989). These 2 groups of insects differ markedly in size, colonization abilities, population dynamics, etc., so they should not be considered equivalent food types, and by extension burned forests and bark-beetle outbreaks should not be considered equivalent habitats.

It often flakes away bark by delivering glancing blows (Short 1974, Goggans et al. 1989), but equally capable of excavating holes in search of wood-boring beetles deeper in the tree (Raphael and White 1984, *HDP*). Farner (1952) commented on the unusual sight of a Black-backed Woodpecker flycatching like a Lewis's Woodpecker.

**Seasonal Activity and Behavior:** They begin nesting in mid-May, eggs are present to mid-Jun, young in the nest to mid-Jul, as indicated by the following dates of observations. A male was excavating 20 May in a burned ponderosa pine forest near Lapine (*HDP*). Nests containing eggs were found 25 May–15 Jun (n= 6) (Bent 1939, Gabrielson and Jewett 1940, OBBA). Nests with young were found 6 Jun–20 Jul (n= 11) (Gabrielson and Jewett 1940, Farner 1952, OBBA). Fledged young were seen 20 Jun–10 Jul (n= 6) (OBBA). The breeding schedule can vary among years by at least 3 wk due to weather conditions (*HDP*), and may begin later at higher elevations (Goggans et al. 1989).

**Detection:** Black-backs are easily detected aurally at three stages: during the breeding season (but particularly early in season), when both sexes drum from snags; during excavation; and during the middle to late nestling stage, when young become vocal and beg virtually continuously from the nest (young audible from 330 ft [100 m] or more) (Dixon and Saab 2000). Adults are easily detected when vocalizing. The call is similar to that of Three-toed Woodpecker; shorter and shriller than Hairy Woodpecker, (*jp!*, lacking "vowel" tones, vs. *peek*). Drum accelerates at end; constant-tempo introduction often longer than Three-toed (*HDP*). The descending rattle (scream-rattle-snarl) (Short 1974) ends with several growling phrases (also given alone), which uniquely identify this species.

When silent, it can be difficult to locate, especially in recent burns, where the lustrous black back matches sooty bark. Observers should suspect Black-backed Woodpecker presence around snags with bark flaked off or many small excavations, but, at least in burns, Hairy and Three-toed Woodpecker make similar foraging signs (*HDP*). On the e. Cascade slope, responds to playbacks of drumming during May (Goggans et al. 1989). Also responds in Jun in Jackson Co. (N. Barrett p.c.). Local recordings produce much greater response than commercial (non-local) recordings (*HDP*).

**Population Status and Conservation:** Black-backed Woodpeckers are closely associated with stand-replacing fire, i.e., fire that kills virtually all of the trees it encompasses (Hutto 1995a, Murphy and Lehnhausen 1998). Stand-replacing fire produces habitats that briefly contain abundant food resources for woodpeckers (McCullough et al. 1998). After 3-5 yr, the majority of insects inhabiting the dead wood emerge as adults and do not recolonize the dead trees (McCullough et al. 1998), resulting in a decrease in food availability and hence habitat suitability for woodpeckers. For this reason, recently burned forests provide high-quality habitat, but any single burn provides good habitat for only a few years.

Despite popular ideas that stand-replacing fire is unnatural and catastrophic, it is the historically dominant form of fire in the Pacific Northwest (Agee 1993). The Black-backed Woodpecker is perhaps the bird species most conspicuously adapted to this kind of forest fire (Hutto 1995a). Fire suppression throughout the 20th century dramatically reduced the area of recently burned forests, and this probably reduced Black-backed Woodpecker populations. The shift in public perception about the value of fire suppression, stirred by the calamitous 2000 and 2002 fire seasons, has increased enthusiasm and funding for forest thinning, controlled burning, and salvage logging. Unfortunately for the Black-backed Woodpecker, adopting these new measures is not likely to improve habitat, because the first two will continue to reduce the amount of recently burned forest available and the third will devalue the habitat that does exist (Hutto 1995a). For this and other fire-dependent animals, it is crucial that forest-management plans find room for stand-replacing fire, and that portions of burned forests are exempted from salvage logging.

In addition to this species' affinity for burned forests, there is good evidence that bark-beetle-killed forests are important habitats in Oregon (Bull 1986, Goggans et al. 1989), and the species also occurs sparingly in unburned, mature forests. The relative value of these three habitats is unknown, in part because gathering data where Black-backed Woodpeckers are rare is difficult. One striking difference among these habitats is food availability, but sound management policies await studies that can evaluate habitat suitability between these types of forest.—*Hugh D. Powell*

## Northern Flicker *Colaptes auratus*

The most ubiquitous and unconventional woodpecker in Oregon. Larger than most, it is primarily lighter shades of brown and gray with black markings: spotted underparts, barred back, and a broad necklace. Its wing linings and undertail range from salmon to yellow, and the rump is white. Males have a red or black mustache. It has a slightly curved bill, feeds mostly on the ground,

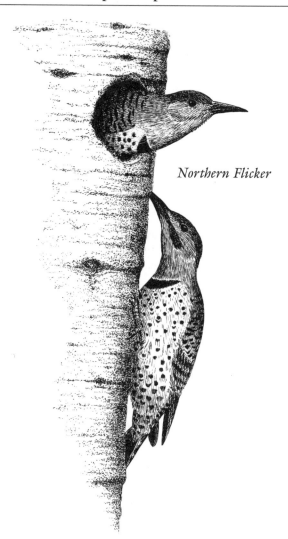

*Northern Flicker*

and nests in a variety of substrates. Previously the red-shafted and yellow-shafted forms were considered separate species.

**General Distribution:** Of four groups of subspecies, the western *cafer* group (red-shafted) breeds from se. Alaska, east to the west edge of the Great Plains, south to Mexico; the eastern *auratus* group (yellow-shafted) breeds from w. and c. Alaska, east of the Rocky Mtns., south to Florida. Both of these groups winter only slightly south of their breeding ranges. Two other groups, *mexicanoides* and *chrysocaulosus*, occur in M. America and Cuba, respectively. Of at least six subspecies, two are identified and a third is tentative in Oregon (*MRB*).

**Oregon Distribution:** A common resident throughout Oregon; found in 417 of 430 hexagons of the OBBA project (Adamus et al. 2001). *C. a. collaris* is found east of the Cascades (e.g., specimens [USNM] from Hood River, Hood River Co.; Bend, Deschutes Co.; several localities in Klamath Co.; Adel, Lake Co.) and in the Rogue R. Valley in Jackson and Josephine counties (SOU). *C. a. cafer* is found in the remaining western parts of the state from the mountains of n. Jackson Co. and Douglas Co. northward (*MRB*). One subspecies of the *auratus* group (yellow-shafted), either *C. a. borealis* or *C. a. auratus* (includes *luteus* as a synonym [Browning 2002]), is known from a small number of specimens (Gabrielson and Jewett 1940, Browning and English 1967b), and probably is a rare winter visitor or transient throughout Oregon. According to Short (1965a) some specimens from Oregon revealed incidences of interbreeding between red- and yellow-shafted groups.

**Habitat and Diet:** Northern Flickers may be encountered in almost any terrestrial habitat, but are generally most abundant in open forests and forest edges adjacent to open country. They venture into nearby habitats, including towns and farms, but typically avoid dense forest (Gabrielson and Jewett 1940, Jackman 1974, Bull 1980, Mannan et al. 1980, Bull et al. 1986, Gilligan et al. 1994, Brett 1997). A greater abundance was noted in old-growth than in managed forests in the Wallowa Mtns. (Mannan 1982). Carey et al. (1991) and Huff and Raley (1991) found Northern Flicker significantly more abundant in stands of increasing age in the Coast Range, but the latter authors found no significant difference in the Cascades. Hagar and Stern (2001) determined that its abundance had a positive correlation with diameter of trees in Willamette Valley oak woodlands. Reinkensmeyer (2000) noted a preference for old-growth vs. mid-successional western juniper in c. Oregon.

Most nests in forested areas are in older open forests, along older forest edges, and in larger-diameter remnant snags. It nests in trees with some decay, often moderate to heavy (Mannan et al. 1980, Morrison and Meslow 1983a, Bull et al. 1986, Nelson 1988, Schreiber and deCalesta 1992, Brett 1997). Bull et al. (1986) found that 71% of nest trees had broken tops and in a study in e. Douglas Co., nests were 4.3 times more likely to be in a broken-topped tree than a tree with an intact top (Brett 1997). Nests have also been noted in nest boxes, earth cut-banks, a coastal sandstone cliff, buildings, fence posts, large sagebrush, and utility poles (Neff 1928, Gabrielson and Jewett 1940, Mattocks et al. 1983, Littlefield 1990a, Gilligan et al. 1994, N. Wander p.c., *DBM*). Nest-box use is often thwarted by European Starlings, but limited successful nesting has occurred (J. Bell p.c., D. Fenske p.c.). Of 68 nests in the Blue Mtns. in forests of all ages, 81% were in ponderosa pine, 13% in Douglas-fir, and 3% each in lodgepole pine and western larch; 95% were in dead trees. The mean dbh, tree height, and cavity height were 22 in (56 cm), 49 ft (15 m), and 26 ft (8 m), respectively (Bull et al. 1986). In aspen in two mountainous areas of sc. Oregon, of 33 nests, the mean dbh, tree height, and cavity height were 13.0 in (33.0 cm), 44.3 ft (13.5

m), and 10.8 ft (3.3 m), respectively (Dobkin et al. 1995, Trombino 1998). Dobkin et al. (1995) found 21 nests at Hart Mtn., 62% in live trees and 38% in snags, and determined that Northern Flicker showed a preference for nesting in snags. Of 63 nests in the s. Cascades, about 52% were in Douglas-fir, 24% in white fir, 11% in hemlock, and 13% in other species. The mean dbh, tree height, and cavity height were 30.6 in (77.7 cm), 64.6 ft (19.7 m), and 46.9 ft (14.3 m), respectively, with larger-diameter trees having a much higher rate of use (Brett 1997). Of 17 nests in young to old-growth Douglas-fir forests in the Coast Range, the average dbh and cavity height were 31 in (79 cm) and 79 ft (24 m), respectively (Mannan et al. 1980, Nelson 1988); of nine nests, the latter author found a mean tree height of 126.6 ft (38.6 m). Of 16 nests in snags in Douglas-fir clearcuts in the Coast Range, mean dbh and tree height were 30 in (75 cm) and 27.6 ft (8.4 m), respectively; mean nest height of 12 nests, was 21.3 ft (6.5 m) (Schreiber 1987).

Densities per 100 ac (40 ha) were < 0.1-1.0 in the Wallowa Mtns. (Mannan 1982), 4.32-5.56 in western juniper and 0.36-0.64 in shrub-steppe/post-burn grassland (Reinkensmeyer 2000), and 0.9-2.8 in ponderosa pine and 0.7-1.2 in Douglas-fir-western hemlock forests on the east and west slopes of the Cascades, respectively (Bate 1995). Maximum densities per 100 ac (40 ha) were 9-12 pairs in western juniper and 3-9 pairs in ponderosa pine forests in c. Oregon (Gashwiler 1977), 13.3 in a forest of mixed hardwoods with some conifer in sw. Oregon (Cross and Simmons 1983), 44 in Oregon white oak in the Willamette Valley (Anderson 1972), and 11 in the c. Coast Range (Mannan et al. 1980, Morrison and Meslow 1983a, Nelson 1988).

Diet based on the contents of 62 stomachs from the Willamette Valley, Rogue R., and Klamath areas consisted of 52.12% animal matter, 44.58% plant matter, and 3.3% "dirt and rubbish." Ants comprised 40.30%; a few stomachs had over 2,000 each. Beetles and their larvae made up 5.24%, and other insects and spiders 6.58%. In the fall some stomachs were completely full with crickets. A variety of fruits, mostly wild, accounted for 29.70%, manzanita berries and seeds and poison oak for 7.50%, and nuts and grain for 6.60% (Neff 1928). Noted eating Pacific madrone and poison oak berries in sw. Oregon and Willamette Valley, respectively (D. Vroman p.c., *MGH*). It visits suet feeders and eats millet and shelled sunflower seeds from seed feeders, typically in winter and occasionally all year (R. Cheek p.c., J. Ciotti p.c., *JS*). Prefers foraging on the ground in open forests and unforested areas, both with lesser amounts of ground cover (Morrison and Meslow 1983a, Bull et al. 1986, Dobkin et al. 1995, Brett 1997); 81% of all feeding sites in the Blue Mtns. were dominated by grasses (Bull et al. 1986). In the Blue Mtns., Bull (1980) noted more than 80% of yearly ground foraging occurred in summer, while starting in the fall they mostly excavated dead and down material. Of trees foraged on, 50% were Douglas-fir, 40% ponderosa pine, 7% western larch, and 3% lodgepole pine (Bull et al. 1986). Snags foraged on in the Coast Range had a mean dbh of 37 in (95 cm), height of 76.1 ft (23.2 m), and 78% were slightly to moderately decayed (Mannan et al. 1980). Of 131 minutes of foraging in the Blue Mtns., 65% was spent foraging on the ground, 16% pecking, 8% excavating, 7% eating seeds, and 4% gleaning (Bull 1980).

**Seasonal Activity and Behavior:** In spring some individuals move to higher elevations and winter visitors leave (Neff 1928, Farner 1952, Bull 1980, Gilligan et al. 1994). A conspicuous influx occurs at Malheur NWR from early Mar to early Apr (Littlefield 1990a). After a "demonstrative" courtship that includes two or three males in "a pantomime of shy advances, retreats, sidling back and forth" for a female (Neff 1928), nest building occurs between late Mar and late Jun (n=9), with the bulk mid-Apr to late May (Gullion 1951, Bull 1980, Adamus et al. 2001). Generally excavate a new cavity, but may re-use an existing one (Bull 1986, Dobkin et al. 1995). Five to 10 eggs are laid (Gabrielson and Jewett 1940) and young are in the nest cavity late Apr to early Aug (n=163); most mid-May to mid-Jul (Griffee and Rapraeger 1937, Gabrielson and Jewett 1940, Bull 1980, Adamus et al. 2001, JS). Fledglings have been noted mid-May to late Jul (n=39); the majority late Jun to late Jul (Bull et al. 1986, Adamus et al. 2001).

Fall movements to lower elevations and migration into Oregon make for decreased numbers in winter at higher elevations and increased fall and winter numbers in farmland, towns, and other areas (Gullion 1951, Farner 1952, Gilligan et al. 1994), such as lowland parts of n. and c. Malheur Co. from Sep to Jan (Contreras and Kindschy 1996), on the west slope of the s. Cascades during late Sep and Oct (Fix 1990a), and at Malheur NWR from mid-Oct to mid-Nov (Littlefield 1990a). Roosting, which may occur at any time of year, has been noted in nest boxes and uninhabited parts of buildings (R. Cheek p.c., J. Ciotti p.c., L. McQueen p.c., S. Shunk p.c., JS).

**Detection:** Aurally conspicuous by its calls and drumming. Calls may be given in flight and on the ground. A weak drummer; may drum on metal (especially on buildings) or other materials that amplify sound (Neff 1928, Farrand 1983b).

**Population Status and Conservation:** Population shows a statistically non-significant decrease of 0.6%/yr for Oregon 1966-2000, based on BBS trend data (Sauer et al. 2001). Oregon CBC data 1959-88 show no significant trends with a decrease of 0.4%/yr. (Sauer

et al. 1996). According to Morrison and Morrison (1983), Northern Flicker is generally decreasing in numbers in the Pacific Northwest; CBCs in Portland and s. Oregon showed significant decreases and increases, respectively, in numbers of observations per party mile from 1952-53 to 1981-82. Thomas, Anderson, et al. (1979) estimated that 38 snags per 100 ac (40 ha) of at least 12 in (30.5 cm) dbh were necessary to support the "maximum population" in forests of the Blue Mtns. and Neitro et al. (1985) calculated that 48.0 snags per 100 ac (40 ha) of at least 17 in (43 cm) dbh were needed in w. Oregon Douglas-fir habitat. Brett (1997) recommended that snags of at least 31 in (80 cm) be left in the Cascades. Northern Flicker requires open space and thus may gain foraging habitat from human-caused changes, including creation of edges, but its need for decayed wood for large nest cavities must be met by managing forests for continual retention of adequate numbers of large excavatable trees and snags (Jackman 1974, Bull 1980, Mannan et al. 1980, Nelson 1988, Dobkin et al. 1995, Brett 1997, Reinkensmeyer 2000).—*Jamie Simmons*

## Pileated Woodpecker *Dryocopus pileatus*

This woodpecker is the largest found in the U.S. and is best recognized by its large, dull black body and red crest. Males are distinguished from females by more red on the crest and a red "moustache" extending back from the bill. Because of its size and strong chisel-shaped bill, this woodpecker is particularly adept at excavating, and uses this ability to construct nest and roost cavities and to find insects in wood. It is most often associated with older stands of trees because of its dependence on large-diameter trees with decay for nesting, roosting, and foraging.

**General Distribution:** Resident through forested e. N. America from e. Canada south to s. Florida, and west to forested river bottoms extending into the Great Plains in e. Texas and Oklahoma, se. Kansas, e. Iowa,

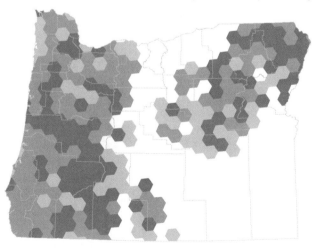

w. Minnesota, and e. N. Dakota; along a forested corridor northwestward across s. Manitoba and c. Saskatchewan, and c. Alberta south through montane regions of w. Montana, n. Idaho, and ne. Oregon; in the Pacific Northwest from c. British Columbia south through Washington and Oregon west of the Cascade summit to c. California. Of four subspecies, *D. p. picinus* is found in Oregon (AOU 1957).

**Oregon Distribution:** An uncommon permanent resident in older forests in the Blue, Cascade, and Klamath Mtns.; Coast Range; and Willamette, Umpqua, and Rogue valleys. Limited altitudinally by habitat availability; higher and lower elevations may lack large enough trees for nesting, roosting, and foraging.

**Habitat and Diet:** Occurs primarily in dense mixed-conifer forests in late seral stages or in deciduous tree stands in valley bottoms. Occasionally seen in younger stands lacking large-diameter trees, particularly in winter. Increasingly seen in urban neighborhoods of metro Portland that have mature trees, especially in vicinity of major parks (*DBM*). Rarely found in stands of pure ponderosa pine. The association with late seral stages stems from the need for large-diameter snags or living trees with decay for nest and roost sites, large-diameter trees and logs for foraging on ants and other arthropods, and a dense canopy to provide cover from predators.

In ne. Oregon, home ranges averaged 1,005 ac (407 ha) for pairs followed 5-10 mos (Bull and Holthausen 1993). In the Coast Range in w. Oregon, areas used by 11 individuals monitored during Jun and Jul ranged from 659 to 2,608 ac (267-1,056 ha) (Mellen et al. 1992).

Each pair excavates a new nest cavity each spring, usually in a dead tree. Nest cavities are quite large (mean diameter of 8 in [21 cm] and depth of 22 in [57 cm]) and are excavated at an average height of 50 ft (15 m) above the ground, so nest trees must have a large girth to contain nest cavities at this height (Bull 1987). Of 105 nest trees located in ne. Oregon, 75% were in ponderosa pine, 25% in western larch and 2% in grand fir; mean dbh and height of trees were 33 in (84 cm) and 93 ft (28 m) (Bull 1987). In the Coast Range in w. Oregon, 73% of nests were in Douglas-fir snags, 20% in red alder snags, and 7% in live Douglas-fir; mean dbh and height were 27 in (69 cm) and 67 ft (20 m) (Mellen 1987). Nests have also been found in Oregon white oak in sw. Oregon (*MGH*) and aspen in sc. Oregon (B. Combs p.c.).

Adults roost at night and during inclement weather inside hollow trees or vacated nest cavities. Of 60 roost trees climbed in ne. Oregon, 95% had a hollow interior created by decay rather than by excavation (Bull, Holthausen, and Henjum 1992). The woodpeckers excavate only the entrance hole to gain access to the hollow interior of the tree and thus conserve energy because an entire cavity is not excavated. Individual radio-tagged birds that were monitored for 3-10 mos used 4-11 different roost trees (Bull, Holthausen, Henjum 1992). In ne. Oregon roosts are typically in a live or dead grand fir with a mean dbh of 28 in (71 cm) (Bull, Holthausen, and Henjum 1992). In the Coast Range Douglas-fir, red alder, western redcedar, and big-leaf maple contained roosts (Mellen 1987).

Diet determined from 330 scat samples collected year-round in ne. Oregon consisted of 68% carpenter ants (*Camponotus* spp.), 29% thatching ants (*Formica* spp.), 0.4% beetles (Coleoptera), and 2% other (Bull, Beckwith, and Holthausen 1992). Wild fruits and nuts are also taken in some parts of its N. American range. It has been observed eating grapes near Grants Pass (J. Contreras p.c.). The most characteristic evidence of foraging of this species are large rectangular excavations in trees or logs. Gleaning, pecking, and scaling bark off trees are also used to search for insects. In the Coast Range, mature stands (> 70 yr) are selected, and younger stands are avoided (Mellen 1987); 44% of the foraging occurred in dead trees, 36% in downed logs, and the remainder in other substrates (Mannan 1984). In contrast, in ne. Oregon, foraging occurred in snags (38%), logs (38%), live trees(18%), and stumps (6%) (Bull and Holthausen 1993). Large-diameter snags and logs with some decay are selected for foraging because carpenter ants select for this kind of material (Torgersen and Bull 1995).

**Seasonal Activity and Behavior:** A pair shares and defends the territory all year against other territorial birds, although floaters are tolerated during the winter. Courtship and intensified territorial activity begin in Feb and Mar in ne. Oregon. Nest excavation occurs from late Mar to early May, eggs (normally 4) are present in May and early Jun, and nestlings are present from late May until early Jul. Nest excavation takes 3-6 wk; incubation lasts about 18 days; nestlings fledge after 24-31 days (Bull and Jackson 1995). Both sexes share in duties of nest excavation, incubation, and rearing of young. No consistent seasonal movements outside the territory are known for adults, although juveniles leave their natal area in the fall.

A variety of vocalizations are given (Bull and Jackson 1995). The most common is a *wok* call uttered in series of up to eight notes which occurs during interactions between individuals. The *wuk* call includes single notes or an irregular series of notes and is used as an alarm call, in interactions at a distance, and for territorial proclamation. A mewing call consists of whining notes given 5-6 times in a series and is given in courtship. Nonvocal sounds include drumming and demonstration tapping (Bull and Jackson 1995). Drumming, a series of 11-30 beats/burst, is usually done on a hard snag which resonates and is primarily used in territorial behavior. Demonstration tapping can be a rapid roll lasting a second and given at prospective nest sites; a series of taps often given within the nest when the mate approaches; or a single or several taps given when the bird is disturbed (Short 1982).

**Detection:** The likelihood of detecting this species can be low because home ranges are large. Most easily detected in the spring prior to nesting when adults are very vocal either advertising territorial boundaries or searching for a mate. Birds are also quite vocal in early Oct, when juveniles disperse from natal ranges. The greatest probability of detecting birds is usually in old-growth stands of mixed conifers. However, individuals are regularly seen in deciduous and coniferous stands that seemingly lack large trees in the three major w. Oregon valleys and foothills, particularly in winter (*DBM, ALC*). It is not known if these birds are floaters or residents or if these habitats serve as population sinks.

**Population Status and Conservation:** Timber harvest has the most significant effect on habitat for this woodpecker. Removal of large-diameter live and dead trees, of down woody material, and of canopy eliminates nest and roost sites, foraging habitat, and protective cover. Forest fragmentation likely reduces population density and makes birds more vulnerable to predation as they fly between forest fragments. Management practices (harvesting and prescribed burning) that eliminate or reduce the number of snags, logs, and cover are detrimental. Conversion of stands dominated by grand fir to an earlier seral stage dominated by ponderosa pine likely reduces the amount of suitable habitat in ne. Oregon. BBS data for 1966-91 show no significant change in w. U.S.—*Evelyn L. Bull*

# Order PASSERIFORMES
## *Family Tyrannidae*

### Subfamily Fluvicolinae

**Olive-sided Flycatcher** *Contopus cooperi*
The Olive-sided Flycatcher is one of the most recognizable breeding birds of Oregon's conifer forests with its resounding, three-syllable, whistled song *quick, three beers*. It is a relatively large, somewhat bulky, large-headed, short-necked flycatcher that perches erect and motionless at the top of a tall tree or snag except when singing or darting out to capture flying insects. The overall olive-gray plumage is generally nondescript except for a whitish stripe down the breast and belly which gives the impression of an unbuttoned vest, and white patches between the wings and lower back.

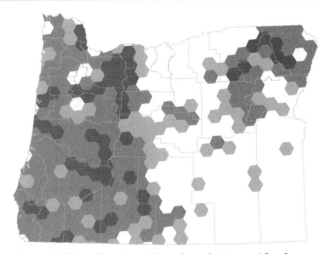

**General Distribution:** Breeds only in conifer forests of N. America. Breeding range extends from near tree line in boreal Alaska and Canada south through the Rocky Mtns. to higher elevations of e. Arizona, w. New Mexico, and w. Texas; in the Sierra Nevada south to n. Baja California; in c. N. America south to n. Wisconsin, Minnesota, and Michigan; and in the east, south to ne. Ohio, nw. Pennsylvania, all of New England, and locally in the Appalachians south to w. N. Carolina (Altman and Sallabanks 2000). Principal migratory route is throughout the forests of w. N. America, Mexico, and M. America (Bent 1942, Gabrielson and Lincoln 1959). Winters primarily in Panama and the Andes of n. and w. S. America, from nw. Venezuela south through Ecuador to se. Peru and n. Bolivia (Fitzpatrick 1980, DeGraaf and Rappole 1995). This species is *Nuttalornis mesoleucus* of Gabrielson and Jewett (1940) and *N. borealis* of AOU (1957). The name *mesoleucus* does not apply to this species, and the names *borealis* and *cooperi* are synonyms (Banks and Browning 1995). Two subspecies, *C. c. cooperi* in Oregon (Pyle 1997, Browning 2002).

**Oregon Distribution:** Breeds in low densities throughout conifer forests in Oregon from near sea level along the coast to timberline in the Cascades and Blue Mtns. Most abundant throughout the Cascades where BBS relative abundance of 5.3 birds/route is the second highest for any physiographic region in U.S. (Sauer et al. 1997). In migration, may occur in any forested habitat including forest patches in desert oases of se. Oregon, urban forest, and deciduous or mixed deciduous/coniferous riparian forest. A most unusual sighting was a bird perched on a steamer vessel approximately 7 mi (11 km) offshore from the Rogue R., 9 Sep 1898 (Loomis 1901).

**Habitat and Diet:** Breeding habitat is conifer forest, particularly in the following circumstances: within forest burns where snags and scattered tall, live trees remain; near water along the wooded shores of streams, lakes, rivers, beaver ponds, marshes, and bogs, often where standing dead trees are present; at the juxtaposition of late- and early-successional forest such as meadows, harvest units, or canyon edges; and in open or semi-open forest stands with a low percentage of canopy cover (Altman and Sallabanks 2000). Association with forest openings and forest edge also has been documented at a landscape scale. In the Coast Range, Olive-sided Flycatchers are more abundant in landscapes containing highly fragmented late-seral forest with high-contrast edges than in less fragmented landscapes (McGarigal and McComb 1995). In the Blue Mtns., territorial birds reported mostly along stream courses and around wet openings (M. Denny p.c.). Tall, prominent trees and snags, which serve as foraging and singing perches, are common features of all nesting habitat. In a nw. Oregon study, the only measured habitat variable significantly associated with nest success was snags >40 ft (12 m) tall (Altman 2000c). Migration habitat use has not been studied, but Olive-sided Flycatchers have been observed in a great diversity of habitats during migration compared to the breeding season, including lowland riparian, mixed or deciduous riparian at higher elevations, and urban woodlots and forest patches (*BA*). For example, migrants are routinely found in tall willow and cottonwood oases in se. Oregon (Littlefield 1990a), and they have been observed moving north through sagebrush flats in Malheur and Harney counties in late May (M. Denny p.c.).

The earliest described nests in the state include two in Klamath Co. in 1913, one at Strawberry L. in Grant Co. in 1915 (Gabrielson and Jewett 1940), and one in 1928 in logged-off land near Valsetz in sw. Polk Co. (Maltby 1931). Research in 1997 and 1998 in the n. Cascades and in the foothills of the east slope of the Coast Range near Salem located 179 nests (Altman 2000c). On the east slope of the Cascades, most nests were in grand fir (52%, n=16) and Douglas-fir (29%, n=9). On the west slope of the Cascades, nests were relatively evenly distributed among western hemlock (20%, n=26), mountain hemlock (21%, n=28), Pacific silver fir (22%, n=29), and noble fir (17%, n=23). In the Coast Range, most nests were in western hemlock (52%, n=11) and Douglas fir (38%, n=8).

Nests are open cup structures placed at varying heights above ground, and generally on a relatively flat cluster of needles on a horizontal branch well out from the trunk of a coniferous tree. In a nw. Oregon study, nest height was variable and ranged from 6-110 ft (2-34 m), with a mean of 37 ft (11.3 m) (n=170) (Altman 2000c). Site fidelity of a few banded birds has been observed on the breeding grounds in California (n=2) (J. Booker p.c.) and Alaska (n=5) (Wright 1997), and on wintering grounds in Belize (Russell 1964). Territories are relatively large for a passerine, up to 100 ac (40-45 ha) per pair, but most often in the range of 35-45 ac (15-20 ha) per pair.

Forages mostly from high, prominent perches at the top of snags or the dead tip or uppermost branch of a live tree. Forages by "sallying" or "hawking" out to snatch a flying insect, and then often returning to the same perch ("yo-yo" flight) or another prominent perch. Foraging behavior as an air-sallying insectivore requires exposed perches and unobstructed air space, thus tall trees or snags and broken canopy provide a better foraging environment than closed-canopy forest. During the early reproductive period (i.e., courtship, nest building, egg laying), males usually forage from the tops of the tallest trees and snags, and females forage at lower heights and near the nest (Altman 2000c).

Preys almost exclusively on flying insects including flying ants, beetles, moths, and dragonflies, but with a particular preference for bees and wasps (Bent 1942). Hymenopterans (bees and wasps) were found in 61 of 63 stomach samples from a number of breeding locations; 26 samples (41%) contained no other food (Beal 1912). In migration in Costa Rica, Hymenopterans comprised 81% of prey items in stomach contents of four birds (Sherry 1984). In contrast, they comprised only 10% of food volume from birds (n=12) in the Sierra Nevada, where principal prey items were beetles (Otvos and Stark 1985).

**Seasonal Activity and Behavior:** Spring migration and arrival of residents well documented because of loud, distinctive song. Spring migration peaks in late May, earlier in sw. and coastal Oregon, and later in e. Oregon. Average arrival date near Corvallis (n=19) is 6 May (A. McGie p.c.), and in e. Oregon near Bend (n=15) 17 May (C. Miller p.c.). Early dates include 4 Apr in the s. Willamette Valley (Evenden 1949), 17 Apr in Coos Co. (Contreras 1998), 20 Apr in Benton Co. (A. McGie p.c.), 24 Apr in Portland (Lillie 1998) and Eugene (Irons 1984b), and in e. Oregon 1 May at Malheur NWR (Littlefield 1990a), 6 May near Bend (C. Miller p.c.), and 12 May at Willow Cr., Morrow Co. (Sullivan PT 1995a). Late migrants occasionally occur at desert oases in early Jun (Gilligan et al. 1994). Apparent migrants (birds present one day but never again) were regularly detected at Toketee Ranger Station to the end of the first week of Jun (D. Fix p.c.).

Territory establishment and pairing begins upon arrival. Nest building most evident during first and second week of Jun, but completed nests have been reported as early as 27 May (Altman 2000c). Nest area aggressively defended by both members of the pair. Monogamous breeder producing 3-4 eggs per clutch and one clutch per pair. Incubation period is 14-15 days, nestling period approximately 19-22 days. Hatching of nestlings from successful first nest occurs mostly in second week of Jul. Will renest after a failed clutch until about 1 Jul. Latest fledging of nestlings is 30 Aug (Altman 2000c). Adults remain with fledglings for up to 2 wk.

Timing of fall migration is less known, but peaks late Aug and into first week of Sep. A few late Sep records include 24 Sep in the Umpqua NF (Gilligan 1992a), and 22 Sep (Sullivan 1997a) and 24 Sep (Littlefield 1990a) at Malheur NWR; latest 28 Sep 1986 at Emigrant L., Jackson Co. (Fix 1987a).

**Detection:** Detectability is high in suitable habitat during spring migration and breeding season because of the loud and distinctive song, and frequency with which it sings. It is often only bird singing on warm afternoons during breeding season. Detectability low during fall migration, and only occasional birds are reported. Reduced detectability when giving call notes, 3-4 trebled notes *pip pip pip*, the first two slightly closer together. The call notes are not as prominent as the song, and can be confused with those of other species such as Red Crossbill and Pygmy Nuthatch. Detected visually by scanning tops of trees and snags at forest edge or in forest openings, and watching for frequent foraging flights outside of and above forest canopy. Visual identification can be confused with Western Wood-Pewee, which occurs in similar forest edge habitats.

**Population Status and Conservation:** Population trends based on BBS data show highly significant declines for all continental (N. America), national (U.S. and Canada), and regional (e. and w. N. America) analyses, and for most state and physiographic region analyses (Sauer et al. 1997). In Oregon, highly significant ($p < 0.01$) statewide decline of 5.1% per year 1966-96.

Speculation on causes of population declines has focused on habitat alteration and loss on the wintering grounds, because declines are relatively consistent throughout the breeding range of the species (Altman and Sallabanks 2000). Nevertheless, factors potentially contributing to declines on the breeding grounds include habitat loss through logging, alteration of habitat from forest management practices (e.g., clearcutting, fire suppression), lack of food resources, and reproductive impacts from nest predation or parasitism.

It has also been speculated that the Olive-sided Flycatcher may depend on early post-fire habitat, and has likely been negatively affected by fire-control policies of the past 50-100 yr (Hutto 1995a). The ability of forest management practices (e.g., selective cutting, clearcutting) to mimic natural disturbance regimes caused by forest fires has been questioned. Habitat created by these forest management scenarios may provide only the appearance of early post-fire habitat, but be lacking in some attributes or resources required by Olive-sided Flycatchers (*BA*).

During the past 50 yr, forest management has resulted in an increase in forest openings and edge habitat, which has seemingly increased habitat for the Olive-sided Flycatcher. However, this dichotomy of increased habitat availability and declining populations may indicate that harvested forest represents an "ecological trap" (Hutto 1995b), where habitat may appear suitable, but reproductive success and/or survival is poor due to factors such as limited food resources, predation, or parasitism. Data from the study in nw. Oregon provide a preliminary examination of the ecological trap hypothesis that supports the importance of post-fire habitat and suggest that some types of harvested forest may be functioning as ecological traps or sink habitat. Mayfield nest success estimates of 61% in post-fire habitat (n=19) were nearly significantly different (and probably would have been with a larger sample size) than the nest success estimates in forest edge habitats (33%, n= 31) and harvest units (39%, n=89). Within harvest units, nest success estimates of 29% in dispersed retention trees (n=26) may be particularly indicative of insufficient productivity (Altman 2000c).

Proportional nest success (53%, n=174) in the nw. Oregon study (Altman 2000c) compares favorably with results from Alaska (50% proportional nest success, n=19) (Wright 1997), and with mean proportional estimates of nest success for open cup nesting passerines that winter in the neotropics (40-45%) (Martin 1992). However, the latter estimates include many species with different reproductive strategies (e.g., double or triple brooding, large clutch size), and they may not be comparable with a species like Olive-sided Flycatcher which is single brooded with a low reproductive capability. Indeed, it has been suggested that flycatchers in general have evolved the need to have a relatively high nest success rate (Murphy 1983). Thus, Olive-sided Flycatchers may need much higher nest success rates than 40-45% to maintain viable populations.—*Bob Altman*

## Western Wood-Pewee *Contopus sordidulus*
The down-slurred *pee-eeer* call of this flycatcher is one of Oregon's most characteristic summertime bird sounds. Wherever there is a canopy of mature deciduous trees, one is likely to hear the call during warm afternoons when most other birds are silent. Because the call can easily be heard from a considerable distance, the Western Wood-Pewee is more often heard than seen. But once heard, it can usually be found perched near the tip of a dead branch from which it frequently flies a short distance to capture a flying insect, or to chase an intruder from its territory.

At 6-6.5 in (15-16.5 cm) it is noticeably larger than all of the *Empidonax* flycatchers, with longer wings that extend halfway down the tail when folded. It is further distinguished by a darker gray-brown back, darker olive-gray sides and breast, and the lack of an

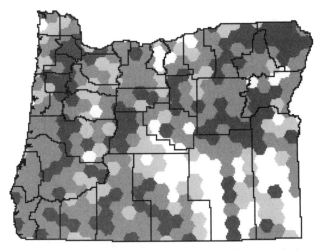

eye-ring. The two pale wing-bars are also much less pronounced.

**General Distribution:** Breeds from ec. Alaska, s. Yukon, s. Mackenzie, n. Alberta, nw. and ec. Saskatchewan, sc. Manitoba, and nw. Minnesota south to s. Baja California and the interior highlands of Mexico and Guatemala to Honduras and (possibly) nc. Nicaragua, and east to c. N. Dakota, w. S. Dakota, w. Kansas, w. Texas, and s. Tamaulipas. Winters from Colombia and Venezuela south to Peru and Bolivia, casually north to Costa Rica. Migrates east to w. Kansas, and south through M. America, occurring in lowlands on both slopes as well as in highlands. Two of three subspecies occur in Oregon.

**Oregon Distribution:** Common migrant and fairly common to common breeder statewide in open groves of trees or along forest edges at all elevations. Rare in landscapes dominated by dense conifer forests in the w. Cascades and Coast Range (Morrison and Meslow 1983b), even in open habitats, but occasionally present along riverine woodlands adjacent to open areas (*MGH*) or at lower elevations. Uncommon summer resident along the northern coast (Gilligan et al. 1994). In e. Oregon, found throughout most open conifer forests and forest edges and in woods (often deciduous) along river courses (Gabrielson and Jewett 1940, Sharp 1985). In vast expanses of agriculture or sagebrush steppe, found only in patches of trees at homesteads and near water. Gabrielson and Jewett (1940) used the specific name *richardsonii*, a name that does not apply to this species (Phillips and Parkes 1955). *C. s. saturatus* breeds west of the Cascades and *veliei* breeds in the remainder of the state; names proposed by Burleigh (1960a) and *veliei* are synonyms (Browning 1977a).

**Habitat and Diet:** Principally breeds in groves of deciduous trees and mixed deciduous/conifer forest with open space below the canopy for perching and watching for flying insects (*FS*). A California study

found that such open space was a critical factor (Beedy 1981). Also uses denser habitats where they are adjacent to open space, such as multi-canopy woods or riparian zones in parks, campgrounds, pastures, and deserts (*FS, MGH*).

Nest usually placed in the open on a horizontal branch 15-30 ft (4.5-9 m) above ground (Bent 1942), but occasionally much higher or lower. In 1973 a nest was found near Salem, Polk Co., 4 ft (1.21 m) above ground, and another in 1996 in Carlton, Yamhill Co., more than 50 ft (15.2 m) high in an oak tree (*FS*).

The wood-pewee is often found in urban parks, near suburban residential communities, and open areas of the Willamette Valley where isolated groves of Oregon white oak provide appropriate habitat. Also common in riparian stands of black cottonwood and Oregon ash throughout w. Oregon (D. Vroman p.c., *FS*) and a summer resident of aspen groves in c. and e. Oregon. (Marshall 1987). According to BBS data it is found only occasionally during breeding season in juniper/sagebrush habitat east of the Cascades (Sauer et al.1999), where it is most likely only in oases of deciduous trees surrounded by juniper/sage (P. Adamus p.c.). Following a forest fire in Wallowa Co., a 5-yr study found that wood-pewees increased (Sallabanks 2000).

Diet consists almost entirely of insects taken in flight. In a study by Beal, the contents of 174 stomachs was 99.93 % animal matter (insects and spiders) and 0.07 % vegetable (Bent 1942). Vegetable matter consisted of a few seeds of elderberries and a piece of fruit skin. Presumably this pattern holds true in Oregon. Observation of this bird while it is capturing insects, and especially while feeding young in the nest, makes it clear that large numbers of prey items are taken in the course of a single day.

**Seasonal Activity and Behavior:** Spring arrival in Oregon is comparatively late. Records compiled by the Audubon Society of Corvallis indicate that first arrivals are typically during first half of May. Early sightings were recorded in Eugene on 23 Apr 1988 (Heinl 1989a), 26 Apr 1984 and at Coos Bay on 28 Apr 1984 (Irons 1984b). Records based on 15 yr of observations in c. Oregon (C. Miller unpbl. data) show the average arrival date there to be 7 May with an early date of 29 Apr. At Malheur NWR, arrival dates range 16 Apr-21 May, with a mean of 10 May (Ivey, Herziger, and Scheuering 1998). Statewide, the peak of passage is typically the latter half of May (D. Fix p.c.), and migrants are noted in se. Oregon into early Jun (D. Irons p.c.). During 1995-99, nest building observed 14 May-17 Jun (n=7); nests with eggs 12 Jun-22 Jul (n=25); and nests with young 22 Jun-20 Aug (n=13) (OBBA). Eggs of this species are occasionally taken by predators. During one such event an Acorn Woodpecker was observed, "perched on the

*Western Wood-Pewee*

nest and eating the egg of a Western Wood-Pewee" (Bryant 1921). Nest site reuse apparently is more common with this species than with most non-colonial, open-nesting passerines (Curson et al. 1996). Such an occurrence was reported from Eugene: "nesting in the same crotch of the same maple tree in Hendricks Park," 1 Jul 1997 and 12 Jun 1998 (D. DeWitt p.c.).

According to most observers reporting on fall migration, many wood-pewees have left the state by Sep and there are very few Oct reports; among the latest are one at Baskett Slough NWR 2 Oct 1989 (Fix and Heinl 1990), one in the Rogue Valley 3 Oct 1984 (Fix 1985f), and one at Malheur NWR P Ranch 8 Oct 1978 (S. Summers unpubl. data).

**Detection:** Usually first detected by voice. A few minutes watching for frequent sallying flights in pursuit of insects, and checking the surface of dead branches, often reveals the location of the bird. During migration can often be observed using a lower perch such as a bush or fence, when it is occasionally confused with Willow Flycatcher. Vocalizations are much less frequent at this time. Nests are often easily visible from below, the location revealed by the adults' habit of flying directly to it from some distance.

**Population Status and Conservation:** The N. American BBS (Sauer et al. 1997) indicated that the Western Wood-Pewee experienced a gradual population decline in w. Oregon during 1968-96. By contrast, in the Blue Mtn. mixed-conifer area of ne. Oregon and the sagebrush steppe area of s. Malheur Co. in extreme se. Oregon there was a slight increase.—*Floyd Schrock*

## Eastern Wood-Pewee *Contopus virens*

This common flycatcher breeds from sc. Canada to Texas eastward and winters from M. America southward. There are very few records west of its regular range. It is closely related to the Western Wood-Pewee and in the field can only be separated from that species with certainty by voice. A singing bird was tape recorded and photographed at Malheur NWR HQ 28-30 May 1994 (Johnson J 1995c). Another singing bird was mist-netted and banded there 28-31 May 1998 (Sullivan 1998b). Monotypic (AOU 1957, Browning 1977a).—*Harry B. Nehls*

## Willow Flycatcher *Empidonax traillii*

This long-distance, relatively late-arriving migrant to Oregon is associated with shrub-dominated habitats, especially riparian willow thickets. The plumage has subtle tones of olive-green and gray; the species is without a visible eye-ring (unlike most *Empidonax*), but the characteristic sneezy, abrupt song reveals its presence. Regarded as a form of Traill's Flycatcher until 1973 when split into Willow and Alder Flycatchers.

**General Distribution:** Most widely distributed *Empidonax* in N. America (Sedgwick 2000). Breeds from coast to coast, mostly in the northern half of the U.S. except for the Great Plains, Sierra Nevada in California, and sw. U.S. Taxonomists recognize four (Unitt 1987) or five (Browning 1993) subspecies, two of which breed in Oregon.

**Oregon Distribution:** *E. t. brewsteri* breeds in w. Oregon from sea level along the coast (e.g., Astoria and Reston [USNM], Tillamook [AMNH]) and interior (Portland and Beaverton [USNM], Corvallis [OSU]) to above 5,000 ft (1,500 m) west of the Cascades summit. In e. Oregon, *E. t. adastus* breeds mostly above 1,000 ft (300 m) (M. Denny p.c.) from Ft. Klamath to Burns (CM), also Lake Co. (CM), Elgin in Union Co. (OSU), and e. Oregon localities listed by Unitt (1987). Both subspecies intergrade near Roseburg

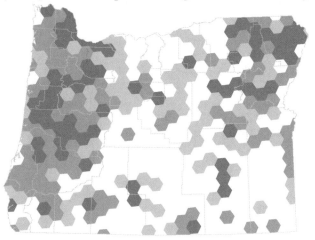

and several localities in Jackson Co. (Browning 1993). Transients, presumably of the breeding subspecies, occur throughout the breeding range.

**Habitat and Diet:** Habitat of breeding Willow Flycatchers is characterized by dense shrubs and/or tall herbaceous plants with scattered openings of shorter herbaceous vegetation. Nesting and migratory habitat in e. and sw. Oregon is almost exclusively riparian zones, typically willows. In nw. Oregon, both riparian and upland habitat is used for nesting, from low-elevation valleys to high mountain areas. Nesting habitat in conifer-dominated forest landscapes occurs in early-seral forest approximately 4-15 yr following timber harvest or natural events that remove most or all of the forest canopy and allow for extensive growth of a shrub layer, as well as in moderate- to high-elevation shrubby wet meadows. Habitat used for nesting in the Willamette Valley includes both riparian shrub and upland thickets of shrubs, particularly patches of exotic Himalayan blackberry and Scotch broom. Upland shrub-dominated sites receive less use during migration, and there is limited fall migratory movement through the Willamette Valley. Riparian habitat used during fall migration in nw. Oregon is primarily moderate- to high-elevation wet meadows with a shrub component (*BA*).

Two studies in se. Oregon revealed dependence on shrubby thickets, especially willow habitats. Along the Blitzen R., Willow Flycatchers occurred almost exclusively at riparian sites with the greatest shrub volume, and they were most abundant on sites with the least amount of grazing pressure (Taylor 1984a). In the Bear and Silvies valleys, Grant Co., they were most abundant in continuous shrub sites vs. discontinuous shrub and herbaceous shrub sites (Sanders and Edge 1998). They were most abundant where willow volume was >70,629 ft³/ac (>5000 m³/ha) and absent when willow volume was <16,767 ft³/ac (<1,187 m³/ha).

This species nests in shrubs or other shrub-level vegetation within a few feet of the ground. Mean nest height in the Willamette Basin was 3.9 ft (1.2 m [range 0.3-2.7, n=147]) (B. Altman unpubl. data). Vegetative cover near nest (i.e., within 16 ft [5 m], n=140) is mostly shrubs (68%), with some herbaceous vegetation (19%) and trees (11%). Nests were located in 17 different plant species, but none in willow. Four species—Himalayan blackberry (n=47), bracken fern (n=21), Scotch broom (n=19), and vine maple (n=19)—accounted for 71.4% of the plant species in which nests were found. Among these four plant species, Mayfield estimates of nest success were lowest in vine maple (17.2%) and highest in bracken fern (78.1%). Nest success was not significantly different between nests in exotic plants (35%, n=71) and native plants (45.9%, n=76).

In three regenerating, early-seral forests in the Willamette R. basin, vine maple and trailing blackberry were important components of nesting habitat (Altman et al. in press). Three other species, Himalayan blackberry, Scotch broom, and bracken fern were significantly associated with nest sites. Species selected against as nesting habitat were California hazel, Douglas-fir, and cascara.

Territories are small and dominated by a mix of shrub and herbaceous vegetation. In a Willamette Basin study, mean territory size was 1.1 ac (0.44 ha), range 0.3-3.6 ac (0.12-1.44 ha, n=49) (*BA*). Mean territory size in early-seral forest was only 0.6 ac (0.24 ha, n=13), much smaller than that in the valley (1.3 ac [0.52 ha], n=36). Mean percent cover of 54 territories was 45% shrubs, 37% herbaceous, and 11% trees.

Forages within shrub patches and often in openings between shrub patches; also over water. In a se. Oregon study, most foraging occurred in cattail marshes adjacent to willow nesting habitat (Sedgwick 2000). Diet has not been studied in Oregon. The Willow Flycatcher is an aerial insectivore that feeds primarily on the wing by sallying out to capture flying insect prey; it occasionally gleans (Sedgwick 2000).

**Seasonal Activity and Behavior:** Most birds arrive in s. Oregon in mid-May, with the peak of migration occurring throughout the state in the last few days of May through the first week of Jun. Late migrants extend to mid-Jun. In w. Oregon, average arrival near Corvallis is 15 May (n=15) (A. McGie p.c.). Early dates include 7 Apr at Fogarty Beach (Crowell and Nehls 1969c), 21 Apr in Multnomah Co. (Gabrielson and Jewett 1940), 25 Apr near Corvallis (A. McGie p.c.), 28 Apr in Applegate Valley (Lillie 1999), and 30 Apr at Mt. Tabor Park in Portland (Lillie 1995). Average arrival date in e. Oregon near Bend is 15 May (n=15) (C. Miller p.c.), and 12 May at Malheur NWR (Littlefield 1990a). Early dates include 29 Apr at Malheur NWR (Littlefield 1990a) and 2 May at Succor Cr., Malheur Co. (Sullivan 1999b).

The earliest reported nests with eggs are 5 and 7 Jun, from the Wallowas (OBBA), and 8 Jun in the Willamette Basin (B. Altman unpubl. data). The height of the nesting period throughout state is from late Jun through mid-Jul (Griffee and Rapraeger 1937, Gabrielson and Jewett 1940, Altman et al. in press, OBBA). In a Willamette Basin study (Altman et al. in press), most nest building and egg laying occurred in mid- to late Jun. The earliest hatch date was 21 Jun and the earliest fledging was 8 Jul. Most hatching occurred in early to mid-Jul and fledging in the last 10 days of Jul and the first week of Aug. Nearly one-third of the nests (31.3%, n=46) were still active in Aug. This included nine nests (20%) that still had eggs. Most of the nests active in Aug fledged during the first week of Aug (69.6%, n=32). The latest fledge date was 22 Aug.

Willow Flycatchers are single brooded with 3-4 eggs/clutch. They are a frequent host species for Brown-headed Cowbirds. In se. Oregon, 23.4% of nests (n=882) were parasitized during a 10-yr period (Sedgwick and Iko 1999). Nest success of parasitized pairs was 50.3% less than that of unparasitized pairs. Of 204 parasitized pairs, 23.5% fledged a cowbird, 8.8% fledged both a cowbird and a flycatcher(s), 27.9% fledged only flycatchers, and 39.7% of the pairs failed to produce any fledglings. In a nw. Oregon study, the rate of cowbird parasitism was low (4%, n=147), and all parasitism occurred within valley habitats (8% of valley nests) (Altman et al. in press). These flycatchers will renest, often using some or all of the nest material from the failed nest (*BA*). They often bury cowbird eggs in the nest lining or abandon the nest.

In a Willamette Basin study, 58.5% of the nests (n=147) were successful with a Mayfield estimate of nest success of 40.5% (Altman et al. in press). Yearly and 2-yr Mayfield estimates were not significantly different between valley (39%, n=75) and forest (42%, n=72) habitats. Two-yr nest success estimates were not significantly different between riparian (44%, n=31) and upland (40%, n=116) habitats; however, nest success was significantly different between riparian and upland habitats within each year, and also for riparian between each year. Among the six habitat nest-location categories, Mayfield estimates were lowest in valley upland (34.1%) and highest in riparian (44.1%).

Fall migration occurs mostly during mid-Aug to mid-Sep with the peak of migration east of the Cascades in late Aug and west of the Cascades in early Sep (Gilligan et al. 1994). Late dates in w. Oregon include 28 Sep in Yamhill Co. (Bayer 1986b), 29 Sep at Creswell (S. Nelson p.c.), 29 Sep along the Rogue R. (J. Alexander p.c.), 1 Oct at Coos Bay (T. Rodenkirk p.c.), and 3 Oct at Harbor, Curry Co. (Heinl and Fix 1989). Late dates in e. Oregon include 25 Sep at Malheur NWR (Littlefield 1990a), 28 Sep at P Ranch on Malheur NWR (Sullivan 1996a), and 29 Sep in the Klamath Basin (E. Olmedo p.c.). Reported to occur in concentrations in early Sep such as 32 on Cape Blanco, Curry Co., and 51 banded in 1 day at a Medford, Jackson Co., banding station (Gilligan et al. 1994).

A most curious record is that of a bird banded in early Jun at PRBO, California, and recovered on 5 Aug of same year at Mike's Meadow in the w. Cascades (S. Dowlan p.c.). It was not in breeding condition at either capture.

**Detection:** Visual identification, as with all flycatchers of the genus *Empidonax*, is difficult. Vocalizations, particularly the song, are most reliable for identification. Many birds alternate the typical *fitz-bew* song with a less well-known song *wre-beer* without the sneezy ending to the first syllable. This has confused a number of observers and generated reports of Alder Flycatcher.

Primary *whit* call note too similar to Dusky and Gray Flycatcher for accurate identification for most observers, although habitat during the breeding season can assist in these distinctions.

**Population Status and Conservation:** *E. t. adastus* was listed as a U.S. Fish and Wildlife Species of Concern in Oregon (J. Dillon p.c.) and a Focal Species for conservation in the Columbia Plateau Bird Conservation Planning Region (Altman and Holmes 2000). Factors indicated as conservation concerns include loss and degradation of the quality of riparian shrub habitats from altered hydrologic regimes, disturbance and loss of habitat from overgrazing, and cowbird parasitism. Proposed objectives for conservation include patches of native shrub vegetation >3 ft (1 m) high and 33 ft$^2$ (10 m$^2$) in size with 40-80% shrub cover. Additionally, it was recommended that conservation sites be >1.6 mi (1 km) from urban/residential areas and >8 mi (5 km) from high-use cowbird areas. Among the conservation strategies suggested are to increase width of riparian shrub zones through plantings, discourage aggregations of livestock near riparian areas through fencing or herd management, and eliminate willow cutting and herbicide spraying in the riparian zone. Population increases in the 1970s and 1980s on Malheur NWR coincided with a dramatic decrease in cattle grazing and the elimination of willow cutting and spraying (Taylor and Littlefield 1986).

*E. t. brewsteri* was listed as State Sensitive (Vulnerable) in 1997 (ODFW 1997) due to concerns about declining populations and a lack of information on species ecology. *E. t. brewsteri* was formerly considered a Federal Candidate species (USFWS 1994a), and a Species of Concern in Oregon by the USFWS (G. Miller p.c.). The Willow Flycatcher is also a Focal Species for conservation in the Westside Lowlands and Valleys Bird Conservation Planning Region (Altman 2000a).

From about the turn of the last century through the mid-1900s, all ornithologists used the word "common" in their description of Willow Flycatcher abundance in the Willamette Valley (e.g., Johnson 1880, Anthony 1886, 1902, Gabrielson and Jewett 1940, Gullion 1951). However, BBS data for the last 30+ yr indicate significant population declines of 3.6%/yr for *E. t. brewsteri* in w. Oregon and Washington and nw. California (Sauer et al. 2000). BBS data for the Willamette Valley (n=11 routes) indicate that the Willow Flycatcher population has declined from a mean of approximately 11-13 birds per route in the early 1970s to 4-5 birds per route throughout the 1990s. An extreme example is a route that borders the valley and foothills near Portland where the mean number of Willow Flycatchers has dropped from 50-70 birds during 1968-72 to 0 birds throughout the 1990s!

Despite significant population declines for *E. t. brewsteri* as indicated by the BBS in Oregon, this subspecies has the highest mean number of Willow Flycatchers per BBS route in N. America (Sauer et al. 2000). The Willow Flycatcher is a fairly common species in early-seral forest habitats in the Willamette Basin. In several studies it ranged from the third to seventh most abundant species (Monthey 1983, Morrison and Meslow 1983b, Vega 1993).

Willow Flycatcher abundance ranges from locally common to rare in the Willamette Valley. One of the largest populations is at Sandy R. delta along the Columbia R. where over 50 pairs are present (*BA*). Moderate populations (10-20 pairs) are present at a few sites, but most Willow Flycatchers in the Willamette Valley occur in small populations of 1-5 pairs patchily distributed across the landscape.

The Sensitive status for the Willamette Valley population of *E. t. brewsteri* seems warranted based on population declines in the valley, lower nest success than in early-seral forest, and continual loss of riparian habitat (Altman et al. in press). Cowbird parasitism does not appear to be a limiting factor for Willow Flycatcher populations in the Willamette Basin.

Altman et al. (in press) proposed several conservation options for *E. t. brewsteri*. Riparian shrub habitat should be emphasized when management for Willow Flycatcher is being considered in the Willamette Valley. If management and restoration actions are scheduled to avoid or minimize impacts on nesting Willow Flycatchers, 15 Aug should be considered the end of the nesting season. In early-seral forest habitats of the Willamette Basin, where there is often management against deciduous shrub vegetation in revegetating clearcuts, removal or killing of deciduous vegetation should be discouraged if management for Willow Flycatcher is a priority. They also recommended that bracken fern should be considered a high priority for retention in early-seral forests if a management goal is to support nesting Willow Flycatchers.—*Bob Altman*

### Least Flycatcher *Empidonax minimus*

This small *Empidonax* breeds from Yukon Territory to n. Washington, and across N. America to the e. coast. It migrates east of the Rocky Mtns. to winter in M. America (Briskie 1994). It closely resembles the Hammond's Flycatcher, but its distinctive voice and choice of habitat help to identify calling birds.

The Least Flycatcher was formerly an unexpected vagrant west of the Rocky Mtns. It was first recorded in Washington during 1958, and has become a fairly regular migrant in the interior of that state since 1974 (Mattocks et al. 1976). In Oregon, not known from specimens. The first Oregon record was of a mist-netted bird on Hart Mt., Lake Co., 1 Jun 1977 (Mewaldt 1977a). Since 1981 it has become recognized as a regular migrant and local summer resident in the state. The spring migration ranges from mid-May to mid-Jun with the majority of sightings from east of the Cascades, especially Harney Co. The fall movement ranges from early Aug to late Sep with sightings reported from both e. and w. Oregon. One bird at Tillamook, 20-28 Dec 1992 was mist-netted, measured, and photographed before being released (Johnson J 1993b). Another was mist-netted and carefully measured at Cape Blanco, Curry Co., 25 Aug 1999 (OBRC, Gilligan 2000).

Territorial birds have been regularly observed during the summer at Clyde Holliday SP, along the John Day R. near Mt. Vernon, Grant Co. Up to five singing males have been reported from there during some summers. On 7 Jul 1985, an adult bird was seen sitting on a nest approximately 30 ft (9 m) up in a black cottonwood. The nest was placed in a fork on a branch off the main trunk (D. Fix and D. Irons p.c., *MGH*). Nesting was also confirmed there during Jul 1995 (*ALC*) and 20 Jun 1997 (Spencer 1998). A territorial pair was on Sauvie I. from 2 Jun to 4 Jul 1991 and was suspected of successfully fledging young (Johnson J 1992a, *HBN*). Singing birds were near Monument, Grant Co., 16 Jun 1996 (Sullivan 1997c); at Bone Cr. Canyon, Malheur Co., 19 Jun 1997 (Denny 1998a); at Page Springs CG, Harney Co., 23-24 Jun 1998 (Spencer 1998) and during the summer of 2000 (Spencer 2000b); at Thornhollow, Umatilla Co., during the summer of 1999 (Spencer 2000a); southeast of Boardman, Morrow Co., 8 Jul 1999 (Spencer 2000a); and at the north end of Agency L., Klamath Co., 8 Jul 2000 (Spencer 2000b).

In Oregon the Least Flycatcher is found in deciduous groves along streams and in wet lowlands. It desires a deciduous overstory with at least some low brushy undergrowth. It nests in the canopy and feeds on insects caught by hawking in the open spaces below the canopy or by gleaning vegetation (*HBN*). Monotypic (AOU 1957).—*Harry B. Nehls*

### Hammond's Flycatcher *Empidonax hammondii*

Although this species is abundant during the nesting season in montane conifer forests, relatively little is known about it. The Hammond's Flycatcher spends much of its time in tall conifer canopies, where its subdued plumage and quiet, monotonous chant let it be easily overlooked. A diligent observer may be able to locate this aerial insectivore on a dead limb just beneath the live crowns of mature conifers, from which it sallies into a canopy gap to capture insect prey on the wing.

**General Distribution:** Breeds in coniferous forests of w. N. America from c. Alaska, throughout Pacific Northwest and Rocky Mtn. regions, south through Sierra Mtns., and to extreme n. Arizona and New

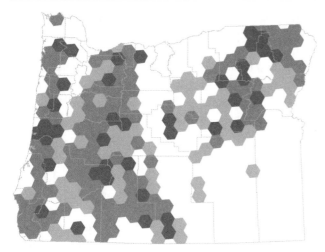

Mexico. Winters from se. Arizona, through highlands of Mexico, and as far south as n. Nicaragua. Monotypic (AOU 1957).

**Oregon Distribution:** Common summer resident of montane coniferous forests throughout state. Gabrielson and Jewett (1940) mention occurrence in the Blue Mtns. and both sides of the Cascade Range. Common on both slopes of the Cascades, with confirmed breeding records on east slope and probable records on the west slope (OBBA), with eggs at Mollala, Clackamas Co., and McMinnville, Yamhill Co., in 1952 and 1954, respectively (Griffee 1954). Described as abundant breeder in closed-canopy conifer forests of the Coast Range based on presence during breeding season (Carey et al. 1991); confirmed and/or probable breeding records for most counties of Coast Range (OBBA). Breeds in true fir and Douglas-fir-dominated forest types in Klamath/Siskiyou Mtns. (Alexander 1999). Present in conifer and riparian forests of isolated mountain ranges of se. Oregon, including Hart and Steens mountains (Gabrielson and Jewett 1940). Mewaldt (1980) described 18 Hammond's Flycatchers captured at Hart Mtn. 1972-79 as migrants. Considering widespread summer presence in western montane forests, additional work can be expected to confirm breeding elsewhere in the state. Breeding specimens have been recorded from Lane, Jackson, Umatilla, Baker, Wheeler, Deschutes, Klamath and Lake counties (Johnson NK 1963). Uncommon spring migrant in conifer and deciduous woods in the Willamette Valley (Gullion 1951, Gillson 1999). Fall migrant specimens have been recorded from Grant, Lake and Harney counties (Johnson 1970a). One winter sight record from Roseburg (Contreras 1997b).

**Habitat and Diet:** Strongly associated with conifer-dominated habitats, especially west of the Cascades. In Blue Mtns., also finds primary breeding and feeding habitat in aspen (Thomas et al. 1979). Often reaches highest abundance in late-seral conifer forests (Gerig 1992, McGarigal and McComb 1995, Anthony et al. 1996). Densities in mature (130-300 yr old) and old-growth (400-450 yr old) forests in the c. Cascades were estimated at 12.5 birds/100 ac (40 ha), compared to 3 birds/100 ac (40 ha) in a small sample (n=2) of young stands (25-35 yr) (Anthony et al. 1996). Avoids clearcuts and young second growth prior to canopy closure, generally <20 yr old (Gerig 1992, Bettinger 1996). Uncommon in managed Douglas-fir stands 20-30 yr old on Detroit RD of Willamette NF (Bettinger 1996). However, abundance may be higher in managed mid-aged forests (approximately 40 yr old) relative to old-growth (Hagar and Starkey 2000). Similarly, Carey et al. (1991) found lower densities in old-growth (>200 yr old; 2.3-3.3 birds/100 ac [40 ha]) than in natural young (40-72 yr old; 9.6-13 birds/100 ac [40 ha]) and mature (80-120 yr old; 8.2 birds/100 ac [40 ha]) stands in the Coast Range. In ne. Oregon, 85- and >200-yr-old mixed conifer forests supported equal densities (Mannan 1982). In grand fir forests of Blue Mtns., more abundant in mid-aged, closed-canopy stands (tree density approximately 11.3 stems/ac >5 in [13 cm] dbh) than in any other successional stage from stand initiation to old forest (Sallabanks et al. 2002). Tree age may be less important than forest structure in determining habitat suitability: gaps in and beneath canopy provide necessary space for aerial foraging, but selects nest sites with large overstory trees that have well-developed canopies (Mannan 1984, Sakai and Noon 1991). Therefore, rare in very dense (>180 trees/ac [72 trees/ha] > 4 in [10 cm] dbh) mid-aged stands (Hagar et al. 1996, Hagar and Howlin 2001), and in very open stands (fewer than 10 trees/ac [4 trees/ha] > 4 in (10 cm) diameter) (Hansen and Hounihan 1996). In Klamath/Siskiyou Mtns., abundance was positively correlated with density of trees >25 in (64 cm) in diameter (Alexander 1999). Shows consistent strong positive response to reduction of tree density through thinning in managed, mid-aged Douglas-fir stands in the Coast Range (Hagar et al. 1996, Hayes et al. 1998) and on the west slope of the Cascades (Hagar and Howlin 2001).

In the Coast Range, more abundant in upslope than riparian habitats (McGarigal and McComb 1992). More abundant in unlogged than logged riparian stands, and not observed in riparian buffers extending < 115 ft (35 m) from stream edge (Hagar 1999a).

Nests are built high above ground in live trees, and well concealed by foliage; tend to be built on small- to medium-diameter branches, well out from tree bole (Sakai and Noon 1991).

Data on diet and foraging specific to Oregon not available. Throughout range, reported as strictly insectivorous, preying mainly on adult and larval butterflies and moths, flies, wasps, and beetles. Forages primarily by sallying out from a perch to catch insects on the wing, returning to perch to consume prey. Typical foraging perch is twig or small dead branch just beneath live conifer canopy (Sedgwick 1994).

**Seasonal Activity and Behavior:** Arrive mid-Apr to early May west of the Cascade crest (Faxon and Bayer 1991, Gillson 1999, Lillie 1999); early dates 7 Apr in Salem (Fix 1990c) and 14 Apr in Corvallis (Gillson 1999). Arrive early to mid-May in e. Oregon (Gabrielson and Jewett 1940); early date 22 Apr at Malheur NWR (Sullivan 2000b). Nest building begins late May. Pair observed building nest 16 Jun in Malheur Co. (Spencer 1998). Adults on nest late May to early Jul (n=8) (Gabrielson and Jewett 1940, Sullivan 1999b, OBBA). Gabrielson and Jewett (1940) report eggs laid in Jun and Jul. Nest with young observed 9 Jul (OBBA).

Little other data on nesting and development of young are available for Oregon, but detailed studies from California (Sakai 1988, Sakai and Noon 1991) and Rocky Mtn. populations (summarized in Sedgwick 1994) report clutch sizes of at least three eggs and a 15-day incubation period. Young fledge 16-18 days after hatching, and remain on parents' territory for about 20 days (Sedgwick 1994). Late dates for 13 yr of fall observations in Lincoln Co. were from 19 Aug to 21 Sep (Faxon and Bayer 1991). Recorded in Malheur NWR into late Sep (Littlefield 1990a). Other late records for east of the Cascades (Harney and Klamath counties) are mid-Oct (Sullivan 2001a).

**Detection:** Most frequently detected and most easily identified by song or call; difficult to visually distinguish from other *Empidonax* flycatchers.

**Population Status and Conservation:** Population trend was stable in Oregon and S. Pacific rainforest region during 1966-2000, and increasing for the Cascades (Sauer et al. 2001). However, Raphael et al. (1988) estimated that populations have decreased by 43% in nw. California relative to pre-settlement levels, due to harvesting of mature forest habitat. Sakai and Noon (1991) suggest that reduction in area of old-growth Douglas-fir/tanoak habitats will decrease density of breeding Hammond's Flycatchers in n. California. May be negatively impacted by harvesting on a large spatial scale due to association with landscapes of less than average fragmentation (McGarigal and McComb 1995). Light thinning of dense, young conifer stands may be a good management strategy for enhancing habitat for this species in young forests of w. Oregon (Hagar et al. 1996, Hayes et al. 1998).—*Joan Hagar*

## Gray Flycatcher *Empidonax wrightii*

Among the least conspicuous of Oregon's birds, this inhabitant of arid country may be found in pine and juniper woodland and sagebrush shrubland. A particularly drab member of the difficult-to-identify *Empidonax* genus, the Gray Flycatcher can most readily be recognized by its downward tail-bobbing motion. Other identification features include its overall gray coloration, its relatively long bill and tail, and a habit of frequently dropping to the ground from low perches in pursuit of food. Gabrielson and Jewett (1940) and Bent (1942) used the binomials *griseus* for Gray Flycatcher and *wrighti* for Dusky but see AOU (1957).

**General Distribution:** Breeds from sc. British Columbia through c. Washington, c. and e. Oregon southward throughout the Great Basin to ne. Arizona and w. and c. New Mexico. Winters in s. Baja California Sur, se. Arizona, and Mexican mainland from Sonora to Oaxaca (AOU 1998, Sterling 1999). Monotypic (AOU 1957).

**Oregon Distribution:** An uncommon to locally fairly common breeder east of the Cascade summit, including the Columbia Plateau southward throughout the Great Basin, with breeding specimens from Haycreek, Jefferson Co., and Burns and The Narrows, Harney Co. (Johnson NK 1963). Breeds in isolated locations in the northeast portion of the state (Gilligan et al. 1994, OBBA, BBS). The accuracy of records outside normal range must be viewed skeptically because identification is challenging. Rare but annual along the west slope of the Cascades during spring migration, including 1-5 individuals detected per year at Detroit Flats, (at upper end of Detroit Res.), Marion Co., since 1995 (*CRM*). Rare in the Rogue Valley and very rare in the Willamette and Umpqua valleys during spring migration. There have been no breeding records west of the Cascade summit, although they have been reported occasionally during breeding season along the west slope of the Cascades (OBBA, *CRM*). Only three s. coastal records (*CRM*). Breeds to elevations

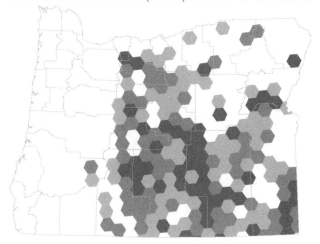

as high as 6,000 ft (1,846 m) (Gilligan et al. 1994). Where present, breeding density averages 51-64 pair/ mi² (20-25/km²) (T. Haislip in Friedmann et al. 1977, Wiens and Rotenberry 1981).

**Habitat and Diet:** Breeds in arid woodlands and shrublands. Exposed ground is a characteristic feature (Johnson 1963). Preferred shrub habitat includes big sagebrush, especially along dry washes, and bitterbrush. Generally less common out in broad sagebrush flats (M. Denny p.c.). Woodland habitat includes mountain-mahogany, old-growth and mid-successional juniper, and open ponderosa pine with an understory of sagebrush or bitterbrush (Gabrielson and Jewett 1940, Sterling 1999, Reinkensmeyer 2000, *CRM*). In se. Deschutes Co. and nw. Klamath Co., commonly nests in sparse lodgepole pine over bitterbrush and sagebrush (D. Fix p.c.). Nest constructed of plant fibers and shredded bark and placed in shrubs or small trees within 6 ft (2 m) of the ground (Gabrielson and Jewett 1940, Ryser 1985). During migration less selective of habitat; often found in riparian areas frequented by other migrating *Empidonax* species (*CRM*). Feeds exclusively on insects in flight, from the ground, or from plants (Sterling 1999).

**Seasonal Activity and Behavior:** Spring migration begins mid- to late Apr and is complete by the end of May (Littlefield 1990a, Gilligan et al. 1994, *CRM*). Most records west of the Cascades are in the last week of Apr and the first week of May. The earliest was in Ashland on 13 Apr 1989 (Heinl 1989b). There appears to be no pronounced peak east of the Cascades, but the largest influx occurs in the first and second weeks of May (Littlefield 1990a, *CRM*). The earliest record east of the Cascades is 16 Apr 1972 at Bend (Gilligan et al. 1994).

Males arrive at breeding areas about a week earlier than females (Johnson 1963). Defends territory by displays and vocalizations. Sings throughout breeding season and throughout the day, but most frequently at dawn. Also sings on moonlit nights in May (D. Fix p.c.). Two typical song types, one a twice-repeated, strong, two-syllable *chlup-chlup* and the other a strong *chlup* followed by a weak higher-pitched *seep*. Alarm *whit* call is similar to that of Dusky Flycatcher. Gives "rattle" call during territorial disputes. Female defends vicinity of nest and often gives distraction (injured bird) display if nest is approached by intruder (Johnson 1963, Sterling 1999). Lays 3-4 cream buff eggs (Gabrielson and Jewett 1940). Lays one egg per day (Sterling 1999). First egg date in Oregon is 8 Jun and the latest is 25 Jul (Gabrielson and Jewett 1940, OBBA). Incubation period 14 days, nestling period 16 days (Russell and Woodbury 1941). Dependent on parents for 14 days after fledging (Russell and Woodbury 1941).

Southward migration extends from mid-Aug to late Sep (Littlefield 1990a, *CRM*). The latest fall record is 2 Oct 1991 at Malheur NWR (Evanich 1992b). The only fall record west of the Cascades was a vagrant reported at Gold Beach on the out-of-season date of 4 Nov 1998 (Gilligan 1999). Two winter reports mentioned by Littlefield (1990a), both on 22 Dec 1940 at different locations by different people are unverified. There are no documented winter records.

**Detection:** Most easily detected by emphatic two-syllable song during breeding season. Blends into surroundings, but frequent movements help draw attention. Habit of perching at medium to low heights also assists detection. Excellent locations to observe this species includes Cabin L. CG north of Fort Rock in sc. Oregon and the juniper stands east of Bend.

**Population Status and Conservation:** BBS data suggest an increasing annual trend of 5% in Oregon since 1966 (Sauer et al. 1999). A dramatic annual population increase of 37% in NFs between 1980 and 1994 has been attributed to deforestation (Sharp 1996). E. Oregon has some of the highest population densities in the species' breeding range, indicated by averages of 40 individuals on the Clover Cr. BBS in Crook Co., and 31.3 from the Wagontire BBS, Harney Co. However, very little is known about ecological relationships and requirements. Utilized habitat is restricted and vulnerable to change. The common practice of juniper and sagebrush removal and crested wheatgrass seeding eliminates essential habitat. Cowbird parasitism is significant; seven of 28 nests found in an Oregon study were parasitized resulting in the death of all young of the host species and three nests successfully fledged cowbirds (T. Haislip in Friedmann et al. 1977).—*Craig R. Miller*

**Dusky Flycatcher** *Empidonax oberholseri*
Formerly known as Wright's Flycatcher (*E. wrighti* ; see Gray Flycatcher) (AOU 1931, Gabrielson and Jewett 1940), the Dusky Flycatcher inhabits open conifers, conifer-hardwoods, or shrubs in the mountains of Oregon. A medium-sized *Empidonax* with a small head and rounded crown. The upperparts are grayish olive to grayish brown; the throat is grayish and the underparts are mostly whitish with an olive-gray wash (sometimes yellowish). The wings have two narrow, usually whitish wingbars. The narrow, white eye ring and pale lores give the appearance of spectacles. The lower mandible is pale orangish at the base with up to 50% dark-colored tip. Outer tail feathers are edged whitish.

**General Distribution:** Breeds from sw. Yukon through c. British Columbia, sw. Alberta, sw. Saskatchewan, Washington, and Oregon (except coastal areas), the

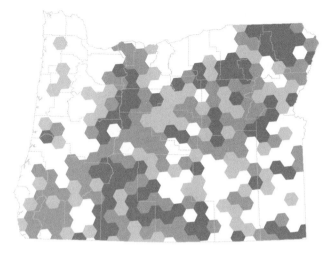

Malheur NWR (USFWS 1981, Littlefield 1990a); Steens Mtn. (Littlefield 1990b); and Owyhee Uplands (Contreras and Kindschy 1996, OBBA) above about 4,500 ft (1,372 m) (M. Denny p.c.).

Fairly common spring migrant and rare to uncommon fall migrant in most lowland valleys in the vicinity of breeding territories (*DPV*). Also a rare migrant in the Willamette Valley (Gullion 1951), Columbia R. estuary (Patterson 1998b), n. coast (Summers and Miller 1993), and c. coast (Sawyer and Hunter 1988). Rare to occasional migrant along s. coast (ODFW 1985, Brown et al. 1996, Contreras 1998).

**Habitat and Diet:** Breeding habitat west of the Cascade summit and Klamath Mtns. is typically open-canopied brushy areas (often clearcuts), typically with scattered small trees (Fix 1989, *DPV*). In sw. Oregon, inhabited clearcuts are typically 5-30 yr old, generally flat to less than 50% slopes, and frequently on ridges and warm, dry slopes (Fix 1989, *DPV*). Associated plant species west of the Cascades include ponderosa, knobcone, sugar, and western white pines, Douglas-fir, incense-cedar, true firs, Pacific madrone, tanoak, canyon live oak, chinquapin, green manzanita, snowbrush, deerbrush, mountain whitethorn, bitter cherry, huckleberry oak, Pacific rhododendron, Sadler oak, currant and gooseberry. East of the Cascades: grand fir, other true firs, ponderosa and lodgepole pine, western juniper, aspen, snowbrush, mountain-mahogany, and sagebrush (*DPV*).

Breeding habitat east of the Cascade summit includes mountain aspen stands, juniper woodlands, open ponderosa and lodgepole pine forests (Follett 1979, Littlefield 1990a, b, Contreras and Kindschy 1996, B. Altman p.c.), or other open mountain areas with scattered trees; openings in grand fir forests (Huff and Brown 1998), and riparian willow thickets. Preferred breeding habitat is broken or disturbed conifer forest, especially ponderosa pine, or aspen and mahogany woods with a shrub understory (Johnson 1966). Spring migration habitat less restrictive (Sedgwick 1993), includes lowland valleys (Evanich 1990, Littlefield 1990a, *DPV*).

Over the range as a whole, Dusky Flycatcher nest placement is generally 3-7 ft (0.9-2.1 m) above ground, maximum 15 ft (4.6 m), in tree or shrub (often well hidden); mainly located next to trunk or in upright fork (Bent 1942, Johnson 1963, Ehrlich et al. 1988, Sedgwick 1993). The nest is a soft, open cup, with the outer part neatly woven of grasses, shredded bark, and sun-bleached weed fibers, and lined with fine weed bark, grasses, animal hair, vegetable down, and feathers; the nest may include small amounts of lichens, pine needles, and human-made materials (Bent 1942, Sedgwick 1993). Near Detroit, Marion Co., a nest was found in an 8-yr-old clearcut (3,500 ft

mountains of California, Rocky Mtn. states and the Colorado Plateau, ne. Nevada and n. Baja California. Winters from s. California, s. Arizona, sw. New Mexico, through mainland Mexico (mostly in the highlands) to nw. Guatemala. Migrates regularly through sw. U.S. (east to w. Texas), casually through coastal Washington and Oregon, to n. Baja California. Monotypic (Browning 1974).

**Oregon Distribution:** The Dusky Flycatcher is an uncommon to common summer resident in most of its breeding range in Oregon. It is found the entire length of the Cascades, but habitat is limited west of the summit in the north (Farner 1952, Fix and Sawyer 1991, Gilligan et al. 1994, USDA 1997, Huff and Brown 1998, S. Dowlan p.c.). Generally found at 3,000-6,000 ft (914-1,829 m) elevation on the west slope of the s. Cascades (Fix 1989); in the Klamath Mtns. (USDI 1993, Dillingham 1994, USDA 1996), generally above 2,900 ft (884 m) (*DPV*). Breeding has been recorded 11 mi (18 km) west of Bend at Tumalo Cr. at 4700 ft (1433 m) and Sisters, Deschutes Co.; south of Mt. Thielsen at 6200 ft (1890 m), Douglas Co.; Crescent L. and 6 mi (10 km) northwest of Ft. Klamath, Klamath Co. (Johnson 1963). Locally uncommon summer resident in the w. Cascades and Rogue-Umpqua Divide in the c. Umpqua Basin (Hunter et at. 1998, USDI undated), west to near Mt. Bolivar, (se. Coos Co. (Evanich and Fix 1983, Tice 1999a, T. Rodenkirk p.c.), and Iron Mtn. (n. Curry Co.), as low as 2,000 ft (610 m) (T. Rodenkirk p.c.). Breeding specimens have been taken from s. Lake Co. and Steens Mtn. 6200-7400 ft (1890-2256 m), near Frenchglen, and other localities in Harney Co. (Johnson 1963).

Also breeds in higher mountains east of the Cascades, including ne. Oregon (except lowlands of Columbia Basin) (Evanich 1992a, ODFW undated checklist [b], OBBA); Blue Mtns. (Thomas 1979, Umatilla NF 1991, Bull and Wisdom 1992, Huff and Brown 1998, OBBA); Klamath Basin (Summers 1993a, USFWS

[1,067 m] elevation) about 4 ft (1.2 m) up in an 8-ft (2.4-m) chinquapin, placed against trunk (K. Bettinger p.c.). A nest found 17 Jun 1990, 5 mi (8 km) west of Sunriver was about 2 ft (0.6 m) up in snowbrush (L. McQueen p.c.). Another was found 7 Jun 1998 near L. Billy Chinook (3,350 ft [1,021 m] elevation) about 8 ft (2.4 m) up in western juniper and placed against the trunk (W. Gross p.c.).

Limited information is available on diet for Dusky Flycatchers; none for Oregon. Diet during breeding season is insects, including wasps and bees, grasshoppers, damselflies; caterpillars, moths and butterflies; percentages not documented (Sedgwick 1993).

**Seasonal Activity and Behavior:** Arrival of spring migrants and establishment of breeding territories appear to overlap statewide; mid-Apr to mid-May. Early arrival dates: Fields 14 Apr 2000 (Maitreya p.c.), Rogue Valley 18 Apr 1976 (S. Summers p.c.) and 23 Apr 1998 (*DPV*), Diamond L. RD 21 Apr (Fix 1990a), Mt. Tabor (Portland) 24 Apr 1998 (H. Nehls p.c.), and Klamath Basin 25 Apr 1980 (S. Summers p.c.). Nest building observed 11 Jun to 14 Jul (n=6); nests with eggs 20 May to 11 Jul (n=12); carrying food 27 May to 19 Jul (n=3); nests with young 6 Jun to 26 Jul (n=5); recent fledged young 26 Jun 1998 and 12 Jul 1997 (OBBA). Departure from breeding territories and fall migration occurs early Aug to early Sep. Late dates include 4 Sep 1998 in the n. Cascades (S. Dowlan p.c.); 9 Sep 1990 near Ashland (Fix 1991); 9 Sep 1992 at Summer L. (S. Summers p.c.); 27 Sep 1986 at Malheur NWR (S. Summers p.c.); and 22 Oct 1963 at Malheur NWR (Littlefield 1990a). There is one unverified mid-Dec sighting thought to be this species near Coos Bay (T. Rodenkirk p.c.).

**Detection:** Vocal upon arrival; detected most often by calls and songs. *Empidonax* flycatchers are difficult to identify without the aid of songs or calls. Field guides and articles by Whitney and Kaufman (1985a, b), Carey et al. (1990), and Sedgwick (1993) are helpful.

**Population Status and Conservation:** Difficulty in identifying this species, especially prior to the mid-1960s, makes past distribution uncertain. East of the Cascades likely little changed since Gabrielson and Jewett (1940). Appears to have increased since the 1940s due to clearcutting of conifer stands; previous to 1940s, wildfire and high-grading timbered stands likely influenced distribution (*DBM*). Populations appear stable to increasing in Oregon.

Oregon populations show 4.9%/yr increase 1980-99 (p=0.02, n=57) (BBS); 4%/yr increase 1980-94 (p<0.05) (Sharp 1996). Breeding season counts 1994-97 in four Klamath Mtn. clearcuts (age 13-30

yr, elevation 2,900-4,400 ft [884-1,341 m]) west and southwest of Grants Pass found average estimated abundance of 0.3 birds/ac (n=15), range 0.2- 0.6 (0.8 birds/ha, range 0.4-1.4) (*DPV*). Huff and Brown (1998) report mean detections of 5.1 (1996) and 4.5 (1997) birds/hr in Ochoco Mtns.; mean detection range of 0.6 to 0.9 birds/hr in the Blue Mtns. (1995-97).

Reduced timber harvest and continuance of fire-suppression practices west of the Cascades may reduce habitat in the future. Reducing stand (crown) densities by thinning, or creating small openings in dense stands, may maintain suitable habitat. Removal of shrubs from natural mountain brushfields would reduce available habitat.—*Dennis P. Vroman*

## Pacific-slope Flycatcher *Empidonax difficilis*

This small greenish flycatcher is easily overlooked in the moist, shady forests where it makes its summer home. Formerly classified as a single species (Western Flycatcher, *E. difficilis*), the two species (AOU 1989) Pacific-slope Flycatcher and Cordilleran Flycatcher differ genetically, vocally, and morphologically in color, shape, and size (Johnson 1980, Johnson and Marten 1988). The two species are sympatric in n. California and s. Oregon (Johnson 1980, Johnson and Marten 1988, Johnson 1994). The term "Western" Flycatcher may be useful for reporting sightings of some birds just as the term "*Empidonax*" is sometimes used for unidentified individuals in the genus.

**General Distribution:** Breeds from se. Alaska and c. British Columbia south through Washington, Oregon, California (Coast Ranges, w. Sierra Nevada, and Channel Is.) and Baja California. Eastern boundary of breeding range and extent of overlap with Cordilleran Flycatcher in zone from se. British Columbia and sw. Alberta through e. Washington and Oregon is uncertain due to difficulty in field identification and inadequate study in that area (Cannings in Lowther 2000, Weber 2000a, Beck 2001). The two forms are sympatric in the Siskiyou Mtns. of n. California (Johnson 1980). Respective winter ranges less well-known than breeding ranges because the species are essentially indistinguishable in the field during winter. They share a combined range from s. Baja California and n. Mexico south to Oaxaca and Yucatan; based on specimens, Pacific-slope Flycatchers likely winter along w. coast of Mexico, Cordilleran Flycatchers in mountains of c. Mexico (Lowther 2000). Pacific-slope Flycatcher has three recognized subspecies; *E. d. difficilis* occurs in Oregon.

**Oregon Distribution:** Common to abundant breeder in forests of Coast Range and w. Cascades below about

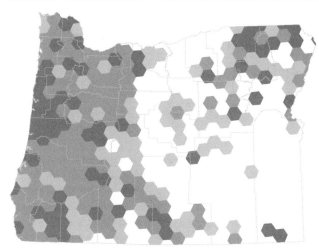

*Distribution map for Pacific-slope Flycatcher and Cordilleran Flycatcher*

4,000 ft (1,200 m) elevation; common transient in w. Oregon. "Western" Flycatchers of uncertain taxonomy are locally common to uncommon breeders in moister forested habitats east of the Cascade crest (e. Cascades and Blue Mtns.). They are uncommon transients in e. Oregon (Gilligan et al. 1994).

**Habitat and Diet:** Common in a variety of low- to mid-elevation forest types in w. Oregon, including Sitka spruce, red alder, western hemlock, Douglas-fir, and western redcedar. At higher elevations, uncommon in Pacific silver fir forests (Gillson 2001a), local at mesic microsites in lower subalpine forests, absent in lodgepole pine forest (Fix 1990a). Favors moist, shaded locations, often near riparian zones. In unmanaged Coast Range forests, abundance is slightly but not significantly higher along streamsides than in upslope stands (McGarigal and McComb 1992). Generally prefers mature forests over younger stands (Raphael et al. 1988, Carey et al. 1991, Manuwal 1991). In the w. Cascades, most common in mature (80- to 190-yr-old) and old-growth (200- to 450-yr-old) stands, but also relatively common in young (30- to 60-yr-old) stands (Hansen et al. 1995). In the w. Cascades, prefers old stands with decayed logs, fern and deciduous shrub cover, western hemlocks and very large western redcedars (Gilbert and Allwine 1991). In the c. Coast Range, abundance was lower in riparian buffer strips (59-246 ft [18-75 m] in width) left after clearcutting than in riparian zones surrounded by mature forest; they were not detected in buffer strips less than 59 ft (18 m) wide (Hagar 1999a). Less abundant in thinned than in unthinned Douglas-fir forest (Hagar et al. 1996).

In e. Oregon "Western" Flycatcher occurs locally in black cottonwood, quaking aspen, ponderosa pine, lodgepole pine, and high-elevation spruce/fir forests, particularly in moist riparian corridors (Johnson 1980); during migration "Western" Flycatcher occurs in a variety of wooded or brushy habitats throughout state, and at oases in arid country east of the Cascades (Gilligan et al. 1994).

Pacific-slope Flycatchers feed primarily on flying insects, usually hawking from a perch or sometimes gleaning from foliage. Diet includes hymenopterans, beetles, moths, caterpillars, flies, and occasionally seeds or berries (Bent 1942).

Pacific-slope Flycatcher nesting data are primarily from California and British Columbia. They nest 0-30 ft (0-9 m) above ground, in sites backed by hard supporting surface, e.g., the crotch of a tree or shrub branch, in moss clumps or behind loose bark on tree trunk (frequently red alder), in tree cavity, in roots of downed tree, or on streambank, cliff ledge, shaded building, or bridge. Nests are composed of moss, lichens, bark, grass, etc.; lined with fine grass, fibers, etc. (Davis et al. 1963).

**Seasonal Activity and Behavior:** Spring migrants usually begin to arrive in w. Oregon in mid- to late Apr, breeders common by mid-May (Fix 1990a, Gilligan et al. 1994, Contreras 1998, Hunter et al. 1998, Janes et al. 2001). Average first arrival in Corvallis 27 Apr (Gillson 2001a). Early dates: 5 Mar 1995 at Pony Slough, N. Bend, Coos Co. (Contreras 1998), 2 Apr in Corvallis; 23 Apr on upper Calapooia R.; 1 May at Lebanon (Gillson 2001a). In e. Oregon first "Western" Flycatcher arrivals in late Apr and early May, peaking in late May and early Jun (Gilligan et al. 1994). At Malheur NWR, spring migrants observed from 23 Apr to 17 Jun, average 14 May (Littlefield 1990a, Ivey, Herziger, and Scheuering 1998). Nest from May to Aug, peak activity in Jun. Nest building takes place primarily in early to mid-Jun (n=2) (OBBA). Nest built by female alone, in 5-6 days (Sakai 1988, Ainsley 1992). Clutch size usually 3-4 eggs. Incubation 13-16 days, by female (Davis et al. 1963, Ainsley 1992). Young observed on nest primarily from late Jun to early Jul, with a late date of 22 Aug (n=6) (OBBA). Both sexes feed young. Time to fledging 14-17 days (Lowther 2000). Fledglings observed late Jun to late Jul (n=5) (OBBA). May raise two broods per year (Harrison 1979). Fall migration peaks in late Aug and early Sep, mostly complete by mid-Sep (Gilligan et al. 1994). Late dates: 20 Sep on upper Calapooia R.; 4 Oct along Beaver Cr. at Lebanon (Gillson 2001a); 8 Nov (Gilligan et al. 1994). At Malheur NWR, fall migrant "Western" Flycatchers observed from 12 Aug to 3 Oct, with peak passage 25 Aug to 15 Sep (Littlefield 1990a). A few winter reports, including one at Grants Pass on 29 Dec 1991 (Gilligan et al. 1994) have accrued, but no winter records have yet been verified (H. Nehls p.c.).

Pacific-slope Flycatchers are interspecifically territorial with Hammond's Flycatcher (Johnson 1980), which overlaps broadly in range with Pacific-slope Flycatcher but tends to occur at higher elevations and is more closely associated with old-growth forest rather than dense, younger stands (Sakai and Noon 1991, *GEC*).

**Detection:** Most easily detected and identified by voice, but incongruence between published descriptions of vocalizations and some birds heard in the field lessens the certainty of identification to species, especially those in e. Oregon.

The position note given by classic Pacific-slope Flycatcher males west of the Cascade crest is a slurred, rising, high-pitched whistle: *pseeweat!*, termed "sinusoidal" by N. K. Johnson (1994b). The full advertising song, generally given upon arrival on the breeding grounds, is a high-pitched, intermittently repeated sequence, usually of three syllables: *ps-SEET ptsick seet!* (Davis et al. 1963); the order may be ambiguous as sequential songs merge together. The *ptsick* syllable has two accented elements, sometimes with a third unaccented element; the two accented elements have a rising "low-high" sequence (Johnson 1980).

Vocalizations of Cordilleran Flycatchers are generally similar to those of Pacific-slope Flycatchers, with subtle distinguishing characteristics (Johnson 1980). The *ptsick* syllable of the Cordilleran advertising song has a falling "high-low" sequence rather than "low-high". Classic Cordilleran males, particularly in the Rocky Mtns., give a distinctly 2-parted position note, with the second note higher: *pit-peet!* However, in e. Oregon and n. California, position notes can be variable or intermediate (Lowther 2000); birds may give the two-parted note, the sinusoidal note, or a slightly two-noted, sharp *pseeet!* or *seeet!* (termed "steeply rising" by N. K. Johnson [1994b]). Birds in the e. Cascades near Crater L. gave a typical Cordilleran "high-low" advertising song; however, at least some of these individuals were "bilingual" in their position notes, delivering both sinusoidal notes characteristic of Pacific-slope Flycatchers and steeply rising or occasionally two-parted notes characteristic of Cordilleran Flycatchers (Johnson NK 1994a). Birds east of the Cascades are reported to give predominantly up-slurred, single-parted position notes (P. T. Sullivan p.c.). In general the two-parted *pit-peet!* position notes that have often been used to identify Cordilleran Flycatchers do not appear to be the norm for e. Oregon birds; such notes have been reported sporadically from the Umatilla R. upstream from Pendleton (Hampton 1997), Burnt R. Canyon in Baker Co. (*ALC*), northwest of Lakeview (R. Hoyer p.c.), east of Lakeview, and southeast of Union (P. T. Sullivan p.c.). However, others have reported that position notes of birds in the Blue Mtns. are primarily Cordilleran-type (Weber 2000b, R. Sallabanks p.c.). It is unclear whether birds that sing a Pacific-slope "low-high" advertising song might also

give a variety of position notes; two-parted position notes have been reported from one bird on the coast near Cascade Head (Pickering 2001).

Because position notes are so variable, the advertising song may be a more reliable distinguishing characteristic. However, differences among songs are subtle and can be difficult to detect in the field without a sonogram (J. Mariani p.c.). Also, songs recorded in e. Washington, British Columbia, and Alberta indicate a cline in characteristics of the distinguishing syllables (Beck 2001, Hunn 2001). Geographic distribution and overlap of "high-low" and "low-high" song types in Oregon are poorly known, so it is unclear whether the Cordilleran pattern predominates in e. Oregon. Further study is needed to determine whether differences in advertising song coincide with genetic structuring of the population.

In many cases birds cannot be identified to species in the field. Females of both Pacific-slope and Cordilleran Flycatchers give similar calls (a thin, high-pitched *seet*), and are apparently indistinguishable in the field. Migrating and wintering birds that do not call also cannot be identified except perhaps by measurement in the hand.

**Population Status and Conservation:** "Western" Flycatchers are common, and BBS data (which combine Pacific-slope and Cordilleran Flycatchers for analysis) indicate no significant rangewide change 1966-2000. However, BBS data in Oregon indicate a significant annual decline of 3.7% (p=0.02) 1966-2000. This decline appears to have steepened in recent decades: 3.1% (p > 0.1) 1966-79, vs. 4.6% (p=0.03) 1980-2000. They are not old-growth obligates, but could be adversely affected by extensive clearcutting of mature forest.—*Grant E. Canterbury*

## Cordilleran Flycatcher *Empidonax occidentalis*

The Cordilleran Flycatcher was recently designated a species distinct from the Pacific-slope Flycatcher (AOU 1989), with which it was formerly lumped under the name Western Flycatcher. The two species are almost identical in appearance, and the population in e. Oregon is in some respects vocally intermediate between the Cordilleran and Pacific-slope types, so the distribution and status of the Cordilleran Flycatcher in Oregon is unclear. Western Flycatchers in e. Oregon are relatively uncommon by comparison to Pacific-slope Flycatchers west of the Cascade crest. For further information see discussion under Pacific-slope Flycatcher.

**General Distribution:** Breeds from sw. Alberta, w. Montana south through the Rocky Mtns. and Great Basin to e. Arizona, c. New Mexico, and mountains of Mexico. Western range boundary and extent of overlap with Pacific-slope Flycatcher is uncertain in a zone from se. British Columbia and sw. Alberta through e. Washington and Oregon due to difficulty of field identification and inadequate study. Cordilleran Flycatcher has two recognized subspecies, *E. o. hellmayri* occurs in Oregon.

**Oregon Distribution:** The identity of populations in e. Oregon is unclear and birds are most safely identified as "Western" Flycatchers. "Western" Flycatchers are locally common to uncommon breeders in e. Cascades (specimen from Ft. Klamath, Klamath Co. [USNM]), and in the Ochoco and Blue mountains. They breed in low numbers at elevations >4,500 ft (1,372 m) in the drier s. Blue Mtns. of Grant, Harney, and Malheur counties, and in the Pueblos and Oregon Canyon mountains (M. Denny p.c.). There are non-breeding specimens from Malheur NWR, Harney Co., and Drews Res., Lake Co. (USNM). The status of Cordilleran Flycatcher in w. Oregon is uncertain; it is likely very rare if it occurs at all. See discussion under Pacific-slope Flycatcher.

**Habitat and Diet:** Generally occurs in drier, higher-elevation forests than Pacific-slope Flycatcher (e.g., black cottonwood, quaking aspen, ponderosa pine, lodgepole pine, high-elevation spruce/fir forest), and is more closely associated with riparian zones (Lowther 2000); it is unclear whether habitat preferences of the two species differ where they sympatric. R. Sallabanks (p.c.) found Cordilleran Flycatchers rare and Pacific-slope Flycatchers absent in grand fir and subalpine fir forests of the Blue Mtns. Mannan (1982) found no Cordilleran or Pacific-Slope Flycatchers on eight study plots covering approximately 950 ac (380 ha) of Douglas-fir/ponderosa pine forest in the Blue Mtns. See discussion under Pacific-slope Flycatcher.

**Seasonal Activity and Behavior:** Nesting biology similar to Pacific-slope Flycatcher, but poorly known in Oregon. Nests often located on rock faces or human-made structures (Lowther 2000). Migrants that do not call cannot be distinguished from Pacific-slope Flycatchers, thus little is known about their migration chronology.

**Detection:** See discussion under Pacific-slope Flycatcher.

**Population Status and Conservation:** Poorly known in Oregon due to difficulty of identification. BBS data do not distinguish between Pacific-slope and Cordilleran Flycatchers, but data for both species indicate a significant decline during 1966-2000 (see Pacific-slope Flycatcher).—*Grant Canterbury*

**Black Phoebe** *Sayornis nigricans*
This medium-sized flycatcher has expanded its breeding range from n. California to sw. Oregon and continues to expand its range in Oregon. First experiences with the species may bring to mind a Slate-colored Junco behaving like a flycatcher. The Black Phoebe is dull, sooty black overall, somewhat paler on the back, with a white belly contrasting with the black breast and sides. Bill, legs, and feet are black. The phoebe dips its tail repeatedly. Tertials and outer tail feathers are often edged grayish-white, and the undertail coverts are white. Juveniles have deep brown wing-bars and some body feathers edged buffy-cinnamon.

**General Distribution:** Breeds from sw. Oregon, California, s. Nevada, s. Utah, n. Arizona, se. Colorado, c. New Mexico, and wc. Texas south to s. Baja California and, mostly in the highlands, through M. America (except the Yucatan Peninsula) to w. Panama, east to n. Venezuela, and south in the Andes from Colombia to nw. Argentina. Partially migratory, with northern populations dispersing after the breeding season. Casual north to s. British Columbia (Vancouver) and w. Washington, east to se. Texas and Florida; sight reports for Idaho and Minnesota. Four subspecies; *S. n. semiatra* occurring in Oregon (AOU 1957).

**Oregon Distribution:** Expanding. Uncommon to common local resident in lowlands of Rogue, Applegate, and Illinois R. valleys and tributaries (Browning 1975a, Gilligan et al. 1994, *DPV*), generally below 2,500 ft (760 m) (*DPV*); s. coast lowlands north to the Coquille R. Valley (more birds in winter) and Coos Bay (Brown et al. 1996, Contreras 1997b, 1998). Rare to irregular (mostly winter reports) in Umpqua Valley (Hunter et al. 1998); nesting confirmed near Sutherlin 26 May 1999 (K. Wilson p.c.); may become resident. Nesting reported near Creswell (Lane Co.) 15 May 1997 (Lillie 1997), but an actual nest was not found (S. Nelson, S. Maulding p.c.). An adult feeding young observed at Simpson Park, Albany (Linn Co.), 10-19 Jul 1998

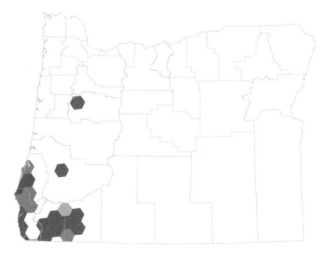

*Black Phoebe*

**Habitat and Diet:** No habitat or diet studies have been conducted in Oregon. Black Phoebes are strongly associated with water. Slow-flowing, idle, or slack water of large rivers, streams, and creeks (*DPV*), ephemeral and permanent ponds, lake shorelines, irrigation ditches (*DPV*), and even water tanks are used. Not strongly associated with any particular vegetative species; generally at riparian edge, or habitats adjacent to water; less restricted during winter (Zeiner et al. 1990, *DPV*). Perch sites are needed for foraging. Phoebes perch on bare limbs, fencelines, or similar open structures over or near water, including rocks at the edge of flowing water (*DPV*). Foraging habitat includes open water near land, flooded fields, open grasslands and pasturelands, lawns, parks, bare ground; females tend to forage inside or at canopy edge while nesting (Wolf 1997). Habitat requirements are similar throughout year; tend to breed on structures, with no special attachment to them in winter.

Black Phoebes require a mud source and specific structural features for nesting (Bent 1942, Wolf 1997). Nest-site criteria include protective ceiling, near or over water, suitable foraging habitat, away from prevailing winds and direct sunlight. Natural nest sites (generally limited) include sheltered rock faces, streamside boulders, dirt banks, hollow tree cavities. Artificial nest sites (generally human structures) include eaves of buildings, concrete bridge stringers, concrete irrigation and drainage culverts, abandoned open wells, sluice boxes (Wolf 1997, *DPV*), ledge above doorway, and rain gutters under eaves (J. Van Hulzen p.c.).

In Oregon, nests are constructed of mud pellets (mud mixed with shredded bark, grass stems, or roots in varying proportions) placed on a vertical (e.g., a bridge) or a horizontal (e.g., eaves) (*DPV*) surface. Nests resemble those of the Barn Swallow. The nest can be lined with plant fibers, strips of bark, animal hair, wool, or occasionally feathers. A range of 41-85% of nests are reportedly built using the previous year's nest structure (Wolf 1997).

Scant documentation is available on this phoebe's diet in Oregon. In the Rogue Valley individuals were observed taking an orange dragonfly 29 Jul 97 (L. Heinze p.c.) and an orange, medium-sized butterfly on 10 Mar 2001 (*DPV*). Phoebes are believed to forage on mayflies in winter when available (V. Zauskey p.c.). Diet consists of insects (99% by volume); mainly flying insects. Stomach contents of California birds (n=344) (Wolf 1997) included wild bees and wasps 31% (59% in Aug), flies 28% (64% in Apr), beetles 13%, damselflies and dragonflies, spiders 6%, true bugs

(Tice 1999a). A nest was located and monitored along the Willamette R., south of Dayton in Yamhill Co. during Jun-Jul 2002 (F. Schrock p.c.). Four eggs were present on 16 Jun, a half-grown nestling and at least two eggs were present on 13 Jul, and the young bird was fledged by 20 Jul (three unhatched eggs were still in the nest) (F. Schrock p.c.). Casual visitor in the Klamath Basin (Summers 1993a) and coastal areas north of Coos Bay (Summers and Miller 1993, Gilligan et al. 1994). Occasional throughout the Willamette Valley to the Columbia R.; about 17 occurrences to date (*Oregon Birds* and *North American Birds*, numerous observations). An individual was observed at Gold L. bog (e. Lane Co.) on 8 Jul 1988 at 4,800 ft (1,463 m) (Anderson 1989d). Great Basin reports include individuals at Fields 20 May 1990 (Anderson DA 1990b), and Malheur NWR 5 Apr 1991 (without details) (Evanich 1991a).

11%, butterflies and moths 8%, and grasshoppers 2%. Small fish and small amounts of berries are taken by some individuals.

**Seasonal Activity and Behavior:** The Black Phoebe's display is a hesitant flight straight up from its perch, with its fanned tail and wings fluttering, sometimes accompanied by song. The song is a repeated two-syllable note, commencing in Feb (*DPV*); they occasionally sing in winter (*ALC*). They regularly sing from courtship through nesting. Singing occurred at Central Point ODFW office pond 17 Feb 2000 (*DPV*), near Sutherlin 13 Mar 1999 (K. Wilson p.c.); singing and display flight observed 8 Feb 2000 along Applegate R. at Fish Hatchery Park (*DPV*). Nest building was observed 30 Mar 1995 along the Applegate R. (J. Van Hulzen p.c.); 8 Apr 1999 north of Merlin (*DPV*); and 17 Apr 1998 near Applegate R. (rebuilding previous year's nest) (J. Van Hulzen p.c.). In Coquille Valley, nesting birds have been reported 20 Mar 1999 (P.T. Sullivan p.c.), 23 Apr 1998 at Sturdivant Park (S. Wilson *fide ALC*) and 17 Apr 1999 (T. Rodenkirk p.c.). Adults were noted feeding young in the nest 26 May 1999 near Sutherlin (K. Wilson p.c.). Nest with young was observed 8 Jul 1996 near the mouth of the Rogue R. (OBBA). An adult carrying food items was seen 12 Apr 1997 (possibly on its way to a female on the nest) in the Coquille Valley (D. Munson p.c.), and feeding recently fledged young 5 Jul 1998 in Coquille Valley (K. A. Bettinger p.c.). A fledgling was observed at Simpson Park near Albany on 10 Jul 1998 (M. Patterson p.c.). An independent juvenile was captured 5 Jul 1997 along the Applegate R. (*DPV*). Fall dispersing individuals were noted 15 Sep 1997 (R. R. Robb p.c.) and 13 Oct 1999 (*DPV*), both in open oak woodland-buckbrush habitat in c. Rogue Valley.

Black Phoebes are solitary, except when in mated pairs (Wolf 1997). The largest groups consist of recently fledged young with adults. Nothing is known of the movements of locally nesting birds after breeding is completed, or the source of winter influxes.

**Detection:** Most frequently detected by song and call. Vocalizations decrease by end of nesting. Single-note call commonly used, described as loud *tseep*. Birds visible while perched or foraging and during display flights.

**Population Status and Conservation:** The historic range of the Black Phoebe in Oregon is poorly documented. Questionable records from the late 1800s indicate possible presence of Black Phoebe in Oregon at that time (Jobanek 1997). Bailey (1924) indicated that the distribution included Oregon. The phoebe was listed as a hypothetical species by Gabrielson and Jewett (1940), based on the uncertainty of past documentation. Occurrence was documented in the s. Willamette Valley in mid-1930s (Evenden et al. 1947, Richardson and Sturges 1964).

Recently, the Black Phoebe's range has been rapidly expanding and populations are clearly on the increase in the sw. interior and s. coastal Oregon (Contreras 1997b). The first record for Coos Co. was in Jan 1982. The species subsequently increased phenomenally as a wintering bird, and was found nesting in the late 1980s. It now commonly breeds and winters in the Coquille Valley and continues to increase in coastal areas to the north (Contreras 1998). Not surprisingly, a 2%/yr increase in Black Phoebe numbers has been seen on BBS routes in California 1966-98 (P=0.03, n=115) (BBS).

Black Phoebe cohabits well with human development that increases nesting sites and foraging habitat (see Habitat and Diet section), but House Sparrows known to destroy nests (J. Van Hulzen p.c.).—*Dennis P. Vroman*

## Eastern Phoebe *Sayornis phoebe*

This rather plain but charismatic tail-wagging flycatcher breeds throughout e. N. America to ne. British Columbia, N. Dakota, and Texas. It migrates east of the Rocky Mtns. to winter in the s. U.S. and M. America. Small numbers regularly winter in coastal California. It is casual to Oregon and Washington. There have been many reported sightings (no specimens) in Oregon (Nehls 1993a), but only 7 have been accepted by the OBRC. Individuals were observed at Independence, Polk Co., 19-20 Feb 1996 (OBRC), Valley of the Rogue SP, 10-12 Jun 1999 (OBRC), and Clarno Bridge, Wheeler Co., 14 May 2000 (Sullivan 2000b). A singing territorial bird was photographed at Falls City, Polk Co., 5-24 Jun 1992 (Tice 1993). Individuals were photographed at Fields, Harney Co., 1-7 Nov 1994 (OBRC); at Buena Vista Station, Malheur NWR, Harney Co., 31 May to 7 Jun 1998 (OBRC); and near Bandon, Coos Co., 30 Dec 1998 to 20 Mar 1999 (OBRC). Monotypic (AOU 1957).—*Harry B. Nehls*

## Say's Phoebe *Sayornis saya*

The arrival of this stalwart flycatcher in Feb prematurely announces spring east of the Cascades. It specializes in the capture of low-flying and ground-dwelling insects, enabling it to survive harsh conditions. Its near-ground niche allows it to reside from the arctic tundra to the deserts of s. Mexico. Its subtle song and coloration fit in well with the open country it occupies. Although not shy, it is easily passed unnoticed by the casual observer. Its black tail contrasting with brownish-gray back, light gray throat and chest gradually blending into cinnamon buff belly and undertail coverts distinguishes this species.

**General Distribution:** Breeds from Alaska and Great Plains to c. Mexico. Disjunct northern breeding

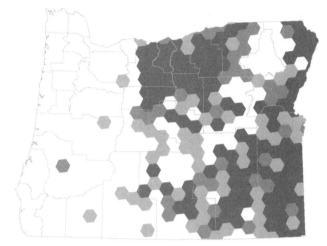

population occupies interior Alaska and Yukon Territory. Southern portion breeds from interior s. British Columbia and s. Saskatchewan south to Baja California and ne. Sonora, Mexico. Winters from n. California to sc. Texas south to s. Mexico (AOU 1998, Schukman and Wolf 1998). Of two subspecies only *S. s. saya* (*yukonensis* is a synonym [Browning 1976]) occurs in Oregon.

**Oregon Distribution:** Breeds from the east base of the Cascades eastward. Common breeder from se. to nc. Oregon and Snake R. in extreme ne. Oregon. Uncommon breeder in sc., c., and ne. Oregon (OBBA, *CRM*). Common migrant east of the Cascades. Uncommon to very uncommon spring and fall migrant west of the Cascade summit to the coast. In most springs 3-4 individuals are reported west of the Cascades, but some years are exceptional, such as 1999, when as many as 31 were reported (Lillie 1999). At the other extreme, no spring migrants were reported 1991-94. Fall migrants west of the Cascades average 2-3/yr; however, as many as 12 were reported in 1998 (Gilligan 1999, *CRM*). Very uncommon but regular winter resident in the Rogue Valley where as many as four have been found. Very uncommon and irregular winter visitant in the Umpqua and Willamette valleys. However, one spent at least five consecutive winters at E.E. Wilson W.A., Benton Co., 1993-94 through 1997-98. Occasional in winter along the southern coast. Occasional winter resident in lowlands east of the Cascades (Gilligan et al. 1994, Contreras 1997b, *CRM*).

**Habitat and Diet:** Breeds in arid, sparsely treed, open country such as sagebrush plains, dry foothills, canyons, rimrock country, and dry farms (Bent 1942, Ryser 1985, Schukman and Wolf 1998). Breeds at elevations from 200 to at least 6,000 ft (60-1,846 m). Requires a sheltered ledge upon which to build its nest, often using cliff face, rimrock, or human-built structure. May use multiple materials to construct nest base such as rocks, plant stems, grasses, moss, wool,

spiderwebs, and hair, and lines cup with materials such as wool, hair, natural and synthetic fibers, paper, and feathers (Gabrielson and Jewett 1940, Schukman and Wolf 1998). Nests may be reused in same or subsequent year. Forages from perches or hover-gleans insects from perches within 3-6 ft (1-2 m) of the ground (Schukman and Wolf 1998). Primary food consists of insects including bees, wasps, flies, beetles, and grasshoppers (Beal 1912, Schukman and Wolf 1998). Diet during Feb, when ground may still be frozen and snow still present, has been open to speculation. Although Littlefield (1990a) suggests "major food is likely seeds," studies (all outside Oregon) consistently reveal that nearly 100% of this phoebe's diet consists of insects, even during winter (Beal 1912, Schukman and Wolf 1998). However Bent (1942) gives an account of a snowbound bird feeding on ivy berries for a week, and Dawson (1923) states dried berries and seeds are sometimes taken during winter. Ryser (1985) suggests its near-ground foraging niche is more amenable to acquiring insects in cold climates than further off the ground, due to a warmer microclimate. Indigestible food parts regurgitated as pellets (Bent 1942). Water needs are supplied by its insectivorous diet, so typically does not drink even if water is available (Weathers 1983, Schukman and Wolf 1998). Outside of breeding season occurs in almost any open habitat including marsh edges, high elevations above treeline, and coastal farmland and dunes.

**Seasonal Activity and Behavior:** Earliest of our insectivorous migrants, first arriving in mid- to late Feb. Spring migration peaks in mid-Mar and continues through mid-Apr, although a few stragglers may continue to arrive into early May (Littlefield 1990a, Gilligan et al. 1994). Although not always possible to distinguish from winter residents, most of the early Feb records likely represent spring migrants. Most migrate singly, males arriving about 1 wk earlier than females (Littlefield 1990a, Schukman and Wolf 1998).

Most studies have been conducted outside Oregon. Say's Phoebes show strong nest-site tenacity. Egg laying begins early to mid-Apr (Gabrielson and Jewett 1940, Littlefield 1990a). Lays 3-7 (usually four or five) pure white eggs occasionally with reddish or dark brown spots (Gabrielson and Jewett 1940, Bent 1942). Incubation period usually 13-17 days and young fledge about 17 days after hatching. Recently hatched young have been found as early as 10 Apr and as late as 16 Jun. Although not studied in Oregon, apparently often has two broods throughout most of its range (Bent 1942, Schukman and Wolf 1998). Only breeding record west of the Cascades is a pair that nested for at least four consecutive yrs at the McKenzie School in Blue R., e. Lane Co. (Kurt Cox p.c.). Success of these breeding attempts is unknown. Late records of individuals in w. Oregon include 17 Jun 1978 at Eugene (Harrington-

Tweit et al. 1978), and 2 Jun 1998 at the north spit of Coos Bay (Tice 1999a).

Southward migration occurs from late Aug to the end of Sep without a discernable peak (Littlefield 1990a, Gilligan et al. 1994). Migrates singly rather than in flocks (Schukman and Wolf 1998). Most records later than Sep (through winter) are west of the Cascades, although single individuals have been reported east of the Cascades most years since 1990 (CBC data, *CRM*).

**Detection:** Its propensity to construct nests in and around human habitations allows easy observation and study, as does its occupation of open country. Often perches on top of shrub, post, or fence line while foraging, and habit of spreading tail, hovering above the ground, and hawking insects in the air quickly identifies it as a flycatcher. A variable and frequently given *phee-eur* vocalization helps draw attention to the species' presence (Schukman and Wolf 1998, *CRM*). However, its soft coloration blends in to surroundings causing many birds to be easily overlooked.

**Population Status and Conservation:** BBS trend data are a poor indicator of population trends for Say's Phoebe because of inadequate coverage and low bird densities along routes. The highest count average in Oregon is 3.33 on the Catlow Rim route. Although the long-term trend for Oregon is positive, the estimation is not statistically significant (Sauer et al. 1999). Throughout its range, BBS trend data showed a strong decline 1966-91, but an increasing trend since then (Schukman and Wolf 1998). Although Gabrielson and Jewett (1940) stated "it is a regular resident of the Rogue, Umpqua, and Willamette Valleys," no supporting information was provided. Breeding records west of the Cascades have been nonexistent in the last half-century with one exception noted above. Major causes of mortality to eggs and young include predation, wind-blown nests, and human destruction (Schukman and Wolf 1998). Parasitism by Brown-headed Cowbirds has not been studied in Oregon, but is rare elsewhere. Human-made structures have provided nest sites, but the effect of these on range and population is unknown.—*Craig R. Miller*

**Vermilion Flycatcher** *Pyrocephalus rubinus*
This brightly colored tropical species is resident as far north as s. California, s. Oklahoma, and c. Texas. It is casual in fall and winter elsewhere in the U.S. A subadult male was photographed at Bend, Deschutes Co., 10-25 Oct 1992 (Crabtree 1993). A bright adult male was observed at Myrtle Point, Coos Co., 6-7 Dec 1992 (OBRC); and an adult male was photographed at Irrigon, Morrow Co., 7 Nov 2000 (Sullivan 2001a). Subspecies unknown.—*Harry B. Nehls*

## Subfamily Tyranninae

**Dusky-capped Flycatcher** *Myiarchus tuberculifer*
This tropical species breeds as far north as Arizona and New Mexico, and winters in M. and S. America. It is casual to c. California, and casually farther north along the coast. One was photographed and its voice recorded at Newport, Lincoln Co., 2-11 Jan 1996 (Dickey 1996).—*Harry B. Nehls*

**Ash-throated Flycatcher** *Myiarchus cinerascens*
With its erect posture and stately manner, the Ash-throated Flycatcher brings a touch of elegance to the oak and juniper woodlands of Oregon. A medium-sized flycatcher, it has a puffy crest and generally pale coloration; sexes are similar. It has gray-brown upperparts, and an ashy gray breast; the throat may appear whiter. Belly and undertail coverts are pale yellow. It has two whitish wing bars, and rufous-colored inner webs of the tail and primaries. Juveniles have more extensively reddish tails.

**General Distribution:** Breeds from sc. Washington, nc. Oregon (not nw. Oregon as in AOU Check-list) southeast to wc. Texas, south to s. Baja California, s. Sonora, and the Mexican highlands to sc. Mexico. Winters from s. California (rarely) and c. Arizona south throughout most of w. and interior Mexico, interior Guatemala, and on the Pacific slope to Honduras. Two subspecies; *M. c. cinerascens* occurs in Oregon (AOU 1957).

**Oregon Distribution:** Uncommon to locally common summer resident in the Rogue and Applegate valleys (Browning 1975a, *DPV*); locally uncommon summer resident in the Illinois (*DPV*) and Umpqua valleys (Hunter et al. 1998). Rare vagrant in the Willamette Valley (Gilligan et al. 1994, Salem Audubon 1995); most regularly sighted at Mt. Pisgah, Lane Co. Fairly common to locally common from Bend-Sisters area

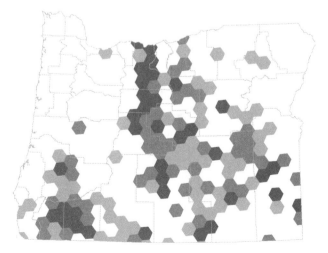

north to The Dalles, including Crooked R. (D. Tracy p.c.), Bear Cr. (OBBA), and mid- to upper John Day Valley (OBBA). Accidental in the n. Blue Mtns. (Grande Ronde Bird Club 1988, Evanich 1992a, M. Denny p.c.). Uncommon summer resident in the s. Blue Mtns. (Thomas 1979), locally in w. and s. Malheur Co. (Contreras and Kindschy 1996, OBBA), Alvord Basin (Evanich 1990), and at Malheur NWR (USFWS 1981, Littlefield 1990a). Fairly common to locally common summer resident in Hart Mtn. N. Antelope R. (USFWS 1986c), Adel and Warner Valley area (OBBA); in the Klamath Basin (Summers 1993a), Summer L. to Silver L. and the Christmas Valley northeast to the Brothers-Hampton area (OBBA). Rare to occasional migrant in coastal Oregon (Summers and Miller 1993, Dillingham 1994, Brown et al. 1996, Contreras 1998, Patterson 1998b). On the same day in Jun 1985, individuals were observed at Brookings and Lone Ranch Beach (D. Irons p.c.). A possible nesting pair was recorded at Brookings into late May 1993 (Gilligan 1993b).

**Habitat and Diet:** Oregon habitat varies with geographic location, but almost always involves some slope. In sw. Oregon, habitat used is predominantly Oregon white oak and California black oak, with some Oregon ash, ponderosa pine, incense-cedar. Undergrowth may include white and greenleaf manzanita, wedgeleaf buckbrush, poison oak, deerbrush, and mountain-mahogany; Douglas-fir and Pacific madrone in small amounts (*DPV*). In Rogue, Applegate, and Illinois valleys, Ash-throated Flycatchers are found in dry lowland and foothill oak-chaparral, oak woodlands, or open mixed hardwood-conifer woodlands; generally below 2,600 ft (792 m; Gilligan et al. 1994, *DPV*). Some undergrowth is desirable in providing foraging and lookout perches in oak woodlands (*DPV*). Present in dry oak woodlands and savannahs in Umpqua Valley (Hunter et al. 1998). Also present in upper to mid-slope foothill oak and madrone-pasture edge (ungrazed) habitat (D. Fix p.c.); exceedingly rare in Pacific madrone-dominated habitat (Cross and Simmons 1983).

East of the Cascades, Ash-throated Flycatchers use semi-arid slopes and canyons with large western juniper (Littlefield 1990a, Contreras and Kindschy 1996, Reinkensmeyer 2000), sometimes with an understory of sagebrush, bitterbrush (S. Shunk p.c.), and/or rabbitbrush (D. McCartney p.c.). Uses oak-pine habitat in the e. Columbia Gorge (*MGH*). Found at 3,500 ft (1,067 m) in the Sisters-Bend area. In dry, mixed woodlands of western juniper, mountain-mahogany, and ponderosa pine in Klamath Basin, or oak woodlands (similar to Rogue Valley) in Klamath R. canyon (Summers 1993a).

There are no published details of nests in Oregon. Elsewhere, nests described as 2-25 ft (0.6-7.6 m)

above ground in a natural cavity or old woodpecker hole (Bent 1942, Ehrlich et al. 1998); occasionally uses large-sized pipe (D. Tracy p.c.) or old mailboxes (Kaufman 1996). Also uses suitably located nest boxes (D. McCartney p.c., *DPV*). One was observed entering a basalt cavity near the Potomic Ranch in Malheur Co. (M. Denny p.c.). Nest trees are typically large oaks in the Rogue Valley, but they may use ash, cottonwoods, or other hardwoods; primarily junipers east of the Cascades. Nest base is dry grass and grass roots; interior hair, fur, feathers, finer grass, occasionally snakeskin (Bent 1942, Ehrlich et al. 1998); may include moss and lichens in Rogue Valley (*DPV*).

Diet consists mainly of insects; in California is 92% animal matter with 8% vegetable (Bent 1942). Animal matter included 27% bees, wasps, and ants; 20% bugs, 19% caterpillars and moths, 14% flies, 5% beetles, 5% grasshoppers, 3% spiders and other insects; tree hoppers and cicadas. Observed feeding on mouse (rare) (Barrett 1987), cicadas, and large lepidoptera larvae (*DPV*) in Rogue Valley. Vegetable matter in diet includes fruit and berries such as elderberries, mistletoe berries, and others in small amounts (Bent 1942). Forages in short flights, most often from different perches. Also hovers and picks insects from foliage, sometimes taking insects from trunks, branches and the ground (*DPV*). May range widely for food (Bent 1942).

**Seasonal Activity and Behavior:** Ash-throateds arrive west of the Cascades from late Apr to early May (Hunter et al. 1998, *DPV*), and east of the Cascades primarily early to mid-May (Littlefield 1990a, Summers 1993a). Early arrival dates include 17 Apr 1992 in the Rogue Valley (*DPV*), 22 Apr 1997 at Summer L. (J. Plissner p.c.), and 21 Apr 1984 Malheur NWR (Littlefield 1990a).

Nest building was observed 6 May 1989 and 14 May 1997 in the Rogue Valley (*DPV*), 8 Jun 1996 at Malheur NWR, and 27 Jun 1996 in the Owyhee Valley (OBBA). Nests with eggs were noted in nest boxes in the Rogue Valley 5 Jun 1988, 20 May 1989, and 26 May 1997 (*DPV*). Nests with eggs were noted 5 and 24 Jun 1997 in John Day Valley (OBBA). The range of annual first egg dates in Wheeler and Grant counties was 27 May to 24 Jun (n=16) (C. Corkran, unpubl. data). A nest with eggs was observed 27 Jun 1997 near Riley, Harney Co. (OBBA). Nests with young were observed 14 Jun 1987 (not fully feathered) and 13 Jul 1991 in the Rogue Valley (*DPV*); 27 Jun 1997 near Silver L.; and 8 Jul 1998 near Redmond (OBBA). Flycatchers carrying food items were noted 15 Jul 1996 in the Rogue Valley (OBBA); and 12 Jul 1999 near Paulina, Crook Co. (D. Tracy p.c.). Fledged young were observed 2 Jul 1992 and 28 Jul 1997 in the Rogue Valley (*DPV*); 5 Jul 1998 in the Klamath Basin; 14 Jul 1998 near Bend; and 2 Aug 1998 in Guano Valley, Lake Co. (OBBA).

After fledging, adults and juveniles leave breeding territories from mid-Jul to mid-Aug. During this time, in the Rogue Valley they may be found in open willow riparian habitat, where they do not breed. Late departures from breeding areas include 18 Aug 1991 and 11 Sep 1997 from the Rogue Valley (*DPV*). Reverse fall migration, or dispersing juveniles, may account for fall coastal and Willamette Valley sightings. There are few winter reports (Contreras 1997b), and none confirmed after Nov (*ALC*).

**Detection:** Ash-throateds are most often detected by calls and song, and are usually vocal late into the day. They are also spotted during foraging flights or while perched. Late fall and winter reports should be carefully distinguished from potential vagrant *Myiarchus* flycatchers.

**Population Status and Conservation:** Limited BBS data in Oregon show a non-significant increasing trend of 1.7%/yr during 1980-98 (BBS). Breeding season counts (May-Jun, 1993-96, n=14) estimated an average of 0.31 birds/ac (0.76/ha), range 0.05-0.51 birds/ac (0.13-1.27/ha), along a 0.7 mi (1.1 km) route in n. Grants Pass oak woodland habitat (*DPV*). Reinkensmeyer (2000) found 0.05 birds/ac (0.12/ha) in mid-successional and 0.04 birds/ac (0.11/ha) in old-growth juniper habitats (May-Jun, 1998-99) in c. Oregon (Deschutes and Lake Co.). Any increase in e. Oregon may be related to expansion of juniper habitat.

The prominent threat to Oregon populations is the loss or modification of essential nesting habitat, particularly removal of large-sized, cavity-bearing oak (w. Oregon) and juniper (e. Oregon). House Sparrows are known to usurp nesting boxes from birds in the Rogue Valley (*DPV*).—*Dennis P. Vroman*

## Tropical Kingbird *Tyrannus melancholicus*

Individuals of this M. and S. American resident regularly disperse northward in the fall. They occur in good numbers along the California coast, but become steadily scarcer northward where they are casual in British Columbia and, exceptionally, Alaska. Numbers involved in this northward movement vary considerably from year to year (Roberson 1983, Small 1994). They can be separated in the field from the very similar Couch's Kingbird, *T. couchii*, only by voice. Many Oregon records of silent birds are assumed to be Tropical Kingbirds since Couch's Kingbird seldom disperses, with very few sightings north of s. Texas (Roberson 1983).

In Oregon, Tropical Kingbirds are most often found in open situations close to the ocean, about an estuary, in pastures, in towns, sitting on a telephone wire or fence line, or on a bare tree branch. The majority of Oregon records occur from late Sep to late Nov (Watson 1989). Outside this period, one was reported from Cape Arago, Coos Co., 18 Feb 1985 (Heinl 1985); another was photographed at Cape Blanco, Curry Co., 26 Jul to 8 Aug 1998 (OBRC). There are few inland sightings. One was photographed at Malheur NWR HQ, Harney Co., 27 Sep 1995 (Sullivan 1996a). Another was photographed and heard calling on Sauvie I., Multnomah Co., 1-17 Nov 1996 (Gilligan 1997). One was observed at Grand I., Polk Co., 11 Oct 1998 (OBRC). There are no specimens from Oregon, but specimens exist from coastal Washington (Burleigh 1954) and n. California (Mall 1956).—*Harry B. Nehls*

## Cassin's Kingbird *Tyrannus vociferans*

This rather dark kingbird breeds from c. California and se. Montana south into Mexico. It winters primarily in M. and S. America. It is seldom reported outside of its regular range. An immature female was collected at Mercer, Lane Co., 4 Aug 1935 (Jewett 1942). It was in the OSU collection in 1973 where Browning (1974) identified the bird as nominate *vociferans*; however, the specimen could not be found in Dec 1988 (Bayer 1989a). An immature was photographed near Canby 10 Oct to mid-Dec 2001 (OBRC).—*Harry B. Nehls*

## Western Kingbird *Tyrannus verticalis*

The vigilant Western Kingbird is a summer resident of open country. As *Tyrannus* suggests, they are known for their fearless and aggressive nature in the nesting season: Gabrielson and Jewett (1940) called them "exceedingly pugnacious," and Littlefield (1990a) describes breeding pairs at Malheur Field Station attacking humans who approached too closely to their nesting site. Often seen perched on telephone wires, tall trees, fence posts, or any upright structure, surveying the surroundings and sallying out to capture airborne insects. Has adapted well to advancing human settlement and frequently nests on utility poles. Formerly known as Arkansas Kingbird, its name was officially changed in 1957 to reflect its range more accurately and to conform to common usage (Gamble and Bergin 1996).

**General Distribution:** Breeds from sw. Canada south through w. U.S. to n. Baja California and eastward to ec. Minnesota, w. Iowa, e. Kansas, Oklahoma, and Texas. Winters in s. Mexico, primarily along the Pacific slope, through M. America to c. and sw. Costa Rica. Smaller numbers winter along Atlantic coast from S. Carolina to s. Florida and west to s. Louisiana. Monotypic (AOU 1957).

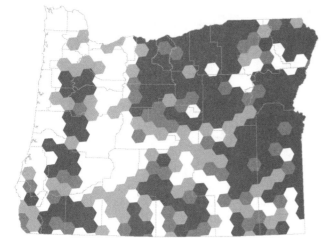

**Oregon Distribution:** Fairly common summer resident east of the Cascades. Range also extends westward through open valleys within the Siskiyou Mtns. and into the Rogue and Umpqua valleys, where it is also fairly common (Hunter et al. 1998). Uncommon to rare in summer in the Willamette Valley but found annually, with more birds and nesting reports from southern locales. In the s. Willamette Valley, Gullion (1951) reported 1-2 birds scattered through season, while D. Irons (p.c.) reports 5+ pairs near Eugene in recent years. Nesting records exist throughout the Willamette Valley (Crowell and Nehls 1973c, Gilligan et al. 1994), but recent breeding has been confirmed only as far north as Marion and Polk counties (OBBA). Rare to very rare breeder along the s. coast north to Coos Co. (Contreras 1998). Regular and rare to locally fairly common transient on the coast at least north to Tillamook. Seen regularly in migration along Elk R. bottomlands, Curry Co., where at least 20 were present in early May 1997 (Lillie 1997), and the same number again in early Jun 1998 (Tice 1999a). Rare spring and casual fall migrant in open areas in the w. Cascades, such as golf courses, pastures, developed (e.g., residential, industrial) areas, and reservoir edges (Fix 1990a, *MGH*). There have been no records for this species in winter in the state.

**Habitat and Diet:** Nests in open country where scattered trees, tall hedgerows, or power poles provide nesting sites; will also nest around buildings, along cottonwood-lined riparian zones, or in the broken tops of fence posts (Gabrielson and Jewett 1940, Gilligan et al. 1994, Hunter et al. 1998). In the Umpqua Valley they have been described as most common along floodplains or on rolling hills in open, grassy oak savannahs (Hunter et al. 1998). Gabrielson and Jewett (1940) described it as particularly abundant in the irrigated croplands of e. Oregon, drawn to the "swarming hordes of insects." Nesting birds at Malheur NWR and vicinity are commonly located near human habitation (including NWR HQ, Malheur Field Station, P-Ranch, and Frenchglen) (Littlefield 1990a).

In extreme e. and ne. Oregon associated with desert areas, farmland, open areas in towns, open woodlands, and riparian areas at low to moderate elevations (Evanich 1992a, Contreras and Kindschy 1996). Commonly places nests on transformers on the utility pole at the end of many rural driveways in e. Oregon (P. T. Sullivan p.c.). Gabrielson and Jewett (1940) recorded an unusual nest site on the face of a rocky cliff on Rock Cr., Gilliam Co. A pair nested on a billboard in downtown Roseburg in the 1980s using string from a mop kept on a nearby dock of a feed store; the mop string hung down 4 ft (1.2 m) (D. Fix p.c.). From a study conducted in w. Nebraska, Western Kingbird nests are described as an open canopy of grass, twigs, and other string-like materials, constructed almost entirely by the female (Bergin 1997). Gabrielson and Jewett (1940) describe their nests as "somewhat untidy," and usually containing four eggs.

Only anecdotal data available on Western Kingbird diet in Oregon. Near Umapine, Umatilla Co., they have been observed feeding on honey and alfalfa bees, flies, and elder beetles (M. Denny p.c.). Studies elsewhere indicate that insects comprise 90-97% of adult diet (Gamble and Bergin 1996). May also take fruits of various plants such as elderberries or hawthorn, though this is uncommon (Gamble and Bergin 1996).

**Seasonal Activity and Behavior:** An unusually early spring arrival was reported on 28 Feb 1947 on the north bank of the Willamette R. at Eugene (Gullion 1948a), though this could have been a more unusual species such as a Tropical Kingbird. Other early dates include 10 Mar 1980 at Union (Watson 1980b), and 18 Mar 1979 at Oakridge (Watson 1979c). In w. Oregon, typically arrives mid- to late Apr. Transients in nonbreeding areas usually gone by the end of May; a late individual was at Bayocean Spit, Tillamook Co., on 15 Jun 1977 (D. Fix p.c., H. Nehls p.c.). At Malheur NWR, average arrival date is 25 Apr, peak of spring migration occurs 5-15 May, and transients have left the area by 25 May (Littlefield 1990a). Nest building is usually in progress by late May through mid-Jun (n=18); young have generally been seen in the nest from mid-Jun to mid-Jul (n=32), and most have fledged by late Jul (n=17), though fledglings have been seen as early as mid-Jun and as late as mid-Aug (OBBA, Gabrielson and Jewett 1940, Littlefield 1990a).

Fall migration at Malheur NWR begins in early Jul, peaking 15-25 Aug, and most have left the refuge by Sep (Littlefield 1990a). It is typically gone from Umatilla Co. by late Aug (M. Denny p.c.). Most have departed the state by early to mid-Sep. Records of late individuals include 13 Oct 1998 near the mouth of the Elk R., Curry Co. (Gilligan 1999), 18 Oct 1985 at Nehalem (Heinl 1986a), and 6 Nov 1982 at Barview (Evanich 1983b).

**Detection:** Conspicuous in suitable habitat within range. Species may often be detected first by strident vocalizations given while defending nesting territory. Fall and winter birds found after mid-Sep should be carefully distinguished from other kingbirds.

**Population Status and Conservation:** The Western Kingbird has expanded the eastern edge of its breeding range in N. America in the 20th century, generally in association with human alteration of habitat, including the erection of structures (e.g., utility poles, signs), clearing of forests, and planting of trees (Gamble and Bergin 1996). In formerly treeless areas, such as most of se. and sc. Oregon's lowland deserts, shade trees planted around dwellings and ranches have allowed this species to move into the area (Littlefield 1990a). Across its breeding range, populations have shown increases 1966-94 (Gamble and Bergin 1996). In Oregon no population increases or declines have been reported.—*Rachel White Scheuering*

### Eastern Kingbird *Tyrannus tyrannus*
The plumage and perching habitats of the Eastern Kingbird make it one of the more conspicuous birds in open habitats of e. Oregon. The plumage is well defined: black on the upperparts and white on the underparts, and a white band on the terminal tip of the tail feathers. It is a relatively large flycatcher, often perching on powerlines, fences, or exposed perches on trees or snags.

**General Distribution:** Breeds from ne. and s. British Columbia east across s. and c. Canada to Nova Scotia, south to ne. California, c. Texas, the Gulf coast, and s. Florida. Winters in S. America from Colombia to n. Chile and Argentina (Campbell et al. 1997). Monotypic (AOU 1957).

**Oregon Distribution:** Breeds throughout non-forest of most of ne. Oregon lowlands, with spotty distribution in c. and se. Oregon. Abundance variable

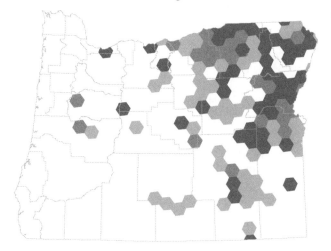

from locally common to rare. Most abundant in irrigated valleys of ne. Oregon, including Umatilla, Morrow, Wallowa, Union, Baker, and ne. Malheur counties; more local in se. Oregon in Harney and Malheur counties (Summers and Miller 1993, Gilligan et al. 1994, OBBA); sparsely distributed in Owyhee Uplands (*MGH*). A specimen was taken 21 May 1930 from near Adel (CM), Lake Co. Migrants may occur throughout open habitats of e. Oregon.

The only documented nesting site in w. Oregon is the Sandy R. delta along the Columbia R. near Portland (Altman 1994a), where one or two pairs have nested each year since 1993, including three pairs in 1999 (*BA*). Previously reported as a rare summer resident near Ashland and in Hoover's Lakes area in Rogue Valley in the early 1960s, although nesting not documented (Browning 1975a). A few individuals occur nearly annually as spring and fall migrants in w. Oregon, particularly along the coast, with some interior valley records (Altman 1994a, Gilligan et al. 1994).

**Habitat and Diet:** In e. Oregon, nests and migrates in open habitats with scattered trees, particularly around irrigated agriculture fields, large ranches, and orchards (all human influenced); and also along the edges of riparian habitat around lakes, streams, and marshes. Essential features are suitable exposed perches for flycatching (e.g., scattered trees or snags) within habitat conducive to abundant insect populations. At Malheur NWR, occurs mostly along willow-bordered watercourses and ponds (Littlefield 1990a).

In w. Oregon, habitat at the nesting site at the Sandy R. delta is upland fields with scattered shrub clumps, primarily Himalayan blackberry, and a few cottonwood trees (*BA*). Sightings elsewhere in w. Oregon have been from similar settings: mostly open agricultural or fallow grasslands with a scattered shrub and/or tree component, in either upland or open wetland/riparian habitats.

Nest substrates are highly variable: typically trees (dead or living), but this kingbird often uses human-made structures (e.g., transmission towers, utility poles, water towers) where available. Nests are open-cupped and most often conspicuously placed in forks or crotches of horizontal branches of trees close to the canopy edge (Murphy 1983). Nests in human-made structures are often placed on flat surface where girders or other materials meet. At Sandy R. delta in w. Oregon, nests have been placed 50-150 ft (15-46 m) above ground on a flat part of the girders of transmission towers (*BA*).

Only anecdotal data are available on the Eastern Kingbird diet in Oregon. In Umatilla Co., they have been observed to take damselflies, sulfer butterflies, stoneflies, and cicadas (M. Denny p.c.). They hawk aerial insects during the breeding season. Forage by sallying out from exposed perch, often powerlines or fence lines. Reported to also eat fruit such as red-osier dogwood berries, particularly during fall migration, and especially by juvenile birds (Cannings et al. 1987, Siderius 1994).

**Seasonal Activity and Behavior:** Typically arrives in late May. In e. Oregon, early arrival dates include 4 May at Malheur NWR (Littlefield 1990a), 5 May in Harney Co. (Gabrielson and Jewett 1940), 11 May near Lakeview (OBBA), 15 May at Malheur NWR (OBBA), and 17 May south of Adrian (Sullivan 1997b).

Rare spring transient in w. Oregon (0-3 birds/yr) with most sightings along the south and central coast. Average arrival date near Corvallis is 7 Jun (n=4) (A. McGie p.c.). The two earliest dates are 25 Apr at E.E. Wilson WMA, and 5 May near the Newport airport (Lillie 1998), both in the same year. Other early dates include 10 May in sw. Portland (Nehls 1987b), 20 May near Waldport (Bayer 1999a), and 23 May near Corvallis (A. McGie p.c.) and Banks (Irons 1984b).

Several records exist from w. Oregon in mid- to late Jun. Most were single birds and one-time sightings, indicating they were late migrants or nonbreeding floaters, but breeding evidence should be looked for in the event of future such observations. Example sightings include 14 Jun in Beaverton (Heinl 1988b), 15 Jun at s. jetty of the Columbia R. (Johnson J 1992a), 18 Jun at South Beach in Lincoln Co. (R. Bayer p.c.), 19 Jun on Tub Run Rd. in Linn Co. (B. Altman p.c.), 25 Jun near Tillamook (Nehls 1988b), and a bird seen for approximately 1 wk at the end of Jun along Elk R. near Cape Blanco (T. J. Wahl p.c.). Four birds were at Powell Butte in Portland on 17 Jun with at least one pair acting as if nesting (Nehls 1992a). A bird reported on 25-26 Jul near Beaver Cr. at Newport (Watson 1981b) may have been an early migrant or postbreeding wanderer.

Eastern Kingbirds are highly territorial, and aggressively defend nests against any intruders, including conspecifics. Courtship, territorial behavior by the male, and nest building occur predominantly in early and mid-Jun (n=9) (OBBA). Clutch size is most often four eggs (Murphy 1996). Nestlings are present throughout latter half of Jun and into Jul; early nestling date, 12 Jun near Ukiah (OBBA), late date for nestlings 10 Jul near Ukiah (OBBA). Fledglings most typically appear after the first week of Jul; two fledgling dates in e. Oregon are 12 and 19 Jul near Black Butte and Hermiston, respectively (OBBA). Fledging occurred 23-25 Jul at the Sandy R. delta in w. Oregon (Altman 1994a).

Migratory movements are much less reported in fall than in spring here in Oregon. Migrates in small to mid-sized flocks unlike most flycatchers (Campbell et al. 1997), and migrates during the day unlike most passerines. At Malheur NWR, fall migration occurs during Aug, and by Sep few birds remain (Littlefield

1990a). Late dates in e. Oregon include 12 Sep at Malheur NWR (Summers 1994a), and 15 Sep in Harney Co. (Gabrielson and Jewett 1940). A late date in w. Oregon is 10 Sep at Seaside (Heinl 1988a).

**Detection:** Eastern Kingbirds are easily observed because of striking black-and-white plumage, occurrence in open country, and habit of conspicuous perching on telephone wires and fencelines. However, if seen in silhouette, or if the white breast and terminal tail band are not seen, they may readily be confused with Western Kingbird or other similar-sized birds that perch conspicuously in open country (e.g., Loggerhead Shrike). Detectability by ear fair to poor due to relatively weak and indistinct vocalizations. Characteristic flight aids in identification: relatively slow with shallow, rapid wing beats. Often vocalizes in flight.

**Population Status and Conservation:** Insufficient sample size for evaluation of BBS state trend. Population trend in the Columbia Plateau BBS Region (includes e. Oregon, e. Washington, s. Idaho, and part of n. Nevada) indicates non-significant declining trends for both long-term (1966-96, 2.1%/yr) and short-term (1980-96, 2.9%/yr) (Sauer et al. 1997). It is noteworthy that the BBS trend specifically e. Washington is significantly (p<0.05) declining for the long-term (1966-96, 3.3%/yr). On Malheur NWR, Eastern Kingbirds reportedly increased in abundance and expanded their range on the refuge during the 1970s and 1980s due to improved nesting habitat resulting from a decrease in grazing in riparian zones (Littlefield 1990a).—*Bob Altman*

## Scissor-tailed Flycatcher *Tyrannus forficatus*

This spectacular flycatcher is a species of open agricultural lands and dry grasslands, breeding from s. Nebraska and se. Colorado south into Mexico. It winters mainly in Mexico. It is casual north of its regular range throughout the U.S. and s. Canada. Unknown from specimens in Oregon. The majority of Oregon sight records are from early May to early Jul. Individuals were observed at Cape Arago, Coos Co., 7 May 1966 (Crowell and Nehls 1966b); at Malheur NWR during 1967 and on 4 Jul 1973 (Littlefield 1990a); photographed at Davis L., Klamath Co., 13 Jun 1978 (Watson 1989); observed at Euchre Cr., Curry Co., 6 Jun 1987 (Heinl 1988b); observed on Cascade Head, Tillamook Co., 16 May 1992; near Fairview, Multnomah Co., 25 May 1992 (Gilligan 1992b); photographed at Yaquina Head, Lincoln Co., 25 May 1995 (Lillie 1995); observed near Cape Blanco, Curry Co., 26 Jun 1992 (Johnson J 1993a)

Individuals in fall were photographed at Otter Rock, Lincoln Co., 11-20 Nov 1993 (*Oregon Birds* 20[1]:cover, Gilligan 1994); observed at Coos Bay 4

Nov 1997; at Beaver Cr., Lincoln Co., 25 Sep 1997; at Cascade Head 27 Sep 1997 (Gilligan 1998); and at Malheur NWR 7 Aug 1998 (OBRC).—*Harry B. Nehls*

## Family *Laniidae*

### Loggerhead Shrike *Lanius ludovicianus*

This striking songbird is best known for its habit of impaling prey on thorns and barbed wire, or wedging items in a v-shaped branch for easier handling and storage—a behavior that earned the unaffectionate nickname "butcherbird." Shrikes are unique among passerines for their ability to kill vertebrate prey by biting the neck and disarticulating cervical vertebrae (Cade 1995). Head and back bluish-gray with black mask extending behind/above eye and narrowing over bill; underparts white or buffy-white, and faintly barred; wings chiefly black with white patches. Tail black with increasing amounts of white on outer tail feathers, which are primarily white. Juvenal plumage retained into fall; similar to adults but barred on head and back, more heavily barred underneath, and washed brown throughout.

**General Distribution:** Breeds from se. Alberta south through California to s. Baja California and eastward throughout most of the U.S. and south through most of Mexico. Northern populations are generally migratory. Most winter south of latitude 40º N through s. U.S. (Yosef 1996) and in Mexico throughout breeding range, irregularly as far south as Chiapas on the Atlantic slope (Howell and Webb 1995). Nine subspecies; *L. l. gambeli* occurs in Oregon (AOU 1957).

**Oregon Distribution:** Breeds in open habitats east of the Cascades where rare but regular in the winter, especially at low-elevation sites (Littlefield 1990a, Summers 1993a). Absent from forested landscapes and higher-elevation sites in the Blue and Wallowa

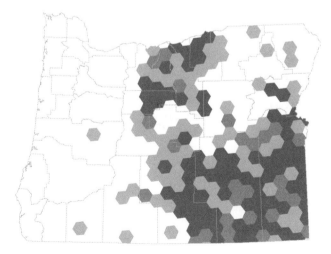

mountains. Uncommon and declining in ne. Oregon where most birds are found in s. Union Co. (Evanich 1992a). West of the Cascades, there are usually a few records each year during fall, winter, and spring in open habitats of the coast and the Willamette, Umpqua, and Rogue valleys (Gilligan et al. 1994).

**Habitat and Diet:** Basic nesting-habitat requirements include elevated perches for singing and hunting, open or grassy areas for hunting, and scattered shrubs or small trees for nesting. Dense stands of shrubs are also used so long as open areas are available close by for foraging. Primary vegetation communities in Oregon breeding areas include big sagebrush, low sagebrush with scattered juniper, black greasewood, and cold desert shrub communities (Wiens and Rotenberry 1981, Holmes and Geupel 1998, *ALH*). In communities with shorter shrubs such as those dominated by Wyoming big sagebrush, favors ravines and bottomlands where deeper soils result in taller shrubs (Leu and Manuwal 1996 [Washington], Holmes and Geupel 1998).

Diet has not been studied in Oregon. Research in other localities suggests opportunistic prey selection (Craig 1978, Yosef 1992). Insects make up the majority of prey items taken during the breeding season, although vertebrates may account for the majority of biomass, and become increasingly important in winter months when insects are scarcer (summarized in Yosef 1996).

**Seasonal Activity and Behavior:** Early migrants in e. Oregon and se. Washington appear in Feb (Gabrielson and Jewett 1940, Littlefield 1990a, Weber and Larrison 1977), with most arriving mid-Mar to 1 Apr (Littlefield 1990a, Poole 1992). Territorial behavior begins upon arrival on the breeding grounds. Birds typically sing from exposed perches and vigorously defend against intruding individuals. Spring song of male is variable and consists of short trills or combinations of clear notes characterized by rhythmic repetition of song units and generally low sound volume (Miller 1931). Both male and female regularly sing territorial song, similar to spring song but with rougher quality. Aggressive encounters that often end with one bird chasing the other off are common early in the breeding season (*ALH*). Nest initiation dates in Morrow Co. ranged 21 Mar to 16 Jul (Holmes and Geupel 1998), which are similar to nest dates reported from the nearby Hanford site in s. Washington where initiation peaked in early to mid-Apr (Poole 1992). In Morrow Co., over a 3-yr period, complete clutches contained a mean of 6.2 eggs (range=5-8, n=113) (Holmes and Geupel 1998). Only a small percentage of successful pairs in the Columbia Basin attempt second broods (Poole 1992, *ALH*). Nestlings fledge from late Apr/early May through mid-Aug for the latest attempts of the season (OBBA data, *ALH*).

*Loggerhead Shrike*

Migrants typically depart the Hanford site by mid-Sep (Poole 1992) and this is probably similar to low-elevation breeding areas in Oregon. Later departure dates to mid-Nov have been published from higher-elevation sites (Gabrielson and Jewett 1940, Littlefield 1990a). However, because this species winters throughout most of its Oregon range in low densities, extreme arrival and departure dates should be interpreted with caution.

**Detection:** Often perches at the top of shrubs or trees, which facilitates detection. Scanning potential perches at the top of shrubs in appropriate habitat is a good strategy for locating birds. Auditory detection is fair. Songs tend to have a low sound volume but several calls, including a buzz and a loud *bzeek bzeek* (Miller 1931) can be heard from some distance. The flight is characterized by faster wing-beats and no undulation, in comparison to the Northern Shrike (D. Irons p.c.).

**Population Status and Conservation:** Declining throughout most of its range. In Oregon, where it is considered a sensitive species, BBS data show a significant 3.4%/yr declining trend 1966-98 (Sauer et al. 1999). Population declines have been attributed to many factors including pesticides, high winter mortality, and changes in agricultural land use (see Yosef 1996 for discussion), although most experts agree that loss and degradation of suitable habitat are the major underlying causes of declines (Cade and Woods 1997). According to recent assessments, shrub-steppe, the primary breeding habitat in Oregon, has experienced the greatest loss of all cover types within the interior Columbia R. basin (Saab and Rich 1997). However, higher-elevation shrub-steppe in se. Oregon has had relatively low rates of conversion to agriculture and exotic grasses, and no decline in shrike populations has been noted there in the past 15 yr (Marshall et al. 1996). Low nest success in degraded shrub-steppe (Holmes and Geupel 1998) supports the notion from other states that reduced productivity may be a factor in declines (Novak 1989). Preventing further loss of shrub-steppe habitats to exotic grasses and agriculture should be a management priority to help conserve populations of this species.—*Aaron L. Holmes*

### Northern Shrike *Lanius excubitor*

This is the larger of Oregon's two shrikes, and the more likely to be seen in winter. Northern Shrikes come from the boreal forests of the arctic and subarctic. Most of those seen in Oregon are hatch-year birds wearing brownish plumage in the fall and graying as winter passes. Adults stand out from young of the year with more crisp gray, black, and white plumage. Shrikes inhabit open landscapes. They resemble and act like small raptors; however, they capture and kill prey with a hooked bill rather than with talons like hawks and owls. Their habit of impaling prey on barbed wire or thorns has given these birds the local name, "butcherbirds."

**General Distribution:** Circumpolar arctic and subarctic breeder of the N. Hemisphere. In the Old World breed as far south as N. Africa, but the southern limits of the N. American breeding range are in n. British Columbia, Alberta, and Manitoba. In N. America winter from the southern end of the breeding range southward to New England, the n. Great Plains, Great Basin, s. Rocky Mtn. region, and California, and casually to the southern states. Two subspecies in N. America: *L. e. invictus* in w. N. America (AOU 1957).

**Oregon Distribution:** Uncommon to locally common winter visitor in open habitats statewide. Absent some years along the southern coast. Rare, only in open areas (e.g., clearcuts, reservoir edges, pastures), in the Coast Range and Cascades (*MGH*). Commonest shrike in winter east of the Cascades except during mild winters when Loggerhead Shrikes remain in warmer areas, e.g., Klamath and Summer L. basins, and Snake R. Valley. This is the only shrike that regularly occurs in nw. Oregon. Less likely to be seen farther south, but Browning (1975a) considered it a "fairly regular winter visitor in the Lower Rogue River and Bear Creek valleys and foothills."

**Habitat and Diet:** Occurs in open areas including fields, grassy sandspits, shrub and juniper steppe, marshes, and occasionally clearings in wooded areas. Small trees, e.g., willows, from which the shrikes hunt, are a necessary structural component of shrike habitat. Therefore, in shrub-steppe, shrikes tend to be associated with riparian areas. Littlefield (1990a) commented that in the Blitzen Valley of the Malheur NWR, where both shrikes sometimes winter, Loggerhead Shrikes most often frequent desert shrub habitat while Northern Shrikes spend the majority of their time along willow-bordered meadows.

Anecdotal observations in Oregon and elsewhere show that Northern Shrikes prey on small mammals, small birds, and insects. Oregon observations include a vole, an American Goldfinch, and a House Finch (M. Denny p.c.). No food habits studies have been made in Oregon.

**Seasonal Activity and Behavior:** A strikingly early arrival in e. Oregon was an immature reported 29 Jul 1962 at Malheur NWR (Scott 1963). In w. Oregon a more expected early sighting was made 27 Sep 1985 at Tillamook (Hunn and Mattocks 1986). Usually arrives early to mid-Oct in ne. Oregon, mid- to late Oct in the Willamette Valley (Gullion 1951), and late Oct to early Nov on the s. coast (Dillingham 1994) and Klamath Basin (Summers 1993a). Littlefield (1990a) noted that the species typically departs by mid-Mar, but has remained as late as 16 Apr on Malheur NWR. Bayer (1995a) showed no Lincoln Co. records after Mar, and Gullion provided a late date of 30 Mar in the Willamette Valley. One was at Warrenton, Clatsop Co., 9 Apr 1966 (Crowell and Nehls 1966b). In e. Oregon, Gabrielson and Jewett (1940) showed extreme dates of 9 Sep in Crook Co. to 9 Apr in Wallowa Co.

In Oregon, Northern Shrikes generally appear individually. They are typically silent and hunt from a perch up to 20 ft (6 m) above the ground using a wait and watch approach. When prey passes by, a shrike will pursue it with flat, fast, undulating flight, sometimes chasing it around and through heavy foliage like a small accipiter.

**Detection:** Frequently seen in valleys east of the Cascades. Most easily found by scanning likely perches in good habitat, or by driving roads in open country with fences or utility lines.

**Population Status and Conservation:** Oregon population numbers unknown. Due to typically low numbers, significant fluctuations or cycles are not easily detected in Oregon CBC data. Nevertheless, general agreement is sometime reached among field observers that some years seem especially noticeable. For example, Fix (1984a) noted that larger than usual numbers appeared in the fall and winter of 1984-85, and during the winter of 2001-02 many observers reported a marked absence of Northern Shrikes in many areas. Oregon counts show an average of 1.32 individuals/100 party hr compared to a continental figure of 0.42 birds/100 party hr.

No conservation problems have been identified for this species, although it is assumed that maintaining riparian growth in arid regions of the state is important.—*Alan L. Contreras*

## Family Vireonidae

### Bell's Vireo *Vireo bellii*

This small, plain-colored, difficult-to-identify, brush-loving vireo breeds through the c. and sw. U.S. and winters in M. America. One was observed at Fields, Harney Co., 22 and 24 May 1980, and another was observed and heard singing there 6 Jun 1998 (OBRC). Subspecies unknown.—*Harry B. Nehls*

### Plumbeous Vireo *Vireo plumbeus*

This dark gray bird with conspicuous white eye-rings and lores breeds from s. Idaho to S. Dakota and south through Nevada to Texas. It winters in Mexico (Heindel 1996). Plumbeous, Cassin's and Blue-headed vireos, formerly considered conspecific (AOU 1986), are separate species (AOU 1997). The status of Plumbeous Vireo in Oregon is not fully understood and care should be taken in distinguishing this bird from Cassin's Vireo (Heindel 1996); there are no specimens. The first Oregon report was a sighting from Plush, Lake Co., 28 May 1976 (Johnson J 1998b). It has been reported from Harney Co. each spring since 1992 (Johnson J 1998b). One was photographed in Catlow Valley, Harney Co., 25 May 1992 (Evanich 1992c). Another, photographed at Fields, Harney Co., was singing and acting territorial from 22 May to well into Jun 1994 (Summers 1994b).

A pair was finishing construction of a nest 6 ft (2 m) up in an incense-cedar along Kelly Cr. south of Lakeview., Lake Co., 13 Jul 1996, but the area was logged shortly thereafter and the vireos were not relocated (Sullivan 1997c, Johnson J 1998b, M. Denny p.c.). One was near Joseph, Wallowa Co., 3 Sep 1993 and at the Enterprise Fish Hatchery, Wallowa Co., 17 Sep 1993 (Summers 1994a, C. Corder p.c.). Singles were at Indian Ford CG, Deschutes Co., 17 Sep 1994 (Johnson J 1998b); Klamath Marsh NWR, Klamath Co., 19 Jun 1998 (Spencer 1999); on Stukel Mt., Klamath Co., 19 Jun 1999; near Ironside, Malheur Co., 5 Jun 1999 (Spencer 2000a); and near Sisters 28 May 2001 (Sullivan 2001b).—*Harry B. Nehls*

## Cassin's Vireo *Vireo cassinii*

The most distinctive features on this gray and greenish vireo are the bright white eye rings and lores, together called "spectacles." Often difficult to see as it forages among the foliage; identification is usually based on hearing its distinctive song. Widespread in migration, when its habitat includes city parks and heavily wooded neighborhoods. Formerly considered conspecific with Blue-headed and Plumbeous Vireos under the name Solitary Vireo (AOU 1997).

**General Distribution:** Breeds British Columbia to Alberta, south to California, Nevada, and to Baja California. Winters extreme s. Arizona to Guatemala. Of two subspecies, *V. c. cassinii* occurs in Oregon (AOU 1998).

**Oregon Distribution:** Uncommon to fairly common summer resident in forests and woodlands, except along immediate coast (Contreras 1998) and rarely in n. Coast Range (OBBA, *HBN*). Not known to breed in se. Oregon east of Hart Mtn. Uncommon transient throughout the state.

**Habitat and Diet:** Because of low densities, habitat associations of this species have rarely been described in detail. Breeds in conifer and mixed conifer-hardwood forests at low to moderate elevations; relatively dry forests with medium or small trees seem to be preferred (Gabrielson and Jewett 1940, Farner 1952, Fix 1990a, Smith et al. 1997). Much more likely to be encountered in coniferous trees than the Warbling Vireo, showing a marked predilection for pines and firs (Merrill 1888, Jewett et al. 1953), but "seems to prefer the deciduous timber, cottonwoods, willows, and alders for nesting" (Jewett et al. 1953). Recorded in eight of nine oak woodlands in a Willamette Valley study (Hagar and Stern 2001).

There is little information on Oregon nests. Nest is a cup attached by its upper edges to the fork of a limb, usually low in bushes or trees, occasionally higher (Gabrielson and Jewett 1940, Bent 1950). Nest composed of dull-colored leaves, grasses, moss, and lichens, lined with dry fine grasses. Outside diameter 3.25 in (82.6 mm), 2.25 in (57.2 mm) high, inside 2.25 in (57.2 mm) diameter and 1.75 in (44.5 mm) deep (Bent 1950).

Foliage-gleaning insectivore (Diem and Zeveloff 1980). Diet almost all insects, primarily Hemiptera. Caterpillars and moths important food source throughout the year (Beal 1907).

**Seasonal Activity and Behavior:** Migration taken individually or in small groups, often with flocks of other species. Main movement mid-Apr through May; earliest west of the Cascades 19 Mar (Browning 1975a), e. Oregon 18 Apr (Ivey, Herziger, and Scheuering 1998).

Monogamous. Possibly two broods per season. Usual clutch four eggs. Both parents incubate and care for young. Male often sings from nest (Baicich and Harrison 1997). Breeds s. Willamette Valley 21 Apr to 25 Jul (Gullion 1951); Portland 14 May to 21 Jun (Griffee and Rapraeger 1937). Nest on Thornton Cr., Lincoln Co., 9 Jul 1974, contained 3 eggs and a newly hatched young (Faxon and Bayer 1991). Nest at Vancouver, Washington, 29 Apr 1934 contained two eggs (Jewett et al. 1953).

Some postbreeding movement to higher elevations (Grinnell and Miller 1944, Farner 1952). Fall migration not conspicuous. Most obvious during Sep with sharply reduced numbers through Oct. Latest at Tillamook, 13 Nov 1974 (Crowell and Nehls 1975a) and Oak Grove, Clackamas Co., 31 Dec 1997 (Tice 1998a).

**Detection:** Sluggishly foraging within the foliage, this species is usually inconspicuous. However, it is a persistent singer that draws attention to itself.

**Population Status and Conservation:** Widespread but unevenly distributed throughout the forest, preferring dry, warm places and is less common in more open, cooler forests (Grinnell and Miller 1944, Smith et al. 1997, Fix 1990a). Mannan (1982) found 4-11 birds per 100 ac (40 ha) in grand fir-mixed forests on the Wallowa-Whitman NF. Oregon population appears stable with no serious conservation problems at this time.—*Harry B. Nehls*

## Blue-headed Vireo *Vireo solitarius*

This mainly eastern vireo breeds from ne. British Columbia across Canada to the e. coast and southward to n. Wisconsin, c. Georgia, and ne. Alabama. It migrates through the e. and c. U.S. to winter from the s. U.S. and the Caribbean south to M. America. Formerly conspecific with Cassin's and Plumbeous Vireos (AOU 1997). It is casual in coastal California, but identification criteria require better definition

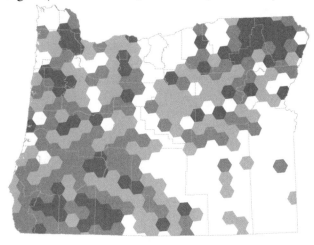

(Erickson and Hamilton 2001). Its status in the Northwest is not fully understood, and care should be taken to distinguish this species from fresh fall-plumaged Cassin's Vireos (Heindel 1996). Oregon sightings of single individuals were on the Bayocean Peninsula, Tillamook Co., 4 Oct 1980 and 5 Oct 1985 (Johnson J 1998b); at Mt. Tabor Park, Portland, Multnomah Co., 29 Mar 1992 (Johnson J 1998b); in the Summer L. basin, Lake Co., 9 Sep 1992 (Summers 1993b) and 13 Sep 1993 (Summers 1994a); in Sawyer Park, Bend, Deschutes Co., 3 Oct 1993 (Summers 1994a); and photographed at Malheur NWR HQ, Harney Co., 9 Sep 1998 (OBRC).—*Harry B. Nehls*

## Hutton's Vireo *Vireo huttoni*

Described as a "quiet, modest, unobtrusive little bird that must be sought to be seen in its shady retreats" (Bent 1946), this little-studied species can easily be overlooked. It is typically associated with oaks and mixed woodlands, where it hops among the foliage hunting for insects. In winter it forages with flocks of chickadees, kinglets, and nuthatches. This is Oregon's only resident vireo, and although it is sometimes referred to as non-migratory, some seasonal movement has been observed (Fix 1985f, 1990a, Gilligan et al. 1994). Similar in appearance and behavior to the more common and widespread Ruby-crowned Kinglet, this winsome little vireo presents an identification challenge to beginning birders. Often first noticed by its characteristic persistent two-syllable song: *zu-wee . . . zu-wee . . . zu-wee* (Davis 1995).

**General Distribution:** Resident from sw. British Columbia south through w. Washington, w. Oregon, and California to nw. Baja California, generally west of the Cascades and Sierra Nevada; very rare visitant east of these mountains. Also found from c. Arizona, sw. New Mexico, and sw. Texas south into the highlands of Mexico. Twelve subspecies (Phillips 1991), one to two in Oregon (Rea *in* Phillips 1991).

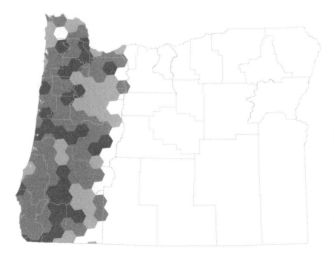

**Oregon Distribution:** Based on Rea (*in* Phillips 1991), *V. h. obscurus* (*contra* Browning 1979) breeds from sw. British Columbia to Oregon (west of the Cascades summit) south to Coos Co., where *obscurus* intergrades with *V. h. parkesi*, a newly proposed subspecies (Rea *in* Phillips 1991) from nw. California. The region from Coos Co., Oregon, to Del Norte Co., California, where specimens were identified by Rea (in Phillips 1991:184) as "variably intermediate towards *obscurus*, is larger than zones of intergration of subspecies recognized elsewhere in Oregon (*MRB*). The species is a fairly common permanent resident occurring almost exclusively west of the Cascade crest. OBBA results found this species in 125 of the 126 hexagons for this part of the state, showing an unusually uniform distribution. Most common at lower elevations, especially in the lowland forests of the Coast Range in sw. Oregon (Gilligan et al. 1994); less regular in the Cascades above the western foothills (Contreras 1997b). Also known to occur in forests of sw. Klamath Co. in small numbers; extremely rare elsewhere in state. Three reports exist for Malheur NWR (Littlefield 1990a); this species has not been recorded elsewhere in e. Oregon.

**Habitat and Diet:** Found most often in mixed woodland, where conifers (usually second-growth) such as Douglas-fir, western hemlock, or western redcedar are intermixed with Oregon white oak, canyon live oak, Pacific madrone, or bigleaf maple (Fix 1990a, Gilligan et al. 1994, Davis 1995). An example of these preferred associations has been well-described for the N. Umpqua R. corridor as "primarily on southerly exposures where conifer growth is somewhat retarded and hardwood intrusion is greatest, resulting in the scrubby, closed-canopy mixed woods the species favors" (Fix 1990a). Also occurs in riparian areas dominated by alder, willows, cottonwood, and/or maple. Breeding and winter habitats are essentially the same, although use of riparian woodlands is more extensive in winter (Gilligan et al. 1994).

Douglas-fir is the most commonly used nesting substrate in Oregon; other recorded substrates include red alder and scouler willow (Davis 1995). Gabrielson and Jewett (1940) described a nest found at Oak Grove, Clackamas Co., 7 ft (2 m) up in an oak. Steve Heinl (p.c.) and Dave Irons (p.c.) have found single nests in one among several planted incense-cedars on Skinners Butte, Eugene. A nest found in a rhododendron at Mt. Tabor Park, Multnomah Co., was constructed of fine lichen filaments and spiderwebs and lined with thin stems of dry grass. It was thimble-shaped, with the exterior completely covered in filamentous lichens (P. Johnston p.c.). In California's coastal mountains, lace lichens were found to be the principal component of most nests, and the availability of these epiphytes may be a factor in selecting breeding habitat (Davis 1995).

Diet has not been studied in Oregon. Elsewhere these vireos are found to subsist mainly on insects and spiders, which they glean from foliage. They also take some plant material including insect galls and fruits of elderberry and poison oak (Davis 1995).

**Seasonal Activity and Behavior:** Begins singing in late Feb or early Mar (Irons 1984b, Fix 1985a). Nesting phenology is not well documented in Oregon. The earliest nest was one found on Skinners Butte in Mar 1985 (D. Fix p.c., S. Heinl p.c.). Otherwise, nest building, in which both sexes take part, has been observed in Oregon from early Apr to mid-Jun (n=4) (P. Johnston p.c., OBBA), A nest found near Medford on 9 Jul contained six vireo eggs and five Brown-headed Cowbird eggs (Browning 1975a), and another found at Oak Grove, Clackamas Co., on 4 Jul contained four newly hatched young (Gabrielson and Jewett 1940); these may have been second attempts. Fledglings have been seen from mid-May to late Jun (n=4) (OBBA).

Information on extent of dispersal and migration is vague. Most populations in U.S. are considered resident but may exhibit erratic local dispersal, such that individuals may be present locally in fall, winter, and spring, but absent in summer (Davis 1995). Correspondingly, the appearance in spring and fall of a small number of birds in riparian habitat at Toketee L. in the s. Cascades, where they do not summer, indicates migrants passing through (Fix 1990a). There is clearly substantial movement away from breeding areas, as evidenced by birds found in Sep in mountainous forest habitat in e. Douglas Co. (Fix 1985f), and a noticeable influx Oct-Feb in western valleys in winter (D. Fix p.c.). In winter joins mixed-species flocks that usually include other foliage gleaners such as chickadees, kinglets, bushtits, and nuthatches.

**Detection:** Easy to miss. Can be found in the proper habitat by listening for distinctive vocalizations. In winter, examination of mixed species flocks might yield a Hutton's Vireo, but careful viewing is needed for identification (Kaufman 1993). Blue-gray legs and feet (vs. orange-yellow in Ruby-crowned Kinglet) can sometimes be a surprisingly conspicuous feature on imperfectly seen birds (D. Fix p.c.).

**Population Status and Conservation:** Slight discrepancies exist among sources regarding abundance of this species in w. Oregon. Gabrielson and Jewett (1940) found it "rather uncommon." Elsewhere it is described as "fairly common but inconspicuous" (Gilligan et al 1994), and "common to very common" in spring when the bird is singing (R. Korpi p.c.). Though the hypothesis has not been tested, it is possible that populations have grown in the past 60 yr along with the increase in second-growth habitat

associated with forestry practices. But because of this species' resemblance to Ruby-crowned Kinglet, it is likely misidentified and underreported, making abundance hard to pinpoint. Population trends are undocumented for Oregon, though rangewide numbers appear to be stable or slightly increasing (Davis 1995). Nothing is known of population regulation mechanisms for this species (Davis 1995), but as a known host of the Brown-headed Cowbird in Oregon (Anderson SH 1970, Browning 1975a), this species warrants investigation into potential impacts of nest parasitism.—*Rachel White Scheuering*

## Warbling Vireo *Vireo gilvus*

Despite being one of the most common songbirds in deciduous and riparian forests throughout Oregon, the Warbling Vireo is frequently overlooked. Its plumage is indistinct: gray-olive upperparts, no wingbars, a white eyebrow stripe, and whitish underparts with yellow wash on the flanks. It tends to forage high in the treetops, moving slowly and deliberately among twigs and leaves gleaning insects. Despite its subtle plumage and habits, familiarity with its song makes this vireo easy to find, and a delight to listen to. Perhaps due to its frequent association with riparian areas, a writer quoted in Bent (1950) wrote of this vireo: "During the flood period of its song the singer is seemingly carried away by his efforts ... the renditions of his song flowing along like the current of a stream."

**General Distribution:** Breeds from se. Alaska across Canada to New Brunswick, including most of U.S., except certain western lowlands and the extreme se. U.S. (Gardali and Ballard 2000). Also breeds in Mexico. Western populations winter in w. and s. Mexico; eastern populations in s. Mexico and n. M. America (Howell and Webb 1995). Rarely winter in extreme s. California and Arizona and in s. Louisiana (Gardali and Ballard 2000). Two subspecies groups recognized by AOU (1998): eastern *gilvus* and western

*Warbling Vireo*

*swainsonii* group. The *swainsonii* group includes 4-5 subspecies of which two occur in Oregon (Browning 1974, 1990, *contra* Phillips 1991).

**Oregon Distribution:** Breeds in moderate densities in deciduous habitat throughout Oregon from sea level to montane areas. Mostly nests along river corridors and low-elevation woodlands where deciduous canopy is more common. Not found in lowland sagebrush-steppe areas in c. and se. Oregon, except where stands of deciduous trees and shrubs are located near water sources or homesteads. Most abundant in c. Coast Range, where 11-30 individuals detected per BBS route (Sauer et al. 2001). Moderately abundant west of the Cascades, with 4-10 individuals per route. In the Cascades and Blue Mtns., 2-3 birds per route, and in se. Oregon <1 bird detected per route. During migration found in almost any deciduous habitat, including areas not typically used for breeding, such as riparian willows not associated with canopy trees. Breeding specimens of *V. g. swainsoni* have been confirmed from Tillamook, Curry, Josephine, and Jackson counties (e.g., USNM), and *V. g. leucopolius* from Warner Valley (CM) and Wallowa Co. (CM, CMNH), but further collecting is required to more precisely define the Oregon distribution of each (*MRB*).

**Habitat and Diet:** Breeds in stands of deciduous trees, or shrubs associated with tall, deciduous canopy trees. Often breeds in riparian areas or near other water sources. East of the Cascades, strongly associated with riparian areas and snowpocket aspen stands.

Abundant breeder in both seral (burned), densely regenerating aspen stands and mature, multi-aged aspen stands. Absent from aspen stands with little regeneration or shrub understory (e.g., heavily grazed stands). Uncommon breeder in willow-dominated riparian areas in e. Oregon (Littlefield 1990a, Heltzel and Earnst 2002). Nests in deciduous stream corridors and woodlands on east slope of the Cascades and in the Blue Mtns., Steens and Hart mountains, and other ranges of se. Oregon (Ryser 1985, Marshall 1987, Littlefield 1990a). Also breeds in residential areas with deciduous trees, often in non-native poplars (*JH, DBM*).

In w. Oregon breeds in deciduous woodlands, riparian areas, and residential areas. Found in red alder, bigleaf maple, Oregon ash, willow, white oak, and black cottonwood stands (Anderson SH 1970, Gilligan et al. 1994, Hagar and Stern 2001). Absent from coniferous forests, except in riparian corridors and openings with deciduous trees (Anderson 1972, McGarigal 1993). On the Olympic Peninsula, more common along larger streams with large areas of deciduous trees than in smaller drainages (Lock and Naiman 1998). In the w. Cascades, breeding pairs found in tall ceanothus and manzanita thickets (S. Dowlan p.c.).

One nest 12 ft (4 m) in alder in Portland found 16 May 1917 with four eggs; another nest found in aspen near Fort Klamath on 30 May 1934 with three eggs (Gabrielson and Jewett 1940). In 2001, 19 nests were located at Hart Mtn. in se. Oregon at elevations of 6,000-6,600 ft (1,800-2,000 m) (Heltzel and Earnst 2002). Eighteen nests were found during nest-searching efforts in 42 ac (16.5 ha) of riparian aspen, and only one nest in 30 ac (12 ha) of riparian willow. Nests were also located in cottonwoods and non-native poplars in the Warner Valley near Hart Mtn. (*JH*). At Hart Mtn., nest heights ranged 5-50 ft (1.5-15 m) in aspen (n=18). Nest in willow was 6.5 ft (2 m) high. Nest heights of 5-122 ft (1.1-37 m) documented (Gardali and Ballard 2000). Based on coastal California data, probably nest in willow, red alder, Oregon ash, and bigleaf maple in w. Oregon (Gardali et al. 2000).

High site fidelity to breeding areas in sw. Oregon based on return of banded individuals (D. Vroman p.c.). In British Columbia, 13 of 13 color-banded birds resighted in same territories 1-2 yr after initial observations (Ward and Smith 2000). Territory size reported to be 1.2-1.5 ac (0.5-0.6 ha) by various authors (summarized in Gardali and Ballard 2000). At Hart Mtn. in 2001, territories were approximately 2.5-3.8 ac (1.0-1.5 ha) in riparian aspen stands.

Woven, basket-like nest suspended from fork in small branches, usually well away from main stem of tree. Occasionally nest low in shrubs. Nest mainly of thin strips of bark, grasses, and spider webbing to bind nest rim to twigs. Nests usually well camouflaged in foliage, but may be located by homing in on a stationary, singing male (*JH*).

Forages in small branches in deciduous canopy trees, gleaning insects mainly from leaves, also twigs. Moves relatively slowly through territory while foraging. Males frequently observed actively foraging and singing simultaneously. "He sings while in constant motion, seeking his food" (Lord 1902). At Hart Mtn., observed foraging on ground and in sagebrush during brood rearing (*JH*).

Diet mainly insects. Chapin (1925) quantified stomach contents of vireos in California Apr-Oct: 43% butterflies and moths (mainly caterpillars), 21% true bugs, 19% ladybug beetles, 7% beetles, 2% spiders, and 1% bees, wasps, and ants. Approximately 3% of diet vegetable matter, mainly elderberries and poison oak seeds taken in Aug and Sept.

**Seasonal Activity and Behavior:** Begin to arrive in w. Oregon in late Apr, peak arrivals in early May (Gilligan et al. 1994). Early arrivals in e. Oregon in early May, peak arrivals in late May, and smaller numbers of birds arrive into early Jun. At Malheur NWR, earliest arrival 24 Apr 1984, average first arrival 11 May. Peak migration 18 May to 2 Jun (Littlefield 1990a).

Territories established upon arrival on breeding grounds. Pairs may be formed prior to arrival (Bent 1950, Howes-Jones 1985a). Pairs sometimes arrive on territories together, or males arrive 1-4 days earlier than females (Howes-Jones 1985a). Territories established in e. Oregon in late May. Early nests built in late May, peak nest building in early Jun. In w. Oregon begin nesting early May. Territory and nest vociferously defended by the pair against intruders, including potential nest predators and cowbirds (Ward and Smith 2000).

Nest built mostly by female, occasionally assisted by male. Nest construction takes approximately 7 days (Gardali and Ballard 2000). Male often follows female closely during nest building to guard against extra-pair copulations. Monogamous, typically produce clutch of four eggs. At Hart Mtn., 12 first egg dates 3-24 Jun (Heltzel and Earnst 2002). In Oregon, nests with eggs observed 2 Jun to 6 Jul (n=14); nests with young 28 May to 14 Jul (n=14) (OBBA). Up to two broods per season, although second broods are not common in the northern portion of its range,

including Oregon. Incubation begins with penultimate egg. Both male and female share in incubation and brooding, although the female spends approximately 50% more time incubating than male (Howes-Jones 1985a). Male develops nearly complete brood patch (Pyle 1997). Male will commonly sing from nest. Incubation 12-14 days, nestling period 13-15 days. Fledglings remain with adults for approximately 2 wk after leaving nest.

Common host to Brown-headed Cowbird. Cowbird eggs frequently hatch before vireo eggs due to shorter incubation period. Even where cowbird and vireo eggs hatch at the same time, cowbirds develop more rapidly than vireos and vireo young starve or are crushed in the nest. Parasitism rate 48-80% in western populations (Gardali and Ballard 2000). At Hart Mtn. in 2001, 6 of 13 (46%) nests found in the egg stage were parasitized. Of the six parasitized nests, two successfully fledged cowbird young, and only one fledged vireo young (Heltzel and Earnst 2002).

Warbling Vireos may abandon nests where clutch size is reduced due to destruction of vireo eggs by cowbirds. Known to puncture and eject cowbird eggs, although this behavior has been less frequently observed in western than in eastern populations, possibly due to larger bill size of eastern subspecies (Sealy et al. 2000).

Fall migration in Oregon Aug to late Sep, with several records in Oct (Gilligan et al. 1994). At Malheur NWR, peak migration 25 Aug to 7 Sep, and latest record 25 Sep 1987 (Littlefield 1990a).

**Detection:** In spring and summer males sing persistently and loudly, often into the afternoon in May and Jun. While the bubbling song is quite familiar, less well known are the diagnostic harsh, nasal *waahh* or *meaahh* call, used as a contact call between sexes while foraging separately on territory, and also frequently heard at nest exchanges, during territory disputes, and while scolding intruders (Howes-Jones 1985b). Call also occasionally heard in fall, when vireos are otherwise difficult to detect.

Frequently sing at edges of territory, from a favorite perch, or from the nest. A reliable way to find a nest is to locate a male singing continuously from one location (he is probably on the nest). Generally visually inconspicuous, although some pairs are obvious while nest building. Not likely to be confused with other species in Oregon, but drab appearance makes a silent vireo easy to overlook.

**Population Status and Conservation:** Gabrielson and Jewett (1940) reported Warbling Vireos to be abundant in riparian areas throughout Oregon, but largely absent from coastal areas. Extensive areas of red alder in coastal and w. Oregon clearcuts probably support higher densities of breeding vireos than were historically found in these areas.

Populations show positive trend in most areas of Oregon. BBS data for 1966-96 show >1.5% increase in numbers detected in most areas of the state, and a slightly smaller increase in coastal areas (Sauer et al. 2001). In Owyhee and Snake R. drainages, populations have decreased by 1.5% in the same time period. Nationwide, population trends are generally positive or stable. In California, several populations appear to be declining due to excessive parasitism by cowbirds (Gardali and Ballard 2000, Gardali et al. 2000).

In se. Oregon in 2001, Mayfield nest success was 44% (n=19) (Heltzel and Earnst 2002). This is comparable with Mayfield nest success rates of 61% in Arizona (Martin and Li 1992) and 52% in Montana (Gardali and Ballard 2000), and significantly greater than 21% success rate in a sink population in coastal California, where annual reproduction is not sufficient to compensate for mortality and the population is declining (Gardali et al. 2000).—*Jeannie Heltzel*

### Philadelphia Vireo *Vireo philadelphicus*

This vireo breeds from c. British Columbia eastward across Canada to the e. coast. It winters in M. America, migrating southeast of the Rocky Mtns. The many coastal California records range from mid-Sep to mid-Jun (Small 1994). There are several unpublished Oregon sight records. A bird was photographed at Fields, Harney Co., 3 Jun 1991 (Tweit and Johnson 1991b, Evanich 1992d). Monotypic (AOU 1957).—*Harry B. Nehls*

### Red-eyed Vireo *Vireo olivaceus*

When walking through riparian areas in certain parts of Oregon in summer, one can often hear "a song which suggests the Robin's but with less volume and energy, and with a greater variety of phrase" (Hoffmann 1927). Yet, when one looks up, the bird is often hidden within the canopy foliage. When found, the Red-eyed Vireo's combination of gray cap with a white supercilium bordered by two black lines distinguish it from other vireos, and its plain olive-green back and white underside reveal why the singer could not be readily found. Returning the next summer to the same spot may reveal no such singer, as the Red-eyed Vireo often shows up one year, but not the next, in parts of its Oregon range.

**General Distribution:** Breeds from extreme sw. Yukon across Canada to the Atlantic Ocean. Probably reaches extreme se. Alaska as an extension of its range from British Columbia (not the Yukon). Found in the N. Cascades and Okanogan Mtns. in Washington, south into Oregon via the Blue and Wallowa mountains, east into Idaho and Montana, and in riparian areas of the Great Plains of the Dakotas, Nebraska, and the Platte

R. Valley of Colorado. From there, a breeding resident across the eastern half of N. America (east of the 100th meridian); also breeds in S. America (Cimprich et al. 2000). N. American birds winter in n. S. America. Two N. American subspecies; *V. o. caniviridis* in Oregon (Behle 1985, Browning 1990, Phillips 1991).

**Oregon Distribution:** Status is not well known, perhaps owing to fluctuations in numbers of birds. Fairly common to rare summer breeder in Wallowa Co.; uncommon to rare breeder in Union Co. (Evanich 1992a), Baker Co. (specimen, Burleigh 1960b), e. Grant, and e. Umatilla counties (Gilligan et al. 1994), and n. Malheur Co. (Contreras and Kindschy 1996). Healthy breeding populations have been noted along lower Grouse Cr. and the Imnaha R., Wallowa Co.; Grand Ronde R. (below Palmer Junction), Union and Wallowa counties; Wall Cr., Grant Co.; North Fork John Day R. (below Camas Cr.), Umatilla and Grant counties; North and South Forks of the Walla Walla R., and on the Umatilla R. (above Mission), Umatilla Co.; and around Richland and Halfway, Baker Co. (M. Denny p.c.). Breeding apparently has also occurred in the Owyhee Valley of Malheur Co. (H. Nehls p.c.), but it does not breed there today (*ALC*).

Elsewhere east of the Cascades, the species' distribution is far less clear. In addition to what is noted above, the species has been reported during the breeding season near the north end of Klamath L. (Lund 1979), in nw. Klamath Co. (OBBA), where a breeding male (MVZ) was found near Ft. Klamath (McCaskie and Benedictis 1964), and in Klamath R. Canyon (Spencer 1999); on several occasions at DeMoss Springs Park, Sherman Co.; and locally in Jefferson and Deschutes counties (OBBA). Summering birds were also found in Harney Co. during the OBBA period (1995-99).

West of the Cascades, the Red-eyed Vireo has a disjunct range and irregular status. As Gilligan et al. (1994) noted about the species' w. Oregon distribution, "some favored sites [support] birds for years at a time, then seem to lose them." These favored

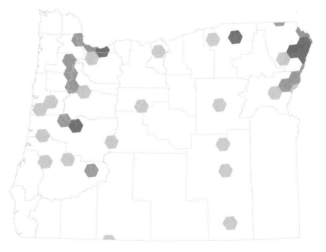

sites are often referred to as "colonies" in local field notes. In the n. Willamette Valley, found from Sauvie I. (with one report from Scappoose, Columbia Co. [Johnson J 1991a]) and Portland (USNM) east along the Columbia R. to the mouth of the Sandy R. Along the Sandy, found upriver to Roslyn L. (Dowlan 1998). A compilation of numerous records taken from the field notes sections of *Oregon Birds* shows records in the Willamette Valley along the Willamette R. at Luckiamute, Polk Co.; Grand I., Yamhill Co.; and near Stayton and Scio in Marion Co., as well as up the S. Santiam R. at Crabtree, Linn Co. A long-standing group up the Middle Fork of the Willamette R. from Jasper Park to Oakridge, Lane Co., has been noted annually from the late 1970s throughout the 1990s, and birds have also been found at Fern Ridge Res., Lane Co. (the above from numerous field notes in *Oregon Birds* and *American Birds*). There are scattered Douglas Co. records for Jun and Jul (Hunter et al. 1998), including a female with a brood patch banded at Kanipe Ranch 16 Jul 1994 (Johnson J 1995a). A small "colony" (10 birds noted) was discovered in Jackson Co. in 1976 at Dodge Bridge on the Rogue R. (Crowell and Nehls 1976d) and persisted at least to 1979 (D. Fix p.c.). A record at Talent, 28 Jun 1994, also suggests possible breeding in the Rogue Valley (Johnson J 1995a). It is casual along the coast in summer; it has been recorded in all Oregon coastal counties except Tillamook.

**Habitat and Diet:** Little has been published of the habitat and diet of the Red-eyed Vireo in the Pacific Northwest. Found in extensive riparian areas during the breeding season. As Dowlan (1998) notes for w. Oregon, "the species is most often detected in riparian forests consisting of large black cottonwood, but stands of Oregon ash, red alder, and various willow species may also provide quality habitat." In Wallowa Co., they are often found in black cottonwood >100 ft (30 m) tall with an understory of chokecherry, willow, alder, hawthorn, and netleaf hackberry, growing over the surface of moving waters (M. Denny p.c.).

Nests are constructed at the fork of a branch, are small and cup-like, and consist primarily of twigs and grasses held together with spider webs (Robb 1998, *RTK*). Such construction is consistent with that found elsewhere in N. America (Cimprich et al. 2000).

No diet information is available for Oregon. They have been observed gleaning caterpillars near the mouth of the Sandy R., on Sauvie I., and in Wallowa Co. (*RTK*). In N. America, consumes primarily insects and spiders (Cimprich et al. 2000).

**Seasonal Activity and Behavior:** Most individuals reaching Oregon probably come north across the Gulf of Mexico and then turn west after overland migration (Cimprich et al. 2000). The late arrival dates in Oregon

and the small number of Rogue Valley, Willamette Valley (away from breeding grounds), and coastal records seem to support this hypothesis.

Found from late May increasingly into Jun in migration. The earliest dates in the state have been 10 May 1988 at Sauvie I. (Mattocks 1988b), and 19 May 1973 at Malheur NWR (Littlefield 1990a). Peaks at Malheur (very few birds) during the first week of Jun, and birds in ne. Oregon often are on territory by this time as well. Arrival dates in the Willamette Valley vary from the second week to the fourth week of Jun.

Migration seems somewhat protracted, although some late birds could be vagrants rather than part of the Northwest breeding population. For instance, migrants have been reported at Malheur NWR as late as 20 Jun (Littlefield 1990a) and have been found at other well-known migration concentration spots such as DeMoss Springs Park, Sherman Co., and Lava L., Santiam Pass, Linn Co., at around the same time (Anderson DA 1990c). The five birds caught at a banding station at Hart Mtn. 1975-79 appeared from 3 Jun to 29 Jun (Mewaldt 1980). The few spring coastal records are about evenly distributed between May and Jun (Bayer 1995a, Contreras 1998).

Nesting activity begins quickly after arrival. The one OBBA confirmation of a nest with eggs in ne. Oregon was found on 1 Jul 1997; more data on ne. Oregon breeding are certainly needed. In the Willamette Valley, nesting has been observed as early as 15 Jun. Males begin singing immediately upon arrival and, as in the e. U.S., will sing continuously into the heat of the afternoon. In the Willamette Valley, tend to stop singing by the end of Jul, and breeding seems to be completed by Aug, though more observation of the timing needs to be obtained. Adults observed feeding young on 7 Aug 1989 on Sauvie I. (Fix and Heinl 1990), and a bird was still singing on territory at Virginia L., Sauvie I., 15 Aug 1999 (*RTK*).

Perhaps most interesting is the pairing of a Red-eyed Vireo (on nest) and Cassin's Vireo (singing and feeding Red-eyed Vireo) in Jasper Park, Lane Co., in Jun-Jul 1997. Mating was observed, and a nest was built, but apparently no offspring were produced. The only egg observed in the nest was believed to be that of a Brown-headed Cowbird (Johnson J 1998a, Robb 1998).

Fall migration, following the opposite pattern from spring migration, starts in early Aug. A great majority of the records are from Malheur NWR and Fields, Harney Co., areas where observers concentrate birding efforts in fall. Malheur NWR records range from 15 Aug to 21 Sep, with no Jul records (Littlefield 1990a); a female (*MRB*) was taken there in late Aug (Kridler and Marshall 1962). Two fall records of hatch-year birds at Hart Mtn. were 8 Sep and 17 Sep (Mewaldt 1980). A late record for e. Oregon was from Frenchglen, Harney Co., 23 Sep 1997 (Sullivan 1998a).

Four coastal records, two each for Jul and Aug (Gilligan 1997, 1998, Johnson J 1998a), as well as some Lane Co. records into late Aug (Gilligan 1997), are difficult to classify. Due to the late arrival of this species, individual summer records may be lingering nonbreeders or vagrants. There seems to be only a single fall record away from the coast and away from suspected breeding locations: one was observed at Tigard, Washington Co., 7 Sep 1989, a fairly late date (Fix and Heinl 1990). Oregon's latest date is 28 Sep 1977 at Sauvie I. (Fix 1977/1978).

**Detection:** Red-eyed Vireos are most often detected by loud, repetitive songs given on the breeding grounds. Because of their use of the upper portion of the canopy, they can often be hard to observe, even when singing (*RTK*). However, they can be easily observed in netleaf hackberry along the Imnaha R., Wallowa Co. (*MGH*).

For less-experienced birders, this, as well as the song's similarity to that of Cassin's Vireo and other woodland species, may cause it to be missed. The red eye is not a reliable field mark; indeed, as Pyle (1997) suggests, some birds may never fully develop a red eye. A well-marked bird observed on 4 Jun 1999 had a brown iris (*RTK*), and fall hatch-year birds will show a brown iris exclusively (Pyle 1997).

**Population Status and Conservation:** BBS data show a drop of 9.1% between 1966 and 1999; however, such trend data are from only nine of 90 Oregon routes, and as Cimprich et al. (2000) note, any determinations made about this species from BBS data should be viewed with caution. Dowlan (1998) notes that a new BBS route was created in 1993 along the Lower Sandy R. to monitor avian activity in the area, and Red-eyed Vireo is certainly a species being watched. Sharp (1990) suggested that the downward negative trend is counter to national increases in the species and that, while wintering habitat problems were a concern, "breeding habitat changes cannot be discounted."

The lack of data is exacerbated somewhat by the species strange "colonial" nature in Oregon. Gabrielson and Jewett (1940) describe that they found the species becoming more common after 1924, noting that "some years, up to a dozen males" could be found in various Columbia R. bottomlands around Portland. The Gabrielson and Jewett (1940) account of the species reads much like the record compiled here: seen at a site for a year or two, then gone, then back. More recently, largely since the early 1970s, people seem to have "discovered" colonies that were there before or that were near where they are found today.

More effort needs to be made to document Red-eyed Vireo occurrence and nesting in all areas of the state, and a more comprehensive effort to account for its historical status throughout the state is needed.—*Raymond T. Korpi*

## Family *Corvidae*

### Gray Jay *Perisoreus canadensis*

Gray Jays are common visitors at mountainous campsites and parks and are commonly known as "camp robbers" for their habit of taking food from humans. Gray Jays in the Blue Mtns. have the top of their heads white, while birds in the Cascades and Coast Ranges have white restricted to the forehead, and Coast Range birds are decidedly browner vs. grayish overall (Gabrielson and Jewett 1940). Appear to be long-lived, as a banded bird collected in Crater L. in 1945 was at least 9 yr old (Farner 1946); the longevity record for Gray Jays is over 15 yr (Klimkiewicz 2000). Very little is known regarding many basic life-history traits of this species in Oregon.

**General Distribution:** Breeds and winters from w. and c. Alaska, across Canada and south into n. Minnesota, n. Wisconsin, and Maine, and south through the Rocky Mtns. and Cascade and Coast Ranges to n. California. Occurs irregularly slightly south of breeding range in winter. Six subspecies, two in Oregon (Strickland and Ouellet 1993).

**Oregon Distribution:** *P. c. obscurus*, formerly considered a distinct species, the Oregon Jay, resides in conifer forests of the Coast and Cascade ranges (Mt. Hood, N. Santiam R., Crater L. NP [USNM]), e. slope of Cascades at Ft. Klamath (USNM), and sw. Oregon (Strickland and Ouellet 1993). It is uncommon to common throughout the Coast and Cascade ranges, but rare to uncommon in sw. Oregon and the Klamath Mtns. (Browning 1975a). The extent to which the species breeds in and near the Willamette Valley is unclear. Although typically most common in higher elevations, many of the breeding records for the state have been at low elevations including in

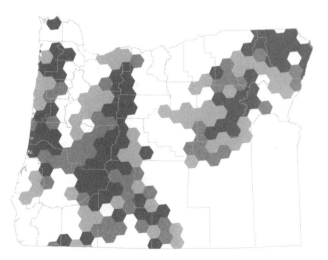

Molalla, Sandy, Beaverton, in Clatsop Co., and near Eugene (Gabrielson and Jewett 1940, Griffee 1954, Mattocks et al. 1983). They occur on the immediate coast from at least s. Lincoln Co. northward (Netarts [AMNH], Tillamook [USNM, AMNH], Seaside [AMNH]), usually in older spruce/alder stands (D. Irons p.c.). Rare on the s. coast (Heinl 1986a, Fix 1991), where they are most regular on forested inland ridges (Contreras 1998). *P. c. bicolor* resides at mid- to high-elevation coniferous forests of the Blue Mtns. (Strickland and Ouellet 1993), where it appears to be uncommon to common (Evanich 1992a, *DBM*). Specimens from Enterprise, Wallowa Co.; Strawberry Mtns., Paradise, and Canyon City, Grant Co.; Maury Mtns. (all USNM); and Howard and Prineville, Crook Co. (SOU).

**Habitat and Diet:** Occurs primarily in conifer forests, including Douglas-fir, western hemlock, mountain hemlock, lodgepole pine, and in true fir, spruce, and mixed-conifer forests (Gabrielson and Jewett 1940, Farner 1952, Browning 1975a). Not recorded in stands dominated by Oregon white oak or in pure red alder stands of w. Washington (Anderson 1972, Stiles 1980).

Studies in the Coast and Cascade ranges of Oregon and Washington reported associations (McGarigal and McComb 1995) and a lack thereof (Carey et al. 1991, Huff and Raley 1991, Manuwal 1991, Brooks 1997) with stand age. There are no clear trends regarding the effects of forest cutting on populations of Gray Jays. In the e. Coast Range of Oregon, abundance was similar in uncut mature stands and stands with small patch cuts, two-story stands, or clearcut stands with retained live and dead trees (Chambers et al. 1999). Gray Jays were present, but uncommon in young (5- to 45-yr-old) stands of the Coast and Cascade Ranges (Bettinger 1996, *JMW*). They were more abundant in unthinned than in thinned young forests of the n. Coast Range, but were similar in abundance in thinned and unthinned stands of the c. Coast Range (Hagar et al. 1996). In the Blue Mtns., abundance did not differ statistically (p=0.35) between structural classes (stand initiation, open and closed canopy stem exclusion, understory reinitiation, young forest multistory, and old forest multistory) (Sallabanks et al. 2002).

Gray Jays were more abundant in unburned than in burned areas 0-3 yr after fire in ne. Washington (Kreisel and Stein 1999).

Very little information exists regarding nest sites in Oregon. Known nest sites, including a few in Oregon, have been in Douglas-fir, western hemlock, red fir, lodgepole pine, larch, and willow (Gabrielson and Jewett 1940, Griffee 1954, Strickland and Ouellet 1993). Most Oregon nest sites are described as being low to the ground (<32 ft [10 m]) in saplings, but one was noted at 75 ft (23 m). Nest is built from twigs, cocoons, bark strips, and arboreal lichens and is lined with feathers or fur (Strickland and Ouellet 1993).

No description of foraging habitat could be found. Omnivorous. Primary items in the stomachs of 67 non-nestlings from a variety of locations (56 from Ontario and Quebec) were arthropods (beetles, true bugs, hymenoptera, caterpillars, flies, crickets, spiders, and centipedes), bones and fur of small mammals, and seeds from berries. Also known to eat carrion, fungi, conifer seeds, and the eggs of other birds. Stored food items during the summer in Alaska included berries, arthropods, and mushrooms. Gray Jays rely on cached food during winter because they stay on their territory year-round, even at high elevations (Strickland and Ouellet 1993). It is not known if jays residing in more moderate climates of Oregon also exhibit extensive caching behaviors or if they breed as early as their northerly counterparts. Caches are stored by coating food items with sticky saliva and then placing them under flakes of bark, in lichen, and in coniferous foliage (Strickland and Ouellet 1993).

Very little information exists regarding habitat use in winter. In unmanaged stands of the s. Washington Cascade Range in winter, were more abundant in late than in mid-seral stands (Huff et al. 1991). In the e. Coast Range, were absent from two-story and clearcuts but were present in low abundance in stands that were uncut and that had small patch cuts (Chambers and McComb 1997).

Gray Jays are territorial year-round. No information for territory size in Oregon, but in Ontario, territory size was 170 ac (69 ha) (Strickland and Ouellet 1993).

**Seasonal Activity and Behavior:** Very little information exists regarding timing of breeding in Oregon. In Oregon, nest building has been observed mid-Mar and late Apr (n=2) and nests with eggs have been found 8 Apr to 8 May (n=7) (Gabrielson and Jewett 1940, Griffee 1954, Contreras 1998). Elsewhere, nesting is reported primarily Mar to early May (Strickland and Ouellet 1993). An adult was observed feeding recently fledged young on 25 Jun near Eugene (Mattocks et al. 1983). Fledged young were reported throughout the state 30 May to 18 Aug (n=26) (OBBA), but juveniles remain close to the adult after fledging and the brown juvenile plumage is held to Jul-Sep (Pyle 1997), thus some of these may have been fledged for several weeks or months. In addition, earlier sightings of recently fledged young may have been missed due to the timing of the OBBA effort. More study is needed to determine the timing of breeding in Oregon.

Very few data regarding territoriality in Oregon. The recapture of one bird near its original banding location 9 yr after banding suggests that the species has very high site fidelity (Farner 1946). Elsewhere, territory boundaries are maintained year-round and may remain constant even if pair members change (Strickland and Ouellet 1993). Elsewhere, the young remain on the territory until approximately Jun when the dominant juvenile ejects all subordinate juveniles from the territory. A small group of birds remains on the territory through winter and includes the breeding pair, the dominant juvenile, and sometimes an unrelated adult (Strickland and Ouellet 1993).

Irruptions have been reported to occur outside of Oregon in winter. It is not clear what individuals may be involved, but it seems likely that they may be adults or juveniles that are not associated with a territory (Strickland and Ouellet 1993).

**Detection:** Generally quiet. Most frequently sighted after it has sneaked up on its observer. Conspicuous when vocalizing as they can be quite loud and have a wide repertoire. The most common calls heard are the single, loud, *whuit* contact call and the two-note *whee-yap* call. Gray Jays sometimes mimic other birds, especially raptors. Mimicked birds are often, but not always, within sight of the bird giving the call (Strickland and Ouellet 1993).

**Population Status and Conservation:** There are no significant population trends in Oregon (Sauer et al. 2000). Strickland and Ouellet (1993) noted that Gray Jays are very vulnerable to traps set for furbearers. No immediate conservation actions appear to be needed, however much still needs to be learned about basic life-history traits of this species in Oregon.—*Jennifer M. Weikel*

## Steller's Jay *Cyanocitta stelleri*

Unmistakable with its charcoal and blue plumage, distinctive crest, and raucous call announcing its presence. Birds in nw. Oregon often have blue streaks on their forehead and throat, while those in sc. Oregon often have pale blue streaking on forehead or throat, and those in the Blue Mtns. typically have white streaking on forehead and a white streak or spot above the eye. Despite their abundance and familiarity, very little information exists regarding the life history of this species in the Pacific Northwest.

**General Distribution:** Resident from se. Alaska to se. British Columbia and sw. Alberta south through the Rocky Mtns. and the mountains of the Southwest through the highlands of M. America (except Belize). Seventeen subspecies are recognized, three of which breed in Oregon (Pyle 1997) and one has occurred during fall and winter in Oregon (*MRB*).

**Oregon Distribution:** Subspecies in nw. Oregon have gone through a number of taxonomic changes (Browning 2002). Gabrielson and Jewett (1940)

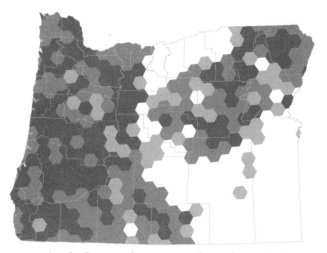

recognized *C. s. carbonacea* as the subspecies in w. Oregon north of the Klamath Mtns. Stevenson (1934) confined *carbonacea* to California and recognized *paralia*, a subspecies proposed by Oberholser (1932), for w. Oregon. AOU (1957) likewise confined *carbonacea* but considered *paralia* as a synonym of *stelleri*, the subspecies at that time recognized as breeding in nw. Oregon. Later, Browning (1979a), without comment, followed Stevenson (1934), Miller (1941), and Aldrich (in Jewett et al. 1953) in recognizing *paralia*. Recognition of *paralia* is further substantiated by Phillips (1986), Weibe (1995), and Browning (2002); the latter placed the southern range as probably Humboldt Co. in nw. California.

*C. s. paralia* is resident from the Coast Range to the Cascade crest excluding the upper Rogue R. Valley region where *paralia* and *frontalis* intergrade (Browning 2002). *C. s. frontalis* is resident from near Bend to Klamath and Lake counties (Gabrielson and Jewett 1940), and intergrades with *paralia* in w. Klamath Co. (specimens at OSU, USNM; *MRB*). *C. s. annectens* is a common resident in conifer forests of the Blue, Wallowa, and Ochoco mountains region (Gabrielson and Jewett 1940) to the east slope of the n. Cascades and intergrades with *paralia* on east slope of the Cascades from slopes of Mt. Hood to Sisters (specimens at OSU, USNM; *MRB*). *C. s. stelleri* has occurred four times (*MRB*): once each in w. Lane Co., Oct (USNM); w. Lincoln Co., Sep (DMNH); Tillamook Co., Nov; and Multnomah Co., Jan (AMNH).

**Habitat and Diet:** Common resident in mesic and dry conifer and mixed conifer-hardwood forests from valley floors to near timberline (Gabrielson and Jewett 1940, Browning 1979a, Greene et al. 1998). In forests of the Coast and Cascade ranges during the breeding season, they are present in conifer stands of all ages (Carey et al. 1991, Gilbert and Allwine 1991, Bettinger 1996, *JMW*). Associations of abundance with stand age are not consistent among studies. In one study in upland, unmanaged stands of the

Cascade Range, abundance increased with increasing stand age (Gilbert and Allwine 1991). However in another study in unmanaged riparian areas of the Coast Range, abundance decreased with increasing forest age (Anthony et al. 1996).

Conflicting evidence also exists with regard to the effects of timber harvest on Steller's Jays. In the Coast Range, Steller's Jays were more abundant in logged than in unlogged riparian sites; abundance increased with increasing buffer width up to about 197 ft (60m), then declined thereafter (Hagar 1999a). Abundance declined in response to conversion of mature closed-canopy forest to two-story and clearcut stands (Chambers et al. 1999). In younger (35- to 45-yr-old) forest, abundance appeared to be similar between moderately thinned and unthinned young Douglas-fir stands, but may have been negatively affected by heavier thinning (Hayes et al. unpubl. ms., J. Hagar p.c.). In the Cascade Range, abundance was highly variable and was typically higher in old-growth stands than in all other stand types (clearcuts, young closed-canopy plantations, and mature forests) except clearcuts with retained live trees (Hansen et al. 1995). In ne. Oregon, abundance did not differ statistically (p=0.12) between forests of different structural classes (stand initiation, open- and closed-canopy stem exclusion, understory reinitiation, young forest-multistory, and old forest-multistory) (Sallabanks et al. 2002). Conflicting results between studies may reflect the typically "generalist" nature of this species (Greene et al. 1998). Whereas overall trends in habitat selection appear not to be consistent over study sites, smaller-scale trends are apparent and may reflect small-scale (and perhaps even short-term) opportunistic use of resources.

Nests in trees or shrubs and often places nest near trunk and within 10-16 ft (3-5 m) from the ground (Gabrielson and Jewett 1940, Greene et al. 1998). The nest is a bulky structure made of sticks, plant fibers, dry leaves, and moss mixed with mud and lined with coarse rootlets, conifer needles, and animal hair (Greene et al. 1998). Several nests located in the Blue Mtns. were about 20 ft (6 m) above the ground in Douglas-fir or ponderosa pine along ridges or above canyons (M. Denny p.c.).

May move into other habitats in winter (Greene et al. 1998). Observed in Oregon white oak from late summer through winter (Anderson 1972, *JMW*). Similar to trends observed during summer, Chambers and McComb (1997) found that Steller's Jays were most abundant in uncut stands and in stands receiving small patch cuts in mature forests of the Coast Range; they were present in low abundance in two-story and clearcut stands during the first 3-6 yr after cutting.

*Steller's Jay*

However, in Sep and Oct in the same two-story stands approximately 10-yr after cutting, groups of 3-6 jays were frequently observed (*JMW*).

No information exists regarding foraging habitat or diet in Oregon. In general, Steller's Jays forage on the ground and in trees and bushes. Omnivorous; eat a variety of animal and plant food including arthropods, small vertebrates including the eggs and young of other birds and small adult birds, seeds, nuts, berries, and fruits. Common visitor to campgrounds and feeders where they consume a large variety of foods (Gabrielson and Jewett 1940, Otvos and Stark 1985, Greene et al. 1998). Steller's Jays cache acorns and seeds among the bark of trees or in the ground for later consumption and will raid food caches placed by Clark's Nutcrackers and Gray Jays (Farner 1952, Greene et al. 1998). They have been observed carrying chinquapin seed pods in the sw. Cascades (N. Barrett p.c., D. Fix p.c.).

Birds exhibit site-related dominance, which is intermediate between territoriality and coloniality. In California, each pair's "zone of dominance" was approximately 394 ft (120 m) across (Greene et al. 1998).

**Seasonal Activity and Behavior:** Nest building observed 8 Apr to 21 Jun (n=6) (OBBA, Gabrielson and Jewett 1940). Greene et al. (1998) report that nest building starts in Mar and peaks in Apr; it is possible that birds in Oregon also follow this pattern and that existing observations have been noted later due to the timing of the OBBA project and recreational birding during the latter months of spring. Nests with eggs have been located 7 Apr to 7 Jul (n=20) and nests with young 28 May to 26 Jul (n=7). Recently fledged young have been observed 13 May to 19 Oct (n=35) (OBBA, Gabrielson and Jewett 1940). Typically lay four or five eggs; only the female broods and the male feeds the female during brooding. Both sexes care for young up to about 1 mo after fledging; young may remain on the adults' territory until fall or winter (Greene et al. 1998).

Jays living in lower-elevation areas likely remain on their home ranges year-round (Greene et al. 1998). Upslope movements have been noted in Crater L. NP in Aug and Sep (Farner 1952). Birds breeding at high elevations typically move downslope in winter (Gabrielson and Jewett 1940, Browning 1979a, Evanich 1992a). A few individuals may move latitudinally or longitudinally (Morrison and Yoder-Williams 1984); *MRB* found that 4% of 273 band recoveries showed movement >60 mi (96 km).

Steller's Jays mimic a variety of local birds and mammals as well as mechanical sounds such as water sprinklers, telephones, and squeaky doors. Most commonly mimic Red-tailed Hawks. Have been observed to mimic Red-shouldered Hawks in Coos Co. (D. Fix p.c.).

Steller's Jays have a complex social structure. They are monogamous and the breeding pair has dominance over all others within its territory. The level of dominance decreases with increasing distance from the nest, resulting in a complex relationship between birds. They also have a complex communication system comprised of an array of vocal, postural, and display signals (Greene et al. 1998).

**Detection:** Detected from great distances by its loud, raucous calls.

**Population Status and Conservation:** No evidence exists to suggest that Steller's Jay populations are declining or that populations are in need of special conservation measures (Greene et al. 1998). However, very little is known regarding basic life history characteristics or effects of different land management practices on this species.—*Jennifer M. Weikel*

## Blue Jay *Cyanocitta cristata*

From s. Canada and throughout much of the e. U.S., one of the characteristic birds of woodlands and city streets is this loud, colorful jay. Its bright blue-and-white plumage, and shrill calls are quite distinctive. It is closely related to the Steller's Jay and hybrid individuals have been noted where their ranges overlap. Both Steller's Jays and Western Scrub-Jays are often called "Blue Jays" by those unfamiliar with this species.

**General Distribution:** Northernmost birds are well-recognized migrants in the Lake States and in the ne. U.S., but mostly resident from ec. British Columbia across Canada to Newfoundland, south through e. U.S., and westward to the Rocky Mtns. Tends to stage impressive flights and gatherings during the fall of some years (Kaufman 1991). Western range expansion began during the 1950s and continues. It reached most western states and s. British Columbia as a rare migrant and winter visitor by 1970 (McCaskie 1970, Mattocks et al. 1976, Nehls 1977a). Four subspecies; Oregon subspecies could not be determined because of lack of specimens.

**Oregon Distribution:** The first two reports of Blue Jay in Oregon both came during the last week of Dec 1973, one at Halfway, Baker Co. (Gashwiler and Gashwiler 1975), and the other at Ontario, Malheur Co. (Hoffman 1980). A major influx to the Northwest during the fall of 1976 brought individuals to many parts of the state (Nehls 1977a). It is now a rare but regular visitor to e. and w. Oregon from late Sep to late Apr.

The Blue Jay has been seen yearly in the Grande Ronde Valley since first arriving there during the fall of 1975. Flocks of up to eight individuals have been reported (B. Dowdy p.c.). Many territorial birds remained for several years, with nesting suspected in many instances (J. Evanich p.c.). Nesting was verified during summer 1977 at Union, Union Co. (Van Horn 1978), and in 1998 at Elgin, Union Co. (F. Conley p.c.). During the spring of 1991 a pair began nesting at Hermiston, Umatilla Co., but the attempt failed when the adults were driven off by resident Black-billed Magpies (Evanich 1991a).

**Habitat and Diet:** Prefers open mixed forests or deciduous groves, and is often found in orchards and parks, and along wooded city streets (Madge and Burn 1994). In the Grande Ronde Valley occurs primarily at forest edges around the perimeter of the valley (B. Dowdy p.c., J. Evanich p.c.). Like other corvids, an opportunistic forager of small animals and invertebrates, but is predominantly a vegetarian (Goodwin 1986). Often joins Steller's and Western Scrub-Jays at bird-feeding stations and other sources of seeds or nuts (McCaskie 1970, *HBN*).

**Seasonal Activity and Behavior:** Unpredictable in its arrival and where it may occur, most remain several days, often through the winter. In many instances two or more birds are seen together.

**Detection:** A noisy and conspicuous bird most of the year, but can be secretive during the breeding season, making it difficult to locate birds and verify nesting. Can be overlooked as "just another jay,"' but easily recognized by its loud distinctive voice, and blue-and-white plumage.

**Population Status and conservation:** Population increasing over most of its range and expanding into new areas (Madge and Burn 1994, Tarvin and Woolfenden 1999). However, it does not appear that a resident population is becoming established or expanding in Oregon at this time. No conservation concerns have been identified.—*Harry B. Nehls*

## Western Scrub-Jay *Aphelocoma californica*

Said to have "one of the most peculiar distributions of any Oregon bird" (Gabrielson and Jewett 1940), the Western Scrub-Jay has been slowly extending its range for decades, possibly taking advantage of changes to the landscape wrought by humans. Its name derives from its preference for "scrub" habitat, consisting chiefly of shrubs or brush intermixed with sparse trees. A crestless jay with a blue head and wings, white throat, gray breast and back and a long blue tail, the scrub-jay provides a flash of color wherever it goes. It calls attention to itself with its raspy metallic shriek. Its harsh voice and fussy, boisterous behavior might lead some to consider the scrub-jay a nuisance. But this bird also possesses abundant character, and like all corvids, is considered to be uncommonly smart and adaptable.

**General Distribution:** Resident from sw. Washington south through wc. Oregon to s. Baja California, and east locally from c. Oregon through s. Idaho into Colorado and south through New Mexico. Also found locally in the Mexican highlands south to Oaxaca. Formerly considered conspecific with Florida Scrub-Jay and Island Scrub-Jay. The number of subspecies is questionable, but they fall into three groups: California Scrub-Jay (on the Pacific coast), Woodhouse's Scrub-Jay (interior w. N. America), and Sumichrast's Scrub-Jay (s. Mexican plateau). Two subspecies in Oregon (Browning 2002).

**Oregon Distribution:** Common permanent resident in western interior valleys and foothills between the Coast Range and Cascades, especially in the Willamette, Umpqua, and Rogue valleys, and less common and more local along the s. coast and in extreme sw. Oregon (Pitelka 1951, Gilligan et al. 1994). In Coos Co., birds occasionally move westward in winter out of the interior valleys as far as Coquille, and occur rarely on

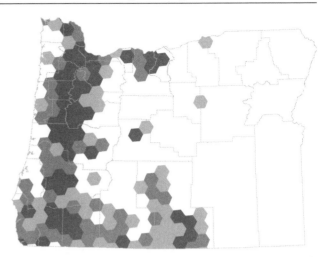

the coast (Contreras 1997b). Rare, but reported with increasing frequency on the c. coast (Johnson 1997b, Gilligan 1998, 1999, Tice 1999b). Recently, range has also expanded west along the Columbia R. to Astoria, where a small population now resides year-round. Breeding was confirmed there in 1992 and 1993 (Gilligan et al. 1994). In the n. Coast Range, an adult was observed in Birkenfeld, and a hatch-year bird just north of there on Fish Hawk Rd., wc. Columbia Co., on 22 Jul 2002 (M. Patterson p.c.). In the w. Cascades, breeding populations occur up to Idleyld Park in the N. Umpqua R. basin (Fix 1990a); Oakridge in the upper Willamette R. basin; and Vida and possibly Blue R. in the McKenzie R. basin (*MGH*).

East of the Cascades, Western Scrub-Jay occurs locally east to The Dalles and Pine Grove (Highway 216), Wasco Co. (D. Lusthoff p.c.); Moro, Sherman Co.; and in the n. Deschutes R. canyon (Korpi 1997, 1998, Sullivan 1997b, 1999a). They have also moved south into Bend, where approximately 25 were present in the early 1990s (Contreras 1997b, Korpi 1999), and 86 were recorded on the 2001 CBC. In spring of 2000 a pair successfully nested and fledged two young near Prineville, Crook Co. (MacDonald 2000). Presumably this same pair was present in 2001-02 and produced at least one young in 2002 (N. MacDonald p.c.). Also occurs with increasing frequency in areas of sc. Oregon (Gabrielson and Jewett 1940, Gilligan et al. 1994, Contreras 1997b).

*A. c. californica* breeds west of the Cascades, with specimens from numerous localities (Pitelka 1951); synonyms include *oocleptica, caurina*, and *immanis* following Phillips (1986) and provisionally *superciliosa* of AOU 1957 (Browning 2002). *A. c. woodhouseii* (includes *nevadae* as a synonym [Phillips 1986]), is a Great Basin subspecies found in the south-central part of the state (Browning 2002).

Scrub-jays are reported as locally common in s. Lake and Klamath counties (Gilligan et al. 1994), especially around Adel (Contreras 1997b) and Lakeview (Korpi 1997a, Sullivan 1998a). Gabrielson and Jewett (1940) reported only two records of *woodhouseii* in Oregon, both from Steens Mtn. It was thought that these marginal records represented irregular wandering rather than the periphery of their range (Pitelka 1951). Specimens collected decades ago from s. Klamath Falls are similar to *californica* and specimens from s. Lake Co. identified as "subspecies?" by Phillips (1986:48) are *woodhouseii* (Browning 2002). However, field reports of both subspecies are now common in sc. Oregon (*ALC*). Given the complex taxonomy of the species (Browning 2002), and the possibility of rapid changes, recent specimens will be required to determine subspecies occurrence and distribution in sc. Oregon.

Western Scrub-Jays are now found in various parts of c. and e. Oregon with increasing frequency, and are rare wanderers to extreme eastern sections of the state, e.g., recorded at Castle Rock, Vale, and near Westfall, all Malheur Co. (Contreras and Kindschy 1996, Korpi 1997). Because of the dynamic nature of this species' range east of the Cascades, birds in these areas could be from either the western population or, less likely, the Great Basin population. Populations established in The Dalles, the n. Deschutes R. canyon, and Bend appear to represent an expansion of *A. c. californica* up the Columbia R., but no specimens have been examined from this region. Also, scrub-jays of unknown subspecies are occasionally seen in fall far out of range in other parts of the state, e.g., at Fish L. in the Cascades of e. Linn Co., at Toketee in the Cascades of e. Douglas Co., and at Summit Meadow in Clackamas Co. (Fix 1990a, *MGH, DBM*).

*A. c. woodhouseii* has been described as shy and secretive, unlike the seemingly fearless *californica*. Genetic and behavioral data suggest that these subspecies may be separate species (Peterson and Burt 1992).

**Habitat and Diet:** Commonly found in open deciduous habitats, especially oak woodland, also brushy hillsides, orchards, and mixed thickets bordering fields. Gabrielson and Jewett (1940) called it "a bird of the manzanita and wild plum thickets, preferring such cover as that of oaks or any other deciduous trees to the coniferous forests." They also use residential areas with urban plantings and riparian woodland. In sw. Oregon, they occur mainly in the broken vegetation of the open, south-facing slopes of river valleys, on the borders of mixed forests of Douglas-fir, tanoak, madrone, and bigleaf maple, and wherever there is a dense understory of ceanothus and other shrubs (Pitelka 1951). Close to the coast, the preferred habitat is characterized by extensive thickets of azalea, cascara, and other shrubs in the vicinity of lodgepole (shore) pine (Pitelka 1951). In sc. Oregon, occurs mainly in the sage-juniper association typical of the region, and in nearby willow thickets. Historically observed near Fort Klamath on hillsides covered with

mountain-mahogany (Pitelka 1951). Near Adel a nest was found in sagebrush (Pitelka 1951). Nests are typically constructed of sticks, sometimes containing moss or grass, and lined with fine rootlets or hairs (Gabrielson and Jewett 1940).

Diet has not been closely studied in Oregon. Generally, it includes insects, invertebrates, small vertebrates, bird eggs, nestlings, and fledglings. In nonbreeding season also relies on acorns, fleshy fruits, seeds, and nuts (Ehrlich et al. 1988, Lanner 1996). The Western Scrub-Jay is among the most routine visitors to bird feeders within the western interior valleys.

**Seasonal Activity and Behavior:** Nest building has been observed 29 Feb to 29 May (n=4) (OBBA). Birds studied in California showed synchronous breeding mainly restricted to the spring months. One instance of fall breeding there was thought to be linked to an abundant crop of acorns and access to a bird feeder (Stanback 1991), though this has not been documented in Oregon. Average nest contains 3-6 eggs (Gabrielson and Jewett 1940). Young in nest have been reported late May to early Jul (n=4) (OBBA). Fledged young typically seen from mid-Jun to mid-Jul (n=12), though they have been seen as early as 7 May and as late as early Aug (OBBA). Often observed Jul-Oct coursing back and forth across the sky carrying nuts and other mast to cache sites (*MGH*). Little is known about seasonal movement. In general, astonishingly little information is available on this common and interesting species in Oregon.

**Detection:** Large size, flashy coloration, and habit of perching prominently make this species easily spotted. Because it does not sing, it is not easily detected by cursory aural surveys, but its loud, harsh calls reveal its presence given a longer listening window.

**Population Status and Conservation:** Once common only in the s. Willamette Valley, the Umpqua and Rogue valleys, and locally in s. Klamath and Lake counties, it is now common throughout the western inland valleys and sc. Oregon, and continues to expand from its traditional range (Gabrielson and Jewett 1940, Gilligan et al. 1994). In the n. Willamette Valley this species has increased markedly since early in the 20th century when Jewett and Gabrielson (1929) reported it uncommon north of Salem and rare in the Portland area except for an established "thriving" colony on Sauvie I. They described the Sauvie I. location as marking the northernmost limits of its range. However, the 1990s brought a large increase to the Puget Sound basin, and numbers have expanded east and west along the Columbia R.

In 1940, the south coast population (formerly Nicasio Jay, *A. c. oocleptica*) had not been seen north of Pistol R., Curry Co., though it was closely watched for (Gabrielson and Jewett 1940); by 1951 it was being reported at Wedderburn, Curry Co., approximately 10 mi (16 km) to the north (Pitelka 1951); in the 1970s the limit was a few miles farther north at Nesika Beach, Curry Co. (J. Rogers p.c.); and in 1994 it was seen at least as far north as Sixes, Curry Co., another 30 mi (48 km) north (Gilligan et al. 1994).

The population of this species has not been quantitatively studied in the state, but considering the scope and success of its range expansion it is safe to assume scrub-jays in Oregon are faring well if not thriving. Human alterations such as clearing of forests have probably aided this bird by increasing areas of suitable habitat (Pitelka 1951). Areas where coniferous forests have been developed or interrupted and secondary communities of shrubs and broad-leaved trees have moved in have become especially advantageous to the adaptable Western Scrub-Jay.—*Rachel White Scheuering*

## Pinyon Jay *Gymnorhinus cyanocephalus*

The haunting cries of these wanderers evoke a variety of reactions from curiosity to wonder. Highly social, this corvid epitomizes the dynamics of flock behavior such as colonial nesting, communal feeding of young, and non-territoriality. Although Pinyon Jays are nomadic and unpredictable, each flock is a tight-knit, integrated unit occupying a home range that does not overlap with other flocks. However, flocks may wander widely outside their home range if sufficient food is not available (Balda and Bateman 1971). Historically known as Blue Crow, Maximilian's Jay, and Piñon Jay, its uniform blue color, short tail, and gregarious habits set it apart from other corvids.

**General Distribution:** Occupies pinyon pine and juniper regions of the Great Basin and the Southwest. Resident from c. Oregon, s. Idaho, c. Montana, w. S. Dakota, and nw. Nebraska south through California to n. Baja California, s. Nevada, ec. Arizona, c. New Mexico, and w. Oklahoma. Highest densities occur in the contiguous pinyon pine woodlands of Nevada, Utah, Colorado, Arizona, and New Mexico. May wander hundreds of miles outside its breeding range (Balda and Bateman 1971, AOU 1998, BBS). Monotypic (AOU 1957).

**Oregon Distribution:** Permanent uncommon to common resident in juniper and ponderosa pine woodlands of c. Oregon (Gabrielson and Jewett 1940, Gilligan et al. 1994). Oregon's known breeding population is confined to the Metolius R. drainage eastward along the s. Ochoco Mtns., south through Bend and east of Newberry Crater to Silver L. basin eastward to the Lost Forest in Lake Co. (OBBA,

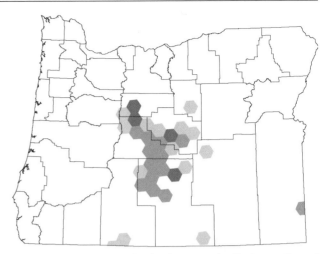

*CRM*). The largest flocks have typically been found in the Cabin L. area, Lake Co., where as many as 500 have been observed (Summers 1993b). Breeding specimens were taken from Deschutes R. and Ft. Klamath (Brodkorb 1936). In Oregon, breeding has not been documented outside c. Oregon in the last half-century, despite the intensive 5-yr OBBA. Rare in the Klamath Basin during breeding season (OBBA, K. Spencer p.c., S. Summers unpubl. data). However, breeding occurs just south of the Klamath Basin in n. California (BBS). A pair observed near Juniper Point south of Jordan Valley in se. Oregon in Jun 1998 was nearer to the populations found in n. Nevada and sw. Idaho than to the c. Oregon population (OBBA, BBS, L. Fish p.c.).

Outside of the breeding season, the range of the Pinyon Jay regularly expands east to Sage Hen Ridge in Harney Co., north to northern foothills of the Ochocos, west to e. Cascade foothills west of Madras, and south to the north edge of the Summer L. basin (*CRM*). Very rare from the Malheur-Harney Basin eastward (Littlefield 1990a). On 18 Oct 1987, one was found well east of its range at Calamity Butte north of Burns. Uncommon and local in the Klamath Basin and sc. Oregon contiguous with northern limit of California population (BBS, OBBA, K. Spencer p.c.). Several large flocks have been observed during Jun on the road between Silver L. and Klamath Marsh (H. Nehls p.c.), and there are two records of individuals near the Sycan Marsh (S. Summers unpubl. data). The highest elevation at which one has been recorded was 8.060 ft (2.480 m) on Garfield Peak at Crater L. NP, Sep 1990 (Anderson 1991a).

Occasional west of the Cascades. Two were in Salem on 21 Dec 1910 (Gabrielson and Jewett 1940). One was collected from a flock of 300 at Gaston, Washington Co., 8 Jan 1936 (Du Bois 1936). Fall 1987 was remarkable for three records: a flock of 40 visited Tiller in the s. Umpqua R. drainage on 16 Sep; one was at Howard Prairie Res. in the sw. Cascades on 4 Oct; and one was northeast of Lebanon on 15 Oct (Heinl 1988a). Additional records from sw. Oregon include eight at Emigrant L. area in the Rogue Valley on 6 Dec 1990 to early Mar 1991 (Johnson J 1991b, Janes et al. 2001), and one in junipers 22 Sep 2001 at Hobart Bluff in the Cascade-Siskiyou National Monument of se. Jackson Co. (Contreras 2002b).

**Habitat and Diet:** Resides in juniper, juniper-ponderosa pine transition, and ponderosa pine edge forests (Gabrielson and Jewett 1940, Ryser 1985, *CRM*). Occurs in pinyon pine woodland over most of its continental range, but this habitat does not exist in Oregon; thus, relevance of studies in this habitat to Oregon populations is unknown. Nests are built by the male and female at a height of 3-85 ft (1-26 m), but usually 8-20 ft (2.5-6 m) in a juniper or pine (Braly 1931, Bent 1946). Nest consists of a "bulky mass of twigs and bleached grasses, well lined with wool, moss, hair, and feathers" (Gabrielson and Jewett 1940).

Pinyon Jays often feed on the ground in leapfrog fashion, where the rear of a flock will fly over the flock and drop down at the front (Ryser 1985). Eat nuts, seeds, or young tender cones of ponderosa pine, wild fruits including juniper berries, various seeds, grain, grasshoppers, beetles and other insects, eggs, and young of small birds (Bent 1946, Ryser 1985). When plentiful, pine nuts are cached where snow is most likely to melt first: on the south side of trees, on south-facing slopes, and open windy areas. (Balda and Bateman 1971, Vander Wall and Balda 1981). This remarkable food-storer may carry as many as 40 pine nuts in its esophagus to deposit at a single cache (Balda and Bateman 1971, Vander Wall and Balda 1981). Extent of dependence on juniper berries is unknown. During winter snow may be the sole source of free water (Balda and Bateman 1971).

**Seasonal Activity and Behavior:** Little is known about the biology of Oregon populations. They spend most of the year in nomadic flocks of up to several hundred; thus, Pinyon Jays may be found in numbers one season and absent the next. In an Arizona study, the home range of one flock was at least 8 mi² (20 km²). Home ranges are not defended and can change depending on food availability (Balda and Bateman 1971, Marzluff and Balda 1992). Monogamous; pairs remain bonded year-round and for life (Balda and Bateman 1971, Ryser 1985). Courtship and pair formation of unmated birds begin in winter or early spring, although most yearlings do not mate (Ryser 1985, Marzluff and Balda 1992). Breeds in loose colonies (occasionally in pairs) from Apr through Jul (Braly 1931, OBBA, *CRM*). Early breeding (during Feb and Mar), reported as typical elsewhere (Vander Wall and Balda 1981), has not been observed in Oregon (OBBA, *CRM*).

Colonial nesting is closely synchronized so that most eggs hatch about the same time, and all young fledge within a week of each other (Balda and Bateman 1971, Marzluff and Balda 1992). Clutch size 2-5, usually four. Incubation lasts about 17 days and young fledge about 3 wk after hatching (Bateman and Balda 1973, Marzluff and Balda 1992). Male feeds female during incubation and feeds female and young the first few days after hatching. Subsequently, young are fed by both parents, sometimes assisted by kin during the last few days in the nest and for about 3 wk after fledging (Marzluff and Balda 1992). Vocal communication is sophisticated, consisting of at least 15 distinct calls, but this species does not have a "song" per se, or a territory (Balda and Bateman 1971, Ryser 1985, Marzluff and Balda 1992). Calls are individually recognized within a flock, and birds can discriminate between calls of their own flock and those of others (Marzluff and Balda 1992). Most extralimital records are during the fall and winter.

**Detection:** Pinyon Jays are found most easily during the postbreeding season when young are still confined to nesting areas. Flocks become nomadic as young become independent, and location becomes unpredictable throughout the fall and winter. During breeding season they can be difficult to find because of decreased vocalizations and lack of territorial song. Excellent locations to find this species include Bend, Cabin L., and Lost Forest, Lake Co.

**Population Status and Conservation:** BBS trend data indicate an annual 3.5% decline throughout its range 1966-99 (Sauer et al. 2000). Oregon's population density is low compared to the majority of its range, which is dominated by pinyon pine. Isolation from core population accentuates vulnerability. BBS trend data are unavailable for Oregon due to limited range and habitat. Usually found only on the Deschutes BBS route in n. Deschutes Co. Although Gabrielson and Jewett (1940) considered numbers "abundant" in Klamath Co., their present status in this region is greatly decreased (OBBA, K. Spencer p.c.). In an Arizona study, nest predation by corvids (American Crows and Common Ravens) caused the highest mortality in its life cycle. Increased crow and raven populations due to human population expansion and open landfills resulted in a decline in flock size over a 12-yr period (Marzluff and Balda 1992). Effect on population of juniper expansion over the past 150 yr has not been studied. Conversely, the consequences of large-scale juniper removal in the breeding range has not been monitored.—*Craig R. Miller*

**Clark's Nutcracker** *Nucifraga columbiana*
On his historic expedition with Meriwether Lewis, Captain William Clark, the bird's namesake, first mistook this species for a woodpecker (Cutright 1969), undoubtedly because of its long, sharp beak. However,

this most specialized member of the N. American crow family uses this apparatus to pry loose its favored seeds from unrelenting cones of several pines, with which the nutcracker has a symbiotic relationship. The whitebark pine, in particular, is totally reliant on Clark's Nutcrackers for seed dispersal and germination (Lanner 1996). Planted by nutcrackers on high, treeless, windswept slopes, these pines ultimately provide shade for hemlock, fir, and spruce establishment, and habitat for many other plants and animals (Lanner 1996). Because their seed-storage behavior affects tree and cone morphology, forest distribution, and population structure, nutcrackers are thought to be keystone mutualists or builders and manipulators of subalpine ecosystems (Lanner 1996). Oregon hikers and mountaineers enjoy the flashing black-and-white wings and tails of these striking ash-gray birds, undulating woodpecker-like in flight, gliding over alpine ridges or fanning over montane forest far below after a wings-folded plummet (Gabrielson and Jewett 1940, Farner 1952, Bent 1946). But few recognize the ecological and artistic service of these raucous caretakers of our most scenic vistas.

**General Distribution:** From Tomback (1998). Resident in mountains of nc. and s. British Columbia, sw. Alberta, and w. U.S. including Rocky, Cascade, Klamath, Warner, Sierra Nevada, and isolated mountains with a disjunct population in Cerro Potosí, Nuevo León, Mexico. Irregular and irruptive, especially in fall and winter, in other mountainous areas (e.g., Olympic Mtns. [Contreras 1997b]) and lower elevations from c. and s. Alaska, along w. coast to Baja California, Mexico, east to the Great Plains and south to Nuevo León. Monotypic (AOU 1957).

**Oregon Distribution:** Resident along the crest of the Cascades, usually above 4,000 ft (1,200 m), lower on the east slope, from the Columbia R. south to the California border, west into the Siskiyous, and east to the Warner Mtns., northeast throughout the Blue and Wallowa mountains (Gabrielson and Jewett

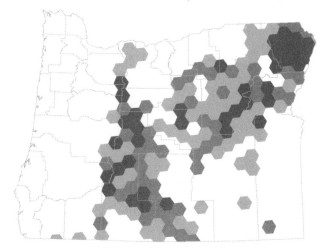

1940, McAllister and Marshall 1945, Browning 1966b, 1975a, Fix 1990a, Evanich 1992a, Summers 1993a, Gilligan et al. 1994), and in the Ironside Mtn./Castle Rock area of Malheur Co. (Contreras and Kindschy 1996). Usually uncommon where resident but common to very common at Crater L. (Farner 1952). In the Blue Mtns., this species is much more common in the drier e. and s. Blues than in the wetter nw. slopes of the Blues north of about Pilot Rock (M. Denny p.c.).

Away from the areas described above, the species is irregular (especially higher points along the Coast Range) and/or irruptive, especially in fall and winter of poor cone crop years, to nearly any part of the state including valleys, basins, coastal areas and major metropolitan areas (Gabrielson and Jewett 1940, Watson 1982, Littlefield 1990a, Contreras 1998, Herlyn 1998, Hunter et al. 1998). Appears not to be resident on Steens Mtn. (Gabrielson and Jewett 1940), likely owing to the absence of pines, but has occurred there as a transient (*DBM*). Observations 19 Jun 1998 and 1 Jul 1999 in the Oregon Canyon Mtns., Malheur Co. (Adamus et al. 2001), are intriguing, but their status is unknown.

**Habitat and Diet:** Breed in open coniferous subalpine forests of pine, spruce, fir and adjacent Douglas-fir above 4,000 ft (1,200 m) during summer, and less often in juniper and ponderosa pine east of the Cascades. They move to lower elevations erratically in winter (Gabrielson and Jewett 1940, Evanich 1992a, Csuti et al. 1997, Tomback 1998). Nest (4 in/11 in [11 cm/29 cm] inner/outer diameter, 3 in/6 in [8 cm/15 cm] inner/outer depth) of Douglas-fir, incense-cedar, or juniper twigs lined with fine strips of bark, grass, moss, animal hair, or mineral soil. In Oregon, diet includes ripe and unripe seeds of whitebark, limber, Jeffrey, and ponderosa pines, Douglas-fir, and Shasta red fir; in addition, black twinberry, spiders, insects, small mammals, carrion, garbage, and offerings from people are taken (Gabrielson and Jewett 1940, Farner 1952). Elsewhere also piñon, bristlecone, and southwestern white pines (Tomback 1998). Large, wingless seeds of white pines are preferred (Lanner 1996, Tomback 1998).

Clark's Nutcrackers extract seeds from cones and transport large loads (Tomback 1978, Vander Wall and Balda 1981) in a sub-lingual pouch (Bock et al. 1973), an ability shared only by their congeneric relative, the Spotted Nutcracker of Eurasia (Tomback 1998). Maximum pouch capacity is >=1 oz (30 g or 28 ml) or 20% of a bird's weight (Vander Wall and Balda 1981), e.g., 35-150 whitebark pine nuts (Tomback 1978), delivered 0-13.6 mi (0-22 km) from parent tree before caching. Nutcrackers typically cache 1-15 seeds 0.5-1.5 in (1-3 cm) deep in mineral soil or crevices by pushing the seeds individually into the ground or crevice with their bill tip or by digging a small trench with their beak. Individuals may store 7,400-98,000 seeds/yr (Tomback 1998), an amount that may exceed their energetic needs by >3 fold (Vander Wall and Balda 1977, Tomback 1982). Nutcrackers have a remarkable spatial memory that allows retrieval of items from tens of thousands of caches known only to the storing individual or observant corvid thieves (Farner 1952, Vander Wall and Balda 1977, Hutchins and Lanner 1982, Tomback 1982, Vander Wall 1982, 1988, 1990, Balda and Kamil 1989, 1992, Kamil and Balda 1990, Dimmick 1993). Some caches lead to clumped stem morphology of mountain-dwelling pines (Linhart and Tomback 1985, Furnier et al. 1987, Carsey and Tomback 1994, Lanner 1996).

**Seasonal Activity and Behavior:** Courtship commences as early as Dec through Apr. Nests are built mid-Mar to mid-Apr, near seed caches of the previous fall, in outer horizontal branches at a fork on the leeward side 6-79 ft (1.8-24 m) high. Two days after nest construction, 2-5 pale green eggs are laid, 1/day. Incubation takes about 18 days and is accomplished by both adults (approximately 80% by the female), each with a brood patch. Nestlings are fed lubricated, shelled seeds from previous fall's caches, as well as insects and arthropods. They fledge at 20 days, remain in family groups until 3.5-4 mos old, and are fed seeds from caches and the new cone crop by adults until late summer. Gathering and storage of conifer seeds at the highest forested elevations begins before cone maturation in summer and continues into early winter on open windswept slopes, and later at lower elevations. Cone crop size affects breeding attempts, nest success, and seasonal movements (Tomback 1998). An individual banded at Crater L. NP on 1 Sep 1950 was recovered 16 Oct 1950 on Mt. Adams, in the s. Washington Cascades (Farner 1952). Another bird banded at Crater L. NP 4 Aug 1952 was recovered there 13 Nov 1969 (Clapp, Klimkiewicz, and Futcher 1983).

**Detection:** Except when near nest, nutcrackers are vociferous, bold, and conspicuous. They most frequently give *kra-a-a* or *char-r-r* (Bent 1946) calls but, like other corvids, have an extensive vocal repertoire (Tomback 1998). Most easily observed at Crater L. N.P., which offers an excellent combination of conditions.

**Population Status and Conservation:** Because Clark's Nutcrackers reside in places we value for scenery, solace, and wilderness, one would think them immune to our influence, perhaps more than any other native N. American bird. But these adaptable birds capitalize upon the habits of humans by utilizing refuse, handouts, and carrion. Not all influence of Euro-American settlement has benefited nutcrackers.

Introduced white pine blister rust continues to devastate whitebark pine throughout much of the tree's range (Tomback 1998) though infection and mortality is lower in Oregon, thus far, than in Washington and Idaho (Kendall 1995). While the pine appears entirely dependent on Clark's Nutcrackers (Lanner 1996) the reverse cannot be said because of the bird's dietary opportunism. Nevertheless, the extent of mutualism between the tree and bird (Lanner 1996, Tomback 1998) clearly predicts an effect on nutcracker numbers, behavior, distribution, and seasonal movements where these forests are lost or damaged by the fungus. Optimistically, should any whitebark pines prove blister-rust resistant, Clark's Nutcrackers will probably be the first to find out and the first to begin this pine's reestablishment because of their propensity to find, distribute, and cache its seeds.—*Keith Swindle*

## Black-billed Magpie *Pica hudsonia*

This is one of the most audacious of Oregon's resident avifauna both in appearance and behavior. Its black coat and streaming tail dappled in blue-green iridescence contrasts starkly with its flashing white wing feathers during flight. Common and conspicuous east of the Cascades, the magpie prefers open areas stippled with dense thickets or trees. They are highly social, often gathering in large flocks. Historically despised and persecuted by hunters, farmers, and ranchers, this trickster has flourished in the tradition of the coyote.

**General Distribution:** Resident range apparently disjunct. Northern region includes s. coastal Alaska southward to sw. Yukon and northwest corner of British Columbia. Southern region includes c. and sc. British Columbia, eastward to eastern edge of Manitoba south to ec. California and eastward including n. Arizona and New Mexico to Kansas, Nebraska and N. Dakota. Notably absent from moist regions west of the Cascades of the Pacific Northwest and Sierra Nevada

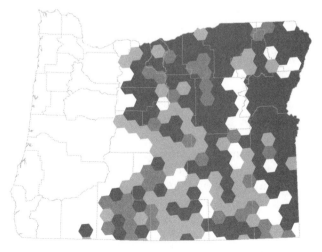

*Black-billed Magpie*

of California (AOU 1998, Trost CH 1999). Eurasian and N. American magpies recognized (AOU 1998) as *P. pica* are two separate species (AOU 2000). The N. American species, *P. hudsonia*, is monotypic.

**Oregon Distribution:** Widespread and common resident east of the Cascades except in coniferous forests and in extreme se. Oregon, where rare. Very uncommon but regular visitant in the Rogue Valley (Gilligan et al. 1994, *CRM*); breeding documented in 1999 (OBBA). About 20 records throughout the Willamette Valley since 1970 (*CRM*). The species is sometimes kept as a pet, thus some records may represent released or escaped birds. There have been at least four coastal records including a "small flock" 8 Oct 1919 in Blaine, Tillamook Co.; 1-4 from 12 Jul to 15 Aug 1982 at Thornton Cr, Lincoln Co.; one at Cape Meares 7 Mar and possibly the same bird again at Manzanita 29 Mar 1988, Tillamook Co. (Gabrielson & Jewett 1940, Heinl 1989a, *CRM*).

**Habitat and Diet:** Predominantly occurs in dry, cold, steppe regions (Linsdale 1946, Cramp and Perrins 1994). Occupies a wide variety of habitats typified by open country including ranch and agricultural lands, juniper woodlands, sagebrush steppe, and open meadows with riparian thickets. Breeds in thickets associated with open areas (Trost CH 1999). Streamsides and other wet areas (e.g., stock ponds) with riparian thickets may be especially important (D. Irons

p.c.). Preferred nest site is in a dense tree or shrub such as juniper, alder, birch, or willow (Linsdale 1946, Littlefield 1990a, *CRM*). The Russian-olive may be the most used species at lower elevations in e. Oregon (M. Denny p.c.). Nest is a domed woven-twig structure about 30 in (75 cm) high by 20 in (50 cm) wide, with entrance on the side (Trost CH 1999). Built from Mar to May, it takes about 43 days to construct, and consists of mud anchor, twig superstructure, mud bowl, and grass lining (Linsdale 1946, Trost CH 1999). May be reused or built on top of previous year's nest, sometimes resulting in a very large structure if reused multiple times such as one in Washington measuring 7 ft (2.15 m) in height (Linsdale 1946).

Like many other corvids, is an omnivorous scavenger. Unique to N. American corvids, insects constitute largest portion of diet (Linsdale 1946), but also includes carrion, small mammals, seeds, and fruit depending on availability and season (Kalmbach 1927, Trost CH 1999). Primarily forages on the ground. Also gleans ticks and other external parasites from ungulates such as elk, deer, and livestock. Has been reported to eat flesh from open sores or cuts of livestock, sometimes so persistently as to cause death (Linsdale 1946, Ryser 1985). Caches food at scattered locations (Trost CH 1999). Forms and regurgitates pellets depending on diet (Reebs and Boag 1987, Trost CH 1999).

**Seasonal Activity and Behavior:** Resident throughout its range, although postbreeding and winter movements can be extensive. Spring "migration" to breeding sites is usually in progress by Feb and extends into Apr (Littlefield 1990a). Vocalizations are harsh call notes, varying in intensity and length depending on degree of excitement or alarm (Birkhead 1991). Male dominance is usually correlated with bill length (Moholt 1989). Nonbreeding birds may constitute as much as 40% of magpie population during the breeding season but have been little studied (Birkhead 1991).

Territoriality is either nonexistent or minimal (Birkhead 1991). Where resource abundance permits, nests are closely spaced, almost colonial (Stone 1992, Trost CH 1999). Female triggers male courtship by calling loudly and frequently while near the nest. Courtship consists of male flashing wings and holding flared tail high while circling female. Pairs often remain together for life and return to the same nest site year after year (Buitron 1988, Trost CH 1999). Lay 4-9 glossy grayish, tan, or olive brown eggs variably marked with brown speckles (Gabrielson and Jewett 1940, Buitron 1988, Birkhead 1991). Earliest laid 21 Mar, most laid Apr and early May (Gabrielson and Jewett 1940). Female incubates eggs while male feeds her (Mugaas and King 1981, Buitron 1988). Incubation period 17-21 days (Linsdale 1946, Buitron 1983). Young fledge from early May through Jul, about 24-30 days after hatching (Gabrielson and Jewett 1940, Buitron 1988, Littlefield 1990a, OBBA). Only attempts a second brood if first is unsuccessful. Young fledge 24-30 days after hatching and remain dependent on parents for another 6-8 wk (Buitron 1988, Birkhead 1991, Trost CH 1999). Young stay in parents' territory 3-4 wk after fledging, then join in a flock with 2-8 families. After young become independent of parents they may disperse individually, although young males often form flocks of up to 40 or more (Linsdale 1946, Trost CH 1999). Even during breeding season, nonbreeders often associate in social flocks (Moholt 1989).

During Oct and Nov, many adult and hatch-year birds have been observed higher up in forested drainages of the west-facing slope of the Blue Mtns. (to 5,400 ft [1,650 m]) in Washington and e. Umatilla Co., looking for and feeding on "gut piles" left by hunters (M. Denny p.c.). Although not reported in Oregon, they are known to spend winter nights in communal roosts, often involving as many as 200 or more magpies (Linsdale 1946, Trost CH 1999).

When a dead magpie is discovered, the finder gives rattle call to alert others in the area and a "funeral" ensues. A flock of as many as 40 gather, some fly to the ground and form a circle around the dead bird, call loudly, walk around the body, and sometimes lightly peck at wings or tail. After 5-15 min the gathered flock silently flies away (Miller and Brigham 1988, Moholt 1989, Trost CH 1999).

**Detection:** Raucous call, distinctive shape, contrasting color pattern and bold behavior all contribute to conspicuous presence. Particularly conspicuous during fall and winter when in flocks.

**Population Status and Conservation:** Numbers appear stable throughout its range, and on the basis of BBS data (Sauer et al. 1999) there have been no significant population trends in Oregon since 1966. Reports by several early naturalists suggest a breeding population in the n. Willamette Valley before 1900 (Jobanek and Marshall 1992). Although Gabrielson and Jewett (1940) had "numerous records of its appearance along the Columbia near Portland," lack of such records since 1940 is unexplained. Has survived well despite concerted efforts by farmers, ranchers, and hunters to eradicate by shooting, trapping, and poisoning 1925-40 (Trost CH 1999). Decreasing numbers in Jackson Co. coincide with the closure or covering of landfills (N. Barrett p.c.).

Although fully protected under the Migratory Species Act, persecution continues in some rural communities (Trost CH 1999, *CRM*). Has been observed to pick at fresh cattle brands, potentially obscuring owner identification (M. Denny p.c.). Nonetheless, human intrusion has actually solidified magpie populations thanks to ranching and agricultural wastes, open landfills, road-killed animals, and other human influences (Linsdale 1946). Magpies will avoid traps if they are observed being baited. They also recognize people who have been perceived as a threat (Trost CH 1999). Despite its reputation among many rural folk as a pest, humans ultimately benefit due to insect consumption and scavenging (Kalmbach 1927, Linsdale 1946).

Among human-caused threats are loss of riparian habitat, use of pesticides for livestock treatments, collisions with automobiles, excessive disturbance at nest sites, and continued persecution (Trost CH 1999, C. Parsons p.c.). Fatal to magpies and still in widespread use is topical application of the organophosphate famphur (Warbex®) used on cattle to control parasites. Exposure occurs from direct contact or by eating contaminated insects, ectoparasites, or hair (Henny, Blus, Kolbe, and Fitzner 1985, Dierauf 1997, C. Parsons p.c.). Mean life expectancy 2-3.5 yr, although long-term survival is much better if survives first year (Birkhead 1991, Trost CH 1999).—*Craig R. Miller*

## American Crow *Corvus brachyrhynchos*

So familiar is the American Crow that it has been said if a person knows only 3 species of birds one of them will be the crow (Bent 1946). Recognized by its coal-black plumage, fan-shaped tail, and nasal *caw* call, it is found throughout most of N. America, and its seemingly mischievious character has been immortalized in folktales and fables. For centuries crows and their habits have been judged unappealing and unworthy of respect: they are thought to be a threat to crops (thus the scarecrow), a harassment to livestock, and an enemy to nesting songbirds. Yet their depredations are almost always overestimated. Furthermore, as Henry Ward Beecher once proclaimed: "If men had wings and bore black feathers, few of them would be clever enough to be crows." These shrewd birds possess a superior intelligence and an ability to learn and make decisions (Kilham 1989, Caffrey 2000). They are also sociable, joining together in large roosts, especially in fall and winter. Able to thrive in a wide variety of environments, crows are expanding into urban areas and habitats created by farming, forestry, and other human alterations.

**General Distribution:** Breeds from extreme se. Alaska across c. Canada and south (except on Pacific coast south to nw. Washington) to extreme nw. Baja California, c. Arizona, s. New Mexico, c. and se. Texas, the Gulf coast, and s. Florida. Winters from s. Canada south throughout the breeding range. Formerly known as the Common Crow. American Crow and

Northwestern Crow are closely related and may be conspecifics (Johnston 1961). Further taxonomic work is needed. Four subspecies; *C. b. hesperis* occurs in Oregon. Nominate *brachyrhynchos* may breed in the Great Basin (Richards 1971) and may intergrade with *hesperis* in e. Oregon (*MRB*). Further work is also needed at the subspecies level.

**Oregon Distribution:** Very common resident west of the Cascades in interior valleys, urban areas, and along the coast; fairly common resident throughout the Coast Range lowlands and in the w. Cascade foothills (Gilligan et al. 1994). Abundant in the s. Willamette Valley, with records distributed evenly throughout the year (Gullion 1951). Occurs in the w. Cascades in areas where it was not present 30 yr ago, e.g., in small towns and residential clusters, e.g., Oakridge, McKenzie Bridge (*MGH*), and near Mt. Hood in Government Camp at 4,000 ft (1,220 m), on Summit Meadow, and at the Trillium L. CG (*DBM*). Farther south, a rare visitor in migration to the Diamond L. area in the w. Cascades (Fix 1990a). East of the Cascades, locally common in summer in areas of human habitation or agriculture. Common in spring and fall and uncommon in summer on Malheur NWR, with generally no more than five pairs nesting on the refuge. Overall less common on the refuge than historically though they are still abundant in summer and fall around Burns, Harney Co. (Littlefield 1990a). In extreme e. Oregon, common breeder in agricultural areas, occasional to rare in desert habitats (Contreras and Kindschy 1996). In winter mainly absent east of the Cascades except in the Klamath Basin, the Bend region, in n. Umatilla Co., and along the Snake R. (mostly from about Brownlee Dam, Baker Co., southward [M. Denny p.c.]), where they are locally common to abundant (Evanich 1984a, Gilligan et al. 1994, Contreras and Kindschy 1996).

**Habitat and Diet:** In general, use woodlands and forests near open country for nesting and roosting, and open or partly open country, such as agricultural lands, urban areas, or tidal flats, for foraging (Gilligan et al. 1994, AOU 1998). Increasing in urban and suburban areas, where omnivorous feeding habits have allowed it to take advantage of various food sources. Pairs near Burns in se. Oregon commonly nest in wooded streambottoms along the Silvies R. floodplain, or among taller trees in the town; the few that nest on Malheur NWR tend to favor willow thickets (Littlefield 1990a). Typically are absent in mountain forest, and are less abundant in arid regions, where restricted mostly to riparian woodlands and/or towns and ranches. Often nest in a crotch of a tree, occasionally on a cliff ledge, where they form a bulky mass of sticks and bark bound together with an inner layer of roots and mud to form a deep bowl lined with grass, leaves, moss, feathers, or rootlets (Gabrielson and Jewett 1940).

During the fall and winter, large, communal roosts are located in foothills adjacent to valleys, or woods in the vicinity of feeding areas (e.g., Amazon Park in Eugene), but roosting habitat has otherwise not been studied in Oregon (*MGH*).

Diet has not been studied specifically in Oregon, though it is widely known as a generalist. Will go after seeds, nuts, berries, caterpillars, frogs, mice, birds' eggs, nestlings, garbage, or carrion (Ehrlich et al. 1988). In Corvallis, birds regularly observed placing large nuts such as walnuts in crevices on streets where cars drive across and crack them open (*MGH*). Crows have also been observed in Salem to drop nuts in order to break them open (P. T. Sullivan p.c.). Both of these habits have also been observed in Portland (H. Nehls p.c.). Urban-dwelling American Crows in c. California open walnuts by repeatedly dropping them on the ground, using greater heights for nuts with harder shells, and decreasing drop height with repeated drops of the same walnut, suggesting that crows adjust for the increasing likelihood that a nut will break (Cristol and Switzer 1999). On the Oregon coast, crows have shown this prey-dropping behavior with live clams, dropping them from 50+ ft (15 m) to break the shell (*MGH*). Additionally, in a show of opportunism and boldness, individual crows in Portland have become pests at bird feeders, consuming great quantities of food in a short time (*DBM*).

**Seasonal Activity and Behavior:** As mating begins in Feb or Mar, winter roosts break up (Gabrielson and Jewett 1940). East of the Cascades, migrants begin returning mid-Mar (Gilligan et al. 1994). Average arrival date at Malheur NWR is 16 Mar, with peak migration in late Mar, and most transients are gone by mid-Apr (Littlefield 1990a). Around the state, OBBA data show nest building occurring mainly early to mid-Apr (n=10) and decreasing by late Apr (n=2), with one anomalous report for 5 Jun (OBBA). Typical clutch contains 4-8 pale green eggs, usually laid in early May (Gabrielson and Jewett 1940). Young in the nest have been observed as early as mid-May (n=2), with a peak in early Jun (n=7), and one in mid-Jul (OBBA). Most reports of fledged young have come in Jun (n=15), although they have been seen as early as late Apr (n=2) and as late as late Jul (n=3) (OBBA).

In general, by Jul family groups begin to congregate at favorable feeding sites (Littlefield 1990a). As Gabrielson and Jewett (1940) noted, "after the nesting season, the birds wander about the country feeding along the stream banks and irrigation ditches and exploring the forests or sage-clad hills for food." In Aug, flocks increase in size until late fall, when roosts reach peak numbers. At Boardman, Morrow Co., a huge summer concentration occurs (1,400 or more birds) well into Oct, where birds hunt the I-84 strip for road kills and litter (M. Denny p.c.). Autumn migration east of the Cascades peaks in Oct: most have left Malheur NWR by mid-Nov (Littlefield 1990a). Winter roosts can contain as many as hundreds or even thousands of birds, especially in colder parts of the state (Contreras 1997b). Scattered birds and small loose flocks flying toward roosts in evening are a common sight at that time of year. Flocks of up to 5,600 have been recorded for the s. Willamette Valley in winter (Gullion 1951). Gabrielson and Jewett (1940) reported that the Snake R. population, on an island near Ontario, reached 50,000 birds in some winters.

**Detection:** Hard to miss in appropriate habitat. Garrulous and somewhat raucous vocalizations, gregarious flocking habits, bold nature, and constant tolerance of benign human activity seemingly beg for attention.

**Population Status and Conservation:** From 1966 to 2000, BBS data for Oregon show a long-term increasing trend in American Crows, averaging +1.5 % per year (BBS). While Gabrielson and Jewett (1940) found it "most at home along the timbered banks of the larger streams, where it nests in cottonwoods and willows," it now clearly thrives in cities and towns as well. Their increase and establishment in urban Portland began in the 1950s and 1960s and continues today (*DBM*). Aside from occasional small-scale control efforts by farmers, American Crows as a population face very few threats in Oregon. Their adaptability, intelligence, and ability to exploit food sources in areas of human habitation virtually guarantee the continued success of this species.— *Rachel White Scheuering*

## Common Raven *Corvus corax*

This largest of corvids in the N. Hemisphere appears in the mythologies of many cultures, but nowhere has it been elevated to the level found in the Pacific Northwest. The raven was considered a god by many American Indian tribes of the region, the creator of the earth, moon, stars, and people; and a trickster who deliberately created an environment meant to make human life more difficult (Heinrich 1989). Ravens are clever, innovative, and entertaining. They quickly exploit human-created opportunities for food and shelter. Their spectacular aerial acrobatics conducted under windy or thermal conditions appear to be an act of fun. The Common Raven's plumage is entirely shiny black like the American Crow, but ravens average 25% larger, have a wedge-shaped tail, and have deeper croaks and other calls than the American Crow.

**General Distribution:** Holarctic; at least 11 recognized subspecies worldwide. Four are recognized by Pyle (1997) in N. America, although he considers the evidence for separation weak. One subspecies in Oregon (AOU 1957).

**Oregon Distribution:** Fairly common widespread resident in many habitats throughout state (OBBA). Population densities are highest east of the Cascades (Gough et al. 1998) and lowest in the western interior valleys. In the Willamette Valley, they are relatively rare in the extreme north and fairly common in the south. The subspecies *C. c. sinuatus* occurs in Oregon, although coastal birds may be intermediates between *C. c. sinuatus* and *C. c. clarionensis* according to Rea (*in* Phillips 1986). Rea places *C. c. clarionensis* along the coast of California north to Humboldt Co.

**Habitat and Diet:** East of the Cascades, the raven is common in agricultural lands, marshes, rimrocks, sagebrush and juniper steppes, and forested areas (M. Denny p.c., *MP*). It is common in all forest types in the Blue Mtns. (M. Denny p.c.). In w. Oregon, distribution is limited along coastal beaches and in agricultural areas because of the need for large trees or rocky outcrops in undisturbed areas for nesting. In mountainous areas in w. Oregon, ravens are largely associated with forest openings, lakes, highways, and recreational sites, but

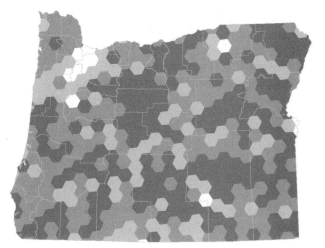

*Common Raven*

ELVA PAULSON
©1997

they occur year-round in remote areas, even in areas of heavy snow cover (*MP*). Nests, which are built of branches and twigs and lined with hair, bark, and other plant material, are built on rock ledges, in trees, windmills, and even abandoned buildings (Littlefield 1990a). Nests observed in the Blue Mtns. have been observed in grand fir, western larch, and Douglas-fir; most trees were >25 inches dbh and live (M. Denny p.c.). Nests are reused and added to in successive years. Breeding territory size has not been studied in Oregon, but ranged 11-18 mi$^2$ (28-47 km$^2$) in populations studied elsewhere (Hooper et al. 1975). Adults generally stay on their territory throughout the year.

Diet varies by season and year. Feeding concentrations regularly occur at landfills, salmon-spawning sites, livestock feedlots, and along coastal beaches where carrion is available. Take fruits and grain, small rodents, crickets, birds, and eggs according to Heinrich (1989). Analysis of 84 adult and nestling raven stomachs taken in early summer at Malheur L. found that 43 contained young rabbits (Nelson 1934). Other items included a variety of birds, small mammals, eggs, insects, and grain. It is not known what percentage of the birds and mammals in these reports constituted carrion. Maser (1975) described ravens team-hunting feral Rock Doves at Succor Cr. Canyon, Malheur Co., driving them into the water as a method of capture. Mike Denny (p.c.) has observed the species team-hunting for eggs and chicks of the Long-billed Curlew and Short-eared Owl. While live prey accounts for some of the raven's diet, especially in the breeding season, carrion is also important. Ravens are often associated with large carnivores, particularly wolves and coyotes (Kilham 1989). They commonly feed on sheep carcasses. Also, they routinely cruise beaches in search of washed-up birds, marine mammals, and invertebrates and highways for road-killed mammals, birds, insects, and amphibians. Scavenging at landfills and campgrounds are common feeding strategies that place them in association with humans (D. Fix p.c., *MP*).

**Seasonal Activity and Behavior:** Adult ravens form permanent pair bonds, and maintain a territory which they defend year-round. Breeding begins in Mar and young fledge in May and Jun (Gabrielson and Jewett 1940, Littlefield 1990a). Recently fledged young remain with parents for about 3 wk (Ehrlich et al. 1988, Heinrich 1989). Postbreeding dispersals of subadult birds spreads them out over most of the state in winter.

Subadult birds roost communally, sometimes in very large groups at well-established sites beginning in Oct with peak occupancy in Jan (Stiehl 1978). Littlefield (1990a) reported more than 800 at some communal roost sites in Harney Basin. Young et al. (1986) reported roost sites of about 2,000 along 380 mi (611 km) of power line near the Snake R. In Harney Basin, Stiehl (1981) found an average foraging radius of about 26 mi

(42 km), with some individuals foraging as far away as 300 mi (483 km) during the course of a winter.

A most curious raven feeding strategy is the practice of subadults alerting other ravens to the presence of carrion in winter. Territorial adults will defend a food source from other individuals, but will not do so if multiple birds appear. Heinrich (1989) conjectures that subadults actively call in "reinforcements" to take advantage of food sources defended by adult pairs. Feeding behavior can also often involve removing food from a site and consuming it elsewhere (*DBM*). Raven cleverness can be illustrated by an observation made by *DBM*, who observed a pair methodically removing paper litter from a garbage can at Saddle Mt. SP, Clatsop Co., to gain access to meat scraps close to the bottom of the can. Raven intelligence is the subject of a book (Heinrich 1999).

**Detection:** Large size, aerial behavior, croaking call, and numerous other vocalizations make them conspicuous and generally easy to identify. The distinctive contact calls of dependent young fledglings are among the most familiar bird sounds in Jun and Jul where ravens are numerous (D. Fix p.c.).

**Population Status and Conservation:** Gabrielson and Jewett (1940) stated that ravens only occasionally occurred in the Willamette Valley and on the coast, but may have been more common prior to Euro-American settlement. They cite early explorers who considered ravens to be common. Ravens were extensively shot or poisoned in the early part of the 20th century because of concern about predation on livestock and game birds and this was likely the cause for their decline. Since the time of Gabrielson and Jewett, populations west of the Cascades have rebounded (Sauer et al. 1997, Shipman 1998).

Gabrielson and Jewett (1940) expressed considerable concern over egg predation by ravens on waterfowl and colonial waterbirds at Malheur NWR. In a study that monitored the fate of 892 Sandhill Crane nests at Malheur NWR from 1966 through 1984, Littlefield (1985) found that the raven was second to the coyote as a predator of crane nests. Of the 399 crane nests destroyed by predators (of a total of 892), 146 were attributed to ravens. Raven-control programs have occasionally been instituted at Malheur NWR (*DBM*).—*Mike Patterson*

## Family Alaudidae

### Horned Lark *Eremophila alpestris*

Wide open spaces generally surround these sparrow-sized, ground-dwelling birds. The upperparts are mostly brownish and the underparts are generally buffy with varying amounts of yellow on the throat.

There is black on the breast and side of the head, but the most unique features are small black "horns." Females and immature birds are duller. Interesting behaviors include aerial displays and "flight songs" during courtship, and propensity to forage and loaf along dirt and gravel roads.

**General Distribution:** Breed throughout most of N. America and winter throughout most of the U.S. and Mexico (Beason 1995). Twenty-one subspecies, with three or four breeding in Oregon; possibly others present in migration and winter. Hubbard (1972) commented that the subspecific taxonomy of adults of this species is in need of a thorough revision; this remains true today (*MRB*).

**Oregon Distribution:** In w. Oregon, *E. a. strigata* breeds (based on sight records) in small, scattered populations throughout the Willamette Valley, with concentrations in the central valley on and near Baskett Slough NWR and in the Waldo Hills area east of Salem (Altman 1999b). Also a local and irregular breeding species (presumed *strigata*) on the n. coast, especially the s. jetty of the Columbia R. (M. Patterson p.c.), and on dredge spoil islands in the Columbia R. such as Rice I. (M. Patterson p.c.), Miller Sands I. (Edwards 1979), and Jim Crow I. (Dorsey 1982). There are breeding specimens of *strigata* from Linn, Polk, Clackamas, Multnomah, and Marion counties (Behle 1942) and specimens (USNM) from Forest Grove, Corvallis, and Salem (*MRB*). Formerly an abundant breeding species in the Rogue Valley (Gabrielson and Jewett 1940), with specimens from Jackson Co. (Behle 1942), and breeding confirmed as late as 1976 (*MRB*), where it now may be extirpated (O. Swisher p.c.). Two sight records in coastal mountains, possibly *E. a. strigata*, may represent migrants or breeding birds: three singing males in the Kalmiopsis Wilderness Area (Vulcan Peak), Curry Co. on 23 May (Gilligan 1993b), and two birds on Sugarloaf Mtn., Polk Co. on 15 May 1992 (Gilligan 1992b).

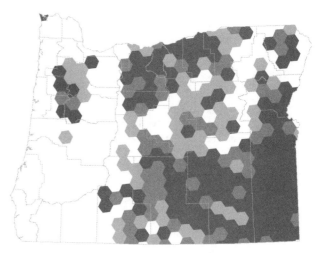

Birds observed breeding above Timberline Lodge on Mt. Hood (G. Gillson p.c, T. Janzen p.c.) have not been identified to subspecies, and possibly are *alpina*, which breeds in the Washington Cascades and Olympics (AOU 1957). A small breeding population occurred on Llao Rock at 7,700 ft (2,347 m) in Crater L. NP in 1950 (Farner 1952), from which three specimens were tentatively identified as *merrilli*. Identification by Duvall (Farner 1952) of a juvenile from Crater L. NP as more like *alpina* than *merrilli* is doubtful because subspecific characters have never been satisfactorily documented (*MRB*). It is unknown if a population persists in Crater L. NP. Juvenile Horned Larks were observed on S. Sister in Aug during several years from 1980 to 2000, indicating possible nesting, but confirmation is needed (D. Fix p.c.).

In e. Oregon, Horned Larks are found in disjunct populations centered on (often large) patches of suitable habitat. Distribution of subspecies is uncertain. Beason (1995) indicated that *E. a. lamprochroma* breeds in the lowlands (i.e., shrub-steppe and agricultural habitats) and *E. a. merrilli* breeds in intermountain valleys. Others also recognized both subspecies (Miller 1941, Behle 1942, AOU 1957). Further study of all subspecies is needed (Dickerman 1964, *MRB*). Locality and habitat data from specimens collected before 1950 by Behle and others (MVZ) are inconsistent with information summarized in Beason (1995). Although habitat may have changed, Behle (1942) should not be doubted (*MRB*). Behle (1942) listed breeding specimens of *lamprochroma* from Lake (Adel, Spanish L., and near Plush), Harney, Umatilla, Wallowa, and Baker counties, and breeding *merrilli* from Sherman, Wasco, Morrow, Klamath, and Lake (Lakeview) counties.

Migrant and wintering birds are present throughout the breeding range in Oregon except not above timberline in winter. Several subspecies, possibly groups of more than one subspecies, are occasionally seen during migration and in winter, but plumage variability and overlap makes field identification of subspecies impossible.

On the s. Oregon coast (Coos Co.), the Horned Lark is a rare but regular fall and winter visitant (Contreras 1998). On the n. Oregon coast, an annual migrant in fall and occasional (irregular) wintering species (M. Patterson p.c.). Occasional migrants reported in open habitats on Coast Range mountain tops (Gilligan et al. 1994).

*E. a. arcticola* is a rare straggler, reported as occasional in winter by Gabrielson and Jewett (1940), with specimens from Wallowa, Umatilla, Morrow, Gilliam, Baker, and Lake counties. Other specimens of *arcticola* from Ft. Klamath in Dec. (Oberholser 1902), Mt Hebo, TillamookCo., at 3,155 ft (962 m) on 4 Sep 1937 (Walker 1940), and a female from Agate Res. region in Jackson Co. on 16 Apr 1976 was identified by N. K. Johnson as an example of either *arcticola* or *alpina*, a similar subspecies from the mountains in Washington (Browning and Cross 1999). Jewett (1943) listed two winter records of *alpina* from the Blue Mtns., but did not indicate if they were sightings or specimens. There is a nonbreeding specimen of *merrilli* from Tillamook Co. (Behle 1942).

**Habitat and Diet:** In the Willamette Valley, mainly occurs in open fields with short (<1 ft [31 cm] tall), herb-dominated ground cover, significant areas of sparse vegetation, and patches of bare ground (Altman 1999b). Absent in fallow fields, where grass height is usually >2 ft (62 cm) tall due to lack of grazing or mowing. Mean territory size 1.9 ac (0.8 ha) (n=3). Territories mostly herb-dominated (83% herb cover) but with substantial amounts of bare ground (17%). Nesting habitat includes native prairie and a wide variety of agricultural lands (e.g., cultivated grass fields, row-crop agriculture, Christmas tree farms 2-5 yr post planting, plowed or burned fields, moderate to heavily grazed pastures) or non-agricultural habitats (e.g., gravel roads or gravel shoulders of lightly traveled paved roads, dirt roads, short grass adjacent to airport runways, and seasonally inundated areas where receding water levels result in dry, cracked mudflats). Foraging occurs in all of the above.

Nest sites (i.e., within 10 m radius) in the Willamette Valley (n=13) characterized mostly by herbaceous cover (62%), but with substantially more bare ground (31%) and litter/residue (11%) than present in territories, and no shrub or tree cover (Altman 1999b). Nest sites also characterized by relatively low vertical cover and nest concealment. Open-cup nest on ground, often placed in a depression such that rim of nest is at ground level. Proportional nest success 39% (n=13), but the Mayfield (1975) estimate of nest success was only 14%. Nest failures were due to abandonment (n=3), predation (n=3), and farming practices (n=2), one plowed over, and another run over by a vehicle.

On the coast and islands in the Columbia R., habitat includes estuarine tidal flats, beaches, dunes, and sparsely vegetated dredge spoils.

In the Cascades, Horned Larks use alpine and pumice habitats. The habitat of the 1950 Crater L. NP breeding population was pumice slope with a few clumps of mountain hemlock and whitebark pine (Farner 1952). On Mt. Hood, one nest found under a large rock, and two in ground-level crevices in rock outcroppings (H. Nehls p.c.).

In e. Oregon, nesting habitat for Horned Lark includes grasslands, mixed grass/sagebrush habitats, large areas of cheatgrass, herbaceous openings amid large patches of sagebrush, plowed fields, the margins of alkaline playas, and agricultural lands such as dryland wheat and ryegrass fields (Gilligan et al. 1994, M. Denny p.c.). In grasslands, they use mixed cover of bunchgrasses, especially Sandberg's bluegrass and Idaho fescue (M. Denny p.c.). In habitats with sagebrush or other shrubs, usually occur where shrubs are relatively short and/or widely dispersed. Habitat on Malheur NWR includes plowed fields, crested wheatgrass seedlings, and expanses of low sagebrush (Littlefield 1990a).

Nonbreeding season habitat is similar to breeding habitat, but includes stubble of various types of harvested fields (e.g., wheat, corn). Fledglings are often seen in groups on roads. In winter in e. Oregon when snow cover is present, they seek out wind blown sites free of snow (*DBM*).

Diet is variable, mostly animal matter in spring and summer, and seeds and waste grain in fall and winter (Beason 1995).

**Seasonal Activity and Behavior:** Limited data from w. Oregon indicate nest building takes place predominantly in mid- to late May, although second broods and renesting initiated throughout Jun (*BA*). Timing of nesting highly variable, and appears dependent on environmental factors. In both Willamette Valley (*BA*) and e. Oregon (M. Denny p.c.), spring rains and/or high water conditions delayed breeding until nesting habitat available in seasonally inundated areas. Usually 3-4 eggs/clutch; often double-brooded. Earliest reported date for nest with eggs is 3 Apr near Portland (Griffee and Rapraeger 1937), although Gabrielson and Jewett (1940) indicated that eggs were found as early as 15 Mar. Late egg dates in the Willamette Valley study include 8 and 11 Jul (*BA*). Late date for nestlings 21 Jul.

In e. Oregon, postbreeding migrant flocks begin forming in Sep on Malheur NWR and reach a peak 5 Oct-5 Nov (Littlefield 1990a). Spring and fall migrant and wintering flocks can number in the hundreds, such as 500 in Gilliam Co. (Korpi 1997), 700 on 4 Apr 1975 on Malheur NWR (Littlefield 1990a), and 1,000 at Antelope Res., Malheur Co., on 28 Aug (Sullivan PT 1995b). Flocks start to break up in Mar and by Apr most birds are paired. Influx of migrants on Malheur NWR between 10 Mar and 10 Apr, but few remain to breed (Littlefield 1990a). A flock of 10 was reported on Mt. Bachelor on 2 Sep (Sullivan 1996a).

In w. Oregon, migrant and wintering flocks are usually smaller than those in e. Oregon. Flocks are variable in size, but noteworthy groups in the Willamette Valley include 100 at William L. Finley NWR on 22 Nov (Gilligan 1999), 100 near Tangent on 19 Oct (Gilligan 1998), 110 at Ankeny NWR in Nov 1985 (Heinl 1986a), 200 on William L. Finley NWR on 14 Jan (Johnson J 1995b), and 300 southeast of Corvallis on 1 Jan (Tice 1999b).

**Detection:** In the breeding season, the distinctive songs and calls of Horned Larks are generally easy to detect in broad landscapes free of background noise. However, in more fragmented habitats, such as many areas in w. Oregon, distant vocalizations of the Horned Lark can be more difficult to detect, as they are weak in volume and high-pitched. Even when the song is heard, visual detection can be difficult because the weak sound can be difficult to pinpoint. Additionally, birds sing from the ground often hidden by vegetation or sing in the air often near the limit of human visibility. Visual detection is enhanced during nonbreeding season by the species' flocking nature, and during both breeding and nonbreeding season by the tendency to occur on roads. Snow cover, particularly in e. Oregon, tends to concentrate flocks on open ground, especially along roads, and enhances detectability.

**Population Status and Conservation:** *E. a. strigata* is listed as State Sensitive (Critical Status) by ODFW because of concerns about declining populations and habitat loss, and limited information on the status and breeding ecology of this form.

Anecdotal information indicates substantial population declines in *E. a. strigata* in the last 40-50 yr. In the 1870s, it was "an abundant summer visitor, nesting very commonly" in the n. Willamette Valley (Johnson 1880). In the late 1800s, it was "a rather common summer resident" in Washington Co. (Anthony 1886), and "not uncommon in suitable localities" around Portland (Anthony 1902). In the early 1900s, it was described as a "common resident in western Oregon and southwestern Washington" (Hoffmann 1927). In the 1930s, it was a "common breeding bird of the open fields in western Oregon, and particularly abundant in the rolling open hills of Polk and Yamhill Counties and in the great, flat pastureland area of Linn, Lane, and Benton Counties, and equally abundant in the rocky grasslands east of Medford, Jackson County" (Gabrielson and Jewett 1940). In the early 1940s, the Horned Lark was regularly found in agricultural areas between Portland and Gresham and in the Columbia R. floodplain north of Portland (*DBM*). In the late 1940s, it was "common permanent resident" in the s. Willamette Valley (Gullion 1951). Currently, numbers encountered at localized breeding areas belie their scarcity overall; it is rare, with a total breeding population estimated to be <200 pairs (*BA*).

There is no evidence that it is currently breeding in the Umpqua Valley (R. Maertz p.c.). In the early 1970s, still considered a "fairly common permanent resident in the White City area" of the Rogue Valley (Browning 1975a), with many breeding season specimens at MVZ (*DBM*), but it has not been considered a breeding species in the Rogue Valley for the last 20 yr (O. Swisher p.c.). The most recent breeding record was of adults and a fledgling 22 May 1976 near Agate Res., Jackson Co. (MVZ).

Statewide BBS trends (includes all breeding subspecies) indicate a non-significant long-term (1968-98) declining trend of 0.8%/yr, and a non-significant short-term (1980-98) declining trend of 2.3%/yr (Sauer et al. 1999). However, in the Columbia Plateau BBS Region (primarily shrub-steppe in e. Oregon) long-term and short-term trends are significantly declining (p<0.05) at 2.8 and 2.2%/yr, respectively. Data are insufficient for analysis of BBS population trends in w. Oregon. Of 11 BBS routes in the Willamette Valley, only four have recorded Horned Lark. Only the Dayton route, west of Salem, consistently records the species, and the number of birds recorded has dropped by about one-half since the late 1970s and early 1980s (i.e., approximately 20 birds/route down to 10 birds/route).

The most intensive effort to determine the breeding status of this species and several other grassland-associated species was conducted during 1996-97 throughout the Willamette Valley (Altman 1999b). Over an entire field season, <150 individuals were recorded during over 1,000 point count censuses (relative abundance=0.14 birds/point count).

Data from CBCs in w. Oregon also indicate declining populations, although subspecies composition at that time of the year is uncertain. In the Willamette Valley, the mean number of birds/count (n=6-8) has dropped from 10-12 during the late 1970s through the late 1980s down to a mean of <4 birds/count in the 1990s. In the Rogue Valley (Medford CBC), the Horned Lark was recorded nearly annually from the late 1950s through the early 1980s, but has been recorded in only 3 yr since 1983. In e. Oregon, it is recorded irregularly on several counts, but most common and regular on the Umatilla Co. CBC, where the average count in the 1990s was >100 birds.

Speculation on factors contributing to the recent (last 40-50 yr) population declines include extensive loss of field habitats to urban/residential development; conversion of suitable agricultural habitat to non-suitable agricultural lands such as rowcrops, orchards, and nurseries; mortality at nests from trampling by livestock; being mowed or run over by vehicles; inundation by flooding; earlier and more frequent mowing/harvesting of fields, which can abort reproduction; increased predation levels from predators associated with semi-urban/residential habitats such as skunks, raccoons, crows, and feral and domestic cats and dogs; and potential reproductive failures from use of pesticides or other contaminants. An additional factor that may be impacting populations is a relatively high likelihood of mortality from moving automobiles because of its propensity to forage and nest on roads (*BA*).

In Christmas tree farms in the Willamette Valley, nest success is potentially compromised by the timing and extent of management activities such as herbaceous vegetation control, tree pruning, and recreation (Altman 1999b). Former nesting along coastal dunes has apparently been impacted by dune stabilization, which results in vegetation too tall for this species (Gilligan et al. 1994). Conversely, in e. Oregon, conversion of sagebrush to exotic crested wheatgrass has likely benefited this species (Littlefield 1990a).

Altman (1999b) provided a list of general recommendations for conservation of *E. a. strigata* and other grassland-associated species in the Willamette Valley. These include: modifications of agricultural practices such as delaying harvesting of fields until after 15 Jul, creating or maintaining patches of bare or sparsely vegetated ground within or adjacent to fields, minimizing agricultural field activities during the breeding season, and controlling grazing levels in pasture to manage for preferred grass heights.

Altman (2000a) provided a list of specific recommendations for *E. a. strigata* including: maintain or provide small patches of suitable habitat within native and agricultural grasslands that have 20-50% cover of bare or sparsely vegetated ground, herbaceous vegetation <12 in (30 cm) tall, and located where minimum human or environmental disturbances occur. A population objective was to establish >10 breeding populations (>20 pairs/population) in the Willamette Valley. Additionally, 11 Grassland Bird Conservation Areas were delineated in the Willamette Valley to focus conservation efforts.

Horned Larks benefit from natural events or agricultural activities that create barren or sparsely vegetated conditions (Owens and Myers 1973). In the years before and just after Euro-American settlement of the Willamette Valley, regular flooding and aboriginal burning of the prairies likely benefited *E. a. strigata*.

Creation of suitable nesting habitat in areas secure from disturbance will reduce the species' vulnerability and potentially increase nest success and population size. It also appears that suitable habitat can support relatively dense populations because of small territory size and propensity to forage communally during the breeding season at good foraging sites.—*Bob Altman*

## Family Hirundinidae

### Subfamily Hirundininae

**Purple Martin** *Progne subis*

All have cause to marvel at the sight of a gorgeous male Purple Martin. Adult males are entirely glossy bluish-purple, although they may look black in poor light. Females and yearling males are grayish below and darker above with a paler forehead and nape. The world's largest swallow, martins are uncommon in Oregon. They nest both solitarily and colonially in nest boxes specially put up for them, in crevices in human-made structures, and in cavities in snags and pilings.

**General Distribution:** Breeds from s. Canada to n. Mexico, mainly east of Rocky Mtns. Distribution is patchy in the western part of its range; along Pacific coast breeds locally from s. British Columbia through w. Washington, w. Oregon, and California to lower Baja California, Mexico. Winters in S. America. Of three subspecies, *P. s. subis* is recognized (*MRB*) provisionally in Oregon; *P. s. arboricola*, a subspecies proposed by Behle (1968) may occur in the Pacific Northwest but further work is needed for a definitive conclusion (Hubbard 1972, Browning 2002).

**Oregon Distribution:** Uncommon local summer resident, principally inhabiting the Coast Range and Willamette Valley. Locally common at Fern Ridge Res., Lane Co., at some coastal estuaries, and at numerous colonies along the Columbia R. from Hood River to Astoria (Horvath 1999). Rarely breeds in the w. Cascades foothills and in the interior Umpqua R. basin (Hunter et al. 1998, Horvath 1999). Transients are rare to uncommon in w. Oregon, and rare to very rare east of the Cascades (Anderson 1989c, Gilligan et al. 1994).

**Habitat and Diet:** Forages diurnally over open areas such as rivers, lakes, marshes, fields, and high above the canopy of forests. Often forages higher than other swallows (Brown 1997), except some Violet-green Swallows (D. Fix p.c.). Nests opportunistically in cavities in open habitats (Lund 1978, Brown 1997, Horvath 1999,). Oregon nest sites include snags in forest clearcuts and burns, snags in coastal dunes, old pilings and nestboxes along estuaries and rivers, gourds set on poles in fields, and crevices beneath docks and bridges (Fouts 1988, Horvath 1999). An inventory of known and recently discovered colonies found that 75% of pairs nested in structures specifically put up for martins, such as single nestboxes, gourds, and multi-compartment bird houses (Horvath 1999). The remaining 25% nested in other sites: under metal caps on pilings, in other human-made structures, in cavities in pilings, and in snags. All sites were quite open, at least 20 ft (7 m) from live trees. May prefer to nest over water as 70% of the colonies in 1998 were over water, but this is not an obligate requirement as some colonies were 3 mi (5 km) from open water. Prior to European colonization, martins nested predominantly in snags (Brown 1997), but in 1998, only 5% of the known Oregon population nested in snags (Horvath 1999). This decline in snag use was likely due to removal of snags by logging and fire prevention programs, and competitive exclusion from the remaining snags by introduced European Starlings (Sharp 1986, Fouts 1988).

Food habits have not yet been studied in the Pacific Northwest. In e. N. America, martins exclusively eat flying insects including beetles, butterflies, dragonflies, flies, bees, winged termites, and others, with an increasing proportion of butterflies and dragonflies later in summer (Brown 1997). No evidence exists that martins normally eat mosquitos (Kale 1968).

**Seasonal Activity and Behavior:** First spring migrants are sometimes seen in Mar (earliest arrival 5 Mar [Bayer 1995a]), but usually arrive in early Apr (Gilligan et al. 1994). Martins continue arriving until early Jun (*EGH*). Where age-specific return schedules have been studied in e. N. America, older birds precede yearlings by about 1 mo (Morton and Derrickson 1990). During late spring, older males circle high above nest sites in predawn hours and sing a far-carrying "dawn song," perhaps to attract yearlings to settle at nearby cavities (Morton et al. 1990). Coloniality in Oregon varies from solitary nesting in single nest boxes or snags, to loosely clumped pairs, to highly colonial situations with multiple pairs inhabiting a single snag or martin house (Horvath 1999). Nests are built from May through Jul, when martins can be seen bringing grass and small green leaves from nearby trees to the nest cavity. Copulation is rarely observed, and apparently occurs mainly at night within the nest cavity (Brown 1980). While usually socially monogamous (one male and one female tending a nest), cuckoldry of yearlings is common in e. N. America (Morton et al. 1990). Nests with eggs have been found from mid-May through late Jul in Oregon (Gabrielson and Jewett 1940, Horvath 1999). Clutch size is typically 3-6 eggs; mean size 4.6 (n=126) in w. Oregon (Horvath 1999). Incubation in e. N. America lasts 15-18 days, the nestling period typically 28-29 days, and one brood per season is standard (Brown 1997). In w. Oregon most young fledge in Jul and early Aug, although some nestlings are still being fed in late Aug (*EGH*). Martins begin departing soon after young fledge, and the last martins are typically seen in the first half of Sep (Gilligan et al. 1994, *EGH*).

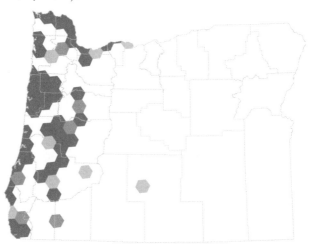

**Detection:** Martins are frequently detected by call long before they are seen, particularly high-flying individuals. Martins are most reliably seen at established colonies in spring and summer when they sing loudly and perch near the nest site. Large, easily observed colonies are found on Sauvie I. and at Yaquina Bay (Horvath 1999). In May and Jun, morning is the best time to see martins at their colonies, since they often forage far away at midday. After the young hatch in Jul, martin activity at colonies remains high throughout the day as adults regularly feed young.

**Population Status and Conservation:** Purple Martins once nested more widely in Oregon, including colonies in the upper Klamath R. basin in se. Jackson Co. (Browning 1975a), at Klamath Falls in Klamath Co. (Gabrielson and Jewett 1940, Lund 1978), and at Drews Res. in se. Lake Co. (Gabrielson and Jewett 1940). Martins nested at the end of Judah Jim St. in Chiloquin, Klamath Co., as late as 1995 (D. Fix p.c.). No martins were found in a 1998 survey of these former sites; they are apparently extirpated as breeders from these regions (Horvath 1999).

While Gabrielson and Jewett (1940) reported martins as uncommon in the early 1900s, Gullion (1951) described martins as common in the 1940s in the s. Willamette Valley. In the early 1950s, in attempt to attract martins to nest boxes in urban locations, Richmond (1953) hand-raised several chicks hatched from eggs transported from Arkansas. Anecdotal reports indicate a drastic population decline from the late 1940s to the 1980s (Sharp 1986). Early in this period, large snags (particularly on ridgetops) were removed to reduce fire danger (Richmond 1953), and in middle and later portions of this period, the European Starling began nesting in abundance (Jobanek 1993). In 1977, Lund (1977) censused 168 pairs of martins in Oregon. While he did not detail his methods or list the areas surveyed, his data are believed to reflect a reasonably thorough attempt at documenting the known statewide population. In 1998, a systematic survey (Horvath 1999) found a minimum of 784 pairs in Oregon. This probably indicates the beginning of a population rebound, likely due to installation of artificial nest structures.

Nest box installation projects begun by Tom Lund in the 1970s and expanded upon by others (e.g., ODFW, Dave Fouts, Eric Horvath) in the 1980s and 1990s are the main hope for re-establishment of martin colonies in much of w. Oregon. In areas where European Starlings are common, erection of starling-resistant nestboxes or gourds (design illustrated in Horvath 1999) will allow martins a more secure future. In areas where starlings are few (e.g., heavily forested areas of the Coast Range and w. Cascades), retention of large snags following timber harvest or wildfire would benefit martins. Indeed, if forest managers recruited more snags, the Oregon martin population might not come to nest exclusively in human-made structures as has happened in the entire e. U.S.—*Eric G. Horvath*

## Tree Swallow *Tachycineta bicolor*

A colorful harbinger of spring, the hardy Tree Swallow arrives from the south during Feb each year. It is a highly social species that is usually observed in large flocks often with Violet-green and other swallow species. It is not colonial but several pairs may nest together if available cavities are clustered. It is a bird of open places near water and is seldom seen in residential neighborhoods or built-up urban areas. It is the only swallow that eats berries and small seeds as well as insects.

**General Distribution:** Widespread breeding bird of N. America from Alaska to Labrador and south to s. California, Oklahoma, and Georgia, casual to the Gulf of Mexico. Winters from c. California and S. Carolina south to the s. U.S. and M. America; irregularly farther north. Monotypic (Browning 1974).

**Oregon Distribution:** Uncommon to locally abundant summer resident and breeding bird throughout Oregon typically near water with adjacent snags. Distribution and population levels are mainly limited by the availability of suitable nesting cavities (Robertson et al. 1992). Avoids dense woods and forests and treeless prairies. Widely scattered and local east of the Cascades due to aridity. Common to abundant migrant in all areas. Irregular in winter in western interior valleys and along the coast. Single birds were at Malheur NWR, Harney Co., 9 Jan 1958 (Marshall 1959) and 22 Dec 1980 (Littlefield 1990a).

**Habitat and Diet:** The Tree Swallow occurs in open areas with nearby trees providing nesting cavities and roosting sites. Readily uses nest boxes when available. It is most common about bodies of water and along rivers and streams, with lesser numbers in drier upland areas including mountain meadows and forest clearcuts (Robertson et al. 1992, *HBN*). The nest is placed in a natural cavity or unused woodpecker nest hole in standing live or dead trees in open areas, usually near water. It readily uses nest boxes placed in open situations. The size and shape of the cavity and type of tree species varies depending on availability. Entrance holes are typically 1.5-3.5 in (4-9cm) in diameter with the cavity 4-8 in (10-20cm) deep (Robertson et al. 1992). The nest is made of grasses and other plant material covering the floor of the cavity. The nest cup is a depression in the grass lined with feathers that are arranged so that the tips curl upward over the eggs (Tyler 1942). The cup is about 2 in (5 cm) in diameter and 0.75-1.5 in (2-4 cm) in depth (Tate and Weaver 1966).

The Tree Swallow is an opportunistic forager of insects taken on the wing from the air, and to a lesser extent from the surface of water, from vegetation, and on the ground (Hobson and Sealy 1987b, Robertson et al. 1992). Large amounts of berries and small seeds are also eaten, especially when insects are not available (Turner and Rose 1989). Gabrielson (Gabrielson and Lincoln 1953) observed a number feeding on bayberries by picking them off while darting past the twigs that held the fruits. Gnats, flies, and beetles form most of the diet, along with smaller numbers of other insects (Beal 1918). Swarming insects such as ants and mayflies are also taken (Tyler 1942). Elliot (1939) found that overwintering birds in New York had eaten crustacea, water boatmen, spiders, and bayberries, plus bulrushes, sedges, smartweed, and other seeds.

**Seasonal Activity and Behavior:** Diurnal migrant. Early birds arrive late Jan or early Feb with the majority moving through w. Oregon from late Feb to mid-Apr (Irons 1984b, Lillie 1997); east of the Cascades from mid-Mar to mid-May (Littlefield 1990a). Females tend to arrive several days after males and younger birds of both sexes several days after the females (Robertson et al. 1992). Flocks of many thousands regularly noted during spring migration.

Competition for nest sites is thought to be the underlying purpose of most Tree Swallow behavior such as early spring arrival, intense territorial defense, and strong aggressive responses to nest site competitors (Turner and Rose 1989, Robertson et al. 1992).

Monogamous. One to two broods per season. Two broods per season are fairly regular in the Willamette Valley (Gullion 1947, *HBN*). Usual clutch size is 5-7 eggs. Tree Swallows select nesting sites on arrival, but egg laying and incubation often delayed until favorable weather, at which time they synchronize laying with other pairs in the vicinity (Turner and Rose 1989). Females do almost all nest building and incubation (Robertson et al. 1992). In Oregon incubation begins during May (Griffee and Rapraeger 1937, Gabrielson

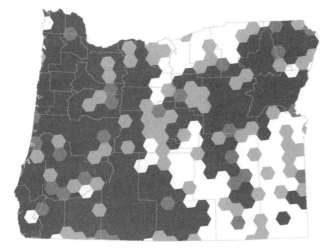

and Jewett 1940). The incubation period is about 14 days. Young fledge about 16-24 days after hatching by flying from the nest and foraging almost immediately (Tyler 1942).

After fledging, young and adults gather into flocks, with most Oregon birds moving south between mid-Jul and mid-Aug (Heinl 1988a). Migrants from farther north pass through Oregon during Aug and Sep with small groups and individuals continuing in diminishing numbers to mid-Dec. Fall flocks seldom exceed 1,000 individuals, but a flock estimated at 1,900 was at Klamath Falls, Klamath Co., 11 Oct 1997 (Sullivan 1998a).

There are numerous late Dec and Jan records but successful overwintering has not been demonstrated. In cold weather individuals will roost close together to conserve heat (Weatherhead et al. 1985), or may even become torpid (Stake and Stake 1983).

**Detection:** Tree swallows are easily detected in flight, but care must be taken to separate them from the similarly plumaged Violet-green Swallow with which they are often seen. The rich, gurgling call-notes of these birds frequently cause them to be heard before they are seen.

The Tree Swallow is unique in that the female may take 2 yr or more to acquire adult plumage, while the male molts directly from juvenal to adult plumage. Young females and juveniles are dark brownish-gray above and dull white below, and may be confused with Northern Rough-winged Swallows (Feb observations of the latter species should be closely scrutinized). A faint brown band across the breast is often dark enough to cause confusion with the Bank Swallow, a smaller species with a much more distinct breast band.

**Population Status and Conservation:** No population estimates exist for Oregon. There has been an increase throughout N. America in recent years with a range expansion into new areas, especially to the south (Robertson et al. 1992). Adverse weather can inflict high mortality, causing periodic sudden drops in breeding populations. Nest-site competition with House Sparrows and European Starlings has limited nesting by Tree Swallows in some areas (Robertson et al. 1992).

Breeding populations are limited by nest-site availability. Placement of nest boxes about wetlands, bluebird nest box trails, and even Wood Duck box projects have increased Tree Swallow populations in local areas (Holroyd 1975). This is temporary, however, and natural cavities must be provided and preserved. Management of the riparian zone around wetlands is important, as is a forest management plan that includes creating and preserving snags (Bull et al. 1980). Maintaining a high population of woodpeckers is also important in the conservation and management of Tree Swallows (Robertson et al. 1992).—*Harry B. Nehls*

## Violet-green Swallow *Tachycineta thalassina*

Dashing and darting about, flashing its bright white underparts, the Violet-green Swallow is one of the characteristic birds of summer. Unlike the Tree Swallow it commonly nests in niches and cavities on urban buildings and readily uses nesting boxes in residential areas. Its soft twittery call notes are a familiar pre-dawn sound as they fly about overhead. A very early spring migrant concentrating about streams and wetlands where emerging insects can be found until warmer weather allows them to move into more upland areas.

**General Distribution:** Breeds in w. N. America from c. Alaska and s. Saskatchewan south into Mexico. Winters s. California and s. Arizona to n. M. America, occasionally farther north. Two subspecies; the northern *T. t. thalassina* occurs in Oregon, following Phillips (1986).

**Oregon Distribution:** Common to abundant summer resident and breeding species throughout most of Oregon, although uncommon in the Klamath Basin (Summers 1993a). This swallow occurs from sea level to high peaks, and is primarily limited by availability of nesting cavities. Has nested within 200 ft (66 m) of the summit of 9,182-ft (3,012-m) Mt. Thielsen, Douglas Co. (Fix 1990a), and a pair was attending a nest at >9,500 ft (2,895 m) on Steens Mtn., between East Rim View and the summit 21 Jul 1975 (D. Fix p.c.). Although a solitary nester, it will form good-sized colonies where suitable cavities are clustered. The largest colonies are found in e. Oregon on streamside rimrock and cliffs where niches and cavities are numerous. Nesting requirements are less restrictive than for the Tree Swallow, allowing this species to be more common and widespread. Abundant migrant in all areas. Occasional in winter in western interior valleys and along the coast.

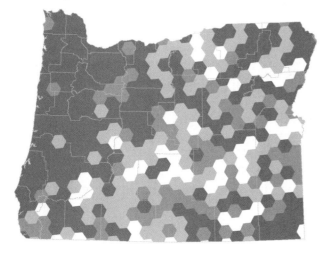

**Habitat and Diet:** Occurs in open areas with nearby trees or cliff faces providing nesting cavities and roosting sites; also about human habitations where nest boxes and niches in buildings provide nesting sites. The nest is placed in a natural cavity or an unused woodpecker nest hole in standing live or dead trees and in cavities in cliff faces. The size and shape of selected cavities are influenced by availability (Brown et al. 1992). Any darkened cavity with an adequate entrance hole or crevice seems suitable (Campbell et al. 1997). The nest is made of grasses and other plant material thickly covering the floor of the cavity. The nest cup is a depression in the grass formed with finer grasses and lined with a generous layer of feathers (Edson 1943, Campbell et al. 1997).

An opportunistic forager of insects taken on the wing. Leafhoppers, leafbugs, flies, ants, and beetles form most of the diet along with smaller numbers of other insects (Beal 1918, Bent 1942). Violet-green Swallows are distinctive for flying far higher while foraging than any other swallow (>5000 ft [1524 m] above ground level) (D. Fix p.c.).

**Seasonal Activity and Behavior:** Diurnal migrant. Early birds arrive in Feb, usually among migrant Tree Swallow flocks. The main movement occurs from early Mar through Apr. Timing and numbers involved are dependent on weather (Bent 1942, Campbell et al. 1997). Movements appear consistent on both sides of the Cascades, with larger numbers to the west (Littlefield 1990a, Sullivan 1996b, Campbell et al. 1997). Although large numbers are often observed in spring, few flocks exceed 200 birds.

Monogamous. One to two broods are raised per season (Brown et al. 1992). Two broods per season are regular in the Willamette Valley (Jewett and Gabrielson 1929, Gullion 1947, *HBN*). Usual clutch size is 4-6 eggs (Turner and Rose 1989, Campbell et al. 1997). Violet-green Swallows visit nest sites on arrival but it may be weeks before nesting begins (Edson 1943, Gullion 1947). The female does almost all nest building, incubation, and feeding of young (Combellack 1954). In Oregon, incubation occurs during May and Jun (Griffee and Rapraeger 1937, Gabrielson and Jewett 1940). The incubation period is about 15 days (Brown et al. 1992); hatching is asynchronous. Young fledge approximately 23 days after hatching (Edson 1943). Parents feed the fledglings for several days after leaving the nest (Turner and Rose 1989, Brown et al. 1992).

After fledging, adults and young gather into flocks, often mixed with other species, and almost immediately migrate. The peak of the fall movement east of the Cascades occurs during Aug-Sep; in w. Oregon it extends through Oct (Edson 1943, Fix 1985f, Heinl 1986a, Fix and Heinl 1990, Littlefield 1990a). Fall swallow flocks are often impressive, with many

*Violet-green Swallow*

thousands of birds on fence lines or on overhead wires. Violet-green Swallows are often the most numerous among these gatherings. A roosting flock of 20,000-40,000 at Rocky Point, on Upper Klamath L., Klamath Co., 29-30 Jul 1989 was primarily this species (Rogers 1989).

Dec and Jan records are few, and it is unknown if the winter visitors are resident or transient. Torpidity has been documented for this species (Lasiewski and Thompson 1966).

**Detection:** Easily observed in flight and detected by call but care must be taken to separate it from the similar Tree Swallow. High-flying individuals often go undetected unless attention is paid to faint calls or the sky is purposely searched for their presence.

**Population Status and Conservation:** The Violet-green Swallow appears to be a very stable species that apparently has changed little from historic levels. Their ability to nest both in remote cliffs and near human habitation may have saved them from harmful human impact (Erskine 1979). Nest site competition with House Sparrows and European Starlings may limit nesting in some areas (Erskine 1979). As with the Tree

Swallow, forest management plans that include creating and preserving snags are important in any conservation plan for this species.—*Harry B. Nehls*

## Northern Rough-winged Swallow
*Stelgidopteryx serripennis*

Rich, warm, unpatterned brown above and dull white below with a dusky throat and breast, the Rough-winged Swallow is inconspicuous and often overlooked when flying with other, more brightly colored, swallows. It is often confused with the similarly plumaged Bank and immature Tree Swallows. It is most often observed flying low over rivers and lakes, rarely high overhead.

**General Distribution:** Summer resident from c. British Columbia across s. Canada to New Brunswick, and south through the U.S. and Mexico to Costa Rica. Winters extreme s. U.S. to Panama. Two N. American subspecies; *S. s. serripennis* occurs in Oregon (AOU 1957).

**Oregon Distribution:** Locally uncommon to common summer resident statewide, most abundant at low to moderate elevations, usually near water. Usually nests singly, but sometimes in small loose colonies (Erskine 1979, Littlefield 1990a), rarely more than three pairs (M. Denny p.c.). Distribution is limited in many areas by lack of suitable nest sites.

**Habitat and Diet:** Nests are usually located along waterways, road-cuts, or quarries with nearby open areas for foraging. Forages primarily low over rivers, lakes, or other waterbodies. They nest in burrows in vertical surfaces, usually in clay, sand, or gravel banks, but occasionally in cavities or crevices in human-made structures (DeJong 1996). They use burrows vacated by other burrow-nesting birds or mammals, but will dig their own burrow if necessary (DeJong 1996).

The burrow entrance is usually horizontally oval with a vertical diameter of 1.6-6 in (4-15 cm);

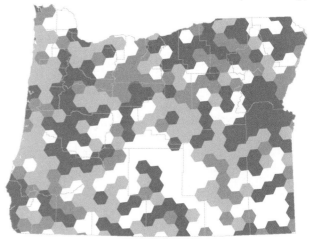

horizontal, 2-4.3 in (5-11 cm) (Campbell et al. 1997). Nest is a large pile of coarse plant material and other debris placed 1-6 ft (30.5-183 cm) inside burrow. A well-shaped cup containing finer and softer material is formed in the pile. Size and shape of nest determined by dimensions of cavity or burrow (DeJong 1996, Baicich and Harrison 1997, Campbell et al. 1997).

Takes flying insects almost exclusively, either from the air or from surface of water or ground (DeJong 1996). Ants, bees, wasps, flies, and beetles form most of the diet, along with smaller numbers of other insects (Beal 1918).

**Seasonal Activities and Behavior:** Diurnal migrant. Spring movement usually in small flocks with other swallow species. Main movement west of the Cascades mid-Mar to mid-Apr (Irons 1984b, Fix 1990b), earliest 24 Feb (Browning 1975a). They return to nesting sites on Diamond L. RD, e. Douglas Co., by mid-Apr (Fix 1990a). The main movement east of the Cascades is early Apr to mid-May, with the earliest date of detection 6 Mar (Littlefield 1990a).

Monogamous. One brood per season. Usual clutch size 6-7 eggs. Female builds nest and incubates; both parents care for young. Incubation period 15-16 days; fledge 23-25 days after hatching (Baicich and Harrison 1997). Little data on Oregon nesting. Nesting apparently begins earlier east of the Cascades than to the west. Nesting at Malheur NWR begins by May with fledged young seen in late Jun to early Jul (Littlefield 1990a). Breeding records in the s. Willamette Valley include 30 May to 10 Jul (Gullion 1951). Nest containing young at Portland 23 Jun (Jewett and Gabrielson 1929). One pair began incubation at Portland 20 Jun (Griffee and Rapraeger 1937). Young were noted in a nest at Crater L. NP 16 Jul (Farner 1952).

Postbreeding staging at Malheur NWR is evident by mid-Jul; 750 there 13 Jul 1967; a late flock of 150 there 15 Sep 1971 (Littlefield 1990a). No such large gathering has been noted anywhere else in Oregon. Southward movement begins late Jul, with most gone by late Aug (Fix 1990a, Littlefield 1990a), though individuals are noted through Sep. Latest Malheur NWR 4 Oct (Littlefield 1990a), Banks, Washington Co., 13 Nov (Crowell and Nehls 1977a). Two were at Ankeny NWR 10 Dec 2000, and one was reported at Albany 3 Feb 2001 (Korpi 2001c).

**Detection:** Northern Rough-winged Swallows are very noticeable along streams and lakes at nesting sites especially when calling, but are more difficult to distinguish when in migration and mixed with other swallow species. Care must be taken to separate this species from Bank and immature Tree Swallows.

**Population Status and Conservation:** Widespread, but unevenly distributed and difficult to estimate population. No estimates available but Oregon population appears stable. Range expansion and population increase documented in e. and c. U.S. (Robbins et al. 1986, DeJong 1996).—*Harry B. Nehls*

## Bank Swallow *Riparia riparia*

This colonial-nesting swallow places its nest at the end of a burrow dug into a soft cliff or bank. The nesting cliff often appears riddled with holes, but not all burrows are used for nesting. A highly social species, the Bank Swallow is usually observed in flocks of its own or with other swallow species. It has dark wings and tail that contrast with the paler brown back. The underparts are whitish except for a distinct brown breastband. Over much of its world range the Bank Swallow is known as the Sand Martin.

**General Distribution:** Widespread breeder throughout much of N. America, Europe, and Asia. Winters Arabia, Africa, s. Asia, and S. America. N. American population breeds from Alaska across c. Canada to Newfoundland and south to n. California, N. Carolina, and Texas. Winters in Mexico and S. America. There are four subspecies, with the widespread *R. r. riparia* the N. American breeding form (Phillips 1986).

**Oregon Distribution:** Generally uncommon, but locally common to abundant summer resident at mid- to low elevations east of the Cascades. Numerous colonies contain 10-100 pairs; a few exceed 500 pairs. Instability of nesting sites regularly forces colonies to move to more suitable nearby locations. Larger colonies often break up into smaller units (Garrison 1999, *HBN*).

A few pairs occasionally nest west of the Cascades, but most colonies are unstable and short-lived (Gabrielson and Jewett 1940, Crowell and Nehls 1969c, Browning 1975a). The only currently known colonies west of the

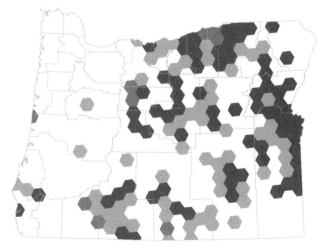

Cascades are in Curry and Clackamas counties. A large colony was present during 1987 along the Chetco R. (Heinl 1988b); by 1991 it was reduced to 7-8 pairs because of erosion of the nesting bank (Johnson J 1992a). By 1994 a large colony had formed at Nesika Beach, 5 mi (8 km) north of the Rogue R. (Tice 1999b). During the 1999 nesting season this colony contained 118 burrows and 80 birds (Tice 2000a). A small colony was observed along the Clackamas R., Clackamas Co., during the summer of 2001 (Lillie 2001), and returned there in 2002 (E. Specht p.c.). Common to abundant migrant east of the Cascades along waterways and about bodies of water. Rare migrant west of the Cascades.

**Habitat and Diet:** Nesting colonies are usually located along waterways, roadcuts, or in sand and gravel quarries where vertical cliffs and bluffs of friable, small-grained soils are exposed. Require relatively large open areas for flying space around nest burrows (Hjertaas 1984). Existing burrows may be reused in ensuing years if suitable, but many are abandoned. Average depth of 29 nest burrows in British Columbia was 35 in (90 cm); average height and width 2.3 x 2.7 in (6 x 7 cm). The nest, placed at the end of the burrow, is composed of grasses, feathers, and other plant material (Campbell et al. 1997).

Takes flying or jumping insects almost exclusively on the wing. Occasionally takes items from surface of water and ground (Garrison 1999). Ants, bees, wasps, flies, and beetles form most of the diet, along with smaller numbers of other insects. Water is also taken on the wing.

**Seasonal Activity and Behavior:** Diurnal migrant. Spring migrants arrive in late Apr with most at nesting sites by mid-May (Littlefield 1990a, Sullivan 1996b, 1997b, Lillie 2000).

Monogamous. One brood per season. Usual clutch size 4-5 eggs. Using bill, feet, and wings, the male digs the burrow (Stoner 1936). Nest building, including preparation of the burrow, takes up to 14 days (Sieber 1980). Both sexes incubate. Incubation period 14-16 days; fledge 18-22 days after hatching (Garrison 1999). Colony at Adel, Lake Co., contained full sets of eggs 26 May 1925, and a colony at Arlington, Gilliam Co., had half-grown young 6 Jun 1926 (Gabrielson and Jewett 1940). At Malheur NWR, Harney Co., young fledge late Jun to early Jul (Littlefield 1990a).

Families disperse and join flocks of other swallows soon after young fledge. Pure flocks of up to 1,000 are often seen during Jul and early Aug east of the Cascades. During Aug 1986 and 1987 up to 1.500 staged at Malheur NWR prior to departure (Littlefield 1990a). By late Jul 1989 over 3.500 were on the refuge (Anderson DA 1990c). On 28 Jul 1990 a concentration

of 3.000 was near Irrigon, Morrow Co. (Tweit et al. 1990). Individuals are occasionally observed within migrant swallow flocks in w. Oregon. Most leave the state by mid-Aug, but migrants are noted through Sep. A late bird was at Malheur NWR 1 Oct 1993 (Summers 1994a), and two were at Kirtland Road sewage ponds, Jackson Co., 8 Oct 1990 (Fix 1991).

**Detection:** Accessibility of colonies is highly variable, therefore some are easy to find and others are quite difficult. Easily observed near colonies and at foraging areas; sometimes detected by their calls. Migrants in mixed swallow flocks are often overlooked. Northern Rough-winged Swallows and immature Tree Swallows are sometimes mistaken for this species.

**Population Status and Conservation:** Accurate data on colony sizes and numbers in Oregon are lacking. Much existing data relies on the number of burrows counted at a site, or surveys taken at the wrong time of year. At most colonies up to half of the burrows are unoccupied (Garrison 1999). Malheur NWR and the vertical banks along the Snake R. around Ontario, Malheur Co., appear to have the largest populations in the state at this time (Gabrielson and Jewett 1940, Rogers 1987a, Anderson 1988d, Littlefield 1990a, Contreras and Kindschy 1996).

This species is highly adaptable and is able to withstand considerable disturbance. There is little indication that populations have dropped from historic levels; the Malheur NWR population has increased in recent years (Anderson DA 1990c, Littlefield 1990a).—*Harry B. Nehls*

## Cliff Swallow *Petrochelidon pyrrhonota*

This chunky swallow is readily recognized by its square tail and orangish rump patch. It nests colonially and has taken to human-made structures so well that it has greatly expanded its range into many areas otherwise not suitable for it. It does not do well in urban settings, however, and quickly disappears when areas become densely settled. The unique gourd-shaped mud nest is often usurped by other species for nesting and is often used for protective roosting sites by rosy-finches and other wintering species.

**General Distribution:** Breeds throughout N. America from Alaska to Nova Scotia and south into Mexico. Winters in S. America from Paraguay and Brazil to c. Argentina, casually farther north. Four subspecies; the northern subspecies *P. p. pyrrhonota* occurs in Oregon (Browning 1992a).

**Oregon Distribution:** Locally common to abundant breeding bird near water throughout most of Oregon. Largest colonies occur on cliff faces along waterways east of the Cascades. Much smaller colonies occur under bridges and overpasses and on other human-made structures. Nests rarely occur singly. Seldom nest in urban areas and rarely at higher elevations. Abundant migrant, usually following valleys and waterways.

**Habitat and Diet:** Occurs in open areas near cliffs, bridges, or other human-made structures that provide suitable nesting sites. Nearby mud is essential for nest building (Emlen 1941, 1952). In recent years nesting under bridges has been preferred over other human-made structures (*HBN*). Nest is a round gourd-like structure attached to a bare vertical surface and protected by an overhanging ledge or roof. Nests colonially with nests abutting one another, often sharing adjacent walls (Emlen 1954). Nests tend to detach and fall from surfaces too smooth or too friable for the mud to adhere (Brown and Brown 1995), if the nest is saturated with water (Brown and Brown 1989), or from vibration (*HBN*). Birds commonly reuse nests of previous years (Brown and Brown 1995). In 1987, a pair at Toketee RS, e. Douglas Co., utilized a nest constructed in 1986 that was originally a Barn Swallow nest "roofed over" in 1985 by the Cliff Swallows (Fix 1990a).

Nests are constructed of mud pellets with some plant fibers and hair added. They may have a projecting neck, which can be up to 5-6 in (13-15 cm) long, or it may be absent. Diameter of typical entrance hole is about 2 in (5 cm). Nest cavity is lined with grasses and other plant material. Nesting cup is a depression in the grass lined with fine fibers and feathers (Emlen 1954).

An opportunistic forager chiefly of insects taken from the air, rarely from the surface of water or the ground. Generally forages in groups with unsuccessful foragers regularly following successful birds to food source (Brown 1986, 1988). Ants, water boatmen, beetles, gnats, and flies were taken in one California study (Beal 1907). The type of insects taken is subject to availability (Brown and Brown 1995).

**Seasonal Activity and Behavior:** Diurnal migrant. Spring migration occurs mid-Mar to early May. Early individuals were at Malheur NWR, Harney Co., 28 Feb 1982 (Littlefield 1990a) and at Yamhill, Yamhill Co., 8 Mar 1989 (Heinl 1989b). Spring flocks seldom exceed 500 birds but an estimated 4,000-5,000 were near White City, Jackson Co., 2-4 May 1963 (Boggs and Boggs 1963c).

Monogamous. Usually one brood per season but two occasionally reported. Usual clutch size 3-5 eggs. Nest building, incubation, and feeding chicks shared equally by both parents (Turner and Rose 1989). Nesting activities synchronized within the colony (Emlen 1952, Brown and Brown 1987). Nest building observed 30 Apr-22 Jun (n=9) (OBBA); takes 1-2 wk to build, occasionally longer. Average nest contains 900-1,200 mud pellets carried one at a time from the source to the nest (Emlen 1954). Observed 5 May-29 Jun in nest (n=77) (OBBA). In Oregon incubation occurs May and Jun (Gabrielson and Jewett 1940); incubation period about 12-14 days. Young observed in nest 20 May-1 Sep, but most during late Jun (n=33) (OBBA). Young fledge about 24 days after hatching (Turner and Rose 1989). Parents feed young 3-5 days after fledging (Brown and Brown 1995).

Cliff Swallows are unique among swallows in that there is considerable brood parasitism within a colony. Residents frequently lay eggs in, or physically transfer by mouth eggs laid in their own nests to, neighboring

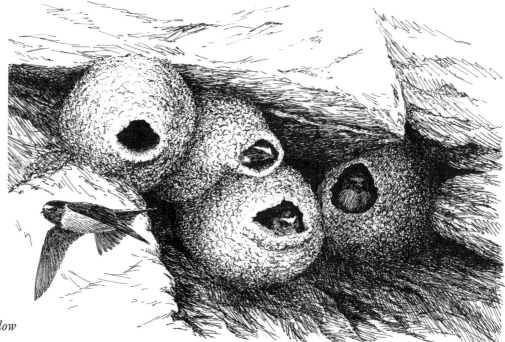

*Cliff Swallow*

nests (Brown 1984, Brown and Brown 1988, 1989). The parasites have their own nests and raise broods themselves, but supplement their reproduction by parasitizing others (Brown and Brown 1995).

After fledging, adults and young disperse from breeding areas almost immediately and gather into flocks, usually mixed with other swallow species. Fall flocks of Cliff Swallows seldom exceed 1,000 birds but 5,000 were at Malheur NWR 13 Jul 1967 (Littlefield 1990a). Fall dispersal and migration occurs from late Jun to early Sep; stragglers are noted through Oct. Late individuals were on Sauvie I., Multnomah Co., 20 Nov 1988 (Heinl and Fix 1989); at Forest Grove, Washington Co., 19 Nov 1995 (Gilligan 1996); and at Wickiup Res., Deschutes Co., 17 Nov 1996 (Sullivan 1997a).

**Detection:** Readily picked out of a large swallow flocks and easily observed at numerous bridges throughout the state.

**Population Status and Conservation:** Breeding population is difficult to census by transect methods since colonies are locally concentrated and tend to move from year to year (Brown and Brown 1995). No information on size of Oregon colonies. Widespread construction of bridges, buildings, and culverts has allowed this species to expand into areas where nesting sites not formerly available. Species overall appears to be stable or increasing throughout its range (Brown and Brown 1995). Cliff Swallows are extremely tolerant of disturbance by humans and rarely abandon their nests unless access is blocked or the nest detaches and falls (Brown and Brown 1995).—*Harry B. Nehls*

## Barn Swallow *Hirundo rustica*

"With its long, forked tail and long wings, it is the most graceful of all land birds and reminds one of the smaller terns not only in shape but in behavior" (Gabrielson and Jewett 1940). The Barn Swallow has taken so completely to nesting on human-made structures that one forgets they were once restricted to caves and rock crevices. Almost every farm in the state has a pair or two nesting in an outbuilding, and very few bridges do not have a pair or two. It is the best known of the swallows.

**General Distribution:** Widespread breeding bird throughout most of N. America, Europe, and Asia. In N. America from Alaska to Labrador and south to s. California and s. Mexico. Winters S. America, Africa, and s. Pacific. In N. America from Mexico through much of S. America to Chile and Argentina. Two vagrant subspecies to N. America (Phillips 1986). A third, *H. r. erythrogaster*, is the only breeding subspecies

in N. America (Patterson 1981, Browning and Cross 1999), and is the subspecies known from Oregon.

**Oregon Distribution:** Fairly common to locally abundant summer resident and breeding bird throughout Oregon. Restricted primarily to human-made structures, especially farm outbuildings, bridges, and homes. Uncommon at higher elevations and in vast forested landscapes where bridges and buildings or open foraging habitats are scarce. Here they are often found at resorts, lodges, and cabins near lakes (e.g., Fix 1990a). Seldom nests in built-up urban areas, likely due to lack of nearby foraging areas (D. Fix p.c.). Although not considered a colonial nesting species, its preference for nesting under bridges, especially low bridges over small streams, has created small to medium sized "colonies" scattered throughout most of the state. Very common to abundant migrant, primarily over valleys and along waterways. Numbers at evening roosts often spectacular. Rare and irregular in winter to western interior valleys and along the coast.

**Habitat and Diet:** Occurs in open areas around bridges or other human-made structures that provide vertical or horizontal walls or beams that are completely covered overhead. Nearby mud supply for nest-building is also necessary. Originally nested in caves and crevices but has moved almost entirely to human-made structures; a few still use natural sites (Brown and Brown 1999).

Nest is an open cup constructed of mud pellets with straw and grasses added for strength. If the nest is attached to a vertical surface the top rim is semicircular in shape. If built on a horizontal surface the rim is more circular (Ryser 1985). The interior cup is about 2 in (5 cm) deep and 3 in (7.5 cm) wide at the rim (Baird et al. 1875). Interior is lined with fine grasses and other soft material (Duffin 1973), and often covered profusely with feathers (Brown and Brown 1999).

This swallow forages well away from nest sites over fields, pastures, and rivers, and is the only swallow often found feeding above ocean beaches and dunes (D. Fix p.c., D. Irons p.c.). Opportunistic foragers of insects taken mainly on the wing. Barn Swallows commonly feed very low to the ground and opportunistically take insects flushed by livestock and humans walking through pastures and other grassy areas (e.g., golf courses). Seem to prefer larger, single insects compared to other swallow species (Brown and Brown 1996). Flies, beetles, water boatmen, leafhoppers, and ants are primary prey (Beal 1918) but will take what is locally available (Hoskyn 1988).

**Seasonal Activities and Behavior:** Diurnal migrant. Early individuals and small flocks arrive during Feb and Mar but remain in low numbers until main flight from late Mar through Apr (Irons 1984b, Heinl 1989b, Littlefield 1990a). Although widespread and common with some concentration about prime feeding areas, no large flocks are reported during the spring movement.

Monogamous. Two, sometimes three broods per season. Usual clutch size 4-5 eggs. Nest building, incubation, and feeding chicks shared equally by both parents, although female does most of incubation. Nest takes 1-2 wk to build. Average nest contains 750-1,400 mud pellets carried one at a time from the source to the nest (Møller 1994). In Oregon incubation typically begins in May but four nests at Malheur NWR, Harney Co., 5 Apr 1962 contained eggs and one newly hatched young (Littlefield 1990a). The nesting season is long and it is not uncommon to find young still being fed in the nest during Sep (Littlefield 1990a, Summers 1994b). Incubation period is about 14 days. Young fledge about 21 days after hatching. Family groups stay together up to 1 wk after fledging with parents feeding young and often returning to the nest (Turner and Rose 1989, Brown and Brown 1999).

Following independence, juveniles travel widely, often visiting other nests or colonies (Bell 1962). By late Jul the southward movement begins with many joining other swallow species to form large conspicuous flocks. The main movement occurs from mid-Aug through Oct with small groups and individuals noted through Nov (Heinl 1986a, Littlefield 1990a). On 21 Aug 1977, an estimated 5,000 passed south over Tillamook Bay, Tillamook Co., during a major movement (Fix 1977c).

Migrants roost in large flocks in marshes and grainfields (Brown and Brown 1999). These evening roosts are often spectacular. One such roost in use for many years south of Dayton, Yamhill Co., contains up to 500,000 birds during late Sep each fall (Fix 1987a, Gilligan 1998).

There are numerous Dec and Jan records but successful overwintering has not been documented. In cold weather, individuals will cluster together in an attempt to conserve heat (Weatherhead et al. 1985).

**Detection:** The chances of detection are very high for this conspicuous species. It can easily be picked out of a large swallow flock by its loud call notes and long forked tail. Juveniles are duller plumaged and have shorter tails but are still distinctive.

**Population Status and Conservation:** Human activity has had strongly positive effects on this species by providing abundant nesting sites, leading to a population much greater than before European settlement (Brown and Brown 1999). With conversion to human-made structures there appears to be an abundance of nesting sites, so population now is probably not regulated by nest-site availability but by

weather-related mortality (Brown and Brown 1999), and accessibility of nearby grassy/open foraging sites (D. Fix p.c.). There is no information on the size of the Oregon population but it appears to be well above historic levels and is fairly stable. Some local decreases in nesting birds have been reported in some years (*HBN*).—*Harry B. Nehls*

## Family Paridae

**Black-capped Chickadee** *Poecile atricapilla*
Noted for its familiar call, *chick-a-dee-dee-dee*, the Black-capped Chickadee is widely heralded as one of Oregon's friendliest and cheeriest residents. Even in the midst of winter, this bird "fairly overflows with good spirits" (Blanchan 1904). The Black-capped Chickadee is distinguished by a black cap and bib, white cheeks, grayish back, darker wings with "frosted" secondaries, dark tail, and tan-colored flanks. Keen observers will note the brightening of the flanks in late summer as adults acquire fresh plumage.

**General Distribution:** Resident from wc. Alaska and Canada east to the Atlantic coast and south to n. California in the west and N. Carolina in the east (Smith 1993). Ten subspecies in N. America (Phillips 1986); *fortuita* (not *fortuitus*, *Poecile* is feminine [AOU 2000]) and *occidentalis* in Oregon (Browning 2002).

**Oregon Distribution:** *P. a. occidentalis* is resident at low to moderate elevations in w. Oregon, from the Willamette Valley and coastal counties (AMNH, USNM) to Douglas Co. (USNM); *P. a. fortuita* is resident in most of e. Oregon from Wallowa L. (USNM) to Klamath Co. (OSU), John Day R. (Duvall 1945a), Enterprise, and Lostine (Behle 1951). Southeast populations assigned by Phillips (1986) to *P. a. nevadensis* were reidentified as *fortuita* by Browning (2002). Intergrades between *fortuita* and *occidentalis*

occur in Rogue R. Valley and in lower Deschutes R. basin just east of the n. Oregon Cascades (Browning 2002).

Although primarily found in suburban areas and deciduous stands in w. Oregon, also found, albeit sparingly, in young conifer forests (with deciduous component) of w. Cascade foothills (*MGH*). Fix (1990a) called Black-capped Chickadees "possibly a very rare permanent resident" of the Diamond L. RD of ne. Douglas Co. Black-caps are considered common in deciduous and suburban areas of ne. Oregon (Evanich 1992a). They are relatively uncommon in grand fir forests of the Blue Mtns. (R. Sallabanks p.c.). They occur as far south as Jordan Valley in Malheur Co. (Contreras and Kindschy 1996). They are not reported from the Fremont NF (McAllister and Marshall 1945) or Sycan Marsh, Lake Co. (Stern, Del Carlo, et al. 1987). Summers (1993a) reported only two sites in the Klamath Basin, but recent sightings suggest more widespread distribution and breeding in the area, likely uncommon along the edge of Upper Klamath L. and Link R., and rare along Lost R. (K. Spencer p.c.). This species is absent in the high Cascades, the treeless areas in the southeast quarter of the state, and deep in conifer forests or high-elevation aspen groves of e. Oregon.

**Habitat and Diet:** Mostly restricted to hardwood-dominated habitats, typically valley bottoms, coastlines, suburban areas, and river corridors in w. Oregon; rarely detected in conifer-dominated sites even at low elevations. Commonly seen at Oregon white oak and cottonwood/willow banding stations in the Willamette Valley (J. Weikel p.c.). Considered abundant and permanent residents of low-elevation Oregon white oak woodlands (Anderson SH 1970, Anderson 1972, Hagar and Stern 2001). In the Klamath Basin, nests have been found in former woodpecker cavities in willow and juniper trees, generally within older willow communities, sometimes including some quaking aspen and black cottonwood (K. Spencer p.c.).

A chickadee study in Portland and Eugene (mostly Chestnut-backed Chickadees, but including 11 Black-capped Chickadees) found that nesting materials were identical between the two species with nests being constructed of mosses, and lined with fur and occasionally with feathers (Gaddis undated [b]). Studies outside of Oregon indicate that nests are excavated by both sexes in partially rotted wood 4-15 ft (1.2-4.6 m) above the ground, but nest contents are arranged exclusively by the female (Forshaw et al. 1994). The species readily uses artificial nest boxes (A. Reid p.c., *DBM*).

The Black-capped Chickadee is omnivorous. Little documentation of foraging habits is available from Oregon, but studies elsewhere estimate that the diet in the breeding season is 80-90% animal (mostly caterpillars; also spiders, small snails and slugs, and centipedes) and 10-20% seeds and fruits, including blackberries, honeysuckle, and blueberries as available (Smith 1993). In the nonbreeding season, the diet may be approximately 50% animal (mostly insects, spiders, and insect eggs and pupae) and 50% plant (primarily seeds, including goldenrod, ragweed, hemlock, and bayberry when available) (Smith 1993).

Studies conducted in other states have found Black-capped Chickadees expert at caching food and remembering the location (Barnea and Nottebohm 1995), and have documented the species as one of the most common and persistent feeder birds, obtaining 21% or more of daily requirements from seeds provided at feeders (Brittingham and Temple 1992b). Supplemental seed at feeders, especially in autumn and winter, increases body mass and overall survival rates (Brittingham and Temple 1988), and does not appear to promote dependency (Brittingham and Temple 1992a).

**Seasonal Activity and Behavior:** There is no obvious courtship stage. Pairs break out of winter flocks for breeding in Mar-Apr (as early as mid-Feb [D. Irons p.c.]) and become intolerant of other chickadees. Female may be approached by the male as she displays wing-quiver. Nest building observed in n. Willamette Valley and Lane Co. begins in late Mar or early Apr with egg laying starting in early or mid-Apr (Gaddis undated [b]). Observations have been reported of nest building, nest and eggs, or birds entering or leaving a probable nest site 16 Apr to 25 Jun (n=43); nestlings 14 May to 29 Jul (n=62). One brood per year is normal, but two broods have been observed (A. Reid p.c.).

Black-caps form loose flocks in winter with flock sizes, population density, and home range size sensitive to available food (Smith and Van Buskirk 1988). Flocks commonly overlap favored foraging areas but engage in few agonistic interactions, reflecting the ability to space themselves when possible (Desrochers and Hannon 1989). In winter, they often form the nucleus of mixed-species flocks that include Hutton's Vireos, creepers, warblers, woodpeckers, kinglets, nuthatches, and Townsend's Warblers (*NKS*). In order to survive cold winter climates, Black-capped Chickadees do not increase body mass or fat stores but are able to enter a state of regulated hypothermia that can reduce nighttime energy expenditure by 32% (Cooper and Swanson 1994).

**Detection:** Easily located by listening for calls and songs. Readily attracted to sunflower seed and suet at bird feeders. Responds emphatically to imitations of owl sounds and often to spishing. An observer may be rewarded by discovering an interesting menagerie of birds moving and feeding together (*NKS*).

**Population Status and Conservation:** CBC data indicate stable populations for Oregon (Brennan and Morrison 1991). BBS trends show slight declines in w. Oregon over the past 30 yr and small declines or increases in patches elsewhere in the state (Sauer et al. 1999). Riparian destruction in e. Oregon probably has resulted in population declines there over the past 100 yr or more. Riparian destruction in w. Oregon also has impacted Black-capped Chickadee habitat, but this may have been offset by creation of habitat in suburban areas. Winter bird feeders are seen as an important component of chickadee "habitat" in suburban areas, especially when temperatures become extremely cold and when natural food supplies may be too widely dispersed or too scarce (Brittingham and Temple 1988, 1992a, 1992b).—*Noah K. Strycker*

### Mountain Chickadee *Poecile gambeli*

An acrobatic flier with a dashing white eye-stripe, the Mountain Chickadee is a common year-round resident of Oregon's high-elevation coniferous and mixed forests. Like its better-known relative, the Black-capped Chickadee, this species has a black cap and bib, whitish cheeks, and grayish back, wings, and tail. This species is distinguished from other N. American chickadees by its white eyebrow, gray flanks, and gray undertail coverts, and by its drawling, hoarse-sounding *chick-a-dee-dee-dee* call.

**General Distribution:** Confined to middle to high elevations in Washington, Oregon, Idaho, California, Montana, Wyoming, Utah, Colorado, New Mexico, and Arizona (McCallum et al. 1999). Six subspecies; *abbreviatus* (with *grinnelli* as a synonym [Snow 1967, *MRB*]) and *inyoensis* in Oregon.

**Oregon Distribution:** Resident in all types of forests from 2-10 mi (3.2-16 km) west of the Cascades summit and east, in the Blue, Siskiyou, Wallowa, and Warner mountains, and on Hart Mtn., Steens Mtn., and other isolated mountains east of the Cascades (McCallum et

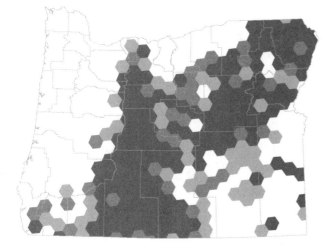

al. 1999). *P. g. inyoensis* in extreme se. Oregon. *P. g. abbreviatus* in the Cascades, possibly Siskiyou Mtns. (AMNH, *MRB*) and northeast counties including Umatilla, Union, Wallowa, and Baker (Behle 1956). Both subspecies winter in their breeding range but may move to lower elevations. Only *abbreviatus* found in coastal localities (Behle 1956). Subspecies limits poorly known and require further study (*MRB*).

Most abundant permanent resident and one of the most abundant breeding species in Crater L. NP (Farner 1952). Abundant resident in the eastern one-third of the Diamond L. RD of ne. Douglas Co.; western limit imperfectly known but probably most common nesting in pine-dominated stands (Fix 1990a). One of the most common species detected in Fremont and Winema NFs of c. Oregon (McAllister and Marshall 1945, Arnett et al. 2001). Very common in grand fir forests of the Blue Mtns. (Sallabanks et al. 2002), and common at Sycan Marsh of sc. Oregon (Stern, Del Carlo, et al. 1987). Breeds throughout Malheur Co., mainly at higher elevations; common in pine and mixed forests in northwest corner of the country, but also breeds in aspen on mountains and in riparian zones in desert canyons (Contreras and Kindschy 1996).

The Mountain Chickadee is a sporadic visitant to Malheur NWR, mostly in scattered localities including the headquarters and the willow-bordered watercourses and juniper woodlands of the s. Blitzen Valley (Littlefield 1990a). They irregularly occur in western valleys in very small numbers in winter (*DBM*), and in irruption years, tens of birds are reported in w. Oregon valleys and the outer coast (CBC, *Oregon Birds* field notes).

**Habitat and Diet:** Breeds in ponderosa pine, lodgepole pine, and other conifer forests (McAllister and Marshall 1945), juniper woodlands (Gilligan and Smith 1980, Reinkensmeyer 2000), high-elevation aspen forests (Contreras 1997b), and mountain-mahogany (M. Denny p.c.). Little detail regarding further habitat preferences in Oregon. Appears to be somewhat of a forest generalist, though its relationship with specific habitat attributes—at least in grand fir forests—is not fully understood (R. Sallabanks p.c.). The dominance of the species in lodgepole pine forests suggests a strong preference for this forest type (Arnett et al. 2001). Studies in the Sierra Nevada of California suggest a preference for mid- to high-elevation ponderosa pine, sugar pine, and white fir (Brennan 1989), with increased use of incense-cedar in winter (Morrison et al. 1985). Also seen in desert riparian cottonwood-willow stands (Myers 1993) and in aspen groves in Oregon. However, in forests of sw. Oregon, showed negative association with number of hardwood trees (Ralph et al. 1991). Nests tend to be low to the ground in naturally occurring crannies, bird-excavated cavities,

*Mountain Chickadee*

ELVA PAULSON
© 1991

and fledglings can take advantage of greater availability of insect prey when new shoots appear (Kleintjes and Dahlsten 1995). Omnivorous. Studies conducted in California suggest Mountain Chickadees favor insects during warm seasons (including moths, caterpillars, sawfly larvae and adults, beetle adults, aphids, scale insects, and spiders) and conifer seeds during cool seasons (McCallum et al. 1999). Crop analysis of captured Mountain Chickadees (n=5) in the Tumalo Res. area of c. Oregon in 1958 yielded insects and weed seeds (Eastman 1960). Use bird feeders year-round, when available (McCallum et al. 1999).

No published documentation of seed-caching behavior in Oregon, but studies elsewhere in N. America, including Colorado and New Mexico, have found Mountain Chickadees expert at hiding seeds and later recovering the cache, most obviously in winter (McCallum et al. 1999).

**Seasonal Activity and Behavior:** Breeding pairs start to establish territories in late winter and early spring, with the male leading the inspection of nesting cavities and the female later selecting a site (McCallum et al. 1999). Nesting activities extend from early May to late Jul. Observations have been reported of nest building, nest and eggs, or birds entering or leaving a probable nest site 4 May to 29 Jul (n=56); nestlings 8 Jun to 9 Jul (n=18); and recently fledged young 14 Jun to 31 Jul (n=27) (OBBA). Generally sedentary species, with some irregular migratory movements downslope in winter (Contreras 1997b), likely driven by the search for food. During peak movement years, may expand to w. Oregon as early as late summer or fall, sometimes later. Form loose nonbreeding flocks in winter, often in common with other small bird species (McCallum et al. 1999).

**Detection:** Easily detected by songs and calls. The best way to locate Mountain Chickadees is to visit a ponderosa pine forest in summer or fall and listen for the familiar call, or try spishing and imitating owl sounds (*NKS*).

nest boxes, and even fallen logs (*DBM*). Soft materials, such as rodent fur, are used for the nest cup.

When their territories overlap those of Black-capped Chickadees, Mountain Chickadees tend to nest in taller trees and larger cavities (Hill and Lein 1988, Floyd 1993). Black-capped Chickadees prefer to forage in deciduous trees, Mountain Chickadees higher in the canopy and in larger trees (Hill and Lein 1988). Mountain Chickadees tend to favor pines and sites with little canopy closure while Chestnut-backed Chickadees utilize moist, dense, closed-canopy forests of Douglas-fir, true fir, spruce, and hemlock (*DBM*).

Opportunistic feeders, perhaps timing their breeding season with the growth of white fir so that nestlings

**Population Status and Conservation:** Long-term population trend is stable throughout Oregon, according to CBC data (Brennan and Morrison 1991). BBS trends show slight declines in w. Oregon over the past 30 yr, small increases in extreme s. and e. Oregon, and patches of declining or increasing populations elsewhere in the state (Sauer et al. 1999). Forest practices that retain snags and placement of nest boxes in areas where cavities are scarce are seen as important management tools for enhancing survival (McCallum et al. 1999).—*Noah K. Strycker*

## Chestnut-backed Chickadee *Poecile rufescens*

Chestnut-backed Chickadees are one of the most common species of bird in conifer forests of w. Oregon (Carey et al. 1991, Gilbert and Allwine 1991). They are distinguished from other chickadees by their chestnut-colored back, lack of an eye-line, and their wheezy song. Like other chickadees, they are frequently observed performing acrobatic maneuvers such as hanging from branch tips while foraging high in the canopy. Also, they frequent bird feeders for suet and sunflower seeds and will nest in boxes if they are placed near groves of conifers.

**General Distribution:** Breeds from sc. Alaska, w. British Columbia, n. Idaho, w. Alberta, and nw. Montana south through the coast ranges to s. California and south through the Cascade Range to c. California. Winters throughout breeding range and inland to se. British Columbia. Three subspecies are recognized; only *P. r. rufescens* occurs in Oregon; *levyi* and *caliginosus*, proposed by Burleigh (1959), and *rufescens*, are synonyms (Phillips 1986).

**Oregon Distribution:** Permanent resident along the coast and throughout most of the Coast Range and Cascades, including foothills in forests dominated by Douglas-fir. Rare to locally uncommon at moderate elevations in the e. Blue and Wallowa mountains (Evanich 1992a). In the Klamath Mtns., uncommon in high-elevation, true fir forests and common up to about 3,500 ft (1,067 m) elevation in mixed-conifer forest.

In winter, absent from drier pine-dominated forests of e. Oregon (Contreras 1997b). Abundant in winter west of the Cascade summit. Winters sparingly in the lower Rogue R. and Bear Cr. valleys (Browning 1975a). Mostly absent from deciduous woods in the Willamette Valley, but flocks occur in riverine forests and in some suburban parks that have conifers or are not more than about 1 mi (1.6 km) from conifer patches (*DBM*).

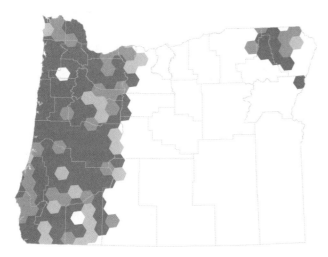

**Habitat and Diet:** Most abundant in moist coniferous forests, especially Douglas-fir and western hemlock forests. They also have been observed in older, pure red alder forests in w. Washington in summer (Stiles 1980). They are unreported from drier pine-dominated forests and stands of pure Oregon white oak in the Willamette Valley in all seasons (Anderson 1972, Hagar and Stern 2001).

In conifer forests, most abundant in older forests (Carey et al. 1991, Gilbert and Allwine 1991, Anthony et al. 1996, Nelson 1988) in Coast and Cascade ranges during the breeding season. In Douglas-fir and western hemlock forests of the Coast Range, Anderson (1972) recorded average densities of 44-198 birds/ac (109-489 birds/ha), peaking in late summer. In the Coast Range, Mannan et al. (1980) recorded densities of 45, 22, 16, and 3 birds/99 ac (40 ha) in forests > 200, 100, 75, and 35 yr old, respectively. No chickadees were recorded in 10-yr-old forests. Present in managed young forests of the Coast and Cascade Ranges; abundance increased with stand age between 5 and 30 yr (Bettinger 1996, Weikel 1997). Abundance was not affected by thinning in young forests of the Coast Range (Hagar et al. 1996, Hayes et al. unpubl. ms.). Abundance declined in clearcut and two-story stands in the Coast Range, but remained stable in uncut control stands and stands that received small, group-selection cuts (Chambers et al. 1999). Chickadees were strongly affected by the size of old-forest patches, being more abundant in large forested patches than in small forested patches (McGarigal and McComb 1995).

Abundance increases with increasing density of large Douglas-fir trees (Nelson 1988, Gilbert and Allwine 1991, Lundquist and Manuwal 1990) and large snags (> 39 in [100 cm]) (Carey et al. 1991).

More abundant upslope than near streamsides (McGarigal and McComb 1992) in the Coast Range. More abundant in unlogged than in logged headwater stream areas of the Coast Range; within logged areas, abundance increased with increasing width of forested stream buffers (Hagar 1999a).

Use old woodpecker cavities or will partially excavate their own cavity in decayed wood for nesting. In unmanaged forests of the Coast Range mean diameter of nest trees ranged from 32 in (81.4 cm) in young forests to 48 in (122.4 cm) in old growth (Mannan et al. 1980, Nelson 1988). In managed young forests of the Coast Range, chickadees nested exclusively in residual snags and stumps from the previous old-growth stand. Mean diameter of nest snags was 41 in (104.9 cm; n=37). All nests appeared to be excavated by chickadees and were in heavily decayed snags, but cavities were located in portions of the snag where the outer core of the wood was still hard (*JMW*). In another study in the Coast Range, chickadees nested in all but the hardest snags and most frequently used snags of moderate decay (Mannan et al. 1980). In old-growth forests, chickadees selected relatively hard snags whereas in young forests they selected more decayed snags. This difference may relate to low abundance of woodpeckers in younger forest and the associated need for highly decayed wood to excavate their own cavities. May collect fur from weathered carnivore droppings for use in nest (Vroman 1994).

Chestnut-backed Chickadees forage in the branches of live trees and capture their prey mostly by gleaning them from the surface of leaves or needles (Lundquist and Manuwal 1990, Weikel and Hayes 1999). Weikel and Hayes (1999) reported that chickadees selected hardwoods over conifers for foraging within young coniferous forests of nw. Oregon. Lundquist and Manuwal (1990) and Weikel and Hayes (1999) reported that chickadees select large-diameter trees for foraging in both young and old-growth forests.

Little information exists on diet. Feed largely on arthropods. In a study conducted in the n. Willamette Valley and in Lane Co., nestling diet comprised mostly caterpillars (58% overall, 95% before 15 Jun). Moths and spiders were also important (Gaddis undated [a]).

Little is known regarding the winter ecology of Chestnut-backed Chickadees. In winter in the Cascade Range, most abundant in older forests (Huff et al. 1991, Anthony et al. 1996). Lundquist and Manuwal (1990) reported that in nw. California, chickadees foraged on all tree species available in spring, but shifted their foraging to western hemlock in the winter.

**Seasonal Activity and Behavior:** Nest building observed late Mar to mid-Jun (n=14, OBBA, *JMW*, Gaddis undated [b]). Egg laying reported as early as 4 Apr (Gaddis undated [b]) and possibly extending as late as 15 Jul when a female was observed with an egg in her oviduct (OBBA). Hatching occurs Jun-Jul and fledging occurs mid-Jun to early Aug (OBBA). Lay 4-10, usually eight eggs and typically incubate for 19 days. May attempt to raise two broods/yr, but the second brood is often less successful than the first (Gaddis undated [b]). Territorial during the breeding season but beginning in mid- to late Jul (especially in fall and winter), occurs in single- or mixed-species flocks with Black-capped Chickadees, Brown Creepers, Red-breasted Nuthatches, Golden-crowned Kinglets, Ruby-crowned Kinglets, Downy Woodpeckers, and Hutton's Vireos (*MGH, DBM*).

Some short-distance movement is likely during nonbreeding seasons, but remains undocumented. Chickadees were much more abundant in riparian areas of the Cascade Range during winter as compared to summer (Anthony et al. 1996).

**Detection:** In spring and summer, Chestnut-backed Chickadees are mostly frequently detected by their relatively high-pitched (compared to other chickadees), wheezy "chick-a-dee-dee" call; however, observers should be aware that the finale of the Golden-crowned Kinglet's song is remarkably similar to this call at a distance (*MGH*). In fall and winter this chickadee is most often detected by its high-pitched, tinkling calls, which also may be confused with similar calls of the Golden-crowned Kinglet, with which it often forages in forest canopies. A good place to look for Chestnut-backed Chickadees is at the edges between coniferous and deciduous patches of forest. Easy to call in during fall and winter by imitating the Northern Pygmy-Owl.

**Population Status and Conservation:** Populations may fluctuate from year to year. Farner (1952) reported that Chestnut-backed Chickadees were unusually common in Crater L. NP during the winter of 1951 (Farner 1952). In addition, a crash in population size was observed in 1999 in young forests of the n. Coast Range following an unusually harsh winter (*JMW*). Gaddis (undated [b]) noted that unusually wet or cold weather during the early breeding season caused unusually high rates of nest failure and abandonment. Of 17 Oregon locations monitored by Brennan and Morrison (1991), population trends were insignificant at 15, significantly positive for one and significantly negative for another; thus, overall Oregon populations appear fairly stable.

Although common, select very large-diameter snags for nesting. It is unclear what, if any, implications the lack of large-diameter wood may have on the ability of chickadees to persist in intensively managed landscapes. Will accept nest boxes (*DBM*). —*Jennifer M. Weikel*

## Oak Titmouse *Baeolophus inornatus*
This species reaches the northern limit of its range in sw. Oregon. Oak and Juniper titmice were formerly conspecific as the Plain Titmouse (*Parus inornatus*), but were recognized as separate species by the AOU (1997). The drab, gray color with distinct crest and chickadee-like calls and behavior characterizes these species. Plumage of sexes is identical. The Oak Titmouse is a friendly, high-spirited, and melodious bird of oak-dominated habitats of interior valleys and lowlands.

**General Distribution:** Resident from sw. Oregon, south in w. Sierra Nevada to s. Baja California; absent in c. Baja California. The AOU (1957) recognized 11 subspecies in what is now the Oak/Juniper Titmouse complex. Cicero (1996) reduced this to six subspecies, with four assigned to the Oak Titmouse; only *B. i. inornatus*, with *sequestratus* as a synonym, was recognized in Oregon by Cicero (2000), but *sequestratus* is provisionally recognized (*MRB*).

**Oregon Distribution:** Common permanent resident in oak woodlands of the interior Rogue Valley (Gabrielson and Jewett 1940, Browning 1975a); rare permanent resident in oak woodlands of Illinois Valley (*DPV*); unverified sightings only in the c. Umpqua Valley (Hunter et al. 1998). Uncommon permanent resident in oak- and juniper-dominated woodlands of the Klamath Basin (Summers 1993a, *DPV*). Identification of Klamath Basin populations is unresolved, but believed to be Oak Titmouse (Gilligan et al. 1994, Contreras 1997b). Cicero (2000) indicates that the Lava Beds National Monument area in n. California (Siskiyou and Modoc Co. boundary) is the only known overlap zone of Oak and Juniper titmice.

**Habitat and Diet:** Inhabits dry habitats of Rogue Valley lowlands dominated by Oregon white and California black oak, generally below 1,500 ft (460 m). Also found in open riparian habitat with oaks; generally absent in dense riparian habitat. Tree size and stand densities vary for foraging, but cavities are required for nesting. Ponderosa pine is a notable habitat component in the Rogue Valley (*DPV*); small amounts of Pacific madrone, incense-cedar and Douglas-fir tolerated (*DPV*). Stands with brushy undergrowth are highly preferred; some grass/forb patches are accepted. Undergrowth species include buckbrush, white manzanita, poison oak, and birch-leaf mountain-mahogany. Summers (1993a) indicated that oak and western juniper/mountain-mahogany habitats were occupied in the Klamath Basin, generally below 4,500 ft (1,370 m). Present in rural residential areas with widely spaced homes, or outer edge of suburban locations with lightly impacted oaks and native vegetation.

Titmice nest in natural tree cavities (trunk, limb), old woodpecker holes, and nest boxes. They also can partially excavate rotten wood (Bent 1946, Harrison 1978, 1979). They generally nest 3-10 ft (0.9-3 m) and up to 32 ft (9.8 m) from the ground (Ehrlich et al. 1988), but no nests have been described in Oregon. Nest material includes mosses, fur, and hair (*DPV*); may include feathers, grasses, and bark.

Titmice chip away bark and decayed wood to search for insects. They forage primarily in oaks (but also brush) for insects, and on the ground for seeds (Oct) (*DPV*). They have been observed hovering outside a tree canopy for insects and foraging at active sapsucker wells on buckbrush 28 Feb 2001 (*DPV*). Diet consists of invertebrates and vegetable food; percentages vary with season (Bent 1946, Martin et al. 1951, Cicero 2000). Invertebrate amounts are greatest during the nesting season: 15-75% by volume (43% average) including true bugs, scales, leaf- and treehoppers, caterpillars, beetles, weevils, ants, wasps, and some spiders and grasshoppers (Cicero 2000). Titmice were observed eating insect larvae from sweet-brier rose galls 15 Jan 1995 (*DPV*). Vegetative food 25-85% by volume (57% average), including acorns, seeds

(ponderosa pine, Douglas-fir, juniper, poison oak, star-thistle, walnuts), oak buds (Dec-Feb[*DPV*]), oak catkins (Mar [*DPV*]), cherries, apples, and oats (Martin et al. 1951, Cicero 2000). Sunflower seed and suet are taken when available. Observed removing seed from ponderosa pine and Douglas-fir cones Sep-Oct (*DPV*). A bird was seen attempting to cache a small acorn beneath the ground on 3 Sep 2000, Rogue Valley (*DPV*). Caching of sunflower seeds has also been noted (*DPV*).

**Seasonal Activity and Behavior:** Territorial singing starts Dec (infrequent) with a definite increase in mid-Feb, peaking Mar-Apr; declines sharply when juveniles fledge mid-Jun to early Jul (*DPV*). Adult wing flutter observed while foraging and singing 8 Feb 1998 and 21 Feb 1999 (*DPV*), likely agonistic behavior (Cicero 2000). Birds roost singly in cavities; female uses nest cavity up to 1 mo before nesting. Adults visit potential nest sites early Feb to late Mar (n=3) (*DPV*). Birds found dead in nesting box 15 Feb 1987 and 26 Apr 1987, perhaps died while roosting (*DPV*).

Observed carrying nest material 25 Mar-16 Apr (n=3), on eggs 28 Apr 1987 (*DPV*). Female sits tight on eggs; hisses loudly if disturbed (*DPV*). Observed carrying food items 23 Apr-21 May (n=6) (*DPV*). Unfeathered young in nest box 6 May 1989, six feathered young 20 May 1989, gone from box 24 May 1989 (*DPV*). Feeding fledglings 21 May-31 Jul (n= 4) (*DPV*). Many fledged juveniles banded (Rogue Valley) mid- to late Jun (*DPV*). Second brood attempt noticed 27 May 1989; nest/eggs abandoned 4 Jun 1989 (*DPV*).

Pairs and fledglings remain together about 1 mo (Cicero 2000). Dispersing juveniles meet resistance when intruding into adult territories. Juveniles searching suitable territories (floaters) likely account for birds found outside normal range. This may account for c. Umpqua Valley sightings (Hunter et al. 1998)

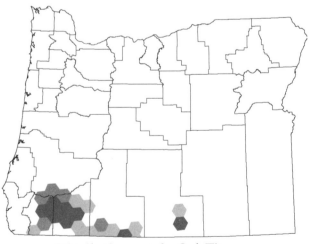

*Distribution map for Oak Titmouse and Juniper Titmouse*

and a bird at Onion Mtn., Siskiyou NF, at 4,000 ft (1,220 m) in an evergreen brushfield 1 Aug 1997 (V. J. Teale p.c.).

Bent (1946) and Harrap and Quinn (1995) discuss seasonal activities. Oak titmice pair for life, and do not form flocks (Cicero 2000). Adult movement is minimal throughout life; remain within territorial boundaries year-round. When mate is lost, remaining bird re-mates within same territory. Pairs join mixed-species flocks within territory, but separate at edge. Territory size (California, San Francisco Bay area) 0.3-1.1 ac (0.8-2.6 ha) (Zeiner et al. 1990).

**Detection:** Easily detected by territorial singing. Two different song-types are used in the Rogue Valley, both repeat same note many times (*DPV*). Although active and usually vocal, can be secretive and difficult to see.

**Population Status and Conservation:** The first published record for Oregon was an inclusion in the AOU (1886) check-list. The historic range appears to have changed little since Gabrielson and Jewett (1940). Klamath Basin populations have not been well documented in the past, but likely are stable. Sedentary adult behavior and specific habitat requirements within a comparatively narrow elevation band appear to limit range expansion. Few Oregon distribution or density data are available. Breeding season point counts (May-Jun, 1993-96) along 0.7-mi (1.1-km) route located in n. Grants Pass found an average of 0.22 birds/ac, range 0-0.36 (n=14) (0.56 birds/ha, range 0-0.89). Winter season counts for the same route (Dec-Feb, 1993-96) found an average of 0.28 birds/ac, range 0.05-0.47 (n=11; 0.68 birds/ha, range 0.13-1.15) (*DPV*).

Hejl (1994) found a significant downward 10- and 24-yr trend (-2.5%/yr, P < 0.10) for Plain Titmouse (Oak and Juniper Titmice) in w. U.S. using BBS data (mostly California data). Although poorly investigated, current populations appear stable in Oregon. CBC data available for Grants Pass, Klamath Falls, and Medford counts indicate no apparent long-term trend. Grants Pass detections averaged 16 (range 2-27, n=18), Klamath Falls averaged six (range 0-18, n=19), and Medford averaged 36 (range 4-75, n=38).

Loss or modification of oak woodland nesting and foraging habitat by human activities and development may pose the greatest threat to Oregon populations.—*Dennis P. Vroman*

## Juniper Titmouse *Baeolophus ridgwayi*

Formerly considered conspecific with Oak Titmouse, to which it is very similar in appearance, the Juniper Titmouse presents the demeanor of a miniature jay with its crest jutted proudly upright. The Juniper Titmouse is a pale gray bird above and underneath, with little

or no brown coloration. Songs and calls are useful in locating hidden titmice. Occurs in pinyon pine-juniper woodlands in the bulk of its range; in se. Oregon the species is confined to juniper woodlands. Very little is known about this species in Oregon.

**General Distribution:** Resident from se. Oregon, ne. Nevada, se. Idaho, s. Wyoming, c. Colorado, and extreme w. Oklahoma south to se. California (east of the Sierra Nevada), c. and se. Arizona, extreme ne. Sonora, s. New Mexico, and extreme w. Texas. The binomial *griseus* for the Juniper Titmouse (AOU 1998) was corrected (Banks et al. 2002) to *ridgwayi*. Two subspecies; *B. r. zaleptus* in Oregon (Cicero 1996, 2000 and others, *contra* Phillips 1959).

**Oregon Distribution:** The Juniper Titmouse occurs in scattered isolated populations east of the s. Cascades to Idaho (Contreras 1997b). It is uncommon to rare and a local permanent resident east of Lakeview and Abert Rim (Evanich 1990), on Hart Mtn. N. Antelope R. (Rogers 1985c, USFWS 1986c), in s. Warner Valley (Bent 1946, Gilligan et al. 1994), and west of Adel, Lake Co. Birds have been found in Kelly Cr. Canyon (Sullivan 1997c) and up Deep Cr. Canyon (Spencer 2000a), both Lake Co. Locally rare north of Silver L., Table Rock area (Summers 1991); a 1999 report near Ironside, Malheur Co. (Adamus et al. 2001), was a data-entry error (C. Brumitt p.c.). Single specimen from Blitzen Canyon, Steens Mtn., 9 Feb 1936 (Gabrielson and Jewett 1940) with no sightings there since (Gilligan et al. 1994). Specimens from near Lorella, Klamath Co., and near Adel, Twentymile Cr. Canyon, and Warner Valley, Lake Co. (Cicero 1996). Not yet reported from Owyhee R. area, but regularly found in Idaho 5 mi (8 km) east of Three Forks, (Malheur Co., along N. Fork Owyhee R. (G. Gillson p.c.) and an individual was observed close to the Oregon border near McDermitt, Nevada (Contreras and Kindschy 1996). Reports in s. Langell Valley, Klamath Co. (K. Spencer p.c.), may be Oak Titmouse (see that species for further discussion) (Gilligan et al. 1994, Contreras 1997b).

**Habitat and Diet:** In Oregon, confined throughout the year to mature western juniper habitats, or stands with small-sized trees mixed with mature trees, generally below 6,000 ft (1,830 m). Inhabits juniper-agricultural (cattle grazing) locations s. Warner Valley; big sagebrush may be present (K. Spencer p.c.). Must have mature juniper stands with cavities during nesting (W. Pyle p.c.). Winters in Hart Mtn. N. Antelope R. and thought to require juniper stands greater than 120 ac (48.6 ha) with abundant berries (W. Pyle p.c.).

Cavity nester (Harrap and Quinn 1995, Cicero 2000). Use of nesting boxes has not been documented in Oregon; boxes are used in pinyon-pine habitat within range of the species (Cicero 2000). Nest is often placed in a crevice of a twisted trunk of large, older junipers (Cicero 2000). An Oregon nest was found 19 Jun 1999 in a western juniper cavity with an entrance hole of about 3 x 1.75 in (7.6 x 4.4 cm) (R. Freeman p.c.). Two nests were found in holes in a dirt wall of a gully in New Mexico (C. Goguen p.c.). No nest material data are available from Oregon; materials used elsewhere within range include rabbit and rodent hair, grass, shredded bark, moss, rootlets and straw (Cicero 2000).

In Oregon, primarily forages in junipers. Diet data are lacking (Cicero 2000). Observed carrying 0.75-in (19-mm) greenish insect larvae to nest cavity in juniper stand west of Adel, Lake Co. (R. Freeman p.c.). Juniper seed is important in the winter diet (W. Pyle p.c.).

**Seasonal Activity and Behavior:** Harrap and Quinn (1995) and Cicero (2000) indicate that activities and behavior are similar to Oak Titmouse (see that species): highly sedentary, pair for life; more prone than Oak Titmouse to form winter flocks. Foraging behavior is probably similar to Oak Titmouse (see that species), but has not been documented (Cicero 2000).

Breeding chronology details are limited for Oregon. Singing birds and wing flutter (possibly agonistic behavior) (Cicero 2000) of a single bird facing another (both thought to be adults) after a short chase were observed west of Adel on 30 May 1999 (D. Tracy p.c.). Nine pairs behaving territorially, visiting potential nest cavities, or carrying nest materials were noted in Hart Mtn. N. Antelope R. Jun to Jul 1985 (Rogers 1985c). An adult was observed feeding young in a cavity 19 Jun 1999 west of Adel (R. Freeman p.c.), and feeding a fledgling 15 Jul 1998 in s. Langell Valley (K. Spencer p.c.). Fall dispersal is restricted to juveniles (Harrap and Quinn 1995). Only one dispersing juvenile was captured at Hart Mtn. N. Antelope R. 30 Sep 1975 during 11 yr (1972-83) of constant-effort banding Apr-Sep (K. Voget p.c.). The Juniper Titmouse joins mixed-species winter flocks (Cicero 2000), especially chickadee flocks; e.g., two birds south of Adel, Oregon, observed with Mountain Chickadees 23 Dec 1998 (S. Kornfeld p.c.).

Juniper Titmouse remains within its territories, and exhibits weaker territorial and sedentary behavior than Oak Titmouse throughout the year (Cicero 2000); studies lacking. No Oregon territory size available. Territory size in pinyon-juniper-ponderosa pine in Arizona averaged 3 ac (1.2 ha) (Zeiner et al. 1990); 3.6 ac (1.3 ha) in w. Nevada (Cicero 2000).

**Detection:** Located by territorial singing in spring and early summer and by calls outside breeding period.

**Population Status and Conservation:** The first documented specimens in Oregon were south of Adel (near California border) 3 May 1930 (Jobanek 1997), and two specimens were collected near this location on 19 May 1932 (Gabrielson and Jewett 1940). The current range is similar to that reported by Gabrielson and Jewett (1940), but the distribution and status of Oregon populations is not well documented past or present. Range expansion is likely limited by sedentary behavior and requirements of expansive mature juniper habitat, especially in winter. No Oregon density data are available; average densities of 0.04-0.2 pairs/ac (0.1-0.5 pairs/ha) were reported near Reno, Nevada (Cicero 2000).

Hejl (1994) found a significant downward 10- and 24-yr trend (-2.5%/yr, P < 0.10) for "Plain Titmouse" (combined Oak and Juniper titmice) throughout the range in w. U.S. using BBS data. Although scantily investigated in Oregon, populations are thought stable. CBC data indicate no long-term winter trend. The Adel CBC averaged 13 birds (range 0-44), and titmice were detected 12 of 14 yr. At the Hart Mtn. CBC, titmice counts averaged 1.4 (range 0-15) birds, and titmice were detected 6 of 26 yr.

The expansion of mature juniper cover in se. Oregon adjacent to presently occupied mature stands would likely benefit the species. Loss or modification of mature western juniper stands within the range of the species (especially large, continuous acreage that provides nesting cavities and foraging habitat) by human development or wildfire may be the greatest threat to Oregon populations.—*Dennis P. Vroman*

## Family Aegithalidae

**Bushtit** *Psaltriparus minimus*
A group of twittering, tiny gray birds streaming through bushes and trees and across openings surely are Bushtits. Females' eyes are pale, males' dark. Highly gregarious except when nesting. The intricately made sock-like nest is unusually large for the size of the bird. Bushtits show a distinct indifference to humans and regularly nest within residential neighborhoods and establish foraging routes throughout many cities. Readily take suet at bird feeding stations and visit backyard birdbaths.

**General Distribution:** Resident from sw. British Columbia, c. Washington and sw. Idaho s. to Texas and Guatemala. Of 11 subspecies, four are found in Oregon.

**Oregon Distribution:** Fairly common to uncommon resident throughout Oregon except Umatilla, Union, and Wallowa counties and at higher elevations of mountain ranges, where it is a rare fall visitant. Oregon ranges have expanded, but with few published data and no specimens. *P. m. minimus*, described as occurring

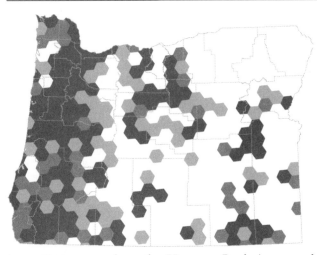

in w. Oregon south to the Umpqua R. drainage and through Coos and Curry counties into California, may be the subspecies which has extended its range into the w. Cascades and east along the Columbia R. to The Dalles. *P. m. californicus* occurs in Josephine and Jackson counties east to s. Klamath and s. Lake counties. The Oregon range of *P. m. plumbeus* was formerly described as being restricted to Harney and Malheur counties north to s. Grant and Baker counties (Phillips 1986). Bushtits subsequently reported or seen elsewhere throughout e. Oregon by Nehls (1978b), Gilligan (1994), and *HBN* are assumed to be *plumbeus*, but no specimens have been taken for verification. *P. m. saturatus*, normally described as occurring in British Columbia, was recorded at Portland once in Apr and Dec (*SMNH, MRB*). Rea (in Phillips 1991:95) reported two spring specimens from Pacific Co., Washington, that "appear to be *saturatus.*"

**Habitat and Diet:** Breeds in open woodlands and brushy places, especially deciduous bottomlands. Clearcutting forests and suppression of range fires allowed range expansion into areas previously unavailable (Nehls 1978b). Meslow and Wight (1975) explained that clearcut coniferous forests are unused by Bushtits the first several years after cutting, but by the eighth year, when shrubs and saplings take over, they move in and breed. After about 7-8 more years the cover gets too heavy, they stop utilizing the area for breeding but will continue to forage into and through the forest. In e. Oregon, control of range fires has allowed junipers to expand into former grasslands and sagebrush flats (Janes 1987). The juniper-sagebrush habitat is ideal nesting habitat for Bushtits, but they will not nest in treeless sagebrush or grasslands. They will forage through these areas, however (*HBN*).

The nest cup is suspended on several root threads 7-10 in (17.3-25.6 cm) below the supporting twig. The outside of the nest and the supporting threads are covered with an outer wall of lichens, mosses, spider web, and other soft materials (Bent 1946b, *HBN*). The cup is lined with soft down or fur. The finished nest is a sack-like pendant 6.6-12 in (16.5-30 cm) long by 2.5-4 in (6.5-10 cm) in diameter with the entrance hole at one side near the top (Harrap and Quinn 1995). The nest is suspended from the end of a twig, often in an open situation, with leaves overhanging the nest. Bent (1946) reports that nests are seldom more than 15 ft (4.6 m) above the ground, but D. Fix (p.c.) has seen one nest at approximately 40 ft (12 m) and many higher than 20 ft (6 m).

Forages by gleaning from foliage and small branches of trees and shrubs but rarely on the ground (Harrap and Quinn 1995). Food comprises mostly insects (mainly plant-lice and bark-lice) and spiders; some vegetable matter is also taken (Bent 1946).

**Seasonal Activity and Behavior:** Pairs leave flocks in Jan and Feb and begin nest building. Bushtits are reportedly monogamous, but several birds are often in the nesting territory and help build the nest and feed the young (Harrap and Quinn 1995). Two broods per season. Usual clutch 4-7 eggs. Both sexes and occasionally a helper incubate. Incubation period 12 days; fledge 14-15 days after hatching (Harrap and Quinn 1995). Nesting mid-Mar to Jul, mostly May and Jun (Gabrielson and Jewett 1940, Irons 1984b, Littlefield 1990a, Sullivan 1996b, 1998b).

After fledging the family remains intact, joining other families to form a flock that remains together until the next nesting season (Harrap and Quinn 1995). Flocks are typically 15-35 birds (D. Irons p.c., *MGH*), and seldom exceed 50 individuals (Littlefield 1990a). Size of the foraging range is based on available food. In suitable habitat with sufficient food, flocks establish a regular foraging pattern within the home range (Harrup and Quinn 1995). In marginal areas and in years of poor food supplies, it appears that flocks may move farther afield and do not establish a foraging patterns (*HBN*). When not nesting, Bushtits may occur anywhere in Oregon, but most move to lower elevations in winter.

**Detection:** Although nesting birds are quiet and unassuming they are not secretive. They are often first detected by their twittering calls. Foraging flocks are widespread and cover large areas.

**Population Status and Conservation:** There is little indication that populations have dropped from historic levels; the breeding range is expanding and numbers appear to be increasing in many areas (*HBN*).—*Harry B. Nehls*

## Family Sittidae

### Subfamily Sittinae

### Red-breasted Nuthatch *Sitta canadensis*

Bent (1948) aptly described this nuthatch as a "happy, jolly little bird, quick and agile in his motions and … seemingly always in a hurry to scramble over the branches." Distinguished from other nuthatches by white eyebrows, black eyelines and cap, reddish breast, and nasal *yank yank* song. Although males have a blacker cap and redder breast than females, distinguishing sexes in the field is difficult. During winter, can be observed foraging in mixed-species flocks with chickadees, Brown Creepers, Golden-crowned Kinglets, Townsend's Warblers, Yellow-rumped Warblers, and Dark-eyed Juncos. Although nuthatches have a reputation for moving downward on trunks of trees, the Red-breasted Nuthatch is just as frequently observed foraging among branches.

**General Distribution:** Breeds from coastal s. and se. Alaska across Canada and south to the mountains of the w. U.S., the Great Lakes states, New England, and into the Appalachians. Monotypic; *S. c. clariterga*, proposed by Burleigh (1960b) is not recognizable (Banks 1970).

**Oregon Distribution:** Breeds and winters throughout Oregon where conifer or mixed conifer-hardwood forests are present, including some urban areas (Gabrielson and Jewett 1940, Browning 1975a, Evanich 1992a). Winters in wooded areas from valley floors to timberline (Gabrielson and Jewett 1940, Evanich 1992a). Migratory individuals are encountered widely in areas where they do not breed (Gilligan et al. 1994).

**Habitat and Diet:** During the breeding season in the Coast and Cascade ranges, most abundant in old-growth and mature conifer forests (Mannan et al. 1980, Nelson 1988, Carey et al. 1991) and occurs in younger coniferous forests at variable densities. Mannan et al. (1980) recorded densities of 19, 5, and 3 nuthatches per 99 ac (40 ha) in 200-, 110-, and 75-yr-old forest, respectively. None were found in 10- and 35-yr-old forests. Others have observed Red-breasted Nuthatches in young (8- to 50-yr-old) forests of the Coast and Cascade Ranges (Bettinger 1996, Hagar et al. 1996, Weikel 1997). Chambers et al. (1999) reported that Red-breasted Nuthatches were negatively affected by conversion of mature stands to clearcuts and two-storied stands in the Coast Range. Effects of thinning in young forests (35-50 yr old) have been variable, but generally numbers have been equal or greater in thinned stands (Hagar et al. 1996, Weikel 1997, Hayes

et al. in press). In forests of the Coast Range, are more abundant upslope than in riparian areas (Anthony et al. 1996).

In e. Oregon, abundance of Red-breasted Nuthatches was similar in young, mature, and old-growth forests, but they were absent from very young stands (Sanderson et al. 1980). In a study of post-fire bird communities in ne. Oregon, abundance 1 yr following fire was similar between unburned areas and those that received low- and medium-intensity burning, but was lower in areas that received high-intensity burning. This was true despite the increased availability of snags in the heavily burned stands (Sallabanks 1995b). In the Blue Mtns., significantly less abundant in stand-initiation forest structure classes compared with older forest types (open- and closed-stem exclusion, understory reinitiation, young forest multi-story, and old forest multi-story) (Sallabanks et al. 2002). In juniper forests of c. Oregon, found in low abundance in both old-growth and mid-successional juniper stands; absent from sagebrush (Reinkensmeyer 2000). Not reported in forests dominated by aspen in Wyoming and Colorado (Finch and Reynolds 1987); status is undetermined in aspen stands of se. Oregon.

Not found in oak-dominated stands in the Willamette Valley in the breeding seasons of the late 1960s but present in low abundance in the late 1990s (Anderson SH 1970, Hagar and Stern 2001, OBBA). Change may be due to encroachment of Douglas-fir into oak stands. Breeds in conifer patches in urban areas (Gabrielson and Jewett 1970).

Nest in cavities in dead trees or in dead limbs of live trees. Reported to nest in Douglas-fir, grand fir, western hemlock, red alder, ponderosa pine, and lodgepole pine (Gabrielson and Jewett 1940, Farner 1952, D. Fix p.c., *JMW*). Most frequently excavate their own cavities, but also use cavities created by woodpeckers and often line the entrance of their nest with pitch. In unmanaged forests of the Coast Range, mean diameter of nest snags ranged from 23 in (58.2 cm) in young forests to 46 in (118 cm) in old-growth forests (Mannan et al. 1980, Nelson 1988). In young

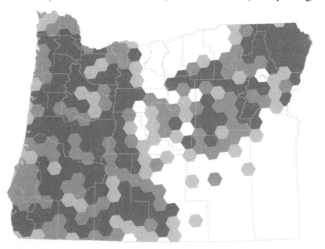

managed forests of the Coast Range, mean diameter of 11 nest snags was 18.1 in (46.1 cm) (*JMW*). Typically nest in snags with moderate amounts of decay (Mannan et al. 1980, *JMW*).

Red-breasted Nuthatches forage along the trunk and amongst the branches of coniferous trees. In old-growth and young forests of the s. Washington Cascade Range and in young forests of the Oregon Coast Range nuthatches selected large-diameter conifers for foraging and foraged roughly equally on branches and trunks (Lundquist and Manuwal 1990, Weikel and Hayes 1999). In the s. Washington Cascade Range in winter, nuthatches shifted their foraging locations on trees inward and to lower portions of the trunk. Corroborating these observations, Anderson (1976) found more bark-dwelling arthropods in their diet in winter as compared to summer. In urban areas in winter, frequent suet and seed feeders and often remove seeds and cache them amongst the bark of nearby trees for later consumption (*JMW*).

In winter, occur throughout coniferous forests and in deciduous woods and urban areas (Evanich 1992a, *JMW*). May occur in atypical habitats such as sagebrush and bulrush during winters when food supplies are scarce in upslope forested areas (Littlefield 1990a).

Anderson (1976) compared the diets between seasons in w. Oregon. In Douglas-fir forests of the Willamette Valley, fed largely on weevils during the breeding season; on weevils, ants, leaf bugs, and earwigs during fall; and on weevils and seeds of sedge during winter. In ponderosa pine forests of the c. Cascade Range, foraged on weevils during the breeding season; weevils, ants, scarab beetles, and click beetles during fall; and weevils, bark beetles, and true bugs during winter. Bark beetles increased from 6 to 12% between fall and winter. Conifer seeds are an important food item outside the breeding season (Harrap and Quinn 1995, Ghalambor and Martin 1999).

**Seasonal Activity and Behavior:** Spring migration at Malheur NWR usually between 23 Apr and 5 May (Littlefield 1990a). Nest building observed 18 Apr to 14 Jun (n=14, OBBA) (*JMW*). Egg laying and incubation likely occur in May and Jun. Nests with young have been observed 7 Jun to 12 Jul (n=11, OBBA) (*JMW*) and fledged young have been observed 14 Jun to 21 Jul (n=12) (OBBA).

Migration and seasonal movements within Oregon are difficult to predict. If food resources are sufficient, a pair may remain on the breeding territory through winter (Harrap and Quinn 1995). Although elevational migrations are typical, migrations within mountain ranges and to new areas are also likely as nuthatches move to areas with productive cone crops. It is well documented that large-scale population changes occur on a year-to-year basis throughout Oregon in both the summer and winter (Farner 1952, Littlefield 1990a,

Evanich 1992a) and that populations will undergo eruptions on a nationwide scale (Davis and Morrison 1987). Timing of fall migration varies. Peak periods at Malheur NWR have occurred as early as Jul and as late as Sep; variability in migration is likely related to year-to-year changes in populations and whether it is an irruption year (Littlefield 1990a).

Winter numbers in lowland w. Oregon and on the outer coast vary markedly from year to year. Some years, no birds were observed on the outer coast whereas hundreds have been found in other years (CBC).

**Detection:** Easily detected by its song, which it sings all year. Commonly attracted to imitations of owls, and often one of the first species to respond.

**Population Status and Conservation:** Although fairly common and somewhat flexible in use of different forest types, may be sensitive to intensive forest management practices, particularly in w. Oregon. Intensive forest management that reduces the amount of large-diameter trees, snags, and structural diversity may result in population declines (Ghalambor and Martin 1999). Forest practices that promote structural diversity and retain sufficient quantities of large-diameter trees and snags may help prevent population declines. May be expanding their range into the Willamette Valley with the increasing encroachment of conifers into oak and grassland-dominated habitats.—*Jennifer M. Weikel*

## White-breasted Nuthatch *Sitta carolinensis*

Among the largest of the world's nuthatches, White-breasted Nuthatches also are noteworthy for an extensive repertoire of unusual behaviors and habits. Unlike most other N. American passerines, White-breasted Nuthatches maintain close pair bonds over most of the year. In the spring, they cement their pair bond by exhibiting a variety of courtship displays. Elaborate display rituals also are used in antagonistic territorial interactions, and distraction displays are used to deter predators. The food-caching behavior of White-breasted Nuthatches is well known, as is their ability to find cached items again. They regularly sanitize their roost cavities by removing feces each morning (Kilham 1971b), and may "sweep" nest cavity entrance with toxic insects to deter potential predators (Kilham 1971c). They also have been known to use tools for foraging (bark flakes used to pry off other pieces of bark) (Mitchell 1993). Deceitful use of alarm calls is practiced to scare other birds from feeders, presumably to reduce competition for food (Tramer 1994). These clever woodland residents are easily recognized by their black caps, white underparts, blue-gray upperparts, and their characteristic pose of clinging upside down on a tree trunk.

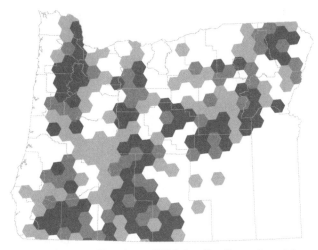

**General Distribution:** Widely distributed resident in woodlands throughout N. America; from Prince Edward I. in the northeast, south along the e. seaboard to n. Florida, west across s. Canada, and to the Pacific coast in California. Reaches the northern extent of its range in British Columbia and Alberta; occurs south into the highlands of s. Mexico. Gaps in distribution occur in treeless parts of the Great Plains, Great Basin, and Sonoran Desert. Although northern and western populations are occasionally irruptive, this species is resident throughout its range and is not known to migrate (Pravosudov and Grubb 1993). Up to 11 subspecies, depending upon the authority, but two occur in Oregon (Aldrich 1944, Hawbecker 1948). Behle (1963) identified birds from the Warner Mtns. as *S. c. nelsoni* but these were reidentified correctly as *S. c. tenuissima* by N. K. Johnson (1970b).

**Oregon Distribution:** *S. c. aculeata* common to uncommon resident in w. Oregon lowlands; most abundant in southwestern interior valleys, with specimens from Salem (USNM) to Jackson Co. (DMNH, SOU). Common resident in oak and mixed forests, nut orchards, and suburban plantings in the Willamette Valley region (Gillson 1999). Occasional summer visitor in Curry Co. but no breeding records (C. Dillingham p.c.). Very rare visitor to Coos Co. in fall and winter, with only three CBC records for mid-Dec (Contreras 1998), and two recorded on 12 Sep 1977 at Coos Head (Mattocks and Hunn 1978a). One record for Florence CBC (Heinl 1985). Largely absent from high-elevation coniferous forests, and most fir forests of the w. Cascades and Coast Ranges. One record in the high Cascades of Linn Co., at Lost L. in 1996 (Gillson 1999). *S. c. tenuissima* common to uncommon in forested areas east of the Cascade summit, with specimens from Sisters and Lapine, Deschutes Co. (SDNHM), and from the east slope of Mt. Hood to Ft. Klamath, and Enterprise in Wallowa Co. (USNM). Breeds in ponderosa pine and mixed-conifer forests in the Blue Mtns. (Thomas, Miller, et al. 1979). Occasional spring and autumn visitor to Malheur NWR (Littlefield 1990a). March visitor (SOU) to Emigrant Res., Jackson Co. (*MRB*). Historical breeding record from Camp Harney (Bendire 1877).

**Habitat and Diet:** Occurs in two main habitat types in Oregon: oak and ponderosa pine (Contreras 1997b). In the Willamette and Umpqua valleys and lower eastern slope of the Coast Range, strongly associated with Oregon white oak (Cross and Simmons 1983, Hagar and Stern 2001). East of the Cascade Range, sympatric with Red-breasted and Pygmy Nuthatches in ponderosa pine forest. In Blue Mtns., feeding and breeding activities primarily confined to mature and old-growth ponderosa pine and mixed-conifer habitats (Hall and Thomas 1979). Population density estimated at 3-6 birds/40 ac (12 ha) in the Willamette Valley oak woodlands (Anderson SH 1970, Hagar and Stern 2001), where associated with large-diameter oaks in semi-open woodlands (Pravosudov and Grubb 1993, Hagar and Stern 2001), and abundance negatively correlated with Douglas-fir cover (Hagar and Stern 2001). Use cavities excavated by woodpeckers or formed by decay in live or dead trees for nesting and roosting. Nests are mainly in live trees, and occasionally in nest boxes (*MGH*). Individuals in the mid-Willamette Valley use more than one cavity for roosting, perhaps to avoid predation or to obtain suitable microclimate (Gumtow-Farrior 1991). Minimum diameter of cavity entrance is 0.79 in (2 cm). Nest lined with fur, bark strips, and feathers found in box on 9-in (22-cm) dbh Oregon white oak in an oak grove in Pierce Co., Washington (Chappell and Williamson 1984).

Forage mainly on large tree limbs and trunks by gleaning from bark surface or probing into crevices (Matthysen 1998). In the winter in w. Oregon, forage on branches and trunks of trees and sometimes on shrubs (Anderson 1976). Frequently cache food by wedging items under bark flake or in bark furrow. Diet varies by habitat and season. Smaller food items taken in oak than in pine habitats of Oregon. In white oak habitats of w. Oregon, weevils make up a large percentage of the diet throughout the year (Anderson 1976). In pine habitats, ants and beetles are major food items during breeding and postbreeding seasons, but booklice and stinkbugs supplement beetles in winter. Favor sunflower seeds and suet at feeders.

**Seasonal Activity and Behavior:** Pairs occupy the same territories year-round. During winter, territories are not vigorously defended, but territoriality increases during breeding season (Matthysen 1998). Even if nesting and roosting habitat is abundant, the strong territorial behavior of this species may limit population densities (McEllin 1979). Intricate courtship behaviors begin at the end of winter (no specific dates available for Oregon), including four distinct courtship

*White-breasted Nuthatch*

©1997
ELVA H PAULSON

May 1983 (Gillson 1999). Incubation lasts about 15 days, and nestlings fledge 16-26 days after hatching (Matthysen 1998). Although only female incubates, male enters nest to feed female during incubation, and both adults feed young (Pravosudov and Grubb 1993). Fledglings typically observed mid-Jun to mid-Jul (n=9) (OBBA). Single brooded, but may replace lost clutches (Harrap and Quinn 1995).

Migrations have been observed in the e. U.S., but this phenomenon has not been documented for western populations. Often found in mixed flocks in winter. Roosts in cavities in winter, often removing feces from roost hole upon exiting in morning (Kilham 1971b).

**Detection:** Easily detected from late summer to early spring, when most vocal; less conspicuous during nesting season. Will visit feeding stations.

**Population Status and Conservation:** Anecdotal (Partners in Flight 2000) and survey (BBS and CBC data, Sauer et al. 1999) data provide substantial evidence of declining population trends throughout w. Oregon and Washington. BBS data for the Willamette Valley indicate a decline in abundance from an average of 2-3 birds/route (bpr) in 1970s to <1 bpr in the early 1990s. Currently nearly extirpated in w. Washington (Partners in Flight 2000). Population decline in w. Oregon and Washington may be attributed to loss of open stands of large-diameter oaks (Gumtow-Farrior 1991, Hagar and Stern 2001). Because oak woodlands in the Willamette Valley historically were maintained by fire, prescribed burning may be an effective tool for discouraging encroachment by shade-tolerant tree species in order to maintain the open stands of oak with which this species is strongly associated.—*Joan Hagar*

## Pygmy Nuthatch *Sitta pygmaea*

A constant chatter of high-pitched staccato *tidi tidi tidi* or *tideet tideet* calls coming from the canopy of ponderosa pine forests east of the Cascade Range is a sure sign of the presence of this tiny, highly active, social nuthatch. Measuring only 3.75-4.5 in (9.5-11.4 cm) long, this stubby mite is the smallest and plainest of the three w. U.S. nuthatches. It has a blackish cap that laterally darkens as a stripe over the eye, bluish-gray upperparts, and white and cream underparts. Like White-breasted and Red-breasted Nuthatches with which it co-exists in Oregon, this is a tree-bark clinger that has a strong woodpecker-like bill for probing bark, opening seeds, and cavity excavation. Unlike the other two nuthatches, the Pygmy Nuthatch forages over all tree surfaces from the trunks to the outer- and top-most needles and cones. The Pygmy Nuthatch also possesses some other unusual passerine behaviors.

vocalizations, courtship feeding, and numerous displays (Kilham 1972). Nest building takes place in Apr and May (n=3) (OBBA). Clutch of 5-10 eggs (Matthysen 1998) laid late Apr to late Jun (Griffee and Rapraeger 1937, Bent 1948, Gillson 1999). Six to eight eggs per clutch were recorded for four nests found near Portland (Griffee and Rapraeger 1937). Young in nest primarily in Jun (n=8), but as early as May (n=2) and as late as Jul (n=4, all east of the Cascades) (OBBA). In Brownsville, Linn Co., five nestlings/fledglings were banded 16-20

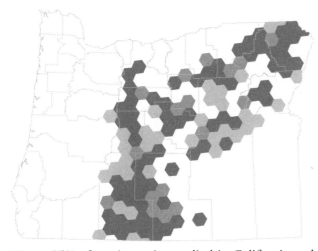

Up to 35% of nesting pairs studied in California and Arizona employed helpers in the form of unmated males to assist with nesting (Norris 1958, Sydeman et al. 1988). To survive cold winter nights, this nuthatch goes into a state of torpor when roosting communally in tree cavities (Knorr 1957, Sydeman and Guntert 1983).

**General Distribution:** Mostly resident of long-needle-type pine forests in w. N. America from s. interior British Columbia east to nw. Nebraska and south to n. Baja California and nc. Mexico. Six subspecies; *S.p. melanotus*, the most widespread, occurs in Oregon (Phillips 1986).

**Oregon Distribution:** Resident of ponderosa pine-dominated forests from the east slopes of the Cascades eastward into the Blue and Warner mountains (Gabrielson and Jewett 1940, Gilligan et al. 1994, numerous reports in *Oregon Birds*). Abundance varies with habitat quality. Following the breeding season, occasionally found just outside edges of ponderosa pine belt, as for example at Hoodoo and Big L., both e. Linn Co. (Gillson 1987, 2001b, Tice 2000b). While generally considered resident, individuals occasionally range >50 mi (80 km) outside breeding ranges following breeding season and on into winter. Littlefield (1990a) mentions 11 records from 23 Jul to 22 Nov over a 35-yr period at Malheur NWR. Gilligan (1993) reported two individuals near Howard Prairie Res., Jackson Co., 3 Aug 1992. A flock of six was reported on 17 Aug 1987 at Applegate, Jackson Co. (Heinl 1988a), and one was at Ashland in Jan and Feb 1991 (Johnson J 1991b). Browning (1975a) cites two occurrences on Medford CBCs, including five individuals on one count. Other examples include two reported near Williams, Josephine/Jackson Co. line (Korpi 2001a), and two at Cape Blanco, Curry Co., 13 Sep 1977 (Mattocks and Hunn 1978a). By 1992 up to five records reported for Curry Co., all in the fall (Rogers D 1982). Most unusual were 1-2 at a bird feeder in s. Salem Dec 1991, Feb 1993, and Jan 1994 (Johnson J 1992b, 1993b, 1994b).

**Habitat and Diet:** In Oregon, occurs in mature and old-growth ponderosa pine or mixed-species forests dominated by ponderosa pine (Gabrielson and Jewett 1940, *DBM*). However, sometimes forages in young ponderosa pines (*DBM*) and in lodgepole pines adjoining or near ponderosa pine stands (Stern, Del Carlo, et al. 1987, Gillson 2001a). Obviously vagrants and wanderers frequent other tree species. Arizona studies show this species reaches highest densities in old-growth ponderosa pine stands because of heavy reliance on cavities for nesting and roosting and high volume of ponderosa pine foliage (Szaro and Balda 1979). Timber harvesting has been demonstrated to significantly reduce densities in Arizona and Colorado with degree of reduction varying with harvest methods (Franzreb 1977, Franzreb and Ohmart 1978, Szaro and Balda 1979, Brawn 1987). No similar Oregon studies.

Nest in cavities in snags or dead portions of live trees (Norris 1958, Hay and Guntert 1983). Bent (1948) reported they typically excavate own nest cavities, often using cracks to gain entrance to a hollow or decaying wood. Likewise, in Marin Co., California, Norris (1958) reported these nuthatches as excavating their own cavities. However, in Colorado, McEllin (1979) found nest cavities (n=26) were usually those excavated by woodpeckers or were natural cavities that were sometimes modified. All were in ponderosa pine snags. Typical nesting cavities in California were 20+ ft (6+ m) from the ground in decaying pines that usually exceeded 20 in (50 cm) dbh (Norris 1958). Cavities were 2-4.5 in (5-11.4 cm) in diameter and 8.6 in (21.8 cm) deep, and were sometimes re-used in successive years (Norris 1958). Ten nest cavities in Arizona were in trees with a mean dbh of 16 in (39.2 cm), 18 ft (5.6 m) from the ground (Hay and Guntert 1983). The nest itself is cup-shaped and constructed of bark shreds, moss, grasses, fur, feathers, and other soft materials (Gabrielson and Jewett 1940, Bent 1948, Norris 1958). High rate of acceptance of artificial nest boxes found in Arizona (Brawn 1988, Brawn and Balda 1988) and Colorado (Bock and Fleck 1995). Nest boxes increased breeding pair densities where timber harvest had taken place in the Colorado study.

Roosting cavities, which are larger than nesting cavities, vary seasonally in size and character of openings according to thermoregulation and ventilation needs (Hay and Guntert 1983). Eight roosting cavities examined in Arizona were in trees with a mean dbh of 28.8 in (73.1 cm) (Hay and Guntert 1983).

Forage particularly on outer branches in upper canopy on needle clusters, cones, and emerging shoots (Norris 1958). Limited foraging occurs on bark of tree trunks and branches, and even on the ground (Manolis 1977). Forage by walking, hopping, and climbing both up and down all parts of the tree in varied positions including both right-side up and upside-down and sideways (Ewell and Cruz 1998). Cache food items. Employ probing, gleaning, picking, sallying, and cracking (in case of seed). Sealy (1984) reported capture of flying carpenter ants and caching them under bark in British Columbia. Diet varies by season and locale, but consists mainly of insects according to data collected in both Oregon and California by Beal (1907), Norris (1958), and Anderson (1976). Species include beetles, wasps, ants, true bugs, and butterfly/ moth larvae. Breeding diet in an Oregon study by volume comprised 45% weevils, 37% leaf beetles, and various ants and bark-dwelling insects (Anderson 1976). The diet switched to 59% leaf beetles and 38% other insects during the postbreeding period and in winter went to 12% leaf beetles, 25% weevils, 12% true bugs, 50% other insects, and 4% seeds. In Marin Co., California, Norris (1958) reported that nestlings were often fed pine seeds with hard outer coat removed. Pygmy Nuthatches can be attracted to bird feeders with suet and sunflower seed (*DBM*).

**Seasonal Activity and Behavior:** Monogamous with pair bonds maintained through the year (Norris 1958). Both sexes participate in cavity excavation and feeding of young. Excavation of nesting cavities likely begins in Mar and can extend over a lengthy period, based on out-of-state reports. Males defend a small territory near the nest; home ranges of nesting pairs can overlap (Norris 1958). OBBA data that show adults entering cavities from 7 Apr through 10 Jul (n=18) have questionable relevance considering that cavities are used year-round. However, the atlas shows presence of nestlings between 9 May and 18 Jul (n=9). Dates for fledged young extended from 13 Jun to 13 Jul (n=9). Incubation done by females (Norris 1958). Males feed females during nesting period. Clutch size typically 5-9, incubation 12-17 days, fledging 19 days (Norris 1958, Kingery and Ghalambor 2001). Both parents, and helpers if present, feed young. No Oregon information on helpers, but nesting pairs in Arizona and California often found to have one or more helpers, usually males produced the previous season that were related to the breeding pair (Sydeman et al. 1988, Sydeman 1989, 1991). Nests with helpers have higher success rate than those without (Sydeman et al. 1988). Second broods, while uncommon, do occur (Norris 1958, Kingery and Ghalambor 2001), and might in part account for the extended nesting period (*DBM*).

After the breeding season, typically occur as small flocks that increase in size through fall as two or more family groups comprising adults, helpers, and fledglings combine (Kingery and Ghalambor 2001). Multiple-family flocks can combine with still additional flocks for roosting during the coldest months. Foraging flock associates in Oregon include Mountain Chickadees, Red-breasted Nuthatches, and Brown Creepers (*DBM*).

To assist with maintaining body heat in winter, roosting individuals bunch together, clinging to the interior of a cavity or forming a pile at the bottom (Sydeman and Guntert 1983). Up to 150 individuals have been found in single cavities in Colorado and Arizona (Knorr 1957, Sydeman and Guntert 1983). Enter a torpid state in which body temperatures are lowered within the roosting cavity (Hay 1983). Distance traveled to roosts recorded up to 1 mi (1.7 km).

**Detection:** Easily and regularly detected by vocalizations. Observing more difficult because of constant movements and usual presence in upper canopy. Readily located where large pines are present in the Camp Sherman, Cold Springs, Black Butte region west of Sisters and in the Wood R. and west side of Upper Klamath L. areas.

**Population Status and Conservation:** No data are available indicating significant population changes since Gabrielson and Jewett (1940), who considered the Pygmy Nuthatch to be common. However, it is likely that since their time population numbers have declined based on habitat deterioration caused by loss of large-diameter snags and replacement of large ponderosa pines with smaller trees and other conifer species through fire control and logging (Agee 1993, Henjum et al. 1994).

Population densities vary between years, seasons, and locales. Densities can almost triple following the breeding season (Kingery and Ghalambor 2001). Matthysen (1998) calculated overall mean of 19.6 breeding pairs /100 ac (40 ha) from "various studies." Brawn (1987) had population densities reach 30 pairs/100 ac (40 ha; n=5) in Arizona through use of nest boxes in thinned ponderosa pine. BBS surveys run in Oregon are inconclusive because of small sample sizes.

Data from Oregon on this species comparable to those from other states are needed. Considering its dependence upon healthy ponderosa pine forests, status of this species should be periodically monitored in order to identify any habitat problems. Habitat needs of this species in many ways duplicate those of the Flammulated Owl and White-headed Woodpecker, which are species of concern for land managers and agencies.—*David B. Marshall*

## Family *Certhiidae*

### Subfamily Certhinae

**Brown Creeper** *Certhia americana*
Brown Creepers are the only N. American birds that rely on both the trunk and bark of trees for both nesting and foraging. They are small birds, about 5 in (13 cm)

in length, and have a long, slender, down-curved bill used to probe for insects hidden in the furrows of tree bark. Their brown back, streaked with white, makes creepers one of the best-camouflaged birds of the forest. They most often forage upward from the base of a tree, using their long, stiff tail for support.

**General Distribution:** Breed in forested regions of sw. and c. Alaska, c. British Columbia, Newfoundland, south to M. America, locally in the Midwest U.S. Winter throughout most of breeding range except for high latitudes and altitudes. Winter range includes areas of e. U.S., s. Texas, the Gulf coast and c. Florida where absent during the breeding season. Formerly *C. familiaris* but see AOU (1998). Nine subspecies are recognized, four of which occur in Oregon (*MRB*).

**Oregon Distribution:** Breeds and winters throughout forested areas of Oregon. *C. a. occidentalis* breeds from the coast to the w. Cascades (AMNH: Tillamook, Lakeside, Forest Grove; USNM: Astoria, McKenzie Bridge, Reston; DMNH: Salem), including specimens from Jackson, e. Douglas that Webster (*in* Phillips 1986) identified as *C. a. zelotes*. Browning (1990) confined the northern limit of *C. a. zelotes* to the east slope of the s. Oregon Cascades. *C. a. zelotes* breeds in Klamath (USNM) and s. Lake (CM) counties. *C. a. montana* breeds in the Blue Mtns. (USNM), and *caurina* on the east slope of the Cascades from n. Oregon to Deschutes Co. (Aldrich 1946). Webster (*in* Phillips 1986) and Pyle (1997) concluded that *caurina* is not distinct from *montana*, but *caurina* is more similar dorsally to *zelotes* and may actually be a paler example of *zelotes*, such as those in California (Browning 1990). Recognition of *caurina* is provisional (*MRB*). Uncommon to common transient, with *occidentalis* found throughout its breeding range and at Ft. Klamath (DMNH), *caurina* in the breeding range and at Anchor, sc. Douglas Co. (Aldrich 1946), Ft. Klamath (CM), and Portland (USNM), and *montana* in the breeding range and at Pendleton, Malheur NWR (USNM), and near Mt. Ashland in Jackson Co. (Unitt

and Rea 1997). Transient (subspecies uncertain) in scattered forest patches in the Columbia Basin, c. and se. Oregon, and throughout the breeding ranges. Winter throughout breeding range, including high-elevation forests, but may be less abundant there in winter (Contreras 1997b).

**Habitat and Diet:** Predominantly found in conifer forests, but also in oak woodlands (Hagar and Stern 2001), cottonwood stands (*JMW*), and in urban areas (*JMW, DBM*), especially during winter. It is not known if creepers occur in pure aspen stands of se. Oregon, but they were present in low numbers in such stands in Wyoming and Colorado (Finch and Reynolds 1987). Also, creepers were found in pure red alder stands >35 yr old in w. Washington (Stiles 1980), and may occur in similar habitat in Oregon. There are no sources describing territory or home range of creepers in the west. In Michigan, territories were 5.8-16 ac (2.3-6.4 ha) (Davis C 1979).

In small forested watersheds of the Coast Range, abundance of creepers was positively associated with the percent of land cover in late-successional forest (McGarigal and McComb 1995, Brooks 1997). In studies of conifer forest age classes in w. Oregon, creepers were more abundant in old-growth and mature woods than in young forests (Nelson 1988, Carey et al. 1991, Gilbert and Allwine 1991). In 80- to 120-yr-old stands in the Coast Range, clearcutting and cutting with live tree retention caused a reduction in abundance of creepers whereas small patch cuts did not affect abundance (Chambers et al. 1999). Creepers have been reported absent or relatively rare in younger managed forests in w. Oregon (Bettinger 1996, Mannan 1980, *JMW*). Creepers have been negatively affected by thinning in young conifer forests (Hayes et al. in press).

In the Blue Mtns., creepers were less abundant in recent clearcuts than in other forest types, but did not differ in abundance among stem exclusion, closed canopy, understory reinitiation, or old-forest multistory stands (Sallabanks et al. unpubl. ms.). Density of creepers was substantially reduced for at least 3 yr following stand-replacing fires in ne. Oregon that removed most live conifer canopy (Sallabanks and McIver 1998).

It is uncertain if fragmentation of late-successional forests affects creepers. McGarigal and McComb (1995) reported that creepers occupied landscapes that were less fragmented than average landscapes in the Coast Range, however, they and Brooks (1997) reported creepers to be associated with some indices that represented higher degrees of fragmentation. More study is needed to clarify this relationship.

In the Coast Range, creepers were more abundant upslope than near streams (McGarigal and McComb 1992) and more abundant in unlogged than in logged

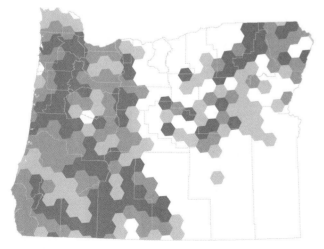

riparian areas (Hagar 1999a). Within logged areas, abundance increased with increasing width of buffers (Hagar 1999a).

In unmanaged Douglas-fir forests of the Coast Range, abundance of creepers in summer was positively related to density of large (> 39 in [100 cm]) snags and trees (Carey et al. 1991). In grand fir forests of ne. Oregon, abundance of creepers was positively associated with height of the canopy and density of trees (Sallabanks et al. unpubl. ms.). In Oregon white oak woodlands, abundance during the breeding season was positively related to height of overstory trees of Oregon white oak and negatively related to the percent overstory cover of Douglas-fir (Hagar and Stern 2001).

The presence of large trees with deeply furrowed bark, such as oaks, giant sequoias, and maples may explain why this "old-growth"-associated species occasionally resides in urban areas. They have been reported to occur in urban areas of ne. Oregon (Evanich 1992a), in the city of Corvallis (*JMW*), and in areas of Portland with old (100 yr) Douglas-fir trees (*DBM*). It is uncertain whether creepers breed in urban areas.

Creepers usually nest under loose, sloughing bark of relatively large-diameter dead trees. In unmanaged forests of the Coast Range, mean dbh of nest trees (n=28) was 42 in (107.4 cm) in old-growth forest, 23.5 in (59.7 cm) (n=14) in mature forest, and 16 in (41.4 cm) (n=8) in young forests (Nelson 1988). Creepers will nest in small-diameter snags if large snags are not available, but the ability to successfully fledge young from these nests is uncertain. Of six nests found in another study in managed young forests of the Coast Range, mean dbh was 11.5 in (29.3 cm); four nests were thought to have been abandoned or destroyed by weather, one was suspected to fledge young, and one successfully fledged young (*JMW*). Nests in small-diameter trees appear to be more susceptible to damage from weather due to the relatively thin bark of those trees. Creepers have been reported to use Douglas-fir, western redcedar, grand fir, bigleaf maple, western white pine, and lodgepole pine for nesting (Gabrielson and Jewett 1940, Nelson 1988, Lundquist and Mariani 1991). Creepers select snags with little to moderate decay (Nelson 1988, *JMW*). May use specially designed nest boxes (Merilees 1987).

During the breeding season, creepers forage on the trunk and to a lesser extent along the branches of live trees (Lundquist and Manuwal 1990, Weikel and Hayes 1999). Creepers selected trees with deep furrows and many dead branches for foraging in young forests of the Coast Range (Weikel and Hayes 1999), and trees >20 in (50 cm) for foraging in both old- and second-growth forests in the s. Washington Cascades (Lundquist and Manuwal 1990). Aspects of epiphytic communities and associated arthropod communities may also be important components of foraging habitat (*MGH*).

Little information is available on winter habitat, but existing studies suggest more general use in winter than summer. In w. Cascade riparian areas, abundance of creepers greater in old-growth than mature forest during summer, but similar during winter (Anthony et al. 1996). In young forests of the c. Coast Range, more abundant in thinned vs. unthinned stands during summer, but no difference in winter (Hagar et al. 1996). In the s. Washington Cascades, foraged almost exclusively on tree trunks during summer, but foraged more generally and used branches more during winter (Lundquist and Manuwal 1990).

No diet information from Oregon. In forests of the s. Cascades in Washington, spiders were present in all six creeper stomachs collected, and abundance of creepers was positively correlated with abundance of spiders (Mariani and Manuwal 1990). Also found in creeper stomachs were larvae and pupae of Lepidoptera, and adult Diptera, Neuroptera, Tricoptera, Lepidoptera, Hemiptera, Homoptera, and Coleoptera. In the Sierra Nevada of California, Otvos and Stark (1985) examined the stomachs of 14 creepers collected from conifer forests experiencing an outbreak of bark beetles. They found that beetles comprised the largest proportion (62.8%) of the diet (by volume) followed by Pseudoscorpionida (9.7%), Hemiptera (7.5%), Arachnida (5.7%), and Elateridae (4.2%). Thus, creeper diet may vary widely throughout their range and they may take advantage of locally abundant prey species.

**Seasonal Activity and Behavior:** Nest building observed early May to mid-Jun (n=6), incubation mid-May to late Jun (n=6), and hatched young mid-Jun to mid-Jul (n=10) (OBBA). Fledged young are most frequently observed in Jul, but have been observed as early as mid- to late May (n=15) (OBBA, Gullion 1951). Little information exists regarding post-fledging behaviors, but a thorough study in Michigan (Davis C 1979) reported that young birds were cared for by both parents after fledging and that the young, without the company of the adults, formed communal night roosts. They have not been reported to raise more than one brood per year, but will renest if the nest is destroyed (Davis C 1979, Harrap and Quinn 1995).

Little information exists regarding seasonal movements, but some localized short-distance movement likely occurs between seasons. Creepers migrate through Malheur NWR: peak passage is 25 Apr to 7 May, the latest arrival 6 Jun. In fall, recorded 1 Oct–13 Nov (Littlefield 1990a). Phillips et al. (1964) found *C. a. caurina* in winter in Arizona, suggesting longer movements of interior populations. During winter, usually found alone, in pairs, or in flocks with chickadees, kinglets, nuthatches, woodpeckers, and other creepers (Bent 1948, Anderson 1972).

**Detection:** Most likely to be detected by hearing their high-pitched *trees, trees, beau-ti-ful trees* song in the spring and summer. In fall and winter, they are most easily detected by their call notes, which are similar to those of Golden-crowned Kinglets, but can be distinguished from them because they usually occur in pairs and sound similar to the two introductory notes of the creeper song. Creepers can be seen by following their calls and looking for the birds as they fly to the base of, or as they creep upward along the bole of a tree.

**Population Status and Conservation:** Although fairly common and somewhat flexible in their use of different forest types, creepers may be sensitive to forest-management practices, particularly in w. Oregon (Chambers et al. 1999, Hayes et al. unpubl. ms.). Intensive forest management that reduces the number of large-diameter snags and live trees and fragments the forest may result in population declines of creepers. However, management that retains sufficient quantities of large-diameter trees and snags may help prevent population declines in managed forests (*JMW*).— *Jennifer M. Weikel*

## Family Troglodytidae

### Rock Wren *Salpinctes obsoletus*

Even in the most barren and desolate reaches of the Great Basin, the cheerful song of this hardy wren will contradict any notion that the desert is devoid of life. This specialist of cracks and crevices can be found almost anywhere there is exposed rock. One of its most unique features is the mysterious pebble path it constructs from its stone-cave nest to the outside entrance. Drab and pale overall, the gray head and back, white to tawny underparts, and gray tail with buff-tipped corners distinguish this species from other wrens.

**General Distribution:** Breeds from sc. British Columbia, s. Alberta, and s. Saskatchewan south throughout w. U.S. to Baja California, east to w. N. Dakota, c. and s. Texas and south to Costa Rica. A few remain within the northern limits of its breeding range, but most winter from n. California, s. Nevada, se. Utah, n. New Mexico and Oklahoma south through southern portions of breeding range. Casual outside breeding range during migration and winter west of Coast Ranges and east to e. Nebraska and e. Texas (AOU 1998, Lowther et al. 2000). Of several subspecies, *S.o. obsoletus* is found in Oregon (Phillips 1986).

**Oregon Distribution:** The Rock Wren is a common breeder east of the Cascade summit, rare breeder west of the Cascade summit. Principal breeding range

is within the Great Basin where abundant. Rare but regular breeder at scattered rocky ridges and summits in the w. Cascades, Rogue Valley, and Siskiyous. Breeds to at least 7,000 ft (2,150 m) and has been found during the breeding season above timberline in the Cascades (though not all are confirmed as breeding). For example, a singing bird was noted at 7,500 ft (2,286 m) on the east side of Mt. Hood and 1was noted on the north side as well (Anderson 1989d); and Rock Wrens are locally common in Crater L. NP (Farner 1952, Follett 1979). Several Rock Wrens, likely postbreeding birds, were observed 18 Aug 1984 at 9,200 ft (2,800 m) on the summit of Mt. McLoughlin in the s. Oregon Cascades (Hunn and Mattocks 1985). Also has been found on top of Steens Mtn. (*CRM*). Extremely rare and irregular breeder in the Willamette Valley and Coast Range (Gilligan et al. 1994, OBBA, *CRM*).

In winter, very uncommon to rare resident east of the Cascades, rare in the Rogue Valley (Gilligan et al. 1994, Contreras 1997b), and generally absent elsewhere. Only three coastal winter records; one at Netarts 27 Dec 1912 (Jewett 1913), one at Yaquina Head 13 Nov-24 Dec 1988 (Heinl and Fix 1989, Johnson 1989b), and one at the Coast Guard Air Facility in Newport 15 Dec 2000-28 Jan 2001 (*CRM*).

**Habitat and Diet:** The principal requirement of Rock Wren habitat is sparsely vegetated or unvegetated surface rich in crevices, interstices, recesses, and confined passageways (Ryser 1985). They are most often found at rock outcroppings, rocky slopes, rimrock, and lava fields, but also at rock quarries, earthen dams, and forest clearcuts, especially west of the Cascade summit (Marshall and Horn 1973, Gilligan et al. 1994). They are best adapted to the shrub-steppe-dominated Basin and Range Ecoregion of se. Oregon. Nests are placed in a crevice or on the ground beneath a rock in a tightly confined space (Ryser 1985, Lowther et al. 2000). The bird paves its nest cavity with 0.5- to 2-in (12- to 50-mm) flat stones (may include other similar-sized objects), topped by

a nest with sticks and bark, lined with fine rootlets, grass, moss, hair, and spider silk (Gabrielson and Jewett 1940, Harrison 1979, Merola 1995, Oppenheimer and Morton 2000). Additionally, unless the nest is close to the entrance, the wren paves a stone walk from nest to the entrance 0-20 in (0-45 cm) in length, sometimes piling rocks at the entrance to form a barrier with a small opening (Bailey 1904, Ryser 1985, Littlefield 1990a, Lowther et al. 2000).

Rock Wrens feed primarily on insects including grasshoppers, crickets, ants, and leafhoppers (Knowlton and Harmston 1942, Holbo 1979, Lowther et al. 2000). They most often forage on open ground, in bunchgrass clumps, and alongside rocks (Mirsky 1976, Lowther et al. 2000). Sufficient water is provided by their diet to meet their needs; Rock Wrens are not known to drink free water (Smyth and Bartholomew 1966). Habitat requirements are essentially unchanged in winter, although elevations must be low enough to provide snow-free access to exposed rocky openings.

**Seasonal Activity and Behavior:** Spring migration extends from early Apr to mid-May, and although generally inconspicuous, peaks in early May (Littlefield 1990a, *CRM*). Territories are set up soon after arrival in the breeding area; individuals often return to previous year's site (Merola 1995). Males are vigilant in defense of territories and mates, both by singing and chasing (Merola 1995). When an intruder enters its territory, the male responds by giving its call, bobbing, and even making physical contact (Lowther et al. 2000). The song repertoire astonishingly can exceed 120 distinct types for a single individual. Frequent use of specific song types is geographically associated (Kroodsma 1975). The male sings while perched on one or another favorite promontory. Nesting begins early to mid-May (Littlefield 1990a). The female lays 4-10 white eggs spotted reddish brown (Bent 1948). There are only two substantial breeding studies, conducted in New Mexico by Merola (1995) and at high elevation in California by Oppenheimer and Morton (2000): eggs were laid at the rate of one per day; incubation performed by female only; eggs hatched in 12-16 days; young fledged in 12-16 days. Both parents assisted in feeding young on the nest and up to a week after fledging; young stayed in the parents territory up to 4 wk after fledging. Up to three broods were observed in a season in a New Mexico study; each brood was raised in a different nest in the same territory (Merola 1995). Multiple broods may occur in Oregon; dependent fledglings were observed 14 Jun to 11 Aug (Farner 1952, OBBA).

Postbreeding dispersal and southward migration extends from mid-Aug to late Oct and peaks in early to mid-Sep (Littlefield 1990a, *CRM*). Family groups may remain together through Oct (Mirsky 1976, *CRM*). A few birds spend at least some winters in the lower elevations east of the Cascades (depending on severity of weather), in the Rogue Valley, and very rarely along the coast.

**Detection:** Usually heard before seen. Most easily found during breeding season when male is sure to be heard singing from the top of a rock perch. Coloration can effectively camouflage the bird even when in full view on exposed rock surface. However, tendency to bob and dip while singing or investigating helps locate the bird. Sharp, slightly trilled *tic-reer* call is frequently the first announcement of its presence (Bent 1948, Lowther et al. 2000). Call may be heard throughout the year and given by either sex (Lowther et al. 2000). Usually not shy, and may approach the observer within a few feet (Holbo 1979, *CRM*).

**Population Status and Conservation:** BBS data have shown no significant population changes in Rock Wren breeding range over the past 30 yr (Sauer et al. 1999). Oregon has some of the highest densities in the U.S. Expansive arid lands of rimrock, talus slopes, and rocky lands provide a unique niche with minimal competition with other avian species. The Warner Valley BBS and nearby Blizzard Gap BBS averaged 39.5 and 34.4 individuals per count respectively (USGS 2001, K. Pardiek p.c.). Rough terrain, inaccessibility, and vast expanses of public land tend to prevent human intrusion and significant loss of critical habitat in its range.—*Craig R. Miller*

## Canyon Wren *Catherpes mexicanus*

This eloquent wren is admired for its sweet, descending, liquid notes that echo off canyon walls. It is distinguished from other wrens by its gleaming white throat set off by gray head, rusty brown underparts and back, and bright rufous tail. Appreciated as it is, this is one of our least-studied birds in part due to its frequently inaccessible habitat: cliffs, rimrock, and deep canyon walls.

**General Distribution:** Resident from sc. British Columbia, w. and s. Idaho, and s. Montana south to wc. Texas, Baja California, and Mexico to Oaxaca. Disjunct populations occur in sw. S. Dakota, ne. Wyoming, and se. Montana (Jones and Dieni 1995). Winters in generally same range, although found in some desert areas where rarely if ever breeding. Length of migration unknown; some individuals may withdraw from high elevations and northern portions of their range (Jones and Dieni 1995, AOU 1998). Of possibly eight subspecies, *C. m. griseus* breeds in Oregon (Phillips 1986); *punctulatus*, recognized by Behle (1943) and Aldrich (1946), and *conspersus* (*contra* AOU 1957) do not occur in Oregon (see Phillips 1986).

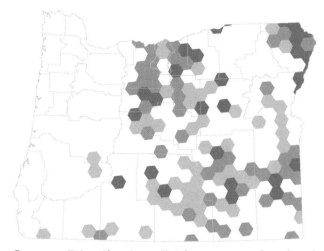

**Oregon Distribution:** Fairly common but local breeder in Oregon east of the Cascade summit; restricted to rocky cliffs or outcrops. Very rare, but possible breeder on the west slope of the s. Cascades (Heinl 1989b, Fix 1990a, Hunter et al. 1998). Rare and sporadic during summer in the Rogue Valley westward (Gilligan et al. 1994, Tice 1999a). Only one coastal record, a singing bird near Wedderburn, Curry Co., 28 Jun 1970 (Gilligan et al. 1994). More dispersed after breeding season as evidenced by a smattering of Aug-Oct records west of known breeding range along the Columbia Gorge, in the Willamette Valley, and in the Cascades (Gilligan et al. 1994, *CRM, MGH, DBM*).

**Habitat and Diet:** Inhabits steep rocky canyon walls, cliff faces, rimrock, and boulder piles in open, arid country (Gilligan et al. 1994, Jones and Dieni 1995). Occupies crevices, interstices, and cracks. Has marginally adapted to human dwellings, and is even known to inhabit occupied homes (Bent 1948, S. Kornfeld p.c., *DBM*). Has no association with any vegetative community (Jones and Dieni 1995). Nest placed in crevice, cave, or abandoned building; a cup constructed with twigs, moss, grasses, and dead leaves and lined with soft materials such as lichens, plant down, cobwebs, and feathers (Jones and Dieni 1995). Feeds on spiders and insects. Forages almost exclusively in cracks, crevices, and under rocks while Rock Wren usually forages on surfaces, explaining ability to coexist despite overlapping habitat and diet (Tramontano 1964, Mirsky 1976). Long, slender bill, flattened skull, and short tarsi are adapted to foraging and locomotion in narrow and confined spaces. Distinctive foraging posture includes spread legs, extended neck, and breast and bill close to the surface. Large feet, long claws, and short tarsi allow upward and downward climbing along vertical rock (Mirsky 1976).

**Seasonal Activity and Behavior:** Some are resident, but there is a minor seasonal migration and dispersal. Spring migration occurs from mid-Mar through Apr

without a discernible peak (Littlefield 1990a, *CRM*). Virtually all the information on the biology of the Canyon Wren has been obtained outside Oregon. Monogamous, possibly mating for life (Tramontano 1964, Mirsky 1976, Jones and Dieni 1995). Song is a series of descending liquid notes ending in a low burry *too-ee*. Although both sexes sing, the song of the female is rarer, shorter, and more buzzy (Tramontano 1964, Jones and Dieni 1995). May sing any time of year from regular perches high on cliff tops to bottom of rock faces. Courtship vocalizations are variable and involve both sexes. Call is a loud, penetrating buzz (Jones and Dieni 1995). Both sexes may attempt to repel Rock Wren, although successful breeding territories sometimes overlap. Lays 3-7 (but usually five) white eggs with a few faint reddish brown dots (Bent 1948, Jones and Dieni 1995). Female incubates eggs 12-18 days (average 15 days), male feeds female during incubation (Tramontano 1964, Verner and Willson 1969, Jones and Dieni 1995). Hatched young fledge in 12-17 days (average 15 days). In Oregon, range of dates for incubating, carrying food, and nest with young 17 May-2 Jul (n=6) (OBBA), and fledge dates 23 May-11 Jul (n=7) (OBBA). Both parents feed nestlings and fledglings (Tramontano 1964, Verner and Willson 1969). Although young may stay with adults as family group for several weeks to several months, they are only fed 5-10 days after fledging (Mirsky 1976, Jones and Dieni 1995).

Fall migration from late Aug through mid-Sep is inconspicuous and usually goes unobserved (Littlefield 1990a, *CRM*). However, Littlefield (1990a) recounts "a pronounced movement" of "several" individuals at the Malheur Field Station on 8-9 Sep 1977. Uncommon but regular in breeding areas during winter. Territory is established year-round by residents, but is smaller during breeding season than winter. In Colorado, average territory increased from 2.2 ac (0.91 ha) during breeding season to 3.6 ac (1.44 ha) in winter (Jones and Dieni 1995).

**Detection:** Canyon Wrens are most easily found during breeding season when actively singing, but alarm call also facilitates detection. Although elusive, they are not particularly shy and may allow approach within a few feet (Bent 1948). Inaccessibility of nest makes study of life history difficult. Good locations to find this species include Smith Rock SP, Fort Rock SP, Wright's Point, and Page Springs CG near Frenchglen, and Succor Cr. Canyon in Malheur Co. (Littlefield 1990a, *CRM, ALC*).

**Population Status and Conservation:** Although BBS data indicate a significant decline on a continent-wide basis, the data do not adequately cover habitat in Oregon. No information is available regarding population trends in Oregon. Competition with other bird species is minimal (Tramontano 1964, Mirsky 1976). The only potential threat identified is local nest disturbance by rock climbers (Jones and Dieni 1995). Smith Rock SP is the only breeding location in Oregon with a significant rock climbing presence.—*Craig R. Miller*

## Bewick's Wren *Thryomanes bewickii*

The song of this wren is often mistaken for that of the Song Sparrow in the thickets and open woodlands where it resides. When in view, however, its long tail, thin bill, and white line above its eye are distinctive. Found in a variety of habitats, it readily takes advantage of cleared forest grown to large shrubs, especially blackberries. Populations have decreased dramatically in the e. U.S., but its population and range have expanded in Oregon.

**General Distribution:** Breeds from sw. British Columbia, w. Washington, w., nc. and sc. Oregon, and California, to sc. Baja, Mexico; in Great Basin and sw. U.S., from ne. California, s. Nevada to w. Colorado; c. U.S. within s. Kansas, Oklahoma; Ozarks; c. Texas; throughout much of c. Mexico; currently, a rare breeder in e. U.S. Winter range is broadly consistent with breeding range. At least 16 subspecies north of Mexico (AOU 1957), with three occurring in Oregon.

**Oregon Distribution:** Permanent resident west of the Cascades, in Klamath and Warner basins, and along the upper Columbia R. and tributaries (Nehls 1981, Gilligan et al. 1994, Contreras 1998). Locally common nester in clearcuts and along forest edges up to 2,000 ft (600 m) elevation in the Coast Range and w. Cascades (Fix 1990a, Gilligan et al. 1994). Historically, Bewick's Wrens were rare at Malheur NWR, with no sightings between the 1870s (Bendire 1877) and 1982 (Littlefield 1990a). However, numerous recent sightings suggest that a population may be re-establishing in the southeast section of the

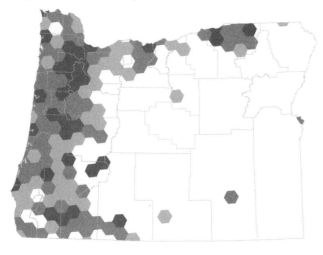

refuge (Littlefield 1990a). Populations have become established in the past 30-40 yr in suitable habitat in the e. Columbia R. basin (Nehls 1981). Birds have been found east to c. Umatilla Co. (Gilligan et al. 1994), and south along the upper stretches of the Deschutes R. and White R. near White R. SP (D. Lusthoff p.c.). In Umatilla Co., Bewick's Wrens are now found year-round in the Umatilla R. and Walla Walla R. drainages, up to 2,800 ft (853 m) in the Blue Mtns. (M. Denny p.c.). Most recently, 25 May 2002, one was observed singing and appearing territorial on Cactus Mtn. above the Snake R. in e. Wallowa Co., (F. Conley p.c.).

Winter birds are mostly found in valley areas below 1,500 ft (455 m), with the largest number wintering west of the Cascades (Gilligan et al. 1994). Bewick's Wrens were rare in winter in the early 1990s in Union and Wallowa counties (Evanich 1992a), but are becoming more regular (M. Denny p.c., F. Conley p.c.).

Subspecific boundaries are not well understood, particularly in sw. Oregon (Browning and Cross 1999). *T. b. calophonus* nests chiefly west of the Cascades from Columbia R. to Coos and Douglas counties (Gabrielson and Jewett 1940, AOU 1957, Nehls 1981); occasionally winters in Rogue Valley (Browning and Cross 1999). *T. b. drymoecus* is found in the Rogue R. Valley and the Klamath Basin (Gabrielson and Jewett 1940, AOU 1957, Browning and Cross 1999). A boundary between *calophonus* and *drymoecus* occurs near Grants Pass, Josephine Co. (Browning and Cross 1999). *T. b. atrestus* apparently is a resident in the Warner Valley and the Klamath basin (CMNH, OSU, Miller 1941, *MRB*). Subspecific determinations have not yet been made for populations expanding into e. Columbia R. basin.

**Habitat and Diet:** Habitats include brushy areas and scrub in open country, riparian and upland forest thickets and edges, clearcuts, and open woodlands; but also around human habitations when enough cover is available. At William L. Finley NWR, Bewick's Wrens are found in dense patches of blackberry and Nootka rose, mixed stands of Douglas-fir and Oregon white oak, and river-bottom habitat of oak or ash overstory with a dense understory (Kroodsma 1973). Found in all 10 oak woodland sites within the Willamette Valley surveyed by Hagar and Stern (2001). In drier climate of sw. Oregon, found in chaparral-oak communities (Browning 1975a, Gilligan et al. 1994).

Nests of Bewick's Wrens are placed in natural or woodpecker-created cavities when available, and on ledges in barns and sheds. Are generally cup shaped (2.0-2.6 in [5.0-6.5 cm] in diameter) (Kennedy and White 1997) and are constructed from a variety of materials of both plant (e.g., rootlets, twigs, leaves, and moss) and animal (e.g., spider webs, feathers, and hair) origin. Nests are typically located within 6.6 ft (2 m) of the ground.

*Bewick's Wren*

Foraging is accomplished in rapid bouts within thickets, gleaning insects from leaves, bark, and occasionally within litter on the ground. Clearly insectivorous, as 97% of food items identified over the course of a year were insects and spiders (Beal 1907). In this California study, 146 stomachs, collected over all months of the year, were examined: true bugs dominated the samples (31%, primarily leaf bugs, stink bugs, shield bugs, leaf hoppers, tree hoppers, and jumping plant lice), followed by beetles (21%; primarily weevils, ladybirds, and leaf beetles), hymenoptera (17%; mainly ants and wasps), caterpillars (11%), grasshoppers (4%), and spiders (5%).

**Seasonal Activity and Behavior:** In areas where birds reside year-round, territories are established as early as Feb (Kroodsma 1972), but territories can also be maintained over winter months (Miller EV 1941, Kroodmsa 1974). Nest building by both sexes begins in early to mid-Mar. Eggs are generally laid (clutch size 3-6) from early Apr through late May (Gabrielson and Jewett 1940, OBBA). Only the female incubates eggs. Fledging takes places mid-late May through late Jul. On William L. Finley NWR, nesting was completed in 13 of 19 nests by mid-Jun (Kroodsma 1973). Fledging occurred in five other nests in Jul; these later nests were parented by first-year males or renesters. Multiple brooding by males appears to be uncommon as only 2 of 30 second-nesting attempts monitored by Kroodsma (1972) resulted in successful broods. After leaving the nest, fledglings are fed by both parents for 2-3 wk; dispersal from their home territory is generally complete within 5 wk of fledging (Kroodsma 1974).

A study in the Willamette Valley found nesting territories to be contiguous but non-overlapping (Kroodsma 1973). Territory size was dependent upon habitat structure; mean territory size was 4.9 ac (2.0 ha), ranging 3.1-9.4 ac (1.3-3.8 ha) in a forest with dense underbrush and 9.4 ac (3.8 ha), ranging 6.1-11.8 ac (2.5-4.8 ha) in an open woodland where suitable shrub habitat was more patchy. Territories overlapped extensively with those of House Wrens, but Bewick's Wrens preferred thicker vegetation while House Wrens generally utilized more open areas. Interspecific competition may also be reduced by slightly different nesting phenologies; peak fledging period of Bewick's Wren was approximately 1 mo before the House Wren's (Kroodsma 1973).

Although generally considered to be monogamous breeders, bigamy has been identified (Kroodsma 1972). On Finley NWR, a male was observed feeding nestlings that were known to be its own plus a family flock of four fledglings on his territory. One day later, the nest fledged and the young birds joined the other fledglings on the territory. Although clearly uncommon, it is not surprising since four of nine species within the wren family are regularly polygamous (Verner and Willson 1969).

**Detection:** Easily detected by songs and calls. It is difficult to find nests in thick brushy habitat, but males are easy to spot while singing from conspicuous perches. These wrens are quite responsive to attractive noises (e.g., spishing and hooting).

**Population Status and Conservation:** Across the U.S., population sizes have fluctuated greatly, with eastern populations decreasing significantly while some western populations have increased substantially (Sauer et al. 1999). Between 1966 and 1999, eastern populations decreased by 12.6% per year; the most significant declines were in W. Virginia (33.5%), Tennessee (19.1%), and Mississippi (15.9%). A possible cause of the decline was competition with the House Wren, which has been observed to displace Bewick's Wrens from territories through aggressive interactions (Root 1969b), and to destroy nests, eggs, and nestlings (Kennedy and White 1996). During that same period, populations in the Basin and Range region of the west increased 52.1% while those on the Columbia Plateau increased 13.3%.

In Oregon, overall population size was found to have increased at a rate of 6.5%/yr 1980-99 (Sauer et al. 1999). Range expansion into the foothills of the Cascades, possibly facilitated by favorable habitat created after timber harvesting (Nehls 1981), likely contributed to this increase. Considerable population expansion into the Columbia R. lowlands has also occurred during the past 40 yr (Lewke 1974, Nehls 1981, Gilligan et al. 1994). Backwaters formed after construction of dams probably led to new riparian habitat suitable for colonization (Nehls 1981).— *Robert Peck*

## House Wren *Troglodytes aedon*

This moderately small wren maintains the frenetic energy that is so obviously typical of this family of birds. It is a summer inhabitant in many parts of Oregon, generally in open woodlands, thickets, and occasionally in residential gardens. Its overall body coloration is light brown with subdued barring on wings and tail. It is distinguished from other wrens by its distinctive song, a lack of obvious markings (such as a distinctive white eyebrow stripe), and a relatively long, often uncocked tail. This wren occurs over the widest latitudinal range of any New World passerine (Johnson LS 1998).

**General Distribution:** Breeds from c. Canada to Tierra del Fuego (Argentina and Chile) (Paynter 1960, Phillips 1986). Winters in the s. U.S. south throughout much of M. and S. America to c. Argentina and c. Chile (DeGraaf and Rappole 1995). Approximately thirty subspecies recognized within five groups (Paynter 1960, Phillips 1986). *T. a. parkmanii* is found in w. U.S. and Oregon.

**Oregon Distribution:** Very uncommon to common transient and summer resident in semi-open woodland habitats throughout the state. In sw. Oregon, most common in oak-chaparral and mixed woodlands of valley foothills and mountains (Browning 1975a, Gilligan et al. 1994). Generally uncommon on west slopes of the Coast Range, except in clearcuts containing snags, where it can be very common (Schreiber 1987). Common in oak and mixed forests of foothills on the east side of the Coast Range (Gilligan et al. 1994). Found in scattered locations in the Willamette Valley, particularly within brushy areas (Kroodsma 1973, Gillson 1999) and oak woodlands (Hagar and Stern 2001). Within the w. Cascades, most often found at natural and clearcut forest openings containing suitable nesting habitat (Fix 1990a). East of the Cascades, found in suitable treed habitats, particularly aspen (Marshall 1987, Evanich 1992a, Gilligan et al. 1994, C. Corkran unpubl. data), but also found in brushy areas in late summer (*DBM*). Common spring and fall migrant and summer nester throughout Malheur Co. (Contreras and Kindschy 1996) but uncommon nester on Malheur NWR (Littlefield 1990a). Occasionally reported in winter but few well-documented records exist (Contreras 1998).

**Habitat and Diet:** Although regionally variable in abundance, the House Wren nests in a wide variety of native and human-influenced habitats, including riparian and upland deciduous woodlands, open conifer forests, clearcuts and thinned conifer stands, rural and urban gardens and city parks (Gilligan et al. 1994, *DBM*). On the Umpqua NF, found to colonize recently burned clearcuts, foraging on open ground or near the base of down logs and stumps (Fix 1990a). This wren nests along stream courses in the Pueblos in s. Harney Co., and in the Mahogany Mtns., Oregon Canyon Mtns., Battle Mtn., and Cedar Mtn., Malheur Co. (M. Denny p.c.).

Nest sites are primarily located within preformed cavities in snags (such as woodpecker-drilled holes), but also are found behind cupped bark on snags, in tall stumps in clearcuts, and in nest boxes. In snags within clearcuts in the c. Oregon Coast Range, Schreiber (1987) found average nest height to be 17.7 ft (5.4 m; range 2.0-4.7 ft [0.6-14.3 m]; n=96 nests). Other odd locations include outhouses and abandoned farm equipment and rock crevices (C. Corkran p.c., *DBM*).

Nest cups described from outside Oregon are generally constructed of grass, fine bark, hair, and feathers, and often built on a platform of small twigs and sticks 2-8 in (5-20 cm) tall (Johnson LS 1998). The size and shape of the stick platform is determined by the dimensions of the cavity and allows the soft nest cup to be built in preferred positions within the cavity. In nest boxes placed in Wheeler and Grant counties, the nest cavity is totally filled with sticks, leaving only a narrow tunnel from the entrance, up over the top of the sticks, and down to the cup in a lower back corner of the box (C. Corkran p.c.). Males often initiate or complete the construction of the stick platform while the female builds the soft lining of the nest (Kennedy and White 1992, Alworth and Scheiber 2000). Nest cavities are commonly reused, but nearly all old nest cups, and some platforms, are removed prior to rebuilding a new nest. Removal of old nests has been suggested as a means of reducing populations of parasitic mites that may overwinter in the nests (Pacejka and Thompson 1996).

Like other wrens, House Wrens feed primarily by gleaning arthropods from surfaces of leaves and woody parts of understory vegetation, but also forages within ground litter. A study in Manitoba identifying contents of stomachs of 88 individuals concluded that birds consume representatives of most invertebrate taxa available (Guinan and Sealy 1987). Other studies of both adults and nestlings also revealed a wide range of prey consumed, including, but not limited to, crickets, beetles, leafhoppers, true bugs, flies, spiders, wasps, ants, and caterpillars (Beal 1907, Morton 1984, Johnson LS 1998).

**Seasonal Activity and Behavior:** Males generally arrive on nesting areas a few days prior to females (late Apr to early May), and immediately begin **claiming**

open nesting cavities and initiating nest construction (Kroodsma 1973, Littlefield 1990a, OBBA). Early dates for the species include 23 Mar 1985 at Corvallis (Fix 1985a), and 30 Mar 1986 at Fern Ridge Res. (Heinl 1986c).

Pairs are predominantly monogamous, although male polygyny has been observed (Johnson and Kermott 1991). Females complete nests within 3-14 days; once the nest is completed, egg laying is initiated (Johnson LS 1998). A survey of 137 nests in bluebird nest boxes in juniper savannah in Wheeler and Grant counties revealed an average clutch size of 6.8 eggs (C. Corkran unpubl. data). Eggs and nestlings are brooded exclusively by the female. Egg incubation usually lasts 12-13 days after the last egg is laid, and the nestling period lasts 17-18 days (Johnson LS 1998).

Double brooding may greatly extend the length of the nesting season. Double brooding is a common phenomenon in the House Wren, but whether it occurs is influenced by location (e.g., elevation, latitude) and possibly reproductive experience (Kendeigh 1941, Johnson LS 1998). It is not clear to what extent double brooding occurs throughout Oregon, but observations of young birds in nests in late Jul and mid-Aug (OBBA) suggest that it may occur. In C. Corkran's (unpubl. data) survey of bluebird boxes, the onset of egg laying was observed as late as 18 Jul. Here, however, House Wrens sometimes only obtained access to nest boxes after young bluebirds had fledged.

Timing of fall migration is not well known, but most birds likely depart between late Aug and late Sep, with few reports by early Oct (McAllister and Marshall 1945, Browning 1975a, Littlefield 1990a, Gilligan et al. 1994). Littlefield (1990a) indicates that fall migration peaks between 20 and 31 Aug on Malheur NWR. Late dates include 25 Oct 1970 at Prineville (Scott OK 1971), 2 on 22 Nov 1981 at Tumalo (Evanich 1982d), and 19 Oct 1986 at Florence and Ashland (Fix 1987a).

Interspecific competition with Bewick's Wren is widely recognized, but the intensity of the interaction appears variable. In California, interspecific territories were well defined, with the House Wren generally displacing Bewick's Wren upon encounter (Root 1969b). In contrast, Kroodsma (1973) found considerable overlap of territories on William L. Finley NWR, with House Wren territories being considerably smaller than those of Bewick's Wren; 2.3 ac (0.9 ha; n=14) vs. 9.4 ac (3.8 ha; n=6), respectively. Population densities, as well as habitat structure, may contribute to the intensity of these interactions.

**Detection**: Easily detected by song during breeding season. Where sympatric, House Wren has been found to mimic the song of Bewick's Wren (Kroodsma 1973). During winter, Marsh Wrens are sometimes mis-identified as House Wrens because of their relatively plain plumage that time of year (MGH).

**Population Status and Conservation:** Population trend estimates from BBS data reveal only minor fluctuations in population sizes. Across U.S. and Canada, a small increase in abundance was detected 1966-99 (1.2% increase per year). In the Pacific Northwest, populations increased in the Cascades (+7.4%) and on the Columbia Plateau (+3.7%) but decreased in the Willamette lowlands (-4.2%). Overall, a small decrease was found in Oregon (-2.7%). None of these changes represent statistically significant departures from zero over time. These data suggest that populations are relatively stable over multiple regions that have experienced a variety of human-caused impacts to habitat. Locally, formerly rare on Sauvie I., but a sharp increase occurred during 1985-87 (Fix 1985a, Tweit and Mattocks 1987a) and it is now abundant there (H. Nehls p.c.). Likely to decrease in forested regions where timber harvest is reduced and fire suppression continued (MGH). Has likely benefited from establishment of nest boxes, most of which were placed for bluebirds, but to what extent is unknown.—Robert Peck

## Winter Wren *Troglodytes troglodytes*

This small, rich-brown wren is only slightly larger than a quarter, and has a tail quite short for a wren. A quiet observer in the forest will see these birds hop in and out and all over logs, snags, shrubs, twigs, and limbs on the forest floor. Gabrielson and Jewett (1940) aptly described this species as "a pert little bit of brown fluff" and "a mouselike mite … that … mounts to the top of a convenient stump and bursts forth in the most amazing, loud, clear song that ever came from a brown protuberance." It has been said that the song of this bird is larger than the bird itself (J. Dewater p.c.).

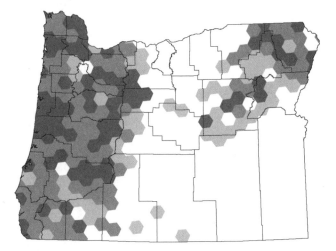

**General Distribution:** In N. America, breeds from s. Alaska to Newfoundland south to c. California, c. Idaho, the Great Lakes area and in the Appalachians to n. Georgia. Also breeds in the Paleartic from Iceland, the Faroe Is., Shetlands, British Isles, n. Scandinavia, n. Russia and c. Siberia south to nw. Africa, the Mediterranean region, Near East, Iran, n. India, c. China and Japan. Winters in N. America along the w. coast, in the desert states, across the se. U.S. and north to New York. In the Paleartic, winters throughout breeding range but extreme northerly populations usually migrate southward. Sixteen N. American subspecies; four occur in Oregon. Subspecies named by Rea [*in* Phillips 1986] were unconfirmed but probably are valid (Browning 1990) and should be recognized (*MRB*).

**Oregon Distribution:** *T. t. muiri* breeds from Coos Co. southward (Rea *in* Phillips 1986). Most breeding in northern coastal regions were assigned to *salebrosus* by Rea but specimens compared by *MRB* are similar to *pacificus*, a subspecies confined to se. Alaska and Queen Charlotte Is. by Rea. *T. t. salebrosus* is resident in e. Oregon (Browning 1990) in the Blue Mtns. (Burleigh 1959), and Steens Mtn. (Rea *in* Phillips 1986); specimens from s. Cascades not compared but Rea identified intergrades between *salebrosus* and *muiri* in Douglas Co. Breeding ranges need further work (*MRB*).

The species retreats from high altitudes in winter where snow pack is heavy (*DBM*); there is an obvious winter movement into lowlands (Gullion 1951, Contreras 1997, Hunter et al. 1998). McAllister and Marshall (1945) did not observe Winter Wrens in the Fremont NF; their absence in this location may have been due to a lack of moist forest conditions (*DBM*). Migration probably occurs throughout the state, but movements are most noticeable in spring and fall at locations such as Malheur NWR (Littlefield 1990) where the species does not breed or winter. *T. t. ochroleucus*, from insular se. Alaska, is a rare winter visitor (late Jan at Tillamook and Corvallis) (Rea *in* Phillips 1986).

**Habitat and Diet:** During all seasons, Winter Wrens are closely associated with moist coniferous forests, but can also be found in older (> 35-yr-old) red alder forests, and in Oregon white oak woodlands (Anderson SH 1970, Stiles 1980).

During the breeding season, occurs in all ages of coniferous forest (Carey et al. 1991, Gilbert and Allwine 1991). Within unmanaged forests of the Coast and Cascade ranges, occurred in all forest ages with similar densities (Carey et al. 1991, Gilbert and Allwine 1991). However, in studies that included both unmanaged and managed stands in the Coast Range (McGarigal and McComb 1995) and the Cascades,

along streams (Anthony et al. 1996), Winter Wrens were associated with late-seral forests. It may be that young stands in the former studies (initiated by fire) had an abundance of down wood making them more suitable than young stands in the latter studies, which were initiated by timber harvest.

McGarigal and McComb (1995) found that Winter Wrens were associated with a landscape less fragmented (by clearcutting) in the Coast Range; abundance was positively associated with the size and core area of late-seral forest patches. In a similar study in n. California, Rosenberg and Raphael (1986) also found that Winter Wrens were positively associated with size of late seral forest patches. In mature Douglas-fir forests of the Coast Range, abundance of Winter Wrens decreased in response to cutting in clearcuts and two-story stands, but not to small 0.49-ac (0.2-ha) group selection cuts (Chambers et al. 1999). After clearcutting in the Cascades, abundance increased with increasing stand age between 5 and 34 yr (Bettinger 1996). Results are especially unclear with regard to thinning in young forests, with Winter Wrens reported to be positively and negatively affected as well as unaffected by thinning (Hagar 1996, Hayes et al. unpubl. ms.). As speculated in the previous paragraph, these differences may indicate that quantity and quality of logs and shrubs may be more important to Winter Wrens than changes in overstory cover (*MGH*).

In the Coast Range, Winter Wrens were more abundant near small streams than in adjacent upslope areas (McGarigal and McComb 1992). Hagar (1999a) found that Winter Wrens were more abundant in unlogged riparian areas than in logged riparian areas and that abundance increased with increasing width of stream buffers.

"Nook and cranny" nesters, Winter Wrens usually build their nests in cavities or holes amongst dead wood, dirt, rocks, or foliage. Of 25 nests found in upslope 35- to 45-yr-old Douglas-fir forests of the n. Coast Range, 16 were under or in logs, six were in cavities in snags or stumps, two were amongst foliage, and one was in a road embankment. Large logs and snags were used; almost all were legacy structures from the previous old-growth stand. Mean diameter of nest logs was 35 in (88.3 cm); mean diameter of nest snags and stumps was 41 in (105 cm). Nests in logs were often near streams and were located either in cavities or at the junction of two logs (*JMW*). In riparian areas of British Columbia, stream banks and upturned root-wads of fallen trees were used more than logs or snags (Waterhouse 1998).

Very little is known regarding habitat use in winter. Chambers and McComb (1997) found that Winter Wren abundance did not differ among uncut, two-story, small patch cut, and clearcut stands in winter. Hagar et al. (1996) found that Winter Wrens were more abundant in thinned than in unthinned stands in winter. In lowlands in winter, present in hardwood stands, parks, and other urban sites having adequate cover (Contreras 1997b, *DBM, JMW*).

Winter Wrens forage on the forest floor, including on logs. Very little is known regarding diet in Oregon. Van Horne and Bader (1990) found that beetles, spiders, flies, and caterpillars were the most common food items found in an analysis of fecal samples of nestlings in the Coast Range.

**Seasonal Activity and Behavior:** Sings year-round. Males in the Cascade Head Experimental Forest had a complex repertoire of songs, averaging 21 different song types per bird (Van Horne 1995). No information could be found regarding territory size of Winter Wrens in Oregon. In w. British Columbia, territories ranged 0.9-5.9 ac (0.37-2.38 ha) in size (Waterhouse 1998). Males build multiple nests. Mating habits in Oregon ranged from monogamy to concurrent or sequential polygyny (Van Horne 1984). Three of 9, and 3 of 13 mated birds studied over 2 yr in the Coast Range of Oregon (Van Horne 1995) had two mates; the remaining birds had one mate. Polygyny rates are not known for birds in other areas of Oregon. Nesting activities occur Apr-Aug. Nest building observed as late as May-Jun (n=20), incubation from early Apr to late Jul (n=27), and hatched young from late Apr to mid-Jul (n=18) (Gabrielson and Jewett 1940, *JMW*, OBBA). Fledged young are most frequently observed Jun and Jul, but have been observed as early as late May (n=15) (JMW, OBBA). Often raise multiple broods each year (Van Horne 1984).

In w. Oregon, increases in lowland wintering sites in late Sep-Oct and decreases Apr-May (Heinl and Hunter 1985, Hunter et al. 1998). At Malheur NWR, fall migrants observed 9 Aug to 1 Nov and spring migrants during Mar and Apr (Littlefield 1990a).

**Detection:** Most easily detected by listening for its long, musical song, or its sharp chip notes. Males are often observed singing from high perches. These wrens, especially juveniles of the species, sometimes approach very closely.

**Population Status and Conservation:** BBS data indicate Oregon populations are stable or increasing (Sauer et al. 2000). However, abundance may be negatively affected by loss of mature and old-growth forest (McGarigal and McComb 1995, Anthony et al. 1996) and the effects of cutting in younger forests are not clear (Hagar 1996, Hayes et al. unpubl. ms.). It is unknown what the impacts will be when old-growth legacies (e.g., large-diameter logs, snags, and stumps) decay and are no longer present in young, intensively managed forests. More study is needed on the effects of forest practices on long-term productivity of Winter Wrens.—*Jennifer M. Weikel*

**Marsh Wren** *Cistothorus palustris*
This pugnacious little wren, formerly known as the Long-billed Marsh Wren, inhabits cattail, bulrush, and other marsh plants. As the only Oregon species of wren that nests over water, it is easy to identify when seen, but sexes are difficult to differentiate in the absence of song due to similar coloration. Cinnamon brown on upper parts and whitish to buffy below; white stripes on the back distinguish it from other wrens. This species has long been of interest to behavioral and evolutionary ecologists due to its polygynous mating system (Verner 1964, 1965a), widespread construction of dummy nests (Leonard and Picman 1987), and the male's complex singing behavior (Verner 1976).

**General Distribution:** Breed in freshwater wetland habitats over much of the U.S. and s. Canada ranging from sw. and c. British Columbia, east to se. Maine; nest primarily in tidally influenced marshes from Delaware south to Florida and Texas (Kroodsma and Verner 1997). Disjunct population nests in c. Mexico (Howell and Webb 1995). Breeding populations absent to rare in plains region of w. N. Dakota, S. Dakota, e. Colorado, e. Montana, and sw. Alberta; southern half of U.S. west of Rocky Mtns; and in California outside of Central Valley and coast. Winters over much of breeding range in w. and s. U.S. where temperatures remain above 25°F (-4°C) and south to c. Mexico. Two phylogenetic lineages recognized, dividing approximately w. Saskatchewan to c. Nebraska. Fourteen subspecies recognized (Phillips 1986) with two found in Oregon.

**Oregon Distribution:** Nests state-wide in appropriate wetland habitats. *C. p. pulverius* is particularly common during breeding season around Malheur NWR, especially in Blitzen Valley, on Malheur L., with a specimen from Burns (Aldrich 1946), near Double O substation, in wetlands of Lake Co. (Summer L.), and in Klamath Basin (Gabriel-son and Jewett 1940) including Klamath Falls (Aldrich 1946); but also locally

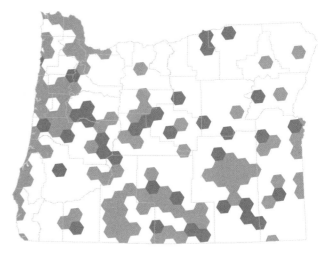

*Marsh Wren*

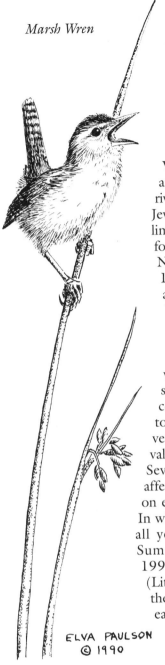

ELVA PAULSON
© 1990

common in lower-elevation marshes and wet meadows of the Blue and Wallowa mountains (Evanich 1992a). Less common breeding populations of *C. p. paludicola* are found along the Columbia R. and in the Willamette Valley, in coastal estuaries, and in s. Oregon coastal river valleys (Gabrielson and Jewett 1940). The southern limit of the breeding range for this subspecies is around Netarts by Rea (*in* Phillips 1986) and somewhere along the central coast by Unitt et al. (1996). More work is needed.

Winter populations are largely restricted to wetlands on the west side of the Cascades; common along the coast to locally fairly common to very uncommon in interior valleys (Gilligan et al. 1994). Severity of winter strongly affects wintering abundance on east side of the Cascades. In winter, at least uncommon all years in Klamath Basin, Summer L. (Gilligan et al. 1994), on Malheur NWR (Littlefield 1990a), and along the Columbia R. from Biggs eastward (M. Denny p.c.).

**Habitat and Diet:** In e. Oregon, breed in marsh habitats but also occasionally in wet meadows. In marshes, nest site locations vary with availability and quality of substrate and with competition from other species. At Malheur NWR, hardstem bulrush was the preferred nesting substrate but nests are also found regularly in cattails, and at least occasionally in flooded greasewood (Littlefield 1990a). At McFadden Marsh, now a part of the William L. Finley NWR, >25 nests found in slough sedge and hardhack in 1947 and 1948 prior to invasion of reed canarygrass (*DBM*, F. G. Evenden field notes). Verner and Engelsen's (1970) research in e. Washington indicated that distribution of nests changed seasonally, as they found a greater number of nests in cattails early in the season while more nests were found in bulrushes later in the season

as the marsh dried out. Gabrielson and Jewett (1940) suggested that a lack of suitable habitat resulted in only scattered nesting pairs or colonies west of the Cascades. However, they did indicate that thick clumps of wild rose bushes along Devils L., Lincoln Co., were frequented. Also found to be common in extensive reed canarygrass at Fern Ridge Res., Lane Co. (*MGH*).

Nests are domed ellipsoids approximately 7 in (17.8 cm) high by 5 in (12.7 cm) wide, woven together with cattails, sedge, or grass (Verner 1965a). Nest height is influenced by timing of construction (affecting water level and height of vegetation), but was found to average 33.7 in (85.6 cm) (n=81) in Washington marshes (Verner 1965a). The outer shell of nests is generally constructed by the male while lining is provided by the female. Lining often consists of strips of vegetation, cattail seeds, and feathers. Dummy nests differ from breeding nests in lacking a significant lining.

Habitat requirements are generally similar in winter although appear more variable. For example, most overwintering individuals at Malheur NWR were found to switch from marsh habitat into riparian zones (Littlefield 1990a). Along the coast, uncommon in dense stands of dune beachgrass (*MGH*).

A generalist feeder of invertebrates associated with marsh vegetation. Primarily gleans prey near water surface; occasionally probes for subsurface invertebrates and sallies for flying insects (Verner 1965a). Stomach analyses indicate that spiders, beetles, bees, ants, wasps, true bugs, flies, leafhoppers, and moths are most frequently consumed (Beal 1907, Welter 1935, Kale 1964).

**Seasonal Activity and Behavior:** Arrival dates on nesting grounds generally differ for populations east and west of the Cascades. Gilligan et al. (1994) generalize that westside birds are on nesting territories by late Mar and Apr while eastside birds arrive on nest sites between mid-Apr and early May, but the latter estimate may be a bit late. At Malheur NWR, Littlefield (1990a) indicates that a major influx of birds occurs in early Mar, and they are abundant and widespread by Apr. In Washington, males generally arrived at nest sites 7-10 days before females (Verner 1965a). Nest building occurs mid-Apr to mid-Jun (n=9) while fledglings are typically found late May to early Aug (n=10) (OBBA). Littlefield (1990a) found fledged young to be abundant in late Jun and Jul. At McFadden's Marsh, newly constructed nests found 8 Apr 1947 and 13 Apr 1948; nest with 3 eggs 13 May 1947 had 7 eggs 20 May 1947 (*DBM*, F. G. Evenden field notes).

Verner's (1965a) detailed study of the nesting behavior and phenology of Washington populations revealed the following points: (1) laying began relatively synchronously within a marsh approximately 3 wk after mean date of first nest construction; (2) clutch size averaged 5.2 eggs/nest (n=79); (3) incubation was solely performed by the female and lasted 15.1 days (n=23); (4) nestlings leave the nest after approximately 14 days; and (5) fledglings obtained food from parents for 23-27 days after leaving the nest.

Breeding territories are established and defended by males while individual nest sites within territories are defended by females. Territory size is highly variable; average size among five marshes in Washington ranged 4,500-18,200 ft$^2$ (413-1,671 m$^2$) (Verner 1965a). Both intraspecific competition and habitat quality influence territory size. Aggressive interactions with other marsh-dwelling birds, particularly Yellow-headed and Red-winged Blackbirds, have also been suggested to limit the ability of a male to defend a territory, influencing both territory placement and size (Verner 1965a, Leonard and Picman 1987).

Notable male behaviors include polygyny and the construction of dummy nests, or nests that are used for purposes other than egg laying. The number of dummy nests built varies among individuals and years, but as many as 20 nests/territory/season have been recorded (Verner 1965a, Verner and Engleson 1970, Leonard and Picman 1987). The purpose of dummy nests is unclear. Polygynous behavior is well developed in some populations, although highly variable. Verner (1965a) found the proportion of males with territories containing multiple females to range 12.5-50%.

**Detection:** In the breeding season, distinctive song easily detected. When silent, especially during the nonbreeding season, often difficult to see. Best seen during the nesting season, when males vocalize from tops of vegetation and females are chasing intruders from breeding territories or searching for food for nestlings. Silent skulkers in coastal dune grass, sometimes mistaken for Savannah or other sparrows, or House Wrens, by inexperienced observers. Males sing abundantly throughout the day and sometimes into the evening, but are particularly vocal during early morning hours.

**Population Status and Conservation:** Few data exist indicating how population sizes may have changed in Oregon since Gabrielson and Jewett (1940). Although wetland habitat may have been reduced overall, limited data do suggest that numbers may be increasing in some areas. Browning (1975a) indicated that a range expansion may have taken place in Jackson Co., where the impression of abundance changed from being a rare winter visitor prior to 1963 to becoming common in the lower Rogue R. and Bear Cr. valleys. Presenting BBS data 1966-94, Kroodsma and Verner (1997) indicated that populations in the w. U.S. region increased at an annual rate of 5.6% and concluded that they saw "no

basis for concern about trends in abundance at this time," particularly with western populations, although cautioned that eastern populations bear vigilance. Numerous studies have shown that populations have decreased in eastern states, largely due to drainage of wetlands (e.g., Brewer et al. 1991, Sibley 1993b).

Overall, prospects for long-term persistence of the species appears good in Oregon since much habitat is maintained on refuges (e.g., Malheur and Klamath NWRs), but persistence of smaller, more localized populations will be dependent upon protection of wetland habitats.—*Robert Peck*

## Family Cinclidae

### American Dipper *Cinclus mexicanus*

Few birds are as astonishing as the American Dipper. This nondescript, dark brown to gray bird is seldom seen more than a few feet from water's edge. Its elaborate song, which can come forth even on cold winter days, is readily heard above the noise of rushing streams. This bird's ability to dive into a rushing stream to forage on aquatic invertebrates and reappear in the same location has elicited wonder and excitement from ornithologists, naturalists, and birders, as well as envy and adoration from fly-fishers. Unique adaptations facilitate the existence of this truly aquatic passerine songbird: long, strong legs and toes tipped with sharp claws grasp slippery bottoms; short, stout wings are used in both air and water for flying; and high hemoglobin concentration increases the oxygen-holding capacity of the blood (Sullivan 1973, Tyler and Ormerod 1994). Dippers are named for their bobbing or dipping behavior. Dips are a quick lowering of the entire body, and are different from head-bobbing or tail-wagging common in other species. Ecological explanations for this behavior remain contested and range from the probable, such as intra-specific communication, or prey detection (Tyler and Ormerod 1994), to the silly (e.g., pumping blood from their feet,

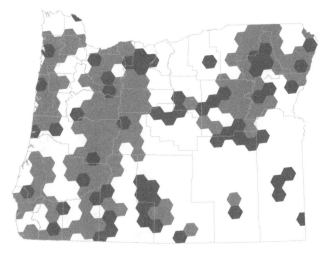

or keeping warm). Dippers often blink during each dip, displaying the white eyelid feathers (not a white nictitating membrane). Dipping rates tend to increase when dippers are agitated or disturbed (*JPL*).

**General Distribution:** Found throughout mountainous regions of w. N. America from the Rocky Mtns. to the Pacific coast, and Alaska to the Isthmus of Panama (Bent 1948, Van Tyne and Berger 1959, Kingery 1996). Most are year-round residents, but latitudinal and altitudinal migration occurs in some areas in response to stream freezing. Five subspecies: *C. m. unicolor* is the only one found north of Mexico (Phillips 1986).

**Oregon Distribution:** Uncommon year-round resident in montane streams and rivers throughout Oregon (Gilligan et al. 1994). Occurrence is likely regulated by the availability of suitable nest sites during the breeding season (Kingery 1996, Loegering 1997). Gabrielson and Jewett (1940) reported they reside from the Cascades west, and in the Blue and Warner mountains, observations that roughly describe the dipper's distribution today. However, the species also breeds in small numbers in se. Oregon, including Hart Mtn., Steens Mtn., Trout Cr. Mtns., and Mahogany Mtn. (Marshall 1987, Littlefield 1990a, Gilligan et al. 1994, Contreras and Kindschy 1996, Adamus et al. 2001). Probable breeding also occurs along the Owyhee R. (Adamus et al. 2001). Found to mouths of coastal streams where sometimes feed in salt water (*ALC*). Some winter movement noted, including to lower elevations from Steens Mtn.(Littlefield 1990a), and to edges of Willamette Valley (CBCs), including to Eugene (*ALC*).

**Habitat and Diet:** Dippers are intimately linked with fast-flowing, clear, and unpolluted stream ecosystems, and occur there throughout the year, provided they are ice-free. Stream habitat ranges from narrow headwater streams <5 ft (1.6 m) wide to broad, wide streams (e.g., McKenzie R. near Eugene, >100 ft [30 m] wide); however, their abundance peaks in mid-sized streams (Loegering and Anthony 1999). Depths are generally < 6 ft (2 m) and are often much shallower. Stream quality and the availability of nest sites appear to be more important factors in determining the presence of dippers than other factors such as character of associated upland habitat (Kingery 1996, Loegering 1997).

Nests are placed over or directly above the edge of the stream; they are inaccessible to predators, above the flood line, and are often sheltered from the weather (Hann 1950, Price and Bock 1983, Kingery 1996). Nests are dome-shaped including a roof, composed of moss, and are 6-10 in (15-25 cm) in diameter. Are built typically on a cliff's narrow ledge; in a cavity of a

horizontal hollow log; on mid-stream boulders, under or within the support structure of bridges (Sullivan 1973, Price and Bock 1983, Kingery 1996); or in nest boxes (Jost 1970, Hawthorne 1979). Nest sites are very near to or overhang the stream's edge (Kingery 1996); all of the 80 nests Loegering (1997) found in Oregon were within 12 in (0.3 m) of the stream's edge despite search efforts up to 16 ft (5 m) from the stream's edge. Use of large wood pieces and logs as nesting structures varies geographically in importance. In the Cascades and Coast Range, and along the Pacific coast, 16%, 32%, and 55%, respectively, of nests were associated with large wood pieces (Loegering 1997).

Dippers readily use human-created nest sites (Hawthorne 1979, Loegering 1997) including boxes, ledges, or cavities. Local abundances can be increased by placing such structures in unoccupied habitats. For example, Loegering (1997) experimentally doubled the abundance of dippers by placing human-constructed nest sites along a 6.2 mi (10 km) stream segment.

Aquatic organisms, primarily adult and larval invertebrates and fish, are predominant food items. Have been observed to feed on water bugs, salmon eggs and fry, tadpoles, marine beach hoppers, black flies, stonefly and mayfly nymphs, and caddisfly larvae (Burcham 1904, Bakus 1959, Sullivan 1973, Hayward and Thoresen 1980, Donnelly and Sullivan 1998). Thut (1970) and Mitchell (1968) found dippers also consumed flies, beetles, and snails, and suggested that dippers were opportunistic generalists. Additionally, Loegering (1997) observed adults feeding nestlings crane flies, true flies, a moth, and a crayfish. Dippers' impact on stream biota is unclear, but Harvey and Marti (1993) noted substantial reductions in prey biomass during late summer.

**Seasonal Activity and Behavior:** Dippers often remain at or near their breeding territories through the year. They are monogamous or polygynous and first breed at 1 yr of age (Kingery 1996, Price and Bock 1973). Males remain on territories and defend them against conspecifics during incubation and brood rearing. Territories, which are centered on the nest, are linear along the stream and 875-1,094 yds (800-1,000 m) long (Ealey 1977, Price and Bock 1983). Breeding activities generally begin first at lower elevations where courtship and nest building can begin in Feb (*JPL*). Nests are constructed by males and females. Four to five eggs are laid mid-Feb to mid-Jun with earliest nesting at lower elevations (J. Kaiser p.c., *JPL*). Only females incubate the eggs and brood the nestlings. Both parents feed the young with equal effort (Loegering 1997) or with the female as the primary food provider (Bakus 1959, Sullivan 1973). Initial broods fledge in late Mar, and second broods generally by early Jul (J. Kaiser p.c., *JPL*). Renesting following egg loss is common, and >50% of pairs at low elevations attempted to raise two broods in a season (*JPL*). Overall nest success is unusually high for a passerine, perhaps because of dippers' unique life-history strategy and nest placement. Reproductive success may vary with nest-site quality (Price and Bock 1983); however, Loegering (1997) found nest and brood survival for all nests to be high (79% and 87%, respectively) in the Oregon Coast Range.

**Detection:** Dippers are readily detected by sight and sound by walking along or within a stream. Streams with ample nest sites have higher abundances. Locations near waterfalls are particularly fruitful. However, even where most abundant, they occur at <1.0 bird / 0.6 mi (1 km) (Loegering 1997, Loegering and Anthony 1999). Dippers show limited avoidance of humans, are approachable to 80-130 ft (25–40 m), and seldom fly >2 m from the water's edge when disturbed (*JPL*). However, become more secretive during late summer when molting and flightless (*JPL*). Are most active and detectable Apr to Jun as they deliver food to nestlings. Silver Cr. Falls SP with its numerous waterfalls and streamside trails is an excellent place to observe this species.

**Population Status and Conservation:** Abundance in Oregon, or throughout their range, has not been well estimated. No convincing evidence is available suggesting that their population has changed from pre-settlement periods. Dippers are infrequently detected on standard surveys (e.g., BBS or CBC). These surveys may underestimate their true abundance given dippers' close association with noisy stream environments that are seldom included in typical songbird surveys. Moreover, systematic surveys of swift mountain streams are uncommon and fraught with difficulties (Loegering 1997). Large landscape-modifying practices afford both detriments and benefits for local populations. Widespread removal of coarse wood from streams in the 1960s and indiscriminate logging practices may have depressed populations; however, bridges constructed during these impacts provided scarce nesting sites for many years. Efforts during the past decade to improve stream habitat for fisheries will generally benefit dippers' prey species.

It is commonly thought that "healthy dipper populations on upland rivers throughout the world indicate healthy river ecosystems" (Tyler and Ormerod 1994). Moreover, it has been proposed that dipper presence be used as a biomonitoring indicator of stream water quality (e.g., Sorace et al. 2002). Although dippers can be a synthetic sampling tool to assess stream invertebrates, and dippers' presence typically indicates good water quality, their absence may simply be a function of other limiting factors, such as available nest sites (Kingery 1996, Loegering 1997).

In a study on tributaries of the upper Willamette R., the eggs and feathers of dippers are being used to more directly assess the status of a specific pollutant, in this case mercury (C. Henny p.c.). Dippers may be a good species for evaluating contaminants including metals in cold headwater streams, because the food they eat comes only from the stream.—*John P. Loegering*

## Family Regulidae

### Golden-crowned Kinglet *Regulus satrapa*

The smallest and hardiest of our resident bird species, Golden-crowned Kinglets are remarkable for their ability to survive through severe northern winters, when most other small insectivores have migrated to warmer climates. Spending winter nights in a squirrel's nest or huddled together in a sheltered spot are strategies this species uses for winter survival. Their high-pitched calls ring like tiny bells from the canopy as they flutter among the branch tips in small flocks, searching for insects wintering in conifer foliage and dead leaves. Because of their small size, muted plumage, and fondness for foraging in the tops of tall trees, Golden-crowned Kinglets are more often heard than seen. Occasionally they descend from the heights of the forest canopy to forage on shrub foliage or lichens on low branches, allowing a glimpse of a flame-bright crown that sharply contrasts with the soft olive-green of their body plumage.

**General Distribution:** Northern limit of breeding range is nearly continuous from Newfoundland to sw. Alaska. Migratory populations breed throughout forested portions of Canada south to n. Great Lakes region in the eastern half of the continent and to s. British Columbia and Alberta in the west. Year-round resident in the northeast, from Newfoundland south through Appalachian Mtns. to N. Carolina, and in w. Michigan. Year-round resident throughout much of w. U.S. and sw. Canada west of the Continental Divide, and discontinuously as far south as Guatemala. Winters

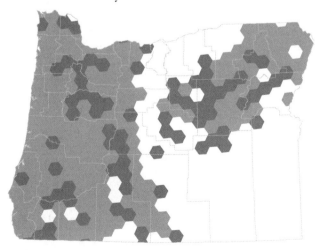

throughout U.S. and sc. Canada, except for c. and s. Florida, and parts of sw. U.S. Some of the greatest breeding and wintering population densities occur in w. Oregon (Ingold and Galati 1997). Four subspecies in N. America provisionally (Phillips 1991); *R. s. olivaceus* in Oregon (Browning in 2002).

**Oregon Distribution:** Very abundant year-round in coniferous forests from the Cascades and west throughout Coast Range and Willamette Valley (OBBA). Within the Cascade Range, more abundant in Mt. Hood NF and Rogue River-Umpqua NF than in the H.J. Andrews Experimental Forest during the breeding season (Gilbert and Allwine 1991). A Dec specimen from Depoe Bay, Lincoln Co., may represent an unnamed subspecies from Queen Charlotte Is., British Columbia (Phillips 1991).

East of the Cascades, breeds primarily in montane spruce and fir zones. In winter, common west of the Cascade crest, and especially abundant along the coast (Gilligan et al. 1994). One of few species to be found in high Cascade forests in winter (*MGH*). Seasonal movements along elevation gradient evidenced by less frequent records in low-elevation habitats in summer than winter (Gullion 1951). In e. Oregon, found in almost any habitat with trees during the remainder of the year; numbers of wintering birds vary substantially on an annual basis east of the Cascades (Gilligan et al. 1994).

**Habitat and Diet:** Among the most abundant breeding birds in low- to mid-elevation conifer forests in w. Oregon (Carey et al. 1991, Hansen et al. 1995, Bettinger 1996). Densities in unmanaged Douglas-fir stands in the Coast Range averaged 54, 74, and 62 birds/100 ac (40 ha) in young, mature, and old-growth, respectively (Carey et al. 1991). Densities on the west slope of the Cascades were estimated at 145.5 birds/100 ac (40 ha) (Wiens and Nussbaum 1975). Strongly associated with conifer canopy cover, density, and basal area during breeding season (Farner 1952, McGarigal and McComb 1992, Bettinger 1996), but niche breadth seems to widen in winter (Marcot 1985) leading to use of a greater variety of habitats (Hagar et al. 1996). For example, uses oak woodlands in the Willamette Valley in winter but not during breeding season (Anderson SH 1970, Anderson 1972, *JCH*). Builds nests close to the trunk of conifer trees, attached to hanging twigs below horizontal branches high in canopy, average 50 ft (16 m) above ground (Ingold and Galati 1997). Uses lower layers of forest vegetation more in winter than in summer (Marcot 1985, *JCH*).

During breeding season, abundance increased with stand age from early post-harvest (5 yr-old) to 34-yr-old Douglas-fir plantations on Willamette N.F. (Bettinger 1996), to reach greatest abundance in

*Golden-crowned Kinglet*

young (30- to 75-yr-old) stands (Manuwal and Huff 1987, Hansen et al. 1995). Declines in breeding abundance following most disturbances that decrease canopy cover, including timber harvesting (Vega 1993, Chambers 1996, Hagar et al. 1996) and fires (Sallabanks 1995b). More abundant in upslope habitats where conifers were dominant than along small streams in late seral forests in the Coast Range (McGarigal and McComb 1992). Abundance decreases in harvested riparian areas, even where buffers have been retained (Kinley and Newhouse 1997, Hagar 1999a). In study of bird communities along small streams in the Coast Range, Golden-crowned Kinglets were observed consistently at unlogged riparian sites, but occurred at logged sites only if riparian buffers were > 107 ft (35 m) wide (Hagar 1999a). Avoided edges in California mature and old-growth stands, and attained higher densities in stands with lowest ratios of edge to interior habitat (Rosenberg and Raphael 1986). Similar negative relationship to edges was not found in the Coast Range (McGarigal and McComb 1995).

No foraging studies from Oregon, but strongly insectivorous throughout range. Feet are uniquely adapted for hanging on to tips of conifer branches, where much time is spent foraging (Ingold and Gallati 1997). Infrequently observed foraging low in canopy or shrubs, especially during winter. Main food items are small soft-bodied arthropods gleaned from tree and shrub foliage, limbs, twigs, dead leaves and from lichens on trees and shrubs (Morrison et al 1985, Ingold and Gallati 1997, JCH).

**Seasonal Activity and Behavior:** Information on breeding and nesting is scarce for Oregon. Gullion (1951) reports nest building on 2 Jun in the s. Willamette Valley. Incubation began 3 and 27 May at two nests with 6-8 eggs found in the n. Willamette Valley (Griffee and Rapraeger 1937). Incubation takes 15 days (Ingold and Galati 1997). One nest with young found on 12 Jun (OBBA). Fledging occurs at 18-19 days (Ingold and Galati 1997). Fledglings observed 19 May to 26 Aug (n=31) (OBBA), with most (87%) observed between mid-Jun and late Jul.

In late Sep in the n. Blue Mtns., huge numbers of these kinglets pass south at elevations >4,000 ft (1,200 m) (M. Denny p.c.).

In winter, often found in pure flocks (Anderson 1972) or with chickadees, Brown Creepers, and/or Red-breasted Nuthatches in mixed-species flocks (e.g., Farner 1952, LaGory et al. 1984). Flocks of Golden-crowned Kinglets appeared in the oak woodland on Pigeon Butte, William L. Finley NWR, beginning in early Oct each year, 1998-2000 (J. Weikel p.c., JCH).

**Detection:** Seems almost omnipresent in forest and woodlands during winter, where foraging flocks are easily detected by their continual high-pitched calling. Calls may be difficult to distinguish from those of species with which it commonly flocks, such as Chestnut-backed Chickadees or Brown Creepers, or may be difficult to hear at all for people with impaired ability to hear high-frequency sounds.

**Population Status and Conservation:** Breeding populations in Oregon declined significantly 1966-99. This trend is consistent with population reductions observed throughout the w. U.S. and Canada (Sauer et al. 2000). Reasons for population decreases are not clear, although Raphael et al. (1988) implicate a loss of mature forest habitat in the wake of decades of timber harvesting as a reason for reduced populations of Golden-crowned Kinglets and other species associated with mature forest in nw. California. More research is needed on population dynamics and habitat relationships in order to understand reasons for decreases in breeding populations in Oregon. CBC data indicate that wintering populations in Oregon were relatively stable 1959-88.—*Joan C. Hagar*

## Ruby-crowned Kinglet *Regulus calendula*

This drab, greenish, diminutive species is similar in appearance to the Hutton's Vireo, and sometimes confused with that species in w. Oregon. Slighter-billed and smaller than the vireo, this little bundle of energy seems always to be moving as it flicks its wings and hops from twig to twig. The male Ruby-crowned Kinglet sports a bright red crown spot, typically visible only when the bird is agitated, and in spring pours forth a delightful melody, surprising for such a small, drab bird.

**General Distribution:** Breeds in forests from Alaska north to tree line across Canada to Newfoundland, south through s. British Columbia, Cascade and Sierra Nevada Mtns. to c. California, and in Rocky Mtns. into n. Arizona. East of Rocky Mtns., south to c. Saskatchewan, sw. Manitoba, ne. Minnesota, n. Wisconsin, s. Ontario, n. New York, and s. Vermont. Isolated population in Black Hills of S. Dakota. In winter, from s. British Columbia through w. Idaho, e. Utah, n. Arizona, across the U.S. north to s. Kansas, s. Illinois, n. Pennsylvania, s. Connecticut, south to Florida and s. Mexico (Ingold and Wallace 1994). Two subspecies; both occur in Oregon (Browning 1979b).

**Oregon Distribution:** The species breeds in high-elevation forests, primarily east of the Cascade crest (OBBA), where it is common in summer, and in the Blue, Wallowa, and locally in the Warner mountains (McAllister and Marshall 1945, Gilligan et al. 1994). Based on specimens, breeding birds are *R. c. calendula* (Browning 1979b, see also Gabrielson and Jewett 1940). Frequently found late in spring in areas where they do not breed. Found throughout in winter (Phillips 1991, *MRB*). Some birds mistnetted in winter were determined to be *R. c. calendula* (M. Patterson p.c.). *R. c. grinnelli* are abundant in winter and as transients throughout w. Oregon, and uncommon at lower elevations east of the Cascades (Gabrielson and Jewett 1940, Contreras 1997b), with specimens from

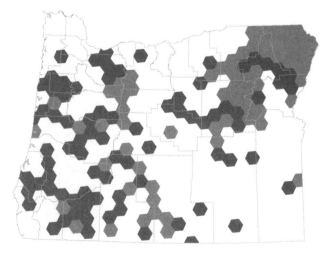

Umatilla and Lake counties in Sep (Phillips 1991), Logan in Clackamas Co. in Jan, and Sauvie I. in Multnomah Co. in Mar (*MRB*). Gilligan et al. (1994) describe the species as a sometimes abundant migrant throughout state.

**Habitat and Diet:** In managed forests of ne. Oregon, nested in small north-facing areas dominated by Douglas-fir, mixed with small numbers of larch and grand fir trees. Less common in old-growth forests in ne. Oregon. Breeding density of 8-11 birds per 100 ac (40.5 ha.) in managed forests, 0.5-2 per 100 ac (40.5 ha) in old-growth (Mannan and Meslow 1984). In Wallowa Mtns., nest in dense coniferous forest above 5,000 ft (1,525 m) elevation, showing a preference for Engelmann spruce, Douglas-fir, and grand fir forest over open ponderosa pine-grassland habitat (F. Conley p.c.). In interior Columbia R. basin of Idaho, e. Washington, e. Oregon, and nw. Montana, associated with coniferous forest and juniper woodlands (Saab and Rich 1997). On eastern slope of the Cascades, occur during nesting season above 5,500 ft (1,676 m), mostly over 6,000 ft (1,830 m), in mixed lodgepole pine, white pine, and fir (B. Altman p.c.). At Crater L. NP, primarily associated with lodgepole pine forests and dry canyons containing conifers, with lower densities occurring in mountain hemlock and ponderosa pine forests (Farner 1952). In w. N. America, most nests located within 40 ft (12 m) of ground. Highest nests were 79-89 ft (24-27 m) from ground (Ingold and Wallace 1994). Gabrielson and Jewett (1940) report a nest constructed of moss. A nest found at Crater L. NP was made of lichen and lined with feathers, built near the end of a lodgepole pine branch 7 ft from the ground (Farner 1952).

In e. Oregon, migrants regularly use old homestead sites and rangeland, foraging in exotic leafy bushes and trees at homestead sites (Bohn et al. 1980). At Malheur NWR, spring and fall migrants concentrate in shrubby thickets, wooded stream bottoms, arid woodlands, and areas around human habitations (Littlefield 1990a). Occasional wintering birds in s. Blitzen Valley inhabit wooded stream bottoms and arid woodlands (Littlefield 1990a). In winter in w. Washington, forage almost exclusively in brushy understory, consisting of wild crabapple, elderberry, Indian plum, salmonberry, willow, and snowberry (LaGory et al. 1984). In w. Oregon, winter resident of Oregon white oak stands (Anderson 1972), as well as many other clumps of bushes and trees (Contreras 1997b). In Rogue Valley, commonly winter in riparian habitat along larger rivers, with smaller numbers in upland oak woodland (D. Vroman p.c.).

Diet not studied in Oregon, but in ne. Oregon managed forests, breeding birds foraged 59% of time in Douglas-fir trees, also showing a preference for western larch and grand fir (Mannan and Meslow 1984). In California and Arizona primary food is arthropods, with small amounts of vegetable matter taken (Beal 1907, Laurenzi et al. 1982). Seems opportunistic, taking whatever food is most abundant (Laurenzi et al. 1982). In California, from Sep to Apr, stomachs contained wasps and ants, bugs, beetles, butterfly and moth adults and larvae, flies, spiders, and pseudoscorpions. Plant material included fruit, weed seeds, poison oak seeds, and leaf galls (Beal 1907).

**Seasonal Activity and Behavior:** Observed singing on wintering grounds in Oregon as early as Feb. Data from across N. America indicate that males arrive on breeding grounds and set up territories before females return (Fairfield and Shirokoff 1978, Swanson et al. 1999). According to banding data from the Rogue Valley, males migrate just ahead of females in spring (D. Vroman p.c.). Wintering birds on n. coast mostly gone by mid-Apr, with latest birds remaining until 15 May (M. Patterson p.c.). In Rogue Valley, most spring migrants move through from late Mar to late Apr, with latest spring departure 11 May (D. Vroman p.c.). In the Siskiyou NF at 2,100 ft (640 m) elevation, latest departure date is 11 May (D. Vroman p.c.). Other late dates for w. Oregon include 22 May at Scoggins Valley Park (Heinl 1989a), 12 Jun at Cape Arago (Harrington-Tweit et al. 1978), and 13 Jun (2 birds) in Corvallis (Crowell and Nehls 1972d).

At Malheur NWR, average date for earliest arrival is 31 Mar, with the earliest migrant recorded 2 Feb. Most migrate 10-27 Apr, with the latest spring record 20 May (Littlefield 1990a). Begin arriving in the Wallowas in late Apr, with peak arrival 15-25 May at 4,500 ft (1,370 m) elevation (F. Conley p.c.). Singing takes place through mid-Jul (n=14) (OBBA). Territorial behavior observed mid-Jun to mid-Jul (n=7) (OBBA). Nest building observed in Ochocos in mid-Jun, and two nests with eggs noted in the Wallowas in mid-Jun (Gabrielson and Jewett 1940). Nest containing young in the Wallowas on 1 Aug 1998 (OBBA). An adult carrying food was seen 21 Jul 1937 at Crater L. NP (Farner 1952). On 25 Jul 1948 a nest found at Sand Cr. in Crater L. NP contained six young which flew from the nest when it was looked into (Farner 1952). Rare host to Brown-headed Cowbirds throughout its range (Boxall 1981).

Common on breeding grounds in the Wallowas through Aug, after which they migrate to lower elevations, with birds leaving elevations over 5,500 ft (1,676 m) by 10 Sep (F. Conley p.c.). At Malheur NWR, earliest fall arrival 3 Sep. Fall migration there peaks 24 Sep to 15 Oct, latest fall migrant recorded 13 Nov, with some winter records, almost all from s. Blitzen Valley (Littlefield 1990a). Earliest fall arrival on n. coast is 12 Sep (M. Patterson p.c.), and in Rogue Valley 17 Sep (D. Vroman p.c.). Females migrate earlier in fall, and winter farther south than males throughout

N. America (Fairfield and Shirokoff 1978, Swanson et al. 1999). Banding data from the Rogue Valley (n=129), primarily of wintering birds, found 62% males and 38% females (D. Vroman p.c.).

Found individually or in mixed-species flocks in winter (*KVS*). An unusually large mixed-species flock along the Willamette R. near Salem on 18 Jan 2001 contained approximately 70 Ruby-crowned Kinglets, along with 90 Bushtits, 20 Golden-crowned Kinglets, 15 Black-capped Chickadees, five Bewick's Wrens, two Winter Wrens, and two Brown Creepers (P. Gallagher p.c.). Flocks in w. Washington often include chickadees, Golden-crowned Kinglet, Downy Woodpecker, Dark-eyed Junco, Yellow-rumped Warbler, Bushtit, and Pine Siskin (LaGory et al. 1984). In s. California, a male was observed occupying and defending a distinct territory in winter, to which it returned the following year (Rea 1970). Along the Applegate R., birds banded during fall migration have been recaptured in subsequent years, indicating some site fidelity in migration or wintering locations occurs in Oregon (D. Vroman p.c.).

**Detection:** Easily seen and heard in winter in w. Oregon, often in mixed-species flocks with chickadees, nuthatches, and Golden-crowned Kinglets (Contreras 1997b). Rapid wing-flicking and movements attract attention, although often remains hidden in foliage. Responds readily to spishing, often approaching to within a few feet of observer. Loud, long song is easily heard during spring migration and on breeding grounds.

**Population Status and Conservation:** Common throughout range. CBC trend data show a slight increase in winter in Oregon (Contreras 1997b). BBS data from Oregon 1966-2000 indicate a significant (P<0.01) declining trend of 7.9 % per year during breeding season (Sauer et al. 2001).—*Karen Viste-Sparkman*

## Family Silviidae

### Subfamily Polioptilinae

### Blue-gray Gnatcatcher *Polioptila caerulea*
S. Oregon is the northwest limit of the breeding range of Blue-gray Gnatcatcher, which, as its name implies, is an active, diminutive blue-gray forager of small insects. It is identified by bluish-gray upperparts (brightest on crown), distinct white eye-ring, dark wings with whitish edging, grayish to white underparts and sides. A black tail with outer feathers edged in white comprises about half the bird's total length. The breeding male has a narrow black area on its forecrown. Female and immature birds are less bluish above. This is an energetic bird, commonly jerking its tail sharply to one side, wings held below, occasionally spreading its tail.

**General Distribution:** Breeds from s. Oregon eastward to s. Maine, south to s. Baja California, Mexico to Belize, s. Florida and the Bahama Is. Winters from c. California southeast to c. Texas, Gulf states and coast to s. Virginia, south to Honduras, w. Greater Antilles and Cayman Is. Casual north of usual range. Seven subspecies, *P. c. obscura* (*amoenissima* is a synonym) found in Oregon (Phillips 1991).

**Oregon Distribution:** Breeds in numerous disjunct localities and may be expanding its range in Oregon (Nehls 1995a). Uncommon to common summer resident in the interior Rogue Valley (Browning 1975a, Gilligan et al. 1994), rare summer resident in Illinois Valley (*DPV*), reported (but unverified) in the s. Umpqua Valley (Hunter et al. 1998). An isolated nesting attempt was observed in the s. Willamette Valley at Mt. Pisgah (Johnson J 1998a). Uncommon summer resident in the Klamath Basin (Summers 1993a); near Summer L. (Summers 1993c, OBBA) and at Hart Mtn. N. Antelope R. (Pyle 1985, USFWS 1986c), south to California (OBBA). Rare, with nesting attempts in Malheur NWR (Littlefield 1990a). A pair built and then abandoned a nest above Page Springs in Jul 1975 (D. Fix p.c.). Nesting was confirmed at Frenchglen in 1995 (Contreras and Kindschy 1996, OBBA) and Page Springs CG area 6 Jun 1997 (Spencer 1998, A. McGie p.c), and in two locations east of Drewsey (Harney-Malheur Co. line) Jun-Jul 1997 (E. Henze p.c., M. LaFaive p.c.). Locations with late spring sightings that may indicate nesting include Cyrus Springs, Crooked R. National Grasslands (Evanich 1992c); Mahogany Mtn., Battle Mtn., and Oregon Canyon Mtns., Malheur Co. (L. Fish p.c.). Casual in early winter in w. Oregon.

**Habitat and Diet:** Favors dry, brushy habitats, generally with widely spaced trees for breeding. In interior Rogue and Illinois valleys uses chaparral-oak communities (Browning 1975a, *DPV*), generally below

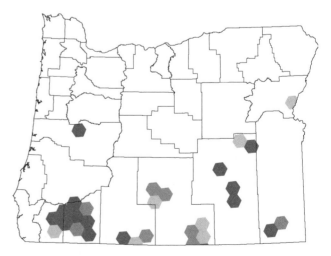

1,800 ft (550 m) elevation (*DPV*); habitat is similar at Mt. Pisgah (T. Mickel p.c.). Dominant habitat feature is narrow-leaved buckbrush, with varied amounts of Oregon white oak, ponderosa pine, white manzanita, and poison oak; California black oak may be present in moist habitats. Pacific madrone, Douglas-fir and birch-leaf mountain-mahogany in small amounts. Migratory habitat in Siskiyou Mtns. includes low-elevation silktassel and birch-leaf mountain-mahogany (W. Gray p.c.). East of the Cascades, Klamath Basin populations breed in mountain-mahogany (Summers 1993a), and Hart Mt. and Great Basin populations use juniper or mountain-mahogany (Littlefield 1990a, Contreras and Kindschy 1996). Mountain-mahogany habitat in se. Oregon can include wild rose, serviceberry, currant, and oceanspray (*MGH*) or ponderosa pine (M. LaFaive p.c.). Juniper habitats may lack tall brush cover.

Six Rogue Valley nests were in 10- to 15-ft (3- to 4.5-m) tall Oregon white oak, 6-8 ft (1.8-2.4 m) from the ground (Lev 1983), and seven nests were in 7-ft (2.1-m) tall buckbrush 3-6 ft (0.9-1.8 m) from ground (Lev 1983, N. Barrett p.c.). Two Applegate Valley nests were observed in white oaks about 15 and 25 ft (4.5 and 7.6 m) above ground (J. Van Hulzen p.c.). A Mt. Pisgah nest in a 20-ft (6-m) tall, solitary Oregon white oak, was 6 ft (1.8 m) above ground (T. Mickel p.c.). A nest west of Frenchglen was 15 ft (4.5 m) above ground in a juniper near the end of a branch (P. T. Sullivan p.c.).

Throughout its range, the Blue-gray Gnatcatcher constructs an open cup nest generally saddled more than halfway out on a limb (Ellison 1992). The outer layer of the nest consists of forb and grass stems, bark strips, while the inner layer is composed of plant down, animal hair, and feathers. The nest is camouflaged with lichens held by spider web or caterpillar silk. A Rogue Valley nest located in May 1975 had a lichen and moss exterior and the grass cup was lined with feathers and animal hair (N. Barrett p.c.).

The gnatcatcher diet consists of small insects and spiders (Bent 1949, Martin et al. 1951, Ellison 1992). The diet of California and Arizona birds consisted of 70 arthropod families, including aphids, leafhoppers, true bugs, beetles, weevils, butterflies, moths, flies, wasps, ants, bees, spiders, and some grasshoppers (Root 1967). The gnatcatcher actively forages on outer twigs (sometimes along branches) of deciduous and evergreen trees and shrubs; forage sites vary with season (Ellison 1992, *DPV*).

**Seasonal Activity and Behavior:** Arrive early to mid-Apr in sw. Oregon (Gilligan et al. 1994); late Apr east of the Cascades (Evanich 1992c, Summers 1993a). Early detection dates: Medford 29 Mar 1970 (Crowell and Nehls 1970b), Rogue Valley 31 Mar 1990 (Fix 1990c), 2 Apr 1992 (W. Gray p.c.), 5 Apr 1987 (captured female, *DPV*); Malheur NWR 28 Apr

1975 (S. Lindsay p.c.); Crooked R. National Grassland 26 Apr 1992 (Evanich 1992c).

Site fidelity is unknown, but a banded gnatcatcher observed (not in hand) 17 Apr 1988 in w. Rogue Valley may have been the bird banded at the same location the previous year (*DPV*). In Rogue Valley, gnatcatchers vocalize upon arrival. Copulation was observed 18 Apr 1983 (Lev 1993); territories were established and nest building observed early May in Rogue Valley (Lev 1983, Speer and Felker 1991). Root (1969a) reported territory size (California chaparral-woodlands) of 2.2-7.4 ac (0.9-3 ha), averaging 4.6 ac (1.9 ha). Nest building was observed 2 Jun 1997 in ne. Harney Co., 5 Jun 1997 in c. Harney Co., and 2 Jul 1999 sw. Malheur Co. (OBBA).

Eggs reported from 19 May to 12 Jul (n=8) (Lev 1983., Speer and Felker 1991, OBBA, N. Barrett p.c.). Both sexes incubate (Ellison 1992); an exchange of adults at Mt. Pisgah nest was observed 12 and 19 Jun 1997 (T. Mickel p.c.). Nests with young were observed 28 May to 30 Jul (n=4) (OBBA, Speer and Felker 1991). Fledglings were observed 30 Jun to 19 Jul 1991 in the Rogue Valley (Speer and Felker 1991) and 29 Jun 1996 in the Klamath Falls area (OBBA). Second nesting attempts occur (Ellison 1992), and have been suspected at Lower Table Rock Preserve (Speer and Felker 1991). Seven of 10 active nests found by 1 Jun 1983 at Lower Table Rock Preserve were gone 17 Jun 1983 (Lev 1983); the cause of the disappearance was not determined.

Gnatcatchers depart breeding areas when young become independent in Aug (Ellison 1992, Gilligan et al. 1994). In nw. California, they are reported to disperse to brushlands and riparian areas (Harris 1996). Nonbreeders were noted in Applegate R. riparian areas on 20 Jun 1995 and 25 Jun 1999 (J. Van Hulzen p.c.). A bird was observed 4 Aug 1998, and a juvenile was captured 11 Sep 1997 in unoccupied breeding habitat in c. Rogue Valley (*DPV*). Late detections in the w. Rogue Valley include 21 Sep 1996 and 20 Sep 1997 (*DPV*).

Reverse fall migration reported on northeast coast of N. America (Ellison 1992). Similar behavior in w. U.S. may account for late fall-winter sightings in Oregon (Nehls 1995a, Contreras 1997b). CBC observations include one on 22 Dec 1979, Salem; 2 on 19 Dec 1993, Grants Pass; and one on 20 Dec 1981, Coos Bay.

**Detection:** Active, commonly visible foraging in outer canopy; vocalizations common. Quiet vocalizations difficult to hear over 160 ft (50 m) (Ellison 1992).

**Population Status and Conservation:** Gabrielson and Jewett (1940) did not report this species as occurring in Oregon. Pruitt (1950) reported sightings in Lane Co. in 1949, stating he did not know of any previously published records for Oregon. However, Bent (1949) reported two specimens in the British Museum, without details or reference, taken 4 Feb 1881 at Ashland.

DeSante and George (1994) reported increasing trend (small increase, with low or very low uncertainty) for 13-yr period (1979-91) based on BBS data from four western states.

No historic data on population status in Oregon, few current data. Lev (1983) found 15 pairs in Lower Table Rock Preserve; Speer and Felker (1991) found eight pairs in census of same location. Known breeding populations appear stable, where habitat remains stable. Three out of seven nests in the Rogue Valley fledged Brown-headed Cowbirds, two of four parasitized nests were abandoned in 1991 (Speer and Felker 1991). Loss or modification of chaparral-oak habitat by human development or other activities is greatest threat to Rogue and Illinois valley populations (*DPV*). Little known about Great Basin populations, but loss or modification of juniper and mountain-mahogany habitat may have a negative impact.—*Dennis P. Vroman*

## Family Turdidae

### Northern Wheatear *Oenanthe oenanthe*

This active, sparrow-sized thrush breeds from ne. Canada across Eurasia into Alaska and Yukon Territory. N. American birds winter in Asia (Gabrielson and Lincoln 1959). It is casual elsewhere in N. America. One was photographed at Malheur NWR, Harney Co., 22 Jun 1977 (Roberson 1980, Watson 1989). One was observed at Finley NWR, Benton Co., 1 Oct 1988 (Heinl and Fix 1989), and another was observed at Tillamook, Tillamook Co., 28 Oct 1995 (OBRC). Subspecies unknown.—*Harry B. Nehls*

### Western Bluebird *Sialia mexicana*

This cavity-nesting thrush is one of three bluebird species found only in N. America. Previously abundant in w. Oregon as expressed in a much-quoted reference— "it vies with the robin for first rank as a dooryard bird" (Gabrielson and Jewett 1940)—the Western Bluebird suffered a precipitous decline through degradation of habitat and avian competition (Gillis 1989). Bluebirds are well represented in art, music, verse, and prose because of their brilliant colors, anthropomorphized behaviors, and nesting in the proximity of people. The male has a cobalt blue head and throat, blue wings and tail edged with dusky brown, russet breast and flanks (the hue sometimes extending across upper back), gray-blue belly and undertail coverts. Female coloration is subdued: head and throat gray, back gray-brown, wings and tail pale blue, breast and flanks pale

russet. Amount and brightness of blue and russet are brighter on older birds. Juvs. are gray-brown above, heavily speckled with white on breast and back, a lighter shade of blue on wings and tail, and have a conspicuous white eye ring.

**General Distribution:** Breeds throughout much of w. N. America: n. Idaho, w. and c. Montana, Washington, Oregon, California, w. Arizona, and New Mexico; s. British Columbia and s. Alberta, Canada; through Baja and Mexico. Winters at low elevations from Washington and w. Montana (rarely as far north as s. British Columbia) south through the breeding range; also into se. California and c. Texas. Six subspecies, of which *S. m. occidentalis* occurs in Oregon (Phillips 1991).

**Oregon Distribution:** Breeds in open habitats with suitable nest cavities and structures throughout forested mountains and patchily in wooded lowlands; most abundant in low- to moderate-elevation foothills in w. Oregon. Rare on c. and n. coast (Gilligan et al. 1994), uncommon to fairly common on s. coast (Dillingham 1994, Contreras 1998). Fairly common on open eastern slopes of Coast Range foothills and other hills intruding the length of the Willamette Valley (Prescott 1979). In interior sw. Oregon, uncommon to common in the Rogue (Browning 1975a) and Umpqua valleys (Hunter et al. 1998). Uncommon to fairly common in early seral clearcuts with snags in the w. Cascades (*MGH*), and rare to locally common in high Cascades (Fix 1990a, *MGH*). Variably rare to locally fairly common east of the Cascades (Gilligan et al. 1994). Rare to very uncommon in Klamath Basin (Summers 1993a). Mostly absent during breeding season from high deserts of se. Oregon, and vagrant summer visitor in vast open country near Malheur NWR (Littlefield 1990a) and Columbia Basin grasslands. In Wheeler and Grant counties nesting in boxes in juniper savannah since 1988 (C. Corkran unpubl. data); otherwise uncommon in the Blue Mtns. (Thomas 1979, Evanich 1992a).

Winters at lower elevations within breeding range, generally in greatly reduced numbers in e. Oregon. Of special interest are two males found dead near Corvallis, 16 and 17 Feb 1985, both banded on breeding grounds near Pateros, nc. Washington (Guinan et al. 2000).

**Habitat and Diet:** Nests in meadows, grasslands abutting forest, juniper and oak savannahs; mixed coniferous transition zones (Thomas 1979, Pinkowski 1981b, W. Dowdy p.c.); deciduous open woodland with sparse understory; and early succession clearcuts. Meslow and Wight (1975) listed Western Bluebirds as nesting predominantly in shrub-sapling stages, and only "using" grass-forb and second-growth. In w. Oregon and Washington, not reported in dense, closed-canopy regenerating forests, young, mature, or old-growth forests, or lightly thinned stands (Mannan 1977, Mannan et al. 1980, Morrison and Meslow 1983b, Manuwal and Huff 1987, Hagar 1992, Hansen et al. 1995). On Diamond L. RD, in the Cascades of e. Douglas Co., "restricted to the availability of recent and barren clearcuts and leave tree cuts, ... preferring expanses of open ground dotted with standing dead trees, ... and in which they find cavities for nesting" (Fix 1990a). In a Coast Range study, found on 10 of 13 clearcuts (<4 yr old; slash-burned, grass-seeded, and planted with Douglas-fir seedlings) with snags (Schreiber and deCalesta 1992). Also in the Coast Range, McGarigal (1993) found Western Bluebirds almost exclusively in grass-forb stage, and rarely in shrub or sapling stages. In w. Oregon, Hansen et al. (1995) reported highest densities of Western Bluebirds at low densities of live overstory trees; estimated mean densities of bluebirds were greatest at about 1.6 trees/ac (4 trees/ha) and declined to 0 at about 8 trees/ac (20 trees/ha, for all stems >4 in [>10 cm]). In juniper savannah in Grant and Wheeler counties, Western Bluebirds used nest boxes in approximately equal proportion to their placement in four tree-density categories: 47% of nests were in nest boxes with 1-5 trees within 50 ft (15 m) radius, 35% with no trees, 17% with 6-10 trees, and 1% with 11+ trees (C. Corkran unpubl. data).

Nests in cavity created by birds (especially woodpeckers) or natural decay in live or dead trees, posts, poles and other human-made structures. Nest cup 1-4 in (1.5-10.2 cm) deep, depending on size of cavity, brood sequence, climatic conditions, and prior experience; composed of neatly woven dry grasses, rootlets, or pine needles; may incorporate horse hair, nylon twine, plastic bits, or a blue or gray feather into cup (*EKE*). Adults choose medium to high territorial perches near nest site for foraging and defense from inter- and intraspecific competition. Snags used for nesting in a Coast Range study (n=18) averaged 28 in (71 cm) dbh, range 9.8- 53.9 in (25-137 cm); 30.2 ft (9.2 m) in height, range 11.8-59.1 ft (3.6-18.0 m); height of cavities on snags (n=14) averaged 21.7 ft (6.6 m), range 7.8-34.4 ft (2.4-10.5 m) (Schreiber 1987, Schreiber and deCalesta 1992).

Wintering flocks in the Willamette Valley occur in most of the open habitats with brushy cover nearby (*DBM*). Will use nest boxes for winter roost. Throughout entire year attracted to water for drinking, for feather maintenance, control of ectoparasites, and cooling (Cromack 1983).

Primarily insectivorous, the Western Bluebird forages for crickets, grasshoppers, spiders, moths, butterflies (including larval and instar stages), ants, beetles, flies, occasionally angleworms (Beal 1915), and sowbugs (Thompson-Cowley et al. 1979, Eltzroth and Cromack 1980, Herlugson 1982, Guinan et al. 2000, C. Corkran unpubl. data). Summer food also consists of cascara (Blackburn 1987, *EKE*), fruits and other berries; in winter mistletoe berries (Eltzroth EK 1987, A. Cromack p.c.); juniper berries east of the Cascades (Contreras 1997b). It is thought that the winter distribution of the Western Bluebird in w. Oregon is highly dependent upon the availability of mistletoe berries (D. Fix p.c.).

**Seasonal Activity and Behavior:** Spring migration is difficult to discern in w. Oregon, but flocks have been observed during Apr in the w. Cascades (*MGH*); spring migration peaks during late Feb at Malheur NWR (Littlefield 1990a).

Pair bonding occurs at foraging sites or established feeders as early as Feb. The male selects a nest cavity and sings a repetitious, soft courtship warble nearby in early morning; it occasionally sings midday or following loss of mate (*EKE*). Males and some females aggressively and physically defend their territory from other pairs and other cavity-nesters (Prescott and Gillis 1985, Altman and Eltzroth 1987), even snapping their bill and emitting a harsh *chuck* to indicate danger or when chasing an intruder.

ELVA H. PAULSON © 1990

*Western Bluebird*

In the Willamette Valley, the female builds a nest and lays eggs beginning in late Mar to early Apr (Sims 1983), and lays 4-6 eggs (mean 5.3, range 3-9, n=1138 clutches), which are unmarked blue, rarely white (*EKE*). Western Bluebirds have 1-3 clutches, the third usually in late Jul. Young have been observed in the nest primarily May-Jul through-out the state (n=33) (OBBA), and occasionally in Aug (in the w. Cascades [*MGH*]). Both adults feed young (Eltzroth 1983, Eltzroth EK 1987), which fledge at 20-21 days. Fledglings have been observed predominantly in late Jun and Jul statewide (n=20) (OBBA). A simple loud *churr* indicates a bird's location or the presence of a food source. A second adult male, possibly related to nesting pair (Altman and Eltzroth l987) or juvenile from previous brood may help at the nest (Toops 1994, Guinan et al. 2000). Violet-green Swallows have also been found helping at a nest (Eltzroth and Robinson 1984).

Western Bluebirds sometimes examine pipes and vents that resemble nest or roost cavities during late summer or early fall (Hurst 1980). In the Willamette Valley, three bluebirds in 1982, one in 1994, and three in 1995 entered an unscreened chimney pipe and died in a wood-burning stove; one entered and was recovered alive 1996 (*EKE*).

Fall migration is not apparent in w. Oregon lowlands, but flocks are occasional in mountainous regions, and more common in desert and agricultural areas of e. Oregon. In e. Oregon, fall migration peaks at Malheur NWR late Sep-Nov (Littlefield 1990a). Recovery of bluebirds banded near Corvallis indicated females traveled significantly farther from natal nest site (n=50, range 0-59.8 mi [0-96.5 km]) than males (n=68, range 0-8.9 mi [0-14.5 km]) (Guinan et al. 2000). The female of a snag-nesting pair located near Deadwood, Lane Co. (T. Mickel p.c.), originally fledged in 1984 from box near Philomath (*EKE*).

**Detection:** Most visible spring and summer where nest boxes or "trails" have been established in suburban or rural subdivisions with 2- to 5-ac (1- to 2-ha) homesites, on TV antennae, on Christmas tree and family farms, and in vineyards. During fall and winter may be seen perched on fence posts, utility poles and wires along rural roads. Distinctive location calls are used to communicate when traveling in small family or large foraging flocks. In winter in w. Oregon and on CBCs, Western Bluebirds are visible in white oak savannahs and trees bearing mistletoe berries, and in open fields and pastures feeding with other species.

**Population Status and Conservation:** The Western Bluebird was prevalent throughout Willamette Valley plains before 1940; however by 1973 bluebirds were regarded as occasional transients nesting only in hilly areas intruding into the Willamette Valley (Prescott

1979, Gillis 1989). Prescott (1979) observed a decline before the widespread use of DDT. Several factors likely contributed to the decline in w. Oregon. Forest practices, in particular the widespread removal of snags, reduced nesting habitat. In the Willamette Valley, after WWII, small family farms with gardens and orchards gave way to intensified high-value monoculture and "wall to wall' farming. House Sparrows were introduced in the mid-1880s, breeding in Portland by 1897, and surged until they were "thoroughly at home throughout Oregon" (Gabrielson and Jewett 1940). House Sparrows usurp natural cavities and nest boxes, destroy eggs, and kill adults and nestlings (*EKE*). European Starlings, which arrived in the 1940s, and began breeding abundantly during the 1960s and 1970s (Prescott 1980, Jobanek 1993), have added to the problem by evicting primary and secondary cavity-nesters in natural habitat. Fortunately, starlings have not been considered a serious threat at most Oregon nest boxes because bluebird boxes are generally constructed with a 1.5-in [38-mm] diameter hole, which starlings cannot fit into. The paucity of natural nesting sites was evident as competition with Violet-green and Tree Swallows was observed to increase at nest boxes (Eltzroth 1983, Gillis l989). In s. Oregon, Ash-throated Flycatchers may be competing for cavities as well (D. Vroman p.c.). Use of boxes in western states by this flycatcher rose from 22 reported in 1991 to 543 in 1997 (Black 1998).

A 2-yr pesticide study of DDT on the reproductive success of Western Bluebirds in e. Oregon (McCluskey et al. 1977) indicated no significant differences in egg production, hatching, mortality, or fledging of young between control and sprayed areas.

Bertrand and Scott (1973b) listed it common only in sw. Oregon. M. S. Eltzroth (1987a) listed it abundant in sw. Oregon and common in three zones of w. Oregon. Increase in bluebird populations was well documented in nest boxes southwest of Portland (Prescott Bluebird Recovery Project 1991-2000); on the west side of the Willamette Valley (Audubon Society of Corvallis 1977-2002) east of the Cascades in Wheeler, Baker, and Union counties (Marshall 1992a); and in the Crooked R. National Grasslands, Jefferson Co., since 1993 (B. Gooding p.c.).

Nestlings are subject to ectoparasitism by blow-fly larvae, feather mites, and louse fly (Guinan et al. 2000). Prolonged inclement weather and cold temperatures are responsible for large numbers of abandoned eggs and nestlings (Gillis 1989, Corkran 1992). Browning (1975a) observed a dramatic decline in numbers during a wk of winter temperatures near 1°F (-17°C). Unexplained deaths of adult bluebirds in 1977 led to necropsies at OSU Veterinary Diagnostics Lab, which revealed the first case of the thorny-headed worm (an acanthocephalan endoparasite) recorded in a Western Bluebird (Thompson-Cowley et al. 1979, Eltzroth et al. 1980). This parasite, coupled with weather-related stress, is associated with diseases diagnosed as enteritis, peritonitis, coccidiosis, and botulism (*clostridium* sp.) in the Western Bluebird (Guinan et al. 2000, Bildfell et al. 2001).

Recommended short-term conservation measures include the use of nest boxes in habitat where nest sites are limited, along with continued maintenance in existing and former ranges to retain a breeding population (Guinan et al. 2000). Long-term forest management options that favor primary cavity nesting species also favor secondary nesters like the bluebird (Herlugson 1975), provided that open-canopied stands are maintained or created through fire or harvest.—*Elsie Kollin Eltzroth*

## Mountain Bluebird *Sialia currucoides*

The graceful short-distance flight of a bright male bluebird is a memorable sight. The Mountain Bluebird haunts open country, providing an "irreplaceable color note in the gray sagebrush landscape; particularly when in migration their brilliant blues flash in the desert sun in startling contrast to the prevailing dull colors of most other birds" (Gabrielson and Jewett 1940). Like other bluebirds it readily accepts nest boxes. This accessibility, along with its sky-blue color, have always endeared it to nature-lovers and made it a favorite of many. Females are generally dull brownish-blue with bright blue tinges on rump, tail, and flight feathers. Its longer wings, longer thinner bill, and upright posture help distinguish it from other bluebird species.

**General Distribution:** Breeds from ec. Alaska southeast through mountains of w. Canada, the Cascades, the Sierra Nevada, and throughout the Rocky Mtn. region north of Mexico. Winters from Pacific Northwest south to n. Baja California, c. Mexico, and s. Texas. The specific name *arctica* revived by Phillips (1991) for this species has not been used for decades and is thus a *nomen oblitem* (Banks and Browning 1995). Monotypic.

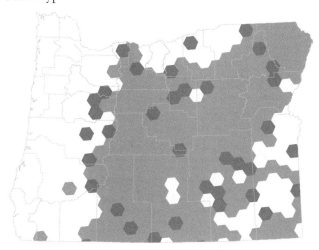

**Oregon Distribution:** Common breeder and transient east of the Cascade summit except in treeless expanses. West of the Cascade summit, breeds locally above 3,500 ft (1,130 m), and in higher elevations in the Siskiyou Mtns. (Fix 1990a, Gilligan et al. 1994). Rare to uncommon migrant in higher w. Cascades (*MGH*).

Uncommon in winter, mainly in sc. Oregon (Contreras 1997b). Occasionally stray during winter into Willamette Valley (Gullion 1951, Tice 1999b) and Rogue Valley (Browning 1975a). Two wintered in the Rogue Valley 1996-97 (Johnson 1997b). Rare winter visitor on coast (Gabrielson and Jewett 1940, Contreras 1997b).

**Habitat and Diet:** Important factors determining habitat selection are availability of suitable nesting cavities and open terrain (Farner 1952). Breed in sagebrush-juniper steppe and high-elevation mountain meadows associated with ponderosa or lodgepole pine forests (Contreras and Kindschy 1996, A. Reid p.c.). Densities of this species are higher in old-growth than mid-successional juniper stands (Reinkensmeyer 2000). In a nest-box study in juniper savannah in Grant and Wheeler counties, birds used nest boxes nearly in proportion to their availability in four tree-density categories, but with a slight preference for fewer trees (C. Corkran unpubl. data). Often breed in aspen groves, which usually occur as narrow riparian belts surrounded by sagebrush steppe (Marshall 1987, Dobkin et al. 1995). Also breed in true fir forest openings in the Siskiyous, from 4,600 ft (1,400 m) to about timberline, where Shasta red fir, white fir, and noble fir dominate (Browning 1975a); and in areas of widely scattered mountain hemlock and whitebark pine (Farner 1952). Associated with burned areas, where fire has created openings but also left standing trees or snags (Farner 1952, Gilligan et al. 1994). Fall flocks may be seen foraging on open pumice flats (Farner 1952).

Abandoned woodpecker cavities are frequently used for nesting (Gabrielson and Jewett 1940, Farner 1952, *LF*). Prefer cavities excavated by Northern Flickers over smaller sapsucker-excavated holes, despite competition with starlings for flicker holes; this may reflect the importance of cavity depth (Dobkin et al. 1995). Birds nesting in natural cavities in sc. Oregon favored live trees and snags with dbh > 9.4 in (24 cm), and avoided any under 7 in (18 cm) dbh (Dobkin et al. 1995). Sometimes nest in mail boxes, fence posts, or a rocky crevice (Gabrielson and Jewett 1940, Littlefield 1990a). In Jackson Cr. Canyon, Malheur Co., this species nested in small lava tubes 10-16 ft (3-5 m) above the base of basalt cliffs, with one nest visible within 1 ft (30 cm) of the entrance (Denny 1998b, M. Denny p.c.). Nest usually constructed of grasses or shredded strips of bark (A. Reid p.c.).

The diet of this primarily insectivorous species has not been extensively studied in Oregon. They forage from utility lines and fence rows in addition to native brush and tree perches (Gabrielson and Jewett 1940, *LF*). They have been observed to take berries from mountain ash, viburnum, and currant (M. Denny p.c.). An early spring migratory flock was observed to feed on flies in saltgrass at the north end of L. Abert, Lake Co. (M. Denny p.c.). During the nestling period, adults in sc. Washington decreased their consumption of larger prey, which they fed to nestlings (Herlugson 1982). In a study in Grant and Wheeler counties, items fed to nestlings were predominantly grasshoppers (40%) and crickets (26%) (n=472) (C. Corkran unpubl. data). Flocks are sometimes found wintering in association with American Robins and Townsend's Solitaires, feeding on juniper berries or other fruits (Contreras 1997b).

**Seasonal Activity and Behavior:** Spring migrants enter Oregon by late Feb (Littlefield 1990a, *LF*); large flocks are often observed in Mar (Gabrielson and Jewett 1940, Gilligan et al. 1994). Mountain Bluebirds give a soft nasal advertising call throughout the day, a low warbled song usually before dawn and during flight, and a high-pitched alarm *tink*, especially on territory or near fledglings (Power and Lombardo 1996). Highly protective of nesting territories (Power and Lombardo 1996, *LF*).

During the 1995-99 OBBA effort, nest building was most often observed mid-Jun (n=5), but as early as 9 May (OBBA, Farner 1952). However, in a study in Grant and Wheeler counties, Corkran (unpubl. data) regularly observed egg laying beginning in mid-Apr, always about 2 wk prior to that of Western Bluebirds. Nests with young have been reported from early May to late Aug, with most records in Jun and Jul (n=37); fledglings have been recorded as early as 20 May, with some in Jun (n=7), and most in Jul (n=18) (Farner 1952, OBBA, A. Reid p.c.).

Gather in large flocks beginning in mid-Aug; sometimes forage in association with juncos, chickadees, Yellow-rumped Warblers, and Cassin's Finches (Farner 1952). In the Blue Mtns., Mountain Bluebirds frequent lithosol meadows during late summer through Oct (M. Denny p.c.). They leave higher elevations in fall to move into open country (Littlefield 1990a). Usually migrate Sep-Oct but linger intermittently; as long as mild weather holds they often overwinter in high desert (Aldrich 1940, Farner 1952, Contreras 1997b, Korpi 1997). Often flock with Western Bluebirds in migration (Contreras and Kindschy 1996).

**Detection:** Easily found by scanning open perches and tree tops, and watching for short flights to the ground. Frequents fence rows and utility lines in open and semi-open country.

**Population Status and Conservation:** Approximately 100 yr ago, A. G. Prill (1892) described Mountain Bluebirds as uncommon in summer near Sweet Home, Linn Co., reporting six pairs in a 6 mi (9.7 km) radius. Gabrielson and Jewett (1940) saw summer birds in every county along the w. Cascade crest. Observed during summers in the 1930s in extensive westside burns with large snags present (*DBM*). These observations suggest that a summer population, some probably nesting, was formerly uncommon at moderate elevations west of the Cascade summit. This species has declined to casual status in these areas, perhaps in association with the decrease in large forest fires, but has remained at higher elevations. BBS data show a 3.3%/yr increase for Oregon 1966-2000, but decreases in the Cascades for this period (Sauer et al. 2001).

In the Great Basin, decades of heavy grazing and fire suppression have greatly reduced the number of large aspen (Dobkin et al. 1995), which provide strongly favored nesting habitat for this species. Starlings compete aggressively for nest cavities in some of these areas, and may exert a negative influence on populations where suitable cavities are limited (Dobkin et al. 1995). Mountain Bluebird production and survival would likely increase with conservation efforts that preserve snags with nest cavities or provide nest boxes of the proper dimensions and locations (*LF*).

At study areas in ne. Oregon, DDT applied aerially over nesting habitat after egg laying showed no measurable short-term effect on nestling survival or fledging success (Thomas and McCluskey 1974, McCluskey et al. 1977). However, 1 yr after DDT application in ne. Oregon, all Mountain Bluebird eggs (n=35) collected contained residual DDT at levels 10 times greater than in Northern Flicker eggs, most likely because this species is a primary insectivore (Henny et al. 1977).—*LeRoy Fish and Rachel White Scheuering*

## Townsend's Solitaire *Myadestes townsendi*

The type specimen for Townsend's Solitaire was collected in Oregon near the mouth of the Columbia R. in 1835 by John Kirk Townsend (AOU 1998). The bold eye-ring, white outer rectrices, and intricate buff wing pattern distinguish this elegant gray thrush at close range. The scaly patterned brown juveniles are quite unique in appearance. The complex song particularly impressed Charles Bendire, who wrote to Thomas Brewer in 1875, "I find it very varied, soft and flute-like at times, strong and powerful at others, and it reminds me, in many respects, of that of the European Skylark"(Gabrielson and Jewett 1940). The call note was described by Bendire as "the occasional sound produced by an axle of a wagon just about commencing to need greasing" (Gabrielson and Jewett 1940). The call carries well, and is a characteristic sound of the winter bird community in juniper woodlands east of the Cascades.

**General Distribution:** Disjunct in mountainous areas of w. N. America. Migratory northern population breeds from ec. Alaska, Yukon Territories, and the McKenzie Mtns. and Nahanni R. in Northwest Territories, south to extreme n. British Columbia. There is a gap in the breeding distribution from 59° to 53° N latitude. Southern breeding population from sc. British Columbia and sw. Alberta, south to Zacatecas, Mexico. Disjunct breeding population in Sierra Madre, Mexico. Winters through most of the breeding range and adjacent lowland areas, eastward onto the Great Plains. Two subspecies; *M. t. townsendi* occurs in the U.S. and Canada (AOU 1957).

**Oregon Distribution:** Widespread but uncommon summer resident in the Coast Range (Mickel 1982, Contreras 1998, Herlyn 1998, OBBA). Nesting was observed in the Coast Range in 1947 and 1948 (Walker 1949) and in w. Lane Co. in 1977 (Egger 1977a); no new nests were reported there during OBBA efforts. Uncommon to locally common summer resident on the west slope of the Cascades and Klamath Mtns. generally above 1,000 ft (300 m) (Fix 1982, Gilligan 1994, OBBA). Uncommon to fairly common summer resident in the e. Cascades and in the Blue Mtns. from timberline down to the ponderosa pine zone (Gabrielson and Jewett 1940, McAllister and Marshall 1945, Gilligan 1994, Contreras 1996a, OBBA). The lack of historical records and evidence from OBBA indicates that the species does not breed in juniper woodlands.

Uncommon migrant in the Coast Range. Rare during fall, winter, and spring west of the Cascades in interior valleys (Mickel 1982, Contreras 1998, Herlyn 1998). Fairly common to abundant migrant and winter resident in juniper woodlands east of the Cascades (Gabrielson and Jewett 1940, Evanich 1992a, Gilligan 1994, Contreras 1998).

**Habitat and Diet:** Breeds in and near open coniferous forest stands, natural forest openings, burned areas, shelterwood cuts and clearcuts to timberline. In

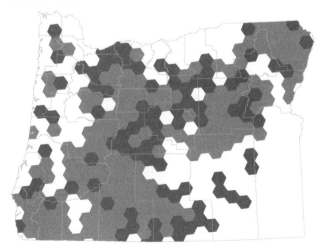

the Coast Range, Mickel (1982) noted the species most frequently at the edges of clearcuts, generally above 1,000 ft (300 m). In the w. Cascades from Lane to Clackamas counties. Fix (1982) most often found the species in recently harvested clearcuts (1-2 yr old), 18-20 ac (7.3- 8.1 ha), 2,000-4,000 ft (600-1,200 m) elevation. Typical sites had been subjected to prescribed burning to remove logging slash, with residual shrubbery (rhododendron, vine maple, western hemlock, and Pacific yew) at the forest interface and low-growing forbs, shrubs, and grasses in the interior. Most birds were seen or heard within the upper half of the site, usually near the perimeter, with no preference for aspect. Farner (1952) noted the species as a common summer resident "wherever there is well-drained terrain with some trees for cover for nest sites and for perches" around Crater L. In serpentine habitat of Klamath Mtns., most common in relatively dense (compared to the usual very open), tall stands of incense-cedar/Jeffrey pine/sugar pine with good numbers of spike tops or dead trees, from which they sing (D. Vroman p.c.). In Union and Wallowa counties, breeds in open coniferous forests at moderate to high elevation (Evanich 1992a).

Nest usually a bulky mass of sticks and pine needles, usually placed on the ground near or on logs or stumps, in tree roots or among rocks. Nests are rarely exposed from above (Bowen 1997). Two nests observed by Fix (1990a) on the Umpqua NF were beneath mats of overhanging rootlets below the tops of road cutbanks; one was lined entirely with cast needles of western white pine. Many nests in the Blue Mtns. have been found in road cuts of forest roads, usually about 24 in (60 cm) below the top of the cut (M. Denny p.c.). In lodgepole pine forest of the c. Oregon pumice zone, nest habitat selection models indicated significantly positive relationships with snags and down logs and significantly negative relationships with percent ground cover and number of saplings (B. Altman p.c.).

In the Coast Range in the breeding season, Mickel (1982) observed solitaires flycatching from exposed perches, and in late summer and fall feeding on red huckleberries, salal, and the fruit of trailing blackberry. Diet may be 100% juniper berries in nonbreeding season, or a variety of berries and other fruit during migration or in winter habitats other than juniper woodlands (Bowen 1997).

**Seasonal Activity and Behavior:** Fix (1990a) reported that the species increased rapidly following arrival in early to mid-Apr. No noteworthy spring influx has been reported elsewhere in w. Oregon. Spring influx around Malheur NWR early Mar, peak abundance 20 Mar to 7 Apr (Littlefield 1990a). Males sing from exposed perches, though are quiet while foraging close to the ground with mates. Aerial songs, part of a distinctive flight song display, are only given by males.

Nest building begins when the ground is sufficiently clear of snow (Bowen 1997). Statewide egg dates range from 21 May to 9 Jul (n=9) (OBBA), though Bailey (reported in Gabrielson and Jewett 1940) found a nest with eggs in Baker Co. as late as 29 Jul 1915. Eggs number 3-6 (Gabrielson and Jewett 1940). Young have been observed in the nest as early as 31 May 1906 in Baker Co. (Gabrielson and Jewett 1940). Observations of nestlings from OBBA range from 7 Jun to 21 Jul (n=9). Farner (1952) found one nest with downy young in Crater L. NP at 5,800 ft (1,760 m) elevation on 1 Jul 1948. Gabrielson collected spotted young "barely able to fly" from a nest at the base of Mt. McLoughlin on 27 Jul 1926 (Gabrielson and Jewett 1940). May be observed in family groups during breeding season (Bowen 1997). Males and females establish winter feeding territories around food supplies. Fledglings typically observed 17 Jun -18 Aug (n=12) (OBBA). Earliest fall transient at Malheur NWR 16 Aug, peak passage in mid-Nov. No significant influx west of the Cascades. Fix (1990a) reported latest fall departure from Diamond L. RD as 7 Nov.

Males sing vigorously for 2 wk in Sep as territories are established, and will sing through winter. May form loose associations with other solitaires and American Robins, sometimes moving into towns to feed on ornamental plantings (Evanich 1992a, Contreras 1997b), though generally solitary when defending winter territories. At Eagle L., California, winter territories were lost due to violent eviction by other solitaires, which resulted in higher winter mortality rates for the losers. Individuals maintain a high degree of site fidelity for winter territories from year to year (Bowen 1997).

**Detection:** Initial detection is usually by song or call. Sometimes flushed from roadsides in forested habitat. Easily overlooked while foraging, often appearing suddenly from between young trees or other low shrubbery. Generally not shy, and may permit close observation (Egger 1977a, *SGD*).

**Population Status and Conservation:** Rangewide, BBS data indicate no significant long- or short-term population trend. A statistically significant increasing trend (4.2% annual increase, p=0.03) has been recorded for Oregon for the years 1966-98. Given the species' preference for forest openings, the long-term increase may be a result of human-caused disturbances, especially logging, in closed-canopy forests west of the Cascades where undisturbed habitat would otherwise be unsuitable. As previously logged conifer forests in the Coast Range and w. Cascades mature and reach a closed-canopy stage, the species may be excluded from these areas until disturbances create new early seral or edge habitat, resulting in local declines on federal forest lands. CBC trend data for Oregon indicate

a 2.5% annual rate of increase for years 1959-89. Around Malheur NWR, winter numbers appear to be dependent on juniper berry crops (Littlefield 1990a). Nests are rarely parasitized by Brown-headed Cowbirds (Bowen 1997).—*Stephen G. Dowlan*

## Veery *Catharus fuscescens*

The Veery is known less for its appearance than for its ethereal song, a series of spiraling, reverberating flutelike notes, each lower in pitch, suggesting the name: *vee-ur, vee-ur, vee-ur*. A patient observer may get a fleeting glimpse of a small thrush with reddish-brown upperparts, pale undersides, and a buffy upper breast with a few darker spots.

**General Distribution:** Breeds from e. Canada to c. British Columbia and through the northern tier of states to the Washington Cascades, south in the Appalachians to W. Virginia, locally to n. Georgia and in the n. Rocky Mtns. to c. Colorado, locally to ec. Arizona and historically to nw. New Mexico (Phillips 1991, Moskoff 1995b). Winters in tropical S. America (Gabrielson and Jewett 1940, Moskoff 1995b). AOU (1957) recognized three subspecies; we follow Phillips (1991), who recognized five. The breeding subspecies in Oregon *C. f. salicicola* is accepted provisionally (*MRB*); Browning (1990) recognized a gray subspecies under the name *C. f. subpallidus*, and recomparisons of specimens, especially types, are needed (*MRB*).

**Oregon Distribution:** Uncommon breeder in lower to middle elevations in the Blue Mtns. where sufficient riparian thickets exist for cover and forage needs. Locally common along watercourses in Union, Wallowa, and e. Umatilla counties; less common in n. and w. Baker Co., uncommon and local in Grant and Crook counties. Occurs irregularly in Wheeler, Morrow (possible breeder), Deschutes, Harney, and Malheur counties, where more observations and documentation are needed (Egger 1977b, Contreras 1979c, 1996a; Gilligan et al. 1994). Casual anywhere

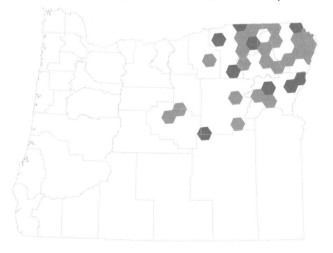

away from breeding locations. There are reports from Deschutes, Lake (Hart Mtn.), Jackson, Josephine, and Curry counties, and elsewhere during migration (Gabrielson and Jewett 1940, Browning 1975a, C. Dillingham p.c.). Rare reports of brighter birds may represent vagrant eastern subspecies, but no specimens of these are known from Oregon.

**Habitat and Diet:** Oregon birds use different habitat than those in e. N. America. Most often found in dense riparian shrub growth, often with adjacent evergreen forest. Often found foraging and singing in stands of dense willow and alder (*ALC*), black hawthorn and blue elderberry along stream courses (M. Denny p.c.). Nests on or very near the ground in low shrubs according to studies done in Canada and the e. U.S. (Dilger 1956b, Moskoff 1995b). Actively forages for arthropods (mainly insects) and fruit, usually within understory cover near the ground. Some seeds and an occasional snail, small frog, and salamander are eaten (Dilger 1956a). Feeding apparently occurs by sight; the birds actively flip ground litter with bill. Minimal flycatching and arboreal searching have been observed; other behavioral feeding moves include: hops, foot-quivering, flights, and hovers (Holmes and Robinson 1988, Yong and Moore 1990, Moskoff 1995b).

**Seasonal Activity and Behavior:** Spring migrants arrive in the e. U.S. during Apr but are not observed on Oregon breeding grounds until late May or early Jun (Gilligan et al. 1994, Moskoff 1995b). Because w. coast and Rocky Mtn. breeding populations are not observed in Mexico and sw. U.S. during spring, Phillips et al. (1964) suggest that Veeries first migrate into the east in spring then circle west across N. America to arrive on their more westerly breeding grounds.

Almost no data exist on nesting chronology in Oregon. In Union and Umatilla counties, they arrive by 25 May and are seldom seen after mid-Aug (M. Denny p.c.). Veeries are likely on eggs in Jun and fledge in late Jul and Aug (one observation 22 Jul 1999) (OBBA). They are thought to depart Oregon by early Sep, but late summer reports are essentially unknown; birds may retrace their eastern migratory route. However, fall transients do appear in Mexico and M. America (Rappole et al. 1983).

**Detection:** Best detected by song and call. Visual observation of Veery usually requires patient watching within riparian vegetation, where its brown plumage makes it difficult to pick out until it hops or flies. *Catharus* thrushes pose some difficulties in identification in Oregon, especially because the *salicicola* subspecies of Veery resembles the *ustulatus* subspecies group of Swainson's Thrush. See major field guides, Phillips (1991), Pyle (1997), and Lane and Jaramillo (2000).

**Population Status and Conservation:** The Ochoco Mtn. breeding colonies have remained relatively small and isolated for at least 30 yr; the nearest known breeding site (with very few birds) is 75 mi (120 km) eastward in c. Grant Co. The Ochoco population is therefore quite sensitive to even moderate habitat loss. Recent reports from the east slope of the Cascade Mtns. have not resulted in any suggestion of breeding (Contreras 1979c, Gilligan et al. 1994). Current population numbers and trends for breeding birds in Oregon remain relatively unknown. Additional observations are needed to improve our current understanding of distribution and occurrence of Veery in Oregon.—*LeRoy Fish and Alan L. Contreras*

### Gray-cheeked Thrush *Catharus minimus*

This thrush of northern coniferous forests of ne. Asia, Alaska, and n. Canada migrates east of the Rocky Mtns. to winter in S. America. It is only casually noted in the w. U.S. Its similarity to other *Catharus* thrushes makes it difficult to identify in the field. One was photographed at Fields, Harney Co., 22 Sep 1984 (Watson 1989). Another was observed at Malheur NWR HQ 26 Sep 1994 (Sullivan 1995b). While all w. U.S. and Oregon records indicate *C. minimus*, the very similar *C. bicknelli* cannot be entirely ruled out, although *bicknelli* has not been reported away from its restricted e. coast breeding and migration range.—*Harry B. Nehls*

### Swainson's Thrush *Catharus ustulatus*

Although they are one of the most abundant breeding birds in forests and woodlands west of the Cascade crest, it can be difficult to actually see Swainson's Thrushes. Drab plumage and the habit of sitting very still hides them from the eyes of would-be predators and birdwatchers alike, especially in the shrubby habitats they favor. However, the beautiful song of this minstrel compensates for a lack of colorful plumage. During the longest days of summer, a chorus of liquid notes rising from the deep shadows each dawn and late afternoon reveals the actual abundance of this species in the conifer forests of w. N. America.

**General Distribution:** Breeds throughout forested regions of Canada and w. U.S., from Black Hills in w. S. Dakota, through Rocky Mtns. south to s. Colorado and west to Pacific coast. Highest breeding abundance recorded by BBS is in Pacific Northwest, from nw. B.C. south to w. Oregon north of Douglas Co. Breeding abundance decreases from common in the northwest to rare in s. California and nw. Arizona. In e. U.S., common breeder in n. New England, from Maine to n. New York; rare breeder in Appalachian Mtns., from Pennsylvania to W. Virginia, and in upper Great

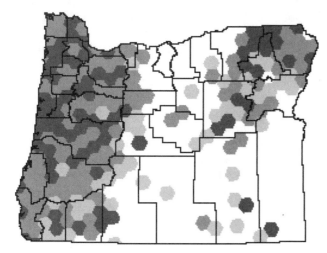

Lakes region. Winters c. Mexico south to Nicaragua (Phillips 1991). Six currently recognized N. American subspecies (see Pyle 1997, Mack and Yong 2000, who recognized *almae* but otherwise followed Ramos [*in* Phillips 1991]), three in the "russet-backed" group and three "olive-backed" (*MRB*, see Phillips 1991). Three subspecies breed in Oregon.

**Oregon Distribution:** The "russet-backed" *C. u. ustulatus* is a very common summer resident in conifer forests throughout the Coast and Cascade ranges (Gabrielson and Jewett 1940) except s. Cascades in Jackson Co. (Browning and Cross 1999). Rare at higher elevations. Common summer resident in mixed woods and riparian areas in the Willamette Valley region. Migrates throughout w. Oregon (Browning and Cross 1999). Another member of the "russet-backed" group, *C. u. oedicus*, breeds in interior sw. Oregon from Jackson Co. to w. Klamath Co. (Browning and Cross 1999) and possibly the Siskiyou Mtns. (*MRB*). An "olive-backed" subspecies *C. u. almae* (*swainsoni* of

Gabrielson and Jewett 1940) breeds in montane forests east of the Cascades (Gabrielson and Jewett 1940) and is a common spring and fall transient in dense shrubs or woods throughout the state. Browning and Cross (1999) report an individual of *almae* possibly breeding with a "russet-backed" subspecies *oedicus* in w. Klamath Co. Birds of unknown subspecies are reported by (Gilligan et al. 1994) as breeding in aspen woodlands in mountain ranges east of the Cascades. Bond (1963) wrote that there are occasional records of migrant *C. u. swainsoni* from Oregon, but this was an error (G. M. Bond p.c.). There are no verified winter records of Swainson's Thrush for the state.

**Habitat and Diet:** Occurs in most seral stages of conifer forest (Carey et al. 1991, Gerig 1992), although most strongly associated with closed canopy forest, especially where midstory and understory composed of deciduous hardwood vegetation (Bettinger 1996, Chambers 1996). Positively associated with density of shrubs, saplings, and seedlings in the Blue Mtns. (Sallabanks et al. 2002). Morrison and Meslow (1983b) reported average of 49 birds/100 ac (40.5 ha) in early-growth clearcuts in w. Oregon. Abundance typically declines following timber harvests that remove all or most of overstory (Chambers 1996), but subsequently increases with stand age (Bettinger 1996) to reach a peak in 30- to 50-yr-old stands (Hansen et al. 1995). Similarly, negatively impacted by fire in ne. Oregon, with decreases in abundance greatest following highest intensity burns (Sallabanks 1995b). Moderate levels of commercial thinning (Hagar and Starkey 2000, Hayes et al. in press) and removal of timber in small patches (1.5 ac [0.6 ha]) (Chambers 1996) do not negatively affect abundance in the short term, and may improve habitat if increase in shrub cover results from disturbance.

More abundant in riparian areas than in upslope habitats, especially along headwater streams in the Coast and Cascade ranges (McGarigal and McComb 1992, Anthony et al. 1996) and in streamside alder thickets (Gillson 1999). In Blue Mtns., riparian areas are primary habitat for reproduction and feeding (Thomas 1979), so this species is most frequently found near streams (Sturges 1957). In the Coast Range, abundance was positively related to riparian buffer width, although abundance in riparian buffers >65 ft (20 m) wide was similar to abundance in unlogged riparian areas (Hagar

ELVA/PAULSON

*Swainson's Thrush*

1999a). Abundance positively correlated with large >16-in (41-cm) logs (Bettinger 1996), which are possibly a source of arthropod prey such as beetles and ants.

Builds open cup nests of woody material or grass lined with moss, leaves, or grass close to ground, usually <10 ft (<3 m) high in thickets of shrubs or conifer saplings (Mack and Yong 2000). Density of red alder, cover of sword fern, and total canopy cover have been positively associated with nest success (unpubl. data cited in Mack and Yong 2000).

Chiefly forages on or near ground, occasionally in mid- to upper forest canopy, for invertebrates and fruits. Nearly 20% of 53 foraging observations involved gleaning from moss or lichens on tree trunks or shrubs (*JCH*). The most frequently encountered arthropod taxa in diet samples (n=56) of breeding Swainson's Thrushes from the c. Coast Range were beetles (80% of samples) and ants (43% of samples) (*JCH*). Spiders, moths and butterflies, and flies also consumed. Fruits taken include elderberry, blackberry, and salmonberry.

**Seasonal Activity and Behavior:** Earliest spring arrival 2 Apr 1972 in Eugene (Crowell and Nehls 1972c). Males arrive before females (Mack and Yong 2000) from early to mid-May (Faxon and Bayer 1991, Gilligan et al. 1994). Peak spring migration late May to early Jun for Willamette Valley (Gullion 1951, Gillson 1999). Arrival averages 26 May at Malheur NWR; earliest 30 Apr (Ivey, Herziger, and Scheuering 1998). May have high fidelity to breeding sites (Johnson and Geupel 1996, Mack and Yong 2000). Breeding records 16 May-29 Jul in w. Oregon (Gullion 1951). Height of nesting season mid- to late Jun; late date 8 Jul. Little information published on nesting behavior and chronology. Nests with eggs most frequent in mid-Jun (Gabrielson and Jewett 1940), and OBBA documented five nests with eggs between 22 Jun and 7 Jul. Average four eggs/clutch (Griffee and Rapraeger 1937). OBBA documented four nests with young between late Jun to mid-Jul, and food carrying was observed from early Jun to mid-Jul (n=9) (OBBA). Young leave nest 10-14 days after hatching. Fledglings typically observed early Jun to late Jul (n=10) (OBBA). Diet becomes less insectivorous and increasingly frugivorous after breeding and during fall migration.

In fall, peak migration of the Swainson's Thrush in the Willamette Valley occurs during mid-Sep (Gullion 1951). Nocturnal migration has been described for the Willamette Valley (*DBM*) and Coast Range as occurring during early Sep to early Oct, when "vast numbers of these birds pass overhead in the darkness, their calls fill[ing] the sky" (Nehls 1978a, Faxon and Bayer 1991). In ideal conditions during mid- to late Sep, D. Irons (p.c.) reports maxima of 15-20 calls/min in Portland, and 40+ calls/min along the immediate coast. This species is typically reported to late Oct. Late dates include one banded 6 Nov 2001 along the Applegate R., Josephine Co. (Contreras 2002b, D. Vroman p.c.); and individuals reported 9 Nov 1987 at Cloverdale (Anderson 1988b), 25 Nov 1981 in Springfield (Hunn and Mattocks 1982a), and 3 Nov to 3 Dec 1974 in Corvallis (Crowell and Nehls 1975a).

**Detection:** During the breeding season, easily detected by song and call in most woodlands and forests throughout its range. Dawn and evening choruses in the Coast Range can be spectacular to hear. After nesting, becomes quiet and increasingly difficult to detect during fall migration. At Pigeon Butte in William L. Finley NWR, this species would have gone undetected during several fall migration mist-netting sessions if it had not been captured (*JCH*). Calm nights with low overcast are best for listening for migrants in flight. While often reported just after dark and pre-dawn, nocturnal migrations can be heard at any time of night (D. Irons p.c.).

**Population Status and Conservation:** Evidence exists of declining populations (BBS data) for Oregon (1966-99 and 1980-99) and S. Pacific rainforests (1966-99). The breeding range has contracted in California, and Alaskan populations are also declining (Mack and Yong 2000). However, the species was found by Hagar and Stern (2001) at three oak woodland sites in the Willamette Valley where they had not been recorded in surveys 30 yr earlier (Anderson SH 1970, 1972), probably in response to increased canopy closure over time. May be vulnerable to nest predation (Chambers 1996, Mack and Yong 2000). Nests may be more prone to depredation by Steller's Jays in riparian buffers <164 ft (<50 m) wide than in unlogged riparian forest (Hagar 1999a). Nest parasitism by Brown-headed Cowbird appears to be rare (Mack and Yong 2000).—*Joan C. Hagar*

# Hermit Thrush *Catharus guttatus*

Rather plain gray to brown with a spotted breast and reddish tail, the unobtrusive Hermit Thrush blends well with the dappled light of the forest understory. It is famous for its sweet, clear, musical song. "It includes three or four passages, separated by considerable intervals and at higher or lower pitch, but each opens with a flute-like note that gives the performance the effect of a chant of sacred music" (Hoffmann 1927). In migration and during winter Hermit Thrushes may be found in some residential areas that have dense stands of shrubs, particularly berry producers, and conifers.

**General Distribution:** Breeds from Alaska across Canada to Labrador and south to Wisconsin and W. Virginia, and from s. British Columbia and w. Montana

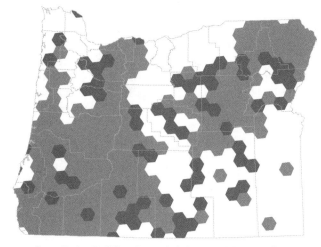

south to Baja California and Arizona. Winters from W. Virginia to Arizona and along the Pacific coast from s. British Columbia to Mexico and M. America. Of nine subspecies listed by Jones and Donovan (1996), three breed in Oregon and four winter or migrate through the state. See Browning (2002) for discussion of nomenclature and ranges of subspecies in Oregon.

**Oregon Distribution:** Uncommon to common summer resident of mature and old-growth forests at mid- to high elevations in the Cascade, Klamath, Blue, and Warner mountains (Sanderson et al. 1980, Fix 1990a, Jones and Donvan 1996); uncommon to common in the s. Coast Range, and rare in the n. Coast Range (Mattocks 1986, Carey et al. 1991, BBS); rare and local in se. Oregon (Marshall 1987, Littlefield 1990a, 1991, Contreras 1996a). *C. g. slevini* breeds west of the Cascades (USNM, MVZ, Browning 2002); *oromelus* breeds from the Cascade crest (Mt. Hood [OSU], Jefferson Co. [USNM], e. Jackson Co. [SMNH]) to Klamath Co. (SMNH) and the Warner Mtns. (CMNH, MVZ). Intergradation between *slevini* and *oromelus* on the w. slope of the Cascades (Aldrich 1968) was not verified (*MRB*). *C. g. auduboni* breeds in ne. Oregon south through Harney and Malheur counties (USNM, SMNH).

The northern subspecies *guttatus* is an uncommon winter visitant throughout the state, primarily west of the Cascades (Gabrielson and Jewett 1940), with specimens from Portland (SMNH) to Salem (University of Utah) in the Willamette Valley, and Prospect in Jackson Co. (SOU). The northern Pacific coastal subspecies *nanus* is a common winter visitant primarily along the coast (University of Utah, SMNH, USNM, DMNH) and irregularly to w. Oregon interior valleys (Gabrielson and Jewett 1940). Other subspecies occuring during nonbreeding months include *vaccinius*, with specimens from Coos Bay in Dec (USNM), Netarts in Feb (SMNH), Prospect in Dec (SOU). An intermediate between *vaccinius* and *oremelus* was collected near Ashland in Dec (SOU, *MRB*).

Migrant and wintering birds avoid deep snows and are found primarily in lowland woods and dense shrubs. The s. coast sustains the highest number of wintering Hermit Thrushes in the state (Contreras 1998, CBC).

**Habitat and Diet:** Breeds in mature forests of all types that provide a shaded understory of brush and small trees (Aldrich 1968). Breeding sites typically have semi-open canopies (D. Irons p.c.), and many areas lack a dense understory, having only minimal shrub cover (D. Fix p.c.). Present in mountain-mahogany thickets, aspen groves, dense juniper woodlands, and dense to moderately open coniferous forests (Ryser 1985). Breeds in north-facing juniper/mountain-mahogany thickets on Steens Mtn. and in the Warm Springs Mtns. (Littlefield 1990a, 1991) and aspen and mountain-mahogany thickets on Pueblo and Oregon Canyon mountains (Marshall 1987). Often seen on the ground or on stumps, boulders, or logs in the shade of the forest (Jewett et al. 1953). Songs are often given from high perches (Jewett et al. 1953, Jones and Donovan 1996).

Nests on the ground, in dense brush, or in small trees (Mannan 1980). Few Oregon nests have been described. Four nests found in the Blue Mtns. were placed in spruce and fir saplings 6-8 ft (1.8-2.4 m) above the ground (Gabrielson and Jewett 1940). One nest at Camp Harney, Harney Co., was on the ground (Bendire 1877). Gabrielson and Lincoln (1959) describe nests in Alaska being "like those of other thrushes, consisting of an outer structure of twigs, weed stems, rootlets, moss, lichens, or strips of bark, lined with fine rootlets, grass and sometimes hair."

In winter, prefers moist and dense cover of woody growth with ready access to insects and berry-bearing vegetation at lower elevations (Aldrich 1968, *HBN*), such as in disturbed woodland edges, and ornamental plantings in urban and semi-urban settings (D. Irons p.c.). Uses edge habitats extensively in migration (D. Fix p.c.).

The Hermit Thrush is primarily an opportunistic ground forager of insects, occasionally amphibians and reptiles (Jones and Donovan 1996). There is little information on the diet of the Hermit Thrush in Oregon. Fruit and berries are taken when available, especially in migration and during the winter. Several near Onion Mtn., Josephine Co., 19 Oct 2001 were eating the berries of silktassel shrubs (D. Vroman p.c.). Observed taking the fruit of blue elderberry, Russian-olive, yew, huckleberries, blackberries, wild raspberry, thimbleberry, and golden currant, as well as moths, stoneflies, and inchworms (M. Denny p.c.).

**Seasonal Activity and Behavior:** Migration is primarily nocturnal (Bent 1949) and inconspicuous. Wintering birds complicate early spring arrivals but clearly by mid-Apr many are moving through the state (Gabrielson and Jewett 1940, Irons 1984b, Lillie 1996). Good numbers continue through early May in w. Oregon at which time numbers leap and birds are present in all sorts of sites (D. Fix p.c.). Fix (1990a) found singing males back on territory at the Diamond L. RD, e. Douglas Co., by the second week of Apr. In e. Oregon, the period of passage may extend longer than w. Oregon, but most are gone from nonbreeding areas by the end of May (Gabrielson and Jewett 1940, Littlefield 1990a, Sullivan PT 1995a, Lillie 1999).

Monogamous. One brood per season. Usual clutch four eggs. Female builds nest and incubates. Both parents care for juveniles (Baicich and Harrison 1997). Laying dates late Apr to late Aug, most May and Jun (Jones and Donovan 1996). Incubation about 12 days, fledge 12 days after hatching (Baicich and Harrison 1997). No information on how long juveniles are dependent on adults.

Nests with eggs reported 13 Jun to 20 Jul (n=4); nests containing young 11 Jun to 17 Jul (n=4); fledglings observed 20 Jun to 18 Aug (n=5) (OBBA). A ground nest at Camp Harney 28 Jun 1875 contained three nearly fledged juveniles and one addled egg (Bendire 1877). A nest near Bourne, Baker Co., 3 Aug 1915 contained three incubated eggs (Jewett 1916a). A nest containing four fresh eggs 19 Jun 1927, one with two eggs 20 Jun 1927, and another with two eggs 20 Jul 1929 were found in the Wallowas (Gabrielson and Jewett 1940). Adults were feeding juveniles at Cold Springs CG, Deschutes Co. 7 Aug 1994 (C. Morrow p.c.).

The fall movement at Malheur NWR begins early in Sep and continues to late Oct (Littlefield 1990a). During 1996 migrants were noted east of the Cascades 3 Aug to 28 Oct (Sullivan 1997a). West of the Cascades migrants and wintering birds begin to appear in the lowlands by mid-Sep with most arriving during Oct and Nov (Gabrielson and Jewett 1940, Contreras 1998).

**Detection:** Though inconspicuous, this species spends much time on the ground and is often more visible than Swainson's Thrush. Its distinctive *chup* call notes often draws attention to the bird.

**Population Status and Conservation:** Widespread but unevenly distributed throughout forests. The Oregon population appears stable. Density in Siuslaw NF was 3-38 birds per 100 ac (40 ha) (Mannan 1977); in the Wallowa Whitman NF, 10-14 birds per 100 ac (40 ha) (Mannan 1982). In the Coast Range there appears to be an ongoing northward range expansion (Gabrielson and Jewett 1940, AOU 1957). Cutting of mature forests and controlled burning of forest understory brush can be detrimental (Meslow and Wight 1975); spring fires are potentially far worse than late summer burns (M. Denny p.c.). There appear to be

no serious conservation problems at this time.—*Harry B. Nehls*

## Wood Thrush *Hylocichla mustelina*

This thrush of e. N. American deciduous woodlands breeds and migrates east of the Rocky Mtns. to winter in M. America. It is only casually noted in the w. U.S. Individuals were observed in the Mahogany Mtns., Malheur Co., 21 May 1980, and at Pike Cr., Harney Co., 27 May 1980 (Rogers 1980c). Another was photographed at Fields, Harney Co., 14 Oct 1989 (Anderson DA 1990a). Monotypic (Browning 1978).—*Harry B. Nehls*

## American Robin *Turdus migratorius*

Arguably the most widely recognized of Oregon's birds, the American Robin is the largest, most abundant, and most widespread thrush in the state. Ranging from sea level to treeline, the robin's loud, musical voice and conspicuous brick-red chest make it unmistakable to even the most casual of observers. The robin thrives in both human-dominated (e.g., suburban and agricultural) and natural (e.g., forest and woodland) landscapes and is considered to be a habitat generalist throughout its range. Considering the robin's natural history, we know most about its diet, which comprises primarily soft invertebrates in the spring and summer and fruit in the fall and winter. Rather surprisingly, we know least about the robin's song (its development, vocal array, and function) and reproductive behavior (mating system).

**General Distribution:** Breeds from nw. Alaska across n. Canada to Newfoundland south to s. California and n. Baja California, across the s. U.S. to the Gulf coast and c. Florida, n. Sonora, and in the mountains of Mexico to c. Oaxaca and wc. Veracruz. Winters from s. Alaska and southernmost Canada and n. U.S. south to s. Baja California, throughout Mexico to Guatemala, and across the s. U.S. to the Gulf coast and s. Florida, Bermuda, w. Cuba, and casually to the n. Bahama Is. Seven subspecies (Sallabanks and James 1999); 2 in Oregon (AOU 1957, Browning 2002).

**Oregon Distribution:** Most abundant in nw. Oregon, where *T. m. caurinus* breeds from Lincoln Co. northward and in the Willamette Valley (AOU 1957). *T. m. propinquus* breeds in sw. Oregon and from the crest of the Cascade Range eastward (Gabrielson and Jewett 1940, Sallabanks and James 1999). The subspecies breeding on the west slope of the Cascades is unknown (*MRB*). The species does not breed in open areas of se. Oregon except in canyons, riparian zones, on ranches, and occasionally near a water hole or trough. Also, in some areas of the wc. Cascades with lots of dense forest, robins can actually be rather scarce on relatively dry slopes and ridges away from open areas and water (*MGH*). Winter populations are likely a mix of both subspecies (Gabrielson and Jewett 1940, Sallabanks and James 1999), with most birds coming from breeding grounds to the north (Contreras 1997b). It is also possible that some birds may travel to the lowlands from higher elevations during winter, but this has not been verified.

**Habitat and Diet:** Occurs in a wide range of habitats, including forest, woodland, and gardens. In lowland valleys, breeds primarily where lawns and other short-grass habitats are interspersed with trees, or at the very least, tall shrubs (e.g., residential areas, towns, farmyards, and parks) (Sallabanks and James 1999). In more natural settings, is common to very common in all except the densest forest habitats, from westside lowland conifer-hardwood forest (e.g., H.J. Andrews Experimental Forest) to subalpine parklands (e.g., Eagle Cap Wilderness Area in the Wallowa Mtns.) (*RS*).

More is known about habitat use in w. than e. Oregon. Four studies conducted in the western hemlock vegetation zone of the Oregon Coast Range provide insights into habitat preferences and potential effects of forest management. McGarigal and McComb (1995) did not find the robin to be associated with late-seral forest (120–140 yr old). It tended to be more abundant in thinned compared to unthinned Douglas-fir forest (Hagar et al. 1996). Robins did not respond to three silvicultural treatments designed to mimic natural disturbance regimes more closely than traditional clearcutting (small-patch group selection, two-story, and a modified clearcut) (Chambers et al. 1999). Neither did abundance differ between logged and unlogged riparian buffers (Hagar 1999a). Hansen et al. (1995) examined data from five studies conducted in the wc. Cascades of Oregon and found the robin generally absent from stands with >182 trees/ac (>450 trees/ha), although abundance did not vary among five stand types examined (clearcut, retention, young, mature, and old growth). In the nw. Cascades, the robin was more abundant in meadows compared with clearcuts and forested habitats (Monthey 1983).

Information from e. Oregon is restricted to mixed conifer forest. In the Blue Mtns., the robin differed significantly in abundance among six forest structural classes in the grand fir vegetation zone, being most common in early seral (i.e., stand initiation and stem exclusion–open canopy) classes compared to mid-late seral (i.e., stem exclusion–closed canopy, understory reinitiation, young forest–multistory, and old forest–multistory) classes (Sallabanks et al. 2002). Relative abundance of robins in stands of grand fir was negatively correlated with shrub density and overstory canopy cover (*RS*). Also in grand fir forest, relative abundance

of this species did not differ between managed and old-growth forest when studied by Mannan and Meslow (1984). In subalpine fir forest 3–5 yr following wildfire in the Wallowa Mtns., the robin was most common in the most heavily burned forest, frequently nesting directly on the top of exposed broken-top snags (*RS*). Also, the robin was more frequently detected in early and mid-successional post-fire forest than in any other major cover type that occurs in the n. Rocky Mtns. (Hutto 1995a).

Nests can be found from ground to treetops but usually saddled on a firm support and sheltered from rain (Sallabanks and James 1999). Of 24 nests monitored in mixed-conifer forest of the Blue and Wallowa mountains, mean nest height was 15.32 ft (4.67 m) with a range of 3.80–39.37 ft (1.16–12.00 m) (*RS*). Nests were primarily located in ponderosa pine (46%, n=11), Douglas-fir (21%, n=5), and grand fir (17%, n=4) trees. Mean height of nest trees was 43.53 ft (13.28 m) with a range of 6.00–118.12 ft (1.83–36.00 m). Mean dbh of nest trees was 21.85 in (55.50 cm) with a range of 2.48–45.28 in (6.30–115.00 cm) (*RS*).

The robin generally forages on the ground during spring and summer in search of invertebrates, with earthworms and beetles (especially Coleoptera and Carabidae) dominating its diet (based upon data from the Pacific coast states and those eastward to Idaho, Nevada, and Arizona [Wheelwright 1986]). In fall and winter months, its diet is primarily fruit-based (especially cherries and hawthorn) (*RS*), though in areas with short or sparse ground cover (e.g., heavily grazed pastures, parks, lawns) they have been observed to feed heavily on earthworms through the winter as long as the ground is moist and unfrozen (D. Irons p.c., *MGH*). Crop analyses of birds collected (n=9) during late summer and fall near Tumalo revealed stomach contents of western juniper berries, insects, ponderosa pine seed, and alfalfa seed; two captive individuals also ate ponderosa pine seed and juniper berries (Eastman 1960). Fruit choice during the winter has been well studied, especially in woodlands of Oregon white oak in the Willamette Valley (Sallabanks 1992b) where the robin acts as the major dispersal agent of the English hawthorn and fruits of this species are a staple food item (Sallabanks 1992a). A number of cues, such as fruit abundance and fruit size, are used to make foraging decisions first among fruiting plants, and then among fruits within plants (Sallabanks 1993c). Typically the robin picks and gleans to harvest fruit, but also may take fruit on the wing (*RS*). Prefers fruits of the English hawthorn to those of the native black hawthorn, possibly contributing to the successful spread of the nonnative species across Oregon (Sallabanks 1993b). It also forages on many other fruits, including English holly, mountain-ash, and cotoneaster. Damage to commercial fruit crops can be significant, especially grapes, cherries, and blueberries (Sallabanks and James 1999). The USFWS issues 6–10 depredation permits annually to Oregon vintners for killing robins (and Cedar Waxwings) (T. Tate-Hall p.c.).

**Seasonal Activity and Behavior:** *T. m. propinquus* that winter in Mexico and M. America move northward through Oregon in Feb; likewise, many *T. m. caurinus* that winter in coastal California arrive in Mar (Sallabanks and James 1999). Generally breeds early Apr through late Jul (Sallabanks and James 1999). Birds defend their breeding territory mid-Mar to mid-Jul (n=35); nest building observed early May to early Aug (n=12); egg laying and incubation early Apr to late Jul (n=53); young are in the nest primarily from mid-Apr to early Aug (n=47); fledglings typically observed mid-May to mid-Aug (n=102) (OBBA). In nw. Oregon range of *T. m. caurinus*, nests with full sets of eggs have been noted from 11 Apr to 8 Jul (Gabrielson and Jewett 1940); and two fledged young were observed in Portland 1 Mar 1984 (Fix 1984a). In the range of *T. m. propinquus*, early activity includes young that fell out of a nest in Ashland 5 Mar 1966 (Crowell and Nehls 1966a); in the Blue and Wallowa mountains of ne. Oregon, nest-building 19 May to 10 Jul; egg laying/incubating 15 May to 6 Jul; hatching/feeding nestlings 2 Jun to 4 Aug; and fledging 8 Jun to 9 Aug (n=24 nests) (*RS*). The species typically raises two broods per season, and sometimes three, especially following nest failure; second brood can fledge approximately five weeks after the first (Sallabanks and James 1999).

The robin is one of the first birds to begin singing in the morning and one of the last birds to be heard singing in the evening (Sallabanks and James 1999). Often make a high-pitched, thin, whining whistle from a high vantage point in the middle of the day, especially during hot weather when birds are generally inactive (*RS*). The whistles may be from males only. Large southerly flights of robins, and sometimes Varied Thrushes, can be observed in the Cascades in fall (e.g., early Oct) (*RS, MGH*).

In general, migratory patterns of the robin in Oregon are poorly understood. For example, there is still much to be known about the source of birds that winter in the Willamette Valley and those that winter in western juniper stands of c. Oregon. During winter months, D. Irons (p.c.) observes that robin numbers may substantially decrease in one area and increase in another, as robins take advantage of local food sources. He also suggests that some winter changes in populations may be following the depletion of food sources to the north and availability of food sources to the south. Wintering birds in the Willamette Valley are known to defend fruit supplies from conspecifics during cold weather (5 to 34°F [-15 to 1°C]) when ground is snow covered (Sallabanks 1993a). Foraging behavior of some individuals is also modified during such conditions; as dusk approaches, fruits are stored in an extendible esophagus, presumably to maximize fuel storage for the cold night ahead (Sallabanks 1997). Winter roosts can be very large (>1,000 birds), especially in orchards, hawthorn thickets, and western juniper stands, although more typical roost sizes are on the order of 20-200 birds (*RS*).

**Detection:** Easily located on a prominent perch by song during spring and summer months, both in suburban and farmland settings as well as in more natural forested habitats. During the nonbreeding season, large flocks of hundreds or thousands of adult birds migrate to lower elevations, where they form loose roosting aggregations that follow the availability of local fruit supplies (*RS*).

**Population Status and Conservation:** Over the 34-yr period 1966–99, BBS data indicate a significant population decline (-1.4%/yr) for the robin in Oregon (Sauer et al. 2000). During 1966-79, the robin population appeared to be stable, but during 1980-99, BBS data reveal a significant decline of -1.5%/yr. Significant declines in Oregon are not typical of other states, provinces, and physiographic regions within the U.S., where population trends for the robin are mostly stable to increasing (Sallabanks and James 1999), and the reason for the decline in Oregon is not known.—*Rex Sallabanks*

**Varied Thrush** *Ixoreus naevius*
When glimpsed in the deep shadows of its preferred densely forested habitat, this secretive thrush resembles a plump robin. But a clearer view will reveal the distinctive fieldmarks of a dark breast band, orange eyebrows, and orange wingbars. As striking as its plumage is its unmistakable song: a succession of single drawn-out, ventriloquial notes, given at different pitches that pierce the fog and dense foliage of its

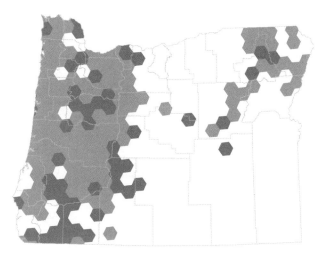

favored haunts in lush coastal and montane old-growth forests.

**General Distribution:** Breeds from n. Alaska south to extreme nw. California, with small isolated breeding population in San Mateo and Santa Cruz counties, sc. California. Breeding range includes n. Rocky Mtns. and Blue Mtns. in Oregon and Washington. Extreme w. Siskiyou Co., California, delimits eastern edge of southern portion of breeding range (George 2000). Winters along Pacific Northwest coast, as far south as San Bernardino Mtns., California. Irregularly winters east to w. Montana, se. Oregon, w. Nevada, sw. California and south to n. Baja (George 2000). Four subspecies; two are known to occur in Oregon (Phillips 1991, George 2000).

**Oregon Distribution:** *I. n. naevius* breeds throughout the Coast Ranges and in the Cascades. Fairly common breeder in low-elevation hemlock and spruce forests along n. coast, but elsewhere only rarely nests in lowland conifer forests (Gabrielson and Jewett 1940). Transient statewide during migration. Fairly common winter resident in low-elevation forests and woodlands, and regularly found in orchards and suburban backyards, especially during severe winter weather (Gilligan et al. 1994). Winter resident below 800 ft (240 m) in the Coast Range, Lincoln Co. (Faxon and Bayer 1991). Often common in winter in the s. Willamette Valley, with daily sightings of 1-20 birds evenly distributed from mid-Oct to late Mar and concentrations of up to 200 birds during infrequent snowfalls (Gullion 1951), but few are seen some years.

*I. n. meruloides* breeds in interior montane forests east of the Cascade crest, and may migrate latitudinally (George 2000). Rare breeder in dry pine forests east of the Cascade crest (Gilligan et al. 1994). Locally common in wet sites throughout the Blue Mtns. above 4,265 ft (1,300 m) (M. Denny p.c.). Uncommon resident in ne. Oregon (Evanich 1992a). May breed in Wheeler, Harney, and Lake counties in c. Oregon, but no confirmed records (OBBA). Common east of the Cascades during winter. Many birds that winter in Oregon may breed farther north (Gilligan et al. 1994).

Two other subspecies, both recently described (Phillips 1991), should be looked for in Oregon. A specimen of *I. n. carlottae*, which breeds in the Queen Charlotte Is., British Columbia, has been taken in California (Phillips 1991). *I. n. godfreii*, which breeds as far south as e. Washington (Phillips 1991), could also be a winter visitor, but a specimen would be required for verification.

**Habitat and Diet:** Varied Thrushes reach their highest breeding abundance in mature or old-growth Douglas-fir forests (Carey et al. 1991, Gilbert and Allwine 1991, Gerig 1992, McGarigal and McComb 1995). Densities in unmanaged Douglas-fir stands in the Coast Range were 4.8, 15.1, and 14.75 birds/100 ac (40 ha) in young, mature, and old-growth, respectively (Carey et al. 1991). Densities on the west slope of the Cascades in conifer stands above 3,000 ft (900 m) elevation were estimated at $365/mi^2$ ($141/km^2=18.8$ birds/40 ha) (Wiens and Nussbaum 1975). Strongly associated with late-seral forest habitats in the Oregon Coast Range (McGarigal and McComb 1995). Varied Thrushes occur in low abundance in young forests and plantations (Hagar 1992, Bettinger 1996, Hagar 1999b), except in the n. Coast Range where they are more abundant (J. Weikel p.c.). Higher densities are reported for old-growth riparian stands relative to mature and young riparian stands (Anthony et al. 1996). Similarly, Varied Thrushes were more abundant in unlogged than logged riparian stands along headwater streams in the Coast Range, where they were never observed in riparian buffers < 130 ft (40 m) wide (Hagar 1999a). May avoid forest edges and small (< 40 ac [16 ha]) forest stands during the breeding season (McGarigal and McComb 1995, George 2000).

Nests in shrub or sapling, occasionally on ground, in second- or old-growth forests. Nest is bulky and usually poorly concealed 6-13 ft (2-4 m) above ground (George 2000), and constructed of conifer

*Varied Thrush*

twigs, covered with moss, and lined with grass (Alcorn 1978). One nest in Oregon was in managed 40-yr-old Douglas-fir stand, 15 ft (3.5 m) up in 11-in (28-cm) diameter tree, braced against bole among bases of several branches, unconcealed by foliage (*MGH*).

During winter, occupies a broader range of habitats than in the breeding season, including riparian habitats, orchards, urban parks, suburban gardens, juniper woodlands, and chaparral. Winter resident in white oak woodlands in the Willamette Valley (Anderson SH 1970).

Diet consists mostly of berries, insects such as beetles, ants, caterpillars, and crickets; and other invertebrates, including millipedes, sowbugs, snails, earthworms, and spiders (Johnson and O'Neil 2001). Little Oregon-specific information on foraging and diet is available. In the Columbia Basin of nc. and ne. Oregon Varied Thrushes winter in and forage on Russian-olive; also eat millet and cracked corn (M. Denny p.c.). However, the following information from a study in n. California (Beck and George 2000) is likely to apply to Oregon because of similarity in forest habitats and plant species composition. Early in the breeding season, mainly forage on ground-dwelling invertebrates. Microsites selected for ground foraging tend to have little vegetation or litter cover. After fledging of young, diet switches to primarily fruit such as huckleberries, thimbleberries, and salmonberries. Winter diet comprises primarily fruit and mast. Fruits of madrone, manzanita, blackberry, snowberry, poison oak, and honeysuckle are important food items, and orchard fruits also are consumed, particularly downed apples (D. Irons p.c.). Winter mast includes seeds and acorns (George 2000). Cyclical variations in abundance may be related to similar cycles in acorn production (Wells et al. 1996). Acorns of tanoak are important food items during winter in n. California (Hagar 1960), therefore may also be important in sw. Oregon where tanoak is abundant.

**Seasonal Activity and Behavior:** Varied Thrushes are sometimes heard singing as early as Jan or Feb (D. Irons p.c.). Elevational migrants return to montane breeding grounds in Mar and Apr (Gilligan et al. 1994). Recorded in winter habitat in the Willamette Valley as late as 2 May (Gullion 1951). Nests with eggs have been found as early as 19 Apr and as late as 20 Jun (Gabrielson and Jewett 1940). Clutches with 1-5 eggs are incubated for 2 wk (George 2000). Young are on the nest primarily from early Jun to mid- Jul (n=8); fledglings typically observed early Jun to late Jul (n=4) (OBBA). Suspected to be double brooded, especially eastern subspecies (Alcorn 1978, George 2000).

Typically arrives on wintering grounds in valleys and foothills in late Sep (Gabrielson and Jewett 1940); an early arrival was 19 Sep (Gullion 1951). It is unknown what proportion of wintering birds are from Oregon's breeding sites or from points north. Typically in Oct, hundreds can sometimes be seen flying south along high elevation ridges and plateaus in the Cascades, often with American Robins (*MGH*).

**Detection:** Can be observed foraging for invertebrates on forest roads, roadsides, and paths before dawn and at twilight during all seasons (*JCH*) and diurnally during winter (George 2000). Can be detected by song in appropriate breeding habitat, although may be difficult to locate because of ventriloquial quality of song, and single notes may be overlooked in cacophony of dawn chorus. Most easily detected in winter when can be seen in a greater variety of habitats and more open habitats than are used for breeding. Also frequents bird feeders during this time, sings occasionally, and sometimes congregates in large flocks near feeding areas during bad weather (Gullion 1951).

**Population Status and Conservation:** Breeding and wintering abundance varies cyclically, peaking synchronously every 2-5 yr (Wells et al. 1996). Overall declining population trends in Oregon, Washington, and n. California 1980-98 are significant (Sauer et al. 1999). Status east of the Cascades is unknown, but declines are significant for west of the Cascades. Habitat loss resulting from fragmentation and loss of mature forest habitat have been cited as possible reasons for population declines (George 2000).—*Joan C. Hagar*

## Family *Timaliidae*

### **Wrentit** *Chamaea fasciata*

This is a mouse-like bird, only occasionally mustering the courage to dart from its shadowy domain. The male and female are generally indistinguishable by external characters. Both sexes are small and brown, with dim streaks on a paler, often pinkish breast; generally paler and grayer in drier regions (Bowers 1960, Browning 1992b). Both sexes sing; the female's repeated single note is easily distinguishable from the male's fast trill

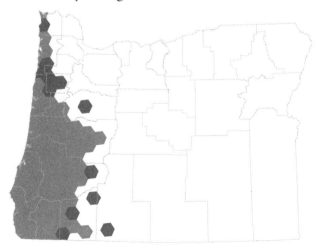

introduced by several individual notes. Despite the dull plumage, a long cocked tail and bushy head with pale eye give the bird a unique appearance. While subtle in its habits, this species has staged a remarkable range expansion to interior w. Oregon over the past 70 yr or more, and continues to expand north, but on the north coast it has not yet crossed the Columbia R. into Washington.

**General Distribution:** Resident from nw. Oregon to nw. Baja California, primarily west of the Cascades and Sierra Nevada. Five subspecies, two in Oregon (Browning 1992b).

**Oregon Distribution:** Expanding. *C. f. phaea* is resident along the coastal slope; in Columbia R. lowlands upstream to Brownsmead, e. Clatsop Co. (M. Patterson p.c.), and in the south inland to w. Klamath Mtns., east of O'Brien, w. Josephine Co. (Gabrielson and Jewett 1940, AOU 1957, Browning 1992b, Gilligan et al. 1994). *C. f. margra* (an endemic population from the northern range of *C. f. henshawi* of AOU 1957) is resident in the Rogue Valley of Jackson and e. Josephine counties; tentatively this subspecies ranges east to near Klamath Falls (Browning 1992b). Birds from Klamath R. Canyon (Summers 1993) have not been identified to subspecies. Those in extreme s. Jackson Co., Oregon, and n. Siskiyou Co., California, intergrade with *C. f. henshawi* (Browning 1992b). Populations of uncertain subspecies are resident from the interior Umpqua R. Valley (Browning 1992b, Hunter et al. 1998) north in the e. Coast Range and foothills to Yamhill Co. (unverified reports from Washington Co. and Columbia Co. [G. Gillson p.c.] (BBS, Gilligan et al. 1994), at the southern edge of the Willamette Valley, and in the w. Cascades and foothills to wc. Linn Co. (Hunter 2002). Cascade populations are reported as far east as Toketee L. in the Umpqua R. basin (Fix 1990a), 10 mi (16 km) northeast of Oakridge in the N. Fk. Willamette R. basin (Hunter 2002), near Vida in the McKenzie R. basin (Hunter 2002), 3 mi (4.8 km) east of Holley in the Calapooia R. basin (Gillson 2001c), and at the valley-foothills interface in the upper reaches of the One Horse Slough drainage, 9 mi (14 km) east of Lebanon, Linn Co. (Gillson 2001c, K. Bettinger p.c.). Reports from the Portland area (Jobanek 1975, 1976) are unconfirmed (H. Nehls p.c.). However, populations may already occur undiscovered in the N. Santiam, Mollala, and Clackamas R. drainages. Residents occur to 4,000 ft (1,219 m) in the Klamath Mtns. (D. Vroman p.c.), and 4,200 ft (1,280 m) in the w. Cascades of Douglas Co. (R. Maertz p.c.), generally at lower elevations in the north (*MGH*). Fall dispersants are uncommon in nonbreeding locations in late summer and fall (D. Vroman p.c., *MGH*).

**Habitat and Diet:** Uses a wide range of habitats depending on the geographic location. In the Rogue R. basin, valley bottom birds use broad riparian corridors with brushy undergrowth consisting of Himalaya blackberry, willow, and other species (D. Vroman p.c.). In adjacent foothills, they occur in riparian areas, powerline rights-of-way, and serpentine habitats and clearcuts with regenerated conifers and abundant brush. Also present in chaparral-oak communities (Browning 1975a, D. Vroman p.c.). At mid-elevations (2,000-3,800 ft [610-1,158 m]), they occur in natural brushfields or regenerating clearcuts, where common plants include Douglas-fir, incense-cedar, ponderosa pine, sugar pine, knobcone pine, Jeffrey pine, Pacific madrone, canyon live oak, huckleberry oak, tanoak, chinquapin, deerbrush, mountain whitethorn, snowbrush, buckbrush, and some others (D. Vroman p.c.). At highest elevations (4,000 ft [1,219 m]), the Wrentit is present in natural brushfields, but not in all habitats that appear suitable, and not in seemingly suitable habitats at higher elevations (D. Vroman p.c.).

Near the coast, Wrentits occur in heavy brush, especially evergreen huckleberry and salal (Gilligan et al. 1994). Among the breeding birds in 12 early-growth clearcuts in the Coast Range, habitat characteristics of Wrentits were most similar to those of Orange-crowned Warblers (Morrison and Meslow 1983b). Habitat occupied by Wrentits was characterized by moderate cover of deciduous trees and moderate height of shrubs. In these clearcuts, Wrentit densities ranged 0-0.08 birds/ac (0-0.20/ha) (Morrison and Meslow 1983b). No Wrentits were found in 14 clearcuts in the c. Coast Range with a shrub layer generally < 3 ft (<1 m) tall (Schreiber 1987).

Generally rare in Coast Range forests, absent in some (Hagar 1992, McGarigal and McComb 1992). Detected at densities of 0.42-0.45/100 ac (40 ha) in young, mature, and old-growth forests in the c. Coast Range (Carey et al. 1991). In a study of thinned and unthinned young conifer forests, Wrentits were rare and only found in unthinned stands (Hagar 1992). It would seem that thinning young stands would encourage growth of shrubs and attract Wrentits, but mechanical damage to shrubs during logging and delay in shrub recovery may explain their absence. Heavier thinning that encouraged brush development would likely attract Wrentits as brush flourished (*MGH*).

In the w. Cascades, Wrentits are found most often in brushy clearcuts (Fix 1990a, *MGH*). In the Umpqua Valley, they are found in "thick, shrubby areas, including both open areas and sparsely wooded areas" (Hunter et al. 1998), including thick Himalaya blackberry under riparian forest (*MGH*). Gullion (1948c) noted two birds in chaparral near Garden Valley, about 5 mi (8 km) northwest of Roseburg; but this habitat no longer occurs in the area (*MGH*).

In Douglas-fir/hardwood forests of sw. Oregon and nw. California, Wrentits were more abundant in older stands than mature, and more abundant in mature than young (Ralph et al. 1991). A positive relationship with stand age was also found in another nw. California study (Raphael 1984). The relationships with forest stand age may be correlated to the openness of the canopy and/or the maturity of the understory shrub layer (*MGH*). In early growth clearcuts in Klamath Mtns., Siskiyou NF, densities were detected up to 0.51/ac (1.27/ha), but averaged <0.20/ac (0.50/ha) (D. Vroman unpubl. data).

Little information is available on the diet of the Wrentit. D. Vroman (p.c.) mist-netted one "drunk" on Himalaya blackberries in the Rogue Valley. The Wrentit likely consumes a variety of berries and invertebrates.

**Seasonal Activity and Behavior:** Wrentits sing year-round. In Josephine Co., an egg was detected in the oviduct of a female 25 May 1995 (OBBA). Eggs were taken at Depoe Bay 11 Jun 1932 (Gabrielson and Jewett 1940). A nest with eggs was observed 13 Jun 1996 in Curry Co. (OBBA). Wrentits were observed carrying food 16 May-17 Aug (n=6) (OBBA); it is expected these primarily indicate feeding of nestlings. Singing may lessen during the nestling period (D. Lauten p.c.). Fledglings have been reported 19 Jun-7 Sep (n=6) (OBBA), but reliability of observations unknown due to lack of plumage differences in adults and young. In late Aug and Sep in sw. Oregon, dispersants, thought to be young of the year, have been detected at nonbreeding locations; singing (by adults?) may increase at this time (D. Vroman p.c.). Similarly, in Aug 2002, L. Cain (p.c.) noted that there were more Wrentits making their ticking calls in Clatsop Co. clearcuts than during the summer. There are at least 10 unpublished mid- to late summer reports of singles or "family groups" of Wrentits in residential Eugene, where they are not known to breed (D. Irons p.c., L. McQueen p.c.). More investigation is needed on dispersal of Wrentits in Oregon. In California, fall dispersants were detected at higher elevations than breeding locations (Verner et al. 1980). Breeders at high elevations (>4,000 ft [1,219 m]) are suspected to retreat to lower elevations during heavy, persistent, winter snow accumulations (D. Vroman p.c.).

**Detection:** Easily detected by song at well over 100 yds (100 m), and by grating, ticking call at close range. Often difficult to see, but respond to spishing and owl imitations. Responds to spishing in pairs more than any other Oregon songbird (D. Fix p.c.).

**Population Status and Conservation:** Ironically, this highly sedentary species has been expanding its range for at least 70 yr in w. Oregon (Hunter 2002). Earliest reports listed the birds only along the Oregon coast (AOU 1931), although specimens were taken in the Rogue Valley as early as 1916 (Gabrielson and Jewett 1940). They were not reported by Shelton (1914) from the Garden Valley area northwest of Roseburg in 1914, but Gullion (1948c) located three birds in the area on 19 Apr 1947. At about the same period Gullion (1951) had three records of individuals in sc. Lane Co. at Walterville, 6 Mar 1938; 1 mi (1.6 km) northeast of Crow, 12 Jun 1946; and on the west side of Cottage Grove Res. 23 Jun 1948 (the latter with Ben H. Pruitt and Fred G. Evenden). Even with several s. Willamette Valley records 30 yr earlier, Wrentits were not recorded on the Eugene CBC until 25 Dec 1967, Corvallis on 28 Dec 1976, and Dallas on 28 Dec 1982 (CBC).

Gullion (1948c) remarked that the northward expansion of the Wrentit was not surprising given the "general northwestward movement of Sonoran birds," which he considered apparent. Nevertheless, the source of interior birds north of the Rogue R. basin remains uncertain (Hunter 2002). Gullion (1948c) described two birds seen at close range 5 mi (8 km) northwest of Roseburg as being grayer and lighter than *C. f. phaea*, and attributed them to *C. f. henshawi*, then the subspecies of the Rogue Valley. However, Browning (1992b) later examined three specimens from s. Douglas Co. and remarked that they were different from either the coast or interior subspecies, and preferred to not assign subspecies until more specimens became available. It seems that the Wrentit could have expanded from the south (*C. f. margra* or *C. f. henshawi*) or through the Coast Range (*C. f. phaea*), perhaps in w. Douglas Co., or both (Hunter 2002).

No significant statewide trends were detectable on Oregon BBS routes 1966-2000 (Sauer et al. 2001). Recent reduction of timber harvest rates along with continued fire suppression will likely reduce habitat for interior populations of this species (*MGH*).—*Matthew G. Hunter*

## Family *Mimidae*

### Gray Catbird *Dumetella carolinensis*

Shadow-colored skulkers in dense riparian growth, catbirds are among the often-heard, less frequently seen denizens of ne. Oregon. They are all dark gray except for a black cap and russet undertail coverts. The song consists of variable melodious warblings with occasional imitations of other birds and off-key noises. A distinct mewing call is often heard.

**General Distribution:** Breed from c. British Columbia eastward across Canada and south through most eastern states, the c. Rocky Mtns, ne. Oregon and locally to c. Arizona. Winters from M. America north to the Gulf states, locally in small numbers to New England, rare inland. Monotypic (Monroe 1968, *MRB*).

**Oregon Distribution:** Fairly common breeder in dense riparian zones of the ne. Blue Mtn. ecoregion; most common and regular in Wallowa and Union counties (Evanich 1992a) and e. Umatilla Co. along the Umatilla R., Pine Cr., and Meacham Cr. (Contreras 1983, OBBA). Breed locally in Baker Co. along the Powder R., Pine Cr., and Burnt R. (Contreras 1983). There is a Jun specimen from Grant Co. (Aldrich 1946). Not found breeding along the lower Burnt R. in the late 1990s, although they used this area in the early 1980s (OBBA, *ALC*).

Rare, irregular breeder in n. Malheur Co. (Peck 1911, Contreras and Kindschy 1996) and probably extreme se. Malheur Co. (OBBA). Birds have recently been reported in the Willow Cr. valley of n. Malheur Co. where Peck found them in 1910, an indicator that riparian restoration projects in the area may be bearing fruit (Crabtree 1995a, location in Gilliam Co. should refer to Malheur Co.; Spencer 1999). Have bred at Malheur NWR and in n. Harney Co. (Sooter 1943, Littlefield 1990a), and possibly in e. and n. Grant Co. (Contreras 1983, OBBA), e.g., near Galena on the Middle Fork John Day R. (M. Denny p.c.). Recently bred in s. Morrow Co. (OBBA), where not previously known to occur.

Recent reports suggest irregular breeding along the Deschutes R. in Deschutes Co. (OBBA) and along Simnasho Cr. (at least 6 yr in same location) and Beaver Cr. in Wasco Co. (OBBA, Sullivan 1997c). Rare elsewhere, mainly in summer; very rare w. of the Cascades; rare spring visitant outside the breeding range.

Casual in winter; one was in Corvallis 9 Jan-17 Feb 1997 (Herlyn 1999) and another was in La Grande in the winter of 1988-89 (Anderson 1989e).

**Habitat and Diet:** In Oregon, uses dense riparian growth, especially willows with an admixture of taller trees such as cottonwood or mountain alder. Not found in residential areas such as used by populations in e. N. America. Sometimes observed in drier habitat during migration (*ALC*). No Oregon dietary studies exist, but the catbird has been observed eating insects and berries (Anderson 1989e, *ALC*), including blue elderberry, black hawthorn, mayflies, and grasshoppers (M. Denny p.c.).

**Seasonal Activity and Behavior:** Migratory movements are among the least-known among Oregon breeders. Arrives late in spring, probably from the east, based on the annual but very small number of records in se. Oregon. Earliest report 19 May (Gilligan et al. 1994), average about 28 May in the w. Blue Mtns. (M. Denny p.c.). Territorial birds observed as late as 4 Jul (Littlefield 1990a) and fledglings as late as 7 Aug (OBBA). It is usually gone from the w. Blue Mtns. by the second week of Sep (M. Denny p.c.). Fall movements are quiet and obscure; most birds thought to move east rather than south from Oregon, as it is very rare at Malheur NWR (latest 10 Oct) and in California in fall (Littlefield 1990a, Rogers and Jaramillo 2002). One was at Grants Pass 18 Sep 2002 (D. Vroman p.c.).

**Detection:** Fairly easy to detect by songs and calls in the core of its range in Union, Wallowa, and e. Umatilla counties, but not always easy to see because of its retiring habits. Quieter in migration and winter but mewing calls are sometimes heard.

**Population Status and Conservation:** Population data are unavailable from Oregon, but anecdotal evidence and OBBA data suggest that it is undergoing a minor expansion in its Oregon range. Because it is highly dependent on dense riparian growth, land management practices that protect such habitat within its range will no doubt assist in maintaining Oregon's population.—*Alan L. Contreras*

## Northern Mockingbird *Mimus polyglottos*

World famous for its loud, persistent singing and mimic abilities, the Mockingbird is highly conspicuous. The white flashes in the wings and tail of this grayish bird identify it in flight. It is primarily a southern species that has, by taking advantage of the environmental changes brought about by the ever-increasing human population, expanded its range northward in recent years (Arnold 1980, Derrickson and Breitwisch 1992). In many parts of the country it is a familiar bird of residential neighborhoods.

**General Distribution:** Primarily resident from s. Canada south through the U.S. to s. Mexico. Northern populations are partially migratory (Derrickson and Breitwisch 1992). One N. American subspecies, *M. m.*

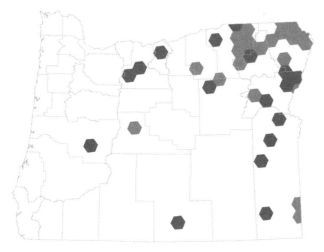

*polyglottos* (includes *leucopterus* as a synonym; Phillips 1961, 1986, *MRB*).

**Oregon Distribution:** Rare permanent resident in the Rogue Valley, especially from Medford north to White City. The first recorded successful nesting was in the Rogue Valley in 1993 (Nehls 1996). Rare but regular during all seasons elsewhere west of the Cascades with no nesting attempts reported. Rare in spring e. Oregon with some territorial birds remaining to summer, including occasional successful nesting; irregular in fall and winter. There have been many reports of territorial pairs, some with juvs., but only four nests have been recorded: at Silver Cr. Marsh CG, Lake Co., 7 Jul 1983 (Nehls 1996); Fields, Harney Co., during the summer of 1994 (Crabtree 1995a, Maitreya p.c.); Bone Cr. Canyon, Malheur Co., 20 Jun 1997 (Denny 1998a); and near Bully Cr. Res., Malheur Co., Jun-Jul 1999 (Zeillemaker 2000).

**Habitat and Diet:** The establishment of urban, suburban, and agricultural areas provided favorable habitat for the Mockingbird and most Oregon reports are from such habitats. The natural habitat of the Mockingbird in California, prior to the arrival of the first European settlers, was desert scrub in the Lower Sonoran Life Zone and the lower chaparral belt of the Upper Sonoran Life Zone (Pitelka 1941). Most e. Oregon summer records and all nests were found in this type of environment. In e. Washington, most sightings (including one nest) have been in areas under >150 KV power lines running through dry areas (M. Denny p.c.).

Nests are placed in low shrubs, seldom over 10 ft (3 m) above the ground, and comprise an open cup of dead twigs lined with fine grasses and roots. Paper, foil, and other human-made objects are often incorporated into the nest (Bent 1948). The Bone Cr. Canyon nest was a "flat, rough stick nest with a fine grassy bowl" in a sagebrush bush not far from patches of willows and roses (Denny 1998a). The nest near Fields was in similar habitat (*HBN*). The Bully Cr. nest was about 3 ft (0.9 m) above the ground and was well hidden in a scraggly 6-ft (1.8 m) plant, in a much more desert-like habitat with widely spaced low-growing desert shrubs (Zeillemaker 2000). The Silver Cr. Marsh nest was in a tall tree 20 ft (6.1 m) above the roadway (B. Tice p.c.), in an open, brushy, ponderosa pine forest (Nehls 1996).

Most w. Oregon records are from urban and suburban areas. In the Rogue Valley, nests and young have been found in heavily vegetated suburban areas with many mowed grass lawns and open fields, but no details have been published (*HBN*).

Forages primarily on bare ground or on short-grass lawns and fields, where it takes large quantities of insects. Native and cultivated fruits and berries are also taken (Beal et al. 1916). Denny (1998a) watched the Bone Cr. Canyon parents bring a large amount of insects to the nest along with one ripe currant berry (M. Denny p.c.). One bird near Bully Cr. Res. 4 Jan 1996 was eating Russian-olive berries (Crabtree 1996b).

**Seasonal Activity and Behavior:** Migrations are individual and not conspicuous (*HBN*). There are noticeable increases in sightings during Apr and May with a peak period during mid- to late May (Summers 1993c, Lillie 1997, 1999). Males appeared on territory in the Rogue Valley 19 May 1989 (Heinl 1989b) and at Fields during late May 1994 (Crabtree 1995a). During Jun and Jul most birds reported are singing males apparently on territory. In many cases they do not attract a mate, stop singing, and disappear during Jul (*HBN*).

Over most of its range the Northern Mockingbird is monogamous, raising 2-3 broods per season. Usual clutch 3-5 eggs (Baicich and Harrison 1997). Female incubates but both parents build nest and care for young (Derrickson and Breitwisch 1992). Incubation period 11-14 days; fledge 12-14 days after hatching (Baicich and Harrison 1997). Parents feed juveniles up to 3 wk after fledging (Derrickson and Breitwisch 1992).

Zeillemaker (2000) observed nest building near Bully Cr. Res. on 23 Jun; observed four eggs in a nest 1 Jul; and found one juvenile and one unhatched egg in a nest 21 Jul. The Bone Cr. Canyon nest contained three juveniles on 20 Jun (Denny 1998a). Parents were feeding noisy young in the nest at Silver Cr. Marsh 7 Jul (Nehls 1996).

There are no noticeable fall movements but individual birds continue to be reported throughout the fall and winter. Most winter reports are from w. Oregon.

**Detection:** Similarities in plumages can cause confusion between this species and a shrike, but the actions and habits of each species are quite different. Conspicuous and noisy much of the year, Mockingbirds often draw attention to themselves, but transient and wintering birds are usually unobtrusive.

**Population Status and Conservation:** Has undergone recent population increases and northward range expansions (Arnold 1980, Stiles 1982). Numbers of sightings and nesting in Oregon correspond with these increases, though the expansion has not been as rapid or as extensive as one might expect. The first Oregon report was of birds found on Steens Mtn. during 1935-36, including a juvenile, indicating possible nesting (Jewett 1937). One was singing at Burns in May 1940 (Hyde 1940), and one was at Malheur NWR 25 Jul 1940 (Sooter 1941a). First reported in the Rogue Valley 18-24 Nov 1958 (Schultz 1959). Away from the Rogue Valley the first w. Oregon reports came 12 Nov 1950 at McMinnville (Fender 1951) and at Nehalem Bay 16 Apr 1952 (Walker 1955). Since 1958 it has increased to be a rare but regular visitant and local breeding species. Increased density and range expansion seems likely in Oregon, as humans alter habitat in ways favorable to mockingbirds (Derrickson and Breitwisch 1992), but current expansion, if any, is very slow. There appears to be no environmental threat to this species, though widespread use of pesticides could be locally detrimental.—*Harry B. Nehls*

## Sage Thrasher *Oreoscoptes montanus*

More often heard than seen, this eloquent singer is the quintessence of the sage-dominated Great Basin. Its pale eye, short bill, brownish-gray back, boldly streaked breast, and long, white-cornered tail distinguish this towhee-sized thrasher. It is often glimpsed darting or running low across the road, tail corners flashing, then disappearing abruptly into the brush. Its aerobatic display flight and tireless vocalizations are its most outstanding features.

**General Distribution:** Breeds principally in sagebrush-dominated deserts from s. interior British Columbia, c. Washington, and sc. Montana south to e. California, n. Arizona, and n. New Mexico. Winters from se. California, c. and s. Arizona, to c. and s. Texas south to s. Baja California, n. and wc. Sonora and from n. Chihuahua and Nuevo Leon south in the interior to Durango (Reynolds et al. 1999). Monotypic (AOU 1957).

**Oregon Distribution:** Breeds in shrub-steppe communities east of the Cascade summit, principally in the Great Basin region of c. and se. Oregon, and occasionally in the northeast portion of the state (Gabrielson and Jewett 1940, OBBA, BBS). Common from vegetated alkaline basin floors to the high plateaus, breeding to elevations as high as 6,500 ft (2,000 m) generally (Reynolds et al. 1999) to 7,500 ft (2,286 m) on Twin Buttes, Oregon Canyon Mtns., Malheur Co. (M. Denny p.c.). Nesting densities range 25-50 per mi² (10-20 per km²) (Rotenberry and Wiens 1980, Wiens and Rotenberry 1985). Absent most winters, with only about 13 records over the past 30 yr (Littlefield 1990a, Gilligan et al. 1994, Contreras 1997b, *CRM*). Winter records are in regions where breeding birds are most numerous; all except one were of single individuals. Rare at all seasons west of the Cascade crest with about 30 records, most during spring. About one-third of the records are coastal and the remainder are inland; all are of individual birds except two instances of two individuals at upper end of Detroit Res., in the w. Cascades of Marion Co. (*CRM*). Five separate spring

records at Detroit Res. are the most from a single location west of the Cascade summit.

**Habitat and Diet:** Preferred breeding habitat is big sagebrush (Reynolds et al. 1999). Although considered a "sage obligate" by Bent (1948) and others, will also breed in other shrub cover such as greasewood, shadscale, and rabbitbrush (Wiens and Rotenberry 1981, Littlefield 1990a, Medin 1990). Nest consists of coarse sticks such as sagebrush twigs and plant stems, grasses, lined with rootlets (Gabrielson and Jewett 1940, Rotenberry and Wiens 1989). Nest is placed either on the ground under a shrub surrounded by dense grass, or above the ground within a dense portion of the shrub, depending on shrub height (Rich 1980b, Rotenberry and Wiens 1989). Protective shrub cover is required, and taller and/or denser plants are preferred (Reynolds and Rich 1978, Rich 1980b), but have been found nesting in low shadscale, stiff sage, and hopsage sites in plants <12 in (30 cm) above ground in the s. Sheephead Mtns., Malheur Co. (M. Denny p.c.). Forages almost exclusively on the ground, mainly on insects, but occasionally consumes other arthropods and plant material (Reynolds et al. 1999). Fond of berries and other small fruit in season (Ryser 1985, Reynolds et al. 1999). Diet of fledglings is almost exclusively arthropods (Rotenberry and Wiens 1989). The winter diet is unknown.

**Seasonal Activity and Behavior:** The few records from mid-Feb to early Mar could either represent very early migrants or winter survivors. The more apparent spring migration begins in mid- to late Mar and peaks in early Apr (Littlefield 1990a, Gilligan et al. 1994, *CRM*). Most w. Oregon vagrants occur mid-Apr through May; however, they have been observed at least once in every month between 18 Mar and 19 Nov.

On breeding grounds, males establish and defend territories a week or more before females arrive (Reynolds et al. 1999). In an Idaho study, territory size

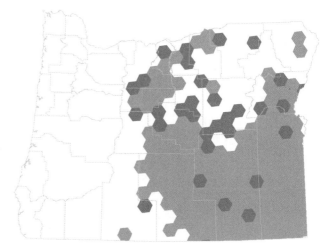

*Sage Thrasher*

ranged 1.9-5.5 ac (0.78-2.24 ha), largely depending on year studied (Reynolds 1981). Male performs a dazzling display flight over its territory. Flight is rapid and undulating from as high as 26 ft (8 m) and dipping below the tops of sagebrush, taking a circular or figure-eight path for as many as 10 revolutions, all the while singing. Wings are extended high over back upon perching, and will repeatedly raise and lower wings similar to the "wing flashing" of some other mimids, all the while singing from perch (Rich 1980a, Ryser 1985, Reynolds et al. 1999). Perches on top of shrub or other higher perch if available. Song is complex and elaborate, averaging 166 sec in an Idaho study, but has been recorded up to 22 min. Although mimics other birds' notes such as Western Meadowlark, Brewer's Sparrow, and Horned Lark, mimicry plays a minor role in song. Although singing routinely begins 45 min before sunrise and continues all day, sometimes continues all night long (Reynolds et al. 1999). Onset of nesting activities may vary from year to year by several weeks (Reynolds 1981). Lays three to five rich blue or greenish-blue eggs densely spotted with brown (Gabrielson and Jewett 1940, Reynolds 1981). Usually lays one egg per day, but sometimes two (Reynolds et al. 1999). Like Sage Sparrows, lays eggs 4-6 wk earlier than Brewer's Sparrows where breeding territories overlap (Rich 1980b). First egg date in Oregon is 6 May, although in sc. Idaho is as early as 12 Apr (Gabrielson and Jewett 1940, Reynolds et al. 1999).

Incubation period 11-13 days; both sexes incubate eggs and brood and feed young. Nestling period 11-14 days (Reynolds 1981, Reynolds et al. 1999). Earliest evidence of hatched young 31 May; first fledged 16 Jun (OBBA). However, in some years fledging could occur a month earlier (Reynolds et al. 1999). Usually has one brood, but in s. Idaho study sometimes had two (Reynolds and Rich 1978). Local dispersal and southward migration begins in Jul and peaks early Aug to mid-Sep (Littlefield 1990a, *CRM*).

**Detection:** Found most easily during and immediately following breeding season. Loud, persistent song from top of perch or during display flight makes detection simple. However, tends to be evasive when approached, often flying close to or running along the ground to elude observers. Increased numbers and less caution of recently fledged young facilitates detection in the postbreeding period.

**Population Status and Conservation:** BBS trend data indicate no significant population changes in Oregon since 1966 (Sauer et al. 1999). Se. Oregon has some of the highest population densities in the breeding range, averaging as many as 126 individuals on the Fandango Canyon BBS (north of Summer L.). Population densities are correlated to the density of shrubs, but may also be affected by climate from year to year (Reynolds 1981, Wiens and Rotenberry 1981). Competition and predation apparently do not substantially affect population densities (Wiens and Rotenberry 1981). Although prefers habitat similar to that of Sage Sparrow and Brewer's Sparrow, there is no evident competition for nest sites among these species and population densities and distribution vary independently of one another (Rich 1980b, Wiens and Rotenberry 1981). Cowbird eggs are readily recognized and rejected in Idaho studies (Rich and Rothstein 1985). Most nest predation occurs on chicks rather than eggs (Reynolds and Rich 1978, Rotenberry and Wiens 1989). Townsend's ground squirrels have been identified as a chief predator (Rotenberry and Wiens 1989). Effects of livestock grazing have been little studied. In an Idaho study, nesting density was diminished in a grazed area compared to ungrazed (Reynolds and Rich 1978). The practice of replacing native sagebrush habitat with crested wheatgrass eliminates this species, as does fire-induced replacement by cheatgrass (Reynolds and Trost 1980, Reynolds et al. 1999).—*Craig R. Miller*

## Brown Thrasher *Toxostoma rufum*

This rusty-brown thrasher is a common resident of s. Canada and the U.S. east of the Rocky Mtns. Northern birds move southward in fall to winter in the U.S. It is most often found in residential neighborhoods, about farms, and in open brushy areas near trees. It is a fairly regular visitant west of the Rocky Mtns. Most Oregon birds are found during the winter and spring. There are 11 winter records, mostly of birds that remained long periods. They were recorded from late Oct to early May; most were photographed. Thirteen records occurred between late May and early Jul; none remained more than 2 days. An early spring bird was collected at Malheur NWR HQ, Harney Co., 7 Mar 1954. The specimen (Marshall 1959) belongs to *T. r. longicauda*, the western subspecies. An ill bird in Portland 6-7 Jun 1987, later found dead (Watson 1989, spec. no. 1409 PSU), has not been identified to subspecies.

Fall records include individuals at Upper Klamath L., Klamath Co., 20 Aug 1940 (Bagg 1941), and at Malheur NWR 6 Sep 1977 (Littlefield 1990a). One was photographed at Malheur NWR HQ 18-26 Sep 1994 (Sullivan PT 1995b). Another was at Glass Butte, Lake Co., 10 Sep 1999 (Sullivan 2000a).—*Harry B. Nehls*

## California Thrasher *Toxostoma redivivum*

This secretive bird is a resident of the dense thickets and chaparral-covered slopes of w. California north to Humboldt and Shasta counties. It is a sedentary resident which exhibits a minimum of wandering after the breeding season (Small 1994). One visited a feeding station near Medford, Jackson Co., from 24 Jul to 20 Oct 1967; it or another was at the same feeders 4-25 Feb 1968 (Browning 1975a). A singing bird was observed 18 Jun 1977 a few miles north of the California border near O'Brien, Josephine Co. (OBRC). One was at Medford, Jackson Co., 17 Sep 1999 (Gilligan 2000). A bird found dead along Table Rock Rd., Jackson Co., 21 May 1996 (Spec. no. 1030, SOU), has not been identified to subspecies.—*Harry B. Nehls*

## *Family Sturnidae*

## European Starling *Sturnus vulgaris*

"When I lived in North Portland, a pair of Starlings would nest in my neighbor's dilapidated back porch every spring, raise some young, then migrate through my yard to the other neighbor's dog run. There, like clockwork, the adults and young would feed on the dry dog food put out for the 90-pound pit-bull mix that lived there" (*RTK*). This sort of opportunism shows why the European Starling has expanded so rapidly and successfully across N. America. Starlings most closely resemble blackbirds, with which they often flock in fall and winter. While both have iridescent plumage, starlings can be told from blackbirds by their two-tone wing pattern—dark upperwing, pale underwing—and

during the breeding season by the bright yellow bill. Starlings adapt readily and quickly to human habitation and are highly efficient and successful breeders. However, the abundance of the bird, the rapidity with which it has spread across N. America, and its propensity to cause damage to crops and native bird populations cause the starling to be disfavored by many and remind us of how much damage an introduced species can cause.

**General Distribution:** Native to n. Eurasia from Britain and Scandinavia across n. Europe into c. Italy, the M. East, and Russia east to Lake Baikal. Winters in many of these areas as well as n. Africa. Introduced into Australia, New Zealand, other parts of Africa, and several islands in the Caribbean (Cabe 1993). In N. America, the species moved across the continent having first been introduced in New York City in 1890 and 1891. It now ranges from ec. Alaska across most of c. and s. Canada down through all 48 of the continental United States. Some winter in the Bahamas, Yucatan, and other parts of Mexico, and their range seems to be expanding southward. Of 11 known subspecies, *S. v. vulgaris* occurs in N. America (AOU 1957).

**Oregon Distribution:** Common to abundant breeder in urban areas, and locally common in agricultural areas through the state where buildings and trees are present (OBBA). Distribution appears highly dependent upon available cavities for nesting. Generally rare in heavily forested regions, especially the w. Cascades (Fix 1990a, *MGH*), and in high desert sagebrush habitat devoid of human structures, particularly in s. Malheur Co. (OBBA). During winter, present throughout breeding range, though often in much larger numbers in lowland valleys and absent from higher elevation sites (*MGH*). During spring and fall, small flocks are regularly noted in areas where they do not breed or breed in smaller numbers (e.g., Fix 1990a).

**Habitat and Diet:** Opportunistic cavity nesters throughout their range, European Starlings use tree cavities, nest boxes, nooks and crannies in houses and structures, street and traffic lights, commercial signs, crevices in tuff formations in the John Day Valley, as well as old burrows on stream banks and road cuts (*RTK*). While generally rare to absent in forest clearcuts, will colonize newly cleared areas, especially where buildings or agricultural areas are present or nearby (*RTK*). Since the mid-1990s, starlings have become more common near Rhododendron and Wildwood Recreation Area, Clackamas Co., as increased development has occurred along Hwy 26 (B. Kott p.c.).

Starlings are opportunistic food gatherers. During spring and summer, feed primarily on insects and small invertebrates such as earthworms. In Oregon, have been noted feeding on "leatherjackets," the larval forms of crane flies, and groups of birds can be seen patrolling lawns, using their long beaks to pull these from the ground (Marsh 1996, *RTK*).

During fall and winter, more plant matter is eaten, and starlings are often seen in pastures and feedlots. Large flocks sometimes forage in holly farms and fruit orchards, maintaining their reputation as a damager of crops, though damage to other agricultural crops seems of less concern than in other parts of the country (Marsh 1996). East of the Cascades, starlings often use Russian-olive berries in fall and winter (Contreras and Kindschy 1996, R. R. Kindschy p.c.). In Umatilla and Morrow counties, they also forage at large cattle feedlots, vineyards, and apple orchards; pick grain out of cattle dung; and forage for invertebrates along the Columbia R. shoreline (M. Denny p.c.). Starlings find food in dumpsters throughout the year and, in urban areas, can often be found scavenging at malls and fast-food restaurants (*RTK*). Large night roosts are located in groves of trees and on structures such as bridges (Contreras 1998; *RTK*).

**Seasonal Activity and Behavior:** Cavity exploration and nest building have been noted as early as the first half of Mar (OBBA). Resident populations of male starlings start looking for suitable nest sites and defending territory in late winter, while migrant populations engage in breeding activities a bit later (Cabe 1993). Migrants have been noted in the w. Cascades in May (Fix 1990a). Most OBBA nesting detections were in May and the first half of Jun, though some breeding activity was observed into Jul. Cabe (1993) suggests that starlings engage in some second brooding as well as polygyny. Neither have been investigated or reported in Oregon.

A distinct pulse of fledged young join postbreeding or nonbreeding adults typically in Jun, but a few flocks can be found as early as May (H. Nehls in Jobanek 1993). These flocks may wander widely, and such movements likely contributed to the species' rapid advance across Oregon in the 1940s and 1950s (Cabe 1999). Further, many OBBA confirmations after 15 Jun were those of fledged young. Since the gray-brown juvenal plumage can be retained into early fall during widespread natal dispersal, observations of "fledglings" are poor evidence of local breeding. During this wandering period from Jun into fall, starlings are frequently observed in areas where they are typically infrequent or in lower numbers at other times of year (Fix 1990a, Gillson 1999, RTK). In e. Oregon, Gilligan et al. (1994) suggested that "there appears to be some migration out of areas east of the Cascades, but many remain." In the higher w. Cascades of e. Douglas Co., small flocks (typically 10-30) appear in fall, usually in Oct (Fix 1990a).

In fall and winter, flocks build to hundreds or thousands (*RTK*). In prime lowland areas flocks of 5,000 to 10,000 are typical at night roosts. CBC numbers in Portland topped the 1-million mark during the 1960s (Jobanek 1993).

**Detection:** Easily detected. The loud raucous calls and songs of male starlings are easily tracked. Notorious mimics, starlings imitate a great number of avian and human-produced noises. Especially noteworthy is its ability to mimic Western Wood-Pewee. Reports of "heard-only" pewees and observations of starlings imitating pewees are common during Mar and early Apr. All observers should be aware of the variety of the starling repertoire. Starling nest cavities can often be detected by the loud begging of the young when adults return with food.

**Population Status and Conservation:** Initially introduced into the Portland area in the late 1880s, but after early initial success, starlings were gone by the late 1920s (Gabrielson and Jewett 1940, Jobanek 1993). The first starling from the westward-moving population from the e. U.S. was found at Malheur NWR, Harney Co., on 10 Dec 1943 (Jobanek 1993). Small groups were first found in w. Oregon on the Eugene and Portland CBCs on 26 and 28 Dec 1947, respectively, and birds were first found at the coast on 15 Dec 1948 at Nestucca Bay, Tillamook Co. (Jobanek 1993). Nesting birds were first found near La Grande, Union Co., in 1950, in several eastern counties in 1957, and west of the Cascades in 1958 (Jobanek 1993, Gilligan et al. 1994).

Counts of over 1 million starlings found in the mid-1960s on the Portland CBC were predominantly from a huge roost that was at a holly farm (formerly Cedar Mill Orchards) in the West Haven area (H. Nehls p.c., J. G. Olson p.c.). Development in the area replaced this farm, and starlings have since left this area. Large numbers still roost on downtown Portland bridges and on the Interstate Bridge between Portland and Vancouver, Washington. Roost numbers seem somewhat reduced in these areas during the breeding season, though there do always seem to be some birds that are roosting rather than breeding (*RTK*).

After the initial large increases, BBS data from 1966 to 1999 show a leveling-off of the starling population (0.5% increase over 30 yr [Sauer et al. 2000]). CBC data also suggest that starling populations are plateauing or declining (Contreras 1997b). Jobanek (1993) suggested that the starling CBC records in Portland and Eugene reflect the bird's population trend across the country: initially small flocks, a first population boom after 5-10 yr, a second sharp increase some years after, then a decline as the population stabilizes. However, since 1995, CBC counts in Portland may also be low because counters are often not at major roost sites at day's end, as was the case in previous years (*RTK*).

Starlings, as an introduced species, are not protected by law, and no active measures are taken to conserve their population; indeed, a recipe for starling stroganoff as a suggested remedy to the problem has appeared in *Oregon Birds* (Dillingham 1996). Large roosts can cause health concerns as well as damage to property, as has occurred several times in the Portland metro area. Their nesting in cavities in buildings with resulting noise and excrement is just one of their disconcerting habits. Clearly the biggest conservation problem with starlings is their effect on native species. Starlings are often blamed for the decrease in native bird populations, especially populations of Lewis's Woodpecker, Acorn Woodpecker (Coos Co. [Contreras 1998]), Western Bluebird, and Purple Martin. Competition for natural nest cavities has been suggested as the cause for the declines (Evanich 1986a). However, most sources suggest a combination of factors for these declines, many of which have been exacerbated by the arrival of the starling (Evanich 1986a, Gilligan et al. 1994, Horvath 1999).—*Raymond T. Korpi*

## Family Motacillidae

### Yellow Wagtail *Motacilla flava*

A colorful wagtail with bright yellow underparts. Breeds across Eurasia to w. and n. Alaska. Winters Africa, India, and Japan. Casual fall transient on w. coast of N. America to California. One accepted Oregon record, a bird at the mouth of Siltcoos R., Lane Co., 31 Aug 1997 (OBRC). Subspecies unknown.—*Harry B. Nehls*

### Black-backed Wagtail *Motacilla lugens*

This distinctive bird with the long expressive tail breeds in Asia and winters in s. Asia and Africa. It is casual along the w. coast of N. America. This and the White Wagtail are almost indistinguishable except for males in alternate plumage and were once considered a single species (Morlan 1981). Their taxonomy and identification continues to be discussed (Erickson and Hamilton 2001). The White Wagtail breeds across Eurasia to w. Alaska and winters in Eurasia and Africa. It is also casual along the w. coast of N. America. Photographs of individuals at Eugene, Lane Co., 3 Feb to 31 Mar 1974 (Watson 1989); at Cape Blanco, Curry Co., 9 Nov 1996 (Gilligan 1997); and at the John Day Dam, Sherman Co., 20 Sep 1997 (Sullivan 1998a) were accepted as Black-backed Wagtails by OBRC. One was observed at Umatilla NWR, Morrow Co., 9 Feb 1975 (OBRC), and another observed at Harris Beach SP, Curry Co., 4 Jun 1980 (OBRC), could have been either White (*M. alba*) or Black-backed Wagtails. Individuals photographed at Gold Beach, Curry Co., 8 Nov 1998 and at North Bend, Coos Co., 23 Feb 1999, appear to be Black-backed Wagtails (*HBN*). Phillips (1991) listed the Black-backed Wagtail as a monotypic species, provisionally separate from White Wagtails. Although the species is possibly polytypic, identifications of photographs to subspecies are not included here, as different authors assign the same populations to different species (Black-backed Wagtail or White Wagtail) (e.g., Vaurie 1965, Cramp 1988).—*Harry B. Nehls*

### American Pipit *Anthus rubescens*

These small, buffy ground-dwellers are often seen in migration as they pass overhead in lisping flocks or as they walk deliberately along a muddy shore, tilled field, or short-grass upland with their tails slowly bobbing. Breeding birds are grayish above and lightly streaked below; winter birds are more heavily streaked below and brownish above. All plumages have cream-buff undersides (brightness varies) and a dark tail with white outer feathers.

**General Distribution:** Breed from e. Siberia across Alaska and n. Canada to the n. Maritime Provinces, south locally on mountaintops to n. New England and to Arizona and New Mexico. N. American breeding populations winter along the coast of N. America and locally inland from the n. U.S. through Mexico to M. America. We follow AOU (1957), which recognized 4 subspecies, *contra* Phillips (1991) who recognized five. Pyle (1997) followed Phillips. Two subspecies occur in Oregon.

**Oregon Distribution:** Considerable individual variation and lack of specimens cloud the subspecies picture. Subspecies *A. r. pacificus* breeds in the Wallowa Mtns. according to A.O.U. (1957); *geophilus*, provisionally recognized by Phillips (1991) as "a rather unsatisfactory race" is a synonym according to AOU (1957) and *MRB*. However, *alticola* was recognized by Phillips (1991) as the subspecies breeding in the Wallowa Mtns. Birds breeding on Steens Mtn. (Littlefield 1991) are believed by Pyle (1997) to belong to *alticola*. Those breeding at Little Belknap, Linn Co. (Anderson 1989a), the Three Sisters, and Diamond Peak (Lorain 1990), and at Paradise Park on Mt. Hood (D. Helzer p.c., *DBM*) have not been identified to subspecies. Not reported as a breeder from Mt. Jefferson, the Strawberry Range, or other high peaks.

Locally common in lowlands in winter, especially in w. Oregon and on the coast. Winter birds in w. Oregon are *pacificus* (AOU 1957). Occasional reports of pale-legged birds may be referable to *japonicus*, a rare vagrant to w. N. America (Pyle 1997), but no reports have yet been verified by thorough documentation or specimens. Hundreds of pipits can be found some years in preferred habitat in the c. Willamette Valley and coastal pastures, e.g., 658 on the Corvallis CBC, 600 on the Brownsville CBC (Gillson 1999), and 363 on the Coquille Valley CBC (Contreras 1998). East of the Cascades, winter numbers are small and generally at lower elevations. Flocks of >300 may occasionally be found in the lower Columbia Basin (M. Denny p.c.).

**Habitat and Diet:** American Pipits are open-country specialists. Breeding habitat is typically very sparse cover of forbs with substantial bare ground or rocks. No studies have been conducted on pipit breeding in Oregon. In a study in the Snake Range of c. Nevada (habitat similar to Steens Mtn.), 3.5-3.7 pairs of pipits per 49 ac (20 ha) were found in the period 1981-83 (Medin 1987).

Birds in winter or migration typically use similar but moister areas compared to the breeding season. Pipits are perfectly at home on bare dirt, gravel pans, mud, or even snow, though they are also fond of short-grass areas. The large flocks that inhabit w. Oregon in migration and winter often use grass-seed fields, pastures, estuarine mudflats, and similar locales. East of the Cascades, where moist unfrozen earth is harder to come by, pipits are especially drawn to mud and gravel bars along rivers (often quite broad in autumn); they are often abundant in fall at such locations as the shores of Malheur L. and the Snake R. at Farewell Bend, Malheur/Baker counties (*ALC*). McKay Cr. NWR, Umatilla Co., may host dozens some winters until complete prolonged freeze-up (M. Denny p.c.).

In migration, pipits will drop into almost any patch of open space available in forested areas. Fix (1990a) noted that in addition to sometimes using clearcut landings, pipits fed on lawns and even buildings at Toketee RS, going so far as to check rain gutters.

Little information is available on diet in Oregon. Anderson (1989a) noted a young bird being fed insects near Little Belknap Crater. Birds often feed on snowfields on Steens Mtn., apparently gleaning moribund insects (*ALC*). Studies conducted elsewhere in N. America show that pipits eat mainly insects, especially in summer, but also use some seeds in fall and even take small marine animals when migrating along the coast (Verbeek and Hendricks 1994).

**Seasonal Activity and Behavior:** Breeding appears to be fairly late in Oregon, no doubt due to heavy snow cover in preferred habitat, but no data are available on arrival on breeding grounds, courtship, or early nesting activities. Transients at nonbreeding locations in the Cascades of e. Douglas Co. occurred 9 Apr-19 May (Fix 1990a), which may reflect an approximate arrival time of the Cascade nesting birds. D. Helzer (p.c.) found an adult feeding a recently fledged young

on 15 Jul 1998 in the Paradise Park area of Mt. Hood. Anderson (1989a) found a recently fledged bird without a fully grown tail near Little Belknap on 27 Jul 1980.

Remarkable summer records include 12 Jul near Phoenix, Jackson Co. (Browning 1975a), and 17 Aug in c. Lane Co. (Gullion 1951). Fall movements begin in late Aug, with peak of passage in late Sep and early Oct. The outer coast and mountaintops typically get the first migrants, as early as 22 Aug in Coos Co. (Contreras 1998), 4 Sep on the ridgetops of Steens Mtn. (moving flocks there suggest migration, not local breeding birds, *ALC*), at Crater L. (Farner 1952), and in e. Douglas Co. (Fix 1990a). Nearby interior lowlands tend to see migrants somewhat later: the earliest record for Benton Co. is 5 Sep (Herlyn 1998), and Malheur NWR has not recorded fall migrants until 11 Sep (Littlefield 1990a). Flocks at Malheur generally number 50 or fewer, but about 1,000 birds were seen there on 19 Sep 1957 (Littlefield 1990a). Several thousand birds were seen over a 2-day period 26-27 Sep 1980 in the Christmas Valley/Fort Rock area (D. Irons p.c.). Latest fall departure from nonbreeding locales in e. Douglas Co. was 17 Nov (Fix 1990a).

Spring movements are extended and involve both small groups and large flocks. The largest flocks reported include 500+ near Brownsville on 4 Apr 1998 (Gillson 1999), while birds have been found in Coos Co. to 14 Apr (Contreras 1998) and in Benton Co. as late as 18 May (Herlyn 1998). East of the Cascades where few birds winter, the average arrival is 27 Mar at Malheur NWR with the earliest record (other than a rare wintering few) 13 Feb and the latest 27 May (Littlefield 1990a).

**Detection:** Pipits are easy to hear and see in appropriate habitat, but are so well-camouflaged that the unwary observer often flushes a flock into the sky before good looks can be had. By standing still in an area where pipits are feeding, close views can sometimes be had. Their clear, soft *teep-it* notes overhead often call attention to their presence, though many such birds remain distant specks without landing, especially along the coast in fall migration.

**Population Status and Conservation:** Breeding populations in Oregon are confined to alpine areas, most of which are in wilderness status. An important exception is Steens Mtn., a major breeding and migratory area that is accessible to vehicles. However, as long as such access to breeding habitat does not increase, the impact of human use on the Steens Mtn. population is unlikely to have much effect.

Migration and winter habitats are either areas not subject to much human disturbance (muddy riverbanks and lakeshores) or areas where human activity actually provides better habitat (e.g. grazed lands such as dairy farms). The advent of large-scale grass-seed farming in the Willamette Valley may have provided more winter and spring habitat than was previously present.—*Alan L. Contreras*

## Family Bombycillidae

**Bohemian Waxwing** *Bombycilla garrulus*
The Bohemian Waxwing is a nomadic species, invading locations with fruit-bearing trees or shrubs. Referred to by Bent (1960) as "roving bands of gypsies," their name reflects this view of their unpredictable and seemingly carefree lifestyle. Very sociable birds, they exhibit pronounced flocking habits in the winter, and frequently give themselves away with their constant, gentle seeping or trilling voice, as their Latin name *garrulus* suggests. Their sleek profile and elegant, almost exotic coloration also distinguish these birds. Gabrielson and Jewett (1940) considered it to be among the most beautiful of all birds in Oregon, noting the silky texture of their plumage and its soft pastel shades. Their velvety gray and brown colors contrast with the bright yellow-tipped tails and the waxy red drops on the secondary wing feathers. Other distinguishing features include a high crest, pointed wings, and rufous undertail coverts (vs. whitish undertail coverts on Cedar Waxwings). Also known as Greater Waxwing (AOU 1998).

**General Distribution:** Breeds from n. Scandinavia east across Russia to n. Siberia, and in N. America from w. and n. Alaska south and southeast through interior British Columbia, south to n. Washington, n. Idaho, and nw. Montana, and east to n. Ontario and extreme wc. Quebec. Winter movements of this irruptive species are highly variable. Found from c. and se. Alaska south and east to s. Quebec and south sporadically to s. California and n. Texas. In some winters invasions extend as far east as W. Virginia and Pennsylvania, and as far south as s. Arizona and s. New Mexico. Two subspecies: *B. g. pallidiceps* regular in Oregon; the Old World subspecies *centralasiae*, recognized following Vaurie (1958) and Phillips (1991), found once (USNM spec. no. 202981, female, Camp Harney, 17 Jan 1876; color of the specimen does not appear to be from postmortem changes [*MRB*]).Only other N. American specimen of *centralasiae* was from Attu I., Aleutians (Phillips 1991).

**Oregon Distribution:** Fairly common winter visitor to mountain valleys in the northeast part of the state. Flocks are reported almost annually from this region, especially in Joseph, Enterprise, La Grande, Pendleton, and John Day, though numbers vary widely from year to year. In general, distribution is likely based on availability of food sources (Bent 1960). During invasion years large flocks may move south into se. Oregon, and/or into western interior valleys (Littlefield 1990a, Gilligan et al. 1994). Numerous records exist of flocks in the vicinity of Malheur NWR, including the Blitzen Valley, Frenchglen, and Fields (Littlefield 1990a, Sullivan 1998a, 1999a).

Bohemian Waxwings are rare and erratic winter visitors west of the Cascades. Fourteen records exist for Benton Co. between 1968 and 1987, with most sightings from Corvallis and Philomath, but also Finley NWR and Marys Peak (Herlyn 1998). Three birds were with a flock of Cedar Waxwings in Medford on 16 Mar 1985 (Fix 1985a). Small flocks of up to about 70 birds have been seen in the Cascades in e. Douglas Co. (Fix 1990a).

One breeding record exists in Oregon, the only documented summer record. Eggs were taken from a nest in Gearhart, Clatsop Co., in 1958, where adults were seen at close range and positively identified (Griffee 1960).

**Habitat and Diet:** Winters in open woodland at low to moderate elevations, also parks and suburbs with fruiting trees and shrubs. Most Oregon records have come from small towns in the northeast part of the state, which collectively feature brushy juniper woodlands, riparian bottomland, hedgerows, and wooded parklands (Evanich 1990). Bendire (1877) found it among willows along the Silvies R., Harney Co.

Birds in Oregon have been reported feeding on juniper berries, mountain ash, rose hips, crabapples, cultivated shrubs such as firethorn and coral berry, and buds of black cottonwood (Gabrielson and Jewett 1940, Bayer 1986b, Littlefield 1990a, D. Fix p.c.). Also listed by Bent (1960) as frequenting Russian-olive trees. In the case of Oregon's one breeding record, the birds nested 7 ft (2.1 m) up in a bushy cedar tree in a residential area (25 ft [7.6 m] from a highway). The nest was constructed of grass, moss, and a few twigs in the cup, lined with moss, fine grass, hemlock needles, and lint (Griffee 1960).

**Seasonal Activity and Behavior:** Generally begin arriving in Oregon in mid-Nov (Gilligan et al. 1994). A sighting of one bird in Umatilla on 9 Sep 1992 (Summers 1993b) was unusual, as were two birds in a group of Cedar Waxwings near Salem on 23 Oct 1995 (Gilligan 1996). Most records at Malheur NWR have occurred from mid-Dec through Feb (Littlefield 1990a). The majority of birds have departed the state by late Mar and Apr, with a few records extending into May. The latest date seen in spring at Malheur NWR is May 2 (1973); there are several records of birds staying into late Mar, and in spring of 1976 several hundred stayed near Burns for 3 wk in Apr (Littlefield 1990a). A small flock was in Portland 23 May 1984 (Irons

1984b). Oregon's only nest had five fresh eggs on 25 Jun (Griffee 1960).

**Detection:** Bohemian Waxwings are typically detected by constant high, thin trilling. Flocking behavior also makes them conspicuous.

**Population Status and Conservation:** Contreras (1997b) suggested a slight decline in the Pacific Northwest, commensurate with slight declines of this species across the continent. Elsewhere increasing numbers have been noted in the variable winter range in recent years (Kaufman 1996). Ambiguity as to population status is unavoidable: as an irruptive species, they are extremely difficult to census. Overall numbers occurring during invasions may not be closely associated with actual population numbers or trends; however, these numbers are still of interest historically. Gabrielson and Jewett (1940) describe an invasion in the winter of 1919-20, with many birds present in Portland, Corvallis, and elsewhere in w. Oregon, as well as over most of the eastern part of the state. Other irruptions to w. Oregon occurred in the winters of 1931-32, 1968-69, 1972-73, 1981-82, and 1986-87 (Gullion 1951, Fix 1990a, Gilligan et al. 1994, Herlyn 1998). Records for Malheur NWR and vicinity include an invasion at Frenchglen in winter 1959, a high of 950 birds in s. Blitzen Valley in spring 1973, and numerous records of much smaller flocks in the region (Littlefield 1990a). A count of well over 1,000 birds recorded in Joseph in winter 2000 (Korpi 2000); in many years peak numbers are closer to several hundred. On 11 Feb 1999, a flock involving >2,000 birds was observed taking drinks in the partially ice-covered Lostine R., between Wallowa and Lostine (M. Denny p.c.).—*Rachel White Scheuering*

## Cedar Waxwing *Bombycilla cedrorum*

One of Oregon's most efficient fruit-eaters and a perennial irritant to cherry, blueberry, and grape growers (J. Brent p.c.), the Cedar Waxwing is a sleek, social resident of mixed forests and urban areas throughout the state (Gabrielson and Jewett 1940). Smooth, tan-brown plumage, a black mask with a small head crest, red waxy wingtips, and a yellow-tipped tail give Cedar Waxwings a distinctive appearance. Waxwings derive their name from the red waxy tips on their wings (Witmer et al. 1997). Sources disagree on the significance of the "cedar" part of the name, with some claiming a preference for cedars (Forshaw et al. 1994) and others arguing no particular preference (Baron and Acorn 1997).

**General Distribution:** Breeds from Canada south to nw. California, sw. Colorado, and w. N. Carolina. Winter range is variable, from southernmost Canada south through the U.S., Mexico, and M. America to Panama. Burleigh (1963) recognized three subspecies. Browning (1990) provisionally accepted one of these, *B. c. larifuga*, which occurs in Oregon, Washington, and Idaho, and is grayer above and has paler crowns than the eastern subspecies.

**Oregon Distribution:** Breeding range covers most of Oregon, except for extensive conifer forests and expansive treeless areas, with greater breeding populations reported in lowlands (Sauer et al. 1999). Common summer resident and migrant in open woodlands and suburban areas at low to middle elevations; uncommon and nomadic in winter (Gabrielson and Jewett 1940). Observed on Oregon CBCs every winter 1942-94 except one, with larger numbers reported in warmer areas (CBC).

**Habitat and Diet:** Nests usually saddled on a horizontal branch or in a fork of a tree or bush in overgrown fields, edge of wooded areas, mixed woodlands, orchards, roadside thickets, urban parks, brushy gardens, and yards (Witmer et al. 1997). Nests are bulky, made of twigs, stems, grasses, lichens, and human-made fibers, lined with finer materials (Gabrielson and Jewett 1940), with 2-5 blue spotted eggs. Nests may be isolated or loosely colonial, e.g., 8.7 nests/ac (22 nests/ha) in one colony (Rothstein 1971).

In an e. U.S. study, annual diet consisted of 84% fruit, 12% insect prey, and 4% flower parts (Witmer et al. 1997). Feeds in spring and summer predominantly on fleshy seasonal fruits, and in winter primarily on berries, especially from European mountain ash and American holly in w. Oregon and western juniper in e. Oregon (Gabrielson and Jewett 1940). Other important food plants in Oregon include the native Pacific madrone, black hawthorn, huckleberry, and serviceberry, as well as introduced plant species, such as firethorn, other hawthorns, Russian-olive, highbush cranberry, and cotoneasters (*DBM*). During breeding season, up to one quarter of diet can consist of insects,

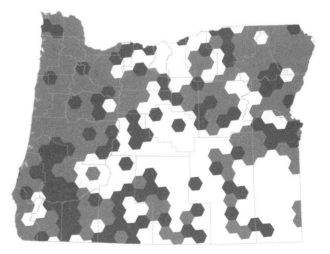

including beetles, ants, flies, caterpillars, grasshoppers, crickets, mayflies, and scale insects. At Malheur NWR, where fruit supplies are scarce, observed to consume quantities of petals from several flowering trees at HQ (Littlefield 1990a). Known to be adversely affected by fermented fruit, sometimes fatally should the bird fly into an object (e.g., building, vehicle) or fall from the sky (Baron and Acorn 1997).

**Seasonal Activity and Behavior:** Cedar Waxwings are not territorial and have a loose migratory pattern that does not conform to regular northern and southern swings of most N. American birds (Bent 1950), but is likely more tied to the availability of food sources. Often cluster in large flocks: one flock at Malheur NWR was estimated at 653 birds (Littlefield 1990a). Although permanent residents in some areas, they are most common in spring and summer, when they breed and feed on seasonal fruits and insects. Numbers in Oregon increase during spring migration in late May, although in some years movement is noted as early as late Mar (Herlyn 1997). Cedar Waxwings perform an interesting courtship ritual in which the couple passes a berry or other object back and forth many times before one of them eats or discards it (Witmer et al. 1997). Nesting activities extend from early to mid-Jun into late Aug; observations have been reported of nest building 15 May to 29 Jul (n=13), nest and eggs 16 Jun to 19 Aug (n=4), nestlings 16 Jun to 31 Aug (n=9), and recently fledged young 17 Jun to 23 Jul (n=14) (OBBA). They commonly raise two broods per year, the first around mid-Jun and the second around mid-Jul to Aug. In mid- to late summer, often seen flycatching over ponds and rivers. Fall migration begins in late Aug, and large numbers usually move through Oregon from late Sep to late Oct; by early Nov most migrants are gone, moving south to warmer areas (Forshaw et al. 1994).

**Detection:** Cedar Waxwings often travel and feed in large noisy flocks. They do not sing, but are easily located by high-pitched *ssee-ssee-ssee* vocalizations (Baron and Acorn 1997). The best technique to find them is to search out likely food sources and look for feeding birds. Keep a sharp eye out for droppings; Cedar Waxwings are notorious for their highly staining, purple, seed-packed excretions (*NKS*).

**Population Status and Conservation:** Reportedly thriving with numbers increasing or stable throughout its range, probably because of a good supply of fruit and berries (Witmer et al. 1997). In Oregon, where native habitat has shifted increasingly to an agricultural/urban base and introduced plant species, from 1966 to 1996 the population trend showed an increase on the east side of the state and a decline on the west side (Sauer

*Cedar Waxwing*

et al. 1999). Though agricultural pesticides are thought to impede nesting success and many birds die from flying into human-made objects such as cars, towers, and windows, the population remains viable, and no conservation measures have been proposed (Witmer et al. 1997).—*Noah K. Strycker*

## Family Ptilogonatidae

**Phainopepla** *Phainopepla nitens*
This dark desert bird with large white wing patches breeds from sw. Texas, s. Utah, and s. Nevada north through foothills adjacent to the Sacramento Valley of California. It tends to disperse south during the fall and move back north during Apr (Small 1994). One collected at Malheur NWR, Harney Co., 17 May 1957 (Marshall 1959, spec. no. 466260 USNM) was of the subspecies *P. n. lepida*. Individuals were observed south of Medford, Jackson Co., 15 Mar 1961 (Browning 1966a); at Lakeview, Lake Co., 26 Sep 1991 (Evanich 1992b); and at Camp Sherman 20 May 2001 and Bend 23-24 May 2001 (Sullivan 2001b). Another was photographed near Gold Hill, Jackson Co., 22 Dec 1988 to 1 Jan 1989 (Johnson 1989b).—*Harry B. Nehls*

## *Family Parulidae*

### Blue-winged Warbler *Vermivora pinus*

The Blue-winged Warbler breeds in the ne. U.S. westward to c. Iowa. It winters in M. America. There are very few records to the west of its range. While there have been Oregon sight records, only two have been accepted by the OBRC, a singing male observed 29 May 1993 at Page Springs CG, Harney Co. (Summers 1993c), and one photographed north of Sisters, Deschutes Co., 24 Jul to 29 Sep 2000 (OBRC). Monotypic (AOU 1957).—*Harry B. Nehls*

### Golden-winged Warbler *Vermivora chrysoptera*

This bird of coniferous woodlands and brushy areas breeds from e. Manitoba eastward to the Atlantic coast and south to S. Carolina. It winters in C. and n. S. America and irregularly to California and other southern states. It is occasionally found in spring elsewhere in N. America. One was at Indian Ford CG, Deschutes Co., 14 Jun 1977 (OBRC), and another was at Malheur NWR, Harney Co., 3-4 Jun 1983 (Watson 1989). Monotypic (AOU 1957).—*Harry B. Nehls*

### Tennessee Warbler *Vermivora peregrina*

This rather plain warbler breeds across Canada from the Atlantic coast to c. British Columbia and s. Alaska. The main migratory route is east of the Rocky Mtns., but small numbers regularly migrate along the w. coast. It winters primarily in M. and n. S. America. Small numbers winter in California and occasionally farther north. The Tennessee Warbler is most often found in deciduous groves or mixed woodlots. It is similar in plumage to the Warbling Vireo, though its habits are more active and warbler-like. Care should also be taken to distinguish this species from gray-headed Orange-crowned Warblers.

Most Oregon records are from early May to late Jun. One was observed near Mirror L. in the Wallowa Mtns., Wallowa Co., 9 Aug 1971 (Littlefield and Anderson 1971); another was observed at Indian Ford CG, Deschutes Co., 29 Jul 1976 (OBRC); and one was observed at Lost L., Linn Co., 24 Jul 1994 (Crabtree 1995a). Fall records are predominantly from late Aug to early Oct. There are nine winter records for w. Oregon of birds that remained for 5 days or less; one was at Corvallis 1-11 Dec 1996 (Johnson 1997b). There are several photographs in the files of the OBRC (Watson 1989). One was collected at Malheur NWR HQ 12 Jun 1963 (Kridler 1965, spec. no. 479637 USNM). Monotypic (AOU 1957).—*Harry B. Nehls*

### Orange-crowned Warbler *Vermivora celata*

This olive-green warbler is one of the drabbest of Oregon's warblers, often showing obscure streaking on the underparts and an indistinct dark eyeline. The species is named for its telltale orange crown spot, but this feature is often hidden, reduced, or absent in immature and female birds, and therefore rarely observed in the field. Orange-crowned Warblers are one of the earliest and most abundant migrants in Oregon. They glean insects from the undersides of leaves and are often seen probing into dead leaf clusters and flower heads. Perhaps this is why they are able to winter farther north than most other warblers (Dunn and Garrett 1997).

**General Distribution:** Breed across the boreal regions of Alaska and Canada and south through the Rocky Mtns., Great Basin, and Pacific coast to Baja California. Winters chiefly in the s. U.S. and Mexico through Guatemala, but is known to regularly occur in small numbers north to sw. British Columbia and the Atlantic states (Sogge et al. 1994, Dunn and Garrett 1997). Tentatively four subspecies; three in Oregon (Browning 2002).

**Oregon Distribution:** *V. c. lutescens* are common to uncommon breeders from the coast (OSU, USNM) to the west slope of the Cascades, and cross the Cascades in lower densities into at least Klamath and Wasco counties; the subspecies in central and northern east slope of the Cascades is unknown. *V. c. orestera* breeds east of the eastern base of the Cascades in mountainous regions up to near timberline; rare to very uncommon in the w. Blue Mtns. in c. Oregon and mountains of se. Oregon (Steens Mtn. [OSU]), and uncommon to fairly common in the Blue and Wallowa mountains of ne. Oregon (Gabrielson and Jewett 1940, Evanich 1992a, Gilligan et al. 1994, OBBA). Note that Gabrielson and Jewett (1940) reluctantly classified e. Oregon birds as *V. c. celata* since *orestera* had been eliminated in the 1931 A.O.U. Check-List, but they stated that

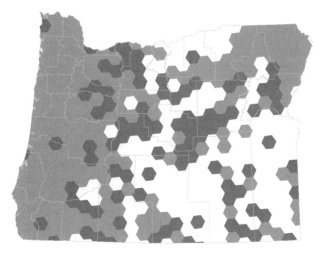

*orestera* fit these birds better than any other taxon available at the time. Recognition of *orestera* here is tentative because the difference in wing and tail lengths between *orestra* and *lutescens* (*celata* is not a breeding bird in Oregon) was based (Oberholser 1905) on a small sample of incorrectly aged specimens (Browning 2002). *V. c. celata* may migrate through the state in spring; a specimen (SOU) was identified by Jewett (1946b) from Prospect, Jackson Co. Orange-crowned Warblers are common in migration throughout the state, even in desert regions; however, subspecific identity of migrants is not well understood.

Orange-crowns are uncommon to rare in winter (Dillingham 1994, Gilligan et al. 1994, Contreras 1998). The peak winter count at a single site is three by D. Fix at the Norway log pond, Coos Co., 3 Dec 1990 (Contreras 1998). The classification of wintering subspecies has not been verified by specimens, thus field identifications are speculative, and generally indicate observations of birds with (*orestera* or *celata*) or without (*lutescens*) gray hoods. *V. c. lutescens* was reported to be the most common wintering subspecies along the coast and Willamette Valley (Fix 1985b). Both *orestera* and *celata* have been reported in winter and are very uncommon winter residents along the coast and w. Oregon inland valleys, and rare east of the Cascades, primarily along the Columbia R. (Fix 1985b, B. Altman unpubl. data, *MGH, CD*). *MGH* believed that half of the approximately 25 he has seen in w. Oregon in winter have been gray-hooded birds, while Fix (1985b) believed that the majority of the ones he has seen in w. Oregon in winter have been *lutescens*, but lists two records for *orestera*, both in Lane Co. A compilation of 16 w. Oregon sightings in winter 2001-02 revealed seven birds that appeared to be *lutescens*, seven that appeared to be *orestera*, one that appeared to be *celata*, and 1 unknown (D. Irons p.c.). Fix (1990a) lists one May sighting thought to have been *orestera* from e. Douglas Co. During spring 2002, M. Patterson (p.c.) banded 65 Orange-crowned Warblers in the Neawanna Natural History Park, Clatsop Co., of which 45 were assigned to *lutescens*, 19 to *orestera*, and one to *celata*, the latter the last Orange-crowned Warbler banded for the season, on 1 Jun 2002 (photographs were taken of birds thought to represent each subspecies).

**Habitat and Diet:** Breeding habitat characteristically includes brushy areas, particularly deciduous growth. In interior Oregon breeds in streamside thickets in canyon bottomlands and in dense quaking aspen, willow, and mountain-mahogany groves to 7,000 ft (2,134 m) (Gilligan et al. 1994). In coastal areas, breeds in riparian thickets and brushy habitats up to 5,000 ft (1,524 m) in elevation. Birds presumed to be *lutescens* especially favor thickets that contain willow

(*CD*). Foraging habits of Orange-crowned Warblers showed generalized and wide niche breadth (used shrub, deciduous, and conifer tree components) in clearcut settings of coastal Lane and Lincoln counties. In habitats that lacked deciduous tree cover, Orange-crowned Warblers spent most of their time foraging in the shrub layer (Morrison 1981). Orange-crowned Warblers foraged lower in non-deciduous woodlands (mean 2.6 ft [0.8 m], S.D. 1.6 ft [0.5 m]) than in deciduous woodlands (5.6 ft [1.7 m], S.D. 0.7 ft [0.2 m]) (Morrison 1981).

In the Cascades of e. Douglas Co., Fix (1990a) found that Orange-crowned Warblers were rare to very uncommon in the local avifauna during the breeding season. Fix believed that the higher altitude and competition with Nashville Warblers limited the density of Orange-crowned Warblers; and observed that Orange-crowned Warblers preferred dense, tangled, fairly mesic brush associations for breeding, while Nashville Warblers accepted drier, sun-parched, semi-open communities such as ceanothus thickets. In a w. Cascades study of bird communities in 5- to 34-yr-old managed Douglas-fir stands, Bettinger (1996) found Orange-crowned Warblers in stands 5-19 yr old, and most abundant in stands 10-14 yr old.

Wintering habitat is usually composed of bare deciduous overstory and a dense understory of brambles, usually Himalayan blackberry (Fix 1985b). Frequent plant associates are cottonwood, hawthorn, willow, and various shrubs. They are most often discovered in thickets that are close to slow-moving or standing water. Fix (1985b) speculated that the temperature-moderating effect of water might lessen the impact of winter weather or cold snaps on this semi-hardy passerine. Such sites probably support a larger and more consistent winter insect fauna than sites removed from water. Mostly insectivorous, but occasionally take fruit, especially in winter. Occasionally come to suet, peanut butter, and even hummingbird feeders at winter feeding stations.

**Seasonal Activity and Behavior:** Spring migration begins in mid-Mar along the s. Oregon coast (Dillingham 1994) and peaks in Apr. Males migrate earlier than females (Otahal 1994). They begin singing in late Mar to early Apr, singing tapers in late Jun and ceases in Jul (*CD*). Males often cease singing after pair bonds are formed (Sogge et al. 1994). Nest building observed in the Blue Mtns. of ne. Oregon late May to mid-Jun (n=3); eggs detected in oviducts of captured birds in w. Oregon mid- to late Jun (n=2); nest with eggs located 20 Jun in se. Oregon; nests with young observed mid-Jun to early Jul (n=3) in ne. and se. Oregon; adult birds observed carrying food Jun through early Jul (n=9) throughout Oregon; fledged young observed from mid-May to early Aug (n=10) throughout Oregon (OBBA).

After nesting and prior to migration (Jul-Aug), Orange-crowned Warblers can be observed dispersing from breeding sites. Some Orange-crowned Warblers move to higher elevations, even to tree line (Sogge et al. 1994, Gaines 1988), where insect populations are probably high that time of year. At high elevations in Curry Co., large numbers of juvs. move into deciduous shrub thickets in early Aug before departing on their southern migration (D. Vroman unpubl. data). Fall migrants peak in early to mid-Sep, and are mostly gone by mid-Oct. Migrants are common in deciduous and brushy habitats statewide, especially at lower elevations (Gilligan et al. 1994).

**Detection:** Dull coloration and habit of foraging through dense brush make Orange-crowned Warblers difficult to detect visually and consequently they are often overlooked (Gabrielson and Jewett 1940). However, their junco-like trill is easy to hear in spring and summer, and familiarity with their thin, clear *chip*-note will allow detection at any time of year. In winter the best technique to find them is to search out likely bottomland willow thickets with a dense bramble understory, *spish* and imitate pygmy-owl calls, and practice keen observation skills.

**Population Status and Conservation:** BBS data (Sauer et al. 1999) indicate the species is most common along the coast and Rogue and Willamette valleys (3-10 birds per survey route). Fewer occur in the w. Cascades (1-3 birds per survey route). Populations around Tillamook and Coos Bay are the highest in the state with 10-30 birds per survey route. The Wallowa Mtns. have more birds per survey route (1-3) than the rest of Oregon east of the Cascades (>1). Survey data suggest populations are relatively stable. There are no significant increases or decreases rangewide or by ecoregion, although small declines have been noted in Oregon (Sogge et al. 1994).—*Colin Dillingham*

## Nashville Warbler *Vermivora ruficapilla*

The foothills of interior sw. Oregon come alive in late Apr with the bold song of this bright yellow warbler. Here it seems every brushy area or mixed conifer/hardwood forest with dense undergrowth has at least one male singing just beyond the reach of binoculars. Although it can be found in many other places in the state and in a variety of habitats, nowhere else is it as common. The Nashville Warbler has attracted surprisingly little attention in the state since being first reported in the late 1800s (Gabrielson and Jewett 1940). Even today, little is known of the natural history of the species in the state. Spring males are bright yellow below with a gray hood. They have a narrow, unbroken white eye-ring. A small chestnut-colored patch on the top of the head is seldom seen in the field. The back is olive-green, and the rump is yellow. It lacks wingbars. Females, fall males, and young birds are similar but slightly duller.

**General Distribution:** There are two disjunct breeding populations, representing two subspecies. The eastern population (*V. r. ruficapilla*) breeds from c. Saskatchewan east to the Maritime Provinces and south to Minnesota and W. Virginia. The western population (*V. r. ridgwayi*) breeds from s. British Columbia, w. Montana, and Idaho south to mountains of s. California (local). Most birds winter in M. America, but a few winter in coastal California.

**Oregon Distribution:** Fairly common breeding species in the interior southwest portion of the state below 4,000 ft (1,200 m) from the Calapooya Divide south, typically in mixed conifer/hardwood forests and regenerating clearcuts. Breeds in Jackson Co. (SOU, OSU) where it is common (Browning 1975, Janes et al. 2001). Southward from the Illinois Valley into California, abundance declines (Ralph et al. 1991). Nashville Warblers also breed regularly in the Columbia Gorge and along the eastern foothills of the Cascades in Wasco and Hood River counties below 3,000 ft (900 m); specimen from Sherman Co. (USNM). Local elsewhere, including drier foothills near the s. Willamette Valley as far north as Benton and Yamhill counties, and the w. Cascades as far north as Santiam Pass (Gilligan et al. 1994). Also breed locally along the coast, away from the outer coast, as far north as Lincoln Co. Although most common at the lower elevations, scattered territorial males can be found in the higher elevations of the Coast Range (Bratz 1950, Sturges 1955) and in subalpine areas of the Cascades (*SWJ*). They are very local in the Blue Mtns., occurring as far west as Wheeler Co. (*SWJ*), but are more widespread in the foothills of the Wallowas (Johnson 1976, Evanich 1992a); also breed in Baker Co. (USNM). Breed sparingly in the mountains east of the Cascades in Klamath, Lake, and possibly Malheur counties (Contreras and Kindschy 1996).

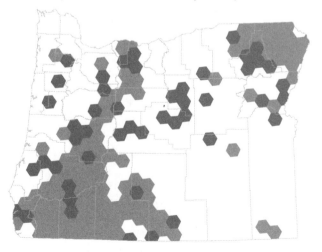

Uncommon during northward migration, but common in late summer especially in thickets at higher elevations. In recent years, it has become apparent that a very few Nashville Warblers linger into winter, with most reports along the coast, in the interior valley lowlands, and in towns.

**Habitat and Diet:** Nashvilles are one of the few warblers in the West to nest on the ground. They occupy diverse shrub communities, often including or adjacent to a relatively short or open tree canopy. In sw. Oregon, distribution coincides closely with Pacific madrone and California black oak, but they are absent from pure stands of Oregon white oak and chaparral. Common in shrubby habitats that follow timber harvest (Fix 1990a) and stand-replacing fires. Among naturally occurring young to old forest stands, Nashville Warblers are most abundant in young, mixed conifer/hardwood forests with a moderately dense understory (Carey et al. 1991, Gilbert and Allwine 1991). In the Badger Cr. Wilderness Area, Mt. Hood NF, Nashvilles occupy forests of short stature, low total foliage volume but with a high-density canopy (*SWJ*). Habitat most often contains both Douglas-fir and Oregon white oak. Singing males occurred as high as 5,600 ft (1,700 m) in subalpine fir and other openings with low woody vegetation (Fix 1990a, Janes 1994b). In se. Oregon, Merry Lynn Denny observed 5-6 territorial birds in mountain-mahogany with an understory of choke cherry on a west-facing talus slope in upper Two Mile Cr. on Battle Mtn., Malheur Co., 4 Jul 1998, but no nests were found (Spencer 1999, M. Denny p.c.). Diet consists of foliage dwelling invertebrates (*SWJ*).

**Seasonal Activity and Behavior:** Early spring arrivals include 3 Mar 1976 at Newport and 12 Mar 1976 at Albany, Linn Co. (Crowell and Nehls 1976b), and 4 Apr 1978 in Portland (Mattocks and Hunn 1978b). Nashvilles typically arrive in abundance in sw. Oregon in mid-Apr. Mean arrival date for the Corvallis area (16 yr) is 16 Apr (A. McGie unpubl. data) and 19 Apr for the Bend area (15 yr) (C. Miller unpubl. data). Most spring sightings for the Malheur NWR are in the first part of May (Littlefield 1990a). Egg dates for Oregon birds range 6 May-10 Jul, and the female performs most if not all of the incubation (Williams 1996). Nest with young observed 4 Jul (n=1), adults carrying food 7 Jun-13 Jul (n=5), fledglings 15 Jun-28 Jul (n=6) (OBBA). Produce one brood of 4-5 young annually (Williams 1996). Following breeding, many move up into the mountains. Individuals and flocks frequent shrubby habitats from 3,000 to 6,000 ft (1,000-2,000 m) beginning as early as mid-Jul. Tend to be an early fall migrant with the major movement in Aug. Scattered individuals may linger until late Sep.

Moves about rapidly in the understory and low in the canopy gleaning prey from leaves. Unlike eastern populations, birds of the western subspecies tend to be tail-bobbers (Dunn and Garrett 1997). Males typically rise to an elevated and exposed perch about 25-40 ft (7.5-12 m) high from which to sing (Grinnell and Miller 1944). Song consists of two parts, an introductory sequence of two-note syllables following by a short, fast series of repeated notes. Song is both loud and fluid. Many warblers including members of the genus *Vermivora* sing songs of two types. No second song has been verified for Nashville Warblers in the west. Nashvilles are one of the first birds to stop singing in the summer; declines may begin in mid-Jun in sw. Oregon, and most singing has ceased elsewhere by mid-Jul (Fix 1990a).

**Detection:** If you are familiar with the song of the Nashville Warbler, they can be easily located in sw. Oregon or along the foothills of the Cascades in Wasco and Hood River counties. In the breeding season, the major difficulty you may encounter is negotiating their dense habitat.

**Population Status and Conservation:** Considering preference for early successional habitats and low-elevation forests where fire has not recently cleared out the understory, the abundance of Nashville Warblers undoubtedly increased in the state during the 20th century. However, changing forest practices including restrictions on clearcuts and the increased use of prescribed burns to reduce fire hazard may eventually lead to some declines. Nashville Warblers are hosts to Brown-headed Cowbirds (Verner and Boss 1980). Rural development with its associated forest fragmentation may have an adverse impact upon this species by bringing warblers and cowbirds into closer contact.—*Stewart W. Janes*

## Virginia's Warbler *Vermivora virginiae*

This grayish warbler breeds at elevations of 4,000-9,000 ft (1,219-2,743 m) from s. Wyoming, s. Idaho, and e. Nevada s. to Arizona and New Mexico. It winters in M. America. It is regular in California, occasional in Oregon, and casual elsewhere in N. America. Most Oregon records have involved presumed transients, but nesting may occur. One was netted, banded, and photographed on Hart Mtn., Lake Co., 29 May 1977 (Mewaldt 1977a, Watson 1989). Another was photographed at Fields, Harney Co., 17 Sep 1988 (OBRC). Individuals were observed at Eugene, Lane Co., 8 Nov 1979 (OBRC); on Stukel Mtn., Klamath Co., 27 Jul and 3 Aug 1980 (OBRC); near Mapleton, Lane Co., 9 Aug 1988 (OBRC); and on Hart Mtn. 5 Aug 1996 (Sullivan 1997a). Two were at Page Springs CG, Harney Co., 26 May 2000 (Sullivan 2000b), and a female was in the Trout Cr. Mtns, Malheur Co., 16 Jul 2000 (Spencer 2000b). One was at Castle Rock, Malheur Co., 16 Jun 2001 (Spencer 2001a).

In 1998, increased search efforts revealed birds in seemingly suitable breeding habitat in se. Oregon, often in mountain-mahogany groves, not far from breeding populations in Nevada. On 18 Jun 1998, two territorial males and one female were found in a remote area of Malheur Co., 10 mi (16.1 km) northeast of McDermitt, Nevada; the songs of one male were recorded (OBRC). Two or more pairs were near Twin Buttes in the Oregon Canyon Mtns., Malheur Co., 19-20 Jun 1998 (OBRC); a male was on Battle Mtn., Malheur Co., 4 Jul 1998 (OBRC); and a singing territorial male was south of Ironside, Malheur Co., 5 Jul 1999 (Spencer 2000a). Nevertheless, subsequent searches in some of the above areas did not turn up this species (P. Adamus p.c., *MGH*), and breeding has not yet been verified in Oregon. Monotypic (AOU 1957).—*Harry B. Nehls*

### Lucy's Warbler *Vermivora luciae*
This desert species breeds along waterways and about ponds from s. California, s. Utah, and s. Nevada south through Arizona into Mexico, New Mexico, and Texas. It winters in Mexico and occasionally to Texas, Arizona, and California. One was photographed along the N. Fork of the Siuslaw R., Lane Co., from 27 Dec 1986 to 25 Jan 1987 (Bond 1987, Watson 1989). Monotypic (AOU 1957).—*Harry B. Nehls*

### Northern Parula *Parula americana*
This colorful bird of coniferous forests and mixed woods is a common breeding species of e. N. America. It winters in the W. Indies and M. America and occasionally in California and the s. U.S. It is a regular migrant in very small numbers in spring and irregular in summer and fall in the sw. U.S. to California (where it has bred a few times) and Oregon, and is occasionally found elsewhere in the West. The majority of Oregon records are from late Apr to late Jun, mostly from east of the Cascades. Individuals were at Malheur NWR, Harney Co., 6 Jul 1980 (Littlefield 1990a); 27 Jul 1995 (OBRC); 27 Aug to 7 Oct 2000 (Sullivan 2001a); and 1-2 Oct 2001 (Sullivan 2002). A male and a female were at Charleston, Coos Co., 9-11 Jul 1984 (OBRC); one was at Tillamook, Tillamook Co., 24 Jul 1993 (Johnson J 1994a). Individuals were on Hart Mtn. 3 Sep 2000 (Sullivan 2001a); at Cascade Head, Tillamook Co., 4 Sep 1980 (OBRC); photographed at Malheur NWR 23-26 Sep 1990 (OBRC); and at Baker City, Baker Co., 18 Oct to 3 Dec 1972 (Rogers 1973a). One was at the mouth of the Winchuck R. 6 Oct 2001 (Contreras 2002b). There are several photographs in the files of the OBRC (Watson 1989).—*Harry B. Nehls*

### Yellow Warbler *Dendroica petechia*
Bringing its cheerful song to streamside thickets throughout the state each breeding season, the bright and active Yellow Warbler seems to be the incarnation of summer. Notable for its vivid color, it has been described as "a rich yellow flame among the opening leaves" (Bent 1953). It was once the most conspicuous breeding warbler in Oregon (Gabrielson and Jewett 1940), and was formerly common in shade trees of urban areas, including w. Oregon, but declined precipitously before the advent of the BBS (*DBM*).

**General Distribution:** Breeds from nw. and nc. Alaska through n. Yukon and southeast across c. Canada to Newfoundland; south to n. Baja California, through the central plateau of Mexico, and east through c. Oklahoma, c. Arkansas, and c. Georgia, to c. N. Carolina. Winters from s. California, sw. Arizona, n. Mexico and the Bahama Is. south through M. and S. America to Peru and Amazonian Brazil. Recent taxonomic review lists 43 subspecies broken into three groups; the *aestiva* group occurs in Oregon (Browning 1994, Dunn and Garrett 1997). Within it are nine subspecies, three of which occur in Oregon.

**Oregon Distribution:** *D. p. morcomi* breeds east of the Cascades (Browning 1994). Birds attributed to *morcomi* are common to abundant breeders on the east slope of the Cascades and in the Blue and Wallowa mountains, though very local above 5,000 ft (1,524 m) (Gilligan et al. 1994). Elsewhere east of the Cascades, common along watercourses, or to a lesser extent, in residential areas (Gilligan et al. 1994). Rare straggler to Crater L. NP (one specimen identified as *morcomi*), but relatively common in the Klamath Basin (Farner 1952). On Malheur NWR, abundant in spring, summer, and fall (Littlefield 1990a). Also common to locally abundant breeder in suitable habitat in extreme se. Oregon (Marshall 1987, Contreras and Kindschy 1996).

*D. p. brewsteri* breeds west of the Cascades (Browning 1994). Birds attributed to *brewsteri* are

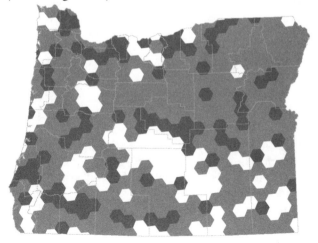

very local and uncommon along the coast and in the Coast Range in summer. They are fairly common to common in western interior valleys, and locally in adjoining foothills to 4,000 ft (1,220 m) (Gilligan et al. 1994). They are uncommon to locally common summer residents in the s. Willamette Valley, and are known to breed at Finley NWR (J. Hagar p.c.). Yellow Warblers are found regularly in small numbers along the N. Umpqua R. in the sw. Cascades in summer, though generally uncommon in this region, usually found in small "colonies" where they do occur (Fix 1990a). Common summer resident throughout Jackson Co. (Browning 1975a).

The species migrates throughout the state. *D. p. banksi* known positively by one specimen (USNM) in May from Jackson Co. (Browning 1994). Based on re-examinations, migrants once identified as *rubiginosus* by Gabrielson and Jewett (1940) and others may be *rubiginosus*, *banksi*, or some other subspecies (see Garrett and Dunn 1997, *MRB*). Several winter reports (subspecies not determined) in the Willamette Valley and Coos Co. but no specimens are available (Gilligan et al. 1994, Contreras 1997b, Gilligan 1999, Tice 1999b).

*Yellow Warbler*

**Habitat and Diet:** Yellow Warblers find preferred nesting habitat among riparian woodlands and thickets, particularly those dominated by willow or cottonwood, though they will accept a variety of species associations, either low or tall (Fix 1990a, Gilligan et al. 1994, Sanders and Edge 1998). Breeding at Snagboat Bend (a disjunct portion of Finley NWR on the Willamette R., Linn Co.) occurs in a cottonwood-willow riparian patch on the east bank of the Willamette R. (J. Hagar p.c.). East of the Cascades, in open country and in the Blue and Wallowa mountains, breeds locally in deciduous riparian growth, including stands of aspen (Gilligan et al. 1994). In se. Oregon, they are most abundant in structurally complex, willow-dominated riparian zones (Sanders and Edge 1998). Preferred nesting habitat at Malheur NWR is found among wooded streambottoms, watercourses bordered by willow and alder, shrubby thickets, and in planted trees and hedges (particularly at refuge HQ) (Littlefield

1990a). In extreme e. Oregon, commonly found in deciduous or mixed woodland and residential areas at low to moderate elevations (Contreras and Kindschy 1996).

Near Diamond L., can be "surprisingly numerous" in the lodgepole pine and sapling Shasta red fir stands of the high mountains for a brief period at the peak of spring passage; and well after spring migration a few regularly appear in nonbreeding habitat at Toketee RS, an administrative complex offering lawns and shrubbery at the confluence of the N. Umpqua and Clearwater rivers (Fix 1990a). Juvs. in early fall may be found in almost any broadleaf thicket (Fix 1990a). Rangewide, during migration tend to concentrate in same habitats used for breeding (Lowther et al. 1999).

Nest is a compact cup of plant fibers, lined with down and feathers, and anchored to a fork in a bush, sapling, or tree within 6.5 ft (2 m) of ground (Gabrielson and Jewett 1940, Taylor and Littlefield 1986). A Colorado study revealed nest site selection to be based on characteristics surrounding the nest bush that favor concealment, rather than characteristics of the nest bush itself (Knopf and Sedgwick 1992). Studies conducted in Manitoba, Illinois, and Utah show diet consisting mainly of insects; proportions of different insect orders and families vary with location (Lowther et al. 1999)

**Seasonal Activity and Behavior:** Spring migrants generally arrive during late Apr, though they occasionally are seen in early or mid-Apr (Gilligan et al. 1994); early dates include 20 Mar 1972 in Portland (Crowell and Nehls 1972b) and 25 Mar 1983 in Grants Pass (Mattocks and Hunn 1983b). The peak of spring migration occurs mid- to late May (Littlefield 1990a, Gilligan et al. 1994). Average spring arrival date at Malheur NWR is 26 Apr, with the majority of transients gone by 1 Jun (Littlefield 1990a). On the Diamond L. RD in the s. Cascades, migratory maximum was 30-50 birds at the upper end of Toketee L. (at 2,450 ft [747 m] elevation) 25 May 89 (Fix 1990a). Banding and recapture data from Malheur NWR headquarters show males returning to the same territory (Littlefield 1990a). Nest building in progress by late May (n=4), and fledglings typically observed early to mid-Jul (n=6), more rarely in late Jul or early Aug (n=3) (OBBA). In response to Brown-headed Cowbird parasitism, Yellow Warblers are known to build a new nest lining over cowbird egg(s) (and any of its own), and to initiate a new clutch on the superimposed nest (Sealy 1995). Yellow Warblers are the only known Brown-headed Cowbird host to use this method of rejection regularly (Sealy 1995), though it has not been documented yet in Oregon.

Fall migration begins early, peaking between mid-Aug to early Sep, and by late Sep they are very uncommon in the state (Gilligan et al. 1994). During late Aug and early Sep, migrants may be noted in areas on the coast where they probably do not breed (D. Fix p.c.). The latest fall record at Malheur NWR is 15 Oct (Littlefield 1990a). Several reports through Dec in w. Oregon (Gilligan et al. 1994, Gilligan 1999, Tice 1999b).

**Detection:** During spring migration and the breeding season, often first detected by song. Highly visible in riparian areas of e. Oregon. By the end of the breeding season, birds become much less apparent. Possible winter sightings should be carefully distinguished from bright Orange-crowned Warblers.

**Population Status and Conservation:** Because of its close association with riparian habitat, this species is vulnerable to habitat destruction, especially by grazing (Taylor and Littlefield 1986, Sanders and Edge 1998). Conversion of forest and scrubland to farms and pastures has benefited the Brown-headed Cowbird, whose brood parasitism can have an adverse effect on Yellow Warbler breeding attempts in some parts of N. America (Ortega and Ortega 2000), though this has not been investigated in Oregon.

Population losses have been documented for the w. U.S. (Ortega and Ortega 2000), and BBS data from Oregon confirm consistent declines: statewide, 1966-2000 showed an average population change of -1.7%/yr (BBS). It was listed by Gabrielson and Jewett (1940) as an "abundant summer resident throughout state," and reported to be common in every county. This is no longer true, especially for w. Oregon. One likely cause has been loss of riparian habitat (Sanders and Edge 1998).

Riparian vegetation on Malheur NWR was reduced during the 1950s, 1960s, and early 1970s, when cattle grazed over virtually every acre of the Blitzen Valley and willows were eliminated with herbicides (Taylor and Littlefield 1986). During this period breeding Yellow Warbler numbers on the refuge reached an all-time low. Only seven birds were recorded on a BBS route including part of the refuge in 1972 (Taylor and Littlefield 1986). As cattle grazing began dramatically decreasing in the mid-1970s and willows and other shrubs began increasing in volume, Yellow Warbler numbers increased correspondingly. By 1986 the same BBS route showed 56 birds (Taylor and Littlefield 1986); from 1986 to 2000 the average for the same route was 61 (BBS). Clearly, improvements to riparian shrub habitat can increase populations of this species in Oregon (Taylor and Littlefield 1986, Sanders and Edge 1998). But while loss of riparian habitat is likely the principal threat, quantifying the impacts of brood parasitism and nest predation, and studying habitat ecology in winter range are also crucial to understanding population dynamics.—*Rachel White Scheuering*

**Chestnut-sided Warbler** *Dendroica pensylvanica*
This inhabitant of riparian thickets and brushy clear-cuts and pastures breeds from ne. British Columbia across s. Canada to the e. coast and south to Georgia. It winters in M. America and occasionally to s. U.S. The main migratory route is east of the Rocky Mtns., but small numbers regularly occur along the w. coast. Small numbers of transients are reported almost yearly in Oregon. Spring records are between mid-May and mid-Jul. There are fewer fall records than in spring, most occurring between mid-Aug and mid-Oct. There are numerous photographs in the files of the OBRC (Watson 1989). Monotypic (AOU 1957).—*Harry B. Nehls*

## Magnolia Warbler *Dendroica magnolia*

This species breeds in brushy forest understory and openings from the e. coast across Canada to c. British Columbia. It winters in M. America. It is casual in winter in the U.S. The main migratory route is east of the Rocky Mtns., but lesser numbers regularly migrate through w. N. America. The state's first, an immature female, was collected at Euchre Cr., Curry Co., 8 Sep 1971 (spec. no. 19291 DEL) (Bayer 1989a); the collection date reported by Browning (1974) was incorrect. Small numbers of transients have been reported almost annually in Oregon since the 1970s, with most occurring east of the Cascades. The spring records occur from late Apr to mid-Jun, and in fall from early Sep to late Oct. One was netted and banded 14 Jul 2000 at Galesville Res., Douglas Co. (Tice 2000a). There are many photographs in the files of the OBRC (Watson 1989). Monotypic (AOU 1957).—*Harry B. Nehls*

## Cape May Warbler *Dendroica tigrina*

This bird of coniferous forests breeds from se. Yukon and e. British Columbia, across Canada and n. U.S. to the e. coast. It winters in M. America and occasionally in the U.S. The main migratory route is east of the Rocky Mtns. with small numbers occurring irregularly along the w. coast. Most Oregon records are from Harney Co. Spring transient records for Harney Co. occur from late May to early Jun. One was observed at Harris Beach SP, Curry Co., 30 May 1992 (OBRC), and photographed near Gold Beach during Mar 2001 (Lillie 2001). The fall records from Harney Co. are from early Sep to early Oct. One was photographed at Tillamook Bay, Tillamook Co., 19 Oct 1980 (Gilligan and Schmidt 1983, Watson 1989). There are several photos in the files of the OBRC (Watson 1989). Monotypic (AOU 1957).—*Harry B. Nehls*

## Black-throated Blue Warbler

*Dendroica caerulescens*

This species breeds in upland deciduous and mixed forests with dense understory from se. Canada south to Georgia. It winters in the Caribbean and M. America, and casually in the U.S. It migrates primarily along the e. coast and regularly in small numbers along the w. coast. It is rare but regular in Oregon during the fall from early Sep to mid-Nov. A male was collected 9 Oct 1957 at Malheur NWR, Harney Co. (Marshall 1959) (spec. no. 466258 US NM). Another was collected there 27 Sep 1960 (Kridler and Marshall 1962). One was photographed at Medford, Jackson Co., 9-30 Jan 1986 (Watson 1989). Another was observed at Powers, Coos Co., 20-29 Jan 1989 (OBRC). It is occasional in spring between early May and late Jun.

One male was observed on territory near Still Cr. CG in the Cascades of Clackamas Co. 23 Jun to 10 Jul 1979 (Harrington-Tweit et al. 1979). Monotypic (*MRB*).—*Harry B. Nehls*

## Yellow-rumped Warbler *Dendroica coronata*

The Yellow-rumped Warbler is perhaps the most familiar warbler in the state. Outside the breeding season, it can be found in almost any habitat from backyard trees in suburban areas to willow thickets in sagebrush country to the deepest coniferous forests. It maintains a presence in the state during the winter when most other warblers have retreated to warmer climates. Unlike the reclusive Hermit and Townsend's Warblers that remain difficult to observe high in the canopy, brightly colored male Yellow-rumped Warblers regularly descend to the lower branches as they dash after insects flushed from the foliage, often at the edge of a mountain lake or in a patch of subalpine fir above timberline. The name "Yellow-rumped Warbler" resulted from combining the former Myrtle Warbler (*D. coronata*) and former Audubon's Warbler (*D. auduboni*), into one species (Hubbard 1969, AOU 1973). Both forms are found in the state, but only the "Audubon's" breeds here. Breeding males of both have a black chest and flashes of white in wing and tail. They also wear splashes of yellow on their rump, sides, and crown. Male "Audubon's" also have a yellow throat. Male "Myrtle" have more limited black on the chest, a white throat, and a white eye stripe. Females are more somber, adorned in shades of brown instead of black and white but still wear a yellow rump and white in the tail. The throat of female "Audubon's" has a yellow wash but is white in the "Myrtle." In winter, males of both wear plumage similar to females.

**General Distribution:** Breeds from the northern edge of the boreal forest south to ne. U.S. in the east, and in the west it breeds south to the mountains of M. America. The "Myrtle" Warbler, *D. c. coronata* (*hooveri* is a synonym [Lowery and Monroe 1968, Hubbard 1970]), breeds in the northern boreal forest of Alaska east to New England while the "Audubon's" Warbler, *D. c. auduboni* (*memorabalis* is a synonym [Grinnell and Miller 1944]), breeds from c. British Columbia southward. The two meet in the Canadian Rocky Mtns. where they hybridize. "Audubon's" Yellow-rumped Warblers winter in the w. U.S. to M. America while "Myrtle" Yellow-rumped Warblers winter in e. N. America south into the Caribbean, and from Washington south to n. Baja California.

**Oregon Distribution:** *D. c. auduboni*, the "Audubon's" Warbler, breeds from sea level to timberline in most conifer forests and aspen throughout the state; uncommon to rare at low elevations, fairly common at higher elevations and in forests with broken canopies (Janes 1994b). Rare in juniper woodland. Common to very common summer residents in the Cascades, Blues, Wallowas, and other mountain forests east of the Cascades (Sturges 1957, Evanich 1990) where Archie and Hudson (1973) found densities of 3-4 pairs/100 ac (8-10 pairs/100 ha). Densities are higher in the southern portion of the Cascades (Gilbert and Allwine 1991) but then decrease into nw. California (Ralph et al. 1991). Uncommon and local breeding residents at higher elevations in the Coast Range (Bratz 1950, Sturges 1957).

Abundant migrant likely to occur in almost any habitat. In winter occur regularly at lower elevations west of the Cascades. Along the coast are common as far north as Lincoln Co., becoming less common farther north (Gilligan et al. 1994). East of the Cascades a few attempt to remain during mild winters. Along the Columbia R. east of the John Day Dam, they frequently winter in good numbers in Russian-olive (M. Denny p.c.).

*D. c. coronata*, the "Myrtle" Warbler, does not breed in the state but is a common migrant and sparse winter resident in interior valleys of w. Oregon; much more common along the coast, where locally abundant, as in outer coastal wax myrtle thickets (D. Fix p.c.). They are uncommon to rare migrants east of the Cascades (Littlefield 1990a).

**Habitat and Diet:** Breeding birds occur in more open forests than other warblers inhabiting coniferous forests and forage closer to the ground. They can be found in most coniferous forests but are most abundant among the true firs of moderate to high elevations. On Steens and Hart mountains they breed in aspen woodlands (Hansen 1956). In the Badger Cr. Wilderness Area east of Mt. Hood, Yellow-rumped Warbler habitat is characterized by forests of relatively short stature and a dense canopy, usually dominated by true firs (*SWJ*). Yellow-rumped Warbler habitat also includes abundant foliage near the forest floor 0-15 ft (0-5 m). Among

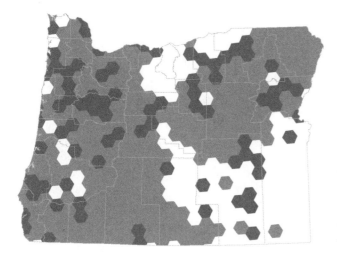

the few breeding bird species in lodgepole pines, where they are often very common (Arnett et al. 1997). In the Siskiyous and s. Oregon Cascades, are most common in white firs above 3,000 ft (1,000 m). Of the many coniferous forest types available to them ranging from ponderosa pine to subalpine fir, are least abundant in Douglas-fir forests (Janes 1994b). Abundance decreases with stand age (40-525 yr) in the Coast Range (Carey et al. 1991). Breed in managed and unmanaged forests but were slightly more abundant in the managed forests in the Blue Mtns. (Mannan 1982). Little information is available regarding nesting in Oregon, but elsewhere typically place an open nest 3-100 ft (1-30 m) above the ground, which usually is screened from above by an overhanging branch (Verner and Boss 1980).

In migration and in winter, open woodlands and hedgerows in agricultural areas at lower elevations west of the Cascades frequently harbor this species. On the coast, most common in patches of wax myrtle, with "Myrtle" Warblers the predominant form.

Diet consists largely of arthropods. Occasionally visits sap wells created by sapsuckers (*SWJ*). In fall and winter may add fruit to their diet and will feed at feeding stations providing suet or a mixture of suet and peanut butter (Hunt and Flaspohler 1998). Observed feeding on poison oak berries in winter in sw. Oregon (D. Vroman p.c.).

**Seasonal Activity and Behavior:** Yellow-rumped Warblers tend to move north earlier and south later than most warblers. The northward movement occurs in w. Oregon from mid-Mar through early May. East of the Cascades, mean arrival date is 2 Apr in the Bend area (C. Miller unpubl. data [15 yr]) and 8 Apr at Malheur NWR (Littlefield 1990a). Migration peaks early Apr to early May. In spring, males seek high perches from which to sing a lively two-part song. Like many other warblers they sing two types of songs, but the two song types are not markedly different (Morse 1989), and have not been verified in Oregon (*SWJ*). Nest building has been observed 11 May-24 Jun (n=7), birds on nests 9 Jun-11 Jul (n=5), nests with young 9 and 14 Jul (n=2), carrying food 16 May-27 Jul (most late Jun to mid-Jul, n=36), and fledglings 12 Jun-16 Aug (mostly late Jun and Jul, n=38) (OBBA). While Yellow-rumped Warblers in the e. U.S. often raise two broods of 4-5 young/yr (Harrison 1978), second broods are rare in the w. U.S. (Hunt and Flaspohler 1998). A postbreeding movement to higher elevations occurs in Jul and Aug. Although southward movement is observed as early as Aug, the major fall movement takes place in late Sept and Oct after most other warblers have departed. D. Vroman (p.c.) reports a recapture of a "Myrtle Warbler" along the Applegate R. on 19 Oct 1999 (banded Oct 1998 in same location), indicating the possibility of routine migration routes. Audubon's and Myrtle Warblers tend to migrate and winter separately, but mixed flocks are occasionally encountered.

In Oregon, Myrtle Warblers forage in vegetation. They use a great array of species, but appear to prefer natives. They almost never forage on the ground (in Oregon) or on human-made substrates (D. Fix p.c.). Conversely, Audubon's Warblers feed in vegetation, on mown grass, in pastures, on barren earth, on manure piles, on stacks of center-pivot irrigation pipe, on wire fences, wooden-rail fences, in raingutters, on electric wires, on sheds and other outbuildings, in cattail marshes, in dunelands, on river cobble, and above timberline. They associate freely, if loosely, with Western Bluebirds in winter, something not observed in Myrtle Warblers (D. Fix p.c.).

**Detection:** In spring, easily detected by song, and not difficult to see though sometimes high perches make observation difficult. During the nonbreeding season when they occupy a wider range of habitats, they are most often detected by following their distinctive call notes, which are more forceful but "duller" than the call notes of most other warblers inhabiting upland sites. With practice, the calls of Myrtle and Audubon's Warblers can be distinguished. Can often be attracted by spishing.

**Population Status and Conservation:** At high elevations where logged areas often grow back to broken or irregular canopies, Yellow-rumped Warblers will likely continue to find suitable breeding habitat. However, at moderate and lower elevations, traditional even-aged silviculture will favor Hermit Warblers and exclude Yellow-rumped Warblers. More diverse and open canopies at moderate and lower elevations may allow sympatry of Hermit and Yellow-rumped Warblers in managed forests (D. Fix p.c.). BBS data indicate stable populations for Audubon's Yellow-rumped Warblers. Although Yellow-rumped Warblers are frequent hosts for Brown-headed Cowbirds in California (Verner and Boss 1980, Airola 1986), a preference for higher elevations reduces risk of cowbird parasitism in Oregon. There is evidence that Yellow-rumped Warblers can recognize and reject cowbird eggs (Dunn and Garrett 1997).—*Stewart W. Janes*

## Black-throated Gray Warbler
*Dendroica nigrescens*

One of the first spring migrants to brighten Oregon woodlands with song is the Black-throated Gray Warbler. As early as the first week in Apr, the distinctive buzzy song announces the male's arrival in habitats from riparian forests to juniper woodlands, chaparral to Douglas-fir forests. It sings even as it darts through the canopy and understory in search of insects. Except for the small yellow spot in front of the eyes, the male is an essay in black, gray, and white. The cap and throat are black, as is the cheek, which is outlined in white. The back is gray, striped with black, and the belly is white with black streaks along the sides. It has white wing bars and outer tail feathers that show clearly when they fly. The female is similar but the black throat patch is usually reduced or absent, and the black cap and face are replaced by dark gray.

**General Distribution:** Breeds from sw. British Columbia and c. Rocky Mtns. south into n. Mexico. Winters in the foothills of the Sierra Madre Occidental of w. Mexico south to the state of Oaxaca. Monotypic (AOU 1957). Morphological characters used by Morrison (1983) are too minor for recognizing subspecies; differences between sonograms of birds from west (Benton Co.) and east (Jefferson Co.) of the Cascades (Morrison and Hardy 1983b, Morrison 1990) suggest, however, that eastern and western populations differ. Further study is needed.

**Oregon Distribution:** Summer resident of the foothills and valley bottoms of w. Oregon though less common in wetter areas along the coast. Extends into Cascades in fingers of riparian forests along major rivers and in young forests, especially adjacent to the riparian corridors (*MGH*). Along the eastern foothills of the Cascades, is locally common in Hood River and Wasco counties, uncommon to rare farther south. Also occurs very locally in the Ochoco, Blue, and Wallowa mountains; more widespread in the mountains and canyons of s. Lake, Harney, and Malheur counties (Contreras and Kindschy 1996). Common spring and fall migrant. Occasional in winter west of the Cascades.

**Habitat and Diet:** Black-throated Gray Warblers occur in many wooded habitats where they glean a variety of invertebrates from foliage. In general, the farther north in the distribution of this species, the more they tend to be associated with conifers. In w. Oregon, they most frequently occur where Oregon white oak mixes with Douglas-fir (Morrison 1982). In Wasco Co. along the eastern foothills of the Cascades, they frequent mature stands of Douglas-fir, often with few or no oaks (Janes 1994b). This habitat is more characteristic of Hermit Warblers west of the Cascades. However, Black-throated Gray Warblers occur in habitat with lower foliage volume and lower canopy density than adjacent Hermit Warblers in both locations. Elsewhere in w. Oregon they can be found in shrubby habitats of regenerating clearcuts, declining in abundance as stands mature (Carey et al. 1991, Gilbert and Allwine 1991, Ralph et al. 1991) as well as riparian habitats containing alder. In sw. Oregon they are common among canyon live-oak and in mature chaparral containing whiteleaf manzanita, Pacific madrone, and

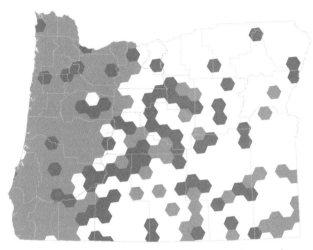

oak. East of the Cascades, they also occur in ponderosa pine with mountain-mahogany, and in se. Oregon they occupy juniper woodlands and stands of mountain-mahogany. On average, the nest is placed 7.5-35 ft (2.3-10.7 m) up and 4-7 ft (1.2-3.0 m) away from the trunk (Guzy and Lowther 1997). Black-throated Gray Warblers are active in both canopy and woody understory. In Douglas-fir, males forage higher (42 ft [12.7 m]) than females (28 ft [8.6 m]) (Morrison 1982). Both forage at similar heights in oak.

**Seasonal Activity and Behavior:** In w. Oregon (Corvallis), earliest arrival 14 Mar 1976 (Crowell and Nehls 1976b), with a few as early as late Mar. Males typically arrive about 12 Apr (A. McGie unpubl. data), with the major influx in mid-Apr and early May. In sw. Oregon, males arrive in the secondsecond week of Apr followed by the females 2 wk later (*SWJ*). East of the Cascades (Bend) they arrive about 2 May (C. Miller unpubl. data) with peak movement at Malheur NWR 5-20 May (Littlefield 1990a). Janes and Ryker (unpubl. ms.) measured mean territory size of 1.75 ac (0.72 ha, n=7) in sw. Oregon. Raise one brood/yr consisting of an average of four eggs (range 2-6) laid in mid-May (Guzy and Lowther 1997). Incubation typically begins in the second or third week of May in sw. Oregon (*SWJ*), fledging in late Jun. Elsewhere in state, observed carrying food 24 May-18 Jul (n=7), and fledglings observed 8 Jun-20 Jul (n=3) (OBBA). Female alone incubates the eggs (Harrison 1978). The major southward movement occurs in late Aug and Sep though a few remain until late Oct; latest 15 Nov 1983 in Bend (Hunn and Mattocks 1984).

Like many warbler species, it sings two types of song (Morrison 1982, 1990, Morrison and Hardy 1983b). Prominent is the loud and distinctive buzzy song that begins with a series of repeated notes and typically ends with a descending slurred note. This is the familiar song to most and does not vary greatly around the state, in contrast to the songs of the Hermit Warbler. A second song type can be heard before dawn, later in the breeding season, and during territorial encounters

(*SWJ*). It is a variable, fluid song that does not have a distinct pattern and lacks the buzziness of the first. It is softer and does not carry as far as the first, so you must be closer to the bird to hear this underappreciated song. Black-throated Gray Warblers are closely related to Hermit and Townsend's Warblers (Mengel 1964) and forage in a similar manner (Morrison 1982). Because of this similarity, they are potential competitors. In many locations where Black-throated Gray and Hermit Warblers occur in close proximity, they regularly respond to the recorded songs of the other species and sometimes maintain separate territories (Janes and Ryker unpubl. ms.). However, Morrison (1982) found them to only respond to songs of the other species in areas where they did not regularly hear each other's songs. Unlike Hermit and Townsend's Warblers, Black-throated Gray Warblers rarely hybridize with their close relatives (Rohwer et al. 2000).

**Detection:** Following the buzzy song of the Black-throated Gray Warbler is the best way to find this active occupant of dense vegetation. At times it will sing from an exposed perch high in the canopy offering a chance for a good view. Songs of some Hermit Warblers can be confused with those of Black-throated Gray Warblers.

**Population Status and Conservation:** This species is a frequent resident of early successional habitats, and as a result its habitat is not in jeopardy, and populations likely increased in w. Oregon during the 20th century. With reduced logging on federal lands, some habitat may disappear in 4-5 decades. In sw. Oregon one of their preferred habitats is mature chaparral with invading madrone and black oak. This habitat has increased in recent decades due to a reduction in the incidence of fire. Land managers concerned about increasing fire hazard are reducing fuel loads through brush cutting. A plan allowing for a mosaic of chaparral patches of varying ages as probably existed prior to human intervention would be beneficial. Black-throated Gray Warblers are frequent hosts of Brown-headed Cowbird young. Rural development and pastures create cowbird foraging habitat in close proximity of much of this species' habitat in w. Oregon. Further rural development may exacerbate this problem.—*Stewart W. Janes*

## Black-throated Green Warbler *Dendroica virens*

This warbler breeds from e. British Columbia across Canada to the e. coast and south to Georgia and S. Carolina. It winters in M. America and irregularly in the U.S. It migrates primarily along the e. coast and regularly through the prairies and into California. It is irregular in spring and occasional in fall in the Pacific Northwest. Oregon spring records range from mid-

May to late Jun with most sightings in Harney Co. An immature male was observed at Corvallis, Benton Co., 21 Sep 1985 (OBRC). One was observed at Malheur NWR, Harney Co., 21 Sep 1987 (Rogers 1988a). An immature was in Eugene 7 Dec 2001 (OBRC). There are several photos of spring birds in the files of the OBRC (Watson 1989, Anderson 1991b). Subspecies unknown.—*Harry B. Nehls*

## Townsend's Warbler *Dendroica townsendi*

A dreary winter day can come alive with a flock of these striking birds foraging quietly in a dark green conifer. Though a common migrant and uncommon winter resident, it breeds largely to the north of Oregon. Gabrielson and Jewett (1940) considered it to be "at least an occasional summer resident that possibly breeds in the state." By the 1960s it was a common breeding bird in the Blue Mtns. It appears to have benefited greatly from fire suppression and a resulting increase in abundance of Douglas-fir and grand fir. Townsend's Warblers are closely related to Hermit and Black-throated Gray Warblers and the Black-throated Green Warbler found east of the Rocky Mtns. (Mengel 1964, Bermingham et al. 1992). Male Townsend's Warblers have a face outlined in yellow as well as a yellow breast. Cap, auriculars, and throat are black while the back is green, streaked with black. Wing bars and outer tail feathers are white. The throat patch of the female is reduced or absent, and for the most part where the feathers are black on the male, the female shows dark gray with greenish tones. Immatures are similar to the female.

**General Distribution:** Breed from se. Alaska and sw. Yukon south to the c. Oregon Cascades and Blue Mtns., and the n. Rocky Mtns. of Montana and Idaho. Most winter in the mountains of w. Mexico south into M. America. Small numbers winter in the lowlands along the Pacific coast from Washington to California. Monotypic (AOU 1957).

**Oregon Distribution:** Common breeder in the Blue and Wallowa mountains of ne. Oregon (Evanich 1992a). Local summer resident in the vicinity of Mt. Hood and in the c. Cascades as far south as Davis L., Klamath Co. (Morrison and Hardy 1983a). Isolated territorial male Townsend's Warblers have been observed in the Coast Range and as far south in the Cascades as Jackson Co. (*SWJ*). Also reported from the Warner Mtns. Townsend's and Hermit Warblers hybridize where ranges meet (Morrison and Hardy 1983a, Rohwer and Wood 1998). In Oregon this is most readily observed in the Santiam Pass area where Townsend's Warblers have extended their range since 1940. Hybrid specimens include birds from the N. Santiam R., Marion Co., and Sisters, Deschutes

Co. (MVZ); Jackson Cr., Jefferson Co. (OSU); and Hamner Butte, nw. Klamath Co. (OSU).

In winter they occur along the Oregon coast, and small numbers can be found throughout the lower elevations in the Willamette and Umpqua valleys. Morphological analysis suggests these wintering birds breed in the Queen Charlotte Is., British Columbia (Morrison 1983). Reported as an uncommon winter visitor in the Rogue Valley (Browning 1975a). Townsend's Warblers are common spring and fall migrants throughout the state in a variety of habitats. Northward migrants are more often seen at lower elevations than Hermit Warblers.

**Habitat and Diet:** Townsend's Warblers breed in a wide range of coniferous forests. In the Blue Mtns. they attain highest abundance in grand fir and larch, usually where a dense understory of grand fir is found (Mannan and Meslow 1984). In the Badger Cr. Wilderness Area of Mt. Hood NF, they frequent habitat similar to that occupied by Hermit Warblers and at similar elevations (4,000-5,600 ft [1,200-1,700 m]) (*SWJ*): tall grand and Pacific silver fir forests with foliage evenly spread among all heights. However, Townsend's Warblers tend to occupy forests with a lower foliage volume, fewer large trees, and a lower canopy density than Hermit Warblers. Males tend to forage higher than females, closer to where they deliver their song (*SWJ*). Gilbert and Allwine (1991) found Townsend's to be more abundant in younger stands in the Cascades. Nests of Townsend's Warblers in the Blue Mtns. were placed in the lower canopy usually 12-66 ft (4-20 m) above the ground and on a horizontal branch 6-16 ft (2-5 m) from the trunk (Mannan et al. 1983). The nest typically had a concealing branch directly above the nest.

During winter, they are found in the coastal lowlands, along the lower Columbia R., and below 1,500 ft (460 m) in the Willamette, Umpqua, and Rogue R. drainages. They are seemingly absent from mountain forests and regrowth in winter (D. Fix p.c.). Favored habitats include the edges of mixed conifer-

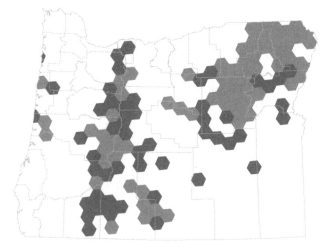

and-hardwood stands; mature riparian zones; near coastal spruce and alder thickets; semi-open groves of full-crowned Douglas-firs or ornamental conifers, as in old cemeteries; varied residential shrubbery mixed with isolated tall trees, wooded city parks, and neglected orchards edged by blackberry thickets (D. Fix p.c.). Scattered single birds may appear in highly urban settings, about the margins of untilled crop stubble, and in suburban gardens; they frequent suet feeders, particularly in cold weather (D. Fix p.c., *DBM*). They feed upon a variety of invertebrates gleaned from canopy foliage, but are also observed foraging on the ground near residential foundations, hedges, and even under eaves (D. Irons p.c.).

**Seasonal Activity and Behavior:** Mean dates for first spring migrants are 1 May for the Bend area (C. Miller unpubl. data) and 8 May at Malheur NWR (Littlefield 1990a). Fairly common to common migrant in w. Oregon from late Apr to early May. Younger males arrive later followed by the females, which arrive in late May (Pearson and Rohwer 1998). Males sing two types of songs as do the closely related Hermit and Black-throated Gray Warblers. Townsend's Warblers in Washington initiated their clutch on average on 7 Jun and laid a mean of 4.9 eggs (Pearson and Rohwer 1998). Rear a single brood a year and only the female incubates the eggs (Wright et al. 1998). Incubation is 11-14 days and nestling period is 9-11 days (Mannan et al. 1983). The major fall movement at Malheur NWR occurs 23 Aug-7 Sep (Littlefield 1990a). Stragglers linger until mid-Oct.

Following the general southward movement of birds from late Aug to Oct, individuals and small flocks may be encountered through the rest of the winter among the roving bands of chickadees, kinglets, Red-breasted Nuthatches, Hutton's Vireos, and similar forest and forest-edge species typical of valley-edge and lower foothill situations (D. Fix p.c.). Wintering birds remaining into early spring may begin singing some weeks prior to the apparent arrival of northbound birds in similar sites (D. Fix p.c.).

**Detection:** As canopy residents, can be hard to observe. Most quickly detected by song or call, but these sometimes difficult or impossible to distinguish from those of the Hermit Warbler. Wintering birds are less predictable, but mature stands of spruce and Douglas-fir close to the coast or mixed western redcedar and bigleaf maple stands inland offer the best chance. Their distinctive but soft call note will help locate them.

**Population Status and Conservation:** The Townsend's Warbler has greatly increased in abundance in the Blue Mtns. over the last century. An increasing understory of Douglas-fir and grand fir in the Blue

*Townsend's Warbler*

Mtns. due to fire suppression has favored this species (Mannan and Meslow 1984), apparently by providing nesting sites and prey. Changing forest management practices in the region may alter this situation. Rohwer and Wood (1998) consider Townsend's Warblers to be competitively superior to Hermit Warblers, and the zone of hybridization appears to be approaching Oregon from the north. It is not known whether the zone of hybridization in the c. Oregon Cascades is expanding. Except for the uncertain consequences of changing forest practices in the Blue Mtns., populations appear to be secure. Townsend's Warblers are known hosts of Brown-headed Cowbirds though cowbirds do not appear to present a significant threat at this time because of Townsend's Warbler preference for dense forests.—*Stewart W. Janes*

## Hermit Warbler *Dendroica occidentalis*

One of the most numerous breeding birds in Douglas-fir and true fir forests of w. Oregon is the Hermit Warbler; yet it is often overlooked. This may be surprising, given the male's bold colors; however, it seldom descends from the higher reaches of the forest canopy. If you are familiar with its song, you can often hear 3-5 males singing on a spring morning from many places in appropriate habitat. The male Hermit Warbler has a bright yellow head, set off by a black throat and nape. The gray back is marked with black stripes that vary in width among birds. Its belly is unmarked white, and it has white wing bars and white outer tail feathers. Females are similar, though the black on the throat is reduced or absent. In areas of overlap, it hybridizes with the Townsend's Warbler (Jewett 1944a, Morrison and Hardy 1983a, Rohwer and Wood 1998), and hybrids show a wide range of

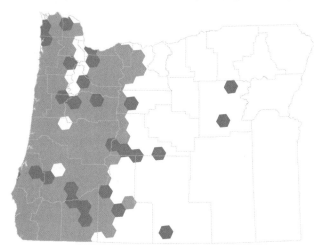

intermediate plumage characteristics (Eckert 2001). Mitochondrial DNA studies have indicated that Hermit and Townsend's Warblers are more closely related than the two populations of Black-throated Gray Warblers, which are sometimes considered separate subspecies (Bermingham et al. 1992).

**General Distribution:** Breeds west of the eastern foothills of the Cascades and Sierra Nevada. Occurs from the c. Washington Cascades and e. Olympic Mtns. in the north to the San Gabriel and San Bernardino Mtns. of s. California where local. Also occurs in the Warner Mtns. of California (Grinnell and Miller 1944). Winters in the mountains of w. Mexico south to Nicaragua. Scattered records from Costa Rica and Panama. A few winter in coastal California. Monotypic (AOU 1957).

**Oregon Distribution:** Common summer resident and migrant of coniferous forests of Coast Range, Klamath Mtns., and Cascades except pure ponderosa pine in the eastern foothills of the Cascades. Wiens and Nussbaum (1975) reported densities of 29-133/100 ac (75-344/km²) in the McKenzie R. drainage. The possibility of scattered breeding birds in the Blue and Wallowa mountains has been reported but not verified (Gilligan et al. 1994). Hybridizes with the Townsend's Warbler from n. Klamath Co. northward (see preceding species). Occasional in winter along the coast and in the Willamette Valley. Rare in e. Oregon during migration (Littlefield 1990a).

**Habitat and Diet:** West of the crest of the Cascades, occupy a variety of conifers but attain greatest densities in Douglas-fir forests. Regular in stands with Douglas-fir trees as young as 20 yr (Bettinger 1996). Adults tend to inhabit older stands than yearlings (Pearson and Manuwal 2000). Though not often found in pine, they occupy ponderosa pine forests in sw. Oregon as long as there is a Douglas-fir understory. Habitat differs along the eastern slopes of the Cascades in Wasco and Hood River counties where they are most abundant in

grand and Pacific silver fir and are largely absent from Douglas-fir (Janes 1994b). Also occur in small numbers in lodgepole pine in e. Lane, Linn, and Douglas counties. Regardless of tree species, prefer forests with a high canopy volume and stands with multiple layers of vegetation including a well-developed understory as opposed to a single layer canopy (Morrison 1982, SWJ). Also show a preference for the tallest stands and stands with the densest canopy in the Badger Cr. Wilderness Area, Mt. Hood NF (SWJ). Nests tend to be placed 30 ft (7 m) up in a conifer and 13 ft (4 m) out from the trunk (Pearson 1997). Unlike many species, Hermit Warblers are seldom seen outside of breeding habitat during migration. They forage on small invertebrates by gleaning from vegetation and occasionally hovering. Like many warblers, male Hermit Warblers tend to forage and sing higher in the canopy than females (Morrison 1982). Females forage lower, closer to the height of the nest.

**Seasonal Activity and Behavior:** Arrive during late Apr with peak movement in early May (Fix 1990a, Hunter et al. 1998, SWJ); early dates 7 Apr in Eugene (Fix 1984a), and 17 Apr in e. Douglas Co. (Fix 1990a). A. McGie (unpubl. data) reports a mean arrival date of 30 Apr for the Corvallis area (13 yr). In se. Oregon, where they do not breed, a late individual was at Fields 3 Jun 1993 (Tweit and Johnson 1993).

In sw. Oregon, and probably elsewhere, females begin arriving during the second week of May, approximately 2 wk after males (SWJ). A mean territory size of 1.6 ac (0.65 ha, n=8) reported from sw. Oregon (Janes and Ryker unpubl. ms.). Nest building observed 5 Jun (OBBA). Egg laying begins in early Jun; average clutch size 4.3; only the female is known to incubate (Pearson 1997, SWJ). A single brood is reared per year (Pearson 1997). Observed carrying food (likely to young in nest) mid-Jun to mid-Jul (n=4) (OBBA); nest with young observed 29 Jun (OBBA). Singing declines abruptly in mid-Jul (Fix 1990a, SWJ). Young predominantly fledge early to late Jul (SWJ), but fledglings reported 13 Jun to 10 Aug (n=18) (OBBA). The major movement south takes place in late Aug with small numbers lingering until late Sep.

Hermit Warblers sing two types of songs. Songs of the first type are typically sung from treetops. This song is heard over much of its range and usually starts with a trill, containing 2-5 intermediate notes, and ends decisively. In some populations the ending is a sharp downward slurred note; in others the final note ascends. Males in the upper Rogue, Umpqua, and Middle Fork Willamette R. drainages sing a unique song without an introductory trill or a distinctive ending. The second song type is sung most often before dawn, later in the breeding season, and during territorial encounters. It, too, begins with a trill, though slightly harsher. After the intermediate notes, it ends on 2-3 repeated notes. A given male typically sings at least 2-3 different songs of the second type. The second song type is also variable with noticeable differences between populations only a few miles apart (*SWJ*).

Hermit Warblers interact with closely related species (Mengel 1964, Bermingham et al. 1992). Hermit and Townsend's Warblers maintain exclusive territories, and male Hermit Warblers frequently respond to the songs of Black-throated Gray Warblers and even exclude them from their territories (Janes and Ryker unpubl. ms.).

**Detection:** Easy to detect by song, but difficult to see. Some songs are difficult to distinguish from those of Townsend's Warblers, and others from those of Black-throated Gray Warblers. Open, low-canopied, Douglas-fir forests or steep country where canopies can be viewed from above offer the best chance to observe this species. They are plentiful at mid-elevations in the Siskiyous and Cascades. In mid- and late summer, isolated springs and intermittent streams with remnant puddles within the forest may offer opportunities for close viewing.

**Population Status and Conservation:** One of the most abundant breeding birds in w. Oregon coniferous forests, and probably the most abundant breeding warbler in w. Oregon, especially at intermediate elevations. May not always have been so plentiful. Gabrielson and Jewett (1940) considered the Hermit Warbler to be a regular but not abundant inhabitant. Since Hermit Warblers reportedly attain greatest density in younger stands in the Coast Range and Cascades (Carey et al 1991, Gilbert and Allwine 1991), timber harvest in recent decades and the abundance of young second-growth may have contributed to greater abundance. However, others have found abundance to increase with stand age (Ralph et al. 1991, Anthony et al. 1996, *SWJ*). Raphael et al. (1988) estimate a 40% decline in nw. California since Euro-American settlement due to changes in the Douglas-fir forests. BBSs have found no recent declines (Pearson 1997).

Hermit Warblers hybridize with Townsend's Warblers. Rohwer and Wood (1998) report three hybrid zones: the Olympic Mtns., the Cascades of s. Washington just across the Columbia R. from Oregon, and in the Santiam Pass area, where Townsend's Warblers have expanded their range in the last 40 yr. However, Fix (1990a) has noted hybrids from Davis L., Klamath Co., north, and S. Heinl (p.c.) observed a singing hybrid male at Gold L., e. Lane Co., on 14 Jul 1984. In early May 2001, Bob Altman, Kevin Sands, C. J. Ralph, and Mike Denny located at least five hybrid birds at Cold Springs CG, Deschutes Co. (M. Denny p.c.). More work in the Oregon Cascades may reveal a more extensive and sophisticated distribution of hybridizing Hermit and Townsend's Warblers. Pearson

and Rohwer (1998) suggest that Townsend's Warblers may be competitively superior to Hermit Warblers. There is evidence that the zone of hybridization in the s. Washington Cascades is moving southward. Hermit Warblers are also hosts to Brown-headed Cowbirds (*SWJ*).—*Stewart W. Janes*

### Blackburnian Warbler *Dendroica fusca*

This colorful warbler breeds in coniferous and mixed forests from e. Alberta east across s. Canada to the e. coast and south to Georgia. It migrates east of the Rocky Mtns. to winter in C. and S. America. It is regular in fall and winter and irregular in spring in California. Elsewhere west of the Rocky Mtns. it is casual. Immatures were at Malheur NWR, Harney Co., 15-18 Sep 1986 (OBRC); and 13 Oct 1994 (Sullivan PT 1995b); an adult male was photographed at Nehalem Meadows, Tillamook Co., from 15 Nov 1987 to after 12 Mar 1988 (Johnson 1988b). One was observed at Malheur NWR 23 May 1994 and a different bird was there 24 May 1994 (Summers 1994b); one was observed at Fields, Harney Co., 7 Jun 1988 (Anderson 1989d); one was photographed at Page Springs CG, Harney Co., 1-2 Jun 1990 (Anderson 1991b); a male was photographed at Fields 16-17 Jun 1998 (Spencer 1999). One was observed at Salem, Marion Co., 19 Oct 1998 (Gilligan 1999). Monotypic (AOU 1957).—*Harry B. Nehls*

### Yellow-throated Warbler *Dendroica dominica*

This common breeding species of the e. U.S. winters from the s. U.S. south into M. America. It is occasionally found elsewhere in N. America. One adult was photographed at Malheur NWR, Harney Co., 9-11 Jun 1985 (Summers 1985a, *Oregon Birds* 13[1]: cover). One was photographed at Fields, Harney Co., 24 Apr 1997 (Sullivan 1997b). Both of these individuals were presumably of the western subspecies *D. d. albilora*. One photographed by several observers at Malheur NWR HQ in early Jun 2002 has not yet been reviewed by the OBRC. One was observed at North Bend, Coos Co., 27 May 1989 (Heinl 1989b).—*Harry B. Nehls*

### Pine Warbler *Dendroica pinus*

This warbler of the pine forests of se. Canada and e. U.S. drops south in winter to the se. U.S. It is occasionally found in winter to s. Canada and elsewhere in the U.S. One was observed at Harbor, Curry Co., 23 Oct 1986 (OBRC). Care is needed in identifying this species because female and immature birds are difficult to separate from similar plumages of Blackpoll and Bay-breasted Warblers in particular. Subspecies unknown.—*Harry B. Nehls*

## Prairie Warbler *Dendroica discolor*

This tail-wagging warbler breeds from se. Canada south through e. U.S. It winters from coastal S. Carolina and Florida south to the W. Indies and M. America. It is regular in small numbers during the fall in California and is occasionally found elsewhere in the U.S. Most Oregon records were found along the coast during the fall. Individuals were observed at South Beach, Lincoln Co., 27 Sep 1981 (OBRC); Bandon, Coos Co., 24 Aug to 3 Sep 1989 (OBRC); aboard a boat 3 mi (4.8 km) west of Brookings, Curry Co., 28 Sep 1991 (OBRC); photographed at Harris Beach SP, Curry Co., 21-25 Sep 1993 (OBRC); observed at Fort Stevens SP, Clatsop Co., 3 Oct 1993 (OBRC); banded and photographed at Cape Blanco, Curry Co., 29 Sep 1994 (Gilligan 1995); photographed at Newport, Lincoln Co., 6-26 Dec 1995 (Johnson 1996b); observed at Brookings 12 Oct 1995 (Gilligan 1996); observed at Newport 16 Sep 1996 (Gilligan 1997); observed at Lone Ranch State Wayside 13-24 Oct 1999 (OBRC). The only inland record was of a male photographed at Malheur NWR HQ, Harney Co., 10 Sep 1999 (OBRC). As this book went to the publisher in fall 2002, additional reports occurred in Sherman, Curry, and Clatsop counties. Subspecies unknown.—*Harry B. Nehls*

## Palm Warbler *Dendroica palmarum*

Palm warblers constantly pump their tails in a down-then-up motion, more so than any other warbler. They also walk and run on the ground more than most warblers. The common name is a misnomer as the species has no particular attraction to palms. A key field mark is the bright yellow undertail coverts which contrast with whiter underparts. Palm Warblers are hardy warblers, migrating early in the spring and late in the fall (Dunn and Garrett 1997).

**General Distribution:** Breeds from extreme ne. British Columbia east across the Canadian Provinces to Nova Scotia. In the central part of the continent the breeding range extends south to the Great Lakes region of Michigan, Minnesota, and Wisconsin. Winters regularly from s. Delaware-Maryland-Virginia peninsula south through easternmost portions of N. Carolina through s. Florida and west through s. Texas (Dunn and Garrett 1997). Two subspecies in N. America; only *D. p. palmarum* (specimen, Gabrielson and Jewett 1940) positively in Oregon.

**Oregon Distribution:** Birds presumably *D. p. palmarum* are regular fall transients on the outer coast and irregularly remain through the winter and spring (Dillingham 1994, Gilligan et al. 1994, Contreras 1998). They are occasional spring and fall transients in the Willamette Valley and have been found wintering in 1994, 1998 and 1999 (Gillson 1999, C. Miller p.c.). They are irregular spring and fall transients east of the Cascades. The only winter record east of the Cascades was at the mouth of the Deschutes R., Sherman Co., on 2 Feb 1992 (S. Russell p.c.).

There are two records that appear to be *D. p. hypochrysea*, but neither were adequately documented. Both were observed in Harney Co.; one at Malheur NWR. on 7 Jun 1985 (Gilligan et al. 1994) and the second at Fields 25-26 Sep 1994 (Sullivan 1994).

**Habitat and Diet:** Coastal brush thickets, weedy fields, forest edges, fencerows, barns, pastures—habitats where one would expect to find sparrows (Wilson 1996). Found most commonly on the outer coast in relatively open areas with exposed flat ground and brushy thickets (*CD*). Largely insectivorous, but also eats seeds and berries during winter (Wilson 1996). It is often seen foraging on open ground, jumping from limb to limb in low shrubs, and flycatching.

**Seasonal Activity and Behavior:** The earliest fall record is from Curry Co., 9 Sep 1993 (Gilligan et al. 1994). The bulk of the Oregon passage occurs in late Sep through Oct (Dillingham 1994, Gilligan et al. 1994, Contreras 1998). Found annually along the coast in recent winters (Dillingham 1994, Gilligan et al. 1994, Contreras 1998). Rare in spring: at least five records from 9 May to 7 Jun (Herlyn 1997, Watson 1979a, C. Miller p.c.). The latest spring record is 7 Jun 1985 (Gilligan et al. 1994). Two records do not fit established migratory patterns; one from 6 Jul 1979 near Forest Grove, Washington Co., (Watson 1979b) and the other from Salem on 1 Aug 1993 (Gilligan 1994).

Migrates at night (Wilson 1996). Length of stay in fall may depend on the weather, with birds moving south rapidly before a severe or sudden cold wave (Griscom and Sprunt 1957).

**Detection:** It is difficult to find this rare fall warbler. They are occasionally found in the company of Yellow-rumped Warblers, or "crowned" sparrows, but more often by themselves. They are frequently detected first by call. They feed more methodically and slower than Yellow-rumped Warblers, with less branch-to-branch flight, and they do not pivot like Yellow-rumped Warblers, but their tail-bobbing behavior is visible at quite a distance (D. Fix p.c., D. Irons p.c., *MGH*).

**Population Status and Conservation:** In 1940 Palm Warblers were not known along the coast of Oregon and the only state record was of a *D. p. palmarum* specimen from the Catlow Valley, Harney Co., 26 Sep 1913 (Gabrielson and Jewett 1940). Not known from Coos Co. until the early 1970s (Contreras 1998). Not known from Curry Co. until one was found 27 Oct

1974 (Crowell and Nehls 1975a). Gilligan et al. (1994) report that since the second state record in 1966, the Palm Warbler has been a regular rare migrant along the coast in fall. Palm Warblers are now uncommon fall visitants, becoming more common in the past 20 yr (Contreras 1998). An extraordinarily heavy fall movement occurred in 1993, when about 120 were reported across the state including a total of 97 birds in Curry Co. (Gilligan 1994).—*Colin Dillingham*

## Bay-breasted Warbler *Dendroica castanea*
This distinctive warbler breeds in coniferous forests from se. Yukon, e. British Columbia across Canada to New England. It migrates east of the Rocky Mtns. to winter in M. and n. S. America. Only two west coast records in the 1960s (Hubbs and Banks 1966), the species is now rare (AOU 1998) but regular in California, especially in fall, and irregular elsewhere in the West. One was collected on the west side of Upper Klamath L., Klamath Co., 7 Jun 1963 (McCaskie and DeBenedictis 1964, spec. no. 14937 MVZ); other records are photographs or sightings. Individuals were at Malheur NWR HQ, Harney Co., 7 Jun 1976 (Littlefield 1980) and 9 Jun 1980 (Littlefield et al. 1985). One was photographed there 25 May 1986 (Summers 1986b, Watson 1989); and 16-18 Sep 1988 (OBRC). Singles were observed at Howard Prairie L., Jackson Co., 22 Jun 1976 (OBRC); at Fields, Harney Co., 27 May 1986 (Summers 1986b); photographed at Page Springs CG, Harney Co., 27 May 1990 (Anderson DA 1990b); observed south of Davis L., Klamath Co., 13 and 22 Aug 1976 (Crowell and Nehls 1977a); and banded and photographed on Hart Mtn. 2 and 23 Aug 1987 (Anderson 1988b). Monotypic (AOU 1957).—*Harry B. Nehls*

## Blackpoll Warbler *Dendroica striata*
This warbler of the boreal forests breeds in Alaska and across n. Canada to the e. coast and south to Pennsylvania. It migrates along the e. coast to winter in S. America. It is a regular transient elsewhere east of the Rocky Mtns. and in California. In Oregon it is reported in small numbers almost annually with most records being immatures from Harney Co. and along the immediate coast. Spring records range from mid-May to early Jun. Two adults accompanying two or three fledged juveniles were on Sauvie I. 24-26 Jul 1969. The adults were observed feeding the young as well as one or two Brown-headed Cowbirds (Crowell and Nehls 1969d). There are twice as many fall records as spring records, fall records occurring between early Sep and late Oct. One was collected at Malheur NWR HQ 7 Sep 1967 (Littlefield and McLaury 1973, spec. no. 530472 USNM). One was photographed on a trawler 47 mi (75.6 km) west of Lincoln Co. 1-3 Oct

1987 (Watson 1989). There are many photographs in the files of the OBRC (Watson 1989). Monotypic.— *Harry B. Nehls*

## Black-and-white Warbler *Mniotilta varia*
This distinctive warbler breeds in deciduous and mixed forests from se. Yukon, e. British Columbia, across Canada and through the e. U.S. It migrates east of the Rocky Mtns. to winter from n. S. America north to the s. U.S. It is a regular transient west of the Rocky Mtns. with many more spring records than fall. Oregon spring records range from early Apr to mid-Jun. with most records during Apr and May. A singing male was at Hilgard Junction SP, Union Co., 11 Jun to 6 Jul 1985 (Summers 1985a). One was observed at Bloomberg Park near Eugene, Lane Co., 9 Jul 1994 (Johnson J 1995a). A male was at Malheur NWR HQ 13 Jun to 5 Jul 2000 (Spencer 2000b). One was banded near Fort Klamath 16 Jul 2001 (Spencer 2001a).

Fall records occur from mid-Aug to late Nov with most records during Sep. A female was collected at Malheur NWR HQ, Harney Co., 17 Sep 1960 (Kridler and Marshall 1962). One was photographed at North Bend, Coos Co., from 17 Dec 1977 to 22 Jan 1978 (OBRC, Hunn and Mattocks 1978). One was at Coos Bay, Coos Co., 19 Feb 1980 (Mattocks and Hunn 1980b). One was at Roseburg, Douglas Co., from 9 Feb into Apr 1996 (Johnson 1996b, Lillie 1996). There are many photographs in the files of the OBRC (Watson 1989). Monotypic (AOU 1957).—*Harry B. Nehls*

## American Redstart *Setophaga ruticilla*
This delicate warbler rewards a diligent observer with a stunning black-and-orange vision hidden among the leaves (adult males) or a more subtle gray-and-gold (females and immatures) in riparian areas within the open forests of ne. Oregon. A sparse, unpredictable, and probably declining breeder in the state, it is sometimes seen at "vagrant traps" such as desert oases and isolated coastal copses during migration.

**General Distribution:** Breeds in most forests of e. N. America, Canada, the northern tiers of states, and the n. Rocky Mtns. Winters in S. America, M. America, and the Caribbean. Two subspecies; provisionally, *S. r. tricolora* is represented on Oregon breeding territories in summer (Browning 2002).

**Oregon Distribution:** Uncommon breeder through the 1980s but now increasingly rare, irregular, and local in ne. Oregon and rarely in the sc. Cascades. Although sometimes thought of as a regular breeder in ne. Oregon, it reaches the edge of its breeding range there in most years, and is not present in all available habitat. It is rare to uncommon (in peak years) and local in Union and Wallowa counties, found most often along the Grande Ronde R. upstream of La Grande (Evanich 1992a), where a nest with four young was found during summer 1981 (Rogers 1981d). Pairs have also been found in ne. Umatilla Co. along the Umatilla R., where as many as eight territorial birds were found in 1985 (Summers 1985a); most often found from Thorn Hollow east to the Bar M Ranch (M. Denny p.c.). Occasionally reported south to c. Baker Co. Irregular and not proven to breed elsewhere in e. Oregon.

The first American Redstart nest in the Cascades was found in 1973 near Davis L., Klamath Co., where single birds had been reported the previous year. They nested there or nearby in the Crescent Cr. area annually through 1977 and sporadically through 1984 (McQueen 1977). No breeding birds have been found there since 1984, though a fresh immature was observed there in early Aug 2000 (D. Irons p.c.). As many as four birds, an adult male, adult female, and 2 juveniles, were observed during the period 1 Jul through Sep along Indian Ford Cr., Squawback Rd., Deschutes Co. (Spencer 2000b, Sullivan 2001a), and a pair that bred was first located there 3-9 Jun 2001 (Spencer 2001a).

The only documented successful nesting west of the Cascade summit was a pair with four young found 2 Jul 1970 along the Rogue R. near Shady Cove, Jackson Co. (Browning 1975a); the nest was collected (OSU, Bertrand and Scott 1973a). The only suggestions of nesting west of the Cascades since 1970 was a pair found about 15 mi (24 km) ne. of Roseburg 6 Jul 1982 (Evanich 1982c), and a failed nesting attempt in Curry Co., Jun 2000 (T. J. Wahl p.c.).

Occasional in winter in w. Oregon, e.g., one in Eugene 19 Dec 1987 (Johnson 1988a), and 2 immatures in North Bend 1-13 Jan 1980 (Mattocks and Hunn 1980b, Contreras 1998).

**Habitat and Diet:** Found in riparian growth along major rivers in ne. Oregon (Evanich 1992a). In areas near La Grande, seen mainly in rather open pine forests with at least some willow understory near water (*ALC*). The Davis L. population used areas of open lodgepole pine interspersed with willows near creeks (McQueen 1977). Nests for which data are available are from the Davis L. population: one in a young pine thicket about 4 ft (3.3 m) above the ground (H. Wisner p.c.), another in a small thicket of lodgepole pine, about 6.5 ft 2.2 m) up, with no willows adjacent (L. McQueen p.c.), and a third about 8 ft (2.7 m) up in a 10-ft alder (S. Gordon p.c.).

There have been no dietary studies on the small Oregon population. They have been observed catching mosquitos and other small flying insects at Davis L. and near La Grande (*ALC*).

**Seasonal Activity and Behavior:** Redstarts are fairly late migrants in spring, typically not appearing on their Oregon breeding grounds until late May or early Jun. Spring migration in this species is hard to describe with any accuracy, as some birds seen in se. Oregon may be en route to local breeding locales while others may be vagrants from eastern populations. There are records nearly every year from such vagrant traps as Malheur NWR HQ and Fields oasis in late May and early Jun. There are also spring records from such nonbreeding locales as Cape Blanco (banded, *fide* L. McQueen), Summer L., Lake Co. (C. Supnet p.c.), Selmac L., Josephine Co. (K. Ward p.c.), and the Lane Co. Coast Range (M. Egger p.c.).

Breeding may occur quite late in summer by warbler standards; an active nest with one fledgling was found at Davis L. on 20 Jul 1974 (D. Gleason, G. Jobanek p.c.).

Fall movements are underway by mid-Aug and are spread across the state, but involve very few birds. Whether these represent southbound Oregon breeders or wanderers from elsewhere is not known. Most reports are from se. Oregon vagrant traps or from the outer coast through mid-Sep based on numerous reports in *Oregon Birds*; also a specimen from Malheur NWR, 8 Sep 1960 (Kridler and Marshall 1960). Late records include 5 Oct 1993 at Gold Beach (Tweit and Gilligan 1994), and 11 Nov 1974 through end of month at Svenson, Clatsop Co. (Crowell and Nehls 1975a).

**Detection:** The song, reminiscent of a thin Yellow Warbler song, is very helpful in locating birds. Beware redstart "imitations" by Yellow Warblers. The small population in the state makes locating birds hard, but if a pair can be found, they are often easily seen because nests are not high and the birds are typically active.

**Population Status and Conservation:** The Oregon population is small and varies in size somewhat from year to year. No useful population data are available from Oregon. Because of its affinity for trees near water, it is somewhat sensitive to loss of riparian habitat, but its actual needs in Oregon are poorly known.—*Alan L. Contreras*

## Prothonotary Warbler *Protonotaria citrea*

This hole-nesting species of deciduous lowland woodlands breeds through the e. U.S. and winters in M. America. It is a regular transient east of the Rocky Mtns. and in California, especially during the fall. It is occasionally found in the Northwest. One was observed at Charleston, Coos Co., 19 Oct 1974 (OBRC); one was banded and photographed at Hart Mtn., Lake Co., 19 Aug 1976 (Mewaldt 1977b); one was photographed at Malheur NWR HQ, Harney Co.,

10-11 Oct 1987 (Anderson 1988b); and 30 May to 3 Jun 1993 (OBRC, *Oregon Birds* 19[4]: cover, Summers 1993c); and another was banded and photographed at Malheur NWR HQ 19-22 Sep 1998 (OBRC). One was at Frenchglen, Harney Co, 7 Oct 1999 (Sullivan 2000a), and one was photographed and banded at Odessa Cr., Upper Klamath L., 2 Jul 2001 (Spencer 2001a). Another was photographed near Halfway, Baker Co., 9-20 Nov 2001 (Sullivan 2002). Monotypic (AOU 1957).—*Harry B. Nehls*

## Worm-eating Warbler *Helmitheros vermivorus*
This distinctive warbler breeds in the e. U.S. and winters in M. America, and occasionally to the s. U.S. It is sporadic west of the Rocky Mtns. One was observed at Malheur NWR HQ, Harney Co., 16 Sep 1990, and 10-11 Jun 2001 (OBRC). One was at the mouth of the Winchuck R., 1 Nov 2001 (OBRC). Monotypic (AOU 1957).—*Harry B. Nehls*

## Ovenbird *Seiurus aurocapillus*
This thrush-like ground-foraging warbler breeds from se. Yukon and e. British Columbia across Canada and south through the e. U.S., and locally elsewhere east of the Rocky Mtns. It migrates east of the Rocky Mtns. to winter in M. America. It is occasionally found in winter in its breeding range and in California. Small numbers regularly occur in w. N. America. Most Oregon records are from the southeast part of the state. One was reported at Ashland, Jackson Co., 4 Mar 1996 (Lillie 1996). Spring records range from early May to mid-Jun. A female collected at Malheur NWR HQ, Malheur Co., 4 Jun 1961 was *S. a. aurocapillus* (spec. no. 478486 USNM, Kridler 1965). The only spring record away from e. Oregon was of a bird that landed on a fishing boat and was photographed 5 mi (8 km) west of Coos Bay 6 Jun 1970 (Crowell and Nehls 1970d, Contreras 1998). There are seven records of singing territorial males in the Cascades during Jun and Jul. No females were noted, nor was nesting suspected at any of these locations. One was singing on the Bayocean Spit, Tillamook Co., 18 Jul 1988 (Mattocks 1989). A male was banded and photographed on Hart Mtn., Lake Co., 10 Jul 1979 (OBRC). Fall records are fewer than in spring, and occur between late Aug and early Sep. There are many photographs in the files of the OBRC (Watson 1989).—*Harry B. Nehls*

## Northern Waterthrush *Seiurus noveboracensis*
One of Oregon's rarest and most local breeders, this vocal but somewhat secretive warbler can be heard and sometimes seen in summer in the sc. Cascades. The patient observer may catch a glimpse of a chunky, dark-backed bird feeding low in dense willows, sometimes showing its pale underparts with dark streaks. It is otherwise a rare migrant or vagrant statewide, mostly in spring.

**General Distribution:** Breeds from the ne. U.S. north and west across much of Canada and Alaska, and in the n. Rocky Mtns. Winters mainly in Latin America and the Caribbean. Monotypic (Eaton 1957, *MRB*).

**Oregon Distribution:** An isolated population of this species has summered and presumably bred in the sc. Cascades since at least 1977 (Greenfield 1977, Egger 1978). The population extends from the Little Deschutes R. north of Gilchrist, Klamath Co., south to the vicinity of Hwy 58, west along Crescent Cr. and to Salt Cr. east of the falls, Lane Co. (Contreras 1988a). One singing bird was in suitable habitat at Lost L., e. Linn Co., in Jun in the late 1980s (D. Irons p.c.), and another singing bird was in suitable habitat near the confluence of Skookum Cr. and the N. Fk. Middle Fk. of the Willamette R. in May or Jun in the early 1990s (*MGH*). No nest has been found in Oregon, owing mainly to the impenetrable habitat. Recent reports (OBBA) suggest that a small population may breed in the upper Wenaha R. area of Union and Wallowa counties, not far from the Idaho colonies along the St. Joe R. Others are reported in late spring and early summer from vagrant traps in e. Oregon. Most of these are likely vagrants vs. migrants to the very limited Oregon breeding populations.

**Habitat and Diet:** Birds along Crescent Cr. are found in dense willows 5-8 ft. (1.7-2.7 m) high with some Sitka alder interspersed, often in standing or slow-moving water. The surrounding forest is lodgepole pine and ponderosa pine. Birds along the Little Deschutes R. are in similar habitat. The Salt Cr. site is a similar riparian willow zone within a forest of Douglas-fir, lodgepole pine, and a few Engelmann spruce (Contreras 1988a). Birds have been observed singing from willows, nearby pines, and pine snags, sometimes quite high (*ALC*).

No dietary studies have been conducted in Oregon. Kaufman (1996) states that the species eats a variety of insects and even such food as snails, crustaceans, and small fish, representative of its wetland habitat.

**Seasonal Activity and Behavior:** The breeding population appears to arrive during early Jun, though there is some variation in reports from year to year. Earliest arrival 13 May 1990 at both Gilchrist and Paulina Marsh (Tweit and Fix 1990b). Birds have been reported carrying nesting material as early as 2 Jun (J. Gilligan p.c.) but in most years are hard to find until the second week of Jun (S. Russell p.c.). Generally gone by late Jul and appear to be absent in Aug (Egger 1978, *ALC*, S. Russell p.c.).

There are a number of fall records statewide from Aug through the season, including individuals on 3 Oct 1993 at Fields, Harney Co. (Summers 1994a) and 28 Nov 1984 at McNary Dam 28 Nov 1984 (Rogers 1988a). There are three winter records: a fresh window kill on 1 Jan 1978 at North Bend (Contreras 1998), specimen to Southwestern Oregon Community College but now cannot be located; 16 Dec 1995 at Tillamook (Johnson 1996b) and 2 Jan 1999 at Warrenton (Gilligan 1999).

**Detection:** The song of this species is very loud and distinctive, making detection of singing birds easy. However, foraging birds are difficult to locate among thick riparian shrubs bordering stream banks. They occasionally sing from exposed perches, thus an observer who is in a territory early in the day and can track down the singer can often see the bird.

**Population Status and Conservation:** No population surveys have been done, but in peak years birds are reported at all riparian access points within the Crescent Cr.-Little Deschutes portion of the range, suggesting the presence of many pairs. L. McQueen (p.c.) located nine singing birds at access points in this breeding area in Jun 1990. The presence of the population for at least 23 yr suggests that quite a few pairs are involved. Much appropriate habitat is not easily accessible.

The central Cascade population appears to occupy essentially the same area that it did in 1977-78, with slight expansions and contractions over the years. Because these birds are dependent on dense riparian willows in Oregon, damage to this habitat would have immediate and extreme consequences for the survival of this species as an Oregon breeder. This is one of the rarest annual breeders in Oregon and efforts should be made to maintain it as part of the state's avifauna.—*Alan L. Contreras*

## Louisiana Waterthrush *Seiurus motacilla*

The Louisiana Waterthrush is a ground-foraging warbler that occurs along shaded, fast-flowing streams. It breeds in the e. U.S. and winters from the s. U.S. to n. S. America. It is casual to s. California. One was photographed and videotaped at Silver Falls SP, Marion Co., 26-30 Nov 1998 (Lawes and Lawes 1999), for the only Oregon record. Monotypic (AOU 1957).—*Harry B. Nehls*

## Kentucky Warbler *Oporornis formosus*

This denizen of deciduous woodlands with dense bushy understory breeds over much of the e. U.S. It winters in M. America and occasionally to California and other southern states. It is a regular spring and fall visitant to California and is occasionally found elsewhere in the West. One was observed at Fields, Harney Co., 16 Jun 1989 (OBRC) and 8 May 2000 (Sullivan 2000b). One was photographed at Frenchglen, Harney Co., 8 Jun 1990 (Anderson 1991b); and one was banded and photographed near Dead Horse L. in the Fremont NF, Lake Co., 3-14 Jul 1996 (Sherman 1997). Monotypic (AOU 1957).—*Harry B. Nehls*

## Mourning Warbler *Oporornis philadelphia*

This shrub-loving bird breeds from ne. British Columbia across s. Canada to the ne. U.S. and south to W. Virginia. It winters in C. and n. S. America. It is occasionally found west of the Rocky Mtns. It is difficult to separate this species from the more common MacGillivray's Warbler. Single birds were at Brothers, Deschutes Co., 8 Jun 1990 (OBRC); at Hills Cr. Res., Lane Co., 12 Jul 1984; one was photographed at Malheur NWR HQ 26 Sep 1982 (OBRC); one was observed near Corvallis, Benton Co., 4 Sep 1983 (OBRC); and another was observed at Malheur NWR HQ 26 May 2001(OBRC). Caution is required in making or accepting sight records of this species (Browning 1995a). Monotypic (AOU 1957).—*Harry B. Nehls*

## MacGillivray's Warbler *Oporornis tolmiei*

During the breeding season, this gray-hooded warbler is conspicuous, singing boldly from riparian thickets, clear-cuts, and roadside brush. However, "when household cares occupy the daylight hours they become elusive as field mice, slipping about through the thickets like shadows, only the sharp alarm note betraying their presence to an intruder" (Gabrielson and Jewett 1940). After many minutes of careful pursuit, an observer is often left with only a brief glimpse of an olive-colored back or a broken white eye-ring. MacGillivray's Warbler is one species that appears to thrive in areas that have been disturbed by industrial forest practices.

**General Distribution:** Breeds from the Alaska panhandle and extreme se. and sc. Yukon south to mountains of s. California, se. Arizona, and sw. New Mexico. Also disjunct populations in sw. S. Dakota and se. Coahuila and s. Nuevo Leon in ec. Mexico. Scattered and local in mountains of coastal California, the Great Basin, and the desert Southwest. Winters from n. Mexico to Panama (Pitocchelli 1995, Dunn and Garrett 1997). Phillips (1947) originally described four subspecies, though only two are now recognized (AOU 1957), both of which occur in Oregon.

**Oregon Distribution:** The MacGillivray's Warbler has been reported from every county (Gabrielson and Jewett 1940, Gilligan et al. 1994). *O. t. tolmiei* is the

breeding subspecies in w. and n. Oregon. It is common in the Coast Range, though rare or absent along the immediate c. and n. coast (Gabrielson and Jewett 1940, Gilligan et al. 1994, Contreras 1998, Herlyn 1998). Fairly common to abundant in the foothills of western interior valleys and Cascades (Gabrielson and Jewett 1940, Farner 1952, Fix and Sawyer 1991, Gillson 1998, *SGD*). Breed throughout Blue Mtns., locally uncommon in Union and Wallowa counties (Evanich 1992a). Common to abundant in the Klamath Basin (Summers 1993a), and noted at several locations in the Fremont NF (McAllister and Marshall 1945).

*O. t. monticola* breeds in se. Oregon; uncommon and local on Steens Mtn. and Mahogany Mtn. (AOU 1957) south through the Trout Cr. Mtns., Pueblo Mtns., and Oregon Canyon Mtns. (Bent 1953, Gilligan and Smith 1980, Marshall 1987, Contreras and Kindschy 1996, *SGD*). Phillips (1947) identified specimens from Roseburg and Grants Pass to be intermediate between *O. t. intermedia* (now a synonym of *monticola*) and *O. t. tolmiei*. Subspecies unknown for Jackson Co. and other localities; further work needed.

**Habitat and Diet:** MacGillivray's Warblers breed in dense brush throughout the state. In humid parts of the range, they breed in forest openings, young clearcuts, road and power-line rights-of-way, open montane chaparral, and shrubby borders of streams and subalpine meadows, where it may be numerous (Gabrielson and Jewett 1940, Farner 1952, Gilligan et al. 1994, *SGD*). In two comparative studies of foraging behavior of western warbler species in early seral clear-cuts on the Siuslaw NF, MacGillivray's Warblers concentrated foraging activity in low shrub cover typically composed of salmonberry, thimbleberry, vine maple, salal, sword fern, tansy ragwort, foxglove, pearly everlasting, and Oregon oxalis (Morrison 1981, Morrison and Meslow 1983b). Foraging height was mostly below 3 ft (1 m) in both deciduous and conifer-dominated forest types (Morrison 1981, Morrison and Meslow 1983b). Territory size averaged 4.2 ac (1.7 ha) for Coast Range clearcuts (Morrison 1981, Morrison

and Meslow 1983b). Gillson (1999) refers to the species as a "common summer resident in ceanothus thickets" in the Hoodoo Butte area of Linn Co.

East of the Cascade summit, MacGillivray's Warblers breed in dense willow thickets around springs and stream bottoms (Gabrielson and Jewett 1940). Noted around springs with willow and aspen in Fremont NF (McAllister and Marshall 1945). Common in riparian habitat in canyon bottoms on Mahogany Mtn., Malheur Co. (Gilligan and Smith 1980). Commonly nests among moist brush tangles and willow-bordered watercourses in the Blue Mtns. and on Steens Mtn., though not on Malheur NWR (Littlefield 1990a, *SGD*). Does not nest in sagebrush habitats (Gilligan et al. 1994). Nest placed in low shrubbery or tall herbaceous cover, constructed and lined with dried grass (Gabrielson and Jewett 1940).

No specific food data for Oregon. Prey items in California include: true bugs, leaf-hoppers, beetles, bees, wasps, and ants during the breeding season (Shuford 1993); click, dung, and flea beetles, alfalfa weevils, and caterpillars elsewhere (Pitocchelli 1995).

**Seasonal Activity and Behavior:** In w. Oregon, spring migrants begin arriving in the latter half of Apr. Early records include 11 Apr 1989 at Eugene and Portland (Heinl 1989b), and 13 Apr 1984 at Eugene (Fix 1984a). Migration peaks early to mid-May. East of the Cascades, first arrivals appear during early May (rarely late Apr), and peaks early to mid-May, with some late migrants through early Jun. Highly territorial, their courtship begins soon after arrival at breeding grounds (Gabrielson and Jewett 1940, Pitocchelli 1995). Earliest complete egg set date is 30 May (no location indicated), latest 18 Jul in Baker Co. (Gabrielson and Jewett 1940). Data from some continuous effort banding stations indicate first fledglings in the third week of Jun at 2,100 ft (640 m) in Josephine Co. (M. Mamone unpubl. data), the third week of Jul at 4,000 ft (1,220 m) in Clackamas Co. (*SGD*) and the third week of Jul at 4,400 ft (1,340 m) in Curry Co. (M. Mamone p.c.). Males on breeding territories were noted to sing in the Cascades of e. Douglas Co. well into Aug (Fix 1990a).

Fall migration occurs statewide from mid-Aug through mid-Sep, with very few birds still present in late Oct (Gilligan et al. 1994), e.g., one late bird at Salem 22 Oct 1984 (Hunn and Mattocks 1985). Fall migration at Malheur NWR begins 7 Aug, peaks 15-25 Aug, with a late date of 10 Oct (Littlefield 1990a). There are at least three mid-winter records: two birds at Eugene, 31 Dec 1967, one of which sheltered in a garage (Contreras 1997b); one bird at Astoria 2 Dec 1989 (Johnson 1990b); and one was found in Eugene from 29 Dec 2001 to 22 Feb 2002 (*ALC*).

**Detection:** "Macs" are inquisitive, usually responding quickly to intrusion or spishing with loud, scolding chip notes. Songs may be heard from low dense shrubs or from tree perches 16-22 ft (4.9-6.7 m) high (Pitocchelli 1995). Flight songs are occasionally observed, during which the male clumsily flies upward while singing, then rapidly descends while giving chip notes. Singing occurs most frequently at dawn and dusk (Pitocchelli 1995). Both sexes may persistently scold intruders near a nest or fledglings, remaining well-concealed while approaching closely.

**Population Status and Conservation:** Breeding range has probably expanded significantly since European settlement of w. N. America (Pitocchelli 1995). BBS data indicate conflicting population trends between states and regions within the Oregon range. Though the species is found in moderate abundance overall, data are not adequate for statistically significant trends to emerge. Density in w. Oregon Coast Range varied from 1.4 to 1.8 birds/ac (3.5-4.5 birds/ha) (Morrison 1981, Morrison and Meslow 1983b). Industrial forest practices in humid western mountains which remove all or most of the forest overstory, road construction in forests, and other disturbances appear to benefit the species, provided shrubland results from the activity. The rate of stand-replacement timber harvest on federal lands in w. Oregon peaked in the 1980s, however, and can be expected to decline considerably if current federal timber harvest policies remain in place. As a result, numbers of this species may decline on federal lands, though populations on private industrial forest land, where short-rotation harvest regimes can be expected to continue, may remain steady or even increase.

East of the Cascades, loss of riparian habitat in drier parts of the range may have resulted in local declines and even extirpation. Forest treatments in older mixed-conifer forest in the Blue Mtns., which are intended to return stand conditions to the relatively open understory conditions of historic times, are also likely to result in local declines. Specifically, intensive grazing, wildfire, prescribed burning, and herbicide treatments have been identified as potential threats to stable populations (Altman 2000b).—*Stephen G. Dowlan*

## Common Yellowthroat *Geothlypis trichas*

The Common Yellowthroat is one of N. America's most widespread warbler species, and its *witchity-witchity-witchity* song is also among the most easily recognized. This skulker may breed in any suitably damp brushy or weedy habitat throughout the state, and can be abundant in extensive marshy habitat. The olive-backed male's distinctive broad black mask, edged white above, and bright yellow chin and under tail coverts are instantly recognizable field marks. Females

are also olive-backed and similarly marked below, but lack the male's mask; they are sufficiently nondescript as to confuse inexperienced observers.

**General Distribution:** Breed from se. Alaska across Canada to the Maritime Provinces and all the mainland states of the U.S. south to Mexico. Winters in the e. U.S. from the Carolinas west across the Gulf states through sc. and coastal Texas, most commonly along the coastal plain; rarely as far north as Newfoundland and around the s. Great Lakes. In w. N. America, winters mainly in s. Arizona, along the Colorado R. and in other suitably marshy areas in s. California; rarely to extreme s. British Columbia and interior western states. Twelve subspecies were recognized by the AOU (1957), at least two of which breed in Oregon.

**Oregon Distribution:** *G. t. arizela* is recognized by AOU (1957) as breeding throughout w. Oregon, including the coast and Cascades to moderate elevations, with specimens from Washington, Benton, and Coos counties (Behle 1950) and from Tillamook and Multnomah counties (Browning 2002). It is fairly common, but is sometimes found in very high densities, especially in coastal lowlands and western interior valleys.

*G. t. occidentalis* breeds throughout most or all of e. Oregon (AOU 1957, Guzy and Ritchison 1999). Common Yellowthroats are described as common to abundant in marshes and wetlands, especially in the Klamath Basin, Malheur NWR (Gabrielson and Jewett 1940, Littlefield 1990a), and around lake and river margins and wet meadows of Malheur Co. (Contreras and Kindschy 1996). This subspecies has been taken from Lake, Malheur, Jefferson, and Sherman counties (Behle 1950), as well as Klamath (AMNH) and Harney (OSU) counties (see Browning 2002). *G. t. campicola*, the breeding subspecies found in se. Washington (AOU 1957, Guzy and Ritchison 1999), is not known from Oregon (Browning 2002). Evanich (1992a) describes the Common Yellowthroat as a common summer resident and spring and fall migrant at lower elevations

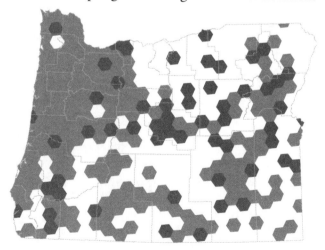

*Common Yellowthroat*

of Union and Wallowa counties, where specimens are needed to confirm subspecies.

Rare (subspecies unknown) in winter in w. Oregon in interior valleys and along the coast, with fewer than 30 records prior to 1994 (Contreras 1997b). Winter sight-ings have increased since then, likely due to increased CBC coverage and observer skill. Thus far, only one winter record exists east of the Cascades, from Grant Co. (Contreras 1997b).

**Habitat and Diet:** Yellowthroats are generally found in wetlands or adjacent shrubby areas. Though they are familiar to nearly all bird enthusiasts, Oregon habitat associations are not well described in the literature. Throughout the range greatest numbers are found in cattails and other dense emergent marsh vegetation (Dunn and Garrett 1997, Guzy and Ritchison 1999). Yellowthroats breed in a wide variety of sites with a dense growth of low vegetation. Along the coast, they are found in wet meadow and edge habitat which may include willows, sedges, twinberry, wax-myrtle, Nootka rose, Scotch broom, and non-native blackberries, as well as cattail marshes. High densities may be found in coastal dairy lands with cultivated hay grasses, willows, and blackberries (Contreras 1998, M. Patterson p.c.). Throughout the state, yellowthroats appear to be most closely associated with cattail marshes. Breeding also occurs in small marshy areas with permanent year-round water that lack the cattail component, but yellowthroats are not always present when this habitat is available (T. Rodenkirk p.c.). Found below 1,000 ft (305 m) in brushy clear-cuts on the east slope of the Coast Range in Polk Co. (Gerig 1992).

Willamette Valley habitat associations include almost any type of tall, dense, continuous herbaceous cover

and nearby edge habitat, as well as in the understory of cottonwood forests if canopy closure is not dense (Ford 1993, B. Altman p.c.). Some preference for marshes with scattered trees and bushes has been noted (Herlyn 1998). In the w. Cascades they are common in riparian areas and wet tangles in lower clearcuts to approximately 3,300 ft (1,000 m, Gillson 1998, *SGD*), and to higher elevations where suitable habitat exists (e.g., Gold L., Lane Co., at 4,800 ft [1,463 m]). Throughout w. Oregon, the yellowthroat commonly breeds in areas dominated by reed canarygrass (*MGH, SGD*).

East of the Cascades in Klamath, Lake, and Harney counties, dense stands of emergent vegetation are preferred (Merrill 1888, Gabrielson and Jewett 1940, Littlefield 1990a). Common in hardstem bulrush at the north end of L. Abert, Lake Co. (Kristensen et al. 1991). McAllister and Marshall (1945) reported yellowthroats at 6,000 ft (1,800 m) at Dog L. in Fremont NF, where the "south end is mostly marshland ... with quaking aspen and willows surrounding the lake." Found in marshes, along lake and river margins, and at wet meadows at low elevations in Union and Wallowa counties (Evanich 1992a). Also found in dense brush, weedy fields, and in such sites as vacant lots and city parks during migration. Winter sightings in w. Oregon are usually in some semblance of typical breeding habitat (*SGD*).

The yellowthroat's nest is usually a deep cup of woven grass, lined with grass and hair, placed on or near ground, usually near water (Gabrielson and Jewett 1940, Alcorn 1978). No information is available specific to Oregon food habits. Generally, yellowthroats feed on insects and invertebrates close to the ground in dense low cover (Guzy and Ritchison 1999).

**Seasonal Activity and Behavior:** Early arrival dates for w. Oregon each year are usually during the last week of Mar, with the average widespread arrival around the first week of Apr (Bayer 1995c, Gillson 1998, Herlyn 1998). Earliest arrival for Malheur NWR has been 13 Apr, with an average for e. Oregon around 1 May (Littlefield 1990a, Contreras 1996a, Ivey, Herziger, and Scheuering 1998). Males arrive about 1 wk ahead of females (Guzy and Ritchison 1999). The species' secretive habits make nest building difficult to observe and nests difficult to locate (*SGD*). OBBA efforts resulted in only a handful of nest observations statewide; nest building on 25 May and 26 May, nests with eggs on 14 May, 7 Jun and 8 Jul, and nests with young on 29 May and 24 Jun. Fledglings were reported as early as 14 May and as late as 3 Aug (OBBA). Eggs 3-5.

In w. Oregon, southbound migration begins in late Aug (Gilligan et al. 1994). It peaks during the last week of Aug and the first two weeks of Sep and declines through mid-Oct. Stragglers, usually immatures, may be seen well into Oct, e.g., 30 Oct 1967 at Baker (Rogers 1968a). At Malheur NWR, adults begin southbound migration before immatures in late Jul (Littlefield 1990a). Here the species is most numerous during the last two weeks of Aug; late date for Malheur NWR 6 Oct (*ALC*). There are no records past Oct for Klamath Co. (Summers 1993a). One male banded at Malheur NWR headquarters on 28 Aug 1985 was recaptured 17 Feb 1986 in Nayarit, Mexico (Littlefield 1990a).

**Detection:** In general, this is an inquisitive species that is easily coaxed into view by spishing and squeaking. Males sing loudly and frequently and are often in view during the breeding season, frequently giving flight songs (Dunn and Garrett 1997). Females can be exceptionally secretive when tending nests, and may disappear in heavy growth well away from the nest and make their way to the nest low in the vegetation (*SGD*). In migration and in winter, call notes are given less frequently.

**Population Status and Conservation:** Populations in the Pacific Northwest are increasing (Guzy and Ritchison 1999). BBS data indicate an increasing trend (p=0.03) for Oregon (Sauer et al. 1999). Frequently breed in areas dominated by non-native species, though nest success and productivity relative to native vegetation has not been evaluated (*SGD*). Local declines may occur due to habitat loss, but newly created habitat may quickly be colonized (Dunn and Garret 1997). Rangewide, the Common Yellowthroat is one of the most frequent cowbird hosts (Hofslund 1957, Dunn and Garrett 1997), though the effect of parasitism on Oregon populations has not been assessed. One study from California indicates that nests in extensive cattail marshes were rarely parasitized, suggesting the importance of larger and more contiguous patches of emergent vegetation which lack trees or shrubs (Spautz 1999). Littlefield (1990a) noted "occasional" losses to cowbird parasitism at Malheur NWR.—*Stephen G. Dowlan*

### Hooded Warbler *Wilsonia citrina*
The Hooded Warbler breeds from e. Texas and Oklahoma to New England and locally north to Michigan. It winters in M. America. Small numbers occur annually in California, mostly in spring. It occasionally occurs in the Northwest. Single males were tape-recorded at Washburn State Wayside, Lane Co., 20 Jul 1974 to the end of the month (OBRC); observed at Malheur NWR HQ 20 May 1977 (OBRC); photographed there 31 May 1992 (OBRC); photographed and sound-recorded at a rest area along Highway 395, 10 mi (16.1 km) south of Canyon City, Grant Co., 11-17 Jul 1982 (OBRC); photographed

along Wildhorse Cr., north of Pendleton, Umatilla Co., 21 Oct and 8 Nov 1983 (OBRC); and observed at Harbor, Curry Co., 28 Aug to 28 Sep 1985 (OBRC). A singing male remained through Sep 1998 at Odessa CG at the south end of Upper Klamath L., Klamath Co. It was mist-netted several times and was banded (Sullivan 1999a, Kevin Spencer p.c.). A male and a female were at Hart Mtn. 13 Aug to 8 Sep 2000 (OBRC); a male and a female were at Malheur NWR HQ 6-11 Oct 2000 (Sullivan 2001a). Two males were at Malheur NWR HQ in Sep 2002 (*ALC*). Monotypic (AOU 1957).—*Harry B. Nehls*

### Wilson's Warbler *Wilsonia pusilla*
The original name, Wilson's Black-capped Fly-catching Warbler (Harrison HH 1984), describes one of the main foraging techniques of the Wilson's Warbler, but does not do justice to its bright plumage. The glossy black cap, or "pileum" inspired the name Pileolated Warbler, the name formerly used for the western subspecies (Harrison HH 1984). The golden-yellow face and breast of the male Wilson's Warbler distinguish it as one of the brightest of Oregon's breeding warblers. Adult females are similar in plumage to males, and may even have a full black cap; however, the caps of females are smaller and duller than those of males, and are flecked with olive-green. These lively warblers nest and forage for insects in tall, dense shrub growth, often within small gaps in mature forests, humid forest understory, or riparian thickets.

**General Distribution:** Breeds across n. N. America from Newfoundland and Nova Scotia south to New England and n. New York, west to Alaska, and south through the Rocky Mtns. to n. New Mexico. Absent as a breeder, it is a regular migrant from most of the U.S. east of the Rocky Mtns. Wilson's Warblers winter in M. America, from n. Mexico (casually as far north as the s. U.S.) south to w. Panama. Three subspecies are recognized, and all have been recorded in Oregon.

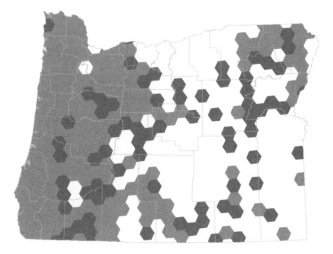

**Oregon Distribution:** *W. p. chryseola* is an abundant breeder in woods and tall shrubs in the Coast Range (example specimens from Tillamook, Tillamook Co.; Depoe Bay and Newport, Lincoln Co.; Mercer, Lane Co. [all USNM]), and is common in the Willamette Valley and w. Cascades. *W. p. pileolata* breeds in the e. Cascades and Blue Mtns., uncommonly in scattered habitat patches in arid regions of Columbia Plateau and Northern Great Basin, with example specimens (USNM) from Maupin, Wasco Co.; Sisters, Deschutes Co.; Ft. Klamath, Klamath Co.; The Narrows, Harney Co.; Homestead and Huntington, Baker Co.; and Ordnance, Umatilla Co. (*MRB*). Occur from low elevation to treeline in appropriate habitat. Summer records exist in Malheur Co. (OBBA), but it is doubtful that they nest there (M. Denny p.c.).

Abundance of the Wilson's Warbler is lower in the Cascades than in the Coast Range, and lower still east of the Cascades (Gabrielson and Jewett 1940, Sauer et al. 1999). Within the Cascade Range, it is more abundant in the Mt. Hood NF than in the Rogue River NF or the Umpqua NF and the H.J. Andrews Experimental Forest (Gilbert and Allwine 1991).

More unusual records include a migrant *chryseola* at Malheur NWR (*USNM*). Two specimens of *W. p. pusilla*, the subspecies that breeds predominantly in e. N. America, were collected on Government I. in the Columbia R. in 1908 (Gabrielson and Jewett 1940) and at Portland in 1944 (Jewett 1945b).

At least six winter records (Dec) in w. Oregon, mainly coastal (Jewett 1945b, Johnson 1997b, Contreras 1998), including a specimen of *W. p. pileolata* collected 6 Dec at Coquille, Coos Co. (Burleigh 1957). One record for e. Oregon, 14 Jan 1990, near Milton-Freewater, Umatilla Co. (Anderson DA 1990d).

**Habitat and Diet:** Wilson's Warblers occur in most forests in Oregon in which there is a well-developed understory of moist-site shrubs. During the breeding season, Wilson's Warblers are among the most abundant species in the Coast Range Douglas-fir/western hemlock forests (Carey et al. 1991, McGarigal 1993), where densities average about 30 birds/100 ac (40 ha) (Morrison and Meslow 1983b, Carey et al. 1991). They also occur in oak woodlands in the Willamette and Umpqua valleys (Anderson SH 1970, Cross and Simmons 1983, Hagar and Stern 2001). Abundance of Wilson's Warblers in w. Oregon has been positively correlated with cover of hardwood shrubs and trees (Hagar 1992, Bettinger 1996, Chambers 1996). In the Blue Mtns., often sing from alder-dominated islands surrounded by conifers; not found in elderberry during the nesting season (M. Denny p.c.). Well-developed understory vegetation is required for concealing nests, which are built on or near the ground (Leupold 1946, Farner 1952, Stewart 1973, Chambers 1996). Wilson's Warblers predominantly used blackberry

as a nesting substrate in coastal California, possibly because its horizontal runners formed supports for nests, overhanging leaves provided concealment, and dense tangles formed by the thorny vines may deter predators (Stewart 1973). Ferns, usually sword fern, are also used to support nests (Stewart et al. 1977, Chambers 1996). Nests are composed of leaves, twigs, or bark shreds lined with hair, moss, dry grass (Leupold 1946, Stewart 1973).

Wilson's Warblers occur in almost all seral stages of forested habitats in Oregon, from shrub to old-growth (Thomas 1979, Gerig 1992), provided shrubs are present. For example, in the Coast Range, they are usually not found in dense conifer plantations in which the shrub layer is inhibited by continuous conifer canopy. In contrast, young stands in which shrubs have developed following thinning of the conifer overstory do provide habitat (Hagar et al. 1996).

These birds may be more abundant in riparian zones than in adjacent upslope habitats in regions where cover of shrubs and deciduous vegetation is concentrated next to streams or other wet areas. For example, they are often associated with willow thickets along mountain streams and wet mountain meadows (McAllister and Marshall 1945, Farner 1952, Stewart et al. 1977). However, in a study in the Coast Range, McGarigal and McComb (1992) found abundance of Wilson's Warblers to be similar in streamside and upslope habitats, probably because shrub cover did not differ between the two habitats.

Wilson's Warblers forage in understory shrubs and trees to within 4.9 ft (1.5 m) of the top of the canopy (Stewart 1973). Stewart et al. (1977) suggested that only the height of the available vegetation limits the height of foraging. Their foraging strategy, which includes hovering, hawking, flycatching, and gleaning from foliage (Bent 1953, Stewart et al. 1977), enables Wilson's Warblers to prey primarily on small winged insects found on the tips and undersurfaces of branches and twigs too small to support the weight of a perched bird. Strongly insectivorous, diet includes spiders, flies, beetles, aphids, wasps, true bugs, and adult and larval moths and butterflies (Beal 1907, Hagar unpubl. data).

**Seasonal Activity and Behavior:** Earliest dates 22 Mar at Grants Pass (Tweit and Heinl 1989), 11 Apr in Lane Co. (Lillie 1998), and 15 Apr in c. Oregon (C. Miller p.c.). Main migration early to late Apr, continuing to late May (Tweit and Heinl 1989). Average first arrival in the Coast Range, Lincoln Co., 17 Apr (range: 4-25 Apr) (Faxon and Bayer 1991). Older males may return to breeding grounds before second-year males (Stewart 1973). Spring migration can involve a staggering number of birds during peaks 25 Apr to 15 May in w. Oregon, and heavy migration is observed in se. Oregon sometimes through the first week of Jun (D.

Fix p.c.). Site fidelity of returning males appears to be high, as they have been observed to defend the same territory in successive years (Stewart 1973, Stewart et al. 1977).

The following information on breeding ecology and behavior is mainly compiled from two detailed studies in California, by Stewart (1973) and Stewart et al. (1977), unless otherwise stated (no such studies have been conducted in Oregon). Pair formation begins about 2 wk after the first males arrive on breeding grounds. Territories 0.5-3.2 ac (0.2-1.3 ha; ave.= 1.3 ac [0.54ha]) in coastal California (Stewart 1973); home ranges larger. Territories 1.7-4.9 ac (0.7-2.0 ha; ave.= 3.0 ac [1.2 ha]) in Sierra Nevada (Stewart et al. 1977). Polygyny has been reported for a population in the Sierra Nevada, California, but typically monogamous. Pair bonds may exceed 1 yr.

Nest building completed in 5 days; first egg laid 2-3 days later. One egg/day laid until clutch is complete. In w. U.S., clutch sizes average 4-5, range 2-7. Incubation begins after last egg is laid, and lasts 12-13 days. In the s. Willamette Valley, breeding and nesting activity reported 30 May to 24 Jul (Gullion 1951). Incubation began 12 Jun at nest near Portland (Griffee and Rapraeger 1937). In the high Cascades, nests with eggs have been observed as late as 1 Jul at Crater L. NP (Farner 1952) and 20 Jul on Mt. Hood (Leupold 1946), > 4,000 ft (1,219 m) elevation. Nestlings present 13 May-9 Jul (n=2) (OBBA). Nest with young was observed 8 Jul at 6,000 ft (1,829 m) in Crater L. NP (Farner 1952). Fledglings observed 25 May-17 Jul (n=7) (OBBA).

Males begin participating in feeding young several days after eggs hatch. Stewart (1973) observed females making more trips to feed the young (41/hr) than males, but males removed 70% of fecal sacs from nest. Young leave the nest 8-10 days after hatching and feed mostly on their own by about 32 days, at which time they begin to leave their parents' territory. At 39-40 days old, brown juvenal feathers are replaced with yellow. Second clutches after successful first broods may be attempted but are uncommon, and only sometimes successful.

After breeding or attempted breeding, territoriality begins to wane and adults begin wandering (Stewart 1973). Dispersal and migration occurs from late Jul to early Oct. The average date of latest sighting 1973-90 in the Lincoln Co. Coast Range was 16 Sep (range 2-27 Sep) (Faxon and Bayer 1991). Other late sightings include 25 Oct in the s. Willamette Valley (Gullion 1951) and 17 Nov at Summer L. (C. Miller p.c.). A few birds have wintered.

**Detection:** Most frequently detected by song or call. The bright plumage and boisterous song of male Wilson's Warblers make them more easily detected than the less conspicuous females. The song of a nearby Wilson's Warbler is loud and distinct enough to be heard over road, engine, and stream noise (D. Irons p.c., *MGH*).

**Population Status and Conservation:** Populations have remained relatively stable, with no significant decreases or increases in Oregon over the past 35 yr (Sauer et al. 1999). Throughout the w. U.S., Wilson's Warblers are common cowbird hosts. In Oregon, cowbird parasitism may be a more serious threat east of the Cascades, where the best habitat for Wilson's Warblers may be in riparian zones, which are frequently subjected to cattle grazing. However, populations in w. Oregon also experience nest parasitism, as evidenced by observations of adult Wilson's Warblers feeding fledgling cowbirds in Lincoln Co. (Faxon and Bayer 1991).

Forest management practices that affect the abundance and cover of shrubs may affect the population status of Wilson's Warblers. For example, the use of herbicide or manual vegetation control to reduce competition of broadleaf shrubs, such as vine maple, with commercially valuable conifers is likely to affect the availability of habitat for Wilson's Warblers (Morrison and Meslow 1983b). Chambers (1996) reported that Wilson's Warblers were associated with mature forest, and that they decreased in abundance following clearcut and two-story harvests. Abundance was unaffected by small patch harvests (removal of one-third of stand volume in 0.5-ac [0.2-ha] circular patches) in Chambers' (1996) study. Hagar (1999a) found that Wilson's Warbler abundance did not differ between logged and unlogged riparian areas in the Oregon Coast Range, but did increase with riparian buffer width.—*Joan C. Hagar*

## Canada Warbler *Wilsonia canadensis*

This warbler breeds from se. Yukon and e. British Columbia across Canada to the e. coast and south to n. Georgia. It winters in n. S. America. It is regular in California, especially in fall. It is casual in the Northwest. Individuals were photographed at Malheur NWR HQ, Harney Co., 25 Sep to 2 Oct 1982 (Watson 1989), 2-4 Sep 1988 (Anderson 1989b), and 8 Sep 2001 (Sullivan 2002). One was observed there 9 Sep 1998 (OBRC). Another was photographed at Seaside, Clatsop Co., 29 Oct to 1 Nov 1989 (OBRC); one struck a window at Gold Hill, Jackson Co., 17 Sep 1990 (Fix 1991, spec. SOU, Ashland; Browning and Cross 1999); and one was photographed near Mt. Tabor Park in Portland, Multnomah Co., 24-25 Jun 1996 (Johnson 1997a). Monotypic (AOU 1957).—*Harry B. Nehls*

## Yellow-breasted Chat *Icteria virens*

"The Chat's coming in the spring is like the arrival of a brass band," says Bailey (1924). Male chats are loud, continuous singers, sometimes heard through the night. Chats inhabit lowland tangles and thickets along rivers and floodplains. This is the largest of N. American warblers, with a heavy black bill, and olive-green to olive-gray upperparts, including the long tail. The throat and breast are bright yellow, while belly and undertail coverts are white. The lores are blackish, and the cheeks are olive-gray with white stripes above eye and under the lores. The female's upperparts, lores, and bill are grayer.

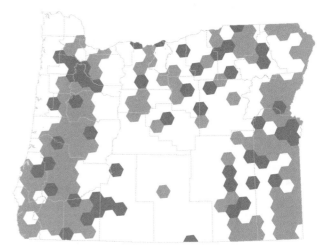

**General Distribution:** Breeds from s. British Columbia eastward to s. Saskatchewan, w. and c. N. Dakota, s. Minnesota eastward to c. New York south to sc. Baja California, on Pacific slope to s. Tamaulipas, and to the Gulf coast and n. Florida. Winters from s. Baja California, s. Sinaloa, s. Texas, s. Louisiana, and s. Florida south through M. America to W. Panama. Two subspecies in N. America but *L. v. longicauda* sometimes recognized; provisionally *I. v. auricollis* breeding in Oregon (Browning 2002). Additional study needed.

**Oregon Distribution:** In w. Oregon, the chat is an uncommon to common summer resident of interior Rogue Valley (Browning 1975a, Gilligan et al. 1994, *DPV*), generally below 1,800 ft (549 m), occasionally to 2,100 ft (640 m) elevation (*DPV*). It is locally uncommon summer resident in the interior Umpqua Valley (Hunter et al. 1998) east to Glide (D. Fix p.c.). In the Willamette Valley it is a locally rare to uncommon summer resident (Gilligan et al. 1994), and rare east to Oakridge (*MGH*), generally below 1,500 ft (457 m) (B. Altman p.c.). Numbers decrease northward to the Columbia R. Rare to uncommon local summer resident in coastal river valleys south of Coos R. (Dillingham 1994, Brown et al. 1996, Contreras 1998), and a rare transient or visitor (possible summer resident) northward (Sawyer and Hunter 1988, Summers and Miller 1993, Siuslaw NF undated) to the Columbia R. estuary (Patterson 1998b). Three verified winter records pre-2000 (Gilligan et al. 1994, Contreras 1997b). More recently, a male was banded 7 Dec 2001 in Ashland (Klamath Bird Observatory), and one bird was photographed in Florence from 27 Dec 2001 to 4 Jan 2002 (D. Pettey p.c.).

In e. Oregon, the chat is a rare spring migrant in Klamath Basin (Summers 1993a); possibly nested in 1999 along Klamath R. near the California border (K. Spencer p.c.). Rare (thought to nest) in Hart Mtn. N. Antelope R. (USFWS 1986c). Locally uncommon summer resident in valley riparian areas of Harney and Malheur counties (Littlefield 1990a, Contreras and Kindschy 1996, OBBA, A. McGie p.c.), the Deschutes and John Day R. systems (OBBA); ne. Oregon valleys (Grande Ronde Bird Club 1988, Umatilla NF 1991, ODFW undated checklist[b]); Snake R. Canyon, Imnaha R., Little Sheep Cr. (OBBA); Grande Ronde, Powder, and Burnt R. systems (OBBA); Walla Walla R. and tributaries, Umatilla R.; Butter, Willow, and Rhea Cr. in Morrow Co. (OBBA). Rare in forested regions of Blue Mtns. (Thomas 1979, OBBA). Locally common in se. and ne. Oregon where habitat is excellent.

**Habitat and Diet:** Occupies edges of large, dense thickets in valley riparian areas and swales, floodplain areas adjacent to streams and rivers, and in unmanaged dense leafy vegetation fringing ponds and swamps (Gabrielson and Jewett 1940, Bent 1953). Open-canopy overstory trees are generally present, except in desert riparian situations. In the Rogue Valley and tributary drainages they are present in large thickets of Himalayan blackberry (major component), willow, Oregon ash, black cottonwood, red alder, California grape and reed canarygrass (*DPV*). In the Willamette Valley, chats are typically in riparian zones consisting of Himalayan blackberry, Oregon ash, willow, red-stemmed dogwood, Douglas spiraea, and small deciduous trees 20 to 30 ft (6 to 9 m) tall; cover typically 55% shrub, 35% forbs, 10% trees (B. Altman p.c.). Singing males have been detected in regenerating clearcuts of w. Cascade foothills (elevation 800 ft [244 m] or less) adjacent to the s. Willamette Valley, usually in conjunction with thick, brushy, deciduous vegetation of small-stream riparian areas (K. Bettinger p.c.). On Malheur NWR chats occupy riparian willow and dogwood (Littlefield 1990a). Riparian areas occupied along the Malheur and Owyhee rivers, upper Willow Cr., Succor Cr. and in the Oregon Canyon Mtns. consist of brushy mature willow and mountain alder (Contreras and Kindschy 1996).

Throughout the breeding range, the nest of the Yellow-breasted Chat is a bulky cup, well-hidden in dense vegetation, usually 2-3 ft (0.6-0.9 m), range 1-8 ft (0.3-2.4 m), above ground (Ehrlich et al. 1988, Dunn and Garrett 1997); generally in impregnable blackberry thickets in Rogue Valley (*DPV*). Constructed of dead leaves, grasses, and weeds, bark shreds; lined with finer material. No recent nest descriptions available for Oregon.

The Oregon diet has not been documented. Diet generally consists primarily of insects: 98% in spring, 65% in summer (Martin et al. 1951). Fall diet includes up to 50% fruit and berries (Kaufman 1996). Insects include ants, bees, and wasps; beetles and weevils; caterpillars, grasshoppers, mayflies, true bugs, and spiders (Bent 1953, Martin et al. 1951). Plant matter consists of fruits, including Pacific madrone, thimbleberry, sumac, dogwood, nightshade (Pacific region) (Martin et al. 1951); berries of many plants and wild grape (Bent 1953, Dunn and Garrett 1997); and a high percentage of Himalayan blackberries in the Rogue Valley (*DPV*).

**Seasonal Activity and Behavior:** Chats arrive in w. Oregon from late Apr to early May; east of the Cascades, from early to mid-May. Early arrival dates include 19 Apr 1989 in the Rogue Valley (*DPV*); 24 Mar 1990 along Bear Cr. south of Prineville Res. (Anderson DA 1990b); 5 Apr 1990 on Hunter Cr., s. Curry Co. (Fix 1990c); 5-12 May at Malheur NWR (Littlefield 1990a); 4 Apr 1997 in the c. Willamette Valley (Plissner 1997); and 21 Apr 1997 in the Applegate Valley (J. Van Hulzen p.c.). A migrant was observed at Fields, Harney Co., on 22 May 1997 (Maitreya p.c.). Chats sing upon arrival. Their song is long and complex, including a series of cackles, rattles, whistles, mews, and squeals. They perform a bizarre display flight. While singing, the chat flies vertically, or horizontally, with slow wing-beats (exposing yellow underwing coverts), legs dangling, while pumping its tail and holding its head high.

Birds recaptured 2-3 yr after banding (five males, one female) in the c. Rogue Valley indicate breeding-site fidelity (*DPV*). Nest building has been observed along the Applegate R. 28 May 1997 (J. Van Hulzen p.c.) and along the Owyhee R. 25 Jun 1998 (OBBA). Chats were observed carrying food on 8 Jun 1996 and 21 Jun 1997 near Powder R. (OBBA), and 13 Jun 1995 near the Applegate R. (J. Van Hulzen p.c.). A nest with young was observed 10 Jul 1998 on the N. Fork John Day R. (OBBA). A local fledgling was captured 6 Jul 1999 near the Applegate R. (*DPV*), and independent juveniles were captured 21 Jul 1997 and 10 Aug 1997 (*DPV*). Dispersing juveniles (and/ or postbreeding adults?) often give a short, mewing catbird-like call (*DPV*). Late dates include 30 Sep 1940 in the s. Willamette Valley (Gullion 1951), 23 Sep 1990 at the s. jetty of the Columbia R. (Fix 1991); 25 Sep 1990 at the mouth of the "D" R. near Lincoln City (Fix 1991); and 22 Sep 1998 and 26 Sep 2000 (captured juvenile) in the c. Rogue Valley (*DPV*).

**Detection:** In breeding areas, the chat's loud continuous song is easily heard until young have fledged, after which only occasional calls are heard. Not easily seen as the birds are shy and skulking, generally staying concealed in thickets, except during singing and display flights.

**Population Status and Conservation:** Yellow-breasted Chats were described as common summer residents in the Columbia R. bottom in the early 20th century (Jewett and Gabrielson 1929). Gabrielson and Jewett (1940) indicated the species was a "common" breeder throughout state (except coast), including the Willamette Valley (Gullion 1951). No historic density data. Thirty birds (in pairs) were detected along the Rogue R. behind Gold Ray Dam during a 2-mi (3.2-km) float trip on 11 Jul 1973 (Crowell and Nehls 1973c). Rates of 8-9 birds/mi (5-5.5 birds/km) were recorded between Joseph and Imnaha (20 mi [32.2 km] length of road) during a 1980 breeding season survey (Rogers 1980d). Willamette Valley territories (n=21) averaged 2.9 ac (1.2 ha), and ranged 1.6-4.7 ac (0.6-1.9 ha). Approximately 100 singing males were estimated in the Willamette Valley during 1999-2000; the majority were at E. E. Wilson W.A. and Fern Ridge Res. (20-25 pairs each) (B. Altman p.c.).

The greatest threat to chat populations is loss or modification (e.g., undergrowth removal, reduced width) of river riparian and floodplain habitat, particularly east of the Cascades. In the Willamette Valley, chat habitat is typically reduced during urban and industrial development, as well as during cover removal in farming areas. In the Willamette Valley, population declines occurred prior to the 1970s, but cannot be quantified (*DBM*). Even since the 1970s, Willamette Valley populations demonstrate a long-term (but statistically non-significant) decline from 1970s to early 1990s (Altman 2000a). Statewide BBS data 1980-98 show an increasing (but statistically non-significant) breeding season trend (2.0%/yr).—*Dennis P. Vroman*

## Family Thraupidae

**Summer Tanager** *Piranga rubra*
This tanager breeds from Nebraska to New Jersey, south through the se. U.S., and from se. California to the Gulf coast. It winters in M. and S. America. It is regular in s. California, but rare and irregular in n. California and Oregon. There are 10 Oregon records between mid-May and mid-Jun, mostly from Harney Co. Outside this period a female was observed at Coos Head, Coos Co., 10 Nov 1981 (OBRC); a male was observed at P Ranch, Harney Co., 30 Sep 1988 (Littlefield 1990a) and 20-24 Sep 2000 (Sullivan 2001a); at Cedar Mill, Washington Co., 10 Jan through 4 Apr 2001 (OBRC);

Portland 7 May 2001 (Lillie 2001); and Coos Bay 27 Jun 2001 (Korpi 2001b). A subadult male was photographed at Bend 17-25 Nov 2001 (Sullivan 2002). Individuals were at Beaverton 28 Sep 2001, and at Portland 13 Oct 2001 (Contreras 2002b). Subspecies unknown.—*Harry B. Nehls*

## Scarlet Tanager *Piranga olivacea*

The Scarlet Tanager breeds from s. Manitoba to Quebec and New Brunswick south to n. Alabama and Georgia. It winters in C. and S. America. It is occasional in s. California with sporadic records elsewhere in the West. An adult male was photographed at Malheur NWR HQ, Harney Co., 31 May 1979 (Littlefield et al. 1985); an adult male was banded and photographed at Hart Mt., Lake Co., 14 Jun 1979 (Delevoryas 1980, Roberson 1980); an adult male was photographed along Trout Cr., Harney Co., 28 May 1980 (OBRC); and a female was photographed at Pike Cr., Harney Co., 31 May 1987 (Anderson 1987f). A first fall male was photographed near Brookings 7-10 Dec 2001 (OBRC). Monotypic (AOU 1957).—*Harry B. Nehls*

## Western Tanager *Piranga ludoviciana*

The bright yellow, red, and black plumage of the male Western Tanager, so conspicuous in open situations, is very obscure in forested areas where it tends to blend into the shaded foliage. The species perhaps is best known in migration when it visits city parks, orchards, and other open urban and suburban areas. It is attracted to birdbaths but seldom to bird feeders.

**General Distribution:** Breeds se. Alaska and nw. Saskatchewan south to s. California and Texas. Winters s. Mexico and M. America, casually north to s. British Columbia and Idaho. An adult banded on the Deschutes NF 25 May 1978 was recovered on the Pacific Slope of Guatemala 11 Nov 1978 (BBL). Monotypic (Browning 1978).

**Oregon Distribution:** Widespread summer resident throughout virtually all conifer forests, especially Douglas-fir and ponderosa pine (Bent 1958, Smith et al. 1997, Hudon 1999). In the w. Cascades, more abundant in Rogue and Umpqua basins than farther north (Gilbert and Allwine 1991). Does not breed in juniper woodlands (Gilligan et al. 1994, *HBN*). Rare in summer in high-elevation aspen woodlands, where breeding has not been confirmed (Marshall 1987). Nonbreeding birds often observed outside breeding areas during mid-summer (Small 1994, BBS).

Common to abundant migrant that may occur anywhere in the state from alpine meadows, sagebrush flats, junipers, and lowland deciduous groves to urban and suburban neighborhoods (Gabrielson and Jewett

1940, Farner 1952, Littlefield 1990a). Casual in winter in w. Oregon interior valleys (Crowell and Nehls 1974a, 1975b, 1976b) and on the s. coast (*ALC*).

**Habitat and Diet:** Breeds in open coniferous forests and mixed coniferous and deciduous woodlands, primarily in mountains (Brown 1985, Hudon 1999). In the w. Cascades, did not show association with forest stand age (Gilbert and Allwine 1991, Bettinger 1996); associated with young forests in s. Coast Range (Carey et al. 1991). Dense, poorly lighted forests are avoided or sparsely occupied, and at other extreme, woodlands are avoided in which trees are so far apart as to necessitate prolonged exposure in flight and high isolation of ground cover and leaf canopy (Grinnell and Miller 1944). In dense forests most common where forest canopy is broken by snags, natural openings, burns, or clearcuts (Jewett et al. 1953, Hansen et al. 1995, Hagar et al. 1996, Smith et al. 1997).

Nest usually in conifer, rarely deciduous trees, at varying heights of 8-60 ft (2.4-18.3 m), usually well out on a branch, often at the fork of a horizontal limb (Baicich and Harrison 1997). The nest is constructed of twigs, rootlets, moss, and coarse grass, lined generally with fine rootlets, occasionally with horse or cow hair (Jewett et al. 1953).

An opportunistic forager of insects, primarily wasps, ants, beetles, and wood borers (Beal 1907, Jewett et al. 1953, Hudon 1999). Spends most time in canopy in trees and shrubs; also occasionally feeds on ground (Oberholser 1974). Seeks insects mostly among larger twigs and branch masses, as well as in air and foliage by flycatching (Grinnell and Miller 1944). Also takes fruits and berries when available (Beal 1907, Hudon 1999).

**Seasonal Activity and Behavior:** Conspicuous spring migrant. Usually found singly or in small groups but occasionally performs spectacular movements (Gabrielson and Jewett 1940, Bent 1958, Hudon 1999, Lillie 1999). Earliest records are in mid-Mar with

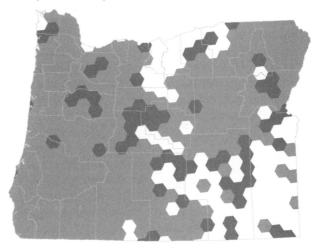

peak numbers west of the Cascades late Apr through May (Gabrielson and Jewett 1940, Lillie 1999). Peak movements east of the Cascades early May to early Jun, latest at Malheur NWR 23 Jun 1966 (Littlefield 1990a).

Monogamous. One brood per season. Female builds nest and incubates. Usual clutch four eggs. Both parents care for young. Incubation period 13 days, young fledge 10-11 days (Baicich and Harrison 1997). Nests primarily in Jun. Bowles (1902) gave outside dates 4-28 Jun. Patterson gave 13 May to 27 Jun for s. Cascades (Gabrielson and Jewett 1940). Griffee and Rapraeger (1937) gave 10 Jul and 18 Jul for two late Portland nests. More recently, nest building observed 2-23 Jun (n=7); nests with eggs 26 May to 6 Jul (n=7); nests with young 8 Jun to 20 Jul (n=11); adults carrying food (likely to nestlings) 11 Jun to 26 Jul (n=27); fledglings mostly early to mid-Jul (n=18) (OBBA). Young dependent on parents for about 2 wk after fledging (Hudon 1999).

Fall movements are inconspicuous involving individuals or small groups passing silently through the trees. Main movement takes place mid-Jul to mid-Sep with peak in late Aug and early Sep. Straggling individuals through Oct, rarely Nov (Fix 1985f, Littlefield 1990a, Gilligan et al. 1994).

**Detection:** Common and easily identified but tends to remain out of view, often first located by distinctive *pit-ick* call notes. Song sometimes confused with American Robin, Cassin's Vireo, or Black-headed Grosbeak.

**Population Status and Conservation:** Oregon population remains steady with significant increases in recent years in ne. Oregon (BBS). Populations unevenly distributed throughout forests in response to preferred canopy cover and successional stage of the forest (Anthony et al. 1996, Hudon 1999). In the conifer forest on the Siuslaw NF, Mannan (1977) found 3-48 birds/100 ac (40 ha); in the grand fir forest on the Wallowa-Whitman NF there were 8-13 pairs/100ac (40 ha) Mannan (1982). There appear to be no conservation problems at this time.—*Harry B. Nehls*

## Family Emberizidae

### Green-tailed Towhee *Pipilo chlorurus*

A large and colorful member of the sparrow family, the Green-tailed Towhee is perhaps more recognizable by its eye-catching chestnut crown than by its less intense green-gray back and olive tail. Its adult plumage is distinctive, and with its slim body and long tail it is unlikely to be confused with most other sparrows. As a ground forager, it spends most of its time on the ground or in thick cover, scratching about industriously

in the leaf litter, and it may go unnoticed. But its catlike mewing call, which it often gives from a brushy perch, is one of the quintessential sounds of the shrublands of the east slope of the Cascades and Great Basin.

**General Distribution:** Breeds from c. Oregon south to s. California, and east to sc. Montana, se. Wyoming, c. Colorado, and s. New Mexico. Winters from s. California east to c. Texas, and south through Baja California and c. Mexico. Monotypic (Miller AH 1941).

**Oregon Distribution:** Locally fairly common east of the Cascades in summer (Gilligan et al. 1994). Most common in n. Great Basin, where it is found in nearly all desert mountain ranges (Marshall 1987, Littlefield 1990a, Gilligan et al. 1994, OBBA). Particularly abundant above 6,500 ft (1,982 m) in Pueblo Mtns. (Marshall 1987). Present but more local in the Blue Mtns. (Littlefield 1990a, OBBA). Rare in nc. Oregon, but known to breed in White R. drainage, and Hood River and Wasco counties (OBBA, Gilligan et al. 1994). Locally uncommon to common on east slope of the Cascades in c. and sc. Oregon, and in the Klamath Basin (McAllister and Marshall 1945, Summers 1982a, Evanich 1990, Reinkensmeyer 2000).

Generally absent west of the Cascade summit, except in parts of sw. Oregon. Locally uncommon on the west slope of the Cascades in Jackson Co. (Browning 1975a). Also in Douglas Co., where a small breeding population is established at Thorn Prairie (Fix 1990a); and breeding has been recorded at Reynolds Ridge (Evanich 1982c). Locally fairly common through higher elevations of the Siskiyou Mtns. (Gabrielson and Jewett 1940, Browning 1975a).

Migrants rarely reported outside of breeding range (Gabrielson and Jewett 1940, Gilligan et al. 1994). Extremely rare in winter: only two records, one from Ashland in Dec 1977 (Browning and Cross 1999), and one from Coos Co. in Dec 1994 (Contreras 1997b).

**Habitat and Diet:** In Oregon and elsewhere in range, prefers vigorous shrub stands with high shrub species diversity (Knopf et al. 1990, *MGH*). Breeding habitat in n. Great Basin includes brushy slopes of desert mountain ranges, where scattered trees such as juniper or aspen intermingle with significant stands of shrubs, particularly mountain-mahogany or snowbrush (Gilligan and Smith 1980, Marshall 1987, Littlefield 1990a). Less abundant in big sagebrush habitat, and most likely to be found where juniper or mountain-mahogany also occur (Contreras and Kindschy 1996). Partial to canyons and rims (Contreras and Kindschy 1996). Also known to use riparian areas in dry open country for nesting (Gilligan et al. 1994). In the Blue Mtns., found mainly in ponderosa pine-sagebrush

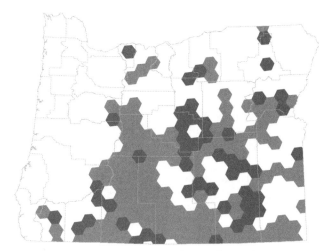

associations in dry, brushy foothills and canyons (Evanich 1992a, Gilligan et al. 1994). In c. Oregon, detected at higher densities in grasslands with 5% shrub cover than in shrub-steppe (Reinkensmeyer 2000), a finding that refutes an earlier characterization of Green-tailed Towhees in the n. Great Basin as sagebrush near-obligates (Braun, Baker et al. 1976). Gashwiler (1977) found a maximum of 4 territories in 100-ac (40.5-ha) plots in juniper in c. Oregon.

Habitats on western slopes of the Cascades resemble structurally the more common habitats of e. Oregon's desert ranges, but are composed of different plant species (Fix 1990a). Use clearcuts on drier sites, with shrub layer including snowbrush, currant, greenleaf manzanita, and/or mountain whitethorn, sometimes with scattered conifer saplings (Fix 1990a). At Crater L. NP, associated with these same shrubs, and to a lesser extent oceanspray or willows (Farner 1952). In the Siskiyous, found in suitable patches within mixed-conifer forest zone, especially near patches of ponderosa pine (Browning 1975a).

Nests in Oregon not well described. Generally located in low bushes close to the ground, woven of grasses and lined with hair, sometimes of porcupine (Gabrielson and Jewett 1940). A nest on ground under a shrub was observed in n. Harney Co. (*MGH*). Also nest in willow (Farner 1952). Outside of Oregon, known nest substrates include juniper, sagebrush, and snowbrush (Dobbs et al. 1999).

Diet in Oregon not known in detail. A study in c. Oregon showed birds eating insects and weed seeds (Eastman 1960). Elsewhere known to eat a wide variety of seeds and insects, including beetles, butterflies, Mormon crickets, grasshoppers, and wasps: also take fruit such as serviceberries, elderberries, and even raspberries (Dobbs et al. 1999).

**Seasonal Activity and Behavior:** Breeding biology not well understood. Spring migrants arrive late Apr to early May (Gabrielson and Jewett 1940, Fix 1990a). At Malheur NWR migrants appear individually, with no apparent peak (Littlefield 1990a).

Nests with eggs found late May to late Jun (OBBA, Marshall 1987). Young in the nest recorded as early as 20 May, but most in Jun to mid-Jul (n=12) (OBBA). Fledglings observed late Jun to early Aug (n=15) (OBBA).

Postbreeding dispersal to higher elevations (as high as timberline) occurs Aug-Sep (Gilligan et al. 1994). Most birds leave late Aug to early Sep; few are seen by mid-Oct (Fix 1990a, Littlefield 1990a, Gilligan et al. 1994).

**Detection:** Often difficult to see, but in the breeding season males located by song (Gabrielson and Jewett 1940). Beware very similar song of Fox Sparrow, which breeds in similar habitat. Distinctive catlike *mew* calls, given during breeding and nonbreeding seasons, also reveal this bird.

**Population Status and Conservation:** Trends difficult to discern. BBS data show marginally significant increases for Oregon 1982-91, but show overall slight decrease (-1.7%/yr) from 1966 to 2000 (Sauer et al. 2001). Interpretations of BBS data vary however, and populations of this species may not be accurately sampled by BBS methods (Dobbs et al. 1999).

Impacts of human-caused alterations to habitat in Oregon are complicated and poorly understood. Across its breeding range, fire suppression in mountain forests may degrade breeding habitat by reducing amount of forest openings with brushy regrowth (Bock and Lynch 1970, Raphael et al. 1987). However, this species may actually benefit from the habitat fragmentation associated with logging, as evidenced by its occurrence in heavily logged and/or clearcut areas in w. Oregon (Browning 1975a, Fix 1990a). Deserves greater attention regarding population trends and conflicting impacts of human activities on its breeding habitat.— *Rachel White Scheuering and Johnny Powell*

## Spotted Towhee *Pipilo maculatus*

This well-known ground-dwelling bird is black above on the male, and brown on the female, including the entire head and upper breast. On both sexes the upperparts are spotted with white on the wings and the long tail. Has rufous sides and a white belly. Breeding subspecies in e. and interior sw. Oregon (*curtatus* and *falcinellus*) have more white spotting than *oregonus* (Gabrielson and Jewett 1940, Greenlaw 1996, Rising 1996). It frequents brushy areas and is common at bird feeders wherever seed is scattered on the ground, but does not feed far from cover. The varied song usually has one to three parts, but geographic distinctions within Oregon are not well known.

**General Distribution:** Breeds from s. Saskatchewan west to s. British Columbia, south through most of the w. U.S. and locally in highlands to Guatemala. Many winter in the breeding range but most withdraw from Canada (except coastal British Columbia) and the n. Great Plains and Rocky Mtns.; also winters in the s. Great Plains, Gulf regions, and Mexican lowlands outside the breeding range (Rising 1996, AOU 1998). Of nine subspecies north of Mexico, three occur in Oregon.

**Oregon Distribution:** Breeds statewide. Winters primarily west of the Cascades and in small numbers in lowland areas east of the Cascades. It is not known which subspecies breeds locally in the high Cascades where *oregonus* and *curtatus* could meet. Most *curtatus* migrate out of Oregon in winter; most *oregonus* and *falcinellus* thought to remain.

*P. m. curtatus* breeds in all ecoregions east of the Cascade summit, being widespread in the e. Cascades and Blue Mtns. and local in the High Lava Plains, Columbia Plateau, and Great Basin (Gabrielson and Jewett 1940, OBBA, specimens listed by Browning [2002]). Breeds locally on Steens Mtn. to at least 7,200 ft (2,400 m) and elsewhere within the southeast part of the state where habitat is available (Hansen 1956, Marshall 1987, Littlefield 1991, OBBA). Birds collected at Crater L. NP in Sep have proven to be this subspecies (Farner 1952) although it is not clear whether these represented upslope movements of nearby breeders or migrants from farther away. A few birds thought to be this subspecies winter in lowland riparian areas (Evanich 1992a, Summers 1993a, CBC) in e. Oregon, and many birds winter from s. California east through Arizona (AOU 1957).

*P. m. oregonus* breeds from the w. Cascades westward (Gabrielson and Jewett 1940, AOU 1957, Browning 2002) except in the Rogue Valley and adjacent foothills. Movements of *oregonus* are poorly known and deserving of additional study. It appears more sedentary than *curtatus*, but in nc. Benton Co. and c. Lincoln Co. the species is distinctly less common in the

lowlands in late summer, and at least in Lincoln Co. is thought to move onto higher ridges in mid-summer (Anderson 1972, Faxon and Bayer 1991) for reasons that are not clear but may relate to the availability of preferred food. *P. m. oregonus* is less common in winter at higher elevations of e. Douglas Co. (Fix 1990a) and in Portland (Jewett and Gabrielson 1929, *DBM*). There is evidence of some southward movement of *oregonus*, as Grinnell and Miller (1944) mention winter specimens of *oregonus* from n. California (where it does not breed) and even one found in Dec on San Clemente I., California (not Santa Catalina, *contra* Greenlaw 1996) in winter. It also occurs occasionally in the Rogue Valley in winter (Gabrielson and Jewett 1940).

The Rogue Valley breeding subspecies is *P. m. falcinellus*, movements of which are essentially unknown. Grinnell and Miller (1944) treat it as resident within its California range, noting postbreeding upslope movements and a retraction to lower elevations in winter. Oregon movements may be similar. Intergrades between *falcinellus* and *oregonus* found at Merlin and Louse Cr. near Grants Pass, Josephine Co. (Browning 2002).

Grinnell and Miller (1944) imply that *P. m. falcifer* occurs to the Oregon line, and Greenlaw (1996) stated that it is a breeding bird in sw. Oregon. However, we are unaware of any breeding season specimens from Oregon and do not recognize this subspecies as a breeder (*MRB*).

**Habitat and Diet:** *P. m. curtatus* breeds mainly in dense shrub cover in riparian situations within wooded areas, with willow thickets commonly used. However, some occur locally where dense riparian growth (e.g., willow, chokecherry, mountain alder) is present in otherwise arid and treeless situations in the Great Basin and Columbia Basin (Marshall 1987, OBBA, *ALC*). Some birds use big sagebrush habitats adjacent to lava flows in c. Malheur Co. (Contreras and Kindschy 1996). In contrast to w. Oregon subspecies, generally absent from early and young-growth forests (Mannan and Meslow 1984). Also generally absent from homogeneous big sage, western juniper, ponderosa pine, and lodgepole pine communities (Gashwiler 1977), being found in more diverse, shrubby patches and riparian areas within these habitats (*MGH*).

*P. m. oregonus* breeds in a variety of settings where dense undergrowth is available, favoring Himalayan blackberry, salal, and willow thickets from the w. Cascades to the coast. It also breeds in urban areas when sufficient cover is available. A study conducted at Pigeon Butte, Benton Co., found 88 birds/100 ac (40 ha) in white oak stands with various understories in late spring and early summer, with 22 birds/100 ac (40 ha) in nearby Douglas-fir stands, and none in western hemlock communities (Anderson 1972). Hagar and

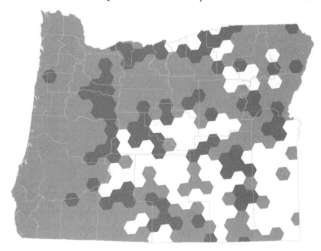

Stern (2001) found towhees in all nine oak woodlands surveyed in the Willamette Valley. Immigrates or increases in density in response to canopy removal in young (40- to 55-yr-old) and mature (80- to 120-yr-old) Douglas-fir forests in the Coast Range during breeding season (Hagar et al. 1996, Chambers et al. 1999) and winter (Chambers and McComb 1997). A study of managed Douglas-fir stands conducted in the w. Cascades of Linn Co. showed that towhees achieved peak numbers in stands 10-14 yr old and were essentially absent once stands reached 20 yr of age and open brushy areas were subsumed (Bettinger 1996). A study in the Coast Range of Polk Co. produced similar results, showing that towhees were most common in open-canopy Douglas-fir forests with significant brushy understory (Gerig 1992). Similarly, Mannan (1977) found towhees in early-growth clearcuts, older partial-cuts, and riparian areas, with a maximum density of 32 birds/100 ac (40 ha) in the early-growth clearcuts.

*P. m. falcinellus* uses the drier shrub types of the Rogue Valley from the valley floor to about 4,000 ft (1,330 m) in the Klamath Mtns. In the valley, found in Himalayan blackberry thickets adjacent to pastureland and in riparian corridors in Himalayan blackberry/willow thickets at edge of cottonwood/ash stands, with reed canarygrass often present. In more upland valley locations such as the Table Rock areas, found in buckbrush, or buckbrush mixed with white manzanita, generally some scattered Oregon white oak and/or madrone, California black oak, and conifers. Other cover used includes: deerbrush, snowbrush,

*Spotted Towhee*

poison oak, mountain-mahogany, whitethorn, scrubby tanoak, and live oak in the valley foothills. In mountainous areas found in early-successional areas, especially brushy clearcuts to 30+ yr of age. Once stands become dense and closed, these towhees are generally absent. Densities are sometimes quite high in brushy serpentine habitats including Jeffrey pine, incense-cedar, Douglas-fir, huckleberry oak, scrubby canyon live-oak, white manzanita, California coffeeberry, some buckbrush, and mountain-mahogany (D. Vroman p.c. for all *falcinellus* habitat). In natural brushfields and shrubby regrowth after timber harvest in Klamath Mtns., 1,900-3,018 ft (579-1,006 m) elevation, densities ranged to 0.51/ac (1.27/ha), typically about 0.2/ac (0.5/ha; D. Vroman unpubl. data).

Nests are placed on the ground or low in shrubs. Although there are few data available for Oregon, nests have been found in Himalayan blackberry (*oregonus* [*ALC*] and *falcinellus* [*MRB*]) and clumps of riparian willow about 10 ft (3 m) tall (*curtatus*) (*ALC*). Nests in other interior parts of the w. U.S. have been "under scrub oak, rose, sage, and mountain-mahogany" (Greenlaw 1996).

Dietary information for Oregon is essentially absent, although the species is observed to eat insects in the breeding season and seeds in winter (*ALC*).

**Seasonal Activity and Behavior:** Some northward movement (presumably of *curtatus*) is noted in the Klamath Basin in mid-Feb, with the bulk of movement beginning in early Mar (Summers 1993a). Average spring arrival at Malheur NWR is 4 Mar, with peak of passage 15 Mar-5 Apr and stragglers through May. A bird banded in Monterey Co., California, on 22 Feb 1956 was found in Baker Co., Oregon, on 14 Apr 1961 (Greenlaw 1996). Breeding season data for birds in the range of *P. m. curtatus* are very limited except for recent OBBA data, which found young in the nest 31 May to 30 Jul (n=9) and fledglings 23 Jun to 8 Aug (n=18), most in mid- to late Jul. Fall peak of passage is from 10 Sep through 5 Oct at Malheur (Littlefield 1990a) and most birds gone from the Klamath Basin by late Oct (Summers 1993a).

In *oregonus*, Gullion (1951) noted breeding activity (defined as nest building through "the latest date for fledglings incompletely feathered or being cared for by their parents") from 25 Apr to 23 Jul in c. Lane Co. Griffee and Rapraeger (1937) indicate that in the Portland area *oregonus* commences incubating on dates from 22 Apr to 2 Jul, with the peak season during which at least 50% of known pairs are incubating 10 May to 3 Jun. OBBA data for the range of *oregonus* show a range of 25 May to 25 Jul for nests with young (n=5) and 19 May to 13 Aug for fledglings (n=18).

Comparable data for birds in the range of *falcinellus* are limited, but OBBA found fledglings from 13 Jun to 18 Aug (n=5).

**Detection:** This species is easily found most of the time throughout its range because of its distinctive sounds and willingness to perch in the open, but becomes somewhat more secretive during the breeding season. It is easy to observe at feeders in winter. E. Oregon *curtatus* are notably more secretive than western subspecies, tending to skulk in dense riparian growth.

**Population Status and Conservation:** This species shows a rate of decrease of 1.0% on Oregon BBS routes 1966-86, a minor shift but perhaps notable because Washington and Idaho (which share sizable populations of the same breeding subspecies with Oregon) both showed increases (4.4% and 4.3%, respectively) for the same time period (BBS).

CBC trend data 1959-88 show a 1.8% rate of increase. Note that BBS and CBC data are not necessarily of the same populations. Winter population size varies from year to year. An analysis of trends on the Coos Bay CBC shows that the species' winter population varies considerably from year to year. From 1973 to 1997 Coos Bay ranged 6-106 with a median of 35. Birds/100 party hours ranged 5.8-154.6, and even birds/100 foot hours (arguably the best measure for towhees) shows a range of 11.6 to 382.1.

This species is likely to be harmed by excessive grazing in riparian areas where such areas represent the bulk of available habitat (as in most of e. Oregon) but probably derive at least short-term benefits from logging practices that provide large areas of brushy habitats during regeneration (Greenlaw 1996). It is not considered threatened in Oregon but is certainly sensitive to land-use patterns that destroy dense shrub forms and adjacent ground cover, especially in riparian areas. Expanding development into brushy areas in the western interior valleys and the trend toward "clean farming" devoid of hedgerows will limit the range of this species.—*Alan L. Contreras*

## California Towhee *Pipilo crissalis*

The California Towhee can be found in chaparral habitats of s. Oregon, quietly flitting in and out of the brush in search of seeds. It is a plain brown bird with a rusty throat patch and undertail coverts, noticeably larger than the Spotted Towhee. Its long slender tail is also a useful identifying feature. Sexes cannot be told apart in the field, but juveniles can be distinguished by the extensive streaking and spotting of the underparts.

**General Distribution:** Found in low-elevation chaparral from Oregon south to Baja California.

Formerly conspecific with the Canyon Towhee, and called the Brown Towhee. Eight subspecies; *P. c. bullatus* occurs in Oregon (Browning 2002).

**Oregon Distribution:** The California Towhee is an uncommon to fairly common permanent resident throughout the Rogue, Applegate, and Illinois valleys. It is an uncommon and very local resident in the Umpqua Valley as far north as Myrtle Cr., and occasional sightings have occurred in and around Roseburg (Shelton 1914, Hunter et al. 1998). In the Klamath Basin it is an uncommon resident on brushy hillsides around Lower Klamath L. and south along the Klamath R. (Grinnell and Behle 1937, Summers 1993a, J. Shelton p.c., K. Spencer p.c.). In summers of 1984-86, five or more pairs were located on Short Lake Mtn., just north of Bonanza, Klamath Co., and may still be present there (M. Denny p.c.). This towhee occurs from elevations of 1,300 ft (396 m) in the Applegate Valley to over 5,000 ft (1524 m) in the Klamath Basin. Woodcock (1902) reported two birds in Corvallis, a singing male was reported in n. Lincoln Co. near Otis (Hand 1960), and one was reported at Mt. Pisgah, Lane Co. (Tice 1999a), but the origin and/or validity of these records are suspect.

**Habitat and Diet:** In the Rogue, Applegate, and Umpqua valleys, found in oak/chaparral complexes, consisting primarily of scattered groves of scrub oak and Pacific madrone, with an understory of ceanothus, whiteleaf manzanita, and poison oak. Preferred habitat in more arid regions is usually adjacent to riparian habitats of alders, willows, cottonwoods, and introduced Himalayan blackberry (Davis 1951, LaBerteaux 1989, Purcell and Verner 1998), however, in Oregon, preferred habitats often occur on drier flats or on hillsides (D. Fix p.c.). In the Klamath Basin this towhee is found in the juniper/sagebrush/bitterbrush steppe. California Towhees are ground foragers, always occurring near stands of woody vegetation, searching in leaf litter or, preferably, adjacent grasses. Nests are placed primarily in thick brush and lower branches of

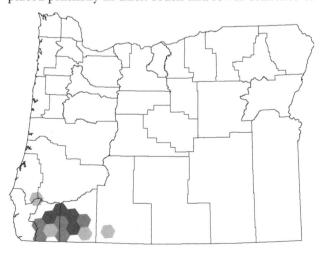

trees near or in riparian areas, typically 2-11 ft (0.6-3.4 m) above ground (LaBerteaux 1989, D. Vroman unpubl. data). Tends to forage in shaded areas during active periods to minimize heat stress and avoids activity at midday. Grass and weed seeds compose the majority (> 51%) of their general diet (Beal 1910) throughout the year; they usually locate them by pecking and gleaning the soil surface (LaBerteaux 1989) or by scratching through leaf litter with both feet together (Marshall 1960). Insects constitute an important part of their diet in the spring and early summer, when protein and fat are especially necessary. Fruits are also utilized when available (Davis 1957).

**Seasonal Activity and Behavior:** Usually paired for life on a permanent territory of about 2-10 ac (1-4 ha) (Marshall 1964, Bent 1968). Extremely sedentary and nonmigratory (Marshall 1964, Purcell and Verner 1998). During breeding season, beginning early Mar (D. Vroman unpubl. data), the unpaired male's song announces that it has a territory and seeks a mate. Once paired, it stops singing abruptly. Male emits piercing chips as it patrols the periphery of its territory. Quaintance (1938) believed loss of song as a function of territorial defense may be due to behavior of patrolling, where in open habitat sight of the owner is the primary warning. Mates usually forage together year-round, giving a locative note when separated and then engaging in a pair-reinforcement squeal duet (Davis 1957). This duet is reduced the longer the pair has been together, eventually to a light perfunctory rendition (Marshall 1964). In s. California nest initiation corresponded to the time at which half the perennial plants had foliated. Nesting dates have not been studied in Oregon, but D. Vroman (unpubl. data) identified two active nests 11 May and 27 Jul. Fledglings observed mid-Jun to mid-Jul (n=3) (OBBA). LaBerteaux (1989) found clutch sizes generally 2-4 and if fledging was successful, only one out of 28 pairs studied attempted a second brood. Adults continued to feed their young for at least 4 wk after fledging. Oregon subspecies reproductive biology is likely to be similar but has not been studied. Williams and Koenig (1980) found them to be diurnal drinkers, flying primarily at dawn and evening to a water source.

**Detection:** Relatively hard to find because of small numbers and dense habitat; often first detected by calls or song. Look in ceanothus adjacent to riparian areas, especially in Jackson Co. surrounding Tables Rocks and along the Rogue R. from Lost Cr. Res. to Gold Ray Dam, and in Josephine Co. at Fish Hatchery Park (J. Shelton p.c., D. Vroman p.c.). Frequents bird feeders if they are located in their territory.

**Population Status and Conservation:** Population status in Oregon unknown. Habitat loss or degradation from development of riparian and adjacent hillsides for suburbanization and agriculture may have reduced breeding habitat as has occurred in California (LaBerteaux 1989). Populations formerly present in the vicinity of Roseburg (Shelton 1914) and in the Umpqua Valley in general (Gabrielson and Jewett 1940) are no longer present except very locally in the southern part of Douglas Co. (Hunter et al. 1998). Hunter et al. (1998) hypothesized a drastic change in shrub abundance and shrubland composition on foothills and riparian areas as important in the change. Domestic and feral cat predation is probably significant. Conversely, Davis (1951) and Ehrlich et al. (1988) found certain California populations have expanded their range due to grazing, logging, farming, and suburbanization that increased edge habitat, while Purcell and Verner (1998) found that grazing also appeared to reduce the number of suitable understory nest sites and forced nesting in the more complex structure of multiple-stemmed trees, thus reducing the effects of density-dependent predation by the Western Scrub-Jay. Medford CBCs 1966-99 indicate a relatively stable population. Of 13 yr sampled, 12 birds were seen in both 1967 and 1999, with a high of 43 in 1983 and a low of 8 in 1988. Average count was 17. No conservation problems have been reported, possibly because this species is uncommon and unobtrusive, and hence often overlooked.—*Guy Tutland*

## American Tree Sparrow *Spizella arborea*

This winter visitor is a study in gray and tan, with a small dark spot on an otherwise gray breast, dull rufous stripes on the side of the head and crown, and brown wings with distinct white stripes. Tree Sparrows visit Oregon only in winter, mainly in lowlands within the Blue Mtn. and Owyhee Upland regions, with a few farther west in some years. They frequent willow clumps in grassy areas and occur occasionally at feeders.

**General Distribution:** Breeds from w. Alaska to ne. Canada, and south to nc. British Columbia and the northern edge of the Prairie Provinces, n. Ontario, and n. Quebec. Winters from the southern edge of Canada south and east to N. Carolina, n. Texas, n. Arizona, the Great Basin and e. Washington. Generally does not winter west of the Cascade-Sierra divide. Two subspecies; *S. a. ochracea* occurs in Oregon (Gabrielson and Jewett 1940, AOU 1957).

**Oregon Distribution:** Winters annually in valleys within and near the Blue Mtns. from n. Morrow Co. south and east to n. Malheur Co. (Evanich 1992a, Gilligan et al. 1994, Contreras 1996a). Most common in Wallowa, Union, and Baker counties (M. Denny p.c.). Not annual but often reported south to Malheur NWR (Littlefield 1990a). Occasional elsewhere east of the Cascades; rare west of the Cascades, where single birds appear irregularly, with reports south to Curry Co. and Ashland (Browning 1975a, Contreras 1998, T. Rodenkirk p.c.). One was banded near Corvallis in Nov 1962 (Strauch 1963).

**Habitat and Diet:** Strongly associated with willow-grown draws near water in open country; also found in hedgerows and occasionally in sagebrush and greasewood (Gabrielson and Jewett 1940, Littlefield 1990a). Winter diet (based on studies outside Oregon) consists mainly of seeds but may also include berries, catkins, and occasional insects; sometimes found at feeders (Naugler 1993).

**Seasonal Activity and Behavior:** Earliest arrival 16 Oct 1993 at Umapine, Umatilla Co. (Summers 1994a). Generally arrives in ne. Oregon in late Oct or early Nov (Gilligan et al. 1994) and reaches Malheur NWR in Dec in years when they occur. Littlefield (1990a) notes that there are few records after mid-Feb at Malheur, with 25 Mar the latest record. The latest spring records for Oregon are 17 May 1947 (Gullion 1951) and 15 May 1971 (C. Watson p.c.) in c. Lane Co., 11 May 1985 at Bay City (Fix 1985a) and 6 May 1995 at Cape Meares (Lillie 1995).

American Tree Sparrows tend to work their way along willow riparian areas or fencelines, picking at the ground for seeds and occasionally perching in shrubs and small trees. They often creep longspur-like along the grassy edges of fields, and seldom perch or forage high in trees (*ALC*).

**Detection:** Tree sparrows are relatively hard to find because they are small, quiet, plain, present in small numbers, not common at feeders in Oregon (more so in the e. U.S.) and tend to skulk in somewhat dense habitat. However, a patient observer who works the willow bottoms, particularly in Union, Wallowa, and Baker counties, and listens for the distinctive tinkling call notes of a flock, is likely to be rewarded.

**Population Status and Conservation:** Oregon data are limited. The longest-running CBC in the species' region of consistent occurrence is Baker Valley, where tree sparrows were found on 60% of counts since 1956, with an average of 13.4 and a high of 251 birds. This species has never been considered common in Oregon although in peak years small flocks appear (Gabrielson and Jewett 1940, Littlefield 1990a, CBC).

Activities that may reduce habitat include elimination of or damage to riparian willows by grazing or land management practices. Any practices that remove hedgerows and wetland edges will tend to limit habitat.—*Alan L. Contreras*

## Chipping Sparrow *Spizella passerina*

The Chipping Sparrow is a small slender sparrow that has a distinctive sharp chip note and simple, trilling song. Breeding adults display a chestnut crown, a black eye-stripe, and a crisp white eyebrow. After nesting season both male and female lose their distinctive bright cap for a streaky dull brown head pattern that is similar to other winter sparrows. Its habit of lining its nest with animal hair led to its former nickname "horse hair bird" (Gabrielson and Jewett 1940), though when automobiles took the place of horses the nickname gradually lost its meaning and disappeared from use.

**General Distribution:** Breeds from ec. Alaska southeast through nc. Canada to sw. Newfoundland and south to n. Baja California, s. Nevada, through c. Texas and the Gulf coast to nw. Florida, also south through highlands of Mexico to nc. Nicaragua. Winters from c. California and s. Nevada east through southwest states to Arkansas, Tennessee, and s. New England south through s. Florida, also south throughout Mexico, and through breeding range south of Chiapas. Two to three subspecies occur in the U.S. depending upon authority (Middleton 1998); based on color, specimens of *borophila* and *arizonae* were not separable (*MRB*) and recognition of subspecies was not supported by mtDNA comparisons (Zink and Dittmann 1993). *S. p. arizonae* occurs in Oregon (AOU 1957).

**Oregon Distribution:** Uncommon to common summer resident in open forests and drier woodland edges throughout the state (Gilligan et al. 1994, *MGH*). Especially abundant in the Blue Mtns. of ne. Oregon (Sauer et al. 2001), though it is generally rare there in north-facing wet grand fir sites >5,000 ft (1,524 m) (M. Denny p.c.). It is common in sw. Oregon (OBBA, Hunter et al. 1998), and locally uncommon in the n. Willamette Valley and the s. Coast Range (OBBA). Breeds in scattered locations in the Cascades (Fix 1990a, OBBA), and throughout higher elevations of e. Oregon (OBBA, Littlefield 1990a, Contreras and Kindschy 1996). Noted as rare in the

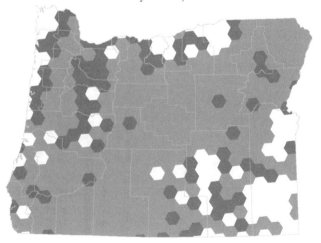

high Pueblos and Oregon Canyon mountains, and on vast sagebrush flats north and east of Basque Station, Malheur Co. (M. Denny p.c.). Generally absent or rare on the coast north of Curry Co. and in densely forested areas of the n. Coast Range (OBBA, Gilligan et al. 1994). Fairly common in migration, when it can appear almost anywhere, though a genuinely rare migrant on much of the coast (D. Fix p.c.). Very rare in winter, most records from the southwest part of the state (Contreras 1997b).

**Habitat and Diet:** In breeding season, prefers open coniferous forests or stands of trees interspersed with grassy spaces or other areas of low foliage suitable for ground foraging (Farner 1952). In the w. Cascades, Chipping Sparrows breed in openings in lodgepole pine forests, and are occasionally observed in grassy, regenerating clearcuts dotted with conifers in the s. Cascades (Fix 1990a). They are generally absent in clearcuts farther north in the w. Cascades and Coast Range (Gilligan et al. 1994, Bettinger 1996). In c. Oregon, they are found in good numbers in juniper, ponderosa pine, and lodgepole pine forests, but are not present in sagebrush communities. Associated with juniper woodlands on Steens Mtn. and in c. Oregon, mixed ponderosa pine forests with grassland edge in the Blue Mtns., and mountain-mahogany stands in extreme e. Oregon (Penderson and Adams 1975, Littlefield 1990a, Contreras and Kindschy 1996, Reinkensmeyer 2000). On the Winema NF in sc. Oregon, the Chipping Sparrow was one of the six most frequently encountered species in lodgepole pine forest, both before and after salvage logging (Arnett et al. 2001). In a study in the Wallowa-Whitman NF, the Chipping Sparrow was more numerous in managed (i.e., thinned) forest than old-growth, presumably because of its preference for open areas for foraging and nesting (Mannan and Meslow 1984). The nest is a neat cup, built of grass and lined with hair or fur (Gabrielson and Jewett 1940).

At Crater L. NP, birds that have formed postbreeding flocks seem to use a broader range of habitats, from treeless pumice flats to fairly dense lodgepole pine stands (Farner 1952). In recent winters small flocks have been found using filbert orchards in the Willamette Valley; it is not clear why this habitat is used (*ALC*).

The diet of this species has not been well studied in Oregon. Gabrielson and Jewett (1940) describe it foraging on the ground collecting insects and seeds to feed young, and a study in c. Oregon revealed its preference for "weed seed" (Eastman 1960). During Apr-Jul in the Blue Mtns., frequently forages on insects, particularly larvae (M. Denny p.c.). Diet studies elsewhere show it feeding primarily on seeds of grasses and other annuals, adding insects and other invertebrates when breeding (Middleton 1998).

**Seasonal Activity and Behavior:** This is one of Oregon's earliest passerine migrants. They begin arriving in w. Oregon in late Mar, though they have been seen as early as 7 Feb (Johnson 1997b). Peak movement occurs mid-Apr in w. Oregon, late Apr in e. Oregon (Irons 1984b, Gilligan et al. 1994). Nest building has been observed mid-May through mid-Jun (n=4) (OBBA); eggs seen in nest as late as 4 Jul, but more typically throughout Jun (n=9), and young in nest have been seen late May through early Jul (n=9) (OBBA). Fledglings have been seen most often mid- to late Jul (n=15), but dates of observations range from early to mid-Jun (n=4) to late Aug (n=2) (OBBA).

Postbreeding birds at Crater L. NP were observed forming flocks beginning in mid-Jul, congregating in open areas and occasionally associating in mixed-species flocks with Mountain Chickadees, Dark-eyed Juncos, Red-breasted Nuthatches, and/or Yellow-rumped Warblers (Farner 1952). High in the Blue Mtns., flocks of 15-20 birds are often observed beginning in early Aug with Vesper Sparrows, Dark-eyed Juncos, Townsend's Warblers, Mountain Bluebirds, and Yellow-rumped Warblers, all feeding around lithosol meadows (M. Denny p.c.). Flocking has also been observed by mid-Jul in the Diamond L. area, Douglas Co., peaking in number before the end of Aug (maximum observed was 30 birds, 18 Aug 1990 [Fix 1990a]). A few birds linger in w. Oregon through the winter, but most are gone by early Oct (Gilligan et al. 1994, Gilligan 1996).

**Detection:** Frequent singing during the breeding season raises detectability (Middleton 1998). Openness of preferred habitat and association with human-associated landscapes make it an accessible species. Outside of breeding season, care should be taken to distinguish from other *Spizella* sparrows.

**Population Status and Conservation:** Despite its familiarity, this species remains under-studied, especially in regard to its breeding biology. Formerly "one of the familiar lawn birds of the valley towns throughout the state" (Gabrielson and Jewett 1940), now quite rare in most Oregon towns (*MGH*). BBS data for Oregon indicate significant declines during 1966-2000, at the rate of -3.9%/yr (Sauer et al. 2001). More specifically, decreases have been reported in the Willamette and Umpqua valleys (Hunter et al. 1998, Hagar and Stern 2001). Chipping Sparrows were once associated with open oak woodlands in the Willamette Valley (Anderson SH 1970), but due to the absence of fire in these habitats, successional advancement has gradually changed open woodlands into closed-canopy habitats, and this species has disappeared from these areas (Hagar and Stern 2001). In other parts of its range, habitat changes have brought on increased risk of cowbird brood parasitism and competition with

House Sparrows and House Finches (Middleton 1998, Ortega and Ortega 2001). These factors may be at play in Oregon as well.—*Rachel White Scheuering*

### Clay-colored Sparrow *Spizella pallida*

This is a sparrow of the dry brushlands. The Clay-colored Sparrow breeds chiefly across the northern prairies from ne. British Columbia east to Michigan and south into Colorado. It winters in the s. U.S. and Mexico. It has expanded its range westward and northward in recent years and is now nesting in small numbers in e. Washington (Roberson 1980, Tweit and Johnson 1994). It was seldom reported west of the Rocky Mtns. prior to 1960. Since that time it has become a regular migrant and wintering bird along the w. coast (Roberson 1980, Knapton 1994).

The first Oregon record was a bird collected at Pleasant Valley, Tillamook Co., 15 Nov. 1953 (spec. no. 11643, OSU). The second was of a singing bird observed along Wildhorse Cr. in the Alvord Basin, Harney Co., 14 Jun 1971 (Kingery 1971). It has since been found to be a regular fall and winter visitant to w. Oregon and an irregular spring and occasional fall visitant to e. Oregon. The majority of records are from mid-Sep through Oct with a few remaining to winter. Spring records have become annual and range from mid-May to mid-Jun. Many of these records are verified by photographs in the files of the OBRC (Watson 1989). An apparent hybrid Clay-colored x Chipping Sparrow was in Eugene, Lane Co., during the winter of 1979-80 (Fix 1988a). Monotypic (AOU 1957).—*Harry B. Nehls*

### Brewer's Sparrow *Spizella breweri*

One of the most nondescript birds found in Oregon, this sparrow makes up for its drab appearance by its extraordinary song. It is by far the most abundant bird breeding in the vast sagebrush expanses of the intermountain West (Rotenberry et al. 1999). The plain brownish upperparts and crown, faint facial markings, and unstreaked whitish breast help distinguish it from other sparrows. Identification challenges are greatest in the late fall and winter when the very similar winter-plumaged Chipping Sparrow and Clay-colored Sparrow are, though rare, the more likely species to be found in Oregon.

**General Distribution:** Two recognized subspecies of Brewer's Sparrow (*S.b. breweri* and *S.b. taverneri*) were originally described as separate species, and some authorities still treat them as such (Sibley and Monroe 1990). *S. b. breweri* breeds from sw. Canada eastward to the west edge of N. Dakota, including Columbia Basin in e. Washington, s. Idaho, se. Alberta, sw. Saskatchewan, and Montana. Its breeding range

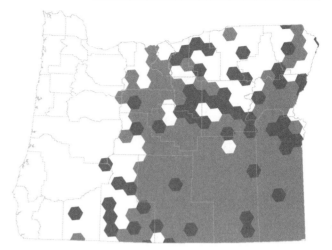

extends southward to s. California, Nevada, n. Arizona and nw. New Mexico, including the west edge of S. Dakota, Oklahoma, and Nebraska. Highest densities occur from se. Oregon to c. Nevada. Winters from the southwest edge of the U.S. to the southern tip of Baja California and c. Mexico (AOU 1998, Rotenberry et al. 1999, Sauer et al. 1999). *S. b. taverneri*, the "Timberline Sparrow," breeds in the mountains above timberline from se. interior Alaska (Doyle 1997), sw. Yukon south to sw. Canada (AOU 1998) and nw. Montana (Walker 2000a), and possibly as far south as n. California (Grinnell et al. 1930). The winter range of *taverneri* is poorly known (AOU 1998). Work on the taxonomy of these forms is in progress (B. Walker p.c.). In Oregon, only *S. b. breweri* is confirmed.

**Oregon Distribution:** The Brewer's Sparrow is an abundant migrant and summer resident east of the Cascades summit, particularly in the southeast quarter of the state among the vast sagebrush communities of the Great Basin shrub-steppe. There is some evidence of local breeding in small numbers in the w. Cascades and in sw. Oregon. Generally a very rare migrant west of the Cascades summit, though can be locally rare to very uncommon in some years (e.g., Fern Ridge Res, Lane Co.). Casual west of the Coast Range where there are only about six records (*CRM*).

Since it was first recorded in 1970, there have been several summer records in old burned-over areas, clearcuts, and other shrub habitat along the west slope of the Cascades (Marshall and Horn 1973, Heinl 1986b, Gilligan et al. 1994) including one documented breeding record: on 1 Jul 1985 a female was photographed on a nest in a clearcut near Emigrant Pass, e. Lane Co. (Heinl 1986b).

Local breeding was also evident at timberline along the summit of the Cascades. Several adult pairs as well as juveniles were found in stunted (variably shrub-sized) mountain hemlock in a low pass just north of Mt. Jefferson in 1992 (Johnson J 1993a, M. Patterson p.c., *ALC*). Because of the odd location and habitat, these birds were thought possibly to be of the

"Timberline" subspecies. However, DNA sequencing of a specimen collected from this area revealed a mitochondrial haplotype consistent with *breweri* (J. Klicka unpubl. data). Sonogram analysis of the songs of the Mt. Jefferson birds and more specimens may be required to clarify the taxonomic status of these birds. Regardless of the status of the Mt. Jefferson population, individuals of the Timberline "subspecies" likely pass through Oregon during their migration in the Pacific Northwest between Canada and Mexico, and should be looked for.

In the Rogue Valley, many Brewer's Sparrows (males, females, juveniles) have been captured in mist-nets at The Nature Conservancy's Whetstone Preserve near Lower Table Rock during Jun and Jul since monitoring began in 1997. A female with an inactive brood patch (i.e., postbreeding) was captured there on 18 Jul 1997. The only recapture was a juvenile captured there on 22 Jul 2000 and recaptured at the same spot 20 days later (Johnson J 1998a, D. Vroman p.c.). This species does not appear to nest there, but uses the area for molting prior to migration (D. Vroman p.c.). Three summer records exist in the Klamath Mtns. of sw. Oregon. A female with an inactive brood patch (likely not breeding there) was captured and banded 12 Jul 1999 at the Horse Cr. MAPS (banding) station, 18 mi (29 km) west of Grants Pass (D. Vroman p.c.). Several birds (including a singing male) were located 7 Jul 2000 at about 6,500-6,800 ft (1,980-2,070 m) elevation in a small patch of sagebrush on a south-facing slope on the high ridge system going west of Mt. Ashland (D. Vroman p.c.), and a singing male (photographed) was found in a clearcut near Happy Camp Sno Park, along Happy Camp Rd. (fairly high elevation) about 10 mi (16 km) south of Cave Junction, 20 Jun 2000 (*CRM*). The status of Brewer's Sparrow at the latter two locations is unknown.

**Habitat and Diet:** Principally breeds in shrublands where the average canopy height is less than 5 ft (1.5 m) (Wiens and Rotenberry 1981). The primary plant association used by the Brewer's Sparrow is big sagebrush; thus there is extensive overlap with the range of Sage Sparrow (Rotenberry et al. 1999). Not limited to sagebrush habitat, however, and utilizes a variety of shrub habitats over a wide elevation range. Other shrub species utilized for breeding in the Great Basin include greasewood, rabbitbrush, and shadscale. Occupies brush patches and thickets such as sagebrush, buckbrush, and mountain whitethorn in the Rogue Valley, buckbrush and sedge in clearcuts, and stunted mountain hemlock in the high mountain sites (Marshall and Horn 1973, Wiens and Rotenberry 1981, M. Patterson p.c., D. Vroman p.c.). Possible nesting pairs were found as high as 6,000 ft (1,850 m) elevation in the Cascades (Gilligan et al. 1994,

M. Patterson p.c.). Nest is placed in thick crowns of sagebrush (H. Nehls p.c.), or low in bush, or in grass clump at base of bush (Rising 1996, B. Walker unpubl. data), and is composed of dry grass and lined with hair (Gabrielson and Jewett 1940). Diet during breeding season consists pri-marily of small insects gleaned from foliage and bark of sagebrush, but may feed on seeds taken from the ground and on insects from other plants or trees (Wiens et al. 1987). Winter diet consists primarily of seeds (Rosenberg et al. 1991).

*Brewer's Sparrow*

E Paulson

**Seasonal Activity and Behavior:** Spring migrants usually arrive from late Apr to early Jun, although in some years a few arrive as early as mid-Apr. Average first arrival date at Malheur NWR is 25 Apr (Littlefield 1990a, Malheur NWR unpubl. data). The earliest in Oregon was a well-described bird 20 Mar 1999 at upper end of Detroit Res. in the w. Cascades in Marion Co. (S. Dowlan p.c.); a report on 8 Mar 1980 did not rule out other *Spizella* sparrows (Watson 1980c). Within the breeding range, the earliest sighting is 2 Apr 1996 at Summer L. W.A. (M. St. Louis p.c.). The date of 23 Mar that Paine (1968) gave as the early arrival date at the Lava Beds National Monument (near the California-Oregon border) without source or citation is questionable. However, Rotenberry et al. (1999) stated that the first migrants arrive in se. Oregon by mid- to late Mar based solely on Paine's date (Rotenberry p.c.).

Males arrive several days before females and establish territories, often tightly packed, ranging 1-6 ac (0.4-2.3 ha) in size (Wiens et al. 1985). Males typically return to territories established in previous years (Petersen and Best 1987, B. Walker unpubl. data). Song prior to pairing is short and individually distinctive, expressed repeatedly. Territorial song is long, consisting of a wide repertoire of variable-pitched buzzes and trills given most vociferously at dawn and during aggressive interactions with other males (Walker 2000b). Both males and females will defend territory by chasing away male competitors.

The onset of nesting activity may vary from year to year by several weeks (Reynolds 1981, Rotenberry et al. 1999). Nest construction begins soon after pair formation in late Apr to early May (Gabrielson and Jewett 1940, Paine 1968, Rotenberry et al. 1999). Paine (1968) gives a range of dates from 18 May to 22 Jul when eggs are laid in Oregon, but laying has been documented as early as 24 Apr in nc. Washington (B. Walker unpubl. data). The Brewer's Sparrow lays eggs 4-6 wk later than the Sage Sparrow and Sage Thrasher where breeding territories overlap (Rich 1980b). Males assist with incubation and brooding of young nestlings (Walker 2000b). Birds hatch after 10-12 days of incubation and fledge 9 days later (Rotenberry et al. 1999). A second brood is sometimes raised and birds will renest if nests are subjected to predation (Rotenberry et al. 1999). Fledging dates range 8 Jun to 16 Aug (Rotenberry et al. 1999, OBBA).

Significant dispersal occurs by mid-Jul and southward migration increases to peak during the last two weeks of Aug. Numbers diminish rapidly during Sep and most leave by mid-Sep. Latest record is 30 Sep 1991 at Summer L., Lake Co. (*CRM*). Reports after Sep are almost nonexistent. One well-documented bird was photographed at "D" R. in Lincoln City on 19 Oct 1999 (P. Pickering p.c.). Two undocumented records from the Umpqua Valley in Douglas Co. are the only winter reports (Hunter et al. 1998).

**Detection:** Detection is best accomplished during the breeding season by recognizing the conspicuous and unique vocalization. Abundance in appropriate habitat coupled with habit of perching on top of a bush while singing help ensure detection. However, wary when approached with a tendency to run on the ground and take flight at a distance. Brooding females remain stationary on nest unless approached to within 1-2 ft (30-60 cm) (Paine 1968). Individuals can be difficult to locate after pair-bond formation due to decreased vocalization (Best and Peterson 1985, Walker 2000b). Away from breeding season and habitat, detection and identification present considerably more difficulty due to similarity to Clay-colored Sparrow and to immature and winter adult Chipping Sparrow (Pyle and Howell 1996). Instances of hybridization with Clay-colored and Chipping Sparrows multiply the challenge (Rising 1996, B. Walker p.c.).

**Population Status and Conservation:** Abundant in primary breeding range, on average composing 55% of all birds in shrub-steppe bird communities (Rotenberry and Wiens 1980). Although habitat preferences are similar to those of Sage Sparrows and Sage Thrashers, no competition is evident for nest sites among these species (Rich 1980b). In se. Oregon and c. Nevada

where densities are highest, 30-40 individuals are normally encountered on BBS routes. However, at least two counts in Oregon average greater than 250 individuals. Although common to abundant in its range, BBS data have shown a significant population decline of about 3.1% per year 1966-98, and in Oregon a decline of 2.6% per year (not statistically significant) during the same time interval (Sauer et al. 1999). The reason for decline is unknown, but fragmentation and loss of habitat from agriculture, cattle grazing, and invasion of exotic annual plants (especially cheatgrass) has been implicated (Braun, Baker et al. 1976, Wiens and Rotenberry 1985, Rotenberry and Wiens 1998). In the Columbia R. basin nearly 60% of native shrub-steppe has been lost to agriculture (Dobler et al. 1996). The status of *S. b. taverneri* in Oregon is unknown.—*Craig R. Miller*

## Black-chinned Sparrow *Spizella atrogularis*

This small sparrow breeds from Mexico and sw. U.S. north to s. Oregon. This species' presence in Oregon is erratic and unpredictable, possibly irruptive, as Oregon is at the north end of its range (Tenney 1997). It is a bird of dry slopes and hillsides covered with tall thick vegetation. Casual in Oregon; most records are from ceanothus- and oak-covered hillsides in sw. Oregon. Two were observed on Roxy Ann Butte, Jackson Co., 7-8 Jun 1970, and a female was banded; three were there 2 Jul 1970 (Crowell and Nehls 1970d); another was there 15 May 1971 (Crowell and Nehls 1971b); a pair was there from late May to 29 Jul 1977, the male photographed (OBRC, Roberson 1980); and a male was there 14 Jul 1979 (Watson 1979a). Two males were on a ceanothus-covered slope 10 mi (16.1 km) northeast of Medford 23 May 1979, with one still there 11 Jun (Harrington-Tweit et al. 1979); a family group was photographed on Stukel Mt., Klamath Co., 17-28 Jul 1990 (OBRC); and a singing male was there 22-28 Jun 1996 (Sullivan and Spencer 1997). One was observed on Glass Butte, Lake Co., 25 May 1996 (Sullivan 1996b). A male was observed 28 Jun 1999 at Blitzen Crossing, Steens Mt., Harney Co. (Spencer 2000a). A singing male was observed in a clearcut near Marquam, Clackamas Co., 12 Jun 1999 (Tice 2000a). Subspecies unknown.—*Harry B. Nehls*

## Vesper Sparrow *Pooecetes gramineus*

The vesper (evening) song of this bird is one of the characteristic sounds of spring evenings in much of the high desert country of e. Oregon. This temperate migrant is a ground-nesting, ground-foraging bird of most of the grassland, agricultural land, and shrub-steppe habitats of Oregon. The streaked brownish plumage of the Vesper Sparrow is similar to that of several small to medium-sized sparrows, except for white outer tail feathers, shown most conspicuously in flight.

**General Distribution:** Breeds from c. Canada south throughout most of the U.S.; winters in the southern part of breeding range and south into c. Mexico. Two of three subspecies breed in Oregon.

**Oregon Distribution:** Oregon subspecies are *P. g. confinis* breeding east of the Cascade crest (e.g., specimens from Ft. Klamath [USNM] and Midland [SOU], Klamath Co., and [USNM] Harney in Harney Co., Heppner in Morrow Co., Meacham in Umatilla Co.) and *P. g. affinis* west of the Cascade crest (e.g., specimen from Douglas Co. [USNM]) (AOU 1957). In e. Oregon, the Vesper Sparrow breeds in open habitats up to 7,000 ft (2,134 m) on desert mountains such as Steens Mtn. and Hart Mtn. (Gilligan et al. 1994). Breed irregularly below 4,000 ft (1,220 m), and abundance in shrub-steppe may be greater at higher elevations (Stepniewski 1994, M. Denny p.c.). For example, it is not present as a breeding species on the relatively low-elevation Boardman Bombing Range near the Columbia R. (Holmes and Geupel 1998). In e. Oregon, fairly common migrant throughout much of breeding range. Rarely encountered in winter.

Breeds west of the Cascades in the Willamette and Umpqua valleys, in foothills and mountains above the Rogue Valley, and in coastal valleys of sw. Oregon from Bandon south in Coos and Curry counties (Gilligan et al. 1994). May also breed on islands in the Columbia R. (e.g., Government I. [*BA*]). Abundance greatest in dry, grassy foothills of Umpqua and Rogue valleys, where it is an uncommon to locally common breeding species (Browning 1975a, Hunter et al. 1998). In the Willamette Valley, rare to locally uncommon in pastures and open foothills in the southern valley, and in Christmas tree farms throughout the valley and foothills (Altman 1999b). Migrants are uncommon to common throughout the breeding range, and are rare in north-coastal lowlands and in the Cascades

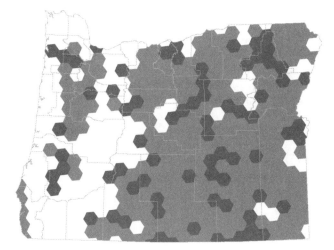

(Fix 1990a, *MGH*). Occasional birds are reported in winter in the s. Willamette Valley and Rogue and Umpqua valleys.

**Habitat and Diet:** General nesting habitat requirements include elevated perches for singing and a grass-dominated understory for foraging and nesting (*BA*). In a Willamette Valley study, primarily associated with two habitat types: (1) lightly grazed pastures with scattered shrubs where grass height < 2 ft (60 cm) high and preferably < 1 ft (30 cm) high, and (2) Christmas tree farms, particularly young farms 2-5 yr post-planting, if extensive grasses and weeds are present (Altman 1999b). Approximately 95% of detections during point count censusing occurred in these habitats, despite <15% of the sampling effort in these habitat types (n=540 point count stations). Only rarely encountered in grass-seed fields. Rarely found in manicured Christmas tree farms where herbaceous vegetation is controlled, but regularly detected in weedy farms with moderate amounts of herbaceous vegetation mixed with bare ground.

In the Willamette Valley study, 46% of territories (n=38) in pastures dominated by grass heights 6-12 in (15-30 cm) (Altman 1999b). Association with shorter grass exemplified by their absence in fallow fields, which often have scattered shrub component, but grass height usually >2 ft (61 cm) tall due to lack of grazing or mowing. Mean territory size 3.1 ac (1.3 ha; range 1.1-13.0 ac [0.4-5.2 ha]), and only one territory greater than 6 ac (2.4 ha). Territories mostly grass dominated (88% cover) with equal amounts of bare ground (6%) and shrubs/trees (6%). Nesting pairs occurred in small areas of habitat (<10 ac [4 ha]) in the Willamette Valley (Altman 1999b), thus small blocks of suitable habitat (e.g., 10-20 ac [4-8 ha]) may provide for a few pairs regardless of surrounding habitat.

Nests on ground, often placed against clump of vegetation, crop residue, clod of dirt, or at base of shrub or small tree (*BA*). Nest sites in the Willamette Valley study characterized by less grass cover (49%), and more bare ground (24%) and litter/residue (21%) than present in the territory (Altman 1999b). Nests found in pasture (n=4), fallow fields (n=3), and Christmas tree farms (n=12). Mayfield (1975) estimate of nest success 30% (n=19). All four nests in pasture successful (i.e., fledged at least one young), but only five of 12 successful in Christmas tree farms. Nest success in Christmas tree farms dependent upon low degree of activity (e.g., herbaceous vegetation control, tree pruning, and recreation) during breeding season (Altman 1999b). Additionally, spraying to control insects that affect Christmas trees (e.g., aphids) may reduce prey base and potentially impact reproductive output.

In the Rogue R. basin, Browning (1975a) reported Vesper Sparrow in open habitats of the mixed-conifer forest zone in the breeding season, and throughout the valley during migration. No other data from sw. Oregon.

In e. Oregon, occurs in a wide range of habitat types including grassland, sagebrush, fallow fields, montane meadows, juniper-steppe, and agricultural cropland such as grain fields. Also occurs in dry, open woodlands and openings in forested habitat such as clearcuts. Breeding abundance greater at higher elevations (e.g., >4,000 ft [1,220 m]) where temperatures are cooler and rainfall slightly higher, which results in increased ground cover of grasses. In sagebrush, mostly use sparse, low vegetation (Wiens 1969). Most abundant in habitats characterized by bunchgrasses and short, stiff sage, and particularly on east- and north-facing slopes (M. Denny p.c.). On and adjacent to Malheur NWR, occurs in sagebrush highlands above 4,100 ft (1,200 m) (Littlefield 1990a). In the Alvord Basin, mostly on slopes high above the basin floor (Liverman 1983). Migration habitat on Malheur NWR described as weedy roadsides, shrubs, and grasslands (Littlefield 1990a).

No diet studies conducted in Oregon. Diet consists of a mix of invertebrates and seeds (Ehrlich et al. 1988), although primarily insectivorous during breeding season, particularly arthropods, and granivorous during winter.

**Seasonal Activity and Behavior:** In Rogue Valley, migrants first arrive in late Feb (Browning 1975a). In the Willamette Valley, early migrants may appear in mid-Mar, but most migration occurs in Apr. Early dates include individuals at Portland early Feb through 24 Mar 1979 (Hunn and Mattocks 1979b, Mattocks 1979), 11 Mar in Yamhill Co. (Bayer 1986b), 19 Mar near Corvallis (A. McGie p.c.), 25 Mar at Finley NWR (Crowell and Nehls 1974a). Mean arrival date in Yamhill Co. 3 Apr (n=30) (Bayer 1986b) and 16 Apr near Corvallis (n=10) (A. McGie p.c.).

In e. Oregon, spring migrants begin to arrive in late Mar and become abundant in early Apr (Gabrielson and Jewett 1940). At Malheur NWR, peak spring passage 15 Apr-1 May, although most abundant after 25 Apr (Littlefield 1990a). Mean arrival date 27 Mar for Malheur NWR, and 3 Apr for c. Oregon (n=15) (C. Miller p.c.). An extremely early date is 28 Feb at Malheur NWR (Littlefield 1990a). Other early dates include 15 Mar in c. Oregon (C. Miller p.c.) and 23 Mar in Klamath Co. (Gabrielson and Jewett 1940).

Singing begins upon arrival on the breeding grounds. Male often sings from exposed perch (e.g., shrubs, trees, power line, fence post), but will also sing from ground if perches are lacking. Limited Oregon data on nest initiation indicate nest building takes place primarily in mid- to late May. Earliest date for nest observed with eggs 13 May near Portland (Griffee and Rapraeger 1937) and 15 May near John Day

(OBBA); late date 18 Jul in the Willamette Valley (*BA*). An apparent early nesting record based on an adult carrying food on 25 Apr near Gold Beach (OBBA) may not be unusual; in e. Washington, 23% of nests (n=77) were initiated before 1 May (M. Vander Haegen p.c.), and Jewett et al. (1953) reports a mean of 10 May for full clutch of eggs, with an early date of 5 Apr. Usually 3-4 eggs/clutch; often double-brooded. Occasional host to Brown-headed Cowbird in e. Washington (M. Vander Haegen p.c.). Most young fledge throughout Jun; early date 5 Jun in the Willamette Valley (*BA*) and 14 Jun near Warm Springs (OBBA). Late fledging date 29 Jul in the Willamette Valley (*BA*).

Fall migration through Rogue Valley mostly late Sep and early Oct (Browning 1975a). Peak fall migration at Malheur NWR early Sep (Littlefield 1990a). Most birds have left the state by early Oct (Gilligan et al. 1994). Late dates include 2 Nov at n. spit, Coos Bay (T. Rodenkirk p.c.), 1 Nov near Eugene (Gullion 1951), and in e. Oregon 23 Sep at Malheur NWR (Littlefield 1990a).

There have been a few confirmed winter records, mainly in westside valleys and primarily near Eugene (Gullion 1951), but most lack verification (Gilligan et al. 1994). The first winter report was from Eugene on 7 Jan 1939, and multiple wintering birds were reported near Fern Ridge Res. in the late 1940s (Gullion 1951). Recorded 10 times on the Eugene CBC, nine times on Corvallis CBC, and twice on Roseburg and Medford CBCs. The 1956 Eugene CBC reported six birds. In e. Oregon, reported twice (1970 and 1971) on the Malheur CBC (Littlefield 1990a), and also have been recorded on the Wallowa County CBC (Gilligan et al. 1994). Nearly all CBC records are prior to the mid-1980s and lack documentation. We think that most of these reports are valid and that winter occurrence of this species has declined in Oregon.

**Detection:** Visual and auditory detection fair. General appearance and habits similar to several small brown sparrows. Juvenile Dark-eyed Juncos sometimes mistaken for Vesper Sparrow by inexperienced observers. Some Savannah Sparrows have pale fringe on outer tail feathers suggesting Vesper Sparrow with a quick look. Sings frequently, but song not particularly distinctive; mixed pattern of notes, trills, and buzzes similar to several other sparrows. Song most frequently confused with Song Sparrow, although sweeter and more musical.

**Population Status and Conservation:** Population trends in Oregon (includes both subspecies) based on BBS data indicate relatively stable long-term (1966-96) trends (1.4%/yr decline, but non-significant), but highly significant (p<0.01) short-term (1980-96) declining trends (2.9%/yr) (Sauer et al. 1997). Declines may be occurring in both subspecies. Population trends in the Columbia Plateau BBS region of e. Oregon and Washington mirror the state trend; relatively stable long-term (1966-96) trends (0.5%/yr decline, but non-significant), but significant (p<0.05) short-term (1980-96) declining trends (1.4%/yr) (Sauer et al. 1997). Insufficient data for analysis of trends during last 30 yr in w. Oregon, but anecdotal information indicates substantial population declines in the last 40-50 yr. In the late 1800s "abundant summer resident, found everywhere in open country" in Washington County (Anthony 1886). In the early 1900s "fairly common on the prairies and grassy fields of western Oregon and Washington" (Hoffmann 1927). In the 1930s "abundant summer resident in the Willamette Valley native and agricultural grasslands, and somewhat less common in other valleys" and "less common in the coastal valleys but can be looked for in open meadow and farm lands where it frequents the fence rows and pasture lands" (Gabrielson and Jewett 1940). In the 1940s "common summer resident" in the s. Willamette Valley (Gullion 1951). By the early 1990s, locally uncommon to rare summer resident in Willamette and Umpqua valleys, and "locally uncommon summer resident only from Bandon, Coos Co., south through Curry Co." (Gilligan et al. 1994). Currently, rare to locally uncommon in widely scattered areas of the Willamette Valley (Altman 1999b), locally uncommon in the Umpqua Valley (Hunter et al. 1998, R. Maertz p.c.), and rare along the immediate coast of s. Coos and Curry counties (T. Rodenkirk p.c.), and not present in coastal valleys.

Speculation on factors contributing to population declines include conversion of native grasslands and shrub-steppe to non-suitable agriculture (e.g., rowcrops), mortality at nests from trampling by livestock, changes in agricultural practices such as early and more frequent mowing/harvesting of fields and reduction in weedy edges and fencerows that are not managed for agriculture, and potential reproductive failures from use of pesticides or other contaminants (Altman 1999b). In w. Oregon, additional factors include extensive habitat loss due to development, particularly in the Willamette Valley, and increased predation levels from mammals associated with semi-urban/residential habitats such as skunks, raccoons, and feral and domestic cats (Altman 1999b). Willamette Valley population listed as "sensitive" by ODFW.—*Bob Altman*

## Lark Sparrow *Chondestes grammacus*

The adult Lark Sparrow is one of the most easily recognized passerines. The head pattern is sharp and crisp, with a chestnut crown and cheek patch surrounded by alternating white and black stripes. White underparts with a small black central spot and a long, blackish tail with conspicuous white wing

corners further aid identification. Courtship behaviors, including turkey-like strutting by males and twig passing during copulation, differ markedly from that of other passerines (Martin and Parrish 2000).

**General Distribution:** Breeds discontinuously from se. British Columbia east to Manitoba, Minnesota, and W. Virginia, south to Baja California Norte and Louisiana (Rising 1996). Winters from sw. Oregon to Oklahoma (casually), south through Baja California Sur, Chiapas, and Veracruz, along the Gulf coast east to Florida (Rising 1996). Recorded in winter rarely as far north as Alberta and New York (Rising 1996). In migration regular along both coasts. Two subspecies; *C. g. strigatus* is found in Oregon (AOU 1957).

**Oregon Distribution:** Uncommon to locally common summer resident and migrant east of the Cascades. Rarely breeds above 6,000 ft (1,829 m) elevation (Gilligan et al. 1994). In w. Oregon, fairly common summer resident in Rogue Valley and foothills (Browning 1975a). Rare and local in summer in Umpqua Valley (Hunter et al. 1998). Rare but regular spring and fall migrant in Lane Co. (Contreras 2002a). Rare migrant elsewhere in the Willamette Valley and along the coast (Gilligan et al. 1994) and in the Cascades (Fix 1990a, *MGH*). Rare winter visitor in the Willamette Valley; the Salem CBC has reported one each past 3 yr (1999-2001). Fairly common to uncommon in Rogue Valley in winter, where flocks of up to 40 may be found. Very rare east of the Cascades in winter; a Feb 1980 record at La Grande was highly unusual (Gilligan et al. 1994).

**Habitat and Diet:** Rangewide, typically breeds in open habitats, usually characterized by ground cover and containing or adjoining scattered shrubs or trees (Martin and Parrish 2000). In e. Oregon, shows strong affinity for shrub-steppe such as sagebrush, often adjoining grasslands, cultivated land, and juniper woodlands (*TAS*). Point counts over 3 yr on the Boardman Bombing Range showed this species nested

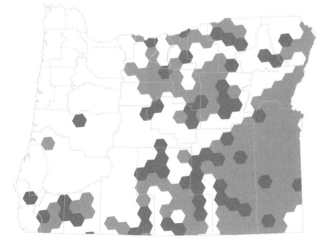

at least once at 50% of points in bitterbrush (n=28), 78% (n=23) of points in grazed basin/Wyoming sagebrush, 53% of points (n=34) in Wyoming sagebrush (grazed), 28% (n=29) of points in ungrazed sagebrush perennial grass, and 6% (n=52) of points in needle and thread grass and/or bluebunch wheatgrass perennial grassland. This species never occurred in annual grasslands (cheatgrass, n=27) (Holmes and Geupel 1998). Holmes and Geupel (1998) concluded that abundance was positively correlated to sagebrush and bare ground and that abundance varied significantly year to year (A. Holmes p.c.).

In sw. Oregon, utilizes open woodlands and grassy terrain with scattered bushes (Gilligan et al. 1994). May occupy sites with poor soils or disturbed by severe overgrazing (Fitch 1958, Zimmerman 1993). Nest-site data from California, Oklahoma, and Texas populations show >50% of nests were constructed on ground (McNair 1985). In one study in greasewood-sagebrush shrub-steppe habitat in Montana, seven of eight ground nests were on ground at base of large sagebrush and one under greasewood (Walcheck 1970). Data from museum oology collections show mean height of nests above ground 1.46 m ± 0.65 SD (n=309) (Baepler 1968, McNair 1982, 1990). Nests above ground usually in woody or herbaceous shrubs and small trees, including juniper, pines, greasewood, and sagebrush. One nest in Josephine Co. was approximately 10 ft (3 m) above ground in fork of bole of 20 to 22 ft (6 to 6.7 m) tall jeffrey pine (D. Vroman p.c.). Prefer elevated perches such as fence posts, tops of shrubs and small trees, telephone wires, and open perches in woody vegetation (McNair 1982, Martin and Parrish 2000).

When found in the Willamette Valley in winter, often with other sparrows in hedgerows, especially Himalayan blackberry, near fields and grasslands (G. Gillson p.c., T. Janzen p.c., S. Dowlan p.c., *TAS*)

No diet studies conducted in Oregon. Over all seasons and locales, diet is approximately 75% granivorous and 25% insectivorous (Baepler 1968). DeGraaf et al. (1985) described this species as a ground-gleaning granivore during the nonbreeding season and a ground-foraging omnivore during the breeding season. Martin and Parrish (2000) also mention foraging on lower portions of shrubs. During breeding season, consumes more insects than seeds, selectively predating with regard to insect size and energy gain/handling time (Kaspari and Joern 1993). Prey selection is diverse and includes arcidid grasshoppers, adult beetles, larval butterflies and moths, horned grasshoppers, bees and ants, bugs, flies, and spittle bugs (Kaspari and Joern 1993). Arthropods, especially grasshoppers, make up the greatest percentage of insect prey and are the sole item fed to nestlings (Baepler 1968, McNair 1990, Kaspari and Joern 1993).

**Seasonal Activity and Behavior:** Males may sing throughout winter and migration (Phillips et al. 1964), although this has not been reported in Oregon. Spring migration in Oregon begins the last 10 days of Mar (Gabrielson and Jewett 1940) and peaks late Apr through mid-May (Gilligan et al. 1994). Males precede females approximately 30 days in returning to breeding territories (Baepler 1968). Earliest arrival date 19 Mar at Malheur NWR; average 26 Apr (Littlefield 1990a). Other early dates presumably representing returning birds are 31 Mar at Lower Table Rock, Jackson Co. (S. Russell p.c.) and 16 Mar in Linn County (Gillson 2001a). Transients noted Mar-May in Lane Co. (Contreras 2002a).

Males on territory sing at all hours of day and into late evening. Nest building observed 26 May to 21 Jun (n=6). Nest with eggs, 20 May to 24 Jun (n=3), and nest with young 6 and 14 Jun (n=2); carrying food, presumably to nestlings 20 May to 9 Jul (n=7); fledglings 3 Jun to 24 Jul (n=15) (OBBA). Commonly attempts to renest, often producing second clutch after first (Baepler 1968, Kaspari and Joern 1993) or renesting near depredated or failed nest (Martin and Parrish 2000). Mean clutch size for all geographic locations 4.09 ± 0.66 SD (n=928) based on museum data and 3.84 ± 0.70 SD (n=209) based on nest research card data. Clutch size 3-6 (McNair 1985). Female alone incubates eggs; male and female care for young. Young capable of flight after 8-9 days (Martin and Parrish 2000). In late Jul and Aug forms foraging flocks, often with other species; often away from breeding areas. Fall migration east of the Cascades peaks in latter half of Aug and early Sep, by mid-Sep few remain, although individuals are rarely noted into early Oct. Rare but regular migrant along coast Sep-Oct (Gilligan et al. 1994). In Lane Co., transients noted Jul-Sep; late date 26 Nov (Contreras 2002a).

**Detection:** Easily detected due to adults' distinctive appearance and males' habit of singing and sitting on exposed perches. Although easily flushed when disturbed, does not dive into cover like other sparrows, rather flies off short distance and perches (Martin and Parrish 2000, *TAS*).

**Population Status and Conservation:** Through at least 1902 was considered an uncommon to common breeder in the Willamette and Umpqua valleys (Gabrielson and Jewett 1940, Hunter et al. 1998). This is not surprising considering that the vast expanses of prairies intermingled with shrubs in these two valleys at the time of Euro-American settlement have been replaced with agricultural crops, especially in the Willamette Valley (Habeck 1962, Franklin and Dyrness 1973, Towle 1974).

Martin and Parrish (2000) cite several studies that describe both positive and negative effects on Lark

Sparrow populations from fire and livestock grazing. It is apparent from these studies that a balance between shrubs, grassland, and even some bare ground is a requirement for this species. Conversion of shrub/grassland to agricultural crops is detrimental. Populations are probably influenced by the availability of arthropods, and local population declines have been attributed to intense grasshopper control measures (Paige and Ritter 1999). Loss of native plant habitat to exotic annuals in the Great Basin also affects populations (Martin and Parrish 2000). Studies of habitat requirements and population status are needed in Oregon. Oregon BBS survey trends show a significant 9.8% decrease for 1966-2000, which is not surprising considering the loss of the described habitat.—*Tim A. Shelmerdine*

## Black-throated Sparrow *Amphispiza bilineata*

This charming sparrow was known as *Wut'-tu-ze-ze* to the Paiute Indians, reflective of its song (Ridgway 1877). The most striking feature is its broad black throat patch and dark gray head, set off by white moustachial stripes and eyelines. This uncommon inhabitant of Oregon's high desert can be a challenge to find unless the observer becomes familiar with its territorial song and preferred habitat. Habitat requirements are specialized and population distribution and densities are highly variable from year to year in Oregon.

**General Distribution:** Resident of the northern half of Mexico and Baja California northward to the southern edge of the U.S. from Texas to California. Regular breeding range extends north to the northern edge of the Great Basin including Oregon, Idaho, and the southern edge of Wyoming (Byers et al. 1995). Breeding has occurred sporadically in the Columbia R. basin as far north as c. Washington (Smith et al. 1997). Of nine subspecies, only *A.b. deserticola* is found in Oregon (AOU 1957).

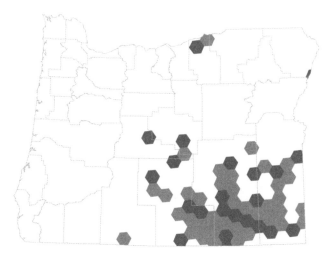

**Oregon Distribution:** Principal breeding range is se. Oregon. In many years apparently restricted to the arid slopes of the Alvord and Warner basins, although could have strongholds in other rarely visited basin areas in the southeast corner of the state. In some years breeding occurs northward to the Harney, Abert, and Summer L. basins and to the east in Malheur Co. (Liverman 1983, Contreras and Kindschy 1996, *CRM*). Breeding is rare north and west of the Great Basin, such as the Painted Hills National Monument in Wheeler Co. (L. Rems p.c.), the Boardman Army Depot in the Columbia R. basin of nc. Oregon (G. Green p.c.), and in the Klamath Basin (Summers 1993a, *CRM*). Breeding was suspected 10 mi (16 km) north of Klamath Falls in 1959 (Brown 1960). It is quite possible that breeding occurs in other portions of the state during influx years, but may go undetected due to lack of field observers. Elsewhere in the state it is an occasional vagrant with about 40 records west of the Cascades (most in spring) and two records in ne. Oregon (Hunn 1978, Gilligan et al. 1994, *CRM*).

**Habitat and Diet:** Occur along boulder-strewn, sparsely vegetated slopes of arid deserts (Ryser 1985). Prefer warm dry sunny south slopes of desert basins. However, in years of high abundance may also be found along west and east-facing slopes and in dune habitat (Smith 1980, Liverman 1983, *CRM*). Primary vegetation communities in Oregon breeding areas include sagebrush, shadscale, saltbush, and greasewood (Liverman 1983, Ryser 1985). Nest is placed low in a thick shrub. Diet consists of dry seeds, fresh green plant material, and insects, depending on time of year and water availability (Smyth and Bartholomew 1966). Possess specially adapted kidneys able to withstand heat and low moisture conditions. Although will drink water when available, they are among few N. American birds able to utilize insects and plants as their only moisture source (Smyth and Bartholomew 1966). It is unknown what limits this species to very local sites in e. Oregon.

**Seasonal Activity and Behavior:** Earliest spring arrival record is 28 Apr 1994 along Abert Rim (S. Summers unpubl. data). The only earlier Oregon record was away from its breeding range in Salem, 13 Mar 1987. Although a few records are from early May, most spring migrants first appear in mid-May with migration peaking by late May (pattern similar for e. and w. Oregon). Males begin to sing on arrival in May, often even before establishing territory (*CRM*). On territory the male typically will perch near the top of preferred bushes where it sings repeatedly. Can be heard singing at any time of day, but most singing occurs from 1 hr before to 4 hr after sunrise (*CRM*). Eggs are pale blue (usually 3-4) and are laid in early to mid-Jun, although a nest still containing eggs was recorded as late as 13

Jul in the Alvord Basin (Liverman 1983, Byers et al. 1995). In Oregon young usually fledge between mid-Jun. and early Jul. Birds are silent after this time and leave on their southward migration by the end of Jul (Smith 1980, *CRM*). Latest record in the breeding range was a juvenile found 12 Aug 1994 at Painted Hills, Wheeler Co. (L. Rems p.c.). The only records past this date are of one found on the s. Oregon coast near Brookings, 26 Sep 1985, and an extraordinary record 24 Jan 2002, also at Brookings (Korpi 2002).

**Detection:** Most easily detected by male's song. Does not occupy prominent perches so even singing birds often visually inconspicuous. Foraging and inactive birds even more difficult to observe among desert shrubs. Habitat tends to be inhospitable and difficult to access, making this one of the state's more challenging breeding birds to find. Their silence and resemblance of immature to Sage Sparrow may help account for the paucity of records past the last week of Jul. The most reliable locations to find this bird include the south- and southeast-facing slopes of the Alvord Basin and west-facing slopes of the Warner Basin at the base of Poker Jim Ridge and Hart Mtn. More accessible but less predictable are the south-facing slopes of Wright's Point near Burns and south Coyote Butte at Malheur NWR.

**Population Status and Conservation:** This species went almost unreported in Oregon during the first half of the 20th century (only two records) and Gabrielson and Jewett (1940) considered them rare stragglers. It is unclear if populations have recently expanded into Oregon or if early ornithologists merely overlooked this species.

Although probably an annual breeder in the state, the Black-throated Sparrow can be extremely rare in some years. More often than not, none are detected on most breeding bird surveys conducted within the breeding range in Oregon, and numbers fluctuate widely on a given survey when detected (Liverman 1983, Sauer et al. 1999), thus population trends are difficult to assess.

On the Warner Valley BBS, where they have been recorded every year since initiated in 1993, total count numbers have been as low as one and as high as 76 (*CRM*). Both 1984 and 1994 were years when notable populations occurred in the breeding range. During years of greater abundance in core breeding areas, breeding expands northward and westward. The most recent large influx (1994) was the same year that breeding records were established in nc. Oregon, at the Painted Hills, and the Boardman Bombing Range.

Vagrant occurrences in Oregon tend to cluster during years of high abundance, usually in May. Of approximately 40 records west of the Cascades, nearly half were established in the years of 1984 (13) and 1994 (5) (Gilligan et al. 1994, *CRM*). Likewise, the

years 1959 and 1970 provided a number of records west of the Cascades (*CRM*). Although the reason for occasional population influxes into Oregon is speculative, it has been suggested that historic vagrancy may increase during periods of either drought or extreme cold in the sw. U.S. (Hunn 1978).

In Oregon, no major threats have been identified (Marshall 1996). However, BBS data indicate an alarming nationwide population decline of about 3.9%/yr over the past 30 yr. In Oregon, alterations of their preferred habitat are due primarily to livestock grazing and off-road vehicle use (*CRM*). Rough terrain, inaccessibility, and vast expanses of public land tend to prevent significant loss of critical habitat in the state.—*Craig R. Miller*

**Sage Sparrow** *Amphispiza belli*
Although common within its range, this handsome sparrow can easily be overlooked. The gray head, black malar stripe, white eyebrow, and prominent black spot set in the middle of a white breast identify the bird. It is widespread throughout the extensive shrub-steppe of c. and e. Oregon.

**General Distribution:** Resident along inner coast ranges of California (far) short of the Oregon border south to c. Baja California and eastward over the southern portion of the Great Basin as far as Colorado. Breeds in the Great Basin from c. Washington to e. California and eastward to Wyoming, Colorado, and w. New Mexico. During winter most interior birds migrate short distances south to occupy c. California, s. Nevada, and w. Texas southward to n. Baja California and Mexico. Of five subspecies, only *A. b. nevadensis* is known to occur in Oregon (AOU 1957).

**Oregon Distribution:** The principal breeding range of Sage Sparrow is se. and c. Oregon. Found throughout the arid expanses of the Great Basin and usually associated with big sage. Common to uncommon from the alkaline basin floors to the high

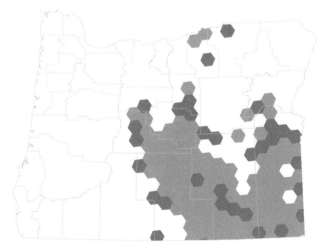

*Sage Sparrow*

Jun, and Aug (*CRM*). Although migration during spring is usually inconspicuous, it can be locally dramatic. On 9 Mar 1998 as many as 200 birds were found along a 1-mi stretch of road in flocks of 10-20 near Fields in se. Oregon (Maitreya p.c.).

Atypical of most passerines, most are already paired upon arrival to their breeding sites. Adults that have bred successfully at a certain location are likely to return there in successive years (Wiens and Rotenberry 1985).

plateaus. Breeds to elevations of 6,800 ft (2,100 m) on Oregon Canyon Mtn. (M. Denny p.c.). Found locally along the Columbia R. basin in nc. Oregon, especially the Boardman Army Depot and irregularly in sagebrush-dominated valleys of the Blue Mtns. in ne. Oregon (Gilligan et al. 1994, G. Green p.c., OBBA). Despite relative abundance e. of the Cascades, strays are remarkably rare west of the Cascades with only about 14 records, mostly in early spring (e.g., Dowlan 2000b); only three extralimital records are coastal (*CRM*). Any sw. Oregon strays should be scrutinized carefully for *A. b. belli*, likely to be split as a separate species (Martin and Carlson 1998). In some years a few Sage Sparrows (flocks rarely more than five) remain throughout the winter in se. and sc. Oregon (Littlefield 1990a, Gilligan et al. 1994), and in the lower Columbia Basin (M. Denny p.c.).

**Habitat and Diet:** Although considered by some authors to be a sagebrush obligate, Sage Sparrows have been found in other plant communities exclusive of sagebrush including rabbitbrush, shadscale, saltbush, and greasewood (Braun, Baker et al. 1976, Green and Smith 1981, Rising 1996). In Oregon they are most commonly associated with big sagebrush communities, sometimes including a mix of other shrubs, or among western juniper. Forages almost exclusively on the ground (Rich 1980c). Food consists primarily of insects when available (from May through Aug) and of seeds during other times of the year (Rotenberry 1980).

**Seasonal Activity and Behavior:** Spring migrants begin to reach Oregon in late Feb to early Mar and numbers peak mid-Mar (Gilligan et al. 1994, *CRM*). Most w. Oregon records are mid-Feb through Apr, concomitant with the main passage in e. Oregon. Otherwise there are single extralimital records in Jan,

However, yearling sparrows tend not to return to their natal locations (Wiens 1982). Territory size is larger than the known size of other N. American sparrows, averaging 11 ac (4.4 ha) in Idaho (Rich 1980c). Male territorial behavior is marked by single bouts of singing from a perch near the top of a bush and flying to a different perch after each bout. Most bouts consist of only a single song, but up to 118 consecutive songs have been recorded (Rich 1980c). Become more vocal as the nesting season proceeds and singing continues until young are fledged (Rich 1980c, *CRM*). Unlike most other sparrows, territorial chasing and visual display are nearly absent (Rich 1980c). Nesting season varies depending on elevation, but ranges from mid-Mar through mid-Jul (Martin and Carlson 1998, OBBA). The nest is placed in the densest portion of a 4- to 39-in (10- to 100-cm) tall bush (Rich 1980b, Peterson and Best 1985). Large, living shrubs are favored, the southwest side of the shrub is avoided, and the northeast side is preferred (Peterson and Best 1985). Nests consist of shredded sagebrush bark and grass. Usually enter and leave nest by walking rather than flying (Peterson and Best 1985). Three to four pale bluish eggs are laid early Apr to mid-May (Gabrielson and Jewett 1940). Brood size correlated with rainfall the previous winter. Fledging dates range 16 Jun to 16 Aug (n=12) (OBBA). Southward migration begins in late Aug and peaks in mid-Sep at Malheur NWR, with some remaining through Nov (Littlefield 1990a).

**Detection:** Elusive. Song is inconspicuous and the bird tends to be secretive. Habit of singing from a perch below the top of the shrub causes blending into the background. Sage Sparrows are most visible from the direction they are facing because of white breast plumage (Rich 1980c). The species is well-described by Gabrielson and Jewett (1940) to have "an almost uncanny ability to slip from one bush to another, keeping out of sight of an intruder as it does so," both by taking short low flights and by running along the ground. However, once familiarity with their song is gained, the chance of detection in appropriate habitat is likely during the breeding season. Excellent locations to find this species include the Alvord, Fort Rock, and Warner basins in se. and sc. Oregon.

**Population Status and Conservation:** The extent of shrub-steppe and alkaline basin habitat under public ownership has prevented wholesale destruction of requisite habitat. BBS data reveal no significant population trends in Oregon or the U.S. in the past 30 yr. However, the practice of replacing sagebrush-dominant habitat with non-native grasses such as crested wheatgrass results in local population declines (Wiens and Rotenberry 1985), and this alteration of the landscape has occurred on large tracts of public lands in se. Oregon. Livestock grazing likely impacts nesting success directly by disturbing nesting birds and damaging nests, and indirectly by enabling cowbird parasitism (Rich 1978, *CRM*). Livestock and fire-induced exotic weed invasion, especially by cheatgrass, poses another threat to viable habitat (Martin and Carlson 1998). On the other hand, livestock grazing and fire suppression has converted much of the grassland habitat in the Great Basin to sagebrush shrubland, creating more habitat favorable to the species. Habitat loss (to agriculture) has had significant impact in the northern part of e. Oregon. Gabrielson and Jewett (1940) described the sparrow as being "abundant" in "the sage-covered sand area of northern Morrow County." Today, the only remnant habitat in the area is found on the Umatilla Army Depot and Boardman Bombing Range where small numbers breed every year (C. Corder p.c., G. Green p.c.).—*Craig R. Miller*

**Lark Bunting** *Calamospiza melanocorys*
The Lark Bunting breeds in the open prairies east of the Rocky Mtns., dropping south to winter in the s. U.S. and Mexico. It is a regular transient and winter visitant to s. California, occasionally in small flocks. Individuals are occasionally found elsewhere in the West. It is a casual visitor to Oregon with the majority of records occurring from mid-May to late Sep. There appears to be no pattern or concentration of occurrences. A male, accompanying a female, was photographed at Bob Cr. in coastal Lane Co. 17 Jul 1983 (OBRC) for the only multiple sighting. One was observed at White City, Jackson Co., 13 Nov 1961 (Boggs and Boggs 1962); another was at Medford, Jackson Co., 30 Jan 1966 (Crowell and Nehls 1966a); and one was collected 5.5 mi (8.8 km) east of Corvallis in Linn

Co. 3 Jan 1967 (Islam 1994, spec. no. FWNO 7597 OSU). A male wintering at a Portland, Multnomah Co., feeder from early Jan to 4 May 1972 changed from full basic to full alternate plumage during its stay (Crowell and Nehls 1972c). Monotypic (AOU 1957).—*Harry B. Nehls*

**Savannah Sparrow** *Passerculus sandwichensis*
The buzzy, insect-like song of the Savannah Sparrow is a characteristic sound of open landscapes dominated by grasslands throughout Oregon. Savannah Sparrows are usually heard or seen when perched atop a fencepost, small shrub, or tall weed, or running on the ground between openings in vegetation. Flights are usually short and often just above the vegetation until the bird abruptly drops down into cover. Despite its relatively common status in suitable grassland habitat, little is known about Savannah Sparrow breeding ecology and subspecies occurrence in Oregon.

**General Distribution:** Breeds throughout most of N. America and winters in the s. U.S., Mexico, Belize, Guatemala, and n. Honduras (AOU 1957, Wheelwright and Rising 1993). Many of the approximately 17 subspecies are difficult to recognize (Wheelwright and Rising 1993); five have been identified from Oregon.

**Oregon Distribution:** Historically there has been confusion as to subspecies identifications within Oregon (Gabrielson and Jewett 1940). *P. s. nevadensis* and *P. s. brooksi* breed in Oregon (AOU 1957, Pyle 1997), although Wheelwright and Rising (1993) do not recognize *brooksi*. Northern breeding subspecies that have occurred as migrants or wintering birds include *crassus* (following Aldrich in Jewett et al. 1953 and Paynter 1970, *contra* AOU 1957), *sandwichensis*, and *anthinus*.

*P. s. nevadensis* is a common breeding subspecies in open grassland habitat in e. Oregon (e.g., specimens from Harney, Malheur, and Klamath counties

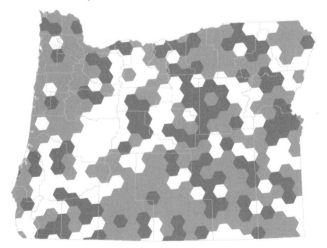

[USNM]). *P. s. brooksi* breeds in the Willamette Valley and along the coast in w. Oregon (Gabrielson and Jewett 1940), and also on islands in the Columbia R. (e.g., Government I., Miller Sands I.) where suitable habitat is present (Dorsey 1982, *BA*). Savannah Sparrows also breed in some montane meadows (usually larger meadows) above 5,000 ft (1,500 m) including the Warner Mtns. (K. Spencer p.c.) and Ochoco Mtns. (*ALC*). It is a rare breeder in the Cascades, such as the south end of Diamond L. (Fix 1990a). The breeding subspecies in the Cascades is unknown, although suspected to be *P. s. nevadensis*, the alpine breeding subspecies in the Washington Cascades (Banks 1960). The Savannah Sparrow is a rare breeder in the Rogue Valley (Gilligan et al. 1994), apparently reduced from its common resident status in the 1960s (Browning 1975a). It is an uncommon breeder in the Umpqua Valley (Hunter et al. 1998)

Migrants of both breeding subspecies occur throughout their Oregon breeding range. Fall migrants also occur in high-elevation montane meadows of the Cascade Mtns. (subspecies uncertain but suspected to be *P. s. nevadensis*) in places where they do not breed (Gabrielson and Jewett 1940, Farner 1952, *BA*). Migrants and some wintering birds of northern breeding *P. s. sandwichensis* occur primarily in w. Oregon (Gabrielson and Jewett 1940, AOU 1957). *P. s. crassus* and *P. s. anthinus* also pass through or winter in the state (Pyle 1997). There are specimens of *crassus* from Ft. Klamath, Klamath Co. (Peters and Griscom 1938) and specimens (USNM) from Mt. Hood, Hood River Co.; Crooked R. (county unknown); Ft. Klamath, Klamath Co.; and Scottsburg in w. Douglas Co. (*MRB*). There are specimens (USNM) of *anthinus* from most e. Oregon counties (*MRB*). During the 1970s, migrants of unknown subspecies were regularly observed at night during spring and especially fall at the lighted driving range at Eastmoreland Golf Course in se. Portland, but not observed there during the day (D. Irons p.c.).

Winter populations throughout most of the state (all subspecies combined) are reduced from that of the breeding season (except Rogue Valley); uncommon to locally common in the Willamette Valley, and uncommon to rare in e. Oregon, and along the coast (Gilligan et al. 1994). Significant winter populations can occur in the Rogue Valley (Contreras 1997b).

**Habitat and Diet:** Suitable breeding habitat in w. Oregon includes most open fields. This includes cultivated fields (e.g., grass seed, alfalfa), pastures, hayfields, airports, weedy fallow fields, and roadsides. In the arid regions of e. Oregon, breeding habitat usually restricted to grasslands, irrigated fields, or the grassy margins of wet areas. Also nests in some large subalpine and alpine meadows dominated by forbs and grasses, and grassy dunes along the coast (*BA*).

Generally requires large areas of habitat for breeding, and will use highly disturbed or weedy habitats if the cover and foraging resource are suitable. Savannah Sparrow was the most abundant species in various agricultural grassland habitats (e.g., grass-seed fields, hayfields) of the Willamette Valley (Altman 1999b). In e. Washington shrub-steppe communities, most abundant in sites with shallow soil in poor condition (Vander Haegen et al. 2000). In se. Oregon and Nevada, Rotenberry and Wiens (1980) reported a positive correlation between Savannah Sparrow abundance and forb cover.

Nests on the ground, often in a slight depression and well concealed by a canopy of dead vegetation or partially tucked under a clump of vegetation. Forages primarily on the ground, but may glean insects and larvae from tree and shrub vegetation (Wheelwright and Rising 1993).

Migration and wintering habitat similar to that of the breeding season, but also includes areas less dominated by grass such as corn fields, log-littered beaches, wetlands, coastal sandspits, and dikes (*BA*).

Diet not studied in Oregon, but highly variable and adaptive. Mostly animal matter (adult insects, larvae, eggs, and other invertebrates) in spring and summer, and seeds and fruits in winter supplemented with insects when available (Wheelwright and Rising 1993).

**Seasonal Activity and Behavior:** In w. Oregon, much overlap between arrival of subspecies in spring (Gabrielson and Jewett 1940). Early arrivals of *P. s. brooksi* and *P. s. sandwichensis* occur in the later half of Mar, but most arrive in early Apr. Migrant flocks can be large and numerous along the coastal dunes in Lane and Lincoln counties in Apr and early May (R. Bayer p.c., *ALC*). Average arrival date 17 Apr (n=21) in Yamhill Co. (Bayer 1986b). Peak migration in the s. Willamette Valley is late Apr (Gullion 1951). *P. s. sandwichensis* is generally through Oregon by mid-May (Gabrielson and Jewett 1940). Spring transients can linger into early Jun (Gilligan et al. 1994).

In e. Oregon, average arrival date at Malheur NWR is 22 Mar with peak of passage 5-25 Apr (Littlefield 1990a). Early dates in e. Oregon include 1 Mar at Malheur NWR (Littlefield 1990a) and 6 Mar at Millican, Deschutes Co. (Sullivan 1999b). Gabrielson and Jewett (1940) indicated that *P. s. nevadensis* arrives in mid-Apr, thus, birds in Mar likely of northern breeding subspecies.

Pair formation and nest building begin in early May. Clutch size 2-6 eggs, most commonly four; usually double brooded. Known to be parasitized by Brown-headed Cowbird, but frequency is low (Friedman and Kiff 1985). Early dates for nest with eggs are 12 May, nest with young 19 May, and fledged young 30 May (OBBA). Nests with young mostly reported in late May and Jun (OBBA). Late date for carrying food (presumably to dependent young) is 11 Aug (OBBA).

Among breeding subspecies, *P. s. nevadensis* generally departs by mid-Aug (Gabrielson and Jewett 1940). At Malheur NWR, fall migration begins in Aug and peaks between 10 Sep and 5 Oct (Littlefield 1990a). Most individuals have left by Nov with an occasional wintering bird. Migration of birds identified by Gullion (1951) as *P. s. brooksi* in the s. Willamette Valley occurred from mid-Sep to mid-Oct with a peak in late Sep. Fall transients of breeding subspecies arrive in Aug (Gilligan et al. 1994). Nonbreeding migrants of *P. s. sandwichensis* arrive in Sep and remain into Nov (Gabrielson and Jewett 1940). Occurs mostly in small to mid-sized flocks in winter (<50 birds), although occasional large flocks reported such as 200-300 birds that wintered south of Albany (Johnson 1997b).

**Detection:** Can be difficult to detect due to weak, insect-like song, and ground-foraging habits within vegetation. Also can be difficult to identify due to relatively indistinct plumage and similarities to other sparrows, especially in winter. Singing perches (e.g., fence posts, shrubs) enhance visual detection and identification.

**Population Status and Conservation:** Slightly declining (-1.6%/yr) but non-significant BBS trend in Oregon over the last 30+ yr (Sauer et al. 1999). Similar non-significant declining trends (-0.9%/yr) in Columbia Plateau BBS physiographic region (*P. s. nevadensis*), but non-significant increasing trend (1.7%/yr) in the Southern Pacific Rainforest physiographic region (*P. s. brooksi*). Highest breeding season densities in Oregon based on BBS data are in the Willamette Valley, Klamath Basin, and Harney Basin (Wheelwright and Rising 1993).

Savannah Sparrows are an adaptable species and have benefitted from several types of human manipulation of the environment. This includes conversion of rangelands in e. Oregon to irrigated agriculture, and conversion of grazed pastures to grass-seed fields in w. Oregon. Conversely, permanent loss of these grasslands to development, especially in the westside valleys, has reduced available habitat (*BA*).

Because of their extensive use of agricultural lands throughout the year, Savannah Sparrows can be affected by a number of agricultural practices. They are regularly exposed to various pesticides; and the effects of these on Savannah Sparrow populations are largely unknown. Additionally, field mowing and other agricultural operations during the breeding season may impact populations through direct mortality of eggs/nestlings or indirect reductions in productivity from disturbance or habitat alteration (*BA*).

It has been noted elsewhere that regional Savannah Sparrow population changes are not closely related to productivity on the breeding grounds, but apparently more due to events during migration or on their wintering ground (Wheelwright and Rising 1993). Several studies in the Midwest (Herkert et al. 1993, Herkert 1994) and east (Vickery et al. 1994) indicate that Savannah Sparrow is highly sensitive to fragmentation, and generally restricted to large, contiguous habitats.—*Bob Altman*

## Grasshopper Sparrow
*Ammodramus savannarum*

The Grasshopper Sparrow is one of the more enigmatic and erratic birds in Oregon. A small population may appear in an area, persist for a few years, and then disappear, only to return at some later time. It is also difficult to detect, because of both its quiet, insect-like song and its reclusive habits. Males sing from elevated perches, such as flower stalks or fenceposts before diving back among the grasses. As careful observation increases our knowledge of this species, we may learn that it is not so much erratic as poorly observed. In profile, Grasshopper Sparrows are dumpy, short-tailed birds with a large bill and a flat-headed appearance. A prominent black eye stands out from an unmarked buff-colored face. Underparts are unstreaked in adults and buff-colored in contrast to the streaked upperparts. The crown has a pale median stripe. At close range the yellow loral spot and bend in the wing might be seen. The breast and sides of the juvenile are buff-colored and streaked.

**General Distribution:** Occurs broadly across N. America from the southern prairies of Canada (Alberta to Ontario) south to the Greater Antilles and Ecuador. It winters from California east across the s. U.S. and south into S. America. *A. s. perpallidus* in Oregon (*bimaculatus* of Gabrielson and Jewett [1940] is a synonym [AOU 1944]).

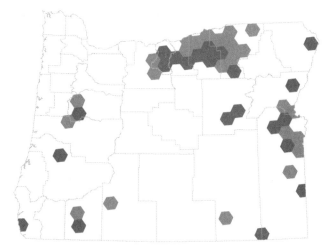

**Oregon Distribution:** The Grasshopper Sparrow is a widespread but very local breeder and rare migrant. It occurs in scattered "colonies" along the unforested northern slopes of the Blue Mtns. (Janes 1983, Evanich 1992a, Sullivan 1992e). Densities in very limited habitat in Morrow Co. varied from 1.1 individuals/100 ac (2.8 individuals/km²) in the Boardman area to 8.2 individuals/100 ac (20.3 individuals/km²) in the Heppner area (Janes 1983). Elsewhere east of the Cascades, they have been observed in Harney Co. at Foster Flats (Gilligan et al. 1994) and locally near Vale and Jordan valley, Malheur Co. (OBBA). West of the Cascades, one small colony has persisted since 1987 in the Rogue Valley (up to six singing males), and since 1998 the species has been observed at several additional sites. Isolated birds have been observed on BBSs in the Umpqua Valley. Singing males have been located in the c. and s. Willamette Valley, including Baskett Slough NWR, near Brownsville and Lebanon, and Fern Ridge Res., Lane Co. (the latter since the early 1970s) (Altman 1994b, 1997, L. McQueen p.c.). At least two winter records exist for Fern Ridge Res. (Contreras 1997b). In addition, one found 4 Jan 1982 near Alton Baker Park, Eugene, was monitored for several days then found dead in its nightly snowcave roost (Evanich 1982d, Mattocks and Hunn 1982a, D. Fix p.c.).

**Habitat and Diet:** Throughout their range, Grasshopper Sparrows occur in grasslands and grainfields in relatively dry habitats. In Oregon their distribution is restricted to grasslands. East of the Cascades they occur in native bunchgrass remnants on north-facing slopes (Janes 1983). This is consistent with observations elsewhere in its breeding range where it has shown a preference for high-quality rangeland with only 20-25% bare soil (Whitmore 1981, Bock and Webb 1984).

Grasshopper Sparrows sing from elevated perches, a critical habitat feature. In Morrow Co. they use the flowering stalks of the large velvet lupine (Janes 1983). However, they are rarely encountered in habitats with abundant woody shrubs, habitat that would seem to offer abundant perches for singing. East of the Cascades, bunchgrass prairies with shrubs tend to be occupied by Brewer's Sparrows, a possible competitor that requires shrubs for nest placement. In the Willamette Valley they frequent lightly grazed pastures with scattered shrubs (Altman 1997). They construct a domed nest on the ground, which is concealed under vegetation (Vickery 1996). No information exists regarding diet of Oregon birds, but elsewhere they feed on both seeds and insects usually gleaned from the ground.

**Seasonal Activity and Behavior:** Singing males have been observed beginning 23 Apr in e. Oregon (Janes 1983), 26 Apr in the Rogue Valley (*SWJ*) and 5 May

in the Willamette Valley (B. Altman p.c.). Little is known of breeding in the state. A pair was observed carrying food on 31 May in Morrow Co. (Janes 1983). Two nests were located in early Jul in the Willamette Valley, and one fledged young between 19 and 21 Jul (Altman 1997). Two other observations of fledglings were also during mid-Jul (OBBA). Elsewhere, they typically produce two or more broods annually each consisting of 4-5 eggs (Vickery 1996), and the Jul nests in the Willamette Valley may represent second broods. Once males cease singing in Jul, they are rarely observed though there are 1 Aug (D. Irons p.c.) and 2 Sep records for the Roseburg area (Altman 1994b, Hunter et al. 1998).

Grasshopper Sparrows are quiet ground dwellers that both hop and run. They are among few sparrows that sing more than one song. The primary song is a *tsick, tsick, tsurrrrr* usually delivered from an elevated perch and reminds some of the song of the Savannah Sparrow. They also sing a sustained song lasting 5-15 sec that may be sung while in flight as well as when perched (Vickery 1996). Grasshopper Sparrows compete with Savannah Sparrows for habitat, and Savannah Sparrows are dominant in these interactions (Wiens 1973).

**Detection:** Besides their restricted distribution and small numbers, Grasshopper Sparrows are difficult to detect even when standing within a territory. The thin, insect-like song is easily overlooked among the medley of louder and more musical inhabitants contributing to the spring chorus. However, once the birder is acquainted with their song and focused on it, the best opportunity is to listen in suitable habitat early in the morning (before 0800) and search potential singing perches. Sullivan (1992e) offers a number of localities in Umatilla and Morrow counties where they can be sought including Deadman's Pass and Emigrant Hill Rds. just east of Pendleton.

**Population Status and Conservation:** Noted for marked annual changes in abundance (Smith 1963). Prior to 1940 the only record for the state was an individual collected in Baker Co. (Gabrielson and Jewett 1940) though the authors anticipated their occurrence among the bunchgrass prairies around the base of the Blue Mtns. Since then, reports of additional territorial males have gradually accrued, spanning widely scattered localities across the state. As Gabrielson and Jewett (1940) predicted, the center of abundance includes the remnants of the perennial grasslands along the northern slopes of the Blue Mtns. (Janes 1983, Evanich 1990, Sullivan 1992e).

Further conversion of bunchgrass prairies to dryland wheat and other crops presents a threat to this species in nc. and ne. Oregon. Many of the existing pairs persist in bunchgrass remnants between cultivated fields or in marginal habitat with soils that are too shallow to plow. Heavily grazed land does not appear to retain the habitat features required by this species. In Utah and Arizona the absence of Grasshopper Sparrows is used as an indicator of overgrazing (Bock and Webb 1984, Behle et al. 1985). Habitat in the Willamette Valley is vulnerable to changing land practices and urban growth. Landowners should be encouraged to protect the limited habitat fragments suitable to this species.—*Stewart W. Janes*

## Le Conte's Sparrow *Ammodramus leconteii*

This sparrow of wet bogs and meadowlands breeds from e. British Columbia across Canada and the n. U.S. It winters in the se. U.S. It is a casual migrant and winter visitant along the w. coast. Immatures were photographed at Fields, Harney Co., 27 Sep 1983 (Gilligan et al. 1984) and 12 Oct 1991 (OBRC). Monotypic (AOU 1957).—*Harry B. Nehls*

## Fox Sparrow *Passerella iliaca*

These big, medium-brown sparrows with variable grayish faces and heavily streaked or blotchy undersides can be found in summer at higher elevations across much of the state except the Coast Range. Darker brown birds from more northerly breeding populations are common to locally abundant in w. Oregon in winter, often coming to feeders, where they scratch like towhees for seed on the ground.

**General Distribution:** Breed from the Maritime Provinces across nc. Canada and c. Alaska, also south at high elevations in the Rockies, in the Cascade and Sierra Nevada ranges, and locally in the Great Basin. Winters in the e. U.S., the desert Southwest and along the Pacific coast to s. British Columbia. Eighteen subspecies, some well marked and with distinctive movements, were recognized by the AOU (1957). A different assemblage of 17, including recently recognized *chilcatensis* (see Webster 1983, Browning 1990) is commonly recognized by banders (Pyle 1997). We recognize *fulva* as a separate subspecies (*contra* Pyle 1997) pending additional research. Thus, we estimate three breeding subspecies and an additional nine or more migrant and wintering subspecies in Oregon.

Subspecies are often treated as three (Swarth 1920) or four (Zink 1986, 1994, Rising 1996, Pyle 1997) general groups. Rising (1996) treats the groups as separate species but the AOU (1998) does not; we follow the AOU.

**Oregon Distribution:** Subspecies distribution below is from Gabrielson and Jewett (1940) and AOU (1957) except as noted. Determinations of subspecies' ranges

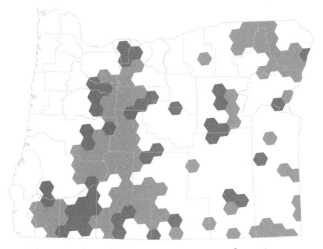

mainly were based on measurements of specimens or in-hand live birds. However, even relatively recent studies such as Zink's (1986) involved few specimens per site (Browning 1995a). More research on subspecies is needed.

*P. i. schistacea* breeds in the Blue Mtns. (until recently including the Ochocos, now appears extirpated) and locally in Malheur Co. Behle and Selander (1951) identified specimens of *schistacea* from Wallowa and Baker counties and AOU (1957) gave the breeding range as e. Oregon including the Cascades to Warmsprings, n. Crook Co. in the Ochoco Mtns., and the Wallowas. Smith et al. (1997b) considered all Blue Mtn. birds as *schistacea* but Aldrich (1943) and AOU (1954) considered *olivacea* to breed in the Blue Mtns. in Oregon; later AOU (1957) confined the southern breeding range to Washington. *P. i. fulva* breed in the e. Cascades from Klamath Co. (e.g., specimens from Annie Cr. in Crater L. NP and Ft. Klamath [USNM]), south and east to the Warner Mtns., Plush, and Hart Mtn. in Lake Co. (USNM), and possibly Steens Mtn. (see discussion below). Also breeds north locally to w. Deschutes Co., less common north to the "breaks of the Columbia R. south of [The Dalles]"; we treat "Bend" in this account of *fulva* as erroneous, actually referable to The Dalles (Gabrielson and Jewett 1940). *P. i. megarhyncha* breed in the Siskiyous (AMNH) west to e. Curry Co. (Cushing 1938, Dillingham 1994, D. Vroman p.c.), east (e.g., specimens from Robinson Butte and Pinehurst, Jackson Co. [USNM]) to the Cascades of sw. Klamath Co. (Zink 1986, *MRB, ALC*) and north probably to e. Lane and at least occasionally to e. Linn Co. (Swarth 1920, Banks 1970, Zink 1986).

Recent banding work on Steens Mtn. (S. Dowlan p.c.) found birds with bill measurements too small for *fulva*, though it was previously thought to be the breeding subspecies there. It is unclear which subspecies, *fulva* or *schistacea*, breed on Steens Mtn., Wagontire Mtn., or in the Pueblo, Trout Cr., or Oregon Canyon ranges. Habitat in these areas is isolated and populations are limited.

USNM specimens from Annie Cr., Ft. Klamath (n. Klamath Co.) and the head of Whiskey Cr. (w. Deschutes Co.) are *fulva* (*MRB*). Specimens from sw. Klamath Co. are within the measurement range for *megarhyncha* (Zink 1986, *ALC*). This suggests that the Klamath Basin lowlands may be a natural break between *fulva* and *megarhyncha*—an intergrade from Keno, Klamath Co., is in the USNM (*MRB*).

Birds of uncertain subspecies breed in the w. Cascades from Lane Co. north to Clackamas Co. and across the summit eastward in adjacent w. Jefferson and w. Wasco counties. Most field measurements of live birds in this region are consistent with the small end of the *megarhyncha/fulva* group (as defined by Pyle 1997, Dowlan 2000a). Birds on both sides of the n. Cascade ridgeline are similar in measurements to each other and are indistinguishable by sight and song (S. Dowlan p.c.). It is possible that *megarhyncha* grades northward into *fulva* in the n. Cascades as suggested by Pyle (1997), or that *fulva* as recognized by previous authorities is expanding its range.

The breeding complex departs the state entirely to winter in California and the Southwest, and is replaced in Oregon during that season by birds that breed in Alaska and w. Canada. These populations overlap somewhat in Oregon but there is some geographic sorting. Fox Sparrows winter abundantly on the coast and in the Coast Range, and include *fuliginosa* (AMNH) and *chilcatensis* (specimen from Tillamook [*MRB*]; see Webster 1983). Swarth (1920) considered *fuliginosa* to be largely sedentary, noting that wintering birds in California are placed "reluctantly" into that subspecies, but see AOU (1957). Also wintering in w. Oregon in smaller numbers are *townsendi* (in coastal localities [University of Michigan, AMNH, USNM]) and *sinuosa* (Netarts in Tillamook Co. [University of Michigan], Klamath Falls in Klamath Co. [AMNH]) (see also Swarth 1920, Gabrielson and Jewett 1940, Zink 1986). Fox Sparrows are common in winter in the western interior valleys, but little information is available about the relative abundance or distribution of the above subspecies. Similarly, a few (unexamined to subspecies) also winter locally into the w. Cascades below the elevation of consistent snowpack, and east of the Cascades as far north as Umatilla Co. (C. Corder p.c.).

Other subspecies that breed north of Oregon pass through as migrants but winter in small numbers or not at all. Among these are *altivagans, unalaschcensis, annectens, insularis,* and *olivacea* (Gabrielson and Jewett 1940, Aldrich 1943, *MRB*). Specimens of *annectens* from Beaverton 27 Feb and Netarts 12 Jan (University of Utah) suggest occasional wintering, as is true of *unalaschcensis,* which has been collected at Nehalem on 14 Jan and 7 Dec (AMNH) and at Carlton on 15 Jan (USNM). Winter specimens of *insularis* are known from Portland, Netarts, and Grants Pass

(*MRB*). Bright, streaky "Red" Fox Sparrows of either the *iliaca* or *zaboria* subspecies are occasionally seen in Oregon, mainly in winter west of the Cascades (*Oregon Birds* field notes, *ALC*), but most are not well documented and there are no specimens.

A thorough review of existing specimens from all seasons and parts of the state, along with additional collecting, is recommended to clarify the identity and status of Oregon populations.

**Habitat and Diet:** Fox Sparrows occur in dense, low shrub growth at all seasons. In Oregon they breed in snowbrush, mountain-mahogany, chokecherry, greenleaf manzanita, willow, red-osier dogwood, sagebrush (at higher elevations), and regenerating 15- to 25-yr-old Douglas-fir and noble fir (Gabrielson and Jewett 1940, Farner 1952, Fix 1990a, Littlefield 1990a, Contreras and Kindschy 1996, S. Dowlan p.c., *MGH*). L. Fish (p.c.) notes that in the Owyhee Uplands they are present "most often in young aspen with manzanita, snowberry and wild rose." Farner (1952) noted that the species used "willows, alders and small firs," but to a lesser extent than manzanita and ceanothus. Evanich (1992a) noted breeding birds in "boggy coniferous forest edges" in ne. Oregon. Nests are placed on the ground or in low shrubs (Rising 1996).

*Fox Sparrow*

Migrant and winter birds use habitat of equivalent structural density. Coastal birds are most abundant in mosaics of red alder, red elderberry, and salmonberry, and in thickets of salal, while those in the western interior valleys reach highest densities in Himalayan blackberry tangles and dense residential shrubbery.

**Seasonal Activity and Behavior:** Birds breeding in the Cascades arrive mid-Apr (Fix 1990a, Dowlan 2000a). At Malheur NWR the average arrival of spring migrants is 10 Apr, with the earliest record 16 Mar (Ivey, Herziger, and Scheuering 1998); peak of passage late Apr and early May (Littlefield 1990a). Studies at Hart Mtn. show that breeding birds are present by the third week of May and that laying occurs as late as 3 Jul (Mewaldt 1980). Wintering birds in w. Oregon begin moving in late Mar (*ALC*) and most are gone by late Apr (Contreras 1998, Gillson 1999). Later migrants still in "winter" habitat commonly sing.

Birds breeding in the s. Cascades depart in Sep (Fix 1990a). Fall movement at Malheur NWR is extended, with birds arriving as early as Aug (earliest 5 Aug), peak of passage 15 Sep to 5 Oct, stragglers occuring into Nov, and only a few in winter (Littlefield 1990a). Migrants from the north appear in late Sep and Oct in w. Oregon (Gullion 1951, Fix 1990a, Gillson 1999, *MRB*), with early arrivals in the second week of Sep (D. Fix p.c.). S. Dowlan (p.c.) noted a peak during the second week of Sep in the nw. Cascades. Farner (1952) noted that *sinuosa* migrates through Crater L. in Sep, though it does not winter there. A "gray-headed" bird of one of the breeding subspecies was noted at Toketee RS, Douglas Co., on 19 Nov 1988, a very late date (Fix 1990a).

**Detection:** The song of the Fox Sparrow is loud, melodious, and easy to distinguish from other species, except for that of the Green-tailed Towhee, with which they sometimes occur. Breeding birds are difficult to see as they dash from shrub to shrub; even perched and singing birds can be difficult to see. Winter birds are far more visible, respond promptly to spishing, and are ubiquitous at feeders and in brushy areas throughout w. Oregon. Breeding races in Oregon are very reluctant to call and have quieter call notes than winter birds, whose heavy *check* can be heard in any westside blackberry tangle. Wintering birds will occasionally sing on warm, sunny days.

**Population Status and Conservation:** Oregon BBS data show a 3% decrease 1966-96 (p=0.06). CBC data (counting a completely different population) show a 5.8% increase 1959-88 (p=<0.01). Breeding Fox Sparrows were not known from the west side of the Cascade summit north of Jackson Co. early in the 20th century (Gabrielson and Jewett 1940). The species was first found at Lava L. in Linn Co. in 1968

(W. Thackaberry p.c.) and is now locally common in brushy clearcuts and old burns from e. Linn Co. north to at least c. Clackamas Co. (S. Dowlan p.c.). While extensive, high-elevation timber harvest beginning in the 1960s certainly has increased habitat for the species, the seeming "expansion" of Fox Sparrows to the w. Cascades in and of itself may just as well be an artifact of recent observer access via logging roads, which were not present early in the previous century.

Clearcut logging has probably benefited forms that breed in w. Oregon by creating suitable shrubland patches among otherwise densely forested landscapes (Webster 1983, *MGH*). However, forest practices typically endeavor to minimize early-seral successional stages, while wildfire burns typically remain in suitable habitat longer. Nevertheless, the reduction in harvest rates in Pacific Northwest forests (USDA/USDI 1994), along with continuing fire suppression policies will likely result in a reduction of habitat for this sparrow in w. Oregon (*MGH*).

In e. and sw. Oregon, open pine forests with dense ground cover such as bitterbrush or currant often support breeding Fox Sparrows and breeding may continue after logging; thus it is probably relatively insensitive to loss of timber, though little information is available to support this. Breeding habitat is much more limited in the Great Basin, and may be more susceptible to disturbance. Overgrazing in sensitive riparian areas or clearing of streamside vegetation could eliminate the species from large areas.—*Alan L. Contreras*

## Song Sparrow *Melospiza melodia*

Although not brilliantly plumaged, the conspicuous Song Sparrow is one of the more regularly seen birds in Oregon. Defensive and curious, when approached it readily announces its presence with loud *chips* and often excitedly rises to a conspicuous perch to confront the interloper. It readily responds to spishing. The Song Sparrow is well named as both male and female have a variety of songs, which may be heard at any time of year, and juvenile birds begin to sing full songs within 2 mo of hatching (Sherwood 1929, Nolan 1968a). This is a grayish-brown bird with a rusty-red and blackish streaked back and heavily streaked head and breast. Birds east of the Cascades are much brighter plumaged than the darker, duller birds to the west.

**General Distribution:** Breeds s. Alaska to Newfoundland south to Georgia and Colorado, and through California and Arizona to Mexico. Withdraws from most of Canada in winter but otherwise winters throughout its breeding range. Of 31 subspecies in N. America, five breed in Oregon and three others migrate through or winter in the state (AOU 1957).

**Oregon Distribution:** *M. m. morphna* is a common and widespread resident of w. Oregon (e.g., specimens [AMNH, USNM] from numerous localities). Postbreeding dispersal, mostly immature, takes many to higher elevations and southward (Gabrielson and Jewett 1940, Farner 1952, Jewett et al. 1953). Some movement to lower elevations in winter with transients and wintering birds from the north increasing numbers to beyond the local breeding population (Jewett 1916b, Gabrielson and Jewett 1940, Jewett et al. 1953, Tompa 1962). *M. m. cleonensis* is restricted to coastal Curry Co. north to Pistol R. (Gabrielson and Jewett 1940), but intergrades with *morphna* have been collected from Lakeside, Coos Co. (AMNH).

Based on comparisons of hundreds of breeding specimens (*MRB, contra* AOU 1957), the Rocky Mtn. subspecies *M. m. montana* breeds in the mountains of se. Oregon in Lake, Harney, and Malheur counties (USNM, AMNH). Intergrades exist between *montana* and *M. m. fisherella* in Klamath (USNM) and Crook counties (MVZ). *M. m. fisherella* is a common resident of riparian areas about marshes, lakes, and streams from Jackson Co. to Klamath Co. (AMNH) *contra* AOU (1957). *M. m. merrelli* breeds in the n. Cascades (Hood River and Wasco counties) and the Blue and Wallowa mountains (*MRB, contra* AOU 1957). The extension of the breeding range of *merrilli* to include Oregon is implied in Jewett et al. (1953).

Most Song Sparrows move to protected riparian areas in winter with some southward movement (Nolan 1968c, Littlefield 1990a). Wintering birds in many areas are not the local breeding birds but migrants from the north according to Rogers (1974a). Gabrielson and Jewett (1940) and Nolan (1968b, 1968e) included only *caurina* as a nonbreeding subspecies in Oregon. However, *caurina* and *inexpectata* (see AOU 1957) and *rufina* (specimens from Portland in Sep [AMNH] and mid-Mar [MCZ], Tillamook in Dec and Jan [MCZ]) have also been identified. *M. m. caurina* was considered to be regular in winter along immediate coastal beaches and headlands (Shelton 1915, Gabrielson and Jewett 1940).

**Habitat and Diet:** The humid climate west of the Cascades allows this moisture-loving species to nest not only in riparian areas but also in upland meadows, fields, urban areas, and even in forests where low, dense thickets are found (Gabrielson and Jewett 1940, Jewett et al. 1953). "Everywhere it keeps fairly close to the ground and in general it remains in wet or marshy places" (Jewett et al. 1953). In the Diamond L. RD of the Douglas Co. Cascades, Fix (1990a) found summering birds "being strongly tied to semi-open brushy swales with persistent surface water in the area."

*M. m. fisherella* are more restricted to the wetter areas of e. Oregon. "Riparian vegetation, marshes, and lake borders" are sought out, for "the combination of dense low cover and surface water with wet ground is essential for this race" (Grinnell and Miller 1944, Dumas 1950). At 7,000 ft (2,133 m) in the Trout Cr. Mtns. Song Sparrows were in willows where water was flowing, not in the occasional willow clumps where no flowing water was present (S. Dowlan p.c.). It commonly nests in the willow thickets within the 6,000-8,000 ft (1,800-2,400 m) elevation subalpine quaking aspen belt on Steens Mtn. (BBS, *HBN*). Birds of the Blue Mtns. prefer streamside willows (Peck 1911) and boggy thickets (*HBN*).

Tompa (1962) studying a dense breeding population on Mondarte I., British Columbia, recorded an average territory size of 3,100 ft² (288 m²) and a home range of 5,091 ft² (473 m²). Nice (1968) recorded 21,528 ft² (2,000 m²) as the minimum territory size in Ohio. Pairs present along Little Blitzen R. on Steens Mtn. appeared to occupy extensive linear territories, as one banded on 28 Jul was observed 295.3 ft (90 m) east of the capture site on 29 Jul (Littlefield 1990b). There are no other data on territory sizes in Oregon.

Most early nests are placed on the ground, usually concealed in heavy brush or grasses. Later many are placed in bushes and shrubs, generally not above 5 ft (1.5 m) (Gabrielson and Jewett 1940, Nolan 1968a, Byers et al. 1995). Kobbe (1900) measured an elevated nest made of grass stems, coarse in the body of the nest, finer in the lining, and found its external diameter was 5 in (125 mm), its internal diameter 3 in (75 mm), its external depth 3.5 in (87.5 mm), and internal depth 2 in (58 mm).

Oregon food data are not available. The Song Sparrow is apparently an opportunistic feeder. Judd (1901) lists a variety of insects, grass and weed seeds, and wild berries and fruit in the diet for the species. Dawson (1923) says that a bird "sometimes seizes and devours small minnows."

**Seasonal Activity and Behavior:** Migratory movements can be obvious but are usually unrecorded. Fix (1990a) noted an influx of Song Sparrows at the Diamond L. RD from late Mar through Apr. There is generally an influx at Malheur NWR 1-15 Mar with most resident birds on territory by 1 Apr (Littlefield 1990a).

Permanent resident males move on territory during Jan and Feb (Hughes 1951, Tompa 1962, Littlefield 1990a), migrants late Feb and Mar (Nolan 1968a, Littlefield 1990a, Byers et al. 1995). Nesting takes place mainly Apr to Jul (Gabrielson and Jewett 1940, Littlefield 1990a). Gullion (1951) gives the extreme nesting dates for the s. Willamette Valley at 28 Feb and 13 Aug. Griffee and Rapraeger (1937) noted the first nesting period in the Portland area from 18 Apr to 22 May, the second period, 16 Jun to 8 Jul. These most likely represent peak breeding periods.

Monogamous. Usually 2-3 broods per season. Usual clutch four eggs. Female builds the nest and incubates. Incubation period 12-14 days; fledge 10-14 days after hatching; independent 18-20 days after fledging (Baicich and Harrison 1997).

Postbreeding dispersal occurs in Aug (Farner 1952, Tompa 1962, Littlefield 1990a). Fall migratory movements at Malheur NWR occur from mid-Sep to mid-Oct with most transients gone by late Nov (Littlefield 1990a). Transients at Diamond L. RD most obvious during late Sep and Oct (Fix 1990a). A conspicuous movement occurred at Tillamook Bay 15 Oct 1972 (*HBN*). Many breeding birds remain on, or near, their territories throughout the year while others migrate south or move to more protected areas, often becoming locally very common (Anderson 1989e, Littlefield 1990a, Korpi 2000). Migrants from farther north join these local wintering birds.

**Detection:** Although a rather nondescript bird, its song and call notes are distinctive. The dark-plumaged birds of w. Oregon are often confused with the wintering dark brown Fox Sparrows by beginning observers. The Song Sparrow has dark brown and gray facial streaks that the Fox Sparrow lacks.

**Population status and conservation:** Common and widespread, the species appears to fill all available habitat. BBS data indicate that the Oregon population is stable. Destruction of riparian habitat is detrimental to this species, especially east of the Cascades (Taylor 1984a). Overgrazing and resulting erosion have seriously reduced the Song Sparrow in some areas (Taylor 1984a, Littlefield 1990b).—*Harry B. Nehls*

## Lincoln's Sparrow *Melospiza lincolnii*

This small tan-and-gray sparrow with a delicately streaked upper breast is found in summer in wet mountain meadows, where its bubbly song can be heard from low shrubs. It winters in brushy lowland areas, where it skulks in tall grass and weeds and is usually seen only for a moment.

**General Distribution:** Breeds from Alaska to Labrador south locally to the northern tier of states and farther south in mountainous regions. Winters from the mid-Mississippi Valley through the Southwest and on the Pacific coast north to s. British Columbia, also south to Honduras. Three subspecies were recognized by AOU (1957), Byers et al. (1995), and Pyle (1997), but *M. l. alticola* and *M. l. lincolnii* are synonyms (Wetmore 1943, Phillips 1959, Rising 1996, *MRB*). In Oregon, *M. l. lincolnii* occurs as a breeder and *M. l. gracilis* as a nonbreeder.

**Oregon Distribution:** Breed locally above 3,000 ft (914 m), with most above 3,500 feet (1,066 m), in the w. Cascades (Gabrielson and Jewett 1940, Voth 1963, Fix 1990a, S. Dowlan p.c., *ALC, DBM, MGH*), south at least to Howard Prairie Res., Jackson Co. (Browning 1974). A few breed at lower elevations in the w. Cascades west to the upper Molalla R. drainage, Clackamas Co. (S. Dowlan. p.c.), in ec. Linn Co. (Gillson 1998), and in ec. Lane Co. (*MGH*). Breed locally in the Klamath Mtns., with evidence from Bolan L. (Gabrielson and Jewett 1940), and at Bigelow Lakes (D. Vroman p.c.). Lincoln's Sparrows breed in the e. Cascades and east to the Gearhart Mtn. area (McAllister and Marshall 1945, C. Miller p.c.), the Warner Mtns. (C. Miller p.c., BBS), and the Blue Mtns. (Miller 1939b, Evanich 1992a). They also breed locally on Steens Mtn. (Fix 1977a, D. Fix p.c., *DBM*) and possibly in the Bowden Hills and Woolhawk Canyon in s. Malheur Co. (Denny 1998c).

Lincoln's Sparrows winter in Oregon mainly in valleys west of the Cascades. Although it is not clear which subspecies winter in the state, Gabrielson and Jewett (1940) indicate that w. Oregon migrants in their collections were of the Alaska-British Columbia breeding form *M. l. gracilis*. Burleigh (1957) found three *gracilis* and collected one at Coos Bay on 7 Dec 1955, suggesting that this may be a wintering subspecies in Oregon. It is not known which subspecies occasionally winters east of the Cascades, but Farner (1952) notes that two Sep specimens from Crater Lake NP proved to be *lincolnii* (identity not confirmed, *MRB*). The species is a rare to fairly common transient throughout the state.

**Habitat and Diet:** Most prevalent in flat or gently sloping mountain meadows where surface water is present (Cicero 1997, *ALC*). In Upper Munson Meadow at Crater L. NP, birds were found breeding in "a wet montane meadow with a lush cover of sedges and forbs; about half of the surface also has a cover of dense willow thickets," with "a few alpine [sic] firs and lodgepole pines … scattered through the area"

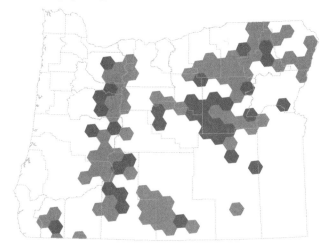

(Farner 1952). In e. Linn Co., they were found feeding "largely [on] aphids" on hellebore in a wet meadow bordered by willow and alder at 4,500 ft (1,371 m) (Voth 1963). In e. Douglas Co., habitat included "lakeshore marshes and persistently wet bogs in which grow low clumps of willows, false hellebore, spiraea, arrowleaf groundsel and the like" (Fix 1990a). In the Siskiyous, Lincoln's Sparrows were found in clumps of Sitka alder in wet meadows above 5,000 ft (1,524 m) (D. Vroman). East of the Cascades it has been found in false hellebore bogs with sedges and willows on Steens Mtn. (Fix 1977a, *DBM*), in willows in wet meadows in the Wallowas (*ALC*), and in a thicket of rose and spirea in s. Malheur Co. (Denny 1998c).

At Munson Meadows in Crater Lake NP pair territory sizes ranged 0.2-1.5 ac (0.08 to 0.60 ha) (Farner 1952). In each year of the two-year study, the smallest territory enclosed the same clump of trees, each territory consisted mainly of willow thickets (usually at least three-quarters of the territory) and each also included a few small conifers, which were used as song perches.

In winter, Lincoln's Sparrows occur in moist weedy sites such as lowland fields and overgrown pastures, uplands adjacent to wetlands, and roadside ditches. Occupied sites usually have tall grass with scattered tall forbs or shrubs, often near water or wet areas. No specific studies have been conducted on winter habitat in Oregon.

Only anecdotal data on Oregon diet are available. In Jul 2001 an adult was observed to bring caterpillars, craneflies, small moths, and damselflies to young in a nest in a meadow at 6,300 ft (1,900 m) in Baker Co. (M. Denny p.c.). In a Wyoming study, mainly arthropods were taken in the breeding season, although seeds were also consumed. Winter food is mainly small seeds (Raley and Anderson 1990).

**Seasonal Activity and Behavior:** An obvious migrant at e. Oregon oasis sites; average spring arrival at Malheur NWR is 24 Apr, with the earliest on record being 22 Mar; peak of passage in the first two weeks of May and stragglers seen through 21 May (Littlefield 1990a). In w. Oregon valleys, birds typically remain through a peak movement in late Apr, with stragglers in early May (Gullion 1951, Heinl and Hunter 1985, Hunter et al. 1998), rarely later in the month (D. Fix p.c.).

The breeding season in Oregon seems to vary somewhat based on snowpack. A juvenile was found 12 Jul 1937 (Farner 1952) at Munson Meadows (elevation about 6,900 ft. [2,103 m]) south of Crater L. rim. Given that incubation (in a Colorado study) takes an average of 11.5 days and fledging an additional 10-11 days (Ammon 1995), it seems likely that nest building was completed and eggs laid no later than mid-Jun. Birds did not arrive at Munson Meadows until 4 Jul 1948 because of late snowmelt, and the

observer found juveniles "scarcely able to fly" on 6 Aug at another site (Farner 1952).

Gillson (1998) reports a bird feeding nestlings on 5 Jun 1998 at the mouth of Crescent Cr. at Lava L., Linn Co. He also notes that nestlings or fledglings were banded in the Parks Cr. area of e. Linn Co. in Jul 1993 and in Jun 1994 and 1996. At Mike's Meadow in e. Clackamas Co., females with brood patches were captured 4 Jun 1997 and 1998 and 18 Jun 1999 (a heavy snowpack year); fledglings were captured at that site 3 Jul 1997, 6 Jul 1998, and 23 Jul 1999 (S. Dowlan p.c.).

The peak of fall passage at Malheur NWR falls between 15 Sep and 1 Oct, with the earliest on 15 Aug and the latest on 23 Oct (Littlefield 1990a). Fix (1990a) notes that the species is a regular migrant in Sep and early Oct at Diamond L., e. Douglas Co. In the Willamette Valley and c. Douglas Co., Lincoln's Sparrows begin appearing in early Sep with most movement in late Sep and Oct (Heinl and Hunter 1985, Hunter et al. 1998). Present in small numbers throughout winter.

**Detection:** On the breeding grounds this bird is best detected by its loud wren-like song, often given from a partly concealed perch low in a willow or small conifer. In migration and winter it is often difficult to see, since when flushed this grass-colored sparrow tends to flit along just above the ground, perch briefly in the open and then disappear for good into the depths of a blackberry patch or grass-shrouded willow. Its distinctive call note, a soft, elongated *eentz* (a similar call is given by the Swamp Sparrow) can alert observers to its presence, as can a *chap* note like a milder version of the "Sooty" Fox Sparrow call heard in winter in w. Oregon. It often responds better to an observer's imitation of a Northern Pygmy-Owl than to spishing.

**Population Status and Conservation:** Oregon BBS trend data are insufficient for a statistically valid trend to emerge for breeding populations. Breeding habitat is rather specialized, but most is at mid- to high elevations, with a considerable portion within existing wilderness or otherwise protected. However, some habitat is subject to grazing with loss of willows in wet meadows. Cicero (1997) found that the species is much less common as a breeder in heavily grazed meadows that otherwise would seem likely to support many breeders. Degradation due to changes in runoff patterns due to logging or road building is also possible, especially at marginal or lower-elevation sites.

Early ornithologists did not find this species wintering in Oregon (Gabrielson and Jewett 1940), perhaps because of its retiring habits, but the wintering population may have increased. CBC trend data show a 4.9 % increase (P=<0.01) compared to decreases in British Columbia, Washington, and the continent as a whole. This may be due in part to the greater experience level of observers who seek the species in its somewhat specialized winter habitat, much of which is in areas where CBC coverage is relatively recent (thus an expected increase in birds per party hour for the state). However, observers who have been in the field for the past 20-30 yr consider the species easier to find today than in the late 1960s and early 1970s. CBCs that have considerable appropriate habitat may record numbers in the 30s and 40s. The winter population of this species would be damaged by draining of sumps, channelization and other activities that reduce wetland edge or shrubs and grassy areas, but habitat is relatively common in w. Oregon at this time.—*Alan L. Contreras*

## Swamp Sparrow *Melospiza georgiana*

First detected in Oregon in 1955, the Swamp Sparrow has been found regularly in w. Oregon since 1975. It uses wet areas that have thick vegetation for cover. Several glimpses of this reclusive bird may be required before it can safely be separated from Lincoln's Sparrow or the more common Song Sparrow, though its distinctive call will give it away to observers familiar with it. Chestnut coloration on the wing coverts helps separate this species from other wintering sparrows.

**General Distribution:** Breeds from British Columbia and Saskatchewan east to Newfoundland, southeast to c. Nebraska and east to Delaware. Winters from Nebraska east to Massachusetts, south to n. Guerrero and c. Veracruz. Also on Bermuda. Small numbers winter in the w. U.S. from Alaska southward. Three subspecies (AOU 1957), *M. g. ericrypta* in Oregon (Burleigh 1957) tentatively (*MRB*). Geographic variation is clinal (Phillips et al. 1964) and named subspecies are not distinct (Paynter 1970).

**Oregon Distribution:** Rare to uncommon spring and fall transient and winter visitant in w. Oregon, particularly along the coast. A Nature Conservancy preserve on Tillamook Bay, Tillamook Co., and the c. Coquille Valley, Coos Co., are well-known wintering areas (Fix 1992). These birds are found primarily at low elevations (Fix 1990a), but migrants have occurred in the w. Cascades in spring (Gilligan 1992b, Lillie 1999) and fall (Fix 1990a, 1990b, Gilligan 2000, *MGH*). They are not detected every year east of the Cascades; probably regular fall migrant and irregular winter visitant. There are few spring records east of the Cascades (all in Mar) of individuals not known to have wintered (Watson 1981c, Rogers 1983b, Evanich 1992c, Contreras and Kindschy 1996). Has wintered at McNary Park, Umatilla Co. (Evanich 1992e) and at Hatfield L., Deschutes Co. (Summers 1993c, Sullivan

1998b, Korpi 2000). May have wintered at Miller I., Klamath Co. (Rogers 1988b) and the Wallowa Fish Hatchery, Enterprise, Wallowa Co. (Crabtree 1994b). Possibly winters in patches of suitable habitat in other locations, but not likely in snow-covered areas. Little is known about the subspecies in Oregon, but *M. g. ericrypta* is the breeding subspecies in British Columbia (Mowbray 1997) and was the subspecies collected at Tillamook in 1955 (Burleigh 1957). At the south jetty of the Columbia R. on 5 May 1990, M. Patterson (p.c.) netted and photographed a bird that also appeared to be *M. g. ericrypta*.

**Habitat and Diet:** In w. Oregon, habitat generally has "dense grassy, weedy, sapling-dotted boggy pockets, often with tangles of blackberry and some standing water" (Irons and Fix 1990). Sites meeting these requirements include shallow marshes of all sizes, wet fields with pockets of dense vegetation, pasture edges, and areas near many sewage ponds. Such habitats in Oregon may contain cattails, canarygrass, bulrushes, blackberry patches, and/or tree saplings such as willow, Oregon ash, and hawthorn (Fix 1992). Along the Columbia R., this species winters in areas that seldom drop below 25°F (-4°C), among dense cattail and blackberry mixed with Russian-olive and willows (M. Denny p.c.). No information on specific foods used in Oregon. Generally eats both insects and seeds, though seeds may constitute the greater portion of the diet in fall and winter. Takes food items from ground, vegetation, and water (Mowbray 1997).

**Seasonal Activity and Behavior:** The earliest arrival is 16 Sep at Diamond L., Douglas Co. (Gilligan 2000). Usually begins arriving late Sep-Oct east of the Cascades and during the last two weeks of Oct west of the Cascades. May be found in "sparrow patches" with other sparrows, or sparrows and finches (Burleigh 1957, Kearney 1991), including Dark-eyed Juncos, Golden-crowned Sparrows (Anderson DA 1990a), Song Sparrows, and House Finches (*BJC*). Usually absent after the first half of Apr. A singing bird was at Shady Cove, Jackson Co., 5 Apr 1969 (Browning 1975a). Latest spring records from coastal Clatsop Co. 5 May 1990 (Fix 1990c, Tweit and Fix 1990b); at the upper end of Detroit Res., Marion Co., 8 May 1999 (Lillie 1999); and a male singing in an alder/willow/sedge bog along Salt Cr., e. Lane Co., 17 May 1992 (Gilligan 1992b, *MGH*).

**Detection:** The Swamp Sparrow is an expert skulker. Most easily detected by hearing its call, a sharp, sweet *teep!* or *seek!* (Fix 1992). Distant call notes of Golden-crowned Sparrows and White-throated Sparrows can be mistaken for Swamp Sparrow calls. Dense vegetation obscuring plumage details may make positive identification difficult.

**Population Status and Conservation:** The first state record was collected at Tillamook, Tillamook Co., 29 Nov 1955 (Burleigh 1957). First record east of the Cascades was 6 Mar 1981 at the Wallowa Fish Hatchery, Enterprise, Wallowa Co. (Watson 1981c). This species has been found regularly since 1975. Reports are usually of single individuals, although as many as 20 have been found at Rain R. Reserve, Tillamook Co. (Johnson 1990b). Not found every year on any single Oregon CBC, perhaps partly because preferred areas may flood and be inaccessible to counters. Reports have increased since the mid-1980s, but fewer than 100 have been reported each season. Whether the increased number of sightings in Oregon is due to winter range expansion or increase in birding activity or both is poorly understood (Mowbray 1997). Low numbers statewide make Oregon a relatively insignificant part of this sparrow's winter range. Wintering needs can be met by habitats that are less threatened than its wetland breeding areas (Mowbray 1997).—*Barbara Combs*

## White-throated Sparrow *Zonotrichia albicollis*

Familiar to anyone from the e. U.S. and Canada, this sparrow is much less common in Oregon. Adults show both a "white-striped" and "tan-striped" morph, while first-year birds resemble tan-striped adults but are typically more heavily streaked underneath. Even the dullest first-year birds have a distinct rectangular white throat patch, often set off with a partial black border.

**General Distribution:** Breeds from nw. Canada eastward to n. Minnesota and the n. Great Lakes and northeast to New England and the Maritime Provinces. Winters throughout the e. U.S. and in smaller numbers to the Southwest and Pacific coast to w. Washington. Monotypic (AOU 1957).

**Oregon Distribution:** Rare to uncommon migrant and winter visitor, mainly in w. Oregon (Gabrielson and Jewett 1940). Rare migrant, most frequent in fall, east of the Cascades. Generally unreported in mountainous areas. In winter, much rarer east of the Cascades, where found mainly in lowland valleys with other wintering sparrows. Most e. Oregon records are from the Columbia and Klamath basins (CBC, Summers 1993a), probably reflecting both habitat availability and observer coverage. White-throateds are progressively rarer farther east in Oregon, with only three records through 1991 in Union and Wallowa counties (Evanich 1992a) and two records in Malheur Co. through 1995 (Contreras and Kindschy 1996). The only winter record for Malheur NWR came on 2 Dec 1960 (Littlefield 1990a), presumably part of a record fall movement that year.

**Habitat and Diet:** In Oregon these birds are typically found along brushy fencerows, in Himalayan blackberry tangles, the edges of agricultural areas and in shrubby willows, but they are also more willing than most sparrows to remain in open wooded areas having sufficient shrub cover. They also use residential areas where cover is available, and are frequently observed at feeders. No diet information from Oregon is available, but feeding patterns resemble those of flockmates.

**Seasonal Activity and Behavior:** First arrives in late Sep, but most seem to arrive from late Oct through Nov, with peak numbers at wintering sites often not seen until early Dec (*ALC*). On rare occasions notable fall movements are reported east of the Cascades, the most impressive of which was 15 birds banded between 11 Sep and 23 Oct, 1960 at Malheur NWR HQ (Littlefield 1990a).

In rural areas, White-throated Sparrows typically flock with other *Zonotrichia* sparrows or juncos. However, this species is at least as common, perhaps more so, in urban and suburban settings, often associating with feeder flocks of juncos (D. Irons p.c.). Summers (1993a) notes that in the Klamath Basin they prefer to flock with Golden-crowned Sparrows. These sparrows show considerable site fidelity and even territoriality in winter (Falls and Kopachena 1994). Spring migration is generally quiet and rarely reported, unsurprising for the small number of birds present in the state. At Malheur NWR spring records fall between 25 Apr and 10 May (Littlefield 1990a). Late records include individuals 20 Jun 1993 at Hunter Cr. (Gilligan et al. 1994), and 21 Jun 1991 at Harbor (Johnson J 1992a), both Curry Co.

**Detection:** This is a relatively easy species to see where present, as its plumage stands out from others of the genus even from behind (when reddish tones of its upperparts are helpful in locating it), and it often feeds on open ground, albeit close to cover. They are best observed at feeders and known wintering sites; less obvious in migration except at se. Oregon oasis sites. Aggregations of 3-4 birds sometimes form in peak years at feeding stations and sparrow concentration areas.

**Population Status and Conservation:** Anderson (1988f) reviewed the Oregon CBC records of this species for the period 1971-85. His evaluation showed a variation from six to 39 birds on Oregon's combined CBCs during that period, with a range of 1-4 birds the norm on counts reporting the species. Since 1990, Oregon CBC totals typically have been more than 50 birds, and trend minima have continued to increase to about 100 in 2000 (NAS 2002). While this increase is undoubtedly in part due to increased participation in

CBCs, the standardized figures (birds per party hour) have also gradually increased, from just under 0.01 prior to 1989 to about 0.025 in 2000 (NAS 2002). The relatively few birds present in the state each year make this a species of minor concern here. Its habitat needs are essentially the same as for such species as Golden-crowned Sparrow.—*Alan L. Contreras*

## Harris's Sparrow *Zonotrichia querula*

This large sparrow is white below and in most plumages has at least some black around the face or throat, more in adults than younger birds. Cheeks are golden-tan in fall and winter and grayish in spring. It is streaked above. It is a winter visitor usually found with other sparrows.

**General Distribution:** Breeds in Canada from the Northwest Territories south and east to nw. Ontario. Most birds winter in the Great Plains. Small numbers winter elsewhere in N. America. Monotypic (AOU 1957).

**Oregon Distribution:** A very rare migrant and rare but regular winter visitor statewide. Numbers vary considerably from year to year but a few birds are typically found in the state every year. They are most regular in the Columbia Basin and in valleys within the e. Blue Mtns. (Evanich 1992a, C. Corder p.c.), but also found almost annually in the Willamette Valley (CBC, *ALC*). One was collected at Nehalem, Tillamook Co., in Jul (Walker 1955), and two at Medford, Jackson Co., in Feb (Gabrielson and Jewett 1940). Irregular migrant and winter visitant in the Umpqua Valley (Hunter et al. 1998). There is a single record of a migrant in the w. Cascades (Fix 1990a). In peak years single birds are found at many sites throughout the state, even reaching the southern coast and Rogue Valley, with small groups of 2-5 birds reported rarely in the eastern half of the state (Kridler and Marshall 1962, J. Johnson p.c., Maitreya p.c., E. Marple p.c.). Five wintered at Malheur NWR in 1974-75 (Littlefield 1990a).

**Habitat and Diet:** Typically found with sparrow flocks in or near dense shrub or bramble cover. May be at edge of woods or in isolated shrubrows. Only anecdotal data are available on Oregon diet; e.g., observed feeding on millet and cracked corn at feeders, and eating Russian thistle and knapweed seed, and picking at downed apples away from feeders (M. Denny p.c.).

**Seasonal Activity and Behavior:** Relatively late fall arrival to Oregon, with birds usually first reported in late Oct (e. Oregon) or early Nov (w. Oregon); earliest 14 Sep 1983 at Mule Shoe Spring, Grant Co. (Evanich 1983a). Birds often remain until Apr (Summers 1995,

Contreras 1998). Notable late records include one collected 10 May 1962 at Ashland (Browning 1975a), one observed on 15 May 1988 at Malheur NWR (Littlefield 1990a), one on 23 May 1998 at Pole Cr. Res. near Brogan, Malheur Co. (Marple 2002), one on 24 May 1994 at OO Ranch (Lillie 1994), and one remained at P Ranch, Malheur NWR, until 25 May 2002 (J. Meredith p.c.).

Relatively sedentary once they arrive, Harris's Sparrows often remain with a chosen sparrow flock for the entire winter. Feeding behavior is dictated somewhat by flock patterns, but these sparrows are more willing than other *Zonotrichia* or smaller sparrows to perch in the open above cover or even occasionally high in trees in the vicinity of feeding groups, a behavior more akin to that of juncos than of other wintering sparrows (*ALC*).

**Detection:** Once these birds settle in for the season they are quite obvious in sparrow flocks, as they are distinctly larger than all other similar sparrows, more like a small towhee than a sparrow. They are often first noticed because of their size, buffy face, very white underparts, and black on the throat.

**Population Status and Conservation:** Anderson (1988f) reviewed Oregon CBC records of this species from 1971 to 1985 and found annual numbers from 1 to 12 for the state as a whole, with an annual average of about 4 birds. Geier (2002) surveyed observers and tallied 43 present during the winter of 2001-02. No conservation concerns are apparent.—*Alan L. Contreras*

## White-crowned Sparrow *Zonotrichia leucophrys*

This large brown sparrow with its handsome black-and-white head pattern (which earned it the nickname "skunk head") is a common breeder in brushy, semi-open country throughout much of the state. In winter, frequently found in large flocks, often in the company of Golden-crowned Sparrows and other seed eaters. White-crowns are easily seen as they feed on the ground, repeatedly dashing back into the cover of dense shrubs before emerging for another foraging bout (Contreras 1997b). Under ideal conditions, the subspecies that occur in Oregon can be separated by head pattern (black versus white lores, pink versus orange bill), back and flank coloration, and song (Dunn et al. 1995).

**General Distribution:** Breeds from n. Newfoundland and Labrador across nc. Canada and most of Alaska west to the Bering Sea, and south through the Rocky Mtns. to n. New Mexico and n. Arizona. Also along the Pacific coast from c. Vancouver I. to s. California, and in the coastal mountains and the Cascade-Sierra ranges

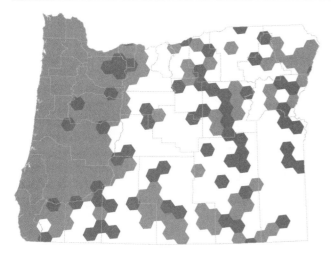

to sc. California and c. Nevada. Winters from sw. British Columbia, Washington, and Idaho across the c. US to s. Massachusetts and south through most of the U.S. (absent from much of the southeastern seaboard and parts of the Florida peninsula) to c. Mexico and s. Baja California. Five subspecies are generally recognized, at least three of which occur in Oregon (AOU 1957).

**Oregon Distribution:** Common breeder, migrant, and winter resident that presents a complex pattern in terms of distribution because of seasonal changes and a mix of migrant and assumed resident populations and subspecies, the movements of which are not fully understood.

As a breeding species, occurs across the state, but distribution is somewhat patchy (Gabrielson and Jewett 1940, Gilligan et al. 1994). As shown by Adamus et al. (2001) and by others as cited, it commonly occurs in summer along the coastal strip, in the Willamette and Umpqua valleys (Gullion 1951, Hunter et al. 1998), in the Coast Range, and at mid- to high-elevation mountain meadows of the Siskiyou Mtns. (D. Vroman p.c.), the Cascades southeast to the Warner Mtns. (McAllister and Marshall 1945, Farner 1952, Browning 1979a, Fix 1990a, Gillson 1999), the Blue Mtn. complex (Evanich 1992a), and high ranges of se. Oregon, e.g. Hart Mtn., Steens Mtn., and the Pueblos, Trout Cr., and Oregon Canyon mountains (Hansen 1956, Mewaldt 1980, Marshall 1987). In the w. valleys south of c. Douglas Co., it becomes increasingly less common and is largely absent from Jackson Co., where Janes et al. (2001) list the species as "rare and irregular" during the summer. Breeding is probable in the Columbia Plateau Ecoregion of nc. Oregon (Adamus et al. 2001).

Fall and spring see an influx of migrants throughout the state, including areas not associated with breeding. Many remain for the winter in valleys lacking snow-cover.

*Z. l. pugetensis* is the breeding subspecies west of the Cascades (AOU 1957), with specimens from coastal counties to interior locations from Multnomah Co. south to Eugene and from w. Josephine Co. into the Cascades (Banks 1964) and other localities in Gabrielson and Jewett (1940). Migrant and winter *pugetensis* are confined to west of the Cascades (Cortopassi and Mewaldt 1965). The range of these subspecies in the high Cascades is unclear (*MGH*). There are no known intergrade specimens between *oriantha* and *pugetensis* (*MRB*).

*Z. l. oriantha* (*leucophrys* of Gabrielson and Jewett [1940]) breeds in most mountain ranges throughout the eastern part of the state (e.g., Hart, Steens and Wallowa mountains [Baptista and King 1980]) and winters to Mexico. Based on available specimens Browning (1974) concluded that further study is required to determine subspecies in se. Oregon.

During migration *Z. l. gambelii* makes up the bulk of migrant White-crowned Sparrows east of the Cascades, while smaller numbers move through w. Oregon (Gabrielson and Jewett 1940); three specimens (USNM) were collected at Crater L. NP in Sep (Farner 1952). Some *gambelii* stay to winter at low elevations in e. Oregon (Gabrielson and Jewett 1940), and have been observed among wintering flocks of *pugetensis* in w. Oregon (Gilligan et al. 1994). Migrant *Z. l. pugetensis* stay west of the Cascades (Cortopassi and Mewaldt 1965). A hatch-year *pugetensis* that was banded near Grants Pass, Josephine Co., on 29 Dec 1989 was recovered southwest of Seattle on 25 Jul 1990 (D. Vroman p.c.). The ranges and movements of various populations of these birds need further study.

**Habitat and Diet:** Generally, breeding birds require three main habitat components: grass cover, bare ground for feeding, and dense shrubs or small conifers (Chilton et al. 1995). In addition, they favor the presence of standing or running water and of tall coniferous trees nearby (DeWolfe and DeWolfe 1962). In w. Oregon, the species breeds abundantly in grass or shrubby headland and dune areas along the immediate coast, in forest clearings in the shrub successional stage in the Coast Range and (less commonly) on the west slope of the Cascades, and in hedgerows and semi-open farmland in the Willamette Valley (Gabrielson and Jewett 1940, Herlyn 1997, Gillson 1999). They are also prominent along freeway rights-of-way even in downtown Portland (*DBM*).

In e. Oregon, breeders are restricted to subalpine meadows, willow and aspen thickets, and riparian areas at higher elevations up to 7,000 ft (2,100 m) (Gabrielson and Jewett 1940). They utilize grassy areas dominated by willow, sagebrush, shrub pine, or aspens, often with taller conifers at the periphery of the breeding territories (DeWolfe and DeWolfe 1962, King and Mewaldt 1987, Adamus et al. 2001). Running water favors denser populations in the mountains (King and Mewaldt 1987).

The nest is usually placed on the ground under a shrub, or above ground in dense shrubs or small conifers. Blanchard (1941) reports that 31% of *pugetensis* nests in California were placed on the ground, with an average height of 39 in (98 cm) for above-grounds nests. At Hart Mtn., 84% of *oriantha* nests were located on the ground, and above-ground nests were placed at an average height of 50 in (127 cm) (King and Mewaldt 1987).

During migration, the species can be found in almost any habitat that provides some open ground for feeding and suitably dense cover nearby. Migrating flocks are especially common along hedgerows, weed patches, and in Himalayan blackberry thickets in w. Oregon, and in sagebrush at lower elevations in e. Oregon. Wintering birds utilize similar habitats as migrating birds, preferring areas with a mix of dense cover and open ground.

Little dietary information exists for Oregon. Generally, all subspecies feed on seeds, buds, grass, fruit, and arthropods during the winter, while diet during

breeding season is predominantly arthropods (mainly insects) and seeds (Chilton et al. 1995). Wintering birds along the Snake R. Canyon in Washington feed mainly on amaranthus seeds in Jan, green plants in Feb, and hackberry buds in Mar (Morton 1967). In winter, most foraging occurs on the ground, rarely more than 6-12 ft (2-4) m away from cover (Pulliam and Mills 1977). During breeding season, forage on the ground, in grass and low shrubbery, and rarely higher in trees. They occasionally hawk for insects. Migrants at Malheur NWR HQ regularly feed on spruce cones in the tree tops at 50 ft (17 m) or more (*HGH*). They also take seed at bird feeders (*DBM*).

**Seasonal Activity and Behavior:** Migratory movement in w. Oregon begins in late Mar and is most noticeable mid-Apr to early May, when the majority of *gambelii* move through (*HGH*). A late migrant *gambelii* in nonbreeding condition was mist-netted at the Horse Cr. MAPS (banding) station, Josephine Co., on 22 Jun 1998 (Dennis Vroman p.c.). Breeding *pugetensis* arrive on territories early to mid-Apr, and laying begins in early May. Gabrielson and Jewett (1940) list 5 May as the earliest date for eggs. Hatching usually begins in late May, and fledging in early Jun (Chilton et al. 1995). Due to the long breeding season, birds in w. Oregon often raise 2-3 broods (Blanchard 1941, Chilton et al. 1995). Birds depart breeding territories by mid- to late Aug, and fall migration in w. Oregon of *pugetensis* is most pronounced from late Sep to early Oct (Gilligan et al. 1994), again coinciding with the passage of *gambelii*.

E. Oregon and California data show breeding *oriantha* arrive mid-May and begin laying from late May to mid-Jun (DeWolfe and DeWolfe 1962, King and Mewaldt 1987, Morton and Pereyra 1994). Hatching begins in mid-Jun and fledging in late Jun (King and Mewaldt 1987). Birds depart the breeding grounds by mid-Sep (Morton and Pereyra 1994).

Migrant arrival (mostly *gambelii*) in e. Oregon begins in late Mar and peaks in mid-Apr (Littlefield 1990a). Autumn migration at Malheur NWR occurs from 15 Aug to 13 Nov, peaking from late Sep until early Oct (Littlefield 1990a).

**Detection:** This species is quite easily detected during most seasons. In the breeding season, its melodious, whistled song gives it away long before it is seen, and singing males often sit on an exposed perch. Later in the season, they often become more secretive, but winter flocks are easily located. Breeding birds in the Warner Mtns. in late Jul and Aug stayed well hidden in streamside willow thickets and showed a marked reluctance to come out into the open (*HGH*).

**Population Status and Conservation:** For the state as a whole, White-crowned Sparrows have shown a

*White-crowned Sparrow*

ELVA PAULSON

significant 4.19%/yr decrease 1966-2000 on BBS routes (Sauer et al. 2001). No significant trends are present in Oregon CBC numbers 1959-88 (Sauer et al. 1996).

Forest clearing likely replaced fire in terms of maintaining habitat in the Coast Range and w. Cascades during the mid-20th century and allowing the species to move higher up the western slope of the Cascades, as is the case in w. Washington (Baptista 1989). Road construction and farming also create new habitat by providing bare ground and grassland in previously wooded regions (Chilton et al. 1995). On the other hand, the clearing of brushland and hedge rows for agricultural purposes may have lead to a habitat reduction at lower elevations. Because of a lack of habitat elements, former breeding in Crater L. NP (Farner 1952) and Ft. Klamath in Klamath Co. (eggs, USNM) could not be confirmed in the 1960s (DeWolfe and DeWolfe 1962).

Isolated montane populations, such as those in e. Oregon, are susceptible to disturbances and habitat destruction through grazing in riparian areas that destroys streamside vegetation (Knopf et al. 1988). King and Mewaldt (1987) determined that reproduction within the isolated Hart Mtn. population was inadequate to maintain the population, and that recruitment was augmented by individuals from outside areas. Overall, the general statement in Chilton et al. (1995) that "no subspecies of White-crowned Sparrow requires management at present time" may hold true for Oregon, although montane populations should be monitored closely.—*Hendrik G. Herlyn*

## Golden-crowned Sparrow *Zonotrichia atricapilla*

Flocks of these big, brown, plain sparrows are a common sight in winter in w. Oregon. By early spring their faded head markings become a beautiful gold, black, and white, and their plaintive descending songs become frequently heard from almost any large brushpile.

**General Distribution:** Breeds from Alaska and Yukon south through British Columbia, sw. Alberta and rarely in extreme n. Washington (Smith et al. 1997, AOU 1998). Winters in a fairly narrow band along the Pacific coast from Alaska south to Baja California, and locally inland to the Southwest. Monotypic (AOU 1957).

**Oregon Distribution:** Abundant migrant in w. Oregon; less common farther east. Abundant in winter throughout the Willamette Valley and locally wherever habitat permits in the Coast Range, lower elevation w. Cascades, along the outer coast, and in valleys of interior sw. Oregon (*ALC*, CBC). It appears that the bulk of migrants move south in the mountains but return north at lower elevations, which is probably

related to the availability of food and the presence of snow cover.

Uncommon in winter (but numbers vary from year to year) in lowlands along the Deschutes R. drainage and in the Klamath Basin, occasional east to Umatilla Co. and c. Lake Co. (CBC), and rare to occasional in the valleys of the Blue Mtns. (CBC, Evanich 1992a) south to n. Malheur Co. (E. Marple p.c.). Rare elsewhere in the Great Basin and Owyhee Uplands in winter (Contreras and Kindschy 1996).

Reported to breed once near Coos Bay in 1982 with four young fledged (Contreras 1998). The report is said to have been by a good observer, but since no further details are available it cannot be confirmed.

**Habitat and Diet:** Preferred winter habitat includes thickets, weed patches, blackberry tangles, the edges of cornfields with nearby cover, and other brushy areas with a nearby food source (Gabrielson and Jewett 1940, *ALC*). High numbers are often present at the suburban/rural fringe. Also uses urban yards when enough cover and food is available. This species, like the White-throated Sparrow, sometimes uses open deciduous woodlands more than does the White-crowned Sparrow (Rising 1996, *ALC*). Fall migrants at high elevations are known to use willows (Farner 1952) and other shrubby vegetation, especially in clearcuts and along roadsides (D. Fix p.c., *MGH*).

Little information is available on Oregon food habits, but it clearly uses seeds and fresh plant growth such as buds. Observed eating ovaries of cherry blossoms in spring (*MGH*). Seems partial to new shoots of grass in spring (*DBM*).

**Seasonal Activity and Behavior:** In fall, outriders occasionally appear in late Aug (Gullion 1951) and reach even s. Oregon by mid-Sep (Browning 1975a, Summers 1993a, Contreras 1998). More typical movements bring birds to mountain ridges of w. Oregon in early Sep, and the species can be locally abundant through early Oct (Farner 1952, Fix 1990a, S. Dowlan p.c., *MGH*). Fix (1990a) noted that the early surge of montane migrants appeared to be mostly hatch-year birds. It is not known whether these birds keep moving south or move down into the valleys. Fewer birds move through e. Oregon. The earliest fall report at Malheur NWR is 6 Sep with a peak between 20 Sept and 5 Oct (Littlefield 1990a).

Winter *Zonotrichia* flocks appear fairly sedentary, as they can be visited repeatedly during the season. They often feed in a "tidal" motion in which sparrows spread out slowly from cover, hopping into a garden, gravel road, or grain field, then all flee back to the blackberry patch when startled, only to begin the same process again. However, little is known about when wintering groups become established, or when they depart.

Spring movements are more extended and feature birds in more colorful plumage. In the w. Cascades, Fix (1990a) noted an earliest arrival of 14 Apr and a latest departure of 17 May. Movements peak in the w. Cascades and Coast Range normally in Apr (Fix 1990a, Faxon and Bayer 1991). On the east side, the highest number recorded at Malheur NWR was 20 on 24 Apr 1940, but single birds or groups of a few are the norm. The earliest spring arrival at the refuge is 19 Mar but the average is 2 May, with a peak between 5 and 12 May (Littlefield 1990a).

Individuals straggle into early summer (Gabrielson and Jewett 1940, Farner 1952, *ALC*). The latest date known from the state (setting aside the 1982 breeding report) is 19 Jun 1990 (Johnson J 1991a). There are other records of very late migrants including 13 Jun 1982 at Cape Arago (Contreras 1998).

**Detection:** This species is easy to see in almost any lowland brushy area in fall, winter, and spring. Winter flocks are sometimes combined with White-crowned Sparrows but are also seen as monotypic foraging groups. Some patience may be required for birds to come out in the open but they can usually be called up by spishing. This species has the most musical chirp of all wintering sparrows; a metallic *zink* that can be heard at a considerable distance. The plaintive three-note descending song is often heard (at least in part) in spring, and sometimes in fall and on sunny winter days.

**Population Status and Conservation:** CBC trend data show almost no change in abundance in 30 yr. Numbers vary widely from year to year, e.g. from 204 to 884 at Salem, a count with relatively constant observer coverage. This species' habitat preferences make it somewhat vulnerable to large-scale clearing of land for development, but to the extent that this leaves openings and brushy edges there is probably little negative effect. Fall movements through the Cascades may be facilitated by the many openings caused by timber harvest. East of the Cascades the maintenance of riparian willow growth would no doubt be of benefit, but this is the edge of the species' range and affects few birds.—*Alan L. Contreras*

### Dark-eyed Junco *Junco hyemalis*

This small, dark-headed sparrow flashing white outer tail feathers is one of the state's most abundant species and one of the easiest to identify. When not nesting it might be seen nearly anywhere in the state. It is a regular visitor to city parks and neighborhood bird feeders. Most juncos occurring in Oregon show dark hoods, dull rusty-brown backs, and pinkish-brown below the wings. Some are grayish, lacking much of the brown tones. They are most often observed in single-species flocks but individuals and small groups often join mixed wintering sparrow flocks.

**General Distribution:** Breeds from the northern limit of trees south to n. U.S., then extends south through the Appalachian Mtns., and from the Rocky Mtns. west to the Pacific coast and south to n. Mexico. Withdraws from most of Alaska and Canada in winter, occurring throughout the U.S. to n. Mexico. Of 15 subspecies, four breed in Oregon and several others migrate through or winter in the state. Subspecies taxonomy follows Phillips (1962), Rea (1983), and Browning (1974, 1978, 2002).

**Oregon Distribution:** *J. h. simillimus* (=*shufeldti* of AOU 1957) is resident from the Columbia R. south to Douglas Co. and from the Cascades to the coast (USNM, Miller 1941). There is some southward movement in winter (Gabrielson and Jewett 1940). Intergrade specimens between *simillimus* and *thurberi* are from Prospect in n. Jackson Co. (SOU) and Glendale in s. Douglas Co. (USNM). *J. h. shufeldti* (=*montanus* of AOU 1957) breeds in the Blue and Wallowa mountains of ne. Oregon south to s. Deschutes, n. Harney, and nw. Malheur counties (USNM). In winter it moves to lower elevations and south throughout e. Oregon and to n. Mexico. *J. h. thurberi* is resident in Coos, Curry, Douglas, and Josephine counties, Siskiyou Mtns., Ashland in Jackson Co. (USNM), and throughout se. Oregon: Crater L. NP (Farner 1952) and Chiloquin in Klamath Co. (USNM) and Warner Mtns. in s. Lake Co. (Miller 1941, AOU 1957). *J. h. caniceps*, mostly pale gray with a reddish back, occasionally has been reported from se. Oregon (Littlefield 1981, Anderson 1988b). On 22 Jun 1999 it was found breeding at 7,600 ft (2,317 m) in the Oregon Canyon Mtns., Malheur Co. (Denny 2000a, 2000b). On 17 Jun 2000 it was present and presumed breeding at 7,000 ft (2,133 m) in the Trout Cr. Mtns., Malheur Co. (S. Dowlan p.c.).

The northern subspecies *J. h. oreganus* found in winter (AOU 1957) regularly west of the Cascades. The mostly gray "slate-colored" *J. h. hyemalis* and *J. h. henshawi* (=*cismontanus* of AOU 1957) are observed regularly during winter in small numbers

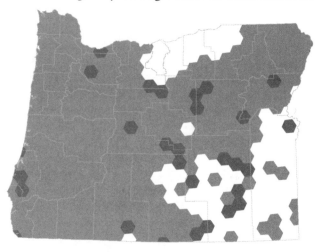

throughout the state. The lone Oregon record of *J. h. aikeni* ("White-winged Junco") was of a bird at a Bend feeder 2 Feb to early Mar 1987 (Crabtree 1987), but characteristics of this bird were within the range of variation of more than one subspecies (Browning 1995a). Individual *J. h. mearnsi* are occasionally reported (Korpi 1998, Sullivan 2001a).

Transient and wintering birds can be found anywhere in the state, even at high elevations, but most concentrate in developed and rural lowlands.

**Habitat and Diet:** Forages and nests on or close to the ground and is associated with forest openings and patches of early seral vegetation (Mannan and Meslow 1984, Kessler and Kogut 1985). Breeds primarily in and about coniferous forests, aspen groves, mixed woodlands, and in small numbers in mature juniper woodlands and urban and suburban areas (Farner 1952, Phelps 1968, Anthony et al. 1990, Reinkensmeyer 2000, *HBN*). A ground cover of grasses, moss, duff, or some broad-leafed herb is usually present. Does not nest in expansive treeless grasslands or desert.

Gabrielson and Lincoln (1959) described typical nesting sites: "nests on the ground, frequently in cutbanks along roads or in the sides of logs, under upturned roots of trees and other places where they are sheltered from above." In more open situations the nest is placed in a depression on the ground and is usually well concealed by surrounding vegetation (Baicich and Harrison 1997, *HBN*). There are several instances of nests placed in bushes and trees, even in cavities and woodpecker holes (Jewett 1928, Griffee 1947, Nikas 1999, Spencer 1999).

Two nests in a railroad cut-bank near Portland were constructed of an outer layer of coarse grasses, then a thick layer of fine grasses, and a lining of cow hair. The inner cavity measured 2.25 in (56.25mm) across and 1.25 in (31.25 mm) deep, while the outer measurements were 2 in (50 mm) across and 2.5 in (62.5 mm) in depth (Bohlman 1903). Hair is the preferred nest lining, but fine grasses or feathers are often used (Phelps 1968).

Apparently an opportunistic ground feeder. Seeds of many plants are the main food. Weed seeds are the primary food item but seeds of Douglas-fir, western white pine, and western larch are also taken (Ellison 1934, Adams 1947). Insects are eaten when available and are an important food during the nesting season (Salt 1953). Jewett (1928) observed birds drinking and bathing in highly mineralized water flowing from small springs near Paulina L., Deschutes Co.

**Seasonal Activity and Behavior:** Spring movements are not conspicuous; there is a slow decline as local breeders move from farms and cities into forests and northern nesting birds begin to migrate. Non-local flocks can often be identified by the presence of a "slate-colored" individual. At Malheur NWR the spring movement begins in late Feb and reaches its peak 10 Mar to 10 Apr with stragglers through May (Littlefield 1990a). This appears to be the pattern throughout the state. At a feeding station in the w. Cascades of e. Douglas Co., a flock of 70 was noted 1 May 1988, and 120 on 26 Apr 1989. These later-occurring birds are thought to perhaps be part of later-breeding northern or mountainous populations (Fix 1990a). The latest date for a "slate-colored junco" was 23 May 1971 at Eugene (Crowell and Nehls 1971b).

Nesting begins earlier at lower elevations than in the mountains (Phelps 1968, Fix 1990a). Nests in sw. Oregon were found from 25 Apr to 7 Jul (Gabrielson and Jewett 1940), in the s. Willamette Valley 9 May to 25 Aug (Gullion 1951), and in the Portland area 22 Apr to 8 Jun (Griffee and Rapraeger 1937). At Crater L. NP Farner (1952) recorded nests from late May to early Aug. Similarly, nests at 4,800 ft (1,463 m) and 6,000 ft (1,829 m) in e. Douglas Co. had full incubated clutches in late Jul (Fix 1990a). A full-grown juvenile was found in Corvallis on 10 Apr (D. Irons p.c.).

Monogamous. Usually two broods per season. Usual clutch four eggs. Female builds nest and incubates. Incubation period 11-12 days, young fledge 11-13 days after hatching. Adults feed young for about 3 wk after fledging (Baicich and Harrison 1997).

Postbreeding dispersals begin in Jul with large flocks often seen, most moving to higher elevations (Farner 1952, Crowell and Nehls 1966c). Most birds remain at higher elevations until fall storms drive them to the lowlands (Phelps 1968, Fix 1990a). Individuals and small family groups of local breeders may appear at lowland cities and farmlands during Jul (*MGH*), but it is Sep before transient flocks arrive from the north and mid-Oct before peak numbers are reached (Littlefield 1990a). The earliest "slate-colored" was 16 Sep near Silver L., Lake Co. (Gabrielson and Jewett 1940).

**Detection:** Common and easily identified. The dull, streaked, brownish juveniles would cause identification problems but for the conspicuous white outer tail feathers. Identification of breeding subspecies in the field is often difficult as differences in plumage characteristics are minor and quite variable.

**Population Status and Conservation:** Common and widespread. BBS data indicate that the Oregon population is stable and may be increasing. Forest thinning, clearcutting and other land use practices that reduce forest canopy cover and allow low shrubs and small trees to develop favor this adaptable species (Hagar et al. 1996, Hagar 1999b). Spring prescribed burns may destroy nests in all breeding areas (M. Denny p.c., *MGH*). Otherwise, there appear to be no extensive conservation problems at this time.—*Harry B. Nehls*

## McCown's Longspur *Calcarius mccownii*

This species breeds on the dry sparse prairies from s. Alberta and Saskatchewan to n. Colorado. It winters in s. California and s. U.S. into Mexico. It is occasionally reported elsewhere in the West. There are no photo or specimen records for Oregon. One was at Malheur NWR, Harney Co., 24 Nov 1956 (Scott 1957); a male was along Highway 20 east of Burns, Harney Co., 8 Aug 1976 (OBRC); a male was among a large flock of Lapland Longspurs and Horned Larks at Lower Klamath NWR, Klamath Co., 31 Jan 1981 (Rogers TH 1918b, OBRC); another, also with Lapland Longspurs, there on 26 Nov 1986 (Anderson 1987b); a male was within a flock of Lapland Longspurs there 13-31 Jan 1990 (OBRC); and six there 19 Feb to 4 Mar 2001 (Spencer 2001b, OBRC). Monotypoic (AOU 1957).—*Harry B. Nehls*

## Lapland Longspur *Calcarius lapponicus*

Within wintering flocks of Horned Larks in valleys of e. Oregon, and along flats bordering coastal estuaries in the fall, it is sometimes possible to find flocks of this large arctic-breeding sparrow. Their habit of running along the ground in a crouch rather than flying makes them a challenge to observe, but in flight their characteristic rattling call is unmistakable. Otherwise, in fall and winter plumage, they appear as brownish streaked sparrows. In flight their dark tail with white sides is conspicuous.

**General Distribution:** Breeds in the arctic tundra of N. America, Greenland, and Eurasia. Winters most commonly in open grassy plains of the Asian subcontinent and Great Plains of N. America. Two breeding (AOU 1957) and one vagrant subspecies (Gibson 1986) occur in N. America; *C. l. alascensis* the western subspecies, has been reported (AOU 1957) for California; Oregon subspecies unknown (no specimens).

**Oregon Distribution:** Along the outer coast, the Lapland Longspur is an uncommon but regular fall migrant, especially at the south jetty of the Columbia R. where flocks of up to 200 occur (Broadbooks 1946b, Contreras 1998, Patterson 1998b). They are irregular on the coast in winter and spring. This longspur is regularly reported in e. Oregon, but numbers vary year to year. For example, during the winter of 1996-97, they were reported from the Oregon-California line in the Klamath Basin, near Ontario, Malheur Co., at Malheur NWR, Adel, Lake Co., and Redmond, Deschutes Co. (Korpi 1997), while in other years e. Oregon reports are missing. Reported during only 12 of the most recent 20 yr of Oregon CBCs, most frequently east of the Cascades (Shipman 1998). Flocks of up to 500 have been reported in winter in

the Klamath Basin (Summers 1993a). Reported most years in *Oregon Birds* from other parts of e. Oregon, especially ne. Oregon. A flock of 50-100 near La Grande through the winter of 1974-75 is an example (Rogers 1975). Casual in Umpqua (Hunter et al. 1998) and Rogue (Browning 1975a) valleys, and in the Willamette Valley (Gilligan et al. 1994).

**Habitat and Diet:** Along the Oregon coast, these longspurs occur in tidal salt marshes with salicornia, seaside plantain, and mixed grasses, as well as nearby dune margins (*MP*). In e. Oregon, they are found in pastures, grasslands, and fields that have been mowed or plowed or are burned stubble. Birds at the s. jetty of the Columbia R. have been observed stripping seeds from seaside plantain and seaside arrow-grass (*MP*), but no other information on food habits is known from Oregon. Byers et al. (1995) reported that the nonbreeding diet consists primarily of seeds of grasses, sedges, and herbs with no specific locale given.

**Seasonal Activity and Behavior:** Fall dispersal from breeding grounds begins in mid-Aug (Dunn and Beadle 1998). While there are some late Aug records for Lapland Longspurs on the Oregon coast, most arrive there in mid-Sep and can be found reliably through Oct. The majority of individuals using the coastal strip leave by the end of Oct. Spring coastal records are from late Apr and early May, but are distinctly few compared to fall. Summer records include a 10 Jul 1984 report from the s. jetty of the Columbia R. (Gilligan et al. 1994) and another for 1 and 8 Jul 1984 at Tillamook Bay (Harrington-Tweit and Mattocks (1984). Wintering birds in e. Oregon are present from Nov to Mar (Gilligan et al. 1994), although there is an early fall record of 29 Aug 1996 at Harney L., Malheur NWR (Anderson 1987b) and late spring sightings of 27 May 1994 along the Double O Ranch Rd., Harney Co., and 25 May 1998 at Pole Cr. Res., near Brogan, Malheur Co. (Marple 2002).

**Detection:** Lapland Longspurs prefer to run or remain still in a low crouch. When startled into flight they typically fly a few meters and drop back to the ground. Although quiet on the ground, in flight they give a noisy string of dry, cricket-like rattles and plaintive *tew* notes. At the peak of migration, flocks in flight are conspicuous. In e. Oregon longspurs should be looked for in flocks of Horned Larks and Snow Buntings (Rogers 1975, Summers 1993a).

**Population Status and Conservation:** Gabrielson and Jewett (1940) identified the "Alaskan Longspur" (*C. l. alascensis*), as "reach[ing] Oregon so infrequently as to become a rare straggler." Most of their records were from east of the Cascades in Dec. They cited only one coastal record, which was near Siltcoos L., Lane

Co., in 1915. Although it can be speculated that the species was overlooked by most early observers, it is suspected the species has became more common in Oregon. Despite the presence of resident biologists at the Malheur NWR who sought new bird findings, the species was not recorded there until 9 Jan 1982 (Littlefield 1990a); thereafter it has been periodically reported. This represents an absence of reports of the species in that region from Bendire's time in the 1870s for the next 108 yr.

Occurrence in Oregon is irruptive, making long-term trends impossible to assess. Breeding-ground habitat is not subject to substantial alteration from human activities. The status of N. American populations is thought to be stable (Rising 1996).—*Mike Patterson*

### Chestnut-collared Longspur *Calcarius ornatus*

This species breeds in grasslands from Alberta and Saskatchewan to n. Colorado. It winters in the s. U.S. and Mexico. Small numbers regularly migrate and winter in California, but is only occasionally observed in the Northwest. A breeding plumage male was photographed at Fern Ridge Res., Lane Co., 1 May 1976 (Watson 1989); one was in the Lower Klamath NWR, Klamath Co., 14 Nov 1981 (Rogers TH 1982a); a male was photographed at the s. jetty of the Columbia R., Clatsop Co., from 17 Jul to 25 Sep 1985 (Watson 1989), during which time it molted from alternate to basic plumage; one was at Bandon, Coos Co., 3 Nov 1985 (Heinl 1986a); one was at the Diamond L. sewage ponds, Douglas Co., 2 Oct 1987 (OBRC); another was there 13 Sep 1989, and a different bird was there on 3 Oct 1989 (Fix 1990a). An immature was video-taped at the south jetty of the Columbia R., 9 Oct to 1 Nov 1998 (OBRC, Gilligan 1999). One was at Cape Blanco, Curry Co., 13-22 Oct 1999 (OBRC) and 9 Oct 2001 (Contreras 2002b). One was on the n. spit of Coos Bay 26 Oct 2001, and one was at Lost Cr. Res., Jackson Co., 9 Nov 2001 (Contreras 2002b). Monotypic (AOU 1957).—*Harry B. Nehls*

### Rustic Bunting *Emberiza rustica*

This Eurasian species breeds from n. Scandinavia through Siberia. It winters in China and Japan. Small numbers regularly occur in the Aleutian Is., and occasionally along the w. coast of N. America to California. A male was observed with other sparrows in downtown Portland, Multnomah Co., 21 Nov 1975 (OBRC); and one remained and was photographed in a Eugene, Lane Co., residential area from 31 Mar to 27 Apr 1994 (Sherrell 1994a). Subspecies unknown.— *Harry B. Nehls*

### Snow Bunting *Plectrophenax nivalis*

The Snow Bunting is a large finch that breeds throughout the high arctic tundra. In winter, many move south, sometimes forming large flocks in open grasslands, steppes, and dunes. When feeding in agricultural fields, these flocks may be hidden among the stubble, but when alarmed they often arise as a group and whirl about in a white cloud before returning to their spot or a nearby one (Gabrielson and Jewett 1940). Oregon is at the southern edge of their winter range, and their wanderings about the state are erratic. In basic plumage, they are buffy and cream-colored with black and white wings.

**General Distribution:** Holarctic. Breeds in arctic across n. N. America, Greenland, and Eurasia. Winters from sw. Alaska east through s. Canada, and south throughout much of Great Plains. The extent of southward incursion varies from year to year, but generally southern limit extends from e. Washington and n. Oregon through n. Utah to c. Kansas, and across to eastern seaboard. Four subspecies recognized worldwide; *P. n. nivalis* occurs in Oregon (AOU 1957).

**Oregon Distribution:** Irruptive. Occasional to locally common winter visitor in ne. Oregon (Evanich 1992a). Large flocks numbering in the hundreds can be found in Wallowa Co. (Contreras 1997b): e.g., 450+ seen near Enterprise in Jan 2001 (Spencer 2001b). Occasionally reported elsewhere in e. Oregon, in much smaller numbers. Recorded several times near Vale, Malheur Co., and recorded almost annually on or near Malheur NWR (Littlefield 1990a, Contreras and Kindschy 1996, Korpi 1997, Sullivan 1998a). Seen as far south as Lower Klamath NWR (Sullivan 1999a).

Rare winter visitor along n. coast (Gilligan et al. 1994). Most often reported in small flocks of up to 30 from the s. jetty of the Columbia R. and at Bayocean Spit, Tillamook Co. (Gilligan et al. 1994, Heinl 1985, *MP*). Occasionally winters at Yaquina Bay jetties (Fix 1985a). There are scattered reports along the coast south of there, including one for Harbor, Curry Co., but it is generally very rare on the s. coast (Gilligan et al. 1994, Gilligan 1996).

Rare and irregular in late fall and winter on bald mountain tops and alpine meadows in the Cascades and Coast Range (Gilligan et al. 1994), e.g., Marys Peak, Benton Co. (Gilligan 1996, Herlyn 1998). Very rare in the Willamette Valley: there are several records of small numbers near Halsey and near Lebanon, both Linn Co.; and at Philomath, Benton Co. (Gilligan 1996, Gilligan 1998, Tice 1999b). Extremely rare to interior sw. Oregon (Contreras 1997b); one near Talent in 1994 is the only record from Rogue Valley (Janes et al. 2001).

**Habitat and Diet:** Open country. Often found on plowed fields in grain or corn stubble (Contreras and Kindschy 1996). In ne. Oregon use "vast, sprawling grasslands" and foothills at low to moderate elevations (Evanich 1992a). Many records from Malheur NWR are from open flats along receding shorelines of Malheur L., and along rocky roadsides in the vicinity (Littlefield 1990a). On coast, found among dunes and on beaches; often at boundary between dune grass and beach, particularly where there is an accumulation of drift debris (Evanich 1990, *MP*).

No diet studies in Oregon. Known winter diet consists of weed and grass seeds and waste grain (Gabrielson and Jewett 1940, Lyon and Montgomerie 1995). In coastal habitats, small crustaceans also important (Lyon and Montgomerie 1995). Always forage on ground (Lyon and Montgomerie 1995).

**Seasonal Activity and Behavior:** Earliest arrival date for Malheur NWR is 29 Oct (Littlefield 1990a), and earliest date on the coast is 1 Oct (Gilligan et al. 1994). Generally first arrives in the state in Nov (Evanich 1990). Most records from Malheur NWR are in Dec and Mar (Littlefield 1990a). In ne. Oregon, particularly Wallowa and Grant counties, most easily seen in Dec and Jan when it often forms huge flocks (P. Sullivan p.c., *MP*). Most leave in Mar, but seen as late as 7 Apr at Malheur NWR, and 14 Apr on the coast (Evanich 1990, Littlefield 1990a, Gilligan et al. 1994).

**Detection:** Along coast, often heard before seen. Call is a characteristic *tee-ew*. A chittery rattle similar to Lapland Longspur is also produced. In e. Oregon regularly form flocks, often with Horned Larks (Gabrielson and Jewett 1940). However, tendency of flocks to wander widely makes their appearance highly unpredictable.

**Population Status and Conservation:** First recorded in Oregon by Bendire (1877) at Camp Harney near present-day Malheur NWR, Harney Co., where the species was rarely seen again until the mid-1980s. It is now recorded there almost annually, usually in small numbers, though flocks of up to 60 have occurred (Littlefield 1990a). Overall, statewide population figures are difficult to track due to irregular nomadic movements of this species in winter. No quantitative data available for impacts of land-use practices on wintering populations; though as heavy users of agricultural fields, this species could be vulnerable to pesticide contamination (Lyon and Mongomerie 1995).—*Mike Patterson and Rachel White Scheuering*

**McKay's Bunting** *Plectrophenax hyperboreus*
This close relative of the Snow Bunting breeds on islands in the Bering Sea and winters along the Bering Sea coast of Alaska. It is accidental south along the Pacific coast to Oregon. Two birds were photographed among a Snow Bunting flock at the south jetty of the Columbia R. 23 Feb to 9 Mar 1980 (Watson 1989). The photos were examined by Dan Gibson of the University of Alaska Museum, who confirmed the identification. Monotypic (AOU 1957).—*Harry B. Nehls*

## *Family Cardinalidae*

### Rose-breasted Grosbeak
*Pheucticus ludovicianus*
This species breeds from ne. British Columbia to Nova Scotia and south to n. Georgia. It winters in M. and n. S. America. Small numbers regularly occur along the w. coast, especially in spring. The majority of Oregon records have occurred from early Mar through Jul, mostly from mid-May to mid-Jun. A pair was at Malheur NWR HQ, Harney Co., 15 Jun 1976 (Littlefield 1980), that pair, or another, was a few miles west at Stinking L., Harney Co., 4 Jul 1976 (Rogers 1976). A subadult male was at a Tillamook, Tillamook Co., feeder 5-13 Mar 1986, when it was found dying (OBRC, spec. Tillamook Co. Museum). A male was photographed at Cape Meares Village, Tillamook Co., 28 May to 12 Jul 1994 (Johnson J 1995a). From 21 Jun to 3 Jul 1976 a territorial male was mated with what was thought to be a female Black-headed Grosbeak at Cold Springs CG, Deschutes Co. A nest was built but no incubation was noted (OBRC). One was at Bend 3 Aug 2001 (Sullivan 2002) and at Astoria 26 Aug 2001 (Contreras 2002b). Individuals are occasionally found from mid-Sep to mid-Jan, mostly birds that remained less than 5 days. Casual in fall and winter. All Dec and Jan records are from w. Oregon. Most w. Oregon birds have been detected at feeders. Monotypic (AOU 1957).—*Harry B. Nehls*

### Black-headed Grosbeak
*Pheucticus melanocephalus*
For many, the rich, melodious song of the Black-headed Grosbeak is the music of springtime in Oregon. The handsome males, with their bold pattern of cinnamon, black, and white, are among our most striking songbirds, and are a familiar sight in parks and gardens as well as in almost every forest type in the state. The buffy, streaked females are less conspicuous, but are also accomplished singers. Yearling males are highly variable, and range from female-like to adult-male-like in plumage.

**General Distribution:** Breeds across w. N. America from sw. Canada east to the Great Plains, and south to s. Mexico. Winters in c. to s. Mexico, where wintering and breeding populations overlap. Two subspecies (Phillips 1994); *P. m. melanocephala* (includes *maculatus* as a synonym) in Oregon.

**Oregon Distribution:** A common to fairly common breeder and common migrant in forested regions throughout the state. Areas where they are relatively scarce include the north coast, riparian areas of nc. and extreme e. Oregon, and extensive conifer forests with little deciduous canopy in the c. Cascades (Gabrielson and Jewett 1940, Gilligan et al. 1994, *MGH*). Casual in winter: there are six w. Oregon records for Dec, with at least two remaining all winter (H. Nehls p.c.). In e. Oregon, one was at Ochoco Res. 23 Dec 1980 (Watson 1981c).

**Habitat and Diet:** Found in a wide variety of habitats, but most abundant in riparian zones and in open mixed conifer and hardwood forests. Optimal conditions are often met in younger forests (Carey et al. 1991, Gilbert and Allwine 1991). Reaches high densities in regenerating clearcuts (10-20 yr old), though they appear to avoid young clearcuts (< 10 yr old) (Hutto et al. 1992). Common in oak woodlands in valleys, around mountain meadows and riparian areas in mountain conifer forests, and in willow and cottonwood thickets in the dry country of e. Oregon. In Willamette Valley foothills, found equally in Douglas-fir and western hemlock-dominated forest types (Anderson 1972), as long as a deciduous component is present. Commonly found as high as 5,000 ft (1,524 m) in the Cascades, and as high as 7,000 ft (2,134 m) in aspen groves on Steens, Pueblo, and Trout Cr. mountains (Hansen 1956, Marshall 1987). Also common in parks and residential areas where there is sufficient cover for nesting. Readily visits bird feeders, including nectar feeders (Hill 1995).

Nests are usually well hidden among foliage, mostly 5-15 ft (2-5 m) above ground. A wide variety of plant

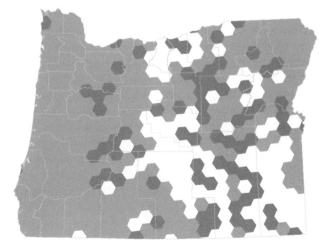

species have been recorded as nest sites in California, of which approximately 80% were deciduous trees and shrubs (Weston 1947). Nests are bulky open cups, loosely constructed of twigs, stems, and rootlets, and lined with finer plant fibers, hair, and green plant material (Weston 1947, Hill 1995).

Has a varied diet during the breeding season, composed of approximately 60% animal material and 40% plant material (McAtee 1908, Beal 1910). Powerful beak allows feeding on hard seeds and insects, including weevils, click beetles, and cicadas (McAtee 1908). Wild and cultivated fruits are eaten, including poison oak, elderberry, blackberry, cherry, and strawberry. Both larvae and adult lepidoptera taken; the wings of adult butterflies and moths are pulled off (and discarded) before consumption (Marshall 1957, Fink and Brower 1981).

Most foraging for insects is by gleaning in foliage (70% of foraging in a California study [Airola and Barrett 1985]), often relatively high in vegetation. Also forages for insects on twigs, captures them in the air, and feeds on seeds on the ground.

**Seasonal Activity and Behavior:** Generally arrive in w. Oregon in mid- to late Apr. Early date 30 Mar 1980 at Philomath, Benton Co. (Gilligan et al. 1994). Arrival east of the Cascades peaks in mid-May, with first arrivals in early May (Ivey, Herziger, and Scheuering 1998). Adult males arrive first, usually all within 4-5 days of each other, followed by the first females 5-7 days after the first males (Weston 1947, Hill 1989). Yearling males arrive last, 12-16 days after adult males (Hill 1989).

Males sing intensely from their arrival in the spring to the completion of the female egg-laying period. Both males and females frequently sing from the nest during incubation. Female songs are typically shorter in duration and simpler in structure than those of males (Ritchison 1983b).

Both members of the pair defend the territory. No data on territory size in Oregon; published averages range from 2 ac (0.79 ha) in New Mexico (Hill 1988) to 6.8 ac (2.7 ha) in Utah (Ritchison 1983a). Pair formation appears to occur very rapidly following female arrival (Weston 1947, Hill 1989). The male's most elaborate display is a courtship flight with the showy plumage spread to great effect, and accompanied by continual loud song (Weston 1947).

Nest construction is entirely or almost entirely by the female, closely accompanied by her mate, who guards her against rival males. Nest construction takes 3-4 days (Weston 1947, Ritchison 1983a), and occurs primarily from late May to mid-Jun in Oregon (n=7) (OBBA). Egg dates have been reported in Oregon 12 May to 4 Jul (Gabrielson and Jewett 1940). Clutch size typically 3-4 (Gabrielson and Jewett 1940, Hill 1995). Incubation period is 12-14 days (Weston 1947,

Ritchison 1983a). Both sexes incubate, spending approximately equal time on the nest during the daylight hours. Black-headed Grosbeaks are infrequent hosts of Brown-headed Cowbirds (Hill 1995).

Young in the nest primarily Jun to early Jul (n=19) (OBBA). The nestling period is 10-14 days in Utah (Ritchison 1983a). Both parents feed and brood the young (Weston 1947, Ritchison 1983a). In Oregon, young observed out of nest Jun and Jul (as late as mid-Aug; n=26) (OBBA). Young spend an extended flightless period of approximately 15 days after leaving the nest. During this period, they remain hidden and silent in thick foliage. Renesting occurs if the first attempt fails, but second broods when the first is successful have not been observed. Males may leave the area before the period of juvenile dependency is over (Weston 1947, Ritchison 1983a).

Fall migration typically begins in early Aug and lasts through mid-Sep, with a peak in late Aug (Gabrielson and Jewett 1940). Males leave first, sometimes as early as late Jul. Females depart 2-4 wk later (Weston 1947), and young of the year are the last to go, often several weeks after the last adult (Hill 1995). Mountain-nesting grosbeaks often move to riparian areas at lower elevations in late summer and may spend several weeks there before departing. A few stragglers have been recorded west of the Cascades into mid-Oct, e.g., a bird 14 Oct 1975 at Sauvie I. (Crowell and Nehls 1976a).

Most females breed in their first spring, but most males do not breed until their second spring (Hill 1988). Only yearling males with bright, adult-like plumage are able to attract mates and breed (Hill 1988). Greatest life span recorded in the wild is 9 yr, 1 mo (Klimkiewicz and Futcher 1987); has lived 25 yr in captivity (Weston 1947).

**Detection:** Readily detected by song during the spring and early summer. Less conspicuous following fledging of the young, when both sexes essentially cease singing, but at this time, especially, the common and distinctive call-note reveals the presence of many dispersing birds that otherwise would go unnoticed. May gather in small groups in late summer at fruiting sources, including plums and other ornamental trees in parks and gardens.

*Black-headed Grosbeak*

**Population Status and Conservation:** Oregon populations have remained stable overall during 1966-99, according to BBS data (Sauer et al. 2000). The trend during 1980-99 has been significantly upward. With its broad ecological range, tolerance of human activity, and apparent preferences for habitat edges and patches, the Black-headed Grosbeak seems well adapted to human-dominated landscapes.—*Pepper W. Trail*

### Blue Grosbeak *Passerina caerulea*

The Blue Grosbeak breeds from c. California across the s. U.S. to Pennsylvania and south through M. America. It breeds annually in the Sacramento Valley of California and in s. Idaho. It is casual in winter in the U.S. A female-plumaged bird was photographed as it visited a Corvallis, Benton Co., feeder 4-17 Jan 1975 (Roberson 1980, Watson 1989); another female-plumaged bird was near Fern Ridge Res., Lane Co., 21 Dec 1980 (OBRC). On 9 Jul 1997 a subadult male and a female were found attending two newly fledged juveniles along Willow Cr., northwest of Brogan, Malheur Co. They remained into Aug for many birders to observe and photograph (Spencer 1998); a female was observed near there 28 Jun 1998 (OBRC). The monotypic genus *Guiraca* was merged with *Passerina* (Banks et al. 2002).—*Harry B. Nehls*

## Lazuli Bunting *Passerina amoena*

All of Oregon's blue-colored birds are appreciated for their dazzling appearance, but the striking plumage of this summer visitor is accompanied by a song described by William Rogers Lord (1902) as "vivacious, varied, well-articulated and sweet." Males are unmistakable when singing from a prominent perch, flashing deep azure upper parts with rich orange-brown breast and flanks, a white belly, and white wing bars. Lord introduced the species in his book by stating, "If it is a question of beauty and coloring, no other bird may hope to surpass to human eyes this little bit of heaven's blue." Females are warm brown and relatively plain, though they share with males the habit of twitching the tail to one side when excited (Hoffmann 1927).

**General Distribution:** Breed from se. British Columbia, s. Alberta, and extreme s. Saskatchewan south through the Great Basin and w. Great Plains to extreme w. Oklahoma and n. Texas panhandle, n. New Mexico and n. Arizona. Western distribution includes the west slope of the Washington Cascades, interior valleys south to the s. coast of Oregon, through California (excluding eastern desert areas) into nw. Baja California. Winters in s. Arizona, s. Baja California, and w. and s. Mexico. Monotypic (AOU 1957).

**Oregon Distribution:** Fairly common in low-elevation dry valleys in Curry Co., becoming uncommon north through the Coquille R. valley. Rare along the immediate coast from n. Coos Co. north to Cascade Head, Lincoln Co. (Gabrielson and Jewett 1940, Gilligan 1994, Contreras 1998, OBBA), occasional northward. Common breeder in the Rogue and Umpqua R. valleys and fairly common in the s. Willamette Valley, becoming less common north to the Columbia R. (Gabrielson and Jewett 1940, Gullion 1951, Browning 1975a, Swanson 1991, Gilligan 1994, Herlyn 1998, Hunter et al. 1998, Gillson 1999). In the north, most frequently found where there are dry, brushy, south-facing aspects, such as in the e. Coast

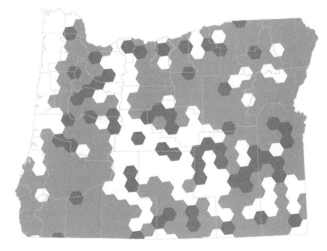

Range. Breed in the w. Cascades with decreasing abundance northward, becoming scarce north of Linn Co. (Gillson 1999, OBBA, *SGD*).

Uncommon to fairly common along the eastern slope of the Cascades through the Klamath Basin (Evanich 1990, Summers 1993a, D. Lusthoff p.c., *SGD*). Breed throughout the mountains of the south-central and southeastern portion of the state, including the Warner Mtns., Hart Mtn., Steens Mtn., and the Trout Cr., Oregon Canyon, and Pueblo mountains (Marshall 1987, Evanich 1990, Littlefield 1990a, Sullivan 1992a). Breed in the Blue Mtns, uncommon to locally abundant in Wallowa and Union counties (Gabrielson 1924, Evanich 1992a). Locally uncommon in canyons and at lower elevations in Malheur Co. (Contreras 1996a, Denny 1998c, 1998b). Migrants are common to uncommon throughout the range (Gilligan et al. 1994), with some irregularity of numbers noted from year to year for Douglas Co. (Fix 1990a). Two winter reports from c. Douglas Co. (Hunter et al. 1998), but no documented winter sightings for the state.

**Habitat and Diet:** In Coos Co., found in brushy fields and hillsides away from the immediate coast (Contreras 1998). In western interior valleys it is generally a grassland-savannah associate where a scattered shrub component occurs (Altman 2000a). Of 50 point-count stations in the Willamette Valley where Lazuli Bunting were detected, 32% also had Vesper Sparrow. Found in Christmas tree farms 4-7 yr post-planting (B. Altman p.c.). Noted by Farner (1952) as a summer resident to 6,500 ft (1,970 m) in Crater L. NP, usually associated with meadows containing willows and bordered with "reasonably tall trees, dead snags ... and pinnacles for song perches." Singing birds noted by Fix (1990a) to 5,800 ft (1,760 m) in Umpqua NF, including clearcuts, brushy "prairies," subalpine meadows, and ridge lines. Occurrence is unpredictable in the northern portion of the w. Cascades though suitably dense ceanothus thickets are present well into Clackamas Co. (*SGD*). One record of a singing bird at Jefferson Park, Marion Co., a subalpine meadow at approximately 5,800 ft (1,758 m) (Gillson 1999).

Widespread east of the Cascades, generally in dense riparian corridors at low elevations. Occasionally found in upland pine-oak stands with well-developed brushy undergrowth along the east slope of the Cascades (Evanich 1990, D. Lusthoff p.c.). In the lower canyons of the Blue Mtns., also found in ornamental plantings (Evanich 1990). In the extreme e. Cascades and Warner Mtns., breed in montane brush fields and regenerating clearcuts, especially where snowbrush is present in dense thickets (Evanich 1990, Summers 1993a, *SGD*). In the canyons of desert mountain ranges, found mainly above 1,100 ft (335 m) (Altman 1999a), also in brushy areas where stands of chokecherry occur (Erickson in Bent 1968, Marshall 1987, Gatchet and

Denny unpubl. ms., *SGD*). Locally abundant in dry riparian canyons of e. Wallowa Co. (Evanich 1992a).

Migrants may be found in a variety of habitats which are atypical for nesting, including "migrant traps" in the w. Cascades, sagebrush and desert oases (Erickson in Bent 1968, Gilligan 1994, Fix 1990a, *SGD*).

No data specific to Oregon nests, which are generally placed approximately 3 ft (1 m) or lower in dense, well-shaded herbaceous weeds, bushes, or saplings (Alcorn 1978, Greene et al. 1996).

**Seasonal Activity and Behavior:** Two early spring records on 15 Mar 1947 and 25 Mar 1977 (Gullion 1951, Gilligan 1994). First spring arrival is usually the last week of Apr in sw. Oregon (Browning 1975a, Hunter et al. 1998), generally appears about a week later east of the Cascades (Gilligan et al. 1994). A group of 35 was observed 17 May 1988 at Toketee RS, Douglas Co. Fix (1990a), the largest concentration reported for spring passage. Rangewide, males arrive on breeding territories 4-6 days before females (Erickson in Bent 1968, Greene et al. 1996). Nest building observed 28 May-16 Jul (n=3) (OBBA) statewide, with egg dates ranging 9 Jun-20 Jul (n=15) (Erickson in Bent 1968). Young in nests were reported 12 Jun-3 Aug (n=8) (OBBA), and fledglings were noted 26 Jun-6 Aug (n=10) (OBBA). Fall passage commences in early Aug. Most birds depart the state by the end of Aug, with a late date of 9 Sep west of the Cascades (Gabrielson and Jewett 1940) and 23 Sep east of the Cascades (Littlefield 1990a). Some dispersal to high-elevation meadows occurs after the breeding season (Gilligan 1994, *SGD*).

**Detection:** Generally easy to locate during the breeding season, when is a persistent and conspicuous singer at least through the middle of Jun (Gabrielson and Jewett 1940, Greene et al. 1996). Though most males sing from conspicuous perches higher than surrounding vegetation, the bright colors of the male may not be visible depending upon angle of view (the blue color is due to refraction rather than pigmentation). May sing for long periods from a single perch, or switch perches frequently (Greene et al. 1996, *SGD*).

**Population Status and Conservation:** Long-term (1966-99) BBS trends in Oregon generally stable (1.3 %/yr decline, but non-significant). Significant declining long-term trend for lowland valleys of Oregon and Washington (Altman 2000a). Historically common to abundant summer resident statewide (Shelton 1917, Jewett and Gabrielson 1929, Gabrielson and Jewett 1940). Currently, fairly common only in the southern reaches of the Willamette Valley, uncommon and local elsewhere to the north. Still common to locally abundant in interior valleys to the south. Population declines west of the Cascades may be due primarily to

extensive habitat loss due to development, particularly in the Willamette Valley, and large-scale conversion of native shrub lands to non-suitable agriculture (e.g., rowcrops). Increased predation levels from mammals associated with semi-urban/residential habitats such as skunks, raccoons, and feral and domestic cats often influences nest success for low nesting species, and is likely to be a contributing factor as well. Seldom breed in urban or suburban neighborhoods, even those well planted with mature vegetation (*SGD*). Although shrubby clearcuts in the northern reach of w. Cascades would appear to provide suitable habitat, the species is irregular even in low-elevation harvest areas where competing vegetation is not intensively managed (*SGD*).

In e. Oregon, habitat degradation or loss from altered hydrological regimes, brush control, and livestock grazing in riparian zones have been identified as issues of concern (Altman 1999b). The species is a frequent host to Brown-headed Cowbirds throughout the range, possibly influencing nest success in e. Oregon cattle country (Greene et al. 1996, Altman 1999b). Data are lacking in all aspects of nesting ecology and habitat relationships for this region.—*Stephen G. Dowlan*

## Indigo Bunting *Passerina cyanea*

The Indigo Bunting breeds primarily from s. Saskatchewan to Texas and east to the e. coast, locally to the Rocky Mtns. and occasionally to the w. coast. It winters in M. and n. S. America, and occasionally in the U.S. It is regular in small numbers along the w. coast in spring with occasional territorial males remaining through Aug. The majority of Oregon records are males that occur from mid-Apr to mid-Jun with territorial males remaining to early Aug. Records are scattered in e. and w. Oregon. A male was collected at Ft. Klamath, Klamath Co., 4 Jul 1941 (OBRC, spec. no. 127505 CM).

Many of these territorial birds attract female Lazuli Buntings and nesting is attempted. This species is closely related to the Lazuli Bunting and both prefer dry open brushlands and brushy roadsides. During late Jul 1986 a male Indigo Bunting, apparently paired with a female Lazuli Bunting, was observed near Roseburg, Douglas Co., feeding a fledgling bunting and a young Brown-headed Cowbird (Mattocks 1986). A territorial male paired with a female Lazuli Bunting was photographed at Bloomberg Park in Eugene, Lane Co., during the summers of 1994 and 1995 (Johnson J 1995a, 1996a). An apparent Lazuli X Indigo hybrid was observed at Mt. Pisgah near Eugene 28 Jun 1997 (Johnson J 1998a).

There appears to be no regular fall movement through Oregon. The only records are a male at Eugene 9 Nov 1977 (Anonymous 1978a); an immature at Eugene 29 Nov to 4 Dec 1975 (Crowell and Nehls 1976b); a female at a Leaburg, Lane Co., feeder 1 Dec 1974 to early Jan 1975 (Crowell and Nehls 1975b, 1976b); a female or young bird was photographed at a Corvallis, Benton Co., feeder 2-7 Nov 1979 (Watson 1989); and one was at Cape Blanco, Curry Co., 19-21 Nov 1999 (Gilligan 2000). Monotypic (AOU 1957).—*Harry B. Nehls*

## Painted Bunting *Passerina ciris*

This brightly colored species breeds from se. New Mexico and s. Missouri to Florida and north to North Carolina. It winters in s. U.S. and M. America. It occasionally occurs elsewhere in the U.S. An adult male of the western subspecies *P. c. pallidior* was collected 2 Jun 1963 at Malheur NWR HQ, Harney Co. (Kridler 1965, spec. no. 479638 USNM). An immature female was observed at Tumalo SP, Deschutes Co., 4 Oct 1981 (OBRC); one was reported without details from Frenchglen 10 Jun 1989 (Anderson DA 1990c); and a green-plumaged bird was photographed at Harbor, Curry Co., 20-29 Nov 1992 (Gilligan 1993a). An adult male was photographed at Idleyld Park, Douglas Co., during Dec 1999 (OBRC). One reported from Malheur NWR HQ 11 Jun 1977 (Nehls 1977b) was not accepted by the OBRC.—*Harry B. Nehls*

## Dickcissel *Spiza americana*

The Dickcissel is a prairie bird that breeds from Montana to the Great Lakes and south through Texas. It winters in M. and n. S. America, and occasionally at feeders in the U.S. It is regular in California but is only occasionally found elsewhere west of the Rocky Mtns. One visited a feeder in Tillamook, Tillamook Co., for several days during late Mar 1959 (Walker 1960); an adult male was photographed at a feeder at Lakeside, Coos Co., 30 Nov to 6 Dec 1979 (Mattocks and Hunn 1980a, Watson 1989); one was observed at Tillamook, 27 Oct 1984 (Fix 1985f); an adult male was photographed at a North Bend, Coos Co., feeder 19 Mar to 18 Apr 1988 (Heinl 1989a); a juvenile male was photographed at Astoria, Clatsop Co., 10 Dec 1988 to 19 Jan 1989 (Johnson 1989b); a male was observed at Manzanita, Tillamook Co., 27 Jan to 25 Feb 1989 (OBRC, Johnson 1989b); a female was photographed at Eagle Point, Jackson Co., 20-29 Oct 1993 (Gilligan 1994); one was photographed in the Ochoco NF, Crook Co., 28 May 1995 (Crabtree 1996a); 1 was at Malheur NWR HQ and at Malheur Field Station, Harney Co., 9-27 Jun 1996 (Sullivan 1997c); and one was photographed at Harbor, Curry Co., 2-5 Jul 2000 (Tice 2000b). Monotypic (AOU 1957).—*Harry B. Nehls*

## Family *Icteridae*

## Bobolink *Dolichonyx oryzivorus*

Bobolinks summer in Oregon's eastern grasslands and meadows, singing what has been described as "a bubbling delirium of ecstatic music that flows from the gifted throat of the bird like sparkling champagne" (Bent 1958). The yellow-brown female, juvenile, or nonbreeding male may at first appear to be a sparrow, but the breeding male has an astonishing and diagnostic backwards tuxedo pattern of buff on the nape and white rump and scapulars on an otherwise black body. Studies of navigation systems of this species suggest that it orients for migration via the earth's magnetic field using iron oxide surrounding the olfactory nerve and bristles projecting into the nasal cavity, then observes stars for navigation (Wittenberger 1978, Martin and Gavin 1995).

**General Distribution:** Nests in Canada and n. U.S. from British Columbia across s. Canada to Newfoundland and as far south as Colorado, usually between 50°N and 39°N; an isolated population exists in Arizona (Martin and Gavin 1995). Winters in S. America, primarily east of Andes from e. Bolivia and sw. Brazil to Paraguay, Argentina, also coastal Peru (Martin and Gavin 1995). Monotypic (AOU 1957).

**Oregon Distribution:** Regular, locally common breeder at Malheur NWR; a few to many scattered pairs occur in ne. Oregon near North Powder, Baker City, and Hereford, Baker Co.; Ironside, Malheur Co.; La Grande, Union Co.; and Enterprise and Wallowa, Wallowa Co.; in the Blue Mtns. near John Day and Prairie City, Grant Co.; at Silvies Valley, Grant and Harney counties; and Van, Harney Co.; as far east as Jordan Valley, Malheur Co., near the Idaho border; and as far southwest as Bonanza, Klamath Co., near the California border (Sullivan 1992d, Gilligan et al. 1994, Jobanek 1994b, Marshall et al. 1996, OBBA). Breeding birds are also present at Mt. Vernon, Grant

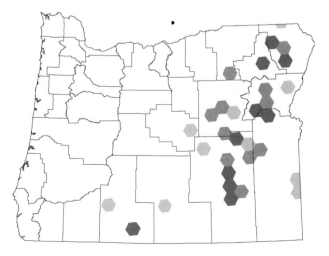

Co.; Catlow and Diamond valleys, Harney Co.; and Juntura, Malheur Co. (Sullivan 1992d, Marshall et al. 1996). West of the Cascades, some rare spring and summer records include singing males in the Willamette Valley near Brooks, Marion Co., and Fern Ridge Res., Lane Co., and a pair was near Ashland in Jun (Eltzroth 1978, Jobanek 1994b). These birds were most likely late-arriving migrants, vs. breeders, as no long stays have been recorded. Casual visitants on the coast in fall, with reports from Gold Beach, Newport, North Bend, mouth of Columbia R., and near Cape Blanco (Eltzroth 1978, Jobanek 1994b).

**Habitat and Diet:** Nests on the ground at Malheur NWR in moist meadows composed of grasses, sedges, and forbs that are mowed in late summer, and grazed in autumn, winter, and formerly in early spring (Wittenberger 1978). Cow parsnip, willows, and fences are used for song perches. Habitat in Bear and Silvies valleys in the Blue Mtns. consists of grasses and forbs in a continuous mesic shrub association (Sanders and Edge 1998). Birds in fall at Malheur NWR are found along weedy fence rows and grassy fields (Littlefield 1990a), often feeding on Canadian thistle (G. Ivey p.c.).

Feeds in irrigated hay meadows and grass-and-forb habitats (Puchy and Marshall 1993). At Malheur NWR in May, males eat primarily dandelion seeds, infrequently cutworms and other insects (Wittenberger 1978). In Jun, diet also includes seeds of cinquefoil, yarrow, Canadian thistle, and false lupine; gathers caterpillars for young from clover, vetch, groundsel, false-Solomon's-seal, and peppergrass. Young at Malheur NWR are fed primarily butterfly and sawfly larvae and grasshoppers (Wittenberger 1982). Birds in migration eat grains, seeds, and occasionally insects (Martin and Gavin 1995).

**Seasonal Activity and Behavior:** The earliest arrival date is 30 Apr 1977 at Malheur NWR (Littlefield 1990a). Average arrival date at Malheur NWR is 19 May, one of the latest for any Oregon breeding species (Ivey, Herziger, and Scheuering 1998). Males arrive about 1 wk before females (Wittenberger 1978). Those from the same breeding area likely migrate to and from the breeding site together (Martin and Gavin 1995). Most males (other than yearlings) return to within 0.6 mi (1 km) of previous year's territory; many females do the same (Wittenberger 1978). Typically, one-third of young have survived from the previous year and comprise half the spring population (Wittenberger 1978).

Females begin egg laying when food becomes abundant, usually in late May to Jun (Wittenberger 1978). Within the loose colonies at Malheur NWR, 30% of the males are polygynous (Wittenberger 1978), and there may be more than one father for each brood

(multiple paternity). The Bobolink was one of the first species documented doing so (Martin and Gavin 1995). Young leave the nest before they can fly, and hide in vegetation for about a week before fledging (Martin and Gavin 1995), usually by the end of Jul at Malheur NWR (Wittenberger 1978). Also in Jul, males begin to molt and resemble females and young. All depart Malheur NWR by mid-Sep (Littlefield 1990a). Most coastal observations are during Sep and Oct. Late fall records include one on 18 Oct 1975 at Yaquina Bay (Crowell and Nehls 1976a), two on 27 Oct 1979 at North Bend, and two birds on 10 Dec 1979 at Myrtle Point, Coos. Co. (Watson 1980a).

Birds from Oregon do not migrate directly south; rather, they journey east across the prairie states, then to S. America, approximately 7,500 mi (12,000 km) round trip (Wittenberger 1978). They arrive at wintering grounds in early Nov (Martin and Gavin 1995).

**Detection:** The tinkling, elaborate song of the male may best be heard at the south end of the Blitzen Valley of Malheur NWR north of P Ranch. Males may occasionally be seen singing on perches or during flight displays; females are rarely observed.

**Population Status and Conservation:** Historically, Bobolinks were shot in southern states because they were considered pests in rice fields. More recently, the U.S. population has been in decline over the last several decades due to land-use changes, and wintering birds are sold as pets in S. America (Martin and Gavin 1995). Management strategies include providing large areas of suitable habitat, controlling succession, and protecting nesting habitat from disturbance (Dechant et al. 1999). Mowing and burning maintains habitat, but may cause mortality of young if done too early (Martin and Gavin 1995).

The Oregon Alpine Club proposed introducing the "joyous" Bobolink before it arrived on its own at Union in 1903; however, the endeavor was not successful (Jobanek 1994b). A state game warden who proposed another effort was enthusiastic, saying, "There are few songsters capable of pouring forth a more acceptable melody than the Bobolink" (Jobanek 1994b). Habitat became available in the s. Blitzen Valley after 1872 when marshes were drained and converted to grazing lands (Wittenberger 1978, Jobanek 1994b). Breeding colonies were first noted at Malheur L. on several dates in the early 1900s, at Brogan in 1910, at Ironside in 1911, and near John Day in 1915. Other historical observations were made in the Wallowa Valley, the Warner Basin, and near Baker City and Halfway, Baker Co. (Jobanek 1994b). The species was recorded for the first time west of the Cascades in 1966 at Medford (Jobanek 1994b). The Malheur NWR population size was 200-350 birds

1972-76 and appeared stable (Wittenberger 1978); it is now the largest known population west of the Great Plains (Marshall et al. 1996). In 1998, 539 males were counted, the highest number since the yearly survey started in 1984, probably due to a large prescribed burn, which provided ideal habitat (G. Ivey p.c.). However, during years with low water supply numbers decrease, distribution changes, and fledging success lowers. Cold or wet weather reduces survival of young and possibly migrating adults (Wittenberger 1978). Also, habitat in the northern portion of Malheur NWR was flooded and unsuitable for about 5 yr during the late 1980s (Malheur NWR files). Numbers have declined in the Wallowa population (Jobanek 1994b), with 10 to 15 pairs each at three colonies; only a few pairs are at other sites (Gilligan et al. 1994). The Bobolink was listed as a Sensitive Species by ODFW (1997) because of limited distribution (Puchy and Marshall 1993), and as a Nongame Species of Management Concern by USFWS (1995a).—*Caroline Herziger*

## Red-winged Blackbird *Agelaius phoeniceus*

The male "red-wing," sentry of the marsh during the breeding season, continually announces its territory to all present with its *oak-a-tee* song, and tenaciously defends against flyby predators. The male is territorial, polygynous, larger than female, and glossy black with a broad bar of red-orange, bordered with yellow, on wing wrist. Females are less conspicuous in behavior, light brown, with a heavily streaked breast, and buffy supercilium. This is one of the most abundant and studied birds in N. America.

**General Distribution:** Breeds from se. Alaska across Canada to sc. Quebec, south to the Caribbean, Mexico, and M. America. Winters from se. Alaska, e. and w. Canada south through breeding range to Gulf coast and Mexico. Sixteen subspecies in N. America (AOU 1957, Browning 1974, 1978); two in Oregon (Browning 1974).

**Oregon Distribution:** *A. p. caurinus* occurs west of the Cascades, with specimens (e.g., USNM, OSU) from coastal and valley localities, and *A. p. nevadensis* east of the Cascades (AOU 1957, Browning 1974), with specimens (USNM) from eastern counties. Intergradation occurs between *caurinus* and *nevadensis* in n. Klamath Co. and Jefferson Co. (Browning 1974). Intergradation between *nevadensis* and *zastereus* (a subspecies from Idaho and w. Montana proposed by Oberholser [1974] and recognized by Browning [1974, 1978, 1990]), known from specimens from Jordan Valley, Malheur Co. (Browning 1974). The Red-winged Blackbird is an abundant breeder in major wetlands and occurs in lesser numbers in small wetlands statewide. Large marshes of sc. and se. Oregon, notably those in Klamath, Lake, and Harney counties, support the largest breeding concentrations (Gabrielson and Jewett 1940). Elsewhere, where marshes are not so extensive, they are a locally common to uncommon breeder in the Willamette (Gullion 1951), Umpqua (Hunter et al. 1998), and Rogue valleys (Browning 1975a), and along the Columbia R. and other major rivers and reservoirs (*DBM, KS*). They are less common along the immediate coast, but are locally conspicuous immediately back from the coast in freshwater marshes (Contreras 1998, Patterson 1998b, *KS*). The redwings summer in meadows of major mountain ranges and intervening valleys from the Cascades east, e.g., Summit Meadow south of Mt. Hood (*DBM*), the Diamond L. area (Fix 1990a), Summit Prairie in the Ochoco Mtns. (C. Gates p.c.), Sycan Marsh (Stern, Del Carlo et al. 1987), Warner Mtns. (*KS*), and elsewhere in Fremont NF (McAllister and Marshall 1945), and in ne. and extreme se. Oregon (Evanich 1992a, Contreras and Kindschy 1996).

The winter distribution of the redwing is reduced from summer range in areas where water freezes. Coastal sites and w. Oregon valleys support thousands in winter (CBCs); as do low-elevation areas of ec. Oregon, such as Boardman, Pendleton, and Hermiston areas (C. Corder p.c.). Limited numbers remain in major inland basins, e.g., Klamath, Summer L., and Harney (Littlefield 1990a, *KS*). CBC high numbers include: 40,263 at Eugene in 1993; 6,799 at Medford in 1988; 3,030 at Klamath Falls in 1980; 2,547 at Umatilla in 1997; 825 at the Columbia estuary in 1991; 806 at Tillamook in 1997; and 241 at Wallowa in 1991.

**Habitat and Diet:** The Red-winged Blackbird breeds in large and small marshes, ditches, hay fields, pastureland, parks and suburban habitat associated with wetlands, and saltwater marshes (Yasukawa and Searcy 1995). They nest in virtually any emergent vegetation and in wetland shrubs and small trees, e.g., willows. They are most abundant in continuous, least abundant in discontinuous, willow communities in streamside riparian areas (Sanders 1995). The nest is a bulky cup of dry emergent vegetation woven into upright stems of taller emergents, including broad-leaved cattail, slough sedge, and grasses (Merrill 1888, Gabrielson and Jewett 1940, Littlefield 1990a, F. G. Evenden unpubl. field notes). Nests are also placed in shrubs such as Douglas spiraea, small Oregon ash, willow, and alder trees (F. G. Evenden unpubl. field notes, D. Lauten p.c.). Females select nest site, males participate, and female builds nest, usually 8-32 in (0.2-0.8 m) above water (Nero 1984, Yasukawa and Searcy 1995).

No Oregon diet information is known. In spring, California diet by volume consisted of 32% cultivated grain, 41% wild seed, 10% grit, 6% ground beetles, and 11% various insects and animals; in summer, ground beetles replaced by water beetles; in winter, diet consisted of 67% cultivated grain, 20% wild seed, 9% grit, 2% ground beetles, and remaining 2% other insects and animals (Crase and DeHaven 1978). In Missouri, nestlings were fed mostly true bugs and flies (Wilson 1978). In Iowa, of total insects fed to nestling, 35% were grasshoppers, 9% moths, 9% larvae, and the remaining percentage various other insects (Gabrielson 1915). Females forage in separate areas to reduce intraspecific competition, and purposely select larger, slower, soft-bodied larvae and nymphs, maximizing feeding efficiency (Wilson 1978).

**Seasonal Activity and Behavior:** Displaying males have been observed occupying territories in early Mar in Sherman and Wheeler counties (Sullivan 1996b) and Klamath and Lake counties (*KS*). Older males (2+ yr) return to breeding sites first, followed by adult females and younger birds (Gabrielson and Jewett 1940). Females nest as yearlings, males not until second year (Skutch 1996). Jaramillo and Burke (1999b) report that yearling females nest after 2(+)-yr-old females, possibly explaining the extended nesting season (F. G. Evenden unpubl. field notes, *DBM*). One of most highly polygynous bird species; up to 15 females have nested on territory of one male. Greater than 50% of females mate with polygynous males. Nearby nesting females reduces predation risk (Yasukawa and Searcy 1995). Mean territory size is 2,000 yd$^2$ (1,625 m$^2$) for marsh, and 3,560 yd$^2$ (2,895 m$^2$) for uplands; female territoriality unclear (Yasukawa and Searcy 1995). In California, displaying males are spaced 20 ft (6 m) apart (Payne 1969). In the Willamette Valley, F. G. Evenden (unpubl. field notes, *DBM*) observed eggs in nests 24 Apr (n=76) to 24 Jun (n="many"), and >100 nests were observed with eggs on 5 May. On 24 Jun, "many new nests, some with young, some with eggs, some with fledged" (F. G. Evenden unpubl. field notes). Egg dates east of the Cascades are 2 May to 20 Jun, peaking near 1 Jun (Gabrielson and Jewett 1940). At Malheur NWR, the earliest nesting was 23 Apr, and the latest fledging was mid-Jul (Littlefield 1990a). Number of eggs typically 3-4; as many as five (F. G. Evenden unpubl. field notes); pale blue-green with streaky blotches or spots of brown or black (Nero 1984).

Incubation by female takes 12 days; young fledge 12 days after hatch (Payne 1969). The last young leave the nest at the end of Jun in e. Washington (Beletsky and Orians 1991). Females feed the young and fledglings; males sometimes feed older nestlings and fledglings (Payne 1969). Fledglings are fed by parents for 30 days after fledging (Payne 1969). Redwings capture insects by gaping, and open their bill to forcibly separate grass sheaths (Yasukawa and Searcy 1995).

Nests have been predated by the Northern Harrier, American Crow, and raccoon; Marsh Wrens also peck eggs (Picman et al. 1988) and nesting success increases with nest dispersion and distance from Marsh Wrens

(Picman et al. 1988). Redwings fearlessly harass buteos, Common Ravens, Black-billed Magpies (Bent 1958), and Sandhill Cranes at Malheur NWR (*DBM*). They use a hawk alarm call, a high-pitched whistle, exclusively as strong alarm during breeding, and a general flocking note in winter (Orians and Christman 1968). They gather in large, sexually separate flocks in agricultural fields such as cut and uncut grain, cut alfalfa, and feedlots, Jul-Sep (*KS*); flocks decrease in e. Oregon late Sep and Oct, reducing to smaller numbers during winter (Gabrielson and Jewett 1940, *KS*). In winter, mixed blackbird flocks in Klamath Basin and Fern Ridge Res., Lane Co., can be seen at dusk moving towards marsh roost sites (*KS, ALC*).

**Detection:** During the breeding season, males are conspicuous and easily located by sight and sound, while females are more elusive. Redwings are conspicuous in large flocks during the nonbreeding season. Worn birds of both sexes may be confused with Tricolored Blackbirds (Jaramillo and Burke 1999b).

**Population Status and Conservation:** The winter population in N. America is estimated at 190 million. Grain fields closest to blackbird roost areas have comparably greater economic losses (Dolbeer 1981). Wheat and barley are consumed in Klamath Basin (*KS*). Conversely, Red-winged Blackbirds eat agricultural insect pests (Bent 1958). Many were killed by traffic while attempting to feed in roads during a ne. Oregon butterfly migration in 1992 (Denny 1994a). Poisoning, wetting agent application, trapping, shooting, or flock harassment by loud noises is allowed by an amendment to the Federal Migratory Bird Treaty Act of 1918 (Nero 1984). Population control, by reducing grain waste, using resistant cultivars and crops less favorable to blackbirds, and timing of agricultural activities, is possibly more effective (Dolbeer 1990). In the Dakotas, redwings have declined due to drought and tilling of breeding areas (Besser et al. 1984).—*Kevin Spencer*

### Tricolored Blackbird *Agelaius tricolor*

The gregarious Tricolored Blackbird is one of N. America's most intensely colonial breeders, forming dense, non-territorial, noisy colonies. A highly synchronized nesting system exploits secure nesting locations and rich food supplies that change from year to year. The male is entirely black, with deep red shoulder patches bordered by white on the wing. The female is blackish brown above, streaked only on the breast, throat, and supercilium.

**General Distribution:** Largely endemic to lowlands of California from the Central Valley and inland coastal lowlands of California south to nw. Baja California, north to sc., nc., and rarely nw. Oregon (local), and, since 1998, sc. Washington. Monotypic (AOU 1957).

**Oregon Distribution:** Tricolored Blackbird breeding colonies are scattered and intermittent at specific locations, though sites used during consecutive years may be in the same general area. The tricolored breeds most consistently in Klamath Co. at Agency L., Klamath Falls, Malin, Lower Klamath, and Alkali L., near Bonanza (Neff 1933, 1937, Sullivan 1997c, Spencer 1998, *KS*), and in Jackson Co. near Medford, Eagle Point, White City, Central Point, Phoenix, and Talent (Richardson C 1961, Richardson and Sturges 1964, Browning 1975a, J. Shelton p.c.). Since the 1960s, small colonies and summering residents have been found in the Willamette Valley in the Columbia R. bottomlands, n. Portland, and Ankeny NWR, near Salem (Crowell and Nehls 1967b, Fix 1984a, Irons 1984b, Gilligan 1991, Evanich 1992d); during fall and winter they have been rare (Crowell and Nehls 1967a, 1968a, Tweit and Mattocks 1987b). Very small local colonies were discovered in 1980s in e. Oregon near Stanfield, Umatilla Co. (Evanich 1992d, Spencer 1998, Crabtree 1996a); Bullgate unit, Summer L., Lake Co. (Evanich 1982a, M. St. Louis p.c.); Wheeler Co., where unknown prior to 1989 (Evanich 1992c, Sullivan 1996b); Wasco Co. (Tweit and Gilligan 1991, Tweit and Johnson 1993); Crook Co. (Tweit and Gilligan 1991, Sullivan 1997c); and Deschutes Co. (Tweit, Lillie, and Mlodinow 1999).

Most retreat south to California in winter, while some remain in Oregon, mainly in the Rogue Valley and Klamath Basin. Tricoloreds were present on the Medford CBC 1957-73 (average 413), then present only 3 yr during 1974-91 (average four birds when present), after which they have been present on about half the counts (average 44 when present 1992-96); highs were 2,000 and 2,067 birds in 1963 and 1964, respectively (Cruickshank 1964). On the Klamath Falls CBC, tricoloreds averaged 175 during 1979-91; the high was 810 in the 1980 CBC (Arbib 1981). Tricoloreds are uncommon to rare in fall and winter elsewhere in e. Oregon, including Prineville, Crook Co.; Powell Butte, Deschutes Co.; Summer L. and Paisley, Lake Co.; and Jefferson Co. (Evanich 1982a, Sullivan 1997a).

**Habitat and Diet:** Oregon breeding colonies occur in hardstem bulrush, cattail, nettles, willows, and Himalayan blackberries (Neff 1937, Gordon 1978, Crabtree 1996a, M. St.Louis p.c., *KS*). Cattail is the preferred nesting substrate but tricoloreds use other dense vegetation types as well, possibly in the event of marsh habitat loss (Neff 1937). At Wood R. Wetlands, Agency L., nests are located in willows 5-10 ft (1.5-3 m) above ground and are constructed of previous year's cattails; also found in blackberries along a canal near Malin, 2-4 ft (0.6-1.2 m) above ground, and constructed of grasses (both Klamath Co.) (*KS*). In California, nests are constructed of wet cattails, sedges, grasses, or other aquatic vegetation (Payne 1969). Productive foraging areas in summer include irrigated pastures, lightly grazed rangelands, and mowed alfalfa (Beedy and Hamilton 1999, *KS*). Tricoloreds have been observed in grain fields or pastures 0.5-1.5 mi (0.8-2.4 km) from nesting locations near Malin, Bonanza, and Wood R. Wetlands (n. Agency L.) in Klamath Co. during summer (*KS*). During fall, winter, and in early spring, they forage in pastures, stubble grain fields, and cattle feedlots. Near Lower Klamath NWR, they forage with cattle along rows of hay cast for feed (*KS*). Little is known about the tricolored's diet in Oregon. Super abundance of insects is an important factor for nest site selection; foraging flocks in California follow nomadic grasshoppers for miles (Payne 1969). The diet of nestlings in California was 86-91% animal matter by volume and included ground beetles, water beetle larvae, grasshoppers and crickets, weevils, moths, flies, and cutworms and loopers (Crase and DeHaven 1977, Skorupa et al. 1980). In California, adults consumed 65% and 91% plant matter by volume in spring and fall; mostly rice and water grass. In summer, insect consumption (mostly ground beetle and water beetle larvae) increased to 24% by volume (Crase and DeHaven 1978). Oats were the primary vegetable food for adults in Merced Co., California (Skorupa et al. 1980). Rice dominated the diet of adults in Sacramento Co., California (Crase and DeHaven 1978).

**Seasonal Activity and Behavior:** Winter populations of tricoloreds increase Feb-Mar in Klamath, Jackson, Deschutes, and Crook counties (Crowell and Nehls 1974a, Gordon 1978, Rogers TH 1981b, Sullivan 1999b, Tweit, Lillie, and Mlodinow 1999), with the largest concentrations noted in Apr. For example, a high of 4,000 was observed in early Apr at Lower Klamath NWR (Rogers 1980c). Based on 12 reports in *Oregon Birds*, *Audubon Field Notes*, and *American*

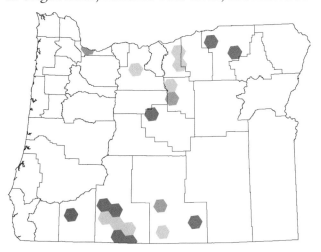

*Birds*, 1967-93, returns to Portland, Salem (not regular), and Wheeler and Wasco counties typically occur in late Mar-Apr. Courting by males includes 17 vocalizations and nine displays (Orians and Christman 1968). In California, after colony nesting and foraging areas are located, males mate with 2-3 females on the same day. Nests are constructed and completed in 3-4 days, often within a foot of each other, and birds may renest within 10 days if the site is abandoned (Payne 1969). At Wood R. Wetlands, Agency L., Klamath Co., nests were completed and occupied 8 Jun 1996 (*KS*). Eggs are incubated by the female for about 12 days, the entire clutch hatches within 24 hr, and the young fledge approximately 12 days after hatching (Payne 1969). Males forage during the nesting period. During two 10- to 15-min observation periods in late May to mid-Jun 1997 at Wood R. Wetlands, more than 1,000 males and a few females were observed to leave the colony site in small groups to forage (*KS*). Near Malin, Klamath Co., fledglings were observed being fed in early to mid-Jun 1993 (*KS*). Tricoloreds disperse from breeding areas in Jul.

**Detection:** Breeding colonies are conspicuous because of the high bird density and continuous loud raspy calls (Orians and Christman 1968). White median coverts on males are evident in flight. Female tricoloreds are darker than female Red-winged Blackbirds. Foraging males depart from and return to breeding colonies in small groups using low direct flight (*KS*). Identification of males and females with worn plumage is sometimes difficult (Jaramillo and Burke 1999a).

**Population Status and Conservation:** The largest and longest-used breeding colonies are found in Klamath and Jackson counties. Gabrielson and Jewett (1940) stated that the only known nesting was at Agency L. (Neff 1937). Nesting has since been confirmed in Jackson Co. in 1958 (Browning 1975a); near Portland in late 1960s (Gilligan et al. 1994); at Summer L. in the early 1980s (M. St. Louis p.c.); near Stanfield, Umatilla Co., in 1990 (Evanich 1992c); and at Painted Cove, Painted Hills unit, Wheeler Co., in 1992 (D. Lusthoff p.c.) and 1996 (Sullivan 1996b). One near Baker City, Baker Co., Apr 2001, may be an indication of a nearby breeding colony (*MGH*).

Observations in the early 1900s have not been widely accepted. Tricoloreds were listed as "near Portland," with specimens, in 1902 (Neff 1937). Peck (1911) reported a considerable breeding colony, at Willow Cr., near Brogan, Malheur Co. in 1910, but Jobanek (1997) questioned Peck's identification, as no Red-winged Blackbirds were listed, and because of the great distance to California populations.

The Tricolored Blackbird is a species of concern in California due to declines following 1930s, 1970s, and 1994 surveys, and due to vulnerability to nesting failures that affect entire colonies (Beedy and Hamilton 1999). The Oregon population of Tricolored Blackbirds was estimated to have declined 22% during the 1980s, but the Oregon population represents only 1% of the total Tricolored Blackbird population (Beedy et al. 1991). Human disturbance is a factor in nesting colony abandonment or failure. At Wood R. Wetlands, Jun 1996, the colony relocated 2 mi (3.2 km) away in another willow grove when the first site was abandoned after heavy truck use on an adjacent gravel road (*KS*). Elimination of habitat, burning, plowing, loss of abundant food source supply, pesticide applications, smaller colony size, and unpredictable shifts in local population abundance may account for the apparent decline in Oregon during 1980s (Payne 1969, Beedy et al. 1991, Beedy and Hamilton 1999).—*Kevin Spencer*

## Western Meadowlark *Sturnella neglecta*

In grass- or sagebrush-dominated habitats throughout the state, the song and striking appearance of the Western Meadowlark create one of the most familiar and endearing avian images in Oregon. With its bold yellow breast and belly with a distinct black V across the chest and its habit of perching on fences along roadsides, the Western Meadowlark is one of Oregon's most recognizable birds. Fittingly, it was chosen as Oregon's state bird by a vote of Oregon schoolchildren ratified by the Legislature in 1927. It is one of the most widely distributed open-country species in Oregon, and one of the most abundant species in the arid desert country of e. Oregon. It can be found in the state year-round, although most birds in e. Oregon migrate out of the state in winter.

**General Distribution:** Breeds in grassland and shrub-grassland habitats south from c. British Columbia, east to w. Ontario and n. Minnesota, Michigan, and Wisconsin, south through the eastern edge of the Great Plains to wc. Texas, and west through nw. Sonora, Mexico to nw. Baja California (Lanyon 1994). Winters in much of its breeding range south of Canada and the northern tier of the U.S., including Washington and Oregon. Monotypic (Blake 1968, *MRB*).

**Oregon Distribution:** The Western Meadowlark breeds in scattered locations along the coast, in w. Oregon valleys, and throughout desert shrub-steppe, grassland, and agricultural areas of e. Oregon. In w. Oregon, it is most common as a breeding species in the Rogue Valley, and common to uncommon in the Umpqua Valley. Now a rare breeding species in the n. Willamette Valley, uncommon in the c. and s. Willamette Valley, but locally common in the se. Willamette Valley between Brownsville and Coburg (Altman 1999b), and around Fern Ridge Res. (Heinl

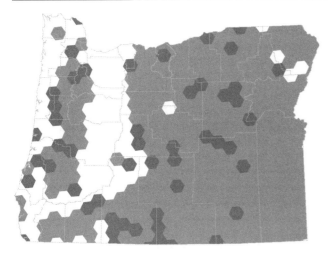

and Hunter 1985). Small breeding populations also occur in a few south-coastal valleys and headlands in Coos Co. (Contreras 1998). They have been reported to breed in Lincoln Co. on the c. coast (Faxon and Bayer 1991), but are not a breeding species on the n. coast (M. Patterson p.c.). In e. Oregon, meadowlarks enjoy a ubiquitous breeding distribution throughout unforested habitat up to 6,000 ft (1,830 m) (Gilligan et al. 1994), and they are one of the most common breeding species in all habitat types in shrub-steppe country.

Wintering populations in w. Oregon are generally higher than breeding populations. The highest wintering concentration in the state is in the Rogue Valley (CBC). Meadowlarks also winter in small flocks along the entire coast. Populations are reduced in winter in e. Oregon, suggesting some birds migrate, but small wintering flocks at low elevations are not uncommon. The highest wintering concentrations in e. Oregon are in Umatilla Co. (CBC).

Migrants are seen both spring and fall throughout the breeding and wintering range, and a few birds stop over in open, grassy areas in the Cascades such as Detroit Flats at the upper end of Detroit Res. and other areas near lakes and reservoirs, clearcuts, residential developments, and the like (Fix 1990a, *MGH*). During the 1970s, regularly observed at night during spring and fall at the lighted driving range at Eastmoreland Golf Course in se. Portland, but not observed there during the day (D. Irons p.c.).

**Habitat and Diet:** Optimal breeding habitat in the Willamette Valley is lightly grazed pastures or fallow fields with grass height 1-2 ft (0.3-0.6 m), and shrub or tree cover <10%. Marginal habitat is hayfields and cultivated grass fields (annual or perennial) with grass height 1-3 ft (0.3-1 m) and shrub or tree cover <25% (Altman 1999b). Cultivated grass fields are used as escape cover and to a lesser extent nesting cover, but have only limited use as foraging habitat. Thus, quality foraging habitat for meadowlarks (e.g., lightly grazed

pastures, fallow fields) needs to be adjacent to or within territories dominated by cultivated grass fields or hayfields in order for the latter habitats to be used for nesting. Singing perches (fencelines, telephone pole, shrubs, trees, boulders) are essential components of all territories.

Breeding habitat in e. Oregon includes all types and conditions of shrub-steppe or rangeland habitat outside of forested areas. On the Boardman Bombing Range in the Columbia Basin, the meadowlark is the most abundant species in all annual grass and shrub habitat types (includes grazed and ungrazed sagebrush, bitterbrush, and other low shrub habitat), but relative abundance is greatest in bitterbrush and ungrazed sagebrush habitats (Holmes and Geupel 1998). Abundance of meadowlarks is greater in bunchgrass and sagebrush habitats that are free from grazing. Holmes and Geupel (1998) noted that the three variables most highly associated with meadowlark abundance were percent open ground (negative association), and shrub height and bitterbrush density (positive associations).

In the Willamette Valley, mean territory size was 14.3 ac (5.7 ha) (range 4.8-35 ac [1.9-14 ha], n=21), with nearly 70% of territories 10-19 ac (4-8 ha) (Altman 1999b). Territories were dominated by grass cover (mean 94%) with minimal amounts of bare ground (3%) and shrub/tree cover (3%). Only 24% of territories included cultivated grass fields, and none were more than 50% cultivated grass field. Nest sites were characterized by relatively high grass cover (mean 84%) and litter/residue (13%), with some bare ground (6%). Nests were well concealed on the ground, and usually partially domed with a roofed runway.

No foraging data are available for Oregon, but the diet is thought to vary depending on the time of year (Lanyon 1994). Western Meadowlarks take mostly insects in late spring and summer, seeds in fall, and where available, grain in winter and early spring. In the Willamette Valley, most foraging during breeding season occurs in pastures, likely due to increased insect availability. Forages mostly in grass fields during the nonbreeding season, likely on seeds and grain (*BA*), but also in dunes, deflation plains, wet pastures, plowed or sprouting earth, airports, and median strips (D. Fix p.c.).

**Seasonal Activity and Behavior:** In w. Oregon valleys and along the coast, wintering flocks increase in size and number in late Feb and throughout Mar during early northward migration. Flocks break up by late Mar, and there is a pulse of migratory movement in early Apr. Most nesting begins in late Apr, with the peak of nesting activity throughout May, although there is an early egg date of 3 Apr (Gabrielson and Jewett 1940). In e. Oregon, migrants first arrive in late Feb and most are on territories by Apr (Gilligan et al. 1994). At Malheur NWR, the earliest spring arrival has been 6 Feb, with the average arrival 27 Feb, peak of passage 10-25 Mar, and earliest nesting 23 Apr (Littlefield 1990a).

Singing begins upon arrival on the breeding grounds, as early as Mar. The male often sings from an exposed perch (e.g., a powerline, fence post), but will also sing from the ground. A male's song is often immediately followed by a "rattle" call, which is a female vocalizing. The meadowlark's mating system is polygynous; males often have two mates concurrently, occasionally three (Lanyon 1994). In the Willamette Valley, about half of males believed to have two mates (*BA*). May renest after a failed nesting attempt, and can produce two broods in one season.

On the Boardman Bombing Range in e. Oregon, nest success (n=80) was poor; proportional nest success was 28% and a Mayfield estimate of nest success (based on days of observation [Mayfield 1975]) was 11% (Holmes and Geupel 1998). In the Willamette Valley, proportional nest success was 50% (n=12), but a Mayfield estimate was 10% (Altman 1999b), similar to that in e. Oregon. Reasons for nest failure in the Willamette Valley included abandonment (n=1), predation (n=3), and field mowing (n=1).

The latest fledging date from w. Oregon is 17 Jul, likely a second brood (*BA*). Fall migrants along the coast begin to appear in dunes and farm fields in late Aug and early Sep (M. Patterson p.c.). In the western valleys, flocks increase in size from Aug through Oct, probably due to arrival of northern migrants. At Malheur NWR, autumn migrants arrive in early Aug and the peak of migration is 20 Aug-20 Sep (Littlefield 1990a). A few linger into Oct and Nov there, with occasional wintering birds. During the nonbreeding season in western valleys, Western Meadowlarks form foraging flocks that may vary from a few to over 100 birds (*BA*). Wintering flocks on the north coast are usually <10 birds (M. Patterson p.c.).

**Detection:** Highly detectable from long distances by song in spring and summer, and conspicuous perches make visual detection easy any time of year. The song is complex and melodious, and generally not confused with others. In winter, the flocking habit makes groups more conspicuous.

**Population Status and Conservation:** Population trends in Oregon based on BBS data indicate relatively stable long-term (1966-96) trends (1%/yr decline, but non-significant), but highly significant (p<0.01) short-term (1980-96) declining trends (2.9%/yr) (Sauer et al. 1997). Most declines appear to be from w. Oregon with highly significant long-term (7.2%/yr) and short-term (6.9%/yr) declines (note: these data include the Puget Lowlands of Washington).

Declines in abundance have been most apparent in the Willamette Valley, where mean number of birds/ BBS route (n=11) dropped from approximately 13 in the early 1970s to <1 in the mid-1990s (Altman 2000a). Populations in the Columbia Plateau BBS Region (includes all non-forest in e. Oregon, e. Washington, and s. Idaho) mirror the Oregon state trend; relatively stable long-term trends (non-significant decline of 0.6%/yr), and highly significant declining short-term trends (2.6%/yr) (Sauer et al. 1997). Despite recent declining trends, Western Meadowlarks remain the most abundant birds throughout Oregon's shrub-steppe habitat.

Population trends based on Christmas Bird Count (CBC) data also indicate declining populations. In the Willamette Valley, the mean number of birds/count (n=6-8 counts/yr) dropped from approximately 100-110 in the late 1970s to 55-65 in the early 1990s. During the same time frame, totals on the Roseburg CBC diminished from more than 150 birds/count to fewer than 50, and the Medford CBC from over 600 birds/count to less than 400. Most current CBCs in e. Oregon also report fewer numbers than throughout the 1970s and 1980s.

Factors suspected to contribute to declines include conversion of native grasslands and shrub-steppe to non-suitable agriculture (e.g., rowcrops); habitat degradation from grazing; mortality at nests from trampling by livestock and agricultural practices such as mowing; a high degree of sensitivity to human disturbance near nest sites; and potential reproductive failures from use of pesticides or other contaminants (Lanyon 1994). In w. Oregon, additional factors include extensive habitat loss due to development, particularly in the Willamette Valley, and increased predation from feral and domestic cats. Conservation in the valleys of w. Oregon is complicated by the need for relatively large areas due to territory size (Altman 1999b).

The Willamette Valley population is listed as "sensitive" by ODFW. The Western Meadowlark has been identified as a species of high concern under all proposed management options for the Interior Columbia Basin (also includes e. Oregon, Idaho, and parts of Montana and Nevada) (Saab and Rich 1997).—*Bob Altman*

## Yellow-headed Blackbird
*Xanthocephalus xanthocephalus*
"The song of the Yellow-head—if song it can be called, as it lacks every musical quality" (Taverner 1934) is a familiar sound in the marshes particularly of c. and se. Oregon. The male, with its yellow head, neck, and breast, black body and wings, and white wing patches, is unmistakable. The female is more subtle with its

dusky or sooty brown body plumage and yellow cheeks, chin, throat and chest, but also is distinctive.

**General Distribution:** Breeds in the wetlands of w. and c. N. America, from British Columbia to Manitoba, south to ne. Baja California and n. Texas, and from Washington and Oregon east to Ontario and nw. Ohio (Orians 1980). Winters from California east to Texas, south through the Mexican Plateau. Recorded in winter rarely as far north as Washington and Minnesota (Twedt and Crawford 1995). Monotypic (Browning 2002).

**Oregon Distribution:** Abundant spring and summer resident in marshes of large alkaline lakes and wetlands in se. Oregon, most notably the Klamath L. and Summer L., Malheur L., and Harney L. basins. Local and uncommon on smaller bodies of water, marshes, and flooded areas east of the Cascade crest. Increasingly rare north to the Columbia R., except in Morrow and Umatilla counties, where it is locally common (M. Denny p.c.). Occurs at elevations up to 5,000 ft (1,500 m) in marshes of mountain lakes just east of the Cascades crest (e.g., Davis L. [Gilligan et al. 1994]). Local and uncommon spring and summer resident at Fern Ridge Res., Lane Co.; near Amity, Yamhill Co.; and Baskett Slough NWR, Polk Co. Irregular breeder near Forest Grove, Gaston (Tualatin R. Valley, Washington Co.), Corvallis, Albany, White City, and Hoover L., the latter two in Jackson Co. (Gilligan et al. 1994). Formerly nested at Delta Park in n. Portland before it was developed as a race track and golf course (H. Nehls p.c.); breeds semi-annually at the Howell House Marsh on Sauvie I. (H. Nehls p.c.). Rare migrant in the sw. Cascades (Fix 1990a), and along the coast (Contreras 1998). Rare in winter in Klamath Basin, Summer L., and other lowland areas east of the Cascades. Irregular in winter west of the Cascades (Gilligan et al. 1994).

**Habitat and Diet:** In Oregon, the Yellow-headed Blackbird nests in common (broadleaf) cattail and

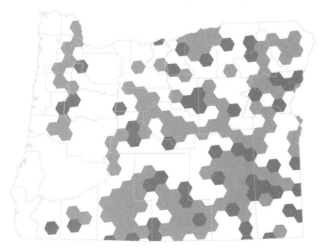

hardstem bulrush standing in deeper water along pond, lake, or marsh edges. It nests less commonly in willows in flooded areas. Establishes territories in emergent vegetation in water 2-4 ft (0.6-1.2 m) deep, rarely deeper, usually at edge of water, field, or desert, where aquatic insect production is highest (Orians and Willson 1964). Avoids nesting along lake or pond edges bordered by trees or high cliffs which project >30 degrees above the horizon (Orians 1980). Densities are variable, reported as high as 25-30 nests in an area of 225 ft² (21 m²) (Orians 1980). Breeding occurs in grouped territories, when most food resources are obtained within the territory, or is loosely colonial when most food is obtained by foraging outside the territory (Twedt and Crawford 1995). Adjacent uplands, agricultural lands, and sagebrush near territories are regularly utilized for foraging during the breeding season.

Diet varies geographically and temporally with availability of food resources (Twedt et al. 1991, Twedt and Crawford 1995). No studies of diet are available for Oregon. In Washington studies, aquatic prey consistently comprised at least 82% of the food items brought to nestlings (Orians 1980). In diet studies in Washington and Utah, insect prey included but was not limited to flies, butterflies and moths, grasshoppers and crickets, bees and ants, beetles and dragonflies, the latter being a preferential food for nestlings (Knowlton and Telford 1947, Orians and Angell 1985). Prey is often taken at the water's edge where adult insects are just emerging from their formerly aquatic larval life, but also from many other foraging sites throughout the day. Aquatic insects constitute the highest proportion of food exploited during the breeding season and cultivated grains and weed seeds are consumed during the fall and winter (Twedt and Crawford 1995).

**Seasonal Activity and Behavior:** Adult males begin to arrive on breeding grounds from mid-Mar to early Apr. At Malheur NWR, the earliest arrival date is 9 Mar, average arrival 27 Mar, with the major influx about mid-Apr (Littlefield 1990a). Adult females arrive 7-14 days after adult males. Second-yr birds arrive after adults, with males arriving about 7 days before females (Twedt and Crawford 1995). Males establish territories upon arrival, defending them against other males and even evicting already established Red-winged Blackbirds from preferred habitat (Willson 1966). Males are polygynous, attracting an average of 1-6 females. In one study on three lakes in Washington (Orians 1980), the mean number of females per territory was 1.7-4.2 (range 0-8). Nest site displays, given in response to the arrival of a female, were given on average a few times per hour. After attracting a female to a suitable nest site within his territory, the male pecked at the nest site or went through the motions of nest building. Females

*Yellow-headed Blackbird*

did not always build nests in the sites pointed out to them. Bowl-shaped nests, attached to vegetation, were built exclusively by the female. Some males, especially second-year males, did not establish territories but become "floaters." Unlike males, females bred in their second year. Males defended territories vigorously against conspecific males, other blackbird species, and predators, and mobbed such predators as the Northern Harrier, the most frequent diurnal aerial predator. They responded aggressively to Marsh Wrens, which punctured unguarded eggs. Females defended their territories against other females while nest building and egg laying.

In Oregon, nest building has been observed 20 and 30 May (OBBA). Egg laying generally initiated 1-2 days after nest building, with one egg laid on successive days until clutch is complete. Clutch size 3-5 (usually four) eggs. In Washington, mean date of first egg laying 18 May (SD=7.1 days, n= 274) (Orians 1980) with earliest date 29 Apr. If first nesting fails, generally due to predation or destruction of nests by weather events, female may attempt a second nest. Female incubates exclusively. Incubation takes 12-13 days. Nestlings observed during Jun in Oregon (n=5) (OBBA). Males may assist in feeding of nestlings. Fledge 9-12 days

after hatching (Fautin 1941); late May to early Aug (n=10) (OBBA). At the age of 3 wk, fledglings can fly up to about 25 yds (23 m) and pursue their parents, begging noisily for food (Fautin 1941).

Little is known about initial dispersal of Yellow-headed Blackbirds from their natal sites. In Jul, nesting areas are abandoned and they gather in large groups in the densest stands of marsh vegetation, emerging to forage in the morning and evening in surrounding agricultural lands. In Aug, after completion of molt, they form large foraging flocks with other blackbird species, roaming widely through pastures, cultivated fields, barnyards, roadsides and even small town streets seeking food (Orians 1980). Southward migration may begin as early as Jul and by late Sep nearly all have left the state, with only a few remaining to winter (Gilligan et al. 1994).

**Detection:** In the breeding season, males are easy to detect from great distances by their loud song and yellow head. Females and young are more subtle and require closer examination. During migration and molt, this species may stay hidden in dense vegetation, making detection much more problematic, although males occasionally vocalize during spring migration.

**Population Status and Conservation:** The Yellow-headed Blackbird has increased noticeably at Malheur NWR since the mid-1970s (Littlefield 1990a). While there is little concern for continental populations, draining of wetlands is currently the most significant threat to this species. Local populations fluctuate with wetland conditions. In periods of drought, populations can be expected to drop, although recovery after such an event is usually rapid. Conversion of native sagebrush and grass uplands to agriculture has probably increased survival of fledged young as well as the number of overwintering birds (Orians and Angell 1985). Local populations may be threatened by the careless use of pesticides, which may reduce aquatic insect populations and lead to starvation of nestlings. Indiscriminate use of herbicides may render wetlands unsuitable for breeding. Although not considered an agricultural pest in Oregon, postbreeding foraging flocks of blackbirds have been suggested for abatement (i.e., by poisoning) in other northern states (Twedt et al. 1991). Use of toxic baits and spray against blackbirds to control crop depredation probably has little long-term impact on regional populations, but could be devastating if directed at breeding or roosting areas (Twedt and Crawford 1995).—*Tim Shelmerdine*

**Rusty Blackbird** *Euphagus carolinus*
This species breeds from Alaska across Canada and south to c. British Columbia and New England. It winters primarily in the se. U.S., and occasionally west

of the Rocky Mtns. Difficulties in separating this species from the closely related Brewer's Blackbird make most sight records questionable. The following records have been accepted by the OBRC: a male (*E. c. carolinus*) (*MRB*) collected at Tillamook, Tillamook Co., 20 Mar 1959 (Walker 1960); a male observed at Baskett Slough NWR, Polk Co., 13 Nov 1977 (Contreras 1978); one photographed at Roseburg, Douglas Co., 24 Jan 1981 (OBRC); a female photographed at Sauvie I., Multnomah Co., 14 Feb to 8 Apr 1987 (Watson 1989); two females photographed there 17-23 Dec 1987 (Johnson 1988a); a female observed there 31 Dec 1993 to 11 Jan 1994 (OBRC); and a female photographed at Gold Beach 2 Feb 2001 (Korpi 2001c).—*Harry B. Nehls*

## Brewer's Blackbird *Euphagus cyanocephalus*

Highly adaptable, this ubiquitous species may be found in habitats as diverse as coastal marshes, sagebrush shrub-steppe, and urban supermarket parking lots. The adult male is blackish, showing a purplish sheen on the head and a greenish sheen on his back; eyes are yellowish to creamy white. Females and juveniles are dusky brown above and grayish brown below, with paler throat and eyebrows, and brown eyes (Skutch 1996).

**General Distribution:** Breeds from British Columbia east to sw. Ontario; south to n. Baja California, east to n. New Mexico and w. Oklahoma. Some populations, including those along the Pacific coast, are resident, otherwise winters w. Washington, sw. Idaho, s. Montana, sw. Nebraska east to Atlantic coast along approximate latitude of Chesapeake Bay. Southern limit of winter range s. Baja California to Veracruz, Mexico, Gulf coast of U.S. to s. Florida (Jaramillo and Burke 1999b). Monotypic.

**Oregon Distribution:** Common permanent resident along coast. West of the Cascades, common to abundant in inland valleys. Within the Cascades, migrant and summer resident in meadows and at human settlements (Fix 1991, *DBM*). East of the Cascades, abundant summer resident and uncommon winter resident. Nests from sea level to above 6,000 ft (1,829 m) elevation. From late summer through winter may be found in mixed flocks with starlings and other blackbirds numbering in thousands in agricultural areas west of the Cascades and in Klamath Basin; uncommon in winter in other agricultural areas east of the Cascades. Uncommon in winter near Malheur NWR, although can border on common near productive feeding areas. Several hundred regularly present on ranches west of refuge headquarters and near Princeton (Littlefield 1990a). Wintering areas may be tied to elevation and especially climate. This species is less common in

areas that receive more than 25 in (63.5 cm.) of snow annually and have protracted periods of snow cover, limiting availability of food (Stepney 1975). Common spring transient throughout the state (Gilligan et al. 1994).

**Habitat and Diet:** No formal studies in Oregon. Found in open areas such as grasslands, pastures, lawns, golf courses, agricultural fields, alpine meadows and beaches; very common in urban areas (Skutch 1996, Jaramillo and Burke 1999b). Commonly feeds along sandy beaches, freshwater ponds, and other marine environments along coast (Jaramillo and Burke 1999b). Utilizes shrubs for nesting, preferring groups of dense conifers or other thickets. Roosts in dense vegetation or marshes (Jaramillo and Burke 1999b). Utilizes a wide variety of breeding habitats; OBBA data indicated strong habitat affinity for salt desert shrubland, grasslands, and coastal shrubland, urban/residential, edges of cropland/pasture/orchard, and streamside/wetland shrubland. Littlefield (1990a) states that this species prefers drier sites than the other marsh-dwelling blackbirds, commonly nesting near human habitations and in arid shrublands. Most nests at Malheur NWR were located low in shrubs and hedges.

Although blackbirds are primarily colonial nesters, Brewer's Blackbirds do not usually nest in colonies as dense as some other icterids, possibly indicating a wider tolerance of habitat requirements (Williams 1958). Fences and overhead wires, as well as trees and bushes used as perches. Nests may be found on ground or up to 150 ft (46 m) high in trees (Williams 1958). At Camp Harney (near present day Burns) in se. Oregon, nests frequently found placed on ground "or rather in the ground, the rim of the nest being flush with the surface" (Bendire 1895).

No diet studies conducted in Oregon. Although omnivorous, studies of stomach contents show Brewer's Blackbird is much more insectivorous than cowbirds or Red-winged Blackbirds (Beecher 1951). A wide variety of feeding strategies utilized; Skutch (1996) mentions some birds may hover over open water, picking floating creatures from the surface; Williams (1952) mentions observing flycatching from the ground or from telephone wires. Commonly occur in foraging flocks, overturning or pushing stones, fragments of wood, cow pats, or other small objects forward with gaping bill to expose food, though not as frequently as other icterids (Orians 1980, Skutch 1996). Is highly adaptive, having learned several new feeding strategies, e.g., picking dead insects off automobile radiator grills or snatching trapped insects off glass walls and windows (Jaramillo and Burke 1999b). Has been to known to kill and feed on other birds; there are at least two recorded instances of feeding on nestlings of other species (Anthony 1923, Jaramillo and Burke 1999b).

Main prey items include damselflies and grasshoppers when available. Highly opportunistic; often eat human food scraps such as popcorn and bread, sometimes softening harder food items by dipping them in water (Skutch 1996). Diet includes plant seeds and cultivated grains (Skutch 1996). Studies in Washington showed that dragonflies and damselflies made up approximately 33% of nestlings' food, moths made up 25%, flies 20%, other insects and spiders the remainder (Orians 1980). A California study of the contents of 285 stomachs taken year-round showed insect prey included members of the following orders: beetles, flies, true bugs, ants and bees, moths and butterflies, grasshoppers, centipedes, and spiders (Soriano 1931).

**Seasonal Activity and Behavior:** Common migrant throughout state late Feb to May (Gilligan et al. 1994). Breeders return to Malheur NWR around 15 Mar (earliest 3 Feb; average 10 Mar), reaching abundant numbers by 20 Mar (Littlefield 1990a). Begins pairing behavior (perching and foraging together, engaging in mutual displays and maintaining a common distance between pair members) as early as late Jan, but may revert to flock behavior until Apr (Williams 1958), but this information not taken from Oregon. Pair bond appears to be long term, with males often consorting with the same females in subsequent years and showing pairing behavior throughout most of the year (Williams 1958). Pairing behavior increases into spring, gradually increasing time spent in pairs and decreasing time spent in flock, until pair members are only rarely separated for brief intervals (Williams 1958). Pairs nest singly, in scattered pairs or in loose colonies (Williams 1958).

Are non-territorial, colonial, and monogamous in e. Washington (Orians 1980), but in California found to be monogamous or polygamous; individuals may change status from year to year (Williams 1952). Sexes arrive on the breeding grounds in Washington already paired (Orians 1980). Nest construction carried out almost completely by female, *contra* Bendire (1895), who stated that "both sexes assist" in nest building. Do not defend foraging or breeding territories, but both sexes may defend nest sites, although females initiate attacks more frequently than males (Williams 1958).

At Malheur NWR, nesting begins early May (Littlefield 1990a). Nest construction to clutch completion usually lasts 10-14 days (Williams 1958). Clutches completed 1 May to 24 Jun (Gabrielson and Jewett 1940). Most common clutch size is 5-6; incubation generally 12-13 days; nestling period 13 days (Williams 1958). First small flocks of fledglings start to appear throughout the state at the end of May (Gabrielson and Jewett 1940). At Malheur NWR young have been observed as early as 18 May, with most young fledging in Jun, although feeding of nestlings has been observed "well into July" (Littlefield

1990a). Late date is a record of a nest containing new hatchlings observed on 17 Jul (Gabrielson and Jewett 1940).

Females may initiate a second brood, especially if first brood unsuccessful and three attempts in one season have been recorded. Females have been observed carrying nesting material while still feeding nestlings (Williams 1958). Gabrielson and Jewett (1940) stated that second broods are frequent in Oregon.

After breeding is complete, usually in Aug, family groups form foraging flocks with other blackbirds and starlings. Numbers most abundant in Sep, by 10 Nov only winter residents remain.

Birds banded in California in winter were later recovered in Oregon and Washington, demonstrating that at least part of the population withdraws southward after the breeding season (Jaramillo and Burke 1999b). Bendire (1895) and Gabrielson and Jewett (1940) state that flocks in winter appear to be composed primarily of males, offering evidence of differential sex migration. Other sources confirm that females tend to migrate farther south than males (Jaramillo and Burke 1999b).

**Detection:** Easily detected due to conspicuous habits and calls. Inexperienced observers may confuse this species with other blackbirds, grackles, and cowbirds.

**Population Status and Conservation:** Probably taking advantage of the clearing of eastern forests, range expansion to Minnesota and Ontario has occurred in the eastern part of the species' range over the past 80 yr and continues (Stepney and Powers 1973, Stepney 1975). Wintering concentrations were virtually absent east of Mississippi R. prior to the middle of the 20th century, but are now found to w. N. and S. Carolina, nw. Georgia and n. Florida (Stepney 1975). Expansion to northwest has also occurred; now regular in s. Alaska (Ketchikan) and has overwintered there. Numbers of wintering birds in Great Basin and mountain states have increased (Stepney 1975, Jaramillo and Burke 1999b). Despite range expansion to the north and the east, BBS data 1966-94 show a negative trend of 1.9% per year. Reasons for this decline are unclear. At Malheur NWR, Littlefield (1990a) considered this species to be the primary cowbird host, finding 1-3 cowbird eggs in most nests.—*Tim Shelmerdine*

## Common Grackle *Quiscalus quiscula*

This species breeds east of the Rocky Mtns. from ne. British Columbia to Texas, across Canada and the U.S. It drops south to winter in se. Canada and e. U.S. Its range has expanded westward in recent years and it now nests in Idaho and Nevada; it appears to still be expanding. Sightings elsewhere in the West have increased in recent years (Peer and Bollinger 1997). The first Oregon record was at Malheur NWR HQ, Harney Co., 28 May 1977 (Summers 1977). Up to five reports are now received annually, mostly from mid-Apr to late Oct. A male was photographed displaying unsuccessfully to female Brewer's Blackbirds at Veneta, Lane Co., 1 May to 19 Jun 1987 (Heinl 1987a). Two individuals were photographed at Port Orford, Curry Co., 6 Jun to 14 Sep 1993 (OBRC, Johnson J 1994a). A male was photographed near Tumalo, Deschutes Co., 7 Dec 1996 to late Feb 1997 (Korpi 1997). Subspecies unknown.—*Harry B. Nehls*

## Great-tailed Grackle *Quiscalus mexicanus*

This is a bird of riparian thickets, farmlands, and towns. Prior to 1900 it ranged from S. America north to Texas, Arizona, and New Mexico, but then expanded its range north into the c. Prairie states. Since 1970 it has moved westward reaching California and Nevada in 1973 and Oregon by 1980 (Littlefield 1983). Since 1980 it has been observed almost annually in Harney Co., usually in numbers less than five. The first verified nesting record came in 1994 when a pair successfully fledged young near the Malheur NWR HQ (Crabtree 1995a). Most Harney Co. records occur from early Apr to late Oct. Individuals were noted near Malheur NWR HQ 23 Dec 1996 and 23 Feb 1997 (Korpi 1997). There are many photographs in the files of the OBRC (Watson 1989).

Away from Harney Co. individuals were in the Grande Ronde Valley of Union Co. 5-6 Jun 1980 (OBRC); photographed at Madras, Jefferson Co., 23-28 May 1992 (Evanich 1992c); Port Orford, Curry Co., 1 Jun 1992 (OBRC); and Fern Ridge Res., Lane Co., 27 Jun 1992 (OBRC). Two were observed at Umatilla NWR, Morrow Co., 24 May 1993 (Summers 1993c); and one at Klamath Falls, Klamath Co., 20 May 1998 (Sullivan 1998b). Individuals were south of Ontario, Malheur Co., 6 Jun 1999, and at Sycan Marsh, Lake Co., 16 Jun 1999 (Spencer 2000a). Up to four were in Ontario during the winter and spring of 2001-02 (OBRC).—*Harry B. Nehls*

## Brown-headed Cowbird *Molothrus ater*

Prior to European settlement, the Brown-headed Cowbird was a species of Great Plains grasslands and was probably closely associated with American Bison. It was referred to in some of the early literature as "buffalo bird" (Bailey 1914), presumably because it commonly foraged on insects flushed under the feet of ungulates. Forest fragmentation and agricultural developments allowed the cowbird to extend its range throughout much of N. America. It is a brood parasite, laying its eggs in nests of other species and leaving the rearing of young to surrogate parents. This has had

serious consequences for many host species within the cowbird's extended range. To mitigate these effects, cowbird removal programs have been implemented in some states with endangered host species (Terborgh 1989).

**General Distribution:** N. America from se. Alaska, c. Canada to n. Mexico. Three subspecies are recognized in N. America, two of which most probably occur in Oregon.

**Oregon Distribution:** Common migrant and breeder in open habitats and woodland edges in all parts of the state. Most abundant in agricultural land, sagebrush and juniper steppe, coastal scrub, riparian zones, and suburban areas. Less frequently found, but present, around larger lakes, meadows, and resort areas of the Cascades (Sauer et al. 1997). Infrequent in clearcuts among extensive conifer forests in the w. Cascades and Coast Range. Wintering cowbirds, which closely associate with other blackbirds, are now regular and common in the western interior valleys.

*M. a. artemisiae* is presumed to comprise e. Oregon breeding populations (Gabrielson and Jewett 1940, Pyle 1997). Rothstein (1994) suggests that cowbirds found in the valleys and coastal regions of w. Oregon may be *M. a. obscurus*. The well-documented advance of *obscurus* through California from the south combined with evidence from analysis of vocalizations support this. Rothstein (1994) recommends data collection of wing length throughout the region to confirm this hypothesis. It is not clear which subspecies is represented in wintering populations, and specimens would be necessary for verification.

**Habitat and Diet:** Cowbirds require woodland/ riparian edges or grass and shrub-steppe for breeding habitat. Studies on cover requirements in Wisconsin (Brittingham and Temple 1996) show a preference for light cover with an open sub-canopy and good ground cover. Evidence also suggests that cowbirds require some kind of perch from which to watch the activity

of potential hosts. Freeman et al. (1990) found that nest predation on Red-winged Blackbirds was higher in areas where perches were available.

Removal of forest cover for residential and agricultural uses and the resulting fragmentation of large areas of native forests and woodlands have aided the range expansion. Cowbirds tend to focus on woodland margins. Penetration into U.S. forests was shown to drop from an average of 1.1 cowbird eggs near forest edges to 0.23 eggs per nest 984 ft (300 m) in the forest interior. As the ratio of forest edge to whole forest increases, the number of cowbirds in an area also increases (Brittingham and Temple 1983).

In winter, cowbirds inhabit many lowland sites, where at least one or two cowbirds may be expected in any large flock of blackbirds. Dairies, pastures, feedlots, and other areas with livestock are often attractive to cowbirds (MGH).

No diet information is available specific to Oregon, but across their range their diet is comprised (by volume) of 94% weed seeds, grass seeds, and grains in winter. In summer that drops to 48% when the birds also forage on grasshoppers, beetles, caterpillars, and other insects (Lowther 1993).

**Seasonal Activity and Behavior:** Cowbirds have a fairly conspicuous arrival in the Willamette Valley in late Mar and early Apr (D. Fix p.c., S. Heinl p.c.). Numbers jump in late Apr, at which time breeding displays begin. In e. Oregon, at Malheur NWR, the cowbird arrives in late Apr or early May (earliest 4 Apr 1982, average 26 Apr), and is most common mid- to late May (Littlefield 1990a). Throughout the range of the species, multiple males often chase a single female. Courting males generally take up a position on a branch below a perched female where they will sing while throwing back the head and ruffling breast feathers.

Cowbirds have been recorded to lay eggs in the nests of 220 N. American species. Of about 9,000 recorded instances of parasitism, the top two hosts were the Yellow Warbler and Song Sparrow. Additional Oregon species among the top 17 included Chipping Sparrow, Spotted Towhee, Common Yellowthroat, Yellow-breasted Chat, Red-winged Blackbird, and Willow Flycatcher (Lowther 1993). Poorly documented but obvious population declines and/or range reductions in several of these species coincided with the arrival of cowbirds in w. Oregon (DBM).

Eggs produced by cowbirds do not closely mimic the eggs produced by host species. It is estimated that only about 3% of eggs laid in host nests are successful, but this is offset by an unusually long reproductive cycle and the production of an average of 80 eggs for each female throughout the breeding season (Ehrlich et al. 1988, Lowther 1993). The combination of a very long reproductive period and a wide assortment of potential host species explains why cowbirds are able

to take over a newly colonized area so rapidly even as some host species decline.

In early Jul at Malheur NWR adults begin congregating and are moving southward by mid-Jul (Littlefield 1990a). In early Jul, juveniles become apparent in e. and w. Oregon, and are usually first seen following their host parent, begging for food soon after fledging (MP). After leaving their foster parent, they regularly join other young cowbirds, forming small single-species flocks. At Malheur NWR, young birds remain until Aug or early Sep (Littlefield 1990a). In both e. and w. Oregon, some birds remain among large flocks of blackbirds, but by Oct the majority of birds have left the state.

Most cowbirds move to the s. U.S. and n. Mexico, where they form large flocks with other blackbirds. Wintering flocks of as many as 300 have been recorded in the Willamette and Rogue valleys (Shipman 1998).

**Detection:** During the breeding season, males can be easily detected sitting on a conspicuous perch singing their high-pitched whistles and gurgles. Females are less easily seen, spending most of their energy skulking through the foliage searching for potential laying sites.

The identification of recently fledged birds is often problematic. Appearing alone, these tawny and streaky birds hop about on the ground behaving as if they were some misplaced vagrant sparrow. Most juveniles complete a pre-basic molt by Aug and take on a more cowbird-like appearance (Pyle 1997).

**Population Status and Conservation:** There is no concern about the welfare of the Brown-headed Cowbird. The N. American population is estimated at 20 to 40 million (Lowther 1993).

Oregon was one of the last areas in N. America to witness the range expansion of the Brown-headed Cowbird. Gabrielson and Jewett (1940) stated that the species was encountered with regularity only in the southeast corner of the state. They first bred west of the Cascades in Eugene in 1946 (Gullion 1951) and Medford (fledgling collected) in 1950 (Thatcher 1953). CBC data show a rapid increase in winter records in the late 1940s, reaching Tillamook Co. by 1969 (Shipman 1998).

Human-caused changes in the environment do not completely explain the expansion of Brown-headed Cowbird into Oregon. There is some evidence to suggest that the range expansion of *obscurus* was underway before substantial change in habitat had occurred (Rothstein 1994). Forest fragmentation and conversion to agriculture provided additional habitat, but range expansion into the Willamette Valley and Oregon coastal areas may have been inevitable.

BBS data suggest that cowbird numbers have stabilized in most of Oregon (Sauer et al. 1997). Conversion of agricultural land to suburban development may also be affecting their winter status, as reflected by a decline in numbers reported from CBCs (Shipman 1998).—*Mike Patterson*

## Orchard Oriole *Icterus spurius*

This small oriole of the e. U.S. breeds from s. Saskatchewan south into Mexico and east to the e. coast. It winters from s. California and Texas south to n. S. America. It is casual elsewhere west of the Rocky Mtns. An immature was photographed at South Beach, Lincoln Co., 27 Sep 1981 (Gilligan and Irons 1987, Watson 1989); another was there 13-16 Oct 2001 (Contreras 2002b). A female was photographed at the Toketee RS, Douglas Co., 8-10 May 1988 (OBRC). A female was photographed at Brookings, Curry Co., 12 Nov to 12 Dec 1990 (OBRC); a female and immature male were there during the winter of 2001-02 (OBRC), and a male was photographed at Fields, Harney Co., 4-7 Jun 1991 (OBRC). Monotypic (AOU 1957).—*Harry B. Nehls*

## Hooded Oriole *Icterus cucullatus*

This colorful oriole breeds from n. California south to Texas and into Mexico. It winters primarily in Mexico and occasionally along the w. coast and sw. U.S. With the settlement of California this southern species extended its breeding range northward, reaching n. California by 1972. At the present time it is a regular breeding species along the nw. California coast (Harris 1991). Known in Oregon from sightings and photographs only. The first Oregon record was from Ashland, Jackson Co., 15 May 1965 (Browning 1966a). It is now an irregular spring visitant from mid-Apr to early Jun, and an irregular rare winter visitant from late Nov to mid-Apr. Nevertheless, the scarcity of palms of any size in Oregon might ultimately deny this species a foothold in the state (D. Fix p.c.).

All wintering records are from w. Oregon. A pair remained at Hunter Cr., Curry Co., through Jun 1987, indicating a possible nesting attempt (Heinl 1988b). Another was at Talent through the summer of 2001 (Contreras 2002b). One was observed at Coos Bay, Coos Co., 31 Aug 1991 (OBRC). Most Oregon records are of birds visiting hummingbird feeders. There are many photographs in the files of the OBRC (Watson 1989). Subspecies unknown.—*Harry B. Nehls*

## Streak-backed Oriole *Icterus pustulatus*

This resident of Mexico and M. America ranges north to s. Arizona and occasionally to s. California. The only record north of this range is of a male photographed feeding at sapsucker wells at Malheur NWR HQ 28 Sep to 1 Oct 1993 (Denny 1994b, Herlyn et al. 1994).—*Harry B. Nehls*

## Baltimore Oriole *Icterus galbula*

This close relative of the Bullock's Oriole breeds from c. Alberta to Nova Scotia and south to Texas and Florida. It winters chiefly from Mexico to n. S. America, and occasionally in California and the e. U.S. Because of widespread hybridization along the east slopes of the Rocky Mtns. this species was joined in 1973 with the Bullock's Oriole to form a single species called the Northern Oriole (AOU 1973). The two forms were returned to full species status in 1995 (AOU 1995). Monotypic.

In California it is regular in spring and irregular at other times of the year. In Oregon it is occasional in spring and sporadic at other times of the year. The majority of records occur between mid-May and mid-Jun, mostly east of the Cascades. A female was collected at Logan, Clackamas Co., 4 Jun 1907 (Browning 1975b) (spec. no. 239a, University of Utah Museum of Zoology); single adult males were collected at Malheur NWR, Harney Co., 1 Jun 1960 (Kridler and Marshall 1962); photographed on the Bayocean Spit, Tillamook Co., 26 Oct 1974 (OBRC); photographed there 16 Sep 1997 (OBRC); and photographed at Brookings, Curry Co., from 29 Nov 1991 to 7 Mar 1992 (OBRC). An immature was photographed at Malheur NWR HQ 16 Sep 1997 (Sullivan 1998a). A subadult male was at Summer Lake, Lake Co., 15 Oct 1998 (OBRC).—*Harry B. Nehls*

## Bullock's Oriole *Icterus bullockii*

A boldly colored medium-sized bird, the Bullock's Oriole builds its characteristic hanging nest in broad-leafed trees and tall shrubs, especially when the trees or shrubs are spaced widely and situated along edges of streams and fields. The Bullock's Oriole is the western counterpart of its similarly orange-colored relative, the Baltimore Oriole, with which it occasionally interbreeds in a few areas in the Great Plains (AOU 1998).

**General Distribution:** Breeds from w. N. Dakota, s. Saskatchewan, and s. British Columbia south to s. Texas, c. Mexico, and s. California. Winters mostly from Mexico to Costa Rica, although scattered individuals linger farther north. Monotypic (Rising 1970).

**Oregon Distribution:** Rare to fairly common breeder, especially along major rivers and around farmsteads (Gabrielson and Jewett 1940, Littlefield 1990a). BBS data indicate this species is most widespread in sw. and ne. Oregon. In particular, on the Derby route in Jackson Co., recorded on an average of 55% of survey points annually 1966-97, vs. 8% on all routes statewide where it occurred. Common in Umpqua Valley (Hunter et al. 1998). In the s. Willamette Valley, detected at 9% of 121 mostly riparian points scattered throughout a 30 mi$^2$ (77 km$^2$) area near the confluence

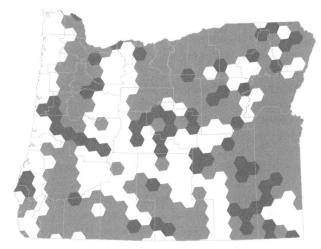

of the McKenzie R. and Willamette R. (Adamus and Fish 2000). Reported uncommon in Linn Co. (Gillson 1999); rare in Benton Co., with only "two or three nests reported annually" (Herlyn 1998). In 1990-91 study of a wide variety of Portland natural habitats, comprised 0.31% of all birds surveyed at over 200 sites (Poracsky et al. 1992). In a 1999 Portland area study, was present in seven (12%) of 54 urban and suburban riparian areas (Hennings 2001).

Tendency to nest along the Oregon coast seems to vary from year to year (Bayer 1993). Generally rare or absent from higher elevations of Coast Range and Cascades. Widespread and uncommon to locally common in lowland riparian areas and in deciduous trees at farmsteads in e. Oregon (Littlefield 1990a, Gilligan et al. 1994, Contreras and Kindschy 1996).

**Habitat and Diet:** Nests primarily in openly spaced cottonwoods, maples, and other tall, forking, broadleaf trees (*PA*). Also nests in junipers (Littlefield 1990a), Douglas-fir (*MGH*), oak-madrone chaparral (Browning 1975a), willows, and orchard trees (*PA*). In arid regions, may nest more extensively where lands are irrigated (Kennedy 1914) and where trees are widely scattered rather than in large closed-canopy blocks (Saab 1999).

In the Willamette Basin 1968-97, recorded at 4.3% (annual range: 1-10%) of the BBS route points in agricultural and other open lands, 2.4% (annual range 0.7-4.0%) in urban/suburban areas, and 1.3% (annual range 0.7 – 2.7%) in forested areas (P. Adamus and C. Lett, unpublished analysis). Tree heights of greater than 50 ft (15 m) and canopy closures of 30-60% have been recommended (Altman 2000a), based partly on findings of Schaefer (1976). The species has not been reported from any of the hundreds of point counts conducted in Oregon's coniferous forests (e.g., Ruggiero et al. 1991, Anthony et al. 1996, Huff and Brown 1998).

Nest is constructed of plant fibers, hair, fine grass, and moss, usually at the end of a branch, is fastened to supporting twigs both at its sides and its top, mostly

about 6-15 ft (1.8-4.6 m), sometimes 6-50 ft (1.8-15.2 m) above ground (Ehrlich et al. 1988). Mainly eats insects (Ehrlich et al. 1988). Forages amid foliage along branches, and less often on the ground or in the air. Also attracted to hummingbird feeders and plantings of red-hot-pokers, consuming their nectar (Gillson 1999).

**Seasonal Activity and Behavior:** In most of w. Oregon, migrants or prospective breeders arrive mid- to late Apr, earliest 11 Apr in Benton Co. (Herlyn 1998), 9 May in Linn Co. (Gillson 1999). Presumed early migrants have been seen as early as 29 Mar in Medford (Browning 1975a). In e. Oregon, birds arrive about a week later, and numbers peak around mid-May (Littlefield 1990a). Earliest arrival is Apr 25 and latest May 14 in vicinity of Malheur NWR (Ivey, Herziger, and Scheuering 1998).

Statewide, nest building has been reported in mid-May, with young detected as early as 1 Jun (Adamus et al. 2001). In s. California, pairs occasionally nest close together, especially if food and nest sites are scarce (Pleasants 1979). Data are lacking for Oregon, but studies elsewhere have reported clutch sizes ranging 3-6. Eggs hatch in about 2 wk, and young leave the nest in another 2 wk. Both parents tend nest, but after young fledge, adult males become solitary (Ehrlich et al. 1988).

In the fall, migrants (i.e., birds seen at locations where they apparently did not breed) are most often reported during the latter half of Aug, with scattered reports until mid-Sep (Gilligan et al. 1994, Gillson 1999). As of 1994, there were 13 winter records; only two from east of the Cascades (Gilligan et al. 1994). In California, increased incidence of wintering birds has been attributed partly to use of nectar feeders (Zeiner et al. 1990).

**Detection:** Quite noticeable as it is boldly colored, occurs in somewhat open habitats, has a moderate-sized home range, and vocalizes loudly during the breeding season. Nests are also easy to spot after deciduous trees have shed their leaves in the autumn.

**Population Status and Conservation:** Bullock's Oriole is one of 44 birds whose statewide distribution is more than 90% on private land (Kagan et al. 1999). Has been proposed as a "focal species" for conservation of large-canopy trees in riparian deciduous woodlands of the Rogue and Umpqua valleys (Altman 2000a). BBS trends for the species are not statistically significant for Oregon or for any ecological regions that overlap Oregon (Sauer et al. 2001).

May be highly vulnerable to use of pesticides because it nests close to residences and farms, and is primarily an insectivore. Along the Blitzen R. (Harney Co.), occurred more commonly in riparian habitats that had been grazed less often (Taylor 1986a). The abandonment of many isolated farmsteads with their accompanying shade trees and gardens also may have affected this species negatively in e. Oregon. In w. Oregon, the recruitment of trees that are essential to this species along riparian edges is probably limited by dense growths of Himalayan blackberry and by abnormal flood regimes associated with river regulation by dams (Adamus and Fish 2000).

Fledglings are preyed on by snakes (Marr 1985) and probably a wide range of other predators. Customary use of edge habitats may make Bullock's Oriole especially vulnerable to predators, as well as to being occasionally parasitized by Brown-headed Cowbird (Smith 1972, Hanka 1984). However, the species apparently has evolved some behaviors to partly cope with cowbird parasitism (Hobson and Sealy 1987a, Rohwer et al. 1989, Neudorf and Sealy 1992, Sealy 1996).—*Paul Adamus*

### Scott's Oriole *Icterus parisorum*

This oriole breeds from c. Nevada, sc. Idaho, and sw. Wyoming south to s. California, Texas, and into Mexico. It winters primarily in Mexico and occasionally to s. California and Texas. It is casual elsewhere in the w. U.S. A female observed at Fields, Harney Co., 4-8 Jun 1991 (OBRC) is the only accepted record for Oregon. Monotypic (AOU 1957).—*Harry B. Nehls*

## Family *Fringillidae*

### Subfamily Fringillinae

### Brambling *Fringilla montifringilla*

This northern finch breeds from Scandinavia across Russia to Kamchatka and winters in Europe, n. Africa to Japan, and to the Philippines. It regularly occurs in migration and winters in Alaska and sporadically elsewhere in N. America. A male was photographed at Portland, Multnomah Co., 22 Nov 1967 to late Mar 1968, during which time it molted from basic to alternate plumage (Watson 1989). Singles were photographed at La Grande, Union Co., 9 Dec 1983 to 24 Jan 1984 (Watson 1989); observed at Dallas, Polk Co., 1 Dec 1985 (Heinl 1986c); photographed at Florence, Lane Co., 25-31 Oct 1990 (Fix 1991); photographed at Aloha, Washington Co., from late Dec 1991 to mid-Mar 1992 (Johnson J 1992b); photographed at Portland 13 Dec 1998 to 5 Jan 1999 (OBRC); observed at Holley, Linn Co. 26 Dec 1998 (OBRC); observed at Umapine, Umatilla Co., 8 Feb 1992 (OBRC); and one remained at Burns during the winter of 2001-02 (OBRC). All Oregon records were at residential feeding stations. Monotypic (Banks 1970).—*Harry B. Nehls*

### Subfamily Carduelinae

## Gray-crowned Rosy-Finch
*Leucosticte tephrocotis*

Rosy-Finches are the highest-altitude breeding birds throughout most of their range. They are long-winged and generally dull-looking unless seen at close range, when the pinkish hues and combinations of brown, gray, and black can be seen. Their conical bill is usually dark during spring and early summer and yellowish especially in fall and winter (Leffingwell and Leffingwell 1931, Johnson 1977). These birds usually perch on ground, but occasionally alight on buildings, trees, bushes, phone, and fence wires (Gabrielson and Jewett 1940). They typically walk rather than hop, but do the latter occasionally. They also swipe with their bill rather than digging with feet as some sparrows and finches do. The taxonomy of this and other *Leucosticte* has been changed a number of times. All rosy-finches were lumped with Asiatic Rosy-Finch (*L. arctoa*) as Rosy-Finch in the 1983 AOU Check-list, and split again in 1998 into three N. American and one Asiatic species.

The Wallowa Mtns. form of this finch, *L. t. wallowa*, was described in 1939 (Miller 1939a), and is one of only two avian taxa endemic to Oregon (see Wrentit for the other). These birds are somewhat darker, less tawny and red-brown overall, than *L. t. littoralis*, which breed in the Blue Mtns. and Cascades (Miller 1939a). However, *littoralis* with intermediate characters (some brownish on otherwise gray cheeks) have been reported in Grant and Baker counties (Johnson 1975). Johnson (1975) suggested that some birds collected from the Wallowas (*L. t. wallowa*) showed intermediate characters as well. Evanich (1992a) reported birds that appeared intermediate between Gray-crowned and Black Rosy-Finches in ne. Oregon, but it is unclear if dark individuals of *wallowa* could be mistaken for such intermediates.

**General Distribution:** Breeds above timberline and near glaciers in much of Alaska, Yukon, British Columbia, and sw. Alberta, south through Rockies to nw. Montana, c. Idaho, and ne. Oregon, and in the Cascades and Sierra Nevada to ec. California. Winters from the Aleutians, s. mainland Alaska (rarely), British Columbia, s. Alberta, and c. Saskatchewan south to w. Oregon, c. and e. California, c. Nevada, c. Utah, n. New Mexico, nw. Nebraska, and sw. N. Dakota. Six subspecies, of which two occur in Oregon.

**Oregon Distribution:** In the Cascades, *L. t. littoralis* was reported to breed in early 1900s on Mt. Hood, Mt. Jefferson, and Three Sisters. It was also found but not confirmed nesting on Mt. McLoughlin, and suspected on Mt. Washington and Three Fingered Jack (Gabrielson and Jewett 1940). It is a common summer resident at Crater L. near snow fields in high open areas (Farner 1952). Juveniles have been observed here, and one or more nests were reported from here without details (Aldrich 1940). Summer observations of rosy-finches were reported during the 1960s and 1970s from Mt. Hood (Baldridge and Crowell 1965, Crowell and Nehls 1966c, 1970c), Mt. Jefferson (Crowell and Nehls 1969d), Big L., Lane Co. (Crowell and Nehls 1973b), South Sister (Crowell and Nehls 1970a), and Crater L. (Baldridge and Crowell 1965, Crowell and Nehls 1972d, Rogers 1974b, 1974c). Recent breeding has been confirmed at Mt. Hood, Crater L. (OBBA), and Three Fingered Jack (S. Shunk p.c.), with additional summer sightings from Three Sisters, Mt. Thielsen, Wallowa Mtns., and Steens Mtn. (OBBA, Fix 1990a). A flock was noted on top of Hamaker Mtn., Klamath Co., in early May 1984, but no breeding evidence was obtained (Gordon 1984a).

New breeding localities for *littoralis* were found in the Blue Mtns. in the 1960s. Several birds were seen and a male in breeding condition was collected in a small patch of alpine habitat at 8,400 ft (2,560 m) on the north slope of Strawberry Mtn., Grant Co., 8 Jul 1967 (Johnson 1975). Johnson suggested that additional habitat may occur 2 mi (3.2 km) to the southeast, at lower elevation, above Little Strawberry L. Breeding birds (a collected female had a fully formed egg, males had enlarged testes) were located 10 Jul 1967 in an alpine enclave on the north face of Rock Cr. Butte, 9,000 ft (2,743 m), Baker Co. A single Jun-Oct record exists from ridges at the head of the S. Fork of the Umatilla R. drainage (Pedersen et al. 1975).

The distinctive Wallowa Mtns. subspecies, *wallowa*, described by Miller (1939a) has been taken from Eagle Cap and Elkhorn Peak (Miller 1939), and at the head of Big Sheep Cr. (Jewett 1924). Gabrielson and Jewett (1940) stated that *L. t. tephrocotis* [=*wallowa*] bred only in highest parts of Wallowa Mtns. from peaks in the vicinity of Steamboat L. to those at head of Big Sheep Cr. and the Imnaha R. In 1970, *DBM* assessed, "While total suitable habitat apparently consists of a strip about 10 miles long, this area has not been altered by man and the bird has probably had this status for hundreds of years" (Rogers 1970b), and the bird remains strictly alpine there in summer (Evanich 1992a). Ten birds assumed to be *wallowa* were seen 26-29 Jul 1970 at Jewett L. and one was seen at Frazier L., a previously unreported location for the bird. Rosy-finches were reported in Aug from the Bonny Lakes area, Wallowa Co. (Evanich 1983c). Also about seven were seen along Thorp Cr., below Sacajawea Peak on 17 Jul 1984 (*DBM*).

The only records suggestive of Gray-crowned Rosy-Finches (subspecies unknown) breeding in se. Oregon are Littlefield's (1990a) mention of

their summer presence on Steens Mtn., and two birds observed in Jun 1999 in suitable habitat in the Oregon Canyon Mtns., Malheur Co. (M. Denny p.c.).

In winter, *littoralis* has been collected in Wallowa, Baker, Union, Umatilla, Grant, Lake, and Malheur counties. *L. t. wallowa* (formerly included in *tephrocotis*) irregularly winters in ne. Oregon; specimens exist from Baker, Grant, Harney, Wallowa, and Lake counties. This subspecies is often found mixed in with the more common *littoralis* (Gabrielson and Jewett 1940). The most distant record of *wallowa* from its breeding grounds is a flock of >50 near Ramsey, Nevada, 15 Nov 1941 (Alcorn 1943) (1 specimen taken: no. 84647 MVZ). Most reports outside the breeding season remain unidentified to subspecies.

In fall and winter, Gray-crowned Rosy-Finches have been found almost annually in the Coast Range on top of Marys Peak, Benton Co., since 1974 (Herlyn 1998). The only other Coast Range records were three in a clearcut near Scoggins Valley Park 21 Jan 1986; five in a clearcut in the same area 31 Jan 1986 (Heinl 1986c); and one at a feeder in Astoria in the early 1990s (photos, M. Patterson p.c.). There are approximately four records for fall through spring in the Willamette Valley (Crowell and Nehls 1974b, Ramsey 1977, Fix 1985e, Heinl 1985).

Rosy-finches have been reported in the Cascades in winter only since development of convenient public access at Mt. Hood and Crater L. For example, 1,000 on 10 Dec 1962, and 100 on 26 Jan 1963 at Timberline Lodge, Mt. Hood (Boggs and Boggs 1963b); a flock of 50 at timberline on Mt. Hood, 27 Dec 1968 (Crowell and Nehls 1969b); and a flock on Mt. Hood 17 Feb 1985 was considered typical (Heinl 1985).

*Gray-crowned Rosy-Finch*

ELVA PAULSON

Flocks were also been observed at Crater L. on 8 Oct 1972 (Crowell and Nehls 1973a), and 200 were there 18 Jan 1986 (Heinl 1986c).

In ne. Oregon, rosy-finches are a rare to locally abundant migrant and winter visitant, their status being highly irregular (Evanich 1992a). They have been reported on a majority of CBCs in Union, Wallowa, and Baker counties, most years reporting >100, with a maximum of 3,033 on the 1983-84 Union Co. count (CBC data). Large numbers are often seen just outside Union and Enterprise (Rogers TH 1981b, Evanich 1984b), and flocks of 100+ are commonly reported near Baker City (Rogers 1960, 1963, 1967a, 1968b, 1970a, Rogers 1973b, Summers 1985b).

Records in the Oregon Columbia Plateau are primarily from sc. Morrow Co.: 11 mi (18 km) up Willow Cr. Rd., east of Heppner, Morrow Co., winter 1970-71 (Kolb 1971); flocks of 100 or more at Heppner, winter 1972-73 (Rogers 1973b); recorded nine of 22 Ruggs-Hardman CBCs ; but also two of 13 Umatilla Co. CBCs. There is one record of 2,030 rosy-finches on the John Day CBC.

In the Great Basin of Oregon, most records of rosy-finches are from Steens Mtn., Hart Mtn., and vicinities (e.g., Rogers TH 1978a, Summers 1986a). CBC records include seven of 26 Hart Mtn. CBCs, one of 13 Adel CBCs, and two of 13 Summer L. CBCs (CBC data). Also there are three Nov-Dec records at Malheur NWR (Littlefield 1990a). Two females were observed Dec 2001 a couple of miles east of Fort Rock, Lake Co., feeding around broken bags of grain (S. Shunk p.c.).

**Habitat and Diet:** Typically breeds in the highest reaches of alpine habitat, usually above timberline, but also "in cirques on the north and east faces of certain peaks that are timbered to their summits, but where deep snow accumulation and shade combine to produce an alpine climate at lower elevations" (Johnson 1975). Nests are located in rock crannies and crevices, typically in cliffs (Jewett 1924, Shaw 1936, Gabrielson and Jewett 1940), but in Yosemite NP, California, nests have also been found in talus slopes and boulder fields (Wheeler 1940). In Yosemite NP, nests in cliffs suffered less predation from Clark's Nutcrackers and chipmunks than nests in talus and boulder fields (Twining 1940).

Nests in Oregon are described as dry grass and roots (Gabrielson and Jewett 1940). Nests in Washington and California included *Usnea* (a tree lichen), rootlets, moss, and/or coarse grass, with a lining of fine grass, feathers, moss, rush culms, goat hair, and/or willow fluff (Shaw 1936, Wheeler 1940); some nests were quite wet (Dixon 1936).

In the Wallowas, birds apparently nesting in cliffs were observed foraging in areas below from the cliffs (Jewett 1924). Similarly, in Yosemite NP parents feeding young at a nest in a talus slope were observed to forage in a meadow "far below" the nest location (Wheeler 1940). Food is carried back to the young, the throat sometimes bulging with food (Twining 1940). Food is apparently stored in the throat during transport, and taken from inside mouth by the young (Shaw 1936). If snow is present, rosy-finches continue to forage along the edge throughout summer, e.g., flocks at the edges of snow at Crater L. NP 11 Aug 1972 (Crowell and Nehls 1972d).

Regarding diet, Gabrielson and Jewett (1940) only mention the Wallowa Mtn. birds foraging on insects on snowfields and glaciers. Farner (1952) reported the smartweed *Polygonum newberryi* as a favorite food item in Crater L. NP, but that a variety of insects are taken, and two were observed feeding on seeding flowers of the composite *Raillardella argentea*, on 11 Aug 1950, at 8,000 ft (2,438 m) on Dutton Ridge. Gullets, stomachs, and fecal sacs, as well as field observations in British Columbia and California, similarly revealed a variety of insect and plant material taken, predominantly insects during nestling and fledgling periods and plant material (seeds, bulbs, shoots, and flower parts) at other times. Items are taken from snow, bare ground, ground vegetation, tree bark, and lake shores (Swarth 1922, Grinnell and Storer 1924, Dixon 1936, Twining 1940).

Winter roosts reported in Oregon include vacant Cliff Swallow nests along Rock Cr., south of Hardman, Morrow Co., and under the eaves of barns and outbuildings near Enterprise, Wallowa Co. (Sullivan 1992c). Winter roosts have been reported in vacant Cliff Swallow nests in se. Washington (Taylor 1923, Leffingwell and Leffingwell 1931), abandoned buildings and piers in Utah (King and Wales 1964), mine shafts in Montana and California (Miller and Twining 1943, Hendricks 1981), and a cave in se. Idaho (French 1959). The Montana mine shaft had fairly constant night-time temperatures of 48-50°F (9-10°C), while the outside temperature nightly was −19.5°F (−28.6°C) (Hendricks 1981). Temperatures in vacant but representative roost sites in abandoned buildings and piers near Salt Lake City, Utah, were about 4-18°F (2-10°C) warmer than outside temperatures; thus roost sites occupied by birds are likely even warmer due to reflected body heat (King and Wales 1964).

In winter in e. Oregon, rosy-finches forage on rocky hillsides and snowy open fields (Gabrielson and Jewett 1940, Evanich 1992a). Birds in se. Washington foraged up to several miles from the night roost. Diet of these birds was found to consist primarily of Russian thistle, wild grass, Jim Hill mustard, tumbleweed, and sunflower. Rosy-finches are commonly reported at winter feeding stations in Montana (Hendricks 1981). Birds came to cracked wheat and corn placed near a winter roost in se. Washington (Leffingwell and

Leffingwell 1931), and with millet in Utah (King and Wales 1964). Birds arriving on breeding grounds early in the season typically forage in patches where wind, snow-slides, or rapid melting have cleared snow to expose bare ground, but also in scattered places on snow (Dixon 1936, Twining 1940, Rogers 1974b).

**Seasonal Activity and Behavior:** Attempts at song, increasing "quarrels," and pairing are usually noted beginning in Feb at a wintering locality in se. Washington; darkening of bills also noted at this time (Leffingwell and Leffingwell 1931). Birds probably arrive on breeding grounds Apr to early Jun. Heavy snow storms early in the season may drive birds temporarily to lower elevations (Dixon 1936). In Crater L. NP, copulating birds were observed 1 Jun 1944 at summit of Dutton Cliff, and 7 Jul 1950 on Videa Ridge (Farner 1952). Pairs were observed at Crater L. on 26 Jun 1949 (Wilson and Norr 1949) and 12 Jun 1996 (OBBA), and males in breeding condition were collected in Jun and Jul (Farner 1952). A pair was observed at Mt. Thielsen 19 Jun 1996 (OBBA). Numerous birds were reported on Park Ridge just north of Mt. Jefferson on 4 Jun 1926 (Gabrielson and Jewett 1940).

No nest building or egg dates for Oregon. Nest building noted 29 Jun to 11 Jul in the Sierra Nevada, California (Dixon 1936, Wheeler 1940). A nest with eggs was observed 17 Jun on Mt. Baker, Washington (Shaw 1936), and incubation occurred 30 Jun, and 7, 9 and 15 Jul in the Sierra Nevada (Dixon 1936, Wheeler 1940). A hatching date of 25 Jun was recorded at Mt. Baker (Shaw 1936). Young were observed in nests on 23 Jul and 21 Aug in the Wallowas (Jewett 1924, Gabrielson and Jewett 1940); 6-13 Jul on Mt. Baker (Shaw 1936); and nestlings were common 6-7 Jul in the Sierra Nevada (Dixon 1936, Wheeler 1940). The nestling period is approximately 2 wk at Mt. Baker (Shaw 1936), and most birds are out of the nest in 10 days in the Sierra Nevada (Dixon 1936). Fledglings were observed 8 Jul on Mt. Baker (Shaw 1936), 23 and 24 Jul in the Wallowas (Jewett 1924, Gabrielson and Jewett 1940), 15 Jul at Crater L. (OBBA), 17 Jul in the Sierra Nevada (Dixon 1936), and 22 Aug on Mt. Rainier, Washington (Shaw 1936). Ten or more juveniles were observed among 83 birds on Dutton Cliff, Crater L., 28 Jul 1951, including one juvenile being fed by an adult (Farner 1952). Late dates of birds in the vicinity of breeding grounds include 25 Aug at Crater L. (Farner 1952); 30 Aug on Mt. McLoughlin; and 17 Sep in the Wallowas (Gabrielson and Jewett 1940).

In Yosemite NP, ephemeral groups of rosy-finches formed while foraging in the vicinity of the breeding grounds (Twining 1940), but larger more cohesive groups primarily formed in fall and winter. In se. Washington, most molt completed before arriving on wintering grounds (Leffingwell and Leffingwell 1931).

In Oregon and the w. U.S., autumn arrival on the wintering grounds is consistently in a 3-wk period in late Oct to mid-Nov, early Nov being the average (Leffingwell and Leffingwell 1931, King and Wales 1964, Herlyn 1999). Similarly, there is a consistent departure from the wintering grounds typically in the last two weeks of Mar, principally the last week (Leffingwell and Leffingwell 1931, Miller and Twining 1943, King and Wales 1964, Hendricks 1981, Herlyn 1999). There are very few post-Mar records at Oregon wintering grounds: e.g., 50 near Ironside, n. Malheur Co., 12 Apr 1987 (Anderson 1987f); one at Eugene 22 Apr 1974 (Crowell and Nehls 1974b); and singles at Marys Peak, Benton Co., 16 Apr 1989 and 14 May 1995 (Herlyn 1999).

In Montana, Washington, Idaho, and Utah, birds typically left winter night-roosts near dawn and well before sunrise (about 0630), and returned in the afternoon 2-3 hr before dusk (1400-1500) (Leffingwell and Leffingwell 1931, French 1959, Hendricks 1981).

**Detection:** In breeding habitat, rosy-finches are often detected by their swift flight over rocky areas, or by their characteristic calls. Nests are located most easily during nest building or hatching stages when adults are flying back and forth to the nest carrying nest material or food for young; adults are most secretive during the egg stage when Clark's Nutcrackers and chipmunks are looking for a meal (Dixon 1936). Foraging birds can be looked for near the interface of receding snow and exposed rock and soil. In winter, flocks may be from several 10s to over 1,000 birds, making the species absent from most of the landscape but present in high densities wherever the flocks occur. Counts can be made at winter roosts.

**Population Status and Conservation:** No population estimates are available. There is likely a much greater wintering population than breeding population in Oregon. In general, winter encounters seem much less frequent than indicated by Gabrielson and Jewett (1940) early in the 20th century. *L. t. wallowa* should be regularly monitored, as the breeding population is likely very small and is endemic to Oregon. While the reality and magnitude of global warming are hotly debated, potential effects such as a reduction or loss of snow fields in breeding areas may impact this species (*DBM*).—*Matthew G. Hunter*

## Black Rosy-Finch *Leucosticte atrata*

This dark, medium-sized finch with gray and pink highlights is the darkest of the rosy-finches and one of Oregon's rarest breeding birds. It is found in summer in montane areas above timberline, where loose swarms of these birds seem to blow like leaves among isolated cirques, cliffs, and hanging snowfields.

**General Distribution:** Breeds locally from c. Idaho and w. Montana and Wyoming south and west to e. Oregon, Nevada, and Utah. Winters within and south of the breeding range at lower elevations, to n. Arizona and New Mexico. Monotypic (AOU 1957).

**Oregon Distribution:** Breeds on Steens Mtn., where first found by Zeillemaker on 19 Jun 1966 (Scott 1966). Two males collected there in breeding condition on 4 Jul 1967 (Johnson 1975) confirmed a breeding presence that has continued (D. Fix *fide* Anonymous 1977a, Littlefield 1991, R. Johnson p.c.). May breed at least occasionally in the Wallowa Mtns. (Gabrielson and Jewett 1940, Johnson 1975, Evanich 1992a), but not proven and birds are not always found when sought. Johnson (p.c.) notes that of 84 rosy-finches collected in the Wallowas by many collectors over many decades, only three have been Black Rosy-Finches. Winter distribution is poorly known, but birds can be found on the lower east side of Steens Mtn. and in the Alvord Desert in winter (Littlefield 1990a, 1991, Contreras 1997b) and rarely in c. Wallowa Co. (Evanich 1990).

**Habitat and Diet:** These birds have one of the most barren and specialized breeding habitats in Oregon. They use bare rock outcroppings, cliffs, and talus for breeding and mainly open ground and snowfields for feeding (French 1954, Johnson 1989b, *ALC*). French (1954) noted that Utah birds make single flights of well over a mile (sometimes in succession) when feeding, and therefore may require a sizable area of appropriate habitat for breeding.

Very little Oregon dietary information is available for this species. They have been observed picking insects from the edges of snowfields and removing seeds from various plants on Steens Mtn. in Sep (*ALC*). An extensive study of diet in Utah birds showed a great variety of seeds and insects taken, with seeds the primary food after mid-Aug (French 1954).

**Seasonal Activity and Behavior:** A Utah study found birds engaged in what appeared to be display behavior at 11,000 ft (3,350 m) elevation by early Apr as long as weather conditions allowed access to rocky areas for foraging. Because the higher reaches of Steens Mtn. are sometimes snow-covered, and in some years still receiving snow until Jun (*ALC*), birds may not return to breeding grounds until later in spring or early summer. Pair formation took place on the breeding grounds in a Utah study (French 1954). Males outnumber females by 6:1 in the larger population (Ehrlich et al. 1988), unusual in birds.

R E Johnson (p.c. to M. Stern) found a nest with young "on northeast facing cliffs at the head of Kiger Gorge" on Steens Mtn. on 2 Aug 1982. Family groups (birds showing recent feathering attended by adults)

have been observed as late as the first week of Sep on Steens Mtn. (*ALC*). David Fix et al. (Anonymous 1977a) observed an adult feeding a young bird at the head of Kiger Gorge 22 Jul 1977.

Birds are thought to move downslope from Steens Mtn. in fall and return in spring, but more study of this movement is needed. The species is often found in Sep along higher Steens Mtn. ridges, with flocks of 80 (*ALC*), 50 (P. T. Sullivan in Anderson 1989b), and up to 150 (Sullivan 1997a) the largest reported. Numbers are usually smaller and sometimes mixed with Gray-crowned Rosy-Finches. Littlefield found a mixed flock of Black and Gray-crowned Rosy-Finches still present at the Steens Mtn. summit on 11-12 Oct 1977 (Rogers TH 1978a).

Birds reported from time to time in ne. Oregon have been within flocks of Gray-crowned Rosy-Finches. Flocks of "500 or more" rosy-finches seen in the Wallowas in early Nov 1967 contained about 10% Black Rosy-Finch, but these birds disappeared within 2 wk (W. Thackaberry in Rogers 1968a). French (1954) found that Utah birds often moved a few hundred miles southward in fall in addition to coming downslope. A report from Indian Rock, Grant Co., on 8 Oct 1994 (Sullivan PT 1995b) was later retracted (Jones 1996).

Winter records in Oregon are few. Littlefield (1991) indicates that at Steens Mtn. the species is "uncommon [in] winter on lower slopes, mostly along east slope among shrub uplands and grasslands." Approximately 20-30 were observed 30 Jan 1994 along the Fields-Denio Rd. near the Alvord Desert, in a large flock of American Goldfinches, Pine Siskins, and Cassin's Finches (D. Copeland p.c.). Evanich (1990) notes that the species has been reported rarely in winter within flocks of Gray-crowned Rosy-Finch in the Crow Cr.-Zumwalt area of Wallowa Co. Evanich (1982d) indicates that one was seen 20 Dec 1981 near Enterprise, Wallowa Co. Winter roosts in Cliff Swallow nests and human-made structures have been reported in Oregon for Gray-crowned (Sullivan 1992c) and in Utah for Black Rosy-Finches (French 1954).

There is a single spring record away from Steens Mtn. One was with four Gray-crowned Rosy-Finches along Hwy 140 west of Doherty Rim, Lake Co. on 1 Apr 1997 (A. Floyd in Sullivan 1997b), which is also the westernmost report for Oregon.

**Detection:** In Oregon the only reliable place to find them is along the edges of snowfields on the summit ridges of Steens Mtn., especially in late summer and early fall. This involves careful searching, sometimes at a distance. The best way to locate them is to walk to the edge of cliffs and look down or across at snowfields. Even small patches of snow may have birds. Fairly reliable sites include the head of Kiger Gorge (west of the parking area) and areas northwest of the east rim parking area. Birds sometimes feed on the sides of cliffs and in weed patches, generally near snow. These birds are unwary, often come near an observer in appropriate habitat, and can be studied at ease. Be aware that American Pipits also breed on Steens Mtn. and many move along the ridges in fall. They sometimes feed on snowfields and can be confused with finches at a distance.

**Population Status and Conservation:** Considered a Sensitive Species by ODFW in Oregon because of its very small, geographically isolated population. Breeding habitat is unlikely to be affected by humans because of its inaccessibility. Winter habitat is not well known, but it is likely that the species uses a range of native and agricultural habitats similar to those used by the Gray-crowned Rosy-Finch. Provided that the upper reaches of Steens Mtn. remain free of development, there is unlikely to be a change in the species' Oregon status. No data allowing population size comparison over time are available for Oregon.

French (1954) noted Clark's Nutcracker, Prairie Falcon, long-tailed weasel and even a chipmunk preying on Black Rosy-Finches in the Rocky Mtns.—*Alan L. Contreras*

## Pine Grosbeak *Pinicola enucleator*

Since the early 1900s this robust finch has been suspected of nesting in the Wallowa Mtns., but breeding evidence has been reported only recently, and a nest has not yet been found in Oregon. Gabrielson and Jewett (1940) commented of wintering birds "While in Oregon, the birds are tame and unsuspicious [sic], usually allowing a close approach as they feed on buds or dried fruits. The soft-gray females and young males, the latter more or less washed with yellow on the head, far outnumber the rosy males, and observers should look carefully for these duller-colored birds." Alarm and contact notes of Pine Grosbeaks are similar throughout much of their range, but location calls vary substantially throughout their range (Adkisson 1981), and these have not been described for Oregon. The song is often described as similar to the Purple Finch, but fuller and with lower pitch. The flight is typically finch-like, but with broad, bounding undulations (Jewett et al. 1953).

**General Distribution:** Breeds in northern boreal forests of N. America from Alaska east through Canada to Nova Scotia, south in Rockies and western mountains to ec. California, se. Arizona, and n. New Mexico. Winters throughout the breeding range except the northern half of the boreal forest. Irruptions bring birds to the northern tier of states from the Rockies east, and occasionally (with less regularity) to lower elevations in the West. Of eight subspecies, two occur in Oregon.

**Oregon Distribution:** *P. e. montana* breeds in the Wallowas, and is suspected to breed in the Blue Mtns. and Cascades. A total of seven sightings were made of individual birds from these ranges during the 1995-99 OBBA. Breeding evidence in the Wallowas include a pair with two young barely capable of flight Jul 1985 in Brownie Basin (D. Lorain p.c.); adults feeding two young about 1 mi (1.6 km) southeast of Aneroid L. in the second week of Jul 2001 (J. Hohmann p.c.); a family of five about 2 mi (3.2 km) east of Bonny L. in Aug in the early 1990s; a family about 0.5 mi (0.8 km) south of Bonny L. in Aug 2001 (F. Conley p.c.); one female and two immatures were near the south end of Aneroid L. on 30 Jul 2002, and a pair was noted the same day on the trail 0.5 mi (0.8 km) below the lake (F. Conley p.c.). In the Wallowas, birds taken along Cliff R., 9 Sep 1915, were badly worn and were probably breeding birds (Gabrielson and Jewett 1940). Pine Grosbeaks were reported previously in Aug from the Bonny Lakes area, Wallowa Mtns. (Evanich 1983c). A pair was observed at Unit L., Wallowa Mtns., on 17 Jul 1968 (*DBM*). The Pine Grosbeak was considered a characteristic bird of the alpine zone in the Wallowas by Booth (1939), but more recently noted as "far from common" by D. Lorain (p.c.) who has logged hundreds of miles in the Wallowas with only a dozen sightings.

In the Blue Mtns, one was observed (unspecified Jun-Oct) at the head of the S. Fk. of the Umatilla R. (Pedersen et al. 1975); and one female or immature was reported 3 Aug 1940 in fir woods at 4,500 ft (1,372 m) near Mt. Emily, Union Co. (Hyde 1942). A pair was observed singing and performing display flights 5 Jun 2000 above upper Summer C., Umatilla NF, Union Co., at about 5,100 ft (1,500m) (Spencer 2000b, M. Denny p.c.). H. Nehls (p.c.) has observed singing pairs at Elk Meadow near Troy, Wallowa Co., and at Starr CG south of Canyon City, Grant Co.

Pine Grosbeaks breed as close as Mt. Rainier in the Cascades of Washington to the north (Jewett et al. 1953), and the Sierra Nevada of California to the south, suggesting the likelihood of breeding in the Oregon Cascades. There are Mar-Aug records in the Cascades of Linn Co. (Gillson 1999), and several summer and early fall records from the c. and s. Cascades (Farner 1952, L. McQueen p.c.). In sw. Oregon, individuals were observed on 30 May 1960 and 30 May 1965 at Howard Prairie Res.; one on 30 Jun 1961 near Mt. Ashland (Browning 1966a); one at Green Springs, east of Ashland, 30 May 1965 (Hesse and Hesse 1965); and one seemingly far out of place near Sutherlin, Douglas Co., 17 May 1968 (Crowell and Nehls 1968b).

In winter, individuals of *P. e. montana* taken from Fort Warner, Lake Co.; Crane, Harney Co.; and La Grande, Union Co. (Gabrielson and Jewett 1940). However, *P. e. alascensis* is the more abundant wintering form in e. Oregon, taken from Wallowa Co., south to Malheur, Harney, and Klamath counties, and recorded from Crook and Deschutes counties; may appear in any community during the winter months (Gabrielson and Jewett 1940). *P. e. flammula* was thought to be the most numerous wintering subspecies in w. Washington (Jewett et al. 1953), thus winter reports in w. Oregon such as two photographed on the Alma-Upper Siuslaw CBC, 19 Dec 1977 (Heilbrun 1978), and 32 reported at an Astoria feeder winter 1989 (LeBaron 1989, M. Patterson p.c.), may include this subspecies (but no specimens are available). An earlier specimen from Ironside, n. Malheur Co., thought to be *flammula* by Gabrielson and Jewett (1940) was reidentified by Browning (1974) as *montana*, who identified two (UCLA, OSU) others from the same flock as *montana* and another (UCLA) as *alascensis.*

Of 10 CBC circles recording Pine Grosbeak in Oregon, over half of the records came from counts in Baker, Wallowa, and Union counties, where they have occurred irregularly on about 20-25% of counts. They have also been recorded one or more times on Hart Mtn., Malheur NWR, Hood River, Mulino, and Oakridge counts, the latter two being in w. Oregon. The median number of Pine Grosbeaks on counts tallying this species is about 10, and the maximum 58 (CBC data).

**Habitat and Diet:** No detailed information on habitat is available from Oregon. During the summer, Pine Grosbeaks observed in the Bonny Lakes area, Wallowa Mtns., were observed in small flocks among the spruces, acting like crossbills or siskins sitting at the pointed tips of trees to give their beautiful warbling song (Evanich 1983c).

On Mt. Baker, Washington, Pine Grosbeaks breed in numbers near timberline at 6,000 ft (1,829 m) in mountain hemlock and subalpine fir; other reports in Washington are 4,000-6,500 ft (1,219-1,981 m) (Jewett et al. 1953). In the Sierra Nevada of California, they are largely restricted to the red fir forest, about 5,577 ft (1,700 m), mainly on the west slope (Ray 1912, Adkisson 1977). Adkisson (1977) observed >=6 pairs during 10 days in a mixed forest of red fir, Jeffrey pine, and lodgepole pine, and found the birds virtually ignoring the pines, only perching in them occasionally, but using the firs constantly for food, nesting, and preening. Ray (1912) reported two nests in the Sierra Nevada, 16 and 35 ft (5 and 11 m) high, and 4 and 8 ft (2.4 and 1.2 m) out from the trunk, respectively, in large red firs.

Information on diet is not available for Pine Grosbeaks in Oregon, except that they have been noted at feeding stations in La Grande in the winter (Evanich 1984b). In the Sierra Nevada, the crop and stomach of one bird taken in the summer contained soft ends of pine and fir needles, as well as seeds and insects

(Ray 1912). In the Washington Cascades, grosbeaks were observed eating huckleberries near ground level 14 Sep (Jewett et al. 1953). Winter foods reported include apples (flesh and seeds), serviceberries and snowberries, fir seeds, weed and bunchgrass seeds, maple, box elder, and white hulled seeds of ponderosa pine (Jewett et al. 1953). Pine Grosbeaks were noted to obtain water from melting icicles on a cabin roof in winter near Anchorage, Alaska (Wolfe 1996). In spring, on the Washington State University campus (then State College of Washington), Pullman, one fed on a honeysuckle bush (Jewett et al. 1953).

**Seasonal Activity and Behavior:** Very little information is available. In the Sierra Nevada, courtship activities were observed 11 and 12 Jun and again during the incubation period, and nests with one or more eggs were located mid-Jun at about 8,000 ft (2,438 m) (Ray 1912). In Washington, a female was observed carrying nest material on 24 Jun, at 4,500 ft (1,372 m) on Miner's Ridge, Bumping L., Yakima Co. (Jewett et al. 1953). Adults were observed feeding young 17 Jul on Mt. Baker (Jewett et al. 1953). In the Sierra Nevada, recent fledglings were observed 29 Jul at about 9,000 ft (2,743 m), and full-grown young in early Aug (Ray 1912). In Oregon, birds are found in winter locations typically mid-Nov to early Mar (Gabrielson and Jewett 1940).

Pine Grosbeaks have been observed to include vocalizations of other species (Hairy Woodpecker, Gray Jay, American Robin, and redpoll) during their whisper song in winter in se. Manitoba (Taylor 1979).

**Detection:** During the breeding season, Pine Grosbeaks are probably best detected by songs and calls, which may sound similar to the Purple Finch. The flight call is typically described as triple-noted, but may not be so in Oregon. More reports are needed.

**Population Status and Conservation:** Clearly, effort needs to be made to determine the breeding status of this species in Oregon. Limited data and high temporal variability make assessment of winter population trends very difficult, but Pine Grosbeaks generally seem less frequent and widespread than in the days of Gabrielson and Jewett (1940). Continent-wide this species shows irruptions every 2-3 yr, but this pattern is much more subdued in the w. U.S. (Bock and Lepthien 1976), and irruptions are not always synchronous in the ne. and nw. U.S. (Arbib 1974). A fall invasion in the w. U.S. was noted in 1963 and simultaneously noted in mountains near Baker in ne. Oregon (Rogers 1964). Five observations totaling 11 birds in the vicinity of the Wallowa Mtns. during the winter of 1980-81 seemed substantial (Rogers TH 1981b). The winter of 1984-85 was also a good finch year in Oregon, when 50 were reported east of Pendleton on 16 Mar; four at

Malheur NWR 15 Dec to 22 Jan; five in Burns 3 Feb; seven along Hwy 395, 8 mi north of Burns; and one at the High Desert Museum, Deschutes Co. 23 Feb (Summers 1985b).—*Matthew G. Hunter*

## Purple Finch *Carpodacus purpureus*

The bubbly warble of this finch is common in w. Oregon conifer forests in summer, while its crossbill-like—but more delicate—*pik* call is heard in lowland valleys in winter. Adult males have a distinctly reddish-colored head, face, rump, throat, and breast, broadly but very faintly streaked brownish-pink sides, and a diffused brownish-red nape, back, and wings. Females and immature males have brownish-olive upperparts, wings, and tail, with contrasting streaking. Underparts buffy-white to off-white with fuzzy, brownish streaking; a dingy pale gray stripe is present above the eye. Males are occasionally heard incorporating a rapid succession of syllables from several species' songs into their own songs (*MGH*).

**General Distribution:** Breeds from s. Yukon and nc. British Columbia eastward across forested portions of s. Canada, Great Lakes, and ne. U.S., south to c. W. Virginia and along the Pacific coast to s. California. Winters from sw. British Columbia south along the Pacific coast to nw. Baja California, and from s. Manitoba, eastward to c. Newfoundland south to ec. Texas, and eastward to n. Florida. Three subspecies; *C. p. californicus* and *C. p. rubidus*, described by Duvall (1945b), are found in Oregon (Rand 1946, *MRB*).

**Oregon Distribution:** *C. p. californicus* breeds west of the Cascades (Duvall 1945b) from Umpqua region (DCM) southward to Jackson Co. (USNM, SOU, *MRB*). *C. p. rubidus* breeds west of the Cascades north of Douglas Co.; birds from w. Klamath Co. have been identified as intergrades (Rand 1946). Subspecific identity of e. Oregon birds remains undetermined (*MRB*).

Fairly common to common transient, summer resident and winter visitor on the west slope of the Cascades and westward (Gabrielson and Jewett 1940, Browning 1975a, Gilligan et al. 1994, Contreras 1997b, Contreras 1998, Hunter et al. 1998). Nests at lower elevations of s. Cascades (Fix 1990a), rare at higher elevations (Farner 1952, Gilligan et al. 1994); generally below 4,000 ft (1,219 m) in Klamath Mtns. while nesting (*DPV*). Uncommon to locally fairly common resident in Klamath Basin (Summers 1993a, Winema NF 1997). Rare to locally fairly common resident on the east slope of the Cascades and local transient and winter visitant elsewhere in e. Oregon (USFWS 1986c, Summers and Miller 1993, Gilligan et al. 1994, Contreras and Kindschy 1996, OBBA). Rare to uncommon summer resident in ne. Oregon

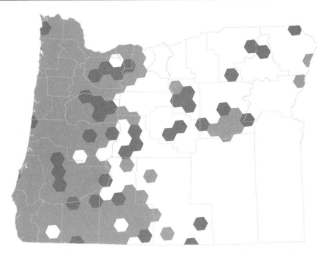

(Grande Ronde Bird Club 1988, Umatilla NF 1991, Bull and Wisdom 1992, Evanich 1992a, Huff and Brown 1998, OBBA) and Blue Mtns. above 6,000 ft (1,829 m) (Thomas 1979). Rare transient in se. Oregon (Littlefield 1990a, Contreras and Kindschy 1996). E. Oregon status needs clarification, as it may have changed in the last few decades; more reporting and documentation is urged (*MGH*).

**Habitat and Diet:** West of the Cascades, the Purple Finch mainly breeds in moderately moist, open or semi-open conifer forests and edge habitat at low to mid-elevations (Gabrielson and Jewett 1940, Fix and Sawyer 1991, Gilligan et al. 1994) and in coastal shore pine (T. Rodenkirk p.c.). Frequently breeds in open, mixed conifer-hardwood forests, deciduous woodlands, riparian corridors, and edge habitat (Cross and Simmons 1983, Fix and Sawyer 1991, Gilligan et al. 1994, *DPV*), or vigorously regenerating clearcuts and forests with partial stand retention (Fix 1990a, Fix and Sawyer 1991, *DPV*); occasionally serpentine forests in the Klamath Mtns. (*DPV*). East of the Cascades found in ponderosa pine-aspen and mature ponderosa pine on the Ochoco NF (Huff and Brown 1998); open forests of ponderosa pine, mixed conifer (Douglas-fir, grand fir, western larch), and riparian and forest edge in the Blue Mtns. (Thomas 1979, Bull and Wisdom 1992). In the Klamath Mtns., bird were recorded at densities of 0.6 birds/ac (1.4 birds/ha) in 1998 following fall 1997 controlled burn of serpentine conifer-brushfield habitat at 2,100 ft (640 m), with no detections the two preceding years (1995-96) (*DPV*).

The nest site is typically on a horizontal branch of a conifer, or sometimes a deciduous tree, 2.5-60 ft (0.75-18.3 m) above ground. The cup nest usually has a base of sticks, twigs, fine roots, grasses and is lined with rootlets, hair, and moss (Wootton 1996).

Postbreeding (late Jul-Aug) habitat in the Klamath Mtns. includes meadows with brushfields and streamside vegetation where berries are plentiful (*DPV*). Winter habitat varies widely, primarily valley lowlands in deciduous woodlands, open conifer-hardwood woodlands, forest edge, orchards, brushy areas, rural or partially wooded residential areas (Browning 1975a, Gilligan et al. 1994, Wootton 1996), also semi-open riparian locations with Oregon ash, alder, and willows (*DPV*).

Diet is mainly vegetative matter; includes a small amount of insects in summer. Reported items include buds, flowers, and fruit of apple, cherry, pear, and apricots; fruit of serviceberry, pyracantha, and juniper; seeds of conifers, maple, elm, and dogwood; weed seeds (hemp, wild radish, dandelion [Martin et al. 1951, Clement et al. 1993, Wootton 1996]). Insects consumed are mainly aphids, caterpillars, beetles, ants, and grasshoppers (Martin et al. 1951, Wootton 1996). Young are fed mostly regurgitated seeds by both parents. In the Rogue Valley, Purple Finches were observed foraging on rose hips (Jan), black and white oak buds (Jan-Mar), developing oak leaves (Apr), flowers of white manzanita (Mar) and Pacific madrone (Apr); fruit of hairy honeysuckle, blackberries, and cascara (Aug), Oregon-grape (Sep), Pacific madrone (Nov) and Oregon ash seed in winter (*DPV*). Additional foods include sunflower and millet seed from feeders, fruit of Oregon crab apple, catkins of red alder and willow (M. Patterson p.c.).

**Seasonal Activity and Behavior:** Spring migratory flocks frequent feeders from Feb into Apr (peak varies annually) in the Rogue Valley (*DPV*), and Apr at Toketee RS in s. Cascades (Fix 1990a). Sing from high perch beginning mid-Feb, continues through nesting season in the Rogue Valley (*DPV*). Nest building and egg laying recorded 8 May to 6 Jul (n=6) west of the Cascade summit and 14 May east of the Cascades (OBBA). Nest with young 16 Jun west of the Cascades, 30 Jun east of the Cascades (OBBA); feeding fledged juveniles recorded 24 May to 20 Aug west of the Cascades (n=6) (OBBA, *DPV*) and 17 Jul east of the Cascades, near Sisters (S. Shunk p.c.). Adult breeding site fidelity weak in the Klamath Mtns. (12-yr banding study) (*DPV*). Fall migration was noted mainly during Oct in the Cascades of e. Douglas Co. 1984-90 (Fix 1990a).

Three Purple Finches banded at or near Grants Pass on 9 Apr 1988, 26 Mar 1990, and 19 Aug 1996 were recovered on 20 Jan 1990 in Ukiah, California; 5 Jun 1990 in Parkland, Washington (Pierce Co.); and 30 Oct 1996 in Willits, California, respectively, suggesting a north-south movement through Oregon (Vroman 2002).

Winter numbers appear erratic; Purple Finches may be common one year, rare the next, likely due to food availability (Clement et al. 1993, Gilligan et al. 1994).

**Detection:** Easily detected by song or calls though sometimes confused with Cassin's and House Finches. Frequently seen at feeders in rural areas or wooded edges of lightly impacted residential areas. The "vireo song" of the female commonly causes confusion with the song of the Cassin's Vireo (D. Fix p.c.).

**Population Status and Conservation:** Reported in early 20th century as one of the most common and widely distributed finches in w. Oregon, but irregular, or not found, east of the Cascades (Gabrielson and Jewett 1940). Breeding populations are declining; Oregon BBS data show significant trend of -6.4%/yr, 1980-1998 (n=46). Oregon CBC data show a non-significant annual trend of -0.5% for winter populations (n=32) (Sauer et al. 1996). Reasons for decline are not known, but clearing of forest and woodland habitat for residential, agricultural, and industrial development and displacement due to increased House Finch populations are suspected (*DBM, MGH*).—*Dennis P. Vroman*

## Cassin's Finch *Carpodacus cassinii*

This finch of montane pine and aspen forests is a surprisingly talented mimic, often incorporating songs and calls of the Mountain Chickadee, American Robin, Western Tanager, White-breasted Nuthatch, and Townsend's Solitaire into its own song (*KAB*). Adult male Cassin's Finches have bright crimson rose-pink caps, slightly paler pink upper chest and rump, and pale pink streaks in the wings. The colorful cap ends abruptly at the brown nape of the neck. Females and first-year males are streaked gray-brown above and below. Because first-year males and females are identical, it is sometimes incorrectly stated that females sing.

**General Distribution:** Breeds in mountainous areas between the eastern face of the Rocky Mtns. and the Cascades, Sierra Nevada, and s. California Coast ranges from sc. British Columbia to n. Baja California (Hahn 1996, AOU 1998). Also breeds in the Klamath Mtns. of sw. Oregon south into the Coast Range of nw. California. Winter range overlaps breeding range and expands to include most of Arizona and New Mexico south through interior nc. Mexico. Some withdrawal occurs from extreme northern portions of its range in winter. Monotypic (AOU 1957).

**Oregon Distribution:** Fairly common to common summer resident from the Cascade summit eastward throughout all mountainous and forested regions of e. Oregon (Browning 1975a, Fix 1990a, Summers 1992, Gilligan et al. 1994). Very uncommon resident at higher elevations of Siskiyou Mtns. in Josephine Co. (Gabrielson and Jewett 1940, Gilligan et al.

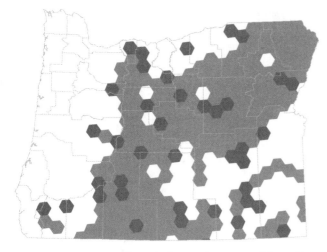

1994). In winter, found through most of breeding range and an uncommon transient and winter visitor to lower elevations. In w. Oregon, very rare winter visitor, often at feeders (Watson 1979c, Evanich 1982d, 1983b, Irons 1984b, Fix 1985a, 1985f, Heinl 1985, 1989a, Johnson 1997b, Lillie 2000). Unusual sighting of a flock of 30 Cassin's Finches reported from Sugarloaf Mt. in the Coast Range, 26 Sep 1994 (Gilligan 1995).

**Habitat and Diet:** Breeds primarily in open, mature coniferous forests of lodgepole and ponderosa pine, but also quaking aspen, subalpine fir, grand fir, and juniper steppe or woodlands (Gashwiler 1977, Sullivan et al. 1986, Huff and Brown 1998, Reinkensmeyer 2000). Occupies burned forest as well (Jewett et al. 1953, Hutto 1995a, Sallabanks 1995a). Habitat used in winter generally the same but with bulk of populations at lower elevations (Hahn 1996). Habitat preference nicely summed up by Jewett et al. (1953): "the Cassin [sic] finch likes best the scattered, open timber rather than the heavy woods."

On both the Fremont and Winema NF, more abundant in salvage-logged stands where dead and down lodgepole pine was removed than in unharvested control stands (Arnett et al. 1997, 2001). No live or dead ponderosa pines or live lodgepole pines were removed from the salvage-logged stands. Cassin's Finch probability of presence was negatively associated with the number of live and dead trees, number of live trees <32.8 ft (<10m) tall, percent seedling cover, percent shrub and grass forb cover, foliage area of live trees, and percent canopy cover. Cassin's Finch probability of presence was positively associated with the number of trees >11.8 in (>30 cm) dbh and the amount of ground debris (Arnett et al. 2001). In a study of seral stages in the n. Blue Mtns., Cassin's Finches were negatively associated with the habitat variables of crown cover and down woody debris, and positively associated with canopy height (Sallabanks 1995a). In a study of unburned to heavily burned forest in the se. Wallowa Mtns., Cassin's Finches increased

with fire (the degree of burn) 1 yr post-burn; this may be a short-term response to take advantage of conifer seeds released by fire (Sallabanks 1995a). They were negatively associated with the amount of understory vegetation. Hutto (1995a) also found Cassin's Finches abundant 1 yr post-fire in the Rocky Mtns., though they dropped off in second year following fire. Cassin's Finches were more abundant in lodgepole stands with active needleminer or mountain pine beetle infestation and in stands dead 1-5 yr from beetle kill than in healthy stands without infestation (Herman 1971, Bull 1983). Reinkensmeyer (2000) found Cassin's Finches to be three times more abundant in old-growth juniper (most trees established pre-1870; sparse shrub layer) than mid-successional juniper stands (most trees established post-1870; intact shrub layer). In the grand fir zone of ne. Oregon, they were more abundant in managed forests than old-growth (Mannan and Meslow 1984). The more open structure of the managed forests is preferred by Cassin's Finches for nesting and allows them to forage on ground.

Nests usually placed well out on lateral branches of larger conifers (i.e., not saplings), often near the end of branch and quite high up (Bent 1968, Hahn 1996). Two nests found during the building stage on the Fremont and Winema NF study in e. Oregon were both in lodgepole pine; one about 50 ft (15 m) high, and the other about 30 ft (9 m) high and part-way out on branch (B. Altman p.c.). A nest found by King (1953) in se. Washington during the building stage was 40.5 ft (12 m) high and 12 ft (3.6 m) from the trunk on a limb of a ponderosa pine. Nests are constructed of fine twigs, weed stems, grass, and rootlets, and frequently contain lichens (Gabrielson and Jewett 1940, Bent 1968). Described by Gabrielson and Jewett as a "thin platform" (1940). The lining is generally rootlets and hair, occasionally shredded bark. Four nests were found in big sagebrush on the Hart Mt. N. Antelope R. in 1984, all of which successfully fledged young (Sullivan et al 1986).

Diet consists of buds, berries, fruit, seeds, and some insects (Hahn 1996). Forages mainly in the tops of trees or on the ground; rarely in shrubs. Not able to open tightly closed cones; in Washington, observed removing seeds from open cones such as ponderosa pine or collecting them from the ground (Hahn 1996). Gleans insects, including Douglas-fir tussock moth larvae and lodgepole needleminer larvae and pupae from conifer foliage (Herman 1971, Torgersen et al. 1984, 1990). Migrating birds seen at Summer L. late Apr 1988 were feeding on Chinese elm buds (Anderson 1988d). Mixed flocks of adult and young Cassin's Finches in Spokane, Washington, Jul 1924 were reported as very common and feeding on cherries (Jewett et al. 1953). In Dec 1920, birds were noted in creek beds near Republic, Washington, feeding on buds of alder and birch, and occasionally working on ponderosa pine cones (Jewett et al. 1953). Often noted foraging with Red Crossbills and Evening Grosbeaks (Bent 1968, Hahn 1996). Cassin's Finches frequently visit mineral deposits on the ground and have been reported eating rock salt spread for deer in the Yellowstone area, and feeding on salt blocks put out for cattle on the Malheur NF (Bent 1968, Hahn 1996, *DBM*).

**Seasonal Activity and Behavior:** An altitudinal migrant. Earliest observation of birds returning to breeding habitat was 9 Apr on Hart Mtn. (Mewaldt and King 1985), and 18 Apr in the w. Cascades of e. Douglas Co. (Fix 1990a). No other dates reported for Oregon, but in Washington leave for higher elevations in Mar (latest date 28 Mar 1941 [Dumas 1949]). Cassin's Finches showed high breeding site fidelity (nearly 100%) in a study in Oregon in an 11-ac (4.5-ha) island of ponderosa pine forest in sagebrush (Mewaldt and King 1985). Fidelity reported to be much lower in other studies in other states (Hahn 1996).

Territory established once pair bond has formed and female begins to test out potential nest sites. Female is the focus of the defended area, which reaches its largest radius of about 51.2 ft (15.6 m) at time of nest completion/clutch initiation (Hahn 1996). Territory defense ends once incubation begins. Do not defend an all-purpose territory and foraging often occurs well away (98-984 ft [30-300 m])from the nest site. Socially monogamous. Evidence suggests long-term pair bonds may be maintained (Hahn 1996).

In Oregon 1995-99, nest-building activity was reported 27 May to 1 Jul (n=10) (OBBA, B. Altman p.c., *KAB*). Nests with eggs were reported 25 May to 11 Jul (n=5) (OBBA). In the Hart Mtn. study, the egg-laying period for 96% of first clutches (n=198) fell between 19 May and 13 Jun with all 5 yr combined, though the laying period in any one year only ranged 16-20 days (Mewaldt and King 1985). Clutch size is usually 4-5 eggs with incubation by the female only. Adults carrying food were reported 27 May to 1 Aug (n=17) (OBBA). Only one nest with young reported (18 Jul) (OBBA). Both parents feed young (Hahn 1996). Fledglings were reported 21 Jun to 15 Aug (n=31) (OBBA, B. Altman p.c., *KAB*). Young leave nesting area immediately after fledging (Mewaldt and King 1985) and while still being fed by parents, family groups may temporarily move to higher elevations by the end of the nesting season. Stay as family group for some time. Adults were reported to still be feeding immature birds in a group seen in Mt. Rainier NP 8 Aug 1919 (Jewett et al. 1953).

Forms small flocks in late summer and typically stays in groups nearly year-round except for the actual nesting period (Bent 1968, Mewaldt and King 1985, Hahn 1996). Flocks of 30 or more reported in early Jul on Hart Mtn. (Mewaldt and King 1985), and 25-30 seen flying above timberline in late summer in Mt. Rainier NP (Jewett et al. 1953). When flocking, may mix with House Finches or Red Crossbills.

Most high-elevation breeders move downslope to lower elevations or into the valleys in fall, though some individuals can still be found in normal breeding areas through fall and winter (Hahn 1996). Noted in the w. Cascades of e. Douglas Co. through early Nov (Fix 1990a). In Washington, birds begin to arrive on the wintering grounds in Nov (earliest date 28 Oct 1939 [Dumas 1949]). Do not defend a territory in winter.

**Detection:** Begins to give full song in Apr, well before nesting. Usually stays silent during cold, overcast weather in spring. Prior to nesting, may sing in flight (Jewett et al. 1953, Bent 1968, Hahn 1996). Stops singing and becomes quiet and inconspicuous by mid-to late Jul (Hahn 1996). According to Jewett et al. (1953) "becomes tame and unsuspicious in winter."

**Population Status and Conservation:** According to BBS data, no change in population in Oregon 1966-91 (Hahn 1996). Forest management practices that open up dense stands of mature timber within the range of the Cassin's Finch likely benefit them.

Cassin's Finches were the most abundant breeding bird on Hart Mtn. 1975-79, with 8-10 pairs/ac (20-25 pairs/ha) in an 11-ac (4.5-ha) relict stand of ponderosa pine forest that measured about 3,280 ft (1,000 m) long and 148 ft (45 m) wide (Mewaldt and King 1985).

Weather in high-elevation regions can be a mortality factor: Jun snow storms, heavy summer rain and hail have been implicated in mortality of females on eggs and young in nest (Bent 1968, Hahn 1996).—*Kelly A. Bettinger*

## House Finch *Carpodacus mexicanus*

The most widespread of Oregon's "red finches." A congenial, cheerful singer from urban areas to desert plateaus. The male has a red forehead, throat, eyebrow, rump and varying amount of red in the breast; may have small amounts of reddish wash in otherwise brownish cheek, hindcrown, nape, and streaked back. In some males, red is replaced with red-orange, orange, yellow-orange, or yellow. The female is drab grayish-brown overall, with indistinct streaking above (face and back); no red. The belly and flank of both sexes (throat and breast of female) is pale buff-gray, streaked with brown. The tail and wings of both sexes are dull brown with inconspicuous buff-white wing bars and covert edges.

**General Distribution:** Breeds from s. Canada south to s. Baja California and most of Mexico. Winters throughout the breeding range. Introduced and established in the Hawaiian Is. and in e. N. America on Long I., New York (early 1950s). Thirteen subspecies throughout the range; four subspecies occur in the w. U.S. (Pyle 1997); two occur in Oregon (Pyle 1997) provisionally (*MRB*).

**Oregon Distribution:** *C. m. frontalis* occurs in w. Oregon, *C. m. solitudinus* in e. Oregon (Pyle 1997). *C. m. solitudinus* and *C. m. frontalis* are synonyms (AOU 1947, 1957) following Grinnell and Miller (1944) and others. Aldrich and Weske (1978) reported variation in size and color of birds from our region consistent with *frontalis* (*MRB*).

Fairly common to locally common resident in lowlands, urban, rural, and agricultural areas throughout Oregon. Absent in closed-canopy conifer forests, associated clearcuts, and arid, open rangeland devoid of trees and residences (Gilligan et al. 1994, Contreras 1997b, OBBA). Locally common resident in ne. and se. Oregon (Evanich 1992a, Contreras and Kindschy 1996, OBBA). Generally occurs below 2,100 ft (640 m) elevation in the Rogue Valley (B. Massey p.c., *DPV*), and at low to moderate elevations in ne. and se. Oregon (Littlefield 1990a, Evanich 1992a, Contreras and Kindschy 1996).

**Habitat and Diet:** House Finches occur in a wide range of open or semi-open habitats in Oregon, including: suburban to highly urbanized areas, coastal dunes (mostly in winter), orchards, farm and ranch lands, oak and juniper woodlands, rangeland and sagebrush steppe with water sources, blackberry thickets, and weedy fields with hedgerows. Dense, continuous conifer forest or woodlands are not occupied.

Prefers sheltered nest site 5-35 ft (1.5-10.7 m) above ground (Ehrlich et al. 1988). Throughout range, locations vary widely and include trees, shrubs, and vines, hanging plants, building ledges, and other building-associated sites. Oregon nest sites include conifer trees and shrubs, buildings, light fixtures, rolled-up window blinds, and grapevine tangles (*DPV*). Nest building is mostly by the female; bad weather may interrupt early-season construction. Nest materials include fine weed and grass stems, leaves, rootlets, thin twigs, vegetative debris, string, wool, hair and feathers; lined with similar materials of finer texture (Bent 1968, Hill 1993, *DPV*).

Through the seasons the diet averages 97% vegetable matter (range 92-100%) based on stomach contents of western specimens (Martin et al. 1951, Hill 1993); includes seeds, buds, and fruits (Hill 1993). Plant food reported in the western range of this species is primarily weed seeds, including filaree, star thistle, other thistles, mustard, amaranth, knotweed, and fiddleneck; fruit of cherry, apricot, peach, pear, plum, strawberry, blackberry, and other berries have been reported to comprise up to 20% of the diet in late summer and fall (Hill 1993). Oregon diet includes Pacific madrone flower parts (Apr), white oak buds (Nov); seeds of turkey mullein, dandelion, poison oak, salsify, and fruit of Himalayan blackberry in Rogue Valley (*DPV*) and Willamette Valley (*DBM*). Young are fed regurgitated vegetable matter exclusively, mostly weed seeds. Animal matter taken is mainly aphids or caterpillars in spring (Martin et al. 1951). Forages mainly on the ground, or by clinging to forage plants; often forages in trees or shrubs for fruit. Visits feeders regularly, with a preference for black oil sunflower seeds.

**Seasonal Activity and Behavior:** House Finches are distinctly gregarious, especially in winter (Hill 1993, Contreras 1997b), when flocks can be >50 birds. Both sexes display strong breeding site fidelity, some wintering site fidelity suspected but not well documented (Hill 1993); neither documented in Oregon. Pairs may nest in close association; male defends only immediate area around nest (Hill 1993). Two broods per year per is common in the Rogue Valley (*DPV*), likely throughout range in Oregon; third brood attempts not documented in Oregon.

Male courtship display consists of singing while following the female, fluttering wings, hopping about female with raised tail and drooped wings, also raising head and crown feathers at times (Ehrlich et al. 1988, *DPV*). Male's song is a lengthy, disorganized jumble of notes, generally ending with an upward sweeping *whee- er* or *che-err*; call is a sweet *cheeet* or *queet*, often given in flight (Clement et al. 1993); female may sing a short song. Singing begins mid-Feb Rogue Valley (*DPV*) and continues to late Jun or Jul. Adult female begging wing-flutter behavior observed 13 Apr and 4 May; copulation observed 26 Apr, 19 May, and 18 Jun Rogue Valley (*DPV*). Nest building occurs mid-Mar to late Jul; early completion date 4 Apr 1999 Rogue Valley (*DPV*), late date 22 Jul 1997 in c. Oregon (OBBA). Nests with eggs observed mid-Apr to mid-Jun; early date 20 Apr 1999 Rogue Valley (*DPV*), late date 17 Jun 1996 from se. Oregon (OBBA). Nest with young early May to early Jul (OBBA); nest with half-grown young 10 May Rogue Valley (*DPV*). Fledglings observed mid-May to mid-Jul (OBBA, *DPV*). Early independent juvenile observed 15 May Rogue Valley (*DPV*).

Juveniles form large foraging flocks in late summer (Hill 1993, *DPV*). Recoveries of four banded Rogue Valley birds demonstrated random directional dispersal occuring from mid-Jul to late Oct, at distances of 2-8 mi (3.2-12.9 km) (*DPV*). A dispersing orange-colored male banded 25 Jan 1986 in Grants Pass was recaptured alive near Portland 15 Jun 1986, 217 mi (349 km) north of the capture site (*DPV*). Migratory behavior has not been documented within Oregon. Winter movement occurs at some cold locations; some individuals remain, while many may relocate to other nearby areas (Littlefield 1990a).

**Detection:** Most often detected by call or song given while flying or perched. Forages unconcerned in the open; flocks are especially noticeable.

**Population Status and Conservation:** Gabrielson and Jewett (1940) indicated the species was "common" in Oregon except west of the Cascades, north of Umpqua Valley. Few pre-1940 records were noted in the Willamette Valley and northward (Jewett 1940b). Marshall (1989b) recounts that Portland area populations increased beginning in 1941. Noted as very common resident in the s. Willamette Valley in late 1940s (Gullion 1951). This species appears to have benefited from human development and should continue to do so. Oregon populations appear stable or increasing within their present range. BBS data indicate an increasing low-level significant trend of 2.1%/yr, 1980-99 (P=0.16, n=59). Contreras (1997b) records a winter increasing annual change of 2.1%/yr based on CBC data (43 Oregon count circles).—*Dennis P. Vroman*

## Red Crossbill *Loxia curvirostra*

The Red Crossbill is aptly named for its unusual bill configuration of crossed upper and lower tips of mandibles, which it uses to pry seeds primarily from native conifer cones. Degree of bill crossing variable depending on wear; can have a right or left cross. Adaptation to varied conifer cone structures and seed sizes has resulted in a diversity in body size, bill size and shape, and palate configurations in Red Crossbills that are correlated with different call types. Juvs are brown with heavy streaked undersides and faint buff wing bars. Mature males red with dark brown flight feathers and tail; first-year males are yellow to orange, all lacking wing-bars. Females overall brown. Almost always found in mature seed-bearing forests in flocks ranging from a few to several hundred individuals.

**General Distribution:** In N. America, occurs irregularly and breeds throughout taiga, montane, and coastal coniferous forests from s. Alaska to e. Canada; south to California and Arizona, New Mexico, Georgia, and the pine forests of M. America. Southward to limits of spruce, pine, Douglas-fir, and western hemlock. Also breeds in Europe, Asia, and n. Africa (Adkisson 1996). Eight subspecies in N. America, with three or four occurring in Oregon. However, recent research indicates that N. American (Groth 1993a, b) and Pacific Northwest (Benkman 1993a) populations may consist of many more subspecies and possibly several species.

**Oregon Distribution:** A nomadic and uncommon to common breeder in coastal and montane coniferous forests across Oregon, but is irregularly detected wherever coniferous stands occur (Sauer et al. 1996, 2000, NAS 2002). *L. c. sitkensis* is resident in the moist forests from the Cascade crest westward. *L. c. bendirei* resident from east slope of the Cascades east to Warner and Blue mountains, wandering occasionally to w. Oregon; *L. c. benti* resident in Rocky Mtns., occasionally wandering in winter to Pacific coast (Gabrielson and Jewett 1940, AOU 1957). Names of subspecies are tentative (Browning 2002).

Groth (1993a, b) contended that Red Crossbills in Oregon have different call-note types that are believed to represent distinct subspecies. Of the 5 call types in Oregon, Type 2 (=*bendirei* or *pusilla*) prefers mainly ponderosa and lodgepole pine areas of e. Oregon, with vocal recordings near Burns and Bend; Type 3 (=*minor*) prefers Sitka spruce and western hemlock of the Coast Ranges; Type 4 (=*neogaea*) frequents Douglas-fir mainly in w. Oregon, but also statewide; Type 5 (=*bendirei* or *pusilla*) prefers lodgepole pine in higher elevation e. Oregon montane forest; Type 7 (=*bendirei* or *pusilla*) prefers Engelmann spruce/lodgepole pine in the same geographic range as Type 5.

**Habitat and Diet:** Breed in every type of coniferous forest. Nest is a cup of twigs, grass, lichen, needles, shredded bark, hair, and feathers placed on conifer branch near trunk 7-66 ft (2-20 m) high and well concealed in dense cover. Use mature conifer forests wherever large cone crops are produced by Douglas-fir, spruce, hemlock, or pine. No references to foraging on seeds of true fir cones or seeds consumed; foraging on true fir cones may be energetically inefficient due to cone structure. Availability of conifer seeds is correlated with local abundance of crossbills; will leave areas of scarce seed for areas of abundant seed (Benkman 1993a, 1993b, Adkisson 1996). Will also opportunistically feed on deciduous leaf buds and cones of alder, birch, and insects, especially aphids on Douglas-fir (Adkisson 1996). Likely requires

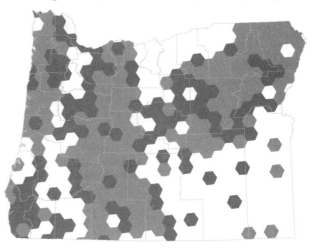

periodic mineral supplementation; has been observed consuming charcoal ash and grit, as well as frozen mammal urine on snow. At least 40 crossbills descended on a barbeque kettle in meadow surrounded by old and mature forest; consumed all of still-warm ash and grit in kettle in less than a few hours Jul 1987, H. J. Andrews Experimental Forest, Blue R. (D. H. Johnson p.c.), and two individuals observed taking ash and grit from active campfire Jul 2001, S. Fk. McKenzie R. (*SMD*). Mortalities observed on winter roads that have been salted and sanded (*SMD*).

In the nearby s. Cascades of Washington, were 30 times more abundant in old forests (>325 yr) than in younger forests (65-140 yr) (Huff et al. 1991). This difference was attributed to western hemlock being the only late-successional conifer (in the forest types examined) to produce seeds during the study (1983-86), and hemlock was of cone-bearing size and age only in the old-growth forests (Manuwal and Huff 1987, Huff et al. 1991). In the drier Douglas-fir forests of ne. Oregon and c. Idaho, Sallabanks (1995a) found the most detections of crossbills in mature and old stands vs. younger age classes.

"Key" conifers hold seeds in partly closed cones through the winter. Crossbills are more efficient at extracting seeds in partly closed cones than any competitor, especially when few seeds remain in the cone (Benkman 1993a). Cone crops are variable among years; the numbers of cones and ripeness can vary both between trees in a locality and among years. Key conifers that produce good cone crops each year typically occur somewhere in the range of each crossbill type. During most winters, some to most of the crossbill populations likely experience selection pressure that is consistent from year to year, so that foraging efficiency of bill type and conifer species is optimized. This indicates that the key conifer species that are characterized as foods are consistently available during late winter, the lean period of food availability (Benkman 1993a).

**Seasonal Activity and Behavior:** Seed availability is a critical factor influencing breeding (Coombs-Hahn 1993). If seed conditions are favorable, may nest late Dec to late Aug, and may have as many as four broods annually (Adkisson 1996). Not strongly territorial, often nest within 50-100 ft (15-30 m) of another (Adkisson 1996). Clutch size usually three eggs (range 2-5), incubation period 12-16 days; fledge 15-25 days, young disperse after about 7 wk. Juvs may be encountered in 10 mo of the year, Jan-Oct, but Hahn (1995) reports breeding may cease, even amid a bumper seed crop, when day length drops below 12 hr. Molt then sets in, and breeding can resume when day length reaches 10.5 hr. High reproductive potential suggests quick recovery from losses due to starvation and emigration (Newton 1967).

*Red Crossbill*

Due to nomadic behavior, most likely nest every year because are likely to find suitable seed source; and fidelity of nesting sites unlikely. Spends much of time paired; pairs have identical flight calls (Groth 1993b).

Crossbills appear to consist of many nomadic subpopulations. Band records have documented repeated colonization of habitat patches containing good seed crops, with individual movements up to 1,250 mi (2,000 km) (Adkisson 1996). As suitable patches become smaller and spatially more isolated, the rate of crossbill colonization may decline, as small patches are more difficult to locate. Due to their nomadic nature, individual crossbills may need to colonize many patches over their lifetime.

**Detection:** Usually obvious when present due to flocking behavior and incessant call notes, usually in the upper crowns of larger trees. When cone crops are low, may be absent from seemingly appropriate habitats. Calling rate of foraging birds may be inversely proportional to quality of foraging (Benkman 1993a). The different subspecies can only be differentiated in the field by call notes, and in hand by bill size and shape.

**Population Status and Conservation:** Numbers and distribution are highly variable from year to year. Can be locally abundant when conditions are suitable (Benkman 1993b, Adkisson 1996, Sauer et al. 1996, 2000, Smith et al. 1997, Holimon et al. 1998). Consequently, short-term trend data may be inadequate to accurately detect changes in population in specific subspecies of Red Crossbills. Irruptions away from forests of moderate cone crops can occur, suggesting an interaction of population size and seed availability that regulates populations (Newton 1967, Benkman 1988a).

BBS data from Oregon showed no significant changes in relative abundance 1966-99 (Sauer et al. 2000). CBC trend data 1958-88 showed a slight but non-significant increase of 1.1 birds/survey circle (Sauer et al. 1996). However, Adkisson (1996) states there are no reliable population estimates available for N. America. The nomadic nature of Red Crossbills and the presence of different subspecies may be masking actual population change among individual crossbill types. Extreme variability of food supply and nomadic behavior means crossbills are sometimes the most abundant bird in a habitat (Benkman 1993a) but are usually or most often absent. Decreases are possible where reduction of mature cone-bearing forests is rapid, as in the Pacific Northwest (Benkman 1993b).

Maximizing the amount of late-successional forest area (the most productive and used habitat) remaining would most benefit Red Crossbills. In w. Oregon, mature and old forest structural diversity allows dominant canopy species (e.g., western hemlock and Douglas-fir) to receive sunlight on a greater crown surface area than younger forests, resulting in enhanced cone production (Spies and Franklin 1991, 1998). Mature western hemlock trees are more prolific cone producers than younger trees, producing good cone crops every 3-4 yr, although some localities may vary 2-8 yr or more (Packee 1990). As forests mature, shade-intolerant Douglas-fir is gradually replaced by western hemlock over long periods of time (Spies and Franklin 1988, 1991, Franklin and Spies 1991). Decreased areas of these most productive cone habitats and diminished cone production as a result of timber harvest could result in a decline of crossbills even within mature forests. Mature and old forest tracts protected for late-successional species (e.g., Spotted Owl) can reduce the chance of complete cone failure in the Pacific Northwest; however, this is a limited part of the Red Crossbill's range. Old forests are scarce in most parts of the landscape due to timber harvest. This suggests that for a specific crossbill type specializing in western hemlock cones, a shortfall of preferred cones in one or multiple seasons is highly likely. This scenario could potentially negatively impact a specific population.

Productive cone crop years for Douglas-fir are generally sporadic, having one heavy and one medium crop roughly every 6-7 yr (Hermann and Lavender 1990). However, even during heavy seed years, only about 25% of the trees produce an appreciable number of cones (Isaac 1943, *ref.* in Hermann and Lavender 1990). In w. Oregon, appreciable cone production of Douglas-fir does not initiate until trees are about 50-60 yr of age. Douglas-fir 200-300 yr of age can produce 20-30 times the number of cones that 50-100-yr-old trees produce (Hermann and Lavender 1990). There is a severe paucity of mature lowland conifer forest in Oregon. Industrial forestry with relatively homogenous species composition and rotation lengths of 45-50 yr is unlikely to produce appreciable cone crops.

Because geographically separated areas often produce asynchronous cone crops, regionally limited reserves for each forest type (e.g., Sitka spruce-hemlock) may not be adequate to support nomadic populations of Red Crossbills. Forest reserves within a region could be located among as many distinct climatological regions as possible to avoid synchronous cone failures among all areas. For example, USDA tree seed zones represent different climates and elevations; areas in which cone crops for a species would potentially differ in a given year. In effect, this would minimize the risk of catastrophic events potentially destroying a reserve of a forest type constrained to a certain region. Reserves that include productive lower-elevation forests will be most beneficial to this species.—*Steven M. Desimone*

## White-winged Crossbill *Loxia leucoptera*

One of the "winter" finches that appear unpredictably in the state, the White-winged Crossbill wanders in flocks year-round searching for food, and may actually be seen in parts of Oregon in any month of the year. Its peculiar twisted bill, specialized for prying seeds out of conifer cones, is smaller than that of Red Crossbill, and it prefers smaller, softer cones, mainly spruce (Benkman 1992). Males are dull pinkish red, with distinctive broad white bars on black wings. Females are dusty brown and dull yellow with blurry streaks.

**General Distribution:** Breeds from wc. Alaska, through nw. and c. Canada east to nc. Labrador and Newfoundland south to ne. Oregon, nw. Wyoming, and across n. U.S. to n. New Hampshire, Maine, and Nova Scotia. Also breeds in the Greater Antilles; and from n. Scandinavia east across n. Russia to n. Siberia, and south to L. Baikal. Winters throughout breeding range, wandering irregularly south to s. Oregon, ne. New Mexico, n. Texas, c. Oklahoma, and east to N. Carolina; and in Old World irregularly south to c. Europe and Japan. Two subspecies; *L. l. leucoptera* occurs in Oregon (AOU 1957).

**Oregon Distribution:** Very rare and erratic visitor (Gilligan et al. 1994). Successful breeding not yet confirmed in Oregon. Only during years of major incursions can this species be expected in numbers in Oregon (Contreras 1997b). May occur at any time of year in ne. Oregon, especially in the Wallowa Valley, but also reported from John Day area, Grant Co.; Langdon L. area, Umatilla Co.; and Anthony Lakes., nw. Baker Co. (Gabrielson and Jewett 1940, Evanich 1992a, Korpi 1997, Sullivan 1998a).

Also occurs in higher elevations in the Cascades in any season (Gilligan et al. 1994). Most reports from Cascades come from central portion along the crest, e.g., Waldo L. area, Lane Co.; Sparks L., McKenzie Pass, and Little Cultus and Big Cultus lakes, all Deschutes Co.; and Odell L., Klamath Co. (Jewett 1954e, Summers 1986a, Evanich 1990, Korpi 1998, Sullivan 1998a, Gilligan 2000, T. McAllister p.c.). Seen as far south as Mt. Bailey area, Douglas Co. (Fix 1990a).

**Habitat and Diet:** Associated with coniferous forests and woodlands; preferring spruce, hemlock, and true fir over pine or Douglas-fir (Evanich 1992a, Contreras 1997b). Found in dense forests of white fir, Engelmann spruce, and larch at high elevations in Wallowa Mtns, and sometimes in ornamental spruces at county courthouse in Enterprise (Evanich 1990). Seen in mountain hemlock and Shasta red fir subalpine forests, mostly above 4,500 ft (1,372 m) in the Cascades (Fix 1990a).

No information on diet in Oregon. Known to eat conifer seeds almost exclusively, especially spruce and larch (Benkman 1992). When these are scarce, will take alternative foods such as insects, buds of various trees, or seeds of pine (Benkman 1992). At Little Cultus L., Deschutes Co., a flock came daily 12-16 Aug 1948 to a campfire ring where they took bits of charcoal, apparently to satisfy a mineral craving (T. McAllister p.c.). Similar behavior has been observed at nearby Waldo L. (*ALC, MGH*). Forages in flocks throughout range (Benkman 1992).

**Seasonal Activity and Behavior:** Throughout range, capable of breeding at any time of year, whenever adequate cone crop is available (Benkman 1992). In 1977 a small flock summered near Enterprise and attempted unsuccessfully to nest (Evanich 1992a). Does not regularly migrate, though often travels long distances in large flocks tracking cone crops (Benkman 1992). In ne. Oregon, seen most often Oct-Mar (Summers 1985b, Evanich 1990, Korpi 1997) and in c. Cascades, most likely in summer or fall (Summers 1986a, Gilligan et al. 1994, Gilligan 2000, Tice 2000b).

**Detection:** Tendency to flock year-round raises visibility. Rapid, chattery call given throughout year, especially in flight (Benkman 1992).

**Population Status and Conservation:** Most likely under-reported for lack of observers in appropriate habitats, especially in winter (Contreras 1997b). This species is too nomadic to be adequately censused by CBCs.

Population trends are closely linked to conifer seed availability. Every three or four years, cone crops fail over much of boreal forest in N. America, forcing crossbills to feed on non-conifer seed, at much reduced foraging efficiency (Benkman 1988b). These periods probably result in high mortality for this species (Benkman 1992). Due to its total dependence on mature, seed-bearing coniferous forests, timber harvest may also have a considerable negative impact on this species.—*Rachel White Scheuering*

## Common Redpoll *Carduelis flammea*

These tiny finches brighten the winter landscape of ne. Oregon in some years. Their tan and ivory streaked with brown is plain enough, but the red forehead, black chin, and breast suffused in pink add a spot of color to snow-covered trees and shrubs.

**General Distribution:** Arctic and subarctic breeder across the continent south as far as nw. British Columbia, Quebec and Newfoundland. Winters over much of breeding range and south, typically at mid to high-elevations, as far as California, the desert southwest states and S. Carolina some years. Three subspecies in N. America; Oregon specimens belong to nominate *flammea*. The name *linaria* used by Gabrielson and Jewett (1940) and *flammea* are synonyms (AOU 1944). Old World populations are now considered a separate species under the name *C. cabaret* (Banks et al. 2002).

**Oregon Distribution:** Uncommon to rare, irregular winter visitant, mainly in lowlands of the e. Blue Mtn. ecoregion. In peak years this species can be locally common in Union, Wallowa, and Baker counties but in other years it is essentially absent (Evanich 1992a, CBC data). Irregular in Umatilla Co. (Gilligan et al. 1994), rare in Grant Co. (T. Winters undated). The winter of 1985-86 brought thousands of this species into the western face of the Blue Mtns. north of the I-84 corridor (Umatilla Co.) (M. Denny p.c.). Rare and irregular south to Malheur NWR and vicinity, where there are at least seven reports, two of which involved 30 birds (Littlefield 1990a). Very rare west to Deschutes and Jefferson counties (Crabtree and Miller 1993, Craig Miller p.c.). Very rare to the Klamath Basin (Summers 1993a).

Very rare in winter to w. Oregon, with records of single birds as far southwest as Eugene (Shelton 1917, Gullion 1951), Florence (CBC), and Medford (Crowell and Nehls 1976b). A "flock of about 150 birds" was near Corvallis on 20 Jan 1900; specimens were collected (Gabrielson and Jewett 1940). This was part of a historically unique movement that also brought hundreds of birds to ne. California, where it is extremely rare (McCaskie et al. 1988). No such large flocks have been reported south or west of ne. Oregon, let alone in the western valleys, since that time, but individuals and small flocks are occasionally reported.

Oregon lies on the edge of this species' winter range; even 100 mi (161 km) north in e. Washington and n. Idaho the species is more regular and occurs on more than half of CBCs (Contreras 1997b).

**Habitat and Diet:** Uses "open brushy country such as fields, farmlands and foothills" according to Evanich (1992a). Oregon dietary data are not available, but diet elsewhere in the country suggests regular use of catkins and small seeds (Kaufman 1996).

**Seasonal Activity and Behavior:** Generally arrives in late Nov or early Dec (when it occurs at all) and remains only through Feb (Littlefield 1990a, J. Evanich p.c.). There are few spring records. The latest records include one at Nehalem sewage ponds 12 May 1991 (Tweit & Gilligan 1991). Even later and remarkable because of the simultaneous occurrence were single birds near Dallas (description from R. Robb p.c.) and at Canyon Cr., Grant Co. (Sullivan 1996b), both on 24 May 1996. One extremely odd record was of two Common Redpolls photographed by Cathie Ray on 11 Jul 2002 at a feeder along Bear Cr. Rd., Bandon, Coos Co.; the birds were present the following day (Simmons 2002).

**Detection:** Because these birds are small, quiet, and often rare, detection even in favorable habitat in the right season is difficult. However, once located they are usually unwary and easy to observe. Seek them in mid-winter in far ne. Oregon in brushy areas and among deciduous trees. This species does not frequent feeders in Oregon (Evanich 1992a) although it is occasionally seen at them (F. Conley p.c.), where it feeds on thistle seed along with siskins and goldfinches (M. Denny p.c.).

**Population Status and Conservation:** CBC data show that the species is irregular and visits in small numbers. The Baker Valley CBC found the species on only eight of 35 counts in the period 1956-91 (including count wk sightings), with a high of 90 and a low of two in years when found.—*Alan L. Contreras*

### Hoary Redpoll *Carduelis hornemanni*
This Arctic species breeds from the Arctic slope and the Bering Sea coast of Alaska across Arctic Canada to Baffin I. and across Arctic Eurasia, being almost completely circumpolar. It winters irregularly south to n. U.S., c. Europe, Asia, and Japan. It is similar in plumage to the Common Redpoll and is very difficult to separate from that species. Up to three were photographed among a Common Redpoll flock at Umapine, Umatilla Co., 21 Jan to 6 Feb 1986 (Schmidt and Crabtree 1987); another was observed among a Common Redpoll flock 9 mi (14.5 km) northwest of Bates, Grant Co., 19 Jan 1990 (OBRC).—*Harry B. Nehls*

### Pine Siskin *Carduelis pinus*
Although a common breeding bird throughout Oregon's mountains, the Pine Siskin retains an air of mystery, due to its highly nomadic and unpredictable movements, and its fondness for the inaccessible conifer canopy. Most familiar in winter through early spring, when flocks descend to foothills and valleys to feed on alder catkin seeds and many mingle with goldfinches in weed patches and at feeders. Readily identified by its heavily streaked plumage and by the yellow wing and tail bars that are especially prominent in flight. Pine Siskins are prone to irruptive movements tied to cone crops, and exhibit little apparent fidelity to breeding areas.

**General Distribution:** Breeds in conifer forest from s. Alaska east to Labrador, and south as a regular breeder to n. New England, Michigan, and Minnesota, throughout the mountains of the w. U.S., n. Baja California and through the Mexican highlands to Guatemala. An irruptive species whose populations fluctuate widely, it may breed far south of its normal range. Three subspecies are recognized, of which *C. p. pinus* occurs in Oregon (*MRB*).

**Oregon Distribution:** Generally common to fairly common resident in conifer forests throughout the state. May occur as a transient and winter visitant anywhere in Oregon. Highly nomadic, resulting in unpredictable population levels.

**Habitat and Diet:** Found primarily in coniferous forest communities, but also frequents deciduous trees, chaparral, grasslands, urban areas, and even sagebrush habitats in the nonbreeding season. Forages in the canopy of conifers and hardwoods, in shrubs, and on the ground. A regular visitor to bird feeders, especially partial to thistle seed. A pugnacious competitor, it often dominates goldfinches and even larger species such as Purple Finches at feeders (Palmer 1968, *PWT*).

Favored nest sites are far out on horizontal limbs of conifers, including fir, Douglas-fir, and pine (Keller 1894, Dawson 1997). Nests in Oregon have also been found in maples and oaks (Keller 1894). Nests are saddled over the limb, and often concealed in the needles. Reported nest heights in Oregon range 8-40 ft (2.4-12.2 m) (Keller 1891, Stryker 1894); the average from nationwide data is 20 ft (6.1 m) (Dawson 1997). Nests are relatively shallow cups, constructed of fine twigs, grasses, rootlets, or lichens, and lined with a thick layer of hair, feathers, moss, or thistle down. This well-insulated nest allows the very early nesting that has been recorded for the species (Dawson 1997).

Diet composed of a wide variety of seeds, with a significant arthropod component. Seeds of small-coned conifers (e.g., western redcedar [*MGH*]) are particularly favored, though siskins have also been observed taking seeds from the large cones of ponderosa pine (Palmer 1968). Regularly feed on a number of small-seeded deciduous trees, particularly alders. Takes a variety of grass and forb seeds, including composites such as dandelions, ragweed, and sunflowers (McAtee 1926, Palmer 1968). Also feeds on buds, alder catkins, and at sapsucker bore-holes (McCabe and McCabe 1929, Batts 1953).

Arthropods taken include aphids, scale insects, sawfly larvae, spiders, and the egg masses, larvae, and pupae of spruce budworm (Torgersen and Campbell 1982, Jennings and Crawford 1983). Arthropods are usually gleaned from conifer needles and bark, but will also capture insects in the air (Rodgers 1937). Animal material estimated to compose one-sixth of diet (McAtee 1926). Like other carduelines, attracted to salty mineral deposits; siskins have been observed pecking at the andesite rocks at Crater L. NP (Farner 1952).

**Seasonal Activity and Behavior:** Gregarious throughout the year. Pair formation occurs in winter flocks. Birds primarily associated in pairs by the second half of Mar in c. California (Rodgers 1937). Often join flocks to forage even during the nesting period (Granlund 1994). Nesting is semi-colonial, with only a small territory (2-6 ft [1-2 m] diameter) around the nest defended during the egg period (Weaver and West 1943).

Has an extended breeding season in the Pacific Northwest. Nesting in British Columbia and Washington has been documented from Mar into Sep (Bowles 1924, Paul 1968, Dawson 1997). Few nest records from Oregon; these document nest building Apr-Jul (n=5) (OBBA) and eggs as early as May 1 (Gabrielson and Jewett 1940). Flocks may remain in lowland valleys away from nesting habitat until mid-Jun (Gilligan et al. 1994). In the Willamette Valley foothills, found in Douglas-fir community in Mar to mid-Apr, moving into western hemlock community by mid-Apr to Jun (Anderson 1972).

Nest building is apparently done entirely by the female, and takes at least 5-6 days (Weaver and West 1943, Howitz 1984). Clutch size is typically 3-4. Incubation entirely by the female, lasts 13 days (Weaver and West 1943). Female is fed on the nest by the male, allowing nearly continual incubation. After hatching, female continues intensive brooding for 8-10 days, by which time nestlings are approaching full size. The male feeds the brooding female on the nest during this period, and the female passes food to nestlings. During the last 4-5 days of the nestling period, both adults forage and bring food to the nestlings (Weaver and West 1943). Fledging occurs in approximately 15 days. Young continue to be fed by parents for approximately 3 wk after fledging, and may disperse considerable distances from the nest site during this period (Peterjohn and Rice 1991). In general, siskins appear to be single-brooded, but will renest if the first clutch is lost. Following breeding, adults and hatch-year birds join into flocks and may wander widely. Flocks in fall and winter may number in the thousands in the w. Cascades (*MGH*). Able to withstand severe winter weather conditions, due to marked winter fat accumulation and to their ability to sustain elevated metabolic rates in cold temperatures (Dawson and Carey 1976, Dawson and Marsh 1986).

Band returns from the e. U.S. suggest little annual fidelity to either breeding or wintering sites (Todd 1940), though some short-term fidelity in wintering areas has been demonstrated (Yunick 1983, Baumgartner and Baumgartner 1992).

**Detection:** Most easily found in winter, when in flocks. In woods and forests, most often detected by vocalizations of flocks in flight or foraging high in the canopy.

**Population Status and Conservation:** Dramatic inter-year fluctuations in numbers are typical of the species in Oregon (Gabrielson and Jewett 1940), as elsewhere (Larson and Bock 1986, Dawson 1997). The causes of Pine Siskin irruptions are not well understood, but appear to be related to failure of cone crops in some areas and their availability elsewhere (Widrlechner and Dragula 1984, Huff et al. 1991). Numbers may increase dramatically in the first year following a forest fire, apparently in response to increased conifer seed availability (Hutto 1995a).

Oregon populations exhibited a declining trend 1966-99, according to BBS data (Sauer et al. 2000). Overall this trend was not statistically significant, but the decline 1980-99 was dramatic (9.2%/yr), and was statistically significant. Population trends in irruptive species are particularly difficult to interpret. Available data on siskin habitat preferences are equivocal, variously suggesting either preference for mature and old-growth forest (Carey et al. 1991, Huff et al. 1991, Hutto et al. 1992), preference for forested areas fragmented by clearcuts (Keller and Anderson 1992), or no clear differences between old-growth and managed conifer forests (Mannan and Meslow 1984). More information on ecology and population levels of Pine Siskins in Oregon is needed to assess the conservation requirements of this species.—*Pepper W. Trail*

## Lesser Goldfinch *Carduelis psaltria*

Formerly known as the Green-backed Goldfinch, this species was either not present or overlooked during the 19th century by most Oregon ornithologists (Gabrielson and Jewett 1940). The male's black forecrown contrasts smartly with the greenish back and bright yellow underparts. Females lack the clear contrasting colors of the males, though the tips of the secondary coverts and the base of the primaries are white in both sexes. Often the plaintive *tee-yee* call reveals the presence of the bird long before it is seen.

**General Distribution:** Breed from extreme sc. Washington south through the w. U.S., Mexico, and M. and S. America. Two subspecies in N. America; *C. p. hesperophila* in Oregon (AOU 1957). Birds reported as "black-backed" in se. Oregon could be *C. p. psaltria* or variation in *hesperophila*; specimens would be necessary for confirmation.

**Oregon Distribution:** In the n. Willamette Valley, the Lesser Goldfinch is a fairly common breeder along the western fringe, less common to the east. Scattered and local in the Portland area (H. Nehls p.c.). Fairly common from the s. Willamette Valley southward through the the Umpqua Valley, reaching greatest abundance in the Rogue Valley. Uncommon summer resident in some interior valleys of the Coast Range north to c. Coos Co. Local and uncommon summer resident in Lake, Harney, and Malheur counties, with nesting verified as far north as Crook Co. (OBBA). Other summer records from Hood River, Wasco, Gilliam, Jefferson, Deschutes, Wheeler, and Grant counties (Gilligan et al. 1994, OBBA). Fairly common permanent resident in s. Klamath Co., though numbers decline in winter (Gilligan et al. 1994).

The birds are most abundant in winter in the Rogue Valley, where flocks of 100 or more have been noted (Gilligan et al. 1994). They are common in the s.

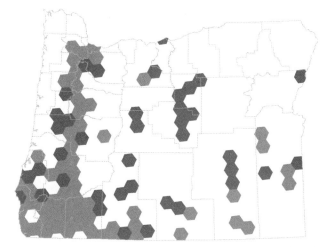

Willamette Valley, less common north to Portland. Flocks of up to 25 have been noted around Corvallis, and up to 45 within the Brownsville CBC circle (Gillson 1999). Found in small numbers (5-15) at a few regular locations within the Salem CBC circle, a situation that is probably prevalent elsewhere in n. Willamette Valley (*SGD*). Occasional on the s. coast, usually absent north of Coos Co. (Contreras 1997b). Casual in e. Oregon (e.g., Summers 1986b, Anderson DA 1990d).

**Habitat and Diet:** Very little study of birds in habitats occupied by this species. In western interior valleys, thought to be associated with oak woodlands, riparian areas, and brushy habitat on the valley floor throughout the year (*SGD*), but not recorded in oak woodland studies, though American Goldfinch was recorded in these studies (Anderson SH 1970, Anderson 1972, Hagar and Stern 2001). May also be common in residential areas. Very rare at low elevation slopes and oak woodlands in the Cascade foothills of the Willamette Valley (*SGD*), though fairly common on the western edge of the valley (Herlyn 1998). Nests to 2,500 ft (760 m) in the mountains around the Rogue Valley (Gilligan et al. 1994). In sw. Oregon, the Lesser Goldfinch is a fairly common permanent resident in chaparral-oak community, and is one of the most common breeding species in wedgeleaf ceanothus and whiteleaf manzanita chaparral (Browning 1975a, Gilligan et al. 1994, Hunter et al. 1998, Altman 2000a).

In e. Oregon, habitat is not well-described and distribution is spotty at best outside of Klamath Co. Nests at 7,000 ft (2,120 m) in junipers around the Blitzen Canyon on Steens Mtn. (Gilligan et al. 1994). Littlefield (1990b) noted the species in junipers along the lower Blitzen R., though Littlefield (1990a) also describes the species distribution around Malheur NWR as limited by the lack of broad-leaved trees. Regular breeder at the Fields oasis (*SGD*) and fairly regular at Frenchglen and Page Springs CG, Harney Co. (*ALC*).

In winter in the Willamette and Umpqua valleys, weedy lots, typically with teasel and Himalayan blackberry, and ornamental birch trees are a favored habitat (Herlyn 1998, *SGD*). No food data for Oregon, though a California study (Beal 1910) found the diet to be over 98% vegetable matter composed mainly of seeds of thistles and other weeds. Other foods include flowers, buds, fruits, and infrequently insects (Watt and Willoughby 1999). Also uses feeders, where it feeds on sunflower and thistle seed.

**Seasonal Activity and Behavior:** Generally resident in the western interior valleys, though pairs may be well scattered throughout suitable habitat. Egg dates statewide range 19 Apr to 21 Jun (n=4) (OBBA, Gabrielson and Jewett 1940). A nest with young was observed 29 Aug in Jackson Co. (OBBA). In some winters, most birds appear to withdraw from the n. and c. Willamette Valley, and the species can then be hard to find (Gilligan et al. 1994, Herlyn 1998, *SGD*). May be found with American Goldfinch, Pine Siskins, and other sparrows and finches in winter in western interior valleys (Browning 1975a, *SGD*).

East of the Cascades, is a common permanent resident only in s. Klamath Co., where numbers decrease somewhat during winter (Gilligan et al. 1994). Numbers are erratic around Malheur NWR and the Blitzen Valley; early spring arrival at Malheur 8 May, with peak numbers 18-22. Fall numbers peak 15-25 Aug, with a late date of 9 Sep (Littlefield 1990a).

**Detection:** To a trained ear, the plaintive *tee-yee* or rough *chup-chup-chup-chup* notes are diagnostic for unseen birds. May permit close approach while feeding in dense weedy patches. May occasionally be found by sorting through quiet winter feeding flocks of *Carduelis* finches, though Lesser and American Goldfinches do not frequently occur in mixed flocks.

**Population Status and Conservation:** Statistically significant long-term declining trends throughout the U.S. range. Oregon BBS data indicate significant declining trends statewide (1966-99, -6.0%/yr, n=18), though occurrence of the species in suburban areas and weedy fields would seem to indicate at least some tolerance for human habitat alteration (Watt and Willoughby 1999).—*Stephen G. Dowlan*

## Lawrence's Goldfinch *Carduelis lawrencei*
This small finch has a local and discontinuous breeding distribution from c. California to Baja, California, and s. Arizona. It is mainly resident with some wandering in winter to Texas and s. Nevada. Individuals were observed in Medford, Jackson Co., 20 Apr 1958 and 7 Jun 1967 (Browning 1975a). An adult male was photographed at a Florence, Lane Co., feeder from 24

Dec 1991 to 11 Jan 1992 (Johnson 1992b); one was observed 15 May 1997 at Lower Table Rock, Jackson Co. (OBRC); a male visited a feeder near Jacksonville, Jackson Co., from late Dec 1997 to 4 Feb 1998 (Tice 1998a). Monotypic (AOU 1957).—*Harry B. Nehls*

## American Goldfinch *Carduelis tristis*
The exuberant bounding flight, musical calls, and flashy yellow and black plumage of breeding-season American Goldfinches make them one of the most recognized and welcome of Oregon birds. Found in flocks nearly year-round, these goldfinches are a familiar sight in riparian woodlands, orchards, weedy fields, and agricultural land. They are among the last of Oregon's songbirds to nest. Highly nomadic in the nonbreeding season. May form mixed flocks with Lesser Goldfinches and Pine Siskins at bird feeders and weed patches throughout Oregon, as well as with Common Redpolls some years in ne. Oregon.

**General Distribution:** Breeds across N. America, from s. British Columbia east to Newfoundland, and south to N. Carolina, n. Louisiana, Oklahoma, c. Colorado, Utah, Nevada, and s. California. Winter range broadly overlaps breeding range, encompassing most of the continental U.S. except the n. Great Plains, and extending into Mexico (to Veracruz on the east and n. Baja California on the west). Four subspecies are recognized, of which two occur in Oregon (AOU 1957).

**Oregon Distribution:** *C. t. jewetti* occurs as a year-round resident west of the Cascades (specimens from Tillamook, Gold Beach, Salem, Eagle Point), particularly in the large interior valleys. Very small numbers in the Cascade and Coast Range mountains; virtually absent there in winter, except at relatively low elevations. Type specimen collected in Ashland (van Rossem 1943). *C. t. pallidus* occurs east of the Cascades. The species is generally common year-round,

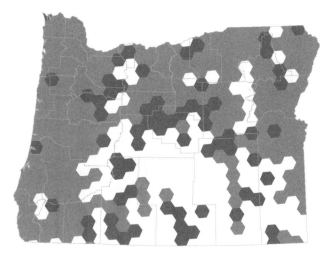

though populations are nomadic in winter, resulting in dramatic fluctuations in local numbers (Gabrielson and Jewett 1940).

**Habitat and Diet:** Found in all types of open country, including grasslands, oak savannahs, cultivated areas, roadsides, gardens, and parks, as well as riparian and early-successional woodlands. Oak habitat associations appear to be particularly favored in w. Oregon (Anderson 1972). Riparian willows are favored in e. Oregon (Gabrielson and Jewett 1940).

Preferred nest sites are deciduous shrubs with clusters of upright, terminal twigs sheltered beneath the leafy canopy, and with open space on at least one side. Nests may also be placed in herbaceous plants and in small conifers, and range in height from near ground level to several meters high (Middleton 1993). Nests are beautifully constructed cups of rootlets and plant fibers lined with thistledown, cottonwood down, or similar material. Nests are so tightly woven that they hold water (Lewis 1952, Berger 1968). The reproductive cycle has been shown to be under the control of photoperiod, but the appearance of flowering composites may stimulate nesting (Stokes 1950, Lynch 1970, Middleton 1978, 1979).

Diet composed almost entirely of seeds, with those of the sunflower family, particularly thistles, strongly preferred. Other important food plants include grasses and small-seeded trees such as elm, alder, and birch. Also feeds opportunistically on insects, buds of fruit trees, birch, and elm, and bark strips from young twigs (Middleton 1993). Unusual among Oregon birds, nestlings are fed almost exclusively seeds. This low-protein diet may explain why Brown-headed Cowbird nestlings fail to survive in goldfinch nests (Middleton 1991).

**Seasonal Activity and Behavior:** Remain in flocks longer than other passerines breeding in Oregon. Pair formation appears to take place in winter flocks, though some evidence suggests that pairs may form immediately before nesting (Stokes 1950, Coultee 1967, Holcomb 1969). Unique among cardueline finches, the American Goldfinch has a spring body molt, which results in the greatest difference between winter and summer plumages of any species in this group. Huge flocks (thousands) gather in Apr and May in the Willamette Valley, most or all in bright spring plumage.

The American Goldfinch is one of the last of Oregon's songbirds to nest each year. Flocks may be present into early Jun (D. Irons, *MGH*). Nest-building dates recorded 1995-99 in Oregon were Jun to late Jul (n=12) (OBBA). Nest construction is entirely by the female, who is closely accompanied by the male (Batts 1948, Stokes 1950, Nickell 1951, Tyler 1968). Egg dates for *C. t. jewetti* in the w. U.S. are 15 Jun to 6

Jul (Gabrielson and Jewett 1940); for *C. t. pallidus* the dates are 24 May to 18 Aug, with a peak of incubation from 20 Jun to 8 Jul (Tyler 1968). Most pairs produce only one clutch in a season, due to the relatively short nesting period. Experienced pairs are sometimes able to produce two broods, but this requires the female to abandon the first brood to her mate and to mate with a new male (Middleton 1993).

Clutch sizes for *C. t. jewetti* average 5-6 eggs, and for *C. t. pallidus* 4-5 eggs (Middleton 1993). Eggs are typically laid at 1-day intervals. Largest clutches are laid early in the nesting season. Incubation is by the female alone, who incubates in long unbroken spells, and is fed on the nest by the male (Middleton 1988). Incubation averages 12-14 days, with considerable variation (Middleton 1979). The female broods nestlings closely for the first 4 days. While on the nest it is fed by the male, and in turn feeds the chicks. After 4 days, female takes active role in feeding chicks. Nestlings fed a sticky regurgitated bolus composed primarily of seeds. Female presence is essential for nest success up to day 8; after this, it can abandon brood without risking its success (Middleton 1979, 1988).

Fledging occurs about 12 days after hatching (range 11-17 days) (Middleton 1993); in Oregon recorded mid-Jun to early Aug, most in Jul (n=8) (OBBA). Young dependent on adults for approximately 3 wk after fledging. Following independence, young birds gather into flocks, often with adult birds, which may number in the hundreds by early fall. Flocks tend to be nomadic during the winter, moving greater or lesser distances depending on food abundance.

Reproductive maturity achieved in the first spring, although young birds attain breeding condition about 2 wk later than adults (Middleton 1978). Maximum documented life span in the wild 11 yr (Middleton and Webb 1984). Female mortality rates are higher than that of males, resulting in a strongly skewed adult sex ratio favoring males 1.6: 1.0 (Prescott et al. 1989).

**Detection:** Nonbreeding flocks are easily noticed in flight, but are sometimes overlooked when perched. In all cases, usually first detected by the rollicking flight call. Nomadic movements of winter flocks may make the species surprisingly hard to find at times. A frequent visitor to bird feeders, especially those stocked with thistle seed. In summer, most often found in riparian habitats, where the songs and bright colors of males make them conspicuous.

**Population Status and Conservation:** Although it remains a common and familiar species, the American Goldfinch showed a significant declining trend of 3.6%/yr in Oregon 1966-99, according to BBS data (Sauer et al. 2000). Reasons for decline are uncertain, but may include loss of open-country habitat in interior valleys to development, the use of agricultural chemicals, and the adoption of "clean" farming practices that reduce the availability of weed seeds eaten by this species.—*Pepper W. Trail*

### Evening Grosbeak *Coccothraustes vespertinus*

In the early 1800s, settlers in the Midwest encountered this bird and named it Evening Grosbeak, erroneously believing it to hide quietly in the forest during the day, coming out to sing only at twilight (Farrand 1992). Because of its unpredictable nomadic movements, which can cause it to be abundant in an area one year and absent the next, the name given by French-speakers was more accurate: *le gros-bec errant*, or the wandering grosbeak. This sturdy-looking bird has a large head, short tail, and massive conical bill adapted for seed eating. The male plumage features bold patches of lemon yellow shading into olive, then brown and black, with white secondaries creating a flashy wing-patch easily seen in flight. The male's bill is chalky white in winter, but changes in early spring to a pale green that matches the new growth at the tips of spruce boughs, where they often nest. Many encounters with this species are of individuals heard flying high overhead, leaving an observer with little else to note, and it is difficult to study during breeding season. As a result, information on its life history is lacking.

**General Distribution:** Breeds from c. British Columbia and n. Alberta southeast across s. Canada to Newfoundland, and south to c. California, through se. Arizona, s. New Mexico, and into the Mexican highlands to wc. Veracruz; and, east of the Rocky Mtns., to sw. S. Dakota and nc. and ne. Minnesota east across n. U.S. to c. Massachusetts. Winters throughout the breeding range and south, sporadically, to s. California, s. Arizona, Oaxaca, w. and c. Texas and the n. portions of the Gulf states to c. Florida. Three subspecies (AOU 1957); *C. v. brooksi*, recognized provisionally (*MRB*), occurs in Oregon.

**Oregon Distribution:** Uncommon to common year-round resident; highly irruptive. Gabrielson and Jewett (1940) found it to be "not an uncommon sight anywhere in Oregon." In general, this species spends the summer in mountainous forests statewide; OBBA data have confirmed breeding in the lowlands of the s. Willamette Valley (near Eugene and south of Corvallis), but other than this, breeding outside of mountainous areas is largely undocumented. Montane mixed forests east of the Cascade crest are perhaps the most consistently occupied habitat in summer (McAllister and Marshall 1945, Stern, Del Carlo, et al. 1987). In the Blue Mtns., breeds at elevations of about 3,200-4,700 ft (1,000-1,400 m), and after breeding wanders up to 6,000 ft (1,800 m) (M. Denny p.c.). Breeds locally near Ironside Mtn., Malheur Co.

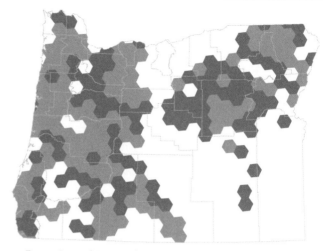

In spring, this grosbeak may be found in significant numbers around towns and cities during large spring incursions in the interior valleys of w. Oregon (Gilligan et al. 1994). Here they are uncommon in fall. Lowland areas in e. Oregon may also see minor spring incursions, and birds can also be found in desert oases during fall and spring (Gilligan et al. 1994). The species is uncommon in spring and occasional in fall at Malheur NWR (Littlefield 1990a), and can be seen anywhere in Malheur Co. during migration (Contreras and Kindschy 1996).

Often moves into lowlands throughout the state in colder months (Littlefield 1990a, Gilligan et al. 1994), though numbers in the lowlands in winter vary significantly from year to year (Gabrielson and Jewett 1940, Littlefield 1990a, Contreras 1997b) and decade to decade (NAS 2002).

**Habitat and Diet:** Found in summer months in coniferous forests at mid- to high elevations (Gilligan et al. 1994). Midsummer birds at Crater L. NP are associated primarily with fir forests (Farner 1952). A study in the Coast Range revealed this species' preference for commercially thinned stands of Douglas-fir (average 146 trees/acre [360 trees/ha]) over unthinned stands (average 200 trees/acre [495 trees/ha]) during the breeding season, possibly because forage shrubs are more accessible in canopy gaps than in continuous conifer cover (Hagar et al. 1996). In general, birds selecting nest sites in Oregon prefer open areas and avoid dense deciduous stands (Bekoff et al. 1987).

In nonbreeding season, most abundant in the lowlands (Gabrielson and Jewett 1940). Attracted to bigleaf maples (Gilligan et al. 1994) and elms (D. Irons p.c.) during spring incursions into western inland valleys. At Crater L. NP, noted in isolated areas of ponderosa pine whenever adequate cones are available; also forage in ponderosa pine-white fir-chaparral associations where there are large open areas including clumps of ceanothus, greenleaf manzanita, and currants (Farner 1952). At Malheur NWR in colder

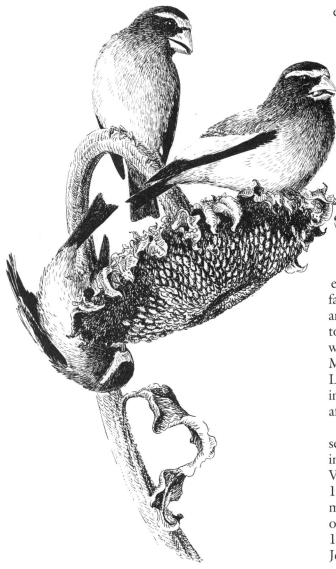

et al 1987). In towns and cities, feed extensively on maple seeds and mountain ash fruits (Gabrielson and Jewett 1940). Often seen (at any time of day) in noisy flocks feeding in tall conifers or riparian trees; very tame when feeding (Gabrielson and Jewett 1940). Attracted to feeding stations, especially in winter, and known to consume large quantities of sunflower seed. Like other coniferous seed-eating species, feed on salt-impregnated dirt or salty gravel (Gabrielson and Jewett 1940).

**Seasonal Activity and Behavior:** Spring incursions into lowlands generally occur from Mar into Jun (Gilligan et al. 1994); typically peaking late Apr and May (*MGH*). In some years, incursions in the Willamette Valley are enormous, involving thousands of birds sometimes at favored foraging sites within one or two city blocks, and perhaps tens of thousands of birds in individual towns (*MGH*). Earliest spring arrival at Malheur NWR was 4 Apr 1971; usually arrive in May, peaking 15-30 May, and remaining well into Jun (Littlefield 1990a). Late migrants and/or nonbreeders sometimes reported into Jun in lowlands, but rarely seen in lower elevations after mid-Jul (Gilligan et al. 1994).

Evening Grosbeaks are secretive during the breeding season, and much of their breeding range and ecology in Oregon is a mystery. Breeding in the s. Willamette Valley has been recorded 19 Jun to 26 Jul (Gullion 1951). Nest building has been observed in early to mid-Jun (n=3) (OBBA). A female with eggs in its oviduct was noted 8 Jul 1997 (OBBA), another shot 16 Jul 1926 also had eggs in oviduct (Gabrielson and Jewett 1940). Fledged young have been seen as early as 29 May and as late as 4 Aug (n=6) (OBBA).

The earliest fall occurrence at Malheur NWR 15 Sep 1971, and the peak of passage is 15-30 Oct (Littlefield 1990a). Most leave the refuge in Nov, while a few stay through much of the winter; though when food supplies become depleted, these birds leave by late Feb (Littlefield 1990a). Flocks have been seen in the Willamette Valley and at Toketee RS in the s. Cascades in late Sep and Oct (Fix 1990a, Gilligan 1999).

**Detection:** Evening Grosbeaks are most conspicuous during large spring incursions into lowland areas. They are often recognized by their distinctive clear, ringing cries, especially when flying high overhead. Foraging flocks are often loud and easily noticed. It is difficult to predict where this species will show up in a given year.

**Population Status and Conservation:** Nomadic behavior makes trends difficult to interpret. BBS numbers for Oregon indicate a population change

months, seen mostly in areas of planted trees, wooded watercourses, juniper woodlands, willow thickets; their arrival in spring usually corresponds with emerging deciduous tree seeds (Littlefield 1990a).

The nest of this chunky bird is a surprisingly frail structure 15-50 ft (4.6-15.2 m) up, of twigs and roots lined with fine materials; usually in a conifer (Gabrielson and Jewett 1940).

The Evening Grosbeak consumes seeds from cones of spruce and fir; also seeds and fruits of deciduous trees, including elm and boxelder seeds, and cottonwood catkins (Littlefield 1990a). Birds studied in c. Oregon preferred seeds of ponderosa pine, and were observed flocking during peak of pine seed crop (Eastman 1960). Buds of deciduous trees and shrubs also favored; e.g., known to feed on buds of California hazel shrubs in the Coast Range (Hagar et al. 1996). General studies outside of Oregon show nestlings fed on insect larvae and fleshy fruits (Ehrlich et al 1988); birds in Colorado and elsewhere well-documented consuming larval stage of spruce budworms (Bekoff of 2.6%/yr 1966-2000, though this is based on somewhat deficient data. CBC data show a relatively consistent presence in e. Oregon as a whole (with multi-year fluctuations), whereas birds per party-hour have decreased significantly from the 1970s to the 1990s in the Willamette Valley and concomitantly increased along the n. coast (NAS 2002).—*Rachel White Scheuering*

## Family Passeridae

### House Sparrow *Passer domesticus*

No other N. American wild bird is so associated with human settlements as the introduced House Sparrow. Its foods are nearly all imports, and its nesting and cover requirements are also human-derived. The House Sparrow and European Starling are the only introduced passerine birds that are thriving in Oregon. For those who know and feed native birds or erect nest boxes in urban or rural areas, the House Sparrow needs no introduction. They can dominate bird feeders at the expense of less-aggressive native species, and utilize nest boxes that were intended for wrens, chickadees, bluebirds, swallows, and in some cases Purple Martins. Their reputation as a pest also comes from their fouling of buildings with excrement. Although the introduction of the House Sparrow outside its native range was unfortunate, people find enjoyment by feeding them in cities where native species are scarce. This Old World sparrow is chunkier than N. American sparrows. Adult breeding males have reddish-brown upper body parts, a gray crown, black bib, and otherwise light gray underparts. The bib is less conspicuous on nonbreeding males and upper parts tend to be more grayish than brown. Females and immatures have brown upperparts with black and ochre streaking and grayish underparts. Formerly known as the "English Sparrow" in the U.S., reflecting its geographic origin.

**General Distribution:** Native from Eurasia south to n. Africa, Arabia, India, and Burma. From introductions, has spread throughout temperate N. America south into S. America. Also introduced to Hawaii, Australia, New Zealand, and s. Africa. Non-migratory in most parts of its range, including N. America. Numerous subspecies: *P. d. domesticus* in N. America (AOU 1957).

**Oregon Distribution:** Statewide around buildings at human developments of adequate size ranging from scattered farmsteads in remote and rural areas to highly populated areas, where most abundant (Gabrielson and Jewett 1940, Gilligan et al. 1994).

Absent to uncommon in the Coast Range and w. Cascades and at most mountain resort areas (*MGH, DBM*). However, dispersants that have not remained visit small communities, as for example, Toketee RS in e. Douglas Co. (Fix 1990a).

**Habitat and Diet:** As above, associated with human settlements, but not always in some residential areas with substantial conifer cover and in some coastal communities. Reach greatest densities where livestock are present at farmsteads, dairies, and large ranches. Also common at landfills, sidewalk cafes, and drive-ins (Campbell et al. 2001, *DBM*). Utilize buildings and thick foliage of shrubs and small deciduous trees for cover, roosting, and perching. Forage mainly on the ground.

In Oregon, nest in crevices and cavities in buildings, in nest boxes, and even in Cliff Swallow nests and Bank Swallow burrows (*DBM*). This pattern, including use of the swallow nests, is similar to that recorded elsewhere in the U.S. (Bent 1958, Lowther and Cink 1992, Campbell et al. 2001). In the absence of cavities, nest in dense vegetation, e.g., English ivy on buildings and power poles (*DBM*). South of Klamath Falls, just north of the California border (H. Nehls p.c.), and in ne. Oregon (M. Denny p.c.), makes round 12-in (30-cm) stick and grass nests in trees. Cavity nests include an untidy cup composed mostly of dried grasses, feathers, and debris; nests in vegetation are covered (Anderson 1978). The OBBA recorded three instances of House Sparrows entering natural cavities.

Consume vegetable matter primarily, but some insects in spring and summer. No studies of diet in Oregon, but foods in U.S. generally universal because of heavy dependence on common introduced plants. Food varies between urban and rural areas (Kalmbach 1940, Gavett and Wakeley 1986, Lowther and Cink 1992). Cereal grains, including corn, oats, and wheat are prominent in rural areas whereas stomachs from urban areas often contain millet and other seeds from commercial wild-bird seed mixes, but seldom unhulled sunflower seeds (they have difficulty cracking these seeds open [*DBM*]). Seeds of weedy herbs and grasses are also important, especially in urban areas. Examples beside weedy grasses include composites, oxalis, smartweeds, and chickweed. Kalmbach (1940) found maximum insect intake occurs in Jun and was 10% by volume. In Gavett and Wakeley study (1986), conducted in Pennsylvania, beetles constituted most of the insect intake, whereas in Missouri, Anderson (1978) found butterfly and moth larvae predominated. Anecdotal observations indicate foods taken in Oregon are similar to those described above (*DBM*).

**Seasonal Activity and Behavior:** Gregarious. Typically occur in small groups of 5-50+ individuals, especially during postbreeding period. Groups often vocalize together, especially when perched in cover of thick bushes or small trees, e.g., hawthorns (Lowther and Cink 1992, *DBM*). In prime habitat nest in small aggregations or loose colonies, but immediate nest site is defended (Lowther and Cink 1992). Males sometimes claim a nest site in the fall. Monogamous, but may switch mates during a season or between years (Sappington 1977). Male advertises for mate at nest site with a noisy continuous *cheep, cheep* vocalization.

Nest construction can begin in Feb (Lowther and Cink 1992) in some parts of the U.S., including Oregon, as illustrated by a nest with eggs on 1 Mar (OBBA). In Brititsh Columbia clutches have been recorded 8 Mar to 11 Aug (n=536) (Campbell et al. 2001). Most often 4-6 eggs with one laid daily. Both sexes participate in incubation and feeding of young (Lowther and Cink 1992); helpers sometimes participate. Hatch 10-14 days after last egg laid (Anderson 1978, Lowther and Cink 1992). Can begin laying subsequent clutches 7-8 days following hatching (Anderson 1978). There are no published data on the number of successive broods in Oregon. In the early 1980s at Eastmoreland Golf Course in Portland, House Sparrows typically had 3 broods (D. Irons p.c.). Three broods were typical in British Columbia (Campbell et al. 2001), and as many as four were recorded in Missouri (Anderson 1978). Raise successive broods using same nests (Anderson 1978, Lowther and Cink 1992), even with successive removals of nest contents (*DBM*). Broods 24 Mar to 25 Aug in British Columbia (Campbell et al. 2001). Results from OBBA show nests with young 26 Apr to 25 Jun (n=36), but the atlas did not adequately cover the lengthy breeding season for this species. Nestlings are independent in 7-10 days; fledge as soon as 14 days (Anderson 1978). Fledglings observed 12 May to 28 Aug (n=24) (OBBA). Immatures gather in small groups and forage in adjoining areas. Adults join them following breeding season to form small to large flocks, which can wander outside breeding areas (*DBM*).

**Detection:** A conspicuous species. Readily detected by distinctive *cheep* and other vocalizations.

**Population Status and Conservation:** Not protected by federal or state statutes. BBS data for Oregon from 1968 do not indicate a significant change, but nationally a decline is shown. Anecdotal information strongly suggests major declines in Oregon since the 1930s and 1940s (DBM). Also believed to have declined prior to that time throughout the U.S. with replacement of horse-drawn equipment with petroleum-powered vehicles (Bent 1958, Lowther and Cink 1992). This eliminated a food source in the form of spilled grain and partially digested seeds in manure associated with horses.

Unlike the Rock Dove, which in the past was often ignored on CBCs, House Sparrows have generally been counted, but as pointed out by Contreras (1997b), observers tend not to look for them. Oregon CBC results show stable populations for 1959-88 (Contreras 1997b).

The House Sparrow joins the European Starling and Rock Dove as three of the world's most successful birds in terms of densities and distribution. Its rapid occupation of N. America following introductions in the 1850s, 1860s, and 1870s from England and Germany was accelerated by subsequent transplants from established U.S. populations (Wing 1943, Robbins 1973). The views of those who extolled the bird's virtues for controlling undesirable insects prevailed over objections from naturalists. It is assumed to have immigrated to Oregon from transplants made outside the state, and possibly to have used railroad corridors with their spilled grain and stations as an avenue (Anthony 1921, Robbins 1973).

In Oregon first reported from Portland, where Finley (1907b) wrote of a nest and pair that was about an "ivy-covered house" in 1889, and suggested the first birds arrived in 1888. Bard (1897) said the species was not strongly established in the state as of 1887 and then only in Portland with an estimated population of 500. Anthony (1921) wrote that House Sparrows by the thousands were present in Burns and had spread to Harney Co. ranches, despite isolation by extensive stretches of desert. Although much was written on control methods (Anonymous 1948), removals are invariably temporary as replacements rapidly move in from nearby areas (DBM).—David B. Marshall

# Chapter 4
## SUPPLEMENTAL SPECIES LIST

by *David B. Marshall* except where otherwise indicated

Like others preparing a state bird book, the editors had to make decisions regarding which species to cover. We decided to include in "Chapter 3: Species Accounts" only those species for which records had been accepted by the Oregon Bird Records Committee (OBRC), sponsored by Oregon Field Ornithologists. Species included in the OBRC list are those for which 1) occurrence has been verified through an identifiable specimen, photograph, or in some cases detailed descriptions by several observers, 2) populations exist that are self-sustaining, and 3) individuals have occurred in Oregon without human assistance. Species that have occurred in Oregon but do not meet all three criteria are commented upon in this chapter. These are predominantly species that have been introduced, domesticated, and/or escaped from captivity. Additionally we discuss a few records that appear in recent ornithological literature but are not accepted by the OBRC. We begin this chapter with Oregon's only completely extirpated species.

## Extirpated Species

### California Condor *Gymnogyps californianus*
This vulture, which was the largest soaring bird in Oregon, formerly ranged from British Columbia to Baja California, but was last seen in Oregon at the beginning of the 1900s with sightings of two in 1903 and four in 1904 near Drain, Douglas Co. (Finley 1908a). Numbers dwindled to the point that the few remaining individuals, all in California, were taken into a captive breeding program in 1987. Captive breeding has been very successful, but released birds have been subjected to the same kinds of mortality problems as initially brought the wild population down. Releases have taken place in s. California and the Grand Canyon area of Arizona (Snyder and Schmitt 2002).

The California Condor must have been fairly common in the Northwest; remains have been found in Indian middens, including 63 birds in a midden at Five Mile Rapids in the Columbia R. Gorge (Miller 1957). Based on available records, Wilbur (1973) found indications of some yearlong residency and a definite movement to the Columbia R. in fall and away in spring. Nesting was not recorded from Oregon, Washington, or British Columbia. Lewis and Clark (1814) found them "not rare" near the mouth of the Columbia R. and abundant at Deer I. in 1805 and 1806. Several specimens were collected during the early 1800s (Wilbur 1973). By 1850 the bird was rare (Newberry 1857). Away from the Columbia R. the condor was observed in the Umpqua R. area during Mar-Oct (Finley 1908a, Douglas 1914, Peale 1957) in addition to the Drain records.

The Oregon Zoo has been approved by the California Condor Recovery Team to participate in the captive breeding program, but whether there are any suitable sites in Oregon to release condors has not been officially determined.—*Harry B. Nehls*

## A Note on Introduced Species

Unfortunately, the history of non-native species in Oregon has been poorly documented in the literature. The number of non-native species that have been introduced to Oregon is unknown. Most introductions with the intent to establish populations have failed. In many cases the number of birds released was small and inadequate in terms of establishing populations even if conditions were suitable. This is no doubt fortunate in view of the potential adverse impact on native species. Biologists generally agree that any further introductions of birds to Oregon should not be made without a careful analysis of possible adverse impacts on native species and agriculture.

### Introduced Domestic Birds
Several domesticated forms of foreign species occur or have occurred in the wild in Oregon and can confuse beginning birders. Note: the scientific names given are for the wild counterparts. The AOU does not provide scientific names for domestic forms.

### Domestic or Barnyard Goose *Anser anser*
This bird was derived centuries ago from the wild Graylag Goose (*Anser anser*) of Eurasia. It occasionally escapes to the wild from parks and farms. Plumage colors vary from browns similar to the Greater White-fronted Goose to partly or mostly white.

### Domestic Muscovy Duck *Cairina moschata*
This heavy-set duck was derived from the wild Muscovy Duck found from extreme s. Texas south into Argentina. It is sometimes found on park ponds; feral populations have become established in some parts of

the U.S. (AOU 1998). Breeding for domestic purposes has created numerous plumage colors which can vary from white to black.

## Domestic Mallard *Anas platyrhynchos*
Domestic ducks derived from the wild Mallard vary in color from dark shades of brown and black to white. Generally they are much heavier than wild birds, and in park situations can interbreed, producing ducks with a variety of plumage colors.

## Common Peafowl *Pavo cristatus*
Feral populations or escapees have been occasionally reported from Oregon, but insofar as is known at this time this showy species is found only about farms, zoos, and public gardens. It is native to Pakistan and India. Males are commonly referred to as "peacocks."

## Introduced or Escaped Wild Waterfowl
Private waterfowl collections exist in Oregon and elsewhere on the Pacific Coast. Zoos, city parks, and wild animal parks also have exotic waterfowl. Those listed below are frequently encountered in Oregon and have at times become established as feral populations.

## Mute Swan *Cygnus olor*
This is the swan that was introduced to parks and zoos from Eurasia for ornamental purposes starting in the mid-1800s (Ciaranca et al. 1997). Because of concerns about competition and conflicts with native waterfowl, Mute Swans were classified as a controlled species by ODFW in 1996, prohibiting import into Oregon and requiring all captive birds be pinioned and cobs neutered.

A distinctive orange bill with a dark base readily separates adult Mute Swans from native N. American swans, which have black bills. Feral Mute Swan populations numbering in the low thousands are established in New York, Maryland, and elsewhere along the Atlantic coast, in Michigan and other states of the upper mid-west, and near Vancouver, British Columbia (Ciaranca et al. 1997, Nelson 1997).

Years of first Oregon introductions are unknown. Six pairs were obtained from Sweden in 1921 for Lithia Park in Ashland (Ashland Park Dept. files), and pinioned individuals were present in parks in Portland during the 1930s or earlier (*DBM*). Introductions to the Deschutes R. in Bend first occurred in the 1940s. Unknown numbers of swans have been purchased from breeders and released on private ponds. Many of these birds were pinioned.

According to Evanich (1986a), six Mute Swans inhabited Devil's L., Lincoln Co. starting in the 1950s until the last one was killed in 1977. These birds also used nearby Siletz Bay. The only recent breeding population has been in Bend where four swans in 1985 expanded to 56 by 1995 including six adult pairs, 19 sub-adults, and 25 cygnets (*CGC*). Population controls were implemented in 1995; eggs were addled, all birds were captured and pinioned, and males were neutered. Sterile and same-sex pairs were relocated to private ponds. As of Jun 2002, two infertile pairs and three unpaired individuals remained on the Deschutes R..

Mute Swans of unknown origin are periodically observed in the state; records are too numerous to record. Recent examples include five at Baskett Slough NWR 4 Jul 2001 and five at Fernhill Wetlands, Washington Co. 19 Jul 2001, which were assumed to be the same birds (Korpi 2001c). Possibly these birds came from a feral population of 500-1,000 in Vancouver, British Columbia, or were escapees from private breeders.—*Chris G. Carey* and *Harry B. Nehls*

## Egyptian Goose *Alopochen aegyptiacus*
Sometime during the late 1980s, this native of N. Africa began showing up along the Umpqua R. between Canyonville and Roseburg (R. and M. Denney, p.c.). Nesting was observed. These birds are believed to have escaped from a nearby wild animal park. According to R. Denney (p.c.), the population eventually grew to about 200 birds in the early 1990s and subsequently declined. Present status along the Umpqua R. is not clear.

B. Combs (p.c.) reported that Egyptian Geese show up in the Eugene area "from time to time." One was sighted at Ankeny NWR in Apr 1988 (S. Dowlan p.c.); and during the same period came a report from R. Korpi of one along the Columbia R. in the mid-1980s. This is a somewhat showy goose having a pink bill and legs, a white fore-wing, dark eye patch, and variable buff and gray coloring on the body. Feral populations have been established in Britain (Madge and Burn 1988) and s. California (Sibley 2000). It appears possible this species could become established in w. Oregon and could compete with resident Canada Geese for nesting sites along rivers (*DBM*).

## Mandarin Duck *Aix galericulata*
This native to e. Asia and relative of the Wood Duck has become established in Britain (Madge and Burn 1988). While it periodically appears in Oregon, specifics are undocumented because it has been assumed these birds were escapees from waterfowl collections, where these colorful ducks are common. However, it is possible that the source of some of these birds could be California, where a feral population appears to be established. D. Yparraguirre (p.c.) reported that the California Waterfowl Association has problems with

Mandarin Ducks using nest boxes intended for Wood Ducks in the Santa Rosa (Sonoma Co.) area; and that controversy exists over whether the mandarins should be "extinguished." W. Mathewson (p.c.) has heard of two being shot by hunters in the Portland area. He saw one in late Feb 2000, 5 mi (8km) south of Amity, Yamhill Co., and in Mar 2001 one with Wood Ducks at a pond in Amity. In the 1990s, a Mandarin Duck resided with park Mallards in Oswego L., Clackamas Co. (*DBM*). A male was observed to have mated with a female Wood Duck at Scappoose, Columbia Co., in Feb 1992 (Johnson J 1992b). It is reasonable to assume that a self-sustaining population of this species could become established in the Willamette Valley or elsewhere in w. Oregon.

## Other Escaped Waterfowl

The appearance of waterfowl species in the wild that are not normally found in Oregon continually raises the question of whether these birds escaped from collections or arrived here without human assistance. The following have periodically occurred in the wild in Oregon: Black Swan (*Cygnus atratus*), Swan (Chinese) Goose (*Anser cygnoides*), Bar-headed Goose (*Anser indicus*), Barnacle Goose (*Branta leucopsis*), Red-breasted Goose (*Branta ruficollis*), Northern Shelduck (*Tadorna tadorna*), and Red-crested Pochard (*Netta rufina*) (Evanich 1986a). All of these birds are popular in private waterfowl collections, which are assumed to be the source of Oregon appearances.

## Introduced Game Birds
### Miscellaneous Species and Subspecies

ODFW files show at least 23 taxa of upland game birds that are not native to Oregon were released from state game farms between 1911 and 1996. They are not listed by scientific names and some of the common names used are not identifiable by available literature, including Delacour (1951) and Madge and McGowan (2002). Among the identifiable species that were unsuccessfully introduced are the following: Red-legged Partridge (*Alectoris rufa*), Kalij Pheasant (*Lophura leucomelanos*), Silver Pheasant (*L. nycthemera*), Reeves Pheasant (*Syrmaticus reevesii*), and Lady Amherst's Pheasant (*Chrysolophus amherstiae*). The authors have not been able to identify three other introduced pheasants, but suspect they are subspecies of the Ring-necked Pheasant. Other unsuccessfully introduced birds include a Tinamou (Tinamidae), an unidentified species of Francolin (*Francolinus* sp.), Bamboo-partridge (*Bambusicola* sp.), and a Guineafowl (Numididae); none of these are native to N. America. A N. American introduction, the Gambel's Quail (*Callipepla gambelii*), introduced in 1933, also

did not succeed. It is too early to determine the outlook for the recent introduction to the Willamette Valley of 18,689 individuals known as "Sichuan" Pheasant (*Phasianus colchicus strauchi*), a Ring-necked Pheasant subspecies, native to c. China. Several other subspecies of Ring-necked Pheasants have been introduced from game farms, but results are unrecorded or they have interbred with subspecies previously introduced (see Ring-necked Pheasant account in Chapter 3). The Common Quail (*Coturnix coturnix*) of Europe was released with various songbirds that are described below.

Species that have reproduced many yrs without assistance include the Gray Partridge, Chukar, two or more subspecies of the Ring-necked Pheasant, Wild Turkey, and Northern Bobwhite, although the long-range outlook for the Northern Bobwhite is now in question (see Chapter 3).

## White-tailed Ptarmigan *Lagopus leucurus*

In the late 1960s, ODFW introduced the White-tailed Ptarmigan to the state. Since the success of this introduction is unknown, the account for this species is included in this chapter.

This small alpine grouse is the only ptarmigan in the lower 48 states. It is the size of a Gray Partridge and is mainly brown with a white belly, wings, and tail in the summer. In winter, it is pure white with feathered feet and has black eyes and bill. They are resident along mountain ranges from c. Alaska, south to New Mexico, east to the n. Rocky Mtns. of British Columbia and Alberta and west to Vancouver I. and south into the Washington Cascades (Johnsgard 1973). Successful introductions have occurred in California, Colorado, Utah, and New Mexico (Braun 1993). There are five subspecies.

Status as an Oregon resident is undetermined. Early explorers reported ptarmigan in the Mt. Hood and Mt. Jefferson regions, but no specimens are known from the state for that period (Gabrielson and Jewett 1940). Ptarmigan were translocated in 1967 and 1969 from Washington and Colorado to the Big Sheep Cr. and Lostine R. drainages of the Wallowa Mtns. The releases involved a total of 110 birds, 45 from Colorado and 65 from Washington. All the transplants, except 16 from Colorado (Apr transplant), were released in Sep. Unbanded solitary birds were seen and photographed above 9,000 ft (2,744 m) Jun 1972 on Hurricane Divide and Jul 1978 on Chief Joseph Mtn., near snowfields with succulent low-growing alpine vegetation (*VLC*). Since all of the original birds were banded, these birds likely were offspring of translocated birds. Up to the late 1990s, periodic reports of ptarmigans emerged from the Billy Jones L. area of the Hurricane Cr. drainage (*VLC*). The final outcome of these transplants has not been determined. The best systematic population survey was conducted in the Lostine R. and Big Sheep Cr. drainages by ODFW biologists in Aug 1992 with Colorado ptarmigan authority, Clait Braun. No birds were located but droppings believed to be from ptarmigan were found near Pete's Peak and on Eagle Cap Mtn. Braun concluded that ptarmigan persisted until at least 1989-90 and may still occur in areas not examined (Braun 1993). Other areas in the Wallowas appear to have adequate habitat, have not been surveyed, and could have ptarmigan.

If ptarmigan were in Oregon at the arrival of early Euro-American explorers, it is assumed they would have been *L. l. rainierensis* and not *L. l. leucurus* as reported by Gabrielson and Jewett (1940). *L. l. rainierensis* resides from Mt. Rainier south to Mt. St. Helens, whereas *leucurus* is found in the Rocky Mtns. including mainland British Columbia south to nw. Washington. Birds introduced to the Wallowa Mtns. in the late 1960s from Washington came from the Cascades at the Washington/British Columbia border (*VC*) and therefore fall within the area where the ranges of *leucurus* and *rainierensis* join (Ridgway and Friedmann 1946). Those from Colorado fall within the range of *altipetens*. Following the eruption of Mt. St. Helens in 1980, ptarmigan were reported from the Mt. Hood area (K. Durbin p.c.). Unverified but impressive accounts of white grouse-like birds seen near Santiam Pass were reported to Robert Jarvis (p.c.) in the 1980s.

Ptarmigan distribution generally conforms to that of alpine tundra, where they prefer cirques and benches with sparse short vegetation above the timberline (Johnsgard 1973). Willow is considered a key winter food item in Colorado (Braun et al. 1976). They utilize willow buds or alder catkins that are above the snow and may descend to avalanche paths that provide feeding areas. Alpine plants, including willow, are important summer foods. Heavy domestic sheep grazing in the late 1800s and early 1900s severely damaged alpine plant communities in the Wallowas and portions of the Cascades. If ptarmigan were historically found in Oregon, this habitat destruction could have eliminated the birds. In conclusion, it is still unknown if ptarmigan were formerly native Oregon residents and their current status in the Wallowas and Cascades is undetermined.—*Victor L. Coggins*

## Introduced Parrots

Feral populations of several species of parrots now occur in the U.S. (AOU 1998), and members of the parrot family commonly escape and are seen in the wild in Oregon (*DBM*). However, only the following species has become established, at least temporarily.

**Monk Parakeet** *Myiopsitta monachus*

Also known as Quaker Parakeet, this green, dove-sized bird with a gray face and breast is native to c. S. America. It is a popular cage bird. It is a hardy species, and escapees have built their large stick nests in many U.S. cities (AOU 1998). Local escapees formed a small colony in se. Portland in 1976. By 1980 several small colonies were established in the Portland area and individuals were reported from other nw. Oregon towns. Only a colony south of the Portland International Airport persists in 2002. The OBRC considers this population unstable and not well established with apparently no more than 25 individuals involved.—*Harry B. Nehls*

## Introduced/Escaped Songbirds

In the late 1880s, Oregon residents who originated from Europe and the east coast formed several organizations that introduced songbirds from their homelands to Portland and the Willamette Valley (Jewett and Gabrielson 1929, Jobanek 1987). Species introduced from Europe included the Sky Lark (*Alauda arvensis*), Wood Lark (*Lullula arborea*), Blackcap (*Sylvia atricapilla*), European Robin (*Erithacus rubecula*), Common Nightingale (*Luscinia megarhynchos*), Eurasian Blackbird (*Turdus merula*), Song Thrush (*Turdus philomelos*), European Starling (*Sturnus vulgaris*), Common Chaffinch (*Fringilla coelebs*), Parrot Crossbill (*Loxia pytyopsittacus*), Eurasian Siskin (*Carduelis spinus*), European Greenfinch (*Carduelis chloris*), European Goldfinch (*Carduelis carduelis*), Eurasian Linnet (*Carduelis cannabina*), and Eurasian Bullfinch (*Pyrrhula pyrrhula*); and from the e. coast Northern Mockingbird (*Mimus polyglottos*), Bobolink (*Dolichonyx oryzivorus*), and Northern Cardinal (*Cardinalis cardinalis*). All of these introductions failed (existing populations of the European Starling arrived later from e. coast introductions). Three Northern Cardinals present near Canyonville, Douglas Co., in 1930, were almost certainly escapees (Jewett 1948), as were those near Cottage Grove in the late 1960s (*ALC*).

Other reports of songbirds of foreign or out-of-state origin that are believed to have escaped occasionally emerge. For example, Fix (1990a) reported on a male European Goldfinch "which fed and flew among Purple Finches and American Goldfinches" 10-12 May 1990, at Toketee Ranger Station, Umpqua NF.

## Unaccepted Records of Wild Birds

Gabrielson and Jewett (1940) provide an annotated list of hypothetical species—that is reports of bird species in the state that they considered questionable. In addition, the field notes sections of *Oregon Birds* contain reports of a number of species that have not been accepted by the OBRC for various reasons. Some of these reports are likely valid, but lack adequate verification. Jobanek (1994a) provides an excellent summary of additional questionable records of a historical nature. In this book, we have not attempted to list all questionable species, but have included some which we feel are worth mentioning, particularly where they were accepted by previous publications or we have reason to believe they may occur in the state.

## Red-billed Tropicbird *Phaethon aethereus*

Gilligan et al. (1994) listed this as an Oregon bird based on three offshore records, but none of the three was submitted to the OBRC for approval nor do we have an accounting of these reports. Since 1994 there have been additional reports, but to the best of our knowledge none of them have been written up for evaluation.

## Baer's Pochard *Aythya baeri*

This scaup-like duck breeds in Manchuria and winters in Korea, e. China, and India. The presence of this species in Oregon is based in part on the following from Palmer (1975): "In our area 2 were taken, about 1841 in 'Oregon' (when the concept of Oregon Territory encompassed more area than the present state); the specimen still extant is no. 12,773 in the National Mus. of Nat. Hist. Coll.; details in Friedmann (1949), who pointed out that the captures were in such a remote area and at so early a time as to preclude the birds having been escaped captives."

The bird was taken by the U.S. Exploring Expedition of 1841, and there is no way to determine if it was taken within the existing state of Oregon. The AOU has not recognized the above record, and there is some doubt as to its identification (R. Banks p.c.). However, Palmer concluded the bird was in fact a Baer's Pochard, as has M. Ralph Browning (p.c.), who has examined the specimen.

## Black Rail *Laterallus jamaicensis*

Gabrielson and Jewett (1940) accepted this species based on the records of Bendire (1877), who reported a specimen and sightings of this bird from the "swamps of Malheur Lake." There is no specimen on record. Despite the reliability of Bendire, this meager information has not been accepted by OBRC; and we are inclined to agree with this conclusion, especially in view of the species not having been found since.

## Gray-tailed Tattler *Heteroscelus brevipes*

This shorebird is listed as having occurred at Coos Bay by Gilligan et al. (1994), but the record was not submitted to or accepted by the OBRC.

## Yellow-bellied Flycatcher *Empidonax flaviventris*

Gilligan et al. (1994) reported on a single record at Malheur NWR, but the record was placed in the OBRC's deferred file (*HBN*).

## Alder Flycatcher *Empidonax alnorum*

During the 1970s and 1980s, the OBRC accepted a series of Alder Flycatcher records based at least in part on voice, but it was subsequently found that these were female Willow Flycatcher territorial calls and songs (Nehls 1995b, *HBN*). The species was removed from the official Oregon list.

## Northwestern Crow *Corvus caurinus*

The Northwestern Crow was originally described by Baird in 1858, and over the next 100 yr its taxonomy was changed no fewer than three times. The most recent change was in 1957, when the AOU designated it a full species based almost entirely on reported behavioral and ecological differences (AOU 1983). Johnston (1961) showed that most of the differences between the Northwestern Crow and the *hesperis* form of American Crow could be explained in terms of a north to south cline. This work did not change the official taxonomic status of the Northwestern Crow, but it did change the views on crow taxonomy of many people in our region. The taxa *caurinus* and *brachyrhynchos* may be conspecific (Johnston 1961, Phillips 1986, AOU 1998).

Early accounts of the Northwestern Crow placed them along the Pacific Coast to s. California, but these claims were not based on verifiable data. Most authorities now agree that phenotypic Northwestern Crows occur along the coast from Alaska through British Columbia. Stragglers and possible intergrades with American Crows probably occur with regularity into the Puget Sound and San Juan Is. of Washington (Pyle 1997). The Washington Breeding Bird Atlas (Smith et al. 1997) considers Northwestern Crow as conspecific with American Crow and combines all breeding records.

Jewett and Gabrielson (1929) first considered all crows along the Columbia R. to Portland to be of this species, based on two specimens. Later, they came to believe that the Northwestern Crow was a rare straggler to Oregon (Gabrielson and Jewett 1940). At least 2 reviews of Oregon specimen records (Johnston 1961, Bayer 1989c) cast serious doubt on the occurrence of Northwestern Crow in Oregon. None of the specimen records could be unequivocally identified to this species (Bayer 1989c, Paulson 1989, *MRB*); many were almost certainly misidentified and are more probably small female or juvenile American Crows. Patterson (1989) measured road-killed crows in Clatsop Co. and found none that met the criteria for Northwestern Crow in a part of the state where they would be most likely to occur. Crows nesting in coastal dunes in Clatsop Co. at Fort Stevens SP were clearly *hesperis* type American Crows (*MP*). See Phillips (1986) for a very good review of skeletal morphometrics, holotypes, paratypes, behavior, etc.

Many have noticed smaller crows with noticeably more rapid wing-beats resident around coastal estuaries. Such crows were frequently identified as Northwestern Crows by a combination of region and smaller size. Given the lack of reliable specimen evidence, it cannot be shown that the Northwestern Crow has ever occurred in Oregon. The OBRC has taken no position on the status of Northwestern Crows owing to the difficulty in sorting out sight records. This policy will probably continue until current research is completed and the AOU provides further guidance.—*Mike Patterson*

## Crested Myna *Acridotheres cristatellus*

Gabrielson and Jewett (1940) accepted this species for their Oregon list based on an individual which Gabrielson observed at a bird feeder in the Mt. Tabor district in Portland in Feb 1922. He concluded from appearance and behavior that it was not an escapee, and probably came from the myna colony in British Columbia. This conclusion has not been accepted by the OBRC.

## Eurasian Tree Sparrow *Passer montanus*

This Eurasian species was introduced and has become well established in Missouri and Illinois. During Dec 1989, a male was observed at an Astoria feeder and at the same time a pair began utilizing a feeder in North Bend. These birds were assumed to have arrived by ship from Asia. The North Bend birds remained several years, nested, and raised young (B. Griffin p.c.).—*Harry B. Nehls*

# Glossary

**Alternate plumage:** The often more colorful plumage worn by many species during the breeding season, often referred to as "breeding plumage," although in some species its use is not restricted to the breeding season.

**Arthropods:** Invertebrates in which adults typically have segmented bodies and many-jointed segmental limbs. Examples include arachnids, crustaceans, and insects.

**Basic plumage:** The often less colorful plumage of a post-juvenile bird, in many species worn outside the breeding season and known colloquially as "winter plumage," although in some species that molt annually its use is not related to seasonality.

**Benthic:** Pertaining to the bed of a body of water.

**California Current:** The southerly ocean current that originates off the Pacific Northwest (moving south from the Subarctic Current) and merges off s. California with the North Equatorial Current.

**Clearcut:** An opening in the forest created by cutting down most or all of the standing trees, usually the result of harvest of trees for sale.

**Columbia Plateau (BBS) physiographic region:** The relatively flat region scored with narrow valleys includes w. Umatilla Co., most of Morrow, Sherman, and Gilliam counties, and e. Wasco Co.

**Congeners:** Species or subspecies within a single taxonomic genus.

**DDE:** Dichlordiphenylethylene, produced during the metabolic breakdown of DDT.

**DDT:** Dichlorodiphenylchloroethane, an insecticide that kills by interfering with insect nervous systems. When it reaches high concentrations, mainly in insect-eating animals and certain predators, this can result in damage including thinning of egg shells in birds.

**Galliform:** An individual of the order Galliformes, an order of chicken-like birds that includes domestic and game birds such as turkeys, pheasants, and quails.

**Hacking:** A procedure whereby a wild pair's clutch that failed to hatch due to pesticide contamination is replaced with eggs or chicks that originated from captive stock. (See Peregrine Falcon account.)

**Hatch year:** The calendar year in which a bird was hatched.

**Holotype:** See Type Specimen.

**Instars:** The period or stage between molts, typically of larval invertebrates, numbered to designate the various periods; e.g., the first instar is the stage between the egg and the first molt.

**Leap-frog migration:** A migration pattern in which a given population may overfly a sedentary population of the same species, or a population of the same species that uses a shorter migration route, to breed or winter farther north or south. Examples include Xantus's Murrelet, Black-crowned Night-Heron, Canada Goose, and Fox Sparrow.

**Leave tree cut:** A clearcut with scattered live trees left.

**Lek:** A traditional area used for courtship display or strutting.

**Lithosol meadows:** A soil type that typically supports grass-forb meadows in the Blue Mtns.

**Littoral:** Relating to the shore, usually of the sea.

**Mayfield estimate of nest success:** An estimate of nest success based on the number of days a nest was under observation. This estimate is considered more accurate at the population level than proportional estimates of nest success (i.e., number of nests monitored relative to number of successful nests). See Mayfield (1975).

**Mean:** A numeric value representing the middle value among a set of such values, e.g., of measurements, found by adding all of the values and dividing by the number of values. Thus among the measurements 2, 3, 4, 5, and 24, the mean is 7.6 (combined values of 38 divided by number of values, 5). Also commonly known as the average.

**Median:** A numeric value occupying the point nearest to halfway between the two extremes among a set of values, with an equal number of values being larger and smaller. Thus among 2, 3, 4, 5, and 24, the median is 4.

**Microarthropod:** A small individual of the phylum of invertebrates.

**Minimum convex polygon:** A polygon formed by connecting the most peripheral of a group of points in such a way that all points are located on or within the polygon boundary. This method is frequently used to calculate animal home ranges.

**Mode:** The commonest value among a series of values, e.g., in the series 2, 3, 4, 4, 4, 5, 6, 7, 8; 4 is the mode.

**Morphotype:** Refers to the phenotypic expression or appearance, often in relation to a particular gradient or fixed set of possibilities.

**MtDNA:** Mitochondrial DNA, used in studies of genetic relationships.

**Multistory stand:** Refers to a forest that has more than one tree canopy layer, e.g., an overstory canopy and a mid-level canopy; or it may have individual tree canopies distributed at many heights.

**Nidifugous:** A precocious bird that is capable of feeding itself.

**Palustrine:** Relating to marshes.

**Pelagic:** Relating to the ocean. In common usage in ornithology, the ocean out of sight of land or not visible by a shore-based observer. Thus an albatross is commonly referred to as a pelagic bird while a Surf Scoter is not.

**Philopatry:** The tendency to return to breed or winter in the same area in successive seasons. *Natal philopatry* refers to breeding in the area where originally hatched.

**Polyandrous:** A female bird having multiple male partners in a single nesting cycle.

**Polygyny:** A male bird having multiple female partners in a single nesting cycle.

**Population sink:** A region or location where birds go that are unable to find appropriate breeding habitat. Such locations, often marginal habitat near a regular or historic breeding area, are incapable of sustaining a breeding population so birds that go there do not reproduce at levels sufficient to sustain a local population in the absence of immigration.

**Precocial, precocious:** Hatchlings that leave the nest almost immediately after hatching but may require feeding. *See also* **Nidifugous**.

**Precommercial thinning:** Refers to thinning (reducing stem density) in young regenerating forests where the trees are too small to be commercially valuable.

**Riparian:** Related to the banks of rivers or less often other bodies of fresh water; in ornithology, generally refers to vegetation along a river or stream.

**Second-year:** A bird in its second calendar year of life. Thus a bird hatched in Jun of 2004 becomes second-year on 1 Jan 2005 and retains that status through 31 Dec of 2005. It is also After Hatch Year as of 1 Jan 2005, a more general status which covers all years after 2004.

**Sere, seral:** Refers to a stage in ecological succession (generally of vegetation and related communities) in a given location, typically of forests after cutting or burning but also any ecological sequence of events in one location over time.

**Shelf break:** In Oregon, the western edge of the continental shelf, at the point where it drops below the 100-fathom (~200-meter) depth. The continental shelf is divided into the nearer-shore "shelf" and the offshore "slope," which ends at 1,000 fm. The shelf break is 20-35 mi (32-56 km) off the coast; deep ocean waters (>1,000 fm) start 45-60 mi (72-97 km) offshore.

**Southern Pacific Rainforest (BBS) physiographic region:** Includes most of western Washington, western Oregon, and northwestern California.

**Stand initiation:** The early stages after disturbance in a forest such as logging or fire, when young trees are only a few years old and grasses, forbs, and shrubs are often common on the site.

**Standard Error (SE):** An estimate of the standard deviation of the mean of a population based on sample values.

**Stem exclusion:** The phase of stand development in a well-stocked forest stand when competition for resources among trees in the stand results in the death of some of the trees.

**Synonym:** Having the same meaning. In ornithology, a taxonomic term meaning that a proposed or current name for a subspecies should be considered to refer to the same taxon as another name also in use because the birds in question are indistinguishable. In such cases the name first proposed takes precedence. Thus *brewsteri* is synonymized with *oocleptica* if these two purported subspecies appear to in fact be one subspecies. If *brewsteri* were proposed in 1922 and *oocleptica* in 1951, *brewsteri* becomes the name in use, at least by taxonomists who agree with the proposed synonymization.

**Thermal cover:** Usually vegetation, which functions to ameliorate otherwise extreme hot or cold temperatures.

**Tippets:** Feather groups standing out from a bird's main contour feathers, e.g., the "horns" on a Horned Grebe.

**Type specimen:** The specimen from which a species or subspecies is designated. Sometimes used informally to mean *Holotype*.

**Understory reinitiation:** The period in the development of some forests in which a secondary set of trees begins to grow in the understory of an already established forest. This often occurs in response to canopy openings or ground-level disturbance, but may also occur as conditions become favorable for germination and growth of shade-tolerant species.

# Appendix A:

## List of Common and Scientific Names of Plants and Animals

Common names were used in the text, when available, and associated scientific names are presented here. In the plants and the vertebrates (fish, other birds, mammals, and amphibians) lists, the scientific names given have been updated to reflect current taxonomy. In the insects and the other invertebrates lists, the scientific names (or taxonomic levels) given are those from the original source cited in bird species accounts. When different organisms were referred to with the same common name in different bird species accounts, the name of the account is specified. In all cases, it is recommended that the reader investigate the source cited in the species account to obtain further information.

## Plants

| Common Names | Scientific Names or Taxa | Alternate Names and Comments |
|---|---|---|
| alder | *Alnus* spp. | |
| alfalfa | *Medicago sativa* | |
| alkali bulrush | *Scirpus maritimus* | *S. paludosus* |
| alkali saltgrass | *Distichlis spicata* | saltgrass |
| alpine fir | *Abies lasiocarpa* | author probably referred to subalpine fir |
| amaranth | *Amaranthus* spp. | |
| American elm | *Ulmus americana* | |
| American holly | *Ilex opaco* | |
| American three-square bulrush | *Scirpus americanus* | |
| annual sunflower | *Helianthus annuus* | |
| apple | *Pyrus malus* | *Malus domestica* |
| apricot species | *Prunus* spp. | |
| arrowleaf groundsel | *Senecio triangularis* | |
| ash | *Fraxinus latifolius* | (in Oregon) |
| ashy (giant) wildrye | *Elymus cinereus* | |
| aspen | *Populus tremuloides* | Oregon native is *Populus tremuloides*, quaking aspen |
| azalea | *Rhododendron occidentale* | |
| baltic rush | *Juncus arcticus* | *Juncus balticus* |
| barley | *Hordeum vulgare* | |
| bayberry | *Myrica* sp. | |
| beaked sedge | *Carex utriculata* | |
| bent-grass | *Agrostis humilis* | |
| big huckleberry | *Vaccinium membranaceum* | |
| big sagebrush | *Artemisia tridentata* | |
| bigleaf maple | *Acer macrophyllum* | |
| birch | *Betula* spp. | |
| birch-leaf mountain-mahogany | *Cercocarpus betuloides* | |
| bitter cherry | *Prunus emarginata* | |
| bitterbrush | *Purshia tridentata* | |
| black cottonwood | *Populus trichocarpa* | |
| black greasewood | *Sarcobatus vermiculatus* | |
| black hawthorn | *Crataegus douglasii* | |
| black twinberry | *Lonicera involucrata* | |
| blackberry | *Rubus* spp. | |
| blue elder | *Sambucus cerulea* | blue elderberry |
| blueberry | *Vaccinium* sp. | |
| bluebunch wheatgrass | *Agropyron spicatum* | |

624

| Common Names | Scientific Names or Taxa | Alternate Names and Comments |
|---|---|---|
| box elder | *Acer negundo* | |
| bracken fern | *Pteridium aquilinum* | |
| bristlecone pine | *Pinus aristata* | |
| broad-fruited burreed (bur-reed) | *Sparganium eurycarpum* | |
| broad-leaf cattail | *Typha latifolia* | |
| buckbrush | *Ceanothus cuneatus* | |
| bulrush | *Scirpus* spp. | |
| bur reed | *Sparganium eurycarpum* | *S. eurycarpum* = broadfruit bur reed |
| | *Sparganium* spp. | *S.* spp. = bur reed |
| California black oak | *Quercus kelloggii* | |
| California grape | *Vitis californica* | |
| California hazel | *Corylus cornuta* | |
| Canadian thistle | *Cirsium arvense* | |
| canyon live oak | *Quercus chrysolepis* | |
| cascara | *Rhamnus purshiana* | |
| cattail | *Typha* spp. | |
| ceanothus | *Ceanothus* spp. | |
| cheatgrass | *Bromus tectorum* | |
| cherry | *Prunus* spp. | |
| chinquapin | *Chrysolepis chrysophylla* | golden chinquapin, *Castanopsis* |
| chokecherry | *Prunus virginiana* | |
| cinquefoil | *Potentilla* spp. | |
| clover | *Trifolium* spp. | |
| cockspur | *Echinochloa* | barnyard grass, millet |
| columbine | *Aquilegia* spp. | |
| common chokecherry | *Prunus virginiana* | |
| common reed | *Phragmites australis* | |
| cord grass | *Spartina* sp. | |
| corn | *Zea mays* | |
| cotoneaster | *Cotoneaster* spp. | |
| cottonwoods | *Populus* spp. | |
| cow parsnip | *Heracleum lanatum* | |
| crabapple | *Malus* spp. | |
| creeping Oregon grape | *Berberis repens* | |
| creeping spike-rush | *Eleocharis palustris* | |
| creeping wild-rye | *Elymus triticoides* | |
| crested wheatgrass | *Agropyron cristatum* | |
| curl-leaf mountain-mahogany | *Cercocarpus ledifolius* | |
| currant | *Ribes* spp. | |
| dandelion | *Taraxacum officinale* | |
| deerbrush | *Ceanothus integerrimus* | |
| desert parsley | *Lomatium* sp. | |
| desert saltgrass | *Distichlis stricta* | |
| dogwood | *Cornus* spp. | |
| Douglas spiraea | *Spiraea douglasii* | |
| Douglas-fir | *Pseudostuga menziesii* | |
| duckweed | *Lemna* sp. | |
| dwarf mistletoe | *Arceuthobium douglasii* | |
| | *Arceuthobium* spp. | |
| eelgrass | *Zostera marina* and others | *Z. marina* and *Z. japonica* currently listed for Oregon |
| eelgrass blight slime mold | *Labyrinthula macrocystis* | |
| elderberry | *Sambucus* spp. | |
| elm | *Ulmus* spp. | |

| Common Names | Scientific Names or Taxa | Alternate Names and Comments |
|---|---|---|
| Engelmann spruce | *Picea engelmannii* | |
| English hawthorn | *Crataegus monogyna* | |
| English holly | *Ilex aquifolium* | |
| English ivy | *Hedera helix* | |
| European beachgrass | *Ammophila arenaria* | |
| European mountain ash | *Sorbus aucuparia* | |
| false hellebore | *Veratrum californicum* | |
| false lupine | *Thermopsis montana* | |
| false Solomon's seal | *Smilacina stellata* | |
| fescue grass | *Festuca* spp. | |
| fiddle neck | *Amsinckia menziesii* | |
| | *Amsinckia* spp. | |
| filaree | *Erodium* spp. | |
| fir | *Abies* spp. | |
| firethorn | *Pyracantha* spp. | |
| flatsedge | *Cyperus* spp. | |
| flixweed tanzy (tanzy mustard) | *Descurainia sophia* | |
| four-winged saltbush | *Atriplex canescens* | |
| foxglove | *Digitalis purpurea* | |
| foxtail | *Setaria* spp. | |
| fuchsia | *Fuchsia* spp. | |
| giant burreed | *Sparganium eurycarpum* | |
| giant sequoia | *Sequoiadendron giganteum* | |
| glasswort or pickleweed | *Salicornia* spp. | |
| golden currant | *Ribes aureum* | |
| goldenrod | *Solidago* sp. | |
| gooseberry | *Ribes* spp. | |
| goosefoots | *Chenopodium* spp. | |
| grand fir | *Abies grandis* | |
| grapes | *Vitis* sp. | |
| greasewood | *Sarcobatus vermiculatus* | |
| Great Basin wild rye | *Elymus cinereus* | |
| green manzanita | *Arctostaphylos patula* | |
| groundsel | *Senecio hydrophilus* | |
| grouse huckleberry | *Vaccinium scoparium* | |
| hackberry | *Celtis douglasii* | |
| hairy honeysuckle | *Lonicera hispidula* | |
| hardhack | *Spiraea douglasii* | |
| hardstem bulrush | *Scirpus acutus* | |
| hawksbeard | *Crepis* spp. | |
| hawthorn | *Crataegus* spp. | |
| hemlock | *Tsuga* spp. | |
| hemp | *Cannabis sativa* | |
| highbush cranberry | *Viburnum edule* | |
| Himalayan blackberry | *Rubus armeniacus* | *R. discolor* |
| honeysuckle | *Lonicera* spp. | |
| hopsage | *Grayia spinosa* | |
| horned pondweed | *Zanichiella palustris* | |
| huckleberry | *Vaccinium* spp. | |
| huckleberry oak | *Quercus vaccinifolia* | |
| Idaho fescue | *Festuca idahoensis* | |
| incense cedar | *Libocedrus decurrens* | |
| indian plum | *Oemleria cerasiformis* | |
| inflated sedge | *Carex vesicaria* | |
| Jeffrey pine | *Pinus jeffreyi* | |

| Common Names | Scientific Names or Taxa | Alternate Names and Comments |
|---|---|---|
| Jim Hill mustard | *Sisymbrium altissimum* | |
| juniper | *Juniperus* spp. | |
| | *Juniperus occidentalis* | |
| knobcone pine | *Pinus attenuata* | |
| knotweed | *Polygonum* spp. | |
| | *Polygonum aviculare* | |
| lace lichen | *Ramalina menziesii* | |
| larkspur | *Delphinium* spp. | |
| Lemmon's alkali grass | *Puccinellia lemmoni* | |
| lewisia | *Lewisia* spp. | |
| lichen | *Alectoria* sp. | |
| | *Usnea* sp. | |
| limber pine | *Pinus flexilis* | |
| live oak | *Quercus* spp. | *Quercus chrysolepsis* in Allen's Hummingbird |
| lodgepole pine | *Pinus contorta* | |
| long-leaf phlox | *Phlox longifolia* | |
| loosestrife | *Lythrum* sp. | |
| low sagebrush | *Artemisia arbuscula* | |
| madrone | *Arbutus* sp. | |
| manzanita | *Arctostaphylos* spp. | *Arctostaphylos viscida* in Anna's Hummingbird |
| maple | *Acer* spp. | |
| medusahead | *Taeniatherum caput-medusae* | |
| milfoil | *Myriophyllum* sp. | watermilfoil |
| milkvetch | *Astragalus* spp. | |
| millet | *Echinochloa* sp. | Cultivated millet is *Panicum miliaceum*, as in the House Sparrow account. Some species of *Echinochloa* and *Millium* have millet as part of the common name. |
| | *Panicum miliaceum* | |
| mint | *Mentha* spp. | |
| mistletoe | *Phoradendron* sp. | |
| | *Phoradendron villosum* | |
| monkey-flower | *Mimulus* spp. | |
| moss | *Eurhynchium* spp. Class Musci (Genus *Antitrichia* was specified in the references for Common Merganser) | |
| mountain agoseris | *Agoseris* spp. | |
| mountain alder | *Alnus tenuifolia* | |
| mountain ash | *Sorbus* spp. | *Sorbus aucuparia* in Evening Grosbeak account |
| mountain big sagebrush | *Artemisia tridentata vaseyana* | |
| mountain hemlock | *Tsuga mertensiana* | |
| mountain mahogany | *Cercocarpus ledifolius* | |
| mountain whitethorn | *Ceanothus cordulatus* | |
| mulberry | *Morus* spp. | |
| muskgrass | Characeae | |
| mustards | *Brassica* spp. | |
| narrow spiked reedgrass | *Calamagrostis inexpansa* | |
| narrowleaf buckbrush, narrow-leaved buckbrush | *Ceanothus cuneatus* | wedgeleaf ceanothus |
| Nebraska sedge | *Carex nebraskensis* | |

| Common Names | Scientific Names or Taxa | Alternate Names and Comments |
|---|---|---|
| needle-and-thread (grass) | *Stipa comata* | |
| netleaf hackberry | *Celtis reticulata* | |
| Nevada bluegrass | *Poa nevadensis* | |
| nightshade | *Solanum* spp. | |
| noble fir | *Abies procera* | |
| Nootka rose | *Rosa nutkana* | |
| oak | *Quercus* sp. | |
| oats | *Avena* sp. | *Avena sativa* in House Sparrow account |
| oceanspray | *Holodiscus discolor* | |
| Oregon ash | *Fraxinus latifolia* | |
| Oregon crab apple | *Malus diversifolia* | |
| Oregon oxalis | *Oxalis oregana* | |
| Oregon sunshine | *Eriophyllum lanatum* | |
| Oregon white oak | *Quercus garryana* | |
| Oregon-grape | *Berberis* spp. | |
| oxalis | *Oxalis* spp. | |
| Pacific madrone | *Arbutus menziesii* | |
| Pacific rhododendron | *Rhododendron macrophyllum* | |
| Pacific silver fir | *Abies amabilis* | |
| Pacific willow | *Salix lasiandra* | |
| Pacific yew | *Taxus brevifola* | |
| paintbrush | *Castilleja* spp. | |
| palms | Arecaceae | several genera |
| peach | *Prunus persica* | |
| pear | *Pyrus* spp. | *P. communis* is the cultivated pear |
| pearly everlasting | *Anaphalis margaritacea* | |
| penstemon | *Penstemon* spp. | |
| pepper grass | *Lepidium perfoliatum* | |
| pine | *Pinus* spp. | |
| piñon pines | *Pinus* spp. | |
| plum | *Prunus* spp. | *Prunus domestica* is the commonly cultivated plum |
| poison oak | *Rhus diversiloba* | *Toxicodendron diversilobum* in the Hutton's Vireo account |
| ponderosa pine | *Pinus ponderosa* | |
| pondweed | *Potamogeton* spp. | |
| Port-Orford Cedar | *Chamaecyparis lawsoniana* | — |
| prairie-star flower | *Lithophragma parviflora* | |
| prickly lettuce | *Lactuca serriola* | |
| pussywillow | *Salix* spp. | |
| pyracantha | *Pyracantha* spp. | |
| quaking aspen | *Populus tremuloides* | |
| rabbitbrush | *Chrysothamnus* spp. | |
| | *Chrysothamnus nauseosus albicaulis* | |
| | *Chrysothamnus viscidiflorus* | |
| ragweed | *Ambrosia* sp. | |
| raspberries | *Rubus* spp. | |
| red alder | *Alnus rubra* | |
| red currant | *Ribes sanguineum* | |
| red elder | *Sambucus racemosa* var. *arborescens* | red elderberry |
| red fir | *Abies magnifica* | |
| red goosefoot | *Chenopodium rubrum* | |
| red huckleberry | *Vaccinium parvifolium* | |

| Common Names | Scientific Names or Taxa | Alternate Names and Comments |
|---|---|---|
| red willow | *Salix lasiandra* | |
| red-hot-pokers | *Kniphofia uvaria* | |
| red-osier dogwood | *Cornus stolonifera* | |
| reed canarygrass | *Phalaris arundinacea* | |
| rhododendron | *Rhododendron macrophyllum* | |
| | *Rhododendron* sp. | |
| rice | *Oryza sativa* | |
| rose (also rose hips) | *Rosa* spp. | *Rosa woodsii* as in Ring-necked Pheasant account |
| rush | *Juncus* spp. | |
| Russian olive | *Elaeagnus angustifolia* | |
| Russian thistle | *Salsola tragus* | |
| Sadler oak | *Quercus sadleriana* | |
| sage | *Salvia* spp. | |
| sagebrush | *Artemisia* spp. | |
| | *Artemisia tridentata* | |
| sago pondweed | *Potamogeton pectinatus* | |
| salal | *Gaultheria shallon* | |
| salicornia | *Salicornia virginica* | |
| salmonberry | *Rubus spectabilis* | |
| salsify | *Tragopogon* spp. | |
| saltbush | *Atriplex* spp. | |
| saltgrass | *Distichlis spicata* | |
| Sandberg's bluegrass | *Poa sandbergii* | |
| scarlet gilia | *Ipomopsis aggregata* | |
| Scots broom | *Cytisus scoparius* | often called Scotch broom |
| scouler willow | *Salix scouleriana* | |
| sea lettuce | *Ulva* spp. | |
| seaside arrow-grass | *Triglochin maritima* | |
| seaside plantain | *Plantago maritima* | |
| sedge | *Carex* spp. | |
| serviceberries | *Amelanchier* spp. | |
| | *Amelanchier alnifolia* | |
| shadscale | *Atriplex confertifolia* | |
| Shasta red fir | *Abies magnifica* var *shastensis* | |
| shore pine | *Pinus contorta* | |
| short-beaked sedge | *Carex simulata* | |
| Siberian elm | *Ulmus pumila* | |
| Sierra rush | *Juncus nevadensis* | |
| silk-tassel | *Garrya* spp. | |
| silver sagebrush | *Artemisia cana* | |
| Sitka alder | *Alnus viridis ssp. sinuata* | |
| Sitka spruce | *Picea sitchensis* | |
| slender phlox | *Phlox gracilis* | |
| slough sedge | *Carex obnupta* | |
| smartweed | *Polygonum* spp. | |
| | *Polygonum lapathifolium* | |
| | *Polygonum hydropiperoides* | |
| smooth cordgrass | *Spartina alterniflora* | |
| snowberry | *Symphoricarpos albus* | |
| | *Symphoricarpos* sp. | |
| snowbrush | *Ceanothus velutinus* | |
| southwestern pine | *Pinus strobiformes* | |
| soybean | *Glycine max* | |
| spikerush | *Eleocharis palustris* | |
| | *Eleocharis* spp. | |

| Common Names | Scientific Names or Taxa | Alternate Names and Comments |
|---|---|---|
| spiraea | *Spiraea* sp. | |
| spruce | *Picea* spp. | |
| starthistle | *Centaurea* spp. | |
| sticktight | *Bidens* | |
| stiff sage | *Artemisia rigida* | |
| stinging nettle | *Urtica dioica* | |
| strawberries | *Fragaria* spp. | |
| subalpine fir | *Abies lasiocarpa* | |
| sugar pine | *Pinus lambertiana* | |
| sumac | *Rhus* spp. | |
| sunflowers | *Helianthus* spp. | |
| | *Helianthus annuus* | |
| surfgrass | *Phyllospadix* spp. | |
| sweet-briar rose | *Rosa eglanteria* | |
| sword fern | *Polystichum munitum* | |
| tanoak | *Lithocarpus densiflorus* | |
| tansy ragwort | *Tanacetum vulgare* | |
| teasle | *Dipsacus sylvestris* | |
| thimbleberry | *Rubus parviflorus* | |
| thistle | *Cirsium* spp. | |
| trailing blackberry | *Rubus ursinus* | |
| tree silktassel | *Garrya elliptica* | |
| true fir | *Abies* spp. | |
| tufted hairgrass | *Deschampsia cespitosa* | |
| tule | *Scirpus acutus* | hardstem bulrush |
| tumbleweed | *Amaranthus graecizans* | *Sisymbrium altissimum* |
| | | *Salsola kali* |
| turkey mullein | *Eremocarpus setigerus* | |
| twinberry | *Lonicera involucrata* | |
| velvet lupine | *Lupinus leucophilus* | |
| vetch | *Vicia americana* | |
| vine maple | *Acer circinatum* | |
| walnut | *Juglans* spp. | |
| wapato | *Sagittaria* sp. | |
| | *Sagittaria latifolia* | |
| watermilfoil | *Myriophyllum* sp. | See also above under milfoil |
| waterweed | *Elodea* sp. | |
| wax currant | *Ribes cereum* | |
| wax-myrtle | *Myrica californica* | |
| wedgeleaf ceanothus | *Ceanothus cuneatus* | |
| western hemlock | *Tsuga heterophylla* | |
| western juniper | *Juniperus occidentalis* | |
| western larch | *Larix occidentalis* | |
| western red-cedar | *Thuja plicata* | |
| western spiked watermilfoil | *Myriophyllum spicatum* | |
| western watermilfoil | *Myriophyllum hippuroides* | |
| western white pine | *Pinus monticola* | |
| western yarrow | *Achillea millefolium* | |
| wheat | *Triticum aestivum* | |
| white fir | *Abies concolor* | |
| white oak | *Quercus garryanna* | |
| white pine blister rust | *Cronartium ribicola* | |
| whitebark pine | *Pinus albicaulis* | |
| white-leaved manzanita, whiteleaf manzanita | *Arctostaphylos viscida* | |

| Common Names | Scientific Names or Taxa | Alternate Names and Comments |
|---|---|---|
| wigeongrass | *Ruppia maritima* | |
| wild buckwheat | *Eriogonum* spp. | |
| wild celery | *Vallisneria* sp. | *Vallisneria spiralis* as named in Black and Surf Scoter accounts |
| wild crabapple | *Pyrus fusca* | |
| wild grass | *Sporobolus cryptandrus* | |
| wild millet | *Echinochloa* sp. | |
| wild plum | *Prunus* sp. | |
| wild radish | *Raphanus sativus* | |
| wild rice | *Zizania aquatica* | |
| wild rose | *Rosa* spp. | |
| willow | *Salix* spp. | |
| witchgrass | *Panicum* | |
| Wyoming big sagebrush | *Artemisia tridentata wyomingensis* | |
| yarrow | *Achillea millefolium* | |
| yellow salsify | *Tragopogon dubius* | |
| yellow starthistle | *Centaurea solstitialis* | |

## Insects

| Common name | Scientific name or taxon/taxa | Common name | Scientific name or taxon/taxa |
|---|---|---|---|
| Alfalfa weevils | Coleoptera | Caterpillars | Lepidoptera |
| Alkali flies | *Ephydra hians* | Cicadas | Homoptera |
| Ants | Formicidae | Click beetles | ElateridaeCrane flies |
| Aphids | Aphididae | Diptera | |
| Aphids and leafhoppers | Homoptera | | Tipulidae (American Dipper) |
| Aquatic beetles | Hydrophilidae, Dytiscidae, Curculionidae | | *Tipula* sp. (Hermit Thrush) |
| Arcidid grasshoppers | Arcididae | | |
| Backswimmers | Notonecta | Crickets | Orthoptera |
| Bark beetles | Scolytidae | Cutworms | Lepidoptera |
| Bark lice | Coccidae | | Noctuidae (Bobolink) |
| Beetles | Coleoptera, Dytiscidae, Gyrinidae, Nitidulidae, Buprestidae, Carabidae, Hydrophilidae, Haliplidae | Damselfly larvae | Odonata |
| | | Dragonfly | Odonata |
| | | Dragonfly (adult) | Anisoptera |
| | | Dung beetles | Coleoptera |
| Black fly | Simuliidae | Earwigs | Forficulidae |
| Black rove beetles | *Cafius seminitens* *Cafius canescens* | Fall webworm | *Platyprepia virginalis* |
| | | Flea beetles | Coleoptera |
| Blow fly | *Protocalliphora* sp. | Flies (larvae and adults) | Diptera |
| Bluethroat argentine | *Nansenia candida* | Fruit flies | Drosophilidae |
| Brine fly (flies) | *Ephydra hians* *Ephydra* spp. | Gnats | Diptera |
| | | | Chironomidae (Horned Grebe) |
| Butterflies | Lepidoptera | | |
| Caddisfly, caddis flies | Trichoptera (multiple families) *Limnephilidae* sp. | Grasshoppers | Orthoptera |
| | | Ground beetles | Coleoptera |
| | | | Carabidae (Lewis's Woodpecker) |
| Carpenter ant(s) | *Companotus* sp. *Crematogaster* sp. *Camponotus herculeanus* (Pygmy Nuthatch) | Hoppers | Homoptera |
| | | Jumping plant lice | Psyllidae |
| | | Katydids | Orthoptera |

| Common name | Scientific name or taxon/taxa |
|---|---|
| Ladybird beetles (ladybirds) | Coccinellidae |
| Leaf beetles | Chrysomelidae |
| Leaf bugs | Miridae |
| Leafhoppers | Homoptera |
| | Cicadellidae (Bewick's Wren) |
| Lodgepole needleminer | Coleotechnites milleri |
| Long-legged flies | Hydrophorus plumbeus |
| Loopers | Lepidoptera |
| Louse fly | Ornithoica sp. |
| Mayfly/mayfly larvae | Ephemeroptera (multiple families) |
| Midge | Chironomidae |
| Mormon cricket | Anabrus simplex |
| Mosquito | Culicidae |
| Moths | Lepidoptera |
| Mountain pine beetle | Dendroctonus ponderosae |
| Other flies | Dolichopodid (Eared Grebe) |
| Plant lice | Aphididae sp. |
| Sawfly | Symphyta suborder |
| Scale insects | Homoptera |
| Scarab beetle | Scarabaeidae |
| Scarabid beetle | Scarabaeidae |
| Shield bugs | Scutelleridae |
| Shore flies | Orbellia sp. |
| Short-horned grasshopper | Acrididae |
| Spittle bugs | Cercopidae |
| Spruce budworm | Choristoneura occidentalis |
| Stink bugs | Pentatomidae |
| Stonefly | Plecoptera (multiple families) |
| Tent caterpillar | Malacosoma spp. |
| Treehoppers | Homoptera |
| True bugs | Hemiptera |
| True flies | Diptera (multiple families) |
| True water bug | Belostomidae |
| Wasps | Hymenoptera |
| Water beetle/larva | Coleoptera |
| Water boatmen | Hemiptera |
| | Corixidae (Bufflehead and Horned Grebe accounts) |
| Water bugs | Hemiptera |
| Water fleas | Moina sp. |
| Water strider | Gerridae |
| Weevils | Coleoptera, Curculionidae, Chrysomelidae |
| Wood ants | Formica sp. |
| Wood borers | Bupestridae |

## Other Invertebrates

| Common name | Scientific name or taxon/taxa |
|---|---|
| Amphipods | Corophium spp. |
| | Anisogammerus confervicolus |
| | Corophium spp. (Western Sandpiper) |
| | Amphipoda (Common Loon, Black Scoter, Surf Scoter) |
| | Hyallela azteca (Eared Grebe) |
| Angleworms | Annelida |
| Annelids | Annelida |
| Baltic clam | Macoma balthica |
| Barnacles | Pollicipes polymerus |
| | Balanus glandula (Surfbird) |
| | Cirripedia (Black Scoter, Surf Scoter) |
| Basket whelk | Nassarius spp. |
| Bent-nose clam | Macoma spp. (Long-tailed Duck) |
| | Macoma nasuta |
| | Tellina spp. |
| Blue mussel | Mytilus californianus |
| Brine shrimp | Artemia sp. (Eared Grebe, Wilson's Phalarope, American Avocet) |
| | Artemia salina (Black-necked Stilt) |
| By-the-wind sailor | Velella velella |
| Cancer crab | Cancer sp. |
| Centipede | Scolapocryptops spp. |
| | Chilopoda (Brewer's Blackbird) |
| Chiton | Polyplacophora |
| Clam | Gastropoda |
| | Pelecypoda (Common Loon) |
| Cockles (Cockle Clams) | Cardium spp. |
| Common Shrimp | Crago vulgaris |
| Crabs | Brachyura |
| | Superorder Eucarida, Order Decapoda, Section Brachyura (Common Loon) |
| Crawfish | Astacura |
| Crayfish | Cambarus |
| | Decapoda (American Dipper) |
| | Potamobius (Pied-billed Grebe) |
| | Astacidae cambarus (Red-shouldered Hawk) |

| Common name | Scientific name or taxon/taxa |
|---|---|
| Crayfish (cont.) | *Pacifastacus leniusculus* (Western Screech-Owl) |
| Crustaceans | Crustacea |
| | Decapods (Pied-billed Grebe) |
| Echinoderms | Echinodermata |
| Gastropods | *Littorina* spp. |
| | *Lacuna* spp. (Surfbird) |
| Gem clam | *Gemma gemma* |
| Ghost shrimp | *Callianassa californiensis* |
| Green shore crab | *Hemigrapsus oregonensis* |
| Horseshoe crab | *Limulus polyphemus* |
| Leeches | Hirudinea |
| Limpets | *Collisella* spp. |
| Lined shore crab | *Pachygrapsus crassipes* |
| Littleneck clam | *Protothaca staminea* |
| Macoma (clam) | *Macoma* ssp. |
| Marine worms | Polychaetes |
| Marine beach hoppers | Amphipoda |
| Market squid | *Loligo opalescens* |
| Mole crab | *Emerita* |
| Mollusk | Molluska |
| Mud crab | Hemigrapsis |
| | *Hemigrapsus oregonensis* (Long-billed Curlew) |
| Mud shrimp | *Upogebia pugettensis* |
| Mussels | *Mytilus* spp. |
| | *Mytilus edulis* |
| | *M. californianus* |
| | *Modiolus rectus* (Surfbird) |
| Native littleneck clam | *Protothaca staminea* |
| Native oyster | Ostrea |
| Nematodes | Phylum Nematoda |
| Olive shell | Olivella |
| Pacific crayfish | *Pacifasticus leniusculus* |
| Pelagic barnacle | *Lepas antifera* |
| Periwinkles | *Littorina* spp. |
| Physid snails | Physidae |
| Polychaete Worms | Class Polychaeta |
| Razor clams | *Siliqua* sp. |
| Rock crab (including Dungeness) | Cancer |
| Sand fleas | Gammarus |
| Scallops | Pecten |
| Shore crabs | *Pachygrapsus crassipes* and *Hemigrapsus nudus* |
| Shrimps | Natantia |
| | Malacostraca, Decapoda, Cragonidae |
| | Crago, Palaemonetes |
| | Order Decapoda, Suborder Natantia (Common Loon) |
| Slipper shell | Crepidula |
| Slugs | Gastropoda (Black-capped Chickadee) |

| Common name | Scientific name or taxon/taxa |
|---|---|
| Snails | Gastropoda (Black-capped Chickadee) |
| | *Juga* sp. |
| Sod webworm | *Chrysoteuchia topiaria* |
| Soft-shelled clam | *Mya* sp. |
| Sowbugs/pillbugs | terrestrial Isopoda |
| Spiders | Arachnida |
| | Araneae (Marsh Wren, Blue-gray Gnatcatcher, Bewick's Wren) |
| | Araneida (Yellow-breasted Chat) |
| Squid | *Loligo* spp. |
| True crabs | Brachyura |
| Thorny-headed Worm | *Plagiorhynchus formosus* |

## Fishes

| Common name | Scientific name or taxon/taxa |
|---|---|
| Alaskan stickleback | *Gasterosteus aculeatus* |
| American shad | *Alosa sapidissima* |
| Anchovy | Engraulidae |
| | *Engraulis* spp. |
| | *Engraulis mordax* (Caspian Tern) |
| | *See* northern anchovy below |
| Anchovies | *Anchoa* sp. (Caspian Tern) |
| Bass | *Micropterus* spp. |
| Bay pipefish | *Syngnathus leptorhynchus* |
| Blennies | Stichaeidae |
| Blue chub | *Gila coerulea* |
| Bluegill | *Lepomis macrochirus* |
| Brook trout | *Salvelinus fontinalis* |
| Brown bullhead | *Ameiurus nebulosus* |
| Bullhead, bullhead catfish | *Ameiurus* spp. |
| Bull trout | *Salvelinus confluentus* |
| California headlight fish | *Diaphus theta* |
| Capelin | *Mallotus villosus* |
| Carp | *Cyprinis carpio* |
| Catfish | Ictaluridae |
| Centrarchids | Centrarchidae |
| Channel catfish | *Ictalurus punctatus* |
| Char | *Salvelinus* spp. |
| Chinook salmon | *Oncorhynchus tshawytscha* |
| Chub | *Gila* spp. |
| Clingfish | Gobiesocidae |
| Cod | *Gadus macrocephalus* |
| Codfishes | Gadidae |
| Coho salmon | *Onchorhynchus kisutch* |
| Common carp | *Cyprinus carpio* |
| Creek chub | *Semotilus atromaculatus* |
| Common name | Scientific name or taxon/taxa |

| | |
|---|---|
| Cutthroat trout | *Salmo clarkii* |
| Dace | *Rhinichthys* sp. |
| Dolly varden | *Salvelinus malma* |
| Eelpouts | Zoarcidae |
| English sole | *Pleuronectes vetulus* |
| Eulachon = Columbia river smelt | *Thaleichthys pacificus* |
| Fathead minnow | *Pimephales promelas* |
| Flatfish | Pleuronectidae |
| Flounder | Pleuronectidae |
| Freshwater drum | *Aplodinotus grunniens* |
| Gizzard shad | *Drosoma cepidianum* |
| Gobies | Gobiidae |
| Grayling | *Thymallus arcticus* |
| Greenling | *Hexagrammos* sp. |
| Grunion | *Leuresthes tenuis* |
| Gunnels | Pholidae |
| Hake | *Merluccius productus* |
| Herring | *Clupea harengus* |
| | *Clupea pallasi* |
| Killifish | *Fundulus* spp. |
| Kokanee salmon | *Oncorhynchus nerka* |
| Lampfish | *Stenobrachius leucopsaurus* |
| | *Lampanyctus* sp. |
| Lanternfish | *Protomyctophum thompsoni* |
| | *Tarletonbeania crenularis* |
| Largescale sucker | *Catostomus macrocheilus* |
| Largemouth bass | *Micropterus salmoides* |
| Longjaw mudsucker | *Gillichthys mirabilis* |
| Marine sculpin | Cottidae |
| Minnows | Cyprinidae |
| Northern anchovy | *Engraulis mordax* |
| Northern pikeminnow | *Ptychocheilus oregonensis* |
| Northern sand lance | *Ammodytes hexapterus* |
| Northern squawfish | *Ptychocheilus oregonensis* |
| Ocean sunfish | *Mola mola* |
| Pacific herring | *Clupea pallasii* |
| Pacific lamprey | *Lampetra tridentata* |
| Pacific sanddab | *Citharichthys sordidus* |
| Pacific sandfish | *Trichodon trichodon* |
| Pacific sand lance (also Sandlance) | *Ammodytes hexapterus* |
| Pacific sardine | *Sardinops sagax* |
| Pacific saury | *Cololabis saira* |
| Pacific staghorn sculpin | *Leptocottus armatus* |
| Pacific tomcod | *Microgadus proximus* |
| Peamouth chub | *Mylocheilus caurinus* |
| Perch | *Perca flavescens* |
| Pipefish | Sygnathidae |
| Plainfin midshipman | *Porichthys notatus* |
| Prickleback, snake-blenny, eelblenny | Stichaeidae |
| | *Lumpenis* spp. |
| Pumpkinseed | *Lepomis gibbosus* |
| Redtail surfperch | *Amphistichus rhodoterus* |
| Rex sole | *Errex zachirus* |

| Common name | Scientific name or taxon/taxa |
|---|---|
| River lamprey | *Lampetra ayresi* |
| Roach | *Hesperoleucus symmetricus* |
| Rock fish | Scorpaenidae |
| | *Sebastes* sp. |
| Saddleback gunnel | *Pholi ornata* |
| Salmon | *Oncorhynchus* spp. |
| Salmonids | Salmonidae |
| Sand dab | *Citharichthys* sp. |
| Sandlance (also Pacific sand lance or sandeel) | *Ammodytes hexapterus* |
| Sardine | *Sardinops sagax* |
| Scorpionfishe | Scorpaenidae |
| Sculpin | Cottidae |
| Sea star | Asteroidea |
| Shiner | Cyprinidae |
| Shiner perch | *Cymatogaster aggregata* |
| Smallmouth bass | *Micropterus dolomieui* |
| Smelts | Osmeridae (see Eulachon) |
| Snake prickleback | *Lumpenus sagitta* |
| Speckled sanddab | *Citharichthys stigmaeus* |
| Squid | Tenthoidea |
| Staghorn sculpin | *Leptocottus armatus* |
| Starry flounder | *Platichtys stellata* |
| Steelhead | *Onchorhynchus mykiss* (formerly *Salmo gairdneri*) |
| Stickleback | Gasterosteidae |
| | *Gasterosteus aculeatus* |
| | *Gasteroseus* spp. |
| Suckers | Catosomidae |
| Sunfish | Centrarchidae |
| Surfperch | Embiotocidae |
| Surf fish | *Cymatogaster* sp. |
| Surf smelt | *Hypomesus* sp. |
| Swordfish | *Xiphias gladius* |
| Tidepool sculpin | *Oligocottus maculosus* |
| Tomcod | *Microgadus* sp. |
| Topsmelt | *Atherinops affinis* |
| Trout | Salmonidae |
| Tui chub | *Gila bicolor* |
| Tuna | *Thunnus* spp. |
| | *Katsuwonus pelamis* |
| Warmouth | *Lepomis gulosus* |
| White bass | *Morone chrysops* |
| White crappie | *Pomoxis annularis* |
| Whitebait smelt | *Allosmerus elongatus* |
| Whitefish | *Coregonus* sp. |
| Yellow perch | *Perca flavescens* |

## Amphibians

| Common name | Scientific name or taxon/taxa |
| --- | --- |
| Bullfrog | *Rana catesbiana* |
| Frog | Anura |
| Pacific treefrog | *Pseudacris regilla* |
| Salamander | Caudata |
| Tadpole | *Amphibia* |

## Other Birds

| Common name | Scientific name or taxon/taxa |
| --- | --- |
| Alder Flycatcher | *Empidonax alnorum* |
| Bicknell's Thrush | *Catharus bicknelli* |
| Brown Skua | *Catharacta antarctica* |
| Common Cuckoo | *Cuculus canorus* |
| Eastern Screech-Owl | *Otus asio* |
| Eurasian Magpie | *Pica pica* |
| Eurasian Pygmy Owl | *Glaucidium passerinum* |
| Florida Scrub-Jay | *Aphelocoma coerulescens* |
| Glossy Ibis | *Plegadis falcinellus* |
| Great-winged Petrel | *Pterodroma macroptera* |
| Gunnison Sage-Grouse | *Centrocercus minimus* |
| Island Scrub-Jay | *Aphelocoma insularis* |
| Jack Snipe | *Limnocryptes minimus* |
| Lesser Nighthawk | *Chordeiles acutipennis* |
| Lesser White-fronted Goose | *Anser erythropus* |
| Manx Shearwater | *Puffinus puffinus* |
| Pacific Gray Duck | *Anas superciliosa* |
| Purple Sandpiper | *Calidris maritime* |
| Solander's Petrel | *Pterodroma solandri* |
| Spotted Nutcracker | *Nucifraga caryocatactes* |
| Subantarctic Skua | *Catharacta antarctica antarctica* |
| White Wagtail | *Motacilla alba* |

## Mammals

| Common name | Scientific name or taxon/taxa |
| --- | --- |
| Badger (American Badger) | *Taxidea taxus* |
| Belding's ground squirrel | *Spermophilus beldingi* |
| Big brown bat | *Eptesicus fuscus* |
| Black-tailed jackrabbit | *Lepus californicus* |
| Brush rabbit | *Sylvilagus bachmani* |
| Bushy-tailed woodrat | *Neotoma cinerea* |
| California ground squirrel | *Spermophilus beecheyi* |
| Chipmunk | *Tamias* spp. |
| Coatimundi (White-nosed coati) | *Nasua narica* |
| Columbian ground squirrel | *Spermophilus columbianus* |
| Cottontail | *Sylvilagus* spp. |
| Coyote | *Canis latrans* |
| Deer mouse/mice | *Peromyscus maniculatus* |
| Domestic cat | *Felis domesticus* |
| Domestic sheep | *Ovis aries* |
| Douglas squirrel | *Tamiasciurus douglasii* |
| Dusky-footed woodrat | *Neotoma fuscipes* |
| Feral cat | *Felis domesticus* |
| Goats | *Capra hircus* |
| Golden-mantled ground squirrel | *Spermophilus lateralis* |
| Gray-tailed vole | *Microtus canicaudus* |
| Great Basin pocket mouse | *Perognathus parvus* |
| Ground squirrels | *Spermophilus* spp. |
| Harvest mice | *Reithrodontomys* spp. |
| Jumping mouse | *Zapus* spp. |
| Kangaroo rats | *Dipodomys* spp. |
| Lemming | N. collared lemming (*Discrostonyx groenlandicus*) *Dicrostonyx* sp. Brown lemming (*Lemmus trimucronatus/sibiricus*) |
| Long-tailed vole | *Microtus longicaudus* |
| Marmot (Yellow-bellied marmot) | *Marmota flaviventris* |
| Meadow mice | *Microtus* spp. |
| Mice | Muridae |
| Microtine vole | *Microtus* spp. |
| Mink | *Mustela vison* |
| Mole | *Scapanus* spp. |
| Montane vole | *Microtus montanus* |
| Mountain cottontail | *Sylvilagus nuttallii* |
| Mountain sheep (Bighorn sheep) | *Ovis canadensis* |
| Mule deer | *Odocoileus hemionus* |
| Muskrat | *Ondatra zibethica* |

| Common name | Scientific name or taxon/taxa |
|---|---|
| Northern flying squirrel | *Glaucomys sabrinus* |
| Northern pocket gopher | *Thomomys talpoides* |
| Pig | *Sus scrofa* |
| Pocket gophers | *Thomomys talpoides* *Thomomys* spp. |
| Pocket mice | *Chaetodipus* spp. |
| Polynesian rat | *Rattus exulans* |
| Porcupine (N. American) | *Erethizon dorsatum* |
| Pronghorn | *Antilocapra americana* |
| Rabbits | *Leporidae* spp. |
| Raccoon (N. raccoon) | *Procyon lotor* |
| Red-backed vole (Southern) | *Clethrionomys gapperi* |
| Red squirrel | *Tamiasciurus hudsonicus* |
| Red tree vole | *Arborimus longicaudus* |
| Sagebrush vole | *Lemmiscus curtatus* (Short-eared Owl) *[not microtus]* |
| Shrew | *Sorex* spp. |
| Snowshoe hare | *Lepus americanus* |
| Townsend's chipmunk | *Tamias townsendii* |
| Townsend's ground squirrel | *Spermophilus townsendi* |
| Voles | *Microtus* spp. Cricetidae (Western Screech-Owl) |
| Western gray squirrel | *Sciurus griseus* |
| Western harvest mouse | *Reithrodontomys megalotis* |
| Yellow-pine chipmunk | *Tamias amoenus* |

# Appendix B:

# Changes in Scientific Bird Names Since Publication of Gabrielson and Jewett (1940)

This list covers scientific names as recognized in Garbrielson and Jewett (1940) and their present equivalents as used in Chapter 3 of this book. For example, the taxon *pacifica* of *Gavia arctica*, now represents a separate species, *Gavia pacifica*. *Gavia arctica*, now also a separate species, was not included in this appendix because it was not known in Oregon by Gabrielson and Jewett (1940). On the other hand, these authors' concept of *Aechmorphorus occidentalis* included both species of the genus. Changes in spelling of scientific names since Gabrielson and Jewett (1940) that corrected gender endings (e.*g.*, *a* vs. *us*) or the addition or subtraction of *i* are not included in this list. Changes in nomenclature since Gabrielson and Jewett (1940) follow the latest AOU check-list (AOU 1998), supplements to the AOU check-list, and other references provided in the species accounts. Sequence of species follows Gabrielson and Jewett (1940). English names are those used in the present book.

| Gabrielson and Jewett (1940) | This book | English Name |
|---|---|---|
| *Gavia arctica pacifica* | *Gavia pacifica* | Pacific Loon |
| *Colymbus grisegena* | *Podiceps grisegena* | Red-necked Grebe |
| *Colymbus auritus* | *Podiceps auritus* | Horned Grebe |
| *Colymbus nigricollis* | *Podiceps nigricollis* | Eared Grebe |
| *Aechmophorus occidentalis* | *Aechmophorus occidentalis* | Western Grebe |
| " | *Aechmophorus clarkii* | Clark's Grebe |
| *Diomedea nigripes* | *Phoebastria nigrepes* | Black-footed Albatross |
| *Diomedea albatrus* | *Phoebastria albatrus* | Short-tailed Albatross |
| *Thyellodroma bulleri* | *Puffinus bulleri* | Buller's Shearwater |
| *Casmerodius albus* | *Ardea alba* | Great Egret |
| *Plegadis guarauna* | *Plegadis chihi* | White-faced Ibis |
| *Branta nigricans* | *Branta orientalis* | Pacific Black Brant |
| *Philacte canagica* | *Chen canagica* | Emperor Goose |
| *Chen hyperborea* | *Chen caerulescens* | Snow Goose |
| *Chaulelasmus streperus* | *Anas strepera* | Gadwall |
| *Mareca penelope* | *Anas penelope* | Eurasian Wigeon |
| *Mareca americana* | *Anas americana* | American Wigeon |
| *Dafila acuta* | *Anas acuta* | Northern Pintail |
| *Nettion carolinense* | *Anas carolinensis* | Green-winged Teal |
| *Querquedula discors* | *Anas discors* | Blue-winged Teal |
| *Querquedula cyanoptera* | *Anas cyanoptera* | Cinnamon Teal |
| *Spatula clypeata* | *Anas clypeata* | Northern Shoveller |
| *Nyroca americana* | *Aythya americana* | Redhead |
| *Nyroca collaris* | *Aythya collaris* | Ring-necked Duck |
| *Nyroca valisineria* | *Aythya valisineria* | Canvasback |
| *Nyroca marila* | *Aythya marila* | Greater Scaup |
| *Nyroca affinis* | *Aythya affinis* | Lesser Scaup |
| *Glaucionetta clangula* | *Bucephala clangula* | Common Goldeneye |
| *Glaucionetta islandica* | *Bucephala islandica* | Barrow's Goldeneye |
| *Charitonetta albeola* | *Bucephala albeola* | Bufflehead |
| *Melanitta deglandi* | *Melanitta fusca deglandi* | White-winged Scoter |
| *Oidemia americana* | *Melanitta nigra americana* | Black Scoter |
| *Erismatura jamaicensis* | *Oxyura jamaicensis* | Ruddy Duck |
| *Astur atricapillus* | *Accipiter gentilis* | Northern Goshawk |
| *Accipiter velox* | *Accipiter striatus velox* | Sharp-shinned Hawk |
| *Buteo borealis* | *Buteo jamaicensis* | Red-tailed Hawk |
| *Circus hudsonius* | *Circus cyaneua* | Northern Harrier |

| Gabrielson and Jewett (1940) | This book | English Name |
|---|---|---|
| *Dendragapus fuliginosus* | *Dendragapus obscurus fuliginosus* | Blue Grouse |
| *Canachites franklini* | *Falcipennis canadensis franklini* | Spruce Grouse |
| *Pediocetes phasianellus* | *Tympanuchus phasianellus* | Sharp-tailed Grouse |
| *Lophortyx californica* | *Callipepla californica* | California Quail |
| *Squatarola squatarola* | *Pluvialis squatarola* | Black-bellied Plover |
| *Charadrius nivosus* | *Charadrius alexandrinus* | Snowy Plover |
| *Oxyechus vociferus* | *Charadrius vociferus* | Killdeer |
| *Capella delicata* | *Gallinago delicata* | Wilson's Snipe |
| *Phaeopus hudsonicus* | *Numenius phaeopus* | Whimbrel |
| *Totanus melanoleucus* | *Tringa melanoleuca* | Greater Yellowlegs |
| *Totanus flavipes* | *Tringa flavipes* | Lesser Yellowlegs |
| *Arquatella ptilocnemis* | *Calidris ptilocnemis* | Rock Sandpiper |
| *Pisobia melanotos* | *Calidris melanotos* | Pectoral Sandpiper |
| *Pisobia bairdi* | *Calidris bairdii* | Baird's Sandpiper |
| *Pisobia minutilla* | *Calidris minutilla* | Least Sandpiper |
| *Pelidna alpina* | *Calidris alpina* | Dunlin |
| *Limnodromus griseus scolopaceus* | *Limnodromus scolopaceus* | Long-billed Dowitcher |
| *Ereunetes mauri* | *Calidris mauri* | Western Sandpiper |
| *Crocethia alba* | *Calidris alba* | Sanderling |
| *Steganopus tricolor* | *Phalaropus tricolor* | Wilson's Phalarope |
| *Lobipes lobatus* | *Phalaropus lobatus* | Red-necked Phalarope |
| *Larus argentatus thayeri* | *Larus thayeri* | Thayer's Gull |
| *Hydroprogne caspia* | *Sterna caspia* | Caspian Tern |
| *Cyclorrhynchus psittacula* | *Aethia psittacula* | Parakeet Auklet |
| *Lunda cirrhata* | *Fratercula cirrhata* | Tufted Puffin |
| *Zenaidura macroura* | *Zenaida macroura* | Mourning Dove |
| *Otus asio* | *Otus kennicottii* | Western Screech-Owl |
| *Nyctea nyctea* | *Nyctea scandiaca* | Snowy Owl |
| *Speotyto cunicularia* | *Athene cunicularia* | Burrowing Owl |
| *Scotiaptex nebulosa* | *Strix nebulosa* | Great Gray Owl |
| *Asio wilsonianus* | *Asio otus* | Long-eared Owl |
| *Cryptoglaux funerea* | *Aegolius funereus* | Boreal Owl |
| *Cryptoglaux acadica* | *Aegolius acadicus* | Northern Saw-whet Owl |
| *Nephoecetes niger* | *Cypseloides niger* | Black Swift |
| *Selasphorus alleni* | *Selasphorus sasin* | Allen's Hummingbird |
| *Megaceryle alcyon* | *Ceryle alcyon* | Belted Kingfisher |
| *Colaptes cafer* | *Colaptes auratus* | Northern Flicker |
| *Ceophloeus pileatus* | *Dryocopus pileatus* | Pileated Woodpecker |
| *Balanosphyra formicivora* | *Melanerpes formicivorus* | Acorn Woodpecker |
| *Asyndesmus lewis* | *Melanerpes lewis* | Lewis's Woodpecker |
| *Sphyrapicus varius nuchalis* | *Sphyrapicus nuchalis* | Red-naped Sapsucker |
| *Sphyrapicus varius ruber* | *Sphyrapicus ruber* | Red-breasted Sapsucker |
| *Sphyrapicus varius daggetti* | *Sphyrapicus ruber* | Red-breasted Sapsucker |
| *Dryobates villosus* | *Picoides villosus* | Hairy Woodpecker |
| *Dryobates pubescens* | *Picoides pubescens* | Downy Woodpecker |
| *Dryobates albolarvatus* | *Picoides albolarvatus* | White-headed Woodpecker |
| *Empidonax wrighti* | *Empidonax oberholseri* | Dusky Flycather |
| *Empidonax griseus* | *Empidonax wrightii* | Gray Flycatcher |
| *Myiochanes richardsoni* | *Contopus sordidulus* | Western Wood-Pewee |
| *Nuttallornis mesoleucus* | *Contopus cooperi* | Olive-sided Flycatcher |
| *Otocoris alpestris* | *Eremophila alpestris* | Horned Lark |
| *Iridoprocne bicolor* | *Tachycineta bicolor* | Tree Swallow |
| *Stelgidopteryx ruficollis serripennis* | *Stelgidopteryx serripennis* | Northern Rough-winged Swallow |
| *Petrochelidon albifrons* | *Petrochelidon pyrrhonota* | Cliff Swallow |

| Gabrielson and Jewett (1940) | This book | English Name |
|---|---|---|
| *Perisoreus obscurus* | *Perisoreus canadensis* | Gray Jay |
| *Pica pica* | *Pica hudsonia* | Black-billed Magpie |
| *Cyanocephalus cyanocephalus* | *Gymnorhinus cyanocephalus* | Pinyon Jay |
| *Penthestes atricapillus* | *Poecile atricapilla* | Black-capped Chickadee |
| *Penthestes gambeli* | *Poecile gambeli* | Mountain Chickadee |
| *Penthestes rufescens* | *Poecile rufescens* | Chestnut-backed Chickadee |
| *Baeolophus inornatus sequestratrus* | *Baeolophus inornatus* | Oak Titmouse |
| *Baeolophus inornatus griseus* | *Baeolophos ridgwayi* | Juniper Titmouse |
| *Certhia familiaris* | *Certhia americana* | Brown Creeper |
| *Nannus hiemalis* | *Troglodytes troglodytes* | Winter Wren |
| *Telmatodytes palustris* | *Cistothorus palustris* | Marsh Wren |
| *Hylocichla guttata* | *Catharus guttatus* | Hermit Thrush |
| *Hylocichla ustulata* | *Catharus ustulatus* | Swainson's Thrush |
| *Hylocichla fuscescens* | *Catharus fuscescens* | Veery |
| *Corthylio calendula* | *Regulus calendula* | Ruby-crowned Kinglet |
| *Anthus spinoletta rubescens* | *Anthus rubescens* | American Pipit |
| *Lanius borealis* | *Lanius excubitor* | Northern Shrike |
| *Vireo solitarius cassini* | *Vireo cassini* | Cassin's Vireo |
| *Dendroica aestiva* | *Dendroica petechia* | Yellow Warbler |
| *Dendroica auduboni auduboni* | *Dendroica coronata* | Yellow-rumped Warbler |
| *Hedymeles melanocephalus* | *Pheucticus melanocephalus* | Black-headed Grosbeak |
| *Hesperiphona vespertina* | *Coccothraustes vespertinus* | Evening Grosbeak |
| *Acanthis linaria* | *Carduelis flammea* | Common Redpoll |
| *Spinus pinus* | *Carduelis pinus* | Pine Siskin |
| *Spinus tristis* | *Carduelis tristis* | American Goldfinch |
| *Spinus psaltria* | *Carduelis psaltria* | Lesser Goldfinch |
| *Oberholseria chlorura* | *Pipilo chlorurus* | Green-tailed Towhee |
| *Pipilo fuscus* | *Pipilo crissalis* | California Towhee |
| *Amphispiza nevadensis*** | *Amphispiza belli* | Sage Sparrow |
| *Junco oreganus* | *Junco hyemalis* | Dark-eyed Junco |
| *Zonotrichia coronata* | *Zonotrichia atricapilla* | Golden-crowned Sparrow |

**AOU 98 treats *nevadensis* as a subspecies of *belli*

# Oregon Breeding Bird Atlas, Christmas Bird Counts, and Breeding Bird Surveys

This book contains numerous references to the above methods for surveying bird population trends. Each has different objectives, advantages, and disadvantages. A description of each method is given below.

## The Oregon Breeding Bird Atlas Project

Much recent information in this book that pertains to breeding status comes from the Oregon Breeding Bird Atlas (OBBA) project (Adamus et al. 2001). The all-volunteer project surveyed birds during the breeding season, 1995-99, and mapped the distribution of each of 275 species among 430 equal-sized units statewide. Aggressively promoted and involving over 800 birders, it was the largest statewide inventory of wildlife ever conducted in Oregon. The project focused on geographic distribution, and did not attempt to estimate relative abundance of any species or determine species-habitat relationships at a fine scale. As is commonplace among similar projects in other states, volunteers were provided with field cards, maps, and a handbook containing standard codes for categorizing breeding evidence. On the resulting species maps, this evidence is summarized as "possible," "probable," or "confirmed" breeding. Drafts of these maps were provided, when requested, to authors of the species accounts in this book.

Most participants in the OBBA project surveyed birds in their local communities, resulting in more intensive coverage near population centers, though the project also provided travel grants for covering the most remote corners of the state, thus ensuring minimally adequate coverage of all areas. Survey effort was focused further by annually providing participants with lists of species found previously in an area, as well as species not yet found but expected to occur based on vegetation types known to exist in the area. In addition, all published bird observations during 1995-99 from non-participants, as well as unpublished observations from government biologists and government-sponsored projects (e.g., Breeding Bird Survey, threatened species surveys) and from many corporate landowners, were incorporated into the database used to generate species maps.

Results from the OBBA project, in addition to being incorporated into maps published in this book, are available on an interactive CD-ROM for use on a personal computer. The CD can be obtained from Oregon Field Ornithologists, P.O. Box 10373, Eugene, OR 97440, www.oregonbirds.org. For each species, the CD includes color photographs, multicolor distribution maps showing relative strength of breeding evidence in each of the 430 spatial units, a list of habitat types with which it is expected to associate during the breeding season and photographs of those habitats, color maps showing distribution of the habitats at approximately 1:1,000,000 scale, bar graphs of breeding chronology as compiled from project data, a statistical analysis, statistical summaries, a listing of all observations of the species during the project period, and a summary of remaining geographic data needs. The CD also includes names of all OBBA project participants, data from the 1983-86 Lane County Breeding Bird Atlas, and data from Oregon Breeding Bird Survey (BBS) routes. A panel of experts reviewed the data for erroneous records before inclusion on the CD.

The OBBA project was sponsored by Oregon Field Ornithologists, the nonprofit statewide birders organization. Financial supporters primarily included Audubon Society of Portland, National Fish & Wildlife Foundation, Oregon Chapter of The Wildlife Society, Oregon Department of Fish & Wildlife (Wildlife Diversity Program), Oregon Field Ornithologists (OFO), Oregon Natural Heritage Program, Ralph L. Smith Foundation, U.S. Bureau of Land Management, U.S. Fish & Wildlife Service, U.S. Environmental Protection Agency, and secondarily the Audubon Society of Corvallis, Grande Ronde Bird Club, Rogue Valley Audubon Society, Salem Audubon Society, Siskiyou Audubon Society, and private individuals. The project was initiated by a few birders who communicated among themselves using the Internet in the early 1990s, and was administered by an unpaid coordinator with help from a steering committee. The project was completed with the hope that OFO will sponsor such a project again in another 10-20 years to help focus birding efforts on priority data gaps (by species and geographic region), to document changes in species ranges, and to provide a cartographic format for publishing updates for undersurveyed species.

Paul Adamus

## Breeding Bird Survey

The North American Breeding Bird Survey was initiated in 1966 by the U.S. Fish and Wildlife Service's Patuxent Wildlife Research Center. Sponsorship was subsequently transferred to the U.S. Geological Survey, which now operates the Center. The Canadian Wildlife Service also participates. The objective of the survey is to monitor the status and trends of North American breeding bird populations.

This is a roadside survey wherein a single observer records numbers of birds by species seen or heard at one-half-mile intervals along a 24.5-mi (39.5-km) stretch of roadside under a very rigid protocol. Its use applies mainly to songbird population trends.

The survey was not initiated in Oregon until 1969, when about 15 routes were begun; thus many of the trend figures reported in this book as 1966-98, etc., based on the USGS analysis (Sauer et al. 1996-2001) actually refer to a range beginning in 1969 or later. There were 103 active routes in the state in 2001. In Oregon, the survey is conducted mainly in June.

## Christmas Bird Counts

The Christmas Bird Count is a semi-formal early-winter survey operated by the National Audubon Society. Individual counts occur during a single day selected by the participants during a 3-wk period around Christmas/New Years Day within a 15-mi- (24-km-) diameter circle. Because the count has been conducted for over 100 years using essentially the same protocol for most of that period, the sheer volume of data makes the results useful even though there is variation in how observers cover their areas, their numbers, and skill levels. The use of raw counts along with party-hours of coverage allows researchers to track population shifts for easily counted species with results comparable to those found by the Breeding Bird Survey.

Oregon conducted 41 counts in 2001, with exceptionally broad geographic and habitat coverage from sea level to the summit of Santiam Pass. Some Oregon counts have operated with few if any breaks for well over 50 yr and therefore provide a substantial database for early-winter distribution. CBC data have provided considerable insight into range expansions in such species as the White-tailed Kite, Red-shouldered Hawk, Black Phoebe, Western Scrub-Jay, Wrentit, and European Starling, as well as contraction and subsequent partial recovery of the Western Bluebird.

# Sources Cited

## Printed and Electronic Material

ABRAHAM, D. M., AND C. D. ANKNEY. 1984. Partitioning of foraging habitat by breeding Sabine's gulls and Arctic Terns. Wilson Bull. 96: 161-172.

ADAMCIK, R. S., AND L. B. KEITH. 1978. Regional movements and mortality of Great Horned Owls in relation to snowshoe hare fluctuations. Can. Field-Nat. 92: 228-234.

ADAMS, L. 1947. Food habits of three common Oregon birds in relation to reforestation. J. Wildl. Manage. 11: 281-282.

ADAMUS, P. R., AND L. FISH. 2000. Biological evaluation of the Willamette River and McKenzie River confluence area, Part II: restoration of wildlife and riparian habitat. McKenzie River Watershed Council, Springfield, OR.

ADAMUS, P. R., K. LARSEN, G. GILLSON, AND C. R. MILLER. 2001. Oregon Breeding Bird Atlas. Oreg. Field Ornithol. [www.oregonbirds.org], Eugene, OR.

ADKISSON, C. S. 1977. Morphological variation in North American Pine Grosbeaks. Wilson Bull. 89: 380-395.

ADKISSON, C. S. 1981. Geographic variation in vocalizations and evolution of North American Pine Grosbeaks. Condor 83: 277-288.

ADKISSON, C. S. 1996. Red Crossbill (*Loxia curvirostra*). *In* The birds of North America, No. 256 (A. Poole and F. Gill, eds). Acad. of Nat. Sci., Philadelphia, and Am. Ornithol. Union, Washington, D.C.

AGEE, J. K. 1991. Fire history along an elevational gradient in the Siskiyou Mountains, Oregon, USA. Northwest Sci. 65: 188-199.

AGEE, J. K. 1993. Fire ecology of Pacific Northwest forests. Island Press, Washington, D.C.

AIKEN, C. E. H., AND E. R. WARREN. 1914. The birds of El Paso County, Colorado. Colorado Coll. Sci. Series 12: 497-603.

AINLEY, D. G. 1976. The occurrence of seabirds in the coastal region of California. West. Birds 7: 33-68.

AINLEY, D. G. 1980. Geographic variation in Leach's Storm-Petrel. Auk 97: 837-853.

AINLEY, D. G. 1990. Farallon seabirds: patterns at the community level. Pp. 394-380 *in* Seabirds of the Farallon Islands (D. G. Ainley and R. J. Boekelheide, eds.). Stanford Univ. Press, Stanford, CA.

AINLEY, D. G., D. W. ANDERSON, AND P. R. KELLY. 1981. Feeding ecology of marine cormorants in southwestern North America. Condor 83: 120-131.

AINLEY, D. G., R. J. BOEKELHEIDE, S. H. MORRELL, AND C. S. STRONG. 1990a. Cassin's Auklet. Pp. 306-338 *in* Seabirds of the Farallon Islands (D. G. Ainley and R. J. Boekelheide, eds.). Stanford Univ. Press, Stanford, CA.

AINLEY, D. G., R. J. BOEKELHEIDE, S. H. MORRELL, AND C. S. STRONG. 1990b. Pigeon Guillemot. Pp. 276-305 *in* Seabirds of the Farallon Islands (D. G. Ainley and R. J. Boekelheide, eds.). Stanford Univ. Press, Stanford, CA.

AINLEY, D. G., R. P. HENDERSON, AND C. STRONG. 1990. Leach's Storm-Petrel and Ashy Storm-Petrel. Pp. 128-162 *in* Seabirds of the Farallon Islands (D. G. Ainley and R. J. Boekelheide, eds.). Stanford Univ. Press, Stanford, CA.

AINLEY, D. G., AND B. MANOLIS. 1979. Occurrence and distribution of the Mottled Petrel. West. Birds 10: 113-123.

AINLEY, D. G., S. H. MORRELL, AND R. J. BOEKELHEIDE. 1990. Rhinoceros Auklet and Tufted Puffin. Pp. 339-348 *in* Seabirds of the Farallon Islands (D. G. Ainley and R. J. Boekelheide, eds.). Stanford Univ. Press, Stanford, CA.

AINLEY, D. G., S. H. MORRELL, AND T. J. LEWIS. 1975. Patterns in the life histories of storm-petrels on the Farallon Islands. Living Bird 13: 295-312.

AINLEY, D. G., AND G. A. SANGER. 1979. Trophic relations of seabirds in the northeastern Pacific Ocean and Bering Sea. *In* Conservation of marine birds of northern North America (J. C. Bartonek and D. N. Nettleship, eds.). U.S. Fish and Wildl. Serv. Res. Rep. 11, Washington, D. C.

AINLEY, D. G., L. B. SPEAR, AND S. G. ALLEN. 1996. Variation in the diet of Cassin's Auklet reveals spatial, seasonal, and decadal occurrence patterns of euphausids off California, U.S.A. Mar. Ecol. Prog. Ser. 137: 1-10.

AINLEY, D. G., W. J. SYDEMAN, S. A. HATCH, AND U. W. WILSON. 1994. Seabird population trends along the west coast of North America: causes and the extent of regional concordance. Stud. in Avian Biol. 15: 119-133.

AINLEY, D. G., W. J. SYDEMAN, AND J. NORTON. 1995. Upper trophic level predators indicate interannual negative and positive anomalies in the California Current food web. Mar. Ecol. Prog. Ser. 118: 69-79.

AINSLEY, D. T. J. 1992. Vocalizations and nesting behaviour of the Pacific-slope Flycatcher, *Empidonax difficilis*. M.S. thesis, Univ. of Victoria, Victoria, B.C.

AIROLA, D. A. 1986. Brown-headed Cowbird parasitism and habitat disturbance in the Sierra Nevada. J. Wildl. Manage. 50: 571-575.

AIROLA, D. A., AND R. H. BARRETT. 1985. Foraging and habitat relationships of insect-gleaning birds in a Sierra Nevada mixed-conifer woodland. Condor 87: 205-216.

AKENSON, H. 1991. Status of the Upland Sandpiper in Umatilla and Union counties, Oregon. Unpubl. rep., Oreg. Dept. Fish and Wildl., Portland.

AKENSON, H. 1993. Upland Sandpiper habitat use and breeding biology at Logan Valley and Marley Creek, Oregon: progress report 1993. Unpubl. rep., Oreg. Dept. Fish and Wildl., Portland.

ALBERICO, J. R. 1993. Drought and predation cause avocet and stilt breeding failure in Nevada. West. Birds 24: 43-51.

ALCORN, G. D. 1978. Northwest birds, distribution and eggs. Western Media Printing and Publ., Tacoma, WA.

ALCORN, J. R. 1943. Additions to the list of Nevada birds. Condor 45: 40.

ALCORN, J. R. 1953. Food of the Common Merganser in Churchill County, Nevada. Condor 55: 151-152.

ALDEN, S. M., AND G. S. MILLS. 1976. White-throated Swifts following farm machinery. Wilson Bull. 88: 675.

ALDRICH, E. C. 1940. Notes on the birds of Crater Lake National Park, Oregon. Condor 42: 89-90.

ALDRICH, J. W. 1939. Geographical variations of the Veery. Auk 56: 338-340.

ALDRICH, J. W. 1943. A new Fox Sparrow from the northwestern United States. Proc. Biol. Soc. Washington 56: 163-166.

ALDRICH, J. W. 1944. Notes on the races of the White-breasted Nuthatch. Auk 61: 592-604.

ALDRICH, J. W. 1946. New subspecies of birds from western North America. Proc. Biol. Soc. Washington 59: 129-136.

ALDRICH, J. W. 1963. Geographic orientation of American Tetraonidae. J. Wildl. Manage. 27: 529-545.

ALDRICH, J. W. 1968. Population characteristics and nomenclature of the Hermit Thrush. Proc. U.S. Natl. Mus. 124(3637): 1-33.

ALDRICH, J. W. 1993. Classification and distribution. Pp. 47-54 in Ecology and management of the Mourning Dove (T. S. Baskett, M. W. Sayre, R. E. Tomlinson, R. E. Mirarchi, and R. E. McCabe, eds.). Stackpole Books, Harrisburg, PA.

ALDRICH, J. W., AND A. J. DUVALL. 1958. Distribution and races of the Mourning Dove. Condor 60: 108-128.

ALDRICH, J. W., AND J. S. WESKE. 1978. Origin and evolution of the eastern House Finch population. Auk 95: 528-536.

ALEGRIA, J., L. FOLLIARD, J. LINT, S. MADSEN, T. MAX., AND L. WEBB. 2002. Southwest Oregon inland survey assessment for Marbled Murrelets. Rogue River Natl. Forest, Siskiyou Natl. Forest, Medford District Bureau of Land Manage., and U. S. Fish and Wildl. Serv.

ALEXANDER, J. D. 1999. Bird-habitat relationships in the Klamath/ Siskiyou Mountains. M.S. thesis, S. Oreg. Univ., Ashland.

ALEXANDER, K., G. ROBERTSON, AND R. GALES. 1997. The incidental mortality of albatrosses in longline fisheries. Australian Antarctic Division, Tasmania.

ALEXANDER, S. A., K. A. HOBSON, C. L. GRATTO-TREVOR, AND A. W. DIAMOND. 1996. Conventional and isotopic determination of shorebird diets at an inland stopover: the importance of invertebrates and Potamogeton pectinatus tubers. Can. J. Zool. 74: 1057-1068.

ALLEN, A. W. 1987. Habitat suitability index models: Barred Owl. U.S. Fish and Wildl. Serv. Biol. Rep. 82(10.143).

ALLEN, R. P. AND F. P. MANGELS. 1940. Studies of the nesting behavior of the Black-crowned Night Heron. Proc. Linn. of Soc. New York 50-51: 1-28.

ALSTROM, P., AND P. COLSTON. 1991. A field guide to the rare birds of Britain and Europe. Harper Collins, London.

ALTMAN, B. 1994a. A documented nesting of the Eastern Kingbird in western Oregon. Oreg. Birds 20: 56-57.

ALTMAN, B. 1994b. Occurrence and population trends of 13 sensitive bird species within the western interior valleys of Oregon. Unpubl. rep., Oreg. Dept. Fish and Wildl., Portland.

ALTMAN, B. 1997. Distribution, abundance, and habitat associations of declining and state sensitive bird species breeding in Willamette Valley grasslands. Unpubl. rep., Oreg. Dept. Fish and Wildl., Corvallis.

ALTMAN, B. 1999a. Conservation strategy for landbirds in the Columbia Plateau of eastern Oregon and Washington. Unpubl. rep., Oregon-Washington Partners in Flight.

ALTMAN, B. 1999b. Status and conservation of grassland birds in the Willamette Valley. Unpubl. rep., Oreg. Dept. Fish and Wildl., Corvallis.

ALTMAN, B. 2000a. Conservation strategy for landbirds in lowlands and valleys of western Oregon and Washington. Version 1.0. March 2000. Am. Bird Conservancy and Oregon-Washington Partners in Flight.

ALTMAN, B. 2000b. Conservation strategy for landbirds in the northern Rocky Mountains of eastern Oregon and Washington. Unpubl. rep., Oregon-Washington Partners in Flight; USFWS, Oregon State Office; USFS, Mt. Hood National Forest; and USBLM, Oregon State Office.

ALTMAN, B. 2000c. Olive-sided flycatcher nest success and habitat relationships in post-fire and harvested forests of western Oregon, 1997-1999. Unpubl. rept. submitted to U.S. Fish and Wildl. Serv., Regional Office, Portland.

ALTMAN, B., M.C. BOULAY, S. DOWLAN, D. CRANNELL, K. RUSSELL, K. BEAL, AND J. DILLON. In press. Willow flycatcher nest success and habitat relationships in the Willamette Basin, Oregon. Stud. in Avian Biol.

ALTMAN, R. L., AND E. K. ELTZROTH. 1987. Observations from a "bluebird field" in western Oregon. Sialia 9: 133-136.

ALTMAN, B., AND A. HOLMES. 2000. Conservation strategy for landbirds in the Columbia Plateau of eastern Oregon and Washington. Version 1.0. March 1999. Am.

Bird Conservancy and Oregon-Washington Partners in Flight.

ALTMAN, B. AND R. SALLABANKS. 2000. Olive-sided Flycatcher (Contopus cooperi). In The birds of North America, No. 502 (A. Poole and F. Gill, eds.). The Birds of N. Am., Inc., Philadelphia, PA.

ALWORTH, T., AND B. R. SCHEIBER. 2000. Female wrens contribute more to nest building. J. Field Ornithol. 71: 409-414.

AMADON, D. 1983. The Bald Eagle and its relatives. Pp. 1-4 in Biology and management of Bald Eagles and Ospreys (D. M. Bird, chief ed.). Harpell Press, Ste. Anne de Bellevue, Quebec.

AMERICAN BIRDING ASSOCIATION (ABA). 1999. Bird sightings from the hotlines, November - December 1998. Winging It 11: 3.

AMERICAN BIRDING ASSOCIATION (ABA). 2000. Bird sightings from the hotlines, January - February 2000. Winging It 12: 13.

AMERICAN ORNITHOLOGISTS' UNION (AOU). 1886. The code of nomenclature and check-list of North American birds. Am. Ornithol. Union, New York.

AMERICAN ORNITHOLOGISTS' UNION (AOU). 1931. Check-list of North American birds. Am. Ornithol. Union, Lancaster, PA.

AMERICAN ORNITHOLOGISTS' UNION (AOU). 1944. Nineteenth supplement to the American Ornithologists' Union check-list of North American birds. Auk 61: 441-464.

AMERICAN ORNITHOLOGISTS' UNION (AOU). 1945. Twentieth supplement to the American Ornithologists' Union check-list of North American birds. Auk 62: 436-449.

AMERICAN ORNITHOLOGISTS' UNION (AOU). 1947. Twenty-second supplement to the American Ornithologists' Union check-list of North American birds. Auk 64: 445-452.

AMERICAN ORNITHOLOGISTS' UNION (AOU). 1954. Twenty-ninth supplement to the American Ornithologists' Union Check-list of North American birds. Auk 71: 310-312.

AMERICAN ORNITHOLOGISTS' UNION (AOU). 1957. Check-list of North American birds. 5th ed. Am. Ornithol. Union, Washington, D.C.

AMERICAN ORNITHOLOGISTS' UNION (AOU). 1973. Thirty-second

supplement to the American Ornithologists' Union check-list of North American Birds. Auk 90: 411-419.

AMERICAN ORNITHOLOGISTS' UNION (AOU). 1983. Check-list of North American birds. 6th ed. Am. Ornithol. Union, Washington, D.C.

AMERICAN ORNITHOLOGISTS' UNION (AOU). 1985. Thirty-fifth supplement to the American Ornithologists' Union check-list of North American Birds. Auk 102: 680-686.

AMERICAN ORNITHOLOGISTS' UNION (AOU). 1989. Thirty-seventh supplement to the American Ornithologists' Union check-list of North American birds. Auk 106: 532-538.

AMERICAN ORNITHOLOGISTS' UNION (AOU). 1995. Fortieth supplement to the American Ornithologists' Union check-list of North American Birds. Auk 112: 819-830.

AMERICAN ORNITHOLOGISTS' UNION (AOU). 1997. Forty-first supplement to the American Ornithologists' Union check-list of North American Birds. Auk 114: 542-552.

AMERICAN ORNITHOLOGISTS' UNION (AOU). 1998. Check-list of North American Birds. 7th ed. Am. Ornithol. Union, Baltimore, MD.

AMERICAN ORNITHOLOGISTS' UNION (AOU). 2000. Forty-second supplement to the American Ornithologists' Union check-list of North American Birds. Auk 117: 847-858.

AMMON, E. 1995. Lincoln's Sparrow (*Melospiza lincolnii*). *In* The birds of North America, No. 191 (A. Poole and F. Gill, eds.). Acad. of Nat. Sci., Philadelphia, and Am. Ornithol. Union, Washington, D.C.

ANDERSON, B. W., M. G. REEDER, AND R. L. TIMKEN. 1974. Notes on the feeding behavior of the Common Merganser *(Mergus merganser)*. Condor 76: 472-476.

ANDERSON, B. W., AND R. L. TIMKEN. 1971. Age and secondary characteristics of Common Mergansers. J. Wildl. Manage. 35: 388-393.

ANDERSON, C. M., AND D. M. BATCHELDER. 1990. First confirmed nesting of the Black-shouldered Kite in Washington. West. Birds 21: 37-38.

ANDERSON, C. M., D. G. ROSENEAU, B. J. WALTON, AND P. J. BENTE. 1988. New evidence of a peregrine migration on the west coast of

North America. Pp. 507-516 *in* Peregrine Falcon populations - their management and recovery (T. J. Cade, J. H. Enderson, C. G. Thelander and C. M. White, eds.). Peregrine Fund, Inc., Boise, ID.

ANDERSON, D. A. 1985. Occurrence of the Rock Wren in Hood River County, Oregon. Oreg. Birds 11: 153-154.

ANDERSON, D. A. 1987a. Checklist of the birds of Hood River County. Oreg. Birds 13: 114-120.

ANDERSON, D. A. 1987b. Field notes: eastern Oregon, August-November 1986. Oreg. Birds 13: 219-225.

ANDERSON, D. A. 1987c. Field notes: eastern Oregon, December 1986-February 1987. Oreg. Birds 13: 306-311.

ANDERSON, D. A. 1987d. Field notes: eastern Oregon, June-July 1986. Oreg. Birds 13: 96-100.

ANDERSON, D. A. 1987e. Site guide: Hood River County. Oreg. Birds 13: 108-113.

ANDERSON, D. A. 1987f. The spring migration: eastern Oregon, March - May 1987. Oreg. Birds 13: 438-447.

ANDERSON, D. A. 1988a. Additional inland turnstone records. Oreg. Birds 14: 389.

ANDERSON, D. A. 1988b. The fall migration: eastern Oregon, August - November 1987. Oreg. Birds 14: 194-206.

ANDERSON, D. A. 1988c. Fieldnotes: eastern Oregon, December 1987-February 1988. Oreg. Birds 14: 276-281.

ANDERSON, D. A. 1988d. Fieldnotes: eastern Oregon, spring 1988. Oreg. Birds 14: 368-375.

ANDERSON, D. A. 1988e. Fieldnotes: eastern Oregon, summer 1987. Oreg. Birds 14: 81-87.

ANDERSON, D. A. 1988f. Winter distribution of Harris' Sparrow and White-throated Sparrows in Oregon. Oreg. Birds 14: 76-79.

ANDERSON, D. A. 1989a. Evidence of nesting by the Water Pipit in the Oregon Cascades. Oreg. Birds 15: 213.

ANDERSON, D. A. 1989b. Field notes: eastern Oregon. Oreg. Birds 15: 113-119.

ANDERSON, D. A. 1989c. Fieldnotes: eastern Oregon, spring 1989. Oreg. Birds 15: 291-297.

ANDERSON, D. A. 1989d. Field notes: eastern Oregon, summer 1988. Oreg. Birds 15: 34-39.

ANDERSON, D. A. 1989e. Field notes: eastern Oregon, winter 1988-89. Oreg. Birds 15: 181-187.

ANDERSON, D. A. 1990a. Fieldnotes: eastern Oregon, fall 1989. Oreg. Birds 16: 171-179.

ANDERSON, D. A. 1990b. Field notes: eastern Oregon, spring 1990. Oreg. Birds 16: 314-321.

ANDERSON, D. A. 1990c. Field notes: eastern Oregon, summer 1989. Oreg. Birds 16: 87-92.

ANDERSON, D. A. 1990d. Field notes: eastern Oregon, winter 1989-90. Oreg. Birds 16: 237-242.

ANDERSON, D. A. 1991a. Fieldnotes: eastern Oregon, fall 1990. Oreg. Birds 17: 51-54.

ANDERSON, D. A. 1991b. Field notes: eastern Oregon, summer 1990. Oreg. Birds 17: 23-26.

ANDERSON, D. A., AND B. BELLIN. 1988. Inland records of Ruddy and Black turnstones in Oregon. Oreg. Birds 14: 47-50.

ANDERSON, D. E. 1990. Nest-defense behavior of Red-tailed Hawks. Condor 92: 991-997.

ANDERSON, D. P., R. G. ANTHONY, AND M. V. ICHISAKA. 1985. Wintering ecology of Bald Eagles on the Lewis River, Washington 1984-1985. Unpubl. rep., Oreg. Coop. Wildl. Res. Unit, Oreg. State Univ., Corvallis.

ANDERSON, D. W., AND I. T. ANDERSON. 1976. Distribution and status of Brown Pelicans in the California Current. Am. Birds 30: 3-12.

ANDERSON, D. W., AND F. GRESS. 1982. Brown Pelicans and the anchovy fishery in southern California. Pp. 128-135 *in* Marine birds: Their feeding ecology and commercial fisheries relationships (D. N. Nettleship, G. A. Sanger, and P. F. Springer, eds.). Can. Wildl. Serv., Ottawa.

ANDERSON, D. W., AND F. GRESS. 1983. Status of a northern population of California Brown Pelicans. Condor 85: 79-88.

ANDERSON, D. W., AND J. J. HICKEY. 1972. Eggshell changes in certain North American birds. Proc. Int. Ornithol. Congress 15: 514-540.

ANDERSON, D. W., J. R. JEHL, JR., R. W. RISEBROUGH, L. A. WOODS JR., L. R. DEWEESE, AND W. G. EDGECOMB. 1975. Brown pelicans: improved reproduction off the southern California coast. Science 190:806-808.

ANDERSON, E. D. Unpubl. data. Coordinated roost counts at Ridgefield NWR and Sauvie Island. Ridgefield NWR Complex, Wash.

ANDERSON, J. D., AND B. BELLIN. 1990. Site guide: Ankeny National Wildlife Refuge. Oreg. Birds 16: 287-295.

ANDERSON, M. G. 1974. American Coots feeding in association with Canvasbacks. Wilson Bull. 86: 462-463.

ANDERSON, R. J. 1985. Bald Eagles and forest management. Pp.189-193 in Forestry and wildlife management in Canada: a symposium. Univ. of British Columbia, Vancouver, B.C.

ANDERSON, S. H. 1970. The avifaunal composition of white oak stands. Condor 72: 417-423.

ANDERSON, S. H. 1972. Seasonal variations in forest birds of western Oregon. Northwest Sci. 46: 194-206.

ANDERSON, S. H. 1976. Comparative food habits of Oregon nuthatches. Northwest Sci. 50: 213-221.

ANDERSON, S. K. In prep. Foraging behavior and colony attendance of Caspian Terns nesting in the Columbia River estuary. M.S. thesis, Oreg. State Univ., Corvallis.

ANDERSON, T. R. 1978. Population studies of European sparrows in North America. Occas. Pap. of the Mus. of Natur. Hist. No. 70: 1-58., Univ. of Kansas, Lawrence.

ANDERSON, W. 1970. A preliminary study of the relationship of salt ponds and wildlife – south San Francisco Bay. Calif. Fish and Game 56: 240-252.

ANDRES, B. A. 1994. The effects of the Exxon Valdez oil spill on Black Oystercatcher's breeding in Prince William Sound, Alaska. Final rep, Exxon Valdez Oil Spill Public Information Office, Anchorage, AK.

ANDRES, B. A., AND B. T. BROWNE. 1998. Spring migration of shorebirds on the Yukutat Forelands, Alaska. Wilson Bull. 110: 326-331.

ANDRES, B. A., AND G. A. FALXA. 1995. Black Oystercatcher (Haematopus bachmani). In The birds of North America, No. 155 (A. Poole and F. Gill, eds.). Acad. of Nat. Sci., Philadelphia, and Am. Ornithol. Union, Washington, D.C.

ANONYMOUS. 1915. Columbian Sharp-tailed Grouse. Oreg. Sportsman 3: 138-140.

ANONYMOUS. 1948. Two home-made traps for English Sparrows. U.S. Fish and Wildl. Serv. Wildl. Leafl. 307.

ANONYMOUS. 1970. Fulvous Ducks in Oregon. Oreg. State Game Commission Bull. June 1970.

ANONYMOUS. 1972. Special interagency task force for the Federal Task Force on Alaska oil development. Environmental setting between Port Valdez, Alaska, and west coast ports. Final Environmental Impact Statement Proposed Trans-Alaska Pipeline. Vol. 3. PB 206 921 3.

ANONYMOUS. 1973. Clean-up crew. Oreg. Wildl. 28: 8.

ANONYMOUS. 1977a. Season's highlights. Oreg. Birds 3(4): 35-36.

ANONYMOUS. 1977b. Season's highlights: August 1 - November 1, 1977. Oreg. Birds 3(5): 40-43.

ANONYMOUS. 1978a. Complete results of the 1978 Oregon Christmas Bird Counts. Oreg. Birds 4(6): 8-27.

ANONYMOUS. 1978b. Season's highlights: October 15 - November 29. Oreg. Birds 3(6): 29-30.

ANONYMOUS. 1983. The California Brown Pelican recovery plan. U.S. Fish and Wildl. Serv., Portland, OR.

ANTHONY, A. W. 1886. Field notes on the birds of Washington County, Oregon. Auk 3: 161-172.

ANTHONY, A. W. 1902. List of the birds in the vicinity of Portland, Oregon. In Handbook of birds of the western United States (F. M. Bailey). Houghton, Mifflin and Company, Boston.

ANTHONY, A. W. 1921. The English Sparrow and the motor vehicle. Auk 38: 605-616.

ANTHONY, A. W. 1923. Predatory Brewer's Blackbirds. Condor 25: 106.

ANTHONY, R. G. 1970. Ecology and reproduction of California Quail in southeastern Washington. Condor 72: 276-287.

ANTHONY, R. G., R. W. FRENZEL, F. B. ISAACS, AND M. G. GARRETT. 1994. Probable causes of nesting failures in Oregon's Bald Eagle population. Wildl. Soc. Bull. 22: 576-582.

ANTHONY, R. G., M. G. GARRETT, AND C. A. SCHULER. 1993. Environmental contaminants in Bald Eagles in the Columbia River estuary. J. Wildl. Manage. 57: 10-19.

ANTHONY, R. G., G. A. GREEN, E. D. FORSMAN, AND S. K. NELSON. 1996. Avian abundance in riparian zones of three forest types in the Cascade Mountains, Oregon. Wilson Bull. 108: 280-291.

ANTHONY, R. G., M. C. HANSEN, M. SANDLER, N. V. MARR, C. A. SCHULER, AND R. S. LUTZ. 1990. Short-term effects of triploid grass carp on waterfowl and Bald Eagles at Devil's Lake, Oregon. Unpubl. rep., Oreg. Coop. Wildl. Res. Unit, Oreg. State Univ., Corvallis.

ANTHONY, R. G., AND F. B. ISAACS. 1989. Characteristics of Bald Eagle nest sites in Oregon. J. Wildl. Manage. 53: 148-159.

ANTHONY, R. G., R. L. KNIGHT, G. T. ALLEN, B. R. MCCLELLAND, AND J. I. HODGES. 1982. Habitat use by nesting and roosting Bald Eagles in the Pacific Northwest. Trans. 47th N. Am. Wildl. and Natur. Resour. Conf. 332-342.

ANTHONY, R. G., A. K. MILES, J. A. ESTES, AND F. B. ISAACS. 1999. Productivity, diets, and environmental contaminants in nesting Bald Eagles from the Aleutian archipelago. Environ. Toxicol. and Chem. 18: 2054-2062.

ANTOLOS, M. In prep. Breeding and foraging ecology of Caspian terns (Sterna caspia) in the mid-Columbia River: predation on juvenile salmonids and management implications. M.S. thesis, Oreg. State Univ., Corvallis.

APFELBAUM, S., AND A. HANEY. 1981. Bird populations before and after wildfire in a Great Lakes pine forest. Condor 83: 347–354.

ARBIB, R. S. 1957. The New York State standards of abundance, frequency, and seasonal occurrence. Audubon Field Notes 11:63-64.

ARBIB, R. S., ED. 1970. Audubon Field Notes discovery award. Audubon Field Notes 24: 654.

ARBIB, R. S., ED. 1974. Seventy-fourth Christmas Bird Count. Am. Birds 28: 145-585.

ARBIB, R. S., ED. 1981. Eighty-first Christmas Bird Count. Am. Birds 35: 696.

ARCHIE, M. A., AND R. A. HUDSON. 1973. Scattered mixed coniferous forests in subalpine meadows and spruce bogs. Am. Birds 27: 955-1019.

ARMSTRONG, D. P. 1987. Economics of breeding territoriality in male Calliope Hummingbirds. Auk 104: 242-253.

ARNETT, E. B., B. ALTMAN, AND W. P. ERICKSON. 1997. Relationships between salvage logging and forest avifauna in lodgepole pine forests of the central Oregon pumice zone. Unpubl. annual rep., Winema and Fremont Natl. Forests.

ARNETT, E. B., B. ALTMAN, W. P. ERICKSON, AND K. A. BETTINGER. 2001. Relationships between salvage logging and forest avifauna in lodgepole pine forests of the central Oregon pumice zone. Unpubl. final rep., Weyerhaeuser Co., Federal Way, WA.

ARNETT, E. B., R. J. ANDERSON, C. SOKOL, F. B. ISAACS, R. G. ANTHONY, AND W. P. ERICKSON. 2001. Relationships between nesting Bald

Eagles and selective logging in southcentral Oregon. Wildl. Soc. Bull. 29: 795-803.

ARNOLD, J. R. 1980. Distribution of the mockingbird in California. West. Birds 11: 97-102.

ARNOLD, T. W. 1993. Factors affecting renesting in American Coots. Condor 95: 273-281.

ASHLEY, J. 1995. Harlequin Duck surveys and tracking in Glacier National Park, Montana. Unpubl. tech. rep., West Glacier, MT.

ASHMOLE, N. P. 1971. Seabird ecology and the marine environment. Pp. 223-286 in Avian biology, Vol.1 (D.S. Farner and J. R. King, eds.). Academic Press, New York and London.

ATKINSON, K. M., AND D. P. HEWITT. 1978. A note on the food consumption of the Red-breasted Merganser. Wildfowl 29: 87-91.

AUDUBON SOCIETY OF CORVALLIS. 1977-2002. The Chat, newsletter of Audubon Society of Corvallis.

AUSTIN, J. E., C. M. CUSTER, AND A. D. AFTON. 1998. Lesser Scaup (Aythya affinis). In The birds of North America, No. 338 (A. Poole and F. Gill, eds.). The Birds of N. Am., Inc., Philadelphia, PA.

AUSTIN, J. E., AND M. R. MILLER. 1995. Northern Pintail (Anas acuta). In The birds of North America, No. 163 (A. Poole and F. Gill, eds.). Acad. of Nat. Sci., Philadelphia, and Am. Ornithol. Union, Washington, D.C.

AUSTING, G. R., J. B. HOLT, AND J. K. TERRES. 1966. The world of the Great Horned Owl. Lippincott, Philadelphia, PA.

BAEPLER, D. H. 1968. Lark Sparrow. Life histories of North American cardinals, grosbeaks, buntings, towhees, finches, sparrows and allies (O. L. Austin, ed.). U.S. Natl. Mus. Bull. 237.

BAGG, A. C. 1941. Brown Thrasher in Oregon. Auk 58: 100.

BAICICH, P. J., AND C. J. O. HARRISON. 1997. Guide to the nests, eggs, and nestlings of North American birds. Academic Press, San Diego, CA.

BAILEY, F. M. 1904. Twelve Rock Wren nests in New Mexico. Condor 6: 68-70.

BAILEY, F. M. 1914. Handbook of birds of the western United States. Houghton Mifflin Co., Boston, MA.

BAILEY, F. M. 1924. Handbook of birds of the Western United States. 9th edition. Houghton Mifflin Co. Boston, MA.

BAILEY, R. G. 1976. Ecoregions of the United States. U.S. Dept. of Agric., Forest Serv. Intermountain Region, Ogden, UT.

BAILEY, R. G. 1978. Description of the ecoregions of the United States. U.S. Dept. of Agric., Forest Serv. Intermountain Region, Ogden, UT.

BAILEY, S., P. PYLE, AND L. SPEAR. 1989. Dark Pterodroma petrels in the North Pacific: identification, status, and North American occurrence. Am. Birds 43: 400-415.

BAILEY, S. F., AND D. SINGER. 1996. Middle Pacific Coast region. Natl. Audubon Soc. Field Notes 50: 218-220.

BAIRD, S. F, J. CASSIN AND G. N. LAWRENCE. 1858. Reports of explorations and survey to ascertain the most practicable and economical route for a railroad from the Mississippi River to the Pacific Ocean. Vol. IX. Part II. General report upon the zoology of the several Pacific Railroad routes: birds. A. O. P. Nicholson, Washington, D.C.

BAIRD, S. F., T. M. BREWER, AND R. RIDGWAY. 1875. A history of North American birds. Vol. 1: land birds. Little, Brown, Boston.

BAKER, J. A., AND R. L. BROOKS. 1981. Raptor and vole populations at an airport. J. Wildl. Manage. 45: 390-394.

BAKUS, G. J. 1959. Observations on the life history of the dipper in Montana. Auk 76: 190-207.

BALDA, R. P., AND G. C. BATEMAN. 1971. Flocking and annual cycle of the Pinyon Jay, Gymnorhinus cyanocephalus. Condor 73: 287-302.

BALDA, R. P., AND A. C. KAMIL. 1989. A comparative study of cache recovery by three corvid species. Anim. Behav. 38: 486-495.

BALDA, R. P., AND A. C. KAMIL. 1992. Long-term spatial memory in Clark's Nutcracker, Nucifraga columbiana. Anim. Behav. 44: 761-769.

BALDA, R. P., B. C. MCKNIGHT, AND C. D. JOHNSON. 1975. Flammulated Owl migration in the southwestern United States. Wilson Bull. 87: 520-533.

BALDASSARRE, G. A., AND E. G. BOLEN. 1994. Waterfowl ecology and management. John Wiley & Sons, Inc. New York.

BALDASSARRE, G. A., AND D. H. FISCHER. 1984. Food habits of fall migrant shorebirds on the Texas high plains. J. Field Ornithol. 55: 220-229.

BALDRIDGE, A. AND J. B. CROWELL. 1965. Northern Pacific Coast region. Audubon Field Notes 19: 570-574.

BALDRIDGE, A. AND J. B. CROWELL. 1966. Northern Pacific Coast region. Audubon Field Notes 20: 81-86.

BALDWIN, E. M. 1964. Geology of Oregon, 2nd ed. Univ. of Oreg. Coop. Bookstore, Eugene.

BALDWIN, J. R., AND J. R. LOVVORN. 1994. Habitats and tidal accessibility of the marine foods of dabbling ducks and Brant in Boundary Bay, British Columbia. Marine Biol. 120: 627-638.

BALDWIN, P. H. 1968. Predator-prey relationships of birds and spruce beetles. Proc. North Central Branch Entomol. Soc. Am. 23: 90–99.

BALGOOYEN, T. G. 1969. Pygmy Owl attacks California Quail. Auk 86: 358.

BALL, I. J., E. L. BOWHAY, AND C. F. YOCOM. 1981. Ecology and management of the western Canada Goose in Washington. Wash. Dept. Game Biol. Bull. No. 17.

BALLAM, J. M. 1984. The use of soaring by the Red-tailed Hawk (Buteo jamaicensis). Auk 101: 519-524.

BALTOSSER, W. H. 1989. Costa's Hummingbird: its distribution and status. West. Birds 20: 41-62.

BALTOSSER, W. H., AND S. M. RUSSELL. 2000. Black-chinned Hummingbird (Archilochus alexandri). In The birds of North America, No. 495 (A. Poole and F. Gill, eds.). The Birds of N. Am., Inc., Philadelphia, PA.

BALTOSSER, W. H., AND P. E. SCOTT. 1996. Costa's Hummingbird (Calypte costae). In The birds of North America, No. 251 (A. Poole and F. Gill, eds.). Acad. of Nat. Sci., Philadelphia, and Am. Ornithol. Union, Washington, D.C.

BALTZ, D. M. AND G. V. MOREJOHN. 1977. Food habits and niche overlap of seabirds wintering on Monterey Bay, California. Auk 94: 526-543.

BANG, B. G., AND S. COBB. 1968. The size of the olfactory bulb in 108 species of birds. Auk 85: 55-61.

BANKO, W. E. 1960. The Trumpeter Swan: its history, habits, and population in the United States. U.S. Fish and Wildl. Serv., Washington, D.C.

BANKS, R. 1960. Notes on birds from Harts Pass, Washington. Condor 62: 70-71.

BANKS, R. 1970. The Fox Sparrow on the west slope of the Oregon Cascades. Condor 72: 369-370.

BANKS, R. C. 1986. Subspecies of the Glaucous Gull, *Larus hyperboreus* (Aves: Charadriiformes). Proc. Biol. Soc. Wash. 99: 149-159.

BANKS, R. C. 1988. Geographic variation in the Yellow-billed Cuckoo. Condor 90: 473-477.

BANKS, R. C., AND M. R. BROWNING. 1995. Comments on the status of revived old names for some North American birds. Auk 112: 633-648.

BANKS, R.C., AND M. R. BROWNING. 1999. Questions about Thayer's Gull. Ontario Birds 17: 124-130.

BANKS, R. C., C. CICERO, J. L. DUNN, A. W. KRATTER, P. C. RASMUSSEN, J. V. REMSEN, JR., J. D. RISING, AND D. F. STOTZ. 2002. Forty-third supplement to the American Ornithologists' Union check-list of North American Birds. Auk 119: 897-906.

BAPTISTA, L. F. 1989. The best studied songbird: White-crowned Sparrows in the wild and in the laboratory. Birds Internatl. 1: 10-21.

BARD, D. C. 1897. Report of the third annual meeting of the Northwestern Ornithological Association. Oreg. Nat. 4: 6-8.

BARKER, M. A., AND D. L. TESSAGLIA-HYMES. 1999. Project feeder watch 1997-98: early results. Birdscope 12: 8-9.

BARNEA, A., AND F. NOTTEBOHM. 1995. Patterns of food storing by Black-capped Chickadees suggest a mnemonic hypothesis. Anim. Behav. 49: 1161-1176.

BARNETT, J. K., AND J. A. CRAWFORD. 1994. Pre-laying nutrition of Sage Grouse hens in Oregon. J. Range Manage. 47: 114-118.

BARON, N., AND J. ACORN. 1997. Birds of the Pacific Northwest Coast. Lone Pine Publishing, Renton, WA.

BARR, J. F. 1986. Population dynamics of the Common Loon (*Gavia immer*) associated with mercury-contaminated waters in northwestern Ontario. Can. Wildl. Serv. Occas. Paper 56.

BARRETT, N. M. 1987. Ash-throated Flycatcher feeding on a mouse. Oreg. Birds. 13: 35.

BARROWCLOUGH, G. F. 1980. Genetic and phenotypic differentiation in a wood warbler (genus *Dendroica*) hybrid zone. Auk 97: 655-668.

BART, J. 1995. Evaluation of population trend estimates calculated using capture-recapture and population projection methods. Ecol. Appl. 5: 662-671.

BARTLE, J., D. HU, J-C. STAHL, P. PYLE, T. SIMONS, AND D. WOODLY. 1993. Status and ecology of gadfly petrels in the temperate North Pacific. Pp. 101-111 *in* The status, ecology, and conservation of marine birds of the North Pacific (K. Vermeer, K. Briggs, K. Morgan, and D. Siegel-Causey, eds.). Can. Wildl. Serv. Spec. Publ., Ottawa.

BASKETT, T. S., AND M. W. SAYRE. 1993. Characteristics and importance. Pp. 1-6 *in* Ecology and management of the Mourning Dove (T. S. Baskett, M. W. Sayre, R. E. Tomlinson, R. E. Mirarchi, and R. E. McCabe, eds.). Stackpole Books, Harrisburg, PA.

BATE, L. J. 1995. Monitoring woodpecker abundance and habitat in the central Oregon Cascades. M.S. thesis, Univ. of Idaho, Moscow.

BATEMAN, G. C., AND R. P. BALDA. 1973. Growth, development, and food habits of young Pinyon Jays. Auk 90: 39-61.

BATT, D. K., A. D. AFTON, M. G. ANDERSON, C. D. ANKENY, D. H. JOHNSON, J. A. KADLEC, AND G. L. KRAPU, EDS. 1992. Ecology and management of breeding waterfowl. Univ. of Minnesota Press, Minneapolis.

BATTERSON, W. 1968. All about Brant. Oreg. State Game Commission Bull. 23: 3-5.

BATTS, H. L. 1948. Some observations on the nesting activities of the Eastern Goldfinch. Jack-Pine Warbler 26: 51-58.

BATTS, H. L. 1953. Siskin and goldfinch feeding at sapsucker tree. Wilson Bull. 65: 198.

BAUER, R. D. 1979. Historical and status report of the Tule White-fronted Goose. Pp. 44-55 *in* Management and biology of Pacific Flyway geese (R. L. Jarvis and J. C. Bartonek, eds.). Oreg. State Univ., Corvallis.

BAUMGARTNER, F. M., AND A. M. BAUMGARTNER. 1992. Oklahoma bird life. Univ. of Oklahoma Press, Norman.

BAYER, R., ED. 1977. Birds Of Lincoln Co. OSU Marine Science Center, Newport, OR.

BAYER, R. D. 1978. Aspects of an Oregon estuarine Great Blue Heron population. *In* Wading birds (A. Sprunt IV, J. Ogden, and S. Winckler, eds.). Natl. Audubon Soc. Res. Rep. 7.

BAYER, R. D. 1980. Birds feeding on herring eggs at the Yaquina estuary, Oregon. Condor 82: 193-98.

BAYER, R. D. 1981. Great Blue Herons "mousing" in western Oregon. Murrelet 62: 91.

BAYER, R. D. 1983a. Seasonal occurrences of ten waterbird species at Yaquina Estuary, Oregon. Murrelet 64: 78-86.

BAYER, R. D. 1983b. Nesting success of Western Gulls at Yaquina Head and on man-made structures in Yaquina estuary, Oregon. Murrelet 64: 87-91.

BAYER, R. D. 1984. Oversummering of Whimbrels, Bonaparte's Gulls, and Caspian Terns at Yaquina Estuary, Oregon. Murrelet 65: 87-90.

BAYER, R. D. 1985a. Bill length of herons and egrets as an estimator of prey size. Colonial Waterbirds 8: 104-109.

BAYER, R. D. 1985b. Nearshore flights of seabirds past Yaquina estuary, Oregon, during the 1982 and 1983 summers. West. Birds 16: 169-173.

BAYER, R. D. 1986a. Breeding success of seabirds along the mid-Oregon coast concurrent with the 1983 El Niño. Murrelet 67: 23-26.

BAYER, R. D. 1986b. A guide to the bird notes of Grace McCormac French of Yamhill County, Oregon. Stud. in Oreg. Ornithol. No. 2. Gahmken Press, Newport, OR.

BAYER, R. D. 1987. Winter observations of Bald Eagles at Yaquina Estuary, Oregon. Murrelet 68: 39-44.

BAYER, R. D. 1988a. The yearly cycle of Common Murres along the Oregon coast. Oreg. Birds 14: 150-151.

BAYER, R. D. 1988b. 1988 bird list for Lincoln County, Oregon. Gahmken Press, Newport, OR.

BAYER, R. D. 1989a. Records of bird skins collected along the Oregon coast. Stud. in Oreg. Ornithol. No. 7. Gahmken Press, Newport, OR.

BAYER, R. D. 1989b. The cormorant/fisherman conflict in Tillamook County, Oregon. Stud. in Oreg. Ornithol. No. 6. Gahmken Press, Newport, OR.

BAYER, R. D. 1989c. Measurements of possible Northwestern Crows from Oregon. Oreg. Birds 15: 281-84.

BAYER, R. D. 1993. Journal of Oregon Ornithology: purpose, publishing issues, baseline and site-specific data, Tolerable Observation Effort (TOE), frequencies, and shortcomings. J. Oreg. Ornithol.1: 1-34.

BAYER, R. D. 1994a. Field notes, July 1994. Sandpiper 15: 7.

BAYER, R. D. 1994b. Harlequin Duck records mostly from Lincoln County, Oregon. J. Oreg. Ornithol. 3: 243-260.

BAYER, R. D. 1995a. Semimonthly bird records through 1992 for Lincoln County Oregon, Part II: records sorted by species. J. Oreg. Ornith. 4: 395-543.

BAYER, R. D. 1995b. Mostly Lincoln County field notes. Sandpiper 16(6).

BAYER, R. D. 1995c. Bird List for the Lincoln City area (Salmon River to Depoe Bay), Lincoln Co. OR. URL = http://www.orednet.org/~rbayer/j/j519-527.htm Accessed 20 Sep 2002.

BAYER, R. D. 1995d. Mostly Lincoln County field notes. Sandpiper Vol. 16(5), May.

BAYER, R. D. 1996a. Censuses of Black Brant at Yaquina estuary, Lincoln County, Oregon. J. Oreg. Ornithol. 6: 723-780.

BAYER, R. D. 1996b. An incomplete compilation of Oregon coast pelagic and beached bird records through 1983. J. Oreg. Ornithol. 5: 601-610.

BAYER, R. D. 1996c. Mostly Lincoln County bird field notes. Sandpiper 17(6).

BAYER, R. D. 1996d. Mostly Lincoln County bird field notes. Sandpiper 27: May 1995.

BAYER, R. D. 1997. Mostly Lincoln County bird field notes. Sandpiper 29: Nov 1997.

BAYER, R. D. 1998a. Mostly Lincoln County field notes. Sandpiper 19(6).

BAYER, R. D. 1998b. Mostly Lincoln County field notes. Sandpiper Vol. 19(5), May.

BAYER, R. D. 1999a. Bird field notes. Sandpiper 20(5).

BAYER, R. D. 1999b. Bird field notes. Sandpiper 20(8).

BAYER, R. D. 1999c. Mostly Lincoln County field notes. Sandpiper 20(1).

BAYER, R. D., ED. 1977. Birds of Lincoln Co. Oreg. State Univ. Marine Science Center, Newport, OR.

BAYER, R. D., J. C. DIRKS-EDMUNDS, J. A. MACNAB, AND D. MCKEY-FENDER. 1994. Bird records for the Saddle Bag Mountain area of Lincoln and Tillamook Counties. J. Oreg. Ornithol. 3: 261-310.

BAYER, R. D., AND R. W. FERRIS. 1987. Reed Ferris' 1930-1943 bird banding records and bird observations for Tillamook County, Oregon. Gahmken Press, Newport, OR.

BAYER, R. D., AND D. L. HERZING. 1985. Pre-laying assemblages of Common Murres on the colony at Yaquina Head. Murrelet 66: 94-95.

BAYER, R. D., AND J. KRABBE. 1984. Christmas Bird Count analysis: comparison of coastal Christmas Bird Counts. Oreg. Birds 10: 115-125.

BAYER, R. D., AND R. W. LOWE. 1988. Waterbird and mammal censuses at Siuslaw Estuary, Lane County, Oregon. Stud. in Oreg. Ornithol. No. 4. Gahmken Press, Newport, OR.

BAYER, R. D., AND R. W. LOWE. 1995. Preliminary report: Double-crested Cormorant flight movements along the Oregon central coast. Unpubl. data. Newport, OR.

BAYER, R. D., R. W. LOWE, AND R. E. LOEFFEL. 1991. Persistent summer mortalities of Common Murres along the Oregon central coast. Condor 93: 516-525.

BAYER, R. D., AND E. MCMAHON. 1981. Colony sizes and hatching synchrony of Great Blue Herons in coastal Oregon. Murrelet 62: 73-79.

BAYER, R. D., AND R. E. OLSON. 1988. Plastic particles in 3 Oregon fulmars. Oreg. Birds 14: 155-156.

BEAL, F. E. L. 1907. Birds of California in relation to the fruit industry. Part 1. U.S. Dept. Agric., Biol. Surv. Bull. 30.

BEAL, F. E. L. 1910. Birds of California in relation to the fruit industry. Part 2. U.S. Dept. Agric., Biol. Surv. Bull. 34: 1-96.

BEAL, F. E. L. 1911. Food of the woodpeckers of the United States. U.S. Dept. Agric., Biol. Surv. Bull. 37.

BEAL, F. E. L. 1912. Food of our more important flycatchers. U.S. Dept. Agric., Biol. Surv. Bull. 44.

BEAL, F. E. L. 1915. Food of robins and bluebirds of the United States. U.S. Dept. Agric. Bull. 171.

BEAL, F. E. L. 1918. Food habits of the swallows, a family of valuable native birds. U.S. Dept. Agric. Bull. 619.

BEAL, F. E. L., W. L. MCATEE, AND E. P. KALMBACH. 1916. Common birds of southeastern United States in relation to agriculture. U.S. Dept. Agric., Farmers' Bull. 755.

BEALL, J. T. 1990. Wood Duck nest box use in southern Puget Sound, Washington. Pp. 259-263 in Proceedings of the 1988 North American Wood Duck Symposium (L. H. Fredrickson, G. V. Burger, S. P. Havera, D. A. Graber, R. E. Kirby, and T. S. Taylor, eds.). St. Louis, MO.

BEASOM, S. L., AND O. H. PATTEE. 1978. Utilization of snails by Rio Grande turkey hens. J. Wildl. Manage. 42: 916-919.

BEASON, R. C. 1995. Horned Lark (Eremophila alpestris). In The birds of North America, No. 195 (A. Poole and F. Gill, eds.). Acad. of Nat. Sci., Philadelphia, and Am. Ornithol. Union, Washington, D.C.

BECHARD, M. J. 1983. Food supply and the occurrence of brood reduction in Swainson's Hawks. Wilson Bull. 95: 233-242.

BECHARD, M. J., AND J. M. SCHMUTZ. 1995. Ferruginous Hawk (Buteo regalis). In The birds of North America, No. 172 (A. Poole and F. Gill, eds.). Acad. of Nat. Sci., Philadelphia, and Am. Ornithol. Union, Washington, D.C.

BECK, B. 2001. Field identification of Western Flycatcher sp. in Alberta. Electronic mail message to ID-Frontiers listserver. 9 May 2001. URL = http://www.virtualbirder.com/bmail/idfrontiers/200105/w2/index.html

BECK, H. H. 1920. The occult senses of birds. Auk 37: 55-59.

BECK, M., AND T. L. GEORGE. 2000. Song post and foraging site characteristics of breeding Varied Thrushes in northwestern California. Condor 102: 93-103.

BEDNARZ, J. C., AND J. J. DINSMORE. 1982. Nest-sites and habitat of Red-shouldered and Red-tailed Hawks in Iowa. Wilson Bull. 94: 31-45.

BEEBE, F. L. 1974. Field studies of the Falconiformes of British Columbia. Occas. Pap. of the B.C. Provincial Mus. No. 17. Victoria, B.C.

BEEBE, F. L. 1976. Hawks, falcons, and falconry. Hancock House Publishers, Ltd., Saanichton, B.C.

BEECHER, N. J. 1951. Adaptations for food-getting in the American blackbirds. Auk 68: 411-440.

BEEDY, E. C. 1981. Bird communities and forest structure in the Sierra Nevada of California. Condor 83: 97-105.

BEEDY, E. C., AND W. J. HAMILTON III. 1999. Tricolored Blackbird (Agelaius tricolor). In The birds of North America, No. 423 (A. Poole and F. Gill, eds.). The Birds of N. Am., Inc., Philadelphia, PA.

BEEDY, E. C., S. D. SANDERS, AND D. A. BLOOM. 1991. Breeding status, distribution, and habitat associations of the Tricolored Blackbird (Agelaius tricolor) 1850-1989. Unpubl. rep., U.S. Fish and Wildl. Serv., Sacramento, CA and Jones and Stokes Associates, Inc., Sacramento, CA.

BEER, J. 1943. Food habits of the Blue Grouse. J. Wildl. Manage. 7: 32-44.

BEHLE, W. H. 1942. Distribution and variation of the Horned Larks of western North America. Univ. Calif. Publ. Zool. 46: 205-316.

BEHLE, W. H. 1943. Birds of the Pine Valley Mountain Region, southwestern Utah. Univ. of Utah Bull. 34, Biol. Ser. 7.

BEHLE, W. H. 1950. Clines in the yellow-throats of western North America. Condor 52: 193-219.

BEHLE, W. H. 1951. A new race of the Black-capped Chickadee from the Rocky Mountain region. Auk 68: 75-79.

BEHLE, W. H. 1956. A systematic review of the Mountain Chickadee. Condor 58: 51-70.

BEHLE, W. H. 1963. Avifaunistic analysis of the Great Basin Region on North America. Proc. XIIIth Internatl. Ornithol. Congr. 2: 1168-1181.

BEHLE, W. H. 1968. A new race of the Purple Martin from Utah. Condor 70: 166-169.

BEHLE, W. H. 1985. Utah birds: geographic distribution and systematics. Utah Mus. Nat. Hist., Occas. Publ. 5.

BEHLE, W. H., AND W. A. GOATES. 1957. Breeding biology of the California Gull. Condor 59: 235-246.

BEHLE, W., AND R. SELANDER. 1951. The systematic relationships of the Fox Sparrows (*Passerella iliaca*) of the Wasatch Mountains, Utah, and the Great Basin. J. of the Washington Acad. of Sci. 41: 364.

BEHLE, W. H., E. D. SORENSON, AND C. M. WHITE. 1985. Utah birds: a revised checklist. Utah Mus. Nat. Hist. Occas. Publ. 4: 1-108.

BEHLE, W. H., AND A. M. WOODBURY. 1952. Results of banding California Gulls (*Larus californicus*) at Farmington Bay, Utah. Utah Acad. Proc. 29: 24-29.

BEISSINGER, S. R. 1995. Population trends of the Marbled Murrelet projected from demographic analyses. Pp. 385-394 *in* Ecology and conservation of the Marbled Murrelet (C. J. Ralph, G. L. Hunt, Jr., M. G. Raphael, and J. F. Piatt, eds.). U.S. Dept. Agric., For. Serv. Gen. Tech. Rep. PSW-152, Albany, CA.

BEKOFF, M., S. A. CAUL, AND D. A. CONNER. 1987. Nonrandom nest-site selection in Evening Grosbeaks. Condor 89: 819-829.

BELETSKY, L. D., AND G. H. ORIANS. 1991. Effects of breeding experience and familiarity on site fidelity in female Red-winged Blackbirds. Ecology 72: 787-796.

BELL, D. A. 1996. Genetic differentiation, geographic variation and the hybridization in gulls of the *Larus glaucescens-occidentalis* complex. Condor 98: 527-546.

BELL, D. A. 1997. Hybridization and reproductive performance in gulls of the *Larus glaucescens-occidentalis* complex. Condor 99: 585-594.

BELL, R. K. 1962. Barn Swallow banding: some results and conclusions. East. Bird Banding News 25: 111-116.

BELLROSE, F. C. 1976. Ducks, geese, and swans of North America. Stackpole Books, Harrisburg, PA.

BELLROSE, F. C. 1980. Ducks, geese and swan of North America. Third edition. Stackpole Books, Harrisburg, PA.

BENDIRE, C. E. 1875/76. Notes on seventy-nine of the birds observed in the neighborhood of Camp Harney, Oregon. Proc. Boston Soc. Nat. Hist. 18: 153-168.

BENDIRE, C. E. 1877. Notes on some of the birds found in southeastern Oregon, particularly in the vicinity of Camp Harney, from November 1874 to January 1877. Proc. Bos. Soc. Nat. Hist. 19: 109-149.

BENDIRE, C. E. 1883. Description of the nest and young of the Pygmy Owl. Bull. Nuttall Ornithol. Club 8: 242.

BENDIRE, C. E. 1888. Notes on the habits, nest and eggs of the genus *Sphyrapicus* Baird. Auk 5: 225-240.

BENDIRE, C. E. 1892. Life histories of North American birds. U.S. Natl. Mus. Spec. Bull. 1.

BENDIRE, C. E. 1895. Life histories of North American Birds. U.S. Natl. Mus. Spec. Bull. 3.

BENEDICT, N. G., S. J. OYLER-MCCANCE, S. E. TAYLOR, C. E. BRAUN, AND T. W. QUINN. Unpubl. ms. Evaluation of the eastern (*Centrocercus urophasianus urophasianus*) and western (*C. u. phaios*) subspecies of Sage Grouse using mitochondrial control-region sequence data.

BENKMAN, C. W. 1988a. Flock size, food dispersion, and the feeding behavior of crossbills. Behav. Ecol. Sociobiol. 23: 167-175.

BENKMAN, C. W. 1988b. Seed handling ability, bill structure, and the cost of specialization for crossbills. Auk 105: 715-719.

BENKMAN, C. W. 1989. On the evolution and ecology of island populations of crossbills. Evolution 43: 1324-1330.

BENKMAN, C. W. 1992. White-winged Crossbill (*Loxia leucoptera*). *In* The birds of North America, No. 27 (A. Poole and F. Gill, eds.). Acad. of Nat. Sci., Philadelphia, and Am. Ornithol. Union, Washington, D.C.

BENKMAN, C. W. 1993a. Adaptation to single resources and the evolution of crossbill (*Loxia*) diversity. Ecol. Monogr. 63: 305-325.

BENKMAN, C. W. 1993b. Logging, conifers, and the conservation of crossbills. Conserv. Biol. 7: 473-479.

BENT, A. C. 1919. Life histories of North American diving birds. U.S. Natl. Mus. Bull. 107. (Reprinted in 1963 by Dover Publ., New York).

BENT, A. C. 1921. Life histories of North American gulls and terns. U.S. Natl. Mus. Bull. 113. (Reprinted in 1963 by Dover Publ., New York).

BENT, A. C. 1922. Life histories of North American petrels and pelicans and their allies. U.S. Natl. Mus. Bull. No. 121. (Reprinted in 1964 by Dover Publ., New York).

BENT, A. C. 1923. Life histories of North American wildfowl, Part I. U.S. Natl. Mus. Bull. 126. (Reprinted in 1962 by Dover Publ., New York).

BENT, A. C. 1925. Life histories of North American wildfowl, Part II. Order Anseres. U.S. Natl. Mus. Bull. 130. (Reprinted in 1962 by Dover Publ., New York).

BENT, A. C. 1926. Life Histories of North American marsh birds. U.S. Natl. Mus. Bull. 135. (Reprinted in 1963 by Dover Publ., New York).

BENT, A. C. 1927. Life histories of North American shore birds, Part I. U.S. Natl. Mus. Bull. 142. (Reprinted in 1962 by Dover Publ., New York).

BENT, A. C. 1929. Life histories of North American shore birds, Part II. U.S. Natl. Mus. Bull 146. (Reprinted in 1962 by Dover Publ., New York).

BENT, A. C. 1932. Life histories of North American gallinaceous birds. U.S. Natl. Mus. Bull. 162. (Reprinted in 1963 by Dover Publ., New York).

BENT, A. C. 1937. Life histories of North American birds of prey, Part I. U.S. Natl. Mus. Bull. 167. (Reprinted in 1961 by Dover Publ., New York).

BENT, A. C. 1938. Life histories of North American birds of prey, Part II. U.S. Natl. Mus. Bull. 170. (Reprinted in 1961 by Dover Publ., New York).

BENT, A. C. 1939. Life histories of North American woodpeckers. U.S. Natl. Mus. Bull. 174. (Reprinted in 1964 by Dover Publ., New York).

BENT, A. C. 1940. Life histories of North American cuckoos, goatsuckers, hummingbirds, and their allies. U.S. Natl. Mus. Bull. 176 (Reprinted in 1964 by Dover Publ., New York).

BENT, A. C. 1942. Life histories of North American flycatchers, larks, swallows and their allies. U.S. Natl. Mus. Bull. 179. (Reprinted in 1963 by Dover Publ., New York).

BENT, A. C. 1946. Life histories of North American jays, crows and titmice, Part II. U.S. Natl. Mus. Bull. 191. (Reprinted in 1964 by Dover Publ., New York).

BENT, A. C. 1948. Life histories of North American nuthatches, wrens, thrashers, and their allies. U.S. Natl. Mus. Bull. 195. (Reprinted in 1964 by Dover Publ., New York).

BENT, A. C. 1949. Life Histories of North American thrushes, kinglets, and their allies. U.S. Natl. Mus. Bull. 196. (Reprinted in 1964 by Dover Publ., New York).

BENT, A. C. 1950. Life Histories of North American wagtails, shrikes, vireos, and their allies. U.S. Natl. Mus. Bull. 197. (Reprinted in 1965 by Dover Publ., New York).

BENT, A. C. 1953. Life histories of North American wood warblers. U.S. Natl. Mus. Bull. 203. (Reprinted in 1963 by Dover Publ., New York)

BENT, A. C. 1958. Life histories of North American blackbirds, orioles, tanagers, and their allies. U.S. Natl. Mus. Bull. 211. (Reprinted in 1965 by Dover Publ., New York).

BENT, A. C. 1960. Life histories of North American birds. Land birds (Vol. II). Harper & Brothers, Publ., New York.

BENT, A. C. 1968. Life histories of North American cardinals, grosbeaks, buntings, towhees, finches, sparrows, and allies. U.S. Natl. Mus. Bull. 237. (Reprinted in 1968 by Dover Publ., New York).

BERGER, A. J. 1968. Clutch size, incubation period, and nesting period of the American Goldfinch. Auk 85: 494-498.

BERGIN, T. M. 1997. Nest reuse by Western Kingbirds. Wilson Bull. 109: 735-737.

BERGMAN, R. D., P. SWAIN, AND M. W. WELLER. 1970. A comparative study of nesting Forster's and Black terns. Wilson Bull. 82: 435-444.

BERMINGHAM, E., S. ROHWER, S. FREEMAN, AND C. WOOD. 1992. Vicariance biogeography in the Pleistocene and speciation in North American wood warblers: A test of Mengel's model. Proc. Natl. Acad. Sci. 89: 6624-6628.

BERRY, M. E., C. E. BOCK, AND S. L. HAIRE. 1998. Abundance of diurnal raptors on open space grasslands in an urbanized landscape. Condor 100: 601-608.

BERTRAM, D. F., G. W. KAISER, AND R. C. YDENBERG. 1991. Patterns in the provisioning and growth of nestling Rhinoceros Auklets. Auk 108: 842-845.

BERTRAND, G. A., AND J. M. SCOTT. 1973a. American Redstart breeding in southwestern Oregon. Murrelet 54: 24.

BERTRAND, G. A., AND J. M. SCOTT. 1973b. Checklist of the birds of Oregon. Oreg. State Univ. Book Stores, Inc.

BESSER, J. F., J. W. DeGRAZIO, J. L. GUARINO, D. F. MOTT, D. L. OTIS, B. R. BESSER, AND C. E. KNITTLE. 1984. Decline in breeding Red-winged Blackbirds in the Dakotas 1965-1981. J. Field Ornithol. 55: 435-443.

BEST, L. B., AND K. L. PETERSON. 1985. Seasonal changes in detectability of Sage and Brewer's sparrows. Condor 87: 556-558.

BETTINGER, K. 1996. Bird communities in 5- to 34-year old managed Douglas-fir stands on the Willamette National Forest, Oregon Cascades. M.S. thesis, Oreg. State Univ., Corvallis.

BILDFELL, R. J., E. K. ELTZROTH, AND J. G. SONGER. 2001. Enteritis as a cause of mortality in the Western Bluebird (*Sialia mexicana*). Avian Diseases 45: 760-763.

BILDSTEIN, K. L., AND K. MEYER. 2000. Sharp-shinned Hawk (*Accipiter striatus*). *In* The birds of North America, No. 482 (A. Poole and F. Gill, eds.). The Birds of N. Am., Inc., Philadelphia, PA.

BIRKHEAD, T. R. 1977. Adaptive significance of the nestling period of guillemots (*Uria aalge*). Ibis 119: 544-49.

BIRKHEAD, T. R. 1978. Attendance patterns of guillemots (*Uria aalge*) at breeding colonies at Skomer Island. Ibis 120: 219-29.

BIRKHEAD, T. R. 1991. The magpies: the ecology and behavior of Black-billed and Yellow-billed magpies. Academic Press, (T&AD Poyser) London.

BIRKHEAD, T. R., AND P. J. HUDSON. 1977. Population parameters for the Common Guillemot (*Uria aalge*). Ornis Scand. 8: 145-154.

BISHOP, L. B. 1910. Two new subspecies of North American birds. Auk 27: 59-61.

BISHOP, M. A., AND N. WARNOCK. 1998. Migration of Western Sandpipers: links between their stopover areas and breeding grounds. Wilson Bull. 110: 457-462.

BLACK, C. C. 1998. 1997 Nesting box report. Sialia 20: 88-93, 101.

BLACKBURN, K. 1987. A bird in the bush. Sialia 9: 61-62.

BLAKE, E. R. 1968. Icteridae. Pp. 138-202 *in* A check-list of birds of the world, Vol. 14 (R. A. Paynter, Jr., ed.). Mus. Comp. Zool., Cambridge, MA.

BLAKE, E. R. 1977. Manual of neotropical birds, vol. 1. Univ. of Chicago Press, Chicago.

BLAKELY, K. L., J. A. CRAWFORD, R. M. OATES, AND K. M. KILBRIDE. 1988. Invertebrate matter in the diet of California Quail in western Oregon. Murrelet 69: 75-78.

BLANCHAN, N. 1904. Bird Neighbors. The Country Life Press.

BLANCHARD, B. D. 1941. The White-crowned Sparrows (*Zonotrichia leucophrys*) of the Pacific seaboard: environment and annual cycle. Univ. Calif. Publ. Zool. 46: 1-178.

BLITHE, J. C., AND C. P. DILLINGHAM. 1997. Rogue River Ospreys. Oreg. Birds 23: 89-101.

BLOOM, P. H. 1980. The status of the Swainson's Hawk in California, 1979. California Dept. Fish and Game Fed. Aid in Wildl. Restoration Project W-54-R-12.

BLOOM, P. H. 1985. Raptor movements in California. Proc. Hawk Migration Conf. 4: 313-323.

BLOOM, P. H. 1994. The biology and current status of the Long-eared Owl in coastal southern California. Bull. S. Calif. Sci. 93: 1-12.

BLOOM, P. H., M. D. MCCRARY, AND M. J. GIBSON. 1993. Red-shouldered Hawk home-range and habitat use in southern California. J. Wildl. Manage. 57: 258-265.

BLUS, L. J., B. A. RATTNER, M. J. MELANCON, AND C. J. HENNY. 1997. Reproduction of Black-crowned Night-Herons related to predation and contaminants in Oregon and Washington, U.S.A. Colonial Waterbirds 20: 185-197.

BOAG, D. A., AND M. A. SCHROEDER. 1992. Spruce Grouse (*Falcipennis canadensis*). *In* The birds of North

America, No. 5 (A. Poole, P. Stettenheim, and F. Gill, eds.). Acad. of Nat. Sci., Philadelphia, and Am. Ornithol. Union, Washington, D.C.

Bock, C. E. 1970. The ecology and behavior of the Lewis' woodpecker (*Asyndesmus lewis*). Univ. Calif. Publ. Zool. 92.

Bock, C. E., and J. H. Bock. 1974. On the geographical ecology and evolution of the three-toed woodpeckers, *Picoides tridactylus* and *P. arcticus*. Am. Midl. Nat. 92: 397–405.

Bock, C. E., and D. C. Fleck. 1995. Avian response to nest box addition in two forests of the Colorado Front Range. J. Field Ornithol. 66: 352-362.

Bock, C. E., and L. W. Lepthien. 1976. Synchronous eruptions of boreal seed-eating birds. Am. Nat. 110: 559-571.

Bock, C. E., and J. F. Lynch. 1970. Breeding bird populations of burned and unburned conifer forest in the Sierra Nevada. Condor 72: 182-189.

Bock, C. E., and B. Webb. 1984. Birds as grazing indicator species in southeastern Arizona. J. Wildl. Manage. 48: 1045-1049.

Bock, W. J., R. P. Balda, and S. B. Vander Wall. 1973. Morphology of the sublingual pouch and tongue musculature in Clark's Nutcracker. Auk 90: 491-519.

Boe, J. S. 1992. Wetland selection by Eared Grebes (*Podiceps nigricollis*). Can. Field-Nat. 106: 480-488.

Boekelheide, R. J., and D. G. Ainley. 1989. Age, resource availability, and breeding effort in Brandt's Cormorant. Auk 106: 389-401.

Boekelheide, R. J., D. G. Ainley, H. R. Huber, and L. T. James. 1990a. Pelagic Cormorant and Double-crested Cormorant, Pp. 195-217 *in* Seabirds of the Farallon Islands (D. G. Ainley and R. J. Boekelheide, eds.). Stanford Univ. Press, Stanford, CA.

Boekelheide, R. J., D. G. Ainley, S. H. Morrell, H. R. Huber, and L. T. James. 1990b. Common Murre, Pp. 245-275 *in* Seabirds of the Farallon Islands (D. G. Ainley and. R. J. Boekelheide, eds.). Stanford Univ. Press, Stanford, CA.

Boekelheide, R. J., D. G. Ainley, S. H. Morrell, and T. J. Lewis. 1990c. Brandt's Cormorant, Pp. 164-194 *in* Seabirds of the Farallon Islands (D. G. Ainley and R. J. Boekelheide, eds.). Stanford Univ. Press, Stanford, CA.

Boersma, P. D., and M. J. Groom. 1993. Conservation of storm-petrels in the North Pacific. *In* The status, ecology, and conservation of marine birds in the North Pacific (K. Vermeer, K. T. Briggs, K. H. Morgan, and D. Siegel-Causey, eds.). Can. Wildl. Serv. Spec. Publ., Ottawa.

Boersma, P. D., and M. C. Silva. 2001. Fork-tailed Storm Petrel (*Oceanodroma furcata*). *In* The birds of North America, No. 569 (A. Poole and F. Gill, eds.). The Birds of N. Am., Inc., Philadelphia, PA.

Boersma, P. D., and N. T. Wheelwright. 1979. Egg neglect in the Procellariiformes: reproductive adaptations in the Fork-tailed Storm-Petrel. Condor 81: 157-165.

Boersma, P. D., N. T. Wheelwright, M. K. Nerini, and E. S. Wheelwright. 1980. The breeding biology of the Fork-tailed Storm-Petrel *Oceanodroma furcata*. Auk.87: 268-282.

Boettcher, R., S. M. Haig, and W. C. Bridges, Jr. 1995. Habitat-related factors affecting the distribution of nonbreeding American Avocets in coastal South Carolina. Condor 97: 68-81.

Boggs, B., and E. Boggs. 1961. Northern Pacific coast region. Audubon Field Notes 15: 487.

Boggs, B., and E. Boggs. 1962. Northern Pacific coast region. Audubon Field Notes 16: 66-69.

Boggs, B., and E. Boggs. 1963a. The fall migration of 1962. Audubon Field Notes 17: 59.

Boggs, B., and E. Boggs. 1963b. Northern Pacific coast region. Audubon Field Notes 17: 351-353.

Boggs, B., and E. Boggs. 1963c. Northern Pacific coast region. Audubon Field Notes 17: 427-429.

Boggs, B., and E. Boggs. 1963d. Northern Pacific coast region. Audubon Field Notes 17: 484.

Boggs, B., and E. Boggs. 1964. Northern Pacific coast region. Audubon Field Notes 18: 480.

Bohlman, H. T. 1903. Nest habits of the Shufeldt Junco. Condor 5: 94-95.

Bohn, C., C. Galen, C. Maser, and J. W. Thomas. 1980. Homesteads – manmade avian habitats in the rangelands of southeastern Oregon. Wildl. Soc. Bull. 8: 332-341.

Boland, J. M. 1988. Ecology of North American shorebirds: latitudinal distributions, community structure, foraging behaviors, and interspecific competition. Ph.D. diss., Univ. of Calif., Los Angeles.

Bollinger, E. K. 1991. Conservation of grassland birds in agricultural areas. Pp. 279-288 *in* Challenges in the conservation of biological resources: a practitioner's guide (D. J. Decker, M. E. Krasny, G. R. Goff, C. R. Smith, and D. W. Gross, eds.). Westview Press, Boulder, CO.

Bond, C. 1987. Oregon's first Lucy's Warbler. Oreg. Birds 13: 292-293.

Bond, G. M. 1963. Geographic variation in the thrush *Hylocichla ustulata*. Proc. U. S. Natl. Mus. 114: 373-387.

Bond, R. M. 1939. Observations on raptorial birds in the lava beds, Tule Lake region of northern California. Condor 41: 54 -61.

Bond, R. M. 1946. The peregrine population of western North America. Condor 48: 101-116.

Boone, D. L. 1985. Breeding biology and early life history of the Tufted Puffin *Fratercula cirrhata*. M.S. thesis, Oreg. State Univ., Corvallis.

Booth, E. S. 1939. Zonal distribution of birds in the Blue Mountain district. Murrelet 20: 14-16.

Booth, E. S. 1952. Ecological distribution of the birds of the Blue Mountains region of southeastern Washington and northeastern Oregon. Walla Walla College Publ. of the Dept. of Biol. Sci. 5: 65-107.

Bordage, D., and J-P. L. Savard. 1995. Black Scoter (*Melanitta nigra*). *In* The birds of North America, No. 177 (A. Poole and F. Gill, eds.). Acad. of Nat. Sci., Philadelphia, and Am. Ornithol. Union, Washington, D.C.

Boula, K. M. 1982. Food habitats and roost sites of Northern Saw-whet Owls in northeastern Oregon. Murrelet 63: 92-93.

Boula, K. M. 1986. Foraging ecology of migrant waterbirds, Lake Abert, Oregon. M.S. thesis, Oreg. State Univ., Corvallis.

Bourne, W. R. P. 1957. Additional notes on the birds of the Cape Verde Islands, with particular reference to *Bulweria mollis* and *Fregata magnificens*. Ibis 99: 182-190.

Bowen, D., and A. Kruse. 1993. Effects of grazing on nesting by Upland Sandpipers in southcentral North Dakota. J. Wildl. Manage. 57: 291-301.

Bowen, R. 1997. Townsend's Solitaire (*Myadestes townsendi*). *In* The birds of North America, No. 269 (A. Poole and F. Gill, eds.). Acad. of Nat. Sci., Philadelphia, and Am. Ornithol. Union, Washington, D.C.

BOWERS, D. E. 1960. Correlation of variation in the Wrentit with environmental gradients. Condor 62: 91-120.

BOWLES, J. H. 1902. The Louisiana Tanager (*Piranga ludoviciana*). Condor 4: 16.

BOWLES, J. H. 1924. Tacoma notes on the spring of 1924. Murrelet 5: 7-8.

BOXALL, P. C. 1981. Ruby-crowned Kinglets (*Regulus calendula*) feeding a Brown-headed Cowbird (*Molothrus ater*). Can. Field-Nat. 95: 99-100.

BOXALL, P. C., AND P. H. R. STEPNEY. 1982. The distribution and status of the Barred Owl in Alberta. Can. Field-Nat. 96: 46-50.

BRAITHWAITE, L. W., AND B. MILLER. 1975. The Mallard and Mallard-Black Duck hybridization. Australian Wildl. Res. 2: 47-61.

BRALY, J. C. 1930. Nesting of the California Pygmy-Owl in Oregon. Condor 32: 304.

BRALY, J. C. 1931. Nesting of the Pinyon Jay in Oregon. Condor 33: 29

BRALY, J. C. 1938. Occurrence of the Marbled Godwit on the coast of Oregon. Condor 40: 88-89.

BRAND, J. 1982. Feeding habits of the Double-Crested Cormorant on three southwest Oregon reservoirs. Oreg. State Univ., Corvallis, and Oreg. Dept. Fish and Wildl., Portland.

BRATZ, R. D. 1950. Avifaunal habitats in the central Coast Mountains of western Oregon. M.S. thesis., Oreg. State Univ., Corvallis.

BRAUN, C. E. 1993. White-tailed Ptarmigan habitat investigations in northeast Oregon. Oreg. Birds 19: 72-73.

BRAUN, C. E. 1994. Band-tailed Pigeon. Pp. 60–74 *in* Migratory shore and upland game bird management in North America (T. C. Tacha and C. E. Braun, eds.). Internatl. Assoc. of Fish and Wildl. Agencies, Washington, D.C.

BRAUN, C. E. 1998. Sage Grouse declines in western North America: what are the problems? Proc. Western Assoc. State Fish and Wildl. Agencies 78: 139-156.

BRAUN C. E., M. F. BAKER, R. L. ENG, J. S. GASHWILER, AND M. H. SCHROEDER. 1976. Conservation committee report on effects of alteration of sagebrush communities on the associated avifauna. Wilson Bull. 88: 165-171.

BRAUN, C. E., D. E. BROWN, J. C. PEDERSON, AND T. P. ZAPATKA. 1975. Results of the Four Corners

cooperative Band-tailed Pigeon investigation. U.S. Fish and Wildl. Serv. Resour. Publ. 126.

BRAUN, C. E., J. H. ENDERSON, C. J. HENNY, H. MENG, AND A. G. NYE, JR. 1977. Falconry: effects on raptor populations and management in North America. Wilson Bull. 89: 360-369.

BRAUN, C. E., R. W. HOFFMAN, AND G. E. ROGERS. 1976. Wintering areas and winter ecology of White-tailed Ptarmigan in Colorado. Colo. Division of Wildl. Spec. Rep. 38.

BRAUN, C. E., AND G. E. ROGERS. 1971. White-tailed Ptarmigan in Colorado. Colo. Game, Fish and Parks Dept. Tech. Publ. 27.

BRAWN, J. D. 1987. Density effects of reproduction of cavity nesters in northern Arizona. Auk 104: 783-787.

BRAWN, J. D. 1988. Selectivity and ecological consequences of cavity nesters using natural versus artificial nests. Auk 105: 789-791.

BRAWN, J. D., AND R. P. BALDA. 1988. Population ecology of cavity nesters in northern Arizona: do nest sites limit breeding densities? Condor 90: 61-71.

BRAZIL, M. A. 1991. The birds of Japan. Smithsonian Inst. Press, Washington, D.C.

BREAULT, A., AND J-P. L. SAVARD. 1991. Status report on the distribution and ecology of Harlequin Ducks in British Columbia. Can. Wildl. Serv. Tech. Rep. Series No.110, Pacific and Yukon Region, Delta.

BRENNAN, L. A. 1989. Comparative use of forest resources by Chestnut-backed and Mountain chickadees in the western Sierra Nevada. Ph.D. diss., Univ. Calif., Berkeley.

BRENNAN, L. A. 1999. Northern Bobwhite (*Colinus virginianus*). *In* The birds of North America, No. 397 (A. Poole and F. Gill, eds.). The Birds of N. Am., Inc., Philadelphia, PA.

BRENNAN, L. A., J. B. BUCHANAN, S. G. HERMAN, AND T. M. JOHNSON. 1985. Interhabitat movements of wintering Dunlins in western Washington. Murrelet 66: 11-16.

BRENNAN, L. A., M. A. FINGER, J. B. BUCHANAN, C. T. SCHICK, AND S. G. HERMAN. 1990. Stomach contents of Dunlins collected in western Washington. Northwest. Nat. 71: 99-102.

BRENNAN, L. A., AND M. L. MORRISON. 1991. Long-term trends of chickadee populations in western North America. Condor 93: 130-137.

BRETT, T. A. 1997. Habitat associations of woodpeckers at multiple scales in managed forest of the southern Oregon Cascades. M.S. thesis, Oreg. State Univ., Corvallis.

BREWER, R., G. A. MCPEEK, AND J. R. J. ADAMS. 1991. The atlas of breeding birds of Michigan. Michigan State Univ. Press, East Lansing.

BREWER, T. M. 1875. Notes on seventy-nine species of birds observed in the neighborhood of Camp Harney, Oregon, compiled from the correspondence of Capt. Charles Bendire, 1st Cavalry U.S.A. Boston Soc. Nat. Hist. Proc. 18: 153-168.

BRIGGS, K. T., K. F. DETTMAN, D. B. LEWIS, AND W. B. TYLER. 1982. Phalarope feeding in relation to autumn upwelling off California. Pp. 51-62 *in* Marine birds: their feeding ecology and commercial fisheries-relationships (D. N. Nettleship, G. A. Sanger, and P. F. Springer, eds.). Can. Wildl. Serv., Ottawa.

BRIGGS, K. T., W. B. TYLER, D. LEWIS, AND D. R. CALSON. 1987. Bird communities at sea off California: 1975-1983. Stud. in Avian Biol. 11: 1-73.

BRIGGS K. T., D. H. VAROUJEAN, W. W. WILLIAMS, R. G. FORD, M. L. BONNELL, AND J. L. CASEY. 1992. Seabirds of the Oregon and Washington OCS (Outer Continental Shelf), 1989-1990. *In:* Oregon and Washington marine mammal and seabird surveys (J. J. Brueggeman, ed.). U.S. Dept. Interior, Minerals Management Service, Pacific OCS Region, OCS Study MMS 91-0093.

BRIGHAM, R. M. 1994. Goatsuckers: just feathered bats? Cordillera 1: 12-17.

BRINKER, D. F., K. E. DUFFY, M. WHALEN, B. D. WATTS, AND K. M. DODGE. 1997. Autumn migration of Northern Saw-whet Owls (*Aegolius acadicus*) in the middle Atlantic and northeastern United States: what observations from 1995 suggest. Pp. 74-89 *in* Biology and conservation of owls of the northern hemisphere (J. R. Duncan, D. H. Johnson, and T. H. Nicholls, eds.). U.S. Dept. Agric., For. Serv. Gen. Tech. Rep. NC-190.

BRISKIE, J. V. 1994. Least Flycatcher (*Empidonax minimus*). *In* The birds of North America, No. 99 (A. Poole and F. Gill, eds.). Acad. of Nat. Sci., Philadelphia, and Am. Ornithol. Union, Washington, D.C.

BRITTINGHAM, M. D., AND S. A. TEMPLE. 1983. Have cowbirds caused forest songbirds to decline? Bioscience 33: 31-35.

Brittingham, M. D., and S. A. Temple. 1988. Impact of supplemental feeding on survival rates of Black-capped Chickadees. Ecology 69: 581-589.

Brittingham, M. D., and S. A. Temple. 1992a. Does winter bird feeding promote dependency? J. Field Ornithol. 63: 190-194.

Brittingham, M. D., and S. A. Temple. 1992b. Use of winter bird feeders by Black-capped Chickadees. J. Wildl. Manage. 56: 103-110.

Brittingham, M. D., and S. A. Temple. 1996. Vegetation around parasitized and non-parasitized nests within deciduous forest. J. Field Ornith. 67: 406-413.

Britton, D. 1980. Identification of Sharp-tailed Sandpipers. British Birds 73: 333-345.

Broadbooks, H. E. 1946a. Anthony Green Heron at Yaquina Bay, Oregon. Murrelet 27: 12.

Broadbooks, H. E. 1946b. Snow Bunting on the Oregon coast. Condor 48: 93.

Broadbooks, H. E. 1961. Ring-billed Gulls nesting on Columbia River islands. Murrelet 42: 7-8.

Brodie, E. D., and C. Maser. 1967. Analysis of Great Horned Owl pellets from Deschutes County, Oregon. Murrelet 48: 11-12.

Brodkorb, P. 1936. Geographical variation in the Pinon Jay. Occas. Papers Mus. Zool. Univ. Michigan, Ann Arbor.

Brodkorb, P. 1940. Some birds from the Bulkley River, British Columbia. Condor 42: 123-124.

Bromley, R. G., and R. L. Jarvis. 1993. Energetics of migration and reproduction of Dusky Canada Geese. Condor 95: 193-210.

Brooks, A. 1923. From field and study. Condor 26: 38.

Brooks, A. 1945. The under-water actions of diving ducks. Auk 62: 517-523.

Brooks, J. P. 1997. Bird-habitat relationships at multiple spatial resolutions in the Oregon Coast Range. M.S. thesis, Oreg. State Univ., Corvallis.

Brown, B. A., J. O. Whitaker, T. W. French, and C. Maser. 1986. Note on food habits of the Screech Owl and the Burrowing Owl of southeastern Oregon. Great Basin Nat. 46: 421-426.

Brown, B. T. 1992. Nesting chronology, density and habitat use of Black-chinned Hummingbirds along the Colorado River, Arizona. J. Field Ornithol. 63: 393-400.

Brown, C. R. 1980. Sleeping behavior of Purple Martins. Condor 82: 170-175.

Brown, C. R. 1984. Laying eggs in a neighbor's nest: benefit and cost of colonial nesting in swallows. Science 244: 518-519.

Brown, C. R. 1986. Cliff Swallow colonies as information centers. Science 234: 83-85.

Brown, C. R. 1988. Social foraging in Cliff Swallows: local enhancement, risk sensitivity, competition and the avoidance of predators. Anim. Behav. 36: 780-792.

Brown, C. R. 1997. Purple Martin (*Progne subis*). *In* The birds of North America, No. 287 (A. Poole and F. Gill, eds.). Acad. of Nat. Sci., Philadelphia, and Am. Ornithol. Union, Washington, D.C.

Brown, C. R., and M. B. Brown. 1987. Group-living in Cliff Swallows as an advantage in avoiding predators. Behav. Ecol. Sociobiol. 21: 97-107.

Brown, C. R., and M. B. Brown. 1988. A new form of reproductive parasitism in Cliff Swallows. Nature 331: 66-68.

Brown, C. R., and M. B. Brown. 1989. Behavioural dynamics of interspecific brood parasitism in colonial Cliff Swallows. Anim. Behav. 37: 777-796.

Brown, C. R., and M. B. Brown. 1995. Cliff Swallow (*Hirundo pyrrhonota*). *In* The birds of North America, No. 149 (A. Poole and F. Gill, eds.). Acad. of Nat. Sci., Philadelphia, and Am. Ornithol. Union, Washington, D.C.

Brown, C. R., and M. B. Brown. 1996. Coloniality in the Cliff Swallow: the effect of group size on social behavior. Univ. of Chicago Press, Chicago.

Brown, C. R., and M. B. Brown. 1999. Barn Swallow (*Hirundo rustica*). *In* The birds of North America, No. 452 (A. Poole and F. Gill, eds.). The Birds of N. Am., Inc., Philadelphia, PA.

Brown, C. R., A. M. Knott, and E. J. Damrose. 1992. Violet-green Swallow (*Tachycineta thalassina*). *In* The birds of North America, No. 14 (A. Poole, P. Stettenheim, and F. Gill, eds.). Acad. of Nat. Sci, Philadelphia, and Am. Ornithol. Union, Washington, D.C.

Brown, E. R., Ed. 1985. Management of wildlife and fish habitats in forests of western Oregon and Washington, U.S. Dept. Agric., For. Serv. R6-F&WL-192-1985, Portland, OR.

Brown, L. 1977. Eagles of the world. Universe Books, New York.

Brown, L., and D. Amadon. 1968. Eagles, hawks, and falcons of the world. 2 Vols. Country Life Books, Hamlyn, Middlesex, U.K.

Brown, P. P, and S. W. Harris. 1988. Foods found in 103 Red-necked Phalaropes. West. Birds 19: 79-80.

Brown, P. W., and L. H. Fredrickson. 1997. White-winged Scoter (*Melanitta fusca*). *In* The birds of North America, No. 274 (A. Poole and F. Gill, eds.). Acad. of Nat. Sci., Philadelphia, and Am. Ornithol. Union, Washington, D.C.

Brown, R. 2000. Thinning, fire and forest restoration: a science-based approach for national forests in the interior northwest. Defenders of Wildlife; Washington, D.C. and Portland, OR.

Brown, R. M. 1960. Black-throated Sparrows in south-central Oregon. Condor 62: 220-221.

Brown, S., J. Crocker, C. Dillingham, T. Mickel, J. Rogers, B. Stotz, and L. Thornburgh. 1996. Birding the southern Oregon coast. The Cape Arago Audubon Soc., Coos Bay, OR.

Browning, M. R. 1966a. Additional records on the birds of southwestern Oregon. Murrelet 47: 76.

Browning, M. R. 1966b. Range additions of several species of birds in southwestern Oregon. Murrelet 47: 50-51.

Browning, M. R. 1971. Second inland specimen of the Ancient Murrelet for Oregon. Murrelet 52: 42.

Browning, M. R. 1973a. Nonbreeding birds observed at Goat Island, Oregon. Murrelet 54: 31-33.

Browning, M. R. 1973b. Bendire's records of Red-shouldered Hawk and Yellow-bellied Sapsucker in Oregon. Murrelet 54: 34-35.

Browning, M. R. 1974. Taxonomic remarks on recently described subspecies of birds that occur in the northwestern United States. Murrelet 55: 32-38.

Browning, M. R. 1975a. The distribution and occurrence of the birds of Jackson County, Oregon and surrounding areas. N. Am. Fauna 70.

Browning, M. R. 1975b. First Oregon specimen of *Icterus galbula galbula*. Auk 92: 162-163.

Browning, M. R. 1976. The status of *Sayornis saya yukonensis* Bishop. Auk 93: 843-846.

Browning, M. R. 1977a. Geographic variation in *Contopus sordidulus* and *C. virens* north of Mexico. Great Basin Nat. 37: 453-456.

Browning, M. R. 1977b. Geographic variation in Dunlins, *Calidris alpina*, of North America. Can. Field-Nat. 91: 391-393.

Browning, M. R. 1977c. Interbreeding members of the *Sphyrapicus varius* group (Aves: picidae) in Oregon. Bull. S. Calif. Sci. 76: 38-41.

Browning, M. R. 1978. An evaluation of the new species and subspecies proposed in Oberholser's Bird Life of Texas. Proc. Biol. Soc. Washington 91: 85-122.

Browning, M. R. 1979a. Type specimens of birds collected in Oregon. Northwest Sci. 53: 132-140.

Browning, M. R. 1979b. A review of geographic variation in continental populations of the Ruby-crowned Kinglet (*Regulus calendula*). Nemouria 21: 1-9.

Browning, M. R. 1990. Taxa of North American birds described from 1957 to 1987. Proc. Biol. Soc. Wash. 103: 432-451.

Browning, M. R. 1991. Taxonomic comments on the Dunlin *Calidris alpina* from northern Alaska and eastern Siberia. Bull. British Ornithol. Club 111: 140-145.

Browning, M. R. 1992a. Geographic variation in *Hirundo pyrrhonota* (Cliff Swallow) from northern North America. West. Birds 23: 21-29.

Browning, M. R. 1992b. A new subspecies of *Chamaea fasciata* (Wrentit) from Oregon (Aves: Timaliinae). Proc. Biol. Soc. Wash. 105: 414-419.

Browning, M. R. 1993. Comments on the taxonomy of *Empidonax traillii* (Willow Flycatcher). West. Birds 24: 241-257.

Browning, M. R. 1994. A taxonomic review of *Dendroica petechia* (Yellow Warbler) (Aves: Parulinae). Proc. Biol. Soc. Wash. 107: 27-51.

Browning, M. R. 1995a. The importance of collecting birds and preserving museum specimens. Oreg. Birds 21: 45.

Browning, M. R. 1995b. Do Downy Woodpeckers migrate? J. Field Ornithol. 66: 12-21.

Browning, M. R. 1997. Taxonomy of *Picoides pubescens* (Downy Woodpecker) from the Pacific Northwest. Pp. 25-33 *in* The era of Allan R. Phillips: a festschrift (R. W. Dickerman, compiler). Horizon Publ., Albuquerque, NM.

Browning, M. R. 2001. A review of birds of the world: a check-list, fifth edition by James F. Clements, 2000 (Ibis Publ. Co., Vista, CA.). Oreg. Birds 23: 98-101.

Browning, M. R. 2002. Taxonomic comments on selected species of birds from the Pacific Northwest. Oreg. Birds 28: 69-82.

Browning, M. R., and R. C. Banks. 1990. The identity of Pennant's "Wapacuthu Owl" and the subspecific name of *Bubo virginianus* from the western Hudson Bay. J. Raptor Res. 24: 80-83.

Browning, M. R., and S. P. Cross. 1994. Third specimen of Nuttall's Woodpecker (*Picoides nuttallii*) in Oregon from Jackson County and comments on earlier records. Oreg. Birds 20: 119-120.

Browning, M. R., and S. P. Cross. 1999. Specimens of birds from Jackson County, Oregon: distribution and taxonomy of selected species. Oreg. Birds 25: 62-71.

Browning, M. R., and W. English. 1967a. Anna's Hummingbird in southwestern Oregon. Condor 69: 89.

Browning, M. R., and W. English. 1967b. Possible Yellow-shafted Flicker in southwestern Oregon. Condor 69: 210.

Browning, M. R., and W. English. 1968. A breeding colony of Cassin's Auklet and possible breeding of the Rhinoceros Auklet on Goat Island, southwestern Oregon. Condor 70: 88.

Browning, M. R., and W. W. English. 1972. Breeding birds of selected coastal islands. Murrelet 53: 1-7.

Bruner, H. 1997. Habitat use and productivity of Harlequin Ducks in the central Cascade Range of Oregon. M.S. thesis, Oreg. State Univ., Corvallis.

Brunton, D. H. 1988. Sexual differences in the time budgets of Killdeer during the breeding season. Anim. Behav. 36: 705-717.

Bryan, T. and E. D. Forsman. 1987. Distribution, abundance, and habitat of Great Gray Owls in southcentral Oregon. Murrelet 68: 45-49.

Bryant, H. C. 1911. The relation of birds to an insect outbreak in northern California during the spring and summer of 1911. Condor 13: 195-208.

Bryant, H. C. 1912. Birds in relation to a grasshopper outbreak in California. Univ. Calif. Publ. Zool 11: 1-20.

Bryant, H. C. 1921. From field and study: California Woodpecker steals eggs of wood pewee. Condor 23: 33.

Buchanan, J. B. 1988a. North American Merlin populations: an analysis using Christmas Bird Count data. Am. Birds 42: 1178-1180.

Buchanan, J. B. 1988b. The effect of kleptoparasitic pressure on hunting behavior and performance of host Merlins. J. Raptor Res. 22: 63-64.

Buchanan, J. B. 1996. A comparison of behavior and success rates of Merlins and Peregrine Falcons when hunting Dunlins in two coastal habitats. J. Raptor Res. 30: 93-98.

Buchanan, J. B. 1999a. Recent changes in the winter distribution and abundance of Rock Sandpipers in North America. West. Birds 30: 193-199.

Buchanan, J. B. 1999b. Shorebirds: plovers, oystercatchers, avocets and stilts, sandpipers, snipes, and phalaropes. *In* Management recommendations for Washington's priority species (E. M. Larsen and N. Nordstrom, eds.). Volume 4: birds. Wash. Dept. Fish and Wildl., Olympia.

Buchanan, J. B. In prep. Flammulated Owl (*Otus flammeolus*). Pp. xxx-xxx *in* The birds of Washington (T. R. Wahl, W. Tweit, and S. G. Mlodinow, eds.). Oreg. State Univ. Press, Corvallis.

Buchanan, J. B., L. A. Brennan, C. T. Schick, M. A. Finger, T. M. Johnson, and S. G. Herman. 1985. Dunlin weight changes in relation to food habits and available prey. J. Field Ornithol. 56: 265-272.

Buchanan, J. B., and J. R. Evenson. 1997. Abundance of shorebirds at Willapa Bay, Washington. West. Birds 28: 158-168.

Buchanan, J. B, C. T. Schick, L. A. Brennan, and S. G. Herman. 1988. Merlin predation on wintering Dunlins: hunting success and Dunlin escape tactics. Wilson Bull. 100: 108-118.

Buck, J. 1999. Changes in productivity and environmental contaminants in Bald Eagles nesting along the lower Columbia River. Final rep., U.S. Fish and Wildl. Serv., Portland, OR.

Buehler, D. A. 2000. Bald Eagle (*Haliaeetus leucocephalus*). *In* The birds of North America, No. 506 (A. Poole and F. Gill, eds.). The Birds of N. Am., Inc., Philadelphia, PA.

Buitron, D. 1983. Extra-pair courtship in Black-billed Magpies. Anim. Behav. 31: 211-220.

BUITRON, D. 1988. Female and male specialization in parental care and its consequences in Black-billed Magpies. Condor 90: 29-39.

BULL, E. L. 1980. Resource partitioning among woodpeckers in northeastern Oregon. Ph.D. diss., Univ. of Idaho, Moscow.

BULL, E. L. 1983. Bird response to beetle-killed lodgepole pine. Murrelet 64: 94-96.

BULL, E. L. 1986. Ecological value of dead trees to cavity nesting birds in northeast Oregon. Oreg. Birds 12: 91-99.

BULL, E. L. 1987. Ecology of the Pileated Woodpecker in northeastern Oregon. J. Wildl. Manage. 51: 472-481.

BULL, E. L. 1991. Summer roosts and roosting behavior of Vaux's Swifts in old-growth forests. Northwest. Nat. 72: 78-82.

BULL, E. L., AND H. A. AKENSON. 1985. Common Barn Owl diet in northeastern Oregon. Murrelet 66: 65-68.

BULL, E. L., AND R. G. ANDERSON. 1978. Notes on Flammulated Owls in northeastern Oregon. Murrelet 59: 26-28.

BULL, E. L., AND R. C. BECKWITH. 1993. Diet and foraging behavior of Vaux's Swifts in northeastern Oregon. Condor 95: 1016-1023.

BULL, E. L., R. C. BECKWITH, AND R. S. HOLTHAUSEN. 1992. Arthropod diet of Pileated Woodpeckers in northeastern Oregon. Northwest. Nat. 73: 42-45.

BULL, E. L., AND A. K. BLUMTON. 1997. Roosting behavior of postfledging Vaux's Swifts in northeastern Oregon. J. Field Ornithol. 68: 302-305.

BULL, E. L., AND C. T. COLLINS. 1993a. Nesting chronology, molt, and ectoparasites of Vaux's Swifts in northeastern Oregon. Avocetta 17: 203-207.

BULL, E. L., AND C. T. COLLINS. 1993b. Vaux's Swift (Chaetura vauxi). In The birds of North America, No. 77 (A. Poole and F. Gill, eds.). Acad. of Nat. Sci., Philadelphia, and Am. Ornithol. Union, Washington, D.C.

BULL, E. L., AND H. D. COOPER. 1991. Vaux's Swift nests in hollow trees. West. Birds 22: 85-91.

BULL, E. L., AND J. R. DUNCAN. 1993. Great Gray Owl (Strix nebulosa). In The birds of North America, No. 41 (A. Poole and F. Gill, eds.). Acad. of Nat. Sci., Philadelphia, and Am. Ornithol. Union, Washington, D.C.

BULL, E. L., AND M. G. HENJUM. 1990. Ecology of the Great Gray Owl. U.S. Dept. Agric., For. Serv. Gen. Tech. Report PNW-GTR-265.

BULL, E. L., M. G. HENJUM, AND R. S. ROHWEDER. 1988a. Home range and dispersal of Great Gray Owls in northeastern Oregon. J. Raptor Res. 22: 101-106.

BULL, E. L., M. G. HENJUM, AND R. S. ROHWEDER. 1988b. Nesting and foraging habitat of Great Gray Owls. J. Raptor Res. 22: 107-115.

BULL, E. L., M. G. HENJUM, AND R. S. ROHWEDER. 1989a. Diet and optimal foraging of Great Gray Owls. J. Wildl. Manage. 53: 42-50.

BULL, E. L., M. G. HENJUM, AND R. S. ROHWEDER. 1989b. Reproduction and mortality of Great Gray Owls in Oregon. Northwest Sci. 63: 38-43.

BULL, E. L., AND J. E. HOHMANN. 1992. The association between Vaux's Swifts and old growth forests in northeastern Oregon. West. Birds 24: 85-91.

BULL, E. L., AND J. H. HOHMANN. 1994. Breeding biology of Northern Goshawks in northeastern Oregon. Stud. in Avian Biol. 16: 103-105.

BULL, E. L., J. E. HOHMANN, AND M. G. HENJUM. 1987. Northern Pygmy-Owl nests in northeastern Oregon. J. Raptor Res. 21: 77-78.

BULL, E. L., AND R. S. HOLTHAUSEN. 1993. Habitat use and management of Pileated Woodpeckers in northeastern Oregon. J. Wildl. Manage. 57: 335-345.

BULL, E. L., R. S. HOLTHAUSEN, AND M. G. HENJUM. 1992. Roost trees used by Pileated Woodpeckers in northeastern Oregon. J. Wildl. Manage. 56: 786-793.

BULL, E. L., AND J. A. JACKSON. 1995. Pileated Woodpecker (Dryocopus pileatus). In The birds of North America, No. 148 (A. Poole and F. Gill, eds.). Acad. of Nat. Sci., Philadelphia, and Am. Ornithol. Union, Washington, D.C.

BULL, E. L., S. R. PETERSON, AND J. W. THOMAS. 1986. Resource partitioning among woodpeckers in northeastern Oregon. U.S. Dept. Agric., For. Serv. Res. Note PNW-444.

BULL, E. L., A. D. TWAMBLY, AND T. M. QUIGLEY. 1980. Perpetuating snags in managed mixed conifer forests of the Blue Mountains, Oregon. Pp. 325-336 in Management of western forests and grasslands for nongame birds (R.M. DeGraff, technical ed.). U.S. Dept. Agric., For. Serv. Gen. Tech. Report INT-86.

BULL, E. L., AND M. J. WISDOM. 1992. Fauna of the Starkey Experimental Forest and Range. U.S. Dept. Agric., For. Serv. Gen. Tech. Report PNW-GTR-291.

BULL, E. L., A. L. WRIGHT, AND M. G. HENJUM. 1989. Nesting and diet of Long-eared Owls in conifer forests, Oregon. Condor 91: 908-912.

BULL, E. L., A. L. WRIGHT, AND M. G. HENJUM. 1990. Nesting habitat of Flammulated Owls in Oregon. J. Raptor Res. 24: 52-55.

BUMP, G., R. DARROW, F. EDMINSTER, AND W. CRISSEY. 1947. The Ruffed Grouse: life history, propagation, management. New York State Cons. Dept., Albany.

BUNN, D. S., A. B. WARBURTON, AND R. D. S. WILSON. 1982. The Barn Owl. Buteo Books, Vermillion, SD.

BURCHAM, J. S. 1904. Notes on the habits of the Water Ouzel (Cinclus mexicanus). Condor 6: 50.

BURGER, A. E. 1997. Behavior and numbers of Marbled Murrelets measured with radar. J. Field Ornithol. 68: 208-223.

BURGER, A. E., J. K. ETZHORN, B. GISBURNE, AND R. PALM. 1998. Influx of Brown Pelicans off southwestern Vancouver Island during the 1997 El Niño. Pacific Seabirds 25: 61-64.

BURGER, A. E., AND D. M. FRY. 1993. Effects of oil pollution on seabirds in the northeastern Pacific. Pp. 254-263 in The status, ecology, and conservation of marine birds in the north Pacific (K. Vermeer, K. T. Briggs, K. H. Morgan, and D. Siegel-Causey, eds.). Can. Wildl. Serv. Spec. Publ., Ottawa.

BURGER, A. E., AND D. W. POWELL. 1990. Diving depths and diet of Cassin's Auklet at Reef Island, British Columbia. Can. J. Zool. 68: 1572-1577.

BURGER, A. E., R. P. WILSON, D. GARNIER, AND M. P. T. WILSON. 1993. Diving depths, diet, and underwater foraging of Rhinoceros Auklets in British Columbia. Can. J. Zool. 71: 2528-40.

BURGER, J. 1973. Competition between American Coots and Franklin's Gulls for nest sites and egg predation by the coots. Wilson Bull. 85: 449-451.

BURGER, J. 1978. Competition between Cattle Egrets and native North American herons, egrets, and ibises. Condor 80: 15-23.

BURGER, J., AND M. GOCHFELD. 1994. Franklin's Gull (Larus pipixcan). In The birds of North America, No. 116 (A. Poole and F. Gill, eds.).

Acad. of Nat. Sci., Philadelphia, and Am. Ornithol. Union, Washington, D.C.

BURGER, J., AND M. HOWE. 1975. Notes on winter feeding behavior and molt in Wilson Phalaropes. Auk 92: 442-451.

BURKETT, E. E. 1995. Marbled Murrelet food habits and prey ecology. Pp. 223-246 in Ecology and conservation of the Marbled Murrelet (C. J. Ralph, G. L. Hunt, Jr., M. G. Raphael, and J. F. Piatt, eds.). U.S. Dept. Agric., For. Serv. Gen. Tech. Rep. PSW-GTR-152.

BURKHARDT, J. W., AND E. W. TISDALE. 1976. Nature and successional status of western juniper vegetation in Idaho. Ecology 57: 264-270.

BURLEIGH, T. D. 1954. Another record for the occurrence of the west Mexican Tropical Kingbird in the state of Washington. Murrelet 35: 49.

BURLEIGH, T. 1957. Unusual early winter records from Oregon. Condor 59: 209.

BURLEIGH, T. D. 1959. Two new subspecies of birds from western North America. Proc. Biol. Soc. Washington 72: 15-18.

BURLEIGH, T. D. 1960a. Geographic variation in the Western Wood-Pewee (Contopus sordidulus). Proc. Biol. Soc. Washington 73: 141-146.

BURLEIGH, T. D. 1960b. Three new subspecies of birds from western North America. Auk 77: 210-215.

BURLEIGH, T. D. 1961. A new subspecies of Downy Woodpecker from the northwest. Murrelet 41: 42-44.

BURLEIGH, T. D. 1963. Geographic variation in the Cedar Waxwing (Bombycilla cedrorum). Proc. Biol. Soc. Wash. 79: 177-180.

BURLEIGH, T. D. 1972. Birds of Idaho. Caxton Press, Caldwell, ID.

BURLEIGH, T. D., AND G. H. LOWERY, JR. 1942. An inland race of Sterna albifrons. Occas. Papers Mus. Zool., Louisiana State Univ. 10: 173-177.

BURNESS, G. P., K. LeFEVRE, AND C. T. COLLINS. 1999. Elegant Tern (Sterna elegans). In The birds of North America, No. 404 (A. Poole and F. Gill, eds.). The Birds of N. Am., Inc., Philadelphia, PA.

BURNHAM, K. P., D. R. ANDERSON, AND G. C. WHITE. 1996. Meta-analysis of vital rates of the Northern Spotted Owl. Pp. 92-101 In Demography of the Northern Spotted Owl (E. D. Forsman, S. DeStefano, M. G. Raphael, and R. J. Gutiérrez, eds.). Stud. in Avian Biol. 17.

BURROUGHS, R. D. 1961. The natural history of the Lewis and Clark expedition. Mich. State Univ. Press, Ann Arbor.

BUTLER, R. G., A. HARFENIST, F. A. LEIGHTON, AND D. B. PEAKALL. 1988. Impact of sublethal oil and emulsion exposure on the reproductive success of Leach's Storm-petrels: short and long term effects. J. Appl. Ecol. 25: 125-143.

BUTLER, R. G., D. B. PEAKALL, F. A. LEIGHTON, J. BORTHWICK, AND R. S. HARMON. 1986. Effects of crude oil exposure on standard metabolic rate of Leach's Storm-Petrel. Condor 88: 248-249.

BUTLER, R. W. 1992. Great Blue Heron (Ardea herodias). In The birds of North America, No. 25 (A. Poole, P. Stettenheim, and F. Gill, eds.). Acad. of Nat. Sci., Philadelphia, and Am. Ornithol. Union, Washington, D.C.

BUTLER, R. W., F. S. DELGADO, H. DE LA CUEVA, V. PULIDO, AND B. K. SANDERCOCK. 1996. Migration routes of the Western Sandpiper. Wilson Bull. 108: 662-672.

BYERS, C., J. CURSON, AND U. OLSSON. 1995. Sparrows and buntings: a guide to the sparrows and buntings of North America and the world. Houghton Mifflin Co., Boston.

CABE, P. R. 1993. European Starling (Sturnus vulgaris). In The birds of North America, No. 48 (A. Poole and F. Gill, eds). Acad. of Nat. Sci., Philadelphia, and Am. Ornithol. Union, Washington, D.C.

CABE, P. R. 1999. Dispersal and population structure in the European Starling. Condor 101: 451-454.

CADE, T. J. 1995. Shrikes as predators. Pp. 1-5 in Shrikes (Laniidae) of the world: biology and conservation (R. Yosef and F. E. Lohrer, eds.). Proceedings of the Western Found. of Vertebr. Zool. 6: 1-343.

CADE, T. J., J. H. ENDERSON, L. F. KIFF, AND C. M. WHITE. 1997. Are there enough good data to justify listing the American Peregrine Falcon? Wildl. Soc. Bull 25: 730-738.

CADE, T. J., J. L. LINCER, C. M. WHITE, D. G. ROSENEAU, AND L. G. SWARTZ. 1971. DDE residues and eggshell changes in Alaskan falcons and hawks. Science 172: 955-957.

CADE, T. J., AND C. P. WOODS. 1997. Changes in distribution and abundance of Loggerhead Shrike. Cons. Biol. 11: 21-31.

CAFFREY, C. 2000. Tool modification and use by an American Crow. Wilson Bull. 112: 283-284.

CAITHAMER, D. F. 2001. Trumpeter Swan population status 2000. Unpubl. rep., U.S. Fish and Wildl. Serv., Office of Migratory Bird Manage., Laurel, MD.

CALDER, W. A. 1993. Rufous Hummingbird (Selasphorus rufus). In The birds of North America, No.53 (A. Poole and F. Gill, eds.). Acad. of Nat. Sci., Philadelphia, and Am. Ornithol. Union, Washington, D.C.

CALDER, W. A., AND L. L. CALDER. 1992. Broad-tailed Hummingbird (Selasphorus platycercus). In The birds of North America, No. 16 (A. Poole and F. Gill, eds.). Acad. of Nat. Sci., Philadelphia, and Am. Ornithol. Union, Washington, D.C.

CALDER, W. A., AND L. L. CALDER. 1994. Calliope Hummingbird (Stellula calliope). In The birds of North America, No. 135 (A. Poole and F. Gill, eds.). Acad. of Nat. Sci., Philadelphia, and Am. Ornithol. Union, Washington, D.C.

CALKINS, J. D., J. C. HAGELIN, AND D. F. LOTT. 1999. California Quail (Callipepla californica). In The birds of North America, No. 473 (A. Poole and F. Gill, eds.). The Birds of N. Am., Inc., Philadelphia, PA.

CAMPBELL, R. W. 1973. Coastal records of the Barred Owl for British Columbia. Murrelet 54: 25.

CAMPBELL, R. W., H. R. CARTER, AND S. G. SEALY. 1979. Nesting of Horned Puffins in British Columbia. Can. Field-Nat. 93: 84-86.

CAMPBELL, R. W., N. K. DAWE, I. McTAGGART-COWAN, J. M. COOPER, G. W. KAISER, AND M. C. E. McNALL. 1990a. The birds of British Columbia, Vol. I: nonpasserines - loons through waterfowl. Univ. of British Columbia Press, Vancouver.

CAMPBELL, R. W., N. K. DAWE, I. McTAGGART-COWAN, J. M. COOPER, G. W. KAISER, AND M. C. E. McNALL. 1990b. The birds of British Columbia, Vol. II: diurnal birds of prey through woodpeckers. Univ. of British Columbia Press, Vancouver.

CAMPBELL, R. W., N. K. DAWE, I. McTAGGART-COWEN, J. M. COOPER, AND G. W. KAISER, C. E. McNALL, AND G. E. J. SMITH. 1997. The birds of British Columbia. Vol. 3: passerines - flycatchers through vireos. Univ. of British Columbia Press, Vancouver.

CAMPBELL, R. W., N. K. DAWE, I. McTAGGART-COWAN, J. M. COOPER, G. W. KAISER, M. C. E. McNALL, AND A. C. STEWART. 2001. The birds of British Columbia, Vol. 4:

passerines - wood-warblers through old world sparrows. Univ. British Columbia Press, Vancouver.

CAMPBELL, R. W., AND P. T. GREGORY. 1976. The Buff-breasted Sandpiper in British Columbia, with notes on its migration in North America. Syesis 9: 123-130.

CANNINGS, R. J. 1987. The breeding biology of the Northern Saw-whet Owl in southern British Columbia. Pp. 193-198 *in* Biology and conservation of northern forest owls (R. W. Nero, R. J. Clark, R. J. Knapton, and R. H. Hamre, eds.). U.S. Dept. Agric., For. Serv. Gen. Tech. Rept. RM-142.

CANNINGS, R. J. 1993. Northern Saw-whet Owl (*Aegolius acadicus*). The birds of North America, No. 42 (A. Poole and F. Gill, eds.). Acad. of Nat. Sci., Philadelphia, and Am. Ornithol. Union, Washington, D.C.

CANNINGS, R. J. 1994. A Flammulated Owl takes vertebrate prey in late fall. Northwest. Nat. 75: 30-31.

CANNINGS, R. J., AND T. ANGELL. 2001. Western Screech-Owl. (*Otus kennicottii*). *In* The birds of North America, No. 597 (A. Poole and F. Gill, eds.). The Birds of N. Am., Inc., Philadelphia, PA.

CANNINGS, R. A., R. J. CANNINGS, AND S. G. CANNINGS. 1987. Birds of the Okanagan Valley, British Columbia. Royal British Columbia Museum, Victoria.

CAPEN, D. E., AND T. J. LEIKER. 1979. DDE residues in blood and other tissues of White-faced Ibis. Environ. Pollut. 19: 163-171.

CARBONERAS, C. 1992a. Family Anatidae (Ducks, Geese, and Swans). Pp. 536-628 *in* Handbook of the birds of the world, Vol. I: ostrich to ducks (J. del Hoyo, A. Elliott, and J. Sargatal, eds.). Lynx Edicions, Barcelona, Spain.

CARBONERAS, C. 1992b. Family Gaviidae (divers). Pp. 162-173 *in* Handbook of the birds of the world, Vol. I: ostrich to ducks (J. del Hoyo, A. Elliott, and J. Sargatal, eds.). Lynx Edicions, Barcelona, Spain.

CAREY, A. B., V. E. CASTELLANO, C. CHAPPELL, R. KUNTZ, R. W. LUNDQUIST, B. G. MARCOT, S. K. NELSON, AND P. SULLIVAN. 1990. Training guide for bird identification in Pacific Northwest Douglas-fir forests. U.S. Dept. Agric., For. Serv. Gen. Tech. Rep. PNW-GTR-260. Portland, OR.

CAREY, A. B., M. M. HARDT, S. P. HORTON, AND B. L. BISWELL. 1991. Spring bird communities in the Oregon Coast Range. Pp. 123-142 *in* Wildlife and vegetation of unmanaged Douglas-fir forests (L. F. Ruggiero, K. B. Aubry, A. B. Carey, and M. H. Huff, tech. coords.). U.S. Dept. Agric., For Serv. Gen. Tech. Rep. PNW-GTR-285. Portland, OR.

CAREY, A. B., S. P. HORTON, AND B. L. BISWELL. 1992. Northern Spotted Owls: influence of prey base and landscape character. Ecol. Monogr. 62: 223-250.

CAREY, C. G., AND L. LIEDBLAD. 2000. Mute Swan control and experimental trumpeter breeding project in urban central Oregon. Pp. 115-117 *in* Proc. and Papers of the Seventeenth Trumpeter Swan Soc. Conf. (R. E. Shea, M. H. Linch, and H. K. Nelson, eds.). The Trumpeter Swan Soc., Maple Plain, MN.

CARLSON, J. 1978. Christmas Bird Count results. Oreg. Birds 4(1): 1-22.

CARLSON, J. 1980. 1979 Oregon Christmas Bird Count results. Oreg. Birds 6: 24-45.

CARLSON, J. 1988. Organizing a pelagic trip. Oreg. Birds 14: 121-127.

CARLSON, J., AND S. GORDON. 1981. 1980 Oregon Christmas Bird Count results. Oreg. Birds 7: 9-37.

CARROLL, J. P. 1993. Gray Partridge (*Perdix perdix*). *In* The birds of North America, No. 58 (A. Poole and F. Gill, eds.). Acad. of Nat. Sci., Philadelphia, and Am. Ornithol. Union, Washington, D.C.

CARSEY, K. S., AND D. F. TOMBACK. 1994. Growth form distribution and genetic relationships in tree clusters of *Pinus flexilis*, a bird-dispersed pine. Oecologia 98: 402-411.

CARTER, H. R., AND R. A. ERICKSON. 1992. Status and conservation of the Marbled Murrelet in California, 1892-1987. Pp. 92-108 *in* Status and conservation of the Marbled Murrelet in North America (H. R. Carter and M. L. Morrison, eds.). Proc. West. Found. Vertebr. Zool. 5.

CARTER, H. R., AND K. A. HOBSON. 1988. Creching behavior of Brandt's Cormorant chicks. Condor 90: 395-400.

CARTER, H. R., K. A. HOBSON, AND S. G. SEALY. 1984. Colony-site selection by Pelagic Cormorants (*Phalacrocorax pelagicus*) in Barklay Sound, British Columbia. Colonial Waterbirds 7: 25-34.

CARTER, H. R., AND K. J. KULETZ. 1995. Mortality of Marbled Murrelets due to oil pollution in North America. Pp. 261-270 *in* Ecology and conservation of the Marbled Murrelet (C. J. Ralph, G. L. Hunt, Jr., M. G. Raphael, and J. F. Piatt, eds.). U.S. Dept. Agric., For. Serv. Gen. Tech. Rept. PSW-GTR-152. Albany, CA.

CARTER, H. R., M. L. C. MCALLISTER, AND M. E. P. ISLEIB. 1995. Mortality of Marbled Murrelets in gill nets in North America. Pp. 271-284 *in* Ecology and conservation of the Marbled Murrelet (C. J. Ralph, G. L. Hunt, Jr., M. G. Raphael, and J. F. Piatt, eds.). U.S. Dept. Agric., For. Serv. Gen. Tech. Rept. PSW-GTR-152. Albany, CA.

CARTER, H. R., G. J. MCCHESNEY, D. L. JAQUES, C. S. STRONG, M. W. PARKER, J. E. TAKEKAWA, D. L. JORY, AND D. L. WHITWORTH. 1992. Breeding seabird populations of California. U.S. Dept. of the Interior, Fish and Wildl. Serv., FWS/OBS.

CARTER, H. R., AND S. G. SEALY. 1986. Year-round use of coastal lakes by Marbled Murrelets. Condor 88: 473-477.

CARTER, H. R., A. L. SOWLS, M. S. RODWAY, U. W. WILSON, R. W. LOWE, G. J. MCCHESNEY, F. GRESS, AND D. W. ANDERSON. 1995. Population size, trends, and conservation problems of the Double-crested Cormorant on the Pacific Coast of North America. Pp. 189-215 *in* The Double-crested Cormorant: biology, conservation and management (D. N. Nettleship and D. C. Duffy, eds.) Colonial Waterbirds 18 (Special Publ. 1).

CARTER, H. R., AND L. B. SPEAR. 1986. Costs of adoption in Western Gulls. Condor 88: 253-256.

CARTER, H. R., AND J. L. STEIN. 1995. Molt and plumages in the annual cycle of the Marbled Murrelet. Pp. 99-109 *in* Ecology and conservation of the Marbled Murrelet (C. J. Ralph, G. L. Hunt, Jr., M. G. Raphael, and J. F. Piatt, eds.). U.S. Dept. Agric., For. Serv. Gen. Tech. Rep. PSW-GTR-152. Albany, CA.

CARTER, H. R., U. W. WILSON, R. W. LOWE, M. S. RODWAY, D. A. MANUWAL, J. E. TAKEKAWA, AND J. L. LEE. 2001. Population trends of the Common Murre (*Uria aalge californica*). Pp. 33-132 *in* Biology and Conservation of the Common Murre in California, Oregon, Washington and British Columbia, Vol. 1 (D. A. Manuwal, H. R. Carter, T. S. Zimmerman, and D. L. Orthmeyer, eds.). U.S. Geol. Survey, Info. and Tech. Rep. USGS/BRD/ITR 2000-0012, Washington D.C.

CASTELEIN, K. A., D. J. LAUTEN, K. J. POPPER, D. C. BAILEY, AND M. A. STERN. 2000. The distribution and reproductive success of the Western Snowy Plover along the Oregon Coast – 2000. Unpubl. rep. to Oreg. Dept. Fish and Wildl., Coos Bay Dist. BLM, Oreg. Dunes Nat. Recreation Area, and U.S. Fish and Wildl. Serv., submitted by The Oregon Natural Heritage Program, Portland, OR.

CASTELEIN, K. A., D. J. LAUTEN, L. N. RENAN, S. R. PIXLEY, AND M. A. STERN. 2001. The distribution and reproductive success of the Western Snowy Plover along the Oregon Coast – 2001. Unpubl. rep. to Coos Bay Dist. BLM, Oreg. Dunes Nat. Recreation Area, and U.S. Fish and Wildl. Serv., Oreg. Dept. Fish and Wildl., and to Oreg. Dept. Parks and Recreation, submitted by The Oregon Natural Heritage Program and The Nature Conservancy, Portland, OR.

CHAMBERS, C. L. 1996. Response of terrestrial vertebrates to three silvicultural treatments in the central Oregon Coast Range. Ph.D. diss., Oreg. State Univ., Corvallis.

CHAMBERS, C. L., AND W. C. McCOMB. 1997. Effects of silvicultural treatments on wintering bird communities in the Oregon Coast Range. Northwest Sci. 71: 298-304.

CHAMBERS, C. L., T. CARRIGAN, T. E. SABIN, J. TAPPEINER, AND W. C. McCOMB. 1997. Use of artificially created Douglas-fir snags by cavity-nesting birds. West. J. Appl. Forestry 12: 93-97.

CHAMBERS, C. L., W. C. McCOMB, AND J. C. TAPPEINER II. 1999. Breeding bird response to three silvicultural treatments in the Oregon Coast Range. Ecol. Appl. 9: 171-185.

CHAMBERS, R. E., AND W. M. SHARP. 1958. Movement and dispersal within a population of Ruffed Grouse. J. Wildl. Manage. 22: 231-239.

CHANTLER, P., AND G. DRIESSENS. 1995. Swifts. Pica Press, East Sussex, UK.

CHAPIN, E .A. 1925. Food habits of the vireos. U.S. Dept. Agric. Bull. 1355.

CHAPMAN, J. A., C. J. HENNY, AND H. M. WIGHT. 1969. The status, population dynamics and harvest of the Dusky Canada Goose. Wildl. Monogr. 18.

CHAPPELL, C. C., AND T. A. WILLIAMSON. 1984. First documented breeding of the White-breasted Nuthatch in western Washington. Murrelet 65: 51-52.

CHILTON, G., M. C. BAKER, C. D. BARRENTINE, AND M. A. CUNNINGHAM. 1995. White-crowned Sparrow (*Zonotrichia leucophrys*). *In* The birds of North America, No. 183 (A. Poole and F. Gill, eds.). Acad. of Nat. Sci., Philadelphia, and Am. Ornithol. Union, Washington, D.C.

CHILTON, G., AND S. G. SEALY. 1987. Species role in mixed species flocks of seabirds. J. Field Ornithol. 58: 456-463.

CHOATE, E. A. 1985. The dictionary of American bird names, revised edition. The Harvard Common Press. Boston, MA.

CHRISTENSEN, G. C. 1970. The Chukar partridge: its introduction, life history, and management. Nev. Dept. Fish and Game Biol. Bull. 4. Reno.

CHRISTENSEN, G. C. 1996. Chukar (*Alectoris chukar*). *In* The birds of North America, No. 258 (A. Poole and F. Gill, eds.). Acad. of Nat. Sci., Philadelphia, and Am. Ornithol. Union, Washington, D.C.

CHRISTMAS BIRD COUNT (CBC). 1982. National Audubon So. URL = http://birdsource.tc.cornell.edu/cbcdata

CHRISTMAS BIRD COUNT DATA. Available from The National Audubon Society at URL = http://www.audubon.org/bird/cbc/index.html Accessed 20 Sep 2002.

CIARANCA, M. A., C. C. ALLIN, AND G. S. JONES. 1997. Mute Swan (*Cygnus olor*). *In* The birds of North America, No. 273 (A. Poole and F. Gill, eds.). Acad. of Nat. Sci., Philadelphia, and Am. Ornithol. Union, Washington, D.C.

CICERO, C. 1996. Sibling species of titmice in the *Parus inornatus* complex (Aves: Paridae). Univ. Calif. Publ. Zool. 128: 1-217.

CICERO, C. 1997. Boggy meadows, livestock grazing, and interspecific interactions: influences on the insular distribution of montane Lincoln's Sparrows (*Melospiza lincolnii alticola*). Great Basin Nat. 57: 104-115.

CICERO, C. 2000. Oak Titmouse (*Baeolophus inornatus*) and Juniper Titmouse (*Baeolophus ridgwayi*). *In* The birds of North America, No. 485 (A. Poole and F. Gill, eds.). The Birds of N. Am., Inc., Philadelphia, PA.

CIMPRICH, D. A., F. R. MOORE, AND M. P. GUILFOYLE. 2000. Red-eyed Vireo (*Vireo olivaceus*). *In* The birds of North America, No. 527 (A. Poole and F. Gill, eds). The Birds of N. Am., Inc., Philadelphia, PA.

CLAPP, R. B., M. K. KLIMKIEWICZ, AND A. G. FUTCHER. 1983. Longevity records of North American birds: Columbidae through Paridae. J. Field Ornithol. 54: 123-137.

CLAPP, R. B., M. K. KLIMKIEWICZ, AND J. H. KENNARD. 1982. Longevity records of North American birds: Gaviidae through Alcidae. J. Field Ornithol. 53: 81-208.

CLAPP, R. B., D. MORGAN-JACOBS, AND R. C. BANKS. 1983. Marine birds of the southeastern United States and Gulf of Mexico, Part. 3: Charadriiformes. U.S. Fish and Wildl. Serv., Biol. Serv., FWS-OBS-83/30. Washington, D. C.

CLEMENT, P., A. HARRIS, AND J. DAVIS. 1993. Finches and sparrows: an identification guide. Princeton Univ. Press, Princeton, NJ.

CLEMENTS, J. F. 2000. Birds of the world: a checklist, 5th ed. Ibis Publ. Co., Vista, CA.

CLINBEARD, D. 1999. The eagle's advocate. URL = http://members. aol.com/CEBLS Accessed 27 May, 2002.

CLOWERS, G. 1996. PGE communal roost study final report. Unpubl. rep., Raven Res. West, Madras, OR.

CLOWERS, G. 1997a. PGE Bald Eagle fall communal roost study, 1997. Unpubl. rep. Raven Res. West, Madras, OR.

CLOWERS, G. 1997b. PGE Bald Eagle food habits study final report, 1997. Unpubl. rep. Raven Res. West, Madras, OR.

COGSWELL, H. L. 1977. Water birds of California. Univ. of Calif Press, Berkeley.

COLE, L. W. 2000. A first Shy Albatross, *Thalassarche cauta*, in California and a critical re-examination of Northern Hemisphere records of the former *Diomedea cauta* complex. N. Am. Birds 54: 124-135.

COLLAR, N. J., M. J. CROSBY, AND A. J. STRATTERSFIELD. 1994. Birds to watch 2: the world list of threatened birds. BirdLife, Cambridge.

COLLINS, C. T., AND R. E. LANDRY. 1977. Artificial nest burrows for Burrowing Owls. N. Am. Bird Bander 2: 151-154.

COLLINS, C. T., W. A. SCHEW, AND E. BURKETT. 1991. Elegant Terns breeding in Orange County, California. Am. Birds 45: 393-395.

COLLIS, K., S. L. ADAMANY, D. D. ROBY, D. P. CRAIG, AND D. E. LYONS. 1999. Avian predation on juvenile salmonids in the lower Columbia

River. 1998 Annual rep. of the Oreg. Coop. Fish and Wildl. Res. Unit, Oreg. State Univ. to Bonneville Power Admin. and U.S. Army Corps of Eng., Portland, OR.

COLLIS, K., D. D. ROBY, D. P. CRAIG, S. L. ADAMANY, J. Y. ADKINS, AND D. E. LYONS. 2002. Colony size and diet composition of piscivorous waterbirds on the lower Columbia River: implications for losses of juvenile salmonids to avian predation. Trans. Am. Fisheries Soc. 131: 537-550.

COLLIS, K., D. D. ROBY, D. P. CRAIG, B. A. RYAN, AND R. D. LEDGERWOOD. 2001. Colonial waterbird predation on juvenile salmonids tagged with passive integrated transponders in the Columbia River estuary: vulnerability of different salmonid species, stocks, and rearing types. Trans. Am. Fisheries Soc. 130: 385-396.

COLLOPY, M. W. 1984. Parental care and feeding ecology of Golden Eagle nestlings. Auk 101: 753-760.

COLLOPY, M. W., AND T. C. EDWARDS. 1989. Territory size, activity budget and role of undulation flight in nesting Golden Eagles. J. Field Ornithol. 60: 43-51.

COLUMBIA BIRD RESEARCH (CBR). Unpubl. data. Columbia River Avian Predation Project, Real Time Research, Bend. URL = www.columbiabirdresearch.org Accessed 20 Sep 2002.

COLWELL, M. A. 2000. A review of territoriality in non-breeding shorebirds (Charadrii). Int. Wader Study Group Bull. 93: 58-66.

COLWELL, M. A., R. H. GERSTENBERG, O. E. WILLIAMS, AND M. G. DODD. 1995. Four Marbled Godwits exceed the North American longevity record for scolopacids. J. Field Ornithol. 66: 181-183.

COLWELL, M. A., AND J. R. JEHL, JR. 1994. Wilson's Phalarope (*Phalaropus tricolor*). *In* The birds of North America, No. 83 (A. Poole and F. Gill, eds.). Acad. of Nat. Sci., Philadelphia, and Am. Ornithol. Union, Washington, D.C.

COLWELL, M. A., AND L. W. ORING. 1988. Breeding biology of Wilson's Phalarope in southcentral Saskatchewan. Wilson Bull. 100: 567-582.

COLWELL, M. A., AND K. D. SUNDEEN. 2000. Shorebird distributions on ocean beaches of northern California. J. Field. Ornithol. 71: 1-15.

COMBELLACK, C. R. B. 1954. A nesting of Violet-green Swallows. Auk 71: 435-442.

COMBS, B. 1981. Oregon Christmas Bird Count record high counts. Oreg Birds 7: 161-168.

CONCANNON, G. 1998. 1988-1998 wildlife studies summary report, Pelton Round Butte Hydroelectric Project, FERC NO. 2030. Portland General Electric Co., Portland, OR.

CONNORS, P. G. 1983. Taxonomy, distribution and evolution of golden-plovers (*Pluvialis dominica* and *Pluvialis fulva*). Auk 100: 607-620.

CONNORS, P. G., B. J. McCAFFEREY, AND J. L. MARON. 1993. Speciation in golden-plovers, *Pluvialis dominica* and *P. fulva*: evidence from the breeding grounds. Auk 110: 9-20.

CONOVER, B. 1943. The races of the Knot (*Calidris canutus*). Condor 45: 226-228.

CONOVER, B. 1944. The races of the Solitary Sandpiper. Auk 61: 537-544.

CONOVER, M. R. 1983. Recent changes in Ring-billed and California Gull populations in the western United States. Wilson Bull. 95: 362-383.

CONOVER, M. R. 1984. Frequency, spatial distribution and nest attendants of supernormal clutches in Ring-billed and California Gulls. Condor 86: 467-471.

CONOVER, M. R., AND G. L. HUNT, JR. 1984. Experimental evidence that female-female pairs in gulls result from a shortage of breeding males. Condor 86: 472-476.

CONTRERAS, A. 1977. Site guide: Coos Bay. SWOC Talk (Oreg. Birds) 3(1): 5-9.

CONTRERAS, A. 1978. Details: Rusty Blackbird. Oreg. Birds 3(6): 31-32.

CONTRERAS, A. 1979a. 1979 coastal birding weekend. Oreg Birds 5(6): 25-31.

CONTRERAS, A. 1979b. 1978 coast birding weekend summary. Oreg. Birds 5(1): 16-17.

CONTRERAS, A. 1979c. Present and historical range of the Veery (*Catharus fuscescens*) in Oregon. Oreg. Birds 6: 62-63.

CONTRERAS, A. 1983. Distribution: Gray Catbird. Oreg. Birds 9: 73-75.

CONTRERAS, A. 1988a. Northern Waterthrush summer range in Oregon. West. Birds 19: 41-42.

CONTRERAS, A. 1988b. A review of the status of the Sharp-tailed Sandpiper in Oregon. Oreg. Birds 14: 383-387.

CONTRERAS, A. 1990. Results of 3 winter bird counts in Oregon in 1988. Oreg. Birds 16: 273-278.

CONTRERAS, A. 1991. Record high totals of individuals on Oregon Christmas Bird Counts. Oreg. Birds 17: 105-108.

CONTRERAS, A. 1992. Winter status of the Sora in the Pacific Northwest. West. Birds 23: 137-142.

CONTRERAS, A. 1993. The Yellow Rail in Oregon. Oreg. Birds 19: 40-44.

CONTRERAS, A. 1995. Oregon's Christmas Bird Count record high counts. Oreg. Birds 21: 108-111.

CONTRERAS, A. 1996a. A pocket guide to Oregon birds. Oreg. Field Ornithol. Sp. Pub. no. 9.

CONTRERAS, A. 1996b. Wampole's 1957-1959 annotated checklist of birds of Coos Bay, Oregon. J. Oreg. Ornithol. 5: 545-557.

CONTRERAS, A. 1997a. Getting the most out of your Christmas Bird Count day. Oreg. Birds 23: 138-141.

CONTRERAS, A. 1997b. Northwest birds in winter. Oreg. State Univ. Press, Corvallis.

CONTRERAS, A. 1998. Birds of Coos County, Oregon: status and distribution. Cape Arago Audubon Soc. and Oreg. Field Ornithol. Spec. Publ. 12, Eugene.

CONTRERAS, A. 1999a. A pocket guide to Oregon birds, 2nd ed. Oreg. Field Ornithol., Spec. Publ. 13, Eugene.

CONTRERAS, A. 1999b. New historic records of Anna's Hummingbird from Oregon. West. Birds 30: 214.

CONTRERAS, A. 2002a. Birds of Lane County, Oregon. Oreg. Field Ornithol. Spec. Pub. 15, Eugene.

CONTRERAS, A. 2002b. Field notes: western Oregon, fall 2001. Oreg. Birds 28: 30-47.

CONTRERAS, A., H. HERLYN, D. DEWITT, AND L. BLOCH. 2001. Oregon's first Eurasian Dotterel. Oreg. Birds 27: 7-9.

CONTRERAS, A., AND R. KINDSCHY. 1996. Birds of Malheur County, Oregon, and the adjacent Snake River islands of Idaho. Oreg. Field Ornithol. Spec. Publ. 8, Eugene.

CONWAY, C. J. 1995. Virginia Rail (*Rallus limicola*). *In* The birds of North America, No. 173 (A. Poole and F. Gill, eds.). Acad. of Nat. Sci., Philadelphia, and Am. Ornithol. Union, Washington, D.C.

CONWAY, C. J., AND T. E. MARTIN. 1993. Habitat suitability for Williamson's Sapsuckers in mixed-conifer forests. J. Wildl. Manage. 57: 322-328.

COOMBS-HAHN, T. 1993. Integration of environmental cues to time reproduction in an opportunistic breeder, the Red Crossbill (*Loxia curvirostra*). Ph.D. diss., Univ. Wash., Seattle.

COOPER, J. 1994. Least Sandpiper (*Calidris minutilla*). *In* The birds of North America, No. 115 (A. Poole and F. Gill, eds.). Acad. of Nat. Sci., Philadelphia, and Am. Ornithol. Union, Washington, D.C.

COOPER, S. J., AND D. L. SWANSON. 1994. Seasonal acclimatization of thermoregulation in the Black-capped Chickadee. Condor 96: 638-646.

COOPEY, R. W. 1938. A census of water bird life on Upper Klamath Lake. M.S. thesis, Oreg. State Univ., Corvallis.

CORKRAN, C. C. 1992. Spring weather can be a killer. Sialia 14: 83-84.

CORKRAN, C. Unpubl. reports and data. N.W. Ecol. Res. Inst., Portland, OR.

CORNELY, J. E. 1982. Waterfowl production at Malheur National Wildlife Refuge, Oregon. Trans. N. Am. Wildl. Conf. 47: 559-571.

CORNELY, J. E., B. H. CAMPBELL, AND R. L. JARVIS. 1985. Productivity, mortality, and population status of Dusky Canada Geese. Trans. N. Am. Wildl. Nat. Resour. Conf. 50: 540-548.

CORNELY, J. E., C. L. FOSTER, M. A. STERN, AND R. S. JOHNSTONE. 1980. Additional record of Ring-necked Duck nesting at Malheur National Wildlife Refuge, Oregon. Murrelet 61: 55-56.

CORNELY, J. E., E. L. MCLAURY, L. D. NAPIER, AND S. P. THOMPSON. 1985. A summary of Trumpeter Swan production on Malheur National Wildlife Refuge, Oregon. Murrelet 66: 50-55.

CORNELY, J. E., M. B. NAUGHTON, M. R. HILLS, AND K. M. RAFTERY. 1998. Distribution of wintering Dusky and Cackling Canada geese in western Oregon and western Washington, 1985-1989. Pp. 221-229 *in* Biology and management of Canada Geese: proceedings of the international Canada Goose symposium (D. H. Rusch, M. D. Samuel, D. D. Humburg, and B. D. Sullivan, eds.). Milwaukee, WI.

CORNELY, J. E., S. P. THOMPSON, C. J. HENNY, AND C. D. LITTLEFIELD. 1993. Nests and eggs of colonial birds nesting in Malheur Lake, Oregon, with notes on DDE. Northwest. Nat. 74: 41-48.

CORTOPASSI, A. J., AND L. R. MEWALDT. 1965. The circumannual distribution of White-crowned Sparrows. Bird-Banding 36: 141-169.

COTTAM, C. 1935. Unusual food habits of California Gulls. Condor 37: 170.

COTTAM, C. 1939. Food habits of North American diving ducks. U.S. Dept. Agric., Tech. Bull. No. 643. Washington, D. C.

COTTAM, C., J. J. LYNCH, AND A. L. NELSON. 1944. Food habits and management of American sea Brant. J. Wildl. Manage. 8: 36-56.

COTTRELL, M. J. 1981. Resource partitioning and reproductive success of three species of hawks (*Buteo* spp.) in an Oregon prairie. M.S. thesis, Oreg. State Univ., Corvallis.

COUCH, A. B. 1966. Feeding ecology of four species of sandpipers in western Washington. Ph.D. diss., Univ. Wash., Seattle.

COULSON, J. C., N. DUNCAN, AND C. THOMAS. 1982. Changes in the breeding biology of the Herring Gull (*Larus argentatus*) induced by reduction in the size and density of the breeding colony. J. Anim.Ecol. 51: 739-756.

COULSON, J. C., AND E. WHITE. 1956. The study of colonies of the kittiwake, *Rissa tridactyla* (L.). Ibis 98: 63-79.

COULTEE, E. L. 1967. Agonistic behavior in the American Goldfinch. Wilson Bull. 79: 89-109.

COULTER, M. C. 1975. Post-breeding movements and mortality in the Western Gull, *Larus occidentalis.* Condor 77: 243-249.

COUPE, M., AND F. COOKE. 1999. Factors affecting the pairing chronology of three species of merganser in southwest British Columbia. Waterbirds 22: 452-458.

COVINGTON, W. W. 2000. Helping western forests heal. Nature 408: 135.

CRABTREE, T. 1983. Distribution: Anna's Hummingbird in eastern Oregon. Oreg. Birds 9: 110-111.

CRABTREE, T. 1987. Oregon's first "White-winged" Junco. Oreg. Birds 13: 296-300.

CRABTREE, T. 1993. Oregon's first Vermilion Flycatcher. Oreg. Birds 19: 31.

CRABTREE, T. 1994a. Fieldnotes: eastern Oregon, summer 1993. Oreg. Birds 20: 30.

CRABTREE, T. 1994b. Fieldnotes: eastern Oregon, winter 1993-94. Oreg. Birds 20: 101-103.

CRABTREE, T. 1995a. Field notes: eastern Oregon, summer 1994. Oreg. Birds 21: 27-29.

CRABTREE, T. 1995b. Fieldnotes: eastern Oregon, winter 1994-95. Oreg. Birds 21: 93-95.

CRABTREE, T. 1996a. Field notes: eastern Oregon, summer 1995. Oreg. Birds 22: 25-27.

CRABTREE, T. 1996b. Fieldnotes: eastern Oregon, winter 1995-1996. Oreg. Birds 22: 89-90.

CRABTREE, T., AND C. MILLER. 1993. Birds of central Oregon. Central Oreg. Audubon Soc. and Oreg. Dept. Fish and Wildl.

CRAIG, R. B. 1978. An analysis of the predatory behavior of the Loggerhead Shrike. Auk 95: 221-234.

CRAIG, T. H., E. H. CRAIG, AND L. R. POWERS. 1985. Food habits of Long-eared Owls (*Asio otus*) at a communal roost site during the nesting season. Auk 102: 193-195.

CRAIG, T. H., AND C. H. TROST. 1979. The biology and nesting density of breeding American Kestrels and Long-eared Owls on the Big Lost River, southeastern Idaho. Wilson Bull. 91: 50-61.

CRAMP, S., ED. 1977. Handbook of the birds of Europe, the Middle East and North Africa, Vol. 1. Oxford Univ. Press, Oxford, U.K.

CRAMP, S., ED. 1985. Handbook of the birds of Europe, the Middle East and North Africa, Vol. 4: the birds of the western Palearctic. Oxford Univ. Press, New York, NY.

CRAMP, S., ED. 1988. Handbook of the birds of Europe, the Middle East and North Africa, Vol. 5. Oxford Univ. Press, Oxford, U.K.

CRAMP, S., AND C. M. PERRINS, EDS. 1994. The birds of the western Palearctic, Vol. 8: crows to finches. Oxford Univ. Press, Oxford.

CRAMP, S., AND K. E. L. SIMMONS, EDS. 1977. Handbook of the birds of Europe, the Middle East and North Africa: the birds of the western Palearctic, Vol. 1. Oxford Univ. Press, Oxford, U.K.

CRAMP, S., AND K. E. L. SIMMONS, EDS. 1983. The birds of the western Palearctic, Vol. 3. Oxford Univ. Press, Oxford.

CRASE, F. T., AND R. W. DEHAVEN. 1977. Food selection of nestling Tricolored Blackbirds. Condor 79: 265-269.

CRASE, F. T., AND R. W. DEHAVEN. 1978. Food selection by five sympatric California blackbird species. Calif. Fish and Game 64: 255-267.

CRAWFORD, J. A. 1987. Incidence of leucism in Blue Grouse from Oregon. Murrelet 68: 27-29.

CRAWFORD, J. A. 1993. Biology and management of California Quail in Oregon. Unpubl. rep., Oreg. Dept. Fish and Wildl. Portland, OR.

CRAWFORD, J. A., AND R. S. LUTZ. 1985. Sage Grouse population trends in Oregon, 1941-1983. Murrelet 66: 69-74.

CRAWFORD, J. A., AND N. SWANSON. 1999. Grouse harvest report, 1998. Unpubl. rep., Oreg. State Univ., Corvallis.

CRAWFORD, J. A., W. V. VAN DYKE, V. COGGINS, AND M. ST. LOUIS. 1986a. Hatching chronology of Blue Grouse in northeastern Oregon. Great Basin Nat. 46: 745-748.

CRAWFORD, J. A., W. V. VAN DYKE, S. M. MEYERS, AND T. F. HAENSLY. 1986b. Fall diet of Blue Grouse in Oregon. Great Basin Nat. 46: 745-748.

CRESCENT RANGER DISTRICT. 1998. Odell Lake Bald Eagle surveys - 1998. Unpubl rep., Crescent Ranger Dist., Deschutes Natl. For., Crescent, OR.

CRISSEY, W. F. 1969. Prairie potholes from a continental viewpoint. Pp. 161-171 in Saskatoon wetlands seminar. Can. Wildl. Serv. Rep. Series 6.

CRISTOL, D. A., AND P. V. SWITZER. 1999. Avian prey-dropping behavior: American Crows and walnuts. Behav. Ecol. 10: 220-226.

CROCKER-BEDFORD, D. C. 1990. Goshawk reproduction and forest management. Wildl. Soc. Bull. 18: 262-269.

CROCOLL, S. T. 1994. Red-shouldered Hawk (*Buteo lineatus*). *In* The birds of North America, No. 107 (A. Poole and F. Gill, eds.). Acad. of Nat. Sci., Philadelphia, and Am. Ornithol. Union, Washington, D.C.

CROMACK, A. S. 1983. A bath for all seasons. Sialia 5: 11-13.

CROSS, S. P., AND J. K. SIMMONS. 1983. Bird populations of the mixed-hardwood forests near Roseburg, Oregon. Oreg. Dept. Fish and Wildl. Nongame Wildl. Prog. Tech. Rep. 82-2-05.

CROSSIN, R. S. 1974. The storm petrels (Hydrobatidae). Pp. 154-203 in Pelagic studies of seabirds in the central and eastern Pacific ocean (W. B. King, ed.). Smithsonian Contrib. Zool. 158.

CROWELL, J. B., AND H. B. NEHLS. 1966a. Northern Pacific Coast region. Audubon Field Notes 20: 449-453.

CROWELL, J. B., AND H. B. NEHLS. 1966b. Northern Pacific Coast region. Audubon Field Notes 20: 539-542.

CROWELL, J. B., AND H. B. NEHLS. 1966c. Northern Pacific Coast region. Audubon Field Notes 20: 591-595.

CROWELL, J. B., AND H. B. NEHLS. 1967a. Northern Pacific Coast region. Audubon Field Notes 21: 71.

CROWELL, J. B., AND H. B. NEHLS. 1967b. Northern Pacific Coast region. Audubon Field Notes 21: 357.

CROWELL, J. B., AND H. B. NEHLS. 1967c. Northern Pacific Coast region. Audubon Field Notes 21: 448-452.

CROWELL, J. B., AND H. B. NEHLS. 1968a. Northern Pacific Coast Region. Audubon Field Notes 22: 471.

CROWELL, J. B., AND H. B. NEHLS. 1968b. Northern Pacific Coast region. Audubon Field Notes 22: 567-571.

CROWELL, J. B., AND H. B. NEHLS. 1968c. Northern Pacific Coast region. Audubon Field Notes 22: 639.

CROWELL, J. B., AND H. B. NEHLS. 1969a. Northern Pacific Coast region. Audubon Field Notes 23: 94-99.

CROWELL, J. B., AND H. B. NEHLS. 1969b. Northern Pacific Coast region. Audubon Field Notes 23: 508-513.

CROWELL, J. B., AND H. B. NEHLS. 1969c. Northern Pacific Coast region. Audubon Field Notes 23: 615-619.

CROWELL, J. B., AND H. B. NEHLS. 1969d. Northern Pacific Coast region. Audubon Field Notes 23: 684-688.

CROWELL, J. B., JR., AND H. B. NEHLS. 1970a. Northern Pacific Coast region. Audubon Field Notes 24: 82-88.

CROWELL, J. B., AND H. B. NEHLS. 1970b. Northern Pacific Coast region. Audubon Field Notes 24: 530-533.

CROWELL, J. B., AND H. B. NEHLS. 1970c. Northern Pacific Coast region. Audubon Field Notes 24: 635-638.

CROWELL, J. B., AND H. B. NEHLS. 1970d. Northern Pacific Coast region. Audubon Field Notes 24: 708-711.

CROWELL, J. B., AND H. B. NEHLS. 1971a. Northern Pacific Coast region. Am. Birds 25: 94-99.

CROWELL, J. B., AND H. B. NEHLS. 1971b. Northern Pacific Coast region. Am. Birds 25: 787-793.

CROWELL, J. B., AND H. B. NEHLS. 1972a. Northern Pacific Coast region. Am. Birds 26: 107-111.

CROWELL, J. B., AND H. B. NEHLS. 1972b. Northern Pacific Coast region. Am. Birds 26: 644-648.

CROWELL, J. B., AND H. B. NEHLS. 1972c. Northern Pacific Coast region. Am. Birds 26: 797-801.

CROWELL, J. B., AND H. B. NEHLS. 1972d. Northern Pacific Coast region. Am. Birds 26: 893-897.

CROWELL, J. B., AND H. B. NEHLS. 1973a. Northern Pacific Coast region. Am. Birds 27: 105-110.

CROWELL, J. B., AND H. B. NEHLS. 1973b. Northern Pacific Coast region. Am. Birds 27: 809-812.

CROWELL, J. B., JR., AND H. B. NEHLS. 1973c. Northern Pacific Coast region. Am. Birds 27: 908-910.

CROWELL, J. B., AND H. B. NEHLS. 1974a. Northern Pacific Coast region. Am. Birds 28: 679-684.

CROWELL, J. B., AND H. B. NEHLS. 1974b. Northern Pacific Coast region. Am. Birds 28: 840-845.

CROWELL, J. B., AND H. B. NEHLS. 1974c. Northern Pacific Coast region. Am. Birds 28: 938-943.

CROWELL, J. B, AND H. B. NEHLS. 1975a. Northern Pacific Coast region. Am. Birds 29: 105-112.

CROWELL, J. B., AND H. B. NEHLS. 1975b. Northern Pacific Coast region. Am. Birds 29: 730-735.

CROWELL, J. B., JR., AND H. B. NEHLS. 1975c. Northern Pacific Coast region. Am. Birds 29: 897-902.

CROWELL, J. B., JR., AND H. B. NEHLS. 1975d. Northern Pacific Coast region. Am. Birds 29: 1020-1025.

CROWELL, J. B., AND H. B. NEHLS. 1976a. Northern Pacific Coast region. Am. Birds 30: 112-117.

CROWELL, J. B., AND H. B. NEHLS. 1976b. Northern Pacific Coast region. Am. Birds 30: 755-760.

CROWELL, J. B., JR., AND H. B. NEHLS. 1976c. Northern Pacific Coast region. Am. Birds 30: 878-882.

CROWELL, J. B., AND H. B. NEHLS. 1976d. Northern Pacific Coast region. Am. Birds 30: 992-996.

CROWELL, J. B., AND H. B. NEHLS. 1977a. Northern Pacific Coast region. Am. Birds 31: 212-216.

CROWELL, J. B., AND H. B. NEHLS. 1977b. Northern Pacific Coast region. Am. Birds 31: 365.

CROWELL, J. B., AND H. B. NEHLS. 1977c. Northern Pacific Coast region. Am. Birds 31: 1037-1041.

CRUICKSHANK, A. D. 1964. Sixty-fourth Christmas Bird Count. Audubon Field Notes 18: 302.

CSADA, R. D., AND R. M. BRIGHAM. 1992. Common Poorwill (*Phalaenoptilus nuttallii*). *In* The birds of North America, No. 32 (A. Poole and F. Gill, eds.). Acad. of Nat. Sci., Philadelphia, and Am. Ornithol. Union, Washington, D.C.

CSUTI, B., A. J. KIMERLING, T. A. O'NEIL, M. M. SHAUGHNESSY, E. P. GAINES, AND M. P. HUSO. 1997. Atlas of Oregon wildlife: distribution, habitat, and natural history. Oreg. State Univ. Press, Corvallis.

CUNNINGHAM, R. 1991. Nesting behavior of the Common Merganser. Loon 63: 188-190.

CURSON, D. R. 1996. Nest predation and brood parasitism of passerine birds in pinyon-juniper woodland in northeast New Mexico. M.S. thesis, Univ. of Wisconsin, Madison.

CURSON, D. R., C. B. GOGUEN, AND N. E. MATTHEWS. 1996. Nest-site reuse in the Western Wood-Pewee. Wilson Bull. 108: 378-379.

CURSON, J., D. QUINN, AND D. BEADLE. 1994. Warblers of the Americas, an identification guide. Houghton Mifflin Co., New York, NY.

CUSHING, J. 1938. The status of the Fox Sparrow of southwestern Oregon. Condor 40: 73-76.

CUSTER, T. W., C. M. BUNCK, AND T. E. KAISER. 1983. Organochlorine residues in Atlantic coast Black-crowned Night-Heron eggs, 1979. Colonial Waterbirds 6: 160-166.

CUSTER, T. W., AND W. E. DAVIS, JR. 1982. Nesting by one-year-old Black-crowned Night Herons on Hope Island, Rhode Island. Auk 99: 784-786.

CUTHBERT, F. J. 1988. Reproductive success and colony-site tenacity in Caspian Terns. Auk 105: 339-344.

CUTHBERT, F. J., AND L. WIRES. 1999. Caspian Tern (*Sterna caspia*). *In* The birds of North America, No. 403 (A. Poole and F. Gill, eds). The Birds of N. Am., Inc., Philadelphia, PA.

CUTRIGHT, P. R. 1969. Lewis and Clark: pioneering naturalists. Univ. of Illinois Press, Urbana, IL.

DAILY, G. C. 1993. Heartwood decay and vertical distribution of Red-naped Sapsucker nest cavities. Wilson Bull. 105: 674-679.

DAILY, G. C., P. R. EHRLICH, AND N. M. HADDAD. 1993. Double keystone bird in a keystone species complex. Proc. Natl. Acad. of Sci. 90(2): 592-594.

DALZELL, P. 1997. The influence of incidental catch and protected species interactions on the management of the Hawaii-based longline fishery. West. Pacific Regional Fishery Manage. Counc., Honolulu, HI.

DARLINGTON, P., JR. 1930. Notes on the senses of vultures. Auk 47: 251-252.

DARK, S. J., R. J. GUTIÉRREZ, AND G. I. GOULD, JR. 1998. The Barred Owl (*Strix varia*) invasion in California. Auk 115: 50-56.

DAU, C. P., AND M. E. HOGAN. 1985. The Black Brant. Pp. 443-447 *in* Audubon wildlife report (R. L. DiSilvestro, ed.). Natl. Audubon Soc., New York.

DAVIDSON, N. C., AND T. PIERSMA. 1992. The migration of knots: conservation needs and implications. Pp. 198-209 *in* The migration of knots (T. Piersma and N. Davidson, eds.). Wader Study Group Bull. 64 (suppl.).

DAVIES, J. 1997. Indigenous wildlife use and management. Chapter 5 *in* Animals for living: indigenous community wildlife management in Australia. Internatl. Inst. for Environ. and Development. London.

DAVIS, C. 1979. A nesting study of the Brown Creeper. Living Bird 17: 237-263.

DAVIS, D. 1979. Morning and evening roosts of Turkey Vultures at Malheur refuge, Oregon. West. Birds 10: 125-130.

DAVIS, D. E., AND M. L. MORRISON. 1987. Changes in cyclic patterns of abundance in four avian species. Am. Birds 41: 1341-1347.

DAVIS, J., G. F. FISLER, AND B. S. DAVIS. 1963. The breeding biology of the Western Flycatcher. Condor 65: 337-382.

DAVIS, J. D. 1951. Distribution and variation of the Brown Towhees. Univ. of California.

DAVIS, J. D. 1957. Comparative foraging behavior of the Spotted and Brown towhees. Auk 74: 129-166.

DAVIS, J. N. 1995. Hutton's Vireo (*Vireo huttoni*). *In* The birds of North America, No. 189 (A. Poole and F. Gill, eds.). Acad. of Nat. Sci., Philadelphia, and Am. Ornithol. Union, Washington, D.C.

DAVIS, W. E., JR. 1986. Effects of old nests on nest-site selection in Black-crowned Night Herons and Snowy Egrets. Wilson Bull. 98: 300-303.

DAVIS, W. E., JR. 1993. Black-crowned Night-Heron (*Nycticorax nycticorax*). *In* The birds of North America, No. 74 (A. Poole and F. Gill, eds.). Acad. of Nat. Sci., Philadelphia, and Am. Ornithol. Union, Washington, D.C.

DAVIS, W. E., JR., AND J. A. KUSHLAN. 1994. Green Heron (*Butorides virescens*). *In* The birds of North America, No. 129 (A. Poole, P. Stettenheim, and F. Gill, eds.). Acad. of Nat. Sci., Philadelphia, and Am. Ornithol. Union, Washington, D.C.

DAWSON, W. 1923. The birds of California, Vol. 2: South Moulton Company, Los Angeles, CA.

DAWSON, W. L. 1908. The bird colonies of the Olympiads. Auk 25: 53-163.

DAWSON, W. R. 1997. Pine Siskin (*Carduelis pinus*). *In* The birds of North America, No. 280 (A. Poole and F. Gill, eds.). Acad. of Nat. Sci., Philadelphia, and Am. Ornithol. Union, Washington, D.C.

DAWSON, W. R., AND C. CAREY. 1976. Seasonal acclimatization to temperature in cardueline finches. I. Insulative and metabolic adjustments. J. Comp. Physiol. 112: 317-333.

DAWSON, W. R., AND R. L. MARSH. 1986. Winter fattening in the American Goldfinch and the possible role of temperature in its regulation. Physiol. Zool. 59: 357-368.

DAY, R. H., I. J. STENHOUSE, AND H. G. GILCHRIST. 2001. Sabine's Gull (*Xema sabini*). *In* The birds of North America, No. 593 (A. Poole and F. Gill, eds.). The Birds of N. Am., Inc., Philadelphia.

DECHANT, J. A., M. L. SONDREAL, D. H. JOHNSON, L. D. IGL, C. M. GOLDADE, A. L. ZIMMERMAN, AND B. R. EULISS. 1999. Effects of management practices on grassland birds: Bobolink. Northern Prairie Wildl. Res. Center, Jamestown, ND.

DEFENDERS OF WILDLIFE, THE NATURE CONSERVANCY, OREGON NATURAL HERITAGE ADVISORY COUNCIL. 1998. Oregon's living landscape. Oregon Biodiversity Project. Defenders of Wildl., Lake Oswego, OR.

DEGANGE, A. 1999. Proposal to remove the Aleutian Canada Goose from the list of endangered and threatened wildlife. Fed. Reg. 64: 42058-42068.

DEGANGE, A. R., R. H. DAY, J. E. TAKEKAWA, AND V. M. MENDENHALL. 1993. Losses of seabirds in gill nets in the North Pacific. Pp. 204-

211 *in* The status, ecology, and conservation of marine birds in the North Pacific (K. Vermeer, K. T. Briggs, K. H. Morgan, and D. Siegel-Causey, eds.). Spec. Publ., Can. Wildl. Serv.

DeGraff, R. M., and J. H. Rappole. 1995. Neotropical migratory birds: natural history, distribution, and population change. Comstock Publ. Assoc., Ithaca, NY.

DeGraaf, R. M., N. G. Tilghman, and S. H. Anderson. 1985. Foraging guilds of North American birds. Environ. Manage. 9: 493-536.

DeJong, M. J. 1996. Northern Rough-winged Swallow (*Stelgidopteryx serripennis*). *In* The birds of North America, No. 234 (A. Poole and F. Gill, eds.). Acad. of Nat. Sci., Philadelphia, and Am. Ornithol. Union, Washington, D.C.

Delacour, J. 1951. The pheasants of the world. Country Life, Ltd., London, and Chas. Scribners' Sons, New York.

Delacour, J. 1954. The waterfowl of the world, Vol 1. Country Life Ltd., London.

Delacour, J. 1959. The waterfowl of the world, Vol 3. Country Life Ltd., London.

Delacour, J., and E. Mayr. 1945. The family Anatidae. Wilson Bull. 57: 3-55.

Delacour, J., and D. Ripley. 1975. Description of a new subspecies of the White-fronted Goose (*Anser albifrons*). Am. Mus. Novitates 2565.

De La Torre, J. 1990. Owls: their life and behavior. Crown Publishers, Inc., New York.

Delevoryas, P. R. 1980. Scarlet and Summer tanager captures, Hart Mountain. Oreg. Birds 6: 118-122.

Del Hoyo, J., A. Elliot, and J. Sargatal, Eds. 1994. Handbook of birds of the world, Vol. 2: New World vultures to guineafowl. Lynx Edicions, Barcelona, Spain.

Del Hoyo, J., A. Elliott, and J. Sargatal, Eds. 1996. Handbook of the birds of the world, Vol. 3: Hoatzin to auks. Lynx Edicions, Barcelona, Spain.

Dellasala, D. A., R. G. Anthony, T. A. Spies, and K. A. Engel. 1998. Management of Bald Eagle communal roosts in fire-adapted mixed-conifer forests. J. Wildl. Manage. 62: 322-333.

Dellasala, D. A., C. L. Thomas, and R. G. Anthony. 1989. Use of domestic sheep carrion by Bald Eagles wintering in the Willamette Valley, Oregon. Northwest Sci. 63: 104-108.

DeLong, A. K. 1993. Relationships between vegetative structure and predation rates of artificial Sage Grouse nests. M.S. thesis, Oreg. State Univ, Corvallis.

DeLong, A. K., J. A. Crawford, and D. C. DeLong, Jr. 1995. Relationships between vegetational structure and predation of artificial Sage Grouse nests. J. Wildl. Manage. 59: 88-92.

Dennis, T. E. 1999. Foraging behavior of sympatric *Picoides* woodpeckers of the Sierra Nevada: the relative importance of competition and habitat structure. Ph.D. diss., Univ. of Virginia, Charlottesville.

Denny, M. 1992. Black Turnstone seen eating millet. Oreg. Birds 18: 74.

Denny, M. 1994a. High bird mortality as a result of painted lady butterfly migration in eastern Oregon, spring 1992. Oreg. Birds 20: 23.

Denny, M. 1994b. Streak-backed Oriole at Malheur NWR, Harney Co., Oregon. Oreg. Birds 20: 41-42.

Denny, M. 1995. Eastern Oregon's Heermann's Gull records. Oreg Birds 21: 112-113.

Denny, M. 1996. Common Poorwill nest behavior near Fields, Harney County, Oregon. Oreg. Birds 21: 15.

Denny, M. 1998a. Bone Creek Canyon, Malheur Co, Oregon. Oreg. Birds 24: 7-9.

Denny, M. 1998b. A day in Jackson Creek Canyon, Malheur Co., Oregon. Oreg. Birds 24: 6.

Denny, M. 1998c. Woolhawk Canyon, Malheur Co. Oregon: Oregon's hidden treasure. Oregon Birds 24: 9.

Denny, M. 2000a. Birding Oregon Canyon, Oregon Canyon Mountains, Malheur County, Oregon. Oreg. Birds 26: 164-165.

Denny, M. 2000b. Gray-headed Junco (*Junco hyemalis caniceps*) found nesting in Oregon Canyon, Malheur Co., Oregon. Oreg. Birds 26: 128-129.

Denton, S. J. 1976. Status of Prairie Falcons breeding in Oregon. M.S. thesis, Oreg. State Univ. Corvallis.

Derksen, D. V., K. S. Bollinger, and D. H. Ward. 1996. Black Brant from Alaska staging and wintering in Japan. Condor 98: 653-657.

Derrickson, K. C., and R. Breitwisch. 1992. Northern Mockingbird (*Mimus polyglottos*). *In* The birds of North America, No. 7 (A. Poole, P. Stettenheim, and F. Gill, eds.). Acad. of Nat. Sci., Philadelphia, and Am. Ornithol. Union, Washington, D.C.

Desimone, S. M. 1997. Occupancy rates and habitat relationships of Northern Goshawks in historic nesting areas in Oregon. M.S. thesis, Oreg. State Univ., Corvallis.

Desante, D. F., and T. L. George. 1994. Population trends in the landbirds of western North America. Pp. 173-190 *in* A century of avifaunal change in western North America (J. R. Jehl, Jr., and N. K. Johnson, eds.). Stud. in Avian Biol. 15: 173-190.

Des Lauriers, J. R., and B. H. Brattstrom. 1965. Cooperative feeding behavior in Red-breasted Mergansers. Auk 82: 639.

DeSmet, K. D. 1987. Organochlorines, predators, and reproductive success of the Red-necked Grebe in southern Manitoba. Condor 89: 460-467.

Desrochers, A., and S. J. Hannon. 1989. Site-related dominance and spacing among winter flocks of Black-capped Chickadees. Condor 91: 317-323.

DeStafano, S., S. K. Dow, S. M. Desimone, and E. C. Meslow. 1994. Density and productivity of Northern Goshawks: implications for monitoring and management. *In* The northern goshawk: ecology and management (W. M. Block, M. L. Morrison, and M. H. Reiser, eds.). Stud. in Avian Biol. 16: 32-40.

DeStefano, S., and J. McCloskey. 1997. Does vegetation structure limit the distribution of Northern Goshawks in the Oregon Coast Ranges? J. Raptor Res. 31: 34-39.

Deusing, M. 1939. Nesting habits of the Pied-billed Grebe. Auk 56: 366-373.

Devillers, P. 1970. Identification and distribution in California of the *Sphyrapicus varius* group of sapsuckers. Calif. Birds 1: 47-76.

DeWolfe, B. B., and R. H. DeWolfe. 1962. Mountain White-crowned Sparrows in California. Condor 64: 378-389.

Dickerman, R. W. 1964. Notes on the Horned Larks of western Minnesota and the Great Plains. Auk 81: 430-432.

Dickerman, R. W. 1973. The Least Bittern in Mexico and Central America. Auk 90: 689-691.

Dickerman, R. W. 1986. Two hitherto unnamed populations of Aechmophorus (Aves:Podicipitidae). Proc. Biol. Soc. Washington 99: 435-436.

Dickerman, R. W. 1991. On the validity of *Bubo virginianus occidentalis* Stone. Auk 108: 964-965.

DICKEY, P. 1996. First Oregon record of Dusky-capped Flycatcher. Oreg. Birds 22: 71-73.

DICKINSON, J. C., JR. 1953. Report on the McCabe collection of British Columbian birds. Bull. Mus. Comp. Zool. 109: 123-205.

DIEM, K. L., AND S. I. ZEVELOFF. 1980. Ponderosa pine bird communities. Pp. 170-197 *in* Management of western forests and grasslands for nongame birds (R. M. DeGraff, tech. ed.). U.S. Dept. Agric., For. Serv. Gen. Tech. Rept. INT 86.

DIERAUF, L. A. 1997. Veterinarians warned about famphur. J. Am. Veterinary Medical Assoc. News URL = http://www.avma.org/onlnews/javma/aug97/s081597e.htm

DI LABIO, B. M. 1996. First record of the Asiatic Marbled Murrelet in Ontario. Ontario Birds 14: 15-22.

DILGER, W. C. 1956a. Adaptive modification and ecological isolating mechanisms in the thrush genera *Catharus* and *Hylocichla*. Wilson Bull. 68: 171-199.

DILGER, W. C. 1956b. Hostile behavior and reproductive isolating mechanisms in the avian genera *Catharus* and *Hylocichla*. Auk 73: 313-353.

DILLER, L.V., AND D. M. THOME. 1999. Population density of Northern Spotted Owls in managed young-growth forests in coastal northern California. J. Raptor Res. 33: 275-286.

DILLINGHAM, C. 1992. Leach's Storm-Petrel. Oreg. Birds 18: 78.

DILLINGHAM, C. 1994. A checklist to the birds of Curry County, Oregon. Oreg. Dept. Fish and Wildl. with Siskiyou Nat. For., Coos Bay Bur. Land Manage., and Kalmiopsis Audubon Soc.

DILLINGHAM, C. 1996. Starling Stroganoff. Oreg. Birds 22: 82-83.

DILLINGHAM, C. 1999. Veery? Curry County. Electronic mail message to Oregon Birders On Line listserver. 13 May 1999. URL = 99.htm http://www.orst.edu/pubs/birds/obolnts/curr99.htm

DILLINGHAM, C., R. MILLER, AND L. WEBB. 1995. Marbled Murrelet distribution in the Siskiyou National Forest of southwestern Oregon. Northwest. Nat. 76: 33-39.

DILLINGHAM, C. P., AND D. P. VROMAN. 1997. Notes on habitat selection and distribution of the Acorn Woodpecker in southwestern Oregon. Oreg. Birds 23: 13-14.

DIMMICK, C. R. 1993. Life history and the development of cache-recovery behaviors in Clark's Nutcracker. Ph.D. diss., Northern Ariz. Univ., Flagstaff, AZ.

DIXON, J. B. 1936. Nesting of the Sierra Nevada Rosy Finch. Condor 38: 3-8.

DIXON, K. R., AND J. A. CHAPMAN. 1980. Harmonic mean measure of animal activity areas. Ecology 61: 1040-1044.

DIXON, R. D. 1995a. Density, nest-site and roost-site characteristics, home range, habitat use, and behavior of White-headed Woodpeckers: Deschutes and Winema National Forests, Oregon. Unpubl. rep., Oreg. Dept. Fish and Wildl., Deschutes and Winema Natl. Forests. Nongame Proj. 93-3-01.

DIXON, R. D. 1995b. Ecology of white-headed woodpeckers in the central Oregon Cascades. M.S. thesis, Univ. of Idaho, Moscow.

DIXON, R. D., AND V. A. SAAB. 2000. Black-backed Woodpecker (*Picoides arcticus*). *In* The birds of North America, No. 509 (A. Poole and F. Gill, eds.). The Birds of N. Am., Inc., Philadelphia, PA.

DOBBS, R. C., P. R. MARTIN, AND T. E. MARTIN. 1999. Green-tailed Towhee (*Pipilo chlorurus*). *In* The birds of North America, No. 368 (A. Poole and F. Gill, eds.). The Birds of N. Am., Inc., Philadelphia, PA.

DOBBS, R. C., T. E. MARTIN, AND C. J. CONWAY. 1997. Williamson's Sapsucker (*Sphyrapicus thyroideus*). *In* The birds of North America, No. 285 (A. Poole and F. Gill, eds.). Acad. of Nat. Sci., Philadelphia, and Am. Ornithol. Union, Washington, D.C.

DOBKIN, D. S., J. A. HOLMES, AND B. A. WILCOX. 1986. Traditional nest-site use by White-throated Swifts. Condor 88: 252-253.

DOBKIN, D. S., A. C. RICH, J. A. PRETARE, AND W. H. PYLE. 1995. Nest-site relationships among cavity-nesting birds of riparian and snowpocket aspen woodlands in the northwestern Great Basin. Condor 97: 694-707.

DOBLER, F. C., J. EBY, C. PERRY, S. RICHARDSON, AND M. VANDER HAEGEN. 1996. Status of Washington's shrub-steppe ecosystem: extent, ownership, and wildlife/vegetation relationships. Res. rep., Wash. Dept. of Fish and Wildl., Olympia.

DOBLER, F. C., AND T. W. SAUVE. 1982. Ancient Murrelet on the Columbia River near Wenatchee, Washington. Murrelet 63: 71-72.

DOBYNS, H. W. 1928. Do Burrowing Owls and coyotes live in the same burrow? Murrelet 9: 45-46.

DODD, S. L., AND M. A. COLWELL. 1996. Seasonal variation in diurnal and nocturnal distributions of nonbreeding shorebirds at North Humboldt Bay, California. Condor 98: 196-207.

DODD, S. L., AND M. A. COLWELL. 1998. Environmental correlates of diurnal and nocturnal foraging patterns of nonbreeding shorebirds. Wilson Bull. 110: 182-189.

DOERGE, K. F. 1978. Aspects of the geographic ecology of the Acorn Woodpecker (*Melanerpes formicivorus*). M.S. thesis, Oreg. State Univ., Corvallis.

DOLBEER, R. A. 1981. Cost-benefit determination of blackbird damage control for cornfields. Wildl. Soc. Bull. 9: 44-51.

DOLBEER, R. A. 1990. Ornithology and integrated pest management: Red-winged Blackbirds (*Agelaius phoeniceus*) and corn. Ibis 132: 309-322.

DOLTON, D. D. 1993. The call-count survey: historic development and current procedures. Pp. 233-252 *in* Ecology and management of the Mourning Dove (T. S. Baskett, M. W. Sayre, R. E. Tomlinson, R. E. Mirarchi, and R. E. McCabe, eds.). Stackpole Books, Harrisburg, PA.

DONNELLY, R. E., AND K. A. SULLIVAN. 1998. Foraging proficiency and body condition of juvenile American Dippers. Condor 100: 385-388.

DOREMUS, H. D., AND J. E. PAGEL. 2001. Why listing may be forever: perspectives on delisting under the U.S. Endangered Species Act. Cons. Biol. 15: 1258-1268.

DORIO, J. C., AND A. H. GREWE. 1979. Nesting and brood rearing habitat of the Upland Sandpiper. J. Minn. Acad. Sci. 45: 8-11.

DORSEY, G. L. 1982. An analysis of avian communities on three islands, Lower Columbia River, Oregon. M.S. thesis. Oreg. State Univ., Corvallis.

DOUGLAS, D. 1829. Observations on some species of the genera *Tetrao* and *Ortyx* natives of North America; with descriptions of four new species of the former, two of the latter genus. Trans. Linn. Soc. of London 16: 133-149.

DOUGLAS, D. 1914. Journal kept by David Douglas during his travels in North America, 1823-1827. Royal Horticultural Society, London.

DOUGLAS, H. D., III. 1998. Response of Eastern Willets (*Catoptrophorus semipalmatus semipalmatus*) to song playbacks of Eastern and Western willets (*C.s. inornatus*). Auk 115: 514-518.

DOW, D. D. 1964. Diving times of wintering water birds. Auk 81: 556-558.

DOWLAN, S. 1996a. The breeding status and distribution of Harlequin Ducks in Oregon: a summary of observations and survey efforts. Oreg. Birds 22: 42-47.

DOWLAN, S. 1996b. A verified breeding record for Wilson's Phalarope at Baskett Slough National Wildlife Refuge, Polk County, Oregon. Oreg. Birds 22: 74.

DOWLAN, S. 1998. Finding Red-eyed Vireos and other breeding birds around the lower Sandy River. Oreg. Birds 24: 47-50.

DOWLAN, S. G. 2000a. The breeding Fox Sparrows (*Passerella iliaca*) of the northern Cascade Mountains of Oregon. Oreg. Birds 26: 200-208.

DOWLAN, S. 2000b. Marion County's first record for Sage Sparrow. Oreg. Birds 26: 162.

DOWLAN, S. 2001. Species profile: Varied Thrush. Bird Conserv. 14: 16.

DOYLE, T. J. 1997. The Timberline Sparrow, *Spizella (breweri) taverneri*, in Alaska, with notes on breeding habitat and vocalizations. West. Birds 28: 1-12.

DRENNAN, S. 1986. Eighty-sixth Christmas Bird Count. Am. Birds. 40: 973.

DRENT, R. H. 1965. Breeding biology of the Pigeon Guillemot *Cepphus columba*. Ardea 53: 99-60.

DRURY, W. H., JR. 1960. Breeding activities of Long-tailed Jaeger, Herring Gull, and Arctic Tern on Bylot Island, Northwest Territories, Canada. Bird-Banding 31: 63-79.

DRURY, W. H. 1984. Gulls. Pp. 132-145 *in* Seabirds of eastern North Pacific and Arctic waters (D. Haley, ed.). Pacific Search Press, Seattle.

DRUT, M. S., J. A. CRAWFORD, AND M. A. GREGG. 1994a. Brood habitat use by Sage Grouse in Oregon. Great Basin Nat. 54: 170-176.

DRUT, M. S., W. H. PYLE, AND J. A. CRAWFORD. 1994b. Technical note: diets and food selection of Sage Grouse chicks in Oregon. J. Range Manage. 47: 90-93.

DRUT, M. S., AND R. E. TROST. 1999. Annual summary of goose population monitoring programs in the Pacific Flyway, 1998-1999. Unpubl. rep., U.S. Fish and Wildl. Serv., Portland, OR.

DRUT, M. S., AND R. E. TROST. 2000. 2000 Pacific Flyway data book: waterfowl harvests and status, hunter participation and success, and certain hunting regulations in the Pacific Flyway and United States. U.S. Fish and Wildl. Serv., Office of Migratory Bird Manage., Portland, OR.

DuBOIS, A. D. 1919. An experience with Horned Grebes (*Colymbus auritus*). Auk 36: 170-180.

Du BOIS, H. M. 1936. A new record for northwestern Oregon. Condor 38: 123.

DUBOWY, P. J. 1996. Northern Shoveler (*Anas clypeata*). *In* The birds of North America, No. 217 (A. Poole and F. Gill, eds.). Acad. of Nat. Sci., Philadelphia, and Am. Ornithol. Union, Washington, D.C.

DUEBBERT, H. F. 1966. Island nesting of the Gadwall in western North Dakota. Wilson Bull. 78: 12-25.

DUFFIN, K. 1973. Barn Swallows use freshwater and marine algae in nest construction. Wilson Bull. 85: 237-238.

DUGGER, B. D., AND K. M. DUGGER. 2002. Long-billed Curlew (*Numenius americanus*). *In* The birds of North America, No. 628 (A. Poole and F. Gill, eds.). The Birds of N. Am., Inc., Philadelphia, PA.

DUGGER, B. D., K. M. DUGGER, AND L. H. FREDRICKSON. 1994. Hooded Merganser (*Lophodytes cucullatus*). *In* The birds of North America, No. 98 (A. Poole and F. Gill, eds.). Acad. of Nat. Sci., Philadelphia, and Am. Ornithol. Union, Washington, D.C.

DUMAS, P. C. 1949. Habitat distribution of birds of southeastern Washington. M.A. thesis, Oreg. State Coll., Corvallis.

DUMAS, P. 1950. Habitat distribution of breeding birds in southeastern Washington. Condor 52: 232-237.

DUNBAR, D. L., B. P. BOOTH, E. D. FORSMAN, A. E. HETHERINGTON, AND D. J. WILSON. 1991. Status of the Spotted Owl, *Strix occidentalis*, and Barred Owl, *Strix varia*, in southwestern British Columbia. Can. Field-Nat. 105:.464-468.

DUNCAN, J. R., AND P. A. LANE. 1988. Great Horned Owl observed "hawking" insects. J. Raptor Res. 22: 93.

DUNK, J. R. 1995. White-tailed Kite (*Elanus leucurus*). *In* The birds of North America, No. 178 (A. Poole and F. Gill, eds.). Acad. of Nat. Sci., Philadelphia, and Am. Ornithol. Union, Washington, D.C.

DUNN, E. H., AND D. J. AGRO. 1995. Black Tern (*Chlidonias niger*). *In* The birds of North America, No. 147 (A. Poole and F. Gill, eds.). Acad. of Nat. Sci., Philadelphia, and Am. Ornithol. Union, Washington, D.C.

DUNN, J. L., AND D. BEADLE. 1998. Longspurs: distribution and identification in basic plumage. Birder's J. 7: 68-93.

DUNN, J. L., AND K. L. GARRETT. 1997. A field guide to warblers of North America. Houghton Mifflin Company, New York, NY.

DUNN, J. L., K. L. GARRETT, AND J. K. ALDERFER. 1995. White-crowned Sparrow subspecies: identification and distribution. Birding 27: 182-200.

DURBIN, K. 1975. California import with a Texas drawl. Oreg. Wildl. 30(4): 8-9.

DURBIN, K. 1979. The forest drummer: a look at the Ruffed Grouse in Oregon. Oreg. Wildl. 3-7.

DUVALL, A. J. 1945a. Distribution and taxonomy of the Black-capped Chickadees of North America. Auk 62: 49-69.

DUVALL, A. J. 1945b. Variation in *Carpodacus purpureus* and *Carpodacus cassinii*. Condor 47: 202-205.

DuWORS, R. M., S. HOUSTON, AND P. W. BROWN. 1984. Inland breeding by the Glaucous-winged Gull. J. Field Ornithol. 55: 380-382.

DWYER, T. J., G. L. KRAPU, AND D. M. JANKE. 1979. Use of prairie pothole habitat by breeding Mallards. J. Wildl. Manage. 43: 526-531.

DZUBIN, A. 1955. Some evidence of home range in waterfowl. Trans. 20th N. Am. Wildl. Conf. 278-298.

EADIE, J. M., J-P. L. SAVARD, AND M. L. MALLORY. 2000. Barrow's Goldeneye (*Bucephala islandica*). *In* The birds of North America, No. 548 (A. Poole and F. Gill, eds.). The Birds of N. Am., Inc., Philadelphia, PA.

EALEY, D. M. 1977. Aspects of the ecology and behaviour of a breeding population of dippers (*Cinclus mexicanus*: Passeriformes) in southern Alberta. M.S. thesis, Univ. of Alberta, Edmonton.

EARHART, C. M., AND N. K. JOHNSON. 1970. Size dimorphism and food habits of North American owls. Condor 72: 251-264.

EARNST, S. L., L. NEEL, G. L. IVEY, AND T. ZIMMERMAN. 1998. Status of the White-faced Ibis: breeding colony dynamics of the Great Basin population, 1985-1997. Colonial Waterbirds 21: 301-476.

EASTMAN, W. R., JR. 1960. Eating of tree seeds by birds in central Oregon. Oreg. Forest Res. Center, Res. Note 42. Corvallis.

EATON, S. W. 1957. Variation in *Seiurus noveboracensis*. Auk 74: 229-239.

EATON, S. W. 1983. Horned Grebes downed by ice storm. Am. Birds 37: 836-837.

ECKERT, T. 2001. A HETO warbler showcase: Hermit/Townsend's warbler hybrids. Birding 33: 342-350.

EDDLEMAN, W. R., F. L. KNOPF, B. MEANLEY, F. A. REID, AND R. ZEMBAL. 1988. Conservation of North American rallids. Wilson Bull. 100: 458-475.

EDDY, G. 1982. Glaucous-winged Gulls nesting on buildings in Seattle, Washington. Murrelet 63: 27-29.

EDSON, J. M. 1942. Poor-will at Bellingham, Washington. Condor 44: 130.

EDSON, J. M. 1943. A study of the Violet-green Swallow. Auk 60: 396-403.

EDWARDS, D. K. 1979. An analysis of avian communities on a dredged material island. M.S. thesis, Oreg. State Univ., Corvallis.

EGGER, M. 1977a. Breeding status of Townsend's Solitaire in the Oregon Coast Range. Oreg. Birds 3(6): 11-13.

EGGER, M. 1977b. Raptors and ruinous roads: adventures in northwestern Oregon in July 1977. Oreg. Birds 3(4): 10-13.

EGGER, M. 1978. A probable nesting record of the Northern Waterthrush in Oregon. West. Birds 9: 83-84.

EGGER, M. 1980. First record of the Hudsonian Godwit for Oregon. West. Birds 11: 53-55.

EHRLICH, P. R., AND G. C. DAILY. 1988. Red-naped Sapsuckers feeding at willow: possible keystone herbivores. Am. Birds 42: 357-365.

EHRLICH, P. R., D. S. DOBKIN, AND D. WHEYE. 1988. The birders handbook: a field guide to the natural history of North American birds. Simon & Schuster, New York, NY.

EINARSEN, A. S. 1945. The pheasant in the Pacific Northwest. Pp. 254-274 *in* The Ring-necked Pheasant and its management in North America (W. L. McAtee, ed.). The Am. Wildl. Inst., Washington, D.C.

EINARSEN, A. S. 1965. Black Brant: sea goose of the Pacific coast. Univ. of Wash. Press, Seattle.

EKLUND, C. R. 1942. Ecological and mortality factors affecting the nesting of the Chinese Pheasant in the Willamette Valley, Oregon. J. Wildl. Manage. 6: 225-230.

ELEY, T. J. E., AND C. L. ELEY. 1972. Use of Crater Lake by waterfowl. Murrelet 53: 27.

ELLINGSON, L. 1988. Inventory of Great Blue Heron colonies in the Willamette River Basin, Oregon, 1988. Oregon Coop. Wildl. Res. Unit, Dept. of Fish. and Wildl., Oreg. State Univ., Corvallis.

ELLIOTT, J. J. 1939. Wintering Tree Swallows at Jones Beach, fall and winter 1938 and 1939. Bird-Lore 41: 11-16.

ELLISON, L. 1934. Notes on food habits of juncos. Condor 36: 176-177.

ELLISON, W. G. 1992. Blue-gray Gnatcatcher (*Polioptila caerulea*). *In* The birds of North America, No. 23 (A. Poole, P. Stettenheim, and F. Gill, eds.). Acad. of Nat. Sci., Philadelphia, and Am. Ornithol. Union, Washington, D.C.

ELSTON, S. F., AND W. E. SOUTHERN. 1983. Effects of intraspecific piracy on breeding Ring-billed Gulls. Auk 100: 217-220.

ELTZROTH, E. K. 1981-1998. USFWS band recovery records.

ELTZROTH, E. K. 1983. Breeding biology and mortality of Western Bluebirds near Corvallis, Oregon. Sialia 5: 83-87.

ELTZROTH, E. K. 1987. Population study and breeding biology of the Western Bluebird *Sialia mexicana*. Oreg. Dept. Fish and Wildl., Nongame Wildl. Prog. Tech. Rep. 86-1-01.

ELTZROTH, E. K. 1989. Trailing the banded bird. Sialia 11: 98, 99.

ELTZROTH, E. K., A. S. CROMACK, AND L. L. THOMPSON-COWLEY. 1980. Endoparasitism in Western Bluebirds of Oregon. Sialia 2: 67-71.

ELTZROTH, E. K., AND S. R. ROBINSON. 1984. Violet-green Swallows help Western Bluebirds at the nest. J. Field Ornithol. 55: 259-261.

ELTZROTH, M. S. 1978. Status of the Bobolink in western Oregon. Oreg. Birds 4(4): 10-12.

ELTZROTH, M. S. 1984. Distribution: Calliope Hummingbird. Oreg. Birds 10: 61-63.

ELTZROTH, M. S. 1987a. Checklist of the birds of Oregon. Oreg. State Univ. Book Stores, Inc.

ELTZROTH, M. S. 1987b. Red-naped Sapsucker in western Oregon. Oreg. Birds 13: 36-37.

ELY, C. R. 1992. Time allocation by Greater White-fronted Geese: influence of diet, energy reserves and predation. Condor 94: 857-870.

ELY, C. R. 1993. Family stability in Greater White-fronted Geese. Auk 110: 425-435.

ELY, C. R., AND A. X. DZUBIN. 1994. Greater White-fronted Goose (*Anser albifrons*). *In* The birds of North America, No. 131 (A. Poole and F. Gill, eds.). Acad. of Nat. Sci., Philadelphia, and Am. Ornithol. Union, Washington, D.C.

ELY, C. R., AND J. Y. TAKEKAWA. 1996. Geographic variation in migratory behavior of Greater White-fronted Geese (*Anser albifrons*). Auk 113: 889-901.

EMLEN, J. T., JR. 1941. Cliff Swallow colonies of the central Sacramento Valley in 1941. Condor 43: 248.

EMLEN, J. T., JR. 1952. Social behavior in nesting Cliff Swallows. Condor 54: 177-199.

EMLEN, J. T., JR. 1954. Territory, nest building, and pair formation in the Cliff Swallow. Auk 71: 16-35.

EMLEN, S. T., AND H. W. AMBROSE, III. 1970. Feeding interactions of Snowy Egrets and Red-breasted Mergansers. Auk 87: 164-165.

ENDERSON, J. H. 1964. A study of the Prairie Falcon in the central Rocky Mountain region. Auk 81: 332-352.

ENDERSON, J. H., W. HEINRICH, L. KIFF, AND C. M. WHITE. 1995. Population changes in North American peregrines. Pp. 142-161 *in* Trans. 60th N. Am. Wildl. and Nat. Resour. Conf.

ENGELMOER, M., AND C. S. ROSELAAR. 1998. Geographical variation in waders. Kluwer Academic Publ., Boston, MA.

ENGILIS, A., JR., L. W. ORING, E. CARRERA, J. W. NELSON, AND A. M. LOPEZ. 1998. Shorebird surveys in Ensenada Pabellones and Bahia Santa Maria, Sinaloa, Mexico: critical winter habitats for Pacific Flyway shorebirds. Wilson Bull. 110: 332-341.

ENGLER, J., AND J. E. BRADY. 2000. Final report: 2000 Greater Sandhill Crane nesting season at Conboy Lake National Wildlife Refuge. Unpubl. rep., U.S. Fish and Wildl. Serv., Ridgefield NWR, Ridgefield, WA.

ENGLISH, S. M. 1978. Distribution and ecology of Great Blue Heron colonies on the Willamette River, Oregon. *In* Wading Birds (A. Sprunt IV, J. Ogden, and S. Winckler, eds). Natl. Audubon Soc. Res. Rep. 7.

ENTICOTT, J., AND D. TIPLING. 1997. Seabirds of the world. Stackpole Books, Mechanicsburg, PA.

ERICKSON, M. M. 1968. Lazuli Bunting (*Passerina amoena*). *In* Life histories of North American cardinals, grosbeaks, buntings, towhees, finches, sparrows, and allies, part 1 (A. C. Bent, ed.). U.S. Natl. Mus. Bull. 237.

ERICKSON, R. A., AND R. A. HAMILTON. 2001. Report of the California Bird Records Committee: 1998 records. West. Birds 32: 13-49.

ERICKSON, R. A., R. A. HAMILTON, S. N. G. HOWELL, P. PYLE, AND M. A. PATTEN. 1995. First record of the Marbled Murrelet and third record of the Ancient Murrelet for Mexico. West. Birds 26: 39-45.

ERICKSON, R. C. 1948. Life history and ecology of the Canvas-back (*Nyroca valisineria*) (Wilson), in southeastern Oregon. Ph.D. diss., Iowa State College, Ames.

ERSKINE, A. J. 1966. Growth, and annual cycles in weights, plumages, and reproductive organs of goosanders in eastern Canada. Ibis 113: 42-58.

ERSKINE, A. J. 1979. Man's influence on potential nesting sites and populations of swallows in Canada. Can. Field-Nat. 93: 371-377.

ERSKINE, A. J. 1992. Atlas of breeding birds of the maritime provinces. Chelsea Green Publ., White River Junction, VT.

ERWIN, R. M. 1980. Censusing waterbird colonies: some sampling experiments. Trans. Linn. Soc. of New York 9: 77-85.

ERWIN, R. M., AND T. W. CUSTER. 1982. Estimating reproductive success in colonial waterbirds: an evaluation. Colonial Waterbirds 5: 49-56.

EVANICH, J. E., JR. 1981a. Broad-tailed Hummingbird: identification and status in Oregon. Oreg. Birds 7: 126-130.

EVANICH, J. 1981b. Preliminary checklist: Washington County. Oreg. Birds 7: 169-171.

EVANICH, J. 1982a. Highlights from the field notes: fall 1982. Oreg. Birds 8: 140-147.

EVANICH, J. 1982b. Highlights from the field notes: spring 1982. Oreg. Birds 8: 48-55.

EVANICH, J. 1982c. Highlights from the field notes: summer 1982. Oreg. Birds 8: 95-101.

EVANICH, J. 1982d. Highlights from the field notes: winter 1981-82. Oreg. Birds 8: 4-10.

EVANICH, J. 1982e. Identification: Western Grebe. Oreg. Birds 8: 164-165.

EVANICH, J. 1983a. Highlights from the field notes: fall 1983. Oreg. Birds 9: 127-130.

EVANICH, J. 1983b. Highlights from the field notes: winter 1982-83. Oreg. Birds 9: 3-10.

EVANICH, J. 1983c. Site guide: Bonny Lakes. Oreg. Birds 9: 16-20.

EVANICH, J. 1984a. 1983 Christmas Bird Count highlights. Oreg. Birds 10: 10-17.

EVANICH, J. 1984b. Highlights from the field notes: winter 1983-1984. Oreg. Birds 10: 45-47.

EVANICH, J. 1985. Ross' goose in northeast Oregon. Oreg. Birds 11: 139-140.

EVANICH, J. E., JR. 1986a. Introduced birds of Oregon. Oreg. Birds 12: 156-186.

EVANICH, J. 1986b. Results of a spring pelagic trip. Oreg. Birds 12: 36-38.

EVANICH, J. 1987. Oregon's first "white-rumped" Whimbrel. Oreg. Birds 12: 281-282.

EVANICH, J. 1989. Identification and status of fulva and dominica golden-plovers. Oreg. Birds 15: 91-95.

EVANICH, J. E., JR. 1990. The birder's guide to Oregon. Portland Audubon Soc., Portland, OR.

EVANICH, J. 1991a. Field notes: Eastern Oregon, spring 1991. Oreg. Birds 17: 124-126.

EVANICH, J. 1991b. Field notes: Eastern Oregon, winter 1990-91, Oreg. Birds 17: 89-94.

EVANICH, J. 1992a. Birds of Northeast Oregon: an annotated checklist for Union and Wallowa counties, second ed. (revised). Oreg. Field Ornithol. Spec. Pub. No. 6, Eugene.

EVANICH, J. 1992b. Fieldnotes: eastern Oregon, fall 1991. Oreg. Birds 18: 58-61.

EVANICH, J. 1992c. Field notes: eastern Oregon, spring 1992. Oreg. Birds 18: 124-127.

EVANICH, J. 1992d. Field notes: eastern Oregon, summer 1991. Oreg. Birds 18: 26-29.

EVANICH, J. 1992e. Field notes: eastern Oregon, winter 1991-1992. Oreg. Birds 18: 87-90.

EVANICH, J. 1992f. Status and spread of the Cattle Egret in Oregon. Oreg. Birds 18: 3-6.

EVANICH, J. 1993. Fieldnotes: eastern Oregon, summer 1992. Oreg. Birds 19: 24-26.

EVANICH, J., AND D. FIX. 1983. Highlights from the field notes: summer 1983. Oreg. Birds 9: 91-99.

EVANS, D. E., W. P. RITCHIE, S. K. NELSON, E. KUO-HARRISON, P. HARRISON, AND T. E. HAMER. 2000. Methods for surveying Marbled Murrelets in forests: an update to the protocol for land management and research. Pacific Seabird Group, Marbled Murrelet Tech. Committee.

EVANS, F. C., AND J. T. EMLEN. 1947. Ecological notes of the prey selected by a Barn Owl. Condor 49: 3-9.

EVANS, R. M., AND K. J. CASH. 1985. Early spring flights of American White Pelicans: timing and functional role in attracting others to the breeding colony. Condor 87: 252-255.

EVANS, R. M., AND F. L. KNOPF. 1993. American White Pelican (*Pelecanus erythrorynchos*). *In* The birds of North America, No. 57 (A. Poole and F. Gill, eds.). Acad. of Nat. Sci., Philadelphia, and Am. Ornithol. Union, Washington, D.C.

EVANS, T. J., AND S. W. HARRIS. 1994. Status and habitat use by American Avocets wintering at Humboldt Bay, California. Condor 96: 178-189.

EVENDEN, F. G. Audubon Field Notes from the 1940s. Mus. Vertebrate Zool., Berkeley.

EVENDEN, F. G. 1947. The Bufflehead nesting in Oregon. Condor 49: 169.

EVENDEN, F. G., JR. 1949. Habitat relations of typical austral and boreal avifauna in the Willamette Valley, Oregon. Ph.D. diss., Oreg. State Coll., Corvallis.

EVENDEN, F. G., JR., P. C. DUMAS, AND K. L. GORDON. 1947. The Black Phoebe in Western Oregon. Condor 49: 212.

EVENDEN, F. G., JR., D. B. MARSHALL, AND T. H. MCALLISTER, JR. 1950. Waterfowl populations of a swamp in western Oregon. Condor 52: 159-163.

EVERETT, W. T., AND R. L. PITMAN. 1993. Status and conservation of shearwaters of the North Pacific. *In* The status, ecology, and conservation of marine birds of the North Pacific (K. Vermeer, K. T. Briggs, K. H. Morgan, and D. Siegel-Causey, eds.). Can. Wildl. Serv., Ottawa.

EWELL, H., AND A. CRUZ. 1998. Foraging behavior of the Pygmy Nuthatch in Colorado ponderosa pine forests. West. Birds 29: 169-173.

EWINS, P. J. 1993. Pigeon Guillemot (*Cepphus columba*). *In* The birds of North America, No. 49 (A. Poole and F. Gills, eds.). Acad. of Nat. Sci., Philadelphia, and Am. Ornithol. Union, Washington, D.C.

EWINS, P. J., H. R. CARTER, AND Y. V. SHIBAEV. 1993 The status, distribution, and ecology of inshore fish-feeding alcids (*Cepphus* guillemots and *Brachyramphus* murrelets) in the North Pacific. *In* The status, ecology, and conservation of marine birds of the North Pacific (K. Vermeer, K. T. Briggs, K. H. Morgan, and D. Siegel-Causey, eds.). Can. Wildl. Serv., Ottawa.

FAABORG, J. 1976. Habitat selection and territorial behavior of the small grebe in North Dakota. Wilson Bull. 88: 391-399.

FAIR, J. M., P. L. KENNEDY, AND L. C. MCEWEN. 1994. Effects of carbaryl grasshopper control on nesting Killdeer in North Dakota. Environ. Toxicol. and Chem. 14: 881-890.

FAIRFIELD, D. M., AND P. A. SHIROKOFF. 1978. Migratory patterns and winter distribution in the Ruby-crowned Kinglet (*Regulus calendula*). Blue Bill (suppl.) 25: 22-25.

FALLS, J., AND J. KOPACHENA. 1994. White-throated Sparrow (*Zonotrichia albicollis*). *In* the birds of North America, No. 128 (A. Poole and F. Gill, eds.). Acad. of Nat. Sci., Philadelphia, and Am. Ornithol. Union, Washington, D.C.

FARNER. D. S. 1946. Recovery of a banded Gray Jay. Nature Notes from Crater Lake Natl. Park 12.

FARNER, D. S. 1952. Birds of Crater Lake National Park. Univ. of Kansas Press, Lawrence.

FARRAND, J., JR., ED. 1983a. The Audubon Society master guide to birding, Vol.1: loons to sandpipers. Alfred A. Knopf, New York.

FARRAND, J., JR., ED. 1983b. The Audubon Society master guide to birding, Vol. 2: gulls to dippers. Alfred A. Knopf, New York.

FARRAND, J. 1992. How the Evening Grosbeak got its name. Am. Birds 46: 1184-1186.

FAUTIN, R. W. 1941. Development of nestling Yellow-headed Blackbirds. Auk 58: 215-232.

FAXON, D. 1990. Lincoln County, Oregon bird field notes. Sandpiper, 24 May, 1990.

FAXON, D. 1995. Site guide: southern Lincoln County. Oreg. Birds 21: 71-74.

FAXON, D., AND R. BAYER. 1991. Birds of the Coast Range of Lincoln County, Oregon, Vol. 1: birds of Thornton Creek. Stud. in Oreg. Ornithol. 8. Gahmken Press, Newport, OR.

FAYT, P. 1999. Available insect prey in bark patches selected by the Three-toed Woodpecker *Picoides tridactylus* prior to reproduction. Ornis Fennica 76: 135-140.

FEDERAL REGISTER. 1993. Determination of threatened status for coast population of the Western Snowy Plover. Vol. 58, No. 42, pp 12864-12874.

FEERER, J. L. 1977. Niche partitioning by Western Grebe polymorphs. M.S. thesis, Humboldt State Univ., Arcata, CA.

FENDER, K. 1951. Notes on the Western Mockingbird. Murrelet 32: 29.

FENNEMAN, N. M. 1931. Physiography of western United States. McGraw-Hill Book Co., New York and London.

FERGUSON, R. S. 1981. Territorial attachment and mate fidelity by Horned Grebe. Wilson Bull. 93: 560-561.

FERGUSON, R. S, AND S. G. SEALY. 1983. Breeding ecology of the Horned Grebe, *Podiceps auritus*, in southwestern Manitoba. Can. Field-Nat. 97: 401-408.

FETZ, T. W., S. W. JANES, AND H. LAUCHSTEDT. Unpubl. ms. Habitat characteristics of Great Gray Owls in the Siskiyou Mountains of southwestern Oregon.

FINCH, D. M., AND R. T. REYNOLDS. 1987. Bird response to understory variation and conifer succession in aspen forests. Pp. 87-96 *in* Issues and technology in the management of impacted wildlife (J. Emerick, S. Q. Foster, L. Hayden-Wing, J. Hodgson, J. W. Monarch, A. Smith, O. Thorne II., and J. Todd, eds.). Thorne Ecol. Inst., Boulder, Colorado.

FINDHOLT, S. L., AND C. H. TROST. 1985. Organochlorine pollutants, eggshell thickness, and reproductive success of Black-crowned Night-Herons in Idaho, 1979. Colonial Waterbirds 8: 32-41.

FINK, L. S., AND L. P. BROWER. 1981. Birds can overcome the cardenolide defense of monarch butterflies in Mexico. Science 291: 67-70.

FINLEY, W. L. 1902. Among the seabirds of the Oregon coast. Condor 4: 53-57.

FINLEY, W. L. 1905. Among the seabirds off the Oregon coast, part I. Condor 7: 119-127.

FINLEY, W. L. 1906. Herons at home. Condor 8: 35-40.

FINLEY, W. L. 1907a. Among the gulls on Klamath Lake. Condor 9: 12.

FINLEY, W. L. 1907b. English Sparrow notes. Condor 9: 108-109.

FINLEY, W. L. 1907c. The grebes of southern Oregon. Condor 9: 97-101.

FINLEY, W. L. 1908a. Life history of the California Condor, part 2. Condor 10: 5-10.

FINLEY, W. L. 1908b. Reports of field agents: report of William L. Finley. Bird-Lore 10: 291-295.

FINLEY, W. L. 1914. Trapping and distributing quail. Oreg. Sportsman. 2: 10-11.

FINNEGAN, S. 1993. Slaty-backed Gull, Sauvie Island, Multnomah Co., Oregon. Oreg. Birds 19: 64.

FISHER, H. K. 1893. The hawks and owls of the United States in their relation to agriculture. U.S. Dept. Agric., Div. Ornithol. and Mammal., Bull. No. 3, Washington, D.C.

FITCH, H. S. 1958. Home ranges, territories, and seasonal movements of vertebrates of the natural history reservation. Univ. Kans. Mus. Nat. Hist. Misc. Publ. 11: 63-326.

FITZNER, R. E., AND R. H. GRAY. 1994. Winter diet and weights of Barrow's and Common goldeneyes in southcentral Washington. Northwest Sci. 68: 172-177.

FITZNER, R. E., E. T. SIPCO, AND R. G. SCHRECKHISE. 1980. American Coot nesting and feeding habits in southeastern Washington. Northwest Sci. 54: 244-252.

FITZPATRICK, J. W. 1980. Wintering of North American tyrant flycatchers in the neotropics. Pp. 67-78 *in* Migrant birds in the neotropics: ecology, behavior, distribution, and conservation (A. Keast and E.S. Morton, eds.). Smithsonian Inst. Press, Washington D.C.

FIX, D. 1977a. Birds of Hart Mountain, Steens Mountain. Oreg. Birds 3(3): 86-91.

FIX, D. 1977b. Details: Mountain Plover. Oreg. Birds 3(6): 33-35.

FIX, D. 1977c. Field report: northwest Oregon. Oreg. Birds 3(5): 25-31.

FIX, D. 1977/1978. Field reports: northwest Oregon. Oreg. Birds 3(6): 39-42.

FIX, D. 1979. Occurrence and identification of the Stilt Sandpiper in Oregon. Oreg. Birds 5(2): 6-13.

FIX, D. 1982. Distribution: Townsend's Solitaire, western Cascades. Oreg. Birds 8: 168-170.

Fix, D. 1983. Parasitic Jaegers soaring. Oreg. Birds 9: 38-39.

Fix, D. 1984a. Northern Pacific Coast region. Am. Birds 38: 948-952.

Fix, D. 1984b. Western Oregon field notes: fall 1984. Oreg. Birds 11: 3-17.

Fix, D. 1985a. Field notes: western Oregon, spring 1985. Oreg. Birds 11: 170-184.

Fix, D. 1985b. Notes on winter Orange-crowned Warblers. Oreg. Birds 11: 159-163.

Fix, D. 1985c. A Poorwill in Douglas County. Oreg. Birds 11: 152.
Fix, D. 1985d. Skinner's Butte, Eugene. Oreg. Birds 11: 121-124.

Fix, D. 1985e. Spencer Butte, Eugene. Oreg. Birds 11: 197-199.

Fix, D. 1985f. Western Oregon field notes: fall 1984. Oreg. Birds 11: 3-17.

Fix, D. 1987a. Field notes: western Oregon, fall 1986. Oreg. Birds 13: 228-248.

Fix, D. 1987b. Flammulated Owls in the western Oregon Cascades. Oreg. Birds 13: 38-40.

Fix, D. 1987c. A record 48 Western Screech-Owls on the Florence CBC. Oreg. Birds 13: 278-280.

Fix, D. 1988a. An apparent Clay-colored Sparrow X Chipping Sparrow hybrid in Oregon. Oreg. Birds 14: 250-252.

Fix, D. 1988b. Notes on spring flyway for White-fronted Geese. Oreg. Birds 14: 243-246.

Fix, D. 1988c. Site Guide: Glenwood gull rocks, Lane County, Oregon. Oreg. Birds 14: 61-64.

Fix, D. 1989. Notes on Dusky Flycatchers in northeastern Douglas County, Oregon. Oreg. Birds 15: 209-213.

Fix, D. 1990a. Birds of Diamond Lake Ranger District. Unpubl. manuscript. URL = http://osu.orst.edu/pubs/birds/county/doug/dlrd/ Accessed 20 Sep 2002.

Fix, D. 1990b. Fieldnotes: western Oregon, fall 1989. Oreg. Birds 16: 188.

Fix, D. 1990c. Field notes: western Oregon, spring 1990. Oreg. Birds 16: 322-340.

Fix, D. 1991. Field notes: western Oregon, fall 1990. Oreg. Birds 17: 55-64.

Fix, D. 1992. Notes on observing Swamp Sparrows. Oreg. Birds 18: 103-104.

Fix, D., and S. Heinl. 1990. Field notes: western Oregon, fall 1989. Oreg. Birds 16: 180-198.

Fix, D., and M. Sawyer. 1991. Checklist: the Douglas County western Cascades. Oreg. Birds 17: 3-10.

Flahaut, M. R. 1949. North Pacific Coast region. Audubon Field Notes 3: 220-222.

Fleischer, J. 2002. Bat-hunting Western Screech-Owls in Albany, Linn County, Oregon. Oreg. Birds 28: 7-8.

Fleischer, R. C. 2001. Taxonomic and evolutionary significant (ESU) status of the western Yellow-billed Cuckoos (*Coccyzus americanus*). Rep. to U.S. Fish and Wildl. Serv. of 22 Apr, 2001. Molecular Genetics Lab., Smithsonian Inst., Washington, D.C.

Floyd, A. A. 1993. Nest-site differentiation by three sympatric chickadees. Northwest Sci. 67: 128.

Follett, D. 1979. Birds of Crater Lake National Park. Crater Lake Natur. Hist. Assoc., Crater Lake.

Follett, W. I., and D. G. Ainley. 1976. Fishes collected by Pigeon Guillemots, *Cepphus columba* (Pallas), nesting on southeast Farallon Island, California. Calif. Fish and Game 62: 28-31.

Forbes, J. E., and D. W. Warner. 1974. Behavior of a radio-tagged Saw-whet Owl. Auk 91: 783-795.

Forbes, L. S., and S. G. Sealy. 1990. Foraging roles of male and female Western Grebes during brood raising. Condor 92: 421-426.

Force, M. P., and P. W. Mattocks. 1986. Northern Pacific Coast region. Am. Birds 40: 316-321.

Force, M. P., R. A. Rowlett, and G. Grace. 1999. A sight record of a Streaked Shearwater in Oregon. West. Birds 30: 49-52.

Ford, M. R. 1993. The effect of riparian corridor width on the relative abundance and relative diversity of avian communities. M.S. thesis, Wash. State Univ., Pullman.

Ford, R. G., G. K. Himes Boor, J. C. Ward. 2001. Seabird mortality resulting from the M/V New Carissa oil spill incident, February and March 1999. Final rep. to U.S. Fish and Wildl. Serv., Oreg. Office. R.G. Ford Consulting Co. Portland, OR.

Ford, T. B., and J. A. Gieg. 1995. Winter behavior of the Common Loon. J. Field Ornithol. 66: 22-29.

Foreman, L. D. 1979. Flock size and density of Common Mergansers in northwestern California. Calif. Fish and Game 65: 124-127.

Forshaw, J., S. Howell, T. Lindsey, and R. Stallcup. 1994. The nature company guides: birding. Time-Life Books.

Forsman, E. D., R. G. Anthony, J. A. Reid, P. J. Loschl, S. G. Sovern, M. Taylor, B. L. Biswell, A. Ellington, E. C. Meslow, G. S. Miller, K. A. Swindle, J. A. Thrailkill, F. F. Wagner, and D. E. Seaman. 2002. Natal and breeding dispersal of Northern Spotted Owls. Wildl. Monogr. 149.

Forsman, E. D., C. R. Bruce, M. A. Walter, and E. C. Meslow. 1987. A current assessment of the Spotted Owl population in Oregon. Murrelet 68: 51-54.

Forsman, E. D., and T. Bryan. 1984. Distribution, abundance and habitat of Great Gray Owls in south-central Oregon. Oreg. Dept. of Fish and Wildl. Non-game Wildl. Project Rep. #84-3-05.

Forsman, E. D., S. DeStefano, M. G. Raphael, and R. J. Gutiérrez, Eds. 1996. Demography of the Northern Spotted Owl. Stud. in Avian Biol. 17.

Forsman, E. D., and A. R. Giese. 1997. Nests of Northern Spotted Owls on the Olympic Peninsula, Washington. Wilson Bull. 109: 28-41.

Forsman, E. D., and C. Maser. 1970. Saw-whet Owl preys on red tree mice. Murrelet 51: 10.

Forsman, E. D., E. C. Meslow, and M. J. Strub. 1977. Spotted Owl abundance in young versus old forests, Oregon. Wildl. Soc. Bull. 5: 43-47.

Forsman, E. D., E. C. Meslow, and H. M Wight. 1984. Distribution and biology of the Spotted Owl in Oregon. Wildl. Monogr. 87.

Forsman, E. D., I. A. Otto, S. G. Sovern, M. Taylor, D. W. Hays, H. Allen, S. L. Roberts, and D. E. Seaman. 2001. Spatial and temporal variation in diets of spotted owls in Washington. J. Raptor Res. 35: 141-150.

Foster, C. L. 1985. Habitat definition of nesting birds in the Double-O Unit, Malheur National Wildlife Refuge, Oregon. M.S. thesis, Humboldt State Univ., Arcata, CA.

Fouts, D. R. 1988. The plight of the Purple Martin in the Pacific Northwest. Purple Martin Update 1(3): 8-10.

Frank, P. W. 1982. Effects of winter feeding on limpets by Black Oystercatchers, *Haematopus bachmani*. Ecology 63: 1352-1362.

FRANK, R., H. LUMSDEN, J. F. BARR, AND H. E. BRAUN. 1983. Residues of organochlorine insecticides, industrial chemicals, and mercury in eggs and tissues taken from healthy and emaciated Common Loons, Ontario, Canada, 1968-1980. Arch. Environ. Contam. Toxicol. 12: 641-654.

FRANKLIN, A. B. 1997. Factors affecting temporal and spatial variation in Northern Spotted Owl populations in northwest California. Ph.D. diss., Colorado State Univ., Ft. Collins.

FRANKLIN, A. B., K. P. BURNHAM, G. C. WHITE, R. G. ANTHONY, E. D. FORSMAN, C. SCHWARZ, J. D. NICHOLS, AND J. HINES. 1999. Range-wide status and trends in Northern Spotted Owl populations. Unpubl. rep., Colorado Coop. Fish and Wildl. Res. Unit, Colorado State Univ., Fort Collins.

FRANKLIN, J. F., AND C. T. DYRNESS. 1973. Natural vegetation of Oregon and Washington. U.S. Dept. Agric., For. Serv. Gen. Tech. Rep. PNW-8.

FRANKLIN, J. F., AND T. A. SPIES. 1991. Composition, function, and structure of old-growth Douglas-fir forests. Pp. 71-80 in Wildlife and vegetation of unmanaged Douglas-fir forests (L. F. Ruggiero, K. B. Aubry, A. B. Carey, and M. H. Huff, tech. coords.). U.S. Dept. Agric., For. Serv. Gen. Tech. Rep. PNW-GTR-285. Portland, OR.

FRANZREB, K. E. 1977. Population changes after timber harvesting of a mixed conifer forest in Arizona. U.S. Dept. Agric., For. Serv. Res. Paper RM-184. Ft. Collins, CO.

FRANZREB, K. E. 1983. A comparison of avian foraging behavior in unlogged and logged mixed-coniferous forest. Wilson Bull. 95: 60-76.

FRANZREB, K. E. 1984. Foraging habits of Ruby-crowned and Golden-crowned kinglets in an Arizona montane forest. Condor 86: 139-145.

FRANZREB, K. E., AND S. A. LAYMON. 1993. A reassessment of the taxonomic status of the Yellow-billed Cuckoo. West. Birds 24: 17-28.

FRANZREB, K. E., AND R. D. OHMART. 1978. The effects of timber harvesting on breeding birds in a mixed-coniferous forest. Condor 80: 431-441.

FREDERICK, G. P., AND T. L. MOORE. 1991. Distribution and habitat of White-headed Woodpeckers (Picoides albolarvatus) in west-central Idaho. Idaho Dept. Fish and Game, Boise.

FREDRICH, L. A. 1961. An occurrence of the Laysan Albatross on the northwestern coast of Oregon. Condor 63: 506.

FREEMAN, S., D. GORI, AND S. ROHWER. 1990. Red-winged Blackbirds and Brown-headed Cowbirds: some aspects of a host-parasite relationship. Condor 92: 336-340.

FRENCH, N. R. 1954. Life history and behavior of the Black Rosy Finch. Ph.D. diss., Univ. of Utah, Salt Lake City.

FRENCH, N. R. 1959. Life history of the Black Rosy Finch. Auk 76: 159-180.

FRENZEL, R. W. 1983. Spacing of nest sites and foraging areas of Bald Eagles. In Proceedings of a workshop on habitat management for nesting and roosting Bald Eagles (R. G. Anthony, F. B. Isaacs, and R. W. Frenzel., eds.). Oreg. Coop. Wildl. Res. Unit, Oreg. State Univ., Corvallis, OR.

FRENZEL, R. W. 1985. Environmental contaminants and ecology of Bald Eagles in southcentral Oregon. Ph.D. diss., Oreg. State Univ., Corvallis.

FRENZEL, R. W. 1988. Home ranges, habitat use, and activity patterns of three Bald Eagles nesting on northwestern Upper Klamath Lake and observations of other Bald Eagles in the vicinity of Pelican Butte, Oregon, 1979-1982. Unpubl. rep., Beak Consultants, Inc.

FRENZEL, R. W. 2000. Nest-sites, nesting success, and turnover-rates of White-headed Woodpeckers on the Deschutes and Winema National Forests, Oregon in 2000. Unpubl. rep., Oreg. Nat. Heritage Program, The Nature Conservancy, Portland.

FRENZEL, R. W., AND R. G. ANTHONY. 1989. Relationship of diets and environmental contaminants in wintering Bald Eagles. J. Wildl. Manage. 53: 792-802.

FRENZEL, R. W., AND K. J. POPPER. 1998. Densities of White-headed Woodpeckers and other woodpeckers in study areas on the Winema and Deschutes National Forests, Oregon in 1997. Unpubl. rep., Oreg. Nat. Heritage Program, The Nature Conservancy, Portland.

FRIEDMANN, H. 1949. The Baer Pochard, a bird new to the North American fauna. Condor 51: 43-44.

FRIEDMANN, H., AND L. F. KIFF. 1985. The parasitic cowbirds and their hosts. Proc. West. Found. Vert. Zool. 2: 225-302.

FRIEDMANN, H., L. F. KIFF, AND S. J. ROTHSTEIN. 1977. A further contribution to knowledge of the host relations of parasitic cowbirds. Smithsonian Contrib. Zool. 235: 1-75.

FRIESEN, V. L., A. J. BAKER, AND J. F. PIATT. 1996a. Phylogenetic relationships within the alcidae (Charadriiformes: Aves) inferred from total molecular evidence. Mol. Biol. Evol. 13: 359-367.

FRIESEN, V. L., J. F. PIATT, AND A. J. BAKER. 1996b. Evidence from cytochrome b sequences and allozymes for a 'new' species of alcid: the Long-billed Murrelet (Brachyramphus perdix). Condor 98: 681-690.

FRITSCH, L. E., AND I. O. BUSS. 1958. Food of the American Merganser in Unakwik Inlet, Alaska. Condor 60: 410-411.

FRITZ, L., M. A. QUILLIAM, J. L. C. WRIGHT, A. M. BEALE, AND T. M. WORK. 1992. An outbreak of domoic acid poisoning attributed to the pennate diatom Pseudonitzscia australis. J. of Phycology 28: 439-442.

FROUNFELKER, C. R. 1977. Prey selection of the Great Horned Owl with reference to habitat and prey availability. M.S. thesis, Univ. of Idaho, Moscow.

FRY, D. M. 1995. Pollution and fishing threats to Marbled Murrelets. Pp. 257-260 in Ecology and conservation of the Marbled Murrelet (C. J. Ralph, G. L. Hunt, Jr., M. G. Raphael, and J. F. Piatt, eds.). U.S. Dept. Agric., For. Serv. Gen. Tech. Rep. PSW-GTR-152. Albany, CA.

FRY, D. M., C. K. TOONE, S. M. SPEICH, AND R. J. PEARD. 1987. Sex ratio skew and breeding patterns of gulls: demographic and toxicological considerations. Stud. in Avian Biol. 10: 26-43.

FULLER, M. R., C. J. HENNY, AND P. B. WOOD. 1995. Raptors. Pp. 65-69 in Our living resources: a report to the nation on the distribution, abundance, and health of U.S. plants, animals, and ecosystems (E. T. LaRoe, G. S. Farris, C. E. Puckett, P. D. Doran, and M. J. Mac, eds.). U.S. Dept. Int., Natl. Biol. Serv., Washington, D.C.

FURNESS, R. W. 1987. The skuas. T. & A. D. Poyser, Calton, U.K.

FURNIER, G. R., P. KNOWLES, M. A. CLYDE, AND B. P. DANCIK. 1987. Effects of avian seed dispersal on the genetic structure of whitebark pine populations. Evolution 41: 607-612.

FURNISS, S. B., E. J. O'NEILL, AND E. McLAURY. 1979. Recovery patterns of northwestern California and southeastern Oregon breeding western Canada Goose populations. Pp. 213-222 in Management and biology of Pacific Flyway geese (R. L. Jarvis and J. C. Bartonek, eds.). Oreg. State Univ. Book Stores, Inc., Corvallis.

FURRER, R. K. 1974. First spring sight record of the Yellow Rail for the Pacific Northwest. Murrelet 55: 25-26.

GABRIELSON, I. N. 1915. Notes on the Red-winged Blackbird. Wilson Bull. 27: 293-302.

GABRIELSON, I. 1924. Notes on the birds of Wallowa County. Auk 41: 552-565.

GABRIELSON, I. N. 1931. The birds of the Rogue River Valley, Oregon. Condor 33: 110-121.

GABRIELSON, I. N., AND S. G. JEWETT. 1940. Birds of Oregon. Oreg. State Coll., Corvallis. (Reprinted in 1970 as Birds of the Pacific Northwest by Dover Publ., New York.)

GABRIELSON, I. N., AND F. C. LINCOLN. 1959. Birds of Alaska. Stackpole Co. and Wildl. Manage. Inst., Harrisburg, PA.

GADDIS, P. K. Undated [a]. Impact of BT on growth and reproductive success of chickadees. Unpubl. rep., N.W. Ecol. Res. Inst., Portland, OR.

GADDIS, P. K. Undated [b]. Reproductive biology of the Chestnut-backed Chickadee. Unpubl. rep., N.W. Ecol. Res. Inst., Portland, OR.

GAINES, D. 1974. Review of the status of the Yellow-billed Cuckoo in California: Sacramento Valley populations. Condor 76: 204-209.

GAINES, D. 1988. Birds of Yosemite and the east slope. Artemisia Press, Lee Vining, CA.

GAINES, D., AND S. A. LAYMON. 1984. Decline, status and preservation of the Yellow-billed Cuckoo in California. West. Birds 15: 49-80.

GALBREATH, D. S., AND R. MORELAND. 1953. The Chukar partridge in Washington. Wash. State Game Dept. Biol. Bull. 11. Olympia, WA.

GALEN, C. 1989. A preliminary assessment of the status of the Lewis' Woodpecker in Wasco County, Oregon. Oreg. Dept. of Fish and Wildl. Tech. Rep. 88-3-01. Portland, OR.

GALUSHA, J. G., AND R. L. CARTER. 1987. Do adult gulls recognize their own young? An experimental test. Stud. in Avian Biol. 10: 75-79.

GALUSHA, J. G., B. VORVICK, M. OPP, AND P. T. VORVICK. 1987. Nesting season censuses of seabirds on Protection Island, Washington. Murrelet 68: 103-107.

GAMBLE, L. R., AND T. M. BERGIN. 1996. Western Kingbird (Tyrannus verticalis). In The birds of North America, No. 227 (A. Poole and F. Gill, eds.). Acad. of Nat. Sci., Philadelphia, and Am. Ornithol. Union, Washington, D.C.

GAMMONLEY, J. H. 1996. Cinnamon Teal (Anas cyanoptera). In The birds of North America, No. 209 (A. Poole and F. Gill, eds.). Acad. of Nat. Sci., Philadelphia, and Am. Ornithol. Union, Washington, D.C.

GAMMONLEY, J. H., AND M. E. HEITMEYER. 1990. Behavior, body condition, and foods of Buffleheads and Lesser Scaups during spring migration through the Klamath Basin, California. Wilson Bull. 102: 672-683.

GANO, K. A., AND W. H. RICKARD. 1982. Small mammals of a bitterbrush-cheatgrass community. Northwest Sci. 56: 1-7.

GARBER, D. P., AND J. R. KOPLIN. 1972. Prolonged and bisexual incubation by California Ospreys. Condor 74: 201-202.

GARCELON, D. K., G. L. SLATER, AND C. D. DANILSON. 1995. Cooperative nesting by a trio of Bald Eagles. J. Raptor Res. 29: 210-213.

GARDALI, T., AND G. BALLARD. 2000. Warbling Vireo (Vireo gilvus). In The birds of North America, No. 551 (A. Poole and F. Gill, eds.). The Birds of N. Am., Inc., Philadelphia, PA.

GARDALI, T., G. BALLARD, N. NUR, AND G. R.GEUPEL. 2000. Demography of a declining population of Warbling Vireos in coastal California. Condor 102: 601-609.

GARNER, D. J. 1982. Nest-site provision experiment for Long-eared Owls. British Birds 75: 376-377.

GARRETT, K. L., M. G. RAPHAEL, AND R. D. DIXON. 1996. White-headed Woodpecker (Picoides albolarvatus). In The birds of North America, No. 252. (A. Poole and F. Gill, eds.). Acad. of Nat. Sci., Philadelphia, and Am. Ornithol. Union, Washington, D.C.

GARRETT, M. G., R. G. ANTHONY, J. W. WATSON, AND K. McGARIGAL. 1988. Ecology of Bald Eagles on the lower Columbia River. Final rep., U.S. Army Corps of Eng., Portland, OR. Contract No. DACW57-84-C-0071.

GARRETT, M. G., J. W. WATSON, AND R. G. ANTHONY. 1993. Bald Eagle home ranges and habitat use in the Columbia River estuary. J. Wildl. Manage. 57: 19-27.

GARRISON, B. A. 1999. Bank Swallow (Riparia riparia). In The birds of North America, No. 414 (A. Poole and F. Gill, eds.). The Birds of N. Am., Inc., Philadelphia, PA.

GASHWILER, J. S. 1977. Bird populations in four vegetational types in central Oregon. U.S. Fish and Wildl. Serv. Spec. Sci. Rep.—Wildl. 205.

GASHWILER, J., AND R. GASHWILER. 1975. A Blue Jay record for Oregon. Murrelet 55: 45.

GASTON, A. J. 1992. The Ancient Murrelet: a natural history in the Queen Charlotte Islands. Academic Press, San Diego, CA.

GASTON, A. J. 1994. Ancient Murrelet (Synthliboramphus antiquus). In The birds of North America, No. 132 (A. Poole and F. Gill, eds.). Acad. of Nat. Sci., Philadelphia, and Am. Ornithol. Union, Washington, D.C.

GASTON, A. J., D. K. CAIRNS, R. D. ELLIOT, AND D. G. NOBLE. 1985. A natural history of Digges Sound. Can. Wildl. Serv. Rep. Series 46.

GASTON, A. J., H. R. CARTER, AND S. G. SEALY. 1993. Winter ecology and diet of Ancient Murrelets off Victoria, British Columbia. Can. J. Zool. 71: 64-70.

GASTON, A. J., AND S. B. C. DECHESNE. 1996. Rhinoceros Auklet (Cerorhinca monocerata). In The birds of North America, No. 212 (A. Poole and F. Gill, eds.). Acad. of Nat. Sci., Philadelphia, and Am. Ornithol. Union, Washington, D.C.

GASTON, A. J., AND R. DECKER. 1985. Interbreeding of Thayer's Gull, Larus thayeri and Kumlien's Gull, Larus glaucoides kumlieni on Southhampton Island, Northwest Territories. Can. Field-Nat. 99: 257-259.

GASTON, A. J., L. DE FOREST, AND D. G. NOBLE. 1993. Egg recognition and egg stealing in murres (Uria spp.). Anim. Behav. 45: 301-306.

GASTON, A. J., AND I. L. JONES. 1998. The Auks Alcidae. Oxford Univ. Press.

GATCHET, J., AND M. DENNY. Unpubl. ms. Birds sighted on Mahogany Mountain, Malheur County, Oregon.

GAUTHIER, G. 1993. Bufflehead (Bucephala albeola). In The birds of North America, No. 67 (A. Poole and F. Gill, eds.). Acad. of Nat. Sci.,

Philadelphia, and Am. Ornithol. Union, Washington, D.C.

GAVETT, A. P., AND J. S. WAKELY. 1986. Diets of House Sparrows in urban and rural habitats. Wilson Bull. 98: 144-147.

GAVIN, T. A., R. A. HOWARD, AND B. MAY. 1991. Allozyme variation among breeding populations of Red-winged Blackbirds: the California conundrum. Auk 108: 602-611.

GEIER, J. 2002. The Harris's Sparrow (*Zonotrichia querula*) irruption of fall and winter, 2001-2002. Oreg. Birds 28: 93.

GENTER, D., D. P. HENDRICKS, AND J. D. REICHEL. 1998. Productivity and adult recruitment for Harlequin Duck in the Rocky Mountains. Unpubl. abstract, 4th biennial Harlequin Duck Working Group, and 1st annual Pacific Flyway Symposium, Otter Crest, OR.

GEORGE, T. L. 2000. Varied Thrush (*Ixoreus naevius*). *In* The birds of North America, No. 541 (A. Poole and F. Gill, eds.). The Birds of N. Am., Inc., Philadelphia, PA.

GERIG, R. 1992. Breeding birds of the Coast Range: a comparison of the species mix in successional forest communities in Polk County. Oreg. Birds 18: 7-10.

GERSTENBERG, R. H., AND S. W. HARRIS. 1970. A California specimen of the Bar-tailed Godwit. Condor 72: 112.

GHALAMBOR, C. K., AND T. E. MARTIN. 1999. Red-breasted Nuthatch (*Sitta canadensis*). *In* The birds of North America, No. 459 (A. Poole and F. Gill, eds). The Birds of N. Am., Inc., Philadelphia, PA.

GIBBS, J. P. 1991. Spatial relationships between nesting colonies and foraging areas of Great Blue Herons. Auk 108: 764-770.

GIBBS, J. P., AND S. M. MELVIN. 1993. Call-response surveys for monitoring breeding waterbirds. J. Wildl. Manage. 57: 27-34.

GIBBS, J. P., S. MELVIN, AND F. A. REID. 1992a. American Bittern (*Botaurus lentiginosus*). *In* The birds of North America, No. 18 (A. Poole and F. Gill, eds.). Acad. of Nat. Sci., Philadelphia, and Am. Ornithol. Union, Washington, D.C.

GIBBS, J. P., F. A. REID, AND S. M. MELVIN. 1992b. Least Bittern (*Ixobrychus exilis*). *In* The birds of North America, No. 17 (A. Poole, P. Stettenheim, and F. Gill, eds.). Acad. of Nat. Sci., Philadelphia, and Am. Ornithol. Union, Washington, D.C.

GIBSON, D. 1977. First North American nest and eggs of the Ruff. West. Birds 8: 25-26.

GIBSON, D. D. 1986. *Calcarius lapponicus coloratus* in the Aleutian Islands, Alaska. Auk 103: 635-636.

GIBSON, D. D., AND B. KESSEL. 1989. Geographic variation in the Marbled Godwit and description of an Alaska subspecies. Condor 91: 436-443.

GIBSON, D. D., AND B. KESSEL. 1992. Seventy-four new avian taxa documented in Alaska 1976-1991. Condor 94: 454-467.

GIBSON, D. D., AND B. KESSEL. 1997. Inventory of the species and subspecies of Alaska birds. West. Birds 28: 45-95.

GIBSON, F. 1971. The breeding biology of the American Avocet (*Recurvirostra americana*) in central Oregon. Condor 73: 444-454.

GIESE, A. R. 1999. Habitat selection by Northern Pygmy-Owls on the Olympic Peninsula, Washington. M.S. thesis, Oreg. State Univ., Corvallis.

GILBERT, F. F., AND R. ALLWINE. 1991. Spring bird communities in the Oregon Cascade Range. Pp. 144-158 *in* Wildlife and vegetation of unmanaged Douglas-fir forests (L. F. Ruggiero, K. B. Aubry, A. B. Carey, and M. H. Huff, eds.). U.S. Dept. Agric., For. Serv. Gen. Tech. Rep. PNW-GTR-285.

GILL, R. E., C. M. HANDEL, AND G. W. PAGE. 1998. Western North American shorebirds. Natl. Biol. Information Infrastructure, national programs, status and trends. URL = http://biology.usgs.gov/s+t/frame/b021.htm Accessed 18 Sep 2002.

GILL, R. E., AND L. R. MEWALDT. 1983. Pacific coast Caspian Terns: dynamics of an expanding population. Auk 100: 369-381.

GILL, R. E., JR., M. R. PETERSEN, AND P. D. JORGENSEN. 1981. Birds of the northcentral Alaska Peninsula, 1976-1980. Arctic 34: 286-306.

GILLESPIE, G. E., AND S. J. WESTRHEIM. 1997. Synopsis of information on marine fishes utilized as prey by marine and shoreline bird of the Queen Charlotte Islands. Pp. 36-55 *in* The ecology, status, and conservation of marine and shoreline birds of the Queen Charlotte Islands (K. Vermeer and K. H. Moran, eds.). Can. Wildl. Serv. Occasional Paper 93, Ottawa.

GILLIGAN, J. 1990. Comments regarding communal roosting of Northern Harriers in winter. Oreg. Birds 16: 262.

GILLIGAN, J. 1991. Field notes: western Oregon. Oreg. Birds 17: 127-128.

GILLIGAN, J. 1992a. Fieldnotes: western Oregon, fall 1991. Oreg. Birds 18: 62-64.

GILLIGAN, J. 1992b. Field notes: western Oregon, spring 1992. Oreg. Birds 18: 128-132.

GILLIGAN, J. 1993a. Field notes: western Oregon - fall 1992. Oreg. Birds 19: 56-60.

GILLIGAN, J. 1993b. Fieldnotes: western Oregon - spring 1993. Oreg. Birds 19: 118-120.

GILLIGAN, J. 1994. Field notes: western Oregon - fall 1993. Oreg. Birds 20: 71-72.

GILLIGAN, J. 1995. Fieldnotes: western Oregon, fall 1994. Oreg. Birds 21: 64-68.

GILLIGAN, J. 1996. Field notes: western Oregon, fall 1995. Oreg. Birds 22: 66-68.

GILLIGAN, J. 1997. Fieldnotes: western Oregon, fall 1996. Oreg. Birds 23: 80-84.

GILLIGAN, J. 1998. Field notes: western Oregon, fall 1997. Oreg. Birds 24: 63-68.

GILLIGAN, J. 1999. Field notes: western Oregon, fall 1998. Oreg. Birds 25: 50-56.

GILLIGAN, J. 2000. Fieldnotes: western Oregon, fall 1999. Oreg. Birds 26: 172-174.

GILLIGAN, J., AND D. IRONS. 1987. Oregon's first Orchard Oriole. Oreg. Birds 13: 296.

GILLIGAN, J., AND O. SCHMIDT. 1980. Identification—non-breeding phalaropes. Oreg. Birds 6: 129-135.

GILLIGAN, J., AND O. SCHMIDT. 1983. First verified Cape May Warbler for Oregon. West. Birds 14: 199-200.

GILLIGAN, J., O. SCHMIDT, D. IRONS, AND R. SMITH. 1984. First record of Le Conte's Sparrow in Oregon. West. Birds 15: 185-186.

GILLIGAN, J., O. SCHMIDT, H. NEHLS, AND D. IRONS. 1987. First record of Long-toed Stint in Oregon. West. Birds 18: 126-128.

GILLIGAN, J., AND M. SMITH. 1980. An ornithological visit to Mahogany Mountain, Malheur Co., Oregon. Oreg. Birds 6: 64.

GILLIGAN, J., M. SMITH, D. ROGERS, AND A. CONTRERAS. 1994. Birds of Oregon: status and distribution. Cinclus Publ., McMinnville, OR.

GILLIS, E. 1989. Western Bluebirds, Tree Swallows, and Violet-green Swallows west of the Cascade Mountains in Oregon, Washington, and Vancouver Island, British Columbia. Sialia 11: 127-130.

GILLSON, G. 1987. Site guide: Linn County. Oreg. Birds 13: 342-347.

GILLSON, G. 1989. Christmas Bird Count data reveals patterns in winter gull distribution in Oregon. Oreg. Birds 15: 255-262.

GILLSON, G. 1994. Tricolored Heron. Oreg. Birds 20: 44.

GILLSON, G. 1998. Birds of Linn County. Unpubl. manuscript. URL = http://thebirdguide.com/blc/blc_00.htm

GILLSON, G. 1999. Birds of Linn County. Unpubl. manuscript. URL = http://thebirdguide.com/blc/blc_00.htm

GILLSON, G. 2000. The Flesh-footed Shearwater (*Puffinus carneipes*) in Oregon. Oreg. Birds. 26: 150-153.

GILLSON, G. 2001a. Birds of Linn County. Unpubl. manuscript. URL = http://thebirdguide.com/blc/blc_00.htm Accessed 20 Sep 2002.

GILLSON, G. 2001b. Hoodoo: birds and birding. Oreg. Birds 27: 1-6.

GILLSON, G. 2001c. Range expansion of Wrentit (*Chamaea fasciata*) to Linn County, Oregon. Oreg. Birds 27: 52.

GILMER, D. S., I. J. BALL, L. M. COWARDIN, J. H. REICHMAN, AND J. R TESTER. 1975. Habitat use and home range of Mallards breeding in Minnesota. J. Wildl. Manage.39: 781-789.

GIUDICE, J. H., AND J. T. RATTI. 2001. Ring-necked Pheasant (*Phasianus colchicus*). *In* The birds of North America, No. 572 (A. Poole and F. Gill, eds.). The Birds of N. Am., Inc., Philadelphia, PA.

GLADING, B., AND C. GLADING. 1970. An instance of a captive Turkey Vulture killing prey. Condor 72: 244-245.

GLADSTONE, D. 1977. Leapfrog feeding in the Great Egret. Auk 94: 596-598.

GLAHN, J. F. 1974. Study of breeding rails with recorded calls in north-central Colorado. Wilson Bull. 86: 206-214.

GLOVER, F. A. 1953. Nesting ecology of the Pied-billed Grebe in northwestern Iowa. Wilson Bull. 65: 32-39.

GODFREY, W. E. 1986. Birds of Canada. Revised ed. Natl. Mus. of Nat. Sci., Natl. Mus. of Can., Ottawa.

GOGGANS, R. 1985. Habitat use by Flammulated Owls in northeastern Oregon. M.S. thesis, Oreg. State Univ., Corvallis.

GOGGANS, R., R. D. DIXON, AND L. C. SEMINARA. 1989. Habitat use by Three-toed and Black-backed Woodpeckers, Deschutes National Forest, Oregon. Oreg. Dept. Fish and Wildl., Nongame Wildl. Rep. 87-3-02, Portland.

GOGGANS, R., AND M. PLATT. 1992. Breeding season observations of Great Gray Owls on the Willamette National Forest, Oregon. Oreg. Birds 18: 35-41.

GOLDSTEIN, M. I., B. WOODBRIDGE, M. E. ZACCAGNINI, AND S. B. CANAVELLI. 1996. An assessment of mortality in Swainson's Hawks on wintering grounds in Argentina. J. Raptor Res. 30: 106-107.

GOLLOP, J. B., AND W. H. MARSHALL. 1954. A guide for aging duck broods in the field. Miss. Flyway Tech. Sect.

GONZALEZ, P. M., T. PIERSMA, AND Y. VERKUIL. 1996. Food, feeding, and refueling of Red Knots during northward migration at San Antonio Oeste, Rio Negro, Argentina. J. Field Ornithol. 67: 575-591.

GOOD, T. P., J. C. ELLIS, C. A. ANNETT, AND R. PIEROTTI. 2000. Bounded hybrid superiority in an avian hybrid zone: effects of mate, diet and habitat choice. Evolution 54: 1774-1783.

GOODRICH, L. J., S. C. CROCOLL, AND S. E. SENNER. 1996. Broad-winged Hawk (*Buteo platypterus*). *In* The birds of North America, No. 218 (A. Poole and F. Gill, eds.). Acad. of Nat. Sci., Philadelphia, and Am. Ornithol. Union, Washington, D.C.

GOODWIN, D. 1986. Crows of the world. 2nd ed. Brit. Mus. of Nat. Hist.

GORDON, S. 1978. Brief note: Ross' Geese and Tri-colored Blackbird in Klamath County. Oreg. Birds 4(2): 40.

GORDON, S. 1979. Big Day in Klamath County. Oreg. Birds 5: 25-27.

GORDON, S. 1980. Summary of the 1979 Oregon Christmas Bird Counts. Oreg. Birds 6: 16-23.

GORDON, S. 1984a. Big days: Klamath County 1984. Oreg. Birds 10: 139-141.

GORDON, S. 1984b. Distribution: Lane County breeding bird atlas. Oreg. Birds 10: 126-133.

GOSS-CUSTARD, J. D., R. E. JONES, AND P. E. NEWBERY. 1977. The ecology of the wash: distribution and diet of wading birds (Charadrii). J. Appl. Ecol. 14: 681-700.

GOSS-CUSTARD, J. D., AND M. E. MOSER. 1988. Rates of change in the numbers of Dunlin, *Calidris alpina*, wintering in British estuaries in relation to the spread of *Spartina anglica*. J. Appl. Ecol. 25: 95-109.

GOUDIE, R. I., AND C. D. ANKNEY. 1986. Body size, activity budgets, and diets of sea ducks wintering in Newfoundland. Ecology 67: 1475-1482.

GOUDIE, R. I., S. BRAULT, B. CONANT, A. V. KONDRATYEV, R. M. PETERSEN, AND K. VERMEER. 1994. The status of sea ducks in the north Pacific rim: toward their conservation and management. Trans. 59th N. Am. Wildl. Nat. Resour. Conf.: 27-49.

GOUGH, G. A., J. R. SAUER, AND M. ILIFF. 1998. Patuxent bird identification infocenter. Version 97.1. Patuxent Wildl. Res. Center, Laurel, MD.

GOWANS, B, G. J. ROBERTSON, AND F. COOKE. 1997. Behavior and chronology of pair formation by Harlequin Ducks *Histrionicus histrionicus*. Wildfowl 48: 135-146.

GRABER, R. R., AND J. W. GRABER. 1962. Weight characteristics of birds killed in nocturnal migration. Wilson Bull. 74: 74-85.

GRAF, W. 1946. Notes on the distribution and habits of Anthony Green Heron. Murrelet 27: 50-51.

GRAHAM, R. T., R. T. REYNOLDS, M. H. REISER, R. L. BASSETT, AND D. A. BOYCE. 1994. Sustaining forest habitat for the Northern Goshawk: a question of scale. Stud. in Avian Biol. 16: 12-17.

GRANDE RONDE BIRD CLUB. 1988. Birds of northeastern Oregon: Union, Baker and Wallowa counties (checklist). La Grande, OR.

GRANLUND, J. 1994. Pine Siskin *Carduelis pinus*. Pp. 335-337 *in* The birds of Michigan (G. A. McPeek and R. J. Adams, eds.). Indiana Univ. Press, Bloomington.

GRANT, J. 1966. The Barred Owl in British Columbia. Murrelet 47: 39-45.

GRANT, K. A., AND V. GRANT. 1967. Effects of hummingbird migration on plant speciation in California flora. Evolution 21: 209-220.

GRANT, P. J. 1986. Gulls, a guide to identification. Buteo Books, Vermillion, SD.

GRATTO-TREVOR, C. L. 1992. Semipalmated Sandpiper (*Calidris pusilla*). *In* The birds of North America, No. 6 (A. Poole, P. Stettenheim, and F. Gill, eds.). Acad. of Nat. Sci., Philadelphia, and Am. Ornithol. Union, Washington, D.C.

GRATTO-TREVOR, C. L. 2000. Marbled Godwit (*Limosa fedoa*). *In* The birds of North America, No. 492 (A. Poole and F. Gill, eds.). The Birds of N. Am., Inc., Philadelphia, PA.

GRAVES, K. 1996. Feeding symbiosis between American Coot and American Wigeon. Oreg. Birds 22: 9.

GRAYBILL, M. 1980. Marine birds and mammals notes. Cape Arago Tattler 4: 1-2.

GRAYBILL, M., AND J. HODDER. 1985. Effects of the 1982-83 El Niño on reproduction of six species of birds in Oregon, Pp. 205-210 in El Niño North: Niño effects in the eastern subarctic Pacific Ocean (W. S. Wooster and D. L. Fluharty, eds.). Wash. Sea Grant Program, Univ. of Wash., Seattle.

GRAYSON, D. K., AND C. MASER. 1978. First record for the Long-tailed Jaeger in eastern Oregon. Murrelet 59: 75-77.

GREEN, B. H., AND H. D. SMITH. 1981. Habitat utilization by Sage Sparrows in mixed desert shrub community. Encyclia 58: 159.

GREEN, G. A. 1978. Summer birds of the Alvord Basin, Oregon. Murrelet 59: 59-69.

GREEN, G. A. 1983. Ecology of breeding Burrowing Owls in the Columbia Basin. M.S. thesis, Oreg. State Univ., Corvallis.

GREEN, G. A., AND R. G. ANTHONY. 1989. Nesting success and habitat relationships of Burrowing Owls in the Columbia Basin, Oregon. Condor 91: 347-354.

GREEN, G. A., AND R. G. ANTHONY. 1997. Ecological considerations for management of breeding Burrowing Owls in the Columbia Basin. J. Raptor Res. Rep. 9: 117-121.

GREEN, G. A., R. E. FITZNER, R. G. ANTHONY, AND L. E. ROGERS. 1993. Comparative diets of Burrowing Owls in Oregon and Washington. Northwest Sci. 67: 88-93.

GREEN, G. A., AND K. B. LIVEZEY. 1999. Integrated natural resources management plan: naval weapons systems training facility. Boardman, OR.

GREEN, G. A., AND M. L. MORRISON. 1983. Nest-site characteristics of sympatric Ferruginous and Swainson's hawks. Murrelet 64: 20-22.

GREENE, E., W. DAVIDSON, AND V. R. MUEHTER. 1998. Steller's Jay (Cyanocitta stelleri). In The birds of North America, No. 343 (A. Poole and F. Gill, eds.). The Birds of N. Am., Inc., Philadelphia, PA.

GREENE, E., R. VINCENT, AND W. DAVISON. 1996. Lazuli Bunting (Passerina amoena). In The birds of

North America, No. 232 (A. Poole and F. Gill, eds.). Acad. of Nat. Sci., Philadelphia, and Am. Ornithol. Union, Washington, D.C.

GREENFIELD, S. 1977. Northern Waterthrush. SWOC Talk (Oreg. Birds) 3(3): 83-84.

GREENLAW, J. 1996. Spotted Towhee (Pipilo maculatus). In The birds of North America, No. 263 (A. Poole and F. Gill, eds.). Acad. of Nat. Sci., Philadelphia, and Am. Ornithol. Union, Washington, D.C.

GREENLAW, J. S., AND R. F. MILLER. 1983. Calculating incubation periods of species that sometimes neglect their last eggs; the case of the Sora. Wilson Bull. 95: 459-461.

GREENWOOD, J. G. 1986. Geographical variation and taxonomy of the Dunlin Calidris alpina (L.). Bull. British Ornithol. Club 106: 43-56.

GREGG, M. A., J. A. CRAWFORD, AND M. S. DRUT. 1993. Summer habitat use and selection by female Sage Grouse (Centrocercus urophasianus) in Oregon. Great Basin Nat. 53: 293-298.

GREGG, M. A., J. A. CRAWFORD, M. S. DRUT, AND A. K. DELONG. 1994. Vegetational cover and predation of Sage Grouse nests in Oregon. J. Wildl. Manage. 58: 162-166.

GRIER, J. W. 1982. Ban of DDT and subsequent recovery of reproduction in Bald Eagles. Science 218: 1232-1235.

GRIFFEE, W. E. 1936. Nesting of the Hooded Merganser at Portland, Oregon. Murrelet 17: 53-54.

GRIFFEE, W. E. 1944. First Oregon nest of Yellow Rail. Murrelet 25: 29.

GRIFFEE, W. E. 1947. A high junco nest. Murrelet 28: 22.

GRIFFEE, W. E. 1954. Some Oregon nesting records. Murrelet 35: 48-49.

GRIFFEE, W. E. 1958. Notes on Oregon nesting of American Merganser and Barrow's Golden-eye. Murrelet 39: 26.

GRIFFEE, W. E. 1960. Bohemian Waxwing nesting in Oregon. Murrelet 41: 44.

GRIFFEE, W. E. 1961a. Bufflehead nesting records for Oregon. Murrelet 42: 5.

GRIFFEE, W. E. 1961b. Nesting of the Northern Vaux Swift in the Willamette Valley. Murrelet 42: 25-26.

GRIFFEE, W. E., AND E. F. RAPRAEGER. 1937. Nesting dates for birds breeding in the vicinity of Portland, Oregon. Murrelet 18: 14-18.

GRIFFITH, J. 1992. Oregon's first Steller's Eider. Oreg. Birds 18: 67.

GRINNELL, G. B. 1901. American duck shooting. Forest and Stream Publ. Co., New York, NY.

GRINNELL, J. 1901. Two races of the Red-breasted Sapsucker. Condor 3: 12.

GRINNELL, J. 1908. The biota of the San Bernadino Mountains. Univ. Calif. Publ. Zool. 5: 1-170.

GRINNELL, J., AND W. H. BEHLE. 1937. A new race of Brown Towhee, from the Kern Basin of California. Condor 39: 177-178.

GRINNELL, J., J. DIXON, AND J. M. LINSDALE. 1930. Vertebrate natural history of a section of northern California through the Lassen Peak region. Univ. Calif. Publ. Zool. 35: 1-594.

GRINNELL, J., AND A. H. MILLER. 1944. The distribution of the birds of California. Pacific Coast Avifauna 27.

GRINNELL, J., AND T. I. STORER. 1924. Animal life in the Yosemite: an account of the mammals, birds, reptiles, and amphibians in a cross-section of the Sierra Nevada. Univ. Calif. Press, Berkeley.

GRISCOM, L., AND A. SPRUNT, JR. 1957. The warblers of North America. Devin-Adair, New York.

GROOMS, S. 1992. The cry of the Sandhill Crane. NorthWord Press, Minoqua, WI.

GROSS, A. O. 1923. The Black-crowned Night Heron (Nycticorax nycticorax naevius) of Sandy Neck. Auk 40: 1-30, 191-214.

GROTH, J. G. 1993a. Call matching and positive assortive mating in Red Crossbills. Auk 110: 398-401.

GROTH, J. G. 1993b. Evolutionary differentiation in morphology, vocalizations, and allozymes among nomadic sibling species in the North American Red Crossbill (Loxia curvirostra) complex. Univ. Calif. Publ. Zool. 127.

GROVE, R. A. 1985. Northern Saw-whet Owl winter food and roosting habits in north-central Washington. Murrelet 66: 21-24.

GROVES, C. R., B. BUTTERFIELD, A. LIPPINCOTT, B. CSUTI, AND J. M. SCOTT. 1997. Atlas of Idaho's wildlife. Idaho Dept. of Fish and Game, Boise.

GROVES, S. 1984. Chick growth, sibling rivalry, and chick production in American Black Oystercatchers. Auk 101: 525-531.

GRUSON, E. S. 1972. Words for birds: a lexicon of North American birds with biographical notes. Quadrangle Books Inc., New York, NY.

GUARD, B. J. 1995. Wetland plants of Oregon and Washington. Lone Pine Publ., Renton, WA.

GUICKING, D. 1999. Pink-footed Shearwaters on Isla Mocha, Chile. World Birdwatch Spec. Issue 21(4).

GUIGUET, C. J. 1956. Enigma of the Pacific. Audubon 58: 164-167, 174.

GUINAN, D. M., AND S. G. SEALY. 1987. Diet of House Wrens (*Troglodytes aedon*) and the abundance of the invertebrate prey in the dune-ridge forest, Delta Marsh, Manitoba. Can. J. Zool. 65: 1587-1596.

GUINAN, J. A., P. A. GOWATY, AND E. K. ELTZROTH. 2000. Western Bluebird (*Sialia mexicana*). *In* The birds of North America, No. 510 (A. Poole and F. Gill, eds). The Birds of N. Am., Inc., Philadelphia, PA.

GULLION, G. W. 1947. Use of artificial nesting sites by Violet-green and Tree swallows. Auk 64: 411-415.

GULLION, G. 1948a. An early record of the Western Kingbird in Lane County, Oregon. Condor 50: 46.

GULLION, G. W. 1948b. A mid-winter record of the Barn Swallow in Lane County, Oregon. Condor 50: 92.

GULLION, G. 1948c. Wren-tits in the Roseburg area, Oregon. Condor 50: 132-133.

GULLION, G. 1948d. Young Short-eared Owl "captured" by plant. Condor 50: 229.

GULLION, G. W. 1951. Birds of the southern Willamette Valley, Oregon. Condor 53: 129-149.

GUMTOW-FARRIOR, D. L. 1991. Cavity resources in Oregon white oak and Douglas-fir in the mid-Willamette Valley, Oregon. M.S. thesis, Oreg. State Univ., Corvallis.

GUSTAFSON, M. E., AND B. G. PETERJOHN. 1994. Adult Slaty-backed Gulls: variability in mantle color and comments on identification. Birding 26: 243-249.

GUTIÉRREZ, R. J., C. E. BRAUN, AND T. P. ZAPATKA. 1975. Reproductive biology of the Band-tailed Pigeon in Colorado and New Mexico. Auk 92: 665–677.

GUTIÉRREZ, R. J., AND D. J. DELEHANTY. 1999. Mountain Quail (*Oreortyx pictus*). *In* The birds of North America, No. 457 (A. Poole and F. Gill, eds.). The Birds of N. Am., Inc., Philadelphia, PA.

GUTIÉRREZ, R. J., A. B. FRANKLIN, AND W. S. LAHAYE. 1995. Spotted Owl (*Strix occidentalis*). *In* The birds of North America, No. 179 (A. Poole and F. Gill, eds.). Acad. of Nat. Sci., Philadelphia, and Am. Ornithol. Union, Washington, D.C.

GUZY, M. J., AND P. E. LOWTHER. 1997. Black-throated Gray Warbler (*Dendroica nigrescens*). *In* The birds of North America, No. 319 (A. Poole and F. Gill, eds.). Acad. of Nat. Sci., Philadelphia, and Am. Ornithol. Union, Washington, D.C.

GUZY, M. J., AND G. RITCHISON. 1999. Common Yellowthroat (*Geothlypis trichas*). *In* The birds of North America, No. 448 (A. Poole and F. Gill, eds.). The Birds of N. Am., Inc., Philadelphia, PA.

HAAK, B. A. 1982a. Foraging ecology of Prairie Falcons in northern California. M.S. thesis, Oreg. State Univ., Corvallis, OR.

HAAK, B. A. 1982b. Population status of Prairie Falcons in northern Lake County, Oregon. Oreg. Dept. of Fish and Wildl., Nongame Wildl. Prog. Tech. Rep. 4T22: 82-5-04B. Portland, OR.

HAAK, B. A., AND S. J. DENTON. 1979. Subterranean nesting by Prairie Falcons. Raptor Res. 13: 117-118.

HABECK, J. R. 1962. Forest succession in Monmouth Township, Polk County, Oregon since 1850. Proc. Mont. Acad. of Sci. 21: 7-17.

HAENSLY, T. F., J. A. CRAWFORD, AND S. M. MEYERS. 1987. Relationships of habitat structure to nest success of Ring-necked Pheasants. J. Wildl. Manage. 51: 421-425.

HAGAR, D. C. 1960. The interrelationships of logging, birds, and timber regeneration in the Douglas-fir region of northwestern California. Ecology 41: 116-125.

HAGAR, J. C. 1992. Bird communities in commercially thinned and unthinned Douglas-fir stands of western Oregon. M.S. thesis., Oreg. State Univ., Corvallis.

HAGAR, J. C. 1999a. Influence of riparian buffer width on bird assemblages in western Oregon. J. Wildl. Manage. 63: 484-496.

HAGAR, J. C. 1999b. Songbird community response to thinning of young Douglas-fir stands in the Oregon Cascades – second year post-treatment results for the Willamette National Forest young stand study. Unpubl. rep. for U.S. Dept. Agric. For. Serv., Willamette Nat. Forest.

HAGAR, J. C., AND S. HOWLIN. 2001. Songbird community response to thinning of young Douglas-fir stands in the Oregon Cascades – third year post-treatment results for the Willamette National Forest young stand thinning and diversity study. Unpubl. rep. for U.S. Dept.

Agric. For. Service, Willamette Nat. Forest. URL = http://www.fsl.orst. edu/ccem/yst/ystd.html Accessed 20 Sep 2002.

HAGAR, J. C., W. C. MCCOMB, AND W. H. EMMINGHAM. 1996. Bird communities in commercially thinned and unthinned Douglas-fir stands of western Oregon. Wildl. Soc. Bull. 24: 353-366.

HAGAR, J. C., AND E. STARKEY. 2000. Trophic relations among birds, arthropods and shrubs. Pp. 35-39 *in* Cooperative Forest Ecosystem Research (CFER) Annual Report 2000. U.S. Geol. Surv. For. and Rangeland Ecosystem Sci. Center. Corvallis, OR.

HAGAR, J., AND M. STERN. 2001. Avifauna in oak woodland habitats of the Willamette Valley, Oregon. Northwest. Nat. 82: 12-25.

HAGENSTEIN, W. M. 1936. Pacific Loon in breeding plumage taken on Puget Sound, Washington. Murrelet 17: 56.

HAHN, T. P. 1995. Integration of photoperiodic and food cures to time changes in reproductive physiology by an opportunistic breeder, the Red Crossbill, *Loxia curvirostra* (Aves: Carduelinae). J. Exp. Zool. 272: 213-226.

HAHN, T. P. 1996. Cassin's Finch (*Carpodacus cassinii*). *In* The birds of North America, No. 240 (A. Poole and F. Gill, eds.). Acad. of Nat. Sci., Philadelphia, and Am. Ornithol. Union, Washington, D.C.

HAIG, S. M., L. W. ORING, P. M. SANZENBACHER, AND O. W. TAFT. 2002. Space use, migratory connectivity, and population segregation among Willets breeding in the western Great Basin. Condor 104: 620-630.

HAIG, S. M., R. S. WAGNER, E. D. FORSMAN, AND T. D. MULLINS. 2001. Geographic variation and genetic structure in Spotted Owls. Cons. Genetics 2: 25-40.

HAIGHT, W. 1992. Status/future of management and recovery of Oregon Peregrine Falcons. Pp. 68-71 *in* Proc. symposium on Peregrine Falcons in the Pacific Northwest (J. E. Pagel, ed.). Rogue River Natl. For., Medford, OR.

HAINLINE, J. L. 1974. The distribution, migration, and breeding of shorebirds in western Nevada. M.S. thesis, Univ. Nev., Reno.

HÄKKINEN, I. 1977. Food catch of the Osprey *Pandion haliaetus* during the breeding season. Ornis Fennica 54: 166-169.

HALE, J. B., AND R. S. DORNEY. 1963. Seasonal movements of Ruffed Grouse in Wisconsin. J. Wildl. Manage. 27: 648-656.

HALL, F. C., AND J. W. THOMAS. 1979. Silvicultural options. Pp. 128-147 in Wildlife habitat in managed forests: the Blue Mountains of Oregon and Washington (J. W. Thomas, tech. ed.). U.S. Dept. Agric., For. Serv. Agric. Handbook 553.

HALL, J. A. 1988. Early chick mobility and brood movements in the Forster's Tern (Sterna forsteri). J. Field Ornithol. 59: 247-251.

HALL, J. A. 1989. Aspects of Forster's Tern (Sterna forsteri) reproduction on cobblestone islands in southcentral Washington. Northwest Sci. 63: 90-95.

HALLETT, C., B. CASLER, AND M. STERN. 1995. Semipalmated Plover nesting on the Oregon coast. West. Birds 26: 161-164.

HALTERMAN, M. D., D. S. GILMER, S. A. LAYMONG, AND G. A. FALXA. 2001. Status of the Yellow-billed Cuckoo in California: 1999-2000. Unpubl. rep., U.S. Geol. Surv., Bio. Res. Div., Dixon, CA.

HAMAS, M. J. 1994. Belted Kingfisher (Ceryle alcyon). In The birds of North America, No. 84 (A. Poole and F. Gill, eds.). Acad. of Nat. Sci., Philadelphia, and Am. Ornithol. Union, Washington, D.C.

HAMER, T. E. 1988. Home range size of the Northern Barred Owl and the Northern Spotted Owl in western Washington. M.S. thesis, West. Wash. Univ., Bellingham, WA.

HAMER, T. E., E. D. FORSMAN, A. D. FUCHS, AND M. L. WALTERS. 1994. Hybridization between Barred and Spotted Owls. Auk 111: 487-492.

HAMER, T. E., D. L. HAYS, AND C. M. SENGER. 1991. A comparison of Barred Owl and Spotted Owl summer food habits. Unpubl. rep., Wash. Dept. Wildl., Olympia.

HAMER, T. E., D. L. HAYS, C. M. SENGER, AND E. D. FORSMAN. 2001. Diets of Northern Barred Owls and Northern Spotted Owls in an area of sympatry. J. Rapt. Res. 35: 221-227.

HAMER, T. E., AND S. K. NELSON. 1995a. Characteristics of Marbled Murrelet nest trees and nesting stand. Pp. 69-82 in Ecology and conservation of the Marbled Murrelet (C. J. Ralph, G. L. Hunt, Jr., M. G. Raphael, and J. F. Piatt, eds.). U.S. Dept. Agric., For. Serv. Gen. Tech. Rep. PSW-GTR-152. Albany, CA.

HAMER, T. E., AND S. K. NELSON. 1995b. Nesting chronology of the Marbled Murrelet. Pp. 49-56 in Ecology and conservation of the Marbled Murrelet (C. J. Ralph, G. L. Hunt, Jr., M. G. Raphael, and J. F. Piatt, eds.). U.S. Dept. Agric., For. Serv. Gen. Tech. Rep. PSW-GTR-152. Albany, CA.

HAMER, T. E., S. G. SEIM, AND K. R. DIXON. 1989. Preliminary report: Northern Spotted Owl and Northern Barred Owl habitat use and home range size in Washington. Unpubl. rep., Wash. Dept. Wildl., Olympia.

HAMILTON, R. B. 1975. Comparative behavior of the American Avocet and the Black-necked Stilt (Recurvirostridae). Ornithol. Monogr. 17.

HAMMAR, M. 2000. An inland June record of Pomarine Jaeger. Oreg. Birds 26: 157.

HAMPTON, S. 1997. Western Flycatcher question. Electronic mail message to Oregon birders On-Line listserver. 25 July 1997. URL: http://osu.orst.edu/pubs/birds/obolnts/spec198.htm

HANCOCK, D. R., T. F. GAUMER, G. B. WILLEKE, G. P. ROBART, AND J. FLYNN. 1979. Subtidal clam populations: distribution, abundance, and ecology. Oreg. State Univ. Sea Grant Coll. Prog. Publ. No. ORESU-T-79-002, Corvallis.

HANCOCK, J., AND H. ELLIOT. 1978. The herons of the world. Harper and Row. New York.

HANCOCK, J., AND J. KUSHLAN. 1984. The herons handbook. Harper and Row. New York.

HAND, R. 1960. A sight record of the Brown Towhee in northwestern Oregon. Murrelet 41: 40.

HANDEL, C., AND R. E. GILL, JR. 1992. Breeding distribution of the Black Turnstone. Wilson Bull. 104: 122-135.

HANDEL, C., AND R. E. GILL. 2001. Black Turnstone (Arenaria melanocephala). In The birds of North America, No. 585 (A. Poole and F. Gill, eds.). The Birds of N. Am., Inc., Philadelphia, PA.

HANEY, J. C. 1986. Seabird affinities for Gulf Stream frontal eddies: responses of mobile marine consumers to episodic upwelling. J. Marine Res. 44: 361-384.

HANEY, J. C. 1997. Spatial incidence of Barred Owl (Strix varia) reproduction in old-growth forest of the Appalachian Plateau. J. Raptor Res. 31: 241-252.

HANF, J. M., P. A. SCHMIDT, AND E. B. GROSHENS. 1994. Sage Grouse in the high desert of central Oregon: results of a study, 1988-1993. U.S. Dept. of Int., Bur. of Land Manage., Series P-SG-01. Prineville Dist.

HANKA, L. R. 1984. A Brown-headed Cowbird parasitizes Northern Orioles. West. Birds 15: 33-34.

HANN, H. W. 1950. Nesting behavior of American Dipper in Colorado. Condor 52: 49-62.

HANNA, W. C. 1909. The White-throated Swifts on Slover Mountain. Condor 11: 77-81.

HANSELL, H. 1983. Aspects of the diving biology of Common Murres. M.S. thesis, Univ. of Oreg., Eugene.

HANSEN, A. J., AND P. HOUNIHAN. 1996. Canopy tree retention and avian diversity in the Oregon Cascades. Pp. 401-421 in Strategies for maintaining biodiversity: theory and practice (R. C. Szaro and D. W. Johnson, eds.). Oxford Univ. Press., New York.

HANSEN, A. J., W. C. MCCOMB, R. VEGA, M. G. RAPHAEL, AND M. HUNTER. 1995. Bird habitat relationships in natural and managed forests in the west Cascades of Oregon. Ecol. Appl. 5: 555-569.

HANSEN, C. G. 1956. An ecological survey of the vertebrate animals on Steen's Mountain, Harney County, Oregon. Ph.D diss., Oreg. State Coll., Corvallis.

HANSEN, H. A., P. E. SHEPARD, J. G. KING, AND W. A. TROYER. 1971. The Trumpeter Swan in Alaska. Wildl. Monogr. 26: 1-83.

HANSON, H. A. 1962. Canada Geese of coastal Alaska. Trans. N. Am. Wildl. Nat. Resour. Conf. 27: 301-320.

HANSON, H. C. 1965. The giant Canada Goose. S. Illinois Univ. Press, Carbondale.

HANSON, W. C., AND L. L. EBERHARDT. 1971. A Columbia River Canada Goose population, 1950-1970. Wildl. Monogr. 28.

HARMATA, A. R., G. J. MONTOPOLI, B. OAKLEAF, P. J. HARMATA, AND M. RESTANI. 1999. Movements and survival of Bald Eagles banded in the Greater Yellowstone Ecosystem. J. Wildl. Manage. 63: 781-793.

HARMATA, A., AND B. OAKLEAF. 1992. Bald Eagles in the Greater Yellowstone Ecosystem: an ecological study with emphasis on the Snake River, Wyoming, Vol. 1. Wyo. Game and Fish Dept., Lander, WY.

HARPER, H. T., B. H. HARRY, AND W. D. BAILEY. 1958. The Chukar Partridge in California. Calif. Fish and Game 44: 5-50.

HARRAP, S., AND D. QUINN. 1995. Chickadees, tits, nuthatches, and treecreepers. Princeton Univ. Press, Princeton, NJ.

HARRINGTON, B. A. 1983. The migration of the Red Knot. Oceanus 26: 44-48.

HARRINGTON, B. A. 2001. Red Knot (*Calidris canutus*). *In* The birds of North America, No. 563 (A. Poole and F. Gill, eds.). The Birds of N. Am., Inc., Philadelphia, PA.

HARRINGTON-TWEIT, B. 1979. A seabird die-off on the Washington coast in mid-winter 1976. West. Birds 10: 49-56.

HARRINGTON-TWEIT, B. 1980. First records of the White-tailed Kite in Washington. West. Birds 11: 151-153.

HARRINGTON-TWEIT, B., P. W. MATTOCKS, JR., AND E. S. HUNN. 1978. Northern Pacific Coast region. Am. Birds 32: 1199-1203.

HARRINGTON-TWEIT, B., P. W. MATTOCKS, AND E. HUNN. 1979. Northern Pacific Coast region. Am. Birds 33: 890-893.

HARRINGTON-TWEIT, B., P. W. MATTOCKS, AND E. HUNN. 1981. Northern Pacific Coast region. Am. Birds 35: 970-973.

HARRINGTON-TWEIT, B., P. W. MATTOCKS, AND E. HUNN. 1982. Northern Pacific Coast region. Am. Birds 36: 1009-1011.

HARRINGTON-TWEIT, B., AND P. W. MATTOCKS, JR. 1984. Northern Pacific Coast region. Am. Birds 38: 1054-1056.

HARRINGTON-TWEIT, B., P. MATTOCKS, AND E. HUNN. 1999. Northern Pacific Coast region. Am. Birds 36: 1009-1011.

HARRIS, S. W. 1974. Status, chronology and ecology of nesting storm petrels in northwest California. Condor 76: 249-261.

HARRIS, S. W. 1991. Northwestern California birds. Humboldt State Univ. Press, Arcata, CA.

HARRIS, S. W. 1996. Northwestern California birds, 2nd edition. Humboldt State Univ. Press, Arcata, CA.

HARRISON, C. 1978. A field guide to the nests, eggs and nestlings of North American birds. W. Collins Sons & Co. Cleveland.

HARRISON, C. S. 1984. Terns. Pp. 146-160 *in* Seabirds of eastern North Pacific and Arctic waters (D. Haley, ed.). Pacific Search Press, Seattle.

HARRISON, C. S. 1990. Seabirds of Hawaii. Comstock/Cornell, Ithaca, NY.

HARRISON, H. H. 1979. A field guide to western birds' nests of 520 species found breeding in the United States west of the Mississippi River. Houghton Mifflin Co., Boston, MA.

HARRISON, H. H. 1984. Wood warblers' world. Simon and Schuster, New York, NY.

HARRISON, N. 1984. Predation on jellyfish and their associates by seabirds. Limnol. Ocean. 29: 1335-1337.

HARRISON, P. 1983. Seabirds: an identification guide. Croom Helm Ltd., London.

HARRISON, P. 1985. Seabirds: an identification guide, revised ed. Houghton Mifflin, Boston.

HART, C. M., O. S. LEE, AND J. B. LOW. 1950. The Sharp-tailed Grouse in Utah. Utah Dept. Fish and Game.

HARTWICK, E. B. 1976. Foraging strategy of the Black Oystercatcher (*Haematopus bachmani* Audubon). Can. J. Zool. 54: 142-155.

HARVEY, B. C., AND C. D. MARTI. 1993. The impact of dipper, *Cinclus mexicanus*, predation on stream benthos. Oikos 68: 431-436.

HASEGAWA, H., AND A. R. DEGANGE. 1982. The Short-tailed Albatross, *Diomedea albatrus*, its status, distribution and natural history. Am. Birds 36: 806-814.

HASKIN, L. 1934. Wildflowers of the Pacific Coast. Binfords and Mort, Portland, OR.

HATCH, J. J. 1995. Changing populations of Double-crested Cormorants. Pp. 8-24 *in* The Double-crested Cormorant: biology, conservation and management (D. N. Nettleship and D. C. Duffy, eds.). Colonial Waterbirds 18 (Special Publ. 1).

HATCH, J. J., AND D. V. WESELOH. 1999. Double-crested Cormorant (*Phalacrocorax auritus*). *In* The birds of North America, No. 441 (A. Poole and F. Gill, eds.). The Birds of N. Am., Inc., Philadelphia, PA.

HATCH, S. A. 1993. Ecology and population status of Northern Fulmars *Fulmarus glacialis* of the North Pacific. *In* The status, ecology, and conservation of marine birds of the North Pacific (K. Vermeer, K. T. Briggs, K. H. Morgan, and D. Siegel-Causey, eds.). Can. Wildl. Serv. Ottawa.

HATCH, S. A., G. V. BYRD, D. B. IRONS, AND G. L. HUNT, JR. 1993. Status and ecology of kittiwakes (*Rissa tridactyla* and *R. brevirostris*) in the North Pacific. *In* The status, ecology, and conservation of marine birds of the North Pacific (K. Vermeer, K. T. Briggs, K. H. Morgan, and D. Siegel-Causey, eds.). Can. Wildl. Serv. Ottawa.

HATCH, S. A., AND M. A. HATCH. 1990. Components of the breeding productivity in a marine bird community: key factors and concordance. Can. J. Zool. 68: 1680-1690.

HAWBECKER, A. C. 1948. Analysis of variation in western races of the White-breasted Nuthatch. Condor 50: 26-39.

HAWKSWORTH, D. L., B. C. SUTTON, AND G. D. AINSWORTH. 1983. Dictionary of the fungi, seventh ed. Commonwealth Mycological Inst., Kew, Surrey, England.

HAWTHORNE, V. M. 1979. Use of nest boxes by dippers on Sagehen Creek, California. West. Birds 10: 215-216.

HAY, D. B. 1983. Physiological and behavioral ecology of communally roosting Pygmy Nuthatches (*Sitta pygmaea*). Ph.D. thesis, N. Ariz. Univ., Flagstaff.

HAY, D. B., AND M. GUNTERT. 1983. Seasonal selection of tree cavities by Pygmy Nuthatches based on cavity characteristics. Pp.117-120 *in* Snag habitat management symposium proceedings (J. W. Davis, G. A. Goodwin, and R. A. Ockenfels, tech. coords.). U.S. Dept. Agric., For. Serv. Gen. Tech. Rep. RM-99.

HAY, D. E., M. C. HEALEY, D. M. WARE, AND N. J. WILIMOVSKY. 1992. Distribution, abundance, and habitat of prey fish on the west coast of Vancouver Island. Pp. 22-29 *in* The ecology, status, and conservation of marine and shoreline birds on the west coast of Vancouver Island (K. Vermeer, R. W. Butler, and K. H. Morgan, eds.). Occas. Paper 75. Can. Wildl. Serv.

HAYES, G. E., AND J. B. BUCHANAN. 2002. Washington state status report for the Peregrine Falcon. Wash. Dept. Fish and Wildl., Olympia.

HAYES, J. P., J. M. WEIKEL, AND M. D. ADAM. 1998. Abundance of breeding birds. Chap. 5 *in* Effects of commercial thinning on stand structure and wildlife populations: a progress report, 1994-1997. Coastal Oreg. Productivity Enhancement (COPE) Prog. Coll. of Forestry, Oreg. State Univ., Corvallis.

HAYES, J. P., J. M. WEIKEL, AND M. M. P. HUSO. In press. Response of birds to thinning young Douglas-fir forests. Ecol. Appl.

HAYMAN, P., J. MARCHANT, AND T. PRATER. 1986. Shorebirds: an identification guide to the waders of the world. Houghton Mifflin Co., Boston.

HAYWARD, G. D. 1988. Resource partitioning among forest owls in the River of No Return Wilderness, Idaho. Oecologia 75: 253-265.

HAYWARD, G. D. 1989. Habitat use and population biology of Boreal Owls in Northern Rocky Mountains, USA. Ph.D diss., Univ. Idaho, Moscow.

HAYWARD, G. D., AND E. O. GARTON. 1983. First nesting record of Boreal Owl in Idaho. Condor 85: 501.

HAYWARD, G. D., AND E. O. GARTON. 1984. Roost habitat selection by three small forest owls. Wilson Bull. 96: 690-692.

HAYWARD, G. D., AND P. H. HAYWARD. 1993. Boreal Owl (Aegolius funereus). In The birds of North America, No. 63 (A. Poole and F. Gill, eds.). Acad. of Nat. Sci., Philadelphia, and Am. Ornithol. Union, Washington, D.C.

HAYWARD, J. L. 1993. Nest-site selection and reproductive success of Ring-billed Gulls at Sprague Lake, Washington. Northwest. Nat. 74: 67-76.

HAYWARD, J. L., J. G. GALUSHA, AND G. FRIAS. 1993. Analysis of Great Horned Owl pellets with Rhinoceros Auklet remains. Auk 110: 133-135.

HAYWARD, J. L., JR., AND A. C. THORESEN. 1980. Dippers in marine habitats in Washington. West. Birds 11: 60.

HEATH, A. C. 1999. Crane Prairie Reservoir, Davis Lake, and Wickiup Reservoir waterbird surveys. Unpubl. data., Oreg. Dept. Fish and Wildl., Bend.

HEBARD, F. V. 1949. Birds of the Fremont National Forest, southcentral Oregon. Condor 51: 151.

HECK, M. K. 1985. The social organization of wintering Killdeer (Charadrius vociferus) flocks. M.S. thesis, N. Carolina St. Univ., Raleigh, N.C.

HEEKIN, P. E., C. A. VOGEL, AND K. P. REESE. 1994. Uncovering the elusive habits of Mountain Quail in Oregon. Quail Unlimited 13: 14-16.

HEIDCAMP, A. 1997. Selasphorus Hummingbirds. Birding 29: 18-29.

HEIDRICH, P. C., C. KÖNIG, AND M. WINK. 1995. Bioakustik, taxonomie und molekulare systematik amerikanischer sperlingskäuze (Strigidae: Glaucidium spp.). Stuttgarter Beitr. Naturk., Ser. A, 534: 1-47.

HEILBRUN, L. H., ED. 1978. The seventy-eighth Audubon Christmas Bird Count. Am. Birds 32: 415-908.

HEINDEL, M. T. 1996. Field identification of the Solitary Vireo complex. Birding 28: 459-471.

HEINL, S. 1985. Field notes: western Oregon. Oreg. Birds 11: 98-109.

HEINL, S. 1986a. Fieldnotes: western Oregon, fall 1985. Oreg. Birds 12: 209-223.

HEINL, S. 1986b. Field notes: western Oregon, summer 1985. Oreg. Birds 12: 133-137.

HEINL, S. 1986c. Fieldnotes: western Oregon winter/spring 1985-1986. Oreg. Birds 12: 353-363.

HEINL, S. 1987a. Field notes: western Oregon, March - May 1987. Oreg. Birds 13: 448-456.

HEINL, S. 1987b. Field notes: western Oregon, summer 1986. Oreg. Birds 13: 101-106.

HEINL, S. 1987c. Field notes: western Oregon, winter 1986-1987. Oreg. Birds 13: 312-318.

HEINL, S. 1988a. Field notes: western Oregon, August - November 1987. Oreg. Birds 14: 284-298.

HEINL, S. 1988b. Field notes: western Oregon, summer 1987. Oreg. Birds 14: 88-92.

HEINL, S. 1989a. Field notes: western Oregon, spring 1988. Oreg. Birds 15: 40-50.

HEINL, S. 1989b. Field notes: western Oregon, spring 1989. Oreg. Birds 15: 298-308.

HEINL, S., AND D. FIX. 1989. Field notes: western Oregon, fall 1988. Oreg. Birds 15: 120-137.

HEINL, S., AND M. HUNTER. 1985. Checklist: birds of Fern Ridge Reservoir. Oreg. Dept. Fish and Wildl.

HEINRICH, B. 1989. Ravens in winter. Vintage Books, New York, NY.

HEINRICH, B. 1999. Mind of the Raven. Cliff Street Books, Harper Collins, New York, NY.

HEJL, S. J. 1994. Human-induced changes in bird populations in coniferous forest in western North America during the past 100 years. Pp. 232-246 in A century of avifaunal change in western North America (J. R. Jehl, Jr. and N. K. Johnson, eds.). Stud. in Avian Biol. 15: 232-246.

HEJL, S. J., M. E. McFADZEN, AND T. E. MARTIN. 2000. Maintaining fire-associated bird species across forest landscapes in the northern Rockies, final report INT 99543 RJVA. U.S. Dept. Agric., For. Serv. RMRS Forestry Sci. Lab. Missoula, MT.

HELBING, G. L. 1977. Maintenance activities in the Black Oystercatcher Haematopus bachmani Audubon, in northwestern California. M.S. thesis, Humboldt State Univ., Arcata, CA.

HELLMAYR, C. E., AND B. CONOVER. 1948. Catalogue of birds of the Americas and adjacent islands. Field Mus. Nat. Hist., Zool. Ser. 13: 1-434.

HELTZEL, J., AND S. L. EARNST. 2002. Nesting success of riparian songbirds on Hart Mountain National Antelope Refuge, southeastern Oregon, part III. Ann. prog. rep., U.S. Geol. Surv., Snake River Field Stat., Boise, ID.

HELZER, C. J., AND D. E. JELINSKI. 1999. The relative importance of patch area and perimeter-area ration to grassland breeding birds. Ecol. Appl. 9: 1448-1458.

HENDERSON, B. A. 1975. Role of the chick's begging behavior in the regulation of parental feeding behavior of Larus glaucescens. Condor 77: 488-492.

HENDRICKS, P. 1981. Observations on a winter roost of rosy finches in Montana. J. Field Ornithol. 52: 235-236.

HENJUM, M. G., J. R. KARR, D. L. BOTTOM, D. A. PERRY, J. C. BEDNARZ, S. G. WRIGHT, S. A. BECKWITH, AND E. BECKWITT. 1994. Interim protection for late-successional forests, fisheries, and watersheds: national forests east of the Cascade crest, Oregon and Washington. Wildl. Soc., Bethesda, MD.

HENNINGS, L. A. 2001. Riparian bird communities in Portland, Oregon: habitat, urbanization, and spatial scale patterns. M.S. thesis, Oreg. State Univ., Corvallis.

HENNY, C. J. 1972. An analysis of the population dynamics of selected avian species with special reference to changes during the modern pesticide era. U.S. Fish and Wildl. Serv., Wildl. Res. Rep. I. Washington, D.C.

HENNY, C. J. 1977a. Birds of prey, DDT and tussock moths in Pacific Northwest. Trans. N. Am. Wildl. Nat. Resour. Conf. 42: 397-411.

HENNY, C. J. 1977b. Research, management and status of Osprey in North America. Pp.199-222 *In* World conference on birds of prey – report of proceedings (R. D. Chancellor, ed.). Internatl. Counc. for Bird Preservation, Vienna, Austria.

HENNY, C. J. 1983. Distribution and abundance of nesting Ospreys in the United States. Pp. 175-186. *In* Biology and management of Bald Eagles and Ospreys (D. M. Bird, ed.). Harpell Press, Ste. Anne de Bellevue, Quebec.

HENNY, C. J. 1988. Large Osprey colony discovered in Oregon in 1899. Murrelet 69: 33-36.

HENNY, C. J. 1990. Wintering localities of Cooper's Hawks nesting in northeastern Oregon. J. Field Ornithol. 61: 104-107.

HENNY, C. J., AND D. W. ANDERSON. 1979. Osprey distribution, abundance, and status in western North America: III. the Baja California and Gulf of California population. Bull. S. Calif. Sci. 78: 89-106.

HENNY, C. J., D. W. ANDERSON, AND C. E. KNODER. 1978. Bald Eagles nesting in Baja California. Auk 95: 424.

HENNY, C. J., AND J. T. ANNEAR. 1978. A White-tailed Kite breeding record for Oregon. West. Birds 9: 131-133.

HENNY, C. J., AND M. R. BETHERS. 1971. Population ecology of the Great Blue Heron with special reference to western Oregon. Can. Field-Nat. 85: 205-209.

HENNY, C. J., AND L. J. BLUS. 1981. Artificial burrows provide new insight into Burrowing Owl nesting behavior. Raptor Res. 15: 82-85.

HENNY, C. J., AND L. J. BLUS. 1986. Radiotelemetry locates wintering grounds of DDE-contaminated Black-crowned Night-Herons. Wildl. Soc. Bull. 14: 236-241.

HENNY, C. J., L. J. BLUS, AND C. S. HULSE. 1985. Trends and effects of organochlorine residues on Oregon and Nevada wading birds, 1979-83. Colonial Waterbirds 8: 117-128.

HENNY, C. J., L. J. BLUS, AND T. E. KAISER. 1984. Heptachlor seed treatment contaminates hawks, owls, and eagles of Columbia Basin, Oregon. Raptor Res. 18: 41-48.

HENNY, C. J., L. J. BLUS, E. J. KOLBE, AND R. E. FITZNER. 1985. Organophosphate insecticide (Famphur) topically applied to cattle kills magpies and hawks. J. Wildl. Manage. 49: 648-658.

HENNY, C. J., L. J. BLUS, A. J. KRYNITSKY, AND C. M. BUNCK. 1984. Current impact of DDE on Black-crowned Night-Herons in the intermountain west. J. Wildl. Manage. 48: 1-13.

HENNY, C. J., L. J. BLUS, AND R. M. PROUTY. 1982. Organochlorine residues and shell thinning in Oregon seabird eggs. Murrelet 63: 15-21.

HENNY, C. J., L. J. BLUS, AND C. J. STAFFORD. 1983. Effects of heptachlor on American Kestrels in the Columbia Basin, Oregon. J. Wildl. Manage. 47: 1080-1087.

HENNY, C. J., AND G. L. BRADY. 1994. Partial migration and wintering localities of American Kestrels nesting in the Pacific Northwest. Northwest. Nat. 75: 37-43.

HENNY, C. J., J. A. COLLINS, AND W. J. DEIBERT. 1978. Osprey distribution, abundance, and status in western North America, II: the Oregon population. Murrelet 59: 14-25.

HENNY, C. J., AND J. E. CORNELY. 1985. Recent Red-shouldered Hawk range expansion north into Oregon including first specimen record. Murrelet 66: 29-31.

HENNY, C. J., AND J. L. KAISER. 1996. Osprey population increase along the Willamette River, Oregon, and the role of utility structures, 1976-93. Pp 97-108 *In* Raptors in human landscapes (D. M.Bird, D. E. Varland, and J. J. Negro, eds.). Academic Press Ltd., London.

HENNY, C. J., J. L. KAISER, R. A. GROVE, V. R. BENTLEY, AND J. E. ELLIOT. 2003. Biomagnification factors (fish to Osprey eggs from the Willamette River, Oregon, U.S.A.) for PCDDs, PCDFs, PCBs, and OC pesticides. Environ. Monitoring and Assessment, in press.

HENNY, C. J., AND T. KAISER. 1977. Organochlorine and mercury residues in hawk eggs from the Pacific Northwest. Murrelet 60: 2-5.

HENNY, C. J., AND J. E. KURTZ. 1978. Great Blue Herons respond to nesting habitat loss. Wildl. Soc. Bull. 6: 35-37.

HENNY, C. J., AND D. L. MEEKER. 1981. An evaluation of blood plasma for monitoring DDE in birds of prey. Environ. Pollution (series A) 25: 291-304.

HENNY, C. J., AND M. W. NELSON. 1981. Decline and present status of Peregrine Falcons in Oregon. Murrelet 62: 43-53.

HENNY, C. J., R. A. OLSON, AND T. L. FLEMING. 1985. Breeding chronology, molt, and measurements of accipiter hawks in northeastern Oregon. J. Field Ornithol. 56: 97-112.

HENNY, C .J., R. A. OLSON, AND D. L. MEEKER. 1977. Residues in Common Flicker and Mountain Bluebird eggs one year after DDT application. Bull. Environ. Contam. Toxicol. 18: 115-122.

HENNY, C. J., D. D. RUDIS, T. J. ROFFE, AND E. ROBINSON-WILSON. 1995. Contaminants and sea ducks in Alaska and the circumpolar region. Environ. Health Perspective 103 (suppl. 4): 41-49.

HENNY, C. J., M. M. SMITH, AND V. D. STOTTS. 1974. The 1973 distribution and abundance of breeding Ospreys in the Chesapeake Bay. Chesapeake Sci. 15: 125-133.

HENNY, C. J., AND H. M. WIGHT. 1972. Population ecology and environmental pollution: Red-tailed and Cooper's hawks. Pp. 229-250 *In* Population ecology of migratory birds–a symposium. U.S. Fish and Wildl. Serv., Wildl. Res. Rept. 2.

HENRY, W. G. 1980. Populations and behavior of Black Brant at Humboldt Bay, California. M.S. thesis, Humboldt State Univ., Arcata, CA.

HENRY, W. G. 1983. Inventory of the Black-shouldered Kite population and habitat in Tillamook County, Oregon. Oreg. Dept. of Fish and Wildl. Nongame Wildl. Prog. Tech. Rep. 83-7-05. Portland.

HENRY, W. G., AND SPRINGER, P. F. 1981. Seasonal abundance and behavior of Black Brant (*Branta bernicla nigricans*) on Humboldt Bay. Estuaries 4: 265 (abstr.).

HERKERT, J. R. 1994. Breeding bird communities of midwestern prairie fragments: the effects of prescribed burning and habitat-area. Nat. Areas J. 14: 128-135.

HERKERT, J. R., R. E. SZAFONI, V. M. KLEEN, AND J. E. SCHWEGMAN. 1993. Habitat establishment, enhancement, and management for forest and grassland birds in Illinois. Ill. Dept. Conserv., Nat. Heritage Tech. Publ. 1.

HERLUGSON, C. J. 1975. Status and distribution of the Western Bluebird and the Mountain Bluebird in the state of Washington. M.S. thesis, Wash. State Univ., Pullman.

HERLUGSON, C. J. 1982. Food of adult and nestling Western and Mountain bluebirds. Murrelet 63: 59-65.

HERLYN, H. 1997. Birds of Benton County, Oregon. Audubon Soc. of Corvallis. http://osu.orst.edu/pubs/birds/county/bent/index.htm

HERLYN, H. 1998. Birds of Benton County, Oregon. Audubon Soc. of Corvallis. http://osu.orst.edu/pubs/birds/county/bent/index.htm

HERLYN, H. 1999. Birds of Benton County, Oregon. Audubon Soc. of Corvallis. http://osu.orst.edu/pubs/birds/county/bent/index.htm Accessed 20 Sep 2002.

HERLYN, H. G., S. JONES, AND J. L. SIMMONS. 1994. Oregon's first Streak-backed Oriole. Oreg. Birds 20: 75-77.

HERMAN, S. G. 1971. The functional and numerical responses of the Cassin's Finch, *Carpodacus cassinii* (Baird), to epidemic numbers of the lodgepole needleminer, *Coleotechnites milleri* (Busck). Wash. J. Biol. 29: 71-80.

HERMAN, S. G., AND J. SCOVILLE. 1988. The Upland Sandpiper in Oregon. Unpubl. rep. to Oreg. Dept. of Fish and Wildl., Portland.

HERMAN, S. G., J. B. BULGER, AND J. B. BUCHANAN. 1988. The Snowy Plover in southeastern Oregon and western Nevada. J. Field Ornithol. 59: 13-21.

HERMAN, S. G., J. SCOVILLE, AND S. WALTCHER. 1985. The Upland Sandpiper in Bear Valley and Logan Valley, Grant County, Oregon. Unpubl. rep. to Oreg. Dept. of Fish and Wildl., Portland.

HERMANN, R. K., AND D. P. LAVENDER. 1990. Douglas-fir *Pseudotsuga menziesii*. Pp. 527-540 *in* Silvics of North America, vol. 1: conifers (R. M. Burns and B. H. Honkala, tech. coords.). U.S. Dept. Agric., For. Serv. Agric. Handbook 654. Washington, D.C.

HERRICK, F. H. 1934. The American Eagle: a study in natural and civil history. D. Appleton-Century Co., Inc., New York.

HERRON, G. B., C. A. MORTIMORE, AND M. S. RAWLINGS. 1985. Nevada raptors. Nev. Dept. Wildl., Biol. Bull. No. 8. Reno.

HERSHEY, K. T., E. C. MESLOW, AND F. L. RAMSEY. 1998. Characteristics of forests at Spotted Owl nest sites in the Pacific Northwest. J. Wildl. Manage. 62: 1398-1410.

HERTER, D. R., AND L. L. HICKS. 2000. Barred Owl and Spotted Owl populations and habitat in the central Cascade Range of Washington. J. Raptor Res. 34: 279-286.

HERZOG, S. K. 1996. Wintering Swainson's Hawks in California's Sacramento-San Joaquin River delta. Condor 98: 876-879.

HESSE, W., AND H. HESSE. 1965. Northern Pacific Coast region. Audubon Field Notes 19: 505-507.

HICKEY, J. J., ED. 1969. Peregrine Falcon populations: their biology and decline. Univ. Wisc. Press, Madison.

HICKEY, J. J., AND D. W. ANDERSON. 1968. Chlorinated hydrocarbons and eggshell changes in raptorial and fish-eating birds. Science 162: 271-273.

HILL, B. G., AND M. R. LEIN. 1988. Ecological relations of sympatric Black-capped and Mountain chickadees in Southwestern Alberta. Condor 90: 875-884.

HILL, G. E. 1988. Age, plumage brightness, territory quality, and reproductive success in the Black-headed Grosbeak. Condor 90: 379-388.

HILL, G. E. 1989. Late spring arrival and dull nuptial plumage: aggression avoidance by yearling males? Anim. Behav. 37: 665-673.

HILL, G. E. 1993. House Finch (*Carpodacus mexicanus*). *In* The birds of North America, No. 46 (A. Poole and F. Gill, eds.). Acad. of Nat. Sci., Philadelphia, and Am. Ornithol. Union, Washington, D.C.

HILL, G. E. 1995. Black-headed Grosbeak (*Pheucticus melanocephalus*). *In* The birds of North America, No. 143 (A. Poole and F. Gill, eds.). Acad. of Nat. Sci., Philadelphia, and Am. Ornithol. Union, Washington, D.C.

HILL, S., AND C. H. FISCUS. 1988. Cephalopod beaks from the stomachs of Northern Fulmars (*Fulmaris glacialis*) found dead on the Washington coast. Murrelet 69: 15-20.

HILL, W. L. 1986. Clutch overlap in American Coots. Condor 88: 96-97.

HILL, W. L. 1988. The effect of food abundance on the reproductive patterns of coots. Condor 90: 324-331.

HILL, W. L., M. BROWNE, AND C. HARDENBERGH. 1995. Composition of Eared Grebe and Western Grebe eggs. Condor 97: 1062-1064.

HILL, W. L., K. J. JONES, C. L. HARDENBERGH, AND M. BROWNE. 1997. Nest distance mediates the costs of coloniality in Eared Grebes. Colonial Waterbirds 20: 470-477.

HILLMAN, C. N., AND W. W. JACKSON. 1973. The Sharp-tailed Grouse in South Dakota. S. Dakota Dept. Game, Fish and Parks. Tech. Bull. 3.

HIRSCH, K. V. 1980. Winter ecology of sea ducks in the inland marine waters of Washington. M.S. thesis, Univ. of Washington, Seattle.

HITCHCOCK, R. R., R. BALCOMB, AND R. J. KENDALL. 1993. Migration chronology of American Wigeon in Washington, Oregon and California. J. Field Ornithol. 64: 96-101.

HJERTAAS, D. G. 1984. Colony site selection in Bank Swallows. M.S. thesis, Univ. of Saskatchewan, Saskatoon.

HJORTH, I. 1970. Reproductive behaviour in Tetraonidae, with special reference to males. Viltrevy 7: 183-596.

HOBSON, K. A. 1997. Pelagic Cormorant (*Phalacrocorax pelagicus*). *In* The birds of North America, No. 282 (A. Poole and F. Gill, eds.). Acad. of Nat. Sci., Philadelphia, and Am. Ornithol. Union, Washington, D.C.

HOBSON, K. A., AND S. G. SEALY. 1985. Diving rhythms and diurnal roosting times of Pelagic Cormorants. Wilson Bull. 97: 116-119.

HOBSON, K. A., AND S. G. SEALY. 1987a. Cowbird egg buried by a Northern Oriole. J. Field Ornithol. 58: 222-224.

HOBSON, K. A., AND S. G. SEALY. 1987b. Foraging, scavenging, and other behavior of swallows on the ground. Wilson Bull. 99: 111-116.

HOBSON, K. A., AND D. WILSON. 1985. Colony establishment by Pelagic Cormorants on man-made structures in southwest coastal British Columbia. Murrelet 66: 84-86.

HOCHBAUM, H. A. 1944. The Canvasback on a prairie marsh. Am. Wildl. Inst., Washington, D.C.

HODDER, J., AND M. R. GRAYBILL. 1985. Reproduction and survival of seabirds in Oregon during the 1982-83 El Niño. Condor 87: 535-541.

HODGES, J. I., J. G. KING, B. CONANT, AND H. A. HANSEN. 1996. Aerial surveys of waterbirds in Alaska 1957-94: population trends and observer variability. Nat. Biol. Serv. Information and Tech. Rep. 4.

HOFFMAN, W. 1972. A sight record of the Sharp-tailed Sandpiper at South Beach, Lincoln County, Oregon. Murrelet 53: 32.

HOFFMAN, W. 1980. Detailed field notes: Blue Jay. Oreg. Birds 6: 187-188.

HOFFMAN, W. E. 1982. White-throated Swift. Oreg. Birds 8: 88.

HOFFMAN, W., AND W. P. ELLIOT. 1974. Occurrence of intergrade Brant in Oregon. West. Birds 5: 91-93.

HOFFMAN, W., W. P. ELLIOT, AND J. M. SCOTT. 1975. The occurrence and status of the Horned Puffin in the western United States. West Birds 6: 87-94.

HOFFMAN, W., J. A. WIENS, AND J. M. SCOTT. 1978. Hybridization between gulls (*Larus glaucescens* and *Larus occidentalis*) in the Pacific Northwest. Auk 95: 441-458.

HOFFMANN, R. 1927. Birds of the Pacific states. Houghton Mifflin Co., Boston, MA.

HOFSLUND, P. B. 1957. Cowbird parasitism of the Northern Yellowthroat. Auk 74: 42-48.

HOHMAN, W. L., AND R. T. EBERHARDT. 1998. Ring-necked Duck (*Aythya collaris*). *In* The birds of North America, No. 329 (A. Poole and F. Gill, eds.). The Birds of N. Am., Inc., Philadelphia, PA.

HOHN, E. O. 1967. Observations on the breeding biology of Wilson's Phalarope *(Steganopus tricolor)* in central Alberta. Auk 84: 220-244.

HOLBO, K. J. 1979. Observations of a Rock Wren nest; Spencer Butte, Lane County. Oreg. Birds 5(5): 1-4.

HOLCOMB, L. C. 1969. Breeding biology of the American Goldfinch in Ohio. Bird-Banding 40: 26-44.

HOLIMON, W. C., C. W. BENKMAN, AND M. F. WILSON. 1998. The importance of mature conifers to Red Crossbills in southeast Alaska. For. Ecol. and Manage. 102: 167-172.

HOLMES, A. L., AND G. R. GEUPEL. 1998. Avian population studies at naval weapons systems training facility Boardman, Oregon. Final rep. to Dept. of Navy, and Oreg. Dept. of Fish and Wildl. PRBO Contr. 844.

HOLMES, R. T., AND S. K. ROBINSON. 1988. Spatial patterns, foraging tactics, and diets of ground-foraging birds in a northern hardwoods forest. Wilson Bull. 100: 377-394.

HOLMES, W. N. 1984. Petroleum pollutants in the marine environment and their possible effects on seabirds. Rev. of Environ. Toxicol. 1: 251-317.

HOLROYD, G. L. 1975. Nest site availability as a factor limiting population size of swallows. Can. Field-Nat. 89: 60-64.

HOLT, D. W., AND S. M. LEASURE. 1993. Short-eared Owl (*Asio flammeus*). *In*

The birds of North America, No. 62 (A. Poole and F. Gill, eds.). Acad. of Nat. Sci., Philadelphia, and Am. Ornithol. Union, Washington, D.C.

HOLT, D. W., AND W. D. NORTON. 1986. Observations of nesting Northern Pygmy-owls. Raptor Res. 20: 39-41.

HOLT, D. W., AND L. A. LEROUX. 1996. Diets of Northern Pygmy-Owls and Northern Saw-whet Owls in west-central Montana. Wilson Bull. 108: 123-128.

HOM, C. W. 1983. Foraging ecology of herons in a southern San Francisco Bay salt marsh. Colonial Waterbirds 6: 37-44.

HOOPER, R. G., H. S. CRAWFORD, D. R. CHAMBERLAIN, AND R. F. HARLOW. 1975. Nesting density of Common Ravens in the Ridgefield Valley region of Virginia. Am. Birds. 29: 931-935.

HORAK, G. J. 1970. A comparative study of the foods of the Sora and Virginia Rail. Wilson Bull. 82: 206-213.

HORN, K. M., AND D. B. MARSHALL. 1975. Status of Poor-will in Oregon and possible extension due to clearcut timber harvest methods. Murrelet 56: 4-5.

HORVATH, E. G. 1999. Distribution, abundance, and nest site characteristics of Purple Martins in Oregon. Oreg. Dept. of Fish and Wildl. Tech. Rep. 99-1-01.

HOSKYN, J. L. 1988. An interspecific comparison of the costs and benefits of coloniality in Barn and Cliff swallows. Senior thesis, Yale Univ., New Haven, CT.

HOUGHTON, L. M., AND L. M. RYMON. 1997. Nesting distribution and population status of United States Ospreys. J. Raptor Res. 31: 44-53.

HOWARD, R., AND A. MOORE. 1991. A complete checklist of the birds of the world, 2nd ed. Academic Press, London.

HOWARD, R. P., AND M. HILLIARD. 1980. Artificial nest structures and grassland raptors. Raptor Res. 14: 41-45.

HOWE, M. A. 1975a. Behavioral aspects of the pair bond in Wilson's Phalarope. Wilson Bull. 87: 248-270.

HOWE, M. A. 1975b. Social interactions in flocks of courting Wilson's Phalaropes *(Phalaropus tricolor)*. Condor 77: 24-33.

HOWE, M. A. 1982. Social organization in a nesting population of eastern Willets (*Catoptrophorus semipalmatus*). Auk 99: 88-102.

HOWELL, S. N. G., AND M. T. ELLIOTT. 2001. Identification and variation of winter adult Thayer's Gulls with comments on taxonomy. Alula 4: 130-144.

HOWELL, S. N. G., R. A. PAYNTER, JR., AND A. L. RAND. 1968. Subfamily carduelinae. Pp. 207-306 *in* Check-list of birds of the world, Vol. 14. (R. A. Paynter, Jr., ed.). Mus. Comp. Zool. Cambridge, MA.

HOWELL, S. N. G., L. B. SPEAR, AND P. PYLE. 1994. Identification of Manx-type shearwaters in the eastern Pacific. West. Birds 25: 169-177.

HOWELL, S. N. G., AND S. WEBB. 1995. A guide to the birds of Mexico and northern Central America. Oxford Univ. Press, New York, NY.

HOWELL, T. R. 1952. Natural history and differentiation in the Yellow-bellied Sapsucker. Condor 54: 237-282.

HOWELL, T. R. 1953. Racial and sexual differences in migration in *Sphyrapicus varius*. Auk 79: 118-126.

HOWES-JONES, D. 1985a. Nesting habits and activity patterns of Warbling Vireos, *Vireo gilvus*, in southern Ontario. Can. Field-Nat. 99: 484-489.

HOWES-JONES, D. 1985b. Relationships among song activity, context, and social behavior in the Warbling Vireo. Wilson Bull. 97: 4-20.

HOWITZ, J. L. 1984. First confirmed nesting of Pine Siskins in southeastern Minnesota. Loon 56: 197-198.

HUBBARD, J. P. 1969. The relationships and evolution of the *Dendroica coronata* complex. Auk 86: 393-432.

HUBBARD, J. P. 1970. Geographical variation in the *Dendroica coronata* complex. Wilson Bull. 82: 355-369.

HUBBARD, J. P. 1972. Notes on Arizona birds. Nemoria No. 5.

HUBBS, C. L., AND R. C. BANKS. 1966. Wandering onto the eastern Pacific Ocean of an eastern North American land bird, the Bay-breasted Warbler. Auk 83: 680-682.

HUDON, J. 1999. Western Tanager (*Piranga ludoviciana*). *In* The birds of North America, No. 432 (A. Poole and F. Gill, eds.). The Birds of N. Am., Inc., Philadelphia, PA.

HUFF, M., AND M. BROWN. 1998. Four years of bird point count monitoring in late-successional conifer forests and riparian areas from the Pacific Northwest National Forests, interim results. U.S. For. Serv., Portland.

HUFF, M. H., D. A. MANUWAL, AND J. A. PUTERA. 1991. Winter bird communities in the southern Washington Cascade Range. Pp. 206-218 *in* Wildlife and vegetation of unmanaged Douglas-fir forests (L. F. Ruggiero, K. B. Aubry, A. B. Carey, and M. H. Huff, tech. coords.). U.S. Dept. Agric., For. Serv. Gen. Tech. Rep. PNW-GTR-285.

HUFF, M. H., AND C. M. RALEY. 1991. Regional patterns of diurnal breeding bird communities in Oregon and Washington. Pp. 177-205 *in* Wildlife and vegetation of unmanaged Douglas-fir forests (L. F. Ruggiero, K. B. Aubry, A. B. Carey, and M. H. Huff, eds.). U.S. Dept. Agric., For. Serv. Gen. Tech. Rep. PNW- GTR-285.

HUGHES, J. M. 1999. Yellow-billed Cuckoo (*Coccyzus americanus*). *In* The birds of North America, No. 418 (A. Poole and F. Gill, eds.). The Birds of N. Am., Inc., Philadelphia, PA.

HUGHES, W. M. 1951. Some observations on the Rusty Song Sparrow *Melospiza melodia morphna* Oberholser. Can. Field-Nat. 65: 186.

HUNN, E. S. 1978. Black-throated Sparrow vagrants in the Pacific northwest. West. Birds 9: 85-89.

HUNN, E. 1983. When is an Allen's not an Allen's? Earthcare Northwest 23: Jul-Aug 1983.

HUNN, E. 2001. University of Washington, Seattle, Washington. Electronic mail message to Tweeters listserver. 7 June 2001.

HUNN, E., AND P. MATTOCKS, JR. 1977. Northern Pacific Coast region. Am. Birds 31: 1178-1183.

HUNN, E. S., AND P. W. MATTOCKS. 1978. Northern Pacific Coast region. Am. Birds 32: 390-394.

HUNN, E. S., AND P. W. MATTOCKS, JR. 1979a. Northern Pacific Coast region. Am. Birds 33: 206-209.

HUNN, E. S., AND P. W. MATTOCKS, JR. 1979b. Northern Pacific Coast region. Am. Birds 33: 799-802.

HUNN, E. S., AND P. W. MATTOCKS, JR. 1981a. Northern Pacific Coast region. Am. Birds 35: 216-219.

HUNN, E. S., AND P. W. MATTOCKS, JR. 1981b. Northern Pacific Coast region. Am. Birds 35: 854-857.

HUNN, E. S., AND P. W. MATTOCKS. 1982a. Northern Pacific Coast region. Am. Birds 36: 208-211.

HUNN, E. S., AND P. W. MATTOCKS. 1982b. Northern Pacific Coast region. Am. Birds 36: 886-888.

HUNN, E. S., AND P. W. MATTOCKS. 1983. Northern Pacific Coast region. Am. Birds 37: 215.

HUNN, E. S., AND P. W. MATTOCKS, JR. 1984. The autumn migration: August 1 - November 30, 1983. Am. Birds 38: 236-240.

HUNN, E. S., AND P. W. MATTOCKS. 1985. Northern Pacific Coast region. Am. Birds 39: 92-96.

HUNN, E. S., AND P. M. MATTOCKS, JR. 1986. Northern Pacific Coast region. Am. Birds 40: 316-324.

HUNT, G. L., AND M. W. HUNT. 1975. Reproductive ecology of the Western Gull: the importance of nest spacing. Auk 92: 270-279.

HUNT, P. D., AND D. J. FLASPOHLER. 1998. Yellow-rumped Warbler (*Dendroica coronata*). *In* The birds of North America, No. 376 (A. Poole and F. Gill, eds.). The Birds of N. Am., Inc., Philadelphia, PA.

HUNTER, M. 1985. Short note: status of Clark's Grebe. Oreg. Birds 11: 136.

HUNTER, M. G. 2000. An at-sea observation of a dark-morph Wedge-tailed Shearwater (*Puffinus pacificus*) in Oregon waters. Oreg. Birds 26: 158-159.

HUNTER, M. G. 2002. The twentieth-century range expansion of the Wrentit (*Chamaea fasciata*) in Oregon. Oreg. Birds 28: 150-163.

HUNTER, M. G., AND D. C. BAILEY. 1997. Oregon's first White-capped Albatross (*Diomedea cauta cauta*). Oreg. Birds 23: 35-39.

HUNTER, M., AND G. GILLSON. 1997. The future of Oregon's oceanic birding. Oreg. Birds 23: 40-46.

HUNTER, M. G., M. M. SAWYER, R. MAERTZ, B. KRUSE, AND K. WILSON. 1998. Birds of Douglas County, Part 3: the hundred valleys of the Umpqua. Oreg. Birds 24: 103-117.

HUNTINGTON, C. E., R. BUTLER, AND R. MAUCK. 1996. Leach's Storm-Petrel (*Oceanodroma leucorhoa*). *In* The birds of North America, No. 233 (A. Poole and F. Gill, eds.). Acad. of Nat. Sci., Philadelphia, and Am. Ornithol. Union, Washington, D.C.

HURD, P. L. 1992. American Coot kills Yellow-headed Blackbird nestlings. Wilson Bull. 104: 552-553.

HURST, G. A. 1980. Stove owner's alert. Sialia 2: 149.

HURST, G. A. 1992. Foods and feeding. Pp. 66-83 *in* The Wild Turkey: biology and management (J.G. Dickson, ed.). Stackpole Books, Harrisburg, PA.

HUTCHINS, H. E., AND R. M. LANNER. 1982. The central role of Clark's Nutcracker in the dispersal and establishment of whitebark pine. Oecologia 55: 192-201.

HUTTO, R. L. 1995a. Composition of bird communities following stand-replacement fires in northern Rocky Mountain U.S.A. conifer forests. Cons. Biol. 9: 1041-1058.

HUTTO, R. L. 1995b. U.S. Forest Service Northern Region songbird monitoring program: distribution and habitat relationships. Contract rep. to U.S. For. Serv. Region 1.

HUTTO, R. L., S. J. HEJL, C. R. PRESTON, AND D. M. FINCH. 1992. Effects of silvicultural treatments on forest birds in the Rocky Mountains: implications and management recommendations. Pp. 386-391 *in* Status and management of neotropical migratory birds (D. M. Finch and P. W. Stangel, eds.). U.S. Dept. Agric., For. Serv. Gen. Tech. Rep. GTR-RM-229.

HYDE, A. S. 1940. Western Mockingbird and Desert Sparrow in southeastern Oregon. Condor 42: 305.

HYDE, A. S. 1942. Notes from northeastern Oregon. Wilson Bull. 54: 51-52.

IDAHO CONSERVATION DATA CENTER. 1997. List of known occurrences for the Upland Sandpiper in Idaho, 21 August 1997.

INDEPENDENT MULTIDISCIPLINARY SCIENCE TEAM (IMST). 1998. Pinniped and seabird predation: implications for recovery of threatened stocks of salmonids in Oregon under the Oregon Plan for Salmon and Watersheds. Tech. Rep. 1998-2 to the Oregon Plan for Salmon and Watersheds. Governor's Nat. Res. Office, Salem.

INGOLD, J. L., AND R. GALATI. 1997. Golden-crowned Kinglet (*Regulus satrapa*). *In* The birds of North America, No. 301 (A. Poole and F. Gill, eds.). Acad. of Nat. Sci., Philadelphia, and Am. Ornithol. Union, Washington, D.C.

INGOLD, J. L., AND G. E. WALLACE. 1994. Ruby-crowned Kinglet (*Regulus calendula*). *In* The birds of North America, No. 119 (A. Poole and F. Gill, eds.). Acad. of Nat. Sci., Philadelphia, and Am. Ornithol. Union, Washington, D.C.

IRONS, D. 1984a. Highlights from the field notes: fall 1983. Oreg. Birds 10: 2-9.

IRONS, D. 1984b. Highlights from the field notes: spring 1984. Oreg. Birds 10: 84-99.

IRONS, D., AND D. FIX. 1990. How to search for passerines more effectively in winter: notes on winter habitat microsites. Oreg. Birds 16: 251-254.

IRONS, D., AND S. HEINL. 1984. Highlights from the field notes: winter 1983-1984, western Oregon. Oreg. Birds 10: 35-43.

IRONS, D., AND C. WATSON. 1984. Oregon Bird Records Committee report: committee actions 1978-1983. Oreg. Birds 11: 18-68.

IRWIN, L., D. F. ROCK, AND G. P. MILLER. 2000. Stand structures used by Northern Spotted Owls in managed forests. J. Raptor Res. 34: 175-186.

ISAAC, L. A. 1943. Reproductive habits of Douglas-fir. Charles Lathrop Pack For. Found., Washington, D.C.

ISAACS, F. B. 2001. 2001 midwinter Bald Eagle survey summary. Oreg. Birds 23: 95.

ISAACS, F. B., AND R. G. ANTHONY. 1987. Abundance, foraging, and roosting of Bald Eagles wintering in the Harney Basin, Oregon. Northwest Sci. 61: 114-121.

ISAACS, F. B., AND R. G. ANTHONY. 2001. Bald Eagle nest locations and history of use in Oregon and the Washington portion of the Columbia River Recovery Zone, 1972 through 2001. Unpubl. rep., Oreg. Coop. Fish and Wildl. Res. Unit, Oreg. State Univ., Corvallis.

ISAACS, F. B., R. G. ANTHONY, AND R. J. ANDERSON. 1983. Distribution and productivity of nesting Bald Eagles in Oregon, 1978-1982. Murrelet 64: 33-38.

ISAACS, F. B., R. G. ANTHONY, M. VANDER HEYDEN, C. D. MILLER, AND W. WEATHERFORD. 1996. Habits of Bald Eagles wintering along the upper John Day River, Oregon. Northwest Sci. 70: 1-9.

ISAACS, F. B., R. GOGGANS, R. G. ANTHONY, AND T. BRYAN. 1993. Habits of Bald Eagles wintering along the Crooked River, Oregon. Northwest Sci. 67: 55-62.

ISAACS, F. B., AND R. R. OPP. 1991. Distribution and productivity of Golden Eagles in Oregon, 1965-1982. Oreg. Birds 17: 40-42.

ISAACS, F. B., S. L. REED, E. R. REED, AND R. G. ANTHONY. 1992. Habits of Bald Eagles wintering in northeastern Oregon and adjacent areas of Washington and Idaho. Unpubl. rep., Oreg. Coop. Wildl. Res. Unit, Oreg. State Univ., Corvallis.

ISLAM, K. 1994. Oregon's first verified record of a Lark Bunting. Oreg. Birds 20: 84.

IVEY, G. L. 1979. Effects of haying and grazing on duck production in the Blitzen Valley (unit 12) of Malheur National Wildlife Refuge, 1979. Unpub. report, Malheur Natl. Wildl. Refuge, Princeton, OR.

IVEY, G. L. 1990. Population status of Trumpeter Swans in southeast Oregon. Pp. 118-122 in Proceedings and papers of the eleventh Trumpeter Swan Society Conference (D. Compton, ed.). The Trumpeter Swan Soc., Maple Plain, MN.

IVEY, G., AND C. BAARS. 1990. A second Semipalmated Plover nest in Oregon. Oreg. Birds 16: 207-208.

IVEY, G. L., AND C. G. CAREY. 1991. A plan to enhance Oregon's Trumpeter Swan population. Pp. 18-23 in Proceedings and papers of the twelfth Trumpeter Swan Society Conference (J. Voigt Englund, ed.). The Trumpeter Swan Soc., Maple Plain, MN.

IVEY, G. L., J. P. CLARK, J. E. CORNELY, C. L. FOSTER, R. L. JARVIS, AND D. G. PAULLIN. 1987. Influence of land use on Cinnamon Teal nesting at Malheur National Wildlife Refuge. Abstr. Proc. Symp. on Ecol. and Manage. of Breeding Waterfowl. Delta Waterfowl and Wetlands Res. Station. Portage la Prairie, Manitoba.

IVEY, G. L., J. E. CORNELY, AND B. D. EHLERS. 1998. Carp impacts on waterfowl at Malheur National Wildlife Refuge, Oregon. Trans. N. Am. Wildl. and Nat. Resource Conference 63: 66-74.

IVEY, G. L., J. E. CORNELY, D. G. PAULLIN, AND S. P. THOMPSON. Unpubl. ms. An evaluation of factors influencing colonial nesting waterbirds in the Harney Basin, Oregon, 1980-98.

IVEY, G. L., S. L. EARNST, E. P. KELCHLIN, L. NEEL, AND D. S. PAUL. 2003. White-faced Ibis status update and management guidelines, Great Basin population. U.S. Fish and Wildl. Serv., Portland, OR.

IVEY, G., K. FOTHERGILL, AND K. YATES-MILLS. 1988. A Semipalmated Plover nest in Oregon. West. Birds 19: 35-36.

IVEY, G. L., AND C. P. HERZIGER. 2000. Distribution of Greater Sandhill Crane pairs in Oregon, 1999/00. Oreg. Dept. Fish and Wildl. Nongame Tech. Rep. #03-01-00, Portland.

IVEY, G. L., AND C. P. HERZIGER. 2001. Distribution of Greater Sandhill Crane pairs in California, 2000. Calif. Dept. Fish and Game, Sacramento.

IVEY, G. L., C. P. HERZIGER, AND E. J. SCHEUERING. 1998. Spring migration dates for birds at Malheur National Wildlife Refuge, Oregon, and surrounding area. Oreg. Birds 24: 18-21.

IVEY, G. L., T. J. HOFFMAN, AND C. P. HERZIGER. Unpubl. ms. Migrational movements of Sandhill Cranes from Ridgefield National Wildlife Refuge, Washington, and Sauvie Island Wildlife Area, Oregon.

IVEY, G. L., AND C. D. LITTLEFIELD. 1986. Colonial waterbird response to recent high water levels in the Malheur-Harney Lakes Basin in southeast Oregon. Proc. Colonial Waterbird Group Meeting, San Francisco, CA.

IVEY, G. L., C. D. LITTLEFIELD, AND D. G. PAULLIN. Unpubl. ms. Abundance and migration patterns of migrant shorebirds in the Harney Basin, Oregon.

IVEY, G. L., AND E. J. SCHEUERING. 1997. Mortality of radio-equipped Sandhill Crane colts at Malheur National Wildlife Refuge, Oregon. Pp. 14-17 in Proceedings of the seventh North American crane workshop (R. P. Urbanek and D. W. Stahlecker, eds.). Proc. N. Am. Crane Workshop 7: 14-17. N. Am. Crane Working Group, Grand Island, NE.

IVEY, G. L., M. A. STERN, AND C. G. CAREY. 1988. An increasing White-faced Ibis population in Oregon. West. Birds 19: 105-108.

IVEY, G. L., M. J. ST. LOUIS, AND B. D. BALES. 2000. The status of the Oregon Trumpeter Swan Program. Pp. 109-114 in Proceedings and papers of the seventeenth Trumpeter Swan Society Conference (R. E. Shea, M. H. Linch, and H. K. Nelson, eds.). The Trumpeter Swan Soc., Maple Plain, MN.

JACKMAN, S. M. 1974. Woodpeckers of the Pacific Northwest: their characteristics and their role in the forests. M.S. thesis, Oregon State Univ., Corvallis.

JACKSON, B. J. S., AND J. A. JACKSON. 2000. Killdeer (Charadrius vociferus). In The birds of North America, No. 517 (A. Poole and F. Gill, eds.). The Birds of N. Am., Inc., Philadelphia, PA.

JACKSON, J., I. PRATHER, R. CONNER, AND S. GABY. 1978. Fishing behavior of Black and Turkey vultures. Wilson Bull. 90: 141-143.

JANES, S. W. 1975. Raptor breeding ecology of the Clarno Basin and Antelope Valley, Oregon. Unpubl. rep.

JANES, S. W. 1979. Some physical and biological factors affecting Red-tailed Hawk productivity. M.S. thesis, Portland State Univ., Portland.

JANES, S. W. 1983. Status, distribution, and habitat selection of the Grasshopper Sparrow in Morrow County, Oregon. Murrelet 64: 51-54.

JANES, S. W. 1984a. Fidelity to breeding territory in a population of Red-tailed Hawks. Condor 86: 200-203.

JANES, S. W. 1984b. Influences of territory composition and interspecific competition on Red-tailed Hawk reproductive success. Ecology 65: 862-870.

JANES, S. W. 1985a. Behavioral interactions and habitat relations among grassland and shrubsteppe raptors. Ph.D. diss., Univ. of Calif., Los Angeles.

JANES, S. W. 1985b. Habitat selection in raptorial birds. Pp. 159-188 in Habitat selection in birds (M. L. Cody, ed.). Academic Press, Inc., New York.

JANES, S. W. 1987. Status and decline of Swainson's Hawks in Oregon: the role of habitat and interspecific competition. Oreg. Birds 13: 165-179.

JANES, S. W. 1994a. Partial loss of Red-tailed Hawk territories to Swainson's Hawks: relations to habitat. Condor 96: 52-57.

JANES, S. W. 1994b. Variation in the species composition and mean body size of an avian foliage-gleaning guild along an elevational gradient: correlation with arthropod body size. Oecologia 98: 369-378.

JANES, S. W. Unpubl. ms.(a). Habitat selection by warblers in unmanaged forests in the northern Oregon Cascades.

JANES, S. W. Unpubl. ms.(b). Intra- and interspecific territorial defense in relation to intruder altitude and identity in three buteo species.

JANES, S. W. Unpubl. ms.(c). Sex role partitioning of territorial defense in Swainson's and Red-tailed Hawks and the evolution of reversed sexual size dimorphism.

JANES, S. W., AND J. M. BARSS. 1985. Predation by three owl species on northern pocket gophers of different body mass. Oecologia 67: 76-81.

JANES, S. W., J. M. BARSS, AND D. P. JANES. (unpubl. ms.). A cooperative attack by Golden Eagles on an incubating Swainson's Hawk.

JANES, S. W., AND P. H. BLOOM. Unpubl. ms. Differences in flight morphology and habitat relations among adult and immature Red-tailed Hawks.

JANES, S. W., AND D. P. JANES. Unpubl. ms. Habitat relations among hawks (Buteo spp.) wintering in central California and a comparison with breeding populations.

JANES, S., J. KEMPER, N. BARRETT, R. CRONBERG, J. LIVAUDAIS, M. MOORE, T. PHILLIPS, H. SANDS, G. SHAFFER, J. SHELTON, AND P. TRAIL. 2001. Birds of Jackson County, Oregon: distribution and abundance. Rogue Valley Audubon Soc.

JANES, S. W., AND L. RYKER. Unpubl. ms. Interspecific song response between Hermit and Black-throated Gray warblers.

JAQUES, D. L. 1994. Range expansion and roosting ecology of non-breeding California Brown Pelicans. M.S. thesis, Univ. Calif., Davis.

JAQUES, D. L., D. W. ANDERSON, AND R. W. LOWE. 1992. Northward range expansion in California Brown Pelicans [abstract]. 1992 Pacific Seabird Group annual meeting. Charleston, OR.

JARAMILLO, A. P. 1993. Wintering Swainson's Hawks in Argentina: food and age segregation. Condor 95: 475-479.

JARAMILLO, A., AND P. BURKE. 1999a. Identification review: Red-winged and Tricolored blackbirds. Birding 31: 320-327.

JARAMILLO, A., AND P. BURKE. 1999b. New world blackbirds: the Icterids. Princeton Univ. Press, Princeton, NJ.

JARVIS, R. L. 1966. Occurrence of European or Aleutian Green-winged Teal in western North America with a recent record. Murrelet 47: 15-18.

JARVIS, R. L., AND R. G. BROMLEY. 1998. Managing racial mixed flocks of Canada Geese. Pp. 413-423 in Biology and management of Canada Geese: proceedings of the International Canada Goose Symposium (D. H. Rusch, M. D. Samuel, D. D. Humburg, and B. D. Sullivan, eds.). Milwaukee, WI.

JARVIS, R., AND H. BRUNER. 1997. Probability of detection, and variance of spring surveys of Harlequin Ducks. Unpubl. typescript. Oreg. State Univ., Corvallis.

JARVIS, R. L., AND J. C. CORNELY. 1988. Recent changes in wintering populations of Canada Geese in western Oregon/southwestern Washington. Pp. 517-528 in Waterfowl in winter (M. W. Weller, ed.). Univ. Minn. Press, MN.

JARVIS, R. L., AND M. F. PASSMORE. 1992. Ecology of Band-tailed Pigeons in Oregon. U.S. Fish and Wildl. Serv., Biol. Rep. 6.

JEHL, D. R., AND J. R. JEHL, JR. 1981. A North American record of the Asiatic Marbled Murrelet (Brachyramphus marmoratus perdix). Am. Birds 35: 911-912.

JEHL, J. R., JR. 1973. Breeding biology and systematic relationships of the Stilt Sandpiper. Wilson Bull. 85: 115-147.

JEHL, J. R., JR. 1987a. Geographic variation and evolution in the California Gull (Larus californicus). Auk 104: 421-428.

JEHL, J. R., JR. 1987b. Moult and moult migration in a transequatorially migrating shorebird: Wilson's Phalarope. Ornis Scand. 18: 173-178.

JEHL, J. R., JR. 1988. Biology of the Eared Grebe and Wilson's Phalarope in the nonbreeding season: a study of adaptations to saline lakes. Stud. in Avian Biol. 12: 1-74.

JEHL, J. R., JR. 1994. Changes in saline and alkaline lake avifaunas in western North America in the past 150 years. Stud. in Avian Biol. 15: 258-272.

JEHL, J. R., JR. 1996. Mass mortality events of Eared Grebes in North America. J. Field Ornithol. 67: 471-476.

JEHL, J. R., JR. 1997. Cyclical changes in body composition in the annual cycle and migration of the Eared Grebe Podiceps nigricollis. Stud. in Avian Biol. 28: 132-142.

JEHL, J. R., JR. 1999. Population studies of Wilson's Phalaropes at fall staging areas, 1980-1997: a challenge for monitoring. Waterbirds 22: 37-46.

JEHL, J. R., JR. 2001. The abundance of the Eared (Black-necked) Grebe as a recent phenomena. Waterbirds 24: 245-249.

JEHL, J. R., JR., AND S. A. MAHONEY. 1983. Possible sexual differences in foraging patterns in California Gulls and their implications for studies of feeding ecology. Colonial Waterbirds 6: 218-220.

JEHL, J. R., JR., AND P. K. YOCHEM. 1986. Movements of Eared Grebe indicated by banding recoveries. J. Field Ornithol. 57: 208-212.

JENKINS, J. M., AND R. E. JACKMAN. 1993. Mate and nest site fidelity in a resident population of Bald Eagles. Condor 95: 1053-1056.

JENKINS, J. M., R. E. JACKMAN, AND W. G. HUNT. 1999. Survival and movements of immature Bald Eagles fledged in northern California. J. Raptor Res. 33: 81-86.

JENNI, D. A., R. L. REDMOND, AND T. K. BICAK. 1981. Behavioral ecology and habitat relationships of Long-billed Curlew in western Idaho. Unpubl. rep., U.S. Dept. of Int., Bur. of Land Manage., Boise Dist., Idaho.

JENNINGS, D. T., AND H. S. CRAWFORD. 1983. Pine Siskin preys on egg masses of the spruce budworm, *Choristoneura fumiferana* (Lepidoptera: Tortricidae). Can. Entom. 115: 439-440.

JEWETT, S. G. 1909. Some birds of Baker County, Oregon. Auk 26: 5-9.

JEWETT, S. G. 1913. Two stragglers on the Oregon Coast. Condor 15: 226.

JEWETT, S. G. 1916a. New and interesting bird records from Oregon. Condor 18: 21-22.

JEWETT, S. G. 1916b. Notes on some land birds of Tillamook County, Oregon. Condor 18: 74-80.

JEWETT, S. G. 1924. Additional records of alpine birds in Oregon. Condor 26: 78.

JEWETT, S. G. 1928. Bird notes from Oregon. Condor 30: 356-358.

JEWETT, S. 1929. Limicolae of Oregon. Auk 46: 219-220.

JEWETT, S. G. 1930. Upland Plovers (*Bartramia longicauda*) in Oregon. Auk 47: 48.

JEWETT, S. 1931a. Nesting of the Pacific Harlequin Duck in Oregon. Condor 33: 255.

JEWETT, S. G. 1931b. Upland Plover apparently established in Oregon. Condor 33: 245.

JEWETT, S. G. 1932. The White-cheeked Goose in Oregon. Condor 34: 136.

JEWETT, S. G. 1933. White-tailed Kite in Oregon. Murrelet 14: 79.

JEWETT, S. G. 1936. Bird notes from Harney County, Oregon during May 1934. Murrelet 17: 41-47.

JEWETT, S. G. 1937. The western Mockingbird in Oregon. Condor 39: 91-92.

JEWETT, S. G. 1940a. The Arctic Tern at Portland and Diamond Lake, Oregon. Condor 42: 164.

JEWETT, S. G. 1940b. The House Finch in western Oregon. Condor 42: 169.

JEWETT, S. 1942. Some new bird records from Oregon. Condor 44: 36-37.

JEWETT, S. G. 1943. A new Horned Lark from the state of Washington. Auk 60: 262-263.

JEWETT, S. G. 1944a. Hybridization of Hermit and Townsend's warblers. Condor 46: 23-24.

JEWETT, S. G. 1944b. The Burrowing Owl in the Portland, Oregon region. Murrelet 25: 9.

JEWETT, S. G. 1945a. Breeding of the Green Heron in northwestern Oregon. Condor 47: 219.

JEWETT, S. G. 1945b. A second specimen of the eastern Pileolated Warbler taken in Oregon. Condor 47: 269.

JEWETT, S. G. 1946a. American Rough-legged Hawk taken in the Portland, Oregon, region. Murrelet 27: 13.

JEWETT, S. G. 1946b. The Orange-crowned Warbler in Oregon. Condor 48: 285.

JEWETT, S. G. 1946c. A Ross' Goose taken in Wallowa County, Oregon. Condor 48: 181.

JEWETT, S. G. 1948a. The cardinal in Oregon – a possible explanation. Condor 50: 142.

JEWETT, S. G. 1948b. A late fall record of the Poor-will in Oregon. Condor 50: 133.

JEWETT, S. G. 1949. The Franklin Gull in Oregon. Condor 51: 189-190.

JEWETT, S. G. 1954a. The Common Teal (*Anas crecca*) taken in Oregon. Murrelet 35: 51.

JEWETT, S. G. 1954b. Northward extension of the range of the California Woodpecker. Murrelet 35: 14.

JEWETT, S. G. 1954c. A specimen record of the Black Duck in Oregon. Murrelet 35: 47.

JEWETT, S. G. 1954d. Two waterfowl species not previously reported from the Klamath Lakes of Oregon. Murrelet 35: 31.

JEWETT, S. G. 1954e. The White-winged Crossbill in the Cascade Mountains of Oregon. Condor 56: 165.

JEWETT, S. G. 1954f. A specimen of the Lesser Sandhill Crane taken near Portland, Oregon. Murrelet 35: 13.

JEWETT, S. G., AND I. N. GABRIELSON. 1929. Birds of the Portland area, Oregon. Pacific Coast Avifauna 19. Cooper Ornithol. Club, Berkeley.

JEWETT, S. G., W. P. TAYLOR, W. T. SHAW, AND J. W. ALDRICH. 1953. Birds of Washington State. Univ. of Wash. Press, Seattle.

JOBANEK, C. 1975. Wrentits in the southern Willamette Valley, Oregon: a problem of subspecies distribution. SWOC Talk (Oreg. Birds) 1(1): 3-4.

JOBANEK, C. 1976. Wrentits in Oregon. SWOC Talk (Oreg. Birds) 2(4): 64-65.

JOBANEK, G. A. 1987. Bringing the old world to the new: the introduction of foreign songbirds into Oregon. Oreg. Birds 13: 59-75.

JOBANEK, G. A. 1988. Early history of the Green-backed Heron in Oregon. Oreg. Birds 14: 43-47.

JOBANEK, G. 1993. The European Starling in Oregon. Oreg. Birds 19: 93-96.

JOBANEK, G. A. 1994a. Dubious records in the early Oregon bird literature. Oreg. Birds 20: 3-22.

JOBANEK, G. A. 1994b. History of the Bobolink in Oregon. Oreg. Birds 20: 50-54.

JOBANEK, G. A. 1994c. Some thoughts on Acorn Woodpeckers in Oregon. Oreg. Birds 20: 124-127.

JOBANEK, G. A. 1997. An annotated bibliography of Oregon bird literature published before 1935. Oregon State Univ. Press, Corvallis.

JOBANEK, G. A., AND D. B. MARSHALL. 1992. John K. Townsend's 1836 report of the birds of the Lower Columbia River Region, Oregon and Washington. Northwest. Nat. 73: 1-14.

JODICE, P. G. R., AND M. W. COLLOPY. 1999. Diving and foraging patterns of Marbled Murrelets: testing predictions from optimal-breathing models. Can. J. Zool. 77: 1409-1418.

JOHNS, J. E. 1969. Field studies of Wilson's Phalarope. Auk 86: 660-670.

JOHNSGARD, P. A. 1965. Handbook of waterfowl behavior. Comstock Publ. Assoc., Ithaca, NY.

JOHNSGARD, P. A. 1973. Grouse and quails of North America. Univ. of Nebr. Press, Lincoln.

JOHNSGARD, P. A. 1975a. North American game birds of upland and shoreline. Univ. of Nebraska Press, Lincoln.

JOHNSGARD, P. 1975b. Waterfowl of North America. Indiana Univ. Press, Bloomington.

JOHNSGARD, P. A. 1979. Birds of the Great Plains: breeding species and their distribution. Univ. of Nebr. Press, Lincoln.

JOHNSGARD, P. A. 1981. The plovers, sandpipers, and snipes of the world. Univ. of Nebr. Press, Lincoln.

JOHNSGARD, P. A. 1983a. Cranes of the world. Indiana Univ. Press, Bloomington.

JOHNSGARD, P. A. 1983b. The grouse of the world. Univ. Nebr. Press, Lincoln.

JOHNSGARD, P. A. 1986a. Birds of the Rocky Mountains, with particular reference to national parks in the northern Rocky Mountain region. Colo. Assoc. Univ. Press, Boulder.

JOHNSGARD, P. A. 1986b. The pheasants of the world. Oxford Univ. Press, New York.

JOHNSGARD, P. A. 1987. Diving birds of North America. Univ. of Nebr. Press, Lincoln.

JOHNSGARD, P. A. 1988. North American owls: biology and natural history. Smithsonian Inst. Press, Washington, D.C.

JOHNSGARD, P. A. 1990. Hawks and eagles of North America. Smithsonian Inst. Press, Washington, D.C. and London.

JOHNSGARD, P. A. 1993. Cormorants, darters, and pelicans of the world. Smithsonian Inst. Press, Washington, D.C.

JOHNSGARD, P. A. 1997. The hummingbirds of North America. Smithsonian Inst. Press, Washington, D.C.

JOHNSGARD, P. A., AND M. CARBONELL. 1996. Ruddy Ducks and other stifftails. Univ. of Okla. Press, Norman.

JOHNSGARD, P. A., AND R. DISILVESTRO. 1976. Seventy-five years of change in Mallard-Black Duck ratios in eastern North America. Am. Birds 30: 904-908.

JOHNSON, C. G., L. A. NICKERSON, AND M. J. BECHARD. 1987. Grasshopper consumption and summer flocks of nonbreeding Swainson's Hawks. Condor 89: 676-678.

JOHNSON, D. H. 1991. Unpubl. data for 290 Barred Owl locations in Oregon. Oreg. Dept. Fish and Wildl., Corvallis.

JOHNSON, D. H. 1993. Spotted Owls, Great Horned Owls, and forest fragmentation in the central Oregon Cascades. M.S. thesis, Oreg. State Univ., Corvallis.

JOHNSON, D. J., AND T. O'NEIL, managing dirs. 2001. Wildlife habitat relationships in Oregon and Washington. CD-ROM, Oreg. State Univ. Press, Corvallis.

JOHNSON, D. M., R. R. PETERSEN, D. R. LYCAN, J. W. SWEET, M. E. NEUHAUS, AND A. L. SCHAEDEL. 1985. Atlas of Oregon lakes. Oreg. State Univ. Press., Corvallis.

JOHNSON, E. M. Unpubl. ms. Granary-site selection by Acorn Woodpeckers in Benton County, Oregon. Undergrad. thesis, Oreg. State Univ, Corvallis.

JOHNSON, G. D., AND M. S. BOYCE. 1990. Survival, growth, and reproduction of captive-reared Sage Grouse. Wildl. Soc. Bull. 19: 88-93.

JOHNSON, J. 1987. Oregon's first Little Stint. Oreg. Birds 13: 283-285.

JOHNSON, J. 1988a. Field notes: western Oregon, winter 1987-88. Oreg. Birds 14: 376-382.

JOHNSON, J. 1988b. First verified record of Blackburnian Warbler for Oregon. Oreg. Birds 14: 232-236.

JOHNSON, J. 1988c. Ruddy Turnstone in full breeding plumage found in January. Oreg. Birds 14: 388.

JOHNSON, J. 1989a. Fieldnotes: western Oregon, summer 1988. Oreg. Birds 15: 52-55.

JOHNSON, J. 1989b. Field notes: western Oregon, winter 1988-89. Oreg. Birds 15: 188-196.

JOHNSON, J. 1990a. Field notes western Oregon, summer 1989. Oreg. Birds 16: 93-98.

JOHNSON, J. 1990b. Fieldnotes: western Oregon, winter 1989-90. Oreg. Birds 16: 243-237.

JOHNSON, J. 1991a. Fieldnotes: western Oregon, summer 1990. Oreg. Birds 17: 27-28.

JOHNSON, J. 1991b. Fieldnotes: western Oregon, winter 1990-91. Oreg. Birds 17: 95-96.

JOHNSON, J. 1992a. Field notes: western Oregon, summer 1991. Oreg. Birds 18: 30-32.

JOHNSON, J. 1992b. Field notes: western Oregon, winter 1991-92. Oreg. Birds 18: 91-96.

JOHNSON, J. 1993a. Field notes: western Oregon, summer 1992. Oreg. Birds 19: 26-28. JOHNSON, J. 1993b. Fieldnotes: western Oregon, winter 1992-93. Oreg. Birds 19: 85-88.

JOHNSON, J. 1994a. Field notes: western Oregon, summer 1993. Oreg. Birds 20: 33-36.

JOHNSON, J. 1994b. Fieldnotes: western Oregon, winter 1993-94. Oreg. Birds 20: 104-108.

JOHNSON, J. 1995a. Field notes: western Oregon, summer 1994. Oreg. Birds 21: 30-32.

JOHNSON, J. 1995b. Field notes: western Oregon, winter 1994-95. Oreg. Birds 21: 96-100.

JOHNSON, J. 1995c. First record of Eastern Wood-Pewee for Oregon. Oreg. Birds 21: 3-4.

JOHNSON, J. 1996a. Field notes: western Oregon, summer 1995. Oreg. Birds 22: 28-32.

JOHNSON, J. 1996b. Field notes: western Oregon, winter 1995-96. Oreg. Birds 22: 91-96.

JOHNSON, J. 1997a. Field notes: western Oregon, summer 1996. Oreg. Birds 23: 30-32.

JOHNSON, J. 1997b. Fieldnotes: western Oregon, winter 1996-97. Oreg. Birds 23: 110-112.

JOHNSON, J. 1998a. Field notes: western Oregon, summer 1997. Oreg. Birds 24: 34-36.

JOHNSON, J. 1998b. Status of Blue-headed and Plumbeous vireos in Oregon. Oreg. Birds 24: 74-76.

JOHNSON, J., AND N. LETHABY. 1991. Garganey: the first Oregon record. Oreg. Birds 17: 38.

JOHNSON, K. 1995. Green-winged Teal (*Anas crecca*). *In* The birds of North America, No. 193 (A. Poole and F. Gill, eds.). Acad. of Nat. Sci., Philadelphia, and Am. Ornithol. Union, Washington, D.C.

JOHNSON, L. S. 1998. House Wren (*Troglodytes aedon*). *In* The birds of North America, No. 380 (A. Poole and F. Gill, eds.). The Birds of N. Am., Inc., Philadelphia, PA.

JOHNSON, L. S., AND L. H. KERMOTT. 1991. Effect of nest-site supplementation on polygynous behavior in the House Wren (*Troglodytes aedon*). Condor 93: 784-787.

JOHNSON, M. D., AND G. R. GEUPEL. 1996. The importance of productivity to the dynamics of a Swainson's Thrush population. Condor 98: 133-141.

JOHNSON, N. K. 1963. Biosystematics of sibling species of flycatchers in the *Empidonax hammondii-oberholseri-wrightii* complex. Univ. Calif. Publ. Zool. 15: 70-87.

JOHNSON, N. K. 1966. Bill size and the question of competition in allopatric and sympatric populations of Dusky and Gray Flycatchers. Syst. Zool. 15: 70-87.

JOHNSON, N. K. 1970a. Fall migration and winter distribution of the Hammond Flycatcher. Bird-Banding 41: 169-190.

JOHNSON, N. K. 1970b. The affinities of the boreal avifauna of the Warner Mountains, California. Biol. Soc. Nevada Occas. Pap. No. 22: 1-11.

JOHNSON, N. K. 1976. Breeding distribution of Nashville and Virginia's warblers. Auk 93: 219-230.

JOHNSON, N. K. 1980. Character variation and evolution of sibling species in the *Empidonax difficilis - flavescens* complex (Aves: Tyrannidae). Univ. Calif. Publ. Zool. 112: 1-151.

JOHNSON, N. K. 1994a. Old-school taxonomy versus modern biosystematics: species-level decisions in *Stelgidopteryx* and *Empidonax*. Auk 111: 773-780.

JOHNSON, N. K. 1994b. Pioneering and natural expansion of breeding distributions in western North American birds. Pp. 27-44 *in* Stud. Avian Biol. 15, A century of avifaunal change in western North America, Cooper Ornithol. Soc.

JOHNSON, N. K., AND J. R. JEHL, JR. 1994. A century of avifaunal changes in western North America: overview. Pp. 1-3 *in* Stud. Avian Biol. 15, A century of avifaunal change in western North America, Cooper Ornithol. Soc.

JOHNSON, N. K., AND C. B. JOHNSON. 1985. Speciation in sapsuckers (*Sphyrapicus*), II: sympatry, hybridization, and mate preference in *S. ruber daggetti* and *S. nuchalis*. Auk 102: 1-15.

JOHNSON, N. K., AND J. A. MARTEN. 1988. Evolutionary genetics of flycatchers, II: differentiation in the *Empidonax difficilis* complex. Auk 105: 177-191.

JOHNSON, O. B. 1880. List of the birds of the Willamette Valley, Oregon. Am. Nat. 14: 485-491, 635-641.

JOHNSON, R. E. 1975. New breeding localities of *Leucosticte* in the contiguous western United States. Auk 92: 586-589.

JOHNSON, R. E. 1977. Seasonal variation in the genus *Leucosticte* in North America. Condor 79: 76-86.

JOHNSTON, D. W. 1955. The Glaucous Gull in western North America south of its breeding range. Condor 57: 202-207.

JOHNSTON, D. W. 1961. The biosystematics of American Crows. Univ. Wash. Press, Seattle.

JOHNSTON, R. F. 1992. Rock Dove (*Columba livia*). *In* The birds of North America, No. 13 (A. Poole, P. Stettenheim, and F. Gill, eds.). Acad. of Nat. Sci., Philadelphia, and Am. Ornithol. Union, Washington, D.C.

JOHNSTON, R. F., AND R. JANIGA. 1995. Feral pigeons. Oxford Univ. Press, New York.

JONES, K. 1996. Corrigenda. Oreg. Birds 22: 125.

JONES, P. W., AND T. M. DONOVAN. 1996. Hermit Thrush (*Catharus guttatus*). *In* The birds of North America, No. 261 (A. Poole and F. Gill, eds.). Acad. of Nat. Sci., Philadelphia, and Am. Ornithol. Union, Washington, D.C.

JONES, S. L., AND J. S. DIENI. 1995. Canyon Wren (*Catherpes mexicanus*). *In* The birds of North America, No. 197 (A. Poole and F. Gill, eds.) Acad. of Nat. Sci., Philadelphia, and Am. Ornithol. Union, Washington, D.C.

JOST, O. 1970. Erfolgreiche Schutzmassnahmen in den Brutevieren der Wassermsel (*Cinclus cinclus*). Angewandte Ornithologie 3: 101-108.

JOYNER, D. E. 1982. Effects of interspecific nest parasitism by Redheads and Ruddy Ducks. J. Wildl. Manage. 40: 33-38.

JUDD, S. D. 1901. The relation of sparrows to agriculture. U.S. Dept. Agric., Biol. Surv. Bull. 15: 80.

JULIN, K. R. 1986. Decline of second-growth Douglas-fir in relation to Great Blue Heron nesting. Northwest Sci. 60: 201-205.

KAGAN, J. S., J. C. HAK, B. CSUTI, C. W. KIILSGAARD, AND E. P. GAINES. 1999. Oregon gap analysis project final report: a geographic approach to planning for biological diversity. Oregon Nat. Heritage Prog., Portland, OR.

KAISER, G. W., D. F. BERTRAM, AND D. POWELL. 1984. A band recovery for the Rhinoceros Auklet. Murrelet 65: 47.

KALE, H. W., II. 1964. Food of the Long-billed Marsh Wren, *Telmatodytes palustris griseus*, in the salt marshes of Sapelo Island, Georgia. Oriole 29: 47-61.

KALE, H. W., II. 1968. The relationship of Purple Martins to mosquito control. Auk 85: 654-661.

KALMBACH, E. R. 1927. The magpie in relation to agriculture. U.S. Dept. Agric., Tech. Rep. 24: 1-29. Govt. Printing Office, Washington, D.C.

KALMBACH, E. R. 1940. Economic status of the English Sparrow in the United States. U.S. Dept. Agric., Tech. Bull 711.

KALMER, A. K., R. M. FUVITA, AND C. F. WURSTER. 1996. Seabird by-catch in longline fisheries. Pacific Seabirds 23: 3-6.

KAMIL A. C., AND R. P. BALDA. 1990. Differential memory for different cache sites by Clark's Nutcrackers (*Nucifraga columbiana*). J. Exp. Psychology: Anim. Behav. Proc. 16: 162-168.

KAMM, J. A. 1973. Biotic factors that affect sod webworms in grass seed fields in Oregon. Environ. Entomol. 2: 94-96.

KAMPFER-LAUENSTEIN, A. 1991. Intraspecific territorial behavior of Tengmalm's Owl (*Aegolius funereus*) in autumn. Ecol. Birds 13: 111-120.

KASPARI, M., AND A. JOERN. 1993. Prey choice by three insectivorous grassland birds: reevaluating opportunism. Oikos 68: 414-430.

KAUFMAN, K. 1987. Pectoral Sandpiper and Sharp-tailed Sandpiper. Am. Birds 41: 1356-1358.

KAUFMAN, K. 1990. Advanced birding. Houghton Mifflin Co., Boston.

KAUFMAN, K. 1991. The changing seasons, autumn 1990. Am. Birds 45: 63-66.

KAUFMAN, K. 1993. Identifying Hutton's Vireo. Am. Birds 47: 460-462.

KAUFMAN, K. 1996. Lives of North American birds. Houghton Mifflin, Boston.

KAUFMANN, G. W. 1987. Growth and development of Sora and Virginia Rail chicks. Wilson Bull. 99: 432-440.

KEARNEY, K. 1991. Site guide: Astoria mitigation area and vicinity, Clatsop County. Oreg. Birds 17: 45-46.

KEAST, A., AND S. SAUNDERS. 1991. Ecomorphology of the North American Ruby-crowned (*Regulus calendula*) and Golden-crowned (*R. satrapa*) kinglets. Auk 108: 880-888.

KEBBE, C. E. 1954. Use of nest boxes by Hooded Mergansers. Murrelet 35: 47.

KEBBE, C. E. 1956a. American Scoter record from eastern Oregon. Murrelet 37: 17.

KEBBE, C. E. 1956b. Nesting record of Wood Duck in southeast Oregon. Murrelet 37: 3.

KEBBE, C. E. 1958a. Ground nesting of the Great Horned Owl. Murrelet 39: 28.

KEBBE, C. E. 1958b. Nesting records of the Red-necked Grebe in Oregon. Murrelet 39: 14.

KEBBE, C. E. 1959. Nesting records of Saw-whet Owls in Oregon. Murrelet 40: 2.

KEEGAN, T. W. 1996. Habitat use and productivity of Rio Grande Wild Turkey hens in southwestern Oregon. Ph.D. diss., Oreg. State Univ., Corvallis.

KEEGAN, T. W., AND J. A. CRAWFORD. 1997. Brood-rearing habitat use by Rio Grande Wild Turkeys in Oregon. Great Basin Nat. 57: 220-230.

KEEGAN, T. W., AND J. A. CRAWFORD. 1999. Reproduction and survival of Rio Grande turkeys in Oregon. J. Wildl. Manage. 63: 204-210.

KEEGAN, T. W., AND J. A. CRAWFORD. 2000. Seasonal habitat use and home ranges of Rio Grande turkeys in Oregon. Proc. Natl. Wild Turkey Symp. 8: 109-116.

KEEGAN, T. W., AND J. A. CRAWFORD. Unpubl. data. Game Bird Prog., Oreg. State Univ., Corvallis.

KEISTER, G. 1991. Survey of birds along the Snake River. Unpubl.

KEISTER, G. P., JR., AND R. G. ANTHONY. 1983. Characteristics of Bald Eagle communal roosts in the Klamath Basin, Oregon and California, J. Wildl. Manage. 47: 1072-1079.

KEISTER, G. P., JR., R. G. ANTHONY, AND E. J. O'NEILL. 1987. Use of communal roosts and foraging areas by Bald Eagles wintering in the Klamath Basin. J. Wildl. Manage. 51: 415-420.

KEISTER, G., AND G. IVEY. 1994. Analysis of raptor surveys in northern Harney County. Oreg. Dept. Fish and Wildl., Nongame Wildl. Tech. Rep. 94-5-02. Portland.

KEITH, A. R. 1968. A summary of the extralimital records of the Varied Thrush, 1848 to 1966. Bird-Banding 39: 245-276.

KELLER, C. L. 1891. Nesting of Spinus pinus in the Northwest. Oologist 8: 31.

KELLER, M. E., AND S. H. ANDERSON. 1992. Avian use of habitat configurations created by forest cutting in southeastern Wyoming. Condor 94: 55-65.

KELLY, E. G. 2001. The range expansion of the Northern Barred Owl: an evaluation of the impact on Spotted Owls. M.S. Thesis, Oreg. State Univ., Corvallis.

KENDALL, K. C. 1995. Whitebark pine: ecosystem in peril. Pp. 228-230 in Our living resources: a report to the nation on the distribution, abundance, and health of United States plants, animals, and ecosystems (E. T. LaRoe, G. S. Farris, C. E. Puckett, P. D. Doran, and M. J. Mac, eds.). U.S. Dept. Int., Nat. Biol. Serv., Washington, D.C.

KENDEIGH, S. C. 1941. Territorial and mating behavior of the House Wren. Illinois Biol. Monogr. 18: 1-120.

KENNEDY, C. H. 1914. The effects of irrigation on bird life in the Yakima Valley, Washington. Condor 16: 250-255.

KENNEDY, E. D., AND D. W. WHITE. 1992. Nestbuilding in House Wrens. Condor. 67: 229-234.

KENNEDY, E. D., AND D. W. WHITE. 1996. Interference competition from House Wrens as a factor in the decline of Bewick's Wrens. Conserv. Biol. 10: 281-284.

KENNEDY, E. D., AND D. W. WHITE. 1997. Bewick's Wren (Thryomanes bewickii). In The birds of North America, No. 315 (A. Poole and F. Gill eds.). Acad. of Nat. Sci., Philadelphia, and Am. Ornithol. Union, Washington, D.C.

KENNEDY, P. L. 1997. The Northern Goshawk (Accipiter gentilis atricapillus): is there evidence of a population decline? J. Raptor Res. 31: 95-106.

KENNEDY, P. L., AND D. W. STAHLECKER. 1993. Responsiveness of nesting Northern Goshawks to taped broadcasts of three conspecific calls. J. Wildl. Manage. 57: 249-257.

KENNY, S. P., AND R. L. KNIGHT. 1992. Flight distances of Black-billed Magpies in different regimes of human density and persecution. Condor 94: 545-547.

KEPPIE, D. M. 1970. The development and evaluation of an audio-index technique for the Band-tailed Pigeon. M.S. thesis, Oreg. State Univ., Corvallis.

KEPPIE, D. M. 1982. A difference in production and associated events in two races of Spruce Grouse. Can. J. Zool. 60: 2116-2123.

KEPPIE, D. M., AND J. TOWERS. 1990. Using phenology to predict commencement of nesting of female Spruce Grouse (Dendragapus canadensis). Am. Midl. Nat. 124: 164-170.

KEPPIE, D. M., H. M. WIGHT, AND W. S. OVERTON. 1970. A proposed Band-tailed Pigeon census—a management need. Trans. of N. Am. Wildl. Nat. Resour. Conf. 35: 157–171.

KERBES, R. H., K. M. MEERES, AND J. E. HINES, EDS. 1999. Distribution, survival, and numbers of Lesser Snow Geese of the western Canadian Arctic and Wrangel Island, Russia. Can. Wildl. Serv. Occas. Paper 98, Ottawa, Ontario.

KEREKES, J., R. TORDON, A. NIEUWBURG, AND L. RISK. 1994. Fish-eating bird abundance in oligotrophic lakes in Kejimkujik National Park, Nova Scotia, Canada. Pp. 57-61 in Aquatic birds in the trophic web of lakes (J. Kerekes and B. Pollard, eds.). Devel. in Hydrobiol. 96.

KERLINGER, P., AND M. R. LEIN. 1988. Causes of mortality, fat condition, and weights of wintering Snowy Owls. J. Field Ornithol. 59: 7-12.

KERLINGER, P., M. R. LEIN, AND B. J. SEVICK. 1985. Distribution and population fluctuations of wintering Snowy Owls (Nyctea scandiaca) in North America. Can. J. Zool. 63: 1829-1834.

KESSLER, W. B., AND T. E. KOGUT. 1985. Habitat orientations of forest birds in southeastern Alaska. Northwest Sci. 59: 58-65.

KILBRIDE, K. M., J. A. CRAWFORD, K. L. BLAKELY, AND B. A. WILLIAMS. 1992. Habitat use by breeding female quail in western Oregon. J. Wildl. Manage. 56: 85-90.

KILHAM, L. 1954. Courtship behavior of the Pied-billed Grebe. Wilson Bull. 66: 65.

KILHAM, L. 1971a. Reproductive behavior of Yellow-bellied Sapsuckers, 1: preference for nesting in Fomes-infected aspens and nest hole interrelations with flying squirrels, raccoons and other animals. Wilson Bull. 83: 159-171.

KILHAM, L. 1971b. Roosting habits of White-breasted Nuthatches. Condor 73: 113-114.

KILHAM, L. 1971c. Use of blister beetle in bill-sweeping by White-breasted Nuthatch. Auk 88: 175-176.

KILHAM, L. 1972. Reproductive behavior of White-breasted Nuthatches, II: courtship. Auk 89: 115-129.

KILHAM, L. 1989. The American Crow and the Common Raven. Texas A & M Univ. Press, College Station.

KINDSCHY, R. R., JR. 1964. Ecological studies on the Rock Dove in southeastern Oregon. Northwest Sci 38: 138-140.

KING, D. T., J. F. GLAHN, AND K. J. ANDREWS. 1995. Daily activity budget and movements of winter roosting Double-crested Cormorants determined by biotelemetry in the Delta Region of Mississippi. Pp. 152-157 in The Double-crested Cormorant: biology, conservation and management (D. N. Nettleship and D. C. Duffy, eds.) Colonial Waterbirds 18 (Spec. Publ. 1).

KING, J. R. 1953. Breeding birds of the central palouse region - southeastern Washington. M.S. thesis, State Coll. of Wash., Pullman.

KING, J. R., AND L. R. MEWALDT. 1987. The summer biology of an unstable insular population of White-crowned Sparrows in Oregon. Condor 89: 549-565.

KING, J. R., AND E. E. WALES, JR. 1964. Observations on migration, ecology, and population flux of wintering rosy finches. Condor 66: 24-31.

KING, K. A., D. L. MEEKER, AND D. M. SWINEFORD. 1980. White-faced Ibis populations and pollutants in Texas, 1969-1976. Southwest Nat. 25: 225-239.

KING, W. B. 1984. Incidental mortality of seabirds in gill nets in the North

Pacific, Pp. 709-712 *in* Status and conservation of the world's seabirds, Vol. 2. (J. P. Croxall, P. G. H. Evans, and R. W. Schreiber, eds.). Internatl. Counc. Bird Preservation (ICBP) Tech. Publ., Cambridge, England.

KINGERY, H. E. 1971. Great Basin - central Rocky Mountain region. Am. Birds 25: 882-888.

KINGERY, H. E. 1972a. Great Basin-central Rocky Mountain region. Am. Birds 26: 92-99.

KINGERY, H. E. 1972b. Great Basin-central Rocky Mountain region. Am. Birds 26: 787-791.

KINGERY, H. E. 1996. American Dipper (*Cinclus mexicanus*). *In* The birds of North America, No. 229 (A. Poole and F. Gill, eds.). Acad. of Nat. Sci., Philadelphia, and Am. Ornithol. Union, Washington, D.C.

KINGERY, H. E., AND C. K. GHALAMBOR. 2001. Pygmy Nuthatch (*Sitta pygmaea*). *In* The birds of North America, No. 567 (A. Poole and F. Gill, eds.). The Birds of N. Am., Inc., Philadelphia, PA.

KINLEY, T. A., AND N. J. NEWHOUSE. 1997. Relationship of riparian reserve zone width to bird density and diversity in southeastern British Columbia. Northwest Sci. 71: 75-86.

KIRK, A. 1995. First confirmed breeding of the Least Bittern in Inyo County, California. West. Birds 26: 165-166.

KIRSCH, L., AND K. HIGGINS. 1976. Upland Sandpiper nesting and management in North Dakota. Wildl. Soc. Bull. 4: 16-20.

KITCHIN, E. A. 1934. Nesting of the Wood Duck with the Hooded Merganser. Murrelet 15: 51-52.

KLAMATH BASIN NATIONAL WILDLIFE REFUGES FILES. Unpubl. data. Tulelake, CA.

KLAMATH BIRD OBSERVATORY. Unpubl. banding data. Ashland, Oregon.

KLEIN, R. 1977. A checklist to the birds of Sauvie Island. Audubon Soc. of Portland.

KLEINTJES, P. K., AND D. L. DAHLSTEN. 1995. Within-season trends in the foraging behavior of the Mountain Chickadee. Wilson Bull. 107: 655-666.

KLICKA, J. Unpubl. data. Mitochondrial DNA sequences of Brewer's Sparrows. Univ. Nevada, Las Vegas.

KLIMA, J., AND J. R. JEHL, JR. 1998. Stilt Sandpiper (*Calidris himantopus*). *In* The birds of North America, No. 341 (A. Poole and F. Gill, eds.). The Birds of N. Am., Inc., Philadelphia, PA.

KLIMKIEWICZ, M. K. 2000. Longevity records of North American birds. Version 2000.1. Patuxent Wildl. Res. Center. Bird Banding Lab. Laurel, MD.

KLIMKIEWICZ, M. K., AND A. G. FUTCHER. 1987. Longevity records of North American birds: Coerebinae through Estrilididae. J. Field Ornithol. 58: 318-333.

KNAPTON, R. W. 1994. Clay-colored Sparrow (*Spizella pallida*). *In* The birds of North America, No. 120 (A. Poole and F. Gill, eds.). Acad. of Nat. Sci., Philadelphia, and Am. Ornithol.Union, Washington, D.C.

KNIGHT, R. L., A. D. EVERY, AND A. W. ERICKSON. 1979. Seasonal food habits of four game bird species in Okanogan County, Washington. Murrelet 60: 58-66.

KNIGHT, R. L., AND R. E. JACKMAN. 1984. Food-niche relationships between Great Horned Owls and common Barn-owls in eastern Washington. Auk 101: 175-179.

KNIGHT, R. L., AND J. SKRILETZ. 1980. Four additional cases of bird mortality on barbed-wire fences. West. Birds 11: 202.

KNIGHT-RIDDER/TRIBUNE NEWS SERVICE. 1997. Semipalmated Sandpiper is one of the fastest-flying shorebirds. Reprint from 1996 original. The Wichita Eagle, Wichita, KS.

KNOPF, F. L. 1975. Schedule of presupplemental molt of White Pelicans with notes on the bill horn. Condor 77: 356-359.

KNOPF, F. L. 1994. Avian assemblages on altered grasslands. Stud. in Avian Biol. 15: 247-257.

KNOPF, F. L. 1996. Prairie legacies-birds. *In* Prairie conservation: preserving North America's most endangered ecosystem (F. B. Sampson and F. L. Knopf, eds.). Island Press, Covelo, CA.

KNOPF, F. L., AND J. L. KENNEDY. 1981. Differential predation by two species of piscivorous birds. Wilson Bull. 93: 554-557.

KNOPF, F. L., AND J. A. SEDGWICK. 1992. An experimental study of nest-site selection by Yellow Warblers. Condor 94: 734-742.

KNOPF, F. L., J. A. SEDGWICK, AND R. W. CANNON. 1988. Guild structure of a riparian avifauna relative to seasonal cattle grazing. J. Wildl. Manage. 52: 280-290.

KNOPF, F. L., J. A. SEDGWICK, AND D. B. INKLEY. 1990. Regional correspondence among shrubsteppe bird habitats. Condor 92: 45-53.

KNORR, O. A. 1957. Communal roosting of the Pygmy Nuthatch. Condor 59: 398.

KNOWLTON, G. F., AND F. C. HARMSTON. 1942. Insect food of the Rock Wren. Great Basin Nat. 3: 22.

KNOWLTON, G. F., AND P. E. TELFORD. 1947. Some insect food of the Yellow-headed Blackbird. Auk 64: 459.

KOBBE, W. H. 1900. Birds of Cape Disappointment, Washington. Auk 17: 349-358.

KOCHERT, M. N. 1980. Golden Eagle reproduction and population changes in relation to jackrabbit cycles: implication to eagle electrocutions. Pp. 71-86 *in* Proceedings of a workshop on raptors and energy developments (R. P. Howard and J. F. Gore, eds.). Idaho Chapt., The Wildl. Soc., Boise, ID.

KOENIG, W. D., AND R. L. MUMME. 1987. Population ecology of the cooperatively breeding Acorn Woodpecker. Monogr. in Population Biol. 24. Princeton Univ. Press, Princeton, NJ.

KOENIG, W. D., P. B. STACEY, M. T. STANBACK, AND R. L. MUMME. 1995. Acorn Woodpecker (*Melanerpes formicivorus*). *In* The birds of North America, No. 194. (A. Poole and F. Gill, eds.). Acad. of Nat. Sci., Philadelphia, and Am. Ornithol. Union, Washington, D.C.

KOLB, H. 1971. Winter bird-population study. Am. Birds 25: 633-664.

KÖNIG, C. 1991. Zur taxonomie und ökologie der Sperlingskäuze (*Glaucidium* spp.) des Andenraumes. Ökol. Vøgel (Ecol. Birds) 13: 15-76.

KÖNIG, C., F. WEICK, AND J. H. BECKING. 1999. Owls: a guide to the owls of the world. Yale Univ. Press, New Haven, CT.

KONYUKHOV, N. B., AND A. S. KITAYSKY. 1995. The Asian race of the Marbled Murrelet. Pp. 23-29 *in* Ecology and conservation of the Marbled Murrelet (C. J. Ralph, G. L. Hunt, Jr., M.G. Raphael, and J. F. Piatt, eds.). U.S. Dept. Agric., For. Serv. Gen. Tech. Rep. PSW-GTR-152. Albany, CA.

KORPI, R. 1997. Field notes: eastern Oregon, winter 1996-97. Oreg. Birds 23: 107-109.

KORPI, R. 1998. Field notes: eastern Oregon, winter 1997-98. Oreg. Birds 24: 93-94.

KORPI, R. 1999. Field notes: eastern Oregon, winter 1998-99. Oreg. Birds 25: 82-85.

KORPI, R. 2000. Field notes: eastern Oregon, winter 1999-2000. Oreg. Birds 26: 180-185.

KORPI, R. 2001a. Field notes: western Oregon, fall 2000. Oreg. Birds 27: 25-36.

KORPI, R. 2001b. Field notes: western Oregon, summer 2001. Oreg. Birds 27: 116-121.

KORPI, R. 2001c. Field notes: western Oregon, winter 2000-2001. Oreg. Birds 27: 59-67.

KORPI, R. 2002. Field notes: western Oregon, winter 2001-2002. Oreg. Birds 28: 94-102.

KORTRIGHT, F. H. 1943. The ducks, geese, and swans of North America. Stackpole Books, Harrisburg, PA.

KOTZLOFF, E. N. 1993. Seashore life of the northern Pacific Coast. Univ. of Wash. Press, Seattle.

KRAPU, G. L. 1974. Feeding ecology of pintail hen during reproduction. Auk 91: 278-290.

KREISEL, K. J., AND S. J. STEIN. 1999. Bird use of burned and unburned coniferous forests during winter. Wilson Bull. 111: 243–250.

KRIDLER, E. 1965. Records, obtained while banding, of birds unusual in southeastern Oregon. Auk 82: 496-497.

KRIDLER, E., AND D. MARSHALL. 1962. Additional bird records from southeastern Oregon. Condor 64: 162-164.

KRISTENSEN, K., M. STERN, AND J. MORAWSKI. 1991. Birds of north Lake Abert, Lake Co., Oregon. Oreg. Birds 17: 67-77.

KROGMAN, B. D. 1979. A systematic study of *Anser albifrons* in California. Pp. 22-43 *in* Management and biology of Pacific Flyway geese (R. L. Jarvis and J. C. Bartonek, eds.). Oreg. State Univ. Bookstores, Corvallis.

KROHN, W. B., R. B. ALLEN, J. R. MORING, AND A. E. HUTCHINSON. 1995. Double-crested Cormorants in New England: population and management histories. Pp. 99-109 *in* The Double-crested Cormorant: biology, conservation and management (D. N. Nettleship and D. C. Duffy, eds.) Colonial Waterbirds 18 (Spec. Publ. 1).

KROODSMA, D. E. 1972. Bigamy in the Bewick's Wren? Auk. 89: 185-187.

KROODSMA, D. E. 1973. Coexistence of Bewick's Wrens and House Wrens in Oregon. Auk 90: 341-352.

KROODSMA, D. E. 1974. Song learning, dialects, and dispersal in the Bewick's Wren. Zeitschrift fur Tierpsychol. 35: 352-380.

KROODSMA, D. E. 1975. Song patterning in the Rock Wren. Condor 77: 294-303.

KROODSMA, D. E., AND J. VERNER. 1997. Marsh Wren (*Cistothorus palustris*). *In* The birds of North America, No. 308 (A. Poole, P. Stettenheim, and F. Gill, eds.). Acad. of Nat. Sci., Philadelphia, and Am. Ornithol. Union, Washington, D.C.

KULETZ, K. J., AND J. F. PIATT. 1999. Juvenile Marbled Murrelet nurseries and the productivity index. Wilson Bull. 111: 257-261.

KURZEJESKI, E. W., AND L. D. VANGILDER. 1992. Population management. Pp. 165-184 *in* The Wild Turkey: biology and management (J. G. Dickson, ed.). Stackpole Books, Harrisburg, PA.

KUSHLAN, J. A. 1972. Aerial feeding in the Snowy Egret. Wilson Bull. 84: 199-200.

KUSHLAN, J. A. 1973. Least Bittern nesting colonially. Auk 90: 685-686.

KUSHLAN, J. A. 1978. Feeding ecology of wading birds. Pp. 249-297 *in* Wading birds (A. Sprunt, IV., J. C. Ogden, and S. Winkler, eds.). Natl. Audubon Soc. Res. Rep. 7, New York.

KVITEK, R. G. 1991. Sequestered paralytic shellfish poisoning toxins mediate Glaucous-winged Gull predation on bivalve prey. Auk 108: 381-392.

LABERTEAUX, D. L. 1989. Morphology, foraging behavior, and nesting biology of the Inyo California Towhee (*Pipilo crissalis eremophilus*). M.S. thesis, N. Ariz. Univ., Flagstaff.

LaFAVE, L. D. 1965. Revised status of Laridae in eastern Washington. Murrelet 46: 7-11.

LAGORY, K. E., M. K. LAGORY, D. M. MEYERS, AND S. G. HERMAN. 1984. Niche relationships in wintering mixed-species flocks in western Washington. Wilson Bull. 96: 108-116.

LAIDIG, K. J., AND D. S. DOBKIN. 1995. Spatial overlap and habitat associations of Barred Owls and Great Horned Owls in southern New Jersey. J. Raptor Res. 29: 151-157.

LANCTOT, R. B., AND C. D. LAREDO. 1994. Buff-breasted Sandpiper (*Tryngites subruficollis*). *In* The birds of North America, No. 91 (A. Poole and F. Gill, eds.). Acad. of Nat. Sci., Philadelphia, and Am. Ornithol. Union, Washington, D.C.

LANDRY, M. R., J. R. POSTEL, W. K. PETERSON, AND J. NEWMAN. 1989. Broad-scale distributional patterns of hydrographic variables on the Washington/Oregon shelf. Pp. 1-40 *in* Coastal oceanography of Washington and Oregon (M. R. Landry and B. M. Hickey, eds.). Elsevier Oceanography Series 47. Elsevier, New York.

LANE, D., AND A. JARAMILLO. 2000. Field identification of *Hylocichla/Catharus* thrushes, Part 2: Veery and Swainson's Thrush. Birding 32: 342-254.

LANNER, R. M. 1982. Adaptations of whitebark pine for seed dispersal by Clark's Nutcracker. Can. J. For. Res. 12: 391-402.

LANNER, R. M. 1996. Made for each other: a symbiosis of birds and pines. Oxford Univ. Press, New York, NY.

LANYON, W. E. 1994. Western Meadowlark (*Sturnella neglecta*). *In* The birds of North America, No. 104 (A. Poole and F. Gill, eds.). Acad. of Nat. Sci., Philadelphia, and Am. Ornithol. Union, Washington, D.C.

LARDY, M. E. 1980. Raptor inventory and Ferruginous Hawk breeding biology in southeastern Oregon. M.S. thesis, Univ. of Idaho, Moscow.

LaRIVERS, I. 1941. The mormon cricket as food for birds. Condor 43: 65-69.

LARSEN, K. J., AND J. G. DIETRICH. 1970. Reduction of a raven population on lambing grounds with DRC-1339. J. Wildl. Mgmt. 34: 200-204.

LARSON, D. L., AND C. E. BOCK. 1986. Eruptions of some North American boreal seed-eating birds, 1901-1980. Ibis 128: 137-140.

LASIEWSKI, R. C., AND H. J. THOMPSON. 1966. Field observation of torpidity in the Violet-green Swallow. Condor 68: 102-103.

LATTA, S. 1992. Distribution and status of the Harlequin Duck (*Histrionicus histrionicus*) in Oregon. Unpubl., U.S. Dept. Agric., For. Serv., Eugene.

LATTA, W. C., AND SHARKEY, R. F. 1966. Feeding behavior of the American Merganser in captivity. J. Wildl. Manage. 30: 17-23.

LAUGHLIN, T. 1950. Wallowa District monthly report, Sept. 1950. Unpubl. rep., Oreg. Dept. Fish and Wildl., Enterprise.

LAURENZI, A.W, B. W. ANDERSON, AND R. D. OHMART. 1982. Wintering biology of Ruby-crowned Kinglets in the lower Colorado River valley. Condor 84: 385-398.

LAUTEN, D. J., AND K. A. CASTELEIN. 2000. Oregon's first spring record of Sharp-tailed Sandpiper (*Calidris acuminata*). Oreg. Birds 26: 217-218.

LAVAL, J. 1947. White-tailed Kites in Oregon. Murrelet 28: 41.

LAVERS, N. 1975. Status of the Harlan's Hawk in Washington, and notes on its identification in the field. West. Birds 6: 55-62.

LAWES, C., AND J. LAWES. 1999. Oregon's first Louisiana Waterthrush. Oreg. Birds 25: 31-33.

LAWRENCE, G. E. 1950. The diving and feeding activity of the Western Grebe on the breeding grounds. Condor 52: 3-16.

LAYMON, S. A. 1983. California Gull catches Barn Swallow in flight. Wilson Bull. 95: 296-297.

LAYMON, S. A., AND M. D. HALTERMAN. 1987. Can the western subspecies of the Yellow-billed Cuckoo be saved from extinction? West. Birds 18: 19-25.

LEAHY, C. W. 1982. The birdwatcher's companion: an encyclopedic handbook of North American birdlife. Bonanza, New York.

LEAL, D. A. 1999. A specimen record of Wedge-tailed Shearwater (*Puffinus pacificus*) for Oregon. Oreg. Birds 25: 96.

LeBARON, G. D., ED. 1989. The ninetieth Christmas Bird Count. Am. Birds 44: 515-1050.

LEEMAN, L. W., M. A. COLWELL, T. S. LEEMAN, AND R. L. MATHIS. 2001. Diets, energy intake, and kleptoparasitism of nonbreeding Long-billed Curlews in a northern California estuary. Wilson Bull. 113: 194-201.

LEEMAN, T. S. 2000. Importance of coastal pastures to Long-billed Curlews (*Numenius americanus*). M.S. thesis, Humboldt State Univ., Arcata.

LEFFINGWELL, D. J., AND A. M. LEFFINGWELL. 1931. Winter habits of the Hepburn Rosy Finch at Clarkston, Washington. Condor 33: 140-150.

LEHMAN, P. 1993. Oregon's first Slaty-backed Gull. Oreg. Birds 19: 63.

LEIN, K. J. 1982. The Red-tailed Hawk on Sauvie Island. M.S. thesis, Portland State Univ., Portland.

LEONARD, D. L., JR. 2001. Three-toed Woodpecker (*Picoides tridactylus*). *In* The birds of North America, No. 588 (A. Poole and F. Gill, eds.). The Birds of N. Am., Inc., Philadelphia, PA.

LEONARD, J. P. 1998. Nesting and foraging ecology of Band-tailed Pigeons in western Oregon. Ph.D. diss., Oreg. State Univ., Corvallis.

LEONARD, M. L., AND J. PICMAN. 1987. The adaptive significance of multiple nest building by male Marsh Wrens. Anim. Behav. 35: 271-277.

LEOPOLD, A. S. 1977. The California Quail. Univ. Calif. Press, Berkeley.

LEOPOLD, A. S., AND R. H. SMITH. 1953. Numbers and winter distribution of Pacific Black Brant in North America. Calif. Fish and Game 39: 95-101.

LESCHACK, C. R., S. K. KNIGHT, AND G. R. HEPP. 1997. Gadwall (*Anas strepera*). *In* The birds of North America, No. 283 (A. Poole and F. Gill, eds.). Acad. of Nat. Sci., Philadelphia, and Am. Ornithol. Union, Washington, D.C.

LESKIW, T., AND R. J. GUTIÉRREZ. 1998. Possible predation of a Spotted Owl by a Barred Owl. West. Birds 29: 225-226.

LETHABY, N. 1990. Communal roosting of Northern Harriers in winter. Oreg. Birds 16: 212.

LETHABY, N. 2000. The identification of Long-billed Murrelets in alternate plumage. Birding 32: 438-444.

LETHABY, N., AND J. GILLIGAN. 1991. An occurrence of the Great Knot in Oregon. Oreg. Birds 17: 35-37.

LETHABY, N., AND J. GILLIGAN. 1992. Great Knot in Oregon. Am. Birds 46: 46-47.

LEU, M., AND D. A. MANUWAL. 1996. Habitat requirements, status, and management of the Loggerhead Shrike on the Yakima Training Center. Final rep., Coll. of For. Res., Univ. of Wash.

LEUPOLD, N. 1946. A nesting record for the Golden Pileolated Warbler. Auk 63: 95.

LEV, E. 1983. Documentation and census of nesting Blue-g ray Gnatcatchers (*Polioptila caerulea*) on the Lower Table Rock Preserve. Rep. to The Nature Conservancy, Medford, OR.

LEVER, C. 1987. Naturalized birds of the world. Longman Scientific & Technical, Harlow, U.K.

LEWIS, H. F. 1929. The natural history of the Double-crested Cormorant (*Phalacrocorax auritus auritus* (Lesson)). Ru-Mi-Lou Books, Ottawa, Ontario.

LEWIS, H. 1952. Thistle-nesting goldfinches. Flicker 24: 105-109.

LEWIS, J. C. 1993. Foods and feeding ecology. Pp. 181-204 *in* Ecology and management of the Mourning Dove (T. S. Baskett, M. W. Sayre, R. E. Tomlinson, R. E. Mirarchi, and R. E. McCabe, eds.). Stackpole Books, Harrisburg, PA.

LEWIS, M., AND W. CLARK. 1814. History of the expedition under the command of Captains Lewis and Clark, to the sources of the Missouri, thence across the Rocky Mountains and down the river Columbia to the Pacific Ocean. 2 vols. Paul Allen ed. Philadelphia.

LEWKE, R. E. 1974. Sight record of Bewick's Wren in eastern Washington. Murrelet 55: 42-43.

LEWKE, R. E. 1982. A comparison of foraging behavior among permanent, summer, and winter resident bird groups. Condor 84: 84-90.

LILLIE, G. 1994. Field notes: western Oregon, spring 1994. Oreg. Birds 20: 137-144.

LILLIE, G. 1995. Field notes: western Oregon, spring 1995. Oreg. Birds 21: 129-132.

LILLIE, G. 1996. Field notes: western Oregon, spring 1996. Oreg. Birds 22: 127-132.

LILLIE, G. 1997. Field notes: western Oregon, spring 1997. Oreg. Birds 23: 150-156.

LILLIE, G. 1998. Fieldnotes: western Oregon, spring 1998. Oreg. Birds 24: 130-136.

LILLIE, G. 1999. Field notes: western Oregon, spring 1999. Oreg. Birds 25: 107-115.

LILLIE, G. 2000. Field notes: western Oregon, spring 2000. Oreg. Birds 26: 195-199.

LILLIE, G. 2001. Field notes: western Oregon, spring 2001. Oreg. Birds 27: 86-91.

LIMPERT, R. J., AND S. L. EARNST. 1994. Tundra Swan (*Cygnus columbianus*). *In* The birds of North America, No. 89 (A. Poole and F. Gill, eds.). Acad. of Nat. Sci., Philadelphia, and Am. Ornithol. Union, Washington, D.C.

LINCOLN, F. C. 1932. The Black Duck in Oregon. Auk 49: 344.

LIND, G. S. 1976. Production, nest site selection and food habits of Ospreys on Deschutes National Forest, Oregon. M.S. thesis, Oreg. State Univ., Corvallis.

LINDBLOOM, A. 1998. Habitat use, reproduction, movements, and survival of Chukar partridge in west-central Idaho. M.S. thesis, Univ. of Idaho, Moscow.

LINDVALL, M. L., AND J. B. LOW. 1982. Nesting ecology and production of Western Grebes at Bear River Migratory Bird Refuge, Utah. Condor 84: 66-70.

LINHART, Y. B., AND D. F. TOMBACK. 1985. Seed dispersal by nutcrackers causes multi-trunk growth form in pines. Oecologia 67: 107-110.

LINSDALE, J. M. 1946. American Magpie (*Pica pica hudsonia*). Pp. 133-155 *in* Life histories of North American jays, crows, and titmice (A. C. Bent, ed.) U.S. Natl. Mus. Bull. 191.

LITTLEFIELD, C. D. 1977/78. Field reports: southeast Oregon. Oreg. Birds 3(6): 42-48.

LITTLEFIELD, C. D. 1979. Breeding season 1978: southeast Oregon. Oreg. Birds 5(1): 9-13.

LITTLEFIELD, C. D. 1980. New bird records from Malheur National Wildlife Refuge, Oregon. West. Birds 11: 181-185.

LITTLEFIELD, C. D. 1981. First Oregon record of the Gray-headed Junco. West. Birds 12: 53.

LITTLEFIELD, C. D. 1983. Oregon's first records of the Great-tailed Grackle. West. Birds 14: 201-202.

LITTLEFIELD, C. D. 1985. Radio-telemetry studies of juvenile Greater Sandhill Cranes on Malheur National Wildlife Refuge, Oregon. Unpubl. rep. to U.S. Fish and Wildl. Serv.

LITTLEFIELD, C. D. 1986. Autumn Sandhill Crane habitat use in southeast Oregon. Wilson Bull. 98: 131-137.

LITTLEFIELD, C. D. 1988. Status of the California Yellow-billed Cuckoo in Klamath County and eastern Oregon. Oreg. Dept. Fish and Wildl. Nongame Tech. Rep. 89-5-01, Portland.

LITTLEFIELD, C. D. 1990a. Birds of Malheur National Wildlife Refuge, Oregon. Oreg. State Univ. Press, Corvallis.

LITTLEFIELD, C. D. 1990b. Bird surveys of the Little Blitzen River in southeast Oregon, summer 1987. Oreg. Birds 16: 147-169.

LITTLEFIELD, C. D. 1991. Steens Mountain, Oregon: bird list. Unpubl., Burns District, U.S. Dept. Int., Bur. Land Manage., Burns, OR.

LITTLEFIELD, C. D. 1995a. Demographics of a declining flock of greater Sandhill Cranes in Oregon. Wilson Bull. 107: 667-674.

LITTLEFIELD, C. D. 1995b. Sandhill Crane nesting habitat, egg predators, and predator history on Malheur National Wildlife Refuge, Oregon. Northwest. Nat. 76: 137-143.

LITTLEFIELD, C. D., AND W. L. ANDERSON. 1971. Tennessee Warbler observations in Oregon. Calif. Birds 2: 137-138.

LITTLEFIELD, C. D., AND J. E. CORNELY. 1984. Fall migration of birds at Malheur National Wildlife Refuge, Oregon. West. Birds 15: 15-22.

LITTLEFIELD, C. D., J. E. CORNELY, AND S. P. THOMPSON. 1985. Recent bird records from Malheur National Wildlife Refuge, Oregon. Murrelet 66: 25-28.

LITTLEFIELD, C. D., AND S. M. LINDSTEDT. 1992. Survival of juvenile Greater Sandhill Cranes at Malheur National Wildlife Refuge, Oregon. *In* 1988 North American Crane Workshop (D. A. Wood, ed.). Florida Game and Freshwater Fish Comm., Nongame Wildl. Prog. Tech. Report 12.

LITTLEFIELD, C. D., AND E. L. McLAURY. 1973. Unusual bird records from southeastern Oregon. Auk 90: 680-682.

LITTLEFIELD, C. D., AND E. L. McLAURY. 1971. Black-throated Blue Warbler records for southeastern Oregon. Calif. Birds 2: 93.

LITTLEFIELD, C. D., AND S. P. THOMPSON. 1981. History and status of the Franklin's Gull on Malheur National Wildlife Refuge, Oregon. Great Basin Nat. 41: 440-444.

LITTLEFIELD, C. D., AND S. P. THOMPSON. 1982. The Pacific Coast population of Lesser Sandhill Cranes in the contiguous United States. Pp. 288-294 *in* Proceedings 1981 Crane Workshop (J. C. Lewis, ed.). Natl. Audubon Soc., Tavernier, FL.

LITTLEFIELD, C. D., AND S. P. THOMPSON. 1987. Winter habitat preferences of Northern Harriers on Malheur National Wildlife Refuge, Oregon. Oreg. Birds 13: 156-164.

LITTLEFIELD, C. D., S. P. THOMPSON, AND B. D. EHLERS. 1984. History and present status of Swainson's Hawks in southeast Oregon. Raptor Res. 18: 1-5.

LITTLEFIELD, C. D., S. P. THOMPSON, AND R. S. JOHNSTONE. 1992. Rough-legged Hawk habitat selection in relation to livestock grazing on Malheur National Wildlife Refuge, Oregon. Northwest. Nat. 73: 80-84.

LITTLEFIELD, C. D., M. A. STERN, AND R. W. SCHLORFF. 1994. Summer distribution, status, and trends of Greater Sandhill Cranes in Oregon and California. Northwest. Nat. 75: 1-10.

LIVERMAN, M. C. 1983. Status of the Black-throated Sparrow (*Amphispiza bilineata deserticola*) in the Alvord Basin, Harney County, Oregon. Oreg. Dept. of Fish and Wildl.,

Nongame Wildl. Prog. Tech. Rep. 82-5-02.

LIVEZEY, B. C. 1991. A phylogenetic analysis and classification of recent dabbling ducks (Tribe Anatini) based on comparative morphology. Auk 108: 471-507.

LOCK, P. A., AND R. J. NAIMAN. 1998. Effects of stream size on bird community structure in coastal temperate forests of the Pacific Northwest, U.S.A. J. Biogeography 25: 773-782.

LOCKLEY, R. M. 1974. Ocean wanderers: the migratory sea birds of the world. Stackpole Books, Harrisburg, PA.

LOEGERING, J. P. 1997. Abundance, habitat association, and foraging ecology of American Dipper and other riparian-associated wildlife in the Oregon Coast Range. Ph.D. diss., Oreg. State Univ., Corvallis.

LOEGERING, J. P., AND R. G. ANTHONY. 1999. Distribution, abundance, and habitat association of riparian-obligate and associated birds in the Oregon Coast Range. Northwest Sci. 73: 168-185.

LONG, J. L. 1981. Introduced birds of the world. David & Charles, London.

LONG, L. L. 1993. The daytime use of agricultural fields by migrating and wintering shorebirds in Humboldt County, California. M.S. thesis, Humboldt State Univ., Arcata, CA.

LOOMIS, L. M. 1901. Birds observed during a steamer voyage from San Francisco to Victoria, British Columbia. Auk 18: 201.

LORD, W. R. 1902. A first book upon the birds of Oregon and Washington. J.K. Gill Co., Portland, OR.

LORAIN, D. 1990. Oregon's high mountain birds. Oreg. Birds 16: 225.

LOVE, M. 1996. Probably more than you want to know about the fishes of the Pacific Coast. Really Big Press, Santa Barbara, CA.

LOVE, T. 1990a. Distributional maps of Pacific Northwest birds using neotropical habitats. Oreg. Birds 16: 56-85.

LOVE, T. 1990b. Oregon birds in the neotropics, or...neotropical birds in Oregon? Oreg. Birds 16: 5-26.

LOWE, R. 1988. Blue-collared swans. Oreg. Birds 14: 42.

LOWE, R. W. 2000. Regional reports. Pacific Seabirds 27: 82.

LOWE, R. W., AND D. S. PITKIN. 1996. Replicate aerial photographic censuses of Oregon Common Murre colonies 1995. Unpubl. rep., U.S. Fish and Wildl. Serv. Oreg. Coastal Refuges, Newport.

LOWERY, G. H., AND B. L. MONROE, JR. 1968. Family parulidae. Pp. 3-93 in Checklist of birds of the world, Vol. 14 (R. A. Paynter, Jr., ed.). Mus. Comp. Zool., Cambridge, MA.

LOWTHER, P. E. 2000. Pacific-slope Flycatcher (Empidonax difficilis) and Cordilleran Flycatcher (Empidonax occidentalis). In The birds of North America, No. 556 (A. Poole and F. Gill, eds.). The Birds of N. Am., Inc., Philadelphia, PA.

LOWTHER, P. E. 1993. Brown-headed Cowbird (Molothrus ater). In The birds of North America, No. 47 (A. Poole and F. Gill, eds.). Acad. of Nat. Sci., Philadelphia, and Am. Ornithol. Union, Washington, D.C.

LOWTHER, P. E., AND C. L. CINK. 1992. House Sparrow (Passer domesticus) In The birds of North America, No. 12 (A. Poole, P. Stettenheim, and F. Gill, eds.). Acad. of Nat. Sci., Philadelphia, and Am. Ornithol. Union, Washington, D.C.

LOWTHER, P. E., C. CELADA, N. K. KLEIN, C. C. RIMMER, AND D. A. SPECTOR. 1999. Yellow Warbler (Dendroica petechia). In The birds of North America, No. 454 (A. Poole and F. Gill, eds.). The Birds of N. Am., Inc., Philadelphia, PA.

LOWTHER, P. E., D. E. KROODSMA, AND G. H. FARLEY. 2000. Rock Wren (Salpinctes obsoletus). In The birds of North America, No. 486 (A. Poole and F. Gill, eds.) The Birds of N. Am., Inc., Philadelphia, PA.

LOWTHER, P. E., H. D. DOUGLASS, III, AND C. L. GRATTO-TREVOR. 2001. Willet (Catoptrophorus semipalmatus). In The birds of North America, No. 579 (A. Poole and F. Gill, eds.). The Birds of N. Am., Inc., Philadelphia, PA.

LOY, W. G., S. ALLAN, C. P. PATTON, R. D. PLANK. 1976. Atlas of Oregon. Univ. of Oreg. Books, Eugene, OR.

LOY, W. G., S. ALLAN, A. R. BUCKLEY, AND J. E. MEACHAM. 2001. Atlas of Oregon, 2nd ed. Univ. Oreg. Press, Eugene, OR.

LUND, T. 1977. Purple Martins in western Oregon, Part I: status and conservation. Oreg. Birds 3(6): 5-10.

LUND, T. 1978. The Purple Martin in the western United States, Part II: it's a question of holes. Oreg. Birds 4(2): 1-9.

LUND, T. 1979. Red-eyed Vireos in the Klamath Basin. Oreg. Birds 4(4): 17-18.

LUNDQUIST, R. W., AND D. MANUWAL. 1990. Seasonal differences in foraging habitat of cavity-nesting birds in the southern Washington Cascades. Stud. in Avian Biol. 13: 218-225.

LUNDQUIST, R. W., AND J. MARIANI. 1991. Nesting habitat and abundance of snag-dependant birds in the southern Washington Cascade Range. Pp. 221-239 in Wildlife and vegetation of unmanaged Douglas-fir forests (L. F. Ruggiero, K. B. Aubry, A. B. Carey, and M. H. Huff, tech. coords.). U.S. Dept. Agric., For. Serv. Gen. Tech. Rep. PNW-GTR-285. Portland, OR.

LUNDSTEN, J. 1993. Breeding bird survey on Steens Mountain, Harney County, Oregon. Oreg. Birds 19: 74-75.

LUNDSTEN, J. 1995. Where to find a Blue Grouse in western Oregon. Oreg. Birds 21: 7.

LUNDSTEN, J. 1996. Solitary Sandpiper nesting in Marion County, Oregon? Oreg. Birds 22: 40-41.

LUNDSTEN, S., AND K. J. POPPER. 2002. Breeding ecology of Yellow Rails at Fourmile Creek, Wood River Wetland, Mares Egg Spring, and additional areas in southern Oregon, 2001. Unpubl. rep. to Lakeview Dist. Bur. of Land Manage., U.S. Fish and Wildl. Serv., Klamath Falls, and Chiloquin Ranger Dist., U.S. For. Serv.

LUTZ, S. L., AND J. A. CRAWFORD. 1987a. Reproductive success and nesting habitat of Merriam's Wild Turkeys in Oregon. J. Wildl. Manage. 51: 783-787.

LUTZ, S. L., AND J. A. CRAWFORD. 1987b. Seasonal use of roost sites by Merriam's Wild Turkey hens and hen-poult flocks in Oregon. Northwest Sci. 61: 174-178.

LYNCH, C. B. 1970. The reproductive strategy of the American Goldfinch, Spinus tristis tristis, in Iowa. Proc. Iowa Acad. Sci. 77: 164-168.

LYON, B., AND R. MONTGOMERIE. 1995. Snow Bunting and McKay's Bunting (Plectrophenax nivalis and Plectrophenax hyberboreus). In The birds of North America, Nos. 198 and 199 (A. Poole and F. Gill, eds.). Acad. of Nat. Sci., Philadelphia, PA, and Am. Ornithol. Union, Washington, D.C.

MABEE, T. J., AND V. B. ESTELLE. 2000. Nest fate and vegetation

characteristics for Snowy Plover and Killdeer in Colorado. Wader Stud. Gr. Bull. 93: 67-72.

MACDONALD, N. 2000. Breeding Western Scrub-Jays in Crook County. Oreg. Birds 26: 212.

MACE, P. M. 1983. Bird predation on juvenile salmonids in the Big Qualicum Estuary, Vancouver Island. Can. Tech. Rep. of Fish and Aquatic Sci. 1176. Vancouver, B.C.

MACK, D. E., AND W. YONG 2000. Swainson's Thrush (Catharus ustulatus). In The birds of North America, No. 540 (A. Poole and F. Gill, eds.). The Birds of N. Am., Inc., Philadelphia.

MACROBERTS, M. H. 1970. Notes on the food habits and food defense of the Acorn Woodpecker. Condor 72: 196-204.

MACROBERTS, M. H., AND B. R. MACROBERTS. 1976. Social organization and behavior of the Acorn Woodpecker in central coastal California. Ornithol. Monogr. 21: 1-115.

MACWHIRTER, R. B., AND K. L. BILDSTEIN. 1996. Northern Harrier (Circus cyaneus). In The birds of North America, No. 210 (A. Poole and F. Gill, eds.). Acad. of. Nat. Sci., Philadelphia, and Am. Ornithol. Union, Washington, D.C.

MADGE, S., AND H. BURN. 1988. Waterfowl: an identification guide to the ducks, geese and swans of the world. Houghton Mifflin Co., Boston.

MADGE, S., AND H. BURN. 1994. Crows and jays: a guide to the crows, jays, and magpies of the world. Houghton Mifflin Co., New York.

MADGE, S., AND P. MCGOWAN. 2002. Pheasants, partridges, and grouse: a guide to the pheasants, partridges, quails, grouse, guineafowl, buttonquails, and sandgrouse of the world. Princeton Univ. Press, Princeton, NJ.

MAHER, W. J. 1984. Skuas and jaegers. In Seabirds of eastern North Pacific and Arctic waters (D. G. Haley, ed.). Pacific Search Press, Seattle, WA.

MAHONEY, S. A., AND J. R. JEHL, JR. 1985a. Adaptations of migratory shorebirds to highly saline and alkaline lakes: Wilson's Phalarope and American Avocet. Condor 87: 520-527.

MAHONEY, S. A., AND J. R. JEHL, JR. 1985b. Avoidance of salt-loading by a diving bird at a hypersaline and alkaline lake: Eared Grebe. Condor 87: 389-397.

MALHEUR NATIONAL WILDLIFE REFUGE FILES. Unpubl. data. Princeton, OR.

MALL, R. E. 1956. Another record of the Tropical Kingbird for California. Condor 58: 163-164.

MALTBY, F. 1931. Experiences afield. Oologist 48: 110-112.

MANNAN, R. W. 1977. Use of snags by birds, Douglas-fir region, western Oregon. M.S. thesis, Oreg. State Univ., Corvallis.

MANNAN, R. W. 1980. Assemblages of bird species in western coniferous old-growth forests. Pp. 375-368 in Management of western forests and grasslands for nongame birds (R. F. DeGraff, tech. coord.). U.S. Dept. Agric., For. Serv. Gen. Tech. Rep. INT-86. Ogden, UT.

MANNAN, R. W. 1982. Bird populations and vegetation characteristics in managed and old-growth forests, northeastern Oregon. Ph.D. diss., Oreg. State Univ., Corvallis.

MANNAN, R. W. 1984. Summer area requirements of Pileated Woodpeckers in western Oregon. Wildl. Soc. Bull. 12: 265- 268.

MANNAN, R. W., B. S. HALE, AND M. L. MORRISON. 1983. Observations of nesting Townsend's Warblers in northeastern Oregon. Murrelet 64: 23-25.

MANNAN, R. W., AND E. C. MESLOW. 1984. Bird populations and vegetation characteristics in managed and old-growth forests, northeastern Oregon. J. Wildl. Manage. 48: 1219-1238.

MANNAN, R. W., E. C. MESLOW, AND H. M. WIGHT. 1980. Use of snags by birds in Douglas-fir forests, western Oregon. J. Wildl. Manage. 44: 787-797.

MANOLIS, T. 1977. Foraging relationships of Mountain Chickadees and Pygmy Nuthatches. West. Birds 8: 13-20.

MANOMET CENTER FOR CONSERVATION SCIENCES, Manomet, MA. 2000. U.S. shorebird conservation plan. Draft shorebird prioritization system. URL = http://www. manomet.org/USSCP/index.htm Accessed 18 Sep 2002.

MANUWAL, D. A. 1974a. Effects of territoriality on breeding in a population of Cassin's Auklet. Ecology 55: 1399-1406.

MANUWAL, D. A. 1974b. The incubation patches of Cassin's Auklet. Condor 76: 481-484.

MANUWAL, D. A. 1974c. The natural history of Cassin's Auklet. Condor 76: 421-431.

MANUWAL, D. 1991. Spring bird communities in the southern Washington Cascade Range. Pp 161-174 in Wildlife and vegetation of unmanaged Douglas-fir forests (L. F. Ruggiero, K. B. Aubry, A. B. Carey, and M. H. Huff, tech. coords.). U.S. Dept. Agric., For. Serv. Gen. Tech. Rep. PNW-GTR-285. Portland, OR.

MANUWAL, D. A., AND H. A. CARTER. 2001. Natural history of the Common Murre (Uria aalge californica). Pp. 1-32 in Biology and Conservation of the Common Murre in California, Oregon, Washington and British Columbia, Vol. 1 (D. A. Manuwal, H. A. Carter, T. S. Zimmerman, and D. L. Orthmeyer, eds.). U.S. Geol. Survey, Info. and Tech. Rept. USGS/BRD/ ITR 2000-0012, Washington, D.C.

MANUWAL, D. A., AND M. H. HUFF. 1987. Spring and winter bird populations in a Douglas-fir forest sere. J. Wildl. Manage. 51: 586-595.

MANUWAL, D. A., P. W. MATTOCKS, JR., AND K. O. RICHTER. 1979. First Arctic Tern colony in the contiguous western United States. Am. Birds 33: 144-145.

MANUWAL, D. A., AND A. C. THORESEN. 1993. Cassin's Auklet (Ptychoramphus aleuticus). In The birds of North America, No. 155 (A. Poole and F. Gill, eds.). Acad. of Nat. Sci., Philadelphia, and Am. Ornithol. Union, Washington, D.C.

MARCH, G. L., AND R. M. F. S. SADLEIR. 1970. Studies on the Band-tailed Pigeon (Columba fasciata) in British Columbia, I: seasonal changes in gonadal development and crop gland activity. Can. J. Zool. 48: 1353–1357.

MARCH, G. L., AND R. M. F. S. SADLEIR. 1972. Studies on the Band-tailed Pigeon (Columba fasciata) in British Columbia, II: food resources and mineral-gravelling activity. Syesis 5: 279–284.

MARCHANT, S., AND P. HIGGINS. 1990. Handbook of Australian, New Zealand, and Antarctic birds, Vol. 1. Oxford Univ. Press, Melbourne.

MARCOT, B. G. 1985. Habitat relationships of birds and young-growth Douglas-fir in northwestern California. Ph.D. diss., Oreg. State Univ., Corvallis.

MARCOT, B. G., AND J. W. THOMAS. 1997. Of Spotted Owls, old growth and new policies: a history since the Interagency Scientific Committee Report. U.S. Dept. Agric., For. Serv. Gen. Tech. Rept. PNW-GTR-408.

MARHEINE, R., G. CONCANNON, AND D. RATLIFF. Unpubl. data. Pelton project miscellaneous wildlife observations, 1988-1999. Portland General Electric, Madras, OR.

MARIANI, J. M., AND D. A. MANUWAL. 1990. Factors influencing Brown Creeper (Certhia americana) abundance patterns in the southern Washington Cascade Range. Stud. in Avian Biol. 13: 53-57.

MARÍN, M. 1997. Some aspects of the breeding biology of the Black Swift. Wilson Bull. 109: 290-306.

MARKS, J. S. 1983. Unusual nest sites of a Western Screech-Owl and an American Kestrel. Murrelet 64: 96-97.

MARKS, J. S. 1986. Nest-site characteristics and reproductive success of Long-eared Owls in southwestern Idaho. Wilson Bull. 98: 547-560.

MARKS, J. S. 1997. Is the Northern Saw-whet Owl (Aegolius acadicus) nomadic? P. 260 in Biology and conservation of owls of the northern hemisphere (J. R. Duncan, D. H. Johnson, and T. H. Nicholls, eds.). U.S. Dept. Agric., For. Serv. Gen. Tech. Rep. NC-GTR-190.

MARKS, J. S., AND J. H. DOREMUS. 1988. Breeding season diet of Northern Saw-whet Owls in southwestern Idaho. Wilson Bull. 100: 690-694.

MARKS, J. S., J. H. DOREMUS, AND R. J. CANNINGS. 1989. Polygyny in the Northern Saw-whet Owl. Auk 106: 732-734.

MARKS, J. S., D. L. EVANS, AND D. W. HOLT. 1994. Long-eared Owl (Asio otus). In The birds of North America, No. 148 (A. Poole and F. Gill, eds.). Acad. of Nat. Sci., Philadelphia, and Am. Ornithol. Union, Washington, D.C.

MARKS, J. S., AND E. YENSEN. 1980. Nest sites and food habits of Long-eared Owls in southwestern Idaho. Murrelet 61: 86-91.

MARPLE, E. 2002. Mini site guide: Pole Creek Reservoir, Malheur County. Oreg. Birds 28: 5.

MARR, N. V. 1985. Gopher snake preys on Northern Oriole nestlings. Murrelet 66: 95-97.

MARR, N. V., W. D. EDGE, R. G. ANTHONY, AND R. VALBURG. 1995. Sheep carcass availability and use by Bald Eagles. Wilson Bull. 107: 251-257.

MARSH, C. P. 1983. The role of avian predators in an Oregon rocky intertidal community. Ph.D. thesis, Oreg. State Univ., Corvallis.

MARSH, C. P. 1986. Rocky intertidal community organization: the impact of avian predators on mussel recruitment. Ecology 67: 771-786.

MARSH, M., ED. 1996. Pesticides monitoring in the northwest. U.S. Environ. Protection Agency Region 10, Seattle, WA. URL = http:// yosemite.epa.gov/r10%5Cecocomm.nsf/ecoweb/

Marshall, D. B. 1959. New bird records from southeastern Oregon. Condor 61: 53-56.

Marshall, D. B. 1962. Additional bird records from southeastern Oregon. Condor 64: 163.

Marshall, D. B. 1969. Endangered plants and animals of Oregon, III: birds. Agric. Exp. Station, Spec. Rep. 278, Oreg. State Univ., Corvallis.

Marshall, D. 1987. Comparative bird observations from Steens, Pueblo, Trout Creek, and Oregon Canyon mountains. Oreg. Birds 13: 193-209.

Marshall, D. B. 1989a. Black-chinned Hummingbird at Portland, Oregon. Oreg. Birds 15: 178-179.

Marshall, D. B. 1989b. Recollections of boyhood birding experiences in and out of Portland, Oregon before World War II. Oreg. Birds 15: 169-177.

Marshall, D. B. 1992a. Sensitive vertebrates of Oregon, first ed. Oreg. Dept. Fish and Wildl., Portland.

Marshall, D. B. 1992b. Status of the Northern Goshawk in Oregon and Washington. Audubon Soc. of Portland, Portland, OR.

Marshall, D. B. 1996. Species at risk. Wildl. Diversity Prog. Oreg. Dept. Fish and Wildl., Portland.

Marshall, D. B. 1997. Status of the White-headed Woodpecker in Oregon and Washington. Audubon Soc. of Portland.

Marshall, D. B., M. W, Chilcote, and H. Weeks. 1996. Species at risk: sensitive, threatened and endangered vertebrates of Oregon, 2nd ed. Oreg. Dept. Fish and Wildl., Portland, OR.

Marshall, D. B., and H. F. Deubbert. 1965. Nesting of the Ring-necked Duck in Oregon in 1963 and 1964. Murrelet 46: 43.

Marshall, D. B., and L. W. Giles. 1953. Recent observations on birds of Anaho Island, Pyramid Lake, Nevada. Condor 55: 105-116.

Marshall, D. B., and K. Horn. 1973. Adaptations of two desert birds to clearcut area in the Oregon Cascades. Murrelet 54: 35-36.

Marshall, D. B., H. Weeks, and M. Chilcote. 1992. Sensitive vertebrates of Oregon, first ed. Oreg, Dept. Fish and Wildl., Portland.

Marshall, J. T. 1957. Birds of the pine-oak woodland in southern Arizona and adjacent Mexico. Pac. Coast Avifauna 32: 1-125.

Marshall, J. T., Jr. 1960. Interrelations of Abert's and Brown towhees. Condor 62: 49-64.

Marshall, J. T., Jr. 1964. Voice in communication and relationships among Brown Towhees. Condor 66: 345-356.

Marshall, J. T. 1967. Parallel variation in North and Middle American Screech-owls. West. Found. Vertebrate Zool., Biol. Monogr. 1.

Marshall, J. T. 1978. Systematics of smaller Asian night birds based on voice. Am. Ornithol. Union Monogr. 25: 1-58.

Martell, M. S., C. J. Henny, P. E. Nye, and M. Solensky. 2001. Fall migration and wintering localities of North American Ospreys as determined by satellite telemetry. Condor 103: 715-724.

Martell, M. S., M. J. Kennedy, C. J. Henny, and P. E. Nye. 1998. Highway to the tropics: using satellite telemetry and the internet to track Ospreys in the Western Hemisphere. Proc. Internatl. Seminar: Migratory Birds Know No Boundaries. Torgos 28: 163-172.

Marti, C. D. 1973. Food consumption and pellet formation rates in four owl species. Wilson Bull. 85: 178-181.

Marti, C. D. 1974. Feeding ecology of four sympatric owls. Condor 76: 45-61.

Marti, C. D. 1976. A review of prey selection by the Long-eared Owl. Condor 78: 331-336.

Marti, C. D. 1992. Barn Owls (Tyto alba). In The birds of North America, No. 1 (A. Poole and F. Gill, eds.). Acad. of Nat. Sci., Philadelphia, and Am. Ornithol. Union, Washington, D.C.

Marti, C. D., and J. S. Marks. 1989. Medium-sized owls. Pp.124-133 in Proceedings western raptor management symposium and workshop. Natl. Wildl. Fed., Washington, D.C.

Martin, D. J. 1973. Selected aspects of Burrowing Owl ecology and behavior. Condor 75: 446-456.

Martin, J. W., and B. A. Carlson. 1998. Sage Sparrow (Amphispiza belli). In The birds of North America, No. 326 (A. Poole, and F. Gill, eds.) The Birds of N. Am., Inc., Philadelphia.

Martin, J. W., and J. R. Parrish. 2000. Lark Sparrow (Chondestes grammacus). In The birds of North America, No. 488 (A. Poole and F. Gill, eds.). The Birds of N. Am., Inc., Philadelphia.

Martin, S. G., and T. A. Gavin. 1995. Bobolink (Dolichonyx oryzivorus). In The birds of North America, No. 176 (A. Poole and F. Gill, eds.). Acad. of Nat. Sci., Philadelphia, and Am. Ornithol. Union, Washington, D.C.

Martin, T. E. 1992. Breeding productivity considerations: what are the appropriate features for management? Pp. 455-473 in Ecology and conservation of neotropical migrant landbirds (J. M. Hagan, III and D. W. Johnston, eds.). Smithsonian Inst. Press.

Martin, T. E., and P. Li. 1992. Life history traits of open-versus cavity-nesting birds. Ecology 73: 579-592.

Martin, A. C., H. S. Zim, and A. L. Nelson. 1951. American wildlife and plants. McGraw-Hill Book Co. (Reprinted in 1961 by Dover Publ., New York).

März, R. 1968. Der Rauhfusskauz. Die Neue Brehm-Bücherei 394. Wittenberg-Lutherstadt.

Marzluff, J. M., and R. P. Balda. 1992. The Pinyon Jay. T. & A.D. Poyser, London.

Marzluff, J. M., L. S. Schueck, M. Vakesy, B. A. Kimsey, M. McFadzen, R. R. Townsend, and J. O. McKinley. 1993. Influence of military training on the behavior of raptors in the Snake River Birds of Prey Area. Pp. 40-125 in Snake River Birds of Prey research project annual report (K. Steenhof, ed.). U.S. Dept. Int., Bur. of Land Manage., Boise, ID.

Maser, C. 1975. Predation by Common Raven on feral Rock Doves. Wilson Bull. 87: 552-553.

Maser, C., and E. D. Brodie. 1966. A study of owl pellet contents from Linn, Benton and Polk counties, Oregon. Murrelet 47: 9-14.

Maser, C., and K. Gordon. 1965. A nesting record of Long-eared Owls in Benton County, Oregon. Murrelet 46: 39.

Maser, C., and E. W. Hammer. 1972. A note of the food habits of Barn Owls in Klamath County, Oregon. Murrelet 53: 28.

Maser, C., E. W. Hammer, and S. H. Anderson. 1970. Comparative food habits of three owl species in central Oregon. Murrelet 51: 29-33.

Maser, C., E. W. Hammer, and S. H. Anderson. 1971. Food habits of the Burrowing Owl in central Oregon. Northwest Sci. 45: 19-26.

Maser, C., E. W. Hammer, and R. Maser. 1971. A note on the food habits of the Short-eared Owl (Asio flammeus) in Klamath County, Oregon. Murrelet 52: 27.

Maser, C., S. Shaver, C. Shaver, and B. Price. 1980. A note of the food habits of the Barn Owl in Malheur County, Oregon. Murrelet 61: 78-80.

Masson, W. V. 1954. Introduction of the Chukar partridge in Oregon. Proc. West. Assoc. State Game and Fish Comm. 34: 251-253.

Massey, B. W. 1976. Vocal differences between American Least Terns and European Little Terns. Auk 93: 760-773.

Master T. L. 1991. Use of tongue-flicking behavior by the Snowy Egret. J. Field Ornithol. 62: 399-402.

Mathewson, W. 1997. Big December Canvasbacks. Sand Lake Press, Amity, OR.

Matthews, D. R. 1983. Feeding ecology of the Common Murre Uria aalge off the Oregon coast. M.S. thesis, Univ. of Oreg., Eugene.

Matthysen, E. 1998. The nuthatches. Academic Press, San Diego.

Mattocks, P. W., Jr. 1979. Northern Pacific Coast region. Am. Birds 33: 305-308.

Mattocks, P. W. 1985a. Northern Pacific Coast region. Am. Birds 39: 201-204.

Mattocks, P. W. 1985b. Northern Pacific Coast region. Am. Birds 39: 340-344.

Mattocks, P. W. 1986. Northern Pacific Coast region. Am. Birds 40: 1244-1248.

Mattocks, P. W., Jr. 1988a. Northern Pacific Coast region. Am. Birds 42: 121-126.

Mattocks, P. W., Jr. 1988b. Northern Pacific Coast region. Am. Birds 42: 1331-1335.

Mattocks, P. W. 1989. Northern Pacific Coast region. Am. Birds 43: 154-157.

Mattocks, P. W., and B. Harrington-Tweit. 1987a. Northern Pacific Coast region. Am. Birds 41: 132-136.

Mattocks, P. W., and B. Harrington-Tweit. 1987b. Northern Pacific

Coast region. Am. Birds 41: 478-482.

Mattocks, P. W., B. Harrington-Tweit, and E. Hunn. 1983. Northern Pacific Coast region. Am. Birds 37: 1019-1022.

Mattocks, P. W., and E. S. Hunn. 1978a. Northern Pacific Coast region. Am. Birds 32: 245-250.

Mattocks, P. W., and E. S. Hunn. 1978b. Northern Pacific Coast region. Am. Birds 32: 1045-1047.

Mattocks, P. W., and E. S. Hunn. 1980a. Northern Pacific Coast region. Am. Birds 34: 191-194.

Mattocks, P. W., and E. S. Hunn. 1980b. Northern Pacific Coast region. Am. Birds 34: 299-302.

Mattocks, P. W., and E. S. Hunn. 1981. Northern Pacific Coast region. Am. Birds 35: 328-331.

Mattocks, P. W., and E. S. Hunn. 1982a. Northern Pacific Coast region. Am. Birds 36: 323-325.

Mattocks, P. W., and E. S. Hunn. 1982b. Northern Pacific Coast region. Am. Birds 36: 886-888.

Mattocks, P. W., and E. S. Hunn. 1983a. Northern Pacific Coast region. Am. Birds 37: 329-332.

Mattocks, P. W., and E. S. Hunn. 1983b. Northern Pacific Coast region. Am. Birds 37: 903-906.

Mattocks, P. W., E. S. Hunn, and T. R. Wahl. 1976. A checklist of the birds of Washington State, with recent changes annotated. West. Birds 7: 1-24.

Mauck, R. A., T. A. Waite, and P. G. Parker. 1995. Monogamy in Leach's Storm-Petrel: DNA-fingerprinting evidence. Auk 112: 473-482.

May, J. B. 1935. The hawks of North America. Natl. Assoc. Audubon Soc., New York.

Maybank, B. 2000. The 1999 big day report and the 1998 list report. Birding 32(3) suppl.

Mayfield, H. 1975. Suggestions for calculating nest success. Wilson Bull. 87: 456-466.

Mayfield, H. F. 1984. Phalaropes. In Seabirds of eastern North Pacific and Arctic waters (D. G. Haley, ed.) Pacific Search Press, Seattle, WA.

Mayr, E. M., and G. W. Cottrell, Eds. 1979. Peters' check-list of birds of the world. Mus. Comp. Zool., Cambridge, MA.

Mayr, E., and L. L. Short. 1970. Species taxa of North American birds. Publ. Nuttall Ornithol. Club 9: 1-127.

McAllister, K. 1995. Washington state recovery plan for the Upland Sandpiper. Rep. to Wash. Dept. of Fish and Wildl.

McAllister, N. 1958. Courtship, hostile behavior, nest-establishment, and egg laying in the Eared Grebe Podiceps caspicus. Auk 75: 290-311.

McAllister, T. H., Jr. 1949. Possible nesting of Blue-winged Teal in Willamette Valley, Oregon. Condor 51: 99.

McAllister, T. 1954. The Laysan Albatross (Diomedea immutabilis) on the Oregon coast. Auk 71: 211.

McAllister, T. 1981. At river's end – logger's private refuge is for the birds. Oreg. J. April 6, 1981.

McAllister, T. H., Jr., and D. B. Marshall. 1945. Birds of Fremont National Forest. Auk 62: 177-189.

McArthur, L. L. 1992. Oregon geographic names. Oreg. Hist. Soc. Press.

McAtee, G. 2001. A new Black Swift nest site near Blue Lake, Lane County, Oregon. Oreg. Birds 27: 15.

McAtee, W. L. 1908. Food habits of the grosbeaks. U.S. Dept. Agric. Biol. Surv. Bull. 32.

McAtee, W. L. 1911. Woodpeckers in relation to trees and wood products. U.S. Dept. Agric. Biol. Surv. Bull. 39.

McAtee, W. L. 1926. The relation of birds to woodlots in New York state. Roosevelt Wild Life Bull. 4: 7-152.

McAtee, W. L. 1935. Food habits of common hawks. U.S. Dept. Agric. Circ. 370.

McCabe, T. T., and E. B. McCabe. 1929. Economic status of Pine Siskin. Condor 31: 126-127.

McCaffery, B. J., C. M. Harwood, and J. R. Morgart. 1997. First breeding records of Slaty-backed Gull (Larus schistisagus) for North America. Pacific Seabirds 24: 70.

McCallum, D. A. 1994a. Conservation status of Flammulated Owls in the United States. Pp 74-79 in Flammulated, Boreal, and Great Gray owls in the United States: a technical conservation assessment (G. D. Hayward and J. Verner, eds.). U.S. Dept. Agric., For. Serv. Gen. Tech. Rep. RM-253.

McCallum, D. A. 1994b. Flammulated Owl (Otus flammeolus). In The birds of North America, No. 93 (A. Poole and F. Gill, eds). Acad. of Nat. Sci., Philadelphia, and Am. Ornithol. Union, Washington, D.C.

McCallum, D. A. 1994b. Review of technical knowledge: Flammulated Owls. Pp. 14-46 in Flammulated, Boreal, and Great Gray owls in the United States: a technical conservation assessment (G. D.

Hayward, and J. Verner, eds.). U.S. Dept. Agric., For. Serv., Gen. Tech. Rep. RM-253.

McCallum, D. A., R. Grundel, and D. L. Dahlsten. 1999. Mountain Chickadee (Poecile gambeli). In The birds of North America, No. 453 (A. Poole and F. Gill, eds.). The Birds of N. Am., Inc., Philadelphia.

McCaskie, G. 1970. Blue Jay in California. Calif. Birds 1: 81-83.

McCaskie, G., and P. DeBenedictis. 1964. Bay-breasted Warbler and Red-eyed Vireo in Klamath County, Oregon. Condor 66: 76.

McCaskie, G., P. DeBenedictis, R. Erickson, and J. Morlan. 1988. Birds of northern California, an annotated field list, second ed. Golden Gate Audubon Soc.

McClelland, B. R., L. S. Young, P. T. McClelland, J. G. Crenshaw, H. L. Allen, and D. S. Shea. 1994. Migration ecology of Bald Eagles from autumn concentrations in Glacier National Park, Montana. Wildl. Monogr. 125.

McCluskey, D. C., J. W. Thomas, and E. C. Meslow. 1977. Effects of aerial application of DDT on reproduction in House Wrens, and Mountain and Western bluebirds. U.S. Dept. Agric., For. Serv. Res. Rep. PNW-228.

McCollough, M. A.1989. Molting sequence and aging of Bald Eagles. Wilson Bull. 101: 1-10.

McCrae, J. 1994. Oregon developmental species, Pacific saury Cololabis saira. Oreg. Dept. Fish and Wildl. URL = http://www.hmsc. orst.edu/odfw/devfish/sp/saury. html Accessed 20 Sep 2002.

McCullough, D. G., R. A. Werner, and D. Neumann. 1998. Fire and insects in northern and boreal forest ecosystems of North America. Annual Rev. Entomol. 43: 107–127.

McDermond, D. K., and K. H. Morgan. 1993. Status and conservation of North Pacific albatrosses. Pp. 70-81 in The status, ecology, and conservation of marine birds of the North Pacific (K. Vermeer, K. T. Briggs, K. H. Morgan, and D. Siegel-Causey, eds.). Can. Wildl. Serv. Publ., Ottawa.

McDonald, S. D. 1968. The courtship and territorial behavior of Franklin's race of the Spruce Grouse. Living Bird 7: 5-25.

McEllin, S. M. 1979. Population demographies, spacing, and foraging behaviours of White—breasted and Pygmy nuthatches in ponderosa pine habitat. Pp. 301-330 in The role of insectivorous birds in forest ecosystems (J. G. Dickson, R. N. Conner, R. R. Fleet, J. C. Kroll, and J. A. Jackson, eds.). Academic Press, London.

McFadden, M. E., and J. M. Marzluff. 1996. Mortality of Prairie Falcons during the fledgling-dependence period. Condor 98: 791-800.

McGarigal, K. 1993. Relationship between landscape structure and avian abundance patterns in the Oregon Coast Range. Ph.D. diss., Oreg. State Univ., Corvallis.

McGarigal, K., R. G. Anthony, and F. B. Isaacs. 1991. Interactions of humans and Bald Eagles on the Columbia River estuary. Wildl. Monogr. 115.

McGarigal, K., and J. D. Fraser. 1985. Barred Owl responses to recorded vocalizations. Condor 87: 552-553.

McGarigal, K., and W. C. McComb. 1992. Streamside versus upslope breeding bird communities in the central Oregon Coast Range. J. Wild. Manage. 56: 10-23.

McGarigal, K., and W. C. McComb. 1995. Relationships between landscape structure and breeding birds in the Oregon Coast Range. Ecol. Monogr. 65: 235-260.

McGillivray, W. B., and G. P. Semenchuk. 1998. Field guide to Alberta birds. The Fed. of Alberta Naturalists. Edmonton.

McGilvrey, F. B. 1966. Nesting of Hooded Mergansers on the Patuxent Wildlife Research Center, Patuxent, Maryland. Auk 83: 477-479.

McGilvrey, F. B. 1967. Food habits of sea ducks from the north-eastern United States. Wildfowl 18: 142-145.

McGowan, J. A., D. R. Cayan, and L. M. Dorman. 1998. Climate-ocean variability and ecosystem response in the northeast Pacific. Science 281: 210-217.

McHugh, J. L. 1950. Increasing abundance of albatrosses off the coast of California. Condor 52: 153-156.

McIntyre, J. W. 1975. Biology and behavior of the Common Loon (Gavia immer) with reference to adaptability in a man-altered environment. Ph.D. diss., Univ. of Minn., Minneapolis.

McIntyre, J. W. 1978. Wintering behavior of Common Loons. Auk 95: 396-403.

McKenzie, P. M., and M. B. Robbins. 1999. Identification of male Rufous and Allen's hummingbirds, with specific comments on dorsal coloration. West. Birds 30: 86-93.

McLaren, E. B. 1991. Clutch size in Pigeon Guillemots: an experimental manipulation and comparisons of reproductive success in one and two egg clutches. M.S. thesis, Univ. of Oreg., Eugene.

McMahon, B. F., and R. M. Evans. 1992. Nocturnal foraging in the American White Pelican. Condor 94: 101-109.

McNair, D. B. 1982. Lark sparrows breed in Richmond County, N.C. Chat 46: 1-8.

McNair, D. B. 1985. A comparison of oology and nest record card data in evaluating the reproductive biology of Lark Sparrows, Chondestes grammacus. Southwest. Nat. 30: 213-224.

McNair, D. B. 1990. Lark Sparrows breed in the Rhine-Luzon drop zone, Camp McKall, Scotland County, N.C. Chat 54: 16-20.

McNicholl, M. K. 1971. The breeding biology and ecology of Forster's Tern (Sterna forsteri) at Delta Marsh, Manitoba. M.S. thesis, Univ. of Manitoba, Winnipeg.

McNicholl, M. K. 1982. Factors affecting reproductive success of Forster's Terns at Delta Marsh, Manitoba. Colonial Waterbirds 5: 32-38.

McQueen, L. B. 1972. Observations on copulatory behavior of a pair of screech owls (Otus asio). Condor 74: 101.

McQueen, L. 1977. Lister's corner: American Redstart. SWOC Talk (Oreg. Birds) 3(3): 71.

Medin, D. 1987. Breeding birds of an alpine habitat in the southern Snake Range, Nevada. West. Birds 18: 163.

Medin, D. E. 1990. Birds of a shadscale (Atriplex confertifolia) habitat in east central Nevada. Great Basin Nat. 50: 295-298.

Medin, D. E., and W. P. Clary. 1991. Breeding bird populations in a grazed and ungrazed riparian habitat in Nevada. U.S. Dept. Agric., For. Serv. Intermountain Res. Sta. Res. Pap. INT-441.

Mehall-Niswander, A. C. 1997. Time budget and habitat use patterns of Marbled Godwits (Limosa fedoa beringiae) breeding on the Alaskan Peninsula. M.S. thesis, Oreg. State Univ., Corvallis.

Mellen, T. K. 1987. Home range and habitat use of Pileated Woodpeckers. M.S. thesis, Oreg. State Univ., Corvallis.

Mellen, T. K., E. C. Meslow, and R. W. Mannan. 1992. Summertime home range and habitat use of Pileated Woodpeckers in western Oregon. J. Wildl. Manage. 56: 96-103.

Melvin, E. F., J. K. Parrish, K. S. Dietrich, and O. S. Hamel. 2001. Solutions to seabird bycatch in Alaska's Demersel Longline Fisheries. URL = http://www.wsg. washington.edu/pubs/seabirds/ execsummary.pdf Accessed 18 Aug 2002.

Melvin, S. M., and J. P Gibbs. 1996. Sora (Porzana carolina). In The birds of North America, No. 250 (A. Poole and F. Gill, eds.). Acad. of Nat. Sci., Philadelphia, and Am. Ornithol. Union, Washington, D.C.

Mendall, H. L. 1936. The home-life and economic status of the Double-crested Cormorant., Phalacrocorax auritus auritus (Lesson). Univ. Maine Stud., Second Ser. 38. Maine Bull. 39(3): 1-159.

Mendall, H. L. 1958. The Ring-necked Duck in the Northeast. Vol. LX, No.16 Univ. of Maine Bull. Univ. Press, Orono, ME.

Mendenhall, V. M. 1970. Studies on the feeding ecology and behavior of the Willet. M.S. thesis, Univ. of Calif., Berkeley.

Mengel, R. M. 1964. The probable history of species formation in some northern wood warblers (Parulidae). Living Bird 3: 9-43.

Menon, G. K. 1981. Cattle Egrets feeding in association with human workers. Wilson Bull. 93: 549-550.

Merliees, B. 1987. A next box for Brown Creepers. Discovery (Vancouver Nat. Hist. Soc.) 16: 16-17.

Merola, M. 1995. Observations on the nesting and breeding behavior of the Rock Wren. Condor 97: 585-587.

Merrifield, K. Unpublished pelagic bird censuses from three Lincoln County, Oregon coastal points.

Merrifield, K. 1993. Eurasian X American wigeon in western Oregon. West. Birds 24: 105-107.

Merrifield, K. J. 1994. Censuses of gulls at two sites along the Oregon central coast. Northwest. Nat. 75: 24-29.

Merrifield, K. J. 1996a. Red-breasted Merganser (Mergus serrator) courtship displays in Lincoln County, Oregon. Northwest. Nat. 77: 19.

Merrifield, K. 1996b. 1992-1995 waterbird and raptor records for Cabell Marsh, William L. Finley National Wildlife Refuge, Benton County, Oregon. J. Oreg. Ornithol. 5: 558-600.

Merrifield, K. 1997. Nearshore flights of seabirds past the Yachats River Mouth, Oregon, April 1991 to March 1992. Northwest. Nat. 78: 93-101.

Merrifield, K. 1998. Waterbird censuses of Yaquina Bay, Oregon. March 1993-February 1994. Oreg. Dept. Fish and Wildl., Wildl. Diversity Prog. Tech. Rep. 98-01-1. Portland.

Merrifield, K. 2001a. April Lincoln County bird notes. Sandpiper 22(4).

Merrifield, K. 2001b. Larid, alcid, and crow censuses of Yaquina Bay, Oregon: June 1997–June 1999. Oreg. Dept. Fish and Wildl., Wildl. Diversity Prog. Rep. 01-05-01. Portland.

Merrill, J. C. 1888. Notes on the birds of Fort Klamath, Oregon, with remarks on certain species by William Brewster. Auk 5: 139-146, 251-262, 357-366.

Merson, M. H., R. E. Byers, and D. E. Kaukeinen. 1984. Residues of the rodenticide brodifacoum in voles and raptors after orchard treatment. J. Wildl. Manage. 48: 212-216.

Meslow, E. C., and H. M. Wight. 1975. Avifauna and succession in Douglas-fir forests of the Pacific Northwest. In Proceedings of the symposium on management of forest and range habitats for non-game birds: May 6-9, 1975, Tucson, Arizona (D. R. Smith, tech. coord.). U.S. Dept. Agric., For. Serv. Gen. Tech. Rep. WO-1. Washington, D.C.

Mewaldt, L. R. 1977a. Details: Least Flycatcher and Virginia's Warblers at Hart Mtn. Oreg. Birds 3(4): 23.

Mewaldt, L. R. 1977b. Prothonotary Warbler in Oregon. West. Birds 8: 63-64.

Mewaldt, L. R. 1980. Unpubl. ms. Birds of Hart Mountain.

Mewaldt, L. R., and J. R. King. 1985. Breeding site faithfulness, reproductive biology, and adult survivorship in an isolated population of Cassin's Finches. Condor 87: 494-510.

Michael, C. W. 1927. Black Swifts nesting in Yosemite National Park. Condor 29: 89-97.

Mickel, T. 1982. Distribution: Townsend's Solitaire, Coast Range. Oreg. Birds 8: 172-174.

Mickel, T., and A. Mickel. 1997. Field notes. Quail Oct.: 6-8.

Mickel, T., and A. Mickel. 2000. Field notes. Quail May-June: 6-8.

Middleton, A. L. A. 1978. The annual cycle of the American Goldfinch. Condor 79: 401-406.

Middleton, A. L. A. 1979. Influence of age and habitat on reproduction by the American Goldfinch. Ecology 60: 418-432.

Middleton, A. L. A. 1988. Polyandry in the mating system of the American Goldfinch, Carduelis tristis. Can. J. Zool. 66: 296-299.

Middleton, A. L. A. 1991. Failure of Brown-headed Cowbird parasitism in nests of the American Goldfinch. J. Field Ornithol. 62: 200-203.

Middleton, A. L. A. 1993. American Goldfinch (Carduelis tristis). In The birds of North America, No. 80 (A. Poole and F. Gill, eds.). Acad. of Nat. Sci., Philadelphia, and Am. Ornithol. Union, Washington, D.C.

Middleton, A. L. A. 1998. Chipping Sparrow (Spizella passerina). In The birds of North America, No. 334 (A. Poole and F. Gill, eds.). The Birds of N. Am., Inc., Philadelphia, PA.

Middleton, A. L. A., and P. Webb. 1984. Longevity in the American Goldfinch. J. Field Ornithol. 55: 383-386.

Mikkola, H. 1983. Owls of Europe. Buteo Books, Vermillion, SD.

Miller, A. H. 1931. Systematic revision and natural history of the American shrikes (Lanius). Univ. Calif. Publ. Zool. 38: 11-242.

Miller, A. H. 1939a. The breeding Leucostictes of the Wallowa Mountains, Oregon. Condor 41: 34-35.

Miller, A. H. 1939b. Status of the breeding Lincoln's Sparrows of Oregon. Auk 56: 342-343.

Miller, A. H. 1941. A review of centers of differentiation for birds in the western Great Basin region. Condor 43: 257-267.

Miller, A. H., and H. Twining. 1943. Winter visitant rosy finches in northeastern California. Condor 45: 78.

Miller, C. 1998. Central Oregon Arrival Dates. Unpubl. data. Bend, OR.

Miller, C. R. Unpubl. database of county rarities in Oregon. Bend, OR.

Miller, C., and T. Crabtree. 1989. It was a Gyrfalcon. Oreg. Birds 15: 133-137.

Miller, E. V. 1941. Behavior of Bewick Wren. Condor. 43: 81-98.

Miller, G. C., and W. D. Graul. 1980. Status of Sharp-tailed Grouse in North America. Pp. 18-28 in Proc. of Prairie Grouse Symp. (P. A. Vohs and F. L. Knopf, eds.), Stillwater, OK.

Miller, L. 1940. Observations on the Black-footed Albatross. Condor 42: 229-238.

Miller, L. 1957. Bird remains from an Oregon Indian midden. Condor 59: 59-63.

Miller, L. H. 1911. Additions to the avifauna of the Pleistocene deposits at Fossil Lake, Oregon. Bull. of Dept. of Geol. 6: 79-87. Univ. Calif. Publ.

Miller, M. R., and D. C. Duncan. 1999. The Northern Pintail in North America: status and conservation needs of a struggling population. Wildl. Soc. Bull. 27: 788-800.

Miller, R. F., and L. L. Eddleman. 2000. Spatial and temporal changes of Sage Grouse habitat in the sagebrush biome. Oreg. State Univ., Ag. Exp. Station Tech. Bull. 151.

Miller, W. R., and R. M. Brigham. 1988. "Ceremonial" gathering of Black-billed Magpies (Pica Pica) after the sudden death of a conspecific. Murrelet 69: 78-79.

Milne, K. A., and S. J. Hejl. 1989. Nest-site characteristics of White-headed Woodpeckers. J. Wildl. Manage. 53: 50-55.

Mirarchi, R. E., and T. S. Baskett. 1994. Mourning Dove (Zenaida macroura). In The birds of North America, No. 117 (A. Poole and F. Gill, eds.). Acad. of Nat. Sci., Philadelphia, and Am. Ornithol. Union, Washington, D.C.

Mirsky, E. N. 1976. Ecology of co-existence in a wren-wrentit-warbler guild. Ph.D. diss., Univ. of Calif., Los Angeles.

Mitchell, C. D. 1994. Trumpeter Swan (Cygnus buccinator). In The birds of North America, No. 105 (A. Poole and F. Gill, eds.). Acad. of Nat. Sci., Philadelphia, and Am. Ornithol. Union, Washington, D.C.

Mitchell, D. E. 2000. Allen's Hummingbird (Selasphorus sasin). In The birds of North America, No. 501 (A. Poole and F. Gill, eds.). The Birds of N. Am., Inc., Philadelphia, PA.

Mitchell, P. A. 1968. The food of the dipper (Cinclus mexicanus Swainson) on two western Montana streams. M.A. thesis, Univ. Montana, Missoula.

Mitchell, T. L. 1993. Tool use by a White-breasted Nuthatch. Bull. of Okla. Ornithol. Soc. 26: 6-7.

Mlodinow, S. G. 1997. The Long-billed Murrelet (Brachyramphus perdix) in North America. Birding 29: 461-475.

Mlodinow, S. G. 2001. Possible anywhere: Sharp-tailed Sandpiper. Birding 33: 330-341.

Mlodinow, S. G., G. Lillie, and B. Tweit. 2000a. Oregon-Washington. N. Am. Birds 54: 318-322.

Mlodinow, S., B. Tice, and B. Tweit. 2000b. Oregon-Washington region. N. Am. Birds 54: 214-216.

Moholt, R. K. 1989. Dominance, predator interactions, and social gatherings of the Black-billed Magpie. M.S. thesis, Idaho State Univ., Pocatello.

Møller, A. P. 1994. Sexual selection of the Barn Swallow. Oxford Univ. Press, Oxford.

Monda, M. J., and J. T. Ratti. 1988. Niche overlap and habitat use by sympatric duck broods in eastern Washington. J. Wildl. Manage. 52: 95-103.

Monroe, B. L., Jr. 1968. A distributional survey of the birds of Honduras. Ornithol. Monogr. No. 7.

Monthey, R. W. 1983. Responses of birds to timber harvesting along meadow edges in northwestern Oregon. Northwest Sci. 57: 283–290.

Moore, K. R., and C. J. Henny. 1983. Nest site characteristics of three coexisting accipiter hawks in northeastern Oregon. Raptor Res. 17: 65-76.

Moore, K. R., and C. J. Henny. 1984. Age-specific productivity and nest site characteristics of Cooper's Hawks (Accipiter cooperii). Northwest Sci. 58: 290-299.

Moorman, C. E., and B. R. Chapman. 1996. Nest-site selection of Red-shouldered and Red-tailed hawks in a managed forest. Wilson Bull. 108: 357-368.

Morgan, K. 2001. Hiroshi Hasegawa. Pacific Seabirds 28: 9-10.

Morizot, D. C., R. G. Anthony, T. G. Grubb, S. W. Hoffman, M. E. Schmidt, and R. E. Ferrell. 1985. Clinal genetic variation at enzyme loci in the Bald Eagle (Haliaeetus leucocephalus) from the western United States. Biochem. Genetics 23: 337-345.

Morlan, J. 1981. Status and identification of forms of White Wagtail in western North America. Continental Birdlife 2: 37-50.

Morrison, M. L. 1981. The structure of western warbler assemblages: analysis of foraging behavior and habitat selection in Oregon. Auk 98: 578-588.

Morrison, M. L. 1982. The structure of western warbler assemblages: ecomorphological analysis of the Black-throated Gray and Hermit warblers. Auk 99: 503-515.

Morrison, M. L. 1983. Analysis of geographic variation in the Townsend's Warbler. Condor 85: 385-391.

Morrison, M. L. 1990. Morphological and vocal variation in the Black-throated Gray Warbler of the Pacific Northwest. Northwest. Nat. 71: 53-58.

Morrison, M. L., and J. W. Hardy. 1983a. Hybridization between Hermit and Townsend's warblers. Murrelet 64: 65-72.

Morrison, M. L., and J. W. Hardy. 1983b. Vocalizations of the Black-throated Gray Warbler. Wilson Bull. 95: 640-643.

Morrison, M. L., and E. C. Meslow. 1983a. Avifauna associated with early-growth vegetation on clearcuts in the Oregon Coast Ranges. U.S. Dept. Agric., For. Serv. Pacific Northwest For. and Range Exp. Station Res. Pap. PNW-305. Portland, OR.

Morrison, M. L., and E. C. Meslow. 1983b. Bird community structure on early-growth clearcuts in western Oregon. Am. Midl. Nat. 110: 129-137.

Morrison, M. L., and S. W. Morrison. 1983. Population trends of woodpeckers in the Pacific Coast region of the United States. Am. Birds 37: 361-363.

Morrison, M. L., I. C. Timossi, K. A. Manley, and P. N. Manley. 1985. Use of tree species by forest birds during winter and summer. J. Wildl. Manage. 49: 1098-1102.

Morrison, M. L., and M. P. Yoder-Williams. 1984. Movements of Steller's Jays in western North America. N. Am. Bird Bander 9: 12-15.

Morrison, R. I. G., R. E. Gill, Jr., B. A. Harrington, S. Skagen, G. W. Page, C. L. Gratto-Trevor, and S. M. Haig. 2000. Population estimates of Nearctic shorebirds. Waterbirds 23: 337-352.

Morrison, R. I. G., R. E. Gill, Jr., B. A. Harrington, S. Skagen, G. W. Page, C. L. Gratto-Trevor, and S. M. Haig. 2001. Estimates of shorebird populations in North America. Occas. Paper 104. Can. Wildl. Serv.

Morse, D. H. 1989. Song patterns of warblers at dawn and dusk. Wilson Bull. 101: 26-35.

Morse, T. E., J. L. Jabosky, and V. P. McCrow. 1969. Some aspects of the breeding biology of the Hooded Merganser. J. Wild. Manage. 33: 596-604.

Morton, C. A. 1984. An experimental study of parental investment in House Wrens. M.S. thesis, Illinois State Univ., Normal.

Morton, E. S., and K. C. Derrickson. 1990. The biological significance of age-specific return schedules in breeding Purple Martins. Condor 92: 1040-1050.

Morton, E. S., L. Forman, and M. Braun. 1990. Extrapair fertilization and the evolution of colonial breeding in Purple Martins. Auk 107: 275-283.

Morton, M. L. 1967. Diurnal feeding patterns in White-crowned Sparrows, Zonotrichia leucophrys gambelii. Condor 69: 491-512.

Morton, M. L., and M. Pereyra. 1994. Autumnal migration departure schedules in Mountain White-crowned Sparrows. Condor 96: 1020-1029.

Moskoff, W. 1995a. Solitary Sandpiper (Tringa solitaria). In The birds of North America, No. 156 (A. Poole and F. Gill, eds.). Acad. of Nat. Sci., Philadelphia, and Am. Ornithol. Union, Washington, D.C.

Moskoff, W. 1995b. Veery (Catharus fuscescens). In The birds of North America, No. 142 (A. Poole and F. Gill, eds.). Acad. of Nat. Sci., Philadelphia, and Am. Ornithol. Union, Washington, D.C.

Mossman, M. J. 1989. Wisconsin Forster's Tern recovery plan. Passenger Pigeon 51: 171-186.

Mowbray, T. B. 1997. Swamp Sparrow (Melospiza georgiana). In The birds of North America, No. 279 (A. Poole and F. Gill, eds.). Acad. of Nat. Sci., Philadelphia, and Am. Ornithol. Union, Washington, D.C.

Moynihan, M. 1958. Notes on the behavior of some North American gulls, III: pairing behavior. Behaviour 13: 112-130.

Mueller, H. 1999. Common Snipe (Gallinago gallinago). In The birds of North America, No. 417 (A. Poole and F. Gill, eds.). The Birds of N. Am., Inc., Philadelphia, PA.

Mueller, H., and D. Berger. 1967. Turkey Vultures attack living prey. Auk 84: 430-431.

Mugaas, J. N., and J. R. King. 1981. Annual variation of daily energy expenditure by the Black-billed Magpie: a study of thermal and behavioral energetics. Stud. in Avian Biol. 5.

Munro, J. A. 1953. Red-legged Kittiwake in Oregon. Murrelet 34: 48.

Munro, J. A., and W. A. Clemens. 1939. The food and feeding habits of the Red-breasted Merganser in British Columbia. J. Wildl. Manage. 3: 46-53.

Murphy, E. C., and W. A. Lehnhausen. 1998. Density and foraging ecology of woodpeckers following a stand-replacement fire. J. Wildl. Manage. 62: 1359-1372.

Murphy, M. T. 1983. Nest success and nesting habits of Eastern Kingbirds and other flycatchers. Condor 85: 208-219.

Murphy, M. T. 1996. Eastern Kingbird (Tyrannus tyrannus). In The birds of North America, No. 253 (A. Poole and F. Gill, eds.). Acad. of Nat. Sci., Philadelphia, and Am. Ornithol. Union, Washington, D.C.

Murray, B. G., Jr. 1983. Notes on the breeding biology of Wilson's Phalarope. Wilson Bull. 95: 472-475.

Murray, G. A. 1976. Geographic variation in the clutch size of seven owl species. Auk 93: 602-613.

Myers, J. P. 1979. Leks, sex, and Buff-breasted Sandpipers. Am. Birds 33: 823-825.

Myers, S. J. 1993. Mountain Chickadees nest in desert riparian forest. West. Birds 24: 103-104.

Naslund, N. L. 1993. Why do Marbled Murrelets attend old-growth forest nesting areas year-round? Auk 110: 594-602.

National Audubon Society (NAS). 2002. The Christmas Bird Count historical results (Online). URL = http://www.audubon.org/bird/cbc Accessed 15 Sep 2002.

National Geographic Society (NGS). 1999. Field guide to the birds of North America. Natl. Geographic Soc.

The Nature Conservancy. 1998. Oregon Natural Heritage Program. Oregon Field Office, Portland. URL = http://www.natureserve.org/nhp/us/or/ Accessed 17 Jun 2002.

Naugler, C. 1993. American Tree Sparrow (Spizella arborea). In The birds of North America, No. 37 (A. Poole, P. Stettenheim, and F. Gill, eds.). Acad. of Nat. Sci., Philadelphia, and Am. Ornithol. Union, Washington, D.C.

Nechaev, V. A., and P. S. Tomkovich. 1988. [A new name for Sakhalin Dunlin (Aves, Charadriidae.] Zool. Zhurnal 67: 1596. In Russian.

Neff, J. A. 1928. A study of the economic status of the common woodpeckers in relation to Oregon horticulture. Free Press Print, Marionville, MO.

Neff, J. A. 1933. The tri-colored Red-wing in Oregon. Auk 35: 234-235.

Neff, J. A. 1937. Nesting distribution of the tri-colored Red-wing. Condor 39: 61-81.

Neff, J. A. 1947. Habits, food, and economic status of the Band-tailed Pigeon. U.S. Fish and Wildl. Serv., N. Am. Fauna 58.

Nehls, H. B. 1972. Oregon Great Blue Heron nesting sites. Unpubl. rep., Portland Audubon Society.

Nehls, H. 1977a. Blue Jay expansion into Oregon. Oreg. Birds 3(4): 16-22.

Nehls, H. 1977b. Details: Painted Bunting. Oreg. Birds 3(4): 24.

Nehls, H. B. 1978a. Autumn migration of the Swainson's Thrush. Oreg. Birds 4(3): 16-18.

Nehls, H. 1978b. Status of the Bushtit in Oregon. Oreg. Birds 4(1): 31-36.

Nehls, H. 1980. Detailed field notes: Ruff and Mongolian Plover. Oreg. Birds 6: 185-186.

Nehls, H. 1981. Status of the Bewick's Wren. Oreg. Birds. 7: 108-113.

Nehls, H. 1986. Field Notes: December 1986. Audubon Warbler 50: 14.

Nehls, H. 1987a. Distribution of the Yellow-bellied type sapsuckers in Oregon. Oreg. Birds. 13: 36-37.

Nehls, H. 1987b. Field Notes: June 1987. Audubon Warbler 51: 6.

Nehls, H. 1987c. Oregon's first Ross' Gull. Oreg. Birds 13: 286-291.

Nehls, H. 1988a. Common Murres in Oregon. Oreg. Birds 14: 152-154.

Nehls, H. 1988b. Field Notes: August 1988. Audubon Warbler 52: 14.

Nehls, H. 1989a. A review of the small sandpipers in Oregon. Oreg. Birds 15: 103-108.

Nehls, H. 1989b. A review of the status and distribution of Dowitchers in Oregon. Oreg. Birds 15: 97.

Nehls, H. 1992a. Field Notes. Audubon Warbler 56: 14.

Nehls, H. B. 1992b. Oregon's only Baikal Teal. Oreg. Birds 18: 68.

Nehls, H. 1993a. Eastern Phoebe. Oreg. Birds 19: 4.

Nehls, H. 1993b. Slaty-backed Gull, 29 December 1992. Oreg. Birds 19: 65.

Nehls, H. B. 1994. Oregon shorebirds: their status and movements. Oreg. Dept. Fish and Wildl., Wildl. Diversity Prog. Rep. 94-1-02. Portland.

Nehls, H. B. 1995a. Unpublished manuscript on Oregon birds.

Nehls, H. 1995b. The records of the Oregon Bird Records Committee, 1994-1995. Oreg. Birds 21: 103-105.

Nehls, H. 1996. The Northern Mockingbird becomes established in the Rogue Valley. Oreg. Birds 22: 75.

Nehls, H. B. 1998. Field Notes. Audubon Warbler 62: 22-23.

Nehls, H. 1999. The records of the Oregon Bird Records Committee, 1998-1999. Oreg. Birds 25: 91-93.

Nehls, H. 2001. Pelicans progress. Audubon Warbler 65: 22-23.

Neitro, W. A., V. W. Binkley, S. P. Cline, R. W. Mannan, B. G. Marcot, D. Taylor, and F. F. Wagner. 1985. Snags (wildlife trees). Pp. 129-168 in Management of wildlife and fish habitats in forests of western Oregon and Washington (E. R. Brown, tech. ed.). U.S. Dept. Agric., For. Serv. R6-F&WL-192-1985. Portland, OR.

Nelson, A. L. 1934. Some early summer food preferences of the American Raven in southeastern Oregon. Condor 36: 10-15.

Nelson, B. 1979. Seabirds: their biology and ecology. A. and W. Publishers, New York.

Nelson, D. A. 1984. Communication of intentions in antagonistic contexts by the Pigeon Guillemot Cepphus columba. Behaviour 88: 145-89.

Nelson, D. A. 1985. The systematic and semantic organization of Pigeon Guillemot Cepphus columba vocal behaviour. Zeitschrift fur Tierpsychol. 67: 97-130.

Nelson, D. A. 1987. Factors influencing colony attendance by Pigeon Guillemots on Southeast Farallon Island, California. Condor 93: 765-768.

Nelson, D. A. 1991. Demography of the Pigeon Guillemot on Southeast Farallon Island, California. Condor 93: 765-768.

Nelson, H. K. 1997. Mute Swan populations, distribution and management issues in the United States and Canada. Pp. 125-132 in Proc. and papers of the sixteenth Trumpeter Swan Soc. Conf. Feb. 3-6, 1997 (J. R. Balcomb, M. H. Linck, and A. L. Price, eds.). The Trumpeter Swan Soc., St. Louis, MO.

Nelson, M. W. 1969. The status of the Peregrine Falcon in the Northwest. Pp. 61-72 in Peregrine Falcon populations: their biology and decline (J. J. Hickey, ed.). Univ. Wisc. Press, Madison.

Nelson, S. K. 1988. Habitat use and densities of cavity-nesting birds in the Oregon Coast Ranges. M.S. thesis, Oreg. State Univ., Corvallis.

Nelson, S. K. 1997. Marbled Murrelet (Brachyramphus marmoratus). In The birds of North America, No. 276 (A. Poole and F. Gill, eds.). Acad. of Nat. Sci., Philadelphia, and Am. Ornithol. Union, Washington, D.C.

Nelson, S. K., Y. Fukuda, and N. Oka. 2002. The status and conservation of the Long-billed Murrelet in Japan. J. Yamashina Inst. Ornithol. 33: 88-106.

Nelson, S. K., and T. E. Hamer. 1995a. Nest success and the effects of predation on Marbled Murrelets. Pp. 89-98 in Ecology and conservation of the Marbled Murrelet (C. J. Ralph, G. L. Hunt, Jr., M. G. Raphael, and J. F. Piatt, eds.). U.S. Dept. Agric., For. Serv. Gen. Tech. Rep. PSW-GTR-152. Albany, CA.

Nelson, S. K., and T. E. Hamer. 1995b. Nesting biology and behavior of the Marbled Murrelet. Pp. 57-68 in Ecology and conservation of the Marbled Murrelet (C. J. Ralph, G. L. Hunt, Jr., M. G. Raphael, and J. F. Piatt, eds.). U.S. Dept. Agric., For. Serv. Gen. Tech. Rep. PSW-GTR-152. Albany, CA.

Nelson, S. K., M. L. C. McAllister, M. A. Stern, D. H. Varoujean, and J. M Scott. 1992. The Marbled Murrelet in Oregon, 1899-1987. Pp. 61-91 in Status and conservation of the Marbled Murrelet in North America (H. R. Carter and M. L. Morrison, eds.). Proc. West. Found. Vert. Zool. 5.

Nelson, S. K., K. Ono, J. N. Fries, and T. E. Hamer. 1997. Searching for the Long-billed Murrelet on Hokkaido Island, Japan. Pacific Seabirds 24: 62-68.

Nelson, S. K., and R. W. Peck. 1995. Behavior of the Marbled Murrelet at nine nest sites in Oregon. Pp. 43-53 in Biology of the Marbled Murrelet: inland and at-sea (S. K. Nelson and S. G. Sealy, eds.). Northwest. Nat. 76(1).

Nelson, S. K., and A. K. Wilson. 2000. Marbled Murrelet habitat characteristics on state lands in western Oregon. Final rep., Oreg. Coop. Fish and Wildl. Res. Unit, Oreg. State Univ., Dept. Fisheries and Wildl., Corvallis.

Nero, R. W. 1984. Redwings. Smithsonian Inst. Press, Washington, D.C.

Nesbitt, S. A. 1974. Foods of the Osprey at Newnans Lake. Florida Field Nat. 2: 45.

Nettleship, D. N. 2000. Ruddy Turnstone (Arenaria interpres). In The birds of North America, No. 537 (A. Poole and F. Gill, eds.). The Birds of N. Am., Inc., Philadelphia, PA.

Nettleship, D. N., and D. C. Duffy. 1995. Cormorants and human interactions: an introduction. Pp. 3-6 in The Double-crested Cormorant: biology, conservation and management (D. N. Nettleship and D. C. Duffy, eds.) Colonial Waterbirds 18 (Spec. Publ. 1).

Neuchterlein, G. L. 1981. Courtship behavior and reproductive isolation between Western Grebe color morphs. Auk 98: 335-369.

Neuchterlein, G. L., and D. P. Buitron. 1989. Diving differences between Western and Clark's grebes. Auk 106: 467-470.

Neuchterlein, G. L., and R. W. Storer. 1982. The pair-formation displays of the Western Grebe. Condor 84: 350-369.

Neuchterlein, G. L., and R. W. Storer. 1989. Mate feeding by Western and Clark's grebes. Condor 91: 37-42.

Neudorf, D. L., and S. G. Sealy. 1992. Reactions of four passerine species to threats of predation and cowbird parasitism: enemy recognition or generalized responses? Behaviour 123: 84-105.

Newberry, J. S. 1857. Report upon the zoology of the route. In Reports of explorations and surveys, to ascertain the most practicable and economical route for a railroad from the Mississippi river to the Pacific Ocean,1854-55, Vol. VI. 33rd Congress, 2nd session. House Document 91.

Newton, I. 1967. The adaptive radiation and feeding ecology of some British finches. Ibis 109: 33-98.

Newton, I. 1979. Population ecology of raptors. Buteo Books, Vermillion, SD.

Nice, M. M. 1968. Mississippi Song Sparrow Melospiza melodia euphonia. Pp. 1513-1525 in Life histories of North American cardinals, grosbeaks, buntings, towhees, finches, sparrows, and allies (O. L. Austin, Jr., ed.). U.S. Natl. Mus. Bull. 237.

Nickell, W. 1951. Studies of habitats, territory, and nests of the Eastern Goldfinch. Auk 68: 447-470.

Nickell, W. P. 1966. The nesting of the Black-crowned Night-Heron and its associates. Jack-Pine Warbler 44: 130-139.

Nicpon, B. D. 1995. Influences of feeding stations on Scrub Jay kleptoparasitism at Acorn Woodpecker granaries. M.S. thesis, S. Oregon State Coll., Ashland.

Niethammer, K. R., T. S. Baskett, and D. H. White. 1984. Organochlorine residues in three heron species as related to diet and age. Bull. Environ. Contam. Toxicol. 33: 491-498.

Nikas, M. 1999. An observation of a cavity-nesting junco. Oreg. Birds 25: 99.

Nilsson, L. 1970. Food-seeking activity of south Swedish diving ducks in the non-breeding season. Oikos 21: 145-154.

Noble, D. G., and J. E. Elliot. 1990. Levels of contaminants in Canadian raptors, 1966 to 1988, effects and temporal trends. Can. Field-Nat. 104: 222-243.

Nolan, V., Jr. 1968a. Eastern Song Sparrow Melospiza melodia melodia. Pp. 1492-1512 in Life histories of North American cardinals, buntings, towhees, finches, sparrows, and allies (O. L. Austin, Jr., ed.). U.S. Natl. Mus. Bull. 237.

Nolan, V., Jr. 1968b. Merrill's Song Sparrow Melospiza melodia merrilli. Pp. 1529-1531 in Life histories of North American cardinals, buntings, towhees, finches, sparrows, and allies (O. L. Austin, Jr., ed.). U.S. Natl. Mus. Bull. 237.

Nolan, V., Jr. 1968c. Modoc Song Sparrow Melospiza melodia fisherella. Pp. 1531-1533 in Life histories of North American cardinals, grosbeaks, buntings, towhees, finches, sparrows, and allies (O. L. Austin, Jr., ed.). U.S. Natl. Mus. Bull. 237.

Nolan, V., Jr. 1968d. Mountain Song Sparrow Melospiza melodia montana. Pp. 1525-1527 in Life histories of North American cardinals, grosbeaks, buntings, towhees, finches, sparrows, and allies (O. L. Austin, Jr., ed.). U.S. Natl. Mus. Bull. 237.

Nolan, V., Jr. 1968e. Yellowhead or Riley Song Sparrow Melospiza melodia inexpectata. Pp. 1527-1529 in Life histories of North American cardinals, grosbeaks, buntings, towhees, finches, sparrows, and allies (O. L. Austin, Jr., ed.). U.S. Natl. Mus. Bull. 237.

Noon, B. R., and A. B. Franklin. 2002. Scientific research and the Spotted Owl (Strix occidentalis):

opportunities for major contributions to avian population ecology. Auk 19: 311-320.

Nordbakke, R. 1980. The diet of a population of Ospreys Pandion haliaetus in south-eastern Norway. Fauna Norv. Series C., Cinclus 3: 1-8.

Norris, R. A. 1958. Comparative biosystematics and life history of the nuthatches Sitta pygmaea and Sitta pusilla. Univ. Calif. Publ. Zool. 56: 119-300.

Novak, P. G. 1989. Breeding ecology and status of the Loggerhead Shrike (Lanius ludovicianus) in New York state. M.S. thesis, Cornell Univ., Ithaca, NY.

Noyes, C. L. B. 1981. An analysis of guild structure of avian communities, Columbia River, Oregon. M.S. thesis, Oreg. State Univ., Corvallis.

Oberholser, H. C. 1902. A review of the larks of the genus Otocoris. Proc. U.S. Natl. Mus. 24: 801-884.

Oberholser, H. C. 1905. The forms of Vermivora celata (Say). Auk 22: 242-247.

Oberholser, H. C. 1918. Notes on the subspecies of Numenius americanus Bechstein. Auk: 35: 188-195.

Oberholser, H. C. 1930. Notes on a collection of birds from Arizona and New Mexico. Sci. Publ. Cleveland Mus. Nat. Hist. 1: 83-124.

Oberholser, H. C. 1974. The bird life of Texas, Vol. 2. Univ. of Texas Press, Austin.

O'Donnell, B. P., N. L. Naslund, and C. J. Ralph. 1995. Patterns of seasonal variation of activity of Marbled Murrelets in forested stands. Pp. 117-128 in Ecology and conservation of the Marbled Murrelet (C. J. Ralph, G. L. Hunt, Jr., M. G. Raphael, and J. F. Piatt, eds.). U.S. Dept. Agric., For. Serv. Gen. Tech. Rep. PSW-GTR-152. Albany, CA.

Ohlendorf, H. M., R. L. Hothem, and D. Welsh. 1989. Nest success, cause-specific nest failure, and hatchability of aquatic birds at selenium-contaminated Kestersen Reservoir and a reference site. Condor 91: 787-796.

Ohlendorf, H. M., D. M. Swineford, and L. N. Locke. 1979. Organochlorine poisoning of herons. Proc. Colonial Waterbird Group 3: 176-185.

Olendorff, R. R. 1976. The food habits of North American Golden Eagles. Am. Midl. Nat. 95: 231-236.

Olendorff, R. R., and J. R. Stoddard, Jr. 1974. The potential for management of grassland raptors. Pp. 47-99 in Management of raptors (F. N. Hamerstrom, Jr., B. E. Harrell, and R. R. Olendorff, eds.). Raptor Res. Rep. No. 2. Raptor Res. Found. Vermillion, SD.

Olenick, B. 1987. Reproductive success of Burrowing Owls using artificial nest burrows in southeastern Idaho. Eyas 10: 38.

Olenick, B. 1990. Breeding biology of Burrowing Owls using artificial nest burrows in southeastern Idaho. M.S. thesis, Univ. Idaho, Pocatello.

Oliver, C. D., L. L. Irwin, and W. H. Knapp. 1994. Eastside forest management practices: historical overview, extent of their applications, and their effects on sustainability of ecosystems. U.S. Dept. Agric., For. Serv. Gen. Tech. Rep. PNW-GTR-324. Portland, OR.

Olsen, K. M., and H. Larsson. 1997. Skuas and jaegers. Yale Univ. Press, New Haven, CT.

Olson, B. 1976. Status report, Columbian Sharp-tailed Grouse. Oreg. Wildl. 3: 10.

Olson, J. G. 1961. First Tufted Duck seen in Oregon. Auk 78: 638-639.

O'Neil, T. A., D. H. Johnson, C. Barrett, M. Trevithick, K. A. Bettinger, C. Kiilsgaard, M. Vander Heyden, E. L. Greda, D. Stinson, B. G. Marcot, P. J. Doran, S. Tank, and L. Wunder. 2001. Matrixes for wildlife-habitat relationship in Oregon and Washington. In Wildlife-habitat relationships in Oregon and Washington (D. H. Johnson and T. A. O'Neil, managing dirs.). Northwest Habitat Inst. Oreg. State Univ. Press, Corvallis, OR.

O'Neill, E. J. 1979. Fourteen years of goose populations and trends at Klamath Basin Refuges. Pp. 316-321 in Management and biology of Pacific Flyway geese (R. L. Jarvis and J. C. Bartonek, eds.). Oreg. State Univ. Book Stores, Inc., Corvallis.

Opp, R. R. 1979. Special report: Oregon's first annual mid-winter Bald Eagle survey January 13-27, 1979. Unpubl. rep., Oreg. Dept. of Fish and Wildl., Portland, OR.

Opp, R. R. 1980a. Status of the Bald Eagle in Oregon - 1980. Pp. 35-41 in Proceedings of the Washington Bald Eagle symposium (R. L Knight, G. T. Allen, M. V. Stalmaster, and C. W. Servheen, eds.). The Nature Conservancy, Seattle, WA.

Opp, R. R. 1980b. Summary of the mid-winter Bald Eagle survey in Oregon, January 1980. Unpubl. rep., Oreg. Dept. of Fish and Wildl., Portland, OR.

Oppenheimer, S. D., and M. L. Morton. 2000. Nesting habits and incubation behavior of the Rock Wren. J. Field Ornithol. 71: 650-657.

Oregon Bird Records Committee (OBRC). 1998. Harry Nehls, secretary. Portland, OR.

Oregon Breeding Bird Atlas (OBBA). Oregon Breeding Bird Atlas data 1995-1999, prior to finalizing and publishing the CD (see Adamus et al. 2001).

Oregon Department of Fish and Wildlife (ODFW). 1985. Birds of Coos County Oregon, checklist. Oreg. Dept. Fish and Wildl., Coos Bay.

Oregon Department of Fish and Wildlife (ODFW). 1997. Oregon Department of Fish and Wildlife sensitive species. Oreg. Dept. of Fish and Wildl., Portland.

Oregon Department of Fish and Wildlife (ODFW). 1999a. Game bird hunting statistics. Oreg. Dept. of Fish and Wildl., Portland.

Oregon Department of Fish and Wildlife (ODFW). 1999b. Oregon turkey harvest and distribution. Game Bird Prog. rep., Portland.

Oregon Department of Fish and Wildlife (ODFW). 2000. 1999 game bird hunting statistics. Oreg. Dept. of Fish and Wildl., Portland.

Oregon Department of Fish and Wildlife (ODFW). 2002. Oregon turkey harvest and distribution. Game Bird Prog. rep., Portland.

Oregon Department of Fish and Wildlife (ODFW). Undated checklist(a). Birds of Fern Ridge Reservoir. Portland, OR.

Oregon Department of Fish and Wildlife (ODFW). Undated checklist(b). Birds of Ladd Marsh Wildlife Area, La Grande, OR.

Oregon Department of Fish and Wildlife (ODFW). Undated checklist(c). Birds of the Summer Lake Wildlife Area. Summer Lake, OR.

Oregon Department of Fish and Wildlife (ODFW). Undated files(a). Black-crowned Night-Heron data. Northeast Region office, LaGrande, OR.

Oregon Department Fish and Wildlife (ODFW). Undated files(b). Southwest Regional office, Roseburg, and State office, Portland, OR.

Oregon Department Fish and Wildlife (ODFW). Undated files(c). Summer Lake Wildlife Area, Summer Lake, OR.

Oregon Department of Forestry (ODF). 1995. Elliott State Forest habitat conservation plan. Oreg. Dept. For., Coos District, Coos Bay, OR.

Oregon Natural heritage Advisory Council (ONHAC). 1988. Oregon Natural Heritage Plan. State Land Board, Salem, OR.

Oregon Natural heritage Advisory Council (ONHAC). 2002. Draft 2003 Oregon Natural Heritage Plan. State Land Board, Salem, OR.

Oregon Natural Heritage Program (ONHP). 1999. Vertebrate characterization abstract. Unpubl. data. Oreg. Nat. Heritage Prog., Portland.

Oregon Progress Board. 2000. Oregon state of the environment report 2000. Oregon Progress Board, Salem.

Oregon State Game Commission. 1971. Oregon game code, 1971-1972. Oreg. State Game Comm., Portland.

Oregonian. 1971. Seagulls 'attack' fish nets. The Oregonian, Saturday, September 18, 1971.

Orians, G. H. 1980. Some adaptations of marsh-nesting blackbirds. Princeton Univ. Press, Princeton, N.J.

Orians, G. H., and T. Angell. 1985. Blackbirds of the Americas. Univ. of Wash. Press, Seattle, WA.

Orians, G. H., and G. M. Christman. 1968. A comparative study of the behavior of Red-winged, Tricolored, and Yellow-headed blackbirds. Univ. Calif. Publ. Zool. 84: 1-81.

Orians, G. H., and M. F. Willson. 1964. Interspecific territories of birds. Ecology 45: 736-744.

Oring, L. W. 1964. Behavior and ecology of certain ducks during the postbreeding period. J. Wildl. Manage. 28: 223-233.

Oring, L., E. Gray, and J. Reed. 1997. Spotted Sandpiper (Actitis macularia). In The birds of North America, No. 289 (A. Poole and F. Gill, eds.). Acad. of Nat. Sci., Philadelphia, and Am. Ornithol. Union, Washington, D.C.

Oring, L. W., and J. M. Reed. 1997. Shorebirds of the western Great Basin of North America: overview and importance to continental populations. Internatl. Wader Stud. 9: 6-12.

Ormiston, J. H. 1966. The food habits, habitat, and movements of Mountain Quail in Idaho. M.S. thesis, Univ. of Idaho, Moscow.

Orr, E. L., W. N. Orr, and E. M. Baldwin. 1992. Geology of Oregon, 4th ed. Kendall/Hunter Publ. Co., Dubuque, IA.

Ortega, C. P., and J. C. Ortega. 2001. Effects of Brown-headed Cowbird on the nesting success of Chipping Sparrows in southwest Colorado. Condor 103: 127-133.

Ortega, J. C., and C. P. Ortega. 2000. Effects of Brown-headed Cowbirds and predators on the nesting success of Yellow Warblers in southwestern Colorado. J. Field Ornithol. 71: 516-524.

Orthmeyer, D. L., J. Y. Takekawa, C. R. Ely, M. L. Wege, and W. E. Newton. 1995. Morphological differences in Pacific Coast populations of Greater White-fronted Geese (Anser albifrons). Condor 97: 123-132.

Otahal, C. D. 1994. Sexual differences in spring migration of Orange-crowned Warblers. N. Am. Bird Bander 19: 140-146.

Otteni, L. C., E. G. Bolen, and C. Cottam. 1972. Predator-prey relationships and reproduction of the Barn Owl. Wilson Bull. 84: 434-438.

Otvos, I. S., and R. W. Stark. 1985. Arthropod food of some forest-inhabiting birds. Can. Entomol. 117: 971-990.

Owen, M. 1980. Wild geese of the world: their life history and ecology. B. T. Bates Ltd., London.

Owens, R. A., and M. T. Myres. 1973. Effects of agriculture on populations of native passerine birds of an Alberta fescue grassland. Can. J. Zool. 51: 697-713.

Pacejka, A. J., and C. F. Thompson. 1996. Does removal of old nests from nestboxes by researchers affect mite populations in subsequent nests of House Wrens? J. Field Ornithol. 67: 558-564.

Pacific Flyway Council. 1987. Pacific Flyway management plan for the Pacific Flyway population of Greater White-fronted Goose. Pacific Flyway Study Subcomm. on the Pacific Flyway population of White-fronted Geese. Unpubl. rep., U.S. Fish and Wildl. Serv. Portland, OR.

Pacific Flyway Council. 1991a. Pacific Coast Brant management plan. Pacific Flyway Counc. Tech. Committee. Rep. to U.S. Fish and Wildl. Serv., Portland, OR.

Pacific Flyway Council. 1991b. Pacific Flyway management plan for the Tule Greater White-fronted Goose. Pacific Flyway Study Subcomm. on the Pacific Flyway population of White-fronted Geese. Unpubl. rep., U.S. Fish and Wildl. Serv. Portland, OR.

Pacific Flyway Council. 1992a. Pacific Flyway management plan for the western Arctic population of Lesser Snow Geese. Pacific Flyway Study Subcomm. on white geese. Unpubl. rep., U.S. Fish and Wildl. Serv. Portland, OR.

Pacific Flyway Council. 1992b. Pacific Flyway management plan for the Wrangel Island population of Lesser Snow Geese. Pacific Flyway Study Subcomm. on white geese. Unpubl. rep., U.S. Fish and Wildl. Serv. Portland, OR.

Pacific Flyway Council. 1994. Pacific Flyway management plan for the Pacific Coast population of Band-tailed Pigeons. Pacific Flyway Counc. Subcomm. on Pacific Coast Band-tailed Pigeon. U.S. Fish and Wildl. Serv. Portland, OR.

Pacific Flyway Council. 1998a. Pacific Flyway management plan for the Pacific Coast population of Trumpeter Swans. Pacific Flyway Study Subcomm. on Pacific Coast Trumpeter Swans. Unpubl. rep., U.S. Fish and Wildl. Serv. Portland, OR.

Pacific Flyway Council. 1998b. Pacific Flyway management plan for the Rocky Mountain population of Trumpeter Swans. Pacific Flyway Study Subcomm. on Rocky Mountain Trumpeter Swans. Unpubl. rep., U.S. Fish and Wildl. Serv. Portland, OR.

Pacific Flyway Council. 2001. Pacific Flyway management plan for the western population of Tundra Swans. Pacific Flyway Study Subcomm. on Tundra Swans. Unpubl. rep., U.S. Fish and Wildl. Serv. Portland, OR.

Packee, E. C. 1990. Tsuga heterophylla Western hemlock. Pp. 613-634 in Silvics of North America, Vol.1: conifers (R. M. Burns, and B. H. Honkala, tech. coords.). U.S. Dept. Agric., For. Serv. Agric. Handbook 654. Washington, D.C.

Paczolt, M. 1987. Winter nesting of Anna's Hummingbird in Medford, Oregon. Oreg. Birds 13: 31-34.

Page, G. W., and R. E. Gill, Jr. 1994. Shorebirds in western North America: late 1800s to late 1900s. Stud. in Avian Biol. 15: 147-160.

Page, G. W., L. E. Stenzel, and J. E. Kjelmyr. 1999. Overview of shorebird abundance and distribution in wetlands of the Pacific Coast of the contiguous United States. Condor 101: 461-471.

Page, G. W., L. E. Stenzel, and C. M. Wolfe. 1979. Aspects of the occurrence of shorebirds on a central California estuary. Stud. in Avian Biol. 2: 15-32.

Page, G. W., M. A. Stern, and P. W. C. Paton. 1995. Differences in wintering areas of Snowy Plovers from inland breeding sites in western North America. Condor 97: 258-262.

Page, G. W., J. S. Warriner, J. C. Warriner, and P. W. C. Paton. 1995. Snowy Plover (Charadrius alexandrinus). In The birds of North America, No. 154 (A. Poole and F. Gill, eds.). Acad. of Nat. Sci., Philadelphia, and Am. Ornithol. Union, Washington, D.C.

Pagel, J. E. 1992. Protocol for observing known and potential Peregrine Falcon eyries in the Pacific Northwest. Pp. 83-96 in Proceedings: symposium on Peregrine Falcons in the Pacific Northwest (J. E. Pagel, ed.). Rogue River Natl. For., Medford, OR.

Pagel, J. E., D. A. Bell, and M. L. Anderson. 1998. When is an endangered species recovery complete: is de-listing the American Peregrine Falcon appropriate? Pp. 463-474 in Transactions of 63rd North American Wildlife and Natural Resource Conference.

Pagel, J. E., D. A. Bell, and B. E. Norton. 1996. Delisting the American Peregrine Falcon (Falco peregrinus anatum): is it premature? Wildl. Soc. Bull. 24: 429-435.

Pagel, J. E., D. A. Bell, and B. E. Norton. 1997. Reply to Cade et al. regarding de-listing the American Peregrine Falcon. Wildl. Soc. Bull. 25: 739-742.

Paige, C., and S. A. Ritter. 1999. Birds in a sagebrush sea: managing sagebrush habitats for bird communities. Partners in Flight, Western Working Group, Boise, ID.

Paine, R. T. 1968. Brewer's Sparrow (Spizella breweri). Pp. 1208-1217 In Life Histories of North American cardinals, grosbeaks, buntings, towhees, finches, sparrows, and allies (A. C. Bent, ed.) U.S. Natl. Mus. Bull. 237.

Palmer, D. A., and J. J. Rawinski. 1986. A technique for locating Boreal Owls in the fall in the Rocky Mountains. Colo. Field Ornithol. J. 20: 38-40. (Reprint in Oreg. Birds 14: 23-26.)

Palmer, D. A., and R. A. Ryder. 1984. The first documented breeding of Boreal Owl in Colorado. Condor 86: 251-217.

Palmer, R. S. 1968. Spinus pinus (Wilson) Pine Siskin. Pp. 424-447 in Life histories of North American cardinals, grosbeaks, buntings, towhees, finches, sparrows, and allies (O. L. Austin, Jr., ed.). U.S. Natl. Mus. Bull. No. 237 (1).

Palmer, R. S., Ed. 1962. Handbook of North American birds, Vol. 1: loons through flamingos. Yale Univ. Press, Conn. and London.

Palmer, R. S., Ed. 1975 (1976 on title page). Handbook of North American birds, Vol. 3: waterfowl (part 2). Yale Univ. Press, New Haven, CT, and London.

Palmer, R. S., Ed. 1976. Handbook of North American birds, Vol. 2: waterfowl (part 1). Yale Univ. Press, New Haven, CT, and London.

Palmer, R. S., Ed. 1988. Handbook of North American birds, Vol. 4-5: diurnal raptors. Yale Univ. Press, New Haven, CT.

Pampush, G. J. 1980. Status report on the Long-billed Curlew in the Columbia and Northern Great Basins. Unpubl. rep., U.S. Fish and Wildl. Serv., Portland, OR.

Pampush, G. J. 1981. Breeding chronology, habitat utilization, and nest site selection of the Long-billed Curlew in northcentral Oregon. M.S. thesis, Oreg. State Univ., Corvallis.

Pampush, G. J., and R. G. Anthony. 1993. Nest success, habitat utilization and nest-site selection of Long-billed Curlews in the Columbia Basin, Oregon. Condor 95: 957-967.

Papish, U. 1993. Black Terns nest at Fern Ridge Reservoir, Lane Co., Oregon. Oreg. Birds 19: 97-98.

Parks, C. G., E. L. Bull, R. O. Timm, J. F. Shepherd, and A. K. Blumton. 1999. Wildlife use of dwarf mistletoe brooms in Douglas-fir in northeastern Oregon. West. J. Appl. Forestry 14: 100-105.

Parmelee, D. F. 1992. Snowy Owl (Nyctea scandiaca). In The birds of North America No. 10 (A. Poole, P. Stettenheim, and F. Gill, eds.). Acad. of Nat. Sci., Philadelphia, and Am. Ornithol. Union, Washington, D.C.

Parrish, J. K., N. Lemberg, and L. South-Oryschyn. 1998. Effects of colony location and nekton abundance on the at-sea distribution of four seabird species. Fisheries Oceanogr. 7: 126-135.

Parrish, J. K., and R. T. Paine. 1996. Ecological interactions and habitat modification in nesting Common Murres, Uria aalge. Biol. Conserv. Internatl. 6: 261-269.

Parsons, K. C., and T. L. Master. 2000. Snowy Egret (Egretta thula). In The birds of North America, No. 489 (A. Poole and F. Gill, eds.). The Birds of N. Am., Inc., Philadelphia.

Partners In Flight. 2000. Westside lowlands and valleys bird conservation plan. URL = http://community.gorge.net/natres/pif/con_plans/west_low/west_low_page1.html Accessed 20 Sep 2002.

Paton, P. W. C. 1994. Survival estimates for Snowy Plovers breeding at Great Salt Lake, Utah. Condor 96: 1106-1109.

Pattee, O. H., and S. R. Wilbur. 1989. Turkey Vulture and California Condor. Pp. 61-65 in Proceedings of western raptor management symposium and workshop. Natl. Wild. Fed., Washington, D.C.

Patterson, M. 1987. Allen's Hummingbird record for the Willamette Valley. Oreg. Birds 13: 350.

Patterson, M. 1988. Possible occurrences of Allen's Hummingbird north of its recognized range. Oreg. Birds 14: 237-240.

Patterson, M. 1989. Untitled. Oreg. Birds 15: 286.

Patterson, M. 1990. Green-backed Selasphorus hummingbirds in Clatsop County, Oregon. Oreg. Birds. 16: 218-222.

Patterson, M. 1998a. The great curlew fallout of 1998. Natl. Audubon Soc. Field Notes 52: 150-155.

Patterson, M. 1998b. A guide to birds and other wildlife on the Columbia River estuary. Oreg. Field Ornithol. Spec. Publ. No. 11, Eugene.

Patterson, R. M. 1981. Latitudinal variation in length of Barn Swallow tails in North America. N. Am. Bird Bander 6: 151-154.

Paul, A. 1968. Pine Siskins in British Columbia. Murrelet 49: 24.

Paullin, D. G. 1981. Habitat definition of nesting birds in the Double-O unit, Malheur National Wildlife Refuge, Oregon, 1981. Unpub. rep., Malheur Natl. Wildl. Refuge, Princeton.

Paullin, D. G. 1987a. Cannibalism in American Coots induced by severe spring weather and avian cholera. Condor 89: 442-443.

Paullin, D. G. 1987b. Recent Trumpeter Swan sightings in Oregon outside Malheur National Wildlife Refuge. Oreg. Birds 13: 41-45.

Paullin, D. G., G. L. Ivey, and C. D. Littlefield. 1988. The re-establishment of American White Pelican nesting in the Malheur-Harney Lakes Basin, Oregon. Murrelet 69: 61-64.

Paullin, D. G., and E. Kridler. 1988. Spring and fall migration of Tundra Swans dyed at Malheur National Wildlife Refuge, Oregon. Murrelet 69: 1-9.

Paulson, D. R. 1988. An incident of Common Loons eating clams. Murrelet 69: 53-54.

Paulson, D. 1989. Northwestern Crow distinction? Maybe not. Oreg. Birds 15: 285-286.

Paulson, D. 1993. Shorebirds of the Pacific Northwest. Univ. of Wash. Press and Seattle Audubon Soc., Seattle.

Payne, R. B. 1969. Breeding seasons and reproductive physiology of Tricolored Blackbirds and Red-winged Blackbirds. Univ. Calif. Publ. Zool. 90: 1-137.

Payne, R. B. 1979. Ardeidae. Pp. 193-244 in Checklist of birds of the world (E. Mayr and G. W. Cottrell, eds.). Misc. Publ. Univ. Michigan Mus. Zool. 150: 1-115.

Paynter, R. A. 1960. Family Troglodytidae. Pp. 379-440 In Check-list of birds of the world, Vol. 9 (E. Mayr and J. C. Greenway, Jr., eds). Mus. Comp. Zool., Cambridge, MA.

Paynter, R. A. 1970. Subfamily Emberizinae. Pp. 3-214 in Check-list of birds of the world, Vol. 13 (R. A. Paynter, Jr., ed.). Mus. Comp. Zool., Cambridge, MA.

Peakall, D. B., T. J. Cade, C. M. White, and J. R. Haugh. 1975. Organochlorine residues in Alaskan peregrines. Pestic. Monit. J. 8: 255-260.

Peale, T. R. 1957. Diary of Titian Ramsay Peale. Los Angeles, Dawson's Book Store.

Pearse, T. 1950. Parasitic birds. Murrelet 31: 14.

Pearson, S. F. 1997. Hermit Warbler (Dendroica occidentalis). In The birds of North America, No. 303 (A. Poole and F. Gill, eds.). Acad.

of Nat. Sci., Philadelphia, and Am. Ornithol. Union, Washington, D.C.

Pearson, S. F., and D. A. Manuwal. 2000. Influence of niche overlap and territoriality on hybridization between Hermit Warblers and Townsend's Warblers. Auk 117: 175-183.

Pearson, S. F., and S. Rohwer. 1998. Influence of breeding phenology and clutch size on hybridization between Hermit and Townsend's warblers. Auk 115: 739-745.

Peck, M. E. 1911. Summer birds of the Willow Creek Valley, Malheur County Oregon. Condor 13: 63-69.

Peck, M. E. 1961. A manual of higher plants in Oregon, second ed. Binfords & Mort, Portland.

Pedersen, R. J., A. W. Adams, and L. D. Bryant. 1975. Observation on birds of the Blue Mountains. Murrelet 56: 7-10.

Peer, B. D., and E. K. Bollinger. 1997. Common Grackle (Quiscalus quiscula). In The birds of North America, No. 271 (A. Poole and F. Gill, eds.). Acad. of Nat. Sci., Philadelphia, and Am. Ornithol. Union, Washington, D.C.

Pelham, P. H., and J. G. Dickson. 1992. Physical characteristics. Pp. 32-45 in The Wild Turkey: biology and management (J. G. Dickson, ed.). Stackpole Books, Harrisburg, PA.

Pelren, E. C. 1996. Blue Grouse winter ecology in northeastern Oregon. Ph.D. diss., Oreg. State Univ., Corvallis.

Pelren, E. C., and J. A. Crawford. 1999. Blue Grouse nesting parameters and habitat associations in northeastern Oregon. Great Basin Nat. 59: 368-373.

Pendergast, B. A., and D. A. Boag. 1970. Seasonal changes in the diet of Spruce Grouse in central Alberta. J. Wildl. Manage. 34: 605-611.

Penderson, R., and A. W. Adams. 1975. Observation on birds of the Blue Mountains. Murrelet 56: 7-10.

Penland, S. 1981. Natural history of the Caspian Tern in Grays Harbor, Washington. Murrelet 62: 66-72.

Penniman, T. M., M. C. Coulter, L. B. Spear, and R. J. Boekelheide. 1990. Western Gull. Pp. 218-243 in Seabirds of the Farallon Islands (D. G. Ainley and R. J. Boekelheide, eds.). Stanford Univ. Press, Stanford, CA.

Peterjohn, B. G., and D. L. Rice. 1991. The Ohio Breeding Bird Atlas. Ohio Dept. Nat. Res., Columbus, OH.

Peters, J. 1940. Check-list of birds of the world. Vol. 1. Mus. Comp. Zool., Cambridge, MA.

Peters, J., and L. Griscom. 1938. Geographical variation in the Savannah Sparrow. Bull. Mus. Comp. Zool. 80: 445-477.

Peters, J. L. 1979. Check-list of birds of the world, 2nd ed.: revision of the work of James Peters (E. Mayr and G. W. Cottrell, eds.). Mus. Comp. Zool., Cambridge, MA.

Peterson, A. T., and D. B. Burt. 1992. A phylogenetic analysis of social evolution and habitat use in the Aphelocoma jays. Anim. Behav. 44: 859-866.

Peterson, K. L., and L. B. Best. 1985. Nest site selection by Sage Sparrows. Condor 87: 217-221.

Peterson, K. L., and L. B. Best. 1987. Effects of prescribed burning on nongame birds in a sagebrush community. Wildl. Soc. Bull. 15: 317-329.

Peterson, M. R., J. A. Schmuts, and R. F. Rockwell. 1994. Emperor Goose (Chen canagica). In The birds of North America, No. 97 (A. Poole and F. Gill, eds.). Acad. of Nat. Sci., Philadelphia, and Am. Ornithol. Union, Washington, D.C.

Peterson, R. T. 1961. A field guide to western birds. Houghton Mifflin Co., Boston.

Peterson, R. T. 1988. Forward. In Peregrine Falcon populations - their management and recovery (T. J. Cade, J. H. Enderson, C. G. Thelander and C. M. White, eds.). Peregrine Fund, Inc., Boise, ID.

Phelps, J. H. 1968. Oregon Junco Junco oreganus. Pp. 1050-1071 in Life histories of North American cardinals, grosbeaks, buntings, towhees, finches, sparrows, and allies part 2 (O. L. Austin, Jr., ed.) U.S. Natl. Mus. Bull. 237.

Phillips, A. R. 1947. The races of MacGillivray's Warbler. Auk 64: 296-300.

Phillips, A. 1959. The nature of avian species. J. Ariz. Acad. Sci. 1: 22.

Phillips, A. R. 1961. Notas sistemáticas sobre aves Mexicanas, I. Anal. Inst. Biol. Méx. 32: 333-381.

Phillips, A. R. 1962. Notas sistemáticas sobre aves Mexicans, II. Anal. Inst. Biol. Méx. 33 (1 and 2): 331-372.

Phillips, A. R. 1986. The known birds of North and Middle America, Part 1: Hirundinidae to Mimidae; Certhiidae. Denver Mus. Nat. Hist., Denver, CO. (also publ. privately).

Phillips, A. R. 1991. The known birds of North and Middle America, Part II. Privately publ., Denver, CO.

Phillips, A. R. 1994. A review of the northern Pheucticus grosbeaks. Bull. British Ornithol. Club 114: 162-114.

Phillips, A. R., J. Marshall, and G. Monson. 1964. The birds of Arizona. Univ. of Ariz. Press, Tucson.

Phillips, A. R., and K. C. Parkes. 1955. Taxonomic comments on the Western Wood Pewee. Condor 57: 244-246.

Phillips, W. J., and K. King. 1923. The corn earworm: its ravages on field corn and suggestions for control. U.S. Dept. Agric., Farmer's Bull. 1310: 12.

Piatt, J. F., C. J. Lensick, W. Butler, M. Kendziorek, and D. R. Nysewander. 1990. Immediate impact of the Exxon Valdez oil spill. Auk 107: 387-397.

Piatt, J. F., and N. L. Naslund. 1995. Abundance, distribution, and population status of Marbled Murrelets in Alaska. Pp. 285-294 in Ecology and conservation of the Marbled Murrelet (C. J. Ralph, G. L. Hunt, Jr., M. G. Raphael, and J. F. Piatt, eds.). U.S. Dept. Agric., For. Serv. Gen. Tech. Rep. PSW-GTR-152. Albany, CA.

Piatt, J. F., and D. Nettleship. 1985. Diving depths of four alcids. Auk 102: 293-297.

Pickering, P. 2000. June sightings of multiple Glaucous Gulls in Oregon, with notes on identification. Oreg. Birds 26: 123-127.

Pickering, P. 2001. Electronic mail message to Oregon Birders On-Line listserver. 26 May 2001.

Pickering, P. Unpubl. data: Boiler Bay seawatches, 1999- 2000.

Picman, J., M. Leonard, and A. Horn. 1988. Antipredation role of clumped nesting by marsh-nesting Red-winged Blackbirds. Behav. Ecol. Sociobiol. 22: 9-15.

Pierotti, R. 1981. Male and female parental roles under different environmental conditions. Auk 98: 532-549.

Pierotti, R. J., and C. A. Annett. 1995. Western Gull (Larus occidentalis). In The birds of North America, No. 174 (A. Poole and F. Gill, eds.). Acad. of Nat. Sci., Philadelphia, and Am. Ornithol. Union, Washington, D.C.

Pierotti, R. J., and T. P. Good. 1994. Herring Gull (Larus argentatus). In The birds of North America, No. 124 (A. Poole and F. Gill, eds.). Acad. of Nat. Sci., Philadelphia, and Am. Ornithol. Union, Washington, D.C.

Piersma, T., and N. C. Davidson. 1992. The migrations and annual cycles of five subspecies of knots in perspective. Pp. 187-197 in The migration of knots (T. Piersma and N. Davidson, eds.). Wader Study Group Bull. 64 (suppl.).

Piersma, T., A. Koolhaas, and A. Dekinga. 1993. Interaction between stomach structure and diet choice in shorebirds. Auk 110: 552-564.

Pierson, B. J., J. M. Pearce, S. L. Talbon, G. F. Shields, and K. T. Scribner. 2000. Molecular genetic status of Aleutian Canada Geese from Buldir and the Semidi Islands, Alaska. Condor 102: 172-280.

Pinkowski, B. C. 1981a. Further notes on Wilson's Phalarope – American Avocet feeding associations. J. Field Ornithol. 52: 147.

Pinkowski, B. 1981b. Ponderosa, the ecology of a tree "made" for bluebirds. Sialia 3: 83-87.

Pitelka, F. A. 1941. Distribution of birds in relation to major biotic communities. Am. Midl. Nat. 25: 113-137.

Pitelka, F. A. 1950. Geographic variation and the species problem of the shore-bird genus Limnodromus. Univ. Calif. Publ. Zool. 50: 1-108

Pitelka, F. A. 1951. Speciation and ecologic distribution in American jays of the genus Aphelocoma. Univ. Calif. Publ. Zool. 50: 195-464.

Pitman, R. L. 1981. Seabird observations off Oregon, March 31, 1981. Oreg. Birds 7: 98.

Pitman, R. L., and M. R. Graybill. 1985. Horned Puffin sightings in the eastern Pacific. West. Birds. 16: 99-102.

Pitman, R. L., J. Hodder, M. R. Graybill, and D. H. Varoujean. 1985. Catalog of Oregon seabird colonies. Unpubl. rep., U.S. Fish and Wildl. Serv., Portland, OR.

Pitocchelli, J. 1995. MacGillivray's Warbler (Oporornis tolmiei). In The birds of North America, No. 159 (A. Poole and F. Gill, eds.). Acad. of Nat. Sci., Philadelphia, and Am. Ornithol. Union, Washington, D.C.

Pleasants, B. 1979. Adaptive significance of the variable dispersion pattern of breeding Northern Orioles. Condor 81: 28-34.

Plissner, J. H., S. M. Haig, and L. W. Oring. 1999. Within- and between-year dispersal of American Avocets among multiple western Great Basin wetlands. Wilson Bull. 111: 314-320.

Plissner, J. H., S. M. Haig, and L. W. Oring. 2000. Postbreeding movements of American Avocets and implications for wetland connectivity in the western Great Basin. Auk 117: 290-298.

Plissner, J. H., L. W. Oring, and S. M. Haig. 2000. Space use of Killdeer at a Great Basin breeding area. J. Wildl. Manage. 64: 421-429.

Plissner, J., Ed. 1997. Field notes. Chat 26: 9. Corvallis Audubon Soc., Corvallis, OR.

Pogson, T. H. 1987. Sandhill Crane banded in Alaska migrates to Oregon and California. N. Am. Bird Bander 12: 90-92.

Pogson, T. H., and S. M. Lindstedt. 1991. Distribution and abundance of large Sandhill Cranes (Grus canadensis tabida) wintering in California's Central Valley. Condor 93: 266-278.

Point Reyes Bird Observatory (PRBO). Unpubl. data. Pacific Flyway Project, Point Reyes Bird Observatory, 4990 Shoreline Highway, Stinson Beach, CA.

Poole, A. F. 1985. Courtship feeding and Osprey reproduction. Auk 102: 479-492.

Poole, A. F. 1989. Ospreys: a natural and unnatural history. Cambridge Univ. Press, Cambridge.

Poole, A. F., and F. Gill, Eds. 1992-ongoing at time of this writing. The birds of North America. The Birds of N. Am. Inc., Philadelphia, PA.

Poole, L. D. 1992. Reproductive success and nesting habitat of Loggerhead Shrike in shrubsteppe communities. M.S. thesis, Oreg. State Univ., Corvallis.

Pope, M. D. 1999. Annual report: Mountain Quail research summary. Unpubl,. Oreg. State Univ.

Popp, D. L., and F. B. Isaacs. 1989. Supplemental feeding of Bald Eagles at Thompson Reservoir, Lake County, Oregon. Unpubl. rep., Oreg. Dept. of Fish and Wildl., Bend, OR.

Popper, K. J., and S. Lundsten. 2001. Breeding ecology of Yellow Rails at Fourmile Creek, Wood River Wetland, Mares Egg Spring, and additional areas in the Klamath Basin of southcentral Oregon, 2000. Unpubl. rep. to Lakeview Dist. Bur. of Land Manage., Oreg. Dept. of Fish and Wildl., Bend, and U.S. Fish and Wildl. Serv., Klamath Falls.

Popper, K. J., E. C. Pelren, and J. A. Crawford. 1996. Summer nocturnal roost sites of Blue Grouse in Oregon. Great Basin Nat. 56: 177-179.

Popper, K. J., and M. A. Stern. 1996. Breeding ecology of Yellow Rails at Jack Spring and Mares Egg Spring, Klamath County, Oregon, 1995-1996. Unpubl. rep. to Winema Natl. For., Bur. of Land Manage. at the Klamath Falls Resource Area, and the Oreg. Dept. of Fish and Wildl., Bend.

Popper, K. J., and M. A. Stern. 2000. Nesting ecology of Yellow Rails in the Klamath Basin. J. Field Ornithol. 71: 460-466.

Poracsky, J., L. Sharp, E. Lev, and M. Scott. 1992. Metropolitan Greenspaces Program data analysis, part 1: field-based biological data. Metro, Portland, OR.

Porter, K. R. 1960. Knot collected inland in Oregon. Auk 77: 219-220.

Porter, R. D., and S. N. Wiemeyer. 1972. Propagation of captive American Kestrels. J. Wildl. Manage. 34: 594-604.

Portnoy, J. W. 1980. Census methods for Gulf Coast waterbirds. Trans. Linn. Soc. of New York 9: 127-133.

Posphala, R. S., D. R. Andersen, and C. J. Henny. 1974. Population ecology of the Mallard II: breeding habitat conditions, size of breeding populations, and production indices. Bur. Sport Fish. & Wildl. Res. Publ. 115.

Pough, R. H. 1957. Audubon western bird guide. Doubleday & Co., Inc., Garden City, NY.

Poulin, R. G., S. D. Grindal, and R. M. Brigham. 1996. Common Nighthawk (Chordeiles minor). In The birds of North America, No. 213 (A. Poole and F. Gill, eds.). Acad. of Nat. Sci., Philadelphia, and Am. Ornithol. Union, Washington, D.C.

Powell, H. D. W. 2000. The influence of prey density on post-fire habitat use of the Black-backed Woodpecker. M.S. thesis, Univ. of Mont., Missoula.

Power, H. W., and M. P. Lombardo. 1996. Mountain Bluebird (Sialia currucoides). In The birds of North America, No. 222 (A. Poole and F. Gill, eds.). Acad. of Nat. Sci., Philadelphia, and Am. Ornithol. Union, Washington, D.C.

Powers, L. C. 1997. Space use of breeding Killdeer (Charadrius vociferus) in Great Basin desert wetlands. M.S. thesis, Univ. Nevada, Reno, NV.

Powers, L. C., and H. A. Glimp. 1997. Impacts of domestic livestock on shorebirds: a review of current information and application to shorebird species in the western Great Basin. Internatl. Wader Stud. 9: 55-63.

Pravosudov, V. V., and T. C. Grubb, Jr. 1993. White-breasted Nuthatch (Sitta carolinensis). In The birds of North America, No. 54 (A. Poole and F. Gill, eds.). Acad. of Nat. Sci., Philadelphia, and Am. Ornithol. Union, Washington, D.C.

Preble, E. A. 1915. Oregon. Smithsonian Inst. Archives. Record Unit 7176. U.S. Fish & Wildl. Serv. 1860-1961 field reps. Box 88, Folder 5. Washington, D.C.

Prescott Bluebird Recovery Project. Newsletters 1991-2000.

Prescott, D. R. C., A. L. A. Middleton, and D. R. Lamble. 1989. Variations in the age and sex ratios of American Goldfinch trapped at baited stations. J. Field Ornithol. 60: 340-349.

Prescott, H. W. 1979. Oregon's Willamette Valley. Sialia 1: 52- 56, 81.

Prescott, H. W. 1980. Causes of decline of the Western Bluebird in Oregon's Willamette Valley. Sialia 2: 131-135.

Prescott, H. W., and E. Gillis. 1985. An analysis of Western Bluebird double and triple nest box research on Chehalem and Parrett Mountains in 1982. Sialia 7: 123-130, 146.

Preston, C. R. 1980. Differential perch-site selection by color morphs of the Red-tailed Hawk (Buteo jamaicensis). Auk 97: 782-789.

Prevost, Y. A. 1983. Osprey distribution and subspecies taxonomy. Pp. 157-174 In Biology and management of Bald Eagles and Ospreys (D. M. Bird, ed.). Harpell Press, Ste. Anne de Bellevue, Quebec.

Price, F. E., and C. E. Bock. 1973. Polygyny in the dipper. Condor 75: 457-459.

Price, F. E., and C. E. Bock. 1983. Population ecology of the dipper (Cinclus mexicanus) in the front range of Colorado. Stud. Avian Biol. 7.

Prill, A. G. 1892. Mountain Bluebird. 768. Sialia arctica (Swains). Oologist 9: 36.

Prill, A. G. 1937. Bird records for Oregon. Wilson Bull. 49: 119.

Pruett, C. L., D. D. Gibson, and K. Winker. 2001. Molecular "cuckoo clock" suggests listing of western Yellow-billed Cuckoos may be warranted. Wilson Bull. 113: 228-231.

Pruitt, B. H. 1950. Gnatcatchers in Oregon. Condor 52: 40.

Puchy, C. A., and D. B. Marshall. 1993. Oregon wildlife diversity plan 1993-1998. Oreg. Dept. Fish and Wildl, Portland.

Pugesek, B. H., K. T. Diem, and C. L. Cordes. 1999. Seasonal movements, migration, and range sizes of subadult and adult Banforth Lake California Gulls. Waterbirds 22: 29-36.

Pulliam, H. R., and G. S. Mills. 1977. The use of space by wintering sparrows. Ecology 58: 1393-1399.

Purcell, K. L., and J. Verner. 1998. Density and reproductive success of California Towhees. Cons. Biol. 12: 442-450.

Purdy, M. A., and E. H. Miller. 1988. Time budget and parental behavior of breeding American Black Oystercatcher (Haematopus bachmani) in British Columbia. Can. J. Zool. 66: 1742-1751.

Pyle, P. 1997. Identification guide to North American birds, Part 1: Columbidae to Ploceidae. Slate Creek Press, Bolinas, CA.

Pyle, P., and S. N. G. Howell. 1996. Spizella Sparrows: intraspecific variation and identification. Birding 28: 374-387.

Pyle, W. H. 1985. The nesting season, June 1-July 31, 1985. Northern Rocky Mountain-intermountain region. Am. Birds 39: 940.

Quaintance, C. W. 1938. Content, meaning and possible origin of male song in the Brown Towhee. Condor 40: 97-101.

Quaintance, C. W. 1944. California Cuckoo collected in eastern Oregon. Condor 46: 89-90.

Quinlan, S. E. 1983. Avian and river otter predation in a storm-petrel colony. J. Wildl. Manage. 47: 1036-1043.

Rabenold, K. N. 1978. Foraging strategies, diversity, and seasonality in bird communities of Appalachian spruce-fir forests. Ecol. Monogr. 48: 397-424.

Racey, K. 1926. Notes on the birds observed in the Alta Lake region, British Columbia. Auk 43: 319-325.

Rainboth, D. 1990. Great Egrets nesting in Coos County, Oregon. Oreg. Birds 16: 95.

Raley, C., and S. Anderson. 1990. Availability and use of arthropod food resources by Wilson's Warblers and Lincoln's Sparrows in southeastern Wyoming. Condor 92: 141-150.

Ralph, C. J., P. W. C. Paton, and C. A. Taylor. 1991. Habitat association patterns of breeding birds and small mammals in Douglas-fir/hardwood stands in northwestern California and southwestern Oregon. Pp. 379-

393 in Wildlife and vegetation of unmanaged Douglas-fir forests (L. F. Ruggiero, K. B. Aubry, A. B. Carey, and M. H. Huff, tech. coords.). U.S. Dept. Agric., For. Serv. Gen. Tech. Rep. PNW-GTR-285. Portland, OR.

Ralph, C. J., S. K. Nelson, M. M. Shaughnessy, S. L. Miller, and T. E. Hamer. 1994. Methods for surveying Marbled Murrelets in forests: a protocol for land management and research. Pacific Seabird Group, U.S. Dept. Agric. For. Serv., Arcata, CA.

Ramer, B. A., G. W. Page, and M. M. Yoklavich. 1991. Seasonal abundance, habitat use, and diet of shorebirds in Elkhorn Slough, California. West. Birds 22: 157-174.

Ramsey, F. 1977. Field notes. The Chat 7(4): 3. Corvallis Audubon Society, Corvallis, OR.

Rand, A. L. 1946. A new race of the Purple Finch. Can. Field-Nat. 60: 95-96.

Randle, W., and R. Austing. 1952. Ecological notes on Long-eared and Saw-whet owls in southwestern Ohio. Ecology 33: 422-426.

Raphael, M. 1984. Wildlife diversity and abundance in relation to stand age and area in Douglas-fir forests of northwestern California. Pp. 259-274 in Fish and wildlife relationships in old-growth forests: proceedings of a symposium, 1982 April 12-15; Juneau, AK (W. R. Meehan, T. R. Merrel, Jr. and T. A. Hanley, eds.). Am. Inst. of Fishery Res. Biol., Morehead City, NC.

Raphael, M. G. 1995. Use of Arbutus menziesii by cavity-nesting birds. Pp. 17-24 in The decline of the Pacific madrone (Arbutus menziesii Pursh): current theory and research directions (A. B. Adams and C. W. Hamilton, eds.). Proc. of April 28, 1995 Symp. for Urban Horticulture, Univ. of Wash., Seattle, WA.

Raphael, M. G., M. L. Morrison, and M. P. Yoder-Williams. 1987. Breeding bird populations during twenty-five years of postfire succession in the Sierra Nevada. Condor 89: 614-626.

Raphael, M. G., K. V. Rosenberg, and B. G. Marcot. 1988. Large-scale changes in bird populations of Douglas-fir forests, northwestern California. Bird Conserv. 3: 63-83.

Raphael, M. G., and M. White. 1984. Use of snags by cavity-nesting birds in the Sierra Nevada. Wildl. Monogr. 86: 1–66.

Rappole, J. H., E. S. Morton, T. E. Lovejoy, III, and J. L. Ruos. 1983. Nearctic avian migrants in the neotropics. U.S. Fish and Wildl. Serv., Washington, D.C.

Rasmussen, P. C. 1988. Apparent sibling cannibalism by a nestling Pigeon Guillemot. Wilson Bull. 100: 136.

Ratcliffe, D. A. 1967. Decrease in eggshell weight in certain birds of prey. Nature 215: 208-210.

Rathbun, S. F. 1925. The Black Swift and its habits. Auk 42: 497-516.

Ratti, J. T. 1979. Reproductive separation and isolating mechanisms between sympatric and dark- and light-phase Western Grebes. Auk 96: 573-586.

Ratti, J. T. 1981. Identification and distribution of Clark's Grebe. West. Birds 12: 41-46.

Ratti, J. T. 1985. A test of water depth niche partitioning by Western Grebe color morphs. Auk 102: 635-637.

Ratti, J. T., T. R. McCabe, and L. M. Smith. 1983. Morphological differences between Western Grebe color morphs. J. Field Ornithol. 54: 424-426.

Ratti, J. T., and D. E. Timm. 1979. Migratory behavior of Vancouver Canada Geese: recovery rate bias. Pp. 208-212 in Management and biology of Pacific Flyway geese (R. L. Jarvis and J. C. Bartonek, eds.). Oreg. State Univ. Book Stores, Inc., Corvallis.

Rawls, C. K. 1954. Reelfoot Lake waterfowl research. Unpubl. rep., Tenn. Game and Fish Comm.

Ray, M. S. 1912. The discovery of the nest and eggs of the California Pine Grosbeak. Condor 14: 157-187.

Rea, A. M. 1970. Winter territoriality in a Ruby-crowned Kinglet. West. Bird Bander 45: 4-7.

Rea, A. 1983. Once a river. Univ. Arizona Press, Tucson.

Recher, H. F., and J. A. Recher. 1972. Herons leaving the water to defecate. Auk 89: 896-897.

Redmond, R. L., and D. A. Jenni. 1985. Note on the diet of Long-billed Curlew chicks in western Idaho. Great Basin Nat. 45: 85-86.

Redmond, R. L., and D. A. Jenni. 1986. Population ecology of the Long-billed Curlew (Numenius americanus) in western Idaho. Auk 103: 755-767.

Reebs, S. G., and D. A. Boag. 1987. Regurgitated pellets in central Alberta. Can. Field-Nat. 101: 108-110.

Reed, C. A. 1965. North American birds eggs. Dover Publications, Inc., New York.

Reed, J. M. 1985. Relative energetics of two foraging behaviors of Forster's Terns. Colonial Waterbirds 8: 79-82.

Reed, J. M., N. Warnock, and L. W. Oring, Eds. 1997. Conservation and management of shorebirds in the western Great Basin of North America. Internatl. Wader Stud. 9.

Reese, K. P., and J. A. Kadlec. 1985. Influence of high density and parental age on the habitat selection and reproduction of Black-billed Magpies. Condor 87: 96-105.

Reeves, H. M., and R. E. McCabe. 1993. Historical perspective. Pp. 7-46 in Ecology and management of the Mourning Dove (T. S. Baskett, M. W. Sayre, R. E. Tomlinson, R. E. Mirarchi, and R. E. McCabe, eds.). Stackpole Books, Harrisburg, PA.

Reeves, H. M., R. E. Tomlinson, and J. C. Bartonek. 1993. Population characteristics and trends in the western management unit. Pp. 341-376 in Ecology and management of the Mourning Dove (T. S. Baskett, M. W. Sayre, R. E. Tomlinson, R. E. Mirarchi, and R. E. McCabe, eds.) Stackpole Books, Harrisburg, PA.

Reid, W. V. 1988. Population dynamics of the Glaucous-winged Gull. J. Wildl. Manage. 52: 763-770.

Reilly, E. M., Jr. 1968. The Audubon illustrated handbook of American birds. McGraw-Hill, New York.

Reinkensmeyer, D. P. 2000. Habitat associations of bird communities in shrub-steppe and western juniper woodlands. M.S. thesis, Oreg. State Univ, Corvallis.

Remsen, J. V., Jr., and L. C. Binford. 1975. Status of the Yellow-billed Loon (Gavia adamsii) in the western United States and Mexico. West. Birds 6: 7-20.

Repenning, R. 1977. Great Egret preys on sandpiper. Auk 94: 171.

Reukema, D. L., and J. H. G. Smith. 1987. Development over 25 yrs of Douglas-fir, western hemlock, and western redcedar planted at various spacings on a very good site in British Columbia. U.S. Dept. Agric., For. Serv. Res. Pap. PNW-RP-381. Portland, OR.

Reynolds, R. T. 1983. Management of western coniferous forest habitat for nesting accipiter hawks. U.S. Dept. Agric., For. Serv. Gen. Tech. Rep. RM-102.

Reynolds, R. T., and E. Forsman. 1971. A recent occurrence of a colony of White-throated Swifts in central Oregon. Murrelet 52: 13-14.

Reynolds, R. T., R. T. Graham, M. H. Reiser, R. L. Bassett, P. L. Kennedy, D. A. Boyce, G. Goodwin, R. Smith, and E. L. Fisher. 1991. Management recommendations for the Northern Goshawk in the southwestern United States. U.S. Dept. Agric., For. Serv., Southwestern Region, Albuquerque, NM.

Reynolds, R. T., and B. D. Linkhart. 1987. The nesting biology of the Flammulated Owl in Colorado. Pp. 239-248 in Biology and conservation of northern forest owls (R. W. Nero, R. J. Clark, R. J. Knapton, and R. H. Hamre, eds.). U.S. Dept. Agric., For. Serv. Gen. Tech. Rep. RM-142.

Reynolds, R. T., and E. C. Meslow. 1984. Partitioning of food and niche characteristics of coexisting accipiter during breeding. Auk 101: 761-769.

Reynolds, R. T., E. C. Meslow, and H. M. Wight. 1982. Nesting habitat of coexisting accipiter in Oregon. J. Wildl. Manage. 46: 124-138.

Reynolds, R. T., R. A. Ryder, and B. D. Linkhart. 1988. Small forest owls. Natl. Wildl. Fed. Tech. Ser. 12: 134-143.

Reynolds, R. T., and H. M. Wight. 1978. Distribution, density, and productivity of accipiter hawks breeding in Oregon. Wilson Bull. 90: 182-196.

Reynolds, T. D. 1981. Nesting of the Sage Thrasher, Sage Sparrow and Brewer's Sparrow in southeastern Idaho. Condor 83: 61-64.

Reynolds, T. D., and T. D. Rich. 1978. Reproductive ecology of the Sage Thrasher (Oreoscoptes montanus) on the Snake River Plain in south-central Idaho. Auk 96: 580-582.

Reynolds, T. D., T. D. Rich, and D. A. Stephens. 1999. Sage Thrasher (Oreoscoptes montanus). In The birds of North America, No. 463 (A. Poole and F. Gill, eds.). The Birds of N. Am., Inc., Philadelphia, PA.

Reynolds, T. D., and C. H. Trost. 1980. The response of native vertebrate populations to crested wheatgrass planting and grazing by sheep. J. Range Manage. 33: 122-125.

Rhoner, C. 1997. Non-territorial 'floaters' in Great Horned Owls: space use during a cyclic peak of snowshoe hares. Anim. Behav. 53: 901-912.

Rich, T. 1978. Cowbird parasitism of Sage and Brewer's sparrows. Condor 80: 348.

Rich, T. D. 1980a. Bilateral wing display in the Sage Thrasher. Wilson Bull. 92: 512-513.

Rich, T. D. 1980b. Nest placement in Sage Thrashers, Sage Sparrow and Brewer's Sparrows. Wilson Bull. 92: 362-368.

Rich, T. 1980c. Territorial behavior of the Sage Sparrow: spatial and random aspects. Wilson Bulletin 92: 425-438.

Rich, T. 1986. Habitat and nest-site selection by Burrowing Owls in the sagebrush steppe of Idaho. J. Wildl. Manage. 50: 548-555.

Rich, T. D., and S. I. Rothstein. 1985. Sage Thrashers reject cowbird eggs. Condor 87: 561-562.

Richards, A. 1988. Birds of the tideline: shorebirds of the northern hemisphere. Dragon's World Ltd., Surrey, Great Britain.

Richards, G. L. 1971. The Common Crow, Corvus brachyrhynchos, in the Great Basin. Condor 73: 116-118.

Richardson, C. 1961. Tricolored Blackbirds nesting in Jackson County, Oregon. Condor 63: 507-508.

Richardson C., and F.W. Sturges. 1964. Bird records from southern Oregon. Condor 66: 514-515.

Richardson, F. 1961. Breeding biology of the Rhinoceros Auklet on Protection Island, Washington. Condor 63: 456-473.

Richardson, S. A., A. E. Potter, K. L. Lehmkuhl, R. Mazaika, M. E. McFadzen, and R. Estes. 2001. Prey of Ferruginous Hawks breeding in Washington. Northwest. Nat. 82: 58-64.

Richmond, S. M. 1953. The attraction of Purple Martins to an urban location in western Oregon. Condor 55: 225-249.

Rickard, W. H., and L. E. Haverfield. 1965. A pitfall trapping survey of darkling beetles in desert steppe vegetation. Ecology 46: 873-875.

Rickerson, E. V. 2002. Nesting ecology of Mallards in the Willamette Valley. M.S. thesis, Oreg. State Univ., Corvallis.

Ricketts, E. F., J. Calvin, and J. W. Hedgpeth. 1968. Between Pacific tides. Stanford Univ. Press, Stanford.

Ridgway, R. 1877. United States geological exploration of the Fortieth Parallel, Part 3: ornithology. U.S. Gov. Printing Office, Washington, D.C.

Ridgway, R. 1919. The birds of North and Middle America, Part 8. U.S. Natl. Mus. Bull. No. 50.

Ridgway, R., and H. Friedman. 1946. The birds of North and Middle America. U.S. Natl. Mus. Bull. 50. Part X.

Ripley, S. D. 1977. Rails of the world. Godine, Boston.

Rising, J. 1996. A guide to the identification and natural history of the sparrows of the United States and Canada. Academic Press, New York.

Rising, J. D. 1970. Morphological variation and evolution in some North American orioles. Syst. Zool. 19: 315-351.

Ritchison, G. 1983a. Breeding biology of the Black-headed Grosbeak in northern Utah. West. Birds 14: 159-167.

Ritchison, G. 1983b. The function of singing in female Black-headed Grosbeaks (Pheucticus melanocephalus): family-group maintenance. Auk 100: 105-116.

Robb, R. 1998. Photos of nest used by Red-eyed and Cassin's Vireo, Lane Co. Oreg. Birds 24: 33.

Robbins, C. S. 1973. Introduction, spread, and present abundance of the House Sparrow in North America. Pp. 3-9 in A symposium on the House Sparrow (Passer domesticus) and European Tree Sparrow (P. montanus) in North America (S. C. Kendeigh, chairman). Ornithol. Monogr. 14, Am. Ornithol. Union.

Robbins, C. S. 1981. Effect of time of day on bird activity. Stud. in Avian Biol. 6: 275-286.

Robbins, C. S., Ed. 1953. Fifty-third Christmas Bird Count. Audubon Field Notes 7: 44-192.

Robbins, C., D. Bystrak, and P. Geissler. 1986. The breeding bird survey: its first fifteen years, 1965-1979. U.S. Fish and Wildl. Serv. Res. Publ. 157.

Roberson, D. 1980. Rare birds of the west coast. Woodcock Publ., Pacific Grove, CA.

Roberson, D. 1983. Introducing the «NEW» ABA birds. Birding 15: 116-130.

Robert, M., L. Cloutier, and P. Laporte. 1997. The summer diet of the Yellow Rail in southern Quebec. Wilson Bull. 109: 702-710.

Roberts, H. B. 1970. Management of the American Osprey on the Deschutes National Forest, Oregon. Raptor Res. News 4: 168-177.

Robertson, G. J., F. Cooke, R. I. Goudie, and W. S. Boyd. 1998. The timing of pair formation in Harlequin Ducks. Condor 100: 551-555.

Robertson, G., and I. Goudie. 1999. Harlequin Duck (Histrionicus histrionicus). In The birds of North America, No. 466 (A. Poole and F. Gill, eds.). The Birds of N. Am., Inc., Philadelphia, PA.

Robertson, I. 1974. The food of nesting Double-crested and Pelagic cormorants at Mandatre Island, British Columbia, with notes on feeding ecology. Condor 76: 346-348.

Robertson, R. J., and N. J. Flood. 1980. Effects of recreational use of shorelines on breeding bird populations. Can. Field-Nat. 94: 131-138.

Robertson, R. J., B. J. Stutchbury, and R. R. Cohen. 1992. Tree Swallow (Tachycineta bicolor). In The birds of North America, No. 11 (A. Poole, P. S. Stettenheim, and F. Gill, eds.). Acad. of Nat. Sci., Philadelphia, and Am. Ornithol. Union, Washington, D.C.

Robinson, J. A., and L. W. Oring. 1997. Natal and breeding dispersal in American Avocets. Auk 114: 416-430.

Robinson, J. A., L. W. Oring, J. P. Skorupa, and R. Boettcher. 1997. American Avocet (Recurvirostra americana). In The birds of North America, No. 275 (A. Poole and F. Gill, eds.). Acad. of Nat. Sci., Philadelphia, and Am. Ornithol. Union, Washington, D.C.

Robinson, J. A., J. M. Reed, J. P. Skorupa, and L. W. Oring. 1999. Black-necked Stilt (Himantopus mexicanus). In The birds of North American, No. 449 (A. Poole and F. Gill, eds.). The Birds of N. Am., Inc., Philadelphia, PA.

Roby, D. D., D. P. Craig, K. Collis, and S. L. Adamany. 1998. Avian predation on juvenile salmonids in the lower Columbia River. 1997 annual rep. to Bonneville Power Admin. and U.S. Army Corps of Eng., Portland, OR.

Roby, D. D., K. Collis, D. E. Lyons, D. P. Craig, J. Y. Adkins, A. M. Myers, and R. M. Suryan. 2002. Effects on colony relocation on diet and productivity of Caspian Terns. J. Wildl. Manage. 66: 662-673.

Rochelle, M. J. 2001. A Turkey Vulture (Cathartes aura) nest in a timber harvest unit in Linn County, Oregon. Oreg. Birds 23: 103.

Rodenkirk, T. 2000. Birding hot spots: Millicoma Marsh, Coos County. Oreg. Birds 26: 209-212.

Rodgers, J. A., Jr., and H. T. Smith. 1995. Little Blue Heron (Egretta caerulea). In The birds of North America, No. 145 (A. Poole and F. Gill, eds.). Acad. of Nat. Sci., Philadelphia, and Am. Ornithol. Union, Washington, D.C.

Rodgers, P. 1993. Field notes. Quail June: 6-10.

Rodgers, T. L. 1937. Behavior of the Pine Siskin. Condor 39: 143-149.

Rodway, M. S. 1990. Attendance patterns, hatching chronology and breeding population of Common Murres on Triangle Island, British Columbia following the Nestucca oil spill. Can. Wildl. Serv. Tech. Rep. Ser. 87.

Rodway, M. S., H. R. Carter, S. G. Sealy, and R. W. Campbell. 1992. Status of the Marbled Murrelet in British Columbia. Pp. 17-41 in Status and conservation of the Marbled Murrelet in North America (H. R. Carter and M. L. Morrison, eds.). Proc. West. Found. Vert. Zool. 5.

Roest, A. I. 1957a. Notes on the American Sparrow Hawk. Auk 74: 1-19.

Roest, A. I. 1957b. Observations on birds of central Oregon. Condor 59: 141-142.

Rogers, D. 1979a. Oldsquaws off Cape Blanco. Oreg. Birds 5(3): 26-27.

Rogers, D. 1979b. Status of the Red-shouldered Hawk in Oregon. Oreg. Birds 5(1): 4-8.

Rogers, D. 1981. 1980 Oregon coastal birding weekend. Oreg. Birds 7: 92-96.

Rogers, D. 1982. Curry County checklist. Oreg. Birds 8: 116-121.

Rogers, G. E. 1969. The Sharp-tailed Grouse in Colorado. Colo. Div. of Game, Fish and Parks. Tech. Rep. 23.

Rogers, J. 1978. Brief notes: White-headed Woodpecker in Curry County. Oreg. Birds 4(5): 34.

Rogers, L. E., and R. E. Fitzner. 1980. Characterization of darkling beetles inhabiting radioecology study areas at the Hanford site in southcentral Washington. Northwest Sci. 54: 202-206.

Rogers, L. E., and J. D. Hedlund. 1980. A comparison of small mammal populations occupying three distinct shrub-steppe communities in eastern Oregon. Northwest Sci. 54: 183-186.

Rogers, M., and A. Jaramillo. 2002. Report of the California Birds Records Committee: 1999 records. West. Birds 33: 1-33.

Rogers, T. 1955. Palouse-northern Rocky Mountain region. Audubon Field Notes 9: 389-392.

Rogers, T. 1960. Northern Rocky Mountain—inter-mountain region. Audubon Field Notes 14: 326-328.

Rogers, T. H. 1963. Northern Rocky Mountain—inter-mountain region. Audubon Field Notes 17: 343-345.

Rogers, T. H. 1964. Northern Rocky Mountain-intermountain region. Audubon Field Notes 18: 57-60.

Rogers, T. H. 1965. Northern Rocky Mountain-intermountain region. Audubon Field Notes 19: 564-567.

Rogers, T. H. 1966. Northern Rocky Mountain–inter-mountain region. Audubon Field Notes 20: 74.

Rogers, T. H. 1967a. Northern Rocky Mountain—inter-mountain region. Audubon Field Notes 21: 440-443.

Rogers, T. H. 1967b. Northern Rocky Mountain—inter-mountain region. Audubon Field Notes 21: 524-527.

Rogers, T. H. 1968a. Northern Rocky Mountain—inter-mountain region. Audubon Field Notes 22: 69-73.

Rogers, T. H. 1968b. Northern Rocky Mountain—inter-mountain region. Audubon Field Notes 22: 460-463.

Rogers, T. H. 1970a. Northern Rocky Mountain—inter-mountain region. Audubon Field Notes 24: 70-74.

Rogers, T. H. 1970b. Northern Rocky Mountain—inter-mountain region. Audubon Field Notes 24: 699-702.

Rogers, T. H. 1973a. Northern Rocky Mountain - intermountain region. Am. Birds 27: 85-91.

Rogers, T. H. 1973b. Northern Rocky Mountain - intermountain region. Am. Birds 27: 639-643.

Rogers, T. H. 1974a. Northern Rocky Mountain - intermountain region. Am. Birds 28: 665-668.

Rogers, T. H. 1974b. Northern Rocky Mountain - intermountain region. Am. Birds 28: 828-832.

Rogers, T. H. 1974c. Northern Rocky Mountain - intermountain region. Am. Birds 28: 925-929.

Rogers, T. H. 1975. Northern Rocky Mountain-intermountain region. Am. Birds 29: 716-720.

Rogers, T. H. 1976. Northern Rocky Mountain-intermountain region. Am. Birds 30: 978-982.

Rogers, T. H. 1977. Northern Rocky Mountain - intermountain region. Am. Birds 31: 1025.

Rogers, T. H. 1978a. Northern Rocky Mountain-intermountain region report. Am. Birds 32: 231-235.

Rogers, T. H. 1978b. Northern Rocky Mountain-intermountain region report. Am. Birds 32: 1186-1190.

Rogers, T. H. 1979a. Northern Rocky Mountain-intermountain region. Am. Birds 33: 196-199.

Rogers, T. H. 1979b. Northern Rocky Mountain-intermountain region. Am. Birds 33: 881-883.

Rogers, T. H. 1980a. Northern Rocky Mountain-intermountain region. Am. Birds 34: 182-184.

Rogers, T. H. 1980b. Northern Rocky Mountain-intermountain region. Am. Birds 34: 291-293.

Rogers, T. H. 1980c. Northern Rocky Mountain-intermountain region. Am. Birds 34: 797-800.

Rogers, T. H. 1980d. Northern Rocky Mountain-intermountain region. Am. Birds 34: 914.

Rogers, T. H. 1981a. Northern Rocky Mountain-intermountain region. Am. Birds 35: 205-208.

Rogers, T. H. 1981b. Northern Rocky Mountain-intermountain region. Am. Birds 35: 319-321.

Rogers, T. H. 1981c. Northern Rocky Mountain-intermountain region. Am. Birds 35: 843-846.

Rogers, T. H. 1981d. Northern Rocky Mountain-intermountain region. Am. Birds 35: 960-963.

Rogers, T. H. 1982a. Northern Rocky Mountain-intermountain region. Am. Birds 36: 198-201.

Rogers, T. H. 1982b. Northern Rocky Mountain-intermountain region. Am. Birds 36: 875-877.

Rogers, T. H. 1982c. Northern Rocky Mountain-intermountain region. Am. Birds 36: 999.

Rogers, T. H. 1983a. Northern Rocky Mountain - intermountain region. Am. Birds 37: 202-204.

Rogers, T. H. 1983b. Northern Rocky Mountain - intermountain region. Am. Birds 37: 892-894.

Rogers, T. H. 1985a. Northern Rocky Mountain-intermountain region. Am. Birds 39: 78-81.

Rogers, T. H. 1985b. Northern Rocky Mountain-intermountain region. Am. Birds 39: 189-191.

Rogers, T. H. 1985c. Northern Rocky Mountain-intermountain region. Am. Birds 39: 938-941.

Rogers, T. H. 1986. Northern Rocky Mountain-intermountain region. Am. Birds 40: 142-145.

Rogers, T. H. 1987a. Northern Rocky Mountain-intermountain region. Am. Birds 41: 463-466.

Rogers, T. H. 1987b. Northern Rocky Mountain-intermountain region. Am. Birds 41: 1464-1466.

Rogers, T. H. 1988a. Northern Rocky Mountain-intermountain region. Am. Birds 42: 104-108.

Rogers, T. H. 1988b. Northern Rocky Mountain-intermountain region. Am. Birds 42: 296-299.

Rogers, T. H. 1988c. Northern Rocky Mountain-intermountain region. Am. Birds 42: 1318.

Rogers, T. H. 1989. Northern Rocky Mountain-intermountain region. Am. birds 43: 1342-1345.

Rogue Valley Audubon Society. 2001. Birds of Jackson County: abundance and distribution. Rogue Valley Audubon Soc., Medford, OR.

Rohwer, S., and C. Wood. 1998. Three hybrid zones between Hermit and Townsend's warblers in Oregon and Washington. Auk 115: 284-310.

Rohwer, S., C. D. Spaw, and E. Roskaft. 1989. Costs to Northern Orioles of puncture-ejecting parasitic cowbird eggs from their nests. Auk 106: 734-738.

Rohwer, S., C. Wood, and E. Berningham. 2000. A new hybrid warbler (Dendroica nigrescens x D. occidentalis) and diagnoses of similar D. townsendi x D. occidentalis recombinants. Condor 102: 713-718.

Romagosa, C. M., and T. McEneaney. 1999. Eurasian Collared Dove in North America and the Caribbean. N. Am. Birds 53: 348-353.

Root, R. B. 1967. The niche exploitation pattern of the Blue-gray Gnatcatcher. Ecol. Monogr. 37: 317-350.

Root, R. B. 1969a. The behavior and reproductive success of the Blue-gray Gnatcatcher. Condor 71: 16-31.

Root, R. B. 1969b. Interspecific territoriality between Bewick's and House wrens. Auk 86: 125-127.

Root, T. 1988. Atlas of wintering North American birds: an analysis of Christmas Bird Count data. Univ. of Chicago Press, Chicago.

Root, T. L., and J. D. Weckstein. 1994. Changes in distribution patterns of select wintering North American birds from 1901 to 1989. Stud. in Avian Biol. 15: 191-201.

Rosenberg, K. V., R. D. Ohmart, W. C. Hunter, AND B. W. Anderson. 1991. Birds of the lower Colorado River valley. Univ. of Ariz. Press, Tucson.

Rosenberg, K. V., and M. G. Raphael. 1986. Effects of forest fragmentation on vertebrates in Douglas-fir forests. Pp. 263-272 in Wildlife 2000: modeling habitat relationships of terrestrial vertebrates (J. Vernier, M. L. Morrison, and C. J. Ralph, eds.). Univ. of Wis. Press, Madison.

Rossair, D., and D. Cottridge. 1995. Photographic guide to the shorebirds of the world. Facts on File, Inc., New York, NY.

Rotenberry, J. T. 1980 Dietary relationships among shrubsteppe passerine birds: competition or opportunism in a variable environment? Ecol. Monogr. 50: 93-110.

Rotenberry, J. T., M. A. Patten, and K. L. Preston. 1999. Brewer's Sparrow (Spizella breweri). In The birds of North America, No. 390 (A. Poole and F. Gill, eds.). The Birds of N. Am., Inc., Philadelphia, PA.

Rotenberry, J. T., and J. A. Wiens. 1980. Temporal variation in habitat structure and shrubsteppe bird dynamics. Oecologia 47: 1-9.

Rotenberry, J. T., and J. A. Wiens. 1989. Reproductive biology of shrubsteppe passerine birds: geographical and temporal variation in clutch size, brood size, and fledging success. Condor 91: 1-14.

Rotenberry, J. T., and J. A. Wiens. 1998. Foraging patch selection by shrubsteppe sparrows. Ecology 79: 1160-1173.

Rothstein, S. I. 1971. High nest density and non-random nest placement in the Cedar Waxwing. Condor 73: 483-485.

Rothstein, S. 1994. Cowbird's invasion of the far west: history, causes and consequences experienced by host species. Stud. in Avian Biol.15: 301-315.

Rowe, R. A. 1943. A record of Emperor Goose in southwest Oregon, April, 1943. Murrelet 24: 29.

Rowe, S. P., and T. Gallion. 1996. Fall migration of Turkey Vultures and raptors through the southern Sierra Nevada, California. West. Birds 27: 48-53.

Rubega, M. A., and J. A. Robinson. 1997. Water salinization and shorebirds: emerging issues. Internatl. Wader Stud. 9: 45-54.

Rudolph, S. G. 1978. Predation ecology of coexisting Great Horned and Barn owls. Wilson Bull. 90: 135-137.

Ruggiero, L. F., K. B. Aubrey, A. B. Carey, and M. H. Huff, Tech. Coords. 1991. Wildlife and vegetation of unmanaged Douglas-fir forests.U.S. Dept. Agric., For. Serv. Gen. Tech. Rep. PNW-GTR-285. Portland, OR.

Rule, M., G. Ivey, D. Johnson, and D. Paullin. 1990. Blitzen Valley Management Plan, Malheur National Wildlife Refuge, Oregon. Malheur Natl. Wildl. Refuge, Princeton, OR.

Rusch, D. H., E. C. Meslow, P. D. Doerr, and L. B. Keith. 1972. Response of Great Horned Owl population to changing prey densities. J. Wildl. Manage. 36: 282-296.

Russell, H. N., and A. M. Woodbury. 1941. Nesting of the Gray Flycatcher. Auk 58: 28-37.

Russell, R. W., and P. E. Lehman. 1994. Spring migration of Pacific Loons through the southern California bight: nearshore flights, seasonal timing and distribution at sea. Condor 96: 300-315.

Russell, S. M. 1964. A distributional study of the birds of British Honduras. Ornithol. Monogr. 1.

Russell, S. M. 1996. Anna's Hummingbird (Calypte anna). In The birds of North America, No. 226 (A. Poole and F. Gill, eds.). Acad. of Nat. Sci., Philadelphia, and Am. Ornithol. Union, Washington, D.C.

Rust, H. J. 1947. Migration and nesting of nighthawks in northern Idaho. Condor 49: 177-188.

Ryan, M. R. 1981. Evasive behavior of American Coots to kleptoparasitism by waterfowl. Wilson Bull. 93: 274-275.

Ryan, M. R., R. B. Renken, and J. J. Dinsmore. 1984. Marbled Godwit habitat selection in the northern prairie region. J. Wildl. Manage. 48: 1206-1218.

Ryan, T. P., and C. T. Collins. 2000. White-throated Swift (Aeronautes saxatalis). In The birds of North America, No. 526 (A. Poole and F. Gill, eds.). The Birds of N. Am., Inc., Philadelphia, PA.

Ryder, J. P. 1993. Ring-billed Gull (Larus delawarensis). In The birds of North America, No. 33 (A. Poole and F. Gill, eds.). Acad. of Nat. Sci., Philadelphia, and Am. Ornithol. Union, Washington, D.C.

Ryder, J. P., and R. T. Alisaukas. 1995. Ross' Goose (Chen rossi). In The birds of North America, No. 162 (A. Poole and F. Gill, eds.). Acad. of Nat. Sci., Philadelphia, and Am. Ornithol. Union, Washington, D.C.

Ryder, R. A. 1967. Distribution, migration and mortality of the White-faced Ibis (Plegadis chihi) in North America. Bird-Banding 38: 257-277.

Ryder, R. A., and D. E. Manry. 1994. White-faced Ibis (Plegadis chihi). In The birds of North America, No. 130 (A. Poole and F. Gill, eds.). Acad. of Nat. Sci., Philadelphia, and Am. Ornithol. Union, Washington, D.C.

Ryser, F. A., Jr. 1985. Birds of the Great Basin: a natural history. Univ. of Nevada Press, Las Vegas.

Saab, V. A. 1999. Importance of spatial scale to habitat use by breeding birds in riparian forests: a hierarchical analysis. Ecol. Appl. 9: 135-151.

Saab, V. A., and T. D. Rich. 1997. Large-scale conservation assessment for neotropical migratory land birds in the interior Columbia River basin. In Interior Columbia Basin ecosystem management project: scientific assessment (T. M. Quigley, ed.). U.S. Dept. Agric., For. Serv. Gen. Tech. Rep. PNW-GTR-399. Portland, OR.

Sadler, D. A. R., and W. J. Maher. 1976. Notes on the Long-billed Curlew in Saskatchewan. Auk 93: 382-384.

Sadler, K. C. 1993. Other natural mortality. Pp. 225-230 in Ecology and management of the Mourning Dove (T. S. Baskett, M. W. Sayre, R. E. Tomlinson, R. E. Mirarchi, and R. E. McCabe, eds.) Stackpole Books, Harrisburg, PA.

Safina, C., and J. Burger. 1988. Prey dynamics and the breeding phenology of Common Terns (Sterna Hirundo). Auk 105: 720-726.

Sakai, H. F. 1988. Breeding biology and behavior of Hammond's and Western flycatchers in northwestern California. West. Birds 19: 49-60.

Sakai, H. F., and B. R. Noon. 1990. Variation in the foraging behaviors of two flycatchers: associations with stage of the breeding cycle. Stud. in Avian Biol. 13: 237-244.

Sakai, H. F., and B. R. Noon. 1991. Nest-site characteristics of Hammond's and Pacific-slope flycatchers in northwestern California. Condor 93: 563-574.

Salem Audubon Society. 1995. Salem bird checklist. Salem Audubon Center, Salem.

Sallabanks, R. 1992a. Fruit fate, frugivory, and fruit characteristics: a study of the hawthorn, Crataegus monogyna (Rosaceae). Oecologia 91: 296–304.

Sallabanks, r. 1992b. Fruits and frugivores: interactions and decision-making mechanisms. Ph.D. diss., Univ. of Oreg., Eugene.

Sallabanks, R. 1993a. Fruit defenders vs. fruit thieves: winter foraging behavior in American Robins. J. Field Ornithol. 64: 42–48.

Sallabanks, R. 1993b. Fruiting plant attractiveness to avian seed dispersers: native vs. invasive Crataegus in western Oregon. Madroño 40: 108–116.

Sallabanks, R. 1993c. Hierarchical mechanisms of fruit selection by an avian frugivore. Ecology 74: 1326–1336.

Sallabanks, R. 1995a. Avian biodiversity and bird-habitat relationships in conifer forest of the inland northwest: an ecosystem management approach. Annual rep. to Boise Cascade Corp., Natl. Fish and Wildl. Found., Natl. Counc. for Air and Stream Improvement, and U.S. For. Serv. Sustainable Ecosystems Inst., Meridian, ID.

Sallabanks, R. 1995b. Effects of wildfire on breeding bird communities in coniferous forests of northeastern Oregon. Annual rep. to The Blue Mountain Nat. Res. Inst.

Sallabanks, R. 1997. Packing fruits at dusk: fuel storage in an American Robin wintering in western Oregon. Northwest. Nat. 78: 62–64.

Sallabanks, R. 2000. Five-year response of forest bird communities to wildfire in the Blue Mountains, Oregon, 1994. Sustainable Ecosystems Inst., Meridian, ID.

Sallabanks, R., and F. C. James. 1999. American Robin (Turdus migratorius). In The birds of North America, No. 462 (A. Poole and F. Gill, eds.). The Birds of N. Am., Inc., Philadelphia, PA.

Sallabanks, R., and J. D. McIver. 1998. Response of breeding bird communities to wildfire in the Oregon Blue Mountains: the first three years following the Twin Lakes Fire, 1995-1997. Pp 85-89 in Wildlife and fire in the Pacific Northwest—research policy and management: proceedings of annual meeting of the northwest section of The Wildl. Soc., Spokane, Washington. April 6-8, 1998.

Sallabanks, R., R. A. Riggs, and L. E. Cobb. 2002. Bird use of forest structural classes in grand fir forests of the Blue Mountains, Oregon. For. Sci. 48: 311-321.

Sallabanks, R., R. A. Riggs, L. E. Cobb, and S. W. Dodson. Unpubl. ms. Bird-habitat relationships in grand fir forests of the Blue Mountains, Oregon. [Submitted to For. Sci.].

Salomonsen, F. 1950. Gronlands fugle. The birds of Greenland. Ejnar Munksgaard, Copenhagen.

Salomonsen, F. 1968. The moult migration. Wildfowl Trust annual rep. 19: 5-24.

Salt, G. W. 1953. An ecologic analysis of three California avifaunas. Condor 55: 258-273.

Salt, G. W., and D. E. Willard. 1971. The hunting behavior and success of Forster's Tern. Ecology 52: 989-998.

Salyer, J. C., II, and K. F. Lagler. 1940. The food and habits of the American Merganser during winter in Michigan, considered in relation to fish management. J. Wildl. Manage. 4: 186-219.

Sanders, T. A. 1995. Breeding bird community composition in relation to riparian vegetation structure in grazed habitat. M.S. thesis, Oreg. State Univ., Corvallis.

Sanders, T. A. 1999. Habitat availability, dietary mineral supplement, and measuring abundance of Band-tailed Pigeons in western Oregon. Ph.D. diss., Oreg. State Univ., Corvallis.

Sanders, T. A., and W. D. Edge. 1998. Breeding bird community composition in relation to riparian vegetation structure in the western United States. J. Wildl. Manage. 62: 461-473.

Sanders, T. A., and R. L. Jarvis. 2000. Do Band-tailed Pigeons seek a calcium supplement at mineral sites? Condor 102: 855-863.

Sanderson, H. R., E. L. Bull, and P. J. Edgerton. 1980. Bird communities in mixed conifer forests of the interior Northwest. Pp. 224-237 in Management of western forests and grasslands for nongame birds (R. M. DeGraff, tech. ed.). U.S. Dept. Agric., For. Serv. Gen. Tech. Rep. INT 86.

Sanger, G. A. 1965. Observations of wildlife off the coast of Washington and Oregon in 1963, with notes on the Laysan Albatross (Diomedea immutabilis) in this area. Murrelet 46: 1-6.

Sanger, G. A. 1970. The seasonal distribution of some seabirds off Washington and Oregon, with notes on their biology and behavior. Condor 72: 339-357.

Sanger, G. A. 1972. Checklist of bird observations from the eastern North Pacific Ocean. Murrelet 53: 16-21.

Sanger, G. A. 1973. Pelagic records of Glaucous-winged and Herring gulls in the North Pacific Ocean. Auk 90: 384-393.

Sangster, G., M. Collinson, A. J. Helbig, A. G. Knox, D. T. Parkin, and T. Prater. 2001. The taxonomic status of Green-winged Teal Anas carolinensis. British Birds 94: 218-226.

Sanzenbacher, P. M., and S. M. Haig. 2001. Killdeer population trends in North America. J. Field Ornithol. 72: 160-169.

Sanzenbacher, P. M., and S. M. Haig. 2002a. Regional fidelity and movement patterns of wintering Killdeer in an agricultural landscape. Waterbirds 25: 16-25.

Sanzenbacher, P. M., and S. M. Haig. 2002b. Residency and movement patterns of wintering Dunlin in the Willamette Valley of Oregon. Condor 104: 271-280.

Sappington, J. N. 1977. Breeding biology of House Sparrows in north Mississippi. Wilson Bull. 89: 300-309.

Sargent, M. C. 1942. Pacific gull color-banding project. Condor 44: 78.

Sater, D. M. 1999. Habitat associations of the Northern Pygmy-owl in Oregon. M.S. thesis, Oreg. State Univ., Corvallis.

Sauer, J. R., S. Schwartz, and B. Hoover. 1996. The Christmas Bird Count home page. Version 95.1. Patuxent Wildl. Res. Center, Laurel, MD. URL = http://www.mbr-pwrc.usgs.gov/bbs/cbc.html Accessed 20 Sep 2002.

Sauer, J. R., J. E. Hines, G. Gough, I. Thomas, and B. G. Peterjohn. 1997. The North American breeding bird survey results and analysis. Version 96.4. Patuxent Wildl. Res. Center, Laurel, MD. URL = http://www.mbr.nbs.gov/bbs/

Sauer, J. R., J. E. Hines, I. Thomas, J. Fallon, and G. Gough. 1999. The North American Breeding Bird Survey, Results and Analysis 1966 - 1998. Version 98.1, USGS Patuxent Wildl. Res. Center, Laurel, MD URL = http://www.mbr-pwrc.usgs.gov/bbs/bbs.html Accessed 20 Sep 2002.

Sauer, J. R., J. E. Hines, I. Thomas, J. Fallon, and G. Gough. 2000. The North American Breeding Bird Survey, Results and Analysis 1966–1999. Version 98.1. Patuxent Res. Center, Laurel, MD. URL = http://www.mbr.nbs.gov/bbs/bbs.html

Sauer, J. R., J. E. Hines, and J. Fallon. 2001. The North American Breeding Bird Survey, Results and Analysis 1966 - 2000. Version 2001.2, USGS Patuxent Wildl. Res. Center, Laurel, MD. URL = http://www.mbr-pwrc.usgs.gov/bbs/bbs.html Accessed 20 Sep 2002.

Savaloja, T. 1981. Yellow Rail. Birding 13: 80-85.

Savard, J.-P. L. 1988. A summary of current knowledge on the distribution of and abundance of moulting sea ducks in the coastal waters of British Columbia. Can. Wildl. Serv. Tech. Rep. Ser. 45, Pacific and Yukon Region, Delta.

Savard, J-P. L, D. Bordage, and A. Reed. 1998. Surf Scoter (Melanitta perspicillata). In The birds of North America, No. 363 (A. Poole and F. Gill, eds.). The Birds of N. Am., Inc., Philadelphia, PA.

Sawyer, M. 1981. Solitary Sandpiper: probable nesting in Oregon. Oreg. Birds 7: 131-133.

Sawyer, M. 1985. Distribution of Calliope Hummingbirds. Oreg. Birds 11: 137.

Sawyer, M., and M. Hunter. 1988. Checklist: Douglas County Coast. Oreg. Birds 14: 95-106.

Sayre, M. W., and N. J. Silvy. 1993. Nesting and production. Pp. 81-104 in Ecology and management of the Mourning Dove (T. S. Baskett, M. W. Sayre, R. E. Tomlinson, R. E. Mirarchi, and R. E. McCabe, eds.). Stackpole Books, Harrisburg, PA.

Schaefer, V. H. 1976. Geographic variation in the placement and structure of oriole nests. Condor 78: 443-448.

Schaeffer, L. 1992. Avian predators at Oregon Department of Fish and Wildlife hatcheries: their identification and control. Tech. Serv. Rep. 92-1. Oreg. Dept. Fish and Wildl., Portland.

Schaffner, F. C. 1984. Elegant Terns as supplementary anchovy stock indicators. Colonial Waterbird Group Newsletter 8: 42.

Schaffner, F. C. 1986. Trends in Elegant Tern and northern anchovy populations in California. Condor 88: 347-354.

Schardien, B. 1981. Behavioral ecology of a southern population of Killdeer. Ph.D. diss., Miss. State Univ., Starkville, MS.

Scharff, J. C. 1944. The Louisiana Heron in Oregon. Condor 46: 124.

Schempf, P. F. 1997. Bald Eagle longevity record from southeastern Alaska. J. Field Ornithol. 68: 150-151.

Schick, C. T., L. A. Brennan, J. B. Buchanan, M. A. Finger, T. M. Johnson, and S. G. Herman. 1987. Organochlorine contamination in shorebirds from Washington state and the significance for their falcon predators. Environ. Monitoring and Assessment. 9: 115-131.

Schirato, G. 1993. A preliminary status report of Harlequin Ducks in Washington: 1993. Pp. 45-48 in Status of Harlequin Ducks in North America (E. F. Cassirer, ed.). Harlequin Duck Working Group, Boise, ID.

Schirato, G., and J. Hardin. 1998. Washington Harlequin Duck population demographics. Unpubl. abstract, 4th biennial Harlequin Duck Working Group and 1st annual Pacific Flyway Symp., Otter Crest, OR.

Schirato, G., and N. Perfito. 1998. Minimum stream survey replicates to determine presence or absence of Harlequin Ducks. Unpubl. abstract, 4th biennial Harlequin Duck Working Group and 1st annual Pacific Flyway Symp., Otter Crest, OR.

Schmidt, O. 1989. Leucistic Mottled Petrel. Oreg. Birds 15: 143-144.

Schmidt, O. 1995. It was a Gyr. Oreg. Birds 21: 126.

Schmidt, O., and T. Crabtree. 1987. Oregon's first Hoary Redpoll. Oreg. Birds 13: 301-304.

Schorger, A. W. 1952. Introduction of the domestic pigeon. Auk 69: 462-463.

Schorger, A. W. 1976. Canada Geese. Pp. 183-234 in Handbook of North American Birds, Vol 2, Part 1 (R. S. Palmer, ed.). Yale Univ. Press, New Haven, CT.

Schreiber, B. 1987. Diurnal bird use of snags on clearcuts in central coastal Oregon. M.S. thesis, Oreg. State Univ., Corvallis.

Schreiber, B., and D. S. deCalesta. 1992. The relationship between cavity-nesting birds and snags on clearcuts in western Oregon. For. Ecol. and Manage. 50: 299-316.

Schroeder, M. A. 1985. Behavioral differences of female Spruce Grouse undertaking short and long migrations. Condor 87: 281-286.

Schroeder, M. A., and D. A. Boag. 1987. Dispersal in Spruce Grouse: is inheritance involved? J. Anim. Behav. 36: 305-307.

Schroeder, M. A., and C. E. Braun. 1993. Movement and philopatry of Band-tailed Pigeons captured in Colorado. J. Wildl. Manage. 57: 103–112.

Schroeder, M. A., J. R. Young, and C. E. Braun. 1999. Sage Grouse (Centrocercus urophasianus). In The birds of North America, No. 425 (A. Poole and F. Gill, eds.). The Birds of N. Am., Inc., Philadelphia, PA.

Schukman, J. M., and B. O. Wolf. 1998. Say's Phoebe (Sayornis saya). In The birds of North America, No. 374 (A. Poole and F. Gill, eds.). The Birds of N. Am., Inc., Philadelphia, PA.

Schultz, Z. 1958. Northern Pacific Coast region. Audubon Field Notes 12: 377-379.

Schultz, Z. M. 1959. North Pacific Coast region. Audubon Field Notes 13: 57-58.

Scott, J. M. 1971. Interbreeding of the Glaucous-winged Gull and Western Gull in the Pacific Northwest. Calif. Birds 2: 129-133.

Scott, J. M. 1973. Resource allocation in four synoptic species of marine diving birds, Ph.D. diss., Oreg. State Univ., Corvallis.

Scott, J. M. 1990. Offshore distributional patterns, feeding habits, and adult-chick interactions of the Common Murre in Oregon. Stud. in Avian Biol. 14: 103-108.

Scott, J. M., J. Butler, W. G. Pearcy, and G. A. Bertrand. 1971. Occurrence of the Xantus' Murrelet off the Oregon Coast. Condor 73: 254.

Scott, J. M., and T. W. Haislip, Jr. 1969. An Oregon record of the Emperor Goose. Murrelet 50: 38.

Scott, J. M., W. Hoffman, D. Ainley, and C. F. Zeillemaker. 1974. Range extension and activity patterns in Rhinoceros Auklets. West. Birds 5: 13-20.

Scott, J. M., and H. B. Nehls. 1974. First Oregon records for Thick-billed Murre. West. Birds 5: 137.

Scott, J. M., W. Thackaberry, and G. A. Bertrand. 1971. A specimen of the Black-throated Sparrow from western Oregon. Murrelet 52: 23.

Scott, O. K. 1957. Great Basin, central Rocky Mountain region. Audubon Field Notes 11: 45-47.

Scott, O. K. 1959. Fall migration. Northern Rocky Mountain-intermountain region. Audubon Field Notes 13: 52.

Scott, O. 1962. Great Basin, central Rocky Mountain region. Audubon Field Notes 16: 435.

Scott, O. K. 1963. Great Basin, central Rocky Mountain region. Audubon Field Notes 17: 53-54.

Scott, O. K. 1965. Great Basin and central Rocky Mountain region. Audubon Field Notes 20: 76-77.

Scott, O. 1966. Great Basin, central Rocky Mountain region. Audubon Field Notes 20: 589.

Scott, O. K. 1971. Great Basin, central Rocky Mountain region. Am. Birds 25: 84.

Scott, T. A. 1994. Irruptive dispersal of Black-shouldered Kites to a coastal island. Condor 96: 197-200.

Scott, V. E., and G. L. Crouch. 1988. Summer birds and mammals of aspen-conifer forests in west-central Colorado. U.S. Dept. Agric., For. Serv. Res. Pap. RM-280.

Scott, V. E., J. A. Whelan, and P. L. Svoboda. 1980. Cavity nesting birds and forest management. Pp. 311-324 in Management of western forests and grasslands for nongame birds (R. M. DeGraff, tech. ed.). U.S. Dept. Agric., For. Serv. Gen. Tech. Rep. INT 86.

Scoville, J. 1991. Census of Upland Sandpipers of Grant, Umatilla, and Union counties, Oregon, 1991. Unpubl. rep. to Oreg. Dep. of Fish and Wildl., Portland.

Sealy, S. G. 1975. Feeding ecology of the Ancient and Marbled murrelets near Langara Island, British Columbia. Can. J. Zool. 53: 418-433.

Sealy, S. G. 1984. Capture and caching of flying carpenter ants by Pygmy Nuthatches. Murrelet 65: 49-51.

Sealy, S. G. 1995. Burial of cowbird eggs by parasitized Yellow Warblers: an empirical and experimental study. Anim. Behav. 49: 877-889.

Sealy, S. G. 1996. Evolution of host defenses against brood parasitism: implications of puncture-ejection by a small passerine. Auk 113: 346-355.

Sealy, S. G., A. J. Banks, and J. F. Chace. 2000. Two subspecies of Warbling Vireo differ in their response to cowbird eggs. West. Birds 31: 190-194.

Sealy, S. G., H. R. Carter, and D. Alison. 1982. Occurrences of the Asiatic Marbled Murrelet [B. m. perdix (Pallas)] in North America. Auk 99: 778-781.

Sealy, S. G., H. R. Carter, W. D. Shuford, K. D. Powers, and C. A. Chase. 1991. Long-distance vagrancy of the Asiatic Marbled Murrelet in North America, 1979-1989. West. Birds 22: 145-155.

Sedgwick, J. A. 1993. Dusky Flycatcher (Empidonax oberholseri). In The birds of North America, No. 78 (A. Poole and F. Gill, eds.). Acad of Nat. Sci., Philadelphia, and Am. Ornithol. Union, Washington, D.C.

Sedgwick, J. A. 1994. Hammond's Flycatcher (Empidonax hammondii). In The birds of North America, No. 109 (A. Poole and F. Gill, eds.).

Acad. of Nat. Sci., Philadelphia, and Am. Ornithol. Union, Washington, D.C.

Sedgwick, J. A. 2000. Willow Flycatcher (Empidonax trailli). In The birds of North America, No. 533 (A. Poole and F. Gill, eds.). The Birds of N. Am., Inc., Philadelphia, PA.

Sedgwick, J. A., and W. M. Iko. 1999. Costs of Brown-headed Cowbird parasitism to Willow Flycatchers. Stud. in Avian Biol. 18: 167-181.

Selander, R. K. 1954. A systematic review of the booming nighthawks of western North America. Condor 56: 57-82.

Senner, S. E., and B. J. McCaffery. 1997. Surfbird (Aphriza virgata). In The birds of North America, No. 266 (A. Poole and F. Gill, eds.). Acad. of Nat. Sci., Philadelphia, and Am. Ornithol. Union, Washington, D.C.

Shallenberger, R. J. 1984. Fulmars, shearwaters, and gadfly petrels. In Seabirds of eastern North Pacific and Arctic waters (D. G. Haley, ed.). Pacific Search Press, Seattle, WA.

Sharp, B. 1985. Avifaunal changes in central Oregon since 1899. West. Birds 16: 63-70.

Sharp, B. 1986. Guidelines for the management of the Purple Martin, Pacific Coast population. Sialia 8: 9-13.

Sharp, B. 1990. Population trends of Oregon's neotropical migrants. Oreg. Birds 16: 27-42.

Sharp, B. E. 1992. Neotropical migrants on national forests in the Pacific Northwest. Unpubl., U.S. For. Serv., Portland, OR.

Sharp, B. E. 1996. Avian population trends in the Pacific Northwest. Bird Populations 3: 26-45.

Sharp, D. U. 1989. Range extension of the Barred Owl in western Washington and first breeding record on the Olympic Peninsula. J. Raptor Res. 23: 179-180.

Sharpe, F. 1995. Return of the killer bubbles: interactions between alcids and fish schools. Pacific Seabirds 22: 43.

Shaw, W. T. 1936. Winter life and nesting studies of Hepburn's Rosy Finch in Washington state. Auk 53: 133-149.

Shea, D. S. 1974. Barred Owl records in Western Montana. Condor 76: 222.

Shelford, V. E. 1945. The relation of Snowy Owl migration to the abundance of collared lemmings. Auk 62: 592-596.

Shelton, A. C. 1914. Report on field work at Roseburg, Douglas County, Oregon, October 20-30, 1914. Unpubl. file, Univ. Oreg. Mus. of Nat. Hist.

Shelton, A. 1915. Yakutat Song Sparrow in Oregon. Condor 17: 60.

Shelton, A. 1917. A distributional list of the land birds of west-central Oregon. Univ. Oreg. Bull. 14(4). Eugene, OR.

Sherman, D. 1997. Kentucky Warbler. Oreg. Birds 23: 28.

Sherrell, P. 1994a. Oregon's first verified Rustic Bunting. Oreg. Birds 20: 111-112.

Sherrell, P. 1994b. Tricolored Heron. Oreg. Birds 20: 43.

Sherrod, S. K. 1979. Behavior of fledgling peregrines. The Peregrine Fund, Boise, ID.

Sherry, T. W. 1984. Comparative dietary ecology of sympatric, insectivorous neotropical flycatchers (Tyrannidae). Ecol. Monogr. 54: 313-338.

Sherwood, W. E. 1929. Immature Song Sparrow in full song. Condor 31: 181.

Shields, M. 2002. Brown Pelican (Pelecanus occidentalis). In The birds of North America, No. 609 (A. Poole and F. Gill, eds.). The Birds of N. Am., Inc., Philadelphia, PA.

Shipman, J. W. 1998. Christmas Bird Count database project. URL = http://www.nmt.edu/~shipman/ z/cbc/homepage.html Accessed 20 Sep 2002.

Short, L. L., Jr. 1965a. Hybridization in the flickers (Colaptes) of North America. Bull. Am. Mus. Nat. Hist. 129: 307-428.

Short, L. L. 1965b. Specimens of Nuttall Woodpecker in Oregon. Condor 67: 269-270.

Short, L. L. 1969. Taxonomic aspects of avian hybridization. Auk 86: 85-105.

Short, L. L. 1974. Habits and interactions of North American three-toed woodpeckers (Picoides arcticus and Picoides tridactylus). Am. Mus. Novitates 2547.

Short, L. L. 1982. Woodpeckers of the world. Delaware Mus. Nat. Hist. Monogr. 4.

Shuford, W. D. 1993. The Marin County breeding bird atlas: a distributional and natural history of coastal California birds. Calif. Avifauna Ser. 1. Bushtit Books, Bolinas, CA.

Shuford, W. D. 1997. Status assessment and conservation plan for the Black Tern (Chlidonias niger surinamensis) in North America-Draft. Unpubl. rep. to U.S. Fish and Wildl. Serv., Denver Fed. Center, Denver, CO.

Shuford, W. D., G. W. Page, J. G. Evens, and L. E. Stenzel. 1989. Seasonal abundance of waterbirds at Point Reyes: a coastal California perspective. West. Birds 20: 137-265.

Shuford, W. D., G. W. Page, and J. E. Kjelmyr. 1998. Patterns and dynamics of shorebird use of California's Central Valley. Condor 100: 227-244.

Shull, R. 1978. Bald Eagle nesting. Unpubl. rep., U.S. For. Serv., Deschutes Natl. For., Bend, OR.

Sibley, C. G., and B. L. Monroe, Jr. 1990. Distribution and taxonomy of birds of the world. Yale Univ. Press, New Haven, CT.

Sibley, D. 1993a. An Asiatic Marbled Murrelet in Ontario. Birders J. 2: 276-277.

Sibley, D. 1993b. The birds of Cape May. New Jersey Audubon Soc., Cape May Bird Point, NJ.

Sibley, D. A. 2000. The Sibley guide to birds. Nat. Audubon Soc. Alfred A. Knopf, New York.

Siderius, J. A. 1994. The relationships between nest defense, nest viability, habitat, and nest success in the Eastern Kingbird (Tyrannus tyrannus). Ph.D. thesis, Simon Fraser Univ., Burnaby, British Columbia.

Sieber, O. 1980. Causal and functional aspects of brood distribution in Sand Martins (Riparia riparia). Zeitschrift fur Tierpsychol. 52: 19-56.

Siegel-Causey, D., and G. L. Hunt, Jr. 1986. Breeding-site selection and colony formation in Double-crested and Pelagic cormorants. Auk 103: 230-234.

Siegfried, W. R., and B. D. J. Batt. 1972. Wilson's Phalaropes forming feeding associations with shovelers. Auk 89: 667-668.

Simmons, J. 2002. Field notes: western Oregon, summer 2002. Oreg. Birds 28:186-193.

Simmons, R. E., P. C. Smith, and R. B. Macwhirter. 1986. Hierarchies among Northern Harrier (Circus cyaneus) harems and the costs of polygyny. J. Anim. Ecol. 55: 755-771.

Simons, T. R. 1981. Behavior and attendance patterns of the Fork-Tailed Storm-Petrel. Auk 98: 145-158.

Simpson, G. S., and R. L. Jarvis. 1979. Comparative ecology of several subspecies of Canada Geese during winter in western Oregon. Pp. 223-241 in Management and biology of Pacific Flyway geese (R. L. Jarvis and J. C. Bartonek, eds.). Oreg. State Univ. Book Stores, Inc., Corvallis.

Sims, M. D. 1983. Breeding success and nest site characteristics of the Western Bluebird on Parrett Mountain. M.S. thesis, Portland State Univ., Portland.

Sisson, L. H. 1968. Calling behavior of Band-tailed Pigeons in reference to a census technique. M.S. thesis, Oreg. State Univ., Corvallis.

Siuslaw National Forest. Undated. Bird checklist for the Oregon Dunes National Recreation Area. Reedsport.

Sivak, J. G., and R. F. Glover. 1986. Anatomy of the avian membrana nicitans. Can. J. Zool. 64: 963-972.

Sivak, J. G., T. Hillebrand, and C. Lebert. 1985. Magnitude and rate of accommodation in diving and nondiving birds. Vision Res. 25: 925-933.

Sjoberg, K. 1985. Foraging activity patterns in the Goosander (Mergus merganser) and the Red-breasted Merganser (M. serrator) in relation to patterns of activity in their major prey species. Oecologia 67: 35-39.

Skeel, M. A., and E. P. Mallory. 1996. Whimbrel (Numenius phaeopus). In The birds of North America, No. 219 (A. Poole and F. Gill, eds). Acad. of Nat. Sci., Philadelphia, and Am. Ornithol. Union, Washington, D.C.

Skillman, R. 1997. Mortality of Laysan and Black-footed Albatrosses in the Hawaii pelagic longline fishery. Pacific Seabirds 24: 23.

Skorupa, J. P., R. L. Hothem, and R. W. DeHaven. 1980. Foods of breeding Tricolored Blackbirds in agricultural areas of Merced Co, California. Condor 82: 465-467.

Skutch, A. 1996. Orioles, blackbirds and their kin: a natural history. Univ. of Ari. Press, Tucson, AZ.

Slater, P. J. B. 1980. Factors affecting the number of guillemots Uria aalge on cliffs. Ornis Scand. 11: 155-163.

Small, A. 1994. California birds, their status and distribution. Ibis Publ. Co., Vista, CA.

Smallwood, K. S. 1998. On the evidence needed for listing Northern Goshawks (Accipiter gentilis) under the Endangered Species Act: a reply to Kennedy. J. Raptor Res. 32: 323-329.

Smith, C., F. Cooke, G. Robertson, R. Goudie, and W. Boyd. 1998. Evidence of long-term pair bonds in Harlequin Ducks, (Histrionicus histrionicus). Unpubl. abstract, 4th biennial Harlequin Duck Working Group and 1st annual Pacific Flyway Symp., Otter Crest, OR.

Smith, C. C., J. L. Hamrick, and C. L. Kramer. 1988. The effects of stand density on frequency of filled seeds and fecundity of lodgepole pine (Pinus contorta Dougl.) Can. J. For. Res. 18: 453-460.

Smith, D. C., and J. Van Buskirk. 1988. Winter territoriality and flock cohesion in the Black-capped Chickadee Parus atricapillus. Anim. Behav. 36: 466-476.

Smith, D. G., and J. R. Murphy. 1978. Breeding ecology of raptors in the eastern Great Basin of Utah. Brigham Young Univ. Sci. Bull. 18: 1-76.

Smith, D. G., J. R. Murphy, and N. D. Woffinden. 1981. Relationships between jackrabbit abundance and Ferruginous Hawk reproduction. Condor 83: 52-56.

Smith, D. G., C. R. Wilson, and H. H. Frost. 1974. History and ecology of a colony of Barn Owls in Utah. Condor 76: 131-136.

Smith, J. P. 2000. Fall 1998 raptor migration study at Dutchman Peak in southwest Oregon. Unpubl., HawkWatch Internatl., Inc. Salt Lake City, UT.

Smith, J. P. 2001. Fall 2000 raptor migration studies at Bonney Butte, Oregon. Unpubl., HawkWatch Internatl., Inc. Salt Lake City, UT.

Smith, M. 1980. Birds associated with the Alvord Basin sand dunes. Pp. 155-160 in An ecological study of the Alvord Basin sand dunes, southeastern Oregon (N. Cobb, N. E. Gruber, A. Flecker, D. Lightfoot, A. Masters, N. McClintock, J. Price, T. Seibert, and M. Smith, eds.). Rep. to Natl. Sci. Found.

Smith, M., T. Steinback, and G. Pampush. 1984. Distribution, foraging relationships and colony dynamics of the American White Pelican (Pelecanus erythrorynchos) in southern Oregon and northeastern California. Oreg. Dept. Fish and Wildl. Nongame Wildl. Tech. Rep. #83-0-04. Oreg. Dept. Fish and Wildl., Portland.

Smith, M. R., P. W. Mattocks, Jr., and K. M. Cassidy. 1997. Breeding birds of Washington state, Vol. 4 in Washington state gap analysis - Final report (K. M. Cassidy, C. E. Grue, M. R. Smith, and K. M. Dvornich, eds.). Seattle Audubon Soc. Publ. in Zool. 1. Seattle.

Smith, P. W. 1987. The Eurasian Collared-Dove arrives in the Americas. Am. Birds 41: 1371-1379.

Smith, R. H., and G. H. Jensen. 1970. Black Brant on the mainland coast of Mexico. Trans. Thirty-fifth N. Am. Wildl. Conf. 227-241.

Smith, R. L. 1963. Some ecological notes on the Grasshopper Sparrow. Wilson Bull. 75: 159-165.

Smith, S. A. 1982. Observations of a captive Turkey Vulture attacking live prey. Murrelet 63: 68-69.

Smith S. A., and R. A. Paselk. 1986. Olfactory sensitivity of the Turkey Vulture (Cathartes aura) to three carrion-associated odorants. Auk 103: 586-592.

Smith, S. M. 1993. Black-capped Chickadee (Parus atricapillus). In The birds of North America, No. 39 (A. Poole, P. Stettenheim, and F. Gill, eds.). Acad. of Nat. Sci., Philadelphia, and Am. Ornithol. Union, Washington, D.C.

Smith, T. S. 1972. Cowbird parasitism of Western Kingbird and Baltimore Oriole nests. Wilson Bull. 84: 497.

Smith, W. J. 1970. Displays and message assortment in Sayornis species. Behavior 37: 85-112.

Smith, W. P. 1983. Cooperative harassment of a Pileated Woodpecker by juvenile Sharp-shinned Hawks. Murrelet 64: 97-98.

Smyth, M., and G. A. Bartholomew. 1966. The water economy of the Black-throated Sparrow and the Rock Wren. Condor 68: 447-458.

Snell, R. R. 1989. Status of Larus gulls at Home Bay, Baffin Island. Colonial Waterbirds 12: 12-23.

Snow, D. W. 1967. Paridae. Pp. 70-124 in Check-list of birds of the world, Vol. 12 (R. A. Paynter, Jr. and E. Mayr, eds.). Mus. Comp. Zool., Cambridge, MA.

Snyder, N. R., and N. J. Schmitt. 2002. California Condor (Gymnogyps californianus). In The birds of North America, No. 610 (A. Poole and F. Gill, eds.). The Birds of N. Am., Inc., Philadelphia, PA.

Snyder, N. F. R., H. A. Snyder, J. L. Lincer, and R. T. Reynolds. 1973. Organochlorines, heavy metals, and the biology of North American accipiters. BioScience 23: 300-305.

Snyder, N. F. R., and J. W. Wiley. 1976. Sexual size dimorphism in hawks and owls of North America. Ornithol. Monogr. 20.

Sodhi, N. S., L. W. Oliphant, P. C. James, and I. G. Warkentin. 1993. Merlin (Falco columbarius). In The birds of North America, No. 44 (A. Poole and F. Gill, eds.). Acad. of Nat. Sci., Philadelphia, and Am. Ornithol. Union, Washington, D.C.

Sogge, M. K., W. M. Gilbert, and C. Van Riper III. 1994. Orange-crowned Warbler (Vermivora celata). In The birds of North America, No. 101 (A. Poole and F. Gill, eds.). Acad. of Nat. Sci., Philadelphia, and Am. Ornithol. Union, Washington, D.C.

Sonnenberg, E. L., and L. R. Powers. 1976. Notes on the food habits of Long-eared Owls (Asio otus) in southwestern Idaho. Murrelet 57: 63-64.

Sooter, C. A. 1941a. Additional records of the Western Mockingbird in Oregon. Condor 43: 157.

Sooter, C. A. 1941b. American Egret, Treganza Heron, and Ring-billed Gull at Malheur Lake in winter. Condor 43: 121.

Sooter, C. A. 1943. Catbirds nesting on the Malheur National Wildlife Refuge in southeast Oregon. Condor 45: 234.

Sorace, A., P. Formichetti, A. Boano, P. Andreani, C. Gramegna, and L. Mancini. 2002. The presence of a river bird, the dipper, in relation to water quality and biotic indices in central Italy. Environmental Pollution 118:89-96.

Sordahl, T. A. 1984. Observations on breeding site fidelity and pair formation in American Avocets and Black-necked Stilts. N. Am. Bird Bander 9: 8-11.

Soriano, P. 1931. Food habits and economic status of Brewer's and Red-winged blackbirds. Calif. Fish and Game 17: 361-395.

Sossinka, R. 1982. Domestication in birds. Avian Biol. 6: 373-403.

Soucy, L. J. 1980. Three long distance recoveries of banded New Jersey Barn Owls. N. Am. Bird Bander 5: 97.

Spautz, H. 1999. Common Yellowthroat brood parasitism and nest success vary with host density and site characteristics. Stud. in Avian Biol. 18: 218-228.

Spear, L. B. 1987. Hybridization of Glaucous and Herring gulls at the MacKenzie Delta, Canada. Auk 104: 123-125.

Spear, L. B. 1988. Dispersal patterns of Western Gulls from southeastern Farallon Islands. Auk 105: 128-141.

Spear, L. B. 1993. Dynamics and effect of Western Gulls feeding in a colony of guillemots and Brandt's Cormorants. J. Anim. Ecol. 62: 399-414.

Spear, L. B,. and D. G. Ainley. 1999. Migration routes of Sooty Shearwaters in the Pacific Ocean. Condor 101: 205-218.

Spear, L. B., D. G. Ainley, and R. P. Henderson. 1986. Post-fledging parental care in the Western Gull. Condor 88: 194-199.

Spear, L. B., M. J. Lewis, M. T. Myres, and R. L. Pyle. 1988. The recent occurrence of Garganey in North America and the Hawaiian Islands. Am. Birds 42: 385-392.

Spear, L. B., T. M. Penniman, J. F. Penniman, H. R. Carter, and D. G. Ainley. 1987. Survivorship and mortality factors in the Western Gull. Stud. in Avian Biol. 10: 26-43.

Spear, L. B., W. J. Sydeman, and P. Pyle.1995. Factors affecting the recruitment age and recruitment probability in the Western Gull Larus occidentalis. Ibis 137: 352-359.

Speer, F., and J. Felker. 1991. Blue-gray Gnatcatcher (Polioptila caerulea) study –Lower Table Rock Preserve. Rep. to The Nature Conservancy, Medford, OR.

Speich, S. M., and T. R. Wahl. 1989. Catalogue of Washington seabird colonies. U.S. Fish and Wildl. Serv. Biol. Rep. Ser. 88(6). Washington, D.C.

Speiser, R., and T. Bosakowski. 1987. Nest site selection by Northern Goshawks in northern New Jersey and southeastern New York. Condor 89: 387-394.

Speiser, R., and T. Bosakowski. 1991. Nesting phenology, site fidelity, and defense behavior of Northern Goshawks in New York and New Jersey. J. Raptor Res. 25: 132-135.

Spencer, K. T. 1998. Field notes: eastern Oregon, summer 1997. Oreg. Birds 24: 29-32.

Spencer, K. T. 1999. Field notes: eastern Oregon, June-July 1998. Oreg. Birds 25: 13-20.

Spencer, K. T. 2000a. Field notes: eastern Oregon, summer 1999. Oreg. Birds 26: 138-143.

Spencer, K. T. 2000b. Field notes: eastern Oregon, summer 2000. Oreg. Birds 26: 221-227.

Spencer, K. 2001a. Field notes: eastern Oregon, summer 2001. Oreg. Birds 27: 112-115.

Spencer, K. 2001b. Field notes: eastern Oregon, winter 2000-2001. Oreg. Birds 27: 56-59.

Spies, T. A., and J. F. Franklin. 1988. Old-growth and forest dynamics in the Douglas-fir region of western Oregon and Washington. Nat. Areas J. 8: 190-201.

Spies, T. A., and J. F. Franklin. 1991. The structure of natural young, mature, and old-growth Douglas-fir forests in Oregon and Washington. Pp. 91-109 in Wildlife and vegetation of unmanaged Douglas-fir forests (L. F. Ruggiero, K. B. Aubry, A. B. Carey, and M. H. Huff, tech. coords.). U.S. Dept. Agric., For. Serv. Gen. Tech. Rep. PNW-GTR-285. Portland, OR.

Springer, P. F., and R. W. Lowe. 1998. Population, distribution, and ecology of migrating and wintering Aleutian Canada Geese. Pp. 425-434 in Biology and management of Canada Geese: proceedings of the International Canada Goose Symposium (D. H. Rusch, M. D. Samuel, D. D. Humburg, and B. D. Sullivan, eds.). Milwaukee, WI.

Squires, J. R., and R. T. Reynolds. 1997. Northern Goshawk (Accipiter gentilis). In The birds of North America, No. 298 (A. Poole and F. Gill, eds.). Acad. of Nat. Sci., Philadelphia, and Am. Ornithol. Union, Washington, D.C.

Stabins, H. C. 1995. Peregrine Falcon predation on an Aleutian Canada Goose. J. Raptor Res. 29: 36.

Stager, K. E. 1964. The role of olfaction in food location by the Turkey Vulture (Cathartes aura). Los Angeles Co. Mus. Contrib. Sci. 81.

Stahl, J.-C., J.-L. Mougin, P. Jouventin, and H. Weimerkirch. 1984. Le Canard d'Eaton, Anas eatoni dryglaskii, des Iles Crozet: systematique, comportment alimentaire et biologie de reproduction. Gerfaut 74: 305-326.

Stake, J. D., and P. E. Stake. 1983. Apparent torpidity in Tree Swallows. Conn. Warbler 3: 36-37.

Stallcup, R. 1990. Ocean birds of the nearshore Pacific. Pt. Reyes Bird Observ., Stinson Beach, CA.

Stallcup, R. 1994. Focus: loons. Pt. Reyes Bird Observ. Newsletter, Fall, 1994: 6,7.

Stalmaster, M. V. 1987. The Bald Eagle. Universe Books, New York.

Stanback, M. T. 1991. Autumnal breeding in the scrub jay. J. Field Ornithol. 62: 94-96.

Steenhof, K. 1998. Prairie Falcon (Falco mexicanus). In The birds of North America, No. 346 (A. Poole and F. Gill, eds.). The Birds of N. Am., Inc., Philadelphia, PA.

Steenhof, K., M. N. Kochert, and M. Q. Moritsch. 1984. Dispersal and migration of southwestern Idaho raptors. J. Field Ornithol. 55: 357-368.

Steenhof, K., AND B. E. Peterson. 1997. Double brooding by American Kestrels in Idaho. J. Raptor Res. 31: 274-276.

Stegen, J. A. 2001. Nest-site characteristics of Red-naped Sapsucker (Sphyrapicus nuchalis) in central Washington. M.S. thesis, Central Wash. Univ., Ellensburg, WA.

Steidl, R. J., and R. G. Anthony. 2000. Experimental effects of human activity on breeding Bald Eagles. Ecol. Appl. 10: 258-269.

Stempniewicz, L. 1995. Feeding ecology of the Long-tailed Duck (Clangula hyemalis) wintering in the Gulf of Gdansk (southern Baltic Sea). Ornis-Svec 5: 133-142.

Stenzel, L. E., H. R. Huber, and G. W. Page. 1976. Feeding behavior and diet of the Long-billed Curlew and Willet. Wilson Bull. 88: 314-332.

Stenzel, L. E., G. W. Page, and J. Young. 1983. The trophic relationships between shorebirds and their prey. Unpub. report of Point Reyes Bird Obs., Stinson Beach, CA.

Stepney, P. H. R. 1975. Wintering distribution of Brewer's Blackbird: historical aspect, recent changes and fluctuations. Bird-Banding 46(2): 106-125.

Stepney, P. H. R., and D. M. Powers. 1973. Analysis of eastern breeding range expansion of Brewer's Blackbird plus general aspects of avian expansions. Wilson Bull. 85: 452-464.

Stepniewski, A. M. 1994. Birds of the Wahluke Slope (Saddle Mountain National Wildlife Refuge/Wahluke Slope Wildlife Area): Hanford site biodiversity inventory. Contract rep. to The Nature Conservancy #WAFO-022094, Seattle Field Office.

Sterling, J. C. 1999. Gray Flycatcher (Empidonax wrightii). In The birds of North America, No. 458 (A. Poole and F. Gill, eds.). The Birds of N. Am., Inc., Philadelphia, PA.

Stern, M. A. 1982. Black Tern habitat utilization and nest success at Sycan Marsh, 1982. Unpubl. rep., The Nature Conservancy, Portland, OR.

Stern, M. A. 1987. Site tenacity, mate retention and sexual dimorphism in Black Terns. M.S. thesis, Oreg. State Univ., Corvallis.

Stern, M. A. 1988. Waterbirds of the Warner Basin, Lake County. Oreg. Dept. of Fish and Wildl., Nongame Wildl. Prog. Tech. Rep. #87-5-02. Portland.

Stern, M., R. Del Carlo, M. Smith, and K. Kristensen. 1987. Birds of Sycan Marsh, Lake County, Oregon. Oreg. Birds 13: 184-192.

Stern, M. A., and R. L. Jarvis. 1991. Sexual dimorphism and assortative mating in Black Terns. Wilson Bull. 103: 266-271.

Stern, M. A., K. A. Kristensen, and J. F. Morawski. 1990. Investigations of Snowy Plovers at Abert Lake, Lake County, Oregon. Unpubl. rep. to Oreg. Dept. Fish and Wildl. The Oreg. Nat. Heritage Prog., Portland, OR.

Stern, M. A., D. J. Lauten, K. A. Castelein, K. J. Popper, and J. A. Fukuda. 2000. Impact assessment of oil spilled from the New Carissa on the Western Snowy Plover along the Oregon Coast. Unpubl. rept. by the Oreg. Nat. Heritage Prog. and The Nature Conservancy to TMM Co., LTD; Coos Bay Dist. of Bur. of Land Manage., Oreg. Dept. of Fish and Wildlife; Dunes Natl. Recreation Area; U.S. Fish and Wildl. Serv.

Stern, M. A., J. S. McIver, and G. A. Rosenberg. 1990. Investigations of the Western Snowy Plover at the Coos Bay North Spit and adjacent sites in Coos and Curry counties, Oregon, 1990. Unpubl. rep. to Oreg. Dept. Fish and Wildl. Oreg. Nat. Heritage Prog., Portland, OR.

Stern, M. A., J. F. Morawski, and G. A. Rosenberg. 1993. Rediscovery and status of a disjunct population of breeding Yellow Rails in southern Oregon. Condor 95: 1024-1027.

Stern, M. A., G. J. Pampush, and R. E. Del Carlo. 1987. Nesting ecology and productivity of Greater Sandhill Cranes at Sycan Marsh, Oregon. Pp. 249-256 in Proceedings of the 1985 crane workshop (J. C. Lewis, ed.). Platte River Whooping Crane Maintenance Trust, Grand Island, NE.

Stern, M. A., G. J. Pampush, K. Kristensen, and R. E. Del Carlo. 1986. Survivorship, causes of mortality and movements of juvenile Sandhill Cranes at Sycan Marsh, Oregon 1984-1985. Unpubl. rep., Oreg. Dept. of Fish and Wildl. Nongame Prog., Portland.

Stern, M., and G. Rosenberg. 1985. Occurrence of a breeding Upland Sandpiper at Sycan Marsh, Oregon. Murrelet 66: 34-35.

Stern, M. A., T. G. Wise, and K. L. Theodore. 1987. Use of a natural cavity by Bufflehead nesting in Oregon. Murrelet 68: 50.

Stevenson, H. M., and B. H. Anderson. 1994. The birdlife of Florida. Univ. Press of Florida, Gainesville.

Stewart, P. A. 1962. Waterfowl populations in the Upper Chesapeake Region. U.S. Fish and Wildl. Serv., Spec. Sci. Rep. Wildl. 65.

Stewart, P. A. 1967. Diving schedules of a Common Loon and a group of Oldsquaws. Auk 84: 122-123.

Stewart, R. E., and H. A. Kantrud. 1972. Population estimates of breeding birds in North Dakota. Auk 89: 766-788.

Stewart, R. M. 1973. Breeding behavior and life history of the Wilson's Warbler. Wilson Bull. 85: 21-30.

Stewart, R. M., R. P. Henderson, and K. Darling. 1977. Breeding ecology of the Wilson's Warbler in the high Sierra Nevada, California. Living Bird 16: 83-102.

Stiehl, R. B. 1978. Aspects of the ecology of the Common Raven in Harney Basin, Oregon. Ph.D. thesis, Portland State Univ., Portland, OR.

Stiehl, R. B. 1981. Observations of a large roost of Common Ravens. Condor 83: 78.

Stiehl, R. B., and S. N. Trautwein. 1991. Variations in diets of nesting Common Ravens. Wilson Bull. 103: 83-92.

Stiles, E. W. 1980. Bird communities in alder forests in Washington. Condor 82: 20-30.

Stiles, E. W. 1982. Expansion of mockingbird and multiflora rose in the northeastern United States and Canada. Am.Birds 36: 358-364.

Stiles, F. G. 1972. Age and sex determination in Rufous and Allen's hummingbirds. Condor. 74: 25-32.

Stiles, F. G., and A. Negret. 1994. The nonbreeding distribution of the Black Swift: a clue from Colombia and unsolved problems. Condor 96: 1091-1094.

St. Louis, M. J. 1995. Whooper Swan at Summer Lake Wildlife Area, Oregon, and California wintering areas. Oreg. Birds 21: 35-36.

Stokes, A. W. 1950. Breeding behavior of the goldfinch. Wilson Bull. 62: 107-127.

Stokes, D. W., and L. Q. Stokes. 1996. Stokes field guide to birds, western region. Little, Brown and Company, Boston.

Stone, E. R. 1992. The socioecology of North American Black-billed Magpies (Pica pica hudsonia). Diss. Abstr. Internatl. 52: 5140-B.

Stoner, D. 1936. Studies on the Bank Swallow, Riparia riparia riparia (Linnaeus) in the Oneida Lake region. Roosevelt Wild Life Annals 4: 126-233.

Storer, R. W. 1952. A comparison of variation, behavior and evolution in the sea bird genera Uria and Cepphus. Univ. Calif. Publ. Zool. 52: 121-222.

Storer, R. W. 1961. Observations of pellet-casting by Horned and Pied-billed grebes. Auk 78: 90-92.

Storer, R. W. 1969. The behavior of the Horned Grebe in spring. Condor, 71: 180-205.

Storer, R. W. 1978. Systematic notes on the loons (Gaviidae: Aves). Breviora 448.

Storer, R. W. 1988. Variation in the Common Loon (Gavia immer). 1987 Conf. Common Loon Res. and Manage., N. Am. Loon Fund, Ithaca, NY.

Storer, R. W., and M. J. Muller. 1999. Pied-billed Grebe (Podilymbus podiceps). In The birds of North America, No. 410 (A. Poole and F. Gill, eds.). The Birds of N. Am., Inc., Philadelphia, PA.

Storer, R. W., and G. L. Neuchterlein. 1992. Western Grebe (Aechmophorus occidentalis), and Clark's Grebe (Aechmophorus clarkii). In The birds of North America, No. 26 (A. Poole, P. Stettenheim and F. Gill, eds.). Acad. of Nat. Sci., Philadelphia, and Am. Ornithol. Union, Washington, D.C.

Storer, R. W., W. R. Siegfried, and J. Kinahan. 1976. Sunbathing in grebes. Living Bird 14: 45-56.

Strauch, J. G., Jr. 1963. A Tree Sparrow in western Oregon. Condor 65: 330.

Strauch, J. G., Jr. 1967. Spring migration of Dunlin in interior western Oregon. Condor 69: 210-212.

Strickland, D., and H. Ouellet. 1993. Gray Jay (Perisoreus canadensis). In The birds of North America, No. 40 (A. Poole, P. Stetterheim, and F. Gill, eds.). Acad. of Nat. Sci., Philadelphia, and Am. Ornithol. Union, Washington, D.C.

Strong, C. S. 1999. Marbled Murrelet monitoring research 1998: studies on the distribution and productivity of Marbled Murrelets at sea in Oregon. Unpubl. rep. to Oreg. Dept. Fish. and Wildl., Portland.

Strong, C. S., B. S. Keitt, W. R. McIver, C. J. Palmer, and I. Gafney. 1995. Distribution and population estimates of Marbled Murrelets at sea in Oregon during the summers of 1992 and 1993. Pp. 339-352 in Ecology and conservation of the Marbled Murrelet (C. J. Ralph, G. L. Hunt, Jr., M. G. Raphael, and J. F. Piatt, eds.). U.S. Dept. Agric., For. Serv. Gen. Tech. Rep. PSW-GTR-152. Albany, CA.

Stryker, G. 1894. My first set of Pine Siskins. Oologist 11: 185-186.

Sturges, F. W. 1955. Habitats and distributions of land vertebrates on the Corvallis watershed, Mary's Peak, Benton County, Oregon. M.A. thesis, Oreg. State Univ. Corvallis.

Sturges, F. W. 1957. Habitat distributions of birds and mammals in Lostine Canyon, Wallowa Mountains, northeastern Oregon. Ph.D. diss., Oreg. State Univ. Corvallis.

Suddaby, D., and N. Ratcliffe. 1997. The effects of fluctuation on food availability on breeding Arctic Terns (Sterna paradisaea). Auk 114: 524-530.

Sullivan, J. O. 1973. Ecology and behavior of the dipper, adaptations of a passerine to an aquatic environment. Ph.D. diss., Univ. Mont., Missoula.

Sullivan, P. 1995. A brief visitor. WOS News, Wash. Ornithol. Soc. Newsletter 35: 1, 16.

Sullivan, P. T. 1988. Pelagic fall migration in Oregon waters. Oreg. Birds 14: 134-143.

Sullivan, P. T. 1990. Site guide: western Grant County. Oreg. Birds 16: 227-230.

Sullivan, P. T. 1992a. Clear Lake Ridge and Devil's Gulch, Wallowa County, Oregon. Oreg. Birds 18: 57.

Sullivan, P. T. 1992b. "Rattlesnake" behavior. Oreg. Birds 18: 56.

Sullivan, P. T. 1992c. Rosy Finch roosting site. Oreg. Birds 18: 101.

Sullivan, P. T. 1992d. Site guide: where to find a Bobolink in Oregon. Oreg. Birds 18: 55.

Sullivan, P. T. 1992e. Where to find a Grasshopper Sparrow in Umatilla and Morrow counties, Oregon. Oreg. Birds 18: 23.

Sullivan, P. T. 1994. Fieldnotes: eastern Oregon, fall 1994. Oreg. Birds 21: 62.

Sullivan, P. T. 1995a. Field notes: eastern Oregon. Oreg. Birds 21: 123-127.

Sullivan, P. T. 1995b. Field notes: eastern Oregon, fall 1994. Oreg. Birds 21: 57-63.

Sullivan, P. T. 1996a. Field notes: eastern Oregon, fall 1995. Oreg. Birds 22: 59-66.

Sullivan, P. T. 1996b. Fieldnotes: eastern Oregon, spring 1996. Oreg. Birds 22: 119-125.

Sullivan, P. T. 1997a. Fieldnotes: eastern Oregon, fall 1996. Oreg. Birds 23: 69-75.

Sullivan, P. T. 1997b. Fieldnotes: eastern Oregon, spring 1997. Oreg. Birds 23: 144-149.

Sullivan, P. T. 1997c. Field notes: eastern Oregon, summer 1996. Oreg. Birds 23: 22-29.

Sullivan, P. T. 1998a. Field notes: eastern Oregon, fall 1997. Oreg. Birds 24: 57-62.

Sullivan, P. T. 1998b. Field notes: eastern Oregon, spring 1998. Oreg. Birds 24: 125-129.

Sullivan, P. T 1999a. Field notes: eastern Oregon, fall 1998. Oreg. Birds 25: 43-49.

Sullivan, P. T. 1999b. Field notes: eastern Oregon, spring 1999. Oreg. Birds 25: 106.

Sullivan, P. T. 2000a. Field notes: eastern Oregon, fall 1999. Oreg. Birds 26: 167-172.

Sullivan, P. T. 2000b. Field notes: eastern Oregon, spring 2000. Oreg. Birds 26: 189-195.

Sullivan, P. T. 2001a. Field notes: eastern Oregon. Oreg. Birds 27: 16-24.

Sullivan, P. T. 2001b. Field notes: eastern Oregon, spring 2001. Oreg. Birds 27: 76-85.

Sullivan, P. T. 2002. Field notes: eastern Oregon-fall 2001. Oreg. Birds 28: 18-29.

Sullivan, P. T., and K. Spencer. 1997. Oregon's sixth Black-chinned Sparrow. Oreg. Birds 23: 27.

Sullivan, S. L., W. H. Pyle, and S. G. Herman. 1986. Cassin's Finch nesting in big sagebrush. Condor 88: 378-379.

Summer Lake Wildlife Area Files. Unpubl. data. Summer Lake, OR.

Summers, S. D. 1977. A Common Grackle record for Oregon. West. Birds 8: 156.

Summers, S. 1978. Field reports: winter season, southern Oregon interior. Oreg. Birds 4(2): 26-28.

Summers, S. 1982a. Klamath County checklist. Oreg. Birds 8: 60-69.

Summers, S. D. 1982b. White Lake Snowy Plover population and production survey. Oreg. Dept. Wildl. Tech. Rep. 82-3-11.

Summers, S. 1985a. Field notes: eastern Oregon, April 1985 to June 1985. Oreg. Birds 11: 190-196.

Summers, S. 1985b. Field notes: eastern Oregon, November 1984 to March 1985. Oreg. Birds 11: 185-189.

Summers, S. 1986a. Fieldnotes: eastern Oregon, August - November 1985. Oreg. Birds 12: 129-133.

Summers, S. 1986b. Fieldnotes: eastern Oregon, December 1985 - May 1986. Oreg. Birds 12: 345-351.

Summers, S. 1991. Field notes: eastern Oregon, spring 1991. Oreg. Birds 17: 126.

Summers, S. D. 1992. Birds of the Sycan River: an avifaunal survey of the Sycan Wild and Scenic River Corridor. Unpubl. rep., U.S. Dept. Agric. For. Serv., Fremont Natl. Forest.

Summers, S. 1993a. A birder's guide to the Klamath Basin. Klamath Basin Audubon Soc., Klamath Falls, OR.

Summers, S. 1993b. Field notes: eastern Oregon, fall 1992. Oreg. Birds 19: 52-55.

Summers, S. 1993c. Field notes: eastern Oregon, spring 1993. Oreg. Birds 19: 113-117.

Summers, S. 1994a. Field notes: eastern Oregon, fall 1993. Oreg. Birds 20: 64-70.

Summers, S. 1994b. Fieldnotes: eastern Oregon, spring 1994. Oreg. Birds 20: 131-136.

Summers, S., and C. Miller. 1993. Preliminary draft: Oregon county checklists and maps. Oreg. Field Ornithol. Spec. Publ. 7.

Sunriver Nature Center. Undated. Birds of the Sunriver area. Sunriver Nat. Center, Sunriver, OR.

Suryan, R. M., D. P. Craig, D. D. Roby, W. D. Shuford, N. D. Chelgren, D. E. Lyons, and K. Collis. Unpubl. manuscript. Redistribution and growth of the Caspian Tern population along the Pacific Coast of North America: a 20-year assessment of population status.

Suthers, H. B. 1987/1988. Old field succession and bird life in the New Jersey sourlands. Records of New Jersey Birds 13: 54-64.

Sutton, G. M. 1936. Food capturing tactics of the Least Bittern. Auk 53: 74-75.

Swanson, D. L. 1991. Birds of McDonald Forest, Benton County, Oregon. Oreg. Birds 17: 80.

Swanson, D. L., E. T. Liknes, and K. L. Dean. 1999. Differences in migratory timing and energetic condition among sex/age classes in migrant Ruby-crowned Kinglets. Wilson Bull. 111: 61-69.

Swanson, G. A., and H. K. Nelson. 1970. Potential influence of fish-rearing programs on waterfowl breeding habitat. Pp. 65-71 in A symposium on the management of midwestern winter-kill lakes (E. Schneberger, ed.). Northcentral Div. of Am. Fish. Soc., Bethesda, MD.

Swanson, G. A., and M. I. Meyer. 1977. Impact of fluctuating water levels on feeding ecology of breeding Blue-winged Teals. J. Wildl. Manage. 41: 426-433.

Swanson, G. A., M. I. Meyer, and J. R. Serie. 1974. Feeding ecology of breeding Blue-winged Teals. J. Wildl. Manage. 38: 396-407.

Swarth, H. 1920. Revision of the avian genus Passerella, with special reference to the distribution and migration of the races in migration. Univ. Calif. Publ. Zool. 21: 75-224.

Swarth, H. S. 1922. Birds and mammals of the Stikine River region of northern British Columbia and southeastern Alaska. Univ. Calif. Publ. Zool. 24: 125-314.

Swarth, H. S. 1935. Systematic status of some northwestern birds (Tringa solitaria). Condor 37: 199-201.

Swarth, H. S., and H. C. Bryant. 1917. A study of the races of the White-fronted Goose (Anser albifrons) occurring in California. Univ. Calif. Publ. Zool. 17: 209-222.

Swennen, C., and P. Duiven. 1977. Size of food objects of three fish-eating seabird species: Uria aalge, Alca torda, and Fratercula arctica. Netherlands J. of Sea Res. 11: 92-98.

Swift, B. L., S. R. Orman, and J. W. Ozard. 1988. Response of Least Bittern to tape-recorded calls. Wilson. Bull. 100: 496-499.

Swisher, O. D. 1978. Poor-wills nesting in southwestern Oregon. N. Am. Bird Bander 3: 152-155.

Swisher, O. D. 1982. Poor-wills nesting in southwestern Oregon: a sequel. N. Am. Bird Bander 7: 18-19.

Sydeman, W. J. 1989. Effects of helpers on nestling care and breeder survival in Pygmy Nuthatches. Condor 91: 147-155.

Sydeman, W. J. 1991. Facultative helping by Pygmy Nuthatches. Auk 108: 173-175.

Sydeman, W. J. 1993. Survivorship of Common Murres on Southeast Farallon Island, California. Ornis Scand. 24: 135-141.

Sydeman, W. J., and M. Guntert. 1983. Winter communal roosting in the Pygmy Nuthatch. Pp. 121-

124 in Snag habitat management symposium proceedings (J. W. Davis, G. A. Goodwin, and R. A. Ockenfels, tech. coords.). U.S. Dept. Agric., For. Serv. Gen. Tech. Rep. RM-99.

Sydeman, W. J., M. Guntert, and R. P. Balda. 1988. Annual reproductive yield in the cooperative Pygmy Nuthatch (Sitta pygmaea). Auk 105: 70-77.

Szaro, R. C., and R. P. Balda. 1979. Bird community dynamics in a ponderosa pine forest. Stud. Avian Biol. 3.

Taber, W. B., Jr. 1928. A theory of how the Turkey Vulture finds its food. Wilson Bull. 40: 221-223.

Taft, O. W., and S. M. Haig. Unpubl. data. Predictors of habitat use for wintering shorebirds: interactions among wetland productivity and landscape structure. USGS - Forest and Rangeland Ecosystem Science Center, 3200 SW Jefferson Way, Corvallis, OR 97331.

Takekawa, J. Y., and N. Warnock. 2000. Long-billed Dowitcher (Limnodromus scolopaceus). In The birds of North America, No. 493 (A. Poole and F. Gill, eds.). The Birds of N. Am., Inc., Philadelphia, PA.

Talent, L. 1984. Food habits of wintering Brandt's Cormorants. Wilson Bull. 96: 130-34.

Talent, L. G., G. L. Krapu, and R. L. Jarvis. 1982. Habitat use by Mallard broods in south central North Dakota. Condor 85: 74-78.

Tangren, G. V. 1982. Feeding behavior of crows and gulls on a Puget Sound beach. West. Birds 13: 1-12.

Taoka, M., T. Sato, T. Kamada, and H. Okumura. 1989. Sexual dimorphism of chatter-calls and vocal sex recognition in Leach's Storm-Petrels Oceanodroma leucorhoa. Auk 106: 498-501.

Tarvin, K. A., and G. E. Woolfenden. 1999. Blue Jay (Cyanocitta crustata). In The birds of North America, No. 469 (A. Poole and F. Gill, eds.). The Birds of N. Am., Inc., Philadelphia, PA.

Tate, J., and D. K. Weaver. 1966. Nest analysis of the Tree Swallow. Jack-Pine Warbler 44: 15-22.

Taverner, P. A. 1934. The birds of Canada. Canada Dept. of Mines, Canada Nat. Mus. Bull. 72.

Taylor, A. L., and E. D. Forsman. 1976. Recent range extensions of the Barred Owl in western North America, including the first records for Oregon. Condor. 78: 560-561.

Taylor, B. 1998. Rails, a guide to the rails, crakes, gallinules and coots of the world. Yale Univ. Press, New Haven and London.

Taylor, D., C. Trost, and B. Jamison. 1992. Abundance and chronology of migrant shorebirds in Idaho. West. Birds 23: 49-78.

Taylor, D. M. 1984a. The effects of cattle grazing and other factors on passerine birds nesting in willow riparian habitat. M.S. thesis, Idaho State Univ., Pocatello.

Taylor, D. M. 1984b. Winter food habits of two sympatric owl species. Murrelet 65: 48-49.

Taylor, D. M. 1986a. Effects of cattle grazing on passerine birds nesting in riparian habitat. J. Range Manage. 39: 254-258.

Taylor, D. M. 1986b. Turkey Vultures decline at a traditional roosting site. Great Basin Nat. 46: 305-306.

Taylor, D. M. 2000. Status of the Yellow-billed Cuckoo in Idaho. West. Birds 31: 252-254.

Taylor, D. M., and C. D. Littlefield. 1986. Willow Flycatcher and Yellow Warbler response to cattle grazing. Am. Birds 40: 1169-1173.

Taylor, G. H., and C. Hannan. 1999. The climate of Oregon: from rainforest to desert. Oreg. State Univ. Press, Corvallis.

Taylor, J. M., and J. W. Kamp. 1985. Feeding activities of the Anna's Hummingbird at subfreezing temperatures. Condor 87: 292-293.

Taylor, P. 1979. Interspecific vocal mimicry by Pine Grosbeaks. Can. Field-Nat. 93: 436-437.

Taylor, P. B. 1996. Family Rallidae. Pp. 108-209 in Handbook of the birds of the world, Vol. 3: Hoatzin to auks. (J. del Hoyo, A. Elliott, J. Sargatal, et al., eds.). Lynx Edicions, Barcelona.

Taylor, W. P. 1923. Unusual shelter of some Hepburn Leucostictes in winter. Condor 25: 69-70.

Teale, V. 1988. Does Boreal Owl breed in Oregon? Oreg. Birds 14: 17-23.

Telfair, R. C. 1994. Cattle Egret (Bubulcus ibis). In The birds of North America, No. 113 (A. Poole and F. Gill, eds.). Acad. of Nat. Sci., Philadelphia, and Am. Ornithol. Union, Washington, D.C.

Temple, S. A. 1972. Systematics and evolution of the North American Merlin. Auk 89: 325-338.

Tenney, C. R. 1997. Black-chinned Sparrow (Spizella atrogularis). In The birds of North America, No. 270 (A. Poole and F. Gill, eds.).

Acad. of Nat. Sci., Philadelphia, and Am. Ornithol. Union, Washington, D.C.

Terborgh, J. 1989. Where have all the birds gone? Princeton Univ. Press, Princeton, NJ.

Terres, J. K. 1980. The Audubon Society encyclopedia of North American birds. Alfred A. Knopf, New York.

Terres, J. K. 1995. Encyclopedia of North American birds. Wings Books, New York, NY.

Terres, J. K. 1996. The Audubon Society encyclopedia of North American birds. Wings Books, New York.

Tershy, B. R., D. Breese, and G. M. Meyer. 1990. Kleptoparasitism of adult and immature Brown Pelicans by Heermann's Gulls. Condor 92: 1076-1077.

Thackaberry, W. 1975. The Seventy-fifth Audubon Christmas Bird Count (R. S. Arbib, Jr., ed.). Am. Birds 29: 553.

Thatcher, V. E. 1953. The cowbird in western Oregon. Condor 55: 318.

Thilenius, J. F. 1964. Synecology of the white oak (Quercus garryana Douglas) woodlands of the Willamette Valley, Oregon. Ph.D. thesis, Oreg. State Univ., Corvallis.

Thiollay, J. M. 1994. Family Accipitridae (hawks and eagles). Pp. 52-205 In Handbook of the birds of the world, Vol. 2: new world vultures to guineafowl (J. Del Hoyo, A. Elliott, J. Sargatal, et al., eds.). Lynx Edicions, Barcelona.

Thomas, C. M. 1997. Environmental contaminants and breeding biology of Great Blue Herons in the Columbia River Basin. M.S. thesis, Oreg. State Univ., Corvallis.

Thomas, C. M., and R. G. Anthony. 1999. Environmental contaminants in Great Blue Herons from the Lower Columbia and Willamette Rivers, Oregon and Washington, U.S.A. Environ. Toxicol. Chem. 18: 2804-2816.

Thomas, E. 1999. The migration of Rufous Hummingbirds: a teenager's experience. Oreg. Birds 25: 1-2.

Thomas, J. W., Tech. Ed. 1979. Wildlife habitats in managed forests: the Blue Mountains of Oregon and Washington. U.S. Dept. Agric., For. Serv., Agric. Handbook 553.

Thomas, J. W., R. G. Anderson, C. Maser, and E. L. Bull. 1979. Snags. Pp. 60-77 in Wildlife habitat in managed forests: the Blue Mountains of Oregon and

Washington (J. W. Thomas, tech. ed.). U.S. Dept. Agric., For. Serv. Agric. Handbook 553.

Thomas, J. W., E. D. Forsman, J. B. Lint, E. C. Meslow, B. R. Noon, and J. Verner. 1990. A conservation strategy for the Northern Spotted Owl: report of the interagency scientific committee to address the conservation of the Northern Spotted Owl. U.S. Dept. Agric., For. Serv. and U.S. Dept. Int. Bur. Land Manage., Portland, OR.

Thomas, J. W., and D. C. McCluskey. 1974. Effects of aerial application of DDT for tussock moth control on nestling survival of Mountain Bluebirds and House Wrens. U.S. Dept. Agric. For. Serv. Res. Pap. PNW-185. Portland, OR.

Thomas, J. W., R. J. Miller, C. Maser, R. G. Anderson, and B. E. Carter. 1979. Plant communities and successional stages. Pp. 22-39 in Wildlife habitat in managed forests: the Blue Mountains of Oregon and Washington (J. W. Thomas, tech. ed.). U.S. Dept. Agric., For. Serv. Agric. Handbook 553.

Thome, D. M., C. J. Zabel, and L. V. Diller. 1999. Forest stand characteristics and reproduction of Northern Spotted Owls in managed north-coastal California forests. J. Wildl. Manage. 63: 44-59.

Thompson, B. C. 1977. Behavior of Vaux's Swifts nesting and roosting in a chimney. Murrelet 58: 73-77.

Thompson, B. C., M. E. Schmidt, S. W. Calhoun, D. C. Morizot, and R. D. Slack. 1992. Subspecific status of Least Tern populations in Texas: North American implications. Wilson Bull. 104: 244-262.

Thompson, B. C., and J. E. Tabor. 1981. Nesting populations and breeding chronologies of gulls, terns, and herons on the Upper Columbia River, Oregon and Washington. Northwest Sci. 55: 209-218.

Thompson, J., R. Goggans, P. Greenlee, and S. Dowlan. 1993. Abundance, distribution and habitat associations of the Harlequin Duck in the Cascades Mountains, Oregon. Unpubl., Oreg. Dept. Fish and Wildl., Corvallis.

Thompson, S. P., and J. E. Cornely. 1982. Nest provisioning behavior by a male Northern Harrier on the death of his mate. Wilson Bull. 94: 564-565.

Thompson, S. P., R. S. Johnstone, and C. D. Littlefield. 1982. Nesting history of Golden Eagles

in Malheur-Harney Lakes Basin, southeastern Oregon. Raptor Res. 16: 116-122.

Thompson, S. P., C. D. Littlefield, and R. A. Ryder. 1979. Historical review and status of colonial nesting birds on Malheur National Wildlife Refuge, Oregon. Proc. Colonial Waterbird Group 3: 156-164.

Thompson, S. P., and D. G. Paullin. 1985. First nesting record of the Cattle Egret in Oregon. Murrelet 66: 28-29.

Thompson, T. Unpubl. data. Seabird records 1988-1992. Commercial fisherman. Newport, OR.

Thompson-Cowley, L. L., D. H. Helfer, G. D. Schmidt, and E. K. Eltzroth. 1979. Acanthocephalan parasitism in the Western Bluebird. Avian Diseases 23: 768-771.

Thomsen, L. 1971. Behavior and ecology of Burrowing Owls on the Oakland Municipal Airport. Condor 73: 177-192.

Thoresen, A. C. 1964. The breeding behavior of the Cassin's Auklet. Condor 66: 456-476.

Thoresen, A. C. 1980. Diurnal land visitations by Rhinoceros Auklets. West. Birds 11: 154.

Thoresen, A. C. 1989. Diving times and behavior of Pigeon Guillemots and Marbled Murrelets off Rosario Head, Washington. West. Birds 20: 33-37.

Thornburgh, L. 1981. Number of aquatic birds seen on the Pony Slough mudflats per count from June 1978 to June 1979. Unpubl. rep. to U.S. Fish and Wildl. Serv. and Oreg. Dept. Fish and Wildl.

Thornburgh, L. 1991. Site guide: Bandon area, Coos County. Oreg. Birds 17: 84-85.

Thrailkill, J. A., and L. S. Andrews. 1996. Presence of breeding Northern Goshawks in the Coast Range of Oregon. J. Raptor Res. 30: 248-249.

Thrailkill, J. A., R. G. Anthony, and E. C. Meslow. 1997. An update of demographic estimates for Northern Spotted Owls (Strix occidentalis caurina) from Oregon's central Coast Ranges. Pp. 432-448 In Biology and conservation of owls of the northern hemisphere (J. R. Duncan, D. H. Johnson, and T. H. Nicholls, eds.). U.S. Dept. Agric., For. Serv. Gen. Tech. Rep. NC-190.

Thut, R. N. 1970. Feeding habits of the dipper in southwestern Washington. Condor 72: 234-235.

Tice, B. 1993. Oregon's first verified Eastern Phoebe. Oreg. Birds 19: 3-4.

Tice, B. 1995. Blue Grouse behavior. Oreg. Birds 21: 5-6.

Tice, B. 1997. Records of Oregon coastal birds inland. Oreg. Birds 23: 48-52.

Tice, B. 1998a. Fieldnotes: western Oregon, winter 1997-1998. Oreg. Birds 24: 96-99.

Tice, B. 1998b. Inland observations of Red-breasted Merganser in Oregon. Oreg. Birds 24: 82-85.

Tice, W. 1999a. Field notes: western Oregon. Oreg. Birds 25: 21-26.

Tice, B. 1999b. Field notes: western Oregon, winter 1998-99. Oreg. Birds 25: 85-90.

Tice, B. 2000a. Field notes: western Oregon, summer 1999. Oreg. Birds 26: 144-146.

Tice, W. 2000b. Field notes: western Oregon, summer 2000. Oreg. Birds 26: 218-221.

Tice, B. 2000c. Field notes: western Oregon, winter 1999-2000. Oreg. Birds 26: 185-189.

Timken, R. T., and B. W. Anderson. 1969. Food habits of Common Mergansers in the northcentral United States. J. Wildl. Manage. 33: 87-91.

Timm, D. E., and C. P. Dau. 1979. Productivity, mortality, distribution, and population status of Pacific Flyway White-fronted Geese. Pp. 280-298 in Management and biology of Pacific Flyway geese (R. L. Jarvis and J. C. Bartonek, eds.). Oreg. State Univ. Bookstores, Corvallis.

Timm, D. E., M. L. Wege, and D. S. Gilmer. 1982. Current status and management challenges for Tule White-fronted Geese. Trans. N. Am. Wildl. Nat. Resour. Conf. 47: 453-463.

Titman, R. 1973. The role of the pursuit flight in the breeding biology of the Mallard. Ph.D. thesis, Univ. of New Brunswick, Fredericton.

Titus, J., J. A. Christy, D. VanderSchaaf, J. S. Kagan, and E. R. Alverson. 1996. Upland plant communities and their biota in the Willamette Valley, Oregon. Phase I project: inventory and assessment report to environmental protection agency, Region X, Seattle, Washington. Willamette Basin Geographic Initiative Prog. Oreg. Nat. Heritage Prog., The Nature Conservancy, Portland, OR.

Titus, K., and J. Mosher. 1980. Turkey Vulture predation of Ruffed Grouse chick. Can. Field-Nat. 94: 327-328.

Tobalske, B. W. 1992. Evaluating habitat suitability using relative abundance and fledging success of Red-naped Sapsuckers. Condor 94: 550-553.

Tobalske, B. 1997. Lewis' Woodpecker (Melanerpes lewis). In The birds of North America, No. 284 (A. Poole and F. Gill, eds.). Acad. of Nat. Sci., Philadelphia, and Am. Ornithol. Union, Washington, D.C.

Todd, W. E. C. 1940. Birds of western Pennsylvania. Univ. of Pittsburgh Press, Pittsburgh, PA.

Todd, W. E. C. 1963. Birds of the Labrador Peninsula and adjacent areas. Univ. Toronto Press.

Tomback, D. F. 1978. Foraging strategies of Clark's Nutcracker. Living Bird 16: 123-161.

Tomback, D. F. 1982. Dispersal of whitebark pine seeds by Clark's Nutcracker: a mutualism hypothesis. J. Anim. Ecol. 51: 451-467.

Tomback, D. F. 1998. Clark's Nutcracker (Nucifraga columbiana). In The birds of North America, No. 331 (A. Poole and F. Gill, eds.). The Birds of N. Am., Inc., Philadelphia, PA.

Tomkovich, P. S. 1990. Analysis of geographical variability in Red Knot (Calidris canutus). Bull. Moscow Soc. Nat., Biol. Div. 95: 59-72. (in Russian with English summary).

Tomkovich, P. S. 1992. An analysis of geographic variability in Knot (Calidris canutus) based on museum skins. Pp. 17-23 in The migration of knots (T. Piersma and N. Davidson, eds.). Wader Study Group Bull. 64 (suppl.).

Tomlinson, R. E. 1993. Migration. Pp. 57-80 in Ecology and management of the Mourning Dove (T. S. Baskett, M. W. Sayre, R. E. Tomlinson, R. E. Mirarchi, and R. E. McCabe, eds.). Stackpole Books, Harrisburg, PA.

Tompa, F. S. 1962. Territorial behavior: the main controlling factor of a local Song Sparrow population. Auk 79: 687-697.

Toops, C. 1994. Family ties. Pp. 48-50 in Bluebirds forever. Voyageur Press, Inc., Stillwater, MN.

Torgersen, T. R., and E. L. Bull. 1995. Down logs as habitat for forest-dwelling ants—the primary prey of Pileated Woodpeckers in northeastern Oregon. Northwest Sci. 69: 294- 303.

Torgersen, T. R., and R. W. Campbell. 1982. Some effects of avian predators on the western spruce budworm in north central Washington. Environ. Entomol. 11: 429-431.

Torgersen, T. R., R. R. Mason, and R. W. Campbell. 1990. Predation by birds and ants on two forest insect pests in the Pacific Northwest. Stud. in Avian. Biol. 13: 14-19.

Torgersen, T. R., R. R. Mason, R. W. Campbell, and D. Van Horn. 1984. Avian predators of Douglas-fir tussock moth, Orgyia pseudotsugata (McDunnough) (Lepidoptera: Lymantriidae) in southwestern Oregon. Environ. Entomol. 13: 1018-1022.

Towle, J. C. 1974. Woodland in the Willamette Valley: an historical geography. Ph.D. diss., Univ. of Oreg., Eugene.

Tramer, E. J. 1994. Feeder access: deceptive use of alarm calls by a White-breasted Nuthatch. Wilson Bull. 106: 573.

Tramontano, J. P. 1964. Comparative studies of the Rock Wren and Canyon Wren. M.S. thesis, Univ. of Ariz., Tucson.

Tremblay, J., and L. N. Ellison. 1979. Effects of human disturbance on breeding of Black-crowned Night-Herons. Auk 96: 364-369.

Trivelpiece, W. Z., R. G. Butler, D. S. Miller, and D. B. Peakall. 1984. Reduced survival of chicks of oil-dosed adult Leach's Storm-Petrels. Condor 86: 81-82.

Trochlell, D. 2000. Idaho-western Montana region. North Am. Birds 54: 77-79.

Trombino, C. L. 1998. Species interactions in the hybrid zone between Red-breasted (Sphyrapicus ruber) and Red-naped (Sphyrapicus nuchalis) sapsuckers: fitness consequences, reproductive character displacement, and nest site selection. Ph.D. diss., Northern Illinois Univ.

Trombino, C. L. 2000. Helping behavior within sapsuckers (Sphyrapicus spp.). Wilson Bull. 112: 273-275.

Trost, C. H. 1999. Black-billed Magpie (Pica pica). In The birds of North America, No. 389 (A. Poole and F. Gill, eds.). The Birds of N. Am., Inc., Philadelphia, PA.

Trost, R. E. 1999. 1999 Pacific Flyway data book: waterfowl harvests and status, hunter participation and success, and certain hunting regulations in the Pacific Flyway and United States. Office of Migratory Bird Manage., U.S. Fish and Wildl. Serv., Portland, OR.

Trost, R. E. 2000. Pacific Flyway 1999-2000 fall and winter waterfowl survey report. Office of Migratory Bird Manage., U.S. Fish and Wildl. Serv., Portland, OR.

Trulio, L. A. 1995. Passive relocation: a method to preserve Burrowing Owls on disturbed sites. J. Field Ornithol. 66: 99-106.

Trulio, L. A. 1997. Strategies for protecting western Burrowing Owls (Speotyto cunicularia hypugaea) from human activities. Pp. 461-465 in Biology and conservation of owls in the northern hemisphere (J. R. Duncan, D. H. Johnson, and T. H. Nicholls, eds.). U.S. Dept. Agric., For. Serv. Gen. Tech. Rep. NC-190. St. Paul, MN.

Turner, A., and C. Rose. 1989. Swallows and martins, an identification guide and handbook. Houghton Mifflin Co., Boston.

Twedt, D. J., W. J. Bleier, and G. M. Linz. 1991. Geographic and temporal variation in the diet of Yellow-headed Blackbirds. Condor 93: 975-986.

Twedt, D. J., W. J. Bleier, and G. M. Linz. 1992. Genetic variation in male Yellow-headed Blackbirds from the northern Great Plains. Can. J. Zool. 70: 2280-2282.

Twedt, D., and R. Crawford. 1995. Yellow-headed Blackbird (Xanthocephalus xanthocephalus). In The birds of North America, No. 192 (A. Poole and F. Gill, eds.). Acad. of Nat. Sci., Philadelphia, and Am. Ornithol. Union, Washington, D.C.

Tweit, B. 1988. Northern Pacific Coast region. Am. Birds 42: 310-313.

Tweit, B. 1989. Northern Pacific Coast region. Am. Birds 43: 356-360.

Tweit, B., and D. Fix. 1990a. Oregon/Washington region. Am. Birds 44: 149-154.

Tweit, B., and D. Fix. 1990b. Oregon/Washington region. Am. Birds 44: 486-490.

Tweit, B., and D. Fix. 1991. Oregon/Washington region. Am. Birds 45: 309-312.

Tweit, B., and J. Gilligan. 1991. Oregon/Washington region. Am. Birds 45: 489-491.

Tweit, B., and J. Gilligan. 1992. Oregon/Washington region. Am. Birds 46: 306-309.

Tweit, B., and J. Gilligan. 1993. Oregon/Washington region. Am. Birds 47: 139-143.

Tweit, B., and J. Gilligan. 1994. Oregon/Washington region. Am. Birds 48: 144-147.

Tweit, B., and J. Gilligan. 1997. Oregon/Washington region. Field Notes 51: 108-113.

Tweit, B., and J. Gilligan. 1998. Oregon/Washington region. Field Notes 52: 114-118.

Tweit, B., J. Gilligan, and S. Mlodinow. 1999. Oregon/Washington region. N. Am. Birds 53: 94-99.

Tweit, B., and S. Heinl. 1989. Northern Pacific Coast region. Am. Birds 43: 527-530.

Tweit, B., and J. Johnson. 1990. Oregon/Washington region. Am. Birds 44: 317-321.

Tweit, B., and J. Johnson. 1991a. Oregon/Washington region. Am. Birds 45: 312- 315.

Tweit, B., and J. Johnson. 1991b. Oregon/Washington region. Am. Birds 45: 1152-1156.

Tweit, B., and J. Johnson. 1992. Oregon/Washington region. Am. Birds 46: 1171-1173.

Tweit, B., and J. Johnson.1993. Oregon/Washington region. Am. Birds. 47: 1143-1145.

Tweit, B., and J. Johnson. 1994. Oregon/Washington region. Am. Birds 48: 982-983.

Tweit, B., and J. Johnson. 1996a. Oregon/Washington region. Natl. Audubon Soc. Field Notes 50: 215.

Tweit, B., and J. Johnson. 1996b. Oregon/Washington region. Natl. Audubon Soc. Field Notes 50: 989-992.

Tweit, B., J. Johnson, and P. W. Mattocks, Jr. 1990. Oregon/Washington region. Am. Birds 44: 1177-1180.

Tweit, B., G. Lillie, and S. Mlodinow. 1999. Oregon/Washington region. N. Am. Birds 53: 320-324.

Tweit, B., and P. Mattocks, Jr. 1987a. Northern Pacific Coast region. Am. Birds 41: 318-321.

Tweit, B., and P. Mattocks, Jr. 1987b. Northern Pacific Coast region. Am. Birds 41: 1478-1480.

Tweit, B., and S. Summers. 1994. Oregon/Washington region. Natl. Audubon Soc. Field Notes 48: 334-337.

Tweit, B., B. Tice, and S. Mlodinow. 1999. Oregon/Washington region. N. Am. Birds 53: 200-203.

Twining, H. 1940. Foraging behavior and survival in the Sierra Nevada Rosy Finch. Condor 42: 64-72.

Tyler, S. J., and S. J. Ormerod. 1994. The dippers. T. & A. D. Poyser Press, London.

Tyler, W. B., K. T. Briggs, D. B. Lewis, and G. Ford. 1993. Seabird distribution and abundance in relation to oceanographic processes in the California Current system.

Pp. 48-60 in The status, ecology, and conservation of marine birds in the North Pacific (K. Vermeer, K. T. Briggs, K. H. Morgan, and D. Siegel-Causey, eds.). Can. Wildl. Serv. Spec. Publ. Ottawa.

Tyler, W. M. 1929. Spotted Sandpiper. in Life histories of North America shorebirds (A. C. Bent, ed.). U.S. Natl. Mus. Bull. 146.

Tyler, W. M. 1942. Tree Swallow. Pp. 384-400 in Life histories of North American flycatchers, larks, swallows and their allies (A. C. Bent, ed.). U.S. Natl. Mus. Bull. 179.

Tyler, W. M. 1968. Spinus tristis tristis (Linnaeus) Eastern American Goldfinch. Pp. 447-466 in Life histories of North American cardinals, grosbeaks, buntings, towhees, finches, sparrows, and allies (O. L. Austin, Jr., ed.). U.S. Natl. Mus. Bull. 237.

Umatilla National Forest. 1991. Birds of the Umatilla National Forest (checklist). U.S. Dept. Agric., For. Serv.,Umatilla Natl. For., Pendleton, OR.

United States Army Corps of Engineers (USACE). 2001. Caspian Tern relocation FY 2001-2002: management plan and pile dike modification to discourage cormorant use, Lower Columbia River, Oregon and Washington. Environ. Assess. and Finding of No Significant Impact. Portland, OR.

United States Department of Agriculture (USDA). 1994. A checklist to the birds of Curry County, Oregon. U.S. Dept. Agric., For. Serv., Region 6, Portland.

United States Department of Agriculture (USDA). 1996. Bird checklist for Siskiyou National Forest. U.S. Dept. Agric., For. Serv., Siskiyou Natl. For., Grants Pass, OR.

United States Department of Agriculture (USDA). 1997. Birds of the Winema National Forest. U.S. Dept. Agric., For. Serv., Winema Natl. For., Klamath Falls, OR.

United States Department of Agriculture and United States Department of the Interior (USDA/USDI). 1993. Forest ecosystem management: an ecological, economic and social assessment. Rep. of the For. Ecosystem Manage. Assess. Team. U.S. Dept. Agric., For. Serv., U.S. Fish and Wildl. Serv., Natl. Marine Fisheries Serv., Natl. Park Serv., Bureau Land Manage., and Environ. Protection Agency. Portland, OR.

United States Department of Agriculture and United States Department of the Interior. (USDA/USDI). 1994. Final supplemental environmental impact statement on management of habitat for late-successional and old-growth forest related species within the range of the Northern Spotted Owl. U.S. Dept. Agric., For. Serv., and U.S. Dept. Int., Bur. Land Manage., Portland, OR.

United States Department of the Interior (USDI). 1968. Birds of the Cold Springs National Wildlife Refuge. Checklist.

United States Department of the Interior (USDI). 1973. Birds of the Umatilla National Wildlife Refuge. Checklist.

United States Department of the Interior (USDI). 1978. Determination of certain Bald Eagle populations as endangered or threatened. Fed. Register 43: 6230-6233.

United States Department of the Interior (USDI). 1988. Supplemental environmental impact statement: issuance of annual regulations permitting the sport hunting of migratory birds. U.S. Fish and Wildl. Serv., Washington, D.C.

United States Department of the Interior (USDI). 1992. Draft recovery plan for the Northern Spotted Owl. U. S. Dept. of Int. Washington, D.C.

United States Department of the Interior (USDI). 1993. Birds of the Medford District (checklist). Bur. of Land Manage., Medford, OR.

United States Department of the Interior (USDI). 1995. Recovery plan for the Mexican Spotted Owl. U.S. Fish and Wildl. Serv. Albuquerque, NM.

United States Department of the Interior (USDI). 1999. Endangered and threatened wildlife and plants; proposed rule to remove the Bald Eagle in the lower 48 states from the list of endangered and threatened wildlife. Fed. Register 64: 36453-36464.

United States Department of the Interior (USDI). Undated. Neotropical bird monitoring program for FY 1993 and 1994. Bur. of Land Manage., Roseburg, OR.

United States Fish and Wildlife Service (USFWS). 1981. Birds of Malheur National Wildlife Refuge Oregon (checklist). Malheur Natl. Wildl. Refuge, Burns.

United States Fish and Wildlife Service (USFWS). 1982. Pacific Flyway management plan for Aleutian Canada geese. Portland, OR.

United States Fish and Wildlife Service (USFWS). 1986a. Pacific Flyway management plan for Cackling Canada Geese. Portland, OR.

United States Fish and Wildlife Service (USFWS). 1986b. Recovery plan for the Pacific Bald Eagle. U.S. Fish and Wildl. Serv. Portland, OR.

United States Fish and Wildlife Service (USFWS). 1986c. Wildlife Hart Mountain National Antelope Refuge (check-list). Washington, D.C.

United States Fish and Wildlife Service (USFWS). 1989. Pacific Flyway management plan for the Pacific population of Western Canada Geese. Portland, OR.

United States Fish and Wildlife Service (USFWS). 1990. Endangered and threatened wildlife and plants: reclassification of the Aleutian Canada Goose from endangered to threatened status. Fed. Reg. 55: 51106-51112.

United States Fish and Wildlife Service (USFWS). 1992. Endangered and threatened wildlife and plants: determination of threatened status for the Washington, Oregon and California population of the Marbled Murrelet. Fed. Reg. 57: 45328-45337.

United States Fish and Wildlife Service (USFWS). 1994a. Endangered and threatened wildlife and plants; animal candidate review for listing as endangered or threatened species; proposed rule. Fed. Reg. 59: 58982-59028.

United States Fish and Wildlife Service (USFWS). 1994b. Wildlife of the Hart Mountain National Antelope Refuge. U.S. Fish and Wildl. Serv. N. Prairie Wildl. Res. Center Home Page, Jamestown, ND. URL = http://www.npwrc.usgs.gov/resource/othrdata/chekbird/r1/hartmtn.htm Accessed 20 Sep 2002.

United States Fish and Wildlife Service (USFWS). 1995a. Migratory nongame birds of management concern in the United States: the 1995 list. Office of Migratory Bird Manage. Washington, D.C.

United States Fish and Wildlife Service (USFWS). 1995b. Wildlife of the Klamath Basin National Wildlife Refuges California/Oregon. Klamath Basin Natl. Wildl. Refuge. Tulelake, CA.

United States Fish and Wildlife Service (USFWS). 1996. Endangered and threatened wildlife and plants; final designation of critical habitat for the Marbled Murrelet. Fed. Reg. 61: 26256-26320.

United States Fish and Wildlife Service (USFWS). 1997a. Pacific Flyway management plan for Dusky Canada geese. Portland, OR.

United States Fish and Wildlife Service (USFWS). 1997b. Recovery plan for the Marbled Murrelet (Brachyramphus marmoratus) in Washington, Oregon and California. U.S. Fish and Wildl. Serv., Portland, OR.

United States Fish and Wildlife Service (USFWS). 2001a. Waterfowl population status, 2001. U.S. Dept. Interior, Washington D.C.

United States Fish and Wildlife Service (USFWS). 2001b. Western Snowy Plover (Charadrius alexandrinus nivosus) Pacific Coast population draft recovery plan. Portland, OR.

United States Fish and Wildlife Service (USFWS). Undated. Division of Migratory Bird Management files. Portland, OR.

United States Fish and Wildlife Service (USFWS). Unpublished data from the 1988 Oregon seabird colony survey. U.S. Fish and Wildl. Serv. Oregon Coastal Refuges Headquarters, Newport, OR.

United States Geological Survey (USGS). 1999. USGS finds that mysterious Arkansas Bald Eagle disease has spread to ducks in eastern states. URL = http://biology.usgs.gov/pr/newsrelease/1999/3-29.html Accessed 7 Jul 2002.

United States Geological Survey (USGS) Patuxent Wildlife Research Center. 2001. North American Breeding Bird Survey Internet data set. URL = http://www.mp2-pwrc.usgs.gov/bbs/retrieval/ Accessed 7 Jul 2002.

Unitt, P. 1987. Empidonax traillii extimus:an endangered subspecies. West. Birds 18: 137-162.

Unitt, P., K. Messer, and M. Thery. 1996. Taxonomy of the Marsh Wren in southern California. Proc. San Diego Soc. Nat. Hist. 31: 1-20.

Unitt, P., and A. M. Rea. 1997. Taxonomy of the Brown Creeper in California. Pp. 177- 185 in The era of Allan R. Phillips: a festschrift (R. W. Dickerman, compiler). Horizon Publ., Albuquerque, NM.

Van Brocklin, M. D. 2000. Swift watch 2000: a fall survey of Vaux's Swifts in the Willamette Valley. Unpubl.

rep. to Oreg. Dept. Fish and Wild., Clackamas.

Van Daele, L. J., and H. A. Van Daele. 1982. Factors affecting the productivity of Ospreys nesting in west-central Idaho. Condor 84: 292-299.

Vander Haegen, W. M., F. C. Dobler, and D. J. Pierce. 2000. Shrubsteppe bird response to habitat and landscape variables in eastern Washington, U.S.A. Cons. Biol. 14: 1145-1160.

Vander Wall, S. B. 1982. An experimental analysis of cache recovery in Clark's Nutcracker. Anim. Behav. 30: 84-94.

Vander Wall, S. B. 1988. Foraging of Clark's Nutcracker on rapidly changing pine seed resources. Condor 90: 621-631.

Vander Wall, S. B. 1990. Food hoarding in animals. Univ. of Chicago Press, Chicago, IL.

Vander Wall, S. B., and R. P. Balda. 1977. Coadaptations of the Clark's Nutcracker and piñon pine for efficient seed harvest and dispersal. Ecol. Monogr. 47: 89-111.

Vander Wall, S. B., and R. P. Balda. 1981. Ecology and evolution of food-storage behavior in conifer-seed-caching corvids. Zeitschrift fur Tierpsychol. 56: 217-242.

Van Gils, J., and P. Wiersma. 1996. Black Turnstone. P. 516 in Handbook of the birds of the world, Vol. 3 (J. del Hoyo, A. Elliott, J. Sargatal, et al., eds.). Lynx Edicions, Barcelona.

Van Horn, D. 1978. First breeding record of a Blue Jay in Oregon. Murrelet 59: 70.

Van Horne, B. 1984. The relationship between mating habits and habitat occupancy in the Winter Wren Troglodytes troglodytes in Oregon coastal coniferous forest. Bull. Ecol. Soc. Am. 65: 70-71.

Van Horne, B. 1995. Assessing vocal variety in the Winter Wren, a bird with a complex repertoire. Condor 97: 39-49.

Van Horne, B., and A. Bader. 1990. Diet of nestling Winter Wrens in relationship to food availability. Condor 92: 413-420.

Van Rossem, A. J. 1943. Description of a race of goldfinch from the Pacific Northwest. Condor 45: 158-159.

Van Tyne, J., and A. J. Berger. 1959. Fundamentals of ornithology. John Wiley and Sons, New York, NY.

Varoujean, D. H. 1985. Abundance and distribution of shorebirds, waterfowl, wading birds, gulls, and crows in Coos Bay, Oregon, 1984-1985. Oregon Dept. of Fish and Wildl. Nongame Wildl. Prog. Tech. Rep. 85-2-01.

Varoujean, D. H., S. D. Sanders, and M. R. Graybill. 1979. Aspects of Common Murre breeding biology. Pacific Seabird Group Bull. 6: 28.

Varoujean, D. H., and W. A. Williams. 1995. Abundance and distribution of Marbled Murrelets in Oregon and Washington based on aerial surveys. Pp. 327-337 in Ecology and conservation of the Marbled Murrelet (C. J. Ralph, G. L. Hunt, Jr., M. G. Raphael, and J. F. Piatt, eds.). U.S. Dept. Agric., For. Serv. Gen. Tech. Rep. PSW-GTR-152. Albany, CA.

Vaurie, C. 1958. Systematic notes on Palearctic birds. No. 32 Oriolidae, Dicruridae, Bombycillidae, Pycnonotidae, Nectariniidae, and Zosteropidae. Am. Mus. Novitates No. 1869.

Vaurie, C. 1961. Systematic notes on Palearctic birds, No. 45: Falconidae, the genus Falco (II). Am. Mus. Novitates 2038.

Vaurie, C. 1965. The birds of the Palearctic fauna. Non- Passeriformes. H. F. and G. Witherby, London.

Vega, R. M. S. 1993. Bird communities in managed conifer stands in the Oregon Cascades: habitat association and nest predation. M.S. thesis, Oreg. State Univ., Corvallis, OR.

Veit, R. R., P. Pyle, and J. A. McGowan. 1996. Ocean warming and long-term change in pelagic bird abundance within the California Current system. Marine Ecol. Prog. Ser. 139: 11-18.

Vekasy, M. S., and J. P. Smith. 2000. Fall 1999 raptor migration study at Bonney Butte, Oregon. HawkWatch Internatl., Salt Lake City, UT.

Velarde, E. 1992. Predation of Heermann's Gull (Larus heermanni) chicks by Yellow-footed Gulls (Larus livens) in dense and scattered nesting sites. Colonial Waterbirds 15: 8-13.

Verbeek, N. A. M. 1966. Wanderings of the Ancient Murrelet: some additional comments. Condor 68: 510-511.

Verbeek, N. A. M. 1986. Aspects of the breeding biology of an expanded population of Glaucous-winged Gulls in British Columbia. J. Field Ornithol. 57: 22-33.

Verbeek, N. A. M. 1993. Glaucous-winged Gull (Larus glaucescens). In The birds of North America, No. 59 (A. Poole and F. Gill, eds.). Acad. of Nat. Sci., Philadelphia, and Am. Ornithol. Union, Washington, D.C.

Verbeek, N., and P. Hendricks. 1994. American Pipit (Anthus rubescens). In The birds of North America, No. 25 (A. Poole and F. Gill, eds). Acad. of Nat. Sci., Philadelphia, and Am. Ornithol. Union, Washington, D.C.

Vermeer, K. 1963. The breeding ecology of the Glaucous-winged Gull (Larus glaucescens) on Mandarte Island, British Columbia. Occas. Papers of the B.C. Provincial Mus. 13: 1-104.

Vermeer, K. 1970. Breeding biology of California and Ring-billed gulls. The Queen's Printer for Canada, Ottawa.

Vermeer, K. 1979. Nesting requirements, food and breeding distribution of Rhinoceros Auklets, Cerorhinca monocerata and Tufted Puffins Lunda cirrhata. Ardea 67: 101-110.

Vermeer, K. 1981. The importance of plankton to Cassin's Auklets during breeding. J. Plankton Res. 3: 315-329.

Vermeer, K. 1982. Comparisons of diet of the Glaucous-winged Gull on the east and west coasts of Vancouver Island. Murrelet 63: 80-85.

Vermeer, K., and K. Devito. 1988. The importance of Paracallisoma coecus and myctophid fishes to nesting storm-petrels in the Queen Charlotte Islands, British Columbia. J. Plankton Res. 10: 63-75.

Vermeer, K., K. Devito, and L. Rankin. 1988. Comparison of nesting biology of Fork-Tailed and Leach's Storm-Petrels. Colonial Waterbirds 11: 46-57.

Vermeer, K. S., J. D. Fulton, and S. G. Sealy. 1985. Differential use of zooplankton prey by Ancient Murrelets and Cassin's Auklets in the Queen Charlotte Islands. J. Plankton Res. 7: 443-459.

Vermeer, K., and D. B. Irons. 1991. The Glaucous-winged Gull on the Pacific Coast of North America. Proc. 20th Intnatl. Ornithol. Congress: 2378-2383.

Vermeer, K., K. H. Morgan, G. E. J. Smith, and R. Hay. 1989. Fall distribution of pelagic birds over the shelf of southwest Vancouver Island. Colonial Waterbirds 12: 207-214.

Vermeer, K., S. Sealy, and G. Sanger. 1987. Feeding ecology of the Alcidae in the eastern North Pacific. Pp. 189-227 in Seabirds: feeding ecology and role in marine systems (J. P. Croxall, ed.). Cambridge Univ. Press.

Vermeer, K., M. Bentley, and K. H. Morgan. 1994. Comparison of the waterbird populations of the Chemainus, Cowichan, and Nanaimo river estuaries. Pp. 44-56 in The abundance and distribution of estuarine birds in the Strait of Georgia, British Columbia (R. W. Butler, and K. Vermeer, eds.). Occas. Paper 83, Canadian Wildl. Serv., Ottawa.

Verner, J. 1963. Song rates and polygamy in the Long-billed Marsh Wren. Proc. Internatl. Ornithol. Congress 13: 299-307.

Verner, J. 1964. Evolution of polygamy in the Long-billed Marsh Wren. Evolution. 18: 252-261.

Verner, J. 1965a. Breeding biology of the Long-billed Marsh Wren. Condor 67: 6-30.

Verner, J. 1965b. Northern limit of the Acorn Woodpecker. Condor 67: 265.

Verner, J. 1976. Complex song repertoire of male Long-billed Marsh Wrens in eastern Washington. Living Bird 14: 263-300.

Verner, J. 1994. Current management situation: Boreal Owls. Pp. 88-91 in Flammulated, Boreal, and Great Gray Owls in the United States: a technical conservation assessment (G. D. Hayward and J. Verner, eds.). U.S. Dept. Int., Gen. Tech. Rep. RM-253, Ft. Collins, CO.

Verner, J., E. C. Beedy, S. L. Granholm, L. V. Ritter, and E. F. Toth. 1980. Birds. Pp. 75-319 in California wildlife and their habitat: western Sierra Nevada (J. Verner and A. S. Boss, eds.). U.S. Dept. Agric., For. Serv. Gen. Tech. Rept. PSW-37. Berkeley, CA.

Verner, J., and A. S. Boss, Eds. 1980. California wildlife and their habitats: western Sierra Nevada. U.S. Dept. Agric., For. Serv. Gen. Tech. Rep. PSW-GTR 37. Berkeley, CA.

Verner, J., and G. H. Engelsen. 1970. Territories, multiple nest building, and polygyny in the Long-billed Marsh Wren. Auk 87: 557-567.

Verner, J., R. J. Gutiérrez, and G. I. Gould, Jr. 1992. The California Spotted Owl: general biology and ecological relations. Pp. 55-78 in The California Spotted Owl: a technical assessment of its current status (J. Verner, K. S. McKelvey, B. R. Noon, R. J. Gutiérrez, G. I. Gould, Jr., and T. W. Beck, eds.). U.S. Dept. Agric., For. Serv. Gen. Tech. Rep. PSW-GTR-133.

Verner, J., and M. F. Willson. 1969. Mating systems, sexual dimorphism, and the role of male North American birds in the nesting cycle. Ornithol. Monogr. 9: 1-76.

Vickery, P. D. 1996. Grasshopper Sparrow (Ammodrammus savannarum). In The birds of North America, No. 239 (A. Poole and F. Gill, eds.). Acad. of Nat. Sci., Philadelphia, and Am. Ornithol. Union, Washington, D.C.

Vickery, P. D., M. L. Hunter, Jr., and S. M. Melvin. 1994. Effects of habitat-area on the distribution of grassland birds in Maine. Cons. Biol. 8: 1087-1097.

Victor, D. 1997. Snowy Owl reports in Cascadia, winter 1996-97. URL = http://www.scn.org/earth/tweeters/snowy.html Accessed 20 Sep 2002.

Villard, P. 1994. Foraging behavior of Black-backed and Three-toed woodpeckers during spring and summer in a Canadian boreal forest. Can. J. Zool. 72: 1957–1959.

Vinicombe, K. 1983. Identification pitfalls and assessment problems: Buff-breasted Sandpiper Tryngites subruficollis. Brit. Birds 76: 203-206.

Vos, D. K., D. A. Ryder, and W. D. Graul. 1985. Response of breeding Great Blue Herons to human disturbances in northcentral Colorado. Colonial Waterbirds 8: 13-22.

Voth, E. 1963. A survey of the vertebrate animals of Mount Jefferson, Oregon. M.S. thesis, Oreg. State Univ., Corvallis.

Vroman, D. P. 1994. Where do chickadees get fur for their nests? Oreg. Birds 20: 122.

Vroman, D. P. Unpubl. ms. North-south movements of Purple Finch (Carpodacus purpureus) banded or recaptured in Oregon.

Wagner, J. L. 1981. Seasonal change in guild structure: oak woodland insectivorous birds. Ecology 62: 973-981.

Wahl, T. R. 1975. Seabirds in Washington's offshore zone. West. Birds 6: 117-134.

Wahl, T. R. 1977. Notes on behavior of California Gulls and South Polar Skuas off the Washington coast. Murrelet 58: 47-49.

Wahl, T. R. 1984. Observations on the diving behavior of the Northern Fulmar. West. Birds 15: 131-133.

Wahl, T. R. 1986. Notes on the feeding behavior of Buller's Shearwater. West. Birds 17: 45-47.

Wahl, T. R., D. G. Ainley, A. H. Benedict, and A. R. DeGange. 1989. Associations between seabirds and water-masses in the northern Pacific Ocean in summer. Marine Biol. 103: 1-11.

Wahl, T. R., K. H. Morgen, and K. Vermeer. 1993. Seabird distribution off British Columbia and Washington. Pp. 39-47 in The status, ecology, and conservation of marine birds of the North Pacific. (K. Vermeer, K. T. Briggs, K. H. Morgan, and D. Siegel-Causey, eds.). Can. Wildl. Serv., Ottawa.

Wahl, T. R., S. M. Speich, D. A. Manuwal, K. V. Hirsch, and C. Miller. 1981. Marine bird populations of the Strait of Juan de Fuca, Strait of Georgia, and adjacent waters in 1978 and 1979. U.S. Environ. Protection Agency. DOC/EPAA Interagency Energy/Environ. R&D Prog. Rep. EPA 600/7-81-156. Washington, D.C.

Wahl, T., and B. Tweit. 2000a. Seabird abundances off Washington, 1972-1998. West. Birds 31: 69-88.

Wahl, T., and B. Tweit. 2000b. Where do Pigeon Guillemots from California go for the winter? West. Birds 31: 203-206.

Walcheck, K. C. 1970. Nesting bird ecology of four plant communities in the Missouri River breaks, Montana. Wilson Bull. 82: 370-382.

Walker, A. 1934. Nuttall Poor-will on the Oregon coast. Condor 36: 178.

Walker, A. 1940. Pallid Horned Lark in the Oregon Coast Range. Murrelet 21: 48.

Walker, A. 1949. Townsend Solitaire in the Coast Range of Oregon. Condor 51: 190.

Walker, A. 1955. Unusual bird records for western Oregon. Murrelet 36: 29.

Walker, A. 1960. The Rusty Blackbird and Dickcissel in Oregon. Condor 62: 140-141.

Walker, A. 1972. The Least Tern in Oregon. Murrelet 53: 52.

Walker, K. 1952. Northward expansion of range of the Acorn Woodpecker in Oregon. Condor 54: 315.

Walker, B. L. 2000a. The distribution, abundance, breeding status, and identification of the Timberline Sparrow (Spizella [breweri] taverneri) in Glacier National Park, 1998-1999. Annual res. rep. to Natl. Park Serv. Glacier Natl. Park, West Glacier, MT.

Walker, B. L. 2000b. The structure, use, and function of song categories in Brewer's Sparrows (Spizella breweri). M.S. thesis, Univ. of Montana. Missoula, MT.

Walkinshaw, L. H. 1939. The Yellow Rail in Michigan. Auk 56: 227-237.

Wallace, E. A. H., and G. E. Wallace. 1998. Brandt's Cormorant (Phalacrocorax penicillatus). In The birds of North America, No. 362 (A. Poole and F. Gill, eds.). The Birds of N. Am., Inc., Philadelphia, PA.

Wallace, W. M. 1961. Scaled Petrel in Oregon. Condor 63: 417.

Wallestad, R. O. 1975. Life history and habitat requirements of Sage Grouse in central Montana. Game Manage. Div., Mont. Dept. Fish and Game.

Walter, H. 2000. Ecology of the Chukar in eastern Oregon. M.S. thesis, Univ. of Idaho, Moscow.

Walton, B. J., C. G. Thelander, and D. L. Harlow. 1988. The status of peregrines nesting in California, Oregon, Washington, and Nevada. Pp. 95-104 in Peregrine Falcon populations - their management and recovery (T. J. Cade, J. H. Enderson, C. G. Thelander and C. M. White, eds.). Peregrine Fund, Inc., Boise, ID.

Wander, N. 1998. Oregon Field Ornithologists birding weekend in Curry County. Oreg. Birds 24: 88-89.

Wanless, S., and M. P. Harris. 1986. Time spent at the colony by male and female guillemots Uria aalge and razorbills Alca torda. Bird Study 33: 168-76.

Wanless, S., M. P. Harris, and S. P. R. Greenstreet. 1998. Summer sand eel consumption by seabirds breeding in the Firth of Forth, south-east Scotland. J. Marine Sci.55: 1141-1151.

Ward, D., and J. N. M. Smith. 2000. Brown-headed Cowbird parasitism results in a sink population in Warbling Vireos. Auk 117: 337-344.

Warnock, N., and M. A. Bishop. 1998. Stopover ecology of migrant Western Sandpipers. Condor 100: 456-467.

Warnock, N., M. A. Bishop, and J. Y. Takekawa. 2002. Spring shorebird migration, Mexico to Alaska: final report 2002. Unpubl. Prog. Rep., Point Reyes Bird Observatory, Stinson Beach, CA, and U.S. Geological Survey, Vallejo, CA.

Warnock, N., and L. W. Oring. 1996. Nocturnal nest attendance of Killdeers: more than meets the eye. Auk 113: 566-569.

Warnock, N., G. W. Page, and L. E. Stenzel. 1995. Non-migratory movements of Dunlin on their California wintering grounds. Wilson Bull. 107: 131-139.

Warnock, N., and S. E. Schwarzbach. 1995. Incidental kill of Dunlin and

Killdeer by strychnine. J. Wildl. Disease 31: 566-569.

Warnock, N., and R. E. Gill, Jr. 1996. Dunlin (Calidris alpina). In The birds of North America, No. 203 (A. Poole and F. Gill, eds.). Acad. of Nat. Sci., Philadelphia, and Am. Ornithol. Union, Washington, D.C.

Warnock, N., S. M. Haig, and L. W. Oring. 1998. Monitoring species richness and abundance of shorebirds in the western Great Basin. Condor 100: 589-600.

Warnock, S. E., and J. Y. Takekawa. 1995. Habitat preferences of wintering shorebirds in a temporally changing environment: Western Sandpipers in the San Francisco Bay estuary. Auk 112: 920-930.

Warnock, S. E., and J. Y. Takekawa. 1996. Wintering site fidelity and movement patterns of Western Sandpipers Calidris mauri in the San Francisco Bay estuary. Ibis 138: 160-167.

Watanuki, Y. 1985. Food of breeding Leach's Storm-Petrel Oceanodroma leucorhoa. Auk 102: 884-887.

Waterhouse, F. L. 1998. Habitat of Winter Wrens in riparian and upland areas of coastal forests. M.S. thesis, Simon Fraser Univ., Burnaby, B.C.

Watkins, W. 1988. Population density and habitat use by Red-necked Grebes on Upper Klamath Lake, Klamath County, Oregon. Oreg. Dept. Fish and Wildl., Nongame Wildl. Prog. Tech. Rep. 88-3-04.

Watson, C. 1979a. Highlights from the field notes - late March through early July, 1979. Oreg. Birds 5(3): 12-19.

Watson, C. 1979b. Highlights from the field notes: summer 1979. Oreg. Birds 5(5): 14-18.

Watson, C. 1979c. Oregon field notes summary: January 1 - March 31, 1979. Oreg. Birds 5(2): 14-19.

Watson, C. 1980a. Highlights from Oregon field notes: fall 1979. Oreg. Birds 6: 46-52.

Watson, C. 1980b. Highlights from Oregon field notes: spring 1980. Oreg. Birds 6(3): 123-128.

Watson, C. 1980c. Highlights from Oregon field notes, winter 1980. Oreg. Birds 6(2): 104-111.

Watson, C. 1981a. Highlights from the field notes: fall 1980. Oreg. Birds 7(1): 38-44.

Watson, C. 1981b. Highlights from the fieldnotes: late spring-fall 1981. Oreg. Birds 7(3): 114-125.

Watson, C. 1981c. Highlights from the field notes: winter/early spring 1981. Oreg. Birds 7(2): 68-74.

Watson, C. H. 1982. Index to Oregon bird reports in Audubon Field Notes and American Birds 1947-1981. Oreg. Field Ornithol. Spec. Publ., 3. Eugene, OR.

Watson, C. 1983. Oregon Bird Records Committee report: June 1982 – June 1983. Oreg. Birds 9(2): 55.

Watson, C. 1984. Oregon Bird Records Committee report: July 1983-July 1984. Oreg Birds 10(2): 51-55.

Watson, C. 1987. Correction to two published records of Oregon birds. Oreg. Birds 13: 436.

Watson, C. 1988. Changes in the checklist of the birds of Oregon. Oreg. Birds 14: 173-192.

Watson, C. 1989. The records of the Oregon Bird Records Committee. Pp. 37-145 in Rare birds of Oregon (O. Schmidt, ed.). Oreg. Field Ornithol. Spec. Pub. 5. Eugene, OR.

Watson, J. W. 1986. Range use by wintering Rough-legged Hawks in southeastern Idaho. Condor 88: 256-258.

Watson, J. W., and R. G. Anthony. 1986. Ecology of Bald Eagles in the Tongue Point area, lower Columbia River. Final Rep., Oreg. Coop. Wildl. Res. Unit, Oreg. State Univ., Corvallis, OR.

Watson, J. W., M. G. Garrett, and R. G. Anthony. 1991. Foraging ecology of Bald Eagles in the Columbia River estuary. J. Wildl. Manage. 55: 492-499.

Watson, J. W., and D. J. Pierce. 1998. Ecology of Bald Eagles in western Washington with an emphasis on the effects of human activity. Final Rep., Wash. Dept. of Fish and Wildl., Olympia, WA.

Watt, D. J., and E. J. Willoughby. 1999. Lesser Goldfinch (Carduelis psaltria). In The birds of North America, No. 392 (A. Poole and F. Gill, eds.). The Birds of N. Am., Inc., Philadelphia, PA.

Weatherhead, P. J., S. G. Sealy, and R. M. R. Barclay. 1985. Risks of clustering in thermally stressed swallows. Condor 87: 443-444.

Weathers, W. W. 1983. Birds of southern California's Deep Canyon. Univ. of Calif. Press, Berkeley.

Weaver, H., and W. L. Haskell. 1967. Some fall foods of Nevada Chukar Partridge. J. Wildl. Manage. 31: 582-584.

Weaver, R. L., and F. H. West. 1943. Notes on the nesting of the Pine Siskin. Auk 60: 492-504.

Webb, B. E., and J. A. Conry. 1979. A Sharp-tailed Sandpiper in Colorado,

with notes on plumage and behavior. West. Birds 10: 86-91.

Weber, J. W. 1985. First specimen record of the Short-billed Dowitcher from eastern Washington; subspecific identification of Idaho specimens. Murrelet 66: 31-34.

Weber, J. W., and E. J. Larrison. 1977. Birds of southeastern Washington. Univ. Press Idaho, Moscow.

Weber, W. 2000a. 13 June online posting to Oregon Birders Online (OBOL).

Weber, W. 2000b. Pacific-slope Flycatcher identification. Electronic mail message to Oregon Birders On-Line listserver. 19 May 2000. URL: http://osu.orst.edu/pubs/birds/obolnts/spec100.htm

Webster, H. M. 1976. The Prairie Falcon. Pp. 129-167 in North American falconry and hunting hawks (F. L. Beebe and H. M. Webster, eds.). World Press, Denver, CO.

Webster, J. D. 1941. The breeding of the Black Oystercatcher. Wilson Bull. 53: 141-156.

Webster, J. D. 1983. A new subspecies of Fox Sparrow from Alaska. Proc. of Biol. Soc. of Wash. 96: 664-668.

Wege, M. L. 1984. Distribution and abundance of the Tule geese in California and southern Oregon. Wildfowl 35: 14-20.

Wehle, D. H. S. 1982. Food of adult and subadult Tufted and Horned puffins. Murrelet 63: 51-58.

Weidensaul, S. 1999. Living on the wind: across the hemisphere with migratory birds. North Point Press, New York.

Weikel, J. M. 1997. Habitat use by cavity-nesting birds in young thinned and unthinned Douglas-fir forests of western Oregon. M.S. thesis, Oreg. State Univ., Corvallis.

Weikel, J. M. Unpubl. data. Nest characteristics of cavity-nesting birds in young (35- to 50-year-old) stands of the Northern Coast Range. Pacific Wildl. Res., Corvallis, OR.

Weikel, J. M., and J. P. Hayes. 1999. Foraging ecology of cavity-nesting birds in young forests of the northern Coast Range of Oregon. Condor 101: 58-66.

Weir, R. D., and A. M. Lein. 1989. Snowy Owl: hinterland who's who. Can. Wildl. Serv. Ottawa.

Weller, M. 1961. Breeding biology of the Least Bittern. Wilson. Bull. 73: 11-35.

Wellham, C. V. J. 1987. Diet and foraging behavior of Ring-billed Gulls breeding at Dog Lake,

Manitoba. Wilson Bull. 99: 233-239.

Wellicome, T. I., G. L. Holroyd, K. Scalise, and E. R. Wiltse. 1997. The effects of predator exclusion and food supplementation on Burrowing Owl (Speotyto cunicularia) population change in Saskatchewan. Pp. 487-497 in Biology and conservation of owls in the northern hemisphere (J. R. Duncan, D. H. Johnson, and T. H. Nicholls, eds.). U.S. Dept. Agric., For. Serv. Gen. Tech. Rep. NC-190. St. Paul, MN.

Wells, J. V., K. V. Rosenberg, D. L. Tessaglia, and A. A. Dhondt. 1996. Population cycles in the Varied Thrush (Ixoreus naevius). Can. J. Zool. 74: 2062-2069.

Welter, W. A. 1935. The natural history of the Long-billed Marsh Wren. Wilson Bull. 47: 3-34.

Wenink, P. W., and A. J. Baker. 1996. Mitochondrial DNA lineages in composite flocks of migratory and wintering Dunlins (Calidris alpina). Auk 113: 744-756.

Wenink, P. W., A. J. Baker, and M. G. J. Tilanus. 1993. Hypervariable control-region sequences reveal global population structuring in a long-distance migrant shorebird, the Dunlin (Calidris alpina). Proc. Natl. Acad. Sci. U.S.A. 90: 94-98.

Wennerberg, L. 2001. Breeding origin and migration pattern of Dunlin (Calidris alpina) revealed by mitochondrial DNA analysis. Mol. Ecol. 10: 1111-1120.

Werschkul, D., E. McMahon, M. Leitschuh, S. English, C. Skibinski, and G. Williamson. 1977. Observations on the reproductive ecology of the Great Blue Heron (Ardea herodias) in western Oregon. Murrelet 58: 7-12.

Weston, H. G. 1947. Breeding behavior of the Black-headed Grosbeak. Condor 49: 54-73.

Wetmore, A. 1920. A peculiar feeding habit of grebes. Condor 22: 18-20.

Wetmore, A. 1924. Food and economic relations of North American grebes. U.S. Dept. Agric. Bull. 1196.

Wetmore, A. 1925. Food of American phalaropes, avocets, and stilts. U.S. Dept. Agric. Bull. 1359.

Wetmore, A. 1943. The birds of southern Veracruz, Mexico. Proc. U.S. Natl. Mus. 93: 215-340.

Wetzel, D. J. 1996. Brant use of Yaquina estuary, Lincoln County, Oregon in the spring of 1976. J. Oreg. Ornithol. 6: 715-722.

Weydemeyer, W. 1927. Some new birds from western Montana. Condor 29: 159.

Weyerhaeuser Company. 1992. Doak Mountain management plan for forest health and eagle habitat. Unpubl. rep., Weyerhaeuser Co., Tacoma, WA.

Wheeler, B. K., and W. S. Clark. 1995. A photographic guide to North American raptors. Academic Press, London.

Wheeler, R. 1940. Nesting habits of the Leucosticte. Condor 42: 133-139.

Wheeler, R. J. 1965. Pioneering of Blue-winged Teal in California, Oregon, Washington and British Columbia. Murrelet 46: 40-42.

Wheelwright, N. T. 1986. The diet of American Robins: an analysis of U.S. Biological Survey records. Auk 103: 710–725.

Wheelwright, N. T., and J. D. Rising. 1993. Savannah Sparrow (Passerculus sandwichensis). In The birds of North America, No. 45 (A. Poole and F. Gill, eds.). Acad. of Nat. Sci., Philadelphia, and Am. Ornithol. Union, Washington, D.C.

Whelton, B. D. 1989. Distribution of the Boreal Owl in eastern Washington and Oregon. Condor 91: 712-716.

White, C. M. 1968. Diagnosis and relationships of the North American tundra-inhabiting Peregrine Falcons. Auk 85: 179-191.

White, C. M. 1994. Population trends and current status of selected western raptors. Stud. in Avian Biol. 15: 161-172.

White, C. M., and D. A. Boyce, Jr. 1988. An overview of Peregrine Falcon subspecies. Pp. 789-810 in Peregrine Falcon populations: their management and recovery (T. J. Cade, J. H. Enderson, C. G. Thelander, and C. M. White, eds.). Peregrine Fund, Inc., Boise, ID.

White, C. M., and T. L. Thurow. 1985. Reproduction of Ferruginous Hawks exposed to controlled disturbance. Condor 87: 14-22.

White, R. 1983. Distribution and habitat preference of the Upland Sandpiper (Bartramia longicauda) in Wisconsin. Am. Birds 37: 16-22.

Whitmore, R. C. 1981. Structural characteristics of Grasshopper Sparrow habitat. J. Wildl. Manage. 45: 811-814.

Whitney, B., and K. Kaufman. 1985a. The Empidonax challenge, Part I: introduction. Birding 17: 151-158.

Whitney, B., and K. Kaufman. 1985b. The Empidonax challenge, Part II: Least, Hammond's, and Dusky flycatchers. Birding 17: 277-287.

Whittow, G. C. 1993a. Black-footed Albatross (Diomedea nigripes). In The birds of North America, No. 65 (A. Poole and F. Gill, eds.). Acad. of Nat. Sci., Philadelphia, and Am. Ornithol. Union, Washington, D.C.

Whittow, G. C. 1993b. Laysan Albatross (Diomedea immutabilis). In The birds of North America, No. 66 (A. Poole and F. Gill, eds.). Acad. of Nat. Sci., Philadelphia, and Am. Ornithol. Union, Washington, D.C.

Widrlechner, M. P., and S. K. Dragula. 1984. Relation of cone-crop size to irruptions of four seed-eating birds in California. Am. Birds 38: 840-846.

Wieland, R. 2000. 4 Jul Online posting to Oregon Birders Online (OBOL).

Wiens, J. A. 1969. An approach to the study of ecological relationships among grassland birds. Ornithol. Monogr. 8.

Wiens, J. A. 1973. Interterritorial variation in Grasshopper and Savannah sparrows. Ecology 54: 877-884.

Wiens, J. A. 1982. Song pattern variation in the Sage Sparrow (Amphispiza belli): dialects or epiphenomena? Auk 99: 208-229

Wiens, J. A., and R. A. Nussbaum. 1975. Model estimation of energy flow in northwestern coniferous forest bird communities. Ecology 56: 547-561.

Wiens, J. A., and J. T. Rotenberry. 1979. Diet niche relationships among North American grassland and shrubsteppe birds. Oecologia 42: 253-292.

Wiens, J. A., and J. T. Rotenberry. 1981. Habitat associations and community structure of birds in shrubsteppe environments. Ecol. Monogr. 51: 21-41

Wiens, J. A., and J. T. Rotenberry. 1985. Response of breeding passerine birds to rangeland alteration in a North American shrubsteppe locality. J. of Appl. Ecol. 22: 655-668.

Wiens, J. A., J. T. Rotenberry, and B. Van Horne. 1985. Territory size variations in shrubsteppe birds. Auk 102: 500-505.

Wiens, J. A., and J. M. Scott. 1975. Model estimation of energy flow in Oregon coastal seabird populations. Condor 77: 439-452.

Wiens, J. A., B. Van Horne, and J. T. Rotenberry. 1987. Temporal and spatial variations in the behavior of shrubsteppe birds. Oecologia 73: 60-70.

Wilbur, S. R. 1973. The California Condor in the Pacific Northwest. Auk 90: 196-197.

Wilbur, S. R. 1978. Turkey Vulture eggshell thinning in California, Florida, and Texas. Wilson Bull. 90: 642-643.

Wilbur, S. R., and C. F. Yocum. 1971. Unusual geese in the Pacific coast states. Murrelet 52: 16-19.

Wiley, J. W., and F. E. Lohrer. 1973. Additional records of non-fish prey taken by Ospreys. Wilson Bull. 85: 468-470.

Willard, D. E. 1976. Herons catch two fish in one strike. Auk 93: 391.

Willett, G. 1919. Bird notes from southeastern Oregon and northeastern California. Condor 21: 194-207.

Williams, G. C. 1953. Wilson's Phalaropes as commensals. Condor 55: 158.

Williams, J. M. 1996. Nashville Warbler (Vermivora ruficapilla). In The birds of North America, No. 205 (A. Poole and F. Gill, eds.). Acad. of Nat. Sci., Philadelphia, and Am. Ornithol. Union, Washington, D.C.

Williams, L. 1927. Notes on the Black Oystercatcher. Condor 29: 80-81.

Williams, L. 1952. Breeding behavior of the Brewer's Blackbird. Condor 54: 3-47.

Williams, L. 1958. Brewer's Blackbird. Pp. 302-334 in Life histories of North American blackbirds, orioles, tanagers, and allies. U.S. Natl. Mus. Bull. 211.

Williams, L. E., Jr. 1984. The voice and vocabulary of the Wild Turkey. Real Turkeys, Gainesville, FL.

Williams, M. L., R. L. Hothem, and H. M. Ohlendorf. 1989. Recruitment failure in American Avocets and Black-necked Stilts nesting at Kesterson Reservoir, California, 1984-1985. Condor 91: 797-802.

Williams, P. L., and W. D. Koening. 1980. Water dependence of birds in a temperate woodland. Auk 97: 339-350.

Williams, W. A. 1992. Changes in blood parameters, muscle myoglobin and muscle lactate dehydrogenase of the Common Murre Uria aalge during maturation. M.S. thesis, Univ. of Oregon, Eugene.

Williamson, F. S., and L. J. Peyton. 1963. Interbreeding of Glaucous-winged and Herring gulls in the Cook Inlet Region, Alaska. Condor 65: 24-28.

Willson, M. F. 1966. Breeding ecology of the Yellow-headed Blackbird. Ecol. Monogr. 36: 51-77.

Wilson, M. V., E. R. Alverson, D. L. Clark, R. H. Hayes, C. A. Ingersoll, and M. B. Naughton. 1995. The Willamette Valley natural areas network. Restoration and Manage. Notes 13: 26-28.

Wilson, S. W. 1978. Food size, food type, and foraging sites of Red-winged Blackbirds. Wilson Bull. 90: 511-520.

Wilson, U. W., and J. B. Atkinson. 1995. Black Brant winter and spring staging use at two Washington coastal areas in relation to eelgrass abundance. Condor 97: 91-98.

Wilson, U. W., and D. A. Manuwal. 1986. Breeding biology of the Rhinoceros Auklet in Washington. Condor 88: 256-261.

Wilson, V. T., and R. H. Norr. 1949. Great Basin-central Rocky Mountain region. Audubon Field Notes 3: 246-247.

Wilson, W. H. 1994. Western Sandpiper (Calidris mauri). In The birds of North America, No. 90 (A. Poole and F. Gill, eds.). Acad. of Nat. Sci., Philadelphia, and Am. Ornithol. Union, Washington, D.C.

Wilson, W. H., Jr. 1996. Palm Warbler (Dendroica palmarum). In The birds of North America, No. 238 (A. Poole and F. Gill, eds.). Acad. of Nat. Sci., Philadelphia, and Am. Ornithol. Union, Washington, D.C.

Winema National Forest. 1997. Birds of the Winema National Forest. U.S. For. Serv., Winema Natl. For., Klamath Falls.

Wing, L. 1943. Spread of the starling and English Sparrow. Auk 60: 74-87.

Winkler, D. 1996. California Gull (Larus californicus). In The birds of North America, No. 259 (A. Poole and F. Gill, eds.). Acad. of Nat. Sci., Philadelphia, and Am. Ornithol. Union, Washington, D.C.

Winkler, D. W., and W. D. Shuford. 1988. Changes in the numbers and locations of California Gulls nesting at Mono Lake, California, in the period 1863-1986. Colonial Waterbirds 11: 263-274.

Winkler, H., D. A. Christie, and D. Nurney. 1995. Woodpeckers: an identification guide to the woodpeckers of the world. Houghton Mifflin Company, Boston.

Winter, A. 1976. Davis Lake migration dates. SWOC Talk (Oreg. Birds) 2(5): 69-70.

Winters, T. Undated. Bird listing of Grant County, OR. Locally printed.

Wires, L. R., and F. J. Cuthbert. 2000. Trends in Caspian Tern numbers and distribution in North America: a review. Waterbirds 23: 388-404.

Wishart, R. A., and S. G. Sealy. 1980. Late summer time budget and feeding behavior of Marbled Godwits (Limosa fedoa) in southern Manitoba. Can. J. Zool. 58: 1277-1282.

Witmer, M. C., D. J. Mountjoy, and L. Elliot. 1997. Cedar Waxwing (Bombycilla cedrorum). In The birds of North American, No. 309 (A. Poole and F. Gill, eds.). Acad. of Nat. Sci., Philadelphia, and Am. Ornithol. Union, Washington, D.C.

Witt, J. W. 1996. Long-term population monitoring of Osprey along the Umpqua River in western Oregon. J. Raptor Res. 30: 62-69.

Witt, J. W. 1998. Notes on activity and characteristics of an inland Marbled Murrelet nest site in Douglas County, Oregon. Northwest. Nat. 79: 27-32.

Wittenberger, J. F. 1978. The breeding biology of an isolated Bobolink population in Oregon. Condor 80: 355-371.

Wittenberger, J. F. 1980. Feeding of secondary nestlings by polygynous male Bobolinks in Oregon. Wilson Bull. 92: 330-340.

Wittenberger, J. F. 1982. Factors affecting how male and female Bobolinks apportion parental investments. Condor 84: 22-39.

Woffinden, N. D., and J. R. Murphy. 1983. Ferruginous Hawk nest site selection. J. Wildl. Manage. 47: 216-219.

Wolf, B. O. 1997. Black Phoebe (Sayornis nigricans). In The birds of North America, No. 268 (A. Poole and F. Gill, eds.). Acad. of Nat. Sci., Philadelphia, and Am. Ornithol. Union, Washington, D.C.

Wolf, B. O., and S. L. Jones. 1989. Great Blue Heron deaths caused by predation on Pacific lamprey. Condor 91: 482-484.

Wolfe, D. F. G. 1996. Opportunistic winter water acquisition by Pine Grosbeaks. Wilson Bull. 108: 186-187.

Wood, C. C. 1985. Food-searching behaviour of the Common Merganser (Mergus merganser) II: choice of foraging location. Can. J. Zool. 63: 1271-1279.

Wood, C. C. 1987. Predation of juvenile Pacific salmon by the Common Merganser (Mergus merganser) on eastern Vancouver Island, I: predation during the seaward migration. Can. J. Fish. and Aquatic Sci. 44: 941-949.

Wood, C. C., and C. M. Hand. 1985. Food-searching behaviour of the Common Merganser (Mergus merganser) I: functional responses to prey and predator density. Can. J. Zool. 63: 1260-1270.

Woodbridge, B., P. Detrich, and P. H. Bloom. 1988. Territory fidelity and habitat use by nesting Northern Goshawks: implications for management. Unpubl. rep., Klamath Natl. For., Macdoel, CA.

Woodbury, A. M., W. H. Behle, and J. W. Sugden. 1946. Color-banding California Gulls at Great Salt Lake. Utah. Bull. Univ. Utah 37, Biol. Ser. 10: 1-15.

Woodbury, A. M., and H. Knight. 1951. Results of the pacific gull color-banding project. Condor 53: 57-77.

Woodcock, A. R. 1902. Annotated list of the birds of Oregon. Oreg. Agric. Exp. Station Bull. 68. Corvallis, OR.

Woodruff, K. 1982. Past, present and future of Sharp-tailed Grouse in Baker County, Oregon. Unpubl. rep., Bur. Land Manage., Baker, OR.

Woolington, D. W., P. F. Springer, and D. R. Yparraguirre. 1979. Migration and wintering distribution of Aleutian Canada Geese. Pp. 299-309 in Management and biology of Pacific Flyway geese (R. L. Jarvis and J. C. Bartonek, eds.). Oreg. State Univ. Book Stores, Inc., Corvallis.

Wootton, J. T. 1996. Purple Finch (Carpodacus purpureus). In The birds of North America, No. 208 (A. Poole and F. Gill, eds.). Acad. of Nat. Sci., Philadelphia, and Am. Ornithol. Union, Washington, D.C.

Wright, A. L., and G. D. Hayward. 1998. Barred Owl range expansion into the central Idaho wilderness. J. Raptor Res. 32: 77-81.

Wright, A. L., G. D. Hayward, and S. M. Matsuoka. 1998. Townsend's Warbler (Dendroica townsendi). In The birds of North America, No. 333 (A. Poole and F. Gill, eds.). The Birds of N. Am., Inc., Philadelphia, PA.

Wright, J. M. 1997. Olive-sided Flycatchers in central Alaska, 1994-1996. Alaska Dept. Fish and Game. Fed. Aid in Wildl. Restoration, Final Rep. Proj. SE-3-4. Juneau.

Wright, K. G., and P. V. Clarkson. 1998. Harlequin Duck moulting ecology and banding synopsis in the Strait of Georgia, British Columbia: 1997 progress report. Unpubl.

rep., Harlequin Conserv. Soc., West Vancouver, B.C.

Wright, K. K. 1997. A multi-trophic level examination of recreational impacts on a National Wild and Scenic River. M.S. thesis, Oreg. State Univ., Corvallis.

Wright, K. K., H. Bruner, J. L. Li, R. Jarvis, and S. Dowlan. 2000. The distribution, phenology, and prey of Harlequin Ducks, Histrionicus histrionicus, in a Cascade Mountain stream, Oregon. Can. Field-Nat. 14: 1-11.

Wright, S. K., D. D. Roby, and R. G. Anthony. 2002. California Brown Pelicans nesting in the Pacific Northwest: potential for a major northward expansion in breeding range [abstract]. 2002 Pacific Seabird Group annual meeting. Santa Barbara, CA.

Wunz, G. A. 1992. Wild Turkeys outside their historic range. Pp. 361-384 in The Wild Turkey: biology and management (J. G. Dickson, ed.). Stackpole Books, Harrisburg, PA.

Wyatt, B. 1963. A Short-tailed Albatross sighted off the Oregon Coast. Condor 65: 163.

Yasukawa, K., and W. A. Searcy. 1995. Red-winged Blackbird (Agelaius phoeniceus). In The birds of North America, No. 184 (A. Poole and F. Gill, eds.). Acad. of Nat. Sci., Philadelphia, and Am. Ornithol. Union, Washington, D.C.

Yates, M. 1999. Satellite and conventional telemetry study of American White Pelicans in northern Nevada. Great Basin Birds 2: 4-9.

Yocom, C. 1947. Notes on the behavior and abundance of the Black-footed Albatross in the Pacific waters off the continental North American shores. Auk 64: 507-523.

Yocum, C. F., and S. W. Harris. 1953. Food habits of Mountain Quail (Oreortyx picta) in eastern Washington. J. Wildl. Manage. 17: 204-207.

Yong, W., and F. R. Moore. 1990. Foot-quivering as a foraging maneuver among migrating Catharus thrushes. Wilson Bull. 102: 542-545.

Yosef, R. 1992. Territoriality, nutritional condition, and conservation in Loggerhead Shrikes (Lanius ludovicianus). Ph.D. diss., Ohio State Univ., Columbus, OH.

Yosef, R. 1996. Loggerhead Shrike (Lanius ludovicianus). In The birds of North America, No. 231 (A.

Poole and F. Gill, eds.). Acad. of Nat. Sci., Philadelphia, PA, and Am. Ornithol. Union, Washington, D.C.

Young, J. R., C. E. Braun, S. J. Oyler-McCance, J. W. Hupp, and T. W. Quinn. 2000. A new species of Sage Grouse (Phasianidae: Centrocercus) from southwestern Colorado. Wilson Bull. 112: 445-453.

Young, L. S., K. A. Engel, and A. Brody. 1986. Implications of communal roosting by Common Ravens and operation and maintenance of the Malin to Midpoint 500 kV transmission line. Res. Proj. Annual Rep. 1986, Snake River Birds of Prey.

Younk, J. V., and M. J. Bechard. 1994. Breeding biology of the Northern Goshawk in high-elevation aspen forests of northern Nevada. Stud. in Avian Biol. 16: 119-121.

Yunick, R. P. 1983. Winter site fidelity of some northern finches (Fringillidae). J. Field Ornithol. 54: 254-258.

Zarnowitz, J. E., and D. A. Manuwal. 1985. The effects of forest management on cavity-nesting birds in northwestern Washington. J. Wildl. Manage. 49: 255-263.

Zeillemaker, F. 2000. First Northern Mockingbird nest for Oregon. Oreg. Birds 26: 156-156.

Zeiner, D. C., W. F. Laudenslayer, Jr., K. E. Mayer, and M. White, Eds. 1990. California's wildlife, Vol. II: birds. Calif. Dept. of Fish and Game, Sacramento, CA.

Zimmerman, D. A. 1973. Range expansion of Anna's Hummingbird. Am. Birds 27: 27-835.

Zimmerman, J. L. 1993. The birds of Konza: the avian ecology of the tallgrass prairie. Univ. of Kansas Press, Lawrence.

Zink, R. 1986. Patterns and evolutionary significance of geographic variation in the schistacea group of the Fox Sparrow (Passerella iliaca). Am. Ornithol. Union Monogr. 40.

Zink, R. 1994. The geography of mitochondrial DNA variation, population structure, hybridization, and species limits in the Fox Sparrow (Passerella iliaca). Evolution 48: 96-111.

Zink, R. M., and D. L. Dittmann. 1993. Population structure and gene flow in the Chipping Sparrow and a hypothesis for evolution in the genus Spizella. Wilson Bull. 105: 399-413.

Zink, R. M., D. F. Lott, and D. W. Anderson. 1987. Genetic variation, population structure, and evolution of California Quail. Condor 89: 395-405.

Zink, R. M., S. Rohwer, A. V. Andreev, and D. L. Dittmann. 1995. Trans-Beringia comparisons of mitochondrial DNA differentiation in birds. Condor 97: 639-649.

Zwarts, L., and A.-M. Blomert. 1992. Why Knot Calidris canutus take medium-size Macoma balthica when six prey species are available. Mar. Ecol. Prog. Ser. 83: 113-128.

Zwickel, F. C. 1992. Blue Grouse (Dendragapus obscurus). In The birds of North America, No. 15 (A. Poole, P. Stettenheim, and F. Gill, eds.). Acad. of Nat. Sci., Philadelphia, and Am. Ornithol. Union, Washington, D.C.

## Personal Communications

Adamus, Paul. See author biographies.

Alexander, John. Klamath Bird Observatory, Ashland, OR.

Allen, Dave. Falconer, Pleasant Hill, OR.

Altman, Bob. See author biographies

Anderson, David. Albatross project coordinator. Associate professor, Wake Forest University, NC.

Anderson, Dan. Dept. of Wildlife, Fish and Conservation Biology, Univ. of Calif., Davis.

Anderson, Jim. Observer, Sisters, OR (formerly of Sunriver, OR).

Anderson, Ralph. Senior Biological Technician, Wallowa-Whitman National Forest, LaGrande, Oregon.

Arnold, Vjera. Observer, Springfield, OR.

Baccus, Don. Photographer and Software Engineer, Portland, OR.

Bales, Bradley. Game Bird Program Manager, Oreg. Dept. Fish and Wildl., Portland, OR.

Banks, Richard C. Taxonomist and chair of the AOU checklist committee, U.S. Natl. Museum, Washington, D C.

Barrett, Norman. Wildlife Biologist, U.S. Forest Service, Shady Cove, OR.

Bayer, Range D. Editor, J. Oregon Ornithol., Lincoln Co., OR.

Beall, Jock. Wildlife Biologist, William L. Finley NWR.

Bell, J. Richard (Dick). Observer, Corvallis, OR

Bettinger, Kelly. See author biographies.

Blackburn, Ian. Rare and Endangered Species Biologist, B.C. Ministry of Water, Land, and Air Protection, Vancouver, B.C.

Bohler, Jeff. District Wildlife Biologist, Diamond Lake Ranger District, Oregon.

Bollinger, Karen. Biological Technician, U.S. Fish and Wildl. Serv., Anchorage, AK.

Bond, Gormon M. Retired Research Assistant to the Secretary of the Smithsonian Inst., Washington, D.C.

Booker, Jim. 1998. Biologist, Big Sur Ornithology Lab, Big Sur, CA.

Bortner, Brad. Migratory Bird Coordinator, Region 1, U.S. Fish & Wildlife Service, Portland, OR.

Bray, Tanya. Observer, Corvallis, OR.

Brazelton, Mark. Observer, Jackson Co., OR.

Brent, Jeff. Wildlife Biologist and Northwest District Supervisor, U.S. Dept. Agric, Wildl. Services Prog.

Brown, Mark. Habitat construction crewleader, Arizona Game and Fish Dept., Flagstaff, AZ.

Bruce, Charles. Wildlife Diversity Biologist, Oreg. Dept. Fish and Wildl., Corvallis and Portland.

Brumitt, Clint. Observer, Medford, OR.

Buchanan, Joseph. See author biographies.

Buckmaster, Aimee. Observer, Grants Pass, OR.

Budeau, Dave A. See author biographies.

Bull, Evelyn. See author biographies.

Byford, Ken. Forest Biologist, Willamette National Forest, US Forest Service.

Byrne, Mike. M.S. Student, Dept. Fish. and Wildl., Oreg. State Univ., Corvallis, OR.

Cady, Wilson. Observer, Washougal, WA.

Cain, Lee. Aquatic biology instructor, Astoria, OR.

Carey, Chris. See author biographies.

Casler, Bruce R. Wildlife Biologist, Midway Island, Hawaiian Is. NWR.

Castelein, Kathy. See author biographies.

Castillo, William (Bill) J. Wildlife Biologist, Oreg. Dept. of Fish and Wildl., Springfield, OR.

Chancey, Fred. Observer, Eugene, OR.

Cheek, Rebecca. Observer, South Beach, OR.

Ciotti, Jorrie. Observer, Waldport, OR.

Clark, Al. Refuge Biologist, Julia Butler Hanson NWR, Cathlamet, WA.

Coggins, Victor L. See author biographies.

Collom, Tom. Wildlife Biologist, Oreg. Dept. Fish and Wildl., Klamath Falls, OR.

Combs, Barbara. See author biographies.

Conley, Frank. Observer, Joseph, OR.

Contreras, Alan L. See editor biographies.

Contreras, John. Observer, Grants Pass, OR.

Cooke, Fred. Retired professor and leader of the Behavioral Ecology Research Group, Dept. of Biological Sci., Simon Fraser Univ., Burnaby, B.C. Now lives in Norfolk, England.

Cooper, Romain. Observer, Cave Junction, OR.

Copeland, David. Observer, Salem, OR.

Corder, Craig. Observer, Hermiston, Umatilla Co., OR.

Corkran, Char. Founder, Northwest Ecological Research Institute, Portland, OR.

Cox, Kurt. Observer, Blue River, OR.

Crabtree, Tom. Observer, Bend, OR.

Craig, David. See author biographies.

Cromack, Angeline S. Former bluebird trail monitor. Corvallis, OR.

Danzenbaker, Jim. Shearwater Journeys. San Jose, CA.

Davis, Dick. District Wildlife Biologist, Willamette National Forest.

Denny, Mike. Field biological technician, U.S. Forest Service, Walla Walla, Washington.

Denny, MerryLynn. Observer, Walla Walla, WA.

DeVaurs, Walt. Wildlife Biologist, BLM, Carson City, NV.

Dewater, Joyce. Observer, Corvallis, OR.

Dewitt, Don. Observer, Eugene, Oregon.

Dillingham, Colin. See author biographies.

Dillon, Jeff. U.S. Fish and Wildlife Service, Portland, OR.

Dorsey, Geoff. Wildlife Biologist, U.S. Army Corps of Engineers, Portland, OR.

Dowdy, William (Bill) M. Grande Ronde Bird Club, LaGrande, OR.

Dowlan, Steve. See author biographies.

Egger, Mark. Observer, formerly of Eugene, OR, now living in Washington state.

Ellingson, Amy. Wildlife Biologist, Kingfisher Ecological, Inc., Corvallis, OR.

Ely, Craig. Wildlife Biologist, USGS, Anchorage, Alaska.

Erickson, Ray C. Retired U.S. Fish and Wildl. Service biologist, Salem, OR.

Evanich, Joe. Oregon birder. Deceased. Author of The Birder's Guide to Oregon, Birds of Northeast Oregon, and many articles and illustrations in Oregon Birds.

Evenden, F. G. Former graduate student at Oreg. State Univ. Former Executive Director of The Wildlife Society. Now deceased.

Evens, Jules. Wildlife Biologist, Avocet Research Associates, Point Reyes, CA.

Evered, Duncan. Manager, Malheur Field Station, Burns, OR.

Fairchild, Jim. Former wildlife field biologist. Philomath, OR.

Farrell, Terry. Wildlife Biologist, Oreg. Dept. Fish and Wildl., Roseburg, OR.

Faxon, Darrel. Observer, Coast Range of Lincoln Co., OR

Fenske, Dan. Observer and falconer, Harrisburg, OR.

Findholt, Scott. See author biographies.

Fish, LeRoy. See author biographies.

Fisher, Mark. Biologist, William L. Finley NWR.

Fix, David. Observer, Arcata, CA.

Flint, Beth. Wildlife Biologist, U.S. Fish and Wildl. Service, Honolulu, HI.

Forsman, Eric. See author biographies.

Freeman, Reid. Observer, Eugene, OR.

Frenzel, Richard W. Researcher for Oreg. Nat. Heritage Program, Sandy, OR.

Gallagher, Patrick. Observer, Salem, OR.

Garcelon, David K. President, Institute for Wildl. Res., Arcata, CA.

Gatchet, John. Observer, now of Calhoun, GA.

Gates, Chuck. Field Ornithologist, Prineville, OR.

Geier, Joel. Observer, Polk Co., Oregon.

Gerig, Roy. Observer, Salem, OR.

Gilligan, Jeff. Observer, Portland, OR.

Gillson, Greg. See author biographies.

Gleason, Barbara. Observer, Eugene, OR.

Gleason, Dan. Observer, Eugene, OR.

Gleason, Tom. Falconer, Olympia, WA.

Godfrey, Brian M. Observer, Corvallis, OR.

Goguen, Christopher. Professor, Univ. of Delaware, Newark, DE.

Gooding, Betty. Nest box monitor, Oreg. Dept. Fish and Wildl., Culver, OR.

Gordon, Steve. Observer, Eugene, OR.

Gray, William. Observer, Takilma, OR.

Graybill, Michael. Manager, South Slough National Estuarine Research Reserve, Charleston, OR.

Green, Greg. See author biographies.

Gregg, Michael A. Wildlife Biologist, Sheldon/Hart Mtn. Natl. Wildl. Refuge Complex, Lakeview, OR.

Gross, Wink. Observer, Portland, OR.

Hagar, Joan C. See author biographies.

Hainline, Jim. Wildlife Biologist, U.S. Fish and Wildl. Service, Tulelake, CA.

Hale, Dean. Observer, Bend, OR.

Harding, Jeff. Observer, Lebanon, OR.

Harding, Patricia. Observer, Lebanon, OR.

Harper, Jim. Biologist, Medford District, BLM, Medford, OR.

Harvey, Dwight. Biologist, U.S. Fish and Wildl. Serv., Sacramento, CA.

Haupt, Dave. Observer, Klamath Falls, OR.

Heath, Corey. Wildlife Biologist, Oreg. Dept. Fish and Wildl., Bend, OR.

Heinl, Steve. Long-time Oregon birder, Oregon Birds Field Notes editor. Currently living in Ketchikan, AK.

Heinze, Linda. Observer, Grants Pass, OR.

Helzer, Dave. Observer, Portland, OR.

Hemker, Tom. Statewide Upland Bird Coordinator, Idaho Dept. Fish and Game, Boise, ID.

Henny, Charles J. See author biographies.

Henze, Eric. Observer, Portland, OR.

Herlyn, Hendrik. Observer, Corvallis, OR.

Herziger, Caroline. See author biographies.

Hoffman, Wayne. Observer, Newport, OR.

Hohmann, Jan. Wildlife biologist and naturalist, Lostine, OR.

Holmes, Aaron. See author biographies.

Holt, Denver W. The Owl Research Inst., Missoula, MT.

Horvath, Eric. See author biographies.

Hoyer, Rich. Field ornithologist, Tucson, AZ.

Hwang, Diana. Biologist, U.S. Fish and Wildl. Serv., Portland, OR.

Irons, David. Birder, Eugene, OR.

Isaacs, Frank. See author biographies.

Ivey, Gary. See author biographies.

Jackman, Ron E. Wildlife Biologist, Predatory Bird Research Group, Univ. Calif., Santa Cruz., CA.

Janes, Stewart W. See author biographies.

Janzen, Tim. See author biographies.

Jaques, Deborah. Crescent Coastal Research, Astoria, OR.

Jarvis, Robert. See author biographies.

Jobanek, George (Chip). Observer and ornithological historian, Eugene, OR.

Johnson, David H. Wildlife biologist, Wash. Dept. Wildl., Olympia, WA.

Johnson, Eric M. Undergraduate student in Bioresource Research, Corvallis, OR.

Johnson, Jim. Observer, Portland, OR.

Johnson, Richard (Dick) E. Emeritus professor of ornithology, Washington State Univ., Pullman, WA.

Johnston, Pamela. Observer, Portland, OR.

Kaiser, James L. USGS Biological Resources Division, Forest and Rangeland Ecosystem Science Center, Corvallis, OR.

Kebbe, Chester E. Deceased, formerly with Oreg. Dept. Fish and Wildl., Portland, OR.

Keister, George. Wildlife Biologist, Oreg. Dept. Fish and Wildl., Baker City, OR.

Keller, Geoff. Cornell Laboratory of Ornithology, Coos Bay, OR.

Kemper, John D. Observer, Medford, OR.

Ketchum, Ron. Observer, Jacksonville, OR.

Kindschy, Robert R. Former District Biologist, BLM, Vale, OR.

Kirkpatrick, Doug. Observer, Medford, OR.

Kirsch, Mark. Wildlife Biologist, Oreg. Dept. Fish and Wildl., Pendleton, OR.

Knutsen, Doug. Observer, Salem, OR.

Kochert, Michael. Raptor Research Program, BLM, Boise, ID.

Kornfeld, Steve. Field Ornithologist, Bend, OR.

Korpi, Ray. See author biographies.

Kott, Barbara. Wildlife Biologist, Mt. Hood National Forest.

Kunzman, Lauri. Observer, Metolius River, OR.

Lafaive, Margaret. Observer, Portland, OR.

Lauten, David J. See author biographies.

Laws, Margaret (Meg). Wildlife Biologist, formerly of Malheur National Wildlife Refuge, now at USFWS Migratory Bird Permit Office, Anchorage, AK.

Lethaby, Nick. Observer, Goleta, CA.

Lindsay, Stephen. Observer, Coeur d'Alene, ID.

Littlefield, Carroll D. See author biographies.

Lorain, Doug. Author of wilderness books, most recently Backpacking Oregon. Beaverton, OR.

Lowe, Roy. Supervisory Wildlife Biologist, Oregon Coastal Refuges, U.S. Fish and Wildl. Service, Newport.

Lundsten, John. Observer, Salem, OR.

Lundsten, Sue. Wildlife Biologist, The Nature Conservancy, Portland, OR.

Lusthoff, Donna. Observer, Beaverton, OR.

MacDonald, Nancy. Observer, Prineville, OR.

Madigan, Richard L. Biologist, Oreg. Dept. Fish and Wildl., Summer L. WA, Summer L., OR.

Madsen, Sarah J. Wildlife Biologist, USDA Forest Serv., Regional Office, Portland, OR.

Maertz, Ronald. Observer, Glide, OR.

Maitreya. Observer, Fields, OR.

Mamone, Marion. Wildlife biologist, Rogue River NF.

Mariani, John. Field ornithologist, Santa Clara County, CA.

Marple, Esther. Observer,Vale, OR.

Marzluff, John. Associate professor in the Ecosystem Sciences Division, Dept. of Forest Resources, Univ. of Washington, Seattle, WA.

Massey, Barbara. Observer, Ashland, OR.

Mathewson, Worth. Outdoor writer, Amity, OR.

Maulding, Sylvia. Observer, Springfield, OR.

Mauser, Dave M. Wildlife Biologist, Klamath Basin National Wildlife Refuge Complex, Tulelake, CA.

McAllister, Tom. Naturalist and retired Outdoor Editor, The Oregonian. Portland, OR.

McCartney, Don. Observer, Bend, OR.

McGie, Alan. See author biographies.

McQueen, Larry. Observer and artist, Eugene, OR.

Meredith, Judy. Observer, Bend, OR.

Messick, Lila. Manager, Malheur Field Station, Burns, OR.

Mickel, Tom. Observer, Eugene, OR.

Miller, Craig. See author biographies.

Miller, Gary. U.S. Fish and Wildlife Service, La Grande, OR.

Moore, Marjorie. Observer, Phoenix/ Medford area, OR.

Morrow, Charles. Observer, Portland, OR.

Morrow, Wayne. Wildlife Biologist, Oreg. Dept. of Fish and Wildl., Eugene, OR.

Mowdy, Jason. Research Associate, Oreg. State Univ., Roseburg, OR.

Muller, Pat. Observer, Portland, OR.

Munson, Don. Observer, Brookings, OR.

Nehls, Harry. See senior contributor biographies.

Nelson, Sally. Observer, Creswell, OR.

Newhouse, Bruce. Botanist, Eugene, OR.

Niehuser, Jerry. Volunteer eagle observer, Oreg. Eagle Found., Bend, OR.

Nugent, Martin. Wildlife Diversity Program Director, Oreg. Dept. Fish and Wildl., Portland, OR.

Olmedo, Eddie. U.S. Forest Service, Mt. Vernon, OR.

Olson, James G. Former compiler, Portland CBC, Portland, OR.

Opp, Ralph R. Retired, Oreg. Dept. of Fish and Wildl., Klamath Falls, OR.

Oring, Lewis W. Professor, Environmental Resource Science, Univ. Nevada, Reno, NV.

Pagel, Joel (Jeep). See author biographies.

Pampush, Andy. Biologist, Bureau of Land Management, Tillamook Resource Area, Tillamook, OR.

Pardieck, Keith L. USGS Patuxent Wildlife Research Center, Laurel, MD.

Parker, Alice. Observer, Roseburg, OR.

Parsons, Cory. Agricultural Agent, Oreg. State Univ. Extension Service, Prineville, OR.

Patterson, Mike. See author biographies.

Paulson, Dennis. Observer, Seattle, WA.

Paynter, Carolyn. Observer, Corvallis, OR.

Pearcy, William (Bill). Professor, Oreg. State Univ., Corvallis, OR.

Pesek, Joe. Wildlife Biologist, West Linn, OR.

Pettey, Diane. Observer, Florence, OR.

Pickering, Phillip. Observer, Lincoln City, OR.

Pinnock, Sarah. Naturalist, Jackson Bottoms Wetlands, Hillsboro, OR.

Pitkin, David. Wildlife Biologist, Oreg. Coast Natl. Wildl. Refuges, Newport, OR.

Plissner, John. Observer, Salem, OR.

Polityka, Charles. Retired, U.S. Department of Interior, Portland, OR.

Popper, Ken J. See author biographies.

Powers, Don. Chair, Dept. of Biology and Chemistry, George Fox Univ., Newberg, OR.

Prigge, Allan. Observer, Eugene, OR.

Pyle, William. Biologist, U.S. Fish and Wildl. Serv., formerly Hart Mtn. Natl. Antelope Refuge, OR.

Reid, Alan. Field observer, Leaburg, OR.

Rems, Lewis. Observer, Bend, OR.

Rible, G. Southwest Oregon observer.

Robb, Roger. Observer, Eugene, OR.

Roby, Daniel D. See author biographies.

Rodecap, Justin. Observer, Corvallis, OR.

Rodenkirk, Tim. Wildlife Biologist, Coos Bay BLM.

Rogers, Dennis. Observer, formerly Curry Co., OR, currently in Costa Rica.

Rogers, Jim. Observer, Curry Co., OR.

Rotenberry, John T. Dept of Biology, Univ. of California, Riverside, CA.

Rothe, Tom. State Waterfowl Coordinator, Alaska Dept. of Fish and Game, Anchorage, AK.

Roy, Rob. Wildlife Biologist, Malheur Natl. Wildl. Refuge, Princeton, OR.

Ruppe, Jerry. Pacificorp, Portland, OR.

Russell, Skip. Observer, Beaverton, OR.

St. Louis, Marty. See author biographies.

Sallabanks, Rex. See author biographies.

Sayre, John. Retired, U.S. Fish and Wildl. Service, Seattle, WA.

Schirato, Greg. Wildlife Biologist, Washington Dept. Fish and Wildl., Olympia, WA.

Schmidt, Owen. Observer, Portland, OR.

Schmitt, John. Western Foundation of Vertebrate Zoology, Los Angeles, CA.

Schrock, Floyd. See author biographies.

Scott, J. Mike. Professor, Dept. of Fish and Wildl. Resources, and Leader of the Idaho Coop. Fish and Wildl. Res. Unit, Univ. of Idaho, Moscow, ID.

Shearwater, Debra. Founder of Shearwater Journeys, Hollister, CA.

Shelton, Joseph. Medford CBC compiler, Medford, OR.

Shunk, Steve. See author biographies.

Simmons, Jamie. See author biographies.

Small, Steve. Wildlife biologist, Bureau of Land Management, formerly at the Medford District, Grants Pass Field Office, Medford, OR.

Sovern, Stan G. Research Associate, Oreg. State Univ. Ellensburg, WA.

Specht, Elmer. Observer, Clackamas Co., OR.

Spencer, Kevin. See author biographies.

Springer, Paul. Retired Leader of Cooperative Wildl. Res. Unit, U.S. Fish and Wildl. Serv. at Humboldt State Univ., Arcata, CA.

Stern, Mark A. See author biographies.

Strong, Craig S. Wildlife Biologist, Crescent Coastal Research, Astoria, OR.

Sullivan, John. Observer, Junction City, OR.

Sullivan, Paul T. Observer, Beaverton, Oregon.

Summers, Steven D. Birder, Cedar City, UT.

Supnet, Candy. Observer, Bend, OR.

Swisher, Otis. Retired professor of biology, Southern Oreg. Univ., Ashland, OR.

Tate-Hall, Tamela. U.S. Fish and Wildl. Serv., Office of Migratory Birds, Permits Div., Portland, OR.

Teale, Verda. Observer, Falls City, OR.

Temple, Stanley A. Dept. of Wildlife Ecology, Univ. Wisconsin, Madison, WI.

Thackaberry, William. Observer, Lebanon, OR.

Thompson, P. Observer, Farmer Road Marsh, OR.

Thompson, Terry. Commercial fisherman, Newport, OR.

Thornton, Todd. Observer, Astoria, OR.

Tice, Bill. Observer, Falls City, OR.

Tracy, David. Observer, Bend, OR.

Vander Haegen, Matthew. Washington Dept. Fish and Wildl., Olympia, WA.

Vanderheul, Paula. Observer, Corvallis, OR.

Van Hulzen, Jean. Observer, Grants Pass/Murphy, OR.

Vesely, Dave. Forest Ecologist, Pacific Wildlife Research, Inc., Corvallis, OR.

Voelzer, James. Biologist, U.S. Fish and Wildl. Service, Portland, OR.

Voget, Ken. Retired, U.S. Fish and Wildl. Serv., Las Vegas, NV.

Vroman, Dennis. See author biographies.

Wahl, Terence (Terry) R. Westport seabirds, Bellingham, WA.

Wahl, Terry J. Observer, Wahl Ranch, Langlois, OR.

Walker, Brett L. Masters student in biology, Univ. of Montana, Missoula, MT.

Walker, William. Observer, Vashon Is., WA.

Wander, Nathaniel. Observer, California. (formerly of Salem, OR.)

Ward, Ken. Observer, Josephine Co., OR.

Watkins, Wedge. Wildlife Biologist, BLM, Klamath Falls, OR.

Watson, Clarice. Observer, Eugene, OR.

Weber, Wayne. Field Ornithologist, Kamloops, B.C.

Weikel, Jennifer M. See author biographies.

Weiland, Linda. Observer, Portland, OR.

Wentworth, Laura. Observer, Sunriver, OR.

Wilson, Katherine. Observer, Sutherlin, OR.

Wisner, Herb. Observer, Eugene, OR.

Wright, Sheran. Observer, Portland, OR.

Zauskey, Vince. Observer, Ashland, OR.

Yparraguirre, Dan. Wildlife Biologist, Wildlife Programs Branch, California Fish and Game Commission, Sacramento, CA.

Zeillemaker, Fred. Retired biologist, U.S. Fish and Wildl. Service. Ola, ID.

# Biographies

**Senior editor David B. Marshall** of Lake Oswego became interested in birds in childhood, and through the Oregon Audubon Society (now Audubon Society of Portland) received guidance from Stanley G. Jewett in making and recording field observations. In 1949, Dave began a 32-year career with the U.S. Fish and Wildlife Service, serving as the resident biologist at several national wildlife refuges in the west, including Malheur. He subsequently became the regional biologist for national wildlife refuges of the Pacific states. After passage of the 1973 Endangered Species Act, he served as one of the first biologists to initiate the Service's endangered species program, first in Washington D.C. and later as staff biologist responsible for the program in the Pacific region. Upon retiring from the Service, he became a consultant to government agencies, conservation organizations, and industry, often specializing in writing status reports on threatened, endangered, and other species of concern.

**Co-editor Matthew G. Hunter** of Corvallis is a consulting wildlife ecologist. His interest in birds and birding began in boyhood as he explored the hills, woods, and meadows on the ranch where he grew up in Umpqua. He later obtained a B.S. in wildlife science and an M.S. in forest science (Oregon State) and worked as a wildlife biologist for several federal and state agencies before moving into private work.

**Co-editor Alan L. Contreras** of Eugene has been interested in birds since grade school. He holds a B.S. and J.D. (Oregon) and his books include *Northwest Birds in Winter*, *Birds of Oregon (Status and Distribution)* with Gilligan, Rogers, and Smith; *Birds of Coos County, Oregon;* and *Birds of Malheur County, Oregon* (with Bob Kindschy). He is administrator of the Oregon Office of Degree Authorization and director of policy and research for the Oregon Student Assistance Commission.

**Senior contributor Harry B. Nehls** of Portland is a retired U.S. Postal Service employee. He is past president of the Audubon Society of Portland and is field notes editor of the society's monthly newsletter, the *Audubon Warbler*. He is state coordinator for the U.S. Fish and Wildlife Service's Breeding Bird Surveys, former co-editor with John B. Crowell Jr. of the Northern Pacific Coast Region for *American Birds,* and currently western Oregon sub-regional editor for *North American Birds*.

**Taxonomic editor M. Ralph Browning**, a native of Jackson Co., Oregon, who has returned home, is retired from the National Biological Survey, Department of Interior, at the Smithsonian, Division of Birds. He spent 25 years learning from John Aldrich, Richard C. Banks, Roxie Laybourne, Burt Monroe, Storrs Olson, Allan R. Phillips, and Alexander Wetmore. He is author of numerous papers on taxonomy, nomenclature, and distribution of birds. His major focus has been on the taxonomy of birds from the Pacific Northwest, especially Oregon. His taxonomic revisions of subspecies include Willow Flycatcher, Tree Swallow, Ruby-crowned Kinglet, and Yellow Warbler. He is still writing, but these days mostly music; he recently completed his Symphony No. 10 and concerto for oboe.

**Editorial Assistant Rachel White Scheuering** has worked as a field biologist at Malheur and Klamath Basin national wildlife refuges, and is currently a freelance writer in Portland.

**Artist Elva Hamerstrom Paulson** is a professional wildlife artist and has lived in Oregon nearly thirty years. The daughter of ornithologists Frederick and Frances Hamerstrom, her interest in birds and art began early. Elva spends a great deal of time sketching in the field, while her husband, Dale, photographs. The illustrations in this book reflect both the many hours she has spent out-of-doors familiarizing herself with the character and habits of the birds she loves to draw, and information from her husband's photographs. Elva has illustrated six previous books, her art has been accepted in the Leigh-Yawkey Woodson Birds in Art Show three times, and twice she has been in the top ten finalists of the Federal Duck Stamp Competition.

**Cartographer Jonathan P. Brooks** of Corvallis is a GIS specialist with the Department of Forest Resources at Oregon State University. In addition to a lifelong interest in birds, he has a B.S. in cartography (Salem State, MA) and an M.S. in forest science (Oregon State).

## Authors

**Paul Adamus**, a birder since his early teens, was coordinator and author of the Oregon Breeding Bird Atlas and compiler of the Maine BBA. He holds a B.S. in wildlife science (Maine), an M.S. in biology (Utah), and a Ph.D. in wildlife science (Oregon State). He has done monitoring and research on wetlands and wildlife on contract to government agencies for 24 years.

**Bob Altman** is Coordinator for the Northern Pacific Rainforest Bird Conservation Region for the American Bird Conservancy. He works with numerous partners to facilitate and coordinate a broad range of bird conservation activities from northwestern California to south-coastal Alaska. Bob was previously an independent contractor conducting bird research and monitoring projects for numerous agency and non-governmental organizations throughout the Pacific Northwest. His ornithological interests focus on avian ecology and conservation, particularly the effect of habitat changes on populations, and the development of management strategies to conserve bird populations.

**Robert G. Anthony** is professor of wildlife ecology and leader, Oregon Cooperative Fish & Wildlife Research Unit, Oregon State University. He has spent 23 years studying Bald Eagles throughout the Pacific Northwest and Alaska. He has served on the Pacific States Bald Eagle Recovery Team and the Bald Eagle Working Team for Oregon and Washington.

**Michelle Antolos** is a graduate research assistant with the Oregon Cooperative Fish & Wildlife Research Unit and the Department of Fisheries and Wildlife at Oregon State University. With Roby, Collis, Lyons, and Craig, she has been studying Caspian Terns along the lower Columbia River since 1996.

**Jenny K. Barnett** is a wildlife biologist on the Sheldon National Wildlife Refuge. She earned an M.S. (Oregon State) while studying sage-grouse in southeastern Oregon. Since then she has worked with sage grouse and other species while serving as a biologist for the Bureau of Land Management and U.S. Fish and Wildlife Service.

**Doug Barrett** is a biologist/botanist with Westside Ecological, Inc. He holds a B.S. in agriculture and environmental studies (Vermont). He has trapped saw-whet owls during fall migration in Cape May, NJ, and Florence, OR.

**Kelly A. Bettinger** holds an M.S. in wildlife biology (Oregon State). She has spent the past 10 years surveying bird communities for research and monitoring projects throughout Oregon, and is currently the director of avian research and monitoring for the Northwest Habitat Institute in Corvallis.

**Kevin L. Blakely** holds a B.S. in wildlife management (Humboldt State) and M.S. in wildlife ecology (Oregon State). His master's degree project involved California Quail in western Oregon. He is currently a Watershed District Manager with the Oregon Department of Fish and Wildlife in Pendleton.

**Luke Bloch,** an Oregon native and graduate of South Eugene High School, is a sophomore at the University of Montana. He has enjoyed studying and photographing birds since childhood.

**Joseph B. Buchanan** began bird-watching while a high-school student in west Portland in the early 1970s. He is a biologist with the Washington Department of Fish and Wildlife where he specializes in forest wildlife management issues, particularly those relating to spotted owls and landscape-level conservation planning efforts.

**David A. Budeau** holds a B.S. in wildlife science (Oregon State) and M.S. in wildlife resources (Idaho). For his master's degree he studied the pre-nesting ecology of Greater White-fronted Geese on the Yukon-Kuskokwim Delta, AK. He currently manages Oregon Department of Fish and Wildlife's E. E. Wilson Wildlife Area.

**Evelyn L. Bull** is a research wildlife biologist with the U.S. Forest Service, Pacific Northwest Research Station, in La Grande, OR. She has conducted research on cavity-nesting birds for the last 25 years, in addition to research on forest owls, forest carnivores, and amphibians.

**Chris Butler** of Beaverton holds a B.S. in natural resources (Cornell) and is currently working on a Ph.D. at the University of Oxford (England), where he is studying the population biology of the introduced Rose-ringed Parakeet in the U.K.

**Grant Canterbury** grew up in Anchorage, AK, and studied biology at Reed College and the University of Minnesota. He currently lives in the Portland area, where he works on endangered species issues for the U.S. Fish and Wildlife Service.

**Christopher G. Carey** holds a B.S. in wildlife science (Oregon State) and has worked for the Oregon Department of Fish and Wildlife in central and southeastern Oregon since 1974. His fields of interest include raptors, swans, woodpeckers, threatened and endangered species, land use management and database management. A lifelong birder, he served as president of Central Oregon Audubon Society from 1998 to 2002.

**Kathleen A. Castelein** holds a bachelor's degree in biology (Rutgers). She is an experienced field observer and researcher and has worked throughout North and South America. Her main bird interests are shorebirds and tropical birds. Kathy is currently working with Snowy Plovers on the southern Oregon coast.

**Victor L. Coggins** holds a degree in wildlife sciences (Oregon State). He has worked for the Oregon Department of Fish and Wildlife for 35 years and is currently the District Wildlife Biologist for the Wallowa District in Enterprise.

**Ken Collis** is a fish and wildlife consultant, Real Time Research, Bend, OR. With Roby, Lyons, Antolos, and Craig, he has been studying the ecology and breeding biology of Caspian Terns along the lower Columbia River since 1996.

**Barbara Combs** wrote her first field notes in New Jersey in 1956, and has been an Oregon birder since 1974. A graduate of Oberlin College, she holds an M.S. (Bucknell) and a Ph.D. (Oregon), both in psychology. She participates in projects concerning Oregon's birds and habitats, and has visited all of the continents in search of birds and other wildlife. To finance her hobbies, she has spent more than 23 years doing policy analysis on telecommunications, energy, and water issues for the Oregon Public Utility Commission.

**David P. Craig** is an assistant professor of biology at Willamette University in Salem, OR. With Roby, Collis, Lyons, and Antolos, he has been studying the ecology and breeding biology of Caspian Terns along the lower Columbia River since 1996.

**Steven M. Desimone** holds a B.S. in zoology (Washington) and M.S. in wildlife science (Oregon State). He has worked extensively in both western and eastern Oregon studying forest birds, mainly raptors. He is currently a wildlife biologist with the Washington Department of Fish and Wildlife, specializing in forest wildlife and forest management issues.

**Colin Dillingham** holds a B.S. in wildlife management (Humboldt State), worked as a wildlife biologist with the U.S. Forest Service from 1989 to 2001 in Curry County, and is currently an ecologist with the U.S. Forest Service in Quincy, California.

**Stephen Dowlan** began birding at age 15 in northwest Pennsylvania, and has since chased birds throughout much of the United States and a little bit of Australia. He is a natural resource specialist with the Bureau of Land Management in Salem, OR. He has worked on studies of the distribution of Harlequin Ducks and Fox Sparrows in Oregon.

**Bruce D. Dugger** is an assistant professor in the Department of Fisheries and Wildlife at Oregon State University. His research interests focus on the ecology, conservation, and management of waterbirds, particularly waterfowl, and their wetland habitats.

**Katie M. Dugger** is an assistant research professor with the Oregon Cooperative Wildlife & Fisheries Research Unit and Department of Fisheries and Wildlife at Oregon State University. Katie's research interests include avian population, foraging, and reproductive ecology, with a special interest in waterbirds.

**Elsie K. Eltzroth** holds a B.S. in zoology (Ohio) and a teaching certificate (Central Missouri). She initiated the Corvallis Bluebird Trail in 1976 in a successful effort to return bluebirds to the Willamette Valley. She has documented breeding biology, behavior, longevity, and causes of mortality including disease and has authored articles, provided data for scientific papers and three nationally published books about bluebirds, and was a co-author for The Birds of North America, Western Bluebird monograph.

**Scott L. Findholt** holds a Ph.D. in zoology and physiology (Wyoming). He is a wildlife research biologist for the Oregon Department of Fish and Wildlife and adjunct associate professor of biology at Eastern Oregon University in La Grande.

**LeRoy Fish** died shortly after completing his work for this book. He held a B.S. and M.A. in biology (Walla Walla College) and a Ph.D. in ecology and wildlife biology (Washington State). He was a field researcher in several states and taught biology at Oakwood College (Alabama) and Southwestern College (Texas) as well as working as a commercial fisherman in Alaska. In recent years he maintained a banding station at Triangle Lake, Oregon.

**Eric D. Forsman** is a research biologist with the U. S. Forest Service, Pacific Northwest Research Station in Corvallis. His primary area of interest is the ecology of forest owls and their prey.

**Christie Galen** has been an avid birder since a Western Tanager distracted her during a college seminar. She studied Lewis's Woodpeckers in the White River Management Area east of Mt. Hood in 1988 while under contract with the Oregon Department of Fish and Wildlife Nongame Wildlife Program. She is currently an ecological consultant at Fishman Environmental Services in Portland, specializing in sensitive species surveys, and habitat assessment, restoration, and monitoring.

**Alan R. Giese** is an ecologist who has worked extensively with birds of prey. His master's degree research project involved the use of radio transmitters to examine home ranges and habitat use of Pygmy Owls in western Washington.

**Greg Gillson** began birding in junior high school in 1972. He is a professional seabird guide and electronics technician and co-author of the Oregon Breeding Bird Atlas.

**Gregory A. Green** is a senior wildlife ecologist with Foster Wheeler Environmental Corporation in Bothell, WA. Most of his career has focused on the ecology of shrub-steppe birds and lizards, marine mammal survey, and forest wildlife management.

**Joan C. Hagar** holds an M.S. in forest ecology (Oregon State) with a thesis on the effects of commercial thinning on forest songbirds. She is currently working on her doctoral research, which investigates diets of forest songbirds, and effects of forest management on food resources for birds.

**Susan Haig** is a professor of wildlife ecology at Oregon State University and a wildlife ecologist at the USGS Forest and Rangeland Ecosystem Science Center in Corvallis. For 20 years, she has studied various shorebird and wetland systems across North America.

**Jeannie Heltzel** has been studying riparian songbirds at Hart Mountain Refuge for the past two years. She recently moved to the Gulf Coast, and will be working as a graduate research assistant at the University of Louisiana, studying songbirds in bottomland hardwood forests.

**Charles J. Henny** is a research zoologist at the USGS Forest and Rangeland Ecosystem Science Center and a courtesy professor of wildlife ecology at Oregon State University. He has spent 32 years, including 26 years in Oregon, researching wildlife contaminant issues. He has written over 150 publications; his studies have primarily involved birds of prey and other fish-eating species.

**Hendrik G. Herlyn** is a native of Germany, where he earned a B.S. in forestry and wildlife science at Freiburg University. He has worked on numerous ornithological projects in Europe and North America and traveled widely in pursuit of his birding hobby. An Oregonian since 1988, he currently resides in Corvallis, where he works as a technical translator.

**Caroline Herziger** gave up her job as office manager of a veterinary hospital to put her degree in environmental studies to work. She was employed at Malheur National Wildlife Refuge as a biological technician and has conducted bird surveys and data analysis for various agencies and organizations in Oregon, Idaho, California, and Washington.

**Janet Hodder** is an associate professor at the University of Oregon's Institute of Marine Biology in Charleston, Oregon. She teaches a summer course on the biology of marine birds and mammals and studies the breeding biology of the seabirds of the Oregon coast.

**Aaron Holmes** is a biologist with the Point Reyes Bird Observatory based in Stinson Beach, CA. His primary research interests relate to conservation of shrub-steppe habitats. Current projects focus on songbird reproductive biology and habitat associations in eastern Oregon.

**Eric G. Horvath** has a degree in zoology (Oregon State) and has led birding tours for The Nature Conservancy since 1990. He lives in Newport and maintains Purple Martin colonies along the coast from Bandon to Nehalem.

**Frank B. Isaacs** is a Senior Faculty Research Assistant at Oregon Cooperative Fish & Wildlife Research Unit, Oregon State University. He has been searching Oregon for Bald Eagles and their nests and night roosts since 1979. Frank is a member and past chairman of the Bald Eagle Working Team for Oregon and Washington, and has worked with Bald Eagles in other areas of the Pacific Northwest and Alaska. Frank is a founder of the Oregon Eagle Foundation.

**Kamal Islam** holds an M.S. and Ph.D. (Oregon State) earned studying Himalayan pheasants. Kamal is currently an assistant professor of ornithology at Ball State University, Muncie, IN. His current research interests include breeding ecology of neotropical migrants, in particular the Cerulean Warbler.

**Gary L. Ivey** spent 20 years of federal service as a wildlife biologist including 15 years at Malheur National Wildlife Refuge. He is currently self-employed, primarily working with avian conservation issues.

**Stewart W. Janes** holds a Ph.D. (UCLA) and is professor of biology at Southern Oregon University, where he teaches ornithology and animal behavior among other classes. He has studied bird of prey ecology, mostly buteos, for more than 25 years, and, more recently, his research has involved interspecific communication and song function in warblers.

**Tim Janzen** is a family practice doctor in Portland and has been an avid birder since 1983. He is a member of the Oregon Bird Records Committee and also leads field trips for the Portland Audubon Society. He particularly enjoys "Big Day" birding trips, for which his teams hold the top two Oregon records.

**Robert L. Jarvis** is professor emeritus of wildlife ecology at Oregon State University, where he and his graduate students have studied Band-tailed Pigeons, waterfowl, and wetland ecology since 1971. He taught a variety of courses including biology of birds, principles of conservation, wildlife ecology, and biology of game birds.

**Joseph R. Jehl, Jr.,** holds a PhD (Michigan) and studied with H. B. Tordoff and R. W. Storer. He served as curator of birds and mammals at the San Diego Natural History Museum and as director of research and senior research biologist at Hubbs Sea World Research Institute. In addition to his recent studies of avian biology in saline lakes, he has conducted major research in subarctic Canada, the coasts and offshore waters of southern S. America, Antarctica, and M. America, focusing on seabirds and shorebirds.

**Thomas W. Keegan** holds a Ph.D. (Oregon State); while a graduate research assistant he studied Rio Grande Wild Turkey habitat use and ecology. He also managed state fish and wildlife agency programs for deer and elk in Oregon and upland game and furbearers in Washington. He is currently regional wildlife manager for Idaho Fish and Game's Salmon Region.

**Elizabeth G. Kelly** holds a B.S. in international environmental studies (Rutgers) and M.S. in wildlife science (Oregon State). She spent four field seasons conducting Spotted Owl surveys for the Oregon Cooperative Wildlife Research Unit. She is currently a fish and wildlife biologist for the U.S. Fish and Wildlife Service in Newport, Oregon.

**Joanna Klima** is a native of Poland and holds an M.S. (Warsaw). Her main interest is population dynamics and behavior of shorebirds, although she has also studied passerines and raptors both on breeding grounds and during migration. She co-authored accounts on Stilt Sandpiper, Short-billed Dowitcher and Hudsonian Godwit for the Birds of North America series. She is currently studying demography and behavior of American Golden-Plovers at Churchill, Manitoba.

**Bob Kindschy** retired after 30 years as a biologist with the Vale District, Bureau of Land Management and is now ranching near Vale. In addition to maintaining thirty years of data for sites such as Batch Lake and Bogus Lakes, he has written extensively about the ecology of southeastern Oregon, including journal articles and chapters in *Wildlife Habitats in Managed Rangelands: the Great Basin of Southeastern Oregon.*

**Raymond T. Korpi** holds a Ph.D. in American studies (Washington State). His primary field of research is the history and evolution of bird field guides. He currently is an instructor of English at Clark College, Vancouver, WA, and an active member of Oregon Field Ornithologists, where he served as President from 1997 to 2000.

**David J. Lauten** has a bachelor's degree in biology (Rutgers) and a master's degree in wildlife ecology (Wisconsin-Madison). He has been involved in bird research since 1989, studying a variety of species from the tundra to the tropics. Dave's main interests are shorebirds, tropical birds, and birdsong. He is an avid birder in both North and South America, and is interested in recording birdsongs of South American birds. He is currently studying Snowy Plovers on the southern Oregon coast.

**C. D. Littlefield** worked for many years as a biologist at Malheur National Wildlife Refuge. He is the author of *Birds of Malheur National Wildlife Refuge* (OSU Press, 1990) and one of the nation's experts on Sandhill Crane biology. He is now a biologist at Muleshoe National Wildlife Refuge in Texas.

**John P. Loegering** is assistant professor of wildlife ecology at the University of Minnesota. His appointment involves undergraduate instruction and advising at the Crookston campus and conducting research and outreach associated with the Department of Fisheries, Wildlife and Conservation Biology on the St. Paul campus.

**Donald E. Lyons** is a graduate research assistant with the Oregon Cooperative Fish & Wildlife Research Unit and the Department of Fisheries and Wildlife at Oregon State University in Corvallis. With Roby, Collis, Antolos, and Craig, he has been studying the ecology and breeding biology of Caspian Terns along the lower Columbia River since 1996.

**R. Kahler Martinson**'s interest in waterfowl dates from his early childhood in western Minnesota. His distinguished career in fish and wildlife management included service with the U.S. Fish and Wildlife Service in Washington D.C. as assistant director for migratory birds and as regional director in Portland for the Pacific region. Kahler remains active in conservation issues with the Audubon Society of Portland and is an avid duck hunter.

**Shelley Espeland Matthews** recently graduated from Portland State with a master's degree in geography: natural resource management. While attending college, she volunteered for the Avian Predation on Juvenile Salmonids project at the mouth of the Columbia River. She has also worked with birds at the Oregon Zoo and the Audubon Society of Portland.

**Gary K. McAtee** holds a B.S. in recreation (Oregon). He ended a Forest Service career on the Middle Fork Ranger District, Willamette National Forest, working with wildlife, primarily raptors and elk habitat.

**Alan McGie** holds B.S. and M.S. degrees in fisheries (Humboldt State). He was employed by the Oregon Department of Fish and Wildlife for 34 years, conducting research on sport, commercial, threatened, and endangered fish populations throughout Oregon before retiring in 1994. He also served on the Oregon Bird Records Committee. Alan has birded in the western United States for over 33 years.

**Kathy Merrifield** first learned about birds, the second love of her life, from Dory Jones, her kindergarten teacher at Vernon School in Portland. In 1980, after years of informal interest, Kathy began waterbird studies involving abundance, flight direction, and behavior. Bryophytes and the invertebrates that inhabit them are her current interest in botany, the first love of her life, and she retains strong ties to vascular plants through her native garden. She currently serves as extension nematologist at Oregon State University.

**Craig R. Miller** has lived in Bend, OR, since 1981, where until recently he worked as a physician. He has for many years been an avid naturalist and "desert rat" spending much of his spare time studying the birds of the Great Basin region. He co-authored the 1993 publication *Oregon Checklists and Maps* with Steve Summers and has collected extensive data on the distribution and occurrence of avifauna in Oregon. He was an active member of the steering committee and contributed technical expertise for the Oregon Breeding Bird Atlas.

**S. Kim Nelson** is a research wildlife biologist and senior faculty research assistant with the Oregon Cooperative Fish & Wildlife Research Unit, Department of Fisheries and Wildlife at Oregon State University. She has been studying the behavior, habitat associations, nest-site characteristics, and nest success rates of the elusive Marbled Murrelet in the forests of western Oregon, Washington, and Alaska since 1988. She also participated in research to determine the nesting status of the Long-billed Murrelet in northern Japan between 1996 and 2000.

**Joel E. (Jeep) Pagel** entered his first Peregrine Falcon nest in 1983 and since that time has worked for the U.S. Forest Service as the principal investigator for the Pacific Northwest interagency Peregrine Falcon project. He holds a B.S. in wildlife management (Wisconsin-Stevens Point) and is a doctoral student at the University of California-Davis, working on issues surrounding recovery, downlisting, and subsequent delisting under the Endangered Species Act. He is also a research associate with the Santa Cruz Predatory Bird Research Group.

**Mike Patterson** holds B.S. degrees in zoology and general science and an M.S. in science (Oregon State). He has studied birds for over 30 years. He is currently a consultant for the North Coast Land Conservancy and the Nature Conservancy on issues related to habitat restoration and operates several bird banding stations in Clatsop County.

**Robert Peck** is an avian ecologist with the Pacific Islands Ecosystem Research Center, Kilauea Field Station, Hawaii. In Corvallis, Oregon, from 1992 to 2002, he studied the nesting biology of Marbled Murrelets (OSU) and forest entomology (USFS). He has a BS in Biology (Minnesota) and an MS in Zoology (Hawaii).

**Eric Pelren** holds a Ph.D. in wildlife science (Oregon State). He currently is an assistant professor of natural resources management in the Department of Agriculture and Natural Resources at the University of Tennessee at Martin.

**Michael Pope** holds an M.S. and Ph.D. in wildlife science (Oregon State). His dissertation was on the ecology of Mountain Quail in Oregon. He is a faculty research associate in the Department of Fisheries and Wildlife at Oregon State University and directs the research activities of the Game Bird Research Program.

**Kenneth J. Popper** currently works as a conservation planner with The Nature Conservancy in Portland, OR, and has a wildlife science degree (Oregon State). He has studied Yellow Rails since 1995, as well as other species, in his previous position as wildlife biologist for The Nature Conservancy's Oregon Natural Heritage Program.

**Hugh Powell** got his B.A. (Alabama) and then worked on the bird banding and nest searching circuit long enough to get Resplendent Quetzal on a point count.

He earned his M.S. (Montana) studying Black-backed Woodpeckers and their prey. He is interested in the role of fire in the West's myriad forest types, and lives in Bend. He is currently managing editor of *Condor*.

**Johnny Powell** is a professor of physics at Reed College in Portland, OR.

**Laura Ratti** is a mom and part-time biologist with Westside Ecological, Inc. She holds a B.S. in wildlife management (Rutgers). She has worked studying Saw-whet Owls in New Jersey and Oregon.

**Eric V. Rickerson** holds a B.S. and M.S. in wildlife science (Oregon State). He has worked extensively with waterfowl and upland game birds in Oregon and is currently the Upland Game Bird Program Manager for the Oregon Department of Fish and Wildlife. His professional interests include development of population survey techniques and restoration programs for upland game birds.

**Daniel D. Roby** is a courtesy associate professor of wildlife ecology at Oregon State University and the assistant unit leader for wildlife in the USGS Oregon Cooperative Fish and Wildlife Research Unit. With Collis, Lyons, Antolos, and Craig, he has been studying the ecology and breeding biology of Caspian Terns along the lower Columbia River since 1996.

**Martin J. St. Louis** has spent most of his career in eastern Oregon working for the U.S. Forest Service and Oregon Department of Fish and Wildlife. He is currently the manager at Summer Lake Wildlife Area, working with wetland habitat management and waterbirds in a position he has held since 1987.

**Rex Sallabanks** is the nongame bird biologist and Partners-in-Flight coordinator with the Idaho Department of Fish and Game in Boise, Idaho. He holds a Ph.D. (Oregon), which he earned while studying the foraging behavior of American Robins wintering in the Willamette Valley.

**Todd A. Sanders** holds B.S., M.S., and Ph.D. degrees (Oregon State) and completed his doctoral research on the ecology of Band-tailed Pigeons. He is a wildlife researcher and representative on the Pacific Flyway Study Committee for the Colorado Division of Wildlife.

**Peter Sanzenbacher** holds an M.S. in wildlife science (Oregon State), which he earned while working on movements of wintering Dunlin and Killdeer in the Willamette Valley. He has also studied breeding and nonbreeding shorebirds in various other regions including the Atlantic Coast, the Caribbean, the Great

Basin, and the Arctic. He is currently affiliated with the USGS Forest and Rangeland Ecosystem Science Center in Corvallis.

**Dawn Sater** is a wildlife biologist who conducted her master's research on the distribution and habitat associations of Pygmy Owls in Oregon. After obtaining her master's degree in wildlife biology she became a Buddhist monk in Portland, OR.

**Eric J. Scheuering** is a zoology data manager with the Oregon Natural Heritage Program. He was previously a wildlife biologist for U.S. Fish and Wildlife Service at Malheur National Wildlife Refuge and for Bureau of Land Management in the Roseburg District. He has a B.A. in environmental biology (Montana).

**Rachel White Scheuering** has worked as a field biologist at Malheur National Wildlife Refuge and Klamath Basin refuges, and is currently a freelance writer in Portland.

**Floyd Schrock** has been watching birds in the Willamette Valley since they first caught his attention in about 1950 at his father's feeders and nest boxes. He taught English as a second language (including assignments in Mexico and Japan), and now is assistant director for international admission at Linfield College. Floyd regularly visits such diverse regions as Asia, Scandinavia, and San Antonio. He has been active in the Audubon Society and other nature-oriented groups, leading and participating in field trips, bird surveys, and conservation projects.

**Tim Shelmerdine** teaches high school Spanish in the Portland area. An avid birder since 1985, he has served as a board member, secretary, and president of Oregon Field Ornithologists, and is a member of several other conservation organizations. His primary interest is in seabirds and he works as a guide on pelagic birding trips.

**Stephen A. Shunk** is a freelance writer, public relations consultant, and birding guide based in Sisters, OR. His passion for field ornithology began while volunteering for the San Francisco Bay Bird Observatory in 1992; he has lived in Oregon since 1997.

**Jamie Simmons** became interested in birds as a youth in upstate New York and has birded in Oregon since 1983. He is a guide on pelagic birding trips and served four years on the board of the Audubon Society of Corvallis. A technical writer in Corvallis, he holds a B.A. in geology (Occidental College) and B.S. and M.S. degrees in science education (Oregon State).

**Stuart Sparkman** teaches advanced mathematics in Salem, OR. He is an avid recreational birder and traveler, and is a member of Oregon Field Ornithologists and Salem Audubon Society.

**Kevin Spencer** has been a naturalist since youth and holds a B.S. in forestry management (Humboldt State). He has been active with point counts, Breeding Bird Surveys, and banding stations in Klamath County since the early 1990s.

**Mark A. Stern** is a wildlife biologist for The Nature Conservancy. He holds an M.S. in wildlife science (Oregon State) and has led numerous studies of birds in Oregon, focusing on Sandhill Cranes, Black Terns, Snowy Plovers, Yellow Rails, songbirds in oak woodlands, and waterbirds in the Warner Valley. He currently directs conservation activities for The Nature Conservancy in the Klamath Basin.

**Noah K. Strycker** is a birder, bird photographer, and bird artist who lives near Creswell. A 15-year-old student at South Eugene High School when he wrote these accounts, he also works part time for the Willamette Valley Projects Office of the U.S. Army Corps of Engineers, conducting bird surveys in addition to other field assignments. He edited the recent Oregon Field Ornithologists' reprint of A. C. Shelton's 1917 bird species distributions in Lane County. His articles, photographs, and drawings have appeared in state, regional, and national publications.

**Keith Swindle** holds a B.S. (Michigan State) and an M.S. (Oregon State). He conducted research on Northern Spotted Owls for 10 years with the Oregon Cooperative Wildlife Research Unit, then worked for the Endangered Species Division of the U.S. Fish and Wildlife Service in Portland. Currently, he is a Special Agent for the U.S. Fish and Wildlife Service, Division of Law Enforcement, in Honolulu, HI.

**Carmen Thomas** holds a B.S. (Wisconsin) and an M.S. (Oregon State). She studied environmental contaminants and breeding biology of Great Blue Herons in Oregon and Washington for 4 years, and worked for the U.S. Fish and Wildlife Service in Sacramento, CA, for 5 years, studying environmental contaminant issues for 3 years, and working on endangered species issues for 2 years. She currently is with the U.S. Fish and Wildlife Service in Boise, Idaho, working on both environmental contaminants and endangered species issues.

**Pepper W. Trail** is the ornithologist for the National Fish and Wildlife Forensics Laboratory of the U.S. Fish and Wildlife Service in Ashland, OR. His interests include the biogeography and conservation of birds in the Klamath-Siskiyou region of southern Oregon and northern California.

**Guy Tutland** is a biology teacher in the Medford School District in southern Oregon.

**Karen Viste-Sparkman** holds a biology degree from Willamette University. Since 1994, she has worked as a field biologist on avian research projects in the Pacific Northwest, Hawaii, the Gulf Coast, and Arizona. Currently she works for the U.S. Fish and Wildlife Service as a biological science technician.

**Dennis Vroman** developed a love of the natural world as a youngster growing up walking the shores of Lake Ontario and visiting the woodlands of northern New York State. He retired from the USDA Forest Service in 1996 after 25 years of service, primarily in silviculture with some wildlife-related tasks. A licensed bird bander since 1985, he continues to operate five mist-net breeding-season monitoring stations in southwest Oregon, including one started in 1989.

**Hanspeter Walter** holds a forestry degree (UC Berkeley) and an M.S. in wildlife management (Idaho). He has worked for the Idaho Department of Fish and Game and is currently an environmental scientist with the California Department of Water Resources. His interests include environmental compliance and policy, and he is also pursuing a J.D. from McGeorge School of Law.

**Nils Warnock** holds a Ph.D. (UC Davis and San Diego State University) in ecology. After periods of work for the U.S. Forest Service and the U.S. Geological Survey in Corvallis, Nils is currently co-director of the Wetlands Program at the Point Reyes Bird Observatory. His research focuses on the ecology and conservation of Pacific Flyway birds with emphases on endangered species, bird migration, wetland habitat restoration, and shorebirds.

**Jennifer Weikel** is a wildlife ecologist with Pacific Wildlife Research, a consulting firm based in Corvallis. She holds an M.S. in forest science (Oregon State). She has conducted research on the foraging ecology of cavity-nesting birds and the effects of commercial thinning on bird populations and has been conducting bird-banding research in the Willamette Valley since 1998.